# PARLIAMENTARY DEBATES

## (HANSARD)

SIXTH SERIES—VOLUME 260

# HOUSE OF COMMONS

### OFFICIAL REPORT

THIRD SESSION OF THE FIFTY-FIRST PARLIAMENT
OF THE UNITED KINGDOM OF GREAT BRITAIN
AND NORTHERN IRELAND
FORTY-FOURTH YEAR OF THE REIGN OF
HER MAJESTY QUEEN ELIZABETH II

**SESSION 1994–95**

COMPRISING PERIOD
15 May—31 May 1995

LONDON

HER MAJESTY'S STATIONERY OFFICE

£90 net

ISBN 0 10 681260 2

# HER MAJESTY'S GOVERNMENT

## MEMBERS OF THE CABINET

### (FORMED BY THE RT. HON. JOHN MAJOR, MP, JULY 1994)

PRIME MINISTER, FIRST LORD OF THE TREASURY AND MINISTER FOR THE CIVIL SERVICE—The Rt. Hon. John Major, MP
LORD CHANCELLOR—The Rt. Hon. Lord Mackay of Clashfern
SECRETARY OF STATE FOR FOREIGN AND COMMONWEALTH AFFAIRS—The Rt. Hon. Douglas Hurd, CBE, MP
CHANCELLOR OF THE EXCHEQUER—The Rt. Hon. Kenneth Clarke, QC, MP
SECRETARY OF STATE FOR THE HOME DEPARTMENT—The Rt. Hon. Michael Howard, QC, MP
PRESIDENT OF THE BOARD OF TRADE (SECRETARY OF STATE FOR TRADE AND INDUSTRY)—The Rt. Hon. Michael Heseltine, MP
SECRETARY OF STATE FOR DEFENCE—The Rt. Hon. Malcolm Rifkind, QC, MP
LORD PRESIDENT OF THE COUNCIL AND LEADER OF THE HOUSE OF COMMONS—The Rt. Hon. Tony Newton, OBE, MP
SECRETARY OF STATE FOR THE ENVIRONMENT—The Rt. Hon. John Gummer, MP
CHANCELLOR OF THE DUCHY OF LANCASTER—The Rt. Hon. David Hunt, MBE, MP
SECRETARY OF STATE FOR SOCIAL SECURITY—The Rt. Hon. Peter Lilley, MP
MINISTER OF AGRICULTURE, FISHERIES AND FOOD—The Rt. Hon. William Waldegrave, MP
SECRETARY OF STATE FOR SCOTLAND—The Rt. Hon. Ian Lang, MP
SECRETARY OF STATE FOR NORTHERN IRELAND—The Rt. Hon. Sir Patrick Mayhew, QC, MP
SECRETARY OF STATE FOR HEALTH—The Rt. Hon. Virginia Bottomley, MP
SECRETARY OF STATE FOR EDUCATION—The Rt. Hon. Gillian Shephard, MP
SECRETARY OF STATE FOR EMPLOYMENT—The Rt. Hon. Michael Portillo, MP
SECRETARY OF STATE FOR WALES—The Rt. Hon. John Redwood, MP
SECRETARY OF STATE FOR TRANSPORT—The Rt. Hon. Dr. Brian Mawhinney, MP
SECRETARY OF STATE FOR NATIONAL HERITAGE—The Rt. Hon. Stephen Dorrell, MP
LORD PRIVY SEAL AND LEADER OF THE HOUSE OF LORDS—The Rt. Hon. The Lord Cecil of Essenden
CHIEF SECRETARY TO THE TREASURY—The Rt. Hon. Jonathan Aitken, MP
MINISTER WITHOUT PORTFOLIO—The Rt. Hon. Jeremy Hanley, MP

## LAW OFFICERS

ATTORNEY-GENERAL—The Rt. Hon. Sir Nicholas Lyell, QC, MP
LORD ADVOCATE—The Rt. Hon. Lord Rodger of Earlsferry, QC
SOLICITOR-GENERAL—Sir Derek Spencer, QC, MP
SOLICITOR-GENERAL FOR SCOTLAND—Donald MacKay, Esq, QC

## MINISTERS NOT IN THE CABINET

PARLIAMENTARY SECRETARY TO THE TREASURY—The Rt. Hon. Richard Ryder, OBE, MP
MINISTERS OF STATE, FOREIGN AND COMMONWEALTH OFFICE—
    Minister for Overseas Development—The Rt. Hon. The Baroness Chalker of Wallasey
    The Rt. Hon. Alastair Goodlad, MP
    The Rt. Hon. Douglas Hogg, QC, MP
    David Davis, Esq, MP
MINISTERS OF STATE, HOME OFFICE—
    David Maclean, Esq, MP
    The Rt. Hon. Michael Forsyth, MP
    The Rt. Hon. The Baroness Blatch, CBE
FINANCIAL SECRETARY TO THE TREASURY—The Rt. Hon. Sir George Young, MP
PAYMASTER GENERAL—David Heathcoat-Amory, Esq, MP
MINISTER OF STATE, TREASURY—Anthony Nelson, Esq, MP
MINISTERS OF STATE, DEPARTMENT OF TRADE AND INDUSTRY—
    Minister for Industry and Energy—The Rt. Hon. Tim Eggar, MP
    Minister for Consumer Affairs and Small Firms—The Rt. Hon. The Earl Ferrers
    Minister for Trade—The Rt. Hon. Richard Needham, MP
MINISTERS OF STATE, MINISTRY OF DEFENCE—
    Minister of State for Defence Procurement—The Rt. Hon. Roger Freeman, MP
    Minister of State for the Armed Forces—The Hon. Nicholas Soames, MP
MINISTERS OF STATE, DEPARTMENT OF THE ENVIRONMENT—
    Minister for Construction and Planning—The Rt. Hon. The Viscount Ullswater
    Minister for the Environment and Countryside—Robert Atkins, Esq, MP
    Minister for Local Government, Housing and Urban Regeneration—David Curry, Esq, MP
MINISTERS OF STATE, DEPARTMENT OF SOCIAL SECURITY—
    Minister for Social Security and Disabled People—William Hague, Esq, MP
    The Lord Mackay of Ardbrecknish
MINISTER OF STATE, MINISTRY OF AGRICULTURE, FISHERIES AND FOOD—Michael Jack, Esq, MP
MINISTER OF STATE, SCOTTISH OFFICE—The Rt. Hon. The Lord Fraser of Carmyllie, QC

MINISTERS OF STATE, NORTHERN IRELAND OFFICE—
    The Rt. Hon. Sir John Wheeler, MP
    Michael Ancram, Esq, MP
MINISTER OF STATE, DEPARTMENT OF HEALTH—
    Minister for Health—Gerald Malone, Esq, MP
MINISTER OF STATE, DEPARTMENT OF EDUCATION—Eric Forth Esq, MP
MINISTER OF STATE, DEPARTMENT OF EMPLOYMENT—Miss Ann Widdecombe, MP
MINISTER OF STATE, DEPARTMENT OF TRANSPORT—
    Minister for Railways and Roads—John Watts, Esq, MP

## DEPARTMENTS OF STATE AND MINISTERS

**Agriculture, Fisheries and Food—**
    MINISTER—The Rt. Hon. William Waldegrave, MP
    MINISTER OF STATE—Michael Jack, Esq, MP
    PARLIAMENTARY SECRETARIES—
      The Earl Howe
      Mrs. Angela Browning, MP
**Defence—**
    SECRETARY OF STATE—The Rt. Hon. Malcolm Rifkind, QC, MP
    MINISTER OF STATE FOR DEFENCE PROCUREMENT—The Rt. Hon. Roger Freeman, MP
    MINISTER OF STATE FOR THE ARMED FORCES—The Hon. Nicholas Soames, MP
    PARLIAMENTARY UNDER-SECRETARY OF STATE—The Lord Henley
**Education—**
    SECRETARY OF STATE—The Rt. Hon. Gillian Shephard, MP
    MINISTER OF STATE—Eric Forth, Esq, MP
    PARLIAMENTARY UNDER-SECRETARY OF STATE FOR SCHOOLS—Robin Squire, Esq, MP
    PARLIAMENTARY UNDER-SECRETARY OF STATE FOR FURTHER AND HIGHER EDUCATION—Timothy Boswell, Esq, MP
**Employment—**
    SECRETARY OF STATE—The Rt. Hon. Michael Portillo, MP
    MINISTER OF STATE—Miss Ann Widdecombe, MP
    PARLIAMENTARY UNDER-SECRETARIES OF STATE—
      James Paice, Esq, MP
      The Hon. Phillip Oppenheim, MP
**Environment—**
    SECRETARY OF STATE—The Rt. Hon. John Gummer, MP
    MINISTERS OF STATE—
      Minister for Construction and Planning—The Rt. Hon. The Viscount Ullswater
      Minister for the Environment and Countryside—Robert Atkins, Esq, MP
      Minister for Local Government, Housing and Urban Regeneration—David Curry, Esq, MP
    PARLIAMENTARY UNDER-SECRETARIES OF STATE—
      Robert B. Jones, Esq, MP
      Sir Paul Beresford, MP
**Foreign and Commonwealth Affairs—**
    SECRETARY OF STATE—The Rt. Hon. Douglas Hurd, CBE, MP
    MINISTERS OF STATE—
      Minister for Overseas Development—The Rt. Hon. The Baroness Chalker of Wallasey
      The Rt. Hon. Alastair Goodlad, MP
      The Rt. Hon. Douglas Hogg, QC, MP
      David Davis, Esq, MP
    PARLIAMENTARY UNDER-SECRETARY OF STATE—Tony Baldry, Esq, MP
**Health—**
    SECRETARY OF STATE FOR HEALTH—The Rt. Hon. Virginia Bottomley, MP
    MINISTER OF STATE—
      Minister for Health—Gerald Malone, Esq, MP
    PARLIAMENTARY UNDER-SECRETARIES OF STATE—
      The Hon. Tom Sackville, MP
      The Baroness Cumberlege, CBE
      John Bowis, Esq, OBE, MP
**Home Office—**
    SECRETARY OF STATE FOR THE HOME DEPARTMENT—The Rt. Hon. Michael Howard, QC, MP
    MINISTERS OF STATE—
      David Maclean, Esq, MP
      The Rt. Hon. Michael Forsyth, MP
      The Rt. Hon. The Baroness Blatch, CBE
    PARLIAMENTARY UNDER-SECRETARY OF STATE—Nicholas Baker, Esq, MP
**Law Officers' Department —**
    ATTORNEY-GENERAL—The Rt. Hon. Sir Nicholas Lyell, QC, MP
    SOLICITOR-GENERAL—Sir Derek Spencer, QC, MP

**Lord Advocate's Department—**
LORD ADVOCATE—The Rt. Hon. The Lord Rodger of Earlsferry, QC
SOLICITOR-GENERAL FOR SCOTLAND—Donald MacKay, Esq, QC

**Lord Chancellor's Department—**
LORD CHANCELLOR—The Rt. Hon. The Lord Mackay of Clashfern
PARLIAMENTARY SECRETARY—John M. Taylor, Esq, MP

**National Heritage—**
SECRETARY OF STATE FOR NATIONAL HERITAGE—The Rt. Hon. Stephen Dorrell, MP
PARLIAMENTARY UNDER-SECRETARIES OF STATE—
Iain Sproat, Esq, MP
The Viscount Astor

**Northern Ireland Office—**
SECRETARY OF STATE FOR NORTHERN IRELAND—The Rt. Hon. Sir Patrick Mayhew, QC, MP
MINISTERS OF STATE—
The Rt. Hon. Sir John Wheeler, MP
Michael Ancram, Esq, MP
PARLIAMENTARY UNDER-SECRETARIES OF STATE—
The Baroness Denton of Wakefield, CBE
Malcolm Moss, Esq, MP

**Paymaster General's Office—**
PAYMASTER GENERAL—David Heathcoat-Amory, Esq, MP

**Privy Council Office—**
LORD PRESIDENT OF THE COUNCIL AND LEADER OF THE HOUSE OF COMMONS—The Rt. Hon. Tony Newton, OBE, MP
LORD PRIVY SEAL AND LEADER OF THE HOUSE OF LORDS—The Rt. Hon. The Lord Cecil of Essenden

**Public Service and Science, Office of—**
CHANCELLOR OF THE DUCHY OF LANCASTER—The Rt. Hon. David Hunt, MBE, MP
PARLIAMENTARY SECRETARY—John Horam, Esq, MP

**Scottish Office—**
SECRETARY OF STATE FOR SCOTLAND—The Rt. Hon. Ian Lang, MP
MINISTER OF STATE—The Rt. Hon. The Lord Fraser of Carmyllie, QC
PARLIAMENTARY UNDER-SECRETARIES OF STATE—
Lord James Douglas-Hamilton, MP
George Kynoch, Esq, MP
Sir Hector Monro, MP

**Social Security—**
SECRETARY OF STATE FOR SOCIAL SECURITY—The Rt. Hon. Peter Lilley, MP
MINISTERS OF STATE—
Minister for Social Security and Disabled People—William Hague, Esq, MP
The Lord Mackay of Ardbrecknish
PARLIAMENTARY UNDER-SECRETARIES OF STATE—
Alistair Burt, Esq, MP
James Arbuthnot, Esq, MP
Roger Evans, Esq, MP

**Trade and Industry—**
PRESIDENT OF THE BOARD OF TRADE (SECRETARY OF STATE FOR TRADE AND INDUSTRY)—The Rt. Hon. Michael Heseltine, MP
MINISTERS OF STATE—
Minister for Industry and Energy—The Rt. Hon. Tim Eggar, MP
Minister for Consumer Affairs and Small Firms—The Rt. Hon. The Earl Ferrers
Minister for Trade—The Rt. Hon. Richard Needham, MP
PARLIAMENTARY UNDER-SECRETARY OF STATE FOR CORPORATE AFFAIRS—Jonathan Evans, Esq, MP
PARLIAMENTARY UNDER-SECRETARY OF STATE FOR INDUSTRY AND ENERGY—Richard Page, Esq, MP
PARLIAMENTARY UNDER-SECRETARY OF STATE FOR TRADE AND TECHNOLOGY—Ian Taylor, Esq, MBE, MP

**Transport—**
SECRETARY OF STATE FOR TRANSPORT—The Rt. Hon. Dr. Brian Mawhinney, MP
MINISTER OF STATE—
Minister for Railways and Roads—John Watts, Esq, MP
PARLIAMENTARY UNDER-SECRETARIES OF STATE—
Steve Norris, Esq, MP (Minister for Transport in London)
The Viscount Goschen (Minister for Aviation and Shipping)

**Treasury—**

PRIME MINISTER, FIRST LORD OF THE TREASURY AND MINISTER FOR THE CIVIL SERVICE—The Rt. Hon. John Major, MP

CHANCELLOR OF THE EXCHEQUER—The Rt. Hon. Kenneth Clarke, QC, MP

CHIEF SECRETARY—The Rt. Hon. Jonathan Aitken, MP

FINANCIAL SECRETARY—The Rt. Hon. Sir George Young, MP

PAYMASTER GENERAL—David Heathcoat-Amory, Esq, MP

MINISTER OF STATE—Anthony Nelson, Esq, MP

PARLIAMENTARY SECRETARY—The Rt. Hon. Richard Ryder, OBE, MP

LORDS COMMISSIONERS—

    Timothy Wood, Esq, MP

    Timothy Kirkhope, Esq, MP

    Andrew Mackay, Esq, MP

    Derek Conway, Esq, MP

    Andrew Mitchell, Esq, MP

ASSISTANT WHIPS—

    Simon Burns, Esq, MP

    David Willetts, Esq, MP

    Michael Bates, Esq, MP

    Dr. Liam Fox, MP

    Bowen Wells, Esq, MP

**Welsh Office—**

SECRETARY OF STATE FOR WALES—The Rt. Hon. John Redwood, MP

PARLIAMENTARY UNDER-SECRETARIES OF STATE—

    Gwilym Jones, Esq, MP

    Roderick Richards, Esq, MP

**Her Majesty's Household—**

LORD CHAMBERLAIN—The Rt. Hon. The Earl of Airlie, KT, GCVO

LORD STEWARD—The Viscount Ridley, KG, GCVO, TD

MASTER OF THE HORSE—The Lord Somerleyton, KCVO

TREASURER—Greg Knight, Esq, MP

COMPTROLLER—David Lightbown, Esq, MP

VICE-CHAMBERLAIN—Sydney Chapman, Esq, MP

CAPTAIN OF THE HONOURABLE CORPS OF GENTLEMEN-AT-ARMS—The Lord Strathclyde

CAPTAIN OF THE QUEEN'S BODYGUARD OF THE YEOMAN OF THE GUARD—The Lord Inglewood

LORDS IN WAITING—The Viscount Long, CBE, The Lord Lucas, The Earl of Lindsay

BARONESSES IN WAITING—

    The Rt. Hon. The Baroness Trumpington

    The Baroness Miller, MBE

---

SECOND CHURCH ESTATES COMMISSIONER, REPRESENTING CHURCH COMMISSIONERS—The Rt. Hon. Michael Alison, MP

# HOUSE OF COMMONS

### PRINCIPAL OFFICERS AND OFFICIALS

THE SPEAKER—The Rt. Hon. Betty Boothroyd, MP

CHAIRMAN OF WAYS AND MEANS—The Rt. Hon. Michael Morris, Esq, MP

FIRST DEPUTY CHAIRMAN OF WAYS AND MEANS—Geoffrey Lofthouse, Esq, MP

SECOND DEPUTY CHAIRMAN OF WAYS AND MEANS—Dame Janet Fookes, MP

CHAIRMEN'S PANEL—
Roland Boyes, Esq, MP, Frank Cook, Esq, MP, Sir Patrick Cormack, MP, Mrs. Gwyneth Dunwoody, MP, Alan Haselhurst, Esq, MP, Robert Hicks, Esq, MP, James Hill, Esq, MP, Norman Hogg, Esq, MP, Roy Hughes, Esq, MP, Sir John Hunt, MP, Barry Jones, Esq, MP, Sir David Knox, MP, John McWilliam, Esq, MP, Michael J. Martin, Esq, MP, John Maxton, Esq, MP, Iain Mills, Esq, MP, Edward O'Hara, Esq, MP, Sir Giles Shaw, MP, Michael Shersby, Esq, MP, Roger Sims, Esq, MP, Patrick Thompson, Esq, MP, Mrs. Ann Winterton, MP, Nicholas Winterton, Esq, MP

HOUSE OF COMMONS COMMISSION—
The Rt. Hon. The Speaker (Chairman), The Rt. Hon. Alan Beith, MP, The Rt. Hon. Paul Channon, MP, John Garrett, Esq, MP, The Rt. Hon. Tony Newton, OBE, MP, Mrs. Ann Taylor, MP

SECRETARY OF THE COMMISSION—R. W. G. Wilson

BOARD OF MANAGEMENT—
D. W. Limon, CB, (Chairman), Sir Alan Urwick, KCVO, CMG, Miss J. B. Tanfield, J. Rodda, FCA, I. D. Church, Mrs. S. J. Harrison

SECRETARY OF THE BOARD OF MANAGEMENT—B. A. Wilson

### OFFICE OF THE SPEAKER

SPEAKER'S SECRETARY—N. Bevan, CB

ASSISTANT SECRETARY TO THE SPEAKER—Mrs. M. E. Thomson

TRAINBEARER—D. J. Lord, MBE

DEPUTY TRAINBEARER—P. L. Warwick

DIARY SECRETARY—Mrs. S. Norvell

SPEAKER'S CHAPLAIN—Rev. Canon D. C. Gray, TD, PhD

### OFFICE OF THE CHAIRMAN OF WAYS AND MEANS

SECRETARY TO THE CHAIRMAN OF WAYS AND MEANS—Ms P. A. Helme

### SPEAKER'S COUNSEL

SPEAKER'S COUNSEL—J. S. Mason, CB, T. J. G. Pratt, CB

SPEAKER'S ASSISTANT COUNSEL—A. Akbar

## DEPARTMENT OF THE CLERK OF THE HOUSE

CLERK OF THE HOUSE OF COMMONS—D. W. Limon, CB
CLERK ASSISTANT—W. R. McKay      CLERK OF COMMITTEES—J. F. Sweetman, CB, TD
PRINCIPAL CLERKS—
    C. B. Winnifrith (Table Office)          D. G. Millar (Select Committees)
    R. B. Sands (Public Bills)               M. R. Jack, PhD (Standing Committees)
    G. Cubie (Overseas Office)               R. W. G. Wilson (Domestic Committees)
    A. J. Hastings (Journal Office)          W. A. Proctor (Financial Committees)
    R. J. Willoughby (Private Bills)         Ms H. E. Irwin (Select Committees)
DEPUTY PRINCIPAL CLERKS—S. A. L. Panton, Mrs. J. Sharpe, Ms A. Milner-Barry, F. A. Cranmer, R. J. Rogers,
    C. R. M. Ward, PhD, D. W. N. Doig, D. L. Natzler, E. P. Silk, A. R. Kennon, L. C. Laurence Smyth, S. J. Patrick,
    D. J. Gerhold, C. J. Poyser, D. F. Harrison, S. J. Priestley, A. H. Doherty, P. A. Evans, R. I. S. Phillips, R. G. James, PhD
    D. R. Lloyd, B. M. Hutton
SENIOR CLERKS—Ms P. A. Helme, J. S. Benger, DPhil, Miss E. C. Samson, N. P. Walker, M. D. Hamlyn,
    P. C. Seaward, DPhil, C. G. Lee, C. D. Stanton, A. Y. A. Azad, C. A. Shaw, Ms L. M. Gardner, K. J. Brown,
    D. Steel (acting), P. E. Bolton (acting), Mrs E. A. J. Attridge (acting), A. M. Kidner (acting)
CLERKS OF DOMESTIC COMMITTEES—P. G. Moon, M. Clark
ASSISTANT CLERKS— P. M. Hensher, F. J. Reid, M. Hennessy, G. R. Devine, Mrs. J. N. St. J. Mulley, T. W. P. Healey,
    Miss S. A. R. Adams, K. C. Fox, J. D. W. Rhys, Ms J. A. Long
SENIOR EXECUTIVE OFFICERS—Miss R. J. Challis, S. D. Barrett, Miss S. J. Fox
COMPUTER SUPPORT OFFICER—G. C. Peek
HIGHER EXECUTIVE OFFICERS—L. L. Kaye, A. P. Hubner, Mrs. P. Fisher, F. McShane, J. D. Whatley, Miss A. M. Loader,
    Miss F. L. Allingham, Mrs. L. M. Nugent, J. A. L. Dresner, M. P. Oxborough, N. P. Wright, Ms C. M. Genis,
    Mrs. C. Oxborough, R. W. A. Barrand, A. Catinella, Miss E. Segal, Miss A. Fuki
SPECIALIST ASSISTANTS—C. B. Dibben, V. A. A. Mengot, R. J. Gartside, A. G. Brazier, R. P. Derecki, R. A. Nash, R. D. May,
    Ms M. Manku, Mrs. C. L. Hand, D. Griffiths
EDITORIAL SUPERVISOR OF THE VOTE—B. Tidball, DEPUTY—Miss L. Lewis, ASSISTANTS—Miss B. Balcomb, J. Puricelli,
    K. B. Wood, P. D. Howlett, Mrs. L. R. Shade, P. A. Jack, P. L. J. Sullivan
SECRETARIES—Mrs. G. E. C. Sclater, MBE (Clerk of the House), Mrs. S. D. Pamphlett, Miss S. P. Chubb, Mrs. D. Gent,
    Miss A. T. Power, Miss D. J. Somers, Mrs. K. J. Georgiou, Miss L. Young, Mrs. H. Agnew, Mrs. J. Stott,
    Mrs. A. M. Douglas, Miss K. McClelland, Mrs. B. Hunter, Mrs. A. M. Allen, Mrs. N. Mulloy, Mrs. S. Marshall
EXAMINERS OF PETITIONS FOR PRIVATE BILLS—R. J. Willoughby, B. P. Keith
REGISTRAR OF MEMBERS' INTERESTS—R. J. Willoughby      TAXING OFFICER—R. J. Willoughby
SUPERINTENDING CLERK—R. A. Broomfield
CHIEF OFFICE CLERKS—J. Hole, Mrs. D. B. Nelson, P. A. Derrett, I. A. Blair, B. Dye, J. H. Davies, Ms E. C. G. Partridge,
    Miss A. Burt (temporary)

**Vote Office—**
DELIVERER OF THE VOTE—H. C. Foster
DEPUTY DELIVERERS OF THE VOTE—J. F. Collins (Distribution), F. W. Hallett (Production)
ASSISTANT DELIVERER OF THE VOTE—O. B. T. Sweeney      BOOKSHOP MANAGER—C. D. Lister
HIGHER EXECUTIVE OFFICER—B. G. Underwood, Ms K. M. Barker
SUPERINTENDING CLERKS—Mrs. S. Fuzio, A. J. Ashton
VOTE OFFICE ASSISTANTS—G. E. Howard, C. P. Williams, P. Hannett, J. Harrington, M. D. Cook, J. E. Lawford,
    Miss V. Frewin, S. Haher, P. Smith, Mrs. J. Forsyth


## DEPARTMENT OF THE SERJEANT AT ARMS

SERJEANT AT ARMS—Sir Alan Urwick, KCVO, CMG
DEPUTY SERJEANT AT ARMS—P. N. W. Jennings
ASSISTANT SERJEANT AT ARMS—M. J. A. Cummins
DEPUTY ASSISTANT SERJEANTS AT ARMS—P. A. J. Wright, J. M. Robertson
CLERK IN CHARGE—Miss S. J. Scott Thomson
ADMISSION ORDER OFFICE—A. Chipperfield, BEM, Mrs. S. J. Warren, A. J. Spencer
PRINCIPAL DOORKEEPER—C. E. Gray      DEPUTY PRINCIPAL DOORKEEPERS—D. Shiels, R. J. Tyack
SENIOR DOORKEEPERS—J. Town, J. W. Kirman, L. Outram, R. G. Sterne, P. E. Overfield
HEAD OFFICE KEEPER—Mrs. J. Pay      SENIOR OFFICE KEEPERS—V. M. Roccia, C. R. Harris, BEM, B. Mulvihill, L. Stockwell
INFORMATION TECHNOLOGY SUPPORT MANAGER—Miss S. John
OCCUPATIONAL HEALTH MANAGER—Mrs. M. Mainland      NURSING SISTER—Miss K. Anderson
PARLIAMENTARY WORKS DIRECTORATE—
    DIRECTOR OF WORKS—H. P. Webber, CEng, FICE      DEPUTY DIRECTOR OF WORKS—B. C. Sewell, ARICS
    PRINCIPAL WORKS OFFICERS—A. Makepeace, R. Bentley, MIFireE, SIRM, G. Goode, B. R. Hall, FRICS,
        C. Hillier, CEng, FIMech.E., MIEE, M. Moone, J. F. Moore, ARICS, M. Trott, M. J. Thompson, CEng, MICE
    SENIOR PROFESSIONAL OFFICERS—C. Brown, ARICS, C. Cowell, RIBA, J. Eaton, CEng, MCIBSE, T. Fox, CEng, MCIBSE,
        S. Howard, T. Jardine, TD, RIBA, B. O'Boyle, J. Stone, FRICS
COMMUNICATIONS MANAGER—A. Blake      DEPUTY COMMUNICATIONS MANAGER—Mrs. S. Morrison
PASS OFFICE—M. Coombs

## DEPARTMENT OF THE LIBRARY

LIBRARIAN—Miss J. B. Tanfield

DEPUTY LIBRARIAN—Miss P. J. Baines, B.Litt

LIBRARY AND RESEARCH—

ASSISTANT LIBRARIANS—S. Z. Young, K. G. Cuninghame

DEPUTY ASSISTANT LIBRARIANS (Heads of Section)—Mrs. J. M. Wainwright, FIInfSc, C. C. Pond, PhD, Mrs. C. B. Andrews, R. C. Clements, Mrs. J. M. Lourie, R. J. Ware, DPhil, C. R. Barclay, Mrs. J. M. Fiddick, Mrs. C. M. Gillie, R. J. Twigger, Mrs. G. L. Allen

LIBRARY CLERKS, SENIOR—Ms F. Poole, T. N. Edmonds, R. J. Cracknell, CStat, Miss O. M. Gay, Miss B. McInnes, B. K. Winetrobe, Miss M. Baber, Ms A. Walker, Mrs. H. V. Holden, Mrs. P. L. Carling, Miss J. Seaton, FLA, A. J. L. Crompton, Miss P. Strickland, Miss V. A. Miller, Ms H. M. Jeffs, M. P. Hillyard, Ms J. Roll, S. A. Wise (period)

ASSISTANT—Ms W. T. Wilson, E. H. Wood, Miss N. J. Chedgey, M. Nawaz, P. Bowers, PhD, T. E. Dodd, A. C. Seely, Ms J. K. Dyson, Miss. F. M. Watson, MPhil, G. Danby, PhD, W. F. Lea, PhD, Miss P. M. Hughes, PhD, B. C. Morgan, Ms K. S. Wright, J. Vernon, Miss L. A. Conway, C. Blair, PhD, Dr. J. E. L. Cushion (period), G. Vidler (temporary)

SENIOR EXECUTIVE OFFICERS—Ms F. Whittle, P. W. Skerratt, J. A. Prince, MLS (acting)

SENIOR LIBRARY EXECUTIVES—K. N. H. Parry, ALA, Miss C. E. Fretten, ALA, Miss I. O. White, ALA, Miss G. L. Cooper, Mrs. D. W. Clark, ALA

EDUCATION OFFICER—Mrs. C. Weeds; ASSISTANT—Mrs. C. C. O'Connor

HIGHER EXECUTIVE OFFICERS—E. L. V. MacGregor, Ms B. A. Rowlands, ALA, J. P. Brevitt, Miss C. M. Owens

HIGHER LIBRARY EXECUTIVES—Mrs. P. V. Wiles, Miss M. H. Fletcher, Mrs. G. C. Brown, Mrs. P. E. Cook, ALA, Ms H. Armstrong, Miss E. J. Jones, ALA, G. Haig, Mrs. E. H. Riley, ALA, Mrs. F. M. Ward, Mrs. M. A. Azim, ALA, T. C. Holmes, C. M. Sear, Ms J. B. Hall, ALA, R. Freebury, ALA, A. D. Parker, ALA, Miss G. Rose, Mrs. J. Priestley, Miss C. M. R. Chambers, Miss C. M. Blair, ALA (acting)

EDITOR, WEEKLY BULLETIN—D. B. Inns

LIBRARY EXECUTIVES—P. E. M. Ward, Mrs. J. M. Smith, ALA, Miss J. Lyall, ALA, Ms Z. A. Smallwood, Miss D. J. Gillings, Miss P. Rix, Miss S. Pepin, ALA, R. O. Steeden, G. G. Newell, Miss A. Hatton, Miss V. S. Spratt, Miss K. E. Susilovic, Ms J. Davies, P. D. Banks, G. Howard, Mrs. A. Brooking (temporary), Miss J. Bacchus (temporary)

EXECUTIVE OFFICERS—Miss N. Harland, Mrs. A. J. H. Mara, D. A. Brown, M. Greenhill (Head Library Attendant), B. Smith, Ms J. Fessey, A. J. Fuller, Miss J. M. Perkes, Mrs. H. Onyskiw, A. Clark, Miss A. Gual, Ms M. A. Moulton, Miss N. M. Sutherland, Mrs. C. Millar, Mrs. P. M. Burnett, P. R. Mann, Miss A. O. Creevy, Ms D. Gallagher, Miss V. J. White, Ms S. K. Priddy, Ms L. F. Magee (acting)

## DEPARTMENT OF FINANCE AND ADMINISTRATION

DIRECTOR—J. Rodda, FCA

FEES OFFICE—

ACCOUNTANT—A. R. Marskell

DEPUTY ACCOUNTANT—M. Fletcher     ASSISTANT ACCOUNTANTS—Mrs. G. Crowther, A. A. Cameron

SENIOR EXECUTIVE OFFICERS—N. P. Crawley, Miss R. Harrison

HIGHER EXECUTIVE OFFICERS—Mrs. J. Peach, Mrs. G. M. Baker, Ms M. R. Morris, G. L. Turner, Miss D. M. McGuire, Mrs. S. M. Chalmers, D. M. Allen

EXECUTIVE OFFICERS—Miss D. E. Johnson, D. J. D. Woods, Ms P. R. Mills, Miss S. V. A. Weaver, P. H. Olden, A. D. Rowlands, P. J. S. French, Miss M. Oliver, R. A. P. Edwards, Mrs. C. J. Stockton, A. C. Martin, I. Montgomery, Miss R. Brooks, V. Fernandez, Ms G. Jessiman (temporary)

FINANCE OFFICE—

HEAD OF OFFICE—M. J. Barram, IPFA, MBCS

ASSISTANT ACCOUNTANT—Ms S. Peterson, IPFA

SENIOR EXECUTIVE OFFICER—Mrs. N. Norman,

HIGHER EXECUTIVE OFFICERS—Ms K. Bigwood, P. F. Barratt

EXECUTIVE OFFICERS—Miss T. D. Ruewell, Miss V. E. Wilson, P. F. Dawson, Ms B. Parekh, Ms S. Pratt, Ms T. Myers, Miss N. J. H. Price, T. White

ESTABLISHMENTS OFFICE—

HEAD OF OFFICE—B. A. Wilson     DEPUTY HEAD OF OFFICE—J. A. Robb

HEAD OF THE POLICY/PROJECT UNIT—Ms S. Leeming, MPhil, FIPM

SENIOR EXECUTIVE OFFICER—Miss P. J. Hurford     HIGHER EXECUTIVE OFFICER—Mrs. J. Leverton

PERSONNEL OFFICE MANAGER—M. Page

PERSONNEL OFFICERS—C. L. Watson, Miss C. E. Jackson, Mrs. R. A. Baker, Mrs. A. McGuinn, Miss T. J. West, Miss J. O'Mahoney

COMPUTER OFFICE—

COMPUTER OFFICER—R. S. Morgan, FBCS, FIInfSc     NETWORK PLANNING OFFICER—J. Fishenden, MIDPN, MIAP

COMPUTER SUPPORT OFFICER—Miss M. Morrison (temporary)     NETWORK SUPPORT OFFICER—Mrs. J. M. Cleveland

COMPUTER SUPPORT MANAGER—M. Luckins (temporary)     EXECUTIVE OFFICERS—C. J. Bumstead, P. D. Welsh

COMMON SERVICES UNIT—

HEAD OF UNIT—J. A. Robb     HIGHER EXECUTIVE OFFICERS—R. Gunn, M. J. H. Caswell

INTERNAL AUDITOR—R. H. A. Russell, ACMA     SENIOR AUDITOR—S. J. Lewis     SENIOR EXECUTIVE OFFICER—Mrs. D. C. Hill

TRAINEE AUDITOR—Miss R. A. Smith

STAFF INSPECTOR—R. C. Collins,     HIGHER EXECUTIVE OFFICER—R. T. Castle     TRADE UNION SIDE ADMINISTRATOR—D. R. Sands

WELFARE OFFICER—Mrs. A. Mossop

## DEPARTMENT OF THE OFFICIAL REPORT

EDITOR—I. D. Church
DEPUTY EDITOR—P. Walker
PRINCIPAL ASSISTANT EDITORS—J. Gourley, W. G. Garland, Miss H. A. Hales, Miss L. Sutherland
ASSISTANT EDITORS—Ms C. V. Grainger, Miss V. A. A. Clarke, S. M. Hutchinson, C. Fogarty, Miss V. A. Widgery, Ms K. Stewart, P. Hadlow
COMMITTEE SUB-EDITORS—D. Crosswell, Mrs. A. M. Browne, Mrs. H. J. G. Natzler, Mrs. A. Street, L. Gilmore, Ms G. Hardgrave, P. Oglethorpe, Miss C. Hanly, M. Watson, J. Ransley, Mrs. E. J. Gregory, Ms J. Dall, Ms P. Kelly, Miss K. Myers, Ms J. Warrington (temporary)
REPORTERS—Miss E. Morris, Ms D. Jones, Mrs. J. Symons, Mrs J. L. Davies, Miss J. Goodman, Miss J. Levy, K. Gall, Ms V. Wilson, A. Roberts, F. A. Minichiello, Ms B. Robins
IT MANAGERS—Miss J. L. Brown, R. Daniels
PRINCIPAL HANSARD ADMINISTRATOR—Miss R. Washington
SENIOR HANSARD ADMINISTRATORS—Mrs. M. J. Harding, J. Brake, S. O'Riordan
HEALTH AND SAFETY MANAGER—Mrs. M. Garland
ANNUNCIATOR SUPERINTENDENT—A. E. Thompson

## REFRESHMENT DEPARTMENT

DIRECTOR OF CATERING SERVICES—Mrs. S. J. Harrison, MHCIMA
OPERATIONS MANAGER—N. M. Hutson, MHCIMA
CATERING ACCOUNTANT—D. R. W. Wood, FCA
EXECUTIVE CHEF—D. Dorricot
PERSONNEL ADMINISTRATOR—Mrs. S. M. Nicholls, FHCIMA, MIPD
CATERING MANAGER, HOUSE OF COMMONS—P. Gale, MHCIMA
HEAD CHEF—L. J. Colmer
CATERING MANAGER, BELLAMY'S—Ms S. Hovells, LHCIMA
BANQUETING MANAGER—C. J. Griffiths
ASSISTANT BANQUETING MANAGER—
ASSISTANT CATERING MANAGER—M. W. E. Johnson
ASSISTANT CATERING ACCOUNTANT—Mrs. B. A. Langley
SYSTEMS MANAGER—D. Capstick, MHCIMA
PERSONAL ASSISTANT TO THE DIRECTOR OF CATERING SERVICES—Ms B. Woodiwiss
ASSISTANT CATERING MANAGER, MILLBANK—M. Simons

---

## OTHER PRINCIPAL OFFICERS

CLERK OF THE CROWN IN CHANCERY—Sir Thomas Legg KCB, QC
COMPTROLLER AND AUDITOR GENERAL—Sir John Bourn KCB
PARLIAMENTARY COMMISSIONER FOR ADMINISTRATION—W. K. Reid CB

---

SHORTHAND WRITER TO THE HOUSE—Mrs. P. J. Woolgar
HEAD OF SECURITY—Superintendent C. M. Harris
DEPUTY HEAD OF SECURITY—Superintendent R. Wood
POSTMASTER—J. Arnold
TRANSPORT MANAGER—J. W. Jones
SUPERVISOR OF PARLIAMENTARY BROADCASTING—Miss M. E. Douglas, OBE
DIRECTOR OF THE PARLIAMENTARY OFFICE OF SCIENCE AND TECHNOLOGY—Dr. M. G. Norton

*15 May 1995*

# THE
# PARLIAMENTARY DEBATES

## OFFICIAL REPORT

IN THE THIRD SESSION OF THE FIFTY–FIRST PARLIAMENT OF THE
UNITED KINGDOM OF GREAT BRITAIN AND NORTHERN IRELAND
[WHICH OPENED 27 APRIL 1992]

### FORTY–FOURTH YEAR OF THE REIGN OF
## HER MAJESTY QUEEN ELIZABETH II

**SIXTH SERIES**  **VOLUME 260**

ELEVENTH VOLUME OF SESSION 1994–95

# House of Commons

*Monday 15 May 1995*

*The House met at half-past Two o'clock*

PRAYERS

[MADAM SPEAKER *in the Chair*]

# Oral Answers to Questions

### NATIONAL HERITAGE

#### National Lottery

1. **Mr. Miller:** To ask the Secretary of State for National Heritage if he will list the sports bodies in Cheshire to which grants from national lottery proceeds have been made and the amounts given. [22464]

**The Parliamentary Under-Secretary of State for National Heritage (Mr. Iain Sproat):** The Sports Council has made five grants in Cheshire: Mobberley cricket club, £2,524; Macclesfield tennis club, £22,200; Davenham cricket club, £16,310; Padgate sports association, £32,402; Moore rugby union football club, £93,400. I understand that a further 15 applications from sports bodies in Cheshire are currently under consideration.

**Mr. Miller:** I thank the Minister for that helpful information, and I am sure that everyone in the House would want to wish those clubs every success with the use of that money. The Minister will recall that, on previous occasions, I have drawn his attention to the shortage of resources in and around my constituency, especially for junior football clubs and for athletics. Will he kindly bring to the attention of the committee, when it considers the next tranche, the existence of that difficult position, which needs rectifying in the interests of everyone in our community?

**Mr. Sproat:** I thank the hon. Gentleman for his generous remarks, and I will certainly draw his comments to the attention of the Sports Council.

**Dr. Spink:** Does my hon. Friend agree that in Cheshire, as elsewhere, priority should be given to distributing those funds to those sporting initiatives that address as many ordinary folk as possible, rather than to focusing large amounts of money on elitist and somewhat esoteric initiatives?

**Mr. Sproat:** I am sure that the Sports Council takes those matters very much into account, especially where they benefit young people and deprived people.

**Mr. Pendry:** The Minister will be aware that the second round of lottery grants from the Sports Council to Cheshire sports clubs was slightly better than the first. Will he nevertheless recognise that the distribution of grants generally is erratic? For instance, the north-west, of which Cheshire is a part, received about £1.25 million in the latest round, whereas the south-west received more than £8 million; the east midlands received 15 grants, the west midlands two. Will the Minister involve himself in giving some direction to the Sports Council so that a fairer distribution may operate, and so that urban areas receive a better deal than is currently the case? Only then will the distribution of grants be considered credible by the public.

**Mr. Sproat:** No. I will not involve myself in that matter, which is a matter for the Sports Council. The House rightly decided to distance itself politically from such decisions. However, I have no doubt that, as time goes by, there will be an even spread throughout the country. The Sports Council is mandated to ensure that that is so.

#### Arts Funding

2. **Mr. Rooney:** To ask the Secretary of State for National Heritage when he last met the Association of

Metropolitan Authorities to discuss the funding of the arts by local authorities. [22465]

**The Secretary of State for National Heritage (Mr. Stephen Dorrell):** I met the Association of Metropolitan Authorities on 24 January 1995 to discuss a number of issues.

**Mr. Rooney:** The Secretary of State will be aware of the increasing pressure on local authority budgets and he will be aware that, sadly, non-statutory sectors are sometimes the first to suffer. Is he not worried, especially, about the danger of charges being levied for entrance to museums and similar activities?

**Mr. Dorrell:** The Government's policy has always been that it is a matter for individual museum organisations to decide whether they want to charge for entrance to museums. Regarding the pressure on local authority finance, the hon. Gentleman will be aware that the Audit Commission, when asked to examine the totality of local authority operations, concluded that £500 million was available to be released from excess administrative costs. I look to local authorities to release that resource to improve the quality of all the services that they are responsible for delivering.

**Mr. Clappison:** When my right hon. Friend meets representatives of local authorities, will he give moral support to Hertsmere borough council in its efforts to bring the world-famous Elstree studios back into film production? Is my right hon. Friend aware of the strong support among all shades of opinion and all parties in Hertsmere for the idea that the present owners of the site should sell it to someone who is interested in film production?

**Mr. Dorrell:** I entirely understand my hon. Friend's concern. I am sure that his hope that the site should continue to be used in the film industry to support the development of the British film industry is an ambition shared by many in all parts of the House. My hon. Friend's point underlines the opportunity that confronts the British film industry. I shall talk about that at greater length when I respond to the report of the Select Committee on National Heritage at the beginning of June.

### Competitive Sport

3. **Mr. Hawkins:** To ask the Secretary of State for National Heritage what further measures he proposes to encourage greater participation in competitive sports by children in schools. [22466]

**Mr. Sproat:** The participation of schoolchildren in competitive sports will be a key element in the sports policy statement paper which my right hon. Friend announced on 23 March. The policy statement will be published in early summer.

**Mr. Hawkins:** I thank my hon. Friend for that answer. Will he give particular attention to the importance of providing sporting opportunities for schoolchildren at primary schools such as Hawes Side and Roseacre schools in my constituency? Roseacre school is an exceptionally good school, but unfortunately it has no sports field, and has never had one, as there is no land on which to build one. During his discussions about developing sports facilities for children, will my hon. Friend consider encouraging

those responsible for lottery funding to provide support for children at schools such as Roseacre to obtain facilities at secondary schools and sports centres in the area?

**Mr. Sproat:** I know of my hon. Friend's energetic pursuit of the interests of Roseacre primary school and I entirely agree that everything should be done to ensure that as many pupils as possible have as much access as possible to high-quality sporting facilities. I am glad to say that, from now on, I understand that the Sports Council will consider as eligible for lottery funds the purchase of a van or a minibus to take pupils to such grounds.

**Mr. Enright:** The Minister will have noticed that, under the present funding of schools, there has been a considerable decrease in the number of cricket pitches available. Cricket pitches are extremely expensive to maintain. Will the Minister make a special effort to ensure that extra funding is given to the annual maintenance of cricket pitches?

**Mr. Sproat:** The hon. Gentleman raises an extremely important point. It is true that cricket is a more difficult sport to deal with because of the size of the field and the quality of treatment that must be given to the square. I hope that the point that he has raised will be dealt with in the sports policy paper.

### Cross-media Ownership

4. **Mr. Lidington:** To ask the Secretary of State for National Heritage when he expects to publish the results of his review of cross-media ownership. [22467]

**Mr. Dorrell:** The Government are currently reviewing their policy on media ownership. I shall announce their conclusions once the process is completed.

**Mr. Lidington:** Does my right hon. Friend agree that it is illogical to have a system of regulation that permits one national newspaper group to have significant broadcasting interests yet bars every other national newspaper group from having more than a small stake in broadcasting interests? Will he examine that problem in his review and seek to bring cross-media ownership more within the remit of general competition policy in a way that allows British media groups to compete with their international counterparts?

**Mr. Dorrell:** My hon. Friend raises one of the issues that has been at the core of the debate about the future of media ownership regulation. It would be wrong of me this afternoon to hint at the direction in which the Government plan to go. Our media ownership regulation must have two objectives: first, to safeguard plurality and diversity in our press and secondly, to allow media businesses the opportunity to develop viably and successfully.

**Mr. Kaufman:** Has the Secretary of State taken note of the massive deal that has been made between News International and the American conglomerate MCI? Has he further noted that BT is a 20 per cent. shareholder in MCI? Does he agree that it is plain daft to have a system in which BT, the British telephone company, is allowed to broadcast television to the United States; American telephone companies, as part-owners of cable companies, are allowed to broadcast television in this country; but BT, the British telephone company, is not allowed to broadcast television in its own country? Is it not intolerable that our major telephone company should be prevented by restrictive legislation from becoming a part of the information super-highway in Britain?

**Mr. Dorrell:** The right hon. Gentleman has made that point to me before and I do not agree that it is plain daft. He cogently illustrates why the policy is right. The interests of the American consumer are served by having a choice of distributors available in the American market—that is provided by encouraging British Telecom to invest in it—and the interests of the British consumer are served by having choice in the delivery of the television signal to British homes. My right hon. Friend the President of the Board of Trade has made it clear that he does not propose to allow British Telecom into that market at present, in order to allow others to develop in competition with the long-term possibility that British Telecom offers.

**Mr. Harry Greenway:** Does my right hon. Friend recall the great Ealing comedies? Will he do all he can to see that they are restored by giving support to Ealing—

**Madam Speaker:** Order. I know that the hon. Gentleman sought to catch my eye on an earlier occasion and was undoubtedly frustrated, but he is way out of order on this question. We shall pass on to Mr. Graham Allen.

**Mr. Greenway** *rose*—

**Madam Speaker:** Order. The question relates to cross-media ownership. I saw that the hon. Gentleman wished to intervene and was frustrated when Ealing was mentioned on an earlier question, but this is not the question to which it relates.

**Mr. Allen:** It is less an Ealing comedy than a Whitehall farce. The delay in the Government bringing forward their proposals on cross-media ownership has led to all sorts of difficulties, not least in the recent Channel 5 round of bids, where bidders were completely unaware of whether they would qualify, were their bid to win. Will the Secretary of State tell the House, and all those who are interested, whether he will reach a decision on cross-media ownership in the near future? Above all, will he put his proposals to the House before we leap into the next major series of changes—digital television? Those in the House and outside need to be clear whether new rules will be in place before the digital revolution allocates new channels, or will the Minister delay and create the Whitehall farce that was alluded to earlier?

**Mr. Dorrell:** I can certainly tell the hon. Gentleman that I hope to bring forward proposals both for the allocation of channels and ownership regulations in the digital world and dealing with media ownership issues among conventional media companies. I hope to bring forward proposals on both those matters within the next few weeks. The hon. Gentleman's charge of delay would hold a great deal more water if, at any time during the past few months, we had heard anything from the Opposition suggesting that they have reached any conclusions on those issues. They are very good at telling us that we have been delaying when we have been considering the issues in a mature fashion. However, we have had almost no advice from the Opposition about the way in which that policy should develop.

## Arts, Suffolk

5. **Mr. Spring:** To ask the Secretary of State for National Heritage what is his assessment of the state of the arts in Suffolk.      [22468]

**Mr. Sproat:** It is for the Arts Council and the regional arts boards to take the lead in making assessments of this kind. I understand that Eastern Arts has a high opinion of the quality and range of arts activity in Suffolk.

**Mr. Spring:** My hon. Friend will be aware of the great success of the Bury St. Edmunds festival in my constituency. Is he aware that, two weekends ago, the Newmarket festival took place, the highlight of which was a concert under the Association for Business Sponsorship of the Arts pairing scheme? Does my hon. Friend agree that it is now possible to hear the finest music outside the metropolitan areas?

**Mr. Sproat:** My hon. Friend rightly draws attention to the success of the Bury St. Edmunds festival, which is celebrating its 10th birthday and has been a wonderful success. In respect of the Newmarket festival, the first time that it was held, it was a great success. I agree that the ABSA scheme, or the pairing scheme, which has brought some £80 million of fresh money into arts in the 10 years that it has existed, has been great success. As something like 78 per cent. of the money goes outside London, my hon. Friend is quite right to say that it allows people all over the country to hear the finest music and see the finest performances.

## National Lottery

6. **Mrs. Angela Knight:** To ask the Secretary of State for National Heritage what representations he has received regarding the distribution of national lottery funds to voluntary organisations for the promotion of sports facilities.      [22469]

**Mr. Sproat:** I have received representations from a variety of individuals and organisations on the subject of national lottery funds for sport.

**Mrs. Knight:** Is my hon. Friend aware that the Nutbrook cricket club near Ilkeston in my constituency, which provides sports facilities for young people in particular, has recently applied to the national lottery sports fund for money to improve its changing facilities? The Sports Council has, quite correctly, asked local organisations for their views and all have been supportive except Erewash borough council, which said that the club's bid would compete with the council's own bid for sports facilities. Does my hon. Friend agree that a local authority should not be able to blight another's bid in that way? What advice can he give to Nutbrook and to the Sports Council about the matter?

**Mr. Sproat:** I congratulate my hon. Friend on her persistence in the matter of the Nutbrook cricket club. She wrote to me on 16 June last year about that subject and I know that she has been disappointed in one or two of her applications to the Sports Council and the Foundation for Sport and the Arts in the meantime. I assure her that whatever Erewash borough council says or does not say will not blight the hopes of Nutbrook cricket club. The Sports Council will make its own decision about that important matter.

**Mr. Illsley:** Will the Minister bear it in mind that some organisations which provide funding for sports facilities are suffering because the money that was formerly distributed to them from pools revenue is falling as the success of the national lottery increases? The Barnsley lawn tennis club in my constituency is unable to secure a grant because of a lack of funds within the Foundation for Sport and the Arts. Will the Minister consider equal funding between the various bodies that provide money for sports facilities so as to make up the grants to those bodies which have been affected by the fall in pools revenue?

**Mr. Sproat:** The hon. Gentleman raises an important point. He will know that my right hon. and learned Friend the Chancellor of the Exchequer cut the duty in order that the Foundation for Sport and the Arts could continue to operate. I believe that that was the right thing to do and I hope that the sports club in the hon. Gentleman's constituency will apply for funding to the foundation, the national lottery, Sportsmatch or any of the other sources of Government sports facility funding.

## Tourism

7. **Mr. Barry Field:** To ask the Secretary of State for National Heritage what assessment he has made of the part that tourism can play in economic regeneration.    [22470]

**Mr. Dorrell:** Tourism plays a key role in the local economy in many parts of the country. Successful tourist development is a powerful engine of economic regeneration.

**Mr. Field:** Does my right hon. Friend agree that tourism provides an opportunity for real growth and that major tourist attractions can apply for funds under the single regeneration budget in conjunction with their local authorities? Will my right hon. Friend ensure that that information is made known as widely as possible, as it is a major embarrassment to the citizens of the Isle of Wight that the Liberal Democrat council did not apply for funds in the first round? That is quite extraordinary.

**Ms Lynne:** Oh!

**Mr. Field:** Perhaps that explains where the hon. Lady was for the first four questions of Question Time today; or perhaps the Liberal Democrats have already sold out to Walworth road—who knows?

Does my right hon. Friend the Secretary of State agree that tourism offers the opportunity of real jobs in the United Kingdom, although the Luddites on the Opposition Benches have still not cottoned on to that fact?

**Mr. Dorrell:** I entirely agree with my hon. Friend on both counts. It is extraordinary that the Liberal Democrat-controlled county council on the Isle of Wight is unaware of the opportunities that the single regeneration budget presents—particularly, as my hon. Friend said, the opportunities that it presents for the tourist sector. My hon. Friend is correct: the tourist sector creates real jobs. In the past 10 years, tourism in Britain has created 25 per cent. more real jobs. That underlines the extent to which the

tourist sector is one of the areas of growth in the British economy which holds out future wealth-creation opportunities.

**Mr. McAvoy:** I agree with the Secretary of State's last statement. Bearing in mind the contribution that the tourist and travel industry makes to the regeneration of Britain, what is the Secretary of State doing to ensure that unfair taxation is not imposed on that industry, which far too often the Government regard as a milch cow for taxation?

**Mr. Dorrell:** That is an interesting question for the hon. Gentleman to raise. If one compares the taxation imposed on a hotel operator in southern Britain with that of a French competitor, the most striking contrast that one will observe is the increased non-wage labour costs that French taxation and the social chapter impose upon the French competitor. If the hon. Gentleman were really interested in comparing the taxes imposed on British operators with those imposed on continental operators, he would make it clear to his Front-Bench team that he opposed the imposition of such an obligation on British operators.

**Mr. Forman:** While it is undeniably true that tourism can economically regenerate many parts of the country, is it not also true that it can environmentally degenerate them unless it is properly controlled? For example, has my right hon. Friend any proposals to put to the Secretary of State for Transport and others about controlling the plethora of tourist buses in central London, which cause serious congestion and air pollution problems?

**Mr. Dorrell:** My hon. Friend raises a serious issue: the tourist industry's impact on the centres of heritage interest that attract tourists. It is obviously a short-sighted policy to promote tourism if that damages exactly the attractions that bring people to Britain in the first place. That is why the Government set up a review of exactly those issues at the beginning of the 1990s, and why my Department has followed, through the English tourist board, a programme of sustainable tourism projects, which we are in the process of assessing. The results of that will be published in the autumn of this year.

## National Lottery

8. **Mr. Gordon Prentice:** To ask the Secretary of State for National Heritage if he will review the criteria used for the allocation of national lottery money.    [22471]

13. **Mr. Tony Banks:** To ask the Secretary of State for National Heritage if he will change the methods by means of which national lottery funds are allocated to good causes.    [22477]

**Mr. Dorrell:** I have repeatedly made it clear that the Government intend to keep the guidelines to lottery distributors under regular review. The allocation of lottery funds, however, began barely eight weeks ago, and therefore I am not yet in a position to revise the guidelines.

**Mr. Prentice:** Is the Minister aware that £680,000 of lottery money has just come to my constituency to fund a sports hall, yet that marvellous news was hijacked by the Liberal Democrats, who broke a press embargo 24 hours before the local elections, distributing thousands of leaflets in the constituency and claiming the credit? Is there not a case for reviewing this matter and ensuring that these sensitive announcements are not made during election periods, because otherwise people like the unscrupulous Liberal Democrats will hijack them and use them for electioneering purposes?

**Mr. Dorrell:** In these days of propriety, it would be improper for me to intervene in the arguments between Opposition parties. What I will say to the hon. Gentleman is that the announcement of the Sports Council distribution to which he referred was made not during an election period, but on the Friday after the election period was over.

**Mr. Banks:** We dream of getting £680,000 of the lottery in my constituency. I do not mind if the Liberals want to make the announcement first. I am an enthusiastic lottery punter and I look forward to winning the biggy so that I can clear off to the Caribbean, but a feeling exists in the east end that Camelot is creaming off far more than we are. Would it not be possible to have local committees that could take the money that goes into the lottery locally? We could then allocate some of the resources to good causes for the localities, rather than the money coming up to central London so that a bunch of toffs can allocate it to well-heeled Tories.

**Mr. Dorrell:** The hon. Gentleman's ambition to win the lottery and go to the Caribbean is widely shared on his behalf. On the suggestion that there should be local committees to distribute lottery proceeds, the different lottery distributors have set up structures to ensure that they are offered advice about the local scene before decisions are made. That is why the Arts Council takes the advice of the regional arts board, and why the Sports Council takes the advice of regional sports councils in making lottery distribution decisions. However, a national lottery needs to have a distribution process that culminates in an identifiable national distributor and that is subject, of course, to all the normal propriety disciplines imposed by the National Audit Office.

**Mr. Jopling:** Is the Secretary of State aware that Cumbria, despite having 20 applications currently under consideration, has so far received nothing from the sport and arts fund? Will he draw to the attention of the great and good who distribute that money that Cumbria is not an offshore island and that it is time that something was done?

**Mr. Dorrell:** My right hon. Friend is an effective advocate of his constituents' interests. I am sure that his point will be taken on board. He will understand that a precise regional balance is not sought in each month's allocation but, taking the distribution programme as a whole, my right hon. Friend is right to say that we must ensure that proper regional balance is observed.

**Mr. Jessel:** Does my right hon. Friend agree that there are far too many reviews? Surely there is no need for any review of the careful, and still recent, decision of the House that one quarter of the lottery's turnover should go to the five sets of good causes—the arts, heritage, sports, charities and the millennium fund. Will my right hon. Friend refuse to listen to the whiners, whingers, complainers and other small-minded and tiresome persons?

**Mr. Dorrell:** I shall certainly try to avoid listening to small-minded and tiresome persons. I agree whole-heartedly with my hon. Friend that we must allow the guidelines time to work before reaching considered judgments in assessing them. I repeat my original reply—that

the Government will keep the guidelines under review. This is a new project, and clearly it is important that, as it matures, we learn the lessons of our experience.

**Mr. Chris Smith:** Would it not be sensible to remove the existing requirement whereby the main distributive bodies are not allowed to seek applications but must simply sit and receive them? That system leads directly to the sort of disastrous decision taken over the Churchill papers. Surely it would be more sensible to take a more strategic approach, whereby the boards could consult widely with local authorities, business, trade unions and voluntary organisations to identify gaps and a proper pattern of provision.

**Mr. Dorrell:** The hon. Gentleman seems slightly at variance with the hon. Member for Newham, North-West (Mr. Banks), who was anxious that there should clearly be local input in the distribution process. One of the best ways is to ensure, before a lottery award is made, that there is clear evidence that the proposal has widespread and deeply felt local support. The most effective method is to ensure that lottery money is available to support local initiatives rather than engage in a kind of "goslot", which seems to be wanted by the hon. Gentleman.

9. **Mr. Steen:** To ask the Secretary of State for National Heritage if he will make a statement as to the way in which grants from the proceeds of the national lottery will be publicised and the speed with which grants are made by the grant-making body set up for that purpose. [22472]

**Mr. Sproat:** The manner in which national lottery awards are publicised is a matter for each of the 11 independent distributing bodies. Distributing bodies are dealing with applications for funding as quickly as possible, given the need to ensure that their systems and procedures are robust and each application receives due consideration.

**Mr. Steen:** I congratulate the Government on a great success story—another one. The public would like a bit more information. Will my hon. Friend the Minister consider providing information about how much money has already been raised for good causes? The public would also like to know how much money has been given to good causes. Would it not be a good idea if the regulator published a list every month of all the awards made by the five agencies, so that the public could have a one-stop shop printout of all the awards made, without having to approach all the agencies that give them?

**Mr. Sproat:** From memory, I can say that £495 million has been given to good causes, of which almost £60 million has already been allocated. As to my hon. Friend's interesting suggestion of collating information about the recipients of lottery awards and their value, if that were to help the House, I would certainly agree. My Department would do that, rather than the regulator. If the House wanted that information, we would certainly be prepared to place it in the Library at regular intervals.

**Ms Armstrong:** Since much of the publicity surrounding the lottery and allocation from the lottery has not been helpful or in the best interests of this country and how it orders its priorities, is it not time that everything was re-examined? Many charities which have worked for years to raise money and ensure the protection of the most vulnerable in our society are now losing millions of pounds because of the way in which money is provided through the lottery and because many people think that, instead of giving directly to charity, spending money on the lottery is okay and the charities will somehow get it anyway.

**Mr. Sproat:** On the first point, it is certainly true that there are lessons to be learned from the way in which the lottery is run. As my right hon. Friend the Secretary of State has said, we shall certainly be reviewing that—perhaps after the first year or whatever seems a sensible time. The Charities Board is in fact a matter for my right hon. and learned Friend the Home Secretary.

### Business Sponsorship of the Arts

10. **Mr. Heald:** To ask the Secretary of State for National Heritage what steps he is taking to promote business sponsorship of the arts.    [22473]

**Mr. Dorrell:** The Government actively encourage private sector support of the arts, particularly through their own pairing scheme, which has brought in more than £87 million in new money since 1984. The budget of the pairing scheme was increased by £750,000 to more than £5.5 million in the current financial year.

**Mr. Heald:** Does my right hon. Friend agree that the business sponsorship incentive scheme has been a huge success for the Government, bringing new money into the arts? What steps will he take to extend the scheme and expand the number of businesses participating in it so that the true partnership between public and private sectors may flourish even more?

**Mr. Dorrell:** My hon. Friend is entirely right. I completely agree with the emphasis that he places on the issue. The pairing scheme, as it is now called, has brought in almost 4,000 first-time sponsors since it was launched and has been responsible for increasing business sponsorship over the 20 years of its operation from a vanishingly small sum to roughly £70 million a year. Business sponsorship is a vital source of support for the arts in Britain. I intend to continue to give active support to the development of the pairing scheme.

**Mr. MacShane:** Does the Secretary of State agree that one of the best ways to get businesses interested in the arts is to give them tax breaks for investment? I refer particularly to the film industry, in which Britain is seriously disadvantaged compared with the rest of Europe and much of the rest of the world. Labour has put forward concrete proposals, and so has the film industry. Will the Secretary of State speak to that other great philistine in the Cabinet, his right hon. and learned Friend the Chancellor of the Exchequer, and provide the British film industry— before the Cannes film festival—with the leadership that it needs so that it may develop?

**Mr. Dorrell:** I congratulate the hon. Gentleman on his ingenuity in getting a film tax question into a question on the Association of Business Sponsorship of the Arts pairing scheme. As the House knows, the future of tax relief for film makers was raised in the Select Committee report on the film industry, to which, as I have already said, I intend to respond at the beginning of June.

### Tourism

11. **Mr. Nigel Evans:** To ask the Secretary of State for National Heritage how many tourists from abroad visited the United Kingdom for the last year for which figures are available.    [22475]

**Mr. Sproat:** In the 12 months between March 1994 and February 1995 there were an estimated 21 million visits to the United Kingdom by tourists from abroad.

**Mr. Evans:** Does my hon. Friend agree that many of those visitors want to visit villages around the country because they are quiet and beautiful? Does he agree, therefore, that those drawing up structure plans ought to think twice before trying to build thousands of new houses in villages such as Whittingham and Calderstones in Whalley in my constituency which would detract from their beauty? Does he further agree that another village in my constituency might now attract many more visitors because it contains the training ground of Blackburn Rovers? Will he send his congratulations to Jack Walker, Alan Shearer, Kenny Dalglish and the rest of the team on winning the championship yesterday?

**Madam Speaker:** Order. The last part of that question was rather out of order.

**Mr. Sproat:** If it is in order, Madam Speaker, I add my congratulations to those offered to Blackburn Rovers on winning the league after 81 years. That is a fine achievement and Blackburn Rovers deserve the credit.

With regard to the first part of my hon. Friend's question, it is extremely important, particularly in the case of the beautiful villages that he described, to ensure that the needs of housing are balanced by the benefits which accrue to the tourism industry. I am aware that my hon. Friend has followed the matter very closely over many months and I congratulate him on that. I will certainly draw the important point that he has made to the attention of my right hon. Friend the Secretary of State for the Environment.

**Mr. William O'Brien:** With regard to the 21 million people who the Minister says visit these isles, will the Minister consider the importance of developing tourism in west Yorkshire, particularly in relation to the Yorkshire mining museum? Will he do all that he can to ensure that we have our fair share of tourism in west Yorkshire so that people can see the heritage of the Yorkshire region?

**Mr. Sproat:** Yes, I am glad to say that the percentage of tourists travelling out of London has been increasing. I very much support the Yorkshire mining museum and I am looking forward to visiting it again very shortly.

### CHURCH COMMISSIONERS

### Pension Funds

27. **Mr. Barnes:** To ask the right hon. Member for Selby, as representing the Church Commissioners what plans the commissioners have to respond to the recent report of the Social Security Committee on the operation of pension funds, the Church Commissioners and Church of England pensions.    [22494]

30. **Mr. Clifton-Brown:** To ask the right hon. Member for Selby, as representing the Church Commissioners if he will make a statement on the findings of the Social Security

Committee in its second report of Session 1994-95, HC 354, in respect of the operation of the Church of England pensions provision.                                        [22497]

**Mr. Michael Alison** (Second Church Estates Commissioner, representing the Church Commissioners): The Church Commissioners welcome the view of the Select Committee on Social Security that a pension fund into which contributions are payable needs to be established and that that will help to protect the continuing scope of the commissioners to contribute towards the pay of clergy in the poorest parishes. That is consistent with the principles for future arrangements, on which discussions with diocesan boards of finance are well advanced. A report is to be made to the Church of England General Synod in the summer, following which the necessary legislation will be drafted.

**Mr. Barnes:** The Select Committee revealed some very serious problems in terms of Church of England pensions—£800 million losses, secrecy, recklessness and foolishness. When shall we reports and accounts for the 44 subsidiary companies, all of which are loss-making? When we deal with the matter further in the House, will the right hon. Gentleman support the notion that it should be dealt with by means of a full Bill which is discussable and amendable, rather than by a 90-minute take-it-or-leave-it statutory instrument?

**Mr. Alison:** On the last point, I am sympathetic towards the hon. Gentleman's idea, but it must be something to which the Church of England would agree as it has the majority interest in the issues being discussed. With regard to the pension side of the matter, I can assure the hon. Gentleman and the House that the assets of the Church Commissioners, which are now in the region of £2.4 billion, are very comfortably able to cover the whole of the past actuarial responsibilities for pensions and future pensions up to the point which is now likely to be cut off by a new contributory fund.

**Mr. Clifton-Brown:** Has my right hon. Friend had a chance to reflect on the full and searching debate which took place in the Chamber on Thursday night, in which it emerged that virtually every mistake in the book had occurred in the management of the Church Commissioners' funds? Does he agree that it is now urgent to establish a properly funded pension scheme so that past members of the clergy will be relieved of any anxiety that their pensions will not be properly paid?

**Mr. Alison:** I can assure my hon. Friend that past liabilities are very comfortably covered, as actuarially computed, by the £2.4 billion of assets in hand. My hon. Friend also referred to the future pensions liability. He will be aware that we have announced that there is to be a new contributory scheme to take account of that.

### Churches

28. **Mr. Fisher:** To ask the right hon. Member for Selby, as representing the Church Commissioners what consideration the Church Commissioners give to local opinion when considering offers of purchase and change of use for churches.                                        [22495]

**Mr. Alison:** The commissioners' policy is governed by the Pastoral Measure 1983. When a Church of England church is closed for worship, the Measure lays emphasis on the diocese seeking a suitable use and that is what is most commonly achieved. Each case is decided by the commissioners on its merits, taking into account the advice of their statutory advisers—the Advisory Board for Redundant Churches—the nature of the building, the options available and the views of the diocese. Dioceses are sensitive to local opinion in seeking uses. Formal objections made to the commissioners about proposed uses are most carefully considered.

**Mr. Fisher:** Does the right hon. Gentleman accept that my constituents in Stoke-on-Trent can see no evidence that the commissioners are seriously taking into account their views in relation to St John's Hanley, which the diocese wishes to sell to a company wishing to establish a climbing centre in a handsome church in the middle of the city? Whose interests are being served there? Will the right hon. Gentleman try to ensure that the local views which have been expressed coherently and sensibly with well thought out alternative ideas are taken into account?

**Mr. Alison:** The hon. Gentleman knows that the climbing centre proposal was a good deal further ahead than the Friends of St John's community centre proposal. However, the climbing centre proposal has not gone ahead and it is still fully open to the Friends of St John's community centre project to be considered fairly alongside it. No final decision has yet been taken, and the hon. Gentleman's own preference may in the event win the day.

### LORD CHANCELLOR'S DEPARTMENT

#### Legal Aid

36. **Mr. Hawkins:** To ask the Parliamentary Secretary, Lord Chancellor's Department what further measures he proposes to control the granting of legal aid to prevent those who should not be entitled to legal aid from receiving it.                                        [22503]

39. **Mr. Waterson:** To ask the Parliamentary Secretary, Lord Chancellor's Department what steps he is proposing to exclude wealthy individuals from legal aid entitlement.                                        [22506]

43. **Mr. John Marshall:** To ask the Parliamentary Secretary, Lord Chancellor's Department what recent representations he has received about the proposed changes in legal aid for the apparently wealthy.   [22511]

**The Parliamentary Secretary, Lord Chancellor's Department (Mr. John M. Taylor):** The Lord Chancellor has announced the measures that he intends to take forward following the consultation exercise on the granting of legal aid to apparently wealthy applicants.

**Mr. Hawkins:** Will my hon. Friend take further the welcome consultation on legal aid for the apparently wealthy by urging that a further look be given at cases in which legal aid is granted to those who have a long record of previous criminal convictions when those people are taking civil cases which are often entirely unmeritorious and constitute a serious nuisance to the law-abiding people who are often the defendants in those cases?

**Mr. Taylor:** I shall certainly pass my hon. Friend's remarks on to the Lord Chancellor. Three of the proposals are that there should be a special investigation unit to handle complex cases, a discretionary power to include the assets of friends, relatives and children where these appear to be material to the life style of the applicant and the power to require an applicant for legal aid to transfer ownership to the legal aid authorities of any assets which he fails to declare in the application.

**Mr. Waterson:** Will my hon. Friend confirm that in many cases apparently wealthy people have their assets frozen by injunctions during protracted and complex litigation? Can more be done following the hopefully successful end of that litigation to extract more money back from the beneficiary of legal aid by way of a statutory charge or other means?

**Mr. Taylor:** I am sure that that is a fruitful line of inquiry to pursue.

**Mr. Marshall:** Does my hon. Friend accept that it is a source of great anger that wealthy parasites such as Ernest Saunders and Roger Levitt should receive legal aid while many people with more modest life styles are refused it? Any action that my hon. Friend takes on that front will be welcomed by hon. Members on both sides of the House and across the country as a whole.

**Mr. Taylor:** My hon. Friend makes his point clearly, as he has done before. I am well aware of his views.

**Mr. Frank Field:** Does the Minister recall a question that I asked him recently requesting that he list the top 10 barristers and top 10 solicitors' firms gaining the most from legal aid funds? As that information must exist, does the Minister think that his departmental officials are being economical with the truth when they say that they cannot produce the information for him and for the House?

**Mr. Taylor:** Perhaps the hon. Gentleman would like to come and see me about that. *[Interruption.]* I am keen that he should be satisfied about the matter, and I shall return to the Dispatch Box to put my answer on record, as the hon. Member for Brent, South (Mr. Boateng) would like it to be.

**Mr. Skinner:** How on earth can the Government justify handing out large sums of taxpayers' money to wealthy people such as Saunders, Selig, Levitt, the Maxwell brothers and Asil Nadir, when someone in my constituency who needs to fight a civil claim in respect of an accident at work was told by one of those tinpot solicitors that he would be looked after and get legal aid, but then halfway through he was told, "Sorry, but the case is not strong enough to win"? Not only are those wealthy people making a small fortune out of the taxpayer, but barristers and all the rest of them are raking it in because they can make a ton of money backing the wealthy but they will not make a great deal looking after some poor constituent with a civil claim.

**Mr. Tony Banks:** Hang all lawyers.

**Mr. Taylor:** Barristers can claim what they like, but they will get what is assessed.

**Mr. Bermingham:** I declare an interest as a lawyer, and I wait for my hon. Friend the Member for Newham, North-West (Mr. Banks) to hang me. Will the Minister not rush headlong into what could be a catastrophic situation which will cost the country money? Much is said about large cases, but in efforts to reassess legal aid will the Minister bear in mind that it is sometimes more economical to grant legal aid at first instance in the magistrates court on the very first day of charging so that a matter is speedily disposed of, rather than to wait over several hearings for legal aid to be granted, with additional cost to the taxpayer and other sources, and achieve the same result in the end? Surely expedition is sometimes profitable.

**Mr. Taylor:** But we cannot disregard the Comptroller and Auditor General or the Public Accounts Committee in determining the circumstances in which legal aid is granted in magistrates courts. I can reassure the hon. Gentleman that I have no reputation for headlong rushing, but he need not wait long for the Green Paper on legal aid. It will be out later this week—on Wednesday.

37. **Mr. William O'Brien:** To ask the Parliamentary Secretary, Lord Chancellor's Department when he last discussed the legal aid recovery procedure with the chief executive of the Legal Aid Board; and if he will make a statement. [22504]

**Mr. John M. Taylor:** I discuss all aspects of the legal aid scheme with the board's chief executive from time to time.

**Mr. O'Brien:** Has the Minister discussed the recovery of payments with the chief executive of the Legal Aid Board? Will he take on board the situation involving a constituent of mine? When the recovery people attended the home, because no one was at home they started making inquiries of neighbours and informing them of the situation. That was totally deplorable and unscrupulous of those agents who are employed by the recovery section of the Legal Aid Board. Will the Minister impress upon the chief executive that such practices must cease and that people should not be subjected to such humiliation in front of their neighbours because agents acting on behalf of the Legal Aid Board behave unscrupulously?

**Mr. Taylor:** I will gladly look at that case if the hon. Gentleman will give me the details. I am not entirely sure whether he is referring to recovery by the Legal Aid Board of costs out of winnings, contribution as agreed at the onset of the grant, or the statutory charge which operates after a case has been concluded. Solicitors are under a duty to explain to their clients how the statutory charge works so that they are left in no doubt. The application form is required to be signed by both the solicitor and the applicant on that score to say that it has been explained and understood.

38. **Mr. Fisher:** To ask the Parliamentary Secretary, Lord Chancellor's Department if he will publish an analysis of the net income levels of those receiving legal aid in the last financial year. [22505]

**Mr. John M. Taylor:** I have no plans to publish the analysis that the hon. Gentleman requests.

**Mr. Fisher:** Will the Minister reconsider? I suspect that any analysis would confirm hon. Members' suspicions and the suspicions put to me constantly by the citizens advice bureau in Stoke-on-Trent that a great number of applications for civil legal aid are being turned down, limited or otherwise impeded. People of quite modest means are being prevented from pursuing rightful cases because of the way in which the civil legal aid system works. That cannot be right, and I suspect that it is of general concern to all hon. Members.

**Mr. Taylor:** The hon. Gentleman refers to net income levels, but it would be very difficult to produce the analysis required because net income is disposable income and in the determination of disposable income many allowances can be made which will depend on the enormous variety of individual circumstances of applicants.

**Mr. Clifton-Brown:** On the other hand, has my hon. Friend observed the type of case that I have come across in my advice surgeries recently, involving people who have previously been reported to be wealthy but who have passed the income assessment and been legally aided by the Legal Aid Board for civil cases? That cannot be right.

**Mr. Taylor:** If an individual case, as my hon. Friend puts it, cannot be right, anyone can challenge a grant of civil legal aid, including my hon. Friend.

**Mr. Boateng:** If the Minister has no plans to analyse the income of those currently denied legal aid, does he have any plans, belatedly, to deal with the issue of restrictive practices within the legal profession? Is he aware that there has been an increase of some 600 per cent. in the cost of legal aid to taxpayers while restrictive practices within the legal profession on the part of the Law Society and the Bar Council go unaddressed? Is it not time to redress the balance of legal aid in favour of the taxpayer and the consumer?

**Mr. Taylor:** That must be an ever-present intention, but the hon. Gentleman should know that the number of people helped under the legal aid scheme—3.5 million in 1994-95—will increase by 25 per cent. by 1997-98. As for restrictive practices, he will know—and I invite him to welcome the fact—that under the Courts and Legal Services Act 1990 monopolies of various kinds of legal practice are being steadily eroded. He will find, I dare say, that among the legal aid proposals will be that legal aid funding will be available to law centres and citizens advice bureaux supported by him. The Green Paper will be out on Wednesday—more then.

### Public Record Office

40. **Mr. Dalyell:** To ask the Parliamentary Secretary, Lord Chancellor's Department what are the procedures and criteria by which papers are transmitted to the Public Record Office.        [22508]

**Mr. John M. Taylor:** The Public Records Acts 1958 and 1967 provide for the transfer, under the guidance of the Keeper of Public Records, of those public records which are to be made available at the Public Record Office normally when they are 30 years old. The procedures and criteria are detailed in the "Manual of Records Administration".

**Mr. Dalyell:** May I ask a question of which I have given the Lord Chancellor's Secretary notice? As the right hon. Member for Southend, West (Mr. Channon) certainly

acted in good faith in March 1989 when he was Secretary of State for Transport, could his background papers relating to Lockerbie be expedited to the public view, along perhaps with those of Sir Charles Powell and the then Prime Minister? Could the Lord Chancellor have a word with his colleagues in the Crown Office, who are not answerable to the House, and tell them not to be so childish in respect of the ridiculous defamation of potential witnesses?

**Mr. Taylor:** I am grateful to the hon. Gentleman for giving me advance notice that he wished to mention the Lockerbie bombing. However, all I can say in answer to his question is that it will be for the relevant Government Department, as advised by the Public Record Office, to decide at the appropriate time which records should be selected for permanent preservation.

**Mr. Lidington:** Will my hon. Friend encourage Government Departments, through the Public Record Office, to make as many documents as possible available not only on paper but on CD-ROM, microfiche and microfilm so that researchers do not always have to travel the inconvenient distance to Kew to inspect these documents?

**Mr. Taylor:** My hon. Friend may like to know that by the end of last year some 25,000 additional records had been released as a result of the open government initiatives. As for the advance of information technology of the type to which he refers, it is not merely inevitable but welcome.

### Courts Service

44. **Mrs. Roche:** To ask the Parliamentary Secretary, Lord Chancellor's Department if he will make a statement about the cost of the Courts Service becoming an executive agency.        [22512]

**Mr. John M. Taylor:** The total cost of the Court Service's move to agency status is approximately £900,000, spread over three years.

**Mrs. Roche:** At a time of crisis in the Courts Service, with long delays and more than 10,000 complaints under the courts charter, is it not a scandalous waste of taxpayers' money when there is no evidence that it is improving access to justice?

**Mr. Taylor:** Far from being a scandalous waste, it is money well spent. The Government believe that generally the more businesslike focus of the agency will lead to greater efficiency, as well as higher standards of service.

### Judges

45. **Mr. Tony Banks:** To ask the Parliamentary Secretary, Lord Chancellor's Department what advice is offered to judges in terms of their comments made in open court.        [22513]

**Mr. John M. Taylor:** Each judge is independent. However, the Judicial Studies Board is responsible for the training of the judiciary. Its courses emphasise the need for care, consideration and sensitivity in court.

**Mr. Banks:** Does the Minister recall a letter that I wrote to the Lord Chancellor arising out of something in the *Fleet News*? A Crown court judge, Recorder Mr. Nicholas M. Atkinson, told two people who were being convicted at Winchester Crown court—I paraphrase rather than quote—"I would jail you if you were wearing Chelsea kit." That was a propos nothing because, so far as I was aware, they were not in any way connected with the right hon. and learned Member for Putney (Mr. Mellor). How can a recorder say something as outrageous and insulting to all decent Chelsea supporters as that? How does the Minister intend to call that individual to account?

**Mr. Taylor:** It is indeed within my knowledge that the hon. Gentleman has raised that case with the Lord Chancellor and I read those press notices as well. I am instructed to say that the Lord Chancellor will reply to the hon. Gentleman as soon as possible.

## Points of Order

3.30 pm

**Mr. Paul Boateng** (Brent, South): On a point of order, Madam Speaker. The Minister repeatedly answered my hon. Friends' questions with words such as, "Watch this space. See the statement on Wednesday," and the like. Does he intend to make a statement to the House on Wednesday? If not, why not and why does he repeatedly refer to such an announcement on Wednesday? Is it in order for him to do so when he apparently has no intention of making a statement to the House?

**Madam Speaker:** It is perfectly in order for the Minister to make the comments that he has made. That is not a point of order for me because I have no responsibility for the order of business on Wednesday, or any other day.

**Mr. Gary Streeter** (Plymouth, Sutton): On a point of order, Madam Speaker. Given the announcement by the rail franchising director this morning that rail prices will be pegged to inflation-only increases or less during the next seven years, have you received a request from the Opposition spokesman on transport to apologise to the House and the country at the Dispatch Box for all the Opposition's scaremongering?

**Madam Speaker:** No.

**Mr. Jeremy Corbyn** (Islington, North): On a point of order, Madam Speaker. I do not know whether you are aware of the fact, but the Office of the Passenger Rail Franchising Director has issued a press release that is not allowed to be taken out of this country. A note to editors says:

"This notice must not be taken to the USA or Canada"

or to certain other European countries. Apparently, use of the notice would make the sale of British Rail's stock and services illegal within those countries because of the level of subsidy involved. It seems extraordinary that private notes should be sent to newspaper editors about what can or cannot be exported, yet the House apparently has no prospect of hearing a statement from the Minister about exactly what he is proposing on such matters. Can you help us?

**Madam Speaker:** Perhaps we shall have to wait until tomorrow to see whether a statement is to be made. As I said earlier, I have no responsibility for the business of this House. If Ministers wish to make statements, they always give me and the House notice in good time and the announcement is always on the annunciator screen by 1 o'clock.

## Orders of the Day

### Gas Bill

*As amended (in the Standing Committee), considered.*

#### New clause 1

COMPENSATION FOR DAMAGE OR LOSS CAUSED BY PUBLIC GAS SUPPLIERS

'Schedule 4 to the 1986 Act (Power of Public Gas Suppliers to break up streets, bridges etc.) shall be amended in paragraph (3) by inserting after the second word "shall" the words "as promptly as possible" and by inserting after the word "any" the words "loss caused or".'.—[*Mr. Thurnham.*]

*Brought up, and read the First time.*

3.33 pm

**Mr. Peter Thurnham** (Bolton, North-East): I beg to move, That the clause be read a Second time.

I am grateful for this opportunity to move new clause 1, which stands in my name and that of a number of hon. Friends and Opposition Members. It deals with the need to provide compensation for small shopkeepers, garage owners and others whose trade is disrupted when the street is dug up in front of their premises.

Under the Water Act 1989, compensation is already provided for water works and this new clause will simply bring the Gas Act 1986 into line with the Water Act to provide compensation in exactly the same way. We are not dealing with compensation for all the other utilities.

It seems surprising that that anomaly should exist—but perhaps not, when we consider the bad old days when the old nationalised industries lost money hand over fist and had to be bailed out by the Treasury. No wonder the Government resisted the making of claims by traders who were losing profit. All that has now changed and the privatised industries are making substantial profits. Instead of losing £50 million a week, they pay more than £50 million a week to the Treasury in corporation tax on the profits that they make. British Gas makes nearly £1 billion profit, and the chief executive is being handsomely rewarded for his duties.

My right hon. Friend the Minister for Industry and Energy has not only duties to ensure that the gas industry and other utilities operate efficiently but much wider duties to ensure that a fair balance is struck between the needs of the industry and those of the community at large. On the one hand, we have privatised industries with their directors and shareholders, and on the other we have the customers and the wider community.

In seeking to achieve that balance, my right hon. Friend has been kind enough to see me on two occasions. I saw him first on my own and secondly with a delegation that included my hon. Friend the Member for Bury St. Edmunds (Mr. Spring) and my constituent, Mr. Cyril Eaton. We had with us representatives from the Forum of Private Business and the Federation of Small Businesses, from which I won a "Helping Hands" award in 1991 for providing more help to small businesses than any other hon. Member. We were also accompanied by representatives of the Association of British Chambers of Commerce.

I note that the Leader of the Opposition was in Aberdeen on Saturday, making all sorts of statements to that organisation. I am not sure whether the old or the new

[*Mr. Peter Thurnham*]

Labour party is here today. To judge from the Standing Committee report, I would say that it is the old Labour party. The delegation also included representatives of North West Water, including its insurance claims manager, Mr. Aldridge, and Jonathan Rogers, formerly of Hamptons but now of Highfield Consultants.

At that meeting, my right hon. Friend the Minister was good enough to listen to the strength of the representations and say that he would keep an open mind in considering the issue further. He will recall that I raised the matter in an intervention on Second Reading on 13 March and, on 25 April in Standing Committee, my hon. Friend the Member for Rutland and Melton (Mr. Duncan) kindly raised the issue on an amendment. I could not be there as I was on the Standing Committee that considered the Child Support Bill.

When I read the Standing Committee report, it is apparent to me that the gas industry representatives have been lobbying hard. The speech of the Opposition spokesman suggests that he was quoting from them rather than representing the wider interests of small businesses. For instance, the Association of British Chambers of Commerce says that it has been trying to change the law for 20 years, and it is supported by the British Retail Consortium and others.

This matter first came to my attention through my constituent, Mr. Cyril Eaton. He is the proprietor of a greetings cards stationery business, and he suffered a great loss in trade when North West Water dug up the street in front of his shop in Kearsley. Under the Water Act 1989, however, he was able to claim compensation under paragraph 1(2) of schedule 12, which calls for compensation to be paid for any loss caused or damage done. That was confirmed in a law case in 1979 between Thames Water and Leonidis, which determined that the "losses" covered economic losses and therefore losses of profit.

North West Water says that that legislation is good legislation. It regards it as only fair that, if it causes disruption to small traders through no fault of their own, it should pay compensation for the loss of that trade. It feels that it is not only equitable but necessary to maintain good community relations. Without the legislation, it would be uncertain of its obligations. With that legislation in place, North West Water naturally tries to schedule its work to cause the minimum disruption to trade; without it, it would be under no such specific obligation.

My right hon. Friend the Minister may remember that Mr. David Aldridge, the insurance claims manager of North West Water, said that 95 per cent. of claims are satisfactorily settled and that the company does not suffer from a mass of small claims. In his letter to me of 28 February he said:

"The requirement to pay compensation has, to some degree, facilitated better scheme planning and the use of less invasive construction techniques. The clarity and certainty which the statutory duty to pay compensation has also brought has reduced friction and disputes about compensation with the business community.

I should emphasise that compensation is not paid when the works are of short duration. That avoids the situation where compensation is being sought each time we carry out a small excavation in the street."

My right hon. Friend will remember that Mr. Aldridge was strongly in favour of the legislation governing the water industry and felt that it should be the rule for other utilities, certainly for British Gas.

My constituent, Mr. Eaton, was able to recover £7,000 in compensation from North West Water. However, he was amazed to find that when his trade was disrupted once again, this time by British Gas, it was under no such obligation to pay such compensation. The Gas Act 1986 allows for compensation only for "damage done" and does not include the three words "or loss caused".

If my constituent is entitled to compensation for the loss caused when North West Water dug up the street in front of his shop, it seems inexplicable that he should not be equally eligible for compensation when British Gas did exactly the same. Both events were totally outside his control. He has invested his hard-earned savings in a business, the rewards from which are limited by competition, only to have his livelihood threatened by a monopoly business, or near monopoly business, which does not face the rigours of keen competition. Why should he have to bear such an unforeseeable, unpredictable and uncontrollable cost when British Gas could so easily budget for such compensation claims on a nationwide basis? Where is the fairness, when the livelihood of my constituent is damaged while the directors of British Gas make handsome earnings, which are 50 times or more greater than my constituent can reasonably earn?

I appeal to my right hon. Friend's sense of good British justice. He spoke in Committee about a possible letter of comfort from the chairman of British Gas, about ex gratia payments, but I propose that proper statutory payments should be made, so that the matter can be dealt with properly. That is how the Department of the Environment approached the matter with the Water Act. I hope that my right hon. Friend is not tempted to listen to a "not invented here" argument from officials in his Department, who may argue that line just because the precedent was set by another Department. We are talking just about the gas industry, not about the rest of the utilities industry. The gas industry should follow the example of the water industry.

I know that my hon. Friend the Member for Southport (Mr. Banks) has already been in touch with my right hon. Friend about a particularly vicious case involving his constituents, Mr. and Mrs. Irwin. The trade of their small shop was savagely disrupted in the 13 weeks running up to Christmas and has not yet recovered, but British Gas has arrogantly dismissed all their claims. I have seen a copy of the letter sent to Mr. and Mrs. Irwin on 22 June from the chairman of British Gas, who said:

"I do not, therefore, consider that there is a case for compensation."

Unless British Gas is subject to a statutory requirement, I believe that it will continue to adopt such an arrogant attitude.

Four other cases have been brought to my attention by Mr. Jonathan Rogers of Highfield Consultants, which specialises in such claims. Johnsons garage of Gainsborough lost £2,200 profits because of water works, but it was fully compensated by Anglian Water under the terms of the Water Act. Mr. Patel of Bristol and Cairneyhill garage of Dunfermline, however, have claimed compensation for substantial losses due to disruption, but both have been dismissed by British Gas, which said that it was not interested in making any payments in either case. The letters that I have read simply repeated time and again:

"British Gas in common with other utilities and authorities should adopt a consistent approach to these matters within the framework of the law. Therefore I am unable in this case to agree any form of compensation".

That is the line that British Gas takes every time.

Further cases have been brought to my attention by the Forum of Private Business. I have three recent cases before me, including two in Hampshire. In the constituency of my hon. Friend the Member for Hampshire, North-West (Sir D. Mitchell), G. Dowling and Son of Whitchurch had access prevented for seven weeks, and claimed £2,400. In east Hampshire, work took place for three months, disrupting the business of Morgan Automation. In the constituency of my hon. Friend the Member for Altrincham and Sale (Sir F. Montgomery), who has supported me in that case, Lucas Bookshop has lost £12,000 as a result of eight months of disruption from the laying of gas pipes followed by sewerage works, and £12,000 is claimed.

3.45 pm

**Mr. Iain Duncan Smith** (Chingford): For the guidance of our right hon. Friend the Minister, does my hon. Friend agree that, when British Gas produces its end-of-year profit figures, a chunk of the profit is transferred profit—that is to say, the small businesses that have been adversely affected have had their profit curtailed and transferred essentially to the gas company, which then declares it as its own? Therefore, in a sense, the gas company is declaring unfair profit—excess profit, which we could deal with today.

**Mr. Thurnham:** I am grateful to my hon. Friend for making the argument as clearly as he does. There is a straight trade-off between the profits of British Gas and the profits of small traders. There would be no cost to the Treasury; at least, I do not envisage any. We are simply considering the need for fairness and equity. That already exists in the law, with the Water Act 1989, so we are asking only for the Gas Bill to come into line with the Water Act.

**Mr. Geoffrey Clifton-Brown** (Cirencester and Tewkesbury): Has my hon. Friend thought of another aspect? If the gas industry is not required to pay proper compensation for loss of business, it will have no incentive to expedite works to minimise that loss.

**Mr. Thurnham:** In the correspondence that I have read, British Gas admits that it might have a liability if it were negligent, but it does not admit any liability otherwise to plan its work.

North West Water, during its representations to my right hon. Friend the Minister, did say that it did everything in its power to minimise those disruptions. It said that it regarded the payment of that compensation as part of good community relations, which it needs.

I am amazed that British Gas should take the attitude that it will not pay that compensation, which is only fair, when it is able to report substantial profits and its directors are able to make substantial earnings. They draw earnings that are considerably greater than those of Ministers, who bear far greater responsibilities, not only for the industries concerned, but for the wider interests of the community.

I should have thought that it would be in the interests of those executives of the utilities to ensure that they conduct their business in a thoroughly honourable way, bearing in mind the needs of the communities affected.

I have with me letters from the Association of British Chambers of Commerce, which tells me that it has been trying to change that law for 20 years. It wrote to me in October, saying:

"we would certainly wish to lend our support to any measures which might close this loophole".

It wrote to me further on 15 March:

"We welcome the opportunity to discuss possible amendments to the Gas Bill with a view . . . to pay compensation to traders for losses sustained for work on the public highway."

The Country Landowners Association has also written to say that it believes that

"The only way in which"

British Gas and other utility companies

"can be obliged to respect the legitimate interests of those who are affected by their works, is to impose a liability of this nature."

There is therefore very broad support for the new clause.

I am surprised that, in Committee, the hon. Member for Clackmannan (Mr. O'Neill), the spokesman for the official Opposition, was unable to support the amendment that was tabled at that stage, and that, in considering that, all he could refer to was the Society of British Gas Industries, Electricity Association Services Ltd. and British Gas. What has the hon. Gentleman done about all the other interests that I mentioned? Is he not interested in small business? Obviously, the old Labour party, with its corporatist interests, is not paying any regard to small business, which the Conservative party has always strongly supported.

I trust that I shall have substantial support, not only from Conservative Members, but from Opposition Members. I look forward to hearing what my right hon. Friend the Minister has to say.

**Mr. Martin O'Neill** (Clackmannan): The Opposition have no major objections to the new clause, but we wonder whether it is the right way to deal with the problem. We do not deny that there is a problem, but the general election will have to come and go before we are in a position to do much about it. By that time, the hon. Member for Bolton, North-East (Mr. Thurnham) will not be with us, given the size of his majority and, as far as I recall, his unwillingness to defend his seat.

The new clause, understandably, deals with the only utility that it can deal with—British Gas; it does not take on the electricity companies. The hon. Gentleman was not altogether fulsome in his presentation of the situation. As I understand it, the Water Act 1989 emanated from the Department of the Environment, which has no responsibility for business and can impose on it whatever obligations it likes.

I can only imagine that when the Water Act was passed, the Department of Trade and Industry was not consulted, or if it was, it felt that the burdens imposed on businesses by water boards' activities were greater than those imposed by gas companies. We believe that other utilities could be involved. The cable companies certainly have some obligations under the New Roads and Street Works Act 1991, but the electricity utilities are as yet unscathed. The lobby that seems to be working away in the undergrowth of British business appears to have been strangely silent at the time of the privatisation of the

[*Mr. Martin O'Neill*]

electricity companies. Perhaps the hon. Member for Bolton, North-East could let us know whether representations were made about the electricity companies. I should have thought that they presented just as much of a problem.

**Mr. Thurnham:** The hon. Gentleman said that he thought that electricity companies represented just as much of a problem. Does he not accept that the scale of disruption is generally greatest with water or sewerage works, and, secondly, with gas works? Cable laying is a quick matter, which is here today and gone tomorrow, and is unlikely to give rise to such claims.

**Mr. O'Neill:** I am not competent to pass quite as swingeing a judgment as the hon. Gentleman, who may well have greater experience of the electricity industry than me. I am under the impression that the regional electricity companies and others spend a great deal of time digging up roads. If their stories are to be believed—I have no reason to doubt them—they invest a great deal of money and effort in improving the quality of electricity connections. One would have thought that they would be engaged in such activities, especially in built-up, urban areas.

There is a legitimate case for legislation, but it would be wrong to deal with only one utility. It would be far more sensible to deal with them all at once so that they could be treated fairly and with due weight.

**Mr. Richard Shepherd** (Aldridge-Brownhills): The Water Act has done that.

Does not the hon. Gentleman feel for the small businesses and other businesses affected by a statutory undertaking with monopoly powers? Businesses are damaged—what is his remedy while we have the Bill before us?

**Mr. O'Neill:** We should deal with the problem in the context of all the utilities; it is not appropriate to take one at a time. We clearly did not take one at a time in the case of water—the Water Act came from the Department of the Environment, not the Department of Trade and Industry. I suspect that the DTI was not consulted at the time. As yet, the voluminous correspondence of the hon. Member for Bolton, North-East with everybody and anybody has uncovered nothing. I discovered that with some simple research.

The Labour party is not prepared to go into the Lobby in support of the new clause, if it reaches a vote. If any of my colleagues wish to do so, that is their decision, but the Opposition do not consider that it is the right time for such a new clause.

It would be more appropriate to deal with a number of cases together. Indeed, there is relevant legislation. The New Roads and Street Works Act 1991 covers certain aspects of the issue. I do not know whether the hon. Member for Bolton, North-East, who claims credit for being the most helpful person on those matters, was involved in that legislation. That would have been the obvious time not just to take into account the important matters of the individual safety of pedestrians or of road safety, but to protect the interests of businesses.

We are not in government—that is a pity—and the hon. Gentleman claims credit for having influence elsewhere and being able to speak to Ministers, but it seems that

Ministers are influenced by him about as much as I am. That is regrettable; perhaps it is due to the manner in which he advocates the case that he puts forward.

The Opposition recognise that there is a problem, but we do not consider that it will be resolved to any extent by the new clause, because other industries are just as important and should be dealt with just as expeditiously. Unless they can be dealt with at one time, we not consider it necessary to deal with them at all.

This evening, we want the Government to say something far more conclusive than what they said in Committee. Frankly, I am not prepared to advocate that my hon. Friends support the new clause, if there is a vote. It is up to the hon. Gentleman to make his own judgment as to whether he wishes to put it to a vote.

**Mr. Duncan Smith:** I have been listening carefully to the hon. Gentleman. In principle, he agrees with the logic of the new clause, but he cannot support it in respect of the Gas Bill. Surely the Opposition should take a position on the issue if they agree in principle, as they allege. They must seize the initiative whenever it arises, as all legislators must do, and surely this is the moment to do so. I do not understand how the hon. Gentleman can agree with something and then say that the Opposition do not support it. It makes no sense.

**Mr. O'Neill:** I repeat our position. As far as we are concerned, the role of public utilities in interfering with people's businesses and the damage that that can cause businesses, especially when they dig up roads, should not be dealt with on a utility-by-utility basis. The Water Act dealt with it in that way primarily because the measure came from a different Department. Since then, there has been other legislation that the Government have singularly failed to utilise.

It is possible that an incoming Labour Government would re-examine the matter on a comprehensive basis, but the approach of Conservative Members, in seeking to use such a narrow issue to deal with a far broader problem, is quite understandable in view of the general campaign that utilities which cause damage to businesses should be subject to the law, as they are not at present. However, we are not prepared to take one utility alone. We would want the cable industry, electricity and gas to be taken together as the three utilities that are, as yet, outside the law. Until they can all be handled at once, this is the wrong way to go about it, so we are not prepared to support the new clause.

**Mr. Richard Shepherd:** I am truly confused by the speech of the hon. Member for Clackmannan (Mr. O'Neill). Presumably, on the basis that there was not a universal all-industry approach to the problem, we would not even have had the relevant clause in the Water Act, which is important to many small businesses.

I must declare an interest in the debate. I was a small grocer before I came to the House, and my brother now runs the company that I founded. The Water Act saved part of our business by allowing compensation to be paid to one of our shops for the lengthy barricading of its premises.

The public utilities—which are very much in the Opposition's searchlight as to their management, pay and the way in which dividends and shares are handed over to directors—have enormous powers. They are common-or-garden utility companies that serve local areas as monopolies. The prices they fix, subject to the regulator, are effectively monopoly prices. They can demand all their costs back through the price mechanism, and very few competitive businesses in the world can demand the return of any level of costs through that method.

4 pm

We have seen how the utility monopolies look after themselves—through the boards that overpay themselves, share deals and so on. I commend my hon. Friend the Member for Bolton, North-East (Mr. Thurnham) for proposing the new clause and I commend those across the country who support it; it seems to be a case of the little people against the monopolies. Under the new clause, public utilities are asked to have regard for the way in which they conduct their business.

In the case of the shop that I mentioned, the southern end of a major thoroughfare—Sloane street in London—was dug up in order to improve the supply of water to London. No one disputes that that action was necessary, and the water board acted in an exemplary fashion. Therefore, should there not be like treatment across the board for all statutory undertakings that have monopolies in local service provision? Why should the water industry quite rightly pay compensation for loss of business and damage done to small employers—who are often sole employers—but the gas industry be saved that expense?

I do not believe that the Opposition are fundamentally opposed to such a payment. I did not understand the comment by the hon. Member for Clackmannan about the curious way in which the measure should be bundled up to apply across the spectrum. The House has a means of addressing the second most important issue—after water, as my hon. Friend pointed out—confronting business people in this regard. Digging up roads in front of business premises can make people bankrupt; that is the essence of the matter.

I do not honestly believe that the Government can oppose the payment of compensation. It seems to me that it is a typical case of a monopoly utility company effectively writing a large section of its own legislation in a trade-off between Whitehall and the monopoly interests involved. That has occurred in the past. For example, British Telecom had a duopoly policy in the old days. In the early stages of the policy's development—which is all that I am alluding to—British Telecom had to fight a fierce battle for the British market. There was a secret agreement about that duopoly, whereby the second company was limited to only 3 per cent. of British Telecom's revenue. That was nonsense, so the Government developed that policy until we reached a more satisfactory arrangement.

I cannot conceive of an argument that requires the Government to treat the new clause in any but the most sympathetic manner. I suggest that the Government do so, as millions of small business men and women and their employees are fed up to the teeth with the arrogance of the utility companies and the often incomprehensible manner in which local utility companies that provide the necessities of life treat businesses and consumers.

There will be no cost to the Treasury. In writing legislation, the Government have the opportunity to consider very carefully whom they represent and to take amendments on board. The vitality of small businesses is crucial to the nation's vitality. That is why the Government should listen very carefully to my hon. Friend's argument in proposing the new clause and should not pay any heed to the Opposition spokesman, who wants to postpone a remedy that can be effected immediately in the Bill.

**Mr. Peter Hain** (Neath): The Conservative Members who have spoken have both made strong cases on behalf of small businesses. All of us who have experienced the difficulties faced by small businesses when confronted with works outside their premises will have a lot of sympathy with them, and I think that that sympathy crosses the House, but I want to address some specific points to those hon. Gentlemen and to ask the Minister whether the new clause is the best way to handle the matter.

From reading the new clause, it seems that its consequences would be to impose unquantifiable risk, not so much on TransCo, which could simply pass the risk on to customers through pricing flow-throughs, but on subcontractors, who often are also, if not small businesses, at least medium-sized businesses. They would have to carry the liability, which may well be reflected in the ultimate price that we pay for gas through the pipeline.

The way in which the new clause is phrased and its impact will impose that unquantifiable burden of risk on subcontractors in particular, who are now the norm in the competitive, deregulated regime to which the gas industry is subjected. A technical problem therefore exists in relation to the way in which the new clause has been phrased.

**Mr. Thurnham:** Perhaps the hon. Gentleman could just clarify his point? I am not aware that water companies, which of course use contractors, as every other utility does, face the difficulties to which he has alluded.

**Mr. Hain:** The water industry legislation, as the hon. Gentleman will find when he reads it, applies somewhat differently. That underlines the point, which I repeat, made by my hon. Friend the Member for Clackmannan (Mr. O'Neill). The issue needs addressing in relation to all the privatised utilities, local authorities, and highways agencies. The impact on small businesses of such street works is significant. The problem is best dealt with in a comprehensive rather than piecemeal fashion, which could create knock-on effects that are technically flawed. We have here, as it were, a backlash from Conservative Members against the very privatised utilities for which they were responsible. They privatised gas and they are backing this flawed and fundamentally wrong competition Bill. They are the ones who initially created privatised monopolies; now they are screaming at the consequences.

**Mr. Richard Shepherd:** I shall not go into the hon. Gentleman's exegesis of the Gas Bill. He makes some assumptions or hypotheses. Is he aware of any problems over the same sort of clause in the Water Act 1989?

**Mr. Hain:** I am not aware of any such problems in the Water Act. I have had many experiences such as those referred to by the hon. Gentlemen in relation to the Water Act. I am simply saying that, in relation to the Gas Bill, the way in which the new clause applies will impose unquantifiable risk on subcontractors in particular. The matter should not be handled in this way. It should be addressed on a comprehensive basis. If the hon.

[Mr. Hain]

Gentleman and his hon. Friend persuaded the Minister to introduce legislation to deal with the problem, we would all be sympathetic to it.

The question of cable companies should not be tossed lightly aside. They are also responsible for a great deal of disruption. Where franchises are held by cable companies—they are making great strides in the city of Birmingham, for example—there is considerable unease and impact on small businesses in particular. The issue needs to be addressed, therefore, on a general, not piecemeal basis.

**Mr. Matthew Banks** (Southport): I shall speak briefly to the new clause. I listened carefully to the remarks of the hon. Member for Neath (Mr. Hain), but he did not satisfactorily explain why the burden would fall on subcontractors. My hon. Friend the Member for Bolton, North-East (Mr. Thurnham) referred to a case in my constituency, mentioning Duke street and my constituent Mr. Irwin. If British Gas had a duty placed upon it to compensate for loss of earnings in that case, I have no doubt that instead of weeks and weeks going by—during which time the British Gas contractor involved was seen spending time in the local pub—there would have been a greater sense of urgency on the part of British Gas to tackle the subcontractor, to tell him to get on with the work. The Berlin wall created around that particular business, which prevented access by the public, would have been done away with and life would have returned to normal.

**Mr. Bernard Jenkin** (Colchester, North): The hon. Member for Neath (Mr. Hain) felt there was some irony in Conservative Members proposing this amendment. Is not it much more ironic that Labour Members are blocking an amendment to serve the consumer—perhaps against the interests of a nationalised industry? Conservative Members are following a long and honourable tradition of making public services responsive to the public.

**Mr. Banks:** My hon. Friend makes a perfectly pertinent point in a satisfactory way. We are concerned about the individual, and those of us who put our names to new clause 1 are addressing that concern now.

**Mr. Kevin Hughes** (Doncaster, North) *rose—*

**Mr. Banks:** I will not give way because I am developing my theme, and I want to speak briefly.

The hon. Member for Clackmannan (Mr. O'Neill) was ahead of his party when he replied to Royal Navy debates as Labour's defence spokesman. Labour got itself into a bit of a pickle over Trident and nuclear policy. I do not believe that the hon. Gentleman, in his heart, entirely agrees with everything that he said at the Dispatch Box this afternoon. How long will we have to wait for a Labour Government? A long time, I suspect. We heard nothing from the hon. Member for Neath about his concerns for the individual and small businesses.

In the case to which I am referring, which has endured for many months if not years, the business has virtually gone bust. The individual has almost lost his business and he may lose his home. I will briefly describe the circumstances of that case, on which my hon. Friend the Member for Bolton, North-East touched. A major gas main needed work and the British Gas subcontractor built what I can only describe as a Berlin wall around the business in question. I observed that over weeks because I happen to live nearby, in Duke street. The work started in the summer of 1993 and it was still continuing after a lengthy recess. When the House returned in the autumn of 1993, I took up the question of compensation with British Gas but did not get anywhere. I met yet another brick wall. Constructively, I arranged a meeting at my home across the street between representatives of British Gas, my constituent Mr. Irwin, and his accountant and legal adviser. After lengthy correspondence, I received a letter from British Gas saying that it had considered even an ex gratia payment, but the answer was firmly no.

To cut the story even shorter, I took the matter up with head office. I was told all too often about the rights of British Gas, but there was never much mention of its responsibilities. All too little attention was paid to the rights of my constituent, who had suffered so badly. I was told clearly by British Gas that it had no liability to make reparations. In financial terms—I choose my words carefully because the last thing that I wish to do is embarrass a constituent of mine—the amount of money of which we were talking was absolutely tiny in the big swim of things. It would not matter, however, if it were £5. If somebody has not got much and is trying to keep his business together, £5—or £10,000—is everything.

I was still not satisfied at that stage so I sought a meeting with the chairman of British Gas. Four weeks after I first contacted him, I received a reply. There would be no meeting. My hon. Friend the Member for Bolton, North-East quoted from a letter of 22 June, in which Mr. Giordano told me:

"I do not, therefore, consider that there is a case for compensation."

Yet the subcontractor working on behalf of British Gas had ring-fenced, with the Berlin wall that I mentioned, his entire business. Nobody could get to it. None of the passing trade could stop, even though there was a large area nearby where cars could pull in. It was a disgrace.

That is but one example in my constituency. My hon. Friends have referred to other examples and there are many other such instances in the country. The case to which I have referred is—I think—one of the worst, and I regret that it has happened in Southport.

4.15 pm

Even though, as Member of the House, I believe that very often we try to legislate too much—I often take the view that we should legislate a little less rather than a little more—I have no doubt whatever that at the very least a proper code of practice should be developed by British Gas to deal properly with the case to which I have referred and other such instances. At the moment, there is no statutory obligation on British Gas. It has taken a line from which it will not waver. I very much hope that my right hon. Friend the Minister will accept the broad thrust of my argument. If we cannot legislate today, we need a proper, effective code of practice to help the little man in the street, my constituent, small business men and women and individuals in their homes who have suffered.

**Mr. Nick Harvey** (North Devon): I shall not detain the House long because the hon. Members who have put their names to new clause 1 have made their case well. Indeed, it is clear from the comments of hon. Members of all parties that there is much sympathy for the underlying point that the new clause tries to make. I think that all hon. Members have seen people at their constituency surgeries or have been contacted through the post in connection with the sort of circumstances about which we have heard.

I listened with interest to the comments of the hon. Member for Clackmannan (Mr. O'Neill), the Opposition spokesman. I agree that such obligation would be ideal across all the utilities, but I am surprised that he extrapolates from that the need to oppose the new clause. His argument suggests an element of two wrongs making a right. Whichever party wins the next election, legislative opportunities to address such a point will not present themselves every day. There is an opportunity here and now to do something about the wrongs that will occur in the gas industry.

In my constituency a great deal of trade is seasonal. On occasions, the gas board has not been as sensitive as it should have been and has carried out work throughout the summer season that could have been dealt with equally well during the winter. If the Bill contained new clause 1, it would be more sensitive to such considerations in future.

The hon. Member for Neath (Mr. Hain), who suggested that resultant additional costs might end up being passed to us in our gas bills. I do not believe that, in the current circumstances, that is particularly likely, because there seems to be plenty of profit to pay for such costs. But that might not always be so. If costs were to end up on our gas bills, however, it would probably be right and just. If gas is being supplied at a price that involves small businesses being disadvantaged unfairly, it would probably be better, even if costs were passed on to the gas consumer, that consideration for small businesses ended up on our bills. In the current circumstances, however, I do not believe that that would happen.

If the hon. Gentleman decides to press the new clause to a Division, I hope that Opposition Members will support it. As five Conservative Members have added their names to the new clause, and bearing in mind the parliamentary arithmetic as it is at the moment, we might have a very interesting vote on the new clause. I wait with interest to see whether the hon. Gentleman will press his new clause to a Division.

**Ms Ann Coffey** (Stockport): If the hon. Member for Bolton, North-East (Mr. Thurnham) presses his new clause to a vote, I would be happy to vote for it. I hope that he does press for a Division, because there are probably a sufficient number of Conservative Members who have added their names to the new clause for him to win.

We could legislate today and ensure that the proposal is accepted if the hon. Gentleman presses his new clause to a vote. I would be interested in his explanation to the people on whose behalf he has campaigned if he does not press the new clause to a vote. At the end of the day, whether the proposal is enacted depends on the attitudes and votes of hon. Members. The hon. Gentleman has an opportunity today to test that. I assure him that I would support his new clause and I look forward to his pressing it to a vote.

The hon. Member for Bolton, North-East represents a north-west constituency, as I do. I am aware, as he is, of the problems that public utilities cause in pursuing their improvements. Part of the problem is that the gas board can dig up a pavement or the frontage of a small shop and then be closely followed by the electricity board, British Telecom and, to finish it off, the cable companies. The argument that the proposal should be comprehensive is very good, because small shops obviously do not suffer from the problems caused by just one utility.

I agree that a great deal of the problem relates to the supervision of subcontractors, for whom British Gas must bear the responsibility. A problem that has been raised with me in my constituency relates to subcontractors beginning work at the crack of dawn and disturbing a client's access to a shop with very little warning.

Another problem that has been raised with me is that of reinstatement of work. Although the utility has six months in which properly to reinstate a frontage, which is the responsibility of the shop owner to maintain and not the responsibility of the highways authority, the frontage is sometimes left in a mess, which particularly deters old people from visiting the shop, and that may result in a loss of business. If British Gas had a statutory responsibility to make recompense in those circumstances, it would be a great deal more careful in organising that work and supervising its subcontractors. That would be helpful for everyone concerned.

The hon. Member for Bolton, North-East said that the issue was backing small business against big business. I hope that the Minister for Industry and Energy has noted the hon. Gentleman's comments. I wait with interest to see whether the Minister will back small business against big business and whether, after the Minister has replied to the debate, the hon. Member for Bolton, North-East will be able to back small business against big business. I hope that he will press his new clause, because it would be very welcome in the north-west.

**The Minister for Industry and Energy (Mr. Tim Eggar):** I thank my hon. Friend the Member for Bolton, North-East (Mr. Thurnham) for bringing this issue to the attention of the House. As he made clear, he has had two formal meetings with me and several less formal meetings. In addition, my hon. Friend the Member for Southport (Mr. Banks) brought a particularly serious constituency case to my attention. I am grateful for that.

We all recognise that the role of the utilities is extremely important. We all rely, in one way or another, on their work and we recognise that, from time to time, it will inevitably involve disruption to streets and common services. It was because of that that the Government introduced the New Roads and Street Works Act 1991 which resulted in the adoption by British Gas of detailed service standards.

It might be helpful if I describe those service standards. There should be notification of major works 20 working days in advance; pedestrian access to all premises while work is in progress; signing and guarding of the works with details of a telephone contact number should problems arise; leaving the site safe and tidy at the end of each working day; and reinstating any excavations promptly when the works are finished.

When we considered the 1991 Act, we specifically looked at the case for a general right to compensation for economic loss which arose from street works, and we came to the conclusion that such a provision would be wrong. The main reason for that was the general principle which underlies the use of streets. Successive

*[Mr. Tim Eggar]*

Governments have taken the view that businesses should not have a right in law to any particular given level of passing trade, and that traders must take the risk of loss due to temporary disruption of traffic flows along with all the other various risks of running a business.

That is an important principle. If one did not have that enshrined in law, where would it stop? Streets must be resurfaced from time to time, they can be made one-way and they may have to be closed. The emergency services can affect traffic also. I stand by the basic principle that the risk of disruption to access along streets must be a risk which a business runs on a normal day-to-day basis.

**Mr. Richard Shepherd:** Does not the Water Act 1989 confound the very principle which my hon. Friend is enunciating? We are trying to address the present piecemeal circumstances, and the Bill will place consequential losses upon traders through loss of trade. All that the House is asking is that the Government remedy that. To talk about a general principle on street works related to an earlier Act may be an interesting sideline, but we are confronted with a real problem. How are we to address it? We think the principle adopted by my hon. Friend the Minister is wrong.

**Mr. Eggar:** I understand my hon. Friend's passion. With regard to the provisions of the Water Act 1989, that is a different case which relates not just to street works but to general economic loss on land not associated with streets. It is the provisions affecting the water industry which are anomalous. My hon. Friend should know the dangers of arguing from the particular to the general.

I stick by the principle. Nonetheless, my hon. Friends the Members for Southport (Mr. Banks) and for Aldridge-Brownhills (Mr. Shepherd) have said that we have a practical problem. The issue is how we address that problem. I have been prompted by the initiative set up by my hon. Friend the Member for Bolton, North-East (Mr. Thurnham), and I have been particularly influenced by the constituency case raised by my hon. Friend the Member for Southport.

I have been in active discussion with the chairman of British Gas to see whether we can develop a way forward which deals with the cases that bear unreasonably upon small businesses. Mr. Giordano has suggested to me in a letter—which I shall place on record through the means of a written reply—that British Gas is going to revise the existing procedures of its transportation arm with a view to improving communication and co-operation with the owners of commercial premises. British Gas will discuss with individual business owners issues such as vehicular access, customer access, special notification and any special requirements which a particular business may have.

Beyond that, and subject to certain conditions which are laid out in the letter, British Gas has given an undertaking with regard to exceptional cases affecting businesses with a turnover of less than £500,000. That is British Gas's definition of a small business, which covers about 90 per cent. of businesses in the United Kingdom. Where such small businesses have a severe and clearly established loss of business for more than a month as a direct result of street works carried out by British Gas or its agents, British Gas will sympathetically consider claims in respect of financial loss on an ex gratia basis.

4.30 pm

Having listened to the particular cases that concern my hon. Friends the Member for Bolton, North-East and for Southport, and also taking into account cases that have been brought to my attention through other means, in particular following my discussions in a formal meeting with my hon. Friend the Member for Bolton, North-East, it seems to me that the undertaking from British Gas, to which the Government expect it to adhere in an appropriate way, will meet almost all the cases of which we are aware have caused concern on a constituency basis.

**Mr. O'Neill:** From what I can gather, there will be no admission by British Gas of any liability of an ex gratia character or the rest. Will the Minister look at the draft standard conditions as they apply to public gas transporters' licences? Condition 14 of the standards of performance provides for compensation for consumers. If, in the course of the extension of the distribution system, standards are not adhered to there will be compensation.

Will the Minister consider the licence as a means of securing an obligation? If he is not prepared to accept the "blunt instrument" of an amendment to the primary legislation, he might want to do so through the fine-tuning facility that is afforded within the conditions of the licence. That would impose an obligation upon the licensee, in this case TransCo, which is most likely to be digging up a road. The licence already contains a reference to compensation when standards are not met. I think that that is what hon. Members are talking about.

**Mr. Eggar:** Without studying that condition with care, I think that I am right in saying that it does not cover that set of circumstances. This Government and previous Governments have believed that the basic principle that underlies the 1991 Act is appropriate. None the less, we recognise—this is why I have entered into discussions with the chairman of British Gas—that, in a small number of instances, the cost of those works, despite the 1991 Act and all the additional undertakings that TransCo has given, may bear unreasonably on small businesses.

We think that the best way of dealing with that—this is why we have discussed it with British Rail—is on a case-by-case basis. In practice, the undertakings that have now been given by the chairman of British Gas, to which we expect British Gas to adhere, will deal with almost all the cases that have been brought to my attention by my hon. Friends and through other means.

For those reasons, I cannot go along with my hon. Friends and accept the new clause. I pay tribute to my hon. Friend the Member for Bolton, North-East for the enthusiasm and dedication with which he has—

**Mr. Duncan Smith:** Will my right hon. Friend give way?

**Mr. Eggar:** If my hon. Friend really wants me to give way.

**Mr. Duncan Smith:** I am grateful to my right hon. Friend. I know that he wishes to wind up the debate, and I understand the reasons for that. However, there is a serious problem with the note from British Gas. If it has defined the size of business that it will compensate, are we not now in grave danger of shuffling off the responsibility to legislate and make that a fact, and passing it across to the courts of law? Should somebody who has a business worth more than £500,000 turnover now wish to be compensated, he will have to take redress through the courts to say that British Gas has no right to define him out of such compensation because his loss is no less great than that of a business below £500,000. We could resolve that today by making that a certain fact in legislation.

**Mr. Eggar:** I thought that I had made it clear that the Government were not prepared to move away from the basic principle behind the 1991 Act. I have sought to deal with the specific nature of the problems brought to my attention by my hon. Friends and others. I am confident that the letter from British Gas deals with almost all the practical cases that have been brought to my attention, and I am sure that British Gas will seek to live up to the spirit as well as the letter of the chairman's communication to me.

**Mr. Thurnham:** I have listened carefully to my right hon. Friend and thank him for the great attention that he has clearly given to the issues presented to him. I am a little disappointed that he is not able to accept the new clause, but it was always apparent that there were difficulties in his Department about accepting legislation affecting one utility which some people might then feel should be extended to further utilities.

I have not yet had an opportunity to read the letter from the chairman of British Gas. Clearly, I should like to see it before coming to a conclusion about how the proposals would work, but I welcome my right hon. Friend's reassurance to the effect that he feels that they would deal with most of the problems that might arise. I shall, however, reserve my opinion until I have seen the letter and perhaps discussed it with those who are anxious that the new clause should be accepted. Perhaps there will be an opportunity for the matter to be discussed in the other place if it is felt that the letter does not go far enough in responding to our legitimate concerns.

I listened with amazement to the speech of the hon. Member for Clackmannan (Mr. O'Neill). He seems to think that, because his party was asleep during the passage of the New Roads and Street Works Act 1991, he can pretend that there is nothing he can do now. He might have missed his opportunity then, but he has a perfectly good opportunity now. However, he seems to have chosen not to use it. The hon. Gentleman was followed by my hon. Friend the Member for Aldridge-Brownhills (Mr. Shepherd) who made an excellent speech. He spoke with great feeling as someone whose small business had been affected by street works. I am sure that the whole House sympathises with his position.

**Mr. Richard Shepherd:** As I have already said, I am grateful to my hon. Friend for tabling this important new clause. I do not think that the problem has been dealt with by a letter from Mr. Giordano or see how it places a statutory requirement on British Gas. Nor do I understand how it will lead to compensation. The House itself has wrestled with the definition of a small business, but it seems that British Gas deems it appropriate to define it as one with a turnover of £500,000, or whatever the figure was. I did not hear the figures given for the water companies or what level of compensation they have had to pay, but, if we wait on crystal mountains or behind

ministerial doors for bad news from small businesses, we shall be in some difficulty. Truthfully, I do not think that a letter from Mr. Giordano is sufficient in this instance.

**Mr. Thurnham:** My hon. Friend makes it clear that there are still doubts. Until I have seen the letter, it is difficult to comment further.

I think that, having listened to the speech of the hon. Member for Clackmannan, British Gas shareholders will be delighted with the work done by its directors and other representatives. The hon. Gentleman could not have done better had he spoken as a representative of British Gas.

I could make little sense of the speech of the hon. Member for Neath (Mr. Hain), who seems blind to the benefits of competition. No doubt if he had his way, the gas industry would still be nationalised and there would be no money with which to pay compensation anyway.

**Mr. Hain** *rose—*

**Mr. Thurnham:** I think that we have heard enough from the hon. Gentleman.

I thank my hon. Friend the Member for Southport (Mr. Banks) for his truly excellent speech. He put his constituent's case very well. Clearly, the case that he outlined today had struck home as my right hon. Friend the Minister had earlier considered it personally and brought it to the attention of the chairman of British Gas for a second time. Obviously, this code of practice would be one important way of dealing with the issues if we do not have legislation.

I was pleased to hear the speech of the hon. Member for North Devon (Mr. Harvey), which again illustrated the benefits of competition. Clearly, the other Opposition party made a better case of addressing the issues than the official Opposition. To that extent, I wish the Liberal Democrats well and hope that they will continue to compete and to stir up some more realistic attitudes on the Opposition Benches.

I listened carefully to the hon. Member for Stockport (Ms Coffey) and thank her for her offer of support for the new clause if it comes to a Division. I am tempted to go to that point, so that we can illustrate the extent of the support for the new clause, but in considering whether to beg leave to withdraw it, I bear in mind the need not to over-embarrass Labour Members, as it is clear that early on a Monday afternoon not many of the colleagues of the hon. Member for Stockport would be around—

**Mr. Kevin Hughes:** About half an hour ago, the hon. Gentleman was championing the cause of small businesses, only to dump them and let them down 40 minutes on. He has chickened out and he will not push the matter to a vote. It is the hon. Gentleman's side that is opposing the new clause, not the Opposition.

**Mr. Thurnham:** I can only assume that the hon. Gentleman's remarks were addressed to his Front-Bench colleagues and that they will listen to him. It is interesting that there are considerably more Conservative Members than Labour Members in the Chamber this afternoon. Obviously, the former are concerned about the gas industry and the position of small businesses when compensation is called for, whereas I can see only half a dozen Labour Members and a sole representative of the Liberal Democrats in the Chamber.

**Mr. Hain** *rose—*

**Mr. Thurnham:** We have already heard enough.

[Mr. Thurnham]

I thank the House for the opportunity to debate the issue at some length. It is now clearly on the record and there will be an opportunity for us to study the letter from the chairman of British Gas. If the concerns that we have aired still exist, I have no doubt that many people will press Members of another place to raise the matter when the Bill passes from this House.

The Bill as a whole is excellent and in principle I wish it all possible success. I thank my right hon. Friend the Minister for Industry and Energy for going as far as he did in addressing my concerns and seek your leave, Madam Deputy Speaker, to withdraw the new clause.

**Madam Deputy Speaker (Dame Janet Fookes):** The hon. Member does not need my leave; he needs that of the House. Is it the House's pleasure that the new clause be withdrawn?

**Hon. Members:** Aye.

*Motion and clause, by leave, withdrawn.*

### New clause 2

#### MATTERS TO BE TAKEN INTO ACCOUNT BY DIRECTOR IN EXERCISING POWERS TO CONTROL GAS PRICES

'(1) The Secretary of State shall from time to time issue guidance to the Director as to the matters he is to take into account in exercising any powers specified in the conditions of a licence granted under section 7 or 7A of the 1986 Act to limit, vary or otherwise control the charges set by a licence holder for the supply, transportation or shipping of gas.

(2) Guidance under subsection (1) above shall include as one of the matters to be taken into account by the Director a reference to the extent to which the remuneration of the executive and non-executive directors of a company which holds such a licence reflects the performance of that company during the year preceding the year to which the remuneration in question relates.

(3) In subsection (2) above—

"remuneration" includes any salaries, fees, benefits in kind or share options; and "performance" includes increased efficiency in the carrying on of the activities to which the licence relates and improvements in the standard of service to consumers.'.—*[Mr. Nigel Griffiths.]*

*Brought up, and read the First time.*

**Mr. Nigel Griffiths** (Edinburgh, South): I beg to move, That the clause be read a Second time.

**Madam Deputy Speaker:** With this, it will be convenient to discuss amendment No. 54, in clause 8, page 12, line 41, at end add—

'(3) Standard conditions under this section shall include a duty on the part of any company which is the holder of a licence under section 7 or 7A of the 1986 Gas Act to publish annually details of the remuneration of the executive and non-executive directors of that company, including any salaries, fees, benefits in kind and share options.'.

**Mr. Griffiths:** The new clause and the amendment deal with some of the key issues that concern the public about gas and the other privatised utilities—corporate greed, boardroom bonanzas and lack of restraint, in spite of the preaching of restraint from somewhat unusual Conservative circles.

New clause 2 would give the President of the Board of Trade powers to issue guidance to the Director General of Gas Supply. The Secretary of State shall and must take some responsibility for ensuring that payments in the boardroom are not completely disproportionate to the performance of the company or the service to consumers. The present director general must be given powers to take certain actions with regard to the remuneration of executive and non-executive directors and the company's performance during the year.

The definition of remuneration in the new clause includes all those things about which we have been reading—not merely at the weekend and in all the editorials today, but in months and years past—but nothing has been done. The definition includes salaries, fees, benefits in kind and share options—the raid on the bank by far too many of those executives. Just as important, performance must include the efficiency of the organisation in carrying out its duties to the public, as well as improvements in the standard of service to consumers.

The new clause also gives the Government the power to tell the director general to take into account the level of executive pay in British Gas when fixing prices for consumers. I hope that the new clause will send a warning to the bosses of all the other utilities that Parliament will not sit back and watch them indulge themselves in the sort of boardroom greed that has brought the utilities to a level of disrepute that they have never suffered before.

4.45 pm

The new clause will ensure that those who complain, such as the hon. Member for Southport (Mr. Banks), who is not in his seat but who has written letters to the chairman of the company, are not powerless in the face of unsatisfactory replies. There must be a crisis of confidence in gas when it takes not a member of the public or even a Member of Parliament to get a suitable response from the chairman but the Minister responsible for key powers over British Gas. That in itself is an indictment.

In the past four years, the performance of British Gas has not presented a glowing picture. Pre-tax profits have declined, earnings per share have been reduced from 21.7p to 13.9p, and the return on capital has reduced from 7.3 per cent. to 5.4 per cent. Indeed, as the company states in its briefings, it has lost 60 per cent. of its industrial customers; so it is not a glowing success story, but one that should be sending shivers down the spines of all shareholders.

When I attend the annual general meeting of British Gas a fortnight on Wednesday and act as a proxy voter, I will certainly raise the sort of questions about performance that are voiced not merely by consumers but that we have heard from the now empty Conservative Benches.

What has been the response of the British Gas board to the falling level of profits and of earnings per share—the indicators that show whether a company is in a healthy state? The chief executive, Cedric Brown, had a 75 per cent. pay rise last September and, on top of that, has been awarded 437,000 executive share options, worth more than £3 a share, and now stands to pick up a bonus of 125 per cent. of his salary, which is nearly £600,000—he is a millionaire in a year.

Other board members who are responsible for scrutinising the workings of British Gas and perhaps for drawing to the chairman's attention any lapse in the company's performance have been noticeably silent. Norman Blacker, who holds 165,000 share options worth £500,000, has been silent. Howard Dalton, who holds

236,000 share options worth £700,000, has been silent. Russell Herbett, who holds 163,000 share options worth about £500,000, has been silent. Philip Rogerson, who holds 237,000 share options worth about £700,000, is another silent voice in the boardroom. Finally, Roy Gardener, the finance director who joined the company last autumn, has been silent—a silence bought at a price of £1.1 million in share options and a salary of £285,000.

In addition, all those people stand to pick up bonuses: Mr. Blacker stands to pick up £984,000; Mr. Dalton, £355,000; Mr. Herbett, £210,000; Mr. Rogerson, £310,000; and Mr. Gardener, £355,000, on top of his £1.1 million in share options and his £285,000 salary. Those bonuses, payments and share options have all been earned on the back of the company's declining performance for its shareholders. However, I am more concerned about the company's performance and duties to the consumers whom it is supposed to serve.

British Gas has made drastic cuts. If we are to believe Mr. Giordano, British Gas is the only business that can make such cuts without an impact on services. The Minister was trapped in Committee, despite, I presume, a previous briefing by Mr. Giordano that those cuts were having no impact. Given that the number of British Gas showrooms has been axed from 426 to 266 and that showrooms have been closing in high streets throughout the country, depriving people of a service that they have enjoyed for many years, it is hardly surprising that consumer dissatisfaction is on the increase. Given that showroom staff levels will have fallen from 4,000 to 1,400 by the end of this year, it is hardly surprising that the public are not getting the personal service about which British Gas was reprimanded by the Minister responsible for the charter marks.

Home service advisers are the subject of a new clause, which we shall discuss today or tomorrow, so I shall not dwell on the matter. The number of home service advisers, who help elderly and disabled people in their homes and ensure that the arthritic and the blind receive practical assistance, cannot be cut from 136 to 78 without impacting on that service in every region that British Gas serves.

This year, the emergency services budget of £9 million to trace gas leaks was cut to £1 million. Spare parts have been removed from the vans of engineers conducting emergency call-outs so that they are left with no choice but to cut off defective appliances at the risk of some unscrupulous landlord or criminal proprietor reconnecting a faulty gas heater or cooker and putting at risk not just themselves and their families but their neighbours. Such a policy contrasts markedly with the lavish handouts in the boardrooms.

If British Gas is so proud of the remuneration package that it offers its key directors, and if it thinks that their performance is at the forefront of British business and an example to everyone, why has it hidden its share options schemes from its shareholders? Amendment No. 54 makes the holder of a licence under the Gas Act 1986 liable

"to publish annually details of the remuneration of the executive and non-executive directors of that company, including any salaries, fees, benefits in kind and share options."

On Friday, I visited one of the biggest investors in British Gas, Standard Life, and this morning I called on the Prudential, the biggest single institution that invests in British Gas. They both confirmed their surprise—I

detected a shade of annoyance—at Mr. Giordano's decision to review in secret the remuneration of directors in January 1994. The fact that that was not mentioned in the annual report in February obviously came as a surprise to them, as it would to most shareholders. The fact that it was not mentioned when the quarterly returns were signed off slightly later that spring also came as a surprise. The remuneration packages were not mentioned at the annual general meeting in April, or even in September when the company signed off the second quarter's results. Nor was it mentioned when it was employing Mr. Gardener with £1.1 million of share options and a high salary.

It was not until the *Financial Times* published the information on 21 November 1994 that shareholders, even institutional shareholders, realised that they had been excluded from those critical decisions. We are talking not about a few employees who hold a few hundred thousand pounds' worth of shares but about those whom I met this morning, who hold more than £300 millions' worth of shares, and those to whom I talked on Friday, who hold some £290 millions' worth of shares. So it is no wonder that the matter is out of control, and a new clause and amendment are needed to ensure that such boardroom excesses are publicised.

All that cosy little arrangement was presided over by a key board member, Lord Peter Walker. He was the Secretary of State for Energy who left the Cabinet on 4 May 1990 and by June—within a month—had joined the board of British Gas. The "revolving door" did not apply to Peter Walker; for him, it was an open door to the boardroom of the very company that he voted to privatise. There was no "decent interval", as Nolan has now recommended, but just an indecent haste to join the fattest cats of them all. There are no checks on them, only cheques to them.

This may have been what the Prime Minister meant when, in response to a question in the House on 9 February, he spoke with unusual insight about peer pressure in the private sector. Perhaps he meant the peers who have left the Government and joined the boardrooms, such as the noble Lord Young, who joined Cable and Wireless having been Secretary of State for Trade and Industry responsible for privatising telecommunications, or Lord Tebbit, who was responsible for privatising British Aerospace and then joined its board. That shows the pressure of peers on the boardrooms—no restraint whatever—and why it is necessary to support the new clause.

We need regulatory pressure on British Gas, the six bosses of which have received nearly £7 million in share options, to ensure that its performance to consumers and shareholders is improved. We need similar regulatory pressure on the water and sewerage companies, the 42 bosses of which have awarded themselves £22 million in share options, and on the regional electricity companies, the 63 bosses of which have given themselves £46 million in share options.

The new clause is a model for exercising the minimum modest restraint on the directors of those utilities. It is no secret to the House that the Opposition have had their differences with the present regulators, but even those regulators should be allowed some discretion to ensure that, where boardroom salaries and share options hit jackpot and national lottery levels, the regulator can at

[*Mr. Griffiths*]

least take a step back and ask what service is being provided to consumers and whether it merits such high boardroom salaries.

It seems obvious that, even if share values rise or remain as high, we must question the soaring number of consumer complaints, which rose by 94 per cent. in the three months from November to January compared with the same period the previous year and by 19 per cent. compared with the previous three months.

All those figures would give any other private company pause for thought. If, for instance, Marks and Spencer or Littlewoods saw the number of consumer complaints soar, even if their share prices were rising into the stratosphere someone on the board would sit back and say, "Wait a minute, we shall lose all our customers if those consumer complaints continue." So the proposals make sound economic, shareholder and consumer sense.

It is important also to look outside this place and beyond the Labour party's opinion. The concerns that the shadow Chancellor, my hon. Friend the Member for Dunfermline, East (Mr. Brown), voiced at the weekend are now echoed in all the newspapers that strongly support the Conservatives. Today's *Daily Mail* talks about the profits made by David Jefferies, chairman of the National Grid, who—

**Madam Deputy Speaker:** Order. I am sorry to interrupt the hon. Gentleman, but I must caution him against going too wide of the subject. The clause deals with gas and, although a passing reference to other utilities is acceptable, I now detect a widening out, which is not acceptable.

**Mr. Griffiths:** Perhaps I will be in order if I quote a better example from *The Sun*, which, today, specifically mentions the gas, water and power bosses. That paper arguably influenced the election and caused the swing that led the Tories to hold on to power, just. Today's editorial, entitled "Greed, Inc." states:

"Gas, water and power bosses who leach millions from their cash-gushing monopolies are little better than licensed thieves.

With nobody to stop them, they just keep returning to the scene of the crime and filling their pockets with extra loot.

They've made fortunes out of pay, perks and pensions."

5 pm

That sums up why the clause is needed. Today's edition of the *Daily Express* also ran an article with the headline "Time to curb fat cat bosses". It states:

"The energy, ingenuity and urgency with which they have arranged to line their pockets would turn the strongest stomach."

That paper, which is not a Labour one, has seen the light. In a possible rebuke to the Minister, it states:

"Any sixth-form economic student knows that monopolies can hardly help doing well, since they lack the competition that would otherwise squeeze profits and provide independent benchmarks of performance . . . the Government simply cannot afford to be passive."

That is exactly why I am urging the Government to support the new clause. That paper also states:

"it certainly will not do for Ministers—like Industry and Energy Minister Tim Eggar—to dismiss the fuss as Labour posturing."

We are not posturing, because our complaint is firmly founded on the concerns of consumers as well as of shareholders.

It is important that a message goes from Parliament to the boardrooms of utilities, to reinforce the message sent by Nolan last week, to the effect that directors cannot continue to cash in their chips at an alarming rate to enrich themselves. Twelve directors of the privatised utilities have become millionaires. Those directors cannot afford to continue in that way and ignore the true needs of their shareholders, their companies and, specifically, the needs of 18 million gas consumers.

**Mr. Hain:** I support new clause 2, because, for successive months, the Government have been engulfed in sleaze involving not just the behaviour of successive Ministers, as well as of certain Back Benchers, but that of the privatised utilities. The Government have been engulfed by that sleaze because of their failure to get to grips with those privatised utilities and the way in which they are taking the country for a ride. After all, the gas bills that we pay enable the gas directors and others to enjoy the life of Riley. As has been exposed in the past year, our money has paid for the successive share options that they have given themselves and their massive salary increases, which have repeatedly rained upon us, month after month.

The new clause is a valuable vehicle because it opens the window on that aspect of Government sleaze. It is obscene that six British Gas directors have been able to award themselves £7 million of share options. They are among the top 50 directors of privatised utilities who have awarded themselves £40 million in share options. Across the board, 131 utility bosses have awarded themselves £100 million-worth of share options.

The new clause would curb that practice, which is particularly reprehensible because it is a form of insider dealing. Those directors are not agreeing to remuneration terms and salary levels that are openly declared and accountable to those attending the annual general meetings. They are stuffing share options in their own back pockets and, at the same time, determining, according to the priorities they set for their company, the value of those shares. They have effectively created a mechanism from which they benefit. That objective is quite different from the other possible business objectives of British Gas, or any other privatised utility. Those directors' performance should be judged by much more rigorous, sensible and acceptable business targets, such as the levels of investment and productivity reached. The extent to which those targets have been met might well lead to the payment of bonuses.

Investment is a critical target for any serious industry such as British Gas. Jacking up the share prices and benefiting from them through freebie share options is in direct conflict with investment, because the more share values are driven up, the higher the dividends that are paid to satisfy the insatiable thirst for higher returns on those shares, which, in turn, results from the short-termist economy that the Government have established. Those payments are made at the expense of the needs of British Gas.

The practice of British Gas directors represents a microcosm of what is wrong with the British economy. The Government have created a short-term, speculative, money-for-nothing economy. The behaviour of the British Gas directors exemplifies that. That small elite, in their privileged position, think that they can simply exploit that economy for all they are worth. The share option manoeuvre is a particularly reprehensible example of such exploitation.

As my hon. Friend the Member for Edinburgh, South (Mr. Griffiths) has said, it is not surprising that the share option manoeuvre is part of the wider picture of Cabinet Ministers leaving the Cabinet room for the boardroom. Lord Walker helped to privatise British Gas and he has now ended up on its board. I do not think that my constituents can understand the extent to which Members of Parliament are indifferent to the sleaze that now grips them.

**Mr. Patrick McLoughlin** (West Derbyshire): The hon. Gentleman has stressed how former Cabinet Ministers have joined the boards of particular companies. If there were a Labour Government at some time in the future, what would he think about sponsored trade union members acquiring ministerial responsibility for those industries by which they had been sponsored?

**Mr. Hain:** I do not think that the hon. Member has the power to invite me to take on a job.

**Mr. McLoughlin** *indicated dissent.*

**Mr. Hain:** The hon. Gentleman is not being as charitable as I thought. Is he seriously trying to suggest that I as a sponsored Member—I represent Post Office interests—might be barred from taking up a post in the unlikely event of being offered such a responsibility? That is nothing like someone in Cabinet, responsible for a privatisation that handed millions of pounds in share options and other means to the board, being invited by that very board to serve on it. That is the old boys network in operation. Those people are systematically lining each others' pockets. That is quite different from the example that the hon. Gentleman quoted.

**Madam Deputy Speaker:** Order. I am not sure that it has anything to do with new clause 2 either. Perhaps the hon. Gentleman would return to the point.

**Mr. Hain:** I am pleased to do so, Madam Deputy Speaker. Your intervention was welcome—*[Interruption.]*—but not for the reasons about which right hon. and hon. Conservative Members are now happily smirking. I am happy to defend my argument, but the hon. Member for West Derbyshire (Mr. McLoughlin) introduced a red herring. Without disobeying your dictum, Madam Deputy Speaker, I should like to say that it was interesting to note the reports in the Sunday newspapers that a number of Ministers were considering pressing the Prime Minister to dismiss them early, so that they could take early retirement and get in before—

**Madam Deputy Speaker:** Order. I have exercised my judgment: the hon. Gentleman is quite out of order.

**Mr. Hain:** I accept your judgment, Madam Deputy Speaker, since I have absolutely no option. I was unreasonably provoked by the hon. Member for West Derbyshire and perhaps you will bear that in mind, in mitigation.

I return to my central argument. Many of my constituents cannot pay their gas bills because they cannot even obtain a supply of gas to their homes. The Minister may be weary of my quoting that example, but many people who live up valleys in my constituency—in the Swansea valley, in villages such as Cwmllynfell and Rhiwfawr and, at the top of the Dulais valley, in Seven Sisters and Banwen—have campaigned for years for gas to be supplied up to their villages, and I have supported their campaign.

Gas has been supplied, in some cases, to places less than a mile away from those villages. British Gas has informed me that the total cost of supplying those villages with gas would be less than £3 million; yet six of its directors have received £7 million in share options—more than twice the cost of supplying gas to those villagers who desperately need it. It is a straight trade-off. My constituents do not understand, and I do not understand, how the Government can possibly defend a position whereby share options are dished out like confetti raining down at a wedding or on some similar occasion, when my constituents cannot obtain a gas supply that would cost half the sum that British Gas directors have awarded themselves in share options.

There is a straight trade-off between the creation of millionaires and the misery resulting. New clause 2 would give the Government the power to instruct the Director General of Gas Supply and ensure that that abuse—that type of insider dealing and lining of pockets by senior utility bosses, specifically of British Gas—should cease.

The gas industry is, yes, a privatised operation now; nevertheless it should, as a national champion, set high ethical standards that are respected by customers throughout the country and that will cause low-income customers especially to understand that they are in a fair society—not an unfair society rigged against them, in which millionaires continue to make money yet, if customers cannot pay their bills, their gas supply is cut off. That type of discrimination and exploitation should end. New clause 2 may give the Government a vehicle for ending it.

**Mr. Clapham:** New clause 2 and amendment No. 54 are enormously important.

New clause 2 seeks to impose price penalties on companies where there is excessive executive pay. My hon. Friends have given many examples to show how needful that is.

Clause 54 requires companies to publish details of executive remuneration as a standard of the licence condition. It seems perfectly fair that people should have access to information about remunerative packages paid to executives of utilities.

In some of the press reports about what is likely to happen in the nuclear industry, it has been suggested that a provision similar to new clause 2 would be part of any new legislation for privatisation of the nuclear industry. Perhaps the Minister will enlighten us as to whether that is correct.

New clause 2 gives the Secretary of State responsibility for directing the regulator as to the way in which executives' salaries should be taken into account when setting maximum charges for gas supply, transportation and shipping. That gives the Government indirect power to solve the problem of excessive executive pay packages—the most prominent example being, I suppose, the doubling of Cedric Brown's basic salary at the same time as British Gas showroom staff were asked to take pay cuts.

[Mr. Clapham]

Subsection (1) of new clause 2, makes it plain that

"The Secretary of State shall from time to time issue guidance to the Director as to the matters he is to take into account in exercising any powers specified in the conditions of a licence granted under section 7 or 7A of the 1986 Act to limit, vary or otherwise control the charges set by a licence holder for the supply, transportation or shipping of gas."

5.15 pm

The Minister will be aware, from the Select Committee on Trade and Industry report on the domestic gas market, that the evidence given to the Committee showed that the cost per therm of gas left little room for competition. The report showed that the cost of gas is likely to be about 21.5p—43 per cent. of the total cost per therm. Those were the figures given by British Gas. Transportation and storage was given as 22.5p—45 per cent. of the cost per therm. The supply and trading costs were given as 6p—12 per cent. of the cost per therm, which is reckoned at 50p. That leaves very little room for any changes to be brought about as a result of competition.

I think it is generally accepted that the cost of gas to all the companies likely to be involved in the domestic market will be very similar. Transportation and storage costs will also be very similar. That leaves only trading costs, in which there is likely to be a great deal of competition.

Therefore, not only is it important that consumers are given the opportunity to evaluate the performance of the companies, which may be reflected in some of the price changes that come about, but it is important that they have access to the information regarding the remuneration packages paid to the directors. That is all the more important when it is obvious that the focus of competition will be on that very small part of the cost of a therm of gas.

The powers set out in new clause 2 would allow the regulator to ensure that directors' pay not justified by performance was funded from shareholders' pockets rather than higher prices.

Relying on the future recommendations of the Greenbury committee—to which the Minister referred during discussion in Committee—is not on, because one might liken the Greenbury committee to putting the mice in charge of the cheese. The committee is made up of millionaires, many of whom draw large salaries from their business activities. If they are to make judgments about the remunerative packages to be paid in the utilities, many Labour Members will not expect the Greenbury committee to come up with dramatic or radical changes to the remunerative packages proposed for executives in the utilities.

The Government's response to new clause 2 will show the general public how serious they are about wishing to tackle the problem of directors who award themselves increases unjustified by performance. If the Government oppose the clause, they will demonstrate that the Prime Minister is unwilling or unable to give any substance to his claims of concern about excesses, and that the Tories remain the party of those who would turn a blind eye to the privatisation rip-off and corporate sleaze.

I would expect the Minister to take new clause 2 and amendment No. 54 on board. As well as being necessary for the regulator to control corporate access, amendment No. 54 is justified on its own merits. Consumers should be able to discover easily how much the directors of public utilities are paid and to assess whether it is a fair amount. Opposition to the new clause is a vote to continue to prevent the utilities from being held accountable to the public.

**Ms Coffey:** The Government's response to the recent outrage over the profits that the chairmen of the public utilities have earned—or rather, not earned, for that is the problem—has been low level. The Government's response demonstrates how out of touch they are with what the ordinary member of the public feels about what is happening.

The public do not regard gas as a just another commodity, even though the Government have been trying hard to persuade them that it is. Gas is not seen as a commodity by the public, but as an essential service for which they have to pay out of their income. Over recent years, most of the public have suffered a cut in their income. They have to manage within a limited income. Their pay may have increased minimally, in line with inflation, but they still have to pay all their bills out of a limited income.

Gas is a service for which the public have to pay. The Government have gone to great pains to explain that the benefits of privatisation have included a decrease in the price of gas, but the decrease has affected some consumers and not others. It is not the price of the service that irritates the public beyond belief, but seeing something which belonged to them, and which was transferred to the private market for their benefit, being used by a few people to line their own pockets. That has caused public outrage.

The money that the directors and chairman have earned is beyond the wildest dreams of most working people in this country and seems out of all proportion to anything that people could reasonably earn by the job that they do. People have rightly asked what the chairman has done to earn so much money. The answer is not that the chairman has done anything to earn the money, but that he has got the money because he is the chairman and is able to award himself the money. The ordinary people of this country—particularly those who have been asked to make sacrifices and those who work in the public sector—do not like that system.

We can compare the earnings and the share options of the chairman of British Gas with what nurses are able to earn and what they have been asked to take in wage increases. The British public regard nurses as just as valuable as the chairman of British Gas. They see an enormous disparity between the two sets of earnings, which they believe to be inequitable and unfair. They cannot understand why the Government are unwilling to do something about that. The Government are not willing to criticise the system or to take action to ensure that the British sense of equity and fairness is not outraged.

The British people ask why, in a privatised industry, one person's contribution should be considered so valuable that he can earn an inordinate amount of money in an annual salary and become a millionaire through the exercise of share options, while other employees who contribute to that industry are rewarded with wage cuts and, in some cases, redundancy. The British people wonder why the chairman is worth so much and an employee is worth so little in comparison. In an industry, everyone contributes and everyone's contribution is valuable and worth while.

The Government's argument has always been that huge salaries are paid and chairmen receive enormous amounts of money through exercising their share options because it is important that a private utility has the best possible chairman. The Government say that they are simply following the practice of the private market. The private market may adopt that practice, but there is a great deal more competition in the private market than in the public utilities.

British Gas is a monopoly, the regional electricity companies are monopolies and the water companies are monopolies. People think that perhaps it is not so hard to manage a monopoly when consumers have no option but to buy the service being sold. The analogy between British Gas and what is happening in the private market elsewhere does not hold up. The public utilities will always be a special case because they sell essential services and they will always have to be open to regulation to ensure that they do not rip off the public through price increases. That is why we have regulation. The public know that, and they bitterly resent what is happening.

The purpose of the new clause is to give to the regulator an opportunity to look at what is happening and to relate the remuneration of the chairman of British Gas and his executives to the company's performance. There must be some sort of performance-related pay. There must be some reason to award oneself hundreds of thousands of pounds in bonus, albeit through share options. The person involved has to have done something to earn the money— it is not just manna from heaven—and it is difficult to see what has been done for such sums to be earned in British Gas.

People might understand the bonus or level of salary if they could see what it had been paid for. A number of criteria for measuring the performance of British Gas could be drawn up. They could include its performance in terms of customer care, in terms of helping low-income customers and in terms of ensuring that services are accessible to the public, its investment record and its relationship with its employees.

As my hon. Friend the Member for Neath (Mr. Hain) said, in this country too much time is spent considering companies' and industries' performances simply in terms of their share prices and their dividend yield. Criteria which go beyond that should be applied in determining the quality of a company. British Gas, the regulator or the Minister could show the lead and apply such criteria to the public utilities to set an example to the rest of British industry. It could be shown that the criteria should involve not merely short-term success, but the long-term health of an industry.

I hope that the Minister will respond positively to the amendment. In previous debates on the subject, he has said that the Opposition have been motivated by the politics of envy and do not like people to earn too much money. We do not like people being awarded too much money when they have not earned it. The important word is "earning". In this country we believe that people should earn what they receive and we believe that everyone's contribution to an industry is important.

The Minister should recognise the public sense of outrage at what is happening. Most members of the public believe that there will be a continuing inequity, and that the gap in earnings between those who do a decent day's work and those who sit in the boardroom is becoming too big. Sitting in the boardroom and good management are important, but gas fitters and the people who do the job are also important. Those people must be justly rewarded. One man or group of people should not be rewarded far in excess of other people.

**Mr. Eggar:** I enjoyed the speech of the hon. Member for Stockport (Ms Coffey), not least because she suddenly had to correct herself a number of times during her prolonged peroration to say that the Labour party is sometimes in favour of management and sometimes in favour of high pay, as if the new Labour piece was getting into her brain and she was remembering the right words so as not to undermine her credibility with the current trend within the Labour party.

New clause 2 is extremely pernicious, for all the words uttered in particular by the hon. Member for Clackmannan (Mr. O'Neill) from the Front Bench. It would fundamentally undermine the basis of the regulatory system as the independence of the regulator is the cornerstone of the way in which regulation is approached, not just here but in virtually every country around the world.

5.30 pm

The reason for and the importance of the regulator's independence is that it removes political interference from the management of the regulated utility. New clause 2, more unashamedly than any previous amendment, seeks to reassert political control over the management of the gas industry.

**Mr. Kevin Hughes:** Hear, hear.

**Mr. Eggar:** "Hear, hear," says the unreconstructed hon. Member for Doncaster, North (Mr. Hughes).

Despite all the honeyed words of the Leader of the Opposition and occasionally other Labour Front Bench spokesmen about their dedication to make industry more effective and their commitment to competition, what they really feel in their hearts is that they want political control over the management not just of the gas industry but all parts of British industry. They have not really put their hearts into a new clause IV, it is all just part of an elaborate con.

**Mr. Nigel Griffiths:** We want to know what new Conservatives are thinking and whether new Conservatives are the same as old Conservatives, backing those with their snouts in the trough, the corporate greed and the absolute abuses that have even brought *The Sun*, the *Daily Mail* and the *Daily Express* on to Labour's side on this issue.

**Mr. Eggar:** That was a pretty feeble attempt by the hon. Gentleman. At least some of the more honourable Labour Members admitted that the Labour party wants to reassert political control of the gas industry. I am delighted to see that the hon. Member for Neath (Mr. Hain) is smiling, as that is straight down his view of where the Labour party should be.

[Mr. Eggar]

The Opposition want to go further than reasserting political control. In the terms of the new clause, they want to do it directly by reintroducing an incomes policy through the back door. That is what lies behind new clause 2.

Neither today nor at any stage in Committee have the Opposition introduced a shred of evidence to suggest that there is any logical reason to relate price caps on the one hand to board pay on the other. The reason for that is quite clear. First, even if one takes the total remuneration package for the whole of the British Gas board, which came to some £2.3 million last year—

**Mr. Kevin Hughes:** Per month?

**Mr. Eggar:** No, per year. That represents a cost of about 1p per month on each gas consumer's bill.

In addition, we heard some absolutely absurd figures from the hon. Member for Edinburgh, South (Mr. Griffiths). If he follows the precedent of the level of research to which he has risen in the debate when he attends the British Gas annual general meeting, as he has promised to do, he really will be made a mockery. He fails to understand that the vast bulk of the share options to which he referred were offered at only 9p per share below today's price on the stock exchange. The vast sums that he mentioned bear no relation to the potential or actual profit that could be exercised today.

**Mr. Nigel Griffiths:** The Minister needs a lesson in accuracy as well as economics. The exercised price was 221p and the latest market price is just over £3—302p or 304p—so the difference is more than 9p.

**Mr. Eggar:** The hon. Gentleman is following his long established tradition in misusing the Short money made available to the Opposition. The vast bulk of those share options were offered at 293.5p and today's price is 302.5p. The difference in broad sums is 9p per share. That is the reality. The hon. Gentleman should at least be honest with the House and accept that those were the terms on which the vast bulk of those share options were made available to current board members.

**Mr. Hain:** The Minister pooh-poohs the impact on ordinary customers of these bloated share options for British Gas directors and says that it is matter of a few pence on bills. No doubt the arithmetic proves his point. How does he explain to my constituents—who were told that British Gas cannot afford to extend supply to the Dulais valley and the Swansea valley as it will cost about £3 million—that six directors are being offered £7 million in share options? That is not a few pence, and it is a straight comparison. How does he explain the justification for that?

**Mr. Eggar:** I must congratulate the hon. Gentleman on his persistence on that particular issue. I assume that the voracity of his local papers is absolutely unlimited, as it is the third or fourth time that he has raised the issue. First, I do not accept his figure in regard to the share options. I suspect that he has failed to take account of the price at which the shares were offered, but that is a minor point.

We have already discussed in Committee the particular problem that his constituents and, to be fair, the constituents of many hon. Members may have with regard to getting on

to the gas grid system. I explained in detail how the provisions of the Bill will make it possible for public gas transporters other than British Gas to access the national grid and to provide a gas grid system into areas previously been isolated from the grid. I also made it clear that the change in the ability to pay effectively by instalments for the capital works associated with the gas grid should also provide vendors of the services—the public gas transporters—and consumers with possibilities which did not previously exist.

As the hon. Gentleman well knows, I cannot say that, as a result of the Bill, those communities will get on to the gas grid system, but there will be opportunities available which did not previously exist. That should at least be some reassurance to him and to his constituents. In fairness to the hon. Gentleman, he has most persistently opposed the Bill. He has always made it clear that he does not support it. I am not quite sure how he squares his opposition to the Bill with the advocacy of the interests of his constituents, when he has at least admitted that the Bill will make it easier for public gas transporters to bring gas to the fairly isolated communities that he represents. Perhaps he and his local paper should reflect on the level of inconsistency in his position with regard to the Bill as a whole.

**Madam Deputy Speaker:** Order. I remind the Minister that we are not dealing with the whole Bill; we are dealing with one clause and one amendment.

**Mr. Eggar:** I fear that I have been led down a path that I should not have followed.

**Mr. Hain:** Enticed.

**Mr. Eggar:** I was enticed—to use the hon. Gentleman's word—by the nature of the intervention. I am grateful to you for setting me straight, Madam Deputy Speaker.

In discussing the board level salaries in British Gas and other entities, an important factor is persistently overlooked. British Gas is regulated according to an RPI minus X formula—in other words, the price at which it sells is the important factor. If the industry's costs rise above the level anticipated or above those of its competitors, the impact will be felt by the shareholders and not by the customers who have the advantage of the RPI minus X formula. The idea that somehow high salaries are awarded to board members at a cost to the customer simply does not stand up against any scrutiny of the way in which the regulatory system works.

When the level of the RPI minus X formula is reviewed, the regulator in this industry, as in others, must take account of whether she regards the level of cost in that organisation—including the total remuneration of the board—as appropriate when setting X. That normally occurs on a five-year basis, although it may be earlier in the case of gas.

**Mr. Nigel Griffiths:** When my colleagues and I met the regulator, she spelled out very clearly that she did not even look at salaries in the boardroom. However, the Minister has implied that she examines that cost in arriving at an RPI minus formula.

**Mr. Eggar:** It is one of the factors that the regulator may wish to take into account when setting the formula. She may choose not to do so; it depends on the way in which she approaches the issue. If new clause 2 were to be supported, it is absolutely clear that there would be political direction of the regulator and political interference in the working of the gas industry and that, in effect, an incomes policy would operate through the back door. The hon. Member for Edinburgh, South shrugs his shoulders; it seems extraordinary that the Labour party, which the shadow Chancellor claims is in favour of competition, should take that line. That cannot be the correct way to proceed.

**Kevin Hughes:** The Minister has referred to an incomes policy. It seems to me that the fat cats already have an incomes policy: grab as much as they can for themselves. Does the Minister seriously think that in excess of £400,000 is a fair salary to receive for three days' work? It is interesting that the first time that Tory Back Benchers spoke in Committee was to defend their mates, the fat cats, and their fat salaries.

**Mr. Eggar:** The decisions that are taken as to the level of salaries are a matter for the board and the remuneration committees. At the end of the day, the shareholders have the ultimate say about salary levels. They can exercise whatever powers they choose. As the hon. Gentleman knows, the Government have made it clear that we will consider the recommendations of the Greenbury committee. If the committee recommends legislation in this area, we shall not hesitate to legislate if we consider that appropriate. We do not rule out legislation in this area.

New clause 2 is fundamentally flawed. It involves the introduction of an incomes policy by the back door and political direction of the gas industry and it completely contradicts the broad thrust of Opposition policy as advanced by the shadow Chancellor.

5.45 pm

**Mr. O'Neill:** It would appear that it becomes a political direction for the regulator when the House decides that the salaries and the conditions of directors should be taken into account, yet it is not a political direction if the regulator is required to take account of environmental factors or social responsibilities in relation to the elderly. Those issues are not considered political, but directors' pay is. Somehow the whole regulatory function is transformed because the pay and conditions of a small group of full-time employees—with the exception of the chairman of the company—must be examined by the regulator when determining price levels.

We know that in most instances salaries can be justified to a certain extent. They cannot be justified publicly because the remuneration committee does not meet in public. As I understand it, when the salary of the present chairman of British Gas was increased above the company's limit for directors' salaries, that decision was not transmitted to the annual general meeting in the year that it was made. As a result of such a lack of transparency, shareholders are unable to establish the basis on which decisions are taken. They may be able to ask questions at the AGM, but they are not told of the rationale behind the decision in the company papers or in the final accounts.

There is no means of ensuring that shareholders are clear about why certain individuals are receiving such pay awards. The awards may be based on some kind of notional performance, but, if so, one would imagine that the stratospheric levels that have been breached by the pay rises that certain individuals have enjoyed of late would somehow be related to the company's performance. In

some instances that has been true, but when producing her figures the regulator is not obliged to separate the regulated areas of business from the unregulated areas. Therefore, she is at a certain disadvantage.

There appears to be a link between profit, performance and pay. We know—no one disputes this fact—that the cost of directors' salaries amounts to about 12p per annum per household. It is not significant in terms of profits; we will not reduce prices significantly by cutting directors' salaries to zero. However, the public are concerned about a company that operates in almost monopoly conditions being able to afford to pay its directors salaries that are beyond the expectations and understanding of most ordinary citizens. What we find offensive is the manner in which pay awards are made and reported to the company's shareholders and the fact that the regulator is powerless to take account of them in calculating whether price rises are acceptable. An element of responsibility must be given to the regulator.

Major investors and people representing pension funds and the like repeatedly tell us, as they told my hon. Friend the Member for Edinburgh, South (Mr. Griffiths) just last week, that they are concerned. We must often explain to them that, when in office, the Labour party will have to recognise the protection of the consumer and of the company, its long-term future and the significance of ensuring a steady stream of investment into the company, so that its activities can be funded by means other than purely increasing its bills. We recognise that those three objectives must be balanced and that, to a certain extent at least, responsibility for doing so rests with the regulator and with the regulatory system.

There is a lack of confidence among consumers. As publicity of the pay rises and share options given to senior British Gas executives has increased, people have said, "If they are getting such big rises and doing such a good job, how come I am not getting the service that I think I am entitled to for the whopping bills I am having to pay?" That is why, in the space of three months, the number of complaints increased by 93 per cent. and why the Cabinet has threatened British Gas with withdrawal of its charter mark.

We find, however, that the regulator can do nothing. She cannot question the manner in which the company is being run. We want her to be given the opportunity to take note of such matters. She should be required to take pay into account, not least because of the effect of a significant pay rise on the running of a firm.

If the public feel that executives are not ensuring a good service and are being paid far too much, someone must be able to blow the whistle. We know that not all investors, and not all those who will attend the AGM with their proxy votes, will be that concerned. Many of them have a vested interest in sustaining the remuneration system that affords directors of British Gas and of the companies that they represent the pay that they receive. This is about not the politics of envy but the politics of greed and the ability of a small coterie of interlocking directorships to scratch each other's backs and to ensure that they all get a bit of the action out of companies for which they have some responsibility.

It is difficult for major shareholders to get on to the board and to have an influence. Attempts were made by unions such as the National Union of Mineworkers to influence the investment policies of certain companies in South Africa. They were told that they could not do so

[*Mr. O'Neill*]

because commercial judgments were the responsibility of investors. It was proven that sustaining investment in South Africa over the years was not the correct investment decision. The decision of investors ultimately to withdraw from South Africa was a major contributory factor in the ending of apartheid.

I am not drawing analogies between the rate of pay for directors in the former utilities and the working of apartheid, but the same supine attitude that was adopted by people who attended board meetings of major investors in South Africa prevails today at general meetings of some of the utilities. The legitimate concerns of small shareholders and of pension fund contributors and the like are being ignored. One of the most satisfactory and easy ways to take those into account is to give responsibility to the regulator to consider remuneration when she considers price and its relationship to profit.

**Ms Coffey:** Does my hon. Friend agree that there appears to be some confusion in the Minister's argument? He said that giving such a responsibility would give some political control to the regulator and that, therefore, he is not prepared to have anything to do with it, but then said that if the Greenbury committee makes recommendations the Government might legislate. In legislating, they would be prepared to take political control. Is it just that the Minister is washing his hands of the problem because it is too difficult?

**Mr. O'Neill:** We shall just have to wait for the Greenbury committee's recommendations. Many of us doubt that it will produce very much. The Prime Minister said:

"we are waiting for recommendations on that, and, when necessary, when the facts are available, we shall decide what action needs to be taken, if necessary, including legislation."—[*Official Report*, 2 March 1995; Vol. 255, c. 1182.]

We all know the genesis of the Greenbury committee. It was proposed by the Confederation of British Industry. Its members include those who have benefited from the working of the system. We will all be surprised if it will be able to be sufficiently objective to make recommendations that will satisfy everyone in the House, or at least that will require the Prime Minister to introduce legislation. Most of us believe that it is a fairly cynical exercise.

We want the Government to take this opportunity. We want the regulatory system to be revised. We have been operating under a series of regulators for about 11 or 12 years. This is the first opportunity to examine legislation on a former nationalised utility and, in the light of experience under private ownership, the effectiveness of the regulatory system. That is why we repeatedly returned in Committee to the question of how the regulatory system operates.

We have clearly identified a major shortcoming in the regulatory system: the regulator does not have to take account of the rewards that companies pay their staff when determining prices. The new clause and the amendment would allow the regulator to take account of that, in the same way as she must take account of other issues that are deemed, in most people's eyes, to be political: the environment, the level of gas supplies and the needs of the disabled and elderly, which we recognise. If those are not political issues, heavens above, I do not know what are.

Members of the public in wheelchairs chained themselves to the gates of the House of Commons because disabled people's rights were not being properly recognised in the House. That is a matter of such controversy by dint of it being political. It is nonsense for the Minister to say that, somehow, the regulator will be drawn into politics if the new clause is accepted. If it is passed, the regulator will be drawn into the real world.

For too long, the major energy regulators in the electricity and gas industries have regarded their areas of responsibility as some sort of free market adventure playground where they can work out their fantasies about perfect competition. That was the kind of thing in which, in the past, only academic economists were able to indulge on the blackboards or whiteboards in their lecture rooms. They were given large, expensive toys with which to play but they did not want to break those toys. They regarded them as being made of porcelain and felt that they should not touch then. Because the system has not been properly considered, it is working against the very people for whom the regulator is supposed to be responsible first and foremost—consumers and shareholders.

6 pm

**Mr. Clapham:** I mentioned a reference in the press to legislation on the privatisation of the nuclear industry containing a clause similar to new clause 2. The Minister did not refute that similarity. Would my hon. Friend like to develop that point?

**Mr. Deputy Speaker (Mr. Geoffrey Lofthouse):** Order. I hope that the hon. Gentleman will not develop that point. This debate concerns the gas industry, not the nuclear industry.

**Mr. O'Neill:** I will not stray, Mr. Deputy Speaker. Suffice to say that, when an industry is privatised, it is difficult to legislate beyond the point of privatisation. A free-standing, independent company is established, whose articles of association are determined not by the privatisation measure but by company law and the regulatory process. The regulatory process under which British Gas operates does not take account of the pay and conditions enjoyed by its directors. The amendment would correct that shortcoming by changing the regulatory regime.

**Mr. Hain:** Does my hon. Friend agree that the regulatory system is being brought into disrepute and that many customers and citizens feel that it is not protecting them because of massive abuses caused by boardroom excess, with directors awarding themselves share options and so on? People think, "This is not for me." The regulator is supposed to protect the consumer but she is turning a blind eye to greed on a massive scale.

**Mr. O'Neill:** I could not agree more, and I go further. That is a problem for not only consumers but small shareholders who, having invested perhaps most of their life savings, are asking themselves, "Have I put my money in the right company? Am I doing the right thing in associating with that company?"

In previous debates on the gas industry, we pointed out that British Gas was once regarded second only to Marks and Spencer as the most popular company in the country. That position prevailed until publicity about the pay and conditions now enjoyed by its directors. There has been a transformation in public esteem for British Gas. Its activities once attracted respect worldwide. When in public ownership, it carried through the changeover to North sea gas, which was one of the biggest civil engineering exercises this country and western Europe have ever seen. British Gas played on that affection, and its directors thought that they could ride to the bank with suitcases full of money from their various remunerative perks. The only way in which such an anomaly can be corrected is if the regulator can cast her eye over the situation.

**Mr. Robert Ainsworth** (Coventry, North-East): My hon. Friend rightly spoke about the direct consequences of excessive executive salaries, but they have a small impact on the price paid by the consumer. Are there not other consequences, such as the effect on pay in the organisation, and the demoralising effect on efficiency, when employees see the people at the top treating themselves in the way that British Gas directors do? The indirect effects on the consumer can also be substantial.

**Mr. O'Neill:** I could not agree more. The argument used to be made that it was not a bad idea to pay the bosses good wages, so that everybody else would be dragged along behind them and that would reflect on the morale of the whole operation. Another company in the energy business, Scottish Nuclear, gave all its staff exactly the same pay rise for the specific purpose of improving morale. British Gas did the opposite.

Gas showrooms were not simply high-street supermarkets but places to which consumers looked both to purchase gas appliances and to obtain advice and information on a range of equipment. If one went to a shopping mall, visited a retail outlet offering a variety of white and brown goods and asked about the energy efficiency of a particular product, it was not unusual to be directed to the gas showroom because only there was the relevant knowledge and information available. That was because gas showroom staff were trained and properly remunerated. I do not mean to speak disparagingly of other shop assistants, but British Gas showroom staff regarded themselves as people who did more than walk off the street and start work in a shop the next day. British Gas provided morale and a sense of worth that have been lost as a consequence of the changing character of its showrooms.

Of equal importance is the obscene way in which British Gas staff pay has been cut while the pay of bosses has mushroomed and gone through the roof. We are considering not just the interests of consumers and shareholders. It is in the long-term interests of the success of British Gas that the regulator has power over those people who appear completely unanswerable to anyone. I mentioned the structure of British Gas AGMs and the votes held by people who participate in them. We in the Labour movement might identify them as being not dissimilar to the old block votes. The big companies scratch each other's backs and protect one another.

The new clause is the best approach that we can suggest at this time. It may have imperfections but the Minister did not mention any. He said that the new clause was somehow political. A number of responsibilities already imposed on the regulator are clearly political, and the new clause is political because it attacks vested interests. It is about not the politics of envy but the politics of greed.

I urge my hon. Friends to vote for the amendment, which can change the character of regulation in this country, restore public faith in the regulatory system and

give the regulator guidance in performing her duties—guidance that she does not seem to have at present and appears unwilling to seek. We will press this amendment to a vote, and I urge all hon. Members who believe in fair remuneration and fair reward for people working in the gas industry to accept that the new clause would achieve that, while ensuring that small shareholders in particular will be given adequate protection.

*Question put,* That the clause be read a Second time:—
*The House divided:* Ayes 234, Noes 271.

**Division No. 146]**                                    **[6.10 pm**

### AYES

| | |
|---|---|
| Abbott, Ms Diane | Davies, Ron *(Caerphilly)* |
| Ainsworth, Robert *(Cov'try NE)* | Denham, John |
| Allen, Graham | Dewar, Donald |
| Alton, David | Dixon, Don |
| Anderson, Donald *(Swansea E)* | Dobson, Frank |
| Anderson, Ms Janet *(Ros'dale)* | Donohoe, Brian H |
| Armstrong, Hilary | Dowd, Jim |
| Ashdown, Rt Hon Paddy | Dunnachie, Jimmy |
| Ashton, Joe | Dunwoody, Mrs Gwyneth |
| Austin-Walker, John | Eagle, Ms Angela |
| Banks, Tony *(Newham NW)* | Eastham, Ken |
| Barnes, Harry | Enright, Derek |
| Barron, Kevin | Etherington, Bill |
| Battle, John | Evans, John *(St Helens N)* |
| Beckett, Rt Hon Margaret | Fatchett, Derek |
| Beith, Rt Hon A J | Field, Frank *(Birkenhead)* |
| Bell, Stuart | Fisher, Mark |
| Benn, Rt Hon Tony | Flynn, Paul |
| Bennett, Andrew F | Foster, Rt Hon Derek |
| Bermingham, Gerald | Foster, Don *(Bath)* |
| Berry, Roger | Foulkes, George |
| Betts, Clive | Fraser, John |
| Blair, Rt Hon Tony | Fyfe, Maria |
| Blunkett, David | Galbraith, Sam |
| Boateng, Paul | Galloway, George |
| Bradley, Keith | Gapes, Mike |
| Bray, Dr Jeremy | Garrett, John |
| Brown, Gordon *(Dunfermline E)* | Gerrard, Neil |
| Brown, N *(N'c'tle upon Tyne E)* | Godman, Dr Norman A |
| Burden, Richard | Godsiff, Roger |
| Byers, Stephen | Golding, Mrs Llin |
| Caborn, Richard | Gordon, Mildred |
| Callaghan, Jim | Graham, Thomas |
| Campbell, Mrs Anne *(C'bridge)* | Grant, Bernie *(Tottenham)* |
| Campbell, Menzies *(Fife NE)* | Griffiths, Nigel *(Edinburgh S)* |
| Cann, Jamie | Griffiths, Win *(Bridgend)* |
| Chisholm, Malcolm | Grocott, Bruce |
| Church, Judith | Gunnell, John |
| Clapham, Michael | Hain, Peter |
| Clark, Dr David *(South Shields)* | Hall, Mike |
| Clarke, Eric *(Midlothian)* | Harman, Ms Harriet |
| Clarke, Tom *(Monklands W)* | Harvey, Nick |
| Clelland, David | Henderson, Doug |
| Clwyd, Mrs Ann | Heppell, John |
| Coffey, Ann | Hill, Keith *(Streatham)* |
| Connarty, Michael | Hinchliffe, David |
| Cook, Frank *(Stockton N)* | Hodge, Margaret |
| Cook, Robin *(Livingston)* | Hoey, Kate |
| Corbett, Robin | Hogg, Norman *(Cumbernauld)* |
| Corbyn, Jeremy | Hood, Jimmy |
| Cousins, Jim | Hoon, Geoffrey |
| Cummings, John | Howarth, George *(Knowsley North)* |
| Cunliffe, Lawrence | Howells, Dr. Kim *(Pontypridd)* |
| Cunningham, Jim *(Covy SE)* | Hoyle, Doug |
| Cunningham, Rt Hon Dr John | Hughes, Kevin *(Doncaster N)* |
| Dafis, Cynog | Hughes, Robert *(Aberdeen N)* |
| Dalyell, Tam | Hughes, Roy *(Newport E)* |
| Davidson, Ian | Hutton, John |
| Davies, Bryan *(Oldham C'tral)* | Illsley, Eric |
| Davies, Rt Hon Denzil *(Llanelli)* | Ingram, Adam |

Jackson, Glenda *(H'stead)*
Jackson, Helen *(Shef'ld, H)*
Jamieson, David
Janner, Greville
Jones, Barry *(Alyn and D'side)*
Jones, Jon Owen *(Cardiff C)*
Jones, Lynne *(B'ham S O)*
Jones, Martyn *(Clwyd, SW)*
Jowell, Tessa
Kaufman, Rt Hon Gerald
Kennedy, Charles *(Ross,C&S)*
Kennedy, Jane *(Lpool Brdgn)*
Khabra, Piara S
Kilfoyle, Peter
Lestor, Joan *(Eccles)*
Lewis, Terry
Litherland, Robert
Livingstone, Ken
Lloyd, Tony *(Stretford)*
Lynne, Ms Liz
McAvoy, Thomas
McCartney, Ian
McCrea, The Reverend William
Macdonald, Calum
McFall, John
Mackinlay, Andrew
McLeish, Henry
McMaster, Gordon
McNamara, Kevin
MacShane, Denis
Madden, Max
Maddock, Diana
Mahon, Alice
Marek, Dr John
Martlew, Eric
Meacher, Michael
Meale, Alan
Michael, Alun
Michie, Bill *(Sheffield Heeley)*
Milburn, Alan
Miller, Andrew
Moonie, Dr Lewis
Morgan, Rhodri
Morley, Elliot
Morris, Rt Hon Alfred *(Wy'nshawe)*
Morris, Estelle *(B'ham Yardley)*
Mowlam, Marjorie
Mudie, George
Mullin, Chris
Murphy, Paul
Oakes, Rt Hon Gordon
O'Brien, Mike *(N W'kshire)*
O'Brien, William *(Normanton)*
O'Hara, Edward
Olner, Bill
O'Neill, Martin
Orme, Rt Hon Stanley
Patchett, Terry
Pearson, Ian

Pendry, Tom
Pike, Peter L
Pope, Greg
Powell, Ray *(Ogmore)*
Prentice, Bridget *(Lew'm E)*
Prentice, Gordon *(Pendle)*
Primarolo, Dawn
Purchase, Ken
Quin, Ms Joyce
Randall, Stuart
Raynsford, Nick
Reid, Dr John
Rendel, David
Robertson, George *(Hamilton)*
Roche, Mrs Barbara
Rogers, Allan
Rooker, Jeff
Rooney, Terry
Ross, Ernie *(Dundee W)*
Rowlands, Ted
Ruddock, Joan
Sedgemore, Brian
Sheerman, Barry
Sheldon, Rt Hon Robert
Shore, Rt Hon Peter
Short, Clare
Simpson, Alan
Skinner, Dennis
Smith, Chris *(Isl'ton S & F'sbury)*
Smith, Llew *(Blaenau Gwent)*
Soley, Clive
Spearing, Nigel
Squire, Rachel *(Dunfermline W)*
Steinberg, Gerry
Stevenson, George
Sutcliffe, Gerry
Taylor, Mrs Ann *(Dewsbury)*
Taylor, Matthew *(Truro)*
Timms, Stephen
Tipping, Paddy
Touhig, Don
Turner, Dennis
Vaz, Keith
Walker, Rt Hon Sir Harold
Walley, Joan
Wareing, Robert N
Watson, Mike
Williams, Rt Hon Alan *(Sw'n W)*
Williams, Alan W *(Carmarthen)*
Winnick, David
Wise, Audrey
Worthington, Tony
Wray, Jimmy
Wright, Dr Tony
Young, David *(Bolton SE)*

**Tellers for the Ayes:**
**Mr. Joe Benton and**
**Mr. Peter Mandelson**

## NOES

Ainsworth, Peter *(East Surrey)*
Aitken, Rt Hon Jonathan
Alison, Rt Hon Michael *(Selby)*
Allason, Rupert *(Torbay)*
Arness, David
Arbuthnot, James
Arnold, Jacques *(Gravesham)*
Arnold, Sir Thomas *(Hazel Grv)*
Ashby, David
Atkins, Robert
Atkinson, David *(Bour'mouth E)*
Atkinson, Peter *(Hexham)*
Baker, Rt Hon Kenneth *(Mole V)*
Baker, Nicholas *(North Dorset)*
Baldry, Tony

Banks, Matthew *(Southport)*
Banks, Robert *(Harrogate)*
Batiste, Spencer
Bendall, Vivian
Beresford, Sir Paul
Biffen, Rt Hon John
Booth, Hartley
Boswell, Tim
Bottomley, Peter *(Eltham)*
Bottomley, Rt Hon Virginia
Bowis, John
Boyson, Rt Hon Sir Rhodes
Brandreth, Gyles
Brazier, Julian
Bright, Sir Graham

Brooke, Rt Hon Peter
Brown, M *(Brigg & Cl'thorpes)*
Browning, Mrs Angela
Budgen, Nicholas
Burt, Alistair
Butcher, John
Butler, Peter
Butterfill, John
Carlisle, Sir Kenneth *(Lincoln)*
Carrington, Matthew
Cash, William
Channon, Rt Hon Paul
Chapman, Sydney
Clappison, James
Clark, Dr Michael *(Rochford)*
Clifton-Brown, Geoffrey
Coe, Sebastian
Conway, Derek
Coombs, Anthony *(Wyre For'st)*
Coombs, Simon *(Swindon)*
Cope, Rt Hon Sir John
Cormack, Sir Patrick
Couchman, James
Cran, James
Currie, Mrs Edwina *(S D'by'ire)*
Curry, David *(Skipton & Ripon)*
Davies, Quentin *(Stamford)*
Day, Stephen
Deva, Nirj Joseph
Dorrell, Rt Hon Stephen
Douglas-Hamilton, Lord James
Dover, Den
Duncan, Alan
Duncan-Smith, Iain
Dunn, Bob
Durant, Sir Anthony
Dykes, Hugh
Eggar, Rt Hon Tim
Elletson, Harold
Emery, Rt Hon Sir Peter
Evans, David *(Welwyn Hatfield)*
Evans, Jonathan *(Brecon)*
Evans, Nigel *(Ribble Valley)*
Evans, Roger *(Monmouth)*
Evennett, David
Faber, David
Fabricant, Michael
Fenner, Dame Peggy
Field, Barry *(Isle of Wight)*
Fishburn, Dudley
Forman, Nigel
Forsyth, Rt Hon Michael *(Stirling)*
Forth, Eric
Fox, Dr Liam *(Woodspring)*
Fox, Sir Marcus *(Shipley)*
Freeman, Rt Hon Roger
French, Douglas
Gale, Roger
Gardiner, Sir George
Garel-Jones, Rt Hon Tristan
Garnier, Edward
Gill, Christopher
Gillan, Cheryl
Goodlad, Rt Hon Alastair
Goodson-Wickes, Dr Charles
Gorst, Sir John
Grant, Sir A *(SW Cambs)*
Greenway, Harry *(Ealing N)*
Greenway, John *(Ryedale)*
Griffiths, Peter *(Portsmouth, N)*
Grylls, Sir Michael
Gummer, Rt Hon John Selwyn
Hague, William
Hampson, Dr Keith
Hanley, Rt Hon Jeremy
Hannam, Sir John

Hargreaves, Andrew
Harris, David
Haselhurst, Alan
Hawkins, Nick
Hayes, Jerry
Heald, Oliver
Heath, Rt Hon Sir Edward
Heathcoat-Amory, David
Hendry, Charles
Hicks, Robert
Hill, James *(Southampton Test)*
Hogg, Rt Hon Douglas *(G'tham)*
Horam, John
Hordern, Rt Hon Sir Peter
Howard, Rt Hon Michael
Howarth, Alan *(Strat'rd-on-A)*
Howell, Rt Hon David *(G'dford)*
Howell, Sir Ralph *(N Norfolk)*
Hughes, Robert G *(Harrow W)*
Hunt, Sir John *(Ravensbourne)*
Hunter, Andrew
Hurd, Rt Hon Douglas
Jack, Michael
Jackson, Robert *(Wantage)*
Jenkin, Bernard
Jessel, Toby
Johnson Smith, Sir Geoffrey
Jones, Gwilym *(Cardiff N)*
Jones, Robert B *(W Hertfdshr)*
Jopling, Rt Hon Michael
Kellett-Bowman, Dame Elaine
King, Rt Hon Tom
Kirkhope, Timothy
Knapman, Roger
Knight, Mrs Angela *(Erewash)*
Knight, Greg *(Derby N)*
Knight, Dame Jill *(Bir'm E'st'n)*
Kynoch, George *(Kincardine)*
Lait, Mrs Jacqui
Lang, Rt Hon Ian
Lawrence, Sir Ivan
Legg, Barry
Leigh, Edward
Lennox-Boyd, Sir Mark
Lester, Jim *(Broxtowe)*
Lidington, David
Lightbown, David
Lilley, Rt Hon Peter
Lloyd, Rt Hon Sir Peter *(Fareham)*
Lord, Michael
Lyell, Rt Hon Sir Nicholas
MacGregor, Rt Hon John
MacKay, Andrew
Maclean, David
McLoughlin, Patrick
McMaster, Gordon
Madel, Sir David
Maitland, Lady Olga
Malone, Gerald
Mans, Keith
Marlow, Tony
Marshall, John *(Hendon S)*
Marshall, Sir Michael *(Arundel)*
Martin, David *(Portsmouth S)*
Mawhinney, Rt Hon Dr Brian
Mellor, Rt Hon David
Merchant, Piers
Mills, Iain
Mitchell, Andrew *(Gedling)*
Mitchell, Sir David *(NW Hants)*
Moate, Sir Roger
Monro, Sir Hector
Montgomery, Sir Fergus
Moss, Malcolm
Needham, Rt Hon Richard
Nelson, Anthony

Neubert, Sir Michael
Newton, Rt Hon Tony
Nicholls, Patrick
Nicholson, David *(Taunton)*
Nicholson, Emma *(Devon West)*
Norris, Steve
Onslow, Rt Hon Sir Cranley
Oppenheim, Phillip
Ottaway, Richard
Patnick, Sir Irvine
Pattie, Rt Hon Sir Geoffrey
Pawsey, James
Peacock, Mrs Elizabeth
Porter, Barry *(Wirral S)*
Porter, David *(Waveney)*
Portillo, Rt Hon Michael
Powell, William *(Corby)*
Redwood, Rt Hon John
Renton, Rt Hon Tim
Riddick, Graham
Robathan, Andrew
Robinson, Mark *(Somerton)*
Roe, Mrs Marion *(Broxbourne)*
Rowe, Andrew *(Mid Kent)*
Rumbold, Rt Hon Dame Angela
Ryder, Rt Hon Richard
Sackville, Tom
Sainsbury, Rt Hon Sir Timothy
Scott, Rt Hon Sir Nicholas
Shaw, David *(Dover)*
Shephard, Rt Hon Gillian
Shepherd, Colin *(Hereford)*
Shepherd, Richard *(Aldridge)*
Shersby, Michael
Sims, Roger
Skeet, Sir Trevor
Smith, Tim *(Beaconsfield)*
Soames, Nicholas
Speed, Sir Keith
Spencer, Sir Derek
Spicer, Michael *(S Worcs)*
Spink, Dr Robert
Spring, Richard
Sproat, Iain
Squire, Robin *(Hornchurch)*
Stanley, Rt Hon Sir John

Steen, Anthony
Stephen, Michael
Stern, Michael
Stewart, Allan
Streeter, Gary
Sumberg, David
Sykes, John
Tapsell, Sir Peter
Taylor, Ian *(Esher)*
Taylor, John M *(Solihull)*
Taylor, Sir Teddy *(Southend, E)*
Temple-Morris, Peter
Thomason, Roy
Thompson, Sir Donald *(C'er V)*
Thompson, Patrick *(Norwich N)*
Thornton, Sir Malcolm
Thurnham, Peter
Townend, John *(Bridlington)*
Townsend, Cyril D *(Bexl'yh'th)*
Tracey, Richard
Trend, Michael
Twinn, Dr Ian
Vaughan, Sir Gerard
Waldegrave, Rt Hon William
Walden, George
Walker, Bill *(N Tayside)*
Waller, Gary
Ward, John
Wardle, Charles *(Bexhill)*
Waterson, Nigel
Watts, John
Wells, Bowen
Whitney, Ray
Whittingdale, John
Widdecombe, Ann
Wilkinson, John
Willetts, David
Wilshire, David
Winterton, Nicholas *(Macc'fld)*
Wolfson, Mark
Wood, Timothy
Yeo, Tim
Young, Rt Hon Sir George

**Tellers for the Noes:**
**Mr. Michael Bates and**
**Mr. Simon Burns.**

*Question accordingly negatived.*

### New clause 3

DUTY OF GAS CONSUMERS' COUNCIL TO MONITOR EFFECTS
ON CONSUMERS OF PROVISIONS OF THE GAS ACT 1995

'After Section 41 of the 1986 Act there shall be inserted the following section—

"(41A). The Council shall be under a duty to monitor and report in accordance with section 41 above on the effects of the provisions of the Gas Act 1995 on the interests of gas consumers, with particular regard to prices charged and other terms of supply, the continuity of supply, the quality of the gas supply services provided, the exercise of rights of entry to premises and the extent of universal access to gas conveyed through pipes.".'.—*[Mr. O'Neill.]*

*Brought up, and read the First time.*

**Mr. O'Neill:** I beg to move, That the clause be read a Second time.

**Mr. Deputy Speaker:** With this, it will be convenient to discuss the following: New clause 8—*Duty of Director to prevent discrimination by gas suppliers against certain classes of consumers—*

'The Director shall be under a duty to ensure that a licensed gas supplier shall not introduce price tariffs or payment arrangements which unreasonably discriminate against consumers by virtue of the location of their home or the manner or place at which they settle their accounts.'.

New clause 9—*Duty of gas supplier to publish terms of supply—*

'(1) A gas supplier licensed under section 7A of the 1986 Act (hereafter referred to as the supplier) shall publish the prices to be charged to consumers for the supply of gas and the associated services he will provide (hereafter referred to as "terms of supply") in such a manner as, after consultation with the Director and the Council, he considers will achieve publicity for his terms of supply among all domestic gas consumers in his licence area.

(2) The supplier shall, in the publishing of his terms of supply, not show undue preference to any person or class of person and shall not exercise any undue discrimination against any person or class of persons.

(3) The supplier shall, on being required to do so by any potential domestic gas consumer in his area, give and continue to give a supply of gas at premises of which that potential customer is an owner, occupier or leaseholder and which is connected by a service pipe to a relevant main.

(4) The supplier shall be required to provide the Director with any information relevant to his duties under section [*Duty of Director to protect interests of consumers*]

(5) In this section, "terms of supply" may be taken to include standards of service and such other services which the supplier is obliged to provide in accordance with standard licence conditions.'.

New clause 10—*Duty of Director to protect interests of consumer—*

'(1) The Director shall have a duty to protect the interests of consumers of gas conveyed through pipes in respect of the prices charged and of other terms of supply as defined in subsection (1) and (5) of section [*Duty of gas supplier to publish terms of supply*], the continuity of supply and the exercise of rights under this part to enter their premises.

(2) The Director shall have a duty to secure effective choice for all classes of consumer.

(3) In performing his duties under subsections (1) and (2) above the Director shall not grant a licence or an extension or restriction under section 7A of the 1986 Act if he is of the opinion that the description or area has been so framed as—

   (a) in the case of the licence or extension to exclude from the licence or extension; or

   (b) in the case of a restriction, artificially to include in the restriction,

an undue proportion of consumers who are disabled or of pensionable age or who are in receipt of a state benefit or to whom he might reasonably expect to supply less than 700 therms per annum.

(4) In performing his duties under subsection (3) above the Director shall have power to require the relevant licence applicant or holder and any body or person likely to be representative of those affected to provide him with information with regard to the customer mix of the licence applicant or holder.

(5) If it appears to the Director that a supplier licensed under section 7A of the 1986 Act has contravened any provision of this section, the Director may impose upon the licence holder a requirement to pay to him a monetary penalty of such amount as may be appropriate, in all the circumstances of the case, in respect of the contravention in question.'.

Amendment No. 44, in clause 1, page 1, line 29, after 'supply', insert

'including the establishment of effective contingency plans to deal with serious breakdowns in supply.'.

Amendment No. 48, in clause 6, page 8, leave out lines 3 to 14.

Amendment No. 50, in clause 8, page 12, line 11, after 'modifications', insert

*[Mr. Deputy Speaker]*

'including those persons or bodies appearing to the Director to be representative of consumers.'.

**Mr. O'Neill:** This group of amendments, starting with new clause 3, seeks to impose a duty on the Gas Consumers Council which gives it responsibility for monitoring prices. When the legislation was being considered, it was assumed that the GCC would not survive the publication of the Bill. It was anticipated that the council's responsibilities would be overtaken by those of the regulator, that the council was merely a relic of the old days of public ownership and that there would be no reason for its continued existence.

There was a some surprise and relief that the GCC survived in its present form. We have yet to see what impact the cuts in the council's budget will have, but the Opposition have confidence in the council, which seeks to represent consumers on gas matters, as it has perhaps more of an arm's-length relationship with the Government than Ofgas appears to have at present. It is no secret, and it is almost inevitable, that when legislation of this character is being drafted, the regulator works closely with the Department to secure a form of words that it considers appropriate for the licensing function that it has to carry out.

We would like the Gas Consumers Council to have clear and explicit responsibilities which, in the first instance, should cover prices. An independent dispassionate body should examine the pricing system and the implications of the regulator's recommendations because, at the end of the day, the regulator is responsible for setting prices. The Government have already said this evening that they wish to interfere with—if that is the correct expression—or pass judgment on the regulator in as few ways as possible. However, we believe that there should be a body which, with status and responsibility, can command widespread respect for its role and functions. We would have thought that the Gas Consumers Council was such a body. Therefore, the purpose of new clause 3 is to impose upon the GCC a number of responsibilities. The first relates to price, while the second deals with the terms of supply and the manner in which the supply would be arranged.

It is clear that the regulator has a number of duties to fulfil, and the determination of the terms of the licence is one of the most important. It is therefore vital that the terms of supply should be considered. The terms can cover a variety of arrangements for supply.

Continuity of supply must be considered. One of the considerations that has been uppermost in the minds of those who have taken an interest in the Bill has been that the individuals seeking licences should have sufficient funds to conduct their business. That means not only that they have sufficient funds to pay their staff and to take account of safety obligations where appropriate, but that they are able to purchase the gas that is to be piped through the system to households. Continuity of supply must be subject to independent non-regulatory monitoring. We would want to ensure that the GCC has the resources and the remit to do that.

6.30 pm

We also want to look at the quality of supply services. We have discussed the problems that British Gas has encountered. A number of instances in which British Gas has been deficient in its services have gained great publicity, but aspects of the running of British Gas, such as remuneration, have focused attention on the organisation. Individuals have now realised that there are people to whom they can direct their complaints. The Government have threatened to withdraw the charter mark from British Gas, and it sees that as a worry because it was with great pride that British Gas accepted that honour. We are not saying that a company such as British Gas cannot bounce back and produce a service that is the envy of the world.

We must look at the potential of some of the newcomers that wish to enter the business. It is clear that there are a number of them operating in public utilities already. It has been suggested that regional electricity companies will come into the frame as new licensees, and a number of them have entered into contracts with gas suppliers. The new companies will doubtless bring to the supply of gas the same high standards that they maintained when they were publicly owned electricity utilities.

Many of us have had opportunities to talk to local electricity companies, and they have expressed willingness to aspire to the standards that they have reached in other fields. Some companies are limited in experience and in their scale of operation, and such companies must be policed and monitored. It is our view that the Gas Consumers Council could do that, and it could inform the regulator and the Secretary of State of any deficiencies in the system. The GCC does that at the moment, but we would like to see that duty enshrined in legislation.

I now come to one of the most sensitive areas in the supply and provision of gas—the right to enter premises. A certain number of individuals who work for the public utilities attract a great deal of affection in the eyes of the public. It is fair to say that a generation brought up on Postman Pat is less likely to question the continued public ownership of the Post Office than people who envisage a committee man or woman in a uniform delivering mail for some tinpot organisation. A degree of trust is extended to postmen. I should perhaps say postpeople, as nowadays there are as many postwomen as postmen. In America, they are called letter carriers, which seems to be a compromise that predates this age of political correctness.

Some British Gas staff have access to people's homes, and they normally wear some form of uniform and have easily legible and intelligible forms of identification. In many instances, due notice has been given that the person would be coming to check the meter or to deal with the other problems related to gas maintenance. There are occasions when there might be an emergency, when no notice can be given before the visit, and there might be cases in which individuals use faked identification.

There ought to be an independent body, which would be able to monitor the exercise of the right of entry to premises. That is in no way an implied criticism of the staff of British Gas. We have all experienced their courtesy when they come to read meters. I realise that you, Mr. Deputy Speaker, may well use coal-fired heating in your house, but I must say that the service that gas users receive is courteous, thoughtful and considerate.

A number of people operating in the gas industry do not necessarily aspire to the high standards laid down by British Gas. One of the recurrent themes in Committee was the inadequacy of some of those who were operating under the overall umbrella of the Council of Registered Gas Installers scheme. Individuals assumed for themselves rights of entry which, under the law, they would probably have been allowed to exercise, but which were not exercised with proper care and attention in a number of instances.

In a deregulated gas market, we would wish a wider range of individuals to be given the opportunity to have the right of entry into premises and people's homes. As a consequence, we should be able to secure some means whereby the public can have the confidence that, should anything go wrong, they will be able to contact the GCC to register their concerns.

As I have said, the Gas Consumers Council has carried out several of those duties in the past. In recent months, it has been extremely active in lobbying the House on several concerns that it perceives relate to consumers' rights. It has been most active in respect of universal access to gas. It has certainly been extremely concerned that one problem of the deregulated gas business is that there will be a lack of enthusiasm on the part of some suppliers to acquire customers who might be problematic—that is, people who live in awkward locations or people whom British Gas has decided are not necessarily cost-effective consumers. We want to ensure that there is someone to whom the rejected potential gas consumer can turn. It would be quite reasonable for the GCC to have the monitoring responsibility and to enshrine it in legislation.

New clause 9 is the public service clause. It is the duty of the gas supplier to publish the terms of supply. The terms of supply relate to the publication of prices. It should be clear that it is in everyone's interests that prices are published in the press and in the areas where gas companies are operating. Prices should be publicised nationally, so that individuals can compare and contrast supply across the country.

We also want to see in the public service clause a duty on the gas supplier not to show undue preference or discriminate against any individuals or groups. We recognise that there is what is known as discriminatory practice. By changing or arranging the terms of purchase or the terms of contract and the like, suppliers can deny certain individuals access to goods or services that should be available.

There is also a requirement to supply those who are at present connected to the main. It should not be the right of a gas supplier to say, "We will take that household but not that household." If someone is connected to the gas supply, he should be entitled to obtain gas from any supplier that has a licence to operate in the area. There have been occasions when such entitlements have been undermined. Bodies such as citizens advice bureaux have investigated such cases. Indeed, many have been brought to our attention as constituency Members.

Recently, the CAB in south Wales reported that British Gas refused to connect the gas supply for a client who was a single parent with three young children, including an eight-week-old baby. They had just moved into rented accommodation, and there was an existing gas supply there, but they were refused because the previous occupant had tampered with the meter. Because of such instances, it is important that a specific body has a duty to gather information and the resources to advertise.

Perhaps gas bills could state that consumers could go to the Gas Consumers Council if they felt that the public service clause was not being adhered to.

We want to ensure not only that the Gas Consumers Council would be involved but that the gas supplier published the terms of supply and gave to Ofgas its information on consumer protection. That consumer protection facility would then be the subject of comparison between one company and another. In its annual reports, Ofgas would be able to draw conclusions as to the quality of services that were being provided. Indeed, the standard of service would always be an important consideration.

6.45 pm

New clause 3 places a duty on the Gas Consumers Council, and new clause 9 places a duty on the gas supplier. We would also like to see enshrined in the legislation a duty on the director general to protect the consumer. We want the Director General of Gas Supply to have a duty in respect of price and a duty to secure effective choice for all classes of customers. The director general would have to take account of the size and nature of an area to which licences applied—for example, to take into account the disabled, pensioners, people on state benefits or people who used fewer than 700 therms per annum. There would be a profile of each area, which would take account of that. It is essential to enshrine that in the legislation.

It is stated in the licences that such duties should be imposed. We would like to think that they will be enshrined in the primary legislation and that proper account will be taken of disadvantaged individuals such as the disabled, pensioners, people in receipt of state benefit and small consumers. Those people are the least attractive and the most expensive for suppliers to serve, and the director general should have an obligation to support and protect them.

We would also like to think that the director general would have a responsibility to ensure that those standards were upheld and that there would be punishment if they were not met. Companies could incur a financial penalty if the standards were not met over a period.

The regulator has several duties, but the protection of the consumer, the prevention of cherry-picking and the public service obligations should be clearly included in the primary legislation. It is for those reasons that we want the new clause.

Conservative Members have been very quick to protect small shopkeepers. Indeed, their numbers seemed to melt away as soon as the shopkeeper protection issue disappeared. However, the issues I have mentioned are at the very heart of the legislation. For example, there is the argument that, through competition, there will be an opportunity not only for lower prices but for better services. To those who back the Bill in its entirety, I stress that it is our view that such claims can be met only if we have a tough, effective and well-resourced Gas Consumers Council that has a clear duty to monitor the affairs of the companies involved, if there is a public service clause that imposes a duty on the gas supplier and if the overall director has a responsibility to ensure that those functions are carried out. The companies must be given proper incentives, in the form of the threat of financial punishment, to meet their obligations.

*[Mr. O'Neill]*

We hope that the new clause is of a character that will enjoy the support of all parties.

**Ms Coffey:** New clause 3 is important because it would help to protect the rights of consumers. It has been said that no one knows what will happen to particular groups of consumers in a fully competitive gas market, which means that proper monitoring is essential. I am especially interested in consumers who have pre-payment meters and who already pay a higher tariff for their gas than those who pay on budget schemes, by direct debit or by cash at a post office or their local gas showroom, if they are lucky.

It is clear from the Gas Consumers Council's statistics that there has been a huge increase in the number of pre-payment meters installed. There has been no problem with that, because having a pre-payment meter is clearly better than having one's gas supply cut off. By December 1994, 192,525 new token meters had been installed. Across the country there were 896,950 consumers with pre-payment meters, and the number of disconnections has decreased.

At present, people with pre-payment meters are paying a higher tariff for their gas. British Gas has not made it clear whether what they pay reflects the cost of supply. In the past, British Gas said that the cost had been cross-subsidised. The question was raised whether, once a competitive gas market was in full swing, those consumers could expect their gas tariff to rise in line with what it cost to supply them. That is worrying, because it might mean that they will not benefit from competition in the way that other consumers will. A gas company could offer to supply them at a higher tariff, because the cost of supply was higher, than it would charge people who wished to pay by direct debit.

The problem is that people with pre-payment meters are low-income customers: often, they are families on benefit or low wages and with young children; they might live on housing estates, have other debts and struggle to make ends meet. The situation merits careful monitoring because there will be pressure on people to accept pre-payment meters from the gas companies. Indeed, condition 10 of the licence says that a licensee can request

"a deposit by way of security for the payment of charges as a condition of making a supply of gas available to the customer".

The company itself will set the level of that deposit.

The Minister is no doubt aware, however, that it is almost impossible for people on income support to pay a deposit. The Department of Social Security will have to pay it for them and then deduct it from their weekly benefit. If they already have deductions made from their benefits—for example, social fund payments—it will be impossible to pay a gas deposit. If they cannot pay such a deposit, the gas company will agree to supply gas, but through a pre-payment meter. The low-income family will therefore have to pay a higher tariff for their gas on a week-by-week basis.

It is not fair that people who have little money should pay more. The problem is that they have too little money to pay a deposit and take advantage of being a direct debit customer or one who pays every three months at a post office. Careful monitoring is essential, because I do not believe that this group of customers will benefit from competition.

I think that gas competitors will fix the tariff for pre-payment customers at the level already charged by British Gas, so there will be no benefit in moving from British Gas to new gas suppliers. At the same time, competitors will offer lower tariffs to better-off customers as the cost of supplying them will be less; they know that they will not have the same problems as British Gas in supplying low-income customers or those in urban areas. There will be little incentive for new gas suppliers to offer lower terms than British Gas on pre-payment meters.

Once the gas market has opened up, I have little doubt that some people will benefit. People like me and the Minister and those who have a bank account will benefit enormously, but I doubt that the same is true of the 896,950 customers with pre-payment meters. Their number will increase as more find that they cannot afford a deposit. That is why it is so important that the duty to monitor set out in the new clause is included in the Bill. It is unfair that poorer people will not benefit from competition relating to an essential service. I think that in two or three years it will be shown—the figures must be produced—that that is the case.

I have no doubt that it will be said that the Government must fulfil their social responsibility by making provision through social security legislation to compensate for the fact that some people have not benefited from the competitive gas market. Any Government who are asked to do that will want to know what has happened and why. The Bill will not remove from the Government—any Government—the responsibility to ensure that people on low incomes or on benefit or young families have essential services such as gas at a price that they can afford.

7 pm

**Ms Hilary Armstrong** (Durham, North-West): I support new clause 8. The terms of the gas and electricity privatisations made it exceptionally difficult for some people who live in rural areas to gain access to basic utilities. I had hoped that the Government would have recognised the case that has been put in the years since privatisation by Members of Parliament and the rural communities' councils for studying that issue. The new clause provides the Government with the opportunity to recognise the problems that were inherent in the means of privatisation and that have made it difficult for remote villages to gain access to utilities such as gas.

In my constituency, three or four villages and some smaller hamlets, mainly in the north Pennines, still have no gas; indeed, those hamlets have neither gas nor electricity. As we approach the millennium, surely that is something that we ought not to tolerate. Some of my constituents simply do not have access to things that we take for granted.

The Bill deals purely with gas and I have met British Gas officials on numerous occasions since being elected and on two or three occasions in the past year to discuss the problem. The village of Whitton-le-Wear does not have gas, but its neighbouring village, Howden-le-Wear, had it put in two years ago—I lit the initial flame. Whitton-le-Wear is only a mile away, but it happens to be over a hill and much smaller.

Gas was accessible to residents of Howden-le-Wear for less than £50 per household, but the price was to be about £2,000 per household for residents of Whitton-le-Wear.

British Gas felt that supplying the village was so out of order that it did not even circulate the proposals to every resident, as it knew that there would be uproar and people would be offended to find out that, if they had lived a mile down the road, they would have had access to gas for about £50. British Gas has, in effect, said that it believes that that village will never have gas.

The way in which British Gas was initially privatised means that it is impossible to offset such costs or to bring together villages to offer the service at an affordable price across them all. As that has not been possible, they do not have access to gas and in future the rules will be even more difficult.

**Mr. Eggar** *indicated dissent.*

**Ms Armstrong:** The Minister denies that, but that is what British Gas officials feel. The supplement that they were able to offer will disappear under the Bill and the rules will become even more difficult, so it is even less likely that such villages will get gas.

Burnhope is another village in my constituency that is without gas, although the next village, which is less than a mile away, has had it for some time. There is a post-war housing estate in Burnhope where the council and the local housing association have been refurbishing houses under a special Government scheme. The council and the housing association agreed to put gas into the houses being refurbished. The cost to anyone whose house was not being refurbished, or who did not live on the council estate, was to be about £1,600.

Burnhope is one of the poorest villages in the county of Durham. I have given the House the figures before. The county now has the lowest incomes in the country, apart from an area of South Glamorgan, but incomes in Burnhope are lower than the average in Durham. If residents wanted gas but did not come under the scheme, they would have had to pay £1,500, so of course the scheme has not gone ahead in the rest of the village.

The irony is that, once gas has been in a street for five years, other people in the street can have access to it without paying that initial cost. People on such streets in Burnhope, who have purchased their houses, will be able to have access to gas in five years' time. The company has not extended the gas supply to the rest of the village, so any extension to other streets would be inordinately expensive. That is unjust, unfair and inequitable.

At a time when we are looking to the more efficient and effective use of gas and electricity, the House should be able to support that case and to say confidently that anyone, anywhere in this country will have a fair deal and be treated equally over access to utility services—in this case, gas.

**Mr. Hain:** I must follow on from the excellent contribution of my hon. Friend the Member for Durham, North-West (Ms Armstrong), who drew the attention of the House to the Bill's consequences and its failure to protect outlying and often poor villages, such as the villages in her constituency—former mining villages, I imagine, which exist in my constituency also.

New clause 8 specifies:

"The Director shall be under a duty to ensure that a licensed gas supplier shall not introduce price tariffs or payment arrangements which unreasonably discriminate against consumers by virtue of the location of their home",

and so forth. Under new clause 10(2),

"The Director shall have a duty to secure effective choice for all classes of consumer."

The great benefit of nationalisation and of the gas structure that was built up over generations was that every consumer had the right to access to gas at the same price. Universal access and uniform price were important principles, but they are both being undermined by the Bill and have been successively undermined by privatisation.

The Minister will be relieved to hear that I will not again detain the House by quoting cases of villages up the valleys in my constituency which have been denied access to gas in the way described by my hon. Friend the Member for Durham, North-West, as I have been over that ground quite a few times.

The Bill will institutionalise cherry-picking and social dumping, the other side of it, not by some accident but as the inevitable result of competition. Why? In this context, which is that of a vital utility service—I am talking not about competition in the ordinary exchange of consumer goods and so forth in the marketplace but about a vital service, which is what gas is to many millions of people—the competition focuses on the area in which suppliers and shippers can make money. Competitors are not going to waste their energies trying to invade markets that are not lucrative. They have a duty to their shareholders and they have to concentrate on where they can make money. Those are the areas in which prices will fall, and that will be at the expense of less lucrative markets, which will be socially dumped and where prices will rise.

For example, British Gas is already telling customers who pay by direct debit that they will pay 5 per cent. less, which will penalise and discriminate against customers who cannot pay by direct debit. Their prices will be 5 per cent. more in real terms. That is significant because, although the proportion of households with a bank or building society account has risen steadily, 19 per cent.— nearly a fifth—of households still have no current account through which they regularly handle their money. Some 40 per cent. of that group are pensioners and a further 40 per cent. are low-income householders with an income of less than £150 a week. It is those people who will be socially dumped.

Those statistics show that a significant proportion of the population will lose out. The regime has already discriminated against those people by denying them direct debit arrangements. A feature of that group is that it tends to be geographically concentrated. That criticism goes to the heart of the Bill, which does not afford protection to groups of householders in low-income areas such as exist in my constituency and those of many of my hon. Friends. Low-income households will be totally ignored by the competitors, which will not want to know about competition moving into such low-income areas. That has already happened in the case of direct debit arrangements, on which British Gas penalises up to a fifth of potential or actual gas consumers.

Another interesting geographical impact is that in Wales, for example, the proportion of gas customers with direct debit arrangements is half the number in the rest of the United Kingdom. Just 15 per cent. of gas customers in Wales pay by direct debit, compared with 28 per cent. in the United Kingdom as a whole because Wales has a much higher proportion of low-income households. It has the lowest gross domestic product per capita in the United Kingdom and, as a result, the cherry-picking and social

[*Mr. Hain*]

dumping that will result from the Bill will significantly discriminate against gas customers in Wales. The direct debit arrangements have provided a dress rehearsal for that.

This issue should be set against a much wider background. For example, citizens advice bureaux have already said that low-income users of gas are required to put down higher deposits or rely on pre-payment systems. As my hon. Friend the Member for Stockport (Ms Coffey) pointed out, those are more expensive than ordinary payment arrangements. They tend to be confined exclusively to low-income households and result in the phenomenon of "voluntary disconnection", as it is euphemistically described.

British Gas—and, once the Bill is enacted, the new suppliers—no longer breaks down people's doors to disconnect their supply. Instead, low-income householders will disconnect themselves through the pre-payment arrangement, thereby hiding a great deal of hardship. That phenomenon will increase because, under this regulatory system, increased competition is designed to lead to cost-related pricing, so those who cannot meet the terms of the competitive regime—in this case, low-income households—will be socially dumped.

The Government have disputed British Gas's assertion that 6 million would gain from cost-related pricing and 10 million would lose. I need only rely on the Monopolies and Mergers Commission report on the gas industry, which found:

"Supply to low-volume users (whose use of gas may be confined to cookers and water heaters and who probably include a high proportion of elderly and poor customers) is currently unprofitable, and may require significant price rises."

The MMC also said:

"We recognise that, while the introduction of competition may well result in a fall in the overall level of prices, some groups may be worse off than at present".

We thus have corroborative evidence from the MMC that cherry-picking will take place and social dumping will be the consequence.

Large users, many of whom are affluent families in large homes, will gain because they are cheaper to serve than the average householder. Some 4 million small users—often, poor households—are more expensive to serve, so their prices could rise significantly. The side effect is that, as many low-income users are on income support, the cost may be passed on to the state.

### 7.15 pm

Against that background, it is important to bear it in mind that the family expenditure survey showed that the poorest 20 per cent. in Britain spend 10 per cent. of their weekly budget on gas and electricity bills, whereas the richest 20 per cent. spend just 3 per cent. That is before the imposition of VAT on fuel and heating, which will make the position worse. Low-income families, who spend much more of their income on gas, will be hit even harder as a result of the competitive regime.

We should take note of evidence given by the citizens advice bureaux. For example, a CAB in Yorkshire reported that a client on income support with two dependent children, who had been paying £15 a week off arrears of £565 through the fuel direct scheme, came off income support having found a part-time job and could

no longer pay through the scheme. Although the family income was roughly the same as when the family was on income support once work-related expenses were taken into account, British Gas demanded a lump sum of £320 before coming to an arrangement to pay off arrears. That is a good example of how competition increasingly bears down on our most vulnerable citizens. Without the protection offered by the new clause, there is no guarantee that the phenomenon will not get worse.

It is essential that every gas customer has universal choice, and that is protected under the legislation. I am concerned about the failure to protect ordinary customers, and I refer to one aspect of the licensing arrangements. Although the director general is required to secure effective competition, she has no corresponding duty to secure universal choice. That duty should be statutorily imposed on the regulator, as the new clause seeks to do, otherwise suppliers will have greater freedom to select the more profitable customers and neglect the least profitable customers.

Standard licensing conditions 13 and 7(3) of the draft suppliers' licence could be dubbed a "cherry-pickers charter". Condition 13, which covers undue preference and undue discrimination, applies only to the dominant supplier. In this case, that is British Gas, and it will probably remain so for some time. The condition does not appear to prevent suppliers from supplying only the consumers they want to supply.

For example, condition 7(3) could allow a supplier to refuse to supply a less attractive consumer if he "claims" that to do so would jeopardise his existing customer base, which he may have attained through highly selective marketing techniques. Although there is a duty on every householder to request supply from any supplying company, there is no duty on those companies to canvass for support and to offer genuine choice to every householder. The failure to provide a statutory right to universal choice is a severe handicap, which will increase cherry-picking. That practice will be institutionalised by the regime that will be created as a result of it.

My suspicions were also aroused when the Minister failed to respond to an amendment tabled in Committee by my hon. Friend the Member for Edinburgh, South (Mr. Griffiths) to extend the protection offered in proposed section 7B(4)(b) to the disabled and those of pensionable age to low-paid and low-income users. It would be easy to identify such low-income users, because they are likely to be in receipt of income support or family credit. I do not want to go into the detail of the proposed section, but it illustrates my argument about cherry-picking and social dumping. Why has protection been offered to disabled people and pensioners and not to low-income users? The answer is: one may be disabled but still be relatively affluent; one may be a pensioner but still be relatively affluent. There are rich pensioners.

Clause 7 could have easily offered similar support to low-income families and householders. That is why the new clauses are even more necessary; they require the regulator to pay particular attention to the needs of low-income householders and to ensure that they do not suffer discrimination through social dumping, while the cherry-picking of lucrative customers goes on as a result of competition.

I strongly believe that the thrust of the regulatory system needs radical reform. It needs to be rejigged to protect low-income users and to give them equal access to gas supplies, to protect the principle of universality and to ensure that those do not suffer from discriminatory pricing regimes. We must have a regulatory system that is geared to the benefit of the common good, not a selected few.

**Mr. Michael Clapham** (Barnsley, West and Penistone): Enough has been said about new clause 8, so I should like to refer in particular to new clauses 3, 9 and 10 and to amendment No. 44. Without the new clauses and amendments, it is clear the consumer will be unprotected. The Government should focus on ensuring that consumers are protected in the deregulated industry, so the Minister should accept new clauses 8 and 3 in particular.

As my hon. Friend the Member for Stockport (Ms Coffey) has said, no one knows where competition in gas will take us. There is a danger that the Bill, unless it is amended, may create competition that focuses on supplying the most attractive customers, who tend to be those who consume a great deal of gas and pay by direct debit. Those people may well gain an advantage unless the new clauses, which ensure that all consumers benefit from the proposed changes, are accepted.

The Minister may recall that in Committee I mentioned that I had had negotiations in my constituency, which is a rural one, with the cable companies and British Gas to see whether gas pipes could be laid at the same time as cables. Apparently, that is not possible in certain areas of my constituency, but it may be possible in other constituencies. Has the Minister explored that possibility? Is he prepared to get cable companies with franchises together with British Gas to explore that possibility so that the gas supply can be connected to other villages? Perhaps the Minister can tell us today whether he has explored that idea.

New clause 3 is designed to give the Gas Consumers Council a duty to monitor the impact of deregulated gas supply. Without that scrutiny, it will be difficult for the council to do its job of protecting consumers' interests. I hope that the Minister is prepared to accept the new clause. Should he feel that its current terms are not quite suitable, perhaps he would be prepared to introduce his own new clause. It is important that the Gas Consumers Council is given that duty.

New clause 9 would ensure that all gas prices and associated services, for example, the terms for supply, are published. It would ensure that all customers have the right to a supply from any supplier and those suppliers do not unduly discriminate against any group of customers. The new clause is vital if we are to prevent cherry-picking. It also imposes a duty on suppliers to specify their standards of service as well as the price of their supply. Customers need that information if they are to make an informed choice between suppliers. I am sure that the Minister would agree that if we are to make this Bill work, customers will need to have information about the costs and prices of varying suppliers. It is important that such information, particularly about prices, is published.

As my hon. Friends have already said, low-income customers with pre-payment meters, who consume large amounts of gas, pay far more for their gas than other customers. Some customers with arrears have requested pre-payment meters in the belief that that will save them money. They must be told that such meters tend to cost

the consumer more. Without the publication, in a standard form, of all the varying prices, including the price per therm and the standing charge, customers will be unable to make the informed choice that is necessary for the market to function effectively. I am sure that the Minister agrees, so he will obviously accept the new clauses.

**Mr. Eggar:** What makes me smile is how well the hon. Gentleman has learnt the language since leaving the National Union of Mineworkers. The idea that the hon. Gentleman should argue for the market to operate effectively is amusing to say the least.

**Mr. Clapham:** The Minister is aware that I am a pragmatist. Although I would like the supply of gas to remain the responsibility of British Gas, I am prepared to accept that there is little the Opposition can do to prevent the Government from enacting the Bill. I am therefore trying to do my best to help my constituents to get betterment from the Bill.

New clause 10 aims to outlaw price discrimination against elderly people, disabled people, people who depend on state benefits and small consumers, and to create a duty on the regulator to give all customers an effective choice of supplier. It is important that all customers are given the opportunity to choose their supplier. Without legal protection, as set out in the new clauses, those groups of vulnerable people may end up paying more for their gas to fund price cuts for wealthy people. We must avoid that at all costs.

7.30 pm

As it stands, the Bill, as has been said by my hon. Friend the Member for Neath (Mr. Hain), is a cherry-pickers charter, as it places an obligation to supply customers without discrimination on British Gas only. As the Minister will be aware from some of the submissions that we received from other gas companies, many of those gas companies were content that the obligation that British Gas already accepts should be placed on them. It is important that we ensure that those standards are maintained.

New clause 10 also provides the regulator with the power to refuse to grant or extend a licence or to fine an existing licence holder if the supplier evades supplying those less attractive customers. The National Association of Citizens Advice Bureaux believes that, without those safeguards, competition in gas supply will fail to benefit all customers.

As my hon. Friend the Member for Neath said, when British Gas gave evidence to the Monopolies and Mergers Commission it said that there might be as many as 12 million losers. I know that, since that time, it has amended its assessment, and its assessment of losers is nowhere near the first figure that it gave the MMC. However, other independent organisations have carried out studies, which suggest that there might be as many as 4 million losers. The people who will lose are those who are the most vulnerable—people on low incomes, people on benefits and so on.

It is important, therefore, that those new clauses are accepted, or, if they are not accepted in their entirety, that the Minister is prepared to have his constitutional draftsmen reword the clauses so that the protection that those clauses seek to provide is incorporated in the Bill.

[*Mr. Clapham*]

Those amendments are important, not only to gas consumers, but to utility customers, as they set out a framework against which the utilities may be judged. Only if the utilities are credible and seen to be credible, will the market be made to work.

**Mr. Eggar:** This is a large group of amendments, covering a disparate number of issues. I shall start by replying to some of the arguments that Opposition Members have made.

First, it has been a theme of the Opposition that the Bill is a cherry-pickers charter. Ultimately, the evidence will emerge of the way in which prices feed through for different groups of consumers. In fairness to the hon. Member for Stockport (Ms Coffey), she recognised that. The entire structure of the Bill is designed to ensure that there is no benefit to supplying companies in targeting consumers who are either of high or low volume in terms of the domestic spread. That has been done largely by the Director General of Gas Supply choosing the relatively low figure of the standing charge of about £15.

The best evidence we have of what happens in a competitive gas market is the evidence of the opening up of the industrial market in excess of 25,000 therms. When we started on the exercise of opening up the market from 25,000 therms upwards, as long ago as 1988, there was much criticism. It was said that some industrial companies would gain far more than others and that the average industrial customer would lose, as against the central pricing mechanism previously put in place by British Gas.

What has actually happened in the industrial market is that, in real terms, there has been a 35 per cent. reduction for the average industrial consumer. I have not heard of a single industrial consumer that has not benefited significantly from the introduction of competition in that market. I am the first to accept that it is not directly replicable in terms of the domestic market, but it is the best available evidence that we have.

The hon. Member for Stockport mentioned the issue of pre-payment meters. She quoted very precisely the number of customers on pre-payment meters at present— a figure of well in excess of 850,000 customers.

From my constituency experience, I know that quite a few consumers opt for a pre-payment meter, although they know that it will cost them slightly more, because they want the reliability of what I would call day by day, week by week budgeting instead of not knowing what the bill will be at the end of the quarter. However, we have that large number of pre-payment customers, the pre-payment meters are there, and I fail to understand why competitor companies should not be as keen to supply in a competitive way—and therefore reduce prices to—those 850,000 customers as they would other groups. They are a known credit risk because they use pre-payment meters.

As technology develops, competitor gas companies may be able to reduce the cost of the administrative side of pre-payment meters, and the gap may therefore close between costs to pre-payment customers and to what are called traditional payment customers.

Further, of course, there are adequate provisions in the standard conditions to ensure that each supplier offers several payment methods and cannot discriminate unduly between people who use those.

**Ms Coffey:** The Minister must accept that his statement that pre-payment customers should benefit and my saying that they possibly will not are, for both of us, a matter of conjecture. In that case, is it not all the more important to create a specific duty to monitor?

**Mr. Eggar:** I concede the hon. Lady's first argument. It is in the nature of a competitive market that no one can be absolutely confident about what will happen in that market. The evidence of competition in other sectors is that it has done exactly what we claimed that it would in the case of pre-payment customers—reduced prices and improved the quality of service.

However, one of the reasons why we are slowly extending the pilot area into which competition will be introduced from 500,000 customers to 2 million, then countrywide, is so that, as we go along, practical experience is gained, and everyone can evaluate the lessons as the operation proceeds in an orderly way.

Opposition Members referred to new clause 3. As far as I can check, everything that is in new clause 3 is already covered by section 40 of the Gas Act 1986, and the new clause is therefore unnecessary.

Regarding new clause 8, anxieties have been expressed about the possibility that competitive suppliers might discriminate in some way or other—several individual hon. Members made different arguments about that— against people, having regard to where they lived or the way in which they paid. We have given that much thought and we have explored the subject fully in Committee.

We also explored in Committee the issue of what I would call gas access to remoter communities. In fact we had an exchange about that today with the hon. Member for Neath (Mr. Hain). As the hon. Member for Durham, North-West (Ms Armstrong) raised the issue, it might be worth putting on record exactly how the Bill will help. The hon. Lady gave the impression that the Bill would work against such access. The Bill will probably favour villages such as the one she mentioned, but we will not know for certain until we see how the system evolves.

The first way in which the new licensing provisions in the Bill will help is that long-term supply and connection contracts are permitted. There has been a hiatus during the Bill's passage, but that will disappear once the Bill is enacted. The public gas transporters—British TransCo and other suppliers—will be able to offer different approaches to payment. At present, because of the way in which the 1986 Act works, British Gas has to demand an up-front, lump-sum payment. Now, neither British Gas nor other suppliers will have to do that and will effectively be able to ask for payment for connection charges over a long period—spread over five or more years. That will help a number of people who want to convert to gas, but who cannot afford the lump sum.

There is another provision—I do not think that it will help the constituents of the hon. Member for Durham, North-West, as she mentioned a village that was a mile away. Subject to the necessary safety provisions, it will be possible for individuals or groups of individuals to connect their properties to the mains. It is sometimes alleged that the capital costs for connection charged by

TransCo are high and that connections could be achieved more cheaply. It will now be possible to make arrangements on a communal basis and so lower costs. Consumers will not have to rely solely on TransCo; other competitors will offer the service. Agas is already doing just that and winning business from TransCo because it is able to make cheaper connections.

New clause 9 deals with the obligation to publish prices on the face of the Bill. We accept that, at least initially, the prices should be published. We want to include that provision in the licence because we think that, at some stage in the future, by common consent, it may be appropriate for the prices not to be publicly available. It is interesting that some of the competitor suppliers to British Gas that are trying to supply the market for above 2,500 therms are already encouraging people to whom they are offering their services to negotiate prices with them as opposed to accepting a postalised price. I feel strongly that, initially at least, there should be published prices, but I want to retain the flexibility to move away from that position were it felt to be in the consumers' interests to do so.

The hon. Member for Clackmannan (Mr. O'Neill) raised the subject of rights of entry. It is adequately dealt with by schedule 2, the Rights of Entry (Gas and Electricity Boards) Act 1954 and the terms of the licences. Those exercising rights of entry will have to be fit and proper people and there will have to be arrangements so that customers can confirm the identity of individual meter readers.

I hope that I have covered the points that have been raised by Opposition Members in what has been a wide-ranging debate. I regret that I cannot accept the new clauses or the amendments because, in the main, those issues are appropriately dealt with in the provisions in the licence conditions.

**Mr. Nigel Griffiths:** The Minister has attempted to answer some of the points that have been made, but not very forcefully. He talked about how prices had fallen in the industrial sector after the Gas Act 1986, but there is a widely held view that the industrial sector was partially subsidising the domestic sector. That is reinforced if we consider the average consumption of between 600 and 800 therms for domestic property and the original 25,000-therm threshold.

It is clear that, under the terms of the original 1986 Act, with the minimum threshold of gas consumption of 25,000 therms, for every 35 houses that had to be visited, every 35 meters that had to be installed and every 35 checks that had to be made every two months on those meters—for every group of 35—the gas supplier had to make just one visit to an industrial unit. It is patently obvious that it is far cheaper to deal with 35 factories all using 25,000 therms or more in one visit than it is to visit 35 houses.

There were obvious savings to be made, and they went to the industries and the commercial ventures, with an adequate profit made by the independent gas suppliers. I am not convinced that the same sort of savings will be realised by opening up the market to individuals, when the individual meters will still have to be read.

7.45 pm

The Minister dwelt on pre-payment meters and their value. As a former member of a local electricity consultative committee in the 1980s, I am aware of the tremendous technological developments of pre-payment meters. They have become an alternative to the court order and disconnection. The big problem is that there is now so much fuel poverty that self-disconnection is a risk. People are forced to take pre-payment meters or sacrifice their supplies. Once they have the pre-payment meter, they have to rationalise their spending.

Often, modern income support benefits do not allow them enough money to keep the house warm and to do the cooking for seven days. On the sixth or seventh day, they do not boil the kettle or have hot meals. That is not an uncommon phenomenon in Britain today. The benefits of pre-payment meters should not be exaggerated. Nor should it be said that there are so many pre-payment meters because residents ask for them. Most people with pre-payment meters have no choice.

New clause 3 places the duty on the Gas Consumers Council to monitor the effects on consumers of the Gas Act. The Gas Consumers Council has been widely praised on both sides of the House and outside the House as an independent body, despite the fact that 99 per cent. of its funding comes from British Gas and only 1 per cent. from the Government. The council has achieved the remarkable feat of establishing itself and its independence so that no one can question it.

It is important when accepting the rationale behind new clause 3 that the list of aspects—the prices to be charged by the new companies, any other terms of supply, the continuity of supply, the quality of services and, as has been stressed by my hon. Friends, the rights of entry into premises—should be monitored, not just by the regulator, but by the Gas Consumers Council. The council is often in the front line of complaints and receives 10 times the number of complaints as the regulator, who is seen as having a firm position on regulation.

New clause 9 involves the publication of the terms of supply. The Minister did not convince the House that placing the terms in the licences rather than in the Gas Bill was a satisfactory solution. At the end of the day, the licences will not be subject to parliamentary scrutiny. We have in six fairly concise lines the terms that require the prices to be charged to consumers for gas supply and any other services to be published and that publication should be consumer friendly. It should be done in consultation with the Director General of Gas Supply and with the Gas Consumers Council with a view to making sure that there is local publicity—if a local area is being served—outlining the terms of supply to all the gas consumers in the area.

We fear that, without new clause 9, there will be a tendency to opt for discriminatory marketing. Although the licensee will hold the franchise for a certain area, the licensee may choose not to market in particular areas, but rather to use what we are familiar with in terms of our own campaigning—profiling techniques to make sure that the right message is getting to the right people. When we deal with our constituents, our approach is discriminatory according to political parties and those who are doubtful.

The problem with new clause 9 is that the companies marketing gas will decide to market only to those houses that look as though they have more bedrooms than others in the geographical area and are likely to use more gas. One meter reading will ensure that the gas supplier will make a larger profit. Therefore, although it will not breach

[*Mr. Nigel Griffiths*]

the licence, as the supply will be available to anyone in the licence area, it will not go out of its way to make sure that people know about it.

New clause 10 places a firm duty on the regulator to protect the interests of the consumer and especially to monitor where there may be discrimination against consumers who are disabled, senior citizens or in receipt of state benefit. The Government and the Opposition are wholly in agreement in those aims. New clause 10 is necessary to ensure that measures outlawing discrimination are given proper effect, and we are not convinced by what the Minister told us were the safeguards in the licences.

It is also important that the director general can impose a definite financial penalty on any new independent gas supplier who contravenes the terms that are widely shared in the House and outside.

Amendment No. 44 outlines the need for effective contingency plans to deal with serious breakdowns in supply. Again, the Gas Consumers Council, which is the major recipient of complaints about breakdowns in supplies, if it did not write to the Minister, has taken up with the Health and Safety Executive and Director of Gas Supply the explosions that occurred during the Christmas period—fortunately without loss of life, but none the less very serious—which may have resulted from the breakdown in supply.

It is important that the Gas Consumers Council, which has knowledge and expertise, is seen as user friendly, has its phone number on every gas bill—we proposed amendments to make sure that it is on every gas bill from any independent supplier—and can vet the contingency plans. The Gas Consumers Council should be assured from its vast database that any contingency plans do not fail due to inexperience or inadvertent omission if it can look back at other examples in its own experience where such contingency plans would not have worked. That is the value of the role of the Gas Consumers Council which can use its body of knowledge and say, "These contingency plans will not work. You may think they are good, but there is a one-in-10,000 chance that they will go wrong, as we saw in 1989 or whenever."

For all those reasons, we have sought to press our arguments so that the Minister is aware of our concerns.

**Mr. O'Neill:** My hon. Friends and I felt that it was important to give due airing to this group of amendments, which we consider lie at the heart of the Bill.

The Bill will be severely diminished unless the consumers are afforded protection and certain clear rights, unless their mouthpiece is given clear duties and the suppliers have clear responsibilities. We introduced the amendments on the basis that we wanted to give the House an opportunity to discuss them. We have had a full and wide-ranging discussion, so with the leave of the House I beg to ask leave to withdraw the motion.

*Motion and clause, by leave, withdrawn.*

### New clause 4

#### Duty of Director to consult on exercise of his functions

'After Section 39 of the 1986 Act there shall be inserted the following section—"(39A) In performing his duties under this Part, the Director shall—

(a) take all reasonable steps to consult persons or bodies appearing to the Director to be representative of persons or bodies likely to be affected by the performance of those duties; and

(b) take all reasonable steps to explain and publicise his reasons for any decision made under this Part.".'.—[*Mr. O'Neill.*]

*Brought up, and read the First time.*

**Mr. O'Neill:** I beg to move, That the clause be read a Second time.

**Mr. Deputy Speaker:** With this, it will be convenient to discuss also the following: New clause 5—*Grounds for removing Director from office*—

'Section 1 of the 1986 Act shall be amended as follows:

(a) In subsection (2) by omitting from the word "years" to the end of the subsection and inserting the words "unless re-appointment can be agreed upon in conjunction with the Gas Consumers Council"; and

(b) In subsection 3 by inserting after the word "misbehaviour" the words "or a demonstrable record of failing to exercise his responsibilities in a manner which protects the interests of consumers; and in considering whether any of these grounds have been established, the Secretary of State shall take account of an annual submission about the performance of the Director which shall be made to the Secretary of State by the Gas Consumers Council.".'.

Amendment No. 46, in clause 1, page 2, line 27, at end insert—

'(3A) In performing their duties under subsections (1) and (2) above the Secretary of State and the Director shall consult with persons or bodies appearing to the Director to be representative of persons likely to be affected.'.

**Mr. O'Neill:** We have been talking about the role of the regulator and the accountability of the director general. Earlier in our debate, I mentioned that one important aspect of the legislation is that it provides us with the opportunity to consider the effectiveness of the regulatory regime which now applies to the gas market.

Although we do not consider that anything produced by the House is inherently imperfect, we nevertheless believe that from time to time opportunities arise for us perhaps to improve on the work of the House.

It is fair to say that the British political system came to regulation fairly late in life, especially when we consider the role of the utilities in other countries—particularly the United States, where the regulatory tradition has grown up certainly over the decades of this century. When we consider the regulation of the railways in the early days, it is clear that the movement for regulation came from both the right and the left of the political spectrum. On the left, there were objections to what were seen as the robber barons of the railways and the cartels that were established. On the right, there were objections to what was seen as an offence to competition and various forms of sharp practice introduced at the expense of the passengers. As a consequence, there was a somewhat uneasy consensus, as from different premises the same logic led to the view that regulation had to play a part in American commercial and business life.

The United Kingdom stumbled on regulation almost as an afterthought, when monopolies were created following the privatisation of the former state monopolies. In a number of instances, those monopolies have existed virtually without question over the past 10 years or so. This is perhaps the first opportunity to assess the effectiveness of the regulatory regime in respect of gas.

Because of the changes in prospect for other aspects of energy provision in Britain, the other energy regulator is also coming under scrutiny.

While I do not wish to stray beyond the bounds of order, there are occasions when analogies can be drawn or links can legitimately be made. I say that by way of prefacing my remarks; I do not wish to stray out of order. Madam Deputy Speaker, I shall try if not to catch your eye then to catch your grimace and return to the main thrust of my argument.

8 pm

New clause 4 seeks to impose upon the regulator a duty to consult, explain and publicise his or her activities. That duty involves accountability, openness and transparency. We believe that it is important to require the regulator to justify any modifications that he or she makes to any previous decisions. At present, the regulator is required to justify any licence modifications. We would like to think that that requirement will be extended to other activities and that a range of organisations will play a consultative role.

In discussing the previous new clause, we referred to the significance of the Gas Consumers Council. It is clear that there is a network involving groups such as the National Consumer Council, the Consumers Association and the Gas Consumers Council. We have seen some co-ordination between those bodies in the lobbying in relation to this legislation. They all seek to represent consumer interests in a different way and we believe that they should be consulted when decisions are taken.

At present the regulator is called to account largely by way of the annual report. We do not think that that is the most satisfactory accountability measure. Indeed, the regulator, Mrs. Spottiswoode, has said that the annual report is a most inadequate means of conveying the full burden of her interests and concerns. Perhaps we should examine the way in which other regulators operate. The chief executives of some electricity companies reported that they submit a sizeable number of papers and reports to the appropriate regulator. Presumably he digests them, meets the companies concerned and, without any real comment, subsequently distributes letters which begin "I am minded that" and contain a series of unjustified conclusions.

I do not believe that that is a satisfactory way for a regulatory regime to operate. I think that it is important that the companies which are being regulated, the consumers whose interests are being protected by the regulator and the investors whose interests often differ from the staff of the regulated companies should be involved—not necessarily individually—in the decision-making process. They should be provided with information sufficient to inform them as to what the regulator is thinking.

Recent changes to the system have not evoked a fulsome response from the regulator. The announcement of the direct debit discount scheme caused considerable controversy. Under the scheme, those customers of British Gas who opted to pay their gas bills by direct debit received an immediate £20 discount. That caused considerable concern among those individuals, many of whom were elderly, who paid their gas bills on time and in full and who never missed any of their instalments. I am sure that you have come across them, Madam Deputy Speaker, as I have when performing my constituency duties. They are the kind of people who like to have things in order, who do not have a lot of money and who have developed very good book-keeping habits over many years. They like to be very precise about their calculations and they never fall behind in their payments or in meeting their financial responsibilities.

Many of those individuals do not have bank accounts—they may have money in the Post Office, but they certainly do not have cheque accounts or the facility to make direct debit arrangements. The whole business of getting a cheque book and a cheque card, trying to remember a personal identification number and so on would have been far too much bother because their system worked very well.

Many people bitterly resented what they considered to be the discrimination that the £20 direct debit discount represented, and the Gas Consumers Council was inundated with 3,293 complaints between 17 November and 8 December. That information was transmitted to the director general and to the regulator, whose reply we are still awaiting. We believe that a controversial issue of that nature requires a more immediate response.

The present tariff formula was arrived at in 1992. It was the subject of some consultation and in the end the RPI minus X formula was established alongside the energy efficiency factor element in the Bill. It was never put out for consideration or discussion; it was a foregone conclusion. It was felt at that time that there could have been more consultation about the matter.

In recent months we have examined the question of the E factor involving that part of the Gas Bill which is to fund the energy efficiency schemes for which the Energy Savings Trust has been given responsibility and which we shall discuss in the context of subsequent amendments. The present regulator inherited the duty from her predecessor and she seems rather reluctant to carry it on. As a former Treasury civil servant, I think that she assumes that she is not responsible for collecting money from companies; she considers that to be a tax-collecting role.

We are very conscious that there has been some difficulty because the regulator was not instructed properly and therefore was reluctant to carry out her duties as she perceived them. She did not consider them to be legitimate duties. We do not believe that there was a clear chain of regulator responsibility or accountability. There have been similar instances recently involving changes in the price formula.

As I said earlier, the price formula is calculated on the basis of the rise in the cost of living less a certain figure. For a number of years, the X in the RPI minus X formula represented five. However, when British Gas had to change its organisation as a consequence of the Monopolies and Mergers Commission report and the new arrangements came into play, the X factor fell from five to four. It was assumed that that was to compensate British Gas for the expense of changing its internal organisation, but that was never made specific or clear.

No means exist, at least at present, whereby the regulator can be called to account and asked in an open way, "Why have you done this?" That lack of transparency and accountability diminishes the regulator's authority. It is fair to say that openness leads to better decision-making. Accountability means that a range of views are seen to be taken seriously by the regulator.

[Mr. O'Neill]

There is some debate about whether the passage of the legislation will result in the continuance of regulation. It is assumed among some of the more exotic plants in the free market garden that, once perfect competition has been established, we will no longer need regulation. That is reminiscent of the arguments that Lenin put forward about the role of the state when he said that, once communism had been achieved in its pure and perfect form, no need would exist for the dictatorship of the proletariat or for the state. Experience has shown that that idealism was misplaced.

The same sort of thinking in relation to perfect competition is probably equally misplaced. That is one of the problems with affording to academics the opportunity of putting their academic ambitions on to the blackboard. Allowing them to put their ideas into practice lends scope for massive errors of judgment. We shall have a regulatory system and regulators for some considerable time and it is important that regulators are accountable and are seen to be open and transparent in the way in which they carry out their duties.

It is equally important that other ways exist of calling regulators to account. There are three standard means of dealing with a regulator, if I may put it that way. The first is to seek a judicial review. That is expensive and often time-consuming. The Minister looks dubious. I suspect that he was a solicitor in his previous incarnation and that he is therefore not so aware as many of us are of the public's anxieties about paying his profession any more money. On the grounds of expense or delay, judicial review is a dubious method of calling regulators to account. It is effective, but it can be dear.

**Mr. Hain:** My hon. Friend might note that, as the Minister is likely to lose his Brecon and Radnor seat to a Labour candidate at the next general election, he will be looking for work as a solicitor, so judicial reviews may come in handy.

**Mr. O'Neill:** I should like to think that, when the Minister leaves the House, he will be able to earn a crust, but we do not want him to earn a cake on the scale that some lawyers seem to earn at present.

A judicial review is one option. The second is a reference to the Monopolies and Mergers Commission. The third is a regulator's failure to be reappointed to the job. Those sanctions are not sufficient. A clearer indication should be given of the grounds on which an individual who is not fulfilling his responsibilities could be removed. The Gas Consumers Council, which we have already spoken about as the most effective monitor and recipient of information about the working of the gas market, should be consulted. That is the burden of new clause 5.

If a demonstrable record exists that an individual has failed to exercise his responsibilities to consumers, that should be grounds for his removal. We should like to think that the Gas Consumers Council report would be given due weight by the Secretary of State for Trade and Industry if the possibility of removal were to arise. I do not consider those remarks to be a reflection on the activities of the present regulator, who has not blotted her copy book in ways that would be grounds for removal under new clause 5.

8.15 pm

On the other aspect of the accountability of the regulator to which we want to draw attention, amendment No. 46 states that the Secretary of State and the director should consult

"with persons or bodies appearing to the Director to be representative of persons likely to be affected."

The emphasis there is slightly different from the emphasis that I placed on the bodies which are deemed to be the natural representatives of consumers—the Gas Consumers Council and the Consumers Association. On occasions, local authorities may be the most appropriate organisation to consult. Where we were dealing with fairly small groups of residents, tenants and housing, residents associations may be the appropriate body. One can envisage local authorities providing gas heating arrangements, which might have to be taken into account.

We are concerned about providing a means whereby the regulator should be more answerable to Ministers and to the community. As I said earlier, regulators will have a role in the British political and economic framework for many years to come. The provision of basic services such as water, electricity and gas have of necessity to be regulated because they are of such significance in the lives of ordinary citizens. As a consequence, we want to ensure that the gas regulation system, which is as far as our remit extends, has within it a degree of accountability, both to the Secretary of State and to consumers, individuals and the bodies that represent them. This group of amendments would extend and lend credibility to the functions of the regulatory process in Britain, and would contribute to the proper working of the gas energy market. For those reasons, we are happy to commend the amendment and new clauses.

**Ms Coffey:** I suppose that the central issue is who regulates the regulator. At present, under the Gas Act 1986 and the proposed Bill, the regulator has a duty to pay special interest to the disabled and pensioners. I understand that it would be difficult for a group of people—perhaps a pensioners group or the Gas Consumers Council—to hold the regulator to account if they felt that she had not paid them special interest, as laid down in her duties to customers. I understand that a pensioners group could not refer the regulator's action to the Monopolies and Mergers Commission.

The only course of action open to it would be to take the regulator to a judicial review, which is an expensive process. Although there is an existing legislative duty on the regulator to consider the needs of those two groups, if he or she failed in that respect, how would those groups challenge the regulator except by the expensive process of judicial review? The market has no conscience, and the gas market will be no different. Conscience is provided by the regulator and the interests of consumers being part of his or her duties.

In Committee, the Minister refused to accept an amendment which would have instructed the director general to take into account not only the disabled and people of pensionable age but consumers on low incomes. That group, to which everyone has referred during the Bill's progress as of particular concern, appears to be missing from the regulator's social conscience role. The regulator has no duty to protect that group.

Because there is no duty on the regulator to protect low-income customers, pressure to do something about British Gas standing charges has not been exerted. I understand that those charges have decreased, but it would be perfectly possible for British Gas not to impose them at all but to incorporate them into the cost of supply, then produce a tariff that was the same for each customer. Standing charges act to the detriment of low-income customers because they account for a disproportionately large part of their bills. If the regulator had a duty to protect low-income customers, there might have been more pressure to abolish standing charges. As that duty does not exist, the regulator cannot be held to account for the problems that have arisen with standing charges. They will continue to pose a problem to low-income customers, who will not benefit from gas competition in the way that other customers will benefit.

The Minister will say that the regulator's role is to be independent, but no regulator is that. The individual regulator has beliefs and experience, and his or her actions have political implications. The intent may not be political, but sometimes the consequences are political. There is no independence from political beliefs—with a small "p"—in the regulatory system, even though there may be independence from party political beliefs.

Accountability therefore becomes crucial. The only way to ensure real accountability is to specify precisely what is expected of the regulator, then hold the regulator to account as to whether he or she has satisfactorily discharged their duties. No such mechanism currently exists. Parliament cannot do that. The regulator is not accountable to Parliament. She may appear before a Select Committee and account for her actions, but she is not accountable to the Committee, to Parliament or to the Minister. Neither is she accountable to consumer groups. If they believe that the regulator has failed in her regulatory duties to protect particular groups, they cannot call her to account, except through expensive judicial review.

Everyone should be accountable. Being accountable to a is another. The new clauses seek to ensure such accountability.

**Mr. Hain:** New clauses 4 and 5 propose increased accountability for the gas regulator. I shall put the arguments in a broader philosophical framework because it is necessary to understand how the Government's approach to regulation differs from that of Labour.

The Government endorse the free market as the agency by which equilibrium will be created and everyone will broadly benefit. Regulation is an afterthought grafted on to that system—from the point of view of the free marketeers, something that started as a monopoly needed regulation. The Government believe, as my hon. Friend the Member for Clackmannan (Mr. O'Neill) said, that, as competition gradually grows more dominant and universal, regulation should wither on the vine. That is one model of regulation—not a principle dynamo of Government policy but a necessary adjunct to the competitive market.

The second approach to regulation—the one that socialists adopt—is quite different. Instead of favouring a free market economy, it favours a democratic economy in which market forces play an important role. An interventionist regulatory mechanism would seek, clearly and deliberately, to promote social good, common good, economic efficiency and strategic interests rather than competition and expecting those social and common goods to spill out as a consequence.

The growing debate on regulation is informed by both perspectives. The existing regulatory system enjoys little support, except from Ministers and their cohorts. Labour spokespersons, the Select Committee on Trade and Industry, National Power's chairman, John Baker, and the gas regulator, Clare Spottiswoode, have all argued for reform of the regulatory system. It has grown like Topsy in the past 10 years. It is now ad hoc, complex, over-technical and deeply flawed. There is no consistency in the decision of regulators as between one industry and another. The regulators within any one industry—and gas is a good example—are not necessarily consistent. Decisions made by Clare Spottiswoode do not necessarily stand in line with those made by her predecessor, Sir James McKinnon. I will return to Sir James, because he is a good example of why the system needs reforming.

It is also important to note—this is why the two new clauses are very important—that the regulatory system in the gas privatisation programme in particular was largely an afterthought. It was the bait to catch the privatisation fish. When the Government realised that they could not privatise monopolies without placing some check on them, they hastily thought up a regulatory system, which was rushed in and ill-thought-out, and which developed under its own momentum rather than being strategically planned from the outset.

In the process of that development, competition has been obsessively elevated above all other possible objectives of the regulator. For example, at a meeting in the Palace of Westminster some months ago, the gas regulator, Clare Spottiswoode, said:

"Regulators can never do as well as competition."

That is very interesting because it informs us about how she sees her role: to promote competition, virtually at all costs, and over and above other strategic or social objectives that a regulator should have responsibility for promoting. If the regulator were subjected to proper accountability under the two new clauses, she would have to have more regard for other matters.

In short, competition drives the regulatory system. The gas regulator sees it as her job to make changes to the pricing formula, to conditions for new market entrants or to the regime under which they operate so as continuously to promote competition and thereby—she believes and the Government obviously accept—create a situation from which gas customers will benefit. Such benefits have clearly not followed. Certainly there is no logical reason in principle why they should, as we heard in the previous debate on cherry-picking and social dumping.

Although competition has been put above all other objectives, it was not the primary objective in the privatisation legislation, such as the Gas Act 1986. Competition was one of a series of other objectives, above which it has been elevated, with the Government's blessing and under the regulator's ideological remit. To that extent, the idea, as the Minister said and as the gas regulator has been heard to argue, that regulators are non-political is total nonsense. They make decisions that advantage certain groups and disadvantage others. That is politics. They are just as political as any Back Bencher— and a lot more powerful to boot. They are political animals. Their decisions are highly political. The idea that, by hiving off regulation to an independent appointee, decisions and policy consequences become non-political is nonsense and a contradiction in terms. I repeat: their

[*Mr. Hain*]

decisions are highly political in their impact on energy policy, because they benefit certain social groups and disadvantage others.

In that context, a particular feature of this regulatory system, which the new clauses would at least go some way to address, is a compartmentalised type of decision making, in which the gas regulator, for example, makes decisions about gas competition while being quite oblivious—at least apparently oblivious—to the consequences for energy policy. I say energy policy, but there is no energy policy. Competition is energy policy, which means we do not have one. All sorts of anomalous consequences result. Within five years, we will have gone from nil to 25 per cent. gas-generated electricity. That will be achieved only by closing pits, at an estimated cost of £1 billion to the taxpayer in unemployment benefit and other costs. That is a consequence of the promotion of competition in gas and of allowing competition in the electricity industry to use gas, for which it is not really suitable.

British Gas has consistently—I do not think that it bothers any more—made clear its opposition to using gas for power station baseload, for which gas is not suitable. Such use will diminish the life of gas reserves in the North sea by 15 years and divert those reserves away from their much more efficient use as an on-the-spot domestic and industrial fuel. Gas should be used like that, yet we are blowing it away.

8.30 pm

When I asked the gas regulator to address that issue, she said that it was nothing to do with her. She has an interest only in promoting competition in gas. Indeed, her decisions have virtually forced British Gas to sell more gas to power stations, which is against the long-term interests of Britain, the gas industry, energy policy and gas customers. It is against our long-term national interest because UK dependence on energy from overseas suppliers raises important strategic issues, about which the regulators do not believe they must be bothered. We already have a big balance of payments burden as a result of importing coal and other energy sources. That will be increased by imports of gas in future, including from very unstable regions in Asia and the middle east.

If the gas regulator were more accountable to public, to Parliament and perhaps to the Select Committee on Trade and Industry, and if she were required to give reasons for her decisions, the use of gas for power stations might have been included in the debate. We could have questioned whether burning it away in power stations was a sensible use of gas or whether we should conserve it and thereby make us less dependent on foreign suppliers.

The gas regulator has—apparently—neither the power, the will nor the interest in intervening to protect the common good as opposed to the private good of the competing gas companies. The promotion of competition in the gas sector has been oblivious to the knock-on consequences for other energy sectors and for the wider industrial structure and economic interest of Britain. It is also interesting to note—I shall not develop the point, because we shall cover it later—that promoting competition in such a way has relegated conservation and the entire environmental agenda to second place at best. There is a crying need to reform the regulatory system to ensure that wider social and strategic interests are met.

It is also important to recognise that the gas regulator, in common with other regulators, has enormous personal discretion.

**Mr. Simon Burns** (Chelmsford): That is right.

**Mr. Hain:** One of the Government Whips mutters from a sedentary position, "That is right." The gas regulator has considerable discretion, which the Government have encouraged. Indeed, they praise it because they say that it removes decisions from the political arena, from Parliament. What are we here for, if it is not to have some influence, as Members of Parliament, over crucial public policy areas such as gas supply and the wider energy context in which that operates?

In considering the degree of discretion, I need quote no more relevant a figure than the previous gas regulator, Sir James McKinnon, who developed a personality cult in the industry, using his discretion to an enormously egotistical degree. In successive press releases, he even described himself as the Santa Claus of the gas industry. Industry commentators started to refer to regulation by press release, counting how many times his name and picture appeared in Ofgas publications. During his tenure, Ofgas performed a series of U-turns on successive issues. He changed his mind three times on the structure of the industry. He veered from supporting the integrated nature of British Gas one year to its complete destruction the next and he finally opposed the limited break-up suggested by the Monopolies and Mergers Commission.

Such policy gymnastics were very destabilising. Perhaps that is why Sir James McKinnon went—perhaps the Minister will reveal all. Clare Spottiswoode has been a much more admirable gas regulator, which is welcome, but there is enormous scope for discretion, which was abused by Sir James McKinnon and could be abused by any other gas regulator.

In that regard, I need seek no greater confirmation than the behaviour of the electricity regulator and the recent intervention of Professor Stephen Littlechild on prices in the power share sales. That discretion challenged the heart of democratic politics. Decisions are being hived off to independent appointees that should properly be brought within the system of political accountability. That should not be confused with operational responsibilities.

I am not arguing that the regulator should be held accountable or forced to consult in respect of every detail of regulatory policy, but I am concerned that the broad political and public policy trajectory of regulation should be much more accountable.

There is no real transparency, as my hon. Friend the Member for Clackmannan so eloquently said. Effectively, the regulators are the high priests of public policy. They make significant decisions and they are more powerful than almost all Back Benchers. They are even more powerful than collective groups, such as Select Committees, with regard to the impact of their decisions.

There is a need for greater accountability. The objectives of the regulators should be changed so that they are given much more responsibility for the social consequences of their decisions and for the strategic implications of regulatory decisions, especially with regard to energy policy and the need for international competition.

At the moment, the regulator's decisions favour domestic competition. They pay very little regard, if any, to the need for international competition. At the moment, just about every foreign-owned or controlled gas supplier is being invited to clean up the British market, but British Gas—the national champion—cannot enter foreign markets on a reciprocal basis. Indeed, under its current structure, the European Union specifically prevents British Gas from getting into Europe in the way that European companies can enter our markets.

Why is the gas regulator not addressing that problem? Why is she not banging on the Minister's door saying, "I want to change the regulatory system in order to make international competition a much greater priority than it is under the present regime"?

8.45 pm

We have become the laughing stock of the international gas community. Our competitors, NOVA in Canada, Gaz de France, American-owned Enron, Italgas, Ruhrgas, Tractebel, Gas Natural, the Russian company Gazprom and BHP in Austria, many of which are state-owned, are gaining a massive world lead at the expense of British Gas. We are not concerned with international competition as the regulator is so obsessed with promoting pygmy competition in the domestic market. There is no regard for the industrial and strategic interests of the British economy, which would be advanced by the promotion of international competition and in respect of which British Gas would be able much more effectively to conquer the world markets and become a world leader and one of the top four or five global gas players, which I believe will happen when the market shakes out.

For those reasons, the regulatory system is fundamentally flawed. My hon. Friend the Member for Stockport (Ms Coffey) asked a question that is becoming increasingly important: who regulates the regulators? No one other than the Government and the existing regulators—and not even all of them—defends the existing system. There should be radical reform, and the new clauses would go some way towards achieving that.

**Mr. Eggar:** We have had another wide-ranging debate. The first issue to be raised was that of the direct debit discount. As is now fairly well known, British Gas, I am told, is planning to introduce a new scheme later this year which will give direct discounts to prompt payers who choose not to pay by direct debit. It justifies the current direct debit discount by arguing that the discount reflects the lower average cost of serving direct debit customers as against other customers.

The hon. Member for Clackmannan (Mr. O'Neill) said that the regulator had not responded to several letters on that issue. It is my understanding that it is her provisional view that the discount does not involve undue discrimination. That is obviously what she has to consider—*[Interruption.]* The hon. Member for Stockport (Ms Coffey) has a marvellous mouth, but to look at it in a totally uninterrupted way is slightly taxing on the eyes.

According to the regulator, the discount does not involve undue discrimination. However, the director general is considering representations, including several letters to the contrary, and at the moment she is not satisfied that there has been any contravention.

We did not spend much time on new clause 5. The implication of the remarks made by the hon. Member for Clackmannan is that even the hon. Member for Edinburgh, South (Mr. Griffiths) recognises that that new clause goes a little too far. The evidence for that is that

not even the Gas Consumers Council, which would be given the powers, actually wants them. It does not believe that it is equipped for that or that that is its role. I enjoyed the elegant way in which the hon. Member for Clackmannan trotted around new clause 5.

It is fair to say that most of the debate has revolved around new clause 4, and in particular the accountability issue alluded to in it. There is perhaps a fundamental difference between the Government and the hon. Member for Neath (Mr. Hain) because, as I listened to him, I could not make up my mind whether he was saying that the regulator should have more powers to take into account issues like international competition, or whether she should have fewer powers because she was not democratically accountable. I was not clear what he meant by democratic accountability.

There is clearly a difficult balancing act. If we are to have a proper system of regulation, it must not be at the beck and call of political intervention by whoever happens to be the Minister of the day. Whether that applies from the Opposition Benches—for example, to ensure that the hon. Member for Neath's valley gets gas, which was the argument he made in Committee—or from the Government Benches to achieve an objective which we felt was particularly attractive from our constituency point of view, any system of regulation must be properly independent from the political process in terms of direct intervention.

Obviously Ministers will be accountable to this place for certain policy issues. An example of that which relates to the structure of the Bill is the standard conditions. We regard the standard conditions as absolutely essential to the structure of the licence because a veto is vested in the Secretary of State. I believe very strongly in the principle of the independence of the regulator, but that independence must lie in a framework, which ultimately must be decided by Ministers.

The judicial review cannot be dismissed lightly. From a Minister's point of view and the exercise of discretion that he may have—not in this respect, but in others—and from a regulator's point of view, judicial review is a very important aspect of accountability. That is not always recognised, because it is not often that there are judicial reviews of Executive decisions. The regulators and I both find that power to be a significant form of accountability. Reference was also made to the Monopolies and Mergers Commission, and the issue of how individual decisions are reached was also raised. I referred to that in terms of the standard conditions. We exercise a veto in that area.

Further scrutiny is afforded by Select Committees, and that is an issue for the House to consider carefully. We must look at the way in which the Select Committees on Trade and Industry, the Environment and Employment have called the gas regulator to account. I am a believer in Select Committees, and I think that the House should use them more effectively. The House should reflect on the relationship between Select Committees and the regulators, although there is no obvious prescription as to how that can be done. Select Committees, like the National Audit Office, provide an important form of accountability.

**Ms Coffey:** The Minister is suggesting that the Select Committees have not held the regulators to be sufficiently accountable. However, the gas regulator said that although the Select Committee can hold her to account—as the

*[Ms Coffey]*

Committee can hold to account a Minister—the regulator is not accountable to the Select Committees. She is accountable in the sense that she has to give an account of her actions, but she is not accountable in the sense that the Select Committee has any direct influence or control over her actions. That is the key point.

**Mr. Eggar:** The hon. Lady and I part company there. She is arguing for politicians—in this case an all-party Select Committee—to have the power to instruct or direct the regulator, whereas I believe strongly in the independence of the regulator. I was not being critical of Select Committees. I was simply saying that that is an issue for the House, because the regulators could be made more accountable to the Select Committee system if a little more thought was given to doing so. I do not see that essentially as a matter for the Government.

I hope that my answer has been useful. I am afraid that, for the reasons I have given, I certainly cannot recommend that new clause 5 be agreed to. I do not think that the Opposition want to press it to a Division. On the other points in the debate, they got the balance right.

**Mr. O'Neill:** The discussion has contained the germ of a good debate. Most of the speeches of my hon. Friends, while emphasising slightly different elements, dealt with the general approach to regulation, which has produced a whole that is greater than the sum of its parts. The Minister has, for once, avoided bluster and has endeavoured to engage in a genuine debate. It is regrettable, therefore, that no other Conservative Member has sought to contribute. A couple of individuals have come into the Chamber as our debate has come to a close, but no one from the Opposition Back Benches has been prepared—

**Mr. Nigel Griffiths:** The Government Back Benches.

**Mr. O'Neill:** I am getting into a habit, but that description will be appropriate before too long.

The point is that no one from the Government is not so much prepared to defend the regulatory system but to discuss it. To that extent, the Minister's remarks are evidence of a lack of thought and discussion. He went through the standard means of accountability of the regulator, including a judicial review. I know that that is a hobby-horse of the Minister's, and we have debated that matter in Committee. His experience is greater than ours, and he believes that the threat of a judicial review is of no small significance in concentrating the minds of individuals.

We have seen references to the Monopolies and Mergers Commission used in much the same manner of megaphone diplomacy in the past. Where we part company with the Minister is on his touching faith in Select Committees. If there is a fundamental flaw in the Select Committee system, it is that it has been grafted on to the House of Commons without a proper separation of powers. Those countries in which the committee system operates most effectively use committees as a check on bodies in which those involved have no direct interest.

Our Select Committees contain individuals who wish to join the Executive at some stage, or those who have been on it and are embittered or indifferent. I do not think that there is a correct relationship between our Select

Committees and the Executive. I am not sure if it would be within the bounds of the proceedings of the House—although given the flexibility of our Standing Orders, pretty well anything is possible—if we were to have a mechanism whereby individuals who were nominated to become regulators could be subject to an interview before their appointment. They would then have to be confirmed in the post by the House. That is not the way in which the House operates at the moment.

During our debates on the Coal Industry Act, we suggested that the chief executive of the Coal Authority would have to be confirmed or interviewed by the Select Committee. In some respects, that was the kind of thing that one does in a Standing Committee—flying a kite. Our Select Committee system is useful for collecting information, but it is never very good at drawing conclusions, because the conclusions tend to be the ultimate compromise.

Some Select Committee conclusions and recommendations are eventually taken on board. Sometimes, in the longer term they have a role in establishing a consensus, but, as a means of dealing with the serious political problems to which my colleagues and I have alluded—for example, the direct debit issue, the establishment of the price formula and so on—if there is to be immediate action, Select Committees are not good at getting the message across. They can inform debate, but ultimately they do not play a conclusive role.

I take the Minister's point about the National Audit Office. Indeed, the Public Accounts Committee can look retrospectively at matters, but it cannot be proactive. In the regulatory sector there might be occasions when proaction is appropriate.

We have had the beginnings of a good debate. I do not suggest that we go on any longer, because we have other business to attend to. It is unfortunate that no Conservative Back Bencher was prepared to take part in the debate. However, the matter has been ventilated. I beg to ask leave to withdraw the motion.

*Motion and clause, by leave, withdrawn.*

### New clause 6

DUTY OF SECRETARY OF STATE AND DIRECTOR TO CONSULT WITH HEALTH AND SAFETY EXECUTIVE ON SAFETY QUALIFICATIONS OF GAS CONTRACTORS

'The Secretary of State and the Director shall each have a duty to consult with the Health and Safety Executive with the objective of securing that any public gas transporter, retailer, shipper or supplier who may have cause to undertake work on any gas supply meter, gas fitting or appliance shall ensure that—

    (a) any employee or third party contractor is suitably qualified in the relevant aspects of gas distribution, installation or service;

    (b) any third party contractor undertaking such work is registered with an appropriate recognised trade body approved by the Health and Safety Executive.'.—*[Mr. Nigel Griffiths.]*

*Brought up, and read the First time.*

**Mr. Nigel Griffiths:** I beg to move, That the clause be read a Second time.

New clause 6 deals with critical safety issues. The House will be aware of the Monopolies and Mergers Commission's report on gas under the Fair Trading Act 1973. The report, published in August 1993, stressed that safety was a major consideration in the removal of the monopoly. If electricity is switched off, it leaves no problems behind. If gas is switched off, pilot lights can remain on. Gas requires greater skill and vigilance.

9 pm

Fortunately, gone are the days when there was widespread fear of gas and when the consequences of gas explosions were felt by all. None the less, there is an alarming number of gas incidents. I am a founder member of Consumer Safety International, which assists people who have lost relatives or suffered injuries abroad because of gas, particularly in Spain, and of CO-GAS, which is a British-based organisation that campaigns for safer gas appliances.

New clause 6 gives the Health and Safety Executive an overview. It would make the Secretary of State and the Director General of Gas Supply duty bound to consult the HSE, to ensure that gas transporters, retailers, shippers or suppliers were suitably qualified.

The Government have had a big drive to encourage people to register with the CORGI scheme. I appreciate the work of CORGI and of its skilled engineers, but there are various estimates—none is below several thousand—of unqualified, unregistered people installing gas supplies in highly dangerous circumstances.

I notice from the Government's statistics that a large number of appliances still have dangerous gas fittings. In 1993-94, for example, 445 dangerous boilers, 44 dangerous water heaters, 330 dangerous gas fires and 112 dangerous cookers were identified. There were a total of 1,467 dangerous appliances, which was an increase of more than 200 on the previous year, and that was an increase of almost 500 on the year before. In the past three years, there has been a trend of a steady increase in the notification of dangerous gas fittings, when the gas for domestic premises was supplied by one gas supplier.

As the market opens up, it is very important that proper safeguards are in place, to ensure that the domestic gas consumer is not put at risk. There are many reasons for faults, and again the available statistics are helpful. For example, in 883 cases, the manner of installation was deemed to be dangerous. Modifications and alterations caused danger in 259 cases. Servicing and maintenance problems occurred in 87 cases and design problems occurred in 32 cases out of the total of 1,467. Far too many dangerous fittings required attention. Once the Bill has been passed and the market has been deregulated, we do not want an alarming upward trend, which is the primary reason why we have tabled the new clause.

The Gas Consumers Council has made representations and runs campaigns for the register of Corgi installers to be made available to consumers and for the literature and leaflets to be user friendly. However, it also wants a proper register established to ensure that third-party contractors or employees of the new independent gas companies are suitably qualified in all aspects of gas distribution, installation and service.

There is a general fear that the installation of gas may become deskilled. Certainly, in the past, gas engineers were not only highly trained, as they still are, but worked to tolerances that did not allow the possibility of accidents in any number. Anyone who talks to gas engineers these days knows that cuts by British Gas, in the face of private sector competition, have meant that, whereas engineers were trained to work to tremendously fine tolerances, standards have slipped a little. I do not intend to alarm

the public—I believe that there are still adequate safeguards—but we do not want any further slippage, and we certainly do not want the new third-party contractors employing unskilled and unqualified people.

I shall be interested to hear what the Minister has to say in defence of not ensuring that any third-party contractor is using suitably qualified personnel. The Government joined us in supporting the CORGI scheme, but we want to ensure that the several thousand people who are currently practising unregistered and unqualified are driven out of business—and quickly.

We know of the tremendous risks not only of explosions but of carbon monoxide poisoning caused by fumes from faulty gas appliances and flues. We want to be sure that, once the gas market has opened up, Ministers, the regulator and the Health and Safety Executive are convinced that companies that succeed in getting a licence and that are involved in the installation and repair of appliances and the distribution of gas are suitably qualified and do not pose a risk to themselves or, more important, to the public.

**Mr. Kevin Hughes:** I, too, welcome the opportunity to debate the safety aspect of the Bill, which is probably one of the most important aspects for the consumer. Safety is probably uppermost in people's minds when gas appliances are installed in their homes. I should like to think that the Government will support new clause 6, but I doubt that they will. The fact that they will not is very unfortunate.

**Mr. Eggar:** How does the hon. Gentleman know?

**Mr. Hughes:** It is a guess, but we shall see at the end of the debate. I would not be able to bet on it at William Hill; the odds would certainly not be good anyway.

It is a pity that the Government will not support the new clause because it is fundamentally about protection and safety. It is designed to secure safety standards and service for consumers in future, under arrangements similar to those enjoyed in the present system, under British Gas. That means that appliances will have to be repaired by fully qualified and trained installers. Preferably, they should be properly registered and be able to provide expertise equal to that provided by TransCo and British Gas at present.

The new clause deals with the proper training of installers who carry out appliance repairs. Under the Bill, TransCo will be called out to deal with any difficulty with supply and will have responsibility for making an appliance safe. The repairs will not be carried out by TransCo, however, which will be responsible only for safety upstream of the meter. Consumers will be left with a list of CORGI-registered suppliers, and will have to arrange for the repair themselves.

There is concern about what the fragmentation of the repair service will mean in practice. Consumers will be left to take pot luck with the list of contractors that is handed to them. At present, British Gas engineers can make arrangements for appliances to be repaired and can leave temporary equipment, such as electric heaters, on loan to customers who may be vulnerable to cold and who do not have any other source of heating. Under the new system, that sort of comprehensive service and the benefits that it brings to consumers might be lost as householders are left to fend for themselves.

*[Mr. Hughes]*

The annual report of the Gas Consumers Council this year pointed out that a register of competent installers that is both accessible and meaningful to domestic consumers and advice agencies has not yet been produced. The Health and Safety Executive is considering that matter as part of its review of the CORGI registration scheme, which is welcome news.

The GCC has consistently pressed for such a register to be made available to gas consumers. At present, such information is not published. The council wants information on the hours and type of work that an installer has CORGI registration to undertake, which is particularly important. When competition is introduced, it is vital that such information is published in an accessible format and is readily available to both suppliers and consumers.

The Minister will remember that in Committee we discussed training for some CORGI scheme members compared with that for TransCo engineers at present. Unfortunately, not all CORGI-registered engineers will be trained in all types of gas appliances. Different levels of registration will apply for CORGI installers, and they may not always have the experience or expertise that British Gas engineers have. That is of concern, because a number of cases were raised in Committee in which mistakes had allegedly been made by CORGI-registered firms, which is deeply worrying.

CORGI-registered installers who work outside the competence for which they are registered are breaking the law, but customers may not know the level of competence of an installer, so adequate information must be available to consumers on that issue. At present, the business rather than the individual is given CORGI registration, which is a further potential source of confusion for the public in the light of the new circumstances that are proposed.

In the event of contracting out and even subcontracting, the parent company is sometimes not aware of who is carrying out the work. In some circumstances, it seems to lose control of who is handling the screwdrivers, spanners or whatever tools are needed to do a particular job. In this case, it could be dangerous if the parent company were not fully aware of who was carrying out repairs to appliances in people's homes.

As the Minister knows, I worked in the mining industry for a long time—

**Mr. Eggar:** How long?

9.15 pm

**Mr. Hughes:** Too long for me to remember, but more than 20 years. The Minister is probably aware of the number of accidents that occurred when outside contractors came to work in the industry. I shall not develop this point, Madam Deputy Speaker, but it is worth noting that the safety record of outside contractors was far worse than that of British Coal. I am worried that, if we start to contract out, as is almost inevitable, a similarly poor safety record may apply to those sent out to fix people's gas appliances. We should make it clear that only CORGI-registered engineers may carry out work on gas appliances. The Health and Safety Executive is looking into that matter in the context of its review.

In Committee, hon. Members expressed concern about the loss of expertise that may result from the fragmentation of repair work. Through working together

and sharing experiences, British Gas engineers have been able to identify potentially dangerous design faults and installation problems and report them to manufacturers when necessary. That good feature will probably be lost. Their combined pool of experience has been valuable and the potential loss of that exchange of information is worrying.

The Health and Safety Commission recognises that problem in its safety framework document and proposes that the Health and Safety Executive discuss with the industry and other parties arrangements for effective investigation into incidents downstream of the meter and for the dissemination of lessons learnt, such as on design faults in appliances.

What I have said shows that much more work will be placed on the Health and Safety Executive as a result of the Bill and how much the Bill's safety aspects depend for their implementation on the HSE's ability to cope with that new work. Opposition Members have consistently pressed the Government to provide additional funding for the Health and Safety Executive, to help it to carry out its responsibilities.

I understand from a letter that was left for me on the board this afternoon that the Minister proposes to provide more than £2.5 million to enable the HSE to carry out that work. The caveat is that that sum is for only three years. While I welcome the fact that the Government have come forward with that sum, which is warranted and necessary, I am concerned about what will happen when it runs out after three years. Will the Health and Safety Executive be forced to cut back or will the Government provide further funding? I hope that the Minister will address that matter when he responds.

I hope that the right hon. Gentleman will seriously consider the new clause, which aims to ensure that safety and standards of service are maintained for gas consumers in their own homes. The issues that I mentioned must be addressed, to guarantee that good safety standards are achieved once the Bill is enacted. Not least, the good work of the HSE must continue. I hope that the £2.5 million will not dry up after three years, because we would then have a serious problem. I hope that the right hon. Gentleman will respond to those important points, which are of particular concern to people because of their effect on their homes.

**Mr. Eggar:** I always listen with particular respect to contributions from the hon. Member for Doncaster, North (Mr. Hughes) on safety. Because of his particular experience in the mining industry, I recognise that safety, of which he has a great deal of knowledge, is close to his heart.

Although the hon. Gentleman would be misguided to put money on whether I would accept new clause 6, I would not have hesitated to do so if I thought that it was necessary to provide a thoroughly safe regime in the new competitive gas market. Clause 2 will insert section 4A(2) in the Gas Act 1986, which places a specific duty on the Secretary of State and the director to consult the HSE on all safety matters and to take into account any advice that it offers. In addition, sections 4A(3) and 4A(4) provide that the director must prepare and lay before the House a memorandum of understanding with the HSE, with the aim of securing co-operation and exchange of information and that, therefore, she must act in accordance with that memorandum. Those provisions cover the vast bulk of the concerns relating to hon. Members' insistence, quite rightly, that the HSE should be involved effectively.

I welcome the slightly grudging praise for the fact that we have produced the necessary funding for the HSE. It does not go beyond three years because the public expenditure system works on a three-year period. We shall address the needs for the fourth year and so on as they come up in the normal cycle of events.

**Mr. Kevin Hughes:** The right hon. Gentleman will probably not have to do that, because we shall be in government by then.

**Mr. Eggar:** Illusions, illusions. I shall allow the hon. Gentleman that little flight of fantasy because I do not want to disappoint him about that at least.

The other matters that the new clause would regulate are dealt with in existing regulations, in particular, the Gas Safety (Installation and Use) Regulations 1994. They require that only competent persons may do work on any gas fitting. That definition of gas fitting includes all appliances and pipe work downstream of the meter and the meter itself. In effect, the regulations mean that the people who do that work must be members of CORGI. Under the Bill, responsibility for safety upstream of the meter lies with the public gas transporter. At present, that operates under the general provisions of the Health and Safety at Work, etc. Act 1974. The HSE is, however, currently preparing draft regulations on more explicit rules in relation to gas pipelines.

**Mr. Clapham:** What steps has the Minister taken to ensure that there is a national register of CORGI-qualified engineers? Many hon. Members know of cases that have caused great concern, because engineers who were not CORGI qualified fitted installations at people's homes. Local authorities, which are particularly relevant because of their housing stock, have no access to a national register to see whether a man contracted by them is CORGI qualified.

**Mr. Eggar:** That matter was mentioned in Committee, and there is anxiety about it. The HSE has responsibility for that, as one would expect. It is important that the independent agency, the tripartite body under the HSE, looks after those matters. It is reviewing the CORGI scheme at present, and I am sure that it will take into account the anxieties that were expressed by the hon. Gentleman and other hon. Members.

In other words, I am convinced that the arrangements that we propose will meet the necessary requirements for safety. That is not only my opinion but that of the HSE. I wish to repeat, for the record, that we regard safety as paramount, for all the reasons mentioned by Opposition Members. We shall not compromise on that. We believe that the present systems and the present proposals in the Bill strike the right balance and will go as far as it is humanly possible to go to achieve the right type of safety regulation in that important industry.

**Mr. Nigel Griffiths:** My hon. Friend the Member for Doncaster, North (Mr. Hughes) speaks with great feeling on this subject, and he made a forceful case. The Minister has not reassured us satisfactorily, so we are especially keen to ensure that the other place has a chance to consider the issue, as it often does, in a less politicised atmosphere.

I beg to ask leave to withdraw the motion.
*Motion and clause, by leave, withdrawn.*

### Clause 1

#### GENERAL DUTIES UNDER 1986 ACT

**Mr. O'Neill:** I beg to move amendment No. 45, in page 2, line 19, at end insert—

'(2A) The Director, in performing his duty under subsection (2)(c) above shall—

(a) have regard to official estimates of the amount of discovered and recoverable reserves of gas, from onshore and on the United Kingdom Continental Shelf;

(b) have regard to the target reductions in carbon dioxide emissions agreed at the United Nations Conference on Environment and Development, held at Rio de Janeiro in June 1992;

(c) in conjunction with the Secretary of State, support an energy savings trust for the promotion and monitoring of energy efficiency.'.

**Madam Deputy Speaker (Dame Janet Fookes):** With this, it will be convenient to discuss amendment No. 51, in clause 8, page 12, line 41, at end add—

'(3) Standard conditions for gas suppliers shall included a duty on licence holders to ensure that details of how to obtain free energy efficiency, bill payment and gas appliance servicing advice is clearly displayed on all written material produced by a gas supplier for use by its customers.'.

**Mr. O'Neill:** The two amendments were in some respects mentioned in Committee, when we discussed matters relating to energy efficiency and conservation. We considered that it would be useful to bring the matter back to the House.

We realise that the hour is somewhat against us, but we want our responsibility for conservation matters and energy efficiency to be more explicitly expressed than the legislation does. It is important that the Director General of Gas Supply has regard to the amount of recoverable reserves of gas offshore and onshore.

The figures on gas reserves are produced annually in the Brown Book. They appear in several categories: proven, probable, proven plus probable, possible and then a maximum. We can sum up the position briefly in respect of gas reserves. The consensus is that between 20 and 35 years' supply of gas is available to us.

It is often said that, in the past 20 years, people have always assumed that there was only 20 years' supply left. That assumption has been due partly to the ingenuity of explorers and partly to the efficiency of companies in extracting gas, but we cannot always assume that there will be an infinite supply of a finite resource simply because of what has happened in the past 20 years. We therefore consider it important that the director general take account of those reserves of gas when advising on specific schemes or when considering systems of generation and the like.

Recently, in the case of electricity, when insufficient attention was given to the construction of gas-fired power stations, some of our coal reserves were lost to the extent that, when certain power stations that depended on specific coal mines closed, the mines in turn closed and we were denied access to supplies of coal. There is a link between the regulatory function and the conservation function. We would like to think that the director general

[*Mr. O'Neill*]

would have an explicit duty to take account of the estimates that are produced annually in what has become known as the Brown Book.

There is also the environmental consideration required of us by the Rio summit. We are committed to reducing our emissions of carbon dioxide. One of the major factors in the production of carbon dioxide is the pattern of our energy consumption. It would be appropriate for the director general to take account of the success or otherwise of our attempts to meet our internationally agreed targets for emissions.

### 9.30 pm

The issue of most basic concern to energy consumers in the United Kingdom is probably the establishment of an Energy Saving Trust that has some legislative basis. At present, the Energy Saving Trust exists in a sort of vacuum. It has been created and is the recipient of moneys, but it does not have the proper status that it merits. The amendment is an attempt—perhaps not a wholly adequate attempt—to give proper legislative recognition to the trust.

It is important to have a national agency that gives leadership on the promotion and monitoring of energy efficiency. If we were to have a competitive market and prices were to fall, it would matter little to those who did not have proper access to information about energy efficiency. We know from the experience of many of our constituents that living in draughty houses that are not properly insulated means that much of the money that residents lay out on electricity bills follows the heat out of the windows into the cold and the money is wasted. It is vital that the Energy Saving Trust enjoys enhanced status, which is why we have referred to such a body in the amendment. There is a clear link between the director general's responsibility for energy efficiency and the trust's work.

Amendment No. 51 states that, in the standard conditions for gas suppliers, the licence holders should be required to provide information on energy efficiency, bill payment and gas appliance servicing advice. That information should be available and should be included in all written materials. We know that certain steps have been taken. British Gas has often given information and sources of information, but that information should be in the standard conditions and should be part and parcel of the companies' responsibility, even if they themselves do not provide that information. It could be argued that, if they do not provide the information, that is all the more reason why organisations such as the Energy Saving Trust and neighbourhood energy action should be drawn to the attention of gas consumers.

Energy efficiency and conservation measures should lie at the heart of the new energy market which is developing. It is not enough merely to deal with matters of price. We should be considering environmental considerations and issues involving energy efficiency—one of the best ways of improving our constituents' quality of life.

I am happy to propose the two amendments in the hope that the Minister will give greater weight to the energy efficiency and conservation responsibilities that he carries, but that really should be shared between him and the director general and her staff.

**Mr. Eggar:** The director general and my right hon. Friend the Secretary of State already have a duty to exercise their functions in the manner that is best calculated to promote the efficient use of gas. The director general also has a specific power to set standards of performance for gas suppliers in connection with the promotion of the efficient use of gas. The licence also sets out minimum requirements for the provision of energy efficiency advice to consumers.

We believe, as distinct from Opposition Members, that the introduction of competition will itself provide a spur to the promotion of energy efficiency, because different suppliers will want to supply gas in the most appropriate way and many consumers will want to buy that gas in an energy-efficient mode; in other words, suppliers will be competing to supply warm houses as against merely therms of gas.

On the specific points that have been raised, the United Kingdom CS point, or the reserve, is fine. In practical terms, the effect of the amendment would be completely to disregard energy efficiency, because gas reserves have gone up year on year. Gas discovered on a proven basis has exceeded gas consumed. We do not believe, therefore, that it is an appropriate factor that the regulator should take into account.

The hon. Gentleman referred to the Energy Saving Trust. He did not say that my right hon. Friend the Secretary of State for the Environment announced last week that his Department was making available an additional £25 million a year to the Energy Saving Trust to promote energy-efficient measures. Had he focused on that, he would have welcomed that move.

**Mr. Clapham:** I am grateful to the Minister for giving way. He referred earlier to the fact that the director general should not have to concern herself with gas reserves. Given that we are using more gas for energy production, and that by the end of century we are likely to be using 40 million tonnes of coal equivalent, will there not be more pressure on prices and, therefore, should the director general not be concerned with these matters?

**Mr. Eggar:** It is true that the domestic consumption of gas is rising; so is the amount of success with gas discoveries. Imports of gas are near their lowest level since we first started importing from Norway. Gas prices are probably at their lowest level in real terms, but we cannot be confident that will continue.

The hon. Member for Clackmannan (Mr. O'Neill) raised the issue of what would be disclosed on bills for domestic customers. The list of disclosures required is long, going far beyond what British Gas is required to do or does as a matter of practice. However, it is reasonable to expect that when gas suppliers are competing for customers they will wish to make people fully aware of the services that they offer. It is best to leave it up to them to decide the best way to do that. For those reasons, I feel unable to accept the amendment.

**Mr. O'Neill:** The Minister has had a brief run around the track, and we recognise the points that he has made. We feel that there is some complacency about the view that, simply because we are getting more gas into Britain and because prices are cheaper, somehow the regulator should not take account of the levels of supply and the reserves.

We do not wish at this stage to push the amendment to a vote. We raised the matter in Committee. Everyone in the House will be grateful that money is now being put in the way of the Energy Saving Trust, because we recognise that it is an important body. I hope that the legitimacy that the funding will afford the trust will be only the first stage of putting it on a proper footing.

The Government have spent a lot of time attacking quangos, although they have created many of them. I am not sure whether the Energy Saving Trust is a quango in the true sense of the word, because it does not have a statutory basis. Although it is vaguely answerable to the Secretary of State for the Environment, a more appropriate person for that role might be the President of the Board of Trade, with his responsibility for trade and industry. However, I do not think that we need to debate that matter this evening. To avoid any further temptation to do so, I beg to ask leave to withdraw the amendment.

*Amendment, by leave, withdrawn.*

## Clause 5

### Licensing of public gas transporters

*Amendments made:* No. 1, in page 5, leave out lines 13 and 14 and insert—

'(b) the conveyance of gas through pipes which—

(i) are situated in an authorised area of his; or

(ii) are situated in an area which was an authorised area of his, or an authorised area of a previous holder of the licence, and were so situated at a time when it was such an area; or'.

No. 2, in page 7, line 1, at end insert—

'( ) references to the carrying on of activities authorised by a licence under this section shall be construed without regard to any exception contained in Schedule 2A to this Act;'.— [*Mr. Eggar.*]

## Clause 6

### Licensing of gas suppliers and gas shippers

**Mr. O'Neill:** I beg to move amendment No. 49, in page 8, line 29, at end insert—

'(2A) In the period before the relevant date the Director shall:

(a) monitor the effect of the granting of a licence under subsections (3) to (5) below on such persons as in his opinion are appropriate; and

(b) consult such persons and organisations as appear to him to represent the interests of persons affected by the granting of a licence under those subsections, and such other persons as he considers appropriate, on the effects of granting such a licence.

(2B) No licence shall be granted under section 7A(1)(a) of the 1986 Act (other than by virtue of subsections (3) to (5) below) until the Secretary of State has laid a report before both Houses of Parliament indicating—

(i) the results of the monitoring and responses to the consultation referred to in subsection (2A) above;

(ii) the effect, in his opinion and in the opinion of the Director, of the granting of licences under subsections (3) to (5) below and Schedule 5 to this Act in the period before the relevant date; and

(iii) the reasons why, in his opinion, it is in the interests of all persons affected that licences under section 7A(1)(a) of the 1986 Act should be granted.'.

In some respects, the amendment is one of the most pertinent with which we shall deal because it relates to what has become known as the pilot areas—those areas in which the competitive gas market will be tested. The amendment is an attempt to require the director general to monitor the effect of granting a licence and to consult organisations and people who appear to represent the interests of the persons affected by the granting of the licence. The amendment also states that no licence shall be granted until a report has been laid before both Houses of Parliament indicating the result of the monitoring and the responses to the consultation.

The only other example of a deregulated gas market comes from Canada and it must be said that the Canadian experience was not wholly successful. As a consequence, many people are anxious about the exercise, and that is evidenced by the Government's testing the water. We welcome the attempt to choose areas in the south-west of England that are among the most controversial. If the exercise is to have any worth, it is vital not only that the pilot areas are studied properly but that the House has the right to pass judgment on whether the scheme should proceed once the pilot has been completed.

Some of my hon. Friends may take the view that it does not really matter because, by the time the reports are completed, there will be another Government and we will take the decisions about those matters. That is as may be, but we must ensure that proper monitoring techniques are put in place and that the director general is able to take full account of them. As I have said, the experience in other countries has not been wholly satisfactory. The Canadian experience caused great difficulty, but perhaps that will not be replicated here with such ferocity in view of the differing climatic conditions in that country.

Nevertheless, the experience could create anxiety among communities who, even now, are extremely vulnerable. Therefore, we believe it is important to ensure that proper monitoring takes place and that the monitoring is reported correctly. At the end of the day, the House should be able to pass judgment on the findings of the report and decide whether we wish to proceed to grant the rest of the licences across the United Kingdom. That approach has wide support. A number of consumer groups—containing people who are in touch with gas consumers—have heard of and are conscious of the problems that could arise; therefore, it is essential that a proper assessment is made of the monitoring process.

I can do no more than quote paragraph 60 of the Select Committee on Trade and Industry report, which states:

"It would be pointless to have a transitional period unless there is a full assessment of its consequences and wide consultation, including parliamentary scrutiny, before further steps are taken."

That is what the amendment would achieve. We want that in relation to the designated pilot areas. That is why the House should have the right to stop and take stock before it takes this big step for the whole British energy market. For those reasons, we are happy to table amendment No. 49.

9.45 pm

**Mr. Harvey:** I support the amendment. I moved one along similar lines in Committee. The amendment is a welcome, if overdue, innovation in Government practice that the Government have chosen to run a pilot scheme.

[Mr. Harvey]

If they had done so in relation to many other areas of legislation, it would have saved them and the public a great deal of pain.

It would serve the Government's purpose far more comprehensively if, having taken the decision to run a pilot scheme, their assessment criteria went far wider than simply technical aspects, which seem to be the scope of their intention to date. The amendment's proposal of giving both Houses a chance to scrutinise the pilot scheme and to assess it is much to be applauded.

**Mr. Eggar:** The Government have previously made it clear that the phased transition to a nationwide competitive system will provide an opportunity to test the necessary technical and administrative systems for the balancing of gas and the transfer of customers. That is essentially a technical operation. That is why we are starting with an area of 500,000 customers in the south-west and moving up to one of 2 million. We want to find out whether additional problems exist as we expand and go nationwide.

The purpose of the pilot scheme and then of the expanded pilot is to allow British Gas TransCo and competing gas suppliers to iron out any problems with their systems while they are still operating on a relatively small scale. That relates particularly to computer and other such systems.

We must be clear, however, that the pilot is not an attempt to test the principle of whether competition will go ahead. That decision has already been made, on Second Reading. An approach that left the question of principle in doubt would cast a shadow of uncertainty over the industry, both onshore and in the North sea. That would be in no one's interests because it might mean that suppliers would not make the investment needed for competition to be a success. The scheme must be planned with a degree of certainty.

In particular, such an approach would make the necessary adjustment of North sea supply positions and contracts impossibly unpredictable. It would be wrong to try to reopen the principle of competition through what I would call the back door, as it would bring in considerable uncertainty, which is the last thing that we need in terms of planning large investments.

Of course, the director general will clearly wish to monitor the progress of competition and expect to seek feedback from consumers and suppliers of their experience of competition during the transitional phase. That was one of the criteria that we asked the areas to comment on when they applied to be pilots. If that monitoring showed that licence conditions were not having the desired effect, the director general could make proposals to change them. The on-going monitoring process will enable Ministers and the director general to report appropriately to the House and to the other place about progress. It is certainly my intention to do just that.

**Mr. O'Neill:** That answer was wholly unsatisfactory. The Minister said that ultimately it is all down to computers and a few pipes, and that if the report is disastrous only a little fine tuning will be required and everything can be changed. We are discussing the big step of reconstructing the energy market and a potentially dangerous fuel, using a number of companies untested in the UK, and many untested worldwide, in the selling of gas.

We are told that if the House had the right to veto further developments until it was satisfied that necessary changes and improvements had been made, that would create such a shadow of uncertainty that there would be fear of investing and an adjustment to North sea contracts. I imagine that we will be debating amendments Nos. 40 and 41 to schedule 5 tomorrow, relating to the consequences of changes to North sea contracts. The Minister will be playing a different tune then.

If monitoring is not undertaken effectively, reports are not presented in the appropriate way and the House is not given the opportunity to pass judgment, the deregulation of the gas market could founder. If the proposal is to survive and is to command the respect and support of both sides of the House and, more important, command consumer confidence, it is essential that monitoring in pilot areas assumes greater significance than simply suggesting that the tweaking of a computer or changing a piping system will resolve all problems.

This matter is of the utmost importance and I am not prepared to withdraw the amendment. We will press the amendment to a Division because, in essence, the House has the right to be able to say, in a matter which is in many respects a leap in the dark, that if we get it wrong with the pilot projects, the proposal should not proceed. The amendment is of sufficient significance for the House to have the opportunity to vote on it. I urge my hon. Friends to join me in the Lobby to support it.

*Question put,* That the amendment be made:—

*The House divided:* Ayes 229, Noes 269.

**Division No. 147]**                                    **[9.53 pm**

### AYES

| | |
|---|---|
| Abbott, Ms Diane | Carlile, Alexander *(Montgomery)* |
| Ainsworth, Robert *(Cov'try NE)* | Chisholm, Malcolm |
| Allen, Graham | Clapham, Michael |
| Alton, David | Clark, Dr David *(South Shields)* |
| Anderson, Donald *(Swansea E)* | Clarke, Eric *(Midlothian)* |
| Anderson, Ms Janet *(Ros'dale)* | Clarke, Tom *(Monklands W)* |
| Armstrong, Hilary | Clelland, David |
| Austin-Walker, John | Clwyd, Mrs Ann |
| Banks, Tony *(Newham NW)* | Coffey, Ann |
| Barnes, Harry | Cohen, Harry |
| Barron, Kevin | Connarty, Michael |
| Battle, John | Cook, Frank *(Stockton N)* |
| Beckett, Rt Hon Margaret | Cook, Robin *(Livingston)* |
| Bell, Stuart | Corbett, Robin |
| Benn, Rt Hon Tony | Cousins, Jim |
| Bennett, Andrew F | Cummings, John |
| Benton, Joe | Cunliffe, Lawrence |
| Bermingham, Gerald | Cunningham, Jim *(Covy SE)* |
| Berry, Roger | Cunningham, Rt Hon Dr John |
| Betts, Clive | Dafis, Cynog |
| Blunkett, David | Dalyell, Tam |
| Boateng, Paul | Davidson, Ian |
| Bradley, Keith | Davies, Bryan *(Oldham C'tral)* |
| Bray, Dr Jeremy | Davies, Ron *(Caerphilly)* |
| Brown, Gordon *(Dunfermline E)* | Denham, John |
| Brown, N *(N'c'tle upon Tyne E)* | Dewar, Donald |
| Burden, Richard | Dixon, Don |
| Byers, Stephen | Dobson, Frank |
| Caborn, Richard | Donohoe, Brian H |
| Callaghan, Jim | Dowd, Jim |
| Campbell, Mrs Anne *(C'bridge)* | Dunnachie, Jimmy |
| Campbell, Menzies *(Fife NE)* | Dunwoody, Mrs Gwyneth |
| Cann, Jamie | Eagle, Ms Angela |

Eastham, Ken
Enright, Derek
Etherington, Bill
Fatchett, Derek
Faulds, Andrew
Field, Frank (Birkenhead)
Fisher, Mark
Flynn, Paul
Foster, Rt Hon Derek
Foster, Don (Bath)
Fraser, John
Fyfe, Maria
Galbraith, Sam
Galloway, George
Gapes, Mike
Garrett, John
Gerrard, Neil
Gilbert, Rt Hon Dr John
Godman, Dr Norman A
Godsiff, Roger
Golding, Mrs Llin
Gordon, Mildred
Graham, Thomas
Grant, Bernie (Tottenham)
Griffiths, Nigel (Edinburgh S)
Griffiths, Win (Bridgend)
Grocott, Bruce
Gunnell, John
Hain, Peter
Hall, Mike
Harman, Ms Harriet
Harvey, Nick
Heppell, John
Hill, Keith (Streatham)
Hinchliffe, David
Hodge, Margaret
Hoey, Kate
Hogg, Norman (Cumbernauld)
Hood, Jimmy
Hoon, Geoffrey
Howarth, George (Knowsley North)
Howells, Dr. Kim (Pontypridd)
Hoyle, Doug
Hughes, Kevin (Doncaster N)
Hughes, Robert (Aberdeen N)
Hughes, Roy (Newport E)
Hutton, John
Illsley, Eric
Ingram, Adam
Jackson, Glenda (H'stead)
Jackson, Helen (Shef'ld, H)
Jamieson, David
Janner, Greville
Jones, Barry (Alyn and D'side)
Jones, Lynne (B'ham S O)
Jones, Martyn (Clwyd, SW)
Jowell, Tessa
Kaufman, Rt Hon Gerald
Kennedy, Charles (Ross,C&S)
Kennedy, Jane (Lpool Brdgn)
Khabra, Piara S
Kilfoyle, Peter
Lestor, Joan (Eccles)
Lewis, Terry
Litherland, Robert
Livingstone, Ken
Lloyd, Tony (Stretford)
Lynne, Ms Liz
McAvoy, Thomas
McCartney, Ian
McCrea, The Reverend William
Macdonald, Calum
McFall, John
Mackinlay, Andrew
McLeish, Henry
McMaster, Gordon

McNamara, Kevin
MacShane, Denis
Madden, Max
Mahon, Alice
Mandelson, Peter
Marek, Dr John
Martlew, Eric
Meacher, Michael
Meale, Alan
Michael, Alun
Michie, Bill (Sheffield Heeley)
Milburn, Alan
Miller, Andrew
Mitchell, Austin (Gt Grimsby)
Moonie, Dr Lewis
Morgan, Rhodri
Morley, Elliot
Morris, Rt Hon Alfred
Morris, Estelle (B'ham Yardley)
Mowlam, Marjorie
Mudie, George
Mullin, Chris
Murphy, Paul
Oakes, Rt Hon Gordon
O'Brien, Mike (N W'kshire)
O'Brien, William (Normanton)
O'Hara, Edward
Olner, Bill
O'Neill, Martin
Orme, Rt Hon Stanley
Paisley, The Reverend Ian
Patchett, Terry
Pearson, Ian
Pendry, Tom
Pike, Peter L
Pope, Greg
Powell, Ray (Ogmore)
Prentice, Bridget (Lew'm E)
Prentice, Gordon (Pendle)
Primarolo, Dawn
Purchase, Ken
Quin, Ms Joyce
Radice, Giles
Randall, Stuart
Raynsford, Nick
Reid, Dr John
Rendel, David
Robertson, George (Hamilton)
Robinson, Geoffrey (Co'try NW)
Robinson, Peter (Belfast E)
Rooker, Jeff
Rooney, Terry
Ross, Ernie (Dundee W)
Rowlands, Ted
Ruddock, Joan
Sedgemore, Brian
Sheerman, Barry
Sheldon, Rt Hon Robert
Shore, Rt Hon Peter
Short, Clare
Simpson, Alan
Skinner, Dennis
Smith, Chris (Isl'ton S & F'sbury)
Smith, Llew (Blaenau Gwent)
Snape, Peter
Soley, Clive
Spearing, Nigel
Squire, Rachel (Dunfermline W)
Steinberg, Gerry
Stevenson, George
Sutcliffe, Gerry
Taylor, Mrs Ann (Dewsbury)
Taylor, Matthew (Truro)
Timms, Stephen
Tipping, Paddy
Touhig, Don

Vaz, Keith
Walker, Rt Hon Sir Harold
Watson, Mike
Wigley, Dafydd
Williams, Rt Hon Alan (Sw'n W)
Williams, Alan W (Carmarthen)
Winnick, David
Wise, Audrey

Worthington, Tony
Wray, Jimmy
Wright, Dr Tony
Young, David (Bolton SE)

**Tellers for the Ayes:**
   Mr. Dennis Turner and
   Mr. Jon Owen Jones.

## NOES

Ainsworth, Peter (East Surrey)
Aitken, Rt Hon Jonathan
Alison, Rt Hon Michael (Selby)
Allason, Rupert (Torbay)
Amess, David
Arbuthnot, James
Arnold, Jacques (Gravesham)
Arnold, Sir Thomas (Hazel Grv)
Ashby, David
Atkins, Robert
Atkinson, David (Bour'mouth E)
Atkinson, Peter (Hexham)
Baker, Rt Hon Kenneth (Mole V)
Baker, Nicholas (North Dorset)
Baldry, Tony
Banks, Matthew (Southport)
Banks, Robert (Harrogate)
Bates, Michael
Batiste, Spencer
Bellingham, Henry
Bendall, Vivian
Beresford, Sir Paul
Biffen, Rt Hon John
Booth, Hartley
Boswell, Tim
Bottomley, Peter (Eltham)
Bottomley, Rt Hon Virginia
Bowis, John
Boyson, Rt Hon Sir Rhodes
Brandreth, Gyles
Brazier, Julian
Bright, Sir Graham
Brooke, Rt Hon Peter
Brown, M (Brigg & Cl'thorpes)
Browning, Mrs Angela
Bruce, Ian (Dorset)
Budgen, Nicholas
Burns, Simon
Burt, Alistair
Butcher, John
Butler, Peter
Butterfill, John
Carlisle, Sir Kenneth (Lincoln)
Carrington, Matthew
Carttiss, Michael
Cash, William
Channon, Rt Hon Paul
Clappison, James
Clark, Dr Michael (Rochford)
Clifton-Brown, Geoffrey
Coe, Sebastian
Conway, Derek
Coombs, Simon (Swindon)
Cope, Rt Hon Sir John
Cormack, Sir Patrick
Couchman, James
Cran, James
Currie, Mrs Edwina (S D'by'ire)
Curry, David (Skipton & Ripon)
Day, Stephen
Deva, Nirj Joseph
Dorrell, Rt Hon Stephen
Douglas-Hamilton, Lord James
Dover, Den
Duncan, Alan
Duncan-Smith, Iain

Dunn, Bob
Durant, Sir Anthony
Dykes, Hugh
Eggar, Rt Hon Tim
Emery, Rt Hon Sir Peter
Evans, David (Welwyn Hatfield)
Evans, Jonathan (Brecon)
Evans, Nigel (Ribble Valley)
Evans, Roger (Monmouth)
Evennett, David
Faber, David
Fabricant, Michael
Fenner, Dame Peggy
Field, Barry (Isle of Wight)
Fishburn, Dudley
Forman, Nigel
Forsyth, Rt Hon Michael (Stirling)
Forth, Eric
Fowler, Rt Hon Sir Norman
Fox, Sir Marcus (Shipley)
Freeman, Rt Hon Roger
French, Douglas
Gale, Roger
Gardiner, Sir George
Garel-Jones, Rt Hon Tristan
Garnier, Edward
Gill, Christopher
Gillan, Cheryl
Goodlad, Rt Hon Alastair
Gorman, Mrs Teresa
Gorst, Sir John
Grant, Sir A (SW Cambs)
Greenway, Harry (Ealing N)
Greenway, John (Ryedale)
Griffiths, Peter (Portsmouth, N)
Grylls, Sir Michael
Gummer, Rt Hon John Selwyn
Hague, William
Hamilton, Neil (Tatton)
Hampson, Dr Keith
Hannam, Sir John
Hargreaves, Andrew
Harris, David
Haselhurst, Alan
Hawkins, Nick
Hayes, Jerry
Heald, Oliver
Heath, Rt Hon Sir Edward
Heathcoat-Amory, David
Hendry, Charles
Hicks, Robert
Hill, James (Southampton Test)
Hogg, Rt Hon Douglas (G'tham)
Horam, John
Hordern, Rt Hon Sir Peter
Howard, Rt Hon Michael
Howarth, Alan (Strat'rd-on-A)
Howell, Rt Hon David (G'dford)
Howell, Sir Ralph (N Norfolk)
Hughes, Robert G (Harrow W)
Hunt, Sir John (Ravensbourne)
Hunter, Andrew
Hurd, Rt Hon Douglas
Jack, Michael
Jackson, Robert (Wantage)
Jenkin, Bernard

Jessel, Toby
Johnson Smith, Sir Geoffrey
Jones, Gwilym *(Cardiff N)*
Jones, Robert B *(W Hertfdshr)*
Jopling, Rt Hon Michael
Kellett-Bowman, Dame Elaine
Kirkhope, Timothy
Knapman, Roger
Knight, Mrs Angela *(Erewash)*
Knight, Greg *(Derby N)*
Kynoch, George *(Kincardine)*
Lait, Mrs Jacqui
Lamont, Rt Hon Norman
Lang, Rt Hon Ian
Lawrence, Sir Ivan
Legg, Barry
Leigh, Edward
Lennox-Boyd, Sir Mark
Lester, Jim *(Broxtowe)*
Lidington, David
Lightbown, David
Lilley, Rt Hon Peter
Lloyd, Rt Hon Sir Peter *(Fareham)*
Lord, Michael
Lyell, Rt Hon Sir Nicholas
MacGregor, Rt Hon John
MacKay, Andrew
Maclean, David
McLoughlin, Patrick
McNair-Wilson, Sir Patrick
Madel, Sir David
Maitland, Lady Olga
Major, Rt Hon John
Malone, Gerald
Mans, Keith
Marlow, Tony
Marshall, Sir Michael *(Arundel)*
Martin, David *(Portsmouth S)*
Mates, Michael
Mawhinney, Rt Hon Dr Brian
Mellor, Rt Hon David
Merchant, Piers
Mills, Iain
Mitchell, Andrew *(Gedling)*
Mitchell, Sir David *(NW Hants)*
Moate, Sir Roger
Monro, Sir Hector
Montgomery, Sir Fergus
Moss, Malcolm
Needham, Rt Hon Richard
Nelson, Anthony
Newton, Rt Hon Tony
Nicholls, Patrick
Nicholson, David *(Taunton)*
Nicholson, Emma *(Devon West)*
Norris, Steve
Onslow, Rt Hon Sir Cranley
Ottaway, Richard
Patnick, Sir Irvine
Pattie, Rt Hon Sir Geoffrey
Pawsey, James
Peacock, Mrs Elizabeth
Pickles, Eric
Porter, Barry *(Wirral S)*
Porter, David *(Waveney)*
Portillo, Rt Hon Michael
Powell, William *(Corby)*
Redwood, Rt Hon John
Renton, Rt Hon Tim
Robathan, Andrew

Robinson, Mark *(Somerton)*
Roe, Mrs Marion *(Broxbourne)*
Rowe, Andrew *(Mid Kent)*
Rumbold, Rt Hon Dame Angela
Ryder, Rt Hon Richard
Sackville, Tom
Sainsbury, Rt Hon Sir Timothy
Scott, Rt Hon Sir Nicholas
Shaw, David *(Dover)*
Shephard, Rt Hon Gillian
Shepherd, Colin *(Hereford)*
Shepherd, Richard *(Aldridge)*
Shersby, Michael
Sims, Roger
Skeet, Sir Trevor
Smith, Tim *(Beaconsfield)*
Soames, Nicholas
Speed, Sir Keith
Spencer, Sir Derek
Spicer, Michael *(S Worcs)*
Spink, Dr Robert
Spring, Richard
Sproat, Iain
Squire, Robin *(Hornchurch)*
Stanley, Rt Hon Sir John
Steen, Anthony
Stephen, Michael
Stern, Michael
Stewart, Allan
Streeter, Gary
Sumberg, David
Sykes, John
Tapsell, Sir Peter
Taylor, Ian *(Esher)*
Taylor, John M *(Solihull)*
Taylor, Sir Teddy *(Southend, E)*
Temple-Morris, Peter
Thomason, Roy
Thompson, Sir Donald *(C'er V)*
Thompson, Patrick *(Norwich N)*
Thornton, Sir Malcolm
Thurnham, Peter
Townend, John *(Bridlington)*
Townsend, Cyril D *(Bexl'yh'th)*
Tracey, Richard
Trend, Michael
Twinn, Dr Ian
Vaughan, Sir Gerard
Viggers, Peter
Waldegrave, Rt Hon William
Walden, George
Walker, Bill
Waller, Gary
Ward, John
Wardle, Charles *(Bexhill)*
Waterson, Nigel
Watts, John
Wells, Bowen
Whitney, Ray
Whittingdale, John
Widdecombe, Ann
Willetts, David
Winterton, Nicholas *(Macc'fld)*
Wolfson, Mark
Wood, Timothy
Yeo, Tim
Young, Rt Hon Sir George

**Tellers for the Noes:**
    **Mr. Sydney Chapman and**
    **Dr. Liam Fox.**

*Question accordingly negatived.*

Further consideration adjourned.—[*Mr. Conway.*]

Bill, *as amended (in the Standing Committee), to be further considered tomorrow.*

**Mr. Gerald Bermingham** (St. Helens, South): On a point of order, Mr. Deputy Speaker. Some days ago, I tabled a series of questions to the Home Secretary about a contract issued in respect of a computer for the probation service. Those questions were duly accepted, and are listed as Nos. 186, 198, 209 and 231 on the Order Paper today.

It is now after 10 o'clock and, in accordance with the normal conventions, those questions which were due for answer today should have been notified to me either by way of a written answer or by being tabled for the press. Neither has happened. It is clear that the answers to those questions will be in *Hansard* tomorrow, and it is also clear that the Home Office—officials of which I have been trying to contact all night—has deliberately avoided answering the questions on the named day. The reason it has done so is undoubtedly suspicious. We are talking here about a £20 million computer contract which may well be—

**Mr. Deputy Speaker (Mr. Geoffrey Lofthouse):** Order. I think that I can help the hon. Gentleman. He must take the matter up with the Minister concerned, as it is not a matter for the Chair at this stage.

**Mr. Bermingham:** Further to that point of order, Mr. Deputy Speaker.

**Mr. Deputy Speaker:** Order. I have ruled on the hon. Gentleman's point of order.

**Mr. Bermingham** *rose*—

**Mr. Deputy Speaker:** Order. I have ruled on it, and there can be no further points of order on that matter.

**Mr. Bermingham:** On a point of order, Mr. Deputy Speaker.

**Mr. Deputy Speaker:** Is it the same point of order?

**Mr. Bermingham:** No. Several times in the past, the Chair has ruled that it is the convention that Members—

**Mr. Deputy Speaker:** Order. The Chair has just ruled, and there can be no further points of order on that subject.

# Legal Services

10.8 pm

**The Parliamentary Secretary, Lord Chancellor's Department (Mr. John M. Taylor):** I beg to move,

That the draft Conditional Fee Agreements Order 1995, which was laid before this House on 20th April, be approved.

**Mr. Deputy Speaker (Mr. Geoffrey Lofthouse):** I understand that with this it will be convenient to discuss the following motion:

That the draft Conditional Fee Agreements Regulations 1995, which were laid before this House on 20th April, be approved.

**Mr. Taylor:** The order and regulations will bring into force the conditional fee provisions of section 58 of the Courts and Legal Services Act 1990. The scheme will greatly widen access to justice by enabling lawyers to act on a "no win, no fee" basis. To reflect the risk that that entails, lawyers will be able to charge an uplift on their normal fees if the litigation is successful. The Courts and Legal Services Act provides that the Lord Chancellor, after consultation with the designated judges and the profession, should prescribe the types of proceedings in which conditional fee agreements would be allowable, the maximum percentage uplift that would be permitted and any other requirements that he considers necessary. Those matters are set out in the draft order and regulations.

**Mr. Alex Carlile** (Montgomery): The Lord Chancellor, with his great expertise in Scottish law, will no doubt have considered the success of similar arrangements that have been available in Scotland for some time. What has been the uptake of those arrangements in Scotland, and how successful have they been?

**Mr. Taylor:** I will come back to that matter, but I can say that an uplift of 100 per cent. is exactly what has been allowed since 1992 under the Scottish speculative fee scheme. *[Interruption.]* I will answer at the end of the debate.

Personal injury litigation would seem particularly well suited to conditional fee agreements because although the uplift or "success fee", as it is often called, is not directly related to the amount of damages recovered, the fact that there will be a monetary award in successful cases will give the litigant the means to pay his lawyer's fees.

In the light of representations made during the consultation exercise to which I have referred, the Lord Chancellor decided to include insolvency proceedings and cases before the European Commission of Human Rights and the European Court of Human Rights. The Lord Chancellor has set the maximum uplift at 100 per cent. That will encourage lawyers to accept cases with a 50:50 chance of success which, if the uplift were lower, they might not be inclined to take. The whole purpose of the new arrangement is to extend access to justice.

I consider that the proposals will prove a valuable addition to the judicial system in this country, and I commend them to the House.

10.10 pm

**Mr. Paul Boateng** (Brent, South): The Minister's failure to respond to the query of my—he is not an hon. Friend yet—the ˙hon. and learned Member for Montgomery (Mr. Carlile) speaks volumes. Was his reticence due to a lack of information on his part? Will it soon be remedied by a flurry of notes and interest from the silent ones, or was it unlikely and, in my respectful submission, unhelpful reticence on the point? Perhaps the response will come any minute now, so I shall of course give way to the hon. Gentleman.

Perhaps the Minister's reticence is due to the fact that in Scotland the self-same regulations—or at least regulations of a sort upon which the measures are based—have not produced any appreciable benefit to the consumer of legal services. It is by those criteria that the Opposition judge the measures. What will be the benefit not to the lawyer but to the consumer of legal services? On that issue, the jury is out.

**Mr. Taylor:** Actually, it is not. I have a letter dated 11 May from Meriel Thorne, the parliamentary officer of the Consumers Association. She states:

"As we made clear in our response to the various consultations from the Lord Chancellor's Department, we warmly support this provision. We support the new arrangements for the improved choice and access to justice they will provide for the large number of people currently prevented from enforcing their legal rights. We welcome"—

this is the Consumers Association—

"the means of support they will offer for those who would otherwise be deterred from pursuing their legal rights by the fear of legal costs."

**The Treasurer of Her Majesty's Household (Mr. Greg Knight):** Withdraw.

**Mr. Boateng:** I hear a cry of "Withdraw" from the usually silent one, but I have no intention of doing so. I repeat, the jury remains out, and the Minister's attempt to rely on a specious majority verdict with the numbers made up by the National Consumer Council is not going to work.

**Sir Ivan Lawrence** (Burton) *rose*—

**Mr. Boateng:** I shall give way in a moment, but I fancy that the hon. and learned Gentleman will be making his own contribution in due course.

Why is it that, despite his intervention, the Minister has failed to answer the question asked by the hon. and learned Member for Montgomery?

**Sir Ivan Lawrence:** What is the hon. Gentleman doing talking about juries? The order will not apply to jury trials.

**Mr. Boateng:** That contribution speaks for itself. Even at this late stage of the evening, one would hope for better from the hon. and learned Gentleman. Still, one lives in hope.

It is not good enough for the Minister to pray in aid the National Consumer Council. He is not alone in having letters from the council—we can all produce and refer to them. The regulations fail to deal with the council's concerns about the particular arrangements for the conditional fees proposed by the Minister and the issue of the 100 per cent. uplift.

The council is not alone in expressing concern about the extent of that uplift. It commends to the Minister that the Law Society should encourage solicitors to put a voluntary cap of 25 per cent. of the total damages as the amount that they take in success fees, even if it is less

[*Mr. Boateng*]

than the agreed success fee. Is that something which the Minister will join the National Consumer Council and the Opposition—

**Mr. John M. Taylor:** At least for the correction of *Hansard,* I repeat that I am reading a letter of unqualified support not from the National Consumer Council, to which the hon. Gentleman refers, but from the Consumers Association. The record should be clear on that.

**Mr. Boateng:** I am grateful to the Minister for that because it did surprise me that he should suggest that the consumers spoke with one voice on this issue. He admits by that intervention that the National Consumer Council's doubts about the measures remain, and they remain unanswered by the Minister.

Is the Minister prepared to join the National Consumer Council in calling on the Law Society to encourage solicitors in every way to impose a voluntary cap? Does he think that that is desirable? The Minister remains silent, so we must conclude that he is not prepared to put the authority of his office and that of the Lord Chancellor behind that modest proposal as a way of safeguarding the consumer.

**Mr. Edward Garnier** (Harborough) *rose—*

**Mr. Spencer Batiste** (Elmet) *rose—*

**Mr. Boateng:** I am glad to see such a flurry of interest from the Conservatives. It is welcome on a matter of such importance. We all look forward to the speeches that they will no doubt make on the issue.

Will the Minister deal with the following matter on behalf of consumers? In 1994, the National Consumer Council's research into client care found communication about costs—even in ordinary arrangements—to be a problem. About one third of privately paying clients surveyed did not receive adequate information about likely costs. Given the greater potential for misunderstanding between client and solicitor over the highly complicated terms of agreement and the variety of possible outcomes envisaged in these regulations, what steps will the Minister undertake to take, here and now, to ensure that the potential for misunderstandings between solicitors and clients is reduced in that regard, as without that Conservative Members and many others will continue to fear the impact of the arrangements on consumers and on their welfare?

**Mr. Batiste:** I am a little confused by what the hon. Gentleman said. It appeared to be self-contradictory. From his early comments on the Scottish experience, I thought that he was saying that conditional fees should be encouraged, but that they had been relatively unsuccessful in capturing the public imagination in Scotland. Yet, by his subsequent proposal that only a 25 per cent. uplift should be allowed, is he not in effect saying that it is unlikely to be successful anywhere, as few people will be prepared to take the risk at those levels?

**Mr. Boateng:** There is no contradiction. Our concern— it must be one that is shared by all people of good will—is that every effort should be made to encourage and support arrangements that improve and enhance the consumer's access to justice. We take that as read. These proposals

have been much vaunted by the right hon. Lord Chancellor and, indeed, by the Minister as an important response to the problem of access to justice.

**Mr. Garnier:** Will the hon. Gentleman give way?

**Mr. Boateng:** Not at the moment.

The Opposition are pointing out that, in the light of the Scottish experience, it would be wrong for us to see these arrangements as some sort of panacea for the problems that exist in promoting access to justice. Now that the regulations have been laid before the House, our concern is to ensure that every encouragement is given to ensure that they work in the interests of the consumer. Hence the concern about the cap, and a recognition of the role of a voluntary cap in some cases, but also, and importantly, the concern about ensuring that consumers of legal services who enter into such agreements with their solicitors are fully aware of all the implications for their relationship with their solicitor. We regard that as important.

**Mr. Garnier:** Will the hon. Gentleman give way?

**Mr. Boateng:** No, not at the moment.

We are anxious to receive assurances from the Minister on a further matter—the potential, which the National Consumer Council has pointed out, for solicitors to exaggerate the difficulties of winning to justify a high success fee, even if it is an open and shut case. Where they can, clients must treat conditional fees like any other business transaction and must be in a position to shop around to get the best deal. That is why we urge the Government to ensure that safeguards are in place for the consumer. As the arrangements are put in place for the first time, we also want the Government to keep them under constant review to ensure that consumers get the best possible deal and to avoid some of the potential dangers that have been identified.

It is important that the Government respond to the concerns about the proposals expressed in the other place and elsewhere by the judiciary. The criticisms of Lord Justice Steyn, Lord Ackner and Lord Simon of Glaisedale in particular require the Government's consideration. I would welcome a sign from the Minister that Lord Steyn's urgings that officials in his Department rethink the proposals have had some effect. It would be wrong of the Minister to ignore the concerns expressed by Lord Steyn, not least the warning that, under the present arrangements, litigants might find all their damages swallowed up in increased fees. Lord Steyn's committee said that the risk applies even if those are increased by only 50 per cent. The risk is that much greater if they are increased by 100 per cent.

**Mr. Garnier:** I am diffident about interrupting the hon. Gentleman because I know that for some years he was a solicitor and for some little while has been a barrister, but will he tell the House what is the Labour party's policy on that measure? Does it support it or not?

**Mr. Boateng:** I had hoped that it would be possible to discuss this measure, raising, as we are bound to raise, the concerns on the part of consumers but, at the same time, not ignoring the importance of exploring, by all reasonable means, the opportunity to give consumers greater access to justice and legal services. I hope that that sets the hon. and learned Gentleman's mind at rest.

**Mr. Garnier** *indicated dissent.*

**Mr. Boateng:** I do not know whether the hon. and learned Gentleman is unduly exercised by the fact that he may be required to wait a little longer to see whether we divide the House on this issue. If that is his concern, as I suspect it may be, I have no intention whatever of putting him out of his misery. He can wait just a little longer.

**Mr. Garnier** *rose*—

**Mr. Boateng:** I do not intend to give way to the hon. and learned Gentleman again.

**Mr. Garnier:** The hon. Gentleman is frightened.

**Mr. Boateng:** I think not.

Our purpose in ensuring that we had a full debate on the issue on the Floor of the House tonight was to seek from the Minister the reassurances that I have outlined. We feel the need to do that given the absence of reassurances so far. When the Lord Chancellor and the Minister were advised about the concerns expressed by the higher judiciary about the proposals, far from saying that they had rethought the scheme, they expressed their determination to persist with it, come what may. That is not the attitude for which we would have hoped from the Minister and the Lord Chancellor. We can only hope that the Minister will be able to offer us some of the reassurances that we seek.

We also seek some assurances about the Law Society's proposals for insurance. It has apparently proposed a scheme under which some clients, but not all, can protect themselves against paying the legal costs of their opponents if they lose. Lord Steyn has said that such a scheme is of great importance, but the Law Society has been singularly unforthcoming in producing the detail about its provisions that one would want. It is by no means clear whether everyone litigating under the no-win, no-fee arrangements would be able to obtain cover.

Has the Minister's Department met representatives of the Law Society to discuss the scheme? What advice has the Law Society been given about the scheme? Will it cover all those who seek to avail themselves of its benefits? Our decision on whether to divide the House on the proposals will depend upon the Minister's responses to those questions. Hope springs eternal—

**Mr. Alex Carlile:** They have all gone home.

**Mr. Boateng:** I am surprised at the hon. and learned Gentleman, whom I sought to support in his earlier humble contribution. It just shows that it would be premature to regard him as a friend. I am surprised that he should make such an unkind remark from a sedentary position, suggesting that all my hon. Friends have gone home. That is far from the truth. Not all of them have—

**Mr. Carlile:** Just two others are here.

**Mr. Boateng:** My hon. Friend the Member for Great Grimsby (Mr. Mitchell) has done distinguished service on the matter. If pushed, I can assure the Minister and

Conservative Members that my hon. Friends will come out of the woodwork to do their duty by the consumers of legal services.

**Sir Ivan Lawrence:** What normally comes out of the woodwork is sap and creepy-crawlies.

**Mr. Boateng:** We look forward to yet more comments from the hon. and learned Gentleman. I hope that we will be treated to speech from him, because, given his current position, it would be a shame if he did not share his wisdom with a wider audience.

We will determine whether to divide the House once we have heard the Minister's response to our queries.

10.32 pm

**Mr. Spencer Batiste** (Elmet): I shall speak briefly, in deference to colleagues and the hour of the night.

Given the potential importance of the subject, it is important that certain things are placed on the record. I speak as a solicitor. Although I have not practised in litigation for many years, I have watched closely developments in the law.

The justice system is currently prone to serious problems, particularly in relation to civil litigation. They relate basically to access to justice and the cost of it. The proposals seek to address those two elements.

The problem that faces most people is that, if they do not qualify for legal aid, they can barely afford litigation. A large proportion of the population is therefore precluded from civil litigation.

There is an even worse injustice. An individual who is sued by a person who has legal aid is in an unenviable position even if he wins. It is often the case that the person being sued—the defendant—is only slightly wealthier than the person who sues him. Those problems must be solved if we are to have a modern justice system.

In the United States, there have been many pitfalls and abuses that do nothing to enhance the United States justice system, but bring it substantially into disrepute. The Government must be congratulated on striking a balance, in the legislation before us, which avoids the pitfalls of the United States and tries to divine the best of the lessons that must be learnt from the American experience while adapting them to the United Kingdom's specific institutions.

It seems to me that many practitioners in the law will be prepared to take on conditional fee litigation in the types of cases where the odds of success are roughly 50:50. It seems to me that they should not take up cases where the odds are significantly less than that, because that tends to lead to the vexatious litigation that takes place extensively in the United States.

However, there are an awful lot of people who, if they are told by their lawyers that they have a 50:50 chance of winning, simply cannot afford to take the risk of litigating. The regulations that we are discussing tackle that problem. In giving an uplift to fees rather than giving a share of damages, one avoids the excesses of the United States, where lawyers have a direct stake in the amount of damages that will be won.

The controls and caps that have been introduced, which will be introduced in detailed regulations by the Law Society and, potentially, by the Government, will avoid the abuses that have been described by the hon. Member for Brent, South (Mr. Boateng).

[*Mr. Spencer Batiste*]

However, it is important that that type of litigation is widely used and available for people who at the moment feel that they have no recourse to justice. If the terms and conditions of the order are made more restrictive than they are now, they will not be used. I believe that the balance is right, and that the legislation should be passed as it is. Obviously, it should be kept under close surveillance. If further adjustments are necessary in future, so be it, but it is an excellent first attempt at what should be an important step in modernising justice in Britain.

10.36 pm

**Mr. Alex Carlile** (Montgomery): I should start by declaring an interest, as a practising barrister who does a certain amount of personal injury litigation in the course of my practice.

There is no reason why new systems should not be introduced which increase the availability of justice and access to justice, as the hon. Member for Elmet (Mr. Batiste) said. If that system will work on that basis, it should be welcomed. The question is, will it work and what will it replace, if anything?

As to whether it will work, the Parliamentary Secretary was kind enough to give way to me during his opening speech, but his response was an extraordinarily skittish one for a Minister speaking from the Dispatch Box. The usual purpose of asking questions of Ministers in the early stages of a debate is so that the debate can be informed. The Parliamentary Secretary deliberately chose not to inform the debate.

**Mr. John M. Taylor** *rose*—

**Mr. Carlile:** I will give way in a moment.

The Minister deliberately chose not to inform the debate during his opening speech in such a way that his answer could be considered during other speeches in the debate. He told us that he would inform the debate of the answer to my question when he came to reply to the debate—if that happens.

I will give way to the Minister in a moment, but I would ask him to tell us what the uptake has been in Scotland. I suggest to him that the uptake in Scotland has been disappointing. Conditional fee arrangements have hardly been used in civil litigation in Scotland. It is incumbent on the Minister to tell the House what the Lord Chancellor's Department has done to try to ensure that the measures are not simply a paper tiger, as they are in Scotland, but bring more people into the courts with their claims.

Now I will give way to the Minister, if he will answer the question.

**Mr. Taylor:** I invited the hon. and learned Gentleman to give way to me a moment ago because I did not want to leave him with the impression that I had sidestepped his question, at the time when he posed it, out of any disrespect for the House or any unwillingness to answer his question. From time to time, there is a place in the House for candour. I did not answer the question at the time because I did not know the answer. I have no statistics in front of me, but I do not think that the hon. and learned Gentleman put his question in a statistical form and I will not reply in a statistical idiom.

I understand, upon advice, that the Scottish experience has been that the take-up of what I think is called the speculative fee system in Scotland has been fairly limited. It has not been overwhelming or encouraging—those involved have not been run over by the weight of the business. But I also say in precisely the same spirit—again, not statistically, but in good faith to the hon. and learned Gentleman—that there is quite a body of anecdotal evidence that there is a willingness in England and Wales to take up the scheme with some enthusiasm. As the hon. Member for Brent, South (Mr. Boateng) asked, am I—the Minister—and the Lord Chancellor's Department prepared to keep matters under review? We certainly are—but we have got to give the scheme a try.

**Mr. Carlile:** I am grateful to the Parliamentary Secretary for his candour. But it seems extraordinary that the Government have brought forward an order and regulations for conditional fee agreements without inquiring fully into the way in which the system works in Scotland and making adjustments to the English and Welsh situation to take into account Scottish experience.

The position is even more dramatic than the Parliamentary Secretary's anecdotal answer suggested. In Scotland, speculative fee agreements are hardly used at all. One could probably count up the number of such agreements that there have been since they were introduced on the fingers of two people's hands.

**Mr. Garnier:** Will the hon. and learned Gentleman give way?

**Mr. Carlile:** I shall give way to the hon. and learned Gentleman in a moment. It is a pleasure to see him present. He is to be congratulated on having recently been admitted to silk. The hon. and learned Gentleman is an expert—indeed, a foremost expert, as has recently been confirmed—in the law of defamation and specialises in that sphere of practice.

One matter which concerns many is that the conditional fee arrangements do not apply to defamation actions of any sort. Legal aid is not available for defamation cases. Many people of modest means find it impossible to bring proceedings, particularly against big guns such as newspapers, when they have been seriously defamed, because legal aid is not available and they cannot find a generous backer for their claim. Does the hon. and learned Gentleman agree that that is an aspect of the regulations which needs to be reconsidered?

**Mr. Garnier:** I am grateful to the hon. and learned Gentleman for his kind words, but the question that I want to ask him does not relate to defamation. He has clearly studied the Scottish position with some care. Can he tell the House, from his studies, what is the position where a lawyer acting for a contingency fee plaintiff is unsuccessful? What happens to the successful defendant? From whom does he recover his costs? Does he recover his costs from the effectively maintained plaintiff, from the maintaining lawyer or not at all?

**Mr. Carlile:** My understanding of the situation in Scotland is that he recovers his costs, and that where he recovers them from depends on the nature of the agreement entered into.

I must reflect a little disappointment that the hon. and learned Gentleman did not answer the question about defamation with which I tempted him.

The agreements referred to in the Conditional Fee Agreements Regulations 1995 are both complex and far from what I think was originally in mind when the Lord Chancellor introduced the proposals which eventually formed the Courts and Legal Services Act 1990. The agreements that will be permitted will not be conditional on the case being successful, either by judgment or by settlement out of court. The agreements include a situation in which the litigant will have to pay certain fees to his or her lawyer in any event. That is clear from regulation 3(c), which provides for payment

"upon partial failure of the specified circumstances . . . irrespective of the specified circumstances . . . and upon termination of the agreement for any reason."

That will put rather unequal power in the hands of lawyers entering into conditional fee agreements because litigants who can find no assistance elsewhere might well find their lawyers placing agreements in front of them that will require payment of the lawyers' costs in part in any event. One does not have equal bargaining power.

I do not know what consultations the Lord Chancellor's Department has had with the Law Society and the General Council of the Bar on these matters, but it is extremely important that the enthusiasm of the Consumers Association should be tempered by such considerations. It is vital that such agreements should be entered into at arm's length, under strict controls and in fair circumstances.

Before I give way to the Minister, I will ask him another question. Can he confirm that, if a plaintiff enters into a conditional fee agreement—for example, in respect of a medical negligence action which may involve enormously expensive expert witnesses, and these days good experts attending court tend to ask for at least £1,000 a day—and that plaintiff wins his case, he will be able to recover all his costs, including the uplift from the other side? If that is the case, and it seems right from the plaintiff's viewpoint that that should be the position, how does the Minister justify to the defendant's side that they may be paying double the costs in such an action? What is the solution to that conundrum?

**Mr. John M. Taylor:** I shall need to reflect on the last point that the hon. and learned Gentleman put to me. On the first point, about the mismatch in bargaining between the lawyer and the client, the hon. and learned Gentleman needs no law lectures from me. His attainment as a lawyer is probably well beyond mine, but he will be familiar with those relationships known as uberrimae fidei, or of the utmost good faith, in which the doctrine of undue influence comes into play. The hon. and learned Gentleman will know from his learned studies that, if a solicitor exploits the relative weakness of his client in those circumstances, the outturn will be determined contra preferentem, or against the person advantaged, or in other words against the solicitor.

**Mr. Carlile:** The hon. Gentleman, from his experience as a high street solicitor—*[Interruption.]* I believe that the address of his office was the high street in Walsall. He will know from his considerable experience and expertise—and it happens to all Members of Parliament—that allegations of undue influence are extremely difficult to prove, although many of us come across them on a regular basis in respect of probate matters which are brought to our constituency surgeries.

The doctrine of uberrimae fidei will not give a great deal of comfort to ordinary litigants. In the fastnesses of Montgomeryshire, people think of nothing but uberrimae fidei as they drink their tea and enjoy the Barra Bridd.

I also suggest to the Minister that there is real concern that proceedings before the civil courts are to be consigned to conditional fee arrangements as civil legal aid is allowed to wither on the vine. Will he give a commitment on the part of the Government that such agreements are not intended to deal with everyday run-of-the-mill cases? Those arrangements are intended to deal with the residue of cases where legal aid may not be available or where the litigant may be just above the legal aid means test limit and is thus deprived of that remedy unless some other mechanism is found.

I turn to proceedings before the European Commission of Human Rights and the European Court of Human Rights. The Minister will know that that is a very specialised and difficult field of practice. It is also a potentially very expensive field of practice because one pays the price for the expertise that one receives. Very few lawyers in this country—I doubt whether there are any in the House—can claim to be expert in those matters, other than possibly the Attorney-General, whose services are not available to the ordinary litigant. I believe that the Attorney-General and the Solicitor-General have appeared before the European Court of Human Rights from time to time.

**Mr. Austin Mitchell** (Great Grimsby): And lost.

**Mr. Carlile:** And lost occasionally, as the hon. Gentleman—who cannot wait to have a go at the lawyers in his usual fashion—says from a sedentary position.

It seems to me that the best and soundest route politically to the European Court of Human Rights is through legal aid rather than a conditional fee arrangement. There is a real risk that conditional fee arrangements will prove a very unsatisfactory way of dealing with such complex matters. Surely our society should be prepared to extend legal aid to those very few cases which make their way to the European Commission and to the even fewer which make their way to the European Court.

In conclusion, I wish to address the types of lawyers—particularly the types of solicitors—who will take on those arrangements. There are some excellent solicitors, some very bad solicitors and a great mass of competent solicitors in the middle. All those who have practised at the Bar over the years will know of the existence of what one might loosely call the "dodgy solicitor".

**Mr. Gary Streeter** (Plymouth, Sutton): Or dodgy barrister.

**Mr. Carlile:** Does the hon. Gentleman wish me to give way or will he withdraw that remark, which I understand was directed at me?

**Mr. Deputy Speaker:** Order. I did not hear the remark as I was speaking to the Clerk at the time. I do not know what the hon. Member for Plymouth, Sutton (Mr. Streeter) is alleged to have said.

**Mr. Carlile:** I will not pursue the matter, Mr. Deputy Speaker.

[*Mr. Carlile*]

There is a real fear that dodgy solicitors, and perhaps occasionally the odd dodgy barrister, may be more prepared than others to take on this type of agreement, and there is thus a risk that lawyers of lesser quality will build practices in this area. I ask the Minister to assure the House that the issue has been or will be discussed with the Law Society as well as the General Council of the Bar.

Despite the criticism which is sometimes very justifiably levelled at lawyers, we are quite proud of the quality of the legal system in this country. The American lawyers who came in droves to advise us about the then Courts and Legal Services Bill which was before Parliament strongly recommended against conditional fee arrangements. Will the Minister give an assurance that the quality issue will be addressed so that real scrutiny can take place and we may ensure that, when the agreements are used, they are used properly?

10.53 pm

**Mr. David Harris** (St. Ives): As a layman, I hesitate to rush in where my honourable and learned colleagues fear to tread. However, I share some of the apprehensions that have been expressed during the debate. My hon. Friend the Member for Elmet (Mr. Batiste) put it well when he said that no hon. Member wishes to rush down the American road in this area. We do not want to see litigation multiply at an alarming rate on the basis that, if a lawyer does not win the case, he or she will not receive a fee. As constituency Members—that is how I approach the issue—we have all come across constituents who believe that they have a right to justice, that they must therefore be supported, usually through legal aid or some other means, and who want to take their case to the ultimate body, which normally means the European Court of Human Rights or the European Court of Justice. They do not know the distinction between the two.

This is my fear about the order. We may end up with litigation which will bog down our courts and buoy up people's expectation that they will win, when they probably will not. We must guard against that danger. As the hon. and learned Member for Montgomery (Mr. Carlile) fairly said however, some people have an absolute right, as we would all agree, to pursue their case, but for one reason or another they cannot do so. That is the dilemma facing the House.

I am minded to vote for the order because the Government have approached it with due caution and have probably struck the right balance in a difficult situation, but I should hate the outcome of the debate to be that the House encourages people to go to a lawyer, saying that perhaps there are dodgy solicitors and barristers—I would not know about these matters—who will take up their case and fight it to the ultimate. As the hon. and learned Gentleman warned, however, there may be a downside and those people may have to pick up part of the bill. We must be careful about that.

I shall vote for the order, but I do so with some trepidation because I do not want us to go down the American road, which has led to increasing litigation, with everyone feeling that they have a right to go to the courts at someone else's expense, although it might be at

their own expense. I do not want that to happen. I shall vote for the Government's proposals, but on the basis that real dangers exist in pursuing the American example.

10.57 pm

**Mr. Austin Mitchell** (Great Grimsby): I speak as a non-lawyer who takes a close interest in these issues. The danger with all legal service matters, particularly here, is that policy and legal services will be formulated exclusively by lawyers, who have a vested interest in maintaining their income. The voice of the consumer—the people—is never heard. That domination by lawyers is damaging.

Admittedly, tonight many lawyers have spent most of their time criticising dodgy lawyers—they should know their own trade. Lawyers always safeguard themselves against each other, but never take account of people's interests, which should be dominant when we approach this important issue.

Tonight, we are expanding the range of available legal services in a way that does not cost much and that will introduce an element of competition to serve the people. In some respects, I am qualified to speak because I have a history in the argument. This debate is like a class reunion of those who attended the debate on the Courts and Legal Services Act 1990. Five years on, the class is as old and as repellent as ever, but it brings together the arguments. The order results from that Act.

When some of us argued for contingency fees on the American pattern, the Lord Chancellor proposed this canny Scottish idea. He said that it would be an alternative to the full flowering of contingency fees and that we should build on the Scottish precedent. I am happy to go down that road. The fact that we first took that road in 1990 but only now are considering the order shows the slowness of change. What the hell has been going on? Why has it taken so long? I can imagine all the grudging discussions and the acquiesence in getting these measures past the judges, but this incredible series of delays shows how difficult it will be to bring the full flowering of legal services to the people.

I argued for contingency fees. When I visited the United States to lecture for the English Speaking Union, I was impressed by the effectiveness of contingency fees in the hands of crusading lawyers. I know that they are much criticised as ambulance chasing but I saw, particularly in the southern states, crusading lawyers who were prepared to push cases at enormous risk and expenditure to themselves, on the basis of contingency fees. Without those fees, the cases would not have been pursued. We need similar endeavour in this country, because that would bring legal services to the people in a way that nothing else can.

We will never return to the days of wide-ranging legal aid services of a few years ago. The Lord Chancellor began brilliantly—and I am still a strong supporter of his—but increasingly he is becoming Treasury-driven. That means meanness towards legal aid. We must accept as a fact of life that legal aid provision will decrease. Legal aid can never work as a full and adequate form of funding as long as it is drained off into the bottomless pit of private practice. As long as we support private practice, it will be expensive to provide legal services to the people. I hope that Labour will spend more on legal aid and will commit itself to wider provision. However, even Labour will never attain the full range of legal services that would obviate the need for some kind of additional service.

Legal aid will never be adequate, so we need measures to defend the causes, interests and concerns of the people. The legal system is pricing itself out of the market. It will never be adequate until we have an employed legal service—a public defender service for criminal matters and an employed legal service at law centres for civil matters. I would like law centres to participate in conditional fee arrangements.

Until we have full provision of legal services, these measures are a beneficial step towards the American system. We have not yet tackled the costs problem. If we are going down the American path, I see no reason for not pursuing the same path in respect of costs. Why should they be allocated against the losing side? A sensible compromise has been reached—to allow a case to go forward without the risk of costs—with which I am happy.

I am happy with the range of uplift, because, since there is a range of cases, a degree of risk and a range of possibilities, it is sensible that fees should approximate to that gradation of risks. I should like all cases to be pursued. I do not see why only those with a 50:50 chance of success should be considered because the boundaries widen all the time. Until we extend those boundaries by taking more risks, we shall never know what cases will be successful or not. Why stop at 50:50? Why not include 60:40 or 70:30 cases? All such cases need pursuing.

I like the word "uplift" in respect of lawyers' fees. The next time that I meet members of the Law Society I shall ask them specially about their uplift. It makes me think of the Church of England, which is a very uplifting institution. The Law Society will clearly become a much more uplifting institution under this new system. It is fair that the uplift is gradated as the regulations provide. The uplift has to be agreed by the client and, indeed, it is subject to an appeal—ultimately, effectively, by the client.

I am worried, however, by the telling point made by the hon. and learned Member for Montgomery (Mr. Carlile). When I consider such matters, my test is, "How will it work in Grimsby?" When people want to pursue a case against a hospital, a medical practice or whatever, they shop around among solicitors. If there is provision for the charging of fees in such cases and if there has to be an agreement, not only on the level of uplift but on what fees are charged, a conspiracy—a ring of lawyers—could develop. Solicitors could say, "Let's charge them this. Let's charge them that. Let's not take any case below a certain level of uplift." That is the danger.

How will the provisions work in a town such as Grimsby? In such a scenario, the less power given to solicitors to increase the uplift and the charges to the client, the better. We must have and encourage full and free access for the people of Grimsby to the legal services they need to defend themselves against powerful major institutions. The more the system becomes one of haggling and quibbling, the greater the potential of a conspiracy against the public and the people of Grimsby.

**Mr. Michael Stephen** (Shoreham): Does the hon. Gentleman accept that he does an injustice to the solicitors of Grimsby? Does he accept that competition between solicitors is very fierce indeed and that, in fact, it is driving charges to the consumer down almost to the point at which some legal practices are becoming non-viable?

**Mr. Mitchell:** There is a conspiracy against people in many respects. There was clearly a conspiracy on fees for conveyancing until it was broken by ending the conveyancing monopoly and introducing fair competition. As long as lawyers have a monopoly, there is danger of a conspiracy. I might be exaggerating, but I do not want to give them any leverage that might enable them to conspire against the people.

In a big city, there is more competition and solicitors might be prepared to stand up and say that they are willing to take a risk, but I do not want the people of Grimsby to have to go to Leeds or Sheffield for legal advice because only there can they find an independent, determined solicitor who will take on the system and exact less demanding terms from them than a local conspiracy of solicitors. Small towns lead to conspiracy. I am afraid that that is true of so many professional services and I do not want to give the legal system any cause to follow suit. The hon. and learned Member for Montgomery was quite right to raise that point.

The system will bring a better legal service to ordinary people than legal aid. Legal aid is, in any case, contracting. It is becoming less adequate and it often tends to be the sort of provision which has fallen off the back of the practice. I am perfectly happy to accept 100 per cent. uplift, if it would mean that cases were pursued which would not otherwise be taken on. That is the important point.

**Mr. Oliver Heald** (Hertfordshire, North): Will the hon. Gentleman give way?

**Mr. Mitchell:** No. I am, believe it or not, grinding to a conclusion.

The hon. and learned Member for Montgomery said that the process was little used in Scotland. Scotland does not have a system that provides for costs like the insurance system in this country. In addition, the system will be used increasingly as the boundaries of legal aid contract. The system will be an attractive alternative and I am happy to support it.

With the right degree of muscle, my hon. Friend the Member for Brent, South (Mr. Boateng) said that we would wait for the Minister's reply. I will not anticipate his reply and I will support the measure whatever the Minister says because it is a step on the way to solving the desperate need to bring more effective legal services to the people of this country.

I do not want the measure to be unduly restrictive, and I am worried about the restrictions that it contains. I regard it not as the end, but as the beginning. It is only a step on the way, but it will allow people to advance cases that would not otherwise be taken up. It is a step on the way to a paid legal service which will reach the parts that conditional fees cannot reach. I still want to move down that track. There is still a need to adopt the full American system of contingency fees where they take a slice of the winnings. Why not do that if it brings legal services to the people?

On the basis that the proposal is an advance and something that can be built on, improved, expanded and developed, we should support it.

[*Mr. Mitchell*]

11.10 pm

**Mr. John M. Taylor:** If there is a Division tonight, it will be interesting to see whether the Labour party fields one Member in each Lobby and, if so, where the Lib-Lab accrual will take place.

On a more serious note, I congratulate my hon. Friend the Member for Elmet (Mr. Batiste), who summed matters up so neatly and eloquently that I shall take *Hansard* tomorrow to read his in-a-nutshell treatment of what the Government are trying to do.

The hon. and learned Member for Montgomery (Mr. Carlile) extended to me the courtesy of endeavouring to deal with some of his questions in interventions during the debate. He also asked me to reassure the House that conditional fees are not intended to supplant legal aid and I am very pleased to do that on behalf of the Government: They are not intended to replace legal aid in any way. They are intended to complement legal aid, to provide an extra choice to the consumer, a greater versatility and a variety of options to people who find it hard, difficult and expensive to go to law.

With regard to the point made by the hon. and learned Member for Montgomery about whether clients would be advised fairly in those circumstances, I draw his attention to the narrow point, which is squarely met however, by regulation 4(2)(a) of the regulations, which states that one of the things that the client must be advised on is whether he or she

"might be entitled to legal aid in respect of the proceedings".

That is, as it were, built into the script.

The hon. and learned Member for Montgomery told us of his experience of American lawyers coming to this country and advising against contingency fees in 1990. He is right. American lawyers advised against contingency fees where the reward to the lawyer is based on the damages. In advancing conditional fees, we are promoting a scheme where the reward to the lawyer is proportionate to the fee agreed with the client or awarded against the other side by the court.

The hon. Member for Brent, South (Mr. Boateng) quite rightly deployed arguments in favour of the protection of the client. While waiting to reply to this debate, I considered whether I should answer his questions by reading a substantial passage from the longer speech that I had thought of using tonight. On reflection, I think that the regulations are far more specific than my text, and I therefore commend to the hon. Gentleman regulations 3 and 4, which set out definitively the protection of a client who is entering into an agreement.

At the risk of saying this twice, I advise the hon. Member for Brent, South and the House of the long-standing doctrine of undue influence, whereby in cases where one party's solicitor is in a greatly advantageous position against the client, the rules of interpretation favour the weaker party, as they should. I have said that we will keep the matters under review.

I was requested to comment on the insurance arrangements. The Lord Chancellor's Department has discussed the insurance scheme with the Law Society, which has made it clear that it is willing to provide details of the scheme to anyone who is interested in it.

My hon. and good Friend the Member for St. Ives (Mr. Harris) usefully made the distinction between the European Court of Human Rights and the European Court of Justice—a distinction that is often overlooked. The different roles, constitutions and cultures of the courts are not widely known.

My hon. Friend also referred to the "American road" down which he feared we were going, and that qualified his welcome for the measure. I understand that, and I thought that he spoke fairly, but the American example is of lawyers' rewards that are geared to damages. We eschew that, and are interested in lawyers' rewards geared to the original base fee agreed, or to the costs awarded in the case by the court.

The hon. Member for Great Grimsby (Mr. Mitchell) is a member of the class of 1990, as I am, and he has a record in these subjects as long as your arm. He possesses creditable form in the issue, and always enlivens these occasions. I am glad that he felt able to support the measures, because in the name of fair play he has been one of the agents of reform. He says that reform has gone too slowly, and that it has taken since 1990 to get to where we are tonight. I understand his taking that view, because he was never content with the pace of progress.

I find myself criticised in some quarters for haste, and in some other quarters for leaden-footedness. I cannot win, which probably means that I will not get a fee. I would like to make secure the order and the regulations tonight.

*Question put and agreed to.*

*Resolved,*

That the draft Conditional Fee Agreements Order 1995, which was laid before this House on 20th April, be approved.

*Resolved,*

That the draft Conditional Fee Agreements Regulations 1995, which were laid before this House on 20th April, be approved.—[*Mr. John M. Taylor*]

# Employment (Waveney)

*Motion made, and Question proposed,* That this House do now adjourn.—*[Dr. Liam Fox.]*

11.12 pm

**Mr. David Porter** (Waveney): I would like to thank Madam Speaker for the opportunity to raise the matter of employment in Waveney, in particular the barriers to employment. I am sorry that the Under-Secretary of State for Employment, my hon. Friend the Member for Cambridgeshire, South-East (Mr. Paice), is unwell and cannot reply to the debate, as he knows something of my constituency in addition to what his officials tell him. I am delighted, however, that my hon. Friend the Minister of State is here to reply, and I am grateful to her.

Clearly, unemployment nationally is falling, but the perception in Waveney is that we are still in dire straits economically. Unemployment in Waveney from March 1994 to March 1995 fell by 3 per cent., but that is not the perception locally. Politics is all about perception, and that is why I want to bring to the attention of the House some aspects of Waveney's particular circumstances. I do not want to be guilty of the same charge that I sometimes level at my local authority of running my area down, but some unique circumstances need attention.

My constituency association recently did a survey in a residential area, and the overriding concern on the doorsteps was local employment. When I visit schools, the overwhelming issue for all youngsters approaching school-leaving age is local employment and the inevitability of having to move away to work. In a constituency where the majority of people are still native born and bred, that is a serious factor in the political equation.

SCEALA, the Standing Conference of East Anglian Local Authorities, found last year that the region is beginning to recover from recession, but the Henley centre for forecasting put Waveney among the worst economic prospects for Britain, along with Liverpool, Gateshead and south Tyneside.

Historically, Waveney developed around the fishing industry at Lowestoft and agriculture in the hinterland. By the 1970s, the whole economy had become dependent on oil and gas offshore, shipbuilding, fishing, food processing and tourism. By 1981, we were the most industrialised district in Suffolk. Since then, there has been a 19 per cent. reduction in the proportion of the work force employed in manufacturing nationally, but a 26 per cent. reduction in Waveney.

We know that no one owes the country a living, so it certainly does not owe Waveney a living. We know that. We know the stark modern facts on industries—that, in general, the time between the sunrise and the sunset of an industry is getting smaller. We know that. We know the reality on national manufacturing figures—7 million jobs in 1979 and 4 million today, but the 4 million make more than the 7 million did, and all because of technology, which we cannot uninvent or even slow down. We know that. But Waveney's dependence then and still on a declining manufacturing base makes prospects seem much bleaker.

The UK national average of manufacturing employees in the work force is 22 per cent.; in Waveney it is 27 per cent. There has been some service and high-tech industrial development, and some firms are doing very well. I should list some of them for the record. They are SLP, Kvaerner Oil and Gas, Birds Eye, Clays of Bungay, Harrod's of Lowestoft, Sanyo, Adnams of Southwold, Bernard Matthews, M and H Plastics, Fibernyle of Beccles, and a host of smaller firms. We know that.

We know that in a vibrant economy, businesses collapse and are taken over, and new ones are born. We know that. Recent contracts won by SLP Engineering and Kvaerner Oil and Gas are very encouraging and welcome, but they cannot solve the problem of the economy being dependent on a small handful of sectors. Help for diversity and training and retraining to diversify is what is needed now.

We also know that we are the most easterly point of the United Kingdom, yet we are only 120 miles from London. In some ways, it might as well be 1,000. I have said that before many times in the House, and the previous time I said it, I was rewarded with a cartoon in the *Lowestoft Journal* portraying me as Indiana Jones trying to get from there to the House.

That is part of the charm of the area—I accept that—but the lack of reasonable roads, either the A12 north to south or the A47 upgraded as a major European route east to west, and the want of the third crossing at Lake Lothing at Lowestoft, all combine to hamper economic growth, compared with other parts of the country. That is the perception of businesses, and of people in the tourist and job-creating sectors of the community whom I talk to and whom I represent in the House.

We have fallen victim to a freezing of the roads programme and a changing of policy on roads, which might be right in national terms, but it is welcomed only by areas that already have reasonable roads. We are just 26 miles from Norwich, which is our regional and economic centre. Norwich itself has suffered enormous job losses recently. Norwich Union is to cut 20 per cent. of its work force during the next 12 months. The Nestlé Rowntree factory is closing, with 900 jobs going. Colemans of Norwich is up for sale.

I do not say that all the Norwich economy is bad—it certainly is not. Again, the picture in Norwich is much the same as that which I have portrayed in Waveney—a host of firms are doing well—but it is the perception that all are not doing well that does not help to boost business confidence. In a sense, the whole of Norfolk and north Suffolk belies the image of prosperous East Anglia which so many people from outside the area have. That is perhaps why many people in the area are unfortunately voting Labour, tragic though that is.

Jonathan Sisson, the president of the Norfolk and Waveney chamber of commerce and industry, recently launched a debate about our local economy. He centred it on two arguments. The first was that it was time to lower the drawbridge on Fortress Norfolk and Waveney and end the view that the isolated nature of the area and the quality of our life compensate for economic stagnation. The second was that the road and rail infrastructure needs to be dealt with. He understands, as we all do, that growth is as essential for the economy locally as it is nationally. When we do not achieve that growth, commensurate with our location, population and assets, something is wrong. When we are 80 miles from the motorway network, and when it is quicker to get to Amsterdam than to London or Birmingham, all is not quite right.

[*Mr. David Porter*]

I hope that my hon. Friend the Minister of State will consider what I am saying from an economic and employment point of view and pass those thoughts to the Department of Transport when the roads programme is reviewed again next year, not so that East Anglia is covered in roads, but to put what we have got on the competitive level of other parts of the country.

From her position, my hon. Friend the Minister will know of the decline in employment. In 1991, the Rural Development Commission identified Waveney as an area likely to suffer further agricultural job losses. She may also realise how much fishing has suffered, too. One hundred years ago, there was a fleet of 500 boats; today, there are fewer than 20 beam trawlers. One thousand jobs have been lost in the fishing industry in the past 12 years alone. I do not blame the Government alone for that. It is part of the global decline of the fishing industry as technology and mechanisation have improved. However, the common fisheries policy, as my hon. Friend the Minister will not be surprised to hear me say, has failed to conserve fish stocks. I believe that it should be scrapped so that we can start again.

Worse than that for Lowestoft is the fact that a plaice swap has been imposed by the Government, which will take £1 million-worth of plaice out of the fish market and run the fleet out of quota by the autumn. As a consequence of the CFP, to which the Government are so wedded, there will be no fishing industry left before long—or perhaps I should say that there will no British fishing industry left before long. It is a further barrier to employment, economic development and business confidence and contributes in many people's minds to the feeling of a spiral of decline and decay. The much-vaunted decommissioning scheme encourages owners to make fishermen redundant and puts merchants into bankruptcy.

Waveney failed to win assisted area status, whereas neighbouring Great Yarmouth succeeded. I am delighted to see my hon. Friend the Member for Great Yarmouth (Mr. Carttiss) here tonight. I do not complain about Great Yarmouth's success in this instance, because, on the day the figures were set, Great Yarmouth's unemployment was greater than that of Waveney. However, my hon. Friend and I put it to the Minister that the areas should have been treated equally—both, or neither, should have received assisted area status. We have, however, been awarded objective 5b money, which could be a very big boost. To be fair, the local authorities, the training and enterprise council and the private sector are coming up with ideas for the money.

The sad thing is that it is now necessary to have that money, that kind of life support. We are pleased that the Government have approved it—the European Union will now give some British taxes back to us—but it would not have been necessary had the Government funded our infrastructure improvements at the same time as those of other parts of the nation.

There is much that we can do to help ourselves, and it is being done. The trade unionists to whom I talked last week, the local authorities, the major employers and the smaller job creators are all singing from the same hymn book, although I wish that our local authorities spent less time employing people on poverty strategies and concentrated more on driving down the council tax.

There is a determination locally to use our natural assets better. Kvaerner has come only recently to Waveney because of its location and the quality of the work force. The Government can lend two helping hands. First, they can keep inflation down, keep interest rates stable and business taxes low, deregulate and privatise, help with training and retraining and resist the minimum wage. All that they are doing but, secondly, they could remove the extra barriers that we have and that other areas of structural decline do not have. I have already mentioned poor road and rail links and the common fisheries policy, but additional barriers are the special assistance schemes to our competitors at our expense and excessively zealous bureaucratic enforcement of rules and regulations. No magic wands are asked for or expected, only a fair deal.

The area is almost the closest part of the United Kingdom to the rest of the single market. We should be able to use that advantage our way. Nobody predicted 25 years ago that tourism would be the great job creator that it is today. In Waveney, about 3,800 jobs—10 per cent. of the work force—are in tourism-related work, even though it is sometimes seasonal, short-term, part-time or low-paid. No one can predict how the future will produce the work that the country needs, including the 4,500 new jobs that Waveney needs in the next 10 years to stand still.

In the meantime, I urge my hon. Friend the Minister to do her best to help Waveney to pull down some of the barriers to employment that need not be there, so that we can fight fair.

11.29 pm

**The Minister of State, Department of Employment (Miss Ann Widdecombe):** I congratulate my hon. Friend the Member for Waveney (Mr. Porter) on securing the debate. I thank him for raising the issue of employment in his constituency. It is only right to record the interest shown in the debate by my hon. Friends the Members for Great Yarmouth (Mr. Carttiss) and for St. Ives (Mr. Harris). The defence of the British fishing industry by my hon. Friend the Member for St. Ives has commanded much respect in the House.

As my hon. Friend the Member for Waveney knows, the number of people out of work fell again in March, to its lowest level since June 1991. That was the 19th month in a row when there had been a fall. Furthermore, throughout the country employment is growing. Nearly 300,000 more jobs were created in the past year, and over 200,000 were in full-time positions. In the United Kingdom as a whole, unemployment has fallen by over 600,000 in the past two years. East Anglia has shared strongly in that improvement. Indeed, it has the lowest unemployment rate of all UK regions.

My hon. Friend paid tribute to the attractive areas of East Anglia, including Waveney, the constituency which he represents. My hon. Friend the Under-Secretary has sadly been prevented from replying to the debate due to a dislocated shoulder. He is familiar with the area and I cannot compete with his familiarity with it. He assures me that it is an area that provides a wide range of wildlife habitats, waterways and tourist attractions, to which my hon. Friend the Member for Waveney referred.

I recognise that Waveney has some special difficulties, and my hon. Friend the Member for Waveney has eloquently described them. At the same time, many positive things can be said about the district in economic terms, to which I shall return to focus upon if time permits.

I know that, for many years, agriculture has been the staple industry in the area. I am aware also that the fishing industry has traditionally played a major part in the prosperity of the local coastal towns. Tourism is also important. I am sure that the seaside resorts on the East Anglian coast are beginning to see the holiday makers emerge as the weather becomes warmer and brighter.

Even in a prosperous region such as East Anglia there will still be areas of high unemployment if the traditional local industries decline, especially if they decline more quickly than new ones grow to replace them. Similarly, all industry needs to modernise and invest to compete at a European and world level. That means that many traditional, existing industries, such as fishing and farming, cannot always be sustained with the same employment levels that they have enjoyed in the past. I am pleased that those problems have been recognised in the granting of assisted area status to Wisbech, Harwich, Great Yarmouth and Clacton. That entitles them to apply for regional selective assistance.

I am sorry that Lowestoft was not successful in its bid for assisted area status. I can assure the House, however, that my Department is aware of the employment situation in the area. There is no single factor that determines eligibility for assisted area status. Decisions on the map were not taken on the basis of an automatic statistical process. Current employment, as well as the unemployment rate over the past five years and the level of long-term unemployment, were taken into account, along with several other factors.

More recently, Lowestoft and parts of the Waveney valley, and three rural areas—the Fens, central rural Norfolk and rural east Suffolk—have been awarded European Union objective 5b status, which will entitle them to £46 million of extra resources over five years for projects to diversify their economic base. I understand that a wide range of organisations in the area, including the TEC and district council, recently submitted bids to make best use of that newly available funding. The European programme PESCA will also assist the fishing industry in Lowestoft to cope with the current structural difficulties by diversifying coastal regions.

We all appreciate that economic change brings difficulties for industries and those who work within them, but change should not always be portrayed as a negative process. The business community in East Anglia and Waveney is resourceful and enterprising and, over the years, a broad economic base has developed with a wide variety of industries, including a high number of manufacturing industries, particularly in the Waveney area. Those are not only vital for local prosperity, which so concerns my hon. Friend, but important for the economy of the UK as a whole.

That is undoubtedly why the region has one of the highest rates of employment in the country. I prefer to say "employment", as my hon. Friend did in his title for this debate. We should all talk much more about employment. That is the important issue, whether it be in Waveney or elsewhere in the country.

We take the problem of long-term unemployment very seriously and it is worth pointing out that between January 1994 and January 1995, the latest period for which we have statistics, the number of people out of work for more than a year fell by 19 per cent. in the eastern region, compared with 15 per cent. across the UK as a whole.

The Government have a number of initiatives to help long-term unemployed people, in addition to the wide-ranging support offered by the Employment Service. For example, we have job plan workshops, work trials and the jobfinder's grant, which we announced in the last Budget. The training for work programme offers more than 1 million training opportunities every year. It is worth mentioning that many of those made unemployed in the eastern region as a result of redundancies in manufacturing, the vehicles industries, and the financial and banking sectors are extremely well qualified and would be in demand by businesses requiring high skills. That is good news for the region's economy as it returns to growth.

My hon. Friend rightly raised the issue of transport infrastructure. We are well aware of the importance of economic growth and the relationship between transport infrastructure and competitiveness. We understand that companies move 90 per cent. of their products by road, and they do it in lorries, rather than buses, trams or on bicycles. The Highways Agency has the task of delivering the roads programme, but I understand that the recent transport supplementary grant settlement for the county is perfectly fair, with 14.8 per cent. of its bid being accepted.

Substantial investment has been made in improving the major routes to and through East Anglia in view of its importance as a region in its own right but also as a major gateway to Europe. Those improvements and the Government's future proposals are an important element in improving the attractiveness and competitiveness of the area for economic development. I understand that Suffolk county council will make a package bid for Lowestoft in this year's transport plans and policies round. It has already been successful with an Ipswich package bid, and substantial progress is being made.

Perhaps I should mention some of the good economic news of which I am aware in the Waveney district. Despite its difficulties, unemployment has fallen in the Waveney constituency and 194 fewer people are registered unemployed than a year ago. We acknowledge that unemployment in the Lowestoft travel-to-work area is still too high. The Employment Service and the TEC will do all that they can to promote enterprise and help local people get back to work. The unemployment rate, which is down 1.1 per cent., has fallen across the East Anglian region and 11,359 fewer people are now registered unemployed than a year ago. As I said, the unemployment rate in the region is the lowest in the country at 6.8 per cent.

New jobs have been created in the region. For example, a multi-million pound offshore contract to design and build a 2,000 tonne accommodation module has been secured by SLP Engineering, which was mentioned by my hon. Friend. That will secure the jobs of 225 workers at Lowestoft and could create new jobs. The Norwegian offshore giant, Kvaerner, is bringing new jobs to its Lowestoft-based operation with a construction contract worth more than £1 million. Around 25 jobs will be created as Kvaerner Oil and Gas services works on a major contract for the port of Felixstowe. Lowestoft-based graphics firm, Supersine, is to become a centre of

[*Miss Ann Widdecombe*]

excellence for screen printing. The recently launched Enterprise 2000 will also help 1,000 people to become their own bosses in the region.

During the past decade, the Rural Development Commission has been actively involved in the Waveney area. It has promoted development so that rural businesses and services can prosper and provide for the varied needs of rural communities. For example, the RDC provided £40,000 in grant aid last year to encourage the refurbishment of 14,000 sq ft of redundant buildings, which is likely to accommodate 40 jobs. That has been a typical level of grant aid.

Since the launch of Norfolk and Waveney TEC's "Train and Gain" initiative in October 1993, 727 people have been placed back in work. It offers training grants to employers taking on people who have been registered unemployed for six months or more. There are also extra payments to encourage national vocational qualification take-up. The TEC is also operating a business expansion loan scheme, in partnership with the Midland bank. The scheme allows small companies to borrow up to £15,000 at low rates to encourage expansion and, with that expansion, new jobs.

We can concentrate on our achievements nationally, regionally and locally. There will always be room for improvement in certain areas, but the way forward to prosperity in every area of the country is through sustainable economic growth. That means the encouragement of employment policies that are not just short-term expedients but long-term solutions with long-term benefits to meet the nation's current and future needs. I believe that Waveney and Great Yarmouth will benefit from the prosperity generated.

*Question put and agreed to.*

*Adjourned accordingly at eighteen minutes to Twelve midnight.*

16 MAY 1995

# House of Commons

*Tuesday 16 May 1995*

*The House met at half-past Two o'clock*

PRAYERS

[MADAM SPEAKER *in the Chair*]

# Oral Answers to Questions

## HEALTH

### Hospital Provision (South-west London)

**1. Dr. Goodson-Wickes:** To ask the Secretary of State for Health what recent consultations she has had concerning the provision of hospitals in south-west London. [22851]

**The Minister for Health (Mr. Gerald Malone):** Local health authorities, national health service trusts and general practitioners in south-west London are considering the future provision of hospital services in the area.

**Dr. Goodson-Wickes:** Does my hon. Friend accept that although the London borough of Merton does not have a general hospital within its boundaries, thanks to Government reforms it already has unrivalled access to three excellent national health service hospitals, St. George's hospital, St. Helier hospital and Kingston hospital? Does he agree that the picture would be completed by the exciting new plans to rebuild the Nelson hospital in Wimbledon, so that my constituents can have access to the highest quality day surgery and out-patient care?

**Mr. Malone:** My hon. Friend has been a staunch advocate of that proposal. It is intended that the review of specialist services, which is under way, will improve services across the area that serves my hon. Friend's constituency. I am sure that his points will be borne in mind by all concerned.

**Mr. Nicholas Brown:** As London has half the number of health centres per person of other major cities in England and fewer GPs, health visitors and district nurses than it had in 1990, and as there has been a decrease of 2 per cent. in the number of GPs per head of the population in inner London in the past decade, how can the Minister claim to be presiding over a shift from hospital services to primary care? Surely he is getting rid of beds without providing alternative services.

**Mr. Malone:** As it is essential to provide excellent health care in London, combine specialist services, improve primary care and continue the Government's investment in primary care, such as the £210 million investment in the London implementation zone scheme, why do the hon. Gentleman and his party want to stop all that in its tracks and call for yet another review?

### Consultant Specialties

**2. Rev. Martin Smyth:** To ask the Secretary of State for Health if she will make a statement on the shortage of staff in consultant specialties in the health service. [22852]

**The Secretary of State for Health (Mrs. Virginia Bottomley):** In the five years to 1993, the number of hospital consultants in England increased by an average of 3 per cent. a year, well above the target of 2 per cent. set in 1987. Over the same period, the number of consultants in Northern Ireland increased by 12 per cent. The Government have established effective mechanisms to ensure that consultant numbers continue to expand to meet demand.

**Rev. Martin Smyth:** If the Government are controlling numbers to meet demand, why are there continuing shortages, particularly among anaesthetists and paediatricians, which mean that operations have been cancelled? Is someone in the Department using new maths and not counting correctly? Is it job protectionism, or are hospitals saving money at the cost of patient care?

**Mrs. Bottomley:** I explained that there has been a substantial increase in the number of consultants, but there are always times when there is particular pressure on certain categories. That is why we have set up a working arrangement with the professions, whereby one committee can monitor and anticipate where there is particular pressure. The hon. Gentleman will be pleased to know that, for example, in paediatrics there was a 5.5 per cent. increase in consultants and in accident and emergency there was a 6.7 per cent. increase. The increase has been above average in both those specialisms.

**Mrs. Roe:** Will my right hon. Friend confirm that the Government are committed to increasing the number of medical students and have taken on board the recommendations to that effect by the Medical Workforce Standing Advisory Committee? Will she also comment on the training of doctors? Can she say anything further about the implementation of the Calman changes?

**Mrs. Bottomley:** I can indeed inform my hon. Friend that, having not only published the first report of the Medical Workforce Standing Advisory Committee but acted on it, we shall shortly produce the second standing advisory committee report. We train about 500 more medical students a year than we did 10 years ago and we anticipate further increases. My hon. Friend referred to the important Calman proposals to improve and accelerate specialist training. We are working on their detailed implementation, from which future generations of consultants will greatly benefit.

**Mrs. Bridget Prentice:** Is the Secretary of State aware of public alarm at the number of casualty departments being temporarily closed—including at least five in London? Is she further aware of concern that—

**Hon. Members:** Order.

**Madam Speaker:** Order. The question has already been widened.

**Mrs. Prentice:** Is the Secretary of State aware that those closures might be due to staff shortages or, more likely, to the Government's policy of permanently closing casualty departments? What guarantee can she give London in particular that such closures will not recur?

**Mrs. Bottomley:** The hon. Lady identifies an area of special focus—accident and emergency departments—in which there has been an 11.1 per cent. increase in consultant appointments because it is moving towards a consultant-led service. That is precisely what underpins the move to larger A and E departments associated with minor injury centres. Junior doctors will increasingly want to staff areas that offer an A and E service according to best practice—well staffed, well equipped and of significant size.

I am sure that the hon. Lady is aware that the Royal College of Surgeons commented recently that placement in an A and E department is not necessary for training. As a result, we are holding discussions with professional groups to ensure that those jobs continue to be attractive. Our job must be to ensure top quality, well-staffed, well-equipped A and E departments for the people of this country.

**Mr. Heald:** Does my right hon. Friend agree that consultant numbers have increased well ahead of target? Will she join me in congratulating North Hertfordshire NHS trust based at Lister hospital on the appointment of a new audiology consultant in September which, together with the new magnetic resonance imaging scanner later this month, will make a huge contribution to improved patient care for my constituents?

**Mrs. Bottomley:** I join my hon. Friend in congratulating his trust, which is a classic example of how trusts have used the opportunities of their status to improve patient services and make them more responsive. I confirm that there have been an extra 300 consultants a year for the last four years. We intend to maintain and improve that impressive record.

### Hospitals

3. **Mr. Turner:** To ask the Secretary of State for Health how many hospitals there were in England in 1979, April 1991 and December 1994.     [22853]

**Mr. Malone:** In 1979 there were 2,023 hospitals in England, and in 1991 there were 1,624. For 1994, NHS Estates, using a different basis of calculation, has estimated the number at 1,440.

**Mr. Turner:** Have not 245 hospitals closed since 1990—one per week since Conservative health reforms were introduced? Does the Minister agree that as a result of record waiting lists, hospital closures and bed losses, the NHS is at breaking point in many parts of the country? Operations have been cancelled, specialist beds have been unavailable and there has been the unholy sight of many people on trolleys waiting hours in casualty departments.

**Mr. Malone:** If the hon. Gentleman were to look at his own constituency, he would see a different picture from that which he painted. In 1989-90, there were 560 waiters over two years; in 1995, there is none. In 1989-90, there were 214 two-year waiters; in 1995 there is none. Investment projects totalling £17 million are under way in the hon. Gentleman's constituency. Of course there have been a number of closures, but substantially better

facilities have been put in their place. Why does not the hon. Gentleman recognise that when it is happening in his constituency?

**Mr. Rowe:** Is my hon. Friend aware that people in my constituency have warmly welcomed the closure—regrettable though it is in some respects—of the oldest hospital in Britain, St. Bart's, and of All Saints hospital, the former workhouse? It is shortly to close, almost entirely owing to the large investment put into the Medway hospitals complex, which will provide unrivalled modern facilities. Does he agree that this counting of hospitals is meaningless?

**Mr. Malone:** My hon. Friend is quite right. The purpose of the health service reforms was to allow services to be provided closer to people. That is precisely what my hon. Friend points out in respect of the reconfiguration of services in his constituency.

**Mrs. Beckett:** Does the Minister accept that we are pleased to learn that he has found out some facts about hospitals, as it is not long since he told us that he did not know how to define one. I hope that that means that the questions that we table will in future be answered. Does he nevertheless accept that there is considerable concern in many parts of the country about the pace of change, and that when Ministers say, as they repeatedly do, that they do not know what is happening in terms of the provision of hospitals and do not know which hospitals or A and E departments are at risk, they add to that concern?

The Secretary of State said a moment ago that Ministers are concerned about standards of hospital care and of accident and emergency provision. How can they know that standards are being met if they do not even know what is happening on the ground?

**Mr. Malone:** The right hon. Lady is well aware that these matters are decided locally. When they are disputed or objected to by community health councils, they come to Ministers for decision. Hence a tremendous amount of reconfiguration of service and change is going on around the country by local agreement.

It is not good enough to be obsessed with old buildings; it is far better to look at the new investment going into the health service. More than 700 schemes costing more than £1 million each have been completed in the course of the past decade. That is the measure of the Government's commitment to an improved health service. I do not understand why the right hon. Lady is obsessed with the past.

### Residential and Nursing Home Care

4. **Mr. Sims:** To ask the Secretary of State for Health what guidance she offers to local authorities in assessing the means of persons in need of residential and nursing home care; and what plans she has to amend the figures on which such calculations are based.     [22854]

**The Parliamentary Under-Secretary of State for Health (Mr. John Bowis):** Comprehensive guidance was issued to local authorities in December 1992 and is regularly updated.

**Mr. Sims:** At present, anyone with capital of more than £3,000 is expected to contribute towards the cost of his care, and anyone with more than £8,000 has to pay in full. Will my hon. Friend confirm that the figures were inherited in 1993 from the income support system and have not been altered since? In fact, they date back to 1990. Does he agree that they are perhaps due for review?

Will my hon. Friend consider clarifying the guidance that he gives local authorities, which take into account the full occupational pension of a person in a residential nursing home? This often means that the spouse left in the family home has no income whatever and may have to resort to income support.

**Mr. Bowis:** My hon. Friend's statement of the figures is correct. They were brought into line with income support figures in 1993, when the threshold was raised from £1,200 to £3,000. We do indeed keep the figures under review and will continue to do so.

As for the occupational pension, local authorities have a discretion to enable a spouse to remain at home with the same standard of living to which he or she has been accustomed. My noble Friend Lord Mackay asked in another place for any evidence that this discretion was not being used properly to be brought to the Government's attention. I repeat that request today; to date we have received no such evidence. We shall, however, consider the matter, as we promised to do, in another place.

**Mrs. Dunwoody:** Is the Minister aware that literally thousands of people are terrified that they will become so frail that they will be removed—forcibly, if need be— from an NHS bed and sent to a private home, leaving their families unable to make up the difference between the fees and the amounts available? That not only frightens large numbers of people but implies that the system is on the verge of breaking down.

**Mr. Bowis:** I refer the hon. Lady to the guidance that we recently issued on continuing care and on discharge; and to one of the conditions of the special transitional grant—that there should be agreement between the social services and hospitals. There has been no change to the system for charging introduced in 1948 by the then Labour Government. This Government introduced the discretion and the requirement that the value of the house be ignored for spouses and other members of a family who may remain at home.

**Mr. Wilkinson:** Will my hon. Friend publish the results of his review? As my hon. Friend the Member for Chislehurst (Mr. Sims) has made clear, in parts of outer London, such as my constituency of Ruislip-Northwood, a place in a residential nursing home can cost several hundred pounds a week, which can lead to a spouse eventually having to sell the family home, causing great distress over and above that of looking after the sick patient. Will my hon. Friend publish the review and re-examine the criteria?

**Mr. Bowis:** There is no review as such. I said that we kept the matter under review. If we decide to make a change, we shall announce it. However, I can reassure my hon. Friend that, where a spouse remains at home, there is no question under this Government of that spouse being turned out of the family home. That is precisely the requirement that we put into law which was not there under the previous Labour Government. We have also

given the discretion to enable that spouse to remain in the family home according to the standard of living to which he or she has been accustomed.

**Mr. Wigley:** Does the Minister accept that people with on-going medical needs are being pressurised to move from hospitals into private nursing homes because of the in-built financial structure of the health care authority and its lack of beds? Surely anyone with an on-going medical need should be able to stay on in an NHS hospital.

**Mr. Bowis:** The hon. Gentleman is correct. If someone is deemed by a doctor to have a continuing in-patient health care need, that should be provided by the NHS, whether in a hospital or a bed purchased by the NHS. It is only if doctors decide that there is no longer an in-patient health need that a patient will be discharged into the community where the community health services will continue to be free to that individual. However, as has been the case since 1948, the social care needs would be paid for by the individual unless that individual's income warrants support by previously the benefit and now the community care system.

**Mr. Sumberg:** Does my hon. Friend recognise that there is considerable concern among elderly people and their relatives that the family home, for which they have saved over many years, may well have to be sold? Will my hon. Friend urgently and radically consider proposals to exempt such homes?

**Mr. Bowis:** My hon. Friend is correct to raise the concern of his constituents. I am happy to give him the assurance that we will continue to review the situation to ensure that the family is looked after. We already have in place assurances that we can give to families, and to spouses in particular, and now we must consider whether the figures that are in place are still adequate to meet the needs.

**Mr. Hinchliffe:** Does the Minister recall that one of the key objectives of the assessment process was the avoidance of unnecessary institutional care? Is it not a fact that many people are still being placed unnecessarily in care homes because of the requirement to spend the bulk of the community care grant in the private sector? Will the Minister make it clear which is more important—the proper assessment of individual needs or propping up the private care market?

**Mr. Bowis:** Yet again, we see the naked hostility to the private sector that has been so apparent from the Labour party ever since we introduced the community care policy. It is clear that the assessment of the individual is central to community care. The individual takes part in that assessment and the individual and the individual's carers take part in discussions on how to meet the needs of that assessment.

It is then a question of whether it is possible to enable the individual to stay at home with a package of care or whether it is better to place the person in residential care. That is a matter for the assessment, which should involve the appropriate medical input. We have no dogmatic view on whether someone should stay at home or go into residential care. We want the individual to receive the best care, irrespective of from which sector that care comes.

### Elective Surgery

5. **Mr. Ottaway:** To ask the Secretary of State for Health what proportion of elective surgery is now carried out on a day-case basis.    [22855]

**The Parliamentary Under-Secretary of State for Health (Mr. Tom Sackville):** Half of all elective surgery is done on a day-care basis.

**Mr. Ottaway:** In the light of that excellent answer, will my hon. Friend pay tribute to Croydon's Mayday healthcare trust? More than half its non-urgent surgery is carried out on a day-care basis, and it has just opened a brand-new paediatric day-case unit. Does my hon. Friend realise that, if he had listened to the Opposition last week, all that would have been put in jeopardy? Is it not the Conservative party that is looking forward, and the Labour party that is looking backward?

**Mr. Sackville:** I can confirm that 90 per cent. of cataract operations carried out at the Mayday hospital, 73 per cent of arthroscopies and 54 per cent. of laparoscopies are performed on a day-case basis. That is good news for patients in my hon. Friend's constituency, and I am glad that he has endorsed and paid tribute to what has been a central policy in my Department.

**Mrs. Mahon:** When the Minister gives figures showing an increase in day-case surgery, does he take into account the extra work load for nurses? Does he not feel just a little ashamed of the fact that those who have made that increase possible are now balloting on whether to take industrial action?

Is it not time that the Minister stopped insulting nurses, and started to pay them a proper rate for the job? At present, nurses are scrabbling about with trusts which do not care, and which are not—as the Minister claimed—offering them a 3 per cent. pay increase: they are offering 1 per cent., or 3 per cent. if extra elements are taken into account. That involves altering nurses' working conditions.

**Mr. Sackville:** Nurses do a wonderful job in day-case units, and it is right and fitting for their pay to reflect that.

### Night Services (General Practitioners)

6. **Mr. Simon Coombs:** To ask the Secretary of State for Health if she will make a statement on the provision of night time services by general practitioners.    [22856]

**Mr. Malone:** Night-time services provided by family doctors are integral to British general practice. On 20 April, after discussions with general practitioner leaders, we proposed changes to strengthen services by increasing the support for local GPs working together to offer high-quality care to patients in their area.

**Mr. Coombs:** No doubt my hon. Friend is aware that the number of night visits by GPs has more than doubled in the four years to last year. Is he fully satisfied that the proposals that the Department has put to the BMA—on which it will vote in the next few days—reflect that fact? How satisfied is he that the BMA will accept what is, on the face of it, a very reasonable proposition?

**Mr. Malone:** It is perhaps not surprising that, when the hours of night cover were extended some years ago, night

fees and the number of night visits increased. About 50 per cent. of the increase in visits is attributable to that increase in hours of cover.

As GPs across the country decide whether to accept the proposal, I ask them to bear two points in mind. First, it is fair to them; secondly, it is fair to their patients. It will encourage the sort of co-operative arrangement that I saw in Reading, which serves my hon. Friend's constituency. That is certainly one of the possible ways forward, providing first-class out-of-hours cover for patients.

**Mr. Bryan Davies:** If the services are satisfactory, will the Minister condemn, and take steps to stamp out, the practice of hotels charging their residents for night-time visits when they are taken ill on the ground that national health service provision is inadequate and private doctors must be called in?

**Mr. Malone:** There is nothing to prevent anyone who is resident in either a hotel or private premises from making his or her own arrangements to seek emergency care.

**Mr. Budgen:** Is my hon. Friend aware that there is, in general, great satisfaction in Wolverhampton about the way in which GPs provide night-time services? Will he pay a sincere compliment to the hon. Member for Wolverhampton, South-East (Mr. Turner)? For 20 years, in all his observations about matters connected with the health service, the hon. Gentleman has screamed that there is a crisis, and has said that the best way of dealing with that crisis is to spend a large amount of someone else's money. Is he not to be commended for the splendid consistency of his views?

**Mr. Malone:** His consistency is the equivalent of others who cry wolf too often and eventually get ignored. My hon. Friend makes a good, substantive point—that care in his constituency is good. The proposals for GP out-of-hours cover are designed to improve on that, to reduce the burden on medical practitioners who wish to undertake fewer night visits and to ensure that the quality of care for patients is improved during that important period when they need to call on medical services.

### GP Fundholding

7. **Mr. Gunnell:** To ask the Secretary of State for Health what research her Department has undertaken into the administrative costs of general practitioner fundholding; and if she will make a statement.    [22857]

**Mrs. Virginia Bottomley:** The management costs of general practitioner fundholding are kept under regular review. In the first three years of the scheme, general practitioner management costs were about 2 per cent. of budgets, which represents excellent value for money for the very real benefits to patients resulting from the scheme.

**Mr. Gunnell:** I am sure that the Secretary of State is aware that the magazine *Fundholding*, which can hardly be said to be unsympathetic to fundholders, has estimated that the amount spent on setting up the scheme and on administration was £98 million, and that the average cost per fundholding practice is more than £80,000. There is also plenty of research to show that this is a much more expensive way of purchasing for district health authorities. Does not she think that the money should have been put into patient care and not into creating an expensive administrative system?

**Mrs. Bottomley:** I do not agree with the hon. Gentleman. I believe, as does the King's Fund, that fundholding has been one of the most exciting aspects of our health service reforms. I recommend to the hon. Gentleman the words of the National Audit Office, the Organisation for Economic Co-operation and Development and Professor Howard Glennerster. They have all confirmed that fundholding has made care much more responsive to patients. The amount spent on management is modest compared with the substantial improvements in patient care and the better value for money that has been achieved by the scheme.

**Mr. Quentin Davies:** Is my right hon. Friend aware that in Lincolnshire well over 50 per cent. of patients are now treated by fundholding general practitioners? Is not that a remarkable tribute to the popularity of fundholding among GPs and patients, and does not it vindicate the Government's decision to go ahead with this proposal despite the consistent opposition of the Labour party?

**Mrs. Bottomley:** I commend the example of Lincolnshire, but perhaps the most interesting example is to be found in Derbyshire. In Derby, South, 78 per cent. of the population have fundholders. That shows how persuasive is the Opposition spokesman on health with her local general practitioners, all of whom totally disregarded her words and decided that there were benefits for their patients by taking up the fundholding option.

**Mrs. Beckett:** Is the Secretary of State aware that managers in some parts of the country are said to be insisting that general practitioners become fundholders and are refusing to provide financial or administrative support to groups of GPs who want to become commissioning GPs although that is a much less expensive and more effective system? Those managers claim to be acting on instructions from the Department of Health. Why?

**Mrs. Bottomley:** Let me make it clear that fundholding is and will remain voluntary. Undoubtedly, fundholding offers much more direct control to the general practitioner for securing, commissioning and monitoring services than joint commissioning. Joint commissioning clearly has a part to play, but in our view it is not as effective as proper GP fundholding. As the right hon. Lady will know, we have now set up 51 total fundholding projects which are being carefully evaluated to see what further lessons can be learned.

**Mr. Evennett:** Does my right hon. Friend agree that GP fundholders are delivering a clear benefit to all patients in their areas? Does she further agree that the waiting time for the patients of GP fundholders tends to be shorter and that the opportunity for a better and more varied service in the surgery is greater?

**Mrs. Bottomley:** I very much agree with my hon. Friend. I hope that he agrees that waiting time for all patients is shorter. Before the reforms there were 200,000 one-year waiters and he will know that there are now only 31,000. That affects all patients, irrespective of whether they have GP fundholders. It is right to say that the

Opposition do not care. They do not want to know the facts because they might get in the way of the rhetoric. I agree not only with my hon. Friend but with the OECD that GP fundholders have been more prepared to challenge hospital practices and demand improvements. The National Audit Office states:

"the direct involvement of general practitioner fundholders in health care purchasing has led to improvements in the service provided for their patients".

### Broadgreen Hospital

8. **Mr. O'Hara:** To ask the Secretary of State for Health if she will make it her policy that the accident and emergency department of Broadgreen hospital will not be closed until adequate alternative facilities are made available.    [22858]

**Mr. Bowis:** It already is.

**Mr. O'Hara:** I am delighted to have that assurance. The Minister will be aware, however, that at the turn of the year the accident and emergency department has almost closed perforce due to lack of recruitment of qualified staff. He will also be aware of leaked reports that it was to be closed on 31 July when the contracts of staff recruited in crisis came to an end. Will he ensure that steps are in place to ensure that Broadgreen accident and emergency department is fully staffed to remain open after 31 July? Otherwise, my constituents in Knowsley, South will continue to live in fear and suspicion that the trust in which they have no trust is trying to engineer the closure of the department before adequate facilities are in place.

**Mr. Bowis:** The hon. Gentleman's constituents can have trust in the trust. One has to consider only the brand new A and E department at Fazakerley hospital, the largest and best equipped not only in this country but in Europe, the £2.7 million extension to the Royal Liverpool University hospital A and E department, and the new £9 million critical care unit at St. Helens and Knowsley hospital, to be completed in April 1996. The pledge is there that the A and E department at Broadgreen hospital will not be phased out until those facilities are in place.

### National Blood Authority

9. **Mr. Illsley:** To ask the Secretary of State for Health when she last met the chairman of the National Blood Authority to discuss rationalisation proposals.    [22859]

**Mr. Sackville:** Ministers meet the chairman of the National Blood Authority regularly.

**Mr. Illsley:** The Minister will be aware of the national blood transfusion service's continued difficulties consequent upon those rationalisation proposals, the latest of which is the purchase by the NBA of blood-testing kits which are regarded as inferior for HIV and hepatitis testing and are banned in many countries. In the past few months, the level of blood donations has decreased in this country, staff employed in the blood transfusion service have been completely demoralised, many skilled staff have left the service and, above all, there has been a complete loss of public confidence in that precious service. Will the Minister advise the chairman of the NBA to abandon the rationalisation proposals once and for all?

**Mr. Sackville:** I am aware of a continuing attempt by the hon. Gentleman to make his political name by undermining the blood service—*[Interruption.]* He has continually claimed that blood donations are down, when they are holding at the level of last year. Demand for blood has gone up by 4 per cent. and donations have gone up by 5 per cent. As he knows, the plans to rationalise the blood service are to do with that fact that it has always been run regionally, so there is too much processing and too much testing. We must reduce those overheads on the service.

**Dame Elaine Kellett-Bowman:** Does my hon. Friend agree that blood centres must be run for the benefit of the donors who give their blood freely and the teams who so devotedly serve them? Does he further agree that nothing whatever in the consultation document, or in anything that Sir Colin Walker has subsequently said, militates against that? Will he further emphasise his comment that the Opposition's political agitation is causing great dismay and is unnecessary?

**Mr. Sackville:** I confirm that, whatever happens, specialist services, such as the anti-D donors, are being retained in Lancaster. My hon. Friend is right: the allegations have been attempts to be undermine the confidence of donors, but they have failed.

### Statistics

10. **Mr. Win Griffiths:** To ask the Secretary of State for Health what plans she has to change the way in which statistics are collected for publication on activities in the NHS. [22860]

**Mr. Sackville:** There are no specific major changes in prospect, but each statistical return is reviewed at least once every three years, and every item is subjected to rigorous examination.

**Mr. Griffiths:** Many people will be disappointed with that reply because a strong case exists for radically overhauling NHS statistics. For instance, does the Minister agree that we should publish statistics on the readmission of patients to hospital so that we can measure the quality of the care that they receive there, the success of the treatment and the availability of good quality community care?

**Mr. Sackville:** The hon. Gentleman is aware that in England we went over from deaths and discharges to a system of finished consultant episodes some years ago. Wales did not follow at that time, but it is now setting up a patient episode database which roughly mirrors our system. That is good news because the new Körner statistics are a proper measure of patient activity.

**Mr. John Marshall:** Does my hon. Friend accept that, however the figures are collated, there is strong evidence of a shortage of beds in London for the mentally ill, as was discussed in the Adjournment debate last Wednesday?

**Mr. Sackville:** We are making considerable progress in the provision of intermediate beds and in all other areas of mental health. The Under-Secretary of State, my hon.

Friend the Member for Battersea (Mr. Bowis), has replied to such debates on numerous occasions and has explained the plans that are in place to ensure that we improve mental health services everywhere in the country.

**Ms Jowell:** The Minister used statistics to defend the Secretary of State's reputation and to obscure the real information about patient care, which only goes to prove that Disraeli was right about statistics. Will the Minister now undertake to publish figures for the number of patients treated by the NHS and not what Ministers' jargon calls finished consultant episodes?

**Mr. Sackville:** I begin by welcoming the hon. Lady to the Opposition Front Bench at Question Time. Unless we have reliable statistics which show the activity all over the health service, we do not know what is happening. There is no point in relying on individual incidents which are entirely unrepresentative of the health service, as the hon. Lady and her friends in the press continually do.

**Mr. Hendry:** Is not the reality that the Opposition parties wish to change the way in which statistics are calculated because they are horrified at the number of additional patients being treated every year and appalled by the fact that waiting lists are falling and the only way they can achieve bad statistics is by changing the basis on which the statistics are collected? Can my hon. Friend confirm that in my constituency we have no patients waiting for more than 12 months for an operation? Is that not the statistic that really matters?

**Mr. Sackville:** My hon. Friend is right. If one ignores the fact that 120 patients are being treated now for every 100 treated before the reforms, which is an embarrassing statistic for the Opposition, it is impossible to measure the success of the reforms.

### Hospital Closures, London

11. **Mrs. Roche:** To ask the Secretary of State for Health how many (a) hospital beds and (b) hospitals have been lost in London since 1990. [22861]

**Mr. Malone:** The number of acute hospital beds in greater London has been reduced by around 1,900 between 1990-91 and 1993-94. The equivalent figure for inner London, including the special health authorities, is around 1,000. Information on the hospitals that have closed is not held centrally.

**Mrs. Roche:** Given that a ward has recently closed in Hornsey central hospital in my constituency without consultation and that waiting lists have increased by 7 per cent. in the Whittington hospital, which also covers my constituency, does the Minister now accept that, although the Government may have won the vote last week, they did not win the argument in the House or with the people in London or in the constituencies?

**Mr. Malone:** I will tell the hon. Lady what we did win last week and that was a vote for better health care in London, for bringing specialist medical care together on fewer sites, and obtaining better value for money and a better quality of health care. We made some progress towards improving London's health care in both the acute and primary care sectors and the Opposition want to call a halt to that progress.

**Dame Jill Knight:** Does my hon. Friend accept that for many of us what is important is not the number of hospitals or beds that are closed but the number of patients treated? In view of the extra primary care being offered, the number of day care patients being treated and the number of patients dealt with by general practitioners, would it not be extraordinary if the number of hospital beds stayed exactly the same?

**Mr. Malone:** My hon. Friend is quite right. The relevant statistic is the number of people treated. What is important is the amount of activity in the health service, not the simple number of beds. As for London, there is no bed target. It is up to individual health authorities to determine from time to time how many beds are necessary to provide care for the people living in their area. My hon. Friend is also right to point out that the Labour party is obsessed with the bricks and mortar of the health service, whereas we want to improve patient care.

## PRIME MINISTER

### Engagements

Q1. **Mr. Nigel Griffiths:** To ask the Prime Minister if he will list his official engagements for Tuesday 16 May.
[22881]

**The Prime Minister (Mr. John Major):** This morning, I had meetings with ministerial colleagues and others. In addition to my duties in the House, I shall be having further meetings later today.

**Mr. Griffiths:** As the vast majority of the British public want to see the accounts of political parties open to maximum public scrutiny, will the Prime Minister join Labour in calling for the Nolan committee to examine all aspects of party political funding? Or what has he got to hide?

**The Prime Minister:** As the whole House knows, within the past 18 months the Home Affairs Select Committee conducted a full inquiry into these matters. Subsequent to that inquiry, the Conservative party has implemented in full the code of practice drawn up by the Committee. The Labour party has refused to do so.

**Mr. Lamont:** Will the Prime Minister take an early opportunity to point out to the public that almost every country in Europe has had to put up taxes to deal with the effect on deficits of the recession? Will he also point out that, even after recent tax increases, the tax burden in this country in the 1990s will be lower than it was in the 1980s, just as it was lower in the 1980s than in the 1970s, including deficits? Will my right hon. Friend also point out that, thanks to Conservative Governments, this country has by a long way one of the lowest tax burdens in Europe?

**The Prime Minister** *rose*—*[Interruption.]* My right hon. Friend is entirely right—*[Interruption.]*

**Madam Speaker:** Order.

**The Prime Minister:** I commend to hon. Members opposite the excellent speech that my right hon. Friend made on this matter on Friday last week. As a result of the recovery, and despite the tax changes that we were compelled by the recession to make, households will actually be about £250 a year better off on average after tax and inflation this year.

**Mr. Blair:** Given the latest pay and perks scandal in the utilities at the weekend and today's massive rise in electricity profits, does the Prime Minister recognise that the utilities have degenerated into an unseemly racket and that the sooner he orders a thorough overhaul of their system of regulation the better? *[Interruption.]*

**Madam Speaker:** Order. I will have no more barracking from sedentary positions by individual Back Benchers. They will be named the next time.

**The Prime Minister:** Everyone wishes to see consumers protected. That is precisely why we have regulators to control prices and why, when necessary, the regulators have acted to control prices. Utility prices have fallen during the period of privatisation.

Although I have not yet had the opportunity to consider in detail the proposals of the shadow Secretary of State for Trade and Industry, I have to say that artificial plans to control profits smack very much of old Labour, not new Labour. The determination of what the Opposition call "reasonable profits" seems to me to be impossible. Who determines their level? Who says what is reasonable? What happens when profits bounce back after a period in which there have been losses? Do they apply just to the utilities or to other industries? These are the sort of questions that we would have asked of the Labour party in the 1970s; now we discover that we must ask them of the Labour party in the 1990s as well.

**Mr. Blair:** Will the Prime Minister confirm the following? Electricity prices in real terms for domestic households have risen since privatisation, as the House of Commons Library confirmed this morning; water charges have risen by more than 40 per cent. since privatisation; gas complaints are up by 150 per cent. in the past year— *[Interruption.]* He can cap rail fares only by promising an open-ended subsidy from the taxpayer to privatised operators. Why does he always stick up for the excess profits and the managers who make themselves into millionaires rather than the hard-pressed consumer, who is forced to use such monopoly services and is fed up with the way they are being run?

**The Prime Minister:** That was very well prepared, but almost entirely inaccurate. The reality is that the nationalised industries once cost the taxpayer £50 million a week and the privatised industries now yield £50 million a week. The average price of domestic electricity to households has fallen by 8.5 per cent. in real terms over the past two years; the price of gas has fallen by more than 20 per cent. in real terms since privatisation; BT's main prices have fallen by more than 35 per cent. in real terms since privatisation; Britain's water is now among the cleanest in Europe—*[Interruption.]* When those industries were all nationalised, prices went up year after year after year. The Opposition would like to control and regulate from the centre; they are determined to go back to when prices went up and not down year after year after year.

**Dr. Spink:** Will my right hon. Friend join me in welcoming yesterday's vote by the police, which showed that they do not wish routinely to carry arms? Does he feel, like me, that the best way in which to protect the police from those who carry arms is to increase the sentences that we can inflict on such people, and will he consider bringing back the death penalty for the murder of police officers?

**The Prime Minister:** I certainly very strongly support the decision not to carry firearms taken by the police in their ballot yesterday. That is wholly in tradition with policing in this country. I believe that it is the right decision and I warmly congratulate the police on having reached it. In recent years, we have increased the penalties for a large number of offences. I shall not retail them all at this moment, but I will willingly set them out in a parliamentary answer if my hon. Friend wishes me to do so. As my hon. Friend knows, I personally do not favour the return of capital punishment.

**Mr. Ashdown:** If the Conservative party has put its house in order on the question of funding, why will the Prime Minister not allow Lord Nolan to look into it? Does not the question of funding of all political parties go to the heart of the public's concern about trust in our political system? Does the Prime Minister not realise that, while he got high marks for establishing the Nolan committee, he will get no marks if he now seeks to turn what he told us was to be the public's bloodhound into the Prime Minister's poodle?

**The Prime Minister:** I do not think that anyone who has studied the membership of the Nolan committee or knows any of its members would remotely recognise the right hon. Gentleman's description of it. As he knows, there are only two ways of funding political parties in a free democracy. One is by subscription or donation freely given, and it is right in an open society that donors, if they wish, should preserve anonymity. *[Interruption.]* The other way is to fund political parties out of taxpayers' money. I do not favour that way and I hope that we shall not go in that direction. What is wrong about funding of political parties is when the funding of a party actually buys influence over its policy. *[Interruption.]* That is what is happening with the Opposition, where trade unions have 70 per cent. of the votes in Labour policy-making bodies, and even the proposal for dramatic reform would only diminish that to 50 per cent.

**Mr. Duncan Smith:** Does my right hon. Friend agree that, although the nuclear non-proliferation treaty has been signed there remains a serious threat of proliferation, and that the possession of a nuclear weapon is a measure of deterrence against those who would possess nuclear devices? Does he not find it absurd that Labour Front-Bench spokesmen say that they would hold Trident but would never use it? Does he think that that would deter anybody?

**The Prime Minister:** I suppose that there is a logical case for saying that one would scrap Trident—although I passionately disagree with that case, as I believe that Trident is necessary as a deterrent—but it is absolutely intellectually unsustainable to say that one would have Trident as a deterrent, but to tell those whom it is there to deter that one would never use it. If that is their position, the Opposition might as well take the money and pour it down the nearest drain.

Q2. **Mr. Win Griffiths:** To ask the Prime Minister if he will list his official engagements for Tuesday 16 May.     [22882]

**The Prime Minister:** I refer the hon. Gentleman to the reply I gave some moments ago.

**Mr. Griffiths:** Can the Prime Minister confirm that there are now an extra 500,000 people, notably those on low incomes, paying tax, principally because of the cuts in the married person's allowance last month, and that, after 16 years of Tory government, there are a record 26.2 million people paying income tax? Is the message not clear: "Tory Governments damage your wallet"?

**The Prime Minister:** First I must tell the hon. Gentleman that, if we had retained the Labour tax regime, there would have been an extra 1 million people in tax today. As for his specific questions, there are two substantive reasons why more people are paying tax this year. One is wage drift upwards. The second is the number of people who were unemployed but who are now in work and paying taxes. I should have thought that the hon. Gentleman would welcome that drop in unemployment.

Q3. **Mr. Jenkin:** To ask the Prime Minister if he will list his official engagements for Tuesday 16 May. [22883]

**The Prime Minister:** I refer my hon. Friend to the reply I gave some moments ago.

**Mr. Jenkin:** Further to the notice that I have given my right hon. Friend, as we approach the 1996 intergovernmental conference in Europe, and more particularly as we approach the 'reflections' group meeting in the summer, will he undertake to publish the Government's contribution to that group? Is it not essential that the IGC should address not stories about square strawberries and straight bananas, but the real public anxieties about growing European Union power—anxieties which the Leader of the Opposition apparently does not share, as he would give away the veto? Like one of his predecessors, the right hon. Gentleman may be fit to become a European Commissioner one day, but he is unfit to lead this nation.

**The Prime Minister:** I am grateful to my hon. Friend for giving me notice of the matter that he proposed to raise. I certainly agree that the European Union needs to be more responsive to the views of its people, with less interference and less red tape. We shall enter the IGC with a positive agenda, providing for more intergovernmental co-operation in a Europe of nation states, including co-operation in foreign policy, in defence and in the international battle against crime.

I believe that the European Union, both at the IGC and beyond, should give more consideration to Europe's place in the world rather than to the internal politics of the nations currently within it. We shall also press for more subsidiarity, more action against fraud and mismanagement, and a strengthened role for national parliaments. We shall not surrender our veto or our opt-outs from the social chapter and the single currency. I will consider my hon. Friend's request that we should publish our paper.

**Q4. Mr. Wicks:** To ask the Prime Minister if he will list his official engagements for Tuesday 16 May.    [22884]

**The Prime Minister:** I refer the hon. Gentleman to the reply I gave some moments ago.

**Mr. Wicks:** Does the Prime Minister agree with the statement of his Health Minister, Baroness Cumberlege, speaking to the Royal College of Nursing, that

"community care clearly isn't working"

and, if so, what does he intend to do about it?

**The Prime Minister:** I understand from my hon. and noble Friend—who is more familiar with the quotation than I am—that the hon. Gentleman has quoted the remark out of context.

**Q5. Mr. Bill Walker:** To ask the Prime Minister if he will list his official engagements for Tuesday 16 May.    [22885]

**The Prime Minister:** I refer my hon. Friend to the answer I gave some moments ago.

**Mr. Walker:** Does my right hon. Friend agree that a tax-raising legislative assembly in Edinburgh which fails to address the West Lothian question and the number of Members from Scotland in this House is bound to be unworkable and will be merely a stepping stone to separation?

**The Prime Minister:** I agree with my hon. Friend. It would be unworkable because some questions about it are unanswered and unanswerable. No one has yet explained why Scottish Members should be able to vote on English matters while English Members would not be able to vote on Scottish matters. There is silence from the Opposition on that. No one has yet explained why people who live in Scotland should pay more tax simply for the pleasure of being in Scotland. Again, there is silence from the Opposition. If the Opposition were serious about the constitution of Scotland, they would long ago have been able to answer a range of questions on the matter. Yet they still cannot answer them. Their policy is bad for Scotland, bad for the economy and bad for the United Kingdom.

# Nuclear Non-proliferation Treaty

3.30 pm

**Madam Speaker:** We now come to a statement—*[Interruption.]* Will Members please leave the Chamber quickly as we have an important statement to hear now?

**The Secretary of State for Foreign and Commonwealth Affairs (Mr. Douglas Hurd):** With permission, Madam Speaker, I would like to make a statement on the outcome of the non-proliferation treaty review and extension conference.

For 25 years, the non-proliferation treaty has helped prevent the spread of nuclear weapons. It is one of the essential foundations of our security. On 11 May the parties to the treaty decided unanimously to extend the treaty indefinitely. That decision is excellent news. A permanent treaty, properly applied, will make the world a safer place. It will provide the stability and predictability essential to continuing efforts towards disarmament and to the peaceful use of nuclear energy.

The conference also agreed by consensus a number of important texts, copies of which will be placed in the Library. The declaration on principles and objectives for nuclear non-proliferation and disarmament calls upon states not party to the treaty, in particular those with unsafeguarded nuclear facilities, to join it as a matter of urgency. It affirms the support of all states parties for the safeguards regime administered by the International Atomic Energy Agency and for efforts to increase the agency's capability to detect undeclared nuclear activities.

The programme of action on disarmament in the declaration stresses the importance of completing negotiations for a universal and verifiable comprehensive nuclear test ban treaty no later than 1996, the early conclusion of negotiations on a convention banning world wide the production of fissile material for nuclear weapons and the determined pursuit by the nuclear weapon states of systematic and progressive efforts to reduce nuclear weapons globally, with the ultimate goal of eliminating those weapons.

The British delegation played a weighty part in negotiating the declaration. The Government endorse it. The objectives it sets are in line with the policies we have pursued and will continue to pursue. When I spoke to the conference on 18 April, I underlined our commitment to early progress on the comprehensive test ban treaty and a cut-off convention. As the House knows, we have dropped our requirement for so-called safety tests and we have stopped production of fissile material for explosive purposes. I made clear in New York our readiness to join multilateral negotiations for the global reduction of nuclear weapons when progressive reductions by the United States and Russia bring their forces to a level comparable with our own minimum deterrent.

The conference decided that the treaty's review mechanism should be strengthened. It agreed that review conferences should be held every five years, that those conferences should be prepared more intensively and that their proceedings should be better structured to make them more effective. We welcome these decisions. It is essential that adherence to the treaty be properly monitored.

The agreements reached in New York were the result of many months of careful and painstaking negotiation. Our delegation was one of 21 in the core negotiating committee convened by the conference chairman. We worked closely with the United States, our European Union partners and other members of the group of western countries. We also collaborated closely with key non-aligned states. I would mention South Africa, in particular, which did outstanding work in achieving a result acceptable to all. The effort was immense and, for example, involved about 150 of our diplomatic posts around the world as they put our case, but it was abundantly worth while.

**Mr. Robin Cook** (Livingston): May I welcome the extension of the non-proliferation treaty, which for two decades has provided an international barrier to the spread of nuclear weapons? May I also welcome the Foreign Secretary's praise for South Africa? Its decision to dismantle its nuclear devices and to play a full part in the non-proliferation treaty shows a commitment to nuclear disarmament on which the Government of South Africa are to be congratulated.

Will the Foreign Secretary admit, however, that the debates at the review conference were much more controversial than his statement acknowledges? Will he confirm that the conference failed to agree the review text on progress under the treaty because most non-aligned countries do not believe that enough has been done by the nuclear weapon powers to honour their commitment under article 6 to pursue negotiations on nuclear disarmament? Will he confirm that the European Union was unable to table a unanimous text because even a number of European countries did not accept that enough had been done under article 6 by both France and Britain?

Does the Foreign Secretary recall stating in January that he did

"not feel any particular pressure from . . . non-nuclear weapon states"

for nuclear disarmament by Britain? Can he honestly repeat that claim after three weeks of such pressure at the review conference? Will he now recognise that the extension of the non-proliferation treaty must not be taken as removing the pressure on the nuclear powers to negotiate towards disarmament?

May I press the Foreign Secretary on what steps the Government are going to take to implement the principles and objectives in the final declaration of the review conference? It may come as a surprise to his Back Benchers, but in his statement he took credit for the weighty part played by Britain in negotiating that declaration. What is Britain going to do now to honour it?

The declaration demands assurances by nuclear weapon powers that they will not use such weapons against countries that do not possess them. Will the British Government therefore abandon the right that they have claimed to use nuclear weapons against countries that have none? Can the Foreign Secretary name the circumstances in which he thinks that it would be justifiable to use nuclear weapons against such countries?

**Mr. Michael Fabricant** (Mid-Staffordshire): So the hon. Gentleman would disarm unilaterally?

**Mr. Cook:** I have to tell the hon. Gentleman that I am quoting from the declaration that the Conservative Government have claimed a weighty part in negotiating. The House wants to know what the Government are going to do to implement the commitments that they made in New York.

The declaration calls for respect for nuclear-free zones. Will the Government respect all such zones and, if so, will they drop their refusal to observe the south Pacific nuclear-free zone? The declaration calls for the detection capability of the International Atomic Energy Agency to be increased. Is the Foreign Secretary aware that the safeguards budget of the agency has been frozen for 10 years? What, therefore, does he propose to do to increase its capability?

Finally, the Foreign Secretary stated that he endorsed the declaration and quoted the commitment in it to the elimination of nuclear weapons. His endorsement of that declaration is welcome, particularly since it has been reported that the British delegation privately lobbied to drop the commitment to the elimination of nuclear weapons. In view of that position in the negotiations, and of the expression of disagreement with it from his Back Benchers, the Government will be judged on their commitment to the elimination of nuclear weapons, not by his statement today, but by their record in the remaining two years available to them, and on what steps they take to working towards a world without nuclear weapons.

**Mr. Hurd:** I can answer some of the hon. Gentleman's specific questions. I am glad that he was glad about the outcome of the conference.

On funding, we agree that every effort should be made to ensure that the International Atomic Energy Agency has the necessary financial and human resources, and we are willing to consider a fully justified and controlled real increase in the agency's regular budget in 1997-98 to strengthen the safeguards regime.

On security assurances, the declaration states that we
"will not use nuclear weapons against non-nuclear weapon states parties to the treaty on the non-proliferation of nuclear weapons except in the case of an invasion or any other attack on the UK, its dependent territories, its armed forces or other troops, its allies, or on a state towards which it has a security commitment, carried out or sustained by such a non-nuclear-weapon state in association or alliance with a nuclear weapon state."
The hon. Gentleman will want to study that declaration, but I think that it gives a reasonable answer to his question.

As I reported to the House when the hon. Gentleman questioned me about it a short time ago, I gave a certain number of undertakings in New York about the steps that we would now take. On a comprehensive test ban treaty, we no longer press for tests on safety grounds because we believe that we can maintain our deterrent without such tests. We have agreed to a cut-off in the production of fissile material and have given the security assurance that I mentioned. I also said that, in a world in which US and Russian nuclear forces were counted in hundreds rather than thousands, Britain would respond to the challenge of multilateral talks on the global reduction of nuclear arms. That corresponds closely to the wording of the declaration that was finally agreed.

The hon. Gentleman is in difficulty here. In the past few weeks, he has spent a good deal of energy setting out at considerable length in the broadsheets which he and his hon. Friends read, and in the *New Statesman and Society,* the reasons why the British Government could not achieve an indefinite extension of the nuclear non-proliferation treaty without making concessions about our deterrent which we were not willing to make. He has been proved entirely wrong. We have managed to join others in notching up this significant achievement for the greater

safety of the world without giving undertakings about our minimum national deterrent, which the hon. Gentleman wrongly said would be indispensable. He is clearly wrong, which is why we had those equivocations today.

We believe that our tactics and strategy were well directed and that we gave undertakings that were necessary, but not further undertakings that would weaken this country's security.

**Mr. David Howell** (Guildford): Does my right hon. Friend accept that the indefinite extension of the treaty is good for the world, and that he and his colleagues in this country have played a significant part in achieving that result? Does he also accept, however, that the problem with all those treaty-based regimes is not so much signing the bits of paper as achieving monitoring, compliance, verification and the underpinning of intelligence, without which none of the treaties will work, because countries will sign them without necessarily complying with them? Will he assure us that resources will be put in place, both nationally and internationally, particularly in the intelligence sphere, to ensure that this treaty-based regime, like those for chemical and biological weapons when those treaties are signed, go forward and are made to work in an increasingly dangerous world?

**Mr. Hurd:** I agree entirely with my right hon. Friend. We need a treaty—we now have one—that is indefinitely extended. But having got the treaty signed, we must ensure that the signatures are worth while. We have anxieties about two countries that have signed the treaty: we have continuing anxieties about North Korea; and we have anxieties about Iran, which have been fairly well documented in recent weeks.

It is important that the IAEA is properly budgeted—the hon. Member for Livingston asked about this—to carry out its duties, and that member states use all their assets and abilities to document the carrying out of the treaty in practice.

**Mr. Menzies Campbell** (Fife, North-East): May I welcome the extension of the treaty, particularly the additional commitment to a test ban treaty? Does the Foreign Secretary share the disappointment of many that, so soon after the decision to extend the treaty, the Chinese Government carried out a nuclear test?

The Foreign Secretary did not refer to the middle east, but he will be aware that that is an area where the proliferation issue is at its most acute. When Israel refuses to acknowledge its possession of nuclear weapons, Iraq has previously signed the non-proliferation treaty but ignored it and Iran is clearly embarked on a programme designed to achieve nuclear capability, how will the treaty assist the issue of nuclear proliferation in the middle east?

**Mr. Hurd:** We noted the Chinese test yesterday. I was not particularly surprised by it, but it shows how far we still have to go. It is worth noting that the Chinese statement includes a clear commitment to abide by a comprehensive test ban treaty when it is agreed. The middle east has been a difficult area of negotiation because of the attitude taken by Israel, which is understandable, but to some extent out of date. The conference passed a resolution on the middle east. It does not single out Israel, but we believe that all non-party states in the middle east—there are several of them—

[*Mr. Hurd*]

should adhere to the treaty and it is particularly important that states with unsafeguarded nuclear facilities should accept safeguards.

**Mr. Nigel Forman** (Carshalton and Wallington): While welcoming the Government's willingness to support extra resources and appropriate personnel for the IAEA, if that proves necessary, will my right hon. Friend say more about the part that we may play in future multilateral negotiations on our strategic deterrent? He mentioned that we may be prepared to join those negotiations if and when the two super-powers, as they were once called, reduce their strategic armoury to roughly our level. Can he confirm that our level represents about 5 per cent., for example, of the American strategic capability?

**Mr. Hurd:** We believe that our level, which has substantially reduced in explosive power in recent years, is the minimum that we need. It is a small proportion of the armoury either of the United States and Russia. As I said in New York and repeated to the House a few minutes ago, a world in which American and Russian nuclear forces were counted in hundreds rather than thousands would be one in which we would respond to the challenge of multinational talks on the global reduction of nuclear arms. That is similar to what the Government have said before. It is reasonable, and it is as far as we could be expected to go.

**Mr. Andrew Faulds** (Warley, East): Perhaps the Foreign Secretary would tell us what is so understandable about Israel's nuclear policy. Other countries could mount exactly identical arguments.

**Mr. Hurd:** It is understandable as, for many years, Israel was surrounded by neighbours who, to varying degrees, were in a state of hostility to her. That has passed, but the policy remains. Israel needs to move, but we can understand the security preoccupations which to some extent hold her back.

**Mr. John Wilkinson** (Ruislip-Northwood): Will my right hon. Friend commend the Government of the Ukraine on their positive programme of dismantling its nuclear forces, thus creating a very satisfactory background for the recent visit of President Clinton, which was an outstanding success? What part did the United Kingdom play in advising Ukrainian authorities on their programme of dismantling their nuclear forces and what part might we and our Western European Union partners play in confidence-building measures to restore Ukraine?

**Mr. Hurd:** My hon. Friend is entirely right. If the Ukraine, which inherited some of the considerable power of the Soviet Union's nuclear weapons stockpile, had acted differently, the whole story would have had a much less happy ending. Ukraine had a political problem and wrestled with it and that was not easy. I and other Foreign Ministers from the west visiting Kiev urged the Ukrainians to move ahead, and they have done so. The result was satisfactory and, as my hon. Friend clearly knows, we and the Americans have given practical help to the Ukraine—for example, in transporting weapons to Russia for decommissioning.

**Mr. David Winnick** (Walsall, North): Should not the Foreign Secretary's words condemning China's nuclear

test yesterday have been stronger? Why is it that, time and time again, excuses are made for that notorious police state? I know that the President of the Board of Trade is in China, but surely—as with South Africa in the past—appeasement does not pay. It is about time we stopped supporting a notorious tyranny.

**Mr. Hurd:** I am not conscious that I was supporting it. I simply explained what happened and what will be the content of the Chinese statement. I hope that the outcome will be a comprehensive test ban treaty that we are prepared to join and by which the Chinese, as they said yesterday, will abide when it is agreed. That is the way to make sure of no more tests of that kind.

**Mr. Harold Elletson** (Blackpool, North): I congratulate my right hon. Friend on the treaty's extension, but is he confident that all its signatories will be as good as their word? Will be specifically comment on the position of the Russian Government, who also signed the conventional forces in Europe treaty but who have completely ignored its provisions, to deploy extra tanks and troops on Russia's southern flank? Russia is also engaged in trying to sell to Iran nuclear reactors capable of producing plutonium.

**Mr. Hurd:** My hon. Friend is, of course, right. One needs the treaty, but one needs also the performance—and that does not necessarily follow the treaty. I cited earlier North Korea and Iran, because we are concerned about the extent to which the treaty is observed in practice in those countries. However, without the treaty, one does not have a leg to stand on in talking to such countries.

I have no reason to doubt Russian good faith, but we and the Russians have a problem in respect of the CFE treaty. I share my hon. Friend's concern about Russia's transactions with Iran, which have to some extent been whittled down as a result of President Clinton's visit to Moscow. Nevertheless, we all continue to feel anxiety about that aspect.

**Mr. Harry Cohen** (Leyton): The treaty requires nuclear weapon states to move towards disarmament. Now that the Government have the indefinite extension that they wanted, how will the disarmament process work? The Defence Select Committee said that Trident was a significant enhancement of the UK's nuclear capacity. If the Foreign Secretary is not to call that Committee a bunch of liars—and I hope not—how will we meet our disarmament obligations?

**Mr. Hurd:** The wording was negotiated with some difficulty and is important. We undertook to take part in working towards a global reduction. It is clear in common sense that the first steps must be taken by countries that have hugely the greatest armouries. That is why I used the phrase in New York and today about the thousands of American and Russian weapons coming down to hundreds. That is a reasonable way of looking at the matter.

In 1998, by comparison with the 1970s, there will be a 59 per cent. reduction in the total explosive power of our deterrent, or 62 per cent. if one leaves maintenance and other stocks out of the calculation. That substantive reduction takes account of the abandonment of nuclear free-fall bombs. No one can seriously argue, unless they are beneath-the-skin devotees of unilateral disarmament, that our deterrent plans can be substantially reduced and yet maintained.

**Mr. Iain Duncan Smith** (Chingford): Now that the treaty has been agreed and signed, does my right hon. Friend acknowledge that the real problem lies with those countries that would proliferate? China, which has just exploded a nuclear device, and North Korea are at the apex, but many scientists are prepared to sell their expertise to countries that have the money, such as Iran. Does my right hon. Friend agree that the real issue is what the west is prepared to do to deter countries that would obtain the technology, develop nuclear weapons and proliferate? Has he established any mechanism for discussing that matter?

**Mr. Hurd:** We consider problems case by case. They certainly exist. China is a nuclear power, so yesterday's test will not be particularly surprising to my hon. Friend or anybody else.

As regards North Korea, there is an agreement with the United States to freeze, and later to dismantle, its nuclear programme. So far, that has been implemented—I emphasise the words "so far".

As for nuclear "professors", of course that is a real problem, particularly out of the Soviet Union, but it is one on which the Russian Government—and all of us—keep a close eye, case by case. So far, the consequences have not been as dangerous as predicted. But my hon. Friend is perfectly right: whether we talk about plutonium or expert knowledge, these are lines of watchfulness that must be carried through.

**Mr. Tam Dalyell** (Linlithgow): In his statement, did we not hear the Foreign Secretary claim that we were working closely with our European Union partners? How come, then, that three members of the EU declined to support any declaration praising Britain and France for our nuclear efforts?

What is being done about French testing in the south Pacific? Should we not give the same support to the Australians, in whose area the testing is being done, as many people in Britain gave the Canadians in the fishing dispute? Why should the Pacific be made filthy by our partners? If we have influence in the Union, why do we not use it?

**Mr. Hurd:** Just as our decision about testing was essentially one for us, so the French decision is one for them. We decided that we no longer need tests in the Nevada desert for the safety of our deterrent—we think there are ways that can be achieved without testing. It was not an easy decision, but we took it on the best advice.

What we aim for—this is true of France and China—is an indefinite ban on testing by which all will abide. The French have the same objective. After the success in New York we need to move forward to get precisely such an agreement.

**Mr. Oliver Heald** (Hertfordshire, North): Does my right hon. Friend agree that the indefinite extension of the treaty is a tremendous success and a vindication of the Government's policy of negotiating from a position of strength? Does he share my concern at the fact that Opposition Members are talking yet again about making one-sided concessions with nothing in return—the old CND, old Labour party? Does he agree that the world is

a safer place because the Government ignored such advice during the 1980s? Will my right hon. Friend continue to ignore it and stand up for Britain's interests?

**Mr. Hurd:** I think that the hon. Member for Livingston (Mr. Cook) and some of his hon. Friends may want to draw a line of forgetfulness under what they have been saying in the past few weeks. They have been proved wrong: my hon. Friend's analysis has been proved right. The only explanation for the excursion by the hon. Member for Livingston into this field has been a dim but fond recollection of the days when he said that Britain should immediately disengage from the nuclear arms race, and that it was nonsense on stilts for Britain to pretend to be a nuclear power. He has had a little nostalgic dream about the fond days of the past when he had a powerful voice but no responsibility. Now, albeit in a shadow way, he has responsibility—and on this occasion he has forgotten it.

**Mrs. Margaret Ewing** (Moray): Of course we all welcome the extension of the treaty, but I would caution the Foreign Secretary that many of us are impatient to see its aims fully implemented.

Will the documents agreed by consensus and to be placed in the Library be backed by a clear list of the countries that assented to or dissented from the consensus, together with the arguments used in each case? Was a baseline set and a timetable laid out for the multilateral negotiations that are to take place once Russia and America agree to reduce their warhead numbers to the minimum deterrent level of the United Kingdom?

**Mr. Hurd:** The answer to the hon. Lady's last question is no. The matter was carried as far as I have explained to the House. I shall see, in answer to the first part of her question, what can be given to her and the House—but the point about a consensus is that everybody agrees.

**Mr. Gary Streeter** (Plymouth, Sutton): Is my right hon. Friend aware that the news that Britain will be retaining its nuclear deterrent will be widely welcomed by all patriots who recognise, albeit reluctantly, that nuclear weapons cannot be uninvented? Does he share my concern that it is obvious from what Opposition Members have said today that the Labour party's commitment to Trident is paper-thin and, in the unlikely event of Labour forming the next Government, they would scrap Trident, leaving Britain unprotected and throwing 4,000 Plymouthians, whose jobs depend on the Trident submarine, out of work?

**Mr. Hurd:** The honest answer to my hon. Friend's question is that nothing about the Opposition's policy on these matters is clear. I thought that it was clear. I really did think until a few months ago that we had a consensus in favour of the Trident programme from all parties in the House. If there were such a consensus, it would be greatly to Britain's advantage. Since then, there has been a lot of cloudiness and a good deal of rowing back and nostalgia for the good old CND days. We look for a clear declaration to sort these matters out.

**Mr. Robert N. Wareing** (Liverpool, West Derby): What encouragement does the Secretary of State believe that he gives to non-nuclear states to stay non-nuclear when he refuses to rule out the first use of our nuclear weapons against a non-nuclear power?

**Mr. Hurd:** That is the argument that the Opposition put before we achieved this agreement. Now that we have

*[Mr. Hurd]*

achieved this agreement, the hon. Gentleman's argument is clearly out of date and wrong. We achieved the agreement without making the concession that he urged on us.

**Mr. Neil Gerrard** (Walthamstow): The Foreign Secretary referred several times to putting our nuclear weapons into multilateral talks when the United States and Russia have reduced their weapon levels to a level similar to ours. Is not the truth of the matter that, on any likely time scale, that will probably happen after Trident has become redundant? So he is saying that Trident will never become part of any multilateral negotiations and that for the next 25 years we will carry on saying to people in the rest of the world who do not have nuclear weapons, "Don't do as we do, do as we say"?

**Mr. Hurd:** The basis of the treaty which has now been indefinitely renewed is the distinction between the five nuclear powers and the non-nuclear powers. That is a matter of history. It is also a matter of fact that, even when START 2 is implemented, British nuclear forces will be considerably less than 10 per cent. of the total nuclear forces available to the United States or Russia. Those are the two countries with the huge armouries.

That is why it is reasonable for us and for the French to say that a world in which American and Russian nuclear forces were no longer counted in thousands but in hundreds would be one where we would be ready to join in multilateral negotiations on the global reduction of nuclear arms. That is a reasonable position. It is not reasonable to ask us, as the Opposition did, to move earlier than that on the subject. They said that only if we moved earlier would we get the indefinite extension of the treaty, and they have been proved wrong.

**Mr. Jeremy Corbyn** (Islington, North): What criticisms were made during the conference, particularly by the Government of Mexico, to the effect that Britain's building, extending, arming and commissioning of the Trident submarine fleet is a breach of the non-proliferation treaty? It is an enormous extension of the seaborne nuclear fire power. Would not Britain's greatest contribution now be to announce that it will decommission its nuclear weapons as part of a progress towards a nuclear-free world?

**Mr. Hurd:** I think that I have answered that question several times. Whatever the Mexicans may say, most people in the House believe that it is in our national interest to have a minimum national deterrent. It was argued that we could not sustain that and renew the treaty indefinitely. We have managed to do so.

**Mr. Paul Flynn** (Newport, West): Has the Foreign Secretary drawn a line of forgetfulness under the written answer that he gave me on 5 April 1990 when, in reply to a request from me to beef up the IAEA inspections of the Iraq nuclear weapons programme, he said that Saddam Hussein was a signatory of the non-proliferation treaty and, as such, the Government had full confidence that he would abide by his international obligations and not work on developing nuclear weapons?

Happily, the Gulf war intervened, or Saddam Hussein would have those nuclear weapons from those three programmes that he was developing despite the NPT. Can the Foreign Secretary give us a guarantee today that the 30 unstable nations in the world that have intercontinental ballistic missiles, which in many cases are run by malign dictators, are not hoodwinking us and the IAEA inspectors in the same way as Saddam Hussein did?

**Mr. Hurd:** Saddam Hussein certainly did do that. It has now been corrected—but at great cost, as the hon. Gentleman rightly points out.

A number of states have not signed the treaty. The hon. Gentleman knows which they are. Obviously, it is desirable for them to do so. A number of states have signed, but we are suspicious about their intentions: I have mentioned two in the House today. That is why we accept that the safeguards of the IAEA should be strengthened, and when there is a considered and costed programme we are prepared to support it.

**Mr. John Hutton** (Barrow and Furness): I welcome the extension of the treaty, but will the Foreign Secretary tell us his view of the legal status of the declaration of principles and objectives that has accompanied its renewal? In particular, what new legal obligations on the United Kingdom Government will result from the extension in relation to a comprehensive test ban treaty and progress towards the global elimination of nuclear weapons?

**Mr. Hurd:** We have given undertakings on both points. I stated those undertakings in New York, and have reported them to the House. They are Government intentions, which we have openly declared.

I do not think that I should chance my arm in regard to the legal status of the declaration. It is not part of the treaty; it is alongside it. I think that it would be sensible if I wrote to the hon. Gentleman with a lawyer's answer. I shall make sure that I get it right, and will place the answer in the Library.

**Mr. Robin Cook:** The Foreign Secretary's reply has clouded the clarity of his opening statement, in which he pointed out that the declaration called for the total elimination of nuclear weapons. He said that he endorsed that declaration; indeed, he even claimed credit for a weighty part in its negotiation.

Unaccountably—although given several opportunities by his own Back Benchers—the Foreign Secretary failed to remind us that his Government are now committed to the total elimination of nuclear weapons. For the avoidance of doubt, will he now tell the House whether he and the Government accept that goal in the declaration and, if so, what specific contribution Britain will make to the elimination of nuclear weapons in the two years that are all that remain to the Government, who will then be out of office?

**Mr. Hurd:** The hon. Gentleman has misquoted me slightly, but only slightly. I reported to the House that the programme of action on disarmament in the declaration stresses the importance of, among other matters, the determined pursuit by the nuclear weapon states of systematic and progressive efforts to reduce nuclear weapons globally, with the ultimate goal of eliminating those weapons. That is true, and it has been true ever since the treaty was signed.

During these exchanges, I have repeatedly answered questions from Opposition Members about how we intend to set about that. What I said about the hundreds of weapons in the United Kingdom and the thousands of weapons possessed by the United States and Russia is the answer to the hon. Gentleman's question.

# Criminal Cases (Evidence Disclosure)

4.7 pm

**The Secretary of State for the Home Department (Mr. Michael Howard):** With permission, Madam Speaker, I would like to make a statement on disclosure of evidence in criminal cases.

The extent to which the law requires the prosecution to disclose evidence in advance of trial has caused increasing concern. It has become more and more apparent that the current arrangements do not serve the interests of justice, and are in need of reform. Today I am publishing a consultation document that sets out the Government's proposals for reforming the law. Subject to that consultation, we intend to legislate to put them into effect as soon as a suitable opportunity occurs.

The current disclosure requirements have given rise to the following problems. First, the sheer volume of material to be disclosed and copied to the defence places a very heavy burden on the police and the prosecuting authorities. The prosecution must make available to the defence large quantities of material, at great expense, much of which may not be relevant to the real issues in the case.

Secondly, under the current arrangements it is difficult to protect from disclosure sensitive material such as the identity of an informant or undercover police officer. The current rules often require disclosure to be made in cases where the actual relevance of that sensitive material may be marginal at best. Disclosure of the identity of an informant may place the informant's life in danger. The prosecution may have to choose between taking that appalling risk and abandoning the case to protect the informant, however strong the other evidence in the case may be.

Let me give an example to illustrate that point. Three individuals were arrested in possession of a number of incendiary devices with which they intended to damage a vehicle used for transporting animals. The evidence against them was overwhelming. Unknown to the police who arrested them, intelligence files were held centrally on the organisation to which the defendants belonged. None of that information was to form part of the prosecution case at the trial, but the trial judge ruled that those files should be disclosed to the defence. Since that would have compromised future investigations, the prosecution decided to offer no evidence rather than comply with the ruling. One of the defendants commented in a statement to the media:

"It was our intention to remove the animals from this vehicle and then damage it. The only reason this trial collapsed was because the prosecution refused to reveal to our defence lawyers material about us held on computer by the police."

Thirdly, the defence is generally not required to disclose anything about its case before the trial. The presentation of a defence at the last minute, with no advance warning to the prosecution, does not contribute to justice. The fact that the defendant has the opportunity to examine the whole of the evidence produced by the prosecution without having to give any indication of his case in advance encourages the manufacture of false defences. That serves to defeat the interests of justice.

The Royal Commission on criminal justice considered what might be done about the current disclosure requirements. The scheme that it devised provides a basis

*[Mr. Michael Howard]*

on which we can build. We agree with it that a statutory disclosure scheme is needed, with the main elements set out in primary legislation underpinned by rules or a code of practice. We also agree with the idea of a phased approach to disclosure, under which the prosecution would disclose certain material at the first stage, the defence would then disclose something of its own case, and additional prosecution disclosure would be related to what the defence had disclosed.

But the test for initial prosecution disclosure that was proposed by the royal commission is very wide-ranging, and would not significantly reduce the current burdens on the police and the prosecuting authorities. The proposals for defence disclosure made by the royal commission are so general that they would not be of any real benefit in narrowing the issues in dispute. In fairness to the royal commission, it did not set out to devise a detailed solution to the problems of disclosure. That is the task of the Government, and it is to the Government's proposals that I now turn.

The task that we have set ourselves is to put in place a system that will reduce the burden of the current disclosure requirements without denying to the defendant access to material to which he should be entitled in the interests of justice. The scheme that I shall set out today would require the investigator to preserve any material gathered or generated during the criminal investigation that led to the charges against the defendant. It would then require the prosecutor to serve on the defence the material upon which he intends to rely at the trial, and also to disclose unused material in his possession, which might undermine the prosecution case.

For example, if part of the prosecution case is a statement by a witness that he saw the accused near the scene of the crime shortly after it was committed, it will be necessary to disclose a statement by another witness that he saw a person of a different description from the accused at the same time and place.

That test for prosecution disclosure is more limited than the current test. It is focused on what the prosecutor knows about the weaknesses in his own case. It does not require him to guess what the defence might be and to disclose anything that may be relevant to any possible defence. The test would also protect sensitive material more effectively than at present. In many cases, information from an informant or the pictures obtained from surveillance equipment are ancillary to the prosecution case and are not needed to prove the charges against the defendant. Such material tends to support the prosecution case rather than to undermine it. Under our proposals, the prosecutor would not need to disclose such material, nor would he need to apply for a court order to protect it.

The second stage in the process would be a requirement for the defendant to provide sufficient particulars of his case to identify the issues in dispute between the defence and the prosecution before the start of the trial. That should include the name and address of any witness whom he proposes to call. That will narrow the issues in dispute and enable the prosecutor to assess whether there is any additional undisclosed material that might assist that defence. If there is, the prosecutor would then be required to disclose it.

This system will work only if there are sanctions to enforce it. The defendant might simply refuse to disclose any details of his defence. If that happens, the prosecution

will be entitled to comment on that failure at trial, and the court will be able to draw whatever inference seems appropriate from it.

That approach will not penalise the defendant who has a genuine defence, who is prepared to disclose it in advance and who maintains it at the trial; nor does it affect the principle that it is the duty of the prosecution to prove the guilt of the defendant beyond reasonable doubt. No defendant will be compelled to incriminate himself. As with the existing provisions on inferences from silence, no one will be convicted simply on the basis of an inference drawn by the court from the response of the defence.

I have set out our proposals in detail in a Command Paper that I have published today. I have placed copies in the Library of the House.

The proposals extend to England and Wales only. My right hon. and learned Friend the Secretary of State for Northern Ireland will be publishing a paper inviting views on the introduction of a similar scheme in Northern Ireland.

There can be no doubt that the current arrangements have undermined public confidence in the criminal justice system by creating a gap between law and justice. My aim is to close that gap. The proposals should prove more effective in convicting the guilty, while continuing to protect the innocent. I commend them to the House.

**Mr. Jack Straw** (Blackburn): The Home Secretary is well aware that, for some time, the current wholly inadequate state of the law on disclosure has been a matter of great concern in this country and in the House. He will also be aware that my right hon. Friend the Leader of the Opposition expressed strong support for the royal commission's proposals when they were originally made two years ago, that my hon. Friend the Member for Cardiff, South and Penarth (Mr. Michael) moved amendments during the passage of Criminal Justice and Public Order Bill seeking better to regulate defence and prosecution disclosure, and that I made proposals to deal with the issue in a speech on 5 April this year to the Police Federation and the British Transport police at their meeting in Southport. The Secretary of State's conversion to the arguments that we have been making for more than two years is therefore welcome.

Public confidence in the criminal justice system is wholly undermined if there is a perception that its procedures and rules inhibit the quest for the truth and result in the innocent being convicted or in the guilty going free. There is widespread public impatience with the present trial process in England and Wales, and a feeling that too much of the system may resemble a game and too little a serious examination of the truth.

Although the overwhelming principle of the criminal justice system must be the protection of the genuinely innocent, does the Secretary of State accept that the whole process of police investigation and the conviction of the guilty would grind to a halt if the identity of informants, sites of surveillance and the identities of members of the public, who often courageously assist such police work, are routinely and gratuitously disclosed to the defence, even though it is not probative of the prosecution case?

Does he further accept that, so great is the current confusion in the law, that, in addition to the examples that the Secretary of State gave, there are a great many other examples of well-founded prosecutions of serious criminals such as armed robbers having to be withdrawn because of the risk to informants' lives or the sites of surveillance, and that there are other occasions when police investigation not probative of the prosecution case could be compromised?

Does the Secretary of State accept that, given that there is a consultative period of almost three months, it would be better if time were taken to reflect on his detailed proposals? May I ask him four specific questions? First, will he give an idea of the time scale that he has in mind for primary legislation? Is it intended to legislate in the next Session of Parliament?

Secondly, relating to that, how does the Secretary of State's time scale in the document relate to the publication and then consideration by the House of the Scott inquiry into the sale of arms to Iraq? As the right hon. and learned Gentleman will know, part of that inquiry deals crucially with the issue of public interest immunity certificates signed by Secretaries of State, which is one means by which relevant evidence can be kept from the court and from the jury.

Thirdly, the Secretary of State said in his statement that there would be a requirement for the defence to disclose the name and address of any witness whom he or she proposed to call. Does he accept that such a requirement could be open to abuse by the prosecution, so there will be strong grounds for there to be safeguards by way of rules about the circumstances, if any, in which such defence witnesses should be approached by the police or the prosecuting authorities?

**Mr. Oliver Heald** (Hertfordshire, North): That is always done in respect of alibis.

**Mr. Straw:** I hear what the hon. Gentleman said, but that is a special circumstance to which the Secretary of State referred.

Fourthly, does the Secretary of State recognise that, while there is no doubt that a new system is needed—something about which I have spoken at length—it is essential that we get the balance right between the needs of the prosecution and the rights of the defence? If we do not, rather than being faced with a strengthening of the process, we shall be faced in future years with more miscarriages of justice. Will the Secretary of State bear it in mind that almost every notorious miscarriage of justice that has come to public attention in recent years has involved a failure of the prosecution at some stage to disclose material evidence?

The Secretary of State said that there would be an obligation on the prosecution, for example, to disclose the statement by another witness that he or she saw a person of a different description from the accused at the same time and place. That is welcome. The Secretary of State also said that there should be sanctions in order to ensure that the system operated. Does he accept that sanctions must apply to the prosecution as well as to the defence and that, where there is a wilful failure by the police or the prosecution to disclose relevant evidence of the type of which he spoke, that should be a matter for the disciplinary rules of the police and the prosecuting authorities and should, in some cases, be made a criminal offence?

**Mr. Howard:** I am grateful to the hon. Gentleman for what I took to be his general welcome for the thrust of the proposals. He asked four specific questions. On the time scale for legislation, he will understand that I cannot go beyond what I said in my statement, which is that, subject to the consultation exercise, we intend to legislate as soon as a suitable opportunity occurs.

As I have no idea what will emerge from the Scott inquiry, the hon. Gentleman will understand that I cannot answer his question about any relationship between what may emerge from the report of that inquiry and these proposals. It must remain entirely a matter for speculation as to whether there will be any relationship between any recommendations in the report and these proposals.

I agree with what was said by my hon. Friend the Member for Hertfordshire, North (Mr. Heald), albeit from a sedentary position, about the requirement for the defence to disclose the names and addresses of witnesses. That is already a requirement in the context of an alibi defence. We propose to build on that and to adopt a similar approach to that which already exists in that context. Therefore, I see no great difficulty there.

Of course we must seek the right balance between the needs of the prosecution and the rights of the defence. We have not had that balance in the past. The system has been weighted too much in favour of the criminal and against the protection of the public, and it is that imbalance which I sought to put right in the Criminal Justice and Public Order Act 1994 and in these proposals.

The hon. Gentleman began his contribution in an extraordinary way. He sought to take credit for having thought of these things first. He talked about the proposals that he put forward in his speech to the British Transport police on 5 April. It would be as well if I reminded the House what those proposals were. He proposed that the matter be sent to the Law Commission. That was the extent of the hon. Gentleman's proposals on 5 April.

As for the amendment moved by the hon. Member for Cardiff, South and Penarth (Mr. Michael) in the Standing Committee debating the Criminal Justice and Public Order Bill, it was not moved as a free-standing change to the law but, as he made absolutely clear when he was moving it, as an alternative to the Government's proposals to provide for inferences to be drawn from the right to silence. He said that the Committee had

"a choice between the Government's proposal to abolish the right to silence"—

he got that wrong—

"and the Opposition's alternative".—[*Official Report, Standing Committee B*, 1 February 1994; c. 351.]

Perhaps the hon. Gentleman will tell us whether he still opposes our proposals on the right to silence or whether he now joins the Government, the police and the Lord Chief Justice, who all think that the changes to the law are sensible, balanced and reasonable.

**Sir Ivan Lawrence** (Burton): Just as my right hon. and learned Friend has already dealt with miscarriages of justice involving the conviction of the innocent, so he is now dealing with those involving the acquittal of the guilty. I think that most people will support the broad thrust of the proposals. In particular, both sides in a criminal trial will welcome any provision that reduces the mass of paper that currently flies about in all directions at great public expense. Also, most people will agree that the defence ought to expose the broad nature of the defence ahead of the trial so that the issues can be narrowed down and the trial shortened.

[*Sir Ivan Lawrence*]

Some care must be taken, however, to provide safeguards when the defence has to disclose the names and addresses of potential witnesses, not all of whom are necessarily people of clean and impeccable background and who might be deterred from giving evidence in the first place, which would be in conflict with justice. There must be protection, and it is not enough for my right hon. and learned Friend to say that we already have that requirement in respect of alibis, because in those circumstances the courts do not require the alibi notice to be given effect in the course of a trial if they do not think that justice will be done. If my right hon. and learned Friend does not want the courts to circumnavigate his proposal, appropriate safeguards must be established.

I welcome the fact that this is a consultation document from which, we hope, all kinds of recommendations will flow and be heard before legislation is implemented.

**Mr. Howard:** I am grateful to my hon. and learned Friend for his general support of the proposals. He of course brings considerable experience and expertise to bear on his consideration of these matters. I note what he says about the proposal that the defence should be required to make available the names and addresses of witnesses. I do not entirely share his concerns in that respect, but he is quite right to point out that the document is to be the basis of a consultation exercise and I shall, of course, listen carefully to all the issues raised during the consultation exercise.

**Mr. Simon Hughes** (Southwark and Bermondsey): I join the general response being given to the Home Secretary's proposals. They go in the right direction, and it is clearly correct that there should be a royal commission set of recommendations, a consultation paper and, eventually, legislation.

The idea that the defence must also assist in the trial and not keep its hand secret to the last is not only right but meets the public's desire to secure a more correct balance.

The matter that probably needs the most careful adjudication—a matter on which the right hon. and learned Gentleman touched and to which he is clearly alert—is that of who determines what material gathered or held by the prosecution may or may not be relevant to the defence and is required to be seen in advance by the defence.

There is, of course, a difference between incidentally held material, as in the example that the Home Secretary gave, which should not be disclosed, and material gathered in the course of investigating a case, which the prosecution may not regard as relevant either to support or undermine the case, but which the defence should see in order to ensure that it knows the full range of the case assembled against it. If that matter can be adjudicated fairly, there will further grounds for belief that the balance will be far better in future.

**Mr. Howard:** I am grateful to the hon. Gentleman for his support for the proposals. I understand the point that he made. He has put his finger on the heart of that part of the set of proposals which will need the most careful consideration. I would suggest to the hon. Gentleman, and I hope that he will accept, that the requirement on the defence to identify the essence of its defence will help to achieve a proper resolution of the considerations to which

he referred. It will help to achieve a better balance in the interests of justice. I entirely agree, however, that we shall have to consider the matter very carefully in the light of the views expressed in the consultation exercise.

**Several hon. Members** *rose—*

**Madam Speaker:** Order. Before we proceed, I remind hon. Members that I have to keep in mind the other business that the House has to conduct today. Therefore, I ask for brisk questions and brisk answers so that we might move on to other business fairly soon.

**Mr. Julian Brazier** (Canterbury): In strongly welcoming the proposals, may I urge my right hon. and learned Friend to look again at section 78 of the Police and Criminal Evidence Act 1984, which is being used to introduce an agent provocateur argument through the back door? Even with the new guidelines, it could still be used to deny juries the opportunity to hear the evidence because the prosecution needs to protect an informer.

**Mr. Howard:** I shall certainly give my hon. Friend an undertaking to look at that section, and I am grateful for the welcome that he gave the proposals.

**Mr. John Fraser** (Norwood): Given escalating costs of criminal defence, will the Home Secretary think twice before introducing disclosure provisions for summary trials, most of which end in convictions in any event? The effect of the proposals in that case would be only to lengthen the process and add to the expense. Is not non-disclosure the crucial issue? Of course we must protect people from intimidation in a society of guns and great amounts of money, but the crucial issue is surely who makes the decision about disclosure and what the sanctions are if he or she gets it wrong.

**Mr. Howard:** I am not sure that I share the hon. Gentleman's concerns about cost. We are all, of course, concerned about cost, but I hope that the effect of the proposals, relieving as they do the police and the prosecution from the voluminous burdens placed on them, will be to reduce the costs of criminal trials. That is one of the questions on which I specifically invite views in the consultation paper. I take the hon. Gentleman's point about the importance of proper disclosure being made by the prosecution. That is, of course, as he is quite right to say, at the heart of the proposals.

**Mr. James Couchman** (Gillingham): My right hon. and learned Friend will be aware that his announcement is very welcome news. He will also be aware that several of our Kent colleagues and I have been conveying to him the views of our chief constable on the question of disclosure. Is he confident that his proposed steps will meet the various concerns of the police as they have been represented to him? There is no doubt whatever that the acquittal of serious criminals—because of the disclosure procedures heretofore—is a major affront to the criminal justice system.

**Mr. Howard:** I am grateful to my hon. Friend for his support. Indeed, I am aware of the views of the chief constable of Kent, not only through representations made by my hon. Friend and other colleagues from Kent, but because the chief constable personally has left me in no doubt of his strong views on the matter. I am not able to report to the House the chief constable's reactions to the proposals, but the president of the Police Superintendents Association of England and Wales has already given them a very warm welcome.

**Mr. David Trimble** (Upper Bann): I am sure that the Home Secretary realises that the proposals are broadly welcomed by myself and my colleagues. He is quite right that the high volume of material can simply lead to mistakes. I became aware of a case in my constituency in recent weeks of a mistake enabling a terrorist organisation to issue direct threats to witnesses, notwithstanding ceasefires.

May I query the procedures with regard to Northern Ireland? Does the Home Secretary realise that, on this matter, the legal system and the law in Northern Ireland are not significantly different? I must therefore query why we must have a separate consultation exercise. Cannot the two proceed in tandem? Cannot the changes be made by one piece of legislation, as is happening with the Criminal Appeal Bill? As he knows, during consultation on that Bill, practitioners in Northern Ireland said that they wanted to be included in the legislation. I worry that a different procedure would enable the Northern Ireland Office to drag its feet, to prevent proper discussion of Northern Ireland matters in the House.

**Mr. Howard:** I am grateful to the hon. Gentleman for his welcome of the proposals, but I do not think that there is any basis for the strictures that he has passed on the Northern Ireland Office. I have said that my right hon. and learned Friend the Secretary of State for Northern Ireland intends to publish similar proposals for Northern Ireland. The hon. Gentleman will understand that I am not in a position today to give him any assurance about the legislative vehicle for such proposals, but I am sure that it will be the intention of my right hon. and learned Friend, as it is mine, to proceed with due expedition on the matter.

**Mr. David Ashby** (Leicestershire, North-West): My right hon. and learned Friend will know that disclosure has reached ridiculous proportions, and that his reconsideration of the subject is welcome. However, he should be mindful of the fact that some of the most notorious cases that have reached the Court of Appeal have resulted from non-disclosure. The Crown Prosecution Service takes a lot of reminding that all its staff and all of us who are prosecutors are administrators of justice, and we must all ensure that justice is done.

One specific matter that I wish to raise is the fact that, despite that great idea about alibis, alibi notices are being ignored. Does my right hon. and learned Friend agree that, if we are to have disclosure by the defence—and that is right—it should perhaps be accompanied by an opening statement by the defence in front of the jury? Would it not assist the jury enormously to hear the prosecution speech and then a defence statement, so that it knew what issues to look for in the evidence?

**Mr. Howard:** I am grateful to my hon. Friend for his support. His precise suggestion goes somewhat beyond the proposals as they stand, but I am perfectly prepared to consider it in the context of the consultation exercise.

**Mr. Chris Mullin** (Sunderland, South): I welcome the Home Secretary's proposals in so far as they are intended to make the criminal trial a process of truth seeking. Does the right hon. and learned Gentleman see that there is a

danger that when the defence case is disclosed in advance, the police or the prosecution may be tempted to try to nobble witnesses—or to "refresh their memories", to use a phrase that I have heard? Does he recall that, in the Guildford case, for example, a key defence witness was seen off by the threat of being charged with the offences with which four innocent people were eventually charged? That disposed of him for 15 years.

**Mr. Howard:** I do not think that it is at all appropriate to infer from particular cases, however serious, generalised allegations about a propensity on the part of the police to behave in the way that the hon. Gentleman has imputed to them. I do not believe that what he suggests would happen. During the consultation exercise, we can consider the importance of putting in place proper safeguards.

**Mr. Michael Stephen** (Shoreham): Does my right hon. and learned Friend accept that his proposals will be widely welcomed both in my constituency and throughout the country? It is surely in the interests of justice that both parties to a criminal trial should know what case they have to meet before the trial begins. My constituents are sick and tired of hardened criminals escaping conviction by springing ambush defences on the prosecution.

**Mr. Howard:** I am grateful to my hon. Friend. I entirely agree with his assessment of the view of the public, and I share that view.

**Mr. Mike O'Brien** (Warwickshire, North): I, too, welcome the Home Secretary's efforts to deal with what has become the farce of disclosure—both in terms of the volume of material, and because of the way in which witnesses for the prosecution can have their names disclosed to the prejudice of the trial. I was also greatly shocked when a senior police officer told me of a murder case that had to be dropped because of such problems.

The importance of dealing with disclosure lies in the detail. Will the Home Secretary give us the assurance that, both during the consultation process and, more importantly, when legislation comes before the House, he and his fellow Ministers will deal with it in the most bipartisan way possible, so that we can get the detail right and provide lasting rules on disclosure, which will avoid miscarriages of justice, and which can be preserved over a long period as good law?

**Mr. Howard:** I am grateful to the hon. Gentleman for his support for the proposals. I am perfectly happy to give him the undertaking that both during the consultation exercise and while any legislation is being taken through Parliament, we shall consider the detailed suggestions made in as clear-headed, receptive and objective a way as possible. Our only aim is to achieve the best possible balance and the best possible system of criminal justice. That is what we regard as the ultimate goal of all our endeavours.

**Mr. John Greenway** (Ryedale): My right hon. and learned Friend knows of my concerns about this matter over many years. Those concerns reflect in particular those of the police about the burdens placed on them by the present arrangements. I am also concerned that, as has been made clear this afternoon, many trials have collapsed as a consequence. Given that the consultation and legislation will take several months, and given that so many of the difficult decisions that have been taken

[*Mr. John Greenway*]

relating to disclosure seem to be matters of interpretation and discretion by the judiciary, can my right hon. and learned Friend tell the House what arrangements he, my right hon. and noble Friend the Lord Chancellor and my right hon. and learned Friend the Attorney-General might have in mind to improve the guidelines to judges for the current disclosure rules? My right hon. and learned Friend will know that there is still some concern about those guidelines and the way in which they are exercised.

**Mr. Howard:** My hon. Friend is entirely right to remind the House of the concerns that he has expressed on the matter for a long period, and I am grateful to him for the suggestions that he made. I fear, however, that I cannot respond as positively as I might like to his invitation to issue guidance to the judiciary. It is not a matter for me, nor is it a matter for my right hon. and noble Friend the Lord Chancellor. It is a matter for the courts, the Court of Appeal and perhaps the Lord Chief Justice.

**Mr. Tam Dalyell** (Linlithgow): With the dark horse in the next Secretary of State for Scotland stakes sitting beside him, could the Home Secretary tell the House what the position is in relation to Scottish law, and in particular to disclosure? The right hon. and learned Gentleman will know of the great anxieties that many serious people have over the biggest case of murder against western civilians since 1945—that is, Lockerbie.

In relation to the English responsibilities—since some evidence was found in England—could the Home Secretary look at Mr. Francovitch's film, which appeared last Thursday night, and ask senior officials at the Home Office whether there are any conclusions relating to the non-disclosure of evidence which the Crown Office said it has, as that is a matter that pertains to the Home Office?

**Mr. Howard:** I am not sure which would be the greater lack of wisdom—to draw inferences from the film to which the hon. Gentleman referred, or for me to try to explain to the House the Scottish law on disclosure. I am certainly aware of my limitations, so I have no intention of responding to the hon. Gentleman's request. I have no doubt that he will raise the matter in due course with my right hon. Friend the Secretary of State for Scotland.

**Mr. Nick Hawkins** (Blackpool, South): I very much welcome what my right hon. and learned Friend has said today, and I particularly welcome his response to the royal commission's comments about the need for the prosecution to provide such vast amounts of material for the defence, particularly in cases in which serious professional criminals can comb through that material in the hope of chancing upon something that might provide a defence. That has been an abuse for many years, and I hope that, after the consultation period, my right hon. and learned Friend will produce legislative proposals to correct that mischief as soon as possible—preferably in the next Session.

On the day when the true attitude of Labour Front-Bench Members has been shown by the attempt of the hon. Member for Brent, South (Mr. Boateng) and his colleagues to compromise the independence of the judiciary by threatening to politicise them, may I once again congratulate my right hon. and learned Friend on ensuring that the guilty are convicted and are not slipping out on technicalities?

**Mr. Howard:** I am grateful to my hon. Friend for his support. We shall look at the point that he made during the consultation exercise, and I share his views. I do not wish to extend the scope of these questions and answers by referring to the proposals made by the hon. Member for Brent, South (Mr. Boateng).

**Mr. Gary Streeter** (Plymouth, Sutton): My right hon. and learned Friend will be aware that much damage has been done to the reputation of the criminal justice system in the past few years by apparently guilty men getting away on legal technicalities. Is he aware that the most important point resulting from his announcement today is that it will start to restore public confidence in the criminal justice system by putting guilty men where they belong—behind bars?

**Mr. Howard:** My hon. Friend is right to put his finger on that point. We must enhance public confidence in the criminal justice system, and everything that I have sought to do in my two years in this job has been designed to achieve that objective. The proposals certainly will play their part in taking that objective forward.

**Mr. Oliver Heald** (Hertfordshire, North): Does my right hon. and learned Friend agree that the importance of the new procedure is that it will have an impact on every criminal case, by narrowing the issues and reducing the amount of disclosure that is required? It will therefore save time, and make the administration of justice in England and Wales much more efficient. Does he accept that the proposals go further and are far better than the amendments tabled by the Labour party in Committee on the Criminal Justice and Public Order Act 1994? Those amendments did not involve any substantial reduction in the amount of disclosure that has to be made, whereas these proposals do. Will not the photocopiers of the Crown Prosecution Service run more quietly as a result?

**Mr. Howard:** My hon. Friend is entirely right. In recognition of the inadequacy of the proposals put forward by the hon. Member for Cardiff, South and Penarth in the Standing Committee, the hon. Member for Blackburn (Mr. Straw) decided that, rather than adopting the course suggested by his hon. Friend, he would send the matter off to the Law Commission. The hon. Member for Blackburn was right to recognise those deficiencies, but we have been able to find a satisfactory solution without the further delay that referring the matter to the Law Commission would involve.

# Points of Order

4.45 pm

**Mr. Richard Tracey** (Surbiton): On a point of order, Madam Speaker. On a number of occasions, I have heard you speak to the House about the use of House of Commons notepaper and the House's portcullis insignia, and all hon. Members have received guidelines on the matter from the Serjeant at Arms. I have before me a letter to a business man on House of Commons notepaper, which promotes a conference involving leading members of the Opposition Front Bench. The letter is signed by one of those hon. Members. Delegates are asked to pay £295 a head for the conference, which is to be organised by professional conference organisers called Hobsbawm Macaulay Communications Ltd., which is obviously a commercial operation.

It seems to me that that is an abuse of House of Commons paper and insignia. In the light of what Lord Nolan has been saying to all of us in the past few days, surely that is the type of abuse that the House should not allow.

**Madam Speaker:** The hon. Gentleman was courteous enough to let me have a copy of the item to which he referred, although I have only been able to glance at it. He knows that the supervision and enforcement of the regulations that govern the use of the portcullis and of House of Commons stationery is a matter for the Serjeant at Arms. I would appreciate it if he let the Serjeant at Arms have a copy of the correspondence to which he referred.

**Mr. Donald Dewar** (Glasgow, Garscadden): On a point of order, Madam Speaker. I understand that an announcement about the jobseeker's allowance was made a short while ago in another place. The other place has been told that the introduction of the allowance has been postponed from April 1996 to October 1996. I have no idea why that has been done. I do not know whether it is due to a systems failure or administrative problems, or whether it is a political and tactical retreat because of the unpopularity of the legislation. But it seems to me that the House should be told, and I wonder whether you have received any indication from Ministers of an intention to come to the House to explain what is a major development in a sensitive area of policy.

**Madam Speaker:** I have not been informed that the Government are seeking to make a statement on the matter, but those on the Treasury Bench will have made a note of what the hon. Gentleman said. I understand that, in due course—I cannot tell the hon. Gentleman when "due course" is—we shall be receiving an amendment from the Lords. I understand the hon. Gentleman's impatience at this time.

**Mrs. Ann Taylor** (Dewsbury): Further to that point of order, Madam Speaker.

**Madam Speaker:** I do not think that there can be anything further to that point of order, as I have made a ruling. I cannot give any more information, although the hon. Lady may have some information to give the House.

**Mrs. Taylor:** May I seek your guidance? Would it be possible, at a suitable point during today's business—perhaps after a vote—for the appropriate Secretary of State to come to the House to make a statement on the matter raised by my hon. Friend the Member for Glasgow, Garscadden (Mr. Dewar)?

**Madam Speaker:** I am always available to a Minister who seeks to inform me that he wishes to make a statement. If that were the case, I would be here in the Chair to deal with that statement.

# Employment of Illegal Immigrants

4.48 pm

**Mr. Nigel Waterson** (Eastbourne): I beg to move,

That leave be given to bring in a Bill to make it unlawful to employ an illegal immigrant; and for connected purposes.

Rarely have so many people been on the move across the globe. Millions of people, both economic migrants and genuine asylum seekers, are abandoning their countries and looking for a better, or at least a safer, life elsewhere. It is a problem faced by every advanced country. The recent reimposition of some border controls in "Schengenland" underlines the problem, which must be faced with both firmness and fairness.

How big is the problem? Estimates vary dramatically. The Home Office is quick to point out that there are no official estimates of the number of illegal immigrants in the United Kingdom. The Home Secretary said recently:

"by its very nature, illegal immigration is difficult to measure and any estimates would be highly speculative."—[*Official Report*, 20 April 1995; Vol. 258, *328*]

We know that, in 1994, 7,240 illegal entrants were detected and, in the same period, 3,670 were removed or departed voluntarily from the UK. In addition, 4,750 persons were issued with a notice of intention to deport.

Mr. Peter Tompkins, the former chief inspector of the immigration service, claimed that almost 40,000 illegal immigrants enter the UK a year. In his view, immigration officers catch only about one in seven illegal immigrants. There has been a sharp growth in the number of cases from eastern Europe and north Africa and, with 1997 looming, there must be worries about potential immigration from Hong Kong.

One of the most worrying statistics is the extent to which asylum is being abused. In 1994, about 80 per cent. of asylum decisions were outright refusals.

A significant number of those employed in hotels and restaurants, in factories or on farms at harvest time will be illegal immigrants. That is not a problem that any responsible Government could ignore and yet, bizarrely—this is the central thrust of my Bill—it is not an offence at present to employ an illegal immigrant and there is no general requirement on employers to satisfy themselves about the immigration status of their employees.

Of course, it is an offence to assist illegal entry, and it has been held that acts to facilitate entry into the United Kingdom can be pursued under that provision, even once the illegal immigrant has already got through the port of entry and perhaps has even started work.

Another existing offence is harbouring. It is an offence knowingly to harbour anyone who one may know, or have reasonable cause for believing, is either an illegal immigrant or an overstayer, or is in breach of a condition not to work or to register with the police. The offence is triable only summarily, with a penalty of a fine or a maximum of six months' imprisonment and prosecutions are rare.

There is clearly a yawning gap in the law. A statutory requirement should be laid on employers of permanent and casual labour that they must check the immigration status of job applicants. If they are not satisfied, they should refuse to employ them and, ideally, pass the relevant information on to the authorities. I do not believe that that would be an onerous burden on employers, for I believe strongly in the Government's deregulation initiative.

Taking a lead from the offence of harbouring, the prosecution should have to show that the employer knew or had reasonable cause to believe that the person he employed was an illegal entrant or an overstayer, or was in breach of conditions. That would give the requisite element of what we lawyers call mens rea. Penalties should be tough—heavy fines and a maximum prison term of up to five years. There should also be a right of trial at the Crown court for serious cases.

I am delighted to have seen recently some press speculation that my right hon. and learned Friend the Secretary of State for the Home Department has it in mind to introduce such legislation in the next Queen's Speech.

My Bill calls for one measure, but I recognise that a range of measures are needed to tackle the growing problem. We must continue to operate our own strict border controls, in line with the 1985 European Union declaration. There must be no question of article 7a of the treaty of Rome being allowed to dilute our determination.

Next, we must develop a more efficient and fraud-proof system for the issue of national insurance numbers. We must also continue to crack down on social security excesses. My right hon. Friend the Secretary of State for Social Security has already gone to great lengths to combat fraud and deter so-called benefit tourists. We have to go further.

As I pointed out, the great majority of applications for asylum are bogus. Furthermore, most asylum seekers originally enter this country as visitors or students and on the basis that they will not become a charge on the public purse. It is only later—sometimes a very short time later—that they claim asylum. That entitles them to claim a range of benefits: income support at 90 per cent. of the full rate, housing benefit, council tax benefit and family credit. An asylum seeker is also allowed free medical treatment under the national health service and, if receiving income support, free prescriptions, medical and dental treatment and concessionary eye treatment.

In 1985, 5,060 asylum seekers were awaiting a decision. That figure had risen to 55,000 last year, of which, statistically, 80 per cent. will turn out to be bogus. Yet, as long as those 55,000 are waiting for a decision, they are entitled to all the benefits that I described. The British have always been a fair and generous people, but enough is enough.

Above all, we must press ahead with a compulsory and comprehensive system of identity cards. They will have many benefits, not least in tracking down illegal immigrants and overstayers.

**Mr. John Spellar** (Warley, West): On a point of order, Mr. Deputy Speaker. None of these issues relate to the Bill as it was outlined on the Order Paper.

**Mr. Deputy Speaker (Mr. Michael Morris):** The most recent contribution was going rather wide of the Bill, and I hope that the hon. Member for Eastbourne (Mr. Waterson) will return to the specifics.

**Mr. Waterson:** To return to the central theme of my Bill, I have no doubt that it will provoke some howls of protest from Opposition Members and from some of the organisations that purport to represent the best interests of ethnic minorities, but I hope that they will come to recognise that the present situation is simply unfair. It is unfair on the indigenous population and it is unfair on legal immigrants—the existing ethnic minorities in this country.

Perhaps above all, it is unfair on those illegal immigrants who are employed in restaurant kitchens, sweatshops and the fields as a modern form of slave labour. They are often paid minimal wages by employers who know that, no matter how harsh the conditions, the workers will not and cannot complain.

Hon. Members may have seen recent press reports about a sweatshop in London employing illegal Turkish workers. Hours are long and conditions basic. There is no canteen and little attempt to ensure health and safety at work. A worker can earn as little as £1.50 an hour and there is no overtime rate. Recently, half the sweatshop's 60 workers walked out in a dispute over piece rates. The Turkish owner called the police and the workers fled— some jumping from second-floor windows. Pay rates for those who remain have been cut in retaliation. We owe it as much to those people as to our own British citizens to put a stop to that sort of practice.

4.57 pm

**Mr. Neil Gerrard** (Walthamstow): The Bill could have been made to sound reasonable, at least to some people outside this House who have been fed myths about the extent of illegal immigration and how easy it is to evade controls.

I will speak briefly against the Bill because it foreshadows a debate that we will probably have at greater length in the next few weeks, if some of the reports that have been trailed in the press recently are anything to go by. We have been told that, even now, Ministers are planning to introduce controls and that the Bill, or something very like it, is one of the options that they have considered.

The comment in *The Guardian* last week summed up what is going on. It said:

"Never have the hurdles to enter Britain been so high, yet ministers are even now planning a series of . . . trip wires to catch the slim numbers of illegal immigrants who do slip through. What's going on? An election is approaching."

That is precisely what the proposed legislation is about. It is being presented as if thousands of illegal immigrants were employed in hotels and sweat shops, but there is no evidence whatsoever to support that claim.

**Mr. Nick Hawkins** (Blackpool, South): Will the hon. Gentleman give way?

**Mr. Gerrard:** No, I wish to be brief.

If it is true—I suspect that it is—that illegal immigrants are working in sweatshops making clothes and the like, the hon. Member for Eastbourne (Mr. Waterson) should have thought of an alternative solution—a minimum wage. Employers would then have no incentive or ability to employ people in sweatshops.

My main concern is what will happen as a consequence of the Bill. If you, Mr. Deputy Speaker, or I were to apply for a job with such legislation in place, we would not be asked about our immigration status for the simple reason that our skin is white, but many of my constituents from Pakistan or the Caribbean—decent, law-abiding British

citizens—will be asked to prove their immigration status. I ask the House to consider what the Bill would do for race relations.

Moreover, how could employers with no expertise in the matter be qualified to make the judgment that the Bill asks them to make? It is not simple to decide someone's immigration status. The result would simply be checks on everyone who is not white, and deteriorating race relations. I do not argue in favour of illegal immigration, although we could argue whether the present immigration laws are fair and reasonable, but that is not what the debate is about.

The Bill is based on prejudice and, if implemented, it would foster prejudice and destroy good race relations. It is a nasty, vicious little proposal, which I hope will get no further in the House.

*Question put, pursuant to Standing Order No. 19 (Motions for leave to bring in Bills and nomination of Select Committees at commencement of public business):—*

*The House divided:* Ayes 74, Noes 65.

**Division No. 148]**                                    **[5.01 pm**

AYES

Allason, Rupert (Torbay)
Ashby, David
Atkinson, David (Bour'mouth E)
Banks, Matthew (Southport)
Batiste, Spencer
Bendall, Vivian
Body, Sir Richard
Booth, Hartley
Butcher, John
Butterfill, John
Carlisle, John (Luton North)
Carrington, Matthew
Carttiss, Michael
Clark, Dr Michael (Rochford)
Clifton-Brown, Geoffrey
Congdon, David
Coombs, Anthony (Wyre For'st)
Cope, Rt Hon Sir John
Couchman, James
Davies, Quentin (Stamford)
Day, Stephen
Deva, Nirj Joseph
Duncan-Smith, Iain
Dunn, Bob
Durant, Sir Anthony
Elletson, Harold
Fabricant, Michael
Fishburn, Dudley
Gardiner, Sir George
Greenway, Harry (Ealing N)
Griffiths, Peter (Portsmouth, N)
Hargreaves, Andrew
Harris, David
Hill, James (Southampton Test)
Howell, Sir Ralph (N Norfolk)
Hunter, Andrew
Jenkin, Bernard
Jessel, Toby
Jones, Nigel (Cheltenham)

Jopling, Rt Hon Michael
Kellett-Bowman, Dame Elaine
Lamont, Rt Hon Norman
McLoughlin, Patrick
Marshall, John (Hendon S)
Marshall, Sir Michael (Arundel)
Mills, Iain
Mitchell, Sir David (NW Hants)
Moate, Sir Roger
Molyneaux, Rt Hon James
Montgomery, Sir Fergus
Neubert, Sir Michael
Pattie, Rt Hon Sir Geoffrey
Porter, David (Waveney)
Powell, William (Corby)
Riddick, Graham
Robathan, Andrew
Shaw, David (Dover)
Smith, Tim (Beaconsfield)
Smyth, The Reverend Martin
Spicer, Sir James (W Dorset)
Spicer, Michael (S Worcs)
Spink, Dr Robert
Spring, Richard
Tapsell, Sir Peter
Thompson, Sir Donald (C'er V)
Thornton, Sir Malcolm
Townend, John (Bridlington)
Vaughan, Sir Gerard
Walker, Bill (N Tayside)
Wardle, Charles (Bexhill)
Waterson, Nigel
Wilshire, David
Winterton, Nicholas (Macc'f'ld)
Yeo, Tim

**Tellers for the Ayes:**
    **Mr. Nick Hawkins and**
    **Mr. John Sykes.**

NOES

Ainsworth, Robert (Cov'try NE)
Austin-Walker, John
Barnes, Harry
Bayley, Hugh
Bennett, Andrew F
Bermingham, Gerald

Caborn, Richard
Campbell, Mrs Anne (C'bridge)
Campbell, Menzies (Fife NE)
Campbell, Ronnie (Blyth V)
Cann, Jamie
Clapham, Michael

Clwyd, Mrs Ann
Connarty, Michael
Cunningham, Jim (Covy SE)
Dalyell, Tam
Donohoe, Brian H
Eagle, Ms Angela
Enright, Derek
Etherington, Bill
Evans, John (St Helens N)
Gapes, Mike
Gerrard, Neil
Godman, Dr Norman A
Godsiff, Roger
Gordon, Mildred
Graham, Thomas
Grant, Bernie (Tottenham)
Gunnell, John
Harvey, Nick
Hughes, Robert (Aberdeen N)
Hutton, John
Jackson, Helen (Shef'ld, H)
Janner, Greville
Jones, Lynne (B'ham S O)
Khabra, Piara S
Lewis, Terry
Livingstone, Ken
McAllion, John
Macdonald, Calum

McMaster, Gordon
McNamara, Kevin
MacShane, Denis
Madden, Max
Mahon, Alice
Michie, Bill (Sheffield Heeley)
Mitchell, Austin (Gt Grimsby)
Morris, Rt Hon Alfred (Wy'nshawe)
Oakes, Rt Hon Gordon
O'Hara, Edward
Parry, Robert
Patchett, Terry
Rendel, David
Rooney, Terry
Ross, Ernie (Dundee W)
Sedgemore, Brian
Skinner, Dennis
Steel, Rt Hon Sir David
Taylor, Matthew (Truro)
Timms, Stephen
Tipping, Paddy
Wicks, Malcolm
Wise, Audrey
Wray, Jimmy
Young, David (Bolton SE)

**Tellers for the Noes:**
   **Mr. Harry Cohen and**
   **Mr. Jeremy Corbyn.**

*Question accordingly agreed to.*

Bill ordered to be brought in by Mr. Nigel Waterson, Dame Elaine Kellett-Bowman, Mrs. Angela Knight, Mr. John Marshall, Mr. John Sykes, Mr. Harold Elletson, Mr. Harry Greenway, Mr. Spencer Batiste, Mr. David Shaw, Mr. James Clappison, Mr. Charles Hendry and Dr. Robert Spink.

### EMPLOYMENT OF ILLEGAL IMMIGRANTS

Mr. Nigel Waterson accordingly presented a Bill to make it unlawful to employ an illegal immigrant; and for connected purposes: And the same was read the First time; and ordered to be read a Second time upon Friday 14 July and to be printed. [Bill 123.]

## SITTINGS OF THE HOUSE

*Motion made, and Question put forthwith, pursuant to Order [19 December],*

That this House, at its rising on Thursday 25th May, do adjourn till Tuesday 6th June.—*[Mr. Bates.]*

*Question agreed to.*

# Orders of the Day
## Gas Bill
*As amended (in the Standing Committee), further considered.*

### Clause 8

STANDARD CONDITIONS OF LICENCES

*Amendment made:* No. 3, in page 11, line 25, leave out 'and 26(1A)' and insert ', 26(1A) and 27(1A)'.— *[Mr. Eggar.]*

5.13 pm

**Mr. Nigel Griffiths** (Edinburgh, South): I beg to move amendment No. 52, in page 12, line 41, at end add—

'(3) Standard conditions for gas suppliers shall include a duty on licence holders to take account of the needs of low income customers in laying down methods of payment and procedures regarding debt and disconnection.'.

**Mr. Deputy Speaker (Mr. Michael Morris):** With this, it will be convenient to discuss amendment No. 53, in page 12, line 41, at end add—

'(3) Standard conditions for gas suppliers shall include a duty on licence holders to provide special services including those services that must be delivered by appropriately qualified home service advisers for meeting the needs of consumers of gas conveyed through pipes who are disabled or aged 60 years and over.'.

**Mr. Griffiths:** The amendments are important because they concern the role of home service advisers who help elderly, disabled and blind people in their homes. At a face-to-face meeting, British Gas told me that it had to cut the budget in that sector to compete with the new firms that the Government seek to bring into the gas market. British Gas envisages that those firms will set low standards, so it has been forced to cut its services in line with them.

I shall spend a few moments telling the House about the people who will suffer because of those terrible cuts by British Gas. Some 18 months ago, British Gas had more 150 home service advisers, who do not only visit schools and teach children about the value of using gas wisely and safely—an issue of danger of which everyone is well aware, especially people of our parents' and grandparents' generation. More importantly, the British Gas home service advisers have developed an unique role. They visit the homes of elderly, blind and disabled people and ensure that the gas fittings are safe and easy to use.

If, for instance, by some misfortune a constituent should become blind and is a gas user, British Gas will send in a home service adviser at no cost to ensure that the appropriate Braille stickers are stuck onto the controls of the cooker to identify the grill, the oven and other parts of the cooker. For those with the misfortune to suffer from arthritis, which afflicts not just the elderly but younger people too, British Gas will send in a home service adviser with a range of adaptations to help them switch on their cooker. If it has small, fiddly knobs larger ones will be fitted so that the controls can be used more easily. If a heater cannot be operated because the control is at an awkward angle or of an awkward size so that arthritic fingers cannot grasp it, the home service adviser will adapt it as necessary.

The amendments seek to ensure that the service is not only preserved, but extended to those entering the gas market, so that new gas companies which seek to cream off domestic customers cannot turn their backs on those who are elderly, disabled or blind. That is vital because British Gas has already begun the process.

Some 18 months ago, British Gas employed 136 home service advisers; now there are 78. It has reduced by about 50 the number of home service advisers so that geographical areas covering thousands of square miles of the country no longer benefit directly from that service. Last autumn, British Gas took away from Inverness, Aberdeen and the north of Scotland the only home service adviser based there. Now, if someone requests that service from British Gas, somebody from Perth, Edinburgh or Glasgow has to travel 100 or 150 miles to Inverness or to Thurso in the north of Scotland. A service that people took for granted a year ago has been cut by British Gas which told me and the Minister that it can no longer afford the £30 million to finance that and other related service.

The amendments seek to ensure that the service is restored. The cuts in Scotland from 10 home service advisers 18 months ago to four now has been universally reflected throughout the United Kingdom. There are now no home service advisers on call in many constituencies. The service may be provided after some delay. If British Gas internal papers are to be believed, it may be provided at a cost, and British Gas has floated the cost of £25 for the service. The service may be withdrawn altogether. We believe that unless it is incorporated in the Bill, we may lose that extremely valuable service. We may lose the advice and help that is given by those highly trained key staff who visit people's homes.

The Minister has already said that he wants the service protected, but under his stewardship, albeit remotely, the number of home service advisers has been cut by some 40 per cent. It is all very well for the Minister to stand at the Dispatch Box and promise us that he wants that tremendous service to continue when he has done nothing to stop British Gas cutting it to the bone.

If the Bill is left unamended, elderly, disabled and blind people will no longer be able to rely on a service that allows them to stay in their homes and that is part of community care. Until the Government insisted on further privatisation, British Gas did that job well. In the face of brutal competition, British Gas has slashed its budget and the number of home advisers.

The Minister will be hard pressed to reassure the House that he can redress the balance and ensure that the elderly, the disabled and the blind enjoy an enhanced level of service. We want a guarantee that the number of advisers will be restored to the number that existed as recently as last autumn. Unless the Minister gives that assurance, we will view all his assurances on the Bill with considerable scepticism.

**The Minister for Industry and Energy (Mr. Tim Eggar):** The hon. Gentleman has gone in yet again for exaggerated rhetoric. It is interesting that, on the day that the right hon. Member for Copeland (Dr. Cunningham) has made a speech allegedly in favour of competition, the hon. Member for Edinburgh, South (Mr. Griffiths) is claiming that the only form of competition is that which preserves in concrete the present situation. That approach is not taken by the Bill. The Government's approach is to maintain or enhance existing standards through licensing. Condition 17 of the gas suppliers licence will require licence holders to provide a series of special services on request and without charge to pensioners and the disabled. Some will require home visits.

There is an obligation to provide on request a free annual safety check of appliances and fittings on the customer's side of the meter. There is an obligation to provide on request a meter reading every quarter when neither the customer nor any other person living with the customer is able to read the meter. There is also an obligation to reposition gas meters. Those are three examples of visits to consumers' homes being required as a matter of practice.

As a general principle, we do not intend to require all gas suppliers to do things exactly the same as British Gas. That is the nature of competition. There may be alternative ways of providing the same or better quality services, which competitors are free to develop and from which customers could doubtless benefit.

The amendment—like so many presented by the hon. Member for Edinburgh, South—seeks to make competition impossible and impracticable. The theme of the Opposition and their amendments is so to curb and confine the area in which competition can occur that there would be no competition. The amendment is the latest and most obvious example of the hon. Gentleman's contributions, and I cannot accept it.

**Ms Ann Coffey** (Stockport): The Minister will doubtless say that the terms of amendment No. 52 are already contained in condition 19 of the standard licence. However, it states that, when customers cannot pay,

"the arrangements shall in relation to any of the licensee's domestic customers who through misfortune or inability to cope with credit terms for the supply of gas for domestic use incurs obligations to pay for gas for such use which he finds difficulty in discharging provide for".

So, provided that that criterion is met, the supplier is obliged to consider certain arrangements for payment. It broadly continues the present arrangements for protecting consumers in debt but the phrase "misfortune or inability" is curious.

How will such a customer be distinguished? Who will make the judgment that the customer is part of the deserving poor rather than of the undeserving poor? It appears that it will be for the supplier to decide whether the consumer is a can't-payer or a won't-payer and whether the supplier has any obligation to the defaulting customer. Defaulting customers have no effective redress in disputes over their rights. If a supplier decides that a customer is not part of the deserving poor, the customer has no way of making any representations against that decision.

It is procedurally unclear who is obliged to take the initiative in bringing the appropriate arrangements into play. Will it be for the supplier to investigate or for the consumer to make his or her case when a debt has accumulated? The conditions leave it to the supplier to nominate conditions of supply, having made the judgment that an individual is part of the undeserving poor. That leaves customers with few rights. The director general would not be involved in any such disputes.

Amendment No. 52 is important in placing an obligation on the director general to make certain that the licence conditions are discharged. Perhaps the director general could intervene in disputes between suppliers and their customers over the terms on which gas is supplied. Although condition 19 is part of the social obligation, its

[Ms Ann Coffey]

drafting is unclear. I presume that the Minister will not accept the amendment but I would like to hear his response to my comments.

**Mr. Nigel Griffiths:** I had expected the Minister to take the opportunity to persuade the House. He ducked the key issue of why it was right for British Gas to cut the number of home service advisers from 136 to 78, and he did not dwell on the valuable function performed by those advisers. The Minister commented on the lunchtime remarks by my right hon. Friend the Member for Copeland (Dr. Cunningham), in which I had a hand. The hon. Gentleman stated that his view of competition is not the same as ours. I say, "Hear, hear" to that. The Minister's approach is to make sure that the elderly or disabled go to the wall. That is the guiding principle of the Government of the day. If we support competition, it will not be at the cost of the poor, elderly, blind or otherwise disabled. If that is the clear blue water between Labour and the Conservative party, I am happy to be standing on this shore, not that one.

*Amendment negatived.*

## Clause 15

### MINOR AND CONSEQUENTIAL AMENDMENTS

*Amendment made:* No. 55, in page 16, line 31, after 'enactments', insert 'and instrument'.—*[Mr. Eggar.]*

## Clause 17

### SHORT TITLE, COMMENCEMENT AND EXTENT

*Amendments made:* No. 56, in page 17, line 11, at end insert—

'( ) Without prejudice to section 13 of the Interpretation Act 1978 (anticipatory exercise of powers), any power conferred on the Secretary of State or the Director by a provision of this Act which comes into force by virtue of subsection (2) above may be exercised before the appointed day provided that nothing done in the exercise of that power has effect before that day.'.

No. 15, in page 17, line 15, after 'Act' insert

', except this section, subsections (1) to (6) of section 11 and paragraph 15 of Schedule 5,'.—*[Mr. Eggar.]*

## Schedule 2

### THE GAS CODE

*Amendments made:* No. 57, in page 19, line 27, leave out

'premises owned or occupied by him'

and insert 'particular premises'.

No. 58, in page 19, line 32, after first 'gas', insert 'conveyed to his premises'.

No. 59, in page 19, line 33, leave out 'his' and insert 'those'.

No. 60, in page 21, line 27, leave out 'Sub-paragraph (3) below applies' and insert

'Sub-paragraphs (3) and (3A) below apply'.

No. 61, in page 21, line 41, at beginning insert

'If no other gas supplier has become a relevant supplier,'.

No. 62, in page 21, line 45, at end insert—

'(3A) If—

    (a) another gas supplier has become a relevant supplier ("the new supplier"); and

    (b) the supplier has assigned to the new supplier his right to recover the charges due to him from the consumer,

sub-paragraph (3) above shall apply as if any reference to the supplier were a reference to the new supplier.'.

No. 63, in page 21, line 46, leave out from beginning to 'shall' in line 48 and insert

'Sub-paragraphs (3) and (3A) above shall have effect subject to any restrictions imposed by conditions of the supplier's licence or, as the case may be, the new supplier's licence; and the powers conferred by those sub-paragraphs'.

No. 64, in page 22, line 7, at end insert—

### 'Deemed contracts in certain cases

7A.—(1) Where a gas supplier supplies gas to a consumer otherwise than in pursuance of a contract, the supplier shall be deemed to have contracted with the consumer for the supply of gas as from the time when he began so to supply gas to the consumer.

(2) Where—

    (a) a gas supplier ceases to supply gas to a consumer by reason of his ceasing to be the owner or occupier of any premises; and

    (b) otherwise than by arrangement with the supplier or another gas supplier, a new owner or occupier of the premises takes a supply of gas,

the supplier shall be deemed to have contracted with the new owner or occupier for the supply of gas as from the time when the new owner or occupier began to take such a supply.

(3) Sub-paragraphs (1) and (2) above shall not apply in any case where gas is supplied or, as the case may be, a supply of gas is taken at a rate which is reasonably expected to exceed 75,000 therms a year.

(4) If a gas supplier at any time so elects, sub-paragraph (3) above shall have effect, so far as relating to him and to supplies begun to be made or taken after that time, as if the reference to 75,000 therms were a reference to 2,500 therms.

(5) If a gas supplier at any time withdraws an election under sub-paragraph (4) above, sub-paragraph (3) above shall have effect, so far as relating to him and to supplies begun to be made or taken after that time, without the modification made by sub-paragraph (4) above.

(6) The express terms and conditions of a contract which, by virtue of sub-paragraph (1) or (2) above, is deemed to have been made shall be provided for by a scheme made under this paragraph.

(7) Each gas supplier shall make, and from time to time revise, a scheme for determining the terms and conditions which are to be incorporated in the contracts which, by virtue of sub-paragraph (1) or (2) above, are to be deemed to have been made.

(8) A scheme under this paragraph may make different provisions for different cases or classes of cases determined by, or in accordance with, the provisions of the scheme.

(9) As soon as practicable after a gas supplier makes a scheme under this paragraph, a revision of such a scheme, an election under sub-paragraph (4) above or a withdrawal under sub-paragraph (5) above of such an election, he shall—

    (a) publish, in such manner as he considers appropriate for bringing it to the attention of persons likely to be affected by it, a notice stating the effect of the scheme, revision, election or withdrawal;

    (b) send a copy of the scheme, revision, election or withdrawal to the Director and to the Council; and

    (c) if so requested by any other person, send such a copy to that person without charge to him.'.

No. 16, in page 22, line 21, leave out 'discontinue' and insert 'cut off'.

No. 65, in page 22, line 29, leave out 'any' and insert 'a consumer's'.

No. 66, in page 22, line 30, leave out 'any' and insert 'a consumer's'.

No. 67, in page 22, line 44, leave out from 'off' to end of line 48 and insert

', the consent of the supplier who cut off the supply, or the consent of a person who is or is about to become a relevant gas supplier'.

No. 68, in page 23, line 22, at end insert—

*'Failure to notify disconnection of meter*

.—(1) This paragraph applies where any meter through which gas has been supplied to any premises is completely disconnected, that is to say, is disconnected both from the service pipe and from all other pipes within the premises.

(2) Except in so far as it is not reasonably practicable for him to do so, the person making the disconnection shall—

(a) ascertain the name and address of the owner of the meter; and

(b) inform that owner of the disconnection and of the address at which the meter will be available for collection.

(3) If any person fails to comply with sub-paragraph (2) above, he shall be guilty of an offence and liable on summary conviction to a fine not exceeding level 2 on the standard scale.'.—*[Mr. Eggar.]*

**Mr. Eggar:** I beg to move amendment No. 17, in page 25, line 2, after 'informed' insert

'by any person ("the informant")'.

**Mr. Deputy Speaker:** With this, it will be convenient to discuss Government amendments Nos. 18 and 19.

**Mr. Eggar:** It might be of assistance to the House if I mentioned that these amendments give effect to a commitment that I gave in Committee, following our debates there.

*Amendment agreed to.*

*Amendments made:* No. 18, in page 25, line 3, leave out from 'gas' to 'to' in line 8 and insert

'(other than one, in the case of a transporter, that he is required by sub-paragraph (1) above to prevent), he passes the information on, without avoidable delay, either—

(a) to a responsible person, that is to say, a person appearing to him—

(i) to be responsible (whether under that sub-paragraph or otherwise) for preventing the escape; or

(ii)''.

No. 19, in page 25, line 9, at end insert 'or

(b) to a nominated person, that is to say, a person nominated by a responsible person to receive information about escapes of gas on his behalf.

(6) There shall be a sufficient compliance with sub-paragraph (5) above if the transporter, supplier or shipper is satisfied that the informant—

(a) intends to pass the information on, without avoidable delay, to a nominated person; and

(b) is in a position to do so.

(7) References in sub-paragraphs (5) and (6) above to the passing on of information to a nominated person are references to the passing on of information to that person in such manner (if any) as may be specified by the responsible person by whom that person was nominated.'

No. 20, in page 26, line 27, leave out 'from the supplier' and insert 'or'.

No. 21, in page 26, line 29, leave out from third 'gas' to end of line 33.

No. 22, in page 26, line 41, leave out 'gas fitting or meter' and insert

'meter or other gas fitting'.

No. 23, in page 26, line 46, at end insert—

*'Entry for removing fittings and meters*

.—(1) This paragraph applies where—

(a) a person occupying premises supplied with gas through a meter or other gas fitting owned by a public gas transporter or gas supplier ceases to take a supply through that meter or fitting; or

(b) a person entering into occupation of any premises previously supplied with gas through a meter or other gas fitting so owned does not take a supply of gas through that meter or fitting.

(2) Any officer authorised by the public gas transporter or gas supplier, after 24 hours' notice to the occupier, or to the owner of the premises if they are unoccupied, may at all reasonable times, on production of some duly authenticated document showing his authority, enter the premises for the purpose of removing the meter or other gas fitting.

(3) Sub-paragraph (3) of paragraph 19 above applies for the purposes of this paragraph as it applies for the purposes of that paragraph.'—*[Mr. Eggar.]*

5.30 pm

**Mr. Nigel Spearing** (Newham, South): I beg to move amendment No. 88, in page 27, line 44, at end add—

*'Duties of relevant gas shipper or supplier in relation to gas fittings*

23. (1) It shall be the duty of any relevant gas shipper or supplier to make arrangements for the supply of spare parts for, or replacements of, any gas fitting or appliance of a type approved under Regulations made under this Act or under any other enactment.

(2) The Secretary of State shall—

(a) make Regulations specifying the nature and extent of the obligations imposed by subsection (1) above upon relevant gas shippers or suppliers; and

(b) monitor the carrying out of those obligations, which may be modified or added to in further Regulations.

(3) Regulations made under subsection (2) above shall be made by statutory instrument which shall be subject to annulment in pursuance of a Resolution of either House of Parliament.'.

We now move to an issue that is also of great importance to the consumers of gas, of whom notionally the Minister is in favour—that is presumably why he has introduced the Bill. I say "notionally", because there is an element of doubt, as we heard during the last debate.

Amendment No. 88, supported by my hon. Friend the Member for Newham, North-East (Mr. Timms), relates to spare parts and the replacement of approved appliances— everything inside the house which is known in the technical jargon as "upstream" of the supply, which means everything the other side of the meter which is the responsibility of the householder who pays for the gas and not of the supplier.

Newham knows all about the production and supply of gas. In Victorian times, and until fairly recently—before North sea gas—we had more than 700 acres of land dedicated to this very purpose. We had Beckton, one of the biggest gas works in the world, 90 miles of railway lines, and a workshop capable of making railway locomotives. So gas skills are indigenous to the area.

The beginnings of the gas industry, from the earliest days of the Gas Light and Coke company, whose works were in Marsham street—those round foundations are reputed to have something to do with original gasholders—were approved in this House. Gas was originally used for lighting; power and heating came later. The rules governing its use were approved in this very House. The interests of the producer were balanced against those of the consumer of a very dangerous but very useful product.

*[Mr. Nigel Spearing]*

Over the years, all the private gas companies linked the safety of their product with the safety and interests of consumers. If a gas appliance goes wrong, or is faulty, the consequences are much greater than with electricity. If a fuse blows, that is inconvenient; if there is a gas leak, or something is wrong with a gas appliance, it is a very different matter.

The historic link between the obligations on the supplier and the safety of the consumer and the general public was a principle well-known to this House. I understand, however, that this Bill disaggregates the two. There is, necessarily, a well-known set of regulations relating to approved appliances. One cannot just connect any appliance from any manufacturer to any supply of gas. The calorific value has to be right; the appliance has to be adjusted correctly and approved. If not, problems will follow. That is only common sense.

Over the years, the Gas Light and Coke Company, or North Thames Gas as it became—British Gas as it now is—prized that link. Many of my constituents were involved in gas servicing and were proud of it. Now, for the first time, the pattern is to be disrupted and possibly even destroyed. Time and again with privatisation measures, the Government have given us assurances that all is well. As I shall show briefly, however, this time things have begun to go wrong even before the legislation leaves this House.

Some 200 of the 700 acres that I have mentioned were used, first by the North Thames gas board and then by British Gas, as a service centre for the whole of London, originally, and then for the whole of south-east England. Until not long ago, that service centre was being expanded. Workshops and depots were being closed as far away as Letchworth and other parts of the south-east, and the plan was to build a depot at Bromley-by-Bow, to the east of the River Lea—in West Ham, not Tower Hamlets. It was a good service site with plenty of roads, space and good workshops.

That integrated site is now to be broken up, under the legislation, into five or six units run by different firms. Wire fences are even being put up on the site. That does not seem to make sense, but the Government think it a good thing. The main point about the site is the giant store. My hon. Friend the Member for Newham, North-East and I have visited it, so we know that it houses no fewer than 20,000 spare parts. No doubt there are various types of each part; the mind boggles at how many bits and pieces are stored there in total—all in giant stacks, serviced by the latest unmanned electronically guided vehicles.

The parts are sent to service engineers and distribution depots all over south-east England in just a few hours. The parts are packed away in trailers which return to the warehouse and take them away overnight to the depots. Like many Londoners, I have personal experience of British Gas's relatively good efficiency. It had a bad time in the conversion period, but since then I have found the company extra-efficient.

Within the company finances, I suspect that the process may be something of a loss leader. As we know, however, loss leaders produce more profits and turnover: that is what they are there for. If the organisation is split up by the Bill into different businesses—to be known, I believe, as service and sales—one section will be left more vulnerable than the other as the two cease to be integrated and each tries to make a profit for itself without any statutory responsibility for the welfare of the other.

**Mr. Stephen Timms** (Newham, North-East): On the basis of our visit, does my hon. Friend agree that the facility at Bromley-by-Bow is an impressive operation which has been the beneficiary of substantial investment by British Gas in the recent past? Does he further agree that there is a link between the uncertainty which now hangs over that operation, and perhaps others like it, which the amendment addresses, and the marked fall in customer confidence in British Gas as reported by the Gas Consumers Council in its 1994 annual report?

**Mr. Spearing:** The fact of rising complaints about the gas industry is well known. I think that I can satisfy my hon. Friend because even before the legislation has completed its passage through the House changes are being made in plans for servicing in particular. Spare parts and servicing go together. If one has an annual inspection of gas appliances—I am not declaring an interest, but all consumers do—if there is something wrong, the service engineer promises to come back the next day or the next week with a spare part. He has got to get it, so it is all part of one thing.

We were told that that giant depot, which I believe is efficient and could have coped with an area larger than south-east England, would be closed—just like that—and 200 or 300 people were to be made redundant, despite their skills and their pride in their work. Pride in service is the sort of thing that Conservative Members are keen on. Those people were not to be made compulsorily redundant: they could have had a job in Derby or Nottingham or somewhere like that. The whole gubbins, the whole bang shoot, was to be dissipated.

I wrote to British Gas to ask what it was all about. I wrote a thesis several pages long, which I will not bore the House with, analysing the Gas Bill. I received a reply from Mr. Norman Blacker, one of the directors of British Gas, who had been allocated the task by Mr. Giordano, who also sent me a short reply. Mr. Blacker said:

"Your letter also asks about our Service and Retail operations. Our new Service Business Unit already operates in a highly competitive market. Our reorganisation is designed to allow us to compete effectively with the other 40,000 or so companies operating in this field. At the same time we will maintain our aim of providing high standards of service throughout the country."

Note that he says "maintain our aim", not "maintain the standards". The letter continued:

"Service will be introducing home-based working for its engineers to help increase our competitiveness by removing the need for expensive depots which are only used for a short period every day. Customers will not notice any adverse effect as a result of the service they receive from our engineers, who will obtain their work information and parts directly, rather than having to make a special journey to a depot . . . This should save time during the working day and make for more efficient operations . . . Details of how this home-based working pattern will be implemented are being discussed with the relevant trade unions."

In other words, men in vans, parked outside their homes, having delivered in all sorts of curious places, would cut out the distribution depots.

**Mr. Ted Rowlands** (Merthyr Tydfil and Rhymney): I draw my hon. Friend's attention to an illustration of exactly that. With a fanfare of trumpets, the noble Lord Walker opened a major depot as part of his valleys initiative. It has now been closed. Instead, the engineers go to a green box at the side of a petrol filling station to pick up their bags and instructions. It may be efficient, but it is completely contradictory to the policy adopted only recently by the noble Lord Walker.

**Mr. Spearing:** I am not surprised to hear what my hon. Friend says. My recollection is that, other than being very successful in public relations as Secretary of State for Wales—

**Mr. Rowlands:** And Secretary of State for Energy.

**Mr. Spearing:**—and Secretary of State for Energy, when I think he was very much concerned with gas, he is some functionary in the gas world. I suppose that he must have come under the scrutiny of another noble Lord in a recent report about which we all know—an interesting link.

5.45 pm

I am grateful to my hon. Friend but, unknown to him, I was coming to same topic. In the *Observer* on 22 January 1995, an article headed

"British Gas engineers go to church for spares"

said:

"British Gas service engineers are using motorway flyovers, pub car parks and church halls as collection points for spare parts, as the company struggles to introduce a new service infrastructure."

**Mr. Rowlands:** And petrol filling stations.

**Mr. Spearing:** And petrol filling stations, as my hon. Friend says. I do not think that the Government can deny that. Is that unconnected with what my hon. Friend the Member for Newham, North-East reminded us of, if we needed reminding—the downturn in service standards and upturn in complaints? Does the Minister deny that the one follows the other? That is before the appointed day and before the 40,000 competing service engineers get going.

I wonder what sort of cut-throat competition there will now be in the industry. Is competition really required? We may disagree with double gas pipes in the ground—that may seem stupid enough—or gas from different suppliers going into one house on a take-it-or-leave-it basis, but is it necessary to have people other than suppliers competing? The Minister must either deny that that is going on or accept it and, I hope, support the amendment.

The depot at Bromley-by-Bow, with the skills and loyalty of its staff who are working all the time, is a symbol of service to the public throughout the nation. The knock-on effect of its closure and its replacement by the church hall, motorway flyover and filling station, about which we have just heard from my hon. Friend the Member for Merthyr Tydfil and Rhymney (Mr. Rowlands), is a symbol of the downturn in the standards of maintenance.

What about the skills in the gas service industry? Many years ago in my other job, I helped to place school pupils—experience outside the House, as Lord Nolan calls it, and very useful—and I found that British Gas apprenticeships were not only the most sought after but were often the start of lifelong careers. Many people from my part of the world and that of my hon. Friend the Member for Newham, North-East served the gas industry for most of their lives and were pleased to do so under the relatively benign regime of the Gas Light and Coke Company and the even better regime of British Gas and the publicly owned sector of it. Their skills and those of

the private contractors under some sort of licence which some think is not good enough, were built up on the apprenticeships of the gas industry. What will happen to those skills?

This is part of so-called privatisation. This commodity, which is of great value to us, is not produced privately. It is publicly owned gas in the middle of the North sea, or thereabouts, piped to us. The gas in the North sea cannot be owned other than by the British people. I see that the Minister nods. Under this legislation, it is being privately distributed by a curious system of competition under the regulator. The obligations on the supplier should be to maintain those services that we have had from private and public gas suppliers alike. I believe that that is incorporated in the amendment.

Even if we do not get very far tonight, I am looking to the Minister to deny any of the facts that I have presented and to say why the obligation in the amendment, perhaps in another form, should not be incorporated in this important Bill, which for the first time disaggregates the obligation of the supplier to supply, maintain and provide—at a reasonable cost, of course—for the safety of the equipment upstream of the meter.

**Mr. Eggar:** I do not want to be unnecessarily unkind to the hon. Member for Newham, South (Mr. Spearing), but at least some of his obiter dicta suggest that he has not read the Bill in its entirety and does not understand the full implications of what is proposed. In fairness to him, however, I concede that he was concentrating on a constituency point.

The hon. Gentleman failed to appreciate that the 40,000 competitors to whom he and, I believe, Mr. Blacker referred have been around for a long time. For years, they—the so-called Corgi-approved operators—have competed with British Gas, including the element of British Gas that looks after appliances "upstream of the meter", as the hon. Gentleman put it. There has never been any obligation on those operators to stock limitless spare parts; like garages, they have developed a system that has allowed them access to warehouses. I believe that they have sometimes had direct access to British Gas warehouses.

The amendment proposes that new suppliers should be obliged to keep a stock of spares for which, in fact, they would have no use. Many of those suppliers supply only gas, and have no desire to supply appliances. They recognise not only that British Gas will continue—presumably—to provide an effective spares service, but that those 40,000 competitors will do the same. The hon. Gentleman's proposal constitutes an imposition on potential suppliers: it is rather like requiring water companies to supply washers to repair leaking taps, which no one has ever suggested.

I entirely understand the hon. Gentleman's concern about employment in his constituency, and appreciate that, as a constituency Member, he must support the interests of his constituents. I must say, however, that the logic of his amendment is fundamentally flawed. The competitive marketplace has provided many sources of servicing and spares, and I have no doubt that it will continue to do so without the need for legislative intervention.

**Mr. Nigel Griffiths:** My hon. Friend the Member for Newham, South (Mr. Spearing) has done the House a service in highlighting the problems that now face gas

[Mr. Nigel Griffiths]

consumers. They are of recent making. British Gas is fearful of the opening of a competitive market, and the impact on the public is clear to my hon. Friend and to me—and, I think, to 8 million gas consumers. It is a good prelude to what will happen when the Bill is enacted.

Before 1 January, British Gas service engineers held a range of spares in their vans. Those spares were held in depots throughout the country, in case engineers were called out in an emergency to cut off cookers or heaters because they contained defective parts. That was part of the service for which customers paid, and it enabled engineers to reconnect many appliances because their vans contained standard stock from the depots.

In Committee, the Minister argued forcefully for an end to that practice. He failed to take on board not just the fact that members of the public might be left without a working cooker or heater—which, of course, is a tremendous imposition on the elderly and disabled—but the fact that an irresponsible or, indeed, criminally negligent person might reconnect the appliance without having it fixed. That would mean a cost to the community: not merely the person concerned, but his or her family and neighbours, might be blown up. In his creditable amendment, my hon. Friend the Member for Newham, South seeks to ensure that gas suppliers supply more than just gas itself.

A very old hand—a former director of British Gas, now retired—told me, "The problem with the gas market now is that you do not have to know anything about it; you just have to have a phone, a desk and a sympathetic bank manager. You order the gas on the phone, at beach-head prices, and agree to supply it somewhere—and British Gas TransCo has to put it down its pipes. You have no social obligations; you have no obligations to hold spares that the public might want."

My hon. Friend the Member for Newham, South focused perceptively on my main fear, eliciting a hopelessly inadequate response from the Minister. I fear that the new gas competitors will merely supply gas, and that people who have problems with their gas appliances—regardless of whether they have been supplied by British Gas—will be left to lump it, no matter how old, poor or crippled they may be. I fear that the new competitors, as private contractors, will be able to walk away from the problem.

My hon. Friend rightly sought to pin the Minister down, and he did so with a degree of cleverness which belied the Minister's own clever view of himself. He pinned the Minister down to saying, "Why should people who are simply supplying gas—for that is what competition is about—supply any additional services? Why should they keep spare parts at all?"

Having discussed the amendment with my hon. Friend, I can say that he knows that this excellent measure is likely to receive a sympathetic hearing from people more thoughtful than the Government.

**Mr. Spearing:** With the leave of the House, Mr. Deputy Speaker—

**Mr. Deputy Speaker:** Order. The hon. Gentleman usually knows the rules of the House in great detail, but I must point out to him that on this occasion he does not need the leave of the House to speak.

**Mr. Spearing:** I am grateful to you, Mr. Deputy Speaker, but I believe in good insurance policies.

I shall, I hope, find it not too difficult to demolish the logic of the Minister, who claims that I am illogical. He began by saying that I had not read the Bill—I confess that I have not read all of it—and that something in the Bill rendered the amendment redundant. Having implied that the evidence was there, however, he did not produce it. He also said, "Of course I forgive the hon. Gentleman, and pat him on the head: he was making a constituency point, which he had to make. We all know about that, ho ho."

In fact, my point applies to 8 million consumers. It is illustrated by what is happening in a depot in West Ham, which is three times the size of a football pitch and which, according to the accountants, will be too costly to maintain. "Oh," says the Minister, "There will be 40,000 contractors, all ready and waiting. Indeed, they are there now." He means the CORGI contractors.

I shall not go into the details, because we must make progress, but there is considerable worry about the standards to which those so-called CORGI contractors operate. That may have been dealt with in other parts of the Bill. Those contractors have been riding on the backs of the gas suppliers, especially in my part of the world, which is covered by North Thames Gas.

The Minister says, "Well, the contractors will be able to provide spares from somewhere else." Owing to various factors and the involvement of other people, however, the cost of the operation will escalate. Showrooms have been mentioned. I recall that someone in another place about which we are not supposed to know wrote a wonderful article about how he tried to obtain a new electric stove.

It was possible to go to a one-stop shop for electrical appliances, which provided advice and a variety of products, but will that be possible in future? Will it be possible to pay bills, obtain advice, examine appliances and secure spare parts? I very much doubt it. There will not be such a service. The Minister said that there would be an imposition on new suppliers, and therein lies the rub. He is defending the new suppliers but is there not an obligation on all public gas suppliers, whether old or new, to make the supply safe for the consumer?

6 pm

The Minister used water supply as an analogy. Perhaps he does not know that many years ago I had a slight connection with the water industry—not, I hasten to add, in terms of income but as a decorative vice-president of the British Waterworks Association. There is all the difference in the world between a leaking tap and a gas leak. A water leak is visible and the supply can be turned off at the main or other action taken. Perhaps the Minister does not know that water companies readily supplied free washers. A consumer could telephone the supplier, who fitted the washer free. It was covered by the water rates, in the old days when we paid water rates and not water charges. The Minister's analogy with the water industry and water taps is therefore wrong.

It is clear that people want gas and are willing to pay for it, but they want it supplied in a safe manner and they want to be assured that equipment and spare parts are available. The Bill will not maintain the standards to which people in this country have been accustomed from the gas industry for perhaps more than a century. I hope that at some later stage in the progress of the Bill that will be understood and rectified. As I know where the Bill goes next, and as the Government may have second thoughts, I beg to ask leave to withdraw the amendment.

*Amendment, by leave, withdrawn.*

### Schedule 3

OTHER AMENDMENTS OF PART I OF 1986 ACT

*Amendments made:* No. 69, in page 28, leave out lines 31 to 35 and insert—

'(4) Subject to subsection (5) below, a consent under subsection (2) above may be given subject to compliance with—

   (a) such modification or other conditions as the Director considers necessary or expedient for the purpose of protecting the interests of consumers; and

   (b) such incidental or consequential modification conditions as he considers necessary or expedient.'.

No. 70, in page 29, line 25, after '4', insert ', 7A'.

No. 71, in page 35, line 13, leave out

'with gas by a gas supplier'

and insert

'by a gas supplier with gas conveyed to particular premises'.

No. 24, in page 30, line 45, leave out 'after consultation with' and insert 'with the consent of'.

No. 25, in page 31, line 30, at end insert—

'( ) the making or maintenance of the connection would involve a new or increased supply of gas to the premises in question;'.

No. 26, in page 31, line 35, leave out 'that rate' and insert

'the new or increased supply'.

No. 27, in page 33, line 35, at end insert—

'( ) The Director may by notice in writing require a public gas transporter to give to the Director, or to any person appointed by him for the purpose, within such time and at such place as may be specified in the notice, such information as the Director may reasonably require for the purpose of making regulations under this section or of giving directions under such regulations.'

No. 28, in page 34, line 18, leave out second 'of' and insert 'owned or occupied by'.

No. 4, in page 36, line 53, leave out 'and (4)' insert 'to (4A)'.

No. 5, in page 37, line 14, leave out 'the stamping of' and insert 'another person to stamp'.

No. 6, in page 37, line 18, leave out

'or authorised to stamp it'.

No. 7, in page 37, line 21, leave out from 'submission' to 'and' in line 22.

No. 8, in page 37, line 24, at end insert—

'(4A) A meter examiner may authorise another person to stamp a meter, notwithstanding that he has not himself examined it, if—

   (a) the meter was manufactured or repaired by that person;

   (b) that person has obtained the consent of the Director to his stamping of the meter; and

   (c) any conditions subject to which the consent was given have been satisfied.'.

No. 29, in page 43, line 9, leave out from beginning to 'with' in line 10 and insert 'he has consulted'.

No. 9, in page 43, line 48, leave out from beginning to 'shall' in line 2 on page 44 and insert

'licences under section 7 above, licences under subsection (1) of section 7A above or licences under subsection (2) of that section, he—

   (a)'.

No. 10, in page 44, line 5, at end insert 'and

   (b) may make such incidental or consequential modifications as he considers necessary or expedient of any conditions of licences under that provision granted before that time.'.

No. 72, in page 46, line 34, leave out 'this section' and insert 'subsection (1A) above'.

No. 11, in page 46, line 48, leave out from 'holder" to 'a' in line 49 and insert—

   '(a) in relation to a reference under subsection (1A) above, means the holder of a licence to which the reference relates;

   (b) in relation to the modification of'.

No. 12, in page 46, line 50, leave out

'a licence holder whose licence'

and insert

'the holder of a licence which'.

No. 30, in page 48, leave out lines 6 to 8 and insert—

   '(b) for paragraph (b) there shall be substituted the following paragraph—

     "(b) the circumstances are as mentioned in section 73(1) of that Act (order on report on merger reference) and at least one of the two or more enterprises which ceased, or (in the application of that provision as it has effect by virtue of section 75(4)(e) of that Act) which would cease, to be distinct enterprises was or, as the case may be, is engaged in the carrying on of activities authorised by a licence;".'.

No. 73, in page 53, leave out lines 1 to 3 and insert—

' "(a) such activities as are mentioned in section 5(1) above; and

   (b) activities ancillary to such activities.".'.

No. 74, in page 54, line 11, leave out from 'activities' to 'and' in line 12 and insert

'to which this subsection applies'.

No. 75, in page 54, leave out lines 22 to 24 and insert 'the carrying on of activities to which this subsection applies'.

No. 76, in page 54, line 26, at end insert—

'( ) Subsections (2) and (3) above apply to—

   (a) activities required or authorised by licences;

   (b) such activities as are mentioned in section 5(1) above, whether or not so authorised; and

   (c) the storage of gas.'.

No. 31, in page 56, line 11, leave out 'road' and insert 'motor'.—*[Mr. Eggar.]*

### Schedule 4

MINOR AND CONSEQUENTIAL AMENDMENTS

*Amendments made:* No. 32, in page 64, line 23, after 'and' insert 'section 22A(1)(b) of and'.

No. 77, in page 66, line 42, at end insert—

*'Central Rating Lists Regulations 1994 (S. I. 1994/3121)*

. In Part 3 of the Schedule to the Central Rating Lists Regulations 1994, for the words "public gas supplier", in both places where they occur, there shall be substituted the words "public gas transporter".'.—*[Mr. Eggar.]*

## Schedule 5

### TRANSITIONAL PROVISIONS AND SAVINGS

**Sir John Hannam** (Exeter): I beg to move amendment No. 40, in page 68, line 19, leave out from 'register' to end of line 22 and insert—

'and

(b) subject to that and to the provisions of any contract entered into before the passing of this Act shall be binding on all persons.'.

**Madam Deputy Speaker (Dame Janet Fookes):** With this, it will be convenient to discuss amendment No. 41, in page 68, line 27, at end insert—

'(7) No provision such as is mentioned in sub-paragraph (4) above shall apply to any contract entered into before the passing of this Act.'.

**Sir John Hannam:** The amendments deal with the assignment of rights and liabilities. Like so many of my hon. Friends, I welcomed the Bill when it was introduced in March. Consumers in the industrial and commercial gas supply market have already benefited by substantial savings of up to 20 per cent. as a result of competitive marketing. In April 1996, when the domestic gas pilot project comes into operation in the south-west, my constituents in and around Exeter will be some of the first domestic users to benefit from the liberalisation of this market.

The anticipated price differential from which my constituents will benefit can be compared with the reductions that occurred in the telecom market when increased competitiveness forced British Telecom to become more efficient, allowing it to narrow its margins in line with the rest of the market. That has been the experience in the supply of gas to the industrial market, almost to the point at which the independent suppliers are now finding it hard to realise a respectable return on their investment in such a competitive marketplace.

When the industrial market was opened up, the composition of the initial supplier or producers of gas from the North sea remained unchanged, as did the size of the marketplace, creating the demand for a supply of gas in factories, smelting works and brick works throughout the United Kingdom's industrial base. Similarly, exploration and production companies will continue to produce gas from the fields that they have been operating for as long as 15 years, and the domestic market will remain constant, or its size and the demand for gas may increase.

For those reasons, I am concerned at the precedent that is being set in paragraph 2 of schedule 5 to the Bill, which effectively invites the renegotiation of gas supply contracts at the well or production end just because the gas supplier at the street or consumer end will possibly change at some time between 1996 and 1998 or beyond.

Historically, most gas sale contracts have been long-term arrangements, typically for the projected life of a field, and they were concluded between the field owners and British Gas. For example, the Hewett field principal agreement was concluded in 1968 and still survives.

Gasfield owners require some certainty that the buyer will buy a certain amount of gas in each contract year, and British Gas required some certainty that the seller would deliver those same amounts each year. Gas sale contracts have been concluded in that way for a number of reasons, principally that, first, gas is not a commodity which can be easily moved around the world like oil. Therefore, a seller's choice of buyer is restricted and for many years the only customer has been British Gas.

Secondly, the cost of offshore operations is such that, as soon as the field is brought on stream, it cannot be economically suspended. The decision to invest hundreds of millions of pounds in a particular asset has been taken on the basis of a secure long-term contract to sell the gas that is produced. I should mention that the capital investment going into that hundreds of millions of pounds development has been raised to commission exploration and development projects, and has been offered by banks on the understanding that repayment would be achieved from a steady revenue stream arising from one long-term contract and one long-term customer: British Gas, which, one would assume, has an exceptional credit and status rating in corporate lending circles.

Paragraph 2 of schedule 5 as currently drafted would permit British Gas to assign gas contracts, without counter-party assent, to an affiliate that may not have the financial means and structure necessary, or even the inclination to meet commitments that British Gas made on freely entering into those contracts, such as take or pay contracts. As written, that could and would include existing gas supply contracts. As the hon. Member for Clackmannan (Mr. O'Neill) said:

"If the going got really rough, British Gas could allow those smaller operations to founder as companies and its obligations would then disappear. The gas suppliers would be left to pick up the tab."—[*Official Report, Standing Committee A*, 27 April 1995; c. 327.]

If the provision were enacted in its current form, it would have profoundly damaging consequences, both in relation to the future development of Britain's offshore oil and gas resources—and hence longer-term gas supply security—and internationally to the sanctity of contracts, a principle that is fundamental to the interests of a country whose offshore sector enjoys such extensive international investment.

By applying the schedule in a retrospective manner, there is a strong chance that the sanctity of contracts, an essential prerequisite of long-run international business, will be threatened. Let us not forget that those contracts were freely entered into by two responsible and consenting parties.

I know that this matter has been discussed to some extent in Committee, when my hon. Friend the Minister likened the guarantees for gas contracts to other items "of varying magnitude" which British Gas purchases. He mentioned everything from computers, to telephones to office cleaners. With all due respect, it is not quite appropriate to compare gas contracts worth millions of pounds with cleaning contracts.

As we know, liberalisation is happening in a phased manner, commencing with a trial area of approximately 2 million homes in the west country around April next year. I can find no valid reason why the assigning of rights and liabilities should not apply to gas contracts negotiated and agreed after the Bill has received Royal Assent.

My proposed amendments avoid the provisions of schedule 5 applying to contracts in existence before Royal Assent. Amendment No. 41 makes the transfer binding on everyone, subject to the consent of anyone whose consent would otherwise be necessary under the terms of the contract. That serves to clarify the position that the amendments, grouped together, attempt to preserve only existing contractual positions.

Any gas supply contracts negotiated after Royal Assent would be subject to liabilities being reassigned, but then at least both parties negotiating would be aware of that extra dimension during negotiation.

In that way, sanctity of contract would be maintained and the future development of Britain's offshore oil and gas resources, and hence longer-term gas supply security, would no longer be threatened. The United Kingdom continental shelf would continue to receive the extensive international investment that it enjoys.

I know that my hon. Friend has had meetings with the United Kingdom Offshore Association in recent days and over the past week and that he is fully aware of the concerns of the gas supply industry. I hope that he will respond to those fears today.

**Mr. O'Neill:** The amendment is broadly the same as the amendment that we debated in Committee, and it is being considered at roughly the same stage in proceedings as that amendment. It is unfortunate that such an important matter should be considered at what is, to all intents and purposes, the fag end of proceedings. It is important, however, that we debate it again, because, in Committee, the Minister did not fully appreciate the concerns that were expressed by the other parties, as it were, in the liberalisation process: the suppliers of gas in the first instance.

Discussions have taken place. It would be useful if the Minister reported on them this evening. I am not sure whether they will necessarily be accepted by everyone in the industry. Like the hon. Member for Exeter (Sir J. Hannam), a number of people from a variety of companies have come to see me. Although there is always a degree of special pleading in these matters, tonight I shall focus only on one important point: the sanctity of contract.

6.15 pm

I can well imagine that, perhaps in about 18 months' time, if a Labour Government were to introduce utilities regulations or changes in arrangements that were seen to favour a major employer who had a fully unionised work force and to whom it was considered the Labour party might be sympathetic, and if some attempt were made to nudge a piece of legislation slightly in that employer's direction, that tilting would be regarded with great suspicion and as something akin to the end of western civilisation. People would say that the Labour party was seeking to distort the law of contract, on which the whole of our business system seems to rest. As a consequence, we would be the subject of opprobrium from the press and everyone else.

The Government may be lucky that they have not attracted such attention, and that the United Kingdom Offshore Operators Association and bodies such as Brindex have been adopting a softly, softly approach, but contracts that were entered into before the original privatisation, which have been running, as has been said,

for the best part of 25 years in one or two instances, still have some time to go, and a number of considerations must be taken into account.

We would like to think that the good name of Britain would not be the subject of international disdain. The United Kingdom continental shelf has still some time to operate as an active oil and gas field. We want to ensure that companies will come to the North sea and to the west of Shetland in the certain knowledge that, when a deal is struck, it is struck in all good faith, and that abrogations will not take place.

We recognise that circumstances have changed and that British Gas does not require gas in the quantities to which it once subscribed. When it entered into some of those contracts, it did not have the Morecambe field at its disposal. It does not need all the gas that it is contracted to purchase, but it might be able to purchase more if it were not taking so much of its gas from the Morecambe field. That is an internal matter that must be the subject of negotiation.

It will be helpful if the Minister tells us what the state of the negotiations are. As was pointed out by the hon. Member for Exeter, in the initial consideration of this matter, the Minister's response was not fully considered or wholly adequate as he drew analogies with other pieces of privatisation legislation that, frankly, were not directly relevant. He also, in relation to British Gas's operation, drew internal analogies that were not appropriate because, as has been pointed out, agreements for office supplies and the like are different from agreements that are entered into on a large financial scale and that relate to important contracts of an international character. I hope that the Minister will be able to give some hope that there will be stability and that negotiations will be entered into, with all sides being able to reach a satisfactory compromise.

It has been argued that the amendment would perhaps tilt the balance too much the other way. In many respects, and quite deservedly so on occasions, the Minister is damned if he does and damned if he doesn't. On this occasion, he has shown favour to a British company for reasons that were not fully appreciated, and that favour could rebound on other British companies at other times. As I said, if a Labour Government had introduced the provision, we would have had the coals of hell heaped on our heads, and probably correctly so, because it would have suggested a degree of favour for one company against another and would undermine the sanctity of contract law.

It is incumbent upon the Minister to tell us now, in terms that he was not able to use in Committee, where he stands. We also need to know, through their trade associations, how satisfied the oil and gas companies have been with some of the undertakings that he has suggested might be the way out of this difficult problem.

**Mr. Robert Banks** (Harrogate): I congratulate my hon. Friend the Member for Exeter (Sir J. Hannam) on tabling the amendment and on the way in which he presented his case. He has drawn support from the Opposition Front Bench, which usually strikes a chord of alarm, but the hon. Member for Clackmannan (Mr. O'Neill) stressed the sanctity of contracts, and that rings true with me because it is why I support the amendment.

As far as possible, I have always resisted retrospective legislation. I believe that contracts undertaken, particularly in this instance, should always be honoured

[*Mr. Robert Banks*]

as best as is possible. I support and fully respect the merits of the Bill. It is a great Bill. It frees up competition and will do a remarkable job in reducing prices for the consumer. It makes British Gas a wholly different animal with the separation of gas supplies from the monopoly over the gas pipeline network.

Although there is full justification for the new arrangement, those companies with long-term investments based on supply contracts with British Gas are disadvantaged because British Gas is not held to the original contracts, as has been expressed, and because gas companies are having to renegotiate from a position of weakness. In the past, British Gas has benefited from the continuity of its supplies at prices which were set under the contractual agreements. As has been said, in some cases those agreements go back over 20 years or more. At the same time, gas companies have had the opportunity to plan and raise finance on a long-term investment programme on the basis of the contracts that have been given.

**Mr. Michael Clapham** (Barnsley, West and Penistone): Is it not a fact that all those contracts are indexed to either the retail prices index or the price of oil?

**Mr. Banks:** I do not know the answer to that because I do not have that information. I imagine that some of the contracts would be indexed and some would not. That is a matter that we could check at a later date.

We must bear in mind not just the on-going revenue that arises from the contracts and the assuredness of the programme of investment that the companies have made and must continue to make, but the dismantling of the gas rigs when they have exhausted their fields. There is a big question mark about how the rigs are to be disposed of. Considerable costs will be involved, and the contracts will become all the more valuable because that must be borne in mind.

The fact that these companies will have to renegotiate the pricing levels of gas while British Gas will have a free hand to place the contracts with one or more of its affiliate companies causes some concern because, as I understand it, those companies do not have the right to voice their opinions as to the viability, competitiveness, competence and financial stability of the affiliate companies. All in all, a great deal of work has to be done to arrive at a position that is fair to the companies that supply British Gas and which will ensure that they get a fair deal in the future. Those companies will naturally want assurances about the companies that will take over the contracts that they had, hitherto, with British Gas. That should be fully understood by British Gas and I should like to see it woven into the legislation in some way.

The length of the contractual obligations and the price structures in the original contracts should be taken into account in the negotiations of new terms which will be necessary as a result of this legislation. We must look carefully at the situation because some companies with substantial infrastructure investments will suffer considerable losses. I accept that we are facing changed circumstances, but there are obligations that must be fulfilled if we are to see the contracts honoured.

Gas companies achieving a high price structure— higher than the market at present—as a result of some of the old contracts could be placed in a more favourable position for the price cutting of the surplus gas that they have available to put on the market. That causes a problem—I recognise that the Minister accepts that— because it would be unrealistic for a company to benefit in that way; to cut out competition and achieve a greater share of the gas market as a result of an overgenerous new price structure.

I hope that the message that will be recorded in *Hansard* will be taken account of, and that their Lordships in another place will take note of our debate on this subject.

I believe that, where decisions have been made on the basis of contracts that have been entered into, those contracts must be recognised and there is an obligation to ensure that those companies do not suffer unnecessarily from the new terms and conditions that will now apply and which will have to be renegotiated.

**Mr. Bill Michie** (Sheffield, Heeley): On a point of order, Madam Deputy Speaker. I wish to inform the House that some members of the Select Committee on Members' Interests have walked out after two votes—

**Madam Deputy Speaker:** Order. That is not a matter for the Chair. If the hon. Gentleman wishes to raise this matter, he must do so in another way. It is not a point of order.

**Mr. Michie:** On a point of order, Madam Speaker.

**Madam Deputy Speaker:** Is it a different point of order?

**Mr. Michie:** It is the same point of order—

**Madam Deputy Speaker:** Order. I have already ruled on that. That is enough.

**Mr. Eggar:** I am grateful to my hon. Friends the Members for Exeter (Sir J. Hannam) and for Harrogate (Mr. Banks) for raising this important subject. I am grateful also for the contribution from the hon. Member for Clackmannan (Mr. O'Neill). Over the past week or so, I have been involved in detailed discussions with individual producer companies as well as with British Gas, UKOOA and Brindex—the trade associations of the independent producers and the offshore operators. They are aware of the general thrust of what I am about to say.

Suggestions have been made that the provisions of schedule 5 would encourage the abrogation of commercial contracts and give an unfair commercial advantage to British Gas. That was the thrust of the remarks of the hon. Member for Clackmannan and was behind the concerns expressed by my hon. Friends. I do not accept that view, but it would be helpful if I described how the Government see the position.

I have said consistently that the successful establishment of a competitive gas supply market will require some adjustment to the contractual arrangements under which gas is produced and delivered to suppliers. British Gas will no longer hold a monopoly and will, inevitably, lose market share to the new suppliers. Some adjustment to the previous contractual arrangements appropriate to a monopoly supplier will be necessary. However, there is no reason why that process should result in disruption of the market if it is carried out in an orderly manner between the commercial interests involved. I want to see British Gas and the producers developing the new contractual framework on an even-handed basis.

I recognise that many companies have made significant investments to support their gas contracts—that was the point made by my hon. Friends—and that they have a legitimate interest in maintaining an acceptable overall position. That in turn should assure the continuation of offshore investment in future gas production, which is extremely important to the United Kingdom.

Schedule 5 closely follows similar provisions in several other statutes so there is ample precedent for the wording of schedule 5. A key feature of the arrangements proposed in the Bill is the separation of the functions of gas transportation and supply. That is to ensure that competing suppliers, including the supply arms of British Gas, use the pipeline network on the same basis.

6.30 pm

It follows, therefore, that provision must be made for a scheme under which British Gas will allocate its various rights and obligations among the different legal entities that it will need to create in order to carry on its business. That is integral to the Bill. I can, however, assure the House that it is not the Government's intention that the provisions should give any commercial interest an unfair advantage over any other. Schedule 5 emphatically does not create a right for British Gas simply to walk away from contracts.

The Government's objective is to ensure a framework for a competitive gas industry in which all can participate on an equitable basis. The Government will be watching the developing commercial discussions very carefully to ensure that this overriding objective is met.

I hope that what I have said has allayed the fears of my hon. Friends and answered some of the points raised by the hon. Member for Clackmannan. It is an important and sensitive matter. Large sums of money are at stake and the future of the gas industry—onshore and offshore—is greatly affected by the terms of the contracts. We do not take the matter lightly, and I know that the producers and British Gas—do not do so. I am confident that, in the light of what I have said, the producers, British Gas and other entities will be able to reach a satisfactory commercial conclusion to the benefit of all involved.

**Sir John Hannam:** I thank my right hon. Friend for his comments which will assist in reassuring the gas supply industry. Certainly, the issue needed to be debated today and will no doubt be debated again in another place. However, in the light of my right hon. Friend's helpful remarks, I beg to ask leave to withdraw the amendment.

*Amendment, by leave, withdrawn.*

*Amendments made:* No. 13, in page 69, line 19, at end insert—

'( ) As soon as practicable after making a scheme under this paragraph, the Secretary of State shall publish the text of each licence which by virtue of the scheme is treated as granted under section 7 or 7A(1) or (2) of the 1986 Act; and any text so published shall be treated as authoritative unless the contrary is shown.'.

No. 78, in page 70, line 19, at end insert—

*'Transfers under paragraph 6: corporation tax*

.—(1) Any shares issued to the public gas supplier by a transferee in pursuance of the scheme under paragraph 2 above shall be treated for the purposes of the Corporation Tax Acts as if they had been issued wholly in consideration of a subscription paid to the transferee (and attributable equally between those shares) of an amount equal to the difference between—

(a) the value, on the appointed day, of the property, rights and liabilities vested in the transferee by paragraph 6 above; and

(b) the principal sum payable under any debentures issued to the supplier by the transferee in pursuance of the scheme.

(2) The value required to be determined for the purposes of sub-paragraph (1)(a) above is market value, as defined in section 272 of the Taxation of Chargeable Gains Act 1992.

(3) Any debenture issued to the public gas supplier by a transferee in pursuance of the scheme under paragraph 2 above shall be treated for the purposes of the Corporation Tax Acts as if it had been issued—

(a) wholly in consideration of a loan made to the transferee of an amount equal to the principal sum payable under the debenture; and

(b) wholly and exclusively for the purposes of the trade or business carried on by the transferee.

(4) For the purposes of Chapter II of Part VI of the Income and Corporation Taxes Act 1988 (definition of distributions), where in the case of any transfer under paragraph 6 above any consideration given or treated as given in respect of a security relating to—

(a) any liability; or

(b) the use of the principal to which any liability, being a liability to interest or an equivalent liability, relates,

would fall (apart from this sub-paragraph) to be regarded for those purposes as new consideration received by the public gas supplier, that consideration shall be treated instead, to the extent that it relates to so much of the liability as falls in consequence of the transfer to be discharged by the transferee, as if it were new consideration received by the transferee.'.

No. 79, in page 70, line 19, at end insert—

*'Transfers under paragraph 6: petroleum revenue tax and gas levy*

. Where any transfer is effected by paragraph 6 above, the transferee shall be treated—

(a) for the purposes of section 10(1)(a) of the Oil Taxation Act 1975; and

(b) for the purposes of the Gas Levy Act 1981,

as if it were the same person as the public gas supplier.'.

No. 80, in page 70, line 19, at end insert—

*'Transfers under paragraph 6: consequential modifications of rating provisions*

.—(1) This paragraph applies where any transfer effected by paragraph 6 above is a transfer of a hereditament which, immediately before the appointed day, falls within the description set out in Part 3 of the Schedule to the Central Rating Lists Regulations 1994.

(2) The Secretary of State may by order make such modifications of that Part of that Schedule, and of the British Gas plc (Rateable Values) Order 1994, as may appear to him necessary or expedient as a consequence of the transfer.

(3) An order under this paragraph which is made after the appointed day may have effect as from that day or any later day.

(4) Where, by virtue of sub-paragraph (3) above, an order under this paragraph has effect from a day earlier than that on which it is made, any necessary alteration shall be made with effect from that earlier day to any central rating list in which the hereditament is shown.

(5) An order under this paragraph shall be made by statutory instrument which shall be subject to annulment in pursuance of a resolution of either House of Parliament.'.

No. 33, in page 70, line 42, leave out '("the gas' and insert '(a "gas'.

No. 34, in page 71, line 4, leave out third 'the' and insert 'each'.

No. 35, in page 71, line 22, at end insert 'concerned'.

No. 36, in page 71, line 22, at end insert—

[*Sir John Hannam*]

'( ) A scheme under this paragraph may make different provisions for different cases or classes of cases determined by, or in accordance with, the provisions of the scheme.

( ) As soon as practicable after making a scheme under this paragraph, the Secretary of State shall publish, as respects each different case or class of case—

(a) the text of any exemption which by virtue of the scheme is treated as granted under section 6A of the 1986 Act; and

(b) the text of any licence which by virtue of the scheme is treated as granted under section 7A(1) or (2) of that Act;

and any text so published shall be treated as authoritative unless the contrary is shown.'

No. 37, in page 71, line 23, leave out second 'the' and insert 'each'.

No. 38, in page 71, line 28, leave out 'the gas supplier' and insert

'such gas suppliers as he considers appropriate'.

No. 39, in page 71, line 29, leave out second 'the' and insert 'each'.

No. 14, in page 71, line 47, leave out

'have effect on and after that day'

and insert

'be treated for the purposes of section 5(1)(c) of the 1986 Act'.

No. 81, in page 71, line 48, after 'supplier's', insert 'transport'.

No. 82, in page 72, line 1, leave out 'paragraph' and insert

'Part of this Schedule "transport'.

No. 83, in page 73, line 42, at end insert—

*'Recovery of gas charges etc.*

.—(1) Where—

(a) such a demand as is mentioned in paragraph 7(5) of Schedule 5 to the 1986 Act (recovery of gas charges etc.) has been made by a public gas supplier; and

(b) the payment demanded is not made before the appointed day,

paragraph 7(1) of Schedule 2B to the 1986 Act shall have effect as if the demand had been made by the supplier's domestic supply successor on the day on which it was made by the supplier.

(2) Where—

(a) such a notice of intention as is mentioned in paragraph 7(5) of Schedule 5 to the 1986 Act has been given by a public gas supplier; and

(b) the supply of gas is not cut off before the appointed day,

paragraph 7(3) of Schedule 2B to the 1986 Act shall have effect as if the notice had been given by the supplier's domestic supply successor on the day on which it was given by the supplier.

(3) In this Part of this Schedule "domestic supply successor", in relation to a public gas supplier, means the person who becomes the holder of a licence under subsection (1) of section 7A of the 1986 Act by virtue of the scheme made by or in relation to that supplier under Part I of this Schedule.'.

No. 84, in page 73, line 42, at end insert—

*'Use of antifluctuators and valves*

. Any notice—

(a) which has been given by a public gas supplier under sub-paragraph (1) or (2) of paragraph 8 (use of antifluctuators and valves) of Schedule 5 to the 1986 Act; and

(b) which is in force immediately before the appointed day,

shall have effect on and after that day as if it had been given on that day under sub-paragraph (1) or, as the case may be, sub-paragraph (2) of paragraph 13 of Schedule 2B to that Act by the supplier's transport successor.'.

No. 85, in page 73, line 42, at end insert—

*'Restoration of supply without consent*

.—(1) Where—

(a) a supply of gas to any premises has been cut off by a public gas supplier under paragraph 8 (use of antifluctuators and valves) or paragraph 9 (improper use of gas) of Schedule 5 to the 1986 Act; and

(b) the supply is not restored before the appointed day,

paragraph 9 of Schedule 2B to that Act shall have effect as if those premises had been disconnected on that day by the supplier's transport successor otherwise than in the exercise of such a power as is mentioned in sub-paragraph (1) of that paragraph.

(2) Where—

(a) a supply of gas to any premises has been cut off by a public gas supplier otherwise than under paragraph 8 or 9 of Schedule 5 to the 1986 Act and otherwise than in the exercise of a power conferred by regulations under section 18(2) of that Act; and

(b) the supply is not restored before the appointed day,

paragraph 9 of Schedule 2B to that Act shall have effect as if a supply of gas to those premises had been cut off on that day by the supplier's domestic supply successor otherwise than in the exercise of such a power as is mentioned in sub-paragraph (1) of that paragraph.'.

No. 86, in page 73, line 42, at end insert—

*'Failure to notify connection or disconnection of service pipe*

. Any notice—

(a) which has been given to a public gas supplier under sub-paragraph (1) of paragraph 12 (failure to notify connection or disconnection of service pipe) of Schedule 5 to the 1986 Act; and

(b) which is in force immediately before the appointed day,

shall have effect on and after that day as if it had been given on that day under sub-paragraph (1) of paragraph 10 of Schedule 2B to that Act to the supplier's transport successor.'.

No. 87, in page 73, line 42, at end insert—

*'Rating provisions*

. Nothing in this Act shall affect the operation of the following, namely—

(a) sections 19 and 33 of and Schedules 3 and 6 to the General Rate Act 1967 and Schedule 3 to the Local Government Act 1974, so far as those provisions of those Acts continue to have effect in relation to periods ending before 1st April 1990;

(b) the Central Rating Lists Regulations 1989, so far as those Regulations continue to have effect in relation to periods ending before 1st April 1995; and

(c) the Central Rating Lists Regulations 1994, so far as those Regulations have effect in relation to periods ending before the appointed day.'.—[*Mr. Eggar.*]

*Order for Third Reading read.*

*Motion made, and Question proposed,* That the Bill be now read the Third time.—[*Mr. Eggar.*]

6.33 pm

**Mr. O'Neill:** On Second Reading, we tabled a reasoned amendment because, although we did not oppose the principle of the Bill, we had misgivings about the way in which it dealt with a number of issues. We expressed a number of qualifications, to which we returned in Committee. We sought additional protection for consumers, especially those on low incomes and income support, and wanted explicit guarantees that the possibility of cherry-picking and social dumping would not be allowed, but we did not get them.

We also asked about postalised pricing. The Minister said last night that he hoped that he could achieve such pricing but thought that it might not last. We were extremely concerned about all aspects of safety and matters relating to the health and safety of those working in the gas industry. In addition, we drew attention to our misgivings about the financial status of people who might be involved in the licensing process and we wanted an undertaking from the Minister about the financial status of the "fit and proper" persons.

There were debates about the concerns of some regional electricity companies, but they were not considered to be of major significance. However, we felt that the Government had not given proper status to energy efficiency or the Energy Saving Trust. Indeed, they paid scant regard to the amendments that the trust offered to the Committee and to both parties.

We were all fortunate in having access to the support and lobbying of a number of groups from the gas industry, including British Gas and the United Kingdom Offshore Operators Association, from individual potential independent gas suppliers and a range of consumer organisations, some of which wanted status in legislation. We recognised that and sought to have them enshrined in the legislation.

We also felt that the Gas Consumers Council, whose future had been in some doubt, should be given certain formal responsibilities to justify its continued existence and to back its claim for additional resources. We were able to secure the interest of the trade unions involved, including Unison, which covers a plethora of different groups in the gas supply industry, and the GMB, which historically organised manual workers in the industry.

All those organisations made their amendments freely available to members of the Committee but, as far as I can recall, they were only twice picked up by Conservatives, perhaps by Back Benchers who were able to make their point and influence Ministers behind the Chair. It certainly did not happen in the Committee itself, where Conservative Back Benchers made the fewest contributions that I can recall. The one exception was the hon. Member for Rutland and Melton (Mr. Duncan), who tabled an amendment that was subsequently defeated by the Government and Labour members of the Committee because we felt that it would endanger certain aspects of the organisation of British Gas.

Never had I been in a Committee or participated in a debate on Report in which there were so few speeches from Conservative Back Benchers, and never has so little been offered by the Government in response to reasoned arguments and debate. Inoffensive amendments were even apparently tabled by the Liberals but they, too, received no support from the Government.

The Bill has been a disappointment. We approached it believing that it was wrong that British Gas should continue to enjoy the last remaining monopoly in the gas market—the domestic market. We recognised that British Gas had enjoyed a monopoly and that the original privatisation legislation included a number of privileges in return for it meeting certain social obligations. Some of those social obligations have been diluted in the Bill because it was conceded that British Gas no longer had a monopoly of domestic gas supply and therefore should not have to carry burdens. None of the burdens or obligations that we have identified has been enshrined in the Bill.

Time after time, my hon. Friend the Member for Edinburgh, South (Mr. Griffiths) has pointed out the dilution of the quality of service that British Gas offers to consumers. There is little prospect of any improvement being made by any of the independent suppliers, either in overall or individual commitment. One group, spearheaded by United Gas, published a paper called "39 Steps and More", but because of the opposition of other independents the "and more" part was quietly dropped and we were back to the 39 undertakings to which British Gas was prepared to agree.

If we had had to consider only that aspect of the Bill, we could have said that vested interests were being taken into account and that the Government were listening to their friends in the City and in business, but there were other areas of concern too.

I should like to touch on the specific area of regulation, to which we returned in Prime Minister's Question Time today, when the division between the views of Conservative and Opposition Members was clear. We have found that division repeatedly when we have sought to address regulation. We felt that, after some nine years of privatisation and nine years of operation of the Office of Gas Supply under two different directors general, it would be appropriate to assess the situation, yet in Committee, on Report and whenever we have debated regulation we have come up against a buffer of complacency, embodied by the Minister for Industry and Energy. He says that there is nothing wrong with the world and that everything is fine. The only thing that the Government say about regulation is that, when perfect competition is achieved, somehow there will be no need for regulators. Indeed, they said last night that, like Lenin's state, regulation will somehow wither when perfect competition arises.

The nature of the market, the commodity it sells and the service that it provides to 18 million households across the country, whereby households may be heated and food may be prepared, cannot be determined exclusively by the regulator or the market alone. A regulator must take account of more than simply market considerations. It has been argued that if we changed the rules, somehow politics would intrude into the market system.

We know that, at the moment, provisions are made for the regulator to take account of the needs of elderly and disabled people, yet not of those who are on income support or low incomes. If two groups can be identified, it would be reasonable to introduce a third. It would be no less political. Indeed, we drew attention last night to the debates and the demonstrations that disabled people have staged inside and outside the Palace of Westminster in recent months. To say that disablement is not a political issue and that the rights of the disadvantaged and those on low pay is a political issue is nonsense.

I realise that there is a desire for us to complete our business this evening, so I shall not detain the House much longer. We entered into the liberalisation debate on gas in a spirit of co-operation and offered constructive criticism of the proposals. None of the issues that we have raised have received a scintilla of support or an ounce of co-operation from the Government; the Government have not travelled an inch along the road towards a compromise. For those reasons, I urge my hon. Friends to vote against Third Reading.

When we take office, we shall certainly wish to attack British Gas's monopoly and legislate for changes in it and in the gas market generally. We do not like the way in which this Bill will regulate the gas market so that 18 million families, who are dependent on gas, will have to

[Mr. O'Neill]

enter the market to attain the means by which they cook their food and heat their homes. For those reasons, I ask my hon. Friends to join me in opposing the Bill.

6.44 pm

**Mr. Rowlands:** This Gas Bill is the third in a trilogy over the past 12 years. As a veteran of the previous two, I should like to consider briefly the contents of this Bill in the context of the evolution of the legislative process of gas privatisation.

I do not think that even the Minister could argue that there has been a logical progression in the gas privatisation process. The three Bills since 1982 have demonstrated in many ways the three contradictory objectives of privatisation: first, the Treasury demanded the maximum money possible; secondly, there was the idea of people's capitalism, with premiums on shares, which meant that the Government were not able to collect as much money; and, thirdly, enshrined in this Bill, there has been the idea of trying to create some new form of competition in what are otherwise monopolies.

As a Front-Bench spokesman on the original 1982 legislation, I remember fascinating debates with Lord Lawson, who envisaged legislation that would create an American-style privatisation—a common carriership and a huge collection of companies drawing off it. That vision was waylaid, as the Minister will be well aware because he too is a veteran of some of the arguments in the 1980s, by the corporatist tendency of Lord Walker. Barons Rooke and Walker got together and did a deal, which constituted the Gas Act of 1986. That deal basically enshrined British Gas's monopoly in the domestic market. The original Lawson legislation never intended to include the last remaining corporatist tendency, which was personified by Lord Walker and led to the 1986 Act. The Bill, as I see it, is trying to return to the original Lawson vision and create some new competition in gas.

I think that we have been very lucky, because the 1986 Act would not have produced anything like the same support for the consumer had it not been for the inspired appointment of the first director general of Ofgas, Sir James McKinnon. McKinnon has been much reviled in many circles, but he was the first regulator to care for consumers. The Littlechilds and the Carsbergs have been more interested in the theory of competition and in models. McKinnon, on behalf of the consumer, tenaciously attacked the monopoly powers of British Gas during his tenure of office.

Before we break up a large public corporation and the dominant share that it has had in domestic gas consumption, I should like to pay it one tribute. The Bill would not have been possible if it had not been for a nationalised public corporation that built the most remarkable, technically efficient natural gas pipeline. It was an amazing success story of professional and technical expertise, which was driven through despite great difficulty.

Whatever occurs in the field of competition as a result of this Bill will be dependent on that amazing exercise in technical proficiency by a nationalised concern. I know that it is now unfashionable to talk about such things— even, to a certain extent, in my party—but I pay tribute to the enormous post-war visionary generation,

represented by an era of professionals, especially technical gas engineers, who built the pipeline that will enable people to develop and thrive.

Two potential absurdities and two concerns arise from the Bill. The first absurdity is already happening and will become even more evident if the Bill proceeds. My hon. Friend the Member for Newham, South (Mr. Spearing) has described it. In future, when a gas engineer attends a safety call at somebody's house, identifies the problem and disconnects the supply, he will no longer be allowed to deal with the problem. He will no longer be able to repair the appliance, as he would have done in the old days. Presumably he now has to hand out a card and say, "This is the list of people you can phone." Instead of being able to deal with the problem, his operation will be ring-fenced and he will be able to deal only with the safety of the supply. In the past, he could have solved the whole problem and restored both the appliance and the supply, but now he will not be allowed to do so.

That is an appalling illustration of the nonsense and absurdity that will arise from the Bill. The second absurdity is the question of who will become the new competitors. I see the Under-Secretary of State for Corporate Affairs on the Government Front Bench, and as he represents Brecon and Radnor, I ask him: who will be the new competitors in south Wales? The margins for such competitors will be very small; who will they be?

In fact, the only competitor to British Gas likely to emerge in south Wales is the monopolistic South Wales Electricity company. What a rich irony, and what an extraordinary situation it would be if the competition came only from another private monopoly supplier of a rival form of energy. That would reveal the absurdity of some aspects of the Bill.

I have two more concerns, one of which involves safety. I am worried not about the powers in the Bill—on safety, those are strong enough—but about the people. We have had safe gas supplies for a generation, because of the fantastic training supplied by the British gas industry since the second world war. A whole generation of gas engineers were brought up properly to care for safety and to do a Rolls-Royce job. But the new generation of gas suppliers will not devote the same effort and money as the gas industry used to devote to developing gas engineers of that quality. In fact, they will draw on the quality of the generations trained by British Gas.

Secondly, as one who represents a valley community a long way from the southern North sea, my second concern is the differential pricing that will result from the Bill. We are reassured that there will be only a 2 per cent. difference, but all the figures are guesstimates. We are told that competition will result in a 10 per cent. saving, but that for communities at the end of the line, such as most of the valley communities, that saving will be only 8 per cent. Certainly the communities in Brecon and Radnor, represented by the Under-Secretary of State, will be at the end of the line.

What will be the scale and character of the differential gas pricing? I do not believe in the 2 per cent. difference; it is a guesstimate. What will happen if the price differentials widen? Our communities will be disadvantaged as a result of the so-called competitive legislation.

I said at the beginning of my speech that this was the third in a trilogy of Gas Bills. I make one prediction: before the end of the century there will be another Gas Bill to put right the wrongs that the Bill before us will have created.

6.52 pm

**Mr. Kevin Hughes** (Doncaster, North): As we all know, the Bill has been comprehensively discussed in Committee and on Report, and the same is now happening on Third Reading. By now, the Minister for Industry and Energy should be well aware of the concerns of hon. Members, not least Opposition Members. Yesterday, uncharacteristically, I was able to welcome his announcement of extra funding for the Health and Safety Executive. That shows that he has at least listened to some of the concerns expressed by Opposition Members—and it puts paid to the rumours that his ears were only painted on.

I also welcomed the Government's decision in Committee to table a subsequent amendment slightly to change the conditions for receipt of the special home services for the elderly. The Ministers knows that I was worried about that, and I am pleased that the Government decided to respond to the concerns about equal treatment for men and women.

The protection in the Bill for low-income customers is minimal. The main requirement relevant to them is that a licence must not be drafted so as to exclude the premises of customers likely to default. For the provision of services for elderly people, the Government have been prepared to give special protection in the Bill. Although I welcome that, I ask the Minister why the two cases are different. The Government have not given a convincing response to that question.

Yesterday, we discussed the possibility of access to services being restricted by requirements for deposits or specific payment methods. The Government said that they did not believe that gas companies would attempt to do that, but in a competitive market one cannot rule out the possibility. Had they offered more support for the Labour amendments, we would have been able to send a clear message to the gas suppliers to ensure that they provided a reasonably low-cost service encompassing proper choice for all who want it.

The practice of offering different prices to similar-volume consumers should not be allowed when competition is introduced into the market. It would be bad for low-income and elderly consumers alike, because they constitute the vast majority of the 20 per cent. of households with no banking facilities.

The Government have not done enough to protect the more vulnerable consumers from the effects of the introduction of full competition into the service. The prospect of cherry-picking remains a problem, and customers will be left to face it alone. The Government have made their position clear, but I hope that they have listened to what has been said about the need to involve consumers and to recognise the special obligations that fall on companies that provide such an important service.

Affordable warmth is too important to be sacrificed to competition. British Gas may be big business, but that carries with it big responsibilities that affect public safety and the quality of people's lives; potential suppliers to the domestic market must recognise that fact. I hope that the Minister will convey our feelings to them.

6.56 pm

**Mr. Clapham:** It will come as no surprise to the Minister to know that I am rather sceptical about the Bill. No one knows where competition in gas will take us, and many people may be disadvantaged. Already in Canada, whose gas industry is deregulated, prices have increased.

That could happen in the United Kingdom, because although there is now an oversupply of gas, the Minister will know that there is an enormous demand for gas within the energy industry. It is predicted that, by the end of the century, we shall be using as much as 40 million tonnes of gas, in coal equivalent. I also understand—the Minister will correct me if I am wrong—that there are now several new applications for gas-fired power stations, and that too will increase the use of gas.

In addition to the deregulation of the domestic market, the increasing marketing risks of gas production may inhibit the development of new gas fields. Those two factors—energy use and the marketing risks—could lead to higher prices. Yet yesterday, the Minister rejected the amendment that would have required the regulator to take account of supply.

The Bill is inadequate without the amendments that were tabled by the Opposition. Unfortunately, neither in Committee nor on Report was the Minister prepared to accept any of those amendments, which would have improved it. Some of them would have given the consumer safeguards. As it stands, the Bill fails to deal with consumer protection, security of supply and, in part, safety. Without new clauses 3, 6, 9 and 10, which the Minister rejected yesterday, the consumer has no statutory protection.

The Gas Consumers Council should be able to monitor the impact of the Bill on customers and to keep an eye on the prices charged and the quality of service delivered. That is fundamental if we are to ensure that the high standards set by British Gas are maintained. It is also essential that information on prices is widely publicised. I pointed out to the Minister yesterday that low-income customers on pre-payment meters consuming large quantities of gas are paying far more than other gas customers. The irony is that some customers with arrears are seeking pre-payment meters in the belief that they will save them money. Without the publication of prices in a standard form, people will not be given the opportunity to make informed choices.

When the Select Committee on Trade and Industry reported on the domestic gas market, it was unsure whether there would be advantages in terms of costs, benefits or risks. It would appear that only a small part of the cost of a therm of gas is likely to be influenced by competition. The standing charge is clearly an important element, and the Minister is aware that the regulator has proposed that the transportation element of the standing charge should be £15. That is possible because of a cross-subsidy from large users to small users. Without that mechanism, there would be millions of losers.

Do the Government intend to ensure that that cross-subsidy will continue without jeopardy? The Select Committee emphasised the need for assurance on that factor. I do not feel that social purposes will be in any way advanced by the Bill, and I urge Conservative Members to support the Opposition.

7.1 pm

**Mr. Nick Harvey** (North Devon): I had considerable sympathy with the plaintive cry of the hon. Member for Clackmannan (Mr. O'Neill) about the Government and the Minister. They were faced with Opposition members of the Committee who were essentially sympathetic to the subject, but having moved about 270 amendments of their own, they did not find it in their hearts to accommodate a few more from the Opposition, not least my own which, as the hon. Gentleman said, were comparatively inoffensive.

The Bill is far from perfect, its most obvious flaw being the primacy it seems to give to the creation of competition in a perfect theoretical framework over the practical interests of serving the consumer. Those points have been put forward by the hon. Member for Edinburgh, South (Mr. Griffiths) and his colleagues at length—often at considerable length.

The Bill seeks to create a competitive framework for the supply of gas to the domestic consumer which will in the long term serve the consumer better than a continuing monopoly—albeit a regulated one. It may well be that, as the hon. Member for Merthyr Tydfil and Rhymney (Mr. Rowlands) mentioned, we will find ourselves returning to legislate again on the gas industry before the end of the century. I hope that that will not be so, and I also hope that those seeking amendments of the sort which have been tabled will have better fortune in another place. But the fact remains that the measure will be in the best interests of domestic gas consumers and, for that reason, I shall be supporting it this evening.

7.5 pm

**Mr. Nigel Griffiths:** First, may I thank you, Madam Deputy Speaker, and the hon. Member for Staffordshire, Moorlands (Sir D. Knox) for chairing the Committee and being so patient with us as we went through a considerable number of amendments? The amendments came mainly from the Government because this is such half-baked legislation.

I also thank my hon. Friends who have spoken today—in particular my hon. Friend the Member for Newham, South (Mr. Spearing)—and my colleagues who have spoken with such conviction on Third Reading, including my hon. Friends the Members for Merthyr Tydfil and Rhymney, for Barnsley, West and Penistone (Mr. Clapham) and for Doncaster, North (Mr. Hughes). My hon. Friends spoke at length on behalf of their constituents and 18 million gas consumers. I should also like to thank my hon. Friends who spoke in Committee, including my hon. Friends the Members for Stockport (Ms Coffey), for Neath (Mr. Hain), for Dulwich (Ms Jowell), for Dagenham (Ms Church) and for Coventry North-East (Mr. Ainsworth).

This is the Third Reading of what Ministers have been trailing in the press as landmark legislation which is taking privatisation through the 1990s and is building on the so-called successes of the 1980s—successes which have turned sour for so many millions of consumers. It is amazing that not one Conservative Member spoke on Third Reading except the Minister. The Government could not get one of their own Back Benchers to stand up and say that the further privatisation of British Gas is worth supporting. It is also worth noting that none of the

hon. Members from the Scottish National party is in the Chamber, and no Scottish nationalist has spoken at all in this important gas debate.

**Mr. Andrew Robathan** (Blaby): Will the hon. Gentleman give way?

**Mr. Griffiths:** I am delighted to see anybody who wishes to defend the SNP, which is a dying breed.

**Mr. Robathan:** I understood that the Labour party wanted to go home at 7 o'clock, and I did not speak for that reason.

**Mr. Griffiths:** The hon. Gentleman is sadly mistaken. We would be happy to fight this Bill until 7 o'clock, 8 o'clock or 10 o'clock at night, but the hon. Gentleman wants to maintain his supine position.

The Bill is supposed to be the flagship of the Government's legislation for this Session and, by giving a free hand to the private sector to lure customers away from British Gas, allows the chancers a chance to get their snouts in the trough. Yet from the hour that the Bill appeared in the Queen's Speech on 16 November, its progress has been a shambles.

Publication was expected in January, but it did not appear. The Bill did not surface at the beginning of February, or at the middle or the end of February. When it did appear in March, the schedules were not ready. We debated the Second Reading without key schedules, which did not appear until the week after the House gave the Bill its Second Reading. The schedules—the blueprint for the detail of the Bill—were simply not available because the Government had an army of civil servants struggling to close all the loopholes in this chancer's charter.

Second reading came and went, and still there were no schedules. It is no wonder the Government delayed producing the schedules. All the things that the Minister promised the House at Second Reading—guaranteed protection for elderly and disabled consumers, safeguards to protect rural gas customers and safeguards for low income groups—are not fully dealt with.

In Committee—a full 17 weeks after the Queen's Speech—the shambles continued. Some 71 amendments were tabled by the Minister to his own Bill. The Minister accuses us of opposing the legislation. Too right, but we could not match his opposition to the Bill, as shown by the number of amendments he had to table to it. He has tabled some 160 amendments to this half-baked legislation. He is saying to the House and to 8 million consumers, "Trust us—the future of gas is safe in our hands."

The Minister told the House yesterday that the poor executives of British Gas were going to make only 9p a share out of their executive options, when the real figure made so far by executives who have ripped off so many consumers is 85p, or about £1 million to the six directors of British Gas. The Minister feared that gas firms would be put off buying into British Gas if there were too many consumer safeguards in the Bill.

British Gas has already axed services and cut staff in preparation for the Bill, but the public outcry has forced the Government to introduce a battery of amendments to make sure that at least there are some consumer protections. However, the protections included are not adequate. That is why a staggering total of 231 amendments to the Government's own legislation have been tabled. The Committee chairman, the hon. Member for Staffordshire, Moorlands, voiced his grave reservations about the number of amendments which had been tabled, and about the fact that the Minister had tabled them so late. With more than 70 amendments tabled in the past few days, we cannot recommend this legislation to 18 million domestic gas consumers.

Who has been absent through all this? It is no wonder that the President of the Board of Trade left the Cabinet on Monday and took a plane to China. He has decided that this legislation is not safe in the Minister's hands.

Let us consider the Government's track record and why we oppose the Bill on principle. The Minister told us that British Gas has cut prices to consumers by 21 per cent., but the price that it has been paying for that gas has fallen by more than 27 per cent. since 1986. We want to know what has happened to the 6 per cent. cut that British Gas has enjoyed, which has not been passed on to consumers.

The Government say that the Bill will guarantee no cuts. It is vital that we challenge that. We challenged the cuts—the loss of 160 gas showrooms and 50 home service advisers for disabled and elderly gas consumers. We know that there will now be no curbs on British Gas or any of its competitor companies. The Government have rejected curbs on executive pay, effective safeguards for elderly and disabled consumers, price guarantees for the future and all the consumer protection that we proposed. We reject the Government and all that they stand for, and I urge the House to reject the Bill.

7.10 pm

**Mr. Eggar:** With the leave of the House, may I first say what a pleasure it was to be in a debate again with the hon. Member for Merthyr Tydfil and Rhymney (Mr. Rowlands)—these debates go back 10 years or so, but I enjoyed this one none the less. May I add my thanks to that given by the hon. Member for Edinburgh, South (Mr. Griffiths) to you, Madam Deputy Speaker, the Chairman of the Standing Committee and everyone who has been involved in preparing and drafting the Bill and helping to steer it through Committee and Report? May I also join with the hon. Member for Clackmannan (Mr. O'Neill), who paid tribute to the various groups outside the House who have played a constructive role as the Bill has been considered?

As the hon. Member for Edinburgh, South pointed out, we have had to introduce a number of technical amendments. Despite the fun that he was having at our expense, I am grateful to him and his colleagues for the sensible way in which we were able to handle those amendments. I would much rather not have had to proceed in that way, but there was no alternative.

The general objective of the Bill remains to build on successful experience in the industrial and commercial gas supply sector and to provide a sound foundation for the phased introduction of the benefits of competition to the 18 million domestic gas customers in the United Kingdom. Conservative Members believe that competition will reduce prices and improve services for consumers.

Opposition Members seem completely unable to grasp that the introduction of competition can benefit customers, whether they move to another independent supplier or stay with British Gas, and that has been a constant theme during the passage of the Bill. The reality is that nothing sharpens up a company and improves its performance

more than the prospect of its customers taking their business elsewhere. Despite that essential truth, the Opposition think that customers need to be protected from having a choice.

The Opposition consistently say that they are concerned about what the hon. Member for Clackmannan calls cherry-picking. They are really concerned about not being able to interfere and dictate the results before the competition commences. The old Labour party is in the ascendant.

I shall deal briefly with the points raised by Opposition Members. They claim that the Bill lacks adequate protection for groups of vulnerable customers. Let us examine that criticism. First, special services for pensioners, the disabled and the blind will continue, just as they have with British Gas. Indeed, the Bill and the licence ensure that those requirements for those groups will be as tough as or tougher than they are at present.

The Opposition have suggested that the social obligations are inadequate because they are not on the face of the Bill, but they simply do not appear to understand that a licence condition, as structured in the Bill, is as legally binding as a provision in the legislation. A large number of the current obligations of British Gas are dealt with in its licence. Of course, the standard conditions of licences cannot be changed without the agreement of the Secretary of State.

Some Opposition Members claimed that the Bill would discriminate against low-income customers, yet the real interest of those customers is in getting cheaper gas. That is what they want and, because prices will come down as a result of the Bill, they will benefit more, proportionately, from price reductions than other customers.

If Opposition Members are really concerned about helping low-income customers, they should have supported the Bill wholeheartedly. In practice, they have opposed it in detail and, had their amendments been carried, they would have made it virtually impossible for competition to arise in any meaningful sense.

I think that there is one thing on which hon. Members on both sides of the House are agreed—we are all concerned to protect the interests of those customers who have genuine difficulties in paying their bills. The Government are as concerned about that as anyone in the House; that is why all suppliers, as a condition of their licences, will have to follow debt and disconnection procedures that are designed to assist those in genuine difficulty.

Today, *The Times* said that the hon. Member for Edinburgh, South

"clearly believes in the formulation of policy on the run."

It also commented:

"fund managers . . . perceive Mr. Griffiths' style to be long on threats and short on debate."

Those of us who were members of the Standing Committee with the hon. Gentleman know that the fund managers are right, but we can go further and say that he is long on prejudice and short on analysis. His speeches have been wrong in almost every regard.

I shall give one example. In Committee, he said:

"the public are concerned that British Gas is proposing to downgrade all the current licence conditions and to review the provision of Braille controls for blind people."

[Mr. Eggar]

He continued:

"I fear that blind, disabled and elderly people will be forced to pick up the bill for such services."—[*Official Report, Standing Committee A*, 21 March 1995; c. 32.]

Either in ignorance or deliberately, he was misleading the Committee, because the truth is that the draft standard conditions of licences make it clear that the existing service requirement will continue. The free gas safety check, special adaptors and controls, passwords and special inquiry facilities for the blind and disabled will all be there and will be guaranteed—all without charge.

The hon. Member for Clackmannan referred, at the beginning of this Third Reading debate, to the regulator and the role of regulation. He referred to the speech that his right hon. Friend the Member for Copeland (Dr. Cunningham) made this afternoon, which I have here. The general thrust was that, at present, the regulator has too much discretionary power.

After reading that analysis, I considered the amendments that the Opposition tabled to the Bill. In some areas, they tabled amendments that would have given the regulator more power, not less. They wanted the regulator to have the power to challenge the terms of consumers' contracts and, in effect, to be involved in decisions on the remuneration of gas company executives. They wanted the regulator to have a duty to secure choice to all consumers and not merely to promote it. Only yesterday, the hon. Member for Neath (Mr. Hain) was inviting the House to agree that the regulator should have regard for the industrial and strategic interests of the British economy.

On the one hand, the right hon. Member for Copeland, who leads his party on these matters, is saying that the regulator has too much discretionary power and, on the other, that the Opposition have been tabling amendments designed to increase that power throughout the passage of the Bill. It is no good the hon. Member for Edinburgh, South just grinning. He claimed earlier in our proceedings that he had written the speech for the right hon. Member for Copeland, so he does not understand either his amendments in Committee or what he has written for the right hon. Member for Copeland. He cannot have it both ways.

The Labour party's attitude to the Bill has been absolutely fascinating. We have seen a battle played out between old Labour—the hon. Members for Bolsover (Mr. Skinner) and for Brent, East (Mr. Livingstone) are in their places—and so-called "new" Labour. The hon. Member for Clackmannan made a speech last November in which he said:

"it is not the function of Labour to defend British Gas as the monopoly supplier of gas to any sector of the UK market."

At that time, new Labour was on top and apparently in favour of competition.

To be fair, on Second Reading the right hon. Member for Copeland endorsed that competition. But official Labour abstained on Second Reading and it was left to the hon. Members for Bolsover, for Falkirk, West (Mr. Canavan), for Islington, North (Mr. Corbyn), for Preston (Mrs. Wise), for Bradford, West (Mr. Madden) and for Halifax (Mrs. Mahon) and the right hon. Member for Chesterfield (Mr. Benn) to vote against Second Reading. In Committee, new Labour prevailed, except the hon. Member for Neath when he bothered to turn up and make speeches for the benefit of his local papers. [*Interruption.*]

**Madam Deputy Speaker:** Order. What started as a series of private conversations has now become a hubbub. I am not prepared to preside over a hubbub. I therefore ask for considerably greater quiet.

**Mr. Eggar:** After hours of debate and a well-trailed speech by the hon. Member for Dunfermline, East (Mr. Brown) in which he extolled the virtues of competition, today on Third Reading the Opposition have a chance to say conclusively whether they are in favour of competition. That is the choice they must make in a few seconds when we go in to the Lobbies. Will the official Opposition represent a victory for new Labour in favour of competition, or for old Labour against competition? If they oppose Third Reading, they will show what we all know: that the Labour party has not changed and is still in favour of state control and against competition. A vote against Third Reading will be a vote for the hon. Member for Bolsover.

*Question put*, That the Bill be now read the Third time:—

*The House divided*: Ayes 297, Noes 228.

**Division No. 149]**                                    **[7.22 pm**

### AYES

| | |
|---|---|
| Ainsworth, Peter (East Surrey) | Carrington, Matthew |
| Aitken, Rt Hon Jonathan | Carttiss, Michael |
| Alison, Rt Hon Michael (Selby) | Cash, William |
| Allason, Rupert (Torbay) | Channon, Rt Hon Paul |
| Alton, David | Chidgey, David |
| Amess, David | Clappison, James |
| Arbuthnot, James | Clark, Dr Michael (Rochford) |
| Arnold, Jacques (Gravesham) | Clifton-Brown, Geoffrey |
| Arnold, Sir Thomas (Hazel Grv) | Coe, Sebastian |
| Ashby, David | Congdon, David |
| Ashdown, Rt Hon Paddy | Conway, Derek |
| Atkins, Robert | Coombs, Anthony (Wyre For'st) |
| Atkinson, David (Bour'mouth E) | Coombs, Simon (Swindon) |
| Atkinson, Peter (Hexham) | Cope, Rt Hon Sir John |
| Baker, Rt Hon Kenneth (Mole V) | Couchman, James |
| Baker, Nicholas (North Dorset) | Cran, James |
| Baldry, Tony | Currie, Mrs Edwina (S D'by'ire) |
| Banks, Matthew (Southport) | Curry, David (Skipton & Ripon) |
| Banks, Robert (Harrogate) | Davies, Quentin (Stamford) |
| Bates, Michael | Davis, David (Boothferry) |
| Batiste, Spencer | Day, Stephen |
| Bendall, Vivian | Deva, Nirj Joseph |
| Beresford, Sir Paul | Dorrell, Rt Hon Stephen |
| Biffen, Rt Hon John | Douglas-Hamilton, Lord James |
| Body, Sir Richard | Dover, Den |
| Booth, Hartley | Duncan, Alan |
| Boswell, Tim | Duncan-Smith, Iain |
| Bottomley, Peter (Eltham) | Dunn, Bob |
| Bottomley, Rt Hon Virginia | Durant, Sir Anthony |
| Bowis, John | Eggar, Rt Hon Tim |
| Boyson, Rt Hon Sir Rhodes | Elletson, Harold |
| Brandreth, Gyles | Emery, Rt Hon Sir Peter |
| Brazier, Julian | Evans, David (Welwyn Hatfield) |
| Bright, Sir Graham | Evans, Jonathan (Brecon) |
| Brooke, Rt Hon Peter | Evans, Nigel (Ribble Valley) |
| Brown, M (Brigg & Cl'thorpes) | Evans, Roger (Monmouth) |
| Browning, Mrs Angela | Evennett, David |
| Bruce, Ian (Dorset) | Faber, David |
| Budgen, Nicholas | Fabricant, Michael |
| Burns, Simon | Fenner, Dame Peggy |
| Burt, Alistair | Field, Barry (Isle of Wight) |
| Butcher, John | Fishburn, Dudley |
| Butler, Peter | Forman, Nigel |
| Butterfill, John | Forsyth, Rt Hon Michael (Stirling) |
| Campbell, Menzies (Fife NE) | Forth, Eric |
| Carlisle, John (Luton North) | Fowler, Rt Hon Sir Norman |
| Carlisle, Sir Kenneth (Lincoln) | Fox, Dr Liam (Woodspring) |

Fox, Sir Marcus (Shipley)
Freeman, Rt Hon Roger
French, Douglas
Gale, Roger
Gallie, Phil
Gardiner, Sir George
Garel-Jones, Rt Hon Tristan
Garnier, Edward
Gill, Christopher
Gillan, Cheryl
Goodlad, Rt Hon Alastair
Goodson-Wickes, Dr Charles
Gorman, Mrs Teresa
Gorst, Sir John
Grant, Sir A (SW Cambs)
Greenway, Harry (Ealing N)
Greenway, John (Ryedale)
Griffiths, Peter (Portsmouth, N)
Grylls, Sir Michael
Gummer, Rt Hon John Selwyn
Hague, William
Hamilton, Rt Hon Sir Archibald
Hamilton, Neil (Tatton)
Hampson, Dr Keith
Hanley, Rt Hon Jeremy
Hannam, Sir John
Hargreaves, Andrew
Harris, David
Harvey, Nick
Haselhurst, Alan
Hawkins, Nick
Hayes, Jerry
Heald, Oliver
Heath, Rt Hon Sir Edward
Heathcoat-Amory, David
Hendry, Charles
Hicks, Robert
Higgins, Rt Hon Sir Terence
Hill, James (Southampton Test)
Hogg, Rt Hon Douglas (G'tham)
Horam, John
Howard, Rt Hon Michael
Howarth, Alan (Strat'rd-on-A)
Howell, Sir Ralph (N Norfolk)
Hughes, Robert G (Harrow W)
Hughes, Simon (Southwark)
Hunt, Sir John (Ravensbourne)
Hunter, Andrew
Hurd, Rt Hon Douglas
Jack, Michael
Jackson, Robert (Wantage)
Jenkin, Bernard
Jessel, Toby
Johnson Smith, Sir Geoffrey
Jones, Gwilym (Cardiff N)
Jones, Nigel (Cheltenham)
Jones, Robert B (W Hertfdshr)
Jopling, Rt Hon Michael
Kellett-Bowman, Dame Elaine
Kennedy, Charles (Ross,C&S)
King, Rt Hon Tom
Kirkhope, Timothy
Knapman, Roger
Knight, Mrs Angela (Erewash)
Knight, Greg (Derby N)
Knight, Dame Jill (Bir'm E'st'n)
Kynoch, George (Kincardine)
Lait, Mrs Jacqui
Lamont, Rt Hon Norman
Lang, Rt Hon Ian
Lawrence, Sir Ivan
Legg, Barry
Leigh, Edward
Lennox-Boyd, Sir Mark
Lester, Jim (Broxtowe)
Lidington, David

Lightbown, David
Lilley, Rt Hon Peter
Lloyd, Rt Hon Sir Peter (Fareham)
Lord, Michael
Lyell, Rt Hon Sir Nicholas
Lynne, Ms Liz
MacGregor, Rt Hon John
MacKay, Andrew
Maclean, David
Maclennan, Robert
McLoughlin, Patrick
McNair-Wilson, Sir Patrick
Madel, Sir David
Maitland, Lady Olga
Malone, Gerald
Mans, Keith
Marlow, Tony
Marshall, John (Hendon S)
Marshall, Sir Michael (Arundel)
Martin, David (Portsmouth S)
Mates, Michael
Mawhinney, Rt Hon Dr Brian
Mellor, Rt Hon David
Merchant, Piers
Michie, Mrs Ray (Argyll & Bute)
Mills, Iain
Mitchell, Andrew (Gedling)
Mitchell, Sir David (NW Hants)
Moate, Sir Roger
Monro, Sir Hector
Montgomery, Sir Fergus
Needham, Rt Hon Richard
Nelson, Anthony
Neubert, Sir Michael
Newton, Rt Hon Tony
Nicholls, Patrick
Nicholson, David
Norris, Steve
Onslow, Rt Hon Sir Cranley
Oppenheim, Phillip
Ottaway, Richard
Page, Richard
Patnick, Sir Irvine
Patten, Rt Hon John
Pattie, Rt Hon Sir Geoffrey
Pawsey, James
Peacock, Mrs Elizabeth
Pickles, Eric
Porter, Barry (Wirral S)
Porter, David (Waveney)
Portillo, Rt Hon Michael
Powell, William (Corby)
Rendel, David
Renton, Rt Hon Tim
Riddick, Graham
Rifkind, Rt Hon Malcolm
Robathan, Andrew
Robinson, Mark (Somerton)
Roe, Mrs Marion (Broxbourne)
Rowe, Andrew (Mid Kent)
Rumbold, Rt Hon Dame Angela
Ryder, Rt Hon Richard
Sackville, Tom
Sainsbury, Rt Hon Sir Timothy
Scott, Rt Hon Sir Nicholas
Shaw, David (Dover)
Shaw, Sir Giles (Pudsey)
Shephard, Rt Hon Gillian
Shepherd, Colin (Hereford)
Shepherd, Richard (Aldridge)
Sims, Roger
Skeet, Sir Trevor
Smith, Tim (Beaconsfield)
Soames, Nicholas
Spencer, Sir Derek
Spicer, Michael (S Worcs)

Spink, Dr Robert
Spring, Richard
Sproat, Iain
Squire, Robin (Hornchurch)
Stanley, Rt Hon Sir John
Steel, Rt Hon Sir David
Steen, Anthony
Stephen, Michael
Stern, Michael
Stewart, Allan
Streeter, Gary
Sumberg, David
Sykes, John
Tapsell, Sir Peter
Taylor, Ian (Esher)
Taylor, John M (Solihull)
Taylor, Matthew (Truro)
Taylor, Sir Teddy (Southend, E)
Temple-Morris, Peter
Thomason, Roy
Thompson, Sir Donald (C'er V)
Thompson, Patrick (Norwich N)
Thornton, Sir Malcolm
Thurnham, Peter
Townend, John (Bridlington)
Townsend, Cyril D (Bexl'yh'th)
Tracey, Richard

Trend, Michael
Twinn, Dr Ian
Vaughan, Sir Gerard
Viggers, Peter
Waldegrave, Rt Hon William
Walden, George
Walker, Bill (N Tayside)
Wallace, James
Waller, Gary
Ward, John
Wardle, Charles (Bexhill)
Waterson, Nigel
Watts, John
Wells, Bowen
Whitney, Ray
Whittingdale, John
Widdecombe, Ann
Wilkinson, John
Willetts, David
Wilshire, David
Winterton, Nicholas (Macc'f'ld)
Wolfson, Mark
Yeo, Tim
Young, Rt Hon Sir George

**Tellers for the Ayes:**
    Mr. Sydney Chapman and
    Mr. Timothy Wood.

## NOES

Abbott, Ms Diane
Ainsworth, Robert (Cov'try NE)
Anderson, Donald (Swansea E)
Anderson, Ms Janet (Rossendale)
Anderson, Ms Janet
Armstrong, Hilary
Ashton, Joe
Austin-Walker, John
Banks, Tony (Newham NW)
Barnes, Harry
Barron, Kevin
Battle, John
Bayley, Hugh
Beckett, Rt Hon Margaret
Bell, Stuart
Bennett, Andrew F
Berry, Roger
Betts, Clive
Blunkett, David
Boateng, Paul
Bradley, Keith
Bray, Dr Jeremy
Brown, N (N'c'tle upon Tyne E)
Burden, Richard
Byers, Stephen
Caborn, Richard
Callaghan, Jim
Campbell, Mrs Anne (C'bridge)
Campbell, Ronnie (Blyth V)
Canavan, Dennis
Cann, Jamie
Chisholm, Malcolm
Church, Judith
Clapham, Michael
Clark, Dr David (South Shields)
Clarke, Eric (Midlothian)
Clarke, Tom (Monklands W)
Clelland, David
Clwyd, Mrs Ann
Coffey, Ann
Cohen, Harry
Connarty, Michael
Cook, Frank (Stockton N)
Cook, Robin (Livingston)
Corbett, Robin
Corbyn, Jeremy

Cousins, Jim
Cummings, John
Cunliffe, Lawrence
Cunningham, Jim (Covy SE)
Dafis, Cynog
Dalyell, Tam
Darling, Alistair
Davies, Bryan (Oldham C'tral)
Davies, Rt Hon Denzil (Llanelli)
Davies, Ron (Caerphilly)
Denham, John
Dewar, Donald
Dixon, Don
Dobson, Frank
Donohoe, Brian H
Dowd, Jim
Dunnachie, Jimmy
Dunwoody, Mrs Gwyneth
Eagle, Ms Angela
Eastham, Ken
Enright, Derek
Etherington, Bill
Evans, John (St Helens N)
Ewing, Mrs Margaret
Faulds, Andrew
Field, Frank (Birkenhead)
Flynn, Paul
Foster, Rt Hon Derek
Foulkes, George
Fraser, John
Fyfe, Maria
Galbraith, Sam
Galloway, George
Gapes, Mike
Garrett, John
Gerrard, Neil
Gilbert, Rt Hon Dr John
Godman, Dr Norman A
Godsiff, Roger
Golding, Mrs Llin
Gordon, Mildred
Graham, Thomas
Grant, Bernie (Tottenham)
Griffiths, Nigel (Edinburgh S)
Griffiths, Win (Bridgend)
Grocott, Bruce

Gunnell, John
Hain, Peter
Hall, Mike
Harman, Ms Harriet
Hattersley, Rt Hon Roy
Heppell, John
Hill, Keith (Streatham)
Hinchliffe, David
Hodge, Margaret
Hoey, Kate
Hogg, Norman (Cumbernauld)
Hood, Jimmy
Hoon, Geoffrey
Howarth, George (Knowsley North)
Howells, Dr. Kim (Pontypridd)
Hoyle, Doug
Hughes, Kevin (Doncaster N)
Hughes, Robert (Aberdeen N)
Hughes, Roy (Newport E)
Hutton, John
Illsley, Eric
Ingram, Adam
Jackson, Glenda (H'stead)
Jackson, Helen (Shef'ld, H)
Jamieson, David
Janner, Greville
Jones, Barry (Alyn and D'side)
Jones, Lynne (B'ham S O)
Jones, Martyn (Clwyd, SW)
Jowell, Tessa
Kennedy, Jane (Lpool Brdgn)
Khabra, Piara S
Kilfoyle, Peter
Lestor, Joan (Eccles)
Lewis, Terry
Litherland, Robert
Livingstone, Ken
Lloyd, Tony (Stretford)
Loyden, Eddie
McAllion, John
McAvoy, Thomas
McCartney, Ian
Macdonald, Calum
McFall, John
Mackinlay, Andrew
McLeish, Henry
McMaster, Gordon
McNamara, Kevin
MacShane, Denis
Madden, Max
Mahon, Alice
Mandelson, Peter
Marek, Dr John
Martlew, Eric
Meacher, Michael
Meale, Alan
Michael, Alun
Michie, Bill (Sheffield Heeley)
Milburn, Alan
Mitchell, Austin (Gt Grimsby)
Moonie, Dr Lewis
Morgan, Rhodri
Morley, Elliot
Morris, Rt Hon Alfred (Wy'nshawe)
Morris, Estelle (B'ham Yardley)
Mudie, George
Mullin, Chris
Murphy, Paul
Oakes, Rt Hon Gordon
O'Brien, William (Normanton)

O'Hara, Edward
Olner, Bill
O'Neill, Martin
Orme, Rt Hon Stanley
Parry, Robert
Pearson, Ian
Pendry, Tom
Pike, Peter L
Pope, Greg
Powell, Ray (Ogmore)
Prentice, Bridget (Lew'm E)
Prentice, Gordon (Pendle)
Prescott, Rt Hon John
Primarolo, Dawn
Purchase, Ken
Quin, Ms Joyce
Randall, Stuart
Raynsford, Nick
Reid, Dr John
Robertson, George (Hamilton)
Robinson, Geoffrey (Co'try NW)
Roche, Mrs Barbara
Rogers, Allan
Rooker, Jeff
Rooney, Terry
Ross, Ernie (Dundee W)
Rowlands, Ted
Ruddock, Joan
Salmond, Alex
Sedgemore, Brian
Sheerman, Barry
Shore, Rt Hon Peter
Short, Clare
Skinner, Dennis
Smith, Andrew (Oxford E)
Smith, Chris (Isl'ton S & F'sbury)
Smith, Llew (Blaenau Gwent)
Snape, Peter
Soley, Clive
Spellar, John
Squire, Rachel (Dunfermline W)
Steinberg, Gerry
Stevenson, George
Stott, Roger
Straw, Jack
Sutcliffe, Gerry
Taylor, Mrs Ann (Dewsbury)
Timms, Stephen
Tipping, Paddy
Touhig, Don
Turner, Dennis
Vaz, Keith
Walker, Rt Hon Sir Harold
Walley, Joan
Wareing, Robert N
Watson, Mike
Welsh, Andrew
Wicks, Malcolm
Williams, Rt Hon Alan (Sw'n W)
Williams, Alan W (Carmarthen)
Wilson, Brian
Winnick, David
Wise, Audrey
Worthington, Tony
Wray, Jimmy
Wright, Dr Tony
Young, David (Bolton SE)

**Tellers for the Noes:**
   Mr. John Owen Jones and
   Mr. Joe Benton.

*Question accordingly agreed to.*

*Bill read the Third time, and passed.*

**Mr. Donald Dewar** (Glasgow, Garscadden): On a point of order, Madam Deputy Speaker. May I briefly ask your advice on a matter of some importance? In another place, Lord Mackay of Ardbrecknish announced that the jobseeker's allowance would not be introduced as planned on 1 April 1996, but would be introduced in October 1996—a delay of six months. Since then, we have obtained a little further information which makes the matter even more important.

In a written answer today, we are told that Ministers

"have concluded that, in order to deliver an excellent service to unemployed people from day one"—

which sounds an interesting euphemism—

"JSA should be introduced in October 1996."

It continues:

"the duration of an unemployed claimant's entitlement to Unemployment Benefit will, from April 1996, be the same as it would have been had JSA been introduced on that date."

In other words, the cut from 12 to six months in entitlement will take effect from 1 April.

I am also told, although I cannot confirm it, that lower rates of unemployment benefit will be introduced as though JSA had been introduced on 1 April and that changes in structure, such as the differential rates for those below and above the age of 25 will be introduced on 1 April. I may be wrong, but it appears that the change in Government intention is a retreat in theory but not in substance, and that, to put it quite frankly, what happened today was a form of deception in terms of an apparent announcement that does not bear examination.

My concern is that, if they mean what they appear to mean, today's changes are extremely important. They also raise important issues about the Government, if they can announce that they do not intend to implement changes and then smuggle them in administratively. There would appear to be no need for a statement in the House or any administrative regulation or legislation in order to change unemployment structures into some kind of ghost of the jobseeker's allowance.

In view of all that, it is important that we have a statement at the earliest possible opportunity. I wonder whether you, Madam Deputy Speaker, have had any intimation of one, or if Ministers can reassure us that these rather mysterious and opaque goings on will be explained to the House so that we can judge them for what they are worth and take the appropriate action.

**Madam Deputy Speaker (Dame Janet Fookes):** I have had no intimation that a statement is to be made, but the Leader of the House is present and no doubt he will have heard what was said. Even if no statement is forthcoming, one can rely on the ingenuity of hon. Members in finding other legitimate ways of raising the issue.

**Mr. Ian McCartney** (Makerfield): On a point of order, Madam Deputy Speaker.

**Madam Deputy Speaker:** Is it the same point of order?

**Mr. McCartney:** No, it is a different point of order. I am the hon. Member who put the questions on the Order Paper on 11 May for written answer on 16 May. The parliamentary questions were delivered to me after they were submitted to the press in the Press Gallery. However, despite that, looking at the detail of the written answers, it is clear that some fundamental questions still require answers. First, the Government did not state in the written answer—

**Madam Deputy Speaker:** Order. It seems to me that the hon. Member is raising the same point of order. I have said that I can deal only with matters that relate to responsibilities of the Chair. This is clearly not the responsibility of the Chair.

**Mr. McCartney:** I am raising a different point of order, Madam Deputy Speaker, relating to whether the Secretary of State has exceeded his powers in respect of the answer that I was given, which requires a response. I apologise if I am delaying the House, but the answer is vital to the business of the House. The position is clear—

**Madam Deputy Speaker:** Order. I am sorry to interrupt the hon. Gentleman but I can deal only with matters that relate to the responsibilities of the Chair. The matters to which the hon. Gentleman refers clearly do not. I must ask the hon. Gentleman to desist.

**Mr. McCartney:** I do not want to incur your wrath, Madam Deputy Speaker, but—

**Madam Deputy Speaker:** Order. I have effectively asked the hon. Gentleman to resume his seat. We must move on.

**Mr. McCartney:** The question that relates to the Chair is whether the Secretary of State's answer of 16 May in respect of my question of 11 May is ultra vires. If so, both the Leader of the House—who is present—and Ministers should come to the House with an explanation.

**Madam Deputy Speaker:** Order. Those matters are not for the Chair. I am not prepared to consider them further.

# STATUTORY INSTRUMENTS, &c.

### FEES AND CHARGES

*Motion made, and Question put forthwith pursuant to Standing Order No. 101(5) (Standing Committees on Statutory Instruments, &c.),*

That the draft Department of Trade and Industry (Fees) (Amendment) Order 1995, which was laid before this House on 3rd April, be approved.—*[Mr. Kirkhope.]*

*Question agreed to.*

### NORTHERN IRELAND

*Motion made, and Question put forthwith pursuant to Standing Order No. 101(5) (Standing Committees on Statutory Instruments, &c.),*

That the draft Historic Monuments and Archaeological Objects (Northern Ireland) Order 1995, which was laid before this House on 3rd April, be approved.—*[Mr. Kirkhope.]*

*Question agreed to.*

# EUROPEAN COMMUNITY DOCUMENTS

### TELECOMMUNICATIONS INFRASTRUCTURE

*Motion made, and Question put forthwith pursuant to Standing Order No. 102(9) (European Standing Committees),*

That this House takes note of European Community Documents Nos. 10589/94 and 4674/95, relating to the liberalisation of telecommunications infrastructure, and the unnumbered Explanatory Memorandum submitted by the Department of Trade and Industry on 28th April 1995, relating to a future regulatory framework for telecommunications, and supports the Government's view that competition in the provision of telecoms services and infrastructure is essential to guarantee the widespread availability of affordable high quality telecoms within the European Community.—*[Mr. Kirkhope.]*

*Question agreed to.*

# RJB (Mining)

*Motion made, and Question proposed,* That this House do now adjourn.—*[Mr. Kirkhope.]*

7.41 pm

**Mr. Clive Betts** (Sheffield, Attercliffe): I want to draw the attention of the House to certain events in my constituency on the Tinsley site and to ask questions of the Minister about the role played by RJB (Mining) and other companies with which its chairman, Richard Budge, has been associated. My questions concern the opencasting of the Tinsley site; the failure to provide an airport there; the role played by Sheffield development corporation, British Coal and its officials, and Ministers; and whether Richard Budge is a fit and proper person to run British Coal operations.

I shall not delve into the history of efforts to provide an airport for Sheffield, which is the largest city in Europe not to have an airport. During the 1980s, another survey of potential sites was made. The site at the top of the list, in terms of commercial viability and Civil Aviation Authority air safety, was Tinsley. Interest in the city, from a council and business perspective, was also being developed.

In 1987, British Coal changed that scenario by indicating that it wanted to opencast at Tinsley. Contrary to statements made from time to time, there has from the beginning been a close link between the opencasting at the site and the airport development, with the gains from the former helping to fund the latter being a key to subsequent events. The first sign of British Coal's wish to opencast was a press release, which stated that opencasting on the site would help to finance the proposed Sheffield airport and would not delay the city's wish to have the short take-off and landing airport in operation by 1991. We are now in 1995, and there is not an aeroplane in sight, let alone a runway. Nevertheless, that press release confirms the early link between the opencasting site and the provision of an airport.

I was not against opencasting on the Tinsley site. There are differences of view among Opposition Members about opencasting, and I oppose it when it is proposed for green-field sites and risks destroying the environment. The Tinsley site was extremely polluted, with the cost of ridding it of chemicals and other pollutants from the former steel works estimated at £20 million. It was badly despoiled but an ideal location, being next to the M1 in Sheffield's industrial corridor. It was a prime site for development.

I declare an interest as a Member of Parliament sponsored by the Transport and General Workers Union, which has members employed in the opencast industry. The site would create jobs, but there were local concerns about dust and pollution. The city council, which was then the planning authority, took steps as part of the planning agreement to ensure controls and constraints on times of working. We were also conscious of the fact that, if we turned down British Coal's proposals, its application for opencasting might have been granted on appeal, yielding none of the potential benefits for the locality.

In general, I support the provision of an airport on the Tinsley site. Again, community concerns about noise and flying hours must be taken into account. I am particularly aware of Phillimore school in my constituency, because recently there has been speculation that a requirement

fully to insulate the school from aircraft noise might be relaxed. I am not in favour of any such relaxation, but want the original proposals for proper insulation to be implemented.

There was full consultation and opinion surveys. I attended public meetings with colleagues and representatives of British Coal Opencast, and a community liaison group was established. By and large, the opencasting operations did not have a massive impact on the community. However, given the profits made from that site, I am concerned about constituents such as Mrs. Lilley, a pensioner. Dust from the site made it necessary to have cleaned her husband's headstone in the local cemetery. That cost her £100, which she could ill afford— and that bill still has not been paid by Richard Budge, his company or anybody else connected with the opencast operations. That sort of meanness is typical of the way in which the city of Sheffield has been ripped off.

There is real anger that British Coal got coal out of the site and Richard Budge got money out of it, but Sheffield still does not have an airport. Many supposed community benefits have not happened.

At the end of the consultation process in 1989, an initial planning agreement was drawn up, which clearly linked the opencast arrangements and the airport. From the beginning, Tony Palmer, British Coal Opencast's regional director, attended meetings that linked the two. He was associated with the press release that I mentioned. I found him to be a fair and open person with whom to do business. I put that on record because his consultation was very thorough. Sheffield city council was still the planning authority and granted the initial permission, and British Coal then placed a contract with A. F. Budge through its subsidiary, A. F. Budge (Mining), to opencast the site.

There were benefits for the community in return. A £250,000 community fund was established and many local groups have been involved in developing projects. A gipsy site was relocated and given improved facilities, which was welcome and important. Five holes of a local golf course were relocated and a new club house provided. There was also the access road to the edge of the site, to be built at a cost of £1.7 million. That, too, would benefit its future development.

There was also an agreement that once the site had been used for opencast mining, the ground would be compacted in such a way as to be suitable for laying a runway. Has the ground been thus compacted? People who worked on the site claim that the job was never done properly—the earth was just tipped back on to the site, and if anyone tried to lay a runway on it, he would end up with the airport equivalent of a traffic calming measure. Bumps would appear as the ground settled.

On 14 July 1989 a contract was agreed between British Coal Opencast and A. F. Budge (Mining) for 800,000 tonnes of coal to be extracted from the site. The planning gains were to be the other side of the coin; but clearly British Coal and A. F. Budge (Mining) were to make large profits from the site—there is no dispute about that. Indeed, just today I received from a Minister at the Department of the Environment a letter accepting the fact that all those community gains were specifically lodged in the original planning agreement, and formed part of it.

Immediately the initial planning agreement was drawn up, planning responsibility transferred from Sheffield city council to Sheffield development corporation. In the recent "Panorama" programme, which included a great deal of excellent information, one of the issues that was not absolutely clear was the fact that, as events unfolded, the responsibility lay not with Sheffield city council but with Sheffield development corporation.

It is clear from the whole affair that the only gains to the community from the entire process were those stipulated in the planning agreement signed by Sheffield city council, which got the matter right and achieved something for the local community. The rest of the problems appeared once the council had left the scene—I shall return to some of the advice given by councillors in due course.

The development corporation was set up against the advice of the city council. We, like the chamber of commerce, opposed it in principle—the latter believed that it could work with us. Sheffield city council had entered into partnerships and joint working arrangements with the private sector in the mid-1980s, so nothing could be further from the truth than the view that Labour councils cannot sit down and talk to business, or that we are against development and against creating new industries and jobs.

The Government's view, however, was that the regeneration of derelict areas, and in particular of an area of Sheffield which had lost 40,000 jobs following the collapse of the steel and engineering industries, was a matter for development corporations. David Trippier, the Minister at the time, came to see me when I was leader of the council and asked what our response would be to a Sheffield development corporation with £50 million to spend.

I said that I thought that the city council, in conjunction with Government and private industry, working on a tripartite basis, would spend the money better and with more democratic accountability. I added that, if the Government were making it a take-it-or-leave-it offer, we would not wish away a development corporation with £50 million, which could benefit local people. Certainly, we opposed it in principle, but once it was established we would sit down and work with it and try to make it as big a success as possible. That was a difficult decision for the council, but none of what follows can be laid at the door of the city council's refusing to work with the development corporation.

We entered into a unique agreement with the corporation, trying to ensure that as much democratic accountability and openness as possible were brought to bear on the proceedings. We sat down with it to work for the benefit of the people of Sheffield. In all that follows, however, it is important to bear it in mind that this was ultimately a non-accountable body—except perhaps to Ministers, who must surely be responsible for what development corporations do, because no one else can be. Supposedly, furthermore, the body was set up not only because local Labour councillors would not work with business but because business acumen was needed to reach the right development decisions on behalf of local people. One can only smile at that in the light of what ensued.

In May 1990 Sheffield development corporation entered into a new agreement with A. F. Budge for the construction and operation of an airport on the site at Tinsley. It was going to be cross-subsidised by the development of adjacent land, by the company, for a business park. In some ways, that seemed a sensible

arrangement. But then, some time later, on 12 March 1991, came an extension to the opencast contract belonging to British Coal and lodged with AFB (Mining). That extension altered the tonnage to be taken from the site, from the 800,000 tonnes that the opencast executive had agreed initially with Sheffield city council, to 1.1 million tonnes.

I have seen communications from Ministers stating that there was no link between the opencast operation and the provision of infrastructure for, and the construction of, the airport. Nevertheless, from the very beginning in 1989, the initial planning agreement linked the two. Now Ministers claim that the extension of the agreement to mine opencast coal on the site was not linked with the further agreement to allow AFB (Mining) to develop the site for an airport. That is a key point in the whole discussion.

I have a letter, dated 15 May, from the office of the chairman of the British Coal Corporation, signed by Mr. Bryn Morris, corporate affairs director, in which he states:

"In May 1990, Sheffield Development Corporation entered into an agreement with A. F. Budge (Mining) Ltd for the construction and operation of the airport and the development of adjacent land".

So far, we do not disagree.

"Subsequently, on 12 March 1991 the opencast contract between British Coal and A. F. Budge (Mining) Ltd was altered, with the tonnage to be extracted from the site increased. This was as a consequence of the agreement between A. F. Budge (Mining) Ltd and the SDC with regard to the airport construction, which extended the time available for the operation of the opencast site."

So British Coal believes that the agreement to build the infrastructure for the airport and the extension of the opencast contract were linked—that, at any rate, is how its corporate affairs director understands the situation.

Ultimately, not the original 800,000 tonnes, nor even the extra 300,000 tonnes, were taken from the site: 1.5 million tonnes of coal were extracted. How was the extraction of the coal assessed? How did 400,000 tonnes more appear, as if by magic, right at the end of the scheme? Who did the calculations; who benefited from them; and what did the community get for the extra coal extracted? It appeared in no agreement, but it just so happens that 1.5 million tonnes was the amount initially requested by British Coal's opencast division back in 1987—a request that Sheffield city council refused to accept in the planning agreement of 1989.

In my mind, and in the minds of local people and of British Coal's opencast division, the airport agreement and the extension of the opencasting agreement were certainly linked, under the same parent company—A. F. Budge (Mining). Will the Minister publish all details of the agreements, so that if there is any dispute about them, the public and Members of the House can see them and come to their own conclusions about the truth of the matter?

On 15 March 1991, three days after the extension of the opencast agreement, another peculiar event took place. The opencast contractor, A. F. Budge (Mining), agreed to take over responsibility for any defects resulting from the improper compacting of the site within five years of the completion of that compacting. In return for taking over and guaranteeing to put right any defects—I should have thought that the contractor should be responsible for defects in any case—British Coal Opencast paid to A. F. Budge (Mining) £1 million. A private contractor

[Mr. Clive Betts]

received £1 million of public money to put right the defects that resulted from its own failure to compact the site properly.

That of itself begs quite a few questions. Given that AFB (Mining) and its subsidiaries have now gone out of business, is British Coal Opencast still responsible for putting right defects on the site? Who is responsible? Having paid £1 million, is British Coal now left with the responsibility for putting right any defects of compaction? In other words, did it hand over £1 million to a private company for no return, or did it transfer those responsibilities in the deal done with RJB (Mining) as part of its takeover of British Coal's responsibilities in Britain? It would be interesting to hear the Minister's response.

What checks were carried out before the sell-off of all the operations on the viability of the work carried out by RJB (Mining) on the site? Was it compacted properly? I have asked the question and I shall repeat it because it is so important. When British Coal gave £1 million to AFB (Mining) in March 1991 for a guarantee that defects would be put right five years after work on compacting finished, just a year or more before the company became insolvent, what checks did British Coal Opencast make on the viability of the company? It is incredible that a public body should have accepted a guarantee from a private company stretching more than five years ahead, yet within 18 months that private company had gone bankrupt. Were any checks on its financial viability carried out?

In March 1992, the A. F. Budge group was restructured and Richard Budge, through his new company, RJB (Mining), bought out AFB (Mining)'s interests. The opencast contract at Tinsley was novated to that new company, but not the airport agreement. That is the crux of the issue. Why was the airport agreement not transferred to the new company when, clearly, all the way along the key issue was that the profits from the opencasting operation would help fund the airport project? Going back to the initial proposals in 1987, there is no doubt about that.

What is in some ways worse about the issue is that the agreement to guarantee any defects of compacting once they had become apparent after the opencasting had finished was not novated along with the rest of the opencast contract to RJB (Mining); it was kept in the A. F. Budge group and eventually novated to Sheffield airport, which was a subsidiary of the AFB group. Therefore, the responsibilities for carrying out the opencasting went to RJB (Mining), with all the profits, but the responsibility for putting the defects right, if there were any at the end of the contract, were left with a different company, which went into liquidation 18 months later.

Why was that allowed to happen? Given that Government approval must have been necessary for the novation of those two contracts to different companies, why was a split allowed at the time? Already, 1 million tonnes of coal had been taken out and half a million tonnes were to be taken out in the next year.

We know from asking questions that the airport arrangements were approved by Ministers. It is also clear from questions that I have asked that, although Ministers say that they did not approve the split of responsibilities between the two companies, they were clearly aware of

it. That split took place in March 1992. An answer that I received today from the Under-Secretary of State for the Environment states:

"My Department was notified in December 1991 of the proposed company restructuring which would separate the mining and airport construction interest within the A. F. Budge group. No approval was required from my Department."

Why not? The Department had approved the initial airport contracts. Therefore, it must have had interest in whether they would go ahead. Yet it allowed that restructuring to take place and the split of responsibilities, including the novating of the compacting defects arrangement to a different company, apparently without any concern from Ministers that something very wrong was about to happen.

Those are all the very arrangements that led to the concerns of and investigations by Coopers and Lybrand into the role of the A. F. Budge directors, including Richard Budge himself, which led to the investigations by the insolvency unit and by the official receiver. Yet, despite the fact that those arrangements subsequently led to all those investigations, at the time Ministers were not concerned. They did not say that it was a matter on which they must take a view because it was so serious. They simply got the information and apparently did nothing with it.

That leads me to a range of questions that have to be answered by Ministers. In the end, we are talking about the spending of public money with no return. Why were the responsibilities allowed to be split in the way that they were—responsibility for the airport and its cost in one company and the benefits of and the profit from opencasting in another company? At that time, could not the problems of the A. F. Budge group have been foreseen? A company that went into liquidation within 18 months would not have given the impression at the time that it was financially sound. What financial checks were done on the companies in question by civil servants? What advice did Ministers get? Why were no cross-guarantees required? Were they even requested from the Budge companies so that one arrangement could support the other in the event of a company failure? What were the contract details? Will Ministers publish them?

At the end of the day, who made the decisions? Was it British Coal Opencast or the Sheffield development corporation? Ministers clearly knew about the arrangements. What advice did they give to the development corporation? If they did not give approval, did they give any advice throughout the whole of this? If they did not give approval, why not? Why did they not take the matter seriously?

What in all this was the role of Richard Budge himself? He was a director of A. F. Budge at the time. He had a 35 per cent. personal stake in the Sheffield airport company. It all looks too convenient, does it not? Somehow he manages to buy out the profitable parts of the business, with all the profits from opencasting, with an extra 300,000 tonnes agreed, which turns into an extra 700,000 tonnes without any particular approval being given, and with the costs of any defect arrangements being transferred to another company, so he is not responsible for them, yet all the responsibilities for providing the airport are left with another company.

Throughout all this, Sheffield city council was not involved because, as I said, from 1989 it ceased to be the planning authority. However, I have seen a brief that Sheffield city council's treasurer's department gave to counsel at the time on the issue, which asks many questions about what was going on at Tinsley, but I simply cannot believe that its staff were the only people with their eyes open asking questions about what was happening.

The brief asks who the opencast mining contract was with—British Coal or R. J. Budge (Mining) Ltd.— because it seems rather confused throughout. What were the main financial provisions of the contract? They were never revealed. Had there been any significant changes in the terms of the original contract? Clearly there had, but it is not clear what they were. Had there been any changes to the parties to the contract or any of the sureties for the performance of the contract? What the sureties were and whether there were any is not clear. Had the contract been satisfactorily performed, operationally and financially? When would it be completed? In what state would the site be left on completion of the contract? That was an important question because of the doubts over compaction.

On the airport contract, the brief asked whether it was with A. F. Budge (Mining) Ltd., now renamed R. J. Budge (Mining) Ltd., with A. F. Budge Ltd. as surety for performance. What were the main financial provisions of the contract? Had there been any significant changes to the terms of the original contract? Why was the contract transferred to Sheffield Airports Ltd. when the R. J. Budge group split off from the A. F. Budge group? Why was the contract not left with RJB (Mining), perhaps retaining the A. F. Budge Ltd. guarantee and obtaining a guarantee from R. J. Budge's new holding company, RJB (Mining) plc? As Sheffield Airports Ltd. was only 65 per cent. owned by A. F. Budge Ltd., was the remaining 35 per cent. owned by Mr. R. J. Budge personally? Were any sureties or guarantees obtained from Mr. R. J. Budge?

How far, if at all, has the contract been fulfilled to date, operationally, financially and so forth? How was the Budge group selected to undertake the opencast mining and the airport contracts? What inquiries were made about the financial status of the Budge group before the contracts were entered into? How were the opencast mining contract and the airport contract linked? Did they stand alone commercially, or were the profits of the opencast mining expected to be ploughed back into the airport construction? Why was it decided to allow the contracts to be split between the two groups of companies?

If the Minister does not take shorthand, I shall be happy to give him that load of questions later; but I do not think that I should have to ask them tonight, or that officers in Sheffield city council should have to ask them. Civil servants should have been briefing Ministers, and Ministers should have considered them and then given advice to Sheffield development corporation. As a result of that advice, responsibility for the provision of the airport and profits from opencasting should not have been split as they were.

**Mr. Dennis Skinner** (Bolsover): Certain factors worsen the position. For instance—in the knowledge that they had not asked all the questions about the crook R. J. Budge, or seemingly had not—the same Government, faced with a bid from the same R. J. Budge to take over all the English pits and 20 other opencast sites, then allowed the man to be a serious bidder. There was no one else in the field, because he had bid for all three regions.

The Government allowed Budge to take the sites for £900 million-odd. Then, when he had them—with, as I have said, no other serious bidder in the field—this negligent Government knocked another £100 million of taxpayers' money off the original successful bid to allow their Tory friend the contract. It is a sorry saga, which started with the Sheffield airport site and the opencast sites and has ended with the success of a man who is likely to pour large sums into Tory party coffers for the next general election while telling miners that they must have a wage freeze.

**Mr. Betts:** As my hon. Friend has said, the whole matter prompts questions about the judgment of Ministers and the propriety of the actions of Mr. Richard Budge. Is he really a fit and proper person to control the future of British mining?

The matter did not end there, however. Not deterred by the fact that the responsibility for Sheffield airport had passed from him, Richard Budge saw the potential for such an airport—provided he did not have to fund it with the profits of his opencast operation.

In January 1993, lo and behold, there was a bid for the open partnership fund, for a Sheffield aerocentre project. That bid came from none other than a company headed by Mr. Richard Budge, whose proposals required £2 million of Government funds and another £1 million from Sheffield development corporation—as well as International Development Association grants of more than £2 million, which have subsequently been agreed.

Having had the money from the site and having separated the profit from that generated by the airport project through RJB (Mining), Mr. Budge then saw the possibility of developing the airport project and the business site associated with it at public expense. Again, questions must be asked about how that could be allowed to happen so soon. The Government eventually turned down the airport bid, but IDA grants to the tune of £2 million have been allocated.

A new company called Glenlivet has now become involved in the Sheffield airport project. As far as I am aware, it is not owned by Richard Budge or connected with him in any way—apart from the fact that the man in charge of the operation, Mr. Mike Shields, just happens to be the person who was in charge of Richard Budge's proposal to build the airport a few months earlier. I am not trying to persuade Ministers that Sheffield airport is not a good idea worthy of Government support. What I am questioning is whether the degree of Government support that will now be necessary is greater than it would have been, because some of the profits from the opencast operation should have gone into the airport rather than Richard Budge's pocket.

Indeed, Ministers might now spell out to us the extra cost to public funds of developing the airport—a cost that would not have been necessary had the original agreements been kept in one company, rather than being split. The responsibility for spending that money remains somewhere between Ministers, Sheffield development corporation and British Coal; Ministers might well expand on where they think it lies.

The role of Richard Budge throughout the affair prompts many questions. First, when the airport and opencast responsibilities were split between the two companies, did not Richard Budge—as a director of A. F. Budge—know the state of the company and its various

*[Mr. Betts]*

offshoots? As a director, was he not aware that the company was in financial difficulties? Should not Ministers ask those questions? Did Richard Budge not know that the airport deal was worth funding? Did he not have plans to retain an interest in it? Did he simply not want the responsibility of putting in his own money, preferring an opportunity to come back for more Government money rather than using the opencast profits?

Did not Richard Budge also cleverly manipulate the situation so that he would not end up with liability for the compaction defects on the site, but—although he was a contractor on the site—the liability would lie with Sheffield Airport Ltd., a subsidiary of the A. F. Budge group, which went into liquidation? Did Richard Budge reach any understanding with people on the site at Tinsley that the ground would not be compacted properly, so that even if money is now given for an airport more will have to be spent on putting right a site that should have been put right as one of the consequences of the original planning agreement? That certainly needs investigation; perhaps, if the Minister cannot give an answer tonight, he will commit the Government to carrying out such an investigation and reporting back.

How far was all this sorry mess taken into account in the determination of whether Richard Budge was a fit and proper person to take over British Coal operations—and, indeed, whether he was a fit and proper person to be a director of any public company? What was the role of Ministers, who clearly knew all about the actions at Tinsley, in deciding the fate of Richard Budge?

Was not their ultimate decision not to take action against him taken against the advice of Coopers and Lybrand, against the advice of the consultancy unit in the Department of Trade and Industry and against the advice of the official receiver? Perhaps Ministers will spell out who advised them of what at various stages. My hon. Friend the Member for Sherwood (Mr. Tipping)—who will probably want to speak later—has written a letter, a copy of which I have seen, asking Ministers to give the precise timetable; it will be interesting when Ministers respond to that.

Is it true that officials involved in the privatisation of British Coal attended meetings of officials in the insolvency unit while discussion of Richard Budge's future was taking place? Did Ministers themselves attend those meetings before final decisions about Richard Budge's future were made? Why was Richard Budge treated differently from the other directors of A. F. Budge, against whom action is apparently being taken? Richard Budge was a director of the same company; apparently, he took illegal loans. There are still question marks over those issues. He was responsible for the restructuring of the arrangements at Tinsley, which allowed him to walk away from his responsibilities to Sheffield airport and the defects in the compacting agreement.

Why did not Ministers tell the House about all those matters, and the various investigations that were taking place, when they presented their privatisation proposals to the House? Why did they leave themselves no alternative—no other companies in the frame that could be considered for the buy-out of British Coal operations? Did they not effectively put themselves in a completely unviable position? If they had disqualified Richard Budge, they would have had no alternative, and the privatisation proposals would have fallen flat on their face.

I am sorry to go on for so long, but these extremely complicated issues need many answers by Ministers. A few matters are crystal clear. The opencasting and the airport were linked from 1987 when British Coal made its first proposals, and they were clearly linked in the first planning agreement in 1989. The council planning agreement at that time contained an arrangement whereby planning gains for the community took various forms and were linked to the start of an airport. That agreement was extended. It was agreed to take an extra amount of coal from the site and extra work was to be carried out on the airport infrastructure.

At some stage, those responsibilities were split, airport responsibilities remaining with the A. F. Budge group and RJB (Mining) taking on board the profitable operations of opencast mining on the site. There is, of course, no link between those two sets of responsibilities. After the split was carried out, no guarantees or sureties were apparently entered into or even asked for by SDC or by Ministers.

It is also clear that 1.5 million tonnes of coal were extracted from the site—nearly twice the amount allowed in the initial planning agreement. It was 400,000 tonnes more than even the extended agreement that was reached subsequently, and all that extra profit went into the pockets probably of British Coal but also of Richard Budge and his company and there was no return to the community.

The precise nature of the unpublished agreements is unclear. Who knew what and who made the decisions on all these matters as between SDC, British Coal and Ministers? What information was sought and what prior investigations were carried out before contracts were entered into with A. F. Budge and RJB (Mining) or any of the other companies involved? Were there any contingency arrangements? Why were guarantees not required and what will be the extra cost to public funds resulting from the collapse of A. F Budge and the fact that the airport will now have to receive more funding from the public purse?

Why has secrecy surrounded all those matters and why is public money being spent and the public interest being involved without proper openness? Was the ground finally properly compacted, and why was the defects agreement separated from the responsibility for opencasting and novated to Sheffield airport instead of RJB (Mining)? Why were the extra 400,000 tonnes of coal extracted and what benefit did that give to the community? What was the role of Richard Budge in all this? How much profit did he make? How many responsibilities did he leave behind that should properly have been paid for out of that profit? What did he know about the whole arrangement throughout?

It is just too convenient for Richard Budge somehow to make an arrangement under which he walks away with all the money while responsibilities for community provision are left behind by another company of which he is a director and which just happens to go into liquidation a few months later. In view of all that, there must be questions as to whether he is a fit and proper person to run the coal industry, bearing in mind all the other questions that have been raised about his role as a director of A. F. Budge at the time.

The history of the matter is a mixture of administrative incompetence, financial ineptitude, negligence and perhaps naivety and lack of accountability. It has all the appearance of sharp practice by the only individual who seemed to know what he was doing in his own interests. That person is Richard Budge, the chairman of RJB (Mining). As the Government, British Coal and SDC appeared to squander public resources or watch while they were being squandered, A. F. Budge collapsed, but Richard Budge walked away with the profits, not from the tonnage as originally agreed but from 1.5 million tonnes, thereby giving himself an even stronger financial base from which to mount his bid to run British Coal.

In my view and the view of my constituents that has left deep unease and concern about the whole situation but especially about Richard Budge and his company. That unease and concern will be addressed only by a full public inquiry into this whole affair. It has to be brought out into the open and must be the subject of full public scrutiny.

**Several hon. Members** *rose—*

**Mr. Deputy Speaker (Mr. Geoffrey Lofthouse):** Order. I understand that the hon. Member for Wallsend (Mr. Byers) has sought the agreement of the hon. Member for Sheffield, Attercliffe (Mr. Betts) and the Minister to take part in the debate. Any other hon. Member hoping to catch my eye must do likewise.

8.24 pm

**Mr. Stephen Byers** (Wallsend): I congratulate my hon. Friend the Member for Sheffield, Attercliffe (Mr. Betts) on securing this debate. He has understandably concentrated on the effect of RJB (Mining) on the Tinsley site in Sheffield and also raised some wider issues about the role of Richard Budge and the part that RJB (Mining) will play now that it has control of what remains of the English coalfield. I want to address those wider issues.

The House will be aware that on 12 October 1994 RJB (Mining) was named by the Government as the preferred bidder for the remains of the English coalfield. As my hon. Friend the Member for Attercliffe said, the chairman of that company is Mr. Richard Budge. Based on information in my possession, I have to say that there must be serious doubts about whether it was appropriate for the Government, in view of what they knew about the conduct of Richard Budge as a former director of A. F. Budge, to name his company as the preferred bidder.

I understand that Richard Budge was named by Coopers and Lybrand in its report and also in the first report by the official receiver. As I shall later show, there were two reports by the official receiver. The first report named Richard Budge as a person whose conduct was such that an application should be made to the court for him to be disqualified from holding a future directorship in any company. These are serious allegations, which I shall seek to support in my contribution.

We need to be aware that at the time of these events two issues were effectively running in parallel. One was the investigation into the collapse of the A. F. Budge group of companies. In addition, the Government's political imperative was to secure the privatisation of the coal industry. In December 1992, administrative receivers were appointed to the A. F. Budge group of companies and Coopers and Lybrand was appointed to report to the

insolvency service, which is part of the Department of Trade and Industry. It was to report on the events surrounding the collapse of A. F. Budge and in particular on the liabilities, responsibilities and conduct of individual directors of the A. F. Budge group.

The Coopers and Lybrand report was submitted to the insolvency service on 28 September 1993. I understand that that report highlights the conduct of, in particular, three former directors of A. F. Budge and questions their fitness to be directors. One of the three named was Mr. Richard Budge. The insolvency service took time to consider the Coopers and Lybrand report and the official receiver reported on 25 July 1994.

I understand that on that date the official receiver recommended that a report be made to the court under the Company Directors Disqualification Act 1986 applying for three former directors of A. F. Budge, one of whom was Mr. Richard Budge, to be disqualified from holding office as directors of any company. That report was not acted upon. Word had begun to circulate in the Department of Trade and Industry and to set alarm bells ringing in the special unit which had been set up to oversee the privatisation of the coal industry. Everything was put on hold until a decision was taken about who the preferred bidder for the coal industry was to be.

Tenders were submitted in September 1994 and, as we know, on 12 October 1994 RJB (Mining) was named as the preferred bidder for the English coalfield. It is of particular interest that no fallback position was announced at the time. It was agreed that RJB (Mining) should be the one and only company to form the substantive part of the preferred bidder. The Government, however, had a problem: what should they do with the official receiver's report of 25 July?

The official receiver was asked to reconsider the position. On 11 November, 14 November and 15 November 1994, he interviewed the three directors named in his original report for disqualification, no doubt to try to find out whether new evidence existed of which he had not been aware before his original report. Mr. Richard Budge was interviewed on the first of those dates. Following those interviews, advice was given by the official receiver to Ministers. On 21 November 1994, the decision was taken to bring disqualification proceedings against just two of those interviewed, and Mr. Richard Budge escaped liability and responsibility. Following that recommendation, on 7 December 1994 a report against the remaining two directors was made to a court for their disqualification as company directors. With one bound, Mr. Richard Budge was free.

Given the Government's commitments to the privatisation of the coal industry, Labour Members will understand why it was so important that some quick solution was found to get Mr. Richard Budge off the hook. In addition to the political imperative, however, he clearly had friends in high places. On no less than seven separate occasions, he met the Minister for Industry and Energy, who is responsible for coal privatisation, to discuss matters relating to that privatisation. Those meetings were all held at important and strategic times: 17 June 1992, 29 June 1992, 1 March 1993, 26 March 1993, 15 April 1993, 15 June 1993 and 7 July 1994. He had access to a Minister that even many Labour Members do not have.

Of course, Mr. Budge has other friends in high places. I am told that people attending Doncaster races on 10 September 1993—I do not know whether you were there,

Mr. Deputy Speaker—were surprised to see a helicopter emblazoned with the RJB (Mining) logo land in the centre of the race track. Mr. Richard Budge got out, which was not unexpected, given that it was his helicopter, but who was he accompanied by? He was with Lord Wakeham, at that time Leader of the House of Lords and a member of the Cabinet, who was out for a day at the races.

**Mr. Paddy Tipping** (Sherwood): Does my hon. Friend recall that the noble Lord was called in during the coal crisis, when the Government wanted to close pits, to sort out the problem, and that he chaired a Cabinet committee to resolve the issue? Was he not therefore a man with real influence?

**Mr. Byers:** My hon. Friend makes an important point. Hon. Members should never forget that it was Lord Wakeham who, when he was a Member of this House and Minister with responsibility for energy, awarded a contract to Rothschild to advise the Government on coal industry privatisation. I shall not discuss the fact that he is now a Rothschild director as that would not be appropriate for this debate.

Clearly, therefore, Mr. Richard Budge is a man with friends in high places. He knows how to operate the system on behalf of RJB (Mining). I was interested to learn that in 1993 he took over Clipstone colliery in Nottinghamshire, that he made a deal, that he effectively reopened it after it had been closed for a fairly short time, and that, as the new owner, he entered into an arrangement with North Nottinghamshire training and enterprise council whereby for every miner he re-employed he would receive a grant of £1,000 for retraining purposes.

In total, in 1993-94, he obtained £150,000 for RJB (Mining) from that TEC. What is of particular interest is that the House of Commons Library informs me that in 1993-94, the same year in which Mr. Budge's company received £150,000 from North Nottinghamshire TEC, he was a director of that TEC.

Many questions need to be answered. The Minister will be pleased to learn that I have just two to add to the list submitted by my hon. Friend the Member for Attercliffe. Will the Minister now publish the Coopers and Lybrand report into the conduct of the former directors of A. F. Budge? Secondly, will he publish the official receiver's initial report of 25 July 1994? Refusal to do so will lead all reasonable people to believe that there is a cover-up and that the Government have something to hide.

All the available information points to this being a shameful and shoddy affair. The issue will not go away. Labour Members will continue to pursue it until we receive some straight answers to those important questions.

8.37 pm

**Mr. Paddy Tipping** (Sherwood): I congratulate my hon. Friend the Member for Sheffield, Attercliffe (Mr. Betts) on securing the debate. I should like to put on the record my thanks to the Minister for allowing me to take part and for his helpful attitude to questions since he became a Minister at the Department of Trade and Industry only a few weeks ago. His openness contrasts with the difficulties that we have had in obtaining information.

I wish the people who have bought the newly privatised industry no harm. I regret the passing of the coal industry into the private sector, but I wish the new coal owners well because they have a monstrous task before them. You, Mr. Deputy Speaker, will recall perhaps better than anyone that contracts with the generators run until 1998. Some of us are have real concerns about what the coal industry faces after that. In view of that, I wish the people who own the industry, and more particularly the people who work in it, well and a good future.

I want to raise issues that some of my colleagues have not dealt with and to extend the debate. I remind the Minister that on 12 October 1994 Mr. Richard Budge was named as the preferred bidder in a blaze of glory at the Tory party conference. We also know that in November 1994 he made a bid of £914 million for the three English coal regions. We know that because I have a copy of the presentation that he took round the City.

At the end of November 1994 I wrote to the Chairman of the Public Accounts Committee to say that I was extremely concerned about the bid. It was far in excess of anybody else's bid and I suspected that there would be negotiations to knock the bid down. A few days later I was proved right because the deal concluded for the sale of the coal industry in England to Mr. Budge was £815 million. My hon. Friend the Member for Bolsover (Mr. Skinner) has already asked the relevant question, but I want to reinforce it: how is it that, in only a few days, the value of the coal industry fell by £99 million? Clear questions need to be asked and clear answers need to be given.

That is not the end of the matter. We know that the deal that Mr. Budge did with the Department of Trade and Industry through all the brokers was to buy the industry, as miners in Nottinghamshire say, on the never-never. All the other bidders were told that they had to pay cash up front. The deal that was eventually concluded allowed RJB (Mining) to buy the industry over three years with deferred payments. So, as well as the £99 million loss, I calculate that the deferred payments over three years will result in a further loss of £116 million.

Some of my hon. Friends have already pointed out that the preferred bidder was named in October. I find it staggering that the other bidders—a wide range of other people could have bought the English coal industry—were told between October and December to go away and not to keep their financing in place. So, from a very early day, the Government were committed to Mr. Budge. Part of the problem now is that the Government walked down the gangplank with Mr. Budge and, when the going got tough and the sea got stormy, they had no alternative but to jump into the water with him.

These are significant issues and I am delighted that the Public Accounts Committee is looking at these matters. I hope that things will be clarified when the Public Accounts Committee receives the report. My only sadness is that it will be the autumn before we know about this. Many of us were raising concerns about the proposed sale in the autumn of last year and it is bizarre that we can examine the matter only in retrospect. That is one of the reasons why I welcome the debate. I hope that the Minister will be open and honest about the dealings and the relationships with RJB (Mining).

There are other issues that concern me. I have looked carefully at the documents that RJB (Mining) has produced over the years. I was interested to see that in its

"Pathfinder" prospectus, which was published in November 1994, it says that the company's chief executive, Mr. Richard Budge, received an annual salary of £235,000. For the year after the purchase of British Coal—the present year—his salary will increase to £290,000 plus a £50,000 acquisition bonus. Put another way, that reflects a salary increase of 45 per cent. The prospectus also shows that the remuneration committee of RJB (Mining) will have a discretionary power to pay a performance-related bonus of up to 100 per cent. at the end of 1995 if the company performs well. In the space of just over a year Mr. Budge's salary could increase to £630,000—an increase of 168 per cent. from November 1994.

What galls the miners in Nottinghamshire, Yorkshire and throughout the country—all those who work for Mr. Budge and RJB (Mining)—is the letter that they received in February. Mr. Budge wrote to the work force saying that there would not be a base rate adjustment in pay until March 1998. He justified that in the letter by saying that, because of the alleged difficult and competitive economic climate, the company could not afford to pay more.

It is staggering that miners throughout England who have worked hard and raised productivity by 150 per cent. in recent years as well as producing coal at half the cost of Germany should be told by their new chief executive, "Times are tough, lads, and you will take a pay freeze until March 1998. However, if things go well for me, my salary will increase to £630,000—an increase of 168 per cent."

RJB (Mining) was purchased by Mr. Budge out of A. F. Budge in a management buy-out in February 1992. It is clear that, even before the buy-out A. F. Budge was facing major financial difficulties. One of the things that concerns me as a taxpayer—I hope that the Minister will pursue this point with the chairman of British Coal—is how in 1991 British Coal could make advance payments of £10.5 million to A. F. Budge for an opencast site at Eastpit near Swansea. That is an unprecedented interest-free loan. It has not been possible at this stage to get to the bottom of the matter with British Coal.

**Mr. Michael Clapham** (Barnsley, West and Penistone): In his research into A. F. Budge, has my hon. Friend come across any contributions to the Conservative party? If so, can he quantify the contributions that have been made over recent years?

**Mr. Tipping:** I shall come to that in a moment.

We ought to acknowledge that the payment of £10.5 million to A. F. Budge in 1991, according to its then chairman and chief executive, Mr. Tony Budge, kept the company afloat for an extra year. There is no doubt about that. In a sense, A. F. Budge was being looked after by the taxpayer. As my hon. Friend the Member for Barnsley, West and Penistone (Mr. Clapham) has just suggested, we need to examine the relationship between A. F. Budge, Mr. Tony Budge and the Conservative party.

There is no doubt that there are clear links. I understand that, despite his difficulties, Mr. Tony Budge is still the vice-president of the Newark Conservative party. I know from experience that Mr. Tony Budge has raised a great deal of money for the Conservative party through fund-raising events and that he was chairman of an east midlands group of industrialists which also raised money

for the Conservative party. Although his company was looked after with £10.5 million, it is clear that he had previously been looking after the Conservatives.

My hon. Friend the Member for Wallsend (Mr. Byers) talked about the process of A. F. Budge going into liquidation and asked a number of specific questions about the timetable of events. When did Ministers receive reports from Coopers and Lybrand and then from the Official Receiver and when were decisions taken to prosecute former directors of A. F. Budge? I find it very difficult to understand why three directors of A. F. Budge—Mr. Tony Budge, his wife, Janet Budge, and a finance director, face court action whereas Mr. Richard Budge does not.

My principal concern relates to the loans that Richard Budge had from the companies with which he has been associated. I have no doubt—indeed, it is documented in the reports that Ministers have received from Coopers and Lybrand—that Mr. Richard Budge had a loan account of £400 million with A. F. Budge.

People like me wanted to know what a loan account is. In simple terms, it means borrowings from a company. One of Mr. Richard Budge's borrowings from A. F. Budge was £12,500 for the hire of a marquee for a family party. In addition, on 30 March 1991, a payment of £10,000 in petty cash was made to him. That is extremely disturbing behaviour, and I believe that Coopers and Lybrand and the liquidators found such payments distressing. As my hon. Friend the Member for Wallsend said, Mr. Richard Budge was criticised in the reports. On a D2 form, it was said that Mr. Richard Budge's behaviour made him unfit to be concerned in the management of a company.

The prospectus issued by RJB Mining in the autumn of last year contains a paragraph which states that Mr. Richard Budge paid back £325,000 to the liquidators, without admitting any liability, in order to pay the loans that he had had with the company. I believe that that payment is in breach of the Companies Acts and that Coopers and Lybrand and the draft report produced by the Insolvency Service took the same view.

There appears to be a record of pathological behaviour because, having bitten once, Mr. Richard Budge bit again. The prospectus also contains the following phrase:

"During the financial period ended 31 December 1992, the company entered into credit transactions with R. J. Budge. In so doing, the company did not comply with the provisions of the Companies Act. The maximum aggregate value of these transactions was £70,442".

Mr. Richard Budge had a loan account of £400,000 with A. F. Budge. He cleared it at the insistence of the liquidators but, as his own company prospectus makes clear, he went on to have a further loan account with his new company amounting to £70,000 in breach of the Companies Acts.

Ministers cannot say that they were unaware of such behaviour as the documents are a matter of public record. Indeed, I would go further and remind the Minister that, in December last year, I wrote to his colleague, the President of the Board of Trade, pointing out a raft of issues that led me to be concerned about the fitness of Mr. Richard Budge to run the deep coal industry.

I wrote to the President of the Board of Trade before the contract to buy the industry was signed on 24 December. I have now written again, asking him to produce a detailed timetable of when reports were

[*Mr. Tipping*]

received from the liquidators, who was involved in making decisions, what advice Ministers received from their civil servants and whether it is true that the DTI unit involved in selling the coal industry was holding meetings in another part of the building with the Insolvency Service to consider what might happen to Mr. Richard Budge?

My hon. Friend the Member for Sheffield, Attercliffe talked about the ingenious financing that enabled the good to be cherry-picked by Mr. Richard Budge's company and the liabilities to be left elsewhere. Let me draw the Minister's attention to a company called Moira Pottery based in Leicester. It was a loss-making company acquired by A. F. Budge which was interested not in pottery but in the opencast reserves that lay underneath the company's premises. We now know, because the record is at Companies house, that when RJB Mining was bought out of A. F. Budge, Moira Pottery was acquired for £1. It was subsequently valued at £1 million. Accusations are being made that there were attempts to transfer A. F. Budge's prime assets out of the company and into a new company, RJB Mining.

People are extremely concerned about those issues. The time has now come for the Minister and his colleagues who were there before him to come clean. I am delighted that the Public Accounts Committee is looking at the matter. I regret that it will take time to report. Many of us want to see a strong, deep coal industry in this country. The men who work in the industry deserve that. For that industry to succeed, it is important that the whole tale is told and that all the secrets are let out of the cupboard so that the coal industry can go forward, into a new future without skeletons. There are enough skeletons in the history of the coal industry without there being more holding it back.

8.59 pm

**The Parliamentary Under-Secretary of State for Industry and Energy (Mr. Richard Page):** May I start by congratulating the hon. Member for Sheffield, Attercliffe (Mr. Betts) on not only his skill in securing this Adjournment debate, but on somehow managing to get it into a time frame in which half an hour has extended to something like two and a half hours? I think that that is only right, however. It is a complicated subject and it is only right that we discuss it and try to clear up some of the misunderstandings and dispel some of the conspiracy theories that seem to be puzzling and worrying Opposition Members.

May I say right at the start that I well understand the concern of the hon. Member for Attercliffe over the failure of the Sheffield city airport project to go ahead. I do not want to damage his political standing in Sheffield. Indeed, the hon. Gentleman and I sat side by side and watched the "Panorama" programme on which he appeared. I thought that he gave a splendid presentation in which he represented, quite justifiably, the concerns of his constituents. Of course the "Panorama" programme had been so edited that it was as jerky as a silent first world war film. But that is by the by.

Before I address the questions raised, I would like to make one or two general points regarding coal privatisation. The Labour party continues to suggest that coal privatisation has been a mistake and a failure. The hon. Member for Bolsover (Mr. Skinner) is not present at

the moment. He came into the House, issued one of his usual rants and has since disappeared. I regret to say that he, among others, will not accept the reality that privatisation has been a considerable success. We set out a clear objective to achieve the largest economically viable coal industry in the long term and to ensure value for money for the taxpayer. As the House knows, the sale was successfully concluded in December, and it was far from being the failure predicted by so many Opposition Members.

**Mr. Clapham:** The Minister must realise that, in 1993, before the coal closure programme was enacted, there were 50 collieries. At the present time, there are some 28 collieries, which were previously part of British Coal, and there are a number of other smaller collieries, which have always been outside the public sector. Those 50 collieries employed 50,000 men. At the present time, around 6,000 men are employed in the industry. In other words, we have seen the loss of 44,000 jobs since 1993. How can he justify that as a success? The other thing that the Minister must remember is that the remaining 28 collieries are high-technology collieries, which were transformed by the public purse. Of course productivity in those collieries is high—purely and simply because of the mining technology which was paid for by the taxpayer.

**Mr. Page:** I do not want to get diverted too far down that route. Otherwise, we would have to be here, if we were allowed, until about 12 o'clock. I must delicately point out to the hon. Gentleman that, if he looks at the history of the coal industry, he would find that his party has closed more mines and put more miners out of work than any other. I commend his courage in allowing me to draw attention to that point.

We have, as I say, created a successful industry and in creating that successful industry, we have received proceeds just short of £1 billion, which is a significant boost for public finances. Competition has been increased, with the transfer of former British Coal mines to a number of companies. RJB (Mining) now operates or is developing a total of 20 collieries, as the hon. Member for Barnsley, West and Penistone (Mr. Clapham) said, across central and northern England—more than British Coal operated or was developing at the time of privatisation. Coal Investments is operating or developing half a dozen collieries. Scottish Coal operates another significant deep-mine complex, and there are management and employee buy-out teams at Tower colliery in south Wales and Hatfield in Yorkshire. Between them, those companies have some 29 former British Coal collieries, twice the number that it had been claimed would survive.

In the new private sector, companies are making a success of their business. New customers are being found. British Steel has bought British-mined coal from Tower colliery in place of imports for the first time for many years. Tower colliery is even selling coal to France. New employment opportunities are opening up with the re-opening of collieries that have been on care and maintenance and the new apprenticeship schemes offer by RJB (Mining). Productivity is improving and costs are coming down.

I shall now talk about the case of RBJ (Mining), and I shall start with Sheffield airport, on which the hon. Gentleman legitimately spent so much of his time. As I said earlier, he has been assiduous in pursuing the matter on behalf of his constituents, and I already understand the acute disappointment that he must feel because the Sheffield airport project has not gone ahead.

The hon. Gentleman started by expressing concern about the splitting of the responsibility for providing the infrastructure for an airport at Tinsley, Sheffield, and about the Government's role. I shall outline some of the essential facts, and do my best to answer as many as I can of the questions that have been asked. But at one stage in the debate the questions were coming like machine-gun bullets, and I shall certainly not be able to answer all of those. However, I assure the hon. Gentleman that I shall read the *Official Report* of the debate afterwards. I hope that *Hansard* has faithfully recorded all the points that he made, and I shall return to him and let him have the details about all the questions that I do not cover tonight.

In May 1990 A. F. Budge (Mining) Ltd.—which subsequently became RJB (Mining) Ltd.—and A. F. Budge Ltd. contracted with Sheffield development corporation for the construction and running of an airport at Tinsley Park, Sheffield, part of which was then being worked as an opencast coal mine by A. F. Budge (Mining) Ltd. under a contract from British Coal.

Such a disposal of a large area of land for what might be described as an unusual use required the consent of the Secretary of State for the Environment. As the hon. Gentleman will know from the answer given to him on 9 May—he has already referred to it—such approval was given. Subsequently several variations in the terms and time scales provided for in the contract were agreed between the parties.

During 1991 discussions took place to separate the Budge mining operations run by Mr. R. J. Budge from the principal Budge construction and other companies run by his brother, Mr. A. F. Budge. That involved, among other things, the formation of a new company—Sheffield Airport Ltd., a subsidiary of A. F. Budge Ltd., the holding company of the Budge Group of companies. Those discussions were concluded in February 1992, when there was a management buy-out, led by Mr. R. J. Budge, of the coal mining operations.

The terms of the airport contract for Tinsley Park were varied, releasing A. F. Budge (Mining) Ltd. and bringing in Sheffield Airport Ltd., which, with A. F. Budge Ltd. as surety, was to undertake the development—although it was my understanding that the intention remained that A. F. Budge (Contractors) Ltd., another A. F. Budge Group company, would carry out the work.

Let us be clear about three things. First, the restructuring of the A. F. Budge Group and the disposal of the coal mining operations were the subject of detailed consideration and reports by solicitors and accountants acting for the parties. The agreements were crawled over by accountants and solicitors.

Secondly, the variation of the Tinsley Park airport contract, releasing A. F. Budge (Mining) Ltd., was agreed to by the Sheffield development corporation. The hon. Member for Attercliffe asked many questions about who had agreed to this and who had agreed to that. I must remind him that Sheffield development corporation was not an innocent party standing on one side. It was in a position to make many of those inquiries and to find out many of the answers before going ahead.

Thirdly, as the hon. Gentleman will also know from the answer given to him on 9 May, although the Department of the Environment was aware of the variations of the

contract, it was not necessary for it to give its approval or otherwise to be involved, as the holding company, A. F. Budge Ltd., continued as surety for the performance of the contract. I am not aware that the administrative receivers or the liquidators for the A. F. Budge Group of companies have sought to challenge the transaction itself.

To complete the history—

**Mr. Betts:** The Minister referred to the fact that the A. F. Budge Group had a surety for Sheffield Airport Ltd. and the provision of the airport. That does not answer the question about the splitting of responsibilities for mining and making a profit and building the airport and incurring expense. The letter from the office of the chairman of British Coal which I read out said that those two matters were linked and that agreements were drawn up.

**Mr. Page:** I am unaware of the contents of the letter that the hon. Gentleman received from British Coal, but the information which he has given suggests that these agreements were not linked and that the Sheffield development corporation agreed to the particular splits which took place. A degree of responsibility for this matter must lie with the Sheffield development corporation.

I wish to complete the history of Tinsley Park, which I recognise is most disappointing to the Sheffield development corporation and the people of Sheffield. The administrative receivers were appointed in relation to A. F. Budge Ltd. in December 1992, and subsequently in relation to other A. F. Budge Group companies.

Clearly the A. F. Budge Group was not in a position to undertake any construction on the site. In March 1993, Sheffield Airport Ltd.—which had no other business assets—formally notified the Sheffield development corporation that it was not able to proceed with the development. Discussions took place between the corporation and the administrative receivers to try to find a solution, but none could be found. The site was eventually handed back to the corporation. Sheffield Airport Ltd. was wound up by the courts in October 1993, with the corporation claiming payments under the contract relating to the purchaser of an area of land adjoining Tinsley Park which the A. F. Budge Group intended to develop as a business complex.

I am told that the notified liabilities of that company total some £407,000, although further claims could come under the contract. The minimal assets of £10,000 are likely to be absorbed by the costs of winding up. The hon. Member for Attercliffe has asked for some form of inquiry, but he will know from the answer given to him by the Under-Secretary of State for the Environment on 9 May that that Department has no plans for a public inquiry into the contract relating to the Tinsley Park airport development.

With regard to the A. F. Budge Group, detailed consideration was given to the restructuring which took place in February 1992, including the disposal of the mining operation by that group, the administrative receivers and the official receivers. That consideration was taken into account in their reports to the Insolvency Service under the Company Directors Disqualification Act 1986. It was also taken into consideration in the service's decision in relation to disqualification proceedings.

[*Mr. Page*]

A few points were raised over the compaction of the site at Tinsley Park. The hon. Gentleman is concerned about what happened to the £1 million paid by British Coal for compaction once the mining had finished and the site had been prepared for the construction of the airport. It is my understanding that the payment to A. F. Budge (Mining) Ltd. went into the A. F. Budge Group account, and was used with other group funds, to finance on-going group operations.

The hon. Gentleman asked what checks were carried out on financial liability, but that is a commercial matter for British Coal.

For accounting purposes, A. F. Budge (Mining) Ltd. was thus shown as owing the £1 million by A. F. Budge Ltd. on an inter-company account.

When the A. F. Budge Group was restructured and its mining operations were bought out in February 1992, Sheffield Airport Ltd. took over some of the obligations of A. F. Budge (Mining) Ltd. in relation to the airport development contract. The inter-company account of £1 million shown as due to A. F. Budge (Mining) Ltd. by A. F. Budge Ltd. was transferred to Sheffield Airport Ltd. As far as I am aware, no cash changed hands. I am sure that the administrative receivers of the A. F. Budge Group and the liquidators of Sheffield Airport Ltd. considered any questions raised about the use of those moneys.

One of the questions raised in the debate dealt with the tender price.

**Mr. Betts:** I have been listening with interest to what the Minister had to say about compaction. He has not said why the obligations to guarantee putting right the defects in compaction work five years after that work had been completed were novated to Sheffield airport, which seems a strange company to take on that responsibility, and not transferred with the novation of the contracts on opencasting to RJB (Mining), which would have seemed a more logical and legitimate place for them to rest.

**Mr. Page:** I cannot say why it went that way. I have had no evidence to suggest that the compacting has not been done correctly. If it has not, in the first instance, it will be a matter for British Coal.

The reduction in the bid by RJB (Mining) was made out to be some sort of back-door deal, but it was not. The tender price was adjusted as envisaged in the information memorandum issued by Rothschilds. The adjustments reflected developments since tenders were submitted in September 1994—or information that was not available to bidders when they submitted their tenders. The adjustments would have been available to any other preferred bidder. As I said, even after those adjustments, RJB's bid was considerably higher than the others.

The hon. Member for Wallsend (Mr. Byers), beguilingly, tried to suggest that, if I could release the reports of the official receivers and Coopers and Lybrand, I would be a decent, open and honest sort of fellow. I am afraid that this is where I am going to be a constant disappointment to the House because those reports are confidential and come under the Company Directors Disqualification Act 1986. If they were not confidential, in future many people would be reluctant to give

information in such cases and the truth of the operations of one or two companies would not, therefore, come to hand and the correct decisions might not be made.

**Mr. Tipping:** Will that report be made available to the National Audit Office, which is acting for the Public Accounts Committee in looking at the sale?

**Mr. Page:** The straight answer is that I do not know. I served for seven years on the Public Accounts Committee and we were most assiduous in trying to get information out of aspects of Government when we thought that we could find out where money had been wasted or spent incorrectly. I am afraid that that is a question that the hon. Gentleman will have to direct to the Comptroller and Auditor General.

The hon. Member for Wallsend tried to work up some sort of conspiracy theory, suggesting that the Government were trying to help one of their friends—all that about secret meetings and Ministers getting involved with people who are involved in the industry. It would have been a peculiar way of doing it and an expensive form of conspiracy if, after one of those conspiratorial meetings, the gentlemen involved paid £200 million plus more than the nearest bidder. The hon. Gentleman also asked me about a timetable and perhaps I can help him a little.

On 9 December 1992, the first A. F. Budge Group company was put into administrative receivership. On 28 September 1993, administrative receivers submitted conduct reports on directors. On 25 July 1994, the official receiver submitted reports of initial investigations, including considerations of administrative receivers' conduct reports. The Treasury solicitors were instructed and counsel was engaged to advise on preparation of the case. Administrative receivers were employed to undertake further inquiries at the direction of the official receiver.

On 12 October, RJB (Mining) was told that it was the preferred bidder. On 21 November, the Insolvency Service decided to instigate proceedings against the three directors, who have already been mentioned, and the decision was endorsed by the Minister. But, as has been made perfectly clear, proceedings were not taken against Mr. Richard Budge and other directors. On 7 December, summonses were served against those three directors and, on 8 February this year, the first hearing of application in the case was outlined to the court. The hearing was then adjourned to a second formal hearing.

**Mr. Tipping:** It is helpful to know that timetable. I thought that I heard the Minister say a few seconds ago that counsel was instructed to take the prosecution forward. Was legal advice taken from just one counsel, or was it taken from a variety of sources?

**Mr. Page:** I shall write to the hon. Gentleman if I am incorrect, but I believe that more than one source of legal advice was obtained.

**Mr. Byers:** The timetable reflects the sequence of events that I outlined. However, the important point is that we had the report from the official receiver on 25 July. Will the Minister confirm that that report recommended that disqualification proceedings should be taken against Mr. Richard Budge because he was not a fit person? On

12 October, he was then declared to be the preferred bidder. He was re-interviewed on 11 November and, lo and behold, on 21 November he was suddenly free and disqualification proceedings were not to be taken against him. That is my interpretation of events. What recommendations did the official receiver make on 25 July concerning Mr. Richard Budge?

**Mr. Page:** As I mentioned earlier, the report is confidential and I cannot reveal its contents. As I was saying, the hon. Gentleman could draw one or two conclusions from the timetable and details that I have given, which any prudent politician would deduce.

**Mr. Betts:** May I help the Minister on that point? He may be trying to tell Opposition Members that if the official receiver's report in July did not recommend that action should be taken against Mr. Richard Budge, there would be no need for further interviews.

**Mr. Page:** The hon. Gentleman must not deduce anything from what I have said.

**Mr. Betts:** I can deduce what I like.

**Mr. Page:** Obviously, the hon. Gentleman can deduce things. That is entirely up to him. It is his privilege. I see nothing peculiar in the various representatives in this matter undertaking a series of interviews with a number of people who have been involved in this matter. In no way does it imply a crime, irresponsible act or shortcoming.

The Department started out with a clear objective to return the British coal mining industry to the private sector to secure the largest economically viable coal industry in the long term while ensuring value for money for taxpayers. That has brought significant improvements. One or two Opposition Members conveniently forget that, since 1979, the coal industry has had stuffed down its throat £19 billion of taxpayers' money. I look forward to the day when it starts to pay some tax back to the people of this country.

*Question put and agreed to.*

*Adjourned accordingly at twenty-four minutes past Nine o'clock.*

# House of Commons

*Wednesday 17 May 1995*

*The House met at Ten o'clock*

PRAYERS

[MADAM SPEAKER *in the Chair*]

## Housing Market

*Motion made, and Question proposed,* That this House do now adjourn.—*[Mr. Lightbown.]*

10.4 am

**Mr. Nicholas Winterton** (Macclesfield): I am delighted to have the opportunity to debate and discuss the housing market. Macclesfield borough is a prosperous and successful borough in the north-west of England and, following the local elections a fortnight ago, is the only borough that has overall Conservative control north of a line from the Wash to the Severn. It is an area where people want to live and where people want to move to live, where businesses want to expand and where new businesses want to locate. So, quite clearly, it is a successful area.

But I know that hon. Members on both sides of the House will agree when I say that housing is fundamental to all 651 constituencies in the United Kingdom, and problems that face home owners affect all 651 constituencies.

I want to start the debate by quoting Lady Thatcher, now in another place, from her book "The Downing Street Years", page 698. She writes:

"I was . . . acutely conscious of what interest rate changes meant for those with mortgages . . . borrowers . . . lives . . . can be shattered overnight by higher interest rates. My economic policy was . . . intended to be a social policy. It was a way to a property-owning democracy. And so the needs of home owners must never be forgotten."

It is because I believe that my Government have forgotten about the importance of home owners that I have asked for this debate today.

Hon. Members on both sides of the House will be aware that my interest in the construction industry is of many years' standing. So concerned have I been by the lack of attention given to its problems and its potential that two years ago I formed, with all-party support, the manufacturing and construction industries alliance in Parliament.

This debate, which I have managed to obtain this morning, has also been warmly welcomed by the House-Builders Federation, the Council of Mortgage Lenders and the Building Societies Association, which all accept the fact that the health of the housing market is now so parlous that to fail to call out for understanding and support could be fatal.

The manufacturing and construction industries alliance, which I have said has all-party support and backing from every sector of industry, including trade unions, exists to move the needs of manufacturing and construction further up the public, political and parliamentary agenda.

Never has that been more necessary than it is today. The housing market has been in recession in the south of England since August 1988 and in the north since around mid-1990. As Joe Dwyer, the group chief executive of George Wimpey plc, told the alliance at its most recent presentation here in the Palace of Westminster immediately following the latest Budget, the housing industry still shows no sign of sharing in the undoubted move out of recession that much of the rest of our economy is now experiencing. That was not my view; that was the view of somebody uniquely, over many years, involved in the housing and construction industry here in the United Kingdom.

While the United Kingdom was in the exchange rate mechanism, things were especially difficult, because the very high interest rates that then prevailed deepened the recession, and the housing market could never recover in those circumstances.

However, since our happy escape from the ERM on "White Wednesday", as it has come to be called, we have been able to enjoy greatly reduced interest rates. Although, sadly, the Governor of the Bank of England appears willing to put at risk the fragile recovery that we are experiencing, there has indeed been a steady improvement in our economy—at least the part of it that is involved in exports.

Ministers have consistently told us that there would also be steady improvements in the housing market. However, after a brief improvement in late 1993 and early 1994, the housing market has again faltered. This year, there are fears that it will do far worse than falter. All the evidence that I have been able to find suggests that the housing market is far weaker than expected and that Ministers cannot—dare not—complacently await its improvement.

Estate agents report that, in the period to the end of April, their sales are almost 20 per cent. less than in the same period last year. House builders, who comprise about 11 per cent. of the market, are maintaining their share of the market, but continue to sell at about 4 per cent. below 1994 levels. Therefore, not surprisingly, total building society new lending is down. For example, the Halifax building society reports that prices are beginning to fall yet again. That is because fewer sales are bound to weaken prices.

**Mr. Oliver Heald** (Hertfordshire, North): Obviously, the evidence is mixed, but in East Anglia the first quarter of the year shows an increase in prices of 1.6 per cent. overall, and there has been an increase of 4.3 per cent. in prices of new properties. In fact, there has been an increase in new property prices in East Anglia in every quarter since the end of 1993. Does my hon. Friend believe that the evidence is slightly more mixed than he suggests?

**Mr. Winterton:** I am not suggesting for a moment that there are not pockets of bright light and of encouragement. I can only go on the information provided to me by house builders, by the House-Builders Federation, the Council of Mortgage Lenders and the Building Societies Association—people who are uniquely in a position to provide that information—who say that the market is

[*Mr. Winterton*]

faltering and that overall, things are bleak for the housing sector and for all those supplying those parts of the economy, which are so important to this country.

**Lady Olga Maitland** (Sutton and Cheam) *rose*—

**Mr. Winterton:** I will not give way again at the moment. I want to develop my argument.

The National House-Building Council reports that new house registrations—that is, new building starts—are 17 per cent. down in the first quarter, and the Brick Development Association, which should know what is going on, advises me that brick deliveries in March were 8 per cent. down on those for March 1994. That is consistent with the major house builders, who say that they are laying off bricklayers and cutting back further on production in direct response to falling sales.

On Friday night, I spoke at a dinner in the Moat House hotel at Wilmslow. After my speech, I was asked a question by a young executive, a young man from Merseyside involved with training. He said that he was deeply worried about the failure to provide jobs for young people after they had received basic training from the various schemes offered by the training and enterprise council. He highlighted especially the problems of the construction industry, which in the past has been such a major employer of young people and semi-skilled people in the Merseyside region.

The weakness of the housing market is starting to knock on to employment and spending power in the domestic economy as a whole. Building workers and building materials, as we know—and as my hon. Friend the Member for Chorley (Mr. Dover) will be more than aware—are only the start. Falling housing transactions are widely reported by retailers as a key factor in the undermining of certain markets. White goods, furnishing, timber, carpets, curtains and do-it-yourself—all are affected.

No one can claim that the condition of the housing market does not fundamentally matter to the economy and to employment in the United Kingdom. It is of great significance to the recovery of the domestic economy and it is of massive significance to the fortunes, dare I say it, of my Government, the Conservative Government.

In my opinion, the Conservative party is, and always has been, the party of home ownership. We can be rightly proud of the fact that we have expanded home ownership since 1979 from about 54 per cent. to 67 per cent. of households. When we ignore the problems of the housing market, we ignore the problems of our strongest supporters and, dare I say it, their greatest asset.

**Mr. Tony Banks** (Newham, North-West): Does not the hon. Gentleman find it disturbing that so much of our country's economic prosperity has to be based on the housing market? I can well understand the way in which it affects the housing market, but the feelgood factor is absent precisely because of the facts that the hon. Gentleman is talking about. As the hon. Gentleman is a great champion of manufacturing industry, does he agree that it would be better to base our wealth and prosperity on that sector rather than on prices in the housing market?

**Mr. Winterton:** I cannot but agree with the opinion expressed by the hon. Gentleman. Indeed, I am not in favour of people investing all their money, all their savings, in property. I was deeply unhappy about the property boom of the late 1980s, resulting from decisions of a Conservative Chancellor, who allowed property inflation to roar away. That factor contributed to many of the economic problems that we experienced shortly thereafter. I want people to be encouraged, by fiscal and other measures, to invest in manufacturing in this country. As the hon. Gentleman knows, I want a massive expansion of our manufacturing base, because only when we do so shall we have a stable, successful economy in the long term.

Every time there is hope of a housing recovery, the Governor of the Bank of England mistakes that for overheating in the economy and urges the Chancellor of the Exchequer to increase interest rates, thus undermining confidence among would-be purchasers even further. Every time he does that, he pushes more home owners and more of the Government's traditional supporters into negative equity.

More worrying still have been the policies pursued by some of my right hon. Friends and the effect that they have had on the whole housing market. The Chancellor of the Exchequer has reduced mortgage interest relief at source for two successive years. He has in that time increased interest rates three times, although I must and do sincerely congratulate him on resisting the siren calls from the Bank of England to do so yet again two weeks ago. I say to him, and make this comment very forcibly, long may he continue to resist, and long may the pound continue to confound those who criticise the Chancellor's decision.

Unfortunately, my right hon. and learned Friend the Chancellor of the Exchequer pretends that those changes in his policy, regarding MIRAS and interest rate increases, are not important to the housing market. He regularly tells house builders that the cost effects of those measures are so trivial that they are not responsible for the weakness of the housing market. In my opinion, that position is untenable, especially as the start of the current dip in the housing market coincided exactly with the first cut in MIRAS in April 1994 and with the beginning of the psychological war being waged by the Bank of England against low interest rates.

**Mr. David Nicholson** (Taunton) *rose*—

**Mr. Winterton:** I shall give way in a moment, but I want to develop my argument further.

The effect of those policies has been a reduction in spending power—as was intended—and a blow to confidence in the housing market.

To add to that, the Secretary of State for Social Security has published proposals to limit mortgage interest support for sick and unemployed people. Every housing market commentator and expert whom I have found and read about has condemned those proposals as being bound to eliminate marginal home buyers from the market and to put some existing and future home owners at risk. They threaten further extension of home ownership to marginal groups, something that I know is dear to the heart of our Prime Minister.

**Mr. Nicholson:** I am listening to my hon. Friend's arguments with substantial agreement and considerable admiration, but, given the fact that, for the past two years, interest rates have been lower than for most of the past

15 years, would not a longer-term benefit of cuts in MIRAS be the avoidance of a return to the position described by the hon. Member for Newham, North-West (Mr. Banks), where people could expand their capital only by investing in housing and not, as my hon. Friend wants, by investing in manufacturing industry?

**Mr. Winterton:** There is some sense and rationale in my hon. Friend's view, but home ownership is fundamental and a way for people to invest in their future. As I said, I do not want second and third houses, which is what resulted from mistaken policies that were implemented some years ago.

We cannot continue to treat the housing market and home owners as we are now. We ignore their problems at our peril, both economically and—perhaps this has more effect on Treasury Ministers—politically. Economically, we must look to a significant strengthening of the domestic economy, and that must be soon. Exports may be benefiting from the devaluation of the pound, made possible by, for example, our exit from the exchange rate mechanism, but the domestic economy is fragile and in danger of faltering. Let us not forget that nearly four times more households are employed in the domestic sector, sadly, than in our export-led economy. I say to my colleagues in the Treasury team that it is the domestic economy and the businesses in it that will produce the employment and the profits that are needed to increase tax revenues and so reduce the public sector borrowing requirement and thus the budget deficit.

**Mr. John Spellar** (Warley, West): May I take the hon. Gentleman back to marginal purchasers in the housing market? Is not one of the fundamental problems in the housing market that a huge swathe of the employed population no longer feel secure in their employment? They feel threatened by the constant references to there being no secure jobs, as if that were a virtue. They are considerably concerned by the Government withdrawing cover in the event of their becoming unemployed. Other major purchases result in a long-term commitment on payments, for example, in the automobile sector, which as we know is also in recession in the domestic market— *[Interruption.]*—not production, if the hon. Member for Sutton and Cheam (Lady Olga Maitland) will listen to what I am saying. Sales of cars are in a serious position in the same way as sales of houses, because no one feels secure in making a long-term commitment.

**Mr. Winterton:** One or two of my colleagues may not like me for saying it, but that is an accurate assessment of the position. It is one of the reasons why we do not have a feelgood factor. On many things in the House, there can be consensus and common ground. I am sure that, in many areas relating to housing, there is common ground between hon. Members on both sides of House.

Any upturn in the domestic economy is being retarded by the housing market weakness. The inevitable consequence of that will be a shortfall in income and corporation tax revenue, making any strategy of tax cuts in the next Budget difficult, if not impossible. Thus, there is a clear link between the weakness of the housing market and the Government's ability to deliver their key policy objective before the next general election.

I say to my colleagues on the Treasury team that, politically, we cannot afford to alienate home owners or to treat their fears or aspirations with contempt or indifference, yet sadly the Government are widely perceived to be doing just that. Voices have been raised by mortgage lenders and house builders complaining that the Government are turning their back on home owners and home ownership as a policy.

How can we have let ourselves get into a position in which articles such as this appear? One in the *Daily Mail* of 3 May had the headline:

"What do the Tories have against the hard pressed homebuyer?"

Another in *The Times* of 5 May stated:

"From subsidy to subsidence: a Tory approach to housing—Janet Bush says the Government is merely aggravating a market already deep in trouble."

That is a sorry state of affairs. Something must be done. I fear, however, that the doleful noises from the Treasury and the Bank of England about the consequences of doing something have frightened the Government into silence. Threats of a return to inflation seem to paralyse us all like rabbits in a car's headlights, yet we all know what happens to the rabbit thus paralysed with fear: he gets squashed anyway. We cannot continue to be frightened of doing what is obvious and necessary by an irrational and obsessive fear of inflation.

Expert opinion is now clear. The housing market is so depressed that a significant increase in transactions is vital immediately to stop it deflating throughout the rest of the year. There is a risk of price falls, now being reported month on month throughout the year by the building societies. I ask my Conservative colleagues—and perhaps colleagues on both sides of the House: how do they think their constituents will react to further falls in house prices?

The Government simply cannot expect to survive such a scenario. That last happened in 1992 and was brought to an end by interest rate reductions after our exit from the ERM. No similar bolthole exists for us today. There is not only a risk of deflation, leading to more home owners in negative equity, but, conversely, there is no risk of a housing market recovery triggering the return of the inflation that Eddie George claims wakes him in the night. We cannot afford to allow our entire economic strategy to be run by a single-issue fanatic sitting in Threadneedle street.

As *The Sunday Times* said on 30 April:

"The Prime Minister . . . appears unaware of the trap his government is falling into: 'The prize of keeping the economy growing steadily, with low inflation, is a prize we have not seen in the past,' he says . . . 'We are here,' he says, 'for the long run' . . . This week's local elections will confirm that it would take only the rash or brave to bet on Mr. Major's long-run hold on power. The more the chancellor, egged on by Eddie George . . . succeeds in slowing the economy, the larger the government's budget deficit and the more difficult for 'prudent' tax cuts to be announced before the election. Without them, the Tories' already slim chance of electoral salvation can be written off."

Again, that is a fairly accurate assessment of how many people feel.

On 30 March this year, I expressed my concern in the House to my right hon. and learned Friend the Chancellor about the crisis in the housing market. He denied that there was any crisis, but did concede, I am pleased to say, that there was a weakness. He went on to say that, regardless of that, any artificial stimulus would have even worse consequences, so he would do nothing but await a natural recovery. I wholly reject that view and would argue that it is the Government who, far from giving

[Mr. Winterton]

artificial stimulus, are kicking the housing market by specific measures that are further weakening it, when it is already facing a serious crisis.

In short, confidence in the housing market continues to suffer as a direct result of a series of Treasury-inspired blows to its head. Measures are urgently needed to avoid the crisis worsening. They must not be half-hearted, such as another stamp duty moratorium. They must put more purchasing power and confidence directly into the housing market. Above all, they cannot wait until the Budget in November. Measures delayed until then will not take effect until next April and, by then, the damage to the Government may well be irreparable. The only step open to the Chancellor is partially to reverse his cuts in MIRAS. He must specifically recognise the problems faced by first-time buyers and the significant increase that they will face in entry costs and in higher mortgage payments, especially if he should give in to the Governor of the Bank of England next month and allow interest rates to rise again.

I put it to the Under-Secretary of State for the Environment, my hon. Friend the Member for Hertfordshire, West (Mr. Jones), that the Chancellor must immediately announce a package putting MIRAS up to £50,000 at the standard rate of 25p in the pound for first-time buyers. That is a constructive proposal. He should not time-limit it, but he should retain the option of withdrawing it once the economy and the market have responded to that stimulus. Such a measure would provide him with an excellent and effective regulator, which would be much more sensitive than interest rates, should the housing market need to be reined back at some future date.

To assist in that move and to restore confidence to first-time buyers and right-to-buy purchasers, the Secretary of State for Social Security should quietly and discreetly ditch the electoral millstone of his proposals to restrict mortgage interest support for the sick and the unemployed. My right hon. Friend the Secretary of State has many good reasons for doing so and I understand that the unpublished study on mortgage arrears and repossessions, which is currently sitting in the Department of the Environment, provides ample evidence of the need for a thorough reappraisal of the proposals that my right hon. Friend has announced.

The housing market stands at a crucial crossroads, and so do our economy and the political future of the Government. All are inextricably linked. Let us recognise that and listen to what the electorate told the Government on 4 May. Let us be clear—the British housing industry is among the best in the world. Hon. Members on both sides of the House know that, not least my hon. Friend the Member for Chorley, who has wide experience of the industry. It offers home owners a wide range of high-quality products at prices that are extremely competitive. Affordability is at good levels.

The main factor that is missing from the equation is confidence, the first emerging breaths of which are repeatedly stifled by policies from the very Government who, in the past, have sought to nurture home ownership as a major electoral asset—and it has been such an asset. This is a bizarre, reckless and, ultimately, politically unsustainable position and I hope that in the coming months the Government will realise the importance of home owners and the need to encourage home ownership, and that policies to encourage and stimulate it will be introduced.

10.32 am

**Mr. Tony Banks** (Newham, North-West): I congratulate the hon. Member for Macclesfield (Mr. Winterton) on a characteristically robust speech. He is one of those hon. Members who speaks the truth as he sees it, which is probably why he has more admirers outside his party than within it.

Housing is a massive problem in my constituency and the hon. Member for Macclesfield identified the problem in other constituencies. In the London borough of Newham, it is at crisis proportions. More than 60 per cent. of all my case work involves housing in the private and public sectors, although essentially we are debating the private sector this morning.

It is difficult to be precise, but the best figures that I have been able to produce show that nearly 60 per cent. of private sector dwellings—about 26,000 in the borough—are unsatisfactory. That is twice as high as in Greater London as a whole. It is distressing to note that the percentage of unsatisfactory dwellings has risen since 1979.

In the latter part of the 20th century it is amazing to note that some 2,000 households in my borough still have outside WCs. I remember outside WCs when I was a young lad—they were a useful way of using up old newspapers, with the nail on the wall and so on. I remember going out in the cold: it was an unpleasant experience and can be spooky for a young kid. The idea that in 1995 2,000 households in my area of east London still have outside WCs is unacceptable. A total of 1,200 have no access to a bath. Overall 3,200 households in the private sector in Newham do not have exclusive use of either a bath or an inside WC.

**Lady Olga Maitland:** I am listening with interest to the hon. Gentleman's remarks about houses with outside lavatories. Will he confirm that people are entitled to a grant to ensure that they have inside sanitation?

**Mr. Banks:** No doubt the hon. Lady speaks with great personal experience of outside dunnies. An outside WC is one of the qualifying factors for a grant as is the absence of an inside bathroom—*[Interruption.]* The hon. Lady has asked the question and is now sitting there answering it, no doubt to her satisfaction but, unfortunately, not to the satisfaction of the rest of us who are trying to take a more objective view. As a result of various cuts, there is no money for improvement grants and there is an enormous backlog in the London borough of Newham. That is one of the complaints that I intended to make. The absence of an inside bathroom or WC is one of the highest qualifying factors for an improvement grant, but if the hon. Lady cares to come to Newham to see the backlog of those who are still waiting for such grants—and Newham is one of the most generous boroughs in the country for making improvement grants—she will realise the problem that we face. If we could solve the problem as easily as the hon. Lady suggests, does she not think that we would have already done it, for heaven's sake? I would not be here complaining and getting myself worked up so early in the morning because of the hon. Lady's facile intervention.

I was about to say something constructive but it has now gone out of my mind. I was going to comment on the fact that the number of houses without inside bathrooms or lavatories has declined since 1981 precisely because of the improvement grants that the London borough of Newham has been able to offer, despite which we still have the highest figure in Greater London.

The problem always comes down to economics. Newham is a poor area with a large low-income sector. A total of 50,000 people in the borough are on income support, many of whom are caught in the poverty trap. Two types of owner suffer disproportionately—the elderly and those with large families. I find it distressing and disgraceful to have to bring such statistics to the House's attention at this stage of our development. A total of 65 per cent. of elderly owners and 58 per cent. of owners with large families live in unsatisfactory housing.

One third of owner-occupiers in my borough have incomes of less than £10,000 a year and more than two thirds have incomes of less than £20,000 a year. Twenty two per cent. of owner-occupiers pay more than 40 per cent. of their net household income in mortgage payments. It is not surprising, therefore, that 10 per cent. find it difficult to meet mortgage payments and a further 19 per cent. find it very difficult. One in eight is in mortgage arrears and an estimated 1,500 households are in serious mortgage arrears.

The hon. Member for Macclesfield mentioned mortgage tax relief being increased. I am not happy about that. I can see what he is trying to say. There is a real problem in the housing sector, but we do not want to encourage taxpayers' subsidy in the owner-occupier sector. All those who have observed the housing market have said that we should reduce mortgage tax relief; therefore, the Government are doing something that other parties would support in general terms. Many devices would boost the housing market and they should be encouraged. For example, the Government could allow local authorities to spend far more of their accumulated receipts from the compulsory sale of council housing. That would give the enormous boost to the housing sector about which the hon. Member for Macclesfield is concerned. I am concerned that we should seek real growth in our economy from the manufacturing sector— the productive areas. People had a false sense of security.

**Mr. Heald:** The hon. Gentleman suggests that if capital receipts were available for building homes, they would in some way help the housing market, but surely the effect of the release of receipts would simply be an improvement in the construction industry. That would not help the underlying problems, described by my hon. Friend the Member for Macclesfield (Mr. Winterton), of negative equity, the lowering of prices and the depressing effect of the present situation.

**Mr. Banks:** It could help for the simple reason that it would free up the whole housing market. It would produce far greater mobility.

People are trapped in substandard private accommodation that their landlords or owners are perhaps loth to improve. If people were able to move out into new public sector housing, landlords or owners would have an incentive to improve the vacant property and put it on the market or employ it in some other productive fashion.

One has to look at the housing market in its totality rather than sector by sector. The fact is that there is little movement in the housing market. People find that they are trapped in the private sector or in the public sector by negative equity or simply because there is not sufficient housing stock available in the areas or sectors in which it is most required. We need to free up the public sector far more. By doing that, we would inject far greater vitality into the private sector as well.

I am concerned that the country's prosperity should not be based on people's feelgood factor and the price of their housing. People like a bit of house price inflation because they can draw on the equity if they are in an advantageous position. That money then moves through the economy. That is precisely how the Government boosted the economy in the 1980s. We are now paying the price, as the hon. Member for Macclesfield said.

What I really want to say in my brief intervention is that I want to see more responsibility in the private sector being taken by the building societies and banks. This evening, I shall speak at the launch of the annual report of the Bow county court advice service. It is an excellent service that helps people without representation in the courts who are suffering from the possibility of mortgage repossession and eviction. Through the intervention of the advice service, many people have been saved from having their house repossessed and being made homeless.

It upsets me when people constantly tell me in my advice surgery that because of the problems in the housing market they have suffered from negative equity, run into mortgage arrears, had their houses repossessed and want the council to rehouse them. The council has a statutory responsibility, but where is the responsibility of the lenders of the mortgage in the first place?

What is the responsibility of the banks and building societies? They just tell people that they have got themselves into a bad position, repossess the house and sell it on to get as much back as they possibly can of their original loan. Negative equity normally affects the person who took out the loan rather than the person or organisation that lent the money in the first place. The lenders get their money back. The council is forced to find housing for people who have been dispossessed of their owner-occupied houses. That pressure and the lack of mobility in the public sector put even greater pressure on local authorities.

I want banks and building societies to face up to their responsibilities. They lent the money in the first place and therefore they should take greater responsibility for trying to keep people in their homes in the private sector rather than throwing them out and leaving the local authority to try to rehouse them.

Housing is a serious matter that affects everyone. All hon. Members are fortunate enough to be well housed, but housing is one of the rights of our people. It is absolutely crazy that, as we approach the end of the 20th century, we still have thousands of families homeless in our cities and yet we have tens of thousands of unemployed construction workers and industries that are being laid to waste because of the failure of the housing market. There surely must be a better way to organise the housing market.

I hope that the Minister will seriously address the points made by the hon. Member for Macclesfield, because, as an independent and fearless hon. Member, he quite often speaks for all of us.

10.46 am

**Mr. Den Dover** (Chorley): I congratulate my hon. Friend the Member for Macclesfield (Mr. Winterton) on raising this very important subject, particularly at this time, because, as he knows, in politics timing is everything.

The key word is "market". Too often, the large-volume house builders—my hon. Friend mentioned Joe Dwyer, the superb chief executive of George Wimpey—assume that there is a big market out there and that they have a God-given right to keep on building more and more houses. The fact is that, at the moment, people want to be able to buy houses, especially new houses. There is a much better market for new houses than for existing, second-hand stock.

However, the house builders must give better and better value for money. Sometimes, in a depressed market, such as we have had for the past few years, home owners are in a better situation. For instance, my stepdaughter and her husband recently purchased a house at the boom of the market for £45,000 in the west midlands. They had to sell it recently for £35,000 but, on the other hand, to upgrade to a house for which they would have had to pay £93,000 or £95,000 during the boom, they have had to pay only £75,000. That has meant that the market has continued to operate. They have been able to upgrade and, indeed, they are probably slightly better off.

In the country at large, there are huge differences. In the south-east, properties in the region have decreased in value by 25 or 30 per cent. There is a slight increase in their values at the moment, but that gap will perhaps never be made up.

On the other hand, out in the more realistic world of the north-west, as my hon. Friend the Member for Macclesfield knows only too well, and especially in the north, the rise in property values took place slightly later than elsewhere and never reached the crazy, ridiculous levels of the south-east.

I accept that there has been a slight reduction in property values in the north-west and north but it has been much smaller, perhaps 5 or 10 per cent. at the maximum. That means that there has been a more realistic approach to the value of properties in those regions. People have not overcommitted themselves and the market is now moving back towards some sort of sense of reality.

As I said, it is up to the builders to give better value for money. There have been all sorts of show house give-aways such as full sets of white goods, fridge-freezers, ovens, kitchen units and full bathroom fittings, as well as sanitary goods. Those offers are absolutely essential. I praise the efforts of the house building industry in getting its act together to give a very competitive product to buyers and in ensuring that it presents that product supremely well in all show houses up and down the country.

I never fail to be impressed by the presentation that house builders give in their show houses; it is a pleasure to go into them. House builders understand the needs of buyers. I am delighted at what they are doing.

The only interest that I have to declare is as a non-executive member of the board of Cosalt plc, which is engaged in the development of a waterfront site with some old, clapped-out factories. It had to reuse the site and decided to put in a new factory and an office block for various public sector tenants and to build four phases

of housing. The company put the deal together during the boom and thought that it was on to a sure-fire winner. However, since then the proposed selling prices of four or five years ago have gone down by 15 or 20 per cent. What is it to do in such circumstances? It has managed to get builders to do the demolition, construction and finishing work at much lower prices than it expected so its original construction budget will not be exceeded four or five years on, even allowing for inflation. In other words, building packages have been bought at much lower prices and that fact is reflected in the selling price.

In the private housing market, everything depends on the rate of sales—how quickly a company can construct a building and get purchasers to commit themselves to minimise its cash flow. I am delighted that the construction industry has been able to turn its operations around even in the difficult market of the past four or five years. Previously, we had runaway inflation and the industry made enormous—even unacceptable—profits. It had it too easy, but it has proved itself lively, on the ball and able to adapt to changes. It now gives better value for money but I would still criticise house builders in one respect.

Up to a couple of years ago, house builders kept buying land as if there were no tomorrow, possibly doubling land values. That was a sure-fire way of ensuring that they would be crippled by having too much land stock without being able to provide houses at affordable prices. In fact, they are their own worst enemies in many cases.

What action can the Government take? We have already heard about the difficult political situation in which the Government find themselves with only two years to go. I join those who say that the reduction in mortgage interest tax relief has been introduced too quickly. To reduce it by 5 per cent. a year on a ratchet system means hardship for some house buyers. However, whereas we reached a peak of mortgage interest rates of 13 per cent., 14 per cent. and even 15 per cent., they are now at a more realistic and acceptable 8 per cent. In other words, buyers are now paying less, even allowing for possible tax increases and the reduction in mortgage interest tax relief, and not doing too badly at the moment.

Should the Government intervene and falsely stir inflation into the equation? I do not think so, although I accept that we all feel better if the value of our house, which is our main asset, is increasing month by month, year by year. I applaud the Chancellor's courage in holding out against further interest rate rises in the past week or so. I hope that sterling's performance against the mark and the dollar confounds all the critics and that we might already have reached the interest rate ceiling of the current cycle. That would be marvellous news.

It is not in the interests of individuals, the housing market or industry for interest rates to continue to increase.

**Mr. Mark Robinson** (Somerton and Frome): Does my hon. Friend agree that the purchaser needs stability and to be sure that interest rates will not change as much as they have over the years, even if it means not reducing them so far? Would it not be better if we perhaps had more stable bands of interest rates as in Germany?

**Mr. Dover:** I could not agree more. If interest rates have already reached their ceiling with three responsible and small interest rate increases in the past few months, I believe that my hon. Friends suggestion would be acceptable to industry at large, to individual home owners and the housing market. I agree that we need stable interest rates and stable inflation, which are closely linked. The Government's targets are set in concrete, so to speak, and we are pursuing and achieving our inflation rate target. We must certainly use the interest rate indicator at all times but we must bear in mind the economy as a whole, not only the financial markets.

I deal now with the definite benefits that flow from home ownership. Home ownership is an investment for a first-time buyer, someone who is upgrading and someone who has reached the peak of his housing ambitions. That contrasts markedly with the plight of people who have spent decades paying rent that has simply gone down the drain.

It is unfortunate that more people cannot be motivated early in life to get on to the house-buying ladder. Any Government action needs to concentrate on first-time buyers, who stimulate demand. I urge people to have confidence and to continue to become home buyers and owners. We can achieve the flexibility that we seek in the housing market without nationwide rented accommodation, although I am all in favour of providing council houses for those who are sick, poor or in urgent need.

I agree with the hon. Member for Newham, North-West (Mr. Banks) as I have always supported the use of capital receipts. They need not necessarily be used to build new local authority housing stock but could certainly be used to improve their existing housing stock. However, if the Government allowed much greater use of capital receipts, would the money be well spent or would it add to public spending and debt and increase interest rates? What would it be used for?

In the local elections, we received the strong message that we were wholly out of favour. Some people argue that we should remove the reins from local authorities and stop capping their spending. I believe that it would be sensible to allow them to use their capital receipts for what they want but it would mean that their deposits of capital receipts, if they have any, would not be earning interest. They would have to convince council tax payers that they were doing something worth while on their behalf because some of their income would be lost and they would undoubtedly have to increase the council tax, which might mean they lost favour.

10.56 am

**Mr. Simon Hughes** (Southwark and Bermondsey): The debate is very welcome, and I am grateful to the hon. Member for Macclesfield (Mr. Winterton), who comes from the proud county of my birth, for speaking so strongly, as people from that part of the world usually do. I hope that this will be a prelude to a longer debate in Government time as housing is probably the issue that most affects people's sense of security. Homes and jobs, which are closely related, are matters of great concern, and probably more so now than for many years. We have heard two contributions from hon. Members representing northern constituencies and I join the hon. Member for Newham, North-West (Mr. Banks) in making a contribution from the south.

My constituency begins literally a mile from here. In Southwark, housing policy across all sectors is nothing short of disastrous. There is a crisis not only for those seeking accommodation in the rented sector, but, increasingly, for those seeking to buy or who have bought. I flag up immediately those who have gone into shared ownership and find that they can no longer sustain it but cannot get out; those who bought under the right-to-buy scheme, some of whom have recently been presented with bills of £27,000 for capital charges—as the people involved are a pensioner couple with no capital, it means that they cannot pay and that their home may cease to be their own—and people who were often forced to buy, thinking that they could just manage the purchase when the market was at its highest in the 1980s but have since seen the value of their homes drop by nearly half in some dockland areas—the price of a terraced house there has dropped from over £100,000 to about £60,000 or £70,000. Their negative equity has turned into not a slight deficit but an extraordinary liability.

The practical problem for many people is whether they will be able to keep their homes as their jobs become less secure. Therefore it is urgent that we get the policy right. The phrase that came to mind, which I suppose was prompted by the VE day background to the debate, was that never have so many owed so much—not to so few, but simply owed so much. People are desperately worried about the implications of that.

We could all cite a litany of problems, but we are here to suggest some solutions, too. There is the problem not only of about 1,000 repossessions a week and the fact that almost 500,000 people are three months behind in their repayments, but that there are increasing bills and the prospect in the autumn of reduced security to help people pay for mortgage interest if they are on income support or other benefits.

Additional uncertainty about interest rates and about the future of mortgage interest relief at source—whatever one's views—does not help.

May I make the point as strongly as I can, from a constituency which is ranked in the top five for unemployment in the country, that the best way to get people back into work is to boost the construction industry? It is proven to be the best way to get more people at all levels of skills back into work more quickly. Self-evidently also, the more people are in work, the more people can better afford their homes. We should encourage not only new build, although the hon. Member for Chorley (Mr. Dover) is right to say that there are some very good newly built properties that are well presented, but renovation, modernisation and home improvement. If we want to reduce unemployment significantly, there is no better way than to boost the housing sector.

There has always been intervention in the housing market, incentives and disincentives and a debate about how to control it. We have never left matters entirely to the marketplace. I was on the Standing Committee on the Housing Bill in 1988 when the Government legislated their policy of reducing subsidy. People predicted then, that instead of subsidy being provided by the Department of the Environment, the Department of Social Security would increasingly have to pick up the bill. All hon. Members now see graphs that show the balance changing from subsidy of the buildings to subsidy of the person. There has been a huge reversal and it is unsustainable in the long term. What should be done?

First, we need a partnership between funding through subsidy by the taxpayer, whether by mortgage tax relief or other forms of subsidy, and funding through the private

[Mr. Simon Hughes]

sector. That partnership, especially in shared ownership and the rented sector, must be achieved to provide long-term security. Secondly—I agree with the speeches of the hon. Members for Macclesfield and for Chorley—the housing market has been nonsensical over the years because the most difficult time to get finance has been when one most needs it: when one starts out. Indeed, getting finance becomes easier for people when they least need it, when their income is more secure and their children are off their hands. Nor do we adequately look after people nearing the end of their lives who do not want responsibility, or cannot afford it, but want to stay in their own homes. We must not forget that issue.

We must ensure that we do not distort incorrigibly in Britain the balance between renting and owner-occupation. We have always made a theological distinction between those two forms of housing in this country, which does not exist in other countries. My party has long argued that people should be given housing credit and that it should be applicable equally to the rented and the private sector. Area by area and local authority by local authority, we must respond to local need and demand. The housing mix and the allocation of land should be influenced by what people want; dependent on whether they want to buy or rent.

I hope that hon. Members will take away the following theme from this debate. We should not only consider people who are taking up the right to buy or have started to buy their own home. What we need most is a policy which provides security and stability. Only in that context can people plan and make commitments. I hope that the Government will seek the widest consensus over the next few weeks and months. People can be overly partisan about housing policy. The best housing policy is one which is secure over the remaining period of this Administration and into future Governments. Only in that way will the voters and those who want, need and buy homes, thank us for being sensible about giving them security for the future.

11.3 am

**Mr. Oliver Heald** (Hertfordshire, North): I congratulate my hon. Friend the Member for Macclesfield (Mr. Winterton) on initiating this important debate. There is no more important issue in politics. Home ownership is one of the most deep-rooted ambitions of many people in Britain. All the surveys for many years have shown that 80 per cent. of the population aspire to owning their own home. One of the successes since 1979 has been the rise in home ownership from 45 per cent. to almost 67 per cent. I do not think that the difficulties of the recession in the housing market and negative equity have changed the essential desire among people in the United Kingdom to buy their own homes. In fact, under the right-to-buy scheme, about 1,000 properties are sold each week.

I could not agree more—unusually—with the hon. Member for Southwark and Bermondsey (Mr. Hughes), who said that, as a country, we owe security and stability to people who have the deep ambition to own a home and have perhaps saved over some years to get together a deposit to buy a house. If the housing market is like a roller-coaster, it will not meet those aspirations. So it is right to go for a policy on housing which provides security and stability.

I do not have enough time to say much about the distress and anxiety felt by those in negative equity. In the eastern region, there are something like 70,000 homes with negative equity. Indeed, we have all seen constituents in surgeries who have found saving up, buying a home and then finding that its value has fallen one of the most distressing events in their lives. I accept the point that my hon. Friend the Member for Chorley (Mr. Dover) makes about moving up in the housing market and the possibilities of lower price. He is right and the lowering of interest rates has been welcome. For the future, we should learn from the lessons of the past. We should try to achieve steady growth in house prices and not an inflationary, expansionary boom, which raises expectations and is—frankly—illusory.

There is some good news. I am not saying that the market has completely rectified itself, but it is noticeable that the number of households with mortgage arrears of more than six months has fallen substantially in the past year. It is down by 21 per cent. Certainly in the eastern region, house prices are beginning to rise. There was a 1.6 per cent. increase in the first quarter of this year. That trend has been continuing for well over a year and it is also reflected in the national figures, which I do not believe are as gloomy as one or two hon. Members have said.

Since the end of 1992, through 1993 and 1994, the Department of the Environment mix-adjusted house price index shows, quarter on quarter, year on year, an increase of between 1 and 2 per cent. Although that is not dramatic, it is in the right direction. For new houses, as my hon. Friend the Member for Chorley said, there has been a more noticeable increase. In the eastern region, in every quarter since the end of 1993, new house prices have been rising and, in the most recent quarter, they have risen by 4.3 per cent.

**Mr. Nicholas Winterton:** I am grateful to my hon. Friend for considering the national position. Perhaps we can do no better than to quote the Halifax building society. Its house price index shows that prices are down by 1.5 per cent. in the year to April 1995 and that there has been a cumulative decline of between 10 and 15 per cent. since 1990. Indeed, the Council of Mortgage Lenders says:

"Depending on the house price index used, between 7 and 10 per cent. of mortgage holders have negative equity."

Surely that shows the serious problem that I was seeking to highlight in my opening remarks.

**Mr. Heald:** I hope that my hon. Friend will agree that I have not sought to minimise the difficulties. If he examines the mix-adjusted house prices indices, which give the recognised national figures, he will see that at the end of 1992 the index stood at 92, whereas it now stands at 94. So far as I can see, it has risen to some extent in every quarter over that period.

**Mr. Nick Raynsford** (Greenwich): The hon. Gentleman must be desperate.

**Mr. Heald:** The figures are provided by the Library, so they cannot be far wrong.

I believe that the real solution lies in sustained economic growth in the economy at large, with low interest rates. I entirely agree that we must have low interest rates in Britain if the housing market is to pick up and the construction industry is to thrive, and I hope that the Chancellor of the Exchequer will continue his robust stance on that matter.

Finally, if we come to the point where tax cuts can be made we should consider whether we can provide married couples with some extra assistance, so that we can build on the building block of the family. Many of the families in negative equity are young married couples, and I should like them to have extra relief.

11.10 am

**Mr. Nick Raynsford** (Greenwich): I begin by declaring an interest as a consultant to HACAS, the social housing consultancy, but I stress that I have no financial interest in the subject of the debate—other than that which, I guess, every other Member of the House shares, as a home owner whose property value may be affected by trends in the market.

I congratulate the hon. Member for Macclesfield (Mr. Winterton) on his success in securing this important debate on the state of the housing market. I agree with almost everything that he said in his analysis, which was a trenchant and accurate assessment of the parlous state into which the housing market has fallen.

We all know that, despite frequent promises of green shoots, the private housing market has failed to show any sustained recovery from the recession. Clearly the market is jittery and consumer confidence is low. The number of transactions has been way below the level that might have been expected, given the historically favourable ratio of house prices to incomes.

That is not simply a case of a recovery being stalled. The evidence from the first three months of 1995 shows falling demand and falling output. New house building starts in the first three months of this year are 8 per cent. down on the equivalent three months of last year—a period which itself delivered a rather disappointing output. Even more worrying is the National House-Building Council's evidence that applications for new starts are 17 per cent. down on the equivalent quarter of 1994.

Those figures reflect a seriously depressed market, and do not support the arguments advanced by the hon. Members for Chorley (Mr. Dover) and for Hertfordshire, North (Mr. Heald), who seemed to assume that the market was making a slow recovery.

**Lady Olga Maitland:** The hon. Gentleman seems determined to prove that the market is collapsing, even in the face of information to the contrary. I wonder whether he is aware of a press release by the estate agent Barnard Marcus, which has conducted a survey of properties in west and south-west London. For each category surveyed Barnard Marcus uses phrases such as:

"Optimism has returned . . . if a house is well presented and realistically priced, it will sell without too much difficulty"

In east Surrey, apparently:

"The market is very active at present",

in south-west London:

"house prices in general have increased",

and in Middlesex:

"New homes sales are increasing".

How does the hon. Gentleman equate all that good news with his attempts to knock the market down?

**Mr. Tony Banks:** That is their selling technique.

**Mr. Raynsford:** Yes, the hon. Lady is confusing two things. One is the selling technique of estate agents in south-west London, and the other is the evidence available from every source, including the corporate estate agents with records from all over the country, that shows demand for housing falling. The hon. Lady is talking nonsense, as usual, and is not reflecting the real state of the housing market.

Why is the market in that parlous state? Essentially, there are three explanations. First, the recession of the early 1990s has had a long-lasting and traumatising effect; in the past five years 295,000 families have lost their homes through repossessions, and 1.2 million are still trapped in negative equity. It is hardly surprising that those human tragedies on a massive scale have cast a long shadow over the market. Hundreds of thousands of families are simply not taking the risk of buying a home or of moving, for fear of falling into debt.

The second factor, as was highlighted by my hon. Friend the Member for Warley, West (Mr. Spellar) in his brief intervention, is the impact of changes in the labour market. Uncertainty is caused by more than the fact of a continuing high level of unemployment; the fear of unemployment runs deep among many people who are currently in work. Few people now feel confident that their job will be around for the 25-year duration of the conventional mortgage. The increasing use of short-term contracts also adds to the uncertainty that inevitably inhibits people from taking on new mortgage commitments.

The third factor is the rising cost of mortgage repayments. Increased interest rates, two cuts in MIRAS and the threatened cut in the income support safety net that will force home owners to take out expensive private insurance, have all contributed to a substantial increase in home owners' costs. The costs involved in servicing a mortgage on the average-priced house will have risen by a staggering £830 between January 1994 and October 1995. With the fear of further interest rate rises adding to the misery, it is hardly surprising that the housing market is now showing a serious downturn.

The Government bear a large measure of the responsibility for that situation. They created the unsustainable boom conditions of the late 1980s, which led inexorably to the disastrous crash of the early 1990s. They encouraged people to buy their own homes, often overstretching themselves in the process, with pledges of continued Government support—pledges that have now clearly been broken, as is pithily stated by the Council of Mortgage Lenders in the evidence that it sent to hon. Members for the debate.

The Government promised to retain MIRAS. Although some commentators would question the wisdom of that pledge, it was nevertheless a firm commitment. To break it now, when so many home owners are in serious financial difficulty and market confidence is so fragile, is not only an act of betrayal but an ill-timed intervention, damaging the market and forcing up home owners' costs.

To add insult to injury, the Secretary of State for Social Security has come up with his half-baked proposals to cut the income support safety net, supposedly to make savings

*[Mr. Raynsford]*

that on closer inspection turn out to be derisory. There are few clearer illustrations of the Government's loss of touch. They seek minuscule short-term savings, while causing immense damage to market confidence and leaving hundreds of thousands of home owners fearful about the future.

To complete the sorry picture, there has been a parallel cut in Britain's social housing programme. Local authorities are now to all intents and purposes prevented from building new homes, and housing association output has been savaged by two successive years' cuts in the Housing Corporation budget. The outcome, hugely damaging to hundreds of thousands of people in need and to our hard-pressed house building industry, has been to reduce the number of new rented housing starts in 1995 to the lowest level since the end of the second world war. As my hon. Friend the Member for Newham, North-West (Mr. Banks) said in his important speech, that has left many people living in unsatisfactory housing conditions, both in Newham and elsewhere.

When the health of the housing market is such a major component in the feelgood factor, and with a general election fast approaching, one would have imagined that the Government, fresh from their remarkable performance in the local elections, might have second thoughts about pursuing what appears to be a suicidal policy.

The truth is that the Government are caught in a time warp, driven by the fear of a lurch back to the bad old boom-bust cycles for which they were largely responsible. They are right to want to avoid unleashing another unsustainable boom, but they are wrong in failing to recognise that economic circumstances in the mid-1990s are light years away from those that applied in the late 1980s boom. The danger in the present situation is not that recovery in the housing market will spark off an unsustainable and damaging inflationary spiral, but that the housing market will not be allowed to recover because Treasury Ministers, like the generals in the first world war, are too busy fighting yesterday's battles rather than understanding today's circumstances.

I do not care if the Treasury mandarins—aided and abetted, as the hon. Member for Macclesfield rightly said, by the Governor of the Bank of England—encourage Tory Ministers to rush lemming-like over the cliff of electoral extinction, hotly pursued by many of those who currently sit on the Government Benches. However, I care passionately about the misery being caused in the lives of millions of our fellow citizens by the callous, incompetent and pig-headed policies being pursued by the Government.

We have a responsibility to act to protect the interests of the hundreds of thousands of home owners laden with debt and in fear of repossession. We have a responsibility to act on behalf of more than 1 million households who are trapped in negative equity and are unable to move home, and who have a continuing millstone of debt around their necks. We have a responsibility to act to rescue the beleaguered house building industry, which has been ravaged by the impact of more than five years of recession in which more than 500,000 construction jobs have been lost.

We have a responsibility to act in the interests of the British economy, in which the house building and construction industries play a crucial part. Restoring confidence in the market and expanding our hopelessly inadequate social housing programme will not just be good for housing in Britain, but it will be good for all those in jobs which, in one way or another, depend on a thriving industry—people who make bricks and tiles; people who manufacture kitchen and bathroom units, central heating boilers and fittings; people who manufacture doors and windows; people who weave carpets and curtains. All these, and many more, stand to benefit from a revived housing market. Many hon Members—including the hon Member for Southwark and Bermondsey (Mr. Hughes)—have rightly pointed that out.

In the interests of Britain and the British people, we call on the Government to reverse their misguided and damaging policies towards the housing market. We urge them to abandon their ill-thought-out proposals to cut income support, and we urge them do the U-turn which is vital to send the signal which the market so desperately seeks. I warn the Government that if they do not do that, they will pay a heavy price.

11.20 am

**The Parliamentary Under-Secretary of State for the Environment (Mr. Robert B. Jones):** It was curious that the hon. Member for Greenwich (Mr. Raynsford) chose to have a swipe at the Governor of the Bank of England in his speech, since his hon. Friend the Member for Dunfermline, East (Mr. Brown) was recently talking about giving the Bank more control—not less—over interest rates and monetary policy. No doubt that debate will take place on another day.

Today's debate has been interesting, and the speeches have highlighted the complex inter-relationship between the many factors which affect the housing market. We heard some thoughtful speeches, particularly from my hon. Friends. But while I did not agree with every point that the hon. Member for Newham, North-West (Mr. Banks) made, I thought that he hit one or two nails firmly on the head. I take seriously the question of housing renovation, and I would welcome a discussion with him on the matter on another occasion. Like the hon. Gentleman, I began life with access only to an outdoor loo. Unlike him, however, I had one other hazard. When I stayed with my great aunt Linda in North Carolina, I had to bang loudly on the outdoor loo with a stick to dislodge the rattlesnakes, which one had to do if one did not want to end up with a greater vulnerability than one would have had in Newham or Bedford.

Perhaps we do not get enough opportunities to discuss the housing market, because it is an important subject. While I recognise the concerns which my hon. Friend the Member for Macclesfield (Mr. Winterton) has set out, I cannot share his overall assessment of the situation. I want to start by reaffirming the Government's complete commitment to sustainable home ownership. Owner-occupation remains the tenure of choice of eight out of 10 households. I am not surprised by that, even after the experience of the recent unsustainable boom.

Buying a home remains a sensible investment for most families. It is an investment not in the speculative, get-rich-quick sense, but an investment in choice, independence and control. It is also an investment in security, particularly later in life when mortgages are repaid. That is why home ownership has grown from 56 per cent. to 68 per cent. of all housing tenures since 1979. That is why it will continue to grow in both market share and volume.

Concern has been expressed this morning about the possible effect of the proposed changes to income support for mortgage interest. There will be an opportunity shortly to debate these proposals more fully when my right hon. Friend the Secretary of State for Social Security places his final proposals before the House. In the meantime, I would like to make two points. First, the existence of an insurance market will of itself help build confidence, and secondly the fact is that even under the present arrangements, an estimated 70 per cent. of home owners would not be entitled to state help.

What is needed is comprehensive, high-quality and reasonably priced insurance products. That need exists even under present arrangements. Until now, these products have not generally been available. Many critics have said that this will not change, and that the insurance industry cannot cope. It is important that the new insurance products which emerge should address the realities of the changing labour market, particularly as we move away from traditional patterns of employment. This represents a significant challenge, but we believe that the industry can and will rise to that challenge.

I am pleased to say that the signs are that, in part prompted by the proposed income support changes, a more positive and innovative approach is emerging from the insurance industry and the house builders. That said, it has been recognised from the outset that insurance can provide cover only for a limited and finite period and cannot cover certain eventualities. My right hon. Friend has made it clear that he will consider very carefully the need to continue to protect those whom insurance cannot reasonably cover.

On the question of mortgage interest tax relief, the staged reduction of the MIRAS rate from 25 per cent. to 15 per cent. has increased monthly mortgage payments by £20 at most. This needs to be compared with a £130 reduction in average monthly mortgage payments resulting from interest rate reductions since October 1990.

I said that we continue to support sustainable home ownership. Indeed it remains our policy to extend home ownership. Through the right to buy, shared ownership, cash incentives and other low-cost home ownership schemes, we are enabling over 200 social sector tenants a day to become home owners. It has been suggested that the success of these and other initiatives to encourage marginal first-time buyers are at risk through the increased costs of owning a home. It is not our policy to encourage people to be unrealistic about what they can afford. That is not sustainable home ownership.

Several hon. Members have referred to first-time buyers, but it is worth making the point that it is clearly not affordability which is restraining the market. The National House-Building Council first-time buyers ability to buy index is at the highest level since its introduction over 20 years ago.

I am very conscious of the problems being experienced by some home owners—particularly those in arrears with their mortgage, and those with negative equity. These problems will not disappear overnight. But the success of Government policies in securing sustained economic growth, increased employment opportunities and low interest rates means that fewer people are now likely to get into difficulty with their mortgage payments, and those in arrears are more likely to be able to pay them off.

Figures published by the Council of Mortgage Lenders show that the number of households in arrears of six months or more at the end of 1994 was down 21 per cent. on a year earlier. The number of households affected by negative equity has fallen by 44 per cent. since the 1992 peak. The number will continue to decline as house prices edge upwards. South-east England, where the negative equity problem is most concentrated, has now seen modest house price increases for six consecutive quarters. In the meantime, I am pleased to note that most of the main mortgage lenders now have arrangements to assist borrowers with negative equity who need to move home.

I know very well that recent market conditions have caused concern to the house building and building materials industries. This is a vast sector of British industry, for some 43 per cent. of the total construction market is housing-related.

There is no doubt that house builders have had a difficult time over the last few years. The total number of new house starts fell by nearly 40 per cent. between 1988 and 1992. Although there have been some improvements since then, the industry has regained nothing like its old confidence. Last year was a good one for the industry, by and large; starts were up by 13 per cent. and the total volume of output increased by 7 per cent., but many builders were hoping for a much more significant upturn.

In the early months of 1995 builders were scanning the horizon for the long-awaited resurgence in the private market. Nobody is suggesting that there is a boom at the moment, or anywhere near that. Housing market activity is generally rather lower than last year, and prices are scarcely moving from month to month.

In the nature of their business, house builders have to make considerable investments—in land, materials, machinery and people—well ahead of public demand. The housing market is not an easy one to judge. Understandably, builders have looked with concern at increased interest rates and changes to MIRAS and benefit arrangements, although these factors alone should not make much difference to the market. Nevertheless, they are part of a pattern of uncertainty, and I recognise that markets are critically sensitive to that. We are emerging from a period of many such uncertainties. The last few years have seen the firm establishment of a low-inflation economy. Housing remains a solid investment, but it is no longer a get-rich-quick gamble. That must be good for house building in the longer term, but the market is taking time to adjust to the new realism.

While unemployment continues to fall, a significant proportion of prospective buyers have been affected by unemployment over the past five years. Many of those in work are adjusting to more flexible employment arrangements, such as fixed-term contracts. In the longer term, these changes are good for the economy and the housing market. Builders need a strong, stable, responsive economy and a healthy and responsible attitude to home ownership. No one should regret it if we do not see so much of boom and bust in future. But there has undoubtedly been a hiatus and the market is taking a long time to pick up—longer than many expected and hoped.

House builders can do much to encourage a new spirit of enthusiasm for home ownership. A good product at a good price will always be the prime incentive, and there

[Mr. Robert B. Jones]

is plenty of evidence from the last few years that new housing is more popular than ever. Builders rightly look to the Government to advance the cause of home ownership for all the undoubted benefits that it brings, and we intend to do our best to encourage it.

# Maritime Industries

11.29 am

**Mr. Ian Davidson** (Glasgow, Govan): This is the first debate that we have had for some time on the shipbuilding, ship repairing and other maritime industries. I hope that it will be the first of several exchanges to take place both here and elsewhere within the House on this important issue, because it is widely recognised that important changes have taken place in the industry over the years: it has been rationalised, privatised and then rationalised again, and it now bears no resemblance to the traditional image of shipbuilding as an old-fashioned rust bucket industry. Instead, it is a high-tech, high-skill, high-investment industry in which Britain needs to play a part in future.

For both industrial and national defence reasons, it is important that we safeguard the shipbuilding industry and do all that we can to ensure its success. Given the projected increase in the world market for shipbuilding, we must ensure that the UK gets its fair share of future orders. Hon. Members on both sides of the House should agree that we need a partnership between the public and private sectors to ensure that the industry does as well as it can. In those circumstances, the private sector's role is to ensure that the industry is efficient, adequately financed and resourced, and in a position to compete and win orders. The public sector's role is to ensure that the competition which the industry enters into is fair and that there are no hidden subsidies or support elsewhere.

Although the privately owned industry is efficient thanks to the efforts of management and unions, the danger is that it will not win orders abroad in the magnitude that its efficiency warrants because of unfair competition. There must be a level playing field or, more appropriately in these circumstances, a level swimming pool. If the effect of a tilted playing field is significant, hon. Members will realise that the impact of a tilted swimming pool is even more substantial if one is trying to swim uphill. We need a market that is fair and regulated, and we must establish that the rules are the same for everyone.

I wish to raise three major areas of concern. First, the world market is likely to be substantially affected by an unwarranted expansion of the Korean shipbuilding industry. South Korea caused a glut in the industry by its tremendous expansion during the 1970s. That led to a refinancing requirement in the 1980s, when the industry had to be bailed out by the South Korean Government. The South Koreans now propose a tremendous increase in their yards, which is not warranted by their financial circumstances. The South Koreans are showing that they are willing to buy market share using Government subsidies, both direct and indirect, which involve free and heavily subsidised financial packages.

Do the Government accept that that is the position and, if so, what do they intend to do about it? There is no point in British industry making great efforts to increase efficiency if it is to be beaten by unfair competition by foreign yards. The South Koreans have clearly decided that they have a strategic industry and want to take their share of the market in shipbuilding, but they should not be allowed to drive out British yards by unfair competition.

My second concern is about state aid in Europe. Germany is clearly prepared to pay a substantial amount for reunification, which involves propping up, modernising and investing in east Germany. The impact of that on the shipbuilding sector is to give German yards an unfair advantage over their competitors. Substantial allegations have been made that German yards are winning orders at, effectively, below real costs. I should be grateful to know whether the Minister accepts that assertion and, if so, what he intends to do about it.

Elsewhere in Europe, publicly owned yards that still operate as part of the nationalised sector, particularly in Spain and Italy, receive concealed Government subsidies to allow them to bid for orders abroad. The Minister will be aware of the current competition for orders from the South African navy. This may not be the appropriate time to discuss the details of that, but there are grave concerns about whether the Spanish competitor has an unfair advantage over Yarrow on Clydeside. I hope that, once that order is resolved, the Minister will be prepared to look into that issue.

Similarly, France has just received substantial assistance, which has been agreed by the EC, for restructuring. The danger is that that money will be used not to restructure but to buy orders. The Minister will be aware of recent reports that the Royal Caribbean order of two vessels at some $270 million each involves a subsidy of approximately $130 million per ship. With that level of subsidy, any British yard seeking to compete without state support cannot do so. That differential is so enormous that fair competition can be achieved only by ensuring that there is equality.

My third area of concern is ship financing schemes. It is widely believed that Norway outside the EC and Germany, Denmark and Spain within it have better finance schemes than those allowed by the UK Government. If the Minister accepts that that is the position, what does he intend to do about it? David Smith, president of the Shipbuilders and Shiprepairers Association, and members of that association have raised that matter with the Minister and intend to meet him in future to pursue that important question. In reflecting the industry's concerns, the shipbuilding industry, its management and unions, are noticeably not asking to be propped up or subsidised. They simply ask the Government to ensure that competition with Europe and the rest of the world is fair because they believe that the strenuous efforts that they have made to make the industry more efficient should be rewarded by the opportunity to compete fairly.

I could go into great detail, but I recognise that this is not the time to do so because many other hon. Members wish to contribute to the debate. I hope that the Minister accepts that it would be more appropriate for him to meet a delegation to discuss those points in detail so that they can be more fully explored.

On military procurement, with the ending of the cold war, this is a time for industrial regrouping and alliance forming throughout Europe and the world. While it is not entirely clear whether that regrouping will be on an international or national basis, or whether it will be because of takeovers, industrial alliances or partnerships, it will none the less take place. The Government have a clear responsibility to ensure that Britain's national defence and strategic interests are protected and that that is not left simply and solely to the market.

**Ms Rachel Squire** (Dunfermline, West): I support my hon. Friend's remarks. Will he join me in welcoming today's expected announcement that two additional submarines are to go to Rosyth royal dockyard for refitting, which will help to guarantee 1,000 jobs? Does he also agree, however, that, first, it is vital for the defence interests of our country that Rosyth receives the contractual guarantees for surface ship work that were promised to it? Secondly, does he agree that the Government should adopt a procurement and industrial policy that secures what is left of our shipbuilding and ship refitting industries and recognises their vital role in the defence of the country?

**Mr. Davidson:** I agree. I hope that the Minister also agrees. It is extremely important that we ensure that any industrial rationalisation guarantees that our industrial and military capacity follows our defence policy and does not lead it. We do not want a repeat of the situation during the Gulf war, when the Belgians refused to sell us ammunition because they disagreed with our policy in that conflict. That decision could have had a horrendous impact upon our ability to exercise what we considered to be our national interest. It is important that our military shipbuilding capacity is preserved so that we can guarantee our ability to implement any policy on which we determine.

Given the limited time available to me, I shall not discuss what will happen at VSEL, but, in future, I hope that the Minister will be prepared to discuss that matter, either privately or in public, with interested Members. My hon. Friend the Member for Dunfermline, West (Ms Squire) has already referred to Rosyth, so I shall say nothing further about it or Devonport.

Sea safety is a relatively minor point compared with the sweep of issues that I have raised, but it is worth considering. It is in our national interest to ensure the highest possible safety standards for our mariners and the cargoes that come to our country. I hope that the Government will press as hard as they can to ensure that those high standards are maintained by all ships that come to our country. I hope that they will also do what they can to ensure that the shipbuilding and ship refitting industries are able to benefit from the commercial opportunities offered by such safety work.

**Rev. Martin Smyth** (Belfast, South): I am following the hon. Gentleman's arguments carefully and I agree with everything that he has said. Does he agree that there is great concern throughout the industry that the Government are not paying enough attention to safety standards? As a result, we could lose our seat at the international conference that established the maritime safety conventions. The Government are failing to safeguard the rights of British people employed in the industry worldwide, who sometimes have to take orders from political commissars in contravention of those conventions. I believe that one of our representatives at the conference is a low-grade civil servant, who has little understanding of the industry. Surely that reflects the Government's concern about safety.

**Mr. Davidson:** I am grateful to the hon. Gentleman for raising that extremely important point. I am sure that the Minister will refer to it in his response, but I hope that he will not do so at such length that the answers to my questions are squeezed out.

The environmental benefits of sea travel are worth noting, particularly when so much concern has been expressed about road traffic and the fumes that it causes.

*[Mr. Davidson]*

People should realise that sea travel, particularly cabotage, is an environmentally friendly method of moving goods around the European Community. The Government should encourage that practice wherever possible and ensure that our shipbuilding and ship repair industries take advantage of the related commercial opportunities.

The fact that so many other hon. Members want to take part in the debate demonstrates the importance that so many of us attach to the shipbuilding industry. I hope that this debate will not be the only occasion when shipbuilding, ship repair and other related industries are discussed in the House.

11.44 am

**Mr. Gary Streeter** (Plymouth, Sutton): It is a pleasure to follow the hon. Member for Glasgow, Govan (Mr. Davidson), who led off this important debate extremely well. I find myself in the rather unusual position of agreeing broadly with almost everything he said—that spells the end of his political career. He was right to refer to competition, which is at the heart of shipbuilding and related maritime industries.

I must declare an interest as I am a partner in the law firm, Foot and Bowden, which has a large shipping department. I am not, however, directly involved in that work.

I am particularly proud to take part in the debate given the vast maritime history of the city of Plymouth. It is the city of Drake and of the Pilgrim Fathers, who set sail from the Mayflower steps. It still has strong maritime connections, because it is the home of the world-famous Devonport dockyard and naval base. It is the city of Millbay docks, from which Brittany Ferries takes passengers to France and Spain. It has a substantial fishing fleet and a waterfront and yachting facilities beyond compare in the United Kingdom. We hope to contribute to that maritime heritage with a national maritime aquarium. That will combine Plymouth's maritime history with our hunger for knowledge and the research carried out by the expanding and extremely successful university of Plymouth. I am sure that that aquarium will become a world-famous focal point. I look forward to its opening.

Maritime history is not just in the blood of Plymouth people but, as an island race, it is in the blood of all of us. Perhaps that is why we have a slightly different concept of the European Union than our continental partners. Perhaps, because of that, we do not want to participate in full economic and political union, unlike some of our European partners. We cannot buck not just the market, but our geography and our history.

I have an enormous sympathy for any hon. Member who represents a community in which an established and traditional industry has declined. That has happened over the centuries for a variety of reasons. Sadly, I represent such a community. When I first arrived in Plymouth in 1980, 13,500 people were employed at Devonport dockyard. That number has now fallen to 4,000. I accept that the industry was subject to overmanning in the old days and that naval requirements have changed, but that does not make it any easier for the people in that local community to cope with such downsizing, as the Americans call it. I understand the anger of the communities that have to cope with the huge impact of the decline of their traditional industries.

It is important to consider the Government's proper role in such circumstances. It is interesting that the hon. Member for Govan did not, to his credit, call for the loss-making industries to be propped up by taxpayer subsidy. He called for fair competition. That is the right approach. It is for the Government to ensure fair competition so that our shipbuilding and ship repair yards operate on a level playing field, or in a non-tilted swimming pool, with other shipyards throughout the world. I am not convinced that that is happening now. It is important that the Government do not allow competitive tenders for naval ship repair work to go to yards outside Britain, because it would be wrong for European shipyards to do such work. There is a real fear that the Government subsidies enjoyed by some shipyards on the continent enable them to compete more fully than our yards.

I was pleased that the hon. Member for Govan mentioned the Korean shipbuilding industry. Let me put down a marker on the subject of global free trade. In theory, we probably all support the concept, and if there were indeed a level playing field—as there doubtless will be in due course—such market conditions would of course be right; but the subsidies provided by other Governments, wage levels in other countries and all sorts of strange working practices make the road to our alleged goal of global free trade a rough and rocky one. Let us have competition by all means, but let it be fair.

I welcome the agreement reached by the Organisation for Economic Co-operation and Development in September 1994, which insists on the phasing out of subsidies for other shipbuilding yards and shipping industries generally. However, we must play our part in ensuring that other nations comply with their obligations. We are fed up with being the one nation that plays by the rules in Europe and the world, while others cock a snook at European directives and agreements. Let us be fair, but let us also ensure that no one takes advantage of us. There is no point in our shipyards and shipping companies being exposed to the full glare of competition and market forces if they must compete in a world in which other countries subsidise their industries.

We in Plymouth are fortunate to have Devonport Management Ltd., a highly successful company with a skilled and motivated work force that has attracted work from overseas and from outside the naval industry. That company now wants a period of stability and consolidation in the shipbuilding and ship repair industry, and fair competition.

Let me raise another constituency issue. British Aerospace Systems and Equipment Ltd., also based in Plymouth and a vital supplier of the naval industry, wants competition among major contractors. As I said on 16 February in the debate on the Royal Navy, it is important to

"encourage competition between British Aerospace, GEC and other major prime contractors, as the best means of ensuring value for money in naval, whole ship and systems procurements".—[*Official Report*, 16 February 1995; Vol. 254, c. 1190.]

I hope that the Government will ensure that that competition is guaranteed.

My final constituency point concerns the excellent service that Brittany Ferries runs from Plymouth. For many years, we have had a very successful roll on/roll off ferry industry: it is possible to enjoy a pleasant cruise to Roscoff in France and Santander in Spain. The industry is now developing, and other routes are being considered. I have used the company's services in recent years, and I can thoroughly recommend starting any holiday from Plymouth. Interestingly, 50 per cent. of British people who go to France and stay for more than four nights spend their time there west of a line from Le Havre to Biarritz. It is entirely wrong to begin a holiday by travelling from Dover to Calais; Plymouth is definitely the right starting place.

Many ferry operators fear that the Dover to Calais service is becoming little more than a floating supermarket. People are, in effect, enjoying an hour of duty-free shopping without even leaving the ship at its destination. Local newspapers are offering promotions enabling people to board such boats for 50p.

**Mrs. Jacqui Lait** (Hastings and Rye): Does my hon. Friend agree that it is now cheaper to buy in France than to shop on the duty-free boats?

**Mr. Streeter:** My hon. Friend may well be right. I have not so far availed myself of that opportunity.

My point is that the impact on other ferry companies that cannot offer such a floating supermarket service is very great. Consumers are entitled to ask why they should pay so much more to travel to France from Portsmouth or Plymouth when they can sail from Dover to Calais for 50p. The answer, of course, is that the service is heavily subsidised by the duty-free shopping.

**Mr. Nicholas Brown** (Newcastle upon Tyne, East): On a point of order, Mr. Deputy Speaker. How much more must we hear about cross-border shopping in a debate about the shipping and shipbuilding industry?

**Mr. Deputy Speaker (Mr. Michael Morris):** The subject is tangential to the debate, but it has some relevance to shipping in general. Nevertheless, I ask the hon. Member for Plymouth, Sutton (Mr. Streeter) to return to the main substance of the debate.

**Mr. Streeter:** The title of the debate on the Order Paper, Mr. Deputy Speaker, includes the words "and other maritime industries".

**Mr. Deputy Speaker:** I am aware of the title. I have ruled, and I hope that the hon. Gentleman will respect my ruling.

**Mr. Streeter:** I certainly will, Mr. Deputy Speaker—and you will be delighted to learn that I am approaching the end of my speech. [HON. MEMBERS: "Hear, Hear."] The ferry companies will be disappointed that Opposition Members do not consider them to be maritime industries; they employ a great many people. *[Interruption.]*

**Mr. Deputy Speaker:** Order. I do not think that that remark was required. If the hon. Gentleman wants to make such remarks, he should go outside.

**Mr. Streeter:** It is disappointing that Opposition Members remain stuck in the past. They see only the industries and businesses with which they are familiar; they forget that the world is changing all the time. My constituents who are employed by Brittany Ferries are concerned about their jobs and futures. They wanted to send me here to speak on their behalf. I am sorry that Opposition Members cannot see beyond the end of their noses.

A number of important issues need to be discussed and fair competition is at the heart of all those issues. The Government must play their part in ensuring that our shipbuilding, ship repair and other maritime industries are not prejudiced by unfair subsidies abroad, and I ask for an assurance from my hon. Friend the Minister that he is paying attention to the interests of those industries.

11.57 am

**Mr. John Hutton** (Barrow and Furness): I congratulate my hon. Friend the Member for Glasgow, Govan (Mr. Davidson) on selecting this subject. As he said, this is the first occasion for some time—certainly the first occasion in the current Parliament—on which we have engaged in a wide-ranging debate about the shipbuilding industry: I welcome that, and I know that my constituents will as well.

It is incontrovertible that, as has already been said, the shipbuilding industry has been in steep decline for more than a generation. The results of that decline have been visible, and many Labour constituencies have lived with the consequences—massive unemployment, the end of apprentice training schemes, a fear of the future and a profound sense that job security is vanishing.

We have also seen the decline of certain famous shipyards—indeed, the disappearance of two: Cammell Laird on Merseyside and Swan Hunter on Tyneside. That is very regrettable, and could have been avoided had the Government shown the commitment and support for our shipbuilding industry that other Governments in the European Union have shown. It is a lasting indictment of the Government's record that they were prepared to sit on their hands and do nothing to support those famous shipyards.

As my hon. Friend the Member for Govan hinted, the reasons for that decline are numerous—they are also complex. They have to do with hidden subsidies, both direct and indirect, which many foreign countries have provided for their shipbuilding industries. The reasons involve the lack of investment in the industry in the 1960s and 1970s.

Whatever the reasons for the decline, it is incumbent on the Government to recognise that we can do something about it, as my hon. Friend the Member for Govan said. The Government must recognise that the prospects for the industry are not all doom and gloom. Most independent analysts expect an increase in demand for new merchant shipping throughout the remaining years of the decade. It is important that the remaining industry, which is a high-tech, state-of-the-art industry, should be able to take advantage of the increase in demand when it comes. There has been significant investment in many of the principal yards in the past 10 years.

There will be increased demand for a number of reasons. The first reason is the increasing age of our merchant shipping fleet, which is nearly 17 years old in Britain, compared with 13 years old throughout the rest of the European Union. Our shipping is ancient and needs to be replaced. There will also be an increased demand because of the improving environmental standards related to the carriage of goods by sea. Another reason for an increase in demand is the requirement for double hulling. Improvements in other aspects of the carriage of goods by sea will also lead to an increase in new merchant shipping orders. There are also chances for British yards to take

[*Mr. John Hutton*]

advantage of increased export opportunities in the naval shipbuilding sector. All those factors should give the Government sufficient grounds to look at the industry again and review the way in which they provide practical support to shipbuilding.

One of the problems bedevilling British shipbuilding over many years has been unfair competition abroad. My hon. Friend the Member for Govan mentioned the South Korean industry, which now accounts for nearly 30 per cent. of the world market for merchant shipbuilding. Some 25 years ago, there was no South Korean shipbuilding industry, but it now accommodates about one quarter of the world demand for merchant shipbuilding.

There is no reason why the British Government should not look at a range of policies to support the British shipbuilding industry and show it the same level of support and patriotism as other countries have shown their shipbuilding industries. In particular, I hope that the Under-Secretary of State for Industry and Energy will look carefully at the capital allowance regime that applies to shipowners' purchasing decisions. It is important that we match the best fiscal policies that apply throughout the European Union; at present, we do not. As a result, British shipowners are less inclined, and have historically been less inclined, to place new orders with British yards for merchant ships. The Minister and his colleagues in the Government should consider that issue directly.

I welcome the ban in the new regime on state subsidies for shipbuilding. It is clearly important that any new fiscal regime should apply to all shipowners who want to place orders. I am not saying that there should be a hidden subsidy just for British shipowners, but I am sure that when we consider the tax rules and the fiscal regime closely, we shall find ways of providing a positive incentive for British shipowners to place new orders and work.

I congratulate my hon. Friend the Member for Govan. I know that there will be widespread interest in the British shipbuilding communities in our debate. We want the Government to give a positive message of support to the industry, to give it practical assistance and encouragement, and to take action to reverse the generation of decline that has caused unemployment and misery throughout the length and breadth of this country.

12.2 pm

**Mrs. Jacqui Lait** (Hastings and Rye): Like my hon. Friend the Member for Plymouth, Sutton (Mr. Streeter), I was impressed by the remarks of the hon. Member for Glasgow, Govan (Mr. Davidson), who could have made his speech from the Conservative Benches. I was worried when the hon. Member for Barrow and Furness (Mr. Hutton) started to go down the old Labour route; he recovered himself to support the call for the Minister to ensure that there is a level playing field in the shipbuilding industry. I say that not just because I spent the first 20 years of my life on Clydeside and saw the decline in shipbuilding, but because for a long time I have wanted world trade organisations and the European Union to ensure that competition is free and fair in all industries. Interestingly, the Transport Commissioner in the European Union may be one of those urging free and fair competition on other countries in the European Union.

My constituency has a long coastline but no traditional shipbuilding or ship repairing. I was attracted to the debate because of the mention in its title of maritime industries. I hope that I shall stay in order as there are a number of what I regard as maritime industries along the coastal strip of Hastings and Rye, all of which add employment to the area. Those industries are expanding and beginning to show that the industries now associated with the sea are not just the old traditional ones of ship repairing and shipbuilding.

One company in my constituency exports 98 per cent. of its products. It produces a propulsion backpack for divers, such as we may remember seeing in the James Bond films. The diving industry is expanding and has grown tenfold in the United Kingdom in 10 years. It is a high-tech industry that operates at the frontiers of technology and it provides an opportunity for wealth and job creation for the residents of Rye.

There has also been a recovery in the boatbuilding industry. That raises the question of definitions of boats and ships. I am talking about the small, leisure boat industry, in which a worldwide recovery is taking place. Companies around our shores have fought their way through a difficult recession. New orders are emerging and companies are developing new boats using new technology and equipment. They operate at the frontiers of technology to export and develop new and attractive packages for the international yachting and sailing world. As we have more leisure time, particularly in the rich west, there is a greater demand for such boats.

I may stray slightly out of order when I mention one developing sector. I am not sure whether it is a maritime industry, but I am sure that you, Mr. Deputy Speaker, will tell me if I stray out of order. The medical world is developing the use of sea water, along with shellfish, to produce a high-tech—

**Mr. Deputy Speaker:** Order. I am married to a general practitioner and can say that the hon. Lady has strayed pretty wide of the subject.

**Mrs. Lait:** I bow to your judgment, Mr. Deputy Speaker.

The more different industries develop, the more difficult we shall find it to define a maritime industry. The opportunities for developing new products, for export, and for creating jobs and wealth may come in different guises from the historic shipbuilding and ship repairing industries, but their long-term contribution to this country could be just as effective. I hope that in future debates we can extend the definition of maritime industries so that I can tell people about sea water and shellfish.

12.7 pm

**Mr. David Chidgey** (Eastleigh): I am grateful to be called in the debate, particularly as so many hon. Members wish to contribute. Hon. Members may not realise that shipbuilding, particularly naval shipbuilding, is a large employer in my constituency, and I want to have the opportunity to press that point.

I fully endorse the remarks of the hon. Member for Glasgow, Govan (Mr. Davidson), particularly the fact that shipbuilding is often dismissed as a sunset industry, incapable of withstanding the demands of worldwide competition. There have, unquestionably, been drastic rationalisations, not least in the warship building industry that interests my constituents. Employment in that part of the industry was running at 21,500 in 1990 and is now down to below half that figure. Now, 11,000 people work in the warship building industry in this country. The decline in shipbuilding and its impact on employment is not confined to the famous yards on the Clyde and the Tyne.

In response to the remarks of the hon. Member for Plymouth, Sutton (Mr. Streeter), I should say that as a young student apprentice working in Portsmouth dockyard I remember that 22,000 people were employed to repair and refit capital and other ships for the Royal Navy. At the same time there were burgeoning shipyards along the coast around Southampton, such as Vosper, Harland and Wolff and Thornycroft. What remains of the Portsmouth dockyard today employs a mere 2,000 people—less than one tenth of the number employed when I worked in engineering as a young man.

Harland and Wolff has long since departed from Southampton waters. Vosper and Thornycroft combined to form a highly successful firm, which has shown what can be done through flexibility, innovation and export-led marketing. United Kingdom shipbuilding can succeed in the global market if we specialise in what we are good at, and I suggest that we are good at building high-value, highly sophisticated, specialised warships.

The Vosper Thornycroft shipyards in Eastleigh have shown that British shipbuilders can take on the world and win. In the past 30 years we have exported 370 ships to more than 34 navies worldwide. That is a magnificent achievement from which our shipbuilding industry can draw strength, but how can the industry benefit from the lessons that have been learned—and learned particularly hard in my constituency? The key to the industry's success is investment in skills and modern machinery, to which the hon. Member for Govan referred in his speech and which has led to increased productivity. The productivity of shipyards in Eastleigh has increased by more than 50 per cent. in the past five years. I challenge any hon. Member to find a more successful example anywhere in the world today.

We must recognise the importance of continued product innovation and move away from the traditional aspects of shipbuilding. Shipyards in my constituency have pioneered glass-reinforced plastic warships and they are leading the design development of Trimaran warships. We must also make a commitment to the motivation of the work force. Some 50 per cent. of the workers in my constituency and in nearby areas have a direct stake in the business of the shipyards for which they work. There has been no industrial disruption in the local shipyards for the past five years. That is a very telling point.

We face increasingly fierce competition in the global market. As the hon. Member for Govan pointed out, the end of the cold war, the decline in defence budgets and the potential for so-called "home competition" from our European Union counterparts have made it much more difficult for the United Kingdom shipbuilding industry. We must now contend with about 40 major competitors worldwide in bidding for orders overseas.

I hope that the Minister will concede that it is absolutely essential that we are able to continue to supply ships to the Royal Navy. It is the vital endorsement of our products at home that enables us to sell to export markets. If the Ministry of Defence is considering inviting shipyards from our European Union counterparts to tender for naval shipbuilding contracts or subcontracting in this country, surely it must first establish whether our shipyards have the same free access to bid for similar contracts in the home markets of our potential competitors. If they do not, competing shipyards should not have the opportunity to compete against our domestic companies.

Fierce competition throughout the world has led our main competitor countries to adopt the policy of choosing a single national champion, which they then support in pursuing export opportunities. I welcome the fact that the MOD has apparently decided to follow suit. The Government's support in global export markets can make the vital difference between success and failure, particularly if we are competing against combined teams of Ministry officials and Departments and shipyards overseas. However, if the Government are to choose a national champion, that decision should be made objectively.

I believe that I am correct in saying that only a handful of shipyards in this country—one of which is located in my constituency—have the capacity to act as prime contractors for naval ship construction. In choosing a national champion that the Government will promote and support in bidding for export opportunities, it is essential that that decision should be based on an objective assessment of a shipyard's capability, export contract record and its knowledge of the market being pursued. Above all, there must be an objective assessment of which company is most likely to succeed in its pursuit of that opportunity.

I know that other hon. Members are anxious to speak in the debate, so I shall summarise my comments. The United Kingdom shipbuilding industry should no longer be considered a sunset industry. Drastic restructuring and rationalisation has already taken place and we have seen huge productivity increases through the investment in state-of-the-art facilities, the development of modern management techniques and full worker participation in the yards.

If we are to succeed in a fiercely competitive market, however, we need the dedicated support of the Government—not just for spasmodic and infrequent major new-build contracts, but for regular refit and repair work. That work should be awarded to the yards that are best able to undertake it, and invariably they will be the firms which designed and built the warships. At the very least, the firms in my constituency should be allowed to compete openly with other firms to refit the ships that they built.

I hope that the Minister will take on board the points that I have raised. I look forward to his assurance that they will be considered because they are vital to the future success of the shipbuilding industry and to the interests of my constituents.

12.16 pm

**Mr. Piers Merchant** (Beckenham): At the outset, I align myself with two important themes to which the hon. Member for Glasgow, Govan (Mr. Davidson) alluded in his speech. First, he said that it was essential that the Government should do all in their power to ensure that British shipbuilding yards are able to operate in a spirit of fair competition. That has been a bugbear in this industry for decades and we must fight zealously for fair

[Mr. Piers Merchant]

competition. Secondly, I entirely support the hon. Gentleman's remarks about the importance of maintaining a strategic warship production industry. Heaven forbid that we should ever need to fall back on it as an absolute requirement, but, if defence is to have any meaning, it is essential that we maintain the means of warship production.

I wish to contribute to the debate for three principal reasons. First, I have a constituency interest. One might not think that the leafy, landlocked constituency of Beckenham is relevant to the shipbuilding industry, but it is. When a recent order—which, sadly, we did not win— was open to tender, I was lobbied by Swan Hunter of Tyneside and by two local companies in Beckenham, both of which would have provided a considerable amount of subcontract work. That shows that shipbuilding is important not only in those areas that have traditionally relied on it, but as a core industry that generates jobs and business elsewhere in the country—perhaps in the most unlikely places.

Secondly, I worked for a company one of whose subsidiaries, Clarke Chapman, was an important part of the shipbuilding industry on the Tyne. I know the importance of the industry to those companies and their employees.

Thirdly, one might say that I have an historic interest in the industry as my former seat of Newcastle upon Tyne, Central was particularly important to the shipbuilding industry of Tyneside. I spent a good deal of time campaigning on behalf of the industry that existed then— sadly, it hardly survives today—and I have maintained my interest in it. Only last year I was presented with a very nice booklet entitled "Swans of the Tyne" which bears the inscription:

"Best wishes on behalf of Swan Hunter Campaign Committee".

I looked nostalgically through the booklet and on the last page I saw a picture of the Ark Royal, which was completed in 1985, sailing down the Tyne. I visited the Ark Royal shortly before it began its sea trials. What a magnificent ship it was. It was a tribute to the productive capabilities and skills of the Tyneside shipbuilding industry—how sad it is that that has been almost entirely lost. It is a very sad story and one that I bitterly regret.

In 1926, 40 per cent. of world demand was met by the British shipbuilding industry: it is now about 1 per cent. In 1960, 44,000 jobs in Tyne and Wear were dependent on the shipbuilding industry: it is now a matter of a few thousand. The amount of merchant tonnage produced in Britain was 1.5 million in 1976. That has fallen to about 250,000 tonnes now. It is a very sad decline.

I want briefly to examine the lessons that can be drawn from that experience. The lessons are many, but they show what we must do to prevent other industries from making the same mistakes.

I do not believe that the decline of the shipbuilding industry was inevitable. It was inevitable that it should suffer from the cycles created by the economy and that the fall in demand should hit the British shipbuilding industry, but that it should have had such a cataclysmic result was avoidable. It is interesting that as the shipbuilding industry recovers, countries such as France and Spain, not Britain, are picking up orders, which says something principally about our structural decline.

I should like to allay the myth that the Government have done nothing to help as that is palpably untrue. Apart from the shipbuilding intervention fund paid by the British Government, which represents the 9 per cent. maximum allowed under the seventh directive, nothing more could be done to help that would be in line with international agreements. The £2 billion that was pumped into the industry between 1977 and 1988 shows that a great deal was done, but, sadly, even that was insufficient to sustain the industry.

The problem arose before then, in the 1960s and early 1970s, when order books were full or pretty near full and production was at a record level. Steps were not taken at that time to deal with the industry's ills. Had they been solved then, the industry would have survived.

I refer briefly to three of the problems. The first was a management failure. I would never blame one side of industry, but there was terrible management failure in the shipbuilding industry—old-fashioned management, a loss of entrepreneurial skills, innovative necrosis, undercapitalisation, organisational chaos and a contempt of the work force. All that was clear on Tyneside in those years. I referred to it at some length in a speech that I made in the House in 1984.

There was also, however, a bad failure of trade union practice. Labour Members have not always been prepared to admit that and I feel that they should. It is undoubtedly true that the number of disputes, the demarcation and inflexibility that led to late and cancelled orders and costly products that therefore failed in competitive terms could have been avoided if only those problems had been addressed. I pay tribute to the work force for addressing those problems, but it did so too late. By the time the problems were put right, the strength of the industry had sapped away. That was a shame.

Nationalisation in the 1970s did not help, as it introduced another organisational dimension and confusion to an industry that was already badly holed under the water. Just about everything that could go wrong with an industry went wrong in the 1960s and 1970s, except the skills, which are still there and are slowly being lost for all time. I deeply regret that.

The House can do nothing about the historic situation, but it can learn. I have no problem with Government intervention when it is necessary for an industry. It happens here and I am perfectly happy to see it continue, but, above all, we must have a duty to put in place measures that affect industry, competition and labour relations to prevent the tragedy that hit the shipbuilding industry from happening elsewhere.

12.24 pm

**Mr. Edward O'Hara** (Knowsley, South): I congratulate my hon. Friend the Member for Glasgow, Govan (Mr. Davidson) on introducing the debate. I take a close personal interest in it as I spent my formative years as a young lad in the docklands area of Liverpool. The lives of my family and friends were closely involved with the fate of the British merchant fleet and, of course, I represent a constituency in Merseyside, a maritime area.

I wish to relate the destiny of the shipbuilding industry to the decline of the merchant fleet. A number of points have been made in that respect and I shall not repeat them. As an island nation, there are two important strategic reasons why we need a strong merchant fleet—for the security of our trade, most of which is carried by sea and, of course, for our defence. I include the merchant fleet in my comments on defence as the Falklands campaign could not have been mounted without the magnificent support of the merchant fleet and the Gulf war amply demonstrated the dangers of losing that capacity and becoming beholden to foreign merchant shippers. Furthermore, a strong merchant fleet supports a strong shipbuilding industry.

**Mr. Eddie Loyden** (Liverpool, Garston): Does my hon. Friend realise that only three of the 104 ships chartered for the Gulf war were British owned and that the rest were either flagged out or foreign?

**Mr. O'Hara:** My hon. Friend is absolutely correct. We were obliged to pay through the nose for those foreign ships.

Reference has been made to the decline in the number of ships. There were 1,305 ships of 500 gross registered tonnes in 1979; by the end of 1993 that figure was down to 258. I do not have the latest statistics, but the trend has been so steady that I doubt it has been reversed.

Reference has also been made to our declining share in the world market from nearly 7 per cent. in 1979 to less than 4 per cent. in 1992, according to the latest statistics in my personal files. We were fourth in the league table of shipping nations in 1979. By 1992 we were 31st, behind such countries as the Bahamas, Cyprus, Singapore, Malta and the Philippines, when seaborne trade was and is increasing by 4 per cent. per annum.

Reference has also been made to the age of the fleet. My hon. Friend the Member for Barrow and Furness (Mr. Hutton) referred to the average age of ships in our merchant fleet as nearly 17 years, which is absolutely true. It was six and a half years in 1979; in other words, there has been hardly any replacement since 1979. The average age of ships registered with our major competitors—Denmark, France, Germany and Japan—is nearer 10 years.

We need an increased fleet because a maritime nation needs an increased fleet, not a declining fleet. We also need a renewed fleet. That is the connection between the destiny of the merchant fleet and that of the shipbuilding industry. Obviously, a strong merchant fleet supports a strong shipbuilding industry. As the British merchant fleet will clearly require massive replacement before the end of the century, it seems crazy that Britain is not retaining the capacity to build those ships, provide those jobs and retain and develop those skills.

It has been suggested to me in discussions with the Chamber of Shipping that it does not really matter whether we retain Britain's shipbuilding capacity. It justifies building abroad on the ground that the hull of the ship is just a small proportion of the total investment in a ship; much of the investment goes into the fitting of the ship and our fitters still fit out hulls that are built abroad. However, when one asks where the engines for such ships come from, it is more reticent.

Many ship fitting skills still exist in my constituency. I was interested recently to discover that a furniture factory had set up on Merseyside because it found a dormant pool of ship fitting skills that could be transferred to furniture making. In a dock road in Liverpool recently, I noticed that, sadly, an instrument maker to the shipping industry from the early 19th century, perhaps the late 18th century, had gone out of business.

Solutions are needed. We do not have a shipbuilding capacity to build the shipping fleet that we need now and will need even more in the future. It is a matter on which owners and trade unions are agreed. I shall mention several measures briefly in passing so that others have time to speak.

We could pay more attention to the rules of cabotage, particularly with regard to coastal shipping, as many of our near neighbours do. We could give fiscal incentives to scrap ships and build new ones. We could improve our safety standards, which would give a boost to the ship repairing industry. We could give more investment to maritime transport, which is the poor relation of transport investment in Britain.

Those points could be developed further but I confine myself in the short time available to those few suggestions about what is wrong and the direction in which solutions may be found.

12.31 pm

**Mr. Nicholas Brown** (Newcastle upon Tyne, East): I am grateful to those Conservative Members who have praised the former shipyard workers of Tyneside, but I cannot truthfully say that I know any former shipyard workers on Tyneside who would return the compliment to a Conservative Member of Parliament.

The shipbuilding community of Tyne and Wear is no more. In 1979, the largest single shipbuilding community in Britain was on Tyne and Wear. It is a measure of the significance to our community of that once great industry that this short debate has been attended at different moments by my hon. Friends the Members for Newcastle upon Tyne, Central (Mr. Cousins), for Wallsend (Mr. Byers), for Gateshead, East (Ms Quin), for Jarrow (Mr. Dixon) and for Sunderland, South (Mr. Mullin).

The industry was the cornerstone of the economy of the communities that we are elected to represent. It used to be commonplace, I suspect, in debates such as this, to say that we are an island nation; that more than 90 per cent. of our trade is carried in ships; that the Royal Navy's international role and the role of the British merchant marine is of enormous importance; that the ability to have officers to serve on our merchant ships as well as with the Royal Navy, and the ability of British citizens to find employment as seafarers, is of huge importance to our nation. More recently, we could add that we have an important and expensive stake in offshore installations, particularly in the North sea, for the purposes of mineral extraction.

It is conventional also for Labour Members to say that, since 1979, the Government have neglected those areas. Frankly, the industry would be in better shape had the Government confined themselves to just neglecting this whole area of our national activity. The truth of the matter, particularly as it obtains to shipbuilding, is that the Government have intervened. Warship procurement decisions are intensely political. The calamity suffered by the community that I represent was entirely the consequence of political decision-making within Government, particularly decisions that have affected procurement decisions of huge strategic importance.

Time is short in the debate. When it was clear that Swan Hunter was doomed, and that every person who wanted to stay in the shipbuilding industry who gravitated to Swan Hunter because it was the last large yard open in

[*Mr. Nicholas Brown*]

Tyne and Wear would be thrown out of work, the Government made certain promises to our community about economic development and alternative employment prospects.

I want to draw to the attention of the House today the fact that not one of the promises made in May 1993 by the Prime Minister from the Dispatch Box at Prime Minister's Question Time has yet been put into effect on Tyneside. If the Minister takes one message away from the community that I represent, it must be that we want the promise of alternative employment opportunities to be kept. We want some action and we desperately need it now. We needed it last year and we certainly need it now.

When Swan Hunter went into receivership it was putting £1 million a week into our economy in wages alone, with the wages of subcontractors as well. It is an enormous blow to our community that that employment base is no longer there. Only another large fabrication project on the Tyne could immediately take people off the unemployment registers in any large numbers. I say that on the very day that scrap metal merchants are in Swan Hunter cutting the yard to pieces to ensure that it can never produce such a project. Something must be done and it must be done now.

12.35 pm

**Mr. Peter Robinson** (Belfast, East): I shall follow the fine example of brevity of the hon. Member for Newcastle upon Tyne, East (Mr. Brown). I should say at the beginning that I have an interest, since I have a modest shareholding in the finest of all shipyards in the world—Harland and Wolff of Belfast.

I congratulate the hon. Member for Glasgow, Govan (Mr. Davidson) on choosing this subject for a short debate. The general principles that he outlined are principles which I can wholeheartedly endorse.

It has been a general thread running through the debate that Members on both sides of the House believe that it is incumbent upon the Government to ensure that we have what has been described as a level playing field. We do not have that at the moment.

Even those yards, particularly in South Korea, which are now putting up their hands and claiming that they are clean and that no subsidies are being given to them, clearly are receiving hidden subsidies. Those who know anything about industry in South Korea will know that it is easy to give hidden subsidies because the people who are building ships are also turning out the steel and doing everything else connected with shipbuilding, so subsidies can be given in relation to other products and materials related to shipbuilding.

This nation must recognise that it is not in a position, certainly at present, to compete in the same market as the South Koreans. The hon. Gentleman is entirely right that the future, at least the near future, for shipbuilding in the United Kingdom must be at the high technology end of the shipbuilding market.

Harland and Wolff was forced into competing in the bulk and tanker market, but it has had to try to find a niche in the high-tech end of the industry. It now has a product far in advance of anything that can be offered anywhere else in the world.

I hope that BP in the North sea and the Gulf of Mexico, where the water levels are such as to allow oil to be pumped using ships, will consider buying British in order to ensure that our industries benefit from the oil in the North sea in particular.

**Mr. Mike Watson** (Glasgow, Central): The hon. Gentleman spoke of the importance of seeking orders in the industry in other directions, linking up with oil, and so forth. One matter which has not been given much airing in the debate is the need, at a time of contraction in the number of military warships and military spending, for defence diversification and perhaps the establishment of a defence diversification agency. That is the policy of my party. What is the hon. Gentleman's view on that policy? Is not that an important way to ensure that skills which cannot be retained in the shipbuilding industry can none the less be used in the future because, as has been said, they include skills at the cutting edge of technology?

**Mr. Robinson:** I am happy to concur with the hon. Gentleman. For instance, the American navy is in our waters frequently, yet it does not come to our shipyards to have repairs done. There is a great deal of work that the Government could do to encourage further use of our shipyards.

Leaving the embarrassment of the Conservatives to one side, many people recognise that there is likely to be a Labour Government, probably fairly shortly. I notice the horror on the Minister's face. I shall pay special attention to the winding-up speech by the hon. Member for Cunninghame, North (Mr. Wilson)—I say that, not by way of a challenge, but by way of interest—to determine the attitude that the Labour party will have to the shipbuilding industry in the United Kingdom as a whole and, from my point of view especially, in Northern Ireland.

12.40 pm

**Dr. Norman A. Godman** (Greenock and Port Glasgow): I must be brief, as you know, Mr. Deputy Speaker.

The hon. Member for Beckenham (Mr. Merchant) took us down memory lane. I think I am right in saying that, along with my hon. Friend the Member for Jarrow (Mr. Dixon), I am one of two former shipyard workers in this place. We both served our time as shipwrights.

I make a plea to the Minister. As I said to him the other evening, it is essential for the many hundreds of my constituents who work at Ferguson in Port Glasgow, at Kvaerner in Govan and at Yarrow of Scotstoun that the shipbuilding intervention fund be continued beyond 31 December 1995—European Union wide.

The Greenpeace occupation of Brent Spar prompts a question. Many of those redundant shipyard workers in Scotland might be re-employed, were the Government to adopt a more radical implementation of part I of the Petroleum Act 1987. If the Brent Spar were brought ashore to be dismantled and its materials recycled, it would provide plenty of work.

Shell Expo gave the game away. It said, in a recent publicity leaflet, that 52,000 man hours would be needed to take that redundant oil storage installation and sink it in deep water whereas, if it were brought ashore, as it should be, about 360,000 man hours would be involved in the process. The Government should be doing the latter.

They have failed the fishing interests and many others in their failure to implement part I of the Petroleum Act 1987 in a more radical way.

12.42 pm

**Mr. Brian Wilson** (Cunninghame, North): We have had a good debate and, like everyone else, I am grateful to my hon. Friend the Member for Glasgow, Govan (Mr. Davidson) for making it possible. It has highlighted the fact that we should debate maritime issues more often and at more length, because there is obviously a great deal of interest and anxiety about them.

Conservative Members made some rather odd contributions about shellfish, sea water and duty frees, and we heard from the hon. Member for Beckenham (Mr. Merchant) a speech that he gave in 1984, which he apparently thought worth recycling 11 years later.

**Mr. Merchant** *indicated dissent.*

**Mr. Wilson:** There has been little sign of understanding from Conservative Members that we are discussing a great national industry, which has been allowed to decline grievously as a result of criminal neglect and downright hostility. It is all very well prattling, as the hon. Member for Plymouth, Sutton (Mr. Streeter) did, about island races and maritime traditions, but those words are meaningless if they are not matched by actions.

For years, we have witnessed the relentless decline, not only of shipbuilding but—incomprehensibly—of the British Merchant Navy. As my hon. Friend the Member for Knowsley South (Mr. O'Hara) said, the issues are linked. We need a British-owned, British-registered, British-crewed Merchant Navy; that is the basis of the potential of the shipbuilding industry.

Everyone knows that there will be many merchant shipbuilding orders in the next few years; the question is whether they will be placed by British owners in British yards and whether there will be enough left of the infrastructure to allow that to happen.

The hon. Member for Beckenham spoke about learning lessons, but the lessons have not been learnt. In the same way that the British capacity to build ships was thoughtlessly, mindlessly run down, the British capacity to build trains is being thoughtlessly, mindlessly run down. In a few years' time, since there will be no York and no Derby, we shall buy trains as well as ships from Korea, Spain and America, because idiots have decided that that industry is not worth saving or helping through a difficult time.

I want to ask a few questions, in the few minutes available to me, for the Minister to answer directly. I want to ask him especially about VSEL, and I should like to know why the delay continues in publishing the Monopolies and Mergers Commission report. That report has important implications, not only for Barrow, but for Yarrow on the Clyde and the entire British naval shipbuilding capacity. If, as is widely predicted, both bids are cleared, the conditions that attach to them may be crucial. I put down that marker today.

Why is there a delay? Why has the report now been with the Department of Trade and Industry for longer than the obligatory 20 days? When may we see that report and obtain some movement on that important issue?

I shall speak briefly about Yarrow, and especially about the delegation that is in South Africa at present. On behalf of all Opposition Members, and I hope Conservative Members, I extend the best wishes of the House to Mr. Murray Easton, Mr. Gavin Laird and the Lord Provost of Glasgow, Tom Dingwall. It would be fitting indeed if Glasgow and the Clyde, with our long and proud record of solidarity with the democratic movement in South Africa, were now at the forefront of re-establishing Britain's trading links with the new South Africa. I seek an assurance from the Minister that the Government are doing everything possible to support the Yarrow bid and to ensure that that order comes to this country, and especially to the Clyde.

I shall briefly discuss a subject that was mentioned by the hon. Member for Belfast, East (Mr. Robinson). I have with me an interesting publication, commissioned by the DTI, about floating production systems. It is a report from the Oil and Gas Projects and Supplies Office. That is a subject of immense importance, not only to shipbuilding but to all the spin-off industries of shipbuilding. It would be worthy of a debate in itself.

I should be interested if the Minister would confirm that there is the prospect, in the next few years, of 30 large hulls being ordered for use in British waters, in the oilfields to the west of Shetland. That offers massive new potential for shipbuilding and marine technology in this country. We want to know today—I shall give assurances from the Opposition—the extent to which the Government will get behind the British shipbuilding industry to ensure that those orders go to British yards, and that the subcontracting goes to British companies. If not, it is distinctly possible that all, or the great majority, of those vessels will be built in Norway, Spain or in any other part of the world.

I visited the shipyard at Harland and Wolff, in the constituency of the hon. Member for Belfast, East. The future of Harland and Wolff and the large-scale employment that exists there is tied up with what is contained in that report about floating production systems. Equally, as the report recognises and as is realised in that part of the country, the prospect of a substantial shipbuilding revival at Swan Hunter is tied up with this new generation of vessels which will be ordered in the next few years.

The report is valuable and sets out the potential and the difficulties. It says that there is a lack of interest or awareness in investment circles in this country in getting behind the creation of an industry in Britain building those vessels for west of Shetland. I have the report and I am glad that it has been commissioned, but, above all, what I want from the Minister, and he can write to me on this, are the detailed responses to the report's recommendations and observations. That is vital for Harland and Wolff and for the old Swan Hunter yard. There is potential in the Clyde. Right through the maritime industries, this is an exciting, large-scale opportunity to talk, not about the past, but about the future.

Those structures will be built somewhere. Will they be built in United Kingdom yards or in overseas yards for use in British waters? I should like, although not today because there is no time for it, a detailed response from the Minister, on which we can base an urgent debate.

Only a few weeks ago, we saw the embarrassing spectacle of the Oriana arriving from a German yard to be named by the Queen in Britain. No matter how it is

*[Mr. Wilson]*

dressed up, it is not a British ship because it was not built in a British yard. It is to the Government's shame that it is no longer possible for such a ship to be built in a British yard when British craftsmen are available to do it and when tens of thousands of people are unemployed in every shipbuilding community.

To some extent, the saving grace was the fact that some 80 per cent. of the equipment on board that ship was made in Britain. I commend the efforts of the maritime supply industries to maintain their export effort and thereby the ability to fit out ships such as the Oriana. They have told me and, no doubt, the Government that they cannot rely indefinitely on the export market for their continuing good health. We need a British Merchant Navy. We need British merchant ships that are built in British yards by British craftsmen and crewed by British seaman. That is a maritime policy worthy of the name for an island nation.

I therefore say to Conservative Members: do not give us any flannel about island races or appeals to sentimental considerations because, unless there is a Merchant Navy and a merchant shipbuilding industry, we betray that proud heritage. The Conservative party likes to wrap itself in the flag, but I cannot comprehend what the Government have done to the red ensign. Let them start to reverse that; let them get seriously behind shipbuilding; let them recognise the urgency and address themselves in particular to the new opportunities that exist in the industry.

12.51 pm

**The Parliamentary Under-Secretary of State for Industry and Energy (Mr. Richard Page):** I add my congratulations to the hon. Member for Glasgow, Govan (Mr. Davidson) on securing the debate. In the 20 years that I have been in the House, I came only third in all the ballots in which I took part, and then I was not reached and called; but enough of that, otherwise I shall be accused of being a rugby selector.

I appreciate the importance of the subject raised by the hon. Member for Govan. He is right to say that we have not had such a debate for some time. I am grateful for the opportunity to respond. I wish I had more time, but a number of hon. Members have made comments. It will not be possible to respond to all of them, but I shall try to respond to one or two questions that have been asked.

As the Opposition spokesman, the hon. Member for Cunninghame, North (Mr. Wilson) suggested, I shall write to him about some of his points. He was a little disingenuous, if I may use that word, in his comments about the Oriana. As he knows, it was not quoted for by any British yard, which is a pity. It was made in Germany. He put the record straight, however, by saying how much British equipment was put into that great ship.

The hon. Gentleman mentioned floating production systems and what can be done in that regard. We are obviously encouraging the whole industry to supply such equipment. We are heartened by Harland and Wolff's interest in the subject. Obviously, we hope that some of those orders will be made and constructed in UK yards.

Before I turn to some of the points made by the hon. Member for Govan, and it is his debate, despite all the other comments made by other hon. Members, it would be helpful if we considered the world and European

perspective. Some comments seemed to push it to one side, as if the real market did not matter. Much of what I shall say will be in agreement with the hon. Gentleman's comments.

As the House and people outside know, as a result of low ordering in recent years, on a global basis there is a significant surplus of world capacity for larger ships. As ships get older, they will be need to be replaced, but the expected upturn has not yet occurred and its timing is highly unpredictable. As one or two hon. Members have mentioned, Korean capacity in particular has been substantially expanding, creating more uncertainty for all manufacturers of such vessels.

In 1975, available capacity worldwide was estimated at some 22.4 million compensated gross tonnes. That had dropped to some 15 million by 1990 and is forecast to increase to about 21 million by 2000. The years 1975 and 2000 are roughly comparable in terms of total capacity, but during that period great changes took place in the share accounted for by individual nations. In the past 20 years, western European, Scandinavian and Japanese yards have taken considerable steps, at no little pain, as everyone in the country recognises, to reduce their shipbuilding capacity. They have sought to restore a healthy market and to reduce the possibility of a repetition of the slump in shipbuilding.

In 1975, western Europe and Japan accounted for approximately 80 per cent. of world merchant shipbuilding capacity and Korea accounted for less than 2 per cent. That is interesting, but it is a fast-moving scene. Some sources in the Korean shipbuilding industry reckon that they have just 10 years of dominance before China takes over and supplants them in turn. Over-capacity is having a dramatic effect on prices. Cash prices are significantly lower than they were five years ago. For example, a 150,000-tonne tanker can be bought today for just $40 million compared with $55 million in 1992.

On western Europe, I am glad to say that some aspects of the UK shipbuilding industry are looking a little healthier. Medium-sized yards are specialising in vehicles such as ferries and tugs, and we are achieving some significant advances.

On the Organisation for Economic Co-operation and Development agreement, I must disappoint the hon. Member for Govan. I do not think it would be advantageous to continue. The European Commission has already carried out investigations. We all know that there have been significant market distortions. By removal of all those subsidies, we will find ourselves in a much fairer market. I shall not go into the hon. Gentleman's mixed metaphors, with his comments on swimming and climbing uphill.

An OECD agreement was signed in December 1994 by representatives of the European Union, the United States of America, Japan, Korea and Norway, which account for some 70 per cent. of world capacity. That enables some control to be kept on the effect of unfair subsidies and unfair competition. The OECD agreement has power to investigate allegations of misconduct and to impose penalties. The agreement is a good one for the UK. Korea has accepted a strong anti-dumping code; Japan will modify its home credit scheme; the United States has made concessions to the applicability of the Jones Act; and the EU is giving up its direct subsidy. I hope, therefore, that we shall have a level playing field. I assure the House that the Government will have no hesitation in chasing up any areas where unfair competition exists.

I should like to turn to some success stories. We build ships, although not as many as I should like. The UK has a substantial repair industry, with a turnover of more than £250 million. It employs up to 7,000 people at peak times and they are located all around the coast. Hon. Members have remembered the contribution of those companies serving their localities—a valuable contribution to the UK economy.

Let us not forget the marine equipment industry, which was mentioned by my hon. Friend the Member for Beckenham (Mr. Merchant) and by the hon. Member for Knowsley, South (Mr. O'Hara). There is UK-made marine radar, paint, propellers, engines, and equipment to service the whole range of maritime activities. Sixty to 70 per cent. of a ship's value is in its equipment. Obviously, we want to ensure that we can expand that industry.

We can do more. Marine equipment companies have not been helped by a reduction in home production, but it would be a mistake to assume that they are no longer a world force. The industry has a substantial order book worth about £2 billion. It retains substantial engineering and design expertise and over 70 per cent. of its output is exported to yards abroad. I hope that in July I shall be leading a delegation of business men from the British marine equipment industry to Japan to continue the dialogue and maintain the momentum of our export initiatives.

I thank the hon. Member for Govan for initiating this debate. It has been valuable and I hope that next time I will have a little bit longer to give a more comprehensive response to his important questions.

# Department of Transport (Property Purchase)

1 pm

**Sir Terence Higgins** (Worthing): I am glad to have this opportunity to raise the issue of the Department of Transport's discretionary purchase of property blighted by proposed road developments. My interest in this, as I shall explain, arises from my constituency experience, but I believe that it is a matter of very much wider importance than that affecting just my constituents.

In my view, the way in which we obtain our transport infrastructure can be described as nothing less than highway robbery at the expense of those who happen to have the misfortune to be near a proposed road development. The reality is that such people are seriously affected and, if the proposals for discretionary purchase were properly implemented, the cost might run into not tens of millions of pounds but hundreds of millions of pounds; therefore, I understand that my hon. Friend the Minister of State may be under some inhibitions from the Treasury when he replies to the debate. I should stress that that would be the gross cost. If initially the discretionary purchase of the properties took place—as I believe that it should—once the road was built it would be possible for the Department to re-sell them to new owners and recoup part of the cost.

Let me stress that I am not concerned with compulsory purchase, which is a far from perfect system and has problems associated with it. I am concerned essentially with discretionary purchase. As my hon. Friend the Minister will know, because I have raised this matter in previous Adjournment debates, it arises from experience in my constituency of Worthing where there is a proposal to develop the A27. For many years, I have maintained that the A27 should have a real bypass, completely avoiding the town of Worthing. The Government's so-called preferred route cuts the town in two and involves the demolition of a number of properties. The scheme's effect on many other properties is considerable.

My hon. Friend the Minister will know that there has been a public inquiry into this matter, and I remain strongly of the view that there should be a real bypass. We are awaiting the inspector's report after the inquiry, which lasted a year or so, and I hope that, in the light of it, we will have a satisfactory decision from my hon. Friend.

The question of discretionary purchase has some impact on the choice of route and the cost of alternative routes. I shall come to that in my concluding remarks.

Over a long time I have pursued with Ministers individual cases of properties affected by the Government's preferred route. I am concerned that such cases should be decided by ministerial discretion and I have received replies from Ministers about many cases. However, some months ago, I discovered that the Highways Agency was proposing to reply instead of a Minister, which was highly objectionable. These issues are not merely ones of finance: whether a property should be purchased may depend on the occupant's need to obtain money at short notice, perhaps to repay debts, or on his need to move to a different place to get a job, or his health might be affected by the construction work or by pollution from the road once it is built.

*[Sir Terence Higgins]*

Decisions ought to be matters for ministerial discretion rather than for official discretion. I am glad that the present Secretary of State has now accepted that, although I understand that he has given the responsibility for dealing with these discretionary matters to the Under-Secretary, my hon. Friend the Member for Epping Forest (Mr. Norris). I am glad that my hon. Friend the Minister for Railways and Roads is to reply today, since he has overall responsibility for the development of the roads programme.

The essential matter that we must consider is the improvement, as it seemed at the time, that was brought about by section 62(2) of the Planning and Compensation Act 1991. It states that the highway authority

"may acquire by agreement land the enjoyment of which will in their opinion be seriously affected by the carrying out of the works or the use of the highway".

Many of the problems we face and the reasons why some of the deserving cases have been turned down stem from the Government's interpretation of that expression in the Act. The interpretation has been extremely restrictive. The Government have said that they will generally consider only those cases where property is within 100 m of the centre line of the proposed road. That proposed road may be six lanes wide. Considering only properties within 100 m of the centre line disregards the impact on those further away.

The legislation refers to whether the development will have serious effect. The Department has interpreted that by asking whether the impact on those in the house will be intolerable. Clearly, "intolerable" is a much tighter criterion than "serious". It is a tougher standard to meet. Instead of abiding by the wording of legislation as it has been approved by the House, the Department has sought to reduce its impact.

I want to refer to a report by the ombudsman, which is typical of a number that I have received on other constituency cases, about the way in which the Department has arrived at the guidelines used to decide whether a property should be purchased. I shall quote from the report and give the flavour of it because I have rarely seen such a damning report. It revealed the internal workings of the Department with regard to the way in which the guidelines were interpreted. I want also to deal with the court case that was decided in June 1994. It also has significant relevance to this issue.

The ombudsman's report said:

"Guidance on the operation of the discretionary scheme was published on 17 January 1992. It seems to have been internally contradictory. On the one hand it said that for property within 100 m of the centre line of the proposed road the presumption should be that it would be seriously affected . . . On the other hand it also said that property within the 100 m zone would be treated as outside the scope"

of the legislation

"if the reasonable expectation was that the levels of traffic noise or construction noise would not be such as to qualify for noise insulation."

The ombudsman found that the discretionary criteria were inconsistent and contradictory.

The report also said that there was an inconsistency between what was published in the highways manual and what was published in the Department's press notice. It said that if constituents sought to fill in form G1, which

is relevant to discretionary purchase, it was wrong if the notes given to them made no reference to the criteria by which a serious effect would be judged.

It was pointed out also in the report that the agreement to purchase would be approved by the headquarters of the Department of Transport but that a decision to reject would be taken only by the regional office; in other words, the rejection cases were not normally going to head office, let alone to Ministers.

It was pointed out that some of the questions that the Department asked constituents to answer were so confusing that even an official who sought to amend matters got things the wrong way round. One of the questions involved a double negative. The ombudsman pointed out that that was not a helpful way of putting questions to applicants. The whole history of the matter shows that the way in which the guidelines were determined can be described only as a shambles. As a result, a number of bad decisions have been made.

Some strange excuses were produced, too. For example, the ombudsman pointed out that the crucial press notice was not withdrawn for five months after its content was found to be seriously flawed. He was told that there were legal reasons why he could not be given a proper explanation, but when he asked to see the legal advice, it turned out not to exist. For all these reasons, I believe that the criteria that have been used are not adequate and that the guidelines clearly need serious revision.

However, the main point concerns a case that has been decided in the courts.

**Mr. Michael Lord** (Suffolk, Central): I am grateful to my right hon. Friend for giving way in this short debate. I shall be brief.

I am dealing with what is probably the worst case that I have ever had as a constituency problem and it involves exactly the point that my right hon. Friend is raising. A man's life has been completely ruined by blight.

As a member of the Parliamentary Commissioner for Administration Select Committee, which looks after the ombudsman, I have looked into the question of redress and compensation even in cases where the letter of the law has been strictly observed.

I point out to my right hon. Friend that both my hon. Friend the Minister of State, Treasury and Sir Patrick Brown, the permanent secretary at the Department of Transport, have made it clear that, even where everything has been done correctly, maladministration can still be shown.

In Committee, I quoted the Minister of State, Treasury as telling a previous meeting of the Committee

"that failure to mitigate the effects of strict adherence to the letter of the law where this produces manifestly inequitable treatment, that will now be an example of maladministration."

I asked Sir Patrick Brown:

"Will you now confirm that?"

He responded:

"Yes, Mr. Nelson was speaking for the Government."

**Sir Terence Higgins:** I understand my hon. Friend's point and I am glad that the Select Committee has looked into that subject. The crux of the matter is that the Department of Transport established certain guidelines, the first of which states:

"The Department will use its discretion to purchase . . . where it judges it would be intolerable for the occupier to remain in the property during works or once the road is open."

The guidelines go on to list a number of other factors that need to be taken into account, but the fact is that the form to be filled in within the Department is much more restrictive. It asks:

"Does the property lie within 100 m of the proposed centre line?"

As I said, I do not believe that that has anything to do with the legislation; it is a purely arbitrary decision by the Department. The form also asks:

"Was the road scheme known at time of purchase of the property?"

The next question is:

"In the Department's view (based mainly on forecast noise levels), will the enjoyment of the property be seriously/intolerably affected?".

If the answer is no, the other criteria are not examined.

In fact, the crucial criterion, which the courts took into account, is what has happened to the value of the property. Clearly, enjoyment of the property is seriously affected if one finds that, as a result of the road scheme—whether the property is 100 m or half a mile away—one cannot sell it at the price that applied before the scheme was introduced. I am happy to say that the courts are also of that view.

In the case of R. *v.* Secretary of State for Transport ex parte Owen and another, the court criticised the Department in a number of respects. The judgment states:

"It seems to me that the question of the effect, serious or otherwise, of the diminution of value was never fully or properly addressed."

A subsidiary judgment states:

"whatever view one takes of the guidelines issued by the Department . . . , and at best they have been characterised as ineptly drawn, they seem to me at least to support one view, which in any event I for my part would readily have arrived at, namely, that any significant depreciation of property consequent upon a road scheme indicates of itself that, looking at the matter prospectively, the scheme has a serious effect on the enjoyment of the land."

In other words, the court decided clearly that, if the value of a property has fallen as a result of a scheme, discretion should be exercised. My hon. Friend the Minister knows that I have a large number of such cases in my constituency.

I understand that the financial implications of accepting this even in my constituency are substantial and are likely to be massive across the country as a whole, although, as I said, one must take into account the eventual net cost rather than the gross cost. There will be resistance from the Treasury, but the cost is merely a reflection of the extent to which individuals living on the line of route are suffering.

I believe, therefore, that the Department should change the guidelines—I understand that they are under review—and must take into account the effects of a scheme on the value of a property. It has nothing to do with whether the property is 100 m from the centre line of the road and nothing to do with the noise or whether it will be intolerable; it has everything to do with whether the value of the property has declined. I hope that my hon. Friend the Minister will be able to accept my view, even recognising the financial consequences. The cost should rightly fall on the public purse; the effect of the Government's decisions should not fall on the unfortunate individuals who just happen to live near the line of route.

I know that time is short, so I shall deal now with another crucial point. The Department has already purchased a number of properties, which is welcome, but the way in which it has handled the affair is far from satisfactory. Even in a small close in my constituency—one with perhaps a dozen houses—it is possible to find that eight have been purchased while four have not. The tenants whom the Department has put in the purchased houses have, in many cases, been highly unsatisfactory. Some have criminal records and have to be evicted, so the area has been run down. I fear that that will continue for a long time.

If it is accepted that discretionary purchases should be made because of the reduction in the value of a property and the other criteria that I have mentioned, there will clearly be important social and economic effects. In fact, the choice of route will depend on how much the Treasury has to pay to purchase the relevant properties.

The public inquiry to which I referred has been examining the arguments for more than a year. I should stress that the bypass route will be largely in tunnels, to avoid possible adverse effects on the downs. The result of the investigation shows that, in purely financial terms, the arguments may seem fairly finely balanced. None the less, I believe that the case for the bypass remains overwhelming. However, if one takes into account the true effect on constituents, or if one were to quantify the cost to the Department of purchasing the properties affected by the road construction and the road itself once it is built, the balance goes very much against the preferred scheme advocated by the Government in favour of the real bypass route.

I hope that a rapid decision will be made in favour of a bypass. Perhaps my hon. Friend the Minister can tell me when he expects the inspector's report to be received and when he expects to make a decision. I hope that it will not be very difficult for him to accept my contention in the light of the court case that the depreciation in value must be taken into account in deciding whether there has been a serious effect on a property, and to accept that the case for the bypass, which would involve the destruction not of vast amounts of property but of only four houses, is now absolutely overwhelming.

1.18 pm

**The Minister for Railways and Roads (Mr. John Watts):** I am grateful to my right hon. Friend the Member for Worthing (Sir T. Higgins) for providing an opportunity to debate such matters, which are of grave importance to his constituents and of great interest to a number of right hon. and hon. Members. I recognise the concern felt and the genuine hardship experienced by those who are affected by proposals to carry out public works in their vicinity.

My right hon. Friend has referred to the statutory provisions for compulsory purchase and to the fact that property owned by some people does not have to be needed for a scheme to be seriously affected by it. It was precisely to deal with such cases that the House extended, by way of the Planning and Compensation Act 1991, the

*[Mr. John Watts]*

discretionary purchase powers, which used to be more limited. Now public bodies and highway authorities may, in advance of a scheme, use their discretion to buy property if the enjoyment of it will, in their opinion, be seriously affected by the scheme.

Since February 1992, the Department of Transport and latterly the Highways Agency have used those powers where they have considered that motorway and trunk road proposals seriously affect nearby properties. The Highways Agency operates the scheme in accordance with guidelines which were first approved by Ministers. It is intended to ensure fairness, consistency and rationality of treatment across the country. As my right hon. Friend knows, my hon. Friend the Minister for Transport in London, who also has responsibilities for local transport and road safety, oversees the operation of the scheme. As my right hon. Friend said, my hon. Friend undertook that responsibility following my right hon. Friend's very powerful representations that there should be ministerial involvement in the final determinations made on applications under the scheme.

My right hon. Friend raised a particular case which was the subject of an investigation by the Parliamentary Commissioner for Administration. I must acknowledge that the Highways Agency was at fault, first, in not processing the application quickly enough, and, secondly, in failing to pay proper heed to the medical condition of the applicant. I am pleased to inform the House that all those matters have since been remedied and the agency has now agreed to purchase the property. Clearly, my right hon. Friend's constituent is owed an apology for the way in which the case was handled and I gladly give that apology today.

Inevitably, some applications under the discretionary scheme have had to be rejected; but I can inform the House that offers to purchase have been made in more than 70 per cent. of the qualifying cases where there has been judged to be a serious effect under the present guidelines.

On the cases associated with the A27 improvement scheme raised by my right hon. Friend, the Department of Transport and the Highways Agency between them have considered 174 fully completed applications for discretionary purchase from my right hon. Friend's constituents. Of those applications, offers to purchase have been made in respect of 118 properties and 47 have been rejected. The balance of nine is accounted for by applications that have not yet been decided.

**Sir Terence Higgins:** Is it the case that, in considering those applications, the Department has not taken into account the question of the depreciation of value in the property, even though the courts have decided that it ought to do so? Unless my hon. Friend amends the guidelines to cover that point, all that will happen, given the court decision, is that all my constituents will have to bring individual cases, saying that the courts have decided that the Department must purchase.

**Mr. Watts:** I shall come shortly to the implications of the judgment in the Owen case, to which my right hon. Friend referred. I have reminded the House that discretionary powers are exercisable only where the enjoyment of the property will be seriously affected. Up until the applications brought by Lieutenant-Colonel

Owen in the Court of Appeal last year, it was generally considered that enjoyment of land and property could be seriously affected only by physical factors, such as noise, dust, and vibration. The current guidelines were based on that premise. The House will know that, in coming to their decision on the Owen case, the Court of Appeal judges concluded that, in addition to physical factors, diminution in value should also be considered when assessing serious effect.

I confirm that the Highways Agency has complied with the Court of Appeal judgment and redetermined Colonel Owen's application. Following that judgment, the Highways Agency undertook to review and revise the discretionary purchase guidelines, taking into account the Court of Appeal judgment relating to diminution in value. That review has taken longer than I would have wished, but I hope that the House will understand our concern to get it right and to have guidelines that can be applied even-handedly to both road and rail proposals. We are in the final stages of considering new guidelines and I hope that an announcement will be made shortly.

The decision-making process in respect of discretionary purchase has two stages. First, we must determine whether serious effect arises. To comply with the Owen judgment, we will in future take account of physical factors and diminution of value in making that initial judgment. The second stage is to determine whether to exercise discretion where an application satisfies the serious effect test. I am not in a position today to say anything more about how that second stage in the decision-making process will be determined, but I hope to do so shortly.

During the period since the Court of Appeal judgment, the Highways Agency has continued to operate the pre-judgment guidelines and to buy property where there has been serious effect from physical factors and severe hardship has arisen from an inability to sell homes at a reasonable price. I reaffirm the advice that I gave to the House on 28 April 1995 that all applications made since the judgment, which have been considered and rejected under the present guidelines, will be reconsidered under the new guidelines when they are published, which, as I have already said, I hope will be very soon. Consideration is also being given to the treatment of applications made and decided before the Owen judgment, and I hope to be able to make an announcement on that aspect, too, in the near future.

My right hon. Friend has rightly drawn attention to the proposal to improve the A27 trunk road between Worthing and Lancing. As he knows all too well, that is a heavily congested stretch of road linking a number of major towns along the south coast and it is the only east-west trunk road in the south-east, south of the M25. Investigations to determine the route began in 1972, but it was not until 1993, after public consultation on four options, that the scheme reached the public inquiry stage, which opened on 28 September 1993 and ended on 24 August 1994.

I understand that the inspector is making good progress and we expect to receive his report early in the new year. It would be inappropriate for me to try to anticipate its contents, but I am sure that my right hon. Friends the

Secretaries of State for Transport and for the Environment will give the findings careful consideration before coming to their decision.

**Sir Terence Higgins:** Is my hon. Friend seriously saying that the inspector will take 18 months to report?

**Mr. Watts:** I am afraid that there is a correlation between the length of the public inquiry and the time that it normally takes for an inspector to consider the evidence presented to him and to reach his conclusions and report on them to my right hon. Friends.

**Mr. Lord:** A few moments ago, I referred to an horrendous case in my constituency. The gentlemen's house was not devalued; it was rendered absolutely unsaleable, which removed his collateral for his business. His house is completely ruined and he is in a desperate state. As my right hon. Friend says, time is of the essence. While we sit talking about it and inspectors are pottering around, such people are waiting for important news to drop through their letter boxes. Please may we have some real urgency?

**Mr. Watts:** Certainly no one would be more pleased than me if the production of inspectors' reports were speeded up so that we could make firm decisions.

My right hon. Friend also suggested that the economic evaluation of the scheme may change as a result of the operation of new guidelines on discretionary purchase. I can assure him that such matters will be reviewed when my right hon. Friends the Secretaries of State for Transport and for the Environment make their decision following receipt of the inspector's report. I assure my right hon. Friend that we shall proceed as rapidly as possible in publishing the guidelines and we shall take full account of the points that he has made in this debate.

# Gibraltar

1.28 pm

**Mr. Andrew Mackinlay** (Thurrock): I regret that the Minister is not yet in his place. The genesis of my interest in Gibraltar to a large extent goes back to an invitation that I received, along with a number of other parliamentarians including my hon. Friend the Member for Bolton, South-East (Mr. Young), to its national day in the autumn. I was profoundly moved by the national identity of the Gibaltarian people and the fact that they wish to continue their association with the United Kingdom.

The style and temper of my remarks may not be shared by all hon. Members, but I know that many will agree with the message that I want to convey to the Minister, because they share my outrage at the conduct of Spain in harassing and frustrating people on the Gibraltarian-Spanish border.

Many hon. Members will share my dismay at the apparent indifference and weakness of the Foreign Office, and to some extent of the Prime Minister, when it comes to promoting the interests of the Gibraltarian people in their various councils and deliberations both bilaterally with Spain and in the European Union.

The most recent event that I want to raise is the use by Spain of the so-called Schengen agreement as an excuse further to frustrate people travelling to and from Gibraltar by imposing renewed and inordinate border controls from 27 March. Incidentally, it must be said that the Gibraltarian Government drew the attention of the Foreign Office to the ramifications of the agreement, even when it was in draft form, as early as September 1991, so I would have expected and hoped that the interests of Gibraltar would, or should, have been taken into account subsequently when such matters were being discussed in the European Union.

Until now, I have referred only to the Gibraltarian people, but the wrongdoing by Spain is not confined to them. It is as relevant to people from Grantham or Grampian, and to people in Huntingdon or Sedgefield. British people who spend their holidays in Spain or reside there want free access to and from Gibraltar yet they and the Gibraltarian people are being frustrated.

What on earth is the Foreign Office doing? What on earth is it for? There cannot be any country in the world that would have tolerated its nationals being stitched up for so many weeks without there being one hell of a row both in the press and in Parliament, and without the Foreign Office demonstrating that such action by another state is intolerable.

**Mr. David Young** (Bolton, South-East): Is not the policy of the present Spanish Government a continuation of the closed-gate policy followed by the former fascist Government of Spain in order to bring Gibraltar into submission? Does my hon. Friend agree that Spain's policy towards Gibraltar is virtually the same as the Argentine policy towards the Falklands, the only difference being that the Falklanders have been able to rely on the support of the British Government, whereas the Gibraltarians have not?

**Mr. Mackinlay:** My hon. Friend makes a number of points with which I agree and which need to be emphasised. What sort of foreign policy is it that leads to our being seen to be weak and craven when our nationals are being stitched up? That sends all the wrong signals around the world, and certainly does not reassure people engaged in delicate negotiations for accommodation and agreement in Northern Ireland. It also sends the wrong signals across the Atlantic, both to the Argentine Government and to the Council of the Falkland Islands. Weakness over Gibraltar has ramifications that affect our foreign policy generally.

**Mr. John Marshall** (Hendon, South): Will the hon. Gentleman give way?

**Mr. Mackinlay:** I shall be delighted to give way to the hon. Member for the Northern line, but then I must move on.

**Mr. Marshall:** The hon. Gentleman will realise that he has much support on both sides of the House, but as Spain and Gibraltar both have socialist Governments has the matter ever been raised in the Socialist International, and if so with what effect?

**Mr. Mackinlay:** Again, that is a good point, although probably not the most relevant. I believe that all channels should be used. I, as the Member of Parliament for Thurrock, am using the constitutional channel available to me by raising the matter on the Floor of the House of Commons. This is the Parliament of the people of Gibraltar too, although they have their own legislature. There is a democratic deficit because they are not represented either here or in the European Union, so it is up to people such as the hon. Member for Romsey and Waterside (Mr. Colvin) and me to raise the matter here.

**Mr. Michael Colvin** (Romsey and Waterside) *rose*—

**Mr. Mackinlay:** I shall give way, but this must be the last time.

**Mr. Colvin:** Yes, Gibraltar is part of the European Union; that is an important point to reiterate. As for the debate about Schengen and the external frontier, Spain cannot regard the border crossing between Spain and Gibraltar as part of the external frontier of the European Union, because Gibraltar is within the EU.

**Mr. Mackinlay:** That is absolutely right. It must be made clear that under the European treaties the Gibraltarian people and people from the United Kingdom living or travelling in Spain have rights of free mobility. The Foreign Office should jealously guard those rights, yet there is no evidence that it is doing so. That is the great charge that must be levelled against the Foreign Office today.

I am also disappointed in Her Majesty's Government because rather than meeting problems head on, they use innuendo to detract from the Gibraltarian Government's stewardship of the colony. This morning, the Select Committee on Foreign Affairs was shown a memorandum—I understand that it has not been made public, but it was made available to members of the Committee. The right hon. Member for Westmorland and Lonsdale (Mr. Jopling) referred to that document as

"a scathing attack on the Gibraltarian Government."

As a matter of justice, its contents should be made publicly available so that the Gibraltar Government can respond and give their own version.

The whole affair illustrates the way in which the Foreign Office says one thing one day to one set of people but a different thing on a different day to another. Of course there are numerous problems with the governance and the economy of Gibraltar. Obviously, the economy is in a delicate state as a result of our accelerated withdrawal from the naval base. Two thirds of the economy was directly dependent on the base. Consequently, we have a moral and economic obligation to buttress that Government and that economy. The Foreign Office is not helping that cause; it is not recognising its duty to protect and promote the interests of British subjects who wish to move in and out of Gibraltar.

On 20 December 1994, the hon. Member for Romsey and Waterside initiated a debate, to which another Minister of State, the right hon. Member for Eddisbury (Mr. Goodlad), replied. He went through the routine speech, reading from a brief that described the additional border controls late last year as "intrusive" and "unacceptable". He said that

"we have made repeated strong protests to the Spanish Government in the last few weeks . . . There must be no question of their"—

that is, the controls—

"being reimposed . . . the present level of checks is a disgrace and it is important that they cease permanently."

That is the sort of thing that Foreign Office Ministers routinely say when—prompted, it must be said, by Back Benchers—they come to the Dispatch Box. Their words have little or no substance, so I shall pay careful attention not only to the Minister of State's words but to his body language too, because so far Ministers have given no demonstration of real outrage or anger about Gibraltar.

We have let the people of Gibraltar down badly. We have had many opportunities to protect their interests, especially when Spain's accession to the European Union was being discussed. We ducked the issue then. Maastricht provided another opportunity. It is now time that the Foreign Office showed some anger.

The right hon. Member for Eddisbury further said in the same debate:

"We have asked the Spanish authorities to substantiate their allegations about Gibraltar as a money-laundering centre and to provide examples where co-operation has been refused. To date we have received nothing."—[*Official Report*, 20 December 1994; Vol. 251, c. 1532-35.]

Has substantiation been received yet? If so, will the Minister tell us what it is and publish it so that the Government of Gibraltar may have the opportunity to rebut it?

In the Select Committee on Foreign Affairs this morning, my hon. Friend the Member for Ilford, South (Mr. Gapes) asked whether it was considered that the most recent turning of the screw against Gibraltar was in some part due to the United Kingdom supporting Canada in the recent fishing dispute. The Minister was somewhat ambivalent in his reply, but I assume that our embassy officials in Madrid buy *El Pais*, the principal newspaper there, which made it clear that Spain intended to hit back at the United Kingdom for supporting our Commonwealth partner during the recent fishing dispute.

I was visited by a courteous man from the Spanish embassy yesterday, who confirmed that the newspaper article reflected in substance the view of the Spanish Foreign Ministry. The headline of the *El Pais* article on

15 May stated that Spain was to put sanctions on Gibraltar and the UK for not helping in the struggle against contraband. The article stated that

"the time has come for the UK to pay, and it is going to pay in Gibraltar."

The article quoted the Spanish Foreign Minister, Javier Solana, as promising to send Britain the bill for its lack of co-operation in the struggle against contraband, and for Britain's lack of support in the dispute with Canada over Greenland halibut. Mr. Solana has yet to decide how much the bill will be.

We know that Spain is contemplating additional sanctions against Gibraltar in about four weeks' time after its municipal elections. For that reason—if for no other—it is time that we drew a line and said that we are not going to tolerate this any further.

**Mr. Colvin:** Additional sanctions have been imposed against Canadian passport holders living in Spain who wish to travel into Gibraltar. It is difficult enough for a British passport holder, but it is twice as hard for a Canadian citizen to get into Gibraltar.

**Mr. Mackinlay:** I am pleased that I gave way, as I did not know that. The House of Commons needs to know that such nonsense is going on. I find it difficult to describe my dismay at the fact that there is not a much bigger row going on about the behaviour of the Spanish authorities. Where else in the world would such a situation prevail?

The British press have failed. They are often preoccupied with unimportant matters, but the freedom of British subjects should be as important to them as it should be to the Foreign Office. The Minister's stewardship is extremely weak. We have a patrician and pathetic Foreign Secretary who is prepared to do some of the apparently "big things", but when it comes to looking after a relatively small group of British subjects he ducks it. He is prepared to make perfunctory noises of irritation and outrage which are not backed up by action.

Great harm is being done to our relations with Spain, because Spain feels that it can try to wear down the British Government and make them uninterested in protecting the right of the Gibraltarian people to remain British. We should have had a statement in the House of Commons initiated by the Foreign Secretary about this matter many weeks ago. It should not be up to Back Benchers to raise the matter. The Foreign Secretary should be thumping the Dispatch Box and saying that we will not tolerate it. Previously, the House has had to depend on the hon. Member for Romsey and Waterside to raise the matter. When will the Foreign Office be proactive in promoting the interests of the Gibraltarian people?

The Foreign Office is prepared to insinuate that the Government of Gibraltar are less than diligent in trying to reduce smuggling, money-laundering and so on. However, the British Government are ultimately the police authority for Gibraltar, and not Chief Minister Bossano. The police are under the authority of the Governor and—ultimately—the Foreign Secretary. A financial services commission has been put in place that ultimately will be the responsibility of the Foreign Office, yet I understand that we are requiring the local legislature to introduce financial services legislation the powers of which exceed the legislation required of other countries in the European Union.

If there is a problem regarding speedboats working out of Gibraltar and smuggling between Morocco and the Spanish mainland, what on earth do we have the Royal Navy for? I should like to see the Royal Navy return to Gibraltar. There would, incidentally, be an economic spin-off. Some of what is left of the Royal Navy should be deployed in Gibraltar to help police to control smuggling in the area. What else is the Navy for? It is unreasonable to expect the Gibraltar Government to create a mini-flotilla to stop the contraband smuggling which clearly goes on, although the scale is exaggerated in relation to the involvement of Gibraltar. It is an excuse used by Spain to turn the screws on Gibraltar, and it provides a diversion from the Foreign Office's inactivity.

1.46 pm

**The Minister of State, Foreign and Commonwealth Office (Mr. David Davis):** I congratulate the hon. Member for Thurrock (Mr. Mackinlay) on his good fortune in securing the debate, and I thank him for raising this important issue. It was a pity that he did not measure up to the importance of the occasion with the accuracy and understanding it deserves.

The hon. Gentleman referred to the dispute between Canada and Spain. When we started dealing with that dispute, there was much ignorant comment from the Opposition about our tactics. Those tactics delivered a good outcome, and were publicly supported by the Canadian Government at a later date. I am afraid that the hon. Gentleman's criticisms today were equally badly informed.

The delays at the Spain-Gibraltar frontier are intolerable and unjustifiable. I shall describe to the House in more detail how they came about, and I shall give some detail on what we have done to deal with the situation. Spain has attempted to justify the delays on the grounds of the Schengen convention, but I will show that that justification is wholly fallacious.

The recent delays for cross-border traffic are, sadly, not the first time that the Spaniards have tried to impede traffic at the Gibraltar frontier. Last October, they imposed a regime of secondary checks. Spain justified the checks on the ground that Gibraltar was not a member of the EC common customs territory. The checks produced delays of up to nine hours for vehicles crossing the border, and two to three hours for those crossing on foot.

The House may well remember the Spanish tactics on that occasion. Documentation was minutely checked, and members of the civil guard demanded to see spare spectacles, breakdown tools, sunglasses, fan-belts and even surgical gloves. Drivers who could not produce the required equipment were fined, and their cars impounded until the fine was paid. On some days, the civil guard relaxed its checks, checking documentation only or waving some cars through without checks. Spain claimed at the time that the checks were justified as an attempt to put an end to the problem of drug smuggling, which the hon. Gentleman mentioned.

I agree that there is a problem. We have our own concerns about it, which we have raised in private discussions with the Government of Gibraltar. My right hon. Friend the Foreign Secretary took up that matter and wider questions with Mr. Bossano on Monday evening, but this is neither the time nor the place to debate those issues. The important point is that none of them justifies

[*Mr. David Davis*]

Spanish attempts to impede overland traffic. The illicit traffic is done by sea in fast launches, carrying drugs from Morocco to Spain. There is no evidence of such smuggling by land; no evidence that the Spain-Gibraltar land frontier plays a role in that trade; and no evidence that controls at the land frontier have an impact on smugglers' activities. Causing delays at the land border can only damage Gibraltar's economic base.

**Mr. Colvin:** My hon. Friend is not quite right; there is evidence of drug smuggling through the land frontier, but it is from Spain into Gibraltar.

**Mr. Davis:** I thank my hon. Friend. I should be interested to see that evidence.

We protested to Spain about the delays and I summoned the Spanish ambassador. The jargon in my profession is that we had a full and frank discussion. The problem was eventually resolved through dialogue. In advance of talks between Foreign Ministers in December under the auspices of the Brussels process, the blockages were lifted. It appears, however, that the Spaniards have returned to their previous tactics of squeezing Gibraltar, now using Schengen rather than customs checks as an excuse. That tactic will not succeed. It did not succeed in December and it will not be allowed to succeed now.

As the House already knows, the Schengen convention came into force on 26 March in seven European Union member states: France; Germany; the Benelux countries; Spain; and Portugal. The United Kingdom is not a party to the convention and has no intention of becoming one for reasons of which hon. Members are fully aware. On 27 March at 14:30, Spanish police began systematic passport checks on vehicle traffic and pedestrians both entering and leaving Gibraltar, causing a substantial build-up of vehicles on the Gibraltar side of the border. As yet there is no hard evidence of discrimination between Schengen and non-Schengen European nationals—discrimination between Spanish and Gibraltarians—which would be illegal, and we are monitoring the position carefully in case that arises.

Spain claims that the extra checks required by the Schengen convention cause those delays, but Schengen can be no excuse. Spain must provide adequate resources to carry out its checks without causing undue delays to European Union citizens. That has happened elsewhere in Spain, where there are no significant delays as a result of Schengen. In an extraordinary move, on 7 April the civil governor of Cadiz even went so far as to predict additional delays caused by the implementation of the Schengen convention over the Easter period, but he took no steps to increase staffing at the frontier to deal with the problem. He also announced that the Gibraltar frontier was an external frontier of Europe. That is nonsense. Gibraltar is part of the European Union.

**Mr. David Young:** Will the Minister give way?

**Mr. Davis:** If the hon. Gentleman will forgive me, I shall not do so as I am short of time.

At one point, there were teething problems with the introduction of the Schengen convention elsewhere in Europe. For example, there were queues at the German-Polish border. But those problems were nothing compared with the problem in Gibraltar. The House will realise how damaging those delays can be for Gibraltar, the economy of which depends to a considerable extent on tourists and day trippers. Delays to traffic now are frequently of one or two hours, and have been of four hours or more. Delays on 19 April were reportedly the longest since the border was reopened in 1985. Sometimes delays are shorter and sometimes the traffic even flows smoothly, but the overall effect on business and business confidence is thoroughly negative.

The Government have already made their position extremely clear to Spain. We do not dispute that Spain has a right to maintain frontier controls to ensure that non-European Union nationals remain subject to immigration controls. The Prime Minister has frequently made it clear that we shall retain our right to impose such frontier controls and we have no problem with Spain doing so. But for European Union nationals, those controls should not amount to more than a light passport or identity card check to confirm that they are indeed European Union nationals. There is no need whatever for that to generate delays. The controls at the Gibraltar frontier go well beyond any such checks. They are as unacceptable because of the extreme delays that they cause.

**Mr. David Young:** Will the Minister give way?

**Mr. Davis:** No, I have only a few minutes left. The hon. Member for Thurrock spoke for four or five minutes longer than I expected.

We do not accept that the present delays at the Gibraltar frontier can be justified by the Schengen agreement. When the civil governor of Cadiz predicted problems over Easter, he implied that Spain would knowingly understaff the Gibraltar border posts. That is unacceptable. I do not know whether that policy was co-ordinated with Madrid. I have no evidence as yet that it was, and I hope that it was not to be taken seriously as an expression of Spanish Government policy. Part of the view from Cadiz appears to be that the Spain-Gibraltar frontier is an external frontier of Europe. As hon. Members know, Gibraltar is an integral part of the European Union and it must be treated as such. Article 227(4) of the European Community treaty extends the application of the treaty to Gibraltar. It states:

"the provisions of this treaty shall apply to European Territories for whose external relations a member state is responsible."

The Schengen convention is an agreement between certain member states of the European Union but it is not a European Union agreement. It cannot supersede the rights of UK citizens, including Gibraltarians, under EC law. There should be no discrimination between Schengen and non-Schengen EU nationals at the border. We are closely monitoring the position to observe that.

Like many hon. Members, including the hon. Member for Thurrock, I saw yesterday's press reports suggesting that the Spanish Government were planning

"to introduce sanctions against Gibraltar for refusing to crack down against the Rock's multi-million pound tobacco and drug smuggling industry".

It is not entirely clear what those sanctions are supposed to entail but press reports suggest that they include

"a partial naval blockade of the Rock, virtual paralysis of the land frontier and fiscal penalties for the many Gibraltarians who commute to Spain".

As the House will understand, I have a habit of not believing everything that I read in the press. Although those reports supposedly quote authoritative sources in Madrid, I have no firm evidence that they represent the latest Spanish Government view. Let me leave the House in no doubt that, if there is any truth in press reports of Spanish intentions, I condemn them. It beggars belief that one European Union member state could even contemplate what amounts to a military blockade and sealing off its frontier with another member state. Those are the politics of the 18th century, not the 20th. I hope that that is the stuff of press speculation, and nothing more.

As the House would expect, the Government have acted promptly. We have stood up for the rights of Gibraltarians. I raised the matter with my Spanish counterpart when he was in London only a week or so ago and our ambassador in Madrid has protested to the Spanish Foreign Ministry. Our representations have had some success: the problem has not escalated further as it threatened to do in early April. I regret to report, however, that I can give little further positive news at this point.

Spain's formal response was to attempt to justify the unjustifiable. If there is no early improvement, we shall make further representations as necessary. As well as monitoring Spanish actions at the frontier, we have taken the matter up with the Schengen states and the European Commission and the Schengen secretariat and presidency. Those approaches have drawn attention to the nature and consequences of Spanish border controls.

We have made it clear to every one of Spain's Schengen partners that Spain's behaviour is unacceptable and discredits Spain. It also discredits the Schengen experiment. The Spanish action of choking the Gibraltar border is unacceptable—Schengen is no excuse. We have protested and the House has my assurance that we will continue to press our case until normal traffic at the border is restored.

## Specialist Education (North London)

1.59 pm

**Mr. Hartley Booth** (Finchley): I pay tribute to the patient parents of autistic children, the fine work of care workers and teachers of autistic children, the outstanding work of the North East London Autistic Society and the pioneering work of the National Autistic Society. I should like to speak, most of all, on behalf of those thousands of people who cannot speak for themselves—those who suffer from autism. I intend to refer to the definition of autism, its history, research into it and recently published reports, and to make some recommendations.

Autism is a controversial disorder, but certain factors are agreed upon. It is a human disability or disorder that is biologically based, but is believed to be caused by organic brain damage. It is a developmental disorder, but lasts throughout life. It is found in those with all levels of IQ, but is commonly accompanied by mental handicap. It is described by Lorna Wing, an acknowledged expert, as

"a severe disorder of communication, socialisation and imagination."

It is estimated that 1 million families in Britain are affected by autism, which affects far more boys than girls. It is found among those of all races, nationalities and social background, but it is reported that it is subject to cultural concealment in some groups.

The way in which autism manifests itself varies, but typical features include resistance to change, wandering about smiling—no reference to politicians—obsessional or ritualistic behaviour such head shaking or spinning, stereotyped movements, high levels of anxiety, lack of motivation, inability to transfer skills from one setting to another, vulnerability and susceptibility to exploitation, anger, depression, challenging behaviour, disregard of people with a closer attention to objects and self-injury. That is quite a daunting list.

The National Autistic Society has summed up what it calls the triad of impairments in autism as the absence or impairment of two-way social interaction; the absence or impairment of comprehension and the use of language and non-verbal communication; and the absence or impairment of true, flexible, imaginative activity, with the substitution of a narrow range of repetitive, stereotyped pursuits.

A psychologist at one of the departments of psychiatry in London, Simon Baron-Cohen, has summed up the condition as one that affects some children from birth or infancy and leaves them unable to form a normal social relationship or develop normal communication. As a result, the child may become isolated from human conduct and absorbed in a world of repetitive obsessional activities.

A parent, Mrs. X, has summed up what it is like to have an autistic child. She said that one has to have a sense of humour, otherwise one would go under. She also said:

"It's being able to eat Sunday lunch while sprinting around the house at a very quick pace. It's telling yourself that nobody has ever died with lack of sleep and life is too short to lie in bed anyway. It's being able to look calm in a packed shop when your child is having a major temper tantrum on the floor. It's being able to smile and be pleasant to people when really you could scream and shout. It's being able to pretend you're deaf when everyone around you is tutting at your child's behaviour. It's being able to say, 'Yes, my child looks beautiful, but that will never make him/her normal, so what does that matter.' And mostly, at the end of a very long day, when you look at your child asleep in bed, it's being able to say, 'I love you'."

*[Mr. Hartley Booth]*

So speaks the mother of a young child, but what of an adult with autism? A case study of a young man called Christopher, aged 24, has just been produced by the National Autistic Society. It says:

"Picture a handsome young 24-year-old accompanying his mother to Sainsbury's to do the weekly shopping. Imagine . . . the alarmed reaction of other shoppers and the acute embarrassment of his mother when Christopher decides to leap down the isles with the trolley, yelling exuberantly the chemical formula for manure ('S H one T' for the uninitiated)".

I hope that that last remark did not pass as unparliamentary language and that it is permitted in the context. The report also asks people to imagine what it is like when that young man, who as a child hated being cuddled or restrained in any way, now wants, in his 20s, to drape his 6 ft 2 in frame over the 5 ft 2 in frame of his mother. It asks us to consider how complete strangers feel when he decides to creep up behind them and shout "hairdryer" very loudly just for the fun of seeing their astonished reaction.

In total, there are about 25,000 children and 120,000 adults with autism in the United Kingdom. I want to consider how we can help them best. Autism was first diagnosed in 1943 by an Austrian psychiatrist, Leo Kamer. Its subsequent study has been dogged by as much misunderstanding as illumination. Autism is not caused as a result of emotional deprivation or emotional stress. It is not a withdrawal into a fantasy world or founded on a wish to avoid social contact. It is not due to parental rejection or "refrigerator" parents. It is not a middle-class disorder. It is not a mental illness, nor is it linked to genius or simply another word for mental handicap or a learning disability.

Although autism is widespread and is an important topic, there has, sadly, never been a debate in the House on it before today. Since 1971, the National Autistic Society has placed several reports in the Library of the House, but it was not until recently that a significant number of parliamentary questions have been tabled on it and reference made to it in debate. It was not, however, mentioned specifically in the Education Acts of 1981 and 1993, or in the code of practice.

The first ever published report on the facilities for autistic children in any region—north London—was published a fortnight ago. It was entitled "Going the Distance". I am pleased to see that my colleague from north London, the hon. Member for Hornsey and Wood Green (Mrs. Roche), is present. I wrote that report and I was ably assisted by Jonathan Bartley. A copy of it has been placed in the Library.

The report covers 52 constituencies in north London. We gathered evidence from 100 different sources, which revealed that there were about 1,500 cases of autism in a population of nearly 1 million. When certain facts are discounted, that means that one child in 450 under the age of 18 suffers from autism. We discounted those suffering from Asperger's syndrome, which is a similar disorder, but included all levels of autism. Of the number recorded, 75 per cent. have severe learning difficulties. That means that 1,100 children need specialist treatment in north London, but there are just 350 places for care. That means that the parents of those children have just a one in three chance of having their difficult children, whom they love, properly helped.

What is desperately needed is a broader knowledge of autism. We must identify what is needed. It is unsatisfactory that Barking and Dagenham, Brent, Camden, Hackney, Haringey, Harrow, Havering, Kensington and Chelsea, Redbridge, Tower Hamlets and Westminster have no specialist facilities. That means that 11 out of 20 north London boroughs offer no facilities for autistic children. Barnet has taken the lead with such care, but, unfortunately, its provision is one third below the London average.

I should like to pay tribute to the outstanding work of teachers and care workers in my constituency. The recent work carried out at Oakleigh school was first class. Peter Carney, the head of Oak Lodge school for the past 20 years, has been outstanding in his work to assist autistic children. This morning, he told me that the expertise of his unit needs to expand to cover all age groups.

It is sad to note that the local council in Barnet treated my report as one about a fringe interest. That is especially sad, because its work for autistic children has been excellent in the past. The report condemns the distances covered by the parents of autistic children and describes it as a national scandal.

What can be done? First, early diagnosis is vital. It permits assessment and proper specialist remedial help, which can dramatically mitigate the effects of autism. Failure to recognise the condition early denies a child the chance to benefit from what help is available, and all too often condemns that child to severely life-limiting effects of the condition. It also sentences the community to paying much higher bills to care for what will be a bigger problem in later life, and condemns thousands of marriages to huge stress while disturbing thousands of siblings.

Secondly, as the report makes clear, far more day and residential facilities for autistic children are needed, in the right place. I was prompted to write the report by the story of a child, Matty Solomon, who was taken on a day's journey to the midlands for his treatment. Others beg, borrow and sell their possessions to send their children to the Higashi unit in Boston, in the United States, or spend seven hours a day travelling across London to take their children to the only help that is available—or, indeed, travel only as far as the waiting rooms provided by local authorities, where they are told that there is no help.

Let me tell the Minister that we need more help in this country now. We need more residential educational facilities, and more respite for parents; we also need to provide more day provision for autistic adults. The Government must begin by reviewing the needs of the forgotten children. I know that my hon. Friend the Minister is concerned about this topic; I hope that he will be able to promise the representatives of autistic children who are listening in the Public Gallery, and others who will hear the debate, that the Government will undertake a proper national review of all care needs for autistic children that goes beyond the report begun in 1992 by Jones and Newson, only the first stage of which was ever produced for the Library of the House.

It is now clear that more early care can be provided and paid for from savings made by early assessment and provision. The Government should use the Cabinet Office to co-ordinate the work of the many Departments that should be involved—the Department of Health, the Department for Education, the Department of Social Security and, indeed, the Department of the Environment, which funds local authorities. I have pledged to raise the money for more residential educational facilities in north London, and—along with colleagues who attended the launch—promised to keep autistic children in the eye of Parliament. They may have been forgotten once, but they must never be forgotten again.

2.12 pm

**The Minister of State, Department for Education (Mr. Eric Forth):** I am grateful to my hon. Friend the Member for Finchley (Mr. Booth) for raising this important issue. I acknowledge that—as my hon. Friend pointed out—it is surprising and disappointing to many that it has not been considered here before; he deserves credit for raising it today.

My officials and I have looked at the recent report "Going the Distance", which my hon. Friend co-authored. I, too, sympathise with the difficulties experienced by relatives and friends of those who suffer from the condition: they need the maximum support and help from schools, local authorities, Government and others.

Before dealing with the position in north London, let me say a little about the broader context. As my hon. Friend has acknowledged, the assessment of autistic children for a statement of special educational need, and then the identification of a suitable school for them, is a statutory responsibility of the local education authority in whose area they live. That is not simply an administrative matter. My hon. Friend's report rightly recognises that autistic children, like others with special educational needs, have widely differing requirements, depending on the nature and severity of their disorder. They require a range of provision to meet those needs; decisions about the provision can only be made locally, in the light of a careful assessment of the needs of each child by professionals who know the child. I am sure that that much is common ground.

As my hon. Friend said, it is not always easy to diagnose children with autism. In cases of severe disorder it is usually clear early in the child's development that something is wrong, and diagnosis may come quickly; for others, however, it may take much longer. Once the condition has been diagnosed, children may be educated in local education authority or grant-maintained special or mainstream schools, or in autistic units attached to special or mainstream schools. They may be educated in independent schools, such as those run by the National Autistic Society, or in non-maintained special schools. Placements at independent and non-maintained special schools are paid for by the LEA when that provision is specified in a child's SEN statement.

The majority of autistic children attend schools and units capable of meeting the needs of children with a range of special educational needs; perhaps one child in eight attends a school or unit that specialises solely in teaching children with autism. It does not necessarily follow that the provision for the majority of autistic children is not appropriate. In particular—as I am sure my hon. Friend is aware—the pros and cons of residential placement for autistic children remain the subject of much professional consideration and discussion.

My hon. Friend's report recommends a Government inquiry into the needs of autistic children, and he repeated that request today. As I know he is aware, the Department of Health and my Department have been sponsoring research by the university of Nottingham into current interventions for children with autism. Stage 1 of the project identified facilities and services in England and Wales that cater for children and adults, and summarised information on the current arrangements for the education, treatment and handling of those with autism. A copy of the report of stage 1 was placed in the Library of the House in 1993.

Stage 2 of the research—which goes more deeply into the main characteristics of the forms of education and treatment identified in stage 1 and evaluates the effects of these approaches on the behaviour and skills of autistic children—is now in its final stages. I hope that the team's report of that work will be available later in the year. My officials and those from the Department of Health are in contact with the NAS about taking forward the results.

The evidence on which my hon. Friend draws is up to date. The fact is, however, that, while his inquiries were being undertaken, schools and LEAs began to revise their procedures to match the new code of practice on the identification and assessment of special educational needs. The code came into force in September last year. It incorporates tight time limits on the procedures under which LEAs and other professionals have to assess children and make statements of SEN where appropriate. In particular, the new arrangements under the Education Act 1993 give parents powerful rights in the selection of the school to be named in their child's statement.

When parents are not satisfied with the statement or with the school named by the LEA, they can appeal to the independent SEN tribunal. Since last September, the tribunal has been handling the first appeals made by parents dissatisfied with aspects of the statementing process, including the school named for their child by the LEA. Although I do not wish to diminish the importance of the case made by my hon. Friend, it is a fact that, of the 559 appeals to the tribunal up to the beginning of May, just 1 per cent. have concerned autistic children. I do not know what conclusions we should draw from that; I simply state it as a fact.

**Sir Michael Neubert** (Romford): Does my hon. Friend agree that that appeals procedure is very important to autistic children and their parents? A case in my constituency, involving Terry Murray junior, involved a tremendous tussle between the parents and the local authority. In making both assessment and provision, an authority can be both judge and jury, and that issue needs to be tackled.

**Mr. Forth:** Indeed. That is why the tribunal was established. It is now an independent and impartial body, to which parents who are not happy with what has happened can go and obtain a judgment independent of the local education authority. Early suggestions are that it will be an enormous step forward, providing new justice and fair treatment for parents of children with differing special educational needs, including autistic children. It goes further than that because part of the code of practice requires that needs specified in a child's statement must be mirrored by a clear statement of the provision that the authority is to make for that child. The link between needs and provision is more clearly established, and LEAs are better placed to judge the extent of any shortfall in provision than ever before.

I want to stress to my hon. Friend that I believe that what is new since last September—although it is early days to judge—is that a new clarity will emerge in the nature, effectiveness, use and targeting of moneys that LEAs establish for special needs provision, both at authority level and in schools. In time, there will emerge a new

*[Mr. Forth]*

understanding at every level of the availability of funds and the availability and provision of places for conditions such as autism. We are now in new territory, and an increasing amount of information will be available of the sort that my hon. Friend will be able to use—and we shall want to look at—to carry forward cases such as the one that we are considering today.

Enfield has recently increased its provision for autistic children; Islington is proposing to increase provision so that it can make regional provision for autistic children in north London. I have heard that yet another LEA in the area may propose to establish a unit for autistic children at a school for pupils with moderate learning difficulties. There is some suggestion that steps are already being taken—I should think partly as a result of the clarity provided by the code of practice.

**Mr. Jeremy Corbyn** (Islington, North): I apologise to the House for not being present for the speech of the hon. Member for Finchley (Mr. Booth).

The Minister of State is talking about expansion facilities. He will be aware that Harborough school in my constituency does excellent work with autistic children, and is a wonderful school in many ways. There are proposals to expand its provisions. What is the Government's attitude towards the expansion of provision to give better facilities? I am well aware that many people successfully appeal against the non-provision of places, but there is no special school available. Although the appeal process is welcome, it is limited if, ultimately, there are no places to be found.

**Mr. Forth:** The hon. Gentleman makes a fair point. The Government's attitude is that we would want to give support and a fair wind to any authority that comes forward with sensible, positive proposals to deal with such need. It is rightly a matter for the authority, with its local knowledge, to decide what should be done. We would not want to stand in the way of well-thought-out and properly designed proposals that meet a clearly identified need in the locality or beyond. I hope that there will be no problem.

Given the spectrum of needs and the range of provision that may be appropriate, it is difficult to pin down a shortfall in the way suggested by my hon. Friend the Member for Finchley. Although many LEAs maintain their own specialist provision for children with autism, there is a danger that some will be tempted to place their own children first. If that means that other autistic pupils are on lengthy waiting lists, the LEAs responsible for those children will have to give serious and early consideration to whether there are alternative approaches to meeting their needs.

Not every LEA will be able to, or need to, make its own specialist provision. In some cases, collaboration between LEAs may well be desirable; but, in the first instance, it is for each LEA to satisfy itself about the adequacy of provision for the children for whom it has responsibility. It would be open to, say, the National Autistic Society to convene discussions with LEAs to seek a common view of the position locally. If those discussions led one or more LEAs to publish statutory proposals for new schools or units, the Secretary of State would want to consider

them carefully, together with any associated bids for capital support—the point made by the hon. Member for Islington, North (Mr. Corbyn).

Another factor in the equation is that 11 of the boroughs in north London are at stage 2 or 3 of the grant-maintained process. That means that the Funding Agency for Schools may also be able to propose new provision. I understand that the FAS is considering carrying out a survey of special educational needs units at grant-maintained schools. If a need were established for more autistic provision, the FAS could have a role in considering how such provision should be made. In any event, I would hope that the FAS could be associated with any local discussions on that subject. Such discussions could be fruitful for all parties involved, and I hope that they will consider that proposal with some urgency.

Another route would be for voluntary bodies or charities to consider establishing, or expanding existing, non-maintained special schools to cater for children with autism. Those are schools run by voluntary bodies on a non-profit-making basis. The voluntary body would need to apply to the Secretary of State to open a school or change the status of an existing school. Such applications are considered sympathetically, but stringently. A non-maintained special school can apply to the Secretary of State for capital grants to improve existing buildings or to build new premises, although I must stress—nobody will be surprised to hear me say it—that the money for such purposes is, of necessity, limited. We try to use it in the most effective way. I would therefore expect most of the money in those cases to come from the charity's private income. The running costs of such schools are normally covered by payments from LEAs that place children at them.

I hope that I have demonstrated to my hon. Friend the Member for Finchley that the Government are well aware of the importance of appropriate provision for autistic children. The Government's job is to ensure that there is a clear framework in which local authorities and other professional services, together with parents, can work out solutions to match each child's needs and to ensure that information is available nationally to help authorities determine best practice. We have achieved that in the Education Act 1993 and the code of practice.

We now have the opportunity to identify the needs more clearly and to match them to the provision. We can judge more clearly the effectiveness of existing funds at every level. There is scope for further action to be taken— perhaps headed by the NAS, and no doubt helped by my hon. Friend the Member for Finchley. That action would involve the LEAs and the FAS and would carry forward my hon. Friend's work, for which I praise him. We must ensure that the provision for this vulnerable group of school-age children—and those who are older—is the best available. We must give every support, not only to the young people involved but to their families. I am sure that we all share that aim.

I hope that my brief remarks have contained some hopeful signs for the future. I wish my hon. Friend well in pursuing the interests that he has brought before the House today.

2.27 pm

*Sitting suspended.*

2.30 pm

*On resuming—*

*It being half past Two o'clock, the motion for the Adjournment of the House lapsed, pursuant to Order [19 December].*

## DEATH OF A MEMBER

**Madam Speaker:** I regret to have to report to the House the death of Geoffrey Kenneth Dickens Esq., the Member for Littleborough and Saddleworth. I am sure that hon. Members on both sides of the House will join me in mourning the loss of a colleague and in extending our sympathy to the hon. Member's family and friends.

## PRIVATE BUSINESS

### BIRMINGHAM ASSAY OFFICE BILL

### MALVERN HILLS BILL *[Lords]*
*As amended, considered; to be read the Third time.*

# Oral Answers to Questions

## ENVIRONMENT

### Opencast Mining

1. **Mr. MacShane:** To ask the Secretary of State for the Environment what steps he is taking to ensure that the environment in areas where opencast mining is permitted is not damaged by the activity of opencast mining operators.　　　　　　　　　[23191]

**The Parliamentary Under-Secretary of State for the Environment (Sir Paul Beresford):** Tight, improved guidelines which upgrade environmental requirements on opencast mining were published last July. They would apply to any new permissions

**Mr. MacShane:** I thank the Minister for his short reply. First, is he aware of the great concern about the incidence of asthma and bronchitic disease that is linked to opencast mining? Secondly, is he aware of concern at the Orgreave site in south Yorkshire, where phenol in the ground may be getting into dust and posing a real contamination problem? Thirdly, is he aware of the concern in Rotherham about a proposed opencast mine near Greasbrough? If the mine is allowed to go ahead, it will destroy the visual amenity of a beautiful green-field site in my constituency. In light of that, will the Minister agree to hold a public inquiry in south Yorkshire to explain the Government's real opencast mining policy and allay my constituents' fears?

**Sir Paul Beresford:** The hon. Gentleman will understand that I cannot pick a particular case for inquiry. I imagine that he is aware that the mineral planning guidance note MPG 3 gives his Labour local authority considerable scope on environmental issues, such as the visual side, noise, blasting, dust—which he mentioned—water, transportation, the built environment, nature conservation, subsidence and restoration. In addition to that, my Department is currently undertaking research into dust, blasting and transport and I hope that the results of that research will assist in alleviating the hon. Gentleman's concerns.

**Mr. Batiste:** Is not the real issue where opencasting should take place? Should not priority be given to areas where dereliction is being cleared up, and should not communities' overall environmental and sustainable development needs be taken into account in a strategic sense when considering individual applications?

**Sir Paul Beresford:** My hon. Friend is absolutely right. Operators will need to demonstrate that real benefits will result from their proposals, particularly if they wish to work in sensitive green-field sites.

**Mr. Illsley:** The Minister will be aware that there is concern that private opencast operators are not meeting their obligations to restore opencast sites. Will the Minister consider some mechanism that will allow the Government to enforce private opencasters' obligation to restore those sites? That would prevent a company from allowing a subsidiary company to go into bankruptcy and thus avoiding its obligation to restore opencast sites, as occurred in the case of Sheffield Airport Ltd.

**Sir Paul Beresford:** The hon. Gentleman will be aware of our concern and we shall certainly look into any individual case about which he may care to write to me.

**Mr. John Marshall:** Will my hon. Friend remind those carrying out a vendetta against opencast mining that it is more economical to produce coal that way, it will lead to lower electricity prices and it will benefit consumers, about whom they do not care?

**Sir Paul Beresford:** My hon. Friend is absolutely right. He will agree that the new requirements on environmental issues protect the community as well as providing employment opportunities.

**Mr. Skinner:** Is the Minister aware that one of the problems that local authorities have nowadays, as opposed to 15 years ago, is that when they are presented with an application for an opencast cite to be developed, they are told by local officials that, in some circumstances, if they oppose the case and it goes to appeal, councillors will be surcharged because, under current planning considerations, the Government have got them by the short and curlies? As a result, although they would like to oppose every single one, in many cases they are frightened to do so because they can be driven out of public office. Why do not the Government change that?

**Sir Paul Beresford:** The hon. Gentleman's imagination always runs away with him. If he looks at MPG 3, he will see the ammunition and strength that local authorities have now to protect local communities, while reflecting upon the environmental improvements on one side, and the economic benefits on the other.

**Sir Donald Thompson:** Will my hon. Friend reflect carefully on what the hon. Member for Barnsley, Central (Mr. Illsley) said? The problem of £100 companies welshing on the deal to reinstate is not a new one; it has happened for generations in gravel extraction and other industries. Surely we are adroit enough to stop it happening here.

**Sir Paul Beresford:** It is fairly obvious that my hon. Friend has a particular case in mind. I would be grateful if he would write to me about it.

### European Regional Funds

2. **Mr. Alton:** To ask the Secretary of State for the Environment how much of the funds for objective 1, designated for the financial year 1994-95, have been spent; how much is retained by the Department; and if he will make a statement. [23192]

**The Minister for Local Government, Housing and Urban Regeneration (Mr. David Curry):** Merseyside's European funding is for the period to 2001. Of the £55 million transferred by the Commission to the United Kingdom, £23.7 million has been authorised for payment. The rest is held by Government under the rules set down by the European Union to make further payments as claims for approved projects are submitted.

**Mr. Alton:** I am grateful to the Minister for that reply. Notwithstanding what he said, does he recognise that there

is some concern that, in the first part of the overall period in which money can be spent, there has been a failure to deliver money to projects which had hoped to be under way by now? Does he agree with the recommendations of the monitoring committee which has been working in partnership with the Government, and does he intend fully to implement its proposals? What will happen to the money that has already been given to the Government by Brussels? Will it accrue to the advantage of the Government or to Merseyside?

**Mr. Curry:** The answer to the final part of the question is that the money takes the form of authorisation for payment. There is no crock of gold in a bank in Merseyside and it does not earn interest, so it cannot earn interest for the Government. It can be spent only on projects which have been approved. Those projects are sufficient to draw down the entire amount that was sent over in the year that we are considering. Only about 20 out of 800 projects have not received final approval because of details that need to be settled, and we are on target for the second tranche of projects for which we should get clearance in July.

**Mr. Wareing:** Is not there a tendency for them to accumulate, because there is a complaint in Liverpool of slothfulness in dealing with the bids?

**Ms Eagle:** And in The Wirral.

**Mr. Wareing:** And in The Wirral, as my hon. Friend the Member for Wallasey (Ms Eagle) says. Should not the Government increase the resources of the secretariat so that the process can be speeded up, or are they quite happy to continue at the same old steady pace?

**Mr. Curry:** The hon. Gentleman is not being reasonable. The Commission released the schemes only last July, so the 1995 schemes could not even begin to be considered until the second half of the year. Nearly 800 of those schemes have been approved. The next tranche will fall due in July. We are on schedule for dealing with them in July. I recognise people's anxiety to get the schemes under way because of Liverpool's particular status, and I shall ensure that the regional office does everything in its power to do so. I spoke to the director again yesterday and he told me how strongly the office is committed to making sure that the schemes progress.

### North Sea Ministerial Conference

3. **Ms Ruddock:** To ask the Secretary of State for the Environment what policy his Department will pursue at the fourth North sea ministerial conference due to take place in Denmark on 8 to 9 June. [23193]

**The Secretary of State for the Environment (Mr. John Gummer):** I have placed a statement of United Kingdom policy objectives for the North sea conference in the Library. I am particularly concerned to achieve protection for species and habitats outside territorial waters; comprehensive measures, within the common fisheries policy, to control over-fishing; internationally co-ordinated research to improve knowledge of the possible effects of some chemicals on reproductive systems; and more effective enforcement of international rules against pollution from shipping.

**Ms Ruddock:** The Secretary of State will recall that under his Government Britain became known as the dirty man of Europe. Does he now want us to be known as the scrap merchant of Europe? Given the Greenpeace protest and Danish determination to raise the issue, what environmental reasons will he give to the North sea conference for permitting the towing of Brent Spar into the Atlantic for dumping rather than bringing it ashore for dismantling, recycling and reuse?

**Mr. Gummer:** I am sorry that the hon. Lady did not watch the television programme in which David Bellamy made it clear that we are now the clean man of Europe and that that is the view of all environmentalists. The hon. Lady should talk to some real and serious environmentalists before trying to make party political comments out of her nation's interest. The national interest is simply that we should be dealing with those matters which pollute the North sea and obeying international agreements. In dealing with our North sea oil rigs, we shall follow to the word the agreements of Paris and Oslo. We shall do precisely what we agreed to do internationally. The hon. Lady should be proud to live in a country that is now leading the world in these matters.

**Mr. Mans:** May I encourage my right hon. Friend to take precisely the same proactive approach at the North sea conference as he did at the conference on climate change? We have proved conclusively that, because we abided by the rules and managed to achieve what we said we would achieve, Britain led and others were forced to follow. May I encourage my right hon. Friend to take precisely the same approach at the North sea conference to ensure that those on the continent enforce what they have signed up to as we have done in the past?

**Mr. Gummer:** We are in the top third for meeting targets set by the previous North sea conference. We are concerned with a number of issues, not least the bad cycle which results from industrial fishing, particularly by the Danes who turn the fish into cow food and feed their cows on it, resulting in considerable agricultural pollution in the North sea. That is something that we want to stop.

### Environment Agency

4. **Mr. Steen:** To ask the Secretary of State for the Environment what is his forecast of the annual running costs of the new environment agency; and what are the current costs of carrying out the same work within existing organisations.     [23194]

**The Minister for the Environment and Countryside (Mr. Robert Atkins):** The work to be transferred to the environment agency is valued at £528 million at 1994-95 prices.

**Mr. Steen:** Although Conservative Members welcome the Government's commitment to protecting the environment, there is just a little concern about the advertisements that appeared in the national papers for the director whose salary will be twice that of Cabinet Ministers and who will have 9,000 staff who will no doubt be serving notices and enforcing summonses. Will not the new agency impact on Britain's business culture by adding cost to our products as a result of the number of civil servants who will be rushing around asking businesses to comply with this or that regulation?

**Mr. Atkins:** There is an old adage that, if you pay peanuts, you get monkeys. We are in the business—

*[Interruption.]* We are in the business of ensuring that we get very large monkeys—[Hon. Members: "Stop digging!"] We are in the business—

**Madam Speaker:** I suggest the Minister starts again.

**Mr. Atkins:** I know exactly where I am, Madam Speaker.

We are in the business of ensuring that, whoever is appointed chief executive of that most important agency, which is a product of far-seeing legislation that the Government are introducing, will be paid the right amount to do an important job. Industry will need to ensure that the people who run that agency can speak the same language as it does, so that the legislation is implemented to the highest standard.

**Mr. Pike:** Will the Minister recognise that, on occasion, the National Rivers Authority has not had the necessary powers or finances to deal with certain river pollution, especially from former mine workings? Can he give the assurance that the Environment Bill will give the authority powers to eradicate that pollution from the parts of the country where it is a major problem?

**Mr. Atkins:** There is a question on the Order Paper about that issue, which I intend to answer, but I can give the hon. Gentleman the assurance that he wants.

**Mr. Sykes:** As an adequately paid Back Bencher, I assure my hon. Friend that the national parks currently operate well under the aegis of the Department of the Environment. One thing that is extremely important is the fact that, under the new arrangements, we shall seek far more professional, and perhaps more local democratic representation in the national parks service. Can my hon. Friend give us an assurance today that, for example, parish councillors will be asked to serve on the new national parks board?

**Mr. Atkins:** My hon. Friend makes an extremely important argument. My right hon. Friend the Secretary of State and I are examining it closely. In discussing the Environment Bill, currently in Committee, we have not reached the provisions relating to the national parks, but I intend to ensure that there is better representation from those who live and work in the parks, who are, in my book, the most important people there.

### Mortgage Arrears (Repossessions)

5. **Mr. O'Hara:** To ask the Secretary of State for the Environment what is his latest estimate of the number of households likely to lose their homes through repossession for mortgage arrears in the next 12 months.     [23195]

**Mr. Curry:** The Government do not make predictions about future repossessions. The latest figures published by the Council of Mortgage Lenders show that the number of properties taken into possession in 1994 was the lowest since 1990 and 35 per cent. lower than the peak in 1991.

**Mr. O'Hara:** Such complacency will bring no comfort to the 250,000 home owners who continue to be more than six months in arrears with their mortgages, the 1.2 million home owners trapped in negative equity in a declining housing market or, importantly, those sick, disabled and unemployed home owners who are under threat of losing their homes—12,000 is the calculation of the Council of Mortgage Lenders—as a result of the proposal to cut their income support when they get into difficulties.

How can the Minister be so complacent, when the Government of which he is a member have collectively and comprehensively made such an unholy mess of private and public housing provision?

**Mr. Curry:** The first thing is that no Conservative Member is complacent about that, but equally, no one who suffers from that problem will be comforted by a political rant on the subject. *[Interruption.]* We are conscious of the difficulties—*[Interruption.]* It would be easy for anyone to stand at the Dispatch Box and exude all sorts of phoney rhetoric.

This is a serious matter. The people in those circumstances are unfortunate and I am anxious that they should recover. That is done by taking that into account in the fixing of interest rates—trying to maintain low interest rates. The level of interest rates is the single most important factor.

One must try to ensure that one has sensible relationships with mortgage lenders so that they are understanding and, when people make an honest attempt to make repayments, they make, and continue, arrangements to accommodate them. One must try to ensure that the economy is managed so that we continue to bring people out of unemployment and into employment and so that we can offer hope to people who now find themselves in difficulties. I am as worried about that as anyone in the House.

**Mr. Thomason:** Will my hon. Friend confirm that people's desire to own their own properties remains as buoyant as ever, notwithstanding the difficulties over repossessions, and that Labour Members' consistent attempts over the years to talk out home ownership have failed again and again? Nearly all the British public want to own their own home.

**Mr. Curry:** About 230 people a day in Great Britain are entering into home ownership thanks to the various schemes that help them to do so. That can be only because a large number of people believe that that form of tenure suits them. The Government will continue to assist them to acquire such tenure.

**Mr. Raynsford:** Will the Minister confirm that approximately 1,000 people a week are losing their homes as a result of repossession, and that his Department has received a report from Dr. Janet Ford of Loughborough university, which, I understand, will be published shortly and which demonstrates that private insurance will not provide an adequate safeguard for many home owners in financial difficulty? Will he therefore press his colleague, the Secretary of State for Social Security, to withdraw his ill-conceived and damaging proposals to limit income support, which are already damaging the market and will lead to an increase in repossessions?

**Mr. Curry:** The report will be published tomorrow, so the hon. Gentleman will have the satisfaction of being able to read it. It is reasonable, however, to ask that private provision should take some of the strain from public provision. The increase in the number of households and the demands on the public purse are such that we must reconsider the frontier that divides the two. My right hon. Friend will have heard what the hon. Gentleman has said. I would be interested to know

whether it is Labour party policy to reverse the changes—that is not clear—and how that sits with the new financial probity that, we are told, has fallen on the Labour party.

**Mr. Nigel Evans:** Does my hon. Friend agree that the best way to minimise the number of repossessions is to ensure that we have, as we do at present, the proper conditions for economic growth? That is shown again by today's announcement that unemployment has fallen for the 20th successive time. Does he further agree that we must ensure that we have not only low interest rates but low inflation levels, and that we must encourage inward investment in this country so that we shall be one million miles away from the social chapter and the minimum wage?

**Mr. Curry:** It is certainly true that low inflation levels, which can be reflected in low interest rates, are one of the prime factors in helping people to resume their payments. Keeping unemployment falling and people finding employment is equally important in enabling people to resume their payments. Many people manage to recover their arrears. That is to be welcomed and is an essential way forward.

### Latham Report

6. **Mr. Gapes:** To ask the Secretary of State for the Environment if he will introduce legislation to implement the recommendations of the Latham report in the current Session of Parliament.    [23196]

**The Parliamentary Under-Secretary of State for the Environment (Mr. Robert B. Jones):** The Government have no plans to introduce legislation in the current Session. My right hon. Friend has today published a consultation paper on Sir Michael Latham's recommendations on fair contract conditions.

**Mr. Gapes:** Is the Minister aware that many companies, including Essex Electrical in my constituency and members of the Electrical Contractors Association, will be bitterly disappointed that the Government have no immediate plans to introduce legislation? Will he give the House an assurance that that is not due to opposition from some of his ministerial colleagues in the Department of Trade and Industry, who have ideological objections to regulation?

**Mr. Jones:** The hon. Gentleman's constituents and indeed everyone else would be astonished if we made such an announcement before the end of the consultation period on the first consultative document, and before we had published the second consultative document. The key to success with the Latham recommendations is that we proceed through consensus throughout industry. That is the Government's target. I hope that that will be supported by consensus in the House.

**Mr. Lester:** Does my hon. Friend consider Sir Michael Latham's work, which I think most of us recognise as thorough and helpful, to be important? Many of us have had problems with subcontractors who have gone bankrupt because they have not been paid for work that they have undertaken. The work of my friend Michael Latham was worth while. I hope that the consultation documents will carry things forward to a satisfactory conclusion.

**Mr. Jones:** I am grateful to my hon. Friend. I have no hesitation in praising the work that Sir Michael Latham has done, but he was not the only one. Many people in the construction industry have done an immense amount of work, taking his reports forward into the proposals that have been issued as consultative documents. As one who worked in the construction industry before I was elected to the House, I have every sympathy with subbies. Poor treatment of subcontractors is in no one's best interest. It does not deliver good projects, a healthy industry or good value for money, and we must combat that.

### Minewater Pollution

7. **Mr. Mullin:** To ask the Secretary of State for the Environment what representations he has received from the National Rivers Authority regarding the allocation of responsibility for the control of minewater pollution; and if he will make a statement.                    [32197]

**Mr. Atkins:** My Department maintains regular contact with the National Rivers Authority about minewater pollution. Responsibility for the control of such pollution lies in the first instance with mine operators.

**Mr. Mullin:** Will the Minister confirm that the National Rivers Authority is anxious that the Coal Authority should be given a statutory responsibility for pollution arising from mines that have been closed? Although it is working well with the Coal Authority now, should the money run out or should there be a change of policy, there is nothing to stop the authority walking away from mine pollution with potentially devastating consequences. Does the Minister plan to do anything about that?

**Mr. Atkins:** I hope that the hon. Gentleman will recognise that we hold similar views on the determination to ensure that abandoned mines do not cause detrimental pollution. The hon. Gentleman will be aware that during a recent visit to Durham by the chairman of the Coal Authority the matter was discussed between county councillors and the Coal Authority. Durham county council was able to issue a favourable press release afterwards saying that a number of concerns had been addressed. The Coal Authority has a continuing commitment to do what is necessary to treat abandoned mines because of the possibility that they may cause pollution and has confirmed that the pumping, where necessary, will continue. That commitment stands firm.

### City Pride

8. **Mr. Enright:** To ask the Secretary of State for the Environment what plans he has to extend the city pride initiative.                    [23198]

**Mr. Gummer:** Birmingham, London and Manchester have made tremendous progress in pursuing city pride. We will look at what they have achieved before extending the initiative.

**Mr. Enright:** Is not the way in which the Government look at special schemes and then set them up, excluding other areas, somewhat arbitrary? I am thinking particularly of the single regeneration initiative, which is not all bad and in which some very good things are happening. However, its arbitrary nature is excluding certain areas. South Elmsall, South Kirkby and Upton have been put together, but Hemsworth in the middle, which has equally desperate needs, is not included and that impedes other initiatives.

**Mr. Gummer:** The single regeneration budget is not in any way arbitrary. People are able to bid for the money

and we try to ensure that the bids which provide the best use of the money are met. We try to help those who have failed in the first round to prepare for the bids in the second round. The hon. Gentleman will find that the mix that is achieved—a mixture of meeting the need and finding the best capacity contra to the money put in by the taxpayer—is valuable.

Birmingham, London and Manchester were not chosen arbitrarily. They are the three largest towns in England and it seemed sensible to spread the choice geographically. We must remember that Birmingham has not yet launched its final draft of city pride, but if we find that those cities produce what we hope that they will, we will look to see whether others want to participate. The scheme does not exclude others. When I first announced it, I said that if cities wanted to start outside the scheme, they could do so in the same position as Birmingham, Manchester and London.

**Mr. McLoughlin:** Will my right hon. Friend consider the possibility of using more private sector involvement in the schemes? I am sure that he is aware of the huge amount of money that the Government are spending on regeneration throughout the country, in both city pride and city challenge. The Government get very little credit for the amount that is spent, perhaps because they usually have to work with hostile Labour local authorities.

**Mr. Gummer:** It would be helpful in this area to recognise the very large amount of money that the taxpayer puts into these schemes and the significant success of bringing in private capital. There ought to be cross-party support for that. If we get at least £4 and sometimes even £5 or £6 from the private sector for every £1 put into these schemes, we get a great deal more money to help people and to provide the things about which both sides of the House ought to be concerned.

It seems to me that we can at least agree that this initiative is sensible and proper and successful. We must see how we can make it more successful and effective. I want to do that by getting greater co-operation.

Let us take the Manchester scheme. Under city pride, for the very first time, Manchester council is working well with the other two authorities that make up Manchester— Manchester council hardly talked to one of those authorities previously, even though it was a Labour-controlled council—and with the urban development corporations, which were damned from the housetops when they started.

**Mr. Vaz:** The whole House realises that city pride is nothing more than a public relations exercise initiated by a beleaguered Secretary of State who has run out of ideas for regeneration policy. Despite that, the Manchester, Birmingham and London pride initiatives have used their own time, efforts and resources to prepare excellent policy documents. How does the Secretary of State intend to turn those vision statements into reality when, as he knows, city pride offers no extra resources to any of those local authorities?

**Mr. Gummer:** I am told by the press that the hon. Gentleman is always a nice man, so I will answer him as nicely as I can, given the total absence of truth in his question. The truth of the matter is that Manchester, London and Birmingham have produced their documents and are very pleased with the co-operation, not only with the Government as a whole but with the Government offices concerned. In one way or another, they have all received significant sums from the single regeneration budget. I am pleased to say that Manchester asked me, as Secretary of State, to launch its scheme, so keen was it on city pride. The hon. Gentleman ought to talk to some of his supporters occasionally.

**Mr. Ian Bruce:** Does my right hon. Friend appreciate that it does not always need Government cash to get those principles in place? Will he look at what Purbeck district council has done in setting up Purbeck Pride, with only private sector money and not a penny from the Government? The council is creating the sort of pride that is bringing more tourism and business into Purbeck without a penny of public subsidy.

**Mr. Gummer:** My hon. Friend will have noticed that the hon. Member for Leicester, East (Mr. Vaz) not only laughed at the activities of Labour councils in Manchester and Birmingham and many of those in London that are working for city pride, but evidently finds any reference to a rural area incredibly comic. The fact is that the Labour party does not care about rural areas at all. My hon. Friend points out that in many rural areas, entirely by private initiative working with local authorities, we are doing a great deal to achieve what must be done to secure better opportunities for jobs and employment in those areas.

### Environment Agency

9. **Mrs. Helen Jackson:** To ask the Secretary of State for the Environment what steps he will take to ensure that the operations of the proposed environment agency are open to public scrutiny.    [23199]

**Sir Paul Beresford:** We will expect the agency to provide clear and readily available information on its work. It will be subject to the Environmental Information Regulations 1992 requirements to maintain public registers of information on activities which it regulates, and it will be expected to meet the requirements of the Government's code of practice on access to Government information.

**Mrs. Jackson:** Does the Minister agree that the public are usually the best environmental watchdogs and that they need to have access to all information? Has he forgotten that it was his Government who made local government comply with access to information regulations? Why will he not ensure that the environment agency will be subject to the same rules of accountability as local government?

**Sir Paul Beresford:** The hon. Lady forgets the points made to her in Standing Committee. There will be no lack of information on the agency's activities, which will be subject to a variety of requirements. I also remind her of the Environmental Information Regulations 1992, the legislation on public registers, the principle of openness set out in the Government's code of practice on access to Government information, the code of best practice for board members and public bodies, the duty to produce an annual report, and public registers to provide information about licences.

The Environmental Information Regulations 1992 provide a duty to respond to environmental information requests and provide for the inspection of public registers which are available free of charge. Copies can be obtained

at a minimal cost. The agency's management statement will ensure public access to meetings of the agency's regional and local committees. Ministers will be accountable to Parliament, too. Finally, the agency can, if it wishes, hold meetings in public. There is a deluge of information.

**Mr. Forman:** Is my hon. Friend aware that his diffident and understated answers will be welcomed by his colleagues? Is he further aware that, in the interests of openness, it is important that the public are reassured about some of the leading environmental problems, especially air pollution? Will he see to it that those problems are tackled with the urgency that they deserve, especially in view of the concern felt by my constituents about the possible link between asthma and air pollution?

**Sir Paul Beresford:** I ask my hon. Friend to consider the Government's reaction to environmental factors. If he follows the progress of the Environment Bill, I think that he will find that we have taken much of that concern on board.

### Co-operative Housing

10. **Ms Hoey:** To ask the Secretary of State for the Environment what support he will give to ensure the increase of housing for co-operative ownership.    [23200]

**Mr. Robert B. Jones:** The Housing Corporation's grants to co-operative housing associations for construction, rehabilitation and repair this year amount to £9.514 million.

**Ms Hoey:** The Minister will be aware of the many successful housing co-ops in my constituency, especially in the Waterloo and Coin street area. However, is he also aware that there was no new allocation for housing co-ops in London this year and that there is a feeling, certainly within the Housing Corporation, that the Government's commitment to housing co-ops is perhaps not quite so strong as it was? What is the Department's commitment to housing co-ops?

**Mr. Jones:** Allocations by the Housing Corporation reflect the priorities that local authorities place on particular bids. There is little doubt that some place issues other than housing co-operatives higher up the priority list. The hon. Lady will be aware that that is sometimes because of hostility on the part of local authorities. She does not need to go back very far to remember the hostility of the Labour-controlled Greater London council to the Coin street co-operative in her area.

**Mr. Congdon:** Does my hon. Friend agree that we should do everything we can to continue the extension of home ownership by whatever means possible, including the extension of shared ownership, the assisted private purchase scheme and, perhaps just as important, the extension of the right to buy to tenants of housing associations?

**Mr. Jones:** The Government remain deeply committed to the idea of sustainable home ownership. In addition to the various measures mentioned by my hon. Friend, we are always anxious to hear of new ideas for promoting home ownership from him or anyone who is interested.

## Wind Farms

**12. Mr. Hutton:** To ask the Secretary of State for the Environment if he will make a statement about planning guidance for wind farms.        [23202]

**Mr. Gummer:** The Government have issued planning guidance for wind farms in planning policy guidance note 22, or PPG 22, which was entitled "Renewable Energy" and published in February 1993.

**Mr. Hutton:** While recognising the important environmental benefits of renewable energy, especially wind farms, is the Secretary of State aware of the concern felt by people living in Askam and Ireleth in my constituency about plans to develop wind farms near there? Will he consider strengthening and amending paragraphs 59 to 69 of PPG 22 with a view to making specific reference to the siting of large wind turbines close to towns and villages?

**Mr. Gummer:** I have to be convinced that we need to tighten it further. I have not yet seen a case in which the local authority has not been able to stop the development of wind farms in circumstances where the intrusion is such as that described by the hon. Gentleman. One of the problems with wind farms is people's failure to recognise that you don't get owt for nowt: wind farms may be a clean way of producing electricity, but they have a real visual and noise impact. Some people who object to another form of energy demonstrate against it and demand wind farms, but as soon as one is proposed they demonstrate against that as well. We have to recognise that wind farms are suitable only in places where they will not have an impact of the type already covered in the planning policy guidance note.

**Mr. Hawkins:** Does my right hon. Friend agree that the irony of the history of wind farms—this is true of Lancashire, Yorkshire, Cumbria and other parts of the United Kingdom—is the way in which the single-issue lobby groups have always dominated the Labour party's agenda, on the environment and everything else? Groups used to call for such things until they realised how unpopular their proposals were. Now they oppose them. That is the way of all single-issue lobby groups: they can never decide whether they are in favour of anything, and as soon as they get something they have campaigned for they realise that they did not want it in the first place.

**Mr. Gummer:** I agree with my hon. Friend. I was never able to attend any kind of meeting on nuclear power, for example, without being told that the real answer was to have windmills. The moment one proposes windmills, however, the real environmental problem arises, to which I shall return. We need a mix of energy supplies and we should recognise that to get energy we must accept disadvantages. Those disadvantages occur even when we consider harnessing wind power.

## Supermarkets

**13. Mr. Battle:** To ask the Secretary of State for the Environment how many planning applications for supermarkets are awaiting his decision for a public inquiry.        [23203]

**Sir Paul Beresford:** Approximately 50 proposals for supermarkets over 4,000 sq m are awaiting decision.

**Mr. Battle:** The Minister may be aware that Leeds development corporation recently approved a large-scale supermarket development in the green Kirkstall valley, despite opposition from the local authority, councillors, residents and businesses, and flying in the face of his recent planning guidance. I urge the Minister to call in the application, even at this late stage. Road access has not been sorted out and the development could jeopardise the town centre of Bramley and close down all its shops. Will the Minister call in the application and put forward a proper scheme which is acceptable to the whole community?

**Sir Paul Beresford:** I am happy to look at it, but if planning permission has been given, there is nothing that the Department or the Government can do.

**Sir Patrick Cormack:** While my hon. Friend is pondering such decisions, will he bear it in mind that the transition from a nation of shopkeepers and small shops to one of supermarket shoppers has not been wholly beneficial?

**Sir Paul Beresford:** Yes, I will. I am sorry that my hon. Friend did not attend the recent debate on that very subject, when all hon. Members were in agreement. In fact the hon. Member for Leicester, East (Mr. Vaz) called it a love-in, which may be the reason why my hon. Friend was not present.

**Mr. Betts:** Is the Minister aware of two planning applications in my constituency which have been treated in completely contradictory manners? At Oxclose farm, the council rightly turned down a planning application for a superstore in a green-field site which was not served by any public transport, but an inspector delegated by the Secretary of State overturned the decision on appeal. At Drakehouse, adjacent to an existing centre, however, when the council proposed to change existing retail permission to food retail, the Secretary of State so disliked the idea that he called in the decision for further review. As the latter site is well served by public transport and adjacent to an existing centre, is it not time the Government turned fine words into practical policies, supported local shopping centres on the ground and stopped undermining them, as Government policy on planning applications appears to do every time?

**Sir Paul Beresford:** The hon. Gentleman would clearly also have benefited if he had come to the debate to which I referred. He would have recognised that Opposition and Government are both going down the road that he mentioned.

## Water Bills

**14. Mrs. Lait:** To ask the Secretary of State for the Environment what proposals there are to end the practice of basing water bills on rateable values.        [23204]

**Mr. Gummer:** On 4 April I announced my intention to enable water companies to continue to use rateable values as a basis for charging for water beyond 2000.

However, I believe that the use of rateable values will gradually reduce as customers and water companies alike decide to switch to water meters.

**Mrs. Lait:** Is my right hon. Friend aware that distortions are emerging in people's water bills due to outdated ratable values? That is compounded by the frustration at the cost of water meters, when electricity and gas meters come free. Is he planning a revaluation of domestic properties?

**Mr. Gummer:** Late-valued new housing—late-valued before 1989—has always tended to have a higher rateable value than other housing. That distinction has existed for some time. There is nothing new about the problem, which is simply that if we do not continue with that system the only alternative would probably be to allow council tax banding to be used. The hon. Member for Truro (Mr. Taylor), who speaks for the Liberal party, seems to be saying yes to that. However, I have examined the figures from Severn Trent Water and 1.4 million of its non-metered water consumers live in houses in bands A or B; in other words, they are the poorest people. Of those, 900,000 would pay more for their water if we changed the basis to council tax banding. Something like half a million of them would pay 50 per cent. more. That is the Liberal policy to replace rateable values. I think that we should keep rateable value until more and more people acquire meters. Metering must be the sustainable development answer.

**Mr. Matthew Taylor:** Notwithstanding the Minister's comments, I have seen pensioners in tears because they cannot pay their current water rates, which can be as much as 15 per cent. of their annual income. They cannot afford that. The council tax banding system, on which the Minister elaborated, would allow many such people to benefit if, as with council tax, help were available for people on low incomes and people living alone. That is why the old rating system was ultimately replaced by council tax and the Government did not revert to it after the poll tax. Given that the same problems occur with water rates, the same solution should surely apply.

**Mr. Gummer:** One of the fascinating things about the hon. Gentleman is that it does not matter what the facts are, he still asks the question that he intended to ask before he heard the facts. The Liberal party must face the facts: if we moved to council tax banding, the people who would be hurt most would be those in the smallest and least taxed houses, many of whom would pay much more. If that is Liberal policy, I am prepared to advertise it widely. Everybody ought to know that the Liberals, having been given the facts, want to make poorer people pay more. That is what they want, and that is what we shall pin them with.

The sensible people in the west country are the Conservative Members who have been pressing the water companies which cover the area to be much more efficient, to ensure that they charge as little as possible and to offer people the alternative of water metering. I hope to see more companies following the example of Southern Water, which has reduced the cost of installing meters. That must be sensible.

**Mr. Patrick Thompson:** My right hon. Friend will be aware that many of my constituents and other people throughout the country are worried about the cost of installing a water meter. However, those who have installed meters usually find that there are considerable reductions in their bills. Can my right hon. Friend make those facts more widely known and do more to encourage water metering, which must be right in terms of conservation, especially in times of drought and difficulty?

**Mr. Gummer:** I am sure that we should consider that idea carefully. In the Anglian region, for example, if we do not opt for a mechanism to restrict the use of water more sensibly, we shall need huge new reservoirs and we shall have to draw down water from half-way across the country—in other words, we shall have to do precisely what any sense of sustainable development would forbid. My hon. Friend is right: I shall look for better ways to advertise the fact to the public and to persuade some of the water companies with high charges for installing meters to change their views.

**Mr. Dobson:** Why does the Secretary of State permit the water regulator to continue to try to force water metering on companies which are reluctant to introduce it and on householders who are even more reluctant? With about 20 million households in the country, would it not cost between £1 billion and £1.5 billion to meter every house in Britain, and are there not better ways of spending that money to benefit the environment?

**Mr. Gummer:** First, I cannot tell the water regulator what to do in any circumstances. That is why he is an independent regulator, and I have no intention of changing that. Secondly, no country in the world that is concerned with sustainable development is not having to face the fact that water is a resource which needs to be metered. The hon. Gentleman would be laughed out of any international conference to which anyone was mistaken enough to send him if he suggested that we should turn our backs on sustainable development for water.

The hon. Gentleman has no reputation in the environment world, and one of the reasons for that is that he will not face up to reality. Even if the figure that he gave were true, that amount would be spent over 25, 30 or 40 years. People would be able to conserve water during those years, which is necessary in parts of the country where we are bringing water long distances. We are building large reservoirs, which the Labour party always opposes on the ground that they are against environmental concerns. The hon. Gentleman has no policy on this issue.

**Mr. Streeter:** Does my right hon. Friend welcome the fact that South West Water has now reduced the cost of installing water meters to below £200? Is that not good news for our constituents in the south west? Will he leave no stone unturned in trying to reduce the general level of water charges in the south west, which remain of great concern to my constituents?

**Mr. Gummer:** I am pleased that water metering charges have gone down by more than one third, and I note that that was the result of a concerted effort by Conservative Members in the south-west. I hope that South West Water will get the charges down even further, and I am sure that there are ways to do so. I hope that it will also look at ways of helping people to amortise the cost of water meter installation over a reasonably long period so that they can get the benefits immediately.

### North Sea Ministerial Conference

**15. Ms Quin:** To ask the Secretary of State for the Environment what proposals he will be making at the forthcoming North sea ministerial conference.     [23205]

**Mr. Gummer:** I refer the hon. Member to my earlier reply to the hon. Member for Lewisham, Deptford (Ms Ruddock).

**Ms Quin:** Has the Secretary of State seen the report in *The Observer* and the study by the World Wide Fund for Nature which claim that the Government are failing to meet their international commitments concerning the reduction of pollution in the North sea? Can the Secretary of State assure me that by the end of this year, the Government—as they are supposed to do—will have met every one of the targets to which they have agreed for all the substances listed?

**Mr. Gummer:** We are already in the top third of the North sea countries in meeting our commitments, and we have met 27 of the 36 targets for the reduction of inputs. We are well on the way to meeting the rest of them, including the 75 per cent. target for mercury and the 70 per cent. for cadmium. It is no wonder that David Bellamy has referred to us as the clean man of Europe.

### Housing Improvement Grants

**16. Mr. Tony Banks:** To ask the Secretary of State for the Environment if he will make more resources available for housing improvement grants.     [23206]

**Mr. Robert B. Jones:** I cannot anticipate the public expenditure round, but local authorities are free to add to renewal allocations from their own resources, particularly where they have gone for a large-scale voluntary transfer.

**Mr. Banks:** With regard to the Minister's reply to my hon. Friend the Member for Vauxhall (Ms Hoey) on Question 10, had it not been for the Greater London council there would be no Coin street development.

I thank the Minister for his offer this morning to come to Newham to discuss the matter of improvement grants, but may I remind him that my borough has 2,000 homes with outside lavatories and 1,200 without inside bathrooms? My local authority is one of the best at providing improvement grants, but 4,000 households are still waiting for grants. There has been a dramatic fall in the number of mandatory grants, and the Government know that. We are still waiting for their long-term proposals on improvement grants. When can the House expect to hear them?

**Mr. Jones:** The hon. Gentleman knows that this is a complex subject, but we hope to announce our proposals before too long. He will know that some local authorities underspend their allocations, just as others find themselves running short. We try to use the underspend to help those authorities which have a problem, and I shall be happy to talk to him about Newham. In the hon. Gentleman's own neighbourhood, Redbridge benefited by an extra £613,000 from the reallocation, while Waltham Forest received an extra £185,000. The constituency of the hon. Member for Greenwich (Mr. Raynsford) benefited by an extra £691,000 and—proving that silence is golden—Sandwell benefited by an extra £2 million.

**Mr. Jenkin:** When my hon. Friend considers such demands for increases in public expenditure, will he remain mindful that it is Government policy to try to reduce public expenditure? Who in his Department is responsible for the fundamental review of public expenditure, and what reductions does he expect his Department to achieve?

**Mr. Jones:** In our Department, as in all others, all Ministers take an interest in that subject under the leadership of my right hon. Friend the Secretary of State. We recognise, as I am sure my hon. Friend does, that the first duty for the maintenance of their homes lies with owner-occupiers. However, I recognise problems will arise with particular individuals and we must pay attention to those.

**Mr. William O'Brien:** In considering the grants procedure, will the Minister ensure that the 2.6 million houses in desperate need of attention will be considered in the mandatory grant which, I hope, will be operated taking account of inflation? Will he ensure that the discretionary grant is well funded and ring-fenced so that local authorities have an opportunity to meet the demands made on them by people living in sub-standard properties?

**Mr. Jones:** I have told the hon. Gentleman before that we have not reached a conclusion about the future regime. His opinions, however, seem to be far removed from the vast majority of Labour-controlled authorities that I have met throughout the country, which want to get away from a mandatory scheme so that they can concentrate their renewal strategy where it is most needed. Even with the present arrangements, however, the reallocation benefit of the underspend to the hon. Gentleman's authority of Wakefield was nearly £500,000.

### Open Spaces

**17. Mr. Harry Greenway:** To ask the Secretary of State for the Environment what steps he is taking to ensure the provision of more open spaces in built-up areas; and if he will make a statement.     [23207]

**Sir Paul Beresford:** We fully recognise the importance of open space for amenity and recreation, and our planning policy guidance encourages its provision.

**Mr. Greenway:** I thank my hon. Friend for that reply. Will he be strong with Labour councils such as Ealing, particularly as an open space and sporting facility which has existed for nearly 100 years is under threat? Does he agree that such a facility should continue to exist and not be built on in any way?

**Sir Paul Beresford:** As my hon. Friend is aware, we are "strong" on exactly that issue. Playing fields should normally be protected, except where additional sports facilities are provided for the area, where there is alternative provision of equivalent benefit elsewhere, or where there is an excess of sports provision—which would be rare or non-existent in my hon. Friend's area.

**Mr. Dobson:** As one who has always strongly supported the provision of more open spaces in urban areas, may I tell the Minister that all decisions by the Labour council about the disposal of sites in Ealing simply reflect previous decisions by the former Tory council, which disposed of many more sites? Does the hon. Member for Ealing, North (Mr. Greenway) accept that we welcome his raising that matter as councils throughout the country are strapped for cash and find themselves having to sell off sites? Even more important, the remaining open spaces are becoming increasingly run down, shabby, ill kept and—because they are no longer staffed—insecure. More resources are needed to stop the sell-offs and improve the condition of open spaces.

**Sir Paul Beresford** *rose—*

**Mr. Greenway:** On a point of order, Madam Speaker. A question has been put to me by the hon. Member for Holborn and St. Pancras (Mr. Dobson). May I answer it?

**Madam Speaker:** Order. The hon. Gentleman has been long enough in this House to know that the answer is no.

**Sir Paul Beresford:** I am continually amazed at Labour Members' lack of knowledge and understanding of inner cities and local councils. One need only go to some Labour authorities to see land requiring regeneration which is wasted because the local authorities do not have the money, gumption, ability, information or imagination to get any regeneration moving.

### Thames (Salmon)

19. **Mr. Duncan:** To ask the Secretary of State for the Environment what research has been presented to his Department about the number of salmon in the Thames. [23209]

**Sir Paul Beresford:** I understand that the National Rivers Authority recorded 238 salmon in the river in 1994, confirming the marked improvements achieved in recent years. The actual number of salmon returning to the river in that year is likely to have been greater.

**Mr. Duncan:** Is my hon. Friend aware that in days gone by sittings of the House were suspended because of the stink from the Thames in summer? Do not the increased numbers of salmon swimming up a clean river to spawn prove beyond doubt that the Thames can rightfully claim to be the cleanest metropolitan river in Europe?

**Sir Paul Beresford:** As ever, my hon. Friend is absolutely right. He may be interested to know that in the past five years the average annual return of salmon to the Thames has been 214. The actual number has tended to vary quite significantly year by year, the highest number recorded being 338 in 1993 and the lowest number being 59 in 1991. My hon. Friend is absolutely correct: the Government's success in cleaning up the rivers, and particularly the Thames, is proved by the fact that he and I can risk opening a window in Committee.

# Points of Order

3.31 pm

**Several hon. Members** *rose*—

**Madam Speaker:** Wait a moment. I have a point of order from the hon. Member for Dewsbury (Mrs. Taylor).

**Mrs. Ann Taylor** (Dewsbury): On a point of order, Madam Speaker. May I seek your guidance on what action should be taken by the House on the fact that the hon. Member for Weston-super-Mare (Sir J. Wiggin) used the name of the hon. Member for Falmouth and Camborne (Mr. Coe) to table an amendment to the Gas Bill? Even more important than that is the fact that the hon. Member for Weston-super-Mare may have done that to avoid drawing attention to the fact that the amendment related to his financial interests. From what the hon. Gentleman has said, the Committee sitting may not be the only occasion on which that happened.

The House has taken action against the hon. Members who took cash for questions, but it now appears that we need to investigate the issue of cash for amendments, because any such action is clearly in breach of the existing rules in "Erskine May".

I appreciate that you, Madam Speaker, may not be able to rule fully on the matter yet, but you will be aware of the growing expectation that the matter may have to be resolved by a reference to the Committee of Privileges, as the Prime Minister indicated this morning. The House would be grateful if you could say how best we should now proceed.

**Madam Speaker:** I already have a letter alleging breach of privilege in this matter. The House knows that the hon. Member for Weston-super-Mare (Sir J. Wiggin) is not in the country at the moment. In spite of that, I am seriously examining the situation and I shall do so with all speed.

**Mr. Peter Hain** (Neath): On a point of order, Madam Speaker. I wonder whether you can advise me what protection I have against the allegations of the hon. Member for Rutland and Melton (Mr. Duncan)—I have given him advance notice of this point of order—made in my presence despite my repeated denials, that I collaborated with the "Dispatches" programme and *The Guardian* over this matter. I emphatically deny that allegation: I had no contact with either during the sittings on the Gas Bill. I put it to you, Madam Speaker, that that allegation is an attempt to produce a smokescreen and to divert attention from the gross abuse of the House's procedures by the cash for amendments scandal that has developed.

**Madam Speaker:** Does the hon. Member for Rutland and Melton (Mr. Duncan) wish to respond?

**Mr. Alan Duncan** (Rutland and Melton): I am grateful for the opportunity to do so. Through you, Madam Speaker, I invite the hon. Member for Neath (Mr. Hain) to celebrate the near anniversary of his first apology to the House by apologising now to me for saying things about me in the Standing Committee which he knew to be untrue, in the knowledge that he could take advantage of qualified parliamentary privilege and in the knowledge that those comments would be broadcast afterwards with no recourse on my part.

**Madam Speaker:** I cannot deal, across the Floor of the House, with personal grievances between hon. Members. They ought to be resolved between those hon. Members, rather than being raised on the Floor of the House. It is a disgrace that they are brought to me in this way.

**Mr. Tony Benn** (Chesterfield): On a point of order, Madam Speaker. When you come to consider the ruling that you make on the matter that has been raised, may I invite you to think carefully about it? Your ruling may have historic importance, and may be studied over many centuries. We are not merely discussing the possible conduct of an individual Member of Parliament, which is normally dealt with by a secret meeting of the Committee of Privileges and a minor suspension and then left; I put it to you, Madam Speaker, that we are discussing a new challenge to the authority of the House.

Your predecessor, Madam Speaker, dealt with the King when he tried to interfere. I believe that commercial interests are now trying to dominate the House of Commons by other means. There are 14 pages of offices that are disqualified from service in Parliament—including that of Steward and Bailiff of the Chiltern Hundreds—on the ground that they might be under the control of the King: the mere fact that they are royal appointments excludes them.

When you give your ruling, Madam Speaker, it should go beyond the conduct of the individual Member of Parliament and begin to open up matters of much deeper importance that it is not appropriate for the Nolan committee to consider, because it is not answerable to the House. It is for the House, and only for the House, to legislate to deal with any abuses that may arise.

**Madam Speaker:** I take what the right hon. Gentleman has said very seriously.

**Mr. Roger Gale** (Thanet, North): On a point of order, Madam Speaker. I have no desire to become embroiled in a personal row between my hon. Friend the Member for Rutland and Melton (Mr. Duncan) and the hon. Member for Neath (Mr. Hain). However—

**Madam Speaker:** Order. I have given my ruling, and I will have no more of this across the Floor of the House. If the hon. Gentleman wishes to raise a different point of order, I will hear it; but there must be no references to points of order that have already been made.

**Mr. Gale:** With respect, Madam Speaker, one of your duties as Speaker of the House—

**Madam Speaker:** Order. I am well aware of my duties in the House. I will give the hon. Gentleman every chance: let me repeat that, if he has a genuine point of order on another matter, he may raise it, but he must not raise again issues on which I have already given a ruling.

**Mr. Gale:** Will you use your influence, Madam Speaker, to prevent hon. Members from using parliamentary privilege to smear the reputations of other hon. Members?

**Madam Speaker:** I believe that hon. Members should be sufficiently mature to conduct their business in a proper and decent way, and that the Speaker should not have to intervene in altercations between Back Benchers.

**Mr. David Winnick** (Walsall, North): On a point of order, Madam Speaker. I wish to raise a separate matter from that raised by my hon. Friend the Member for Neath (Mr. Hain). I hope that you will appreciate that it does not relate to a specific case.

What concerns me—and, obviously, must concern you, Madam Speaker—is the reputation of Parliament as a whole. I emphasise that I am not referring to a particular case. I am concerned about the impression that is created— understandably—that this Parliament is hopelessly sleaze-ridden. Is there any way in which we can demonstrate that many of us—many Opposition Members, certainly—have no outside financial interests? Is it not important for people to recognise that we are not all on the make? We are not all acting as consultants, lobbyists and so forth.

**Madam Speaker:** That is barely a point of order for me, but I am sure that it will be not only touched on but, perhaps, developed during Thursday's debate.

**Mr. Paul Flynn** (Newport, West): On a point of order, Madam Speaker. May I raise an entirely different matter— what appears to be the manipulation of Question Time for party political advantage? There have been two examples.

You will recall, Madam Speaker, that in his answer to Question 15 this afternoon the Secretary of State for the Environment gave no information, referring my hon. Friend the Member for Gateshead, East (Ms Quin) to the answer that he gave my hon. Friend the Member for Lewisham, Deptford (Ms Ruddock) in response to Question 3. We should ask why those questions were not linked.

Questions to the Church Commissioners are allotted only five minutes, and normally only two or three questions are answered. That was the case on Monday: only three questions were answered. The Department linked Question 1 with Question 4, and Question 3 was not put to the House. It so happened that Question 4 was put by a Conservative Member. When Ministers link questions they say, "With permission, Madam Speaker", so I presume that it is a matter for you, Madam Speaker. Can you ensure that such linking is not used to silence hon. Members' questions?

**Madam Speaker:** I am sure that the House is well aware that I do not give permission for the linking of questions. It is nothing to do with me and it is up to the Minister involved to decide whether questions are linked. I am sure that those on the Government Front Bench have noted what the hon. Gentleman has had to say.

**Mr. Jeremy Corbyn** (Islington, North): On a point of order, Madam Speaker. On an entirely different matter— have you received a request from a Defence Minister to come to the House and make a statement on the raid that took place earlier today on the offices of Greenpeace? The raid took place on an application to the court from the Ministry of Defence after the non-proliferation treaty had

been completed in order not to draw attention to the fact that Greenpeace has been campaigning vigorously for nuclear disarmament and states that the Trident nuclear missile system is itself a proliferation.

**Madam Speaker:** If a statement were being made today, we should all have known about it by 1 o'clock as it would have been shown on the annunciator screens.

**Mr. Tony Banks** (Newham, North-West): On a point of order, Madam Speaker. It arises out of the point of order raised by my hon. Friend the Member for Newport, West (Mr. Flynn)—

**Madam Speaker:** Order. There can be no other point of order. I do not give permission for the linking of questions—that is done by Ministers. If the hon. Gentleman has a new point of order, of course I must hear it.

**Mr. Banks:** It is.

**Madam Speaker:** In that case, the hon. Gentleman should not have stated that it was related to a previous point of order.

**Mr. Banks:** Madam Speaker, I want further clarification on a matter on which I want you to give a ruling. As permission is sought, if an hon. Member shouts "Object", is it true that the Minister cannot link the questions?

**Madam Speaker:** That is not the case. Ministers have got into the habit over many years—long before I became Speaker—of saying, "With permission". They do so when they link questions and when they make statements, but they do not require my permission to do so. Perhaps we can leave it at that and get on with the ten-minute Bill.

**Mr. Roger Knapman** (Stroud): On a point of order, Madam Speaker. It is probably true that members of the Labour party are safe from allegations of sleaze, because who on earth would employ them outside this place?

**Madam Speaker:** Order. If the hon. Gentleman has a point of order, I want to hear it straight away.

**Mr. Knapman:** The hon. Member for Neath (Mr. Hain) has twice in the past 12 months made allegations of sleaze and has rightly had to come before the House to grovel and apologise to you, Madam Speaker. How many times can an hon. Member do that? If the hon. Gentleman has already had to come before the House twice, having made misleading allegations, should he be allowed to do it yet again this afternoon?

**Madam Speaker:** I hope very much that hon. Members will bear in mind what I have said today and take it seriously.

**Several hon. Members** rose—

**Madam Speaker:** I am taking no further points of order. The electorate and the British public outside the House expect better behaviour and better conduct from the House. It is about time that every Member of the House realised what is expected of us and behaved accordingly. We must now proceed to the ten-minute Bill and I shall take no further points of order from anyone today.

# Commonhold

3.43 pm

**Mr. Dudley Fishburn** (Kensington): I beg to move,

That leave be given to bring in a Bill to introduce a system of commonhold property tenure; and for connected purposes.

The Bill involves a new form of land tenure that will allow flat-dwellers to own their individual flats on a freehold rather than a leasehold basis. It will allow new buildings, whether commercial or residential, to bypass the leasehold system—properties could be sold as commonholds from the outset, with the new law spelling out the obligations and rights of each unit in relation to the whole.

There is nothing controversial in the proposal, which will merely bring to England and Wales a form of tenure available in every other western country—the condominium of the United States, the "strata" title of Australian flats and the system of co-propriété used throughout the continent. Millions of flat-dwellers live under that system throughout the world—some in Scotland, but none in England or Wales, where leasehold has, until now, been the only law recognised in the land for those sharing a common building.

The fact that this country has, extraordinarily, been without such a system has long worried both flat-dwellers and the property industry. At the moment, many thousands of people who own both a leasehold and a share in the underlying freehold—one of the attendants in the House is in exactly that position—have no alternative but to operate both systems in parallel. Under my proposals, that attendant would, with his neighbours, be able to adopt a commonhold tenure that would free him from those complications. It would also increase the value and the marketability of his flat. Most importantly, it would give him exactly the same tenure as for every commonhold flat in the country. Gone would be the endless variations and small print of leasehold; instead he would have full ownership of a property in which all his obligations and rights were spelt out—and spelt out in terms identical to all commonhold flats.

Changes in the property market sparked in part, but only in part, by the Leasehold Reform, Housing and Urban Development Act 1993, have led to a large increase in the number of people who own both a leasehold and a share of the underlying freehold. Many owners of residual freeholds realise that the best thing to do these days is to sell their freehold back to the leaseholders who own the major stake in the building. Yet those people are saddled with a highly complicated form of ownership, having to run a separate freehold company to administer the running of the building.

The leasehold reform Act raised many passions. In 1992 I was made radical of the year for pushing that legislation to the fore through a number of ten-minute Bills and debates, although much of the credit rested with my predecessor, the late Brandon Rhys Williams.

This legislation is more likely to earn me the title—much more difficult to attain because of the greater competition—of bore of the year because no one could possibly oppose it. The commonhold proposal has been penned in part by the Grosvenor Estate. You may recall, Madam Speaker, that the Duke of Westminster left the Conservative party in high dudgeon because of the leasehold reform Bill. Commonhold may bring him

back—I hope so. It has the support of the building societies' Council of Mortgage Lenders, which sees at first hand the problems of lending money to purchase flats on the complicated leasehold-freehold system. It also has the support of the Consumers Association and the Law Commission, which first produced a working commonhold paper in 1987. A new slimline commonhold proposal is now in near final draft.

The sponsors of my Bill include many Members of Parliament from inner London constituencies who know the need for this new form of tenure well enough—for example, my right hon. Friends the Members for City of London and Westminster, South (Mr. Brooke) and for Chelsea (Sir N. Scott) and my hon. Friend the Member for Fulham (Mr. Carrington). They also include Members of Parliament who were vocal in their opposition to leasehold reform. They spoke out against the leasehold Bill because they believed that it was retrospective legislation which involved compulsory purchase and confiscation.

Critical as those hon. Members were of me then, they are happy to sponsor this Bill on the issue of commonhold. They recognise that commonhold is a voluntary system which is overdue in coming to the statute book and which contains no element of confiscation. I welcome the support of my right hon. Friend the Member for Westmorland and Lonsdale (Mr. Jopling), who was once an opponent but who is now an ally in this matter.

Things move slowly in matters of property law. On 12 July 1991 the Government announced that they would bring a system of commonhold before the House based on the 1987 Law Commission report, the 1988 draft legislation and the 1990 consultation paper that produced more than 1,000 replies. It was promised too in the Conservative party manifesto—I know, because I wrote the phrase. But nothing happened. When the leasehold Bill was announced, commonhold was left out. Why? It is because the leasehold Bill came from the Department of the Environment, while commonhold comes from the Lord Chancellor's Department—it seems that Whitehall Department shall not talk unto Whitehall Department.

Throughout the passage of the leasehold Bill, Opposition Front-Bench spokesmen criticised the Government for not introducing commonhold. I am pleased that the hon. Member for Greenwich (Mr. Raynsford), who is a Labour Front-Bench spokesman on housing, is a sponsor of my Bill. Yet the urban dweller waits while so much common agreement produces so little common action. Here is a Bill that is tailor-made for an uncontroversial Queen's Speech; there need be no Division on Second Reading. It could fit excellently into the Jellicoe procedure, by which uncontroversial Bills dealing with legal matters begin in another place.

Commonhold would be entirely voluntary. That is essential. It would be available for those who wished to use it as an alternative form of tenure. If it worked—and it would—it would gradually replace large chunks of leasehold. By gradually, I mean over a generation. A commonhold flat would become London's standard form of ownership. Good tenure would drive out bad.

A commonhold property would soon hold a premium over a leasehold property. The market would do with an invisible hand what politicians failed to do with a big stick.

*[Mr. Dudley Fishburn]*

Most countries recognised a generation ago the need for commonhold as a proper form of land tenure in a modern city. I hope that this modest ten-minute Bill will help bring my proposals to the statute book.

*Question put and agreed to.*

Bill ordered to be brought in by Mr. Dudley Fishburn, Mr. Peter Brooke, Mr. Michael Jopling, Sir Nicholas Scott, Mr. Matthew Carrington, Mr. Nigel Forman, Mr. Henry Bellingham, Mr. Gyles Brandreth and Mr. Nick Raynsford.

### COMMONHOLD

Mr. Dudley Fishburn accordingly presented a Bill to introduce a system of commonhold property tenure; and for connected purposes: And the same was read the First time; and ordered to be read a Second time upon Friday 14 July and to be printed. [Bill 124.]

# Opposition Day

[12TH ALLOTTED DAY]

## Rail Services

**Madam Speaker:** Before we move on to rail services under privatisation, I should inform the House that I have selected the amendment standing in the name of the Prime Minister.

3.51 pm.

**Mr. Michael Meacher** (Oldham, West): I beg to move,

That this House, noting that the threat of rail privatisation is leading to a blight of investment, lowered reliability and punctuality of services, and higher public subsidies to private operators, calls on the Government to improve and increase investment in a publicly owned and publicly accountable rail system which best serves the public interest and the needs of the British economy.

Since 1992, when the Government introduced their rail privatisation proposals, virtually every index of rail performance has shown a sharp decline. The most dramatic and damaging in its long-term effects is the fall in investment. According to the Government's own figures, in 1992, investment in the existing rail network, excluding the channel tunnel, stood at £1,060 million at today's prices. This year, it is expected to be about £490 million. That is a staggering cut of 54 per cent. in three years.

The meaning of the halving of rail investment to below £500 million in the present year is revealed by the fact that Sir Bob Reid, the former chairman of British Rail, recently said:

"To keep the railway in a good steady state we need to be spending in the region of £900 million to £1 billion a year."

To fall below that bottom line for several years running is an obvious false economy. To halve the amount is surely irresponsible and dangerous.

The consequence has been a decline on the railways that is unprecedented for 50 years. Last year, for the first time since the war, there were no orders for new rolling stock. That seems bound to continue this year because of the uncertainties over privatisation. No new signalling or electrification projects were ordered in the two years to April 1994 and Railtrack has placed only one significant contract since being set up that month.

The value of rolling stock orders completed has plummeted by half in the past two years, while signalling turnover has fallen by one third.

**Mr. Patrick McLoughlin** (West Derbyshire): Will the hon. Gentleman give way?

**Mr. Meacher:** I shall give way in a moment, but I want to make one or two points first.

Routine track renewal of £200 million a year is necessary to maintain its condition, yet track renewal has now slowed to such an extent that engineers must assume that rails have a working life of 90 years, which is far beyond what is either realistic or safe. Thank God there has been no really serious accident yet. But I believe that that is much more by luck than by judgment.

**Mr. McLoughlin:** A few minutes ago the hon. Gentleman quoted Sir Bob Reid's estimate of £900 million. Is he saying that if he was Secretary of State for

Transport, he would always do what the chairman of a nationalised industry requested? Is he now committing himself to spending an extra £400 million or £500 million a year on the railways?

**Mr. Meacher:** That is a rather silly point. It is not a matter of doing what the chairman of British Rail says; it is a matter of doing what is sensible. Any reasonable Government would listen to what a chairman of British Rail, whom they appointed, said. To produce an investment record scarcely better than half of what he believes to be the minimum necessary simply to maintain a good steady state is an utter condemnation of the Government's rail investment policy, in which I hope the hon. Gentleman will join.

**Dr. Robert Spink** (Castle Point): Will the hon. Gentleman give way?

**Mr. Meacher:** No, I want to make a little progress.

Altogether, it has been estimated that British Rail now has more than 2,500 carriages and locomotives that need replacing in the near future. Yet no orders are being placed. In the Kent Coast fleet, 475 carriages are more than 40 years old—as the long-suffering Kent commuters know only too well—well beyond their maximum working life. Yet the Government prefer to allow ABB at York to go into liquidation at a cost of 750 jobs rather than bring forward even a limited follow-on order. That is the state of Britain's railways today under this policy.

The result of all that has been that service quality has gone through the floor. In the past year alone, 20,000 trains were cancelled—that is more than 80 a day on average. Overcrowding on commuter lines in the south-east is now so acute that the number of standing passengers on slam-door trains is up to three times the number recommended by the Hidden committee after the Clapham train disaster.

In the past year since British Rail was reorganised for privatisation, delays have soared. Of 102 train service groups covering punctuality and reliability, in the past year two thirds did worse than in the previous year. I shall not detain the House by going into more detail, but those examples are typical of the drift, muddle, make-do and breakdown that is now occurring across the rail network.

It is not as if the Secretary of State has not had personal experience of that himself. I understand that last month he went by train to Leeds, and I take up the story as it was lovingly recorded in one of the newspapers.

"Chuff chuff chuff, until just outside Leeds, when the train stopped with a groan. Points problems, the customers were told. Dr. Mawhinney got out at Leeds, where he cut short the greetings from assorted local management with a sharpish demand to know what had happened to the points and how long there had been problems. The senior British Rail man dropped his kid gloves too: 'It's because of lack of investment, Minister.'"

**Mr. Gyles Brandreth** (City of Chester): Will the hon. Gentleman give way on that very point?

**Mr. Meacher:** I shall be very surprised if it is on that very point, but let us see.

**Mr. Brandreth:** It is on that very point. Obviously, the hon. Gentleman is painting something of a caricature. It certainly does not reflect the line between London and Chester. The hon. Gentleman is a good 10 minutes into his speech, painting a dismal picture, but he has said nothing about the level of investment that he would settle

on or whether he has plans to renationalise. Will he give us some answers as well as telling us how terrible it all appears from his perspective? What are his specific solutions? What should the level of investment be? What are the plans for renationalisation?

**Mr. Meacher:** I well understand the hon. Gentleman's anxiety to leave the subject of the debate. I remind him that the debate is about the further erosion of rail services due to privatisation. That is what we are debating, and that is exactly what I have described.

If the hon. Gentleman wishes to know the Labour party's policy, I shall say something about that before I conclude. However, I can put him out of his misery by saying three things. First, we would substantially increase investment in rail to make up for the huge decline in investment that has taken place for years under the policy of Conservative Governments. Secondly, we believe that rail has a very significant role to play in an overall transport policy. Thirdly, we do not have the visceral hostility to the public sector that emerges from every speech that the Secretary of State and his hon. Friends make.

**Mr. Gary Streeter** (Plymouth, Sutton): Will the hon. Gentleman gave way?

**Mr. Meacher:** No, I will not.

**Mr. James Clappison** (Hertsmere): Will the hon. Gentleman give way?

**Mr. Meacher:** No, I will not. I want to make a few more arguments in my own speech.

Perhaps the best illustration of the great Mawhinney railway revolution is that it appears that damaged trains are now taken for repair by road. ScotRail, for example, found that it would cost £20,000 to £30,000 per train to take two flood-damaged trains from Glasgow to ABB's Derby workshops by lorry, but that renting a special towing locomotive and paying Railtrack's extra charges for using lines between the Scottish border and the midlands would be as much as 20 per cent. more expensive. I hardly need tell the House that, under the old British Rail network, the cost of moving trains by rail would have been absorbed; it would have been at marginal cost in the system.

When I read that in *The Daily Telegraph*—which of course the Secretary of State was reading on his way to Leeds—I congratulated him on giving a new twist to the privatisation saga. None of us had realised that he meant that, under his privatisation proposals, trains would in future travel by private lorry. Things have descended to that farcical level because the privatisation process is pitted with tensions and inconsistencies that cannot be resolved, and there is no leadership from the centre to stop the rot.

The Secretary of State excels as the weather vane Secretary of State; the invisible man of policy. He is the general who has been put in to sound the retreat—not to create a transport policy, but to withdraw from every trace of it. He is the man who has abandoned the M25 widening, who has dropped motorway tolling and who has rejected congestion pricing, but who has produced nothing recognisable as a roads policy. He is the man who kicked into touch the runway capacity in the south-east report on airport development and who put off action on ferry safety until the next decade.

*[Mr. Meacher]*

The Secretary of State is the man who dropped the reduction in through-ticketing stations like a hot brick when the political row became too great for him. He is the man who was prepared to sell ABB down the river and withdraw from Ministers' repeated commitments to a £500 million modernisation programme for the Kent Coast rail fleet. He is the man who scuppered his predecessors' promises to bring in automatic train protection.

The Secretary of State is the man who, after the then Minister of State, the right hon. Member for Kettering (Mr. Freeman), said in January 1993:

"There must be no hiatus in railway investment during a transition to a franchised railway",

has presided over the deepest and longest investment blight in modern railway history. There was no problem about getting rid of all the embarrassing baggage of Tory transport policy; there was just a vacuum where policy should be.

**Mr. Streeter:** Will the hon. Gentleman give way?

**Mr. Meacher:** I take it that it is about the arguments that I have made.

**Mr. Streeter:** Yes. I am grateful to the hon. Gentleman for giving way. He has now met his sound bite quota for the day in full, but the House really wants to know, would the Labour party renationalise British Rail—yes or no?

**Mr. Henry McLeish** (Fife, Central): The Government have not privatised anything yet.

**Mr. Meacher:** As my hon. Friend says, the first question, which is an interesting one, is whether the Government will succeed in privatising anything. Apart from a ballast quarry in Devon or somewhere, I do not think that they have succeeded in privatising anything so far. For reasons that I shall give later, I would be surprised if they succeeded in privatising more than a small part of the system. If and when they do so, we shall make it clear how we shall deal with it and how we shall return to a publicly owned and accountable rail system.

In all this anxiety to scuttle, the alleged goals of privatisation have all been stampeded under foot. The Secretary of State has often proclaimed that one of the objectives is to reduce public subsidies to the rail system.

**The Secretary of State for Transport (Dr. Brian Mawhinney):** That is not true.

**Mr. Meacher:** I am sure that the right hon. Gentleman is on record as saying that one of the results will be that subsidies will be reduced and that the system will be more dependent on the market. It is now clear, however, that public subsidies will be massively increased. Not only has the public service grant been nearly doubled to £1.7 billion a year to pay for track access charges to Railtrack—money that is intended, as public subsidy, to go eventually to Railtrack shareholders—but a public subsidy of at least £330 million to £500 million a year will have to be paid to private train operators to compensate them for their loss of revenue under the cap and to pay for their profits.

It is becoming clear that, far from the market operating unfettered, privatisation will mean a huge enlargement of public subsidies to private operators in the biggest market-rigging operation in modern rail history. Even that is without the £1.4 billion write-off of Railtrack debts as a sweetener for investors, as has happened with every other privatisation before this one.

**Dr. Mawhinney:** The hon. Gentleman has quoted a number of figures this week. He started out on Monday with £1 billion. He seems to have moved a little since then. For our better understanding, will he explain how he calculated those figures?

**Mr. Meacher:** Perhaps I could do a deal with the Secretary of State. If he will tell me what his figures are, I shall be pleased to tell him how we reach our figures. If that is a deal, let me start by saying that we calculated them on a clear basis. In the past, I think, 10 years, under Government edict revenue to British Rail has increased every year by a figure of between 2 and 3 per cent. above inflation. Train operators will lose that revenue under the rail fares cap. In addition, if they are going to buy those investments, they will expect what perhaps I could delicately call a decent profit. I suspect that the going rate in the City is about 10 to 15 per cent. If one calculates both those figures on the basis of fares revenue across the rail network, there will be a need for a subsidy of between at least £330 million and up to £500 million. Those are tight figures, so there may be a need for more to finance the franchisees if they are to make a bid.

Now that I have clearly told the Secretary of State how we reached those figures—I shall be pleased to set them out mathematically for him if he wishes—perhaps he can now tell us what his figure is for the extra public subsidy that will be required as a result of his policy, announced on Monday, for a rail fares cap. I would be pleased to give way to him. He asked me what my figures were and how they were calculated. I have told him. Perhaps he can now tell the House what his figures are. [HON. MEMBERS: "Come on."] The right hon. Gentleman is remarkably coy. In the past two or three days, I have listened to him around the circuit and this is the first time that he seems to be frightened to jump to his feet. I am doing my best to help him. I shall give him another chance. Does he think that the amount will be more or less than £500 million a year? Will he tell us just that?

I am not sure whether the right hon. Gentleman is glued to his seat, but he seems to be thinking very deeply. The Department of Transport did not have a figure when the policy was announced on Monday and it seems clear from the uncharacteristic silence of the Secretary of State that it still does not have a figure. It seems remarkable that he can announce a policy without having a figure.

We know that the Government were in enormous confusion about the policy because it was due to be announced on Friday. The Secretary of State wanted to exclude supersavers and Apex tickets, but the Prime Minister wanted them all to be included. That is why there was a delay until Monday. It still seems that there is no certainty about what the policy will cost.

I am offering the Secretary of State one last chance to come clean. If I am wrong about how this political hotch-potch was achieved, perhaps he will put me right. His silence is significant.

**Mr. Peter Snape** (West Bromwich, East): To be fair, perhaps my hon. Friend is addressing that question to the wrong person. The intellectual justification for the rail privatisation exercise is being driven by the Secretary of State's parliamentary private secretary, the hon. Member for Hayes and Harlington (Mr. Dicks), who is sitting behind him.

**Mr. Meacher:** If the Secretary of State is the ventriloquist's dummy, it explains his silence.

The Secretary of State's second claim is that, even if the passenger service requirements are 20 to 30 per cent. below the level of current timetables, commercial operators will have a strong incentive to improve on the cutbacks. That is the line that he has taken regularly. It is no wonder that he has been tipped as the next Tory party chairman if, as we saw yesterday, he is prepared to allow major cuts on the London to Peterborough line on the basis of that arrangement. I admire either his folly or his courage—I am not sure which.

The truth is that private operators will have neither the incentive nor the resources to improve on the passenger service requirements allowed them because the fares cap will squeeze their revenues and, as we learnt today, because franchise holders will have to put up 15 per cent. of their expected turnover as a guarantee against financial failure. That will tie up a further £500 million across the network.

Perhaps the best comment on the Secretary of State's fantasy comes from James Sherwood, who has expressed a specific interest in purchasing the franchise for South West Trains. He said:

"There will be no incentive for the franchisee to invest or maintain standards. His only incentive will be to provide the minimum service which the Franchising Director will tolerate and thus squeeze every penny of profit out of a deteriorating asset base."

That is not a comment from the Labour party spokesman. James Sherwood is a hard-nosed operator if ever there was one and it shows what idle fantasy the Secretary of State has been talking.

The Secretary of State's third claim, which he has repeated endlessly in the media in the past couple of days, is that fewer subsidies will be needed because if fares are lowered, more people will travel on the trains. That is wrong on two counts. First, as the Secretary of State must surely know—he must at least have been briefed—the elasticities simply do not work like that. If one knocks a pound off the fare, one gets back only about 60p in the increased number of passengers attracted. The retail prices index minus 1 per cent. formula will lose revenue, not raise it.

Secondly, the right hon. Gentleman has been saying that there is more than enough subsidy in the system already because the Government have substantially increased the public service grant to about £1.7 billion a year. The Secretary of State has not told us that a third of that—about £600 million—has to be repaid each year under the Treasury rules by British Rail and Railtrack as an external financing limit contribution to the Treasury. The remaining £1.1 billion is more than taken up with having to meet track access charges and train-leasing costs, as well as the reimbursement for social lines being

kept open. So there is not enough subsidy in the system already. Indeed, more—I would say a great deal more—will be needed.

The right hon. Gentleman's fourth claim is that, even if the passenger service requirements are lower than the present timetable—and they are by an average of 20 per cent. to 30 per cent., but by up to 50 per cent. on some lines—at least that lower level of service is guaranteed. In an earlier debate, I remember the right hon. Gentleman straying from the main point by reiterating that that guarantee was an innovation, but it is not true.

The Office of Passenger Rail Franchising document entitled "Passenger Service Requirements: An Explanatory Note" states:

"If, at any point in future, the Franchising Director's budget were to be reduced to a level which was not sufficient to meet the support commitments contained within Franchise Agreements, then the Franchising Director would need to use this changed procedure to negotiate new passenger service requirements which reflected the reduced amount of money available to support them."

In other words, far from being guaranteed, those services are distinctly tenuous because they are entirely dependent on the vagaries of Government budgeting. Indeed, there is no absolute guarantee that there will be a train service at all.

My final quotation comes from Sir Bob Reid, the former chairman of British Rail. In a recent interview he said:

"It would be quite possible for the franchise director to ensure that if an operator wanted to close a line, it would have to run buses instead."

That is a pretty interesting observation. It may, I suppose, be incorrect and I should be glad if the Secretary of State could give an assurance that, if a line was closed, the franchising director could not turn it over to a bus service. Most of us had previously considered such a notion impossible.

The problem is not only the somewhat mystical nature—if I can politely call it that—of the right hon. Gentleman's claims or even the way he makes them, but the manner in which he clings to ideas and statements that he knows to be untrue. The whole idea of rail privatisation is now so universally detested across the country that the only way he could think of to give it a facelift was to link it to a cap on fares. However, he knows that the fares cap has nothing whatever to do with the logic of privatisation and everything to do with trying to buy cheap popularity for a failing cause.

The Secretary of State knows perfectly well that it was the Government's policy to allow rail fares to rise by 22 per cent. above inflation in the past 10 years. Indeed, the hypocrisy of the right hon. Gentleman now trying to claim that he believes in low fares is revealed by the way in which the Government moved heaven and earth to break the Greater London council's "Fares Fair" policy, which was based on exactly that principle and by the way in which they destroyed the South Yorkshire passenger transport executive's cheap fare policy in the same period, even threatening the withdrawal of the £8 million transport supplementary grant to force it to give up the subsidy. Only this Secretary of State and his accomplice, the Prime Minister, would have the brass neck to appropriate as a sweetener a subsidy regime that they have spent the past 10 years contemptuously and vigorously repudiating.

*[Mr. Meacher]*

Finally, it is touching, even if also rather pathetic, that the right hon. Gentleman continues to cling to the notion that he will privatise 51 per cent. of the train-operating companies and Railtrack by April next year. It is now clear beyond doubt that he cannot and will not, and that the flagship target of rail privatisation is doomed. I say that for the following reasons. Final bids for the first three lines, accounting for some 20 per cent. of turnover, will not be in until the autumn and even an accelerated assessment period will certainly take until January or February next year at the earliest. Bids for the next four lines, accounting for another 25 per cent., will be at least two months behind. That is the quickest that it could be done. The right hon. Gentleman cannot pass the 51 per cent. target within that time limit, and all hope of doing so—I have to tell him and he must know himself—has disappeared.

Earlier talk by the Secretary of State of letting a contract for design and build in mid-1995 for the west coast main line has now vanished and Railtrack has shifted its interest into a new signalling and train control centre instead. Who will really want to buy into Railtrack if at least a majority of private train operators are not in place? It will be extremely difficult to achieve the flotation of Railtrack by that date. Indeed, I believe that it is clear that it is now impossible.

**Mr. Eric Martlew** (Carlisle): With regard to the west coast main line, is my hon. Friend aware that yesterday the Office of Passenger Rail Franchising released statistics on the subsidies to be given to sleeper services? I understand that the situation concerning Fort William is sub judice, so I shall not comment on it. The subsidy for Edinburgh is £79 per passenger, for Aberdeen it is £69 and for Inverness it is £140. I agree with those subsidies and I am pleased that those services will continue. But the subsidy for Carlisle is only £38. Is it right that ScotRail has been vindictively—

**Mr. Deputy Speaker (Mr. Geoffrey Lofthouse):** Order. The hon. Member knows full well that interventions have to be brief and to the point. That was a mini-speech.

**Mr. Meacher:** My hon. Friend makes a very clear point, which the Secretary of State should consider. I hope that either the right hon. Gentleman or the Minister who makes the winding-up speech will answer that question seriously. We are very concerned, not only about the impact of the decision in the Scottish courts, but because a number of other sleeper services, which we are determined should continue, have been allocated lower rates of subsidy.

With the collapse of the April 1996 deadline, the privatisation project is in very deep trouble. Despite bribes to senior management, there is almost nobody who now believes that privatisation is either desirable or practicable. Already 88 per cent. of the electorate are against it, which leaves even a majority of Conservatives opposed to it and only, I suppose, hard-core Thatcherites still in favour. The Secretary of State—I give him credit for this—has had the courage to drop every other millstone of the Government's transport policy. It is now time that he drops this one.

4.22 pm

**The Secretary of State for Transport (Dr. Brian Mawhinney):** I beg to move, to leave out from "House" to the end of the Question and to add instead thereof:

"applauds the record levels of investment in the railways in recent years, including more than £6 billion over the last five years; notes that since nationalisation, despite investment of more than £54 billion in the railways, the proportion of travel undertaken by train has steadily decreased; believes that the railways will be better placed to offer an improved service in the private sector; welcomes recent announcements by the Franchising Director, which represent significant milestones on the path to a privatised railway; supports the new rail fares regime, which will see ticket prices regulated on every line in the country and will produce real fare reductions; believes that the Franchising Director's announcement struck a proper balance between the interests of the passenger and train operators; and condemns the continued failure of Her Majesty's Opposition to offer any policy to stem the relative decline in railway use.".

I listened to the hon. Member for Oldham, West (Mr. Meacher) with interest. This is the third debate in our series and so far the Labour party is batting two-nil down. I must tell the hon. Gentleman that, having listened to his speech, the Labour party is going to be three-nil down.

The hon. Member for Oldham, West made a number of comments, accusations, allegations and predictions, so I must start by testing their credibility. It seemed that the best way to do so would be to examine his track record—if the House will forgive the expression—thus far. I looked back at our debate in January, when the hon. Gentleman had the following to say about through ticketing:

"The thrust of the document"—

the regulator's document—

"is about eroding the number of through-ticketing stations and the only argument is about how far and how fast that can be achieved. The document is consultative in name only."—[*Official Report*, 18 January 1995; Vol. 252, c. 716-17.]

I stood at the Dispatch Box and sought to persuade the hon. Gentleman that it was a consultation document. I told him that there were three options and I reaffirmed Ministers' commitment to through ticketing, but he would have none of it.

What happened? As of today, 1,300 stations will operate through ticketing. Why? Because the document was consultative and out of three options that was exactly what the public said they wanted. We heard a declaration—indeed, a declamation—from the hon. Gentleman that proved to be nonsense.

Let us see what the hon. Gentleman said about investment. In the second debate in our series, on 7 February, he said:

"I have repeatedly made it clear that we believe in increased investment in the rail infrastructure by comparison with that of the present Government."—[*Official Report*, 7 February 1995; Vol. 254, c. 203.]

He said much the same today.

That made me wonder. It sounds terribly like a Labour party spending commitment, and we all know how hard it is to get one of those. I referred back to find out what Labour had spent in office to compare it with what we have spent, in order to determine what the hon. Member for Oldham, West was telling us in those elliptical terms. I discovered that, at constant prices, the Labour Government spent on average £926 million a year on British Rail. We have averaged just over £1 billion a year, so we now have the first firm Labour party spending commitment for the next general election. A Labour Government will invest a minimum of £80 million a year more—and they will not get away with that, because the hon. Gentleman's high-flown rhetoric will drive the figure up even further.

Sir Bob Reid said that we needed to spend £1 billion on the railways this year. The hon. Member for Oldham, West will be encouraged to know that this year's figure for investment in British Rail is £1 billion. He will also be interested to know that Sir Bob Reid and Bob Horton have said that the railways have enough money this year to run as they should. I hope that he is encouraged by that too.

**Sir Russell Johnston** (Inverness, Nairn and Lochaber): Surely if we are talking about comparative investment figures, the basic comparison should be between what we have spent in this country and what has been spent in France and Germany. Between 1980 and 1989, Germany spent £14 billion and France £10 billion: this country spent £3 billion.

**Dr. Mawhinney:** If the hon. Gentleman does not like the Labour Front-Bench spokesman's argument, he must take that up with him. The hon. Member for Oldham, West compared investment in this country, so I responded to that. The House knows that, given the sniff of a vote anywhere, Liberal Democrats will promise another penny on income tax to try to meet the cost of the commitment, so I shall try to do some calculations for the hon. Gentleman and find out how much expenditure his intervention has committed the Liberal Democrat party to.

The third part of the credibility test for the hon. Member for Oldham, West concerns potential operators. He showed a touching concern for the private sector, which I welcome. In our debate on 18 January, he said:

"The fact is that there is such investor apathy about the sales that minimising the conditions that franchisees must meet . . . is a vital part of the exercise, and the interests of the passengers come absolutely nowhere".—[*Official Report*, 18 January 1995; Vol. 252, c. 722.]

We have heard from potential bidders this week— people who have identified themselves as potential bidders, although for reasons of confidentiality I shall neither confirm nor deny the details. The hon. Member for Oldham, West will understand that. Talking of the fares announcement on Monday, Mr. Watt of British Bus said:

"It's still very early days, we're assessing the bids or assessing the information that the Government are providing, and this is simply another parameter that comes into the whole bidding process".

James Sherwood said:

"I don't think they're sending any message at all to the franchisees, I think they're trying to comfort the general public who is worried that the privatisation process is going to result in fares increasing by more than inflation. So . . . this is not a problem for the franchisees. I assure you that fares will not go up in any event, even if there was no cap, by more than inflation".

Ken Irvine, from Prism development, said:

"There are areas where we think we can make our profits through improved efficiency, through new ideas in terms of the operations, and improving the marketing and quality of service to the customer."

A British Rail manager with an interest in a management buy-out said:

"It's fantastic at last to have a policy which will actually encourage more people on to trains at peak times."

The House must decide whether it believes the hon. Member for Oldham, West—whose credibility decreases when we examine what he has said in previous debates— or those who have identified themselves as potential bidders. In my mind, there is no question but that the bidders know what they are talking about, and the hon. Gentleman can take that any way he wishes.

**Mr. Meacher:** If the right hon. Gentleman was so satisfied with the responses to his invitation to tender, why did he extend the pre-qualification registration period for the first three franchises by another month, and for the next five by another three months? Why was he so concerned during his recent visits to Japan for four days and to Korea for four days with trying to drum up interest in far eastern train operators buying into this country's rail system?

**Dr. Mawhinney:** I understand the hon. Gentleman's embarrassment, and the House sympathises with him. He is free-floating. One day he tells us that nobody will be interested in purchasing the franchises, but the next he is told that 37 companies have expressed an interest and that there have been more than 160 expressions of interest in the first eight franchises. He does not want this to succeed, and we all understand that, but a smidgen of intellectual rigour in his argument would impress the House a good deal more.

The hon. Member for Oldham, West issued a press release last Friday that was wisely ignored by the media. Let me give his press release a little airing on his behalf— I am always happy to help the hon. Gentleman. It said that I was to cap only standard fares and season tickets: wrong. He added "or all fares" just to be on the safe side: wrong. It continued:

"In fact it is a disaster . . . it makes the sale of most franchises difficult—if not impossible":

wrong, as we have heard from four self-styled potential bidders.

"The fares announcement will mean cuts in investment":

wrong. It went on:

"The Government's entire privatisation programme is now threatened":

wrong. It is so threatened that today the invitations to tender for the first three franchises went out. My goodness, it feels like a very threatened privatisation.

To help the public deal with their confusion, the hon. Gentleman told "Today" on Monday that if we capped the revenue of operators

"and therefore their profits, frankly I think this is the last straw, so the Government will be forced to provide a huge subsidy paid for by the taxpayer".

That is a large last straw. It is interesting—[*Interruption.*] Opposition Members must allow me to make my speech in my way, as my colleagues and I allowed the hon. Member for Oldham, West to make his speech in his way.

It is interesting that an arch advocate of what is gently referred to as "towards the left" of the Labour party suddenly wants to appear in the eyes of the great British public as being concerned about profits for private operators. A few weeks ago, the hon. Member for Oldham, West was saying that there were not going to be any profits. That was why there would be no bidders. It is a slide across credibility that defies analysis, much less acceptability. Or perhaps it is a reflection of the greatest economic miracle that this country has ever seen. For the

*[Dr. Mawhinney]*

Labour party to move, in the space of two or three weeks, from no profits to profits so high that it wants to cap them would make the mind of the Chancellor of the Exchequer boggle.

On subsidy—

**Several hon. Members** *rose*—

**Dr. Mawhinney:** The hon. Member for Oldham, West has encouraged me to talk about subsidy, so I shall do so.

The first point to make about subsidy is that if the hon. Member for Oldham, West goes back to the White Paper, all the debates on the Bill and all the comments afterwards he will see that everyone recognised that there had to be a continuing subsidy from the taxpayer. As he has reminded me on other occasions, that is true of every railway in the world, and it is true of ours too. If we have no subsidies, we cannot protect services, particularly those on commercially non-viable lines that are deemed to be important. On that point, we have a degree of commonality. The railway was restructured so that there would be one point of entry for subsidy: the franchising director.

Let me explain again to the hon. Gentleman that, in essence, we are franchising against a criterion of information about what subsidy people will need to run various franchises. It is not possible, therefore, to predict, as we sit here today, the level of subsidy.

**Mr. Meacher:** Why not?

**Dr. Mawhinney:** I shall tell the hon. Gentleman why not. First, we have a competitive bidding process and even the hon. Gentleman, with his tenuous grasp of the market, will understand that its effect will be to reduce rather than increase bids. Secondly—I would not expect the hon. Gentleman to understand this point—the difference between what is happening now and what will happen in the future is that we are restructuring the railway to generate efficiencies by moving from the public sector to the private sector—efficiencies that have characterised every previous privatisation. I would go even further and say that the efficiencies that have emerged following previous privatisations have been greater than many people predicted at the time of privatisation.

The hon. Gentleman needs to understand—forgive me, he does not need to as he has managed to get thus far without understanding—

**Mr. McLeish:** That is patronising.

**Dr. Mawhinney:** The hon. Gentleman is right. It sounded patronising and, whatever else I may do, I do not wish to sound patronising.

I hope that the hon. Member for Oldham, West accepts that a fundamental change is in the offing for the railways, from which benefits will flow. Unlike the hon. Gentleman, I believe that the benefits should be shared between passengers and private sector train operators. I should have thought that that would be common ground between us but, having listened to him over the past few weeks, I am no longer sure that it is.

**Mr. Meacher:** The Minister has made an important statement. He said that it is not possible to predict the subsidy that will be required for private operators. From

some experience of government, I believe that the Treasury would never permit such a policy to be adopted and announced without putting at least a rough estimate on what would be permitted. The Treasury would certainly never offer an open cheque book. Within what parameters does the Minister expect that subsidy to settle?

**Dr. Mawhinney:** The parameters are those that have been laid down on many occasions.

I remind the hon. Gentleman of what I said on Monday:

"The Government remains firmly committed to the franchising process and to providing the subsidy needed to support passenger railway services, including the effects of the new policy on fares."

I am not at all clear whether the Labour party has switched from its demand that more and more taxpayers' money should be spent and now believes that less and less of their money should be spent. We are talking about a franchising, competitive bidding process, initiated today for the first three franchises. We will have to see what emerges, but I remain a good deal more sanguine than the hon. Member for Oldham, West.

**Mr. Bruce Grocott** (The Wrekin): The right hon. Gentleman has said a great deal about intellectual rigour in his usual helpful manner. May we ask for just a little bit more of that from him? We are not asking for the parameters. Given his academic skills, the vast resources available to him at the Department of Transport and all the computers through which he can run the figures, will he please tell us the figures on which he has made his calculations about the subsidy that will be needed?

**Dr. Mawhinney:** I have not told the House that I have made any calculations. I have told the House about the bidding process. I have encouraged the House by quoting the potential operators, who understand, because they are in the marketplace, that the certainty of a seven-year fares regime, which most of them were not expecting, will allow them to make judgments about fares in the commercial framework. That certainty will enable them to appreciate the opportunities open to them in the fares structure and the provision of services structure to attract more people on to the railways. The opportunity to make such judgments will emerge from the efficiencies that will be generated by moving from the public to the private sector—something with which the Labour party has not even come to terms.

Let us consider the credibility test of the hon. Member for Oldham, West. On Monday, Sue MacGregor asked him:

"But what do you plan to do about fares?"

He replied:

"Well on fares, as I said, we have a very different philosophy. What the Government have done is to put their money into road building and cars, it has produced congestion and pollution. I think a much better alternative is to switch money steadily in the transport budget out of road building into investment in both the quality and the quantity of public transport."

Sue MacGregor again asked him what he intended to do about fares and he said:

"That would certainly enable us to reduce, or certainly to hold fares, and hopefully to reduce fares steadily in off-peak hours, and I think that is a way of restoring patronage in public transport, but the really key point is, the difference between us and the Government, is that it would not be necessary in our case to have huge swingeing increases in taxpayers subsidies to pay for it."

If I am clear, the hon. Gentleman is saying that the Opposition will decimate the roads budget and put it into the railways. The end result will be

"to hold fares, and hopefully to reduce fares steadily in off-peak hours".

**Mr. Michael Trend** (Windsor and Maidenhead): We have done better than that.

**Dr. Mawhinney:** My hon. Friend is far too generous to the Opposition—we have done much better than that. The people will understand that. What about the credibility test on punctuality and reliability? The hon. Member for Oldham, West made much of that, but against the doom and gloom he offered to the House, he will be encouraged to know that in the first period of 1995-96 performance not only increased, but 88 per cent. of the passenger charter measurements were above the annual average.

Let us consider the credibility of the Opposition Front-Bench team. The hon. Member for Fife, Central (Mr. McLeish)—

**Mr. Snape:** Talk about the railways.

**Dr. Mawhinney:** I know that the hon. Gentleman does not like it, but if anyone was tempted to take seriously the contents of the speech of the hon. Member for Oldham, West, we need to know how much confidence we have can in them.

The hon. Member for Fife, Central also issued a press release on Wednesday. The press ignored it, as they did the one issued on Friday by the hon. Member for Oldham, West. I should like to be helpful to the hon. Member for Fife, Central by referring to it. In it, he said that the new fares structure was aimed at

"protecting politically sensitive areas but exposing the majority of travellers to potentially unlimited fare rises."

That was wrong. It also stated that the announcement of

"Tendering arrangements for the first three franchises to be privatised"

had been "postponed indefinitely". That was on Wednesday; the arrangements have now been made public. According to the press release, the announcement of the new fare structure had been "postponed indefinitely"; it went out on Monday. Last Wednesday, the setting of minimum service standards for four further lines was "postponed indefinitely". That information went out on Tuesday.

I understand the embarrassment of the hon. Member for Fife, Central, but the country needs to know what he wanted it to know last Wednesday. Last Wednesday, he wanted the country to know that the establishment of a fares regime had been postponed indefinitely; the information went out on Monday. Service requirements for the next four franchises had also been postponed indefinitely; the information went out on Tuesday. Tendering for the first three franchises had been postponed indefinitely; that went out on Wednesday. Such is the credibility that we now attach to the utterances of Opposition Front Benchers.

Let me remind the House of the process in which we are engaged. I shall begin by setting down some common ground. In 1953, 17 per cent. of journeys in this country were made by train; today the figure is 5 per cent., and falling. In 1953, 24 per cent. of goods were transported by train; today the figure is 5 per cent., and falling.

Conservative Members, at least—and I shall go so far as to say that I believe that the hon. Member for Oldham, West agrees—want that relative decline to be halted, and then reversed. There is only one argument to address: can that be done in the public sector alone? The answer is clear; it is—after 40 years of relative decline—no.

**Mr. Alex Salmond** (Banff and Buchan): Will the Secretary of State give way?

**Dr. Mawhinney:** No.

Let us consider past privatisations. The injection of private finance and investment decisions, private management skills and private sector sensitivity to customer needs has transformed those businesses and industries, to the benefit of their customers. No one, least of all Opposition Front Benchers, has produced any argument to suggest that rail privatisation differs fundamentally and qualitatively from other privatisations.

**Mr. Hugh Bayley** (York): Will the Secretary of State give way?

**Dr. Mawhinney:** No, I must make progress.

We are told that, if we had to privatise, we did so in the wrong way. European Commission railways policy, in directive 91/440, supports the division of railway business into more commercially oriented infrastructure companies, and separate passenger and freight service operations. That is exactly what we are doing. What is happening in Europe today? The German Government have split the operation of track infrastructure from passenger and freight services by establishing separate profit centres. The Dutch railway is to be split into four independent businesses covering passenger services, freight, infrastructure and capacity management. The Austrian railways were restructured in 1994 to separate infrastructure and train operations, and to make the full cost of operation transparent. The Danish railway has been organised into infrastructure, passenger and freight companies.

In other words, we are genuinely leading the world in separating infrastructure from the provision of services, and recognising the benefits that the passenger can gain from the injection of private sector finance. Labour's problem—clause IV or no clause IV—is that it is rooted in the demonology of trade unions circa 1960. I must tell the hon. Member for Oldham, West that there is no question of an erosion of services; quite the opposite.

My hon. Friends noticed, as I did, that the hon. Gentleman did not offer any alternatives. I need to say a quick word or two about that before I conclude. The country has a right to know what those who purport to be the next Government would do to the railways. I do not want to embarrass the hon. Member for Oldham, West; I want to look at the party's leadership. What does its leader say? He comes to the House on Tuesdays and Thursdays and says that he leads his party. Let us see what he says.

In October 1994 he said:

"Railways should stay in public ownership."

But in January 1995 he said:

"I'm not going to get into a situation where I am declaiming that the Labour Government is going to commit sums of money to renationalisation."

[*Dr. Mawhinney*]

But also in January 1995, through his spokesman Alastair Campbell, he said:

"If the railways are privatised . . . we have plans that under a Labour Government the railways will be publicly owned, publicly run railways."

[HON. MEMBERS: "Hear, hear."] I hope that *Hansard* will record growls of approval from the Opposition Front Bench.

In March 1995 the right hon. Member for Sedgefield (Mr. Blair) said:

"Our goal is clear. It is to ensure that we continue to have a publicly owned, publicly accountable, properly planned network. Nothing else will do."

I was getting confused, as are my hon. Friends. The policies are here today, gone tomorrow. I wrote to the right hon. Gentleman on 3 May. I said:

"I wrote to you on 13 January asking six questions about Labour's policy for the railways. You did not reply."

He did not even have the courtesy to acknowledge my letter. I continued:

"I assumed that this was because you were unable to answer the questions before the outcome of Labour's debate on Clause 4. Now that your Party has expressed a definitive view on state ownership, I am writing to ask for answers to my questions. I asked you:

Do you intend to renationalise the railways?

If you do, would compensation be paid to the shareholders of Railtrack?

Precisely how would passenger services be brought back under state control, bearing in mind the legal franchises and contracts which will govern the use of the railways?

If you do not plan to renationalise, what changes would you make to the way the railways are run?

How would you fulfil Labour's commitment to encourage more passengers and freight onto the railways?

Would you invest more in the railways and, if so, how much?"

I must amend that now to ask how much more it would be than the £80 million a year to which the hon. Member for Oldham, West has just committed his party.

My letter continued:

"Your campaign against railway privatisation will continue to lack credibility until you tell the British people what plans you have for the railways. I look forward to receiving your response."

I put those questions to the hon. Member for Oldham, West in the first of our series of debates when the Labour party went one-nil down. After the second debate, the Labour party was two-nil down and after today it will be three-nil down. I was generous to the hon. Gentleman, as I invited him six times to attempt to answer even one elementary question about what might fleetingly be referred to as a smidgen of Labour party policy on the railways. The result was: nada, nothing, just a great big black hole.

I received no reply from the right hon. Member for Sedgefield in January, February, March or April. I wrote to him again in May and have received no reply thus far. I promise that I shall keep the House informed of the progress of the non-correspondence.

Today we have listened with interest to what the hon. Member for Oldham, West has had to say. Leadership—what leadership? Policy—what policy? Vision—what vision? As I sit here each time, I try to think who it is that the hon. Gentleman reminds me of. The last time he reminded me of one of those old-fashioned railway announcers who make plenty of noise but who do not say anything intelligible. Today he reminded me of Violet Elizabeth Bott, Just William's friend. When she had nothing constructive to contribute and when she did not get her own way, she would say, "I'll thcweam and I'll thcweam and I'll thcweam." We have been entertained today by the hon. Gentleman's thcweam. That sums up the Labour party's policy on rail privatisation: a frustrated thcweam. I suggest that Labour Members continue to thcweam and we will deliver the benefits that the rail passengers of this country are crying out for and will receive.

4.55 pm

**Mr. Peter Snape** (West Bromwich, East): That was not so much a speech by the Secretary of State as an audition for a new job. It was the most deplorable speech that I have heard him deliver in the House. Having heard it, I shall proffer some advice to the Conservative party as a disinterested observer. The Conservatives would be better off sticking with the incompetence of the incumbent rather than putting up with that sort of behaviour. The Secretary of State did not mention the railway's present or future state; he simply made a series of cheap jibes reminiscent of a sixth form public school debate which were unworthy of a proper debate about the future of the railway industry. The Secretary of State should be ashamed of himself.

The state of our railway industry concerns many who have worked in that industry, and I must declare a passing interest as a member of the National Union of Rail, Maritime and Transport Workers. It also concerns those who rely on the railway industry for transportation of themselves or their goods and those who supply the industry with wagons, rolling stock and signalling equipment. It is interesting to see what those people have to say about privatisation. When the Bill to privatise the industry was first published, the Railway Industry Association made a submission to the Select Committee on Transport, in which it said:

"The impact of rail privatisation, arriving during the continuing severe recession and at a point when order books are at an all-time low, poses a frightening risk to the railway supply industry. The fundamental danger is that the vital need for continuing investment—in both rolling stock and track signalling and electrification infrastructure—will be lost amid continuing political debate and organisational uncertainties about the new railway administrative structures and the passage of the Rail Privatisation Bill."

The Railway Industry Association recently submitted another paper to the same Committee, with the benefit of a year's experience of what has taken place since the passage of the Bill. It said:

"Despite repeated past ministerial assurances that our anxiety over privatisation causing a hiatus in investment was unfounded, the opposite now seems to be accepted as inevitable, almost as policy in some quarters. With all its faults, the pre-privatisation process of public funding for railway investment gave both the operational railway and the supply industry some basis on which to plan production and investment strategy".

That is what the Railway Industry Association is now saying about privatisation, yet the Secretary of State did not refer to the plight of that industry or that of railway administration. In his hackneyed collection of cliches, he referred to the efficiency of moving from the public sector to the private sector. It is interesting to examine what has happened since track and infrastructure were separated from the main railway business when Railtrack was created.

In its recent evidence to the Transport Select Committee examining railway finances, the Passenger Transport Executive Group listed examples of cost increases which have occurred since the supposedly wonderfully efficient system was introduced, particularly since Railtrack assumed responsibility for infrastructure projects in April last year.

Centro, the passenger transport authority covering my area, pointed out that Railtrack's site supervision and possession costs amount to 48 per cent. of the contract cost at Five Ways station just outside Birmingham, compared with BR's figure of 21 per cent. at University station or 27 per cent. at Longbridge. Is that the promised land?

In Greater Manchester, electrification from Castlefield to Salford Crescent was originally estimated by BR at £2 million; Railtrack now estimates the cost at between £4.2 million and £5.8 million. Is that the promised land?

In Merseyside, erection of a waiting shelter at Waterloo on the Southport line, to keep the rain off the passengers or customers, originally attracted no design costs because it would have been done in-house by BR. Railtrack's design estimate for a waiting shelter is £53,000.

The original InterCity 250 project in 1990 for the west coast main line was estimated to cost £750 million to provide new trains for the route and to carry out track alterations, including speed improvements and resignalling south of Weaver Junction. The current project is estimated at £1 billion for the entire route to Glasgow, but that figure excludes rolling stock and cab signalling equipment on trains.

Recently, I accompanied a delegation to see the Minister of State about the west coast main line. It did not get very far because he did not give the impression of having much idea about what we were talking about or when the scheme would commence.

**Mr. Nigel Evans** (Ribble Valley): On a point of order, Mr. Deputy Speaker. Considering what has occurred in the House in the past few weeks, would it not be appropriate if hon. Members who had something to declare did so at the beginning of their speeches? I notice that the hon. Member for West Bromwich, East (Mr. Snape) has listed in the Register of Members' Interests that he has remunerated directorships of West Midland Travel plc, Stage Carriage and Express Coach Services and Travel Agency.

**Mr. Deputy Speaker:** All right hon. and hon. Members know, or should know, the rules with regard to Members' interests. It is a matter for individual hon. Members.

**Mr. Snape:** In reply to that pretty cheap jibe, I declared an interest as a member of the RMT. The debate is about railways, so I do not see what relevance a directorship of a stage carriage bus service in Birmingham has to the debate.

**Mr. Evans:** A lot.

**Mr. Snape:** The hon. Gentleman says, "A lot"— *[Interruption.]*

**Mr. Deputy Speaker:** Order. Will hon. Members quieten down and get on with the debate?

**Mr. Snape:** By the pretty loose standards of the Conservative party, it probably is a lot.

I was talking about the attitude of the Minister of State towards a particular project on the west coast main line. When I pointed out that the £1 billion to which I referred did not include a sum for locomotives and rolling stock, he gave us the impression that they were not necessary. I pointed out then, and I do so again now, that, if the project gets off the ground, it makes no sense to install a brand new cab signalling system in 25-year-old electric locomotives. I presume that modernising the west coast main line could, would or should include the provision of new rolling stock and locomotives.

The hiatus to which the Railway Industry Association referred, and to which I referred earlier, is occurring right now. There is a continual decline in the standard of service being provided by what is still known as British Rail, and no conceivable sign, particularly in respect of equipment and resignalling, of the much vaunted private finance initiative doing anything about it.

My hon. Friend the Member for Oldham, West (Mr. Meacher) detailed the collapse in investment in railway expenditure. Excluding channel tunnel expenditure, the Secretary of State is halving the money available for expenditure on the railway industry in the next couple of financial years. He shakes his head, but the figures are there. His own Department gave them recently to the Transport Select Committee. The total rail expenditure in 1994-95 of £1.1 billion includes an estimate of at least half that towards the channel tunnel and the remaining £615 million, which is my personal estimate of what will remain, represents almost a halving of the money available.

The Secretary of State's much vaunted policy announcements about reversing the drift of passengers and freight from rail to road will not be enhanced given those figures. Although he seemed tentatively to go back on that pledge in a television interview last Sunday, presumably it still stands.

Both sides of the House accept that Ministers did not actually intend the hiatus in railway investment to which I referred when plans for privatisation were formulated, but it is about time they accepted that it is happening. If my hon. Friend the Member for York (Mr. Bayley) catches your eye, Mr. Deputy Speaker, I am sure he will refer to that hiatus in respect of his constituency and the future of ABB Transportation.

Restructuring the industry and uncertainties over future funding resulted in fewer infrastructure projects being developed and fewer started. In 1990, 10 resignalling schemes were brought before Ministers for approval. In the current year, there is one. As far as I am aware, none is scheduled for next year.

*[Mr. Snape]*

The Secretary of State presumably travels by train. Why does he not take a cab ride from Euston up the west coast main line? With the exception of new power signalling installation at Crewe, he will find a mixture of 1960s power boxes, early BR equipment and some London, Midland and Scottish equipment. If he passes through my home town of Stockport—I invite him to do so when he comes to see his constituency football team— he will see a series of Victorian signal boxes that were erected in the 1880s. There is no lack of signalling projects on which money should be spent, but money is not being spent. Far from those projects being considered for future investment, they appear to have disappeared completely.

I referred earlier to the private finance initiative, which failed to deliver any new projects apart from the Northern line rolling stock deal. The Heathrow express and the Networker leasing deal were set up before PFI was established under Sir Alastair Morton. Decisions have yet to be made on the channel tunnel rail link, west coast main line, crossrail or Thameslink. All that work is crying out for decisions and investment, but there is no sign of the go-ahead from the Department. Within the restructured industry, there is no strategy or focus for planning that embraces track, trains and stations and Railtrack has still to publish its 10-year plan.

The whole chapter of railway privatisation has been a disaster. It will take more than blustering from the Secretary of State to convince us differently and it is about time that the Government recognise that the project will not work and drop the whole silly idea.

5.6 pm

**Dr. Robert Spink** (Castle Point): I wish to speak in support of the amendment in the name of my right hon. Friend the Prime Minister and I shall immediately inform the House why.

Rail was first nationalised in 1948. I remember it extremely well because it was the year in which I was born. Since that time, some £54 billion of public money has been invested in the rail service.

We should examine the impact of nationalisation and that £54 billion investment. The story is not at all good. The Opposition are in error in painting a picture of the golden heyday of a nationalised British Rail service. No such time existed.

Rail did not flourish or prosper—quite the contrary. Services were awful. They were unreliable. Management was pitiful and customer care was non-existent. The railways were run for the benefit of the unions and the workers, rather than for the benefit of the public.

**Mr. McLeish:** Was the hon. Gentleman's speech written by Conservative central office, or does he have his own views?

**Dr. Spink:** The hon. Gentleman will be pleased to learn that I have sat here and written a few notes simply to remind me when I was born and what has happened to British Rail since then. Central office did not provide me

with any information whatsoever. I was not even planning to speak until I heard the disgraceful comments from the Labour Front Bench.

**Mr. Jacques Arnold** (Gravesham): Does my hon. Friend not find it rather odd for a Labour Front-Bench spokesman to suggest that my hon. Friend is using notes from Conservative central office, when all his information was collated by the research assistants and goodness knows what else in Walworth road which exist to support a Front Bencher? It comes ill from the hon. Gentleman on the Front Bench, who uses other people's notes, to make such a comment about a well-informed Back Bencher.

**Dr. Spink:** We have already heard that the hon. Member for West Bromwich, East (Mr. Snape) is sponsored by one of the rail unions. The hon. Member for York (Mr. Bayley) is also sponsored by a rail union. The hon. Member for Hampstead and Highgate (Ms Jackson), who is hoping to speak—

**Mr. Deputy Speaker:** Order. This is all very well and interesting, but let us get on with some responsible debate, please.

**Dr. Spink:** I take your advice, of course, Mr. Deputy Speaker.

The result of the nationalisation of rail services since 1948 and the investment in them of public money has been a deplorable fall-off in the share of journeys on rail. In 1953, rail had 17 per cent. of all journeys. Today, that figure stands at a miserable 5 per cent. Clearly, the Government had to act to reverse that trend and to redress the situation.

I suspect that the Opposition will continue to call for more public investment to subsidise rail. I shall come to that later; first, I want to put the record straight on recent capital investment, which has been at record levels in recent years—£6 billion during the past five years. I congratulate the Government on that achievement. They have done extremely well by my rail service, to which I shall also come in a moment.

The investment of more and more public money has not resolved, and could not resolve in the future, the difficulties, and deliver the improving standards, reliability in service and increase in passenger numbers that are so much needed and that would lead to a better and more vibrant rail service at lower cost to the public purse.

I want today to concentrate on the line that serves the majority of my constituents—the London-Tilbury-Southend line or the Fenchurch Street line. The majority of people who travel on that line use Benfleet station. The LTS line will, I suspect, be a microcosm of what will happen throughout British Rail as a result of the Government's initiatives. I welcome the excellent recent news for rail travellers.

The scene is now set, certainly in Castle Point, for a dramatic increase in passengers travelling on the Fenchurch Street line in coming years. I hope that we can climb back from the current level of passengers on the line, at about 22,500 passengers a day, and beat the peak number of passengers, which was more than 30,000. I hope that, by the millennium, we can reach a level of 35,000 to 40,000 passengers a day travelling on the Fenchurch Street line.

Let me say how we can achieve that. Passengers will be attracted by a range of factors. The most important of those is the real terms reduction in fares that can now be expected as a result of the Government's excellent strategy to hold fares at the level of inflation for three years and then to reduce fares below the retail prices index by 1 per cent. during the following four years, which should lead to a 4 per cent. overall reduction in fares in real terms by the year 2003. *[Interruption.]* That is not laughed at by my constituents as it is by Opposition Members. It is important to my constituents because they need to plan ahead. They need to decide how they will travel up to London, to the City or docklands, in order to work.

In addition, during the past two years there has been a continued improvement in service reliability. That is remarkable, particularly when one takes into account changes on those lines. Omelettes cannot be made without cracking eggs and the line has suffered disruption as a result of an important resignalling investment. Despite such disruption, dramatic improvements have been achieved on the line.

The Government have invested £150 million in the resignalling project, which started about 15 months ago and is now almost complete. It is delivering the goods. It will improve reliability tremendously. I am delighted to see the hon. Member for Fife, Central (Mr. McLeish) nodding in agreement. Why then did the hon. Member for Oldham, West (Mr. Meacher) not allow me to intervene when he said that investment in resignalling has been cut by two thirds? He did not because he is running scared of his own false information.

That is not the only improvement on the Fenchurch Street line. In about a year's time, we will have 25, 317 sliding-door trains to replace the 35-year-old slam-door trains. That will deliver further improvements in rolling stock. All those factors will help to bring people back on to the line.

**Sir Michael Grylls** (Surrey, North-West): I am following my hon. Friend with great care and I am sure that he is right to say that privatisation, if it works properly, will attract more passengers on to the railways. Whatever our political point of view in the House, with the crowded roads and everything else, it must be everyone's wish to see more passengers on the railways. There is a huge incentive in privatisation for businesses to grow by attracting more passengers and by providing a better and better service. It is a classic service industry that needs to be in the private sector. It is amazing that the Opposition have not learnt that.

**Dr. Spink:** I am indebted to my hon. Friend who speaks with his characteristic wisdom on the matter. I shall come to the direct impact of privatisation and the new management and worker culture that that will bring with it, and the positive impact of that on customer care, service levels and innovation, providing, for example, new off-peak services which will also help to get passenger numbers up.

I introduced the subject by discussing the investment that my line has seen as a result of sound Government policy in this area. My hon. Friend the Member for Basildon (Mr. Amess) has been one of the prime movers who have pushed for investment in the line. He takes a great interest in what will happen in the franchise deal. I know that he continues to see Ministers. I believe that he saw a Minister last night on the subject to press the case of his constituents in Basildon. He is an assiduous worker for his constituents, as we all know.

**Mr. Nigel Evans:** Does my hon. Friend find it somewhat bizarre that this is an Opposition day debate on the privatisation of the railways, yet only five Opposition Back Benchers are present and all of them are sponsored by the Transport and General Workers Union, the National Union of Rail, Maritime and Transport Workers or the Associated Society of Locomotive Engineers and Firemen? Where are all the others if they are so concerned about the railways?

**Mr. Deputy Speaker:** Order. I have already pointed out the limited time available. Seven hon. Members hope to catch my eye in the next hour and interventions of that nature do not help.

**Dr. Spink:** In that case, Mr. Deputy Speaker, I shall chug along.

Through ticketing is now offered by hundreds of stations, one of which is Benfleet in my constituency, the station which serves the greatest number of passengers who use that line. My constituents welcome that and are grateful to the Secretary of State.

We all read what the franchising director, Roger Salmon, said yesterday about passenger service requirements. Private operators, including those on the LTS line, will run more trains. We can look forward to innovative off-peak developments which will boost passenger numbers after line privatisation. I hope that the LTS line capacity will be increased by 13 per cent., as foreshadowed by the passenger service requirements announcement yesterday. That is good news for the people of Essex.

All that will lead to more passengers. More passengers will lead, naturally, to lower subsidies and less demand on the public purse. An increase in passengers will take vehicles off the road, which will help us environmentally and economically. Therefore, I very much welcome all those initiatives and strategies, all coming together this week, which is what I regard as a very positive week for rail for the people of Essex.

The current London-Tilbury-Southend line management are bidding, with some of their employees, for the franchise deal. The management have shaken off the "misery line" tag that was attached to the Fenchurch Street line and, in spite of all the disruption of the resignalling, have performed exceptionally well recently.

During the passage of the Railways Bill, I argued strongly with Ministers that local management and employee teams should be able to bid for franchises. I was delighted that provisions to that effect were included in the Bill in the end. I understand that a significant number of local rail employees, many of whom are my constituents, are interested in investing in and supporting the bid by the management and employees for the franchise. I say no more about that, because I might embarrass my right hon. Friend the Secretary of State, but the future has never appeared rosier for rail in Essex.

I shall now briefly discuss the national scene. We all want a more successful rail network, reducing public subsidy and helping to improve the environment. We all know that Conservative policy is delivering that. The policy, as applied to my local line, is an exemplar of that phenomenon. However, we do not know the Opposition's

[*Dr. Spink*]

policies. The Opposition owe it to the people to stop being dishonest and to tell us those policies, because they have, on that as on everything else, no policies. They are doubly dishonest on that, as on everything else.

On the elusive, job-destroying minimum wage, for instance, Labour Members promise the public everything, but will they say what amount it would be? No, of course not. They have no policies. The leader of the Labour party has no answers to the questions about levels of investment or the renationalisation of rail. He has a policy vacuum. Apart from confirming that, during the past two decades, he and the Labour party have been entirely wrong and we have been entirely right, he has nothing to offer. The Labour leader is frozen in our headlights like "Blair rabbit", with no original ideas. If Opposition Members want more investment, will they be honest—will they intervene on me now? I shall sit down and take an intervention. Will they tell me how much more investment they want?

**Mr. Deputy Speaker:** Order. Do not tell him.

**Dr. Spink:** Will the hon. Member for Ashfield (Mr. Hoon) tell me how much more investment he wants? Will he tell me where the money is coming from? Will he tell me which other services he would cut to provide that investment? Will he tell me which taxes he will raise to provide that investment? Of course not, because Labour Members are too dishonest. They are doubly dishonest.

Labour Members consider that the people of Essex are fools and do not understand that. The people of Essex will show them at the next general election, as they did at the last general election and the one before that and the one before that and the one before that. They are not fools, and they will not accept the Opposition vacuum.

5.22 pm

**Mr. Paul Tyler** (North Cornwall): One can always detect when a Minister expects to be reshuffled because he starts giving hostages to fortune with reckless abandon, confident that someone else will have to live with the consequences.

The Secretary of State said a few minutes ago:

"there is no question of an erosion of services; quite the opposite".

That was almost the only positive statement in his speech, which was mostly good knockabout stuff about the Opposition. As the motion is all about Government policies, it is curious that he felt it necessary to spend so much time talking about the credibility of the Opposition.

As the right hon. Gentleman is the first Secretary of State for Transport in living memory to be perceived as being on the way up rather than on the way out, those hostages have an absurdly optimistic look about them. His statements in the past few days have forecast a dramatic improvement in passenger loading, in revenue and in profitability, and he repeated that forecast at the end of his speech.

The Secretary of State even suggested that that improvement will outweigh the cost of fare capping in the seven years that it will affect. I am sorry that the Secretary of State is no longer in his place as I wanted to test whether, on his criteria, there was credibility in the statement that capping rail fares

"would mean the taxpayer having to provide more money for subsidies to British Rail and a bigger burden on the taxpayer."

Those were the words of the previous Minister for Public Transport, the right hon. Member for Kettering (Mr. Freeman). When the Minister for Railways and Roads, his successor, replies to the debate, I should like to hear whether he continues to agree with the right hon. Member for Kettering, because if so, everything that we have heard from the Secretary of State in the media and in the House today appears pretty silly.

**Dr. Spink:** Will the hon. Gentleman give way?

**Mr. Tyler:** No, I have hardly started. The hon. Gentleman took so long that he has cut down the time available to everyone else.

**Mr. Deputy Speaker** *indicated assent.*

**Mr. Tyler:** I see that you agree, Mr. Deputy Speaker.

That statement was reported in *The Times* yesterday. The report concludes:

"The credibility of Brian Mawhinney, the Transport Secretary, rests on him shelving the sale of Railtrack . . . Mr. Freeman's remark may become Dr. Mawhinney's political epitaph."

That is what has happened in the past few days—the Secretary of State, with reckless abandon, has turned the promises and assumptions of his predecessors on their head. It flies in the face of all the expert analysis and all the empirical evidence from this country and other countries. A more realistic projection would show that only about half the shortfall from fare capping can be made up in that way; however, by the time he is found out the Secretary of State will have got out of the hot seat—he will be out of the driver's cab.

That is the second lesson of the week. Despite all the ministerial wriggling both within and outside the House, denying direct responsibility for any of the uncomfortable truths that have emerged, the Secretary of State and his colleagues remain in hands-on charge of the railway system. Sitting next to the franchising director at the press conference, looking as though he was working the puppet on the string, was the Secretary of State. All the pretence that he has nothing to do with what is happening on important operational issues has been blown to smithereens.

Another lesson can be learnt from the events of the past two or three days. Again, we have had government by press release. The Secretary of State had an opportunity to explain in the House his rationale for all the statements that have emerged from the Department of Transport. Did he take it? Of course he did not. He simply had a go at the Opposition. This was the opportunity to come to the House of Commons and explain to sceptical Conservative Back Benchers as well as Opposition Members what is in his mind. Instead, what does he do? He softens up the public with a series of major media events. That is what is called managing the media. Then the Secretary of State ducked out of sight as soon as there was bad news to be told to the House or to the nation about his doom-laden enterprise.

The news is not good. There is no need to take my word for it. Listen to this, Mr. Deputy Speaker:

"The new and very different regime that we are putting in place is bound to involve a significant period of adjustment before you can expect everything to be working smoothly."

And then:

"we need to take stock and decide whether even the direction in which we have been going is the right one for the future".

Who was that? It was not a Liberal Democrat, nor a Labour spokesman, nor a sceptical Conservative—there are plenty of those on that issue—but the new chairman of British Rail, Mr. John Welsby, just appointed by the Secretary of State to carry through that enterprise. Obviously, that opinion may be influenced by the failure of Ministers to consult properly before changing all the privatisation signals.

I suspect that many of the key participants, the people whose business is affected by those changes of track, such as London Transport and British Rail, were given no forewarning of the events of the weekend and the statement on Monday although it affects all their budgeting and, indeed, everything that they do. Is it any wonder that people wonder what is happening?

Whatever the reason for that deep-seated lack of confidence within the industry, it is now obvious to everyone both within and outside it that the preparation for privatisation has resulted in a large and ever-growing hiatus in necessary investment. One can bandy figures around, but it is clear that there has been a hiatus in the past few months and in the past year. Whether an extra £500 million is required, or whether it is more or less, everyone accepts that there has been a hiatus.

Mr. Welsby assures us that, having slipped on the privatisation banana skin, the railways are recovering their poise. That is all very well, but surely it is always preferable to avoid the banana skin in the first place—and why the wanton and deliberate distribution of banana skins throughout the industry?

The most obvious way in which the travelling public are affected is in terms of punctuality and reliability. If we consider just the south-east, the blight is already apparent. The worst deterioration in reliability is on the Northampton line, where the percentage of trains cancelled has gone up by 219 per cent. The North London line has the largest number of cancellations—4,039 on that line alone, with nearly one service in 20 affected. The North London line also has the biggest increase in cancellations overall—1,253, up 34 per cent. on the previous year.

**Mr. Streeter:** I am not sure whether the hon. Gentleman is making a case for or against privatisation—it is possible that he may not make up his mind until the end of his speech—but is he aware that the Liberal Democrat-controlled council on the Isle of Wight has welcomed the fact that the Isle of Wight will be one of the first regions to have rail franchises? Does he agree with the council?

**Mr. Tyler:** I recognise that the hon. Gentleman does not often attend transport debates. If he did, he would have heard me answer that point on two occasions, I believe. We have never resisted the case for franchising individual services. We have always said that Railtrack is the key to an adequate and effective public service in the public interest.

Punctuality and reliability figures are not the whole story. Evidence of the myriad other ways in which the privatisation programme is devastating the network is piecemeal and anecdotal, but when it is all put together the picture is of a network already at sixes and sevens. I cite a trivial example which nevertheless illustrates the overall mind set that is taking such alarming hold on the

system. In Bolton, the Greater Manchester passenger transport executive had been planning to install new toilet facilities. Now, according to a spokesman, it cannot do so because

"of the changes in procedures and organisations in the run-up to privatisation".

Replying to a passenger who complained about that, the spokesman said:

"I am sure that you realise that it would be invidious if the investment of public money in funding improvements led to an increased demand for subsidy from the operators".

That is an extraordinary statement, and it has been replicated throughout the system. I wonder whether that spokesman will have to reconsider his comments following the Secretary of State's statement on Monday.

Up and down the country, people are finding it impossible to discover how to get from A to B—the prerequisite of a user-friendly rail network. If one travels from Bury St. Edmunds to London, one can go via Ipswich to Liverpool Street or via Cambridge to Kings Cross, but if one consults the timetable at Bury St. Edmunds or at Liverpool Street, one will find no evidence of the Cambridge trains. They are ghost trains; they do not exist, even though some of them are faster than other trains. Stranger still, at Kings Cross one will find no mention of the Cambridge trains either. That has presumably led many an unsuspecting, unwary passenger to slog across a bit of London to Liverpool Street, ignorant of the fact that there was a better train waiting just along the way.

That lunacy come about because the services via Ipswich are operated by Anglia, while those via Cambridge are operated by the West Anglia Great Northern line, and the two companies seem to have no great desire to co-operate. A WAGN line spokeswoman said:

"it must be taken into consideration that during the restructuring for privatisation, British Railways was split into separate companies. Consequently, we have no more jurisdiction over a fellow train-operating company, such as Regional Railways, than we have over London Underground or any other public transport company".

It is no wonder that the travelling public think that the rail network is disintegrating because that is precisely what is happening.

**Sir Russell Johnston:** Will my hon. Friend allow me to give another example? He will know that on the 28th of this month all motorail services in the United Kingdom are to be terminated without any consultation. They used to carry 40,000 cars a year within what was InterCity, when Chris Green was the manager of InterCity, which made an overall profit. Is that not scandalous?

**Mr. Tyler:** I agree with my hon. Friend. His comment applies also to a number of sleeper services. I refer not to the one before the courts, but to other sleeper services. I hope that the Minister will deal with that point.

The position is deteriorating. The co-operation that the Minister claimed would be there is simply not there. I think that all hon. Members are grateful to Christian Wolmar and *The Independent* for their series on great railway disasters, which has pointed up some of the ways in which services are deteriorating. If some of the examples were not so tragic for passengers, many of them would be hilarious.

[*Mr. Tyler*]

It is no wonder that British Rail is worried because it is likely to have to pick up the bits from this mess. As is widely known, in its evidence to the Select Committee on Transport, which has already been mentioned in the debate, British Rail expressed grave anxiety about the effects of the hiatus on the future of the railways. Investment in resignalling, which was its top priority, is way below desirable levels. The same is true of rolling stock, where little or no prospect exists of new orders. I hope that the Minister will tell us how much rolling stock has been ordered this year, and how much is in prospect for the next financial year.

Meanwhile, perhaps most serious of all, essential maintenance requirements are not being met, or people are just scraping by. Repairs that would once have been carried out on the same day are now delayed or are dropped in favour of supposedly temporary lash-ups. It is not commonly known that cracked rails, for example, are often clamped together rather than fully mended, and no one is sure what the fatigue life of those clamps may be. Speed and weight restrictions result. They last longer, are more common and have a more devastating effect. The east coast main line is a noteworthy victim, but other main lines are at risk.

I am glad to see that the hon. Member for St. Ives (Mr. Harris) is here as he and I share an interest in the main line through Cornwall. He may be interested to know that data from internal memoranda that I have seen suggest that an on-going decline in track standards is taking place on the Great Western main line. On the Plymouth to Penzance line in recent months, there have been major restrictions: 30 mph between Menheniot and Liskeard, 20 mph between Par and St. Austell, and 40 mph between Long Rock and St. Erth. That is having a devastating effect on the reliability of the timetable and is threatening the long-term future, whatever happens to the franchise, of the main line 125 express services through Cornwall. The hon. Gentleman knows all too well what effect that would have on the economy and, specifically, on the holiday industry.

Speed and weight restrictions are alarming in themselves, but if safety risks follow, the situation is obviously even more serious. Ministers profess ignorance, but the signs are not reassuring. Despite all that, it seems as though the early bidders for the train operating unit franchises may still find that they are offered enough sweeteners to make it all apparently worth while. Pumped-up subsidies and a benevolent interpretation of passenger service requirements could make bidding an attractive prospect for the first tranche. Ministers aim to have 51 per cent. of services in private hands by April next year, but there is still the other 49 per cent. and Railtrack. What sweeteners can the Secretary of State possibly offer to make that pig's ear look like a silk purse, or is he keeping his fingers crossed that he will by then have moved on and someone else will have to square the circle?

It is rather like the cases involving the first fundholding general practitioners or the first opt-out schools. They were attractive to start with, but latecomers did not receive so much and did not find it such an attractive prospect.

For years, Ministers have told us that fares must rise to cut subsidies. This week, however, we are told that fare cuts will attract so many new passengers on to the railways that that will lead to subsidy cuts. The Secretary of State appeared to say that again this afternoon. We are all left wondering why, if that magic formula exists, Ministers did not find it many years ago.

5.39 pm

**Mr. James Clappison** (Hertsmere): I welcome the opportunity to make a brief contribution to the debate. My interest is on behalf of my constituents who use the railways, particularly those who commute every day from Potters Bar, Radlett, Elstree, Borehamwood, and other destinations on those lines.

The debate was opened by the Opposition in a way that is familiar to those of us who have attended other pre-privatisation debates. The general theme is that privatisation never works and that it will be a disaster. The hon. Member for Oldham, West (Mr. Meacher) went into some detail about that. What the hon. Member for Oldham, West said today belies the experience of other privatisations and what we have been told about new Labour. We have been told that new Labour is friendly to private enterprise, friendly to the market and friendly to private ownership, but there was nothing to distinguish what was said from the Labour Front Bench today from what has been said so many times since 1979 about so many other privatisations. It was a continuation of the same old socialist arguments. There was not even a dressing of new Labour to cover it up.

The reaction of both the Labour party and the Liberal Democrats to the announcement about fares was disappointing. Opposition Front-Bench Members could have found it in themselves to welcome the news that fares will be pegged over the next seven years. They should have welcomed the fact that there will be a real terms benefit to my constituents who use the railway as well as to other rail users, including their constituents. I did not hear a single word of welcome for that. Instead, what we saw clearly was disappointment etched on the faces of the spokesmen for both the Labour party and the Liberal Democrats about the good news that rail fares are to be held down—*[Interruption.]* The reaction of the Liberal Democrat spokesman was of equal disappointment. I can tell him that my constituents in Hertfordshire, including those who are told perpetually by the Liberal Democrats that rail fares should be held down, are pleased that they are being held down. They would rather hear that than hear complaints about toilet facilities in Manchester and the other long list of complaints that the hon. Gentleman gave.

The fact that the price of fares is to be held down is of interest to the Central rail users consultative committee. Major General Lennox Napier of that committee welcomed that as good news for passengers. He speaks for commuters. He said:

"This announcement marks a turning point in policy. Holding fare rises down will increase the attractiveness of the railway and stimulate greater use. We have been calling for years for fare rises to be linked to inflation and quality of service. I am delighted that the Franchising Director, supported by extra Government subsidy, has adopted a policy which could result in a real fall in the cost of rail travel."

**Mr. Tyler:** Will the hon. Gentleman give way?

**Mr. Clappison:** I will not give way, because as the hon. Gentleman said in his speech, time is short.

Throughout the debate Opposition Front-Bench Members have been chanting from a sedentary position that fares have increased by 22 per cent. in real terms over the past 10 years. I must admit that that is right. If Opposition Members look a little further back, they will find that over the past 16 years of Conservative Government fares have increased in real terms by 29 per cent. As we have said, we want to change that. However, I warn Opposition Members, particularly the hon. Member for Oldham, West, not to go back any further because—*[Interruption.]* Well, I might be tempted. According to the figures supplied to me by the House of Commons Library, between 1974 and 1979 there was a real terms increase in rail fares of 31 per cent. That is more in five years under Labour than in 16 years under the Conservatives.

Another instructive feature of the statistics is that the figures that are not adjusted for inflation—the nominal increase—show that under the last Labour Government rail fares rose by over 170 per cent. That drives me to the conclusion that Opposition Members are no more entitled to lecture us on rail fares than they are on inflation.

Another argument used by Opposition Members is the lack of investment. The statistics seem to be at odds with what they are saying. The hon. Member for Oldham, West went into some detail on investment, but the statistics with which I have been supplied from the Library support what has been said by Conservative Members. Over the past 16 years the average investment in railways has been in excess of £1 billion, markedly higher than between 1974 and 1979.

The hon. Member for Oldham, West told us about the east coast main line. He used his experience of that line to illustrate his argument about the lack of investment. He mentioned particularly the line between London and Leeds. If Opposition Members want to choose any line to illustrate a lack of investment, they should not choose that one. They will know that over the past 16 years that line has been electrified and that the service has been considerably improved. Since the hon. Member for Oldham, West finished his speech I have been told by the Library that when his party left office in 1979 the fastest journey time between London and Leeds was just under two and a half hours. Today, the fastest service time between London and Leeds is just under two hours. The hon. Member for Fife, Central (Mr. McLeish) may laugh, but that is of interest to those who use the line.

The hon. Member for Oldham, West complained about a points failure on that line. The only points failure came at the beginning of his speech when he was asked, quite properly, by my hon. Friends about whether he would nationalise the railways and he said that he would return to that later. I was expecting an express journey to the end of his speech where he would tell us what he thought should happen. Instead, he did not reach his destination. We had a points change, a gentle shunt and ended up going backwards to where the hon. Gentleman had begun with a long list of complaints. We have no inkling what the hon. Gentleman would do about railway services.

What will be of interest to my constituents, apart from the good news about fares being held down, is that under privatisation they can look forward to a better quality of service and a greater sensitivity towards the needs of customers, which has been a characteristic of every other privatisation. I hope that in the coming years we will see the sensitivity that has been applied to fares being applied to other parts of the service. I am thinking particularly about car parking charges. That is a matter of great concern to my constituents.

The cost of parking must be considered when we look at the cost of travel. On that point I must be critical. Over a number of years, certainly over the past five years, British Rail has insensitively increased parking charges way above the level of inflation. The increase has been an imposition on my constituents. This year alone there has been a 40 per cent. increase in charges for my constituents in Elstree and a 25 per cent. increase for my constituents who use the car park at Radlett.

I am told by my constituents in Radlett that since 1989 the cost of parking has more than doubled. Off-peak parking, which is particularly valued by my constituents in Radlett, was free before 1989; it then had a charge put upon it and has now increased to the full level. That causes considerable annoyance to my constituents. I have received many representations about that from individual constituents as well as from business people and local residents who are inconvenienced by the wider traffic implications and problems caused by the increased charges. I have received a particularly strong representation from the Radlett Society which I endorse fully.

When I took up the matter with British Rail its response was unsatisfactory. I was told that the increases were being imposed as a quid pro quo for improvements in service such as the introduction of closed circuit television. Those improvements have yet to come about and I have been told that no decision has been taken in principle to install closed circuit television in Radlett. Those are matters of concern to my constituents.

I expect such problems to be remedied by the greater sensitivity to customer needs that will come about after privatisation. We know from successive privatisations, beginning with British Airways in 1979, that once private sector management skills are introduced and there is access to the resources of private finance, there is a sea change in attitudes to the customer. In this case, not only will those factors be at work but the service will be backed by the stringent passenger service requirement agreed between the franchisee and the authority.

We expect a much better service. We have put out our proposals to improve services but have heard nothing at all from the Opposition about theirs. We heard nothing about how they would move to public ownership or about the compensation that might be payable in that event. My worry, on behalf of my constituents, is that the Opposition are determined on a course that will take us back to a declining railway service, that will require huge amounts of compensation and public money and from which my constituents will receive no benefit whatsoever.

5.50 pm

**Mr. Hugh Bayley** (York): I am sponsored by the National Union of Rail, Maritime and Transport Workers, RMT. However, after the announcement last week of the closure of the York carriage works, I am sure that I speak on behalf of all my constituents when I tell the House that the mood in York is one of bitterness, anger and betrayal at what the Government have done to York with their rail privatisation measures.

[Mr. Hugh Bayley]

There is bitterness because the Government promised that there would be no hiatus in rail investment, but there has been a hiatus and the works are closing as a result. There is anger at the comment that the Prime Minister made on the day that the closure was announced last week. He said that rail privatisation was no more to blame for the closure than it was to blame for an outbreak of measles. That flippant and foolish comment will hang round his neck and haunt him and the Conservative party in north Yorkshire for many years to come.

People in York, especially those at the carriage works, feel betrayed because the company, ABB Transportation, has done everything that the Government asked. It bought into the railways and invested £50 million in the York works. The workers have done everything that is necessary to double productivity and, together with the management, to design and build the most modern aluminium railway carriage body shell that is built in Europe—the only one that has the European Commission's full safety certification. They have done all that was asked of them and their hopes have been dashed by the closure, which has been brought about by the freeze in rail investment in the run-up to privatisation.

Two years ago the House debated the Railways Bill. When rail privatisation started, 4,687 people worked for British Rail or for ABB in my constituency. By the end of this year, on the basis of jobs that have gone already or redundancies that have already been announced, that number will have fallen by almost half to 2,583.

When he addressed the House, the Secretary of State sang the praises of privatisations in other industries. However, even he did not have the gall to mention the privatisation that was the stalking horse or pilot study for rail privatisation—the privatisation of British Rail Engineering Ltd. It was sold off in 1989 and since then, it has faced never-ending decline.

That is a disaster for the company that invested in the city of York, Derby and Crewe and a disaster for the work force. When the Railways Bill was going through the House, 1,600 people were employed at the York carriage works; now that number is down to 750. In the light of last week's announcement, by the end of this year, the last man will have walked through the factory gates for the last time. That will be it. After 150 years of building trains at York, it will all be over. Those 1,600 men, who helped to modernise the company to make it competitive and to design new products, which the Government said were wanted, will be cast on to the scrap heap.

Some weeks ago, I met a man who was made redundant from the York works in October 1993. Since then, he has had just nine weeks' work: four weeks one Christmas at one of York's chocolate factories and five weeks as a storeman at a local supermarket.

I have invited the Minister in the past to come to the York works to see what was threatened by rail privatisation and to meet the work force whose jobs are on the line. If he met that man or any of the other 750 still employed at the York works, could he honestly look them in the eye and tell them that rail privatisation was a success, that it was good for them or for the travelling public?

Nobody can say that the Government were not warned what rail privatisation would do. The Transport Select Committee called on the Government to

"address the problem of the hiatus in rail investment."

The Government promised the House that there would be no such hiatus.

On BBC television, in December, Sir Bob Reid, then chairman of British Rail, said:

"There is a hiatus. The question is, how short can that hiatus be kept? If that hiatus can be kept short, ABB will still be around to build trains."

Earlier this year, Eric Drewery, the chairman of ABB, warned the Transport Select Committee that if an order was not received extremely quickly, the York works would close and said:

"To close down highly productive world-class manufacturing facilities is like a stab in the heart."

The Government have stabbed and the York works are bleeding to death.

On Friday, the day after the closure announcement, I met the company's managing director and asked him if there was anything that could be done at this late stage to save the York works. He said that there was only one thing: the Government could tell British Rail to authorise the follow-on order clause in its current contract. That, and that alone, could save the York works, because no other order could come in time to keep people in production. He gave a guarantee that if the Government took that action, his company would feel honour bound to continue production at the York works.

Why will not the Government act? Such action is affordable. It would cost the Government nothing this financial year, probably nothing in the next financial year and there would be a leasing charge of £10 million or £15 million in the following financial year.

The trains are needed. The Transport Select Committee received evidence that 2,500 London commuter carriages urgently need replacing. If the Government asked the Kent or Hertfordshire commuters whether new rolling stock was needed, they would get a resounding yes.

We also need action for the sake of industry. Other European countries are facing up to the need to reinvest in their railways and to maintain their manufacturing bases. Deutschebahn in Germany has placed orders for new rolling stock worth £4.6 billion; in Italy, orders in excess of £5 billion have been placed.

Those other members of the European Union are laughing all the way to the bank because, aided by ABB's main competitor GEC, they too are getting a large share of the new rolling stock orders that have been placed in this country. GEC won the contract to build the new trains for London Underground's north London line. It cannot build the aluminium body shells; there is only one company in Britain that builds modern aluminium body shells—ABB. GEC had to subcontract the work. ABB had bid for work and offered the lowest price but did not get the contract, which went instead to a GEC subsidiary in Spain.

By 1990, there was a £28 million deficit in the UK balance of trade in rolling stock. By last year, the deficit had risen to £126 million. With the loss of the ABB works in York, it will be even higher. Even if orders were only at the level of the past few years, there would be a net reduction of £150 million a year on that balance of trade. We cannot afford the current deficit in industrial terms, or in railway terms.

Since the closure announcement, York city council has put up £50,000 and the North Yorkshire training and enterprise council has put up a similar sum in order to find alternative jobs for the redundant workers. The trade unions have talked to local engineering employers, and I hope and believe that they have found places so that at least the 20 apprentices can finish their training. However, the Government caused the problem and the Government must be part of the solution.

Will the Minister give an undertaking that the Government will put money into the York economy to find new jobs for the men whom they have placed on the scrap heap? There is no way that the existing economy there can find jobs for the 750 men who have been made redundant. Indeed, local employers have not been able to provide alternative jobs for the 1,100 people made redundant in the past two years. New jobs are needed in York. The Government could respond through their single regeneration budget and I ask them to say now what they are going to do to solve the employment crisis that rail privatisation has created in York.

6.1 pm

**Mr. Tim Smith** (Beaconsfield): Like all hon. Members, I am a customer of British Rail, and so are most of my constituents. My interest in this debate relates to the quality of customer services provided by the railways and I believe that if we get that right, the employment that we seek will follow automatically. The important thing is to get the quality of service and the reliability right.

Nationalisation has been a great disappointment. In 1948, when the private railway undertakings were nationalised by the Labour Government, there were high hopes that bringing together all the businesses into British Rail would somehow improve the quality of service, reduce fares and increase the number of people using the railways. As we know, in the intervening period—almost 50 years—the proportion of people using the railways has fallen decade after decade and the proportion of freight being carried by rail has fallen too, as my right hon. Friend the Secretary of State told the House.

One of the main problems was the sheer size of the undertaking. British Rail was a massive organisation and its size made it difficult to manage. Ten or more years ago, the Government introduced private sector management into the organisation, since when there has been a succession of chairmen who have been some of our leading industrialists. Among the most successful, for example, was Bob Reid, the former chairman and chief executive of Shell UK. He was brought in to run British Rail but found it simply impossible to change things from the top down. The reason was that the culture of British Rail was so deeply ingrained that it was never going to be possible for one person, however skilled in management, to change it.

I strongly support the changes that are coming with privatisation, especially those in British Rail's structure. It is especially important to reduce the organisation to units that are easier to manage in human terms and more likely to relate to customers. There have already been changes, certainly on the two lines that serve my constituency.

I met the manager of the Chiltern line last week to talk about the changes being made in anticipation of privatisation. Apparently, it is still not possible to discover the line's turnover—how much it generates in fares and how much subsidy it receives. British Rail used to put all these things together in its accounts and even it did not necessarily know the subsidy for a particular commuter service although, clearly, it would know the income from fares. From 1 April a new company has been established under the Companies Acts which will run the line and, some time after the end of the financial year next March, we shall discover the line's turnover for the first time and what revenue subsidy it is receiving.

The good news is that the turnover is already starting to increase, the service is already more responsive to customers and the manager has brought in management from the private sector. I believe that the key management skill is marketing. With privatisation, there is a real opportunity to increase sales, contrary to what the hon. Member for Oldham, West (Mr. Meacher) said.

Basically, the railway business is a fixed-cost business. The fixed costs are the payments to Railtrack for the use of the system and the payments for the lease of the trains but, after that, it is up to the individual company to extract the maximum possible from the assets being used and to generate more business. I also believe that there are tremendous opportunities for increased efficiency. In every privatisation, we have tended to underestimate the scope for improved efficiency but, in this instance, there is also an opportunity to improve the quality of customer service and profitability and, at the same time, to reduce the subsidy paid by the taxpayer.

I greatly welcome the decisions made by the Government in the past three or four months, including that on through ticketing. It was right that there should be a proper debate on the matter. The more through ticketing there is, the greater the costs involved, but the public felt strongly that it should be maintained and I am glad that the Government decided not to change the present level of service.

I also welcome the more recent decision to peg fares for the next seven years. We have become used to that under previous privatisations and seen massive reductions in prices. I do not suppose that there will be such reductions in this industry but, if we have no real terms increases, that in itself will be a major step forward because, as we have heard, fares have increased by 22 per cent. in real terms over the past 16 years and, in the five years before that, by some 31 per cent. according to my hon. Friend the Member for Hertsmere (Mr. Clappison).

**Mr. Peter Ainsworth** (Surrey, East): Like me, my hon. Friend represents part of the south-east where there is a great deal of concern about overcrowding on the roads and about the environmental damage done by cars. Does he agree that the decision to control fare increases on the railways might play a significant part in encouraging people out of their cars and back on to the rail network where that proves to be a sensible option?

**Mr. Smith:** There are two important matters when it comes to providing a decent rail service, and one is price. The hon. Member for Oldham, West was dismissive about that, but my hon. Friend is entirely right. Anyone examining the options will weigh up the price and possible benefits.

[Mr. Smith]

The other key characteristic—it is impossible to overstate its importance to a rail service—is reliability. My constituents want to know that the train will turn up at the time advertised in the timetable and arrive at its destination at the time advertised in the timetable. Indeed, every day a huge proportion of trains on the Chiltern line fulfil that desire. When the services are privatised, the incentive to ensure a reliable service will be greater than it has ever been.

Two characteristics will bring people back to using rail: first, the knowledge that prices will be pegged—they will not rise in real terms so people will be able to plan accordingly, as my hon. Friend the Member for Surrey, East (Mr. Ainsworth) said—and secondly, reliability. Those are the two most important aspects of customer service.

**Mr. Tyler:** If the Chiltern line is improving its reliability, does the hon. Gentleman accept that it is the exception that proves the rule? The figures published just two weeks ago showed that the reliability factors had deteriorated markedly on a national basis while privatisation has hung like a threat over the industry.

**Mr. Smith:** We are in a transitional period, as is inevitable with any privatisation. Of course the Opposition always exploit the situation. Once the process is complete, the service will improve. Management will have a major incentive to improve reliability because it is the key characteristic of a railway service. For that reason, I support the Government's proposals.

6.10 pm

**Ms Glenda Jackson** (Hampstead and Highgate): I declare an interest as I am sponsored by the rail drivers' union, the Associated Society of Locomotive Engineers and Firemen. I regret that the Secretary of State is not in his place. That he chose to approach this debate with a marked lack of gravity and seriousness, demeaned not only himself and the great office of state that he holds— although that is of no particular consequence—but a great industry and thousands of dedicated people who, in many instances, gave their lives in its service. I regret that he is not present to hear what I say, but no doubt he will be able to read it in the *Official Report*.

The hon. Member for Beaconsfield (Mr. Smith) referred, as did his hon. Friend the Member for Hertsmere (Mr. Clappison), to the capping of rail fares. I find it ironic that Conservative Members have attempted to present the capping of rail fares as anathema to Opposition Members. During Transport questions in January 1993, the then Minister for Public Transport, the right hon. Member for Kettering (Mr. Freeman), said in response to a question of mine that if I wished to see fare increases moderated and reduced, it would mean

"the taxpayer having to provide more money for subsidies to British Rail".—[*Official Report*, 11 January 1993; Vol. 216, c. 597.]

He said that the difference between the Opposition and the Government was that the Government believed that rail passengers should pay the real fare for travelling on railways. I have no doubt that that reply was cheered to the echo by Conservative Members.

Yesterday, the minimum service standards that will be required of potential private rail operators were announced. The House will recall that the concept of minimum service standards was proudly trumpeted by the Secretary of State for Transport as a guarantee of levels of service to rail passengers for the very first time. However, when it was pointed out to him that those standards would lead to a 20 per cent. reduction in current service levels, the right hon. Gentleman attempted to reassure the public by saying that those minimum standards would not in fact ever be implemented. The Secretary of State must be one of the first politicians to have sought to convince people of the merits of his policy by pledging that it would never see the light of day.

This week we have again seen Ministers' efforts at describing the utopia set to greet rail passengers once they board the great rail privatisation express undermined by that boring old killjoy reality. The Prime Minister pledged in the House that rail privatisation would lead to better services for passengers. But if the standards outlined by the Secretary of State were ever to be implemented— perhaps the hon. Member for Castle Point (Dr. Spink) could inform his hon. Friend the Member for Basildon (Mr. Amess) of this fact as he is clearly not aware of it— peak services from Basildon to London would be cut by almost 60 per cent., peak services from Reading to London would be cut by almost 50 per cent. and Epsom commuters would face peak services cuts of 67 per cent.

This week's announcement on service levels was a disaster for the passengers who rely on Britain's rail network. The assault on the hard-pressed commuter, however, did not end with the publication of the passenger service requirement. Today, the franchising director published his invitations to tender. As the departing British Rail chairman Sir Bob Reid pointed out, an invitation to play a part in what is fast becoming the most shambolic privatisation of the past 16 years will be regarded by many as the most unwelcome invitation since the spider threw open his parlour to the fly.

In that document of invitations, potential bidders were warned about the London travelcard. It said:

"Should London Underground, and/or any relevant bus operator introduce competing travelcards which do not include the option of travel on rail services, this may have a detrimental effect on their"—

the potential bidders—

"revenue".

That same travelcard, which Ministers were pledging last year would be safe from rail, bus or even tube privatisation, could, according to the franchising director, be facing the axe, with the result that rail commuters will no longer be able to integrate their travel with the rest of the public transport system. Are Ministers also claiming that the abolition of the London travelcard and other travelcards around the country will constitute an improved service for commuters?

I cited the Secretary of State for Transport and his pledge that privatisation would lead to an improved and guaranteed quality of service. I wonder if, since he made that comment, he has had a chance to speak to his right hon. Friend the Member for St. Albans (Mr. Lilley). Last month, I had the pleasure of visiting St. Albans and experienced in particular the local rail service which links it to Watford, known locally as the Abbey Flyer. In 1988, North London railways spent more than £675,000 electrifying the Abbey Flyer route and improving the service. When I visited it, that good work was about to be reversed. Due to shortages of rolling stock and no money to buy more, North London railways was being forced to remove the electric rolling stock from the line and replace it with old, less reliable diesel units. In addition, because of the extra costs of the new access charging regime, St. Albans council tax payers, who subsidise the Sunday Flyer service, were facing a bill for another £50,000 a year to keep it operating.

Thankfully, as a result of the campaign by the local Labour party and local commuter groups, North London railways announced last week that it had abandoned plans to replace the electric units, but the extra costs of keeping that service running will still have to be borne by the council tax payers of St. Albans and a reduction in late-night services is proposed. Elsewhere on the network, other commuters will still be rattling around behind 30 year-old diesel trains. That is the reality of rail privatisation: higher costs, for poorer services.

On Monday, the Secretary of State attempted to buy some good publicity for privatisation by announcing that he would be capping fares. As we all read in our newspapers on Tuesday, that attempt failed miserably. It did not fail because the idea was wrong in principle; there are good arguments for encouraging greater use of our public transport system by holding fares at reasonable levels. What tripped up the Secretary of State as he attempted his fares U-turn was once again the realities of the flawed rail privatisation policy that he was trying to sell.

If the Secretary of State had been seeking to cap fares in a public rail service, it would have cost approximately £35 million each year over the next three years, but, because of privatisation, that cost has leapt to more than £350 million over the same period. If one adds to that the estimated £1.25 billion overall cost of privatisation itself, one can see that instead of saving commuters' money through lower fares, the Secretary of State is costing them almost £1.5 billion in higher taxation.

That is the reality of privatisation from which the Secretary of State cannot escape. Those are the facts that cannot be hidden. At a time when hon. Members on the Back Benches behind him are desperately trying to clutch at the straws of tax cuts to save them from electoral oblivion, I humbly suggest that it will not be much longer before rail privatisation catches up with him and his Government for good.

6.19 pm

**Mr. Henry McLeish** (Fife, Central): It is a pity that the Secretary of State is not in his place, because he cast a blight over the debate by refusing to take any of the issues seriously. The country and the House are not in the mood to be lectured to by a Secretary of State who is overseeing the most monumentally stupid piece of public policy since the war, overseeing the destruction of a nationally integrated rail network and overseeing a privatisation that is nothing but a shambles.

If the privatisation were a shambles simply because the Government were not achieving any of their objectives, that would be bad enough. But the down side of the whole process is the fact that in the Government's search and in their obsession with privatisation they are causing immense damage to the fabric of the network and to the morale of the people who work in it.

It is extraordinary that when the Secretary of State was asked earlier how much his policy would cost, he simply did not know. That is a rich irony. The first cheque book is being taken out and the price is no object. The Government are saying that there is no price that they will not pay to implement that crazy privatisation process. If that is not irresponsible I do not know what is.

In Scotland we say that a person has "a guid conceit of himself", and it is ludicrous for a Secretary of State, who comes to the Dispatch Box to lecture us on a failing policy, to act in such a patronising manner. That is unforgivable, and I hope that if the Secretary of State does not arrive in time for the remainder of the debate, he will at least read the *Official Report* tomorrow.

As my hon. Friend the Member for Hampstead and Highgate (Ms Jackson) has said, the real tragedy is that of the men and women who work in the rail industry. Is it not sad that no one on the Government Benches is willing to raise the morale of those people by saying that they are doing a good job? We hear many comments about the failures of nationalisation over the past 50 years, and of course we do not have a perfect rail network. But surely there is a difference between saying that, and failing to give credit where it is due to the management and the work force of that great industry.

In the time available I shall concentrate on the evidence that we are submitting about the shambles and the mess that the Government have got themselves into. The passengers of this country, the people of this country— and, at some time in the future the electors of this country—will want to see that evidence.

The first great debacle was about the sleeper services. Is it not amazing that Government policy is now shaped in the courts rather than on ministerial desks? Why is there so much buck-passing, and why will no one take responsibility for anything? The Government tried to con the Scottish people over the costs, the local authority appealed and the matter is now before the courts. The British Railways Board's appeal will be heard on 1 June. I hope that British Rail will now withdraw its appeal. It must start listening to the travelling public instead of to the Government, because the Government are hell-bent on destroying the network. Surely the British Railways Board is the custodian charged with the responsibility of ensuring that the network continues.

As if the court case about the sleepers were not bad enough, my hon. Friend the Member for York (Mr. Bayley) has highlighted the tragedy of ABB. He asked the Government a simple question: why do they not intervene? The Secretary of State says that he is willing to pay any price for subsidies to put into franchises, but when we ask him to restore the domestic market for rolling stock, he does not care.

Of course we would not wish to use such a subsidy. As my hon. Friend said, the affair involves not subsidies but future leasing costs. The Government stand condemned for having put 750 people out of work, and they simply do not care. I challenge the Minister for Railways and Roads, when he replies, to tell the House why he does not care. But perhaps he will surprise us by telling us that he does care. If so, will he now order the British Railways Board to specify rolling stock requirements that will at least allow ABB to be a player in the domestic market? The whole business is a disgrace, and my hon. Friend has eloquently made the case for his local area.

*[Mr. Henry McLeish]*

The franchises are the third cause for concern. This morning the franchising director heralded a new dawn, and the Secretary of State said that we were now genuinely moving forward on privatisation. But that is late too. If those franchises go ahead—there is no guarantee that they will—they will not be operable until next year. We were promised that 51 per cent. of the franchises for the 25 train operators would be completed by May 1996. Once again, the timetable is in disarray. The Minister may want to give excuses and explain why the programme will not meet the targets. Now that the 51 per cent. has disappeared, what new target will the Government set?

The other issue is safety. How many logs are regularly leaked from Railtrack revealing that trains are still going through danger signals on to single tracks? We are spending £1.25 billion on the nonsense of privatisation, yet passenger safety is at risk throughout the country because of a lack of investment. Let us forget the politics; there is a huge moral issue at stake here. Can we let people travel on our railways in certain parts of the country when we are not employing proper safety procedures because the Government, like a drunken sailor, want to squander money on privatisation and politics rather than on people and safety? That is the issue that the Minister should deal with this evening. *[Interruption.]* I heard the hon. Member for Hertford and Stortford ( Mr. Wells) say, from a sedentary position, "Humbug." I want it to be recorded in *Hansard* that the people who sit on the Conservative Front Bench think that the issue of safety is simply humbug—*[Interruption.]* And I want it recorded that not only was safety described as humbug, but there was then a systematic bout of laughter.

**The Minister for Railways and Roads (Mr. John Watts):** What the record should show, Mr. Deputy Speaker, is that my normally silent hon. Friend was describing the hon. Gentleman's argument rather than the importance of safety on the railways.

**Mr. McLeish:** The Minister's attempt to rescue the situation will also be recorded in *Hansard* as a dismal failure.

Apart from safety, the main issue that the Secretary of State dwelt on today was fares. I am pleased to see that the right hon. Gentleman has now returned to the Chamber. When the Government announced fare capping this week they thought that they would get a good press. But in every editorial in the quality newspapers the Secretary of State was hung, drawn and quartered—[HON. MEMBERS: "No."] I suggest that Conservative Members read the editorials before commenting from a sedentary position.

It is right that the Government should be pilloried, because their fare capping is a con. We now know that only 50 per cent. of the fares in Britain will be regulated, and it is important to realise which fares will not be subject to regulation. They are: all first-class fares, cheap day returns, supersavers, Advance, Super Advance, Apex, Super Apex, Shuttle Advance, Shuttle Superadvance, and Network Awaybreak and Network Stayaway, which operate in the south-east.

So now we know that that great fare-capping initiative was a political exercise designed to silence the powerful arguments of commuters throughout the country, some of whom voted Conservative at the last general election, although they may not do so next time. We know that 50 per cent. of the fares paid by the travelling public will not be covered by the capping scheme.

The Secretary of State's performance when he was asked to tell the House how much the extra subsidy would cost was worrying. How often have the Opposition heard the Government say, "What would Labour do?", "Isn't that a spending commitment?" and, "Won't that mean an increase in taxation?" What hypocrisy. What humbug— to coin a phrase. We now know, partly from what he said today, that the Secretary of State has apparently been given an open cheque book. There is no subsidy that he will not pay.

It is important to challenge the right hon. Gentleman again on that issue. Will the cost be £300 million over seven years? Will it be £400 million, or £500 million? The answer is simple: the cost does not matter to the Government. The privatisation policy is in such free fall that the Government are willing to use any part of the taxpayers' contribution to bail it out. The Government should be wary of using "tax and spend" as an attack on us in the future. The Secretary of State came to the Dispatch Box, allowed himself to be drawn into an issue and failed to rescue himself. He did not address the central question of what it will cost to ensure that the privatisation takes place.

Another issue of grave concern is the passenger service requirements. These were introduced with a fanfare of publicity, and the Government thought that they would get credit for them. But there are three passenger service requirements now confirmed, and we find that 15 per cent. to 20 per cent. of all services are to be axed. The Secretary of State says that that will provide the minimum, and that the commercial entrepreneurs lurking out there who are desperate to get their hands on a franchise will deliver improved services. Not only will they reinstate that 15 per cent. to 20 per cent., they will give us more services. That is a policy on a wing and a prayer which does not satisfy any of the passengers.

**Mr. Nigel Forman** (Carshalton and Wallington): Is the hon. Gentleman aware of the parallel with British Airways which moved from the public to the private sector and began to expand its services in both range and quality?

**Mr. McLeish** *rose—*

**Dr. Mawhinney:** He does not want to know the truth.

**Mr. McLeish:** The Secretary of State may say that, but let me address the comparison between this privatisation and any of the others. The Government took British Rail and smashed it into 95 pieces. They now want to sell all of the individual pieces under the guise of a nationally integrated rail network. One does not have to be a genius to work out that this privatisation bears no relationship to any other.

If one believes in the privatisation of British Rail—I do not—one must see that the Government could not have picked a worse method. Not only are they ideologically wrong, they have picked a method which beggars belief. No one can understand why, after going down the privatisation road, the Government then have sought to sabotage it by picking the silliest way possible to privatise.

The question of the invitation to tender was raised by several of my hon. Friends. This matter is seen by the Secretary of State as the start to the privatisation. It is important for this House, the press and the public to understand that this is all being done in secrecy. The Treasury's rules of commercial confidence mean that the director of franchising, Roger Salmon, has £2.1 billion tucked away. Vital services in three franchises are now going out to tender and the issue will be debated behind closed doors.

The British Railways Board did not even get the tender documentation which went out with the bids. It only runs the service at present, so obviously that was an oversight. The fact is that this is being done in secrecy, and the Minister should explain that to the House when he replies. Are we so concerned about whether Brian Souter of Stagecoach might bid 10p or 50p more than someone else when we come to consider ScotRail? The answer is obvious. The Government simply do not want anyone to look into a process which is a major mess.

If one thing above all characterises this privatisation, it is the question of buck-passing. One of the issues which concerns the Labour party, and I am sure the Liberal Democrats, is that of who takes responsibility. The Secretary of State seems to try to work it out on this basis. If he is dealing with an unpopular issue—such as fares—he will not only jump on the director of franchising, but will allow himself to be attacked by the Prime Minister, who has read material on the matter on the way back from Paris. If it is a sensitive issue and the politics are important enough, the Secretary of State will intervene.

If the issue is the Fort William sleeper service, on the other hand, does the Secretary of State really care? A judgment is made. He says, "It is a sleeper service on the periphery of the country which costs £2.5 million on the Government's figures. I will not intervene." We have the director of franchising, the rail regulator, the Minister responsible for railways, the Secretary of State for Transport and the Secretary of State for Scotland, but no one wants to take responsibility. That is shirking responsibility, and the Secretary of State should say whether he is in charge of his transport brief or whether his is only a selective responsibility when the issue suits his purposes.

In my possession I have the Great Britain passenger rail timetable. This will be a collector's item soon. But to add poignancy to the points which I have made this evening, the front cover of the timetable contains tracks, but no trains. That is a significant comment on where we are going. I ask the Minister to start to address the issues and to ignore the politics and the ideology of this crazy adventure.

When will someone in the Government have the courage to dump this whole exercise? How much taxpayers' money has to be squandered? How many jobs—such as those at ABB—will have to go? How many services do we have to lose? How much manipulation of British Rail accounts will be needed to soften and sweeten parts of the industry? What are the Government doing about Railtrack behind the scenes to fatten it up? *[Interruption.]* The Secretary of State winked at that point, which is significant.

If common sense prevails, the privatisation should end. We will work towards that, and I shall finish on a buoyant note. The Government are making such a hash of their own programme that I believe that there will be very little

for us to deal with in terms of what has been moved into the private sector. That will be important when we take over in government in 18 months or two years' time.

6.36 pm

**The Minister for Railways and Roads (Mr. John Watts):** May I begin by reassuring the hon. Member for Fife, Central (Mr. McLeish) that the Great Britain timetable will continue in the privatised railway?

The Labour party has pursued rail privatisation policy through three debates of its own choosing rather like a hunt looking for a fox that finds that all the foxes have been shot. First came the scare about through ticketing; then came the wild allegations that passenger service requirements would lead to the decimation of services. Labour's motion today states that the threat of rail privatisation is leading to a "blight of investment".

Let us examine the facts. If the prospects of privatisation were blighting investment, we would expect to see that reflected in investment expenditure since we embarked on the process of preparing for privatisation. Figures show that in each of the past four years—a reasonable period in which to consider preparations for the privatisation programme—under this Government investment has been higher than in any year under the previous Labour Government. The average under that Labour Government between 1974 and 1978-79 was £924 million a year.

**Mr. McLeish:** Is that at today's prices?

**Mr. Watts:** Yes. I am not using any accountant's sleight of hand by not taking account of inflation.

In the past four years, investment expenditure has been: in 1990-91, £1,216 million; in 1991-92, £1,442 million; in 1992-93, £1,552 million; and in 1993-94, £1,188 million. That makes an average of £1,350 million in each of those years. The increase in real terms in average spend when comparing those four years with the last four years of the previous Labour Government is 46 per cent.

**Mr. Meacher:** Will the Minister give the figures excluding channel tunnel and European Passenger Services expenditure? Will he confirm that over the past four years there has been a steady decline in expenditure on the existing rail network, which, if we take into account expenditure this year, is about half what it was in real terms four years ago?

**Mr. Watts:** The hon. Gentleman has a strange idea of what constitutes a real railway. Does he suggest that the improved facilities between London and the channel tunnel are not part of the real rail infrastructure? One can exclude from an argument anything that is detrimental to one's own argument, but regular users of Eurostar and businesses that use freight services through the channel tunnel know all too well that the investment, which the hon. Gentleman rightly says includes investment to improve continental services through the channel tunnel, is very much real investment and it has led to real infrastructure.

I was asked about the current position. In 1994-95, investment was sustained at more than £1 billion and it continues at that level in the current year. My right hon. Friend the Secretary of State was asked how much Railtrack is investing. In the current year, Railtrack's investment programme is £625 million, an increase of 10

[Mr. Watts]

per cent. over the previous year. The Government need no lectures from the Opposition about the investment needs of the railway.

**Dr. John Reid** (Motherwell, North): I know that the Minister is honest and straightforward so I shall take his statistics at face value. I simply want to be clear about what he is telling the British people. Is he telling them, contrary to what we say, that the Government are spending more of their money to invest more in the railways in order that, when they are privatised, they will make more money, which will go back to the private sector? Is that what he is boasting about?

**Mr. Watts:** No. What I am boasting about, if "boasting" is the right term, is that, in the years of preparation for privatisation, which the Opposition's motion claims has been blighting investment, we have spent—

**Dr. Reid:** No, you have not. The taxpayers have spent.

**Mr. Watts:** The hon. Gentleman is right to make that point. Taxpayers, through the Government, have been providing British Rail and Railtrack with expenditure that is on average 46 per cent. up in real terms compared with the period when Labour was last in government.

**Dr. Reid** *rose—*

**Mr. Watts:** I cannot give way again as I must seek to reply to a number of points.

A key feature of the privatisation policy is that the privatised railway, freed from public expenditure constraints—although they have not been as constraining as they were under the last Labour Government—will have access to the private sector to raise funds for investment. That will be important both for Railtrack and the rolling stock leasing companies.

I know that Opposition Members have an antipathy to looking at the success of privatisation policies, so I shall give them just one example. There is every realistic expectation that, after privatisation, investment will be higher. I refer Opposition Members to BAA, our airport operator, which, every year since it has been in the private sector has invested on average three times as much as it did when it was in public ownership.

The hon. Member for York (Mr. Bayley) referred to the proposed closure of the ABB works at York. I pay tribute to the hon. Gentleman, to my hon. Friend the Member for Ryedale (Mr. Greenway) and to my right hon. Friend the Member for Selby (Mr. Alison) for their efforts to ensure that their constituents who work at ABB would have the prospect of future work. I hope that the hon. Member for York will be generous enough to acknowledge that I have not been an entirely passive observer of those events. He will know that in March, although British Rail had concluded that it had no pressing commercial need to order further rolling stock, in recognition of the order position facing the manufacturing industry it issued an invitation to tender to ABB and to GEC Alsthom for a further supply of Networker trains for Kent services. Tenders are due in from those two manufacturers on 26 May.

The hon. Member for York will recognise that one reason why British Rail was prepared to offer such an invitation to tender was that it recognised the problems facing the industry and was aware of the concerns that the hon. Gentleman and my right hon. and hon Friends had been expressing on behalf of their constituents. However, no manufacturer can expect the right to supply what it wants to supply when it wants to supply it, regardless of the customer's requirements. British Rail does not want to order trains identical to those currently being constructed under the special £150 million leasing deal put together last year. Moreover, ABB must compete for whatever contracts are available in the marketplace. Part of ABB's problem is that it has failed to win enough of the contracts in the marketplace to secure the work load that it needs.

I know that we shall have a further opportunity to debate those issues next week in a debate which the hon. Member for York has requested, so I shall not go into further detail now. I must move on to other points.

Matters related to the creation of alternative employment opportunities, although not primarily a matter for my Department, will certainly be of concern to other Departments and I shall discuss with my ministerial colleagues in the relevant Departments the hon. Gentleman's point about the need to address employment problems in York.

**Mr. Bayley:** I acknowledge that the Minister put pressure on British Rail to seek tenders for orders in March, but does he acknowledge that that was too late? Last May, the Minister's predecessor, the right hon. Member for Kettering (Mr. Freeman), attended the York Rail Forum. He said:

"There is a prima facie case for Kent Coast rolling stock. . . . in the period July-September 1994 the question of who places the order and who owns the stock and the train operating lease will be resolved."

Does the Minister recognise that, had the Government stuck to the timetable set down by the then Minister of State, we would not now have the crisis that has led to the closure of the York works?

**Mr. Watts:** As I have just explained, that would depend partly on whether ABB was successful in securing the order. Frankly, one of the major problems that ABB has faced is its failure to secure the orders that are available— for example, the order for Northern line trains worth £400 million, which was placed earlier this year, and last year the contract for the supply of Heathrow Express trains.

The hon. Member for Fife, Central expressed his concerns about passenger services. He seemed to think that there was something sinister about invitations to tender. He will be aware that there is no secrecy about passenger service requirements, which set out the guaranteed services for passengers. Invitations to tender are a matter of commercial negotiation but there is nothing sinister about that. Yesterday's announcement of the final PSRs for the first three franchises following consultation show that the consultation process on passenger service requirements is genuine.

The franchising director has announced a number of improved specifications to provide better services to passengers. For example, on the Great Western line, direct services are now to be specified from Reading and Swindon to Chippenham, Bath, Bristol and Cardiff. That will be welcome news to many of my right hon. and hon. Friends. Similar arrangements will be made for services to Didcot. Additional safeguards are being provided for first and last trains, such as an early-morning arrival at Exeter. Maximum journey times are to be tightened and there is to be at least one "flagship" service both from south Wales and the west country, meeting the current best performance times.

As well as the rigorous requirements set out by the franchising director, Great Western Trains has announced that it is introducing an additional early-morning train from Penzance to Paddington with the introduction of the new summertime timetable. The night riviera sleeper service will now run to Waterloo to provide connections with Eurostar.

**Mr. Tyler** *rose*—

**Mr. Watts:** I am sorry, I cannot give way because I am pressed for time.

The times of the first and last trains on South West Trains have been adjusted to provide earlier and later services. Stops on certain services have been guaranteed at Vauxhall, Clapham Junction, Wimbledon and Woking to facilitate connections to airports and London Underground. Seating capacity has been specified on peak period services from Salisbury to Exeter and from Reading. Extra connections have been specified at Basingstoke for the last train from Exeter. There will be an extra Sunday service from London to Exeter and an extra early morning arrival at Weymouth.

My hon. Friend the Member for Castle Point (Dr. Spink) expressed his confidence that the improved services for his constituents will encourage more people to travel by train. He is right that they will be attracted by real terms reductions in fares over the next seven years. He may be interested to know that I shall visit the London-Tilbury-Southend line tomorrow morning. My hon. Friend reminded us that services for his constituents have improved because of a £150 million investment in new signalling and the prospect of new rolling stock.

My hon. Friend the Member for Castle Point will be aware that the passenger service requirement announced yesterday provides improved safeguards for first and last trains on every route and full frequency services to Limehouse, which will provide an interchange with the docklands light railway. The PSR provides a new obligation on the Ockenden to Tilbury service to connect with the Tilbury ferry. *[Interruption.]* I am sorry if Opposition Members find the details of those service improvements boring, but as they continually claim that services are to be decimated it is important to set the record straight.

My hon. Friends the Members for Basildon (Mr. Amess), for Castle Point and others who represent Essex will also know that the new summer timetable, to be introduced later this month, will provide additional services between Upminster and Grays, which will serve the new station at Chafford Hundred. Their constituents will therefore have the environmentally friendly option of shopping at Lakeside and travelling there by train rather than having to use their cars.

**Dr. Reid:** What about toilets?

**Mr. Watts:** I have described improvements in services to passengers, but the hon. Gentleman asks me about toilets. I leave hon. Members to draw their own conclusion from that.

In addition to the new services I have mentioned, the new summer timetable includes several new services—for example, an hourly service from south Humberside to Doncaster, Sheffield and Manchester airport. That will operate in addition to the existing extensive range of rail connections to Manchester. New direct services will run from Brighton to Lewes, Eastbourne, Hastings and Ashford. They will provide direct connections with Eurostar trains when the international station at Ashford is open next year.

**Mr. McLeish:** Will Minister give way?

**Mr. Watts:** No, I cannot.

A through service will operate from Tunbridge Wells and Tonbridge to Redhill, Croydon and Victoria. A through service will also operate from Brighton, Worthing, Chichester and Havant to Fareham, Winchester, Basingstoke and Reading, which provides a practical and environmentally friendly alternative to using the M25 and A27.

Those improvements to PSRs and the additional services that are being introduced by British Rail create a different picture from that painted by Opposition Members. Far from being a rundown and running down railway system, it suggests a railway system that is gearing up to meet the opportunities and challenges of privatisation, and doing so with enthusiasm. I believe that managers in the railways and those who work on the railways—it is right to record our thanks to them for the sterling work that they have done for many years—will seize those new opportunities with great enthusiasm.

My hon. Friend the Member for Beaconsfield (Mr. Smith) recognised that there will be opportunity and incentive to develop services further and thus to increase revenue. That is how the private sector will respond.

My hon. Friend the Member for Hertsmere (Mr. Clappison) was right to welcome the new fares policy, on behalf of his constituents, which was spelt out earlier this week. Much to the embarrassment of Opposition Members, he reminded the House of the Labour Government's contrasting and appalling record on rail fares. He also raised the important issue of car parking at Radlett and other stations in his constituency. I am sure that his comments will be noted by British Rail and, more particularly, by those in the private sector who may eventually bid for the franchise.

The hon. Member for Fife, Central claimed that few fares would be controlled. In the course of a week, Opposition Members have gone from speaking about 100 per cent. control to little control. If the Opposition Front-Bench spokesman is right that few fares will be controlled, how can his hon. Friend the Member for Hampstead and Highgate (Ms Jackson) be right when she suggested that the cost of keeping down a small number of fares could lead to an extra subsidy of £350 million a year?

**Mr. McLeish:** Will the Minister confirm that 50 per cent. of the rail network will be unregulated? Will he also confirm the extent of subsidy to finance fare capping? The Secretary of State managed to avoid answering that question.

**Mr. Watts:** The proportion of fares controlled on each line will vary from line to line. It will also vary as between the amount of revenue that is controlled and the number of journeys subject to control. The policy is to control key

[Mr. Watts]

fares for commuters and other users rather than to regulate every fare. The hon. Gentleman will understand that, for example, if the saver fare is controlled, that will set a limit on the extent to which the cheaper and more heavily discounted, but more restricted fares can also be increased. If there was no significant differential between a saver and a supersaver, why would any passenger want to buy a supersaver? It is not necessary to control every fare to achieve broad regulation of fares across the railways.

Opposition Members must understand that the amount of subsidy will depend on the competitive bidding process in the letting of franchises. Unlike a monolithic nationalised industry, where increasing a subsidy merely means money is poured into a bottomless pit, competition between rival operators to secure the right to run rail services will effectively put a cap on the demands made for subsidy.

As my hon. Friend the Member for Beaconsfield reminded us, private sector operators will be looking for every opportunity to increase their revenue which, in itself, will reduce their demands for subsidy. They will not go to the franchising director and, like Oliver Twist, ask for more. They will seek to pitch their bids for subsidy at a level that secures for them the right to operate the services that they find attractive.

We are implementing a policy to arrest the long-term decline of the railway industry that we have seen ever since it was nationalised. From the Labour Government of 1964 to today, the proportion of passengers carried on the railways has reduced by 2 per cent. a decade. My hon. Friend the Member for Beaconsfield stressed the need for a new structure. That was not a criticism of the people who have worked in the railway industry through the dark days of nationalisation, but a recognition of the fact that the existing structure has failed them.

The Labour party may have buried clause IV in favour of voter-friendly language about the market economy, but its commitment to state ownership and control remains clear in the motion that it has tabled today. The command economy may be dead in eastern Europe, but it is alive and kicking in Walworth road.

*Question put,* That the original words stand part of the Question:—

*The House divided:* Ayes 255, Noes 279.

**Division No. 150]**                                    **[6.59 pm**

### AYES

Abbott, Ms Diane
Allen, Graham
Alton, David
Anderson, Donald (Swansea E)
Anderson, Ms Janet (Ros'dale)
Armstrong, Hilary
Ashdown, Rt Hon Paddy
Ashton, Joe
Austin-Walker, John
Banks, Tony (Newham NW)
Barnes, Harry
Barron, Kevin
Battle, John
Bayley, Hugh
Beckett, Rt Hon Margaret
Beggs, Roy
Beith, Rt Hon A J
Bell, Stuart

Benn, Rt Hon Tony
Bennett, Andrew F
Benton, Joe
Bermingham, Gerald
Berry, Roger
Betts, Clive
Blair, Rt Hon Tony
Boateng, Paul
Bradley, Keith
Bray, Dr Jeremy
Brown, Gordon (Dunfermline E)
Brown, N (N'c'tle upon Tyne E)
Bruce, Malcolm (Gordon)
Burden, Richard
Caborn, Richard
Callaghan, Jim
Campbell, Mrs Anne (C'bridge)
Campbell, Menzies (Fife NE)

Canavan, Dennis
Chidgey, David
Chisholm, Malcolm
Church, Judith
Clapham, Michael
Clark, Dr David (South Shields)
Clarke, Eric (Midlothian)
Clarke, Tom (Monklands W)
Clelland, David
Clwyd, Mrs Ann
Coffey, Ann
Cohen, Harry
Connarty, Michael
Cook, Frank (Stockton N)
Cook, Robin (Livingston)
Corbett, Robin
Corbyn, Jeremy
Cousins, Jim
Cummings, John
Cunliffe, Lawrence
Cunningham, Jim (Covy SE)
Cunningham, Rt Hon Dr John
Dalyell, Tam
Davidson, Ian
Davies, Bryan (Oldham C'tral)
Davies, Rt Hon Denzil (Llanelli)
Davies, Ron (Caerphilly)
Denham, John
Dewar, Donald
Dixon, Don
Donohoe, Brian H
Dowd, Jim
Dunnachie, Jimmy
Dunwoody, Mrs Gwyneth
Eastham, Ken
Enright, Derek
Etherington, Bill
Evans, John (St Helens N)
Ewing, Mrs Margaret
Fatchett, Derek
Field, Frank (Birkenhead)
Flynn, Paul
Forsythe, Clifford (S Antrim)
Foster, Rt Hon Derek
Foster, Don (Bath)
Foulkes, George
Fraser, John
Fyfe, Maria
Galbraith, Sam
Galloway, George
Gapes, Mike
Garrett, John
Gerrard, Neil
Gilbert, Rt Hon Dr John
Godman, Dr Norman A
Godsiff, Roger
Golding, Mrs Llin
Gordon, Mildred
Graham, Thomas
Grant, Bernie (Tottenham)
Griffiths, Nigel (Edinburgh S)
Griffiths, Win (Bridgend)
Grocott, Bruce
Hain, Peter
Hall, Mike
Harvey, Nick
Hattersley, Rt Hon Roy
Henderson, Doug
Heppell, John
Hill, Keith (Streatham)
Hinchliffe, David
Hodge, Margaret
Hoey, Kate
Hogg, Norman (Cumbernauld)
Hood, Jimmy
Hoon, Geoffrey

Howarth, George (Knowsley North)
Howells, Dr. Kim (Pontypridd)
Hoyle, Doug
Hughes, Kevin (Doncaster N)
Hughes, Robert (Aberdeen N)
Hughes, Roy (Newport E)
Hughes, Simon (Southwark)
Hutton, John
Illsley, Eric
Ingram, Adam
Jackson, Glenda (H'stead)
Jackson, Helen (Shef'ld, H)
Jamieson, David
Janner, Greville
Johnston, Sir Russell
Jones, Barry (Alyn and D'side)
Jones, Jon Owen (Cardiff C)
Jones, Lynne (B'ham S O)
Jones, Martyn (Clwyd, SW)
Jowell, Tessa
Kaufman, Rt Hon Gerald
Keen, Alan
Kennedy, Charles (Ross,C&S)
Kennedy, Jane (Lpool Brdgn)
Khabra, Piara S
Kilfoyle, Peter
Kirkwood, Archy
Lestor, Joan (Eccles)
Lewis, Terry
Litherland, Robert
Livingstone, Ken
Lloyd, Tony (Stretford)
Loyden, Eddie
McAllion, John
McAvoy, Thomas
McCartney, Ian
McCrea, The Reverend William
Macdonald, Calum
McFall, John
McKelvey, William
Mackinlay, Andrew
McLeish, Henry
Maclennan, Robert
McMaster, Gordon
McNamara, Kevin
MacShane, Denis
Madden, Max
Maddock, Diana
Maginnis, Ken
Mahon, Alice
Mandelson, Peter
Marek, Dr John
Martin, Michael J (Springburn)
Martlew, Eric
Meacher, Michael
Michael, Alun
Michie, Bill (Sheffield Heeley)
Michie, Mrs Ray (Argyll & Bute)
Milburn, Alan
Miller, Andrew
Morgan, Rhodri
Morley, Elliot
Morris, Rt Hon Alfred (Wy'nshawe)
Morris, Estelle (B'ham Yardley)
Morris, Rt Hon John (Aberavon)
Mowlam, Marjorie
Mudie, George
Mullin, Chris
Murphy, Paul
Oakes, Rt Hon Gordon
O'Brien, William (Normanton)
O'Hara, Edward
Olner, Bill
O'Neill, Martin
Orme, Rt Hon Stanley
Parry, Robert

Ministers now seem prepared to sell anything, even the most sensitive of industries, to plug the hole in Treasury coffers.

The consumer is offered what looks like a sweetener—cash for not asking questions: the £20 that is allegedly to be cut from domestic bills. It is a con—the political equivalent of the three-card trick. The £20 off—the 8 per cent. reduction in electricity prices—has been trumpeted by the Tory party and held up in the private Tory party briefing for Conservative Members as the major argument for the privatisation. That sweetener has nothing to do with privatisation. Ending the fossil fuel levy has nothing to do—

**Mr. Phil Gallie** (Ayr): Will the hon. Gentleman give way?

**Mr. Robertson:** How can I resist the hon. Gentleman?

**Mr. Gallie:** Does the hon. Gentleman agree that nuclear engineering and nuclear generation are desirable? If they are, does he believe that there should be another nuclear power station built in the United Kingdom? If he believes that, could he suggest a cost for it and say whether a Labour Government would ever find the cash to supply such a station?

**Mr. Robertson:** The hon. Gentleman might check what his own party is saying about the matter, as it happens to be the Government temporarily. The privatisation reveals that there will be no more public finance in order to build nuclear power stations. The Government are ending the nuclear build programme. It appears that the Whips and the Scottish Office Ministers have spoken to the hon. Gentleman who rebelled a couple of weeks ago in Scotland—perhaps he rebels all the time now—and, as a consequence, he is crawling around attempting to support a case that he knows deep down is not worth sustaining.

Ending the fossil fuel levy has nothing to do with flogging off the nuclear reactors of Britain to whoever wants to buy them. It is a cynical and serious matter to deceive the electorate by pretending that it is largesse resulting from privatisation. Perhaps the Secretary of State for Scotland will confirm whether the 8 per cent. price reduction and the £20 that the Government claim will be cut from electricity bills could have been achieved while retaining the nuclear industry within the public sector.

Will the Secretary of State concede that point? I shall give way to allow him to answer that relatively simple question. Could not those price cuts—that sweetener—have been made without privatisation? I shall give way to allow the right hon. Gentleman to answer that simple and important question. Will he tell the House and the country the answer? Is he not able to tell us; does he not know the answer? Is it not a fact that, if he stood at the Dispatch Box, he would be forced to admit that the sweetener has nothing to do with privatising the nuclear power industry but has to do with a fossil fuel levy that could have been cut off at any point? By his silence, the Secretary of State reveals the weakness of the Government's case. We can draw only one conclusion from his silence.

**Dr. Michael Clark** (Rochford): Perhaps I could attempt to assist the hon. Gentleman by answering the question that he has put several times. He will know that the nuclear levy has been withdrawn because the liberalised and semi-privatised nuclear industry, which has been run very effectively as a separate company, has

raised enough cash to pay for decommissioning the nuclear power stations in due course. The next step is to privatise them so that they will become even more efficient and effective. The money has been raised by the efficient working of the nuclear industry since the initial privatisation took place.

**Mr. Robertson:** The hon. Gentleman is normally authoritative about these matters, and I admire his courage in wandering into the firing line when a member of the Cabinet sits rooted to his seat when confronted with that relatively simple question. However, there is no evidence to suggest that the hon. Gentleman is correct. Last Wednesday, the *Financial Times* made exactly that point in an analysis which was cruel from the Government's point of view. It said:

"unless the government can come up with a convincing explanation of how the money will be found, the assumption must be that the cost"—

of decommissioning—after all, that is what the nuclear component of the fossil fuel levy was all about—

"will ultimately fall on the taxpayer".

The reality is that the Government are going to privatise the nuclear power industry and quite separately—it is irrelevant to the privatisation process—are going to cut off one part of the fossil fuel levy and give the people their money back as a free gift.

**Dr. Robert Spink** (Castle Point): Will the hon. Gentleman give way?

**Mr. Robertson:** No, I shall make some progress.

The Government intend to bribe the people with their own money, which was to go towards paying the vast and indeterminate costs of decommissioning Britain's power stations. As the *Financial Times* correctly points out, that money will have to be raised from the next generation of taxpayers. As usual, the taxpayers will suffer as the new shareholders get a bargain.

The Government's nuclear sums simply do not add up. The Government claim that the Magnox liabilities for Scottish Nuclear and Nuclear Electric amount to £8.5 billion. Will the Secretary of State confirm that that is less than the combined total worth of the two companies as is stated in their annual reports? How does he explain the discrepancy between the Government's figure and what is in the annual reports? What piece of creative accountancy can justify that discrepancy? Will he make available to the House a full detailed breakdown of the Government's new estimates so that hon. Members can decide for themselves?

**Dr. Spink:** Is the hon. Gentleman aware that the first phase of decommissioning the Berkeley Magnox plant has been completed and that it cost one third less than was estimated? Other research shows that the decommissioning costs will be much lower than assumed initially. Will the hon. Gentleman acknowledge those facts?

**Mr. Robertson:** The hon. Gentleman uses one example to make one point, but there are plenty of other examples. The industry experts know that the decommissioning costs will be much greater than the Government estimate. If the Government are willing to publish the details in full, perhaps Opposition Members will be persuaded by the Government's argument.

[Mr. Robertson]

On the basis of the Government's own figures, £5.9 billion has been raised so far to meet the liabilities. Will the Secretary of State confirm that, even according to the Government's published figures, a £2.6 billion funding gap remains? Will he confirm also that even the £5.9 billion figure includes speculative projected savings of 10 per cent. in Magnox liability costs that may or may not materialise? If they do not, the gap in the Government's nuclear sums will increase to £3.5 billion.

There is no guarantee that the Government will raise even that amount from privatisation. Some of the estimates that we have seen so far have been as low as £2 billion. Even if all the cash raised from privatisation were put aside to pay for decommissioning, there is no guarantee that it would meet the full minimum costs of the Magnox liabilities. Of course, it will not be put aside for decommissioning; it will be used to pay for tax bribes to save a dying Government.

Once again, future generations will be forced to clean up the mess that is left by the Government. The public will pay twice because the money that was supposed to pay for decommissioning was spent instead on Sizewell B and the income from Sizewell B that was supposed to help to finance the liabilities of the Magnox plants will be hived off. In other words, the private shareholders will get the assets and the taxpayers will get all the liabilities and they will pay twice. That is some deal for the taxpayers.

Although much attention has correctly been focused on the Magnox liabilities, I would like to pursue the Secretary of State—if he ever decides to answer a question—on the issue of the other liabilities that the private sector will have to accept. Perhaps he is currently being briefed about my first question. It seems pointless to ask questions of him if he does not even bother to listen to them.

What guarantees can the Government give that the taxpayers might not in future have to foot the bill for decommissioning Britain's advanced gas-cooled reactors and pressurised water reactors? Given the difficulty of quantifying decommissioning costs, does the Secretary of State expect the private sector to accept such massive, open-ended liabilities? Of course he does not; no one does.

The *Financial Times* said:

"The City is likely to demand a premium for investing in nuclear power . . . Investors will want reassurance about the liabilities for clean-up costs."

Of course, the implicit deal is that the public will get stuck with the bill. The financial risks involved in investing in the nuclear industry will be massive. If the operators are persuaded to buy the industry, frankly, it will have to be at car boot sale prices, and a boot sale bargain is precisely what it will be. The new Sizewell B reactor cost almost £3 billion to complete, so, in effect, investors in the nuclear power industry are buying into a new holding company and they will get the other seven reactors for free—eight nuclear reactors for the price of one. Once again, the bottom line is that the Government are selling off public assets at a massive discount to the City and a massive loss to the country.

What happens if the privatised company falls into financial difficulty? After all, it will not be just any old company. It cannot board up the windows of nuclear power stations and put up a "To Let" sign. We are talking about nuclear reactors. If the privatised company does not make sufficient provision for decommissioning, the taxpayer will have to pick up the tab as a last resort. Will the Secretary of State for Scotland tell us tonight that that is not true and that, in the deep recesses of the future, the decommissioning costs will be picked up by the private buyers?

It is no use the Government saying that a segregated fund for decommissioning will do the trick. A private company, whose entire raison d'être is to maximise returns to shareholders, will not want to set aside money for decommissioning. Heaven knows, the short-termism in the City of London is such that most investors are concerned with the next five to 10 years at most, never mind liabilities that may arise 100 years down the line. What real incentive will a private company have to put aside the necessary money?

Of course, nobody knows what the final bill will be. In respect of Sizewell B, for example, nobody has ever decommissioned a pressurised water reactor before. How do we know how much it will cost to decommission Sizewell B? The answer is that we do not know. However, we know that Scottish Nuclear is budgeting £10 million this year alone to start decommissioning Hunterston A in Ayrshire.

We do not even know how the Government plan to dispose of old stations and their waste because Ministers have swept the issue under the carpet until after privatisation. What else will be swept under the carpet? What other rabbits will the President of the Board of Trade pull out of his hat once the shares have been sold? What guarantees do investors have that they will not be sold another false prospectus by the Government? Investors know that it has happened before and they have a right to know now what the prospectus will be. Far from offering the nuclear industry a bright future, nuclear privatisation is just another way for the Government to further absolve themselves of the responsibility for Britain's long-term energy needs.

Ministers are quick enough to criticise Labour for refusing to invest in new nuclear power stations, but I say to the hon. Member for Ayr (Mr. Gallie), who should know better—perhaps he was put up to ask the question—that the Government are not prepared to invest in new generating capacity either; they are not prepared to put their money where their mouth is.

The inevitable consequence is that any privatised nuclear company unable to find money for a new nuclear power station will want to diversify into gas-fired generation. Everybody says it and everybody knows it. *The Times* put it succinctly last Wednesday:

"That could mean that a private nuclear industry would by slow degree cease to be nuclear at all."

What future is that for the nuclear industry or, for that matter, for the coal industry that was decimated by the previous dash for gas? Do not Ministers care at all about the long-term mix of energy resources?

Roger Hayes, director-general of the British Nuclear Forum, said:

"It is . . . unfortunate that the Government appears to believe our energy needs can be left entirely to that the short-termism of market forces. They cannot."

The same free market in energy that brought about the dash for gas and ruined the coal industry will wreck the nuclear industry, too. What will that do for investment, research and development and jobs?

**Mr. Matthew Taylor** (Truro): I understand the criticisms that the hon. Gentleman is making of the Government's position on the long-term future of the nuclear industry, but I do not understand them in the context of the Labour party's manifesto commitment not to build new nuclear power stations and the environmental policy document published just today which makes the same statement.

**Mr. Robertson:** If the hon. Gentleman is confessing that he does not understand, I am stating that the Government's position is being undermined by their own policies. The Labour party has made its position absolutely clear in regard to the need for a long-term mix in the energy needs of the country.

I return to the crucial issue of jobs. Some 70,000 jobs have been lost in the gas, water and electricity industries in Britain since privatisation, so why should the nuclear industry be any different? Why should it expect anything different from privatisation?

The Conservative party briefing for Back Benchers, which no doubt we shall hear repeated to the House this evening, is careful and economic with the language it uses in respect of jobs. It says:

"Privatisation will offer new opportunities for staff and management, and is expected to create at least 100 extra jobs in Scotland."

That is a critical argument. There will be no extra jobs anywhere else and jobs will be created in Scotland by a paper transfer across the border. That is just another promise in line with other promises that have been made and betrayed in the past.

The privatisation bears all the hallmarks of previous sell-offs. If it goes ahead, we can expect a rerun of what happened in all the other privatised utilities—massive job losses, huge price increases and directors making themselves obscenely rich at the expense of the consumer.

Privatisation simply is not needed to make the nuclear industry more efficient. After all, Ministers spent the past five years telling us that it was already the very model of efficiency. At the time of the coal review, they never tired of telling us about the improvements in productivity that had taken place, and that is confirmed in the White Paper. Profits are up, productivity is up and costs are down. If the nuclear industry can improve efficiency so dramatically in the public sector, why is there any need to privatise it? If it ain't broke, why are they trying to fix it?

How can privatisation possibly enhance competition when more than a quarter of Britain's electricity generating capacity will be in the hands of one company and when the other two generators and generating companies in England and Wales—National Power and PowerGen—are asked to divest themselves of significant generating capacity?

The regulator himself argued against the creation of a large nuclear monolith. He also expressed concern that Nuclear Electric's current market power

"may have restricted choice and increased prices."

Why are the Government giving it even more market power when even the Electricity Consumers Council says that customers have been massively overcharged for their electricity since privatisation? How will less competition benefit the consumer? Given that the combined company will account for 23 per cent. of electricity generation in the United Kingdom, how can the Secretary of State—I hope that he will take note of this and return to it in his speech—and the Government guarantee that any flotation would not be affected by a possible reference to the Monopolies and Mergers Commission in future?

The shotgun wedding of Nuclear Electric and Scottish Nuclear has nothing to do with the future of the Scottish nuclear industry, and everyone north of the border knows that. It has everything to do with raising as much cash as possible as quickly as possible to plug the gap in the Treasury coffers.

Ministers' claims that the merged company will be able to compete on the world stage simply do not hold water. Adding Scottish Nuclear's two AGRs still leaves the combined company nowhere near the size of Electricité de France, one of its chief rivals. Most experts agree that the key to winning overseas orders is not size but reactor design and a track record in running the reactor type in question. How, then, will adding two AGRs to its generating capacity help Nuclear Electric to win any Taiwanese PWR deal?

The nuclear fusion of Nuclear Electric and Scottish Nuclear is a shoddy betrayal of Scotland's interests. Government guarantees are little more than a cruel confidence trick designed to buy off yet another Tory Back-Bench revolt. Only half the number in revolt is here this evening, and that might even be on the generous side.

While the Scottish Office spin doctors—there seem to be rather a lot of them—have been trumpeting the jobs as a triumph for the Secretary of State for Scotland, the press release from Scottish Nuclear said it all:

"Scottish Nuclear welcomes the decision if it secures future jobs in Scotland."

That is a mighty important "if". Scottish Nuclear is right to be sceptical. After the previous experience of those of us in Scotland of Britoil and the Guinness takeover of Distillers, that if is a pretty big and important "if".

It is therefore no surprise that Sir Donald Miller, hardly the friend of the left in Scottish politics, the former chairman of the South of Scotland electricity board and Scottish Power, described the new brass plate destined for somewhere in Scotland as merely a sop and called the merger a breach of faith.

Do the Government not realise that paper guarantees are not good enough? Why should anyone in Scotland believe the Government's words? The Secretary of State for Scotland wrote to me last week about the triple lock of the establishment of the substantive headquarters in Scotland well in advance of privatisation, incorporation of the key features in the memorandum and articles of association and specific protection of those key features through special shares.

How many times in the past 16 years have we heard about the golden shares, the special shares, the locks, and how many of them are still intact today? None at all. No one in Scotland and no one in the rest of the country believes a word that the Government say.

Then there is the crucial and vital matter of safety. The publicly owned British nuclear industry has an excellent safety record—one of the best in the world. That is a tribute to the management and work force as well as to the fine work of the nuclear installations inspectorate.

*[Mr. Robertson]*

Why, then, should Britain want to jeopardise that record with these dangerous plans? Not only is there a conflict between short-term private profit and the long-term interests of public safety and the environment but there is a real concern that the inspectorate is not properly equipped to regulate a privately owned nuclear industry.

We must recognise that there are substantial costs relating to the regulation of nuclear safety. In the United Kingdom, safety is clearly the responsibility of the nuclear operator. In essence, the onus is on the operator to prove the safety case to a small specialist staff.

In the United States, where the industry is largely in private hands, the demands of the private sector shareholders have ensured that the nuclear utilities take the view that safety is not their responsibility and that regulation is not for them but for the regulator. As a consequence, the American equivalent of the nuclear installations inspectorate is large, bureaucratic and expensive. That expense will have to be borne by the taxpayer if we go down the American route of a privatised industry.

I give this warning now: if the industry is privatised, we will put in place the toughest, strongest, most stringent nuclear safety regime to be found in the world.

**The Secretary of State for Scotland (Mr. Ian Lang):** We have that now.

**Mr. Robertson:** Yes, we have, and there are precious few people in the country who believe for a moment that in order to get rid of the industry on the private market there will not be a weakening in the safety regime. No one believes that. I am simply making it clear that we will put in place the toughest regime that is possible here. Given the apprehensions that exist about nuclear power stations in the private sector, that is a commitment that should be noticed by the public and by the market.

This is the most ill-conceived privatisation of all. It is unwanted and unnecessary. Once again, public assets will be sold, probably at a knock-down price, and while the shareholders and directors of the new company my make themselves rich on the profits, the consumer and the taxpayer will be forced to pick up the tab in the end.

The Government's guarantees about the future of Scottish Nuclear are no more than a fraudulent fig leaf. I urge the hon. Member for Ayr, since he appears to be the only one of the former rebels who is now even interested, to be serious about the whole question of Scottish jobs and a great Scottish company, and not to be bought off with such cheap promises. I invite him to join us in the Lobby tonight and to take a stand for sense, safety and efficiency in this unique and most important of industries.

7.45 pm

**The Secretary of State for Scotland (Mr. Ian Lang):** I beg to move, to leave out from "House" to the end of the Question and to add instead thereof:

"welcomes the outcome of the Government's Nuclear Review; applauds the improvements in performance by the nuclear generators since the privatisation of the rest of the electricity supply industry, including the reduction of decommissioning costs achieved so far; welcomes the proposals for more cost-effective management of Magnox liabilities; welcomes the Government's decision to privatise the industry's seven AGR stations and one PWR station during the course of 1996; endorses the decision to create a holding company, with its headquarters located in Scotland, with the parts of Nuclear Electric and Scottish Nuclear that are to be privatised as its wholly owned subsidiaries; notes that safety will continue to be of paramount importance when the industry is in the private sector; and applauds the benefits to consumers in terms of lower electricity prices which the early end to the nuclear element of the fossil fuel levy in England and Wales and to the premium price in the Nuclear Energy Agreement in Scotland will bring.".

I listened with great interest and even greater curiosity as the hon. Member for Hamilton (Mr. Robertson) poured forth about the future of our nuclear industry. The bogus nature of the sentiments that he expressed and the inherently fraudulent prospectus for the future of the nuclear industry that he offered the House will become clear if I remind the House of the manifesto on which he and his colleagues fought the last general election. It said:

"We will not invest in new nuclear power stations . . . or extend the lives of existing nuclear stations beyond their safe lifespan. Britain's dependence on nuclear power will therefore steadily diminish."

That is the reality of the twilight world of decline and decay, with jobs and technology withering and disappearing, to which the Opposition stand committed.

Nor have the Opposition changed their view since then. The hon. Member for Clackmannan (Mr. O'Neill), whom I see in his seat, Labour's energy spokesman, speaking earlier this year, said:

"Labour's position remains as it was at the last general election."

Therefore, a public sector nuclear industry would know exactly what to expect from a Labour Government: decline and decay leading to demise.

**Mr. Andrew Miller** (Ellesmere Port and Neston): Will the Secretary of State give way?

**Mr. Lang:** Yes. Perhaps the hon. Gentleman will recant on behalf of his party.

**Mr. Miller:** The right hon. Gentleman will know my position on nuclear power. Will he be specific and tell the House how many jobs there are now in the nuclear industry and how many there were, say, 10 years ago? Is it not true that there has been a rapid decline in the number of real jobs in the industry and that that is all down to the Government's failure to develop a proper energy policy?

**Mr. Lang:** There has been a rapid improvement in productivity and efficiency in the industry, which has enabled costs to come down and privatisation to be contemplated. Under the Opposition, however, there will ultimately be no jobs at all in the industry, and that should concern the hon. Gentleman.

The only thing that was clear from the speech made by the hon. Member for Hamilton was that Labour has not abandoned its knee-jerk reaction to every privatisation ever proposed, even though it claims to have abandoned clause IV. I say "claims" because the very day after voting to abandon clause IV in Scotland, Labour's Scottish conference voted to nationalise every single public utility. Does that extend, one wonders, to the privatised nuclear industry? Or would that be the only public utility in Scotland that Labour would not renationalise? I listened throughout the 31 minutes for which the hon. Gentleman spoke to hear that commitment. Perhaps he would like to clarify the position now. I will gladly give way to him if he would like to do so.

**The Minister for Industry and Energy (Mr. Tim Eggar):** Sit down and give him a try.

**Mr. Lang:** The hon. Member for Cunninghame, North (Mr. Wilson) will have another opportunity. Perhaps the Opposition would like to think about it for a little while.

The Government's decisions on the nuclear generating industry were announced by my right hon. Friend the President of the Board of Trade on 9 May 1995, and I welcome the opportunity to explain them once again. Indeed, I wonder whether the hon. Member for Hamilton listened to anything that was said that day. The proposals were unalloyed good news for the industry and its employees, for the taxpayer and for electricity consumers. Unlike the Labour party's plans, they offer the industry a vibrant and enduring future, freed from the constraints of nationalised ownership.

Of course I understand that Opposition Members and the country at large want reassurance on safety—rightly so—and I am happy to give it. The nuclear generation industry in this country has an excellent safety record. I assure the House, as my right hon. Friend the President of the Board of Trade did at the time of his statement, that safety has been a paramount consideration throughout the nuclear review. Our commitment to safety will not be diminished or compromised when the industry is privatised. We shall continue to have, in the public sector, the robust and vigorous safety standards and disciplines for which the country is rightly renowned.

It is irresponsible for the Labour party or other commentators to suggest that the privatised industry will be anything other than totally committed to maintaining the excellent safety record already established by Nuclear Electric and Scottish Nuclear.

**Mr. Tam Dalyell** (Linlithgow): Will the right hon. Gentleman give way?

**Mr. Lang:** I will give way, but perhaps I may finish the argument about safety first.

The Health and Safety Commission has advised that there is no reason to change the licensing and monitoring regime for nuclear sites in any fundamental way to deal with the new structure to be privatised. That regime will remain transparent, rigorous and robust. The Government will not permit any weakening of a regulatory regime or of the safety standards currently in force. The HSC worked with the Government in preparing its timetable. The HSC will continue its independent role as regulator. In that role it will carefully consider all proposals for relicensing consistent with the Government's proposed structure for the privatisation. So we have taken steps. Both public and private sector operators will continue to be subject to the same rigorous safety regime as now applies. Our commitment to that remains absolute.

**Mr. Dalyell:** The question that I asked the President of the Board of Trade on his statement was this: is there to be no member for safety on the main board, and will the safety establishment be at Peel park? Frankly, any idea of Scottish headquarters is not very convincing without a

clear indication that the safety headquarters and all that goes with it will be at the Scottish headquarters, which most of us would like to see at Peel park.

**Mr. Lang:** I give the hon. Gentleman the answer that my right hon. Friend the President of the Board of Trade gave him. That is a matter for the Health and Safety Executive and for the nuclear installations inspectorate and will no doubt be considered as they consider the various stages of progress towards privatisation. It is not a matter for the Government to lay down; it is a matter for the health and safety authorities to satisfy themselves on, and I am certain that they will do so.

It is clear, from the motion and from the speech of the hon. Member for Hamilton, that the Opposition like to live in the past. They are aware of no reason to move on from the perception of 1989, when the nuclear stations had to be excluded from privatisation because of anxiety that was in large part about the risks of those costs and liabilities increasing unpredictably.

**Mr. John Sykes** (Scarborough) *rose*—

**Mr. Llew Smith** (Blaenau Gwent) *rose*—

**Mr. Lang:** I give way to my hon. Friend the Member for Scarborough (Mr. Sykes).

**Mr. Sykes:** Before the Secretary of State leaves the issue of safety, is it not grossly irresponsible of Labour Members to prattle on about safety, as they have done time and again, in relation to every privatisation? I think especially of gas. We have never had to nationalise ICI, a leading chemical company in this country, because of safety problems. It has produced some very dangerous chemicals indeed, but it has proved extremely able to run itself without having to be nationalised. Is it not therefore grossly irresponsible of the Labour party to talk about safety in that way?

**Mr. Lang:** My hon. Friend is absolutely right and he makes the argument very well. There are a substantial number of private nuclear sites already licensed—licensed, in some cases, by the Labour party—in the United Kingdom. To imply that safety is in any way compromised or diminished as a result of the industry entering the private sector is completely wrong and misleading. I hope that the extensive comments that I have made this evening will reassure the House about that.

**Mr. Llew Smith** *rose*—

**Mr. Brian Wilson** (Cunninghame, North) *rose*—

**Mr. Lang:** No, I must move on as I want to mention costs and liabilities.

**Mr. Wilson:** Will the Secretary of State give way on safety?

**Mr. Lang:** I will on that point.

**Mr. Wilson:** The Secretary of State will appreciate that the nuclear installations inspectorate and Her Majesty's inspectorate of pollution have each said that it will take a minimum of 12 to 14 months to go through all the relicensing procedures. Will he give an absolute assurance that no pressure will be brought to bear to truncate that process and that if that time scale proves inadequate no political pressure will be brought to bear to stay within that time scale?

[*Mr. Wilson*]

Will the Secretary of State address himself especially to the problem of the division of ownership within sites, which we have not had previously in this country, and which at Hunterston in my constituency, for instance, will give rise to new questions about the licensing procedures?

**Mr. Lang:** There is absolutely no question of the Government putting pressure on the Health and Safety Executive. It is outrageous that the hon. Gentleman should suggest that, and it is discourteous to all the safety and security organisations in the country to imply that they would be in the slightest way susceptible to such pressure.

On costs and liabilities, since 1989 uncertainties and risks surrounding the costs of decommissioning nuclear stations and managing spent fuel have in reality been substantially reduced. Experience in decommissioning has been going—

**Mr. Llew Smith:** Will the Secretary of State give way?

**Mr. Lang:** No, I should like to press on, if the hon. Gentleman will forgive me.

Experience in decommissioning has been gained at Berkeley and Hunterston A, which have both completed stage 1 of the decommissioning process ahead of schedule, and the work done so far has, as my hon. Friend the Member for Castle Point (Dr. Spink) said, been brought in at well below the estimated cost.

Moreover, both Nuclear Electric and Scottish Nuclear have agreed new fuel cycle contracts with British Nuclear Fuels plc. They are now in a much better position than they were in 1989 to demonstrate that the estimates that they have made of their long-term liabilities are robust. They have been making provision for their liabilities in a much more informed way.

Let me say a word about what Scottish Nuclear and Nuclear Electric have achieved since they were vested in 1990. Both companies have secured very substantial improvements in their financial and operational performance. Output has increased; costs have decreased. Productivity has very significantly increased. They should receive our congratulations on that. That success, driven in part by their ambition to be privatised, has facilitated the Government's decision to privatise the most modern nuclear stations.

Our decision to privatise the advanced gas-cooled reactor and pressurised water reactor power stations is therefore backed up, not only by the vastly improved performance of the AGRs but by reduction of uncertainty about long-term liabilities.

**Mr. Adam Ingram** (East Kilbride): In terms of the achievements of Nuclear Electric and Scottish Nuclear, how would the Secretary of State tackle the issue of utilisation of those stations? Those stations are running at maximum capacity, to try to achieve the best terms pre-privatisation, with both companies wanting to achieve privatisation. If that utilisation rate continues, the life span of the nuclear stations will be considerably shortened.

**Mr. Lang:** The hon. Gentleman puts his finger on precisely the type of point that the management of those companies will need to take into account as they consider the future development of the company and the future employment of their assets. I am talking at the moment about the liabilities associated with the stations to be privatised, and they will all be transferred to the private sector. It will be the Government's aim to ensure—

**Mr. Alan W. Williams** (Carmarthen) *rose—*

**Mr. Michael Clapham** (Barnsley, West and Penistone) *rose—*

**Mr. Lang:** I must make further progress.

It will be the Government's aim to ensure that the privatised companies meet their obligations in full. Specifically, they must make sufficient financial provision to meet their liabilities so that the costs of meeting them do not fall on the taxpayer by default. We believe that the setting up of segregated funds is the best way of ensuring public confidence that that will be so. We shall therefore discuss with the industry the detailed implications of setting up the segregated funds necessary.

Our decision to privatise the more modern stations does not mean that the Magnox stations have been ignored—far from it. The nuclear review identified opportunities for reducing the costs of discharging their liabilities, which potentially fall to the taxpayer. All the Magnox stations and all Magnox liabilities will be held by a single company, which will remain in the public sector. Its operating Magnox stations will meet about 8 per cent. of demand for electricity in England and Wales, thus creating a fourth major generator in that market. The company will also be responsible for decommissioning Berkeley and Hunterston A.

It is intended that that company will eventually be transferred to BNFL, and that will give a clear incentive to maximise revenue from generation by optimising the economic lives of the remaining stations and by minimising costs of Magnox reprocessing and decommissioning. We believe that very significant sums can be saved in that way.

**Mr. Dafydd Wigley** (Caernarfon): Will the Secretary of State give way?

**Mr. Lang:** In a moment.

Substantial sums can be saved in that way, in addition to the money that will be earned from continuing to operate the stations.

We welcome the new long-term agreements between BNFL and the nuclear generators and their intention to improve arrangements for dealing with the various categories of Magnox liabilities.

**Mr. Wigley:** The Secretary of State will be aware of my interest from the point of view of the decommissioning of the Trawsfynydd power station in my constituency. In relation to the changes that he has described, will he give an assurance that if the professional scientific advice is that it would best to keep the structure as it is for 30 years, to allow the intensity of the radioactivity to decay, and thereafter to demolish it, nothing in his financial provisions will make that a less favoured option? Will the scientifically advisable option be adopted?

**Mr. Lang:** All options are open, but I will certainly give the hon. Gentleman the assurance that nothing would be done to compromise safety and that, obviously, such scientific advice would have to be taken seriously.

As a result of the arrangements that I have described, BNFL's key role in the UK nuclear industry will be enhanced. Once the transfer to it of the Magnox stations is complete, it will become a significant new generator, with about 8 per cent. of the market in England and Wales.

In addition, BNFL's key role as the primary provider of nuclear fuel cycle services will be enhanced. It is a leader in the international market for those services and in the nuclear transport market. The Government confirm that BNFL will continue to offer the full range of those services as long as the market continues to demand them. We recognise that a major challenge for BNFL is to develop its business in the overseas markets where growth is stronger and to win further long-term contracts. I hope that that will reassure staff at BNFL as to their important long-term future.

In all this, we have not forgotten the electricity consumer. Privatisation will provide a powerful incentive for the two subsidiary companies to benefit their customers by raising efficiency and reducing costs still further. Domestic electricity prices are lower in real terms, even after value added tax, than two years ago. Further reductions are in prospect. The price paid by industrial consumers of electricity has also fallen significantly since 1989.

**Mr. Brian H. Donohoe** (Cunninghame, South): Will the Secretary of State give way?

**Mr. Lang:** If the hon. Gentleman will forgive me, I must make some further progress as I have a lot of information to lay before the House.

We are, however, taking such steps as are open to Government to accelerate and bring forward those benefits to consumers. In England and Wales, that part of the fossil fuel levy paid to Nuclear Electric will cease at privatisation. In Scotland, where domestic electricity prices are on average 3 per cent. lower than in England and Wales, the element of the premium price that Scottish Nuclear receives from its customers will also end then.

Those developments will result in further reductions in electricity prices both north and south of the border. The scale of the changes will be comparable—about 8 per cent. over the period—for all those who benefit. What we are doing is improving the efficiency of the industry and exerting further downward pressure on prices. That can only be good news for electricity consumers. It will help the industry to be more competitive. If Opposition Members had their way, consumers would be denied the benefits that privatisation will undoubtedly bring them.

**Mr. George Robertson** *rose—*

**Mr. Lang:** If the hon. Gentleman is going to tell me that he will or will not renationalise the industry, I shall happily give way.

**Mr. Robertson:** As the Secretary of State found out this morning, we are not allowed to attach strings to interventions. May I bring the Secretary of State back to the question that I asked and that he refused to answer? He has put forward a bribe from the Dispatch Box this evening. Will he confirm that that reduction in price could have taken place without privatisation, yes or no?

**Mr. Lang:** The hon. Gentleman puts a question in a way that does not make sense. It is because we are

privatising the industry, changing its structure and enabling new management and new ownership to take over that the existing non-fossil fuel obligation and the existing nuclear energy agreement premium can be changed in that way and their termination can be brought forward, with the benefits to consumers that have already been described.

As the House is aware, the Government have decided to privatise Nuclear Electric and Scottish Nuclear as two wholly owned subsidiaries of a new holding company that will be located in Scotland. On 9 May, my right hon. Friend the President of the Board of Trade announced that the holding company will be responsible for all key functions for the group as a whole. As well as support for the holding company board, those functions will include the company secretariat, group finance, personnel, corporate communications and pensions administration. In addition, two separate subsidiaries, also based in Scotland, will handle international marketing for the group and the management of the segregated funds.

The new company is, as I said, to be headquartered in and run from Scotland. I am delighted to be able to announce that Mr. John Robb has agreed to serve as its chairman. He was a distinguished chairman of Wellcome. His strong links with Scotland will help to ensure that the holding company will exert real influence from its new base. The present chairmen of Scottish Nuclear and Nuclear Electric, James Hann and John Collier, have agreed to serve as deputy chairmen of the holding company. Executive directors will be appointed as soon as possible, and a non-executive director from each of the subsidiary companies will serve on the main board.

That structure provides a strong foundation for the new company's future. Sir Peter Middleton, chairman of Barclays de Zoete Wedd, has expressed his company's firm view that the structure will be perceived as both credible and workable by future investors and that, subject to normal financial considerations, potential exists for a successful flotation.

**Several hon. Members** *rose—*

**Mr. Lang:** I shall not give way at the moment.

It is disappointing that the Opposition continue to snipe and to suggest that the new arrangements will not stick, particularly in Scotland—we heard it again from the hon. Member for Hamilton today. The structure that we are creating is designed to be permanent. Three separate mechanisms will interlock to ensure that that is so.

First, the headquarters structure, which I have just outlined, will be well established in advance of privatisation. Secondly, key features of its structure will be incorporated into the company's memorandum and articles of association. Thirdly, those parts of the memorandum and articles will be explicitly protected by a special share that I will hold jointly with my right hon. Friend the President of the Board of Trade.

**Mr. Alex Salmond** (Banff and Buchan): May I test the Secretary of State's seriousness on the question of the special share? If he had held the golden share in Britoil in 1988, would he have exercised it to stop the takeover by BP, which subsequently resulted in the closure of the Glasgow office?

**Mr. Lang:** The analogy is totally inadequate because the circumstances were different and the precise purposes

[*Mr. Lang*]

of the share were different on that occasion. Indeed, the golden share had expired before a change in the circumstances took place that might have given rise to its being exercised.

What I have described will create a triple lock of the sort that I have mentioned. Last week, my right hon. Friend the President of the Board of Trade rightly called the arrangements a cast-iron guarantee for Scotland. It is evidence of the excellent deal that this represents for Scotland that Opposition Members have been reduced to claiming it is a transitory fig leaf. Had that been so, I would not have accepted the proposals.

Consistent with their enthusiasm for indulging in knocking copy, Scottish Members see only the scope for scaremongering. They worked hard during the nuclear review. First, they claimed that 300 jobs would be lost, then 400 and then the hon. Member for Hamilton even suggested that 1,000 jobs would be lost at East Kilbride. He may have impressed his colleagues on the Opposition Benches with the scale of that claim, but he forgot just one small thing—only 450 people are employed at East Kilbride.

The facts are that Scottish Nuclear and Nuclear Electric will continue as separate entities with their own boards. Their continued existence will be protected by separate special shares, of which the holder of my office will hold one—no doubt the hon. Gentleman still aspires to that— in Scottish Nuclear and the President of the Board of Trade the other in Nuclear Electric. The functions currently performed at East Kilbride by Scottish Nuclear will continue to be performed there. In addition, and once the nuclear installations inspectorate is satisfied with arrangements for the transfer, certain engineering functions within the two subsidiary companies will be reorganised to bring more jobs to Scotland. Overall, the new structure, far from leading to the loss of hundreds of jobs, as the Labour party claimed, will actually bring at least 100 jobs to Scotland.

**Mr. Gallie:** My right hon. Friend is just in his comments but he raised a slight concern with me. He has pointed out that, if the nation had an aberration and the lot opposite took control of the Government, the hon. Member for Hamilton (Mr. Robertson) might have control of the golden share. Will my right hon. Friend confirm that that golden share will last 10 years? If that is the case, we should have no cause for concern.

**Mr. Lang:** I assure my hon. Friend on a number of points. First, the special share is without a time limit but must last at least 10 years. Secondly, I hope that his anxiety will steel his resolve to work still harder to ensure, with me and my right hon. and hon. Friends, that the Labour party will never be in a position to exercise the golden share.

The proposals that we have announced are intended to secure and, indeed, to strengthen the future of the nuclear industry in this country. They will secure for it a bright, long-term future, freed from control from Whitehall and freed from the financial constraints of the public sector. Far from leading to the loss of control of an important Scottish company, they will preserve the identities of both existing companies and bring a major new company headquarters to Scotland. In private ownership, that company will be free to compete in domestic and overseas

markets. That is the context in which the new company will be able to make its own investment decisions. Those decisions will be based on commercial factors and not on the dead hand of the state. It opens the way for nuclear generation to compete for its future in the marketplace. Privatisation will be, for this industry as for so many others, the gateway to a bright and prosperous future.

Time and again over the years we have heard the Labour party whine and grumble about the Government's plans for privatisation. There have been countless scare stories, always disproved by subsequent events.

The hon. Member for Glasgow, Garscadden (Mr. Dewar)—I welcome him to our deliberations—started the ball rolling as long ago as 1979, when he claimed that British Airways

"will be the pantomime horse of capitalism if it is anything at all."— [*Official Report*, 19 November 1979; Vol. 974, c. 125.]

Well, that horse has won the Grand National, the St. Leger, the Oaks and just about every other race around the world.

**Mr. Thomas Graham** (Renfrew, West and Inverclyde): Has the Secretary of state consulted the workers in the industry? They are telling us loud and clear that they do not want their industry to be privatised. In my area we have big disused quarries and the local folk are concerned that there is a possibility that low-level radioactive waste could be dumped there, putting them under threat. I am not saying that the industry is unsafe, but the waste is a problem. Will that problem be dumped in my disused quarries?

**Mr. Lang:** The hon. Gentleman should get together with his hon. Friend the Member for Garscadden because they are both so out of touch. The hon. Member for Garscadden could be the front legs of the pantomime horse and the hon. Gentleman could just be himself.

**Mr. Wilson:** Will the Secretary of State give way?

**Mr. Lang:** No, I will not.

Next we had the claim that the privatisation of British Telecom would lead to the extinction of the public telephone box. The reality is that the number of BT call boxes has increased by over 50 per cent. since privatisation. Add to that over £1,000 invested for every household in the country and a 35 per cent. fall in average real prices and one gets the true picture of a successful privatisation.

Never one to miss stealing an idea or two, the right hon. Member for Sedgefield (Mr. Blair) had to get in on the act. I served on the Committee opposite the right hon. Gentleman when the Electricity Bill went through Parliament—at least I think I did; in fact, he was hardly ever there as he kept going out to brush his teeth ready to sparkle for the next sound bite. He said then:

"it is barely an issue that prices will rise because of privatisation."— [*Official Report*, 12 December 1988; Vol.143, c. 684.]

In reality, the cost of domestic electricity has fallen by more than 8 per cent. in real terms in the past two years, more than cancelling out the additional cost of VAT.

Privatisation has benefited not just the consumers of these services but taxpayers as well. In 1979 nationalised industries cost the taxpayer around £50 million every week. Now, as privatised companies, they contribute around £50 million every week in taxes to the Exchequer. There is little doubt that the Opposition have been forced to ditch clause IV because of the success of the Government's privatisation programme. However, their supposed conversion will remain skin deep until they actually support a privatisation. When will we ever see or hear from new or old Labour support for the transfer of any activity from the public to the private sector?

I am confident that our proposals for the privatisation of the nuclear generators will bring significant benefits to taxpayer and consumer alike. A great deal of detailed work needs to be done and we remain determined that the safety standards for which the industry is renowned should be rigorously maintained. We are determined to make the privatisation a great success. I urge the House to reject the motion and support the Government's amendment.

8.13 pm

**Mr. Adam Ingram** (East Kilbride): I enter the debate as a lifelong—that is probably an exaggeration—certainly a long-term supporter of the nuclear industry. I do not remember not supporting the industry. At one time I worked in the electricity supply industry. Also, I speak as the hon. Member for East Kilbride, which is the location of the headquarters of Scottish Nuclear, at which 300 direct staff are employed together with about 200 indirect staff. There is some variation in those figures depending on the number of indirect staff. As the Secretary of State said, there are about 450 jobs in total.

I believe firmly that nuclear energy has a vital role to play in the economy of this country. It offers a safe, reliable and effective source of energy. It is an industry with significant export potential, with a global market of £500 billion over the next 25 years. I genuinely believe that it offers diversity of supply in the context of a balanced energy policy—a policy that I have advocated for as long as I have been politically active in trade unions or the Labour party. Therefore, this is not the knee-jerk reaction of someone who is opposed to privatisation. I hope that my contribution will be considered against that background.

My considered view of the Government's proposals is that they are wrong for energy and the environment. They are bad for the consumer and the taxpayer and for those currently employed at the headquarters of Scottish Nuclear in East Kilbride. In the long term, they will be bad for many of those employed by Nuclear Electric. What is proposed in the White Paper is a wrong decision by a wrongheaded Government.

**Mr. Gallie:** Will the hon. Gentleman give way?

**Mr. Ingram:** The hon. Gentleman made several interventions during the Secretary of State's speech and he did not make many valid points then. He may get a chance to speak later if he catches Madam Speaker's eye.

The decision is wrong for energy because I do not believe for one moment that a privatised nuclear energy industry will build another nuclear station in this country. One needs only to look at the Government's White Paper—not the conclusions, but the analyses, which are ignored in the conclusions. Paragraph 4.24 says:

"On the basis of the evidence presented to the review, the Government concludes that it is unlikely in current market conditions and at current gas prices, that Sizewell C"—

the next new nuclear power station to which reference has been made—

"can provide a rate of return competitive with the main alternative, a CCGT station."

I believe that if we have a privatised nuclear energy industry in this country, it will opt not for nuclear power stations but for gas.

Paragraph 4.25 of the White Paper says:

"The market will in the end be the judge."

So on the basis of current prices and rate of return, no nuclear station would be built. The choice would undoubtedly be gas.

**Mr. Eggar:** The hon. Gentleman has summarised the Government's White Paper. When he stood for Labour at the previous general election, did he specifically disclaim the Labour party's manifesto commitment, which said—I remind him of it—that the Labour party would not invest in new nuclear power stations?

**Mr. Ingram:** We should not be diverted from the central issue of the debate, but in any political party there are people with differing views. The Minister's party is riven from top to bottom on Europe. Many Conservative Members stood on a policy of no tax increases and no increases in VAT, yet the first thing the Government did was to implement those very policies as soon as they got into power. I hold firmly to my view on this. Many of my hon. Friends hold a similar view and many hold differing views. I hope that the debate within the Labour party will bring about a change in our energy policy. That is the democracy within the Labour party and I hope that my view will eventually prevail.

As I was saying, if the industry is privatised, it will not build a nuclear power station in the foreseeable future. I am glad that the Minister has accepted my analysis of the Government's White Paper.

I believe that if no new nuclear power station is built, that will have a major knock-on effect on not just the Scottish economy but the United Kingdom economy. There are many large-scale employers in the United Kingdom—Weirs of Cathcart and Babcock Power in Scotland alone are dependent on an expanding nuclear energy programme. If no nuclear stations are built, many thousands of jobs will be at risk. I believe that that will be the direct consequence of what is proposed in the White Paper.

I said in my opening remarks that the Government's decision was flawed and bad in environmental terms. The White Paper is entitled "The Prospects for Nuclear Power in the UK", but it ducks one of the central issues, which is that of the fuel route and what happens when a station is decommissioned. As I understand it, the Secretary of State for the Environment is not happy with the decision and said that the Government would defer the decision on the fuel route and decommissioning cycle for five years or more. That must be wrong. A White Paper that sets out to deal with the nuclear industry cannot ignore one of its fundamental aspects, that is, the decommissioning and downstream fuel route.

As my hon. Friend the Member for Hamilton (Mr. Robertson) said, I am sure that electricity consumers will not be conned by the £20 per annum reduction in their bills that they have been told will be the result of the levy being abandoned in England and Wales and the withdrawal of the nuclear energy agreement in Scotland. Not many consumers will read the *Financial Times*, but I think that they would agree with one of the points in its leading article the day after the Government's announcement. It stated:

*[Mr. Ingram]*

"the proposed privatisation of the UK's two nuclear generating companies is to be shaped by political pressures and the interests of future shareholders, not by the needs of electricity consumers."

That is an accurate statement. The leading article goes on to make many other trenchant criticisms of the White Paper.

Every year since electricity was privatised, electricity consumers have been paying approximately £1 billion by way of a levy, the purpose of which was, of course, to pay the decommissioning costs, although the total was never going to meet the full cost. However, the levy had to be imposed because the previous generator—the Central Electricity Generating Board—and the Government had not laid aside any of the money coming through the income stream for that purpose. The levy was therefore part of an historical cost and intended to meet part of the future costs.

In other words, consumers have been paying a heavy price for mistakes made in energy production and a heavy price for electricity privatisation, too. They will not be conned. They know what the Government are up to. The reduction in their bills is a small sop—£20 per annum—and it will not convince them to come on side.

Although the consumer will lose out, in the longer term the taxpayer will also be financially clobbered if privatisation goes ahead. It is clear that the underlying purpose of the privatisation proposals is to provide short-term cash for tax bribes. Every independent commentator identifies that as the case and has criticised the Government's proposals accordingly. Only the Government and their supporters are arguing that the reduction is anything other than a way of generating short-term cash for tax bribes.

The problem is that, in the longer term, taxpayers will have to pay the consequences of those bribes. There will be a sizeable debt to pick up. Taxpayers will have to underwrite the decommissioning costs not only of the nuclear stations that remain in the public sector but probably of those that enter the private sector.

In summing up, will the Minister consider what will happen if the privatised company goes bust? If two or three nuclear stations have to close because of the tight regulatory regime, there will be no income and the insurance bond will not pay the decommissioning costs. Who will pay them? It will be not the private sector but the taxpayers. At the same time, taxpayers will have to pick up sizeable decommissioning costs because of the Magnox stations that remain in the public sector.

**Mr. Piers Merchant** (Beckenham) *rose*—

**Mr. Ingram:** I should like to give way, but time is short and other hon. Members wish to speak.

I deal finally with those who are currently employed in the industry. It should come as no surprise to the Minister, the Secretary of State or, I hope, Conservative Members in general, that the overwhelming majority of those employed by Scottish Nuclear and, I suspect, a large number of those employed by Nuclear Electric, are opposed to the proposals for the holding company and the merger of the two companies.

Will the Minister say something about the guarantee that has been given in relation to the corporate headquarters? I asked the President of the Board of Trade

about that when he presented the White Paper, but I did not get a satisfactory answer. I hope that the Minister will provide one. Will the same guarantee be given to those currently employed at Scottish Nuclear headquarters and those currently employed at Nuclear Electric? Will there be a 10-year minimum guarantee of job security for them, just as there is in relation to the jobs that have been transferred to the corporate headquarters?

The fundamental reason why those employed by Scottish Nuclear do not accept the Government's proposals is that they know that the merged company will not make good economic sense. Which company in this country has a corporate headquarters and two separate operating headquarters, with all the duplication of administration, the cost of maintaining pensions for all the staff and the other support costs associated with it?

There may be 100 jobs to be moved around the country, but the reality is that there will be a consolidation of jobs and, therefore, job losses. This year alone another 65 jobs are to be cut at Scottish Nuclear so, although 100 jobs may be coming, there has already been a massive reduction in jobs. Employees do not believe a word that the Government say. They do not accept any of the guarantees that the Government maintain will be delivered, as announced by the Secretary of State.

If a privatised company says that it wants to close one of its operating headquarters because it is not generating enough income as one or two stations are not being utilised to the full, or because one or two have had to be closed as they are cracking and the safety regime insists on it, I do not think that the Secretary of State or the President of the Board of Trade will tell the holding company to keep the two operating headquarters open. If the company can save millions of pounds by closing one of them, so be it.

That is the reality facing the work force at Scottish Nuclear, which is why it does not accept the proposals and why I hope that the House will support the Labour motion.

8.27 pm

**Dr. Michael Clark** (Rochford): I am pleased to be able to follow the hon. Member for East Kilbride (Mr. Ingram). He and I served together on the Select Committee on Trade and Industry for some time and discussed nuclear matters privately on several occasions.

I welcome the Government's proposals to privatise the advanced gas-cooled reactors and the pressurised water reactor. That is in contrast to a speech that I made in the House on 12 December 1988, when I spoke strongly against privatising the nuclear industry along with the rest of the electricity industry of that time.

The reason why I spoke against nuclear privatisation just over six years ago was, first, that the cost of decommissioning was not clearly known. Secondly, I wished us to maintain a sizeable nuclear industry and I could not be certain that, if the nuclear industry had been privatised then, we would have maintained the percentage of nuclear generation that I thought right for this country.

Thirdly, I thought it right to take the nuclear element out of the privatisation so that we could obtain the best possible price for National Power and PowerGen. Fourthly, I wanted to maintain a centre of excellence in the nuclear industry in Scotland and, indeed, in Britain in the constituency of my hon. Friend the Member for Gloucester (Mr. French).

Fifthly, I thought that it was right and proper that we should try to identify the true costs of nuclear energy before we ever absorbed nuclear energy into another large power-generating company or, indeed, privatised it at that time. Finally, and perhaps most important of all, I thought that there was still some public concern about safety and that until the public were confident about nuclear safety, it would not be appropriate to put the nuclear industry into the private sector.

I recall that on the same evening my hon. Friend the Member for Bedfordshire, North (Sir T. Skeet) made a similar speech with similar conclusions. However, both he and I were ignored—our conclusions were ignored at least—and it was decided that the nuclear industry would be privatised along with all coal, gas and oil-fired power stations.

Several months later, a new Secretary of State pulled out the nuclear element from the privatisation, justifying—I think—the stance that my hon. Friend the Member for Bedfordshire, North and myself had taken. As a result of including the nuclear power stations in the initial privatisation plan, however, we were left with one power company, National Power, which was larger than it otherwise would have been. It was made large so that it would be able to accommodate the nuclear element designed to go with it. With a large, conventional generating capacity, it would have adequate cash flow and sufficient profits to be able to counter the nuclear side, which would be less profitable, indeed, probably unprofitable. Having decided rather belatedly not to privatise the nuclear side, we had a skew in the size of our power-generating companies: an over-large National Power and probably the right size for PowerGen.

The hesitation that I had just over six years ago has gone. Decommissioning costs are known and we have the technology to decommission nuclear power stations. In any event, the Magnox stations are outside the privatisation proposal. They will be decommissioned within a separate company, as the Secretary of State for Scotland made clear in his opening speech. Nuclear power generation is now very efficient and represents between 20 and 25 per cent. of electricity generated in England, and a far higher percentage—almost 50 per cent.—in Scotland. National Power and PowerGen were sold at a satisfactory price and are operating very well. We have centres of excellence for research and development, where we can develop operating techniques and maintain and develop the skills of work forces. Indeed, we have centres that are also capable of providing training for operatives and employees at two locations, in Gloucester and East Kilbride.

**Mr. Dalyell:** As the hon. Gentleman knows a great deal about this subject, is he relaxed about the idea that the key safety core of Nuclear Electric should move, as it would have to, to a new headquarters in Scotland?

**Dr. Clark:** I wonder whether the hon. Gentleman would be kind enough to allow me to address that point in due course, because I shall argue in a moment that it should not move to Scotland, which would answer his question. On the intervention that the hon. Gentleman made earlier about the need for a director of safety, of course we want someone—

**Mr. Dalyell:** On the holding board.

**Dr. Clark:** On the holding board, indeed. I am sure that the hon. Gentleman will agree, however, that for something as important as safety, no employee, whether he be the most lowly sweeper or the production or finance director, can ever say, "I will not take note of safety because there is a safety director who does it all." Safety, as we all know if we have worked in industry, is a responsibility for every one of us at every stage in the hierarchy. There is nothing wrong with the belt and braces approach of the hon. Gentleman's proposal for a safety director, but a safety director does not absolve any employee from safety consciousness in all that he or she does in the place of employment.

Before the hon. Member for Linlithgow (Mr. Dalyell) intervened, I was saying that we now have transparency of nuclear costs that was not apparent six years ago. Therefore, my right hon. Friends the Secretary of State for Scotland and the Minister for Industry and Energy have been able to propose that we remove the nuclear levy at the same time as proposing privatisation.

**Mr. Alan W. Williams:** I accept that in the past five years the nuclear industry has become much more economic, but the hon. Gentleman must acknowledge that nuclear power stations operate at a distinct advantage because they have a guaranteed base load provision and therefore a guaranteed market for their product. Does he think that that would be fair in a privatised industry, where it should compete with National Power and PowerGen? Does he, as I would assume, think that access to that regular, guaranteed market constitutes unfair competition?

**Dr. Clark:** There is a base load offer to nuclear power stations at the moment, as the hon. Gentleman rightly said. I am not entirely sure what is proposed for the private sector. I would hope that as far as possible we would have true competition in the private sector, in which case market forces would operate and nuclear power would have to compete in the same way as any other power. I do not know what is being proposed. The hon. Gentleman asked me what I would like to happen and I have told him.

I was talking about safety. There is now far greater public confidence in the safety of nuclear power stations. I believe that that has been achieved largely by publicity, openness, visits to nuclear power stations and, indeed, the performance of the power stations themselves. Since the criteria that I put forward in 1988 against the privatisation of nuclear power stations have been removed, it is only natural that I should welcome proposals to privatise the nuclear element—the AGRs and the PWR—and, at the same time, as has already been said, get rid of the nuclear levy.

If we privatise as one large company—I come now to the point made by the hon. Member for Linlithgow—we shall have three principal generators in this country. I know that there are other smaller generators as well. There will be PowerGen, which is probably about the right size, and National Power, which I have already said is larger than it would have been, had other plans been drawn up initially, rather than the plans to include nuclear power stations. Indeed, National Power is already so large that a reference to the Monopolies and Mergers Commission was considered at one time. There is still a possibility that it will be referred to the MMC at some future date.

One such large nuclear electric company would undoubtedly—I agree with the hon. Member for East Kilbride—expand into combined cycle gas turbine power

*[Dr. Clark]*

generation. Even if it did not expand that way, it would expand into another nuclear power station. The one thing on which we all agree is that it will expand, whether into gas or nuclear or whether it buys some of the surplus coal-fired generating capacity from PowerGen or National Power. If that one large company expands, it will become almost as large as National Power and we shall have two giants and one medium-sized company, which will reduce competition.

My right hon. and hon. Friends on the Front Bench should think again about having one large company. I suggest that they consider two companies: the north and south option, not necessarily one Scottish and one English company, but what is called by some the "for and for" option. That would increase competition. It would mean that we could avoid references to the Monopolies and Mergers Commission in future. We got it wrong in 1989 and had to correct it. Do not let us get it wrong now so that we have to correct it in future when the company is referred to the MMC.

Finally, if we have just one company with its headquarters in East Kilbride, we shall please neither Scottish Nuclear, which wishes to remain an individual company, nor Nuclear Electric, which wishes to keep its headquarters in Gloucestershire and not move to Scotland. If we had two companies, we could please both the existing companies and probably most of the employees, and we could maintain and perhaps even increase competition.

8.39 pm

**Mr. Matthew Taylor** (Truro): The Liberal Democrats' position on this issue is clear. We oppose privatisation of the nuclear industry. We have from time to time supported the Government on privatisation and competition measures, such as the changes to British Gas, so we oppose the measure from a perspective not of outright opposition to change but of what is best for the taxpayer and for the environment.

We have heard more than once tonight about the other occasion when the Government, under the previous Prime Minister, considered privatising the nuclear industry. They abandoned that sell-off because

"nuclear power—although in private hands—would have remained effectively in the public sector".

Today, the same Government propose to sell the profitable parts of the industry but to leave the liabilities in the public sector—in effect acknowledging the reason given for not privatising it last time, but coming to a slightly different conclusion and making what they are doing more apparent.

According to the same criteria, I believe that the Government were right the first time and that they are wrong now. The previous attempt at privatisation clarified what had always until then been denied by the nuclear sector—that it was not profitable and could not compete with other forms of power generation, despite having originally been proposed as the cheap form of power for the future. The extraordinary fact is that now, similarly, in the present Government document and plans, we see the clarification of the fact that for the foreseeable future, even according to the Government, nuclear power stations cannot be built, because they cannot possibly generate a sufficient rate of return to allow them to be competitive.

In effect that announces, in any circumstances that we or the Government can foresee, the gradual phasing-out and the end of the nuclear industry. It has changed from being a developing industry building new power stations to one that manages the results of mistaken decisions on previous investment and waste problems.

**Mr. Gallie:** Will the hon. Gentleman give way?

**Mr. Taylor:** I shall make some progress, and then give way to the hon. Gentleman.

The White Paper makes it clear that nuclear power is economically unviable. Indeed, it confirms that the private sector will not build new power stations. Nuclear Electric itself concedes, on purely commercial criteria and given current market conditions, that new nuclear capacity is not competitive with conventional generating stations, so new stations would be unviable. Investment in new nuclear plant would not be justified.

The truth is that, under privatisation, investment in the industry is coming to an end for the foreseeable future.

**Mr. Merchant:** Will the hon. Gentleman give way?

**Mr. Taylor:** I shall do so in a moment.

Indeed, the French nuclear industry has effectively confirmed that verdict by making it clear in reports issued in the past week that it will not invest in the British nuclear privatisation because it believes that without Government support the industry is in steady decline.

**Mr. Gallie:** Section 4.49 of the report that we are discussing contains a different conclusion on the prospects for building new nuclear generating stations. It seems to me that there is no chance of such a station being built in the public sector, but that, according to investigations that Nuclear Electric is pursuing, there may be hope that that will come about in the private sector.

**Mr. Taylor:** The hon. Gentleman speaks more from hope than from experience, and that is not the conclusion in the document. When the Minister made the statement announcing the policy he conceded that what I have said is correct. Of course he held out the possibility that things might change at some indefinite point in the future that could not be foreseen, but I do not believe that that will happen. Ironically, as policy stands and as things are now, a Conservative Government are to all intents and purposes phasing out the nuclear industry.

Indeed, it is common knowledge—although no public announcement has been made—that the nuclear industry is considering investing in non-nuclear generating capacity and taking part in the dash for gas. So much for the nuclear industry's confidence in its own future.

Amazingly, in view of past history, the Conservative party has announced decisions that will inevitably lead to a cessation of nuclear generation in this country, and to the conversion of the nuclear industry to one that manages waste. Of course, there is the potential for an important role in doing the same for eastern Europe and other parts of the world, so this is not necessarily the end of jobs in the sector, but it is a big change.

The other irony is that the Labour party now seems most confused about what it wants for the future of the nuclear industry. The Labour Members who are here represent a fair selection of those who support the nuclear industry within that party. We do not see many members of the environmental lobby within the Labour party, which is committed to phasing out the power stations.

It is unsurprising, therefore, that when I or Conservative Members have questioned Labour Members, they managed comprehensively to avoid giving a proper answer to the question whether the Labour party planned to phase out the nuclear industry, as had been stated, or whether it meant to keep it or even to develop it. The 1992 Labour manifesto was clear.

"We will not invest in new nuclear power stations, continue with those in the planning process or extend the lives of existing nuclear stations beyond their safe lifespan. Britain's dependence on nuclear power will therefore steadily diminish."

That, however, does not seem to stop Labour spokesmen. The right hon. Member for Copeland (Dr. Cunningham), the shadow spokesman on trade and industry—I notice that he is not here tonight—said on "North of Westminster" in mid-January:

"I have always supported the civil nuclear industry . . . we mustn't let people, I mean the anti nuclear people of course, have one objective and that is to close down and wreck the nuclear industry",

despite the fact that that appears to be Labour's official policy.

The right hon. Member for Sedgefield (Mr. Blair) recently assured the environmentalists that Labour's green policy, "In Trust for Tomorrow", was still party policy, that he stood by it and that it formed the basis of the current Labour approach to the environment. It says:

"Labour's energy research effort will be channelled away from the nuclear sector and into clean coal, (as well as renewables) . . . There remain serious environmental problems associated with nuclear power generation".

The document also refers to

"not building any new nuclear power stations".

Yet the hon. Member for Clackmannan (Mr. O'Neill), the shadow energy spokesperson, said in an interview in *British Nuclear Forum* last autumn that the energy policy set out in "In Trust for Tomorrow"

"isn't the last word as far as Labour's energy policy is concerned".

He followed that up on Radio 4 by saying that commissioning new nuclear power stations remained an option for any future Labour Government.

On 14 March 1995, on Second Reading of the Atomic Energy Authority Bill, Labour's science and technology spokesperson, the hon. Member for Kirkcaldy (Dr. Moonie), said in response to the question whether the new Labour party would build new nuclear power stations:

"I do not know the answer."—[*Official Report*, 14 March 1995; Vol. 256, c. 715.]

That, at least, was more accurate than what most of the rest of the Labour party has been saying.

**Mr. Martin O'Neill** (Clackmannan): I believe that the hon. Gentleman appreciates that there is richness in diversity. Would he say that there is a monolithic view among the Liberal Democrats? Will he tell us about the views of the hon. Member for Caithness and Sutherland (Mr. Maclennan), who normally attends all debates relating to nuclear matters? Has he been banned from the Chamber this evening?

**Mr. Taylor:** The Liberal Democrats' position is clear. I have put it on record, which is more than any Labour Member has been prepared to do tonight. If the hon.

Member for Clackmannan wishes to do so later, he can. My party wants to phase out nuclear power. We would continue research into it—we can see the need to do so— but we do not believe that the present nuclear generation capacity is necessary, and we will remove it. I do not think that we could be any clearer than that. I would welcome the hon. Gentleman clarifying Labour's position.

I have no dispute with Labour Back Benchers who have maintained a consistent and clear position and who have argued that they would like Labour policy to be different, but I do criticise Labour Front Benchers who will not say whether they would phase out the industry. They will not say whether they support the policy that they present to environmentalists, or the policy that they present to the British Nuclear Forum. They are saying different things to different people.

**Mr. Ingram:** It may help the hon. Gentleman if I restate the position in relation to the debate that takes place in the Labour party. I was a delegate at the Labour party conference when "In Place of Trust" was passed. I was a delegate from the Transport and General Workers Union, which voted against that policy and will continue to argue against it. I do not speak for that union, which was not the only union to take that position. There is a clear movement towards change, which I expressed and which I hope will prevail. The hon. Member for Caithness and Sutherland (Mr. Maclennan) holds a similar view to me on the matter, and he may be able to convince the Liberal Democrats to take a more sensible approach.

**Mr. Taylor:** I make no criticism of the hon. Gentleman, who makes his position and that of the Labour party clear, but Labour Front Benchers are not prepared to do so. Labour looks in two different directions depending on which audience it is addressing, and it is time that it sorted that out.

**Mr. Eggar:** The hon. Gentleman has stated the Liberal Democrat party's position, and a document released today clearly says that it is in favour of phasing out nuclear power. When it says "phasing out" nuclear power, does it mean phasing out nuclear stations at the end of their natural lives—as approved by the nuclear inspectorate— or closing them before that?

**Mr. Taylor:** We have argued that nuclear power should be phased out by 2020. We accept that the industry could not be closed overnight, and it would be inappropriate to suggest that. We argue for a phasing out over that time.

**Mr. Alan W. Williams:** Will the hon. Gentleman give way?

**Mr. Taylor:** I must make progress, and the hon. Gentleman will agree that I have given way a number of times. I am conscious of the pressure of time.

The Labour party does not have a monopoly of confusion on the matter. The Government, while accepting that there is likely to be no new build, still argue the importance of nuclear power and say that taxpayers will benefit from the changes following privatisation. They also argue that the burdens of the nuclear industry will be lifted from the taxpayer and transferred to the private sector. That is comprehensively untrue, and they are not prepared to give figures either.

*[Mr. Taylor]*

We are told that the liabilities will no longer fall on the taxpayer, but the full range of potential nuclear accident costs is enormous. For example, the accident at Chernobyl cost £200 billion for immediate damages alone, and funds still cannot be raised to tackle the long-term problems. Similar costs were incurred in the Three Mile island incident.

The overwhelming proportion of such liabilities, however, are not internalised in Britain, because Nuclear Electric need only have liability insurance up to a financial limit of £140 million per accident. The rest is covered by the taxpayer, with the costs of possible accidents falling on our children. If a company has only limited liability for its errors and something goes wrong, it is clear that its liabilities cannot be described as having been internalised.

Most crucially, the Government cannot explain the true profit and loss account facing the taxpayer. When I asked the Minister at the time of the statement what total costs will fall on the taxpayer in future, what the Government's best estimate of the costs associated with cleaning up Magnox are and what revenues are anticipated from privatisation, he was unable to respond. In other words, it is unclear whether this is a profitable exercise for the taxpayer.

The Government intend to end the nuclear levy two years early, reducing domestic electricity bills by 8 per cent. and providing a sweetener to gain public support for privatisation. The justification for the sweetener is that because of increased efficiency the decommissioning costs of Britain's ageing nuclear reactors are one third lower than when the levy was launched, yet the Government concede that they will still have to make up the difference of more than £2 billion, and possibly substantially more if the lower costs suggested are not gained.

In an attempt to allay concern that the taxpayer will have to pay again for decommissioning, Department of Trade and Industry officials said that a combination of cash sources and savings would be sufficient to meet the Magnox liabilities, and that £2.6 billion worth of privatisation proceeds will be used to meet the Magnox liabilities, yet from our knowledge of the costs of decommissioning we know that that cannot be true. We have some idea of the early costs of decommissioning the old Magnox reactors, but we do not have a long-term solution for the most highly radioactive materials. That is still being reviewed and researched.

We have no experience of decommissioning PWRs, and we have no realistic idea of how much it will cost. We do not know when that process will end, or how it will end. Moreover, unless a clear commitment is made to set up a proper segregated Magnox decommissioning fund, the potential cash source of privatisation proceeds may be used for other purposes, such as tax cuts at a general election.

Future taxpayers will be left to foot the huge bill for decommissioning and dealing with radioactive waste. That is effectively what will happen, and the idea that anything else will take place is sheer nonsense. The White Paper says that

"there is no practical benefit from a segregated fund to meet nuclear liabilities".

The truth is that funds from privatisation will be treated as general Government revenue, and will be part of the Government's general accounts. The Government will therefore allow short-term tax cuts at the expense of long-term liabilities for our children.

Even the CBI cannot support that proposal. The Director General of the CBI said in *The Guardian* on 10 May:

"We would urge the Government to put the money already raised into a special account to pay for decommissioning the older nuclear stations. As the levy was expected to continue to 1998, we would ask the Government to top up the fund by some of the sale proceeds."

Of course the Government cannot rely on the substantial amounts of money from the nuclear levy that has been paid because they have been invested not in decommissioning but in building Sizewell B. The taxpayer will thus be asked to pay twice, yet the benefits of any profit accruing to Sizewell B, once all its liabilities are removed, will accrue to the private sector.

The public have already paid for decommissioning Magnox through the fossil fuel levy on electricity bills, but £1.6 billion was diverted to Sizewell B. It is more than likely that the net income to the Government from this privatisation will be less than the sum invested in Sizewell B, let alone the other advanced gas-cooled reactors that the Government will sell off with it.

Privatisation leaves future generations of taxpayers to foot the bill for decommissioning Magnox stations; to take the risk that decommissioning the others will cost much more than anticipated; to take the risk of how to dispose of highly radioactive material in the future; and to take the risks if there are any accidents—and all to fund the Government's tax cuts now. That cannot be justified.

Future generations are being asked to take one further risk. For the most part, I do not argue that the private sector is necessarily less safe. Provided the highest autonomy is given to the nuclear inspectorate and others, I believe that every effort will continue to be made to keep nuclear power stations safe. The record of those in the industry is good, not just in this country but, in one respect, in others. After all, it was the people who ran Chernobyl who stayed there to stop a much more serious accident at the cost of their own lives.

**Mr. Llew Smith:** But those people died as a result.

**Mr. Taylor:** Absolutely. The courage that they showed is nevertheless an example to people.

I do not make personalised attacks on the approach that individuals take but I am concerned about the pressures that the Government are building into the privatisation process. The life of the Magnox stations has already been extended from 25 to 30 years; their average life expectancy is now estimated to be 37 years. In their White Paper, the Government encourage BNFL to

"optimise the economic life of the stations."

The pressure is on further to extend the unsafe use of nuclear power stations. Despite the commitment that individual members of staff may have—at Chernobyl, people lost their lives as a result of that personal commitment to saving others—when such pressure is applied overall and the industry is structured in such a way that the Government seek to extend the life of nuclear stations and cut costs, risks are inevitably taken. By trying to get a return from Magnox stations well beyond their design life and the safe limits of use, lives are put at risk. The very structure of the privatisation is, in the Minister's words, designed to "optimise" the economic lives of the stations and thus extend them beyond what is safe.

This is not a good privatisation. It is not a good deal for the taxpayer. It will cost the taxpayer and potentially put lives at risk. The Government should stop it now and I hope that they will listen to the strength of public opinion in opposition to it.

9 2 pm

**Mr. John Whittingdale** (Colchester, South and Maldon): First, I congratulate the Government on their boldness and wisdom in deciding to privatise two nuclear generating companies. I was originally going to say "courage", but I do not wish to alarm my right hon. Friend the Minister too much.

I had feared that, after the setback which my right hon. Friend the President of the Board of Trade received over his proposal to privatise the Post Office, he might be reluctant to take the risk again. In many ways, the case for privatising nuclear generation is similar to that for privatising the Post Office. Like the Post Office, Nuclear Electric and Scottish Nuclear have dramatically improved their performance in recent years. They have also reached the point where the fetters of state ownership are proving a real constraint on the development of their business.

It would no doubt have been possible to relax the controls to permit greater commercial freedom for the nuclear companies while keeping them in state ownership, but just as that is a second-best solution for the Post Office, it would have been an unsatisfactory solution for the nuclear generators and would still have left them unable to enjoy the full benefits of private sector ownership. The Government are therefore entirely right to opt for full privatisation and I hope that there may yet come a time when the Post Office, too, can enjoy the freedoms that that brings.

**Mr. Llew Smith:** If a privatised nuclear company decides to reprocess its spent nuclear fuel at THORP, might not the company, whose only reason for existence is to make money, be tempted to sell off plutonium to the highest bidder? Might not that nuclear sell-off lead to private proliferation? Could we learn something from the trial going on in Germany this week, involving plutonium being smuggled in from Russia purely for profit motives?

**Mr. Whittingdale:** I see no reason why that need be the case; it is an example of the kind of scaremongering that is bedevilling the debate. There are rigorous controls against such practice and I do not believe that they will be changed by the privatisation of the nuclear companies.

The privatisation of Nuclear Electric and Scottish Nuclear will be good for the companies; good for the electricity industry; good for electricity consumers and good for the United Kingdom. As a Member representing an English constituency, I should first like to pay tribute to Nuclear Electric on the remarkable turnaround that it has achieved in the past four years. There is no doubt that the company was not in a position to be privatised along with the rest of the industry in 1990. As has already been said, however, since that time output has increased by almost 45 per cent., productivity has doubled and the unit cost of nuclear-generated electricity is down by 40 per cent.

Nuclear Electric is a very different company from the one it was four years ago and there is no longer any doubt that it can be sold. The company has also made a strong case that it should be sold, because it needs full commercial freedom to compete effectively with other generators; to take advantage of the opportunities that exist and to invest for the future.

**Mr. Merchant:** Does my hon. Friend agree that Nuclear Electric has shown such a dramatic improvement in the past few years because it has been inspired by the possibility of becoming a private company and realises the benefits to it and the industry from doing so?

**Mr. Whittingdale:** My hon. Friend is absolutely right. The company has always made it clear that it believes that it will do better in the private sector and I have no doubt that it has aimed for that objective, with great success, in the past few years.

Privatisation will also be good for the entire electricity industry. Electricity privatisation has been an enormous success and the competition in generation that it has created has brought great benefits to consumers and the companies. The recent success of Nuclear Electric, however, has allowed it to increase its market share to the extent that there has been a creeping renationalisation of electricity supply. Nuclear Electric has already overtaken PowerGen in terms of market share and it may well have soon overtaken National Power if the latter's market share continued to fall. The result of that would have been that the largest electricity generator in the United Kingdom would once again have been publicly owned. That would have posed a real and growing threat to fair competition.

The Government's proposals will mean that the proportion of electricity generated by state-owned companies will now fall to just 8 per cent. and will decline further as the Magnox stations are phased out. The proposals will increase competition in the industry still further. In future there will be competition for the provision of base load supply as well. Both the privatised Nuclear Electric and the Magnox stations will supply the English and Welsh electricity base load and compete against each other.

I understand that some have argued that the amalgamation of Nuclear Electric and Scottish Nuclear will have the effect of reducing competition, but I do not believe that is significantly the case. The Scottish electricity market is largely distinct from the English and Welsh market and the transfer of power through the interconnector is not that great. The additional competition created by splitting the Magnox stations from the other nuclear plant will outweigh the marginal effect caused by the merger.

The increase in competition will also be good news for the electricity consumer. Just as increased competition in the gas industry—the Gas Bill successfully completed its passage through the House yesterday—will exert downward pressure on prices, the same will apply equally to electricity. A more immediate benefit, to which reference has already been made, will also be apparent. The early removal of the fossil fuel levy—itself a tribute to Nuclear Electric's success—will allow electricity prices to fall by a further 8 per cent. It is ironic that that will almost entirely negate the effect of VAT on electricity bills, which will now be substantially lower than they were before electricity privatisation.

*[Mr. Whittingdale]*

The United Kingdom will benefit from privatisation as Nuclear Electric will be well placed to take advantage of the growing international market for the construction of nuclear generating plant. The British Nuclear Forum has estimated that market to be worth about £500 billion over the next 25 years.

As we know, more and more countries are turning to nuclear power, particularly on the Pacific rim. Nuclear Electric already has an extremely good record, and can point with pride at such achievements as the completion of Sizewell B, on time and below budget. With BNFL, it is rightly seen to be at the forefront of nuclear technology. If Nuclear Electric succeeds in its bid to build a similar power plant in Taiwan, in conjunction with Westinghouse, that alone will create 5,000 jobs for British firms.

Hon. Members have expressed fears that safety could be compromised in a privately owned nuclear company. I reject that argument. The British nuclear industry is one of the most tightly regulated in the world, and that will remain the case. When I get up each morning in my constituency and look out of my bedroom window, the dominant feature of the landscape that I see just three or four miles away is Bradwell nuclear power station: I am therefore extremely conscious of the importance of nuclear safety.

I have also had an opportunity to see at first hand the rigorous inspections and checks that took place at Bradwell before it was granted a 10-year extension of its operational life by the nuclear installations inspectorate. To achieve that, Nuclear Electric had to design and build new equipment such as the "snake", which allows remote ultrasonic inspection of the welds on the pressure vessel. I was pleased to be able to sponsor an exhibition in the Upper Waiting Hall quite recently, which enabled hon. Members to see something of the technology involved.

I understand and accept the reasons why Magnox stations such as Bradwell cannot be included in the privatisation. Inevitably, they are now reaching the end of their lives, and substantial costs will need to be met in their decommissioning. Bradwell is the oldest Nuclear Electric station that is now operational, having generated electricity since 1962. Those who work there know that it will have to close in due course—although I hope that it will be kept running for as long as that is safe and economically viable.

I am encouraged by the assurance that BNFL—which will in due course assume responsibility for the Magnox stations—has already given in that regard. I hope that the new position will allow the station a slightly longer life than it would have had if it had remained part of Nuclear Electric. Even when it does close, the decommissioning process itself will generate continuing employment at the station.

Let me end by repeating the concern that I raised last week with my right hon. Friend the President of the Board of Trade. Today, 397 people—many of whom are my constituents—work at Bradwell power station.

**Dr. Michael Clark:** Some are my constituents.

**Mr. Whittingdale:** I acknowledge that. Those people have never doubted that the station will close in the foreseeable future; however, they are highly skilled people, many of whom will wish to continue to work in the nuclear industry. They represent a body of expertise that the country cannot afford to lose. Transfer to BNFL may open up new job opportunities, but they currently feel that they are being cut adrift from their parent company and that future employment opportunities—opportunities that they previously had—may be jeopardised.

It would clearly be impossible to guarantee those people jobs at BNFL, Nuclear Electric or any other company. I hope, however, that my right hon. Friend the Minister will consider ways of ensuring that they are not disadvantaged by the transfer. They should have the same opportunity to apply for other jobs within Nuclear Electric as they would have had if they had continued to be part of the company. I accept that the details will need to be worked out, but I ask my right hon. Friend to bear my points in mind in the coming months as he implements a policy that I strongly support.

9.13 pm

**Mr. Alan Simpson** (Nottingham, South): I was amazed at the parallels drawn by the hon. Member for Colchester, South and Maldon (Mr. Whittingdale), who has just spoken. In his opening remarks he made connections between the proposals for privatisation of the Post Office and those relating to the nuclear industry. Although the hon. Gentleman may find it difficult to understand the difference, members of the public, however, have no difficulty in understanding the distinction between having a post office at the end of the street and having a nuclear power station there—or the relative desirability of having one rather than the other.

I welcome this debate in one important respect. I do so as an implacable opponent of the nuclear industry as a whole. The debate, however, allows us to explore the shabby and fraudulent financial basis on which the industry is constructed. The Government may be glibly off in pursuit of what they see as short-term pay-offs for the sale of the industry, but if we compare those with the long-term costs and consequences that the public will have to pay, we find that the pay-offs are dwarfed by the long-term costs.

I am grateful to the hon. Member for Truro (Mr. Taylor), who sought to provide some sort of profit and loss analysis of the transaction. For any sale in the world outside one would do exactly the same; taking stock of the money obtained in return for current capital assets and trying to cover the costs, at least, of the residual responsibilities that have to be borne.

We are told that the Government hope that privatisation will raise about £3 billion. It is against this figure that we must compare costs and losses. I am grateful to Scottish Nuclear for its clear calculations on the current construction costs of the nuclear power stations. It has said that the cost for Hunterston B would be £1 billion and Torness, £2.7 billion. I had to turn to the Government's figures for the current construction costs for Sizewell B, which amount to about £4 billion.

Beyond that, it has been difficult to gain any idea of the current construction costs for Nuclear Electric's advanced gas-cooled reactors from the figures in its annual accounts. If I am generous and assume that they would be only of the order of the lower costs of Scottish Nuclear's Hunterston B plant, we are still talking about a further £5 billion. That would require a break-even point on the transaction of £12.7 billion. If we add into this account the residual clean-up costs that the Government will retain, in terms of the disposal and decommissioning of the Magnox reactors, we must add the Government figure of a further £9 billion.

If we consider the rudimentary exchange which one would expect to find in the marketplace, we realise that, in exchange for cash receipts today of £3 billion, the Government are prepared to write off £19 billion. That is simply the capital cost. If we then build in the continuing costs that will have to be met, the figure is even worse. On page 54 of the report that the Government issued in advance of their proposals they make it clear that the National Audit Office report on the costs of decommissioning nuclear facilities published in 1993 estimated that

"the gross lifetime cost of discharging nuclear liabilities is well in excess of £40 billion."

In response, we are told by the Government that privatisation will reduce the costs of future liabilities. Reality suggests that those costs have always been hidden, will always be rising and will always be higher than we have ever been willing to acknowledge. Those costs will accumulate for the next 100 years at least. At this point I was reminded of the words of Mr. Micawber in "David Copperfield". He said:

"Annual income twenty pounds, annual expenditure nineteen nineteen six, result happiness. Annual income twenty pounds, annual expenditure twenty pounds ought and six, result misery."

If Mr. Micawber was looking at these figures, however, he would be talking not about misery, but of madness. That is the scale of the costs that the public will have to face, not simply in my children's lifetime, but for generations to come.

The costs are bizarre and unacceptable, and to offset them the Government are offering the public a £20 sweetener. We should set that sweetener in context. The fossil fuel levy is being cancelled only 18 months before it was due to run out anyway. Let us examine the scale of the Government's generosity. The Library has provided me with figures about the amount of money that the levy has raised. It pointed out that in the years from 1990-91 to 1993-94, the levy raised £1.17 billion, £1.32 billion, £1.34 billion and £1.23 billion respectively.

In that period, in excess of £5 billion has been paid to Nuclear Electric for decommissioning. It is interesting that those levy payments appear in the accounts of Nuclear Electric not in the form of a fund to deal with decommissioning, but as part of its current profit and loss statements. The money has not been set aside for decommissioning purposes. Anyone who has any doubts about that should read the answer that the Minister gave during the debate on 2 March this year when he explained clearly that Nuclear Electric's income from the fossil fuel levy was not hypothecated to any particular activities. That means that the money has not been put aside to cover decommissioning; it has been used to meet current costs.

We have also been told that the nuclear industry is extremely profitable, with a turnover of more than £1 billion per year. At this point, I draw the attention of the House to an analysis provided by Greenpeace. It states:

"Nuclear Electric alone has liabilities of over £27 billion for its nuclear waste and decommissioning . . . Every penny that the industry would ever earn is already spoken for to deal with the radioactive mess".

That means that, if the proceeds of privatisation are spent on tax cuts, the taxpayer will have to find the money again. In fact, I suspect that the taxpayer will pay for it again and again and again, because the money has not been put aside for decommissioning.

We are also told that we may be able to defer the decommissioning issue; that it is a 100-year issue. The sad truth is that it may not be. Less than a month ago, on 26 April, we remembered the ninth anniversary of the Chernobyl disaster. I wish to put on record the cost of that disaster in cash and human terms. Some 8,000 people in the Kiev area have died as a result of the Chernobyl explosion. Some 250,000 people are disabled or seriously ill. Thyroid cancers have risen 800-fold and one in four children born since Chernobyl has birth defects. Orphanages in the country are full of children whose parents could not cope or who simply died. More than 2,000 towns and villages in Belarus have had to be evacuated and 84,000 people from the region still await resettlement. A further 16,000—the lucky ones—have been squeezed into high-rise apartments in Minsk. That is the human cost of the disaster.

In addition to that, the Government of the Ukraine are having real difficulties meeting the commitments that they made to close down the entire Chernobyl plant by 2000 because they cannot afford to meet the cost. They face that cost today. Would the City bear such a cost in the Government's proposed privatisation? I remind the House that on 7 March this year when the electricity regulator, Stephen Littlechild, referred to a proposal to review electricity prices there was an immediate 17 per cent. fall in the share prices of the electricity utilities. Capital does a runner when anything threatens the profits; when anyone mentions increased responsibilities, the profiteers do a bunk. That is what would happen in a privatised nuclear industry.

**Mr. Llew Smith:** On the question of profits, does my hon. Friend agree with the hon. Member for Colchester, South and Maldon (Mr. Whittingdale), who said that the safeguards were strong enough to prevent the sale of plutonium to the highest bidder? Does my hon. Friend think that we have something to learn from the alleged smuggling of plutonium into Germany?

**Mr. Simpson:** The experience of what happened in Germany and the trial that is taking place of those who attempted to smuggle enriched uranium and plutonium out of the Soviet Union is an object lesson to us all and we should be terrified. I feel no safer because of those security guarantees.

There will be no guarantees, however, that the City will meet the costs of the long-term obligations for decommissioning that are inevitably and inextricably linked with the industry. The threatened privatisation of the nuclear industry is an act of irresponsibility verging on lunacy, and for that reason the proposals must be opposed in the House and stopped in the country.

I am absolutely clear that outside this Chamber the public reaction will call a halt to the madness of privatising the nuclear industry, and the notion that we can discharge the nation's long-term responsibilities and sacrifice them on the altar of the short-term profitability that the Government are seeking.

It may be the lifeline that the Government need to survive, but the public have already drawn a line against this. They would not continue to pretend that the nuclear industry would ever be viable if it were separated from the

*[Mr. Simpson]*

nuclear weapons industry and linked instead to the long-term environmental costs that it has to bear. The public would say, as we do, that the proposed privatisation is no more than an attempt to sell a nuclear pig in an everlasting environmental poke. Such folly is not acceptable in the House or in the country.

9.25 pm

**Mr. Douglas French** (Gloucester): At the centre of the privatisation, if I am allowed to view it from England rather than Scotland, is Nuclear Electric, and at the centre of Nuclear Electric are my 900 constituents working at the headquarters in Barnwood in Gloucester.

My right hon. Friends the President of the Board of Trade and the Minister of State will know from my discussions with them in the past week how dismayed I have been at the lack of reliable and unambiguous information about the future of the work force at Barnwood. My views reflect the anxieties of my constituents and it is not surprising that they feel anxious.

My constituents waited a long time for the nuclear review, but when it arrived, nowhere in its 93 pages did Barnwood get a mention. My right hon. Friend the President of the Board of Trade made a statement in the House on 9 May. Nowhere in that statement was any mention made of Barnwood.

The statement was strong on the commercial case for privatisation, which I accept is persuasive, but the business consists also of people—skilful, loyal, hardworking and dedicated people who should not be taken for granted. Without their past efforts, the business would not be where it is. Without their future efforts and skills, privatisation will not succeed.

Hon. Members have referred to the success story of Nuclear Electric in the past five or six years. It is worth reflecting that in 1989 the performance of AGRs was very poor; now it is the best in the world. In 1989, the company faced the considerable hurdle of constructing and operating Sizewell B—it was a step into the unknown. Six years later, Sizewell B has been built to time at the cost anticipated and successfully commissioned.

In those six years, the unit costs for electricity, which were 5.2p per kWh, have been reduced to 2.7p per kWh. Output per man at Nuclear Electric has virtually doubled and the operating loss, which was about £1.1 billion six years ago, is now down to £35 million and destined to go into surplus.

The business has certainly achieved considerable success.

**Mr. Clapham:** Does the hon. Gentleman agree that the facts he has just advanced support the argument that the social purposes cannot be advanced by introducing a profit incentive in the industry?

**Mr. French:** No, I do not accept that argument at all and I shall explain why in a moment.

I was pointing out the considerable success that the business has achieved as a result of the substantial efforts of the people who work for it. I was pleased that that was acknowledged in broader terms at paragraph 9.14 of the review. But the success has not happened by accident. It has happened because of the considerable efforts of the employees at Barnwood.

For many of those employees, that success has been achieved against a background of great uncertainty and dislocation. Many of them had an unsettling time when the changeover took place from the Central Electricity Generating Board. Some had a spell at National Power. Some have moved several times within Nuclear Electric, especially from Knutsford. They have seen the number of jobs steadily shrinking while waiting for the review. They had a legitimate expectation that the review would map out a clear future. Arguably, it does commercially, but for the people who have been dogged by uncertainty up to now, it marks the beginning of a further period of uncertainty and they are entitled to know where they stand.

**Mr. Dalyell:** Will the hon. Gentleman give way?

**Mr. French:** If the hon. Gentleman will forgive me, I will not because I have to conclude by a particular time.

We have been told that 100 jobs will be created in Scotland to cover the financial and legal functions of head office. I seek from my right hon. Friend the Minister tonight an assurance that a significant proportion of that 100 will be additional local Scottish recruitment and that 100 new jobs in Scotland does not automatically mean 100 lost jobs at Barnwood.

I seek an assurance also that there is no validity in the claim that 300 people are about to lose their jobs in Barnwood. I know of no basis in fact to substantiate that claim, but it has gained currency. I should like an assurance that there is no basis in fact.

I also need an assurance from my right hon. Friend that deep and careful thought will be given to the future of Magnox and those who work on it. I realise that it is difficult to privatise Magnox stations because they will not generate enough cash during their remaining lifetime to meet accrued liabilities. I see risks in Magnox being a stand-alone company because, once the AGRs and the PWRs are split off, the income stream will be insufficient to meet liability. It would have been preferable for Nuclear Electric to contract to run the publicly owned Magnox stations on behalf of the Government. I share the disappointment of the chairman, John Collier, that that formula was not adopted.

I do know, however, that decommissioning Magnox requires expertise that is available only at Barnwood. Therefore, I ask my right hon. Friend for an assurance that every possible effort will be made to keep that expertise at Barnwood. Whether Magnox is a stand-alone public company or in time comes to be linked to British Nuclear Fuels Ltd., there is nothing to stop it being located in Gloucester and every reason why it should be located there.

All privatised companies have spread their wings in overseas markets. There is a growing international market for nuclear power, as my hon. Friend the Member for Colchester, South and Maldon (Mr. Whittingdale) spelt out so clearly. There are bids to build a nuclear power station in Taiwan, and that is only the beginning of the possible export opportunities. South Korea, China, the Pacific rim, as my hon. Friend pointed out, are all exciting opportunities.

**Mr. Merchant:** Latin America, too.

**Mr. French:** Latin America, as well.

If those opportunities are seized, the business overall will be immensely strengthened and jobs made much more secure. But an essential prerequisite for getting the business will be technical expertise. I therefore seek an assurance from my right hon. Friend the Minister that a battle will be fought to win export business because that is the way to strengthen job opportunities for those who have technical expertise, and technical expertise is essential if export business is to be won.

I believe that Nuclear Electric's business is likely to be more successful in the private sector than in the public sector. I certainly do not support the Opposition's disgraceful motion, which strikes me as a blindly political diatribe in clause IV mode, and which does not begin to map out a future for Nuclear Electric but seeks only to cling to the past.

I know that my right hon. Friend the Minister will appreciate that I need some reliable assurances on the issues that I have drawn to the House's attention before I can support him in the Lobby tonight.

9.34 pm

**Mr. Martin O'Neill** (Clackmannan): The short debate has enabled several hon. Members to express legitimate constituency worries. Indeed, the hon. Member for Gloucester (Mr. French) has just expressed anxieties about certain aspects of the merger from a different angle from that which Opposition Members would choose—but legitimate none the less.

What was interesting in the debate was the absence of any of the usual arguments in favour of privatisation. No Minister or Conservative Member has argued that the work force should be cut because the nuclear power industry is a bloated, overstaffed nationalised industry. We know that, since it was split off from the Central Electricity Generating Board, the work force has been cut by about 50 per cent. for the English stations and 25 per cent. for Scottish Nuclear. Indeed, there have been about 8,000 voluntary redundancies, so the labour force issue does not arise.

The issue of inefficiency in the public sector does not arise. The most up-to-date figures, published by Scottish Nuclear a few days ago, show that unit generating costs have decreased to 2.2p per kWh from 2.9p per kWh in 1993-94. Power output has increased to an all-time record of 16.9 TWh and output per employee has increased by about 32 per cent. in that time.

In some respects that is because, for the first time, the nuclear industry has been free of the shackles of the CEGB and has been able to concentrate on its own affairs and to tackle the genuine problems of the advanced gas-cooled reactor and to make it an efficient and safe form of generating nuclear power.

The Government repeatedly trot out arguments in favour of privatisation to the effect that the companies will cease to be a burden on the taxpayer. The short-sightedness of the Government is revealed by the fact that those companies contribute about £100 million per annum to the taxpayer.

We are told on occasions that we need privatisation to introduce good, commercial management, yet the figures that I have quoted would not exist, were it not for the quality of the management and the way in which they have been able to work with the labour force to produce the achievements that I described.

The hon. Member for Gloucester mentioned the freedom to seek business abroad, yet Nuclear Electric has been working with American consortiums to secure a Taiwanese contract. They were "down to the wire", as the saying goes, and they have now been told that they must rebid, but it was obvious that Nuclear Electric in the public sector was perfectly capable of associating with private companies abroad and of making a great success of one of the most highly competitive contract processes that has ever occurred in the energy business.

We hope that, regardless of who owns Nuclear Electric, that work will come to Britain, because it is vital not only for people who work in the power stations but for those who work in the electricity supply and equipment supply industries, in which there are so many manufacturing jobs throughout the country.

Should there be freedom to seek investment in the market? Paragraph 4.41 of the White Paper refers to the fact that, with borrowing in the public sector at 8 per cent., if a new power station were built, the price of its electricity would be 2.9p per kWh. However, we know that that money will not be forthcoming from the Government. If the industry goes to the market, it will have to borrow at an interest rate of at least 11 per cent., which would put the price of a unit of electricity in a new power station at about 3.7p per kWh. No one has suggested tonight that anyone will invest in new nuclear power stations if the price of electricity is that envisaged in those figures. The Government have said:

"Private finance for a new nuclear station is unlikely to be forthcoming without a transfer of nuclear specific risks away from private investors to another party in the project."

The other party in the project would have to be the taxpayer, and it would have to be at substantial subsidy. No one is prepared to advocate that case.

Faced with such quantifiable problems, the Government have decided to keep the ageing Magnox stations in the public sector, with us, the taxpayers, picking up the bill for decommissioning and waste management. Let us face it— that will be no paltry sum. The Engineers and Managers Association, the trade union of the power station bosses, has noted that the nuclear liabilities of the two companies amount to about £10 billion. That discounted figure was largely accounted for by Magnox decommissioning.

The money that electricity consumers paid to fund the work has been swallowed up, either by Sizewell B or by work on the advanced gas-cooled reactors, to which I referred earlier. Some of it may have been paid to the national loans fund and found its way into the financing of tax cuts.

The likely sum to be raised from privatisation is about £2 billion to £3 billion. That would probably afford a 1.5p cut in the tax rate. Taxpayers will be left to fund some £10 billion in decommissioning liabilities. That will work out at a cost of about £700 for every household in the land. We will be left with a holding company, supposedly based in Scotland, and perhaps in Edinburgh, although my hon. Friend the Member for Linlithgow (Mr. Dalyell) understandably argued that it should be based at Peel park, and there seems to be some logic to that.

Consideration must be given to the fact that, apparently, there will be premises in Gloucester and in London. If there were a split in the management structure, it would be attractive for the new management team to base itself ultimately in London, although the new chairman, Mr. John Robb, whose appointment was announced this

[*Mr. Martin O'Neill*]

evening, comes from Edinburgh. He seems to be eminently qualified to operate the nuclear industry's accounting system, in so far as he is chairman of Horserace Betting Levy Board. I do not know what other qualities he brings to these matters. We shall have to wait to see how long he is in post, because the holding companies have a somewhat chequered history.

If the stations are to achieve any further reductions in operations, and if the new chairman is to be able to deliver the goods, I suspect that the first casualties of the new order will be the same casualties that have emerged in the other energy privatisations—the research and development functions. They are important in that, in the nuclear industry, they have been closely linked to safety arrangements.

In Britain, the research that has been undertaken and the safety culture that has been a feature of the industry have been the real successes of the nuclear industry. Some speeches tonight, especially that of the hon. Member for Truro (Mr. Taylor), were scaremongering and alarmist about the nature of the nuclear industry. Flippant comparisons have been made between the nuclear industry in Britain and that in the former Soviet Union. It is like comparing a Jaguar car at its best with an inefficient, clapped-out old Lada, with exactly the same care and attention given to the safety and maintenance of Ladas as are showered on cars such as Jaguars.

In part, the safety culture will remain—we do not deny that, but we doubt whether the research and development emphasis will be what it was in the past. If that culture and the mass of big science abilities are not kept together, the nuclear installations inspectorate will encounter difficulties in trying to maintain high safety levels, which will be expensive and dangerous to secure. In the United States, the industry operates in a different way. Its safety regulatory body is now a massive bureaucracy.

We need assurances from the Government that they will insist that the science and research elements which are critical to the industry will remain. The Government have used a great deal of ingenuity and have given a great deal of attention to triple-locking arrangements for the location of an office. Many of us are anxious that they should give as much attention to the location of the laboratories and the safety centres which are such an integral part of our industry.

**Mr. Miller:** I am sure that my hon. Friend will acknowledge the point made by the hon. Member for Gloucester (Mr. French) about the skills of the Magnox staff at Barnwood. Does my hon. Friend share my concern at the fact that we have heard very little from the Government about their intentions for the science base at Berkeley technology centre?

**Mr. O'Neill:** I understand my hon. Friend's concern because that is an important employer in the north-west and it is—

**Mr. Miller:** It is in the south-east.

**Mr. O'Neill:** I apologise. I am so accustomed to my hon. Friend defending the rights of his constituents that I assumed that that part of the nuclear industry was located in his constituency.

My point remains; we are talking about big science and important research projects. We are talking about spin-offs which relate directly to nuclear safety—an area in which Britain can claim some credit for having a good record and not being complacent.

We want to know whether those things will be sustained and whether other problems will be dealt with. Will the competition issue be dealt with? I do not look to the Minister for much consolation there, but I look to the Director General of Electricity Supply. He ducked out the last time when the second tranche of PowerGen and National Power was being floated. He should have made a reference to the Monopolies and Mergers Commission, but he did not. He is now trying to make the best of a bad job by persuading them to divest themselves of some power stations to try to create more competition. If he wants competition, he should ensure that the privatisation scheme is subject to a view from the Monopolies and Mergers Commission.

We must take account of the arrangements that exist in Scotland where the must-take arrangement will be transferred from a public sector company to a private sector company. It will be interesting to see whether the North of Scotland Hydro-Electric Board and Scottish Power will be as keen to operate under the must-take arrangements regardless of price and whether they will seek a judicial review. It is reasonable to assume that there will be a number of legal or quasi-judicial obstacles in the way of this privatisation if the interests of the taxpayer and electricity consumers are to be properly protected.

We do not believe that the privatisation of the industry will make no difference. We believe that it is essential that the industry remains in the public sector. We know that the public have deep-seated, if not always correct, views on the issue of nuclear safety. What is more, we want to be certain that this debate will not be the last opportunity that the House has to debate the privatisation of the nuclear industry.

We recognise that this is the last gasp attempt of the Government to rustle up a few bob in the short term to provide money for bribes before an election. I do not think that the public will be taken in by that. As hon. Members go about the country and hear what their constituents feel about this privatisation, they will be clamouring for another vote. Before the Minister sits down, we want him to tell us that there will be other votes on this issue and that there will be the broadest possible consultation, such as that to which the Prime Minister referred when he came to Scotland last week. Before any subsequent votes, we want to see that there is still an opportunity for us to finish this debate and to finish privatisation. We will do that by going through the Lobby this evening to ensure that we get the vote that we want and end any threat of privatisation to an industry that is currently serving the country very well.

9.49 pm

**The Minister for Industry and Energy (Mr. Tim Eggar):** The remarkable thing about the speech of the hon. Member for Clackmannan (Mr. O'Neill), like that of his hon. Friend the Member for Hamilton (Mr. Robertson), was that he said not a word about the Labour party's policy on nuclear power. Indeed, he was about as forthcoming and knowledgeable on Labour party policy on nuclear power as he was about the geography of the United Kingdom when he seemed to think that Berkeley was in the north-west.

My hon. Friend the Member for Gloucester (Mr. French) is understandably concerned about the interests of his constituents at Barnwood. He also rightly—and almost alone among hon. Members—paid tribute to the work done by the management and staff of Nuclear Electric. He asked me for certain assurances about the staff at Barnwood. First, I can tell him quite categorically that the transfer of work from England to Scotland with regard to Barnwood certainly represents fewer than 50 jobs which might go to Scotland. Secondly, he was concerned about the rumours which had apparently got round at Barnwood about some 300 job losses. I can tell him that those rumours are completely unfounded.

My hon. Friend also raised the issue of the location of the headquarters of the new Magnox company and the employees who would support it. I have taken very careful note of what my hon. Friend said tonight and what he has said to me and my right hon. Friend the President of the Board of Trade during the past few days. I have raised this matter with Nuclear Electric, which has assured me that it will pay the greatest attention to the welfare and convenience of staff in taking decisions about locations.

I also assure my hon. Friend that he and his constituents will get an opportunity to argue their case as part of Nuclear Electric's normal consultative processes. I will also draw his concern to the attention of the chairmen of the holding company and of the new company, when it is established, which will deal with the Magnox stations.

My hon. Friend the Member for Colchester, South and Maldon (Mr. Whittingdale) also raised concerns of behalf of his constituents. I assure him that I have taken careful note of them and will reflect them in my discussions with management.

My hon. Friend the Member for Gloucester asked about the future of the export business. I attach tremendous importance to export opportunities, both for Nuclear Electric and for BNFL and I regard that as a major opportunity for the UK.

My hon. Friend the Member for Colchester, South and Maldon and, in particular, my hon. Friend the Member for Rochford (Dr. Clark), raised issues and expressed concern about competition. The Scottish electricity market, in effect, operates separately from the electricity market in England and Wales. The nuclear generators operate in the base load element of that market, and in practice base load competition in England and Wales will be increased as a result of the spinning out of the new Magnox company. Far from competition being reduced, it is my very strong belief that these proposals will enhance it.

The hon. Member for Cunninghame, North (Mr. Wilson) also raised that issue. He, of course, did not say that he had received a letter from Professor Littlechild on the subject when he indicated, broadly speaking—and I stress broadly—that he accepted the argument about increased base load competition in England and Wales. Getting more competition in generation, especially in marginal plants, and setting the pool price remains an important objective. The undertakings that the director general negotiated last year with National Power and PowerGen about the disposal of plant are an important

part of that process. I support the initiatives that the director general took then and look forward to a successful outcome.

Much has been said about safety in this debate. Some Opposition Members have attempted to raise what I can only call safety scares. That is despite the fact that the Government have said clearly, and my right hon. Friend the Secretary of State has said specifically, that safety will be paramount and despite the fact that the nuclear installations inspectorate serves under the tripartite Health and Safety Commission on which, of course, the unions are represented.

The HSC's evidence to the nuclear review made it clear that the safety regime could cope with any restructuring of the industry. Indeed, the nuclear installations inspectorate has made it clear that the safety regime already operates at private sector nuclear sites. Such sites have been operating under the present regime for a number of years, including the period when the right hon. Member for Chesterfield (Mr. Benn) was Secretary of State for Energy.

Much has been said about the alleged threat to Scotland and to Scottish Nuclear from our proposals. Where is that threat? The creation of 100 high-quality jobs in Scotland is certainly no threat. A new world-class company is to be headquartered in Scotland and there will be an effective triple guarantee that the company will stay in Scotland. A Scottish chairman has also been appointed to the holding company. That is no threat to Scotland. There is a reduction in electricity prices for domestic consumers in Scotland—where is the threat in that? My right hon. Friend's announcement is good news for Scotland.

The Labour party has consistently opposed privatisation and the benefits which have flowed to the consumers from it. I will spell out to Opposition Members what those benefits are. First, they will benefit from the lifting of the nuclear levy. In England and Wales, domestic electricity consumers will save on average more than £20 as a result of the announcement. Consumers are already paying £13 less in real terms than they were before privatisation. Another £11 reduction in their bills is in the pipeline, and that is before any further tightening of price controls. The newspapers also tell us that the flotation of the National Grid could bring a one-off bonus of around £30 to consumers.

To sum up, therefore, our privatisation policy for the nuclear industry and for the traditional non-fossil fuel generating industry could eventually produce a saving of no less than £75 for the average electricity consumer in England and Wales in this year alone. Put into perspective, that amounts to 25 per cent. of the average electricity bill in England and Wales saved in one year. That saving would not have been made but for the Government's commitment to the privatisation of the electricity industry and the additional privatisation of nuclear electricity.

We know that the Labour party opposes privatisation for the sake of old socialist dogma, but we do not know what the Labour party's policy is on nuclear power. Its manifesto states:

"We will not invest in new nuclear power stations".

To be fair to the hon. Member for East Kilbride (Mr. Ingram), he made it clear that he stood as a Labour party candidate at the last election while not believing a word of his own party's manifesto with regard to nuclear power.

[*Mr. Tim Eggar*]

He said that he would fight and fight again to change Labour party policy. The hon. Member for Hamilton refused to say what Labour party policy was, as did the hon. Member for Clackmannan. The only honest man on the Opposition Benches seems to be the hon. Member for Kirkcaldy (Dr. Moonie): when I pressed him on Labour party nuclear policy in a previous debate, he said that he did not know the answer.

Privatisation is good for the consumer, good for the nuclear industry and it should be approved by this House.

*Question put,* That the original words stand part of the Question:—

*The House divided:* Ayes 252, Noes 284.

**Division No. 151]** **[10.00 pm**

### AYES

Abbott, Ms Diane
Allen, Graham
Anderson, Donald (Swansea E)
Anderson, Ms Janet (Ros'dale)
Armstrong, Hilary
Ashdown, Rt Hon Paddy
Ashton, Joe
Austin-Walker, John
Banks, Tony (Newham NW)
Barnes, Harry
Barron, Kevin
Battle, John
Bayley, Hugh
Beckett, Rt Hon Margaret
Beggs, Roy
Beith, Rt Hon A J
Bell, Stuart
Benn, Rt Hon Tony
Bennett, Andrew F
Bermingham, Gerald
Berry, Roger
Betts, Clive
Boateng, Paul
Bradley, Keith
Bray, Dr Jeremy
Brown, Gordon (Dunfermline E)
Brown, N (N'c'tle upon Tyne E)
Bruce, Malcolm (Gordon)
Burden, Richard
Byers, Stephen
Caborn, Richard
Callaghan, Jim
Campbell, Mrs Anne (C'bridge)
Campbell, Menzies (Fife NE)
Canavan, Dennis
Chidgey, David
Chisholm, Malcolm
Church, Judith
Clapham, Michael
Clark, Dr David (South Shields)
Clarke, Eric (Midlothian)
Clarke, Tom (Monklands W)
Clelland, David
Clwyd, Mrs Ann
Coffey, Ann
Cohen, Harry
Connarty, Michael
Cook, Frank (Stockton N)
Cook, Robin (Livingston)
Corbett, Robin
Corbyn, Jeremy
Cousins, Jim
Cox, Tom

Cummings, John
Cunliffe, Lawrence
Cunningham, Jim (Covy SE)
Cunningham, Rt Hon Dr John
Dalyell, Tam
Davidson, Ian
Davies, Bryan (Oldham C'tral)
Davies, Rt Hon Denzil (Llanelli)
Davies, Ron (Caerphilly)
Denham, John
Dewar, Donald
Dixon, Don
Donohoe, Brian H
Dowd, Jim
Dunnachie, Jimmy
Dunwoody, Mrs Gwyneth
Eastham, Ken
Enright, Derek
Etherington, Bill
Evans, John (St Helens N)
Ewing, Mrs Margaret
Fatchett, Derek
Faulds, Andrew
Field, Frank (Birkenhead)
Flynn, Paul
Foster, Rt Hon Derek
Foster, Don (Bath)
Foulkes, George
Fraser, John
Fyfe, Maria
Galbraith, Sam
Galloway, George
Gapes, Mike
Garrett, John
Gerrard, Neil
Gilbert, Rt Hon Dr John
Godman, Dr Norman A
Godsiff, Roger
Golding, Mrs Llin
Gordon, Mildred
Graham, Thomas
Grant, Bernie (Tottenham)
Griffiths, Nigel (Edinburgh S)
Griffiths, Win (Bridgend)
Grocott, Bruce
Hain, Peter
Hall, Mike
Hardy, Peter
Harvey, Nick
Hattersley, Rt Hon Roy
Henderson, Doug
Heppell, John
Hill, Keith (Streatham)

Hinchliffe, David
Hodge, Margaret
Hoey, Kate
Hogg, Norman (Cumbernauld)
Home Robertson, John
Hood, Jimmy
Hoon, Geoffrey
Howarth, George (Knowsley North)
Howells, Dr. Kim (Pontypridd)
Hoyle, Doug
Hughes, Kevin (Doncaster N)
Hughes, Robert (Aberdeen N)
Hughes, Roy (Newport E)
Hughes, Simon (Southwark)
Hutton, John
Illsley, Eric
Ingram, Adam
Jackson, Glenda (H'stead)
Jackson, Helen (Shef'ld, H)
Jamieson, David
Janner, Greville
Jones, Barry (Alyn and D'side)
Jones, Jon Owen (Cardiff C)
Jones, Lynne (B'ham S O)
Jones, Martyn (Clwyd, SW)
Jowell, Tessa
Kaufman, Rt Hon Gerald
Keen, Alan
Kennedy, Charles (Ross,C&S)
Kennedy, Jane (Lpool Brdgn)
Khabra, Piara S
Kilfoyle, Peter
Kirkwood, Archy
Lestor, Joan (Eccles)
Lewis, Terry
Litherland, Robert
Livingstone, Ken
Lloyd, Tony (Stretford)
Loyden, Eddie
McAllion, John
McAvoy, Thomas
McCartney, Ian
McCrea, The Reverend William
Macdonald, Calum
McFall, John
McKelvey, William
Mackinlay, Andrew
McLeish, Henry
Maclennan, Robert
McMaster, Gordon
McNamara, Kevin
MacShane, Denis
McWilliam, John
Madden, Max
Mahon, Alice
Mandelson, Peter
Marek, Dr John
Martin, Michael J (Springburn)
Martlew, Eric
Meacher, Michael
Michael, Alun
Michie, Bill (Sheffield Heeley)
Michie, Mrs Ray (Argyll & Bute)
Milburn, Alan
Miller, Andrew
Morgan, Rhodri
Morley, Elliot
Morris, Rt Hon Alfred (Wy'nshawe)
Morris, Estelle (B'ham Yardley)
Morris, Rt Hon John (Aberavon)
Mowlam, Marjorie
Mudie, George
Mullin, Chris
Murphy, Paul
Oakes, Rt Hon Gordon

O'Brien, William (Normanton)
O'Hara, Edward
Olner, Bill
O'Neill, Martin
Orme, Rt Hon Stanley
Parry, Robert
Pearson, Ian
Pike, Peter L
Pope, Greg
Powell, Ray (Ogmore)
Prentice, Bridget (Lew'm E)
Prentice, Gordon (Pendle)
Prescott, Rt Hon John
Primarolo, Dawn
Quin, Ms Joyce
Randall, Stuart
Raynsford, Nick
Reid, Dr John
Rendel, David
Robertson, George (Hamilton)
Robinson, Geoffrey (Co'try NW)
Roche, Mrs Barbara
Rogers, Allan
Rooker, Jeff
Rooney, Terry
Ross, Ernie (Dundee W)
Rowlands, Ted
Salmond, Alex
Sedgemore, Brian
Sheerman, Barry
Sheldon, Rt Hon Robert
Shore, Rt Hon Peter
Short, Clare
Simpson, Alan
Skinner, Dennis
Smith, Andrew (Oxford E)
Smith, Chris (Isl'ton S & F'sbury)
Smith, Llew (Blaenau Gwent)
Smyth, The Reverend Martin
Soley, Clive
Spearing, Nigel
Spellar, John
Squire, Rachel (Dunfermline W)
Steinberg, Gerry
Stevenson, George
Stott, Roger
Strang, Dr. Gavin
Sutcliffe, Gerry
Taylor, Mrs Ann (Dewsbury)
Taylor, Matthew (Truro)
Thompson, Jack (Wansbeck)
Timms, Stephen
Touhig, Don
Tyler, Paul
Vaz, Keith
Walker, Rt Hon Sir Harold
Wallace, James
Walley, Joan
Wareing, Robert N
Watson, Mike
Wicks, Malcolm
Wigley, Dafydd
Williams, Rt Hon Alan (Sw'n W)
Williams, Alan W (Carmarthen)
Wilson, Brian
Winnick, David
Wise, Audrey
Worthington, Tony
Wray, Jimmy
Wright, Dr Tony
Young, David (Bolton SE)

**Tellers for the Ayes:**
  **Mr. Joe Benton and**
  **Mr. Robert Ainsworth.**

## NOES

Ainsworth, Peter (East Surrey)
Aitken, Rt Hon Jonathan
Alison, Rt Hon Michael (Selby)
Allason, Rupert (Torbay)
Amess, David
Arbuthnot, James
Arnold, Jacques (Gravesham)
Arnold, Sir Thomas (Hazel Grv)
Ashby, David
Atkins, Robert
Atkinson, David (Bour'mouth E)
Atkinson, Peter (Hexham)
Baker, Rt Hon Kenneth (Mole V)
Baker, Nicholas (North Dorset)
Baldry, Tony
Banks, Matthew (Southport)
Bates, Michael
Batiste, Spencer
Bellingham, Henry
Bendall, Vivian
Beresford, Sir Paul
Biffen, Rt Hon John
Booth, Hartley
Boswell, Tim
Bottomley, Peter (Eltham)
Bottomley, Rt Hon Virginia
Bowden, Sir Andrew
Bowis, John
Boyson, Rt Hon Sir Rhodes
Brandreth, Gyles
Brazier, Julian
Bright, Sir Graham
Brooke, Rt Hon Peter
Brown, M (Brigg & Cl'thorpes)
Browning, Mrs Angela
Bruce, Ian (Dorset)
Budgen, Nicholas
Burns, Simon
Burt, Alistair
Butcher, John
Butler, Peter
Butterfill, John
Carlisle, John (Luton North)
Carlisle, Sir Kenneth (Lincoln)
Carrington, Matthew
Carttiss, Michael
Cash, William
Channon, Rt Hon Paul
Clappison, James
Clark, Dr Michael (Rochford)
Clifton-Brown, Geoffrey
Coe, Sebastian
Colvin, Michael
Congdon, David
Conway, Derek
Cope, Rt Hon Sir John
Cormack, Sir Patrick
Couchman, James
Cran, James
Currie, Mrs Edwina (S D'by'ire)
Curry, David (Skipton & Ripon)
Davies, Quentin (Stamford)
Davis, David (Boothferry)
Day, Stephen
Deva, Nirj Joseph
Devlin, Tim
Dicks, Terry
Dorrell, Rt Hon Stephen
Douglas-Hamilton, Lord James
Dover, Den
Duncan, Alan
Duncan-Smith, Iain
Dunn, Bob
Durant, Sir Anthony

Eggar, Rt Hon Tim
Elletson, Harold
Emery, Rt Hon Sir Peter
Evans, David (Welwyn Hatfield)
Evans, Jonathan (Brecon)
Evans, Nigel (Ribble Valley)
Evans, Roger (Monmouth)
Evennett, David
Faber, David
Fabricant, Michael
Fenner, Dame Peggy
Field, Barry (Isle of Wight)
Fishburn, Dudley
Forman, Nigel
Forth, Eric
Fox, Dr Liam (Woodspring)
Fox, Sir Marcus (Shipley)
Freeman, Rt Hon Roger
French, Douglas
Gale, Roger
Gallie, Phil
Gardiner, Sir George
Garel-Jones, Rt Hon Tristan
Garnier, Edward
Gill, Christopher
Gillan, Cheryl
Goodlad, Rt Hon Alastair
Goodson-Wickes, Dr Charles
Gorman, Mrs Teresa
Gorst, Sir John
Grant, Sir A (SW Cambs)
Greenway, Harry (Ealing N)
Griffiths, Peter (Portsmouth, N)
Grylls, Sir Michael
Gummer, Rt Hon John Selwyn
Hague, William
Hamilton, Rt Hon Sir Archibald
Hamilton, Neil (Tatton)
Hampson, Dr Keith
Hanley, Rt Hon Jeremy
Hannam, Sir John
Hargreaves, Andrew
Harris, David
Haselhurst, Alan
Hawkins, Nick
Hayes, Jerry
Heald, Oliver
Heath, Rt Hon Sir Edward
Heathcoat-Amory, David
Hendry, Charles
Hicks, Robert
Higgins, Rt Hon Sir Terence
Hill, James (Southampton Test)
Hogg, Rt Hon Douglas (G'tham)
Horam, John
Hordern, Rt Hon Sir Peter
Howard, Rt Hon Michael
Howarth, Alan (Strat'rd-on-A)
Howell, Rt Hon David (G'dford)
Howell, Sir Ralph (N Norfolk)
Hughes, Robert G (Harrow W)
Hunt, Sir John (Ravensbourne)
Hunter, Andrew
Jack, Michael
Jenkin, Bernard
Jessel, Toby
Johnson Smith, Sir Geoffrey
Jones, Gwilym (Cardiff N)
Jones, Robert B (W Hertfdshr)
Jopling, Rt Hon Michael
Kellett-Bowman, Dame Elaine
Key, Robert
King, Rt Hon Tom
Kirkhope, Timothy

Knapman, Roger
Knight, Mrs Angela (Erewash)
Knight, Greg (Derby N)
Knox, Sir David
Kynoch, George (Kincardine)
Lait, Mrs Jacqui
Lamont, Rt Hon Norman
Lang, Rt Hon Ian
Lawrence, Sir Ivan
Legg, Barry
Leigh, Edward
Lennox-Boyd, Sir Mark
Lester, Jim (Broxtowe)
Lidington, David
Lightbown, David
Lilley, Rt Hon Peter
Lloyd, Rt Hon Sir Peter (Fareham)
Lord, Michael
Lyell, Rt Hon Sir Nicholas
MacGregor, Rt Hon John
MacKay, Andrew
Maclean, David
McLoughlin, Patrick
McNair-Wilson, Sir Patrick
Madel, Sir David
Maitland, Lady Olga
Major, Rt Hon John
Malone, Gerald
Mans, Keith
Marlow, Tony
Marshall, John (Hendon S)
Marshall, Sir Michael (Arundel)
Martin, David (Portsmouth S)
Mates, Michael
Mawhinney, Rt Hon Dr Brian
Mayhew, Rt Hon Sir Patrick
Mellor, Rt Hon David
Merchant, Piers
Mills, Iain
Mitchell, Andrew (Gedling)
Mitchell, Sir David (NW Hants)
Moate, Sir Roger
Monro, Sir Hector
Montgomery, Sir Fergus
Needham, Rt Hon Richard
Nelson, Anthony
Neubert, Sir Michael
Newton, Rt Hon Tony
Nicholls, Patrick
Nicholson, David (Taunton)
Norris, Steve
Onslow, Rt Hon Sir Cranley
Oppenheim, Phillip
Ottaway, Richard
Page, Richard
Pattie, Rt Hon Sir Geoffrey
Pawsey, James
Peacock, Mrs Elizabeth
Pickles, Eric
Porter, Barry (Wirral S)
Porter, David (Waveney)
Portillo, Rt Hon Michael
Powell, William (Corby)
Rathbone, Tim
Redwood, Rt Hon John
Renton, Rt Hon Tim
Rifkind, Rt Hon Malcolm
Robathan, Andrew
Robinson, Mark (Somerton)
Roe, Mrs Marion (Broxbourne)

Rumbold, Rt Hon Dame Angela
Ryder, Rt Hon Richard
Sackville, Tom
Sainsbury, Rt Hon Sir Timothy
Scott, Rt Hon Sir Nicholas
Shaw, David (Dover)
Shaw, Sir Giles (Pudsey)
Shephard, Rt Hon Gillian
Shepherd, Colin (Hereford)
Shepherd, Richard (Aldridge)
Sims, Roger
Smith, Sir Dudley (Warwick)
Smith, Tim (Beaconsfield)
Soames, Nicholas
Speed, Sir Keith
Spencer, Sir Derek
Spicer, Sir James (W Dorset)
Spicer, Michael (S Worcs)
Spink, Dr Robert
Spring, Richard
Sproat, Iain
Squire, Robin (Hornchurch)
Stanley, Rt Hon Sir John
Steen, Anthony
Stephen, Michael
Stern, Michael
Stewart, Allan
Streeter, Gary
Sumberg, David
Sykes, John
Tapsell, Sir Peter
Taylor, Ian (Esher)
Taylor, John M (Solihull)
Taylor, Sir Teddy (Southend, E)
Temple-Morris, Peter
Thomason, Roy
Thompson, Sir Donald (C'er V)
Thompson, Patrick (Norwich N)
Thornton, Sir Malcolm
Thurnham, Peter
Townend, John (Bridlington)
Townsend, Cyril D (Bexl'yh'th)
Tracey, Richard
Trend, Michael
Trotter, Neville
Twinn, Dr Ian
Vaughan, Sir Gerard
Viggers, Peter
Waldegrave, Rt Hon William
Walden, George
Walker, Bill (N Tayside)
Waller, Gary
Ward, John
Wardle, Charles (Bexhill)
Waterson, Nigel
Watts, John
Whitney, Ray
Whittingdale, John
Widdecombe, Ann
Wilkinson, John
Willetts, David
Wilshire, David
Wolfson, Mark
Wood, Timothy
Yeo, Tim
Young, Rt Hon Sir George

**Tellers for the Noes:**
   **Mr. Sydney Chapman and**
   **Mr. Bowen Wells.**

*Question accordingly negatived.*

*Question,* That the proposed words be there added, *put forthwith pursuant to Standing Order No. 30 (Questions on amendments):—*

The House divided: Ayes 272, Noes 251.

**Division No. 152]**                                    **[10.15 pm**

### AYES

Ainsworth, Peter (East Surrey)
Aitken, Rt Hon Jonathan
Alison, Rt Hon Michael (Selby)
Amess, David
Arbuthnot, James
Arnold, Jacques (Gravesham)
Arnold, Sir Thomas (Hazel Grv)
Ashby, David
Atkins, Robert
Atkinson, David (Bour'mouth E)
Baker, Rt Hon Kenneth (Mole V)
Baker, Nicholas (North Dorset)
Baldry, Tony
Banks, Matthew (Southport)
Bates, Michael
Batiste, Spencer
Bellingham, Henry
Beresford, Sir Paul
Biffen, Rt Hon John
Booth, Hartley
Boswell, Tim
Bottomley, Peter (Eltham)
Bottomley, Rt Hon Virginia
Bowden, Sir Andrew
Bowis, John
Boyson, Rt Hon Sir Rhodes
Brandreth, Gyles
Brazier, Julian
Bright, Sir Graham
Brooke, Rt Hon Peter
Brown, M (Brigg & Cl'thorpes)
Browning, Mrs Angela
Bruce, Ian (Dorset)
Budgen, Nicholas
Burns, Simon
Burt, Alistair
Butcher, John
Butler, Peter
Butterfill, John
Carlisle, John (Luton North)
Carlisle, Sir Kenneth (Lincoln)
Carrington, Matthew
Carttiss, Michael
Cash, William
Channon, Rt Hon Paul
Clappison, James
Clark, Dr Michael (Rochford)
Clifton-Brown, Geoffrey
Coe, Sebastian
Colvin, Michael
Congdon, David
Conway, Derek
Cope, Rt Hon Sir John
Cormack, Sir Patrick
Couchman, James
Cran, James
Curry, David (Skipton & Ripon)
Davies, Quentin (Stamford)
Davis, David (Boothferry)
Day, Stephen
Deva, Nirj Joseph
Devlin, Tim
Dicks, Terry
Dorrell, Rt Hon Stephen
Douglas-Hamilton, Lord James
Dover, Den
Duncan, Alan

Duncan-Smith, Iain
Dunn, Bob
Durant, Sir Anthony
Eggar, Rt Hon Tim
Elletson, Harold
Emery, Rt Hon Sir Peter
Evans, David (Welwyn Hatfield)
Evans, Jonathan (Brecon)
Evans, Nigel (Ribble Valley)
Evans, Roger (Monmouth)
Evennett, David
Faber, David
Fabricant, Michael
Fenner, Dame Peggy
Field, Barry (Isle of Wight)
Forman, Nigel
Forth, Eric
Fox, Dr Liam (Woodspring)
Fox, Sir Marcus (Shipley)
Freeman, Rt Hon Roger
Gale, Roger
Gallie, Phil
Gardiner, Sir George
Garel-Jones, Rt Hon Tristan
Garnier, Edward
Gill, Christopher
Gillan, Cheryl
Goodlad, Rt Hon Alastair
Goodson-Wickes, Dr Charles
Gorman, Mrs Teresa
Gorst, Sir John
Grant, Sir A (SW Cambs)
Greenway, Harry (Ealing N)
Griffiths, Peter (Portsmouth, N)
Grylls, Sir Michael
Gummer, Rt Hon John Selwyn
Hague, William
Hamilton, Rt Hon Sir Archibald
Hamilton, Neil (Tatton)
Hampson, Dr Keith
Hanley, Rt Hon Jeremy
Hannam, Sir John
Hargreaves, Andrew
Harris, David
Haselhurst, Alan
Hawkins, Nick
Hayes, Jerry
Heald, Oliver
Heath, Rt Hon Sir Edward
Heathcoat-Amory, David
Hendry, Charles
Hicks, Robert
Higgins, Rt Hon Sir Terence
Hill, James (Southampton Test)
Hogg, Rt Hon Douglas (G'tham)
Horam, John
Hordern, Rt Hon Sir Peter
Howard, Rt Hon Michael
Howarth, Alan (Strat'rd-on-A)
Howell, Rt Hon David (G'dford)
Howell, Sir Ralph (N Norfolk)
Hughes, Robert G (Harrow W)
Hunter, Andrew
Jack, Michael
Jenkin, Bernard
Jessel, Toby
Johnson Smith, Sir Geoffrey

Jones, Gwilym (Cardiff N)
Jones, Robert B (W Hertfdshr)
Jopling, Rt Hon Michael
Kellett-Bowman, Dame Elaine
Key, Robert
Kirkhope, Timothy
Knapman, Roger
Knight, Mrs Angela (Erewash)
Knight, Greg (Derby N)
Knox, Sir David
Kynoch, George (Kincardine)
Lait, Mrs Jacqui
Lang, Rt Hon Ian
Lawrence, Sir Ivan
Legg, Barry
Leigh, Edward
Lennox-Boyd, Sir Mark
Lester, Jim (Broxtowe)
Lidington, David
Lightbown, David
Lilley, Rt Hon Peter
Lloyd, Rt Hon Sir Peter (Fareham)
Lord, Michael
Lyell, Rt Hon Sir Nicholas
MacGregor, Rt Hon John
MacKay, Andrew
Maclean, David
McLoughlin, Patrick
McNair-Wilson, Sir Patrick
Madel, Sir David
Maitland, Lady Olga
Major, Rt Hon John
Malone, Gerald
Mans, Keith
Marlow, Tony
Marshall, John (Hendon S)
Marshall, Sir Michael (Arundel)
Martin, David (Portsmouth S)
Mates, Michael
Mawhinney, Rt Hon Dr Brian
Mayhew, Rt Hon Sir Patrick
Mellor, Rt Hon David
Merchant, Piers
Mills, Iain
Mitchell, Andrew (Gedling)
Mitchell, Sir David (NW Hants)
Moate, Sir Roger
Monro, Sir Hector
Montgomery, Sir Fergus
Needham, Rt Hon Richard
Nelson, Anthony
Neubert, Sir Michael
Newton, Rt Hon Tony
Nicholls, Patrick
Nicholson, David (Taunton)
Norris, Steve
Onslow, Rt Hon Sir Cranley
Oppenheim, Phillip
Ottaway, Richard
Page, Richard
Pattie, Rt Hon Sir Geoffrey
Pawsey, James
Peacock, Mrs Elizabeth
Pickles, Eric
Porter, Barry (Wirral S)
Porter, David (Waveney)
Portillo, Rt Hon Michael
Powell, William (Corby)
Rathbone, Tim
Redwood, Rt Hon John
Renton, Rt Hon Tim

Rifkind, Rt Hon Malcolm
Robathan, Andrew
Robinson, Mark (Somerton)
Roe, Mrs Marion (Broxbourne)
Rumbold, Rt Hon Dame Angela
Ryder, Rt Hon Richard
Sackville, Tom
Scott, Rt Hon Sir Nicholas
Shaw, David (Dover)
Shaw, Sir Giles (Pudsey)
Shephard, Rt Hon Gillian
Shepherd, Colin (Hereford)
Shepherd, Richard (Aldridge)
Sims, Roger
Smith, Sir Dudley (Warwick)
Smith, Tim (Beaconsfield)
Soames, Nicholas
Speed, Sir Keith
Spencer, Sir Derek
Spicer, Sir James (W Dorset)
Spicer, Michael (S Worcs)
Spink, Dr Robert
Spring, Richard
Sproat, Iain
Squire, Robin (Hornchurch)
Stanley, Rt Hon Sir John
Steen, Anthony
Stephen, Michael
Stern, Michael
Stewart, Allan
Streeter, Gary
Sumberg, David
Sykes, John
Tapsell, Sir Peter
Taylor, Ian (Esher)
Taylor, John M (Solihull)
Taylor, Sir Teddy (Southend, E)
Temple-Morris, Peter
Thomason, Roy
Thompson, Sir Donald (C'er V)
Thompson, Patrick (Norwich N)
Thornton, Sir Malcolm
Thurnham, Peter
Townsend, Cyril D (Bexl'yh'th)
Tracey, Richard
Trend, Michael
Trotter, Neville
Twinn, Dr Ian
Vaughan, Sir Gerard
Viggers, Peter
Waldegrave, Rt Hon William
Walker, Bill (N Tayside)
Waller, Gary
Ward, John
Wardle, Charles (Bexhill)
Waterson, Nigel
Watts, John
Whitney, Ray
Whittingdale, John
Widdecombe, Ann
Wilkinson, John
Willetts, David
Wilshire, David
Wolfson, Mark
Wood, Timothy
Yeo, Tim
Young, Rt Hon Sir George

**Tellers for the Ayes:**
    **Mr. Sydney Chapman and**
    **Mr. Bowen Wells.**

### NOES

Abbott, Ms Diane
Allen, Graham
Anderson, Donald (Swansea E)
Anderson, Ms Janet (Ros'dale)
Armstrong, Hilary
Ashdown, Rt Hon Paddy
Ashton, Joe
Austin-Walker, John
Banks, Tony (Newham NW)
Barnes, Harry
Barron, Kevin
Battle, John
Bayley, Hugh
Beckett, Rt Hon Margaret
Beggs, Roy
Beith, Rt Hon A J
Bell, Stuart
Benn, Rt Hon Tony
Bennett, Andrew F
Bermingham, Gerald
Berry, Roger
Betts, Clive
Boateng, Paul
Bradley, Keith
Bray, Dr Jeremy
Brown, Gordon (Dunfermline E)
Brown, N (N'c'tle upon Tyne E)
Bruce, Malcolm (Gordon)
Burden, Richard
Byers, Stephen
Caborn, Richard
Callaghan, Jim
Campbell, Mrs Anne (C'bridge)
Campbell, Menzies (Fife NE)
Canavan, Dennis
Chidgey, David
Chisholm, Malcolm
Church, Judith
Clapham, Michael
Clark, Dr David (South Shields)
Clarke, Eric (Midlothian)
Clarke, Tom (Monklands W)
Clelland, David
Clwyd, Mrs Ann
Coffey, Ann
Cohen, Harry
Connarty, Michael
Cook, Frank (Stockton N)
Cook, Robin (Livingston)
Corbett, Robin
Corbyn, Jeremy
Cousins, Jim
Cox, Tom
Cummings, John
Cunliffe, Lawrence
Cunningham, Jim (Covy SE)
Cunningham, Rt Hon Dr John
Dalyell, Tam
Davidson, Ian
Davies, Bryan (Oldham C'tral)
Davies, Rt Hon Denzil (Llanelli)
Davies, Ron (Caerphilly)
Denham, John
Dewar, Donald
Dixon, Don
Donohoe, Brian H
Dowd, Jim
Dunnachie, Jimmy
Dunwoody, Mrs Gwyneth
Eastham, Ken
Enright, Derek
Etherington, Bill
Evans, John (St Helens N)
Ewing, Mrs Margaret
Fatchett, Derek
Faulds, Andrew

Field, Frank (Birkenhead)
Flynn, Paul
Foster, Rt Hon Derek
Foster, Don (Bath)
Foulkes, George
Fraser, John
Fyfe, Maria
Galbraith, Sam
Galloway, George
Gapes, Mike
Garrett, John
Gerrard, Neil
Gilbert, Rt Hon Dr John
Godman, Dr Norman A
Godsiff, Roger
Golding, Mrs Llin
Gordon, Mildred
Graham, Thomas
Grant, Bernie (Tottenham)
Griffiths, Nigel (Edinburgh S)
Griffiths, Win (Bridgend)
Grocott, Bruce
Hain, Peter
Hall, Mike
Hardy, Peter
Harvey, Nick
Hattersley, Rt Hon Roy
Henderson, Doug
Heppell, John
Hill, Keith (Streatham)
Hinchliffe, David
Hodge, Margaret
Hoey, Kate
Hogg, Norman (Cumbernauld)
Home Robertson, John
Hood, Jimmy
Hoon, Geoffrey
Howarth, George (Knowsley North)
Howells, Dr. Kim (Pontypridd)
Hoyle, Doug
Hughes, Kevin (Doncaster N)
Hughes, Robert (Aberdeen N)
Hughes, Roy (Newport E)
Hughes, Simon (Southwark)
Hutton, John
Illsley, Eric
Ingram, Adam
Jackson, Glenda (H'stead)
Jackson, Helen (Shef'ld, H)
Jamieson, David
Janner, Greville
Jones, Barry (Alyn and D'side)
Jones, Jon Owen (Cardiff C)
Jones, Lynne (B'ham S O)
Jones, Martyn (Clwyd, SW)
Jowell, Tessa
Kaufman, Rt Hon Gerald
Keen, Alan
Kennedy, Charles (Ross,C&S)
Kennedy, Jane (Lpool Brdgn)
Khabra, Piara S
Kilfoyle, Peter
Kirkwood, Archy
Lestor, Joan (Eccles)
Lewis, Terry
Litherland, Robert
Livingstone, Ken
Lloyd, Tony (Stretford)
Loyden, Eddie
McAllion, John
McAvoy, Thomas
McCartney, Ian
McCrea, The Reverend William
Macdonald, Calum
McFall, John
McKelvey, William

Mackinlay, Andrew
McLeish, Henry
Maclennan, Robert
McMaster, Gordon
McNamara, Kevin
MacShane, Denis
McWilliam, John
Madden, Max
Mahon, Alice
Mandelson, Peter
Marek, Dr John
Martin, Michael J (Springburn)
Martlew, Eric
Meacher, Michael
Michael, Alun
Michie, Bill (Sheffield Heeley)
Michie, Mrs Ray (Argyll & Bute)
Milburn, Alan
Miller, Andrew
Morgan, Rhodri
Morley, Elliot
Morris, Rt Hon Alfred (Wy'nshawe)
Morris, Estelle (B'ham Yardley)
Morris, Rt Hon John (Aberavon)
Mowlam, Marjorie
Mudie, George
Mullin, Chris
Murphy, Paul
Oakes, Rt Hon Gordon
O'Brien, William (Normanton)
O'Hara, Edward
Olner, Bill
O'Neill, Martin
Orme, Rt Hon Stanley
Parry, Robert
Pearson, Ian
Pike, Peter L
Pope, Greg
Powell, Ray (Ogmore)
Prentice, Bridget (Lew'm E)
Prentice, Gordon (Pendle)
Primarolo, Dawn
Prescott, Rt Hon John
Quin, Ms Joyce
Randall, Stuart
Raynsford, Nick
Reid, Dr John
Rendel, David
Robertson, George (Hamilton)
Robinson, Geoffrey (Co'try NW)
Roche, Mrs Barbara

Rogers, Allan
Rooker, Jeff
Rooney, Terry
Ross, Ernie (Dundee W)
Rowlands, Ted
Salmond, Alex
Sedgemore, Brian
Sheerman, Barry
Sheldon, Rt Hon Robert
Short, Clare
Simpson, Alan
Skinner, Dennis
Smith, Andrew (Oxford E)
Smith, Chris (Isl'ton S & F'sbury)
Smith, Llew (Blaenau Gwent)
Smyth, The Reverend Martin
Soley, Clive
Spearing, Nigel
Spellar, John
Squire, Rachel (Dunfermline W)
Steinberg, Gerry
Stevenson, George
Stott, Roger
Strang, Dr. Gavin
Sutcliffe, Gerry
Taylor, Mrs Ann (Dewsbury)
Taylor, Matthew (Truro)
Thompson, Jack (Wansbeck)
Timms, Stephen
Touhig, Don
Tyler, Paul
Vaz, Keith
Walker, Rt Hon Sir Harold
Wallace, James
Walley, Joan
Wareing, Robert N
Watson, Mike
Wicks, Malcolm
Wigley, Dafydd
Williams, Rt Hon Alan (Sw'n W)
Williams, Alan W (Carmarthen)
Wilson, Brian
Winnick, David
Wise, Audrey
Worthington, Tony
Wray, Jimmy
Wright, Dr Tony
Young, David (Bolton SE)

**Tellers for the Noes:**
  **Mr. Joe Benton and**
  **Mr. Robert Ainsworth**

*Question accordingly agreed to.*

Mr. Deputy Speaker *forthwith declared the main Question, as amended, to be agreed to.*

*Resolved,*

That this House welcomes the outcome of the Government's Nuclear Review; applauds the improvements in performance by the nuclear generators since the privatisation of the rest of the electricity supply industry, including the reduction of decommissioning costs achieved so far; welcomes the proposals for more cost-effective management of Magnox liabilities; welcomes the Government's decision to privatise the industry's seven AGR stations and one PWR station during the course of 1996; endorses the decision to create a holding company, with its headquarters located in Scotland, with the parts of Nuclear Electric and Scottish Nuclear that are to be privatised as its wholly owned subsidiaries; notes that safety will continue to be of paramount importance when the industry is in the private sector; and applauds the benefits to consumers in terms of lower electricity prices which the early end to the nuclear element of the fossil fuel levy in England and Wales and to the premium price in the Nuclear Energy Agreement in Scotland will bring.

# Flight PK 268

*Motion made, and Question proposed,* That this House do now adjourn.—*[Mr. Willetts.]*

10.26 pm

**Mr. Nigel Waterson** (Eastbourne): Sadly, about a thousand people a year are killed in aeroplane crashes. Each of those deaths involves a deep personal tragedy for the loved ones left behind. This is the story of one of them.

I was approached by my constituents, Michael and Nesta Peate. They are typical decent, law-abiding citizens: Mr. Peate is a respected local optician. They had a daughter, Louise. Aged 31, she had just completed six years' training and had qualified as a clinical psychologist. She went trekking in the Himalayas to celebrate her success, and also to have a break before starting a new job. She was one of the passengers on Pakistan International Airlines flight PK 268 from Karachi to Kathmandu in Nepal on 28 September 1992. The A300 Airbus carried 167 passengers and crew, including 34 Britons such as Louise. Many were also young and talented, with everything in life to look forward to.

At 14:30 hours local time, the aircraft struck a mountain during its approach to Kathmandu airport. It was flying some 1,500 ft too low when it crashed. Everyone on board was killed. As is normal in such cases, a commission was appointed by the Government of Nepal to investigate the accident. It is somewhat ironic, in view of later developments, that it was stated to be

"for the purpose of advancing aviation safety."

The United Kingdom volunteered Mr. Gordon Matthews and Mr. Jeremy Barnett of the air accident investigation branch at Farnborough to lead the investigation. In due course, they produced a thorough and detailed report. I shall return to its main findings in a moment. It is a staggering fact, however, that the report has never been officially published—and, indeed, has been suppressed by both the Nepalese Government and the airline.

Far from being available to advance aviation safety throughout other airlines and airports, the report has officially never seen the light of day. It is not available for use by the families in any litigation. Moreover, the inquest held in London was somewhat farcical, because the report could not be officially admitted in evidence—although most people in the court had access to unofficial copies.

As my hon. Friend the Minister will know, I have pursued this aspect of the case through the Foreign and Commonwealth Office. On 24 January last year, I asked what representations had been made to the Government of Nepal concerning publication of the report. I was told in a reply that no representations had been made, but that copies of the report had been distributed to relatives of the British victims and "interested parties". That is all very well, but I have already explained why the copies of the report now circulating have no official status.

I hope that the Minister will renew pressure on the FCO to press the Nepalese for formal publication. Surely, it must be right that such a report should be published as a matter of course when there is such a tragedy. I have seen a copy of the report on the crash of flight PK 268. Essentially, it blames the pilots of the Pakistan International Airlines flight for

"consistently failing to follow the approach procedure".

There is also criticism of air traffic control at Kathmandu because of

"a missed opportunity to prevent the accident"

when it failed to challenge the low altitude report by the pilots.

The report concluded that some of the air traffic controllers

"had a low self esteem and were reluctant to intervene in piloting matters."

There were also criticisms of PIA's training of its crews for the difficult approach to Kathmandu, as well as the route checking and flight operations inspections procedures. There was also criticism of the ground proximity warning system that

"failed to warn the crew of impending flight towards high ground because of the combination of elderly equipment and rugged terrain".

In all, the report makes 21 recommendations, mostly involving the airline and the Nepalese authorities.

I shall later discuss compensation, but before doing so, I should make it clear that people such as my constituents, the Peates, are not particularly concerned about monetary compensation. They simply do not wish the parents of other young people to have to go through this personal hell. I can do no better than to quote from one of their early letters to me. It stated:

"As deeply grieving parents of a very special talented daughter all we can hope is by our actions to prevent other families enduring similar needless destruction. We were dismayed at the Inquest when PIA were asked by a relative if they intended to implement the safety recommendations that there was no reply."

The system for compensation for air crashes is based on the Warsaw convention, which was formulated as long ago as 1929. At that time, flying was rightly regarded as extremely hazardous, hence the argument for introducing a cap on the amount of liability for death or injury.

I am indebted to Mr. Nigel Taylor, a solicitor who represents the Peates, among others, and who specialises in representing air crash victims. I shall quote more than once from his excellent article in the "Journal of Personal Injury Litigation", entitled "Limitation of Liability of Air Carriers to Air Crash Victims—Has the Warsaw Convention Reached its Retirement Age?"

The limit for carriers registered in countries that have signed only the Warsaw convention would be about £7,000 at current exchange rates. Many countries have signed The Hague protocol that amends the original Warsaw convention. It came into force in 1963 and the maximum compensation can be as little as £13,633.40—and that for the loss of a human life. To its credit, the United Kingdom has signed up to the Montreal protocol, which raised the limit to about £95,000. Pakistan has not signed up to that more recent protocol. All air carriers flying into the United States of America, as well as US-registered carriers, subscribe voluntarily to a maximum limit of $75,000, including legal costs, in the event of loss of life. I understand that that limit is often waived when planes crash in the United States.

Mr. Taylor states in his excellent article:

"A 40 year old executive earning £75,000 a year survived by a wife and two young children, could anticipate compensation of £500,000. If killed in a road traffic accident, this would be fully recoverable. If killed on board an aircraft operated by a carrier which was not contracted for limits in excess of the Warsaw-Hague minimum, the recovery could be as little as £13,633.40, i.e. less than 3 per cent. of the full value of the claim."

It has been argued that the cap on damages is a quid pro quo for what is said to be the strict liability upon a carrier under the Warsaw system. Mr. Taylor describes that as "a common misconception" and he points out various technical defences that are available to lawyers acting for an airline. Article 25 of the convention in principle imposes unlimited liability on a carrier

"if it is proved that the damage resulted from an act or omission of the carrier, his servants or agents, done with intent to cause damage or recklessly and with knowledge that damage would probably result; provided that, in the case of such act or omission of a servant or agent, it is also proved that he was acting within the scope of his employment".

As a lawyer, I can see at a glance that that imposes a pretty heavy burden of proof upon a claimant. As Mr. Taylor says,

"in this country there are no reported cases where an injury or death claimant has successfully discharged the burden that arises".

Indeed, the subjectivity of the test is such that it has been said that the pilot would almost have to leave a suicide note before unlimited liability could be sustained.

What can be done to improve that patchwork of outdated and inadequate compensation? In my correspondence with him, the former Under-Secretary of State for Transport, the noble Lord Mackay, conceded that the current limits

"are now very out of date".

He also pointed out that unilateral action by the United Kingdom would

"not help families like the Peates whose daughter was lost on a flight by a non-UK registered aircraft".

One solution is to obtain international agreement to increase very substantially the liability limit, certainly to its 1975 value of about 250,000 special drawing rights. In October 1992, the European Union issued a consultation paper, but progress through the European Civil Aviation Conference has been slow. The International Air Transport Association has now had approved an application for anti-trust immunity so as to permit inter-carrier discussions. It is also arguing for higher levels of compensation within the same basic framework.

I believe that something more dramatic is required— possibly scrapping the Warsaw system altogether. After all, the last time that a Government—in that case, the United States of America—threatened to denounce the convention, the airlines were put under so much pressure that they agreed a much improved regime in the shape of the 1966 Montreal inter-carrier agreement. Another brave step forward was that taken by the Japanese airlines which in 1992 abolished the artificial limits in most circumstances. It is now about time that some western airlines followed their example.

I have already made the point that this rather creaking system came in at a time when air travel was pretty dangerous. Now it is infinitely more dangerous to drive to the airport than it is to fly to most parts of the world. In Mr. Taylor's words,

"If it was suggested that a bus or coach company should be permitted to limit their financial liability to £13,000 when they kill people, there would be a public outcry".

That is particularly true when one considers that about 1,000 fatalities a year are involved. Admittedly, some of those killed—but by no means all—would be able to claim very large damages in jurisdictions such as the USA. Even so, the amounts involved ought to be insurable in the ordinary way and must be insignificant when compared to the turnover of airlines worldwide.

Finally, there are two other issues relating to compensation. Under English law, it is still the position that if someone over 18 is killed without any dependants—as was true of many of the passengers, including Louise Peate—no substantial damages will be payable on death. Bereavement damages are allowed under English law only in respect of a spouse or a child under 18 years of age. I am aware that that is not part of my hon. Friend's responsibility. I understand that the Law Commission has been looking at this issue and I hope that we shall see some change in the future.

There is no provision to compensate families for the cost of annual trips to a distant crash site to visit the graves of their loved ones. In the case of the Peates, their daughter's body was flown back to this country. The many unidentified victims were buried in a mass grave in Kathmandu. Some of the families make regular visits to the memorial garden there and they have to pay for those visits out of their own pockets. I understand that PIA has been unprepared to commit itself to the long-term upkeep of the memorial garden. In all conscience, that is unacceptable from an airline which has regular flights out of London and Manchester and carries 50,000 or 60,000 passengers a year from the United Kingdom.

Finally, air travel has been one of the great success stories of this century. It enables millions of people to traverse the globe, either on business or for pleasure, often at modest cost and in relative safety and comfort. On the few occasions when pilot error or other circumstances cause a tragic loss of life, it is surely wrong to continue to deny proper investigation and compensation to the families of the victims, for whom it is part of the natural grieving process.

10.40 pm

**The Parliamentary Under-Secretary of State for Transport (Mr. Steve Norris):** I congratulate my hon. Friend the Member for Eastbourne (Mr. Waterson) on his assiduity in pursuing the matter that he has brought to the attention of the House tonight—the tragedy of the loss of Pakistan International Airlines flight 268, which crashed in Nepal en route from Karachi to Kathmandu on 28 September 1992. It was a tragic accident, and it is quite right that my hon. Friend has once again taken the opportunity to draw attention to the decision of the Nepalese authorities not to publish the report of the investigation into the accident.

As I shall explain, the unpublished version of the report has been circulated widely, but—I agree with my hon. Friend—not in a manner that will fully satisfy the relatives of victims of the crash. That is why we are still pressing for full publication of the report.

My hon. Friend also raises the issue of compensation and the Warsaw convention. Obviously, relatives of victims of such disasters, such as Mr. and Mrs. Peate, are not primarily concerned with monetary compensation, but the issue will inevitably arise in the aftermath of such tragedies. As my hon. Friend said, the subject of

[Mr. Steve Norris]

compensation has added poignancy in the case of the loss of flight PK 268, as the only comfort available to many of the families is to visit the memorial garden at the site of the crash near Kathmandu.

I understand that, although Pakistan International Airlines made arrangements for many of the relatives in the United Kingdom to visit the memorial garden shortly after it was completed, the airline has not offered to fund any further visits. That obviously adds to the distress of relatives, who need the comfort and solace of visiting the graves of their loved ones. I shall go further into the issue of compensation in a moment, but first I shall deal with the investigation and the subsequent accident report.

As my hon. Friend said, the single largest group of victims in that tragic crash were British. Because of the number of British fatalities, the United Kingdom's air accident investigation branch offered assistance to the Nepalese authorities in carrying out an investigation into the causes of the crash. The Nepalese subsequently asked the International Civil Aviation Organisation for assistance, and specifically asked that the international team be led by the AAIB from Britain. The international team also included investigators from Canada and Australia.

The team was, in effect, seconded to the Nepalese Government to advise the Nepalese commission of inquiry that was convened to examine the circumstances of the accident. The findings of the investigation team formed the basis of the Nepalese commission's final report.

During that investigation, the Nepalese commission indicated that it would publish the report at the conclusion of the investigation. In accordance with its normal practice, the AAIB sought permission to publish the Nepalese report in the United Kingdom. That permission was not forthcoming.

As my hon. Friend quite correctly said, the report has not yet been formally published. We pressed the Nepalese to publish the report, and the Nepalese commission of inquiry eventually agreed to release the final report to interested parties in August 1993. The AAIB received its copy on 8 September that year.

Recognising their concern and their need for full details, the AAIB provided copies of the report to the families of those who died in the accident as soon as they had received it from the Nepalese. In addition, it arranged for the families to visit the AAIB at Farnborough to receive a briefing on the technical content of the report, and to have the opportunity to ask questions of the inspectors who participated in the investigation.

Under the provisions of annexe 13 to the Chicago convention, which lays down the safety standards for international aviation, circulation of an accident report cannot take place until the state conducting the investigation has released the final report. Although ICAO has recommended that reports should be published, there is no legal requirement on a member state to do so. Since the crash, the United Kingdom has pressed ICAO to upgrade the provision on publication, and ICAO has now agreed that publication of accident reports should be a standard practice implemented by all member states.

Despite extensive efforts, the Government have been unable to persuade the Nepalese authorities to publish the accident report more widely. However, a copy has been submitted, as required, to ICAO, which publishes quarterly summaries of all the air accident reports received from member states. Those summaries are sent to all member states—183 in total—and include details of the circumstances of the accident with causal factors and recommended action.

Although that falls short of full publication, it brings the findings of the Nepalese report to the attention of those who are best placed to help prevent similar tragedies in the future. However, I assure my hon. Friend that we are continuing to press the Nepalese authorities through diplomatic channels for full publication of the report.

A variety of recommendations were directed at Pakistan. Some pertain directly to the complex nature of the Kathmandu approach, with which I know my hon. Friend is familiar. But other recommendations showed some areas of more general airline practice where improvements were necessary—for example, improved route checking and expanded training of flight crew. The implementation of those recommendations will lead to improvements in PIA's operational practice, but it should be noted that there is nothing in the accident report which has given the Department any cause to question the airline's competence to continue to operate to airports in this country. I make that clear and put it on the record. The Civil Aviation Authority of Pakistan has confirmed that it is regulating its airline to ensure its adherence to ICAO safety standards.

Under the Chicago convention, we are expected to accept the assurances already given both to us and to ICAO, since the convention—I know that my hon. Friend is expert in these matters and he will forgive me if I narrate this for the important sake of the record—is clear that it is for each contracting state to regulate its own airlines, and that other states must accept the certificates of competence issued by contracting states.

It is true that it took a long time to obtain details from Pakistan, but it should be remembered that the United Kingdom has no locus to insist. ICAO, too, had seen the report and could have acted if it had identified serious failings. Nor have we had any indications of problems with flights to the United Kingdom. No complaints about safety or procedures have been passed to us by the Civil Aviation Authority, airport authorities or passengers.

As to the provisions of the Warsaw convention, I agree with my hon. Friend that the limits set on carriers' liability by the original convention, and the amending Hague protocol, are now obviously out of date. The United Kingdom Government thought so in 1975—my hon. Friend was kind enough to give credit to our predecessors at that time—and that is why they signed the 1975 Montreal protocols, increasing the limit, as he said, to about £93,000, or 100,000 SDRs, and have constantly urged other states to do likewise. However, the new limit and the other changes made by the protocols have never come into force because insufficient states have ratified them. My hon. Friend knows well the situation with which that presents us.

The United Kingdom adopted the higher limit for its carriers in 1979, but unfortunately only about 20 other states have followed our example and neither Pakistan nor Nepal is among that number.

By late 1992, we and other member states of the European Civil Aviation Conference concluded that, although we would continue to want the Montreal protocols to come into force, some other action would have to be taken if we wanted an improvement in the immediate future. ECAC therefore began discussions, in which the UK has been actively involved, on possible alternative ways of increasing the Warsaw convention limits.

The outcome of those discussions was a recommendation by ECAC that airlines registered in ECAC member states should be encouraged to enter into a voluntary inter-carrier arrangement similar to that which already applies to carriers flying in the United States. That agreement should, inter alia, increase those limits to at least the current equivalent value of the Montreal protocol limits. The agreement could at this stage apply only in Europe—I have to add that qualification—although the aim would be to extend it eventually throughout the international aviation community.

That is the agreement currently being considered by IATA, following the granting by the United States of an exemption from the US anti-trust laws. It is a large task for any organisation to undertake, but I am confident that IATA will be able to accomplish it.

The United Kingdom Government's opinion is that such a voluntary arrangement offers the best and most readily available means to update the Warsaw convention effectively. We believe that the convention should be retained, because it provides the essential basis for a global system for the compensation of passengers or their families when killed or injured on an international flight. Without it, carriers would not be bound to make even the present "no fault" payments.

The Warsaw convention does not and cannot absolve airlines from their liability to compensate people bereaved or injured as a result of an air crash. The limits that it sets are only on the amounts that an airline must pay regardless of the cause of the crash, and without the bereaved or injured people having to take legal action. Under the convention as at present in force, there is no limit on the amounts that a court may award if an airline is successfully sued. That is why, for example, relatives of American citizens who have died in air crashes have been awarded rather larger sums in compensation than the convention limits.

I do understand that that is all of small comfort to bereaved relatives who must, until the Montreal protocols come into force, take such legal action in the country either of registration of the aircraft or of the crash. In many cases, both countries are too distant for the relatives to be able to travel there often enough to visit graves, let alone visit in order to conduct legal action. The United Kingdom Government could, in such cases, make strong representations to the Government or Governments of the states involved to assist the passengers' families but, in the final analysis, it is for the airline involved to acknowledge its responsibilities to its passengers and make appropriate compensation payments to them or their families when due.

I echo my hon. Friend's sentiments about the especially tragic circumstances of the dreadful accident that befell the gifted daughter of Mr. and Mrs. Peate, lost to them in the prime of life. My sympathies also go out to the parents and relatives of all the other victims, many of whom have written to the Department. I want to assure them and my hon. Friend that the Department is doing all that it can to press for an amendment to update the international conventions governing the levels of available compensation, so that we may ensure that other families in future tragedies are spared similar distress.

*Question put and agreed to.*

*Adjourned accordingly at six minutes to Eleven o'clock.*

# House of Commons

*Thursday 18 May 1995*

*The House met at half-past Two o'clock*

### PRAYERS

[MADAM SPEAKER *in the Chair*]

### PRIVATE BUSINESS

LONDON LOCAL AUTHORITIES (No. 2) BILL *[Lords]*

CITY OF WESTMINSTER BILL *[Lords]* (*By Order*)
*Orders for consideration, as amended, read.*
*To be considered on Thursday 25 May.*

# Oral Answers to Questions

## HOME DEPARTMENT

### Asylum Seekers

1. **Mr. Norman Hogg:** To ask the Secretary of State for the Home Department if he will make a statement regarding delays in assessing the cases of asylum seekers. [23546]

**The Secretary of State for the Home Department (Mr. Michael Howard):** The Asylum and Immigration Appeals Act 1993 has reduced significantly the average time taken to decide applications made since the Act came into force, but delays persist as a result of a large and continuing increase in the number of asylum applications. Earlier this year, I announced substantial additional resources to speed up asylum determination and the appeal system. I hope to announce shortly proposals for further improvement.

**Mr. Hogg:** The right hon. and learned Gentleman will recall that, in an answer to my hon. Friend the Member for Hornsey and Wood Green (Mrs. Roche) last November, we were told that some 129 people had been imprisoned or kept in detention centres or police stations for more than six months. Does he agree that that is scarcely consistent with the country's best traditions in dealing with asylum seekers, that it does not reflect well on the Government or, more important, on the nation and that he should try to do better?

**Mr. Howard:** I certainly do not agree with the hon. Gentleman. More than 90 per cent. of people who have been detained for the period to which he refers have already had their asylum applications refused. The proportion of asylum seekers who are detained is a tiny proportion of the people who apply for asylum. Only those who cannot be trusted not to melt away into the general population, never to be seen again, are so detained. I entirely reject the basis of his question.

**Mr. Congdon:** It appears that a sizeable number of people claim asylum some time after they have been in this country to avoid our immigration controls. Under the 1993 Act, how long after they have been here can they still apply for asylum?

**Mr. Howard:** There is no time limit, but that is one of the matters that we are considering. It is clear, from the questions of both my hon. Friend and the hon. Member for Cumbernauld and Kilsyth (Mr. Hogg), that, while the Government are determined to take the necessary measures to deal with bogus asylum seeking, Labour would run away from the problem and not take any action to deal with it were it ever in a position to do so.

**Dr. Howells:** Will the Secretary of State explain why, at the culmination of 16 years of Tory Home Office administration, hundreds of people are being detained at centres such as Campsfield, at enormous cost to the British taxpayer—tens of millions of pounds every year—and why Group 4 is having to train a riot squad because conditions at Campsfield have become so miserable and dangerous? Is not that the most vivid indictment of this squalid regime?

**Mr. Howard:** Conditions are Campsfield are neither dangerous nor miserable, but we will take whatever action is necessary to deal with bogus asylum seeking, which has become a problem that needs firm and effective action. All that we get from Labour is criticism without any idea of what it would do, should it ever find itself in government. See no policies, hear no policies, speak no policies—that is what we get from the Opposition.

### Public Houses (Closing Hours)

2. **Mr. Fabricant:** To ask the Secretary of State for the Home Department what analysis he has made of the incidence of crime arising from uniform night public house closing hours; and if he will make a statement. [23547]

**The Minister of State, Home Office (Mr. Michael Forsyth):** A number of studies show that violent and disorderly offences occur near pubs and clubs at closing time, particularly on Friday and Saturday evenings.

**Mr. Fabricant:** I congratulate my right hon. Friend on the changes that he has made to the licensing laws, permitting drinking in the afternoons and introducing the Licensing (Sunday Hours) Bill, which is currently proceeding in the other place and which will allow drinking on Sunday afternoons. Does he not think, however, that it is about time that we considered evening closing times?

Does my right hon. Friend agree that people living in towns and cities such as Lichfield are terrified to go out late at night on Fridays and Saturdays, when drinkers all pour on to the streets at the same time because all the pubs close at the same time—11 pm? Should it not be left to the local licensing justices to decide when pubs should close?

**Mr. Forsyth:** We are currently considering whether pubs should be allowed to remain open later on Friday and Saturday evenings. I agree with my hon. Friend that there may be merit in allowing magistrates discretion, but he is making the case for staggered hours, which is not the same as the case for extended hours.

## Active Citizenship

**4. Dr. Goodson-Wickes:** To ask the Secretary of State for the Home Department what recent consultations he has had to promote the concept of active citizenship. [23549]

**Mr. Howard:** I am determined to do all that I can to encourage active citizenship, including volunteering. In March 1994 I launched the Government's "Make a Difference" volunteering initiative. The "Make a Difference" team, which includes representatives of key volunteering organisations, has been developing a United Kingdom-wide strategy for volunteering.

In addition, in September 1994 I launched the "Partners Against Crime" initiative, which encourages partnership against crime in the field of crime prevention.

**Dr. Goodson-Wickes:** I acknowledge the merit of that answer. Does my right hon. and learned Friend recognise, however, that the promotion of active citizenship has perhaps lacked momentum? At a time when we seem preoccupied with material matters, will he take this opportunity to commend the enormous amount of good work done by the voluntary sector in all our constituencies, on an entirely unpaid basis? Will he reinvigorate the initiative, on the basis that the state is not the universal provider?

**Mr. Howard:** I am certainly happy to commend those who engage in voluntary activity, in accordance with my hon. Friend's suggestion, but I do not entirely accept the first part of his question. There has, in fact, been a substantial growth in volunteering in recent years—an increase of about 15 per cent. between 1981 and 1991—and about 17 million people engage in the kind of voluntary activity to which my hon. Friend and I attach such importance.

**Mr. Gordon Prentice:** May I ask the Home Secretary about two very active citizens—the Fayed brothers? Why has their application for British citizenship been turned down, with no reasons being given? Has it not been rejected for crude and base political reasons? *[Interruption.]*

**Madam Speaker:** Order. I do not think that that was within the scope of the question.

**Mr. David Nicholson:** In accordance with the concept of volunteering, will my right hon. and learned Friend give all the backing that he can to those of our citizens who volunteer, either regularly or occasionally, to combat crime? Will he ensure that citizens who see a crime taking place in the street and "have a go" are given all possible support, and are not penalised?

**Mr. Howard:** I am extremely keen to encourage citizens to help the police in a number of ways—through neighbourhood watch and street watch schemes, and by becoming special constables. I do not think that it is necessarily wise for them to "have a go", however. They can play a very active part in combating and preventing crime by helping the police without "having a go" themselves. Increasing numbers of people are taking part in one or other of those schemes, and I am sure that their numbers will continue to rise.

## Stolen Vehicles

**5. Mr. Robert Ainsworth:** To ask the Secretary of State for the Home Department if he will make a statement on United Kingdom stolen vehicle recovery rates. [23550]

**The Minister of State, Home Office (Mr. David Maclean):** In England and Wales 62 per cent. of stolen vehicles were recovered in 1994—3 per cent. more than in 1993—and vehicle thefts were down 11 per cent. last year. I congratulate the police on those excellent achievements.

**Mr. Ainsworth:** Having treated us to the usual nauseating trumpeting of a one-year drop in vehicle crime, will the Minister tell us where he gets his figures from? I believe that there has been a consistent drop in the vehicle recovery rate, from 69 per cent. in 1989 to 55 per cent. last year, and that we suffer the worst vehicle crime in the western world. Is he not thoroughly ashamed of that after 16 years of stewardship of policy and what on earth is he going to do about it?

**Mr. Maclean:** I get these figures from the police service in England and Wales and I shall ensure that the police service in England and Wales has its attention drawn to the hon. Gentleman's comments because they seemed to betray some of the attitudes of other Labour Members. The crime figures, which showed the biggest drop in 40 years, have not been changed one iota in their calculation by the Government in 15 years. They are exactly the same figures as the Labour party used to trumpet every minute they were going up and about which it is deeply embarrassed now that they are going down.

**Dr. Spink:** Will my hon. Friend join me in welcoming the very sound part that closed circuit television cameras have played in deterring vehicle theft and vehicle crime? Will he call on British Rail, in particular, to install such devices in its stations?

**Mr. Maclean:** I encourage all organisations and individuals, towns, car parks, and British Rail to take advantage of the tremendous benefits of CCTV. In doing so, they could complement the £5 million that we gave to special schemes last year, levering in £13.8 million from other quarters. The net result of that Government initiative should be about 1,000 extra cameras. That could mean many, many fewer victims of crime, a safer society and a greatly reduced fear of crime.

## Chain Gangs

**6. Mr. Cox:** To ask the Secretary of State for the Home Department what discussions he will have with the Governor of the state of Alabama on the recently introduced policy of prison inmates working in chain gangs; and if he will make a statement. [23551]

**Mr. Michael Forsyth:** I have no plans at present to meet the Governor of Alabama to discuss his policy of reintroducing chain gangs.

**Mr. Cox:** In view of that reply and as the Home Office is increasingly introducing American penal systems such as boot camps and tougher prison regimes—none of which has succeeded in the states where they are used— does the Minister's reply assure us that under no circumstances will the penal systems of the state of Alabama be introduced in Britain?

**Mr. Forsyth:** The hon. Gentleman is talking nonsense. There are many examples in the United States of very successful regimes that have ensured that youngsters are less likely to re-offend. Although those regimes cannot be translated exactly to our system, the Government are open-minded and prepared to take whatever measures are necessary to make prisons more effective.

On the issue of work gangs, I see no difficulty whatsoever in having prisoners engaged in work that is useful to the community. The need to chain them together is a security consideration. I understand that the state of Alabama believes that it is cheaper to chain prisoners together from the point of view of supervision. We do not anticipate a need for chains, but I do anticipate the scope for gangs of prisoners doing useful work in the community, which I am sure most sensible people would welcome.

**Mr. Batiste:** If my right hon. Friend should have the opportunity of discussing prison policy with the Governor of Alabama, will he reflect on the fact that there, as in Britain, prison officers often have to perform acts of conspicuous bravery well beyond the call of duty? Would it make sense to consider introducing a medal similar to the police medal to reward those acts of bravery and to recognise the very brave men who perform them?

**Mr. Forsyth:** My hon. Friend makes a very sensible suggestion that I am happy to consider further. I entirely agree that the service that our prison officers give to the country is much under-recognised. Every day, they have to deal with some 51,000 of the most difficult people in our country and they do so with great courage and determination. That is one of the reasons why yesterday we increased the powers available to governors to take disciplinary action to maintain order in our prisons. I very much hope that where prison officers are attacked, the Crown Prosecution Service will take action and that the courts will impose substantial penalties, because our prison officers deserve to be supported and protected.

**Mr. Beith:** Before the Minister even thinks about ordering the chains and fetters, will he devote some attention to ensuring that a higher proportion of prisoners have more work to do more of the time? Does he recognise that part of the problem is that not enough work is being organised in prisons and that far too many prisoners spend far too long banged up in cells when they should be being prepared for constructive work when they get out—something that many prison officers seek to do every day?

**Mr. Forsyth:** I agree that there need to be more opportunities for constructive work in prison. I should tell the hon. Member for Tooting (Mr. Cox) that one of the very good things that I saw in the United States last month was a prison that, in partnership with the private sector, was able to produce goods that were being sold in the marketplace, thus providing revenue towards the cost of running the prison. That meant that prisoners were doing

a day's work and were able to earn wages that they could use to look after their families rather than expecting, as many do, the taxpayer to take on that task. I hope that the Director General of the Prison Service will seek to involve the private sector to a greater extent in providing opportunities for real work in prisons. That task is now in hand.

### Juvenile Offenders

7. **Mr. Booth:** To ask the Secretary of State for the Home Department what steps he is taking to help the police and courts to deal with the most persistent juvenile offenders.     [23552]

**Mr. Maclean:** The Criminal Justice and Public Order Act 1994 contains important new measures to deal with juvenile criminals. The secure training order will provide a vigorous regime based on education and discipline for persistent juvenile offenders. Invitations to tender for the first two secure training centres were issued at the end of March.

**Mr. Booth:** Does my hon. Friend agree that much of the recent success in tackling juvenile crime has resulted from the implementation of our policies, following sensible advice from the police that we should target the young lads most likely to commit crime? If the Labour party had been in power, we would not have achieved such success, not least because, time after time, it votes against our sensible reforms.

**Mr. Maclean:** That is absolutely true. Last week I visited a police service where, in one division alone, there had been 946 burglaries in 1993 but only eight last year. That was due to the policy of targeting the individuals involved and the imprisonment of four persistent burglars responsible. However, we all remember the howls of outrage from the Labour party when my right hon. and learned Friend the Home Secretary said that prison works. It certainly worked by taking those persistent burglars out of circulation.

**Mr. Michael:** Will the Minister set aside his complacency and accept that it is about time that he did something to cut juvenile crime by providing the legal framework for an active partnership involving the police, local authorities and local communities to tackle crime, by accepting our proposals to nip problems in the bud in respect of young offenders and by providing the secure places that we were promised in February 1991 but which have still not been provided?

**Mr. Maclean:** It is no wonder that the whole country understands what is meant when we say that the Labour party is a policy-free zone. If someone were to interpret what the hon. Gentleman just said, I might like some of it. He fails to tell the House that the Opposition have consistently voted against all the key laws that we have passed to tackle crime and offending. In the Criminal Justice and Public Order Act 1994, we took the powers to deal with offending on bail and to do drug tests in prison while the Labour party, which says that it wants to be tough on crime and the causes of crime, abstained on Second Reading and toughly abstained on Third Reading.

**Sir Ivan Lawrence:** Does my hon. Friend agree that bad families and bad peer influence has a considerable effect on juvenile delinquency and that the success in dealing with juvenile delinquents in the United States has required taking youngsters away from their bad backgrounds for rather longer than is contemplated in the secure training orders? Will he keep an open mind about the effectiveness of that course of action and keep a close watch on the successes that are appearing in some parts of the United States?

**Mr. Maclean:** My hon. and learned Friend may be absolutely right. I seem to recall that when the Criminal Justice and Public Order Bill was going through the House we were under pressure from some quarters to have much shorter periods of secure detention. We rightly made the point that if the period was too short it would not be possible to achieve anything with a youngster, to educate him or her or to rehabilitate youngsters. I shall certainly bear in mind what my hon. and learned Friend has said. If we can take persistent troublemakers out of circulation and keep them out for long enough, not only will the public get respite from their awful offending but there will be a chance to make something of them.

### Combat 18

8. **Mr. Janner:** To ask the Secretary of State for the Home Department if he will make a statement concerning the activities of Combat 18. [23553]

**Mr. Howard:** Combat 18 is the name adopted by a loose collection of violent activists with extreme right-wing views, a small number of whom have been convicted of public order offences and crimes involving violence. The Government deplore the activities of Combat 18, and any other group that advocates racism, violence or intimidation.

**Mr. Janner:** I thank the Minister for that reply. I am sure that the Government deplore this activity but what do they intend to do about it? For example, does the Home Secretary know that members of this violent organisation or of that ilk recently made three attacks on the newly opened office of the immigration advisory service in Cardiff, smashing windows with bullets and abusing staff? Surely the time has come for the Home Secretary to rally his Ministers and the police to take vigorous action against these people to prevent them from doing what we all deplore so much.

**Mr. Howard:** The hon. and learned Gentleman will know that we amended the law under the Criminal Justice and Public Order Act 1994 so as to deal more effectively with serious cases of incitement to racial hatred and deliberate racial harassment. Of course, he will know that the activities to which he refers are already criminal offences. Inquiries are being vigorously pursued by the police and I share the hon. and learned Gentleman's hope that those responsible can be brought to justice.

**Sir Donald Thompson:** As my right hon. and learned Friend will agree, Combat 18 is a very evil group, but will he tell hunt saboteurs and animal rights activists that one cannot pick and choose with violence?

**Mr. Howard:** I agree that the law is indivisible and invisible and that it must apply equally to those who

commit offences. That is why we made changes under the Criminal Justice and Public Order Act to deal with the abuses to which my hon. Friend refers.

**Mr. Straw:** Does the Secretary of State accept that the Oklahoma bombing served as an awful reminder that some seemingly insignificant extreme right-wing groups can indeed have deadly intent? Does he accept the need to maintain the highest vigilance against Combat 18 in this country and against similar groups? Does he agree that politicians of all parties have a heavy duty not in any circumstances to play the race card in politics and so give encouragement, however indirect, to groups such as Combat 18?

**Mr. Howard:** I certainly agree with the hon. Gentleman about the dangers arising from organisations of that kind and about the supreme importance of maintaining our vigilance. As I have said, we have taken steps to make the law more effective. His comments about the race card are absolutely right. Conservatives have always set their faces against anything of that kind. We accept that to keep race relations as good as they have been in this country for a long time we must also have firm and fair immigration policies. We shall continue to have both.

### Policing Costs (Football Matches)

9. **Mr. Carrington:** To ask the Secretary of State for the Home Department what estimates he has of the annual cost of policing football matches. [23554]

**Mr. Maclean:** This information is not held centrally and individual police forces could provide it only at disproportionate cost.

**Mr. Carrington:** My hon. Friend will know that the major cost to the police of looking after football matches lies outside the ground and that it is increased by the somewhat arbitrary way in which fixtures are now frequently moved to Sundays at the behest of television companies, which pay extra fees to clubs for moving matches. Will my hon. Friend ensure that some of the extra profit that goes to football clubs is used to offset the increased cost to police forces of providing security outside grounds on Sundays?

**Mr. Maclean:** I do not think that my hon. Friend is right in asserting that the bulk of cost arises from policing outside the ground. I understand that it arises from policing inside the ground, depending on the type of match, for which the football clubs pay. It has been a long-standing practice that the police do not charge for policing outside football grounds, where their duty is to maintain law and order. I do not wish to depart from that practice. It is up to the police service, in discussion with football clubs, to arrange policing inside the ground and reach an accommodation on cost to cover the bulk of the policing costs.

**Mr. Pike:** Does the Minister accept that, as he said, most football clubs come to sensible arrangements for policing and stewarding inside their grounds to minimise problems? We should recognise that only a handful of clubs make massive profits and we should ensure that in protecting spectators we do not destroy the sport of football.

**Mr. Maclean:** I agree entirely, and nowhere is that more true than in Burnley—I sympathise with the hon. Gentleman about the relegation that his club has suffered. I generally accept the thrust of his point. If I were deeply concerned about the costs of policing football matches, I would wish to take more action. The present arrangements are generally satisfactory, but if a time comes when the police wish to make representations to me, I shall be happy to reconsider the matter.

**Mr. Hawkins:** Does my hon. Friend agree that one of the most effective means of combating football violence, committed by those who are not remotely interested in the sport and who just go to major matches to cause trouble, is the work of the football intelligence unit of the national criminal intelligence service? In that connection, would my hon. Friend have a careful look at a transcript of this morning's "Inside Out" programme on Radio 4 so that he may read views expressed by people who have committed such crimes? They regard the facilities in our prisons as being sufficiently attractive to represent no deterrent against committing further offences. Will he ensure that, in future policy, the view of our right hon. and learned Friend the Secretary of State, which the public support, that prisons should be fair but austere, is followed through?

**Mr. Maclean:** My right hon. Friend the Minister of State has heard the comments of my hon. Friend and no doubt he will organise suitable punishment in the community for gangs of football hooligans should the need arise. I shall certainly pay attention to the transcript, but first, more importantly, I pass on my high regard and the thanks of the whole House to the football unit at NCIS for the tremendous work that it does. It is quite noticeable than when other foreign countries wholeheartedly participate with NCIS, problems have been reduced. We would encourage many other countries in the world where our football supporters or hooligans may go to co-operate with NCIS and to sign bilateral agreements with us. Then, much more can be done.

### Football Violence

10. **Mr. Madden:** To ask the Secretary of State for the Home Department how many people are currently subject to restriction orders made under legislation introduced to combat football violence. [23556]

**Mr. Maclean:** Two.

**Mr. Madden:** Is that not an extraordinary situation? The figure has not changed since the middle of February, when the riot occurred in Dublin before, during and after the England *v.* Ireland match? Does it not show that the courts treat the legislation with contempt? What are the Government doing in the face of mounting evidence that British Nazis are co-operating with European Nazis to turn the forthcoming European football championships into an orgy of violence and serious public disorder?

**Mr. Maclean:** Although only two restriction orders are currently in force, the courts have made use of thousands of exclusion orders. I do not agree that the courts are treating the matter with contempt, but I think that they do

not fully understand the powers available and how they could use them much more—and better perhaps. We therefore intend to send out a reminder in the next few weeks of how the powers can be used. More generally, we are looking at the whole question of exclusion and restriction orders to see whether we can bring about further tightening and simplification of the law and make it easier for the courts to use them.

**Mr. John Carlisle:** Does my hon. Friend agree that the level of football violence has dropped considerably in this country because of the various measures adopted, with some courage, by the Government, including the Criminal Justice and Public Order Act 1994? Does he also agree that the situation has not been helped by the soft community order issued to Mr. Eric Cantona, probably the biggest football hooligan of the lot, who has become something of a folk hero among young people because he is now mixing with them in a rather pleasant way?

**Mr. Maclean:** I cannot comment on an individual sentence imposed by the courts, but my right hon. and learned Friend the Home Secretary has considerably toughened community sentences in general with the new national guidance that has been issued to ensure that community punishments are genuinely punishments in the community, and are tough. That is what my hon. Friends and the whole House want.

### "In the Line of Fire"

11. **Mr. Heppell:** To ask the Secretary of State for the Home Department what is his response to the Audit Commission report "In the Line of Fire". [23557]

**The Parliamentary Under-Secretary of State for the Home Department (Mr. Nicholas Baker):** The Government welcome the report as an important and challenging document, which provides an admirable basis upon which future change in the fire service can be considered and planned.

**Mr. Heppell:** Is the Minister aware of a specific problem highlighted by the report concerning the firefighters pension fund, which is directing resources away from firefighting? How does he propose to deal with that problem?

**Mr. Baker:** The Audit Commission report gives further guidance to brigades on the scope for potential savings which will be very helpful to them. As for the specific question about pensions, we recognise the concern about the increasing net costs of the firefighters pension scheme which, like most schemes in the public service, does not have a pension fund. Its provisions are under review, but even if it were changed the savings would not become available for many years.

**Mr. Sykes:** As the Minister will know, almost a year has passed since the Richmond hotel in my constituency caught fire, yet, even as we speak, there is a proposal on his desk to cut the number of fire engines in Scarborough and Whitby. "In the Line of Fire" recognises the life-threatening inadequacies of the present minimum standards. Will the Minister promise today to prevent the ridiculous suggestion that we cut the number of fire engines in Scarborough and Whitby from going ahead?

**Mr. Baker:** The management of the fire service in my hon. Friend's constituency is a matter for his local fire service authority, but I point out to him and to the fire authority that since 1988 the number of emergency calls handled has increased by 24 per cent. while the number of firefighters in post has increased by only 1 per cent. The Audit Commission report shows many ways in which savings and greater efficiency can be achieved.

**Mr. George Howarth:** Can the Minister confirm that, as the Audit Commission report highlighted, there are serious problems with the finances of fire authorities, which will get worse between now and the end of the century? Will he give an undertaking to move quickly to consult the fire authorities on how to deal with those problems, and will he assure the House that that vital emergency service will not be starved of resources to the point where its effectiveness is compromised?

**Mr. Baker:** There is no question of that important emergency service being starved of resources. As I think the hon. Gentleman recognises, the Audit Commission report is an in-depth study of value for money in the fire service. That is the whole point of it, and it should help brigades to carry out their responsibilities with no diminution of standards in the most cost-effective manner possible.

### Criminal Justice and Public Order Act 1994

12. **Mr. Heald:** To ask the Secretary of State for the Home Department what representations he has received from the police regarding the Criminal Justice and Public Order Act 1994.                                    [23558]

**Mr. Howard:** The representations we have received from the police have warmly welcomed the Act. The chief constable of West Mercia, the chairman of the Association of Chief Police Officers crime committee, has said:

"the provisions . . . in the Act are balanced, rational and fair and they are welcome by the police service."

**Mr. Heald:** Does my right hon. and learned Friend agree that despite the gloomy picture of the Police Federation presented by the hon. Member for Blackburn (Mr. Straw) this morning, in fact the federation has warmly welcomed the Act? Yesterday Mr. Fred Broughton described it as the first Act for years to turn the tide. Is it not then astonishing that the Labour party did not have the guts to back the legislation when it was before the House as a Bill?

**Mr. Howard:** I entirely agree with my hon. Friend. It is also astonishing that the hon. Member for Blackburn went to the Police Federation this morning and pretended to be tough on crime. He did not tell the federation that Labour tried to wreck the bail provisions in the Criminal Justice and Public Order Act. He talked about the courts being soft on sentences, but did not tell the federation that Labour consistently voted against legislation that gave the Attorney-General the right to refer lenient sentences to the Court of Appeal. The hon. Gentleman did not tell the federation about Labour's attempts to vote against changes to right to silence.

**Mr. Michael:** Untrue.

**Mr. Howard:** The hon. Gentleman says, "Untrue," from a sedentary position, but his gesticulations are untrue. It is about time the Opposition started owning up, and they should tell the truth about their attempts to wreck our efforts to fight crime.

**Mr. Straw:** No, Madam Speaker, I did not tell the Police Federation any of those things, because most of them are not true. I told the Police Federation the truth—that crime in this country has more than doubled under this Government, but that the number of convictions and cautions has dropped in absolute terms by 7 per cent. That is a scandal. I also told them that the number—[HON. MEMBERS: "Question."] I also told them that the number of cases discontinued and dropped—*[Interruption.]* That is scarcely a laughing matter for constituents. I said that the number of cases discontinued and dropped by the Crown Prosecution Service has risen by nearly 50 per cent. in eight years, and that the acquittal rate in the Crown courts—*[Interruption.]*

**Madam Speaker:** Order. The Secretary of State widened the question, and the hon. Gentleman has the right to a defence.

**Mr. Straw:** I repeat the point, because the public need to know. Crime has doubled in the past 15 years, while the number of convictions and cautions has gone down by 7 per cent. The number of cases dropped by the CPS has risen by nearly 50 per cent., and the acquittal rate has risen by 60 per cent. Does that not show that there is a serious crisis of confidence in the Crown Prosecution Service, and that reform of that service is urgently needed?

**Mr. Howard:** What the public understand only too well is that criminals are increasingly exploiting loopholes in the criminal justice system. The public also understand that the Government have acted to block the loopholes, and that the Opposition have consistently tried to wreck our efforts to do so.

**Mr. Key:** Does my right hon. and learned Friend accept that my constituents are grateful that the number of police officers in my constituency has gone up and the amount of crime has gone down? Will he support the all-party application—which is supported by the local police—for an exclusion zone around Stonehenge, so that my constituents can go about their lawful duty unhindered and in peace?

**Mr. Howard:** I will, of course, look at the proposal for an exclusion zone around Stonehenge. The first part of my hon. Friend's question shows that he is in touch with what is happening in the fight against crime, and that the Opposition are posturing in a way that deceives no one.

### Closed Circuit Television

13. **Ms Hoey:** To ask the Secretary of State for the Home Department what further resources are being made available to allow more CCTV to be installed in inner-city areas.                                    [23559]

**Mr. Maclean:** The recent CCTV challenge competition has injected £5 million into local CCTV schemes, generating up to £13.8 million in other funding. The possibility of further competitions in the future has not been ruled out, but it is too early to give a firm commitment.

**Ms Hoey:** Does the Minister think that the scheme should be funded by a form of competition? My borough has a high level of crime, and also a high level of fear of crime, and there is full support among the three party leaders in the borough of Lambeth, the police and the community for CCTV to be used more in the area. Will the Minister meet a delegation from my borough and give some support to inner-city areas? Will he make sure that that money does not just go to areas that are seen as slightly safer?

**Mr. Maclean:** There is nothing to stop the hon. Lady's authority pushing ahead with CCTV. The CCTV challenge scheme was successful because £5 million of taxpayers' money levered in almost £14 million of other money. Inner cities have received generous funding from the Government and will continue to do so. Over the next three years, almost £4 billion will be spent on the single regeneration budget, all going to inner cities. It is right that this time we spread the CCTV money around the whole country so that smaller towns and cities can benefit from it.

**Mr. David Atkinson:** I congratulate my hon. Friend on his CCTV initiative, which has matched pound for pound the sum raised by businesses in my constituency, which has now rendered Boscombe high street much safer for shoppers and shop staff alike. Can he make a clearer commitment to extend that scheme to residential and business areas throughout the country to places that the police believe will benefit from it?

**Mr. Maclean:** There is no doubt that the whole country benefits from CCTV. I want to make it clear that the police service totally supports CCTV schemes, which supplement and help police efforts rather than diminish them, and that police numbers will be reduced by not a single policeman because of CCTV. I cannot at present give my hon. Friend the commitment that he seeks. We have noted the tremendous benefit of CCTV and I shall look carefully at whether we can fund future schemes.

## PRIME MINISTER

### Engagements

Q1. **Mr. John Marshall:** To ask the Prime Minister if he will list his official engagements for Thursday 18 May.                                                        [23576]

**The Prime Minister (Mr. John Major):** This morning, I presided at a meeting of the Cabinet and had meetings with ministerial colleagues and others. In addition to my duties in the House, I shall have further meetings later today.

**Mr. Marshall:** Will my right hon. Friend join me in welcoming the reduction in unemployment announced yesterday? Is he aware that it is the 24th reduction in the monthly rate to be announced since the hon. Member for Dunfermline, East (Mr. Brown) said that unemployment would rise month after month after month? How does Britain's unemployment rate compare with those in France and Spain, the Governments of which have adopted the policies recommended by the right hon. Member for Sedgefield (Mr. Blair)?

**The Prime Minister:** My hon. Friend is right to welcome the fall in unemployment and, of course, the growth in employment, particularly in manufacturing. Unemployment has now fallen by well over 600,000 since 1992 and by nearly 19,000 in the past month—the 20th successive monthly fall. As my hon. Friend intimated, the unemployment rate is substantially higher in Spain and France. In France it is around 12.75 per cent. and in Spain around 20 per cent. It is no accident that they have policies like the minimum wage, the social chapter and other policies that damage employment.

**Mr. Blair:** The Prime Minister has indicated that he accepts the broad thrust of Nolan. Does he accept the recommendation that Members of Parliament with consultancies should disclose the agreement under which they are paid and how much they are paid?

**The Prime Minister:** I established the Nolan committee because I am determined to see higher standards in public life. I believe that that is important. It is important not only that we ensure high standards but that the people of this country see for themselves that this House adopts high standards.

On the specific point which the right hon. Gentleman puts to me, we must wait to see what the House has to say about that. That is the purpose of the debate this afternoon. We wish to hear the views of the House and take those into account before we reach final decisions on those matters.

On matters related to the Government, we made it clear that we broadly accept those recommendations, and my right hon. Friends will elaborate on that this afternoon.

**Mr. Blair:** What is the Prime Minister's own view about that recommendation?

**The Prime Minister:** The Government will have to table motions on the Order Paper. Not least as a courtesy to the House, we should listen to the views of the House.

**Mr. Blair:** Of course. But is the right hon. Gentleman seriously suggesting that the debate may lead him to overrule the independent recommendation of his own committee? If the right hon. Gentleman is not prepared to say whether he supports the disclosure of payments to Members of Parliament, and as he is refusing point blank to allow the committee to investigate payments to political parties, may I tell him that his support for Nolan will ring more than a little hollow?

**The Prime Minister:** As far as political parties are concerned, I repeat the point that I made earlier this week. When the right hon. Gentleman and the Labour party meet those points set out by the Select Committee on Members' Interests, a Committee of the House, then, perhaps, they might be in a position to lecture other people on political parties.

As for matters relating to Back-Bench Members, I repeat the point that I made a moment ago. It is right to listen to the views of the House before reaching a conclusion on the House. If, after such a brief period of

Front-Bench authority, the right hon. Gentleman is so arrogant that he no longer wishes to hear the views of the House, he will live to regret that.

**Mr. Cash:** Given my right hon. Friend's enthusiasm for consultation with regard to Government policies and given that the European Commission and Mr. Santer have just published the Commission's White Paper regarding the future of Europe in so far as it affects the intergovernmental conference, can my right hon. Friend give an absolute assurance to the House that in good time and as soon as possible—before the summer recess—we can have a White Paper on European policy as it affects the United Kingdom in relation to that intergovernmental conference?

**The Prime Minister:** I have made it clear to the House on a number of occasions that we are now examining in detail, in Cabinet sub-committees, the British position as to how we will approach the intergovernmental conference. When we have concluded that detailed consideration, it will, of course, be a matter for discussion in the House. That was the case before the Maastricht treaty and it will be the case before the next intergovernmental conference.

**Q2. Mr. Winnick:** To ask the Prime Minister if he will list his official engagements for Thursday 18 May. [23577]

**The Prime Minister:** I refer the hon. Member to the answer I gave some moments ago.

**Mr. Winnick:** In view of the latest developments on sleaze in the House, is it not now clear that the recommendations of the Nolan committee are the very minimum that need to be put into effect as quickly as possible in aid of the reputation of the House of Commons? Does the Prime Minister accept—perhaps he does not—that Members of Parliament are not elected to be hired as paid lobbyists or consultants and that it is about time the practice was put to an end?

**The Prime Minister:** Of course, the House will have the opportunity to debate the Nolan committee this afternoon. As I said to the House a few moments ago, and as I have said on previous occasions, I set up the Nolan committee because I am determined that the House not only has the highest standards, but is seen to have those standards. If the hon. Gentleman is concerned about the highest standards in politics as a whole, I hope that he will also support the suggestion that the Nolan committee should subsequently look at the position in local government. I hope that he will support that. Since the Opposition are so keen on openness in local government, perhaps the leader of the Labour party will hold in public those inquiries into Labour party activities that he is now holding in private.

**Q3. Mr. Harry Greenway:** To ask the Prime Minister if he will list his official engagements for Thursday 18 May. [23578]

**The Prime Minister:** I refer my hon. Friend to the answer I gave some moments ago.

**Mr. Greenway:** Does my right hon. Friend agree that a minimum wage, whatever the level, would destroy jobs? Does he have any intention of proposing such a policy,

not setting a level before the next election and wanting to pass the buck to a union-packed quango, as the Labour party proposes?

**The Prime Minister:** Of course I can confirm that a minimum wage would destroy jobs. The House has that on the excellent authority of the deputy leader of the Labour party, who said on one memorable occasion, "Any silly fool knows that." There is no doubt about it, so of course I can confirm that. For the Labour party these days, a quango a day keeps policy away, because it has announced three so far this week. *[Interruption.]* Yes, a new quango on Monday, a new quango on Tuesday and a new quango on Wednesday. We await today's developments with some interest.

**Q4. Mr. Martyn Jones:** To ask the Prime Minister if he will list his official engagements for Thursday 18 May. [23579]

**The Prime Minister:** I refer the hon. Member to the answer I gave some moments ago.

**Mr. Jones:** Given that the Prime Minister's objection to publicising the source of Tory party income is that he would not like to expose anonymous donors, what is to stop him publishing the list of non-anonymous donors and also the list of donations and their amounts?

**The Prime Minister:** I sometimes wonder whether some Opposition Members understand the importance of privacy in any way on any occasion. In a free and open society, people have the right to donate anonymously if they wish. What is potentially corrupt is when donations buy favours or determine policy. That emphatically does not happen in my party. It emphatically does happen in the Labour party as a part of its constitution.

**Q5. Sir John Hannam:** To ask the Prime Minister if he will list his official engagements for Thursday 18 May. [23580]

**The Prime Minister:** I refer my hon. Friend to the answer I gave some moments ago.

**Sir John Hannam:** Is my right hon. Friend aware that, in my Devon constituency area, unemployment has dropped by more than 20 per cent. since 1992, that crime figures have decreased by 10 per cent. this year and last year, that a new hospital costing more than £50 million is nearing completion and that hospital waiting lists have been reduced to a maximum of nine months? Does not all that, combined with the growing economy, show that Conservative policies are working well in the west country?

**The Prime Minister:** My hon. Friend refers again to the minimum wage, with good reason. There is no doubt that the minimum wage costs jobs. I now see that the Labour party proposes to keep the minimum wage, but not set the level of the minimum wage until after the general election. That will be devolved to someone else.

The House might recall the deputy leader of the Labour party saying—*[Interruption.]* I do not know why they laugh at the deputy leader of the Labour party. We are rather fond of him. He said:

"Some party colleagues have advocated a minimum wage without having the courage of their convictions to state an amount that would make the original commitment meaningful".

I wonder who the right hon. Gentleman might have had in mind.

**Mr. John Evans:** Will the Prime Minister take the opportunity of acknowledging that what has fallen in this country is the number of unemployed benefit claimants, that the number of people in this country who are without a job remains as great as ever, and that it is impossible to compare unemployment statistics in Britain, France, Spain or any other European country, because they use entirely different methods of counting?

**The Prime Minister:** I know the hon. Gentleman would not like the Government to have any credit for anything, even the fall in unemployment, but the fact is that not only has unemployment fallen more dramatically in this country than in any other country in western Europe—far more dramatically than any Opposition Member proposed when the Opposition were talking about unemployment increasing to 5 million—but the number in work has increased.

### Ministerial Visits

Q6. **Mr. Clifton-Brown:** To ask the Prime Minister when he next plans to visit Cirencester and Tewkesbury. [23581]

**The Prime Minister:** I have no immediate plans to do so.

**Mr. Clifton-Brown:** If my right hon. Friend were to visit my constituency, he would discover that a large majority of people would prefer a Europe of nation states rather than a European super-state. Will he therefore undertake, at the intergovernmental conference next year, to resist vigorously giving up our opt-outs and the restriction of our veto, which both the President of the European Commission and the Labour party would like to give up?

**The Prime Minister:** I can give my hon. Friend that assurance. It is for national Governments, not the European Commission, to take decisions on Europe's future at the intergovernmental conference. We will certainly maintain the national veto and we will certainly not accept any attempt to end the opt-outs that I negotiated in the Maastricht treaty.

I look to see the European Union succeed, but on the basis of close co-operation between independent sovereign states. I do not believe that, in the long term, the European Union could or would succeed on any other basis. I believe that the proposition for a substantial amount of further centralisation in Europe would do great damage to Europe. It would split it asunder and it should be resisted.

### Engagements

Q7. **Mr. Simon Hughes:** To ask the Prime Minister if he will list his official engagements for Thursday 18 May. [23582]

**The Prime Minister:** I refer the hon. Gentleman to the reply I gave some moments ago.

**Mr. Hughes:** In this 50th anniversary year of VE day and VJ day and in view of the widespread support across the House, will the Prime Minister meet soon with a deputation from the Royal British Legion to hear the case as to how, at very little cost to the public purse, the four remaining injustices for war widows or service people may be corrected this year? War widows and service people often lose housing benefit or council tax; they may be ineligible for legal aid to pursue claims for injury; they may be unable to hold on to their pensions if they remarry following the death of their spouses who were killed in active service in the past 20 years; and, if they marry someone subsequent to that person's war service, they cannot inherit their spouse's pension.

**The Prime Minister:** I think that the hon. Gentleman knows the extent to which we have taken care over the years to ensure that war widows and others who faced particular difficulty during the war are treated fairly. In 1979, the Conservative Government corrected many of the anomalies that the previous Government had left untouched for a very long time. If the hon. Gentleman will give me details of those four points, I shall examine them.

# Business of the House

3.30 pm

**Mrs. Ann Taylor** (Dewsbury): May I ask the Leader of the House for details of future business?

**The Lord President of the Council and Leader of the House of Commons (Mr. Tony Newton):** The business for next week will be as follows:

MONDAY 22 MAY—Remaining stages of the Child Support Bill.

TUESDAY 23 MAY—Second reading of the Criminal Injuries Compensation Bill.

WEDNESDAY 24 MAY—Until 2.30 pm there will be debates on the motion for the Adjournment of the House, the first of which will be the three-hour replacement of the old recess Adjournment motion.

Opposition Day (13th allotted day). There will be a debate entitled "Social Division and Low Pay" on an Opposition motion.

Motion in the name of the honourable Member for Wantage (Mr. Jackson) relating to disclosure of specified Select Committee papers.

THURSDAY 25 MAY—Motion on the Coal Industry (Restructuring Grants) Order.

Motion on the Pneumoconiosis etc., (Workers' Compensation) (Payment of Claims) (Amendment) Regulations.

FRIDAY 26 MAY—The House will not be sitting.

The House will also wish to know that European Standing Committees will meet on Tuesday 23 May and Wednesday 24 May at 10.30 am to consider European Community documents as follows:

*[Tuesday 23 May:*

*European Standing Committee A—Relevant European Community documents: 5489/95 Reform of the Community Document; Relevant European Legislation Committee Reports HC 70-xii (1994-95) and HC 70-xv (1994-95).*

*Wednesday 17 May:*

*European Standing Committee B—Relevant European Community documents: 8693/94 and 8943/94 Relations with Central and Eastern Europe; 5928/95 Industrial Co-operation with Central and Eastern Europe; Relevant European Legislation Committee Reports HC 70-iv (1994-95) and HC 70-xiv (1994-95). ]*

The House will return, following the Whitsun recess, on 6 June and I expect to give full details of business for that week when I make a statement this time next week. I anticipate a possible need to take Government business until 7 pm on Thursday 8 June. On Friday 9 June, which is a Government Friday, I anticipate a debate on a motion for the Adjournment.

**Mrs. Taylor:** I thank the Leader of the House for that information. I wish to press him on two points that I raised last week: future economic debates in Government time; and whether he has reconsidered the answer that he gave last week about the appropriateness of a debate to mark the 25th anniversary of the Chronically Sick and Disabled Persons Act 1970. The answer that he gave last week was uncharacteristically unsympathetic and I wonder whether the Leader of the House has reconsidered the matter.

With what degree of seriousness should we treat the rather petulant remarks of the Minister for Health about scrapping the nurses' pay review board? Is that the Government's intention, or is it just another example of the yah-boo school of politics that we have come to expect? If there are proposals of that kind, will there be a statement in the House?

Finally, may I ask the Leader of the House about the confusion that the Government have created surrounding the Jobseekers Bill? The right hon. Gentleman will be aware of the points of order raised on the Floor this week, and of the fact that the jobseeker's allowance is to be delayed for six months, from April 1996 to October 1996. As the Government have said in written answers that benefit cuts will still be implemented in April 1996, considerable confusion that needs clearing up remains. We must press the Minister on why there has not been a statement in the House by the Secretary of State for Employment or the Secretary of State for Social Security. The Bill cannot go any further unless and until this matter is fully clarified.

**Mr. Newton:** I cannot at the moment give the hon. Lady further information about economic debates in Government time later this year, but I shall seek to do so as soon as possible.

If my remarks last week about the Chronically Sick and Disabled Persons Act sounded unsympathetic, it was entirely unintentional. No one who listened to my speech at the opening of the exhibition to mark the anniversary on Monday would have thought that I was unsympathetic. Of course I shall continue to bear the hon. Lady's request in mind.

Had the hon. Lady read the letter from the Minister for Health—I suspect that she may not have done—she would have seen that it makes it clear that the Government value the independent review body, value the professional job nurses do, and want nurses to be fairly paid. He certainly did not say—nor would I—that we wanted the body to be disbanded.

I believe that the jobseeker's allowance was handled in exactly the right way. A statement was made in another place, because it was considering the Bill at the time and it was clearly right that their Lordships should have the information. The same information was conveyed to this House in a written answer, at roughly the same time and in an entirely proper way. My right hon. Friend the Secretary of State for Social Security and I did the hon. Member for Glasgow, Garscadden (Mr. Dewar) the courtesy—having been made aware in advance—of attending to listen to his points of order. I am sure that any further clarification requested will be provided.

**Sir Dudley Smith** (Warwick and Leamington): I note that my right hon. Friend did not mention the implementation of the Boundary Commission proposals. When are we likely to get the relevant legislation?

**Mr. Newton:** I cannot give a precise date at the moment, but I am aware that there is concern in the House to see the matter resolved and clarified as soon as possible.

**Mr. Simon Hughes** (Southwark and Bermondsey): Now that the Northern Ireland initiative has proceeded to the stage of talks across all sectors of the community—I realise that there will be no debate next week—after the recess may we have an opportunity in Government time to debate the state of the process in Northern Ireland, to ensure that it goes ahead with the widest possible support in the House and to maximise the chances of a conclusion as soon as possible?

**Mr. Newton:** I am grateful for the hon. Gentleman's tone, which makes me all the more inclined to give consideration, without commitment, to his request.

**Mr. Bob Dunn** (Dartford): May we have an early and urgent debate on the public conduct of Labour-dominated Kent county council, which earlier today used a procedural motion to stifle a Conservative debate on the need to fund in full the teachers' pay settlement from an underspend of £17 million? Will my right hon. Friend condemn this sort of practice by the Labour-Liberal Democrat-dominated council, conducted against free speech in Kent and elsewhere?

**Mr. Newton:** I very much take note of my hon. Friend's comments. Education questions next Tuesday may give him an opportunity to raise the matter with my right hon. Friend.

**Mrs. Gwyneth Dunwoody** (Crewe and Nantwich): Will the Leader of the House make a strong effort to get a Minister from the Foreign Office or the Department of Health to make a statement next week on exactly how much emergency aid is being sent from the United Kingdom directly to Zaire? We have all the products that could aid barrier nursing and protect not only doctors and nurses but volunteers, who are at direct risk. Those products could be on the next aeroplane if the Government would make the effort. Will the right hon. Gentleman make a clear statement that that is what the Government intend to do?

**Mr. Newton:** If I am right in interpreting the hon. Lady's question as a strong representation, I undertake to bring that representation to the attention of my right hon. and hon. Friends.

**Mr. Nicholas Winterton** (Macclesfield): Some sad decisions have been taken by the Royal College of Nursing this week in Harrogate. Would it be possible to have a debate on nursing and the national health service? It seems desperately sad that the independent pay review body structure, which has done so much for nursing, should be in jeopardy, despite what my right hon. Friend has said. It appears that the Government will gain little from local pay bargaining. If we are to have a national system for doctors and consultants, let it be recognised that nurses are just as professional and essential to the health service. Why does not the House have an opportunity to discuss the matter?

**Mr. Newton:** I should make it clear that I do not wholly share my hon. Friend's views in quite the way in which he put them. There has been a fair number of opportunities for the matter to be raised in the House, and I am certain that there will be more.

**Mr. Seamus Mallon** (Newry and Armagh): The Leader of the House will be aware that in 1989 the Government appointed the then chief constable of Cambridge, John Stevens, to inquire into allegations of collusion between members of the security services and loyalist terrorist groupings. Will the right hon. Gentleman make time available to enable the Government to assure the House that the investigations undertaken by Chief Constable Stevens

resulted in cases being brought to the Director of Public Prosecutions against four members of the security services, to give us an opportunity of being updated on the progress of those cases and to give the Government an opportunity to put before the House the findings of the latter stages of the Stevens inquiry, which have not yet been made public?

**Mr. Newton:** All that I can do now is to take note of the hon. Gentleman's request and to bring it, and the representations implicit in his question, to the attention of my right hon. and hon. Friends.

**Mr. James Clappison** (Hertsmere): Is my right hon. Friend aware that fairly soon the House will be debating the annual order relating to the assisted places scheme, the terms of which are somewhat limited? Will my right hon. Friend find time for a wider debate on the scheme, so that we can debate its value to hundreds of pupils in my constituency from lower-income families, and to thousands throughout the country? A wider debate would enable us also to examine the consequences of abolishing the scheme, as the Opposition would do if in government. Its abolition would deprive future generations of children of a similar opportunity, including the brothers and sisters of those who are already on the scheme, who would be deprived of the opportunity to go to the same schools.

**Mr. Newton:** The idea of providing time for the arguments so effectively advanced by my hon. Friend to be more fully deployed is attractive and I shall certainly bear it in mind.

**Mr. Peter Hardy** (Wentworth): The Leader of the House will be aware that earlier this week the Western European Union Council of Ministers issued the Lisbon declaration. The proposals may be perfectly adequate, but the declaration may involve significant additional commitments from the United Kingdom. Would it not therefore be highly appropriate for the House to consider the recommendations at an early date?

**Mr. Newton:** As always, I shall consider the hon. Gentleman's request. I would not wish to encourage too high hopes.

**Mr. Jacques Arnold** (Gravesham): May I support the call for a debate on the funding of education in Kent? It is an urgent matter because due to the incompetence of management of the county council there is a surplus of £17 million as a result of underspend last year, and as little as £3.8 million of this would fully fund the schools this year. Thanks to the Labour-Liberal Democrat coalition putting off such funding into the future, the schools now strapped for cash may have to make economies, including getting rid of some of the teachers who are educating our children. We are witnessing cynical political opportunism on the part of the Labour and Liberal Democrat parties and we need an early debate about the matter in the House.

**Mr. Newton:** Like my hon. Friend the Member for Dartford (Mr. Dunn), my hon. Friend makes an important point. Clearly, I cannot find time for a debate next week, or the week after, given that that is a recess, but there will be an opportunity in Education questions next week.

**Mr. Gordon McMaster** (Paisley, South): Following the welcome statement of the Leader of the House last week that the Government are to consider banning the gel formulation of Temazepam, will the Leader of the House find time next week to make a statement on whether the Government will accept the recommendation of the Advisory Council on the Misuse of Drugs to reschedule Temazepam from schedule 4 to schedule 3?

**Mr. Newton:** I am grateful for the hon. Gentleman's reference to the statement that I made when I launched the Government's White Paper on drugs, but I cannot add to what I then said about continuing consideration being given to the recommendations of the advisory council. I also said last week that I had it in mind to seek to provide time for a debate on drugs when a suitable opportunity arises.

**Mr. John Wilkinson** (Ruislip-Northwood): My right hon. Friend has announced Government business for Thursday 8 June. Will he allow the House to debate civil air transport on a substantive motion calling for Her Majesty's Government to insist that the negotiation of civil air transport agreements between countries remains a national responsibility, against the wishes of Transport Commissioner Kinnock and the European Union who want to arrogate to themselves a function which is properly ours and ours alone?

**Mr. Newton:** That was not quite the business that I had in mind for the first half of that Thursday, and a Government substantive motion may not be overwhelmingly popular on the second half of a Thursday. But the subject that my hon. Friend raises is undoubtedly important. I shall bear his request in mind and he need have no doubt of the firmness of the Government's own position.

**Ms Angela Eagle** (Wallasey): As we shall be debating the Nolan report on a motion for the Adjournment of the House today, will the Leader of the House provide time to debate resolutions that will begin to put the recommendations of that report into practice? As Nolan wishes us to have entirely new systems up and running by November, we will have little parliamentary time between now and the summer to get the business through the House.

**Mr. Newton:** As my right hon. Friend the Prime Minister said at Prime Minister's questions, the purpose of today's debate is to gauge feeling in the House in order to assist decisions about how best to proceed. Clearly, that implies further discussion following today's debate, but shaped in the light of today's debate.

**Mr. Bernard Jenkin** (Colchester, North): I rise more in sorrow than in anger. Is my right hon. Friend aware that the Reflections Group of the European Union considering the forthcoming intergovernmental conference is meeting on 2 June and, notwithstanding my right hon. Friend the Prime Minister's consideration of publication of our contribution to that group, will he confirm that the position at present is that the Government will be tabling a secret document to that Reflections Group meeting and there will be no debate in the House in advance of that meeting on what the Government may be doing? Does not that sit rather uneasily with the Government's determination to strengthen the role of national Parliaments?

**Mr. Newton:** My hon. Friend, of whose interest in these matters I am very much aware, will have heard what my right hon. Friend the Prime Minister said at Prime Minister's questions and I am not in a position to add to that.

**Mr. Tony Banks** (Newham, North-West): May we have an early debate on Members' interests? I am talking not about the financial interests that we will be considering when we debate the Nolan report later, but the far more interesting juicier interests that Government Whips apparently record in a book in their office about which I have been reading in the newspapers. How thick is the book? Is it true that it has now gone into a second volume and the Whips are contemplating a loose-leaf format? In the interests of open government, that book should be published so that we can all see it and have a good laugh.

**Mr. Newton:** As a former Whip myself, I am more than well aware of the dangers that I would face were I to answer the hon. Gentleman's questions, so I shall not.

**Mr. Harry Greenway** (Ealing, North): May we have a debate next week on Chiltern Railways' proposals for west London's summer service, so that I may bring to the House's attention the cut of the 5.18 train to Northolt Park in my constituency, the cut of other highly popular trains at important periods, and the deteriorating service to my constituents? The House should know about it and something should be done.

**Mr. Newton:** I can best point my hon. Friend to the fact that it is Transport questions on Monday.

**Mr. Jeremy Corbyn** (Islington, North): Has the Leader of the House had a chance to consider early-day motion 1143, which relates to yesterday's Ministry of Defence raid on Greenpeace offices, and a similar motion tabled by my hon. Friend the Member for Leyton (Mr. Cohen)?

[*That this House deplores the raid on Greenpeace offices as an infringement of their right to campaign against nuclear weapons and the dangers from nuclear power; and notes that this comes after the conclusion of the Nuclear Non-Proliferation Treaty negotiations and demonstrates the paranoia of the Ministry of Defence about peace organisations.*]

Does the right hon. Gentleman believe that it is important that the matter be fully debated and discussed in the House? Had that raid occurred in any other part of world, with a Government sending their MOD police force into the offices of an organisation that had been openly critical of nuclear proliferation and the development of the THORP fast breeder reactor system, our Government would have been the first to condemn that Government for their action. Does it not smack of something very nasty when a Government try to shut down an organisation that is dedicated to peace and openness, rather than accept the arguments that it is putting forward?

**Mr. Newton:** As I understand it, criminal damage had been committed, and a search was being conducted for evidence related to that criminal damage. Of course, the Government always defend the rights of peaceful protesters, whatever their cause, but they will also defend the position that demonstrators who commit a criminal act should be dealt with under the law.

**Mr. Nigel Evans** (Ribble Valley): May we have a debate as early as possible on employment creation in the

UK as so much good news is occurring in that sector that it is unlikely that the Opposition will choose one of their Opposition days to discuss that matter? We could consider the successive drops in unemployment, today's good news that Iceland Foods has announced the creation of 5,000 jobs, 1,000 of which will be created this year, and the announcement by Whitbread, which has a brewery close to my constituency and where some of my constituents work, that it is to create 5,000 extra jobs, 1,000 of which will be created in the north-west, with an investment of £15 million.

**Mr. Newton:** I am delighted to hear that further practical evidence of good news on the employment front, not least in my hon. Friend's constituency. He will have heard the points that my right hon. Friend the Prime Minister made earlier in response to my hon. Friend the Member for Hendon, North (Sir J. Gorst).

**Mrs. Alice Mahon** (Halifax): Will the Leader of the House reconsider his reply both to the hon. Member for Macclesfield (Mr. Winterton) and to my hon. Friend the Member for Dewsbury (Mrs. Taylor) and grant time for a debate on the injustice being meted out to nurses? I have read the intimidatory letter sent by the Minister for Health, and nurses will never abandon their patients in the way that this Government have abandoned the national health service. Is it not time that nurses received the 3 per cent. pay rise, that they got justice and that fewer threats were made against them?

**Mr. Newton:** When one looks at the figures that are frequently given about the increased resources going to the NHS, and the huge capital building programme that is under way, it is absurd to suggest that, in some sense, the NHS has been abandoned.

**Mr. Patrick McLoughlin** (West Derbyshire): May I join my hon. Friend the Member for Dartford (Mr. Dunn) in calling for a debate on local government? Is my right hon. Friend aware that, in relation to education, local government in Derbyshire holds back £720 per pupil? If we had a national education funding formula, that money could go straight into the schools.

**Mr. Newton:** That was another good point. It sounds to me as if the entire period of Education questions next Tuesday can be fruitfully employed.

**Mr. Alan Simpson** (Nottingham, South): Will the Leader of the House arrange for a debate on new housing policies in Britain, given the report published by the National House-Building Council, which points out that, in the past month, applications by house builders for new housing starts were 16 per cent. down on the previous year and, in the preceding three months, they were 17 per cent. down on the previous year? If he could arrange for such a debate in Government time, it would give the House the chance to endorse the comments of the hon. Member for Macclesfield (Mr. Winterton) in his Adjournment debate yesterday criticising the Treasury-led damage caused by undermining the confidence of the British housing market.

**Mr. Newton:** I cannot promise a debate, but I assure the hon. Gentleman that the Government, will continue with their efforts, among other things, to encourage greater private investment in the social housing sector.

**Mr. John Marshall** (Hendon, South): If I show a certain lack of practice in asking business questions, I apologise.

Under the National Lottery etc. Act 1993, it is possible for the House to vote annually on the distribution of the proceeds of the lottery. Many of us are concerned about the fact that only 6p in the pound goes to charity; can my right hon. Friend tell us when it is likely that we can engage in such a vote?

**Mr. Newton:** I am afraid that, notwithstanding all the good will that I bear my hon. Friend, I cannot give him a date for a debate of that kind. I shall certainly consider the point that he has raised, however.

**Mr. Harry Barnes** (Derbyshire, North-East): When the Leader of the House opened an exhibition in the main Committee Corridor marking the anniversary of the Chronically Sick and Disabled Persons Act 1979, he will have noticed a reference to the Civil Rights (Disabled Persons) Bill, which is currently going through the House. If he had popped along the Corridor, he might also have noted that the Bill's progress back to the Floor of the House is being considerably delayed. The same applies to other Bills, such as the Wild Mammals (Protection) Bill, which has not yet gone into Committee to be duly considered. Will the Leader of the House examine the problems currently affecting private Members' Bills?

**Mr. Newton:** If the hon. Gentleman heard the speech that I made upstairs, he will know that I went to some lengths to avoid becoming embroiled in current controversies, as distinct from marking the achievements of the past 25 years. I shall stay in that mode now. My concern is to ensure that we make further progress by means of the Government's Disability Discrimination Bill.

**Mr. Oliver Heald** (Hertfordshire, North): My right hon. Friend is aware of Conservative concern about the Opposition's policy in regard to a statutory minimum wage, and the huge job losses that would result from its implementation. Will he assure us that the scope of next Wednesday's debate will be wide enough for Conservative Members to express their concern, and also to point out that the cynical deal that seems to have been put together with the unions does not fool anyone? We all know what the level of the statutory minimum wage will be: it will be what the unions want. They pay for all Opposition Front Benchers, they pay for all their offices and they pay for their party.

**Mr. Newton:** So far we have seen only the title of next Wednesday's debate, not the wording of the motion; but the title certainly seems wide enough to embrace the point made by my hon. Friend.

**Mrs. Anne Campbell** (Cambridge): Given the Prime Minister's stated determination to drive out sleaze from public life, is it not about time that we had a debate on the use of private management consultants by Government Departments—particularly Prowess Management, which I understand has been used by Departments to find appointees to quangos without having to resort to

[Mrs. Anne Campbell]

competitive tender? There has been a strong recommendation to that effect from the Chancellor of the Duchy of Lancaster to all Departments.

**Mr. Newton:** As my right hon. Friend the Chancellor of the Duchy of Lancaster is visibly sitting next to me, I shall merely say that those representations have already been drawn to his attention.

**Mr. Gary Streeter** (Plymouth, Sutton): Will the House have an opportunity next week to consider the proposition that an Opposition Leader who is sponsored by the Transport and General Workers Union, and whose private office is funded by the Industrial Research Trust—which is partly funded by the TGWU—could ever, in office, resist the demands of the TGWU for a minimum wage of £4.10, which would throw millions of people on to the scrap heap?

**Mr. Newton:** Again, Madam Speaker, I am invited slightly to take over your role in judging what will and will not be in order during a debate. I think, however, that my hon. Friend has a good chance of being in order if he makes that point.

**Mr. Paul Flynn** (Newport, West): Has the Leader of the House had an opportunity to study the points of order that were raised yesterday, in particular the one that drew attention to a possible manipulation of our procedures by Ministers for their own party advantage? The example given was the way in which, on Monday and yesterday, they had linked questions in one case and not in another, to the great advantage of Conservative Back Benchers and to the disadvantage of Opposition Back Benchers.

As the House cannot intervene in such matters— although it is always said that questions are linked with the permission of the House—will my right hon. Friend ensure that the practice, which constitutes an abuse of democracy and our parliamentary procedures, is ended?

**Mr. Newton:** I was present when the hon. Gentleman raised his point of order. If I may say so, Madam Speaker, I thought that you dealt with it admirably.

**Mr. Dennis Skinner** (Bolsover): Is the Leader of the House aware that if we had a debate on education, as proposed by the hon. Member for West Derbyshire (Mr. McLoughlin), we would be able to point out that Derbyshire local education authority does not have the spare money that was suggested? That money is held back to pay for school meals because, unlike some other local education authorities in which schools administer and pay for school meals and other administrative overheads, in Derbyshire the schools decided to have the money kept centrally. There is no spare money. I have a suggestion for the right hon. Gentleman. If all the 200 Tory Members who have six, seven, eight and nine jobs gave all the money that they get from moonlighting, we could make up the pay shortfalls, not just for teachers but for nurses, too.

**Mr. Newton:** I am not sure whether the hon. Gentleman's contribution is intended as an advance on today's debate or on next Tuesday's Education questions. I will leave him to make up his mind.

**Mr. John Evans** (St. Helens, North): Does the Leader of the House agree that because the Nolan committee did not deal with the funding of political parties, if hon. Members seek to raise that subject in today's debate, they are likely to be ruled out of order? In view of the widespread concern about the matter, especially as expressed by the hon. Members for Hertfordshire, North (Mr. Heald) and for Plymouth, Sutton (Mr. Streeter), will the right hon. Gentleman arrange a debate about the funding of political parties immediately on our return from the recess? Does he accept that, as someone who was chair of the Labour party's finance committee for five years, I will be prepared to ensure that every aspect of the Labour party's finances is presented in the House, if the right hon. Gentleman will guarantee that the appropriate person in the Tory party presents all their figures in the House?

**Mr. Newton:** Perhaps as a gesture of good will in this context, the hon. Gentleman might care to pick up my right hon. Friend the Prime Minister's suggestion that the Labour party could start by conforming with the rules suggested by the Home Affairs Select Committee.

**Mr. Tom Clarke** (Monklands, West): Is the Leader of the House aware that the application of the Hague convention could lead in my constituency to a case whereby a child of 14 months, Lucia Johnson, could be taken from her mother by sheriff officers, placed in custody and put on a plane to Spain without anybody from her family being in her company? Does the right hon. Gentleman agree that if that happens, it would run counter to the principles of the Children Act 1989 and the Children (Scotland) Bill, which is being discussed by Parliament, which rightly assert that the future of the child is paramount? Will he therefore insist that the Secretary of State for Scotland makes a statement to the House or, at least, introduce a debate so that we can decide whether there is a conflict between our perceived international obligations and the clear will of the House on child welfare?

**Mr. Newton:** The hon. Gentleman has understandably raised a point of importance, not least to the individuals concerned. The hon. Gentleman will acknowledge that, without being more fully aware of the circumstances, I could not properly comment, beyond saying that my right hon. Friend the Secretary of State for Scotland is due to answer questions next Wednesday and I will bring that point to his attention.

**Mr. Eric Martlew** (Carlisle): Will the Leader of the House allow in the near future a debate on the vindictive decision of ScotRail to withdraw the dedicated sleeper service to my constituency? That is despite an assurance given to me in January that if the Fort William sleeper service was not withdrawn, the Carlisle service would continue. Yesterday, official figures showed that the subsidy to the Carlisle service was far less than that to any other sleeper destination. May we have an urgent debate on the matter?

**Mr. Newton:** It sounds to me as if the hon. Gentleman's point would be an appropriate subject for representations in relation to the recently issued proposals for passenger service requirements. I am sure that he will make his representations.

# Committee on Standards in Public Life

*Motion made, and Question proposed,* That this House do now adjourn.—*[Dr. Liam Fox.]*

**Madam Speaker:** Before I call the Minister, I have to inform the House that because of the number of Members who wish to speak in the debate, I have had to limit speeches between the hours of 7 pm and 9 pm to 10 minutes.

4 3 pm

**The Chancellor of the Duchy of Lancaster (Mr. David Hunt):** Hon. Members on both sides of the House will, I am sure, welcome this early opportunity to debate the first report of the Nolan Committee on Standards in Public Life, which was published by my right hon. Friend the Prime Minister last Thursday. I commend the committee for the openness of its approach, the unanimity of its conclusions and recommendations and the speed with which it produced its report.

The central reason for setting up the Nolan committee was, of course, the growing public concern about standards in public life. Right hon. and hon. Members will therefore be reassured by the key conclusion of the committee, which states that

"much of the public anxiety about standards of conduct in public life is based on perceptions and beliefs which are not supported by the facts. Taking the evidence as a whole, we believe that the great majority of men and women in British public life are honest and hard-working and observe high ethical standards".

I very much welcome that finding and so, I believe, will the vast majority of people, especially those who serve the public and who know that they are working to the highest standards of efficiency, effectiveness and, above all, integrity, whether they are elected, appointed or employed in the public sector.

The report's recommendations aim to reinforce public confidence in the holders of public office. Wherever existing guidelines may have seemed open to varying interpretation, they seek to restore clarity of direction. Above all, we must ensure that that objective is secured. The Government fully support those aims and welcome the broad thrust of the recommendations in so far as they affect the Government and are ready to take early action on them.

The House will, however, recognise that the report raises many complex matters of detail and many difficult issues. We must ensure, therefore, that the recommendations would achieve their aims. We shall have to examine these issues carefully and resolve any difficulties before we move to implement those recommendations.

**Mr. Tristan Garel-Jones** (Watford): Like my right hon. Friend, I warmly welcome the Nolan report. I am interested in the point that he is making about clarity. Does he agree that, if the House were governed by statute and we were to seek to introduce a Bill to implement the report's recommendations, the drafting of that Bill would be a lengthy and rather complex procedure?

There is one particular aspect of the report about which I have some doubt. Does my right hon. Friend agree that we ought to refer these matters to a senior Committee of the House to "build on the foundation" provided by Lord Nolan? In order to restore public confidence and assist

hon. Members, we must have rules that are clear and that the public and hon. Members understand. It is absolutely crucial that that is done with clarity and care.

**Mr. Hunt:** In responding to my right hon. Friend, let me reiterate the fact that the committee examined a number of matters, and three in particular: first, hon. Members; secondly, Ministers and civil servants; and thirdly, non-departmental public bodies. In opening this debate, I am primarily concerned to give the Government's response to the recommendations affecting Ministers and civil servants and non-departmental public bodies.

As my right hon. Friend pointed out, the first set of recommendations affects right hon. and hon. Members and the procedures of the House and the report does indeed make a number of proposals. Some are straightforward and do not require clarification, such as the restating of the 1947 resolution on hon. Members and outside contractual agreements. But others need to be looked at carefully to ensure that the improvements in the rules and procedures are carried forward in the most effective way with the least room for grey areas. That important point, which was made by my right hon. Friend, deserves reiteration time and again.

We must examine these issues very carefully and, as I said, resolve any difficulties before implementation. The public expect us to get this right: it is too important to get wrong.

**Mr. Nicholas Budgen** (Wolverhampton, South-West): My right hon. Friend did not answer the question about a statute. If the terms upon which hon. Members serve are to be materially changed, is not it right for them to be decided by statute with all the slowness, deliberation and public discussion that that brings rather than in panic in response to particular circumstances? After all, the worst legislation that the House has passed was the Dangerous Dogs Act 1991 and the Single European Act. They were passed in a hurry—

**Mr. Michael Trend** (Windsor and Maidenhead): But Maastricht was not.

**Mr. Budgen:** In my opinion that was not done slowly enough but that is a different point.

If the terms upon which we serve here are to be changed it would be wise, would it not, for that to be done by statute which would perhaps bite at the beginning of the next Parliament?

**Mr. Hunt:** My hon. Friend proposes a fundamental constitutional change because the conduct of the House is not a matter of statute, and if the terms upon which hon. Members serve were to be encompassed in statute, it would be a fundamental constitutional change.

**Several hon. Members** *rose—*

**Mr. Hunt:** I shall give way in a moment, but I should like to answer my hon. Friend. What he said has been heard by my colleagues on the Treasury Bench and my right hon. Friend the Leader of the House will be responding to the debate. However, I hope that my hon. Friend will allow us to hear whether there are any other views, particularly those to the contrary, on the rather fundamental constitutional change that he has suggested.

**Mrs. Ann Taylor** (Dewsbury): Will the Chancellor of the Duchy of Lancaster confirm that it was the

[*Mrs. Ann Taylor*]

Prime Minister, because of the urgency and the great weight of expressed public concern, who asked Lord Nolan to make his first report within six months? If it was important for Lord Nolan to report in that time, surely it is important for the House to take action as quickly as possible. The right hon. Gentleman talked slightly complacently about the problems not being too great. Does he acknowledge that Lord Nolan said:

"unless the strictest standards are maintained and where necessary restored, corruption and malpractice can become part of the way of life. The threat at the moment is not great. Action needs to be taken before it becomes so."?

Surely that action needs to be taken on the time scale that was recommended by Lord Nolan.

**Mr. Hunt:** There was a general welcome for the announcement that my right hon. Friend the Prime Minister was setting up this committee. The Prime Minister made it clear that the central reason for setting it up was the increase in public concern about conduct in public life. Therefore, I hope that the hon. Lady will think again about what she has said in the light of the central conclusion of the Nolan committee that

"much of the public anxiety"—

to which of course my right hon. Friend the Prime Minister referred at the time—

"about standards of conduct in public life is based upon perceptions and beliefs which are not supported by the facts."

Of course, the hon. Lady is right, and I shall come to the action to be taken by the Government on the proposals as they affect the Government.

**Mr. Iain Duncan Smith** (Chingford): Will my right hon. Friend give way?

**Mr. Hunt:** Of course, in one moment. Equally, is it not right that the Government, having arranged for this debate to take place, should listen carefully to views expressed by hon. Members of all parties before moving to the next stage?

**Ms Angela Eagle** (Wallasey): Does the right hon. Gentleman agree with the deliberate time scale that Lord Nolan has put into his report? Lord Nolan uses the categories of A, B and C. If we are considering the recommendations that apply particularly to hon. Members—down that list some quite fundamental changes in the rules with which we are to govern ourselves are suggested—most of them fall into the A category, on which Lord Nolan wants to see immediate action and most of the rest of them fall into the B category, which means that action should be taken and new committees should be in place by November. Does the right hon. Gentleman not realise how quickly we would have to act to fulfil that timetable and thus restore public confidence?

**Mr. Hunt:** I say to the hon. Lady that these are very important issues on which I hope that all hon. Members will reflect carefully in their speeches. It is important to get the facts right. If the hon. Lady would turn to pages—

**Sir Geoffrey Johnson Smith** (Wealden): Will my right hon. Friend give way?

**Mr. Hunt:** In a second. If the hon. Lady turns to pages 7, 8 and 9, she will see that what she has just said is incorrect.

**Sir Geoffrey Johnson Smith:** No one wants anyone to procrastinate, but is my right hon. Friend aware that it is vital to get the detail right and that the job of clarifying rules and regulations should not be done overnight?

**Mr. Hunt:** As I have said on more than one occasion, these are very important issues for this House. Therefore, I think that Opposition Members—

**Mr. Paul Flynn** (Newport, West): Will the right hon. Gentleman give way?

**Mr. Hunt:** Just one moment. Opposition Members do a grave injustice to the Nolan committee if they seek to make this a party political issue. I believe— [*Interruption.*] Let me just make this point. I believe that Lord Nolan's committee has given us—

**Ms Eagle:** On a point of order, Madam Speaker. I have just looked down the list of recommendations that the right hon. Gentleman said were all classified C— [*Interruption.*]

**Madam Speaker:** Order. Let me deal with this matter. It must be a genuine point of order and not a matter for debate. The hon. Member made a long intervention. So many Members want to participate in this debate, and this House and the country want to hear their views. Let us make some progress. Is it a genuine point of order and not a matter of argument?

**Ms Eagle:** I am concerned that the House has been given a misleading impression by what was said, because 19 out of 20 recommendations—

**Madam Speaker:** Order. That is not a point of order. There has been no breach of our Standing Orders or our procedures. The hon. Member is arguing with the Minister, who has the Floor.

**Mr. Hunt:** As the hon. Lady is seeking to continue to dispute the fact, which is rather a waste of time, I ask her to look at page 7. From that she would think that she was correct. But instead of confining herself to page 7, if she turned to page 8, she would see that the majority of the proposals there were Bs. If she recalls, she said at the outset that the majority of the proposals were classified A. On pages 8 and 9, not one proposal is classified A. They are B and in one case C. Therefore—

**Ms Eagle** *rose—*

**Mr. Hunt:** If the hon. Lady examines the record carefully, she will see exactly what she said. I do not understand why we are spending time on a matter that is so clear in the report.

**Mr. Duncan Smith:** At the outset, so that we may get the matter absolutely straight, will my right hon. Friend confirm for the Opposition Front-Bench team and all hon. Members that the matters concerning Members of Parliament are for Members of Parliament to decide and that what will be implemented has nothing to do with the opinion of the Front-Bench teams of either party? Will he confirm that what will be implemented will be up to this House and this House alone and the opinions of either Front-Bench team have absolutely no bearing on the matter?

**Mr. Hunt:** I agree—

**Mr. John Garrett** (Norwich, South): On a point of order, Madam Speaker. This is a genuine point of order. Will you tell us how the Standing Order relates to declarations of interest in the course of the debate? Should hon. Members announce their interest when they speak—and, more particularly, when they intervene?

**Madam Speaker:** It has never been required that hon. Members declare their interests when intervening, but I shall think it very wise if all hon. Members taking part in the debate carry out our usual procedures and say at the very start of their speeches what their interests are.

**Mr. Hunt:** I agree with my hon. Friend the Member for Chingford (Mr. Duncan Smith) that it is arrogant of the Opposition Front-Bench spokesmen to seek to dictate to the House what the response of right hon. and hon. Members in the Chamber should be to these very detailed recommendations.

To return to what I was saying a few moments ago, these are serious issues for the House. I believe that Lord Nolan's committee has given us an excellent opportunity to re-establish public confidence in the system now. We should seize that opportunity and not seek to divert the debate down a particular party political channel. We should rise above that debate in order to deliberate on the real issues that face us.

**Mr. Tony Benn** (Chesterfield): Will the Minister give serious consideration to the answer that he gave about the use of statute? Far from the use of statute being a radical proposal, the House has always dealt with membership and its rules by using the House of Commons Disqualification Act 1975. There are 400 disqualifying offices, and although there may be differences on some issues, many people believe that such matters should be dealt with by statute rather than through a commissioner who would deal with Members. We could say, "If you are within the law you are all right, and if you are outside the law you will be taken to court." So I hope that the Minister will not rule out statute as the proper way of dealing with the matter. He might find that it had a far wider range of support than he believes.

**Mr. Hunt:** When my hon. Friend the Member for Wolverhampton, South-West (Mr. Budgen) raised a similar point, I said that that was an interesting issue but that it raised fundamental constitutional questions. Of course the right hon. Member for Chesterfield (Mr. Benn) is right to refer to the House of Commons Disqualification Act. And of course that is a statute. But the way in which we conduct matters within the House has never been primarily a matter for statute. If it were to become so, that would be a significant move that would require the fullest possible debate in the Chamber.

**Mr. Edward Leigh** (Gainsborough and Horncastle): I agree with the right hon. Gentleman—

**Mr. Garrett:** On a point of order, Madam Speaker. Am I right in believing that the Chancellor of the Duchy of Lancaster did not declare his interests in opening his speech, and could have done so once you had given that ruling?

**Madam Speaker:** I am sure that if the Chancellor of the Duchy of Lancaster has an interest to declare, he will take the opportunity to do so before he takes the intervention.

**Mr. Hunt:** My interest is declared in the Register of Members' Interests—[Hon. Members: "Tell us."]—as a partner in a firm of solicitors and as an underwriting member of Lloyd's. That is widely known, but it has no direct relevance to what we are debating. [Hon. Members: "Oh."] Nevertheless I make it absolutely clear, for the avoidance of doubt.

**Mr. Budgen:** Does my right hon. Friend agree—
*[Interruption.]*

**Madam Speaker:** Order. Let us have some decorum and order in the debate.

**Mr. Budgen:** The Nolan suggestions—and they are only suggestions—do not impinge upon the procedures of the House or on how we behave here. They are suggestions about what are really the terms of our employment. Surely if our terms of employment are to be restricted in some way, that should be set out in statute. Is that not quite different from the old custom of our unwritten constitution, that the procedures of the House and the way in which we behave here are ordered within the House, with no statutory backing?

**Mr. Hunt:** My hon. Friend raises some interesting points, which I hope will find a context in the debate. There are arguments either way, as I have been seeking to demonstrate.

To reiterate, the issues need clarification and we must examine all the difficulties that arise before the House moves to implementation. We are having the debate today so that hon. Members on both sides of the House can deal with the issues, and to allow hon. Members to express their personal opinions in the Chamber.

**Dr. Tony Wright** (Cannock and Burntwood): Has the Chancellor of the Duchy of Lancaster reflected on the fact that the assurances that he gave to the Nolan committee in evidence were comprehensively dismissed by that committee? Is not it the case that the Prime Minister, in setting up the Nolan committee, said that this was a matter of extreme urgency and that the public's trust in those in public life was at stake? Is not the origin of the problem the failure of the House to reform itself? If the House now prevaricates, will not that compound the problem that the Nolan committee was set up to resolve?

**Mr. Hunt:** I am not aware that anything suggested by the hon. Gentleman has ever been said by any of my right

*[Mr. Hunt]*

hon. and hon. Friends. It is important that we get this right. With regard to my evidence, I am coming to the rules affecting Ministers when they leave office. If I may make a little progress, I shall deal with that matter.

**Mr. Geoffrey Clifton-Brown** (Cirencester and Tewkesbury): Does my right hon. Friend agree that sensational cases make bad law? Does he recall Edmund Burke's statement that one owes to one's electorate a duty to one's judgment and not to one's industry? If the judgment of Members of Parliament is so suspect that— for the first time—this place must be judged by somebody else, democracy will be irredeemably damaged.

**Mr. Hunt:** I agree with my hon. Friend, and I recall that someone from Bristol said that a Member of Parliament owes to his constituents his industry, but must never sacrifice his judgment to his opinion, and I agree.

**Mr. Leigh:** I tried to intervene earlier, as I wanted to agree with the right hon. Member for Chesterfield (Mr. Benn). Does my right hon. Friend also agree with the right hon. Gentleman? The right hon. Gentleman made a serious point that, for 700 years, this House has taken the view that in order to safeguard the liberty of the people, the Executive could have no control over the House. If the House is to be regulated in this tight way—which may or may not be the right thing to do—it should be by statute. Hon. Members should know exactly where they stand, and should not be bound by a commissioner effectively appointed by the Executive to oversee independent Members of Parliament.

**Mr. Hunt:** These are all serious points, some of which could involve fundamental changes. It is important today to listen to the views expressed in the Chamber. In all cases, this House will have the final say.

**Mr. Garel-Jones:** The point made by the right hon. Member for Chesterfield (Mr. Benn) and supported by my hon. Friend the Member for Gainsborough and Horncastle (Mr. Leigh) is interesting. But if we were to go down the route to statute, would not that delay the matter much more than if the House dealt with it itself? Would not such a process involve the introduction of a Bill? If we were to have a statute, would not we be handing over the scrutiny of this House to the judges and to legal interpretation? That may or may not be a good thing, but it is certainly something that the House should consider.

**Mr. Hunt:** This will be an interesting debate. We are entering an area that the Nolan committee does not address in its report in detail, and no doubt hon. Members who have views on that aspect will put them forward. My right hon. Friend the Leader of the House will seek to catch your eye, Madam Speaker, at the conclusion of the debate. Like all of us, he will want to consider carefully the contributions made by right hon. and hon. Members.

**Mr. Dennis Skinner** (Bolsover): Will the Minister answer the question that people outside have constantly put in the past few weeks? When Back Benchers become Ministers, 80 or so of whom form a Government, they must then get rid of their consultancies, directorships and all the rest. If that applies to Ministers, why cannot it apply to Back Benchers? One reason why the Government must wrestle with that problem is that, when Thatcher came to power, she allowed those Back Benchers to make as much money as they liked provided that they turned up here at 10 o'clock to get the legislation through. It was the age of materialism and now the Government are having to pay for it.

**Mr. Hunt** *rose—*

**Mr. Budgen:** Will my right hon. Friend give way?

**Madam Speaker:** Order. Not until the Minister has responded.

**Mr. Hunt:** I think that my hon. Friend anticipated that there was nothing serious to respond to.

**Mr. Budgen:** Does my right hon. Friend agree that there is a serious misconception here? There is a great distinction between the role of the Back Bencher and that of the Back Bencher who becomes a Minister. No Back Bencher is forced to become a Minister; if he does so, it is on the terms on which that employment is offered to him. If every Back Bencher is to be bound by new onerous and radical terms of employment, that becomes a matter for the whole nation as it is the basis on which we serve in this Parliament. That must be a matter for legislation.

**Mr. Hunt:** I have already acknowledged that that view is a serious contribution to a wide-ranging debate. The question of statute law as opposed to rules of procedure of the House is fundamental and I look forward to contributions on that subject.

May I deal with the recommendations addressed to the Government, that is, those on Ministers and civil servants? During its review, the committee looked at "Questions of Procedure for Ministers"—guidance that the Prime Minister and the Government have made public for the first time ever. It had not previously been in the public domain. The committee made a number of suggestions to improve the guidance. It says that we should draw out the ethical principles and seek to formulate a code of conduct either within the guidance or as a free-standing document. The committee also recommends new arrangements to extend records of gifts to include hospitality accepted by Ministers in their official capacity.

It is self-evident that the integrity of Ministers must not be open to doubt, whether during their service to the nation or in what they do afterwards. So I make it absolutely clear to the House that the Government intend to implement Lord Nolan's recommendation that proposals by former Ministers to take up appointments after they leave public office should be brought within the scope of Lord Carlisle's Advisory Committee on Business Appointments.

As Lord Nolan recognised, some important points of detail must be put in place before clear ground rules can be established. For example, should the three-month waiting period proposed in the report apply to Ministers who return to an earlier occupation or profession, which may be largely unconnected with their work in government, such as running a business, returning to office as a paid trade union official, returning to lecture at a university, or returning to work as a schoolteacher? How do we strike the right balance between openness and privacy? I would welcome any views that the House wishes to express before we make final proposals for the detailed scheme.

The hon. Member for Cannock and Burntwood (Dr. Wright) asked me about the evidence that I gave to the Nolan committee, so let me explain what I said. I told Lord Nolan that I thought that the existing rules for Ministers were sufficient to uphold the standards of public life, but that the Government would consider very carefully what he recommended.

Lord Nolan's report finds that those standards remain high and that the problem lies mainly in public perception rather than in the facts. I accept that. I also accept the need to rebuild public confidence. We are therefore glad to accept Lord Nolan's recommendation, which will reinforce confidence that British public life maintains the highest possible standards.

On the civil service, the Nolan committee has been able to build on the welcome common ground that exists between all the political parties in the House. The Nolan committee supports the action that we are taking, for instance, to introduce a new code for civil servants, as set out in our response to Nolan and in our White Paper, "The Civil Service: Taking Forward Continuity and Change". That code, which will be a document of great value, arises directly as a result of a recommendation made by the all-party Select Committee on the Treasury and Civil Service. It sets out concisely what is expected of civil servants and introduces a new right of external appeal.

The Government will look constructively at the further points that the Nolan committee has raised and will take them all into account in the consultation exercise that we are currently conducting with the civil service staff and unions. The Opposition spokesmen and the Select Committee on the Treasury and Civil Service have also been invited to offer their views.

**Ms Joan Walley** (Stoke-on-Trent, North): Will that consultation exercise specifically consider the position of Opposition Front-Bench spokesmen and women of whichever party and in whichever Government? The Chairmen of the Select Committees are given specific help, unlike the Opposition spokesmen and women who shadow Ministers, who, in turn, have all the resources of the civil service available to them. When considering how to resource Members of Parliament properly, we should take into account not just their constituency business, but their role in scrutinising parliamentary legislation.

**Mr. Hunt:** The hon. Lady is arguing for more resources through the Short mechanism, which currently provides funds for the party in opposition. That does not relate directly to the point that I was making about the civil service, but should the hon. Lady catch your eye, Madam Deputy Speaker, I am sure that she will raise that issue again in the debate.

When we complete the consultation process with the staff and unions of the civil service, the Opposition and the Select Committee, we shall introduce the code, because I am convinced by the Nolan committee's recommendation that we should not wait for legislation to do that. As hon. Members will know, I have already said that our mind is open on whether such legislation should be introduced, but we agree with Lord Nolan that we need not wait. We shall therefore introduce that code when we have completed the consultation process.

The Nolan committee report also considers the appointment procedures and propriety in the workings of executive non-departmental public bodies and national health service bodies. Non-departmental public bodies are

an integral part of public service. The need for integrity on their part is as great as it is for Ministers, the civil service and elsewhere. It is therefore reassuring to note that, on this issue, too, the committee explicitly rules out the idea that there has been any decline in standards.

The report highlights the continuing tradition of voluntary service by those many thousands of public-spirited individuals in positions that are often unpaid or paid at rates far below those that their skills could attract elsewhere. I should like to add my tribute to the many people who serve in those positions. I hope that they will all accept and that the House will accept that the Nolan committee's report offers a conclusive rebuttal of the allegations hurled, without any evidence or justification, at people who give their time and energy to serve the nation in a public capacity.

**Mr. Robert Sheldon** (Ashton-under-Lyne): Some of the most serious shortcomings to which the Public Accounts Committee drew attention in its eighth report were in non-departmental public bodies. There were some very serious shortcomings indeed, which led to a unique report, of a type that had never been produced by the Public Accounts Committee.

The Nolan report is proposing that auditors from the commercial sector should continue to carry out the audit of some of those non-departmental public bodies. At present, two thirds of non-departmental public bodies are audited by the National Audit Office. I believe, and the Committee believes, that it is important that all those non-departmental public bodies should be audited by the National Audit Office.

Commercial auditors today—we have witnessed some examples of it recently—have an advantage in obtaining so much of their money from consultancy work, and they make very low bids to obtain that. The only organisation that has no interest in those matters is the National Audit Office, which can be answerable to the Public Accounts Committee and can retain those standards. It is important that the standards that exist in the Government service as a whole be applied throughout those non-departmental public bodies.

**Madam Deputy Speaker (Dame Janet Fookes):** Order. Before the Minister continues, may I remind both sides of the House that interventions, by their nature, should be short?

**Mr. Hunt:** I have a great deal of sympathy with several of the arguments made by the right hon. Gentleman. Indeed, one of the Nolan committee's recommendations is that audit arrangements should be reviewed, to ensure that the best practice applies to all public bodies.

I shall discuss appointments and then auditing arrangements and propriety. The Nolan committee does indeed endorse the key principles underlying the existing appointments system—that ultimate responsibility for public appointments must remain with Ministers, all appointments should be subject to the overriding principle of appointment on merit and public bodies should have a balance of skills and backgrounds in their membership.

The Government are already taking steps to improve the transparency and independence of the appointments process. We have reviewed the central guidance and there is increasing use, in the national health service and other

[*Mr. Hunt*]

public services, of advisory panels or committees with one or more independent members. Many of the committee's recommendations build on those initiatives.

**Mr. Barry Sheerman** (Huddersfield): Will the right hon. Gentleman give way?

**Mr. Hunt:** Of course I will give way, but I shall first reply to the argument of the right hon. Member for Ashton-under-Lyne (Mr. Sheldon).

The Government welcome the proposal for a new independent commissioner for public appointments, who would monitor, regulate and approve departmental appointment procedures. We also accept the case for an extension of the role of independent advisory committees. We are developing formal plans now to implement those proposals.

We need to consider very carefully what the exact functions of the commissioner should be. It appears sensible not to finalise the details until we have appointed someone of the highest integrity and listened to his or her opinions.

The committee also examined the standards of conduct, as the right hon. Member for Ashton-under-Lyne says. The report says:

"in general, the board members of executive non-departmental public bodies and national health service bodies are committed to the principles and values of public service and perform their duties to high standards of integrity".

To provide additional reassurance, we are ready to tighten procedures, as recommended in the report. In that way, we aim to show beyond doubt that the rules are being followed. Specifically, we accept that we should review the legal framework governing propriety and accountability in a wide range of public bodies. I am happy to tell the right hon. Member for Ashton-under-Lyne that work on that review by members of the Cabinet Office and the Treasury is already under way.

The committee also suggested that the Treasury "Code of Best Practice for Board Members," issued, I think, in June 1994, should act as a model for mandatory codes of conduct for each executive non-departmental public body. Although the Treasury model is indeed at the moment principally intended to cover non-departmental public bodies, it is not mandatory. I have an open mind about that. Perhaps it should be; or perhaps we need to tackle it in some other way, more responsive to the needs of each individual body. That issue merits very careful consideration.

National health service bodies, for example, have their own codes of conduct and accountability, which are already mandatory on all boards; and compliance is a condition of appointment.

**Mr. Sheerman** *rose*—

**Mr. Hunt:** I shall mention the committee's final recommendations, and then I shall give way.

The committee's final recommendations propose the adoption of the 1994 "Code of Practice on Access to Government Information", together with the committee's own guidelines, throughout executive non-departmental public bodies.

We wholeheartedly endorse those proposals, because greater openness in public life is an important objective of the Government. I believe that our code of practice has already been a notable milestone in meeting that objective. We are also introducing an openness code for the national health service, under which the health service ombudsman will be asked to investigate individual complaints.

**Mr. Sheerman:** The openness that my constituents want is an openness about who is appointed to public bodies. So many good people in this country of ours want to give public service, but, time and again, listen to people such as Baroness Denton, who says that she has never knowingly appointed anyone who is not a member or a supporter of the Conservative party. That is the great unrest among constituents of mine, who want to serve.

**Mr. Hunt:** Baroness Denton has already said that she was misquoted and did not say that.

I would hope that, had the hon. Gentleman listened to what I said, he would have been reassured that the Government have said that, in certain instances, we accept the recommendations set out in the report, and in others the recommendations need careful consideration.

**Mr. John Morris** (Aberavon): In his evidence to the Nolan committee, did the Chancellor of the Duchy of Lancaster discuss the role of the Government Chief Whip, and say that that was to be different from now on?

**Mr. Hunt:** I did give written evidence to the Nolan committee, in setting out the new procedure on appointments, that there would be a lessening role for the Government Chief Whip. I made that clear to the committee, and nothing came down from above to strike me down when I uttered those words.

I have outlined the Government's preliminary response to the Nolan committee's first report. Its subject is of the utmost importance to the Government. We believe that people engaged in public service must work with integrity and to the highest standards, and be seen to do so.

**Mr. David Nicholson** (Taunton): I am grateful to my right hon. Friend. Earlier he was subject to several interventions—from both sides of the House, surprisingly—that might have implied delay in carrying out the recommendations of the report.

Does my right hon. Friend agree that, subject to clarification of certain important matters in the report and subject to a free vote of Back-Bench Members of the House, indeed all Members of the House, there would be high risk to the reputation of Parliament and to the legitimate representation of interests in our processes—which is very important—if there were undue delay in implementing most of the proposals?

**Mr. Hunt:** On my hon. Friend's first point, I have always believed that, in matters governing issues that affect the House, one should give way on every possible and conceivable occasion. If there were any misconceptions, I hope that they have been dispersed by the way in which, on behalf of the Government, I have so clearly welcomed the broad thrust of the recommendations in so far as they affect the Government.

As far as Parliament is concerned, it must be for Parliament to determine the way to proceed. I very much hope that all those who feel that they have an opinion to express will find time, Madam Deputy Speaker, to make their contribution. That is why I should like to bring my remarks to a close by saying that—

**Mr. Anthony Steen** (South Hams): In the spirit of openness which the Government are most concerned to exploit to the full, will my right hon. Friend ensure that there is a cost-compliance assessment of the additional costs of the rules and regulations that will flow from the report and of all the additional staff who will have to be employed at a cost to the taxpayer? That information should be made available to the House and to the nation.

**Mr. Hunt:** I am sure that the consequences in terms of the cost of any proposals will be considered very carefully. At the end of the day, we are here to undertake a task that Lord Nolan's committee has given us every opportunity to accomplish: to re-establish public confidence in the system.

**Mr. Robert Maclennan** (Caithness and Sutherland): I am extremely grateful to the Minister for giving way. While I certainly wish to acquit him of charges of evasiveness about those parts of the report that deal with the Houses of Parliament and while I recognise the Government's desire to hear the views of the House and perhaps of another place in due course, will the Minister at least confirm that the Government accept the underlying thrust of the Nolan committee's report concerning the urgency of the timing of those matters that touch upon the business of the House and the need to act within the time scale that the committee sets out?

**Mr. Hunt:** I hope that I have already established beyond doubt the Government's determination to respond to the recommendations that affect the Government. I believe that the recommendations that the committee has singled out for early implementation should be treated in the same way as we treat the recommendations of a Select Committee: we must provide a detailed response within the usual two-month period. I have already indicated that we are taking action in a number of areas, but that a detailed response will be provided before the summer recess. As to the hon. Gentleman's point about Parliament, that must be a matter for Parliament to decide.

Above all, I hope that we will remember one thing: while formal procedures are vital, in the end the individual's personal position must be beyond reproach. I made that point to the committee when I gave oral evidence to it. I said then that no individual should act in a way that calls into question his or her integrity. Adherence to that principle and to the others set out in the Nolan report—selflessness, objectivity, accountability, openness, honesty and leadership, together with integrity—must remain the foundation of our public life.

I believe that integrity must remain our watchword. We all share responsibility—in this House and elsewhere— for reinforcing the public's confidence in the public service. The Government will do everything necessary to ensure that the quality of the British public service remains, and is clearly seen to be, the best in the world.

4.52 pm

**Mrs. Ann Taylor** (Dewsbury): I start by declaring my interests as they appear in the Register of Members' Interests. I am a sponsored member of the General, Municipal, Boilermakers and Allied Trades Union and I receive research assistance from the Association of Teachers and Lecturers and from Unison. I had intended to begin my remarks by welcoming the fact that we are debating this matter as soon as possible after the publication of the Nolan committee report. I had thought that that showed that the Government were treating the matter seriously and urgently. However, in view of the remarks during Prime Minister's Question Time and the speech by the Chancellor of the Duchy of Lancaster this afternoon, I am beginning to wonder whether I drew the correct inference from this early debate.

**Mr. Jacques Arnold** (Gravesham): Will the hon. Lady give way?

**Mrs. Taylor:** I have just started my speech; I shall make some progress first. I certainly do not wish to do anything that would delay the implementation of the Nolan committee's recommendations, and I shall turn to some practical suggestions a little later. It is important to remind the House why it was necessary to set up the Nolan committee in the first place. Having listened to the remarks of the Chancellor of the Duchy of Lancaster, I think that some hon. Members might be wondering why he thought that the Prime Minister established the Nolan committee. At the time of its establishment, the Prime Minister said:

"In the present atmosphere, there is public disquiet about standards of public life".—[*Official Report*, 25 October 1994; Vol. 248, c. 758.]

Upon reflection on the events that led to the committee being set up, I do not think that history will accuse the Prime Minister of overstatement. In the weeks leading to the establishment of the Nolan inquiry, the House and the public witnessed the cash for questions episode, more than one ministerial resignation and a host of other allegations. I do not intend to go into the details of those matters this afternoon, not least because they are still the subject of some Committee inquiries.

**Mr. Arnold:** In declaring her interests earlier, can the hon. Lady tell us why she did not refer to her remunerated employment? Perhaps she can inform the House of the nature of that remunerated employment.

**Mrs. Taylor:** The entry in the Register of Members' Interests is entirely accurate. My interests appear there: sponsorship by the GMB and research assistance from ATL and Unison. That is a complete entry.

**Mr. Arnold:** Nothing in section 2?

**Mrs. Taylor:** There is nothing to declare in any other section and thus there is no other entry. If the hon. Gentleman wishes to take up that point in any other way, he may do so.

**Mr. Steen:** On a point of order, Madam Deputy Speaker. In the Register of Members' Interests, 22 May 1974 to June 1993 edition, it says that the hon. Member for Dewsbury (Mrs. Taylor) is adviser to the Association of Teachers and Lecturers. Is that true or false?

**Madam Deputy Speaker:** Order. It is entirely a matter for the hon. Member making the declaration to decide

*[Madam Deputy Speaker]*

what it is appropriate to declare. I know of nothing that requires an hon. Member to declare an interest that he or she no longer has.

**Mrs. Taylor:** I have mentioned ATL. I hope that the Whips' briefing to Conservative Members is more accurate on other matters.

**Mr. Steen:** Further to that point of order, Madam Deputy Speaker. This is the Register of Members' Interests as at 30 January 1995. As the Chancellor of the Duchy of Lancaster had to give full details of his interests to the House a moment ago because of Opposition Members' complaints, we ask the hon. Member for Dewsbury to do the same thing when she makes a speech.

**Madam Deputy Speaker:** Order. I have already explained that it is up to the hon. Members concerned to declare such interests as they consider are appropriate to the matter in hand.

**Mr. Garrett:** On a point of order, Madam Deputy Speaker. I raised a similar point of order with the Speaker when she was in the Chair and she said that at the start of every speech—but not an intervention—the hon. Member concerned should state his or her interests as they appear in the Register of Members' Interests. In opening the debate, the Minister failed to do that and I was forced to provoke him into admitting what his interests were.

**Madam Deputy Speaker:** Order. I understand that hon. Members should declare interests that are relevant to the matter under consideration.

**Mrs. Taylor:** Before I continue my speech, may I point out on that point of order—

**Mr. Garrett:** On a point of order, Madam Deputy Speaker.

**Madam Deputy Speaker:** Is it a different point of order?

**Mr. Garrett:** It is an absolutely genuine point of order. How can there be any difference between a statement of interests that are relevant to this debate and what appears in the Register of Members' Interests, because this is a debate about Members' interests, among other things?

**Madam Deputy Speaker:** I have already said absolutely that it is for the hon. Member concerned to declare any interests that he or she considers appropriate.

**Mrs. Taylor:** Not only have I declared every interest that I consider proper, but I have declared every interest that I have.

The point that I was making—it seems to cause significant embarrassment to Conservative Members— was that many people hoped that the establishment of the Nolan committee would mean a reduction in the number of allegations being made. We were hopeful that there would be a clean start and that significant progress could be made. Perhaps I should remind the House of Nolan's terms of reference. They were:

"To examine current concerns about standards of conduct of all holders of public office, including arrangements relating to financial and commercial activities, and make recommendations as to any changes in present arrangements which might be required to ensure the highest standards of propriety in public life".

Those terms of reference imply that the House will take action on any suggestions that the Committee makes.

When the committee's establishment was announced, my right hon. Friend the Leader of the Opposition described it as a plainly sensible and fully necessary move, and promised our full co-operation. I can agree with one thing that the Chancellor of the Duchy said today—we should congratulate the Nolan committee on quickly setting about its task and defining its initial priorities.

I want to deal with the three areas that form the subject of the report published last week. They are: Members' interests; the vexed issue of the employment of former Ministers on the boards of companies, and especially privatised companies with which they had dealings as Ministers; and the issue of patronage which has been exercised in a partisan way when making appointments, particularly to quangos.

The committee took evidence from a wide range of people, in person and in writing. It also took evidence from the Chancellor of the Duchy of Lancaster, from the Leader of the House, from me and from colleagues. We should place on record our thanks for, and admiration and recognition of, the Committee's work.

The report does not contain all the answers to the problems that face us, but then it does not claim to. It is an important first step. The report was unanimous. Lord Nolan sets great store by that fact, and so should we when we come to consider his recommendations.

This must have been a rather strange day for the Chancellor of the Duchy, because he has been forced to accept the thrust of the Nolan report, yet all its conclusions reject the approach that he took when he gave evidence on 7 February. His evidence that day was amazingly complacent. He dismissed, as he did at times this afternoon, many of the concerns as slurs, innuendo and often downright lies. He said that he believed that the Government should be

"determined to ensure that standards of conduct in public service are maintained".

He seemed to be satisfied to leave it there. It is precisely that satisfaction with existing standards that most worries us. No one could, no one should, and I hope no one would issue a blanket condemnation of all Members of Parliament. It is simply not true to say that they all behave as badly as the few who have brought the House into disrepute. But to imply, as the right hon. Gentleman has, that there was no real problem is to do our reputation no good at all.

**Mr. Nigel Spearing** (Newham, South): Surely the real problem is that too many Members of the House regard a seat here as a negotiable asset for private gain, instead of a basis for a vocation. At the same time, they vote and urge others to vote to obstruct those with a vocation, such as doctors, nurses and teachers, and to press them into being short-term monetary contractors. Does that not go against the principles of Parliament and their Christian basis? If it is pursued too far, it could destroy both.

**Mrs. Taylor:** My hon. Friend is right to draw attention to that. In a way, he reinforces the real dangers, outlined by Lord Nolan, that could arise if we did not take action now.

**Mr. Duncan Smith:** Does the hon. Lady agree with the remark in chapter 1 of the report to the effect that much of the anxiety about standards in public life is not supported by the facts?

**Mrs. Taylor:** I have already said that, but I should add that too much of the anxiety has been caused by real problems—such as cash for questions and cash for amendments. It is no use pretending that there is not a real problem.

Giving evidence to the Nolan committee, the Leader of the House acknowledged that there was a real problem to which we had to attend. I want to deal this afternoon with the committee's specific recommendations and outline what our response should be. Then, if time allows, I should like to say a few words about the future work of the committee.

The Chancellor mentioned procedure for Ministers and the fact that the report is now a public document. But, when he gave evidence on 7 February this year, the right hon. Gentleman's attention was drawn by Lord Nolan to an interview that the former had given in which he was asked whether he wanted a change in the rules governing the taking up of outside employment by former Ministers. The Chancellor said:

"I have to say that I believe, and the Government believes, that it is still right to leave decisions about these matters to the judgement of individuals."

Pressed by Nolan to discover whether that meant that the Government wanted no change, the Chancellor reiterated his belief that the current rules were adequate, suggesting that all was well. I am glad that today he has backed down and said that the Government will accept the Nolan recommendations on the employment of former Ministers. I am not convinced that those recommendations can be the last word on the subject, however. We shall want to monitor developments and return to the matter when necessary, to see whether further changes have to be made.

Quangos were included in the inquiry because of the significant concern about them, to which hon. Members have already alluded. Of course there have always been quangos, but they have mushroomed in recent years, spending vast amounts of public money. In the past, there have been unwritten rules determining their balance, and they have never been the subject of such public concern before. That is not surprising, given the facts. Hon. Members have already referred to what Baroness Denton said about not knowingly appointing Labour nominees. Such issues give rise to great concern—not least because they tally with the experience of many of our constituents.

The Nolan recommendations on changing the appointments procedure for members of quangos will make a difference. Quite how significant that difference will be I am not sure, but it is important to realise that it is not, in itself, the answer to the growing problem of the quango state. The Chancellor and other Ministers must acknowledge that public anxiety is not just about who serves on quangos; it is also about their power and spending ability.

The Chancellor of the Duchy, in his evidence to the Nolan inquiry, said that quangos were a good form of accountability. I presume that he has never tried tabling a question about something for which a quango has responsibility. There is amazing complacency about the accountability of quangos. That complacency appeared,

surprisingly, to be shared by the Leader of the House during his statement on drugs last week, in which he said that the chief executives of the health authorities would take the lead in some respect because that form of quango gave the best form of accountability. Quangos may be accountable to the Government but they are not accountable to Parliament, and they are certainly not accountable to the public.

**Mr. Michael Shersby** (Uxbridge): I am sure that the hon. Lady will be aware that the Public Accounts Committee takes a close interest in the work of all quangos and has all the necessary powers to summon their representatives to appear to give evidence. Indeed, the PAC has done so, and its reports are published and debated in the House.

**Mrs. Taylor:** Yes, but there are still problems with auditing, which were referred to earlier. Indeed, the Nolan report touches on those problems. If anybody is to be complacent and claim that changes to the appointment system will remove all the problems that exist within a quango state, he will be deluding himself. He will not, however, delude the public.

**Mr. Alan Williams** (Swansea, West): Will my hon. Friend bear in mind the fact that if the PAC devoted all its hearings over the next 10 years to quangos, it would at the end of that period have discussed only a fraction of them?

**Mrs. Taylor:** That is probably the case. Even if the assiduous members of the Committee were to sit every day of the week, there would still be a monitoring problem.

**Mr. Shersby:** This is an extremely important matter. The hon. Lady has said that there are problems in auditing quangos' accounts. Having served on the PAC for 13 years, I can only say that the auditing of quangos' accounts by the National Audit Office is probably carried out to the highest standards that apply anywhere else in the world.

**Mrs. Taylor:** I am not criticising the NAO, but it can audit only a third of quangos' accounts. There is a real problem in auditing public money. I hope that the hon. Gentleman, who is obviously interested in these matters, will read the Nolan report again, and especially the concerns that Lord Nolan himself expresses about them. The public have a right to know what happens to their money. We must examine how they can be reassured that there will be better auditing procedures in future.

I move on to Members' interests. I shall make some specific suggestions in terms of a timetable that I hope the House will take on board in its consideration of where we should go from here. I accept the recommendations set out in the Nolan report. It is important that the House should move quickly. I am pleased that Lord Nolan has accepted many of the suggestions that I made when I gave evidence to his committee. I said—I believe that this is Lord Nolan's recommendation—that the Register of Members' Interests must be improved.

Contracts of external interest should be registered and available for public scrutiny. The amounts that Members are paid should be disclosed in broad terms. It is extremely important that these recommendations are implemented with all possible speed. Indeed, I believe

[*Mrs. Taylor*]

that the process must be started within the next few weeks. I want to see the framework for the new arrangements in place by the autumn. That means that the House must make positive decisions before the summer recess—indeed, as early as possible.

**Mr. Garel-Jones:** I agree broadly with what the hon. Lady is saying. Do I take it that she, like me, does not agree with the interesting suggestion made by my hon. Friend the Member for Wolverhampton, South-West (Mr. Budgen) and by the right hon. Member for Chesterfield (Mr. Benn) that the House should proceed by way of statute rather than through its own mechanisms, not least because adopting a statutory approach would cause greater delay?

**Mrs. Taylor:** The right hon. Gentleman makes a fair point. By resolution of the House, we can make many of the changes that Lord Nolan suggests. The House will need to consider these matters quickly after the Whitsun recess. We should aim at making the necessary changes as soon as possible.

**Mr. Budgen:** The House may not have objected to the original arrangements for registration, but the Nolan suggestions go a great deal further. They are designed not to deal with the way in which we serve in the House but to set down the terms and conditions of that service and to influence the way in which we behave outside the House. The House might have decided not to be difficult about registration, but if we are to take a major and radical step forward, which is said to be necessary, surely we should do so on the basis of something that is set out in statute so that for the future people will know the terms on which they will serve in this place.

**Mrs. Taylor:** If we make the changes that I shall suggest, anyone who wants to put himself forward at the next general election will be clear about the terms and conditions of his employment as a Member. The hon. Gentleman is making a bogus point that should not delay us.

**Mr. Patrick Nicholls** (Teignbridge): Will the hon. Lady explain—this is not explained in the Nolan report— the difference between income that is derived from advising a respectable organisation about its relationship with government and other forms of income? Why should income that is derived from advising such organisations be declared when the work of the right hon. Member for Birmingham, Sparkbrook (Mr. Hattersley) or that of my hon. Friend the Member for Derbyshire, South (Mrs. Currie), who publish works that no one would read apart from the fact that it is thought that they carry some authority because they are produced by Members—the hon. Member for Great Grimsby (Mr. Mitchell), who is a broadcaster, provides another example—need not be declared? There are, of course, parliamentary silks on both sides of the House. Why should uniquely the money from one source be published but not that from the other? Would it have anything to do—I offer this to the hon. Lady in the spirit of helpfulness—with the fact that there are more parliamentary advisers on the Conservative

Benches than on the Opposition Benches and at least as many parliamentary silks on the Opposition Benches as on the Conservative Benches?

**Mrs. Taylor:** The hon. Gentleman may be pushing some of my hon. Friends into saying, "Publish the lot." I think that Lord Nolan was trying to make it clear that our first responsibility is to ensure that the public know of any income that we receive only because we are Members. That is one of the keys.

**Mr. Nicholls** *rose*—

**Mrs. Taylor:** I may be helpful to the hon. Gentleman. I shall deal with the point in more detail. The hon. Gentleman is not known for his patience, but it would be helpful if in this instance he were patient. I want to make what I hope are some constructive and positive suggestions about the way in which we should proceed.

**Mrs. Teresa Gorman** (Billericay): Will the hon. Lady give way before she moves on?

**Mrs. Taylor:** Yes.

**Mrs. Gorman:** Does the hon. Lady agree that it is important for Members who receive research assistance that is paid for by outside bodies such as trade unions— for example, Unison, which I understand is sponsoring many research assistants for members of the Opposition Front Bench—to make a declaration?

**Mrs. Taylor:** It is clear that the hon. Lady has not read the register in much detail. Money of the sort to which she refers is declared. It should be in the register, and under the new system the amounts involved should be there. We on the Opposition Benches are happy with that proposal and willing to comply with it.

The most important question for us to consider is how we proceed from this point. The way in which we move to implement the Nolan recommendations is the most important issue facing us. The House must take an early decision on the principles of the changes to the register as recommended by Lord Nolan, including the full disclosure of contracts and payments.

The vote on the principle of that has to be separated from the definition of some of the details and, perhaps, the income bandings that would apply, because Lord Nolan has made suggestions and given guidance but not exact definitions. The fact that details have to be established is no excuse for delay. The Select Committee on Members' Interests may well be able to do that and, in normal circumstances, that is the approach that the House would consider.

**Mr. Garel-Jones:** Given that, like her, I think that the whole House wants to be certain that the resolutions that are put to the House are clear not only to Members but to the public, would the hon. Lady think it helpful if the matter, rather than being referred to the Members' Interests Select Committee—which, she is right, is the obvious place—were considered by a committee of senior Members who have already announced their intention to leave the House in this Parliament? [*Interruption.*] I suggest that because such Members would not only command the respect of the House but may command respect outside the House with the general public on the ground that they are unlikely to be thought to have any personal and continuing interest in the matter.

**Mrs. Taylor:** If we were starting from scratch and considering the matter for the first time, that might be a way forward, but we are not. We have Lord Nolan's suggestions and framework. I fear that the right hon. Gentleman's suggestion would be a mechanism for delay, and that is what we cannot have. I hope that the House agrees that we must have an early decision to accept Lord Nolan's recommendations in principle and then move to the mechanisms for working out the necessary detail.

I come now to the need for a code of conduct. I am firmly of the belief that the rules that guide our behaviour as Members of Parliament are in "Erskine May" and we, as Members of Parliament, should all be aware of them. Lord Nolan draws attention to the decisions of the Privileges Committee, going back as far as 1947, which are still the basis of those rules. It is clear to anyone who reads "Erskine May" on aspects relevant to Members' interests that Members of Parliament are not allowed to take cash for questions, amendments, speeches or anything of that kind.

If some hon. Members feel that that is not clear—I accept that not all hon. Members have always consulted "Erskine May"—it may be wise, as I suggested to Lord Nolan, to draw up a code of conduct. Again, we can move on that quickly. I suggest that we ask the Clerk of the House of Commons to draft a code of conduct based on the provisions in "Erskine May" which could then be discussed, amended if necessary, and adopted by the House. I hope that the Clerk of the House would consider that appropriate and I think that the House would appreciate such guidance from such a respected quarter. I hope that there can be cross-party agreement on that.

Another aspect of the Nolan proposals that needs to be acted upon quickly is the suggestion that there should be a parliamentary commissioner for standards. The Nolan report states:

"By analogy with the Comptroller and Auditor General, the House should appoint as Parliamentary Commissioner for Standards, a person of independent standing who will take over responsibility for maintaining the Register of Members' Interests; for advice and guidance to MPs on matters of conduct; for advising on the Code of Conduct; and for investigating allegations of misconduct. The Commissioners' conclusions on such matters would be published."

I accept that suggestion. Such an independent element is vital to restore public confidence in the workings of the House.

**Sir Terence Higgins** (Worthing): Does the hon. Lady think that the recommendations should be published before or after they have been considered by the Privileges Committee?

**Mrs. Taylor:** If a recommendation from the ethics officer, or whatever he is called—*[Interruption.]* I do not see why such a person should not be called an ethics officer or the parliamentary commissioner for standards. If hon. Members say that they are worried about the name, they are creating a smokescreen. Conservative Members may not welcome independent scrutiny, but it is the least that the public are entitled to. Any recommendation by an independent officer concerning a particular Member that

is not accepted by the Committee and any indiscretions that have taken place should be made public. That is important.

**Mr. Nicholls:** My recollection may be entirely false, but I seem to recall that the hon. Lady once worked as a consultant for a firm of parliamentary advisers. Can she confirm that that is so? Why was she presumably content to be a parliamentary adviser then, but apparently now feels embarrassed about it? If she did publish her earnings at the time—or perhaps if she did not—why is she now so keen that everybody else should?

**Mrs. Taylor:** The hon. Gentleman really should take the issue more seriously. The right hon. Member for Worthing (Sir T. Higgins) asked a significant question on the detail of how the parliamentary commissioner for standards would work. We should concentrate on that. Do we want to make constructive progress as a result of the debate or do Conservative Members want to create a smokescreen so that they can bury the Nolan report and its recommendations?

**Mr. Nicholls:** On a point of order, Madam Deputy Speaker. I made a specific allegation that the hon. Member for Dewsbury (Mrs. Taylor) once worked for a parliamentary lobbyist. There is nothing wrong with that. I did as well. But we need an answer to the question.

**Madam Deputy Speaker:** That is not a point of order for the Chair, as the hon. Gentleman should well know. I do not expect to hear anything further from him on that point.

**Mrs. Taylor:** I repeat, ad nauseam, that my interests are in the register. If we are to have a serious discussion about this, let us move on.

The right hon. Member for Worthing (Mr. Higgins) asked about the parliamentary commissioner for standards. I hope that hon. Members will accept in principle that such an independent officer is necessary to restore public confidence in our system. It is important, not least because of the many difficulties that have occurred when Members have tried to investigate complaints, either those lodged with the Members' Interests Select Committee or those serious complaints that have been brought before the Privileges Committee.

**Mr. Patrick McLoughlin** (West Derbyshire): The hon. Lady said a moment ago that she believed that the findings of the parliamentary commissioner for standards should be made public even where they have been rejected by a Committee of the House. Does that mean that an outsider coming in might choose, as Lord Nolan did on arriving in the House, to announce at the beginning of his hearing one of his principal findings and that that should eventually be made public before any evidence has been heard?

**Mrs. Taylor:** The hon. Gentleman clearly has not read the Nolan report and recommendations. That is not what Lord Nolan is suggesting.

**Mr. Julian Brazier** (Canterbury): It was the hon. Lady's answer—not Nolan.

**Mrs. Taylor:** The hon. Member for West Derbyshire (Mr. McLoughlin) doth protest too much. The fact that he has not read the report and its recommendations, and so does not know the context in which I am speaking, is his

[*Mrs. Taylor*]

failing. I would have thought that he should do his homework before coming to such an important debate. Lord Nolan makes clear the circumstances in which such hearings should be published. One of the things that pleases the Opposition and that we appreciate about Lord Nolan's report is that he accepts our case that, wherever possible, the Privileges Committee should sit in public. That is a significant step forward.

**Sir Peter Hordern** (Horsham): Will the hon. Lady take into account the fact that many complaints are lodged before the Comptroller and Auditor General about his work in the public sector and that most of those never see the light of day? I assume that she is proposing that, if complaints are lodged against hon. Members, the official, whoever it may be, would work in a similar way to the CAG, that he would sift out what was necessary to refer to the Privileges Committee, as the CAG does in relation to the Public Accounts Committee, that he would make his report, but that it would always be up to the Privileges Committee to decide whether there was substance in that report.

**Mrs. Taylor:** The right hon. Gentleman understands the position completely. He also understands the concept of an appointment, which other Members do not. The officer would sift every inquiry. The officer would be charged with recommending to the Privileges Committee or to the Sub-Committee which Lord Nolan suggests whether there was a prima facie case. Any inquiry would be made only in those circumstances, and several layers of suggestion are recommended in the Nolan report, but, at the end of the day, Lord Nolan says that evidence and decisions must be made in public.

**Mr. Leigh:** Will the hon. Lady give way?

**Mrs. Taylor:** No. I must make some progress and some other suggestions.

It seems that some Conservative Members do not want to have a serious debate on this matter, but we need to make some positive suggestions about what should happen. Some hon. Members are under a misapprehension about the proposal for a parliamentary commissioner for standards. I have heard it said that such a proposal would undermine the sovereignty of the House. That is not the case. It is being suggested not that Parliament's sovereignty should be diminished but that our work should be assisted by someone who is independent and in whom the public can have a high degree of confidence.

**Ms Eagle:** Does my hon. Friend agree that it is a good idea to work on these proposals, as the Select Committee on Members' Interests sometimes has difficulty gathering evidence? The fact that it has limited resources to do so in relation to issues that are often of great importance to the Members concerned must be borne in mind.

**Mrs. Taylor:** My hon. Friend has significant experience of the difficulties of serving as a member of that Committee. Its members, who have had to deal with many complaints in the recent past, have found it difficult. I recognise the problem there. It would be helpful to them

or to their successors in the Sub-Committee of the Privileges Committee if they had the assistance of someone of that sort.

**Mr. Leigh:** Will the hon. Lady give way?

**Mrs. Taylor:** We should move on to consider what sort of person and what sort of position this is. My suggestion to the Nolan committee, and the suggestion that is in its report, is that we should consider the position with regard to the Comptroller and Auditor General, who is appointed by letters patent on the advice of the Prime Minister following consultation with the Chairman of the Public Accounts Committee. We could consider the way in which the parliamentary ombudsmen is appointed. It is extremely important that we should move very quickly. We should aim to have someone in place by the beginning of the new parliamentary Session in the autumn.

**Mr. Steen:** I deeply resent the implication in Nolan that all of us are crooks. Does the hon. Lady believe that appointing an ethics officer, as she is implying, will solve the whole problem for the nation, and that all the problems that she says exist will disappear as soon as that officer is appointed? Why does she think that that will happen?

**Mrs. Taylor:** The hon. Gentleman clearly has not read Lord Nolan's report or his recommendations. That is a slur on Lord Nolan and all the members of the committee. There is no suggestion in the report that all Members of the House are crooks. Hon. Members resent Members on any side making such allegations. I hope that the hon. Gentleman will reconsider what he has said.

**Mr. Leigh** *rose—*

**Mrs. Taylor:** I must move on because I have a serious point to make. I sometimes think that Conservative Members are not interested in serious points.

The changes that have been recommended by Lord Nolan could come into place relatively quickly. There are other changes that will take a little longer and will need some discussion—for example, those to our Committee procedure, including changes in relation to the Privileges Committee and the possible establishment of a Sub-Committee. That is important. One of the factors that we must bear in mind is that those changes must not be allowed to cause any hiatus by which any of the outstanding matters subject to investigation by Committees fall by the wayside. Important investigations are still being undertaken by the Privileges Committee and by the Select Committee on Members' Interests. We must protect those investigations, despite the difficulties and, sometimes, inadequacies of our procedures. We must ensure that that happens. It is important to ensure that all those outstanding investigations are completed in a proper way.

As I said, there is a need for urgency on this matter—I cannot stress that enough. The public will not understand why, having received Lord Nolan's report, we do not accept it and move on from there. It was extraordinary to listen to the Prime Minister's responses at Question Time to the questions of my right hon. Friend the Leader of the Opposition. The Prime Minister set up an independent review body to investigate standards of conduct in public life, not least because of the concern caused by some of his own Back Benchers. The Nolan committee has recommended that Members of Parliament should reveal their interests, including the amount that they are paid by outside bodies. That is one of the Nolan committee's most central points, and we accept that recommendation.

Today, however, the Prime Minister announced not only that he did not have a view as to whether those central recommendations should be accepted by the House but that he was now prepared to leave the decision to the very same Back Benchers whose financial interests brought the House into disrepute in the first place. That is a remarkable admission by the Prime Minister and it shows perhaps that his concern about our image and the workings of the House is skin-deep.

**Mr. Garrett:** Does my hon. Friend recognise that there will be great pressure on a future Labour Government to increase restraints on outside earnings by Members of Parliament, whatever the hardship that that causes among those on the Conservative Benches, and that we should think hard about what we are going to do, so that we can produce policies that enable Members on both sides of the House who fear such restraints to refrain from running in the next election?

**Mrs. Taylor:** My hon. Friend is right. Whatever we decide today—and, indeed, any action that we take as a consequence of Lord Nolan's recommendations—will not constitute the last word. Problems remain, and we shall have to return to them on other occasions.

I wanted to discuss the future work of the Nolan committee in connection with the need for a register in the House of Lords, the need for an inquiry into local government and the urgent need for an inquiry into party political funding. We shall have to deal with those issues at a later date. I have, however, made positive suggestions in regard to how the House could amend the Register of Members' Interests so that interests and payments are fully declared. I have also suggested a code of conduct for hon. Members, the work being led by the Clerk of the House, and the appointment of a parliamentary commissioner for standards.

Those are things that the House can do in the near future. If we are to begin to restore public confidence in our democracy, our parliamentary system and the House of Commons, we must get on with them as quickly as possible.

5.40 pm

**Sir Edward Heath** (Old Bexley and Sidcup): Before Madam Speaker left the Chair, she asked two things of us: that we declare our interests, and that we speak briefly. I immediately declare my interests, which are set out on the record that was filled in, in the usual way, at the beginning of the year. It is absolutely accurate, and I regret to say that there has been no increase since it was written.

I shall endeavour to be brief. I do not intend to discuss many aspects of the report—particularly the civil service; it has always had its orders, instructions and regulations, and they must be reviewed from time to time. I must emphasise, however, that the number of cases involving lack of integrity in our civil service is minimal compared with that in other countries. Our civil service is the envy of most of the rest of the world.

I agree that we should look at quangos. I am not in favour of increasing the number of quangos; I am in favour of reducing it. They have taken over many of the proper occupations of elected members of local government, and that can be dealt with. As for the audit, I always greatly respect what is said by the right hon. Member for Ashton-under-Lyne (Mr. Sheldon), and his views should be given serious consideration.

Let me again declare an interest: I am a member of the public review board of Arthur Andersen, the world's largest firm of accountants, and I am aware of the relationship between accountants and their clients. Our accountants are not allowed to have lunch with their clients, because they might then be accused of being influenced by those clients when reaching the conclusions in their reports. I do not propose to discuss that in detail, however; I propose to discuss matters which affect the House.

I have seldom found myself in greater disagreement with the hon. Member for Dewsbury (Mrs. Taylor) than I have this evening. She constantly emphasised the question of public unease. I must confess that public unease about this matter will not have been lessened by the conduct of the House during the debate. Moreover, the part played by the House in public unease—of which I am fully aware, as it is constantly demonstrated in reports of public opinion—is minute in comparison with public unease about other aspects of our national life. I immediately recognise those other aspects of public unease, and they must be put right, but they do not involve the House.

The hon. Member for Dewsbury constantly emphasised the need for haste. What is necessary is proper consideration. When haste overtakes proper consideration, we often end up with the wrong answer. I have criticised our own Government for that: they rush in and make decisions without proper consideration. The House should not fall prey to such an approach.

When I entered the House 45 years ago, in 1950, we recognised every Member of Parliament—man or woman—as a person of integrity. That was the attitude, and it was fully accepted. We have now reached a stage at which every man and woman in the House is an object of suspicion. Why has that come about? I do not consider it healthy or satisfactory, and we must not fall prey to that approach either.

In those days, chairmen of major companies were Members of Parliament, as were trade union leaders. Both groups made important contributions and, I believe, benefited from being here, mixing with other right hon. and hon. Members and hearing debates at first hand. I was sorry when the trade union movement ruled that union leaders could no longer become Members of Parliament. I think that that was a grave mistake: the unions lost by it, and we in the House of Commons lost by it.

When a company chairman addressed the House, he would merely say, "I remind the House that I am chairman of such and such a company, which is engaged in such and such activities." All that was accepted; we knew about it anyway. It was not necessary to make such a declaration at Question Time, because it took up time unnecessarily. That is how the system operated, and it operated satisfactorily. We now have an entirely different situation, which I think is regrettable.

How often, during my time here, have we had a major problem? We had a problem in the mid-1970s, involving three Members of Parliament. The Committee of Privileges had its hearings; Reggie Maudling was

[*Sir Edward Heath*]

exonerated, another Member resigned and a verdict was delivered on the third. That was that: everyone recognised that we had done our duty, and done it properly.

Recently, two Members of Parliament were set up by a national newspaper and unfortunately fell wrong. The case was investigated immediately; a conclusion was reached, the House debated it and action was taken. The Members were suspended for two different terms, and lost their remuneration during that time.

There is no reason for anxiety about that. We were carrying out our duty, and doing it properly: there were no problems. So where are all the other cases? In 45 years, I can recall only those two instances, one involving three Members and the other two. We ought to pride ourselves on the fact that we dealt with those cases at once. It is now proposed that we set up a bureaucratic organisation—for it is bound to be bureaucratic. What will it be able to do to find out what is going on? We in the House know far more about what is going on with our fellow Members than any bureaucrat brought in from outside. We have our own machinery for dealing with such matters. We all have a Whips Office, and we can suggest the necessary action.

**Ms Eagle:** Will the right hon. Gentleman give way?

**Sir Edward Heath:** Not for a moment. I want to finish what I am saying.

What can that gentleman do? He cannot go into the Smoking Room and say, "By the way, have you heard such and such about so and so? Do you think that I should look into it?" This is a practical problem. What saddens me about Lord Nolan is that, although he is an admirable judge, he seems to lack a certain worldliness—an ability to realise what actually goes on in this world of ours. We must be careful not to fall into that trap.

The next question is how much we should include in the register. I fully accept that Opposition Members, and perhaps some Conservative Members, are in anguish about the fact that all this information is not public and published. Let me relieve them of their anguish: nothing whatever—legal, political, party or domestic—prevents any of them from publishing every detail of their public and private lives. They can publish all their earnings, their wives' earnings and their family earnings; they can publish the amount that they give in housekeeping money, where they go for their holidays and who pays for their meals. They can publish everything. I do not know why they hesitate. They would be in a very strong position: they could say, "This is the new Labour party—we publish it all." One might add, "Please don't write to the wife saying that she ought to get more housekeeping money." One could add such provisos the whole time. All those things can be printed. I guarantee that if every Opposition Member, in anguish, now gives full details of their public and private lives, I will get a publisher, and I will put that in the register as an interest—a very close interest.

We must be sensible about the matter. There is such a thing as the privacy of the individual. I have always understood that that was one of the important tenets of the philosophy of the Labour party. It believes in the privacy of the individual: very well, then—let it support that in this House. What shall we gain by setting out all that information? It will be a serious blow to democracy in this country. [*Interruption.*] There is nothing to laugh at, because there are examples of what has happened elsewhere.

There is the example, in particular, of the United States after Watergate, when the behaviour of the press and others to the families involved was so appalling that many people whom I know in the United States said that they would never put themselves in a position where the privacy of their families could be destroyed as it was destroyed for those who were involved in Watergate. The result has been that such people have not gone into American public life. That is plain to see for anyone who has studied the subject. I do not want that to happen in Britain. People will say that they are not prepared to be subjected to the sort of inquiries that the new bureaucrat would carry out, the results of which would lead to the information being put in the register. It is bad enough as it is.

I shall give a personal example. Last year, there was a row over Lloyd's, which is still being misrepresented in this week's press. It is said that we deliberately confronted the Members' Interests Committee and refused to do what it wanted. We did not do that. We asked for a discussion and we got one. My hon. Friend the Member for Wealden (Sir G. Johnson Smith), the Chairman of that Committee, is here. After nearly two hours of discussion, the Committee realised that the situation was not what it had thought when it had discussed the matter alone and it quite properly changed its view. That was the proper procedure to follow.

Yet that story still appears. The press and *The Guardian* have not yet apologised. They took my photograph outside today, so perhaps that will lead to something. There were other accusations about our losses and debts meaning that we would have to leave Parliament. I have no debts to Lloyd's. Why should I be tied up with losses of £22 million? That is the sort of thing that is happening. It will be much worse if we start trying to put all that into the register.

It has been suggested that the arrangements should be specified, or even put into statute. That is not humanly possible. There are so many cases to consider. If I have lunch with a friend in business and that friend is then made chairman of a firm, what am I to do about it? Do I have to stop lunching with him? What happens if an *Evening Standard* correspondent sees us lunching together in some restaurant and then writes that I will do what the chairman of that company wants? It is an impossible position. [Hon. Members: "That is trivialising the debate."] It is Opposition Members who are trivialising it.

**Mr. Spearing:** Will the right hon. Gentleman give way?

**Sir Edward Heath:** I am sorry, but I am doing rather well and I do not want to be interrupted.

I recently entertained a diplomat and others at lunch. We had a happy party. He sent me a nice letter of thanks and a bottle of port. What should I do? Should I immediately ask that it be published in the register that I received a bottle of port? Or should I tell the diplomat, "I am awfully sorry; you are very kind, but I am afraid that I have to return it to you. Otherwise, it will be alleged that I will help the company with its problems." Rightly or wrongly, I decided to do neither. All that I did was to write thanking him very much for a bottle of 1970 port, although I would have much preferred 1927.

The great danger is that the Nolan report will damage the House. It will also damage the Labour party, because the new members being sought for the new Labour party in the hope of forming a new Government will not be attracted by the kind of proposals to which the hon. Member for Dewsbury has given her full consent.

The leader of the Labour party said some astonishing things this afternoon. He said that the Nolan committee is the Prime Minister's committee. It is nothing of the sort: it is an independent committee. The right hon. Gentleman also said that because the committee had reported we must accept it and put its proposals into operation straight away. It is not for a moment the job of the House automatically to accept committee reports. The report has to be thoroughly examined and dealt with. If we do that, people outside who understand such things will say that we have acted rather sensibly. It will then lie in our hands to deal with the problems which really cause public unease.

**Mr. Spearing:** The right hon. Gentleman talks about public unease and the changes between the 1950s and the 1990s. Does he agree that the real reason for public unease is the devaluation of the ethic of public service, of public services and, by a few hon. Members, of the office of Member of Parliament? That is the trouble.

**Sir Edward Heath:** I have dealt with Members of Parliament. We dealt with those problems at once and satisfactorily in the House and people realise that.

One matter to which the hon. Member for Dewsbury referred in rather covert form, and which has caused public unease over the past two or three years, is the question of sexual behaviour, which Nolan does not mention. However, the chap in the pub does not talk about setting up an extra bureaucrat to deal with these things; he talks about hon. Members and their sexual behaviour. That has caused a great deal of public unease.

Lord Nolan can do nothing about that problem. He can set out requirements, one of which concerns ethics, but how will he define "ethical"? Hon. Members have many different ethical beliefs, and that is rightly so. To try to typify that and say what every Member of Parliament has to adhere to, believe in and accept as ethical bears no resemblance to human life or the world at large.

I hope that every hon. Member will give the matter serious thought and consideration. Let us abandon inter-party warfare and get down to the things that really affect the public.

5.57 pm

**Mr. Peter Shore** (Bethnal Green and Stepney): It is a pleasure to follow the right hon. Member for Old Bexley and Sidcup (Sir E. Heath). As Father of the House, he speaks with special authority on those matters that particularly concern the House and which have been dealt with in the Nolan report.

I must say to the right hon. Gentleman, with all proper respect, that I think that he has misjudged two things. First, there is the extent of public unease about the things that have been going on in the House. To describe that public unease as small is, frankly, not to recognise the unhappy truth of the matter. I wish, indeed, that it was so. I wish that the matter could be swept aside, because, like all hon. Members, I have a keen regard for the reputation of House and believe that its reputation is essential to the proper working of our democracy.

Secondly, I disagree with what the right hon. Gentleman said about the changes since 1950, when he first came into the House—not that there have not been huge changes, and the right hon. Gentleman described some of them fairly and well. He missed one of the most significant things that has occurred during the past 20 or 25 years: the growth of consultancies. I am talking not about the increase in the number of Members of Parliament having outside jobs and interests, much of which, I think, adds to the experience and authority of the House, but about the practice of Members of Parliament hiring themselves out to external interests in return for reward.

Those Members are trading not their accumulated knowledge and wisdom gained from whatever occupations they had previously and are continuing but the special privilege that they have precisely because they are Members of Parliament—access to Ministers and the undoubtedly greater opportunity that they have to further and favour particular causes. That, in my view, is what lies at the centre of the concern about Members of Parliament. I shall come back to that issue in a moment.

The right hon. Member for Old Bexley and Sidcup said that the demand for openness is often carried much too far. He is certainly right to warn us about following the American route. The idea that we should all publish our income tax returns is nonsense. It does nothing to improve public confidence in Members of Parliament but does much to undermine their own self-respect and standing in the community.

There is no proposal in the Nolan report that Members of Parliament should, as it were, reveal any income derived from any source, other than that which they earn for being Members of Parliament and thus employed by consultancies. No one is saying that a farmer, insurance agent, stockbroker, artist or author will have to declare his income. We are concerned only with those incomes related to what happens in the House.

**Mr. McLoughlin** *rose—*

**Mr. Shore:** No. I now put that point to one side.

I deal now with the most serious point made by a number of hon. Members and which was touched on by the right hon. Member for Old Bexley and Sidcup, especially in an interview that he gave this morning on Radio 4. A number of writers have also dealt with it, including Mr. Simon Heffer who wrote in *The Daily Telegraph* yesterday that Nolan's recommendations involve the

"over-arching constitutional danger of Parliament surrendering the right to regulate itself to a committee".

Clearly, that refers to the proposal to appoint a parliamentary commissioner for standards. It is true that he would have the power to investigate complaints made to him and to initiate inquiries. However, serious complaints would be referred by him, as the report makes plain, to a Committee of the House. The most appropriate Committee would appear to be the Privileges Committee or a sub-Committee of it, as the report suggests.

That Committee would, as now, carry out investigations into allegations of misconduct and decide what, if any, penalties were appropriate. In other words, a Committee of the House—the Privileges Committee—would decide, not someone from outside. It would continue to make the decisions and recommendations and the House would

[*Mr. Shore*]

retain the right to say yea or nay to the Privileges Committee. There is a big difference between that and the impression that has been given that the commissioner for standards would do something on his own account to take over the workings of the House.

**Mr. Leigh** *rose*—

**Mr. Shore:** No, not yet.

The analogies that the committee had in mind when that proposal was made were with the Comptroller and Auditor General and the Parliamentary Commissioner for Administration, to whom my hon. Friend the Member for Dewsbury (Mrs. Taylor) has already referred. Indeed, the Comptroller and Auditor General today has considerable power of investigation, but he works to and assists the Public Accounts Committee, which has the on-going responsibility to invigilate Government expenditure. Similarly, it is Members of Parliament who hold the Executive and the Executive's servants to account for what they do, but they are assisted in this work by the Parliamentary Commissioner for Administration, who also has independent powers of investigation. No one seriously suggests that the appointment of either the Comptroller and Auditor General or the Commissioner has involved the surrender of parliamentary rights and duties. That analogy must be considered seriously in judging this proposal. The job of the Parliamentary Commissioner for Standards would be to assist, not replace, responsibilities in the House of Commons already exercised by the relevant Select Committees and the House itself.

I hope that what I have said has allayed some anxieties.

**Sir Edward Heath:** I think that the right hon. Gentleman has missed the point, but we clearly disagree. What I object to is someone from outside cross-questioning us as Members of Parliament and then deciding whether there is something that he should refer to a committee. That is out of the question; Members of Parliament should deal with matters as they do at the moment.

**Mr. Shore:** It is more of a procedural matter. We can go into it in detail. I am very much in favour of further detailed consideration by the House, perhaps in the form of a motion moved by the Leader of the House or in the relevant Select Committees. What we are dealing with in this Second Reading debate, if it can be so described, is the broad proposition which is analogous with the role of the Comptroller and Auditor General and the Parliamentary Commissioner for Administration.

**Mr. Shersby:** Does the right hon. Gentleman agree that the responsibility of the Comptroller and Auditor General is for matters of economy, efficiency and effectiveness in Government Departments and by the accounting officers for those Departments—or, in other words, the civil service? The Comptroller and Auditor General has no remit whatever to supervise the economy, efficiency and effectiveness of this sovereign Parliament, so I suggest that the right hon. Gentleman's analogy is not strictly correct.

**Mr. Shore:** I willingly concede that it is not too precise, but the Parliamentary Commissioner for Administration investigates individual complaints and comes up with information that Members of Parliament have probably tried to find themselves. They have probably found it impossible to get and are therefore assisted by the Parliamentary Commissioner.

I wish to comment on one or two general points that have emerged from the debate so far. I was relatively pleased with the opening speech of the Chancellor of the Duchy of Lancaster. It is good to know that the Government have accepted a number of the proposals without demur. It is important that we should go ahead with the proposals for scrutinising the appointment of ex-Ministers who are applying for jobs immediately after they have left office. That is right. It works very well with senior civil servants and I see no reason why it should not work well with ex-Ministers.

I am also pleased that the code of conduct for civil servants is to go ahead and that new channels, as it were, of appeal will be made available. That is very important.

On the general question of quangos, I am sure that the new procedures will help. My hon. Friend the Member for Dewsbury made the much larger point that the very role of quangos needs to be reconsidered, but that was not a matter for the Nolan committee. We were dealing above all with how members were appointed to quangos and whether the procedures could be made less vulnerable to criticism and less prone—I put it no more strongly—to the exercise of political patronage than quangos inevitably are today. I think that the suggested procedures will help.

**Mr. McLoughlin:** May I take the right hon. Gentleman back a little to what he said about the way in which the Nolan committee, of which he was a distinguished member, came to its conclusion on which payments to hon. Members should be published? How did the committee distinguish between remuneration from a newspaper article written by a Member of Parliament as a result of his membership of the House and remuneration of a Member of Parliament for his appointment as a non-executive director of a company, offered to him simply because he was a Member of the House and had some influence?

**Mr. Shore:** We can debate that in detail later, but common sense should tell the hon. Gentleman that there is a difference between a Member of Parliament writing an article and being paid for it and a Member of Parliament receiving an undeclared sum of money to use his influence on behalf of a commercial firm or enterprise. He ought to understand that difference, but, if he does not, we are in some trouble.

I shall devote the remainder of my speech to the issue of consultancies, which is very much at the heart of our concerns. There is a class of consultancies which the Nolan committee thinks is sufficiently clear and objectionable to recommend a straightforward ban. In paragraph 55 under the heading "General consultancies" the committee states,

"we can see no justification for consultancy agreements between Members and public relations or lobbying firms, which are themselves acting as advisers and advocates for a constantly changing range of miscellaneous and often undisclosed interests . . . We consider that this is precisely the situation which the Prime Minister has described as 'a hiring fair'."

So much for the moment for that class of consultancies, but that does not settle the matter. According to figures derived from the 1995 Register of Members' Interests, only 26 hon. Members have consultancy agreements with public relations or lobbying firms, while a further 142 have consultancies with other types of companies or with trade associations. In addition, 27 hon. Members have paid consultancies with trade unions, including the Police Federation. They are generally unions not affiliated to the Labour party but those that are affiliated support, through a different form of sponsorship, some 184 hon. Members by making payments to their constituency parties and to their general election funds. Those trade union arrangements may well have to be scrutinised, but I do not think that I am being partisan when I say that it is the 142 paid consultancies with companies and trade associations which are the focus of public concern.

What are the rules affecting these and other consultancies? The rules of Parliament are far from clear. Reference has been made to the 1947 resolution which stated that there should be,

"no contractual agreement with an outside body controlling or limiting the Member's complete independence or stipulating that he should act in any way as a representative of such an outside body."

That seems clear enough in dealing with contractual agreements that have been entered into by an hon. Member with an outside financial interest. But then the question arises: what about paid consultancies which are not binding in the sense of the words that are used in the 1947 resolution but which nevertheless involved a Member using his influence voluntarily but not contractually for the same ends? What about consultancies that are wholly or mainly advisory in which a Member of Parliament undertakes not to initiate any action in the House but consents only to give general advice to an outside body on parliamentary affairs?

An attempt to stiffen the rules on consultancies was made in 1969 by the Strauss committee which was also a committee on Members' interests. Its recommendation is worth reading because it is very important. It stated:

"it is contrary to the usage and dignity of the House that a Member should bring forward by any speech or question, or advocate in this House or among his fellow Members any Bill, Motion, matter or cause for a fee, payment, retainer or reward, direct or indirect, which he has received, is receiving or expects to receive."

That is a strong recommendation, and perhaps that explains why the Strauss committee resolution was never debated and the Front Benches of both parties agreed to put it on one side.

The Strauss approach draws a clear line between advocacy, using the facilities of the House, and advice given to people externally, and recommends that we should be very severe against advocacy. That approach is rather attractive, but it is by no means easy, as the House will recognise, to define with precision the difference between advocacy and advice. They tend to overlap.

**Mr. Garel-Jones:** As the right hon. Gentleman says, the devil in this matter is in the detail. I shall give my own case. I work as an adviser for British Petroleum. Before signing a contract with the company, I had an exchange of letters in which it was made perfectly clear that on no account would I raise questions, lobby or be active for it in the House. My activities for the company are entirely confined to Latin America. It would be naive to think that a company such as BP does not have a public affairs department. There is an inevitable interface with Parliament and Government, and from time to time people

in the public affairs department telephone me and ask for my advice on a particular matter. Naturally, I give my advice.

I hope that the House will be careful and will speedily implement Nolan's recommendations and that, above all, it will be detailed. I am sure that I speak for many of my hon. Friends when I say that I want clear guidance. I want to know where I stand and if the guidance that the House gives is not acceptable to me I shall take the consequences, and so will the House.

**Mr. Shore:** I am grateful to the right hon. Gentleman for that intervention because it clearly illustrates the difference between consultancies. The one that he describes is clearly aimed at giving information and advice outside, and the right hon. Gentleman is not being used to achieve particular objectives for the company. The House must seriously explore consultancies to see whether a line can be firmly drawn or whether it must be drawn elsewhere.

There is another complication. Must a distinction be drawn between the commercial sponsorship of Members of Parliament and charitable, professional and trade union bodies which also appoint Members of Parliament as consultants on the general understanding that, while they are not bound by their sponsor's wishes, they will usually be willing to support their sponsor's interests? That is another category of agreement to which we must attend and try to reach a conclusion about.

Finally, in examining the history of how Parliament has attempted from 1947 to deal with these matters of concern, I shall look at the Register of Members' Interests. Consultancy agreements come third in the separate categories of registrable interests that are demanded. Under the heading of "clients" which is category 3, it states that Members must disclose the names of clients,

"for whom they provide services which depend essentially upon or arrive out of, membership of the House; for example, sponsoring functions in the parliamentary buildings, making representations to Government Departments or providing advice on parliamentary or public affairs."

The demands by the register clearly contemplate that a Member may have received material benefits,

"which might reasonably be thought by others to influence his or her actions, speeches or votes in Parliament",

and which, in the case of consultancy agreements, may involve Members being paid for making representations to Government Departments on issues which inevitably will normally be concerned with matters to be transacted in Parliament. The Nolan committee correctly comments:

"the contrast between the 1947 Resolution and the rules governing the register is in our view totally unsatisfactory. It is small wonder that it has given rise to confusion in the minds of Members of Parliament themselves".

On that great range of consultancies, other than that defined group which I mentioned at the beginning of my speech, the Nolan committee has not come to any definite conclusion.

**Mr. Mark Wolfson** (Sevenoaks): Will the right hon. Gentleman give way?

**Mr. Shore:** No. Indeed, it has been said—I have some sympathy with this—that the committee has passed the buck back to Parliament for its advice and consideration. The Nolan committee recommends, however, that much

*[Mr. Shore]*

more information should in future be supplied to the register than is now available. First, it says that the detail of consultancy agreements be recorded—of the nature to which the right hon. Member for Watford (Mr. Garel-Jones) referred—and, secondly, that the moneys received in respect of consultancies should be declared.

Those recommendations will undoubtedly greatly increase public knowledge of what consultancies entail. No doubt, the House and its Committees will want to consider very seriously whether consultancies should be allowed to continue or whether, in part or in whole, some of them should be banned. The Nolan committee for its part has expressly stated that it will return to the issue after the House has debated the matter and in the light of the enhanced flow of information.

**Sir David Mitchell** (Hampshire, North-West): When an interest is declared and there for everybody to see in some detail, will the right hon. Gentleman explain what difference it would make if the remuneration were £1,000, £5,000 or £10,000? As long as it is clear that there is an interest and that that interest is properly declared, what additional benefit does the House or anyone else gain from knowing the precise amount?

**Mr. Peter Shore** (Bethnal Green and Stepney): That raises many questions, but I think that, in judging the importance of consultancies and paid outside interests, it is relevant that the actual amount be declared. There is a real distinction between the receipt of £1,000 a year for some small service and the receipt of £10,000 or more for other services. Those payments which are related to what we do and are able to do because we are Members of Parliament should be made publicly available.

It is crucial to the success, stability and reputation of our democracy that Ministers and elected representatives are not only animated, but are seen to be animated by their desire to serve the public interest and not personal gain or advantage. The vast majority of Members of the House are indeed honourable Members. There are very few who—sadly—fall below the high standards that the House expects and the House must deal firmly with those who transgress. There is also a need, as I hope that I have demonstrated, for greater clarity in the House's own rules on personal conduct. It is my hope that the Nolan committee's first report will assist the House in the task of re-examining its own rules and in restoring public confidence in the integrity of our democracy.

6.22 pm

**Mr. Tom King** (Bridgwater): I likewise declare my interests, as declared in the Register of Members' Interests. Unlike my right hon. Friend the Member for Old Bexley and Sidcup (Sir E. Heath) I think that the interests are reducing somewhat. I think that the House should be grateful to my right hon. Friend, the Father of the House, and, indeed, to the right hon. Member for Bethnal Green and Stepney (Mr. Shore) for raising the tone of the debate and enabling matters to be addressed with the seriousness that they deserve. This is a House of Commons matter. It is not something that should be lost in party-political squabble. I do not think that it was helpful—I say no more than this—that the Leader of Opposition chose to ask such a question at Prime Minister's Question Time, to which the hon. Member for Dewsbury (Mrs. Taylor) referred. It

might have got the debate off on precisely the wrong foot. It is important that we consider these matters. The Father of the House has done a great service by setting before hon. Members some of the real issues that have to be addressed and the right hon. Member for Bethnal Green and Stepney has made clear that they are very difficult.

The House owes itself the duty to read the report. It is well written. One letter that Lord Nolan received—I do not think that he will mind me disclosing it—said that it takes an Irishman to write English. Whether that is true or false, it is a serious report and it contains a number, not of diktats, not of instructions, but of recommendations which it asks the House to consider. Not all are for the House to consider because, of course, it invites the Government to consider some recommendations as well.

I pay tribute to Lord Nolan and the staff working with him: Alan Riddell, our secretary, and his team. I also pay tribute to my fellow members of the Nolan committee, who managed to rise above party politics in considering some very difficult issues to try to approach the matter seriously. I know that my colleagues on the committee would not object to one man being singled out. So to those who rise too fast to say that we are seeing the end of sovereignty and the traditions of the House, I say that I would like to pay tribute to Sir Clifford Boulton, who is not about to betray this House of Commons in the early moments of his retirement from it. His contribution to the committee was extremely valuable.

The House should approach these issues with seriousness. We are trustees and guardians of a very precious tradition. The mother of Parliaments is temporarily in our hands. We meet here in a week in which the Senate has decided to resume its investigations into the conduct of the President of the United States; the United States Attorney-General has just announced that she will begin investigations into the previous conduct of a fellow member of the Cabinet, the US Trade Secretary; a French Cabinet Minister, who had resigned from the Cabinet because of charges made against him, has been sentenced to gaol; and 20 per cent. of the Italian Parliament—that is a pretty significant number if one looks around—are awaiting trial on criminal charges. Such issues ought not to be taken lightly.

Indeed, when the right hon. Member for Ashton-under-Lyne (Mr. Sheldon) appeared before the committee, he made a telling point. He said that of some 184 members of the United Nations at the present time, he felt that only a handful had managed to maintain the sort of standards of conduct in public life that we treasure. We know that once it is lost, how difficult it is to regain. Those hon. Members of all parties, who I know feel aggrieved about some aspects of the report, should recognise first that we heard a lot of evidence in the Nolan committee. We worked pretty hard in those six months. It bears comparison with another inquiry that is taking place at the present time, whose only contribution appears to be an announcement of a further postponement of its findings. From our hearings came the statement, which was quoted in the House, that while there are problems that need to be addressed, the standards of public life expected in the country are high and the overwhelming majority of Members of the House and people in public life seek to aspire to them and, indeed, to maintain them.

So, that is the challenge that we face. The price of freedom is eternal vigilance; so it is to maintain high standards in public life. Eternal vigilance is necessary. If we say that we believe that we seek to maintain high public standards, we must recognise one thing. My right hon. Friend the Member for Old Bexley and Sidcup asked what has changed. One thing has undoubtedly changed. I shall not theorise on the reasons for it today. The public perception of this House has gone down and down and down.

The very first witness that the committee called to try to get some feeling for public perception of conduct of Members in public life said that 64 per cent. of the public believe that most Members of Parliament make a lot of money by using public office improperly. He confirmed that when a similar poll was taken nine years ago, exactly the same question was asked and the figure was 46 per cent. I and other members of the committee asked each person who came in, such as newspaper editors, and Professor Ivor Crewe, who gave that evidence, whether they believed that the statement was true. Professor Crewe said no, as did a succession of other witnesses. Yet the public perception is that it is true. It is the perception that is untrue, and it needs to be tackled, because if the House does not command the confidence of the British people there is a serious threat to our parliamentary democracy.

It is against that background that we have made our recommendations.

**Sir Geoffrey Johnson Smith:** Will my right hon. Friend give way?

**Mr. King:** May I go on and reach a point on which my hon. Friend may well wish to intervene?

**Sir Geoffrey Johnson Smith:** I want to comment on something that my right hon. Friend has just said.

**Mr. King:** I am sure that there will be lots more before I have finished. I shall certainly give way to my hon. Friend later, but first I want to say something else on the same subject.

I do not want to speak for long, because we have written our report and now it is for the House to speak. I want to listen to the views put forward on our recommendations. I shall deal first with the recommendations for the Government, and first of all with those concerning quangos.

The Committee was set up in the face of a barrage of allegations about the practice of making appointments to quangos. It was said that all appointees were Conservative placemen and that appointments were entirely a matter of political prejudice. We took a lot of evidence, and if hon. Members read the report they will see that we did not find that those allegations were conclusively proved. We found, indeed, that the evidence was inconclusive and that the Government had already made certain proposals to try to improve the arrangements for appointing people to public bodies.

The system does not work well enough. The range is too limited; the same names keep cropping up. This is not a party political point; there is simply not an efficient system for selecting people. There is some resentment in local government that the usual nominations on a bipartisan basis and the normal appointments of a number of people—"Buggins' turn" on the local authority round—are not coming up, because we have changed that system for appointing the members of quangos.

We want good competent people. We have proposed to the Government that, in order to regain public confidence, there should be a public appointments commissioner—not to make the appointments but to regulate and monitor, to report on the progress of the system of making appointments, and to check that the Departments are acting fairly.

As Nolan emphasises, it is essential that Ministers take responsibility for the appointments that they make. In the final analysis they must answer for them. If a Minister sees somebody competent with the ability, energy and drive that he considers necessary for a particular appointment, there is nothing to prevent him from seeking to have that person appointed. But at the end of the day he must be prepared to take the responsibility for the appointment that he has made. Our proposals are an attempt to give greater public confidence in that area, and I hope that that will be achieved.

We already have a system relating to Ministers' conduct and the standards according to which they operate. Many hon. and right hon. Members will be familiar with "Questions of Procedure for Ministers", the contents of which have grown up over the years. It is not sufficiently clear and comprehensive, and we suggest that clearer and more comprehensive guidance, entitled "Conduct and Procedure for Ministers" should be given to every new Minister. My right hon. Friend the Chancellor of the Duchy of Lancaster has already said that a code for civil servants will be introduced, and our suggestion would parallel that, with a proper guide being given to Ministers.

Another question that we addressed was the problem that arises when a Minister is thought to have behaved incorrectly in relation to the code of conduct and procedure, and how that should be investigated. It is no secret that there have been problems. There have been two examples in recent years, and the role of the Cabinet Secretary should be carefully considered. When it is his duty to advise the Prime Minister, should he be the person to conduct the investigations too? I shall not delay the House further, but hon. Members may like to read the conclusions that we drew on the subject. It is essential that there be an effective system.

I shall now mention another aspect that has caused concern—Ministers leaving office and taking up outside appointments. There is no question about the fact that individual Ministers who leave office are capable of making an effective contribution and can bring considerable ability to bear, to the advantage of our country. We must ensure that that channel is not obstructed by political correctness to an extent that becomes unfair to the people concerned and disadvantages our country.

None the less, there must be public confidence that Ministers, like civil servants, are not allowed to take special advantage of information that they have acquired during their period in Government and exploit it for their own personal advantage or for the advantage of an organisation that they may join. When I was Secretary of State for Defence I used to approve or give advice on the terms under which senior civil servants leaving office could or could not take up certain appointments, yet there were no rules for Ministers at all. At present there is nothing to stop a Minister walking straight out and taking any job, although a week beforehand he may have denied his permanent secretary or another senior official in his Department the opportunity to take up a particular employment.

**Mr. Quentin Davies** (Stamford and Spalding): Will my right hon. Friend give way?

**Mr. King:** May I finish this point first?

It is fair that Ministers should be expected to take the advice of the advisory committee now chaired by Lord Carlisle—a group of 10 experienced senior people who can ensure that appointments that former Ministers may take up do not invite allegations of impropriety.

I was glad to see that my right hon. Friends the Members for Sutton Coldfield (Mr. Fowler) and for Norfolk, South (Mr. MacGregor) supported that proposal when they gave evidence before the Committee. It could be a defence and a protection for Ministers in such circumstances.

My colleagues and I were anxious to ensure that it was recognised that Ministers and civil servants are not in the same position. The situation is not the same for a senior civil servant retiring at 60 on a full pension, who has anticipated his retirement and knows when he is going, as it is for a Minister who may be about 40 with three or four children, who finds himself, perhaps to his surprise, no longer in such demand as he was. *[Laughter.]* That reaction is interesting. I do not think that, if the situation changed, Opposition Members would hold quite the same view as they hold now—because it does not happen to be fair. I believe that in the end they would recognise that.

I believe that the changes are sensible. We propose that for Cabinet Ministers, as for permanent secretaries, there should be an automatic three-month waiting period, but that for Ministers below Cabinet level and for Whips there should be no automatic waiting period.

I shall now give way to my hon. Friend the Member for Wealden (Sir G. Johnson Smith), as I promised.

**Sir Geoffrey Johnson Smith:** May I take my right hon. Friend back to the beginning of his speech, when he gave us some interesting figures about the public perception of Members of the House of Commons. He told us that when those who produced the evidence that we were held in low esteem were asked whether they agreed with that opinion, they said that they did not. How does my right hon. Friend account for the gap in perception between those who gave the evidence and the public?

**Mr. King:** I shall not detain the House with my opinion on that, because we all have our views on it. However, it is a fact; I am not sure whether my hon. Friend is challenging it. We all share the concern about the public view of Members of Parliament. The people who do not share it may be those who organised the polls and the commentators who commented on them. That is the public perception which, while it may be unfair and fed by the media, is something we must recognise as damaging to democracy.

I now turn to the issue of Members of Parliament. I shall be helped in my remarks by the clear exposition given by the right hon. Member for Bethnal Green and Stepney, who made clear that there are difficult decisions to be made about how consultancies are to be handled in future. Some members of the committee wondered whether not just lobbyists but all consultancies should be banned completely, and the report addresses that issue.

Exceptions and anomalies have come out in the speeches and interventions which colleagues have made, and the House must address such points. We must ensure that the House does not depend on a mono-cultural stream of people coming through a politically correct net into the House. There must be the widest possible range of access to the House, so that Members have experience and interest in a wide range of fields. The House will be better for that.

The difficulty is how we make that happen in a way which also ensures that we protect ourselves from the other extreme of problem. Every Member knows that there are those who have used their membership of the House to provide services in a way that has invited considerable criticism and which has not brought credit on the House. It will be for the House to draw up the difficult resolutions on that subject.

Some people have asked me what is to happen after this debate. The House must take the report's recommendations forward, and decide how to address the issues. We must ensure that we maintain access to people outside the House, and we must respect the fact that lobbying is an essential part of the democratic process. We do not want debates to be uninformed or to have Members who do not know what they are talking about. We must ensure that we have the mechanisms of democracy without inviting the criticisms which have been attracted to it.

The House must have a way of ensuring that whatever it decides is maintained. I strongly endorse what the right hon. Member for Bethnal Green and Stepney said about a parliamentary commissioner for standards. That person could be the registrar of Members' Interests under another name, as we propose the abolition of that post. We also propose merging the Committee of Privileges and the Committee on Members' Interests into a single committee. Those who think that that would be a gross intrusion into the wonderful system that we have at the moment might like to talk to the two Members who recently experienced the present system. They warmly welcome the introduction of a new system which could contain within it the elements of natural justice, efficiency and promptness which some might feel the two Members were denied under the present hallowed system.

A gentleman—or a lady, I hasten to say—of independence and stature could be appointed by the House, chosen by House, voted in to his post by the House and would be an Officer of the House. I do not see how the appointment of such a person could be a great undermining of the sovereignty of the House. Such a commissioner could report to a sub-committee, and would have some powers of investigation. I see in the proposals protection for men of repute from unfounded allegations.

Individual Members could go to an independent commissioner when allegations and smears are made against them. The commissioner would be able to investigate the allegations privately, and he could have the authority to determine whether they justify further investigation. Hon. Members have said that that would be a considerable strength, as they have nothing of that sort at present. We all have odd constituents who can make some wild allegations, but we have no protection against them at all. Someone who could command confidence in that field would be a reassurance and a benefit.

Another point in the proposals may seem outrageous to some. We propose that the commissioner should be responsible for the guidance of Members, and could operate some form of induction training for Members on conduct and procedures. When I came to the House, I stood between Lord Whitelaw and somebody who I have now forgotten, marched up to the Chair, signed a piece of paper, got my writ and I was in. It was thought that I must know what I was supposed to do. I was elected at a by-election, but nobody told me where anything was.

People may say that we are considering some appalling new professionalism, but certain facilities and improvements in this field will be genuinely helpful. If we want to maintain standards, it would be helpful if the standards which the House expects of Members were clearly set out.

I recognise, as did the right hon. Member for Bethnal Green and Stepney, that we have in a sense passed the buck to the House. We have done that in the knowledge that the Nolan committee believes that it is not only allowable but valuable for Members to have outside interests and involvements because that widens the experience that a Member brings to this House. We believe there are none the less challenges which the House has to face. Abuses and pressures in the field of consultancies and lobbying must be addressed.

One or two comments from hon. Members have given me the worry that some people have felt that they could walk away from this matter, and that they could leave it and everybody would forget about it. All of the evidence that I listened to during the proceedings of the Nolan committee, and all that I have been exposed to in my constituency and in my public life suggests that that would be profoundly unwise.

I hope that the House accepts the responsibility to address the issues and to recognise the difficult dividing lines. The House must come up with proposals which can build on the recommendations which we made in the report, and do so in a way which commands the widest public confidence. We must restore public confidence in this mother of Parliaments which we all cherish and hold dear.

**Mr. Deputy Speaker (Mr. Michael Morris):** Before I call the next hon. Member to speak, may I remind the House that Madam Speaker has declared that speeches from 7 o'clock shall be restricted to 10 minutes?

6.48 pm

**Mr. Robert Maclennan** (Caithness and Sutherland): Following the precedent established during the debate, I shall begin by declaring the interests that I set out in the register in my name. I must express to the right hon. Member for Bridgwater (Mr. King) my belief that he has made an extremely persuasive speech to which we must all listen and upon which we must reflect. He was right to emphasise at the beginning that, compared with standards of conduct observed in public life in other countries, Britain stands out as being gratifyingly clean. It is not pharisaical to note how rarely corruption cases break through the surface of the expansive activities of Government in this country. It is not pious complacency to take pride in the altruism and selflessness of the numberless people who spend their lives working in the public service. Our purpose in Parliament should be to seek to underpin the high standards which the public are entitled to expect and on which, for the most part, they can rely.

In some ways, it is regrettable that today's debate is necessary; but necessary it is. In reflecting that Lord Nolan was not as worldly as he might be to understand the workings of the House and how things are done, the Father of the House was reflecting the judgments of an earlier age and was not sufficiently in tune with the public's perception of the work that is done in the House, nor with the urgent need to seek to affect those public perceptions. I have not served in the House for as long as the Father of the House, but I am in my 30th year of service. Even in my time, I am aware of the changes that have taken place, not least in the accumulation of consultancies, to which the right hon. Member for Bethnal Green and Stepney (Mr. Shore) referred.

One should ask why that has happened. I believe that it has happened at least partly because the remuneration of Members of Parliament during that period has not kept pace with the rise in earnings of others in society. The Nolan committee refers to that fact.

**Mr. Duncan Smith:** Is not it strange, therefore, that the Nolan committee reached no conclusion about the link between the increase in consultancies and the decrease in the purchasing power of hon. Members' pay? Does he not find that a matter of concern?

**Mr. Maclennan:** No. The committee was properly aware of the limitations of its remit. It was not invited to consider the remuneration of Members of Parliament generally and, although it was correct to allude to the issue, it would have been wrong to take a final view about it. However, we can properly consider the link in this debate and form our own judgments on it.

A number of recent episodes have sadly besmirched the reputation of the institutions to which the individuals involved belong. They have raised in the public's mind questions about whether there is a sickness in our political system. I do not wish to linger on the background to setting up the committee, but it will be recalled that a succession of episodes in different areas gave rise to anxiety. Those include the Asil Nadir affair; the circumstances of the arms sales to Iraq, which are currently under investigation by the Scott committee; the resignation of at least one junior Minister who failed to declare a financial interest before his becoming a Minister; the activities of certain political lobbying firms; the accommodation of ex-Cabinet Ministers in the boardrooms of companies that they had a hand in privatising; and, as charted by the Public Accounts Committee in a number of reports, the disreputable conduct of certain individuals who operate within quangos.

Too often, the proper conduct of public business is secured only by ill-defined conventions and self-restraints. Today's abuses are testimony to the frailty of those protections of the public interest. Written constitutions alone manifestly do not eliminate improprieties from public life. None the less, constitutional provisions that defined the public rights and duties of the citizen—and the citizen in public service—and rendered those rights and duties enforceable in the courts would modernise our democracy. They would provide necessary checks and balances, secure greater transparency in public transactions and offer legal remedies where breaches occurred. Under such a constitutional system, Members of Parliament would not have the last word for they would be subject to the constitution. The Liberal Democrats believe that, ultimately, this country should move along that road.

*[Mr. Maclennan]*

The need for the Nolan committee's appointment was, however, urgent and although the effect of its recommendations is far-reaching, it is a very British response to the defacing episodes that I mentioned earlier. The report is a masterly compendium of proposals. If adopted in their entirety, they should help to diminish public anxiety. Wisely, as the need for immediate action is clear, the committee proposes a process—not yet a statutory framework—to be implemented and scrutinised for its effectiveness over a period of time. Members of Parliament are particularly indebted to the committee for the speed and thoroughness with which it accumulated its evidence and formulated cogent proposals.

The underlying principles that the committee advances seem to be compelling. First, those in public life should be guided by certain standards which, when considered together, put the public good before private personal advantage. Secondly, those who choose the course of public service must take responsibility for their own actions and should be guided in those actions by clear codes of conduct to which they and their peers have given assent. Thirdly, as it is not reassuring to people at large that those public servants should be prosecutor, judge, jury and executioner in their own causes, it is right to appoint independent outside officers to oversee and advise on the effectiveness of the self-regulatory system. Fourthly, it is recognised that corruption does not live in the sunlight. The blinds must be lifted.

The recommendations of the Nolan committee founded on those principles seem to be sensible and the immediate necessary step to remove justifiable public concern. Regrettably, however, there are two omissions. The first was alluded to by the Chairman of the Public Accounts Committee, the right hon. Member for Ashton-under-Lyne (Mr. Sheldon), and I shall not linger on it. Non-departmental public bodies should all be subject to scrutiny, by either the National Audit Office or the Audit Commission. I welcome the recognition in the Nolan committee report that

"The absence of automatic public scrutiny does seem to us to represent an anomaly."

I hope that that will be dealt with in the committee's future work.

The second major omission was imposed on the committee by the Prime Minister: consideration of the funding of political parties. All political parties should, in the public interest, be required to disclose substantial funding by individual trusts, private companies and others not required by law to seek the consent of shareholders or members to political donations. The existing arrangements are a potential source of corruption. It has been argued that such bodies and individuals have a right to privacy and to withhold their identification from the public. I cannot see why people should be embarrassed about giving financial support to a political party. The democratic process needs to be funded. The public right to know should override an individual's sensitivity about the revelation of his identity. I take it that few individuals would be reluctant to reveal their identity to the party being funded. The purchase of influence or reward is unacceptable and it is an evil that can be stopped only by openness. No doubt the policing of an open system would present problems, but they are not insurmountable.

I welcome and support the committee's particular recommendation about the Register of Members' Interests. I believe that Parliament is helped by the direct knowledge that Members can bring to it from their personal involvement with the outside world. If all hon. Members spoke only with second-hand experience, our debates would be somewhat diminished. There is, however, a consequent need to declare clearly the nature, extent and value to a Member of his outside connections.

Perhaps a more controversial recommendation, and certainly the most controversial one according to today's debate, is the appointment of a parliamentary commissioner for standards. His proposed role would assist Members of Parliament to perform their duties and in no way supplant their responsibilities. He would assist in drawing up the code of conduct and by maintaining the register, advising new Members and conducting preliminary investigations into complaints. I can only speculate about what effect the presence of such an officer would have had upon some of the more colourful episodes that we have observed, even within the past 48 hours, and that have been described before a rather astonished public.

The proposed amendments to the adjudicating role of the Select Committee on Privileges should help to ensure that the rules of natural justice are followed.

Liberal Democrats have advocated that changes should be made to the rules governing the employment of Ministers after they leave public office. I believe that the Chancellor of the Duchy of Lancaster was somewhat too complacent when he said to the committee:

"It is still right to leave decisions about these matters to the judgment of the individuals concerned."

The life of a Minister may be "nasty, brutish and short", but that is taken into account by politicians when they embark upon that course. From my rather modest experience in that sphere, I do not believe that Ministers become unemployable after they demit office, but the appropriateness of the employment should be subject to external scrutiny. I therefore welcome what the Government have said about that today.

The arrangements for potential whistleblowers in the civil service are also to be welcomed. They will help to limit any attempts to bring improper political pressure to bear upon their independence. Liberal Democrats are unhappy about the growth in Government reliance upon quangos and the evident abuse of powers of political patronage not only to ensure that those quangos are run by agents of like mind to the Government, which is certainly understandable, but that they are used to reward political cronies. The proposals to require the disclosure of political activity and independently to oversee the appointments processes in all Departments is therefore to be welcomed warmly.

Although many of the jobs in the hands of the quangos should be carried out properly by accountable, elected individuals—a point on which I am in complete agreement with the Father of the House—the proposed changes should help to change the more unattractive aspects of the quango culture.

The Nolan committee's recommendations should be accepted. When the Leader of the House replies to the debate, I hope that he will suggest how he proposes to put the issues for decision before the House, particularly those affecting the conduct of Members of Parliament. Of course I understand the desire of the Government to hear the views of the House, but we are entitled to hear from the right hon. Gentleman, as Leader of the House, how he proposes to scrutinise the proposals in detail and give effect to them with a view to meeting the timetable recommended by the Nolan committee. Great importance should be attached to that timetable because an integral part of the committee's recommendations was that matters should be dealt with urgently.

I do not think that there is any point in arguing about whether nine tenths or three tenths of the proposals are capable of being implemented before the end of the year. What is clear is that the Nolan committee expected Parliament to act speedily.

The Ministers who are participating in the debate do so in a double role—as Members of the House, who are leading the discussions in the House, but also as members of the Government. We are entitled to hear their answers to our questions in both those roles.

On behalf of my party, I endorse warmly the work of the committee and express my thanks to all those who clearly laboured long and hard to produce this valuable report.

7.4 pm

**Sir Terence Higgins** (Worthing): I begin by declaring the interests that I have recorded in the Register of Members' Interests.

In many respects, I agree with the suggestions in the Nolan committee's report, but I feel bound to say that if they are accepted in isolation, there is a serious danger that, far from raising standards in public life, they may lower them because, at the end of the day, it is the individuals who take public office who set the standards. I believe that the House is already facing a considerable recruitment problem. Given the implications of the report, that matter cannot be divorced from the issue of Members' and Ministers' pay. That issue is extremely relevant if we are to recruit to the House people of adequate standard. I shall return to that later.

I should like to stress one simple point right at the beginning. The expression "full-time Member of Parliament", which has been bandied today and even appears in the report, is misleading. I doubt that there is a single Member of the House who is not full time in the sense that he fulfils what is a normal working week according to any normal outside standard. Many of those Members with outside interests put in the greatest amount of work in this place, not least, for example, because of their membership of Select Committees, which are an increasingly effective means of holding the Government to account.

I am glad that the Nolan committee has accepted what I suggested in my evidence, when I said that the present arrangements for scrutinising breaches—if I can put it like that—of the normal standards of the House were not working. The split between the Privileges Committee and the Select Committee on Members' Interests is not satisfactory. The Privileges Committee, with its huge membership, takes far too long to convene between one meeting and another. The Select Committee on Members' Interests is not the appropriate body to deal with such breaches.

The Nolan committee's suggestion that we should appoint a Sub-Committee of the Privileges Committee to deal with the matter is entirely right. We must, however, give the structure an opportunity to work. Despite the persuasive arguments of my right hon. Friend the Member for Bridgwater (Mr. King), I am, therefore, not convinced that the proposal for a parliamentary commissioner for standards is appropriate.

I entirely go along with the initial proposal about the parliamentary commissioner's duties. I agree with the idea that he should be an improved registrar of Members' interests and give advice. The idea that he should carry out independent investigations, however, is not appropriate. I am particularly concerned that page 44 of the report states:

"the commissioner should be able to send for persons, papers and records, and will therefore need to be supported by the authority of a Select Committee with the necessary powers. To give the powers personally to the Commissioner would require primary legislation".

I do not like the way in which the committee suggests we should get around that particular business. The power to send for persons and papers should not be delegated by a Committee of the House to some outside individual, however distinguished. I believe that that proposal poses considerable dangers and I sought to explain some of them to the Opposition spokesman, the hon. Member for Dewsbury (Mrs. Taylor).

It is dangerous to have someone independently carrying out inquiries into all types of allegations, and then perhaps publishing his opinions, without the Privileges Committee having a grip on the thing. A new Sub-Committee of the Privileges Committee, able to work quickly and effectively, with all the powers to obtain any evidence that it needs about allegations, should be given a trial before we go along with that other suggestion, which has considerable dangers.

I am quoted in the report with approval as saying that transparency in respect of Members' interests is all-important. I profoundly believe that. However, it is the declaration of interests that is important to the House. The House is able to discount accordingly a speech by an hon. Member declaring an interest, the way in which he votes, and so on. That is the way in which we have always gone.

A Member either has an interest or does not. I am therefore doubtful about the proposition that it is necessary to quantify. It is not very effective, because what to one person is a large amount of money by way of a consultancy fee may be mere pocket money to another.

Perhaps one should quantify with regard to consultancies that arise from the House, but, as the Nolan committee says, not with regard to outside interests that do not arise from the House. That will be a very difficult line to draw. It will be necessary for the House, and perhaps a Committee of the House, to consider the matter and make proposals to tackle that problem. I doubt that the link between the Front Benchers is an appropriate way of doing it.

I return to my main argument. As the Nolan committee recognises, implementation of its proposals will have a significant effect on Members' ability to have outside income. I believe that, in many ways, the proposals will act as something of a deterrent, especially to those who are elected after the next general election. Therefore, one must consider the matter in its context, and it must be related to Members' pay.

I do not suggest that we should have full-time, well-paid Members of Parliament with no outside interests. They need to have both a sensible level of pay and the ability to have outside interests unconnected with their membership of the House.

*[Sir Terence Higgins]*

In that respect, I repeat the evidence and the figures that I gave with regard to what has happened to pay generally. Since I entered the House, real incomes have increased by 80 per cent. Meanwhile, Members' pay has just returned to the level at which it was when I came to this place, and has been below that level, sometimes substantially, throughout the intervening time.

Ministers' pay has declined dramatically—the figures are quoted in the report. That of Ministers has declined by 60 per cent. and that of the Prime Minister by 59 per cent. Present Ministers, in real terms, allowing for inflation, are paid half what Harold Wilson and his Cabinet Ministers were paid. That is the extent of the decline.

We want people to enter the House who are of the quality to become Ministers. We cannot expect them to do so at present levels of pay. That is a serious problem. The amount that one would now need to pay to recruit that type of person as a commercial director in a middling-size plc is double or more what we pay the Prime Minister.

If we are to attract people of real ability into the House, we must consider the fact that someone—perhaps a president of the union—with a good second-class or first-class university degree, who might previously have usually come into this place, can go into the City now and earn more than a Member of Parliament in two years, with the prospect of earning vastly more later.

As the Nolan committee says—indeed, it was said in the final question posed to me when I appeared before it—surely service to the country and to public life is important. Yes; it is profoundly important, and I regard my membership of the House as the greatest honour. Nevertheless, when recruiting people, one cannot disregard the fact that, if one had remained in outside occupation, one would probably be earning five times as much as one has earned in this place—perhaps more. People need to have regard to their family circumstances, and so on.

On timing, it is vital that the proposals in the report should be related to a fundamental review of what is happening to remuneration in this place.

There is a great deal of fuzziness in the report. Many of the issues are not clearly defined. Therefore it is necessary, not for the usual channels, but for a committee to consider carefully the way in which those matters are drafted and the way in which resolutions might be placed before the House.

I make a final argument, because I am running out of time. It is much more important that we should get the matter right than that we should act fast, and it requires very careful consideration indeed by the House and its Committee.

**Mr. Deputy Speaker:** Order.

7.14 pm

**Mr. John Morris** (Aberavon): First, I declare my interests, in the same way as the right hon. Member for Worthing (Sir T. Higgins) did, as recorded in the Register of Members' Interests. I agree entirely with his observations on the way in which Members' and Ministers' pay has fallen back. The new chief executive

of a middle-ranking unitary authority in local government will be paid as much as, if not more than, the Chancellor of the Exchequer. That must be wholly wrong.

When I became Secretary of State for Wales, seven of the chief executives of county councils in Wales were paid more than the person who was the chief civil servant in Wales. There is something wrong.

I express my gratitude to Lord Nolan and his committee and to my right hon. Friend the Member for Bethnal Green and Stepney (Mr. Shore) and the right hon. Member for Bridgwater (Mr. King), who are members of it, whom I congratulate on their speeches. I was curious why the committee had to set out "the seven principles of public life" in more than 200 words. I should have thought that we should all know the difference between "right and wrong" and "right and wrong" as public representatives. The fact that Lord Nolan and his committee felt the need to state that does, in itself, no credit to public life.

Despite all the criticisms, I am confident that probably all of us, when we come to the House, come with the highest possible aims. What is regrettable is the steady erosion of understanding of what should be acceptable. Nolan has rightly made us take stock.

As I told the committee in my written observations, when I entered the House, the political consultant was hardly known. The first that I heard of them was in relation to teachers and the police, and now 30 per cent. of eligible Members are registered paid parliamentary consultants.

Nolan has grasped the nettle as regards multi-client consultancies in recommending that the involvement of Members in such consultancies should be immediately banned. I agree. They epitomise "the hiring fair" that the Prime Minister described.

Nolan has kicked into touch the problem of parliamentary consultancies in themselves. I concede, on reflection, that there is at least an argument for distinguishing paid advice from paid advocacy, and I want to hear more about that. I believe, however, that to be paid as an advocate in the House by an outside interest is incompatible with being a Member of the House. The Member is no more than a hired gun.

I do not blame the Nolan committee for wanting to hear more from Parliament. It has not heard a great deal so far. In any event, it intends to return to the matter in a year's time to review the position.

I wrote to Nolan in the following terms:

"Your committee may wish to consider what difference there is between hard cash for an immediate specified return and a consultant who may book a room for a dinner, make an appointment with a Minister, or even perhaps put down an occasional question."

The House has approved the recommendation of the Privileges Committee, in the recent cases before it, as regards the behaviour that we felt fell short of the standards that the House was entitled to expect of its Members. The Privileges Committee said:

"We see no sustainable distinction between a payment of £1,000 for tabling a parliamentary question and a consultancy for which the fee is £1,000 and the only requirement is the tabling of a parliamentary question".

Personally, I would go further: I see no distinction between being paid to table a parliamentary question either on its own or as part of one's paid duties as a consultant. It is the same concept of a "hired gun".

The Privileges Committee has deferred its consideration of that part of the remit from Madam Speaker dealing with a general position on the need to clarify the law of Parliament regarding consultancies. We did so pending the Nolan report. Lord Nolan and his committee have come and gone on that aspect for the moment. I suppose that the Privileges Committee, either as part of its original remit or as a result of further instructions from the House, must now return to it; hence, I have gained the impression that Nolan has kicked the ball into touch on that issue.

I find the delicacy on the part of the Nolan committee in this difficult to reconcile with the fact that it had the temerity to give birth to a draft code of conduct for Members of Parliament. On page 39, under the heading "Financial Interests", the report states:

"A Member must not promote any matter in Parliament in return for payment."

Subject to clarification as to what "in Parliament" means, that is ample to cover the whole range of parliamentary consultants, be they single or multi—otherwise, what was Nolan up to? I applaud the committee's ingenuity. I take on board the observations of the right hon. Member for Worthing, who referred to the constitutional powers of the independent commissioner. It is a good idea to ensure at least that control remains with Parliament in the form of the Privileges Committee, warts and all. I welcome the recommendation for the Committee to meet in public, and in debate a fortnight ago I suggested that the Committee should be much smaller.

I turn to the employment of ex-Ministers. The Chancellor of the Duchy of Lancaster—I am glad that he is in the Chamber—must feel pretty sore, having received a black eye from the committee over his bland assumption that all was well or steady as she goes. As we were reminded this afternoon, he gave that evidence on behalf of the Government. I find it deeply offensive that Ministers who have played a major part in privatising an industry or in establishing quangos can take up a major paid role in those bodies, scarcely before the ink is dry on the statute that created them. There should be a firm cordon sanitaire for that kind of employment.

We are talking not about employment generally but about jobs that Ministers have created themselves. That is what we are talking about; let us not confuse it with hon. Members who are looking for work to feed their children. What is necessary for civil servants should be necessary also for Ministers. The minimum waiting period before seeking other employment is two years, and perhaps it should be three. I see no distinction between Cabinet Ministers and junior Ministers in that regard.

As to quangos, the present situation is intolerable. I wish that Lord Nolan and his committee had examined the situation in Wales, of which the Chancellor of the Duchy of Lancaster is well aware. I was glad to hear the Chancellor confirm that the Chief Whip—the Patronage Secretary—will play a much lesser role. The Chief Whip is the conduit for political influence when making appointments and I am glad that his role is to change.

In the 11 years that I served as a Minister, I was never conscious of receiving any guidance from on high, offered by the Chief Whip or anyone else, when making appointments. I performed the same role as the Chancellor of the Duchy of Lancaster in his previous office. Any appointments that I made, right or wrong, were my decisions and mine alone. The Chief Whip did not play a part in that process.

In Wales and elsewhere, we have seen wives of Members, wives of Ministers, ex-Members of Parliament and ex-Members of the European Parliament appointed to quangos. They may be very worthy appointments; indeed, I am sure that they are. However, would they have been appointed but for the fact of who they are? I am glad that there will be an independent aspect to appointing people to serve on quangos.

7.24 pm

**Sir Archibald Hamilton** (Epsom and Ewell): I, too, declare my interests, which appear in the Register of Members' Interests. They include a number of consultancies and directorships. Unlike most hon. Members who have spoken in the debate today, I am rather disappointed by the Nolan report. I thought that it represented an opportunity to clarify some extremely complex and difficult areas and I am not certain that it has done that.

My right hon. Friend the Member for Bridgwater (Mr. King) recognised the public disquiet about standards of behaviour in public life, while acknowledging that some expert witnesses had appeared before the committee and said that that disquiet was unjustified. However, he did nothing to attribute blame for the gap between the two positions. It may have something to do with the media, which insist upon reporting everything in the most unfavourable terms possible. We are becoming so cowed by the media that we rarely dare to speak out against them in any way.

My right hon. Friend the Member for Bridgwater also spelled out clearly to the House what an incredibly incorruptible political system we have compared with many other countries. He illustrated his point graphically by referring to the number of Italian parliamentarians who face being put in the slammer and so on. It would have been useful to include that information in the report. It is extremely important to put in context the problems that we are discussing today, because they are minuscule compared with the problems facing parliaments and democracies all over the western world.

We have an admirable civil service. The permanent under-secretary is the accounting officer in any Department and there is a clear division of responsibilities. I think that that is one of the reasons why our system is extremely difficult to corrupt through financial fraud and so on. I believe that the report should have paid tribute to that fact.

I agree with my right hon. Friend the Member for Worthing (Sir T. Higgins), who said that we cannot view the issues in isolation without considering the salaries of Members of Parliament. We must attract professional middle-class people to this House as they have a tremendous amount to offer. But if they are told—as I suspect Labour Members will tell them—that they will receive a salary of £32,000 per annum, they will not come.

Lord Nolan entered chambers in 1953 and was married in that same year. I am informed that he became a tax barrister and I am sure that his earnings, in today's terms, were well in excess of £32,000. He managed to educate his son at a public school and I suspect that he educated

[Sir Archibald Hamilton]

his two daughters in the same way. I assure him that one cannot do that today on £32,000. At one stage perhaps Lord Nolan contemplated becoming a Member of Parliament and came to the conclusion that the salary was too small for him to consider so doing. We must put the issues into perspective and remember that a number of hon. Members, not unnaturally, have aspirations to earn more than £32,000 per annum. They do not consider that to be a fortune—although I have no doubt that their constituents might think that it is.

We must also look hard at the question of a waiting period for Ministers before taking up employment after leaving office. I do not believe that Ministers are comparable with civil servants. As my right hon. Friend the Member for Bridgwater said, civil servants are able to anticipate their retirement and they receive generous pensions with which to retire. It is quite different when a Minister leaves office. It may be an involuntary act anyway, and he may still be young and burdened with heavy expenses. We should bear in mind the fact that the House has decided that redundancy pay for Ministers should be set at three months' salary. If we then make them wait two years before they can pick up another job, it is clear that the whole question of redundancy money will have to be reviewed—in particular, whether it should last much longer.

My other criticism of the report concerns its findings on disclosing remuneration. That is just a ploy to embarrass in front of our constituents those of us who receive consultancy fees. The argument seems based on the idea that if I earn £1,000 a year as a consultant I shall not be doing much in the House for that, but if I earn £20,000 a year in consultancy fees I must be doing infinitely more in the House. In fact, the reverse is true: many consultancy agreements involving large sums of money mean that much more is being asked of Members in terms of work outside the House. Consultancy agreements often mean representing companies which go in for a wide range of activities. I work for an American defence contractor, and I spend some of my time looking for companies over here for it to acquire—that has nothing to do with Parliament.

I turn next to the vexed issue of the distinction between advocacy and advice. It is thought wrong to be paid to be an advocate. Let us face it, Nolan has made it clear—as a long-term recommendation—that there should be a total ban on all forms of advocacy in the House by hon. Members who may be pursuing the interests of bodies with which they have entered into consultancy or sponsorship agreements. What is the difference between someone with a consultancy agreement and someone who is a lawyer or a solicitor tabling amendments to a Criminal Justice Bill? In principle I see no difference at all. The latter will be employed, perhaps, by a firm of solicitors; if he failed to table the amendments or failed to press the case that the partnership thought important, the firm could sack him.

If we press ahead in this way we shall remove professionals who have something to say about the law and something to contribute to Criminal Justice Bills. As my right hon. Friend the Member for Watford (Mr. Garel-Jones) believes, too, farmers would not be able to speak about agriculture, or accountants about Finance Bills, and Members sponsored by trade unions would be unable to comment on labour relations legislation. Even Opposition Members who are lecturers would be unable to comment on education Bills. That is the logical conclusion of banning paid advocacy in the House. We cannot draw the line between a Member with a consultancy agreement and a Member who is paid by a particular profession. We need to get away from glib assumptions about a division between advocacy and advice, because it will be extremely difficult to make such distinctions without removing the expertise that we need in this House for commenting on legislation.

I shall end by discussing the commissioner for standards. Many of us are worried that we may create an independent post that will end up being responsible to no one and creating mayhem in this place—even though we may have voted to set up the post in the first place. The solution to the problem is to make Madam Speaker the commissioner for standards. I am sure that she has many other things to do besides inquiring into whether Members of Parliament are behaving properly, so if she does not want to take on the responsibility herself I suggest that she appoint someone who is answerable to her. The role would then become part of the Speaker's Office and would be clearly seen to be independent and answerable to the House. That would remove many of our fears about an independent commissioner over whom, once we had appointed him or her, we would have no control at all.

7.34 pm

**Mr. Tony Benn** (Chesterfield): I, like others, declare my interests: as a writer, broadcaster and shareholder. I should also announce that I have been a paid consultant for 45 years, first for Bristol, South-East and then for Chesterfield. The idea that a Member of Parliament can be a consultant only on behalf of companies or individuals—and be paid especially for that—is an illusion.

This is not really a new problem. I am alarmed when I am told that we have had a marvellous system hitherto. Lloyd George, whom I met nearly 60 years ago, sold titles. Then we had the Marconi scandal—not to mention 10,000 Enclosure Acts, under which this House handed over the common land to rich farmers. So let us not mislead ourselves: there has always been a problem, but it has always been limited in terms of the numbers of people involved.

The House is in such difficulties now not because one or two Members have done what they have done but because the House failed to take seriously its responsibility to lay down what our standards should be. So the Prime Minister used, of all things, the royal prerogative to set up a royal commission to examine the conduct of the House of Commons—clean contrary to article 9 of the Bill of Rights, which stipulates that no one from outside may presume to regulate what we do here. [Interruption.] Of course Lord Nolan's committee is a permanent royal commission, set up by the Prime Minister without consulting the House—he just announced it—to examine what we should do next. When the House is treated in that way, surely it must begin to take seriously what it has failed to do.

My argument is a simple one and is already known, but I wish to spell it out to the House in some detail: we should lay down what it is lawful for a Member to do and a Member who does not stay within the law will not be eligible to be a Member.

I am very doubtful about an ethics commissioner. When I first heard about "ethics man" taking over our affairs, I wondered whether the speaker had a lisp. I have 40,000 ethics commissioners in my constituency and if I act illegally I am answerable to them. We have heard talk of an induction scheme. Are we going to insist on qualifications for getting into the House of Commons? Many Members who have spoken today seem not to understand that democracy is not about qualifications. No one needs to have any qualifications whatever to get into Parliament; if we insisted on them, many people would never get in here. It is, however, much harder to get elected than to pass an exam. We are answerable to our constituents—that is what democracy is about.

**Mr. Budgen:** Does the right hon. Gentleman agree that all this talk about the seven principles of public life—

**Mr. Benn:** I have just realised that I have only 10 minutes in which to speak, so I am afraid that I cannot allow the hon. Gentleman to read out the seven principles. I hope that he will forgive any discourtesy.

There are 400 classes of person who are disqualified from sitting in this House of Commons—I know because I have been through them all. Judges cannot sit here—Lord Nolan could not sit. Roman Catholic priests cannot sit here. No one has suggested that they should be allowed to do so provided we have a "religious commissioner" to determine whether they are qualified. They were excluded because in the old, prejudiced days it was thought that the Pope ran every Catholic priest. That is not true any more, of course. Anglican Ministers cannot sit here either.

I repeat that we should state what behaviour we object to and then make it illegal. Without wanting to get at anyone, I object to the thought that people who are elected to serve their constituents and pursue their convictions should act, for money, to promote the economic interests of a company. I have no objection to people representing bodies like the Police Federation, or to people being barristers or writers—how could I, when I am one myself—but when I hear a Member advancing an argument in the House I want to know that it is his own argument, or that he is representing his constituency, and not that he is being paid to put an argument to the House. His electors are entitled to the same reassurance.

I have drafted an early-day motion which appears on today's Order Paper and which one or two Members may have seen. It would add to the list of disqualifying offices

"any person . . . who is specifically paid to promote or seek to promote the financial, commercial or industrial interests of a company inside Parliament or in dealings with Government Departments".

That could not be clearer. That is different from being on a board and advising on this or that. Being a company director is different from being in this place and being paid to book a room and to use it—

**Sir David Mitchell:** Will the right hon. Gentleman give way?

**Mr. Benn:** I cannot give way because I do not have time.

Being a company director is different from being in this place and booking a room or seeing the appropriate Minister to arrange something. Such activity in this place should be a disqualification.

Against that background, there is no need for an ethics commissioner. If someone breaks the law, he or she will be taken to court. The hearing will take place in public, unlike the hearings of the Privileges Committee, which take place in private. The hearing takes place and the Member will be liable to disqualification. As for classes of person, that is a matter of judgment. I am not committed to that form of words. If there is a wish to ban trade union representatives, let those who take that view make the case and try to carry the day. The same applies to solicitors and writers, for example. Whatever we do, the procedures must be embodied in law: let us not start with the idea of there being some administrator who will take us aside.

Ethics cover more than personal conduct. For example, would an ethics commissioner say, "Mr. Benn, you should not have supported the poll tax protestors"? Are we not to do this or that? Before we know where we are, democracy will be subordinated to some allegedly objective test.

I was amused when the right hon. Member for Bexley and Sidcup (Sir E. Heath) said that he objected to a commissioner. He said, "Parliament can decide." He should apply that argument to our attitude towards Brussels. He has expressed the very objection that some of us have to the European Commission. He objects to the attitude of the Commission being applied to him.

I return to the point of order that I made yesterday. We are not facing the situation which confronted the country 300 years ago when the then king tried to arrest the five Members. Instead, the business community is trying to buy the five Members. If we do not take a strong line against the commercial corruption of Parliament, as exemplified by the strong line that was taken years ago against the attempt by the then monarch to control Parliament, we should give up.

We are in the present mess because as the House of Commons we have lost our self-respect. We should have dealt with the problem years ago. We should not have left it to emerge as it did so that the Nolan report would be imposed upon us by a worried Prime Minister. We should have taken action ourselves. Now that the issue has arisen, we should take our own action. Let us proceed by law. The law should be set out so that everyone knows what it is. Our constituents can then introduce ethical elements.

I am disappointed that the Nolan report does not contain a recommendation that every voter should receive from his returning officer, with his polling card, information about the interests of every candidate and not only those of the outgoing Member. If that information were available, everyone who voted would know that they were voting for an official of the Transport and General Workers Union or for someone sitting on 10 boards. Let the electors choose: it is one of the characteristics of a democracy that they should decide. This is not a little club that we protect with little rules. That is not what it is about. We are not here because we like one another: we are in this place because we have been sent here, and the ultimate discipline on our conduct is the view that those who sent us here take when they decide to return us or to send us packing.

7.43 pm

**Sir Giles Shaw** (Pudsey): It is splendid to be able to take up the remarks of the right hon. Member for

*[Sir Giles Shaw]*

Chesterfield (Mr. Benn) on one of his high days. He made an extremely interesting and exciting contribution to the debate. I fear that I would not have been able to enter Parliament under the stiff criteria that he laid down. I came from the humble world of industry. I was with a company that was making fruit gums, After Eight mints and other lovely products of that sort. There was a wish to improve the lot of other people and, above all, to create wealth. We wished also to create employment. We all wished to be members of a company that contributed to about one fifth of the working population of York. That is something rather different from that which is represented by the hon. Member for Newcastle upon Tyne, North (Mr. Henderson). Both of us know about the company that I am talking about.

One of the strands of this place is that its Members are all from different backgrounds. We come from different places and we have different attitudes. That fabric makes this place, a place that has survived for hundreds of years. We must be extremely careful that we do not unpick it in a moment of deep penitence or one of deep-seated madness. Whatever else, we must work out correctly the problem that is before us. We must not panic. We must not say, "We cannot touch that which now exists." It is only right that we must react to any problem that confronts us.

My right hon. Friend the Member for Old Bexley and Sidcup (Sir E. Heath), the Father of the House, reminded us of the position in 1947 and referred to the report of the Strauss committee. As I understand it, that was the last occasion on which such issues were considered. It is only right that they should be examined again. Equally, it is right that the Nolan report should give us the opportunity to do so. As the right hon. Member for Chesterfield admirably stated, the outcome must be decided by the House and by no other authority.

Under the heading "Members' Financial Interests", which begins with paragraph 9, the good Nolan committee states:

"The reasons for the public's reduced confidence in the financial probity of Members of Parliament are not hard to identify. The public reads extensive press reporting of cases in which Members have accepted money for asking parliamentary questions, are said to have stayed at expensive hotels at others' expense without declaring an interest and are employed by multi-client lobbying firms".

There is all that huff and puff about what goes on in this place, but there is little grain of substance. We know full well from the sittings of the Privileges Committee—I am sorry that the right hon. and learned Member for Aberavon (Mr. Morris) is not in his place—what happened when it examined the two Members and money for questions. The newspaper that was involved had been given information by an unknown business man and the names of four Members. It found nothing during its investigation to substantiate the allegations relating to those Members. It then set out to try to entrap two Members.

If that is the basis for huge public disquiet and embarrassment, I greatly regret it. We cannot consider these issues without taking into account the fact that some aspects of investigative journalism have started to replace some of the aspects of reporting facts. If that is the way in which the world lives, it is not surprising that we should find ourselves caught up in the present position. As my right hon. Friend the Member for Bridgwater (Mr. King)

said in his excellent speech, we are faced with problems with which we must deal in a way that is best for the interests of the House as a whole.

I have not properly declared my interest. I shall do so straightaway and as it is laid down in the good book. I have a non-executive directorship. That might worry the right hon. Member for Chesterfield. I had two such directorships but I resigned from one, finding it difficult to get to the meetings and deal with the issues that are the responsibility of non-executive directors because of the pressures in this place and the various activities that relate to it.

I understand why it is felt that consultancies are difficult. They are difficult to understand because people do not realise the importance of them. Those who have had management and industrial backgrounds find especially that consultancies are the natural route through which their interests can be expressed outside the House.

As my right hon. Friend the Member for Epsom and Ewell (Sir A. Hamilton) said, lawyers have a remarkable capacity to earn money anywhere. They can earn money by their sheer skills. If someone has been involved in a background of manufacturing enterprise, it is not unreasonable that he should take an interest outside the House in sustaining manufacturing enterprises. Many manufacturing enterprises in Britain need the assistance of those who can help them to learn what it is to deal with the complexities of the rubric of the society in which they live, with the complexities of law and legislation or of getting export credit and everything that happens when trading overseas. All these aspects of business life affect small companies that are trying to make their way and, indeed, large ones. They look to many sources of advice, and sometimes they select Members.

When it comes to the declaration of interests, including consultancies, I understand the recommendations of the Nolan committee. I understand also that lobbying must be of maximum interest to the committee. It is a difficult matter, but, on the other hand, lobbying Members has been endemic to the House ever since its foundation. In the press, the Members' Lobby is seen as an exchange of information of various sorts. That results in reputations being made in print and sometimes rising circulations. It would appear that those results are all to the benefit of newspapers. Members use the Lobby and the Lobby is the entrepôt of ideas that are subsequently exploited. Perhaps money does not change hands. Indeed, I doubt whether it ever does. But once we have such a system it is not surprising that we become involved with outside interests that are seeking to find ways of procuring an influence, perhaps at a modest level. Nevertheless, they seek to procure influence.

But it is quite unreasonable for the committee to say that there should be a statement of the earnings from consultancies, but not a statement of the earnings from all other sources of external interest. It is inevitable that if the matter is dealt with only on the basis of consultancies, investigative journalists will have a field day. They will say, "Ah, Member X is getting a consultancy worth Y. What else is he getting?" They will look at his other interests and find out. They will find a way to expose a Member's external income.

That would be a travesty of the way in which we should react to the problem with which we are trying to deal. There must be a compensatory amount of privacy if there is to be a disclosure of pecuniary advantage. We must balance those two things. Some privacy is pretty crucial for a Member seeking to discharge his public office at a time such as this when we have media interest, 24 hours a day from all over the world, in what Members of Parliament may or may not be doing.

We must move slowly on the matter. We must take serious counsel. I was attracted by the suggestion of my right hon. Friend the Member for Watford (Mr. Garel-Jones) that a committee of Privy Councillors from both sides of the House might be a conduit through which Nolan can be rationalised into what is practical, and what is practical can be applied without the distortions that may happen if the work is done at speed.

I also understand that we must merge the Privileges Committee with the Select Committee on Members' Interests. That is an excellent suggestion and if it is a smaller committee thereby, I for one would be delighted because the 17-man Privileges Committee that we now have is far too substantial for the efforts that we have to make.

I respect what Nolan advises us to do. I understand his keenness to see change. I recognise that there are areas which must be changed. But if we are seriously to preserve our inheritance and not reduce the total panoply of the House for attracting people of talent and enterprise, those changes must be carefully worked out over time in order to be made practical and applicable to our Parliament, and then we can decide ourselves—no one else—to implement them.

7.51 pm

**Mr. Alfred Morris** (Manchester, Wythenshawe): The only interest that I have to declare—I do so with pride—is that I have long had the honour of sponsorship as a parliamentary candidate by the Co-operative Movement. As the House knows, I am also a member of the Committee of Privileges, but, of course, there is no financial interest there.

I shall not be speaking at length. My main purpose is most warmly to welcome Nolan's vindication of those who think it wrong for the Privileges Committee to be continuing to sit wholly in private at a time when Ministers talk of their commitment to open dealing and when, virtually by common consent of the major organs of opinion, the British people now want to see what is being done at Westminster in their name.

From the moment the Privileges Committee was reconstituted last July, I made plain my view that, wherever it could be avoided, we should no longer meet behind closed doors. The caveat "whenever it could be avoided" was to allow for occasions when, for some compelling reason, more especially one involving any possible breach of natural justice, the Committee ought to meet in camera. Yet we still meet in secret even when there is no conceivable legal or other reason for so doing and even when a witness specifically requests to be heard in public, as Peter Preston has done in the case of his impending appearance before the Committee.

The Prime Minister's insistence on secrecy, he told me, is based on precedent. "That's how it has always been" is his attitude. But if precedent had always been strictly adhered to, the Privileges Committee would still be meeting by candlelight and threatening, even imposing, fierce penalties against any journalist who dared to anticipate its reports. We heard earlier that Lord Nolan

had looked at proceedings in the Privileges Committee going back to 1947. What some of its present members have done is to look back to the Committee's proceedings as long ago as the 17th century, and to do so is to crave further modernisation.

I hope very much that this first report of the Nolan committee will now very soon bring our proceedings out of the shadows and into the 20th century while there are still a few years of it left. That would remove a demeaning stain on the reputation of the House; at the same time it would improve the quality of justice dispensed by its most powerful Committee.

The decision now, as I understand the Chancellor of the Duchy of Lancaster, will be one for the House as a whole, free from any pressure from the Government, or from anyone else, and of that I approve. We ought never avoidably now to meet in secret in Committees of the House, not because it is unpopular with, in fact deeply resented by, the British people, but because it is patently wrong to do so.

For the same reason I hope that the Nolan committee will urgently reconsider and reverse its decision not to tackle the funding of political parties. It is indefensible that one political party, at a moment of unprecedented unpopularity, should be allowed a veto on this crucially important issue. Surely no inquiry into standards in public life, properly so-called, can possibly avoid the core issue of party funding. As Simon Jenkins, its former editor, said in *The Times* yesterday:

"It is hard to imagine anything more corrupting than party cash handed over in secret, whether from a property dealer, an Arab Prince or a banker desperate for a peerage."

For his part, speaking last Sunday on BBC television, Lord Nolan said of his committee:

"We are cast in the traditional role of an auditor, a watchdog not a bloodhound, and if a watchdog sees something which needs looking into, it should bark."

That gave the impression that he was determined to stand his ground on party funding, but his bark seems to have been silenced by the Government. That is damaging to his committee's reputation and extremely disappointing to those of us who were encouraged by some of the recommendations in his report.

The Prime Minister's first reaction to the report was to accept its "broad thrust", but he has gone no further since then. We must hope that those two words mean more than that he is prepared to endorse only the principles of acceptable conduct in public life set out in the report:

"selflessness, integrity, objectivity, accountability, openness, honesty and leadership."

Some might say that for the Prime Minister even to accept the report's principles is an important step forward. Certainly some of them are not much in fashion in Whitehall now. Take accountability, openness and leadership. Our attempts to let the public see as much as possible of the Privilege Committee's proceedings was all about accountability and openness and it was leadership we were asking for in pressing the Prime Minister to depart from the ancient precedent to which he still clings in defence of secrecy.

The public now want not only to hear talk about precepts but to see them matched by practice. They are entitled to see beyond the doors of the Committee Rooms of the House, to know what is happening as it happens and to hear the Nolan committee barking loudly for full disclosure of all donations to all political parties.

[*Mr. Alfred Morris*]

I have only one other brief comment to make as a member of the Privileges Committee. In picturesque language, Lord Nolan's report says:

"The Committee is assisted by a small secretariat."

It then goes on to list the names of 12 people who have assisted its work. Those who have criticised the pace of the Privileges Committee's work may like to know that our staffing consists of the admirable Jim Hastings, the Committee's clerk; one third of the time of Paul Derrett, a Committee assistant; and what is called "access" to a shared secretary. What word other than "small" would Lord Nolan use to describe a secretariat as small as that? He might like to come and bark in our forest or, alternatively, perhaps we should start barking too.

*7.59 pm*

**Sir David Mitchell** (Hampshire, North-West): I start by declaring my interest. I have been a Member of this House for 31 years and, for 22 of those, I have been a practising wine merchant.

Important and serious issues have arisen today. I identify three of them. The first is the extent to which we regulate ourselves. I am uneasy about upsetting the delicate balance between the judiciary, Parliament and the Executive. I firmly believe in self-regulation, but we must do that as effectively as is practicable.

The second issue is whether we should go for legalistic rules or a set of principles with a code of practice. Again, I am firmly in favour of the latter. I agree with my right hon. Friend the Member for Bridgwater (Mr. King) that an adviser of one sort or another would be enormously helpful. When I came into the House, an older Member drew me a little map on the back of an envelope that showed where the Chamber, the dining room and the loo were, and he said, "That will do you for the first week." That was the whole induction course that I had on arriving in the House. There is something to be said for helping new Members particularly, and for making available to Members at any time someone who is what the Canadian Parliament would call an ethical adviser but, please, let us not call him a commissioner—that would not give the right sense at all.

Thirdly, there is far more right with our system than is being given credit for. But recent events have identified problems and clearly Lord Nolan has drawn attention to matters of uncertainty and confusion, and the need for clarification. I want to draw attention to two of those matters and to make two practical suggestions.

The first concerns the declaration of Members' interests. I fear that, too often, the declaration of those interests has become an alibi for half covering them up. When tabling questions, writing to Ministers or speaking in the House, Members assume that, because they have registered their interest in the register, that is sufficient, but it is not. People do not go around with a copy of the Register of Members' Interests in their pockets. Interests must be declared at the relevant time. If one is to make a speech that has some relevance to one's interests, one should declare that. If one tables a parliamentary question or writes to a Minister and one has an interest, that interest should be declared.

I put forward one practical, brief suggestion that could be implemented almost immediately. When a Member tables an early-day motion and has a paid interest, he has to put an "R" on the Order Paper to indicate that interest. Either that or the letters IDI—I declare an interest—should be put alongside a parliamentary question when a Member is in a paid position in relation to that question. That would be a practical and useful step forward. We on the Privileges Committee had the unhappy experience of dealing with two hon. Members. In that case, such a proposal would have helped to clarify the position.

The second change that I propose is this. At present, one must put an entry in the Register of Members' Interests within a month of acquiring that interest. I cannot for the life of me understand why there should be such a delay. If a Member has something to register, he should do so before he writes to Ministers, lobbies in any form, asks questions or makes speeches. That would have prevented one of the two cases before the Privileges Committee from occurring.

I hope that the House will consider those two practical suggestions. The first is that a paid consultancy should be identified on a parliamentary question, and the second is that nothing should be done in relation to using the benefit of an interest until it has been put on the register.

We are all grateful to Lord Nolan for his work. He has done an immense amount in relation to hon. Members. I hope that he will not fail to turn his attention to the interests of Members in the upper House, who, in exactly the same way, can be influenced by the possible effect of a consultancy.

I come now to the vexed question of consultancies. They appear to be in two forms. The first relates to Members who watch Bills, watch draft regulations and the like, and generally advise a trade union, trade association or a large company. They perform an important role. These days, there are too many regulations, directives, and pieces of legislation, and companies often need someone to interpret, to guide and to show them the way through them, and to explain the effect on their business of what is going on.

I gingerly raise the possibility that was put to me by a much respected former Member, Sir Robin Maxwell-Hyslop. When Members act on behalf of companies and, as a result, table parliamentary questions, incurring public expenditure, perhaps we should consider whether that company should make some contribution to those costs. I am not sure, but that is a matter for further exploration. There is a big difference between a Member advising a company and, crossing a silent line, a company advising him about what it wants raised in the House. That invisible line divides what is acceptable and what is not acceptable. I should like to ban the latter, but I recognise that there is a thin line between the two, and that it is almost impossible for someone outside to discern whether that line has been crossed.

The best way that the House can help itself is to ensure that transparency exists, that, when someone has an interest, it is declared and available for everyone to consider and, most particularly, that it is declared when it is relevant to the business in hand.

The question of the declaration of the amount of money paid for a consultancy has been raised. Once it is on the register that someone is being paid, that should be sufficient. I do not think that it really matters whether the Member is paid £5,000 or £10,000.

**Mr. Doug Hoyle** (Warrington, North): Oh yes it does.

**Sir David Mitchell:** The hon. Gentleman says, "Yes it does." No one in the debate has yet given a good reason—perhaps we shall hear one later—why amounts should be declared. What is important is that when a Member does not act entirely as a freelance operator, when he is in some way financially benefiting from what he is doing, that should be declared. That it is declared is sufficient to give Members the warning that they ought to have.

In relation to Members' earnings from consultancies and the like, we cannot ignore the fact that Members are paid extraordinarily little for what they do. When I came into the House, I think that we were paid £3,800 a year; now it is over £30,000, but the purchasing power is within £100 of what it was 30 years ago. I do not know of any other profession that has seen no real increase in the value of its take-home salary over 30 years, a period in which the work load has gone up many times—from 25 or 30 letters a week to 200 letters a week. There is a multitude of other work, such as the Committees of the House. It was a part-time operation when I came in, but it is no longer so. It is very much a full-time one today.

I draw hon. Members' attention to the fact that, on 23 November 1994, I asked for a list of those Officers of the House who earn more than we do. Is it really right for nearly 150 of those who look after us to be paid more than we are? Are Members of Parliament really worth so much less than our excellent staff? Are they really worth so much less than those who administer the Palace of Westminster or service the House in many ways, and do it so very well for us?

During—

**Mr. Deputy Speaker:** Order.

8.9 pm

**Mr. Doug Hoyle** (Warrington, North): First, I must declare my interests—although they are all in the register. I am sponsored by the Manufacturing, Science and Finance union; I am an unpaid consultant to the Prison Officers Association; and I am an unpaid adviser to the National Association of Licensed House Managers. *[Interruption.]* I am sorry; I did not catch what was said by the hon. Member for Eltham (Mr. Bottomley).

**Mr. Peter Bottomley** (Eltham) *rose*—

**Mr. Hoyle:** I do not want to be interrupted by the hon. Gentleman, however. I have only 10 minutes in which to speak.

**Mr. Garrett:** He said, "Where do you get your election expenses from?"

**Mr. Hoyle:** It is all in the register; I have nothing to hide. The hon. Member for Eltham need only look in the register. Indeed, he probably has it with him. I am pleased to be able to say that I have nothing to be ashamed of.

In such circumstances, the House finds itself in difficulty because it is complacent about itself. It is time that the House faced up to its low standing with the public. The right hon. Member for Bridgwater (Mr. King) gave two figures from a Gallup poll: he said that 64 per cent. of the public believed that most Members of Parliament make a lot of money using public office improperly, and he said that the figure nine years ago was 46 per cent. He could have gone on to quote the other figures: he could have told us that 77 per cent. of the public believe that Members of Parliament care more about special interests than about people like themselves—which is a real condemnation—and that only 28 per cent. of the public think that Members of Parliament have a high personal moral code.

We ought to be extremely concerned about that. I am sorry that the hon. Member for Pudsey (Sir G. Shaw) is not present, because he mentioned the Privileges Committee and cash for questions and pointed out that only two Members of Parliament were involved. In fact, only 20 Members were surveyed; two of them accepted the money, while another was prepared to take it and then give it to charity. That is not a good record—and what would have been revealed had the investigation gone further? Moreover, it was alleged that other Members, who were not named, had been taking money for quite a while.

We should be concerned about all this. There is a gravy train in the House—and, amazingly, Conservative Members are involved. *[Interruption.]* The hon. Member for Ribble Valley (Mr. Evans), with his little interests in a shop, can laugh; he comes from south Wales. Let me put it this way to him, and to the hon. Member for Hampshire, North-West (Sir D. Mitchell): Conservative Members have 766 outside sources of income. One Conservative Member has 16 such sources, another has 12, two have 11, one has nine, one has eight and one has six.

If we assume that those consultancies are worth £10,000 a time—some are worth more; some may be worth a little less—the Member with 16 of them will earn £160,000, quite apart from his £30,000 salary. Something is wrong. No wonder the public believe that there is sleaze in the House if that is going on. We must know how much Members of Parliament are being paid for all those consultancies. Their constituents have a right to know as well. We have heard a good deal from hon. Members along the lines of, "The public do not want to know; they want to believe that Members of Parliament are honest." I suggest that, at election time, Members of Parliament do not go around saying, "I have 16 consultancies, and I am paid n thousand a time." None of them does that—and, when it comes to making a declaration of what they are receiving, we see them moving away from Nolan.

I have always believed that being a Member of Parliament should be a full-time job, but I also agree with the right hon. Member for Worthing (Sir T. Higgins). One reason why Members of Parliament, particularly Conservative Members, accept consultancies and the retainers that go with them may be that their basic salaries are far too low. We should certainly pay Members a salary that is commensurate with their duties—although Nolan did not make that point.

In recommending the appointment of a parliamentary commissioner for standards, Nolan did not suggest that such responsibilities should be taken away from the House, which would be wrong. He suggested that such a commissioner could report to a smaller version of the Privileges Committee, which would meet in public—which Labour members of the Privileges Committee have advocated. I was very pleased that Nolan recommended that such a Sub-Committee should meet in public whenever possible, and should report to the full Privileges Committee. An aggrieved Member could appeal to the full Committee, and if necessary the matter would be dealt with by the House of Commons as a whole.

*[Mr. Hoyle]*

I do not think that anyone wishing to dispel public unease about the activities of Members of Parliament could disagree with any of those proposals. We should not only be transparent; we should be prepared to put on record what we do and what we earn. If we are not prepared to do that, the public have a right to ask what Members of Parliament have to hide. That is the cause of much of the unease—the sweeping under the carpet, and the cosy club atmosphere that many Members of Parliament want. I believe that those days have gone.

I always appreciate the speeches of the Father of the House, the right hon. Member for Old Bexley and Sidcup (Sir E. Heath), and what he said today was very humorous; but he spoke of matters that belong to the past. Time has moved on. Public unease has grown since the 1950s. My right hon. Friend the Member for Chesterfield (Mr. Benn), however, reminded us that there were scandals in the past as well. We must put our House in order; we have taken far too long in reaching that conclusion. Standards have deteriorated since 1979, but only now is the House prepared to get to grips with that.

The Chancellor of the Duchy of Lancaster was extremely complacent. Given that the Nolan committee was set up by the Prime Minister, I expected him to say, "We must examine these proposals on an urgent basis, and act on them." If we delay as long as he suggested before debating the matter again, we shall find ourselves in the summer recess, and we shall not be able to begin to implement even the recommendations that Nolan believes should be implemented immediately until autumn or even the end of the year.

I hope that the Leader of the House will take account of that in his reply. If we are to restore public confidence in the House, the Nolan recommendations must be acted on as urgently as possible—and I believe that they should all be implemented in full.

8.18 pm

**Sir Dudley Smith** (Warwick and Leamington): The hon. Member for Warrington, North (Mr. Hoyle) will not be surprised to learn that I am diametrically opposed to much of what he said. I hope to pick up some of the points that he made in what must necessarily be a brief speech.

I have been a management consultant for the past 21 years but I have never felt uneasy about operating in the House. I have given political and governmental advice, although some of my work had nothing whatever to do with politics. However, I have never acted in a covert way and I suppose that my activities are perhaps more in line with those outlined by my right hon. Friend the Member for Watford (Mr. Garel-Jones) in his interesting interjection.

As time is short, I shall confine myself mainly to the proposals affecting Members of Parliament, but I agree that we should outlaw the situation that allows Members of Parliament to be employed cavalierly by lobbyists to press the case for a new railway or road and to be paid a large sum of money to canvas and speak to that end. As I understand the Nolan report, that is to be outlawed.

I am also worried about the recommendation relating to Ministers. Goodness knows we have heard how badly paid they are, and I do not think that we can put them in cold storage for two years after they have left office and

expect them not to have a proper job. A minimum interim period should be established, but the matter needs to be examined carefully before a decision is made.

I part company from the two right hon. Members who were members of the Nolan committee—my right hon. Friend the Member for Bridgwater (Mr. King) and the right hon. Member for Bethnal Green and Stepney (Mr. Shore)—when it comes to parliamentary consultancies in general. The report condemns them and recommends the abolition of some, but also suggests strongly that they should in fact be phased out. As we have heard, it demands that the amounts earned should be declared. The hon. Member for Warrington, North said that there is a large difference between the amounts earned by different hon. Members, but I disagree.

What about directors, writers, broadcasters, solicitors and trade union advisers, all of whom in some way owe their jobs to the fact that they are Members of Parliament? Are we to treat some hon. Members differently from others? Is there to be a small core of hon. Members who become the lepers of the House because they have to declare their earnings whereas others, who probably earn much more, get away without doing so? I should not have thought that partial discrimination was the way for the Executive to proceed. I hope that the Government will pay heed to that.

If there is to be financial declaration, it should be total and every hon. Member with an outside interest should declare what he or she earns. There should be either a total declaration or no declaration at all, but there cannot be discrimination.

Of course, we know that the situation would be exploited by the media, who would have a field day if we had to make complete disclosure of such information. Hon. Members would be pilloried by the media, locally and nationally.

I see an inexorable move towards the "full-time" Member of Parliament. My right hon. Friend the Member for Worthing (Sir T. Higgins) said that we are all full-time Members of Parliament but those with outside interests work harder than others.

If we are unlucky enough to have a Labour Government after the next election, I anticipate an accelerated move to full-time Members of Parliament with no outside interests, but who are chained to the House, with no further opportunities, and all for about £32,000. There will be great pressure because the public already think that we should receive only half what we get now. The issue will be fudged by the Government of the day, whether Conservative or Labour. Any increase will be small and will not make up for what is lost with the abolition of outside interests.

I am glad that I am in the later stages of my time here. If I were in my 30s or 40s, I should not want to stay after what I have heard here today and elsewhere. The parliamentary climate is deteriorating. My advice to all contemplating a political career is to think very seriously about it because I can envisage a new authoritarian atmosphere which will not be conducive to their making the best of their abilities.

The Opposition may laugh, but the Nolan committee came about because of "sleaze". If we are unlucky enough to have a Labour Government, they will find that they will receive the same media attention and accusations of sleaze will be directed at them. They should not think that they will get away with anything. They will have a very rough time and should bear that in mind.

The most disturbing aspect of the debate is not the personal feelings or individual cases that hon. Members have used to illustrate their speeches, however, but the fact that Parliament's sovereignty is being undermined. I do not accept what has been said today by the two members of the Nolan committee. The sovereignty of Parliament is being undermined, and that was borne out by the remarks by my right hon. Friend the Member for Old Bexley and Sidcup (Sir E. Heath).

We are to have a commissioner on standards, or ethics officer, as the hon. Member for Dewsbury (Mrs. Taylor) so neatly put it. He will be a veritable gauleiter with strong powers to make recommendations. It is true that he will report to a sub-committee, but it will be his poodle. It is hard to imagine that it will reject his recommendations which will in fact be decisions. The committee would not dare do so. The commissioner will submit his proposals and they will be accepted.

The Nolan report is bullish and I do not like its tone. I know what Lord Nolan was trying to achieve and that he was dealing with serious problems, but the thrust of the report is authoritarian. It implies that the committee has come to stay as an institution in its own right, to monitor, judge and instruct. If we are not careful, it will be Parliament's over-zealous headmaster and will monitor public life in general. That would be very much against the interests of democracy.

The truth is that, for good or ill, Parliament must police itself. The public decide whether they like us and, if they do not, they throw us out. That process must not be subverted by the frenzied, unscrupulous media or for short-term political gain, the attractions of which are clear and have been illustrated by many speeches from Opposition Members. Parliament is the highest court in the land and cannot be ruled by a High Court judge, however eminent, or by a registrar, however qualified or respectable.

The Nolan report is not holy writ. We do not have to obey its timetable or respond to the demand for early action. A period for consideration is very important. Parliament must safeguard its sovereignty and deal with the situation circumspectly. There should be no rush to judgment.

8.27 pm

**Mr. John Garrett** (Norwich, South): I confess that I am an occasional lecturer and author. In fact, I am the author of a book on the effectiveness of the House and the chapter that deals with this particular issue converted me to the idea that something must be done. It has always seemed to me that Conservative Members in particular should declare their lack of interest as well as their interests. For example, in debates on state education and health, they should make it clear that they use neither.

I congratulate the Prime Minister on setting up the Nolan committee and trust that he will accept its recommendations, with a few exceptions. I find that I agree more with Conservatives than with my hon. Friends about what is wrong with the Nolan report. For example, I think that the Speaker should be the commissioner for standards and that the recommendations should be embodied in law.

It is right that the committee should move on to examine the funding of political parties. The Prime Minister and the chairman of the Conservative party say that the giving of personal donations to the Tory party should be confidential and that donors should be guaranteed anonymity. That does not seem unreasonable, so let Nolan tell us about private donors to political parties—their nationality, the amounts that they give and what they appear to receive in return—without revealing their identity. We should then be able to resolve a mystery of the Tory party funding—the gap between total receipts and corporate and other declared donations—but donors would not be exposed. I urge the Government to consider that proposal.

One Nolan recommendation with which I disagree is that the commissioner for standards should be a person of independent standing. It seems ridiculous that we cannot at least put the supervision of parliamentary standards in the hands of the Speaker.

I can see the virtue of having some outside people on the commission for standards rather than on the sub-committee that is proposed by Nolan. However, as one who has long argued for a new and independent role for the Speaker, it seems to me that the holder of that office should chair the commission. That would mean that we would have constant access to the guardian of our standards. Some people say that the Speaker could not cope with that extra burden but there is a simple way round that and I have been advocating it for a long time. It is that the House should have a chief executive. That would remove the managerial responsibilities from the Speaker and the Clerk, and the Speaker would be able to handle the new responsibility.

Hon. Members should declare their incomes from all sources, should be banned from using their capacity as hon. Members to make money, and banned from working for bodies providing parliamentary services and from accepting contracts of employment. What other employer would allow an employee to take a contract of employment with another employer? That does not go anything like as far as the arrangements for American and French legislators.

Conservative Members have said, and I agree, that there has always been a massive amount of hypocrisy about Members' remuneration. The payment of Members of Parliament was reintroduced in 1911 by Lloyd George after a period of some hundreds of years during which they were not paid at all. He described the pay of Members of Parliament as,

"not a remuneration, but a recompense, not a salary but an allowance. The only principle of payment in the public service is that you should make an allowance to a man to enable him to maintain himself confidently and honourably, but not luxuriously, during the time he is rendering service to the State. That is the only principle, and it is the principle on which we have proceeded."

Lloyd George introduced a payment of £400 a year. By that precedent the idea grew up that a Member's pay was an allowance for broken time from a regular job, and for too many it still is. I was in the House when a Conservative Member of Parliament, the director of a famous civil engineering company, said how grateful he was that his company allowed him time off to attend Parliament.

Nowadays the job of an assiduous Member of Parliament is clearly full time. The idea that we collectively benefit from the wisdom of those hon.

[Mr. John Garrett]

Members in all parts of the House who spend a significant proportion of their time in the everyday world of the courts and the City is totally false. Some of the efforts by hon. Members to acquire interests are demeaning to us all. There was not only the money-for-questions scam because the House will remember the case of the Conservative Member who advertised for employment in the parliamentary *House Magazine*, stating:

"it was one way of drawing the nation's attention to the fact that I only had one consultancy and could take on more".

I also object to the provision of research assistants to Members by lobbying or commercial interests. I do not know how widespread that is but Nolan should investigate it. It occurs throughout the House and it is quite wrong. The present office costs allowance is perfectly adequate for the secretarial and research costs of a Back-Bench Member, and Front-Bench Members get Short money.

We need a proper, professional evaluation of the work of a Member of Parliament—a job evaluation. That was carried out very successfully by professional consultants in 1983 but was disregarded by the Government who pegged Members' pay at 89 per cent. of that of a grade 6 civil servant. That is the top end of middle management, a senior Library Clerk in the House or an assistant accountant employed by the Fees Office. The 1983 exercise needs to be carried out again and the most stringent limits placed on outside earnings. In evidence to Nolan, an hon. Member said:

"It is a great honour and a privilege to be an MP but that does not feed, educate or clothe one's wife or husband or children."

He could have fooled me! It was an extraordinarily insensitive remark to make in public when one considers what many of our constituents are paid—those of them who have jobs.

The whole area of Members' work and outside employment is an embarrassment and must be cleared up. The requirements relating to Members' interests should be enshrined in law and not left as an unenforceable code of conduct. We could start with a code of conduct and then put the matter into law.

The relationships of Ministers and civil servants should also be specified by statute. The report in November by the Select Committee on the Treasury and Civil Service proposed legislation to govern the employment of civil servants rather than control via the royal prerogative, which is simply government by proclamation. That legislation could cover the civil servant who had to report wrongdoing by a Minister, and the appropriate outside body for that seems to be the Civil Service Commission.

The legislation would also cover Nolan's proposed commissioner for public appointments instead of having appointments to quangos made by the royal prerogative. Select Committees should have the right to examine prospective appointees to top jobs in quangos. We could not cover them all but simply having the right to do that would put fear into everybody else. My party has been as guilty as any other in creating quangos but now quangos are out of hand. When I first came to the House they were advisory bodies but now they are executive bodies. Wales is a well-known example. There are more members of quangos in Wales than there are local councillors, and they spend more. The whole area needs a clean-up with a view to making as many quangos as possible democratically accountable to elected bodies.

This is the thin end of a very big wedge. Perhaps it will not happen during my time in the House but I hope that during my lifetime outside interests will be on the way out. There will be a proper, settled payment for being an MP and hon. Members will not be able to have employment that in any way derives from their membership of the House. They will be made to declare their incomes and the idea of outside employment will wither away. Nolan has usefully taken the lid off a can of worms and I hope that the debate will move from sleaze, which taints the House—all of us—and on to major constitutional questions. The report is a useful first step.

8.35 pm

**Sir Geoffrey Johnson Smith** (Wealden): I shall speak in a personal capacity and not as the Chairman of the Select Committee on Members' Interests. I declare the interest that is contained in the Register of Members' Interests. I first got involved with the Committee and the matters that we are debating in 1975. It was the first Committee to be set up to look at the whole question of registration and Members' interests. We have come a long way since then and I am proud of the progress that we have made.

When I became Chairman in 1979, some of the Committee's activities were greatly resented and I had to twist the arms of some hon. Members to get them to register. They felt that they should not register because they were not statutorily required to do so and a resolution was not good enough. That view was shared by Mr. Enoch Powell, at that time a distinguished and highly respected right hon. Member, who refused to register. The trouble was that other people who were incarnations of Enoch Powell tried to do the same. They got short shrift.

I shall not enter into an argument about a statute because a resolution of the House presents no difficulty and I no longer have to twist arms to get people to register. Entering the area of statutes would be like entering a hornet's nest.

Over many years, I have tried to use two principles when helping to guide the Committee. The first was transparency and the second was compliance. Openness has been the golden thread running through our deliberations and those of Nolan. However, the need for people to comply willingly with the regulations has been of paramount importance.

Two thoughts were in my mind when considering compliance. First, the Committee should have regard to the traditions and practices of the House and to the nature of the people who are elected to it. On the whole, those people have a strong sense of dedication and vocation. Secondly, if our regulations do not match the spirit of the place because they are thought to be too intrusive or bureaucratic, they are doomed. Instead of showing willing compliance, Members will not respect the regulations and will attempt to circumvent them.

I am grateful to Lord Nolan and those who served so conscientiously on his committee and who rightly responded to the challenge. I do not agree with all that is in the report, but I can go along with much of it. I am glad that hon. Members are not cut off from the rest of life. That is contrary to Opposition opinion, which probably reflects the true voice of the Labour party. Nolan is right to come down on the side of those who believe that hon. Members should be allowed to have outside interests and that, far from diminishing proceedings of the House, they would enhance the contributions to the collective wisdom of the House.

I am also pleased that the Nolan committee recognises the difference between councillors and Ministers who have executive responsibilities. As Back Benchers, we do not have such responsibilities, and it is an important distinction to make. The report was right to recommend that hon. Members should not be paid for acting on behalf of lobbying companies. I do not say that because I have anything against lobbying. I know that it is an integral part of the democratic process. Indeed, I have benefited very much from the briefing that I have received from lobbying companies from time to time.

In my verbal submission to the Nolan committee, I said that the Select Committee on Members' Interests lacked the powers and the expertise to act as an investigative tribunal and that, in an adjudicating role, it left something to be desired. I had in mind the more serious cases that have come before us and are before us. I therefore welcome the appointment of an independent commissioner for standards, who will report to a Sub-Committee of the existing Privileges Committee, thus retaining the absolute right of Parliament to be the sole judge of a Member's conduct.

I am not sure that we have got it right. The powers that the independent commissioner would be given are too extensive. Indeed, they have been criticised by many hon. Members in this debate. Some have suggested the Speaker for the job. Frankly, I think that our Speaker is busy enough. The powers are certainly too great. I also worry about the cost and about creating a new bureaucracy. Nevertheless, I like the idea of using an independent adviser. Certainly, it will help the Sub-Committee to consider the more serious complaints when Members have to face the somewhat daunting experience of being questioned and cross-examined by their colleagues. It is right that such Members should be allowed to call up advisers to help them when they are questioned. If not, it will increasingly be found to appear to be and act like a kangaroo court.

The commissioner and the new arrangements are supposed to be put in place by the beginning of the new Session in November. I do not want to procrastinate, as I said in one of my interventions, but there is much to be thought out. We are in awful danger of underestimating some of the complications, not in setting up the bureaucracy but in deciding what should and should not be registered and what agreements should and should not be put on the register. I feel bound to say that I am not convinced that the Government would be wise to rush into the matter. Many hurdles on the way must be overcome.

A new commissioner, for example, must have a pretty good working knowledge and understanding of the House and its Members, not least because compiling the new register will impose additional information, some of which is controversial. I have no problem with facing up to the need for greater clarity in the register. We have had a stab at it, goodness know how many times, as members of the Committee. But there is no reason why we should not try again. No one should underestimate the complexity of that task alone. It is not just a question of semantics.

The report picks up consultancies as the greatest cause for public concern and recommends immediate prohibition of Members from dealing with organisations providing "paid Parliamentary services to multiple clients".

In the first instance, the report presumably aims at Members with consultancy agreements with public relations or lobbying firms. That category may not be as easy to define as some people think. How and on what criteria are such consultancies to be distinguished from, say, advertising agencies, financial advisers, management consultants, trade associations or, indeed, legal practices, all of which have clients of their own?

In paragraph 55, Nolan also appears to regard consultancies in general as the category that, more than any other, might be thought to influence a Member's conduct in Parliament. He appears to believe that, therefore, they should be registered with greater transparency to include disclosure of income. Is that necessarily true? Why is a consultancy more likely to be influential than, for example, holding certain kinds of directorships, or continuing to practise a particular profession? In short, one could interpret the report as suggesting that a consultant, say, to a financial services company with many clients, would have to register, but if he were a non-executive director, he would not. I do not mean to be pedantic, but I know from experience that the more grey areas are left, the more difficult it becomes for the registrar or even the new commissioner to implement the House's decisions.

Registering financial agreements between Members and firms that employ them and the level of detail which will have to be addressed should not be regarded as easy, either. There is also the question of trade union sponsorship, which is an area of professional influence. Are those receiving such sponsorship supposed to register along with those who have consultancies? Is it regarded as a fact that such sponsorships influence parties and Members? That of course brings in the whole question of political funding. In that respect, the Nolan committee has strayed beyond its immediate remit.

On the principle of disclosure, the report recommends that the remuneration of financial considerations received by a Member for parliamentary services or by way of sponsorship should be entered into the register, possibly in banded form. We are all familiar with the fact that the Nolan committee asserted that a Member who gets £1,000 a year as a parliamentary adviser is less likely to be influenced by the prospect of losing the money than one who receives £20,000. I disagree. To require Members to report into which bands their additional income falls would suggest that the amount of their outside income has some overwhelming significance and influence. It ignores other influences.

All of us know that our constituents are among the big influences in our lives. They know something about us. We do not want them to know anything about, or to appear to do something or do something of which we would be ashamed and which would affect our reputation if they knew about it. Constituents have influence because they have the power to elect us. The local party organisation also has influence; it has the power to de-select. Those are very important influences. The report seems to assume that all Members start from the same financial position—

**Madam Deputy Speaker (Dame Janet Fookes):** Order. I am sorry to interrupt the hon. Gentleman, but the time is up.

8.46 pm

**Mr. John Gunnell** (Morley and Leeds, South): I shall be very rapid. My interests are declared in the Register of Members' Interests. I have a considerable number of them, as people will see. I thought that the hon. Member for Warrington, North (Mr. Hoyle) was referring to me, because 14 non-executive directorships are listed, although nine of those are unremunerated. I am also sponsored by GMB, which pays £600 a year to my constituency.

In his opening speech, the Chancellor of the Duchy of Lancaster drew a distinction between aspects affecting Members' interests, which he said had to be decided by the House, aspects affecting Ministers and those that affect quangos. I was glad to hear him say that the Government would be introducing measures that dealt with Ministers and quangos, but I was disappointed that he seemed to accept that it was for Members of the House themselves to bring forward proposals relating to their Nolan recommendations.

For any proposals to come through, there must be a timetable. The will to keep to the timetable recommended by Nolan has been expressed. I would have thought, therefore, that it was the Government's responsibility to find time during which Members were able to debate these issues. Over the past few weeks, the Leader of the House has not seemed to be enormously pressed for time. I hope that time will be found for the issues to be discussed.

Under what format will that happen? Our debate has shown that the issues are complex and that people have different reactions to them. In the A, B and C category time scale for the recommendations on Members, there are three in category A, seven in category B and one in the category C. I would have thought that it would be perfectly possible for the Government, in Government time, to introduce the three measures in category A, so that the House may debate and decide them, and then cover the measures in category B in a number of separate debates. I hope that it will be possible in the time scale that Nolan suggests to discuss his recommendations and the general issues involved in Government time, during which debate Members would be free to table amendments. I realise that that would take some time, but the issue has proved important and I hope that we will be able to make enough progress in the time scale envisaged.

The two major outside interests that I hold are two non-executive chairmanships. I have held one since 1989, and although I took up the other—the chairmanship of Yorkshire Enterprise—only in the last financial year, it was a job I was returning to, having done it for eight years before I became a Member of Parliament. Those jobs were not given to me because I am a Member of Parliament but are related to my earlier work in the west Yorkshire economy. If those organisations wish me to do those jobs, I am happy to be involved directly in those matters, doing public-private sector work in the west Yorkshire economy.

However, there are other demands in one's life that one must satisfy before accepting any other responsibilities. One has to be satisfied that taking a job will not interfere with one's responsibilities to Parliament. We have responsibilities not only to Parliament but to our constituents, and it is enormously important that those responsibilities are completely fulfilled.

One also must fulfil one's responsibilities to one's party. The work we do must be consistent with the principles of our party and with what one wishes to stand for. It would be wrong to speak directly in the interests of certain bodies here, but it would be wrong also to be involved in an organisation if it worked inconsistently with the principles for which one spoke in the party and in Parliament.

That is why, although the only roles that I have taken after entering the House were not directly derived from my being here, they are connected with my interests here. One of my jobs is concerned with housing, so I spoke to the then Labour spokesperson on housing to ensure that doing it was consistent, in his view, with my membership of the House and of the parliamentary Labour party.

The other decision that I have had to make is about money. I acknowledge that it is a matter of individual conscience, but I am perfectly happy with the idea that the financial figures are set down. It might be more consistent if, as one or two other hon. Members have suggested, we followed the principle of total disclosure of all earnings from outside sources. I certainly believe that there is value in setting down exactly the total amount of cash each Member gains from each appointment, rather than using a banding system.

It is up to us as individuals to decide what our outside earnings should be used for. I try to ensure that I use the money either for additional office costs, for funding other aspects of my job as a Member of Parliament for which we are not recompensed, or for the benefit of other causes that I wish to support. In my case, those are usually causes associated with or supported by the Labour party. But that is entirely a matter for an individual Member and his own philosophy.

It is important to move forward on the proposals, so I hope that the Leader of the House will assure us that time will be found for those that would affect Members to be discussed and decided on by Members. We recognise that these must be decisions of the whole House, and I hope that they can be taken in the time scale that Nolan suggests.

8.54 pm

**Mr. Iain Duncan Smith** (Chingford): I realise that other hon. Members still want to speak, so I shall make my comments brief. I start by making a declaration—that I have not much to declare. I have a little broadcasting and journalism; apart from that, according to the gauge cited by an Opposition Member, who described Members with 16, 17 or 20 consultancies, I must be something of a failure, for I have none. However, having come from industry, I believe that I have some understanding of what is necessary to contribute in the House on what helps that process.

I start by asking: what is this all about? It struck me when the Nolan committee was set up, and I make no bones about repeating it now, that I do not recall ever having voted for the Committee to be set up in the first place. I agree with the right hon. Member for Chesterfield (Mr. Benn) that it was done by prerogative. My views on the position of Parliament mean that I should like to have had some say in deciding what would be set up.

However, the water has gone under that bridge, and now I shall examine what Nolan was all about. The committee was asked to examine the problems caused by a perception of a lack of probity in public life; yet when I read through the results, especially the evidence, I kept coming up against the fact that the committee found that the public perception was far from the facts demonstrating the level of probity in public life—including standards among Members of Parliament, civil servants and Ministers.

The committee was asked to investigate very few cases over that period. Most of them concerned allegations about Members of Parliament, and none could be demonstrated or proven against Ministers or civil servants. The committee made some fairly general statements about that fact, and early in the report the point is made that there is a gap. My hon. Friend the Member for Wealden (Sir G. Johnson Smith) asked my right hon. Friend the Member for Bridgwater (Mr. King) what problem had created the gap between perception and reality. That, more than anything else, is the question that needs answering. The report deals with the reality, yet the perception is otherwise.

I have been in the House only three years, although it has been a pretty interesting three years. I have not had as long as others to see a decline in anything, but in view of the torrid state of affairs over the past three years I wonder what things could have been like for those who have been here for 30 years. I can hardly believe that they can have seen more change than I have.

I shall now mention some of the aspects of the report with which I agree; I shall return to the gap in perception later. As I said in my evidence, I believe that it is legitimate for Members of Parliament to have outside interests. However, I also believe that we require transparency. Our constituents and others should be able to look and see what we do, and when we speak we must make it clear if we have a general interest out there.

I am against any Member making a speech simply because somebody out there has paid him to do so. That is wrong—Nolan makes that clear to some degree—and transparency would put an end to that. I say to the Opposition that I have no objection to Members having direct involvement with trade unions, as it is important that that side of the argument is heard as much as that of commerce and industry. That involvement must, however, be well known.

I would like to know, however, where the mention of lawyers was during this committee process. It now appears that two classes of people are developing who can exist in this place. We may be in serious danger of saying that any involvement with commercial activities or the wealth-creating sector here only infects and taints, while anything to do with the professions somehow uplifts and makes us better; therefore, those involved with the latter are better than those who may be involved with the former.

Another problem is that Nolan seemed to say that if one made money before one came here, that was okay; one could then afford to be a good Member of Parliament, because one could afford the extra costs. If one inherits money, that is also okay. I am worried that a gap is developing between the different types of Members of Parliament, and I gave evidence on that matter.

Although the argument for banning lobbyists may be tremendously persuasive and have much support in the House, I am not certain how we would achieve such a ban. We can ban one thing today, but it would erupt somewhere else under a different guise. A lobby company may be a rogue company which will find some other mechanism. A lobby company that has someone to represent it here should list on the Register of Members' Interests every company that it represents, and that would have a sobering effect.

The draft code of conduct referred to on page 38 of the report says that, although it is accepted that Members should have outside interests, when those interests come up in a Standing Committee of the House the Member must immediately take himself off the Committee. That negates the idea that such outside interests bring anything to the House, and is a strange straddling of two stools.

I find it difficult to agree with the idea of a parliamentary commissioner for standards. I believe absolutely that Parliament should be the ultimate home of discretion for us all, and that our judges should lie within this body. I feel that having a commissioner would be another act of folly, as we would push the jurisdiction of the House outside to some passing judge of no fixed commitment or abode.

As the number of those who transgress is very small, we do not need somebody from outside to act. We want someone from this place, or a group of people, who accept the fact that this is not a party political issue, and that whoever is looked at should be looked at with fairness and with a sense of natural justice. If, however, we are forced to go down the road of having a commissioner, I would say to Madam Speaker that such an appointee must come solely from her office. There is no way that I will vote for somebody from outside this place, who does not know of the pressures and the work of the House, to sit in judgment on Members. I will not accept another judge coming in to declare on us all. Who, more than judges, are more distant from the population whom we serve? We are the elected Members. I would prefer to keep this matter within the House.

The real problem is that we have become careless with democracy. Most of the developments here have resulted in power seeping away from this Chamber, to Whitehall and to Europe or in statutory instruments. For example, when the Nolan report was made public, I was concerned to hear members of the Opposition and the Government pronouncing on what they thought of it. The Government said that they essentially accepted the broad thrust of the report, while Opposition Front Benchers said that the Government had to accept the report in full.

I do not care what Front Benchers from either side of the House thought of the report, because it is to be debated and decided by Members here in this place. It is an indictment of the Executive and the shadow Executive that they immediately think that they can coerce Members into accepting a decision on the report. Members must decide, and it is not for the Executive or the shadow Executive to tell us what to do.

Whatever we decide to implement will be of no worth if the media do not agree to sign up to what we agree. As long as we go on saying that we will publish reports and findings, the media will go on saying that that is not enough. As long we go on saying that we believe in certain aspects of what we do, we will find the media crawling down our backs, saying that we are nothing but a group of sleazy people acting in our own interests. The media must recognise that they have responsibilities in this matter. They are often referred to as the fourth estate, and they have a huge amount of power and influence.

[*Mr. Iain Duncan Smith*]

They influence people to make laws and regulations and they influence the way in which taxpayers' money is spent.

I urge the Nolan committee now to consider where the media's influences come from: who pays their lunches and bills; who sends them on trips; who coerces them to write articles; and what motivates them. Without some idea of what they do and some recognition that they have a responsibility in this matter, whatever we decide here tonight or on any other day will never be of use to anyone.

9.4 pm

**Ms Angela Eagle** (Wallasey): I declare that I am a sponsored member of Unison, which entails no personal remuneration but a payment of £600 a year to my constituency in accordance with the Hastings agreement, which is also a published document.

I commend the work of the Nolan committee, particularly the speed with which it has done its work, the clarity with which it has expressed itself, the openness of its deliberations and the fairness with which it has approached its task. I also commend the right hon. Members for Bridgwater (Mr. King) and for Bethnal Green and Stepney (Mr. Shore), who sat on the committee, for their speeches tonight, both of which were extremely thought provoking and raised important questions of detail with which the House will have to grapple—I hope, shortly.

I welcome the report and its recommendations. I also welcome the three-year remit that the Prime Minister has given the Nolan committee and the fact that it can return to these issues if the House makes no progress.

I wish to concentrate mainly on the section of the report that deals with Members of Parliament. That means not that I underestimate the importance of the rest of the report but that tonight I wish to concentrate on an area about which the Chancellor of the Duchy of Lancaster said very little in his opening speech. He properly dealt with the Government's and the Executive's view, but the crux of many of the issues lies within the House and concerns the conduct of hon. Members.

I hope that, in replying to the debate, the Leader of the House will outline the mechanism by which he proposes to make progress on some of those recommendations— the time scale, perhaps—and the Government's view. I recognise that it is a matter for hon. Members to decide, but the Government must have a view and I should like to know what it is.

The Nolan committee was right express concern about "the very substantial increase in the number of Members of Parliament employed as consultants".

The report identifies the fact that 168 Members share 356 consultancies between them. That is a relatively new matter, which seems to be snowballing with the growth of lobbying firms. We must ensure that the mechanisms that we have in place are modern and efficient enough to deal with changes that occur outside the House. Although we sometimes need to cherish our traditions, we must be ready to change them if the need arises.

I support the proposed ban on multi-client lobbying companies, which was long overdue. The idea of transparency when a company has a multiplicity of clients is

almost impossible to achieve and I hope that the House will take immediate action to put that into effect. I also welcome the recommendation that the House should set in hand without delay a broader consideration of the merits of parliamentary consultancies. My instinct, although I wish to listen to the debate, is that they, too, should be banned. I agree with Nolan that we should look at three quid pro quos if there is to be a ban. First, resourcing for Opposition parties should be much better so that they do not have to rely as much on briefings from lobbying companies. That is done in Germany, for example, where the civil service helps to service opposition parties as well as the Government. We need to look at that issue as legislation becomes increasingly complex.

Secondly, we must consider higher remuneration for Members of Parliament, an issue referred to today by hon. Members on both sides of the House.

Thirdly, we must consider the wider issue of proper resourcing for this legislature. The Executive spends massive sums; I believe that it spends more on advertising than it costs to run the whole of Parliament. I do not see how we can do our job as a legislature properly, looking after how the Executive runs the country, when we have, as a member of the Privileges Committee pointed out, such tiny resources to do that job.

I also agree with the suggestion that the agreement between anyone who has an arrangement with an outside commercial interest and remuneration received as a result should be disclosed. Most of our constituents would not accept the argument that the size of the payment has anything but a direct bearing on the potential strength of that interest. Our constituents are looking for us to make those declarations.

It may seem a rather odd thing for a member of the Select Committee on Members' Interests to say, but I whole-heartedly and unreservedly welcome Lord Nolan's recommendation that the Committee should be abolished. I do not say that with any great joy, but I have served on that Committee since I was elected and it has been a tough and unpleasant duty. Many other members of the Committee probably share that feeling. I cannot go into detail about what is going on on that Committee, but it has been wrecked by the Government's decision to appoint a Whip to it. As a result, we are without an effective system of policing the Register of Members' Interests, just at the time when we most need it. The independent element suggested by the Nolan Committee, albeit sublimated by a Sub-Committee of the Privileges Committee, is an ingenious means of trying to deal with the real difficulty that we have come across in the past few months. Those months have been difficult for me and every member of the Committee.

You might be interested to know, Madam Speaker, that you are being touted as the new commissioner for ethics. That is an interesting proposal, but I am also attracted by Lord Nolan's solution. The main thing about which I am concerned is that Parliament should take fast action to implement some of the extremely important Nolan committee recommendations.

The Strauss committee sat in 1969 and produced a relevant recommendation, which was not even debated in the House. That is why it is important that we are seen by the public, who expect us to take action on the Nolan recommendations, to be serious in our approach. We do not have to be sloppy or look like we are panicking, but we must make faster progress than the House is used to making on such issues. We must fight to reach a consensus on how to deal with them seriously. If it all comes down to party politicking, on one side of the House or on the other, we are doomed to failure. We must strive for consensus to make rapid progress.

The report of the Nolan committee gives us the chance to make such progress. It is no longer acceptable for Members to serve in the House but not to take the necessary action for years. Such action would leave festering resentments and some misapprehensions among our constituents to destroy the foundation of our democracy and our legitimacy in this place.

I would welcome an assurance from the Leader of the House that the extremely tight, but good, timetable for the implementation of the recommendations relating to the House and with reference to Members of Parliament, will be adhered to. Lord Nolan wants 21 of the 32 recommendations to be put into effect now and 10 of them to be put into effect by the beginning of the next Session. That will include setting up new committees and some difficult detailed work, which I hope that the Select Committee on Members' Interests will be able to undertake. Lord Nolan asks for just one recommendation to be implemented by next year.

I hope that we will stick to that timetable. I look forward to the Leader of the House offering us a serious plan of how we will proceed now the debate has been held.

9.13 pm

**Mr. Quentin Davies** (Stamford and Spalding): I remind the House of the interests that I have declared in the Register of Members' Interests.

Two absolutely fundamental principles should underlie this debate and one would hope that they are shared across the House. First, we have an absolute fiduciary responsibility to those who sent us here to act in the interests of our constituents and in the public interest. From time to time there may be trade-offs between those two interests and trade-offs between the short-term and the longer-term national interest. We must handle those trade-offs and make honest judgments about them.

But one thing is clear. No other influences—no private interests or partial affections, to use the words that are used here every day at 2.30 pm—should influence our deliberations or decisions in any way. That is an absolute principle. Therefore there should be no ambiguity about the question whether it is proper for outside bodies—to use the evocative phrase used by my hon. Friend the Member for Hampshire, North-West (Sir D. Mitchell)— to advise Members of Parliament as to the way in which they should conduct themselves in this place, what questions they should table and what matters they should speak about, let alone the way in which they should vote. For that reason, I was grateful to the Nolan committee for drawing my attention to the recommendations of the Strauss committee. Reading those recommendations on that subject, I wished that they had been accepted when they were made. I hope that they will be.

The other fundamental principle must be that the regulation of the House—establishing proper rules of conduct and enforcing them, when necessary—must be the responsibility of the House alone. It is wrong to suppose that that responsibility can be assumed by the Executive branch of Government. It was shocking that the Leader of

the Opposition appeared to consider today that it was a responsibility of the Prime Minister. To slough off our responsibility on to the Executive branch would be a subversion—indeed, a perversion—of the constitutional balance. The Leader of the Opposition's question today gave us a horrifying preview of the attitude that a future Labour Government would take to Parliament and to the constitution.

As it is our responsibility, we must get this issue right and, as has been eloquently said on both sides of the House, we must not act in haste and repent at leisure. We need to use the Nolan report as something of, as it were, a consultant's report—if I am still allowed to use that word in a positive sense in the debate. Any institution, any business, any organisation, may from time to time wish to appoint outside consultants to advise it on the future conduct or course of its business.

The report should form, not the whole agenda, but part of the agenda for a careful examination of these issues by a competent House of Commons committee. That might be the Privileges Committee, the Select Committee on Members' Interests, a merged committee involving both of them, or a new ad hoc committee. We need to consider those matters in considerable detail and on the basis that decisions must be made in the House—they cannot be abdicated to an outside committee or commission, no matter how distinguished a member of the judiciary heads it, or to the Executive.

I have said the most important thing that I wanted to say. Having said that, perhaps I may add some brief comments to the suggestions made by the Nolan committee. The committee has obviously done some thorough work on the subject, and its conclusions need to be treated seriously but, as I have said, that can in no way relieve us of the responsibility for considering the merits of those proposals and considering the issues in the broadest possible way.

First, I have some hesitation about publishing the financial earnings of Members of Parliament derived from activities relating in some way to advice on politics or on Parliament. I suspect that that recommendation is driven more by the media's thirst for prurient information of a personal kind than by any other consideration. The essential thing is that interests should be declared; the amount of remuneration is not especially material.

Secondly, it is difficult to maintain the distinction, suggested in the report, between consultancies, or activities outside the House that have some political or parliamentary aspect, and other outside activities.

When I entered the House, I continued for some time to do my previous job as a director of a merchant bank in the City. In no way was my job changed, except in the time I spent on it. Many of the clients with whom I dealt would not have had the faintest idea that I was a Member of Parliament. If one is sitting at the boardroom table and a fellow board member says, "You are a politician, you must have some idea about Government policy on this matter or on that Bill which is due to come before Parliament", one cannot say, "I am afraid that part of my contract makes it illegal for you to ask me that question". I think that it will be extremely difficult to maintain this distinction, and I hope that the Committee of the House which examines the matters in detail will consider that point very carefully.

*[Mr. Quentin Davies]*

Finally, I am particularly concerned about the recommendations on the composition of Standing Committees. I must declare an immediate interest as I have been delighted to serve for a number of years on the Finance Bill Committee. If the Nolan proposals were adopted, I—with my City background and other interests—would presumably be excluded from serving on that Committee, as would accountants, tax lawyers and others with a professional background in finance. We would be excluded from contributing to that legislation.

I can only assume that the recommendation was made by a committee whose members have never bothered to pick up a Finance Bill. If they had, they would realise that only a very specialised category of the human race is likely to take an intelligent interest in a matter that is so dry and so technical. If we were prevented from contributing to debates about subjects of which we have professional knowledge, we would be a great deal less useful to the public whom we are here to serve.

9.20 pm

**Mr. Harry Barnes** (Derbyshire, North-East): I have two interests to declare which appear in the Register of Members' Interests: I travelled to Dublin as a guest of the Irish Government and I visited Malta as a guest of the Maltese Government. Anyone who knows me will know that I am not in either Government's pocket.

I wish to raise a matter which has not been discussed in the debate today, although it was alluded to by my hon. Friends the Members for Norwich, South (Mr. Garrett) and for Warrington, North (Mr. Hoyle). There is a serious argument that hon. Members should be full-time Members of Parliament with no paid outside interests. That would alleviate the problem of outside influence and pressure from commercial and professional bodies. A majority of the public sent that message to the Nolan committee, but only one Member of Parliament—me—put that view to the committee.

Time is short, as the Front-Bench spokesmen wish to sum up the debate. I therefore simply refer hon. Members to the evidence that I gave to the Nolan committee. The case for having full-time Members is a solid one, and four main arguments have been produced against the counter-view which appears in the Nolan report. They suggest that the committee is wrong to reject the notion that Members of Parliament should not accept employment outside the House. I think that we should have full-time Members of Parliament in a modern democracy.

9.22 pm

**Mr. Jeff Rooker** (Birmingham, Perry Barr): I am glad that my hon. Friend the Member for Derbyshire, North-East (Mr. Barnes) has had an opportunity to refer to the question of full-time Members of Parliament. He was able to speak for only a few minutes, but he raised an issue to which no one has alluded in the entire debate. There was a time when I might have agreed with my hon. Friend and I discussed the issue when I gave evidence to the Nolan committee. It is certainly worthy of debate and it should not be dismissed out of hand. There is a case to be made for having full-time Members of Parliament and I am glad that my hon. Friend has had a chance to put it on the record.

I attended six or seven of the morning sittings of the Nolan committee and I listened to the evidence of about 18 witnesses. Having listened to the questions, it did not take long to work out which way the committee would jump. In many ways, therefore, its recommendations did not come as a complete surprise. It was similar to Select Committee proceedings, where one can work out how Committee members are thinking from the questions that they ask.

I only wish that the Chancellor of the Duchy had attended more often, instead of coming along only to the session at which he gave evidence. It would have been useful for him to listen to the questions asked by the committee and the answers given by the witnesses. Had he done so, he would not have made the speech that he gave today. I wish, too, that the right hon. Member for Old Bexley and Sidcup (Sir E. Heath)—the Father of the House—had sat and listened to the evidence sessions of the Nolan committee. Clearly, he does not even understand the present rules governing the Register of Members' Interests. I respect and admire the right hon. Gentleman, but he trivialised the beginning of today's debate with arguments about the price of a bottle of port, which was ludicrous and demeaning on the part of a former Prime Minister.

I refer to the speech by the right hon. Member for Bridgwater (Mr. King). Like some of my hon. Friends, I was on the receiving end of questions from the right hon. Gentleman when we gave evidence to the Nolan committee, and I learned a good deal from his questioning. I was advancing proposals for a much more rigorous register than the current or the proposed one, but I too was searching for something that was practical and acceptable to the House. It is no good going for the extreme view; the House would not stand for it. Nor can we carve up a solution between Front Benchers—nobody would want that. The right hon. Member for Bridgwater did a first-class selling job for the work of the Nolan committee. Towards the end of his speech he said, tellingly, that the House cannot walk away from this issue. That is a crucial point. We walk away from it at our peril.

This has not been a partisan debate. It is only natural, as the Government have been in power for 16 years, that there should be more Conservative Members with consultancies and hence more Conservative Members who feel aggrieved and under threat. They should not feel threatened by the Nolan report's recommendations. The House can take a sensible view and then implement it quickly. Taken together, the changes proposed are sensible.

This is probably the most important constitutional change since I entered the House 21 years ago. It may even be the most important since the granting of the universal franchise. We in this House expect our fellow citizens to obey laws whether they agree with them or not; yet for several years the House, while expecting Members to obey its resolutions, has crucially failed on occasion to take action when its rules have been disobeyed. We all know of such cases. By and large, we have proved ourselves incapable of putting our own house in order. That is the ultimate proof that self-regulation can be self-delusion.

The public are anxious about Members of Parliament in general, even though they support us in our constituencies. We cannot escape the fact that 64 per cent. of people believe that we are on the make, even though that is not true. Certainly I would not claim that it was true. This view that the public have has arisen out of isolated incidents, and that is the problem that we all have to face. I can think of no other reason for the public perception than the fact that there has been the odd case of impropriety in recent years.

This view has arisen not just because there is now more openness about our proceedings, which are carried on the wireless and on television. There must be another reason, and it is the fact that we have neglected the fundamentals. While we insist on knowing all the details of legislation and on poring over every dot and comma, while we pass—too many—laws to restrict and instruct our fellow citizens, as a Parliament and as the supposed grand inquisitor of the nation we have continued to live with old-fashioned procedures and modern myths. One of those myths is the idea that ours is the oldest and most democratic Parliament in the world. People repeat that ad nauseam, but although we may once have been the mother of Parliaments, the world has changed since then and we have failed to change with it.

It was said earlier that we are the highest court in the land, so we should be left alone. I would argue that we are the highest court in the land, but we should not be a law unto ourselves because we are the law makers. That is the distinction that I draw. I do not understand why some hon. Members find the House under threat if we look for something other than complete self-regulation.

Time is short, but I shall refer to paragraphs 57 to 59 in the report. They are to be found on page 31. It is not easy to find one's way through the report because the paragraph numbers start differently at each chapter. Paragraph 57 reads:

"We are well aware that some will consider that we are over-reacting to a few isolated cases . . . Others will feel we should have gone further, and moved immediately".

Paragraph 58 states:

"It is clear that, while some cases have been so bad as to require direct action even under the existing rules, there are problems of principle and practice over the separation of public and private interests, which damage the standing of Parliament. Neither we nor the media have invented the problems."

That is the reality. The Nolan committee did not invent the problems, and the media did not invent them either.

Paragraph 58 continues to remind us that

"the 1969 Strauss report was shelved without debate".

I remind the House that the 1976 Salmon royal commission was shelved without a debate. The introduction of the Register of Members' Interests was resisted until the Poulson scandal forced the hand of the then Labour Government of 1974. It has taken 20 years since then to get the register fully operational, even though we may criticise it now. We know that in recent years some senior Members have refused to comply with the register.

Paragraph 58 adds:

"The overall picture is not one of an institution whose Members have been quick to recognise or respond to public concern."

Paragraph 59 reads:

"On the other hand we do not believe that the position is so grave that it has to be addressed outside the framework of the House's own rules."

That is my point. I do not think that we are going outside those rules. It is true, of course, that there must be checks and balances.

The original discussion paper of the Nolan committee, entitled "Issues and Questions", led it to be concerned about parliamentary sovereignty. As I said in my evidence to the Nolan committee, I do not want to be misunderstood by anybody. I am honoured to be a Member of this place and to represent the area where I was born and raised, but I do not accept that Parliament should be sovereign over all matters. I am for a written constitution and reform. In a unitary state, political power should be divided and should not reside in one institution, however old and democratic it may be. There should be written codes agreed and enforced by the House and written laws agreed and enforced by the courts, and both should apply to Members.

I was pleased to read in the Nolan report that the committee had taken up the point that the Salmon commission raised in 1976, which is that there appears— there is a dispute about this—to be a gap in statute law, with the result that the bribery, or attempted bribery, of a Member in his or her parliamentary capacity is outside that law. We were asked to take up the matter in 1976 but we never debated the Salmon report. That was a scandal. I raised the issue as a Back-Bench Member when the Labour Government were in office. I raised it again when there was a change of Government in 1979. The issue has remained with us for 20 years and I hope that the Government will now take it on board. The Nolan report asks us to review the matter.

We seek to retain power at the centre of government, in what is still one of the most secretive government systems. As a result, defects in our system have not been taken up. Instead, they have built up in the absence of a relief valve. The pressure has increased. The defects have become worse and worse over the years.

Last Friday, *The Daily Telegraph* reported:

"a moment of panic following a spat of minor scandals involving Tory backbenchers and Ministers last year, causing the Prime Minister to establish the Nolan Committee."

My argument is that we have not examined these issues for years, with the result that "minor scandals" have caused a blunderbuss of a commission to be established. I believe that standards have been falling for years and the time is long overdue for them to be reconsidered.

The Nolan inquiry has done an excellent job. I shall not argue about whether the report goes far enough. The report is a package. It has been assembled by a committee of people who have experience of public life both inside and outside the House. They have submitted unanimous recommendations for us to take account of and act upon for the good of the public. We would be crazy to dismiss their recommendations or try to put them into a siding.

The report has shown that in respect of the civil service and the quango state there has been something wrong in the conduct of public affairs. The committee has done civil servants a real service. I have read the report from cover to cover. Civil servants can work more easily and have a greater comfort factor in the way in which they carry out their functions if all the Nolan report's recommendations are implemented, along with, of course, the changes introduced by the Government. I accept that they are taken in tandem, but that is a great bonus for our civil servants.

Our argument, as *The Times* said on Friday, is that the regulation that we are being asked to accept as Members of the House is minimal. *The Times* described it as a "light touch", although one would not think so from some of the

[*Mr. Jeff Rooker*]

extreme language, based on old-fashioned myths, suggesting that somehow 700 years of parliamentary sovereignty is under attack. That myth is peddled by those who seek to mislead people outside the House about the powers of the House and the nature of British society.

Even so, I accept that this is the first outside interference in hundreds of years in the conduct of the House, but in a very narrow area. However, the changes do not interfere with our prime functions. First, they do not interfere with our ability to represent our constituents in the House. Secondly, they do not interfere with our ability to hold the Government and the Executive to account. Thirdly, they do not interfere with our ability to be the forum of the nation where ideas good, bad and tasteless can be tossed around this cockpit of debate. Nolan interferes with none of that in any way, shape or form, so I cannot see why extreme language describing the House as being under attack is being used.

Acceptance of the Nolan recommendations means, as I told the inquiry, that Parliament ceases to be the absolute arbiter of the public interest boundaries. We have no right, as 651 elected citizens on behalf of our fellow citizens, to be the sole arbiter of the public interest boundaries in every walk of life in Britain. It is not on, it is unacceptable and we are not qualified, even by election, to carry out that function. We have to share that and it has to be shared between ourselves and other interest bodies in society.

Society has become more complex and technical. It is as though over the years the House has not wanted to know about that or be part of it. That is one reason why, over the years, the House has ceded so much power to Whitehall over the decades—it can deal with the technicalities, so do not bother us with that kind of change in society. That has been partly caused by the make-up of the House not being full of people like myself—qualified engineers. Therefore, we should embrace change and do so quickly. We should agree the detailed changes to the Standing Orders and related matters well before the House rises for the summer recess.

One change that we must make, which I do not think is mentioned specifically in the Nolan report but which is crucial in view of its recommendations about the Privileges Committee, is that that Privileges Committee must be given the power to sit during a recess. It is unbelievable that, as far as I am aware, it is the only Select Committee that has no authority to sit when the House is not sitting. The delay that the two Members in the recent cash for questions affair suffered was one reason why they felt an injustice. The matter was raised last June or July, but it was Easter before the House dealt with it. Why? Because for all the weeks that the House does not sit, the Committee of Privileges was not doing any work because it had no power or authority from the House to do so. That must be corrected forthwith. It could be corrected by a motion tabled by the Leader of the House next week. It is crazy not to make that change in the new situation.

**Mr. Sheldon:** Will my hon. Friend give way?

**Mr. Rooker:** No, I am sorry; I apologise, but I shall be taking time from the Minister.

**Mr. Sheldon:** Will my hon. Friend give way?

**Mr. Rooker:** Yes, briefly.

**Mr. Sheldon:** Please, will my hon. Friend include the Public Accounts Committee, which also does not have the power to sit when the House is not sitting?

**Mr. Rooker:** As it is the only Select Committee on which I have ever served in 21 years, yes. I learned more about the machinery of Government in my two years on that Committee than I have in a decade or more on the Opposition Front Bench. Yes, of course that must be the case.

I also believe that the House should regularly review the changes that we institute. We should begin ourselves to think about the implications of the changes for current and future Members. We should not have to wait for someone else to do that. We can think ahead and see the implications of the changes, because that will be important to the way in which we do our work.

I hope that Ministers will not fall over when I say that I do not put all the blame on the Government. Like some of my hon. Friends, I have experience of sitting on both sides of the Chamber. We are a transient group of Members, holding our places on trust on behalf of the people, and no one, from the highest to the lowest, has anything to gain by seeking to make cheap, narrow and partisan points in relation to the changes that we debate, the changes that we propose to introduce and the changes that I hope we shall introduce following Nolan. Nothing is to be gained from such behaviour; we would merely further demean ourselves in the eyes of the public and raise the percentage of those who think we are on the make from 64 to 74 per cent.

The evidence from Nolan is that the public have seen through us and that they do not like what they see. The conduct of policy and the conduct of politics must change and be seen to change. Failure on our part will have the consequence of tearing at the fabric of society. That is a measure of the esteem in which we are held. If we do not do these things, people outside. will be torn asunder. They may not think much of us, but they will think a lot less of us if we do not deal with the changes.

The current membership of the House must be able, with honesty, rightly to claim that we left the political process in better health than we found it. We can start by implementing Lord Nolan's recommendation.

9.40 pm

**The Lord President of the Council and Leader of the House of Commons (Mr. Tony Newton):** When proposing this debate a week ago, I had envisaged and intended that it would provide the opportunity for a wide-ranging debate. I am not sure that I had anticipated it ranging quite as wide as occurred in the speech of the hon. Member for Birmingham, Perry Barr (Mr. Rooker). It went well beyond some of the matters that were covered by the Nolan committee, but it was entertaining for all that, and it would have given many people, apart from myself, pause for thought. I can say only that it is clear that he is a well-qualified engineer.

I especially agree with the hon. Gentleman's point about enabling the Privileges Committee not to get into the position that it was in during the last summer recess. I hope that I carry with me at least one its members who

I can see in my sights. There are, however, obvious difficulties, which we should not ignore, about getting together during the summer recess a body that consists of 17 people. There is no magic answer, but the hon. Gentleman's point needs and deserves further consideration.

**Mr. Sheldon:** The Public Accounts Committee as well.

**Mr. Newton:** If that is a bid for further action from the Chairman of the Public Accounts Committee, having said what I have just said about the Privileges Committee, it would be ungracious of me not to undertake to consider any proposal that he might make.

Following today's debate, one thing that I am clear about is that it was right for the debate to take place as soon as possible after the Nolan committee report was published a week ago. It was also right to have an opportunity to gauge reaction, as we have had this afternoon and evening, before making firm decisions about how to proceed. My speech will seek to reflect the spirit in which many right hon. and hon. Members on both sides of the House have taken part in the debate.

**Mr. Quentin Davies:** Does my right hon. Friend agree that the matters that we have been discussing are extremely complex? We have had an interesting and wide-ranging debate, but many hon. Members have not been able to take part. Does he agree that there has not been sufficient and full consideration by the House of all the matters before us, and that it would be sensible to set up a committee of the House, or to charge the Select Committee on Members' Interests or the Privileges Committees with considering the matter in detail, taking what evidence they think is relevant and returning to the House with considered recommendations?

**Mr. Newton:** My hon. Friend is anticipating a point that I wish to come to later in relation to how we might proceed from here. I shall return to it later.

There is no point in disguising the fact that, during the debate, many different points and perspectives have emerged. To a significant degree, however, I am encouraged by what I take to be the three strands of fairly general—I certainly cannot say universal—agreement that have emerged. The first point would certainly not have universal agreement as a number of hon. Members, including the right hon. Member for Chesterfield (Mr. Benn), my hon. Friends the Members for Wolverhampton, South-West (Mr. Budgen) and for Gainsborough and Horncastle (Mr. Leigh), and the hon. Member for Norwich, South (Mr. Garrett) have suggested putting everything in statute, which would go well beyond the Nolan committee's suggestion.

Apart from that, there has been a general welcome for and endorsement of the importance of self-regulation in the House. It has, perhaps, not been fully recognised today that that is persistently stressed in the Nolan report. Paragraph 1 of its conclusions, for instance, places heavy emphasis on the importance of self-regulation and the committee's wish for it to continue. It states:

"Those standards have always been self-imposed and self-regulated because Parliament is our supreme institution."

That is an important recognition of both the position and the reasons.

Other parts of the report make, in effect, the same point. Paragraph 59 states:

"we do not believe that the position is so grave that it has to be addressed outside the framework of the House's own rules."

Paragraph 89 strongly recommends that the House should draw up a code of conduct setting out the broad principles that should govern the conduct of Members.

Paragraph 92 makes an important point, and I shall quote it in full:

"One of the consequences of privilege is therefore that the House of Commons regulates the activities of its Members itself. Where Parliamentary business is concerned, they are answerable to the House and not to the Courts. Because Parliamentary privilege is important for reasons entirely unconnected with the standards of conduct of individual Members of Parliament, we believe that it would be highly desirable for self-regulation to continue."

I believe that that view is widely, and rightly, shared in the House.

**Mr. Budgen:** Does my right hon. Friend agree that there is a world of difference between regulating the procedures of the House and imposing—by means of a motion in the House—a particular and new condition on all persons who wish to become Members of Parliament? For instance, it would have been wrong, would it not, for the House of Commons to say that no Member of Parliament could be a clergyman in the Church of England. That, rightly, is decided by statute.

Surely, when we reach the stage of regulating through the registration of Members' interests—which changes all the terms and conditions of employment—the nation will have an interest in the matter. We are not doing this just for ourselves, as a private club; it must surely be done by the House of Commons—by the legislature, acting on behalf of the whole nation.

**Mr. Newton:** My hon. Friend links two slightly different points, on which I want to make different comments. First, it has historically been the case for centuries that the House has had rules governing the procedures and conduct of its Members, in various forms. We should think very hard before moving away from that position, especially in the light of the comments made in the report. Secondly—I might have said this to the right hon. Member for Chesterfield (Mr. Benn) had I had a little more time—there is a clear distinction between putting into law, as the House of Commons Disqualification Act 1975 does, a list of offices held that disqualify, and what would come much closer to a list of criteria needing to be interpreted and considered by the courts before it could be decided what was and was not in order. I hope that I have made my concern reasonably clear without labouring it too much, because I must now make progress.

My second encouraging conclusion is that there is a general acceptance of a need for change, in the direction—I choose my words carefully—of the report's recommendations. Substantial reservations are expressed about particular proposals, and considerable emphasis is placed on the need for clarification; but few would argue for no action at all. There has been much echoing of the words of my right hon. Friend the Member for Bridgwater (Mr. King) today, and one phrase that has been quoted more than once since he spoke is, "We cannot walk away from it."

Thirdly, the debate has pointed to a whole range of questions arising from the report's recommendations which have to be addressed and answered before specific resolutions in a clear and workable form can be put to the House for debate and decision.

[*Mr. Newton*]

I took that to be fairly clearly recognised by the right hon. Member for Bethnal Green and Stepney (Mr. Shore) in a reference that he made to discussing the detail on resolutions. That was echoed in a number of speeches right through the debate, not least in the speech of my hon. Friend the Member for Wealden (Sir G. Johnson Smith), the importance of which should be recognised, given the experience which my hon. Friend has had as Chairman of the Select Committee on Members' Interests. He struck a cautionary note about the difficulties of dealing with some of these matters and the need to take care in proceeding with them.

Perhaps that was inevitable because, although tribute has been rightly paid to the Nolan committee for having produced this very substantial report in the short space of six months, it was inevitably unable to address some of the definitional difficulties such as the distinction referred to by the right hon. Member for Bethnal Green and Stepney between advocacy and the giving of advice. It could not address some of those questions as fully as it might have wished had it had more time and as fully as some of them would need to be addressed if we were talking about devising specific resolutions to put before the House. There are a number of such points that I could make.

I would say to the hon. Member for Dewsbury (Mrs. Taylor) that some of the concerns expressed about the need to refine the detail more than was possible for those devising the report, whatever we may think the points of detail are, are not something that can be simply dismissed or waved away. I emphasise that an important part of the thrust of the report is its criticism of the lack of clarity in our existing rules and procedures. We would be doing no service to anyone inside or outside the House by rushing ahead to replace the current set of uncertainties and grey areas with a new set because we have failed to think the problems and difficulties through.

A key question, and again this is a phrase that has echoed through the debate, is to decide how best the work can be carried forward with proper care but without undesirable delay. As many hon. Members have said, we have to get it right.

Before I come back to offer a tentative answer to that question, it might be sensible to say something briefly about the categories of recommendation made in the report: category A, those for implementation with the minimum of delay; and category B, those which, in the committee's view, could be implemented or on which significant progress could be made by the end of the year. The hon. Member for Wallasey (Ms Eagle) rather exaggerated the extent to which the report assumes that everything can be done between now and the end of the year. There is specifically a saving clause in that recommendation. Finally, there is category C, which deals with the longer term.

There is only one recommendation in category C, which, uniquely in this part of the report, is directed to the Government rather than the House. It is that the Government should take steps to clarify the law relating to bribery of, or receipt of a bribe by, a Member of Parliament. Given that that recommendation is directed to the Government, it is something that will be considered in the context of the Government response to which my right hon. Friend the Chancellor of the Duchy of Lancaster referred earlier.

I will therefore focus principally on the recommendations categorised as A and B. For the category A recommendations—the shortest-term ones—there does not appear to be any great problem. The first is a proposition that Members of Parliament should remain free to have paid employment unrelated to their role as Members of Parliament. It clearly requires no further action. That has been implicitly accepted in the course of the debate.

The second recommendation in category A is that the House should restate the 1947 resolution, which I will not rehearse. That plainly presents no great difficulty because it is there already and we would be doing no more than reminding people of it. If that is felt to be appropriate, clearly it can be considered.

The fourth category A recommendation is the setting in hand of a broader consideration of the merits of parliamentary consultancies generally, taking account—I think that is the phrase—of the financial and political funding implications of change. That, again, seems to be reasonably straightforward, which is not to say that the consideration itself would be straightforward, and would seem to point either to referring the matter to one of our existing Committees or, as I am inclined to think may be preferable, to establish one specifically for that purpose.

Before deciding precisely what is right in that respect, it is necessary to spend a moment considering how to proceed with the bulk of the recommendations, which are those falling in category B and which have been the principal focus of most of today's contributions. One possibility would be for me to suggest resolutions following discussion in the usual channels, but my doubts about that have been reinforced by some comments made today. I have grave doubts about whether the House would think that process appropriate or right.

Some understandable suspicion has been expressed, articulated perhaps most clearly, but not only, by my hon. Friend the Member for Chingford (Mr. Duncan Smith), about an attempted diktat by members of the Government Front Bench or of proposals based on a deal between members of the two Front Benches. I am inclined to think—this picks up a comment made a few moments ago by my hon. Friend the Member for Stamford and Spalding (Mr. Davies)—that the appropriate course is to operate according to the House's normal procedure in such circumstances, which is to ask a group of senior and respected Members of Parliament to make recommendations on how we should proceed in the light of the report and to make specific proposals for resolutions that might be put to the House having considered some, many or all of the points raised in today's debate.

That would be more consistent not only with the House's usual practice but with the report itself which, as the two members of the Nolan committee recognised today, has to a significant extent provided a basis for consideration of action by the House. A phrase that they both used but that I do not think was mine was that the committee had in some respects passed the buck to the House. That implies that we now need a proper House mechanism for considering how to proceed.

**Mr. Benn:** Will it be contemplated that such a committee could meet in public so that the flow of argument could be better understood? There are no grounds for it meeting in private when the arguments are what would be interesting.

**Mr. Newton:** That is no doubt something that could be considered and might be appropriate for the committee, were it to be established. My approach in my curtailed response is that I am not seeking to make snap decisions about matters that should be the subject of wide consultation.

In response to the hon. Member for Dewsbury, I must say that I believe that the approach that I have sketched might well be more, rather than less, likely to achieve the pace of progress towards decisions that many of us desire. As has been said repeatedly today, most forcefully by my right hon. Friend the Member for Watford (Mr. Garel-Jones), the devil is in the detail. Frankly, if we attempt to have debates on principle, they will inescapably be debates in which people will say that they do not want to make decisions until they have a clearer idea of shape and detail. Decisions in principle will not mean very much without detail. Only when the detail has been worked out can practical changes occur. In my view, the sooner we get on with it, the better.

If it were felt right to proceed in that way, the question would be whether an existing committee or a new one established for the purpose would be the right course. The latter would probably be preferable, not least for the reason mentioned by the hon. Member for Dewsbury. Regardless of whatever else might be said about their difficulties, the existing committees—the Privileges Committee and the Select Committee on Members' Interests—already have other work on their plate which the House would not like to see pushed to one side.

**Mrs. Ann Taylor:** Is the Leader of the House suggesting that the remit of the committee should be to consider Lord Nolan's proposals or to work out how to implement them?

**Mr. Newton:** I would want to embrace both thoughts. Questions that have been raised today about the specific proposals have to be dealt with before one can say that the only purpose of the committee is to implement them exactly as they stand. That is particularly true with regard to some of the points made about the commissioner for standards. If the hon. Lady is going to suggest that that is an attempt to delay or avoid acting on the proposals in the report, I should have to resist that suggestion. However, the work needs to be carefully and thoroughly done before specific proposals are put to the House.

I believe that such an approach would give the best chance of proceeding in a way that the House would wish. That embraces something that I had not entirely expected to hear from the hon. Member for Wallasey (Ms Eagle), which was the powerful demand for consensus, something that I have not always sensed in her contributions to our proceedings. I strongly believe, and I hope that everything that I have said in the debate—apart from anything that I have said in my previous years as Leader of the House— has shown that I have no doubt whatever that this place and its rules work best when we move forward in a careful and considered way and seek to achieve the maximum consensus. That is the basis on which I hope we can proceed in this instance.

As everyone reflects on the debate and if that approach finds favour, I propose to undertake early consultation in appropriate ways—and I do not mean just through the usual channels—with a view to presenting a specific proposal to the House.

*It being Ten o'clock, the motion for the Adjournment of the House lapsed, without Question put.*

## Schools (North Warwickshire)

*Motion made, and Question proposed,* That this House do now adjourn.—*[Mr. Burns.]*

10 pm

**Mr. Mike O'Brien** (Warwickshire, North): Warwickshire's schools are in crisis. Parents in my constituency are rightly angry at the damage being done to the education of their children by the Government's financial settlement on local authorities. The Secretary of State for Education has described the local authority settlement as tough. That is right. It is tough on children and on the education opportunities that will be given to them. Children have only one chance of a decent education and it is morally wrong to sacrifice it on the altar of storing up a money chest for pre-election tax cuts.

A couple of months ago a march in London showed just how angry the people of Warwickshire are about education cuts. Parents of all political persuasions and of none joined to protest against the cuts, and many of them came from my constituency. It was an angry shout from middle England, which the Government will ignore at their peril.

As I said, those parents were of all political persuasions—and they included people who had been Conservatives. In Warwickshire opposition to Government policy on the funding of schools is not a party political issue: it unites all the parties and the people against the Government. None of the usual Government excuses applies to Warwickshire. The county is a prudent authority with an excellent auditor's report on administration. Yes, it was poll tax-capped twice some years ago, but at that time it was under Tory control. Whether under Conservative or the present Labour control, the councillors and Warwickshire Members have united in saying that the county is broadly well run, and that the Government's calculation of the standard spending assessment and of capping is unfair, unjustifiable and damaging to children's education.

I shall give some examples from north Warwickshire of the impact of education cuts. St. Edward's primary school in Coleshill will have 205 pupils in September, an increase of 25, and a cut in staffing. Mrs. Gill Owen, an excellent head teacher who tries to run a high-quality school, told me today that she will have to cope with a mixed-ability class of 39, two classes of 36 and three of more than 30. The school repair budget is overstretched and its buildings are dilapidated.

Governors are so angry that they have set a deficit needs budget, as up to 20 schools in the county have done. Although I do not approve of deficit budgets, the anger of all the governors is shown by the fact that the chairman of governors describes himself as previously a lifelong Tory voter. A Conservative councillor who is a governor also voted for the deficit budget. The governors did that because they were angry. The capitation fee for pupils, for example, for books and equipment was already too low at £30, but next year it will fall to £10. Those governors believed that education standards were threatened at the school and they wanted to protest. I do not justify those governors, who regarded themselves as Conservatives, breaking the law, but cannot the Minister understand why they did?

In Bedworth, at Nicholas Chamberlain secondary school, 13 teacher posts are to go. Kevin Scott, the excellent new head teacher, said today that he had the problem of a £280,000 deficit on his £2.4 million budget. Class sizes will rise, pupils will have fewer subject choices and practical classes will exceed 25 pupils—in classrooms that were not designed for practical classes of that size. He fears significant health and safety dangers. There will be fewer books, building maintenance will be cut—the school library has already closed—and information technology provision will deteriorate further.

The school expects to have a deficit carry-over from this year of £30,000 due to the underfunding of last year's teachers pay award. This year, the county cannot fund the pay award, which will put another £50,000 on the schools budget. SSA cuts will amount to £70,000. All that means that there will be no extra income, for example, to cover teachers who go sick. Colleagues will have to cover for the sick, adding to already heavily stressed teaching loads. That will also unnecessarily endanger the standard of education.

The Office for Standards in Education has told the school that, as a result of local management of schools, it must now fill an administrative post that it deliberately left vacant from April last year to save money. Governors are dealing with the obvious anger of teachers who will lose jobs, while Ofsted says that administrative assistance is needed because of LMS budgets. I could list the problems at school after school in my constituency. Polesworth high school is losing £112,000 and is gaining an extra 62 pupils. Coleshill high school has a substantial budget shortfall, too.

The list could go on. It is significant, however, that no one blames the local county council. Everyone knows that the Government's SSA education criteria are £10 million below what the schools really need. How in all conscience can the Government justify what they are doing to Warwickshire schoolchildren? Even local Conservative councillors will not justify it.

I repeat: none of the usual Government excuses for cuts in Warwickshire applies. Is there too much administration? There is not in Warwickshire. The auditors say that there is not. The council spends 73.1 per cent. of the English county average on administration. It has already sliced £1.6 million off budgets in recent years. Not even the Conservative leader on the county council believes that any more can be cut without significantly endangering financial prudence in administration.

Should Warwickshire remove surplus places? The Secretary of State has already praised Warwickshire for its planning, to which I shall return. Should it remove discretionary elements in the budget? Warwickshire has not been awarding discretionary grants for years. The youth service has been decimated. Only nursery education funding is maintained. If the Minister really wants nurseries to close, he must say so clearly and explain how that fits in with the Prime Minister's promises on nursery education.

Should school balances be used? In Warwickshire, that is not really a practical option. Many schools threatened with cuts have no balances. Half of them could not meet the cuts imposed from their balances anyway and others are already eating into provision for repairs and emergencies. The larger balances are concentrated in a minority of schools and not in the schools most directly threatened by the cuts. Should Warwickshire cut management perks in administration? The Audit Commission says that many management perks, as they might be called, are already in the lower quartile.

In December, an Education Minister—not the Under-Secretary of State for Schools, who is on the Front Bench—said that, in September, Warwickshire had appointed an extra 500 staff. I remember it well, because the chairman of the education committee was in the Strangers Gallery. I looked up at him and he waved his arms and could not imagine how that could possibly be. When he checked the figures that the other Minister had used, he found that they were the figures for the one-year contracts that had been granted and for the provision of ancillary staff. Moreover, they were September to December figures, which always show an increase simply because people are moving from one post to another.

That incident did not show that Warwickshire had taken on 500 extra staff; that simply was not true. It showed that Ministers used that argument because there was such a paucity of genuine argument to justify and defend their actions.

Warwickshire needs three things. First, the Government should lift the cap. It is not only Opposition Members who say that; it has been said by Conservative Members, too. If the cap were lifted, local people could decide how much they wanted their councillors to impose in council tax. I hope that they would decide that they wanted sufficient tax to fund their schools properly.

We also want fair treatment for Warwickshire in the standard spending assessment. That is not fair at the moment, and has not been fair for a long time. The Government must accept that. The reason is clear, and the Minister can check it with Conservative councillors in the county. No doubt they will agree with me.

Way back at the beginning of the poll tax, the Conservatives who then controlled the county decided to implement the promises on which they had been elected and cut spending in Warwickshire. And for the first year of the poll tax that is what they did. The following year, the Government used the expenditure for that previous year as the base for setting the SSA and capping. Everyone in Warwickshire agrees that, as a result, the county has been unfairly treated since then, and expenditure has been ratcheted down in an entirely wrong way. As a result, damage is being inflicted on the children of the county.

We have also asked the Government to raise the education disregard to cover the costs of reorganisation. I therefore ask the Minister to consider those three things: lift the cap; give the county fair treatment over its SSA; and raise the education disregard to cover the cost of reorganisation.

There is one important thing to say about education reorganisation. The Secretary of State has been telling councils across the country to remove surplus places. But I warn other councils to expect more than a simple refusal to lift the education disregard to fund the reorganisation that will remove surplus places. In Warwickshire's case, that reorganisation has been jeopardised by the Government's delay in making a decision on the second tranche of the changes.

The chief education officer tells me that the county is on the brink of being forced to pull the plug on the reorganisation because of Government prevarication. The delay is bringing us the prospect of chaos. Building contracts need to be made and new teaching posts sorted out. Will the Minister tell me when the decision will be made? Or will he confirm that his Department has legal problems as a result of the decision by Mr. Justice Sedley

in the High Court on 12 April in the case of Regina *v.* Secretary of State for Education ex parte Skitt? The Government had bungled the closure for Beacon school in Walsall by accepting advice from inspectors of schools on which parents had no opportunity to comment. Have they done the same with the Warwickshire reorganisation? Is that the reason for the delay?

Partly through incompetence and partly through a failure to listen not only to the Opposition but to Conservative Members who speak for Warwickshire, the Department for Education is now imposing damage upon Warwickshire children that cannot be justified. I exclude mendacity, because I absolve the Ministers at the Department for Education of that—although I have my doubts about Ministers at the Treasury and at the Department of the Environment. Will the Minister now act to lift the cap for Warwickshire? Will he reform the SSA, or at least adjust the education disregard?

I ask not just on behalf of my constituents, but on behalf of those who have the most to lose from the Government's shambles—the children in Warwickshire schools.

10.14 pm

**The Parliamentary Under-Secretary of State for Schools (Mr. Robin Squire):** I welcome the opportunity provided by the hon. Member for Warwickshire, North (Mr. O'Brien) to discuss education in the county of Warwickshire. While the hon. Gentleman would not expect me to agree with every one of his comments, I welcome the way in which he raised the issue.

The hon. Gentleman started by expressing particular concern about the level of resources made available by the Government for education this year. Let me make clear from the start that, so far as education expenditure is concerned, Warwickshire county council—like every other local authority—is responsible for setting its own budget and deciding its priorities between and within services. It is the council which has the final say on how much is spent on education and how much is spent on other services. It is also the council which determines, by its local management of schools scheme, exactly how much local schools receive.

It has been said by some—although not by the hon. Gentleman—that Warwickshire has been forced to cut its education budget by 3 per cent. in the current financial year. There is no reason why this should happen. The Government have provided for Warwickshire's education standard spending assessment to increase by 1.2 per cent. this year, and under the capping rules it can spend 0.5 per cent. more in 1995-1996 than it did in 1994-95. In total, Warwickshire is able to spend over £273 million on all services this year.

What does the talk about "cuts" actually mean? The county council is certainly not cutting what it is actually spending, although, most importantly it has decided to spend less of its total budget on education. Warwickshire has drawn up a shopping list of additional spending—it is not alone in that respect—and is then cutting back on what it would ideally like to spend if it could buy all the items on that list. Everyone in the public sector and in business faces the same problem, and the solution of course is to become more efficient. To say or imply that there must be full cover for all wage and price increases is to say that there is no scope for efficiency gains, which must be untrue.

[*Mr. Robin Squire*]

It is not unreasonable for Ministers to expect authorities to help fund education by becoming more efficient. Authorities continue to spend vast amounts of money on running their education departments. A recent Audit Commission report found scope for saving over £500 million on the pay bill of local authorities' administrative and clerical staff. In addition, a previous report by the commission found that there was scope for saving over £30 million by rationalising special schools.

It is also not unreasonable for the Government to expect schools to use some of their balances to help offset the cost of providing education. I accept what the hon. Gentleman said about all schools not having available balances, and I hope that he accepts that some do. No information on individual school balances at the end of 1994-1995 is yet available, but at the end of 1993-1994 primary schools in Warwickshire had balances which in total amounted to 6.3 per cent. of their budget shares. Secondary schools had 6.7 per cent.

All schools need to consider what balances they should sensibly hold as a result of planning, not merely casual accrual. They can scarcely complain, given those reserves, that they were underfunded during that time. If reserves are not available for particular schools then they need to pay particular attention to their management of resources. They may also wish to suggest to the authority that its LMS scheme might be amended for future years in order to change the distribution of funds.

I know that Warwickshire schools, like schools in other areas, are concerned about meeting the cost of the teachers' pay award. The Government accepted the award of 2.7 per cent. on the recommendation of the school teachers' pay review body. That body acknowledged the fact that financial provision had been set on the basis that pay increases should be offset, or more than offset, by efficiency gains and increased productivity. We have acknowledged—the hon. Gentleman highlighted it in his comments—that the current settlement is tough. There is no resiling from that statement. Nevertheless, many authorities have been able to achieve an increase in their budgets which matches or outstrips the teachers' pay award and have said that they will meet the pay award in full.

It is worth making the point that, although many local authorities claim that they cannot afford the teachers' pay award, they have reached separately a voluntary pay settlement of their own of over 2 per cent. for clerical and manual staff.

I acknowledge that the award will place local authority budgets under pressure. But, in fairness, local authorities are large and financially complex organisations and they have a variety of means of realising the efficiency gains that are needed.

**Mr. Mike O'Brien:** Will the Minister give way?

**Mr. Squire:** I hope that the hon. Gentleman will recognise that I usually give way. I am willing to do so if I make progress in my speech. He would wish me to reach reorganisation proposals and I am anxious to cover those in considerable detail. If there is time, I promise the hon. Gentleman that I shall give way to him.

The Government consider that teachers thoroughly deserve the increase, in recognition of the excellent work that they carry out in raising standards in our schools.

Governors, teachers and parents, as well as the Government, are entitled to look to local authorities to give priority to front-line services such as schools. I hope and trust that the county council will do so.

I thought that the hon. Gentleman would raise the question of Warwickshire's SSA. I am aware that its SSA per pupil is lower than the average, albeit higher than nine other authorities. But, as the hon. Member is aware, the SSA system sets out to provide funding for a standard level of service nationwide. Comparisons with other local education authorities are not necessarily appropriate because the costs of providing a standard level of education across the country inevitably vary. Some of the factors that need to be taken into account are the costs of educating children in sparsely populated areas, the costs of educating children in areas that are socially or economically disadvantaged, and the high labour costs in London and the south-east. Not all authorities will have such high costs or special circumstances as other LEAs do and, therefore, the "poundage per pupil" must vary from LEA to LEA.

The hon. Gentleman also referred to deficit school budgets. Under section 37 of the Education Reform Act 1988, a local education authority may suspend a governing body's right to a delegated budget if the governors fail to comply with the requirements of the local education authority's local management of schools scheme, or more generally, if they appear to manage the school's finances unsatisfactorily.

Where a governing body refuses to set a balanced budget, the LEA will no doubt wish to consider whether to intervene on either or both those grounds. In the event, we have been notified by Warwickshire that it has suspended delegation in the case of four schools, one of which is in the hon. Member's constituency. I hope that the hon. Gentleman understands that that is as much as I can say: under section 37, governing bodies can appeal to my right hon. Friend the Secretary of State for Education against the suspension of delegation, and it would clearly be inappropriate in these circumstances for me to comment one way or the other at this stage on the action which the authority has taken.

As hon. Members will know, local education authorities have a great deal of discretion in how they arrange their local management of schools schemes. It is important to realise what LMS is about. Above all, it is not about the total of spending on schools; it is about the distribution of that expenditure—the balance between centrally retained items and funds delegated to schools, and the distribution of those delegated funds between individual schools. How much Warwickshire spends on its schools is a decision for the LEA, to be taken in the light of its other commitments, both in education and other services.

I note for the record, however, that, according to Warwickshire's LMS statement for 1995-96, the funding which schools are receiving in their delegated budgets amounts, on average, to £1,382 per pupil in primary and middle schools and £1,961 per pupil in secondary schools. Although we do not yet have comprehensive comparative figures across the country, it is safe to say that those are by no means the lowest in the country.

In any case, the amount which schools receive in their delegated budgets will depend—obviously—on what proportion of the available resources the authority chooses to delegate. I note that Warwickshire's 1994-95 budget statement indicated that the authority was planning to delegate 85.7 per cent. of its potential schools budget—about 1 per cent. below the national average. For 1995-96, the percentage of PSB to be delegated has risen to 88.4 per cent., but am I advised that that is simply because the PSB has been redefined. If the effect of that is discounted, it looks as though the level of delegation in Warwickshire may even have fallen slightly.

As to the important question of Warwickshire's reorganisation proposals, I completely resist the hon. Gentleman's allegation of Government incompetence. I am sure that he will appreciate that as the proposals are currently before the Secretary of State for Education, I cannot comment on them in detail, school by school. The Secretary of State will consider the proposals on their merits, taking account of all views for and against those proposals and all the educational issues involved.

I appreciate that the uncertainty over the future of the schools affected by the proposals is causing considerable anxiety locally. As the hon. Member is aware, I have met a number of deputations expressing either support for or opposition to aspects of the proposals. I can assure the House that the proposals will be determined as quickly as is compatible with a full and careful consideration of the issues. The House might be interested to know that Warwickshire's proposals represent one of the largest reorganisation schemes to come before the Secretary of State. It affects 177 schools, while eight governing bodies have also published proposals for the acquisition of grant-maintained status. Seven of the GM proposals conflict with closure proposals published by the local education authority.

The Education Act 1993 requires the Secretary of State to consider the reorganisation proposals and the GM applications together, but she is required to reach a decision on the GM proposals, on their merits, first. That ensures, in practice, that both the GM and rationalisation proposals are properly considered. The hon. Member will understand that we owe it to the parents, pupils and teachers concerned to give those proposals our very closest attention. I submit that we cannot rush them.

Although there is no legal duty to consider statutory proposals within a set period of time, Ministers have, as hon. Members know, given a public undertaking, where possible, to reach a decision on most statutory proposals, including those published under sections 12 or 13 of the Education Act 1980, within five months of the date of publication. For some complex reorganisation proposals, like those from Warwickshire, a longer period may be necessary to allow Ministers to give full consideration to the proposals.

The hon. Member referred to the ruling of Mr. Justice Sedley on 12 April 1995 concerning the proposed closure of the Beacon special school in Walsall. In essence, it said that, in fairness, interested parties should be given an opportunity to comment on new issues raised by Her Majesty's inspectorate in its advice to the Secretary of State on a statutory proposal. We are urgently considering the implications of the judgment for the Department's handling of statutory proposals, which includes, of course, the Warwickshire scheme.

Although I cannot supply an exact date as to when Ministers will determine the proposals, we hope to have the matter resolved, or all but resolved, by the end of next month. To put that in context, three months from the publication of the last of the GM proposals equals the date of 9 May. When the hon. Member looks at the dates, I hope that, on reflection, he will consider that the timescale is some way short of the imputation he made against the Department about unreasonable delay. In the meantime, I assure all parents and teachers whose schools are the subject of the proposals that I am well aware of the anxieties which they may currently feel. I shall seek to resolve all the outstanding issues at the earliest possible moment.

The hon. Member also argued that in order to allow the council to borrow sufficient resources to implement the proposals, its capping limit should be raised. If the statutory proposals are approved, the authority will receive extra SSA credit to reflect the cost of the reorganisation. The extra SSA credit does not, however, translate into extra spending power, just more revenue support grant. That is because Warwickshire is already spending above the level of its SSA, as the hon. Member implied. Capping rules are designed to bite on such authorities. Failure to relax the cap should not prevent the council from financing the costs of its reorganisation. Other councils, for example Leeds and Wakefield, have been able to carry out large-scale reorganisations, which remove surplus places, without receiving—

**Mr. O'Brien:** Will the Minister give way?

**Mr. Squire:** In fairness to the hon. Member, I must finish my remarks. I am willing to take up other matters with him after the debate. I still wish to put certain facts on record in the last half minute left to me.

As I said, other councils have been able to carry out large scale reorganisations without a relaxation in their capping limits. May I add that capping remains necessary to ensure that all authorities play their part in the restraint of public expenditure.

*The motion having been made at Ten o'clock and the debate having continued for half an hour,* Madam Deputy Speaker *adjourned the House without Question put, pursuant to the Standing Order.*

*Adjourned at half-past Ten o'clock till Monday 22 May.*

# House of Commons

*Monday 22 May 1995*

*The House met at half-past Two o'clock*

PRAYERS

[MADAM SPEAKER *in the Chair*]

# Oral Answers to Questions

## TRANSPORT

### Vehicle Emissions

1. **Mr. Clifton-Brown:** To ask the Secretary of State for Transport what were the total vehicle emissions in the United Kingdom for carbon monoxide, hydrocarbons and oxides of nitrogen (a) in 1970 and (b) at the latest available date. [23878]

**The Minister for Transport in London (Mr. Steve Norris):** Road transport emissions of carbon monoxide were 2.4 million tonnes in 1970 and 5.1 million tonnes in 1993; emissions of nitrogen oxides were 0.6 million tonnes in 1970 and 1.1 million tonnes in 1993; emissions of volatile organic compounds were 0.6 million tonnes in 1970 and 0.9 million tonnes in 1993.

Over the same period, total traffic rose from 200 billion to 410 billion vehicle kilometres.

**Mr. Clifton-Brown:** Do not those figures prove not only that we can meet our existing targets on emissions for the year 2005, but that if the 20-point plan outlined in the document "Air Quality: Meeting the Challenge"— commissioned jointly by the Departments of Transport and of the Environment—were implemented in full, we should do considerably better than that? Does that not show that ours is the only party with realistic policies to deal with such difficult environmental problems, and that the Labour party is bereft of such policies?

**Mr. Norris:** My hon. Friend is entirely right. The Conservative party has consistently shown itself to be the only party prepared to grapple with the genuinely difficult issues involved in air quality. He is also right that the air quality statement produced by the Government will enable us to fulfil our Rio targets.

**Ms Walley:** It is difficult to understand how the Government can claim such credit when they are merely looking through rose-tinted spectacles. People throughout the country are concerned about pollution, just as people were concerned about smog years ago. We have still heard nothing about how the Government intend to monitor emissions of PM10, which is clearly a major pollutant. What powers will now be given to local authorities so that we can start to improve the quality of life for people in both urban and rural areas?

**Mr. Norris:** The facts are quite the reverse. As the hon. Lady knows, it is the Government who are introducing tighter emission standards more than a year before the date when we are required to do so by the European Commission, and that it is her hon. Friend the well-known working-class Member for Oldham, West (Mr. Meacher) who has consistently refused to commit himself to any air quality policy; he is frightfully good at defining the problem, but pretty poor when it comes to the solution.

**Sir Peter Emery:** I declare an interest as chairman of the National Asthma Campaign. Will my hon. Friend consult Ministers at the Department of Health to ensure that, when there are major inversions in the weather and we experience the problem encountered four weeks ago, the Government can warn people about the conditions that are likely to result from monoxides in the air? It would be helpful if the Government took the lead.

**Mr. Norris:** As my right hon. Friend will know, the Committee of Medical Experts on Air Pollution study set up by the Department of Health, with input from the Department of Transport, is addressing that important question. My right hon. Friend the Secretary of State has made it clear that, given his experience of health matters, he gives high priority to this aspect of pollution control.

As for powers to control specific episodes of high pollution, my right hon. Friend the Secretary of State for the Environment has accepted that we should explore the possibilities and ensure that the appropriate powers are in place, with one caveat: we ought not to consider only how to deal with the rare occasions on which air quality deteriorates badly because of atmospheric conditions—we need long-term measures to improve air quality permanently.

### Bus Companies, London

2. **Ms Hoey:** To ask the Secretary of State for Transport what recent assessment he has made of the performance of bus companies in London. [23879]

**Mr. Norris:** The overall quality of bus services in London is continuing to improve.

**Ms Hoey:** Has the Minister seen the excellent report by the Lambeth public transport group on route No. 133, which is the only direct route through south London to the City? Is he aware that that report refers to high staff turnover and to demoralisation among staff, leading to a decline in service on that route? Does he agree that that is a direct result of a tendering process which is not open and accountable and which leaves the public no opportunity to see the facts of the tender that was won by London General?

**Mr. Norris:** What I know about that report is that it is produced by the Lambeth public transport group, which is funded by that magnificent organisation, Lambeth borough council. I suspect that few objective observers will be surprised to know that that group sets all the difficulties on route No. 133—principally traffic congestion on the A23—at the door of the dastardly robber barons who own the London bus companies. The reality is quite the opposite, but the report is an interesting insight into what the priorities of a Labour Administration might be for bus services: pay the trade union members a great deal more money and all the other problems will go away. That is nonsense.

**Mr. Harry Greenway:** I congratulate my hon. Friend and all concerned on the definite improvement in London's bus services, but does he accept that one-person operated buses sometimes delay traffic enormously while the driver takes the fares of people getting on? Will he bring back the clippies on busy bus routes, and does not he think that that would have other advantages as well?

**Mr. Norris:** I shall ponder on my hon. Friend's last point, which raises a fascinating prospect. What my hon. Friend says is important and he is quite right to say that one-person operation tends to reduce the speed.

**Madam Speaker:** Order. I should be glad if the Minister would address the House and particularly the Chair. Too many Ministers turn towards the Member asking the question because they think that that is courteous, but it is not: the courtesy is to address the House and the Chair.

**Mr. Norris:** Thank you, Madam Speaker. I know that you, too, are interested in one-person operated buses and I am happy to follow your direction. I apologise for the discourtesy.

In London about 70 per cent. of fares do not involve cash but travelcards or elderly persons' cards. The way to develop the service is through cashless technology which allows for more rapid entry rather than going back to the inefficient days of two-man operation.

**Mr. Meacher:** Will the Minister confirm that, since deregulation, passenger trips in London—where bus services were not deregulated—have scarcely fallen at all, while in all the metropolitan areas which were deregulated passenger trips have fallen by more than 35 per cent.? Will he acknowledge that deregulation has saddled Britain with a bus industry that is costing passengers more, providing a poorer service for those who need it most and using buses which are generally older, less well maintained and more polluting? Staff are disgruntled and worse off, and deregulation has virtually led to the demise of Britain's bus-building industry. When will the Minister admit that deregulation has been a disaster and that the sooner we have re-regulated bus services under a Labour Government the better?

**Mr. Norris:** Once again, by their words shall they be judged: I am happy to leave any objective observer to think on what the hon. Gentleman has invited me to say. The hon. Gentleman's question proves that he knows nothing about bus services. He does not appreciate the huge difference between the London market and the out-of-London market. It is perfectly straightforward: in London, the inability of those who would otherwise commute by car to find parking spaces determines the consistently high level of bus use, while outside London increasing car ownership has led to less bus use—a feature which is common throughout the European Community. However, there is now clear evidence that the process of deregulation has arrested the rate of decline and, as the hon. Gentleman knows, has led to a halving of subsidy, a reduction of a third in operating costs and 20 per cent. more route miles.

**Mr. Heald:** In assessing the performance of London's buses, will my hon. Friend also look at their environmental performance? Is he aware that Johnson Matthey in my constituency has developed a diesel autocatalyst which is currently being piloted on some of London's buses? Will he see what can be done to spread this excellent initiative across all bus services?

**Mr. Norris:** I did indeed go to a demonstration of the continuous recircling trap product developed by Johnson Matthey. It illustrates the fact that in respect of diesel emissions, which were thought for a long time to be relatively benign, we now realise that those 10 micron particles are among the most dangerous emissions and we welcome any technical development which allows us to eliminate them from diesel engines.

### Railway Rolling Stock

4. **Mr. Gunnell:** To ask the Secretary of State for Transport when he now expects the companies set up for the purchase of rolling stock to be able to place firm orders. [23881]

**The Minister for Railways and Roads (Mr. John Watts):** No companies have been set up specifically to purchase rolling stock. The purchase of new rolling stock remains a matter for British Rail until the rolling stock leasing companies are sold later this year.

**Mr. Gunnell:** Is the Minister aware that the Transport Select Committee and BR chairman Bob Reid both recognise that we have the longest hiatus that we have ever had in producing rolling stock and that this year, for the first time since 1948, there has been no budget for new rolling stock? Is that not why jobs are being lost in York, Hunslet and Wakefield and what does the Minister intend to do about it? It is not sufficient to give the pat answers that we have heard today.

**Mr. Watts:** UK trains currently on order include Networkers for British Rail, mail trains for the Post Office, Heathrow express and channel tunnel trains and new trains for the Jubilee line and the Northern line. Once the rolling stock companies are privatised, of course, they will have access to the private capital markets and will be able to take a longer-term view of investment needs.

**Mr. Bill Walker:** Does my hon. Friend agree that the experience of the bus industry demonstrates clearly that when the private sector becomes involved it invests very heavily in new modern rolling stock? Indeed, in one instance, it has invested more in new vehicles in one year than had been previously been invested in 10 years. That surely demonstrates that the same will happen with the railways because new vehicles cost less to maintain.

**Mr. Watts:** My hon. Friend is right, although I should remind him that British Rail has invested more than £4 billion in new rolling stock since 1979 and that in the past 10 years more than 4,000 new vehicles and locomotives have been brought into use.

### Roads Programme

5. **Mr. Mudie:** To ask the Secretary of State for Transport what progress has been made in the Government's review of the roads programme, following the report of the standing advisory committee on trunk road assessment. [23882]

**Mr. Watts:** All schemes in the planning stages are being reassessed at their next key decision stage.

**Mr. Mudie:** The Minister will be aware that the House welcomed the sensible conclusions of the advisory committee that continuous road building was no answer to congestion. How long will it be before the Department brings forward a serious response to the problem, particularly the pollution and environmental aspects of road building?

**Mr. Watts:** Last December my Department accepted the key recommendations of the SACTRA report. As I have said, we are assessing all schemes in their planning stages for the possibility of traffic generation. The committee did not conclude, as the hon. Gentleman suggests, that road building leads only to congestion.

**Mr. Hicks:** Does my hon. Friend agree that while it may be fashionable in some quarters not to approve of new road schemes there are two improvement schemes for the A38 trunk road in south-east Cornwall which are not only needed but for which there is unanimous support? Can my hon. Friend give an assurance that where people want such schemes, that fact will be taken into consideration?

**Mr. Watts:** It has become clear to me since I have had my present job that there are many more road schemes throughout the country which are welcome both to my hon. Friends and, indeed, to Opposition Members and their constituents than there are schemes which cause them concern.

### Private Vehicles, London

6. **Mr. Tony Banks:** To ask the Secretary of State for Transport if he will bring forward proposals to limit the use of private vehicles in central London. [23883]

**Mr. Norris:** Our approach is already laid down in the document, "Traffic Management and Parking Guidance", which we issued in 1993.

**Mr. Banks:** That simply is not good enough. Does the Minister share the concern of the Opposition—and, I am sure, that of Tory Members—about the appalling air quality in London? There is congestion in the streets, with clapped-out old buses, lorries and cars spewing filth into the atmosphere which we then have to breathe. What are the Government doing about that? Where are the monitoring stations? What is being done about checking the emissions from filthy cars, lorries and buses and taking them off the roads? Is the Minister waiting for people to start dropping dead in the streets of London before he acts?

**Mr. Norris:** If the hon. Gentleman wants to tackle the issues, he must accept that campaigning on the slogan that one is about to restrict the use of private cars in London is unlikely to make him attractive even to the electors of Newham. The reality is that we have to ensure that economic and social activity continues while we come to terms with the very real issues of air quality and congestion that he raises which, as is widely accepted not only by the political parties but by the pressure groups, need to be resolved by using the carrot and the stick, by ensuring the accessibility of public transport and a number of measures to manage traffic demand in a way that improves air quality and the quality of life. I do not believe that arbitrary bans on the number of vehicles coming into major cities is either right or acceptable.

**Mr. Peter Bottomley:** How about closing the House of Commons car park for an experimental period, giving each hon. Member a week's bus pass and putting a bus lane up and down Whitehall?

**Mr. Norris:** Someone told me that when my hon. Friend was a Northern Ireland Minister he once jumped out of his ministerial car to ask a couple of taxi drivers to put on their seat belts. That same brave attitude towards policy formulation perhaps lies behind his offer today, which I will leave on the table for hon. Members to consider.

**Mr. Corbyn:** Would the Minister consider a number of proposals, such as making parts of central London entirely car free and tackling the questions of tax relief for business motoring in and out of the centre of London, car parking in central London and a subsidy for public transport so that people are encouraged to use it rather than facing the current exorbitant fares?

**Mr. Norris:** Subject to the fact that there is already a substantial subsidy for public transport—the largest that there has ever been—to assist operations such as London Underground and London Buses, it might surprise the hon. Gentleman to know that my answer to his question is yes. All the matters that he raises need to be properly explored; I only wish that he would put some pressure on his Front-Bench colleagues to start talking seriously about them rather than hiding behind a great mountain of waffle.

### Network SouthEast

7. **Dr. Spink:** To ask the Secretary of State for Transport when he will next visit Network SouthEast. [23884]

**Mr. Watts:** As part of the Government's plans for privatisation, Network SouthEast was reorganised into 12 separate train operating units on 1 April 1994. I visited the London-Tilbury-Southend train operating unit last Thursday.

**Dr. Spink:** Does my hon. Friend agree that rail travel in south-east Essex, especially on the Fenchurch Street line that he visited, has never been rosier following the £150 million investment in resignalling that was completed last year and in view of the 25 replacement trains coming next year and the new management and worker ethos which is bringing so many benefits? Does he agree that since 1948, when it was nationalised, the line has suffered and failed? What hope can he bring to my constituents that, after franchising, the line will never be renationalised?

**Mr. Watts:** I am sure that none of my hon. Friend's constituents would want the line renationalised once they have tasted the benefits of privatisation. On my visit, I, like my hon. Friend, was impressed by the benefits that will come to his constituents from the investment in the new signalling and other management improvements introduced into LTS Rail.

**Mr. Mackinlay:** Will the Minister assure commuters on the London-Tilbury-Southend line that, following franchising, there will always be as many trains as there are under the current timetable and that all the stations and the Tilbury loop will be maintained?

**Mr. Watts:** As the hon. Gentleman knows, passenger service requirements will protect every station and route, including the LTS line. He will also know that PSRs are not timetables. He will be aware, however, that far from looking to reduce the services provided, the management of LTS Rail is looking for opportunities to develop them further.

**Mr. Gale:** When my hon. Friend next meets Network SouthEast, will he ask for reassurance that the recent sound bite offered to Meridian Television by the hon. Member for Oldham, West (Mr. Meacher) concerning Networker trains was wholly fallacious? Will my right hon. Friend confirm that the Networker trains ordered for the coast line are on schedule and will be in service by the end of the year and that the remaining trains are out to tender? Is that not very good news for Kent commuters?

**Mr. Watts:** My hon. Friend is absolutely right. He will be aware that there is a further invitation to tender for 44 Networker train sets. Those tenders are due to be returned by the end of this week.

### Rail Franchising

8. **Mr. Jacques Arnold:** To ask the Secretary of State for Transport if he will make a statement on progress in the franchising of rail services. [23885]

**The Secretary of State for Transport (Dr. Brian Mawhinney):** On 17 May the franchising director issued invitations to tender for the first three franchises. He expects to issue invitations to tender in respect of five further franchises later in the year.

**Mr. Arnold:** My right hon. Friend will know that the nationalised British Rail has a very warm place in the heart of the British nation. For decades it has been the butt of jokes about leaves on the line resulting in train cancellations, or trains not running due to staff shortages despite considerable unemployment. Moreover, the record of the nationalised British Rail has been, and clearly still is, close to the heart of the Labour party. Does my right hon. Friend agree that once privatisation comes and the British people see proper private sector companies bringing about improvements—such as those brought about by British Airways and by long-distance bus services—they will never again want a return to nationalisation and the Labour party will then claim that privatisation was all its own idea in the first place?

**Dr. Mawhinney:** It would be difficult for the Labour party to make such a claim. However, I agree that the injection of private finance and investment decisions, private management skills and the private sector's well-known sensitivity to what the customer actually wants will produce, over time, a better railway which is more focused on bringing benefits to the passengers. I assume that that will be welcomed across the House.

**Mr. Snape:** If artificially holding down fares in the newly privatised sectors of British Rail will bring about greater passenger use of the railways, why have the Government been doing exactly the opposite for the past 16 years?

**Dr. Mawhinney:** I hope that the House has noted the hon. Gentleman's antagonistic reaction to passengers benefiting from the unique benefits which will flow, for the first time, from the railways moving from the public sector to the private sector. I understand that Labour Members have difficulty in getting their minds around the concept that great benefits will flow from privatisation. Even ignoring the history of every other privatisation since 1979, they should accept that it is from the very act of privatisation that benefits will flow, and that those benefits should be shared by the passengers. That is our view, but we note that it is not the view of the Labour party.

**Mr. Haselhurst:** Does my right hon. Friend think that the franchisees in the new railway sector will attract more customers if they can achieve the right balance between security at their station car parks and the charges that they make to park there? Should not the name of the game be getting more people to travel on the railways in the sure knowledge that their cars will be safe?

**Dr. Mawhinney:** I share that perception with my hon. Friend. I think that I am right in saying that in those car parks where British Rail has installed an element of security the phenomenon referred to by my hon. Friend has already been observed.

**Mr. Tyler:** Will the right hon. Gentleman confirm that under the instructions issued to the franchising director by his predecessor in accordance with section 5 of the Railways Act 1993—that the service specifications for loss-making lines and services must be included in criteria which are put to the Secretary of State, agreed by him and then published—have been carried out and will be completed, including publication?

**Dr. Mawhinney:** I can confirm that all the arrangements which are duly in place for moving forward the privatisation of the railways are being carried through.

**Mr. Waterson:** Will my right hon. Friend confirm that a level of public subsidy has always been part of the Government's privatisation plans and that it is more than likely that, with a cap on fares charged to passengers, revenues will increase due to greater use?

**Dr. Mawhinney:** My hon. Friend is absolutely right. As I told the House in the debate last Wednesday, subsidy was always part of the privatisation process, as was made clear in the White Paper, in the debates on legislation and by Ministers subsequently. Conservative Members recognise that subsidies are very important. Only the hon. Member for Oldham, West (Mr. Meacher) is raising questions about the continuation of subsidy in the unlikely event of a Labour Government.

**Mr. Meacher:** Will the right hon. Gentleman explain why, in the bidding for the channel tunnel rail link, he permitted a bid to proceed from Eurorail which broke the terms of the tender document? Is he aware that the rules of the process, which were published last year, state unequivocally that all tenderers must submit a document on the basis of the reference specifications; yet Eurorail failed to do so and there was no mention in the rules of any tenderer being allowed to submit a fresh bid. Is it not clear that the Secretary of State bent the rules by allowing Eurorail to make a fresh bid because the consortium is led by one of the Government's friends and associates, Lord Parkinson?

**Dr. Mawhinney:** First, that has nothing to do with the question before the House. Secondly, as I should have thought the hon. Gentleman understood, all those documents are commercial in confidence—[HON. MEMBERS: "Ah."] I hope that the *Hansard* will record that surge of contempt for legal contracts signed by those who have a desire to take part in a channel tunnel rail link project. Unlike the hon. Member for Oldham, West, I am not going to flirt with the law in that regard.

## Rail Privatisation

9. **Mr. David Shaw:** To ask the Secretary of State for Transport if he will make a statement on the privatisation of British Rail. [23886]

**Dr. Mawhinney:** Privatisation is moving forward. Most of the restructuring of British Rail is now complete. During the next 18 months or so, most of the railway will be transferred to the private sector.

**Mr. Shaw:** Can my right hon. Friend assure me that the time-keeping problems on the south Kent coastal route, the quality of service and the lack of up-to-date rolling stock will be dealt with by privatisation? My constituents are fed up with the public sector British Rail and want a privatised British Rail.

**Dr. Mawhinney:** I am sure that my hon. Friend is absolutely right that passengers are looking for maximum benefit from the railway services to which they contribute through their taxes and fares and on which so many are dependent. I am greatly encouraged by his support to move the railway into the private sector as quickly as possible and, on behalf of his constituents and those of other right hon and hon. Members, I will do just that.

**Mr. Dalyell:** Even though we have just been told that it is not the Secretary of State's style to flirt with the law, how does he get his mind around the considered judgment of senior judges of the Court of Session in Edinburgh that what happened in relation to the London to Fort William sleeper service was illegal? What are the Government's reflections on that?

**Dr. Mawhinney:** Were I even tempted to answer that question, Madam Speaker, I think that you would remind me that the matter is sub judice.

**Mr. Garnier:** Has my right hon. Friend had the misfortune to see the press release issued by the hon. Member for Oldham, West (Mr. Meacher) on passenger service requirements? Does he agree that that press release was no more than black scaremongering propaganda and will he confirm that his Department and the Government fully confirm that the rail network is a public service and that it will continue, not only for the use of people throughout the United Kingdom, but particularly for my constituents in Market Harborough?

**Dr. Mawhinney:** My hon. and learned Friend is right. I have seen that press release, just as I have heard about a press release about Peterborough, issued by the hon. Member for Hampstead and Highgate (Ms Jackson), in which she even got the date wrong. Last Wednesday week, Opposition Front-Bench Members issued a press statement which said that a new fares structure for the railways had been postponed indefinitely. It was announced the following Monday. They said that new passenger service requirements for four further lines had been postponed indefinitely; they were announced last Tuesday. They also said that the tendering arrangements for the first three franchises had been postponed indefinitely; they were announced last Wednesday. Given that record of accuracy, my hon. and learned Friend can reassure his constituents that, as everyone on this side of the House already knows, they should not be even remotely worried by what the Opposition Front Bench says.

**Dr. Marek:** Is the Secretary of State aware that the travelling public would be much more likely to have a better deal if British Rail was allowed to bid for the first three franchises? The fact that it is not allowed to do so shows that the Government and the franchising director care not one whit for the benefits that accrue to the travelling public.

**Dr. Mawhinney:** The declamation does not constitute evidence. The franchising director has taken a view, and I am very comfortable with it.

**Mr. Hawkins:** Does my right hon. Friend agree that, as privatisation proceeds, as the travelling public and our constituents want, it is crucial that all those in the private sector who wish to run trains should have the fullest opportunity to develop their services? Will he look carefully at the proposals by Statesman Railways to re-introduce the direct through service to Blackpool, which was withdrawn by nationalised British Rail?

**Dr. Mawhinney:** My hon. Friend is right that passengers will want to see the maximum benefit to them arising from the privatisation process. He will understand that those interested in making a bid will be able to do so in the normal and appropriate way.

**Mr. Llwyd:** The Secretary of State has given assurances that fares will be pegged in line with inflation for the next four years. What assurances has he had from the Treasury? If the cash is not there, will not it mean a cut in services?

**Dr. Mawhinney:** I am not sure where the hon. Gentleman has been for the last week, but I have made it clear on a number of occasions, not least in last Wednesday's debate, that the Government will provide the appropriate and necessary subsidy, including that arising from the fares policy.

## Aston Clinton Bypass

10. **Mr. Lidington:** To ask the Secretary of State for Transport when he expects to publish his inspector's report on the A41 Aston Clinton bypass. [23887]

**Mr. Watts:** The inspector's report will be published concurrently with the decision following last November's public inquiry. The announcement will be made as soon as possible.

**Mr. Lidington:** May I remind my hon. Friend that that bypass was first proposed by his predecessor in 1937 and that my constituents in Aston Clinton have had to put up with vastly increased volumes of traffic through their village since his Department completed the Hemel Hempstead and Berkhamsted bypasses? May I urge him and his officials in the Highways Agency to give that project the highest possible priority?

**Mr. Watts:** My hon. Friend reinforces the point that I made earlier about the popularity of many schemes in the programme.

## Manchester Airport

11. **Mr. Nigel Evans:** To ask the Secretary of State for Transport how many passengers used Manchester airport in 1994. [23888]

**Dr. Mawhinney:** The number is 14.3 million.

**Mr. Evans:** Manchester airport is one of the finest regional airports in Europe. Its popularity can be evidenced by that figure, which is due to grow to 15.5 million by next year. I was extremely gratified when my right hon. Friend announced the open skies policy with the United States of America last year as it is good news for regional airports. Will he take the liberalising spirit a step further and extend the open skies policy to the rest of the world so that more aircraft can use airports like Manchester?

**Dr. Mawhinney:** I agree with my hon. Friend that Manchester is a very fine airport and that it has a bright future. Like him, I am pleased that Continental has announced its plans to initiate a flight between Newark and Manchester, arising out of the liberalisation process that I announced last October. That will be good news for passengers and for the Greater Manchester region and its economy. I shall certainly consider carefully any other suggestions that are made to me in that regard.

**Mr. O'Hara:** The hon. Member for Ribble Valley (Mr. Evans) referred to the expected increase in traffic through Manchester airport in the next decade. Manchester airport seeks a second runway to cater for that capacity. It pitches the capacity of its present runway at 18 million whereas Gatwick copes with 24 million passengers on one runway.

Would not it make more sense, instead of building a new runway in Manchester where there will be at most 12 million or possibly only 6 million extra passengers, to develop Liverpool airport, where there is already a runway that can cope with 12 million passengers, and where meteorological conditions and safety conditions are better? There is less environmental impact, and 20 per cent. of the people who use Manchester airport find it as convenient, or more convenient, to go to Liverpool.

**Dr. Mawhinney:** At least the hon. Gentleman's constituents will recognise that he is doing the job that he was sent to this place to do on their behalf. The House will understand that public inquiries are in place relating to both Manchester airport and Liverpool airport, and I am one of only two people in the country who cannot comment about either at the moment.

## ATTORNEY-GENERAL

### Crown Prosecution Service

29. **Mr. Hendry:** To ask the Attorney-General what assessment he has made of the effectiveness of the working relationship between the police and the Crown Prosecution Service.        [23908]

**The Attorney-General (Sir Nicholas Lyell):** It is of fundamental importance to the Crown Prosecution Service that there should be close co-operation between each of its 104 branches and the local police, usually via their crime support units, and that is becoming increasingly effective.

**Mr. Hendry:** Does my right hon. and learned Friend agree that the relationship between the CPS and the police depends on openness and respect for the truth? Does he agree that, when the shadow Home Secretary makes a speech littered with half-truths and inaccuracies to the Police Federation conference, as he did last week, it cannot help that relationship? Is not that a disgrace, and should he not withdraw them at the earliest opportunity?

**The Attorney-General:** I must agree with my hon. Friend and deplore the thoroughly inaccurate, irresponsible and misleading speech made to the Police Federation by the shadow Home Secretary last week. I was astonished that, among other things, he sought to wind up his audience by criticising a judicial sentencing decision, and then failed to draw to the attention of that audience the fact that that sentence had been properly referred, as unduly lenient, to the Court of Appeal.

**Mr. John Morris:** The Attorney-General knows that I supported the setting up of the CPS and have always been anxious that both the CPS and the Serious Fraud Office are seen to be working well, but does he accept that there are continuing anxieties on the part of judges, lawyers and the police, and is not the disclosure by the *Sunday Times* of the CPS employing solicitors who have been disciplined for deliberately or recklessly deceiving clients or incompetence, a matter of grave concern?

In the proposed reorganisation of police force and local authority areas, has the assurance given by the then Home Secretary, in introducing the Prosecution of Offences Bill in 1985, that there would be chief Crown prosecutors for the most part covering a police area, been thrown overboard?

I suggested a review after five years to discover whether we had got it right. Would it not be valuable now to have an independent review to examine the effectiveness of the CPS?

**The Attorney-General:** I would be inclined to acquit the right hon. and learned Gentleman of any part in the speech by his hon. Friend last week, but I doubt whether it would have been made had there been close liaison between them. The speech was very unwise in suggesting that the service should be pulled—

**Mr. Olner:** Outrageous.

**Madam Speaker:** Order. The question that the Opposition Front Bench spokesman has asked the Minister must be answered.

**The Attorney-General:** The speech was very unwise—*[Interruption.]* I am answering the question if hon. Members will listen. The speech was unwise to suggest that the service should be pulled up by the roots. As I made clear the following day, there are 104 branches in the Crown Prosecution Service, and they seek to keep a close liaison with their local police. It is important to ensure effective liaison over discontinuances, which have been coming down over the past two years.

To answer the second part of the right hon. and learned Gentleman's question, the CPS is careful about who it employs. The picture given in the recent press article was by no means complete. The CPS would certainly not keep on anyone whose conduct did not merit him being employed by a public service.

**Mr. Jessel:** On the role of both the police and the Crown Prosecution Service in relation to the War Crimes Act 1991, can my right hon. and learned Friend confirm that, in view of the stark enormity of the murder of 6 million people in concentration camps, the CPS and the police will not be inhibited by the passage of time?

**The Attorney-General:** Any prosecution decision in relation to war crimes will be taken on proper principles. But it will have regard to the will of the House as expressed in the War Crimes Act. This would not cause the mere fact of the passage of 50 years to be taken into account when deciding not to prosecute. I have answered a number of questions in writing recently on the progress of investigations, which are being carried forward with great care.

### Incitement to Racial Hatred

30. **Mr. Soley:** To ask the Attorney-General what assessment he has made of the operation of the law of incitement to racial hatred with particular reference to section 18 of the Public Order Act 1986.    [23910]

**The Solicitor-General (Sir Derek Spencer):** The offences created by part III of the Public Order Act 1986, of which section 18 is but one, provide very full powers for investigation, prosecution and punishment of incitement to racial hatred.

**Mr. Soley:** Will the Attorney-General confirm that he is looking at the additional information that I have sent to him about Mr. Bernard Manning and his comments to the police in Manchester? Will he also confirm that the House passed the amendment, as it was then, to the 1986 Act, as it is now, with the precise intention that the Attorney-General should intervene in cases of racial incitement? Will he also confirm that, in such a case, the Attorney-General has the important duty to intervene and help the police in order to take the necessary prosecution, otherwise we would have passed the Act for no purpose?

**The Solicitor-General:** I am very surprised at the hon. Gentleman's comment in view of the fact that on 3 May my right hon. and learned Friend the Attorney-General, in a written reply, invited the hon. Gentleman to send any evidence he had about a criminal offence to the chief officer of police involved. When I inquired this morning whether any such letter had been received, I was notified that none had. In case the hon. Gentleman does not appreciate it, the Attorney-General's role in the Public Order Act is to give consent in appropriate cases; it is the function of the police to investigate.

**Mr. Garnier:** Will my hon. and learned Friend confirm that 16 out of 21 applications put to his chambers by the prosecuting authorities under section 18 have been accepted? Will he also confirm that his Department and all prosecuting authorities will do their best to ensure that, if the evidence exists, those who are guilty of offences are prosecuted?

**The Solicitor-General:** I can assure my hon. and learned Friend that there is no lack of will to prosecute. The up-to-date figures in respect of applications under part III of the Public Order Act are as follows: There have been 21 applications, 16 have been granted, four were declined and one is under consideration. The House will be aware that in the everyday experience of the courts, most racially-motivated crime falls into the category of criminal damage, assaults or offences under part I of the Act. Offences under part III of the Act are only a small proportion of the whole.

### Mr. Nick Leeson

31. **Mr. MacShane:** To ask the Attorney-General when he expects Mr. Nick Leeson to be interviewed by the appropriate criminal investigative authorities.    [23912]

**The Attorney-General:** The investigation by the Director of the Serious Fraud Office, in conjunction with the City of London police, is not yet concluded and it would be inappropriate at this stage to give details of operational matters.

**Mr. MacShane:** Is the Attorney-General aware that barely an hour's flight from here sits Mr. Nick Leeson, who lost £1 million to the Queen as well as the savings of many investors and caused a major bank to shut down, and no one has asked him one simple question about the matter? Is the Attorney-General further aware that, given the hangman state in Singapore which is seeking to bring Mr. Leeson to account through its form of justice, many people in this country believe that the lack of interest or concern on the part of the criminal investigation authorities borders on a cover-up?

**The Attorney-General:** I am very surprised that the hon. Gentleman, who claims to have some connections with the City of London, should make such an allegation. The matter is being examined with great care by the Serious Fraud Office and by the authorities in Singapore. The Serious Fraud Office has made an application to the courts in Singapore for detailed information which it requires in order to take forward its investigations. The application was not granted at that stage and the office continues to pursue its inquiries.

### OVERSEAS DEVELOPMENT

#### Kenya

36. **Sir David Steel:** To ask the Secretary of State for Foreign and Commonwealth Affairs if he will make a statement on multilateral aid to Kenya following recent political developments.    [23919]

**The Parliamentary Under-Secretary of State for Foreign and Commonwealth Affairs (Mr. Tony Baldry):** There is no direct connection between the levels of support provided by the International Monetary Fund/World bank and political developments. The IMF and World bank have both had recent concerns about some aspects of the economic programme, which they are continuing to discuss with the Government of Kenya.

**Sir David Steel:** The Minister is surely aware of recent events in Kenya, including the arrest and harassment of Opposition Members of Parliament and the interference with the presses which publish *Finance* magazine and *People Weekly*. Will he undertake to consider those matters alongside the economic issues at the Paris Club meeting of donors on 26 July? Will he confirm that the international community cannot be expected to continue to assist Governments which act in that repressive manner?

**Mr. Baldry:** I agree with the broad thrust of the right hon. Gentleman's comments. I know of his long-standing interest in the welfare of Kenya and of course we share his concerns about the deterioration of the political atmosphere in that country in recent months, particularly the arrest of Opposition Members of Parliament and the destruction of the free press.

At the Kenya donors meeting in December last year the United Kingdom delegation made it clear that the future provision of balance of payments aid was subject not only to continued implementation of economic reform but to continued improvement in the overall political situation and progress in the fight against corruption. As the right hon. Gentleman said, there will be a meeting of Kenya aid donors in July. We will attend, as will the Government of Kenya. The right hon. Gentleman and the House may be assured that there will be some very frank talking at that meeting.

### North Africa

37. **Mr. Janner:** To ask the Secretary of State for Foreign and Commonwealth Affairs what proposals he has for the provision of aid to countries on the north coast of Africa. [23920]

**Mr. Baldry:** In the current financial year we propose to provide aid through our bilateral programme to Egypt, Morocco, Tunisia and Algeria. Those countries also receive substantial multilateral aid, in particular through the European Community.

**Mr. Janner:** Can the Minister please look with special generosity at Morocco, whose people are suffering as a result of a catastrophic harvest and which is a pivot of political stability in a very fragile area?

**Mr. Baldry:** Morocco receives significant European Community aid and in the past four years EC aid to Morocco has increased by 35 per cent. The hon. Gentleman takes a particular interest in North Africa and Morocco and I think that he knows that we are also keen to help Morocco by promoting trade and allowing it greater access to European Union markets. A mandate for a partnership agreement with Morocco was agreed by the European Community in December 1993. That agreement aims to create a free trade zone with Europe progressively over the next 12 years. I am sure that the whole House wants to see maximum stability in North Africa and to prevent any other countries in that region from sliding into civil war.

**Mr. Key:** May I encourage my hon. Friend seriously to examine aid to north Africa with our European Union partners? I am convinced that it is in Britain's interest that we should seek to minimise economic migration and the flow of people in north Africa and between north Africa and Europe. One good way of doing that is by investment in jobs, homes and economic prosperity in North Africa to minimise the differences.

**Mr. Baldry:** I entirely agree with my hon. Friend. We want to promote economic stability and economic growth in north Africa. We can do that through the bilateral aid budget and by ensuring that there is greater access for trade from north Africa into the European Union.

### UNESCO

38. **Mr. Alan W. Williams:** To ask the Secretary of State for Foreign and Commonwealth Affairs if the Government will review their policy towards membership of the United Nations Educational, Scientific and Cultural Organisation. [23921]

**Mr. Baldry:** We are continuing to keep the issue under review.

**Mr. Williams:** Will the Minister remind us why Britain withdrew from UNESCO? I remember that at the time it

was an extremely controversial decision and deeply disappointing to all the aid and third world agencies. As the United Nations is celebrating its 50th anniversary this year, would it not be an appropriate time to review and rejoin?

**Mr. Baldry:** It is helpful to remember that we left UNESCO because of its bureaucracy, overspending, mismanagement, inefficiency and political bias. Since we left 10 years ago, there has been some progress, but not enough. It is fair to say that UNESCO is not an aid programme, but a bureaucracy as 75 per cent. of all UNESCO staff are employed in Paris and only 25 per cent. are actually out in the field. The Organisation for Economic Co-operation and Development estimates that only 6.6 per cent. of spending by UNESCO can be considered as development aid to developing countries.

**Miss Lestor:** May I remind the Minister, as my hon. Friend the Member for Carmarthen (Mr. Williams) did, that it is the 50th anniversary of the United Nations? The Government say with many fine words that they are committed to the United Nations and they are joining the celebrations, but in reality they do the opposite. They recently reduced the contribution to UNICEF and I detect a harder line on UNESCO than previously, when they said that some progress had been made. There is enormous pressure from both sides of the House for Britain to rejoin UNESCO. It is not a party political matter. If the Minister wants to express real support for the United Nations in this anniversary year, he should now cut out all the red tape and announce that we shall rejoin UNESCO at the earliest possible moment.

**Mr. Baldry:** We need no lectures on support for the United Nations. The United Kingdom fully supports the UN and its agencies. We pay in full and promptly, and we support 26 UN agencies, as well as other UN bodies, with funds and programmes. In addition, we are one of the main donors to UN peacekeeping. Recently, we increased our grant to UNICEF and gave it an extra £3.4 million in supplementary funding mostly in response to emergency appeals. The hon. Lady should consider whether it makes any sense at all, in the name of development policies, to give money to an organisation when 75 per cent. of its staff are locked up in Paris and only 6.6 per cent. of its total budget is spent on development aid to developing countries.

### Pakistan Cotton Crop

39. **Mr. Pike:** To ask the Secretary of State for Foreign and Commonwealth Affairs what assistance has been given to Pakistan to overcome problems with cotton crop production. [23922]

**Mr. Baldry:** The ODA, through the Natural Resources Institute, has been assisting the Government of Pakistan since 1985 in identifying ways of improving the control of cotton pests in an environmentally benign manner. Assistance is also being provided by the Asian development bank, the European Commission, the United Nations Food and Agriculture Organisation, the World bank and agro-chemical companies.

**Mr. Pike:** As the Minister knows, for the past two years the cotton crop in Pakistan has been affected by a peculiar virus and has reduced by more than half to less than 6 million bales a year. In Pakistan's own view, it is a crisis. What help is being given to Pakistan in terms of expertise and finance to overcome that particular problem?

**Mr. Baldry:** We have an excellent organisation called the Natural Resources Institute, which is funded by the ODA. Through the Natural Resources Institute, we have spent £1 million in recent years on research into cotton pest control in Pakistan. As the hon. Gentleman said, cotton is Pakistan's most important crop. In recent years it has been attacked by viruses, pest infestations and floods, and we have been working extremely hard with the Pakistan Government and with best science in this country to ensure that much of the crop is saved for the benefit of the people of Pakistan.

### Rwanda

40. **Mr. Simon Hughes:** To ask the Secretary of State for Foreign and Commonwealth Affairs what assistance is planned by Her Majesty's Government between now and the end of the year for Rwanda.     [23924]

**Mr. Baldry:** Britain has provided £8 million since January for relief and rehabilitation. Over the coming months that will be used to resettle those displaced from Kibeho, support human rights monitors, and to strengthen the legal sector and the Government's economic policy-making capacity. We are looking at how we might help further.

**Mr. Hughes:** That answer is welcome. Does the Minister agree that it is a great consolation to the people of Rwanda and of other countries that suffer such huge traumas to know that the United Nations will be on hand when needed to respond quickly, act strongly and continue its presence to ensure that human rights are upheld—which is continuing to be necessary, as the Minister said—and to intervene to prevent any further escalation of inter-tribal violence and warfare?

**Mr. Baldry:** I agree that all those objectives are desirable, which is why we support the UN fully and pay our subscription on time. As a country, we are contributing more peacekeeping forces to the UN than practically any other country in the world. It is often forgotten that, for example, in Angola at present there are 600 members of the Royal Logistics corps sorting out the food chain. We will continue to support and to work with the UN.

# Competitiveness

3.30 pm

**The President of the Board of Trade and Secretary of State for Trade and Industry (Mr. Michael Heseltine):** A year ago, the Government published the White Paper "Competitiveness: Helping Business to Win"—the first comprehensive audit of the United Kingdom's industrial and commercial competitiveness. That White Paper was widely welcomed by business. Today, we publish our second report on competitiveness.

This year's White Paper is designed to report on changes in our performance over the past year, describe the action that the Government have taken to improve United Kingdom competitiveness over that period and set out our plans for further progress, making a number of significant announcements today. The White Paper contains new, more extensive analysis of our competitive position. It looks at the competitiveness of key sectors, regional developments and to the future, as well as reporting on changes in our performance over the past year in each of the main factors of competitiveness that we identified last year.

The White Paper reports in detail on the progress that the Government have made in fulfilling the commitments—more than 300 of them—in the 1994 White Paper. It shows promises kept and action taken. For the future, it contains 70 new initiatives and commits more than £240 million extra, of which £165 million is additional Government expenditure. In addition, my right hon. Friend the Chancellor of the Duchy of Lancaster is announcing today, in response to a question from my hon. Friend the Member for Chesham and Amersham (Mrs. Gillan), that he is publishing the report of the technology foresight steering group and the 1995 "Forward Look" of Government-funded science, engineering and technology. My right hon. Friend is also publishing the efficiency scrutiny report on resource management systems in Government. My right hon. and learned Friend the Chancellor of Exchequer is today publishing a White Paper on public procurement, and when the markets open tomorrow morning, my right hon. Friend the Secretary of State for National Heritage will be announcing the Government's conclusions on media ownership issues, followed by a statement to the House in the afternoon.

This White Paper reports good news. Last year, output rose by 4 per cent., manufacturing productivity by more than 4 per cent. and exports by 11 per cent.—increasing our share of world trade. Unemployment fell by 300,000. In the last quarter of the year, investment surged by 8 per cent. and is set to increase still further this year. The balance of payments deficit fell sharply and underlying inflation was at the lowest sustained level for 30 years.

That year-on-year performance is impressive and maintains the turnround in our economic performance started in 1979. But the competitiveness agenda is on-going and long term. Our task is to reverse more than a century of relative decline. Last year's White Paper showed how, during the 1980s, we stopped falling behind the rest of the world. We closed the productivity gap with our main competitors, put strikes into the history books and stabilised the decline in our share of world trade in manufacturing.

Today's White Paper takes the analysis forward. Overall manufacturing productivity is now close to that in Germany and France and continues to catch up the United States of America and Japan. At the same time, British companies have regained their reputation for first-class, world quality in manufacturing and services.

The United Kingdom economy's competitiveness is nowhere better illustrated than in our ability to attract inward investment. The UK accounts for one third of all inward investment in the European Union. That investment is worth more than £130 billion, and it has created and safeguarded nearly 700,000 jobs since 1979.

Our exports too are a huge success. They reached record levels last year, and the Confederation of British Industry reports that orders are growing at their fastest ever rate. Last year, Ministers led more than 80 trade promotion missions, accompanied by more than 1,000 business people, to more than 50 countries. I am delighted to tell the House that the business men and women who accompanied me to China last week were able to strike deals totalling more than £1 billion.

I said that competitiveness was on-going. The White Paper makes clear our determination to seek continued improvement. We shall seek it in management. We have as many world-class firms as Germany, but we have a higher proportion of poor performers. Among a raft of new measures to help companies—particularly small and medium-sized ones—learn from the experience of the best, the Government will make available nearly £100 million extra through business links for locally designed business development programmes.

On improvement in exports, despite the success that I have just described, only 100,000 of our 2.8 million UK firms export. We can do better. Today, therefore, we are setting a target of introducing 30,000 new exporting firms to foreign markets by the year 2000. To achieve that, my Department will spend nearly £40 million extra on support for exporters over the next four years. In addition, my right hon. Friend the Secretary of State for Foreign and Commonwealth Affairs has already announced a significant strengthening of Foreign and Commonwealth Office support for commercial work overseas, involving more than 100 new commercial officers, particularly in key, emerging markets.

On improvement in education and training, the Government's reforms—the national curriculum, publication of schools' performance, devolution of management to local level—have already transformed our education system. One third of our young people now go on into higher education. There is, however, no room for complacency. Our aim is for Britain to have the best qualified work force in Europe. The White Paper sets out the steps that we are taking to achieve that aim. Today, the Government are endorsing new targets for achievement in education and training drawn up by the National Advisory Council for Education Training and Targets. Those set new, challenging standards. To ensure that we meet them, we will conduct a major review of our education and training effort, benchmarking it against our leading competitors and identifying where improvement is necessary.

On improvement in innovation, we match the best in inventiveness but not in bringing products to market. Some of the best ideas are born here. We must ensure that more are exploited here. To help, the Government will spend an extra £70 million over four years to support innovation and technology.

In addition, today's report on the technology foresight programme identifies sectors that we need to develop to stay in the top league of industrial nations. The

Government's initial response is given in this year's "Forward Look". Foresight will influence spending priorities in Government and the universities. The Government will also encourage industry to respond through a foresight challenge, which will provide £80 million—half from industry, half from Government—for collaborative projects over the next three years,

British businesses have already benefited from the huge structural reforms undertaken by the Government since 1979. We shall build on our programme of radical reform: Nuclear Electric and Scottish Nuclear are to be privatised; the gas supply industry is to be liberalised; and today, I am announcing more than 100 deregulatory proposals on which we shall take early action and new measures to make enforcement procedures more business friendly. In terms of regulations alone, more than 1,000 have now been identified for amendment or repeal.

Today's White Paper adds up to a comprehensive agenda for action: action that will help business extend its growing success, action to improve the support that Government can give to the wealth-creating sector, action to equip our companies with the skills, resources and entrepreneurial drive to challenge the best in the world in the century ahead. I commend the White Paper to the House.

**Dr. John Cunningham** (Copeland): We thank the President for making a statement in advance of a wider launch of the White Paper.

We recognise that Britain must survive and prosper in an increasingly competitive global market. There can be no protected Britain and no Fortress Europe. Is the right hon. Gentleman aware that the essentials for success in that market are much better and more sustained investment in skills, education and training, much better support for technological innovation and much longer-term investment in our manufacturing base? Although the modest announcement that he has made is welcome, in several respects it makes good only the planned reductions in spending which his Department announced in its annual statement for the year. There is little new Government money in what the right hon. Gentleman had to say.

Even allowing for two years of relatively successful growth, the right hon. Gentleman and his right hon. Friends will have to do much more to make up for 16 years of devastation of our industrial base. Contrary to what he said, our position has not improved relative to 1979. Manufacturing investment has become worse. Our position in respect of trade and manufactured goods is worse and training now is worse than in 1979. Perhaps we can give a modest welcome to the right hon. Gentleman's belated recognition, after 16 years in office, that some form of industrial strategy is necessary for us to compete in a global market.

The right hon. Gentleman said that his White Paper of a year ago was widely welcomed by industry. We were all reminded by the Director-General of the CBI today in the *Financial Times* that that was far from the truth. The director-general said that industry gave last year's White Paper two out of 10—hardly widely welcoming. The reality is that again many searching questions will be asked by those in industry and commerce about today's statement.

What happened to the much-vaunted industrial financial initiative that the right hon. Gentleman announced at about this stage last year? We all know that it was supposed to be directed to short-termism and the amount of money paid in dividends. That initiative was pole-axed by Lord Hanson. The right hon. Member for Loughborough (Mr. Dorrell), who was then a member of the Treasury team, was moved to the Department of National Heritage and the idea was quietly shelved.

When will the President recognise that unit labour costs matter, not wage rates, when it comes to increasing our productivity and competitiveness? When will he and his right hon. Friends recognise that cutting the training budget by one quarter is not the way to tackle the problem? Reducing training places for work by 55,000 this year over last year is not the way to tackle the problem. Having a training programme in which 50 per cent. of youth trainees achieve no qualifications is not the way to tackle the problem.

The right hon. Gentleman mentioned his recent trip to China. We welcome his endeavours. I remind him that those endeavours are certainly needed because in 1979 we had a balance of trade surplus with China whereas last year we had a deficit of £800 million. That is a measure of what his policies have done to our trade with the People's Republic of China.

The fact is that, far from making ground, Britain is falling behind our international competitors. Growth, since 1979, at 1.6 per cent. is the worst performance in the Group of Seven. Unemployment remains persistently high. Britain has lower productivity than any of our main competitors; lower skills, worse capital equipment and depressed investment. It is no wonder that our competitive position is so awful compared with Japan, China, the United States and others.

As the right hon. Gentleman talked about reducing burdens and getting rid of regulations, perhaps he will tell the House how many of the 1,000 regulations that he has identified for scrapping were introduced by his own right hon. and hon. Friends in the past 16 years.

On burdens, what has the right hon. Gentleman to say to industry and commerce about the record levels of taxation that the Government have introduced, despite all their election promises? Last year, he produced a White Paper of some 160 pages. This year his White Paper has an additional 100 pages—like the right hon. Gentleman, no doubt very long on rhetoric and very short on content.

The right hon. Gentleman had something to say about support for industrial innovation, and as he has announced some modern improvement, I welcome that, but the reality is that page 61 of his Department's annual report shows that his planned support for industrial innovation is to decline in real terms. He is just barely making that decline good. Fifteen sector panels on technology foresight have reported. How will his Department build on and back those strategic areas? The reality is, with very little Government effort or support.

All in all, this is yet another attempt at a relaunch by a failed and discredited Conservative Government, by a man who gives all the impression of taking the lead; but the lead that he really wants to take is the job of the right hon. Gentleman the Prime Minister sitting next to him.

**Mr. Heseltine:** Perhaps the next time that the right hon. Member for Copeland (Dr. Cunningham) responds to a statement, he might find it helpful to read it—a copy was given to him in advance—before he prepares his response.

*[Mr. Heseltine]*

He will have recognised that all the issues on which he took issue with me were covered comprehensively in my statement.

I do not find it too easy to take lectures from the right hon. Gentleman on matters to do with wage rates and unit costs. I thought that the Labour party was committed to the social contract, to giving back power to trade unions and to introducing a minimum wage. Yet Opposition Members are telling us about unit costs. The Labour party is designing policies that would have one express consequence: to increase the unit costs of British industry. The right hon. Gentleman obviously has not understood, when he runs Britain down in so comprehensive a way—

**Dr. Cunningham:** I did not do that.

**Mr. Heseltine:** The right hon. Gentleman says that he did not do that. I heard him use the words "falling behind". That is of an economy that is attracting 40 per cent. of all the inward investment coming into the European Union, an economy with record levels of exports, with the best inflation record for 30 years and with an industrial relations record that we have not seen equalled for 100 years. I do not call that falling behind.

I must say to the cognoscenti of the House, of whom there are many even on the Opposition Benches, that the right hon. Gentleman trespassed a little on the speeches that are now being made by the Leader of the Opposition. The Leader of the Opposition apparently is telling us—I think he did so only today, and I am told that there is, God help us, another lecture coming tonight—that the old Labour days of tax and spend are over. Yet when I announce £165 million of money, the right hon. Gentleman says that it is very little new money. Just exactly how much would Labour's big money be? What will the leader of the Labour party say about the amount of extra money to which, by implication, the right hon. Member for Copeland refers?

I was fascinated by the right hon. Gentleman's references to the comments of the Director-General of the CBI on last year's White Paper. He clearly did not entirely understand what the Director-General had said. He said that the White Paper had been received with "deux points"—I appreciate that my accent may not be all that it should be; there is a limit to the ability even of a Euro-fanatic such as myself to speak French.

I have done some research, and I am told that "deux points" is something to do with a thing called the Eurovision song contest. I understand that the maximum score is 15, so "deux points" is not good news. The problem was, I think, that the Director-General of the CBI thought that the maximum score was "trois points".

The complexities of the translation, given the current exchange rates in France and Britain, may be beyond the right hon. Gentleman's comprehension; but I feel that he should establish whether we are trying to rate the country's performance against a record of serious economic advance or to trivialise it by referring to something to do with the Eurovision song contest. Let us get down to the hard core of the matter. If the Government's track record, economic policy and achievements are as awful as the right hon. Gentleman suggested, why is the leader of the Labour party hawking himself around the country's industrial and commercial communities trying to pretend that nothing much would change if there were a Labour Government?

The reason is that we have got it right, and the only policies that Labour Members can dream up are intended to bring them as close as possible to us without splitting their party in half.

**Sir Timothy Sainsbury** (Hove): The White Paper will provide a welcome opportunity for us to build on the success of the 1994 White Paper in improving understanding of the vital importance of competitiveness to wealth creation in a competitive global economy. Does my right hon. Friend agree, however, that much work remains to be done? It would help, for example, if the media took more interest in the achievements of British industry and, indeed, showed more understanding. As my right hon. Friend has already demonstrated, there is also much work to be done with Her Majesty's Opposition.

Does my right hon. Friend agree that there will be a widespread welcome for the proposal to benchmark our educational achievements against those of our best competitors? Will he assure us that, when he carries out that exercise, he will have particular regard to what has been achieved in encouraging more of our best and brightest students to undertake courses in science and engineering, thus raising the skill base of our economy?

**Mr. Heseltine:** My right hon. Friend is absolutely right. He himself has played a distinguished part in helping to advance the competitiveness of our export activities in particular. My right hon. Friend the Chancellor of the Duchy of Lancaster will have heard what he said, and he can be assured that we take the matter extremely seriously.

As for the role of the media, none of us in the House expects the media to do other than criticise when it is appropriate, but a sense of balance is needed. Every time Britain's achievements are disparaged or ignored, it sends a message to the men and women on whose success we all depend. We need a greater recognition and a fairer representation of Britain's achievements by the British media.

**Mr. Nick Harvey** (North Devon): Will the President say a little more about investment? He spoke of an improvement in the last quarter, but investment is still not leading recovery here as strongly as it is in our competitor economies, or as strongly as it did after the recession of the 1980s. What proposals has the right hon. Gentleman to promote investment further?

**Mr. Heseltine:** The overall requirement is to preserve the stability of the macro-economy. However, the hon. Gentleman will be as pleased as I was to learn that the latest CBI surveys show encouraging indications for investment. We intend to preserve the economic background that will allow that to continue.

**Sir Peter Hordern** (Horsham): Does my right hon. Friend agree that the achievement of such a high level of inward investment is very creditable? Does he recall that 16 years ago corporation tax was at 52 per cent., and exchange controls meant that companies had to get permission before being allowed to invest overseas? Does my right hon. Friend recognise that there have been substantial improvements in the performance of British industry since those days and that there is still room for improvement in the conduct of business for small companies, particularly in terms of the late payment of debt?

**Mr. Heseltine:** My right hon. Friend is right. There has been a transformation, and the only people who do not appreciate that are the Opposition. There is no greater indication of that than the decisions by leading German industrialists to invest in this country rather than in their own, let alone the decisions of the Japanese, the Americans and the Koreans, who are increasingly choosing this country as the home base for their European expansion proposals. The record is important and we can be proud of it. In coincidence with the publication of the White Paper, there is a summary document designed to advise people who are in contact with small firms. I hope that all hon. Members will take the opportunity to disseminate the messages in that document. It is designed specifically for small firms.

**Mr. Richard Caborn** (Sheffield, Central): When the President dealt with last year's White Paper one of the weaknesses that many people criticised related to private financing. The industry finance initiative was set up at that time and it was said that there would be a report on that. First, why has that report not been produced? Secondly, Friday's report by the Select Committee on Trade and Industry on finance for industry again saw that as a structural weakness and mentioned short-termism. I think that that was accepted by the Financial Secretary to the Treasury when he attended the Select Committee. Paragraphs 52, 53 and 54 of the summary show that that structural weakness has not been addressed. The President has dealt with inward investment. What further financial initiatives indigenous to the UK will the President take, because on this issue the Government have a poor record?

**Mr. Heseltine:** The hon. Gentleman will know that we have not responded to the Select Committee report. However, we shall certainly do so with our customary care. A number of proposals are outlined in the White Paper and in the summary document for small firms. For example, one is to use business links to create a chain of advice to help small businesses to gain access to the financial markets. The House will be aware of the changes that we made to permit building societies to operate in that area. We should bear in mind the fact that there are now some 900,000 more small businesses in Britain than there were in 1979 and that they have been able to finance their survival and development within the existing regimes. We are all anxious to try to improve on that, but by and large the problem that affected the small business sector was the recession of the late 1980s.

**Mr. Nigel Forman** (Carshalton and Wallington): Is my right hon. Friend aware that we regard his statement on competitiveness as good news? We should like to see even more done to help small businesses. One of our main competitors, Germany, has five times as many small and medium manufacturers as Britain. Will he assure the House that his efforts, especially on business links and related schemes, will assist that part of our economy because upon it depends much of our future employment and export prospects?

**Mr. Heseltine:** My hon. Friend is right. The White Paper contains a proposal to co-operate with the leading organisations representing small and medium companies so as to promote a national consultative process. We shall involve those organisations in that so as to draw the views of their members to the attention of Government. In that way we shall know exactly what are their high priority needs. That process will unfold in the course of the year.

**Mr. James Molyneaux** (Lagan Valley): Is the President of the Board of Trade aware that some of the matters in his statement are in line with the discussions that the Prime Minister had last week with the two main Northern Ireland parties? Is he further aware that business and industry in Northern Ireland will welcome his intention to streamline the fair employment legislation? No one doubts its objectives, but the problem, as some of his right hon. Friends know, is that the legislation imposes a crushing financial burden, mainly on foreign investors in Northern Ireland who have to meet hideous legal costs to defend themselves against frivolous complaints.

**Mr. Heseltine:** I shall draw the attention of my right hon. and learned Friend the Secretary of State for Northern Ireland to the right hon. Gentleman's remarks. It is fair to say that the initiative of the Prime Minister and of my right hon. and learned Friend the Secretary of State in augmenting the peace process in Northern Ireland has been one of the best bits of news for industry and commerce in Northern Ireland in a generation.

**Mr. Tony Marlow** (Northampton, North): How Euro-fanatic is my right hon. Friend? He has been talking about deregulation and he will be aware that an increasing amount of regulation comes from European institutions, either through qualified majority voting or in areas where we did not think that we had given competence to European institutions. Will my right hon. Friend strive strenuously to return to this House powers which this House should never have lost?

**Mr. Heseltine:** My reference to Euro-fanaticism was a joke. For the benefit of those who take these matters seriously, I am advised that that means a "plaisanterie", but I could have got that wrong, so that might be another joke.

I understand the purpose behind my hon. Friend's question. The purpose of my right hon. and noble Friend Lady Thatcher in the mid-1980s was to create a single market which had rules and it is that which led her to send my right hon. and noble Friend Lord Cockfield as a Commissioner to Brussels to make sure that there were standard rules that everyone would keep to. That undoubtedly caused an enormous process of indigestion when the agenda of 300 items was introduced in the Parliaments of the European Union. That process is now behind us. There is no longer the enormous weight of change that has taken place, but we have to recognise that, as a result of that change, our trade with our partners in the European Union has significantly increased. The opportunities for British industry are very large and they are there partially because there is now a common standard of behaviour.

**Mr. Dennis Skinner** (Bolsover): Have not this Minister and the Government got a cheek to talk about the successes in Britain's industrial trade and base when we consider that in the past 16 years they have shut down nearly every shipyard and closed most of the coal mines? Hardly any steel works can be found and one third of the manufacturing base has been destroyed. About the only people who have made anything out of that are those members of Lloyd's who, we have learned today, have

*[Mr. Dennis Skinner]*

had £2.75 billion written off their tax payments? That money has been lost to the Chancellor of the Exchequer. He has got a cheek to talk about wonderful Britain under the Tories. They have created more havoc than Hitler did in the second world war.

**Mr. Heseltine:** If I may paraphrase the party political broadcast, that was new Labour speaking.

**Dr. Keith Hampson** (Leeds, North-West): Is my right hon. Friend aware that his statement today in particularly welcome because it acknowledges that the prime responsibility for improving industrial competitiveness rests with company management, but that its efforts can be helped or hindered by Government? In that context, is my right hon. Friend aware that I counted seven reports in the 1970s in which the Labour Government acknowledged what we needed to do on education, training and continuing education, with a national curriculum and more further education, and that if they had done anything at all about it, we would now have more maths teachers in our schools and we would not have had the skill-based weaknesses that we have.

**Mr. Heseltine:** My hon. Friend is right to point out that virtually every one of the major changes that have been brought about to the benefit of the United Kingdom economy in the 1980s was forced through the House by the Government in the teeth of the union-dominated attitudes of the Labour party.

**Mr. Malcolm Chisholm** (Edinburgh, Leith): Does the President agree with last week's Select Committee report that the level of dividends in this country is too high and that far more of the money should go into R and D and other investment? Why did the Government give up their finance into industry initiative last year—was it just because Lord Hanson called the previous Financial Secretary a socialist or was it because the Government have no intention of doing anything about the problem?

**Mr. Heseltine:** The hon. Gentleman is fully aware that the Government have introduced a range of changes— principally the reduction in corporation tax—to ensure that companies enjoy the use of more of their own money. Those changes enable alternative sources of finance to be made available to small companies and, above all, we have presided over a climate in which there has been a very large increase in the number of small and medium-sized companies. That proves beyond peradventure that our policy of supporting that wealth-creating sector has been working. It is all very well for the Labour party to talk about these matters, but its policy proposals are all designed either to put more costs on or remove more money from the wealth-creating sector.

**Mr. John Butterfill** (Bournemouth, West): Does my right hon. Friend accept that Conservative members of the Select Committee on Trade and Industry greatly welcome the energy and enthusiasm with which he has addressed many of its recommendations and especially his commitment to assist many more small businesses to become exporters? Does he, however, agree that the single most damaging thing that we could do and which would reduce our competitiveness would be to adopt a national minimum wage? Does he therefore share my hope that the recent reported statements of the Leader of

the Opposition that he does not now intend to proceed with a national minimum wage will not be diverted by his trade union bosses?

**Mr. Heseltine:** I have been abroad and might have missed something, but what I thought the Leader of the Opposition was saying was that he was not going to tell us what the national minimum wage would be until after he became leader of a Government, were that unfortunate event ever to occur. It means that he will do a deal with the trade unions and no one will know what the national minimum wage will be until after he is elected. If he were to be elected, everyone would pay the price in lost jobs, but we shall help the public to understand the risks involved in that deception.

**Ms Ann Coffey** (Stockport): As the President will be aware, the enterprise allowance scheme has helped thousands of start-up businesses through financial and counselling support. That scheme was abolished by the Secretary of State for Employment in April this year and the business link scheme, which is based on recharging businesses for businesses, is not going to offer the same financial support. Does he not feel that there will be a gap and that start-up businesses will in future be offered less support than previously?

**Mr. Heseltine:** The hon. Lady raises an important point. In fact, the single regeneration budget led to a bidding process in which this form of support did not attract locally the degree of priority that it had previously enjoyed. However, when the hon. Lady and other hon. Members read the texts, they will find that we have introduced a new support system to fill part of the gap that has occurred.

**Mr. Den Dover** (Chorley): Does my right hon. Friend agree that, if inward investment and investment in the United Kingdom is to continue to increase, there needs to be more competitiveness in the construction industry? Can he report whether his officials in the deregulation unit have dropped any opposition that they had to the implementation of Sir Michael Latham's proposals?

**Mr. Heseltine:** We greatly admire the work that Sir Michael has done and welcome the sponsorship role that the Department of the Environment is pursuing in partnership with the construction industry. I shall have a further look at what may or may not be happening in my Department in relation to my hon. Friend's question.

**Mr. D. N. Campbell-Savours** (Workington): The President referred to the Government's so-called successes since 1992. Does he attribute any of those so-called successes to the panic devaluation of September that year?

**Mr. Heseltine:** As the whole House knows, the history of the past 50 years has been one of a constantly depreciating currency. In the short term, that always gives a relative advantage to the country whose currency depreciates. The problem is that, time and time again, we have thrown away that advantage by pursuing domestic inflationary policies that undid what temporary gain there was. The strength of the Government's position is that we are not prepared to see that happen again.

**Mr. Harold Elletson** (Blackpool, North): I congratulate my right hon. Friend on his achievements in boosting United Kingdom competitiveness and creating a sustained export-led growth. Is he aware that one of his Department's initiatives, which has been most successful in that regard, is the export promoters scheme? It has been widely applauded by industry and has significantly boosted UK competitiveness. Will he take this opportunity to thank those companies that have taken part in the scheme and will he ensure that it is extended?

**Mr. Heseltine:** I am most grateful to my hon. Friend for providing me with such an opportunity. About 100 export promoters are now seconded to the Department and they are helping to create a change of culture in relationships between the public and private sectors, as well as adding to the significant export achievements of this country.

**Mr. Ken Eastham** (Manchester, Blackley): When the President was trotting out the catalogue of improvements in training, output and production, was he aware that only two weeks ago the Select Committee on Employment was told that the budget for training by training and enterprise councils has been reduced from £3 billion to just over £1.5 billion since 1990? Was he further aware that only a few weeks ago the Engineering Employers Federation issued a document showing that engineering production in the north-west is only 24 per cent. of capacity? What sort of successes are those?

**Mr. Heseltine:** The hon. Gentleman will recognise that unemployment is falling by 1,000 people a day. Therefore, it is not surprising that public-supported training may not be at the same level as it has been. I shall certainly draw the attention of my right hon. Friend the Secretary of State for Employment to the specific points raised by the hon. Gentleman.

**Mr. Anthony Steen** (South Hams): My right hon. Friend's statement is good news, as every right-thinking person should realise. Will he consider the problem of small businesses that are trading with Europe, which is that although the rules and regulations are rigorously enforced in this country by our officials, they are not rigorously enforced in other European Union countries. The result is that our small firms have on-costs and therefore face more problems in competing. Small firms in other countries do not have those on-costs or the enforcement of rules and regulations.

**Mr. Heseltine:** I can only ask my hon. Friend to let me have the evidence. I have a range of officials whose task is to examine specific cases, but I have to tell the House that evidence is a great deal harder to obtain than anecdotal suggestions indicate. We will examine every piece of evidence put before us.

**Mr. Andrew Miller** (Ellesmere Port and Neston): The President will be aware that a number of his hon. Friends are concerned about their future employment and their potential retirement. Will he explain what is meant by the section on page 71, which makes it clear that the Government no longer believe that the state will help people in their old age?

**Mr. Heseltine:** The hon. Gentleman must realise that that is fiction.

**Mr. Miller:** That is what it says.

**Mr. David Shaw** (Dover): Is my right hon. Friend aware that the global market in information technology

and multi-media services is forecast to grow to $1 trillion by the year 2000? Has he considered, in relation to his White Paper, whether British industry will be able to take a leading role in that market? Will he do everything to ensure that as many British jobs as possible are created in that important market?

**Mr. Heseltine:** One of the success stories of the past few years has been deregulation in that very important area, as a result of which we now have huge investment programmes by both multinationals and a growing number of small and medium-sized British companies. My hon. Friend is absolutely right in what he says.

**Mr. George Mudie** (Leeds, East): The President has rightly drawn our attention to the importance of education and training. As a member of a Cabinet that was told by the Secretary of State for Education that there was insufficient money in this year's budget to fund all teachers, can he specifically tell us how much of the £165 million package will go to education?

**Mr. Heseltine:** The public expenditure figures for education have already been announced. The specific package that I have announced today relates to programmes in the Department of my right hon. Friend the Chancellor of the Duchy of Lancaster and the Department of Trade and Industry.

**Mr. Michael Fabricant** (Mid-Staffordshire): Does my right hon. Friend realise how much his statement will be welcomed by exporters throughout the land, with more than 100 initiatives demonstrating that he and his Department are going full steam ahead with fresh ideas? My right hon. Friend mentioned the £40 million extra that he will provide to exporters. Does he realise how important it is for exporters, especially small firms, to attend trade exhibitions abroad? Can he outline whether any of that £40 million is to be used for that purpose?

**Mr. Heseltine:** I am pleased to tell my hon. Friend that, as part of the package of measures that I announced, we intend to increase the number of missions and trade exhibitions to a record level.

**Mr. Tam Dalyell** (Linlithgow): In his opening statement, the President of the Board of Trade referred to Scottish Nuclear and Nuclear Electric. In the debate last Wednesday, two rather different things were said. First, we were told that the headquarters would be coming to Scotland, with all the supposed advantages to Scottish Nuclear. At the end of the debate, however, in answer to the hon. Member for Gloucester (Mr. French), who was reflecting legitimate constituency interests, we were told that Barnwood need not worry, no one was going to move and that there might be 50 extra positions. Which is it?

**Mr. Heseltine:** This matter was fully debated in the House last week. I was extremely grateful to the Opposition for providing the opportunity for such an early debate and I was immensely impressed by the scale of the Government's majority in both Divisions.

**Mr. John Fraser** (Norwood): It is more than three years since the right hon. Gentleman's Department proposed changes in competition law. When will he do something to resolve the discrepancies between European

[*Mr. John Fraser*]

and United Kingdom competition law and to make it easier for the victims of anti-competitive behaviour to get an effective remedy?

**Mr. Heseltine:** The hon. Gentleman raises an important issue and it is a matter of finding parliamentary time.

**Lady Olga Maitland** (Sutton and Cheam): Is my right hon. Friend aware that small and medium-sized businesses in my constituency have thrived and become very competitive as a result of Government policies? Is he also aware of their nervousness of pressures from the Opposition to make the Government sign up to the social chapter, as such a move would cripple them and destroy all their hard work?

**Mr. Heseltine:** My hon. Friend is right and that will become more apparent as the political debate unfolds, especially when it is added to the dangers of the minimum wage.

**Mr. Harry Barnes** (Derbyshire, North-East): Will the President of the Board of Trade confirm that the White Paper states on page 71 that, in old age, people will see no improvement in their living standards from public funds. What does he think that old-age pensioners will think about that provision?

**Mr. Heseltine:** What the paragraph says, as the hon. Gentleman knows full well, is that, if one destroys the wealth-creating process and over-taxes society, it will affect the ability of a society to fund its welfare provisions. That is the context and sense of the observation. It is the most classic extreme of the behaviour of the Opposition to suggest that there is any implication whatsoever that the normal welfare provisions that the Government provide are at risk.

**Mrs. Margaret Ewing** (Moray): May I ask for clarification from the President of the Board of Trade in connection with paragraph 6.5 of the companion booklet entitled, "Helping Smaller Firms", which refers to the preparation of an export development strategy for Scotland. Does he mean the facility to have a distinctive and autonomous Scottish export unit, with its own budget and facilities to make direct contacts overseas?

**Mr. Heseltine:** Of course, that is the position and it will remain the position.

**Mr. Peter L. Pike** (Burnley): Does the President of the Board of Trade agree that it is regrettable that many of the new educational and training standards are still lower than those of our competitor countries? Is not that because the overriding factor that determined the standards was what was attainable rather than what was desirable?

**Mr. Heseltine:** One of the reasons why we have such education problems is that all the reforms which the Government have introduced have been fought tooth and nail by the Opposition. Every attempt that we have made to extend power to parents, publish a national curriculum and introduce testing of children has been resisted. Once we have introduced those reforms, the Opposition once again admit that they would not change them because they know that we are right and simply lacked the guts to do it themselves.

**Mr. Bernard Jenkin** (Colchester, North): Does my right hon. Friend agree that, if we are considering our productivity record over the past 16 years and lamenting the fact that we may still be behind some of our competitors on productivity, it is worth remembering where we started in 1979: flat on our backs at the end of a period of Labour Government? Will he confirm that, over the past 16 years, we have had the highest growth in productivity of all the G7 nations?

**Mr. Heseltine:** I am most grateful to my hon. Friend. That is precisely why White Papers on competitiveness are so valuable: they show the regular annual improvement. We started from a low base. We were behind, but we are catching up. If we go on in that way, the prospect for the country's economy is exciting. The easy way to bring it to an end is not to re-elect a Conservative Government.

**Mr. Barry Jones** (Alyn and Deeside): Does the right hon. Gentleman propose grants to British Aerospace specifically for research and development of wing technology? How does he see the future of the European Airbus Industrie project? Are the jobs of my constituents who work on that project safe?

**Mr. Heseltine:** The Airbus project is at the heart of the country's industrial aerospace strategy. The hon. Gentleman will know that my right hon. Friend the Prime Minister made clear our interest in the future large aircraft project, which will take forward the wing technology in which British Aerospace is the European leader.

**Mr. Denis MacShane** (Rotherham): Does the President agree that, in the case of British Steel, it would be helpful if the £13 million in share option profits announced today were invested in the company? Page 169 shows that Britain in general would then have a higher level of investment and a dividend level that was not twice that of France, three times that of Germany and nearly six times that of Japan.

**Mr. Heseltine:** One of the last announcements that I remember from British Steel was of a major expansion at Llanwern. As I travel the world, I am also aware of the contracts which British Steel is winning. The reason why it is winning is that it is now a world-class private sector company.

**Mr. Mike O'Brien** (Warwickshire, North): Will the President of the Board of Trade now read the document that he has put before the House? Does he accept that page 71 does say that individuals will not be able to look to the state to fund improvements in their living standards in old age? What does the President mean by that statement, which will cause considerable worry to many pensioners throughout the country.

**Mr. Heseltine:** It will cause no worry unless the Labour party indulge in their scare techniques to frighten people when it is not justified. *[Interruption.]* I shall tell hon. Members what it says. It says that if the economy is not run properly, as a Labour Government would not run the economy properly, improvements in living standards cannot be offered to people. Even the Labour party should understand that.

**Mr. Peter Hain** (Neath): How is our industry supposed to remain competitive when it is required to produce punitively higher rates of return—much higher than our competitor countries? What will the President of the Board of Trade do about that?

**Mr. Heseltine:** I shall go on helping British exporters to secure the highest export level that they have ever had, even with the problems to which the hon. Gentleman referred. How is it that we are doing so well if things are so wrong? There is no answer except that things are not as wrong as the Opposition constantly try to suggest.

# Personal Statement

4.23 pm

**Sir Jerry Wiggin** (Weston-super-Mare): With your permission, Madam Speaker, I should like to make a personal statement.

I wish unreservedly to apologise to my hon. Friend the Member for Falmouth and Camborne (Mr. Coe) and to the House for having tabled amendments to a Bill in Standing Committee in his name but without his knowledge or consent.

I act as parliamentary adviser to the British Holiday and Home Parks Association, a fact which is declared in the Register of Members' Interests and of which my hon. Friend is aware. I thought that he would be supportive of the amendments, so I wrote to him, and we spoke the following day. As soon as he informed me that he was not willing to move them, I apologised to him and withdrew the amendments from the Standing Committee's amendment paper. They never came before the Committee. Nevertheless, I repeat my apologies to the House and to my hon. Friend, for an action which I acknowledge was at odds with the proper expectations of the House.

I am aware too that suspicions have been voiced that my motive in tabling the amendments in the name of a colleague was to avoid the declaration of a financial interest that I possess and he does not. I accept that the amendments would have benefited the association for which I act as parliamentary adviser. My purpose in tabling the amendments in the name of a member of the Standing Committee was, however, to improve their chances of being considered, as I was not in a position to move them myself in Committee.

There was no intention to deceive, but I accept that my actions were open to other interpretations and I wish to apologise to the House without reservation for any harm that they may have done to its reputation.

**Madam Speaker:** I have a short statement to make. The House has now heard the hon. Member for Weston-super-Mare (Sir J. Wiggin) make an apology for his conduct. We do not debate or comment on such statements, but I make the point that, whatever structures and procedures we have in the House, we cannot legislate for integrity, and individual Members should act in such a manner whereby their integrity is not called into question.

I trust that this is the last distasteful occasion on which the Speaker is obliged to inquire into the conduct of an hon. Member.

**Mr. Dennis Skinner** (Bolsover): So has he got away with it then?

# Points of Order

4.26 pm

**Mr. Peter Bottomley** (Eltham): On a point of order, Madam Speaker. It is best to resolve minor difficulties without bothering the House or the Speaker, but would you, Madam Speaker, consider that it would be helpful to the House to remind us of the expected courtesies when an hon. Member advises another Member before going into their constituency on a public visit or to make a controversial speech?

**Madam Speaker:** My postbag is inundated these days with letters from Back Benchers, complaining of other Back Benchers who visit their constituencies without notification. It takes up a great deal of my time to try to resolve those matters. Hon. Members should attempt to resolve them themselves. I think the House knows full well my views on this matter. I cannot enforce them. I merely ask that the consideration and courtesy should be extended to each other which I find lacking these days.

**Mr. Peter Hain** (Neath): On a point of order, Madam Speaker. What action can be taken to investigate the press allegations of the widespread practice of questions and amendments being tabled in other Members' names in order to conceal their commercial origins? Surely too many Members of Parliament are now regarded by members of the public as Arthur Daley lookalikes.

**Madam Speaker:** The hon. Gentleman may seek to refer this matter to the Committee on Members' Interests, which may wish to pursue the point that he is making.

**Mr. Max Madden** (Bradford, West): On a point of order, Madam Speaker. Last Wednesday, you told my hon. Friend the Member for Dewsbury (Mrs. Taylor) that you had received a letter alleging breach of privilege, and you continued:

"I am seriously examining the situation and I shall do so with all speed."—[*Official Report*, 17 May 1995; Vol. 260, c. 335.]

I wonder whether you could say whether you intend referring that complaint to the Committee of Privileges now, or at a later date.

**Madam Speaker:** I did consider the matter with all speed. The House will understand that I had to wait for the hon. Member for Weston-super-Mare to come back and to see me. That was only natural justice.

I have written to the hon. Member for Neath (Mr. Hain), who sent me the letter alleging a breach of privilege. I have indicated the action that I have taken to him. That letter was sent to me; it is not yet in the public domain. It was an exchange of letters between the hon. Member and myself. If he wishes to put it in the public domain, I have no desire to oppose him on that issue.

**Mr. Dennis Skinner** (Bolsover): It seems an odd state of affairs. A few weeks ago, two Tory Members of Parliament were told that they were going to get 10 days' and 20 days' suspension—

**Madam Speaker:** Is this a point of order?

**Mr. Skinner:** Yes.

**Madam Speaker:** Perhaps the hon. Gentleman would come to the point that is for me to deal with.

**Mr. Skinner:** I do not understand how, in those two instances and others—

**Madam Speaker:** Order. The hon. Gentleman has been in the House long enough to know how to put a point of order if he wants to do so. I shall do my best to respond if the hon. Gentleman has a genuine point of order. At the moment, he is putting an opinion.

**Mr. Skinner:** My point of order is this: you, Madam Speaker, have just made a statement to the House. We cannot comment on the fact that the hon. Member for Weston-super-Mare (Sir J. Wiggin) has made a personal statement, but your statement follows on from the fact that it appears that the personal statement will be the end of the matter. The fact that two Tory Members of Parliament were suspended for 10 and 20 days for attempting to take money and not receiving it, seems to contrast with the treatment of the hon. Member for Weston-super-Mare, who is still getting the money.

**Madam Speaker:** Order. There is nothing to contrast. The hon. Gentleman knows the procedures of the House; we do not comment after a personal statement. At this stage in our proceedings and in light of the difficulties that the House is experiencing, I am sure that the House will understand and be supportive if I give four or five lines of my beliefs to the House once in a while.

**Mr. Michael Clapham** (Barnsley, West and Penistone): On a different point of order, Madam Speaker. The *Daily Mirror* this morning published a dossier showing that the Government have wasted £35 billion— ranging from £245 million spent on a Ministry of Defence building to £25,000 which was wasted on the cones hotline. Has a Minister indicated that he or she will come to the House and make a statement on the matter?

**Madam Speaker:** That is not the case. The hon. Gentleman would have seen it on the annunciator screen at 1 o'clock when the other statements were announced.

**Mr. David Winnick** (Walsall, North): One of the themes in last Thursday's debate on the Nolan report was self-regulation. Are we to take it that self-regulation means, in effect, what we have heard today from the hon. Member for Weston-super-Mare (Sir J. Wiggin) and that will be the end of the affair? May I assure you, Madam Speaker, that many people outside the House will not understand the position.

**Madam Speaker:** The House must decide for itself what procedures it will adopt. I am a servant of the House and I will follow those procedures.

**Mr. Nigel Spearing** (Newham, South): On a point of order, Madam Speaker. A few moments ago you told the House that you had sent a letter to a Member of the House who had raised a matter on a point of privilege. You further kindly informed us that if that hon. Member so wished it, the letter's content could be made public. My understanding until now has been that a matter sent to you alleging breach of privilege is not referred to, either by the person sending it or by you, unless, in your opinion, the matter raised is a matter of privilege, in which case you would make your decision known to the House. It appears that your decision on today's matter is in the hands of the hon. Member and only he can now tell us what you may have decided. If I am incorrect, will you correct me? If I am correct, is there a precedent for the way in which the matter has been dealt with, which did not include a statement from you?

**Madam Speaker:** It is not the normal procedure. If the House wishes, I shall certainly give it the information that I have given to the hon. Member as soon as I have a copy of the letter to hand.

**Mr. David Hanson** (Delyn): On a point of order, Madam Speaker. I have written to you stating my intention to raise this point of order on the appointment of part-time non-executive members of new health authorities in Wales. The Secretary of State for Wales advertised in local papers in my constituency on 11 May for members to be appointed to new health authorities in Wales. The Bill establishing those health authorities in Wales has not yet completed its parliamentary progress. I wonder whether you, Madam Speaker, have a view on whether the Secretary of State for Wales should spend public money on adverts and pre-empt the wishes of the House before legislation has been passed by the House. I would hope that you would uphold the right of the House and that the Secretary of State should not spend public money on advertising positions that the House has yet to authorise.

**Madam Speaker:** As a result of the constituency Friday, I have not seen the letter from the hon. Member for Delyn (Mr. Hanson). I shall certainly examine it and give the hon. Gentleman a reply.

**Mr. Gordon Prentice** (Pendle): On a point of order, Madam Speaker. Is it open to individual members of the House to refer the actions of other hon. Members to the Committee of Privileges?

**Madam Speaker:** It is a matter for the House, and a resolution of the House must be obtained.

[*Following is the text of Madam Speaker's letter to Mr. Hain:*

Dear Peter:

You wrote twice to me on 17 May asking that precedence be given to a Motion to refer to the Privileges Committee the action of Sir Jerry Wiggin in tabling amendments to the Gas Bill in Standing Committee in the name of Sebastian Coe but without his knowledge or agreement.

You will have heard Jerry Wiggin's personal statement this afternoon. It is my view that the statement disposes of this unpleasant matter, and no interests of the House would be served by a reference to the Privileges Committee. There are two reasons for this. In the first place, there is no dispute about the facts. Secondly, it is the practice of the House to accept without further demur the *bona fides* and candour of a Member who makes a personal statement. That being so, it is hard to see what task the Privileges Committee would be asked to do.

You may of course take on your own account any parliamentary action within our rules of order which you think appropriate, including the tabling of an Early Day Motion.]

# Orders of the Day

## Child Support Bill

*As amended (in the Standing Committee), considered.*
*Ordered,*

That the Child Support Bill, as amended, be considered in the following order, namely, new Clauses, amendments to Clause 1, amendments to Schedule 1, amendments to Clauses 2 to 6, amendments to Schedule 2, remaining amendments to Clauses, new Schedules and remaining amendments to Schedules.—[*Mr. Burt*]

### New clause 3

CHILD MAINTENANCE DISREGARD (NO. 2)

'(1) In section 136(5) of the Social Security Contributions and Benefits Act 1992, after paragraph (b), there shall be inserted the following paragraph—

"(bb) in calculating the income of a person claiming income support, a prescribed amount of any payment or payments of maintenance made or due to be made by—

(i) the claimant's former partner, or the claimant's partner's former partner; or

(ii) the parent of a child who is a member of the claimant's family, except where that parent is the claimant or the claimant's partner,

shall be disregarded;".

(2) At the end of that section, there shall be added the following subsection—

"(6) In this section 'partner' shall have the meaning prescribed.".'.—[*Mr. Bradley.*]

*Brought up, and read the First time.*

4.35 pm

**Mr. Keith Bradley** (Manchester, Withington): I beg to move, That the clause be read a Second time.

Throughout the passage of the Bill, whether on the Floor of the House or in Committee, the Labour party has attempted to be constructive. In that spirit, I have moved new clause 3, which would introduce a child maintenance disregard into the legislation.

As I am sure you are aware, Madam Speaker, this is the fourth time that we have tried to insert a child maintenance disregard into the Bill. We first attempted to do so by way of a reasoned amendment to the Second Reading debate, and we tried to introduce it in two different ways in Committee. We are now attempting on Report to introduce the disregard, which we believe is a crucial omission from the legislation.

As we have made three previous attempts to introduce a disregard, I do not intend to range over all the issues involved this afternoon. We have always intended to be constructive in the debates, and I hope that our proposals will at last find favour with the Government. However, I proceed with some trepidation, as I do not know whether the Secretary of State, who is lined up against me in the debate, will be persuaded by the logic of the arguments in support of the disregard.

Under the current arrangements, any maintenance that is paid to the parent with care who is in receipt of income support is deducted pound for pound from that income support. Therefore, the parent with care—normally the mother—and subsequently the children do not receive a single penny from any maintenance payment. Despite all the changes that have been made to the Child Support Act 1991 at various stages through the regulations and through

[Mr. Keith Bradley]

this legislation, the situation will not alter, and the arrangements whereby income support is reduced pound for pound will remain in place.

However, the situation could be rectified if income support claimants were able to keep a small amount of every maintenance payment, which would be known as the maintenance disregard. We are attempting to establish the principle of such a disregard in new clause 3. If the Government were to accept that principle this afternoon, we would welcome their views about the level at which to set the disregard, which would then be debated subsequently as part of the regulations and the provisions in the Bill.

Such a child maintenance disregard would essentially have two effects. First, the poorest children would gain from maintenance payments. Secondly, the so-called absent parents—I accept that that definition is not satisfactory, but it is the terminology used in the Bill, so I shall use it for the purposes of the debate—would have an incentive to pay, and parents with care would have an incentive to apply for maintenance through the Child Support Agency.

Let me put the proposal in some overall context. According to official statistics, seven out of 10, or 70 per cent., of one-parent families claim income support. In February 1994, 42 per cent. of all claimants having benefit deducted to replace social fund loans were lone parents, and in 1993, 46 per cent. of parents with care on benefit were repaying fuel debts. Those and other official statistics show that lone parents on income support face particular financial hardship. The child maintenance disregard proposed by the Labour party is an attempt to address the problem.

The Government consistently oppose the proposal, because they do not wish to incorporate any work disincentives into the benefit system; hence their proposal in the Bill to introduce a child maintenance bonus instead. However, that proposal is inadequate.

Like the back-to-work bonus in the new jobseeker's allowance, it does not benefit families at the point of real need, but instead promises help, probably in future but perhaps never, as it may take as long as four years of consistent eligibility to reach full entitlement to the new bonus. We believe strongly that split families, with one parent caring for children, need help immediately, not at some future date.

The Government should recognise that many factors are involved in the decision to seek work, particularly when the needs of young children or other responsibilities, such as caring for sick or disabled relatives or friends, have to be taken into account. Those acting in a caring capacity may not be able to seek work. Even if such a person were available for work, there is clearly no guarantee that work would be available.

Throughout our deliberations on the matter, the Government have been unable to provide clear evidence that introducing a maintenance disregard on income support creates a disincentive to work. I should be grateful if they could provide that evidence this afternoon.

However, to allay the Government's fears on that point, it may be possible to run the small weekly disregard alongside the child maintenance bonus in order to help people back to work, thus enabling lone parents on income support perhaps to take part-time work, and therefore immediately reducing the social security bill and the cost of the disregard, and allowing lone parents to obtain skills and ultimately move into full-time work in the longer term, when their children become less dependent.

In addition, a small disregard provides protection against the complete loss of income support that may be associated with maintenance payments, and other losses, such as free school meals and other benefits, that lead to the classic poverty trap, where someone might end up far worse off through the loss of their total entitlement to income support and insufficient compensation.

It must be stressed that the introduction of such a child maintenance disregard is not the only answer in addressing the enormous problems associated with child poverty, but we believe that it is a clear and proper step in the right direction. The Government, on the other hand, believe that only if lone parents return to work will the problems of poverty really be overcome.

It is interesting to note that, in one of our debates in Committee on that point, there was an exchange of views between my hon. Friend the Member for Croydon, North-West (Mr. Wicks) and the Minister. When he was asked how many people were lifted off benefit by the proposals so far, the Minister recognised that, despite the massive £9 billion currently paid in support of lone parents, only 8,000 out of 1 million people—or less than 1 per cent.—had been lifted off benefit. That shows that more must be done to effect the changes that the Government intend.

4.45 pm

The Opposition are clear that it is not enough to look only at in-work benefits. We have to consider the reality for lone parents who are out of work, their availability for benefit, and the amount of money they should be given to ensure proper care for their children. Many organisations, such as the Child Poverty Action Group, the citizens advice bureaux and many others representing lone parents and single people living in poverty, identified that the Government's approach is far too simplistic, and that we cannot look at work as the only way out of poverty.

There are many reasons why it may not be possible to obtain paid employment. Lone parents with young children may feel it more appropriate to remain at home to care for their children, particularly in their early years.

By refusing to accept the need for a small maintenance disregard, the Government are perpetuating the anomaly whereby children of lone parents who cannot take employment do not gain from the payment of child maintenance. According to the Child Support Agency's own statistics, they represent not only the great majority of CSA clients, but the poorest of those clients.

In Committee, the Government claimed that the welfare of the child was at the heart of the legislation. If that is the case, they would surely wish to accept new clause 3. It would give more money to the children of parents with care; it would act as an incentive to co-operate with the agency; it would provide an incentive for so-called absent parents to pay maintenance; and it would help restore public confidence in the agency by showing people on income support that the Treasury was not the only gainer and that, crucially, the children would also gain, as was clearly envisaged by the Government's White Paper entitled "Children Come First".

I hope that, even at this late stage in our deliberations, the Government will accept that there is clear merit in introducing the child maintenance disregard. If they accept that, they will clearly wish to add new clause 3 to the Bill.

**Ms Mildred Gordon** (Bow and Poplar): I support what my hon. Friend the Member for Manchester, Withington (Mr. Bradley) has said. Lone parents with care represent the majority of those on income support, and nothing in the Bill will give immediate help to that group of parents.

All the organisations that support lone parents—those that have attacked the Bill as well as those that feel that the Child Support Agency can do something—are united in asking for a disregard. As has been said, lone parents on income support are often deeply in debt, with rent arrears, debts for utilities and debts for the repayment of social fund loans. They need help now to stop them going under.

Organisations that support lone parents report that they are unable to give their children adequate diets, and that mothers in particular often go hungry, damaging their health and that of their children. Those parents may never be able to return to work successfully, even when their children are of school age, because they will have got into such difficulties. If they are not helped now, the Bill will postpone long-term solutions, not provide them.

The maintenance bonus, which will take some years to accrue fully, could be paid in addition to a disregard. I see no contradiction. The immediate need to alleviate child poverty remains. The Government argue that the way to get lone parents off income support is to make them all go out to work, usually in low-paid jobs—but no paid work is available in many areas.

Employers are often prejudiced against mothers with small children, thinking that their home responsibilities will prevent them from giving full attention to their job. Women often have multiple responsibilities, such as caring for aged or disabled parents, relatives or neighbours. Mothers often do not want to leave children under five years of age. The Government always claim to favour choice, so they should give women the choice whether to leave their children under five to do low-paid jobs or to look after their children themselves.

I have always advocated a nursery place for every child that can benefit from one, but not every child will do so. When I collected my own son from a nursery all day for the first time, I asked him whether he liked it. He said, "It was very nice, but I don't want to go every day." I respected the fact that he was not ready, at the age of three, to leave his mother, be dragged out come rain or shine, and be left with strangers all day.

When my son reached school age, I left secondary teaching to teach in a primary school. It always worried me, when the new intake arrived, to hear some children screaming for weeks on end, making themselves sick. When teachers said that such children had settled down, I often felt that they had given up in despair, and that really they were not ready to be separated from their mothers if they were to grow up as secure, stable individuals. It is wrong to drive all mothers out to work and not give them the chance to enjoy decent living standards while looking after their young children at home.

One third of our children live in households having less than half the average income. If the Child Support Act 1991 and the Bill are to have any effect, they must address, and do something positive to alleviate, child poverty. If the Government ensured that, the public would not think that they were totally uncaring, and huge crowds of angry people would not come to see us, write to us and attend meetings throughout the country because they feel that they are being conned and that the Government do not care about child welfare.

Improving the legislation would have a positive effect on the non-resident fathers, who we want to provide support for their children. Although there may be a few rascals, most fathers care about their children. If they knew that the mothers would enjoy some benefit and be able to raise their income above the level of income support, they would be more eager to pay. For all those reasons, I ask the Government to think again, and to include in the Bill a disregard for parents with care on income support.

**Mr. Stephen Timms** (Newham, North-East): All of us are aware of the enormous problems caused by child support legislation, and many believe that the changes that we are now considering offer the last chance to get the system right and in a form that will be defensible, widely supported and able to function properly. I had hoped and expected that there would be serious scrutiny of the proposals in Committee and an attempt to reach an all-party consensus, so that all hon. Members could have confidence in a supportable way forward.

I am a relatively new Member of the House, so perhaps I was hoping for more than was possible, but no such all-party consensus emerged. Not one speech in Committee was made by a Conservative Back Bencher. Conservative Members made four brief interventions, but that was the sum total of their contribution. I note that those hon. Members are not present in the Chamber.

I am extremely puzzled that so little interest was shown by Conservative Members, that they remain unconcerned about getting the changes right, and that they have failed to display a give-and-take approach that might have led to changes in which we could all have confidence. Not one substantive Opposition amendment has been accepted by the Government. We have before us only the changes that the Government first thought of, which were whipped through the Committee without the serious scrutiny that I had anticipated.

One major reason for the anger surrounding the legislation is that, in many cases, not a penny of the maintenance paid goes to the children who are intended to be the beneficiaries of the child support regime. As 80 per cent. of the agency's caseload is parents with care who are on income support, they account for a high proportion of the total.

The child maintenance bonus offers some prospect of eventually benefiting the children involved, but that payment will not be made immediately. The bonus will anyway be capped and have a fixed maximum value, and many parents with care will never be in a position to receive it.

Despite the changes made by the Bill, we will end up with a child support regime that remains unsupportable and that will continue to provoke immense fury among the people affected by it. The fact that none of the payments will benefit most of the children involved is a major part of the regime's unacceptability. I hope that the Government will accept the new clause, which would be a big step towards creating a defensible system, which all of us want to achieve.

**5 pm**

**Ms Liz Lynne** (Rochdale): I shall not speak on all the groups of amendments, not out of any particular consideration to right hon. and hon. Members—even though, of course, I have that consideration—or out of any satisfaction with the Bill, which is a poor measure and falls far short of what we would wish to be enacted, but because I do not believe that the Government will move on any of the amendments. It is a waste of time for all of us to sit here and try to make the Government see some sense. I should like the wholesale scrapping of the Child Support Act 1991, but, unfortunately, we are not debating that today.

Parents with care will have their benefit clawed back by the Government, pound for pound. That hardly seems fair or just. The case has been well aired and well argued both on Second Reading and in Committee, so I shall not detain the House for long. I should like to point out, however, that some inconsistency exists between what the Minister has been saying and his position. I heard him say that he deplored children of lone parents living in poverty. The new clause would help to get those children out of that poverty, and they form the bulk of the people we dealt with in the Child Support Act.

The new clause would not do a great deal—that would depend on how we set the maintenance disregard—but it would help. To a certain extent, lone parents and their children would be helped out of poverty

Over and again, the Minister says that he wants to get those parents back to work, which seems to be his argument against granting a maintenance disregard. We shall find out whether that is the case when we debate child care costs later this evening. If he accepts the proposal, perhaps I will believe him, but I doubt that he will. He certainly did not accept it in Committee.

We must realise that some lone parents cannot find work. The Minister knows that other ways exist of getting people out of poverty apart from making them go back into work. A maintenance disregard is one of those ways. If a lone parent wants work and finds it, that is great. No one is against that; everyone would support it. In a way, the maintenance bonus will help them to achieve that, but it does not go far enough.

We must ensure that lone parents and their children are not suffering too much. Therefore, we also need the maintenance disregard. If parents without care felt that their children were benefiting, that would encourage them to co-operate with the Child Support Agency law. I am totally opposed to the Act, but I know that the Government will not move on it, so we must find some way of making it just a little better.

I have not heard the Minister or anyone else advance any convincing arguments against a maintenance disregard. I do not know whether he will suddenly come up with some convincing arguments today, but I doubt it. The proposal would also encourage parents with care to co-operate as they would feel that their children were going to benefit and they know that when income support goes, passported benefit and free school meals go. The maintenance disregard would help to offset that clawback of money.

Voluntary organisations and the Law Society want the new clause to go through. I hope that the Secretary of State and the Minister will accept it. They must ask themselves why all these people want the maintenance disregard, and why everyone recognises the reasons for it except the Government Front-Bench team. The Child Poverty Action Group, for instance, points out that the maintenance bonus is one of the few things proposed to help lone parents with children.

Even though the White Paper says that children come first—and we have said that over and again in Committee—they do not come first in the Bill or the Child Support Act. The Treasury comes first. The Government do not really want to put children first. If they did, they would accept the new clause. The Minister and the Secretary of State can prove that they want children to come first merely by accepting the new clause now.

**Dr. Norman A. Godman** (Greenock and Port Glasgow): As always, I promise to be brief, but I should like to ask the Minister a couple of questions. I have long supported child support legislation, but I was always critical of existing legislation, and, indeed, of this Bill. I support new clause 3 and the comments of the hon. Member for Rochdale (Ms Lynne).

I have a number of concerns about the legislation and the way in which it is implemented. What deeply concerns me is the apparent dilatoriness of officials in Falkirk Child Support Agency office, and the often off-hand way in which they treat my constituents.

On Friday evening, a young woman came to see me at my surgery. She is precisely caught up in the circumstances that the new clause seeks to deal with. She has had little or no help from the Falkirk office in more than a year. I intervened on her behalf more than a year ago.

That decent, honourable, poor woman—and she is a poor woman—is living in abject poverty. On Friday evening, she came back to my surgery to complain about what I have just called the apparent dilatoriness of the officials in Falkirk. I would happily bring the details of that case to the Minister's attention, because I know that he will pursue the matter with Miss Chant and her officials.

That young woman is seeking to bring up a child in a rough, tough part of Greenock. She is having an enormously difficult time of it, and she would be helped by better and more courteous assistance from the Falkirk office. She is in difficult circumstances, and, like many others, she would benefit from such support.

I have yet to meet a constituent who, under the extant legislation, is defined as an absent parent and seeks to avoid his obligations to his child or children. Some of them may avoid not only their obligations but my surgeries, knowing that I speak in a fairly straightforward manner on these issues. The overwhelming majority of those people—whose wives may be on income support, and hence would be helped by the acceptance of the new clause—readily acknowledge that they have a duty to protect their children.

Given that the Minister will reject the new clause, may I ask what guidelines are given to local officers in relation to applications made by such mothers for community care grants from the social fund? If they are not to be assisted through a maintenance disregard, why not assist them by way of another disregard: by telling them that they will not be given a crisis loan when they seek assistance to purchase essential resources for the house, but that they will always be considered sympathetically for a community care grant?

Why cannot women caught up in such circumstances be offered community care grants instead of crisis loans? The Minister will resist new clause 3, but if such emphasis were given in relation to parents with care seeking financial assistance from the local Benefits Agency, that would be of some help.

I know of a young person who made such an application to the Benefits Agency in Greenock. She wanted a community care grant, not a loan that she would have to pay back out of her social security income. The young woman concerned had no complaints against the staff of the agency at Greenock. Indeed, the agency is to receive an award in a fortnight's time from Renfrewshire Enterprise because of its business plan and the work that it carries out in the area. Nevertheless, the young woman did not receive a community care grant. My advice to local officials is that, in such circumstances, they should help claimants by offering a community care grant rather than a loan.

If it is custom and practice that a community care grant is usually made available rather than a crisis loan, has that principle been established in local offices? I hope that the Minister will respond positively to my question. For most women—in this instance, we are talking mainly about women—it would be of help to know that they can obtain a community care grant rather than being offered a loan. If it is not custom and practice that such preferential treatment is offered, will the Minister give serious consideration to issuing appropriate guidelines by amending the criteria on which grants and loans are assessed?

I do not want to drift off course, Mr. Deputy Speaker, if you will forgive that maritime metaphor, in anticipation of the Minister's rejection of the new clause. I wish only to make a plea of mitigation. If the new clause is rejected, my question should be given serious attention.

In Australia, disregard is an established practice. I was recently speaking to people who are concerned with child support legislation in South Australia. They assured me that it is working well. The Minister will say, "The hon. Gentleman is bound to say that." I accept that there have been difficulties in implementing that legislation in Australia, but I was told that, in the state of South Australia, it seems to be working well. I am told that, to some extent, it meets the needs of women who are caring for children while living in inadequate housing and being unable to provide their children with the resources that other children come to expect as the normal scheme of things.

In the new clause, we are not asking for a great deal. Surely a compassionate Government should accept it in its entirety. We are not talking about an enormous number of women or a huge amount of money. If the new clause were accepted, some compensation would be made available to those whose lives are at best sparse and at worst characterised by sheer misery.

**Mr. Malcolm Wicks** (Croydon, North-West): I support the new clause. I shall start by reflecting on why child support legislation has become controversial, which has necessitated, among other things, the Bill that is before us. That controversy relates directly to the issue which the new clause seeks to take up. It is legislation designed to bring about a cultural change—some might say a cultural revolution—after many years during which fathers were often able to escape financial responsibilities for their children.

Governments worldwide, and certainly in the United Kingdom—rightly, in my view—are seeking to promote the principle of parental responsibility. After many years during which fathers escaped their responsibilities—when court orders were not enforced—our child support legislation perhaps constitutes a major cultural revolution.

5.15 pm

The Government are seeking to respond to two major trends that are affecting the family, both of which are extremely controversial. The first is large-scale separation and divorce, which means that more and more people—adults and children—are living in one-parent families.

Secondly, there is the increasing phenomenon of single-never-married women with children, something to which the House needs to return on another occasion. The phenomenon is to be found in other European nations, but I think that Britain is ahead—I do not use that word in an approving way—and at the top of the league table. Single-never-married women represent the fastest-rising category of single parents in the United Kingdom. They are the group most likely to be dependent on income support.

The divorce phenomenon and the phenomenon of never-married-single women are controversial and would tax any Government. These phenomena have often become controversial also because of maladministration. There is controversy also because a public wider than those immediately concerned are cynical in believing that the Bill is not a true child support measure. When we are presented with evidence that the vast majority of one-parent families—those on income support—are not receiving extra benefit from child support, we can understand the public's cynicism. That is why the new clause should be taken seriously by the House.

Although I have used the term, I am not an Exchequer supporter. I do not disregard the interests of the taxpayer generally. I am struck by the fact, as are my colleagues, I am sure, that many of the families who come to see us at our surgeries are intact families where the marriage has survived. They are two-parent families that are often struggling against the odds, often in difficult economic times and in a difficult job market, to maintain their own children.

One of the difficulties for the Government is that they are presiding over record levels of taxation and at the same time record levels of social security expenditure. They are doing so—this is the paradox that we need to unravel and understand—at a time when there is a record level of social insecurity, in my judgment.

We must not make the mistake of saying—this certainly applies to my right hon. and hon. Friends—that there is an association between social security spending—state benefit spending—and true social security in the community. We need to think through the implications of that. If they can be avoided, I do not want to impose greater burdens on taxpayers who are looking after their own children. At the same time, however, a balance must be struck. In my judgment, a disregard—in other words, enabling one-parent families on income support to receive some of the benefit of child maintenance—is a part of the balance that should be introduced into the system.

If child poverty, not the Treasury, had been at the centre of concern when framing child support legislation, we would have had better social policy. These are always controversial matters, as evidence from various societies shows. At the same time, I think that a wider concern would have produced better social policy.

We need to get to grips with the fact that the rise of one-parent families is perhaps now the major cause—it is certainly a major cause—of child poverty in this country. The Secretary of State will have seen the recent report on low income statistics from the Social Security Committee,

[*Mr. Malcolm Wicks*]

which contains a table that shows the total number of children—our children, really—on income support in Great Britain. It is extraordinary in terms of the total number, but what strikes me as important about those data is that, increasingly, it is the one-parent family that is associated with poverty.

Opposition Members—perfectly rightly—say a great deal about unemployment, but in 1992, whereas 865,000 children of parents who were unemployed were on income support, the number of children on income support in lone-parent families was 1,750,000, a much larger number. That is the group that is growing most rapidly. When unemployment goes up and down—we can argue about how far it will go—at least it brings down the number of children in poverty for employment reasons.

As far as I can judge, the rise in the number of lone-parent families is somewhat impervious to changes in the economic cycle. It is certainly on the increase at the present time, even when official unemployment statistics point in the other direction. That major contributor to child poverty is of relevance to the new clause, because in a modest way it is saying, "If we can address the poverty of the children of families on income support, at least that will improve the welfare of those children." The welfare of those children must be at the heart of this measure.

I think that the Government will reply—we shall judge soon—that they do not consider a maintenance disregard as the way to tackle poverty, that evidence shows that we need to enable one-parent families to get into the labour market—to get jobs, in simple terms. I do not think that I and my hon. Friends would largely disagree with that broad analysis. Certainly, when one thinks about public expenditure priorities in the future, it is difficult to envisage any Government finding the resources to increase income support to such a level that one would seriously dent the poverty that those children face.

I would argue that the Government are now pushing that analysis too far. If one could devise a strategy to include employment, training, child care and the rest, that would be a good thing, and I would encourage it. In fact, I would encourage the Government to go rather further in that direction. By saying no to the disregard but yes to the child support bonus, which borrows heavily from the Jobseekers Bill—once one gets a job, one gets some benefit from the extra maintenance—the Government are in a curious position for the traditional "party of the family". There are lots of inverted commas in that phrase. They are now saying—not about all mothers—that a lone mother's place is in the job market.

I find that rather interesting, as I have been a student of Tory family politics for a number of years. Whereas, a decade and a half ago, the Tory party of the family was very much persuaded that a woman's place was in the home, and did not really like all the trendy new feminist stuff about careers and so on, there came a time when it came to recognise that perhaps women did have rights in the labour market, and a good thing too.

I had assumed, until I attended the recent Committee that considered the Bill, that the party of the family at least supported the idea of choice. I think that choice is important, and I commend the principle of choice to the Secretary of State. I should have thought that we should be saying to lone mothers on income support, particularly when there are young children, "Although we might give you certain incentives and programmes to get into the labour market, nevertheless, as a mother of a child of four or five, you have a choice: whether to stay at home to look after your own child or to get a job."

Is the Secretary of State an advocate of choice in that area? I hope he is. I am bound to say that the force of this social policy is to push lone mothers into the labour market. If one stays on income support, one does not get any net benefit from child support. That is a serious point.

My hon. Friend the Member for Manchester, Withington (Mr. Bradley) made the point that very few lone mothers are coming off income support because of child benefit. A figure of 8,000 in one year has been cited, against 1 million families involved. I should like to ask the Secretary of State about choice, or whether indeed there is now no choice for lone mothers on income support except to stay in poverty. Is he really now saying that the mothers of England who are on income support have to get jobs, because the Government will not offer any more?

I support my hon. Friends' arguments for a disregard, because those of us who support child support and who did so before we knew that the Government were to introduce it are wrestling with the difficult task of trying to save decent principle from bad practice. That is what it is about.

We have rehearsed some of the likely history of this before. We know that a former Prime Minister, Margaret Thatcher, whom I read about in the public prints only today, announced the policy of child support and parental responsibility. My guess is that the official records one day will reveal that the Department of Social Security probably wanted a disregard, because there is some wisdom in that Department, or there certainly used to be, but, of course, the Treasury saw an opportunity.

The Treasury looked anew at public expenditure targets and projections, it won the battle with the Department of Social Security about the disregard, and it said, "You are not having it. We can't afford it." The original Child Support Bill was therefore a Bill deformed at birth.

That is the difficulty that we have had ever since. If only we could have had a disregard, we could have faced up to the critics of the Bill, including some, not all, of the nastier elements in British life who send obscene and dangerous communications to the staff of the Child Support Agency, and said, "No, this is child support not just in name. We can now point to evidence that children in the most impoverished circumstances are getting extra benefit."

One could point to data such as those in Australia, which show that children are getting more money. At least this is making an impression on child poverty, as caused by those circumstances. But I am afraid that the Treasury, which I have always regarded as a social policy literacy-free zone, got its claws into it and attempted to destroy it at birth. Therefore, some of us have been trying to help the Secretary of State and his colleagues to rescue it ever since by proposing changes and tabling amendments.

I repeat that the taxpayer has an interest—I know that from my advice surgeries, and how poor some of the families paying tax are—but the introduction of a disregard would have brought some social balance into the scheme. Although one or two of us have had this argument before, cross-party, and to some extent we have exhausted the arguments, I hope that Parliament might think again today. I hope that the Secretary of State will have listened carefully to the arguments and will recognise that, if we are to create social policy out of this child support measure, a disregard is a modest but essential step in that direction.

5.30 pm

**Mr. George Stevenson** (Stoke-on-Trent, South): On Friday, I attended a meeting in Stoke-on-Trent involving people who had been seriously affected by the ignominious activities of the Child Support Agency. One reason for their continuing anger is their belief—justified, in my view—that any resources acquired by the agency are, in the main, not being passed on to the children whom, according to the Government, the whole mechanism is designed to support. The new clause is intended to deal with a fundamental contradiction that the Government, for some reason, have failed to recognise since the agency was set up a few years ago.

No doubt the Secretary of State will try to justify the Government's rejection of the new clause. I cannot see for the life of me—I know that the same applies to my hon. Friends—why the Government apparently intend, rather than supporting a maintenance disregard, merely to disregard the strength of our argument. If the fundamental principle is to ensure that children receive support, where is the sense in continuing to support a mechanism that will not achieve that? The new clause begins to address this serious anomaly.

The new clause was discussed in detail during that meeting on Friday. The result was a clear message to the Government: they are making a big mistake if they believe that changes that have been wrung out of them in a Bill forced on a reluctant Secretary of State—no doubt in the face of strong Treasury resistance—and will be drip-fed into the system created by the original legislation and the agency's activities, along with their rejection of a very reasonable new clause, will melt away the anger about the fundamental injustices that remain. Until such injustices are dealt with—new clause 3 tries to deal with one of them, albeit in a small way—the campaign, the justifiable protests and the anger that is felt throughout the country will not only remain but intensify.

**Mr. Derek Enright** (Hemsworth): I have surgeries or appointments every week, and not a week has gone by without someone complaining to me about the unjust workings of the Child Support Act. They do not complain about the Act itself; most fathers admit that they have a duty to pay what their children require to receive a decent upbringing. They are complaining about the fact that the payment formula has been worked out in such a way that the poorest sections of the population are badly hit.

In particular, second families in which the husband is dutifully paying what he is required to pay have suddenly been made to double their payments. That is a major problem in low-wage areas such as the one that I represent: it is entirely wrong for those bringing up children on poverty wages suddenly to have sub-poverty wages thrust on them, and the exemptions demanded by the new clause would make a considerable difference.

It is not as if the Child Support Agency were currently at its most efficient. We were assured that the calculations affecting both the single partner requiring maintenance— male or female—and those paying the maintenance would be made more efficiently, but that has not happened. The cases that infuriate me most involve ladies whose husbands have left them and their children to fend for themselves: the agency personnel say that they cannot possibly deal with those cases within two years, and are making no effort to find husbands who are not low earners but are, in fact, doing extraordinarily well. Where is the stretching of manpower that the Government claimed would be achieved?

It is a question of natural justice—of the recognition that families fall apart, and that we must do our best to foster the new relationships that result without exacerbating difficulties between former partners. Previously, when wives—predominantly—were left on their own, they and their children received allowances in addition to other allowances; now they do not. The allowances are cut to a minimum, so that parents cannot bring up their children decently. Moreover, such parents are unable to secure even the part-time jobs that exist in my constituency, because they are so poorly paid that the money would make no difference to their allowances.

No doubt the Government will reject the new clause, but I hope that they will show themselves to be flexible and imaginative. The Bill has its roots in cross-party co-operation: the ideals that inspired it are essentially cross-party, and those ideals remain.

I hope that, even at this late stage, the Government will feel able to examine the position and do what they can. I hope that they will understand the difficulties experienced by a woman with one, two or three children who is shut up on her own because it is not worth her while to go out and get a job, and the effect that those difficulties will have on her children. That applies particularly in an area such as mine, where there are few diversions that provide opportunities to meet other people. Jobs often provide the only chance for people to come together. The Bill is a disincentive for families to take jobs.

Laying down a rate and taking a fixed amount from a man's wage makes the abandoned family, if we may call it that, no better off, but makes the new family infinitely worse off. That is precisely what is happening in terms of the marginal levels. We have made a meagre suggestion to try to alleviate some of the difficulties. It is not a massive step, and we may be criticised for not tabling a more substantial amendment. However, that meagre measure should be considered. It would cost the Treasury scarcely anything, if anything at all when one considers the way that crime could be prevented by a sensible use of this measure. The Government should accept it.

**The Secretary of State for Social Security (Mr. Peter Lilley):** The new clause deals with an area that has been the main cause of disagreement. However, disagreement has not been characteristic. On the contrary, I endorse the remark by the Opposition Front-Bench spokesman, the hon. Member for Glasgow, Garscadden (Mr. Dewar) that the Opposition have been supportive, co-operative and constructive. I welcome that, and may have the opportunity to say more about it later. That attitude is in marked contrast to that of the Liberal party, which has been fundamentally irresponsible and negative in this matter.

Before coming to my overall reply, I should like to mention one or two points raised by hon. Members. The hon. Member for Greenock and Port Glasgow (Dr. Godman) spoke about problems that he has encountered at Falkirk. I shall certainly respond to his specific points if he pursues them with me or with my hon. Friend the Under-Secretary.

[*Mr. Peter Lilley*]

The hon. Gentleman asked whether community care grants could be an alternative to a maintenance disregard. It would not be possible or sensible to give privileged access to community care grants to people who were getting maintenance, and the new clause would give them the right to higher benefit. The Child Support Agency does not give advice on access to community grants. That would be delivered by the Benefits Agency, which is often housed in the same building, and would be in accordance with existing criteria.

As always, the hon. Member for Croydon, North-West (Mr. Wicks) made an interesting contribution. He has always been robust in his support of the Bill's underlying principles—even when he disagrees with us on the detail. He suggested that the choice of the mother to return to work was at stake. By its nature and through its rules, income support loads the choice against taking up work, because it means that, for every £1 earned above the first few pounds, one is paid £1 less benefit. To try to restore the balance, we have introduced maintenance credit. The new clause would intensify the disincentive, and bias the choice against work.

The hon. Member for Stoke-on-Trent, South (Mr. Stevenson) and some other hon. Members said that the resources raised by the Child Support Agency go mainly to the Treasury. But the Treasury has no money. All the maintenance is paid to the mother and belongs to her. To the extent that benefit is offset by that, money is returned to the taxpayer who is the source of all public finance. We should never forget that.

5.45 pm

Although I have carefully considered the arguments for a maintenance disregard as set out in the new clause and as argued in Committee, I reject the proposal for three basic reasons. First, the best way to help lone parents raise the standard of living of themselves and their children is to help them to return to work. Most of them wish to do that. The disregard would effectively pay people more to refrain from working. It raises the hurdle that they have to vault if they are to get back into work and the amount they have to earn to make that worth while. It is precisely the wrong approach.

We have put the £15 disregard into the benefits that help people who are seeking work or are in work. They are: family credit, disability working allowance, housing benefit and council tax benefit. On top of that, we have increased the incentive to get off income support and back into work by introducing the maintenance credit, which is worth up to £1,000 and is payable when people get back into work.

The hon. Member for Hemsworth (Mr. Enright) asked us to be flexible and imaginative if we could not accept the new clause. Ours is a flexible and imaginative response, and it was certainly not expected until we presented the Bill. The proposal to introduce a maintenance disregard is particularly odd, because it would give extra only to those who get maintenance, and nothing to those who get none. It would be hard to justify to those who were in that unfortunate position.

Secondly, I do not support the proposal because we are sceptical about the claim, by the Opposition in general and by the hon. Member for Bow and Poplar (Ms Gordon) in particular, that a disregard would persuade absent parents who were otherwise resisting paying maintenance to pay up with more enthusiasm. There is no evidence that, because parents with care receive a £15 disregard in the in-work benefits, absent parents would be less reluctant or more willing to pay maintenance.

If there is any such effect, the maintenance credit, which enables a parent with care and the child to benefit by up to £1,000 in maintenance from the absent parent, should act as a spur. It should encourage the parent with care to go back to work, and if she does that she may share part of the financial responsibility of maintenance and reduce the assessment of the absent parent. Because of the maintenance credit, the absent parent should be more willing to pay than he was in the past.

By contrast, the disregard would discourage parents from returning to work. I regret to say that that has been a major source of friction, because the absent parent sees the parent with care staying at home on benefit, and resents the fact that that parent is not working.

In any case, the changes that we have made through the package of measures introduced by regulations from the beginning of April and incorporated in the Bill will go a long way to reduce the genuine resentments that caused many absent parents to be reluctant to co-operate with the agency and to pay maintenance. I hope that we will undermine resistance in that way rather than by the introduction of a maintenance disregard.

The final reason for rejecting the proposal for a maintenance disregard is the cost to the taxpayer. The administration cost alone would be some £40 million a year. At the level that the hon. Member for Glasgow, Garscadden (Mr. Dewar) originally proposed, it would cost in total some £340 million, including administration costs. His last proposal would cost some £245 million a year, including administration costs.

Certainly, whatever the Opposition are talking about—and they are not specific in the new clause—they are talking about hundreds of millions of pounds extra for the taxpayer to pay. This very day, the Leader of the Opposition in his Mais lecture is claiming that the Labour party has abandoned the politics of tax and spend, yet the new clause is down on the Order Paper in his name. We have to ask whether he is aware of that, or whether it has been put down by his hon. Friends without his knowledge.

If so, I have to say that it is a fairly frequent occurrence. I have today listed and published 20 spending commitments in the social security sphere alone, the bulk of them put down in the name of Leader of the Opposition, that have been debated in this Parliament and to which we may suppose that the Labour party is committed. They effectively amount to the rejection of the average £4 billion a year of savings that I proposed, as a result of my Mais lecture, in social security spending by the end of the decade, and £14 billion a year in the next century.

We know that the average working family—married couples and self-supporting lone parents—on average pay around £1,500 a year in extra tax to meet the cost of supporting lone parents on benefit. I do not believe that they want to spend hundreds of millions of pounds more on top of that, yet that is what the new clause would mean. They certainly will not believe any Labour leader who claims that he is against tax and spend while advocating that sort of policy.

The Leader of the Opposition claims that he is clothing his party in the robes of fiscal responsibility, but the new clause shows that the emperor has no clothes. The Labour party has no clothes; it is not so much new Labour as nude Labour. The proposals that we have before us today are typical of old Labour—throwing money at any problem and encouraging dependency.

**Mr. Wicks:** I regret interrupting the sound bites. To get back to reality and, if I am allowed, to the new clause, am I right to say that it was under this Government that the amount of maintenance collected under the old regime declined and declined, at huge public cost, and that it is under this Government that the proportion of one-parent families dependent on income support, at great public cost, has risen and risen? The Government have spent and, as a consequence, they have had to tax.

**Mr. Lilley:** There has been a trend under Governments of both parties, in this country and in many others, towards the break-up of the family and towards having children out of wedlock, both of which have contributed to the growth of lone parenthood, in Britain and abroad. We believe that that was aggravated by the old system of judgments that were made, but often not enforced, by the courts in cases where proper maintenance was not paid. That is why we, and the whole House, agreed to replace the old system with this system—with, I have to say, the honourable and straightforward support of the hon. Member for Croydon, North-West (Mr. Wicks).

We believe that it is right to do so, because, ultimately, the responsibility for supporting children is that of both parents. Even if they split up, the taxpayer should come in only to the extent that the parents do not have the means to support their children. The Child Support Agency exists to assess whether parents have those means, and to ensure that they pay if they do. Where parents do not have the means, of course, the taxpayer has to bear much of the cost.

**Mr. Wicks:** I am not in the business of always defending the last Labour Government, but my recollection is that, in the late 1970s, about four out of 10 one-parent families were on income support. That is a huge proportion, but it is now seven out of 10. The public expenditure implications of that are obvious to us.

**Mr. Lilley:** Surely that is a reason for supporting the proposals which we have put forward and which are inherent in the Bill, not for increasing the level of benefit, which would encourage more people to remain on benefit and fewer to work.

One of the reasons for the trend that the hon. Member mentioned is that, over that period, whereas more married women have gone out to work, fewer women lone parents have gone out to work. The number has declined. That must be for the very incentive reasons which I spelled out earlier, and which would be exacerbated were we to accept the new clause.

For all those reasons, I believe that it is much better that we rely on maintenance credit and on the disregard in the in-work benefits, rather than on increasing the level of benefit arbitrarily for those who are receiving maintenance, thereby discouraging a return to work, costing the taxpayer money, and, not, I believe, leading to any measurable increase in compliance with the Child Support Agency.

**Mr. Bradley:** I am grateful for the Secretary of State's opening remarks, but his speech went downhill from that point. We have always tried to be constructive, to try to get equity into the system. The changes that have been made most recently in regulations and in the Bill have basically favoured the so-called absent parent. I do not argue with that, but the new clause attempts to bring in a disregard to try to get fairness and equity in the changes, and to give more support to parents with care.

I am grateful for the contributions of my hon. Friends, which, as always through the passage of the Bill, have been extremely thoughtful and positive, particularly on the matter of a disregard.

I am also grateful for the support of the Liberal Democrats for this proposal, but we have heard again tonight that their basic position is to scrap the Bill and replace it with family courts. I am pleased that, during the debate on new clause 4, which proposes an advisory committee and relates to family courts, their spokesperson will have the opportunity to give details about how family courts would work. They promised during the passage of the Bill that they would give us that detail. However, I will not stray into that now.

It must be stressed again that, under the current arrangements parents with care on income support lose, pound for pound, for any maintenance paid. The sole intention of the new clause is to try to give more money to the poorest parents to help their children. It is not a case of the Labour party having no clothes. We are trying to ensure through the new clause that the parents with care can afford the clothes their children deserve. That is why we are trying to improve the financial situation of parents with care who have to rely on benefit.

In his summing up, the Secretary of State said that there was a clear disincentive against going back to work, but he also, I think, said that many parents with care wanted to go back to work. I asked him about evidence of that disincentive. He did not provide any, but I hope that he will do so after the debate.

The Secretary of State also repeated the arguments made in Committee and on Second Reading, that the way to alleviate poverty for lone parents is to enable them to return to work. I would not argue with that as a long-term aspiration, but lone parents, especially those with young children, should have the choice of bringing up their children themselves and remaining at home on a decent level of income. They may be on benefit, so the need for a disregard is paramount, to ensure that we raise marginally the level of income of those parents caring for children at home.

6 pm

My hon. Friend the Member for Croydon, North-West (Mr. Wicks) said that he remembers the Tories advocating a family policy to enable mums to remain at home to look after their children. The headlines were reinforced by Tory propaganda about latchkey children. The Bill attempts to return to the situation in which lone parents are forced to return to work when they do not have adequate child care provision. The sole purpose of the new clause is to introduce a disregard, and bring those vital extra pennies into the family to support children.

We strongly believe that a disregard would be an incentive to co-operate with the agency and pay what is required. It would mean that the public had confidence that the Child Support Agency was making money available to support children. The new clause puts children first and would give more money to the poorest

[Mr. Bradley]

families to enable them to support their children. I urge the House to support us in our attempt to protect and support children, by supporting the new clause.

*Question put,* That the clause be read a Second time:—
*The House divided:* Ayes 211, Noes 259.

**Division No. 153]**                                    **[6.01 pm**

### AYES

Abbott, Ms Diane
Adams, Mrs Irene
Ainger, Nick
Ainsworth, Robert (Cov'try NE)
Allen, Graham
Alton, David
Anderson, Donald (Swansea E)
Ashton, Joe
Austin-Walker, John
Banks, Tony (Newham NW)
Barnes, Harry
Barron, Kevin
Battle, John
Bayley, Hugh
Beckett, Rt Hon Margaret
Beith, Rt Hon A J
Bell, Stuart
Benn, Rt Hon Tony
Berry, Roger
Boateng, Paul
Bradley, Keith
Brown, N (N'c'tle upon Tyne E)
Bruce, Malcolm (Gordon)
Burden, Richard
Byers, Stephen
Caborn, Richard
Callaghan, Jim
Campbell, Mrs Anne (C'bridge)
Campbell, Menzies (Fife NE)
Campbell, Ronnie (Blyth V)
Campbell-Savours, D N
Cann, Jamie
Chisholm, Malcolm
Clapham, Michael
Clark, Dr David (South Shields)
Clarke, Tom (Monklands W)
Clelland, David
Clwyd, Mrs Ann
Coffey, Ann
Cohen, Harry
Cook, Frank (Stockton N)
Cook, Robin (Livingston)
Corston, Jean
Cousins, Jim
Cummings, John
Cunliffe, Lawrence
Cunningham, Rt Hon Dr John
Dafis, Cynog
Dalyell, Tam
Davies, Bryan (Oldham C'tral)
Davies, Rt Hon Denzil (Llanelli)
Davies, Ron (Caerphilly)
Denham, John
Dewar, Donald
Dixon, Don
Dobson, Frank
Donohoe, Brian H
Dowd, Jim
Dunwoody, Mrs Gwyneth
Eagle, Ms Angela
Eastham, Ken
Enright, Derek
Etherington, Bill

Evans, John (St Helens N)
Ewing, Mrs Margaret
Fatchett, Derek
Field, Frank (Birkenhead)
Flynn, Paul
Foster, Rt Hon Derek
Foulkes, George
Fyfe, Maria
Galloway, George
Garrett, John
George, Bruce
Gerrard, Neil
Gilbert, Rt Hon Dr John
Godman, Dr Norman A
Golding, Mrs Llin
Gordon, Mildred
Graham, Thomas
Griffiths, Nigel (Edinburgh S)
Griffiths, Win (Bridgend)
Grocott, Bruce
Gunnell, John
Hain, Peter
Hall, Mike
Hanson, David
Harvey, Nick
Hattersley, Rt Hon Roy
Henderson, Doug
Heppell, John
Hinchliffe, David
Hodge, Margaret
Hoey, Kate
Hogg, Norman (Cumbernauld)
Hoon, Geoffrey
Howarth, George (Knowsley North)
Howells, Dr. Kim (Pontypridd)
Hoyle, Doug
Hughes, Kevin (Doncaster N)
Hughes, Robert (Aberdeen N)
Hughes, Simon (Southwark)
Illsley, Eric
Ingram, Adam
Jackson, Helen (Shef'ld, H)
Jamieson, David
Janner, Greville
Jones, Barry (Alyn and D'side)
Jones, Jon Owen (Cardiff C)
Jones, Lynne (B'ham S O)
Jones, Martyn (Clwyd, SW)
Jowell, Tessa
Keen, Alan
Kennedy, Jane (Lpool Brdgn)
Khabra, Piara S
Kilfoyle, Peter
Lestor, Joan (Eccles)
Lewis, Terry
Litherland, Robert
Livingstone, Ken
Lloyd, Tony (Stretford)
Llwyd, Elfyn
Lynne, Ms Liz
McAvoy, Thomas
McCartney, Ian
Macdonald, Calum

McKelvey, William
Mackinlay, Andrew
McLeish, Henry
McMaster, Gordon
MacShane, Denis
Madden, Max
Mahon, Alice
Marek, Dr John
Marshall, David (Shettleston)
Marshall, Jim (Leicester, S)
Martlew, Eric
Meacher, Michael
Meale, Alan
Michael, Alun
Michie, Bill (Sheffield Heeley)
Milburn, Alan
Miller, Andrew
Molyneaux, Rt Hon James
Moonie, Dr Lewis
Morgan, Rhodri
Morris, Rt Hon Alfred (Wy'nshawe)
Morris, Estelle (B'ham Yardley)
Morris, Rt Hon John (Aberavon)
Mullin, Chris
Murphy, Paul
Oakes, Rt Hon Gordon
O'Brien, Mike (N W'kshire)
O'Brien, William (Normanton)
O'Hara, Edward
Olner, Bill
Orme, Rt Hon Stanley
Paisley, The Reverend Ian
Pickthall, Colin
Pike, Peter L
Pope, Greg
Powell, Ray (Ogmore)
Prentice, Bridget (Lew'm E)
Prentice, Gordon (Pendle)
Primarolo, Dawn
Purchase, Ken
Quin, Ms Joyce
Radice, Giles
Randall, Stuart
Raynsford, Nick

Rendel, David
Robinson, Geoffrey (Co'try NW)
Roche, Mrs Barbara
Rogers, Allan
Rooker, Jeff
Rooney, Terry
Ross, Ernie (Dundee West)
Ruddock, Joan
Sedgemore, Brian
Sheerman, Barry
Sheldon, Rt Hon Robert
Short, Clare
Simpson, Alan
Skinner, Dennis
Smith, Andrew (Oxford E)
Smith, Chris (Isl'ton S & F'sbury)
Smith, Llew (Blaenau Gwent)
Spearing, Nigel
Spellar, John
Steinberg, Gerry
Stevenson, George
Stott, Roger
Strang, Dr. Gavin
Sutcliffe, Gerry
Taylor, Mrs Ann (Dewsbury)
Taylor, Matthew (Truro)
Timms, Stephen
Tipping, Paddy
Touhig, Don
Turner, Dennis
Tyler, Paul
Vaz, Keith
Walley, Joan
Wicks, Malcolm
Williams, Rt Hon Alan (Sw'n W)
Williams, Alan W (Carmarthen)
Winnick, David
Worthington, Tony
Wright, Dr Tony
Young, David (Bolton SE)

**Tellers for the Ayes:**
    Mr. Peter Mandelson and
    Mr. George Mudie.

### NOES

Ainsworth, Peter (East Surrey)
Aitken, Rt Hon Jonathan
Alexander, Richard
Alison, Rt Hon Michael (Selby)
Allason, Rupert (Torbay)
Amess, David
Ancram, Michael
Arbuthnot, James
Arnold, Jacques (Gravesham)
Arnold, Sir Thomas (Hazel Grv)
Atkins, Robert
Atkinson, David (Bour'mouth E)
Atkinson, Peter (Hexham)
Baker, Nicholas (North Dorset)
Banks, Matthew (Southport)
Banks, Robert (Harrogate)
Bates, Michael
Batiste, Spencer
Bendall, Vivian
Beresford, Sir Paul
Bonsor, Sir Nicholas
Booth, Hartley
Boswell, Tim
Bottomley, Peter (Eltham)
Bottomley, Rt Hon Virginia
Bowden, Sir Andrew
Boyson, Rt Hon Sir Rhodes
Brandreth, Gyles
Brazier, Julian
Bright, Sir Graham

Brooke, Rt Hon Peter
Brown, M (Brigg & Cl'thorpes)
Browning, Mrs Angela
Budgen, Nicholas
Burns, Simon
Burt, Alistair
Butterfill, John
Carlisle, John (Luton North)
Carlisle, Sir Kenneth (Lincoln)
Carrington, Matthew
Channon, Rt Hon Paul
Churchill, Mr
Clappison, James
Clark, Dr Michael (Rochford)
Clifton-Brown, Geoffrey
Coe, Sebastian
Colvin, Michael
Congdon, David
Coombs, Anthony (Wyre For'st)
Coombs, Simon (Swindon)
Cormack, Sir Patrick
Couchman, James
Cran, James
Currie, Mrs Edwina (S D'by'ire)
Curry, David (Skipton & Ripon)
Davies, Quentin (Stamford)
Davis, David (Boothferry)
Day, Stephen
Deva, Nirj Joseph
Devlin, Tim

Dicks, Terry
Douglas-Hamilton, Lord James
Dover, Den
Duncan, Alan
Duncan-Smith, Iain
Dunn, Bob
Durant, Sir Anthony
Elletson, Harold
Emery, Rt Hon Sir Peter
Evans, David (Welwyn Hatfield)
Evans, Nigel (Ribble Valley)
Evans, Roger (Monmouth)
Evennett, David
Faber, David
Fabricant, Michael
Field, Barry (Isle of Wight)
Fishburn, Dudley
Forsyth, Rt Hon Michael (Stirling)
Forth, Eric
Fowler, Rt Hon Sir Norman
Fox, Dr Liam (Woodspring)
Fox, Sir Marcus (Shipley)
French, Douglas
Fry, Sir Peter
Gale, Roger
Gallie, Phil
Gardiner, Sir George
Garnier, Edward
Gill, Christopher
Gillan, Cheryl
Goodlad, Rt Hon Alastair
Goodson-Wickes, Dr Charles
Gorman, Mrs Teresa
Gorst, Sir John
Grant, Sir A (SW Cambs)
Greenway, Harry (Ealing N)
Griffiths, Peter (Portsmouth, N)
Hague, William
Hamilton, Rt Hon Sir Archibald
Hamilton, Neil (Tatton)
Hampson, Dr Keith
Hanley, Rt Hon Jeremy
Hannam, Sir John
Hargreaves, Andrew
Harris, David
Haselhurst, Alan
Hawkins, Nick
Hawksley, Warren
Hayes, Jerry
Heald, Oliver
Heath, Rt Hon Sir Edward
Heathcoat-Amory, David
Hendry, Charles
Higgins, Rt Hon Sir Terence
Hill, James (Southampton Test)
Hogg, Rt Hon Douglas (G'tham)
Horam, John
Hordern, Rt Hon Sir Peter
Howard, Rt Hon Michael
Howarth, Alan (Strat'rd-on-A)
Howell, Sir Ralph (N Norfolk)
Hughes, Robert G (Harrow W)
Hunt, Rt Hon David (Wirral W)
Hunt, Sir John (Ravensbourne)
Hunter, Andrew
Hurd, Rt Hon Douglas
Jack, Michael
Jackson, Robert (Wantage)
Jenkin, Bernard
Jessel, Toby
Johnson Smith, Sir Geoffrey
Jones, Gwilym (Cardiff N)
Kellett-Bowman, Dame Elaine
Key, Robert
Knapman, Roger
Knight, Mrs Angela (Erewash)

Knight, Greg (Derby N)
Knight, Dame Jill (Bir'm E'st'n)
Knox, Sir David
Kynoch, George (Kincardine)
Lait, Mrs Jacqui
Legg, Barry
Leigh, Edward
Lennox-Boyd, Sir Mark
Lidington, David
Lightbown, David
Lilley, Rt Hon Peter
Lloyd, Rt Hon Sir Peter (Fareham)
Lord, Michael
Luff, Peter
Lyell, Rt Hon Sir Nicholas
MacKay, Andrew
Maclean, David
McLoughlin, Patrick
McNair-Wilson, Sir Patrick
Madel, Sir David
Maitland, Lady Olga
Malone, Gerald
Mans, Keith
Marland, Paul
Marlow, Tony
Marshall, John (Hendon S)
Marshall, Sir Michael (Arundel)
Martin, David (Portsmouth S)
Mates, Michael
Mawhinney, Rt Hon Dr Brian
Merchant, Piers
Mills, Iain
Mitchell, Andrew (Gedling)
Mitchell, Sir David (NW Hants)
Monro, Sir Hector
Montgomery, Sir Fergus
Moss, Malcolm
Neubert, Sir Michael
Newton, Rt Hon Tony
Nicholls, Patrick
Nicholson, David (Taunton)
Nicholson, Emma (Devon West)
Norris, Steve
Onslow, Rt Hon Sir Cranley
Ottaway, Richard
Patnick, Sir Irvine
Pawsey, James
Pickles, Eric
Porter, Barry (Wirral S)
Porter, David (Waveney)
Portillo, Rt Hon Michael
Powell, William (Corby)
Rathbone, Tim
Riddick, Graham
Robathan, Andrew
Robinson, Mark (Somerton)
Roe, Mrs Marion (Broxbourne)
Rowe, Andrew (Mid Kent)
Rumbold, Rt Hon Dame Angela
Ryder, Rt Hon Richard
Sackville, Tom
Sainsbury, Rt Hon Sir Timothy
Shaw, David (Dover)
Shaw, Sir Giles (Pudsey)
Shephard, Rt Hon Gillian
Shepherd, Richard (Aldridge)
Shersby, Michael
Sims, Roger
Skeet, Sir Trevor
Smith, Sir Dudley (Warwick)
Smith, Tim (Beaconsfield)
Soames, Nicholas
Spencer, Sir Derek
Spicer, Sir James (W Dorset)
Spicer, Michael (S Worcs)
Spink, Dr Robert

Spring, Richard
Sproat, Iain
Squire, Robin (Hornchurch)
Steen, Anthony
Stephen, Michael
Stern, Michael
Stewart, Allan
Streeter, Gary
Sweeney, Walter
Sykes, John
Tapsell, Sir Peter
Taylor, John M (Solihull)
Taylor, Sir Teddy (Southend, E)
Temple-Morris, Peter
Thomason, Roy
Thompson, Sir Donald (C'er V)
Thompson, Patrick (Norwich N)
Thurnham, Peter
Townend, John (Bridlington)
Townsend, Cyril D (Bexl'yh'th)
Tracey, Richard
Trend, Michael
Trotter, Neville
Vaughan, Sir Gerard
Viggers, Peter

Waldegrave, Rt Hon William
Walden, George
Walker, Bill (N Tayside)
Waller, Gary
Ward, John
Waterson, Nigel
Watts, John
Wells, Bowen
Wheeler, Rt Hon Sir John
Whitney, Ray
Whittingdale, John
Widdecombe, Ann
Wiggin, Sir Jerry
Wilkinson, John
Willetts, David
Wilshire, David
Winterton, Mrs Ann (Congleton)
Winterton, Nicholas (Macc'fld)
Wolfson, Mark
Wood, Timothy
Yeo, Tim
Young, Rt Hon Sir George

**Tellers for the Noes:**
Mr. Sydney Chapman and
Mr. Timothy Kirkhope.

*Question accordingly negatived.*

## New clause 4

### CHILD SUPPORT ADVISORY COMMITTEE (NO. 2)

' .—(1) There shall be a body to be called the Child Support Advisory Committee ("the Committee").

(2) The Committee shall consist of not less than eight and not more than fifteen members appointed by the Secretary of State.

(3) The Secretary of State shall appoint one member of the Committee to chair its proceedings.

(4) In appointing the members of the committee, the Secretary of State shall have regard to the desirability of appointing persons with experience and knowledge of—

    (a) family proceedings and the work of family courts;

    (b) child support legislation; and

    (c) the welfare of children.

(5) It shall be the duty of the Committee to advise the Secretary of State on the working of child support legislation, and to make recommendations, when it sees fit, for amending such legislation.

(6) It shall be the duty of the Committee to prepare an annual report and to submit it to the Secretary of State.

(7) The report prepared under subsection (6) above shall include—

    (a) details of the number of child maintenance assessments made in the year, and an analysis of their effect on child welfare;

    (b) details of the number of departure directions made in the year, and an analysis of their impact on the effectiveness of child maintenance;

    (c) details of the number of reviews undertaken by child support officers in the year, and an analysis of the results of these reviews;

    (d) details of the number of appeals made to child support appeal tribunals in the year together with an analysis of the grounds of appeals and the findings of the tribunals, and its assessment of any implications of that analysis for the reform of child support legislation; and

    (e) any other matters which the Committee considers appropriate.

(8) The Secretary of State shall lay copies of each report made to him under subsection (6) above before both Houses of Parliament.

(9) Any expenses incurred by the members of the Committee appointed under this section may be reimbursed by the Secretary of State out of moneys provided by Parliament.'.—*[Mr. Dewar.]*

*Brought up, and read the First time.*

**Mr. Donald Dewar** (Glasgow, Garscadden): I beg to move, That the clause be read a Second time.

I am delighted to move the new clause and I assure the Secretary of State that my right hon. Friend the Leader of the Opposition and I are as one on this matter, as we are on most matters.

**Mr. Lilley:** Equally to blame.

**Mr. Dewar:** The right hon. Gentleman can put it that way if he wants, but we will let the nation judge.

During the last minute or two I have managed to obtain a copy of the press release referred to by the right hon. Gentleman. I will not go into the detail because others will no doubt wish to do so. However, it begins with what is positively the most offensive pun, in terms of taste, that I have seen for a long time. It is an extraordinary production.

However, I am glad to see that of the 20 major and decisive spending commitments that I am accused of making—which apparently will change the whole tide of fiscal history in the United Kingdom—the 20th is the new clause that we are about to discuss. That puts the matter into some sort of perspective. Apparently, the appointment of an advisory body is evidence of the fiscal irresponsibility upon which the right hon. Gentleman founds his case. I need hardly tell him that we will be looking carefully at the list and will want to comment on it in due course. I find it a remarkably unconvincing indictment and it is not one that could be taken to a higher court, never mind the high court of Parliament, by a politician with any sense of perspective.

I suppose that, in a way, I am flattered, but it seems lunatic for the Secretary of State to assume, for example, that because one tables a question seeking information, in which one asks for the costing of a development at varying levels, one is making a spending commitment at the level of the highest variable. That does not do the Secretary of State's credibility much good.

**Mr. Lilley:** It would be simple for the hon. Gentleman to tell us how much he would give in a maintenance disregard, or any of the other items to which he referred. Since he is always prepared to bandy numbers about but not to commit himself, he cannot complain if others put an obvious construction on the numbers that he uses.

**Mr. Dewar:** It is not an obvious construction. To put it as charitably as possible, the right hon. Gentleman has been in Government too long. When he arrives on the Opposition Benches I wonder whether he will hesitate, saying, "I would like that information, but my goodness if I ask for it, the Government are entitled to say that that is a spending commitment." No sensible person would take that approach. I suggest that he should reconsider his position.

I do not want to proceed too far down that line, Mr. Deputy Speaker, and will confine myself to saying that I would be genuinely surprised to discover that I am as generous a Santa Claus figure as the Secretary of State imagines. It would come as an even greater surprise to the many lobbying groups that have come to me looking for promises and discovered that they are not easy to obtain, for good hard-headed and practical reasons—that is, the problems that the Labour Government are likely to inherit. If the Secretary of State wants something to worry about today, he might consider one sentence in the White Paper on competitiveness.

**Mr. Deputy Speaker (Mr. Michael Morris):** Order. Does the one sentence refer to the child support advisory committee?

**Mr. Dewar:** I—

**Mr. Deputy Speaker:** The answer is either yes or no.

**Mr. Dewar:** Even for someone in your impartial position, Mr. Deputy Speaker, answers of yes or no are dangerous. I will merely suggest that the Secretary of State might worry about the Government's inability to help raise living standards in old age, which is mentioned in the White Paper, and the more interesting suggestion that taxation policy is totally out of the Government's control because of global movements of capital across national frontiers.

Item 20 on the Secretary of State's list is the interesting and important new clause that we are discussing. The new clause has been tabled because the child support advisory committee is a genuine subject for discussion and debate. I have no doubt that the Under-Secretary of State for Social Security, who is replying to the debate, will say that the committee is unnecessary because we already have the Select Committees on Social Security and on the Parliamentary Commissioner for Administration—the ombudsman—the Social Security Advisory Committee and the chief child support officer.

I accept that a range of people deal, on an ad hoc or occasional basis, with the facts, figures and development of the Child Support Agency. The trouble is that even they should be redundant if the agency were producing the sort of overall and comprehensive figure in its annual reports that would allow one to take a clear view of what is happening, but I am afraid that that is not the case. The agency has become a special case in many ways, but especially in view of its daunting and, at times, depressing record—a fact that Ministers have conceded. After every allowance is made for special circumstances, every alibi weighed in the balance and every explanation explored, the deplorable fact remains that, in many ways, the agency has been an administrative nightmare. Arguably, it has missed many of its social targets—I say arguably because the figures are obscure.

I must make it clear that the Opposition recognise that the task of the agency, and no doubt of the Department, has been greatly hampered by people who have not co-operated. On occasions, non co-operation has been taken to lengths that I condemn and from which I would distance my party. Having said that, many people have commented on the failure to learn by past mistakes, such as the introduction of the disability living allowance. We are in the sad situation that many people who are in touch with the agency see its administrative record and the policy framework within which it operates as adding insult to perceived injury.

I will give one or two brief examples, as I do not want to delay the House. I referred to the chief child support officer who has a remit under section 13 of the Child Support Act 1991. According to the foreword of his recent report the remit includes

"the making, review or cancellation of maintenance assessments . . . by Child Support Officers . . . within the Child Support Agency".

The figures that he produced, which will be familiar to many hon. Members—certainly to the Under-Secretary of State for Social Security—were remarkable. Of the 1,188 maintenance assessments examined and taken for analysis, 157 were found to be correct, 545 to be incorrect and there was insufficient evidence to tell whether the other 486 were correct or incorrect. I rehearse those as an aide-memoire to hon. Members about the scale of the problems that we have been facing. Only 157 assessments out of 1,188 could possibly be said—on the face of the file—to be accurate and as they should have been.

Of course, a series of reports from the Select Committees on Social Security and on the Parliamentary Commissioner for Administration have commented harshly on what has been happening and it is important to remember that great efforts are being made to improve the position. There have been changes at the top in the Child Support Agency and there is no doubt about that. I talked to the new chief executive, Ann Chant, and I appreciate that the agency is trying to make some sort of order out of what appears to have been a good deal of chaos.

I hope that this is not evidence of individual human frailty on my part, but as far as I am concerned it is still extremely difficult to discover with any accuracy what the position is. I am thinking, for example, of the amount of money that the agency takes in maintenance and in other ways as a result of maintenance assessments, the benefit savings and their definition, the liable relative carry-over and what percentage it is of the total, the amount going to children who live in families and the amount going in benefit savings to the Treasury, the number of parents with care who have been floated off—the term that has become jargon—benefit and the number of good cause cases that have not been accepted when there is some dispute as to whether information is being withheld, either properly or improperly, by parents with care at the start of the process.

In March, I made determined efforts to establish some of those things, on the basis that we were about to have the Second Reading of the Bill. I looked—with advice and some help—at the Child Support Agency's annual report and the various parliamentary questions available to us. It was due only to the fact that the chief executive of the agency readily conceded a meeting that I subsequently got a memorandum that tried to deal with some of those fundamental statistics and I pay tribute to her for that. I think that it was agreed, by implication, that the statistics could not have been collected in any other way because they were not generally available. I have before me the three-page memorandum that I received in March. Even then, it threw up a good number of questions when I tried to move the debate on and satisfy myself that I had good grounds for making various points.

6.30 pm

It is easy to say, "That is a simple, basic list of questions. You should be able to get that information easily out of a parliamentary question." It is not so. May I take a simple example and ask for the comments of the Under-Secretary of State, whom we have in our line of sight? It is not a case of trying to shoot the poor man down. He has enough troubles without our adding to them, but this is a good opportunity to get him to elucidate a recent parliamentary question. I recently asked for the average maintenance assessment, excluding those who were on income support, and the answer was £43.46.

That is an interesting figure because it is the average weekly maintenance payable by absent parents who receive income from employment, but it excludes people who may also be on income support. I think that it includes an average of families with one, two or three children, so it is not per capita but per family unit. I presume that that average figure will fall further as a result of the administrative changes that went through in April. I believe that a drop of £5 to £10 is expected, as there was a parliamentary answer to that effect. Unlike the Secretary of State, I do not immediately assume that it will be a £10 drop. I am prepared to accept that the drop may be of only £5, but it will greatly reduce the figure of £43.46.

This is relevant to the new clause, as I am trying to establish why, exceptionally, there is a case for a review body and an outside assessment. I draw the attention of the House to a parliamentary answer obtained by my hon. Friend the Member for Newham, North-East (Mr. Timms) on 18 May. This may be a moment of curiosity on my part. It may not raise a major issue of principle, but I should have expected that the answer to my hon. Friend would have been in the form of a letter from Miss Ann Chant. Although it clearly deals with agency statistics, it has apparently been answered by the Under-Secretary and the Ministry and I am puzzled as to why that has happened. I hasten to say that I do not object. If it is a trend, I am prepared to endorse and welcome it. This will be another area for common ground for an all-party alliance, which is what the Secretary of State is always striving to achieve. Will he say a word or two in explanation?

I hurry over the first table in the parliamentary answer, which deals with

"Benefit Status of Parent with Care and Absent Parent at 11 March 1995"—[*Official Report*, 18 May 1995; Vol. 260, c. *331.*]—

because, with the best will in the world, I cannot understand it. I have asked several people more versed in statistics than me to explain it. I intimated that I was concerned and puzzled about the figures, so perhaps the Under-Secretary has been taking advice and we shall have the benefit of it in a moment.

Will the Under-Secretary look at some of the other figures in the parliamentary answer, which I understand but cannot easily explain? The table at the top of column 332 shows that the average maintenance assessment, which is a full assessment excluding interim maintenance assessments, for absent parents not on income support— what I prefer to call "liable parents not on income support"—is £37.22. That is significantly lower than the £43.46 but the explanation, which I accept, is that the higher figure refers to liable parents who are not in receipt of income support but who have income from employment, whereas the lower figure refers to all absent parents who are not in receipt of income support but who may receive another state benefit or have no income. I see that that might slightly reduce the average figure.

However, as the Minister will see from the maintenance assessments, which fall between £0 and £2.30, that sum is paid by 24.4 per cent. of the total number of people who pay maintenance or are assessed for maintenance purposes. I do not doubt the accuracy of the figure because it is in a parliamentary answer but I should like a comment on it because, as the House will remember, those people are not on income support. Most of them are in employment, so it seems remarkable that 24.4 per cent. of them should pay below the minimum figure expected from someone on income support. I simply do not understand how that figure can be so high. It is not a case

[*Mr. Dewar*]

of what they pay but what they are being asked to pay. For one in four people who are not on income support, most of whom are in employment, to pay less than £2.30 is astonishing and I do not understand how it happens.

The table also shows the full maintenance assessment for liable parents on income support, which is very clear. My understanding always was—clearly, I have got it wrong and should perhaps appear in sackcloth and ashes—that people on income support paid a minimum of £2.30, which has just been uprated to £2.34. The average maintenance assessment—not what is paid—for people on income support is £0.93, which is an awful lot short of £2.34. We also see that 58.9 per cent. of people on income support who have been assessed have a nil assessment. I do not understand that. I do not necessarily object to it because, if there is a good explanation—

**The Parliamentary Under-Secretary of State for Social Security (Mr. Alistair Burt):** The second table to which the hon. Gentleman refers relates to people with second families. Those on income support but with a second family have a nil assessment.

**Mr. Dewar:** Is the Minister saying that as many as 60 per cent. of those on income support fall into that category?

**Mr. Burt:** Yes.

**Mr. Dewar:** Right. I shall think about that, but it seems to be a remarkable statistic.

**Mr. Burt** *rose*—

**Mr. Dewar:** The Under-Secretary may want to comment later. I hope that the House does not think that I am making too much of this matter. I merely use this as an illustration, as it is the most recent information to reach me, because it throws up an enormous number of questions which are not easily answered and which suggest that something is out of sync and out of balance in the results that are being produced.

**Mr. Burt:** May I help the hon. Gentleman on that table? We were asked for a snapshot of current figures, which is what the table represents. Many of the cases that have already been cleared were the simplest to deal with. Where information comes back and someone is on benefit, it is often simple and straightforward to deal with the administration. A number of cases pending are those where there is a dispute about earnings, where the agency is seeking verification of earnings, or where the person is self-employed. If we were to take all the cases currently on the books, whether or not an assessment has been made, we would expect those figures to change. The proportion of those who are on income support is therefore greater in the assessments that have been cleared than would be expected once all the work has been done. That is why there is now an imbalance. If the hon. Gentleman were to ask for the same figures in 12 or 24 months' time, we suspect that the answers and proportions would be different.

**Mr. Dewar:** That makes the case for monitoring closely, and in a way that is more constructive than exchanges across the Floor of the House or the somewhat one-sided process of parliamentary questioning.

I have to say to the Under-Secretary of State that it is an eloquent comment on what has been happening that, two and a quarter years into the agency system, he is able to advance, as an explanation for what are obviously very skewed results, the fact that it has been difficult to deal with difficult cases.

**Mr. Burt** *indicated assent.*

**Mr. Dewar:** It may be true, but it is an unfortunate comment. It appears to me to make the case that I am trying—perhaps rather laboriously—to establish for a review body of the type suggested in the new clause.

After all, at the moment the number of maintenance assessments that show no employment income is 43.8 per cent.—a very large percentage indeed—and, if 60 per cent. of those parents make a nil contribution, it says something interesting about the way in which the scheme is proceeding. I do not know whether the Minister wants to comment further, but we can, and doubtless will, pursue those matters by letter.

In any event, I contend that the figures show how difficult it has been to establish the administration of the agency on a proper basis. I hope—as I quite often do—that I am wrong, but I suspect that there may be difficult passages ahead of us. I do not want to be ungracious for a moment about change that we demanded, and which is now on the way. It is not what we wanted; it is certainly not all that we wanted. However, we were keen to have a procedure whereby one could apply for a departure from the usual financial formula, and now it is important that that works well, that it responds quickly in cases where it is needed and that it is seen to be injecting a measure of fairness into a system that is perceived as unfair. Monitoring and adjusting will be key, and in that respect I envisage the child support advisory committee having a useful role.

That is also true of clean break settlements, which, as you will remember, Mr. Deputy Speaker, apply only to agreements made before April 1993, and which are based on what was reasonably directly called "a broad brush approach" in the White Paper. There is also the vexed question of travel costs. Those will throw up many difficulties. I hope that they will throw up, in the longer term, solutions to some of our problems, but in the teething period there will be frustrations and perhaps mysteries about the way in which the system works. Therefore the need for monitoring is repeatedly proved by experience, and will be proved again.

There are unexpected aspects in which policy advice from an outside source that perhaps was seen as not being contaminated by contact with the Opposition Benches might, one hopes, bring about some improvement.

I received a parliamentary answer—perhaps I should have updated it, and I apologise to the House. It is for 1994-95, but it runs from April 1994 to the end of January 1995. It produced what, to me, was another astonishing figure—that special payments for financial redress have been made only 34 times in that period.

I know the experience of Conservative Members because it has been voiced in the past. There is a very thin turn-out today, but in the past Conservative Members have expressed many complaints and anxieties about the number of angry scenes, confrontations, complaints and anxieties and the amount of stress and strain that the system has caused. It is remarkable that the compensation system is so hedged and circumscribed that it produced only 34 payments for financial redress.

Select Committees have made many other criticisms of the way in which matters have developed, as has the Parliamentary Ombudsman for Administration, who, as my colleagues will remember, reached the conclusion that he could not take on any more cases unless they produced some new point of principle because of the flood of complaints that he was receiving. He made it clear, as did the Select Committee on the Parliamentary Commissioner for Administration, that he saw much of the seed of that discontent in mistakes by Ministers. I quote the Committee:

"We are in no doubt that maladministration in the CSA cannot be divorced from the responsibility of Ministers for the framework within which it operated"

and that

"any policy deficiency was cruelly exacerbated by administrative incompetence".

That is from paragraphs 27 and 35 of House of Commons paper 199.

I hope that I have established that there is anxiety that the system needs a great deal of monitoring. It should receive that monitoring. Co-ordinated scrutiny is needed—we do not want the "dipstick" approach—and it should be carried out by a group of the type that we recommend, which will involve individuals of experience with a wide background and knowledge of the area.

6.45 pm

I am not trying to land the Secretary of State with professional critics; I seek tough, realistic assessors. I do not seek a hanging party, a lynch party—unless the circumstances justify that. There is every advantage in a committee that can examine things impartially, to lend some perspective to what I think everyone will see from the record has become the rather blinkered approach of those in command politically.

**Mr. Timms:** In supporting the case made by my hon. Friend the Member for Glasgow, Garscadden (Mr. Dewar) for a child support advisory committee, I wish to concentrate on one aspect of the system that has been created—the formula by which maintenance assessments from absent parents are calculated, and especially the protected income provisions.

I am grateful for work that has been carried out by Christopher Allen of the London Business School, which he has shown me. He has considered the maintenance formula system as part of the taxation system and drawn some conclusions about it, many of which are striking. I wish to draw them to the attention of the House.

The protected income provisions in the formula are intended to ensure that an absent parent is better off working than on income support. The formula assessment compares the maintenance demand with that protected income figure and, if necessary, the maintenance assessment is reduced to allow the absent parent to retain their protected income level.

The protected income provisions were made considerably more generous in February 1994, the last time that the attempt was made to repair that system. Since then, the arrangements have allowed for £30 earned income in excess of income support levels, plus 15 per cent. of a new partner's income. The provisions have undoubtedly had some impact because, as the figures provided in the parliamentary answer to which my hon. Friend the Member for Garscadden referred show, about

10 and a half per cent. of full maintenance assessments for non-benefit cases are now assessed at a zero contribution. That is considerably more than was the case when the social security statistics were published, the date to which those apply being June 1994.

Paradoxically, that increased generosity has considerably worsened the poverty trap for those people who earn slightly more than the protected income threshold, because the post-maintenance income of people earning between £30 and £60 above the exempt income level will be reduced to the protected income level. That represents a 100 per cent. marginal tax rate on their income. Remarkably, the figures in the written answer show that about one third—32.8 per cent.—of the non-benefit cases with which the agency is dealing fall in that category.

I can explain how that system works. The research paper 94/20, which the House of Commons Library produced last year before the changes were made last February, states:

"If paying the proposed maintenance would reduce the absent parent and any new family to a level of income below the protected income, the child maintenance payable is decreased so that the absent parent is left with the protected level of income."

Conversely, if the absent parent's income increases because of additional overtime payments or other such factors, the child maintenance payable is increased. The marginal increase in income—all 100 per cent.—is taken away by the formula. That is an extraordinary system, and, taken together with the benefit system, it means that absent parents are no better off, and may be worse off, if they take a better job or work additional overtime.

I wonder how that position has arisen. It was suggested earlier that the Treasury had intervened in some aspects of the system. The Treasury certainly has not intervened in the formula. The arrangements that have been reached appear to be entirely contrary to the Government's normal taxation policies.

A large proportion of maintenance assessments—one third of them—fall within the range. If we take 100 per cent. of the marginal income increases of people on relatively low and modest incomes, the system becomes insupportable. I have no confidence that we will not be here in a year's time trying to do yet another desperate repair job on a system that is breaking down. For that reason I strongly believe that we need the monitoring arrangements described by my hon. Friend the Member for Garscadden. We need a committee that can investigate what is going on and that can propose changes to create a sustainable and supportable system. We have not yet achieved such a system.

I shall say a few words about those who fall beyond the £30 to £60 band. The effect of the protected income system are clearly the most aggressive aspects of the maintenance system, but even without those provisions the system is extremely regressive. Up to the payment in full of the maintenance allowance, the marginal rate on take-home income is 50 per cent. If we take into account national insurance contributions and the 25 per cent. income tax level, the overall marginal tax plus maintenance rate over that range is 77 per cent. The absent parent will keep only 23 per cent. of additional earnings. The position might be acceptable if the money represented a transfer of money to improve the children's welfare, but, as we have heard, it does not. That is one specific example, but it is by no means the only one.

*[Mr. Timms]*

The system towards which we are moving still contains severe anomalies and insupportable elements that will require further attention. The changes that are proposed in the Bill are helpful, but as I understand it, they increase the scope of protected and exempt income and push the problems that I have been describing up the income scale. There will still be a large proportion of agency cases who suffer 100 per cent. marginal payment rates in maintenance plus tax. That problem and others like it require the monitoring arrangements proposed by my hon. Friend.

**Mr. Burt:** The hon. Member for Glasgow, Garscadden (Mr. Dewar) introduced the new clause in an entertaining manner and tried to divert the attention of the House away from the excellent press release that my right hon. Friend the Secretary of State published today. On this occasion, as on all others, I wholly subscribe to the views of my right hon. Friend. The easiest way for the hon. Member for Garscadden to clear up any confusion about what his party intends to do and how it intends to finance it is for him to come clean now about my right hon. Friend's statements and deal with the matter once and for all. I suspect that we will be unable to deal with that matter simply today, as we have been asking for a long time for evidence of what the Labour party intends to do should it come to office, and the answers are always fudged.

I remember the celebrated exchange in Committee when the hon. Member for Manchester, Withington (Mr. Bradley) asked the Government to provide more substantial child care support through family credit—a subject to which he might return today. I asked him how much and he gave an extremely evasive answer. I suspect that my right hon. Friend the Secretary of State's efforts to get answers on the subject will have limited success. However, that subject is not the substance of our discussions today and I shall hurry on to deal with the new clause.

The hon. Member for Garscadden also described some of the advice groups that give information to all of us about the effects of the Child Support Agency. He was right to draw a distinction between some of the groups that give us reasonable and straightforward advice and some that appear to have gone slightly too far in some of their activities and the way in which they object to the CSA.

I am grateful that the hon. Gentleman dissociated himself and his party from some of the more extreme activities that we have seen. I am afraid that those activities still continue. The group, Network Against the Child Support Act, in its current periodical clearly suggests to its members that they should lie to the agency to get information and that they should seek to make life difficult for the officers of the CSA simply in order to disrupt the system. They then wonder why we feel aggrieved at such action and suggest that it does not help anyone. I am grateful to the hon. Gentleman for dissociating himself from such groups and hope that he continues to do so.

As the hon. Gentleman has explained, the new clause provides for an advisory committee to advise the Secretary of State on the workings of the child support scheme. We value consultation; there was a wide-ranging consultation exercise before regulations were made under the 1991 Act. We have always taken careful note of the advice of the Select Committee on Social Security and the views of other interested parties in developing the improvements to the child support scheme of which the Bill's provisions form a key part.

We have also had a constructive dialogue with many representatives of absent parents, parents with care and those with experience of family law issues. In developing the changes that we announced in January, we consulted eminent family lawyers and we correspond frequently about the child support scheme with many organisations, including the National Council for One Parent Families, Child Poverty Action Group, citizens advice bureaux and the Law Society. Whatever problems we may have had with child support, they have not been for lack of consultation and it is not clear how the new clause can assist. The Government's main concern is not so much that the new clause and its implications will add to consultation, but that it will obscure existing responsibilities—the hon. Gentleman acknowledged at the beginning of his remarks that that was the main flaw in his argument.

In addition to the function of overseeing legislation—analogous to that of the Social Security Advisory Committee—the proposed child support advisory committee would be required to monitor operational aspects of child support. It is on that subject that the committee's proposed annual reports would focus. In that respect, the committee would duplicate the role, not only of the Select Committee on Social Security, but of the Parliamentary Commissioner for Administration, the National Audit Office and the chief child support officer.

Both the Select Committee on the Parliamentary Commissioner for Administration and the National Audit Office have reported on the operation of the child support scheme. They have drawn attention to problems with those operations and, in response, Ministers have indicated the steps that are being taken to address those problems—in particular, by improved methods within the agency for measuring accuracy, additional checking and enhanced training for staff.

The hon. Gentleman concentrated briefly on the report of the chief child support officer and he was correct to deal with the shortcomings of the agency which the chief child support officer found. However, I remind all hon. Members that, although comments were raised in 86 per cent. of the sample, that does not mean that the assessment was incorrect in every case. We agree that the accuracy rate has been poor and inadequate and we are exerting a great deal of effort to put it right. The agency aims to reduce that comment rate, which was previously 86 per cent of the sample, to 40 per cent. of the sample as soon as possible. That is a particularly demanding target which has been chosen to reflect the importance that the agency attaches to the judgment of its performance by independent bodies.

There is great determination to reach that target in 1995-96 and to deal with the problems that have caused that high figure. Action taken to date includes remedial action on accuracy and quality initiatives. The agency's second-year plan has dealt with many problems. There has been a reorganisation of reviews and appeal work and we have developed staff training further. We have taken serious notice of the reports by the chief child support officer. He is part of the vital monitoring equipment that is built into the work of the Child Support Agency. That is his job, and it is another reason why we do not believe that the superfluous committee that has been mentioned this evening is necessary.

Many of the changes announced in the White Paper entitled "Improving Child Support" are also aimed at improving the operation of the child support scheme. I have no doubt that both the Parliamentary Commissioner and the National Audit Office will continue to provide valuable information about areas where we can improve the scheme and that Ministers will continue to respond positively to that feedback.

Hon. Members will be aware that the post of the chief child support officer was set up under the Child Support Act 1991 to advise child support officers on the performance of their duties. His functions, which he discharges independently of Ministers or the Department of Social Security, include monitoring child support adjudication and reporting annually on performance. His annual reports contain much that is of use in identifying areas where further work is needed and I know that he and agency managers are committed to working together to improve performance.

7 pm

The Department and the agency are involved in an on-going process of evaluating the effectiveness of child support policy and operations. That goes beyond responding to external comment and advice; the agency is seeking the views of key stakeholders by means of regular meetings and it has set challenging charter standards that will be monitored carefully. Officials will continue to monitor the policy, particularly the changes introduced in April and those introduced in the Bill. In addition, the departure system will be piloted before its full introduction in order to identify and solve any unforeseen complications.

There is already considerable overlap between the functions of those who advise about child support and the tasks of a proposed child support advisory committee. In my view, the inevitable overlap would seriously hamper the effectiveness of an advisory committee in the child support field. There is simply no distinct role for a new quango such as the child support advisory committee, either in advising about areas where legislation could be improved or in monitoring the performance of the Child Support Agency.

There was an exchange across the Floor of the House in relation to a question raised by the hon. Member for Newham, North-East (Mr. Timms). He referred to a table that he had particular difficulty following. It would be a cheap shot if I were to say that I cannot see where his difficulty lies. I will not say that, because the table requires quite careful interpretation. Once the hon. Gentleman spots the key, he will find it easy to understand; but one needs to spot the key first. I shall try to assist the hon. Gentleman and other hon. Members who may wish to examine the table in more detail.

The table seeks to illustrate the total number of parents with care—488,000—and to show how many of them are in receipt of benefit. That figure comprises the 391,000 parents with care who are on income support, 63,600 on family credit and 33,400 who receive no benefit. The table then relates each of those figures to the absent parents and their benefit status. For example, of the 391,000 parents with care who are on income support, 77,800 absent parents receive income support, 18,200 are on invalidity benefit,

138,900 are not on benefit and for 156,100 the benefit status is unknown. That is how the table works: it seeks to relate parents with care to the benefit status of absent parents. The benefit status of absent parents is the column on the right and the parent-with-care column is on the left. I must admit that I can see where the hon. Gentleman's confusion lies at first glance. However, I hope that I have made the situation a little clearer. If he wishes to take up the matter with me later, I shall explain it further.

The hon. Member for Newham, North-East raised some questions in relation to protected income and the like. He did not give me previous notice of the figures, which I shall examine. I make it clear that protected income is designed to ensure that there is adequate support for the absent parent and his family. That is not the element that ensures that he is better off in work; the element that ensures that the absent parent is better off in work is the amount over and above that element which is built into the formula to make sure that the parent is not simply existing on benefit. The marginal deduction rate is not as high as 100 per cent. when one adds in that figure—it is something like 85 per cent. That is a high figure, but it is not the 100 per cent. figure that the hon. Gentleman cited. I will examine the figures that he has cited tonight and give him a full answer.

The fact that those questions can be asked and answered by the agency and by Department of Social Security Ministers together with the other equipment that is already built into the system to monitor and control the operations of the Child Support Agency demonstrate that there are enough mechanisms to deal with any queries. The House seeks to ensure that the system works. After two and a half years of live running, we know much more than we knew at the start of the process. Hon. Members have said many times that those who have established agencies similar to ours in other countries have faced similar difficulties. One cannot know a great deal until one gets started.

We are now determined to make sure that the system works better and more efficiently in order to deal with the problems that our constituents raise. I take each problem extremely seriously and the monitoring process to which hon. Members contribute is extremely important to the future of the agency. I ask hon. Members to recognise the monitoring equipment that is already in place and to accept my assurances that an extra committee is not necessary. I ask the House to reject new clause 4.

**Mr. Dewar:** I am grateful to the Minister for his courtesy in trying to deal with the various points that I raised. Even when offered the key, I still find the table somewhat complex. The Minister will be glad to know that he has helped me; he will be able to enter the field of education after the next election if he does not wish to return to his solicitor's office—we dream dreams. I now understand that parents with care are in the first column of the table and that that column is then broken down across the other four columns. I am glad that I now understand the table.

**Mr. Burt:** No charge.

**Mr. Dewar:** I am sure that there is no charge. I pay taxes which help to pay the wages of the civil servants who instruct the Minister. I do not need to feel at all guilty. I will not continue this rather informal conversation as I am sure that it would test your patience, Mr. Deputy Speaker.

*[Mr. Dewar]*

I am still unclear as to where in the table we find those parents with care who work. The Minister says sotto voce that there are "very few". The benefit status of 203,000 absent parents is not known. Does that figure include parents who work? Presumably, quite a number of absent parents are in employment. That seems to be of interest.

**Mr. Burt:** The whole point of the statistics relating to the parents with care is to emphasise that more than 90 per cent. of parents with care who are in the system are in receipt of benefit. That is a measure of the extent of the burden being carried by the community at large, and of why a contribution from absent parents to improve the position of those parents with care is so desperately needed. It was one of the major reasons why the agency was set up in the first place.

**Mr. Dewar:** I am tempted to say that that sounds like a good argument for a disregard, but that would relate to the previous amendment and I must not stray into that.

I assume that there must be a number of absent parents in work. Presumably, they appear in the "benefit status not known" column, which seems a little odd as the figure is so high.

The mysteries can be pursued at another level and on another basis. I remain unconvinced by the Minister's arguments. I recognise, however, that quangos are not popular and that Governments introduce quangos, advisory bodies, non-departmental public bodies and so on only when there is a clear case and a clear need for them. I began by saying that I thought that it was a special case and the somewhat arcane discussion about parliamentary answers was an attempt to establish that. It could probably be more effectively established by the cries of pain from the many people who feel ill-used by the system. Some of them may have a special point of view, but there is no doubt that there is still a perception of injustice about, and that alone would have merited at least consideration of the committee proposed in the new clause.

The Minister, however, possibly because he wishes to be at one with his senior colleague, has hardened his heart. I was touched by his assurance that he supported everything that the Secretary of State did. I believe that politicians ought to have two personae. Inevitably, one has to support loyalties and collective decisions, but one should not commit oneself heart and soul laminated to one's senior colleague, however admirable one may consider him to be. I shall not inquire into quite how admirable the Minister thinks the Secretary of State is, but it seemed that a moral absolute was being proclaimed that will do the Minister's reputation no good.

The Under-Secretary of State has always been seen as a little wet and well intentioned. Although it may be an embarrassment within the Department, it stands him in good stead, at least with public opinion, and he should not sacrifice it too easily.

In any event, I have listened to the arguments and I do not wish to divide the House. We can return to the matter on another occasion, and no doubt we shall do so. As my hon. Friend the Member for Newham, North-East (Mr. Timms) said, I do not believe for a moment that this is the last time that we shall debate the Child Support Act. I am certain that we shall return to it many more times

and I look forward to that pleasure. No doubt the Minister, having noted we are not taking the matter to a vote will note that amendment No. 20 on the Secretary of State's list had better be deleted.

*Question put and negatived.*

## Schedule 1

### DEPARTURE DIRECTIONS

*Amendment made:* No. 38, in page 24, line 21, leave out from beginning to end of line 27 and insert—

'8.—(1) Regulations may provide for two or more departure applications with respect to the same current assessment to be considered together.

(2) A child support appeal tribunal considering—

(a) a departure application referred to it under section 28D(1)(b), or

(b) an appeal under section 28H,

may consider it at the same time as hearing an appeal under section 20 in respect of the current assessment, if it considers that to be appropriate.'.—*[Mr. Burt.]*

## Clause 6

### DEPARTURE DIRECTIONS

*Amendment made:* No. 12, in page 5, line 21, leave out from '(1)' to 'the' in line 22.

**Mr. Bradley:** I beg to move amendment No. 39, in page 5, line 23, after 'State', insert—

'(a) shall give a departure direction, if he is satisfied that the case is one which falls within the provisions relating to child care costs as set out in paragraph 1A of Part I of Schedule 4B; or

(b)'.

**Mr. Deputy Speaker:** With this, it will be convenient to discuss also the following amendments: No. 5, in page 5, line 25, after 'in', insert

'paragraphs 2 to 4 of'.

No. 6, in page 5, line 30, at end insert—

'(1A) Subsections (2) and (3) below shall not apply to departure directions relating to child care costs to be made in accordance with the provisions of subsection (1)(a) above and paragraph 1A of Schedule 4B.'.

No. 7, in page 5, line 47, at end insert—

'(3A) The Secretary of State shall, by regulations, make provision as to the circumstances in which he would have just cause to decline to make a departure direction under the provisions of paragraph 1A of Schedule 4B.'.

No. 8, in schedule 2, page 25, line 12, at end insert—
*'Child care expenses—*

1A. Unless the Secretary of State can show just cause to do otherwise, on the application of a person with care, a departure direction shall be given with respect to expenses of the applicant necessarily incurred to provide child care required to enable the applicant to take up, or remain in, full-time or part-time employment, which were not, and could not have been, taken into account in determining the current assessment in accordance with the provisions of, or made under, Part I of Schedule 1.'.

No. 9, in page 27, line 21, leave out 'special'.

No. 10, in page 27, line 22, leave out 'paragraph' and insert 'paragraphs 1A or'.

No. 11, in schedule 3, page 29, line 30, after 'insert" ', insert '28F(3A),'.

**Mr. Bradley:** The amendment relates to schedule 2, entitled "Departure Directions". Although we welcome the main thrust of the Bill, to introduce departure directions for special cases, the amendment seeks to include the cost of child care in the six-point menu of items in schedule 2 that identifies the special expenses that can be used by absent parents, and also by parents with care, to seek a departure direction.

The amendment specifies the parent with care, but it could apply equally to the absent parent. Throughout our deliberations on the Bill, we have always tried to strike a balance between the interests of parents with care and the so-called absent parent, and amendment No. 39 attempts to strike that balance on a measure that may be used, particularly by the parent with care, for the departure direction.

**7.15 pm**

Throughout the passage of the Bill, we recognised that the emphasis should remain on the formula for the maintenance assessments and that the departure direction should be used only in special cases. However, we do not believe that adding child care costs undermines that principle. It could be argued that the items already in the menu of special expenses are more likely to be used by the absent parents, whereas child care costs are more relevant to the parent with care; therefore, the amendment represents another attempt to redress the balance between those competing interests and to introduce equity and fairness to the departure direction system.

There are many reasons why the Government should accept the amendment. It is clear from our debates earlier today that they consider that the most appropriate way to alleviate family poverty is for the lone parent to return to work, hence the arguments behind their rejection of the child maintenance disregard and their proposal to introduce the child maintenance bonus. However, it seems to us that they want it both ways by denying the fact that child care costs are a significant element in a decision to return to work. If the Government were consistent in their argument that the best way to alleviate poverty is for people to return to work, they should examine every possibility of enhancing that opportunity, and particular to that is the need to take into account child care costs in the departure formula.

It is a similar argument to one that the Government rightly accepted—that travel-to-work costs should provide a ground for departure, in addition to the provision currently available in the formula. The argument of trying to avoid work disincentives, and even to increase incentives, applies to child care costs in the same way as it does to travel-to-work costs, which the Government accepted.

The issues raised by the amendment were well explored in Committee, when the Government set out their objections to the proposal, but, as we made quite clear in Committee, that did not stop our attempts to change the Government's mind. We hope that they gave the matter further consideration in the period between the end of our deliberations in Committee and those on Report and that, on reflection, they consider it relevant to include child care costs in the list of special expenses.

It will be worth while briefly exploring the Government's reasons for rejection. It was never clear in Committee how the definitive list of six items in the special expenses list was determined. Schedule 2 shows them as the costs incurred in travelling to work; costs incurred by an absent parent in maintaining contact with the child; costs attributable to a long-term illness or disability of the applicant or of a dependant of the applicant; debts incurred before the absent parent became an absent parent in relation to a child with respect to whom the current assessment was made, with significant amendments; pre-1993 financial commitments from which it is impossible for the parent concerned to withdraw or from which it would be unreasonable for the parent to withdraw; and costs incurred by a parent in supporting a child who is not his child but who is part of his family.

I would be grateful if the Minister will elaborate on the basis on which those items were chosen. What research was undertaken on those exclusions—and of child care costs, for them to be specifically excluded from the departure direction? The Minister said in Committee that there was considerable research. I hope that he will provide further information tonight.

The Government claim that an addition for child care costs would have little effect on the overall assessment. Many organisations, including the Law Society and Child Poverty Action Group, believe that pre-empts the way in which regulations may be framed and departure officers handle individual cases. The purpose of the appeal for departure is surely to consider special expenses in the context of the whole individual case, to ensure fairness to both parties. When the departure procedure is used, it is important to give genuine consideration to special expenses. There should be the opportunity for both parties to include child care costs.

The Government argue that child care costs are already represented by various components of the formula, and for family credit payments in the calculation of the benefit. Our amendment provides for taking into account only costs not already covered by the formula. Those matters are debateable and, as we pointed out in Committee, need to be clarified in the regulations. Although part or all of the adult personal allowance of £46.50 is included at the first step of the formula, only one quarter of persons with care receive that amount. The final level of the assessment and the family's disposable income, including any benefits received, are the relevant factors. We ranged over that aspect in some detail in Committee. The Minister held to the view that the £46.50 allowance was the contribution to child care costs. In fact, only elements of child care costs appear in the final assessment and they should be taken into account more significantly, by allowing the departure direction to include them.

The proportion of the £46.50 received bears little relationship to the child care costs of the parent with care. In Committee, the Government made great play of the child care component in family credit. Although we welcome that, there is strong evidence that the maximum payable has little relationship to real child care costs. I know that the Government will study the effect of the child care disregard in family credit, but I hope that, since Committee, the Minister has examined more carefully the wide variety of child care costs.

In many ways, the amount available through family credit does not meet the real costs. At this stage, we are asking only for those elements to be kept under review, and for a proper assessment of the way in which amounts in family credit are applied to child care costs—taking into account in the average figures the fact that many people make informal child care arrangements with other family members and friends, which rather skews the

[Mr. Bradley]

information available to help provide the amount of money needed for genuine child care, so that parents with care have the opportunity to return to work, as the Government insist that they do. Departure should be used in cases where the standard formula does not reflect the needs or expenses of a particular family. We hope that the Government will include child care costs in special expenses.

One of the Government's aims is to help lone parents to take employment, by providing a floor of maintenance on which to build. The current formula acts as a disincentive to increasing hours or wages above a certain limit, when the income of the parent with care begins to reduce the maintenance payable. That is surely contrary to the scheme's intention and is particularly damaging to parents for whom child care costs represent a significant proportion of take-home wages. The amendment would ameliorate that effect and, coupled with other measures, would help to increase the disposable income of families in work.

Although we have attempted, as always, to be constructive during the passage of the Bill, in an attempt to restore public confidence in the agency, we met with few concessions in Committee. The argument for child care costs commanded support from all Opposition parties, and it would have a significant impact on furthering the Government's intention to alleviate family poverty. If lone parents' proper child care costs are met, that would allow them to go back to work. I hope that the Government will consider carefully how our proposal harmonises most effectively with other special expenses—particularly travel-to-work costs. The amendment would go a significant way towards redressing the balance between absent parents and parents with care, introduce further equity into the system and restore further public confidence in the agency.

**Ms Lynne:** The Minister opposed the maintenance disregard because he felt that lone parents ought to be encouraged to go back to work. This group of amendments would help lone parents to do that, but they deal with the parent without care as well. The formula is inflexible, but the proposal would free it up just a little. The Minister has acknowledged that there are problems with the Child Support Act 1991, as he has already brought forward departures in certain areas. The principle has been established, for instance, in travel-to-work costs. The Government have also recognised the principle in other social security legislation, particularly in the provisions on family credit. I know that family credit child care costs are not enough and do not nearly meet the real costs of child care, but the principle has been established there.

The amendments seek to add a further departure. They propose that child care costs for the lone parent and for the so-called absent parent are taken into account. There is no difference between the costs in this group of amendments and travel-to-work costs. The amendments have been introduced to enable the parent with care to get back into work.

7.30 pm

If no child care is available, that parent will not be able to go back to work. It stands to reason that, if child care costs are not met, there is no way in which parents can

start working again. So-called absent parents have difficulties because their child care costs are not taken into account when their assessment is made. The amendment would also encourage them to work.

Often, those people have a second family, and both parents are working. Child care costs must be taken into account. It is only fair to treat the parent with care and the parent without care equally. The parent without care would be able to pay the assessed maintenance. The amendment would enable the parent with care to take up work and to get off benefit. Surely that is what the Government have been talking about. The amendment would help people to do that.

The main reasons why lone parents—parents with care—do not work is that they cannot find work or there is nothing that they can do for their children. They do not have relatives around or friends who can look after their child at no cost. If they could employ a child minder to look after that child, they could go back into the work force. That would help not only them but the absent parent.

The Minister says that he wants to lift parents out of poverty. The amendment is a way to do it. I urge him not to reject it yet again. He rejected it in Committee and he keeps rejecting it, but he cannot reject the maintenance disregard and child care costs. It does not make sense. As I said, the proposal affects not only the parent with care but the parent without care. We need a child care cost departure to enable parents to work if they want to.

I am asking not for an automatic right to child care costs but for an application for departure. I am not saying that, if a parent with care has a highly paid job and expensive child care costs, those should be met; of course they should not. It would not be reasonable to expect them to be met within the maintenance formula.

As the Minister accepts, the majority of lone parents are on income support and cannot get back into the work place, so the floodgates will not be opened by the amendment, but it will help those who want to work. I stress again: surely that is what the Government want.

We must avoid the situation where people are better off out of work. If the Minister did not agree to the amendments, he would be accepting the principle that people were better off out of work. I hope that he will change his mind and agree to the amendments.

**Mr. Stevenson:** In arguing for this element to be considered for departure, we aim to instil a further degree of fairness in the starting point, otherwise the whole system becomes the subject of further suspicion. The inclusion of child care costs would enhance that aim. As has been stated, in the main such costs are borne by lone parents. The Government may be worried that accepting the proposal will open the floodgates, but I do not believe that that will happen.

Many lone parents are not employed, but research shows that, of those lone parents who are employed, about 29 per cent. have the additional burden of child care costs—not an insignificant figure, so we are considering an important issue. Particularly for lone parents on low disposable incomes, those costs are not a marginal issue, but an extremely important one. Some would argue that it is a vital issue.

I find it a little perplexing that the Government seem to have accepted travel-to-work costs as grounds for departure, yet they resist child care costs. Travel-to-work costs as grounds for departure are in addition to existing provision. I assume that the motivation behind that is to avoid work disincentives. Surely the arguments apply equally to child care costs.

The Government seem to object to the addition on the ground that it may have little effect on overall assessments. At the very least, that argument pre-empts the form any regulations may take and the discretion that may be used by the departure officer.

The Government argue in terms of cost and say that child care costs are represented already in the components contained in the present formula. From reading the amendment, I understand that it is concerned with costs that are not covered by the present formula. The Government may feel that the amendment duplicates what is already there, but it does not.

If the Government were prepared to concede the amendment, there would be a need for clarification in the regulations—that is accepted—but it is the principle that is vital, and hon. Members have already referred to that. The final level of the assessment and disposable income, including benefits, are important factors in the equation. The current formula is a disincentive to work, because wages above a certain level become a penalty. Surely that is contrary to the Government's stated policies and objectives. The addition of child care costs to the disregard system would not, therefore, be contrary to what the Government are arguing for. It would enhance their objectives. It is also consistent with similar changes that they have made in other sectors, such as family benefit, and with the travel-to-work costs element, which, in certain circumstances, would be subject to the disregard.

**Mr. Wicks:** I am in favour of the proposal for departure, which in this instance means to take out of account child care costs. It is a modest proposal in many respects but it could be important, especially for mothers in one-parent families, or for fathers who are caring for their children.

We talked earlier about the Government's clear strategy to encourage more and more one-parent families away from dependence on income support into independence in the labour market. We had a quarrel about how maintenance disregard might fit into that strategy, but many of my right hon. and hon. Friends agree that if so many families, including many children, are to be moved out of poverty, it must be via jobs and, we hope, high-quality jobs. That is why child care is so important.

We need to think through the implications of the Government's strategy and our arguments about child care, which have been so ably advanced by my hon. Friend the Member for Manchester, Withington (Mr. Bradley) from the Opposition Front Bench. At present, there are many formidable barriers to one-parent families on income support who wish to seek independence. Those who think that we must shift resources in social policy away from family breakdown services—I regard income support as essentially a family breakdown service—towards investment so that people move from dependency towards independence must recognise the barriers standing in the way of one-parent families.

Unfortunately, those barriers are formidable. They include, of course, low wages. Many of us would argue that the Government have enabled lower wages to be paid, which has led to social security chickens, in terms of costs, coming home to roost. That is one reason why the social security budget is at a record level. That has resulted not because we are a more socially secure society—that is not why we are spending more on state benefits—but because we are now a more socially insecure society. That is the paradox at the heart of the Government's social policies.

There is the low wages barrier and, for one-parent families, there is the means testing barrier. A Government who have lived by means testing will die by it because of their failure successfully to pursue the strategy of moving one parent families into the independence of the labour market. Unfortunately, that policy has been unsuccessful. We know that in one year only 8,000 one-parent families moved off income support because of the child support element. It is necessary to repeat the same statistic. We know that seven out of 10 one-parent families are dependent on income support. The means-test mountain is a formidable barrier to independence. Indeed, it is a mountain that most one-parent families fail to climb, often because it is impossible to do so.

That brings me to the other barrier of child care. We are all aware of the relevant arithmetic. One-parent families that are seeking work—many would seek part-time work because, like other mothers, or parents generally, that is the only way in which they can make sense of their dual responsibilities within the family and in employment—are aware that wages for part-time work or, indeed, for full-time work, are only slightly in excess of the moneys that they would receive through income support. The extra moneys are eaten up if it is necessary to pay for child care. That is why the amendment is vital. I am surprised that we are having to make such heavy weather of the arguments that lie behind it, given that we are trying to help the Government implement their strategy of moving people back into the labour market.

Let us concede that the Government's policy, as announced in their Budget a year or two back, of allowing for a child care element in family credit is to be welcomed. In a sense, we are trying to pursue the logic of their policy. I should emphasise that we are talking about quality child care, not child care per se. If we are to provide more assistance for all parents, not only one-parent families, we must recognise that the best social policies apply to all families. We must understand that many parents may have to sort out the problem for themselves by providing a lower quality of child care than many of us would accept for our children. That is my worry.

We must at some stage switch the debate from child care to quality of care. If we fail to do so, I predict that we shall soon hear about more cases of children not being looked after properly, and sometimes being neglected or abused because parents were not able to afford adequate child care. Let us not go for child care on the cheap. That is not always better than no child care.

The Minister may now agree that the arguments in support of a modest proposal for a departure for child care costs fit into the logic behind what the Government are claiming that they are trying to do. We, too, would like more one-parent families, if they choose to take the course, to be more independent in the labour market, and enabled to be independent by a range of training and employment measures, a parcel into which child care fits as a crucial element.

7.45 pm

**Mr. Burt:** Opposition Members have proposed that persons with care responsibilities should be able to seek a departure direction where they necessarily incur child care costs in taking up or remaining in employment. I appreciate their comments. I refer to the hon. Member for Manchester, Withington (Mr. Bradley) and his colleagues and to the hon. Member for Rochdale (Ms Lynne). The hon. Lady has so far resisted the requests of the hon. Member for Withington to enlighten us by setting out her alternative to the child support system that we are discussing. She has had several opportunities to present it to us. There is still time, and I am sure that the hon. Member for Withington and I share the view that it would be interesting to consider it in more detail later. In the meantime, we must await her alternative with bated breath.

As hon. Members on both sides of the Chamber will appreciate, I understand the sentiments that lie behind this flawed amendment. The Government share the objective of improving work opportunities for women with children. That is why we have introduced the child care disregard in the in-work benefits, such as family credit, disability working allowance and housing benefit, and in council tax benefit, which was introduced in October.

The hon. Member for Withington asked why we decided to opt for certain expenditures in the departure system and not others. After some consideration of the way in which the child support system works, we accepted that one of the flaws was perhaps that the system was too rigid and that there should be room for an element of discretion within it.

We made it clear throughout consideration of the Bill in Committee—I think that to a great extent we were joined by Opposition Members—that if the system was to work properly, it was important to keep the gateways reasonably tight at first for the departure system. After due consideration, we decided that it will always be possible to extend the gateways. Once an opportunity has been created, it is always extremely difficult to restrict it or to bring it to an end. If the discretionary system, coupled with the system in which the majority of us—beyond the hon. Member for Rochdale and her colleagues—believe, is to work and the formula is to work in the majority of cases, it is important that the element of departure should now be relatively tight.

We considered carefully where the greatest pressure points were to be found in the system before coming to a decision on the expenses that we should allow, and that the hon. Member for Withington enumerated. We trawled carefully the representations that were made by constituents through their Members in correspondence. We considered carefully what was being said to us by various organisations. During our review, which took place largely in the autumn, we examined as carefully as we could the various pressure points.

The list of special expenses that we propose to allow reflects the consideration that I have described. With the exception of one or two interested groups and fairly recent interest, the issue of child care for parents with care responsibilities was not a serious one when compared with the clean-break argument or travel expenses, for example. All Members will remember the representations that they received on those matters. I ask them to consider whether the same pressure was raised on child care costs for parents with care responsibilities. I have to say that

that was not my experience and I do not really feel that similar pressure was there. Given the amount of concern, we felt it unnecessary to include those costs in a scheme that was primarily intended as a safety valve to relieve the areas of greatest pressure.

**Mr. Bradley:** Will the Minister give me an assurance that the research that he undertook included groups representing the so-called "absent parent" as well as the parent with care, because quite clearly the child care cost may refer more reasonably to the parent with care and less so to the so-called absent parent?

**Mr. Burt:** Yes, of course. As the hon. Gentleman appreciates, representations in relation to child support come from all sides, but often the interests of the parties are quite different. A number of the cases where departure was argued for by those representing the so-called absent parent would be diametrically opposed to the interests of the parents with care. The Government understand that, because, peculiarly—almost uniquely—one of the aims of the system that the Government have set up is to hold the ring between those competing interests. I shall refer to that point later. We received representations from all sides.

As I made clear from the start in Committee, and as the Government have made clear from the beginning of the reform process, the departure system is genuinely designed to deal with the issues that have been of major concern since the Child Support Act 1991 came into operation. It is not our intention to allow any conceivable expense to be cited as grounds for a departure order. To do so would be to run the risk of there being a return to a discretion-based free-for-all.

We believe quite strongly that the current legislation already makes some provision for child care costs. If I may, I shall explain this again briefly to the House. The first step in assessing liability under the formula assessment is to calculate what is known as the "maintenance requirement". That is the amount calculated as representing the basic needs of a child and is based on income support rates. The maintenance requirement includes an amount in respect of the fact that a child needs to be cared for. The carer element is currently £46.50 if the youngest child is under 11 years of age. That compares well with the average cost to families of professional child care of some £42.40 a week. The carer element is designed to cover either the parent with care's own cost if she stays at home and provides care, or the cost of providing for that care if she chooses to work. Thus, the formula already makes a significant contribution towards any child care that may be incurred.

We believe that we have already provided significant help towards child care costs and not just through the benefit system, although of course the changes made to family credit last year are a genuine development of the policy, which we all share, towards assisting women who want to go back into work. Where a working person with care is eligible for family credit, disability working allowance, housing benefit or council tax benefit, costs of up to £40 a week can be disregarded in assessing entitlement to those benefits. The combined effect of those allowances means that working parents can be better off by up to £38.20 a week. We have now seen some 17,000 claims to family credit under that particular system.

I should also point out that those benefits allow for the disregard of the first £15 of maintenance received. That is in addition to the child care disregard and may be used towards the cost of child care, where such costs are incurred.

One can go wider. The hon. Member for Croydon, North-West (Mr. Wicks), who is always thoughtful and always well worth listening to on family issues, asked about the Government's policy and intention. Scattered across the system now—from the Department of Employment, the Department of Social Security and through to the Department of Health—is a whole variety of provision for child care costs, on a level unheard of under any previous Government. It is a great determination that we have and I believe that the contribution and support that we are giving, from tax relief to the expansion of day nurseries, is really quite substantial.

**Mr. Wicks:** I am grateful to the Minister. Has the Department done any computer modelling recently to allow not only for the support that the Government are now giving through family credit, as the Minister said, but the likely wages that mothers might receive in either part-time or full-time work, to see what the net gain to those mothers would be if they returned to the labour market?

**Mr. Burt:** The Department carries out a large amount of modelling, but I do not have that model with me at the moment.

The hon. Gentleman mentioned the barrier caused to progress through low pay. As he knows, we would consider an even greater barrier to low pay to be that of no job whatever, which a minimum wage—the policy of the hon. Gentleman and his party—would introduce. If he is seriously concerned about that issue, that is something that he must bear in mind. I believe that the deputy leader of the Labour party has already recognised that. Therefore, I do not accept the need for the amendments. The carer element in the formula and the maintenance and child care disregards in family credit provide sufficient help for those expenses.

There is a further point, which I must raise as it concerns perhaps a slightly greater flaw than anything else. Uniquely, in the list of special expenses, it seems that the Opposition's amendment would make departure mandatory, in that the normal just and equitable provisions, which are there for the special expenses, appear to have been excluded. It is a serious and important point. I am not saying this dismissively. Under the amendment, the Secretary of State, unless he has just cause to rule it out, should otherwise allow it. The hon. Gentleman made a point of saying that, because he was tailoring it to any costs not covered by the formula, only in cases where a higher amount of child care costs had been incurred would the special allowance and departure be considered. The mandatory element of the amendment suggests that, providing that a parent with care could come along and show that she was genuinely incurring virtually any child care costs that she was prepared to put before the tribunal, the mandatory element of the amendment would require it to be taken into account and awarded, with the burden falling on an absent parent.

**Mr. Bradley:** If that is the only argument against the amendment—I accept the technical flaw—and if the Minister will accept the principle of including child care costs, I would accept a redrafted amendment tabled in the Lords.

**Mr. Burt:** That was a good attempt to deal with one of the two major flaws of the argument, but not, alas, the second, which was what I referred to earlier: our contention that the child care element is there.

I shall return now, if I may, to the point that I made right at the start about holding the ring and holding the balance. It is wholly laudatory for the Government to attempt in a variety of different ways to ease the transition of women back into work. I maintain that the Government seek to do that not only through the element in the formula or through the family credit disregard but in a variety of other provisions as well. However, the provision would place an extra unbalanced burden on the absent parent. We are holding the ring here. We are already asking the absent parent to make a contribution to child care through the formula. To ask the absent parent to make a further contribution to child care—double provision—does not seem to us to be right.

It is correct, therefore, to try to ensure the ability of women to go back into work, and we seek to do that in a variety of ways. It is for the Government to find ways to do that, and we shall continue to do so. It seems to me that the way to do that is not through this provision. It is not through an extra burden on the absent parent or through an extra mandatory requirement. For those reasons, I ask the House to reject the amendment.

**Mr. Bradley:** I am grateful for the response from the Minister, although, clearly, I am disappointed that he has not accepted the arguments that I and my hon. Friends have made in support of including child care costs in the departure formula.

As has been clearly pointed out, it was a particularly modest proposal. We accept the principle that the formula should be used in the majority of cases, but the amendment proposed that the departure direction should be used only in special cases, and it was our intention—as it was in Committee—to retain responsibility for that by not including a whole range of options in the departure formula. For that very reason, we specifically moved amendments in Committee that included training elements and child care costs. It was not our intention at any stage to use that procedure to open up the floodgates to allow everyone to apply for departure. We were looking specifically at a matter that we think is of major concern, particularly to the parents with care.

We believe that the way in which the departure directions will be used will be of particular advantage to absent parents: I do not argue with that. We are, however, trying to introduce equity and fairness by including child care costs—particularly for parents with care—in the departure formula. Throughout our deliberations, we have tried to strike that balance, to ensure that all parties involved in the agency's operations retain confidence in the system through the introduction of the appeals system that we have discussed—a system that has been requested by the Opposition throughout our proceedings on the Bill. We are disappointed that the Government are not prepared to accept our modest proposal. I feel that the views of the House should be tested, and I urge it to divide on the amendment.

8 pm

*Question put,* That the amendment be made:—

*The House divided:* Ayes 210, Noes 261.

**Division No. 154]**                                [8.01 pm

### AYES

Abbott, Ms Diane
Adams, Mrs Irene
Ainger, Nick
Allen, Graham
Alton, David
Anderson, Donald (Swansea E)
Ashton, Joe
Austin-Walker, John
Banks, Tony (Newham NW)
Barnes, Harry
Barron, Kevin
Battle, John
Bayley, Hugh
Beckett, Rt Hon Margaret
Beith, Rt Hon A J
Bell, Stuart
Benn, Rt Hon Tony
Berry, Roger
Bradley, Keith
Brown, N (N'c'tle upon Tyne E)
Burden, Richard
Byers, Stephen
Caborn, Richard
Callaghan, Jim
Campbell, Mrs Anne (C'bridge)
Campbell, Menzies (Fife NE)
Campbell, Ronnie (Blyth V)
Campbell-Savours, D N
Cann, Jamie
Carlile, Alexander (Montgomery)
Chidgey, David
Chisholm, Malcolm
Clark, Dr David (South Shields)
Clarke, Tom (Monklands W)
Clelland, David
Clwyd, Mrs Ann
Coffey, Ann
Cook, Frank (Stockton N)
Cook, Robin (Livingston)
Corston, Jean
Cousins, Jim
Cummings, John
Cunliffe, Lawrence
Cunningham, Rt Hon Dr John
Dafis, Cynog
Dalyell, Tam
Davies, Bryan (Oldham C'tral)
Davies, Rt Hon Denzil (Llanelli)
Davies, Ron (Caerphilly)
Denham, John
Dewar, Donald
Dixon, Don
Donohoe, Brian H
Dowd, Jim
Dunwoody, Mrs Gwyneth
Eagle, Ms Angela
Eastham, Ken
Enright, Derek
Etherington, Bill
Evans, John (St Helens N)
Ewing, Mrs Margaret
Fatchett, Derek
Faulds, Andrew
Flynn, Paul
Foster, Rt Hon Derek
Foster, Don (Bath)
Foulkes, George
Fraser, John
Fyfe, Maria
Galloway, George
Garrett, John
George, Bruce
Gerrard, Neil

Gilbert, Rt Hon Dr John
Godman, Dr Norman A
Golding, Mrs Llin
Gordon, Mildred
Graham, Thomas
Grant, Bernie (Tottenham)
Griffiths, Nigel (Edinburgh S)
Griffiths, Win (Bridgend)
Grocott, Bruce
Gunnell, John
Hain, Peter
Hall, Mike
Hanson, David
Harvey, Nick
Hattersley, Rt Hon Roy
Henderson, Doug
Heppell, John
Hinchliffe, David
Hodge, Margaret
Hogg, Norman (Cumbernauld)
Hoon, Geoffrey
Howarth, George (Knowsley North)
Howells, Dr. Kim (Pontypridd)
Hoyle, Doug
Hughes, Kevin (Doncaster N)
Hughes, Robert (Aberdeen N)
Illsley, Eric
Ingram, Adam
Jackson, Helen (Shef'ld, H)
Jamieson, David
Janner, Greville
Jones, Barry (Alyn and D'side)
Jones, Ieuan Wyn (Ynys Môn)
Jones, Lynne (B'ham S O)
Jones, Martyn (Clwyd, SW)
Jowell, Tessa
Keen, Alan
Kennedy, Jane (Lpool Brdgn)
Khabra, Piara S
Kilfoyle, Peter
Lestor, Joan (Eccles)
Lewis, Terry
Litherland, Robert
Livingstone, Ken
Lloyd, Tony (Stretford)
Llwyd, Elfyn
Lynne, Ms Liz
McAvoy, Thomas
McCartney, Ian
Macdonald, Calum
McKelvey, William
Mackinlay, Andrew
McLeish, Henry
McMaster, Gordon
McNamara, Kevin
MacShane, Denis
Madden, Max
Maddock, Diana
Mahon, Alice
Mandelson, Peter
Marek, Dr John
Marshall, David (Shettleston)
Marshall, Jim (Leicester, S)
Martlew, Eric
Meacher, Michael
Meale, Alan
Michael, Alun
Michie, Bill (Sheffield Heeley)
Milburn, Alan
Miller, Andrew
Moonie, Dr Lewis
Morgan, Rhodri
Morley, Elliot

Morris, Estelle (B'ham Yardley)
Mudie, George
Mullin, Chris
Murphy, Paul
Oakes, Rt Hon Gordon
O'Brien, Mike (N W'kshire)
O'Brien, William (Normanton)
O'Hara, Edward
Olner, Bill
Orme, Rt Hon Stanley
Paisley, The Reverend Ian
Pickthall, Colin
Pike, Peter L
Pope, Greg
Powell, Ray (Ogmore)
Prentice, Bridget (Lew'm E)
Prentice, Gordon (Pendle)
Primarolo, Dawn
Purchase, Ken
Quin, Ms Joyce
Radice, Giles
Randall, Stuart
Raynsford, Nick
Rendel, David
Robinson, Geoffrey (Co'try NW)
Roche, Mrs Barbara
Rogers, Allan
Rooker, Jeff
Rooney, Terry
Ross, Ernie (Dundee W)
Ruddock, Joan
Sedgemore, Brian
Sheerman, Barry
Sheldon, Rt Hon Robert

Short, Clare
Simpson, Alan
Skinner, Dennis
Smith, Andrew (Oxford E)
Smith, Llew (Blaenau Gwent)
Snape, Peter
Spearing, Nigel
Spellar, John
Steinberg, Gerry
Stevenson, George
Stott, Roger
Strang, Dr. Gavin
Sutcliffe, Gerry
Taylor, Mrs Ann (Dewsbury)
Taylor, Matthew (Truro)
Timms, Stephen
Tipping, Paddy
Touhig, Don
Turner, Dennis
Tyler, Paul
Vaz, Keith
Walley, Joan
Wardell, Gareth (Gower)
Wicks, Malcolm
Williams, Rt Hon Alan (Sw'n W)
Williams, Alan W (Carmarthen)
Winnick, David
Worthington, Tony
Wright, Dr Tony
Young, David (Bolton SE)

**Tellers for the Ayes:**
    Mr. Robert Ainsworth and
    Mr. Jon Owen Jones.

### NOES

Ainsworth, Peter (East Surrey)
Aitken, Rt Hon Jonathan
Alexander, Richard
Alison, Rt Hon Michael (Selby)
Allason, Rupert (Torbay)
Amess, David
Ancram, Michael
Arbuthnot, James
Arnold, Jacques (Gravesham)
Arnold, Sir Thomas (Hazel Grv)
Atkins, Robert
Atkinson, David (Bour'mouth E)
Atkinson, Peter (Hexham)
Baker, Rt Hon Kenneth (Mole V)
Baker, Nicholas (North Dorset)
Banks, Matthew (Southport)
Banks, Robert (Harrogate)
Bates, Michael
Batiste, Spencer
Bendall, Vivian
Biffen, Rt Hon John
Bonsor, Sir Nicholas
Booth, Hartley
Boswell, Tim
Bottomley, Peter (Eltham)
Bottomley, Rt Hon Virginia
Bowden, Sir Andrew
Boyson, Rt Hon Sir Rhodes
Brandreth, Gyles
Brazier, Julian
Bright, Sir Graham
Brooke, Rt Hon Peter
Brown, M (Brigg & Cl'thorpes)
Browning, Mrs Angela
Budgen, Nicholas
Burns, Simon
Burt, Alistair
Butcher, John
Butterfill, John
Carlisle, John (Luton North)

Carlisle, Sir Kenneth (Lincoln)
Carrington, Matthew
Carttiss, Michael
Cash, William
Chapman, Sydney
Churchill, Mr
Clark, Dr Michael (Rochford)
Clifton-Brown, Geoffrey
Coe, Sebastian
Colvin, Michael
Congdon, David
Coombs, Anthony (Wyre For'st)
Coombs, Simon (Swindon)
Cormack, Sir Patrick
Couchman, James
Cran, James
Currie, Mrs Edwina (S D'by'ire)
Curry, David (Skipton & Ripon)
Davies, Quentin (Stamford)
Davis, David (Boothferry)
Day, Stephen
Deva, Nirj Joseph
Devlin, Tim
Dicks, Terry
Douglas-Hamilton, Lord James
Dover, Den
Duncan, Alan
Duncan-Smith, Iain
Dunn, Bob
Durant, Sir Anthony
Dykes, Hugh
Elletson, Harold
Emery, Rt Hon Sir Peter
Evans, David (Welwyn Hatfield)
Evans, Nigel (Ribble Valley)
Evans, Roger (Monmouth)
Evennett, David
Faber, David
Fabricant, Michael
Field, Barry (Isle of Wight)

Forsyth, Rt Hon Michael (Stirling)
Forth, Eric
Fowler, Rt Hon Sir Norman
Fox, Dr Liam (Woodspring)
French, Douglas
Fry, Sir Peter
Gale, Roger
Gallie, Phil
Gardiner, Sir George
Garnier, Edward
Gill, Christopher
Gillan, Cheryl
Goodson-Wickes, Dr Charles
Gorman, Mrs Teresa
Gorst, Sir John
Grant, Sir A (SW Cambs)
Greenway, Harry (Ealing N)
Griffiths, Peter (Portsmouth, N)
Hague, William
Hamilton, Rt Hon Sir Archibald
Hamilton, Neil (Tatton)
Hampson, Dr Keith
Hanley, Rt Hon Jeremy
Hannam, Sir John
Hargreaves, Andrew
Harris, David
Haselhurst, Alan
Hawkins, Nick
Hawksley, Warren
Hayes, Jerry
Heald, Oliver
Heath, Rt Hon Sir Edward
Heathcoat-Amory, David
Hendry, Charles
Higgins, Rt Hon Sir Terence
Hill, James (Southampton Test)
Hogg, Rt Hon Douglas (G'tham)
Horam, John
Hordern, Rt Hon Sir Peter
Howard, Rt Hon Michael
Howarth, Alan (Strat'rd-on-A)
Howell, Sir Ralph (N Norfolk)
Hughes, Robert G (Harrow W)
Hunt, Rt Hon David (Wirral W)
Hunt, Sir John (Ravensbourne)
Hunter, Andrew
Hurd, Rt Hon Douglas
Jack, Michael
Jackson, Robert (Wantage)
Jenkin, Bernard
Jessel, Toby
Johnson Smith, Sir Geoffrey
Jones, Gwilym (Cardiff N)
Kellett-Bowman, Dame Elaine
Key, Robert
King, Rt Hon Tom
Kirkhope, Timothy
Knapman, Roger
Knight, Mrs Angela (Erewash)
Knight, Greg (Derby N)
Knight, Dame Jill (Bir'm E'st'n)
Knox, Sir David
Kynoch, George (Kincardine)
Lait, Mrs Jacqui
Leigh, Edward
Lidington, David
Lightbown, David
Lilley, Rt Hon Peter
Lloyd, Rt Hon Sir Peter (Fareham)
Lord, Michael
Luff, Peter
MacKay, Andrew
Maclean, David
McLoughlin, Patrick
McNair-Wilson, Sir Patrick
Madel, Sir David

Maitland, Lady Olga
Malone, Gerald
Mans, Keith
Marland, Paul
Marlow, Tony
Marshall, John (Hendon S)
Marshall, Sir Michael (Arundel)
Martin, David (Portsmouth S)
Mates, Michael
Merchant, Piers
Mills, Iain
Mitchell, Sir David (NW Hants)
Monro, Sir Hector
Montgomery, Sir Fergus
Moss, Malcolm
Neubert, Sir Michael
Newton, Rt Hon Tony
Nicholls, Patrick
Nicholson, David (Taunton)
Nicholson, Emma (Devon West)
Norris, Steve
Onslow, Rt Hon Sir Cranley
Oppenheim, Phillip
Ottaway, Richard
Patnick, Sir Irvine
Pattie, Rt Hon Sir Geoffrey
Pawsey, James
Peacock, Mrs Elizabeth
Pickles, Eric
Porter, Barry (Wirral S)
Porter, David (Waveney)
Portillo, Rt Hon Michael
Powell, William (Corby)
Rathbone, Tim
Redwood, Rt Hon John
Renton, Rt Hon Tim
Riddick, Graham
Robathan, Andrew
Robinson, Mark (Somerton)
Roe, Mrs Marion (Broxbourne)
Rumbold, Rt Hon Dame Angela
Ryder, Rt Hon Richard
Sackville, Tom
Sainsbury, Rt Hon Sir Timothy
Scott, Rt Hon Sir Nicholas
Shaw, David (Dover)
Shaw, Sir Giles (Pudsey)
Shephard, Rt Hon Gillian
Shepherd, Richard (Aldridge)
Shersby, Michael
Sims, Roger
Skeet, Sir Trevor
Smith, Sir Dudley (Warwick)
Smith, Tim (Beaconsfield)
Soames, Nicholas
Spencer, Sir Derek
Spicer, Sir James (W Dorset)
Spicer, Michael (S Worcs)
Spink, Dr Robert
Spring, Richard
Sproat, Iain
Squire, Robin (Hornchurch)
Steen, Anthony
Stephen, Michael
Stern, Michael
Stewart, Allan
Streeter, Gary
Sweeney, Walter
Sykes, John
Tapsell, Sir Peter
Taylor, John M (Solihull)
Taylor, Sir Teddy (Southend, E)
Temple-Morris, Peter
Thomason, Roy
Thompson, Sir Donald (C'er V)
Thompson, Patrick (Norwich N)

Thurnham, Peter
Townend, John (Bridlington)
Townsend, Cyril D (Bexl'yh'th)
Tracey, Richard
Trend, Michael
Trotter, Neville
Twinn, Dr Ian
Viggers, Peter
Waldegrave, Rt Hon William
Walden, George
Walker, Bill (N Tayside)
Waller, Gary
Ward, John
Wardle, Charles (Bexhill)
Waterson, Nigel
Wells, Bowen

Wheeler, Rt Hon Sir John
Whitney, Ray
Whittingdale, John
Widdecombe, Ann
Wiggin, Sir Jerry
Wilkinson, John
Wilshire, David
Winterton, Mrs Ann (Congleton)
Winterton, Nicholas (Macc'f'ld)
Wolfson, Mark
Wood, Timothy
Yeo, Tim
Young, Rt Hon Sir George

**Tellers for the Noes:**
    Mr. Andrew Mitchell and
    Mr David Willetts.

*Question accordingly negatived.*

*Amendments made:* No. 13, in page 5, line 23, leave out 'such a' and insert 'a departure'.

No. 14, in page 5, line 30, leave out 'the proposed' and insert 'a departure'.—*[Mr. Arbuthnot.]*

### Schedule 2

DEPARTURE DIRECTIONS: THE CASES AND CONTROLS

*Amendments made:* No. 37, in page 26, line 8, leave out 'the commitment was' and insert 'they were'.

No. 28, in page 26, line 19, after 'and' insert 'either'.

No. 29, in page 26, line 20, after 'made' insert

'or the child, or any of the children, with respect to whom that assessment was made'.

No. 30, in page 26, line 21, leave out 'between them'.

No. 31, in page 26, line 21, after 'kind' insert

'between the absent parent and any of those persons'.

No. 32, in page 26, line 23, leave out 'made between them'.

No. 33, in page 26, line 27, leave out 'is' and insert 'was'.

No. 34, in page 26, line 38, at end insert—

'.—(1) A departure direction may be given if—

(a) before 5th April 1993—

(i) a court order of a prescribed kind was in force with respect to the absent parent and either the person with care with respect to whom the current assessment was made or the child, or any of the children, with respect to whom that assessment was made; or

(ii) an agreement of a prescribed kind between the absent parent and any of those persons was in force;

(b) in pursuance of the court order or agreement, the absent parent has made one or more transfers of property of a prescribed kind;

(c) the amount payable by the absent parent by way of maintenance was not reduced as a result of that transfer or those transfers;

(d) the amount payable by the absent parent by way of child support maintenance under the current assessment has been reduced as a result of that transfer or those transfers, in accordance with provisions of or made under this Act; and

(e) it is nevertheless inappropriate, having regard to the purposes for which the transfer or transfers was or were made, for that reduction to have been made.

(2) For the purposes of sub-paragraph (1)(c), "maintenance" means periodical payments of maintenance made (otherwise than under this Act) with respect to the child, or any of the children, with respect to whom the current assessment was made.'.—*[Mr. Arbuthnot.]*

## Clause 8

### APPEALS

*Amendment made:* No. 15, in page 7, line 37, leave out from beginning to end of line 39.—*[Mr. Arbuthnot.]*

## Clause 10

### THE CHILD MAINTENANCE BONUS

*Amendments made:* No. 16, in page 9, line 19, after 'treating' insert 'the whole or'.

No. 17, in page 9, line 26, after 'paid' insert

'in such circumstances as may be prescribed'.

No. 18, in page 9, line 26, leave out 'entitled to the bonus' and insert

'who is or had been in receipt of child maintenance'.— *[Mr. Arbuthnot.]*

## Clause 12

### REVIEWS ON CHANGE OF CIRCUMSTANCES

*Amendments made:* No. 19, in page 11, line 6, after 'subsection (6)' insert '—

(a)'.

No. 20, in page 11, line 7, at end insert—

'(b) after "maintenance assessment" insert "by reference to the circumstances of the case as at the date of the application under this section" '.—*[Mr. Arbuthnot.]*

## Clause 14

### CANCELLATION OF MAINTENANCE ASSESSMENTS ON REVIEW

*Amendment made:* No. 21, in page 11, line 28, leave out from first 'the' to end of line 30 and insert

'maintenance assessment in question was not validly made he may cancel it with effect from the date on which it took effect." '.—*[Mr. Arbuthnot.]*

## Clause 19

### NON-REFERRAL OF APPLICATIONS FOR MAINTENANCE ASSESSMENTS

*Amendments made:* No. 22, in page 15, line 14, after 'shall' insert 'subject to subsection (1B)'.

No. 23, in page 15, line 15, leave out from beginning to 'shall', in line 17 and insert—

'(1B) If it appears to the Secretary of State that subsection (10) of section 4 would not have prevented the person with care concerned from making an application for a maintenance assessment under that section he shall—

(a) notify her of the effect of this subsection, and

(b) if, before the end of the period of 28 days beginning with the day on which notice was sent to her, she asks him to do so, treat the application as having been made not under section 6 but under section 4.

(1C) Where the application is not preserved under subsection (1B) (and so is treated as not having been made) the Secretary of State'.—*[Mr. Arbuthnot.]*

## Clause 21

### FEES FOR SCIENTIFIC TESTS

**The Parliamentary Under-Secretary of State for Social Security (Mr. James Arbuthnot):** I beg to move amendment No. 24, in page 16, line 22, leave out from 'made' to 'is', in line 24, and insert 'or a maintenance assessment'.

Clause 21 enables the Secretary of State to recover from alleged parents those fees for DNA tests which the Secretary of State previously paid in connection with a paternity dispute. The amendment fulfils a commitment that I gave to the hon. Member for Manchester, Withington (Mr. Bradley) in Committee, and allows recovery to be made in cases where benefit is not an issue as well as in benefit cases.

In relation to paternity, Opposition Members suggested that we should introduce a presumption of parentage on marriage in disputed paternity cases in England and Wales, similar to that which applies in Scotland. They also moved an amendment so that a declaration of parentage by the courts would have effect for any other proceedings involving the qualifying child.

On the face of it, both those proposals have merit, but the implications are far reaching and could affect other areas of law, such as adoption and surrogacy, registration of births, parental responsibility, immigration and residence and contact issues. These matters will need to be fully considered by several Departments.

The Lord Chancellor has general policy responsibility for family law issues, and I am pleased to say that he has agreed to take forward a consultation exercise on both those matters. Such an exercise may involve public consultation, and could clearly not be concluded in time for any changes in the law to be introduced in the current Bill. However, it will establish the need for and the desirability of making the changes suggested by Opposition Members as and when the opportunity arises. I commend the amendment to the House.

**Mr. Bradley:** I am grateful to the Minister for his response to our amendments in Committee. They recognised that there may be a need for wider consultation not only within Departments but with the wider public. I appreciate the fact that the Minister has now got agreement through the Lord Chancellor for such a procedure to be undertaken. We shall give our views during that process, and we look forward to any subsequent amendments or changes in the legislation that may be appropriate as a result of the consultation. We welcome the Minister's statement.

*Amendment agreed to.*

## Clause 26

### REGULATIONS AND ORDERS

*Amendment made:* No. 25, in page 21, line 22, leave out from beginning to 'order' in line 23 and insert—

'(4) Subsection (4A) applies to—

(a) the first regulations made under section 10;

(b) any order made under section 18(5);

(c) the first regulations made under section 24.

(4A) No regulations or order to which this subsection applies shall be made unless a draft of the statutory instrument containing the regulations or'.—*[Mr. Arbuthnot.]*

## Schedule 3

### MINOR AND CONSEQUENTIAL AMENDMENTS

*Amendments made:* No. 35, in page 27, line 38, at end insert—

' "(ae) compensation payments made under regulations under section 24 of the Child Support Act 1995 or under any corresponding enactment having effect with respect to Northern Ireland;" '.

No. 36, in page 29, line 30, after 'insert' insert '28C(2)(b), 28F(3)'.—*[Mr. Arbuthnot.]*

*Order for Third Reading read.*

8.19 pm

**Mr. Lilley:** I beg to move, That the Bill be now read the Third time.

I am delighted to move the Third Reading, for a number of reasons. First, my officials inform me that this marks the 25th occasion that I have had the opportunity to debate with the hon. Member for Glasgow, Garscadden (Mr. Dewar)—not a moment too many. None the less, despite it being the 25th such occasion, it is my maiden Third Reading speech. I have looked it up to see what is required, and I see that brevity can be of the essence. One of my predecessors managed it in two sentences. However, I have been told that I have a moment or two longer than that.

I want to use the opportunity to congratulate the Committee on the Bill's smooth passage, which reflects the cross-party support for the basic principles that underlie it. I am grateful to the hon. Member for Garscadden for fulfilling his promise that there would be no trench warfare because he wanted the improvements made by the Bill as much as we did.

As a non-participant, I can objectively praise the whole Committee: the Chairmen—the hon. Member for Blaydon (Mr. McWilliam) and my hon. Friend the Member for Cornwall, South-East (Mr. Hicks)—and the constructive contributions from Opposition Members such as the hon. Members for Manchester, Withington (Mr. Bradley) and for Liverpool, Broadgreen (Mrs. Kennedy), and especially those from the hon. Member for Croydon, North-West (Mr. Wicks).

Above all, I have to thank my hon. Friends the Under-Secretaries of State for taking the Bill through, especially my hon. Friend the Member for Bury, North (Mr. Burt). If any one hon. Member has gained in credit, standing and esteem on both sides of the House from this fraught and rather difficult subject, it is my hon. Friend; I am immensely grateful to him for all he has done, both in the context of the Bill and before that.

I wish that I could extend my thanks and congratulations to the Liberal party, too. Despite the great personal charm of the hon. Member for Rochdale (Ms Lynne), I am afraid that I cannot, because she has associated her party with some of the nastiest elements in British politics, and, in proposing to overthrow the Child Support Agency, has actively sought the support of the Network Against the Child Support Act and people like that. They have returned that support with delight.

I have here NACSA's latest report, which states:

"There is no doubt that the Liberal Democrats are delighted with the sudden input of support for their party from NACSA supporters. Campaigners in many areas"—

that is, NACSA campaigners—

"helped them during the council elections. Word from Lib Dem HQ and the ecstatic Liz Lynne is that they have already had a foot high stack of support pledges from NACSA supporters."

These are people who, a page or two later, advise people to lie and to harass. They say:

"Around 150 NACSA stalwarts turned out at Brierley Hill to harass the life out of the inmates of Dudley CSAC."

The report goes on to say:

"You should try and get hold of copies of the CSA business plan. Order one for yourself. Don't say you're from NACSA or whatever, try saying something like you are a welfare rights adviser. You might have better luck."

I would be happy to give way to the hon. Member for Rochdale if she wants to disassociate herself and her party from those undesirable people. However, she does not; she stands, or rather sits, condemned as a result.

I shall deal now with the basic approach of the Bill. We identified the key problem that we have faced since introducing it, and the main area of legitimate concern, as the failure to take into account fully in the formula the impact of past property settlements. That could not be permanently resolved through a formula system, although we have introduced the broad-brush approach to deal with it in the immediate future. It needed the opportunity to depart from the formula system, and that is how we decided to proceed. Primary legislation was necessary, which enabled us to introduce the departure system, and therefore to tackle a limited range of other problems which could not be covered through the formula system itself.

I welcome the fact that the official Opposition have not tried to widen the gateways too far, which would give people departures from the formula. As primary legislation was necessary, we were able also to tackle the take-on of non-benefit cases where there was a past property settlement, and to introduce the child maintenance bonus.

However, the Bill has to be seen as complementary to the secondary legislative changes which we introduced: the broad-brush element in the formula dealing with past property settlements and with travel to work; the changes dealing with housing costs where there were second families; and compensation for family credit and disability working allowance losers as a result of changes elsewhere in the formula. The most important single change introduced by secondary legislation was the 30 per cent. cap on the net income which could be taken by maintenance out of people's net income.

Those changes came in at the beginning of April, over the Easter weekend. They were introduced and implemented in a very few days. The whole operation was virtually hitch-free, and I congratulate the agency on carrying it out so smoothly. It was a massive achievement. It meant major information technology changes in the whole computer system; it meant examining some 1.25 million cases that are stored on the computer system; and it meant contacting some 675,000 customers of the agency.

As a result, about a third of those who have assessments have had their payments reduced by, on average, about £8 a week, or roughly £400 a year. Some have had reductions of as much as £22 a week as a result of the changes.

The two main causes of reduction in numerical terms are the 30 per cent. rule and the shared housing cost, spreading the cost of housing of all members of second households in a way that was not previously done by the formula.

The agency has notified everyone who might be affected that they can seek changes through the formula to reflect past property settlements or travel-to-work arrangements. So far, it has been rather underwhelmed by the response. By early May, there had been some 13,000 requests for such recognition in the formula for either property or travel-to-work expenses. Such applications have to be in by

*[Mr. Lilley]*

18 July, three months after the change was introduced. There is a continual stream coming in, and I reiterate that we welcome those applications up to 18 July.

The other issue which is complementary to the primary and secondary legislation is the improvement in the agency's performance, partly as a result of regulatory changes enabling it to operate more smoothly. The success in introducing the April changes is reassuring. It was, as I say, a major change, and not everyone would have backed with their shirt the certainty of it all working out as well as it did.

I hope that hon. Members are also seeing a steady improvement in the service provided by the agency to them and their constituents. Certainly we have had far fewer complaints to the agency, far speedier replies have been going out to hon. Members, and there has been a four fifths reduction in the number of queries via the direct line compared with the peak.

I hope that the overall package of reforms that we have introduced—administrative reforms, regulatory reforms and primary legislative reforms—are working out properly. I believe that it was necessary and right to introduce them all. They have been well received outside, as well as inside, the House. The changes, I believe, have smoothed many of the rough edges which were identified in the first 18 months of experience of the agency.

The changes will mean that those with a genuine grievance will be able to seek departure from the formula. As a result, I hope that the formula used and the assessments made by the agency will be seen to be fairer, and that it will therefore be possible to obtain greater compliance with those assessments, which will be better for the parents with care, and for the taxpayer.

Overall, I believe that the changes will benefit children, parents and taxpayers, and I commend the Bill to the House.

8.30 pm

**Mr. Dewar:** This debate has something of the atmosphere of a private function. I note that even the right hon. Member for Chelsea (Sir N. Scott) has come back to haunt us for a few minutes. The Secretary of State told me that this is the 25th time that we have faced each other across the Dispatch Box. It will be a somewhat shorter event than our previous exchanges. It is a curious fact that if our exchanges have become habit forming, the right hon. Gentleman could be added to the membership of the Pensions Bill Committee for its last month of sittings, which would allow him to raise the average considerably—although I doubt whether an enjoyment factor would play a prominent part.

I accept that much of what is happening is what we have requested and we are grateful for that. I know that the Bill had a constructive Committee stage. I do not pretend to have read all the *Hansards*, but I have tried to keep in touch with what has been happening. I am glad that the Bill has come through all its stages, although we would have liked there to have been more changes. I must stress that because I do not want to give the impression in these pleasantries that we are satisfied and that we did not look for a great deal more change.

I was glad to hear the right hon. Gentleman's tribute to the Under-Secretary, the hon. Member for Bury, North (Mr. Burt). Who knows, some day he may get his ticket to leave. He may be allowed to leave the treadmill and move to pastures green. He certainly tholed his assize—

**Mr. Piers Merchant** (Beckenham): What is that?

**Mr. Dewar:** I understand that it is an English legal term. It is not one of my strange Scottish gaucheries, which occasionally trouble the *Hansard* reporters.

Mention has been made of the Liberal Democrat party. It is unfortunate that we have not heard a little more about its plans for an alternative to the Child Support Agency. In a few minutes, the hon. Member for Rochdale (Ms Lynne) will have her last chance to sketch for us what I am sure must be well-advanced plans for the replacement of the current system. She has been pressed on those plans on more than one occasion, but presumably she has been waiting for the right moment. I hope that Third Reading is that moment—*[Interruption.]* Perhaps, at some future date, a discreet pamphlet with a pleasant typeface will emerge and explain all.

I reiterate that there is no interest among Labour Members in seeing chaos, confusion and misery arising from any social initiative. It is probably too optimistic to assume that this will be the last time that we consider the CSA. Indeed, I am anxious to stress that we will want to return to it on other occasions. It is important that the changes being introduced are worked through and introduced speedily. I hope that they will help to tackle some of the problems that have undoubtedly given rise to genuine distress about the way that the system has operated. Much will depend on the small print and the way in which the new policies are implemented.

I want to cite what may be an obvious example, but I have chosen it because it was the subject of correspondence that I was dealing with yesterday. It is the suggestion that in certain cases arrears will not be enforced for a period longer than six months. That point is important because many people have substantial arrears, often of 12 months or more. We know from the agency's figures that that is quite common. It will be important how the caveats that surround that proposition work in practice. The White Paper states:

"Where the Agency causes a delay in setting maintenance, consideration will be given to not enforcing more than six months' worth of arrears, provided the absent parent gives a commitment to meet his on-going liability."

It will be interesting to find out whether that is in fact an important and significant concession or whether it is simply decoration. It is a distinction of some moment.

There is no doubt that in the past—I referred earlier to the compensation procedures for delay—what has appeared to be quite an important concession has turned out to be the merest and feeblest of gestures. I hope that that will not prove to be the case about the contents of this Bill and the other parts of the package, of which the Bill is the core component. I know that I cannot go beyond the contents of the Bill, but I wanted to make that point.

Other important changes are still to come. We have always taken the view that capital and financial settlements, which presently come into play—even on a broad-brush approach—only if they were concluded before April 1993, could, with a little imagination, be extended to future circumstances. Again, I pray in aid the system presently operating in Australia.

As the Minister rightly recognised, the centrepiece of the Bill is the provision for departure from the financial formula where circumstances justify that. I certainly did not want an open door that would tempt everyone to go to appeal and to second-guess the system and the formula. However, it is important that the hard cases—and there are still hard cases—are dealt with sympathetically, that there is a speedy response and that the process does not get bogged down and fossilised, as so often happens in Chancery courts and other corners of the legal world. I have played my part in that. I used to do a great deal of industrial tribunal work and I started out with the assumption that it revolved around the merits of the case and looking at the facts. I then discovered that the other lawyers came to the tribunals carting case law by the tome and that if I did not also do so I was likely to be bowled middle stump. I hope that we will not go down that road with this Bill.

This is an important area and there is nothing more important than trying to re-establish a degree of public confidence in the system. I do not want to go into detail on one matter that is not in the Bill, but should have been, but it is well known, and has been argued tonight, that there should be a disregard. There is something unsatisfactory about a system under which children living in families that are most financially at risk—that is, those on income support—are the least likely to benefit from maintenance. I give notice that that argument will continue, no matter how many lists the Secretary of State compiles or how often he ridicules our efforts.

I believe that we speak for the majority of people who are involved with the system and who have followed the arguments about it. It is, perhaps, one of the few arguments that unite those who are violently opposed to the system and those who have doubts about its ability to delivery effectively for the parent with care. Both extremes of the argument agree that common sense and common humanity dictate that a disregard would strengthen the present position. I shall leave it at that. We have made some little progress and it is not unfair to say that Ministers were put under considerable pressure. I hope that the House, and the Opposition in particular, had a not dishonourable role in doing that. We have seen some movement as a result. It is not the total that is required and I am sure that we will come back to the matter, but I hope that the Bill will at least do something to bring a little fairness and a perception of justice to a system that has been terribly battered by the experiences of the past two and a half years and which we all want to be established on a true and genuine basis of public confidence.

8.39 pm

**Ms Lynne:** This is the last opportunity for us to debate the Bill before it goes to another place and I want to make very clear my position on it and the Child Support Act 1991, which it is supposed to amend.

The Bill does not address the real problems. Like other recent Government Bills, most notably the Disability Discrimination Bill, the Government have recognised that something needs to be done because of the extent of opposition throughout the country, but we have got half-hearted measures and that is what we have again today. Most of the Bills go some way towards a remedy, but do not cure the problem and this Bill is a case in point.

The Bill goes some way towards improving the deplorable situation in which many people—both parents with care and those without care—find themselves. Perhaps it relieves the distress a little, but it is a very small step. What we need to do and what I believe that we will do in the long term, even though we are not debating it tonight, is to repeal the 1991 Act because it will come back to the House time and again until the Government and the official Opposition recognise that that is the only way out. Then we may be able to start the process of getting a genuinely fair maintenance system.

The Government and the official Opposition—they are in collusion here—will find that opposition to the Child Support Act will not go away just because the Government have introduced the Bill and the official Opposition support them in it. The Child Support Act has not achieved its purpose—to put children first.

We all know that the Child Support Agency is in disarray. It might have got a little better recently, but it is still in disarray. The opposition is overwhelming throughout the country and has not gone away. The agency has had to defer taking on cases, to abandon other cases and to replace the chief executive. Now we have this Bill.

The Government have not learnt many lessons from what happened with the poll tax. They cannot just impose legislation on people, if it does not have their broad support, however grudging that support might be. The Child Support Act does not even have grudging support. Legislation is not generally opposed unless it is an affront to the people it affects, which is what has happened with the Child Support Act. Plenty of legislation has been unpopular, but the majority of people will abide by the law. The Government should have noted the extent of the opposition to the Child Support Act, which is almost as unpopular as the poll tax.

Many Labour Members have said that I am being opportunistic. Was it opportunistic to oppose the poll tax? We opposed it with all our strength and, after a by-election defeat, the Government decided to scrap it. The Labour party opposed it too. Perhaps new Labour would have branded opposition to the poll tax as opportunism, in the same way as my opposition to the Child Support Act is branded opportunistic. Perhaps new Labour would have supported the Government on the poll tax, as they are supporting them today, and have been during the past few months and years over the Child Support Act.

**Mr. Burt:** The House would listen to the hon. Lady with more interest and without such outrage and incredulity if at any stage during the past few months, while she has held her present position, she had enlightened the Standing Committee or the House with any alternative, but we have heard nothing and I suspect that we will hear nothing more. She rightly coined the term opportunism because I am afraid that until now that is all that we have heard.

**Ms Lynne:** I cannot say that I am grateful for the Minister's intervention. He should have listened to what I have said in the past. We have talked of a unified family court system—that was even mentioned during the passage of the Children Act 1989—and of bringing family law under one court. Surely most people cannot object to that. [HON. MEMBERS: "Details."] Hon. Members may say give us the details, but the problem with the Child Support

*[Ms Lynne]*

Act is that the Government did not consult properly. We have to consult properly about a unified family court system and then introduce those measures. We cannot have the half-baked ideas that the Government have put before us tonight. We need full and proper consultation. If the official Opposition would join us, and if they had opposed the Child Support Act instead of propping up the Government, we might get—

**Mr. Dewar:** Will the hon. Lady give way?

**Ms Lynne:** The official Opposition are propping up the Government with the Child Support Act and I will give way to the hon. Gentleman with pleasure.

**Mr. Dewar:** Does the hon. Lady intend to vote against the Bill tonight? She has said that she recognises that it improves matters. If she does not vote against it, is she not in danger of propping up the Government?

**Ms Lynne:** I have every intention of voting against the Bill tonight to ensure that our opposition to the Child Support Act is recognised, and members of the hon. Gentleman's party will be joining me in the Lobby. Not all of the official Opposition agree with the Front-Bench line. Perhaps the hon. Gentleman should listen to some of his Back-Bench colleagues.

None of us is opposed to the principle of both parents paying for their children—that is not in dispute and never has been. All parents must pay for their children's upkeep.

**Mr. Oliver Heald** (Hertfordshire, North): The principle is all very fine and good, but how does one make it work in practice? We tried the court system and it failed. Why does the hon. Lady believe that her unified court system would be any different, as it is the same thing? The point about the Child Support Act 1991 was that it laid down a formula, which means that many absent fathers have been paying for the first time.

**Ms Lynne:** If the 1991 Act meant that absent fathers were paying for the first time, some people might view it differently. What it does is to make so-called absent parents who are paying, pay more. The Government are not chasing parents who have not paid.

**Mr. Heald:** Under the old system, a father might pay £10 a week for a child, which is nothing when compared with the costs. Is the hon. Lady seriously trying to justify that?

**Ms Lynne:** Certainly not. That is why we want a unified family courts system. We do not want to return to the system of so-called family courts; we want a unified system that would encompass the Children Act and bring all family law under one umbrella. We are studying and consulting on that and those are the proposals that we will introduce in our own good time—not in the good time of the official Opposition or of the Government.

**Mr. Bradley:** Roughly when?

**Ms Lynne:** I will not respond to that. If the hon. Gentleman would say when he intends to introduce his policies on anything I might listen to him, but he and his party do not propose policies on anything. We are the ones who have been proposing policies. During the passage of the Child Support Bill, all the official Opposition could say was, "We support the Government."

The Child Support Act is just not working. It is not good enough to introduce a Bill that tinkers at the edges of a discredited Act, which the changes before us today do nothing substantially to change. Neither the Government nor their partners in the official Opposition have brought forward any radical changes. Why do not they now come out against the Act, given that the amendments which they discussed so eloquently in Committee were not accepted?

My predecessor warned the Minister more than a year ago that Liberal Democrat support was conditional on wholesale changes. The Bill is a sorry disappointment. My main criticism of the Act is that it introduced a rigid formula, and the departure system in the Bill does not substantially change that.

**Mr. Burt:** May I remind the hon. Lady that the original Act provided a rigid formula, and that original Act was supported by her party?

**Ms Lynne:** As the spokesman on social security for the Liberal Democrats, my predecessor made it clear in that debate, as the Minister will see if he looks at *Hansard*, that he would like to see the Act amended.

Instead of discussing what was or was not said in the past, we should look at the future. [*Laughter.*] Hon. Members may laugh, but we are talking about the future of children, which is not a laughing matter. Whether children have a proper support system is extremely serious.

**Mr. Burt:** The hon. Lady is being unfair, as hon. Members are laughing not about the future of children but at her attempts to get out of what happened. We have all been looking at the future. We have spent the past few months looking at the future, trying to devise the right system, with to-ing and fro-ing between the Government and the Opposition and without complete agreement. The Opposition sometimes challenged us to get it more right and asked us for things that we could not give. We have been looking at the future and working for it. During all that time, the hon. Lady might have made a constructive contribution but she did not. That is what her party stands accused of, and why there are wry smiles on both sides of the House.

**Ms Lynne:** The Minister must accept that the Child Support Act is not working. If he could say that it was, that would be fine and my position might be wrong. But the Act does not take into account individual circumstances and, however much the Bill amends the formula, it will still mean that many lone parents will be worse off because their passported benefits will be taken away; so-called "absent parents"—I cannot stand that term, which should not have been used in the original Bill—

**Mr. Dewar:** I genuinely want some information and am not trying to snipe. In the past, the court system has always considered the interests of the two parties to an action and the interests of the child in reaching a financial solution. One of the characteristics of the agency is that it recognises the state's right—I use that word neutrally for the purpose of this question—to recover income support. Would the hon. Lady keep that feature in her new system?

**Ms Lynne:** It is up to the court to decide in each individual case. That is the whole point of having separate assessments and not sticking to a rigid formula. That is the whole point of a unified family court system.

**Mr. Dewar:** The hon. Lady, I am sure unintentionally, has missed my point: that there is a new element in the Act, which is the recovery of benefit savings. That has not been a feature of matrimonial transactions in the past. Would the hon Lady want to retain that feature in her unified courts? It is a fundamental matter of principle. I do not prejudge whether it is right or wrong but simply ask her view on it.

**Ms Lynne:** Obviously, that feature could be retained in a unified family court system. I see no problem with that. I am talking about individual cases, which should be judged on their circumstances. Otherwise lone parents, so-called "absent parents" and second families will all suffer and that will continue to lead to family breakdown, which no one in the House wants.

I shall continue to press the Government to repeal the Act. I wish that the official Opposition Front Bench would do the same. We need a proper process of consultation so that all these arguments can be discussed at great length. We are not in the business of introducing something like the Government have brought forward without proper thought. We want a proper unified family court system that will work and will benefit children above all.

Opposition to the Act will not go away. Ultimately, it will have to be scrapped. *[Interruption.]* Hon. Members and right hon. Members who laugh may realise, in a few years' time when we have tried again and again to amend the discredited Child Support Act, that they got it wrong and will have to repeal it. They will then look back at this debate and realise that what we are saying is right: the Child Support Act must be scrapped.

8.55 pm

**Ms Mildred Gordon** (Bow and Poplar): I intend to vote against the Bill because, although it contains some concessions, which have been forced on the Government, it does not change the position for millions of families. Hon. Members on both sides of the House know that from their post bags.

The Government have rejected a disregard that would lift children out of poverty. They have not included the abolition of the benefit penalty, which threatens with penury thousands of mothers who feel that they have strong reasons for not giving authorisation. The Bill does not abolish maintenance deductions from unemployed men's benefits, which cost more to collect than they are worth, and disability benefits are still taken into account when reckoning income.

The opposition to the Bill in Parliament is a pale reflection of the movement of women, men and children outside Parliament against the Government's child support policy. Hon. Members ignore that movement at the risk of bringing Parliament into further disrepute. People expect to see their deepest feelings and experiences reflected in decisions made in the House. The Bill ignores them and I shall therefore vote against it.

*Question put,* That the Bill be now read the Third time:—

*The House divided:* Ayes 208, Noes 46.

**Division No. 155]**             **[8.57 pm**

### AYES

| | |
|---|---|
| Ainsworth, Peter (East Surrey) | Gorst, Sir John |
| Alexander, Richard | Grant, Sir A (SW Cambs) |
| Alison, Rt Hon Michael (Selby) | Griffiths, Peter (Portsmouth, N) |
| Allason, Rupert (Torbay) | Hague, William |
| Amess, David | Hamilton, Rt Hon Sir Archibald |
| Ancram, Michael | Hamilton, Neil (Tatton) |
| Arbuthnot, James | Hampson, Dr Keith |
| Arnold, Jacques (Gravesham) | Hanley, Rt Hon Jeremy |
| Arnold, Sir Thomas (Hazel Grv) | Hannam, Sir John |
| Atkino, Robert | Hargreaves, Andrew |
| Atkinson, David (Bour'mouth E) | Harris, David |
| Atkinson, Peter (Hexham) | Hawkins, Nick |
| Baker, Rt Hon Kenneth (Mole V) | Hawksley, Warren |
| Baker, Nicholas (North Dorset) | Hayes, Jerry |
| Bates, Michael | Heald, Oliver |
| Batiste, Spencer | Hendry, Charles |
| Biffen, Rt Hon John | Hill, James (Southampton Test) |
| Bonsor, Sir Nicholas | Horam, John |
| Booth, Hartley | Hughes, Robert G (Harrow W) |
| Boswell, Tim | Hunt, Rt Hon David (Wirral W) |
| Bowden, Sir Andrew | Hunt, Sir John (Ravensbourne) |
| Boyson, Rt Hon Sir Rhodes | Hunter, Andrew |
| Brandreth, Gyles | Jack, Michael |
| Brazier, Julian | Jessel, Toby |
| Bright, Sir Graham | Jones, Gwilym (Cardiff N) |
| Brooke, Rt Hon Peter | Kellett-Bowman, Dame Elaine |
| Browning, Mrs Angela | Key, Robert |
| Budgen, Nicholas | King, Rt Hon Tom |
| Burt, Alistair | Kirkhope, Timothy |
| Butcher, John | Knapman, Roger |
| Carlisle, John (Luton North) | Knight, Mrs Angela (Erewash) |
| Carlisle, Sir Kenneth (Lincoln) | Knight, Greg (Derby N) |
| Carrington, Matthew | Knight, Dame Jill (Bir'm E'st'n) |
| Carttiss, Michael | Knox, Sir David |
| Cash, William | Kynoch, George (Kincardine) |
| Chapman, Sydney | Lait, Mrs Jacqui |
| Churchill, Mr | Legg, Barry |
| Clappison, James | Leigh, Edward |
| Coe, Sebastian | Lidington, David |
| Congdon, David | Lightbown, David |
| Coombs, Anthony (Wyre For'st) | Lilley, Rt Hon Peter |
| Coombs, Simon (Swindon) | Lloyd, Rt Hon Sir Peter (Fareham) |
| Cormack, Sir Patrick | Lord, Michael |
| Couchman, James | Luff, Peter |
| Cran, James | Lyell, Rt Hon Sir Nicholas |
| Currie, Mrs Edwina (S D'by'ire) | MacKay, Andrew |
| Davies, Quentin (Stamford) | Maclean, David |
| Davis, David (Boothferry) | McLoughlin, Patrick |
| Day, Stephen | Madel, Sir David |
| Deva, Nirj Joseph | Maitland, Lady Olga |
| Devlin, Tim | Malone, Gerald |
| Douglas-Hamilton, Lord James | Mans, Keith |
| Dover, Den | Marland, Paul |
| Duncan, Alan | Marlow, Tony |
| Duncan-Smith, Iain | Marshall, John (Hendon S) |
| Durant, Sir Anthony | Marshall, Sir Michael (Arundel) |
| Dykes, Hugh | Martin, David (Portsmouth S) |
| Elletson, Harold | Merchant, Piers |
| Emery, Rt Hon Sir Peter | Mitchell, Andrew (Gedling) |
| Evans, David (Welwyn Hatfield) | Mitchell, Sir David (NW Hants) |
| Evans, Nigel (Ribble Valley) | Monro, Sir Hector |
| Evans, Roger (Monmouth) | Montgomery, Sir Fergus |
| Evennett, David | Moss, Malcolm |
| Fabricant, Michael | Newton, Rt Hon Tony |
| Field, Barry (Isle of Wight) | Nicholls, Patrick |
| Fishburn, Dudley | Nicholson, David (Taunton) |
| Forsyth, Rt Hon Michael (Stirling) | Norris, Steve |
| Forth, Eric | Onslow, Rt Hon Sir Cranley |
| French, Douglas | Ottaway, Richard |
| Fry, Sir Peter | Patnick, Sir Irvine |
| Gallie, Phil | Pattie, Rt Hon Sir Geoffrey |
| Goodson-Wickes, Dr Charles | Pawsey, James |
| Gorman, Mrs Teresa | Peacock, Mrs Elizabeth |

Pickles, Eric
Porter, Barry (Wirral S)
Porter, David (Waveney)
Portillo, Rt Hon Michael
Powell, William (Corby)
Redwood, Rt Hon John
Riddick, Graham
Roe, Mrs Marion (Broxbourne)
Rowe, Andrew (Mid Kent)
Sackville, Tom
Sainsbury, Rt Hon Sir Timothy
Shaw, David (Dover)
Shaw, Sir Giles (Pudsey)
Shephard, Rt Hon Gillian
Shepherd, Richard (Aldridge)
Shersby, Michael
Sims, Roger
Skeet, Sir Trevor
Smith, Sir Dudley (Warwick)
Smith, Tim (Beaconsfield)
Spencer, Sir Derek
Spicer, Sir James (W Dorset)
Spicer, Michael (S Worcs)
Spink, Dr Robert
Spring, Richard
Sproat, Iain
Squire, Robin (Hornchurch)
Steen, Anthony
Stephen, Michael
Stewart, Allan
Streeter, Gary
Sweeney, Walter
Sykes, John

Taylor, John M (Solihull)
Taylor, Sir Teddy (Southend, E)
Temple-Morris, Peter
Thomason, Roy
Thompson, Sir Donald (C'er V)
Thompson, Patrick (Norwich N)
Thurnham, Peter
Townend, John (Bridlington)
Townsend, Cyril D (Bexl'yh'th)
Trend, Michael
Twinn, Dr Ian
Viggers, Peter
Walker, Bill (N Tayside)
Waller, Gary
Wardle, Charles (Bexhill)
Waterson, Nigel
Watts, John
Wells, Bowen
Wheeler, Rt Hon Sir John
Whittingdale, John
Widdecombe, Ann
Willetts, David
Wilshire, David
Winterton, Mrs Ann (Congleton)
Winterton, Nicholas (Macc'f'ld)
Wolfson, Mark
Wood, Timothy
Yeo, Tim
Young, Rt Hon Sir George

**Tellers for the Ayes:**
   **Mr. Simon Burns and**
   **Dr. Liam Fox.**

### NOES

Alton, David
Austin-Walker, John
Barnes, Harry
Beith, Rt Hon A J
Benn, Rt Hon Tony
Campbell, Ronnie (Blyth V)
Carlile, Alexander (Montgomery)
Clapham, Michael
Clwyd, Mrs Ann
Cook, Frank (Stockton N)
Corbyn, Jeremy
Corston, Jean
Foster, Don (Bath)
Gerrard, Neil
Gordon, Mildred
Graham, Thomas
Hall, Mike
Hardy, Peter
Harvey, Nick
Henderson, Doug
Heppell, John
Hinchliffe, David
Hodge, Margaret
Jones, Ieuan Wyn (Ynys Môn)
Lewis, Terry

Lynne, Ms Liz
McCartney, Ian
Mackinlay, Andrew
Maddock, Diana
Mahon, Alice
Marek, Dr John
Marshall, Jim (Leicester, S)
Michie, Bill (Sheffield Heeley)
Oakes, Rt Hon Gordon
Olner, Bill
Paisley, The Reverend Ian
Pickthall, Colin
Sedgemore, Brian
Simpson, Alan
Skinner, Dennis
Spearing, Nigel
Steinberg, Gerry
Sutcliffe, Gerry
Tipping, Paddy
Tyler, Paul
Vaz, Keith

**Tellers for the Noes:**
   **Mr. David Rendel and**
   **Mr. David Chidgey.**

*Question accordingly agreed to.*
*Bill read the Third time, and passed.*

## BUSINESS OF THE HOUSE

*Ordered,*

That, at the sitting on Wednesday 24th May, the Speaker shall, not later than one and a half hours after their commencement, put the Questions necessary to dispose of proceedings on the Motion in the name of Mr. Robert Jackson relating to Disclosure of Select Committee Papers, &c.; and the said Motion may be entered upon and proceeded with, though opposed, after Ten o'clock.—*[Mr. Wells.]*

## NORTHERN IRELAND

*Ordered,*

That Mr. James Cran be discharged from the Northern Ireland Affairs Committee and Mr. Richard Spring be added to the Committee.—*[Sir Fergus Montgomery, on behalf of the Committee of Selection.]*

## Meat Products (Imports)

*Motion made, and Question proposed,* That this House do now adjourn.—*[Mr. Wells.]*

9.9 pm

**Mr. Paul Tyler** (North Cornwall): In recent months we have heard a great deal about the export of livestock. Consumers, producers and all those who are concerned with animal welfare should be examining the implications of that controversy for the import of meat and meat products. My text tonight is as follows:

"Some people, led by some supermarkets, are selling veal that may be imported but take great care to ensure that it comes from humane rearing sources in Holland and elsewhere. I hope that nothing that we say today will diminish our commitment to that type of effort because, every time that a supermarket does that, it helps us to ensure that animals are reared humanely before we manage to change the law to ensure that they are reared humanely."—*[Official Report,* 22 February 1995; Vol. 255 , c. 295.]

I think that we would all agree with that. Who made those remarks? It was none other than the Minister of Agriculture, Fisheries and Food in a debate in this place on 22 February. He went on to say that the case for such a selective attitude to imports was "interesting and powerful". The question is why he does not follow his point to its logical conclusion and take action to exclude products that do not meet our own standards of animal welfare and hygiene.

That is the real debate that should be occurring, and the furore in Plymouth, Brightlingsea, Shoreham and elsewhere has surely distracted attention from it. The fact is that farm animal welfare standards in the United Kingdom are unparalleled anywhere in Europe and probably in the world. Instead of vilifying our farmers we should be celebrating their achievements and considering how best to export our standards to the rest of the European Union.

The real issues are three-fold: first, promoting the highest possible standards of farm animal welfare, including poultry, and meat hygiene across the whole of the European Union; secondly, sustaining and promoting the development of a vibrant, prosperous and innovative agricultural community in the United Kingdom and throughout the European Union; and, thirdly, ensuring that fair competition takes place in a genuine single market. Obviously those three issues are closely related.

The public demands meat that has been produced in the most humane fashion possible and that is as hygienic and of as high a quality as can be achieved. If consumers think that they are getting less than that from domestic producers, they will buy elsewhere and our farmers will suffer accordingly. As most farmers know, in that way the highest standards of animal welfare and hygiene are not just an irksome burden, but the bedrock of their trade and a vital marketing tool.

Equally, it must be the business of government to work at every level to ensure that those objectives are met. It is emphatically not sufficient merely to set up new mechanisms to introduce new policies in the United Kingdom. For example, policing the quality of domestically produced meat is a key weapon in the battle to ensure that British produce maintains and increases its competitive edge, but it is not enough. Just as important is working to promote those same virtues across the whole European Union. All too often at present the Government seem to be hell-bent on doing the opposite: punishing our farmers for their success in raising standards.

Let us take Britain's pig producers as an example. New Government regulations mean that they will have to phase out the use of sow stalls by 1998. Although it is not without controversy, I believe that it is a welcome move that will lead to a marked improvement in animal welfare standards. There is wide agreement, even in other European states, that it is the way to go. However, the policy has been introduced in the kind of unilateral fashion that Ministers oppose so vehemently with regard to livestock exports. There has been no effective attempt to persuade fellow member states to follow our lead.

Worse still, there has been no attempt to assist domestic producers with the costs involved in making the necessary changes—at least, not in mainland Britain. In Northern Ireland, Ministers have recognised that the regulations will impose extra costs that are unique to our domestic producers and which therefore threaten to diminish their advantage over continental competitors. Accordingly, there is a system of European Union and national grant to help Northern Ireland pig producers through the transition, as I was able to disclose to the House recently.

In Scotland, Wales and England, however, the same Government Ministers see no such justification and refuse to give even a penny of assistance. Meanwhile, across the channel, our competitors are laughing all the way to the bank. Producers in Denmark and the Netherlands, who supply the lion's share of United Kingdom bacon imports, are under no such obligation to improve their standards; instead they enjoy a massively increased competitive advantage as United Kingdom producers struggle to meet the costs of conversion. If anything, the gap is widening, not narrowing.

The result is inevitable. Despite, indeed because of their uniquely high standards, British pig farmers are going out of business. A recent National Farmers Union survey showed that one in 10 pig producers could leave the industry after the introduction of the ban and that United Kingdom sow stocks could be reduced by as many as 93,000 animals. The NFU survey further estimated that that could mean a loss to the British economy of some £141 million, with 3,000 jobs slashed in the agricultural community.

The solution is not to go back on the sow stall regulations. Very few would advocate that and I certainly would not support it, but we cannot support ministerial idleness while pig producers go to the wall. The solution has to be to persuade our continental competitors to follow our lead, and the best way to do that would be to require their imports to meet our own standards. That surely is logical and reasonable and there is a powerful case for it.

When I asked the Minister, who, I am glad to see, is to respond to the debate, whether she was able to restrict the import of inhumanely reared pig meat, her answer was blithely dismissive:

"It is not apparent that it would be feasible to identify the production methods used for the imported goods mentioned."—*[Official Report,* 2 February 1995; Vol. 253, c. *848.*]

Many things in life are not apparent until one starts looking for them. That must be the experience of all Administrations and all Ministers. I would respectfully suggest that it is the job of the Minister, the Ministry and the Government to delve a little deeper into the issue. The

*[Mr. Paul Tyler]*

Minister's glib answer was merely another indication of how far removed many Ministers appear to be from the traditional rural constituencies that they claim to represent.

Imports that fail to meet our standards are not simply matters of animal welfare; they involve real dangers of hygiene and purity. In particular, there is a danger that United Kingdom consumers are being fed imported meat that contains illegally high chemical residues.

Clearly, the legal advice that the Minister and the RSPCA have received in relation to livestock exports is relevant. The obligations and responsibilities of our national Government to our national citizens to protect our consumers have a legal resonance way beyond that claimed for the treatment of animals once they leave our shores. It must be the responsibility of Government to protect our citizens, and the treaty of Rome and all other European treaties recognise that national responsibility.

I would instance the particular problem that was brought to light recently by the Consumers Association, which revealed how EU legislation on the use of hormones in livestock rearing was being routinely flouted on the continent. In tests on beef, traces of illegal synthetic hormone were found in 21 states from 10 countries and in liver samples from 11 out of 21 countries.

The drugs found, such as clenbuterol, are growth-promoting hormones and have been banned by the European Union since 1988. Their implications for human health are largely unknown but are certainly worrying. As the Consumers Association says:

"some of the samples had concentrations of clenbuterol nearly high enough to be a single medicinal dose for humans."

I have no doubt that United Kingdom farmers are not entirely blameless. One or two traces of hormones may well be found in United Kingdom produce. However, UK farmers are always at or near the top of the hygiene safety league table. Unfortunately, the same cannot be said of some continental competitors. Belgian beef liver produced nearly eight times as many positive results, and Spanish beef liver was 12 times more likely to contain traces of illegal drugs. More than one third of all Spanish beef liver sampled was found to contain traces of clenbuterol. No wonder the Consumers Association concluded that

"we advise you not to eat Spanish calf's liver or beef liver."

That is surely a worrying sign for a Government who are protecting their citizens.

The implication is that UK consumers are unwittingly eating meat that is illegally contaminated and possibly dangerous, and that many continental farmers are routinely getting away with the use of illegal drugs—thereby gaining an important competitive and economic advantage over their more scrupulous UK colleagues. The answer must be to crack down on the importing of meat that does not meet our national standards. Unlike the problem of lower welfare standards, where there may be a question mark over whether it would be legal selectively to ban the import of certain products, this case is clear cut. The chemicals involved are illegal and their use cannot be tolerated.

Luckily, we now have a body that is well placed to stop contaminated meat reaching consumers—the Meat Hygiene Service. By giving it the task of cracking down on the clenbuterol cowboys, we could score a double whammy—safeguarding public health and protecting our farmers from unfair competition. If the MHS has any useful additional role to justify the replacement of the local inspection system, that must be it. At a time when many people in the agricultural community are less than happy with the MHS—rightly so, given that its charges are dramatically higher than under the old system—such a change could not come soon enough. Otherwise, many people will ask whether the service is anything more than just another wing of the quangocracy.

The importance of urgently taking action cannot be overstated. Late at night, it may seem a peripheral problem of interest only to a few livestock farmers—but meat imports into the United Kingdom total £1.9 billion every year, while exports are worth only some £900 million. That is a £1 billion trade deficit, and the gap is growing remorselessly. The gap in bacon alone is more than £400 million, and many UK bacon producers have gone out of business.

Ministry inaction in the face of the growing livestock crisis must cease. Here is a positive way forward that would be supported by the farming industry and have the backing of animal pressure groups. The Royal Society for the Prevention of Cruelty to Animals recently reiterated that it is critically important to keep re-emphasising the long-term objective of Europe-wide improvements in animal welfare.

The stark lesson is irrefutable. Boycotting one's own exports is unlikely to cause one's competitors anything more than bemused entertainment. An entirely legal boycott of their substandard products exported to our country is far more likely to produce real economic results. Demonstrating for that purpose may have less emotional appeal, but it would have far more practical effect.

9.23 pm

**The Parliamentary Secretary to the Ministry of Agriculture, Fisheries and Food (Mrs. Angela Browning):** The hon. Member for North Cornwall (Mr. Tyler) chose for his Adjournment debate a subject about which we all care—the welfare of farm animals. His concern that some food imported into this country might not have been produced in accordance with the animal welfare standards that apply here is shared by many other people. As the hon. Gentleman acknowledged, this country has high standards of farm animal welfare. We have a strong framework of legislation in the form of the Agriculture (Miscellaneous Provisions) Act 1968 and its subordinate regulations and welfare codes. We also provide advice to farmers and conduct publicity campaigns on specific welfare issues.

To ensure that our decisions are firmly based, we have the benefit of the recommendations of the Farm Animal Welfare Council, which provides independent advice, and we carry out extensive programmes of research. Given the long history and depth of interest in this country, and the efforts that we have devoted to the issue, it is hardly surprising that some of our animal welfare requirements set higher standards than apply elsewhere.

As the hon. Member for North Cornwall has mentioned, the veal crate issue is of concern. In 1990, we banned those crates, and close confinement stalls and tethers for pigs will have to be phased out by 1999. As I am sure the hon. Gentleman must be aware, in both those cases, in 1991 the Council of Ministers regrettably refused to agree that our high standards should be included as requirements in the directive that laid down minimum standards for calves and pigs.

Unlike some other members of his party, the hon. Gentleman has been supportive of the need for the live animal export trade to continue.

**Mr. David Harris** (St. Ives): Not all that party's members.

**Mrs. Browning:** Not all its members, as my hon. Friend says, but the hon. Gentleman has publicly and openly gone on record as saying that he understands the argument. I hope that his understanding is not just based on the need to maintain a legal trade, which of course it is.

I hope that the hon. Gentleman also understands European law in relation to specific directives that allow other countries to produce under systems that we have made or will make illegal in this country. When the hon. Gentleman talks about banning specific meat imports from the European Community on the ground of the welfare conditions under which the meat has been reared, he must also understand that the same ruling would apply. It is legal in that country and we are a single market. Of all parties in the House, the federalist party that he represents surely understands the intricacies and detail of the single market, European rules, and the fact that, when a European directive applies, it does so throughout the Community; it is not selective in the way in which it applies. Instead of making cheap jibes at me about being glib, I hope that he would have the grace, therefore, to understand the law that he and his party constantly advocate should apply: we should have a single market and we should all agree to European rulings.

**Mr. Tyler:** The Minister may have missed my point about the different legality of the two positions. As I understand it, the Government of the member state is entitled to take a view about the protection of their consumers in a way that would not apply to the export of products to another country. It is a different legal situation. As I understand it, both the advice to the Royal Society for the Prevention of Cruelty to Animals and to the Minister, which we have not seen the detail of, makes that distinction.

**Mrs. Browning:** The hon. Gentleman may not have seen that advice, but he will be aware that today my right hon. Friend the Minister of Agriculture, Fisheries and Food has made a statement about the legal advice that the RSPCA has asked us to consider. In the further consideration of that legal advice, we have not changed our view; nor has the legal advice suggested to us that we should change it. As my right hon. Friend has said more than once to the House, it stands that we would be in serious trouble if we tried to contravene that legislation. That still holds good.

**Mr. Harris:** Will my hon. Friend confirm that some other members of the Liberal Democrats have actively campaigned to stop the export of animals to the continent? What are her views on that?

**Mrs. Browning:** My hon. Friend is right. We are all aware of early-day motions on the Order Paper which contain the signatures of some of the hon. Gentleman's

friends. If he really wants to start at home in convincing people about animal welfare and the legalities that apply in this matter, he could do as well to start in his own party.

**Mr. Tyler:** I honestly do not think—I hope that the Minister will agree with this—that it will be helpful if we cast aspersions across the Floor. The hon. Member for Brighton, Kemptown (Sir A. Bowden), who is a member of the party of the Minister and of the hon. Member for St. Ives (Mr. Harris), has been a vociferous advocate of a ban on all exports of livestock. I understand that there are people who take a different view. This evening, I hope that we will agree that, if we can find some way of exerting real pressure on other continental producers in the way that I have suggested, that will be helpful to all interests.

**Mrs. Browning:** After a rather personal attack on me, including the way in which I have answered questions and dealt with these matters in the past, it is no good the hon. Gentleman playing the Liberal Democrat trick of saying that we all want to work together and to be constructive. It is not possible to take that attitude after setting down a marker that he intends to be personal. If the hon. Gentleman cannot take it, he should not dish it out. I shall continue my speech.

Earlier this year, we secured the Commission's agreement to bring forward the review of the veal calves' directive, which was due originally in 1997. I hope that the hon. Gentleman will take note of that when he accuses us of doing nothing and suggests that suddenly he has had the bright idea that things should be done and that the Government have dragged their feet. My officials and I have visited European capitals to impress upon Governments the weight of scientific evidence against the close confinement of veal calves and for a diet that includes roughage and adequate iron. The scientific veterinary committee is considering all the evidence and will report to the Commission later this year.

In the meantime, there are real concerns that the impact of the two important United Kingdom measures on the welfare of calves and pigs has been limited because they do not extend to the rest of Europe and elsewhere. I should mention that, although the ban on veal crates is not part of European requirements, a number of other member states, such as Germany, have standards that are in line with our own. It is true, nevertheless, that there are some important producers that do not, and that is why we are working to have the directive amended.

There are two concerns about the use of veal crates. First, as has been discussed in the House on many occasions, there is concern about calves transported from the United Kingdom to be reared in veal crates. Secondly, there is the concern voiced by the hon. Gentleman that imports from countries with lower welfare standards continue to be accepted despite the worries about the conditions in which animals were raised. The same concern also will apply in due course to imports of pork and pork products.

The hon. Gentleman has called for action on such imports and, as I have explained, we are taking action to have our standards adopted throughout the Community. He has suggested, however, action of a slightly different sort—a ban on the import of meat and meat products from those countries with less rigorous standards than our own. It is not that simple. I am advised that selective import restrictions of the sort proposed would not be compatible

*[Mrs. Browning]*

with Community law. As I have explained, the UK is part of the single European market and we must accept products that comply with the laws of the European Community.

**Mr. Martyn Jones** (Clwyd, South-West): Will the Minister give way?

**Mrs. Browning:** Yes, if the hon. Gentleman is extremely quick.

**Mr. Jones:** I am grateful. Of course, the debate can continue until 10.30 pm. Urgency is not as great as it usually is on these occasions.

Might the Ministry not take another tack, notwithstanding the regulations that we must follow within the single market? Would it not be possible legally to provide aid to our producers to enable them, for example, to label their products as welfare friendly? That would enable them to get around the problem and ensure that we do not import welfare-unfriendly products.

**Mrs. Browning:** The hon. Gentleman has hit the nail on the head. What he has suggested is encouragingly happening in the marketplace. Consumers are becoming aware of welfare-friendly methods of rearing animals when they take decisions in butchers' shops and supermarkets to buy meat.

The hon. Member for North Cornwall seemed to suggest that consumers automatically made that choice. I think that there is quite a deal of work yet to be done to persuade consumers to be prepared to make the choice at the point of sale. I have been enormously encouraged by the supermarkets and butchers who have been talking to the Ministry about ways in which they can flag up on packaging the fact that an animal has been reared welfare-friendly conditions. I hope that we shall see more and more action to reinforce that trend.

The hon. Member for Clwyd, South-West (Mr. Jones) is right to say that such labelling informs the consumer. I hope that the consumer will be prepared to seek it out and to pay for welfare. Although we hear a great deal of noise about animal welfare, sadly that is not translated as much as we would like at the point of sale.

**Mr. Tyler:** On that point about information for consumers, will the Minister confirm that it is no longer possible to insist that the country of origin is put on a label, which might help in the circumstances about which she and I are worried?

**Mrs. Browning:** The hon. Gentleman is quite right, although in one case it is easy—for example, if one is shopping for bacon, it is pretty easy to mark out Danish bacon. That will be quite an issue once the ban on sow stalls and tethers comes into effect, because in the discussions that I have been having with the trade, undoubtedly the message to the pig farmers from the purchasers is that they will be actively sourcing pigmeat that has been reared in those conditions. I think that that is very encouraging for the pigmeat trade as a whole. So, certainly in those areas, there is a precedent that it is very clear and easy to define. In many cases, although it is not mandatory, many producers and retailers are seeing the benefit of voluntarily flagging up on the label the country of origin. The United

Kingdom is becoming known to the UK consumer as the country that does apply high welfare standards, and we are doing all that we can to encourage that and to ensure that consumers actively seek it out when purchasing from their butchers or supermarkets.

As well as Community purchases, I know that there is concern about imports from outside the Community. In particular, many people are anxious about the effect of the new general agreement on tariffs and trade and are worried that it will have a detrimental affect on welfare standards. I understand that; at the same time, we should not overestimate the risks. GATT has been in existence for close on 50 years. In all that time, there has never been a successful challenge of the farm animal welfare safeguards applied by the member Governments of GATT. Nor does the new agreement impose any obstacles to the negotiation of bilateral agreements between the European Union and its third-country suppliers of meat and live animals. Indeed, the sanitary and phytosanitary code encourages the voluntary negotiation of "equitable agreements" between member Governments, where each agrees to recognise the health and hygiene requirements of the other where these have broadly the same effect.

The Commission has made clear that, in negotiating agreements of this kind on behalf of the EU, it will want to include animal welfare. That, I am sure, is the right way forward for the time being. It will take some time to build the same consensus internationally that we have at home about the need to respect animal welfare safeguards throughout the production chain. As a result, it will be premature to try to force the issue on to the agenda of the World Trade Organisation now. Were we to do so, we would end up with international standards far below our own and far below what are needed. I am sure that the best way to achieve our objectives is to build agreement in Europe and with our trading partners outside.

I must tell the hon. Member for North Cornwall, who has raised this important debate this evening, that getting a European-wide agreement and bringing the standards of other European partner countries up to our level has been and will continue to be a major part of the work that my right hon. Friend does in his negotiations with our partners.

I have dwelt until now on the legal issues, and although I do not pretend that our task will be easy, we will continue to work towards a position where the law as it applies within the European Union and in relation to its trading partners does not require us to contemplate what to do about lower standards—because it simply will not be relevant. There is, of course, other action that we can take while that process is going on. We are already looking at the prospects for developing the welfare-friendly veal market in the UK. We held a seminar on the subject in February and are also funding a demonstration farm, where producers can see how veal can be produced in systems with the highest welfare standards, and also suggesting to caterers that they should consider using welfare-friendly veal produced under the sort of conditions that we require in this country. I recognise that welfare-friendly veal is and will continue to be a specialist market which will account for a relatively small number of calves. Nevertheless, precisely because it is a small market, the work in which MAFF and the Meat and Livestock Commission are engaged can make a difference.

I would also hope that our pig industry will seize the opportunity provided by the forthcoming ban on sow stalls and tethers, and emphasise to consumers the high welfare conditions under which British pigs are produced. When last week I attended the pig and poultry fair at Stoneleigh, I had many discussions with people in the industry. It was very encouraging to see that the people who purchase the pigmeat, the retailers and others, are very conscious of the fact that they will be demanding these high standards if they are to purchase in the future. That will automatically exclude imports from countries that do not raise their standards to the level demanded by the United Kingdom.

Consumers also need to be encouraged to look for British pork—especially bacon, which has already been mentioned this evening. Bacon has a guarantee of high welfare standards and high quality, 85 per cent. of British pigs being in the top two quality grades. At present much of the production in other member states from which we import pigmeat—mainly bacon—relies on systems that will be banned here by 1999. I think that consumers should be made aware of that.

As I have said, retailers are also conscious of the high-quality health and welfare standards that British pigmeat guarantees them. We have encouraged the development of the British quality assured pigmeat initiative, and announced recently that the Government would continue to run the pig assurance scheme—the farm assurance part of the BQAPI—and hold fees at current levels for three years. I hope that that will prove helpful to the pigmeat industry.

In recent months, retailers have made encouraging statements. I hope that those statements will come to fruition, and they will buy all their pigmeat from systems that meet our welfare standards.

Promotion of British meat and meat products is a major responsibility of the Meat and Livestock Commission, and it does a very good job. Hon. Members will have seen the entertaining and highly successful television campaign entitled "Recipe for Love". Retailers need to be encouraged to identify and promote British meat to consumers, so that all the awareness of the quality and value being built up can be fully exploited.

The hon. Gentleman also mentioned the question of meat products coming into the United Kingdom and the possibility that they may contain veterinary medicine residues, hormone growth promoters and other types of drug which—as the hon. Gentleman rightly points out—would be a matter of great concern. Intra-Community trade in meat and animal products has now largely been harmonised: red meat and poultry products must be health marked, and accompanied by commercial documentation confirming that the consignments are in accordance with both public and animal health trade rules. Consignments of other animal products must currently be accompanied by official health certificates confirming compliance with Community or national rules, pending the introduction of new arrangements similar to those applying to red meat and meat products and poultry meat.

We take very seriously the need to test and monitor meat products that come into this country. The hon. Gentleman mentioned clenbuterol. I am aware that traces of clenbuterol have been found in meat; we are investigating the specific case that the hon. Gentleman cited, to ensure that we obtain all the facts and are able to discover how the information came through the Consumers Association and, if necessary, take action.

We should beware of complacency. The Ministry is working hard to secure EC-wide agreements to ensure that standards equal our own—not just so that people are not disadvantaged commercially; we genuinely believe in the need to raise animal welfare standards throughout the Community.

I am encouraged by what I have seen in my visits to countries in Europe. I believe that we have led the way, and that we are making some progress. I do not deny that in some cases it may be a long haul, but Britain has led the way. Farmers, the food industry and consumers also have a part to play. The Government, meanwhile, will continue to maintain the safety and quality of our meat here at home, and will do our best to ensure that standards in other EC countries are brought up to the level of ours.

# Point of Order

9.44 pm

**Mr. Nigel Spearing** (Newham, South): On a point of order, Mr. Deputy Speaker. You may know that earlier today Madam Speaker replied to me on a point of order about the contents of a letter that she sent to my hon. Friend the Member for Neath (Mr. Hain) in connection with a matter of privilege which he raised. I should be grateful if you could relay these points to Madam Speaker on the points of order on which she graciously replied to me.

First, I take it that, because she did not say what was in the letter, it was not a ruling from the Chair in the normal sense and does not preclude any further ruling in respect of this matter. Secondly, unprecedented conduct, or possible unprecedented conduct, may require unprecedented procedures. In her letter, Madam Speaker told my hon. Friend that an early-day motion would be a possibility. However, this Session has shown that a debate arising from such a motion could not easily be instigated from the Back Benches. That is because, whereas in the last Session there were 12 occasions on which a Member winning the ballot would have been able to have a debate on such a motion, because of the Jopling arrangements there is none available in this Session. Therefore, I suggest that conditions have changed.

An early-day motion on this matter has been signed by 60 hon. Members. Will you ask Madam Speaker whether hon. Members should be able not only to defend but perhaps to explain such matters, which are of the privilege of the public rather than of the House?

**Mr. Deputy Speaker (Mr. Geoffrey Lofthouse):** The hon. Gentleman will appreciate that I am not able to deal with this tonight. I assure him that his comments will have been noted.

*Question put and agreed to.*

*Adjourned accordingly at fourteen minutes to Ten o'clock.*

# House of Commons

*Tuesday 23 May 1995*

*The House met at half-past Two o'clock*

## PRAYERS

[MADAM SPEAKER *in the Chair*]

## NEW WRIT

For North Down, in the room of Sir James Kilfedder, deceased.—[*Mr. Kirkhope.*]

## PRIVATE BUSINESS

BIRMINGHAM ASSAY OFFICE BILL

MALVERN HILLS BILL [*Lords*]
*Read the Third time, and passed.*

# Oral Answers to Questions

## EDUCATION

### Nursery Schools

1. **Mr. MacShane:** To ask the Secretary of State for Education what percentage of three to five-year-olds have pre-school places in publicly funded schools or nursery schools in (a) Great Britain and (b) France.     [23809]

**The Secretary of State for Education (Mrs. Gillian Shephard):** In 1992 all three to five-year-olds in France attended some form of schooling, including private, compared with 68 per cent. in the United Kingdom. Of the other European Union member states, only Belgium, Italy and Spain have a higher percentage attendance than the United Kingdom.

**Mr. MacShane:** I thank the Secretary of State for her answer. I hope that she will take this opportunity to deny the report in yesterday's *Daily Mail* that she plans to introduce a crazy right-wing voucher scheme which will create kiddies farms for middle-class parents. I know that she loves France as much as I do and my more serious point is, why three to five-year-olds in France get a better deal from their Government than my three to five-year-olds get from theirs. I speak as one with two children under that age.

**Mrs. Shephard:** I note that the hon. Gentleman prepared his indignation in advance. Nine out of 10 three and four-year-olds in this country have some form of pre-school education. Just over half attend nursery schools or nursery reception classes in primary schools; and 41 per cent. are registered with a play group. The hon. Gentleman spoke about assertions in the *Daily Mail*. I remind him that we have made it clear that in due course we shall announce our proposals for new places with new

money for children under five. When we make that announcement the mechanisms by which those places will be provided will become clear.

**Sir David Madel:** As local education authorities steadily expand nursery school provision, does my right hon. Friend agree that the Pre-school Playgroups Organisation also plays a vital role in preparing children for compulsory years at school?

**Mrs. Shephard:** My hon. Friend is right. Our announcement will make it clear that we are promoting good quality, and choice and diversity for parents. Our objective is most specifically not to put private or voluntary providers out of business.

**Mr. Don Foster:** Further to the Secretary of State's response to the hon. Member for Rotherham (Mr. MacShane) may I ask her to tell the House a bit more precisely when she is likely to make her announcement about the expansion of nursery education? Does she agree that a voucher system would not provide the necessary resources for places for children in terms of physical facilities, or the training for the high-quality teachers needed for high-quality nursery education?

**Mrs. Shephard:** I say again that we shall make the announcement when the policies are ready. The delivery mechanisms will be part of that announcement. I have already said this afternoon—and on many other occasions—that our plans will promote good quality and choice and diversity; obviously good quality includes the right qualifications and training.

**Mr. Riddick:** Does my right hon. Friend agree that the provision of nursery places for all four-year-olds provides the Government with an excellent opportunity to do something popular—to provide vouchers to parents and thereby give them more choice? Will she take this opportunity to say that she does have sympathy with the article in the *Daily Mail*; and that she will not adopt the sort of hotchpotch compromise trailed in some newspapers, or the sort of scheme that the DFE has some expertise in creating?

**Mrs. Shephard:** I thank my hon. Friend. The delivery mechanisms, including vouchers, bidding systems and so on, are part of the policy considerations that we are currently looking at. Nothing has been ruled in and nothing ruled out.

**Mr. Kilfoyle:** Does the Secretary of State recall the Chief Secretary's speech on nursery vouchers to the Centre for Policy Studies on 15 March, when he described himself as a
"heavy handed Chief Secretary pre-empting the proper process of Government decision making"?
In view of yesterday's *Daily Mail* article, will she tell the House who determines education policy for the Government—the Secretary of State or the Chief Secretary?

**Mrs. Shephard:** I am sure that the editor and proprietor of the *Daily Mail* will be enchanted to know that the paper's every word is so carefully perused by Opposition Members.

As for the Chief Secretary's words at the seminar, I am not sure that I recall them too clearly, but I must tell the hon. Gentleman that I and my team of Ministers are in charge of education policy.

## Stamford Endowed Schools

**2. Mr. Quentin Davies:** To ask the Secretary of State for Education if she will make a statement on future access to the Stamford endowed schools.        [23810]

**The Parliamentary Under-Secretary of State for Schools (Mr. Robin Squire):** I understand that Lincolnshire county council is consulting on a proposal to phase out its scholarship scheme for 25 boys and 25 girls to attend the two Stamford endowed schools.

**Mr. Davies:** Is my hon. Friend aware that these county scholarships, which have enabled children who qualify academically in Stamford to go to the Stamford school and the high school—both excellent schools—irrespective of their parents' means, have been a priceless educational asset to generations of Stamford children? Is he further aware that the only reasons why the county council is planning to abolish the scholarship scheme are ideological prejudice and sheer malice? *[Interruption.]* Does my hon. Friend agree that the behaviour of Opposition Front Benchers, who are shouting now, is contemptible? They take advantage of educational choice for their own children in London, yet when they come to power with their Liberal poodles in Lincolnshire they try to destroy parental choice there.

**Mr. Squire:** My hon. Friend has touched on a sensitive point with Opposition Members. I am sure that he is right about the many boys and girls in Lincolnshire who have benefited in past years, but I am afraid that this is a matter for Lincolnshire county council alone to determine. My right hon. Friend has no jurisdiction, provided that there are sufficient other places for school pupils in the area. I note, however, that the headmaster of Stamford school has described the proposal as social and educational vandalism.

## Grant-maintained Schools

**3. Mr. Waterson:** To ask the Secretary of State for Education how many grant-maintained schools there are in the south-east.        [23811]

**Mr. Robin Squire:** There are 300 grant-maintained schools in London and south-east England, including nearly half the maintained secondary schools in the region.

**Mr. Waterson:** Can my hon. Friend confirm that there is not a single grant-maintained school in east Sussex? Does he agree that that is a great shame; and will he undertake, with his ministerial colleagues, to do everything in his power to communicate to parents, governors and teachers the tangible benefits of GM status?

**Mr. Squire:** I willingly give an assurance to my hon. Friend in answer to his question. He will recognise that the growth of grant-maintained schools is determined by parental ballots and I am afraid that only three out of about 250 governing bodies have so far consulted parents by such a ballot. None is yet benefiting from the improvements that grant-maintained status brings. I have some good news for my hon. Friend. Earlier this year I approved the first grant-maintained school in west Sussex and I strongly suspect that its good influence will waft across the border in the very near future.

**Mr. Tony Banks:** The Minister will recall that there is only one grant-maintained school in the London borough of Newham—Stratford school, which has been judged to be failing. The Secretary of State has now sacked the chairman of governors and the governors and put her own people in. When will the Minister be prepared to sit down with the local education authority to discuss the educational welfare of the children at Stratford school, or is he going to continue, for party political purposes, to throw money at Stratford school, despite the fact that it is failing and will continue to fail?

**Mr. Squire:** First, I must clarify something that the hon. Gentleman said. The former chairman of governors resigned; he was not sacked. On the more substantial point, I trust that the hon. Gentleman shares our wish to see education improve in that school. It is recognised that it is not at the level that it should be and the Government, through the newly appointed governors, are taking steps to ensure that standards will improve at that school, which will benefit all pupils there now and, indeed, in the future.

**Mr. Gale:** My hon. Friend knows that as a result of the Government's policy, Kent county has a very wide range of choice of schools, including excellent grant-maintained schools. He also knows that those schools are staffed by excellent and dedicated teaching staff. Is it not right that those teachers should be paid properly and is it not a disgrace that the Labour and Liberal administration that runs Kent county council is refusing to pay them to score party political points while knowing that it has the money to do so?

**Mr. Squire:** My hon. Friend makes a serious point. I note that other of our hon. Friends from Kent have made similar comments recently in the House. If it is true, that through mismanagement, Kent has discovered that it has significant sums with which it could have fully funded the teachers' pay rise, it is very important that all the people of Kent know exactly where the finger of guilt should be pointed, and that is certainly at Kent LEA.

## Special Needs

**4. Mr. Austin-Walker:** To ask the Secretary of State for Education if she plans to review the resources available for education for children with special needs.
        [23812]

**Mrs. Gillian Shephard:** The special educational needs code of practice, which came into effect in September 1994, will encourage schools to make more effective use of their budgets for pupils with those needs. How each local education authority determines its priorities is a matter for the authority concerned.

**Mr. Austin-Walker:** Will the Secretary of State confirm that the special educational needs tribunal has heard only about 50 of the 500 appeals before it and will she ensure that the tribunal has sufficient resources to clear the backlog? Further, while Opposition Members welcome the code of practice, we recognise that resources are needed for it to be put into place.

Is the Secretary of State aware that many local authorities are not meeting the six months timetable for statementing because of the shortage of educational psychologists? Will she make the resources available to ensure that that can be rectified and provide additional resources in 1996-97 for the additional training that will be needed for special educational needs co-ordinators?

**Mrs. Shephard:** Local education authorities have a duty to provide for the education of statemented pupils. They should provide additional weighting for pupils with special needs. The hon. Gentleman may not be aware that an Audit Commission survey in 1992 found that two thirds of head teachers did not know how much was in their budgets for special educational needs, hence the need for greater transparency was made mandatory under the code. I certainly agree that the work of tribunals has some backlog at the moment, partly because this is a new system.

The hon. Gentleman also mentioned training. He should know that GEST, the grant for education, support and training, amounts to £27.8 million this year, an increase of £4 million on last year, and makes provision to support training for educational psychologists, among other things.

**Mrs. Peacock:** My right hon. Friend will be aware of the unacceptable delays that have occurred in the past in respect of some appeals to her Department. Will she tell me and the House how long it will take the SEN tribunal to deal with the case that I am about to put to it which involves a very bright child who does not have a school to go to in September?

**Mrs. Shephard:** In that case, I should hope that the tribunal would deal with the matter with all dispatch. It is clearly urgent.

### Vandalism

5. **Mr. Janner:** To ask the Secretary of State for Education if she will make a statement on the level of vandalism in schools.     [23813]

**The Minister of State, Department for Education (Mr. Eric Forth):** The Department for Education survey of security in schools shows that vandalism accounts for 80 per cent. of the incidents of school crime.

**Mr. Janner:** Does the Minister know that there is a serious plague of vandalism in the city of Leicester, with no fewer than 796 incidents in my constituency alone in the past financial year? Is he aware of my very useful and constructive conversation with the Secretary of State and her promise to come to Leicester to see the results of that vandalism and talk to the people on the ground? Will she be kind enough to let us know when we are likely to have the pleasure of welcoming her and whether the Department has done anything about helping schools to cope with vandalism since our conversation?

**Mr. Forth:** My right hon. Friend hopes to visit very soon. When she does, I hope that she will learn from the schools affected and from the local education authority about the measures that they are taking within their remit to ensure that this serious problem is tackled. There are many possibilities open to schools and local authorities. For example, GEST funding and supplementary credit approvals may be given, single regeneration budget

money may be made available and closed circuit television is proving to be very successful in reducing vandalism to zero where it was previously often pernicious. I hope that local people will describe to my right hon. Friend what they are doing to tackle this difficult problem.

**Mr. Jacques Arnold:** Does my hon. Friend consider it a quite extraordinary act of vandalism that the school budgets in Kent should have been shortchanged by £3.8 million by the Liberal county council—*[Interruption.]*

**Madam Speaker:** Order. The hon. Gentleman must relate his question to that on the Order Paper, which is not concerned with finance. The hon. Gentleman had the chance to raise that earlier.

**Mr. Arnold:** Is not it a remarkable bit of vandalism that, although there is a surplus of £17 million, our schools are shortchanged?

**Madam Speaker:** Order. The hon. Gentleman has abused the procedure. I hope that the Minister will answer according to the original question and not as widened by the hon. Gentleman.

**Mr. Forth:** That echoes the remarks made by my hon. Friend the Member for Stamford and Spalding (Mr. Davies), who referred to the latest act of socialist vandalism by his LEA. It seems to be an increasing but regrettable feature of some local education authorities.

**Mr. Barry Jones** *rose—*

**Madam Speaker:** Perhaps the hon. Member for Alyn and Deeside (Mr. Jones) can make a better stab at it.

**Mr. Jones:** Is not there a link between rampant vandalism and 16 years of Conservative Government?

**Madam Speaker:** Order. I think that that is known as a quid pro quo, and the Minister is not answering.

### Standard Spending Assessment

6. **Mr. David Atkinson:** To ask the Secretary of State for Education what plans she has to change the present education standard spending assessment formula. [23814]

**Mr. Robin Squire:** My hon. Friend the Minister for Local Government, Housing and Urban Regeneration is reviewing the area cost adjustment. We also keep under review the education factors in the standard spending assessment methodology. Before making any changes, we will take careful account of the views of the local authority associations.

**Mr. Atkinson:** I thank my hon. Friend for responding positively to the representations that I and my Dorset colleagues made to him recently about the adverse comparisons between neighbouring LEAs. Will any new LEA funding formulas be more transparent and demonstrate to governors and parents that they reflect fairly the actual costs of providing education in our schools?

**Mr. Squire:** My hon. Friend refers to the alluring prospect of some simple formula involving a sum per pupil. In practice, there would always have to be some way of allowing for the inevitably higher costs of educating pupils in certain circumstances and areas. As the House will be aware, we are looking at the possibility of a national funding formula, but I would not want to mislead the House by suggesting that it is imminent. Significant practical difficulties have to be overcome.

**Mr. William O'Brien:** When considering a review of the education SSAs, will the Minister take into consideration the need to provide more resources to make available a general educational facility for nursery schools? When adjusting the SSAs, will he also take into consideration consultation with parent and teacher organisations?

**Mr. Squire:** As the hon. Gentleman knows, the SSA is ultimately simply a distribution mechanism. The total size of the budget is determined in discussion with other Government colleagues. If the hon. Gentleman is adding his name and suggestion to the growing list of Labour commitments, we would simply note it.

**Sir Malcolm Thornton:** Is my hon. Friend aware that there will be widespread support, especially at school level, for the prospect of a re-think of the way in which we fund our schools and that there is overwhelming evidence that needs-led funding requires active consideration? Is he also aware that the Select Committee on Education has done some work on that subject and has produced a report, which would not be a blueprint but would nevertheless add to the debate on the possibilities of a national funding formula and which I commend to him?

**Mr. Squire:** I am grateful to my hon. Friend, whose work as Chairman of the Select Committee on Education is so good, sound and gives us many practical suggestions, as indeed, is the work of the Select Committee as a whole. From his position, he will know how true were my earlier comments about the difficulties that attend such a change.

**Mr. Bryan Davies:** Even if it were conceivable that the Government were to move swiftly to change the formula, how soon would they be able to repair the damage done to the fabric of our education system this year? The National Association of Head Teachers has pointed out that already more than 2,500 teachers' jobs have gone, £300 million has been stripped from schools' budgets and the Government's depredation, to refer to an earlier question, has been much more damaging than that which any vandals could do.

**Mr. Squire:** The hon. Gentleman makes no reference to the rising standards in our schools, which is the key point of education. He also makes no reference to the significantly increased sums of capital build in the forthcoming year. If he is suggesting that he would spend significantly greater sums were his party in government, let him come up with a figure, say what it is and get the approval of the hon. Member for Dunfermline, East (Mr. Brown), then we will start to take his criticism seriously.

### Grant-maintained Schools

7. **Mr. Thurnham:** To ask the Secretary of State for Education how many grant-maintained schools there are in the north-west.      [23815]

**Mr. Robin Squire:** There are currently 84 grant-maintained schools in the north-west of England.

**Mr. Thurnham:** When we next have a ballot in the north-west, will my hon. Friend address parents on the very great benefits of grant-maintained schools and invite the Leader of the Opposition to join him on the platform so that the right hon. Gentleman can condemn all the rubbish put out by the Labour party in the north-west?

**Mr. Squire:** I sense that if I were to go to a school and speak about the undoubted benefits of GM status during a ballot, I might find subsequently a small problem or two, vis-à-vis legal advice. The serious point that my hon. Friend makes is worth making. It is not that we even know the Opposition policy on opt-out schools. In this month alone, we have been asked to choose between the comments of the hon. Member for Sheffield, Brightside (Mr. Blunkett), who says that he is in favour of opt-out schools but says nothing specific, and those of the shadow spokesman for Wales, who has said that all the Labour party members in Wales are totally against opt-out schools. Which one speaks for the Labour party?

**Mr. Pike:** Does not the Minister recognise that the majority of parents in Lancashire and the north-west do not want GM schools? All they want are schools provided by the local education authority which have sufficient funding to provide the right quality and standard of education for our children.

**Mr. Squire:** As my earlier answer to my hon. Friend the Member for Bolton, North-East (Mr. Thurnham) indicated, significant numbers of parents want grant-maintained schools in the north-west. They are enjoying them, and they would enjoy even more of them if the hon. Gentleman and his colleagues were not so innately opposed to them.

**Mr. Dover:** Does the Minister acknowledge that the Labour-controlled county council in Lancashire has transformed a 1 per cent. real increase in last November's budget into a 5.5 per cent. cut in the county? Does my hon. Friend agree that the only way to get real increased cash resources to schools is to have a much wider provision of grant-maintained schools?

**Mr. Squire:** Undoubtedly, one of the many benefits of grant-maintained status is that by devolving control of all the budget to the school governors, one gets better value for money and less need for bureaucracy in town or county hall. My hon. Friend is right.

### Capping

8. **Mr. Jamieson:** To ask the Secretary of State for Education if she will make a statement about the effects of capping on schools.      [23816]

**Mrs. Gillian Shephard:** The capping limits allow all local education authorities to increase their budgets. They have discretion over funding for their schools within the level of their cap.

**Mr. Jamieson:** Will the Secretary of State tell the House what recommendations she will make to her right hon. and hon. Friends in the Department of the Environment regarding Devon's cap, following the meeting between the Under-Secretary of State for Schools, myself and a delegation from Devon county council? Will she tell the House whether she agrees with Tory Members in the south-west, such as the hon. Members for Taunton (Mr. Nicholson) and for Exeter (Sir J. Hannam)—and even the hon. Member for Castle Point (Dr. Spink)—who believe that caps should be raised, or whether she agrees with those Conservative Members in Devon who are fully committed to lowering standards in local schools by keeping the caps in place?

**Mrs. Shephard:** I am well aware that Conservative county councillors in Devon gave an additional £4.4 million to the education service in their draft budget, within the cap. We are at present considering the appeals submitted by capped authorities and we shall take decisions in the light of available information.

**Sir Peter Emery:** Does my right hon. Friend realise that the Labour and Liberal Democrat-controlled county council in Devon three times turned down the Conservative budget which provided the money that the hon. Member for Plymouth, Devonport (Mr. Jamieson) accused us of not giving? Does my right hon. Friend also realise that the local education authority takes 28 per cent. of the standard spending assessment to run its headquarters operation? That money could go to the local schools if Devon was not so vociferous about the way in which it wishes to spend money.

**Mrs. Shephard:** My right hon. Friend makes a good point. He and some of my other hon. Friends representing constituencies in Devon have frequently made such points. Devon receives more per pupil in its education SSA than 35 other local education authorities.

## Assisted Places

10. **Mr. David Martin:** To ask the Secretary of State for Education how many children have an assisted place at a private school.                                    [23819]

**Mrs. Gillian Shephard:** Almost 29,800 children hold Government-assisted places in independent schools in England in the current year. In addition, other children are supported in independent schools by local education authorities.

**Mr. Martin:** Can my right hon. Friend confirm that the assisted places scheme is popular with parents because of its educational value and the opportunities provided, not least by places given to pupils in Portsmouth? Will she take every opportunity to point out the fact that the vindictive educational vandals on the Labour and Liberal Democrat Benches would abolish the assisted places scheme if the British people were ever foolish enough to elect a Labour Government?

**Mrs. Shephard:** The assisted places scheme has helped more than 70,000 children since its inception. It is a success and it is popular. The Government believe in encouraging choice and diversity in education, a policy consistently opposed by the Opposition who, if they have a position on the matter, seem to believe that they can exercise as parents choices that they vote to deny to others.

**Mr. O'Hara:** Is not the assisted places scheme more to do with propping up a foundering private system than with the opportunities it gives to the children whom it is draining from the state system, together with resources? Is not it a fact that the value that is vaunted for the assisted places scheme is certainly not borne out by the examination results achieved by the children involved?

**Mrs. Shephard:** Oh, how wrong the hon. Gentleman is. The assisted places scheme is about the extension of choice and about excellent examination results. Assisted places scheme pupils in 1994 had pass rates of more than 90 per cent. in both GCSE and A-levels. The scheme also encourages a high stay-on rate. It is an investment in opportunity which the Opposition would lose no time in abolishing.

**Mr. Anthony Coombs:** Given that the incomes of 60 per cent. of the parents of children with assisted places are less than the national average and that the head of the headmasters conference said that the cost to the Exchequer of the assisted places scheme was less than the average for a state school, does my right hon. Friend agree that the Labour party's opposition to the assisted places scheme is based not on logic or on good education but purely on ideology and envy?

**Mrs. Shephard:** Given that the aim of the scheme is to widen the choice of able children from less well-off families, one would have hoped that Opposition Members would support it. Their attitudes are to do with class envy, as my hon. Friend remarks.

**Mr. Bryan Davies:** Will the Secretary of State confirm that, if the money devoted to the assisted places scheme were devoted to the state sector, 5,000 additional teachers could be employed to assist in reducing the class sizes which she seems determined to drive up?

**Mrs. Shephard:** The hon. Gentleman has forgotten that pupils transfer with their funding, which is unfortunate given that he occupies a place on the Opposition Front Bench. It would be interesting if the hon. Gentleman would confirm that his party intends to abolish the scheme in the unlikely event of the Labour party ever attaining power.

## Parental Choice

11. **Mr. Pawsey:** To ask the Secretary of State for Education what assessment she has made of the contribution of choice and diversity to the quality of education and the contribution of grammar schools, city technology colleges and grant-maintained schools to parental choice and the quality of education.     [23820]

**Mr. Robin Squire:** The exercise of informed parental choice has a key role to play in raising standards. Grammar schools, grant-maintained schools, city technology colleges and specialist colleges mean greater diversity in the kinds of schools to which parents can apply, and high-quality education to large numbers of pupils.

**Mr. Pawsey:** Does my hon. Friend agree that the overwhelming majority of the nation's parents want greater freedom of choice and diversity in education? *[Laughter.]* Does he further agree that Opposition Members—who are currently laughing about education and do not see it as an important matter, as we do—would abolish grant-maintained schools, grammar schools and the assisted places scheme, all of which are in demand by parents? Would not the cost of abolishing those schemes come from the scarce resources in the education budget? Would that not represent a total waste?

**Mr. Squire:** Not only is my hon. Friend right but, unusually, he understates. We can see from the answer to a previous question that a further group of schools will be threatened should the lot opposite come to power. The

Government want all schools to develop their own identity, while the Opposition are motivated more by dogma and are prepared to attack excellent schools in the name of that dogma.

**Mr. Sheerman:** If the Minister is going to talk about the proper use of taxpayers' money, will he defend the information he gave to me in a written answer, that his Department is spending millions of pounds on brainwashing parents in favour of grant-maintained status, including producing a free video which is placed on every seat at every vote? That is not about choice, and it should be paid for by Conservative central office.

**Mr. Squire:** I would have hoped that the hon. Gentleman would share our wish that all ballots should take place in an informed and accurate way. The publicity to which he referred must comply with the proper codes of government conduct, and it is not the equivalent of party propaganda. I certainly bow to the hon. Gentleman's greater knowledge of that subject.

**Sir Teddy Taylor:** Is the Minister aware of the remarkable educational achievements of Southend's four grammar schools, which are unique in offering free education to one quarter of all children from Southend-on-Sea? What steps can he take to protect those schools from Lib-Lab-controlled Essex county council's appalling proposal to abolish free school transport, which will mean that freedom of choice will be available only to the upper-income groups? Would not Keir Hardie, who was a remarkable, truthful socialist, turn in his grave at the thought of that appalling proposal?

**Mr. Squire:** As my hon. Friend is aware, I have considerable knowledge of the achievements of Southend schools to which he rightly refers. I was particularly saddened to read about the proposals of Essex local education authority, which, as my hon. Friend implies, can result only in ensuring that the children who go to those schools in the future are likely to be from better-off families than at present—now, they are drawn simply on the basis of their educational merit.

**Mr. Campbell-Savours:** If state schools are now so superb, is it not time that Conservative Members of Parliament took their children out of the private sector and sent them into the public sector? Furthermore, if these schools are so good, is it not about time that a member of the royal family sent his or her children into the public sector?

**Mr. Squire:** Well, there was a lot of bile there, was there not, Madam Speaker? First, as a state-educated pupil, I have no reason to apologise for the state of my education then or, more important, the state of education in our maintained schools now. It is improving, but it must improve more. How the hon. Gentleman has the gall to talk about private education, given the nature of the Leader of the Opposition, I simply do not understand.

### A-levels

12. **Lady Olga Maitland:** To ask the Secretary of State for Education what comparisons she has made between this year's GCE A-level results and those from previous years.     [23821]

**The Parliamentary Under-Secretary of State for Further and Higher Education (Mr. Tim Boswell):** Since 1980, the proportion of 18-year-olds achieving two or more GCE A-levels has doubled from 14 per cent. to 28 per cent.

**Lady Olga Maitland:** I thank my hon. Friend for that excellent news about the increase in GCE A-level passes. Of course, it is due to successful Government education policies. Will my hon. Friend tell the House what steps he intends to take to maintain the rigorous standards of A-levels and thus public confidence in them?

**Mr. Boswell:** We are absolutely committed to the maintenance of standards and rigour in A-levels and that is fundamental to the remit that we have given to Sir Ron Dearing's review of the qualifications framework from age 16 to 19. My right hon. Friend the Secretary of State has also invited the Office of Standards in Education to undertake a further inspection of GCE A-levels and to report in 1996. That inspection will deal with such matters as consistency of standards in GCE A-levels over time.

**Mrs. Jane Kennedy:** Does the Minister accept that a proper comparison of A-level successes could be made only if other qualifications on offer to older students were also taken into consideration, including the higher national certificate? Will he take the earliest opportunity to consult his hon. Friend the Minister for Merseyside to find out whether a way can be found to save the theatre wardrobe course in Liverpool—a higher national certificate course of the highest quality, which is a great success and attracts students from throughout the country, but which, unfortunately, is due to close?

**Mr. Boswell:** I can report to the House that, alongside the success of GCE A-levels, there has been a massive expansion in the range and quality of vocational qualifications. I advise the hon. Lady, however, not to smuggle in a question about a particular course, which I am empowered neither to provide nor to withdraw, although I recognise her concern. I cannot answer at the Box for that suggestion.

**Dame Elaine Kellett-Bowman:** Does my hon. Friend agree that grant-maintained schools in the north-west have done especially well in their results and that no grant-maintained school in Lancaster or Cumbria has had to declare any permanent teacher redundant?

**Mr. Boswell:** I agree with my hon. Friend in every respect, save that her encomiums for grant-maintained schools are characteristically confined to the north-west, whereas we on the Government Front Bench would apply them to the entire country. They are successful schools with very high standards.

### Special Needs

13. **Ms Lynne:** To ask the Secretary of State for Education what new plans she has to meet the special educational needs of children.     [23822]

**Mr. Forth:** The Education Act 1993 and the code of practice that came into force last September provide an improved framework for meeting special educational needs. The Department has in place a range of measures to support and monitor the implementation of the code.

**Ms Lynne:** Does the Minister accept that one of the advantages of nursery education is that a child's special educational needs can be diagnosed at an early stage? Does he agree that the proposed voucher scheme will mean that children from poorer families will be disadvantaged and their special educational needs will not be diagnosed at such an early stage?

**Mr. Forth:** No, I cannot agree with the point that the hon. Lady makes. With expanded pre-five provision, there is the potential that many special educational needs could and should be diagnosed much earlier. Whatever delivery mechanism is eventually determined, those advantages could, would, should and will be spread to everybody, regardless of his or her means.

**Mr. McLoughlin:** Does my hon. Friend agree that there seems to be a wide divergence throughout the country in terms of the amount of money spent on special educational needs? Is he aware of the growing support on the Conservative Benches for a national funding formula for education, so that we can have transparency in educational funding throughout the country rather than some of the money being salted away by local education authorities?

**Mr. Forth:** Yes. My hon. Friend, typically, has hit on an important point. One of the great advantages of the code of practice and the procedures surrounding it is that, for the first time, we can see much more clearly where special needs money is directed, what use is made of it and who is doing what. As we see that increasingly clearly, authorities that shortchange parents and pupils, particularly those with special educational needs, will be identified, flushed out and shamed into doing something significantly better.

## PRIME MINISTER

### Engagements

Q1. **Mr. Jenkin:** To ask the Prime Minister if he will list his official engagements for Tuesday 23 May. [23839]

**The Prime Minister (Mr. John Major):** This morning, I had meetings with ministerial colleagues and others. In addition to my duties in the House, I shall have further meetings later today.

**Mr. Jenkin:** Further to the prior notice that I have given my right hon. Friend on the subject of the forthcoming intergovernmental conference, will he reassure the House that, contrary to indications in *The Sunday Times* this week, the Government will bid for a net retrieval of power from the European institutions? Is not our resolve in this matter an increasingly defining issue between the Government and the Opposition? Does he agree that our determination to secure the powers of the nation state contrast utterly with the Leader of the Opposition, who has nothing but a soundbite and a submissive smile—*[Interruption.]*

**Madam Speaker:** Order. Let us make some progress.

**Mr. Jenkin:** I see that the yobs are out in force today, Madam Speaker. As I was saying, the Leader of the Opposition's idea of a nation state is Europe.

**The Prime Minister:** I am grateful to my hon. Friend for giving me notice of the broad subject that he intended to raise. I did read the speculative story in *The Sunday Times*, which is speculating on decisions and matters that

are still under discussion, which have not remotely been concluded and will not be concluded for some time. The general approach that the Government will take has been set out on many occasions. We believe that Community action should be used only where it is necessary and valuable and should not include going into what my right hon. Friend the Foreign Secretary has called the nooks and crannies of daily life. At the IGC, I shall block any attempt to extend Community competence into intergovernmental areas such as foreign affairs, defence and home affairs and I shall aim to strengthen subsidiarity, which has already led to a reduction in Commission activity. My hon. Friend is entirely right about the differences between the Conservative party and the Opposition, and they become clearer.

**Mr. Blair:** I welcome the Prime Minister's assurance that the new committee on Nolan will look at how, not whether, it implements the Nolan recommendations. Can I take it that that includes the specific recommendation that the amount paid to Members of Parliament under outside consultancies will be included?

**The Prime Minister:** Let me make it entirely clear to the right hon. Gentleman what I said in the House, without any dissent from him or any other hon. Member, when I set up the committee. I said then:

"Recommendations affecting the Members and procedures of this House will, of course, be for the House to decide."—[*Official Report*, 25 October 1994; Vol. 248, c. 759.]

We have now seen the report. I have said repeatedly that I favour greater transparency and accept the broad principles of the Nolan committee. We need to examine how those principles will work and what their implications will be for Parliament. I hope that that can be done on an all-party basis, which would be in the interests of the House, so that the country can see that the House is seeking to live up to the highest standards which I wish it to have and which, I believe, the right hon. Gentleman has also said he wishes it to have.

**Mr. Blair:** I welcome that and I take it that that answer ensures that the new committee will look at how but not whether the recommendations are implemented. Can the Prime Minister therefore say whether it is his understanding that the new committee will report before the long summer recess its recommendations on how the Nolan recommendations are to be implemented?

**The Prime Minister:** We have set out some detailed proposals on what might be the remit of the committee and they are the subject of current discussion with the hon. Member for Dewsbury (Mrs. Taylor). Those discussions must continue with my right hon. Friend the Leader of the House in the hope that an agreement on that remit is reached.

On the speed of reporting to the House, I certainly anticipate that the committee will make rapid progress. I hope that agreement could be reached on publishing at least an interim report before the House rises for the summer recess. The committee itself must determine how rapidly it can discuss the matters in question.

There is no doubt among those hon. Members who have taken the trouble to read the Nolan committee report that it refers to many matters of great difficulty, on which the Nolan committee believes the House should decide how they are carried forward. This is a matter of great importance to the future of the House and it is vital that it is properly examined and got right.

Q2. **Mr. John Marshall:** To ask the Prime Minister if he will list his official engagements for Tuesday 23 May. [23840]

**The Prime Minister:** I refer my hon. Friend to the answer I gave some moments ago.

**Mr. Marshall:** My right hon. Friend will be aware that, at 6 o'clock last night, the House rejected a Labour-inspired amendment that would have cost the taxpayer £250 million. Is he also aware that, at 6 o'clock last night, the Leader of the Opposition was addressing an audience of City fat cats—*[Interruption.]*—and promised to renounce the high tax and spend policies that have characterised every Labour Government since the war? Is my right hon. Friend aware that that was the fifth time the right hon. Gentleman has admitted that he was wrong? He was wrong on the Common Market; wrong on defence; wrong on industrial relations reform; and wrong on privatisation. Five wrongs do not make a right leader for the country.

**The Prime Minister:** I was not aware of the coincidence of timing between the Opposition amendment, designed to spend more public money, and the right hon. Gentleman's proposal to cut inflation and cut down on public spending. I have to say to the House that I am unsurprised by that contradiction, which is by no means the only contradiction between what the leader of the Labour party says and what the Labour party does. Every time we have dealt with monetary policy to restrain inflation, we have been criticised by the Opposition for putting interest rates up. Every time there has been a dispute of some sort, they wish to spend more money on it. Every time we have tried to restrain expenditure, they have called for more expenditure. There is, to put it kindly, a disconjunction between what they say and what they do.

Q3. **Mr. Livingstone:** To ask the Prime Minister if he will list his official engagements for Tuesday 23 May. [23841]

**The Prime Minister:** I refer the hon. Gentleman to the answer I gave some moments ago.

**Mr. Livingstone:** Has the Prime Minister had time today to read the latest edition of the "Socialist Economic Bulletin"—*[Laughter]*—which demonstrates that, since 1979, dividend payments as a proportion of gross domestic product have increased by £22 billion per annum, while manufacturing investment last year was only £12 billion? What can the Government do to ensure that increased dividend payments do not squeeze out productive investment?

**The Prime Minister:** The hon. Gentleman will be less surprised than others to know that I have, in fact, read the "Socialist Economic Bulletin"—not least because he invited me to do so before answering his question this afternoon. *[Laughter.]* Old Lambeth connections die hard.

I believe that the hon. Gentleman understates the importance of dividends, which, with capital growth, are the reason why people invest in the first place. We have at the moment perhaps the best environment for investment in this country that we have had for very many years. Three years of steady growth with low inflation has given companies the stability to take investment decisions in a secure economic environment. We can see now that investment is increasing, and the Confederation of British Industry forecasts manufacturing investment growth of 8 per cent. in the next year.

Since 1980, United Kingdom investment has grown quite substantially. In the present economic environment, I would expect it to continue to do so.

**Mr. Trotter:** Does my right hon. Friend agree that there is great anxiety about organised crime in this country? Is he aware that the Leader of the Opposition is shortly to take a Labour roadshow to north Tyneside, and would it not be appropriate if that entertainment included the Labour leader's opinions on the current police investigation into serious allegations of corruption and organised crime in the north Tyneside Labour party?

**The Prime Minister:** I am not aware of the details to which my hon. Friend refers, but I know the enthusiasm with which the Labour party likes to see matters examined and debated publicly, so no doubt the party itself will wish to hold a public inquiry into any allegations against any aspect of the Labour party.

Q4. **Mr. Bill Michie:** To ask the Prime Minister if he will list his official engagements for Tuesday 23 May. [23842]

**The Prime Minister:** I refer the hon. Gentleman to the reply I gave some moments ago.

**Mr. Michie:** Bearing in mind the sleaze and the conduct of this place, which is a debate that has been going on for some time, if the Prime Minister really wants to demonstrate to the public at large that we are going to get our act together in this place, will he ask the Conservative members of the Select Committee on Members' Interests to stop blocking the consideration of evidence and remove the Tory Whip, so that we can proceed in a proper, democratic way?

**The Prime Minister:** The hon. Gentleman knows the powers, influence and independence of Committees such as the Members' Interests Select Committee.

**Mr. Campbell-Savours:** And the Whip.

**The Prime Minister:** Before the hon. Gentleman shouts himself into trouble, I should like to say that he also knows that the membership of that Committee is approved by the House before it sits.

**Mr. Robert G. Hughes:** Does my right hon. Friend agree that it is ludicrous to try to set economic tax rates by taking the international average? Was not the import of the Leader of the Opposition's speech last night simply to try to disguise, in his characteristic way, his intention of increasing income tax rates? I take that because most Organisation for Economic Co-operation and Development countries have a higher rate of tax than this country. Instead of saying it directly, as usual the Leader of the Opposition tried to disguise it behind words.

**The Prime Minister:** It is clear that there was a certain lack of transparency in what the right hon. Gentleman said last night. There is no doubt that the UK top rate of income tax and national insurance contributions is the lowest of any country in the European Union, and we have every intention of keeping it that way. We also have the lowest main rate of corporation tax among the major industrial countries, and the burden of taxes on business in the UK is lower than in any other G7 country except Canada. That is in spite of the increases in taxation that we have had to undertake in the past few years to deal with the expenses following on the recession.

However, as the right hon. Gentleman is obviously worried about tax levels, I hope that he will demonstrate that, if and when we are able to reduce taxes, by joining us in the Lobby when we do so.

Q5. **Mr. Tony Banks:** To ask the Prime Minister if he will list his official engagements for Tuesday 23 May.                                        [23843]

**The Prime Minister:** I refer the hon. Gentleman to the reply I gave some moments ago.

**Mr. Banks:** Would it come as a surprise to the Prime Minister to learn that I am one of his admirers—indeed, I might be his only admirer? In that capacity, does he accept my great anger at the outrageous attack made upon him by Margaret Thatcher who, in her book, likens him to some sort of incompetent train spotter? That is a disgraceful attack and I think that we all feel very strongly about it. Will the Prime Minister take this opportunity to damn all Mrs. Thatcher's policies that have got him and his Government into the appalling mess in which they now find themselves?

**The Prime Minister:** The fraternity that exists between former Lambeth councillors perhaps does not entirely extend to the hon. Gentleman. It is less of a surprise to hear that he may be an admirer of mine than a shock and a disappointment.

**Mr. Brazier:** Is my right hon. Friend aware of the concern among some Conservative Members at the idea that homosexuals may shortly be admitted to the armed forces? Is it not true that a barrack room or a ship are not just places of work for service personnel but their homes? Should we not take account of the wishes of service personnel in making that decision? I ask for my right hon. Friend's assurance that he will uphold the promises that were given to the House before legislation to remove the criminal offence of homosexual activity in the armed forces went through Parliament without a vote. Will he assure the House that, if the present court case overturns the status quo, the matter will be brought to the House so that we have the opportunity to reverse the decision?

**The Prime Minister:** The House reached a decision some time ago and I do not wish to anticipate the result of the current court case. Clearly, if it produced a different set of circumstances, we would have to examine it.

As to the first part of my hon. Friend's question, I think that the service chiefs have made their view clear about the matter, and I share that view.

# Cross-media Ownership

3.31 pm

**The Secretary of State for National Heritage (Mr. Stephen Dorrell):** With permission, Madam Speaker, I should like to make a statement about media ownership.

Because of the extreme market sensitivity of this issue, I arranged for the substance of the Government's decisions to be announced by my Department before the stock exchange opened for business this morning. I am making this statement at the earliest opportunity thereafter. I hope that the House will accept this way of proceeding, for which there are clear precedents and which I discussed last week with the hon. Member for Islington, South and Finsbury (Mr. Smith), as well as the hon. Member for Caithness and Sutherland (Mr. Maclennan) and the right hon. Member for Manchester, Gorton (Mr. Kaufman).

Following the relaxation of some of the restraints on the ownership of ITV companies in December 1993, the Government announced in January 1994 that they were to review the existing rules governing media ownership. Today I have published a policy document which sets out our proposals, copies of which are available in the Vote Office. In developing the proposals, we have taken account of advice, ideas and comments from a wide variety of sources. I am grateful to all those who wrote to us and participated in the constructive debate on the issue.

Media ownership policy must balance two key objectives. First, it must underpin the diversity of viewpoint that is necessary in any healthy democracy. The Government believe that that requires additional safeguards on plurality of ownership beyond those required by competition law alone. Secondly, it must ensure that the media industry is able to respond to the changing demands of the marketplace and, in particular, that it is able to take advantage of the market opportunities which flow from accelerating technological change.

Technological convergence is not only bringing together functions that have traditionally been separated, but creating an enormous variety of new products and markets. It is inevitably difficult to predict the exact nature and pace of that change, but as different media sectors converge, media ownership regulation needs to look at the media market as a whole, if its core objectives are to be delivered.

The importance of developing a new approach will be reinforced by the introduction of digital broadcasting over the next few years. That will lead to more channels, more choice for viewers and listeners and more opportunities for media companies. The Government will follow up my announcement today by publishing their proposals for digital broadcasting later in the summer.

Against the background of those changes, I am putting forward for consultation a long-term proposal for the future regulation of media ownership which has three main features. First, the media market would be treated as a whole. Secondly, market share thresholds would be established, below which media ownership would be regulated only by normal competition law. Thirdly, a regulator would be established, who would be empowered to restrict concentration above the thresholds where he or she deemed such concentration to be contrary to the public interest.

For the purposes of consultation, I propose total media market share thresholds at 10 per cent. of the national media market, 20 per cent. of a regional market and 20 per cent. of the individual press, radio or television sectors.

Such a model would provide a flexible and durable framework, which would better accommodate the dynamic of the media industry, while continuing to safeguard the public interest in diversity and plurality. I also believe, however, that the substitution of the existing structure by an entirely new framework of rules must be based on full consultation and widespread acceptance that the new structure is fair. I shall therefore welcome views from all interested parties on the proposal.

In the meantime, however, action is required now. The Government therefore propose to introduce a package of immediate measures to remove unnecessary restrictions on the growth of media businesses. It will contain two elements.

First, I am today introducing a package of proposals for change through secondary legislation. I am laying before the House an amendment to the Broadcasting (Restrictions on the Holding of Licences) Order 1991, which, subject to the overarching 15 per cent. threshold set by the points system set out in part IV of that order, will raise the number of local radio licences that may be held by a single person from 20 to 35 and relax the subsidiary limits on the holdings of radio licences in urban areas with a population of between 1 and 4.5 million.

I am also consulting the Independent Television Commission and the BBC with a view to amending the Broadcasting (Independent Productions) Order 1991. I propose to raise the equity ceiling between independent producers and broadcasters from 15 per cent. to 25 per cent. and to amend the definition of an independent producer, so that the ownership of any broadcasting interests outside the European Union does not disqualify an EU company from independent status within the United Kingdom.

In addition, my right hon. Friend the President of the Board of Trade has agreed to amend the newspaper merger provisions of the Fair Trading Act 1973 by doubling the threshold for automatic reference to the Monopolies and Mergers Commission from a circulation of 25,000 to a circulation of 50,000.

The changes will allow greater consolidation within the radio industry, encourage greater investment and stability within the independent production sector and reduce the costs of small mergers within the newspaper industry. The remaining short-term changes that I am proposing today will require primary legislation, which will be brought forward at the earliest available opportunity.

Subject to two important safeguards, the Government propose that newspaper companies with under 20 per cent. of national newspaper circulation will be able to control up to 15 per cent. of the television market, including up to two regional ITV licences or one regional ITV licence and the Channel 5 licence. Newspaper companies with more than 20 per cent. of circulation share will be free to expand in satellite and cable up to 15 per cent. of the total television market, but regulation will continue to prevent them from owning more than 20 per cent. of any terrestrial ITV or Channel 5 licence.

The new rules will also apply reciprocally, allowing television companies to acquire interests in newspapers on the same basis.

Proposals for cross-control between television and newspaper companies will be subject to safeguards. First, any such investment will require the consent of the ITC, which will have the power to restrict transactions which it deems to be contrary to the public interest. Secondly, no cross-control will be allowed between newspaper and television companies where the newspaper company's regional titles account for more than 30 per cent. of regional newspaper circulation in the relevant ITV region.

The Government also propose that the arrangements to liberalise cross-investment between newspaper and television companies should be replicated for cross-investment in the radio sector. In addition, the Government will take the opportunity to remove the numerical limits on the holding of local radio licences, but retain the overall 15 per cent. limit on the number of points in the radio ownership system.

The Government will also abolish the rules that limit ownership between terrestrial television, satellite and cable. Terrestrial broadcasters will therefore be allowed to have controlling interests in satellite and cable companies, provided that their total interests do not exceed 15 per cent. of the total television market. Satellite and cable companies will also be able to have outright ownership of ITV or Channel 5 licences, subject to the 15 per cent. market limit and the two-licence limit.

These principles will apply subject to one condition. The current rules for ownership of non-domestic satellite broadcasters and cable operators have already allowed for a much higher level of investment by newspapers in those sectors than in terrestrial television. The Government therefore propose that satellite and cable companies that are more than 20 per cent. owned by a newspaper group with a national circulation share of more than 20 per cent. should continue to be restricted to a 20 per cent. holding in one ITV or Channel 5 licence, and 5 per cent. in any further ITV or Channel 5 licence.

Finally, as part of the review, the Government have looked again at the ownership arrangements for ITN. We have decided that the principles underpinning the Broadcasting Act 1990 remain sound, and that the 20 per cent. limit on individual stakes in ITN should remain. However, in order to give more ITV companies the opportunity to invest in ITN, we shall remove the 50 per cent. limit on total ITV holdings.

Our media industry is on the threshold of a new era. We cannot pretend that the changes in technology, and their impact on the marketplace, are not happening. We have an obligation to create the legislative framework that will allow the industry to respond to those changes. At the same time, we must protect the diversity of our media, which is an essential element of our democracy.

The approach that I have outlined today does two things. First, it suggests a fundamental long-term reform of media ownership in Britain, and allows time for the implications of this proposal to be properly considered. Secondly, it proposes some more immediate changes which balance more liberal ownership regulation with the introduction of a new provision for public interest scrutiny of the growth of media businesses. I commend it to the House.

**Mr. Chris Smith** (Islington, South and Finsbury): I welcome the document, which is long overdue. Why has there been such a long delay? In particular, why could we not have heard these announcements before the Channel 5 process was put in hand, rather than after?

Opposition Members welcome the broad, long-term approach of viewing the whole spread of the media, adopting a points system to do so, and insisting that no one company can secure a dominant position. While the principles set out by the Government in the document are broadly right, however, we believe that the practice leaves much to be desired.

Does the Secretary of State understand that he is putting enormous power into the hands of his proposed independent regulator? That regulator will have very wide discretion: he or she will have the power to make or break companies. The regulator will determine what happens to the ownership of national newspapers and television stations. But who appoints the regulator? Who will it be, and to whom will that person be accountable? Those are crucial questions, which the document leaves up in the air.

We believe that the regulator must not be "doubled up" with the Director General of Fair Trading or the ITC. Given the enormous scope and importance of the regulator's role, this must be the only thing that he or she does: he or she must not be moonlighting from other private or public responsibilities.

May we also have an assurance that the normal operation of competition policy through the Monopolies and Mergers Commission will continue alongside the new rules? Surely both must apply: one must not be a substitute for the other.

How has the Secretary of State arrived at his inadequate definition of the public interest, which will be the regulator's crucial remit? I carefully searched paragraph 6.19 of the document for the Government's definition. Diversity, accuracy, economic benefit and efficiency are all rightly included, but I sought in vain for one crucial and overwhelmingly important word—"quality". Surely quality of programme making must be at the top of the list of criteria.

In the more immediate future, is there not also a serious danger of a flurry of takeover and merger activity for hitherto independent ITV stations? If national newspaper companies with a national focus and interests seek to take over regional ITV stations, will there not be a serious danger of harming the regional character of those stations?

A sense of regional identity has been one of the glories of the ITV network since its inception. Is not the Secretary of State putting that at risk? What safeguards will he put in place? Why does the document contain no specific provisions in relation to foreign-owned media companies? Surely precisely the same rules should apply across the board, whether companies are foreign or domestically owned.

What account have the Government taken of the future of community radio stations which may lose out as new radio licences go to bigger commercial companies? There is nothing necessarily wrong with commercial radio expanding, but surely there must be simultaneous provision to protect community radio interests. Why is the document silent on conditional access and the power of media gatekeeping? It states that that issue caused concern during the consultations, but why do the Government proposals not address it at all?

Why does the entire document have about it the sense that it is trying to legislate for an old era rather than a new? It deliberately excludes digital terrestrial television, says little about subscription services, and does not

[*Mr. Chris Smith*]

address the vital issue of access by the public to broadcast sports events. Those are the new growth areas of the media world, and they are remarkable by their relative absence from the document.

The principles are surely clear. They are: diversity, plurality, quality and the best possible programmes for the viewer and listener. The rules are to make sure that there is not excessive dominance by any one commercial provider. The Government have set out some of that in their document, but there is a trail of unanswered questions and concerns over much of the detail. Ultimately, the document will not do much to benefit the ordinary viewer and listener.

**Mr. Dorrell:** I was not entirely clear whether the hon. Gentleman was welcoming the document or attacking it. As he started by saying that he welcomed it I shall take him at his word. He said that there was a trail of unanswered questions. Some of the questions that he listed are in the document in interrogative form because the document starts a consultation process on precisely the questions that the hon. Gentleman raises. Perhaps I may go through his points one by one.

The hon. Gentleman asked why it has taken so long to produce the document. The issue is important, and it is important to address it in the short and long-term contexts. I make no apology for spending time thinking through the document's short and long-term proposals.

Secondly, the hon. Gentleman asked me—presumably this was one of his trail of unanswered questions—about the shape of the regulator. That question is avowedly unanswered in the document, which sets out the need for a regulator and invites opinions on the precise shape that the regulator should take. One way of approaching that would be to vest the power in the Director General of Fair Trading and the MMC. Another way is the one which the hon. Gentleman suggested—I take that as an early response to the consultation process.

The hon. Gentleman asked me whether normal competition rules will continue to apply alongside any specific regulation of media ownership. The answer is yes.

The hon. Gentleman then asked me about the public interest in quality. He was on to an important point, even though it is not directly germane to the regulation of media ownership. We focus on quality in our television system through the ITC, through the channel allocation system, and through the conditions imposed on allocation. The document examines the whole media sector.

I am sure that the hon. Gentleman would not seriously argue for the introduction of statutory machinery to regulate quality in the newspaper sector, which is just as important a part of the media industry as television. The answer to the hon. Gentleman's question about quality is that all those provisions remain unchanged by these proposals—including the provisions in the ITC to protect the regional character of the ITV licensees.

There are no proposals to change existing arrangements governing foreign-owned companies. The Government do not believe that there is any need to change them, so we have introduced no proposals.

Community radio is an important success story from the last round of liberalisation of the radio industry; I look forward to similar success stories in other parts of the media industry, coming on the back of the deregulation that I have announced today.

The hon. Gentleman suggested that the document is silent on the subject of conditional access. It actually devotes a whole page to the subject, between paragraphs 5.12 and 5.16, where it sets out clearly the Government's position. That is that protecting the fair operation of conditional access is fully and adequately achieved by existing competition law arrangements. The DGFT has already demonstrated his willingness to use his powers in that area this year.

So I disagreed with the hon. Gentleman's concluding comments about the balance between the old and the new. The document consciously sets out to deal with today's problems and to show the direction in which we go tomorrow, and I welcome his support for that approach.

**Mr. Peter Bottomley** (Eltham): Will my right hon. Friend accept my welcome for his response to some of the open lobbying and the results of some of the seminars run by the Department? There will be great pleasure at this announcement on the part of the Pearson group, Associated Newspapers, *The Guardian* and The Telegraph Group—perhaps not shared by the Mirror Group and News International.

Will the lobbying by Channel 4 lead in time to an end to the subsidy for Channel 3 interest payments and dividends? Does my right hon. Friend expect a future paper to deal with the unnecessary restrictions that prevent British Telecom from putting television signals down telephone lines?

With the absence of scarcity, does my right hon. Friend soon expect to allow usual fair trading and monopolies and mergers conditions to apply to the newspaper business? The predatory pricing of *The Times* seems to many of us to have increased the losses of that business and to represent an unfair attack on other broadsheets.

**Mr. Dorrell:** My hon. Friend describes the document in terms that I do not recognise, and then goes on to demonstrate the importance of what it seeks to do: to concentrate on the policy objectives that we set ourselves.

The document concentrates on two key interests—plurality and diversity in the media market, and the equal and equivalent interest that the public have in strong and healthy media businesses. The proposals in the document are designed to change media ownership regulation in the service of those two objectives.

The important principle behind the funding mechanism for Channel 4 is that the people who signed contracts when the Channel 3 licences were awarded in the belief that they ran the risk of covering deficits in Channel 4, and in return for that participated in Channel 4 profits, should be entitled to the Government's protecting that interest, which formed part of the contract that they signed when the licences were awarded.

As for BT getting into broadcasting, the House will know that the Government's position is that it is important to restrain the growth of BT in that sector in the short to medium term at least, to allow other operators to set up competing distribution systems.

If my hon. Friend wishes to pursue the question of predatory pricing by individual newspapers, he will know that there are clear provisions in competition law within which that can be pursued. I am sure that the Director General of Fair Trading will look forward to hearing my hon. Friend's evidence.

**Mr. Gerald Kaufman** (Manchester, Gorton): I was concerned at the right hon. Gentleman's response to the hon. Member for Eltham (Mr. Bottomley) on the issue of Channel 4 funding, because it appeared to pre-empt his response to the Select Committee report on the British film industry. I very much hope that his mind is still open on that matter.

In support of my hon. Friend the Member for Islington, South and Finsbury (Mr. Smith), I may say that the proposals for the immediate future that the right hon. Gentleman puts before the House will arouse little controversy, and, I am sure, will be widely acceptable. On the other hand, I ask the Secretary of State to accept that what the consultation document says about the longer-term regulatory arrangements is almost certainly impracticable and quite certainly unrealistic.

It is simply not possible to regulate the technology of the future in the way that the right hon. Gentleman describes in his document. He said that we were on the threshold of a new era, but one would never have thought it from the way in which he looked at the possibility, or from the omission from his document of a policy to enable the free market to operate in the interests of the consumer.

Is the right hon. Gentleman aware that, while he includes in his document arrangements to allow newspaper groups greater freedom to cross-invest in television, television companies greater freedom to cross-invest in newspapers, and cable companies greater freedom to cross-invest in terrestrial television, he once again excludes British Telecom from the ability to compete in broadcasting television to Britain against American telephone companies, which are involved in cable in this country? While he is obstinate about that, I put it to the right hon. Gentleman that he is being a King Canute on the matter. The change has got to come, and the sooner it comes the better.

**Mr. Dorrell:** In what I had to say on the Channel 4 funding formula, I have undertaken to respond to the right hon. Gentleman's Select Committee on the question of the film industry in full within the relevant period, and I shall do that. I shall certainly set out clearly in that document a reconsidered view on the Channel 4 funding formula.

The comments that I made in response to my hon. Friend the Member for Eltham (Mr. Bottomley) reflect the basis on which the Government reached their decision at the end of last year, and that will be reconsidered in the course of the response to the Select Committee. However, I am not certain that there will be widespread expectation of a fundamental review so soon after the decision was originally announced.

I welcome the fact that the right hon. Gentleman regards the short-term changes in both primary and secondary legislation that I propose as relatively uncontroversial. I am grateful for his support on that.

In his concern about the long term, the right hon. Gentleman returns to a theme that has been a familiar subject of discussion between us: the position of British Telecom. My position, and that of the Government, on that has been clear for some time. We believe that there is a strong public interest in the establishment of competing networks alongside BT, and that is the reason why we are constricting the growth of BT into that sector against the published deadline.

**Sir Peter Emery** (Honiton): Will my right hon. Friend take congratulations on moving a long way towards dealing with this difficult position? We all welcome the part of the report that does that.

On the matter of ownership, will my right hon. Friend explain whether he has considered—and if so, why he rejected—the lesson that we might learn from France, where newspapers and other aspects of the media have to be owned by Frenchmen or French-dominated companies? Is that not something that we could emulate?

**Mr. Dorrell:** That is, of course, a subject that is regularly discussed in the context of media ownership. I am bound to say that I find that the comparison between us and the French—and, indeed, between us and many other countries—in respect of foreigners owning aspects of our media tells to our benefit. It is more attractive to have a more liberal regime such as ours, rather than the constricting type prevalent in France and elsewhere. I also observe that it is hardly a new position, but has been fundamental to newspaper economics in this country for the best part of a century.

**Mr. Robert Maclennan** (Caithness and Sutherland): In so far as the policy document will foster diversity and pluralism in broadcasting, it will be wholly welcome. I make no complaint at all about the time that it has taken to come forward with these measures, in a complex and rapidly changing technological environment. May I, however, raise two matters where I doubt that the Secretary of State's proposals will foster diversity and pluralism?

The first concerns the need to regulate the television access systems covering encroaching subscription and cable. The right hon. Gentleman will have noted what Mr. David Glencross, the chief executive of the ITC, said about the need to legislate in this sphere, but the paper speaks only of maintaining a review. Secondly, is it really satisfactory to allow the owner of 30 per cent. of newspaper coverage in a region to acquire a Channel 3 licence? It seems that there is a serious risk of regional dominance by a single owner, which would be unacceptable.

Finally, may I express my satisfaction that the Government have at last agreed to lift the restrictions on ITN ownership above the 50 per cent. level, which always seemed artificial?

**Mr. Dorrell:** I am grateful to the hon. Gentleman for his last point. As for conditional access, I can only repeat what I said earlier. I have not been persuaded that there is any need to go beyond the existing provisions of normal competition law, which require people operating conditional access systems in Britain to operate in a way that is not anti-competitive, and which satisfies normal competition law requirements. I see no need to go beyond those provisions.

I accept that the degree of regional newspaper concentration that is acceptable in the hands of someone who also controls the relevant Channel 3 licence is a matter of judgment, although I think that the 30 per cent. level that I have proposed strikes a fair balance between the interests of diversity and allowing strong and healthy media businesses to grow.

**Several hon. Members** *rose—*

**Madam Speaker:** Order. I must remind the House that, in addition to a Second Reading debate, we have another important statement. May I ask for the co-operation of the House and request brief questions and brief answers, so that we can make some progress?

**Mr. Toby Jessel** (Twickenham): Far from complaining about the delay, like the hon. Member for Islington, South and Finsbury (Mr. Smith), could I ask my right hon. Friend whether he is willing to enlarge to the House and to the country on why it is necessary to make these changes at all? Why could not things just have been left as they were?

**Mr. Dorrell:** The short answer is that real pressures are building up in the marketplace, and media businesses quite properly remind us that the existing provisions are preventing them from taking advantage of the commercial opportunities available, but no public interest is served by maintaining that regulation. Those who are in charge of a regulatory system should have to rejustify the regulation rather than have to justify lifting it.

**Mr. Tony Worthington** (Clydebank and Milngavie): Will the Secretary of State tell us which of his proposals will stimulate good-quality programme making in Scotland, Northern Ireland, Wales and the regions of England? One of the great problems about this country is its metropolitan bias.

**Mr. Dorrell:** The key issue of quality is always served, in my view, by ensuring that those who are responsible for media activity are healthy, strong businesses. I cannot see that the interest of quality is served by unnecessarily and artificially constricting the growth of a business. Having said that, and as I said in answer to the hon. Member for Islington, South and Finsbury (Mr. Smith), the key provisions for regulating the nature of the output of television and radio broadcasters are germane not to the ownership of those companies, but to the conditions on which the licence is granted. That issue is not addressed in the paper.

**Mr. Patrick McLoughlin** (West Derbyshire): Will my right hon. Friend confirm that there is nothing to stop British Telecom offering video on demand, and, indeed, owning cable companies? Why has he not brought forward proposals to ensure that the BBC puts Radios 1, 2 and 3 out to open, competitive tender? Looking at the share of the audience attracted by radio shown in the document, one sees that a far greater share of the nation's population listens to Classic FM than Radio 3, whose service could be provided by the commercial sector.

**Mr. Dorrell:** My hon. Friend's first point is right. With regard to competition in the BBC, my hon. Friend will know that the Government brought forward a White Paper on the future of the BBC during the previous summer. I would not seek to reopen those issues. The clear conclusion of that paper was that we shall continue with the present structure of the BBC, but we shall seek to reinforce the accountability mechanisms which work within it, through the agreement and the pledge to audiences, which the BBC governors will be responsible for issuing each year. The accountability of the BBC is important. I have no proposals to change its status.

**Mr. Chris Mullin** (Sunderland, South): Will the Secretary of State confirm that the document leaves

unscathed the Murdoch empire's control of 37 per cent. of national newspaper circulation, Mr. Murdoch's considerable interest in television and his monopoly of the encryption system? Will he also confirm that the document does not extend to satellite the restrictions on domestic content which apply to commercial television? How quickly does he anticipate that Carlton and Granada will be asked to disgorge their extra 18 per cent. ownership of ITN?

**Mr. Dorrell:** In answer to the last point, the enforcement of the now confirmed provisions of the Broadcasting Act 1990 is a matter for the Independent Television Commission. It will clearly proceed with the enforcement of the provision which has existed since that Act. With regard to the effect of my proposals on Mr. Murdoch's business—or, come to that, any other media business—I confirm that I do not anticipate, as a result of the Green Paper, a dramatic change in Mr. Murdoch's business—or, come to that, anybody else's business.

I am concerned to allow businesses to grow in a way which allows them to respond to legitimate market opportunities, but which subjects them to public interest scrutiny when they get above a certain size in the market. That seems to be the legitimate way in which a regulator should go about his business. I am much more concerned with the principles than I am with the specifics of a particular operator.

**Mr. Nicholas Winterton** (Macclesfield): I congratulate my right hon. Friend on his statement, which to me certainly highlights the importance of plurality, diversity and quality. With such quality clearly comes quality of programmes and regional content of programmes in the development of television.

Does my right hon. Friend accept that one of the main reasons for his statement was to give the United Kingdom media industry the opportunity to compete in the almost unlimited media market internationally, in which we can do so well? Would he answer the question put to him by the hon. Member for Islington, South and Finsbury (Mr. Smith) about the effect of the proposals on community radio, which to many people is of growing importance and which may well be adversely affected by one of the proposals that he has announced this afternoon?

**Mr. Dorrell:** I do not agree that the community radio success story is threatened by what I have announced this afternoon. I would argue that the further liberalisation I have announced is a further step down the road of liberalisation which was introduced some years ago and which made possible the growth of community radio, which my hon. Friend welcomes and which I welcome. I look for an opportunity for other small-scale operators to develop in the radio and other sectors. The proposals on digital, which I shall introduce later in the year, will also have an effect on that aspect of activity.

My hon. Friend is absolutely right to stress the huge opportunities for British media businesses that have critical mass here to exploit their skills and expertise in overseas markets. That is one of the opportunities that is further opened up by this document. I re-emphasise the point that the regulation of quality, through the Independent Television Commission and the Radio Authority, is unaffected by anything that I have done today.

**Mr. John Fraser** (Norwood): Many people will regard with incredulity the right hon. Gentleman's complacency about gatekeeping, or what he calls conditional access. He must be aware that no coherent set of principles applies to these matters, and that nobody knows from one case to another whether a complaint to the Office of Fair Trading will work. Surely the right thing is to have a coherent set of principles and something more like the arbitration system that works under the Copyright, Designs and Patents Act 1988.

**Mr. Dorrell:** One of the first Committees on which I served, with the hon. Gentleman, was the Committee considering the Bill that became the Competition Act 1980. That Act sets out precisely a coherent framework of constraints on anti-competitive practice, and it applies through the normal process of competition law to the conditional access regime that operates in Britain. That is exactly the coherent approach for which the hon. Gentleman asks; it is provided by the competition law approach that I advocate.

**Mr. Alan Howarth** (Stratford-on-Avon): Does my right hon. Friend accept that the media, in their role in mediating our democratic debates, are effectively a part of our constitution? If so, is he not right, as he proposes, to establish a policy framework which both encourages technological pluralism and sets particularly stringent safeguards against monopoly and the abuse of monopoly power in the field of the media?

**Mr. Dorrell:** I am grateful to my hon. Friend, and I agree with his point. In a healthy democracy, it is important that a diversity of voice is available through all the different forms of the media. Plural ownership—that is, ensuring that there is not excessive concentration of ownership—is one of the means of safeguarding that diversity of view.

**Mr. Dennis Skinner** (Bolsover): Does the Secretary of State agree that this statement is set against the background of the Berlusconi scandal in Italy? When the statement was drawn up, did the Government take into account trying to prevent a similar situation from happening in Britain? Apart from the 40 per cent. that goes to the BBC, could a Berlusconi type be stopped as a result of the statement?

Is it conceivable that somebody with political, television and other media strength could emerge—or could be prevented from emerging—as a result of the statement? The truth is that, taking into account the percentage they have now, six Murdoch types could arise as a result of what the Secretary of State has said. Will the Secretary of State give me a straight answer: could a Berlusconi-type scandal emerge in Britain as a result of the statement?

**Mr. Dorrell:** The hon. Gentleman asks me two straight questions, to which I shall give two straight answers. Could a Berlusconi figure emerge as a result of the statement? No. Could a Berlusconi be prevented from emerging? Yes.

**Mr. Anthony Coombs** (Wyre Forest): I recognise the importance of diversity, and I welcome the tentative liberalisation that the statement suggests. However, can my right hon. Friend tell me why it seems to be important to set a long-term target of 10 per cent. of the UK market, especially given the fact that, with digital television, satellite television and more and more interactive communication, it will be far more difficult to measure the total market, let alone to regulate it?

**Mr. Dorrell:** My hon. Friend describes the 10 per cent. envisaged in the long-term scheme as a target. That is not the word that I would use; I would describe it as a threshold. It is fair to say that, if someone owns more than 10 per cent. of the audience share of the media voice in the community, there is the potential for a public interest issue to arise. Once an operator gets beyond the 10 per cent. threshold, he will be subject to public interest regulation. That is not the same as saying that he would be prevented in all circumstances from growing above that level.

**Mr. Tam Dalyell** (Linlithgow): Is the Secretary of State aware of the genuine concerns in Scotland? Should not national newspaper sales be taken into account when assessing the eligibility for acquiring regional and local radio and television interests?

**Mr. Dorrell:** That is exactly what I propose. National newspaper circulation should be the criterion which limits the group of newspaper operators able to invest in Channel 3 and Channel 5 licences. The answer to the hon. Gentleman is that we are going in the same direction.

**Mr. Peter Atkinson** (Hexham): I welcome my right hon. Friend's proposals for liberalisation, but in the long term he must listen carefully to consultation. As he said in his statement, the media market is changing worldwide, and we need strong and significant news groups, such as the Mirror Group and News International, to compete worldwide. Would it not be a pity if those efficient groups were restricted by over-regulation by the Government?

**Mr. Dorrell:** I entirely agree that we have a clear public and national interest in strong, healthy and growing media businesses. The purpose of the paper is to encourage the growth of such businesses, while balancing the continuing and legitimate public concerns about the over-concentration of media ownership in a single hand or a few hands. My hon. Friend is right to draw attention to the importance of minimum regulation, which is necessary to deliver that important public policy objective.

**Mr. Stephen Timms** (Newham, North-East): The Secretary of State's proposals deal with regulating the media market at a regional level. How important does he regard the retention of regional identities in media terms, and how important was that consideration during the framing of the proposals? Does he accept that, if we are to secure the retention of those identities in the long term, proposals will have to be brought to this House which go further than those he has produced this afternoon?

**Mr. Dorrell:** I am a strong advocate of the propositions that regional identity is important and that regional media have an important role to play in fostering a sense of regional identity. I suspect that there is no disagreement on that matter in any part of the House.

*[Mr. Dorrell]*

The proposals do not address that issue directly, because it is not germane to the precise issue which the paper addresses—the regulation of media ownership. Concerns about regional identity in the BBC are handled through the BBC's pledge to audiences, and in the independent sector through the conditions attached to the award of licences by the ITC and the Radio Authority. That issue is not directly germane to the ownership of the companies which ultimately operate those licences.

**Mr. Nigel Forman** (Carshalton and Wallington): In an increasingly multi-media age, when the combination of technological convergence and market liberalisation—factors to which my right hon. Friend has referred—are pointing towards a seamless market in this area, should we not look carefully in the medium term at the idea of an overall regulatory system to avoid the regulatory overload and regulatory arbitrage which could follow from having a plethora of organisations minding the business of the parts of the overall sector?

**Mr. Dorrell:** My hon. Friend makes an interesting and important point which is germane to one of the important points raised by the hon. Member for Islington, South and Finsbury about the shape of the regulator proposed in the long-term scheme. There will no doubt be substantial public discussion about that, and I look forward to pursuing the matter with my hon. Friend.

**Mr. Peter Hain** (Neath): Given the technological convergence accelerated by digitalisation, and alliances such as that between Rupert Murdoch's News Corp and the American communications operator MCI—20 per cent. of which is owned by BT—are not the Secretary of State's proposals for regulation already obsolete? Should we not be looking for a merger of the telecommunications and broadcasting regulations, to create a new and common regulatory system?

**Mr. Dorrell:** That is an interesting thought that we might wish to pursue, but it is not necessary at this stage in the process, for precisely the reason that I have given in more than one answer this afternoon—it is important for us not to confuse the telecommunications industry, development of which is an important national interest, with the existing structure of the broadcast mass communications industries. There is certainly convergence between them, but we are not yet in a world where they are the same, and if we seek to leap into that, we are likely to end up with confused policy objectives.

**Mr. John Butcher** (Coventry, South-West): Does my right hon. Friend feel that the perpetual and contrived hysteria that now obtains on Radio 1 complies with any definition that he might have of public service broadcasting? Should that sort of stuff be paid for by a more or less compulsory levy on the public? As a result of today's announcement, can he reassure those of us who are fugitives from the four terrestrial television channels that the satellite channels will remain a Melvyn Bragg-free zone?

**Mr. Dorrell:** My hon. Friend asks an important question about satellite television—a matter to which the hon. Member for Islington, South and Finsbury also referred. I am with my hon. Friend rather than the hon. Gentleman. If we are to encourage the development of the new technologies of cable and satellite, it is important that we do not import into each and every cable and satellite station the same sort of objectives that we define for the mainstream terrestrial broadcasters. To do so would be to limit dramatically the growth of those new technologies, in a way that would serve no public interest and would be undesirable from an economic point of view.

**Mr. John Whittingdale** (Colchester, South and Maldon): Does my hon. Friend accept that the liberalisation that he has announced will allow the necessary investment to come forward, if we are to take full advantage of the opportunities for technological development in the broadcasting industry? Does he also accept that, as technology allows the further proliferation of channels, it may be possible to relax the rules still further, and that, in due course, the media can be governed by the same rules that govern every other industry?

**Mr. Dorrell:** My hon. Friend has argued that case for some time, and I am aware of his views. For reasons that I have already given, I do not believe that we are in a world—or likely to be for the foreseeable future—in which monopoly regulation alone is sufficient control on concentration in the media market. Further restriction is necessary, but I also believe strongly that anyone who advocates further regulation, which is what I am advocating, needs to rejustify that and to retest the proposition regularly.

# VSEL

4.22 pm

**The President of the Board of Trade and Secretary of State for Trade and Industry (Mr. Michael Heseltine):** I would like to make a statement about the proposed acquisition of VSEL.

I released to the House and to the stock exchange this morning my decisions on regulatory approval for the proposed acquisition of VSEL by either British Aerospace or GEC. I shall now make a statement on the basis for my decisions in the two cases.

Because both bids satisfied the turnover criteria of the European Community merger regulation, the question of regulatory approval would normally have been a matter exclusively for the European Commission, but VSEL's facilities for the construction of nuclear submarines and other warships are plainly vital for United Kingdom national security. Accordingly, the Government took action, through the use of article 223 of the EC treaty, to assert UK jurisdiction over the two merger proposals in so far as they related to the military activities of VSEL. That was the first occasion on which the United Kingdom had invoked the procedure. In practice, the civil component of VSEL's activities is very small, but at the end of last year the EC Commission gave its approval for the acquisition of the non-military component by either British Aerospace or GEC.

The United Kingdom reserved for itself a judgment on how the Royal Navy's requirements for submarine and warship procurement would be affected by a prospective change in the ownership of VSEL. I referred both bids to the Monopolies and Mergers Commission because, given the nature of the target company, I felt it right to have a comprehensive analysis of the UK public interest in both cases, and because I was conscious of potential competition concerns in relation to the GEC bid.

I am grateful to the MMC for the thorough exercise that it has undertaken. Complex issues are involved, as is shown by the fact that the MMC Group did not reach a unanimous view on the GEC bid. But the reports have provided me with a sound basis of analysis from which I can proceed to make the decisions that fall to me under the Fair Trading Act 1973.

The MMC identified no adverse effects for the UK public interest in relation to an acquisition by British Aerospace. The British Aerospace bid is thus cleared to proceed.

The MMC was unable to agree its view in relation to the GEC bid. The majority, consisting of four out of six members, found that there would be adverse effects resulting from a GEC acquisition. Their view was that those effects would arise from a reduction in competition at both prime contractor and subcontractor levels with consequent risks to innovation and to the Ministry of Defence's ability to achieve the best value for money. The recommendation from the majority was, therefore, that the GEC bid should be blocked.

The minority view taken by the remaining two of the MMC Group was that, because of the Ministry of Defence's skills as a monopsony buyer, the GEC acquisition would make no significant difference to the degree of competition in the industries involved in warship making and would contribute to the ease of an ultimately necessary industrial rationalisation.

The advice from the Ministry of Defence to the MMC took the same view as the minority report. As the United Kingdom had claimed jurisdiction over those mergers in the light of our defence interests, I also had to give particular weight to the views of the Ministry of Defence as the customer. As will be seen from the report, the Ministry of Defence judged that the imminent bidding process for Trafalgar class submarines and type 23 frigates would be largely unaffected by a GEC acquisition. It was also confident that it had the resources and means to extract the best value for money, whoever acquired VSEL.

In the light of those considerations, I have decided to allow the GEC bid for VSEL to proceed. I take no view on whether British Aerospace or GEC should prevail. I note the assurance given to the Ministry of Defence by Lord Weinstock that, if GEC wins the competition for the next type 23 frigates, those vessels will in any event be built at Yarrow. The Government will of course be ready to use their well-established arrangements to support British Aerospace or GEC, whichever acquires VSEL, in seeking additional exports of warships to buttress declining domestic demand.

I recognise that it is unusual to set aside an adverse finding by the MMC on a prospective merger. But it is my responsibility under the Fair Trading Act to look at the UK public interest in the round, having regard to all relevant factors, including, in this case, the United Kingdom's defence interests. I have concluded that the public interest will be best served by allowing the market to determine the future ownership of VSEL and hence the industrial structure best adapted to meet the UK's foreseeable naval defence needs.

**Dr. John Cunningham** (Copeland): The President of the Board of Trade is right to assert to the House that those important matters touch on Britain's defence capability and the skills and jobs of many thousands of workers at Barrow-in-Furness, on the Clyde and, for that matter, at Vosper Thornycroft in Southampton. We welcome his decision to make a statement in response to my repeated request that he should do so.

Like the right hon. Gentleman, we have never taken sides in the matter but have pressed for both bids to be referred to the Monopolies and Mergers Commission. The President of the Board of Trade was right to make such a reference. But the first and perhaps central question that he must answer after what is an almost unprecedented decision and statement today is: why has he not accepted the decision of the Monopolies and Mergers Commission? There was little of substance in his statement to justify his decision to reject a clear and emphatic majority decision by the MMC. It is worth asking the right hon. Gentleman what in his arguments can counteract the conclusions and recommendations of the MMC that

"retaining the pressure of competition between prime contractors would be even more effective in promoting change and securing value for money . . . We see no reason to sacrifice the benefits of competition now in the hope that, if the merger were allowed to proceed,"—

this is in respect of GEC—

"there would then be possible benefits . . .

We conclude that the proposed merger may be expected to operate against the public interest."

*[Dr. John Cunningham]*

Is the right hon. Gentleman aware that those conclusions are emphatic? The MMC also stated:

"As we are unable to identify any appropriate remedies for the detriments we have identified we recommend that the proposed merger should not be allowed to proceed."

That is what the MMC concluded after a long and thorough study. The right hon. Gentleman needs to offer the House more of an argument than that in his statement about why those emphatic, clear and unequivocal recommendations should not be accepted.

What is the status of the assurances that GEC has apparently given? Were they given to the MMC or simply to the Ministry of Defence? Can the right hon. Gentleman specifically tell the House what those assurances are and what they amount to? Will those assurances be legally binding or will GEC be able to negotiate them away as events unfold? Those important questions remain, as yet, unanswered.

In allowing the bid from British Aerospace to proceed—and quite rightly—did the President of the Board of Trade or his right hon. and learned Friend the Secretary of State for Defence seek any assurances from British Aerospace about predatory pricing policy? Will there be complete transparency of bids for warship contracts in the future, whoever may emerge as the successful bidder for VSEL?

The right hon. Gentleman and the Government have decided to leave the matter completely to the market—so much for the right hon. Gentleman's apparent commitment to and belief in stringent competition policy in the United Kingdom, which he reiterated to the House yesterday. The right hon. Gentleman has taken no strategic view on the maintenance of jobs or skills in our defence industries nor, apparently, have he or his colleagues taken any strategic view on maintaining our defence capability for the future. Those two requirements are left to the market and could easily be under threat as a result.

**Mr. Heseltine:** I am grateful to the right hon. Gentleman for some of the generous things that he said at the beginning of his statement.

I do not think that the right hon. Gentleman fully appreciated what I said in my statement. If the MMC had come forward with an emphatic, clear and unequivocal recommendation, unanimously reached, I would, of course, have recognised it as part of the evidence that I had to consider. It is quite apparent, however, that the MMC found it as difficult a decision as it undoubtedly is, and as the right hon. Gentleman recognised. The fact is that the MMC divided 4:2 on the issue—the chairman is a member of the committee. If one comes down to simple numbers, one is talking about one person's view, because if one of the four had changed his mind, the outcome would have been three all. The MMC obviously reached a narrow decision.

**Mr. Derek Fatchett** (Leeds, Central): If another had changed his mind, it would have been 4:2 the other way—so what?

**Mr. Heseltine:** That is perfectly right. The division merely reveals that the MMC report does not represent an emphatic, clear and unequivocal set of advice to me. It is a majority-minority view.

I have also had to take into account the views of the Ministry of Defence. We went to Europe to claim jurisdiction over this particular case because of the essential defence interests as we saw them. The MOD told me—its view was clearly expressed to the MMC—that it believes that both bids should be allowed to proceed, because the MOD, which is the custodian of our defence interests, believes that it could handle the competitive issues involved in the process. I was influenced by its views; I believe that it is appropriate that I should be.

It is not just a question of the assurances given by GEC, because the MOD places the contracts. It is in a position to ensure that any assurances given by Lord Weinstock are honoured. He gave clear assurances that if Yarrow wins the type 23 frigate order, those frigates will be built at Yarrow. The MOD is in a position to ensure that that happens—not that I would like to cast any doubt on the integrity of Lord Weinstock's assurances.

**Mr. Barry Sheerman** (Huddersfield): What about small and medium-sized contractors if GEC gets the yard?

**Mr. Heseltine:** The hon. Gentleman asked a question from a sedentary position. If he asks it formally, I shall answer it.

The Ministry of Defence has every interest in securing the transparency of the competitive process. The Ministry of Defence is a customer. I know from experience that it does that job with great concern and care, and it has every interest in ensuring that it obtains the best value for money. It will continue to do so, and the minority view clearly made the point that it is expert in doing that.

I hope that the right hon. Gentleman will recognise that, as I said, this is not an easy decision. I take very seriously the opinions of the MMC, but I think that, in view of the fact that it was a split decision, and in view of the fact that the Ministry of Defence had such clear opinions about what the interests of the customer were, it is right to allow either of those two bids to proceed, and right for the market to determine what happens. I have no preferences one way or another. I have no knowledge whether either or both the bids will proceed.

**Mr. Peter Viggers** (Gosport): Bearing in mind the fact that the market for warships has inevitably shrunk in recent years; that, increasingly, the electronic and support systems of warships are becoming proportionately more important, so the hulls are becoming less important in the manufacture of warships; that there are other yards where warships—steel ships—can be built, including Vosper Thornycroft, which has been extremely successful in recent years, and indeed Harland and Wolff; and bearing in mind the increasing internationalisation of defence procurement regarding issues such as the Horizon frigate, does my right hon. Friend agree that it would have been unwise and artificial to prevent VSEL merging with the company that eventually emerges as the most successful of those bidding for it, and that that would not have been a wise way to proceed in international competition?

**Mr. Heseltine:** I am grateful to my hon. Friend, who represents the constituency in which Vosper is based. I have had the pleasure of visiting that company and, as everyone is, I was much impressed by the work that is going on there.

My hon. Friend makes an important argument about the nature of the purchaser of large defence procurement orders of that type. The purchaser will insist on the break-up of the contract into very large numbers of individual parts, to ensure that there is competition between subcontractors for specific items, amounting to a very large proportion of the total contract.

The Ministry of Defence is expert at doing that. It must face British Aerospace, which is the only source of our military fighter aircraft. It must deal with Rolls-Royce, which is the key supplier of engines for the defence budget. So the Ministry of Defence is very experienced at ensuring that it obtains value for money compatible with the quality that it wants.

**Mr. Nick Harvey** (North Devon): The President of the Board of Trade made a statement in the House yesterday about competitiveness, but if GEC should go ahead and acquire VSEL, where will the competition come from for the type 23s or for other future big projects? The right hon. Gentleman rightly paid tribute to Vosper, which will be in a position to bid on some occasions, but if the Government believe in competitive tendering, where will the competitive tenders come from for the big projects?

**Mr. Heseltine:** The two competitions that are likely in the immediate future—for the type 23 and the batch 2 Trafalgar class submarines—are imminent, so the competitive arrangements are likely to be in place in the event of either of those two bids proceeding. In the longer term—one is talking about, for example, project Horizon, which is the new generation frigate, as my hon. Friend the Member for Gosport (Mr. Viggers) has just said— Yarrow will be a potential competitor, as it is today.

However, I would be the first to recognise that, although in the short term the MMC says that it does not think that there are implications for the existing orders in the existing yards, in the longer term there may be rationalisation, and that has always been the dilemma that has confronted Defence Secretaries or those of us interested in competition policy.

**Mr. Phil Gallie** (Ayr): My right hon. Friend put great store on the Ministry of Defence's comments about competitiveness and on the three undertakings given by Lord Weinstock if GEC were to take over. How one can split the bids of Yarrow and VSEL to ensure that there is competition when they belong to the same company? When there are bids for subcontractors to supply those contracts, how will the interests of one company be sustained?

**Mr. Heseltine:** My hon. Friend will realise that the urgent and imminent competitions will involve the continuation of the existing teams that are at work at present and that will shortly submit the tenders that the Ministry of Defence is contemplating. That division exists already.

I do not know what length of time my hon. Friend is thinking about, but there has been a falling order book— a fall in demand—that may well lead to some rationalisation. If one considers project Horizon, the bid does not involve Vosper, which has the capability—albeit one that is perhaps spread over a longer period than other yards—to become involved in the process. Lord Weinstock has given assurances about the existence of the two teams in the immediate future for the competitions that will take place.

**Mr. Richard Caborn** (Sheffield, Central): Does the President of the Board of Trade believe that his decision

to reject the Monopolies and Mergers Commission's proposal is sound? Many people are concerned about the basis upon which the decision has been taken—value for money for the Ministry of Defence rather than competition. That is a concern as we downsize the military budget and possibly change the landscape of British industry. Will the right hon. Gentleman assure the House that that decision will not trigger a potential takeover of British Aerospace and leave only one major company to compete in Europe? In rejecting the MMC decision, the President of the Board of Trade has signalled a reorganisation of that part of British industry. Many people are concerned that we shall not receive the value for money that the right hon. Gentleman has said will flow from his decision.

**Mr. Heseltine:** I understand the difficulties associated with my decision, and many people have agonised over the various choices. That is why I have had to recognise the fact that the MMC was not able to reach a unanimous view about the matter. Therefore, I take considerable note of the views of the customer—the Ministry of Defence— which believes that it is correct to move in the direction that is possible in the light of the two bids.

**Mr. Frank Field** (Birkenhead): While the House is naturally concerned about the strategic needs of the country and, more specifically, the Government's procurement requirements, is the President of the Board of Trade aware that, when the Government announced their privatisation proposals, his Cabinet colleague, the right hon. Member for Wirral, West (Mr. Hunt), and I tried to persuade GEC to break up the Government's preferred bidding so that it could buy the Cammell Laird yard? Is the President of the Board of Trade aware of our concerns about the long-term future of Laird if VSEL were to acquire it? When the future owners of VSEL emerge and the dust has settled, will he remind the new owners that the people of the Wirral peninsula will be waiting for that company to join with local forces, to try to recreate the skilled jobs that VSEL felt that it had to destroy?

**Mr. Heseltine:** I know the hon. Gentleman's concern about his constituency and the wider region. I hope that he will understand when I say that I have tried, to the limits of my endeavour, to find a buyer or to find work for Cammell. I have done the same thing for Swan— *[Interruption.]* No. The fact is that my Department and I have literally travelled the world trying to find a solution to Swan Hunter's problems. We have not found a solution—I do not like to tell the House that, but I must do so. We have explored every practical suggestion or alternative that we could think of, without success in that case. We all know that demand has diminished.

I have looked up the sorts of speeches that Labour Ministers in my position made in order to justify nationalising the aircraft and shipbuilding industries—I shall not weary the House with the details, unless hon. Members wish me to do so. Nevertheless, Labour Ministers explained to the House as clearly as I have done the need to take difficult decisions in changing circumstances.

**Dr. Norman A. Godman** (Greenock and Port Glasgow): Many of my constituents who are employed at Yarrow in Scotstoun will be keenly interested in the statement by the President of the Board of Trade. He will not be surprised to hear me say that I sincerely hope that

[*Dr. Norman A. Godman*]

Yarrow wins the order for the type 23s. I must point out to him a misleading statement that appears in paragraph 2.10 of the document. It is entirely wrong when it talks about VSEL being the only United Kingdom shipyard that has the capacity to build warships of more than 7,000 tonnes. The President of the Board of Trade knows as well as I do that Kvaerner of Govan is building the hull for the landing platform for helicopters.

Will the right hon. Gentleman assure the House that, if Yarrow and VSEL seek to secure orders for the bigger warships, he and his right hon. and learned Friend the Secretary of State for Defence will remember that Kvaerner, as a subcontracting yard, has the capacity to build such hulls?

**Mr. Heseltine:** I fully understand the hon. Gentleman's views and his representations on behalf of his constituency. He will have noticed already that my right hon. and learned Friend has heard what he said. I shall make it my business to forward the hon. Gentleman's views to the MMC in the light of his observations about its report.

**Mr. Tony Worthington** (Clydebank and Milngavie): I obviously also speak on behalf of many of my constituents who work for Yarrow. I invite the President of the Board of Trade to make it absolutely clear what assurances have been given to him or to the Monopolies and Mergers Commission about the future of the Yarrow yard should the GEC bid be successful.

**Mr. Heseltine:** I think that we have covered that ground. Lord Weinstock has made it absolutely clear that, if his group wins the order, the type 23s will be built at the Yarrow yard. I hope that Lord Weinstock's assurance will be sufficient in those circumstances. The Ministry of Defence is also in a position to insist that the contract be fulfilled at Yarrow.

**Mr. Barry Jones** (Alyn and Deeside): Does the right hon. Gentleman acknowledge that British Aerospace plc has a magnificent exporting record and that it is the largest employer of skilled labour in this country? Does he also know that 2,000 aerospace jobs have been lost in my constituency in the past two years? My constituents would like to know what consequences the statement that he has made today will have for them.

**Mr. Heseltine:** I am proud to say that I think that I have helped British Aerospace to conclude the largest overseas contract ever won by any company in this country. I was proud to negotiate with British Aerospace the conclusion of the European fighter aircraft deal, which I think was the largest international contract that this country has ever entered into.

I have every sympathy for British Aerospace's position. I do not know whether it will continue its bid or whether it will be successful. British Aerospace has not been prejudiced in any way; it is a matter for British Aerospace to decide how it wishes to expand its activities.

**Mr. Tam Dalyell** (Linlithgow): Although I do not doubt Lord Weinstock's good faith, the fact remains that he, like the rest of us, is not immortal. The President of the Board of Trade has told us about assurances; is there any way in which such assurances could be made legally binding, even for a limited period? I realise that it is unrealistic to insist that they should be legally binding for ever, but is there not an argument that they should be legally binding at least in the medium term?

**Mr. Heseltine:** I think that the hon. Gentleman can rest upon the assurances, particularly in the light of the fact that the customer happens to be a Government Department—the Ministry of Defence. Perhaps the House should be aware of another fact. Yarrow already has the first of class of the CNGF, the common new generation frigate, so from the point of view of GEC, there is every interest in filling the work load of Yarrow until it can compete for the common new generation frigate.

**Mr. Brian H. Donohoe** (Cunninghame, South): What assurances can the President give my constituents who work at Jetstream in Prestwick?

**Mr. Heseltine:** I am not sure whether it will be affected by the decision of either of the companies to bid for VSEL. I would have to have specific information as to any concerns that exist, but I do not immediately see them.

## Points of Order

4.50 pm

**Mr. Jacques Arnold** (Gravesham): On a point of order, Madam Speaker. What can be done to protect the House from the incessant and inaccurate torrent of accusations of sleaze from the hon. Member for Neath (Mr. Hain), which has now descended into peddling accusations of sleazy deals against you on "Newsnight" last night? That cannot continue. What should be done about it?

**Madam Speaker:** I would refer all hon. Members to my short statement yesterday about all of us having to have a great deal of integrity. As I said yesterday, we cannot legislate for integrity and we cannot legislate for human behaviour. We all have to live up to the high standards that people outside the House expect of us, and the time has come when we must all look again at our consciences and address the manner in which we, as individuals, deal with each other in the House.

## Naming Ceremonies and Parental Responsibilities

4.51 pm

**Mr. Frank Field** (Birkenhead): I beg to move,

That leave be given to bring in a Bill to empower registrars of births to conduct civil naming ceremonies and to require registrars to make available to certain mothers and fathers parental responsibility agreements.

In seeking leave to introduce a naming ceremonies Bill, I assure the House that it is not a panic measure in response to the discovery that certain of our colleagues in the House seem unaware of the names by which most of us know them. It attempts to deal with a much longer-term trend in our society.

Long before we had any sense of nationhood, long before we had any comprehension of what statehood meant and even before we saw signs of government in Britain, parents would present their children for baptism. The Church taught that it was a sacrament. In those days, parents as easily understood what that meant as parents today find it difficult to comprehend the meaning of such events.

As well as celebrating a sacrament, baptism was an event to welcome a child into the community. As we have had a statement today on the remains of our great warship building yards, it is perhaps appropriate that I draw examples from our sea-going power to illustrate what has happened to the numbers being presented for baptism.

When the British expeditionary forces set sail in the first world war, practically every person in that contingent would have been baptised. When the boats left for the D-day landing, again practically every soldier and sailor would have been baptised. When we went down to the sea in great ships to engage in the Falklands war, only one third of those engaging in that conflict had been baptised.

The reasons for such a dramatic change are twofold. All organisations in decline have a tendency to be caught by fundamentalists, and the established Church is no exception. Priests increasingly refuse to baptise children who are presented by their parents. For example, last week a priest refused to baptise a child because the parents were not married, as if the position of the parent were relevant to what was to be discharged to the child. There is also a more important factor that Matthew Arnold described as the great roar as the tide went out on belief in this country.

The Bill does not pretend that it can deal with those mighty forces at work in our society, but it is an attempt to put in place an alternative to baptism, which is less frequently used than hitherto. It is a short Bill, which would allow registrars at registry offices to carry out civil naming ceremonies.

First, the Bill lists the powers of the registrar. Secondly, it lists where civil naming ceremonies can take place. Thirdly, it lists the duties and the rights of parents. That is particularly important, as increasing numbers of parents who present their children for baptism are not married. It is crucial that fathers who sign birth certificates know that, should the cohabitation split up, their legal rights would be far inferior to legally married fathers.

Although the Bill does not specify it, such a ceremony would be an occasion for both sides of the family to come together and celebrate the great event of the birth of a child and to welcome that child into the community.

[Mr. Frank Field]

It is not my idea. In a week when it is important for us all to declare the sources of the information that we use, I am happy to put it on record that the idea comes from Michael Young, who is known in the other place as Lord Young of Dartington. He is the great social entrepreneur of this century. Among his ideas, he thought of the Consumers Association, the Open university and perhaps 1,000 other useful social inventions. He also played a part in bringing forth the Family Covenant Association, whose raison d'être is to encourage ideas and make available information about alternative naming ceremonies.

Finally, the Bill is not an attempt to force people to use it as an alternative to baptism. I regret that the Bill is necessary, but it is an attempt to widen choice and, above all, to take the best from the baptismal service into the secular, to ensure that each and every child is welcomed into the wider community and that parents and sponsors are aware of their duties to that child.

*Question put and agreed to.*

Bill ordered to be brought in by Mr. Frank Field, Ms Angela Eagle, Mr. Greg Pope, Ms Diane Abbott, Mr. Alan Howarth, Mr. Malcolm Wicks, Mr. Hugh Bayley and Mrs. Diana Maddock.

NAMING CEREMONIES AND PARENTAL RESPONSIBILITIES

Mr. Frank Field accordingly presented a Bill to empower registrars of births to conduct civil naming ceremonies and to require registrars to make available to certain mothers and fathers parental responsibility agreements: And the same was read the First time; and ordered to be read a Second time upon Friday 14 July, and to be printed. [Bill 125.]

# Orders of the Day

## Criminal Injuries Compensation Bill

*Order for Second Reading read.*

**Mr. Deputy Speaker (Mr. Geoffrey Lofthouse):** I should inform the House that Madam Speaker has selected the amendment in the name of the Leader of the Opposition.

4.57 pm

**The Secretary of State for the Home Department (Mr. Michael Howard):** I beg to move, That the Bill be now read a Second time.

This is an important Bill which will make statutory provision to pay compensation to people who have had the misfortune to become victims of violent crime. It paves the way for an enhanced tariff scheme, which provides the right balance between providing for the needs of victims and protecting the interests of taxpayers by concentrating on a simple tariff approach for the majority of victims, while ensuring generous compensation for those most seriously injured.

As the House knows, we have had a non-statutory criminal injuries compensation scheme since 1964. It provides payment from public funds to the blameless victims of crimes of violence and those injured in attempting to apprehend criminals or prevent crime.

When the scheme was introduced, the Government of the day made it clear that they did not accept that the state was liable for injuries caused to people by the criminal acts of others, but they believed that the public felt a sense of responsibility for and sympathy with the innocent victim and that it was, therefore, right for that feeling to be given practical expression by the provision of a monetary award on behalf of the community. We remain of that opinion.

For the past 30 years, the scheme has been run by the Criminal Injuries Compensation Board. In the first full year of the scheme's full operation, 1965-66, the board received 2,452 applications and made 1,164 awards totalling £403,000, or about £4 million at today's prices. In 1993-94—the last full year for which audited figures are available—the board received 73,473 applications, and made 65,293 awards totalling over £165 million. That was more than double the cost in real terms only six years previously.

Under the current scheme, awards are assessed by the board on the basis of common law damages—what an applicant could expect to be awarded in a successful civil suit. Calculation of awards on that basis requires finely judged assessments of the degree of suffering and financial loss. That makes speedy decision making more difficult, and makes it hard to predict and control the future costs of the scheme. Under the able and energetic chairmanship of my right hon. and noble Friend Lord Carlisle, the board has made determined efforts to improve the workings of the scheme over the years—efforts that have met with some success. We are very grateful to Lord Carlisle and his colleagues for all that they have done.

None the less, despite those efforts and despite large increases in administrative resources, the number of unresolved eases has risen inexorably, and now stands at well over 100,000. At the same time, the costs have continued to escalate rapidly in a way that is unsustainable for a scheme funded by the taxpayer.

**Dr. Norman A. Godman** (Greenock and Port Glasgow): Can the Home Secretary confirm that the Bill would allow claims to be dealt with more expeditiously? A constituent of mine, Mr. Roberts, has been treated in a disgraceful and dilatory way by the board in regard to his entirely legitimate claim. Would the proposed scheme have provided him with a more expeditious response?

**Mr. Howard:** That is certainly our expectation. One of the main purposes of the change—although not the only purpose—is to improve the service given to claimants and to ensure that their claims are dealt with more expeditiously.

It was against the background that I have described that we decided to introduce a new, tariff-based scheme in April 1994. That scheme moved away from the one based on individual assessment and provided for payments to be made on the basis of a tariff of awards that grouped together injuries of comparable severity and allocated a financial value to them, based on awards made previously by the board.

The new scheme operated from 1 April 1994 to 5 April 1995, when the Judicial Committee of the House of Lords ruled that the method of the tariff scheme's introduction had been unlawful. That judgment, of course, related solely to the method of the tariff scheme's introduction, not its merits. The tariff scheme was therefore withdrawn immediately and the old scheme reinstated.

However, we remain firmly of the view that a tariff-based approach is the right way forward. Such an approach is easier for applicants to understand and easier to operate, with the result that—as I told the hon. Member for Greenock and Port Glasgow (Dr. Godman)—applications can be dealt with more quickly. It also enables costs to be controlled and more easily predicted.

We have nevertheless considered very carefully all the concerns that have been expressed in this House, in another place and elsewhere about the effect that a simple tariff approach can have on those who are most seriously injured. We all have immense sympathy for such victims, and it is right that we should do what we reasonably can to help them. We have therefore concluded that the tariff-based approach should be enhanced to provide payment for loss of earnings and special care for those most seriously affected by their injury. We also think it right to add payment for loss of dependency and loss of support to the lump sum award payable to family members when, tragically, the victim loses his or her life.

The Bill is accordingly intended to provide the framework for a new, enhanced tariff scheme. It sets the broad parameters for the scheme, making it clear that it is a tariff-based scheme, and leaves the detail to be set out separately. The more important details—those relating to the tariff itself, and other provisions bearing on quantum—will be subject to parliamentary scrutiny, and will require the affirmative resolution of both Houses before they can be included in the scheme.

The Bill will repeal the provisions in the Criminal Justice Act 1988 which would have made the common law damages scheme statutory. It is intended that the Bill should come into force on Royal Assent and that,

following parliamentary approval of the details to which I have just referred, the new scheme itself should start on or about 1 April 1996.

I have already placed outline details of the enhanced tariff scheme and the proposed new tariff in the Library of the House, but, for the convenience of hon. Members who may not yet have had the opportunity of seeing them, it may be helpful if I run through the main features.

There will be a basic tariff of awards. Each injury description is allocated to one of 25 specific levels which will attract a fixed payment. All successful applicants will receive an award from the tariff. In addition, those who are incapacitated as a result of their injury for more than 28 weeks will be entitled to separate payment for their loss of earnings. As under the present common law damages scheme, the payment will be subject to a cap of one and a half times the national average industrial wage. The qualifying period of 28 weeks is tied to the period for which statutory sick pay is payable. That is, we believe, the most appropriate and reasonable way of triggering special consideration for those who have been most affected by their injuries, and for whom we therefore want to make additional provision.

In cases of incapacity for more than 28 weeks, there will also be payment for special care to cover actual costs, from the date of injury, and future costs reasonably incurred. That will cover the same sort of expense for which compensation is payable under the present scheme. For example, the cost of private medical treatment would be payable if, in all the circumstances, both treatment and cost were reasonable. Payment could also cover the costs of home mobility equipment and fittings, special wheelchairs and fees for care in a nursing home.

In fatal cases, reasonable funeral expenses will continue to be reimbursed and a fixed payment will continue be made. Under the previous tariff scheme, the fatal award of £10,000 was shared between all qualifying claimants, of whom there could have been several, but, under the new arrangements, each qualifying claimant will receive an award of £5,000 unless there is only one qualifying claimant, who will receive the full £10,000. In addition, where it is appropriate, there will also be payment for loss of dependency—the family breadwinner's wages—and loss of mother's support. Here again, payment for dependency, as under the present scheme, will be capped at one and a half times the national average industrial wage. Under the enhanced tariff scheme, the upper limit for awards will be £500,000, double that payable under the old tariff scheme.

The final feature of the new arrangements is that there will be provision for payment by what is known as "structured settlement". For higher-value awards, that will enable the victim to opt for payment by the purchase of annuities, which will provide a guaranteed, index-linked stream of non-taxable payments for life, or another specified period. That should have the effect of significantly increasing the net value of the award to the victim.

**Mr. Mike O'Brien** (Warwickshire, North): I am sure that the Home Secretary does not wish to mislead the House. When people refer to the old scheme, they normally mean the scheme based on compensation for personal injuries. I presume that the Home Secretary is not claiming that the new amount is double what would be received in those circumstances; indeed, £500,000

[*Mr. Mike O'Brien*]

might be only a fraction of the sum provided under the old scheme. The Home Secretary is talking about the 1994 tariff scheme, which was, in fact, unlawful. Is not the new sum only a doubling of the sum provided under that scheme?

**Mr. Howard:** I made that absolutely clear. If the hon. Gentleman had been even half awake and half listening, he would realise that. He would also know that in only a handful of cases did the award exceed the £500,000 maximum provided by the new scheme.

**Mr. Simon Hughes** (Southwark and Bermondsey): Will the Home Secretary deal with the concern that has been expressed to all of us—it is, indeed, an obvious concern—about anomalies and discrepancies in the scheme? While an adult with a dislocated finger might receive £1,250 under the tariff scheme, a youngster who had suffered a sexual assault would receive only £1,000. Society would consider that very unbalanced. Would not independent adjudication of the tariff amounts throughout the operation of the scheme—which the Home Secretary has been asked to consider—deal with the criticisms that are being made?

**Mr. Howard:** I am not entirely sure what the hon. Gentleman means by "independent adjudication" of the tariff system. The basis on which the tariff awards have been drawn up has been made clear. As I am sure the hon. Gentleman understands, the figures were not plucked from the air. They were based on an assessment of awards that had been made under the old common law damages scheme for injuries of that kind. The tariff is the result of a very careful exercise. Of course it is not written in stone, and I am prepared to consider representations about it to see to what extent it is possible to respond to them. The hon. Gentleman will understand that, in looking at such representations, it will be important to maintain the integrity of the tariff scheme and its firm basis in awards that have been made in the past under the old common law damages scheme.

**Mr. John Morris** (Aberavon): Before he was interrupted, the Home Secretary spoke about loss of earnings. Will he explain how that applies to the self-employed?

**Mr. Howard:** It applies to the self-employed in exactly the same way as to the employed. That was the case under the old common law damages scheme.

**Mr. Edward Garnier** (Harborough): The hon. Member for Warwickshire, North (Mr. O'Brien) gave the impression that my right hon. and learned Friend the Home Secretary had personally committed some hideous offence. There were mumblings of "Unlawful, unlawful" by some Opposition Members. Will my right hon. and learned Friend confirm that in their speeches not one of the Law Lords in the Judicial Committee in the other place impugned his integrity? In the opening speech, Lord Keith of Kinkel said:

"In the present case no rights have been taken away from anyone, nor has the Minister acted unfairly towards anyone. While no doubt many members of the public may be expected to have hoped that sections 108 to 117 . . . would be brought into force, they had no right to have them brought into force. In any event, the doctrine of legitimate expectation cannot reasonably be extended to the public at large, as opposed to the particular individuals or bodies who are directly affected by certain executive actions."

Is it not an appalling abuse of the House's proceedings for Opposition Members to accuse the Home Secretary of acting unlawfully when they fail to understand the nature of the judgment in question?

**Mr. Howard:** That is no more than I would expect from Opposition Members. My hon. and learned Friend's assessment of the situation is entirely accurate. He will be perfectly aware that 10 judges considered this matter and five held in my favour while the other five held against. [*Interruption.*] That may be a matter for mirth among Opposition Members, but it clearly demonstrates that these matters are not easy to anticipate thoroughly correctly. We are in a grey area of the law in which it is perfectly possible not only for reasonable Secretaries of State but for judges, of the High Court and above, to come to different conclusions.

**Mrs. Bridget Prentice** (Lewisham, East): If five of the Law Lords found in the Secretary of State's favour, why has he brought in the Bill?

**Mr. Howard:** The hon. Lady misunderstands. It was not five Law Lords but 10 judges who considered the matter. Five of them found in my favour at different stages of the proceedings and five found against. If the hon. Lady cares to look at the record, she will understand that.

**Mr. Alun Michael** (Cardiff, South and Penarth): Perhaps the Home Secretary would cast his mind back and remember that he was repeatedly warned in the House and outside that he was acting illegally. The House of Lords has found that he was acting illegally.

**Mr. Howard:** That is more or less what I said about five minutes ago.

As I said to the hon. Member for Southwark and Bermondsey (Mr. Hughes) the tariff is based on that used in the earlier tariff scheme which has now been withdrawn. That tariff was derived from an analysis of nearly 20,000 awards made previously by the board.

Experience of operating the tariff in 1994-95 showed that some adjustments needed to be made to it, for example to incorporate injuries not previously identified and to provide for a greater range of awards in some cases. Therefore, the new tariff has been augmented by nearly 100 additional or changed injury descriptions, and now lists more than 300 injuries.

The intention is that the enhanced tariff scheme will be administered by a body similar to the Criminal Injuries Compensation Authority which administered the earlier tariff scheme. But the Bill envisages the possibility of the administration of the scheme being market-tested at some future date, although there are no immediate plans for that. As under the former tariff scheme, the Bill provides for a two-stage appeals process.

**Mr. Jack Straw** (Blackburn): Will the Secretary of State confirm that the position of scheme manager is mentioned in clauses 1 and 3 to enable the Secretary of State, if he so wishes, to appoint a private company to run the scheme?

**Mr. Howard:** I made it absolutely clear a few moments ago that we want to hold open the possibility of market testing in due course. That is because we believe in taking all necessary steps to take advantage of potential competition in the interests of the taxpayer. The Labour party has declared that it is firmly committed to the abolition of competitive tendering in local government. That shows how Labour remains in the pockets of the trade unions and how uninterested it is in the taxpayer and in how much people have to pay for their services from public bodies. We take a different view.

As under the former tariff scheme, the Bill provides for a two-stage appeals process. If a claimant is dissatisfied with the initial decision, he may ask for a review of his case by a more senior official of the body administering the scheme. If he remains dissatisfied after the review, he will have a right of appeal to an independent appeals panel, which will now come under the supervision of the Council on Tribunals.

The rules of eligibility and the procedures for making applications will remain very much as they were under the earlier tariff scheme, which itself closely mirrored the rules and procedures of the common law damages scheme. However, the time limit for making applications will be extended from the earlier tariff scheme's one year to two years. As before, the authority will have discretion to waive the time limit in exceptional cases.

Finally, I turn to costs. We have made no secret of the fact that one of the main reasons for introducing the tariff scheme last year was to contain the costs of the scheme, which were increasing rapidly. That is not just because the number of applications has been increasing by some 8 per cent. a year but because the average award has been going up each year by some 5 per cent. above inflation. Without reform, we estimate that the annual liability to compensation under the scheme based on common law damages would, by the year 2000-01, be about £460 million. The cumulative liability in the five years 1996-97 to 2000-01 would be about £1.8 billion. That level of expenditure is simply not sustainable.

Under the arrangements envisaged in the Bill, the annual liability will continue to rise year by year with no cuts and no reductions, so that by 2001 it should be about £260 million, and the five-year cumulative liability should be about £1.1 billion. That is still an enormous amount. Indeed, it is some £230 million more than the withdrawn tariff scheme would have cost. Therefore, it is not surprising that our compensation scheme is the most generous in the world, paying out more compensation than the USA, and more than all the other countries in Europe added together. I have no doubt that that will continue to happen under the proposed new arrangements.

I turn now to the reasoned amendment in the name of the Leader of the Opposition. Last week, the hon. Member for Dunfermline, East (Mr. Brown) presented himself as the iron shadow Chancellor. Yesterday evening, the Leader of the Opposition promised that he would be tough on public spending. Today, we see the other face of the Labour party. Its reasoned amendment complains about the "adequacy" of our proposals. We know what that means. It means a call for more public spending.

Victims of crime are, of course, extremely worthy recipients of taxpayers' money. That is precisely why we have, and will continue to have, by far the most generous victims' compensation scheme in the world. But there are limits to how much can be afforded for any group in society, however deserving. Being tough on public spending means being prepared to take unpopular decisions. There is no escape from that.

**Mr. Michael Stephen** (Shoreham): Would my right hon. and learned Friend accept that the financial policy of the Labour party on this and all other matters can be summed up in the words of the late Wilfred Pickles, "Give 'em the money, Barney"?

**Mr. Howard:** My hon. Friend is absolutely right. The Labour party promises the earth to every conceivable interest group: it cannot have it both ways. The same idea was put, almost as eloquently as my hon. Friend puts it, by the right hon. Member for Birmingham, Sparkbrook (Mr. Hattersley) just two months ago. Writing in *The Guardian*, he said:

"Labour now has a clear choice. It can be either the party of higher taxation and proud of it, or the party of higher taxes which it is ashamed to describe, afraid to admit and incapable of calculating with any accuracy. It cannot be the low taxation party."

That would be the honest path for the Labour party. The other would be genuinely to abandon its old tax-and-spend ways. Instead, as ever, the Labour party faces both ways at once. We have no intention of letting the Opposition get away with it. We want clear answers, and we want them now.

The Leader of the Opposition and the hon. Member for Blackburn (Mr. Straw) have tabled a reasoned amendment. Are they prepared to accept its public spending consequences? The question must be answered. Unless the hon. Member for Blackburn is prepared to answer it, he need not bother to get up to address the House; his words will not deserve a single moment of its attention.

**Mr. Michael Shersby** (Uxbridge): Does my right hon. and learned Friend agree that the reasoned amendment is simply inaccurate? It begins:

"That this House declines to give a Second Reading to the Criminal Injuries Compensation Bill because it is based on cutting the cash available to compensate victims".

It is not.

**Mr. Howard:** My hon. Friend is of course right— [*Interruption.*] I would not expect anyone as economically illiterate as the hon. Member for Cardiff, South and Penarth (Mr. Michael) to understand that, but it is manifest, for reasons that I explained earlier.

I believe that the enhanced tariff scheme provides the right balance between the needs of victims and the interests of taxpayers. It combines the benefits of a tariff-based approach, to ensure that the majority of claimants can get their compensation quickly and without undue fuss, with elements of common law damages to ensure that the needs of the most seriously injured victims are properly met.

I hope that the House will recognise that we have listened carefully to the criticisms of the earlier scheme and have made every effort to meet them as far as is reasonably possible, given the resource limitations to which any prudent Government must sensibly pay heed. The enhanced tariff scheme is a good one for victims and for the taxpayer. The Bill provides the necessary framework for that scheme, and I commend it to the House.

5.22 pm

**Mr. Jack Straw** (Blackburn): I beg to move, to leave out from 'That' to the end of the Question, and to add instead thereof:

"this House declines to give a Second Reading to the Criminal Injuries Compensation Bill because it is based on cutting the cash available to compensate victims; because the information provided by the Home Secretary is not sufficient to enable the House to judge the Bill's likely consequences for all classes of victims; because it is being introduced without proper consultation; because its proposals fail adequately to reflect society's obligations to assist victims to recover from their experience of crime; and because it fails to place victims at the centre of the criminal justice system, since it fails to require greater consideration towards them by the Crown Prosecution Service, better information about the progress of prosecutions, greater attention to the needs of victims in court, protection and help for witnesses, support for the provision of counselling and other services by voluntary organisations, and positive action by the Government to tackle the continued rise in crimes of violence."

I learned from yesterday's edition of *The Daily Telegraph* that today is the second anniversary of the right hon. and learned Gentleman's appointment as Home Secretary. In the intervening two years, confidence in the Conservatives' ability to deal with the rising tide of crime has plummeted and the Home Secretary has achieved an unenviable record as the most unpopular member of the Government—apart from the Secretary of State for Health and the chairman of the Conservative party. Little wonder, therefore, that he complained to *The Daily Telegraph* yesterday that he had received "a hard pounding".

If the right hon. and learned Gentleman is wondering why such a misfortune has befallen him he need look no further than his handling of the criminal injuries compensation scheme, for on this he has shown an arrogant disregard for the proper procedures of Parliament and a contempt for the victims of violent crime, whose numbers have risen as a direct result of the Government's failure to control the increase in violent crime.

It was, after all, the humane and acceptable face of the Conservative party—the Leader of the House—who this March warned the Prime Minister that the Government were on the

"wrong side of an argument about the treatment of the victims of violent crime",

and it is the Home Secretary who, almost singlehandedly, has placed the Government in this position.

The Secretary of State's misjudgment was his view that he could ride roughshod over established parliamentary procedures and implement fundamental changes to the 1964 scheme, not by statute approved by both Houses of Parliament but by exercise of the royal prerogative approved by neither. In taking such action, as my hon. Friend the Member for Cardiff, South and Penarth (Mr. Michael) has just pointed out, the Secretary of State cannot complain that he was not warned of the probable consequences. In March last year the distinguished former Law Lord, Lord Ackner, told the other place that he found it difficult to imagine a more arrogant refusal by a

Minister to carry out his duty. He said that he awaited with interest the first set of legal proceedings for judicial review to test the legality of the Government's action.

**Mr. Garnier:** Just for the record, will the hon. Gentleman tell us whether he agrees with the recently cited remarks by the right hon. Member for Birmingham, Sparkbrook (Mr. Hattersley)?

**Mr. Straw:** That is a matter for another debate; I shall come to costs in due course—the hon. and learned Gentleman will just have to wait with baited breath.

**Mr. Stephen:** Does the hon. Gentleman accept that Lord Ackner's language, which he has just quoted with approval, was rather strong and unjustified? The hon. Gentleman and Lord Ackner may be expressing one point of view about this rather arcane legal question, which was eventually decided by the House of Lords, but, as my right hon. and learned Friend has pointed out, no fewer than five of Her Majesty's judges took the opposite point of view.

**Mr. Straw:** The hon. Gentleman has asked me two questions: about whether the language was strong, and about whether it was justified. The answer to both is yes—it was strong and it was justified.

Warnings came not only from Law Lords and respected Members of the other place but from the shadow Home Secretary of the time, now the Leader of the Opposition, who said that if the Home Secretary's action proved unlawful,

"then the Government will have committed its worst blunder yet on its law and order package."

He too was correct.

The right hon. and learned Gentleman duly committed his blunder. Both the Court of Appeal and the Judicial Committee of the Lords found against him. The Lords concluded that his actions were not just unlawful but an

"abuse of the prerogative power".

The language used by the learned judges against the Secretary of State in both forums was strong, although it did not have to be, as was their condemnation of his actions.

As we have heard this afternoon, instead of gracefully accepting defeat in the Lords the Home Secretary and the Minister of State compounded their offence by blithely asserting that this was just a complicated technical matter and by claiming that, while five judges had found against the Secretary of State, five had found in his favour—implying some sort of draw.

The right hon. and learned Gentleman often lectures others about the need to face up to the consequences of their actions—I have a file full of his speeches to that effect—but before he examines the mote in others' eyes he should perhaps start with the beam in his own. Our judicial system, as he well knows, is based on a hierarchy of laws and/or courts. Decisions are not made, as it were, on goal aggregate; they are made after careful argument, with the superior courts necessarily able to overrule decisions of the lower courts. The fact of the matter is that both the Court of Appeal and the Judicial Committee of the Lords found that the Secretary of State had acted unlawfully.

The right hon. and learned Gentleman's response has been not to say sorry but to put up his deputy on television to make a fool of himself—as he did—by inventing a new doctrine to trivialise the decisions of the highest court in the land.

Before 23 May 1993 dawned, the Secretary of State used to be Secretary of State for the Environment, when I had the happy pleasure of opposing him. In that capacity, I recall that he never used to give up any opportunity to lecture Labour local councils on the prudent spending of public money. The wholly unnecessary court action in which he has been involved has cost the taxpayer an estimated £150,000—at least. I suggest—given the weight of opinion against him from the start and all the warnings issued by counsel—that if such sums had been spent by a Labour council the Secretary of State would have clamoured for the district auditor to be brought in. It is extremely fortunate for the Home Secretary that surcharge and disqualification do not apply to Ministers of the Crown.

The Home Secretary, unlike some badly briefed Conservative Back Benchers, at least understands that the Bill cuts the amount available for criminal injuries compensation. What else could its purpose be?

**Mr. Gary Streeter** (Plymouth, Sutton): The hon. Gentleman spoke of upholding court decisions. If he is such a firm upholder of court decisions, why did he refer in his speech to the Police Federation last Thursday to a sentence passed by the courts without telling the Police Federation members present that it had been referred to my right hon. and learned Friend the Attorney-General for being unduly lenient?

**Mr. Deputy Speaker:** Order. The hon. Gentleman is going rather wide of the debate.

**Mr. Streeter** *rose—*

**Mr. Deputy Speaker:** I have ruled that that is rather wide of the debate.

**Mr. Straw:** I was talking about Conservative Members who are badly briefed and here we have one. Parenthetically and speedily, Mr. Deputy Speaker, I may say that I made no point in my speech to the Police Federation about whether that decision had been referred to the Court of Appeal. I read out a very angry letter that had been written to one of my hon. Friends by the police officer concerned, expressing his deep concern about the way in which he had been treated by the court of first instance. I will get on, if I may.

**Mr. Streeter:** On a point of order, Mr. Deputy Speaker. I am sure that you would not like to let pass an instance of an hon. Member, perhaps inadvertently, misleading the House. I have a transcript of the hon. Gentleman's speech to the Police Federation.

**Mr. Deputy Speaker:** Order. I have already ruled that that is going wide of the debate. There the matter stands, and that also applies to hon. Member for Blackburn (Mr. Straw).

**Mr. Straw:** Thank you, Mr. Deputy Speaker. I am astonished that so many hon. Members have been excited by my speech criticising the Crown Prosecution Service.

If the Attorney-General would like to arrange time for a full debate on the matter and on other aspects of what I said to the Police Federation—

**Mr. Deputy Speaker:** Order. Let us get down to the speech that the hon. Gentleman is making today, rather than the one that he made the other day.

**Mr. Straw:** The part of my speech where I mentioned the criminal injuries compensation scheme was well received, too. I shall quote with approval the views of the Police Federation about the new scheme in a moment.

I shall return to the point that I was making before the intervention of the hon. Member for Plymouth, Sutton (Mr. Streeter), who was so badly briefed about other speeches that I have made. The Home Secretary has at least had the grace to recognise that the whole purpose of the Bill is to cut the compensation available. Why else should it be introduced?

The Bill cuts the total projected budget by more than £700 million, or 40 per cent., over a five-year period. Such cuts are bound to result in much lower awards for many victims, despite the concessions that have been forced out of the Home Secretary and which are contained in the Bill.

The Home Secretary had the cheek to talk a moment ago about the issue of honesty. Our first objection to the Government's proposals is that the Government have no mandate whatever for what they have done. They have been dishonest with the electorate. Indeed, the only mandate that could possibly be perceived from what they were saying before the election was one to continue the previous common law scheme.

Right up to and through the last election, the Conservative party never ceased to congratulate themselves on the existing, more generous common law scheme. The 1991 Conservative campaign guide, with all the accuracy that we have come to expect of Conservative central office, boasted that the existing scheme

"has been placed on a statutory basis"—

with the implication that it was already in operation—

"giving victims who suffer significant injuries an automatic right to compensation for the first time."

The 1992 Conservative campaign guide repeated that error, claiming that

"when a crime has taken place, the Government gives the utmost priority to supporting the victims."

The Conservative manifesto made similar extravagant claims.

There was not a word in any of those pre-election documents about the Conservatives' intention to slash compensation even though we now know that Ministers were considering such cuts before the last election.

In a speech that the Home Secretary made just four days before the Law Lords decision of 5 April, he said that the

"only party which truly believes in responsibility and duty is the Conservative party."

When I noticed that the date of that speech was 1 April and that the newspaper that reported it was *The Guardian*, I assumed that it was *The Guardian's* awful spoof.

**Dame Elaine Kellett-Bowman** (Lancaster): The hon. Gentleman has used that before.

**Mr. Straw:** I have not used it before because this is the first occasion on which I have read this speech.

*[Mr. Straw]*

I have now seen the Conservative central office text of the Home Secretary's speech. I wonder whether it has occurred to the right hon. and learned Gentleman, who sprays around speeches about responsibility, that responsibility and duty might have required the Conservative party to have been straight with the electorate at the last election. Of course, it would know nothing about that.

Our second objection to the proposals is that the increase in costs has arisen not by accident or act of God but out of the failure of one Government policy and as a direct consequence of another. The policy failure is their failure to control the relentless rise in violent crime. The Conservative party came to power in 1979 on a promise to control law and order and it has palpably failed to do so. Since 1979, the risk of becoming a victim of crime has not doubled but trebled: from one in 213 when Labour was last in office to 1 in 64 today. Offences of violence are still rising. Last year alone they rose by 7 per cent. "Ah" says the Home Secretary, "but that does not explain the whole of the increase in the costs of the criminal injures compensation scheme." He is right to point to a significant increase in the value of awards and in the number of applications.

**Mr. Stephen:** The hon. Gentleman will be aware that crime has been rising throughout the western world since 1979. Does he suggest that the British Government are responsible for that?

**Mr. Straw:** I had better not take any more interventions from the hon. Gentleman in order to protect him from himself. It is unfortunate that he mentions that, because if he looks at the table published by the Home Office he will see that between 1979 and 1993 this country had the worst rise of any country but one for crime, and that between 1987 and 1993 it took the jackpot. I am entitled to say that the Government promised greater law and order and to control crime in this country and have palpably failed to do so.

The Secretary of State's explanation is that the increase in the costs of the criminal injuries compensation scheme cannot be put at the door of rising crime. Of course, that is correct. There are other matters to which he draws attention, such as the increase in value of awards and the number of applications outpacing the rise in crime.

The recorded crime statistics give little detail about the severity of violent crime and whether that has changed along with the total numbers. I suspect that the increased value of awards may partly reflect an increase in the severity of the crimes committed. The Home Secretary needs to recognise that the increase in the overall number of applications is almost certainly a natural consequence of his Government's actions in publicising far more effectively the availability of compensation.

The one epitaph for the Government will be their publication of charters—citizens charters, passengers charters and victims charters. The victims charter gives pride of place to the criminal injuries compensation scheme. I wonder if it ever occurred to the Home Secretary that if the scheme was better publicised, more applications might result. Did the right hon. and learned Gentleman or his predecessor ever estimate the likely consequences of their actions when they produced the

victims charter in 1988 and republicised in 1990? Or was the charter one of the long list of cynical pre-election ploys designed to give the impression before polling day of concern for victims in the sure but secret knowledge that this insinuation of concern could be dumped once the election was out of the way?

It is no wonder, against the background of implied promises held out in the victims charter and the fact that there was no mandate whatever for these cuts, that the public no more trust the Tories on law and order than they do on tax. Even after the election, the Government's actions to change the scheme have been characterised by evasion and double-speak.

The White Paper issued in December 1993 was one of the most disingenuous documents produced by the Government and there is a long list of competitors for that title. "Wretchedly deceptive" was the verdict of my right hon. Friend the Member for Sedgefield (Mr. Blair) on that document.

The White Paper sought to pretend that its purpose was

"to provide a better service to claimants."

We have had more of such nonsense today.

We have also witnessed Ministers having to stand on their heads. To gain any kind of parliamentary approval for the Bill, they have had to make concessions in respect of loss of earnings and medical care to which, on their merit as well as on their cost, they were wholly opposed just a few months ago. On 16 June last year, Earl Ferrers said that

"a hybrid scheme would retain the worst elements of common law damages—that is, loss of earnings—and would make for great complexities and delay."—*[Official Report, House of Lords*, 16 June 1994; Vol. 555, c. 1847.]

The Secretary of State said:

"We have looked carefully at the possibility of such a hybrid scheme, but I must tell my hon. Friend"—

the hon. Member for Bury, South (Mr. Sumberg)—

"that the practical difficulties which it would involve would be insurmountable."—*[Official Report*, 20 October 1994; Vol. 248, c. 448.]

It is strange that those practical difficulties, which were insurmountable only a few months before, should have suddenly been overcome and that the worst element of common law damages—loss of earnings—should suddenly take pride of place in the scheme.

**Mr. Howard:** The hon. Gentleman misunderstands the reference to a hybrid scheme. What was being proposed by way of a hybrid scheme and what was being urged on us, especially in another place, was a scheme under which the tariff would be the only method of compensation up to a certain level and the old common law scheme—unchanged—would apply above that level. That was being advanced as a hybrid scheme. I said then that it would be unworkable, and I remain of that view.

**Mr. Straw:** That was one of the hybrid schemes but the other had a tariff plus an element for loss of earnings. I can only read out the words on the page; I am not misquoting the Secretary of State or Earl Ferrers, who said that the scheme

"would retain the worst elements of common law damages—that is, loss of earnings—and would make for great complexities and delay."

If this scheme is not a hybrid scheme—it combines a tariff with loss of earnings—I do not know what to call it but, in order to save his blushes, perhaps the Secretary of State has thought of a new title for it.

I shall outline some of our detailed objections to the Bill in a moment but I deal first with the issue of cost, which was raised by the Home Secretary. Throughout his sorry stewardship, he has always tried to shift the blame for unpopular policies or events on to someone else. We saw that earlier this year in his handling of trouble within the Prison Service and we see it now in his handling of the compensation scheme. If it has not been the victims of crime who are to blame for the cuts, it has been the Labour party.

The Secretary of State has suggested from the Dispatch Box that we are as implicated as him because we have not guaranteed that a future Labour Government would make good the cuts in the scheme which he has made. We welcome his expectation of an imminent Labour Government—that is thoroughly to be welcomed—but that Government may be two Conservative Budgets away and two public spending rounds away. He cannot even tell me what the Chancellor of the Exchequer is going to do tomorrow—indeed, the Chancellor of the Exchequer cannot even tell me that—still less what will be in his Budget in November 1995 or November 1996, so he can hardly expect a responsible Opposition to say what their spending plans will be six months after that.

What is more, we have always had the gravest doubts about the assumptions behind the escalating estimates given for maintaining the existing scheme. The Secretary of State states in the explanatory and financial memorandum to the Bill, and has repeated it since, that the cost by the year 2001 would be £460 million. I do not know whether he realises that the cost estimate for the year 2001 has already dropped by £110 million in the space of just 12 months.

Who are we to believe? Just 12 months ago, in the 1994 campaign guide, Conservative central office said—I assume that this was on the basis of information provided by the Secretary of State's special adviser and checked with the Home Office—that

"without the changes now being made, spending would have increased to around £570 million by the year 2000."

Who are we to believe—Conservative central office last year or the Home Secretary today?

I am not saying that the Secretary of State has made up the arithmetic but the figures are a moving target. They have come down by £110 million in the past 12 months, so how are we to know that they will not come down even more in the next 12 months, especially given the great sensitivity in his calculations, which I have studied carefully, to the very substantial percentage increases that are assumed in the value and number of awards likely to be made in the next five years?

**Mr. Howard:** The hon. Gentleman says that he cannot make a commitment to reinstate the scheme because the prospect of a Labour Government is so distant. Indeed, I would argue that it is considerably more distant than he suggests. However, if he says that he cannot commit a Labour Government to reinstating the current scheme on those grounds, why on earth has he tabled a reasoned amendment suggesting that the proposed scheme is inadequate? If he believes that it is inadequate, he must make a commitment to put in place a more adequate

scheme that will cost more. If he is not prepared to make such a commitment, he should not have tabled a reasoned amendment such as this.

**Mr. Straw:** I was just about to deal with the purpose of the reasoned amendment, which is to sustain the current scheme. If the Home Secretary were to join us and keep the present scheme going at the proposed budgeted level—a level which, by the way, we think, is an overestimate—and if there were a proper public expenditure survey allocation, I can think of no circumstances in which we would seek to worsen the compensation available under this scheme and no circumstances at all in which we would do that without a clear election mandate. However, if the money to pay for the scheme has gone—if there is no PES allocation—no such guarantee can be given.

If the Home Secretary squanders the money over the next two years—my hon. Friend the shadow Chief Secretary pointed out yesterday that a great deal of cash has been squandered elsewhere—we shall not have it to spend but, if he ensures that the money is there, we should not dream of changing the scheme.

I note that, in his intervention, the Secretary of State did not mention the appalling and astonishing discrepancy between the cost estimate that he now puts to the House—£460 million by the year 2000—and that given by Conservative central office this time last year of £570 million. Who do we believe—Conservative central office or him?

**Mr. Howard:** The former is a more up-to-date estimate. The hon. Gentleman may not have noticed that inflation has gone down, which is one of the factors taken into account. In addition, the average amount of each award has decreased, which is also taken into account.

What is significant is that the hon. Gentleman did not reply to my point about the Opposition's reasoned amendment. He suggested that its purpose is to maintain the old common law damages scheme for the next two years. I made it clear in the explanatory and financial memorandum to the Bill how much more that would cost. The inescapable inference therefore is that, if a Labour Government were in power for the next two years, taxation would be commensurately higher under them than under the present Government. No other inference is possible.

**Mr. Straw:** That is a silly point. The inescapable conclusion is that if we were in power we would not have duped the electorate by implying that we would keep the scheme going and then breaking the promise within about a year of coming to power.

The estimate of costs is crucial and the right hon. and learned Gentleman makes my point by admitting that they have changed. He has embarrassed himself, and reduced his popularity in the country and his standing in the House by allowing himself, twice before the two most senior courts in the land, to have his actions declared unlawful, and all because of changes in the law that he tried to force through on the basis of wholly inadequate estimates which are now coming down.

**Mr. Garnier:** What would be the financial consequences of the amendment?

**Mr. Straw:** I have already dealt with that. We want some honesty in politics. When a party goes to the country

[*Mr. Straw*]

with express promises—in this case, I am talking about the maintenance of this scheme as outlined in the campaign guide to which I referred—we want it to follow them through when it is in power. If the Government wanted to change the scheme, and as they knew full well what the estimates were before the previous election, they should have included their proposals in their manifesto. Our purpose is to ensure that the party now in power keeps its word, which it gave to the electorate at the previous election.

**Mr. Walter Sweeney** (Vale of Glamorgan): Will the hon. Gentleman give way?

**Mr. Straw:** I hope that the hon. Gentleman will excuse me but I have already given way enough.

We have a number of detailed objections to the revised scheme. I have already said that £700 million is being taken out of the scheme over five years, which is a very large sum. As a result, thousands of victims of violent crime will receive less compensation than they would have received under the old scheme. The saving is generated in part by the setting of a tariff, which is very low in some cases and is especially mean in relation to sexual offences. The tariff that is due to be implemented in April 1996 is very similar to the scheme introduced in April 1994. By the end of the first financial year of the new scheme's awards therefore, claimants will have already lost value to the tune of three years' inflation.

In addition, although the Secretary of State has been forced into accepting that some recompense has to be made for loss of earnings, his proposals are markedly less generous than those under the common law scheme. Many individuals will be adversely affected by the decision to pay loss of earnings only after 28 weeks, as my right hon. and learned Friend the Member for Aberavon (Mr. Morris), the shadow Attorney-General, said. That period was chosen because, as the Secretary of State explained, it is the period for which statutory sick pay is payable.

I do not know whether the Secretary of State has properly appreciated just how unfair it is to set a minimum period of 28 weeks before any account is taken of loss of earnings. Estimates prepared by the research division of the Library draw attention to the fact that if 24 million people in total were employees or self-employed, at least 9 million people would not have any entitlement to sick pay during their first 28 weeks off sick. That particularly applies to the low-paid, to those on short-term contracts and to the self-employed.

It so happens that today a lobby of newsagents—self-employed shopkeepers who used to be natural supporters of the Conservative party—are complaining about another abuse of their position and the way in which the Conservatives have allowed large wholesalers to undermine their business. Once again, the Government's rhetorical claim to care for small businesses is contradicted by their actions. Small business people, such as shopkeepers, are often subject to the worst crimes of violence when thugs rob their shops and they are least able, given the paucity of their earnings, to insure themselves to cover that first seven months of unemployment.

**Mr. Howard:** The hon. Gentleman is entirely right to make the point that self-employed people are not entitled

to statutory sick pay, but I hope that he is not going to leave that passage of his speech without reminding the House that such people are entitled to incapacity benefit.

**Mr. Straw:** They are not entitled to loss of earnings to cover that 28-week period and they will be the subject of discrimination under the scheme. Even those employees who have occupational sick pay schemes will not necessarily obtain anything approaching their full salary when unable to work. Indeed, I have obtained evidence showing that most employees in most private sector schemes will have to have worked continuously for one employer for five years before receiving anything like full entitlement to sick pay from their occupational salary.

It is extraordinary that, having failed to consult any victim organisations or indeed the Criminal Injuries Compensation Board before introducing his first and ill-fated tariff scheme, the Secretary of State has failed to do so again. The hon. Member for Sutton mentioned my fine speech to the Police Federation, but in an even finer speech on the day that the Secretary of State spoke to the Police Federation, Mr. Fred Broughton the chairman of the Police Federation said:

"we very much regret that there has been no consultation about the revisions"

made by the Secretary of State. Mr. Broughton continued:

"The major change in the scheme to which we still object very strongly, is the failure to differentiate between the individual circumstances of victims. It cannot be right that, just because they have suffered an identical injury, the young breadwinner with his or her whole life to look forward to, is treated in the same way as the elderly person with no dependents."

I must ask the Secretary of State again: why is he so afraid to consult those who know more about the issue than he does? After the debacle of his first attempt, it would have been far better to have spent some time in discussion with those who understand the impact of compensation on victims and to have got it right this time.

The proposals fail adequately to recognise the experience which victims have suffered or to assist them to recover from that experience and live as normal a life as possible. The Secretary of State has undoubtedly introduced some improvements in the scheme which has been so derided. The changes have occurred not because of his great concern to improve the lot of victims, but because of his great desire to save his own political skin. The changes do not go far enough, which is why we tabled the reasoned amendment and why we shall seek to improve the Bill in Committee.

The Secretary of State said in September in yet another of his lecturing speeches that the scales of justice had tilted too far in favour of offenders. He said:

"Victims have had a raw deal. I want to redress that balance."

His actions belie his words. He has sought to cut victims' compensation by half and to cut the compensation available to some victims—the most severely injured—to a tenth of what they would have received. If the courts had not intervened to stop him, the Secretary of State would have succeeded in cutting compensation in such a way. The right hon. and learned Gentleman has failed effectively to tackle the relentless rise in violent crime and is now making the victims of that violence pay for his failures. The scheme is unacceptable and I urge the House to vote against the Bill and for our reasoned amendment.

5.54 pm

**Mr. Michael Shersby** (Uxbridge): I wish to declare two interests. I am president of the Uxbridge branch of Victim Support, which is a voluntary activity on my part and is unpaid. I am also parliamentary adviser to the Police Federation of England and Wales jointly with the hon. Member for Warwickshire, North (Mr. O'Brien).

The revised criminal injuries compensation scheme proposed by my right hon. and learned Friend the Secretary of State in the Bill is a great improvement on the tariff scheme that he introduced last year, for several reasons. He has clearly listened to the views of his parliamentary colleagues, their constituents and organisations with a special interest in this very important matter. Victim Support was critical of a number of features of the tariff scheme which was introduced last year. One of its principal objections, which was shared by the police, lawyers and many others, was that it did not properly take account of loss of earnings. Apart from the notional average amount, the tariff contained no provisions for loss of earnings and other financial loss.

In the opinion of Victim Support, one of the most serious defects in the tariff scheme remained, as compensation awards were still counted as capital by the Department of Social Security when calculating means-tested benefits such as income support, so that some victims lost all benefits until the award was spent. That point still concerns my local branch of Victim Support, which points out that victims on low wages have compensation deducted from social security benefit. If a victim receives compensation of more than £3,000, for example, it is deducted from benefit. If a victim receives more than £8,000, he or she loses benefit altogether. I draw those matters to the attention of my right hon. and learned Friend.

Victim Support has, however, welcomed a number of aspects of the Bill, but it still has some concerns which I am sure can be discussed in Committee. One important point is that the entitlement to loss of earnings applies to victims who are off work for 28 weeks. Victim Support wants to know how the provisions will apply to self-employed people and those in part-time, low-paid or temporary work. My right hon. and learned Friend the Secretary of State touched on that issue in response to a point raised by the hon. Member for Blackburn (Mr. Straw). My right hon. and learned Friend made the point that such people would be able to rely on incapacity benefit. Members of the Standing Committee will probably wish to explore that matter in a little more detail so that they may compare the amounts available under incapacity benefit.

Victim Support set up an independent working party on compensation and put forward a number of principles on which it felt that the scheme should be based. It wanted a tariff to be based on clear principles and adequate provision for reducing earning capacity or loss of support in the case of homicide. It wanted no reduction or withdrawal of benefit because of the compensation. It also wanted no judgment about a victim's previous conduct if unrelated to the current crime. It wanted a regular, independent review of levels of compensation, and clear and prompt operation of the scheme. It also wanted compensation to be available for all injuries that were more serious than minor cuts or bruises, and for the psychological equivalent. I hope very much that my right hon. and learned Friend the Secretary of State, as he gives his customary careful consideration to the views of such an important organisation as Victim Support, will listen sympathetically as the Bill passes through Parliament.

I have naturally also had discussions on this with the Police Federation. The federation welcomes the fact that, following the Lords' judgment, the Home Secretary has introduced a Bill rather than seeking to alter the tariff scheme by means of the royal prerogative. The federation takes the view that it is right that the scheme should have the force of statute and I share that view. It is clear from the recent public pronouncements by Mr. Fred Broughton, the chairman of the Police Federation, that in announcing revisions to the tariff scheme my right hon. and learned Friend has moved a long way towards meeting the strong criticisms of it made by the federation, by Victim Support and by trade unions whose members include potential claimants.

The police are especially pleased, as are many of my constituents in Uxbridge, that loss of earnings will continue to be compensated for and that awards will cover special medical care and attention in long-term cases. It would be helpful to have the scope of the provisions spelled out in the Bill in a little more detail. The increase in the amounts that can be paid in awards to £500,000 is most welcome. I must ask, however, whether my right hon. and learned Friend considers that that amount would be sufficient to provide full medical care and attention for the small minority of very serious and tragic cases of which those of us who have read the Criminal Injuries Compensation Board's reports are aware.

Can my right hon. and learned Friend the Secretary of State or my hon. Friend the Minister of State tell us whether it is the Government's view that the cost of such care and attention should be paid for by the improved value of the higher awards because they will be able to provide a guaranteed, index-linked, tax-free income for life? If so, has the Department made any estimate of the improved value of the maximum award to, say, a young man or woman in his or her 20s with normal life expectancy?

The changes proposed in the Bill do not increase the scope of compensation for victims of violent crime compared with the scope of the non-statutory scheme operated by the Criminal Injuries Compensation Board. However, the Bill will bring about a change in the overall costs. As there is no evidence that awards to victims have been unduly generous, we must ask ourselves the reason. The reason was given, quite candidly and properly, by my right hon. and learned Friend the Secretary of State in an earlier debate on the matter. He made the point that the ever-rising cost to taxpayers, based on forward projections of claims, would be too expensive for them to bear in the longer term.

As has already been pointed out in this debate, the reforms proposed in the Bill will not cut expenditure on compensation for criminal injuries, but will simply help to keep rising costs under control. My right hon. and learned Friend the Secretary of State has given, in his excellent speech, a projection of the figures to 2001 which illustrate that point well. He can still claim with absolute justification, however, that the scheme provided for in the Bill will be the best available in the world. It is beyond doubt that the United Kingdom pays out more compensation than the United States and more than all the

*[Mr. Michael Shersby]*

European countries put together. I believe that that is a record of which our country can be proud and I hope that that view is shared by all hon. Members.

It was because many groups, notably the police and Victim Support, felt that the former statutory scheme was the best way to meet society's obligations to victims that they strongly supported it, regardless of the costs. Many of us who read the gripping and often horrifying reports published by the Criminal Injuries Compensation Board felt that we were discharging our obligations to people unfortunate enough to become victims of violent crime. I suspect, however, that few of us realised the extent to which the costs would escalate.

The police accepted that a tariff-based scheme was appropriate for lesser cases involving straightforward injuries. They accepted that such a scheme could mean less bureaucracy and that compensation would reach victims sooner. Speed of compensation is an important point in our consideration of the whole matter. The police have, however, always felt that in cases of homicide, permanent disablement, mutilation and disfigurement, there should continue to be a subjective judgment which takes account of all the consequences of the attack on a victim. The Police Federation therefore regrets the passing of the Criminal Injuries Compensation Board. It also points out that the proposed new scheme will be administered by civil servants instead of the old board staff and that the claimant's right of appeal appears to be limited. Those points need to be investigated and clarified in Committee.

Another issue that needs to be examined is the time limit for submitting a claim. I suggest that it should continue to be the limit which applies to a claim in the courts—three years from the date of the incident. That point is important for some victims who suffer psychological injuries or who have suffered sexual attacks.

The new scheme does not appear to distinguish between individuals and I ask why that is. It seems rather illogical to regard the loss or damage suffered by victims as identical just because they have suffered the same kind of injury. A young person, perhaps a child, who is blinded and who will have to cope with that handicap for the rest of his or her life will be given the same compensation as an elderly person with a short life expectancy. I hope that my right hon. and learned Friend will seriously consider that point. Perhaps he will be willing to consider regarding the proposed tariff as the base for compensation and allowing an assessor to vary awards according to the degree of harm suffered by the claimant.

What is the position of victims who have suffered more than one injury? Should not the new scheme be more generous in respect of a second or further injury than the 1994 scheme was? Perhaps my hon. Friend the Minister of State will respond to that point when he winds up. The new scheme should also specify how awards will be uprated to take account of the effects of inflation. That and a number of other questions need to be considered further in Committee.

As the House knows, I have a special interest in police officers who are, all too often, the victims of violent crimes. It is an unhappy fact that in 1995 the police will sustain about 18,000 serious injuries. However, awards to police claimants have always been abated by the extent of their entitlements under the police regulations and the police pension scheme.

The persons most likely to be worried about the scheme are probably those about whom Victim Support is concerned. They are those who are not covered by occupational injury and pension schemes and who are, by definition, often the weakest and most vulnerable in our society. All of us represent some of those people.

While I fully acknowledge that my right hon. and learned Friend the Secretary of State has responded in his customary positive way to the criticisms made of the 1994 tariff scheme, I hope that he will keep an open mind and that he will be ready to consider some further improvements to the proposed new scheme as the Bill passes through Parliament.

It is important that the tariff scheme is reviewed at regular intervals. The 1994 scheme provided for a review every three years, and it would be sensible for the proposed new scheme also to be reviewed at three-yearly intervals, so that the effects of inflation—albeit the low level that we are experiencing today—can be taken fully into account, and so that the value of awards will not depreciate.

I welcome the Bill and I shall certainly support my right hon. and learned Friend in the Lobby tonight. I hope that he will be able to take account of some of the points that I have made in the debate.

6.9 pm

**Mr. John Morris** (Aberavon): The hon. Member for Uxbridge (Mr. Shersby) made a careful speech, in which he analysed some of the defects of the Bill. Given the totality of those defects, I wonder how he can vote to support the Bill in the Lobby tonight.

I shall make a short speech. The Home Secretary has been forced to introduce this Bill because he adopted a high-handed approach to Parliament. As Lord Denning once said, however high a man is, no man is above the law—not even the Home Secretary.

The right hon. and learned Gentleman cannot say that he was not warned from all sides. My hon. Friend the Member for Blackburn (Mr. Straw) warned him, as did Lord Ackner. In a debate on 20 October 1994, I said that the attitude of the Government was

"an affront to Parliament . . . The Bill ignores the 1988 Act . . . It is not even repealed. It will lie idle on the statute book. Instead, we have a non-statutory scheme and the Government have played ducks and drakes with Parliament and the time that Parliament gave to passing the 1988 Act."—[*Official Report*, 20 October 1994; Vol. 248, c. 466.]

My hon. Friend the Member for Blackburn commented on the goal average approach of the Home Secretary. The right hon. and learned Gentleman lost in the Court of Appeal, and lost in the Judicial Committee of the other place. The Home Secretary has undoubtedly abused his prerogative power, and he and his advisers should have known better.

The Home Secretary has brought forward an amended scheme with a double objective—first to satisfy the courts, and secondly to placate the other place in its legislative capacity. Although there are some improvements, it is still a far from satisfactory measure.

Many of the victims of crime will get much less. I trust that not even this arrogant and brazen Government will lay claim to being the friends of the victims of crime.

**Mr. Sweeney:** Does the right hon. and learned Gentleman agree that, while many people will be worse off, 60 per cent. of claimants will be no worse off?

**Mr. Morris:** I do not accept that figure, which is not put forward by the Government. The bulk of the victims—as regards the totality of their claims—will be less well-off than they would have been under the original scheme. The hon. Member for Vale of Glamorgan (Mr. Sweeney) may be making a comparison not with the new scheme, but with another one.

We have complained about the proposed tariff, and particularly that no allowance was made for loss of earnings. It is now proposed that victims of serious crime who are off work for more than 28 weeks will be eligible for an allowance for loss of earnings up to a maximum of one and a half times the average industrial wage.

Such an allowance for loss of earnings was opposed adamantly by the Government when they brought the original proposals before the House. I am sure that the hon. Member for Uxbridge and others will want to follow in detail the reply that the Home Secretary gives about the self-employed, and I hope that the difficulties in that subject can be clarified in Committee.

A high earner's loss is bound to be higher than that of a low earner. That is common sense. But if one insists on a tariff—this is what the hon. Member for Vale of Glamorgan may not have fully grasped—the high earner will still be a loser. That is the failure of the tariff, which makes no allowance for the consequences as they affect different people.

For example, the consequences for a young girl—let alone a model—with a scarred face will be different from the consequences for a middle-aged man with a similar injury. If there is a flat-rate tariff, the same allowance will go to the young model and to the older man who unfortunately suffer similar injuries.

**The Minister of State, Home Office (Mr. David Maclean):** Before the right hon. and learned Gentleman moves on from that point, will he tell the House under which principle he thinks it right for the taxpayer to pay less to a man who is scarred than to a woman with a similar injury?

**Mr. Morris:** The principle is clear. The original prerogative scheme was based on common law, whereby the common law sought to put the loser back in the position in which he was originally. That was the basis of the scheme, and the Home Secretary referred to it this afternoon. The Minister may not have been listening. The common law would assess the damages, assuming the case was being heard in court. For a young model of 21 with a distinguished career in front of her who unfortunately has her face scarred so that she is never able to work again, the damages would be enormous.

Regrettably, it would be different if someone like myself, or perhaps the hon. Member for Uxbridge, suffered the same calamity. The hon. Gentleman and I are not models—no one would pretend that we were. We are much older, and our expectation of life is, unhappily, shorter. The damages in any common law court would be wholly different from those given to the young model. If

the Minister has not grasped that, he has a great deal to learn about the way in which the common law seeks to right a wrong.

**Mr. Maclean:** I understand the way in which the common law works. I am merely asking whether the right hon. and learned Gentleman thinks that it is right that a taxpayer-funded scheme which is not attempting to right all wrongs but attempting to make payments to victims who have suffered injuries should discriminate against some people because of their age, or because they may be ugly.

**Mr. Morris:** Under Governments of different colours, and ever since the Criminal Injuries Compensation Board was set up, the taxpayer has awarded damages on that basis. It is only the blinding light which has struck the Government in the past two years that is changing the whole situation. In no manifesto of the Conservative party has the change been put before the electorate. That is the basis on which the CICB has been working all these years, and I and the overwhelming number of electors who were not told otherwise were satisfied with that approach.

The tariff is fundamentally flawed, and takes no account of age, sex or occupation. There are also no allowances—I can be corrected if I am wrong—for inflation until another review takes place. The Government are getting away with murder, because the tariffs for the new scheme to be introduced in April 1996 are at the same level as the original tariff proposed in April 1994. If I am wrong, I am sure that the Minister can correct me in his reply. If there is no allowance for future inflation and for giving realistic amounts to victims, the scheme will wither on the vine.

There is concern about how the tariffs were arrived at. The Home Secretary clutches some figures for some assessments and cases, but would it not have been better if an independent outside source had confirmed what the tariffs should be, rather than having an inquiry within the Home Office? If the Home Secretary had then wanted to reduce them, we would have known the foundation.

Concern has already been expressed about the differences in valuations. People are worried about the low awards in the tariff for sexual cases. Why is £1,000 proposed for a child who is sexually assaulted, and £1,250 for an adult who suffers a dislocated finger? I am sure that the Standing Committee will want to explore those examples, and to find out the basis for that approach.

Finally, the poorest victims will suffer. People who receive more than £3,000 will have deductions made from their income support, and those who receive more than £8,000 will lose their entitlement altogether. If that is so, and if the rule is to survive, perhaps hon. Members who will be exploring such matters in Committee will want to consider the way in which clause 8 deals with the income tax position for annuities.

Under that clause, awards will not be regarded as income for tax purposes, but that will not be the case when it comes to any family income support scheme. I agree with Victim Support that criminal injuries compensation should be exempt under the capital rules of the Department of Social Security.

If we have to have this scheme, let there at least be regular reviews of compensation levels, and let every victim of crime be given the health warning, "A Tory Government will damage your expectation of compensation."

6.22 pm

**Mr. Edward Garnier** (Harborough): I must take the right hon. and learned Member for Aberavon (Mr. Morris) up on one point—the little argument that we seem to be having about the number of judges who decided one way and the number who decided the other. Surely, given that five eminent lawyers decided one way on the matter and five the other, we should simply forget the argument about the hierarchical structure of the courts, as it was a matter of—

**Mr. Michael:** What a silly argument.

**Mr. Garnier:** The hon. Gentleman does himself no good by making that sort of fatuous remark. If he will allow me to finish the sentence, I will make my point.

Surely the important thing is that that decision tells us that it was an important and extremely complicated matter, that had vexed other judges and lawyers. Of course no one is arguing that we have a hierarchical courts system, or that, because the decision was 3:2 in the House of Lords, that is what the law was found to be. Surely the simple point is the one that I adumbrated—that the issue is highly complex, and no one can produce any evidence to impugn the motives of my right hon. and learned Friend the Home Secretary.

**Mr. Streeter:** Does my hon. and learned Friend agree that, now that the Labour party thinks only in terms of soundbites, Labour Members would not know a complicated legal argument if it leaped up and bit them on the nose?

**Mr. Garnier:** I will study Opposition Members' nasal probosces with interest.

**Mr. Michael:** Perhaps I can heighten the quality—

**Mr. Garnier:** I have not said that I would give way.

**Mr. Michael:** Will the hon. and learned Gentleman give way?

**Mr. Garnier:** Most certainly.

**Mr. Michael:** I am very grateful. Perhaps we could lift the standard of debate. Does the hon. and learned Gentleman acknowledge that the Home Secretary was warned by Back-Bench and Front-Bench Members in the House, by people outside the House who specialise in the law and in the Lords long before the judgment, that he ignored them, and that they advised him that the course of action that he proposed to take would indeed breach the law?

**Mr. Garnier:** I think that the hon. Gentleman has misunderstood the argument, which was twofold. First, what was the law? The House of Lords reached a decision on that, and on how the prerogative should be exercised. Secondly, what was the best way to approach Parliament? My right hon. and learned Friend the Home Secretary was given plenty of warnings. People made political points— I am sure that the hon. Gentleman was foremost among them—saying that, politically, it would be more advisable if my right hon. and learned Friend did this, that or the other, but the intellectual debate on a matter of law was evenly balanced, and that is the only point that I am making. If the hon. Gentleman is not prepared to accept that, it tells us more about him than about anything else.

It would be helpful to place today's Second Reading debate and the Bill in the context of the criminal injuries compensation system. The Government established a scheme 31 years ago to compensate out of public funds the victims of criminal violence. The scheme was brought into existence through the exercise of the royal prerogative, and the payments were made ex gratia. There was no statutory authority for the scheme, although the necessary funds were voted annually by Parliament, and the victims had no right in law to claim payment.

Compensation was given in the shape of a lump sum, which was arrived at in the same way as a civil award of damages for personal injury caused by a tort—a civil wrong—subject to an upper limit on the amount attributable to the loss of earnings. The scheme was administered by the Criminal Injuries Compensation Board, which comprised a chairman and a panel of eminent lawyers.

At first, the scheme operated on a modest scale, but by 1978 the number of awards had increased twelvefold. In that year, the Royal Commission on civil liability and compensation for personal injury recommended that compensation for criminal injuries should continue to be based on tort damages, but that the scheme, which had originally been experimental, should be put on a statutory basis. The Government, however, preferred to wait until more experience had been gained.

Although, as the years passed, some important changes were made, the scheme retained its original shape, but its scale and costs increased remorselessly. In the first year, the board paid out £400,000. By 1984, the annual amount had risen to more than £35 million, and the backlog was approaching 50,000 claims.

At that point, the Government decided that the time had come to put the scheme into statutory form, and they appointed an interdepartmental working party to consider how that should be done. The working party made numerous recommendations, which the Government largely accepted. The most important was that compensation should continue to be given to the victims of criminal violence on the basis of civil damages.

Accepting that among other recommendations, the then Secretary of State, my right hon. Friend the Secretary of State for Foreign and Commonwealth Affairs, announced in Parliament that legislation would be introduced accordingly, and that considerable extra public funds would be made available. Within a few years, the promised legislation materialised, in the Criminal Justice Act 1988, together with its dependent schedules.

It was decided that, when it was brought into force, the scheme would be administered by a statutory body appointed by the Home Secretary and that it would not be a servant or agent of the Crown. The Home Secretary would defray the expenses incurred by the board, and, subject to certain exceptions and limitations, claims for compensation were to be determined and amounts payable assessed in accordance with the way in which a claim in tort was determined. Of course, there was to be a right of appeal from a determination of the board, to the High Court or the Court of Session.

In the years that immediately followed the passing of the 1988 Act, it seemed probable that, whether or not the statutory scheme took effect, the compensation regime would continue as before. Indeed, as recently as December 1991, my right hon. Friend the Member for Mole Valley (Mr. Baker), then the Home Secretary, announced to Parliament an increase in the lower limit of entitlement, without suggesting that the general principles of the scheme might be under reconsideration. He also took the opportunity to report even greater increases in the amounts of the annual payments and the costs of running the scheme.

In November 1992, my right hon. and learned Friend the Member for Rushcliffe (Mr. Clarke) gave notice of his intention to replace the existing scheme with a new tariff scheme with effect from 1994. At that time, the White Paper, "Compensating victims of violent crime: changes to the Criminal Injuries Compensation Scheme", was presented to Parliament.

Certain paragraphs of the White Paper are relevant to today's debate. For example, paragraph 10 suggested:

"There is no obvious or logical way of matching a particular sum of money precisely to the degree of pain and hurt suffered by an injured person. Even under common law damages the award of damages is not an exact science. Judgments tend to be made pragmatically on the facts of the case and with regard to precedent. But the assessment is essentially subjective and any amount awarded must to some extent be regarded as artificial. There is no exactly right answer."

The White Paper also suggested:

"Such factors have been major elements in the consideration that led the Government to decide that awards based on common law damages are no longer appropriate for a state financed compensation scheme. Since there is no absolute or right figure for an award, the Government does not consider it appropriate to attempt the very difficult and time-consuming task of trying to assign a precisely calculated but essentially arbitrary sum to the injury suffered . . . The new system will accordingly be based on a tariff or scale of awards under which injuries of comparable severity will be grouped together in bands for which a single fixed payment is made. This means that people with similar injuries will get the same payment."

The White Paper suggested:

"Under the current scheme loss of earnings and costs of future medical care can be paid as separate heads of damage"

under the current civil law scheme.

"That is a feature of the common law system, though the necessary calculations can often prove to be very difficult and time consuming to make. The tariff scheme will, however, break the link with common law damages".

That is common ground between both sides of the House.

The White Paper also said:

"the aim will no longer be to provide finely calculated 'compensation' . . . Instead a simple lump sum award related to the severity of the injury will be paid. That removes the subjective element of assessment and substitutes a more objective test which is easier to apply.

The severance of the link to common law damages and the introduction of a straightforward tariff scheme, under which payments are made from a scale of awards related to the nature of the injury, means that the specialist skills of senior lawyers with experience of personal injury casework will no longer be needed and that cases can be decided administratively. There will accordingly be no longer term role for the present Board to play under the tariff arrangements.

If the applicant is dissatisfied with the initial decision he may request reconsideration of his case by the Criminal Injuries Compensation Authority. This will be an internal review of the case conducted by a more senior member of the administration.

If the claimant remains dissatisfied after this review of his case, he will be able to appeal to an appeals panel"

independent of both the authority and the Home Secretary.

Finally, the White Paper pointed out—again, this must be common ground:

"The present scheme is non-statutory and payments are made on an ex-gratia basis. Provision was made in the Criminal Justice Act 1988 for the scheme to be placed on a statutory footing. However,

at the request of the Board the relevant provisions were not brought into force, because this would have disrupted their efforts to deal with the heavy work load."

Hon. Members may have seen in the last Parliament evidence to the Home Affairs Select Committee from the noble Lord Carlisle, which supported that suggestion. The White Paper noted:

"With the impending demise of the current scheme the provisions in the 1988 Act will not now be implemented."

The tariff scheme departs from the basic principles of the old scheme and the statutory scheme. First, the assessment of compensation is no longer based on common law principles. There is no point in hiding behind wise or complicated words, as that is a fact, but it need not necessarily be a worry. Nowadays, there is a movement in modern law jurisdictions to codify law rather than rely wholly on common law.

I believe that the Law Commission is to bring before those interested, and certainly before Parliament, suggestions that the whole of the criminal law should be codified, and that other aspects of the current common legal system should be codified to provide a much simpler and certain legal system. On those grounds, the fact that we are moving away from a common law-based system to a tariff system is not wrong in principle.

The second distinction is that awards are assessed according to a fixed scale of tariffs without taking account of a victim's individual circumstances. I agree with the points made by my hon. Friend the Member for Uxbridge (Mr. Shersby) and the right hon. and learned Member for Aberavon (Mr. Morris), and I urge my hon. Friend the Minister to take those points on board. There will be a number of difficult cases, which may be sorted out or be capable of being sorted out.

This is not simply party political fencing across the Chamber. Those cases give rise to proper and deeply felt intellectual concern about the effects on claimants of differing ages and earning capacities. I hope that the scheme in its final form will take account of the points made by my hon. Friend and the right hon. and learned Member.

The third difference is that awards will be made on behalf of the authority by persons who need not be qualified lawyers, although qualified lawyers may be involved in the hearing of appeals. That seems to be a good idea. There is in the public mind a movement away from a reliance on lawyers' formality on all occasions. Alternative dispute resolutions, taking cases to the small claims court in the county court where claimants and defendants can appear without representation, seems to be a far better way to deal with most of the ordinary cases that now come before county courts, which could more sensibly be dealt with more informally.

I hope that the proposed scheme will attract the commendation not only of the House but of the public at large, who will, after all, have to make use of it. It is common ground that, in some cases, particularly where serious injuries involve prolonged loss of earnings, the sum payable to a victim under the tariff scheme will be substantially less than he would have received under the old scheme or the statutory scheme. When considering their final view on the set-up, I urge the Government to keep an open mind and, if an injustice or injustices should flow from a high earner suffering a disproportionate loss, to bear those changes in mind.

[*Mr. Garnier*]

The general scheme of the Bill, which has been introduced to overcome what I may describe as a little local difficulty in another place not so long ago, is to be welcomed. Although we shall argue over the details, I commend it and invite all those on Conservative Benches and as many as possible on Opposition Benches to join us in supporting its Second Reading this evening.

6.37 pm

**Mr. Simon Hughes** (Southwark and Bermondsey): The beginning and end of the speech of the hon. and learned Member for Harborough (Mr. Garnier) were welcome. The middle sounded like a Government brief to explain how we got here. Although it was a perfectly valid contribution to the debate and we had not heard it before, none the less it did not bear the hallmark of original thought.

There are two themes to the debate. The first is the theme of the series of legal proceedings that drove us to this pass and the other is the much more important theme of how we deal with victims of crime.

I have a limited amount to say on the issue of how we got here. I am glad that at last the issue is being dealt with by statute and not by royal prerogative; it is a nonsense that in 1995, we hold on to the powers of the royal prerogative and we give as much royal prerogative to Ministers of the Crown as we do. Things should be dealt with in a democratic way—via debate in the democratic assemblies of the country. There is a great danger in royal prerogative.

Legislation can be bad enough when it goes through the House of Commons. If we can get things wrong with the Child Support Act 1991, how much more wrong can we get legislation if we do not have the opportunity to examine proposals? It is therefore a good thing that the House of Lords ruled that the Home Secretary was out of order—not for the first time. Although we do not have a Bill of Rights and a proper constitution, it is good that we at least have a House of Lords that occasionally intervenes to establish some principles. It is good that the legal system can occasionally intervene to stop the Government doing what they like. It is a good thing that the House has been driven back to re-examine the criminal injuries scheme and that the Home Secretary has been forced to think the system through again.

We are here to debate what we can do for those who become victims. The precondition to the debate is, of course, the existence of victims. Crime, being sin, will always be with us, so, sadly, there will always be victims of crime. The most important issue that lies behind the debate is the need to reduce the number of victims. According to any objective analysis, the Government cannot be proud of their record on that. I hope that they will not be either complacent or simplistic about that aim.

We all accept that it is not easy to reduce the level of crime, but for the Government to set their face against any argument that there might be a link between high unemployment among young people and crime strikes me as ignoring self-evident truths. If there are so many idle hands, as there are in many of our constituencies, it is not surprising that those people turn to making their living from criminal activity. That activity often becomes that which interferes with the liberties of others. The number

of victims is the first and most important consideration in our debate. I hope that the Government will appreciate that the fewer victims and the fewer crimes committed, the less the taxpayer will be asked to pay.

The second issue is the extent to which the rights of victims are put at the centre of our criminal justice system. The Labour party is right to make that the theme of its reasoned amendment. I believe that we are still miles from putting victims at the centre of our criminal justice system. The most recent example of that failure in London concerns the rights of the survivors and bereaved relatives of those who died when the Marchioness sank. According to the recent coroner's inquest, those who died when that boat sank were unlawfully killed. Had we not, at the last moment, been able to persuade the Lord Chancellor that the survivors and relatives should be legally represented through the legal aid system, they would have been denied the opportunity to be represented and to put their questions at the inquest.

I remember when a young man who lived a couple of doors from me in Bermondsey was attacked on new year's eve. I remember the date in particular because it was the year when I was elected, 1983. He died at Guy's hospital as a result of the injuries that he suffered. When the trial of his assailants took place, the family sat, irrelevant to the proceedings, in the gallery of the Old Bailey. The charges were subsequently reduced to less serious ones on the charge sheet and convictions on those charges led to relatively short sentences. As a result, the family felt not just deprived of a rightful verdict, but that they had had no opportunity to participate in the trial.

The Home Office has only recently decided to allow victims and the families of victims to make representations about sentencing, particularly sentences on appeal. Although I am grateful for that change, it is a minor one. Victims who survive often do not know what happens to their case. At court they are often treated exceptionally badly, like second-class citizens and often have no opportunity to participate in the process of criminal justice. The opportunity to feel part of the system of justice delivered is as important as giving victims any amount of money.

About two years ago, a pensioner constituent of mine, Mrs. H, had her car stolen by a 15-year-old. The local magistrates court at Camberwell eventually ordered that the culprit should pay £25 compensation as well as serve a sentence. To date, not just months but more than a year later, that woman has not even received that £25. No one appears to be doing much to chase that youngster to deliver the money or, if he has not got it, to chase his parents to deliver it. My constituent has probably lost £1,000 and the use of a car. I do not believe that she has replaced it. She is a victim whom we have not looked after.

As a lawyer, I used to appear occasionally at hearings at the Criminal Injuries Compensation Board. I agree with the hon. and learned Member for Harborough that it should not be a lawyers' forum. I have also appeared at that board with people since I have been a Member of Parliament. I have therefore heard the details of most unfair cases. For example, my constituent, whose husband was killed in a pub shooting in Walworth in 1990, has not only failed to receive any compensation yet, but she was told that any money that she inherited by virtue of payments to her as a widow, as a result of her husband's pension scheme, would be counted in as opposed to discounted for the purpose of assessing her income. That decision will therefore reduce the amount of compensation paid to her for the criminal injury that resulted in the death of her husband. The way in which the system has operated in that case is monstrous. If her husband had died of a heart attack, she would have got the money. He went out for a quiet drink with his wife and was shot in a pub, but his widow has not been given any money.

**Mr. Garnier:** When the hon. Gentleman mentioned that he used to practise at the Bar, it reminded me that when I spoke, I should have declared that I am a practising member of the Bar, albeit that I do not do any criminal work. I apologise for interrupting the hon. Gentleman's speech.

**Mr. Hughes:** Those of us in the Chamber understand that declaration and register it. We are all so careful now about what we declare that I would not want to stop the hon. and learned Gentleman declaring anything. I notice that the hon. Member for Uxbridge (Mr. Shersby) declared that he is the voluntary and unpaid president of Victim Support, but he did not declare whether he is paid as an adviser to the Police Federation. I assume that he is and he might have done the House a service by saying that. I hope that we shall soon have to declare how much we are paid for any other work that we do as well as just saying whether we are paid for it.

The steady rise in the number of criminal injuries payments has meant that the Government have acted, but it is fair to say that their overriding concern has been to act to limit the amount of the payments rather than for other purposes. One other issue with which we desperately need to deal is how to ensure that the criminal injuries compensation scheme acts quickly. Justice is not justice if it is denied for years and years. I am sure that the Minister would acknowledge that. The backlog of compensation claims is rather like that held by the Child Support Agency, because the Criminal Injuries Compensation Board has files and files of outstanding cases. I hope that the new system will cut through that delay and offer speedy remedies. It is no good that those who have been badly injured or whatever have to wait years and years for payments.

There appears to be a growing consensus in the House about how the criminal injuries compensation scheme should operate. I should like to offer a tick list of what we need to do. First, the Government must tell the nation, Parliament and, in due course, the Standing Committee more about the principles upon which they are establishing the scheme. We have been offered a piece of outline legislation, but the scheme will be introduced as a result of secondary, delegated legislation, which is a dangerous route to follow. We need to be told about a few more principles that will govern the new scheme. We pass far too much legislation that says that certain things will be done, but that fails to set out the objectives clearly.

We are driven to accept that there will be a tariff-plus system. The parallel under the old civil law is the general and special damages system. One cannot, however, ignore entirely some of the personal circumstances in cases. One cannot ignore the effect on the income of the victim. If someone was earning x and was deprived of work as a result of his injury, compensation must recognise that; and the nature of society is that we do not all earn the same amount, so there will be different payments. People do

not seek to make a profit; they seek to have the money reinstated that they would otherwise have been able to earn.

I do not want to become involved in the debate that we were in danger of getting into, as to whether a 21-year-old female model is worth more than an approximately 60-year-old Queen's counsel Member of Parliament. However, we should consider whether age should be a factor and whether the impact of the injury should be a factor.

Some things in the tariff list are a nonsense. For example, no distinction appears to be made between an injury to one's writing hand or using hand and an injury to a hand that is not. Obviously, that is a highly relevant consideration. No consideration appears to be given to the correctness of the relativity of the tariffs. I made that argument to the Home Secretary in my intervention.

There needs to be an objective way of setting the tariff. That can be done externally of the Home Office and externally of Ministers, and it should be perpetually under review. Many hon. Members will find it odd that we are considering compensating someone more for a dislocated finger that gets better, than for sexual abuse. We cannot allow that anomaly to pass through the system unamended.

I shall be troubled if the tariff does not come up for regular review, and I shall be troubled if we cannot debate and amend it in this place.

Let me add a P.S. on the amounts of compensation that should be paid. If someone is, tragically, murdered, that murder often causes a loss of income to the family, for which compensation should be paid. It is no substitute, but when a relative loses someone, not just out of work but out of life, he should be compensated for the income that the victim was expected to go on to earn.

I made the case for my constituent, the payment of whose husband's pension or entitlement meant that she would lose some of her compensation. Criminal injuries compensation should be a capital payment, not taken into account for the purpose of benefits and Department of Social Security payments. It should be separately regarded and fairly treated.

The lower limit should be lowered. At the moment, it is proposed that it should start from £1,000 only and increase. If someone is beaten up—as people all too often are in London and elsewhere—and is badly bruised, he may not need £1,000, but he may be off work for several days and have to receive medication and so on. We should be less prescriptive about that.

We must not be so prescriptive about a previous criminal record. I had better be careful what I say, but in constituencies such as mine in south London, there are plenty of people who are perfectly proper claimants who do not have an unblemished record—and, as we know, most crime is committed, not on elderly pensioners but among young people on their way out of the pub and going home at 2 o'clock on a Sunday morning. It is unacceptable that because, as happened in a case about which I went to the Criminal Injuries Compensation Board, a 25-year-old had once in the past been involved in an incident and had been arrested and convicted, he was at severe risk of losing all compensation—the lot, unqualifiedly, because of that blemished record. That is unjustifiable.

Other colleagues, including the hon. Member for Blackburn (Mr. Straw), have rightly argued that it is nonsense that the first 28 weeks should be disregarded

[*Mr. Hughes*]

for someone who is self-employed or lacks the statutory entitlements. Twenty-eight weeks without pay can make an incredible difference to one's survival, one's sanity, and probably one's ability not to think of ending one's life in certain circumstances.

I support entirely the argument of the right hon. and learned Member for Aberavon (Mr. Morris)—which I think was also made by the hon. and learned Member for Harborough—that people should be able to apply for three years from the date of the incident, as one can if one is a civil claimant.

People are willing to accept the broad thrust of the legislation, but considerable work needs to be done to make it fair. There was a more or less fair system. We then got a dire system until the House of Lords intervened. We now have a better system again. It is not yet right, but if we work hard it may become more so.

Justice needs to be done and to be seen to be done.

**Mr. Maclean:** The hon. Gentleman said that we had a fair system in the common law damages system, but a few moments before, he criticised the awards in the tariff for sexual abuse and damage to a finger, condemning them as being unfair or not being relatively correct. Does he not realise that those awards in the tariff were based on exactly what the board had allocated beforehand through the common law system, which he thought was fair?

**Mr. Hughes:** Of course I do. I understand that 20,000 cases were examined and the work was done. When I said that we had a fair system, that had a double meaning; I should have been more specific. Perhaps I should have said that the old system was "not bad". I am sorry; I did not mean to mislead the Minister or the House.

The old system was not bad, but it was rough and ready. We then had the tariff system under the temporary arrangements, which were brought to a speedy end. That was a bad system. We now have a better proposal. I accept the process by which we arrived at the system, but it does end up with some anomalies. That is why it should be perpetually open to review and independent of the Government. I hope that that will be better.

We must not have something that is perceived as a criminal justice lottery system, in which for certain things one gets the jackpot and for other things one gets one's £10, one's £1 or even worse. I hope that we end up with a system which recognises how important it is to people and which processes the applications quickly, but which does not preclude the opportunity of the individual's circumstances being submitted, considered and taken into account. However, at the end of the day, it is much more important that the Government take steps to reduce crime and make the reduction of crime their priority, rather than concentrating on victims. The victims need an enormous amount of support—far more than they have had—but the nation is calling on all politicians to make the reduction of crime their priority.

6.56 pm

**Mr. Gary Streeter** (Plymouth, Sutton): I am pleased to take part in the debate and to follow the hon. Member for Southwark and Bermondsey (Mr. Hughes), whose speech I much appreciated. The House recognises that he has long been a champion of the underdog, and his speech reflected that.

If I am fortunate enough to serve on the Standing Committee that will examine the measure, it will certainly—

**Mr. Simon Hughes:** The hon. Gentlemen means that he wants to be on it.

**Mr. Streeter:** It will certainly be my intention to liaise very closely with the victim support group in Plymouth. It does excellent work in supporting victims, and I know that it holds strong opinions about the way in which the Government can improve the lot of victims, which is what we all wish to do. I shall consider the measure carefully if I am fortunate enough to be selected, although I broadly— [*Interruption.*] I would not wish to presume. I support the measure firmly, but there is no legislation that cannot be improved in Committee, and I am sure that we shall all seek opportunities to do that.

I welcome the scheme, especially its flexibility and simplicity, compared with the rather cumbersome, rather bureaucratic, rather slow machinery that we have come to know for so many years in the criminal injuries compensation scheme and the Criminal Injuries Compensation Board.

When victims have suffered the pain, humiliation and indignity of being on the receiving end of crime, they really want a fast procedure whereby whatever money is coming their way is delivered swiftly, without quibble, to meet their special needs. The measure will help us to go firmly along that track.

There are benefits set out in the Bill that are worth pondering on in detail. I welcome the fact that those claimants incapable of work for more than 28 weeks will qualify for payments to cover the cost of special care from the date of the injury and loss of earnings from the end of the initial 28 weeks. There has been some criticism of the 28-week period, but the measure must be viewed in the context of welfare provision generally. Other forms of compensation and support are also available to help people through difficult periods. I welcome the fact that the maximum compensation payable has increased from £250,000 to £500,000. That gives the lie to the claim by some Labour Members that the legislation is a cost-cutting measure—nothing could be further from the truth.

I welcome the fact that in fatal cases payments will include elements for dependency and loss of mother's support fixed at £2,000 per year with a multiplier. The fatality payment will be a minimum of £10,000 per family. Where there are two or more qualifying claimants, they will each receive £5,000. I also welcome the fact that it will be possible to make structured settlements in the case of large awards. They will provide a guaranteed, index-linked, tax-free annual payment that will enhance the net value of the award. These are constructive measures.

The victims of crime want to receive justice from the courts. In a moment, I shall develop some thoughts about the measure. We must recognise that our first priority as legislators is to ensure that justice is delivered through our legal system. It adds insult to injury if families who have been the victims of crime feel that inadequate sentences are passed by the courts.

I raise again the constituency case that grieved me so much two years ago. Jonathan Roberts was killed at age 17 by a young thug who was stealing from a supermarket at which Jonathan worked to fill in his out-of-school hours. It was a brutal killing, although the young thug had no intention of committing murder. He was convicted of manslaughter and sentenced to five years in prison.

Mr. and Mrs. Roberts, with whom I have spent a lot of time since the incident, are not interested in money; they do not seek compensation of that kind. However, they want to feel that justice has been done: they want to know that their son's killer has been severely punished. They do not believe that his sentence is sufficient, and nor do I. I think it is important to put on record that the most crucial way of supporting victims is by ensuring that the punishment fits the crime.

It is important to recognise that we have introduced the unduly lenient sentence measures which are being actively applied. The victim support compensation is very important as a third tier of assistance. Clause 2(3) is the heart of the Bill and I shall refer to it in some detail. It states:

"Provision shall be made for the standard amount to be determined—

(a) in accordance with a table ("the Tariff") prepared by the Secretary of State as part of the Scheme and such other provisions of the Scheme as may be relevant".

Clause 2 does two things, which are important to understand fully. It sets out the basis on which compensation payable under the scheme shall be determined: first, by way of the tariff, to which I have referred; and, secondly, through the provision of the payment of additional amounts of compensation in cases of fatal injury and in respect of loss of earnings or special expenses.

I welcome the coming together of those two separate measures: the tariff system, which is easy to understand and administer in relation to straightforward compensation claims, and a sensible additional provision which compensates on a greater scale. Labour Members have referred to it as a hybrid system. I do not care what they call it; I know that it is a common sense system which meets the needs of victims in our society.

As I have listened to the debate this afternoon I have been slightly worried by some of the attacks on the measure. Labour Members said that it should have been announced before the last general election, as though a party in office must do strictly and to the letter only those things that are set out in its manifesto. That suggestion was made by a party that tells us that it wishes to embrace a minimum wage if it wins the next election but refuses to tell us at what level the minimum wage should be set. It is an exercise in utter hypocrisy for Labour Members to criticise us for not including the changes in our last manifesto. We all know that in relation to a minimum wage—

**Mr. Deputy Speaker (Mr. Michael Morris):** Order. An allusion is acceptable, but it does not need to be developed in this Second Reading debate.

**Mr. Streeter:** I am grateful for your guidance, Mr. Deputy Speaker. The argument that we should have placed the measure in our manifesto is spurious. I cannot imagine that the Labour party said in its 1974 manifesto that within two or three years it would call in the International Monetary Fund to run the country, having made such a mess of running it itself. Governments are not restricted to introducing measures that are set out in their manifestos; parties must deal with the circumstances

that arise when in government. We are elected to be prudent legislators and to introduce measures to meet the needs of the time. That is what the Government have done on this occasion. I shall leave the matter at that point.

**Mr. Maclean:** I am very grateful for my hon. Friend's comments. I checked the Conservative campaign guide and it points out that we have the most generous compensation system in the world. In 1989 the board paid out £91 million to victims of violent crime and last year it paid out £165 million. We continue to maintain the most generous scheme in the world. My hon. Friend should not be ashamed to quote from the manifesto and the campaign guide.

**Mr. Streeter:** I am very grateful to my hon. Friend. My point has taken on an even greater dimension than I expected and I am glad that it is on the record.

**Mr. Mike O'Brien:** I have listened with interest to the hon. Gentleman's comments. Will he tell the House what importance he attaches to the promises that his party makes at election time? Does the electorate have any reason to believe what his party says, or is it irrelevant?

**Mr. Deputy Speaker:** Order. It is perfectly acceptable for the hon. Member for Plymouth, Sutton (Mr. Streeter) to answer in relation to the criminal injuries compensation scheme, but we are not engaging this evening in a wide Second Reading debate about manifestos.

**Mr. Streeter:** Mr. Deputy Speaker, I am very grateful for your guidance on that point. I simply emphasise that we are not restricted, as a Government, to only those issues, matters and policies that are set out in a manifesto if events develop during our period in office. I think that it is critical that every Government and every party should stand by the firm promises that they make at the time of general elections, and we have always done that.

I turn to loss of earnings to which I referred earlier. It is important that our compensation provisions should recognise the risk taken by those people in our society who create wealth and jobs—I refer, of course, to the self-employed. The point was developed earlier in the debate and I would address it very carefully in Committee. It is important that we should not ignore their need to be compensated for loss of earnings and profits as a result of violent crime.

Self-employed people are risk-takers; they create wealth. If we relied only on the public sector to create wealth, we would be in a sorry state. I am delighted that, at this stage in our country's history, small businesses are developing and flourishing. They are creating jobs and reducing unemployment. It is important that our compensation system recognises financial loss as well as physical pain and loss.

I have examined carefully the Labour party's reasoned amendment to the Second Reading which appears on the Order Paper. It criticises the Government's measure for failing adequately to reflect society's obligations. The Labour party is calling for more money to be pumped into the scheme. As has been said earlier in the debate, it simply will not do for Labour Members to appear on television day after day and say that spending and taxation will not increase under any future Labour Government and then to come to the House week after week and call for more taxpayers' money to be pumped into provisions such as the criminal injuries compensation scheme.

[*Mr. Streeter*]

It seems that too many Labour Members have a short-circuit in their minds. They do not understand that what the Government spend must be linked to what the Government raise through tax or borrowing. It will not wash to say that they want to spend more but it will not cost the country or the taxpayer anything. I wish that Labour Members would learn the lessons of the 1970s and understand that they cannot spend or tax their way out of difficulties.

I look forward to hearing answers to the questions that have been put to Labour Front Benchers. How much more money should be pumped into the scheme? They must tell us. From where will that money come? Have they costed those pledges and claims? By how much will they increase the burden of taxation? Unless they can answer those questions in the winding-up speech tonight, they will demonstrate yet again that they are unfit to govern the nation. That applies not only to this measure but to a related measure that we were discussing a few weeks ago in respect of legal aid.

**Mr. Deputy Speaker:** Order. We may have been discussing it a few weeks ago, but we are not discussing it tonight.

**Mr. Streeter:** I am grateful for your guidance, Mr. Deputy Speaker. Labour Members told us today that not enough cash, dosh or loot is being put into the criminal injuries compensation scheme, but they do not have the guts to say how much should be pumped in and where it should come from.

The scheme, even as we have shaped and focused it in the Bill, remains the best criminal injuries compensation scheme in the world. My hon. Friend the Minister of State was right to encourage me to be proud of the scheme. It is a better scheme than those in all the European countries put together. We hear so often that Britain has the best pension scheme for our elderly citizens, the best national health service and the best student support scheme. Now we learn tonight that we have the best scheme for compensating criminal injuries.

The Opposition seek to run us down and rubbish us, but they should consider the facts. It is a scheme of which we can be proud and Conservative Members are proud of it.

7.12 pm

**Mrs. Bridget Prentice** (Lewisham, East): I am delighted to follow the fascinating fairy tale that the hon. Member for Plymouth, Sutton (Mr. Streeter) told us about the wonderful things that are happening in Britain, but I want seriously to discuss why the Bill should have been unnecessary, and why it is inadequate.

The Bill should have been unnecessary because the original scheme that was set up in 1964 with all-party support was a serious attempt to compensate those people who had been tragically injured by criminal acts. Each case was assessed individually using the common law. Unfortunately, the scheme before us tonight attempts to put too many people in simple categories. Individuals cannot be assessed in that way.

The scheme that the Secretary of State introduced last year was obviously intended to cut costs and it is outrageous that Conservative Members are now trying to

deny that. If they had listened to the Secretary of State's speech in opening today's Second Reading debate, they would have heard the implication that it was part of the reasoning behind the Bill. It was not intended to help victims, or to improve the service; if anything, victims were being used to pay for the Government's failed economic policies.

Fortunately, the Bill includes some concessions, as a result of the response of lobby groups, victim support groups and points that my right hon. and hon. Friends have raised in the past. For example, there is an important concession on compensation for loss of earnings, although we are not happy that it does not apply until after 28 weeks. It is important that dependency and loss of support in some fatal cases are included, as are structured settlements.

**Mr. Hartley Booth** (Finchley): I have been listening carefully to the hon. Lady. Will she explain how victims are paying for Government policy? Will she make that point?

**Mrs. Prentice:** I am sorry, but I missed the hon. Gentleman's question.

**Mr. Booth:** The hon. Lady alleges that victims are paying for Government policy. How could that be?

**Mrs. Prentice:** If the hon. Gentleman had been here at the beginning of the debate instead of wandering in a couple of minutes ago, he might have understood my point. I shall repeat it. If the Government reduce the money available for victims of crime, those victims lose out financially. I believe that part of the reason why the Government are reducing the money available to victims of crime is their failed economic policies, and that they are trying to square the circle.

There are several problems with the Bill. It sets specific and inflexible figures for some specific injuries. We have heard examples from the hon. Member for Southwark and Bermondsey (Mr. Hughes), among others. For example, right and left hands are treated in the same way, but for those of us who are right-handed, an injury to the left hand would not be as devastating as an injury to the right hand, and vice versa.

Different people are affected in different ways. For example, the public might consider that the loss of an eye to a police officer would require greater compensation than the loss of an eye to a Member of Parliament. The public might consider that a severe injury to the hand of an artist might deserve greater compensation than if such an injury had been suffered by a Member of Parliament, as we would have other means by which we could continue to do our job.

**Mr. Streeter:** Does the hon. Lady not understand that an artist who loses the use of the hand with which he draws or paints would be entitled to loss of earnings compensation that would not apply to Members of Parliament, as we could still do our job, so there would be compensation for such an injury?

**Mrs. Prentice:** To some extent, there would, but in those circumstances there is much better compensation in civil law. I remind the hon. Gentleman that loss of earnings compensation does not apply until after 28 weeks. The Criminal Injuries Compensation Board stated that the "effect on an individual varies so widely that a tariff, even with the gradations proposed is in practice unworkable".

The maximum levels of compensation available are much lower than under the common law scheme. I make no apology for using the same example as my hon. Friends. The public would find it difficult to understand that a child who has been sexually assaulted is entitled to only £1,000 and that an adult who has a dislocated finger is entitled to £1,250.

The Secretary of State has made the measure too rigid and inflexible and has produced a scheme that the public will not consider fair and equitable. I have a number of questions in respect of the gaps in the Bill and I hope that the Minister will answer them. Why are people not compensated in the same way they would be if they sued their assailant in court? Why are the tariff levels not to be determined by an independent body of experts? We have not yet heard whether the tariff levels will rise in line with inflation. If they will, why has that not been incorporated in the Bill?

The Bill also gives no clear definition of the likely time limits involved. Other Labour Members have recommended an extension to three years, and I think that that is probably right. Of course, we cannot have an open-ended commitment, but the present common law limit of three years seems entirely reasonable. Nor does the Bill make room for exceptional cases in which the victim might apply when time had run out: a child who had suffered sexual or physical abuse, for instance, might not be able—or psychologically ready—to complain to the police until many years later.

An anomaly in the Bill relating to multiple injuries highlights the unfairness and lack of flexibility of tariff schemes. Loss of sight in one eye will attract compensation of £20,000, while loss of hearing in one ear will be worth £15,000. A victim who suffers both injuries, however, will receive only £21,500. That is not adequate compensation.

The hon. Member for Southwark and Bermondsey cited a number of constituency cases, and many of us who represent London constituencies could give similar examples. One in 43 people in London is likely to be a victim of violent crime—the highest proportion in the country. London Members therefore take the Bill very seriously.

The aim of the scheme is to cut the money available to compensate victims of violent crime, which is economically illogical as well as mean-spirited. Cutting such compensation will probably force us to exert pressure on social and health service expenditure. The hon. Member for Southwark and Bermondsey welcomed the statutory framework, saying that it would mean less use of the royal prerogative; I too welcome that, but I hope that the Home Secretary will make an early announcement about the qualification rules for the new scheme. Will they be subject to parliamentary approval?

The Labour party's reasoned amendment reflects the needs of victims in our criminal justice system. I have mentioned the cutting of the cash available to victims and the lack of consultation, among other problems. Although I am pleased that the Home Secretary has had to return to the House to present a change to the scheme that he originally intended, that change is inadequate: if we really want to put victims at the centre of our criminal justice system, we shall have to consider it in detail in

Committee. Victims of crime have enough problems in recovering without having to worry about inadequate financial settlements.

Labour Members—and, no doubt, Conservative Members—could give many examples. Let me simply repeat that victims of crime should be at the centre of the criminal justice system. They should not have to pay for the inadequacies of the system, mentally, physically or financially; it is the job of Government and Parliament to ensure that they are protected. I do not believe that the Bill goes far enough in that regard, and I hope that in Committee we have an opportunity to make detailed amendments and ensure that the scheme reflects our responsibilities to the victims of our criminal system.

7.24 pm

**Mr. Hartley Booth** (Finchley): It is a pleasure to follow the Member for Lewisham, East (Mrs. Prentice), who has shown that she is indeed concerned about victims of crime—as I assume every hon. Member participating in the debate to be.

When it is claimed that the Government have a poor record in this regard, my hon. Friend the Minister and, indeed, my hon. Friend the Member for Plymouth, Sutton (Mr. Streeter) reply that we have the best compensation scheme in the world. I shall say more about that shortly; first, I must declare some relevant interests—none of which, sadly, involves payment. I am a trustee of the Police Dependants Trust Appeal. Policemen are frequently victims of violent crime; they are compensated by the trust fund, and I hope that the Bill will result in further compensation. I dealt with matters of this kind as a practising barrister, and also with the compensation referred to by the hon. Member for Lewisham, East in civil cases. I have been concerned about the issue for some time, and have even written a booklet on the subject.

The remarks of the hon. Member for Southwark and Bermondsey (Mr. Hughes) were enough to spark me into life. He began by saying that we had done very little for victims. If so, why does the Bill refer to a necessary repeal of legislation passed as recently as 1988? We are so anxious to help victims in our legislation that we have taken parliamentary time to legislate twice in the past seven years, and we are now trying to improve what is already a generous scheme. The hon. Member for Southwark and Bermondsey criticised the ignoring of the initial 28 weeks, but that is a false criticism: we have a generous welfare benefits system for everyone who is injured, which helps people during those 28 weeks.

The common law system has been described as complicated. It is not yet clear how the tariff scheme will operate. Clause 10 explains that the Home Secretary will be able to legislate for the calculation involved in the scheme. I am sorry that I could not be present for the first part of the debate—I came in during the speech of my hon. and learned Friend the Member for Harborough (Mr. Garnier)—but we have heard that the tariff scheme will involve a set of monetary amounts calculated in accordance with the description of an injury. For the first time we shall have a codified set of compensatory amounts. That is a useful reform, which could well be copied later for the purposes of the civil courts. To predict

*[Mr. Hartley Booth]*

that there will be other legislation on this subject over the next 10 years would be a digression, but it helps me to welcome the Bill.

**Mr. Peter Ainsworth** (Surrey, East): My hon. Friend makes a good and interesting point. Does he agree that to some extent compensation paid by the courts is something of a lottery? A tariff scheme such as that proposed in the Bill would put an end to such uncertainties.

**Mr. Booth:** I was beginning to develop that point. Hundreds, or perhaps thousands, of lawyers are daily involved in the complicated exercise of calculating someone's loss after injury. That is another form of lottery. Although the Home Secretary will have power to make changes, he has made an honest stab at determining a once-and-for-all compensatory calculation. That is welcome, because it will not only clarify obfuscation but give victims compensation within a reasonable time.

It has been suggested that Conservative Members do not think about victims. If that were so, why would clause 7 bother to go into detail about the awards being inalienable? The Bill seeks to help only the victim. Some commentators have suggested that it is merely a tinkering exercise, but it is more than fine tuning. It will introduce an excellent scheme although to some extent it may be inchoate because clause 10 allows the Home Secretary to progress only some aspects of the Bill. Perhaps he can elaborate on that towards the end of the debate. The big question is whether the House again trusts the Home Secretary to introduce regulations that will flesh out the Bill. Conservative Members certainly trust him.

It would be wrong to say that welcoming the Bill is the end of the matter because the House should always try to push reform. I agree with hon. Members who have said that we should always put the victim first. The Minister and I have had discussions on how to frame legislation that would make it the first duty of every criminal court to consider the victim. Perhaps now or in Committee the Government will use the analysis of criminal compensation to stress the absolute priority of the victim's needs.

An infinite number of consequences would flow from the addition of a clause to put the victim first. I do not need to go into detail because hon. Members can visualise the results of such a clause. It would make sure that a person who had been found guilty of an offence would be assessed to find out how much he could pay in compensation. There is a gap in the Bill and I should like to see it filled. Perhaps it is too late to include in the Bill a provision to the effect that, where possible, the culprit should pay compensation to the victim. Such a link should be enshrined in statute law and this is an admirable opportunity for the Government to create such a link.

The Bill is part of the excellent matrix of help that we are offering victims. I hope that I have pointed the way to further help for victims and that the Bill is only a staging point for much more help. I welcome the measure and I hope that it has Opposition support.

7.35 pm

**Mr. David Trimble** (Upper Bann): As I shall later make a number of criticisms of the Bill, it is perhaps appropriate to start by welcoming two aspects of it. I am pleased to see that the Home Secretary is back in his place. I am glad to note that the Bill represents two small but significant U-turns by the Home Secretary—one voluntary and the other involuntary. The voluntary change, which I welcome, is that we are to have what the Home Secretary calls an enhanced tariff scheme that will, to some extent, take account of loss of earnings and other expenses that might be incurred by victims. I am pleased to see that some provision—although, regrettably, it is inadequate—has been made.

The involuntary change is that the Bill is here at all. Its presence results from the decision by the Judicial Committee of the House of Lords on this matter. Some hon. Members counted judges and balanced one thing against another, and it was interesting to note that in speaking about the legality of his action the Home Secretary said that it was a grey area. I admit that there is a grey area because there is uncertainty about whether the action was lawful. We are dealing with matters of significant constitutional import, but rather than coming before the House and making sure that his action was lawful and constitutional, the Home Secretary decided to try to push ahead and chance his arm to see how far he could go.

**Mr. Howard:** The hon. Gentleman, most uncharacteristically, misunderstands. It was only as a result of the court decisions that it was appreciated that this was a grey area. When I looked at the matter in advance I took advice and went into it very carefully. I took the view, and I was supported by the judgments that were delivered in the case as it went through its various stages—as the hon. Gentleman will discover if he reads them all, although it may take him a long time—that it was not a grey area. My view was that I was clearly entitled to do what I did. The statutory provisions of the Criminal Justice Act 1988 had never been brought into force and, just as the existing scheme was operating perfectly adequately under the royal prerogative, my view was that a new scheme could so operate. As a result of what happened in the courts I am now obliged to accept that it is a grey area.

**Mr. Trimble:** The Home Secretary is right to say that I misunderstood him. I thought from what he said that he had been of the opinion before he launched on what we can call the 1994 tariff scheme that he was dealing with a grey area. He now says that it was only as a result of court decisions that he discovered that he had been in a grey area.

I am even more appalled by what the right hon. and learned Gentleman has just said. He has said that the advice he was given before he started the 1994 scheme—and hence his view of it—was that what he was doing was perfectly lawful. I am astounded to learn that that was the advice given him by the Home Office. I should have thought that any lawyer familiar with the Padfield case would have realised that the Home Secretary was acting dangerously by ignoring what Parliament specified in the 1988 Act. My only surprise is that so many lawyers were not prepared to conclude that the Home Secretary's action was unconstitutional, as I had no doubt it was. I am amazed to hear that he did not receive advice along those lines. The Home Secretary should perhaps carefully consider the quality of the advice that he has been receiving on this matter.

I am happy to see the Bill here. The 1988 Act was not enough; there should have been legislation even before that, because the 1964 scheme was itself operating in a grey area. As long ago as 1983 Lord Elwyn-Jones commented that the non-statutory scheme was a constitutional anomaly. He was right. Remarkably, the scheme operated under the royal prerogative without statutory authority. It should have been put on the statute book and I am glad that it now will be—although I intend to comment on the Bill's defects presently.

The chief feature of this scheme is that it operates with a tariff. In principle there may be nothing wrong with that. To some extent the courts operate to a tariff. Common law damages cover a number of items—pain and suffering, loss of amenity and then loss of earnings. For pain and suffering and loss of amenity the courts have worked out what are sometimes referred to as a conventional scale of damages. Looking through common law decisions to assess damages in tort actions one can identify the conventional sums paid in respect of pain and suffering and loss of amenity, so the idea of a conventional sum is not unusual.

The proposed tariff is based on tort compensation. I was surprised to hear some hon. Members claim that we were moving away from the common law scheme: we are not. The Criminal Injuries Compensation Board operated on common law principles. The tariff is derived from its decisions, or rather from a survey of its decisions, so ultimately it derives from common law damages, but in a curious way. The tariff does not try to identify the conventional sum paid for loss of amenity and pain and suffering. The survey of the board's decisions took into account not just the conventional sum but the extent to which there would be compensation for loss of earnings.

Thus, with the 1994 scheme and the unenhanced tariff, the Government justified the latter by saying that it already included an element of loss of earnings. Now, with the enhanced tariff, there remains conceptual confusion over how we are proceeding. I could understand it if the tariff operated by reference to the conventional sums that the courts have worked out for loss of amenity and pain and suffering, adding loss of earnings to that; but now that that is not to happen, we seem to be operating in some confusion.

What is more, the procedure is too rigid and inflexible. In a debate in the other place Lord Carlisle criticised the scheme, saying that

"a tariff of its nature, for example, means that no regard can be had to such fundamental matters as the age, sex, occupation or way of life of the victim, all of which are reflected enormously in the effect which an injury may have on an individual."—[*Official Report, House of Lords*, 2 March 1994; Vol. 552, c. 1081.]

Loss of earnings is a separate issue, but the effect of an injury leading to loss of amenity will vary tremendously depending on the age and circumstances of a victim. The tariff makes no allowance for that.

Would it have been possible to set out some form of tariff that did make such allowance? The survey of CICB cases, we were told in the White Paper of a couple of years ago, resulted in a median being selected as the amount to go for. Was that possible because the claims identified fell into a narrow range? Would it have been possible to formulate the tariff in terms of a range? There is nothing unusual in guidelines, after all. The courts lay them down for sentencing, and for tort cases they use a conventional scale which is not rigid and which can vary depending on circumstances.

I well appreciate that any element of individual judgment of this sort may include an element of delay and of cost, and one of the Bill's objectives is to reduce delays and costs. I appreciate that there may be a trade-off, but I believe that there may be problems with the precision in the proposed tariff.

I mentioned earlier my pleasure at noting that some provision for loss of earnings is being made, but it is wholly inadequate. It is not just a question of one and a half times average earnings, or of arguing about people getting disability allowance or other statutory benefits during the first 28 weeks; it is a question of the actual loss of earnings that a person may suffer. People with high incomes will suffer the most in this respect. Statutory benefits will be of no significant recompense to them while they suffer loss of earnings, and those who suffer the greatest loss will lose out most under this scheme. It is likely that they will have commitments that they cannot meet because the compensation that they receive is inadequate.

When this issue was raised before, the Home Secretary defended his approach by saying that people with high earnings should take out insurance to cover themselves against the possibility of loss of earnings arising out of a criminal injury. I doubt whether that is a viable option, and that is a serious flaw in the whole scheme. The provision made in the legislation will not suffice for people who suffer the heaviest losses, and the points that have been made about the self-employed serve to reinforce that.

**Mr. Howard:** I think that the hon. Gentleman is referring to the cap of one and a half times average earnings, but that is a feature not only of the proposed scheme but of the current common law-based scheme. It is not a new feature resulting from a tariff.

**Mr. Trimble:** My point is that people will lose out during the 28 weeks when they are reduced to statutory benefits alone, and that they will lose out because of the one and a half times earnings cap. The right hon. and learned Gentleman says that the same applied to the previous scheme, which I am happy to say was different from the one with which I am most familiar: the scheme in Northern Ireland, the best in the world. That is another reason for my desire not to have the legislation extended to Northern Ireland in any circumstances—it is much worse than our scheme.

These points alone would incline my right hon. and hon. Friends and me to oppose the scheme, but I oppose it on other grounds as well. The whole Bill is defective. The hon. Member for Southwark and Bermondsey (Mr. Hughes) mentioned the mistakes the House made in the legislation on child support. We agreed to a framework Act; the meat was in the regulations, and they in turn did not get it right. We have had a lot of difficulty since then trying to get the legislation right and to correct past mistakes. Much the same could happen with this Bill, which is merely a framework or outline. The meat will be in the scheme, which we do not have before us. While the Bill gives statutory authority to the scheme, it does not put it on the statute book. That is a fundamental flaw and a bad way to legislate.

There is an element of parliamentary control over the scheme. Clause 10 provides that certain matters have to be approved by resolution of this House. That is not adequate parliamentary control. There will be a brief debate before the resolution is passed.

[*Mr. Trimble*]

The procedure will be very similar to the debates we have in respect of Northern Ireland Orders in Council. Those debates are extremely frustrating because one cannot discuss detail, make changes or have the equivalent of a Committee hearing. I was interested to hear hon. Members on both sides of the House say that they will look at this or that aspect in Committee, but the meat of the Bill will not be considered in Committee. The meat of the legislation is in the scheme and that will not be subject to line-by-line examination in Committee. That manner of legislating effectively bypasses Committee consideration in this House. That is wrong in principle as a form of legislation. A serious mistake has been made.

Important matters will be in the scheme and we know what some of them will be. Paragraph 27 of 1993 White Paper said:

"The Government believes that these basic criteria have stood the test of time and worked well in practice. No fundamental changes to the current rules are therefore proposed."

When the scheme came into operation in 1994 some of those basic fundamental rules were repeated such as the provision that personal injury must be "directly attributable" to a crime of violence and the provisions for withholding awards where persons fail to take all reasonable steps to inform or co-operate with the police or have failed to give reasonable assistance to the authority or where there is a problem about the conduct of the applicant.

Those provisions existed under the old common law scheme and under the first tariff scheme and, presumably, will be carried forward into the new scheme. They are familiar to me because they are in the Northern Ireland legislation. Indeed, Northern Ireland case law contains scores of cases on the interpretation of the phrase "directly attributable". Such provisions are in Northern Ireland legislation. Why will they not be on the statute book in respect of this legislation? There is no reason why these basic principles, which were contained in the previous schemes, cannot be included in the Bill.

Those provisions will not be subject to any form of parliamentary scrutiny because the provisions in clause 10 on what shall be subject to parliamentary scrutiny are drawn very tightly and leave out the basic provisions about qualification, entitlement and the conditions in which people may have their compensation reduced or disallowed. The administrative provisions are also left out. Such provisions should be in the Bill and for that reason, the legislation is defective.

I have a further example. Hon. Members have referred to the three-year time limit of the original scheme, which was dropped to one year under the first tariff scheme. The Home Secretary announced a two-year time limit. I looked back over the note that he give us, entitled "Proposals for a Tariff-based Scheme". I did not read it in that note. Perhaps it has been published elsewhere or perhaps it was announced for the first time in the Home Secretary's speech. It is nowhere in the material before us, as far as I am aware. That is a fundamentally wrong way to proceed.

There are other questions that I could ask but I will content myself with one more. Frequent reference was made by Conservative Members to their belief that this is the most generous scheme in the world. That is not quite accurate. It is an understandable mistake in the sense that it follows the tradition of the House of always ignoring Northern Ireland, because the most generous scheme exists in Northern Ireland and long may that continue. Apart from that, it is accurate to say that this is the most generous scheme in Europe. Certainly, the old scheme was and the proposed scheme probably will be.

I hope that the Minister will deal with the question of whether the scheme is entirely in accordance with the European convention on the compensation of victims of violent crime, which the United Kingdom ratified in 1991. I think that the scheme is within its provisions but I want an assurance that no derogation from the convention's provisions is intended in the scheme. However, the scheme is more generous than those elsewhere in Europe. It is good that that is being continued, even if not quite as generously as heretofore. It is not as good as that in Northern Ireland. I trust that the Northern Ireland scheme will be left alone.

For the reasons that I gave earlier about the defective way in which we are legislating and because of the failure to deal adequately with the loss of earnings issue, I cannot support the Bill. I will vote for Labour's reasoned amendment.

7.57 pm

**Mr. Peter Ainsworth** (Surrey, East): I shall not follow the hon. Member for Upper Bann (Mr. Trimble) into the Lobby tonight, though he speaks on these matters with great authority.

The hon. Gentleman questioned whether this was the most generous scheme in the world. I looked at the figures produced by the Library, which tend to support the suggestion that it is indeed the most generous scheme, although the hon. Gentleman is right that there is a very generous scheme in Northern Ireland. The scheme is the most generous scheme in the world, including the United States of America. One could argue about these figures indefinitely if one chose to do so. I rely for my information on that provided by the House of Commons Library.

I very much welcome the Bill, which I believe will establish a faster system of payment to the victims of crime. It will also be fairer due to the greater transparency which will result from the tariff system introduced by the Bill.

I congratulate my right hon. and learned Friend the Secretary of State not just on coming up with a scheme based on a clear and transparent tariff but on his persistence, because the proposal has not been without its detractors, both in another place and here. It has not been without its setbacks, either, although it is important to remember that the principal setback that the proposal suffered was not from criticism of the principle but from a matter of detail. My right hon. and learned Friend therefore deserves congratulations on perseverance.

There will always be immense problems in trying to devise an entirely satisfactory scheme which tries to match physical injury with monetary value because no scheme that anybody can or ever will devise can truly place an accurate monetary value on the loss of a limb, life or happiness. It cannot be done. The best that one can do is to look clearly and objectively at cases and come up with a tariff of the type that my right hon. and learned Friend envisages.

**Mr. Mike O'Brien:** The hon. Gentleman makes an important point, but is he suggesting that the common law basis on which personal injuries are now assessed in the civil courts must be changed as well? Is that what he is advocating that the Government should do?

**Mr. Ainsworth:** The hon. Gentleman was present when my hon. Friend the Member for Finchley (Mr. Booth) made that suggestion. I said at the time, and I say again now, that there is some merit in considering the idea because of the lottery element which currently exists under common law. I concede that, for the sake of clarity and consistency, there would be some merit in considering a switch to that line of thought.

It says a great deal about our culture that increasingly we seem to be weighing monetary value against the physical damage caused not only, as in this case, by criminal activity but by misfortune and accidents. In considering the Bill, I was reminded of a case which appeared in the newspapers about 18 months ago. A gentleman had gone for a walk along the Cobb at Lyme Regis which, if we have read our Jane Austen, we know can be a dangerous place. In any event, he fell off and damaged his leg. He took the local district council to court over the damage that he suffered and local council tax payers ended up giving him some £75,000 in compensation, if my memory serves me correctly.

The lottery aspect of common law, to which the hon. Member for Warwickshire, North (Mr. O'Brien) is apparently oblivious, is graphically illustrated by that example. The man damaged his leg while walking in a place where hundreds of people have walked for hundreds of years. Yet he was able to take the taxpayer to task for £75,000 while the surviving members of the family of a person who has been murdered will receive a minimum of £10,000, although it can be a great deal more. That illustrates the immense difficulty of placing a monetary value on physical loss and damage.

I am not saying that the answer to the anomaly is necessarily to increase massively the amounts paid under the compensation arrangements for criminal injury. I would suggest that the answer is to have in place a more sensible system for awarding damages in those cases dealt with under common law. The criminal compensation scheme is clearly very different from that which applies in common law cases and in cases of accidental damage. It has been accepted for very many years that society as a whole has a responsibility to shoulder in cases of criminal injury.

**Mr. Booth:** My hon. Friend is developing the important point that we must focus always on achieving some clarity in the definition of compensation for injury. Does he agree that it is also important to deal with the other head of damages, or loss of earnings, which is much easier to quantify?

**Mr. Ainsworth:** My hon. Friend is right. It is a welcome innovation that the Bill deals with precisely that matter.

Given that we accept, probably rightly, the approach that "We Are All Guilty", to quote the title of a novella by Kingsley Amis—a title probably used with a degree of irony—the system set out in the Bill is sensible and fair. However, I welcome especially the changes that have been introduced since the proposal first saw the light of day. The proposal is now more generous to those who lose earnings as a result of becoming victims of criminal activity. I welcome the introduction of an element to deal

with dependency costs and the fact that the number of qualifying injury descriptions has been substantially increased to the tune of about 100. As I said, no amount of money can ever truly compensate for the loss or damage caused by criminal behaviour—there is no matching the two—but I believe that the Bill, with its clear tariff and reasonable terms for victims, is a sensible way forward.

The key issue for the Government—for any Government—is to crack down on violent crime in the first place. As I and my colleagues know, my right hon. and learned Friend the Home Secretary is engaged in a far-reaching and radical reform of the criminal justice system which will do exactly that. It will crack down on those who perpetrate violent crime and it will lead to tougher sentences; it will mean more police, better use of high technology in detection and higher levels of detection. That is what will lead ultimately to a reduction in violent crime, which is what we are united in wishing to see.

8.5 pm

**Mr. Mike O'Brien** (Warwickshire, North): I agree with the hon. Member for Surrey, East (Mr. Ainsworth) that we need to be tough in dealing with criminals. Unfortunately, however, it seems that the Home Secretary is being tough on victims of crime, which is not what Members of Parliament are supposed to be about.

I must declare that I am a parliamentary adviser to the Police Federation. Although I receive no personal income from that position, I receive help with research and office expenses, and it is right that I should declare that fact. The views of the Police Federation have been eloquently expressed by the hon. Member for Uxbridge (Mr. Shersby), who also has the honour of advising the federation. Suffice it to say that the federation, which represents 126,000 police officers, regards the Bill as deeply flawed and in need of substantial amendment. I associate myself entirely with those criticisms of the Bill expressed by the hon. Member for Uxbridge, but I have some further points to make.

The Home Secretary keeps telling us that his new tariff scheme will be the most generous in the world. The problem is that we already have the most generous scheme and the Government intend to make it much less generous. That is not something of which they should be proud.

The hon. Member for Surrey, East has some interesting ideas, and it is important that the Minister who winds up the debate should comment on some of them, especially the notion that the civil courts should perhaps look again at the way in which they award personal injury compensation and should consider doing so on the basis of a tariff scheme. The hon. Gentleman rightly suggested that there is a certain consistency in introducing the tariff scheme in the awarding of other personal injuries. I shall be interested to hear what the Minister has to say.

**Mr. Peter Ainsworth:** I hesitate to say this, but now that my right hon. and learned Friend the Home Secretary has left the Chamber, albeit briefly, perhaps I could say that not the least benefit of moving to a tariff scheme in civil cases would be a reduction in lawyers' fees. I am aware, of course, that the hon. Member for Warwickshire, North (Mr. O'Brien) is also a lawyer.

**Mr. O'Brien:** Yes, I am, as are many other hon. Members. However, I do not practise at the moment, so I would not benefit from such a change.

I acknowledge openly that the Bill is not so bad as the scheme originally suggested by the Home Secretary. It is, however, a defective Bill which will make many potential victims of crime worse off. The fundamental problem with a tariff-based system is that victims are not treated as individuals. The Home Secretary seems more intent on setting up a cheap administrative system than on responding to the very reason why the scheme was set up in the first place—the fact that society has sympathy with the victims of crime and wants to help them to recover from their injuries. It is right that individuals should be treated as individuals when compensation is assessed, certainly when injuries are very serious. To deny victims their individuality—the reality of very different expectations and losses—is to make them victims of a bureaucratic injustice.

A provision for loss of earnings is welcome, but what of the provision for those who are off work for fewer than 28 weeks? Cannot we acknowledge them as deserving victims? Why must they rely on statutory sick pay? Why must self-employed people fend for themselves? Although the overall cap of £500,000 sounds a lot—it is double the amount that the Home Secretary originally wanted under his unlawful scheme—we must remember that a 20-year-old breadwinner with a family, who is the victim of a very serious criminal assault leaving him or her a quadriplegic or with serious brain damage, may well have to struggle on £500,000 to provide for the family for the next 60 years. For an 80-year-old pensioner £500,000 may be some compensation, but for a 20-year-old breadwinner it is not.

There are three criticisms of the Bill. First, it is a cynical attempt to save money at the expense of victims. The Home Office estimated that under the original common law scheme compensation would rise to £500 million by the turn of the century, compared with a rise to £260 million under the new tariff scheme. That is out of a criminal justice budget of around £10 billion. Victim Support said:

"it is not justified considering the small proportion of the criminal justice budget currently available to victims".

Will the Minister say why spending only one twentieth of his budget on the victims of crime is too much?

**Mr. Maclean:** Before I answer that, will the hon. Gentleman tell me what other part of the budget I should cut?

**Mr. O'Brien:** The Minister might look at all the various schemes for privatisation, for creating boot camps, which he is considering, and at all the various reports that he has commissioned to get the private sector involved— all of which will lead to bad practice in prisons and in the criminal justice system generally. Let him also look at the organisation of the Crown Prosecution Service and at the various ways in which our criminal justice system is inefficiently and ineffectively administered. Let him look at the way in which the victims of crime are not dealt with sensibly when they get to court and how they are required to wait for long periods at great loss to

themselves. Let him look at the cost to the police service of having officers sitting around for long periods, which he has allowed to occur for many years.

**Mr. Sweeney:** Will the hon. Gentleman give way?

**Mr. O'Brien:** Perhaps the hon. Gentleman will allow me to reply to the Minister, who has asked me an important question.

Let the Minister deal with the amount of time that prison officers waste waiting around in courts. Let him deal with the time during which courts lie empty or are kept open when they should not be. Let him deal with those inefficiencies in the criminal justice system before he starts cutting the budget available for the victims of crime.

The second criticism is that the amended scheme will lead to unfairness.

**Mr. Sweeney:** How long has the hon. Gentleman been out of practice? I suspect that if he had been in court recently he would have seen that the Government are addressing issues such as the conditions in which witnesses and victims have to wait, the waiting periods generally and the organisation of the courts to which he referred. All those matters are being addressed—no doubt at considerable expense. Will the hon. Gentleman now respond to the Minister's inquiry about which areas of expenditure he would cut to increase the amount spent on victims?

**Mr. O'Brien:** I would certainly seek to cut crime, which the Minister has had great difficulty in doing. It is three years since I practised regularly in the criminal courts. I am a full-time Member of Parliament. I remind the hon. Member for Vale of Glamorgan (Mr. Sweeney) that the Government have been in power for an awful long time. How long has it taken them to deal with those inefficiencies? How long have victims needed to wait before the Government have responded to the inefficiencies which have caused victims such inconvenience in court? How long will police officers have to wait before they are no longer required to hang around courts for long hours? The Government have had ample opportunity over the years to deal with such problems and they have simply failed to do so.

I return to the second criticism of the Bill. I was commenting on the general unfairness of the way in which the system will operate. A system which does not distinguish between injuries to dominant and non-dominant hands or arms, which, self-evidently, will affect people in different ways depending on whether they are left-handed or right-handed, raises questions of unfairness. A system which does not distinguish between the life expectancy of a young person who has been blinded, perhaps, and that of an elderly person and his very different needs leads to unfairness.

The Home Secretary has already had to increase the list of basic injuries from 187 in his unlawful scheme to 310 in his new Bill. That is a reflection of his recognition that increased flexibility is needed, but I suspect that, as we proceed, other categories will have to be added to the 310 to cope with the various cases of unfairness which will inevitably arise. Will the Minister confirm that he will be prepared to add to that list if unfairnesses become obvious? It is important, as I am sure that he will accept, that we try to minimise unfairness if we are to have a tariff system. Will he therefore adopt an open mind on increasing that list?

The basic unfairness of the Bill lies between the present victims of crime and future victims of crime. Recently I heard the story of a young man from Hillingdon, Mr. Andrew Hay, who was attacked by three masked robbers during a night-time break-in three years ago in which his girlfriend was also terrorised. He received £12,000 under the old criminal injuries compensation scheme and his girlfriend Susan received £6,000. Under the Home Secretary's new scheme, Mr. Hay would be awarded £2,000 and his girlfriend would get nothing. A victim of rape received £75,000 under the common law system but would receive only about £15,000 under the new scheme. Why is one victim worth a certain sum now but a similar victim will be worth a fraction of that sum in future? That is a fundamental unfairness which the Government must answer.

The third problem is that the Bill raises several administrative concerns. Will the Minister confirm that decisions on amounts and on tariffs will be made by relatively junior civil servants? The taking of such decisions is not a problem when it is a straightforward case. If we operate a tariff system, presumably a junior civil servant will be able to make the decision. However, many cases are very complex and difficult. For example, should a claim for compensation be discounted because of provocation or failure fully to co-operate with the police and, if so, by how much? Problematical judgments need to be made and junior civil servants are not suitable arbiters in such contentious situations.

What of cases in which there is multiple injury, psychiatric injury or the consequences of sexual attack? Will the Minister say how those decisions will be dealt with? The Criminal Injuries Compensation Board included experienced personal injury practitioners, but the people who are to run the new system will not have the benefit of the same degree of experience when assessing various claims.

The Bill is not about helping victims; it is about cutting the cost to the Government of helping victims. Despite changes in policy, it remains a callous and unpleasant little Bill. It is not just that it puts the Government on the wrong side of the argument about the victims of crime— the phrase used by the Leader of the House. It is that it communicates to people outside this place that the British Parliament cares less about the victims of crime than it used to do because they have got too expensive for the Government.

The Home Secretary mouths an awful lot of pious statements about his concern for victims, but he cuts their compensation to fund the Treasury's wrongdoings in economic policy. We have a Government who talk tough on crime, but who have presided over the biggest crime rise in history during the past 16 years. The Government have done some very shabby things in the past 16 years, but cutting compensation to victims of crime must be right down there among the worst of them. We do not do enough for victims in our criminal justice system and if the Bill is passed we shall do even less.

8.20 pm

**Mr. Walter Sweeney** (Vale of Glamorgan): I begin by declaring an interest as a solicitor, albeit only in very occasional practice, who could conceivably act for a claimant under the new scheme.

I warmly congratulate my right hon. and learned Friend the Home Secretary on introducing the Bill. I welcomed his original scheme, and I was sorry to see its enforced withdrawal. The extra wait forced on the Government by the courts has proved helpful, in that we now have an even better scheme. The new scheme will provide quicker and more transparent payments to more people than the old common law scheme, and will enable loss of earnings and other important factors to be taken into account.

It was interesting to hear the hon. Member for Blackburn (Mr. Straw) deride the levels of proposed payments to victims. It was interesting partly because it demonstrated, as so rightly pointed out by my hon. Friend the Member for Shoreham (Mr. Stephen), that the Labour party has still not learnt, after 16 years in opposition, that throwing more and more of other people's money at problems is not good for taxpayers, and not good for the economy.

The remarks by the hon. Member for Blackburn were also interesting for the insight they gave into the way in which the Labour party's consciousness is blind to its own failings in the past. To listen to the hon. Gentleman—

**Mr. Mike O'Brien:** I am a little concerned about the impression that the hon. Gentleman may be giving; I am sure that it is not his intention. He spoke about throwing money at other people's problems. Does he accept that the victims of crime are the problem of all of us?

**Mr. Sweeney:** The problems of all of us are the criminals who are hurting the victims. It is a mistake to see the Government in the role of a criminal who is being forced to pay compensation. The Government do not commit these crimes. The Government provide an ex gratia system of compensation which is designed to help victims, and that system, as I shall explain, is extremely generous.

Listening to the hon. Member for Blackburn, an innocent bystander who knew nothing of Labour's record in the 1970s would assume that, when Labour was in office, it was far more generous to victims than the Government now plan to be. Not so. In 1978-79, £15.7 million of compensation was paid to 17,460 victims of crime. That represents an average award of £2,258 at 1994-95 prices. In 1996-97, the average award is likely to be £2,500 at 1994-95 prices, but the number of awards is predicted to be 55,100.

In other words, even after allowing for inflation, each victim is likely to receive slightly more than when Labour was in power. The big difference is that more than three times as many victims will be compensated. It is true that the average payment to each victim will be substantially less than in recent years, but, given the big increase in the number of payments made, only an irresponsible Government would fail to look for ways in which to slow down the growth in the total amount of compensation paid.

I was interested in the contribution by the right hon. and learned Member for Aberavon (Mr. Morris), in which he suggested that a young girl should receive more compensation for facial injuries than should a middle-aged man. I am pleased that he at least is not

*[Mr. Sweeney]*

obsessed with political correctness as are so many of his political colleagues, and that he is prepared to risk their wrath by being sexist and agist at the same time.

I am inclined to agree with the right hon. and learned Gentleman that, in an ideal world, assessment of damages under the common law would more fairly reflect the needs of victims in terms of the amount of compensation paid. If claims are dealt with individually, the principle of common law compensation—as far as possible, putting people back in the position they were in before the act complained of—can be applied more accurately.

If the victim of a crime brings a civil action against a wealthy criminal, that principle should be applied. However, the right hon. and learned Gentleman has misunderstood the nature of criminal injuries compensation. As I said earlier in response to an intervention, these payments are made not by the guilty parties, but by the state on an ex gratia basis. The important factors in a state compensation scheme are that payments should be prompt, that there should be transparency, and that individual payments should be generous, but tempered by concern for public funds.

A number of hon. Members have rightly pointed out that Great Britain has the most generous criminal injuries compensation scheme in the world. The hon. Member for Upper Bann (Mr. Trimble) claimed that Northern Ireland deserved the laurels. Indeed, its figure of £26.6 million paid out in 1993-94 represents more in terms of the size of the population than the figure for Great Britain.

Some £165.1 million was paid out in the same year, which represents 36.2 per cent. of the total amount of compensation paid to victims in the whole world. Our wealthiest competitors, Germany and Japan, pay only 1.4 per cent. and 0.5 per cent. respectively of the total. Even the United States, with almost five times the population, pays out less than we do. In that context, we can be proud of the Bill, which will enable us to continue to provide the best help for victims in the world.

The right hon. and learned Member for Aberavon did not agree when I intervened to say that 60 per cent. of claimants would be at least as well off under the new scheme. I shall make the basis of my contention clear.

The average award under the new scheme will be lower, but only because the average under the old scheme was raised by a small number of very high awards, which will be lower in future. Under the old scheme, most people received less than the average, which means that most claimants under the new scheme will receive as much as or more than before. Claimants who receive less will have the not inconsiderable consolation of receiving their money much more quickly. Under the old scheme, some claimants had to wait years for their money.

The hon. Member for Warwickshire, North (Mr. O'Brien) acknowledged that we had the most generous compensation scheme in the world, and criticised the Government for making it less generous. The overall bill for compensation is likely to rise, not fall. It is not true, as the hon. Gentleman suggested, that the Home Office spends only one twentieth of its budget on victims. With respect to the hon. Member, the reality is that the whole of the Home Office budget—leaving aside the funds for the fire service—is spent on the victim, and we are all potential victims. The Home Office is doing a good job,

and is at last reversing the rising trend in crime, unlike many other countries worldwide. I commend this Bill, and will support it.

8.29 pm

**Mr. Robin Corbett** (Birmingham, Erdington): First, I apologise to the House for not being here earlier.

The Minister of State typically interrupted my hon. Friend the Member for Warwickshire, North (Mr. O'Brien)—in doing so, he implicitly acknowledged that this is a skinflint scheme—to ask where the money would come from if we were to make the scheme more generous. I can tell the Minister where the money would come from, and he knows the answer. The way to ensure that the costs of the criminal injuries compensation scheme are contained is for the Government to put the lid on rising crime. The cost of the scheme has escalated over the years because the Government have virtually abandoned any serious attempt to contain, prevent and detect crime.

The Minister will know that the risk of becoming a victim of a crime of violence was about one in 213 in 1979. It is now one in 64. The Minister should not take comfort from a fall in some categories of recorded crime. Recorded offences of violence against the person are still rising, and rose by 7 per cent. last year.

I find it deeply offensive for the hon. Member for Vale of Glamorgan (Mr. Sweeney) or anyone else to bandy around average figures. Victims of crime are not average. They are unique, and dividing sums of money to get an average result is totally meaningless. However, that is what lies at the heart of the new scheme. The Government say that every victim of crime who has suffered an unwanted injury is exactly the same as any other victim. That is patently not true.

My right hon. and learned Friend the Member for Aberavon (Mr. Morris) sensibly made the point that a young woman of 20 who suffers a severe facial disfigurement after an attack will suffer more serious consequences than a man of my age or older who suffers a similar facial injury. The notion of the tariff goes against the grain of what the system should be, although there may well be problems with the common law basis for an assessment of damages.

Can the Minister, who is so keen on bobbing up to the Dispatch Box, tell us how many victims of crime who have received compensation payments under the present scheme he has met and spoken to? I take it that the answer is none. That is what I suspected. I doubt very much whether any of his officials have done so either. I have spoken to such victims, as I shall tell the Minister and the House in a moment.

I find it offensive for the Home Secretary to issue press releases boasting that we have the most generous compensation scheme in the world, and that the Government are providing more money than the United States and the rest of the European Union. So what? Victims of crime who are knocked about and who have their lives threatened live here. Those violent crimes are carried out against our citizens here, and not in the United States or in other countries in the European Union. Those comparisons are totally irrelevant. *[Interruption.]*

The Minister is mumbling again. He can get up at any time to explain why crime has trebled under the Government, why crimes against the person are still rising, and why the Government show no sign of getting a handle on crime.

In the story that I shall tell the House, I shall not use my constituent's full name. It would not be fair, as I have not sought explicit permission to refer to the case. I hope that the facts will speak for themselves, and that the Minister will look at the matter when he winds up.

My constituent is self-employed, and works with her husband running an off-licence. I understand that, under the proposals in the Bill, loss of earnings can—on second thoughts—be taken into account in compensation scheme awards. Does that mean full loss of earnings for self-employed people and, if so, will those lost earnings be substantiated on the basis of the normal business tax returns which those people submit to the Inland Revenue? If the answer is no, on what basis will the scheme be assessed? Under the scheme that the Government are proposing, the self-employed will suffer.

We will call my constituent Mrs. A. She and her husband run an off-licence in a residential part of Erdington, within a few hundred yards of a parish church. In 1988, she and her husband were in the off-licence when a youth came in and found that he did not have enough money to pay for his beer. He then produced a knife and stabbed my constituent through the heart. It is only by accident that Mrs. A is still alive. She was taken to Queen Elizabeth hospital, such was the seriousness of her injury.

It was said that there were probably only two heart surgeons in the country with the necessary skills and experience to carry out such an emergency operation. By good chance—or perhaps it was something else—one of those surgeons happened to be visiting a friend in the city of Birmingham that weekend. He was asked whether he would attend the operating theatre. He did so, and literally snatched back the life of my constituent for her.

I do not know what level of compensation it would be proper to award in such circumstances. I find it wholly impossible to put a sum to that. My instinct would be to see Mrs. A., offer her a cheque book, sign it, fill in her name and tell her to put a figure on it, because I do not know what it is worth. Of course, I am not arguing that as a serious point, but that is one reaction to such an horrendous attack.

The Minister and the hon. Member for Vale of Glamorgan should not insult my constituent by mentioning average compensation figures to her, either for those horrendous injuries or for loss of earnings. She has still not got over that attack—that will surprise no one—and is unable ever again to serve behind the counter of the shop, which is wired up like Fort Knox and has closed circuit television cameras.

As is typical with such small businesses, the family live over the shop. Most of the time, my constituent lives in real terror—terror from the dreadful memories of what happened to her on that night, and terror because of the gangs of aimless youths who gather nearby, and it is not the only off-licence where that happens. Occasionally, the youths get up to mischievous pranks, but in the past few months the pranks have become more serious, and an adult was assaulted within a hundred yards of the off-licence. Frankly, I wonder how the family can go on in those circumstances.

**Mr. Stephen:** There can be no hon. Member who would not share the hon. Gentleman's sympathy for his constituent. Many of our constituents have suffered similarly. As he said, however, no amount of money can compensate that lady for what she suffered. Does he not agree, therefore, that the allocation of any sum of money on behalf of the taxpayer must, of necessity, be a somewhat artificial process that can never really express what society wants to express to her?

**Mr. Corbett:** I am grateful for that intervention, because the hon. Gentleman makes my point very nicely. I cannot agree with him. Of course I acknowledge that compensation for the horrendous injury is exceptionally difficult to determine. At the time of the accident, the lady was in her early 50s. I have described her injuries, and it is difficult to put a figure on them. I would find it virtually impossible to do so.

The point is that loss of earnings, which can be measured, is swept away under the Government's tariff scheme. That loss is of particular importance to the self-employed such as my constituent Mrs. A. Under this most generous scheme in the world, such arguments are bound to arise.

As I explained, my constituent was in hospital for a long time and received treatment for much longer. It was necessary to hire additional staff to keep the business going, because she was unable to help her husband to run the shop. The cost of the extra staff is known and it is quantifiable, as was demonstrated to the Criminal Injuries Compensation Board under this most generous scheme in the world. The figures are there and there is no argument about them.

The claim for what is known as special damages amounted to £37,405.82. The House will quickly detect that both a lawyer and an accountant had been involved to arrive at such a precise figure. In its wisdom, however, the board decided that the entitlement by way of special damages should be only £16,898. That demonstrates a problem with the existing non-tariff scheme, and I took the matter up with the board and its distinguished chairman, as any other hon. Member would have done.

Figures were provided to demonstrate the extra costs incurred running the business—in some senses, it was the reverse of loss of earnings—because my constituent was unable to play her proper part, for understandable reasons. I do not think that any hon. Member would criticise my constituent. That is the reality of the situation, and it is inconceivable that anyone who had suffered such an experience could go back behind the counter in what is necessarily a vulnerable position still, despite all the security precautions that have to be taken. In an off-licence, as with many other types of shop, large areas have to be open to customers, who want to walk around and select their purchases.

I do not think that there is any argument about the figures. To be fair, I do not think that the Criminal Injuries Compensation Board disputed the amount of the claim for special damages. The figures were real, those amounts had to be paid, and that fact was demonstrated. The board still felt unable, however, to compensate Mrs. A. and her husband fully for the extra cost of keeping the business going, which is in fact the same as loss of earnings.

In the light of some of the comments of Conservative Members, it is my strong feeling and that of my right hon. and hon. Friends that we have a collective duty to people who have been the victims of the most violent crimes—crimes from which we have collectively failed to protect them. Let us take the responsibility on all our shoulders.

There is no argument about the fact that the crime happened, and it is not good enough for the Minister and his right hon. and hon. Friends to say, "Okay, we

[Mr. Corbett]

recognise that something has to be done. We'll come up with an average figure. Think yourselves lucky." As one of the Minister's hon. Friends acknowledged, 40 out of every 100 people will get a lot less than they would have done under the original scheme, and it is not good enough the Government saying, "That's tough: just get on with it."

I have berated the Government for their lack of action to deter and to detect crime, and, in some ways, that is a party political point. I regret the fact that the criminal injuries compensation scheme has had to become a party political football.

The Minister was unable to tell me that he had consulted one victim of crime who had been awarded compensation by the Criminal Injuries Compensation Board. Outside the House, a range of organisations have criticised the Government for not consulting them about the proposals in the Bill, which I very much regret. No doubt the Minister will go through his ritual performance when he replies, but he must not be surprised that the Opposition are critical, if that is the way in which he goes about his business.

My constituent, Mrs. A., and other people out there who now have a one-in-64 chance of becoming victims of crime, simply will not understand why the Government did not listen first to their experiences. They will not understand why the Government have rolled the figures up into averages and said, "This crime affects everybody in the same way," regardless of their age or sex, which is patent nonsense.

While violent crime continues to increase, the bill will increase, and the Government should be ashamed that, since they cannot get a handle on violent crime, which is still rising, they are making the victims of crime pay for their neglect and mistakes.

8.47 pm

**Mr. Michael Stephen** (Shoreham): Clearly, it is the duty of any Government to protect their citizens against crime, but none of us is so unworldly as to suppose that any Government could eliminate crime entirely. There will always be criminals and victims of crime.

It is also clear that no amount of money can compensate a victim of crime for the injury that he or she has suffered. Money is merely a token that society can offer as some form of compensation. Of necessity, the amount must be calculated by a rather artificial process.

When the criminal injuries compensation scheme was set up, 30 years ago, £400,000 of taxpayers' money was spent on compensating the victims of crime. Last year, £165 million were spent in Great Britain, plus a further £26.6 million in Northern Ireland. It is projected that £175 million will be spent in Great Britain next year. Although those are large sums, the word "generous" would not be appropriate. We are not being generous to our fellow citizens when we compensate them for crime; we are simply offering them a token of our understanding of the injury that they have suffered.

The money paid to victims of crime has doubled since 1988. Our concern for the victims of crime compares extremely favourably with that in other countries which can reasonably be compared with ours. For example, France spends £27 million and Germany a mere £6.2

million. Although it is immaterial to victims of crime who have suffered their injuries in this country what the German or French Governments pay their injured citizens, when the House is considering the allocation of our national resources and the proportion that should be spent on the victims of crime, it is right and relevant, no matter what Opposition Members say, to make international comparisons. The Opposition are always ready to make international comparisons when those would reflect badly on this country, but they are more reluctant to make them when they reflect well. We spend more than all the other members of the European Union put together.

I am sure that the whole House wishes that we could spend more on compensating victims of crime, but we have a responsibility to consider and represent not only the recipients of the money but those who pay, the taxpayers. The Opposition speak as though the Government somehow seek to save their own money. They should realise that Governments have no money of their own; the only money they have is taken from the pockets of our constituents, and we must consider them as well.

Under common law, if the perpetrator of the tort or crime is to pay, money is no object and he must be forced to pay to the full extent of his personal resources. But if the taxpayer is to pay, he has not committed a crime and has no legal responsibility to pay; he has only a moral responsibility to pay, and his resources and ability to pay must be taken into account. Parliament would be abdicating its responsibilities to taxpayers if it did not consider their interests.

It is easy for the Opposition to say that we should spend more. Almost every point that I have heard from Opposition Members today could be met by getting out the national cheque book, but that would be too easy. One can do that in opposition, but Governments must find the cash. I consider that our constituents already pay too much tax, for a wide variety of reasons which you, Madam Deputy Speaker, would not permit me to go into this evening. I would be extremely reluctant to increase without good reason the burden that taxpayers already face. I notice that no Opposition Member has said that he has the authority of his Front-Bench economic spokesman to commit his party to greater expenditure on compensating victims of crime.

We must consider not just the taxpayer but the allocation of resources. Every pound that we spend on the criminal injuries compensation scheme is not available to spend on the national health service, education or all the other things that our constituents want. The money that the Government give to the criminal injuries compensation scheme is not the whole story. Victim Support, an organisation to which I give my whole-hearted support, received £10.8 million this year from the Government—or, more accurately, from our fellow citizens, the taxpayers. That sum is 8 per cent. more than last year, when it rose by 20 per cent. on the previous year.

The most effective way to help victims is to protect them from criminals, and I am pleased that we at last have a Home Secretary who is determined to roll back the half-baked left-wing attitudes to crime which have caused so many problems over the past 30 years. A major start has been made to protect people from crime. We spend more on the police than ever before in our history. They are better paid, better manned and better equipped than ever before. Last year in my county of Sussex, the Government allocated a huge increase in resources to our police authority. We have taken action against bail bandits through my private Member's Bill, followed by the Government's provisions in the Criminal Justice and Public Order Act 1994. We are introducing secure schools to deal with young hoodlums who are running out of control. We have introduced DNA testing and dealt with the so-called right of silence. It is absurd that a man can refuse to answer questions in the police station and that fact is kept from the jury, if the case goes to trial.

Opposition Members, particularly Labour Members, say that they are tough on crime and the causes of crime, but when it comes to the crunch and they must go into the Lobby to support measures introduced by the Government to protect people from criminals, we must judge them by their deeds.

**Mr. Michael:** I am sure that the hon. Gentleman would not wish to be ungenerous. Does he recall that Labour Front Benchers supported his Bail (Amendment) Bill and ensured that it did not die?

**Mr. Stephen** *rose*—

**Madam Deputy Speaker (Dame Janet Fookes):** Order. Before the hon. Gentleman continues his speech, I remind him of the content of the Bill which we are currently giving a Second Reading. He is now straying wide of that remit.

**Mr. Stephen:** I am grateful to you, Madam Deputy Speaker. But during the debate, the issue has arisen of how the money available to the Home Office is spent. It is therefore relevant to point out that the most effective way of spending money to benefit victims of crime is to protect them from criminals in the first place.

I acknowledge the support from Labour Front Benchers, particularly the hon. Member for Cardiff, South and Penarth (Mr. Michael), which enabled my Bail (Amendment) Bill to pass through the House. But on other occasions, especially when the Criminal Justice and Public Order Bill was being considered, Opposition support was less than whole-hearted. Money that is spent on the police and on measures to protect victims of crime from crime is, therefore, money well spent.

The Opposition have argued that the crime rate is now higher than when the Conservative party came to office in 1979. I pointed out to the Opposition spokesman, the hon. Member for Blackburn (Mr. Straw), that that is a worldwide phenomenon and that, since that time, crime has risen inexorably in all the developed countries of the western world. He dodged that point by quoting selectively from the period covering 1979 to 1983. He did not deal with my argument, and I submit that he cannot, that rising crime is a worldwide phenomenon. It is no use trying to blame the British Government for that, even if some specific argument were made for why the British Government are to blame. However, argument on that issue from the Opposition came there none.

There are complex reasons for our current high level of crime. If I might trespass on your patience, Madam Deputy Speaker, but not too far, I should like to mention some of them briefly. Those reasons include the breakdown of respect between citizens—between men and women and parents and children—which started in the 1960s and has carried on inexorably, as well as

people's lack of respect for all forms of authority. The rise in crime is also to do with the breakdown of religion, drugs and the effect of television when, night after night, low standards of personal behaviour are portrayed on our screens. The rise in crime is also due to greater mobility among criminals and, finally, poverty. It is, of course, the responsibility of all Governments to manage the economy in such a way that people are—

**Dame Elaine Kellett-Bowman:** Does my hon. Friend also agree that crime has risen because of the breakdown of discipline in schools in many areas, but thankfully not in mine?

**Mr. Stephen:** My hon. Friend makes a valid point. Child-centred education has a lot to answer for. If one teaches a child that he is the centre of the universe, one must not be surprised if he then finds it difficult to comply with the rules that society expects him to obey.

In addition to the financial support that the Government give to Victim Support, they have introduced the victims charter. It is derided by the Opposition because it does not involve large sums of money. It is a mission statement for those involved in the criminal justice process in the courts, the police and the Crown Prosecution Service. It tells them what the public are entitled to expect from them and enables us, as democratically elected representatives of the people, to keep them up to the mark if they fall below those standards. I talk a great deal to those involved in victim support organisations and they tell me that the victims charter is working in their local areas. It still has some way to go, because it has not been entirely successful, but we are getting there. Victims and witnesses are now treated much better.

I was a practising barrister for 15 years and, although I do not practise any more, I was involved in a good many personal injury cases when I was at the Bar. I saw that it was a costly business to ascertain the correct amount of compensation to be paid to a plaintiff. Perhaps I am ashamed to admit that a good deal of that money went into my own pocket as a lawyer. That money should have been better spent on compensating the injured parties rather than being paid to lawyers, even though I was one of them.

I also noticed from my experience that the time it took to resolve those cases was impossibly long. We, as practitioners, did our best to reduce that time scale, but we failed because all too often we had to await medical reports. Doctors also had to wait until the prognosis was clearer and sometimes they wanted to review their opinion. There were a host of reasons why cases could not be resolved quickly. That delay was not the fault of lawyers and doctors, but was inevitable given the methods that we adopted under the old system of criminal injuries compensation, and that are still adopted in the civil courts to ascertain the amount of damages to be paid.

Under the old system, the cost of ascertainment amounted to 10 per cent. of the total cost—I am sure that the Minister will correct me if I am wrong—which represented a substantial sum of public money. I would have preferred to see it going to the victims of crime, not lawyers. For that reason, I was prepared to consider the tariff scheme constructively when it was introduced by my right hon. and learned Friend the Home Secretary. We must admit that it is an inflexible scheme—that is the nature of tariff schemes. Opposition Members have argued for more flexibility, and perhaps there are some

[*Mr. Stephen*]

areas where we can offer that; but if we introduced too much flexibility, we would be back to the old expensive, time-consuming system.

I talk to victims of crime and many say, "I would have settled for a lot less money if I'd got it quickly. The time I needed it was in the few weeks and months after my injury, not years later when I'd more or less recovered." The speedy delivery of the money to the victim is therefore vital.

I should say something about the allegation that my right hon. and learned Friend acted unlawfully when he sought to change the non-statutory scheme for another non-statutory one. I do not blame Opposition Members for seizing on that, going on television and talking as though the Home Secretary had been caught with his fingers in the till, doing something that any one of us would have recognised as unlawful. Of course he did not do that.

The Home Secretary drew attention to the fact that, on that rather arcane question of constitutional law, five of Her Majesty's judges took one view and five took another. He is not suggesting that our court system is one where the number of judges should be totted up and the largest number carry the day—the courts are not as democratic as that. The argument that he made, which appears to have been lost on Opposition Members, was that, if five of Her Majesty's judges thought that the Home Secretary was right in doing what he was doing and had the power to do it, he himself—a mere lawyer, and a non-practising one at that—can hardly be blamed if he was of the opinion that it was in his power.

I confess that, if I had been in the Home Secretary's position, I would probably have thought so, too. He was not seeking to overturn a statute, because one cannot do that—one must return to Parliament and obtain the passage of another statute. He sought simply to change one non-statutory scheme into another non-statutory scheme. The fact that there was on the statute book a statutory scheme that was not implemented would have seemed to me, in his position, to be irrelevant.

The Home Secretary did not start the lengthy, costly process of litigation. That was forced on him by the Fire Brigades Union, which took him to court. The divisional court, which was the first court that considered the case, found for the Home Secretary. It said, "Yes, you do have the power to do this." It was not he who embarked on the second stage, in the Court of Appeal, but the Fire Brigades Union. It took him to the Court of Appeal, and won.

Having one court saying that he is right and one court saying that he is wrong, what is the Home Secretary to do? He gets the matter decided by going to the House of Lords, which will decide it once and for all. Having obtained that decision, what does the Home Secretary do? Of course he abides by the decision of the court, which is why the Bill has been brought before the House today.

I do not think that the Home Secretary can be charged with having behaved high-handedly. Even though he received what are described as warnings from Opposition Members and others, they were no more than expressions of a point of view at the time, albeit a point of view which five of the 10 judges eventually held to be correct.

No victim of crime has suffered, because all will be paid under the original scheme until the new scheme that we are debating comes into force—if and when it does.

Indeed, some people have benefited, because those who have received more than they would have received will not be asked to pay the difference back. Those who received less than they would have received will have their compensation made up.

I am pleased to see that, under the new scheme before the House today, greater recognition will be given to those who have suffered loss of earnings. Even under the previous scheme, which the House of Lords ruled against, there was an element in the compensation for loss of earnings, because the tariff figures had been fixed, not by considering the damages awarded in the civil courts or by the Criminal Injuries Compensation Board for pain, suffering and loss of amenity only, but by considering the total award, including an element, in many cases, for loss of earnings.

Under the new scheme, those who are out of work for more than 28 weeks will receive an additional element reflecting their actual loss of earnings up to a limit which has to be imposed in view of the ability of the taxpayer to pay.

Uncharacteristically, Opposition Members have complained on behalf of the high rollers of this world— the high earners—the people who, under the new scheme, will receive less by way of compensation than they would have suffered in loss of earnings. However, as has been said, the high earners are the very people who are in a position to insure themselves, should they so wish. They are adults and they must make their own decisions, but the opportunity is there for them to do so.

I would pose a question to my hon. Friend the Minister, however. Will he assist the House in understanding when a self-employed person is deemed to be off work for the purpose of compensation for loss of earnings?

Incapacity benefit will often be paid, so the compensation for loss of earnings under the scheme is not the only source of benefit. I would hope that the period of 28 weeks will be reduced, if and when the economy develops to the point when the taxpayer can afford it.

In some occupations, such as the police force, compensation is paid under employment contracts in addition to the money provided by the state. I am glad to see that the tariff for rape victims will increase from £7,500—which I always considered to be a wholly inadequate sum—to £17,500 in certain circumstances. Under the common law scheme operating in civil courts, often a nominal conventional amount is awarded for bereavement. I welcome the increased payment of £5,000 for each qualifying dependant and £10,000 when there is only one such dependant.

We should keep the tariff under review, and hon. Members on both sides of the House have pointed to anomalies. For example, should not a right-handed man who loses his right hand receive more by way of compensation than if he loses his left hand? Should not young people receive more compensation than older people? Should not the system keep pace with inflation and should not the civil servant who administers the scheme be encouraged to refer difficult decisions to more senior people?

As to income support deductions, I see no case for making a deduction from the money awarded for pain, suffering and loss of amenity. However, in so far as a sum is awarded for loss of earnings, an applicant would be compensated twice if he were compensated by the scheme for loss of earnings and also received income support. I think that there is a case for set-off, in that instance. However, some taxpayers will say, "My duty as a taxpayer is to support this man only if he cannot support himself and I do not believe that he cannot support himself if he has £50,000 sitting in the bank." We will have to answer to those taxpayers if we decide to go down that road.

I must mention the plight of rape victims who in the past have been reluctant to pursue their cases to criminal trial. It must be an horrendous experience not only to be raped but to have to endure a criminal trial to the point of conviction. I can well understand why many rape victims could not bring themselves to do that. Under the new scheme, I hope that we will be very sympathetic to women in that position—it usually is women—and that we will not force them to go through with a criminal trial or lose their entitlement to compensation. I hope also that when the economy improves—it is already showing signs of improvement—we will be able to reduce the £1,000 limit to £500 or so to allow those who have suffered minor but important injuries to receive compensation.

I believe that our scheme was, and will continue to be, the best in the world. The Government, on behalf of the taxpayers, have struck the right balance between the interests of those who pay compensation and those who receive it. I think that it is a scheme that we can explain to our constituents and of which we can proud. I shall support the Government in the Division Lobby this evening.

9.13 pm

**Mr. John Gunnell** (Morley and Leeds, South): I was interested to hear the hon. Member for Shoreham (Mr. Stephen) say that a relative of this scheme suffered as a result of decisions by the courts. He was at pains to demonstrate that the Home Secretary had behaved in a perfectly proper manner—I think that the Home Secretary behaved in the way that was expected of him. I liken the right hon. and learned Gentleman's experience to that of boxers who enter the ring looking for a points victory and who are prepared to accept any degree of punishment along the way. He has certainly demonstrated persistence, stubbornness and meanness of spirit. One could use a number of other descriptions, such as obduracy.

I was on the Standing Committee on the Criminal Justice and Public Order Bill, and I heard the earlier proposals mauled in Committee and pilloried on Report. They were defeated in the Lords and that decision was reversed again in the Commons. There were four debates on the earlier measures. On each occasion there were reactions and a clear focus to the Government's intentions.

It has been obvious throughout that the purpose of changing the scheme has been to save money. The Home Secretary made that clear to the House. The hon. Member for Shoreham said that compensation was only a token. However, token is not the right word. We are not talking about a gift or a birthday offering, where such tokens are frequently received.

The purpose of compensation is to aid victims and to provide some recognition of the difficulties that they have encountered, the injuries that they have suffered or the experience that they have undergone, and to compensate them financially. For those who suffer real loss of

earnings, compensation is an essential part of their standard of living thereafter. That was true while loss of earnings compensation was provided as part of the scheme, and it is much less so now, but it is not reasonable to describe it as a token, except in the sense that a token is frequently less than it should be.

Certainly in material terms, saving money on the scheme has reduced its quality and the assistance that it gives victims. That motivation has been clear throughout. It is clear in the Bill, it is among the reasons in our reasoned amendment for rejecting the Bill and it is central to the debate.

The second theme that is central to the debate is the unfairness to victims of reducing a more generous scheme to the one before us now. The Government have made some U-turns; they have not gone far enough, but they have increased the provisions in certain respects. Although we welcome that, we do not consider those increases to be sufficient. The scheme remains mean in comparison with the present system, which the Government thought had been abolished when the earlier measure was passed.

**Mr. Stephen:** I understand the thrust of the hon. Gentleman's remarks and I agree that we would all like to be more generous to the victims of crime, but he cannot avoid the issue. Does he have a commitment from the shadow Chancellor to make the necessary money available to put into practice his pious hopes—perhaps that would be a churlish way of putting it—the generous wishes that he has expressed? How will they be put into practice?

**Mr. Gunnell:** We must take the whole thrust of the policy into account. The leadership of my party is committed to a law and order policy that will reverse the trend in crime levels that has persisted for so long. As we have pointed out, the number of victims has increased enormously: it has increased by a third. That is one of the factors in the inflation of the cost of the present scheme. The scheme costs far more because there are far more victims of crime, which means that more people must be compensated.

I believe that our policy, which is based on tackling the causes of crime, will reduce the incidence of crime and, in so doing, lower the costs of a compensation scheme. My answer to the hon. Member for Shoreham is that the policy—the whole policy—that we shall implement will provide the cash to finance a scheme of the sort that currently exists; although, of course, it is not for me to commit my Front Bench to specific amounts of compensation. The downgrading of the existing scheme and the rigidity of its successor would not feature under a Labour Government, who would not have tampered with the current scheme in this way.

There has been an increasing public reaction against the scheme. It is all very well for the hon. Member for Shoreham to talk about the financial implications; it must be pointed out that the £700 million that will be saved over the next five years as a result of the change will be taken from victims. I do not believe that spending should always be squeezed at the expense of those who least deserve to bear the burden—but that is the thrust of Government policy: when money is to be saved, it must be taken from those who are most in need. Pensioners, for instance, lose a disproportionate amount of income in comparison with other groups.

*[Mr. Gunnell]*

It is not just natural supporters of the Labour party who consider this a mean scheme; indeed, there is clearly dissent in the Government ranks. The Leader of the House warned the Government that they were on the wrong side of the argument about the treatment of victims of crime, but the Government clearly have not noted even those words.

I urge the House to support our reasoned amendment, which deals with some of the most unsatisfactory features of the Bill.

9.23 pm

**Mr. Alun Michael** (Cardiff, South and Penarth): In October 1994, I warned the Home Secretary that he was acting wrongly, unfairly and illegally in trying to cut compensation for crime victims without seeking the approval of Parliament. During that debate, I also warned the House that the Government's new scheme would have a dramatic effect on those who were most seriously injured in criminal attacks; and I warned Conservative Members that

"Neither the Government nor the Conservative party will ever again be able to claim concern for the victims of crime in future when they are treating them so callously today."

I put it on record that

"No Conservative Members of Parliament will be able to claim an interest in victims in their speeches or election material if they vote to disagree with the Lords amendment today."—[*Official Report*, 20 October 1994; Vol. 248, c. 457.]

Time and again we gave Conservative Members the chance to join us in voting for victims. Not a single Tory Member backed them or us, and neither will any of them tonight. The failure of Conservative Members to stand up for victims in that debate was overshadowed by news of more scandal and sleaze at the heart of government. But it returns to haunt them today.

The Bill has been produced for only two reasons. First, it is before us because the courts and the Law Lords declared that the Home Secretary had acted unlawfully and, secondly, because Ministers are determined to slash the cash that is spent on compensating the victims of crime.

During the debate, Conservative Members have tried to dress up as a technicality the fact that the Home Secretary was found to be ignoring the law. But as my right hon. and learned Friend the Member for Aberavon (Mr. Morris) said when he castigated the right hon. and learned Gentleman, the Home Secretary presented an affront to Parliament for which he has never apologised. This measure does not expunge that failure and, as my right hon. and learned Friend rightly said, the Government are arrogant and brazen and are failing to listen.

The Home Secretary's action was not just a minor infringement of the law: it has been described as an abuse of prerogative power. Just as Conservative Members seem not to understand being greedy and sleazy, they seem not to understand that they are guilty of abusing power in government. Equally outrageous was the attempt to dupe the House and the public about the Home Secretary's plan to cut compensation. Incredibly, as recently as March the Home Secretary was trying to pretend that he was not cutting the cash at all. On 9 March I said:

"Does the Home Secretary still not realise that his rhetoric about victims has no effect when people can see the indelible effect of his one genuine policy, which is to cut the total sum available to victims, and especially to cut the level of compensation available for the victims of the most horrific crimes?"

The right hon. and learned Gentleman's response was shameless because he said:

"Far from being cut, the sum will continue to increase."— [*Official Report*, 9 March 1995; Vol. 256, c. 443.]

When he spoke those words and made that wild claim, the Home Secretary had already published his annual report projecting swingeing cuts in compensation this year and for each of the next three years. After his partial U-turn, which appears in the Bill, of conceding some compensation for loss of earnings, on his own admission the Bill contains a cut of £200 million a year.

The hon. Member for Plymouth, Sutton (Mr. Streeter) made a bizarre contribution to the debate. He implied that the cut in compensation arose because the Government were buffeted by unforeseen events.

**Mr. Straw:** They were back in government.

**Mr. Michael:** The Conservatives were planning the cut even before the last general election and perhaps, as my hon. Friend the Member for Blackburn (Mr. Straw) suggests, the buffeting by events was unexpectedly finding themselves back in government.

The hon. Member for Sutton said that the Conservative party keeps election promises. What a set of promises it has kept! In home affairs, where were the 1,000 extra police that it promised for the year following the general election? Where are the real measures to tackle crime? The hon. Gentleman asked for more money to be pumped into the criminal injuries compensation scheme and challenged us about our intentions. We have a simple summary and I shall set it out in case Conservative Members have not yet understood it. It is, "If you do not cut the scheme, we will not."

We have made it clear that the future is in the Government's hands. There is no problem for the Opposition, but there is a problem for the Government because they are setting out to cut the scheme while we have made our position clear. The Minister's response to the hon. Member for Sutton was that the Conservatives have maintained a generous scheme. If the Minister is so proud of maintaining a generous scheme, why is he cutting it? It is made explicit in the Bill that money for the compensation of victims will be cut. But that is not the only betrayal of victims perpetrated by the Conservatives. My hon. Friend the Member for Blackburn laid bare the failures in the Bill. In Committee we shall try to improve it, but at its heart is the intention to cut.

What is as bad, if not worse, is the fact that so many people become victims because of the Government's failure to tackle crime and its causes. My hon. Friend the Member for Birmingham, Erdington (Mr. Corbett) was right to highlight the increase in violence. Violence against the person was up 7 per cent. again last year.

Victims of crime, he said, are not just statistics but people—a point that escaped all Conservative Members who contributed to this debate. My hon. Friend made a powerful speech about the plight of victims.

By contrast, the Home Secretary treated us to a calculation of the rising cost of the old scheme over the next five years. That calculation appears on the face of the Bill too, but on what are the increases based? My hon. Friend the Member for Blackburn asked the right hon. and learned Gentleman that, but there was no answer. Did the Home Secretary undertake a detailed analysis of crime and its impact on victims? Did he look at the fact that violent crime continues to rise by 7 per cent. a year? Has he made a calculation based on facts? Has he looked at any facts at all?

The answer is no, because the Home Secretary does not have the facts. That is revealed in answers to parliamentary questions that I have asked him. The right hon. and learned Gentleman looks puzzled, as he often does. Perhaps he is unaware of the answers provided by his ministerial colleague to a number of serious questions. What was the average award for rape plus serious injury given under the criminal injuries compensation tariff scheme operated from April 1994? He was asked to list for each of the past five years the number of claimants for criminal injuries compensation incapacitated for more than 28 weeks, and the percentage that they represented of the total number of claimants—and the total cost of claims in each of those years. I asked about the number of awards, and the total value of awards made in respect of rape, and of rape plus serious injury, in each of the past six financial years. Those were all facts on which we could base an understanding of the costs of the present scheme and of the Home Secretary's intentions for the future.

The answers were very short and very simple—that the information was not recorded centrally. In other words, Ministers do not have a clue. So how did the right hon. and learned Gentleman reach what my hon. Friend the Member for Blackburn has described as the moving target?

**Dr. Kim Howells** (Pontypridd): He made it up.

**Mr. Michael:** As they say in Pontypridd, he made it up. More technically, it was an extrapolation of cash figures leading to a cash-driven policy instead of one driven by concern for victims. That led in turn to a misunderstanding of the nature of the problem. In short, the Home Secretary based his new policy on unsound information.

**Mr. Howard:** Will the hon. Gentleman withdraw his slur on the people of Pontypridd? They have a very clear understanding of the difference between making up figures—as the hon. Gentleman, without a scintilla of evidence, alleges we did—and extrapolation, which we have always made clear was the basis for our estimates. It is a perfectly sensible basis which I am sure will be recognised and approved by the people of Pontypridd.

**Mr. Michael:** The Home Secretary's methods are so well respected that they keep changing every time he gives us an estimate. The people of Pontypridd, so ably represented by my hon. Friend, will see the matter with as much clarity as he does. They will also see how the Home Secretary dragged out events all the way to the House of Lords even though it was clear that he was wrong.

It adds insult to injury and neglect when the Conservative lie machine time and again repeats untruths that the Ministers here today must know are untruths. Not just victims of crime but communities throughout Britain are calling out to Ministers to face up to the facts of their failure and to stop using crime as a political football. They want them to join Labour in confronting the real issues.

As our reasoned amendment makes clear, criminal injuries compensation is only one aspect of the Government's failure adequately to deal with the needs of victims, support for victims and the protection of the public from the danger of becoming victims. The Government must do much more to put the victim at the heart of the criminal justice system. As we say in our reasoned amendment, the Government fail to require greater consideration towards victims from the Crown Prosecution Service. Last year, we put forward an amendment, which was rejected by the Government, to require the CPS to keep people informed and consult victims before dropping or downgrading the charges against their attackers. My hon. Friend the Member for Blackburn has highlighted many other problems with the CPS in recent weeks.

We have urged the Government to do more to give greater attention to the needs of victims in court, to protect and help witnesses and to support the provision of counselling and other services by voluntary organisations. We have managed to embarrass the Government into keeping some of their promises to Victim Support, but still the victims are not placed at the heart of the criminal justice system.

As we say in our reasoned amendment, above all, the Government have failed to take positive action to tackle the continued rise in crimes of violence. The Labour party has exposed that failure on many, many occasions but we have gone further. We have come forward time and again with positive proposals to deal with crime, from faster intervention with young offenders to increased penalties for weapons offences.

I could give a whole series of well-documented examples, but as the Conservative party's lie machine has made the Criminal Justice and Public Order Act 1994 the test, let us get the record straight. The Labour party opposed what was bad in that legislation and supported what was good. We sought to replace ill-considered and half-baked clauses with effective provisions to deal with crime and the causes of crime and made a number of new and practical suggestions.

When it comes to violent crime, the contrast between the Conservative party and the Labour party is clearest of all. There was nothing in the Criminal Justice and Public Order Bill to deal with violence, drugs or drug-related crime or to punish firearms offenders until Labour proposed amendments. Violent crime was so far from the Government's mind that increased penalties could be brought only by tacking additions on to the sea fisheries and shellfish legislation. It is important that that should be clear.

[*Mr. Michael*]

Conservative Members and the Home Secretary should understand that he has been rumbled. That is what happened with the Criminal Justice and Public Order Act last year.

**Mr. Howard** *rose*—

**Mr. Michael:** As ever, the tough talk from the Tories was exposed as meaningless and it was Labour Members who were willing to engage in serious debate in Committee, based on their practical experience of co-operating with the—

**Mr. Howard** *rose*—

**Madam Deputy Speaker:** Order. The rules of the House are well known. If the hon. Member who has the Floor does not give way, the other hon. Member must resume his seat and that includes the Home Secretary.

**Mr. Michael:** I shall gave way in a moment, but this is a sentence that the Home Secretary should hear.

It was Labour Members who were willing to engage in serious debate in Committee based on their practical experience of co-operating with police and local authorities in their constituencies, to tackle the scourge of crime that affects our people in our areas and so often devastates their lives. We did that. It was a pity that the Ministers who took part in the Committee were not willing so to engage.

**Mr. Howard:** The hon. Gentleman's attempts to rewrite history are based on fantasy. Before he pursues that path, he ought to have a word with his right hon. Friend the Leader of the Opposition because the line that he is taking strays radically from that taken by his right hon. Friend.

The centrepiece of the Criminal Justice and Public Order Act was the 27 points that I announced in my speech to the Conservative party conference. *[Interruption.]* It is interesting that the Labour party mocks them, when a moment ago the hon. Gentleman was trying to take credit for them. Those 27 points were denounced by the Leader of the Opposition as a set of gimmicks. The Opposition cannot have it both ways. Are they gimmicks or do they support them?

**Mr. Michael:** I understand the Home Secretary's need to try to intervene because he does not like what he is being told, which is the truth. He reminds us that that Bill brought in the 27 points, or 27 gimmicks, that he put forward in his conference speech. It was the Michael Howard conference speech implementation Bill. When we came forward with serious proposals that would have tackled and cut crime, protected people, helped victims, nipped in the bud problems with young offenders and dealt with weapons and violent offences, what did the Home Secretary and his team do? They rejected them, voted against them and ignored them. It is the Home Secretary who is seeking to rewrite history, but he has failed. He should apologise for what he said. He has shown disrespect for the way in which we are trying to tackle crime properly.

We see in the Bill a series of complications with which we shall have to deal in Committee. The hon. Member for Uxbridge (Mr. Shersby) referred to serious concerns about the cost of the lifetime care and attention to be given to a person after an attack. There are serious questions about when the tariff will be updated. It is clear, again from parliamentary answers, that the Home Secretary intends to bring in the tariff as outlined in his advisory note, which is already two years out of date and will be three years out of date when the system comes into operation. A parliamentary question answered today states:

"It is intended that the tariff levels will be reviewed every three years",

not annually. It continues:

"No criteria for such review have yet been set, but might be expected to include reference to inflation more generally and other pressures on public expenditure."

The Home Secretary has not thought the issues through.

Adjudicators will be appointed and controlled by the Home Secretary, yet he disclaims responsibility for them. Clause 5 on page 4 of the Bill states:

"The Scheme may include provision—

(a) for adjudicators to be appointed."

It continues:

"Any person appointed . . . under this section by the Secretary of State—

(a) shall be appointed on such terms and conditions as the Secretary of State considers appropriate; but

(b) shall not be regarded as having been appointed to exercise functions of the Secretary of State or to act on his behalf.

(5) No decision taken by an adjudicator shall be regarded as having been undertaken by, or on behalf of, the Secretary of State."

In the Bill, the Secretary of State seeks in advance to clear himself of any responsibility for those who are appointed by or responsible to him. He does not want to take responsibility for anything in future.

The contributions made to the debate by Conservative Members have often been ill-founded and fractious interventions revealing the malaise that lies at the heart of the Government. Last Thursday, we saw Conservative Members reacting with shock and horror at the prospect of having their trough taken away from them. They clearly did not understand why the public were so outraged.

Today, Conservative Members have sounded ludicrous as they tried to pretend that the Home Secretary had not really been defeated in the House of Lords. The President of the Board of Trade was turning over the entrails of another decision earlier today. It seems that the rule now is that the Government set up a system and then, if they do not like it, they do not change the system properly, but pretend that it happened differently.

The public know the central truth about the Bill. We shall consider it clause by clause and seek to improve it in Committee. We welcome the partial U-turn that the Home Secretary has already undertaken, but the public know that the measure is about cutting costs and doing less to help victims. Today, the Home Secretary and those around him are failing to grasp the depth of their own failure to tackle crime and protect victims, but the public understand all too well. I know that the Conservatives do not, but the public understand that only the Labour party will be tough on crime and tough on the causes of crime. Only Labour will put the victims where they should be— at the heart of the criminal justice system.

9.43 pm

**The Minister of State, Home Office (Mr. David Maclean):** The House has just been treated to an outrageous charade by the hon. Member for Cardiff, South and Penarth (Mr. Michael). Sadly, it made him look silly, as one can see from the faces of his colleagues behind him.

The party that professes to be tough on crime is the party that voted against almost every criminal justice measure in the 1980s and always voted against the prevention of terrorism Act. The key elements of the latest criminal justice legislation related to bail bandits but Labour tried to tear the guts out of it. We sought to lock up young hoodlums but Labour tried to tear the guts out of that proposal. It also opposed our reform of the right to silence.

The hon. Member for Cardiff, South and Penarth said that most of the Criminal Justice and Public Order Act 1994 was the Labour party's invention. If so, why did it abstain on Third Reading? He cannot have it every way.

Some interesting points were made by hon. Members on both sides of the House. I assure my hon. Friend the Member for Uxbridge (Mr. Shersby) that of course we shall want to monitor the enhanced tariff scheme, and I take on board his support for the Bill. He asked whether the money available will be sufficient to deal with victims properly in future. I refer him to the structural settlement scheme, which is a recent innovation in damages litigation and which is terribly important. Under the structured settlements provided in the Bill, payments will be tax exempt. It is possible that at today's prices that could mean an award of up to £20,000 index-linked, tax free for life for the most seriously injured victims. That is a very sensible provision.

My hon. Friend the Member for Uxbridge asked about multiple injuries under the tariff. We shall treat multiple injuries under the enhanced tariff scheme in largely the same manner as they were treated under the common law damages scheme: 100 per cent. award for the most serious injury, 10 per cent. more for the second most serious injury and 5 per cent. more for the third most serious injury. That is no real change of substance from the present modus operandi. We propose to uprate that scheme about every three years. I hope that that assurance satisfies my hon. Friend.

I note that my hon. Friend the Member for Plymouth, Sutton (Mr. Streeter) volunteered to serve on the Committee. He should consider himself nominated. He rightly pointed out that during the 28-week period a range of welfare arrangements are available. He was right to expose the hypocrisy of the Labour party in calling for more money for practically every good cause and at the same time saying that it will not increase expenditure.

My hon. Friend the Member for Surrey, East (Mr. Ainsworth) and other hon. Friends were right to point out that the tariff scheme is the most generous in the world, and more generous than the schemes of all the countries in Europe put together. We are proud of that fact. [*Interruption.*] It is a fact that the scheme is more generous than the compensation available in every other country in Europe put together. That will continue to be the case under the new, enhanced tariff scheme unless every other country in Europe does something drastic to increase its payments.

The hon. Member for Upper Bann (Mr. Trimble) made some important points. He asked whether we would lay all the details before Parliament. We will lay all the most important elements of the scheme before Parliament and they will be subject to parliamentary control and affirmative resolution. It would not be a good use of Parliament's time to lay all the minutiae before it. We shall, however, ensure that the key elements are laid before Parliament.

The hon. Member for Upper Bann also suggested that the tariff scheme was illogical as it included an element for loss of earnings beneath the 28-week period, although that is now paid separately. It is true that tariff payments include an unquantified element for loss of earnings. We considered shaving that off but decided that it would be better to leave the levels as they are. Many people who are incapacitated for fewer than 28 weeks will in fact receive some element of compensation for loss of earnings. It also explains why the tariff levels have not been uprated since 1994. In effect, they contain that cushion already: the loss of earnings which we have not shaved off.

The hon. Member for Warwickshire, North (Mr. O'Brien) asked whether the scheme would be kept under review. Of course the tariff scheme will be kept under review. He was worried about the level of civil servants who will be dealing with cases. The civil service has a structure and difficult cases are passed upwards so that senior management may deal with them. Some of us may complain that, at times, too many senior managers are involved in paperwork on files going upwards, but there is of course a structure.

**Mr. Mike O'Brien:** The other point that I made was about the number of injuries on the basic list of injuries, which has been increased to 310. Will the Minister keep an open mind on increasing that number further as unfairness becomes evident?

**Mr. Maclean:** Yes, of course. That is one of the benefits of not having the tariff scheme on the face of the Bill but in statutory arrangements or in regulations. It allows us to change according to circumstances, new ailments or injuries. It is a very sensible provision.

The hon. Member for Birmingham, Erdington (Mr. Corbett) was concerned about loss of earnings for the self-employed. Those losses will be calculated from examination of business accounts and Inland Revenue returns. We can even employ forensic accountants, if necessary, to analyse those returns. The loss to be taken into account will be the same as under the present scheme—one and a half times national industrial average earnings. I hope that that offers some reassurance to the hon. Gentleman.

I now turn to the comments made by the hon. Member for Blackburn (Mr. Straw). I shoot down straight away his assertion that the only reason why the cost of the scheme is rising is rising crime. That is nonsense. There is no clear correlation between crime figures and the number of applications under the scheme. In 1964, when the scheme was introduced—

**Mr. Straw:** I can spare the Minister's breath. I did not say what he claims. I said that the rise in crime was one of the factors that led to the increase in the cost of the scheme. I also said that the other factors were the increase in the severity of individual crimes and that other matters had to be taken into account.

**Mr. Maclean:** The hon. Gentleman put great stress on the crime rise, but I happily apologise to him for misrepresenting his point of view.

[Mr. Maclean]

Since 1964, when the scheme was introduced, violent crime has increased by 500 per cent. The number of applicants under the scheme has increased by 3,000 per cent. and the amount of compensation paid has increased by no less than 40,000 per cent. It is because of that enormous increase in the amount of compensation—way over and above the level of inflation—that the Government believe that we must have not only a fair scheme for victims, but some sensible controls.

The hon. Member for Blackburn quoted, highly selectively, from the speech made by Fred Broughton, the president of the Police Federation. Perhaps you will permit me, Madam Speaker, to give some other quotations from Fred Broughton's speech. Turning to my right hon. and learned Friend the Home Secretary, he said:

"You've conceded one of our main points which was that loss of earnings should continue to be taken into account. You have also agreed that payments can be made in respect of special medical care and long-term cases. You have agreed to increase some of the maximum awards for various types of injury from those you intended to impose and you have agreed to double the proposed maximum limit on any award from £250,000 to £500,000. We are able to give a qualified welcome to your revised proposals."

That puts a slightly different light on the speech.

The hon. Member for Blackburn did not quote at all from the news release issued by the Law Society, which said:

"The new scheme will combine some of the administrative advantages of the tariff, particularly for smaller claims, with the greater fairness of individual assessment of awards in larger cases. This should mean that the victims with the more serious injuries will receive much larger awards than under the tariff, including compensation for loss of earnings and medical care costs."

The heading on that news release reads:

"Law Society welcomes new criminal injuries compensation scheme."

The hon. Gentleman did not mention that.

I shall now deal with one of the key questions and one of the key myths that has been bandied about by the Opposition today—the so-called cuts in compensation. Let us go back only 10 years to 1985. This Tory Government paid out £41 million in 1985, then £48 million, then £52 million, then £69 million, then £72 million, then £109 million, then £143 million, then £152 million and, last year, £165 million—some cuts!

What are we planning to do in future? We expect—this is on the face of the Bill—to make provision for liabilities of £176 million, then £190 million, then £205 million, then £240 million and then £260 million. Let us have no more lies about cuts in compensation for victims. There are no cuts; that is more cash from the taxpayer—

**Mr. Michael:** Lies from where?

**Mr. Maclean:** Those who are responsible will know what I mean—*[Interruption.]*

I am proud to quote from the Conservative campaign guide, the key boast in which is:

"The criminal injuries compensation scheme is now one of the most generous in the world."

**Mr. Michael:** Does the Minister share the view of the Home Secretary, who points a finger at Opposition Members from a sedentary position, or does he accept that we have stated our position truly and clearly during the debate?

**Mr. Maclean:** That was a silly intervention—rather like the hon. Gentleman's speech earlier.

The Conservative campaign guide pointed out our proud boast that we had the most generous victim compensation scheme in the world, and we stated what we paid out in 1989. I can tell the hon. Member for Cardiff, South and Penarth that we can make that boast for 1990, 1991, 1992, 1993, 1994 and 1995. We shall be making that boast in our next manifesto, because the scheme will still be the most generous in the world. It will pay out more than the amounts paid out by every country in Europe put together.

Let us look at the diversity of view within the Labour party on what we should do with victims and how much we should pay out. Last night—I had the pleasure of reading the speech today—the Leader of the Opposition called himself "an unashamed long termist", but even as he was speaking his Front-Bench team was tabling an amendment condemning the world's most generous criminal injuries compensation scheme as not generous enough. For the Labour party, it seems that the long term is the time it takes for a soundbite to travel around the airwaves.

Last night, the Leader of the Opposition spoke of the "long and gruelling slog" to control public expenditure, but today his lieutenants call for more spending. The "long and gruelling slog" which the Leader of the Opposition was talking about is him trying to get anyone else in his party to take him seriously on economic policy. We all know that increasingly he is a one-man band, and we have seen once again tonight that the right hon. Gentleman is on his own in calling for restraint. He has no troops behind him who will back that.

Last night, the Leader of the Opposition could talk of the failure of Keynesian economics, but does anyone seriously believe that the shadow Chancellor, the shadow Foreign Secretary and the deputy leader of the Labour party share his apparent conversion to Milton Friedman economics?

We have heard a lot today from the Opposition about their concern for victims. They have positively oozed compassion and high-minded rhetoric, and they have scattered caring soundbites through every speech like golden hailstones, but we have not heard what they would do. Let me remind the House of the Government's position, which is crystal clear. We will have an enhanced tariff scheme with a separate calculation for loss of earnings for serious cases. We estimate that the cost of that in each of the next five years will be £175 million, £190 million, £205 million, £240 million and £260 million, making a grand total of £1,070 million. There is no bluster and no equivocation there—we are honestly putting up front the costs—but today we have heard not a single word from the Opposition about how much they would spend.

When we announced the tariff scheme, the hon. Member for Blackburn—he does not want to listen, as it is embarrassing for him—said:

"These concessions are nothing like enough".

So there we have it. The £1 billion which we expect to pay out is "nothing like enough" according to the shadow Home Secretary, but he did not tell us what would be enough. Would it be £1.5 billion, £2 billion or £2.5 billion? Of course, he would not tell us because—like all shadow spokesmen—he has had to swear a pledge to the shadow Chancellor, the doctor of Dunfermline, East (Mr. Brown): "I swear that all my promises of a golden tomorrow will have no price tag attached which Tory central office can cost."

That is why the Labour party is now a policy-free zone. If there are no policies, my right hon. Friend the Chief Secretary cannot total up the costs so we can all find out how much taxes will need to go up to pay for them. But Labour Members will have to produce policies some time, and end their empty waffle calling for more investment in education, housing, health, transport, people, communities, the infrastructure, the environment and the planet. At some time, they will have to tell the British people what they would do and how much it will cost. That is the question that they did not answer tonight— what is it going to cost?

The Opposition have condemned our plans as mean and niggardly. Every one of them has suggested that we should spend more money, but this Government will spend more than £1 billion. We say that that is exceptionally generous—the most generous scheme in the world—but that it is all that we can afford. Unless they tell us how much they would spend, we shall be entitled to assume that it would the full amount of the old, unreformed scheme.

By voting against the Bill, the Opposition are committing themselves to £700 million of extra expenditure. By voting against, they are showing that they will not put their principles where their mouths are. That is not surprising because the new, vacuous, soundbite Labour party has no ideas, no policies and no principles, which is why I invite my hon. Friends to support me in the Lobby tonight.

*Question put,* That the amendment be made:—
*The House divided:* Ayes 229, Noes 274.

**Division No. 156]**                                    **[10.00 pm**

### AYES

| | |
|---|---|
| Abbott, Ms Diane | Campbell, Ronnie (Blyth V) |
| Adams, Mrs Irene | Campbell-Savours, D N |
| Ainger, Nick | Cann, Jamie |
| Allen, Graham | Carlile, Alexander (Montgomery) |
| Anderson, Donald (Swansea E) | Chidgey, David |
| Armstrong, Hilary | Chisholm, Malcolm |
| Ashton, Joe | Clapham, Michael |
| Austin-Walker, John | Clarke, Eric (Midlothian) |
| Banks, Tony (Newham NW) | Clelland, David |
| Barnes, Harry | Clwyd, Mrs Ann |
| Barron, Kevin | Coffey, Ann |
| Battle, John | Cohen, Harry |
| Bayley, Hugh | Cook, Frank (Stockton N) |
| Beckett, Rt Hon Margaret | Cook, Robin (Livingston) |
| Benn, Rt Hon Tony | Corbett, Robin |
| Bennett, Andrew F | Corbyn, Jeremy |
| Berry, Roger | Corston, Jean |
| Blair, Rt Hon Tony | Cousins, Jim |
| Boateng, Paul | Cox, Tom |
| Bradley, Keith | Cunliffe, Lawrence |
| Brown, Gordon (Dunfermline E) | Cunningham, Rt Hon Dr John |
| Brown, N (N'c'tle upon Tyne E) | Dafis, Cynog |
| Burden, Richard | Dalyell, Tam |
| Byers, Stephen | Darling, Alistair |
| Caborn, Richard | Davies, Bryan (Oldham C'tral) |
| Callaghan, Jim | Davies, Rt Hon Denzil (Llanelli) |
| Campbell, Mrs Anne (C'bridge) | Davies, Ron (Caerphilly) |

| | |
|---|---|
| Davis, Terry (B'ham, H'dge H'l) | Lloyd, Tony (Stretford) |
| Denham, John | Llwyd, Elfyn |
| Dewar, Donald | Lynne, Ms Liz |
| Dixon, Don | McAllion, John |
| Dobson, Frank | McAvoy, Thomas |
| Donohoe, Brian H | McCartney, Ian |
| Dowd, Jim | Macdonald, Calum |
| Dunwoody, Mrs Gwyneth | McKelvey, William |
| Eagle, Ms Angela | Mackinlay, Andrew |
| Eastham, Ken | McMaster, Gordon |
| Enright, Derek | MacShane, Denis |
| Etherington, Bill | McWilliam, John |
| Ewing, Mrs Margaret | Madden, Max |
| Fatchett, Derek | Maddock, Diana |
| Faulds, Andrew | Mahon, Alice |
| Field, Frank (Birkenhead) | Mandelson, Peter |
| Flynn, Paul | Marek, Dr John |
| Foster, Rt Hon Derek | Marshall, David (Shettleston) |
| Foster, Don (Bath) | Marshall, Jim (Leicester, S) |
| Foulkes, George | Martlew, Eric |
| Fraser, John | Meacher, Michael |
| Fyfe, Maria | Meale, Alan |
| Galbraith, Sam | Michael, Alun |
| Galloway, George | Michie, Bill (Sheffield Heeley) |
| Garrett, John | Milburn, Alan |
| George, Bruce | Miller, Andrew |
| Gerrard, Neil | Moonie, Dr Lewis |
| Gilbert, Rt Hon Dr John | Morgan, Rhodri |
| Godman, Dr Norman A | Morley, Elliot |
| Golding, Mrs Llin | Morris, Rt Hon Alfred (Wy'nshawe) |
| Gordon, Mildred | Morris, Estelle (B'ham Yardley) |
| Grant, Bernie (Tottenham) | Morris, Rt Hon John (Aberavon) |
| Griffiths, Nigel (Edinburgh S) | Mudie, George |
| Griffiths, Win (Bridgend) | Mullin, Chris |
| Grocott, Bruce | Murphy, Paul |
| Gunnell, John | Oakes, Rt Hon Gordon |
| Hain, Peter | O'Brien, Mike (N W'kshire) |
| Hall, Mike | O'Brien, William (Normanton) |
| Hanson, David | O'Hara, Edward |
| Harman, Ms Harriet | Olner, Bill |
| Harvey, Nick | Orme, Rt Hon Stanley |
| Henderson, Doug | Pickthall, Colin |
| Heppell, John | Pike, Peter L |
| Hill, Keith (Streatham) | Pope, Greg |
| Hinchliffe, David | Powell, Ray (Ogmore) |
| Hoey, Kate | Prentice, Bridget (Lew'm E) |
| Hogg, Norman (Cumbernauld) | Prentice, Gordon (Pendle) |
| Hood, Jimmy | Prescott, Rt Hon John |
| Hoon, Geoffrey | Primarolo, Dawn |
| Howarth, George (Knowsley North) | Purchase, Ken |
| Howells, Dr. Kim (Pontypridd) | Quin, Ms Joyce |
| Hoyle, Doug | Randall, Stuart |
| Hughes, Kevin (Doncaster N) | Raynsford, Nick |
| Hughes, Robert (Aberdeen N) | Rendel, David |
| Hughes, Simon (Southwark) | Robinson, Geoffrey (Cov NW) |
| Illsley, Eric | Roche, Mrs Barbara |
| Ingram, Adam | Rogers, Allan |
| Jackson, Glenda (H'stead) | Rooker, Jeff |
| Jackson, Helen (Shef'ld, H) | Rooney, Terry |
| Jamieson, David | Ross, Ernie (Dundee W) |
| Janner, Greville | Ruddock, Joan |
| Jones, Barry (Alyn and D'side) | Sedgemore, Brian |
| Jones, Ieuan Wyn (Ynys Môn) | Sheerman, Barry |
| Jones, Jon Owen (Cardiff C) | Sheldon, Rt Hon Robert |
| Jones, Lynne (B'ham S O) | Short, Clare |
| Jones, Martyn (Clwyd, SW) | Skinner, Dennis |
| Jowell, Tessa | Smith, Andrew (Oxford E) |
| Kaufman, Rt Hon Gerald | Smith, Chris (Isl'ton S & F'sbury) |
| Keen, Alan | Smith, Llew (Blaenau Gwent) |
| Kennedy, Jane (Lpool Brdgn) | Smyth, The Reverend Martin |
| Khabra, Piara S | Snape, Peter |
| Kilfoyle, Peter | Soley, Clive |
| Lestor, Joan (Eccles) | Spearing, Nigel |
| Lewis, Terry | Spellar, John |
| Litherland, Robert | Steinberg, Gerry |
| Livingstone, Ken | Stevenson, George |

Stott, Roger
Straw, Jack
Sutcliffe, Gerry
Taylor, Mrs Ann (Dewsbury)
Timms, Stephen
Tipping, Paddy
Touhig, Don
Trimble, David
Walker, A Cecil (Belfast N)
Wallace, James
Walley, Joan
Watson, Mike
Wicks, Malcolm

Wigley, Dafydd
Williams, Rt Hon Alan (Sw'n W)
Williams, Alan W (Carmarthen)
Wilson, Brian
Winnick, David
Wise, Audrey
Worthington, Tony
Wray, Jimmy
Wright, Dr Tony
Young, Rt Hon Sir George

**Tellers for the Ayes:**
**Mr. Dennis Turner and**
**Mr. Robert Ainsworth.**

## NOES

Ainsworth, Peter (East Surrey)
Aitken, Rt Hon Jonathan
Alexander, Richard
Alison, Rt Hon Michael (Selby)
Allason, Rupert (Torbay)
Amess, David
Arbuthnot, James
Arnold, Jacques (Gravesham)
Arnold, Sir Thomas (Hazel Grv)
Atkins, Robert
Atkinson, David (Bour'mouth E)
Atkinson, Peter (Hexham)
Baker, Rt Hon Kenneth (Mole V)
Baker, Nicholas (North Dorset)
Baldry, Tony
Banks, Matthew (Southport)
Banks, Robert (Harrogate)
Bates, Michael
Batiste, Spencer
Bellingham, Henry
Beresford, Sir Paul
Biffen, Rt Hon John
Body, Sir Richard
Bonsor, Sir Nicholas
Booth, Hartley
Boswell, Tim
Bottomley, Peter (Eltham)
Bottomley, Rt Hon Virginia
Bowden, Sir Andrew
Bowis, John
Boyson, Rt Hon Sir Rhodes
Brandreth, Gyles
Brazier, Julian
Bright, Sir Graham
Brown, M (Brigg & Cl'thorpes)
Browning, Mrs Angela
Budgen, Nicholas
Burns, Simon
Burt, Alistair
Butcher, John
Butterfill, John
Carlisle, John (Luton North)
Carlisle, Sir Kenneth (Lincoln)
Carrington, Matthew
Carttiss, Michael
Cash, William
Channon, Rt Hon Paul
Chapman, Sydney
Churchill, Mr
Clappison, James
Clark, Dr Michael (Rochford)
Clarke, Rt Hon Kenneth (Ru'clif)
Clifton-Brown, Geoffrey
Coe, Sebastian
Colvin, Michael
Congdon, David
Coombs, Anthony (Wyre For'st)
Coombs, Simon (Swindon)
Couchman, James
Currie, Mrs Edwina (S D'by'ire)

Curry, David (Skipton & Ripon)
Davies, Quentin (Stamford)
Davis, David (Boothferry)
Day, Stephen
Deva, Nirj Joseph
Devlin, Tim
Dicks, Terry
Douglas-Hamilton, Lord James
Dover, Den
Duncan, Alan
Duncan-Smith, Iain
Durant, Sir Anthony
Dykes, Hugh
Elletson, Harold
Emery, Rt Hon Sir Peter
Evans, David (Welwyn Hatfield)
Evans, Jonathan (Brecon)
Evans, Nigel (Ribble Valley)
Evans, Roger (Monmouth)
Evennett, David
Faber, David
Fabricant, Michael
Fenner, Dame Peggy
Field, Barry (Isle of Wight)
Fishburn, Dudley
Forman, Nigel
Forsyth, Rt Hon Michael (Stirling)
Forth, Eric
Fox, Dr Liam (Woodspring)
Fox, Sir Marcus (Shipley)
Freeman, Rt Hon Roger
French, Douglas
Fry, Sir Peter
Gale, Roger
Gallie, Phil
Gardiner, Sir George
Garel-Jones, Rt Hon Tristan
Garnier, Edward
Gill, Christopher
Gillan, Cheryl
Goodlad, Rt Hon Alastair
Goodson-Wickes, Dr Charles
Gorman, Mrs Teresa
Gorst, Sir John
Grant, Sir A (SW Cambs)
Greenway, Harry (Ealing N)
Griffiths, Peter (Portsmouth, N)
Grylls, Sir Michael
Hague, William
Hamilton, Rt Hon Sir Archibald
Hamilton, Neil (Tatton)
Hampson, Dr Keith
Hannam, Sir John
Hargreaves, Andrew
Harris, David
Haselhurst, Alan
Hawkins, Nick
Hawksley, Warren
Hayes, Jerry
Heald, Oliver

Heath, Rt Hon Sir Edward
Heathcoat-Amory, David
Hendry, Charles
Heseltine, Rt Hon Michael
Hicks, Robert
Higgins, Rt Hon Sir Terence
Hill, James (Southampton Test)
Horam, John
Hordern, Rt Hon Sir Peter
Howard, Rt Hon Michael
Howarth, Alan (Strat'rd-on-A)
Howell, Sir Ralph (N Norfolk)
Hughes, Robert G (Harrow W)
Hunt, Rt Hon David (Wirral W)
Hunt, Sir John (Ravensbourne)
Hunter, Andrew
Jack, Michael
Jackson, Robert (Wantage)
Jenkin, Bernard
Jessel, Toby
Johnson Smith, Sir Geoffrey
Jones, Gwilym (Cardiff N)
Jones, Robert B (W Hertfdshr)
Kellett-Bowman, Dame Elaine
Key, Robert
King, Rt Hon Tom
Kirkhope, Timothy
Knapman, Roger
Knight, Mrs Angela (Erewash)
Knight, Greg (Derby N)
Knox, Sir David
Kynoch, George (Kincardine)
Lait, Mrs Jacqui
Lamont, Rt Hon Norman
Lang, Rt Hon Ian
Legg, Barry
Leigh, Edward
Lennox-Boyd, Sir Mark
Lidington, David
Lilley, Rt Hon Peter
Lloyd, Rt Hon Sir Peter (Fareham)
Lord, Michael
Luff, Peter
Lyell, Rt Hon Sir Nicholas
MacKay, Andrew
Maclean, David
McNair-Wilson, Sir Patrick
Madel, Sir David
Maitland, Lady Olga
Malone, Gerald
Mans, Keith
Marland, Paul
Marlow, Tony
Marshall, John (Hendon S)
Marshall, Sir Michael (Arundel)
Martin, David (Portsmouth S)
Mates, Michael
Merchant, Piers
Mills, Iain
Mitchell, Andrew (Gedling)
Mitchell, Sir David (NW Hants)
Monro, Sir Hector
Montgomery, Sir Fergus
Needham, Rt Hon Richard
Neubert, Sir Michael
Newton, Rt Hon Tony
Nicholls, Patrick
Nicholson, David (Taunton)
Onslow, Rt Hon Sir Cranley
Ottaway, Richard
Page, Richard
Patnick, Sir Irvine
Patten, Rt Hon John
Pattie, Rt Hon Sir Geoffrey

Pawsey, James
Peacock, Mrs Elizabeth
Pickles, Eric
Porter, Barry (Wirral S)
Porter, David (Waveney)
Powell, William (Corby)
Renton, Rt Hon Tim
Richards, Rod
Riddick, Graham
Rifkind, Rt Hon Malcolm
Robathan, Andrew
Roberts, Rt Hon Sir Wyn
Robinson, Mark (Somerton)
Roe, Mrs Marion (Broxbourne)
Rowe, Andrew (Mid Kent)
Rumbold, Rt Hon Dame Angela
Ryder, Rt Hon Richard
Sackville, Tom
Sainsbury, Rt Hon Sir Timothy
Scott, Rt Hon Sir Nicholas
Shaw, David (Dover)
Shaw, Sir Giles (Pudsey)
Shephard, Rt Hon Gillian
Shepherd, Richard (Aldridge)
Shersby, Michael
Skeet, Sir Trevor
Smith, Tim (Beaconsfield)
Soames, Nicholas
Spencer, Sir Derek
Spicer, Sir James (W Dorset)
Spicer, Michael (S Worcs)
Spink, Dr Robert
Spring, Richard
Sproat, Iain
Squire, Robin (Hornchurch)
Steen, Anthony
Stephen, Michael
Stern, Michael
Stewart, Allan
Streeter, Gary
Sweeney, Walter
Sykes, John
Tapsell, Sir Peter
Taylor, John M (Solihull)
Taylor, Sir Teddy (Southend, E)
Temple-Morris, Peter
Thomason, Roy
Thompson, Patrick (Norwich N)
Thornton, Sir Malcolm
Thurnham, Peter
Townend, John (Bridlington)
Townsend, Cyril D (Bexl'yh'th)
Tracey, Richard
Tredinnick, David
Trend, Michael
Trotter, Neville
Twinn, Dr Ian
Vaughan, Sir Gerard
Viggers, Peter
Waldegrave, Rt Hon William
Walden, George
Walker, Bill (N Tayside)
Waller, Gary
Ward, John
Wardle, Charles (Bexhill)
Waterson, Nigel
Watts, John
Wells, Bowen
Wheeler, Rt Hon Sir John
Whitney, Ray
Whittingdale, John
Widdecombe, Ann
Wiggin, Sir Jerry
Wilkinson, John

Willetts, David
Wilshire, David
Winterton, Mrs Ann (Congleton)
Winterton, Nicholas (Macc'fld)
Wolfson, Mark

Young, Rt Hon Sir George

**Tellers for the Noes:**
   **Mr. Timothy Wood and**
   **Mr. David Lightbown.**

*Question accordingly negatived.*

*Main Question put forthwith, pursuant to Standing Order No. 60 (Amendment on Second or Third Reading), and agreed to.*

*Bill read a Second time, and committed to a Standing Committee, pursuant to Standing Order No. 61 (Committal of Bills).*

### CRIMINAL INJURIES COMPENSATION BILL
#### [MONEY]

*Queen's recommendation having been signified—*

*Motion made, and Question put forthwith, pursuant to Order [19 December],*

That, for the purposes of any Act resulting from the Criminal Injuries Compensation Bill, it is expedient to authorise—

  (a) the payment out of money provided by Parliament of sums required by the Secretary of State in respect of—

  (i) compensation payable in accordance with the provisions of the Criminal Injuries Compensation Scheme established under the Act;

  (ii) payments to or in respect of persons appointed under the Act;

  (iii) any other expenditure incurred by him under or by virtue of the Act;

  (b) payments into the Consolidated Fund—*[Mr. Burns.]*

*Question agreed to.*

### LAW REFORM (SUCCESSION) BILL [LORDS]

*Bill read a Second time, and committed to a Standing Committee, pursuant to Standing Order No. 61 (Committal of Bills).*

## Age Discrimination

*Motion made, and Question proposed,* That this House do now adjourn.—*[Mr. Burns.]*

10.17 pm

**Mr. Richard Ottaway** (Croydon, South): I wish to raise the subject of agism. It is a matter of great concern in my constituency, which has many professional middle-class people who have had the misfortune to find themselves redundant and who, as a result of their age, are unable to work their way back into the job market.

Legislation has been considered by the House in relatively recent times against discrimination in the workplace on the grounds of disability, gender, sexual orientation and ethnic origin. I am sure that the entire House shares the widespread public distaste for any act of discrimination, and I am sure that the majority of employers in the United Kingdom have come to realise the foolishness of allowing such prejudice in the workplace.

Legislation does not mean that discrimination has been overcome. Ethnic minorities in this country continue to experience higher rates of unemployment, people with disabilities continue to feel that they are regarded as second-class citizens in the workplace, and there are still too few women in senior positions in the UK.

However, a primary cause of prejudice in the workplace, agism, remains an accepted practice, unregulated in law, with no commission responsible for tackling the problem and no formal course of redress for those discriminated against on the ground of age. It is ironic that one cause of discrimination that can affect all of us at one time or another is the one that has been given the lowest priority by Governments and employers.

I am delighted that my hon. Friend the Minister of State, Department of Employment is to reply to the debate, since she herself said:

"We know that as many as 40 per cent of employers discriminate simply on the grounds of age. They set age bars to recruitment—sometimes as low as forty, or even thirty in some occupations. They refuse to promote or train older workers and they select the oldest first for redundancy".

My hon. Friend attempted to address the problem with her Department's campaign "Getting On", which sought to highlight the unfairness of age discrimination and to persuade decision makers at all levels that we must solve that problem if we are to have a healthy and a thriving economy. I recognise and welcome the efforts of the Government in that regard, and I applaud my hon. Friend for finally getting the matter on the agenda where it belongs.

Although the Government and other institutions, such as the Institute of Personnel Management, argue that age should not be used as a primary discriminator, research suggests that such discrimination at the point of recruitment is still widespread. Recent advertisements suggested that an audio secretary in Scotland and an assistant manager of a department store in Nottingham should be in the 23 to 35 age group. To be a secretary for a firm of accountants in central London, one would be considered past it if one had reached the grand old age of 26.

People who happen to be 26 may feel comforted by the knowledge that they are in the most desired age group, as more than 69 per cent. of employers stated in a recent

[*Mr. Richard Ottaway*]

survey that they were seeking candidates of that age. However, if one is unfortunate enough to be 45 years old, one is six times less likely to be considered for employment than one's younger counterparts.

A recent survey undertaken by Labour Research found that 46 per cent. of job advertisements effectively excluded applicants aged more than 40 years. Out of 250 advertisements open to the middle age band, a 26-year-old was deemed to be eligible for 173; a 34-year-old had access to 133; but the chances of 36-year-olds were already diminishing, with only 93 jobs open to people of that age.

I recently visited the Victoria street job centre in Westminster. Of 16 advertisements for clerical jobs in February, four specified an age range from 21 to no more than 28 years—more than 35 years from retirement age, and one is already considered too old to be employed in a clerical position.

**Mrs. Teresa Gorman** (Billericay): Does my hon. Friend not agree that, despite the very best efforts and the extreme good will of our hon. Friend the Minister, age discrimination exists in the Westminster employment agency here on the Back Benches? Many people who are more than 50 years old come to this place and find that their talents are ignored because of their age.

**Mr. Ottaway:** I must disagree with my hon. Friend. I have no idea how old she is—perhaps thirty-something— but her talents are well recognised on the Back Benches. I think that she is underestimating her talents and those of her colleagues who are of a similar age.

I have been informed that job centres now encourage employers to advertise job vacancies without a specific age criterion. When employers refuse to do that, I am assured that the job centre will send any suitably qualified person for an interview, regardless of whether he or she falls within the age range sought by an employer. Reasonably often, that supposedly unsuitable candidate is appointed to the position. I think that that clearly shows the folly of age specifications in advertisements and the fact that the requirement that candidates be of a certain age is based purely on prejudice.

I have spoken to many people in their early 40s or 50s who feel that their age has been a serious disadvantage when seeking employment, especially if they are trying to find work after a period of unemployment. After several unsuccessful interviews, omitting information or even lying about their age on a curriculum vitae or application form became an accepted practice in an attempt to overcome age prejudice.

My constituent Mr. Todd has been unable to get back into the job market, having been made redundant at just over the age of 50. [*Interruption.*]

**Madam Deputy Speaker (Dame Janet Fookes):** Order. The hon. Members for Billericay (Mrs. Gorman) and for Workington (Mr. Campbell-Savours) are quite old enough to know that I deplore seated interventions.

**Mr. D. N. Campbell-Savours** (Workington): She is winding me up.

**Madam Deputy Speaker:** That is a very feeble excuse.

**Mr. Ottaway:** Perhaps my hon. Friend the Member for Billericay (Mrs. Gorman) and the hon. Member for Workington (Mr. Campbell-Savours) are feeling their age.

The Institute of Personnel Management recently stated that all its 50,000 members should be aware that decisions based on age are never justifiable, are based on fallible suppositions and lead to the ineffective use of human resources. Although, within 15 years, more of the population will be over 60 than in the 16-to-44 age group, most commentators would agree that the position is getting worse.

The problem, however, is not limited merely to vacancies. The same stereotyped attitudes often prevent management from selecting older workers for training programmes or promotion. The idea that older workers are harder to train and the adage "You can't teach an old dog new tricks" are quite ridiculous.

A senior employee with perhaps 30 years' service has probably altered his way of working several times over the years, and is usually more than capable of learning new skills and techniques. Older workers bring the welcome addition of experience and maturity to training courses.

Early retirement packages are considered preferable to redundancy programmes, yet they are often the sole method of reducing staffing levels, and they directly target older workers. However, it is not all bad news. Some employers, notably B and Q, W. H. Smith, the Nationwide building society and Sainsbury, recognise the waste produced by agism, and are starting to take advantage of the untapped potential in the unemployed aged 40 to 50 who have been overlooked by other employers in favour of younger workers.

In 1989, B and Q reassessed its employment policy and decided to target older workers. Its store in Macclesfield was set up as an experiment, using staff all over the age of 50. The managers who developed the plan hoped that such a move would provide the company with a stock of experienced and customer-friendly staff. Their faith in older workers was repaid threefold. In the words of B and Q's personnel manager, the workers were found to be

"reliable, conscientious staff who have shown a built-in regard for customer service".

No significant productivity difference was discovered and, although some workers were perhaps slower than others, that was more than compensated for by the greater likelihood of older workers getting things right first time, and the lower risk of accidents due to their taking greater care.

The entire work force benefited from the presence of older workers. Relationships with younger members of staff were good, particularly when the older employee took on the role of mentor to his younger colleague. Another store has since been opened along the lines of the one in Macclesfield and the chain is seeking to increase the number of older workers in all its outlets throughout the country.

**Dr. Robert Spink** (Castle Point): Can my hon. Friend confirm that the experiment found that sickness and other absence was actually lower?

**Mr. Ottaway:** I can confirm that trend. Older workers tend to be more reliable. Having been trained, they stay longer and there is less absenteeism.

In my opinion, companies such as B and Q deserve praise for having the foresight to develop such schemes. They do not, however, deserve our thanks. They are not doing society a service by taking on older workers; they are making a sound business decision by doing so, and their businesses are becoming fitter and more profitable for it.

**Mr. Campbell-Savours:** Does that mean that the hon. Member for Billericay (Mrs. Gorman) will not only be a purchaser from B and Q DIY departments, but she will be able to work for one when she leaves the House after the next election?

**Mr. Ottaway:** Following the theme of the debate, I hope that anyone of any age and of any party will be able to work for B and Q after the next election. It is dangerous for the hon. Gentleman to count his chickens before they are hatched.

The Carnegie Third Age Programme inquiry was set up to examine the specific problems of people aged 50 to 70. It discussed at length whether to press for immediate legislation against age discrimination, as operates in the United States, but concluded that the best approach would be first to do everything possible on a voluntary basis, and to press for legislation only when it was clear that employers had failed effectively to deal with discrimination.

I feel strongly that enough time and energy has been spent in recent years trying to promote such a voluntary approach. Despite the efforts of my hon. Friend the Minister, it has been only a partial success. The time has now come to legislate against such foolish and bigoted practice.

There is a great need to raise public awareness of agism to the same level as that of discrimination on any other grounds, such as gender or race. That need can be met only by legislation against agism, in a form that will demonstrate society's disapproval of such morally unacceptable behaviour.

I do not argue that changes in the law will in themselves eradicate discrimination, just as I would not argue that the presence of the criminal law has eliminated burglaries and assaults. The fact that the problems may still exist after legislation, however, is not a valid argument against seeking change.

Other acts of discrimination are, unfortunately, still taking place regularly in our society, but that would not be seen as a valid reason to repeal the Race Relations Act 1976 or the Sex Discrimination Acts. Just as a job advertisement must not specify gender or racial exclusions, so it should no longer be possible to specify an age range.

**Mr. Malcolm Wicks** (Croydon, North-West): I apologise for missing the opening of the hon. Gentleman's speech, but I hope that I may intervene on my Member of Parliament. Is he concerned about the fact that employment rates among older workers have declined during the last 15 years of Conservative government?

**Mr. Ottaway:** Of course one would be concerned about that. If the hon. Gentleman had been present for the earlier part of mmy speech, he would know that I initiated the debate precisely because I believe that there is prejudice against older workers who have been forced into redundancy and are finding it difficult to get back into the job market.

The vital role that the law can play in discrimination cases is to allow any individual the opportunity to seek redress through an industrial tribunal or court. Those who

are treated prejudicially owing to gender or race are already afforded that right; it is now time to ensure that those who suffer the same discrimination through agism are given the same standing in law.

10.31 pm

**The Minister of State, Department of Employment (Miss Ann Widdecombe):** I congratulate my hon. Friend the Member for Croydon, South (Mr. Ottaway) on obtaining the debate, and on raising such an important subject. It has generated far more interest than debates of this kind, at this hour, usually generate. I should record the presence throughout the debate of the hon. Member for Workington (Mr. Campbell-Savours), and the presence of the hon. Member for Croydon, some compass point that I never get right—

**Mr. Wicks:** North-West. Labour gain in 1992.

**Miss Widdecombe:** Labour gain in 1992; Conservative gain later in the 1990s, whenever it may be.

My hon. Friends the Members for Billericay (Mrs. Gorman), for Castle Point (Dr. Spink) and for Colne Valley (Mr. Riddick) have also come along, because they recognise the supreme importance of the subject. There have, indeed, been many interventions. My hon. Friend the Member for Billericay suggested that there was age discrimination even in the House. I always give the same advice to people who complain to me about age discrimination: never, ever give up. I commend that advice to my hon. Friend.

The hon. Member for Croydon, North-West (Mr. Wicks) interrupted at a late stage to say that there had been a decline in the employment of older workers under the Conservative Government. He should distinguish between unemployment and economic inactivity. He will, I am sure, appreciate that there has been a rising tide of early retirement. Whether or not he makes a value judgment on that one way or the other, it is not the same as unemployment, and does not necessarily stem from redundancy or forced early retirement.

Let me turn to the main thesis of my hon. Friend the Member for Croydon, South, who set out the problem so ably. Despite the light-heartedness of some of tonight's debate—I think that all the participants should have declared their interest; we are all of a certain age—a serious problem exists. By the year 2000, some 40 per cent. of the work force will be aged 45 or over.

But we know from surveys that about 40 per cent. of employers openly admit to practising some form of age discrimination—and those are only the ones who openly admit it. It is practised primarily in recruitment, but also in promotion, and certainly in training and in retention policies when putting redundancy programmes into effect.

Such discrimination is bad for the individual who faces being on what is sometimes popularly called the scrap heap. It is also bad for the economy, because if we do not make use of our older workers, we will be sentencing to economic inactivity a growing percentage of our work force because of the way demographics are moving. It is also extremely bad for British business and for employers, who are missing a great wealth of talent and a great deal of experience. Therefore, it is essential for us to address this problem.

There are great myths about employing older workers, the first of which is that somehow they are not trainable. I recently ran a nationwide competition to find older

*[Miss Widdecombe]*

trainees, not people training at home in the hope of getting work or people taking an Open university course, but people who were in work, whose employers believed that they were a worthwhile investment, and who were training for a qualification. We found many people in their late 50s and early 60s. Furthermore, they were training in quite unusual subjects, such as information technology, which employers sometimes, quite erroneously, believe older workers cannot be trained in. Therefore, I know it is not true that people cannot be trained in later life.

Some people hold the view that somehow older people are unfit and cannot keep going quite as long as their younger counterparts. I ran another competition to find the oldest worker in Britain, and found that the oldest male worker who was still working six days a week and giving full satisfaction to his employer was aged 93. The oldest female worker, also working six days a week and giving full satisfaction, was 92. If people of 92 and 93 can give satisfaction to their employers, what is the problem about taking on people who are 40 years younger? The point of that campaign was not to persuade people to work into their 90s but to be able to say to employers, "If people in their 90s can do well, what is your problem with people in their 50s?"

The other great myth is that somehow older workers are not as committed as younger people, that the employer will not get as long a work period out of them. But precisely because it is so difficult for older workers to find a job, particularly if they are in their late 50s, those who have jobs tend to be extremely committed to them. An employer who takes on a man of 55 is likely still to have him at the age of 65. Statistically, it cannot necessarily be said that a man taken on at the age of 20 is likely to be with that employer when he is 30.

My hon. Friend the Member for Croydon, South proposed legislation as the answer. I disagree, but I do not do so lightly or because of some preconceived notion. We carefully studied some 20 countries, and looked particularly at those which have some form of anti-agism legislation. We particularly studied the United States, which has just about the most comprehensive anti-agism package of them all. The United States has approximately the same percentage of unemployed older workers as Britain, so that legislation is not delivering. We took the view of people in those countries with legislation, and their view was that it was not delivering.

I am not interested in cluttering up the statute book for the sake of it. I want to persuade employers to change their minds and to see the errors of their ways. That is what has informed my "Getting On" campaign. To put it cynically, if the way to convince an employer of the desirability of doing something is by commercial advantage, then all employers should be convinced of the advantages of a mixed-age work force.

The campaign that I launched so far has consisted of a very successful booklet giving advice to employers—not advice from Ministers, but advice from other employers who have already got mixed-age work forces and who have found solid business benefits from them. They have them not because they are a nice thing to have but because they bring them solid benefits: customer satisfaction, productivity, the use of experience. That is what the first part of the campaign was about.

**Mr. Wicks:** I agree with the Minister and my hon. Friend—he is my friend—the Member for Croydon, South, (Mr. Ottaway) but I disagree with her about legislation. Inevitably, the state has an interest; despite the Minister's campaign, economic activity rates, especially among male older workers, are in decline. If, because of so-called downsizing, people are retiring or being made redundant— there is a fine balance between the two—in their early 50s, they may be retired people for a third of their lives. That in turn has major implications for state expenditure.

Perhaps the Minister should therefore think again about the implications for legislation.

**Miss Widdecombe:** Indeed the state does have an interest, and, as I was saying, the British economy too has an interest in using the talents and experience of older workers. So far, we can agree.

The hon. Gentleman is a little ungenerous to say, however, that my campaign has not worked. He should spare me a little; I launched it in 1993, and we are not even halfway through 1995 yet. He will well know that statistics are not precise over that sort of period, but we know that surveys done three years ago were showing 40 per cent. of employers openly practising discrimination, whereas a survey done at the end of last year showed that about three quarters of employers expect to take on older workers in the foreseeable future.

I do not suggest that there has been a swing of that order of magnitude—the surveys were not done in exactly the same way, or with the same groups—but we can see that employers are becoming seized of the problem and expect to have to change their ways. So a little patience is called for before we start rushing into legislation, which has not worked elsewhere.

The second stage of my campaign was to give older workers the advice that I gave my hon. Friend the Member for Billericay: never give up. It came in one of the Department's best-ever selling booklets, called "Too Old . . . Who Says?" It is aimed at employees, not employers, giving them advice on what to do.

The next part of the campaign will be aimed at recruitment agencies, which is where many of the problems start. Advertisements for people to work as recruitment consultants include stringent age bars, so it is not surprising that they work through into employers' recruitment policies.

Finally, the Government have tried to be our own best example of what we want. We have raised training for work from an upper age limit of 59 to 63. We have scrapped age limits in central civil service recruitment. We have instructed our job centres to resist age bars in advertisements. When they have no choice but to take an advertisement, we have instructed them to send along people outwith the specification as well as those within it. I take every opportunity I have to promote the older worker. It is this sort of campaign which I believe will work. At any rate, we ought to try it, and to do so seriously, before we rush into legislation which may prove to be more decorative than useful.

*Question put and agreed to.*
*Adjourned accordingly at sixteen minutes to Eleven o'clock.*

24 MAY 1995

# House of Commons

*Wednesday 24 May 1995*

*The House met at Ten o'clock*

## PRAYERS

[MADAM SPEAKER *in the Chair*]

10.4 am

**Madam Speaker:** The House will wish to know of the arrangements made for today's sitting following the death of the former Prime Minister, Lord Wilson of Rievaulx. This morning's proceedings on the motion for the Adjournment will go ahead in the normal way. There will be questions at 2.30 pm and an opportunity for statements at 3.30 pm. Immediately after that, there will be tributes to Lord Wilson and it will be proposed that the House then adjourns.

## Adjournment of the House

*Motion made, and Question proposed,* That this House do now adjourn.—[*Mr. Chapman.*]

10.5 am

**Mr. Jacques Arnold** (Gravesham): I believe that the House should not adjourn before hon. Members have considered the important matter of the underfunding of school budgets. Yesterday, the House heard from my right hon. Friend the Member for Honiton (Sir P. Emery) about school budgets in Devon being underfunded by the Lib-Lab county council, and about the fact that Conservative county councillors there have proposed a motion that the £4 million odd should be restored and have shown the ways and means by which that could be done. That proposal was turned down by the Lib-Lab county councillors in Devon.

The position in Kent should be raised this morning. My hon. Friends representing Kent and I have raised it incessantly. At the risk of boring hon. Members, I shall remind them that the Labour and Liberal Democrat groups on Kent county council at first intended to provide for no increase in school funding for this year, despite knowing that a settlement for an increase in teachers' pay had been rightly approved. That creates an intolerable position for our schools and it has occurred at a time when Kent county council has received a 2 per cent. increase in financial support from the Government, and when the Labour and Liberal Democrat groups have approved a budget that has hit Kent council tax payers with an increase of more than 5 per cent. in their council tax.

When one considers that 2 per cent. increase in Government funding and the fact that council tax payers are contributing another 5 per cent., it is an absolute outrage that schools in our county were confined to budgets that showed no increase to take account of teachers' pay or of inflation. Needless to say, that caused outrage in Kent and the Lib-Labs conceded the point to the extent that they introduced a 1 per cent. increase. That has nevertheless left our schools with problems in relation to their budgets and how they manage their finances. In a small number of cases, those problems could lead to the loss of teaching posts, which is outrageous.

The county council's Conservative group proposed an alternative budget that showed ways in which, by a rearrangement of spending, money could be concentrated on schools, thereby increasing funds to cover the teachers' pay settlement and making up for inflation. That could have reversed the wanton imposition of a £700,000 cut in adult education by the Labour and Liberal Democrat groups and could have kept a fund going for discretionary grants for post-16 education, which the Labour and Liberal Democrat parties have totally cut.

In a neighbouring constituency to mine, we have a case of a young girl who has an exceptional talent in dance. She would normally have looked to the county council for a discretionary grant to develop that talent in her education, but the application was turned down flat by the council on the ground that it has no budget for that. That has never happened in Kent before, but it is what happens when large authorities such as Kent are in the hands of a coalition between the Labour party and the Liberal Democrats. What will happen to the education of that talented youngster and the development of her talent? They care not a bit.

[Mr. Jacques Arnold]

Those two groups use the usual range of excuses, saying that it is because of the Government's actions and that it is all so unfair. Originally, I put it down to inexperience, incompetence or a mixture of both. That seemed quite a reasonable answer to their extraordinary behaviour. However, I am coming increasingly to the view that not only is it a conspiracy at the expense of the people of Kent and the education of all our children, but that that conspiracy extends far further. We have heard what has happened in Devon, where budgets have been deliberately underfunded despite the alternative budget presented by experienced Conservative county councillors. Hon. Members will know of case after case of similar goings on in councils up and down the country.

The conspiracy between the Labour party and the Liberal Democrats seems to be based on the belief that if they short-change the schools and bleat about Government cuts, parents will rise up and blame the Government. That may have had a little to do with the local election results earlier this month. So on that score it was cynically successful. What is left in the wake of that conspiracy is the wreckage of our youngsters' education—including that talented girl to whom I referred—and pressures on schools that they should not have to face when the money is available. I increasingly think that we are dealing with a political, cynical conspiracy.

What strengthens my view? Recently the accountants for Kent county council announced that there was an underspend of £17 million in the revenue budget for the council, let alone the underspend of £24 million in the capital budget. Although it is now the second month of the financial year, Conservative county councillors in Kent quite properly tabled an amendment asking that £3.8 million of that £17 million underspend—that is all that is required—be put into the school budgets in Kent so that they would know that the funding was available and so that, in the minority of cases, they would not have to take the drastic action of dismissing teachers. That is a sensible solution based on the best for the education of our children in Kent.

A detailed budget was laid out by the Conservative group on Kent county council, but it was curtailed without proper debate and was voted down by the Labour and Liberal Democrat groups.

What happened to the amendment to harness £3.8 million from the £17 million underspend of last year? The Labour and Liberal Democrat groups—it is easy to confuse them given the way in which they carry out their so-called work in Kent—decided that they did not want to debate it. However, they dare not turn it down because it is so logical and is supported by the people of Kent. They decided to filibuster and fob it off to a committee. The next meeting is on 22 June. That means that it will be a month before our schools know whether a solution will be found for their problems.

As you know, Madam Speaker, I am the last to complain about the party politics in which we indulge ourselves from time to time, but we are talking about the education of our children—I mean "our children" because my children attend state schools in Kent, as do the children of other hon. Members up and down the county and the country. We should not play politics with the education of our children and that is what the Labour and Liberal Democrat groups are doing in Kent.

I hope that the Labour and Liberal Democrat spokesmen will roundly condemn what has happened in Kent and that at the very least they will instruct their groups in Kent to look at this matter and put the money that is available into our schools for the education of our children.

10.14 am

**Mrs. Diana Maddock** (Christchurch): I am sure that hon. Members will join me in sending our sincere sympathies to the friends and family of those who lost their lives or were injured in the tragic coach crash yesterday. I am sure that hon. Members are aware that a coach carrying 29 members of Christchurch Royal British Legion overturned after they had been out for a pleasant day in Wales. I hope that the Leader of the House will ensure that certain matters are looked into before the recess.

I had given notice that I intended to ask a private notice question later today. However, in view of the sad death of a previous Prime Minister, I thought that it would be more appropriate to raise the matter this morning and I thank you, Madam Speaker, for allowing me to do so.

Only two weeks ago I was celebrating VE day in Christchurch with many of those who were involved in the accident. Various questions arise in our minds as a result of the accident. Over some time, questions have been asked in general about coach safety. Often an accident has nothing to do with roadworthiness, but I should like to draw the House's attention to some figures provided last year in answer to parliamentary questions about coach safety. Unacceptable numbers of coaches failed the annual test; in the last year for which I have figures, 73,000 tests were carried out. Initially, there were over 27,000 failures and the final number of failures was over 13,000. I hope that the Minister responsible will look into that now that we have had yet another tragic accident.

Much has been said about seat belts and, at the moment, we do not know exactly what happened yesterday. It would be premature to say what we think happened when we do not know the truth. We hear that there were some seat belts fitted to the coach, but the impact yesterday was such that the roof of the coach was crushed. That raises questions about the strength of the upper structure of our coaches. The coach involved was about nine years old and I hope that the Minister will look at the existing regulations dealing with the strength of coach roofs.

In view of yet another tragic accident, there are three matters that need to be considered. First, we need to know why so many of our coaches fail their annual tests. Secondly, we need to know why the roof of this coach was crushed and, thirdly, we need to know whether seat belts play a role. I know that that was looked at last year and I understand that there are certain difficulties over legislation in Europe.

It is particularly poignant that those who survived the last war have lost their lives in this tragic way and I hope that the Minister will look into the matter with great urgency and set things in motion before the Whitsun recess.

**Madam Speaker:** I call Mr. Amess. *[Interruption.]* Does the hon. Member wish to speak, or is he just moving around the Chamber?

**Mr. David Amess** (Basildon): I am not ready yet.

**Madam Speaker:** In that case, I shall call Mr. Clappison.

10.19 am

**Mr. James Clappison** (Hertsmere): I welcome the opportunity to speak in this debate on a matter that is of particular importance to my constituents, that is, the future of the assisted places scheme. Currently, 29,000 pupils nationally are helped by the scheme. There is a concentration of places in my constituency, where 411 pupils enjoy its benefits. I admit that not all of them come from my constituency, but a substantial number of them do. In any case, wherever they come from, they are all being educated in my constituency. Also, a number of children from my constituency go to schools outside it to enjoy the benefits of the scheme. Therefore, I am anxious to emphasise the value of the scheme to my constituents and also to highlight its importance nationally.

When we last debated the matter in the House, the Opposition spokesman complained, among other things, that there was little public awareness of the scheme and that not enough members of the public even knew of its existence. He quoted an opinion poll showing that only 40 per cent. of the public had heard of the scheme. Of course, it is a matter of subjective judgment, but I happen to think that 40 per cent. is a rather large proportion of those interviewed in any opinion poll actually being aware of the matter being surveyed.

The Opposition spokesman omitted to mention another opinion poll finding—it may have come from the same poll—relating to public approval of the scheme. The poll showed that of those who were aware of its existence, a substantial majority approved of it. When the figures were broken down by party affiliation, they showed a clear majority of supporters of all parties expressing approval. Indeed, 55 per cent. of Labour party supporters said that they approved of the scheme, while only 27 per cent. said that they disapproved—a clear majority of 2:1.

**Mr. Michael Fabricant** (Mid-Staffordshire): Does my hon. Friend think it ironic that the Labour party opposes the assisted places scheme, even though it is one of the most egalitarian schemes in education? Did he read the column written by Matthew Parris in *The Times* today? He pointed out an interesting dichotomy when he said that the Labour party claimed that if the scheme was discontinued, thousands of pounds would be available for the employment of more teachers, yet it failed to understand that the pupils who currently benefit from the scheme would then have to go into the state education sector, so those additional teachers would be required anyway—resulting in no net saving.

**Mr. Clappison:** I am tempted to say that great minds think alike, but I am not sure who the great minds are in this case because my hon. Friend has anticipated some of the points that I had intended to make—and in particular my next point, which he put so succinctly.

It is the supporters of the Labour party who benefit particularly and considerably from the scheme. Why does the Labour party want to do away with the scheme when so many of its supporters benefit from it? Left-wing commentators and Labour Members have tried to construct an elaborate sociological analysis to show that it is not Labour party supporters who benefit from the scheme. One survey quoted described those who benefit as culturally middle class. Other people have said that they are middle-class, single-parent families—horror of horrors.

That may or may not be so, but it is certainly true that those on the left wing of academic politics are far more inclined than Conservative Members to pin labels on people. I am not especially interested in the cultural, social or any other feature of the backgrounds of those who benefit from the scheme. The important point for the Conservative party is that they are people who would not otherwise have had the opportunity to benefit. It should be clearly understood that the scheme benefits people whose incomes are not especially high by today's standards—some 80 per cent. have below average income. I was told yesterday in a parliamentary answer that 42 per cent. of parents get free places on the scheme because their income is less than £9,300. I am sure that hon. Members will agree that that is a very moderate income. Therefore, the sociological arguments do not carry much weight.

The Labour party's economic arguments are not much better. During Education questions yesterday, Labour Members said that the scheme was a way of propping up foundering private schools. That argument has been used before and conveniently ignores the fact that many of the schools in the scheme are extremely popular and massively oversubscribed. In my constituency, about 350 of the 411 places are offered by the Haberdasher's schools for boys and for girls. I am delighted to say that my hon. Friend the Member for Aylesbury (Mr. Lidington), who is in the Chamber, was educated at Haberdasher's. Indeed, a number of hon. Members on both sides of the House have attended that eminent institution.

My personal knowledge of the Haberdasher's schools is that they could fill their assisted places many times over with pupils whose parents could afford to pay the full fees. However, the schools value the assisted places for a number of important reasons and they are prepared to play a full part in the scheme. The argument of Labour Members simply does not hold water. I could cite a list of schools taking part in the scheme—St. Paul's, Westminster and Dulwich college are a few examples of schools in reasonably close proximity to my constituency—that are of such quality that they attract huge numbers of applicants, so it is certainly not a case of propping up foundering schools.

I come now to the argument about the cost of the scheme, which my hon. Friend the Member for Mid-Staffordshire (Mr. Fabricant) just mentioned. The Opposition spokesman said yesterday that if the scheme were scrapped, state schools could employ an additional 5,000 teachers. That figure is wrong because the entire cost of the scheme could not possibly provide that number of teachers. It was a gross underestimate of the cost of providing a teacher. The Opposition also ignore the fact that pupils being educated under the scheme would have to be educated in the maintained sector if the scheme were scrapped.

We need to examine the true difference between the cost of an assisted place and the cost of a place in the maintained sector. That has varied over the years and sometimes the difference in cost has not been very great. Even when there is a difference in cost, as there is currently, I believe that that cost is well worth paying to provide choice, opportunity and diversity in our education system. I am sure that if that view was put to the fair-minded people who were interviewed in the opinion poll to which I referred earlier, most of them would agree.

[Mr. Clappison]

Assisted places are a welcome contribution to educational choice and diversity in my constituency. Those who have the benefit of such places, whom I meet through my surgeries and otherwise, tell me of the importance and value that they put on those places. They are provided in addition to a great deal of other educational diversity and excellence in my constituency. More than 6,000 pupils attend grant-maintained schools, with some of them coming from as far afield as Islington. Many of those schools are excellent and are receiving good reports from Ofsted.

The Opposition have put the assisted places scheme under direct threat. It is ironic that their only firm pledge on education—out of all the pledges that they could have made—is to abolish the assisted places scheme. That is a shame and it is very sad. Indeed, in many ways it is out of keeping with the old Labour tradition of trying to create the opportunity of a good education for people who would not otherwise have received one.

The Opposition's attitude is also ironic in view of the number of people on low incomes who benefit from the scheme. When the hon. Member for Sheffield, Brightside (Mr. Blunkett) proposed putting VAT on school fees, which would have affected people on higher incomes who could afford to pay the full fees, there was an outcry and the proposal was rapidly withdrawn. The Labour party will not withdraw its pledge to abolish the scheme, which helps people on lower incomes, which is sad. Indeed, if that policy were ever implemented, it would be sad for future generations on lower incomes in my constituency, who would have the opportunity of attending certain schools taken away from them.

In future generations, if Opposition Members were in a position to carry out their intentions, brothers and sisters of children who obtain assisted places would lose the opportunity to go to the same school as their siblings. Opposition Members would deprive children of opportunities that they would otherwise enjoy. That would be rather a shame, as I am sure my constituents would agree.

I put on record my support for the assisted places scheme. The opposition of Labour Members to the scheme deserves to be highlighted. People on lower incomes and Labour supporters, 2:1 of whom are in favour of the scheme, have a right to know that the Labour party is bent on taking away their opportunities for no good reason, as I hope that I have demonstrated. Its arguments are not the real reason for the party's hostility to the assisted places scheme. The real reason is sheer ideological hostility towards independent education, which in the case of assisted places would take away valuable opportunities that the Conservative Government have provided.

10.31 am

**Dr. Norman A. Godman** (Greenock and Port Glasgow): I assure the hon. Member for Hertsmere (Mr. Clappison) that as someone who failed his 11-plus, known in Scotland as the quallies, I shall certainly not be discussing my early academic career.

Before the House adjourns, I hope that the Leader of the House, with his customary courtesy, will attempt to deal with a couple of questions about the Brent Spar

incident and the Greenpeace occupation of the installation. The right hon. Gentleman will not be able to answer the questions himself, but I should be grateful if he would pass them to his right hon. and hon. Friends in the Department of Trade and Industry.

I should like to ask about the Government's proposed framework policy document on abandonment programmes for offshore installations. Will the right hon. Gentleman ensure consultation with interested parties in Scotland, such as the Scottish Fishermen's Federation, which have most to lose or gain from an abandonment proposal?

Will the right hon. Gentleman pass on my concern about the recent decision of the Minister for Industry and Energy to relax to 5 m the minimum water clearance above any platform remaining in situ in the North sea, compared with the 75 m currently obtaining but applied in only one case so far? That could have a disastrous effect for our fishermen. This morning's edition of *The Herald* carries a large article on the Greenpeace occupation of Brent Spar, which is entitled:

"Oil Company Reclaims Brent Spar".

That reclamation was achieved with the assistance of Grampian police officers. The article says:

"Mr. Heinz Rothermund, Shell's managing director, said Greenpeace and other organisations pointed to problems and Shell respected that.

Many things were being done world-wide thanks to the fact that problems had been pointed out, but as industrial organisations they were paid to find solutions and compromise and evaluations were required."

Mr. Rothermund is speaking with a forked tongue because the conduct of his company in the gulf of Mexico is entirely different from its proposed conduct in the disposal of Brent Spar. I accuse the company, its board of directors and senior executives of sheer hypocrisy. It has removed completely 20 installations from the gulf of Mexico. It is American federal law to remove redundant installations from such waters.

Shell has had to comply with American law, but because of the British Government's lax implementation of part I of the Petroleum Act 1987 such companies, with Shell leading, will leave their installations in the North sea, to the detriment of our fishermen. Fishermen have been treated very badly in this affair. The Government are accused of adopting an astonishingly lenient approach to the removal of such structures. Brent Spar should be brought ashore, dismantled and its recyclable elements recycled. Shell is trying to get away with a cheap option. The Government's failure in that regard and the disgraceful behaviour of Shell's senior executives provoked the Greenpeace occupation of Brent Spar.

Brent Spar is an old, redundant oil storage tank, which from the sea bed to the surface extends to some 109 m. It contains a dreadful toxic chemical mix that Shell cannot analyse but is happy to put into what it says are safe deep waters. For such materials, there is no such thing as a safe deep-water burial. In a written answer to a question that I tabled, the Minister for Industry and Energy said:

"In accordance with section 4 of the Petroleum Act 1987 the President of the Board of Trade approved the Brent Spar abandonment programme on 20 December 1994."—[*Official Report*, 15 May 1995; Vol. 260, c. 27.]

He went on to claim that environmental considerations and possible interference with navigation and fisheries had been analysed and there had been a comparative assessment of risk, technical feasibility and cost.

The question of cost looms large in abandonment programmes. The Government encourage international oil and gas companies to leave their structures—or many of them—in place. They are not, however, encouraging such practice in the southern areas of the North sea, where the waters are shallower and the technical difficulties of removing the structures are much less complicated. Installations should be removed from those waters and the beds should be swept clean so that our fishermen, who have fished the waters for hundreds of years, may return to fish their traditional fishing grounds. That is especially important given what is happening elsewhere in the fishing industry.

Shell Expro, aided and abetted by the Government, is seeking to dodge its obligations. Coming from a fishing family, I obviously have a special interest in the matter, but I hasten to assure you, Madam Speaker, and the House that no money whatever is involved, just strong family ties. A brother of mine is currently fishing off the northern coast of Norway on one of our freezer trawlers. Shell Expro has chosen the cheap option for dumping the huge Brent Spar installation. It gave the game away in a publication which it produced some time ago, in which it said:

"Onshore scrapping would require some 360,000 man-hours of work. The complexity and labour intensive nature of the operations means that they would be very costly and expose personnel to greater risk."

Yet in the gulf of Mexico, Shell has removed more than 900 installations from those admittedly shallow waters. Some of the structures in the gulf of Mexico are akin to some of those on our continental shelf, such as the type in Norwegian waters. That is what the company is concerned about. Bringing the installation ashore would cost 360,000 man hours of work whereas, to use the company's words:

"The environmental impact of the sunken Spar will be limited and contained. The site of the sinking is likely to be in water over 2,000 metres deep and more than 240 kms from land."

From my knowledge of the fishing industry, I can tell the House that no trawler anywhere in the north Atlantic fishes in water that deep, but the eventual dispersal of toxic materials will damage marine life.

The document states that dispersal at sea—the dumping in deep water—will require 52,000 man hours of work. That difference in man hours is obviously focusing the minds of Shell's directors and chief executives, who are saving money, having made many millions of pounds out of the offshore industry. It has been estimated, incidentally, that bringing the installation ashore would cost about £46 million. Since the mid-1980s, Shell has been involved in a £1.3 billion renovation programme of its offshore operations, so £46 million would not figure very largely in its costs.

I have argued ever since enactment of the Petroleum Act 1987 that such structures should be completely removed from the marine environment. The late Alick Buchanan-Smith was a fine man and a fair-minded adversary who was popular in Scotland and, indeed, south of the border. As a member of the Standing Committee that considered the Petroleum Bill I told him—I thought that he would be here for many more years—that, while I was in the House, I would campaign for the complete removal of such structures, which is permitted under part I of the 1987 Act, which he steered through Committee.

The Government have failed the people of Scotland by their refusal to ensure that installations are removed. We are talking about as many as 20 or 30 a year during the next few years, as there are more than 200 in our waters. Contrast our Government's attitude with the American legislative view and the way in which the Norwegians handle such matters.

There is hypocrisy in Shell's actions. The company behaves one way in our waters but, because American federal law forces it to behave in another way, it complies with that law in the gulf of Mexico. The Norwegian Government said that they wanted an installation similar to Brent Spar—N.V. Frigg—brought ashore for dismantling and recycling If it is good enough for the Norwegians and their fishermen, why not for Scotland and its fishermen?

Greenpeace has informed me that complete removal of the installation would cost £46 million, which represents only 3.5 per cent. of the money that Shell is spending in the Brent field. We must remember that Shell has assets of more than $11 billion. My fear is that, if Shell is allowed to get away with this unsavoury decision, an unfortunate precedent will be established for others to follow.

Hamilton Oil and Gas demonstrated what should be done plainly enough by the complete removal of the Forbes platform. It plans to remove completely the bigger Esmond platform and ancillary facilities, so it can be done. We shall have to face up to that fact when the time comes for those 200-odd structures to be abandoned. They will be removed from the central and southern North sea and they should be removed from northern waters.

I come from a fishing family and I fully support the view of the Scottish Fishermen's Federation on the matter. In a recently published document, it states:

"Politicians of all Parties will hopefully be reasonably familiar with the long history of difficulty which has been the lot of our Fishermen in competing for access to the waters of the UK Continental Shelf with the North Sea Oil and Gas Industry and with our policy that our forbearance and co-operation with the Oil Operators should be recognised by the acceptance of both them and the Government of an obligation to remove entirely from the sea all installations which cease to be in use. That standpoint has regrettably never been accepted as a general principle and in recent years changes in International Law, heavily influenced by the UK Government, have reached the stage where partial removal of offshore installations will be permitted upon their Abandonment".

Alick Buchanan-Smith said that, where possible, such structures should be removed. He pointed out to me that concrete structures are enormously difficult to move, which I accept; it is a fact of life. The Norwegians are finding similar difficulty with the removal of some of their massive concrete structures, but there has been genuine consultation between the Norwegian Government and associations representing Norwegian fishermen who fish in their waters. There has not been any genuine consultation between the UK Government and the National Federation of Fishermen's Organisations or, more importantly in this regard, with the Scottish Fishermen's Federation.

The issue is very important and it is causing a great deal of concern in Scotland, not merely among Greenpeace activists but in small fishing communities where there are no, or very few, alternative employment opportunities.

I am sure that the Leader of the House would agree that the fishermen have played the game. They said that it was important for oil and gas to be brought ashore. It has helped the Shetland economy enormously over the years,

[*Dr. Norman A. Godman*]

as it has also helped elsewhere—one thinks of Orkney, Fraserburgh and Peterhead and, indeed, of Aberdeen. Many thousands of people are working in the industry.

In my constituency, two rigs are being converted. I hope to see as many as 11 rigs coming into the firth of Clyde in the next two years for conversion work. No one has to tell me, or our fishermen, how important the offshore oil and gas industry is and has been to our economy. We could debate how the money has had to be spent—on the massive number of unemployed people—but that is another story.

Part I of the 1987 Act should be used more radically to ensure the complete removal not merely of the installations but of redundant pipeline networks. They, too, prevent fishermen from fishing the waters that they and their fathers, grandfathers and great-grandfathers fished.

Peter Morrison—a Minister who followed on from the late Alick Buchanan-Smith—said in a speech in Aberdeen, which was widely publicised in Scotland, that the abandonment programmes for the installations could generate many thousands of jobs along the east coast of Scotland and later on the west coast. He said that redundant shipyard workers and others might find employment in such programmes, but that simply has not happened.

The American experience is entirely different. More than 900 installations have been completely removed from the gulf of Mexico. We have the shabby sight of Shell, BP and the other companies that used those natural resources to make massive profits seedily dodging their obligations to other users of the maritime environment, particularly fishermen.

Following enactment of the Petroleum Act, I had hoped that we could say to our fishermen that one day they could fish those waters again. I hoped that the seas would be swept clean of structures and redundant pipeline networks, and that they would be able to drop their gear on to the sea bed without it becoming snagged, as often happens today, by materials from the hugely important offshore industry.

I hope that the consultation exercise that the Government are planning will be genuine, and not the kind of thing that the Scottish Office—under its present regime—undertakes. I hope that there will be genuine consultation with fishermen and others so that we can decide which installations may have to stay in place, such as the concrete structures. I hope that a radical implementation of the 1987 Act will mean that other structures can be removed and brought ashore in the interests of our fishermen. They deserve nothing less.

10.50 am

**Mr. David Amess** (Basildon): I am glad to be called, Madam Speaker, as I felt earlier as though I had been caught out making a false bid at an auction.

I join colleagues in paying tribute to the noble Lord Wilson of Rievaulx who dominated political affairs in this country when I was a child. In every sense he was a great politician.

I should like the House to consider four matters, the first of which is identity cards. Some years ago, I successfully moved a ten-minute Bill to allow the introduction of voluntary identity cards. That was the first occasion on which the House did not oppose the concept of identity cards. I proposed a system of voluntary identity cards because I felt that if the House and the country were not prepared for a compulsory system, a voluntary system would be better than nothing.

People accept that they must have birth certificates and death certificates, but I cannot understand why the bit in between is not recorded. When we knock on doors—as we recently did during the local elections—we find that the general public are concerned about crime. There is no doubt in my mind that identity cards will help in the fight against crime. I shall be astonished if it is true that new Labour is going to oppose the introduction of such cards.

**Mr. Peter L. Pike** (Burnley): Does the hon. Gentleman recall that the 1951 Conservative Government scrapped identity cards as the last remnant of the socialist Government that had been in power from 1945 to 1951?

**Mr. Amess:** My difficulty is that I was born in 1952, so I cannot personally recall that. I am looking to the future, and I do not think that what happened in 1951 is paramount in the minds of the British public at the moment.

**Mr. Barry Field** (Isle of Wight): Does my hon. Friend agree that even en ventre de sa mère he was a Tory?

**Mr. Amess:** There is no answer to that. The Conservative Government have not claimed credit for the national lottery, but I hope that we will claim credit for the sensible introduction of a compulsory identity card.

My second point is well timed, because I see that my right hon. Friend the Secretary of State for Transport is present. The Fenchurch Street line is notorious for offering a poor and inadequate service to my constituents and others in Essex. I am accused of being obsessed with my constituency, but it seems that Opposition Members and Front-Bench spokesmen are becoming increasingly obsessed with it. They have recently visited Basildon to talk about the privatisation of the Fenchurch Street line. They have not done so in an honest and realistic fashion, and have spread things that are not true. I deplore the way in which they have recently been scaremongering in my constituency.

My constituents could not care less who runs the Fenchurch Street line so long as the trains arrive on time, the carriages are comfortable, the fares are reasonable and the line's operators are mindful of security. That is what they are concerned about, and the privatisation of the Fenchurch Street line will deliver those things.

I must say to my right hon. Friend the Secretary of State that I am not entirely happy with the procedures that have been followed hitherto regarding precisely who is being allowed to tender for the line. The wild rumour is that there will be a management buy-out. As a local Member of Parliament, I would not be in favour of that. Some hon. Friends and I took part in a notorious journey five years ago with the present chairman of British Rail, when we were told to catch a train at the wrong time at a station at which the train did not arrive. During that journey, the chairman did not want to talk about services.

I believe in leading from the front, and I do not think that the present management of British Rail can reassure my constituents that they are the best people to run the railway line. I am totally in favour of the privatisation of the Fenchurch Street line, but I am not in favour of a management buy-out, which I believe will be an unfortunate method of embarking upon privatisation. Many other companies are more capable of delivering a fine service to my constituents, and they should be treated in a fair and even-handed fashion.

The third of my four points concerns the concept of education, which some of my hon. Friends have mentioned this morning. I have set myself a target in the past year of visiting every educational establishment in my constituency. That may seem an easy task, but there are 54 of them. I am delighted to tell the House that I have only three more to visit.

Although I shall wait until the end of my visits to produce a paper on how education in Basildon has shaped up in the past year, I wish to take this opportunity to pay a warm tribute to all the people involved in education in my constituency. Some weeks ago, the heads of the schools in my constituency met the Secretary of State for Education, and described to my right hon. Friend the issues that were concerning them. All of them welcomed the constructive debate that took place.

Only last Thursday I was privileged to present 51 certificates at Basildon college at the culmination of the college's adult learners' week. It was a moving event, at which 51 people were presented with certificates for achieving great things. They were not getting degrees from Oxford or Cambridge universities, but the awards were every bit as good as any other award that I have been privileged to hand out.

The House needs to concentrate on parenting. This is a difficult subject, and it is a difficult message for any politician to deliver. The majority of parents do a wonderful job for their children, but there is no doubt that some parents need help to understand the full responsibilities of what it entails to have children. The problems that hon. Members hear in their surgeries—on housing, education, crime or general welfare—can all be traced back to problems in parenting. I hope that my party will take that fact on board. The Opposition are always setting up commissions and two years down the line we get some paper on them. I hope that my party will now embark on a national campaign to deliver some sort of assistance in parenting.

I have an axe to grind about nursery education. The Leader of the House, my right hon. Friend the Member for Braintree (Mr. Newton), and I share the same county council—Essex county council—which is trying to deliver nursery education. That is all well and good but, as I have two children who were born in September, I want something done about rising fives. The current demand for nursery education, apart from the problems faced by parents who must go to work, encapsulates the difficulties that some people experience in coping with the responsibility of being parents. I hope that the House will consider carefully how we can put right the failures of past Governments, past teaching methods and past liberal attitudes, and ensure that every couple who decide to have children accept that that decision brings huge responsibilities.

Some hon. Members may think that this is an unfortunate occasion on which to be partisan but I feel that I must comment on new and old Labour. The crux of my remarks concerns hung councils. I am pleased to see in his place my hon. Friend the Member for Romford (Sir M. Neubert) because his constituency makes up a third of the London borough of Havering, which has a hung council. My right hon. Friend the Leader of the House shares with me Essex county council, which is a hung council. As from last Thursday, my constituency, which shares the local authority of Basildon with my hon. Friend the Member for Billericay (Mrs. Gorman), also has a hung council.

Having read the election addresses carefully, I feel that many socialist candidates who stood under the ticket of the Labour and Liberal Democrat parties were deceiving the general public for various reasons. Essex county council, which has been a hung council for two years, has been an absolute disaster and people in Essex are rapidly regretting it. With no consultation whatever, it has thrown out community care, which had been well established by the Conservatives in consultation with six of the bodies involved. As a result, the constituencies of many of my Essex colleagues are now suffering from bed-blocking. People cannot get the right accommodation; waiting lists for operations are getting longer; and waiting times in hospitals are constantly increasing.

Never mind new or old Labour, it is about time that they and the Liberal Democrats accepted responsibility when they are in power. Given the number of county and district councils that they control and European seats which they occupy, they can no longer blame the Government but must accept responsibility for their inadequacies. What they have done in Essex is wicked.

**Sir Michael Neubert** (Romford): My hon. Friend has good reason to be personally aggrieved at the activities of certain prominent Labour personalities on Havering council. Is not one unfortunate consequence of hung councils and coalition politics that they allow minority parties access to public funds, which are used in anti-Government and therefore effectively party political propaganda, as has happened in Havering? To explain away the consequences of its overspending, Havering council implied, with widespread publicity, that Government grant had been cut by £17 million. When that is combined with the development of a machine at the town hall and investment of £500,000 a year—

**Mr. Deputy Speaker** (Mr. Geoffrey Lofthouse): Order. Many hon. Members are hoping to catch my eye in the debate. Interventions are supposed to be brief and to the point.

**Sir Michael Neubert:** With that investment, personality cults develop, such as we saw in the last days of the Greater London council at county hall across the river. Does not a danger to democracy lie in all that?

**Mr. Amess:** I entirely agree with my hon. Friend. What is happening in Havering council is causing great distress to many residents. I am sure that they voted for candidates thinking that they would enjoy good, sensible local government, and the result has been far from that. I thank my hon. Friend for the sympathy that he offered me about a particular difficulty. Unfortunately, some Basildon socialists work for Havering authority. For instance, the deputy chief executive used to be the leader of Basildon district council. I agree with every word that my hon. Friend said.

[*Mr. Amess*]

The cuts by socialist-controlled Essex county council in selective school transport are a disgrace and have been made for reasons of pure dogma. County councillor David Rex describes the ruling as

"totally divisive and unfair. If children gain places by their own merit at one of our Grammar Schools they should not suffer discrimination because their parents cannot pay for them to get there. Even if a contribution is made to travelling expenses to parents who receive income support or family credit, many other families will still be unable to meet travelling costs and their children will be deprived of the opportunity which their ability and industry has given them".

My hon. Friend the Member for Erith and Crayford (Mr. Evennett) and I served together on Redbridge council, where we retained an excellent grammar school. Southend has four grammar schools; Colchester has two; and Chelmsford has two. They are all excellent. The socialists on the council have told us that the supposed savings from cutting free school transport will be £1.6 million over 10 years, and the treasurer revised that costing to £1.3 million. However, it has been completely forgotten that Southend will be granted unitary status, so the idea that there will be savings is nonsense. I happen to know that the socialists are being overwhelmed with protests from local parents and I entirely agree with those protests.

When there were difficulties with the policing which Essex county council provided at Brightlingsea, the socialists—whether the alliance or new or old Labour—made some disgraceful statements, which made the job of policing even more difficult.

My final point is about the circumstances in which I find myself on Basildon district council, which covers my constituency and that of my hon. Friend the Member for Billericay. On the Thursday before last, we had local elections. I now have eight Conservative district councillors in my constituency. My hon. Friend the Member for Billericay has six Conservative district councillors in hers. In total, there are 14 Conservatives on Basildon district council, 16 Labour and 12 alliance councillors.

When the Labour and alliance candidates were campaigning during the local elections, it was drawn to my attention that there did not appear to be much mention of local issues. Local candidates said that they would be in a position to do something about national taxation, the national health service and the defence of the country. That was dishonest. They should have campaigned on local issues. Of course, the electors have rapidly been disappointed.

I live in the Nethermayne ward. I went to the Towngate theatre to hear the results declared and, when the Nethermayne result was declared, I witnessed the leader of the Labour group, whom I defeated in the general election, and the leader of the alliance group, whom I also defeated in the general election, hug one another—and the result meant that an alliance councillor had been elected. It occurs to me that, far from there being a hung council, it had already been agreed that Labour and alliance would share power. It happens all the time.

Alliance councillors are often so gutless that they abstain on issues, but let there be no doubt about it—new Labour, for which I have no respect, old Labour, for

which I have every respect, and the alliance party, for which I have no respect, have gone into coalition in Basildon.

I intend, for the remaining time of this Parliament, to take every opportunity to bring to the House's attention the consequences of socialist misrule by Basildon district council, socialist misrule by Essex county council and socialist misrule in Europe. I intend to ensure that, as a result, the general public, when they are given the opportunity to vote in a general election, do not make the mistake of being deceived and electing the horror of a socialist Government.

**Several hon. Members** *rose*—

**Mr. Deputy Speaker:** Order. Eight hon. Members are hoping to catch my eye in the time remaining in the debate. If the speeches are as long as the last two, someone will be disappointed.

11.12 am

**Mr. George Mudie** (Leeds, East): Before the House adjourns, I have the opportunity to mention a disturbing case of Government inactivity and insensitivity on an important matter. I hope that the Leader of the House will return to his seat at some point, because he is very much the human face of the Government and I would not wish to miss the opportunity to make the case directly.

**The Lord President of the Council and Leader of the House of Commons (Mr. Tony Newton):** As the hon. Gentleman observed, I was about to take a short break but, in view of his comments, he has made it impossible for me to leave for the moment.

**Mr. Mudie:** I am grateful that the Lord President is staying in his seat, and I hope that neither his situation nor my speech is too uncomfortable.

The important matter to which I refer is the fact that more than 3,000 people suffering from haemophilia are infected with the hepatitis C virus, as a result of being given contaminated blood. For those people in the Chamber who do not know the effect of the hepatitis C virus, it attacks the liver and is potentially life-threatening. Although there is an uncertain medical prognosis, current medical opinion estimates that as many as 80 per cent. of those infected will develop chronic liver disease. Between 10 and 20 per cent. of those people will develop cirrhosis of the liver and many of those, sadly, will develop liver cancer. The progression to severe liver disease can take between 20 and 40 years. Many people with haemophilia have already been infected for more than 20 years.

In 1986, clotting factor concentrates were heat-treated to deactivate the acquired immune deficiency syndrome virus. By coincidence, but largely unrecognised at the time, it had the same effect on the hepatitis C virus. In 1991—good news, in a way, for those suffering from hepatitis C—a test for that virus, for HCV antibody, was developed. The bad news was that, as the haemophiliac population began to be tested, it became apparent, incredibly, that almost everyone suffering from haemophilia who had been treated with clotting factor concentrates before 1986 was infected with the hepatitis C virus.

The Government—I praise them and I praise the Prime Minister especially—acted with regard to those with the AIDS virus. Through the Macfarlane Trust, Government financial help is available to haemophiliac AIDS virus patients and their families, and more than £14 million has been given out in addition to special grants of more than £66 million.

Those are the facts. It is against that background that the Haemophilia Society is campaigning straightforwardly, and I hope understandably, for similar arrangements to be made regarding haemophiliacs who contracted the HCV virus—the hepatitis C virus—to those made regarding haemophiliacs who contracted the AIDS virus from contaminated blood through the national health service.

Everyone accepts the many similarities between haemophiliacs with HCV and haemophiliacs with the AIDS virus, and it is difficult to envisage how the Government can long resist the argument to give more equitable treatment.

I shall list some of the similarities. The route of infection for both HIV and HCV was contaminated blood given as part of NHS treatment. The infection for both viruses took place before the date in 1986 when heat treatment was introduced. Like the AIDS virus, the hepatitis C virus will place additional medical, social and financial burdens on those who already had a life-threatening condition. All will have to cope with the uncertainty and anxiety of not knowing whether they will be one of the 20 per cent. who will experience cirrhosis or the smaller number who may suffer early death from liver cancer.

All will have the worry of possible transmission to sexual partners, transmission to an unborn child and transmission to other members of the household through blood to blood contact. All will experience difficulties in obtaining life insurance, or can receive it only at prohibitive rates or for a short time. Many may suffer disruption to their education and employment as they become ill and some will lose their jobs and their earnings as a result of the illness. Some people, as a result of the ignorance of others, will be confronted by discrimination and ostracism in the workplace, in school and in society in general.

In spite of those similarities, it is accepted that the two cases are not the same. As Baroness Cumberlege said in the other place—somewhat tactlessly, I felt—those with the AIDS virus

"were all expected to die very shortly."—[*Official Report, House of Lords*, 15 March 1995; Vol. 562, c. 864.]

She also outlined other social differences, but nothing on a scale on which to base a strong case for withholding help from those with the hepatitis C virus.

What do the Haemophilia Society and those suffering from the hepatitis C virus ask for? They ask for three things. First, they ask for an across-the-board ex gratia payment, on the same basis as that paid to those haemophiliacs suffering from the AIDS virus, to all those infected with hepatitis through contaminated blood products—not compensation, but an ex gratia payment on the same basis. Such a payment will avoid the spectacle of 3,000 people, already unfortunate enough to have the problem of haemophilia, pursuing the Government through the courts, arguing a case about being treated with infected blood in the national health service.

Secondly, the Haemophilia Society wants those who become ill and the dependants of those who die to have access to the hardship fund of the Macfarlane Trust on the same basis as infected haemophiliacs. Thirdly, as a matter of urgency, it has requested that payments should be made to those who are already ill and to the dependants of those who have died. It has been put to the Department of Health that the deeds of the Macfarlane Trust—set up to assist those haemophiliacs with the AIDS virus—could be changed to extend the work of that excellent and well-respected trust to deal with the larger but similar group of people now suffering from the hepatitis C virus.

The Haemophilia Society would also like those people to be offered many other things, including better counselling and support. But I am aware of your request, Mr. Deputy Speaker, so I must cut my remarks short in fairness to the many other hon. Members who want to speak. I would regret it if my case were harmed by either my presentation or the lack of time available to me. If either were so, it would be unforgivable.

Those of us who are fortunate in health and with children similarly blessed can only marvel at the courage and strength of those who, born with the terrible disease of haemophilia, are struck so unfairly by the second dreadful virus, hepatitis C. I cannot see how anyone other than a blinkered Treasury bureaucrat would not feel that some assistance should be offered to those people.

I remember that it was the Prime Minister who stopped the unseemly wrangle over help to haemophiliacs with AIDS. He acted with compassion and purpose. I hope that the Leader of the House will ask the Prime Minister to extend that compassion and rediscover that sense of purpose to help those who are now asking for his assistance.

If anyone doubts the awfulness of the disease and its effect, let me conclude by quoting from a letter from one of my constituents, who wrote:

"As parents we have seen our 13-year-old son suffer with haemophilia but to give him this virus as well, I feel very depressed.

I went to a meeting this year about the hepatitis and I felt the sky coming down round me as the people were medical and parents and they were talking about liver transplants and bleeding in the stomach, the side-effects of the drug Inferon. I came out the meeting very shocked.

Please help us. I am sorry I cannot put it over how desperate we are, but we love our son and I feel very scared over my boy's future."

I appeal to the House and the Leader of the House to give those parents, that youngster and all those in the same circumstances some help and some hope.

11.22 am

**Mr. David Shaw** (Dover): I pay tribute to the hon. Member for Leeds, East (Mr. Mudie), because I know that we must seriously address the issue that he has raised. Some constituents recently approached me about the same problem. I hope that it can be dealt with on an all-party basis, because it strikes me that it is something that has gone wrong in our society. It should not be a party political issue, but the Government of the day must address it. It is clear that a great deal of injustice is easily capable of being suffered, if that has not already happened. I hope that we will address that issue in a proper debate in the House in the weeks ahead.

I should like to raise a number of issues affecting my constituency as well as one or two national interests that should be considered by the House before it adjourns. Education in Kent has already been referred to today by my hon. Friend the Member for Gravesham (Mr. Arnold), so I need not repeat everything he said.

[Mr. David Shaw]

As I have gone around the schools in my constituency, I have heard concern expressed about the way in which the county council, with the authority of the Liberal-Labour group controlling it, has issued to those schools a number of newsletters which lack any form of independent financial analysis and are extremely biased. Although the director of education and certain politicians who are playing political games with our schools suggested that the schools should send out those newsletters to parents, most of the schools in my area, if not all of them, have resisted that recommendation. They have refused because they have argued that the documents were political, misleading, offered no real accounting sense and sought to make political capital out of what we all accept has been a tight financial settlement for local government. The settlement does, however, allow schools to be funded properly, provided that local authorities are willing to do that and to be more efficient. I am concerned at the way in which the Liberal-Labour group on Kent county council is misusing its position of power and is not acting in the interests of my constituents, in particular, those who have children at school.

Last year, the county council underspent by £17 million. That happens to many county councils, because although they plan for a certain amount of expenditure, some of that spending is not required, for whatever reason. The Liberal-Labour group has refused to apply any of that money or to use any of the consequential underspend that may result this year on funding schools. As a consequence, schools in my constituency have not received the full amount to which they are entitled, which is a tragedy. Kent county council has the necessary money and could plan its expenditure to make it available to the schools, but it has refused to do so. It is playing a political football game with the schools.

Not every school in my constituency is experiencing such financial difficulties, because those that are grant-maintained operate more efficiently. Many of them have greatly increased the number of teaching assistants in their schools because they are better managers of their finances than other schools. One of the results of the politicisation of education in Kent may be more applications for grant-maintained status. I am sure that the House would consider that to be entirely appropriate in the circumstances. Just because Kent county council has become Liberal-Labour controlled, we cannot allow it to play political football with our children's education. That is unacceptable.

We should also debate as soon as possible the channel tunnel rail link proposals. Although that matter is being dealt with by a Committee of the House—so I will not go into a lot of detail—certain important issues should be discussed by the House. The Committee considering the Channel Tunnel Rail Link Bill seems to be having difficulty in considering the financial viability of the channel tunnel rail link, let alone the financial viability of the channel tunnel. That is extremely important to my constituents because, if massive amounts of subsidy were given to either the rail link or the channel tunnel, that would affect Dover port and the ferry industry, which still employ 6,500 people in my constituency and the surrounding areas.

Certain serious questions must be addressed. For example, is the channel tunnel rail link financially viable? Is the channel tunnel financially viable? So far, the company has had to go back to its shareholders on a number of occasions for additional finances. So far, it has not been able to perform as it should have done and it has not worked according to the plan set out in the company's financial forecasts.

**Mr. Dennis Skinner** (Bolsover): We told the hon. Gentleman that.

**Mr. Shaw:** The hon. Gentleman and I rarely agree on matters, but on this issue we have agreed consistently, right back to 1987 when I entered the House. The hon. Gentleman gave me the honour of coming into my part of the Lobby when I divided the House on the channel tunnel issue not long after I was elected here.

**Mr. Skinner:** The Lobby belongs to everyone.

**Mr. Shaw:** Nevertheless, I am still grateful for the fact that the hon. Gentleman came into my Lobby not long after I was elected to the House. I was one of the Tellers who called for the Division. I know that the hon. Gentleman has a long history of questioning the principles that lie behind the channel tunnel project.

**Mr. Skinner:** In the last two years or whatever of this dying Tory Government, in the event that the Government decided to come up with taxpayers' money, whether small amounts or large, to help bail out the people running the channel tunnel, would the hon. Gentleman join me in my Lobby to vote against handing out large sums of taxpayers' money? Will he give me that guarantee?

**Mr. Shaw:** I assure the hon. Gentleman that I shall vote against any public bail-out of the channel tunnel; I make that crystal clear. However, that will not necessarily occur. Although the channel tunnel is in enormous financial difficulty, the private sector may have the means and the ability to sustain it. I shall not support any Government, whether Conservative or Labour, who propose to bail out the channel tunnel with public finances.

I think that the hon. Member for Bolsover (Mr. Skinner) has received the answer that he desires. I do not know whether he will divide the House on the issue and be a Teller in the Division Lobby, but I certainly hope that he will have a Front-Bench role in the new Labour party. I have always believed that he should lead the Labour party—he certainly has a unique ability to make the points for Labour that his colleagues are too frightened to make.

I also draw the attention of the House to the intergovernmental conference which will be held in Europe next year. I do not think that the House should adjourn until we have had the opportunity to discuss the convergence criteria. Although the criteria set out in the Maastricht treaty are quite simple and straightforward— they deal with Government deficits and the proportion of Government debt to gross domestic product—they do not take account of the differences in social security systems in Europe.

People are now beginning to focus on the issue of unfunded pension liabilities, which I first raised in 1991. Governments in Europe have very real debts. The Swedish Government are unable to support their social security system and they have been borrowing for 12 years on the international markets. Those markets are now signalling that they are fed up and that they do not wish to carry any more Swedish debt. They have said that they will no longer fund Swedish employment levels or the expensive Swedish state structure.

The Swedish social security system is under enormous pressure as a result of its international funding being called into question. The Swedish Government certainly cannot fund it from their own highly taxed system. Italy and other European countries, including France, face a similar problem, and the implications are quite horrendous for any financial proposals—such as the single currency—that come before the IGC next year. I believe that the House should debate those issues as soon as possible.

The currency markets continue to build up the deutschmark in an unrealistic and an unreasonable manner. We should have a public debate about the demographics in Germany. The aging of the German population will peak in 2005 and will worsen further in proportion to the number of people in work; as a consequence, the German economy will require a greater level of funding in order to sustain its social security system. If there were to be a single currency, Britain would have to contribute towards subsidising the German social security system. That is totally unacceptable. We should debate those issues and their implications both on the Floor of the House and in the wider community.

**Mr. Oliver Heald** (Hertfordshire, North): Does my hon. Friend agree that one reason why Sweden is in difficulty is that it has done many of the things that the Joseph Rowntree Foundation report in February this year suggested that we should do in this country—such as extra investment in social security, housing and the labour market; direct provision of employment opportunities; state-paid child care; more subsidies to employers to encourage them to take on the unemployed; and indexing benefits above the retail prices index? What does my hon. Friend think would happen if we were to take that advice?

**Mr. Shaw:** If we were to take that advice, like Sweden we would have to borrow from the financial markets rather than try to fund those measures out of taxation—which Sweden can no longer do because its taxation rates are already too high. As a consequence, we would increase national debt and the debt that we owe overseas. We would then be, in effect, bankrupt. Sweden is on the brink of bankruptcy, as are Italy and France, and probably Germany come the year 2005.

We must face the fact that the Joseph Rowntree Foundation recommendations are misguided. The foundation is not conducting balanced political and social research. It is sad that the foundation should be so irresponsible as to advance principles that I doubt that Joseph Rowntree would have supported in his business, personal or public life. Foundations should be much more responsible in the way in which they conduct their research.

I draw a final matter to the attention of the House which I think should be examined before we adjourn. The issue of trade union accounting should be debated on the Floor of the House of Commons. I cannot recall when the last debate on that subject occurred—we have not debated it while I have been a Member of Parliament. It would be interesting to debate the issue of political funds of trade unions.

As a chartered accountant, I have done some research into that matter. I recently reviewed some trade union accounts and found a lack of consistency in the way in which political funds are accounted for. No code of conduct appears to be followed when drawing up accounts of political funds and there seems to be a lack of disclosure regarding so-called "political panels" which appear in trade union accounts. There is no suggestion as to what they are or how they operate.

It is remarkable that one cannot reconcile the finances of the political panels. One cannot see whether the funds are used to support Members of Parliament or how the amounts shown in the trade union accounts may be reconciled with the disclosures in the Register of Members' Interests. According to the accounts of the Union of Communication Workers, its political panel spends some £70,000 each year. The purpose of that political panel is not clear from the union's accounts and we are unsure what demands are made on the people who benefit from that panel.

I have tried to reconcile the accounts with the Register of Members' Interests, and I have found that three Members of Parliament receive money from that political panel. I pay credit to one hon. Member—I shall not mention him by name as I have not given him notice of my intention to do so—who discloses in the Register of Members' Interests that his political association receives £8,000 per year from the UCW, although his declaration does not state that that money comes from the political panel.

That is a significant sum. It is interesting that a Member of Parliament should receive that level of income. I certainly do not derive that sort of sum from any one donation or area. We are often told that no personal benefit is derived from such donations, but I have to attend many rubber chicken lunches and dinners in my constituency to raise funds for my political association. I would be very grateful if some white knight would appear on the horizon and donate £8,000 to my political association with no strings attached. However, I would be concerned that there might be strings attached. I doubt that the Union of Communication Workers would give me £8,000 without requiring me to take a certain political line.

Another hon. Member uses similar words in the Register of Members' Interests but does not disclose the figure of £8,000. That makes a total of £16,000. When I take away £16,000 from £70,000, which is the total amount that the UCW spends on its political panel, my maths tells me that that leaves some £54,000. If that is the case and it is all going to one Member of the House of Commons, that really is quite something.

**Mr. Jeff Rooker** (Birmingham, Perry Barr): Obviously, I will comment on the hon. Gentleman's speech when I wind up, but the purpose of the political panel of the UCW is the political education of its trade union members. That union does more in the political education of its members—about the way in which our democracy works—than most other trade unions put together. The hon. Gentleman implies that the money goes to one Member of the House of Commons. It does not; it is used for the purposes of political education, and I am sure that the hon. Gentleman knows that.

**Mr. Shaw:** There may be a slight problem here, perhaps because I have been using the word "political". I should point out to the hon. Gentleman that the political panel, or, if one likes, the panel, which is part of the political fund, is actually described in the accounts as the "parliamentary" panel. So within the political fund, it is, if one likes, the political parliamentary panel. I would

[*Mr. Shaw*]

certainly be interested to know whether there is any education expenditure there, but I think that it is designed to go towards the work that is done in Parliament on behalf of the union.

**Mr. Rooker:** No.

**Mr. Shaw:** The hon. Gentleman says no, but it would be very welcome if there were a reconciliation of the trade union accounts. He is giving me all the reasons why there should be more disclosure and more information in the trade union accounts on how those items are put together, why they are often described as parliamentary panels, and what their purposes are. If I have been led to conclude wrongly that one Member of the House of Commons is getting some £50,000 a year of support to his parliamentary constituency, I am certainly open to have that position corrected. I really hold no particular brief for arguing something that is incorrect, and I would welcome the opportunity for that trade union, or any other, to disclose where the money in the parliamentary panel part of the political fund accounts goes.

**Mr. Robert Ainsworth** (Coventry, North-East): Can I take it from the hon. Gentleman's comments that he will vote for the full disclosure of all moneys coming from all sources to Members of the House?

**Mr. Shaw:** I think that we might be arriving at a very interesting position. There is an interesting argument, although it is separate from the one that I am making today, on whether we should have more disclosure or whether we should accept that Members of Parliament should be treated like members of the public and have the same rights to privacy. I, for one, do not particularly have any great difficulty with increasing the level of disclosure over time, but that raises the question of how one makes a fair disclosure.

**Mr. George Galloway** (Glasgow, Hillhead): That is a fulsome endorsement.

**Mr. Shaw:** The hon. Gentleman needs to look at his own position and life style and whether he discloses everything about his life style in the way that he should.

**Mr. Galloway:** On a point of order, Mr. Deputy Speaker. That was a very clear assertion that there is something in my life style or my income that I should be disclosing to the House but am not. I really think that that was out of order. If it was not out of order, it was certainly just about the meanest, lowest, most gratuitous insult that anyone has ever paid to me in the House.

**Mr. Deputy Speaker:** The House can well do without personalising things of that nature. It does not do the debate any good and it does not do any good to the image of the House of those outside this place.

**Mr. Shaw:** The hon. Member for Glasgow, Hillhead (Mr. Galloway) was remarkably sensitive in getting to his feet at that point. I think that, if he looks back at comments in the House, he will see that he has not at all times been civil towards me. I have tried, in every way that I possibly can, to be civil towards him. We do not want to go down the path that he has invited me to go down, because that would not do the House much good.

In finalising my point about trade union accounts and trade union disclosure, I draw the attention of the House to the 1995 annual report of the Communication Managers Association. It is an interesting report, showing that the union has three parliamentary advisers. I notice that one of them is even a Conservative Member of Parliament. I am not certain that a Conservative Member of Parliament would want to be associated with all aspects of the report. I feel that perhaps I should go to my colleague and ask him whether he is aware that some £26,000, which comes out of the political fund of the Communication Managers Association, went to the Campaign Against Privatisation of the Post Office— CAPPO, as it is known.

It is obviously reasonable if a trade union wants to fund a campaign against the privatisation of the Post Office. I suppose that that is the sort of thing that a trade union might be expected to do. It might not fund something that is to the benefit of the Post Office consumers, or the people who use the Post Office's services, but I can understand if a trade union wants to fund something that is, perhaps, against the consumer's interest, and supports the current position of the Post Office. I am interested in a sentence in the CMA's annual report under "Parliamentary Advisers", which says:

"In addition, and as reported last year, special arrangements are made in respect of the Leader of the Opposition and we make a donation of £7,000 towards the upkeep of his office."

I feel that the annual report should detail what those special arrangements are. It suggests to me that there is a lack of financial disclosure, and perhaps a lack of proper disclosure, in the trade union's accounts when we do not know what the so-called "special arrangements" are in respect of the Leader of the Opposition and how they are meant to operate.

**Mr. Rooker:** What is it to do with the hon. Gentleman?

**Mr. Shaw:** If there are special arrangements in an organisation that is campaigning politically and those arrangements affect the Leader of the Opposition, I think that we should know, not only as members of the public but as Members of Parliament, what those arrangements are. The Leader of the Opposition discloses in his entry in the Register of Members' Interests something called the Industrial Research Trust. I want to know what is in that trust, what is the purpose behind it, and why money seems to be going into a pot—we do not know where it is coming from or what it is spent on. The money does not seem to be available to every Member of the House of Commons.

One must also question whether there are taxation implications. Is the trust properly set up from a taxation point of view? Is it a device to avoid or evade income tax? Are personal benefits involved? Are conditions attached to it? What special arrangements does the union consider exist?

**Mr. Heald:** What sort of industrial research does my hon. Friend think that that body will be doing in the Labour leader's office?

**Mr. Shaw:** I agree with my hon. Friend. Those are the questions that have to be answered. There is a real issue here as to why some £7,000 a year from the Communication Managers Association—we understand that other sums are also involved—goes into the Industrial Research Trust. Why are those sums necessary? What are the special arrangements? Are they buying support for a particular policy? Is that policy of interest to all members of society, or is it of interest only to a small group in society? We have to know whether hon. Members are able to act in the interests of all members, customers, consumers and citizens of this country—all 57 million people—or whether they are acting on behalf of a small group of people whom they are financed to support.

**Mr. Heald:** I am very grateful to my hon. Friend for giving way. He is being most generous. Does he have any idea who pays into that research fund and who the trustees are? They are nothing to do with the Labour party, are they?

**Mr. Shaw:** I have been informed that some of the trustees of the Industrial Research Trust are members of the other House, and therefore I cannot go into detail about their names or positions, although there has been a suggestion that they are Labour peers. In consequence, it may be that if my hon. Friend or I applied for a grant from the trust, we would not get one if a political judgment about its management were involved. That raises interesting questions about the trust's purpose, the amount of money that goes into it, who benefits, how they benefit, in what circumstances they benefit, the special arrangements that exist and whether people who benefit from that money are able to exercise proper and fair judgment in the House of Commons, untainted by any financial interest or financial support.

There are a number of issues that the House should discuss. I just wonder on this occasion whether, however much hon. Members feel that we need a break, these issues are of such importance to the British nation that we should be prepared to give up some of our break next week to discuss them.

**Several hon. Members** *rose*—

**Mr. Deputy Speaker:** Order. It is a great advantage in debates of this nature to hear as many hon. Members as possible. I have already pointed out that long speeches may prevent other hon. Members from speaking. It appears that my advice is being ignored, and the Chair does not like to be ignored.

11.49 am

**Mr. Robert Ainsworth** (Coventry, North-East): I am grateful for the opportunity before the House adjourns to raise a couple of related issues and the legal framework which has presented problems to the police in dealing with important problems in my constituency: first, the level of car crime in my constituency and nationally; and secondly, the illegal use of motor bikes, which is becoming a real problem in Coventry, North-East and elsewhere, and with which the police have difficulties in dealing within the current legal framework.

Many hon. Members will be surprised, as I was, to discover that it is not an offence for a person to remove the identification marks from a motor vehicle. People can be done for tampering with a motor vehicle, but to remove such marks is not in itself an offence. In addition, there is no enforceable legal obligation on the owners of a motor vehicle to maintain proof of ownership. That situation is causing real problems for the police in their attempts to tackle vehicle-related crime.

My concerns about the issue arise from an analysis of the national situation and from a serious and on-going problem in my constituency. As vice-chairman of the European Secure Vehicle Alliance, in view of all the comments flying around at the moment I should make it clear to the House that that position is entirely unremunerated.

Vehicle theft in England and Wales is higher than in any other country in the western world and our recovery rate for stolen vehicles has fallen substantially since 1989. In 1993, 600,000 vehicles were stolen, of which 250,000 were never recovered. In 1994 there was some improvement in the stolen vehicle rate, but the overall picture is still bleak. Recovery rates have fallen from 69 per cent. in 1989 to a reported figure of 62 per cent. in 1994. I do not altogether accept that figure of 62 per cent. yet. A provisional figure of 55 per cent. was produced, showing a drastic fall in the recovery rate of stolen vehicles, but the final figure came out at 62 per cent. Far be it from me to say that there is anything wrong with the figures, but in view of the Government's track record on other figures I am not prepared to accept that figure until I have had time to analyse it. There is a considerable discrepancy between the provisional figure of 55 per cent. and the eventual figure of 62 per cent. Even taking that into account, however, if we accept the figures as reported at face value we still have a serious situation: only 62 per cent. of stolen vehicles in Britain are recovered.

Much has been said in the House and elsewhere about the problem of so-called joy riders. The figures show clearly that we have a serious problem of permanent crime and unrecovered stolen vehicles. It is generally accepted that the number of unrecovered vehicles is due in part to a growth in organised car crime, where vehicles are either dismantled for their valuable components or have their identification marks doctored so that they can be sold as legitimate cars—a process known as ringing.

The cost of all that vehicle crime falls on the motorist, and it falls disproportionately on those who live in inner cities or the less affluent parts of our towns and cities. Motor insurance premiums have risen by 75 per cent. since 1989 and competition in the insurance market, combined with new abilities to target risks, means that someone deemed to have a high-risk address can be charged three or four times as much for insurance as people living in other parts of the same city. Theft is not the only factor which has caused premiums to rise, but it has made a large contribution. The result is that people in some areas increasingly cannot afford to drive, own or use a motor vehicle legally. They have become the indirect victims of our astronomical levels of vehicle crime.

My constituency has a specific problem with motor bikes being driven on and off the road, through housing estates, at all times of the day and night and at all speeds. During the past two years, a number of pedestrians have been injured. One incident resulted in a woman being admitted to hospital with serious injuries. Some of the bikes are being used to perpetrate serious crime. The police cannot catch the perpetrators in the act, despite using police motor bikes and a police helicopter, and if they manage to track them down to their homes they often find that the bikes have had all the identification marks removed and are in the possession of people who will not say where they got them. Often they cannot prove their ownership in any way and decline to show any receipts. Yet the police cannot confiscate the property. That is astonishing.

When a Kawasaki with all the identification marks removed was seized from someone whom the police described as a "known, prolific criminal" and that person

[*Mr. Robert Ainsworth*]

was unable to produce a receipt or any other document to prove that he had obtained the bike legally, the police's own legal department outlined three options open to them: to incur the cost of taking the matter to court under the Police (Property) Act 1897, but expect the bench to return the motor cycle to the only claimant; to dispose of the motor cycle without the support of the court, but expect civil proceedings against the chief constable to recover the claimant's valuation of the motor cycle; or to return the motor cycle to the claimant. Needless to say, with such legal advice, the motor cycle was returned to the person claiming to own it.

That is the problem facing the police in my constituency and elsewhere when they try to deal with a serious problem that is blighting the lives of many people. The existing law does nothing to help them.

Those problems are not confined to Coventry. Salford metropolitan borough, which was concerned at the number of uninsured, untaxed and often stolen motor bikes being used in the city, recently raised the matter with the Association of Metropolitan Authorities to obtain a national assessment of the problem.

The motor industry is also calling for action to deal with the problem. The core and advanced security group of the Ford Motor Company Ltd. wrote to the European secure vehicle alliance saying:

"One long standing concern has been the ability of car ringers to remove all identification marks and avoid prosecution."

The letter continues:

"Any vehicle whose original identity could not be proved by the police was usually handed back"

to the thief or ringer. The group calls for examination of the Japanese system of marking major vehicle components and storing car identification numbers in a central database.

If we are to reduce the problems of vehicle theft, we need to strengthen the law in this area. We should oblige owners to maintain proof of ownership and make it a criminal offence to remove vehicle identification numbers. I know that there are currently consultations about the tightening of vehicle registration, but that in itself is not enough and will not address the problems that I have outlined today.

Vehicle theft is costing our economy a fortune. The costs fall on the motorist, and disproportionately on poorer motorists. Our crime rate is an indictment of a do-nothing Government who are heavy on rhetoric but light on action. Let us give the police a tool that they can use in tackling these important problems and let us start immediately during the consultation process.

**12 noon**

**Mr. Barry Field** (Isle of Wight): First, I apologise to you, Mr. Deputy Speaker, and to the hon. Member for Christchurch (Mrs. Maddock) for not observing the usual niceties of the House by informing the hon. Lady in advance that I would be mentioning her constituency. However, I am certain that the people of the Isle of Wight, and not least the Isle of Wight county branch of the Royal British Legion, would like me to extend their condolences to the people of Christchurch in respect of the tragedy that

they have suffered. There are many associations between our two constituencies, as hon. Members would expect, and I ought to put that on record before I commence.

I do not intend to go down the route that my hon. Friend the Member for Dover (Mr. Shaw) followed, but I have to say, in the presence of my right hon. Friend the Lord President of the Council, that I allow myself a slightly wry smile in looking at the recommendations of the Nolan committee. The House has for many years directed millions of pounds of taxpayers' money, which is known as Short money, to political parties.

I am open to correction by Opposition Members, but I understand that the Labour party has always voluntarily accounted for that money and published the way in which it uses it. However, it has always been something of an interesting political mystery to me that the Liberal party, which makes so much of open government, has never published how it applies Short money. If any other organisation in the United Kingdom distributed such large sums of money without there being a standing requirement to show how that money was spent, we would be down on it like a ton of bricks. Yet this tradition has gone on for some years in the House and it is impossible to find any transparency. However, that is not what I intended to raise—I merely put it on record and I am sure that my right hon. Friend the Lord President will make a note of it.

My hon. Friend the Member for Gravesham (Mr. Arnold) started this debate by talking about education, and it is along those lines that my concern lies. My hon. Friend expressed the view that there was something of a political conspiracy between the Opposition parties on education in Kent.

The late Sir John Nicholson, who was a well-known figure in the City as well as the Isle of Wight, always told me that the Isle of Wight would never lack for anecdotal evidence. Since I have been its Member of Parliament, I have tried to sift the information which comes to me rather than always believing that there is some great political conspiracy. However, I did happen to notice that a number of Liberal Democrat-controlled authorities have done away with their chief executives and not bothered to replace them.

As hon. Members know, we have a new unitary authority on the Isle of Wight, but we still do not have a chief executive. I have to rely somewhat on hearsay evidence for this because I have not entirely authenticated the figure, but I am told that something like £1.5 million has been spent on the basis of the chairman's decision without referral to committees. That concerns me.

I am not concerned that there should be delegated powers to spend—when I was a councillor, I argued for raising them to a substantial figure—but I am concerned that it has occurred since we have not had a chief executive. I hope that the new unitary council, under the political control of the Liberal Democrats, will address that problem. In a small island community such as ours, feelings run high on many issues and we need someone to hold the ring in a professional way and give thrust to policy as decided by the Liberal Democrats. We are the poorer for not having such a person. I shall return to that subject in future if we are not successful in getting a chief executive appointed.

Over the years, we have always had problems with school admissions on the island. We have only five high schools and some parents want their children to go to schools outside their areas. I have always managed to resolve such problems privately with the chairman of the education committee, Councillor Maureen Stolworthy, for whom I have the utmost regard. I congratulate her on her appointment as the first chairman of the new unitary authority. However, on this occasion that process has not happened. I also find that it is not happening in Hampshire, which is a separate education authority.

I begin to get a slight feeling that perhaps the Liberal Democrats have a new policy to frustrate parental choice in schools—I put it no higher than that—as I have found a ludicrous situation in which two talented students on the Isle of Wight want to study Latin, but they can do so only at Carisbrooke high school, to which they have been refused entrance. There is also a pupil, both of whose parents work for the county council, or unitary authority as it now is, in Newport. They want their child to attend Carisbrooke high school, but their catchment area is Sandown and admission has been refused. However, Sandown high is bursting at the seams. Such illogical enforcement of the rules is beginning to frustrate people on the Isle of Wight.

I have a letter from John Groves, chairman of the governors of Solent middle school. He says:

"It is our opinion that the LEA has mismanaged the admissions process"—

he is referring specifically to his school—

"and has put the school into a position where financially it now needs more children."

The letter was sent to every councillor and continues:

"Please bring your common sense to bear on this problem so that it may be resolved at the earliest opportunity."

I hope that that will happen, and I have written to the new education committee chairman. I hope that the tradition on the Isle of Wight of not using education as a political football will continue and that pragmatism and common sense will prevail.

12.7 pm

**Mr. Peter L. Pike** (Burnley): As a party organiser, I had to work on many occasions with Harold Wilson and I wish to be associated with the tributes that will be paid to him later today. Certainly, the effects and the results of his Labour Governments, such as the Open university, will stand as a tribute to his administration for many years.

Mr. Deputy Speaker, I shall be brief on the issue that I want to raise because you have asked for that and because it would be premature to raise a number of issues that relate to the point that I want to deal with.

The Leader of the House knows of my concern about pension funds. The Pensions Bill is currently going through Parliament. I have constituents who have been affected in the widest sense by pension fund problems, not only in respect of the Maxwell fund but in respect of Astra Holdings, Sycamore Holdings and Bellings pension funds. The Leader of the House knows that I have raised the matter with him and other Ministers on many occasions in the House.

I wish to concentrate today on the Bellings fund, in which there has clearly been fraud and abuse on the widest scale comparable to the Maxwell situation. I hope that the week's recess will give the Government a final opportunity to look at some of the gaps that are not being plugged in legislation so that problems with pension funds

do not occur in future. In the years ahead, no hon. Member should need to tell the House that a pension fund is not able to honour its commitments to its pensioners. Negotiations are still going on over Bellings and for that reason, some things are best not said in the House.

There is, however, one point that the Leader of the House should put to the Minister for Social Security and Disabled People, who has responsibility for pensions, and to the Prime Minister. When I asked the Prime Minister a question on the first day back after the Easter recess, he said exactly the same as the Minister had said. The Prime Minister and the Minister say that because not as many people have been affected by the Bellings pension fund as were affected by the Maxwell fund, the Government will not help them in the same way.

I, any reasonable person and the people who are members of the Bellings fund say that the suffering of the fund members has been identical to the suffering of those in the Maxwell fund and in other funds. The number of people involved is not relevant and the Bellings pension fund members do not take kindly to being told that their problem is not the same. It is, of course, not just a matter of numbers. The Maxwells were well known and the media gave the problems with the Maxwell fund much wider publicity.

I ask the Leader of the House to urge his colleagues in the Department of Social Security to think again. Any help that the Government were willing to give to the Maxwell pension fund members should be given to the Bellings pension fund members and to any others who are in a similar situation, because the procedures have not safeguarded the pension funds of which they are members.

12.12 pm

**Mr. Anthony Coombs** (Wyre Forest): I take this opportunity on the Adjournment of the House to raise three matters concerning education, especially in connection with the Office of Standards in Education report, which raises important matters. The Government's reforms of education have undoubtedly improved education standards in our schools. The GCSE results, the A-level results, the proportion of students staying on at school and the number of people going into higher education—I shall not quote the statistics—are significant evidence of improvement. Our test results will gradually become evidence of that as well.

There are two crucial strands of policy on which I should like the Government to build. The first relates to making schools more directly accountable to parents. A recent public attitude survey found that no fewer than 87 per cent. of parents welcomed the greater control that they had over their local schools and the greater information that they had through the league tables, all of which were a result of the Government's reforms. Secondly, it is important that, through the governing bodies, parents have been given greater powers to control school budgets. Nowadays, even non-grant-maintained schools have 90 per cent. of their budget available to use as they wish.

Even more important is the way in which the secret garden of education—the curriculum—has been opened up, not only by testing, but by the new Ofsted inspections, which are far more comprehensive and far more frequent than used to be the case. In the past, the average secondary school had a comprehensive inspection from outside its

[Mr. Anthony Coombs]

local authority once every 50 years; there is now an inspection once every four years and 6,000 take place each year. That has allowed us to move the education debate away from what I have always regarded as the sterile ground of looking at schools as if they were sausage machines and of believing that the more resources one put in, the more one would get out, to looking in more detail at the education process and at the quality of teaching and education in our schools.

It is sad—it may be ruing this—that the Labour party voted against the Education (No. 2) Act 1986, the Education Reform Act 1988 and the Education Act 1994, which gave parents more access to the information that has opened up the secret garden in a constructive way.

The Ofsted report to which I referred shows that 40 per cent. of 14-year-olds did not meet the required standards last year in English, mathematics and science. Some 25 per cent. of seven-year-olds did not meet the required standards in the three Rs. The report also showed that 20 per cent. of schools—one in five—were not teaching properly something as basic as English.

It behoves us to consider the reasons for those figures. The reasons are not just curriculum organisation and the management of schools. The figures may be related to the basic skills of teachers, and according to Ofsted, which is objective in the matter, that has proved to be the case. Two out of every three newly trained primary teachers, in the opinion of Ofsted, did not know how to teach reading. Only one in 10 primary teachers had a proper grasp of mathematics.

I argue today for two things. First, not on a statutory basis, but on the basis of encouraging every local education authority, there should be criteria by which schools would be judged during visits by inspectors. There should be a clearly laid down system of appraisal of teachers in every local education authority and, more importantly, in every school; it happens in some schools already. The system works well, it is constructive and it is not a hire-or-fire policy, but a way in which the weaknesses of various teachers can be improved. The next stage should be that the Government insist that each school erects such a system so that problems with teachers can be dealt with.

Secondly, there is no point in having such an appraisal system unless head teachers and heads of departments know how properly to use it. I know that head teacher training, especially for new heads, is being improved by the Department for Education. I believe, however, that the retraining of heads on a national basis is important. There should be retraining in terms of general management skills, which many head teachers do not have when they are appointed, and in terms of using the appraisal system. That system would identify weaknesses and would be a significant way in which to motivate teachers.

There is no point in giving schools greater opportunities to appraise teachers and to manage them if we do not give them flexibility in terms of pay. There is only one state school in the country—the Oratory school, to which the Leader of the Opposition is shortly to send his son—which has moved away from the mandatory system of teachers' pay being negotiated on a national basis. It is crazy that teaching is one of the few markets in which pay does not reflect local labour market conditions and which does not give schools the opportunity to reward teachers in a flexible way. We should move to a recommended system of national pay bargaining rather than a mandatory system. That would underpin the improvement of standards that we have seen recently in our schools.

12.17 pm

**Mr. George Galloway** (Glasgow, Hillhead): The House should not adjourn without discussing the current crisis in Kashmir, where two heavily armed countries, both probably in possession of nuclear weapons, are squared up to each other in an atmosphere of escalating tension and where general hostilities may break out at any time. That would have catastrophic consequences for the Indian-Pakistani sub-continent, for the broader area and for the world as a whole.

I declare an interest in the matter. As a long-standing and close associate of the Pakistan People's party, I spent an abstemious Hogmanay in Islamabad as a guest of the Pakistan People's party Government and of Benazir Bhutto personally. It was a very abstemious Hogmanay, but my visit was an interest that I should declare in this debate.

The immediate cause of the crisis has been the escalation from a six or seven-year low-intensity struggle between the Indian occupation force in Kashmir and the indigenous resistance to that occupation into a qualitatively different and more dangerous situation, with the burning of the shrine at Charar-i-Sharif. The flames are still licking around the ruins of the 650-year-old holy shrine, the adjacent mosque and the adjacent houses, all of which were destroyed in a firefight between the Indian occupation forces and people who were taking sanctuary in the shrine. As a result of that firefight, an ancient and revered site has been reduced to ash and ruins. The consequent increase in the political temperature on both sides of the border, and in the occupied and disputed area itself, is real and palpable. The House and, indeed, the Government should recognise it.

The Indian Defence Minister publicly threatened that India would invade the area known as Azad Kashmir, which is currently outside Indian control and in a semi-detached relationship with Pakistan. He said that India would teach Pakistan a lesson. There is a general alert in the area: soldiers and populations are bracing themselves for a new, much more damaging and dangerous military altercation.

The ultimate cause of all the tension—which has meant that two countries where people often go hungry and many millions experience deep poverty spend 60 per cent. of their budgets on armaments and defence—is the unresolved status of the area of Jammu and Kashmir. In a sense, that is a British responsibility: it is unfinished business following partition. It was mishandled at the time of partition, and has never been resolved. The United Nations resolutions of 1948 and 1949, which call for the people of Jammu and Kashmir to decide on their future by plebiscite, have never been implemented; and the United Nations charter that gives every people the right to self-determination has also never been implemented in the area.

India must learn that simply pouring more and more soldiers—650,000 now—and more and more firepower into the occupied territory, the valley of Kashmir, which used to be known as "paradise on earth", and creating increasing aggression on the ground, will not lead to quiescence among the occupied people. Indeed, it merely adds fuel to the fires that we have seen over the past few weeks. There must be a peace process.

My early-day motion 1126, entitled "Need for a negotiated settlement in Kashmir", has been widely supported by members of all parties. It asks for a peace process to begin, and Britain is in an ideal position to begin it. She has good relations with both India and Pakistan, both of which are members of the Commonwealth. Britain is in a position to initiate contacts of some kind, perhaps through an eminent persons group. There are many redundant statespeople in the Houses of Parliament, some of whom were very eminent once. They could be put to constructive work trying to broker the beginning of a peace settlement, bringing to the table the Governments of India and Pakistan and those who represented the people of Jammu and Kashmir at the Hurryat conference.

I do not understand why Britain does not want to play that role. It would bring to a peaceful, negotiated end the long running sore that has cost thousands of lives, has caused three wars and is in danger of causing a fourth. It has led to mass intimidation, rape as an instrument of political oppression, shooting in the streets, torture in the prisons, exile, refugees and all the dreadful panoply that accompanies such a conflict. Britain could do itself a great deal of good in the area, the Commonwealth and the world by beginning a peace process.

Benazir Bhutto and her Government hold the line against extremism in that part of the world. They are a democratic Government of an Islamic country—moderate, not threatening to any neighbours or anyone else; but, for as long as the Kashmir issue remains unresolved, they are in danger. If Benazir Bhutto goes, the dark forces that will step into the government of Pakistan will certainly not be in the interests of the people of the area, this country or the community more generally.

12.24 pm

**Mr. Oliver Heald** (Hertfordshire, North): Before we adjourn, perhaps it would be possible to discuss a range of transport issues, and also low pay.

Johnson Matthey in my constituency has developed a diesel auto-catalyst that has a remarkable effect in removing dangerous particles from exhaust fumes. I know that my hon. Friend the Minister for Transport in London has seen the device in operation, and I hope that more discussion of it will be possible in the House. There is no doubt that, if it were fitted to all the diesel engines in Britain, environmental pollution would be much reduced.

There is much concern about roads in my constituency. The A10 between Royston and Buntingford has become an accident black spot. I am very pleased that my hon. Friend the Minister for Railways and Roads has been able to introduce, through the county council, a range of measures to improve safety on that road. What is most shocking, however, is that most of the accidents have been caused by drivers travelling far too fast and overtaking where road signs make it clear that overtaking is not possible. Accident follows accident, despite the marvellous efforts of the local police, who have prosecuted 120 people in this year alone. I hope that a further campaign can be launched to persuade motorists to cut their speed and obey road signs.

Baldock badly needs a bypass, and I hope that my hon. Friend the Minister will proceed with that programme once the public inquiry has been completed.

Let me turn from local issues to low pay. I am disappointed not to have received an answer to the question that I put to the hon. Member for Glasgow, Garscadden (Mr. Dewar) on 14 February. I asked him whether he endorsed the analysis of the Joseph Rowntree Foundation report, and whether he accepted that its conclusions were sound. He said that he endorsed the analysis, and accepted that many of the conclusions were sound; but he would not say which of those conclusions a Labour Government would implement.

**Mr. Andrew Robathan** (Blaby): Typical.

**Mr. Heald:** It was not a tremendous surprise. It is worth considering, however, what analysis the hon. Member for Garscadden was endorsing. The report said that, since the mid-1970s, income inequality and wealth distribution inequality had grown. That, however, was a period of high inflation and high taxation: anyone with any savings saw those savings eroded year after year, until they had no substantial value. The gap narrowed between such people and those with no savings at all.

It is true that the difference between the highest and the lowest earner was narrower during the mid-1970s, but that was because all wage rates were falling and taxation was penal. If the hon. Member for Garscadden accepts the analysis, surely he must say which of the report's conclusions he would put into practice. Those conclusions were that there should be extra investment in training and education, social security, housing and the labour market, direct provision of employment opportunities, state-paid child care, more subsidies to employers to take on the unemployed, indexing of benefits above the retail prices index, social fund grants, not loans, and a reversal of the reduction in the jobseeker's allowance to six months. When we debated those issues in February, many Labour Members said that those were the changes that they wanted, yet the Opposition do not say what they would do. We hear many claims that the Government are following the wrong path, but the only way in which the public can judge those issues is if the Labour party says what it would do.

All the measures that I have read out involve spending more money. I should like to know how that squares with the Leader of the Opposition's comments in his Mais lecture, when he said:

"In Government, controlling public spending is a long and gruelling slog. But the alternative is far worse".

If he is saying such things—which is a move in the right direction—how can his Front-Bench spokesmen stand there and say that they accept the conclusions of a report that involves spending and more spending? It just will not do.

The report also makes a proposal for a minimum wage, no doubt at the level that the trade unions want. Was it not in November that Denis Healey said that that would enable the trade unions to build a new tower on the platform of the minimum wage? If it is right that that would happen and that all the differentials would move up, how can the Leader of the Opposition say:

"Controlling inflation is not only an objective in itself. It is an essential prerequisite for sustainable economic growth on a scale sufficient to attain the social and political aims of the Labour Party"?

What could be more inflationary than every wage level being pushed up on the platform of a minimum wage? I hope that we can debate those issues before we adjourn and obtain some real answers for a change.

*[Mr. Heald]*

12.31 pm

**Mr. David Winnick** (Walsall, North): Later today, tributes will, I understand, be paid in the usual way to Harold Wilson. Winning four out of five elections as party leader is a remarkable score. I speak as one who, in a sense, benefited from his leadership. I won an election for another seat in 1966 by a majority of 81, and had it not been for the climate at the time I doubt whether even all my hard efforts and those of my supporters would have secured victory. Over many years, Harold Wilson played a significant role in the life of the Labour party. It is right and proper that we should pay tribute to him today.

I want to deal with the importance of making progress on the Nolan recommendations before the long summer recess. It was interesting, as those who have read the press in the last few days will have noted, that in last Thursday's debate the view—almost exclusively expressed by Tory Members—that the Nolan recommendations should not be implemented in whole and that there should be no disclosures of outside financial interests received a hostile press. I may be wrong—I may have missed one or two newspapers—but, literally, not one newspaper echoed the theme of the Tory critics in that debate.

The Prime Minister was right to set up the Nolan committee. As I said during Prime Minister's questions last Thursday, it is important that its recommendations should be implemented quickly. There is no reason why—and I have argued this over many years—disclosure of outside financial interests should not be made in the Register of Members' Interests. At present, the register gives no insight into how much is involved. The Nolan committee's recommendations are constructive.

I know that some of my hon. Friends are in favour of a total ban on outside interests, but I am not. Such a ban would not be right or practical. I have never argued anything along those lines. As Members of the Parliament, however, we have a responsibility to be perfectly frank about what we do outside and what income we receive. We should not conceal it from our colleagues in the House of Commons or from the electorate.

My interests are in the register. My union pays a contribution.

**Mr. Jacques Arnold:** How much?

**Mr. Winnick:** How much is in the register. I have made sure that that is so. The union pays my constituency party £300 each year. It pays me no money, and rightly so. It also pays a proportion of my election expenses. It is all in the register, apart from one other entry that anyone can check.

It has been a matter of regret that the reputation of the House of Commons has been lowered, particularly as a result of what has happened in the past six or nine months. It is important for us to put our House in order. There have always been people who have argued against change and reform. In the last century, they argued against measures to tackle corruption. Even the Reform Act 1832 was rigorously opposed, but those changes were considered to be necessary.

I was in the House of Commons before there was a Register of Members' Interests. When it was suggested that such a register should be introduced, there were protests—mostly, of course, from Conservative Members—that it would be an intrusion into privacy and that it would be wrong. No one argues that now. The register is accepted, even by those critics in the debate last Thursday. Not one single Tory said that there should not be a register. It was, nevertheless, a subject of much controversy before it was introduced.

Once the Nolan recommendations are put into effect, with the source of outside income being disclosed, after a period of time they too will be accepted. No one is likely to argue against them. I ask the Leader of the House: when will the suggested Committee be set up, when will it report, are the Government determined not to dilute Nolan, and will they find excuses as to why those recommendations should not be put into effect?

The recommendations should be put into effect as quickly as possible. There should be firm recommendations before the House embarks on the summer recess. Delay is not permissible. Undoubtedly, delay would not be understood outside. In the country at large, widespread support exists for the changes that we know are necessary to clean up our act and to ensure that the reputation of the House is what it should be. For those reasons, the Leader of the House should give a firm assurance today that the promise that we require will be given.

12.37 pm

**Mr. Jeff Rooker** (Birmingham, Perry Barr): This morning, 14 hon. Members have taken part in the debate—somewhat fewer than we had for the last recess Wednesday debate, in which about 21 took part. One of the reasons for that is that, as you, Mr. Deputy Speaker, have observed, some of the speeches have been far too long. We need a safety valve—a zero hour—to allow us to raise urgent issues, but hon. Members coming to the House during Adjournment debates when they cannot obtain a reply from a Minister causes a bit of a problem for the Leader of the House.

Nevertheless, some interesting points have been made. In the time available, I cannot touch on them all. Obviously, a good many Conservative Members are still shellshocked from the results of 4 May and the consequences of the change ordered by the electorate in the management and governance of their local authorities. They cannot quite come to terms with the fact that, at the request of the electorate, another political approach is being taken in relation to the delivery of services, whether they be social services or education. The first two speeches by Conservative Members dealt with that.

The hon. Member for Christchurch (Mrs. Maddock) was rightly in her place this morning, and she would have been there this afternoon if our business had been as arranged. Following yesterday's accident, we all share the distress, trauma and bereavement that has been caused to many families. These accidents do not happen very often on our roads. We have an intensively used motorway network. There are always many reasons why accidents happen. It would be wrong for the House to rush to a judgment, and we do not wish to do so. We must learn lessons from each of these tragedies so that the experience and knowledge gained can be used to prevent accidents in the future.

I know that the hon. Member for Christchurch and my hon. Friend the Member for Stoke-on-Trent, North (Ms Walley) contacted the Speaker's Office this morning requesting a private notice question. I am sure that Madam Speaker would have granted their request or the Secretary of State for Transport would have made a statement to the House. Obviously, that is not possible because of the sad death of Lord Wilson, our former Prime Minister. We must make it clear that, notwithstanding that terrible tragedy, we have a good safety record on our roads and we have responsible coach operators.

The answer is not to be found by concentrating on a single issue, whether it be seat belts or the structure and integrity of the bodywork of the coach. We must reassure the travelling public that everything will be done by the inspection and investigation agencies to ensure that all the lessons are learnt from the tragedy. I am sure that the House will return to this matter on some other day.

I must confess that I missed part of the speech made by my hon. Friend the Member for Greenock and Port Glasgow (Dr. Godman), but my good friend the deputy Chief Whip told me that he had raised the important issue of the dismantling of offshore equipment in the North sea. We have exploited the natural resource in the North sea to the great advantage of the United Kingdom—and I emphasise, to the advantage of the United Kingdom—in the past 20 years. It has involved an enormous number of jobs, new technologies and an enormous amount of wealth. We can argue about the way in which the wealth has been used, either public or private but, as we are moving further out into the North sea and the Atlantic, the equipment near the shore should not be left in such a state that it affects the ability of hundreds of other people to carry out their normal occupation—fishing.

There is a cost to be met for exploiting the natural resources of the planet, whether it is the coal mines or beneath the sea bed. The cost of that exploitation must be restoration as far as is practicable so that we do not damage opportunities for future generations.

**Mr. Jacques Arnold:** Will the hon. Gentleman tell us how he can justify the new political order to which he referred in view of the contents of my speech, which dealt with Labour and Liberal Democrat-controlled Kent county council? Although that council has more than one source of money available, it short-changes our schools. I asked whether Opposition spokesmen could justify that and whether they would instruct their groups on the council to put the money into schools.

**Mr. Rooker:** I am not keeping a count of this and I cannot refer to every speech, but I believe that I am dealing with the fourth or fifth speech and I do not intend to go back.

The issue raised by my hon. Friend the Member for Greenock and Port Glasgow needs to be addressed and I believe that it will come before the House on many occasions in the future. It affects not just the occupation but the life of those involved in the fishing industry.

The cost of exploitation must be considered under the polluter pays principle. We and the oil industry have polluted the infrastructure of the North sea and we should not allow that to prevent other people from carrying out their normal occupations.

The hon. Member for Basildon (Mr. Amess), who has just arrived back in the Chamber, did a 50 yd sprint along the Benches this morning because the first time he was called to speak he was separated from his notes, so Madam Speaker went on to call another hon. Member. However, when he did make his speech, he seemed to be having some difficulty coming to terms with the catastrophic implications for Tory Members of the results of the elections on 4 May.

I shall not go into detail about the issues that the hon. Gentleman raised about local government in Essex and Basildon, but he should not seek always seek to undermine the concept of independent local government. The House has a real problem with some people who claim that we are sovereign over everything and that we have the answers to everything. We do not, and we should not pretend that we do. If we genuinely believe in independent local government, we will not always agree with what our colleagues in local government do, from whichever side of the political divide they come. We can raise the issues on behalf of our constituents—that is our prime function—but we should not seek to undermine the concept of local government.

The hon. Gentleman mentioned the Fenchurch Street line. I have done some campaigning in Basildon so I suspect that I have travelled on that line in the past.

The hon. Gentleman talked about identity cards. I hope that this will not cause a problem and I hope that he does not fall over, but I should tell him that I am predisposed towards the concept of identity cards and I am not alone on the Opposition Benches. It is not an issue on which there is a narrow party divide. One of the biggest tragedies facing us is that we have a Home Secretary who seeks to make a party issue out of every serious home affairs matter. *[Interruption.]* I do not agree with sedentary interruptions.

I do not agree with the concept of compulsory identity cards and I do not agree with putting DNA information on such cards. I believe that citizens have a right to assert their identity and that is my starting point. They have a right to do that regardless of their position in society, whether it is at home, in the office, getting a travelcard or even if they are stopped in the street. They should be able to tell the police, "Naff off. I have asserted my identity and that is the end of the matter." That right does not exist now. I have a pocket full of credit cards and hon. Members cannot move around the House without a photo-identity pass because we cannot open some of the doors without them. There is a genuine issue to be addressed.

The driving licence may be the way to go. I agree with the chief constable in my area who believes that identity cards should contain not just a photograph but a fingerprint. That would go an enormous way towards dealing with the issue raised by my hon. Friend the Member for Coventry, North-East (Mr. Ainsworth), who spoke of motor crime. In fact, if it were not for motor vehicles, we probably would not need as many police because at least half of all crime is related to motor vehicles in one way or another. That issue must be considered seriously.

My hon. Friend the Member for Leeds, East (Mr. Mudie) raised an important issue. Sometimes there is a downside to the use of modern technology, particularly in the health service, whether one looks back to the thalidomide issue or haemophiliacs and the AIDS virus. We must address this issue. We cannot leave it to the

[*Mr. Rooker*]

courts or to individual citizens to take on the NHS or the drug companies. We should not leave people to go, apparently, begging to the Government.

To our disgrace, we do not have a system of no-fault compensation in this country. The Government would have the full support of the Opposition if they adopted the same attitude to the hepatitis C virus as they did to haemophiliacs and the AIDS virus. The number of people involved is small and it will not be the last time. There will always be such issues because of the use of technology in the health service. Such people need our help before they have to go knocking on doors. Their mothers and fathers need help as do others who take care of them.

The hon. Member for Dover (Mr. Shaw) made a very long speech and I cannot deal with all of it. He also talked about education and complained about local government publicity. If a local authority is breaking the law on political propaganda, the hon. Gentleman should use the mechanisms in the Local Government Act 1988, which the House put in place for hon. Members to operate. He should not just come here and complain about it.

The hon. Gentleman also talked about the Channel Tunnel Rail Link Bill. I should declare an interest: I have no intention of ever using the channel tunnel because I do not think that it is safe enough. I accept that that view is prejudiced, but that is my belief. The Opposition have no predisposition to use public money to save the private investors. On the other hand, we cannot ignore the fact that it is there. The hon. Gentleman rightly declared his vested interest and I suspect that the financing of the channel tunnel will come back to haunt the House and the country for some time, particularly when one considers our inability to provide the necessary infrastructure to go with it.

The main part of the hon. Gentleman's speech was on the political funds of the Union of Communication Workers. As I said in an intervention, political education in that union is far in advance of and more detailed than in any other trade union of which I am aware and the political panel is the structure for doing that.

The political panel does not just relate to the Members of Parliament who happen to be here; it relates to those who aspire to be Members of Parliament and who have to go through the training processes and is part of the funding for their education. It has to come out of the political fund. It certainly does not have the implication suggested by the hon. Gentleman that the money he cannot account for has ended up as £50,000 sponsorship for one of my hon. Friends. I can assure him, without even checking up on the matter, that that is not the case because I know the way in which that union operates.

My hon. Friend the Member for Coventry, North-East raised an issue that he had intended to raise later today under the ten-minute Bill procedure. I was astonished by the fact that two thirds of stolen vehicles are never recovered. It is an astonishing figure bearing in mind the amount of police time occupied in dealing with vehicle crime.

My hon. Friend the Member for Glasgow, Hillhead (Mr. Galloway) was the only person to raise an international issue and he spoke about the continuing and worsening position in Kashmir. As he said, our nation is in a unique position to offer more help to both the

Pakistan and Indian Governments than we have hitherto given. We must not follow the rhetoric that Pakistan does not want an independent Kashmir—I am well aware of that from my constituents in Birmingham. The conflict must be resolved without going to war for the fourth time, and it can be resolved only by talking. That is what this Government should be encouraging.

12.51 pm

**The Lord President of the Council and Leader of the House of Commons (Mr. Tony Newton):** The House will understand that I wish to begin my remarks by expressing the regret that we all feel at the death of Lord Wilson. Whatever political disagreements there may have been, he was undoubtedly one of the substantial political figures of our time. We can all think of some of his memorable phrases that will probably be part of British politics for all time, and which may be referred to when proper tribute is paid to him later today.

This has been another interesting revised Adjournment debate occasion, now known as "Matters to be considered". As the hon. Member for Birmingham, Perry Barr (Mr. Rooker) said, there have not been as many speakers as there were on the last occasion, but rather more than appeared to be likely when Mr. Deputy Speaker spoke so sternly from the Chair about one and a half hours ago—since when the proceedings have speeded up considerably.

My main feeling is one of envy for the freedom with which the hon. Member for Perry Bar felt able to speak from the Dispatch Box. I detected only a rather tenuous connection between what he said and the policies that he is supposed to advocate. Indeed, there must be some risk of a headline in tomorrow's newspapers, "Opposition denounce channel tunnel"—[*Interruption.*] The hon. Gentleman probably said that it was a personal view, but nevertheless I envy his freedom to scatter such comments from the Front Bench. He also used one or two phrases that I would not care to use from the Front Bench, but that is life.

Obviously, I will not have time to deal with all the speeches, any more than the hon. Gentleman was able to do so. I am sure that the House will understand if I start slightly out of order with the hon. Member for Christchurch (Mrs. Maddock), who spoke about the terrible and tragic accident that happened yesterday and which affected many of her constituents. As my hon. Friend the Member for Isle of Wight (Mr. Field) said, it also affected many people with whom he and his constituents are connected.

I hope that the hon. Lady will not mind me saying that my right hon. Friend the Secretary of State for Transport made a special visit to the House this morning to hear what she had to say. I understand that he has been in touch with her and that they had a helpful discussion in which he made clear the sympathy we all feel for the families of those who were killed or injured. I am sure that we all wish to pay tribute to the emergency services for their prompt response.

The hon. Lady fairly said that she did not expect me, or my right hon. Friend, had he been able to answer a private notice question, to make any assumption about the cause of the accident. However, I understand that my right hon. Friend has assured her that he will look at the report that has been commissioned from the Vehicle Inspectorate against the background of the points that she raised this morning.

I want to comment briefly on as many speeches as possible. My hon. Friend the Member for Gravesham (Mr. Arnold) made a number of points about education and he was later echoed by my hon. Friends the Members for Dover (Mr. Shaw) in relation to Kent and for Basildon (Mr. Amess) in relation to Essex. Indeed, education was the single strongest theme running through the debate.

My hon. Friend the Member for Gravesham made a number of comments to which I cannot respond in detail. However, he made an interesting point about the underspend on the revenue budget in Kent and the suggestion of Conservative members of the county council to use that to overcome the problems with the education budget. I am sure that we all hope that that proposition will be carefully considered.

I am glad to note that in Essex, where there were similar problems, the Conservative group had rather greater success. Against a background of division between the Labour and Liberal Democrat coalition, it proposed a plan that successfully prevented the damage that would otherwise have been done by the coalition's original proposals.

I am always reluctant to use the Dispatch Box to air constituency matters and I will not do so now, other than to say that I am finding exactly the position outlined by my hon. Friend the Member for Basildon relating to community care in Essex and bed-blocking. There is also what I can call only the deplorable proposal to withdraw transport to selective schools. That can only damage the least well-off with able children. I very much hope that Essex will decide not to proceed with that proposal when it considers it again next month.

My hon. Friend the Member for Hertsmere (Mr. Clappison) made some important points about the assisted places scheme, which in many ways echo what I have just said about transport to selective schools. Once again, the Labour party is attacking something that has widened educational opportunities for least well-off people in society and which has helped more than 70,000 children since its inception. I hope that the Opposition collectively, not just in any particular area, will reconsider their policies and proposals in that area.

I stayed in the House to listen to the speech of the hon. Member for Leeds, East (Mr. Mudie). He knows that I understand many of the points that he raised because of the time that I served both as a Health Minister and as a Social Security Minister, when a system was put in place to help those who had contracted AIDS from infected blood transfusions. The hon. Gentleman will understand that I cannot add to the various exchanges on those matters, but I am sure that my right hon. Friends the Secretary of State for Health and the Prime Minister will study what he has said this morning with great care.

I hope that people will study if not all at least part of what my hon. Friend the Member for Dover said. He had obviously done a great deal of research into trade union accounts and the Industrial Research Trust. He asked a number of questions that I am sure he would not expect me to answer, but which we all expect others in other places to consider and then provide answers.

The hon. Member for Coventry, North-East (Mr. Ainsworth) made some important and interesting points about car crime and I shall ensure that they are drawn to the attention of my right hon. and learned Friend the Home Secretary.

I shall draw the thoughtful and constructive points made by my hon. Friend the Member for Isle of Wight, on a number of matters, to the attention of my various colleagues.

I cannot add to the exchanges that the hon. Member for Burnley (Mr. Pike) and I have had during business questions and on other occasions. However, our very recognition of the problem of pension funds, which was revealed most dramatically by the Maxwell case, underlies the Pensions Bill that is currently in Committee. At the very least, the Bill is clear recognition of the concern that is felt, which the Government share and which we are seeking to address through changes in the law.

My hon. Friend the Member for Wyre Forest (Mr. Coombs) echoed others' comments, including those of my hon. Friend the Member for Basildon, about the involvement of parents in the educational process. My hon. Friend the Member for Wyre Forest will know that a great deal of effort has been put into securing such involvement and I am sure that his suggestions will be carefully considered.

I am sure, too, that all the points made by my hon. Friend the Member for Hertfordshire, North (Mr. Heald), the hon. Member for Glasgow, Hillhead (Mr. Galloway) and, not least, the hon. Member for Greenock and Port Glasgow (Dr. Godman) about the current consultation exercise, in which the fishermen will have an opportunity to have their say, will be carefully considered by Ministers. In anticipation of that, I hope that all hon. Members who have made points will depart tomorrow reasonably peacefully for a happy and contented recess.

## Anglo-German Relations

1 pm

**Mr. Mike Watson** (Glasgow, Central): On a point of order, Mr. Deputy Speaker. Will you rule that the apt title for the debate that is about to begin is "British-German Relations" or "United Kingdom-German Relations"? I do not wish to delay the debate—indeed, I am secretary of the British-German all-party parliamentary group, and I look forward to it—but it is irritating for those of us in the House who are Scottish, Irish or Welsh continually to hear talk of the Anglo-Irish Agreement, and so on. May we please get the terminology right in future?

**Mr. Deputy Speaker (Mr. Michael Morris):** We must wait to hear what the debate is about before we decide whether the title is appropriate.

1.1 pm

**Mr. Giles Radice** (Durham, North): I entirely agree with the point of order raised by my hon. Friend the Member for Glasgow, Central (Mr. Watson). He is absolutely right. The debate should have been entitled "British-German Relations". The purpose of my debate is to argue the case, before the Anglo-German summit later this week, for a much closer and stronger Anglo-German alliance. I am sure that my hon. Friend would agree with that.

My visits to Germany recently have convinced me that there are some very strong common interests between the two countries. I have been fortunate enough to visit Germany and speak to well over 100 leading and representative Germans during the past two years in gathering material for a book, about which modesty prevents me from saying anything more. I am indebted, however, to the Ebert Stiftung and the Deutsche-Englische Gesellschaft for enabling me to make the trips, and I also thank the Treasury and Civil Service Select Committee for giving me the opportunity to meet three successive presidents of the Bundesbank.

In November 1993, Klaus Kinkel, the German Foreign Secretary, described the relationship with London as "unspectacular . . . solid, dependable, professional". A correspondent of *The Times* commented that Kinkel might have been describing his relationship with his dentist. My case this afternoon is that, given the joint experience, common interest and common problems of the two countries, something warmer than a dentist-patient relationship is needed. Positive and sustained steps, especially by the British side, should be taken to strengthen Anglo-German understanding.

Sadly, British attitudes to Germany and the Germans are far too often characterised by misunderstanding, envy and sometimes downright ignorance. Despite all the good work of the various British-German institutions, including those in which my hon. Friend the Member for Glasgow, Central is involved, the British know very little about modern Germany. German is almost never the first foreign language taught in schools. Few learn subsequently about German politics, institutions or culture, and most British tourists go not to Germany but to France and the Mediterranean countries for their holidays. Indeed, a recent *Financial Times* poll showed that only 5 per cent. of British people have recently been to Germany, although 20 per cent. of Germans have recently been to Britain.

As a result, British views about Germany are shaped not by direct contact, as they ought to be, but by an unhappy combination of national stereotyping, memories of two world wars and half-digested scraps of information. Such poor information is basically due, with some notable exceptions, to the rather inadequate coverage of Germany even in the quality press, while the treatment of Germany by the tabloids is—frankly—a national disgrace.

In the political class, there is, I fear, an element of envy. Germans seems to have done so much better than us in the post-war world. British politicians, especially on the right, fear the German economy when it is strong and criticise it when it is weak. There are totally unjustified concerns about the prospect of an over-powerful Germany. That underlying assumption coloured Mrs. Thatcher's attitude to unification, which, as we know, was extremely hostile and very bad for British-German relations.

It is time that we treated the Germans as allies and friends. They have earned our trust and respect by the way in which they have conducted themselves over the past 50 years.

**Mr. Michael Fabricant** (Mid-Staffordshire): In connection with what the hon. Gentleman has just said and his earlier statements about the fact that German is not taught as our first foreign language, does he agree that a student gains greater satisfaction from learning German rather than French because it is far more easy for an Englishman—nay, even a Scotsman—to speak German with a convincing accent? Indeed, German grammar enables one to understand English grammar, which, given that Latin is no longer studied at school, is very useful.

**Mr. Radice:** We ought to learn both.

**Mr. Denis MacShane** (Rotherham): English and German?

**Mr. Radice:** We ought to learn German and French. I hope that one or two of us know a little English already.

What are the facts about modern Germany? The federal republic, now extended eastward through unification, has been the most successful regime in German history, not only economically but socially and democratically. Drawing on British and American experience and advice, playing to German strengths, and above all learning the lessons of the past, the founding fathers have devised a set of democratic rules and institutions which, over 40 years, have stood the test of time. They include the federal structure, the system of political consensus—shaped partly by proportional representation, the 5 per cent. hurdle, strong political parties, and so on—the social market institutions, which introduce considerable consensus into economic and industrial decision making, and, of course, a long-term perspective, which has been such a feature of German economic success.

We should note that it is remarkable how successful the federal republic has been in tackling the huge twin problems of unification and the restructuring of the German economy within the existing democratic and social consensus framework. The process of unification may have taken longer than the optimists expected, but most fair-minded observers conclude that there will be blooming landscapes, as promised by Chancellor Kohl at the Frauenkirche in Dresden in 1990. Of course, the process has taken much longer than he expected.

At the same time as proving its democratic credentials internally, Germany has showed itself to be a very good neighbour. It is significant that the new unity of Germany, firmly tied to the west and with no enemies and territorial claims to the east—the fruits of Ostpolitik—has been accepted by its European neighbours, including, in the end, if reluctantly, by the British.

Far more unites the United Kingdom and Germany than separates them. The two countries are now economically almost entirely interdependent. Germany is Britain's largest export market, while Britain is Germany's fourth largest export market. Germany is one of the largest investors in Britain. There are 1,000 German firms located here, which bring with them hundreds of thousands of jobs. Britain is a substantial investor in Germany, including the eastern Länder. A stable and prosperous Germany is a key British interest, just as a stable and prosperous Britain is a key German interest. To put it very basically, jobs in the United Kingdom and Germany depend on each other's markets, which is real interdependence.

At the same time, we have close defence links. Both countries have been members of NATO and allies for 40 years. As the United States cuts its forces on the European mainland, British-German defence co-operation will assume an even greater importance. It is impossible to imagine defending the mainland of Europe without that strong alliance between the British and the Germans.

We are both key members of the European Union. Sadly, our relationship has been marred by quarrels and spats, especially following Britain's humiliating exit from the exchange rate mechanism, but there again, we have substantial common interests. They include: a commitment to free markets; an open European Union; extending EU membership to the east; and support for subsidiarity. I submit that a more positive line in Europe by the British Government would bring out those shared views and assumptions.

Given those common interests, it is essential that positive and sustained steps should be taken to strengthen the Anglo-German relationship. The most important priority is improved knowledge of each other's countries. Lack of knowledge allows prejudice to gain hold and, as opinion polls show, it also generates distrust. Last year, a disturbing poll showed that 48 per cent. of Germans distrusted the British, and 50 per cent. of Britons distrusted the Germans. In both cases, that was the highest percentage for attitudes to another major country. That ought to give Ministers some cause for concern.

The key is to expand existing systems of educational and youth exchanges, which are both too small and without sufficient financial backing, especially on the British side. A mass programme of exchanges is required on the Franco-German model. While doing research for my book, I found out that 10 times more is spent on Franco-German exchanges than on Anglo-German exchanges. Something must be done there.

German language teaching should be stepped up dramatically in British schools, as should the number of German courses at British universities. It is interesting and significant that a new centre for German studies at Birmingham university has mainly been financed by German, not British, firms. It is essential for young Germans and Britons to have an informed view of one another.

Industry has a responsibility. British and German firms, which depend so much on each other's markets, ought to be more proactive in expanding awareness of each other's countries. Building on the work of the many Anglo-German institutions, voluntary organisations, political parties and trades unions ought to be expanding their co-operation with their opposite numbers.

Despite all that is sometimes said about twinning, there is a lot to be said for more of it at town, city and regional levels. Two towns in my constituency are twinned with German towns, and it is about much more than just town councillors' junketing. For example, there are youth and school exchanges and so forth, which do a power of good on both sides.

Above all, we need a Government lead, especially by the British Government. I want to hear British Ministers heralding German social democratic and economic achievements. I would like to hear them say a little more often that the Germans are good democrats and have been—have proved themselves to be—good neighbours. I would like to hear them say that it is in Britain's interests to have a strong, prosperous and democratic Germany, playing a leading role in Europe.

I am sure that the Anglo-German summit communiqué will include a number of worthy, but minor, measures. I suspect, however, that the time has come for some more symbolic act of friendship. In 1963, the French and Germans signed a treaty, which was a defining moment in modern European political history. In 1995, there is surely a case for an Anglo-German—I should more properly say British-German—state treaty, which would put British-German relations on a new and more constructive footing. Such an initiative would be good not only for Britain and Germany but for Europe as well.

1.14 pm

**The Parliamentary Under-Secretary of State for Foreign and Commonwealth Affairs (Mr. Tony Baldry):** We are all very grateful to the hon. Member for Durham, North (Mr. Radice) for his timely raising of such an important subject in the House this week. It is a pity that we have only half an hour in which to debate the subject, as a number of hon. Members clearly take an interest, and I fear that there will not be time to allow them to take part.

On Friday, my right hon. Friends the Prime Minister and the Secretary of State for Foreign and Commonwealth Affairs will have some discussions with the German Chancellor and Foreign Minister in Bonn. That will be the culmination of a series of meetings between Ministers of finance, trade, economy and defence, and I therefore welcome this opportunity to review the state of our bilateral relationship with such a close and important partner in Europe as Germany.

The debate is also timely because, as the hon. Gentleman said, he has just published a book on the subject. He was overly modest about it. I would be slightly suspicious of a book that had an endorsement from the right hon. Member for Yeovil (Mr. Ashdown) on its dust cover, but the hon. Member for Durham, North more than redeems himself by frequent and accurate references within it to my right hon. Friend the Prime Minister. Indeed, the hon. Gentleman reminds us of my right hon. Friend's commitment for Britain

"to be where we belong, at the very heart of Europe, working with our partners in building the future."

*[Mr. Tony Baldry]*

It may encourage the hon. Gentleman to know that we have acquired a copy of his book for the Foreign Office library. Having read it, I can say that it is certainly a useful contribution to Anglo-German relations.

**Mr. Radice:** I must correct the Minister: the leader of the Liberal party made a nice comment about a previous book, not that one.

**Mr. Baldry:** I would be suspicious of any author of any book about which the leader of the Liberal party makes nice comments.

This partnership is perhaps most obvious to the business community. When Britain joined the European Economic Community in 1973, bilateral British-German trade totalled £2.2 billion in both directions. In 1994, by contrast, we exported some £17.7 billion worth of goods to Germany and imported £22.7 billion. Germany was our biggest trading partner in the European Union, and only just second to the United States worldwide.

In the same year, Britain was the top attraction for German investors, who invested more than £1.5 billion in the United Kingdom, which is well ahead of German investment in the United States. Our industry is benefiting from German investment, of which BMW's purchase of Rover is but one example.

In the other direction, Britain was the fourth largest investor in Germany, with some £282 million. Around 1,000 British companies have subsidiaries in Germany. British companies have been among the leaders investing in the new German states of the former East Germany. Governments encourage, while companies take the decisions. Economically, our present and future relations are closely intertwined. That is the case politically as well.

**Mr. MacShane:** Will the Minister give way?

**Mr. Baldry:** If the hon. Gentleman will forgive me, I will not give way, because we have had one lengthy intervention in a short debate. This is a half-hour Adjournment debate, and, in fairness to the contribution of the hon. Member for Durham, North, I have a lot that I would like to say.

We recently commemorated 50 years of peace and reconciliation in Europe. Germany is a fully fledged and sovereign partner within the Union, with which we have, and will continue to have, the closest possible relations. We have been close to Germany because of the presence of British troops since the end of the war in the old West Germany; because of Britain's contribution to the establishment of democracy in the new Germany in the early years after the war; and because of our thinking on a range of issues, from the need to promote non-protectionist trade worldwide to the need to extend security and prosperity to the states of central and eastern Europe. That is all dictated by the same concerns.

The presence here of the German Chancellor and German Federal President on 6 and 7 May, and the Prime Minister's presence at commemorations in Berlin on 8 May, have served to emphasise that closeness. I am glad to say that it has also found a warm echo in the public and media response in both countries. I very much agree with the hon. Gentleman's comments about the role of the media in ensuring a responsible approach to the way in which we view not only Germany but other countries.

The year 1995 has already been memorable in Anglo-German relations. Not all the memories were comfortable, but I am glad to say that we were both able to commemorate the end of world war two in the most appropriate way—for example, in Dresden, Hamburg, London and Berlin.

Britain and Germany are, and will remain, key players in setting out how Europe will develop over the coming years. This concerns not only the institutions of the European Union, but the Union's relationship, and our two countries' relationships, with the rest of Europe—especially with Russia and its former allies. Too much attention has been focused on the differences between Germany and the United Kingdom on certain European issues, but we are sufficiently mature democracies to accept that it is unrealistic to agree on absolutely everything. Instead, we should capitalise on the benefits we gain from a dynamic relationship.

Together we want to see a strong Europe and a free Europe. Britain and Germany are the two main bulwarks against a fortress Europe. We are both concerned about the dangers of instability in central Europe; about competitiveness at home in the face of challenges from outside Europe; about the need for a Europe which is deregulated internally and adheres strictly to the principles of subsidiarity; about the need for financial discipline in the budget; and about the need for a cohesive common foreign and security policy. These are all issues on which we have a common concern and approach.

On a large number of the fundamentals of European policy, Britain and Germany agree. Naturally, there are some aspects of the European Union on which we do not agree. Our geography, history and constitutional experiences are different. In some ways, even our ways of thinking are different. It is natural that there should be intense debate about the future of Europe. The development of the European Union is taking place at the frontier of politics. We are inventing something quite new and unique, and debate is therefore essential.

A successful Europe for the future needs to be competitive in its business and trade, strong and active in its defence and security arrangements, flexible in the development of its institutions and, above all, in touch with its peoples. Britain and Germany share these concerns.

We believe in a Europe which holds its own in the open markets of the world. The protectionist blueprint is an illusion which will not protect but destroy jobs. Free trade brings growth and prosperity. That is why we need a single market free of unnecessary regulation. Britain and Germany have together put their shoulders energetically to this wheel, with the establishment of an Anglo-German deregulation group at last year's summit. I hope that, later this week, we shall be able to explain more fully the actions which we have taken to keep this subject high on the European agenda.

On European security, we stand side by side in our convictions. We believe in a European security architecture which rests on firm foundations—the alliance's collective security guarantee and the United States' commitment. But we need to build on those solid foundations. The German constitutional court's decision last July on the possible deployment of the Bundeswehr out of area increases the scope for Germany to play her part. It also widened the range—already considerable—over which we can co-operate in defence.

Several initiatives have been implemented following last year's British-German summit to assist the countries of central and eastern Europe. For example, we jointly organised a seminar in January attended by nine of those countries, and preparation for a trilateral peacekeeping exercise with Hungary is well in hand. Indeed, there is the closest possible relationship between our armed forces. Again, I hope there will be more to say about that after the summit meeting later this week.

Britain and Germany have set much of the agenda for Europe in the last decade on issues such as budgetary discipline, subsidiarity, deregulation, tackling fraud and promoting free trade. These are things which matter to our people in their daily lives. They matter to our prosperity. It is wrong to pretend that Europe has just one motor. There are several, and the British-German motor is one of the more important. It runs rather quietly, as good motors usually do, but is none the less powerful.

Consultation and co-operation with German colleagues at official level has become an inherent part of our lives. In the case of my own Department and the diplomatic service, for example, there are two members of the German foreign service working in the FCO, and two British diplomats working in the German foreign ministry in Bonn. Overseas, our embassies work closely together to our mutual benefit, sharing information and—in one or two places—sharing premises.

For Ministers, too, a close relationship and consultation exists. This week, for example, the federal German Minister for education, science, research and technology has been visiting the UK for talks with my right hon. Friend the Chancellor of the Duchy of Lancaster. Ministers of finance, trade and economy and defence have had profitable discussions in recent weeks, of which the Prime Minister and Chancellor Kohl will take account in this week's summit.

My right hon. Friends have been much encouraged by the pragmatism of our German partners. The results of those deliberations should be announced on Friday, especially on defence and on increasing mutual public awareness, particularly among young people. I agree very much with what the hon. Gentleman said about the importance of ensuring that there is the greatest understanding between our two countries, particularly among young people.

So much for official co-operation. The Anglo-German relationship does not rest solely on contacts between Governments. What about links between communities? A directory of British-German co-operation put out jointly by the German embassy and the FCO earlier this year lists more than 12 pages of towns with twins in Germany. I suspect that the constituency towns of most hon. Members are linked with towns in Germany, and the towns sometimes exchange strange things. For example, Banbury is twinned with Hennef, which has a British post box, telephone box and other artefacts in its main square. We have received similar gifts from Hennef.

Latest estimates suggest that there are around 8,000 Germans studying at British universities, and around 2,500 British students in Germany. Although at school level there are no central statistics, a best guess would be that around 20,000 schoolchildren are involved in school exchanges each year.

Yet despite this solid foundation, in the subjective field of attitudes and mutual perceptions, both countries seem sometimes to be stuck in a time warp. It is human nature to prefer familiar prejudices to new facts, and to keep existing opinions rather than look at the evidence. Germany, more than most, suffers the effects of this in the UK. As the hon. Gentleman said, opinion polls show that there is still too much mistrust between Britons and Germans. That is regrettable.

My right hon. Friend the Prime Minister intends to discuss with Chancellor Kohl what further steps the two Governments might take to help expose old stereotypes for what they are. There are a number of measures to be considered, with the objective of improving access to information on each other's countries, and increasing contacts and exchanges still further.

Just as we must ensure that there is clear understanding among the people of our two countries of the realities of life, so we must ensure that there is a clear understanding between politicians of both countries. Among politicians, there is sometimes a temptation to create bogeys where Germany is concerned. One of those bogeys is that our views and the views of Germany are diametrically opposed.

I do not think that that is the case. We do not agree on everything with the Germans—nor does any other member state. Each nation has its own traditions and its own objectives for the forthcoming intergovernmental conference, the outcome of which must be agreed by all. But there is much on which we do agree with the Germans.

We both believe in a liberal, free-trading and competitive Europe. We both believe in an outward-looking Europe, and in the importance of enlarging Europe. We both believe in the importance of subsidiarity in Europe, and we both want to deregulate Europe. As substantial net contributors, both Germany and ourselves want to see value for money in the European Union, and proper financial control.

Another bogey raised too often about Germany among politicians in this country is that the Germans will pursue a federalist agenda in 1996. I suspect that there are some in Germany who still subscribe to a vision of the future of the European Union as a federal super-state. But it is more important to look at what German politicians have been saying. Chancellor Kohl made it clear when he said:

"We do not want a European 'superstate' . . . In a Europe of the future, we will remain Germans, Britons, Italians or Frenchmen."

He clearly subscribes to a Europe of nation states. Only last week, Werner Hoyer, the German Minister of State for Europe and study group representative, said of the IGC:

"The wheel does not have to be reinvented. But the bearings . . . have to be checked to ensure that they are functioning . . . properly".

That does not sound like a bid for radical federalism to me. The people of Europe do not want a centralised, interventionist Europe, and it is not what their economies need. That is why we have made it clear that, if such proposals are made at the intergovernmental conference, we shall not accept them.

In 1995, we have shown how far our two countries have been reconciled since the war, and how much progress has been made. Now is the time to build on that progress and move forward. I hope that I have shown how the Government are doing exactly that. It is right that we

[*Mr. Baldry*]

should be aware of Germany's economic and political strengths in Europe. We can acknowledge how far Germany has come—

**Mr. Deputy Speaker:** Order. We now move to the debate on the smuggling of tobacco and alcohol.

# Tobacco and Alcohol Smuggling

1.30 pm

**Mrs. Jacqui Lait** (Hastings and Rye): I am delighted to have this opportunity to continue to remind the Treasury and my hon. Friend the Paymaster General of the concern that a number of my hon. Friends and I feel about the smuggling of tobacco and alcohol.

In the current climate, it is difficult to balance the various claims. Some claim that the supply of tobacco and alcohol to vulnerable groups has not increased. But those of us who know of this problem are very much aware that more and more cheap tobacco and alcohol is available for consumption by them. Our high tax policy has been effective and successful in the past—the UK is one of the few countries in the world where the consumption of tobacco has gone down largely because of that policy—but if no tax is paid, that deterrent effect disappears.

The tobacco and alcohol lobby is crying foul because of the volume of smuggled tobacco and alcohol, while the health lobby seems to say that there is no noticeable impact on vulnerable groups. We must also try to balance the fact that we have low official claims by the Inland Revenue of the amount that is lost through the smuggling of tobacco and alcohol with the fact that the tobacco and alcohol lobby alleges, and in some cases can prove, huge effects on our revenue.

My personal interest in this matter came about not because of those conflicting claims but because, in my constituency on the south coast, I see the direct effects of smuggling on many people and businesses. Newsagents find that their sales of rolling tobacco papers have shot up, while they are selling small quantities of hand-rolling tobacco.

Off-licences tell me of the offers of cheap and obviously smuggled alcohol which turn up at their back doors. Pubs and clubs also say that they have had knocks on the back door with offers of cheap alcohol. It is difficult for them to resist when they know that, in these hard times, their competitors down the road may be succumbing to the temptation of cheap supplies and making larger profits. I have no difficulty in understanding the problems that people have and the temptations to which they succumb, and I make no moral statement of what is right or wrong, especially given that the south coast, particularly my constituency, has a history of smuggling that goes back to the 18th century.

I wanted to bring this issue to the attention of the House today because I recently received a witty company report from the Tobacco Alliance about a company called Tobacco Smugglers and Co. It went through the profit and loss account of a mythical company that was making approximately one trip abroad every day, and estimated that the company could make a profit of £5 million a year. That is not an insubstantial sum of money, and it brought home the issues surrounding the importation of cheap tobacco and alcohol.

Evidence of my eyes and ears has, more than anything else, made me more and more concerned about the subject. I am particularly concerned about the health of those who can get cheap supplies. I am fascinated that those involved in lobbying on health issues find it so difficult to come to terms with the fact that vulnerable groups such as the young, among whom tobacco smoking is increasing, have access to much cheaper cigarettes. They cannot seem to grasp the threat which that poses to young people's health in the long term.

One of the most profitable and easily smuggled forms of tobacco is hand-rolling tobacco, which goes to a different group: those who already smoke. I suspect that, the more that such people have access to cheap hand-rolling tobacco, the more they will smoke. In the long run, GPs' surgeries and hospitals throughout the country will find an increase in chest diseases, lung cancers, and all the diseases that we have tried so hard to reduce by means of high taxation.

I should like the various health charities to reconsider their policies to take account of what is happening on the ground. A recently published occasional paper from the Centre for Health Economics at York university, entitled "Should cross-border shopping affect tax policy?", concludes:

"Incentives to engage in CBS"—

cross-border shopping—

"are small, available data does not indicate a large increase in cross-channel journeys or sharp falls in UK sales, the economic effects of substantial tax cuts are uncertain and may have detrimental health and social consequences."

That smacks of an ostrich-like attitude.

We must also look at the associated effects on the rule of law. If there is one country that prides itself on being ruled, as far as possible, by a legal system that is approved by its citizens, it is the United Kingdom. But because of the ease with which tobacco and alcohol can be smuggled, we are undermining that law.

It is easy for the licensed trade to get hold of cheap alcohol and tobacco, and it affects honest traders. When we go around rest homes, schools and industrial estates, we see the availability of that cheap source of supply. It makes a mockery of both police and customs when the general population can get their hands on what they well know are illegal and smuggled products.

We must ensure that never again do I sit at a table having lunch with nice, middle-class people, four of whom smoke and admit to the fact that they do not pay the full price for cigarettes. If the middle class admits that, we are returning to the abuse and undermining of the rule of law that existed in the 18th century.

If we are lucky, we see small articles in our national papers about prosecutions, such as when the Eastbourne cigarette smuggler was sent down, or the group of Barnsley miners were caught. Trade papers may cover those matters better, but they do not reach the national consciousness, and the bulk of people are coming to believe that smuggling is legitimate.

Unfortunately, I must also tell my hon. Friend the Paymaster General that, while efforts at prevention are admirable, in the long term they are ineffective. I base that on research that I have done into the history of smuggling in the 18th century, and on current costs. I should be grateful if my hon. Friend would disprove those statements some time, because I would be less sceptical about prevention if I knew that it was cost-effective.

It has been shown that, historically, the valiant and complex arrangements that were made to try to prevent the smuggling of tea, brandy, lace and all the other goods that are so romantically associated with smuggling, cost considerably more than the goods that were ever prevented from entering this country. I fear that we are going down that route again.

The latest figures that I have been able to find show that the employment costs of the increased number of excise verification officers whom Customs and Excise has rightly hired are about £7.2 million a year. The revenue value of the goods recovered, at the latest date that I have been able to find—in more than a year—is slightly more than £6 million. We are obviously already losing money on our prevention system.

I very much hope that my hon. Friend will be able to disprove those figures, but if not, we need to consider carefully whether prevention is working and how cost-effective it is.

There are many Members in the Chamber who would agree with me that the anecdotal evidence of the ineffectiveness of prevention continues to encourage the public to believe that they can get away with smuggling. Anyone who has gone to Calais will tell of the 40-tonne trucks returning from the continent empty, picking up beer and moving it through Dover.

I am told by my hon. Friend the Member for Dover (Mr. Shaw) that there is a constant trail of Transits coming through the docks, often with three or four people, many of them saying, "This is for personal consumption"— which is quite all right, and I have no quarrel with that— "This is for my daughter's wedding," "This is for the great party we have promised ourselves for our 25th wedding anniversary," or whatever.

However, the ordinary member of the public sees vast quantities of wine, spirits, cigarettes and hand-rolling tobacco going through Dover docks unhindered, unchecked. That cannot be helpful for the image of customs officers, who are trying hard to do a good job in difficult circumstances.

I realise that many of the more sophisticated smugglers are checked up on and followed outside the docks to try to obtain a better picture of the distribution pattern, so that one is able to arrest those who are involved in smuggling on a much more serious and substantial scale. However, the image that the public have of the acceptability of vast quantities of tobacco and alcohol coming in unchecked, which most people suspect will be sold on, one way or another, greatly damages the role and authority of customs.

We also have, as an extension of the way round the controls, the current controversy on tobacco by post from companies based outside the United Kingdom. We expect a pronouncement on that case on Friday. I suspect that, whichever way that pronouncement goes—I know that the Government and the European Commission agree that tobacco by post should be opposed—any judgment will be pursued much further up the line for final decision.

Whichever way that goes, if there is any loophole by which tobacco and alcohol can be sold direct to the customer by post, one suspects—indeed knows—that the large tobacco and alcohol companies will feel that they must join in. It is not only cheeky young entrepreneurs who will feel that they can get away with it. The larger companies will go down the same route, to protect themselves. That reduces the single market, and the policy of high taxation, to farce.

The tobacco subsidies paid by the European Commission to farmers in several countries in the European Union are also farcical. In 1994, nearly £1 billion was paid in subsidies. We do know that many jobs depend on the continuing farming of tobacco, and the

*[Mrs. Jacqui Lait]*

Spanish embassy tells me that, in Spain alone, more than 800,000 people are engaged in tobacco farming. Equally, I welcome the fact that there is no longer any intervention provision for tobacco in the European Union, and that subsidies are no longer available for destroying unusable and unwanted tobacco.

I ask my hon. Friend the Paymaster General to urge on the Agriculture Ministers a reform of the common agricultural policy to end those subsidies, and perhaps to use that money to help farmers to adjust to producing new products that are so new that they may not already receive CAP subsidies. We can then start to change the CAP and bring it closer to the market. What better way to start than by abolishing tobacco farming?

I have outlined the problems. It is always easy to produce problems, but I also want to offer a few solutions. I am sure that they will not be new to my hon. Friend.

The few solutions that I produce are, of course, not the only ones. The parliamentary beer group is investigating the issue, and doubtless will come up with further solutions. I know that many other organisations and groups are seeking how best to amend the rules and regulations to end this unfortunate trade.

I have said that, in my opinion, prevention is not cost-effective. Having said that, in the short run there is nothing else that we can do but continue to use it, and make it more cost-effective.

I urge on my hon. Friend the thought that it should be made more obvious to the general public that, if one indulges in illegal importation, there is a much greater chance that one will be caught for small amounts. Larger smugglers should have much higher-profile prosecutions, so that the national papers carry more than an inch of coverage of the outcome of the case.

I would, in the longer term, draw parallels with what happened in the 18th century. Smuggling died away only after Sir Robert Peel, Disraeli and Gladstone reduced the duties. I fear that, in principle, we must go down that route. We have built a new and lucrative smuggling trade and it is up to us to dismantle it. It is obviously difficult because there are cultural and taxation differences, and Spain, France, Portugal and Belgium will see no need to increase their duties.

However, I want the health lobby to become much more proactive in urging its opposite numbers on the continent to go down the route of a high taxation policy. I was pleased to notice that Action on Smoking and Health suggested precisely that. It must persuade not only its counterparts but the other lobbies in this country to do so. The Department of Health should also raise the profile of the issue on the continent, so that it becomes much more politically and culturally acceptable for tobacco and alcohol duty to increase.

We must ensure that the European Commission does its work. I understand that we continue to await proposals from the Commission for ways to tackle the problem, and I hope that my hon. Friend the Paymaster General will be able to give me some positive news of what is happening in that regard.

Only when national Governments act together to work out a solution which takes the profit out of smuggling will we be able to solve the problem. It is not an entirely British one, because other countries also need to face the reality of the threat to health that we have faced for so long and to work together to try to solve the smuggling problem.

In the coming Budget, I hope that the Treasury will no longer continue to use excise duty as the milch cow to solve all its revenue problems. Even the Institute for Fiscal Studies is changing its mind and beginning to realise that, apart from beer duty, no increase in revenue would be obtained by an increase in excise duty. It was not quite so firm about that a few months ago.

We must, please, ensure that we change our mindset, as I have urged the health lobby to do, in terms of the revenue that comes from tobacco and alcohol. We must move towards a system where the profit is taken out of smuggling and we get rid of that lucrative but distressing trade.

**1.50 pm**

**The Paymaster General (Mr. David Heathcoat-Amory):** My hon. Friend the Member for Hastings and Rye (Mrs. Lait) has taken a close interest in this subject. She has been active in trying to protect the legitimate interests of her constituents, and of the alcohol and tobacco trade more generally, for at least as long as she has been a Member of the House. She has shown by her speech that she knows a great deal about the subject.

I am sure that my hon. Friend will agree that the single market in Europe has brought great benefits to the British economy. The abolition of routine frontier controls has led to administrative savings, and also brought about greater freedoms of movement for goods and people. It has also created problems, or highlighted existing ones, particularly connected with cross-border shopping and the smuggling of excise duty goods.

It is important to distinguish between commercial imports, which are taxed at United Kingdom rates in the normal way; legitimate cross-border shopping, where private individuals bring back goods for their own use and consumption; and those who illegally abuse cross-border shopping—what we call bootlegging or smuggling. We are most anxious to do something about that last category.

My hon. Friend mentioned the differences in the estimates given by the trade, Customs and Excise and other bodies when trying to assess the amount of revenue lost through cross-border shopping or smuggling. It is a statistical minefield, but I am glad to say that considerable progress is being made in reconciling the differences, which are frequently due to differences of definition rather than differences in the underlying data. We hope to publish that work later in the summer.

It is important to recognise that the duty receipts from tobacco and alcohol are holding up quite well, but I concede that, although our duty receipts are firm, some individual traders can be seriously hit. They represent one of the direct effects of smuggling described so well by my hon. Friend. I do not wish to be complacent about the difficulties faced by some parts of the trade.

As for smuggling, we have to be clear that the goods in question are not brought back into this country for personal consumption, but are sold on. That is a crime, which we take seriously.

My hon. Friend made a fair point about the health effects of smuggling. Certainly, higher tobacco prices have helped to reduce consumption, which has had a good effect on the nation's health. Perhaps we should be alert to a secondary effect of the pricing, because, if tobacco is bought cheaply from abroad or smuggled in and sold in uncontrolled outlets, that may have an opposite effect on health, particularly if that tobacco is hand-rolling tobacco, which tends to be stronger.

My hon. Friend also raised an important point about the CAP tobacco regime. It is one of the dottier features of the European Union that substantial amounts of European taxpayers' money is used to subsidise the production of tobacco, which tends to be of a particularly harmful type, while the Commission at the same time is concerned about health and lung cancer. The tobacco regime currently costs about £940 million a year. I am advised that tobacco is the most heavily subsidised crop per hectare in Europe, and receives a subsidy more than 20 times that for cereals. That regime is to be reconsidered in 1996, when the Government will press for its reform.

As for our own responsibilities in countering smuggling, I wish to emphasise to my hon. Friend—I think that she knows it, but I should like to put it on the record—that we take our task extremely seriously. To that end, excise verification officers, or EVOs, have been appointed to carry out visits, particularly inland, to pubs, clubs, markets, restaurants and so on to check for smuggled alcohol or tobacco that perhaps is being resold. Those EVOs work closely with the police and local trading standards officers.

There are about 250 single market excise officers, and during the financial year 1994-95 they made nearly 3,000 detections, including goods with a revenue value of just over £6 million. They have so far successfully prosecuted 466 people, and prison sentences of up to 27 months and fines of up to £10,000 have been imposed. So far, 717 vehicles engaged in such activities have been seized. The goods intercepted are also seized. Civil penalties are available for less serious offences, but more serious ones are taken through the criminal courts.

A successful 24-hour hot line has also been launched, so that people can give information in confidence to Customs and Excise. My hon. Friend mentioned people who are aware of smuggling, and I hope that they, whether ordinary members of the public or in the trade, will not hesitate to give information in confidence to Customs and Excise via that hot line number, which has been widely advertised.

We are aware, of course, that it is the duty differential between this country and the continent which provides the incentive for much of the cross-border shopping and smuggling. We would welcome moves towards greater approximation with other member states, but we must be realistic and recognise that that will be a slow process, because those member states take different positions on that.

A radical and immediate fall in our higher duty rates would be extremely expensive. For example, it would cost some £6.5 billion per year to reduce our tobacco and alcohol rates to French levels. I think that my hon. Friend would agree that that is unrealistic in present fiscal circumstances.

We are fully aware of the difficulties, and we are determined to do all we can to crack down on the illegal and anti-social smuggling of tobacco and alcohol products that undermines the legitimate trade which my hon. Friend has done so much to support.

# York Carriageworks

1.59 pm

**Mr. Hugh Bayley** (York): The news that broke today that neither ABB nor GEC Alsthom will be submitting bids to build the next tranche of Networker trains for London commuters is the latest twist in the long and sorry saga of the sacrifice of Britain's manufacturing industry on the altar of rail privatisation. The Minister knows from the debate that we had on this subject a week ago that York feels betrayed by the unnecessary closure of the York carriageworks. ABB, which owns the works, feels betrayed because it invested £50 million against Department of Transport expectations that a large number of new commuter trains would be needed. As a result of today's announcement, Kent commuters will feel betrayed because they were promised that they would continue to receive new trains after the first 16 are delivered this autumn—they are being built at York—until all 800 antiquated vehicles in the Kent Coast fleet are replaced. That will not occur now because neither ABB nor its competitor GEC is prepared to submit a tender under the terms that the British Railways Board and the Government have laid down in the tender documents.

Since December last year when British Rail announced, to everyone's surprise, that it could see no business case for ordering new trains for the Kent Coast line, the Government have engaged in a cynical exercise to convince the public that rail privatisation is not the cause of the problem, but that the fault lies with British Rail for dragging its feet and with ABB for failing to submit competitive bids. Last week the Minister told the House that he had been pressing for an order in recent months. He said:

"I hope that the hon. Member for York will be generous enough to acknowledge that I have not been an entirely passive observer of those events".—[*Official Report*, 17 May 1995; Vol. 260, c. 385.]

I acknowledged that fact and perhaps I was mistaken in doing so. In time-honoured fashion, this morning I received, anonymously, a draft of a letter that I believe was sent yesterday to the Minister by the director of the Railway Industry Association. In it, the director, Mr. Gillan, says:

"In the light of the current dearth of orders for rolling stock and in particular of the recent announcement by ABB to close their York works you may be surprised at the decision of our two members not to bid for this much needed order.

However, the simple fact is that the terms under which bids have been invited are so unreasonable as to effectively preclude the making of compliant bids.

In particular the requirement that the train leasing period could be for a maximum of seven years, with no assurances as to the likely usage of the trains for the rest of their working lives of up to 40 years, meant that no one could reasonably have been expected to bid. Indeed such are the terms that we are left to wonder what the point of the exercise was."

Similar comments were made in the statement that ABB communicated to employees at the York factory yesterday. It said:

"Of particular concern is the duration of the lease where the Customer is unable to guarantee a lease period beyond the year 2004. This coupled with the uncertainty surrounding the forthcoming privatisation of the Rolling Stock Leasing Companies . . . and the future leasing market, means that we are unable to guarantee recovering our capital build costs, and it is clearly not good business sense to undertake orders on this basis."

I support the use of private finance to build rolling stock. Indeed, it was my right hon. Friend the Member for Kingston upon Hull, East (Mr. Prescott) who first proposed leasing as a means of providing finance for new rolling stock. The latest developments revealed in the correspondence that I have just read to the House show that the Government's private finance initiative has been hijacked by the Treasury and turned into an excuse for cutting public investment, while at the same time preventing private investment in public services.

One has only to look at the Department of Transport's two most recent annual reports to see the scale of the squeeze on public resources that are available to the railway. Last year's departmental expenditure plans anticipated a cut of £292 million in the external financing limit for the railways. As a result of the Chancellor's statement last November, the funding gap has increased. That is recorded in this year's departmental expenditure plans, which show that the cut has been increased to £424 million for the railways this year.

That would not matter if the private finance initiative was making up the difference, but it is not. That is the cause of the problem: the private finance initiative should be freed from the Treasury's shackles. What is the Department doing about that? I also repeat a question that I asked in the debate last Wednesday but to which I did not receive an answer. How will the Government respond to ABB's statement that the only way to save the York works is to agree to a follow-on order for more trains of the type that it is building at the moment, which are the trains that were specified and ordered for the Kent Coast line? That is the only way to save the York works from closure and it is the only way that the Government can fulfil their promise to Kent commuters to provide the new trains that they need so desperately.

The response in York to the closure announcement of less than a fortnight ago has been immediate and involves a wide range of agencies. The city council, North Yorkshire training and enterprise council and ABB have pledged large sums of money to try to deal with the immediate problems. But the scale of those problems is enormous. The Government have created the hiatus in investment that they said would not result from rail privatisation. That has occurred and now the Government must help the local elected authority and other local agencies to find a solution. The problem needs a multi-departmental response from the Government.

I have a number of questions, some of which are directed to the Department of Transport, and I hope that the Minister will answer them today; others are addressed to other Government Departments. I hope that the Minister will undertake to refer those questions to the appropriate Ministers so that I may receive a response.

When the Railways Bill came before the House, York city council commissioned Steer, Davis, Gleave, a firm of transport consultants, to produce a report estimating the impact of rail privatisation on rail employment in York. It anticipated very substantial job losses. At the time, the right hon. Member for Kettering (Mr. Freeman), the then Minister of State, disputed the figures. He said that York was running scared and he agreed to establish the York Rail Forum, which he attended on a number of occasions, together with representatives of the local business community and elected representatives of all parties from the York area.

Since the present Minister was appointed, there has been one meeting of the York Rail Forum. We urgently need to hold another meeting, which the Minister will attend, to address the problems. I hope that the Minister will agree to invite a representative from the Government's Yorkshire and Humberside office so that we receive a response on a genuinely cross-departmental basis.

In 1992, when the House was considering the Railways Bill 4,690 people were employed by the railways in York—3,090 by British Rail and 1,600 by the carriageworks owned by ABB. By the end of last year, that figure had fallen by 1,190 to 2,750 employed by British Rail and 750 at the York works. If the works close, by the end of this year the figure will have fallen to about 2,500, taking account of the British Rail jobs that have already been declared redundant this year.

York is highly dependent on the rail industry. At the start of the process, about one job in 12 in the city was a railway job. What will the Department do to ensure that some of the new railway agencies created as part of the privatisation process are relocated in York, so that the jobs that have been lost will be replaced by other railway jobs? Will he consider the possibility of the Department of Transport moving some of its own jobs to the city of York? Other Government Departments—the Department for Education, the Land Registry, the Crown Prosecution Service and the Ministry of Agriculture, Fisheries and Food—have done so because of its central location and its good communications and because it is a sensible place to base public servants.

York, through its own efforts, has attracted a considerable amount of inward investment and jobs in the past few years. The city council opened a one-stop business advice shop in 1986, well before the Government's business links ideas, and its partnership for prosperity campaign, which it runs jointly with the chamber of commerce, has attracted some 2,000 new jobs to York since 1989. In addition to the jobs from Government agencies, investment came from Nestlé, which has invested £150 million in its York factory, from ABB, which has invested £50 million, from General Accident, which has invested £15 million and from the Shepherd Building Group, which is building its new corporate headquarters in the city. Other companies, such as Smith and Nephew and Samsung, have opened major centres of employment in the York area—Samsung has opened a factory and Smith and Nephew has opened a research centre. The College of Law has opened a new campus in the city of York.

That success must be set against a background of massive job losses in York's traditional industries. Between 1992—when rail privatisation started—and 1995, unemployment nationally has fallen by 13 per cent. In York, during the same period, it has increased by 5 per cent. In 1992, unemployment in York was below the national average: now it is above the national average—8.5 per cent., according to the Government's benefit count, and 12.1 per cent. according to their labour force survey.

The York economy also has structural problems. The loss of manufacturing jobs has been more than twice as fast in York than the national average, and so too has the loss of jobs in construction. York is now more dependent on part-time jobs than the national average. In Great Britain as a whole in 1991, 26 per cent. of the work force was part time—roughly one in four. In York, the figure was 32.1 per cent. Almost a third of the jobs that remain in York are now part time.

We need assistance from the Government, both to rebuild and to restructure the local economy. We need Government Departments to work together and not to pull in different directions. The regional allocation for the training for work scheme does not allow resources to be diverted to the city of York because of our present problems. North Yorkshire training and enterprise council therefore gets no additional resources as a result of the ABB closure. That is a matter on which the Department of Employment could act to make changes and I hope that it will.

York does not have assisted area status, although the areas that are in receipt of the benefits of assisted area status are being reviewed. I hope that the Government will look favourably on including York as an assisted area as a result of the current review. We are eligible for support under the Government's single regeneration budget. I hope that that support will be forthcoming, although the city council has a particular problem in putting together an application, because the outline applications have to be in by next month.

We could get help from the Department of the Environment, through English partnerships, to generate new uses for redundant railway land, not just ABB land but other land around York station. The Department of the Environment should reflect York's pressing needs in its standard spending assessment for future years. At the moment, the city of York is not eligible for EU objective 2 funds, the criteria for which include the following reference. They are for areas

"which have recorded substantial job losses over the last three years or are experiencing or are threatened with such losses in industrial sectors of decisive importance for their economic development, including those losses brought about by industrial changes and changes in production systems, with a consequent serious worsening of unemployment in those areas."

All those factors are reflected in York's current need for jobs in view of the dramatic and unnecessary decline that we face in manufacturing. I hope that the Government will support York's bid for objective 2 status.

Part of the job losses in the area are a result of the "Options for Change" downsizing of the armed forces. We have lost 230 pay corps jobs at Imphal barracks. We have seen the closure of the Royal Electrical and Mechanical Engineers workshop at Strensall and the engineering park at Hessay, on the outskirts of York. The Government have been allocated £74 million by the European Union under the KONVER programme and they will announce later this year how that money is to be split between local areas. I hope that the overall employment situation in York will mean that a fair share of resources come to York, because it will be that much harder for redundant MOD employees to find replacement jobs.

The Department of Trade and Industry must work with York city council and the Yorkshire and Humberside development association to direct overseas investment to York. The Government have a key role to play in identifying leads for people locally to follow up and in influencing decisions. If the York works close, for all the wrong reasons 400,000 sq ft of newly refurbished industrial premises and new offices will come on the market at the same time as 750 skilled engineering

[Mr. Hugh Bayley]

workers. That provides an opportunity for the Government to help the city of York locally to pick up the pieces from the closure by marketing the opportunity of premises and skilled workers. The DTI should play an active part with the local authority and the company, of course, in marketing the site.

York is a great city. It is facing enormous economic problems at the moment. It is doing a great deal to help itself, but it needs help from the Government, because the scale of the problems is so great. I must ask the Minister: will the Government step away from their laissez-faire attitude, because they have, particularly on railways and defence, precipitated those job losses and they must work with the local agencies to help the city of York to replace them?

2.19 pm

**The Minister for Railways and Roads (Mr. John Watts):** The hon. Member for York (Mr. Bayley) was right to secure this further debate on the York carriageworks, although both he and I regret the need for it. I acknowledge his efforts and those of my hon. Friend the Member for Ryedale (Mr. Greenway) and my right hon. Friend the Member for Selby (Mr. Alison) on behalf of York and ABB's employees. I know that they have campaigned hard to avert the closure and that last week's announcement was a great disappointment.

ABB's decision is very sad news for the work force and the city of York. I recognise the proud railway tradition in the city and the importance of rail engineering to the local economy. The hon. Gentleman and I disagree fundamentally about railway privatisation but we can certainly agree on what a blow the redundancies are.

The closure of the York works is a commercial decision by ABB. It reflects the company's need to rationalise its sites following the completion of major contracts for Central line trains and Eurotrams, the failure to win recent orders for Jubilee line, Northern line and Heathrow express trains, and a cyclical fall in orders following the peak of investment in the late 1980s and early 1990s.

The fact is that the company does not have sufficient work to keep open all three of its present works. Nor, with the recent exception of the Eurotrams order, has it been able to attract sufficient export orders for York to supplement domestic orders won in a very competitive market.

I understand that the company could not justify retaining all its plants when either the York or Derby plant is likely to have sufficient capacity to meet forecast demand for new trains. The scale of surplus capacity is such that the company considers that one plant can accommodate all likely opportunities.

In the late 1980s, British Rail benefited from the boom conditions affecting the London economy. Central London employment levels and high personal disposable incomes helped to drive up Network SouthEast's revenues in real terms by more than 10 per cent. between 1986-87 and 1989-90.

British Rail's projections then of the need for new Networkers were made in good faith but were blown off course by the recession. In 1990-91, it was evident that the boom was ending and there followed three consecutive years in which revenues fell in real terms.

Commuting into central London fell by 20 per cent. and was to reach a 20-year low in 1993-94; only recently have there been signs that the tide may have turned. That is the background to the lower than expected orders for new Networker trains.

No manufacturer can expect the right to supply what it wants to supply when it wants to supply it, regardless of the customer's requirements. ABB must compete for whatever contracts are available in the marketplace. Part of ABB's problem is that it has failed to win enough of the orders in the marketplace to secure the work that it needs.

Faced with that situation, the company decided to concentrate its efforts in Derby where it has its headquarters. ABB's announcement emphasised that it was still very much in the United Kingdom train building business, and that it would compete aggressively for orders at home and abroad. It retains the capacity to build new trains when demand increases and it can win orders. Orders still under construction by ABB consist of the current £150 million Networker order for BR, and a £60 million contract for mail trains for the Post Office.

As the hon. Gentleman knows, in recognition of the United Kingdom industry's position, BR issued invitations to tender for a further tranche of Networker trains in March. That decision provided the opportunity for manufacturers to make competitive bids that meet the criteria of the private finance initiative. An opportunity to tender was created, but it was up to manufacturers to take advantage of it. One can lead a horse to water but one cannot make it drink.

The hon. Gentleman questioned whether the private finance initiative can work. I must refer him to the successful conclusion of the £400 million contract for the supply of trains for the Northern line. That was the private finance initiative in action, and it worked.

The hon. Gentleman also referred to the basis on which bidders were invited to tender. It was a demanding specification for a substantial transfer of risk, but bidders who put in a compliant bid were also able to propose alternative packages, particularly with regard to the length of lease, and so on, if they wished to do so. They could also have sought undertakings from the franchising director to underwrite the continued use of trains under such leasing arrangements under the provisions of the Railways Act 1993.

The hon. Gentleman pressed me again to direct BR to reopen the option attached to the existing contract. I understand that the extension to June of the follow-up option was offered unilaterally by ABB and accepted by the British Railways Board without any commitment. I can understand why the hon. Gentleman makes that request again but it would not be appropriate for me to direct BR in that way. It must be a matter for BR's commercial judgment as to when and on what terms it procures rolling stock.

The present £150 million leasing deal was a transitional measure which it was recognised at the time did not meet the full requirements of the private finance initiative. In particular, the residual value risk transferred fell well short of private finance initiative requirements. In addition, as the hon. Gentleman knows, BR concluded earlier this year that there was no commercial justification for the immediate placing of an order for replacement of the Kent Coast fleet, at least if the contractual terms on offer were no different from and no better than those under which the earlier £150 million leasing deal had been concluded.

It has been suggested that changes to the vehicle specification in the present tender invitation would have extended the time scale for completing the tenders or constructing the trains, but that is not the case either.

The recent invitation to tender was based firmly on the specification of the existing Networker express trains under construction by ABB, and it attached a premium to proven designs. It was open to bidders, at their own choice, to offer variations to that specification if they believed a better or cheaper train could thereby be produced.

During the debate on rail services last Wednesday I said in reply to the hon. Gentleman that I would discuss with my ministerial colleagues in the relevant Departments the need to address employment problems in York. In addition, I shall consider further the suggestions made today and I shall write to the hon. Gentleman and to my right hon. Friend the Member for Selby and my hon. Friend the Member for Ryedale in due course. The day after the debate I wrote to my colleagues in other Departments. In addition, my Department is liaising with the Government office for Yorkshire and Humberside and with the Employment Service.

For some time the local office of the Employment Service and North Yorkshire training and enterprise council have been in close contact with ABB and other agencies. I understand that the Employment Service and the TEC have since recognised that this is a large-scale redundancy and therefore eligibility can be relaxed for Employment Service programmes and training for work. They stand ready to give the maximum possible assistance to all those who will be affected by the job losses. That assistance will supplement the help that ABB, the TEC and York city council are providing.

As regards the single regeneration budget, I understand that the Government office for Yorkshire and Humberside has already shown its willingness to discuss any proposals which the partners in York may have, at the earliest possible stage.

I assure the hon. Gentleman that I shall continue to take a close interest, with my colleagues in other Departments, in the ways in which we can, across Departments, help the city of York to tackle the problems that have arisen from these most unwelcome redundancies. I assure him that he will not see a laissez-faire reaction from the Government on the issue.

**Mr. Bayley:** Will the Minister say whether he would attend an urgent meeting of the York Rail Forum and whether the Government are willing to allow a representative from the Government office for Yorkshire and Humberside to attend?

**Mr. Watts:** I would certainly be willing to attend a meeting of the York Rail Forum. The attendance of someone from the Government office is not directly a matter for me. I will certainly put that, with the hon. Gentleman's other suggestions, to my colleagues in the relevant Departments.

2.28 pm
*Sitting suspended.*

2.30 pm
*On resuming—*
*It being half past Two o'clock, the motion for the Adjournment of the House lapsed, pursuant to Order [19 December].*

### PRIVATE BUSINESS

ACCOMMODATION LEVEL CROSSINGS BILL *[Lords]*
*Order for Third Reading read.*
*To be read the Third time on Thursday 25 May.*

# Oral Answers to Questions

## SCOTLAND

### Whisky Industry

1. **Mrs. Ewing:** To ask the Secretary of State for Scotland what is the total number of people employed in the Scotch whisky industry currently; and how many were employed in 1990.                                    [24221]

**The Parliamentary Under-Secretary of State for Scotland (Mr. George Kynoch):** The Scotch Whisky Association, in its latest annual review, states that 13,804 people in 1994 were employed by its member companies in the Scottish whisky industry, compared with 16,376 in 1990.

**Mrs. Ewing:** Will the Minister confirm that the figures that he has just given are taken from the Scottish register of employment, which takes no account of establishments that employ 11 or fewer employees? In that context, does he accept that the rise in the excise duty on Scotch whisky since the Government came to power has been about 30 per cent. and that the decline in the home market has sent out the wrong message to foreign markets? Does he therefore agree that we have to take tender steps to ensure that the Scotch whisky industry is protected and that there will be no further mothballing as there has been at Tamnavulin, Tullibardine and Bruichladdich?

**Mr. Kynoch:** I think that the hon. Lady was, unfortunately, not listening to my reply. I said clearly that the Scotch Whisky Association gave those figures in its latest annual review. They were not from the source to which she referred. The hon. Lady might also be aware of the fact that, in the past 10 years, the real rate of duty on spirits has fallen by some 16 per cent. in real terms. I think that she is giving a slightly distorted story. In the industry in general, since 1980, exports have gone up from £746 million in 1980 to over £2 billion in 1994. I believe that the industry is attacking its markets very aggressively and successfully.

**Mr. Bill Walker:** Does my hon. Friend agree that it is not the Government's job to second-guess the Scotch whisky industry on how it should run its business but that it most certainly is the Government's job to create a tax environment at home, and to influence the tax environment in Europe, to enable the Scotch whisky industry to continue to be Scotland's greatest exporter, excluding oil and gas? That will continue, provided that we have a tax regime that encourages the industry to expand and not to contract.

**Mr. Kynoch:** My hon. Friend is right. It is not the Government's job to intervene in production scheduling in the industry. With regard to taxation, I am sure that my hon. Friend is aware that my right hon. and learned Friend the Chancellor of the Exchequer, in a speech in the House on 13 December last year, said that he was very sympathetic to the case for removing distortion of the duties charged on, for example, wine as opposed to spirits and to maintaining a freeze on alcohol duties for the benefit of the Scotch whisky industry. He reaffirmed his intention to continue along the road to revising duty differentials following the increase in the 1994 Budget that he had forced upon him by some hon. Members.

**Mr. McKelvey:** Is the Minister aware that Saturday the 27th of this month marks the quincentennial celebration of the discovery or the invention of Scotch whisky? To assist the Scotch whisky industry with all its magnificent efforts in exports, the Government should remind the Chancellor that he put the 25p après-Budget additional tax on whisky in a fit of pique because the House democratically voted not to allow him to put the second tranche of VAT on fuel.

**Mr. Kynoch:** I am glad that the hon. Gentleman referred to the 27th of this month because I gather that there will be an open day at many distilleries, and that the hon. Gentleman will be leading the visitations to some of them. He referred to taxation and to what the Chancellor had to do in his second run at the Budget. What he had to do was something that the Labour party is totally incapable of doing—balance the Budget. The Labour party has proposals for a tax-raising Scottish Parliament, which would mean that it would have to address the problem of balancing the Budget. If it could say clearly to Scottish business and to the Scottish people that they would definitely not face a taxation increase, the hon. Gentleman might address taxation issues in a more responsible manner.

### Electricity and Gas Industries

2. **Mr. Ingram:** To ask the Secretary of State for Scotland if he will give the numbers of jobs lost in Scotland in (a) the electricity supply industry and (b) the gas industry since privatisation; and if he will make a statement.                                    [24223]

**The Secretary of State for Scotland (Mr. Ian Lang):** It is a matter for the private utility companies to structure their organisations and working practices in a way that best meets consumer and commercial interests.

**Mr. Ingram:** What the Secretary of State has not told us is that many hundreds of jobs have been lost as a result of the privatisation of the electricity and gas industries. If the Secretary of State had given those figures, they would have proven sufficient reason for those currently employed at Scottish Nuclear to fear its privatisation. Will the Secretary of State give one simple guarantee to the work force based at the headquarters of Scottish Nuclear in East Kilbride? Will he give them the same guarantee of a minimum of 10 years' future employment as has been given to the staff of the new corporate headquarters?

**Mr. Lang:** I think that the hon. Gentleman is already well aware that, as a result of the Government's proposals for the future of the nuclear electricity generating industry, there will be a net increase in jobs in Scotland arising from the various head office functions coming to Scotland. The nuclear industry, like the rest of the electricity industry, has, of course, been rationalising itself to get costs down, to be competitive and to be efficient. The benefit of that to the Scottish economy is considerable. Scottish Hydro-Electric has been increasing jobs, with a net increase of 94 jobs, which is so important in the Perthshire economy. For the rest of the industry, there has been a 120,000 net increase in employment over the past 10 years. That is the product of a more efficient economy, to which lower energy prices contribute.

**Mrs. Lait:** Will my right hon. Friend confirm that Scottish Nuclear was set up, after electricity privatisation, in the constituency of the hon. Member for East Kilbride (Mr. Ingram)? Is not it ungracious of him to complain when additional, high-tech engineering jobs will come into Scottish Nuclear after it, too, is privatised?

**Mr. Lang:** My hon. Friend is absolutely right. It is not just a matter of jobs coming into Scottish Nuclear the nuclear electricity industry—in East Kilbride. It is the fact that a substantial number of new jobs in other industries are coming in. Unemployment in the constituency of the hon. Member for East Kilbride (Mr. Ingram) has fallen by 18 per cent. in the past year alone.

**Mr. Wilson:** Will the Secretary of State accept that the appointment of a two-day-a-week Tory, who is paid £100,000 and who continues to live in Surrey, is one job that we could all very well do without? Will he accept that, in my constituency, that is not accepted as any sort of substitute for the strong, successful public sector company that Scottish Nuclear is?

**Mr. Lang:** Under the Labour party, the Scottish nuclear industry would have disappeared with the loss of all jobs and of a major technology. We have given a future for that company and that industry which is full of promise and the prospect of growth and expansion—under a business leader of considerable distinction whose politics I know not but who, I am certain, will act as a very fine chairman of the industry.

### Monklands Hospital Trust

3. **Mr. Tom Clarke:** To ask the Secretary of State for Scotland when he next intends to visit Monklands hospital trust; and if he will make a statement.        [24224]

**The Parliamentary Under-Secretary of State for Scotland (Lord James Douglas-Hamilton):** My right hon. Friend has no immediate plans to visit the Monklands and Bellshill hospitals NHS trust. However, my right hon. and learned Friend the Minister of State meets the chairmen of trusts regularly, when a range of issues are discussed.

**Mr. Clarke:** Does the Minister agree that the national health service staff in Monklands should continue to consider themselves as such, employed by a national health service trust and enjoying national terms and conditions within the national health service? Alternatively, are the Government planning to privatise such services in Monklands and elsewhere in Scotland, as they already plan to do at Stonehaven? Does the Minister agree that national health service Scotland funding should be on the basis of the British Government making resources available, based on national negotiations, and should not exploit people who offer themselves for employment in poor areas with great health problems? Finally, does the Minister accept that from Coatbridge to Kinross and from Perth to Peebles, people want the national health service that we once enjoyed, and that is being slowly destroyed by the present Government?

**Lord James Douglas-Hamilton:** Some £4,000 million is being made available to the NHS in Scotland this year.

That is a record figure, constituting an increase of £143 million. The hon. Gentleman will also be encouraged to learn that the new chairman of Monklands NHS trust is Mr. David Millan, the well-known former chief executive of Cumbernauld development corporation.

I endorse what the hon. Member for Hamilton (Mr. Robertson) said in January:

"We are not opposed to public/private partnerships—they bring in much needed money for the NHS".

The test must be the provision of a better standard of care for NHS patients. I can confirm that, with private sector involvement, as with all NHS projects, NHS providers will be asked to seek private finance to design, build and service any new facilities.

The hon. Gentleman will be glad to learn that Monklands and Bellshill NHS hospitals trust has made an offer of 3 per cent., subject to certain conditions.

### Rural Roads

4. **Mrs. Ray Michie:** To ask the Secretary of State for Scotland what representations he has received on the detrunking of roads in rural areas of Scotland.        [24225]

**The Parliamentary Under-Secretary of State for Scotland (Sir Hector Monro):** My right hon. Friend has received a number of representations on the detrunking of roads in rural Scotland, particularly in response to the recent consultation exercise "Shaping the Trunk Road Network". The Government's response was published on 27 April.

**Mrs. Michie:** Has not the Minister rejected many of the representations made to him about roads in rural Scotland—in particular, those from Argyll and Bute and from Strathclyde—concerning the determination to detrunk the road between Lochgilphead and Ballachuilish? The road serves the requirements set out in the Minister's document for the trunk road network relating to industry, commerce, agriculture and tourism. Will he assure us that the new Argyll and Bute council will have the funds that are required to maintain the road and to build along the long-awaited and long-promised Creagan bridge?

**Sir Hector Monro:** The hon. Lady has raised a number of points. The Creagan bridge project is still under consideration. Naturally, I expect the new council to have adequate funds to fulfil its responsibilities—bearing in mind the Government's position at the time in relation to the block grant.

The hon. Lady mentioned the detrunking of a certain road in her constituency, particularly between Campbeltown and Ballachuilish. The main road from Lochgilphead is trunked to the national network, as are the roads to Oban and Fort William. We believe that the road linking those three towns independently should be the responsibility of the local authority. Councils are always wanting further responsibility, and this is a very good chance for them to undertake it.

**Mr. Gallie:** I welcome the Government's response to the most recent consultation paper on the trunk road system. I am especially pleased that, for the first time, the A70 southern route to the A74/M74 is shown as a real possibility. What progress has been made by the "access to Ayrshire" group, which is considering the matter? Will my hon. Friend also comment on the progress currently being made on the upgrading of the A77 to motorway standard?

**Sir Hector Monro:** I assure my hon. Friend that we shall never forget the roads in Ayrshire while he is such an effective Member of Parliament for the Ayr constituency. Naturally, we are continuing the consultations on a link road to the M74. That will be an important decision when it comes, as will be the decision on further progress in upgrading the road from Glasgow to Ayrshire.

### Scottish Homes Rents

5. **Sir David Steel:** To ask the Secretary of State for Scotland if he will make a statement on the increase in Scottish Homes rents in the borders; and for what reasons this increase is greater than the current notional rate of inflation indicated in the Government's guidelines. [24226]

**Lord James Douglas-Hamilton:** In December 1994, the Scottish Homes board decided to increase its rents for 1995-96 throughout Scotland by an average of 4.2 per cent., but actual increases will vary in accordance with size, type and situation of house. Increases on this basis were applied to its stock in the borders as well as its stock in other parts of the country. It is for Scottish Homes to review rents, taking into consideration the resources required to manage and maintain its housing stock.

**Sir David Steel:** How can the Minister possibly justify rent increases in the public sector of almost 5 per cent. in my constituency when the Government are trying to hold down wage claims and offering nurses in my constituency an increase of 2.5 per cent.? Surely there must be some consistency in Government policy, or are we to await the arrival of the right hon. Member for Stirling (Mr. Forsyth) for a change of policy?

**Lord James Douglas-Hamilton:** As the right hon. Gentleman knows, housing benefit to the extent of £900 million is being made payable this year to those tenants who need assistance. The actual average increase in rents in Scotland is 28.78p per week, which is certainly well below the English figure, which is almost £10 more per week. The real reason is that, if the relevant housing association wishes to spend sufficient funds on management and maintenance, it will put up rents accordingly. It is for the Scottish Homes board to decide what the level of rents should be for Scottish Homes stock. No direction is given by Ministers.

### Rail Sleeper Services

6. **Mr. Tyler:** To ask the Secretary of State for Scotland what are the implications for the Scottish economy of the decisions taken to date on the continuation of rail sleeper services from other parts of the United Kingdom. [24227]

10. **Mr. Galbraith:** To ask the Secretary of State for Scotland when he last met the directors of ScotRail to discuss rail closures. [24234]

**Mr. Lang:** Although responsibility for railway matters rests with my right hon. Friend the Secretary of State for Transport, I have been taking a close interest in these matters. My right hon. Friend and I agree that the Scottish economy will continue to derive substantial benefit from the continuation of rail sleeper services to and from Scotland and that such sleeper services remain important. I met the director of ScotRail on 28 March 1995. We discussed a wide range of matters relating to rail services in Scotland.

**Mr. Tyler:** If the Secretary of State has been taking such a close interest in the future of sleepers, will he consider the problem of the sleeper service between the west country and Scotland which, according to the timetable which we now have in our hands, is to disappear this weekend, yet which his colleagues in the Department of Transport have said carries 32,000 people a year, requires a minimal subsidy to maintain it and is of huge importance to the tourist industry at both ends of the line?

Can the Secretary of State explain why there has been minimum consultation with the tourist boards and why the economic effects of the closure have not been properly identified either by him or by his colleagues in the Department of Transport? Is it not a scandal that the service is to disappear this very weekend?

**Mr. Lang:** The hon. Gentleman will be aware that the subsidy on the Plymouth sleeper is about £44 per passenger per trip. That amounts to about £1.4 million per annum for a sleeper service that is roughly half occupied most of the time. However, he will be reassured to know that the London-Penzance sleeper is included in the public service requirement for the Great Western franchise.

**Mr. Galbraith:** The Secretary of State may have been taking a close interest in these matters, but he does not seem to be doing anything about them. Does he realise that not only the sleeper services but the overnight seating service to Scotland are being affected? Does he realise that there will be cuts in the west coast line, the highland line and the Kyle of Lochalsh line? Does he realise that privatisation means not only cuts but an increase in charges? When will he stand up for the railways and stop lying down in front of the privatisation express?

**Mr. Lang:** The hon. Gentleman will have the opportunity to put all those relevant points during the consultation process that is now in train. The hon. Gentleman talks about rising costs, but I have to point out that rail fares rose by 22 per cent. more than inflation in the past 10 years. As a result of the arrangements that are now being made for the future, they will fall in real terms in the years ahead.

**Mr. Macdonald:** Does the Secretary of State not realise that, unless he seizes the opportunity, which he now has, thanks to Highland regional council, to save and to develop the sleeper service to Fort William, he is really saying that he does not care if—

**Madam Speaker:** Order. I think that the hon. Gentleman and the House are aware that the hearing on this matter has been set down for 1 June. The matter is therefore sub judice. I just caution hon. Members as to the questions that they may put. Having given that caution, I will hear the hon. Gentleman.

**Mr. Macdonald:** Is the Secretary of State aware that the message that he must give to the people of Scotland is that, in transport terms, all parts of Scotland, including in particular regions such as the highlands and far north-west Scotland, must be connected on equal terms with the rest of the UK? If he does not send that message, he is saying that he does not care about the highlands' social and economic future.

**Mr. Lang:** I care very much about the social and economic future of the highlands, as of the rest of Scotland. That is why I warmly welcome the decrease in unemployment, which is continuing after a fall for three consecutive years, and the growth in new employment and economic activity throughout the highlands and the rest of Scotland. The hon. Gentleman will, of course, have the opportunity to make the points that he has raised in the consultation process, but the announcement by the director of franchising underlines, for the first time, the continuing guarantee attached to the vast and overwhelming majority of rail services in Scotland. They have never had that before.

**Mr. McFall:** In Perth and Kinross, the Prime Minister and the Secretary of State have been banging on about the integrity of the Union. Does the Secretary of State accept that the logic of that statement means that there should be adequate rail access to all parts of the UK, including the highlands? Recent decisions threaten both day and overnight services, tourism and the economic prosperity and livelihood of the inhabitants of the region. Does he agree with the Scottish people that, if the Prime Minister is sincere in his desire to listen to people, he will do so and immediately abandon the folly of rail privatisation in Scotland?

**Mr. Lang:** The hon. Gentleman seems to be completely unaware that the decline in the quality of this country's rail services began when they were nationalised. Nationalised ownership and the starvation of resources undermined the quality of rail services. We are now creating not only a basic guarantee of almost all existing services, but the opportunity for new investment, new commercial management and an improved commitment to the delivery of a quality service. That should lead to a service that is not only cheaper, but better.

### Hospital Wages and Service Provisions

7. **Mr. Foulkes:** To ask the Secretary of State for Scotland when he last met the chairs of NHS trusts in Scotland to discuss wages and service provision in Scottish hospitals. [24229]

**Lord James Douglas-Hamilton:** My noble and learned Friend the Minister of State last met NHS trust chairmen on 20 January 1995 to discuss a range of issues.

**Mr. Foulkes:** Will the Minister admit that his written answer to me yesterday shows that the Government's claim that nurses across Scotland would be offered 3 per cent. is entirely bogus? The truth is total chaos and disarray, with only eight of 47 trusts offering 3 per cent. without strings, and all the others seeking to reduce nurses' conditions of service by removing statutory holidays or making other changes? Will he now reintroduce collective bargaining on a national basis, and give all nurses the increase that they richly deserve— without strings and without delay?

**Lord James Douglas-Hamilton:** The answer is no, but the hon. Gentleman will be glad to hear that the three trusts in Ayrshire have said that they intend to offer 3 per cent., dependent on local negotiations. The great advantage of local negotiations is that local pay can be an important step towards making services more responsive to local needs. Local pay does not necessarily mean less pay; it means fair pay, taking local circumstances properly into account.

**Mr. Ernie Ross:** Once the actual pay round is settled, what evidence does the Minister have that national health

service trusts will take account of service provision? The model used by the Scottish Office to get rid of acute beds is under severe strain, particularly in Dundee. We were originally given assurances that Kings Cross hospital would be used as a back-up if the economic model for acute beds did not work out. We are now told that Dundee Teaching Hospitals NHS trust has considered closing that hospital. What evidence does the Minister have that NHS trusts have taken account of the fact that the economic model used by the Scottish Office to get rid of acute beds may not work?

**Lord James Douglas-Hamilton:** The principle is clear: no patient should be discharged from hospital unless there is a bed provided within the local community. Ministers are not entitled to play any part in clinical decisions which are necessarily matters for the health service. The hon. Gentleman will be pleased to see that Dundee Healthcare trust made an offer of 3 per cent. with conditions. The £143 million extra for the health service this year will provide considerable assistance towards settling these matters satisfactorily.

**Mr. George Robertson:** When the Minister last met the chairmen of the health trusts, did he express any shame about the fact that his Department is now pushing the NHS towards privatisation in Scotland? Is not the evidence for that seen in what is happening in Stonehaven today, where Grampian health board is being obliged by the Scottish Office to offer any or all hospital services or even the entire new hospital to the private profit-making sector? When the Prime Minister told the Tory party conference in 1991 that there would be

"no . . . privatisation of health care, neither piecemeal, nor in part, nor as a whole",

people listened to him. Now, they will concentrate on what is happening in Stonehaven. Has not the contrast between those words and the reality of privatisation in the health service led the Conservative party in Scotland into electoral freefall?

**Lord James Douglas-Hamilton:** If the hon. Gentleman feels like that, why did he say in January

"We are not opposed to public/private partnerships"?

That is precisely what we are talking about, together with improved services. The great advantage of introducing private sector finance is to make public sector funds go much further while providing improved services.

On Stonehaven, Grampian health board is consulting on the way forward. It intends to take the lead and to tender for the service. It is likely to involve local trusts and general practitioners, but there is the possibility of opening up the tender to private providers. That has not been ruled out. The decision as to who wins will depend upon the level of services and the provision of a better service for patients.

### Skillseekers Training Programme

8. **Mr. Connarty:** To ask the Secretary of State for Scotland what is the budget estimate for the skillseekers training programme for 1995-96; and how many jobs with training the programme is expected to provide. [24231]

**Mr. Kynoch:** The 1995-96 budget for youth training in Scotland, which includes the skillseekers training programme, is over £98 million. It is estimated that, for

1995-96, the percentage of young people training under skillseekers who will have employed status will be around 50 per cent.

**Mr. Connarty:** That is a very vague answer from the Minister. I was given better figures by Scottish Enterprise, which estimates that £70 million will go into the skillseekers programme, and it is looking for 30,000 jobs with training. Does the Minister share with me the concern of everyone to whom I have spoken in the past month that the vouchers-for-training scheme is just the beginning of Tory party dogma—the thin end of the wedge—of vouchers for nurseries and vouchers for education? Young people will be out in the market grasping their vouchers and those who will be taking them on will be thinking, "How can I get this person through this job with the least money coming from the employer?" Every person to whom I have spoken has said that there is no increase in money for monitoring. How do the Government expect young people to obtain decent training without anybody supporting them? Why is there no more money for monitoring to ensure that the skillseekers programme is not just another youth rip-off scheme?

**Mr. Kynoch:** The hon. Gentleman might be interested to know that between Scottish Enterprise and Highlands and Islands Enterprise, the total figure estimated for 1995-96, excluding modern apprenticeships, is 35,000. The hon. Gentleman is a little out of date with his figures.

I understand that, on Friday, the hon. Gentleman is due to visit his local enterprise company, Forth Valley Enterprise, which started the skillseekers programme in April. If the hon. Gentleman were to consult more widely, he would find that it has been widely accepted by employers around the country. Local enterprise companies have considerable flexibility in the way in which they can operate within specified guidelines.

Just the other day, I introduced a new pilot scheme in Fife. It is called fast track and trainees will be able to undertake full-time education as well. On monitoring, payment will be made only after very stringent checks against the stringent standards that will have been set by the enterprise companies.

**Mr. Stewart:** Does my hon. Friend agree that skillseekers, which started in Grampian in his area, has been a marked success throughout Scotland? Is it not significant that this, together with every other training initiative introduced by the Government, has been automatically opposed by the Labour party?

**Mr. Kynoch:** My hon. Friend is absolutely correct. The Opposition are full of words, but little action. My hon. Friend referred to skillseekers being piloted in Grampian. He would be interested to learn that in Grampian the number of young people with employed status has risen from 422 at the end of December 1991, under the youth training scheme, to 3,726 at the end of March 1995 under skillseekers. That speaks louder than words.

### Farm Land

9. **Mr. Harry Greenway:** To ask the Secretary of State for Scotland how many acres of Scotland are currently farmed; how many farm acres are currently set aside; at what cost; and if he will make a statement.    [24233]

**Sir Hector Monro:** In 1994, there were just over 6 million hectares of agricultural land in Scotland. About 93,000 hectares were in set-aside. Payments amounted to £25.7 million.

**Mr. Greenway:** I thank my hon. Friend for that reply. Does he agree that farmers and farm workers in Perthshire are enjoying increasing prosperity? Would that not be put at risk by a tax-raising Scottish Assembly?

**Sir Hector Monro:** My hon. Friend is absolutely right to suggest that Scottish farm incomes have risen substantially. Last year, they increased by no less than 25 per cent. to £454 million, the highest figure for 17 years. As he said, Perth and Kinross is the sort of area that benefits substantially from the money going into both less-favoured areas and non-LFA areas. The future looks good, provided people make the right decision tomorrow.

### Nuclear Waste

11. **Mr. Khabra:** To ask the Secretary of State for Scotland what assessment has been made of the safe disposal of nuclear waste generated in Scotland; its current and future costs; and if he will make a statement.    [24235]

**Sir Hector Monro:** A White Paper which sets out the conclusions to the Government's review of radioactive waste management policy and covers wastes arising in Scotland is to be published in the summer.

**Mr. Khabra:** The Minister failed to identify radioactive waste disposal locations in his reply. Is it not utterly irresponsible of the Government to sell the nuclear industry to finance tax bribes, while neglecting the safety of the people of Scotland? Will he give an assurance that enough is being done for the people of Scotland?

**Sir Hector Monro:** The hon. Gentleman's supplementary question shows that he has been misinformed. His main question related to nuclear waste generated in Scotland, and there is no problem with that. Low-level waste from Hunterston, Torness and Chapelcross is taken to Drigg. High-level waste is retained on site for 50 years. There is no problem because, whoever is the owner or manager of Scottish Nuclear's output from its generating stations, the whole process is carried out extremely safely.

### Unemployment, Perth and Kinross

12. **Mr. John Marshall:** To ask the Secretary of State for Scotland what is the number of unemployed in Perth and Kinross; and what the figure was in December 1992.    [24236]

**Mr. Kynoch:** Unadjusted claimant unemployment in the parliamentary constituency of Perth and Kinross stood at 2,647 in April 1995. In December 1992, the figure was 2,791.

**Mr. Marshall:** Does my hon. Friend agree that the most important employer in Perth is General Accident? Has that company not made it clear that a tax regime resulting from a tax-raising Scottish Assembly or the higher taxes of an independent Scotland would cause it to reconsider its employment policy in Perth?

**Mr. Kynoch:** My hon. Friend mentioned just one of the major employers in Perth and Kinross. He was right to imply that the people of Perth and Kinross have to decide clearly what they believe to be best for the future, not only for Perth and Kinross but for Scotland. There is no doubt that the proposals for a tax-raising Parliament and for an independent Scotland would severely jeopardise prospects not just for indigenous industry but for inward investment in both Scotland generally and Perth and Kinross in particular.

**Mrs. Fyfe:** There is no one more accident prone in Perth and Kinross than the Tory candidate. Has the Minister taken the trouble to read the House of Commons research paper that tells him that in April 1990 there were 2,143 claimants in Perth and Kinross and by April 1994 the number had risen to 2,647? A whole year later there is no change for the better. Does he realise that that is an increase of 24 per cent. and that today 11 people chase every job advertised in Perth town centre? Is that not why the Tories are in meltdown in Perth and Kinross?

**Mr. Kynoch:** The hon. Lady is in her usual negative mode. I had rather hoped that she might talk about some significant good news. For example, Monax Glass, the manufacturer of engineering and scientific glassware in Perth, announced an investment of £250,000 last month, creating 40 jobs in Perth. Indeed, Perth Fresh Meats Ltd., which I visited last week and which is part of the Beck Food group, announced that it was to create more than 110 new jobs in Perth. The hon. Lady is in her usual negative mode. If she were to talk Scotland and Perth and Kinross up, she might do a little better for Scotland.

**Mr. Gallie:** Does my hon. Friend agree that training for jobseekers is just as important in Perth and Kinross as it is in other parts of Scotland? Will my hon. Friend consider just what the minimum wage on offer from the Opposition would do to the Government's training programmes?

**Mr. Kynoch:** My hon. Friend is exactly right. The policies on the minimum wage and other employment characteristics, which are supported by all Opposition parties, would be severely detrimental to Scottish business and the Scottish economy as a whole.

### Transport Network

13. **Mr. Eric Clarke:** To ask the Secretary of State for Scotland what plans he has to meet the Scottish Trades Union Congress to discuss Scotland's transport network.                                    [24237]

**Mr. Lang:** I meet the Scottish TUC from time to time to discuss a variety of issues relating to the Scottish economy, including transport matters.

**Mr. Clarke:** Is the Secretary of State aware that people in Scotland fear that the Government are opting out of the transport network in privatising British Rail? Will the subsidies and the guarantees of fares being kept down in the south of England be the same for the whole of Scotland?

**Mr. Lang:** The fares guarantee will apply to the whole of the United Kingdom. As to the Government opting out, on the contrary, we are privatising the rail network because we believe that there is need for improvement which can be provided only by the private sector. The past

few years have not demonstrated that the public sector has the capacity to deliver the quality of rail service that this country needs.

**Mr. McLoughlin:** When my right hon. Friend next meets the TUC, will he point out the great advantages that are being brought about by air liberalisation and allowing competition to take place between British Midland and British Airways, to the benefit of all passengers in Scotland who use those routes?

**Mr. Lang:** My hon. Friend is absolutely right. One of the encouraging features of the rising prosperity in this country is the increasing use of various air routes around the United Kingdom. That is reflected in massive new investment at Glasgow and Edinburgh airports of £30 million and £100 million respectively.

**Mr. Wallace:** In discharging responsibilities with regard to the Scottish transport network, the Secretary of State will know that under section 5 of the Railways Act 1993 the Secretary of State for Transport can give directions to the franchising director, Mr. Salmon, including a direction that Mr. Salmon must submit to the Department of Transport the criteria that he will apply when he puts loss-making services into the passenger service obligation. Has the Secretary of State been involved in discussing those criteria? If so, when will that happen and what are the criteria?

**Mr. Lang:** Surely the hon. Gentleman knows by now that internal discussions between Ministers are not made public. He will wish to address his point to my right hon. Friend the Secretary of State for Transport.

**Mr. McAvoy:** The Secretary of State will be aware that the rail services provided in the Strathclyde regional council area, part-funded by that council, are a key part of Scotland's transport network. But is he aware that the Argyll line services to Cambuslang, Rutherglen and Halfway have been effectively closed over the past few months because of flooding of the line? Despite the efforts of Strathclyde region to get together with ScotRail to try to come up with alternatives to that closed service, ScotRail does not seem to be moving. If the Secretary of State is really concerned about Scotland's rail network, will he ensure that ScotRail co-operates with Strathclyde regional council to re-establish that rail service?

**Mr. Lang:** As the hon. Gentleman rightly says, those are matters for Strathclyde passenger transport executive to negotiate with ScotRail. If he wants to send me any further details, however, I shall see whether there is any way in which I can help him.

**Rev. Martin Smyth:** In discussions with the Scottish TUC and others, has the Secretary of State examined the impact on the transport network in Scotland of upgrading the Stranraer, Larne and Belfast facilities? Will he undertake to have a discussion with the Secretary of State for Transport? He cannot tell us publicly what he has discussed, but could he not use his influence to upgrade facilities at Stranraer?

**Mr. Lang:** The hon. Gentleman will understand why I share his close interest in such matters. I am glad to be able to tell him that a major new investment at Stranraer was announced only this week. It comes on top of the various commitments, on both road and rail, to upgrade the transport network in that important part of Scotland.

**Mr. George Robertson:** Would the Secretary of State give a warm welcome to the right hon. Member for Stirling (Mr. Forsyth), who is lurking suspiciously at the end of the Government Front Bench? While he is doing so, could he bring to mind the prophetic words of his late colleague, Mr. Robert Adley, who described railway privatisation as the poll tax on wheels? Does he not realise that privatising the railways in Scotland will be as wasteful, costly and electorally devastating as the poll tax was to turn out to be? Is it not time that the Secretary of State put Scotland before Tory ideology and, perhaps, put the people of Scotland and their interests before his career plans in the Cabinet?

**Mr. Lang:** We are sweeping away the remnants of the socialist ideology and dogma that led to so many public utilities being brought into the public sector, thereby denying them the resources and investment that they needed to stay efficient and modern. Now we are giving them the opportunity to break free from that constraint, just as we have done with telephones, the airlines, gas and electricity and so many other industries. Where they relied before on Government subsidies of £50 million a week, they are now profitable, successful, more efficient and generating revenue to the Exchequer of around £50 million a week. I have no doubt that railway privatisation will lead to massive improvements for the people of this country.

### Elderly Care Beds

14. **Mr. Chisholm:** To ask the Secretary of State for Scotland how many NHS continuing care beds for the elderly there were in 1985; how many there are now; and how many he expects there to be in 10 years' time. [24238]

**Lord James Douglas-Hamilton:** In 1985, there were 12,064 geriatric and psycho-geriatric beds in Scotland. There are now 12,950 beds in those categories. There has, however, been a reclassification of beds over that period. There are no centrally imposed targets for long-stay bed provision in the NHS.

**Mr. Chisholm:** Does the Under-Secretary realise that there is fear and dismay in Lothian because the number of long-stay beds for the elderly is to be more than halved by the end of the century, with the prospect of eight beds in 10 disappearing by 2005? Does he accept that the main result will be not more care in the community but more elderly people paying for nursing home care? Having paid once through tax and national insurance contributions, why should many elderly people have to pay yet again, some having to sell their homes to do so?

**Lord James Douglas-Hamilton:** I welcome the fact that Lothian health board and the relevant NHS trusts are looking carefully within Lothian at all elderly, long-stay admissions to hospitals and, where appropriate, arranging for suitable placements in the community. Clearly, however, elderly people who need long-stay NHS care will receive it. Guidance has been issued on the subject and, if an element of patients' needs cannot be readily met, quite simply they should not and will not be discharged. We are to consult shortly on Scottish provisions on the NHS role in continuing care and on

provision for appeals against a clinician's assessment for continuing NHS in-patient care, because, on occasions, some of the disputes relate to decisions made by clinicians. I shall bear in mind the hon. Gentleman's points, as will my right hon. and learned Friend the Minister of State.

**Mr. Kirkwood:** In the consultation that the hon. Gentleman has just announced, will he take into account the concern that is felt by many people who occupy NHS continuing care beds, who face the prospect of being transferred into the social work care in the community package and who, in the course of so doing, have not only their needs assessed but their means tested? Will he give a categorical assurance that Scottish health boards will have enough finance to ensure that transitional protection elements are in place, so that there are no costs to existing patients in continuing care in the NHS? During the consultations, will he undertake a review to ensure that benefit thresholds are relaxed so that people's inheritances do not in future have to pay for their continuing care?

**Lord James Douglas-Hamilton:** Some of the matters that the hon. Gentleman raises should be addressed to the Department of Social Security, but we regard it as extremely important that sufficient resources are made available. There has been enhanced mainstream funding of £158 million this year from the transfer of former DSS funds. Some £14 million has been transferred under the mental illness specific grant scheme, and £50 million has been transferred from the health boards to the local authorities. We anticipate that the transfer could be about some £200 million early in the next decade. We cannot state the exact sum at this stage because much of what happens will depend on the judgment of clinicians.

**Mr. Stewart:** My hon. Friend will be aware that in my constituency Greater Glasgow health board has increased the number of continuing care beds compared with its original plans. Does that not show that health boards are responding in real terms to the consultation and constructive points made by communities?

**Lord James Douglas-Hamilton:** My hon. Friend is right. Greater Glasgow health board received a general allocation for revenue expenditure this year of £585.66 million which, together with efficiency savings, gives an increase of 3.76 per cent. over the year before. I am delighted that such progress has been made in my hon. Friend's constituency.

**Mr. McAllion:** Will the Minister try to understand that the quality of those NHS continuing care beds that do survive depends entirely on the people who staff those beds—the doctors, nurses, radiologists, ancillary workers and other NHS workers? Will he try to understand above all that those dedicated people will not be bought and sold like cattle in a marketplace? We need a guarantee from the Minister that no NHS job will be put up for sale to the private sector in open competition in Stonehaven or anywhere else in Scotland. It is simple: either he rules out or he rules in privatising the people who are the NHS in Scotland. Which is it to be?

**Lord James Douglas-Hamilton:** The private finance initiative is certainly not about privatising the health service. It involves sharing the risk with the private sector, giving incentives for better performance and providing services as well as capital to support the NHS. The whole purpose of the scheme is to make public sector funds go much further by bringing in private sector funds to make it certain that high standards will be implemented.

**Mr. McAllion:** What about the people?

**Lord James Douglas-Hamilton:** It is the best service for the people who are being served—the patients. The interests of those at the sharp end of the system must be constantly kept in mind.

### Ambulance Service

15. **Dr. Godman:** To ask the Secretary of State for Scotland what plans he has to meet the chief executive of the Scottish ambulance service NHS trust to discuss the adequacy of the service in Renfrewshire.    [24239]

**Lord James Douglas-Hamilton:** My right hon. Friend has no present plans to meet the chief executive of the Scottish ambulance service NHS trust to discuss the adequacy of the service in Renfrewshire. The provision of emergency ambulance services is the subject of agreements between the Scottish ambulance service NHS trust and health boards. The performance of the Scottish ambulance service against agreed targets is monitored by the health boards as well as by the Scottish Office Home and Health Department.

**Dr. Godman:** Despite the unhelpful and dimwitted remarks made by the chief executive in a letter to a colleague, I seek neither to rubbish the ambulance service nor to cause more distress to the family of a constituent who was severely injured in a recent traffic accident and had to wait 30 minutes for an ambulance. I have every respect for ambulance crews, and I do not agree that there is a problem with the local management and control of the service. Will the Minister initiate an investigation into the management and control of the service in Renfrewshire?

**Lord James Douglas-Hamilton:** I can reassure the hon. Gentleman that that has been done. The Minister of State has asked the chief executive to review the level of cover in that area and to identify any measures that can be taken to improve the response times, particularly in circumstances of exceptional demand.

The targets for Paisley and Greenock are for an ambulance to arrive within eight minutes for 50 per cent. of emergency calls and within 18 minutes for 95 per cent. of calls. In 1994-95, the Greenock station consistently met those targets, but a review is being undertaken, as the hon. Gentleman has requested.

### Sunday Trading (Garden Centres)

16. **Mr. Fabricant:** To ask the Secretary of State for Scotland what plans he has to alter the hours of trading of garden centres on Sunday; and if he will make a statement.    [24240]

**Mr. Kynoch:** I am pleased to be able to tell my hon. Friend that there are no general statutory restrictions on Sunday trading in Scotland. The questions whether and when to trade on a Sunday therefore remain matters for individual and corporate traders to decide. We have no intention of regulating hours of trading on a Sunday for garden centres or any other business in Scotland.

**Mr. Fabricant:** How wise that answer was. May I ask my hon. Friend to give an unequivocal assurance that he has no intention of closing garden centres on Easter Sunday? Is he aware of how disastrous that has been in mid-Staffordshire not only for garden centres—

**Madam Speaker:** Order. The question should relate to Scotland, not Staffordshire.

**Mr. Fabricant:** Does not Scotland lead the way, and should not England and Wales follow? Last Easter Sunday, 15 million people in England and Wales who wanted to buy plants and other products were turned away from garden centres.

**Mr. Kynoch:** I thank my hon. Friend for his opening flattery. Matters relating to south of the border are for my right hon. and learned Friend the Home Secretary.

### Tourism

17. **Mr. Bill Walker:** To ask the Secretary of State for Scotland if he will make a statement on the method available to hon. Members to obtain details of tourism-related capital projects in their constituencies which receive support from public funds.    [24241]

**Mr. Kynoch:** Any hon. Member who wishes to obtain details of tourism-related capital projects in his or her constituency, which have received support from public funds, should contact the appropriate local enterprise company.

**Mr. Walker:** I thank my hon. Friend for that very unhelpful reply. Is he aware that one of the most important things that this House does is to vote Supply, and that the cornerstone of our unwritten constitution is a Member's right to ask questions and have them answered? It may therefore come as a surprise to him to know that I have been unable to get the information required. If it requires legislation, will he consider it so that hon. Members can get answers, as they are entitled to expect?

**Mr. Kynoch:** I think that I know what my hon. Friend is talking about. I accept that local enterprise companies in the Scottish Enterprise area have probably set a greater premium on commercial confidentiality than the Scottish tourist board before them or local enterprise companies in the highlands and islands. He might be interested to know that, while the Scottish Affairs Select Committee has made some recommendations in its report, which Ministers are considering, local enterprise companies in the Scottish Enterprise area are now advising applicants that certain details of financial assistance to individual projects may be made public in the future. I hope that that is a helpful answer to my hon. Friend.

**Mr. Maclennan:** Will the Minister undertake to explain the methodology that he and his colleagues, particularly the Secretary of State, have so misleadingly employed with respect to the passenger subsidy for Scottish rail services? Many people believe that the figures that have been produced for sleepers, for example, are entirely unreliable and are designed to deceive the Scottish public about the cost of those vital services.

**Mr. Kynoch:** That is an ingenious way of getting the question in. The hon. Gentleman can use the consultation period on the passenger service requirement to put his points forward.

## Homelessness

**19. Mr. Welsh:** To ask the Secretary of State for Scotland what is his latest estimate of the level of homelessness in (a) Scotland and (b) Tayside; and if he will make a statement. [24243]

**Lord James Douglas-Hamilton:** In 1992-93, the latest year for which complete figures for Tayside are available, 29,000 households in Scotland and 1,643 households in Tayside were found to be homeless or at risk of homelessness.

**Mr. Welsh:** Does the Minister accept that current levels of homelessness are unacceptable in any civilised society? Will he admit that housing associations alone cannot cope, and will he explain why he is starving local authorities of the resources required to solve that problem?

**Lord James Douglas-Hamilton:** I am not. This year, some £900 million will be invested in housing. It is one of the top priorities for all district authorities in Scotland, which have strategic responsibility. We have given a considerable amount of grant to voluntary organisations, concentrating on prevention rather than cure, and have allocated £29 million for special schemes to assist with homelessness. In addition, we recently issued a consultation paper on a subject in which the hon. Gentleman is interested—anti-social tenants. He is welcome to make observations during the consultation period.

**Dr. Reid:** Is it not true that, under the present Government, both public and private sector housing starts have been crucified? When will the Minister stop the policy of taking away with one hand what he allows with the other to local authorities for public expenditure on housing? Is it not an indictment of the Government's economic policy and their crucifying of the building industry and of their lack of moral imperatives in the way in which they treat the homeless? If he had attended to both economic policy and moral imperatives, would not the Minister and his party stand a chance—just a chance—of avoiding the humiliation that confronts them at the Perth and Kinross by-election?

**Lord James Douglas-Hamilton:** The hon. Gentleman forgets that the most recent Labour Government cut capital expenditure on housing to the bone. As I mentioned, about £900 million will be provided this year in housing investment. We anticipate that, some time during the year, the 300,000th house will be built since 1979, which is a considerable achievement, much of it by the private sector but some by the public sector.

## Hospital Beds

**20. Mr. David Marshall:** To ask the Secretary of State for Scotland what plans he has to improve hospital bed provision in Scotland; and if he will make a statement. [24244]

**Lord James Douglas-Hamilton:** It is for each health board in Scotland to ensure that the needs of the population in its area are matched by appropriate health and health care services. That includes discussing with the NHS trusts and other providers of health services from which it purchases care, the number of hospital beds that should be available.

**Mr. Marshall:** Does the Minister accept the fact that the east end of Glasgow has some of the worst health statistics in Scotland and in the United Kingdom? Will he therefore deplore the proposals to close Belvidere hospital in Parkhead, which cares for elderly people in my constituency—or is he happy for it to be sold off or privatised à la Stonehaven? Just when will he start putting patient care before profit?

**Lord James Douglas-Hamilton:** Any proposal for closure arising from the acute and maternity reviews will require the consent of the Secretary of State. Before the Secretary of State were to give approval for any such proposal, he would have to be satisfied that an equally good, if not better, system of care was put in place. However, I will certainly ensure that the Minister of State is made aware of the hon. Gentleman's opinions.

**Mr. Robert Hughes:** Does the Minister recall that it is but a few years since he was trumpeting the virtues of the national health service trust system? Is he aware that he has now contradicted himself by choosing private tendering for the replacement of Stonehaven hospital? Is he aware that, last night, there was a well-attended meeting in Stonehaven, organised by the Stonehaven and district community council, which voted by an overwhelming margin—by more than 2:1—against privatisation? Will he take heed of that, and abandon that dangerous heresy?

**Lord James Douglas-Hamilton:** The hon. Gentleman must appreciate that there will be consultation. I wish to make it quite clear that, since trusts have been established, waiting times have shortened, more people are receiving treatment and there has been increased investment in improving hospitals. However, as I explained earlier, the purpose of the private finance initiative is to ensure that public sector funds go very much further, with higher standards for the patients.

## Highlands and Islands

**21. Mr. Macdonald:** To ask the Secretary of State for Scotland if he will make a statement on the economic prospects for the highlands and islands. [24245]

**Lord James Douglas-Hamilton:** The success of the Government's economic policies means that the prospects for continuing growth towards long-term economic prosperity in the highlands look very encouraging.

**Mr. Macdonald:** Is the Minister aware that investment in education is crucial to the economic future of the highlands? Is he aware that a recent report into a school in my constituency, Bayble school, by Her Majesty's inspectorate said that it was dangerous, smelly and suffering from chronic disrepair? Is that not the case throughout the highlands, and is that not a telling indictment of 15 years of chronic underinvestment and neglect by Tory Governments?

**Lord James Douglas-Hamilton:** No. Approaching £70 million is made available this year for capital investment in schools and school buildings. When we have the annual spending round this autumn, we shall take a hard look at the issue—not just in the hon. Gentleman's constituency, of which I am aware, but in many other parts of Scotland. We shall consider with great care the condition of school buildings throughout the length and breadth of Scotland.

### Scottish Economy

**22. Dr. Reid:** To ask the Secretary of State for Scotland when he last met the chairman of Scottish Enterprise to discuss the Scottish economy; and if he will make a statement. [24246]

**Mr. Kynoch:** My right hon. Friend last met the chairman of Scottish Enterprise to discuss economic issues on 1 March 1995.

**Dr. Reid:** Is it not crucial for the Scottish economy to maintain and develop research and development and skilled jobs at the forefront of technology? In the light of that, what does the Minister have to say to those Rolls-Royce workers who are today in London to protest against not only the loss of 600 skilled jobs but the transfer of technology out of Scotland and possibly out of Britain? Is it not a damning indictment of the Government's inactivity and uninterest that they have stood idly by while those jobs and that potential have disappeared from Scotland?

**Mr. Kynoch:** Obviously, no one likes to see jobs go. Unfortunately, Rolls-Royce has had to face the conditions that are prevalent in the aerospace industry The hon. Gentleman is perfectly well aware of the much larger job losses that are suffered elsewhere within that industry. The Government believe in ensuring that the right economic conditions are in place to guarantee continuing drops in unemployment, continuing increases in inward investment and the best possible employment prospects for the people of Scotland in the future.

# Lord Wilson (Tributes)

3.30 pm

**The Prime Minister (Mr. John Major):** I beg to move, That this House do now adjourn.

This morning we heard the sad news of the death of Lord Wilson. As the House well knows, Lord Wilson had been ill for a very long time and had endured that illness with courage and with great good humour. I know that the whole House would wish to join me in sending our sincerest condolences to Mary Wilson, who nursed and cared for him with such devotion for so long, and also to his sons, Robin and Giles.

I did not know Harold Wilson personally when he was at the height of his powers, but I knew him from afar as a formidable political opponent. I believe that history will remember him for the sharpness and shrewdness of his mind; for his two periods of service as Prime Minister in difficult circumstances; and for his energy and enthusiasm, as well as for his many achievements. And also, perhaps here of all places, he will be remembered for his wit and his humour—often shown to such devastating effect on the Floor of the House. But that is the public man. His friends who knew him well speak also of the private man—of his great personal kindnesses and generosity. He expected loyalty from those around him and he offered it in full measure in return.

Harold Wilson was a Yorkshireman whose roots mattered to him. His background motivated his politics. His family's experience during the depression, when his father was unemployed, shaped his politics, his thinking and his future policies. In becoming Prime Minister, he broke through many of the traditional class barriers of the day.

I do not believe that it is too generous to describe Harold Wilson as one of the most brilliant men of his generation. He gained an outstanding first-class degree at Oxford. He was an exceptionally young and able don at New college and then a fellow at University college. He worked for William Beveridge on his great study of unemployment. His ability as a statistician was legendary and those who knew him well will recall his remarkable memory, which was displayed with such pleasure so often and to such good effect.

At the outbreak of war, Harold Wilson's capacity for incisive thought and rigorous analysis took him to the economic section of the Cabinet Office and then to the Ministry of Fuel and Power. Over the years, by his remarkable work in those positions, he caught the attention of leading Labour party figures such as Clem Attlee. Then, in 1945, at the relatively young age of 28, he was elected for the first time to the House as the Member for Ormskirk. He was quickly given a ministerial post and a mere two years later he became President of the Board of Trade, the youngest Cabinet Minister in the House since 1806.

As a Minister, Harold Wilson quickly established a strong reputation. He was responsible for the removal of the rationing controls on clothes and textiles that had remained from the war and also for the relaxation of dozens of other regulations. He was active, far beyond his time, in opening up important trade links with Russia.

In 1950, following boundary changes, Harold Wilson was elected to the seat of Huyton, which he was to represent with great distinction for another 33 years. In 1951 he resigned from the Front Bench over the imposition of health charges before Labour's election defeat, which, for him, led to 13 long years in opposition. It was in that time that he developed from the brilliant academic to become the sparkling political figure of later years.

The tragic, untimely death of Hugh Gaitskell brought Harold Wilson to the leadership of his party earlier than he might have expected. His election was widely welcomed. He was recognised as a man of both intellectual and political skills. In choosing his first shadow Cabinet, he displayed his willingness to select people of ability, whether or not they agreed with his point of view. That ability to conciliate—often a scorned attribute, but a necessary one—was displayed continually throughout his leadership of the Labour party. He narrowly won election as Prime Minister in 1964 and secured a large majority in 1966. In government he placed a strong emphasis on technology and innovation, to be carried through with a new emphasis on state planning. His social policies embodied the liberal spirit of the time.

During six years of government, Harold Wilson faced many difficult problems—the ever-present currency crisis; Northern Ireland; the Rhodesia crisis; controversy over whether British troops should become involved in the war in Vietnam; the uncertainty over whether Britain would or would not join the then European Community; and industrial unrest, particularly in the docks. Those problems faced him continually as Prime Minister. I believe that history will judge that Harold Wilson kept a clear and a cool head in the face of those difficulties. For my generation at least, as observers through television and from a distance, his ever-present pipe became a symbol of tranquillity in times of some turmoil.

Harold Wilson had much to his credit in those days. He was responsible for the rapid expansion of higher education, including the development of the polytechnics. He was personally involved in, and rightly proud of, setting up the Open university. He was aware of the dangers of excessive concentration of trade union power and he was brave enough to tackle it, alas without the complete support of many of his colleagues at the time. Of course, he was the only British Prime Minister to preside over England's winning the World cup. He was a remarkable man. He was not ready to give up as Labour leader following defeat in 1970. He was right, and he proved it with two further election victories in 1974. With them, he became the only Prime Minister this century to have emerged victorious from four general elections.

When Harold Wilson stood down as Prime Minister in 1976, many were surprised, even shocked. Why had he done it? What did he mean by it? The fuss was considerable, and how much he must have enjoyed it at the time. Even those who had tried for so long to unseat him could not accept that he had stood down of his own accord; but he had. He had served longer than any Prime Minister before him this century and it was perfectly natural that he would wish to enjoy his retirement.

What was Harold Wilson really like? I have formed my judgment. He was a complex man, certainly, a clever man, a sensitive man, a man who could be bruised and hurt and who never wore the armadillo skin of the fictional politician. He was a man of many achievements and, perhaps above all, a very human man who served his country well and honourably and who has earned, by that, a secure place in its history. In the ledger of life, his credit balance is very high. It is a privilege for me, as one, nominally, of his political opponents, to pay him this tribute and I do so unreservedly.

3.39 pm

**Mr. Tony Blair** (Sedgefield): I thank the Prime Minister for that generous tribute. It is my privilege to join in our tribute to Harold Wilson and in sending our sympathy to Mary and to Harold and Mary's two sons and their families.

I was barely 11 years old when Harold Wilson became Prime Minister. It was a new era, in which the British people were looking forward in a spirit of hope and optimism. Harold Wilson, in a sense, was to politics what the Beatles were to popular culture. He simply dominated the nation's political landscape, and he personified the new era, not stuffy or hidebound but classless, forward-looking, modern. Even his enemies and detractors, and there were a few, could not deny his brilliance, his brain and the intelligence born of natural wit, not social background. But neither were his friends slow to point to his immense generosity, his warmth, his profound human sympathy.

Harold Wilson was born into a very typical non-conformist, lower middle-class northern family. His parents were active in the local church, and Harold Wilson himself was very active in the local scouts. Indeed, some have said that he was, and in some ways remained, the Huddersfield boy scout—respectable, bright, determined. His academic record, as the Prime Minister said, was outstanding—his first-class honours degree, his photographic memory, his period as a research assistant to Sir William Beveridge. When he was elected to Parliament, and then just over two years into being a Member of Parliament became a Cabinet Minister, his was a reputation that was growing day by day.

Harold Wilson resigned in 1951 over what he regarded as excessive defence spending, and I think that it is fair to say that, for the next 13 years, his career was sometimes up and down. He was a Bevanite, regarded with some considerable alarm from time to time by the then party establishment. But his gifts were so undeniable that, whatever the views of whatever party establishment, he was bound to rise to the top. He was known, rightly, as one of the great parliamentary performers, as a stump orator of genius, devastating in repartee. But contrary to legend, that was not natural, but the result of painstaking work and care.

By all accounts, the Cabinet Minister of the Attlee Government was rather a dull speaker, though massively well informed, but Harold Wilson set out to become the best and he did. By 1956, when he became shadow Chancellor, his speeches were acclaimed as parliamentary masterpieces, and he simply got better and better as time went on. In particular, he raised dealing with hecklers, or interruptions at public meetings, to something of an art form. When a young boy hit him in the eye with a stink bomb at an open-air meeting and was marched off by the police, Harold, whose eye was none the less smarting, looked up and said, "Don't lock him up. With an arm like that he should be bowling for England."

At the height of the 1964 election campaign, when a lady got up to carry out a crying child, Harold Wilson turned to her and said, "Let him stay, madam. This is all about his future." He did not always get the best of his tormentors, and one of the good things about him were the stories that he would tell against himself. The best, I believe, was when he was at a vast public meeting. Speaking about the Navy, "I will always defend the Navy," he said, "and why do I say that?" "Because you're in Chatham," shouted a voice from the crowd. Knowing that he was beaten, he joined in the laughter and moved on.

When Hugh Gaitskell died in 1963, Harold became the leader of the Labour party. He stayed leader for 13 years, won four out of five elections and retired in 1976 at a time and in a manner of his own choosing. It is hardly surprising that succeeding Labour leaders look upon him with envy and admiration. Indeed, he is, I believe, the only politician to have won four general elections. My party has been in power this century for something over 20 years and 11 of them were delivered by Harold Wilson.

In 1964, Harold Wilson symbolised the new mood of change. There had been 13 years of unbroken Conservative rule, the memories of war were becoming more distant, technology and science were revolutionising people's lives, and a cultural transformation in popular arts was waiting to happen. It was an age for meritocracy, for sweeping away the old and ringing in the new, and Harold Wilson captured it.

Harold Wilson's speech at the 1963 Labour conference about the new Britain to be forged in the white heat of the technological revolution, where there would be no room, as he said, for restrictive practices or outdated methods on either side of industry, encapsulated the spirit of the time. All the forces of change—political, industrial, cultural—propelled him into office, but his was the victory because in him those forces were personified.

It was a time of hope and opportunity, and although the judgment has occasionally been harsh, it was a time of achievement, too. When Harold Wilson lost office in 1970, Britain had enjoyed low unemployment and low inflation and its finances were in sound and balanced order. No Government have achieved that since. By the end of six years, three times as many people were going into higher education. He created and drove through the Open university, which has given to tens of thousands of people the chance of a university degree. He introduced the first legislation against discrimination in respect of women and racial minorities.

It is no doubt fashionable now to knock the '60s and, like any age, it had its share of faults, but for many, let us not forget, it was a time when opportunity began, horizons opened and ambition and aspiration were spread to a multitude of people previously denied them.

The defeat of 1970 was a bitter blow, but Harold Wilson came back. He won two elections in 1974. This time, the majority was small, and I think that it is right to say that the impending fracture between right and left within our party grew. He had to deal with the problems that eventually boiled over in the 1980s and whose resolution has been the single most outstanding change since Wilson's day.

Although known, sometimes dismissively, as, above all, a party manager of skill, it was, it is fair to say, Harold Wilson who advised his party to accept "In Place of Strife" in 1969 and, again, had his advice been accepted, who knows what the future course of history could have been.

[Mr. Tony Blair]

Even with his difficulties, Harold Wilson achieved much in that Government. He improved pensions. He passed the Sex Discrimination Act 1975. He started to plan child benefit. He set up the National Consumer Council.

No tribute to Harold Wilson would be complete without a word about the foreign policy. Again, the challenges were immense. He had to withdraw defence obligations east of Suez, a difficult but necessary task. He negotiated Britain's remaining in the European Community. He had the painful task of trying to end UDI in Rhodesia. He kept Britain out of the Vietnam war. He was an unrelenting opponent of apartheid and the South African regime. He founded War on Want. He established the Overseas Development Ministry. It is an impressive record. When we look back over those years, there is much of which to be proud.

The end of Harold Wilson's life was often spent in illness and I would like to pay special tribute to Mary, his wife, who cared for him in the last years. She was a source of love and comfort beyond compare.

I believe that in time the perception of Harold Wilson and his years in government will change and, indeed, already is changing. To many, he is defined as a clever politician—and he was. Yet it would be most unfair to let that eclipse his real character and his deep commitment. He had, in the end, a very simple belief in the virtues of social justice and equality and, by and large, throughout his time in politics, he applied them. He once said:

"The Labour party is a moral crusade, or it is nothing."

That should be his real epitaph and long may it remain so.

3.49 pm

**Mr. Paddy Ashdown** (Yeovil): I wish to associate myself and all in my party with the very full and, if I may say so, moving tributes made by the Prime Minister and the leader of the Labour party.

I am sure that most politicians, certainly most party leaders, would recognise that politics can, from time to time, be pretty tough going. To have led one's party for a handful of years, against the pressure of what Macmillan called events, the attack of the press and the business to which one always has to attend of party management, is a success in itself; but to have led one's party—a great party in the state—for 13 years is a remarkable achievement in its own right and an extraordinary testimony to human endurance. By the same token, to have won one election is a triumph; to have won four, it seems to me, is a remarkable achievement.

Harold Wilson, as the Prime Minister and the Leader of the Opposition said, often regarded holding his party together as one of his main achievements. Leading a divided party might at times look messy and manipulative to contemporaries in one's political time and in the press of the moment, but although it is easy to pillory pragmatism as lack of principle, it is nevertheless not the issue by which a politician and a party leader will be judged. History highlights results, and four election victories out of five campaigns is a historic achievement by any standards.

Lord Wilson was Prime Minister through times, as the Prime Minister and the Leader of the Opposition said, of great social change in this country. There were

disappointments—of course there were; that is the way of politics—but there were also great achievements. In particular, the caring and progressive outlook of the personality of Harold Wilson shines through that wide range of the social achievements of his Governments—from equal opportunities legislation to the introduction of redundancy payments and to his own personal pride and joy, the Open university, which changed the nature of education in this country and has been such an assistance to so many who would never otherwise have had access to higher education.

This is a sad day for the House. It is a sad day for our country. But, in particular, our thoughts and our prayers at this moment must be with Lord Wilson's family.

3.52 pm

**Sir Edward Heath** (Old Bexley and Sidcup): Harold Wilson was a true House of Commons man. He knew, loved, enjoyed and respected its traditions. Throughout his life, he spent a great deal of time here, not only in the Chamber, but in the Smoking Room, the Tea Room and the Library, talking to his colleagues and to all who enjoyed talking to him, regardless of party. In that, he showed a touch which earned him great respect and admiration.

Harold Wilson never hesitated to tackle problems and he saw them very clearly. He saw the problem of sterling in the late 1960s. He saw the problem of Rhodesia and tried to resolve it. He not only kept us out of Vietnam, but he saw the problems there and tried to bring peace. He saw the problems of joining the European Community. My greatest regret was that we were never able to come to an agreement about that key policy issue.

Harold Wilson was also a master of the media—all of them, television, radio and the press. Occasionally, he had a slight quarrel with a press correspondent whom he regarded as disagreeable, but he was always on top of every medium in which he was performing. That gave him great influence with the general public which he, quite naturally, used to the advantage of his party. But what really endeared the people of this country to him was that they knew from his background, his upbringing and his own life, in which there was hardship, that he was a compassionate man who understood their needs and who was doing his best, often in difficult circumstances, as we have heard, to meet those needs and to ensure that people had a better life. That was his philosophy and his purpose in coming into the House, in being in opposition and in being a Minister.

We were together for 35 years—in confrontation, some would say, for more than 10 years as leaders of our respective parties. I would not say that it was confrontation during that time. It was facing each other and arguing about the problems. I like to think that we were constrained. We were not abusing each other and we were not trying to get cheap results quickly from each other. That was proved by the fact that behind the scenes, we had frequent exchanges about his intentions, the problems and the sorts of things which one cannot always discuss publicly, but which the leader of the other party ought to know about. In that, Harold Wilson was absolutely faithful and we always knew what the purpose of each other's intentions was.

It is sad that at the end of his life, Harold Wilson's illness lasted so long. In regretting his death, we can only be glad that he no longer suffers in that way. We can share the joy of Mary and his family that they, too, know that his achievements are recognised by the House and that, with help from the historians, they will be recognised in due course by the country and by the rest of the world. This country owes a great deal to him. We are grateful and we would like Mary and the family to know that today.

3.56 pm

**Mr. James Molyneaux** (Lagan Valley): In the mid-1970s, when no one party had a clear majority, it was necessary for me to co-operate with the then Prime Minister, Lord Wilson. We had a kind of unspoken understanding that we did not always take the most direct route to any particular objective and that gained for both of us a distinct reputation. That was illustrated one evening in the Cafeteria, when I had ordered a rather exotic dish of scrambled eggs on toast and Harold had picked up a salad from the other cabinet. He said to me, "Jim, would you mind if I bypassed you up to the cash desk?" I took my empty tray from the rails, did a military two steps back, bowed and said, "Prime Minister, I am delighted to yield to an expert in the art of bypassing." Harold was vastly amused at that, took it as a compliment and invited me to share his table when my scrambled eggs eventually arrived.

This morning, some commentators have been rather less than fair in implying that Lord Wilson had only one guiding principle, that of keeping his party together and keeping it united. There is nothing disreputable about that objective; it is just that some of us are more successful than others.

As the Leader of the Opposition said, Lord Wilson had other principles, mostly based on his non-conformist Christian background. There was, for example, a deep respect for this place, for the traditions of Parliament and for democracy itself. Another principle was revealed to me shortly after he became Prime Minister in 1974. One evening, he invited me to meet him on a one-to-one basis to discuss the position in Ulster arising from the massive electoral rejection of the Sunningdale agreement. I had been stressing the need for sensitivity and caution in a rather volatile situation: there was, for example, talk of a protest strike getting under way. Interrupting all that with a flourish of his pipe, Harold said, "Jim, let me explain that I did not become the Queen's First Minister for the purpose of using the forces of the Crown to suppress the verdict of the ballot box."

Those are not the words of a man with little faith and few principles.

4 pm

**Mr. Tony Benn** (Chesterfield): May I also associate myself with the moving speeches made by the Prime Minister, the Leader of the Opposition and the Father of the House about Harold Wilson? May I add a point about Mary Wilson—who, happily, is with us? She supported him throughout his life, and suffered with him all the pains that come to families in public life. I have a feeling that his retirement was a time to which she looked forward. It is sad that he did not enjoy those years of retirement in good health; but she nursed him and cared for him. Therefore, our feelings are rather personal.

Everyone looks back on those whom they knew with their own perspectives. When I arrived in the House, Harold Wilson was President of the Board of Trade. He was never a Back Bencher: that was actually one of his great problems. He did not serve on the Back Benches until he retired. I made that point at his farewell dinner at No. 10. He put that right in the end, however.

Harold Wilson was passionately committed to British industry and technology. He set up the National Research and Development Corporation. He was very keen on that, and also—as the Prime Minister rightly pointed out—on east-west trade. He thought that trade might well have eased the problems of the cold war.

I heard Harold Wilson's resignation speech—only the Father of the House and I will have heard it. He said that the defence burdens that we had been asked to bear were too heavy. I believe that he was right, and that we paid a heavy price; but that is for historians to assess. He then went through a period in the wilderness, which people hardly mention. He was vilified. Hugh Dalton, who spoke very plainly, described him as "Nye's little dog" because he worked with Aneurin Bevan. He stuck it out, however, and always remained loyal to the friends who supported him during that period—including Lady Falkender, who helped him at a time when he had very few friends in the House.

Then Harold Wilson became leader of the party. He made a series of speeches—including the "new Britain" speeches—which were not soundbites but substantial speeches on every subject. I remember him saying to me—I have never forgotten it—"Tony, in the post-industrial age social expenditure will be the engine of economic progress." I think that a very profound comment. He also made a speech that was much laughed at, in which he spoke of the white heat of the technological revolution. He was not saying that he would put on a white coat, go around with a blowlamp and modernise the economy; he was saying something quite different. He was saying, "If we do not have socialist planning of technical change, there will be mass unemployment, and we shall be burnt up in it." History may well record his judgment to be right.

When Harold Wilson became Prime Minister, he renewed his interest in British industry. He really did believe that public investment and public planning were a necessary part of maintaining a manufacturing base, and I am sure that history will see sense in that.

Undoubtedly, as has been said, Harold Wilson will be remembered in future centuries for the Open university, which he fought through against great opposition. Arnold Goodman, who died the other day, was used to help Jennie Lee to bring that about. As the Prime Minister said, the Open university provided opportunities for people who would never have had access to higher education, including pensioners.

Harold Wilson worked with all wings of the party. Every Prime Minister must think that his Cabinet is difficult, but think of Harold's Cabinet. Two of its members were former members of the Communist party—Lord Healey and Edmund Dell. Two deputy leaders left the party—Roy Jenkins and George Brown. His Minister of Transport, Dick Marsh, joined the Tory party; Christopher Mayhew joined the Liberal party. He stuck it out.

*[Mr. Tony Benn]*

Harold believed in close links with trade unions. He appointed the general secretary of the Transport and General Workers Union to be his first Minister of Technology. He believed what Ian Mikardo always said, that, "Every bird needs a left wing and a right wing and it can't fly on its right wing alone."

I had fierce arguments with Harold Wilson, but when I look back, they were family rows in a spirit of great friendship, and I look back on him with enormous affection because all my ministerial offices, except for the last one, I owe to him.

Like all Prime Ministers, Harold Wilson worried about plots. That is not uncommon. I asked him once, when the plot stories were thickening, "Harold, what shall we do if you are knocked down by a bus?" and Harold said, "Find out who was driving the bus."

### 4.5 pm

**Mr. Gerald Kaufman** (Manchester, Gorton): I would first like to join other right hon. Members in expressing my sympathy to Mary Wilson. She has gone through a very long period of great stress, and the months and years that preceded Harold's death have not been easy for her. Now she has to live with her bereavement, and I am sure that the House will want her to know that all our thoughts are with her.

I suppose that, of the people who are now present in the House, I knew Harold Wilson better than anyone. For five years, as a member of his staff in No. 10 Downing street, I spent almost every day with him, conversing with him, enjoying his confidence, sharing that mutual loyalty that Harold provided for those very few people whom he trusted completely.

It did mean that one had to go through certain ordeals. One of them was Harold's pipe. Stories arose in the press that Harold in private never smoked a pipe but that he smoked cigars instead. I only wish that that had been true. To get out of a sleeping compartment of a train in the early hours of the morning and enter a closed car with Harold lighting up immediately was not the best way to start a day. I remember Mary saying on many occasions, "Oh, Harold, do stop kippering us," but he never paid attention to her.

The other aspect of Harold's private life that was both legendary and true was HP Sauce. He was bewildered by the propensity of Roy Jenkins to go out and have dinner in fashionable restaurants. He could not understand why anyone would want anything more than to sit down at a table in the Downing street kitchen with a plate of steak and chips smothered with HP Sauce.

Unlike many politicians who have followed him, Harold wrote his own speeches. He used to stride up and down the study in No. 10 Downing street, dictating to a succession of secretaries. When the transcript was brought in to him, he would correct it with the green ink that he had always used ever since he was first in the Cabinet. Harold prepared his speeches with meticulous care, and was always extremely careful about the effect that he could create with them.

When Harold was having one of his not infrequent differences of opinion with the BBC, he prepared a speech at the Labour party conference, rose to his feet as leader and Prime Minister, and was greeted with the most enormous ovation by the assembled delegates. Then, after waiting carefully for every last vestige of applause to die down, he said, "I suppose the BBC news tonight will describe that as a cool reception." He then got another ovation.

Harold planned ahead in many ways. The right hon. Member for Old Bexley and Sidcup (Sir E. Heath) may remember receiving a letter that I sent to him when I was a junior Minister at the Department of the Environment in charge of the Government car service—possibly the most powerful position in any Government apart from that of Prime Minister.

I received a direct minute from the Prime Minister—it was very rare for the Prime Minister to send such a minute to a junior Minister—instructing me to write to all former Prime Ministers still living offering them a car and a chauffeur. I then realised that Harold had definitely decided to resign.

Harold was an extremely accessible Prime Minister. Every Tuesday and Thursday, after Question Time at 3.30 pm, his door was open for two hours to any Labour Member who cared to call upon him. I believe that he was ready to see Conservatives as well in certain circumstances. He was an extraordinarily kind man. During one reshuffle, he had decided to sack from the Government for a lack of highly visible competence a junior Minister called Charlie Loughlin. He then heard that Charlie's daughter had died in a car crash. That was the end of the sacking of Charlie Loughlin.

Harold had great ideals. He had an enormous love for the state of Israel. In his latter years, he wrote a book about it and sent his son to a kibbutz there. He had a great affinity with the then Prime Minister, Golda Meir.

Of all the things that have been said about him, and of all the things that he has done, the achievement of which Harold was most proud was that he was the first Prime Minister this century under whom expenditure on education became greater than expenditure on defence. He believed in education, and he believed in Parliament. He believed in democracy, and he left democracy firmer and more secure then when he first became Prime Minister.

### 4.12 pm

**Mr. David Harris** (St. Ives): As is well known, Harold and Mary Wilson have had a house on the Isles of Scilly in my constituency for many years, and I know that my constituents, the Scillonians, would like me to pay tribute to Lord Wilson, and to echo the words of the right hon. Member for Chesterfield (Mr. Benn), who paid tribute to the way in which Lady Wilson nursed Lord Wilson through the last sad years of his life. It was my privilege and pleasure on a number of occasions to call at the bungalow on St. Mary's, the standard of Trinity house flying proudly above it, to see both of them.

I can tell you and the House, Madam Speaker, that the people of the Isles of Scilly love Lady Wilson. She has made a truly remarkable impact on them. They hold her very dear. Of course, they always saw the value of Lord Wilson, particularly during his premiership, because he was a major tourist asset to the islands. I am not sure that that persuaded quite all of them to vote Labour in various elections. Lady Wilson is not just respected, but held in the highest regard.

To give just one personal reminiscence; when I was a very young reporter, I had my first big break covering the 1964 general election. I followed Harold Wilson literally everywhere around the country. Strange as it may seem now, in those days very few newspapers or television cameras did that. I was present at the famous meeting in Chatham to which the Leader of the Opposition referred.

At the end of the campaign, when the results were coming through, we were in the Adelphi hotel. One can see how times have changed, because the few of us who had followed Harold Wilson around were in his bedroom. He was stretched out on the bed, and I think that he was puffing on his pipe. He turned to me and said, "David, you have followed me all around the country, and you are still a damned Tory." In that, as in some other things, he was right.

4.14 pm

**Mr. Alfred Morris** (Manchester, Wythenshawe): This is indeed a day of deep sadness for everyone who knew Harold and had the privilege of working with him. In a very brief tribute, I want to start with a statement of fact. The Chronically Sick and Disabled Persons Act 1970, whose 25th anniversary is being celebrated in many parts of Britain this week, would never have become law had it not been for Harold Wilson. He gave the Bill a very powerful helping hand. In a moment of decisive importance, he decided on the dissolution that ended the 1966-67 Parliament, and gave the Bill preference over many others, including seven of his own, in order to ensure the Bill's enactment.

The late and much respected James Margach, the parliamentary correspondent for many years of *The Sunday Times*, spoke of the utter genuineness of Harold Wilson's concern to make life better for disabled people, their families and their carers. He was utterly right to do so.

In his memoirs, Harold made it clear that the entirely new initiatives he took as Prime Minister to enhance the status and improve the well-being of the weak and vulnerable gave him more satisfaction than any other initiative he took over the whole area of social policy. For that, his death will be widely mourned among severely disabled and other needful people. As my right hon. Friend the Member for Manchester, Gorton (Mr. Kaufman) said, he was an extraordinarily caring man, and his memory will be cherished by us all.

I hope that Mary and the family will be comforted by the deeply heartfelt tributes that have come this afternoon from all parts of the House.

4.16 pm

**Mr. Doug Hoyle** (Warrington, North): Above all, Harold Wilson was a unifying force. He took over a divided party in 1962, but by 1964 he had turned it into a party of government. One reason for that was that he was prepared to accept people from all sides. He had in his Cabinet people who he knew were not admirers of him, but whom he had selected for their ability. It was a question not of friendship, but of whether they were the right people for the job.

Before the 1964 election, Harold made a number of keynote speeches. One party had been in government for a long time, and the country was looking for a change. However, he did not simply allow it to drift into change:

he embraced the features of the day—in particular, new technology and science. In a speech, he showed how they could be harnessed for the benefit of people, rather than putting people on to the scrap heap.

Harold Wilson was trusted by ordinary people. He believed that a great deal of talent had gone to waste. That is why, as has been said today, among his memorials will be the Open university, which gave many people a chance in life that they had not previously had. It allowed them to develop and fulfil their capabilities.

Harold Wilson also had a great knowledge covering many areas. Many people from the arts and from sport visited him while he was at No. 10. He was knowledgeable about Yorkshire cricket, and once referred to Fred Trueman as the greatest living Yorkshireman.

I remember that Harold came to help me in 1979. He said, "What are we doing?" It was about lunchtime, so I said we would go in the pub for a pint and a pie. In the pub were many people on a break from their offices or factories, and they came to join us. He spoke to many of them. I introduced him to a young woman, aged about 25, from Huddersfield, and he showed his knowledge not only of Huddersfield, but of Huddersfield football. He referred to the three great Huddersfield teams of the 1920s, but when he began to name each member of those teams, I am afraid that the young lady's eyes glazed over, and everybody left the table.

Harold Wilson never forgot whence he came. That was his great attribute. He has been described as a pragmatist, but he was also a man of great beliefs. He had a great understanding of ordinary people, and people trusted him and, in fact, related to him when he was Prime Minister. I shall remember the ordinary things that he did. His pipe has been referred to, but along with his pipe went his raincoat. They became symbols of a caricature, but one that related to ordinary people and their lives.

Throughout Harold's extremely distinguished career, even before he became a politician, he was always interested in ordinary people. Imprinted on him were the hard times that people went through in the 1930s. Indeed, Harold's father, despite the fact that he was a scientist, lost his job in the recession, and times were very difficult for the Wilson family. He believed that, in the post-war era, people should never again suffer the indignities of unemployment or the difficulties caused to families under those conditions.

I join the tribute paid to Mary. Her devotion to Harold all through his life, especially in the latter years when he was not very well, was dedicated and caring. We all owe a debt to her for what she did for Harold. As for Harold, he not only won four elections: he carved for himself a niche in history. As we reflect on his years and what he did for the country, his stature will grow and grow, and he will be remembered as one of the great Prime Ministers of the century.

4.21 pm

**Mrs. Margaret Ewing** (Moray): I wish to associate my hon. Friends in the Scottish National party and our colleagues in its sister party Plaid Cymru with the genuine and heartfelt tributes paid to Lord Wilson. We send our kind thoughts and sympathy to Lady Wilson and her family.

*[Mrs. Margaret Ewing]*

I remember being a Member in the early 1970s when Sir Harold was Prime Minister. People have already recounted the kindness that he extended to people in his party and other parties. I too remember that kindness. I also remember many of the phrases he used from the Dispatch Box, which have become part of modern political vocabulary and are part of the inheritance that we owe to him.

Tribute has rightly been paid to the Open university, the creation of which Sir Harold and Jennie Lee steered through the House, and which has been welcomed by so many thousands of people, not least in more remote areas such as my constituency, where the facility to study through the Open university has been a great boon to our communities.

I would also like to mention—it has not been said already—that in 1965, under the premiership of Sir Harold, the Highlands and Islands development board was established, which many of us in Scotland remember with great affection. The board was—I think—the brainchild of the late Willie Ross, whom many of us called basso profondo when he was Secretary of State for Scotland, but it was established under the premiership of Sir Harold.

Many of us in the highlands and islands have a great respect and affection for that organisation. The appointment of Tom Fraser as its first chairman may have caused a by-election result in 1967 which Sir Harold did not enjoy, but at the end of the day, the establishment of the HIDB and its successor body was very welcome in our area of Scotland.

4.23 pm

**Mr. Edward O'Hara** (Knowsley, South): In associating myself with the condolences and the eloquent and deserved tributes which have been paid so far, may I express a few remarks on behalf of the people of my home town of Huyton, whom Harold represented with such distinction for so many years, and of Knowsley, South constituency Labour party—my home party—the successor party to Huyton.

Harold Wilson was synonymous with Huyton, as I have found in many places, no matter how far afield. Say "Huyton", and the immediate response is "Harold Wilson". Harold was loved by the people of Huyton, no less than he was admired by them. What endeared him to them? He had a common touch and a ready wit, and perhaps one of the greatest tributes that can be paid to him was that the wit of Harold Wilson, the Yorkshireman, was so widely admired by Scousers.

I remember much badinage in private in the bar of Huyton Labour club, but I fear that, if I repeated it in the House, it might not pass your rules on parliamentary language, Madam Speaker. Harold Wilson had no side and no false humility, but he had remarkable attributes. He understood the people of Huyton and the ordinary people of this country, their lives and concerns, and was superbly equipped as a Member of Parliament and as a Prime Minister with intellect, political skills and a deep social commitment to addressing those concerns, as has been said.

Many ordinary people in this country today perhaps do not adequately realise what they owe him. My right hon. Friend the Member for Sedgefield (Mr. Blair) gave an

impressive list of Harold Wilson's achievements, which it behoves us all to recognise this day, but they were his achievements on behalf of the ordinary people, which gave them benefits and opportunities that we hope that they will recognise today—benefits in work, their social lives and educational opportunities.

Harold Wilson was a product of the state education system, and I know from talking to him in Huyton that education was always high among his political priorities. Indeed, when I asked him what was his proudest achievement, he said without hesitation, "The Open university," which gives so many people opportunities today.

I will not detain the House overlong, but I wish to say that, to me, Harold Wilson was a man of the people. He lived for the people, and was loved by the people—the ordinary people, by whom he will be sadly mourned this day, and no more so than by the people of Knowsley, South and Huyton.

4.27 pm

**Mr. George Howarth** (Knowsley, North): I first joined the Labour party in Huyton in the 1960s, and a substantial part of my constituency came from the old Huyton constituency, when it was formed in 1983. The greater part of that constituency went to Knowsley, South.

Harold Wilson was held in enormous respect and affection in Knowsley, both for his achievements nationally, to which many hon. Members have referred, and for his work as a constituency Member of Parliament. It is the measure of that affection that he was always known locally simply as "Harold". Although originating from Yorkshire, he became intimately associated with Merseyside and with the spirit of the 1960s and all that that period held, particularly for the people of Liverpool and the surrounding area.

Despite his achievements, Harold Wilson remained a man wholly without affectation. It was for that quality that the people of Huyton and Merseyside held him so dear, and for those reasons that he will be missed so much.

4.29 pm

**Mr. Barry Sheerman** (Huddersfield): I was a young student at the London School of Economics in 1962 when Harold Wilson became the leader of the Labour party, and many of us forget what enormous charisma and power Harold had for my generation. He brought me and many others of my generation into the Labour party with his vision of a classless society, and an end to a society that depended more on connections than on ability.

Harold touched my life in another way, because I was one of the original Open university tutors, and I was grateful to Harold when I was a young and struggling university teacher. When I became the Member of Parliament for Huddersfield, it was with some surprise that I was adopted by Harold. He took a great interest in Huddersfield, and I tried to live up to his expectations. I looked for his maiden speech when I arrived here to get some clues, but he never made one. His first speech in the House was as a Minister, on Members' pay and allowances.

Everyone knew of Harold's fondness for Huddersfield, and many people have referred to it. I was privileged, because he often came to the town. Following a phone call, Mary would kindly organise the visit, and we had some splendid days together. I can remember one occasion in a Huddersfield hotel when Harold was trying to get the autograph of Bill Owen—Compo in "Last of the Summer Wine"—while Bill Owen tried to get Harold's autograph.

Harold would meet people with whom he had gone to Royds Hall grammar school, and people who had lived on the same street as him. He had a phenomenal memory for their backgrounds, their relatives and everything about them. As everyone has said today, he had that common touch. Many people become famous and move on—they might refer on "Desert Island Discs" to their place of origin—but Harold made sure that he went back and helped.

There would not have been a polytechnic in Huddersfield, which is now a thriving university, if it had not been for Harold making darn sure that there was one, and it is the largest wealth-creating institution in my town today. I saw that the people of Huddersfield loved him, and he loved them.

Harold Wilson was able to carry out the work that he did only with the support of Mary and his family. The last time I saw Harold was at the silver anniversary of the Open university. He was then very ill, but he was there, and he was proud. His family were proud with him, and I pay tribute to them and to him today.

4.32 pm

**Mr. Nicholas Winterton** (Macclesfield): As a long-serving Conservative Back-Bench Member, I should like to pay tribute to Lord Wilson, and to express my sympathy to Mary and to his family. As the right hon. Member for Chesterfield (Mr. Benn) said, Lord Wilson served for very few years on the Back Benches. But I can say—as an evergreen Back Bencher—that Harold Wilson valued Back Benchers in this House. Harold Wilson understood this House. Harold Wilson commanded this House. Harold Wilson was a compassionate and caring man, who was highly respected and will be long remembered.

4.33 pm

**Mr. Colin Pickthall** (Lancashire, West): I am grateful for the opportunity to say a word about Harold Wilson on behalf of the people of Ormskirk, where—as the Prime Minister rightly pointed out—Lord Wilson began his parliamentary career. Many older people in my constituency remember Harold Wilson not as a pre-eminent politician, but as the young candidate in 1945 and the young Member of Parliament thereafter.

People in the rural areas of my constituency, and in small villages and hamlets such as Banks and Scarisbrick, recall Harold Wilson standing on soap boxes in the middle of nowhere and conjuring up street meetings. That habit died down thereafter, but it was revived again in 1992 with some success.

Elderly people in the area will open their drawers and get out faded photographs from those days of themselves in their gardens with Harold Wilson. He is remembered in the Ormskirk area with enormous affection for his courteous approach to everybody and his down-to-earth manner. He never lost the ability to relate closely to the working people he represented.

The last time I spoke to Lord Wilson was in the 1983 general election campaign, when I chaired a public meeting in Ormskirk, to which he returned to speak on behalf of the then candidate, Josie Farrington, now Baroness Farrington. As he came in, somebody said, "It's not Harold Wilson, it's Mike Yarwood," and he said, "Yes, that's right," and left everyone in total confusion for the rest of the evening. Despite his failing health on that evening, he made a superb and witty speech. His memory had not failed, and he recalled in detail both the geography of the area from 30 years before and the people in the Ormskirk district. He had a clear grasp of its economic difficulties, and he answered questions with much of his old flair.

My right hon. Friend the leader of the Labour party mentioned Harold Wilson's response to the lady with the crying baby in one of his audiences. I must tell my right hon. Friend that he used that line again at that meeting in 1983. Furthermore, I have used it since, and I have heard Baroness Farrington use it, which goes to show that, when one has a good line, one should not let go of it.

Many of us will remember many of Harold Wilson's good lines. I am sure that many Labour Members have sat at the front of Labour party meetings, and will remember Harold's great line when he was in trouble at conference: "I know what's going on: I'm going on."

Lord Wilson was a distinguished Yorkshireman, but his political life was centred in west Lancashire and Merseyside. In our area, we remain proud of our association with him and of what he achieved and became. We remember with enormous satisfaction that he managed to win four elections for the Labour party. Those of us who were young in the 1960s will always associate those exciting and stimulating years with his premiership.

Like other speakers this afternoon, I wish to extend the deep sympathies of the people of west Lancashire to Mary and his family.

**Madam Speaker:** Thank you.

The House has heard the tributes to Lord Wilson, and I wish to make only one point, which has been touched on by many right hon. and hon. Members today. In my view, one of Harold Wilson's lasting achievements was to bring into being the Open university, of which I have the honour to be the current chancellor.

*Question put and agreed to.*

*Adjourned accordingly at twenty-four minutes to Five o'clock.*

# House of Commons

*Thursday 25 May 1995*

*The House met at half-past Two o'clock*

## PRAYERS

[MADAM SPEAKER *in the Chair*]

## PRIVATE BUSINESS

ACCOMMODATION LEVEL CROSSINGS BILL *[Lords]*
(*By Order*)
*Order for Third Reading read.*
*To be read the Third time on Thursday 8 June.*

CITY OF WESTMINSTER BILL *[Lords]* (*By Order*)

LONDON LOCAL AUTHORITIES (No. 2) BILL *[Lords]*
(*By Order*)
*Orders for consideration, as amended, read.*
*To be considered on Thursday 8 June.*

# Oral Answers to Questions

## NORTHERN IRELAND

### Peace Process

1. **Mr. Winnick:** To ask the Secretary of State for Northern Ireland if he will make a statement on the latest developments in the peace process.                    [24620]

10. **Mr. Canavan:** To ask the Secretary of State for Northern Ireland what recent meetings he has had about the peace process; and if he will make a statement.        [24630]

**The Minister of State, Northern Ireland Office (Mr. Michael Ancram):** Since I last answered questions in the House, there has been one further meeting of exploratory dialogue with the loyalist parties and there have been two with Sinn Fein. On each of those occasions, I have led the Government team. My right hon. and learned Friend the Secretary of State also had an informal meeting with Mr. Adams of Sinn Fein in Washington yesterday. On each of those occasions, we emphasised our commitment to the peace process and the key importance to that process of a substantial decommissioning of illegally held weapons together with progress on a range of other issues.

**Mr. Winnick:** I am grateful for that answer. Does the Minister agree that the White House conference on investment in Northern Ireland is a very good idea and that, indeed, the White House should be congratulated on holding that conference, which the Secretary of State and my hon. Friend the Member for Redcar (Ms Mowlam) are attending? Was not the meeting yesterday between the Secretary of State and the president of Sinn Fein inevitable at some stage, now that terrorism has,

fortunately, ended in Northern Ireland? Will not such talks be on an on-going basis, bearing in mind the qualification made by the Minister?

**Mr. Ancram:** First, I agree with the hon. Gentleman that the White House has acted very constructively in holding a conference, which follows the investment conference held by my right hon. Friend the Prime Minister in Belfast in December. It is being held to try to bring jobs and investment to Northern Ireland, which is indeed a very important purpose. It is quite clear also that that purpose will best be achieved by the establishment of a permanent peace. In the context of the conference in Washington, it was proper that my right hon. and learned Friend the Secretary of State met Mr. Adams to make clear the relationship between peace, economic investment and jobs and to make it clear that the only way in which peace can be founded soundly is by seeing the decommissioning of illegally held arms taking place.

**Mr. Wilkinson:** Can my hon. Friend and Her Majesty's Government do everything in their power to ensure that in their objective of appeasing or seeking the acquiescence of the minority of the minority community, they do not alienate the law-abiding majority on whose support the long-term political future of democratic institutions and stability in the Province depend?

**Mr. Ancram:** I can assure my hon. Friend that I am not in the business either of alienating or of appeasing. I am seeking to build on a situation in which there is a cessation of violence to try to ensure, through exploratory dialogue, that we can see the beginning of a genuine decommissioning of illegally held arms. There is not a Member of the House who would not agree that, at the end of day, peace must be established on the basis of illegally held arms being taken out of the Northern Ireland equation. We have made it quite clear to those to whom we are speaking in Sinn Fein and the loyalist parties that if they wish to proceed to substantive political dialogue in Northern Ireland, substantial decommissioning of arms would have to take place.

**Rev. Martin Smyth:** Is the Minister concerned with the changing stance of Dick Spring from that in December 1993 and June 1994, when he talked not only about a cessation of violence but about a handing over of weapons, along with the statement of Albert Reynolds, who is calling for the decommissioning of legally held firearms by servants of the state? Why did the Minister suggest pulling out of talks with representatives of a loyalist paramilitary faction because they were threatening to shoot drug dealers, while continuing to talk with representatives of those who had shot a drug dealer just two weeks ago?

**Mr. Ancram:** I have made it clear all along that the basis of exploratory dialogue is that it is carried out with parties that do not condone or support the use of violence. When there has been any such suggestion, I have challenged the parties about it. Indeed, earlier this week, when there were suggestions that intimidatory action might be being taken in one quarter, I made it clear that I would not speak to parties that in any way appeared to condone it. Certainly, one of the parties and, I suspect, both, have since said that they do not condone such violence. It is right that we make it clear that, in a civilised society, there is no justification for anyone taking the law into his own hands at any time.

On the first part of the hon. Gentleman's question, it is the agreed position of both Governments that, if we are to achieve a settlement and arrive at inclusive talks—including parties such as Sinn Fein—there has to be a substantial decommissioning of weapons. The Taoiseach said in the Dail on 25 April:

"It is a very important principle of parity of esteem in democratic dialogue that everybody should approach discussion on the same basis, solely on that of their electoral mandate and not by reference to any implied pressure they can exert because of the existence of arms in the hands of associated organisations. In order to achieve parity of esteem and position those arms must be taken out of commission."

I do not believe that the Irish Government could have made their position clearer than that.

**Mr. Bellingham:** Does my hon. Friend agree that, although there has been a welcome abatement of terrorism, it is ridiculous for the hon. Member for Walsall, North (Mr. Winnick) to talk about an end to terrorism, because the IRA clearly still has a massive arsenal and could easily redeploy it in a matter of hours? Does my hon. Friend accept that it is essential that, before the IRA is admitted to round table talks, the decommissioning process should be well under way?

**Mr. Ancram:** I am grateful to my hon. Friend for reminding the House that any steps taken since the cessation of violence have been taken as a direct response to the lowering of the security risk in Northern Ireland. None of them is irreversible, and that is an important part of the response that has been made.

As for the talks, we have made it clear that to move from exploratory dialogue to substantive bilateral dialogue will require a tangible beginning to the process of decommissioning and that to move to inclusive talks around the table will require substantial decommissioning. The reason is not one of doctrine but the fact that others will not sit around the table with a party that still has associations with a fully armed and operational organisation of the sort that the IRA is.

**Mr. Worthington:** May I present the apologies of my hon. Friend the Member for Redcar (Ms Mowlam), who is attending the investment conference in Washington?

Of course, we completely concur with the Government on the importance of decommissioning of arms, but what other matters have been discussed in the talks between the Secretary of State for Northern Ireland and the leader of Sinn Fein and in the Minister's talks with other members of Sinn Fein? Can the Minister update us on those talks? For example, have any assurances been given by Sinn Fein that it is using all its influence to eliminate punishment beatings or to take other steps to improve the quality of the peace being developed in Northern Ireland?

The Minister will have noticed the optimistic annual report of the Chief Constable of the RUC who expresses the belief that both sides of the paramilitary are set to go down a "peaceful road" but that, at the same time, the

"military machines are up, they are cohesive. If they decide . . . to go again they could do so".

What promises have been given that those machines will be stood down?

**Mr. Ancram:** At the moment, we are in an exploratory dialogue, the purpose of which is to explore such questions. The two sessions that I have had with Sinn Fein have concentrated largely not only on how decommissioning might take place but on the reason for it and why it is an essential part of the peace process. As the hon. Gentleman knows, those talks are not on a single-issue agenda; other topics can be, and have been, raised. I have told Sinn Fein and the loyalists that there are other topics that I believe they will wish to raise with me, and exploratory dialogue will continue in the future.

On punishment beatings, on a number of occasions I have made it clear that the Government are not prepared to accept any form of taking the law into one's own hands. We have explained to Sinn Fein that participation in normal political life implies responsibilities as well as rights, and that a party that is fully committed to constitutional means and objectives does not intimidate and threaten the population, does not encourage people to take the law into their own hands and does not condone breaking people's bones with iron bars. We shall continue to make that clear at every possible opportunity.

### Economy

2. **Mr. Mackinlay:** To ask the Secretary of State for Northern Ireland what are his plans for expanding the economy of Northern Ireland during the next 12 months.       [24621]

**The Minister of State, Northern Ireland Office (Sir John Wheeler):** Government's role is to provide the right conditions and the right support for the private sector to create economic growth. In Northern Ireland, we are helping companies to become more competitive, building up management and work force skills, supporting innovation, developing an enterprise culture and encouraging inward investment and tourism.

**Mr. Mackinlay:** How very interesting. Why is the Minister not prepared to proclaim these plans for inward investment and enterprise culture on behalf of the Conservative candidate in the North Down by-election? Can the right hon. Gentleman tell us which Minister from the Northern Ireland team is going to support the Conservative candidate in that by-election on those and other policies? Is it not a fact that Conservative candidates now choose what party policies they support à la carte and Tory Ministers now choose which Conservative candidates to support à la carte?

**Sir John Wheeler:** I am grateful that the hon. Gentleman finds the Government's economic achievements in Northern Ireland interesting. They are, indeed, interesting. Northern Ireland's economy has outpaced the rest of the United Kingdom during the past five years, and the Department of Economic Development envisages even greater achievements in ensuing years. I believe that the hon. Gentleman has chosen to refer to some remarks in a gossip column in a newspaper. I have not been consulted about that gossip column. I certainly have no comment to make on it, and I have no comment to make now, either.

**Rev. Ian Paisley:** What decisions have been made so far about the European Union special fund, and to what projects will that money go? What percentage of the money will be allocated to each programme? Will the money that is allocated internally to Northern Ireland be spent in Northern Ireland on projects decided by the people of Northern Ireland, or will Dublin's voice be heeded? Will Dublin have a say in how that money is spent, although it has its own percentage of money for its own internal affairs?

**Sir John Wheeler:** I am unable to give the hon. Gentleman the precise information that he seeks because not all the matters have yet been decided. It will be welcome if there is additional funding available for the people of Northern Ireland and the island of Ireland as a whole, and in particular the cross-border areas which have important commercial interactions with the Northern Ireland economy. In due course, my Department will make known the precise details of the funding arrangements, but I can say to the hon. Gentleman that that part of the funding which relates to Northern Ireland will be decided by the proper authorities in Northern Ireland.

**Mr. John D. Taylor:** Since the MacBride principles involve positive discrimination and are also contrary to fair employment legislation in Northern Ireland, and since the Government have always campaigned against the MacBride principles, can the Minister assure the people of Northern Ireland that the Government and their agencies, such as the Industrial Development Board, will give no grants whatsoever to any American firm that operates the MacBride principles against the existing legislation in Northern Ireland?

**Sir John Wheeler:** I can understand why the hon. Gentleman couches his question in such a way. Even as we discuss these matters this afternoon, my right hon. and learned Friend is at work in Washington at the investment conference, putting forward the case for investment in Northern Ireland and emphasising the fairness of our employment practices and the opportunities for employing a well-educated and proficient work force in Northern Ireland. We shall adhere to our previously published policies and objectives about the MacBride principles. I am sure that my noble Friend will take into account his own strictures on the matter.

**Mr. John Marshall:** Does my right hon. Friend agree that, although the peace process should encourage substantial inward investment in Northern Ireland, we could handicap that if we adopted restrictions on industry, such as a national minimum wage or the social chapter, as suggested by the Labour party?

**Sir John Wheeler:** My hon. Friend is absolutely right that such practices would greatly discourage investment in the United Kingdom and in Northern Ireland in particular and would lose us jobs, which the people of Northern Ireland seek. He is right once again to draw the attention of the House to such a disastrous policy.

### Teaching

3. **Mr. Harry Greenway:** To ask the Secretary of State for Northern Ireland what guidance he gives teachers on methods of teaching; and if he will make a statement.     [24622]

**Mr. Ancram:** It is the responsibility of the education and library boards to provide the necessary support for

schools and in-service training for teachers to enable them to delivery the school curriculum. The Government give no direct guidance.

**Mr. Greenway:** Is my right hon. Friend aware of the pressure over the years from socialist education idealogues for mixed ability teaching and of its damaging results? I certainly never practised it here and would not do so anywhere else. Will he advise teachers in Northern Ireland and everywhere else that such teaching methods would be disastrous and that sound learning comes only from sound discipline, which must be achieved?

**Mr. Ancram:** I hear what my hon. Friend says and have some sympathy with his comments. I do not have his professional background, so I would not presume to comment in a more professional way. We give no direct guidance to teachers as such.

The Northern Ireland education system, which is particular and unique to Northern Ireland, as my hon. Friend knows, produces very good results. School pupils in Northern Ireland continue to perform better than their English counterparts. In 1992-93, 85 per cent. of A-level pupils in Northern Ireland achieved two or more A-levels compared to 74 per cent. in England, while the proportion of year 12 pupils with no GCSEs was 6 per cent. compared to 7 per cent. in England; so we can take some satisfaction from the fact that the Northern Ireland education system is working, and working well.

**Ms Hoey:** As a product of the Northern Ireland education system, I have to agree. On teaching methods in integrated schools, which are obviously excellent, can the Minister give the House any news on further progress in making the special unit on Rathlin island an integrated school?

**Mr. Ancram:** I can only repeat what I have told the hon. Lady on another occasion. Any proposal for integrated education is considered by my Department according to strict criteria, to ensure that such schools have a chance of being viable and of succeeding. The criteria are carefully laid out and proposals are made to me. When the criteria are met, unless there are specific reasons, we normally support the proposals. When they are not met, I have had, on occasion, to turn them down.

### Inward Investment

4. **Mr. Nigel Evans:** To ask the Secretary of State for Northern Ireland what level of inward investment has been attracted to Northern Ireland for the latest year for which figures are available.     [24623]

**Mr. Ancram:** During 1994-95, the Industrial Development Board secured 10 inward investment projects, with an employment potential of nearly 2,000 jobs and planned investments of £130 million.

**Mr. Evans:** I welcome the Washington conference on investment in Northern Ireland. Will my hon. Friend confirm that we have some particularly good news—between April and August last year 39 potential investors visited Northern Ireland, whereas 96 such investors visited Northern Ireland between September and January this year? Will my hon. Friend confirm that those figures would be further enhanced if we could get the decommissioning of arms by the IRA, and that the message to Sinn Fein, the IRA and the people of Northern Ireland is simple—it is a case of guns out and jobs in?

**Mr. Ancram:** I am grateful to my hon. Friend. That was the message that came through very clearly from my right hon. and learned Friend the Secretary of State last night in Washington. It is a point that we must continue to make because, although the figures to which my hon. Friend rightly alluded are very encouraging, there is no doubt that investment and prosperity in Northern Ireland will depend not only on a cessation of violence but on the confidence that peace will last and, indeed, on the political settlement which I hope will create political stability following on that.

I totally support what my hon. Friend said, but the figures are now rather better than those that he gave. There were 163 visits by potential investors in 1994-95 compared with 146 in the preceding year. Investment inquiries, which are a very good indicator, were up as well, at 743 in the six months to 31 March 1995 compared to only 189 in the corresponding period in the previous year. These are, indeed, encouraging signs.

**Mr. Clifford Forsythe:** The Minister will be aware of my strong support for overseas firms coming into my constituency, although I am very concerned at the extra financial burden placed on those firms by the fair employment legislation. Would the Minister join me to help investigate the unofficial embargo that has been placed by a Government department on a certain product produced in a factory in my constituency?

**Mr. Ancram:** As the hon. Member knows, that is not one of the departments for which I have responsibility in Northern Ireland, although I answer for it in the House. If the hon. Gentleman writes to me giving details, I shall pass them on to my noble Friend Lady Denton and she will reply to him in due course. I know that the hon. Gentleman works very hard in his constituency to ensure that inward investment is forthcoming and that, in the past three years, there has been some significant inward investment.

**Mr. Worthington:** While in the United States, will the Secretary of State see Senator Jesse Helms, the chair of the Senate Foreign Relations Committee, who is against all US aid, including aid for the International Fund for Ireland, to persuade him that this would be exactly the wrong moment to withdraw assistance to Ireland? If we can get money for the International Fund for Ireland, will the Secretary of State ensure that a good proportion of it goes into community-based initiatives so that the people of Northern Ireland can get a sense of ownership of the economy in the Province?

**Mr. Ancram:** My right hon. and learned Friend is in Washington to promote investment into Northern Ireland because that is the purpose of the conference. Certainly, he and my noble Friend Lady Denton and the Under-Secretary, my hon. Friend the Member for Cambridgeshire, North-East (Mr. Moss), will spend their time making sure that that message comes across clearly and strongly to all those at that conference. The purpose of the conference is, however, to attract investment. The reason for attracting private investment is that it can create

jobs, which are, at the end of the day, the best underpinners of prosperity and of the standard and quality of life in Northern Ireland.

**Mr. Sykes:** Does not my hon. Friend find it strange that the hon. Member for Thurrock (Mr. Mackinlay) seems to be more interested in gossip than in facts? Perhaps he is in a hurry to get back to the Chelsea flower show. Will my hon. Friend explain to Opposition Members that it is the social chapter, the minimum wage and state control that affect inward investment and that the reason why British firms have been so successful in attracting inward investment is exactly the absence of those things?

**Mr. Ancram:** I fully agree with my hon. Friend. That is why the Government have taken a firm view on the social chapter. However, in Northern Ireland there has been, as my hon. Friend knows, a particular disadvantage, and that has been the troubled situation that has existed for 25 years. We are now trying to establish peace not only in the short term but in the long term because that will bring even more badly needed jobs to Northern Ireland. As for gossip and the hon. Member for Thurrock (Mr. Mackinlay), one of the occupations of the House in the 20 years in which I have been here, on and off, has always been to indulge, in certain respects, in gossip.

### Peace Process

5. **Mr. Gordon Prentice:** To ask the Secretary of State for Northern Ireland what progress he has made in taking the peace process forward in his talks with representatives of Sinn Fein.        [24624]

**Mr. Ancram:** I met representatives of Sinn Fein at meetings in exploratory dialogue on 10 May and yesterday. At the first meeting, we explored the decommissioning of illegally held weapons and we agreed to discuss it at a future meeting on the basis of a detailed paper tabled by the Government at that time.

Yesterday, we explored in depth the relevance of decommissioning to the peace process and our differences of approach to this. My right hon. and learned Friend held an informal meeting with Mr. Adams of Sinn Fein in Washington last night when the relevance of peace to economic prospects in Northern Ireland was underlined.

**Mr. Prentice:** Now that the Minister has met representatives of Sinn Fein, does he believe that Gerry Adams and the Sinn Fein leadership have the authority and the influence to insist that all IRA brigades decommission their arms and explosives? If not, does he believe that the Government are pressing Sinn Fein to do something on which it cannot necessarily deliver?

**Mr. Ancram:** Sinn Fein has agreed that it was its influence that created the situation that led to the cessation of violence on 31 August last year. I understand, in talking to Sinn Fein, that it has admitted that it has an influence over the question of decommissioning as well. What I am doing—it is absolutely clear—is making it abundantly clear to Sinn Fein that, if it wishes to move from exploratory dialogue to substantive dialogue, not just words but actions in terms of decommissioning will be required. I know that Sinn Fein has taken careful note of what I have said and I am sure that we shall return to the matter again at future meetings.

**Mr. Molyneaux:** Given that the IRA has halted only one aspect of terrorism, that it has actually increased other criminal activities, including murder, recently and that it has continued the very worrying feature of targeting police families and public figures, do Ministers not now realise that they have the backing of the entire community for demanding that the IRA ends its terrorism and that it sets about deactivating its hideous terrorist apparatus for good?

**Mr. Ancram:** I am grateful to the right hon. Gentleman for what he says because it is important that we realise what our objectives are. Our objectives are to take violence, intimidation and terrorism out of the situation in Northern Ireland. What we are doing is making it clear to those who say to us that they wish to become part of the political process that it is no part of a democratic party to condone the use of violence for political purposes. It is no part of a democratic party to condone the use of violence for intimidatory purposes and it is no part of a democratic party to have associations with fully armed and potentially terrorist organisations. We have made it clear that, if this process is to move forward with the participation of Sinn Fein and, indeed, of the loyalist paramilitary representatives, we have to see those problems resolved.

**Mr. Peter Bottomley:** Does my hon. Friend accept that there will be widespread support throughout the House both for what the right hon. Member for Lagan Valley (Mr. Molyneaux) said and for what he said in reply? Will he confirm that, for years, the House has expected elected councillors from constitutional parties to sit in the same chamber as Sinn Fein and that the key point that needs to be made to Sinn Fein is that, whereas talking with Ministers is not frightfully complicated, the most important issue is creating the conditions in which other parties are willing to sit down with Sinn Fein to discuss the future of Northern Ireland within the United Kingdom?

**Mr. Ancram:** I agree with my hon. Friend. That is why the basis for exploratory dialogue was threefold from the start. One part of it was the consequences of the cessation of violence, which included aspects such as the decommissioning of arms. Another was the bringing of Sinn Fein back into the full democratic process within Northern Ireland, in terms not just of electing councillors but of the work that those councillors do. The third was finding the basis for Sinn Fein to become involved in the political discussions and the constitutional discussions on the future of Northern Ireland. My hon. Friend is right to say that if Sinn Fein wishes to achieve that status, it must do so on the basis that all other parties do, which is that they are armed with their electoral mandates and with nothing else.

### Tourism, Banbridge

7. **Mr. Trimble:** To ask the Secretary of State for Northern Ireland what proposals he has to facilitate tourism in the Banbridge district.    [24626]

**Sir John Wheeler:** The Northern Ireland tourist board is taking action in conjunction with the local industry on a number of fronts, particularly marketing, quality and accommodation, to facilitate the development of tourism across all parts of Northern Ireland, including Banbridge.

**Mr. Trimble:** Does the Minister accept that the provision of bed-and-breakfast accommodation in rural areas, by conversion or new build, is a desirable objective

but that it is being frustrated by an over-rigid approach by planning authorities? Does he accept that the people of Banbridge would be delighted if there were major hotel development in the town but that they will be extremely angry with the Government if it turns out that the true reason for the mooted closure of Banbridge hospital is to sell it off for such development?

**Sir John Wheeler:** I know that the hon. Gentleman takes an informed and dedicated interest in the commercial interests of his constituents, not least in the promotion and development of tourism. The provision of quality accommodation has been identified by the Northern Ireland tourist board as an important development for Northern Ireland and the board may be able to provide some form of assistance. I have no knowledge of what the hon. Gentleman suggests in respect of the national health service but if my hon. Friend who is responsible for health knows about that point I am sure that he will communicate with the hon. Gentleman. Planning permission for bed-and-breakfast accommodation is a matter for the divisional planning officer, but I should hope that such decisions would be based on the economic needs as well as the environmental interests of the locality.

### Terrorist Prisoners

8. **Mr. Mike O'Brien:** To ask the Secretary of State for Northern Ireland how many prisoners in Northern Ireland gaols are classified as members of (a) nationalist terrorist organisations and in each case which one and (b) loyalist terrorist organisations and in each case which one.    [24627]

**Sir John Wheeler:** The terrorist affiliation of prisoners is recorded for prison management purposes, not for classification. Approximately 35 per cent. of sentenced prisoners are republican, 23 per cent. are loyalist, and 42 per cent. are not affiliated or are untraced.

**Mr. O'Brien:** Has the Minister had an opportunity to read the report by the Northern Ireland Association for the Care and Resettlement of Offenders concerning the early release of prisoners? Will it form a topic for discussion during his talks with Northern Irish parties?

**Sir John Wheeler:** I welcome the hon. Gentleman's reference to the report and work of NIACRO, which I regard extremely highly. I have regular opportunities to meet representatives of NIACRO and I listen to their points of view and objectives carefully. It is a forward-thinking, highly responsible organisation on which I place much credit. Its observations weigh in my mind when I consider those important and complicated matters and in the course of discussion with others, too.

**Mr. Brazier:** When are the cases of prisoners Fisher and Wright likely to be reviewed, and when is next month's review of the sentence of Private Lee Clegg likely to be completed?

**Sir John Wheeler:** I cannot comment on the cases of the two offenders to whom my hon. Friend referred, other than to say that they are part of the normal process and procedure for the Prison Service in Northern Ireland and will be subject to those procedures in precisely the same way as any other prisoners. The life sentence review board will begin to review Private Lee Clegg's case in June and a report will come to my notice in due course.

**Mr. A. Cecil Walker:** When will the statement of 16 March be implemented to allow financially assisted visits for low-income families of prisoners?

**Sir John Wheeler:** The hon. Gentleman takes a detailed and considered interest in those matters. The Northern Ireland Prison Service is considering a number of proposals to enhance the regime of prisons in Northern Ireland and that is certainly one of them. The Prison Service must take into account the serious cost implications as it balances the different economic needs of the management of prisons.

### Terrorist Disarmament

9. **Mr. Nicholas Winterton:** To ask the Secretary of State for Northern Ireland if he will make a statement on the progress he has made to date in bringing about the disarming of republican terrorist organisations.     [24628]

**Sir John Wheeler:** Substantial progress on decommissioning paramilitary weapons, and on other issues, is needed if Sinn Fein is to enter normal political life in Northern Ireland. We will continue to pursue this matter vigorously during exploratory dialogue. The RUC and Garda will also continue to seek out all illegal terrorist weapons, as recent successes in Northern Ireland and the Republic amply demonstrate.

**Mr. Winterton:** Although I fully support the peace initiative, is my right hon. Friend aware that there are Members who deeply regret the meeting that took place between the Secretary of State and Gerry Adams yesterday in Washington, because it gives credibility to Mr. Adams and his cause, which is totally unjustified? Does he accept that if the Government are to retain the confidence of the overwhelming majority of people in Northern Ireland, who support the Union, including the Unionist parties in Northern Ireland, they must make no further concessions to republican terrorism and we must have a substantial decommissioning of IRA weapons?

**Sir John Wheeler:** I fully understand why my hon. Friend views with distaste the encounter between my right hon. and learned Friend and the president of Sinn Fein. Perhaps he will be pleased to know that that encounter enabled my right hon. and learned Friend to make clear to the president of Sinn Fein that if Sinn Fein is to be a normal political party, it must understand the importance of the decommissioning process and it must agree, through the exploratory talks mechanism that my hon. Friend the Member for Devizes (Mr. Ancram) is conducting, with the modalities of decommissioning if it is to make progress.

My hon. Friend the Member for Macclesfield (Mr. Winterton) urges that the Government should not concede, to use his word, any further leeway to Sinn Fein. I can assure him that the decommissioning principle, which has been so vigorously announced by the Government, will be adhered to.

**Mr. Maginnis:** Is it not somewhat peculiar that the right hon. Member for Westminster, North (Sir J. Wheeler) answered that question instead of the hon. Member for Devizes, who has responsibility, apparently,

for bringing the disarmament process to a conclusion? Has not the hon. Member for Devizes been somewhat coy about his on-going relationship with Sinn Fein-IRA? Is it not a fact that although every demand by Sinn Fein-IRA as to who they will meet and when they will meet them has been met so far, not a single solitary gun has been produced, and nor have we moved to discuss in detail the modalities and methods for disarmament? Is it true that progress on that issue has been made with loyalist paramilitary organisations? Is not the dalliance of the hon. Member for Devizes with Sinn Fein-IRA becoming a sordid little affair?

**Sir John Wheeler:** I can assure the hon. Gentleman that there is no difference in any way between my hon. Friend the Member for Devizes and me on the issue of decommissioning. We stand shoulder to shoulder in our determination to see that process carried forward. The hon. Gentleman is quite right to say that the exploratory talks that my hon. Friend has been holding with various organisations, down but a single track, have shown some to be swifter in their journey than others. The fact remains that, even as we talk of such matters, in Washington my right hon. and learned Friend is urging the decommissioning process, because if investors are to invest in Northern Ireland with confidence, they, like other people, cannot look into the minds of terrorists and their political associates, who speak about permanence of peace, until they look to see the evidence of a standing down of terrorist gangs. When that happens, people will know that decommissioning has indeed been achieved.

**Mr. Cyril D. Townsend:** What plans have the Government to involve either other countries or other organisations in the process of removing and destroying arms, ammunition and explosives that may be seized in due course?

**Sir John Wheeler:** It remains to be seen precisely what procedures are necessary to achieve the successful and actual decommissioning of the substantial amounts of weapons and explosives that are held by the Provisional IRA and others. It is always possible that contributions to the process can be made by other people, although firmly within the control and the jurisdiction of the United Kingdom and the Government of the Republic.

### PRIME MINISTER

#### Engagements

Q1. **Ms Hoey:** To ask the Prime Minister if he will list his official engagements for Thursday 25 May.     [24650]

**The Prime Minister (Mr. John Major):** This morning I presided at a meeting of the Cabinet and had meetings with ministerial colleagues and others. In addition to my duties in the House, I shall be having further meetings later today.

**Ms Hoey:** Has the Prime Minister any understanding of the deep anger that will be felt in the country at the way in which the directors of the privatised National Grid have used tax avoidance measures to ensure that their wives will have hundreds of thousands of bonus shares? What message does that send to pensioners in my constituency who are struggling to make ends meet?

**The Prime Minister:** The hon. Lady may not be wholly aware of what has happened. I have made inquiries to clarify the position.

I understand that the only share options granted by the National Grid have been granted to its own directors and staff; but, having exercised those options and purchased the shares, directors have then given them to their wives. As the hon. Lady may know, it is a fundamental principle that transfers of property between husband and wife are free of tax, as they have been for a long time.

If the hon. Lady and the deputy leader of the Labour party wish to change the position, are they saying that they want to make transfers of property between husband and wife taxable? Are they saying that the independent taxation of men and women should be abolished? Are they saying that widows should no longer be able to inherit property from their husbands free of tax? [HON MEMBERS: "Answer".] That is the inevitable principle that follows from the point put by the hon. Lady. Once again, Opposition Members are trying to use a particular issue for their own advantage without understanding the implications of what they say.

**Rev. Ian Paisley:** I am sure that the Prime Minister has heard of the result of yesterday's meeting in America between his right hon. and learned Friend the Secretary of State for Northern Ireland and the leader of IRA-Sinn Fein. I am sure that he has noted what the leader of IRA-Sinn Fein said: that there can be no progress towards decommissioning until there is complete demilitarisation of everyone—that is, the surrender of arms by Army, police and those who have guns to protect themselves— and that all prisoners must be released. Are the Government prepared to negotiate with the leader of Sinn Fein on those terms?

**The Prime Minister:** As the hon. Gentleman knows, my right hon. and learned Friend met the leader of Sinn Fein yesterday to make a point that was very important for both the hon. Gentleman's constituents and others in Northern Ireland: that the best contribution that Sinn Fein could make to the conference and to Northern Ireland's prosperity would be to promote peace, and therefore to secure the decommissioning of the IRA's arms and explosives. That remains the Government's position.

Until, in these exploratory talks, there have been practical movements forward in the decommissioning of arms, it will not be possible for Sinn Fein to move to full-scale political talks either with the Government or, I suspect, the hon. Gentleman's party or any other political party in Northern Ireland. That is the point that we have made repeatedly to Sinn Fein, and it remains our position. As the hon. Gentleman knows, our objective is to move towards taking the gun entirely out of the politics of Northern Ireland. In that, I believe that we have the support of all the mainstream political parties in Northern Ireland and all the people of Northern Ireland.

**Mr. Blair:** To return to National Grid, is the Prime Minister aware—[HON. MEMBERS: "Oh."] They wanted us to answer the point and now they do not want us to raise it. Is the Prime Minister aware that the issue is not independent taxation between men and women, but remuneration being paid by way of share options so as to avoid income tax? That is what is actually happening in this case. Is the Prime Minister prepared to say that that abuse is wrong and is he prepared to put a stop to it?

**The Prime Minister:** Let me say to the right hon. Gentleman that I favour employee share options and I favour executive share options. I hope that the right hon. Gentleman does too, because that is a direct quote from his hon. Friend the shadow Chancellor. There is no dispute between the right hon. Gentleman and I or between the two major parties about the desirability of share options.

In this instance, the hon. Member for Vauxhall (Ms Hoey) has raised a point that has been the subject of publicity today. Having exercised the share options and purchased shares, a husband passed his own property— the shares—to his wife. The leader of the Labour party seems to be saying that if, having done something of which the leader of the Labour party approves—accepted share options—the husband then does what has been done for many years and passes them to his wife, that should now be taxable. That is quite unlike anything that has happened in the past. If that is Labour's policy, let the Leader of the Opposition please make it clear.

**Mr. Blair:** No, that is not the policy. The only reason why the directors transfer shares to their spouses is that the remuneration is paid by way of share options in order to avoid income tax. That is why they do it. That is the issue: it is not whether share options are wrong or right, it is whether they are taxed as income or as capital gains. Is the Prime Minister prepared to say that, where remuneration is effectively given by way of share options to avoid income tax and only pay capital gains tax, he will put a stop to it?

**The Prime Minister:** Capital gains are taxed at the marginal rate when the capital gain is realised. The right hon. Gentleman is effectively saying that he does not wish husbands to pass those rights on to their wives. The transfer of property between husbands and wives—be it shares, property or capital—is tax free.

Although the right hon. Gentleman is now wriggling because his hon. Friend the shadow Chancellor changed his position mid morning because he realised what he had said and what he had done, the truth is revealed yet again by what the right hon. Gentleman has said: Labour hates privatisation and it hates profit. It cannot stand share ownership. Old Labour lurks there as clearly as it ever did. Labour Members cannot stand the fact that some people receive share options and exercise share options as part of their employment remuneration.

**Mr. Blair:** Perhaps the Prime Minister does not realise that the National Grid has admitted that it used share options to avoid paying income tax. Why does not the Prime Minister stop defending the greed of a privileged few and stand up for the vast majority of decent British people?

**The Prime Minister:** The right hon. Gentleman had better decide whether he is really in favour of share options. The glaring divide between the shadow Chancellor and the leader of the Labour party becomes more apparent day by day. They may sit close together, but clearly they never speak.

**Mr. Lidington:** Will my right hon. Friend join me in welcoming today's announcement of further measures to target taxpayers' money on making state schools more effective and improving standards? Will he confirm that the Government's objective is to ensure that all parents are entitled to a good-quality, high-standard state education for their children, not only if they happen to live a couple of boroughs away from a convenient grant-maintained school?

**The Prime Minister:** I can certainly confirm that point. I believe that the proposals announced by my right hon. Friend the Secretary of State for Education will be widely welcomed up and down the country.

**Mr. Ashdown:** Does the Prime Minister agree that the deadlines in Sarajevo represent a critical moment for the authority of the United Nations and its commanders in Bosnia? Will he ensure that, if our commanders on the ground in Bosnia conclude that decisive action must be taken, they will receive the full and unswerving backing of not only the Government but the United Nations in New York?

**The Prime Minister:** I share the right hon. Gentleman's view about the importance of the present situation. I am happy to tell him that we have already given that assurance to our commanders on the ground. We made that clear in New York last night and they are aware of our position. The United Nations has also reiterated its full support—by that I mean our commanders will have support for whatever action they may consider necessary in the light of the events of the past day or so.

Let me add to that point in view of the present situation. We very much wish the United Nations protection forces to continue performing their role. They have saved many lives delivering aid and containing the fighting. I believe the reason for maintaining a force on the ground remains as compelling today as it has been in the past, but all the parties need to be aware that if they continue ground fighting and accelerate it, they may render it impossible for the United Nations protection forces satisfactorily to carry out the mandate that they have been given. I hope that point is fully understood. At present, General Smith and the United Nations forces are very much in our thoughts. They most assuredly have our total support.

### Official Visits

Q2. **Mr. Dunn:** To ask the Prime Minister what plans he has to visit Southfleet, Kent.     [24651]

**The Prime Minister:** I have no current plans to do so.

**Mr. Dunn:** What advice would the Prime Minister give the leadership of the trade union, Unison, which may be about to inflict a vicious national strike on the British people? The last time Unison inflicted a strike on the British people—

**Mr. Mackinlay:** What has this to do with Kent?

**Mr. Dunn:** People are concerned about it in Southfleet.

The last time Unison inflicted a national strike on British people, hospitals were closed, schools were shut down, operations were cancelled and the dead were left unburied.

**The Prime Minister:** I believe that any form of industrial action in the health service would be bound to harm patients. It is difficult to see how it could do

anything else. My hon. Friend has provided a graphic reminder of what happened on a previous occasion. I am perfectly certain that no professional nurse would wish to pursue such action, and I very much hope that that will be the overwhelming view. I hope that the few people involved will set aside the language of trade union confrontation, look at the fair offer that has been made to them by the vast majority of NHS trusts up and down the country, accept it and put the issue behind us.

### Engagements

Q3. **Mr. Illsley:** To ask the Prime Minister if he will list his official engagements for Thursday 25 May.     [24652]

**The Prime Minister:** I refer the hon. Gentleman to the reply I gave some moments ago.

**Mr. Illsley:** From the Government's overwhelming defeat in the local elections last month, it is clear that the electorate totally rejected their local government policies. In particular, people rejected the Government notion that Labour authorities are high taxing and high spending. Will the Government now abandon plans to cap the expenditure of local authorities this year?

**The Prime Minister:** I have very great doubts about whether people have abandoned the notion that Labour means high taxes, both nationally and locally. If one looks band for band at local taxation last year, one finds that in band C, for example—I take the figures from memory, but I think that they are right—Labour councils taxed about £160 more than Conservative councils. That point will be understood increasingly as people examine their tax bills.

**Mr. Robathan:** In the course of his busy day, has my right hon. Friend had an opportunity to read the report on Islington's social services? If so, he will have found that the Labour party in Islington put political correctness above the needs of the vulnerable and of the children in its care, and above common sense. Does he agree that, in the same way, the Labour party in general puts women-only shortlists and other forms of positive discrimination and political correctness above the interests of the nation—

**Madam Speaker:** Order. What other parties do is not the responsibility of the Prime Minister. I have told the House time and time again that Ministers at the Dispatch Box answer for their policies, not for what other people do. Perhaps the Prime Minister can give some answer to the first part of the hon. Gentleman's question, but I hope that the House will remember in future that Ministers are to be questioned about their responsibilities, not about anything else.

**The Prime Minister:** The substantive part of the question followed on nicely from the question asked by the hon. Member for Barnsley, Central (Mr. Illsley) a moment ago. Like everyone in the House—I would hope—I read the reports about what apparently happened in Islington council and found them extremely disturbing. They show what happens when political correctness runs riot. I believe that tolerance, in that environment, becomes excess. It causes untold suffering for those in need of help. This was a sad example of what happens when the Labour party is in power. The hon. Member for Barnsley, Central neglected to mention the activities that went on in Islington, so I am grateful to my hon. Friend for bringing them to my attention.

Q4. **Ms Quin:** To ask the Prime Minister if he will list his official engagements for Thursday 25 May.　　[24653]

**The Prime Minister:** I refer the hon. Lady to the answer I gave some moments ago.

**Ms Quin:** Does the Prime Minister recall his prediction at the 1991 Conservative party conference that Labour would introduce eight new taxes if it took office? How does that claim look now in the light of the 20 new taxes that he and the Government have introduced?

**The Prime Minister:** Perhaps the hon. Lady should glance at the list of new taxes to which Opposition Front Benchers have committed themselves if they come to government—[Hon. Members: "Rubbish."] Opposition Members are right: most of the taxes that they propose are rubbish. Labour is now and always has been the party of high taxation at national and local levels, and while the Opposition continue to commit themselves to more spending on every occasion, they always will be the party of high taxation.

# Business of the House

3.31 pm

**Mrs. Ann Taylor** (Dewsbury): Will the Leader of the House give us the details of future business?

**The Lord President of the Council and Leader of the House of Commons (Mr. Tony Newton):** The business for the first week back after the spring Adjournment will be as follows:

TUESDAY 6 JUNE—Second Reading of the Crown Agents Bill [Lords].

WEDNESDAY 7 JUNE—Until 2.30 pm, there will be debates on the motion for the Adjournment of the House.

Remaining stages of the Criminal Justice (Scotland) Bill [Lords].

THURSDAY 8 JUNE—Motion in the name of the hon. Member for Wantage relating to disclosure of specified Select Committee papers.

Motions on the European Communities (Definition of Treaties) (Partnership and co-operation agreement between the European communities and their member states and the Russian Federation) order and the European Communities (Definition of Treaties) (Partnership and co-operation agreement between the European communities and their member states, and Ukraine) order.

FRIDAY 9 JUNE—Debate on the White Paper entitled "Tackling Drugs Together"—A Strategy for England 1995-98" on a motion for the Adjournment of the House.

The House will also wish to know that European Standing Committee B will meet at 10.30 am on Wednesday 7 June to consider European Community Document 4069/95, relating to Consumer Protection: Unit Pricing.

MONDAY 12 JUNE—Motion on the Northern Ireland (Emergency and Prevention of Terrorism provisions) (Continuance) order.

Remaining stages of the Medical (Professional Performance) Bill.

I expect to provide for Opposition time on either Tuesday 13 June or Wednesday 14 June, and to take Government business during the first part of Thursday 15 June. Friday 16 June is a non-sitting Friday.

**Mrs. Ann Taylor:** I thank the Leader of the House for that information. Will he confirm that he will be tabling a motion today to enable a Select Committee to work to clarify and implement the recommendations of the Nolan committee on the rules and procedures of the House? I hope that the House will welcome that development, as I am sure those outside it will. I hope especially that a welcome will be given to the movement by the Government over the past seven days on the Nolan report, which I believe has been in the public interest and the best interests of this Parliament.

Will the right hon. Gentleman confirm that the motion that he tables today will be before the House next week and that the Select Committee will meet as soon as possible? Will that Committee be required to make an interim report by 7 July for debate before the summer recess?

The Leader of the House has not scheduled an Opposition Supply day for the first week after the forthcoming recess, although he has promised us one during the week after that. I ask him to remind us of the number of Supply days remaining and give us an assurance that the remaining Supply days will be spread evenly throughout the remainder of the Session.

Last week, the Leader of the House promised information about economic debates in Government time as soon as possible. Is he yet able to say when those debates might be, or will the disagreements between the Chancellor of the Exchequer and the Governor of the Bank of England determine the time scale of economic debates in the House?

**Mr. Newton:** The timing of economic debates, details of which I still cannot give the hon. Lady, will be determined by what seems sensible and the convenience of the House.

The hon. Lady will realise that the problem with Opposition days is partly that the Opposition day debate that should have taken place yesterday was cancelled for reasons that we all understand and appreciate. That led to the tributes yesterday which we all heard—admirable tributes, if I may say so—and which slightly complicated matters. My recollection is that that Supply day will be the 13th and that there are eight such days yet to come. I shall do my best to ensure that they are as evenly spread as is consistent with securing the reasonable passage of Government business.

It may be that by now the motion on the Nolan report has been laid. If not, that will happen shortly. It makes provisions—I shall not read the full text of the terms of reference—for how the principal recommendations that relate to the House might be clarified and implemented and recommends specific resolutions for decision by the House. It is also required by the terms of reference that I am tabling that there should be an interim report, not later than Friday 7 July. As the hon. Lady knows, the purpose of setting that date is to provide an opportunity for debate were debate to be occasioned by the interim report.

As for when the resolution will be brought before the House, I expect and intend that that will happen the first week back after the recess. We shall want the Select Committee to meet as soon as it can after its terms of membership and reference have been agreed.

**Mr. John Biffen** (Shropshire, North): I appreciate that the business announced covers relations with Russia and the Ukraine but it does not mention Shropshire. May I inquire of my right hon. Friend that one may know soon that the Government have accepted the balanced and wise budgets determined by Shropshire county council and endorsed by the hon. Member for The Wrekin (Mr. Grocott) and my hon. Friend the Member for Ludlow (Mr. Gill) and myself, or is it still their intention to pursue confrontationally their original budget?

**Mr. Newton:** I had better say to my right hon. Friend that I would like to bring his question to the attention of my right hon. Friend the Secretary of State for the Environment.

**Mr. A. J. Beith** (Berwick-upon-Tweed): When may we have a debate on the Green Paper proposals on identity cards, so that those of us who think that they are an unwelcome addition to the powers of the state over the individual and that they are wide open to fraud and error can make that view clear? When we get that debate, will those members of the Cabinet who agree with my view of this matter be allowed to speak?

**Mr. Newton:** I rather doubt whether there is any member of the Cabinet who would put any point in quite the same way as the right hon. Gentleman, but, in any event, I will certainly bear in mind the request for a debate on the identity card Green Paper.

**Sir Terence Higgins** (Worthing): Should not my right hon. Friend point out to the hon. Member for Dewsbury (Mrs. Taylor) that we abolished Supply days some years ago and that we have Opposition days nowadays? Could we have some time for debates on Select Committee reports, as there are a number of reports now outstanding which deserve time to be debated on the Floor of the House?

**Mr. Newton:** As always, I shall bear in mind my right hon. Friend's courteously put requests. I would just make the point that I acted extremely promptly in response to a request from one Select Committee Chairman, and others recently, to provide time for the debate that took place on the affairs of the Church Commissioners.

**Mr. Alfred Morris** (Manchester, Wythenshawe): The Leader of the House knows that I speak as chairman of the managing trustees of the parliamentary contributory pension fund. If not in the first week back, when can we now expect to debate the senior salaries review board's recent recommendations on parliamentary pensions?

**Mr. Newton:** I cannot give a precise date at the moment, but the right hon. Gentleman above all will know that my task is to consult the trustees in advance of that, and that I hope to do fairly soon after the recess.

**Mr. Nicholas Winterton** (Macclesfield): In fully supporting the views just expressed by the right hon. Member for Manchester, Wythenshawe (Mr. Morris), may I also pick up a point raised by the hon. Member for Dewsbury (Mrs. Taylor)? It would be very helpful indeed if the House could have a full economic debate to enable Conservative Members to display to the House the amazing amount of good news about the United Kingdom economy, and at the same time enable Conservative Members who wish to do so to provide some very positive and helpful suggestions to the Chancellor of the Exchequer and the Government that will help the Conservatives to win the next general election.

**Mr. Newton:** I always particularly enjoy my hon. Friend's helpful and positive suggestions.

**Mrs. Gwyneth Dunwoody** (Crewe and Nantwich): Has the Leader of the House seen the statement by GEC Alsthom and ABB, both of which are rolling stock manufacturers, which says that the Government's attitude towards private finance for railway privatisation is a totally pointless exercise? Will he therefore arrange, since hundreds of jobs are at risk in railway rolling stock in this country, for us to have an urgent debate, as soon as the House reassembles, on the total chaos that is being created in the railway industry by the utterly unwarranted nonsense of privatisation?

**Mr. Newton:** I do not accept either half of the hon. Lady's propositions about the effects of rail privatisation, or, indeed, its interrelationship with the private finance initiative, but I will of course draw her remarks to the attention of my right hon. Friend.

**Mr. Jacques Arnold** (Gravesham): When we return, may we have a teach-in on share options, because there

seems to be considerable ignorance in the House on the mechanics and working of share options, which was particularly well displayed by the Leader of the Opposition, who knows about the proceeds of share options because they financed his leadership campaign?

**Mr. Newton:** There seemed to be a good deal of misunderstanding, but my right hon. Friend the Prime Minister more than adequately corrected it.

**Mr. Dennis Skinner** (Bolsover): As the business for the week after the holiday is not exactly fizzing with ideas, would it not be a good opportunity to have a debate about nurses' pay, especially taking into account the fact that the Prime Minister, within five minutes, was justifying share options of more than £250,000 while attacking nurses who are struggling to get 3 per cent? It is high time that we were able to declare to the people out there that nurses do not want to go on strike, they just want justice. If a minimum rate of pay is good enough for Members of Parliament, it should be good enough for nurses up and down the country.

**Mr. Newton:** The notion that my right hon. Friend was in any way attacking nurses is totally inconsistent with anything that he said this afternoon or on any other occasion. I remind the hon. Gentleman that it was the present Government who gave the nurses the independent pay review body that they had always wished to have.

**Mr. Andrew Rowe** (Mid-Kent): My right hon. Friend will be aware that in the debates that have followed the Nolan committee report it has become clear that the interaction between some of the recommendations and the possible composition of this place is close. In the possible debate on the subject, will my right hon. Friend allow us to discuss the nature of the House of Commons that is required in the 21st century and to make some suggestions as to what Nolan might look at next, such as the undisclosed financial interests of a number of journalists?

**Mr. Newton:** I am sure that the Nolan committee will note my hon. Friend's latter suggestion. It would be for the Chair to judge what might or might not be in order in such a debate, but I suspect that my hon. Friend would find his own ingenious way into it.

**Mr. Tony Banks** (Newham, North-West): Will the Leader of the House arrange for the Minister responsible to make a statement to the House following the meeting of the International Whaling Commission in Dublin between 29 May and 2 June? When he relays that request, will he also ask whether there is any truth in the rumour that a deal has been done between the British whaling commissioner and the Faroese over not raising in the plenary session the issue of pilot whale slaughter? Those Faroese who are slaughtering the pilot whales are murdering scum. If any deal has been done between the British commissioner and the Faroese there will be an awful lot of anger in Britain.

**Mr. Newton:** I am sure that my right hon. Friend responsible for those matters will note the hon. Gentleman's comments and, of course, attribute to them the weight that his serious interest in these matters over a long period of time would rightly merit. I cannot make any promises about a statement, but I shall certainly bring the request to my right hon. Friend's attention.

**Mrs. Teresa Gorman** (Billericay): Will my right hon. Friend find time for us to debate early-day motion 1175 on the shocking report about child abuse in Islington?

[*That this House deplores the behaviour of the honourable Member for Barking in seeking to shuffle the blame onto others for the findings of the independent White Report; condemns Islington Borough Council which, during the period when the honourable Member for Barking was its leader, betrayed the children in its care, exposing them to severe abuse in council-run homes, failed to investigate such abuses and allowed those responsible to escape unpunished; believes that the stain of political correctness and corruption ingrained in Labour-run local authorities like Islington led to this scandal; and calls upon the honourable Member to accept her share of the responsibility and to apologise without reservation to the victims.*]

Such a debate would enable us to establish whether the matter should be brought before the appropriate Select Committee so that those involved can be closely questioned, including the hon. Member for Barking (Ms Hodge), who was leader of the council at the time and dismissed the report when it was brought to her as simply sensationalist journalism.

**Mr. Newton:** The question of what a Select Committee should consider is for the Select Committee itself, in this case the Select Committee on Health, and I have no doubt that that suggestion will be noted. My hon. Friend will have heard what my right hon. Friend the Prime Minister said a few moments ago about the fact that the reports of what has occurred obviously cause considerable concern. I hope that Islington borough council will act swiftly on the recommendation in the White report that the council should review its equal opportunities policy in its application to child care.

**Mr. Harry Cohen** (Leyton): Will the Leader of the House give consideration to how it is proposed to enact the European Community data protection directive, which goes way beyond the Data Protection Act 1984 passed by the House? If the Government are to enact it, should not it be via primary legislation rather than piecemeal reserve powers?

**Mr. Newton:** As always, I shall give consideration to a point that the hon. Gentleman raises, but I am not in a position to speculate on that consideration at the moment.

**Mr. Piers Merchant** (Beckenham): In view of the tragic bus accident on the M4 earlier this week in which, sadly, 10 people lost their lives, will my right hon. Friend find an early opportunity for a debate on coach safety and, in particular, the fitting of safety belts on Britain's coach fleet and whether the present maximum speed limits are satisfactory for coaches?

**Mr. Newton:** My hon. Friend will know that, as I said in the House yesterday morning, my right hon. Friend the Secretary of State for Transport has asked for an urgent report on the accident and it is being looked into by the Vehicle Inspectorate. Any question of a debate might sensibly await the outcome of those investigations.

**Mrs. Alice Mahon** (Halifax): Will the Leader of the House make time for a debate on the national lottery? He will be aware that a national lottery was justified by the fact that it would provide money for good causes. Would

not it be good if we could debate the fact that £13 million has gone into the back pocket of a Tory Member of Parliament and huge profits are now going into private pockets? It is not time that we had a look at where that money is going?

**Mr. Newton:** It may be appropriate in due course to debate the early experience of the lottery, but we are talking about very early experience. It is clear from further distributions this week, for example, among the arts, especially at regional level, that many of the causes in which I am sure that the hon. Lady is interested are benefiting.

**Mr. Edward Garnier** (Harborough): Will my right hon. Friend arrange an early debate on local authority market rights? Is he aware that Labour-controlled Leicester city council, owing to the six and one third mile rule, has prevented citizens in Oadby and Wigston in my constituency from holding a market to celebrate the 350th anniversary of the civil war in Leicestershire? Does he not agree that it is wholly undemocratic that socialists in the city of Leicester can control the rights of people who cannot even vote for them?

**Mr. Newton:** I had better confess that I was not fully informed about the precise circumstances in Leicestershire that my hon. Friend has described, but I shall ensure that the matter is drawn to the attention of my right hon. Friend the Secretary of State for the Environment and others.

**Mr. Roy Thomason** (Bromsgrove): Does my right hon. Friend think it appropriate to have an early debate on the future of capping of local authority expenditure, with a view to reviewing whether caps should continue, while retaining some system of control to ensure that there is not excessive expenditure and demands made by profligate Labour local authorities?

**Mr. Newton:** The whole way in which Labour authorities use money, to which my right hon. Friend the Prime Minister adverted at Prime Minister's Question Time, may merit debate, but I regret that I cannot propose such a debate next week.

**Mr. Max Madden** (Bradford, West): Will the Leader of the House confirm that the terms of reference of the committee set up to consider the Nolan recommendations will be debatable? Will he give an undertaking that there will be a specific allocation of time for such a debate? In referring to the terms of reference, the right hon. Gentleman mentioned resolutions. If resolutions are introduced, will he ensure that the Committee is invited to consider what would happen to Members who consistently defy such resolutions? As he will know, some hon. Members consistently refuse to observe resolutions relating to Members' interests—as have some former hon. Members—and nothing is ever done about it. Will he ensure that next time we are advised on what would happen if hon. Members refused to observe such resolutions?

**Mr. Newton:** The question of a debate would normally be discussed through the usual channels, of which I would expect to take account. The particular aspects of the Nolan recommendations to which the hon. Gentleman referred are for the Committee to consider, along with all the other Nolan recommendations in relation to the House.

**Mr. Paddy Tipping** (Sherwood): May we have an early opportunity to discuss the problems of endangered species? The Leader of the House will understand the urgency of that request since today's opinion poll shows that the popularity of the Conservatives is at a record low?

**Mr. Newton:** The hon. Gentleman will have, no doubt, made such a point on a number of earlier occasions. As I have said several times in the House, that point was pretty frequently made two years before the last election and look what happened then.

**Mr. Patrick Thompson** (Norwich, North): Bearing in mind the welcome given by many of my constituents and others in the country for the consultation paper on identity cards, may I support the request of the right hon. Member for Berwick-upon-Tweed (Mr. Beith) for an early debate on the subject? Will not such a debate provide an opportunity to rebut some of the phoney arguments against the cards' introduction?

**Mr. Newton:** I am almost being invited to take every side in the debate before we even have it, but I note that further request for such a debate.

**Mr. Andrew Mackinlay** (Thurrock): Will the Leader of the House consider having a debate on the problems of thousands of householders caused by negative equity? Does he realise that negative equity is causing great anxiety to many families, including those in Braintree, Macclesfield, Thurrock and elsewhere? The Government and the Opposition have to deal with the problem because it is jeopardising our economy and blighting the lives of many thousands of families.

**Mr. Newton:** The most effective contribution that the Government can make over a period is to ensure that the present economic recovery is sustained. That is what we are doing and will continue to do.

**Mr. David Shaw** (Dover): Will my right hon. Friend arrange for a debate on the abilities of those who make decisions in the Ministry of Defence? Will he explain how anyone with any ability can close the Royal Marines school of music when independent accountants said that the Ministry of Defence's figures are wrong, when independent chartered surveyors acting as valuers said they are wrong and when some 300 jobs are likely to be lost from the largest employer in Deal? Surely it is about time that we had proper financial decision-making in Government and not that undertaken by the Ministry of Defence.

**Mr. Newton:** My hon. Friend has rightly, honourably and properly made his point about the Royal Marines music school at Deal for a long time. I know, and my right hon. and learned Friend the Secretary of State for Defence will know, how disappointing the decision is to the people of Deal, and I am sure that my right hon. Friend will consider what my hon. Friend has said.

**Mr. Mike O'Brien** (Warwickshire, North): May we have an early debate on the Government's policy of removing surplus places from schools? Is he aware that one of the biggest schemes has been in Warwickshire which has been thrown into chaos and where the plug may have to be pulled on part of the reorganisation because of delays by the Government and the Department for Education in making decisions? They got their procedures wrong and have had to be hauled before the courts to be told that they have not only shortchanged the children of Warwickshire in terms of school funding but messed up the administration of the whole reorganisation scheme.

**Mr. Newton:** I cannot make a quick, off-the-cuff comment on what the hon. Gentleman says, but I shall, of course, bring it to the attention of my right hon. Friend the Secretary of State for Education.

**Mr. Iain Duncan Smith** (Chingford): Will my right hon. Friend find time for a debate on Britain's nuclear deterrent? Although they are clear about our policy, a number of my constituents are concerned that there seems to be a difference of opinion in the Labour party. Labour Back Benchers think that we should get rid of our nuclear deterrent whereas members of Labour's Front Bench want to hang on to it but never use it. Is there not a need for a debate so that Labour Front Benchers may have the opportunity to explain to the Great British public why they intend to waste money on what they will not use while we see the necessity for a deterrent?

**Mr. Newton:** If the time existed in the parliamentary timetable, I would be tempted to have as a match for every Opposition day a Government day when we could debate what the Opposition do not want to talk about, and that would be one of the topics.

**Mr. Harry Barnes** (Derbyshire, North-East): Today, probably at this very moment, the House of Lords is discussing electoral registration and the fact that the electoral register is in an utter mess because between 3 million and 4 million are missing from it. If the unelected House can discuss this key issue, why cannot this House do the same, given that we are directly elected?

**Mr. Newton:** Despite the hon. Gentleman's rather aggressive style from time to time, I always consider what he says, but my positive and constructive suggestion to him, as to my hon. Friend the Member for Macclesfield (Mr. Winterton), is that he might consider raising the issue on a Wednesday morning.

**Mr. Harry Greenway** (Ealing, North): Will my right hon. Friend provide time for a debate on inheritance tax immediately after the recess so that we can investigate what the effect on nurses and others would be of the Labour party's proposals apparently to tax the passing of gifts from one spouse to another? Should not the House consider what Labour is proposing?

**Mr. Newton:** My hon. Friend echoes a point that my right hon. Friend the Prime Minister made, and he presents a further attractive possibility for a debate.

**Mr. Andrew Miller** (Ellesmere Port and Neston): Will the Leader of the House ask the Secretary of State for Education to come to the House to make a statement about education expenditure? Will he specifically ask her to clarify the contradiction which exists between her Department's position and that of Cheshire county council—which is Conservative and Liberal-controlled—over SSA expenditure on education? Either one party or the other is right, but both parties involved are the Conservative party. Only one approach can be right—which is it?

**Mr. Newton:** I always seek to provide clarification where I can, and I note the hon. Gentleman's request in this case.

**Mr. John Wilkinson** (Ruislip-Northwood): May I reiterate to my right hon. Friend my previous pleas for an early debate on the European aspects of civil air transport policy? Will he find time on our first Thursday back—in addition to the debates on Russia and Ukraine—to discuss the proposed European flight time limitations, about which the British Air Line Pilots Association has severe reservations?

**Mr. Newton:** I note my hon. Friend's reservation and while I cannot make promises, I shall keep it in mind.

**Mr. Paul Flynn** (Newport, West): While it is right that we should debate the awful tragedy on the M4 this week in which 10 people died, should not we also debate the 60 deaths a week which occur on the roads of this country? The people killed include Anne Carrinton, who was killed on 1 February in Fleet, Hampshire, and Susan Gardiner, who was killed on 12 February in Brentwood, both of whose families asked me to bring those deaths to the attention of the House because they believe that they were caused in collisions with slow-moving vehicles carrying bull bars. Is not it right that we consider what opportunities there are for us to reduce the terrible number of 60 deaths a week by practical methods, such as daylight saving, compulsory seat belts and banning bull bars?

**Mr. Newton:** Either the hon. Gentleman or someone else—I apologise for my memory not being clearer—has put this point to my right hon. Friend the Prime Minister. *[Interruption.]* It was the hon. Gentleman. In that case, he will recall that my right hon. Friend undertook to look into the matter. No doubt he is doing so, and he will respond to the hon. Gentleman in due course.

**Lady Olga Maitland** (Sutton and Cheam): Will my right hon. Friend consider having a debate on equal opportunities for both men and women? I raise the matter because serious concerns have arisen that women are being offered positive discrimination in the selection of Labour candidates for parliamentary seats. That is demeaning, insulting and undemocratic.

**Mr. Newton:** My hon. Friend's view about the matter is widely shared, not least by many other women.

**Mr. Rhodri Morgan** (Cardiff, West): Will the Leader of the House arrange for an early debate on the extraordinary admission tucked away discreetly in Monday's written questions that the Government have had to approve retrospectively and on an extra-statutory basis £165 million worth of managerial expenses paid unlawfully by the Government between 1 April 1991, when the new NHS internal market reforms came in, and 1 April 1995? Does the right hon. Gentleman agree that a totally unprecedented breakdown of public expenditure control has occurred? Should not any Government who take pride in looking after the public finances and the rule of law as governed by the House recognise that something terribly serious has gone wrong? Has not the matter been given a fig leaf of parliamentary respectability by the extra-statutory payments authorisation? Does not the matter require a debate as to whether the original law was

defective or deliberately deceptive because the Government wished to hide the rampant growth in managerialism following the new legislation?

**Mr. Newton:** I cannot judge whether the matter requires a debate at the moment, but there are various ways of looking at such matters. In any event, I would first want to draw the hon. Gentleman's question to the attention of my right hon. Friend the Secretary of State for Health.

**Mr. Bernard Jenkin** (Colchester, North): Does my right hon. Friend recall that, when we used to have the Budget in March, there used to be a separate public expenditure White Paper in the autumn and a series of debates devoted to that topic? Echoing the request of the hon. Member for Dewsbury (Mrs. Taylor), would not it be useful to have a debate about public expenditure, so that the Government could demonstrate how Conservatives are manfully striving to control it, whereas every policy statement by the Opposition shows that they are determined to increase it whatever they may be pretending?

**Mr. Newton:** That appears to be another good candidate for the putative Government days to which I referred and I will bear it in mind. It also adds to the strength of the case for the economic day for which the hon. Member for Dewsbury (Mrs. Taylor) asked.

**Mr. Gordon Prentice** (Pendle): May we have an early debate on the unfolding scandal of the Churchill papers? May I draw the attention of the Leader of the House to column *647* in yesterday's *Hansard* where, in reply to questions that I tabled, the Heritage Secretary confirmed that the £12.5 million valuation was conjured out of the air by an antiquarian bookseller and that the collection has not even been fully catalogued? Is not that a grotesque scandal and a waste of money?

**Mr. Newton:** I am sure that the board in question took the best possible advice before coming to its conclusion and I do not think that anything that the hon. Gentleman has said in the past few moments calls that into question.

**Mr. James Clappison** (Hertsmere): May I support the request of my hon. Friend the Member for Colchester, North (Mr. Jenkin) for a debate on spending, which the Opposition ought to welcome? Is my right hon. Friend aware that, earlier this week, the Leader of the Opposition promised a long and gruelling slog to control public expenditure while, in the past three weeks alone, Opposition Front-Bench spokesmen on health, transport and industry have made commitments at the Dispatch Box to increase spending? Could we have a debate to clear up any misunderstanding about that and to find out who is going on the gruelling slog, or whether the Leader of the Opposition will be going off on a frolic of his own and the rest of the Labour party have dropped out already?

**Mr. Newton:** If I can combine the debate that my hon. Friend the Member for Colchester, North (Mr. Jenkin) wanted with the more closely targeted debate that my hon. Friend has just advocated, I would be happy to find time for it and will bear it very much in mind.

**Mr. Nigel Evans** (Ribble Valley): May I support the call by the hon. Member for Crewe and Nantwich (Mrs. Dunwoody) for a debate on rail privatisation? It was a great shame that, in the debate the other day, only five of her comrades turned up—all sponsored by one transport union or the other. Such a debate would give us an opportunity to concentrate on the statement by Jimmy Knapp that, if his members do not get a 6 per cent. pay rise, they will embark on another damaging strike. Perhaps this time we can get across the message that, if they do so, the only people whom it will damage will be the people they are there to serve—their customers.

**Mr. Newton:** I very much agree with my hon. Friend and I hope that his words will be borne in mind by those at whom they were directed.

**Mr. John Marshall** (Hendon, South): As one of the sponsors, may I echo the plea for an early debate on early-day motion 1175? Does my right hon. Friend agree that that is one of the biggest scandals in local government in London? Will he congratulate the *Evening Standard* on its persistent and responsible campaign which unmasked this scandal, and will he condemn the indifference of the Labour party to that scandal in the home of new Labour—Islington?

**Mr. Newton:** From what I have seen, I would certainly want to join my hon. Friend in congratulating the *Evening Standard* on bringing that matter to the public's attention. I have already made some observations about what I hope those concerned with the affairs of Islington borough council will do about it.

# Coal Industry

4.8 pm

**The Parliamentary Under-Secretary of State for Industry and Energy (Mr. Richard Page):** I beg to move,

That the draft Coal Industry (Restructuring Grants) Order 1995, which was laid before this House on 1st May, be approved.

This will be the ninth annual order under section 3 of the Coal Industry Act 1987, and it has two purposes. First, it specifies the kind of restructuring expenditure incurred by British Coal in the present financial year for which grant may be paid. Those are: redundancy and early retirement; retraining through the job and career exchange scheme; and, new employment. The latter includes the costs incurred by British Coal Enterprise in promoting new job opportunities in areas affected by pit closures.

Those are the same categories of expenditure as was specified in last year's order, except for transfer allowances, which are not included in this year's order, since British Coal will not be incurring any expenditure in that area this year.

Secondly, the order sets at 90 per cent.—as last year—the maximum percentage of restructuring costs which can be met by restructuring grant in the current financial year.

Restructuring grant has proved to be an essential part of the Government's assistance to British Coal. It has helped the industry to adapt to changing circumstances, by supporting generous redundancy terms for miners and staff who are losing jobs as a result of closures and efficiency improvements. British Coal Enterprise estimates that it has created over 120,000 job opportunities, and retrained and resettled, mostly in alternative employment, some 57,000 people since 1984.

The order will allow the Government to continue to support the industry for a further year. The main expenditures this year will be related to retraining and new employment.

I commend the order to the House.

4.10 pm

**Mr. Stuart Bell** (Middlesbrough): I am grateful for the opportunity of responding to the Minister on this matter.

It is perhaps fitting that you, Mr. Deputy Speaker, are in the Chair. I should like briefly to refer to the death yesterday of Harold Wilson, because I have here a book that he wrote in 1945, entitled "A Plan for Coal". This book was sent by him to Will Lawther, who was president of the National Union of Mineworkers and who was kind enough to pass it on to me.

With your mining background, Mr. Deputy Speaker, you will appreciate that Harold Wilson was a great friend of the industry and the miners. He regularly attended the big meeting days, and made major speeches before them. I remember how in 1965, when he came to the Durham miners' gala, it poured down all day, and the crowds could not assemble. He nevertheless passed out his speech to the press as if he had read it, and enjoyed the festivities as best he could.

It is fitting that, in discussing this mining industry order, he should be remembered today as he was yesterday, and that the work that he carried out half a century ago in "A Plan for Coal" is remembered and placed on the record.

[*Mr. Stuart Bell*]

I am grateful to the Minister for taking us through the order. It may be the last day before the recess, and the day of a by-election, and it may be eighth or ninth order which the Minister and Government have brought to the House, but nevertheless it would have been helpful if the Minister had taken a little longer to go through it. We on this side of the House will seek to rectify that for him.

As the Minister said in his brief introduction, under section 3 of the Coal Industry Act 1987, the Secretary of State can, and does, make grants to British Coal to cover some of the costs incurred as a result of the restructuring of the coal industry. In October 1992, the Government announced what they described as a substantial and wide-ranging package of new measures to assist the coalfield communities. They included extra help for inward investment, promotion and additional activity in British Coal Enterprise.

We fully recognise the role that BCE has played in helping to create over 120,000 job opportunities in coalfield areas across the country—a role which covers business funding, the workplace and outplacement. We also recognise that the £93 million that BCE has committed to job creation projects has attracted from other funders a further £670 million of inward investment into the coalfields. The future existence of BCE, however, remains uncertain, notwithstanding the commitments in the Government's White Paper.

I am glad to see that I am in very good company today, with my hon. Friends the Members for Bolsover (Mr. Skinner), for Barnsley, West and Penistone (Mr. Clapham), for Barnsley, Central (Mr. Illsley), for Midlothian (Mr. Clarke), for Sunderland, North (Mr. Etherington), for Sherwood (Mr. Tipping), for Wentworth (Mr. Hardy) and for Wansbeck (Mr. Thompson), to name but a few.

We want to debate the order and to consider the future of British Coal Enterprise and its work force, who did not know, for example, until February of this year that the grants given for 1995-96 by this statutory instrument would be forthcoming. Consultation is never a high priority in the Government's mind. To this day, the staff of British Coal Enterprise do not know whether they will be in a job this time next year.

The staff of British Coal Enterprise are not alone in the uncertainty they feel about their jobs. Many of us meet constituents who tell us that they are on short-term contracts. We meet constituents who are casual workers and whose jobs do not provide holiday pay or sickness benefit. Those people cannot feel the so-called feel-good factor, because they do not know whether they will be in a job in a year's time, and they do not know whether they will have a roof over their heads. Low morale afflicts the country, so it is not surprising that morale at British Coal Enterprise is extremely low.

Low morale can affect not only the individual concerned, but the services that that individual renders. From all the information we are getting, it is clear that many ex-mining staff still need long-term assistance. A report produced by the Coalfield Communities Campaign, after surveying almost 900 ex-miners from five pits that ceased production in October 1992—the figures are supported by an independent CBI survey and by a survey conducted by Derbyshire county council—showed that

only 44 per cent. were in employment. Some 46 per cent. were unemployed, and 9 per cent. were in training or education.

Of those who were unemployed, 80 per cent. had had no work since leaving the industry. Those who were in employment earned much less than they had as miners. On average, they earned £70 a week less than they had in the mining industry. Overall, 89 per cent. were worse off at the time of the survey than they had been when they worked in the pits.

We submit to the House that there is much hidden unemployment among ex-miners. Some 30 per cent. were claiming sickness benefit which did not show up on the unemployment register. That is a higher proportion than one would expect, as a result of the unhealthy effects of working down a pit, especially as the average age of those surveyed was 38. Those surveyed were in the prime of their working lives.

The survey shows that morale is low among redundant miners, and that low morale can lead to illness. It shows that the hope of getting a job is so small that it is not surprising that morale is low. With low morale and so few job prospects, as in all such circumstances, it is the small, niggling things in life which attain greater importance.

If we take an overview of the economy based on the survey and assume similar levels of unemployment and low pay throughout mining areas, we can see that spending power of more than £300 million a year has been lost to coalfield communities as a result of the job losses since October 1992.

As my hon. Friends know, I come from a mining area. I have written a book about colliery life, which is not as famous as other books that I have written in my time. My father spent 51 years in the pits, and I began my working life in the colliery office.

I can testify to the House that there is a keen sense of community spirit in the mining areas, as you know well, Mr. Deputy Speaker. The former pitmen have a great desire to be independent and to pay their own way through life. With that background, that desire, a sense of independence and a sense of community spirit, how fertile is the prospect for regeneration. Even under this Government, it would not take a great deal, if they brought all the assistance together, for the former miners to be able to help themselves.

We shall not let the Government forget their 1992 White Paper, in which they declared that they would increase the amount available for regeneration measures up to £200 million. It announced that the funds would allow important new major projects to go ahead, which would promote new employment opportunities.

The Opposition are entitled to ask where the money has gone. It has gone into training and enterprise councils, and industrial estates. We have seen, somewhat tardily, two enterprise zones, and a third has only just opened. But that is not new money, and it is not conditional. How often have we sat in the House and heard the President of the Board of Trade tell us that he is putting new money into the economy? It turns out to be the same money as he announced in last year's White Paper, and the same money that the Chancellor of the Exchequer announced in the Budget.

The £200 million which the Government talked about was already allocated to training and enterprise councils, English Estates and even the Welsh Development

Agency. Among the Government's other great attributes, they are able to launder money. They have used the same money time and again, but they say in their White Papers that it is new money.

Apart from laundering money, what else have the Government been doing in terms of energy policy? What other nefarious activities have they been up to? As Opposition Members know, and as the mining communities know better than anyone, the Government have no energy policy other than a dash for gas. They have set miners and mining communities aside, as tools to be disposed of at will. The Government's higgledy-piggledy approach to energy created those circumstances in the first place. Miners who have not found work and who are on the dole must look askance at the so-called "fat cats" in the energy industry, who line not only their own pockets with monumental fees and share options but the pockets of their wives.

Those of us who watched the extraordinary exchange between the Prime Minister and the Leader of the Opposition will have noticed that the one thing which the Prime Minister has not learnt is Lord Healey's adage: "When you are in a hole, you should stop digging." The Prime Minister kept digging throughout the exchanges. He talked about independent taxation and gifts inter vivos. Obviously, that was over the heads of all those who listened and watched it on television.

I remember as a child learning a poem about the mining industry, which told of how the pitman was wakened in the early morning and made his way to the coalface.

**Mr. Eric Illsley** (Barnsley, Central): Tell it to us.

**Mr. Bell:** As my hon. Friend the Member for Barnsley, Central (Mr. Illsley) will know, he was wakened by the coaler's knock on the window. He went to the coalface to batter at the grimy rock, and he thought of all those pampered ones sleeping in what he described as the "midnight sable gloom". And he thought of all those who were above sleeping, and how they could safely bloom.

What does a former miner who is unemployed see as he looks around him at those who run the energy industry—and even at their wives? Not only are they taking home lavish pay packets and enjoying wonderful share option schemes, but their wives are dipping in, too. What we saw was not a dash for gas but a dash for greed—[Hon. Members: "A dash for cash."] It is cash for questions, cash for gas, but no cash for unemployed miners.

We acknowledge and accept the considerable help from the European Union's RECHAR fund to help coalfields across the European Union. The first phase brought £135 million of European Union funding to the United Kingdom, and the second phase was recently agreed. However, that will only begin to deal with the scale of the effort needed to regenerate coalfield economies. If the Government were to allow British Coal Enterprise to go, and if they fail to honour their commitments in the 1992 White Paper, the United Kingdom would be the only coal producer in Europe without a regeneration programme in the coalfields.

In helping coalfields regenerate, we are a poor second to France and Belgium. In the Flemish coalfield, closures were phased over 10 years, to allow a proper transition within the local economy. In this country, the coal industry has had the best vocational training and education schemes. The old National Coal Board was among the best in that respect.

One personnel director began as an apprentice electrician in the industry at the age of 15. He worked his way to the metaphorical top because of a training scheme. Another man, who became director of the north-east area of British Coal, also began working in the industry at the age of 15.

Miners have shown a willingness to undertake training, to learn new skills, to develop new enterprises and to be part of the changing economic scene. They need help over and above that offered by the order. They do not need any rhetoric, although we certainly did not get any from the Minister. They need assistance; they do not need promises. They need certainty; they do not need doubt and confusion.

Since the original pit closures were announced on 13 October 1992, the Government and British Coal have closed 34 of the 50 deep-mine pits then in operation. That led to the loss of 40,000 jobs directly—half the number of those at Wembley stadium watching the cup final on Saturday. Tens of thousands of other ancillary and support jobs were also lost. Before that announcement, 150,000 jobs had been lost from the industry in the previous 10 years. Wembley stadium could be filled twice over with unemployed miners.

The industry now has to cope with the uncertainty about British Coal Enterprise. If the Government had a heart and the will, they would stir themselves within the Department of Trade and Industry. If they cared, they would bring together various strands of policy aimed at regeneration. If they cared, they would create a coherent regional development policy that drew upon the strengths of the coalfields. If they cared, they would replace pessimism with hope, and offer a fair deal to former miners to help themselves.

Although the Opposition welcome the order, as we have welcomed other orders introduced in the past few years, the Government, might, just might, give the impression to the coalfield communities that they care.

4.26 pm

**Mr. Peter Hardy** (Wentworth): I agree with my hon. Friend the Member for Middlesbrough (Mr. Bell) that, since the order is providing some resources for the mining industry and mining communities, it would be illogical for the Opposition to vote against it. That does not mean that we should allow the debate to pass without drawing attention to the grievous scale of need that exists in the coalfield communities.

As my hon. Friend has said, we have seen an enormous contraction in the industry. Coal is not being mined in my constituency, for the first time in more than three and a half centuries. When I entered the House there were 12 collieries in my constituency, and other related industries; now we have none. We are now witnessing the consequences of the destruction of jobs on a scale not seen at any other time in our industrial history. That loss emphasises the need to which my hon. Friend has referred and is why I endorse what he said about the importance of maintaining British Coal Enterprise.

We were fortunate, I suppose, to receive recycled, or laundered, money to finance the Dearne valley city grant, which was one of the first such schemes to be established.

[*Mr. Peter Hardy*]

It has been relatively successful, but it is not far from the end of its projected lifespan. If our local authorities continue to be subject to existing capping procedures, they will be unable to fund that project and carry on the work that the Government exhorted us to undertake.

British Coal Enterprise is one agency that could assist in guaranteeing that work. I have considerable respect for Mr. Philip Andrew, the leader of that undertaking. I believe that security of tenure should be offered to Mr. Andrew and his organisation, because that would at least enable those of us who represent constituencies covered by city grant schemes to be certain that mechanisms will be created to allow the substantial investments that have already been made to be brought to fruition.

It has cost thousands of pounds per acre to reclaim some of the land used in such schemes. The Government would surely be idiotic if they allowed such investment to be made but did not fund the agencies that would ensure that it bore fruit.

That is particularly true in the Dearne valley, which has benefited from one of the first city grant schemes—now coming to an end—and one of the two enterprise zones to which my hon. Friend the Member for Middlesbrough (Mr. Bell) referred. We were promised that enterprise zone a long time ago, but it has only just been authorised. The loss of the agencies or any organisation that could help to develop the enterprise zones would constitute a betrayal of areas in enormous need.

I remind the Minister that, in the 1960s, when some of us wanted economic diversification in our area because our eggs were all in the baskets of coal and steel, public bodies such as the regional civil service told us that ours must be the major coal reservoir in the British Isles. They specifically discouraged economic diversification. Following the decision to inflict rapid contraction on our industry, there must be a national obligation of some kind.

If that constitutes wisdom, the obligation is even greater. The miners may have received redundancy pay, but the jobs have disappeared. The outlook for the younger generation in areas such as ours is very bleak. Ministers should understand that they have an obligation to serve the whole country, even areas that have rejected the Government decisively.

As I have said, in our Dearne valley enterprise zone, substantial amounts of public money have been spent on reclaiming land and preparing it for the economic development that we so desperately need. Immediately south of the enterprise zone and the Dearne valley reclamation area is a portion of green belt. It is green belt because the local authority has taken cognisance of the local community, and because it needs to be green belt: it is attractive, although it is adjacent to hundreds of acres of dereliction. British Coal, however, refuses to fulfil its promise to sell that farm land to the farmer, as many of us expected it would, because it is going to try to sell it as development land.

I ask the Minister to comment on the sanity of spending public money to reclaim devastated, derelict industrial land at enormous expense when British Coal wants to take neighbouring green belt land out of the green belt and sell it for development—thus negating the investment in the reclamation just a few yards away, and making a particularly pleasant farm unviable by reducing the acreage to below the minimum required.

I wrote to British Coal about the matter, and was told, "British Coal believes that it should be development land"—although the local authority and the local community believe that the land should remain in the green belt. We have little enough attractive green belt land as it is; I see no point in taking any away when 1,200 or 1,400 acres of land are being reclaimed under the city grant scheme.

I then wrote to the Minister, pointing out that the decision appeared to constitute a broken promise and an example of irresponsibility that disdained the public investment that—

**Mr. Deputy Speaker (Mr. Geoffrey Lofthouse):** Order. Has the hon. Gentleman's letter to the Minister anything to do with the order? I hope that he will return to that subject.

**Mr. Hardy:** Let me explain, Mr. Deputy Speaker. British Coal seeks not only to obtain the money that the order makes available, but to obtain more than it should from the sale of green belt land. That is perfectly logical—but let me take your advice, Mr. Deputy Speaker, and say that I hope the Minister will ensure that the Government are not so parsimonious that British Coal must go around selling green belt land to make money when it ought to sell it for the much lesser sum that would be available if the tenant farmer were given the opportunity he should enjoy.

Finally, let me remind the Minister of a point I made earlier. A few months ago, the Church of England Children's Society brought some young people to the House to see me. They were ordinary boys and girls of about 15 years of age who were not the sorts of kids who would go into higher education. I do not suggest that they were below average ability, but they were the sorts of boys and girls who would become skilled and semi-skilled workers—the backbone of our society. In the previous two centuries, they would have been employed in the coal and steel industries. But those jobs have now gone.

The worst moment of my 25 years' service in the House of Commons came when I talked to those ordinary kids of 15 about their outlook, prospects and hopes for the future. The Minister should understand that they have no hope, and they see few prospects or opportunities. Therefore, we are not begging the Minister to provide crumbs for the coal areas and the coalfield communities; we are telling the Minister that a wise Government will ensure that the hope that has been blighted in the past 20 years is somehow restored. This measure will provide a little of the assistance that those people need.

4.35 pm

**Mr. Dennis Skinner** (Bolsover): The draft Coal Industry (Restructuring Grants) Order is set against the very bleak background to which my hon. Friends the Members for Wentworth (Mr. Hardy) and for Middlesbrough (Mr. Bell) have referred. It is probably the bleakest period in all of my years in this place.

We have talked about the possibility of mass unemployment, and I suppose that on many occasions we have made what some would consider to be idle threats about it. The truth is that mass unemployment has now reached devastating proportions, and that it affects every constituency. The scale of the problem is almost unbelievable. Unless this or a future Government address their task properly and provide adequate restructuring grants, they will be unable to deal with the difficult social climate and the devastated social fabric of coalfield communities. That is a terrifying prospect.

Whatever little money will result from the grants for retraining, retirement packages and new industries or from the puny efforts of British Coal Enterprise Ltd.—which I am afraid I cannot laud to the skies; we must emphasise that job opportunities are not jobs—it will be infinitesimal compared with the job in hand.

There are no pits left in my constituency or in the whole of north Derbyshire, and the prospects of attracting new industry on any reasonable scale pale into insignificance when compared with the 1960s, which my hon. Friend the Member for Wentworth mentioned. I saw pits close in my local authority area. It was possible for most of those miners—or a good proportion of them—to find work in other pits, because there were other pits to go to.

However, there are no pits to go to now. Probably only 10 per cent. of miners are able to find work in the few pits that remain. A survey conducted by the county council—we can see it also from a head count of local people—found that more than 50 per cent. of miners and all the inhabitants of some pit villages are unemployed. The situation is not improving. Whatever the feel-good factor may be in the rest of Britain, those people are not feeling it. They are becoming more disillusioned with every week that passes.

We have some responsibility to try to find a way out of that predicament. Assuming that the Government are not interested—apart from passing today's relatively minor order—we must have a plan ready on this side of the House to try to combat that mass unemployment. My hon. Friend the Member for Wentworth referred to what happened in the 1960s. I was a part of that. Some 700 miners and 700 other staff used to work in a big factory in Pit lane. We thought we were great, and we were. Industry was on the move in the 1960s.

It was possible to attract industry by establishing special enterprise areas. Our claim to fame was that we attracted industry that would otherwise have gone to the continent, by getting an industrial development certificate. However, those certificates would not amount to a great deal today—first, because industry is not on the move; and, secondly, as a result of technology, there are no jobs, anyway. If five sheds on a big industrial estate have about 30 people working in them, they have done exceptionally well. We have to turn our attention to the background of the restructuring grants in an attempt to get round the problem.

We must be careful about opencast. In many cases, if opencast is agreed to in the pit environs, the prospect of introducing anything else is held back for another decade. Apart from the environmental shambles that it creates, opencast in all the coalfields will prevent the operations to which my hon. Friend the Member for Wentworth referred.

Unless we examine the prospects for what we can do, we all have to acknowledge that, even if we had 10 per cent. of the manufacturing increase that occurred in the 1960s when pits closed, we would be doing exceptionally well. We have to consider where the rest of the jobs are to come from. Assuming that we are returned to office, the Labour party has to get back to the idea of sharing work, and everyone working shorter hours to make more work available.

In all our constituencies, thousands of what would have been young miners receive neither training nor retraining. They do not even have the chance to go to the old Coal Board workshops or anywhere.

As my hon. Friend the Member for Middlesbrough said, notwithstanding the restructuring grants, the amount of money circulating in the economy has reduced dramatically. The chances of creating more jobs as a result of people spending what bit of money they have are not very good. I should say in passing that now we have a wage freeze for the miners but a 23 per cent. increase for Richard Budge, the man running the English pits. That will also reduce the money available.

The grants do not address the real issues. We read every day, and it has been said in the House, that the grants should be applied to the problem of the water that is pouring out without control in every coalfield. There should be no more pumping. None of the money will be used for that. Land slicks are occurring in almost every coalfield; methane is pouring out of some of the old pits, and nobody gives two hoots. The grants should be applied to that in future, and there should be many more of them. That is the bleak picture, and we all know about it in our communities.

Of course we shall vote for the grants today, but they do not add up to a row of beans compared with the problems we face. They are set against the background that we forecast two or three years ago, when it was proposed to close the 31 pits—never mind the others. The world price of coal was already likely to rise, and it has already started to move.

What a crazy economic policy that was. We all know that it was the revenge of the Tory Government, and it has accelerated and accentuated the problems in our constituencies. We shall have to turn our attention to it in a year or two, and we had better ensure those on our Front Bench get some decent plans ready, because mass unemployment brings all kinds of problems in its wake.

4.43 pm

**Mr. Paddy Tipping** (Sherwood): The Minister says that we are discussing the ninth such order. We do not know whether it will be the last, but it is important and significant as it votes money to British Coal Enterprise. The Minister will need no reminding that during the passage of the Coal Industry Act 1994 the Government gave a commitment that British Coal Enterprise would survive the privatisation of British Coal and continue for some time after that. I am dismayed by the ad hoc arrangements that appear to have been made for British Coal Enterprise.

The order votes money for British Coal Enterprise in the current year, but I am well aware that there has been a protracted struggle to agree its future. It is important as it is the only economic development agency that focuses primarily and principally on the coalfield. It brings venture capital to companies in coalfield areas, it attracts new business and £78.6 million has been invested in business in coalfield areas. It has brought workshops to the areas. We needed the £40 million that enabled us to create 1.3 million sq ft of factory space on 47 sites. Most importantly, it is a partner for economic development. It can work with others such as the local authorities, to bring new jobs, new investment and a new future to coalfield communities.

That partnership has been blighted, however, by the lack of clarity about the long-term future of British Coal

[*Mr. Paddy Tipping*]

Enterprise. One does not take a partner that could die at the end of the current financial year, and that is a real possibility for British Coal Enterprise.

I remind the Minister of the report that British Coal and the Department of Trade and Industry commissioned on the future of British Coal Enterprise entitled,

"Market Opportunities and Structural Options",

that was produced in November 1994. I am disappointed that the report was never published. It sets out four options for the future of British Coal Enterprise, but as yet there is no clear way forward.

It is important that we agree a timetable. It is important that all of us who are actors in the coalfield and want to create a new future know what the platforms will be and who the actors are because there is still a need in coalfield areas. In 1980, there were 40,000 miners in Nottinghamshire; today there are fewer than 3,000. To put it another way, in 15 years, more than nine out of 10 mining jobs have gone.

Unemployment is reaching dangerously high peaks. The gap between unemployment in the United Kingdom and that in the coalfield communities is constantly increasing. Inequalities are being created. In April 1991, the gap between United Kingdom unemployment and the employment in the Mansfield travel-to-work area, which covers a large part of the Nottinghamshire coalfield was 2.1 per cent. By April 1995, that gap had grown to 6 per cent.

There is a clear divergence. Unemployment is worsening in pockets of the coalfield communities while nationally it is reducing. We have to take action on that and ensure that a clear timetable spelling out the future of British Coal Enterprise is discussed and agreed quickly. I understand that the Department and British Coal have Samuel Montagu and Co. Ltd. working on the issue now, but it is important that they come clean and that early decisions are made. People can live with decisions, but they cannot live with uncertainty.

Some former miners have found jobs. My hon. Friend the Member for Middlesbrough talked about the work of the Coalfield Communities Campaign, which found that half the miners have found work, but are paid one third less than when they worked for British Coal. This year, Derbyshire county council produced a report with similar findings, showing that miners earn half what they earned down the pit, so there are real and continuing problems.

There is a severe loss of income into the local economy. One has only to walk around coalfield communities to see the number of shops that have shut to see how difficult things are.

Some miners have been more fortunate. I have with me the minutes of a meeting held on 11 January 1993. It was agreed at the meeting that the former miner concerned was to receive good redundancy terms and excellent pension arrangements from British Coal, together with a car and a new house. He has gone on to be appointed by the Government to work on industrial tribunals at £80 a day, and has been appointed to the Coal Authority at £5,500 a year. He is also employed by the Prince's Youth Business Trust as a business advisor at £20,000 a year. That post is funded by British Coal Enterprises. As well as his redundancy package, this gentleman is now receiving nearly £30,000: he has been well looked after.

The man in question, Roy Lynk, is the former president of the Union of Democratic Mineworkers. I find it astonishing that he should get his pension and a house and a car and yet be paid nearly £30,000 from Government funds. There are people in the coal industry who say that he is being well looked after. I wish that the Government were looking after the other miners who have lost their jobs and who feel betrayed as well as they look after Mr. Roy Lynk.

I hope that the Minister will reflect on this and give another group of people a fair chance for the future. He will perhaps know that the British Association of Colliery Management is holding its annual conference at the moment. He has received letters from the president of the BACM about a small group of people who are members of what is known as the triple-S scheme—the staff superannuation scheme. They worked for British Coal right to the end of its life and were then transferred to new employers. They, like their colleagues, can get their pensions at 50 if they leave their jobs in, or are made redundant by, the successor company. But if they move from the successor company to another firm and then lose their jobs, they cannot take their pensions at 50.

Fewer than 3,000 people make up this small group. I hope that the Minister will treat them with equity and examine ways of enabling them to take their pensions at 50, like their colleagues do. The money is already there—it is in the pension fund. I hope that the Minister will therefore consider my suggestion, and take this opportunity to respond to an invitation from the BACM and the pension fund trustees to discuss the issue. I am dismayed to learn that he has so far not met them. The conference meets tomorrow. I hope that the Minister will take a step forward and announce that he is prepared to discuss the future with the conference.

Tonight we are discussing that future. There is a strong feeling in the coalfield communities that the Government have buried the deep coal industry deep and then tried to walk away from it. We in the coalfield communities are pragmatic and hardworking. We want more for our children than we have had. We need to invest in jobs and infrastructure to create a better future for them.

4.53 pm

**Mr. Kevin Hughes** (Doncaster, North): After one false start we finally get to the blocks, as it were.

I welcome the opportunity to discuss this order, which will permit funding to be released for the costs of retirements, redundancies, retraining and new employment following the changes in the coal industry resulting from the privatisation of British Coal. The full cost of that privatisation in terms of jobs has been immense. Before privatisation the Government spent years encouraging the industry to run itself down to a small rump in preparation for the goal of selling it off. The Government's closure programme finished off the last two pits in my constituency—Bentley and Hatfield—and they had already closed down the Askern and Brodsworth collieries a couple of years before.

Taken together, the closures were nothing short of industrial vandalism on a massive scale. Closing profitable pits such as Bentley was economic madness. The jobs lost at Hatfield numbered 700, and 600 were lost at Bentley. That was a further blow to Doncaster's already damaged economy which, in the 1970s, relied on 10 pits and 18,000 mining jobs, not to mention all the other industries that worked in and about the mining industry.

Now the town is having to rebuild. I suppose that the little money from these orders will go towards helping it to do so. Incidentally, the Hatfield pit has reopened under a private management buy-out scheme, and is doing quite well selling coal that the Government said could not be mined or sold economically. The team at the colliery is doing well. I wish its members well and I hope that they will build on their success.

There has thus been some relief in the way of jobs, but not much. Only 200 people work at the pit, but every job is encouraging. Still, the unemployment rate remains well above the national average. What towns like Doncaster need is Government support to make up for the difficulties of the closures. We need more retraining and the creation of new jobs by attracting firms to Doncaster. The local authority has done a great deal in this respect. The town's amenities have been improved; it has good road links in the form of the M1, the M18, the M62 and the A1. The east coast main line runs through Doncaster, and we are developing a railport so that we can key into European railfreight.

**Mr. Jack Thompson** (Wansbeck): My constituency is slightly further north than my hon. Friend's but I regularly travel through Doncaster on the main line. Indeed, my hon. Friend and I often travel north together on the train from King's Cross. Has he noticed, as I have, the huge industrial and commercial developments around Peterborough and Grantham? I think that, with the right sort of support from the Government, they could have been located in Doncaster, Wansbeck or other parts north. There is no particular reason why they should have ended up in the home counties. Under the old industrial development certificate arrangements such industries did come to areas such as ours.

**Mr. Hughes:** My hon. Friend's point is perfectly valid. Each time I travel on the east coast main line—I look forward to doing so again later today—I notice those developments at Peterborough. We need Government help for such projects in Doncaster and Wansbeck.

To the east, west, north and south Doncaster has good road and rail links which will prove a key feature of the council's attempts to rebuild—

**Mr. Deputy Speaker:** Order. I hesitate to interrupt, but the hon. Gentleman has strayed rather wide of the order. Will he now come back to it? I am sure that he is well aware of what it contains.

**Mr. Hughes:** I am grateful for your guidance, Mr. Deputy Speaker. My point is that the money granted in these orders could and should have been used in the areas that I have described to replace the jobs that have been lost in mining. Certainly, the Government have put some of the money into Doncaster, but at the same time they have cut spending on the town, which makes life difficult for the local authority. The local authority, however, is working with the private sector. There are successful partnerships that will be able properly to use the funding that will flow from the order, as well as funding from other sources.

If the Government want to help Doncaster, they could support its attempts to secure RAF Finningley as a commercial airport after the RAF pulls out next year. That

could help them to solve the problems surrounding the fifth terminal at Heathrow. After all, Doncaster is only one and a half hours away from London by train. It takes almost that time to travel from this place to Heathrow. Another consideration is that Manchester is only a short drive from Doncaster across the M62.

**Mr. Deputy Speaker:** That may well be, but the hon. Member must direct his remarks to the order.

**Mr. Hughes:** I am grateful to you, Mr Deputy Speaker. I am talking about the order in terms of training and helping to reskill the work force in Doncaster in assisting it to find new jobs.

Doncaster has been lucky to have the benefit of British Coal Enterprise Ltd., which is mentioned in the order. The House will know that BCE has worked alongside the industry to help it reskill and to place former mining employees in new work with new opportunities.

I am concerned about BCE's future, which is still in the balance. The Government have not decided specifically what they intend to do with BCE in the long term. If the Minister is able to do so, he should tell the House of his intentions.

The Government made an allocation of £3 million for retraining when the Bentley and Hatfield collieries closed. The moneys were allocated to the Barnsley and Doncaster training and enterprise council. Unfortunately, in my opinion, the TEC spent the money in a different area of Doncaster. The areas most directly affected by the closures, which should have received the money that the Government brought forward and which should receive the money that will be made available by the order, did not receive their fair share.

The TEC is well aware of my concerns because I have talked about them to its representatives on many occasions. My latest information is that the area covered by the constituency of Doncaster, North received only a third of the £3 million that was made available.

I have corresponded with Ministers about the designation of other moneys that have been allocated to try to ease the difficulties caused by pit closures, including the economic difficulties that have been faced by Doncaster generally. Of the £8 million allocated to English Partnerships, most of the funding has been directed to projects on the other side of Doncaster from my constituency. The areas in which pits have closed, which should be receiving moneys from the order, as well as from other sources, have seen funding go elsewhere. A derelict land grant has been made available to clean up the Askern site, but the majority of the funding has been spent elsewhere. Some of the money should have been used to help areas north of Doncaster in my constituency where mines have closed and where unemployment is especially bad.

April figures show that in one ward in my constituency there is almost 18 per cent. unemployment. Other wards have unemployment of 13 and 14 per cent. Within these wards are pockets where unemployment is as high as 20 per cent. and over. The moneys that will be made available by the order should be used to help unemployed people reskill and retrain for other work that the council is trying to bring into the town.

Against that background, the Government have cut the training-for-work budget by over £100 million for the next financial year. That is difficult to understand. By

*[Mr. Hughes]*

1997, the budget will have been cut by as much as 12 per cent. That is madness when 11 per cent. of firms nationally are reporting that it is difficult to fill job vacancies. I understand that in Doncaster we have already lost 1,200 places. Indeed, more are likely to be lost. Without training, how are towns such as Doncaster expected to make the best use of the human resources that are available to them?

The Government admit that the cost to the economy of keeping someone unemployed is £9,000 a year. In Doncaster, North alone, that means that £50.5 million will be spent on subsistence for the unemployed this year. It is criminal to spend thousands of millions of pounds each year to keep people unemployed while at the same time reducing the opportunities for them to earn money for themselves in employment. The Government's approach creates a huge burden for the taxpayer instead of using Government money to encourage success. The Government should not be financing economic failure. We should be giving people a hand up, not a hand out. That is what they want and that is what they need if they are to equip themselves with the skills that they require to ensure that they get back into work.

5.7 pm

**Mr. Michael Clapham** (Barnsley, West and Penistone): The order gives the Department of Trade and Industry authority to fund 90 per cent. of British Coal's redundancy costs for 1995-96 and to meet the operating losses of British Coal Enterprise Ltd. for that year.

The first aim of meeting British Coal's redundancy, retraining and relocation costs that have been caused by closures is relatively unimportant because the corporation has already disposed of all its mining operations and the majority of its non-mining activities. It is welcome, however, that the order will provide for redundancy arrangements for the staff who are left with British Coal to dispose of the residual holdings.

The second aim of the order is much more important because it concerns the future of BCE. My hon. Friend the Member for Middlesbrough (Mr. Bell) was right to concentrate on the need for secure funding for BCE as well as on a coherent approach to regional policy. We require a fair deal for the coalfields to ensure regeneration of the areas. It is clear that the coalfield areas have not had a fair deal when we set the order in the context of the 1993 DTI White Paper, "The Prospects for Coal", which set out the measures that would be taken in coalfield areas.

We were told, for example, that Barnsley and Doncaster, as well as Mansfield, would have assisted area status. The White Paper informed us that there would be assistance from the Economic Union. We were told that there would be a concentration on infrastructure aid from English Estates. It was said that there would be assistance from the jobs service and the training and enterprise councils. It appeared that there would be set up a coalfield areas fund of £244 million. We were to have new enterprise zones, extra help for inward investment and additional assistance for BCE.

The Government's record leaves much to be desired. Despite a substantial programme since 1985, they have yet to devise a framework for coalfield regeneration. When we talk about that closure programme, it must be

borne in mind that we are talking about the closure of 140 collieries, with 160,000 men being made redundant. That has had an enormous impact.

The Government's approach contrasts starkly with that of our European partners. For example, Belgium, France and Germany have a strategy for phased closure of surplus coal capacity that is linked to a regeneration framework that empowers local communities. The French Government are contemplating the closure of the Lorraine coalfield and have set a date of 2005 for doing so. Since 1993, the French national Government, in partnership with the local region, departments and communities, have worked on a framework that will help to regenerate the community, so that as the coal mines are closed other jobs will be available.

That has not happened in any of our coalfields, and the Government introduced a package in 1993 only after a public outcry over colliery closures. One could question whether it could be described as a coherent approach. It certainly does not have the coherence that one would expect in the light of the enormous colliery closure programme since 1985.

Let us look at what we were promised, and it does relate to the grant, which is important, as it provides a little extra help. We were promised, for example, assisted area status. That has been granted, but it would have been granted to any area with unemployment that was created by the closures, so it is not as though it is extra help.

What about European Union assistance? The RECHAR programme, which has been of enormous help, was promoted not by the Government but by local authorities. Indeed, as we have seen many times, the programme has been obstructed by the Government, and only after arguments have they accepted additionality.

What about English Estates? It has made some improvement in the provision of business sites, the effect of which has been limited by the lack of a coherent strategy. The same is true of jobs and services from training and enterprise councils.

The record of the programmes supported by the coalfield fund, mainly through TECs and English Enterprise, does not support the argument that the fund was used to provide additional services. Those additional services have not been forthcoming. Perhaps the Minister will tell us what further assistance is likely to be available through the coalfield fund.

Enterprise zones were offered to the coalfields but they are still not fully operational—they certainly were not at the beginning of this year. I understand that the enterprise zone for the Dearne valley in south Yorkshire still has not been designated, but perhaps the Minister will be able to enlighten us on that.

It is important to consider three main aspects in relation to British Coal Enterprise. The provision of start-up finance is important for coalfield communities, because if we are to create jobs we shall do so in small and medium-sized enterprises. We must therefore concentrate on that sector.

Secondly, we must consider the provision of workspace units. Jobs will be created in smaller, growing industries within coalfield communities, so we must concentrate on them. Thirdly, we must consider the outplacing and retraining of redundant coal staff.

Those three aspects are the major part of the second aim of the grant. It is important that the Minister realises that BCE has helped in creating jobs in coalfield communities, although there is some anxiety that it may not continue to do so. Is funding for BCE likely to continue after the order expires in 10 months' time? We do not know whether the grant will continue and, therefore, whether BCE will be able to continue.

Let us consider the situation that former mining communities face every day. My hon. Friends have already made the point that there are pockets of unemployment. In areas such as Worsbrough or Grimethorpe, as many as 40 per cent. of the male population of working age are unemployed. Poor infrastructure has resulted from a concentration on mining, with little diversification. The engineering industry that grew up around mining was very much allied to the mining industry. Consequently, as mines closed, the engineering industry also closed. Two city challenge bids have already been made to try to reverse that situation in the Dearne valley.

We need an appropriate skills base. There is a lower level of skills among some of our young people and we need to be able to lift that, which means concentrating on the appropriate skills to attract the industry that we require into coalfield communities. If we are able to offer the skills that our young people need, perhaps some of them will be able to move to work in areas such as Sheffield, Leeds and Manchester. It is important that we concentrate on the skills that are required for the future.

Environmental degradation has resulted from coal mining. The enormous problem that we face from mine water pollution has been mentioned. If I may, I shall refer to the Minister—within the context of the grant, Mr. Deputy Speaker. Not so long ago, he visited the Koyo factory at Dodworth in my constituency. If he had taken the time to travel one and a half miles beyond that, or if his schedule had allowed him to do so, he would have been in Silkstone, where, as he crossed the Silkstone beck, he would have noted just how polluted it is. The beck is orange. The local garden centre can no longer use the water from the beck for irrigation. Four rivers in my constituency are badly polluted—

**Mr. Deputy Speaker:** This is all very interesting and no doubt correct, but I am having difficulty understanding what it has to do with the order. Perhaps the hon. Gentleman will enlighten me.

**Mr. Clapham:** The point that I am making is that we require more grant to tackle some of the problems in our mining communities. We need more money for training, for business finance, to deal with contamination from polluted mine water and to develop the infrastructure.

Although Opposition Members have some reservations about the extent of the order, because of the limitation on the finance that is to be available, we shall not vote against it. We would, however, like the Minister to assure us that finance will continue after the order expires, which would allow BCE to continue.

5.19 pm

**Mr. Page:** This has been an interesting debate although, I confess, it has been a little short on the substance of the order and fairly long on constituency problems. However, I see no harm in that. Part of the skill of any interested Member of Parliament is, wherever possible, to raise constituency problems. It is a matter of a battle of wits with the occupant of the Chair to see whether one can float in and out of order to convey one's message.

I had a most enjoyable visit to the Koyo bearing factory in the constituency of the hon. Member for Barnsley, West and Penistone (Mr. Clapham). I was most impressed by it. It is a classic and shining example of the Government's inward investment scheme, which has brought several hundred jobs to the hon. Gentleman's constituency. No doubt he will thank the Government for that significant move in the right direction.

As I said in my opening remarks, the purpose of the order is to allow the Government to continue supporting the coal industry for a further year in order to help it to adapt to changed circumstances. The main restructuring expenditures to be charged against British Coal's accounts this year will be in respect of retraining and the job creation activities of British Coal Enterprise.

I admired the way in which the hon. Member for Wentworth (Mr. Hardy) raised a constituency problem. I shall not respond to it, but I shall make some inquiries and come back to him on his particular difficulty.

Nor shall I respond to the unwarranted and, I thought, unjustifiable attack by the hon. Member for Sherwood (Mr. Tipping) on Mr. Lynk, who is carrying out valuable and important work for the coal communities. The hon. Gentleman seemed to be upset by the fact that Mr. Lynk is getting less money than a Member of Parliament. We all have our ways of approaching these matters.

I come now to the eulogy of the hon. Member for Middlesbrough (Mr. Bell) in respect of BCE, which was echoed by other Members of Parliament. I commend its valuable work. It might be churlish of me to remind hon. Members that when BCE was first created Opposition Members were rather hostile to it. However, I am quite prepared to be churlish when the occasion demands. [Hon. Members: "No."] Yes, hon. Members were.

**Mr. Hardy:** I was not.

**Mr. Page:** I accept that the hon. Gentleman has a way of ploughing his own furrow with distinction. However, there was not the uniform enthusiasm when BCE was first created that was apparent in the House today.

It is well to remember that, since its inception in 1984, overall net financial assistance for BCE has totalled some £167 million—roughly £100 million for economic regeneration and some £65 million for resettlement of former British Coal employees. I reassure the House, particularly the hon. Member for Wentworth, that the Government are conscious of the need to ensure best value for money from the substantial investments that BCE has already made.

Options for the future have been raised by several hon. Members. It is important to ensure access to funding to allow the activities of BCE to continue. Access to European funding will be of prime importance. However, the availability of European regional development fund grant for coal areas is not dependent on the role of BCE. Applications from those areas can come from other sources such as local authorities and a range of other regeneration bodies.

In addition to the structural funds in eligible areas, the Government secured the highest allocation of any member state from the RECHAR II initiative. That money will make an important contribution to the economic regeneration of the coalfield communities.

Contrary to the impression that the hon. Member for Middlesbrough may wish to give the House and the nation, the Government have recognised, and do

[Mr. Page]

recognise, that during the past decade BCE has made a valuable contribution in assisting the regeneration of areas affected by coal closures. The Government and British Coal continue to explore the future options for BCE. I recognise the need expressed by the hon. Member for Sherwood for an early decision and, despite the detour around terminal 5, I recognise the point made by the hon. Member for Doncaster, North (Mr. Hughes).

**Mr. Kevin Hughes:** Will the Minister give way?

**Mr. Page:** No, I am running out of time and I want to put these last few points on to the record.

No final decision has been made but the Government have agreed to continue to provide funding for all BCE's activities, including the workspace and business funding activities in order to allow them to continue during the current financial year.

That course of action, recommended by Mr. Neil Clarke, chairman of British Coal, will allow time for British Coal and its advisers to identify future strategies and make recommendations for meeting the needs of the coalfield communities during the longer term. Consideration is being given to the full range of options, including forms of partnership with other regeneration bodies at national and local level. All options require careful consideration before any firm decision is made, as I am sure all hon. Members will agree.

I can assure the House that I am acutely aware of the difficulties faced by many in the coalfield areas and I shall take careful account of all the points raised in coming to a decision on this important issue.

*Question put and agreed to.*

*Resolved,*

That the draft Coal Industry (Restructuring Grants) Order 1995, which was laid before this House on 1st May, be approved.

## Pneumoconiosis

5.25 pm

**The Minister of State, Department of Employment (Miss Ann Widdecombe):** I beg to move,

That the draft Pneumoconiosis etc. (Workers' Compensation) (Payment of Claims) (Amendment) Regulations 1995, which were laid before this House on 1st May, be approved.

The regulations will be made under the Pneumoconiosis etc. (Workers' Compensation) Act 1979. The purpose of the regulations is to increase by 2.2 per cent. the amounts of compensation paid under the Act to those who first satisfy all the conditions of entitlement on or after 1 July 1995.

**Mr. Elfyn Llwyd** (Meirionnydd Nant Conwy): Bearing in mind the fact that inflation is running at 3.3 per cent and that there was no review last year, does the Minister consider that that is an appropriate payment?

**Miss Widdecombe:** I consider it a very appropriate payment because, during the lifetime of the Act from 1980, the cumulative increase in the level of payments had reached 138.3 per cent., but the cumulative interest in the retail prices index during that time has reached 134.7 per cent. Therefore, there has been a real-terms increase. It is precisely because it was running so far ahead that there was no increase last year.

I briefly remind the House of the purpose of the Act. People suffering from industrial diseases have the right to sue the employer concerned for damages, but certain dust-related diseases take a long time to develop, and may not be diagnosed until 20 to 40 years or more after exposure. Because of that, sufferers and their dependants can experience considerable difficulty in obtaining compensation. By the time the disease is diagnosed, the employer responsible may no longer exist.

The 1979 Act set up a scheme to provide a measure of compensation to those who cannot claim it in the usual way through the courts. It provides lump sum payments to sufferers from certain dust-related diseases, or, when the sufferers have died, to their dependants. But it has never been the intention of the Act to provide an alternative to taking civil action in the courts.

Three basic conditions of entitlement must be satisfied before a payment can be made: that there is no relevant employer who can be sued; that no court action has been brought nor compensation received in respect of the disease; and that industrial injuries disablement benefit has been awarded.

My Department does all it can to administer the Act in a sympathetic way. It is necessary to ensure that payment conditions are met, but it is also recognised that each case is an individual disaster, and the Department is therefore as generous as the legislation allows.

Since the Act came into force in 1980, more than 7,800 applicants have made a claim, and 75 per cent. of those have received payment. The total cost to date has been some £39 million. Payments under the Act are additional to any industrial injuries disablement benefit awarded.

The Government have given an undertaking to Parliament to review the amounts payable regularly in order to maintain their value, and the regulations aim to fulfil that commitment.

I feel sure that the House would agree that the circumstances leading to payments are very much to be regretted. They reflect the conditions under which some people worked many years ago. Action taken by the Government to control the use of asbestos and other hazardous substances should prevent such suffering for present and future generations of workers. Nevertheless, I very much welcome the opportunity provided by the regulations to maintain the value of the compensation.

All of us will recognise that no amount of money will ever compensate individuals and families for their loss, but at least the regulations allow us to give some practical and some material help. I therefore commend the uprating of the payment scales to the House, and ask its approval to implement them.

**Mr. Deputy Speaker (Mr. Geoffrey Lofthouse):** I should like to make a brief point before I call the hon. Member for Makerfield (Mr. McCartney).

I think that I have shown that my patience on some occasions knows no bounds. The draft regulations before us, as the House will appreciate, further amend the Pneumoconiosis etc. (Workers' Compensation) (Payment of Claims) Regulations 1988 by increasing the amount of payments to persons disabled by a disease, to which the parent Act applies, by 2.2 per cent., rounded up or down to the nearest £1 as appropriate. The debate must address that particular item.

5.30 pm

**Mr. Ian McCartney** (Makerfield): I am sure that your point, Mr. Deputy Speaker, was a general piece of advice, and not aimed in particular at my speech.

My hon. Friends and I want to relate the motion to a series of interrelated issues with a common approach and purpose, which underlines the need to recognise the terrible tragedies at work and to bring in a far wider regime of compensation and prevention. During my short speech, I shall deal with those issues and how they relate to the regulations.

For the Minister to give an impression that the proposed payments are anything other than paltry is a disgrace— indeed, it is disingenuous. The Government do not intend an annual uprating of this benefit. If the benefit were uprated in line with inflation, the Government would have proposed an uprating of around 5.75 per cent. They are, of course, offering an uprating of 2.2 per cent. In real terms, that represents not an increase but a decrease over the past few years. The Minister has no justification for such a mean-fisted approach.

My hon. Friends and I will also refer to the Government's hostility in a range of areas toward injured workers—

**Miss Widdecombe** rose—

**Mr. McCartney:** I shall give way to the hon. Lady in a moment. I enjoy having a discussion with her. I would like to ask the Minister a number of questions which— perhaps—she can answer when she intervenes.

The coal industry scheme is not directly affected by the amendment; however, there are a number of issues with which the Minister could assist in the context of the draft regulations.

When was the last uprating of the coal miners' pneumoconiosis scheme? When will the Government bring forward regulations to uprate it, even if it is in line with the uprating of the regulations before us? The coal industry pneumoconiosis regulations allow for the

opportunity for reassessment, ensuring that, if there is a deterioration as a direct result of the prescribed illness, levels of compensation may be adjusted accordingly. As I understand the regulations, however, no such facility exists for non-coal mining employees.

Under the amended pneumoconiosis regulations before the House, a 50-year-old who is assessed as 10 per cent. disabled is entitled to £10,888 as a full and final settlement. If the pneumoconiosis is diagnosed three years on, however, by which time the sufferer may be 50 per cent. disabled—that is a reasonable assumption, given the cohort of cases about which we already know—his disability will entitle him to £30,006. That is a hypothetical example, but such cases occur all the time.

Entitlement for a disabled person and his or her dependants could vary by as much as £19,118 or even more, simply because of the timing of the diagnosis. That is ridiculous and inequitable. Will the Minister bring forward proposals to allow for reassessment when we next discuss the regulations?

**Miss Widdecombe:** I am intervening on the hon. Gentleman on the point that he was making when I tried initially to intervene. He said—I heard him quite distinctly—that we have not maintained the value of the compensation over the past three years. Will the hon. Gentleman confirm that, in April 1991, the increase in the compensation was 9 per cent. against a retail prices index of 8.2 per cent., that the following year it was increased by 5 per cent. against an RPI of 4 per cent., and that the following year it rose by 2.5 per cent. in comparison to an RPI of 1.7 per cent.?

That is why there was no increase last year. This increase therefore maintains the value of the compensation against inflation. Over the three years that he quoted, we have increased compensation above the rate of inflation.

**Mr. McCartney:** The hon. Lady is being disingenuous, and I shall explain why. Dust-related diseases, by their very nature, do not always become apparent straight away. Many cases, therefore, under the regulations, are new cases or potential new cases. For the people affected, the regulations do not represent an uprating, which is why I presented the proposed uprating in the context of the past three years. Many people whose illnesses relate to 1979 or 1980 have since died. We are trying to calculate a benefit not for the deceased, but for the living. In that respect, the hon. Lady is wrong and we are right.

The overwhelming bulk of benefit recipients under the pneumoconiosis regulations are former asbestos workers. Deaths from asbestos-related cancers are expected to triple over the next 30 years. Despite the strict controls that govern the use of asbestos today, disease rates will continue to rise because of the long incubation period for such cancers.

Asbestos-related diseases already kill more than 3,000 people a year in the United Kingdom. In Clydeside, Merseyside, Tyneside, Wales, the midlands and every region of the country, there is a time bomb of dust-related diseases. The cancers are the most deadly known. There is no possibility of survival in the medium or long term. Asbestosis causes the most appalling deaths. Dust-related diseases are painful and debilitating.

I pay tribute to my hon. Friend the Member for Clydebank and Milngavie (Mr. Worthington), who, with hon. Members of all Opposition parties, has conducted a

*[Mr. McCartney]*

campaign on behalf of the sufferers of asbestosis and those who care for them. That campaign has been not only about the recognition of the disease and the necessity to uprate benefits, but about the consequences of the Government's notorious compensation recovery unit.

How can the Minister say dispassionately that the Government are concerned to ensure that the sufferers of asbestos are compensated throughout their lives? This year alone, the Government are taking almost £1 million away from sufferers of asbestosis through the compensation recovery unit. They are the same Government who, in a matter of minutes, are able to give R. J. Budge a £1 million sweetener to take over the British coal industry.

It beggars belief that, having recognised the nature of the disease and the need to provide compensation, the Government claw back through the compensation recovery unit compensation provided by employers. As I said, £1 million has been clawed back this year, and more will follow. Even at the point of death, when settlements are made, the Government attempt to claw back money from the mourning dependants. It is a scandal, and the Government are attacking those who have been injured at work. It is about time that they gave a commitment to end the notorious activities of the compensation recovery unit. In one instance, £84,000 was recovered from a sufferer by the compensation recovery unit, but the Government still say that they are concerned about the economic well-being of asbestosis sufferers.

The same double standards apply to the Government's approach to prevention. The Minister said that the Government were interested in work to prevent others from suffering such terrible diseases, but, under this Government, the number of visits of inspection of relevant companies and activities has dropped. The number of inspections of asbestos removal companies has declined from 2,709 in 1985 to just 805 in 1994. In other words, the number of visits has dropped by two thirds in only a decade, despite the evidence of an increase in asbestosis caused by industrial injury, and years of neglect by Government and industry.

A number of my colleagues want to speak, so I shall move on to an issue that is causing grave concern to mining communities across the country—how the Government effectively operate the regulations. On the one hand, the Government give the impression that the regulations benefit sufferers of pneumoconiosis, chronic bronchitis and emphysema, but, on the other, the application of the regulations means that a substantial number of sufferers of industrial disease have no access to any benefits.

In my constituency, 90 per cent. of miners with chronic bronchitis and emphysema have been denied access to any benefits. It is a matter of urgency that the Government consider why the application of the regulations should lead to such a lack of access to benefits for the most vulnerable disabled people.

If the Government are serious about their responsibilities to tens of thousands of people who, because of their environmental and working conditions, suffer a life of disability, they will take steps to alter the operation of the recovery unit and amend the emphysema and chronic bronchitis regulations. They will also take steps to ensure that pneumoconiosis benefit is genuinely uprated, not as the Minister suggests.

I now give the views of three of my constituents who suffer daily because of Government's callous pneumoconiosis regulations. One states:

"I had to take early retirement because of this disease. I spent the majority of my life mining coal underground, and destroyed my health as a result, but the personal cost of my contribution is being denied."

Another told me:

"I've never smoked and don't drink, and just can't comprehend how the agency can distance my illness from my occupation—I feel sickened by the falseness of the Government's 'concern'."

A third said:

"I am severely disabled through my employment, diagnosed long ago as a sufferer of chronic bronchitis. I'm angry that the Government gave the introduction of this benefit such high profile to show the recognition of miners sacrifice, knowing that so few of us would actually qualify for the benefit because of the severity of the criteria. It's all been a sham."

The regulations fail to meet the challenges created by occupational chronic ill-health. The meagre 2.2 per cent. award pales into oblivion when compared with the sums handed by the Tories under privatisation to their friends and supporters in the City. The Minister should be more generous to sufferers of chronic bronchitis, asbestosis and related diseases. If the Government were as generous to them as they are to their friends in the City, we should not have to complain today.

5.43 pm

**Mr. Eric Illsley** (Barnsley, Central): I shall not detain the House long, but I wish to echo what my hon. Friend the Member for Makerfield (Mr. McCartney) said about staged payments, which do not appear to be part of the scheme. They are included in the coal miners' pneumoconiosis scheme, under which, if a sufferer is reassessed and deemed to have a higher percentage of industrial disability, he is awarded a further payment to compensate for the increase in his disablement.

I am currently dealing with the case of a constituent— a coal miner—who suffered for a number of years, although he was never diagnosed as suffering from pneumoconiosis. Whenever he applied and was X-rayed, he joined the high failure—or refusal—rate referred to by my hon. Friend. When my constituent died, the post mortem revealed that he was suffering from pneumoconiosis. As the Minister knows, pneumoconiosis can be diagnosed definitely only on death, when a biopsy can show the condition of the lung section.

The post mortem found that the chap had been suffering from pneumoconiosis since 1982, but under the terms of the scheme applicable to him—which I understand are to be replicated in this scheme—he qualified only for the rate of compensation applicable at the level of disablement that he suffered in 1982 and for the increased payments from that time as his percentage of disablement increased, based on an estimate made by the pneumoconiosis medical panel.

Although that man had suffered desperately for the final 13 years of his life, he received no compensation. On his death, an artificially low payment was made. It was artificially low because it was based on the initial assessment of a 10 per cent. disability as at 1982 and, sadly, the increased payments are only £200. I believe that, under the coal miners pneumoconiosis scheme, those payments should be increased and included in the scheme to which I have referred. There is a case to be made for the increases in assessments to be reflected in increased compensation.

I referred to the difficulty of diagnosis. In the cases of chronic bronchitis and emphysema, the failure rate is 90 per cent. The rate in respect of pneumoconiosis is also high, but not 90 per cent. The two rates are linked because one of the requirements for claiming compensation for chronic bronchitis is that a coal miner has to have evidence of pneumoconiosis in his X-ray. The X-ray evidence has caused difficulties for years.

We are now reaching the stage at which the Government must consider the X-ray qualification, and either instruct the adjudicating bodies to have soft exposure X-rays, as my hon. Friend the Member for Barnsley, West and Penistone (Mr. Clapham) will probably mention, undertaken in all cases of assessment for pneumoconiosis, or relax the qualification rules so that the judgment of the medical practitioner is accepted in place of the arbitrary X-ray and the forced expiratory velocity test of one litre.

We should have a system whereby diagnosis is based on medical opinion, which would probably have avoided some of the suffering inflicted on my constituent, who suffered from pneumoconiosis for 13 years but received no compensation, and whose widow will receive only a very small sum.

The failure rate in diagnosing pneumoconiosis, chronic bronchitis and emphysema makes a mockery of the suggestion that the scheme, the 2.2 per cent. increase now, or the 138 per cent. increase over the past few years are or have been generous. Any percentage increase does not matter very much if people cannot qualify for compensation in the first place.

I sat on the Committee that dealt with the legislation to introduce the compensation recovery unit and increased recovery from 50 per cent. to 100 per cent. of any benefit. It is diabolical to recoup 100 per cent. Beveridge, and the 1947 and 1948 legislation, did not intend that to be the case. It was always taken as 50:50 between the employer and the employee, in view of the national insurance contribution of both sides. The recovery rate should not have been increased.

5.49 pm

**Mr. Elfyn Llwyd** (Meirionnydd Nant Conwy): First, I welcome the opportunity of having a debate on this important subject today. I have the honour to represent a constituency in north Wales in which there are several working slate quarries, and the subject is of great importance to many hundreds of my constituents. I welcome the opportunity to remind the House that it was continued pressure from my party which brought in the legislation on the matter in 1979. That is a fact of which I am proud.

As at December last year, total expenditure under the Pneumoconiosis etc. (Workers' Compensation) Act 1979 amounted to about £38.1 million, with some 5,700 people receiving payments under the Act. Those facts are worthy of acknowledgement, but it must be said that the current system is failing as many people as it is assisting. Perhaps the system itself could best be described as rough justice.

The principle in compensation law is encapsulated in the Latin maxim "restitutio in integrum". One can never put a person suffering from pneumoconiosis, emphysema or chronic bronchitis back to where he should be. That is as plain as a pikestaff. The legislation was introduced to make the lives of sufferers less of a misery than they currently are. I am afraid that the Government are failing in their duty.

In saying that the system is failing those in need, I refer first to the scale that is applied to applicants seeking compensation. The scale is devoid of flexibility, and an assessment of 10 per cent. disability—that is all too common—for a 40-year-old is as little as £8,742. If that person dies at the age of 60, the amount is lowered to £2,107.

When an assessment of 10 per cent. has been made, it remains at that level, despite the fact that a person's health fails with the onset of old age. Should there not be a statutory form of periodical review—say, every five years at the upper limit—so that these poor people are tested automatically? That would be fair, and the present process does not deliver a just result.

That brings me to my second point. Pneumoconiosis is often linked to other diseases, such as emphysema and chronic bronchitis. To a layman like myself, it is matter of inescapable common sense that there is a direct link between slate dust and other respiratory diseases, such as those I have mentioned. Alas, common sense makes little headway with the Government.

In 1992, the Industrial Injuries Advisory Council recommended that chronic bronchitis and emphysema in underground coal miners should be added to the prescribed list of compensatable diseases. The council looked carefully for evidence of a link between pneumoconiosis and the other two diseases, and evidence showed that air-flow limitation in coal miners who had experienced heavy exposure to coal dust was more likely than not to have been caused by their work. That is an obvious point, which we would all accept. On that basis, the council therefore recommended that those two diseases should be prescribed under the scheme and should become compensatory diseases.

I plead on behalf of slate quarrymen that that same qualification should be applied for them. There is no basis in logic or common sense for that not to occur. There is abundant evidence of a causal link, and it only needs collating evidence. It behoves any responsible Government to initiate a full epidemiological survey.

At present, the collection of data is haphazard in the extreme. People may have their cases referred by the odd GP who takes an interest, or even by an employer—although I doubt whether many employers would volunteer the information. People are being let down, and the Government should understand that. I call on the Government to tackle the issue, and to do so without further delay. Delay—as has been said—is very often fatal for people suffering from these debilitating and horrible diseases. The Government must do something about that.

Clearly the uprating is welcome, but only as far as it goes. It has been more than two years since the last uprating, and I have had discussions with the Minister about that. With respect to her, I do not accept what she says. Even if there have been over-generous payments in years gone by, that does not justify making cuts now. We are dealing with people who can hardly move and hardly breathe, and who are in a living hell. The Minister can say that the Government will cut the scheme by 1 or 2 per cent., and that they will not give an extra pound here and there. That is obscene.

*[Mr. Elfyn Llwyd]*

I do not accept the Government's figures, either. In the past two years, the retail prices index has gone up by 5.75 per cent, while a 2.2 per cent. uprating has been offered. Since April 1989, the upratings have amounted to 37 per cent., while price increases have amounted to 33 per cent. There has been a 4 per cent. differential in the figures since 1989. That does not justify cutting back or offering a less generous settlement. I will not dwell on that point, as I am not going to agree with the Minister on it.

I do not accept the reasoning behind the Minister's statement, and the inescapable conclusion is that these people are being sold short by the Government. I therefore urge the Government to consider a far more generous uprating for next year, and to introduce a detailed study to extend the diseases referred to and have them listed as compensatable diseases.

In conclusion—and constrained by your initial warning, Mr. Deputy Speaker—I should like to mention one brief matter. I draw the attention of the House to an iniquitous situation regarding how the social security regulations cover compensation for coal dust victims.

It is ludicrous, if not obscene, to confine payments to those who have worked for at least 20 years underground and who pass the threshold test of having the use of only one third of one lung. That is an obscenity, but it is the law. I call on the Government to publish the Industrial Injuries Advisory Council review of disablement benefit, and for a speedy rectification of the issue.

The Minister is a reasonable person, and I ask her to consider the matters that I have raised tonight. They are important to many thousands of people in Britain, and many hundreds in my constituency, who are suffering. They are good, hard-working people who have worked all their lives. They deserve better than this.

5.57 pm

**Mr. Eric Clarke** (Midlothian): I thank the Minister for bringing the matter to the House, although I am disappointed that we are debating it at the very end of term. There are few Members in the House, and it is a reflection on both the people suffering from these diseases and on the mining industry that these two motions have been tagged on at the very end.

I represent many people who suffer from pneumoconiosis, and many others who are applying for benefit as suffering from emphysema or bronchitis. In the job I had before entering the House, I dealt with the problems related to those diseases. I appeal to the Minister to allow such people the dignity, and the financial dignity, of having this benefit. We cannot restore the health of those suffering a tortuous illness. They face a long and lingering illness before they die, and they look at it on a living death.

We are asking for compassion, and I hope that the Minister takes on board some of the comments made by previous speakers, and by me. In the past, people have been dismissed because they did not have sufficient fibrosis of the lung to qualify for benefit as suffering from pneumoconiosis. The argument was that they had chronic bronchitis and emphysema. When those same individuals have applied under the new scheme, they have been turned down. Some had to leave the industry because they were disabled by the combined diseases. An academic

medical argument then went on. It is not an exact science. As someone said, the only exact science is when a post mortem takes place, and it is horrendous that, to qualify for a widow's pension, a widow should have to allow a post mortem on her husband. All I am asking is for the cases to be reassessed.

Had I drawn a number in the ballot on first coming to the House, my private Member's Bill would have put emphysema and chronic bronchitis on the agenda immediately. I was over the moon that the Government were going to give us this breakthrough, but in Scotland only 5 per cent. of the people who apply qualify—there are so many disqualifications.

Some of those who were disqualified have since died. Many families are appealing posthumously, but I think that we are wasting our time. Many other people do not apply at all. They say, "Why should we? It seems to be a waste of time." Many others do not appeal when they get their first knock back.

As an ex-miner, I have many friends and relations who are suffering from these diseases. Although mining is no longer a great industry, a great army of people in the mining communities, as well as many people in other industries, are suffering from these diseases. There are also many other industrial diseases.

As a nation, we seem to be in a backwater when it comes to industrial medicine. Analysing industrial processes and continually assessing people in employment are not a priority for this nation. I do not know why, but I know that that is happening in other nations.

I am using this short speech to make a plea for the Government to reconsider the qualifying periods. I agree with my colleagues, especially my hon. Friend the Member for Makerfield (Mr. McCartney), who is on the Front Bench, about the 2.2 per cent. increase, which is disappointing. I also laughed when I read the words:

"rounded up or down to the nearest £1 as appropriate."

That sounds like the old negotiating tactics, when we were on piece-rate earnings in the pit. We always found that it was appropriate for the management, but never for the people whom I represented. I hope that that is not the case on this occasion.

Putting that anomaly to one side, it has to be said that 2.2 per cent. is not a great deal of money—nor is the total amount—but it makes a difference. The ex-miners and their families are worried not about the diagnosis, but about qualifying for the pensions concerned. That is the main thing. They know that the person is ill. They do not know why and cannot make a diagnosis—that is up to the medical people—and it is academic to them, but they want to make life a bit more comfortable and tolerable for themselves because they have to give constant care.

I hope that the Minister will consider the matter seriously. Yesterday's *Hansard* contains a written answer giving the statistics for people with emphysema or bronchitis who have claimed during the past two years. It is a damning indictment of the scheme. I hope that the Government will reassess the qualifications necessary. I cannot emphasise that enough, as it is so important to my constituents and to other people throughout the country.

6.3 pm

**Mr. Michael Clapham** (Barnsley, West and Penistone): As the Minister said, the regulation applies generally to people who are outside the mining industry. The hon. Member for Meirionnydd Nant Conway (Mr. Llwyd) mentioned slate quarrying, for example.

However, there will be circumstances in which the regulation applies to mining. If a private mine owner who has taken out employer's liability insurance for a small colliery, for example in Wales, goes out of business, he will have to be traced at some later date, to find out whether claims can be pursued through his insurance. If not, the case would be decided under this regulation.

I want to explore with the Minister the interrelationship between the regulation and the Employers Liability (Compulsory Insurance) Act 1969. There is a relationship by virtue of the fact that only when the previous employer cannot be traced, or there is no insurance, can someone be paid under the regulation. The intention of the 1969 Act was that every employer in the United Kingdom would ensure that all his employees were insured. There would have been notable exceptions—for example, the utilities and British Coal—for which the Government would have underwritten the insurance.

The 1969 Act provided for inspectors to visit works to ensure that the certificate of insurance is displayed in a prominent place and that all the employees are aware that the employer has taken it out. Obviously, that does not always happen and people are not informed of what the certificate means. The idea was to protect employees by requiring the certificate to be placed in a prominent position in the workplace, but that does not always give employees the sort of protection that was envisaged when the Act was introduced.

I have discussed the situation with lawyers who deal with common law damages and I am told that they are experiencing extreme difficulties, especially as they are looking back to 1969 and beyond with asbestosis cases. One of the difficulties seems to have come about because there is no requirement that details of the insurance certificate should be deposited in a central office. Consequently, even when employers are traced, they cannot always remember whether they were insured, or the name of the insurer.

Perhaps the legislation could be amended to require employers to register details of such insurances in a central office, so that they would be available to the public for scrutiny. That would certainly help and I hope that the Minister will take the suggestion on board.

It is not merely a question of forgetting the name of the insurance company. If a company has gone into liquidation, it is almost impossible to trace the insurer, especially if we are talking about looking back more than 20 years. Even when an employer has complied with his obligations under the Act, one is not always able to trace the insurance. That means that we perhaps need to go beyond a central office for depositing details of certificates. It seems eminently sensible to consider the possibility of amending the legislation to require every employer, whether a company by incorporation, a partnership or an individual, to file an insurance return at a central point each year when the insurance is taken out.

There should be a central register, which, as I said, should be open to the public to scrutinise. The issue may become more important as we move into the next century because, as the Minister knows, some reports, especially that in *The Lancet*, which was drawn up by statisticians employed by the Health and Safety Executive, show that by 2020 there are likely to be 3,000 deaths per year

through asbestosis. The number of claims that will be pursued is likely to be in excess of the current number. It is therefore pressing to consider the idea of a central office where details of insurers and insurance premiums can be registered.

I am also told that there are certain other problems. Lawyers tell me that even if an employer can be traced, there are ways in which it can get round its responsibility. For example, in some circumstances, the employer will refuse to pass on a letter of claim to the insurer. The employer may hang on to the letter until such time as the insurer is not prepared to accept the claim. We could get around that problem by imposing a duty on employers to ensure that when they receive a letter of claim in cases of asbestosis, pneumoconiosis and byssinosis, it is passed on to the insurer.

I would suggest to the Minister that that principle is already established because sections 51 and 52 of the Road Traffic Act 1988 specifically provide that once an insurer has given insurance, it must meet its obligation even if a thief were driving the car. There is insurance cover even when there is an accident involving a stolen car that is being driven by the person who has stolen it. It is only one short step to relate that argument to the Employers' Liability (Compulsory Insurance) Act 1969 and consequently to these regulations. Payments would be made from insurance premiums rather having to be made by the taxpayer.

**Mr. McCartney:** My hon. Friend is right, but there is one critical fact that he may want to put to the Minister. Under the regulations that govern the compensation recovery unit, insurers are 100 per cent. non-liable. They know that they need only offer a payment that is less than the cost of benefits already paid and that the state cannot recover that money from them. Therefore, not only do people lose access to benefits to which they are rightly entitled because of their industrial injuries, but the state ends up paying everything and insurers walk away having paid nothing. The compensation recovery unit is a scandal because of the damage and harm done to people by employers and because the insurance companies are being subsidised by the Government's proposals, which take benefits off recipients and do not take anything from the insurance companies.

**Mr. Clapham:** I take my hon. Friend's point, which has already been made clear by my hon. Friend the Member for Barnsley, Central (Mr. Illsley). It is a scandal that the recovery unit takes back every penny. The Minister will be aware that the 1948 legislation set the principle that national insurance contributions were paid 50 per cent. by the employer and 50 per cent. by the employee. That was always an accepted principle up to 1980s under common law in cases of assessing disablement and deductions from disablement assessments. It certainly appears to be a scandal. I hope that the Minister would be prepared to agree that the deduction should be no more than 50 per cent.

**Mr. Illsley:** From working on personal injury compensation claims, my hon. Friend and I know the whole history of the compensation recovery unit and the clawback. The compensation recovery unit gave the green light to the insurance companies because it meant that solicitors had to advise clients to accept minimal claims to avoid a substantial recovery by the CRU. The insurance companies got away with murder because they were

[*Mr. Illsley*]

paying minimal payments and avoided massive compensation payments where a clawback was involved. It was an insurance companies' charter.

**Mr. Clapham:** I take my hon. Friend's point. The Minister should realise from my hon. Friend's intervention that there must be some changes, and not only the change that I suggested for a central office for depositing details of insurance certificates. Unless we start to look at reducing the amount that the CRU takes back, all that will happen as we move into the next century is that employers that want to be helpful to their employees will disappear. There will be no trace that they were in business. Unless the insurance certificates have been deposited, there will be little chance of tracing them. Employers may even find ways around depositing their insurance certificates to help their employees. The 100 per cent. recovery of payments made becomes self-defeating.

I think that the Minister has taken on board the principle that we should have a central office where insurance details should be deposited. That would certainly help and, as I said, that principle is already established. Only when such safeguards are in being will working people feel safe in the knowledge that there is proper insurance protection.

6.17 pm

**Miss Widdecombe:** This has been an interesting debate and many hon. Members have spoken movingly of their constituents, and others, who suffer from these diseases. Indeed, I think it would be a shared view that it is quite impossible to overestimate the degree of suffering that people go through. As I said in my opening speech, it is not possible to compensate sufferers or their dependants for loss of health and, ultimately, loss of life.

Various points of detail were raised in the debate and, in particular, I would like, in reverse order, to reply to the hon. Member for Barnsley, West and Penistone (Mr. Clapham), who raised several points about the problems of enforcing employers' liabilities.

You will be relieved to hear, Mr. Deputy Speaker, that I am not an expert on the Road Traffic Act 1988. I cannot therefore comment one way or the other on the principle that has allegedly been established. I can say that the Government are aware of both of the main issues that the hon. Gentleman raised.

The first issue is simply that of the disappearance of records of with whom the insurance was held and the second is that of employers not putting in claims to their insurers. I am sure that the hon. Gentleman will be aware that the Government are currently reviewing the Employers' Liability (Compulsory Insurance) Act 1969 and that we are consulting interested parties on possible changes to the legislation. I cannot speculate on the outcome of that review, but I can say that the consultation document was issued in April and that comments should be received by the end of July. If the hon. Gentleman wishes to enlarge on any of his comments which, incidentally, I shall ensure that I take into account, I should be interested to receive details either by way of a meeting or in writing.

The specific issues that the hon. Gentleman has raised—records of insurance and the problem of employers having insurance, but not putting in claims—

have both formed part of the consultation, and we have sought views on them. I am genuinely grateful to him for bringing these issues out in parliamentary debate because they are extremely important.

The hon. Member for Midlothian (Mr. Clarke) also made a moving contribution to the debate. I am rather sad that he suggested that we tagged this debate on at the end of the Session, thus revealing that we did not consider it to be important. Once the decision on uprating was taken, we believed that it was important to avoid any further delay and we thought that it was important to have this debate before the House rose. For that reason, the debate was scheduled for today. I hope that the hon. Gentleman will take that point as made in good faith. The debate was not tagged on at the end because it was considered to be unimportant.

Several speakers raised the issue of chronic bronchitis and emphysema. The hon. Member for Meirionnydd Nant Conwy (Mr. Llwyd)—I am sure that I have not pronounced the constituency properly—mentioned slate quarry workers. The Industrial Injuries Advisory Council is an independent statutory body. It advises the Secretary of State on matters that relate to the industrial injuries scheme and it keeps developments in occupational diseases under review. The major part of its time is spent in considering whether the list of prescribed diseases for which industrial injuries disablement benefit may be paid should be enlarged or amended. The council will recommend a disease for prescription only when it considers that there is sufficient scientific evidence to establish the link between the disease and the occupation. In the case of chronic bronchitis and emphysema, the council is satisfied that the link exists for coal miners who have worked underground for 20 years and who satisfy certain medical criteria. I understand the hon. Gentleman's point that the criteria are strict, but I point out that that is the council's scientific view.

The council also believes that it has not received sufficient scientific evidence to suggest that bronchitis and emphysema should be recommended for prescription in relation to slate quarry workers. I can only suggest to the hon. Member for Meirionnydd Nant Conwy that if he is aware of such evidence, he should ensure that it is presented, regularly updated and re-presented to the council so that it can take his views into account. The council is an independent statutory body and we follow its advice.

The hon. Members for Makerfield (Mr. McCartney) and for Barnsley, Central (Mr. Illsley) commented on reassessment, which is available under the British Coal scheme, and on allowance for changes in the nature of the disability or the disease. Payments are weighted—I have an extremely complex table with which I shall not weary the House—to take account of the risk of deterioration and that is built into the scheme. On more than one occasion, the question was raised of why benefits should be recovered from compensation payments.

**Mr. McCartney:** When the regulation was debated two years ago in Committee, my hon. Friend the Member for Strathkelvin and Bearsden (Mr. Galbraith) raised the point about someone dying before the benefit proposal was approved. In such a case, the consequent award is reduced by half; there is a 50 per cent. cut on the basis of death. At the time, we asked the Department to reconsider the proposal as the compensation related to loss of earnings and other matters. We felt that the reduction was unfair. Has the Minister considered the matter and, if so, what decision has she come to?

**Miss Widdecombe:** I am not sure whether the hon. Gentleman is asking me whether the principle of reduction to take account of death when compensation is paid to dependants is wrong in itself and whether it should be the same as that paid to sufferers or whether he was relating his intervention to my point and talking about a change in the nature of the severity.

**Mr. McCartney·** I am making a different point. The Minister talked about weighting. We disagree with her comments because the regulations dealing with pneumoconiosis in miners are different and there is an assessment procedure. There is a recognition in law of deterioration and that should apply here. Why is it that there is a reduction in compensation on death? There seems no validity in law for that. Has the Department considered the matter since the previous discussion and if so, what was its view?

**Miss Widdecombe:** I refer the hon. Gentleman back even further to the origins of the regulations, which I always carry round with me, and to the debate in December 1979 when my right hon. and learned Friend the Member for Tunbridge Wells (Sir P. Mayhew), who was then the Under-Secretary of State for Employment, discussed why the regulations were structured so that there should be a difference between dependants and sufferers. He referred to the pattern that had already been established under the National Coal Board scheme and he pointed out that the regulations followed that pattern exactly. The Pneumoconiosis etc. (Workers' Compensation) Act 1979, which was passed by a Labour Government, made a clear distinction between categories. We followed a long-established, recognised difference between the two.

More than one speaker challenged me to say why benefit payments were recovered from compensation. The Government have long held the view that negligent employers and other compensators should not have their liabilities met through the social security system and that victims should not be compensated twice for the same incident. Those tenets led to the formation of the compensation recovery unit. The principle is, therefore, well established. In a former incarnation in the Department of Social Security, I took part in various debates on the underlying principles and I do not think that I can add much to my comments then.

**Mr. McCartney:** Will the Minister give way?

**Miss Widdecombe:** I would like to make some progress. I have tried to address the various points raised and I am aware that time is a little pressing—

**Mr. McCartney:** I have nowhere to go.

**Miss Widdecombe:** The hon. Gentleman may not have anywhere to go. I suspect that others, including some of his colleagues, may.

There has been some discussion about the failure rate of claims. I believe that a system that pays out on 75 per cent. of claims does not raise the spectre of an unduly high failure rate. The only point on which I shall seek leave not to respond but to write—

**Mr. Illsley:** What about pneumoconiosis?

**Miss Widdecombe:** I shall disregard that intervention because it was a sedentary one. The one point on which I shall write further is the one raised by the hon. Member for Barnsley, Central, who has somewhere to go—[HON. MEMBERS: "He is here."] So he is. He raised the point about the quality of X-rays and about the adequacy of X-rays to be a determining factor. I shall respond on that matter in due course.

I have tried to answer the major points raised in this debate, although I could not answer the entire rant of the hon. Member for Makerfield. It has been a sensible and sensitive debate, and I commend the Order to the House.

*Resolved,*

That the draft Pneumoconiosis etc. (Workers' Compensation) (Payment of Claims) (Amendment) Regulations 1995, which were laid before this House on 1st May, be approved.—*[Dr. Liam Fox.]*

## Statutory Instruments, &c.

*Motion made, and Question put forthwith pursuant to Standing Order No. 101(5) (Standing Committees on Statutory Instruments, &c.).*

### CONTRACTING OUT

That the draft Contracting Out (Functions of the Official Receiver) Order 1995, which was laid before this House on 28th April, be approved.—*[Dr. Liam Fox.]*

*Question agreed to.*

*Motion made, and Question put forthwith pursuant to Standing Order No. 102(9) (European Standing Committees),*

### ENERGY POLICY

That this House takes note of European Community Document No. 4523/95, relating to European Union energy policy, and supports the Government's view that, while welcoming the consultation process, the Community should focus its efforts on completing the single market.

### COTTON REGIME

That this House takes note of European Community Document No. 5489/95, relating to reform of the cotton regime; and supports the Government in its intention to continue to press for a rigorous reform of the cotton regime and, in particular, to reduce the level of subsidisation and to tackle fraud.—*[Dr. Liam Fox.]*

*Question agreed to.*

## Crime in Ribble Valley

*Motion made, and Question proposed,* That this House do now adjourn.—*[Dr. Liam Fox.]*

6.29 pm

**Mr. Nigel Evans** (Ribble Valley): I am extremely grateful for the opportunity to raise this subject this evening, especially as it is still daylight. I trust that it will still be daylight when we finish the debate.

The last Adjournment debate that I had just before a recess was on organ donors and I was asking for a computer so that all that information could be held centrally. I was delighted when, 12 months later, I was successful in gaining that central register, so the nation will be holding its breath to see what I shall ask for this time. I have no doubt that, within a short time, the Government will deliver.

The subject of tonight's debate, "Crime in Ribble Valley", sounds like an Agatha Christie novel such as "Murder She Wrote", "Death of the Tickled Trout" or "Whodunit at Gisburn". Although the debate's title suggests that Ribble Valley is riddled with crime, that is not the case. We do not have an appalling crime rate and we want to keep it that way.

May I start by describing Ribble Valley to put it in context? Just because that beautiful rural area does not suffer from as much crime as other areas, it does not mean that we should be forgotten. It is a personal tragedy for anyone who suffers crime and we should see what we can do to eradicate even the small amount of crime that exists within Ribble valley. My hon. Friend the Minister will know the area well as it is not far from his constituency. My constituency consists of a number of beautiful villages; Clitheroe, which is a larger area; and Fullwood, which is the urban side of Preston. So it has a mix of urban and rural areas. The Ordnance Survey people who make maps tell me that Ribble Valley is at the centre of the United Kingdom. Much is said about middle England these days; if one wants to know what the people of middle United Kingdom think, one need go no further than my constituency.

Since I have been a Member of Parliament I have held three public meetings on law and order, which have all been well attended. People have been vociferous on law and order, not just because they have been victims or know others who have been victims of crime but because they hold strong views on law and order in the United Kingdom generally and want to help eradicate crime throughout the country. The perception is that crime is more widespread than it is, but that does not mean that people should not be worried. Just because news bulletins are not riddled with stories of shootings in Ribble Valley, it does not mean that we should not be concerned about crime there. There is a great community spirit within Ribble Valley which I wish could be extended to some other parts of the country.

I recently sent out a number of surveys on law and order and I have some of the forms with me today. People want to become involved and make suggestions to the Government, and I shall pass the pile of forms to my hon. Friend the Minister, who will be anxious to read the suggestions made on them and see what further measures the Government could take. He may be interested to know that I asked a specific question on identity cards, on which an announcement was made yesterday. I found that 87 per cent. of those who responded want the introduction of some form of identity card because they believe that it will help to crack down on fraud and crime, and I therefore support their call.

I recently had a chat with Alistair Lyons, chief executive of National and Provincial, which issues its own credit and cheque cards. It gives people the option of having their photograph on the front and etched signature on the back. The vast majority of people with National and Provincial cards now choose to have their photograph on them. I applaud National and Provincial for that initiative. It does not charge people for the card, unlike many credit card companies, which take none of those preventive measures. I call on the banks and all card-issuing companies to take that step and allow people to have their photographs and laser-etched signatures on cards. They could all do a little more to contribute towards combating crime.

Those who responded to my survey also believe that identity cards could be used to prevent social security fraud, which has been estimated at about £1 billion. People who pick up cheques at the post office or sign on should have some form of identification to prove who they are. If identity cards would help us to cut down on such fraud, we should take that step. They would also be useful to youngsters who need to prove their age. A card with the young person's photograph, signature and age would mean that off licences, pubs and clubs would no longer have the excuse that the young person looked 18 whereas he or she was only 14 or 13. When I was 20, I was still being refused the purchase of drink in Swansea because I looked so young. An identity card would have proved that I was older than I looked, which would have come in handy for me. So identity cards would be multi-faceted and beneficial in many ways.

**Dr. Robert Spink** (Castle Point): I congratulate my hon. Friend on distributing the Viewfinder Survey, which I see on the Bench before me and which he will pass on to the Minister. In the survey, he asks his constituents a number of questions including whether they favour the introduction of a national identity card. The form that I have picked up says "Yes". Will my hon. Friend let us know at some stage—he may not have analysed the forms yet—how many of his constituents favour the introduction of a national identity card?

**Mr. Evans:** I am glad to tell my hon. Friend, who is interested in law and order issues and has spoken in the House many times on measures that would help to tackle crime, that a staggering 87 per cent. of people in Ribble Valley want identity cards. All the cries from Liberty that identity cards would be a terrible invasion of people's privacy are nonsense. It is an invasion of people's privacy when their houses are broken into, their cars are wrecked and money is stolen from the taxpayer. We should take that relatively simple measure to combat such crimes.

Yesterday I spoke at length with police officers in Clitheroe about burglary and theft, particularly in the villages in my constituency. Sergeant Kirk told me that the vast majority of such crimes are committed by people from outside Ribble Valley. As a result of the Government's continuing investment in the roads programme, we now have a good infrastructure with the M6, the M61 and other motorways. But it means that criminals can come to the area from Manchester,

Liverpool or other urban areas, perpetrate their crimes, put the goods into the back of their vans and disappear down the M6 before we know where we are. We are victims of commuter crime. One of the police officers said that, if only we could build a wall around Ribble Valley, crime would be reduced by 80 per cent. I do not suggest that we build a wall around Ribble Valley, but that shows the sort of problems faced by rural areas.

When I first moved into Ribble Valley I lived in a beautiful village called Downham. It is a relatively small village owned by Lord Clitheroe and it has barely altered throughout the years. "Whistle Down the Wind" was filmed there. Having come from Swansea, I found it remarkable that people knew that I was coming before I arrived. They know when people get up, when they go bed and who has called at houses. They know everything about the village because they take an interest in the community. That type of community spirit is absolutely wonderful.

Such community spirit also helps community policing, because policemen know people who live in the village. They recognise strangers and note those who look suspicious. They are therefore able to go up to such people and ask one or two questions. In many cases that alerts would-be criminals that Ribble Valley is not the place for them.

I was told yesterday how the police went to another beautiful village in my constituency, Sawley, and saw a vehicle that looked a bit suspicious. They had a chat with the people in it and it was not long before it had turned round and was on its way back down to the M6. Such community policing plays a valuable role when combined with the efforts of people who live in the community. We can all benefit from that partnership.

Much of the crime committed in my constituency and indigenous to it is the type of crime about which we all get upset—mindless vandalism, graffiti, broken windows and damage to cars. That is not the stuff of Agatha Christie novels, but it upsets locals, especially shop owners, who find that their windows are put through for no good reason. It is not as though all the shops that are vandalised sell jewellery—most of them use shutters—but even fruit shops are attacked. One could hardly believe that people would throw bricks through windows to steal fruit. We want to eradicate such mindless vandalism.

A camera shop, which stocked a lot of valuable products and had spent a lot of money on reinforced plate windows, was also subject to mindless vandalism. It was open just one day when someone took the trouble to try several times to break the windows. Those attempts left deep marks on the windows and the owner of that shop had to get them replaced.

Shops in my village, Longridge, have suffered from huge amounts of graffiti and traders are fed up with it all. One would think that some parents would ask where their children had been at 1 o'clock or 2 o'clock in the morning. After all, we are not just talking about 18 or 19-year-olds, because some of the youngsters who perpetrate that crime are a lot younger.

I thank the Government for the £28,500 grant they have given to Clitheroe for the closed circuit television scheme. That grant is wonderful news. I know that my hon. Friend will be interested to learn that that scheme will be operational from next month. Those cameras will help to reduce the mindless vandalism, graffiti and damage to cars that occurs in town centres. The scheme will be a

success, so why can we not extend it to some of the neighbouring villages? I know that Longridge has applied for cameras to be installed and it would be wonderful if that application was agreed because it would help the police to eradicate mindless crime committed there. I am 100 per cent. in favour of the CCTV scheme and I hope that my hon. Friend will consider some of the applications for its installation in rural areas in particular, which would help the police. I was also pleased to learn that, instead of sticking trained police in front of CCTV screens, civilians will monitor them. Those civilians will help the trained police to catch the criminals.

Lancashire police have also taken delivery of a helicopter and Ribble Valley has benefited from that. That may seem far-fetched, but, this morning, Superintendent Clarke of Fulwood police station listed a catalogue of incidents where the helicopter has been used. It has been particularly useful at night when the use of thermal imaging equipment means that the crew of the helicopter have been able to give directions to the police on the ground to catch criminals. That is absolutely amazing. I was sceptical when I first heard that Lancashire police intended to buy a helicopter because I thought that £1 million could buy a lot of other equipment. It has already been used to good effect, however, and even the police on the beat are using their walkie-talkies so that they can get in touch with their station and request helicopter assistance. That helicopter can get to the scene in no time at all. That saves a lot of police time because several vehicles from all over the place do not have to chase the criminals. Quite a few criminals have been caught as a result of helicopter assistance.

My hon. Friend will know that I warmly supported the introduction of the side-handled baton, which has also been used to good effect recently in Ribble Valley, when a number of people spilled out of a pub at the same time and a fight broke out. The Clitheroe police were able to call in a special team which has been trained in the use of side-handled batons and within a short time that crowd had been dispersed. It would not have been possible had those officers been using the old truncheons. I am delighted that the police are already using the new batons. I know that trials are being conducted on the use of CS gas and, should they prove successful, I would support its use by the police.

**Dr. Spink:** Is my hon. Friend aware that about two weeks ago the police voted 4:1 against being routinely armed? Does he welcome that decision? Does he think that we should impose stiffer penalties on those who intend to commit felonies while carrying arms, particularly those who kill police officers? Would he welcome the reintroduction of hanging? Is he aware that Lord Tebbit has asked the Government—

**Madam Deputy Speaker (Dame Janet Fookes):** Order. This is becoming a speech: interventions should be short.

**Mr. Evans:** I understand the thrust of my hon. Friend's questions. I asked Sergeant Kirk of Clitheroe and Superintendent Clarke of Fulwood about arming the police. They both felt that that was wrong and they did not want the police to be armed. The last time a police officer was shot, I wrote to Lancashire police to ask it what sort of body armour its officers wanted and whether it was happy that it had received enough resources to buy it. Officers told me that they are looking carefully at the

[Mr. Evans]

body armour that will be made available to them. The current body armour is fine if worn for a short time, but in the summer the police would be unable to wear it all day. I would support the provision of flexible body armour to the police as soon as possible to give them protection, because, after all, they are protecting us.

Superintendent Clarke also told me how much she welcomes the new initiative on DNA sampling. It will be a great boon for the police to be able to build up a database of known criminals, because when evidence is left at the scene of crime it will point to those who perpetrated it. Those who argue about liberty have said that such sampling is a dreadful invasion of privacy. Not at all. I support it if it means that serious criminals will be caught. Superintendent Clarke wanted to know why that sampling could not be introduced retrospectively so that samples could be taken from those already in prison—known criminals. That is a good idea.

I could not make a speech about law and order in Ribble Valley without offering my thanks to all those involved in neighbourhood watch, who do a superb job not only in my area but throughout the country. They have given a commitment and they take the time and trouble to go around their communities to ensure that they are that much safer. They give a lot of support to the police and work side by side with them. I have been told of one initiative that was taken in Ribchester, which suffers from a lot of car crime. Those in the local neighbourhood watch, working with the police, sent out leaflets suggesting the measures that people could take to make their cars safer. People responded and the amount of car crime committed in Ribchester has dropped. That is a perfect working example of where the police and neighbourhood watch are working hand in hand. Such crime prevention will also help people to cut the amount of car insurance they have to pay in the long term.

I also applaud the work of the specials, a dedicated group of people who supplement the work of the police. They give up a lot of their time to ensure that law and order is kept in Ribble Valley. They are also supported by some local firms, for instance, British Aerospace, which has given the specials the use of a car in order to liaise with neighbourhood watch. It is a perfect example of a firm in the community supporting that community with something more than just words—a financial commitment. One of my local garages, Syd Brown, is also supporting the specials by providing a car. I applaud both those organisations and other commercial organisations that are backing the specials and neighbourhood watch with money.

I also welcome the fact that the police are going into schools under community action programmes. Superintendent Clarke told me that a dedicated officer goes around the schools talking to the youngsters. They organise poster competitions and quizzes in primary schools, trying to make the youngsters suggest ways of cutting crime and protecting themselves from criminals. It is important to start such education early, and I recommend the tactic to other police areas that are not already using it.

Clitheroe station has recently been refurbished, and new cells have been provided. That is welcome in a small community such as ours, because it means that police time is no longer wasted. Formerly two police officers had to accompany a prisoner to another area; now the prisoner can be put into a cell immediately, and those policemen can walk the beat. A number of respondents to my "viewfinder" said that they wanted more policemen walking the beat.

The old Clitheroe court was above the police station for a long time, but, unfortunately, it closed last year because of efficiency savings. It has now moved to Blackburn. That means that the police must now go to Blackburn, which takes up a good deal of time. Rural community courts should be kept open, even for only one day a week: the administration can be carried out anywhere, but police time should not be wasted.

I am also concerned about drug and solvent abuse. Will my hon. Friend the Minister make a fresh commitment to the Government's determination not to knuckle under and give in to calls from some of the "softheads"—as I call them—for the decriminalising of soft drugs? That is the last thing that we want, because it would make drugs cheaper and more easily available. No benefits would result. We must crack down on people who take drugs, and in particular those who push them—especially those who sell them to youngsters.

Earlier in the year, I was saddened to read that two youngsters aged 15 had been caught taking soft drugs in a school in my constituency. I shall not name the school, because I know that the headmistress is working hard to tackle such problems; it is a great shame that the governors did not support her in this instance. The youngsters were given a second chance, but were subsequently caught again. The headmistress expelled them. The governing body, however, overturned her decision and gave them a third chance. That gave the wrong message to youngsters who go to the school in question, who now have the impression that the school is not all that fussed about drugs. But we are fussed about young people who become involved with drugs. Only one message should be given to them: they will wreck their lives. We will not cave in to calls for the decriminalisation of drugs.

We must take a further step, however. We must ensure that school children are educated about the damage done by drug and solvent abuse. I am involved with a charity called Life Education; it has a number of small units which visit schools throughout the country, supported by community action groups such as Rotary. They talk to youngsters, in language that they understand, about substances that are harmful if they put them into their bodies.

The other day I visited one of the units in London. It was superb to see youngsters responding to the message conveyed by Life Education members. There should be such units throughout the country, educating children as young as four and five: at that age they can be influenced. The same applies to solvent abuse. Last week a 15-year-old died in Preston as a result of such abuse; what a criminal waste of a young life. I agree with the *Lancashire Evening Post* that we should consider measures to restrict the sale of solvents to young people.

I own a retail store, where my sister imposes her own rule that purchasers of butane gas must be over 21. We must look afresh at ways of restricting access to solvents that can kill young people. I support the newspaper's campaign, and I have sent some relevant papers to my right hon. and learned Friend the Home Secretary. I hope that he will seriously consider new ways of tackling the problem.

We must also ensure that the sentence fits the crime. A shop owner in Clitheroe wrote to me saying that two of her windows had been broken. That had cost her £1,000: the excess on her insurance cost her £250, and the insurance company forced her to install shutters, which cost £600. About £300-worth of goods were stolen. She got most of them back, but some were unsaleable.

So what happened to the person responsible? He was fined £53.40 and given a conditional discharge. I do not want sentencing of that kind in Ribble Valley, and I have already written to the Blackburn courts asking what went wrong. We should be getting tough with such people. Mrs. Carter, who came to my surgery, despairs of the situation. I hope that we will act to ensure that magistrates impose sentences appropriate to the crimes involved, so that others are deterred; but that can be done only through stiffer penalties, which were supported by Ribble Valley "viewfinder".

I have made my views public in my constituency: my constituents know that I am fairly hard on sentencing. I want stiffer sentences, and I think that parents should pay more attention to where their youngsters are. I believe that the use of the cane should be reintroduced in schools. My hon. Friend the Member for Castle Point (Dr. Spink) mentioned the death penalty earlier; last year I voted twice for its reintroduction in cases in which it is appropriate. I support the introduction of boot camps for young thugs, which has been proved to reduce the incidence of reoffending by 50 per cent. in the United States.

I was delighted when we acted to stop sentences for young thugs that involved cruises to Egypt or safari trips to Africa. The victims of their crimes must have wondered what the heck was going on; their taxes were paying for those junkets.

Since becoming Member of Parliament for Ribble Valley, I have been—on visits, I hasten to add—to Strangeways, Lancaster Farms and Fulwood prisons, and I support the work that is going on in those three institutions. Someone said to me the other day, "We are condemned for having more prisoners per head of population than any other European country, but when they are in prison we know that they are not on the streets committing crimes."

**Dr. Spink:** Does my hon. Friend agree that there should be glass shutters separating inmates from visitors, and more barbed wire and fewer video games and golf courses in prisons?

**Mr. Evans:** Indeed. The prison regime should be austere. It has been proved that contact between prisoners and their families or girl friends has enabled them to acquire drugs, and I believe that we should act swiftly to ensure that that never happens again.

I know that the county council structure plan is not in the domain of my hon. Friend the Minister, but it is relevant. I have described the rural nature of much of my constituency: it contains small villages, where there is a community life style. There is a community policeman, and people look after each other. The county council is considering the introduction of new houses on a scale that is not appropriate to Ribble Valley in Whittingham, the site of an old mental institution—it is thinking of putting

1,000 houses into an area that currently contains only 500—and in Whalley Calderstones, where it plans to put at least 1,000 houses. That would fundamentally alter the character of the villages, and would make it much more difficult for them to maintain their good record on law and order.

I back calls that are made when new houses are being built for crime prevention to be taken into account in the design of houses and estates. That, too, helps the police. I praise the work of others who help them—members of neighbourhood watch schemes, special constables and businesses that take the time and trouble, and contribute the money, to assist.

Crime is a war and there can be no conscientious objectors in that battle. In the Ribble Valley the people and the police work as one. Obviously, that does not mean that there is no crime; it means that we will not succumb to crime. We will fight crime wherever it exists and we will support the police when they are defending us. We will defeat the scourge of our society: the criminals who despoil our quality of life.

The Government have the support of the people of the Ribble Valley in the measures that they are taking to tackle the problem. The people of the Ribble Valley will continue to make suggestions to Government and to prod and to push for stiffer action in order to combat the criminals. Middle England has had enough; now is the time to hit back.

7 pm

**The Minister of State, Home Office (Mr. David Maclean):** I congratulate my hon. Friend the Member for Ribble Valley (Mr. Evans) on an excellent and informative speech, in which he drew the House's attention to the problems facing his constituency in the war against crime and to the achievements of the police, the community and the neighbourhood watch scheme in reducing crime. Having listened to my hon. Friend's comments on sentencing, I wish only that he was a senior judge.

My hon. Friend mentioned the possibility of death at the Tickled Trout. I have eaten some of its excellent food on a few occasions and I understand that death through over-indulgence at the Tickled Trout is a very real prospect. I am rather disappointed that, although the closed circuit television scheme, which I was very pleased to fund, opens next month, I cannot find my invitation to perform the opening ceremony and enjoy lunch at the Tickled Trout.

My hon. Friend made a number of interesting points that he believes could help us win the war against crime in the future, not only in Ribble Valley but in the country as a whole. Before dealing with the specific points made by my hon. Friend, I re-emphasise the fact that crime is falling in Ribble Valley. I share my hon. Friend's view that we cannot be complacent about that; we cannot say that we have won the battle and that it is time to go home, because even one crime is a crime too many. Even if we lowered the crime rate, it would still be far too high.

None the less, in the past two years we have had considerable success in cutting crime in this country and I believe that we can regard Ribble Valley as a success story. It is a success that I very much hope will continue; I look forward to hearing from my hon. Friend in a future debate that there has been a further and welcome fall in the crime rate in his constituency.

[Mr. David Maclean]

I am well acquainted with the attractions of my hon. Friend's constituency. Reaching Ribble Valley from Penrith is just a matter of going down the M6 and turning left—and I do not often turn left. I shall try to help hon. Members who are not familiar with it to picture the area. Ribble Valley is delightful. It is largely a rural area and 70 per cent. of the Ribble Valley has been designated as being of outstanding natural beauty.

It has undulating countryside, hills, valleys, gushing streams, lots of sheep, excellent pubs with good beer, and—of prime importance—an outstanding Member of Parliament. With all that, it has a population of just over 50,000—although it increases in the summer months as, not surprisingly, a growing tourist trade is attracted there by good motorway communications. But there is a down side: the motorway network also brings criminals from outside the area. I do not think that my hon. Friend will disagree when I say that the Ribble Valley has some home-grown criminals as well.

As my hon. Friend has reminded us, the major centre in Ribble Valley is Clitheroe, a bustling market town which has certainly shown itself to be wide awake when it comes to crime prevention. I am pleased to say that crime prevention throughout the Ribble Valley is paying off: figures for reported crime in the first four and a half months of the year show a substantial reduction compared with 1994.

Burglary is one of the crimes about which most people worry. Our latest figures run from the beginning of the year to May, and they show that there were just 100 domestic burglaries during that period—a decrease of 70 on the same period last year. Vehicle crime in Ribble Valley has also shown a substantial reduction. During the same five-month period, it fell from 356 to 306 cases. Regrettably, there was a slight increase in violent crimes from 20 to 23 cases, although I am pleased to say that none of them was classified as serious. There were 14 additional cases of non-domestic burglary.

Even taking the increase in those two categories into account, overall there has been a 13 per cent. fall in crime figures in Ribble Valley so far this year, with a total of 818 crimes reported to the police. I am sure that all my hon. Friends will join me in hoping that the improvement will be maintained and in congratulating Lancashire constabulary on its excellent success.

The House should draw encouragement from the fact that the improvement in crime figures for the Ribble Valley is part of the wider improvement that we have experienced nationally. I remind the House that recorded crime in England and Wales fell by 5 per cent. in 1994. Taken with the 1 per cent. fall in 1993, it is the largest percentage fall over a two-year period for 40 years. Lancashire as a whole also had a 5 per cent. drop. That proves that, provided we work together, we can reduce crime. That is why measures to tackle crime remain at the top of the Government's agenda.

Our strategy for dealing with crime is clear and is based on four main strands. First, we must do all that we can to prevent crime. Secondly, we must do all that we can to help the police to catch criminals. Thirdly, we must ensure that when suspects have been caught they are tried fairly and speedily. Fourthly, we must ensure that, if criminals are convicted, the courts have the powers that they need to deal with them appropriately and effectively.

The Government believe that crime prevention should involve everyone in the community: it is not something that can be left to the police or to other specialists. This is why the Government have promoted the partnership approach to crime prevention, encouraging local communities—including local authorities, business and the voluntary sector—to work alongside the police to try to reduce crime.

In response to guidance, support and encouragement from the Government, many successful local crime prevention partnerships have been formed. I am pleased to say that that is precisely what is happening in Lancashire as a whole and in the Ribble Valley. The Lancashire Partnership Against Crime was formed in 1992 as the major crime prevention initiative within the county, with the objective of bringing together commercial companies and local authorities to increase participation in crime reduction work.

The partnership is managed by a board that is made up of representatives from member organisations and it has been involved in a variety of initiatives, including steps to improve hospital security, anti-burglary measures and running community safety patrols. It has also helped to produce security advice for licensees.

A total of 28 police officers work full time on crime prevention in Lancashire and two senior crime prevention panels organise a number of local campaigns. Lancashire constabulary employs a full-time co-ordinator to run the partnership from police headquarters. I have met the co-ordinator and he is a superb operator.

The county also has an initiative to involve young people in community safety. School community action teams, known as SCATs, are proving successful. There are 53 SCATs in the county and I will briefly outline projects that they have undertaken in Ribble Valley. It is by no means a comprehensive list. West Craven high school has adopted and painted a vandalised bus shelter. The school has also had a property marking scheme which encourages people to put their postcodes on their property. At Clitheroe high school five students have undertaken a survey of drug use and abuse, which I am told was "excellent." The police have also asked children in a local school for those with learning difficulties—although I believe that it is outside my hon. Friend's constituency—to help with the clerical tasks involved in one of their crime prevention campaigns.

Other schools in the area, including Ribblesdale high school, have been involved in promoting the vehicle watch scheme and the 25 scheme. I remind the House that the vehicle watch scheme encourages motorists who do not expect to use their cars between midnight and 5 am to put special stickers on the front and rear windows of their vehicles. If the police notice a vehicle with a sticker on the road at that time, they are authorised to stop the vehicle and to question the driver.

The 25 scheme is similar. It involves putting a sticker in the window of a vehicle when a driver under the age of 25 is not normally expected to use that car. I think that the schools should be commended for taking part in that project—although I would not recommend it to my youthful-looking hon. Friend, who would be stopped all the time because the police are bound to think that he is under 25.

An important part of the partnership approach to fighting crime is the use of special constables, and my hon. Friend was correct to mention them. I understand that in Ribble Valley both they and traffic wardens are playing an important role in preventing vehicle crime. While on patrol, special constables and traffic wardens who notice that a car has been left insecure or with valuables visible note the car's details so that the owner can be sent a letter giving him or her details of how to improve vehicle security measures.

The Government have set a target of increasing special constables from 20,000 to 30,000. We consider them an excellent supplement to the regular police force. They are not a replacement, and there is no question of reducing the regular police force if we recruit specials, but it is good for people to volunteer. Next to joining the volunteer reserve forces, serving as a volunteer constable is the highest level of volunteering that any British citizen can do. They are a great body of men and women. I pay the highest tribute to special constables up and down the country.

My hon. Friend said that technology is also being used to fight crime in Clitheroe. The CCTV system, consisting of 13 cameras, is currently being installed in Clitheroe, and that was funded partly through the Home Office CCTV competition that I instituted. I understand that the local police are optimistic that the scheme will deter crime in the town centre and help them to apprehend suspects. They should be optimistic as in every other place where I have seen CCTV schemes in operation—in big cities and smaller towns—it clearly deters criminals, catches criminals and, by God, it helps to convict them. Newcastle police tell me that of 350 people—of course, the figure goes up every week—who they had arrested in the city centre because they had caught them on video, 347 pleaded guilty and had not a leg to stand on. Not only is justice being done, but it saves the courts some considerable time and effort and, no doubt, helps the legal aid fund as well.

There are also plans to provide local shops most likely to experience shoplifting with two-way radios. I have seen similar systems in operation and they are excellent. It will enable shopkeepers to alert the police, each other and the monitoring station if they notice suspicious behaviour.

My hon. Friend suggested that the scheme should be introduced in Longridge. I understand that that is under local consideration, but the Government have always maintained that CCTV should be targeted where it is most needed. It is a long-term commitment involving the local authority, local enterprise and the police.

Clitheroe was successful in gaining funding through the CCTV challenge. The criteria for bids were set out in guidance issued to all local authorities and police forces last November. Under the terms of the challenge, bids are to be matched by local funding, including private sector funding where appropriate. The quality of the bids was very high. No one factor was decisive in the final choice and there were 106 winners all told, including 13 from the north-west. There is nothing to stop Longridge going ahead with a CCTV scheme, but my hon. Friend will understand that I cannot promise any additional funding at present or say whether we will instigate similar challenge schemes.

My hon. Friend mentioned funding in Lancashire. I am sure that hon. Members agree that the realistic expectation of being caught is one of the best deterrents against crime. An additional £9.82 million has been made available to Lancashire for policing purposes this year—an increase of 6.7 per cent. which compares very favourably with the national increase, and even that was way above the level of inflation. Not every other Government Department or local council services department can say that its funding has been a generous as we made police funding this year because we recognise the importance of law and order. It is a good settlement for the police at a time of constraint on public expenditure.

My hon. Friend mentioned the helicopter. I am a great enthusiast for police helicopters, and I encourage him to boast about it publicly. Other police forces must not be shy about telling people that they have a helicopter. It is not an expensive waste of money or an expensive toy; it is an essential policing tool to apprehend today's highly mobile criminals. I have seen the figures, I read the statistics and I have seen police helicopters in operation.

No armed robber escapes from a police helicopter. Once the equipment on a police helicopter locks on to a car, no vehicle can outpace it. I know that one or two Porsches might go faster, but a helicopter can cut the corners.

Not only are helicopters good at catching criminals, but they reduce the chance of high-speed chases. They lower the accident rate and have other features, such as thermal imaging, so that on dark nights they can find people who have wandered off or had accidents. They act as mobile command platforms if there is a major incident or accident. They are wonderful pieces of kit. The Government are keen to fund as many as possible. We have expanded the number over the past few years and I advise police forces not to be embarrassed if they have a helicopter; it is a vital policing tool these days.

My hon. Friend also mentioned secure design or improving design. I spent most of today in Staffordshire opening the county's first industrial park, which has been awarded a "secured by design" certificate. "Secured by design" is a wonderful concept that I would encourage every architect and builder to follow. It is no more expensive to build a house securely with proper locks or to build an entire housing estate with a sensible, decent design instead of the ghastly structures that people build, which no doubt win design awards but have rabbit runs or rat runs everywhere, front doors backing on to back doors and cars scattered all over the place.

Some of those designs encourage crime, as we saw from the ghastly 1960s and 1970s housing with archways and pedestrian walkways that are now—at great cost—being demolished, redesigned and returned to a sensible structure. I pay tribute to those who dreamt up the secured by design project and I intend to host a conference later this year of police architectural liaison officers and more architects and designers to encourage them when they are designing housing estates or ordinary buildings, factories and office blocks to think about security at the design stage, as it is cheaper in the long run.

My hon. Friend mentioned DNA sampling. The Government have been responsible for a number of other measures that are designed to enable the police to do their job more effectively. I am keen on using all forms of technology. The Criminal Justice and Public Order Act 1994 introduced the possibility of DNA sampling. The world's first national DNA database is now up and running, and once again little old Britain got there first. In so many cases, whether it is automated fingerprint computer recognition systems, where the Americans may have the computer, but we invented the data which make it work, or DNA sampling, the British police service is in

[Mr. David Maclean]

the lead the world over. Our database has now come on stream and will result in many people being caught and convicted and people regard it as the greatest policing breakthrough since fingerprints. It is the greatest tool that the police can have.

My hon. Friend mentioned the risks that serving police officers take in their operations against crime. My right hon. and learned Friend the Home Secretary and I share his concern. It is terribly important for officers to have suitable protection against those dangers.

One of the first jobs that my right hon. and learned Friend the Home Secretary did when he came to the Home Office two years and three days ago was to authorise proper scientific assessment of the side-handled baton. Street trials of the expandable version were encouraging, and in June 1994 it was formally approved by the Home Secretary. In November, the Home Secretary, as the police authority for the Metropolitan police, agreed to the issue of straight batons up to 26 in long, and he has given his support to the side-handled baton following a proper programme of evaluation to ensure that it meets officers' needs. At the same time, he gave his support to other chief constables who wished to introduce similar batons.

Since last year, most police forces have replaced the little, short traditional truncheon. I understand that Lancashire has had a programme running for the past four or five months to train officers in the use of side-handled batons and that has been widely welcomed in the force. The new batons can make a big difference to an officer's ability to carry out his duties, both in terms of the protection they offer and the greater confidence that results from it.

We welcome the side-handled batons and the extendable ones. We are receiving information now and we shall collate it. Much of it is anecdotal as the batons have been issued only recently, but we understand that injuries to officers in situations where they would normally have anticipated injuries have declined, that more prisoners are coming quietly and that some minor riots and disturbances have been avoided because the officer appears with a worthwhile baton rather than the tickling stick that the police had for 100 years.

My hon. Friend mentioned body armour. Of course, we are concerned scientifically to evaluate the best possible armour, but despite some of the claims in certain magazines I must tell my hon. Friend that no one has yet invented a body armour that protects against both bullets and stab wounds. There are some good vests which are bullet resistant; there are others which are stab resistant. So far, putting the two together has not resulted in anything that a bobby could wear for more than half an hour at a time. We shall continue to evaluate all kit so that chief constables will be able to know which body armour works and what its limitations are. They can then ensure that their officers are as well protected as possible.

Sentencing is important too. Effective action against crime does not stop with apprehending the suspect. We have ensured that the courts have all the powers they need to deal appropriately with offenders who come before them. My hon. Friends have supported us in the Division Lobby time after time on this issue. Parliament has taken its responsibility seriously to ensure that the powers are available to the courts—if only they would use them.

Severe sentences are available for serious crimes. I shall be careful about what I say when discussing the Executive and the judiciary, but it has been noticeable—judging by the public and the press outcry—that most of our constituents think not that Parliament has failed in its duty to provide adequate sentences but that lenient sentences are handed out. That dismays people; and if the House had not introduced powers to refer over-lenient sentences to the Attorney-General, they would be even more dismayed.

The clear message to those responsible for sentencing is that they must not disappoint the people of this country, who will get very indignant if they feel that sentences are inadequate.

My hon. Friend also mentioned capital punishment. He knows that I am an awful wet on that issue. My wife is much more robust, and starts with hanging for those who have double parked. I would begin with more serious offences—and with those who have been found guilty. My hon. Friend knows that the subject has been debated in the House, and that I share his view that we should have the ultimate deterrent.

My hon. Friend drew the attention of the House to another side of youth culture in his constituency. Unfortunately it appears that there is a problem with solvent abuse in some schools, and my hon. Friend has called for a change in the law. Under existing law, the Intoxicating Substances (Supply) Act 1985 makes it an offence for a person to sell a substance such as glue to a person under 18 if he knows that the substance or its fumes are likely to be inhaled for the purpose of causing intoxication. It was interesting to learn that my hon. Friend's sister sets the limit at the higher age of 21. The primary purpose of the law is to counter the activities of unscrupulous retailers. Enforcement is a matter for the police. By 1993 there had been 70 prosecutions under the Act, 45 of which resulted in findings of guilt.

On this and many other technical matters to do with drugs, the Government are advised by the Advisory Council on the Misuse of Drugs, which recently published a report on volatile substance abuse. The report makes no recommendations for changing the law, but I am happy to look at all the information from the campaign on solvent abuse which my hon. Friend is leading. I will happily study it and bring it to the attention of my colleagues who are responsible for drugs in the Home Office.

The one firm assurance that I can give my hon. Friend—and will always give the House as long as I am a Minister and my right hon. and learned Friend is Home Secretary—is that we shall never legalise any drugs that are currently banned. I know that there are sophisticated trendies who say that they can smoke a bit of pot after dinner parties in Hampstead—they can handle it. No doubt they can. Many people can handle a few glasses of port after dinner, but millions cannot. It is no good telling our kids that some drugs are really bad for them, some are in the middle and some are all right. That is a confusing message. Our message is simple: all drugs are harmful. It is nonsense to say that cannabis is not harmful. It may not be as bad as cocaine, but it is still harmful.

Many kids at the moment are able to resist drugs because they can say that they are illegal—they do not want to do something illegal. That can provide their excuse when they are refusing drugs offered by other kids. We shall never undermine those kids by removing the legal sanction. I remind the House that not a single chief constable among the 43 police forces of England and Wales for which I am responsible thinks that we should legalise drugs.

My hon. Friend went on to mention ID cards, suggesting that they could help to solve the problem of solvent abuse, and other crimes. We know that there is widespread public interest in the issue and that there is a wide range of views on what they would achieve and on how any scheme should operate. So much is clear from today's press articles. The Green Paper that we published yesterday will allow a full national debate before any final decision is taken. I agree with my hon. Friend that ID cards could help to prevent the illegal sale of age-restricted goods such as solvents, as well as helping to prevent crimes involving the use of a false identity, such as cheque and credit card fraud. But the Government do not believe that ID cards would be a general panacea for all crime—let us not kid ourselves about that.

That is why we need to consider the issue carefully and explore all its aspects. This is a genuine consultation exercise of the kind that we always intended to hold. The Government are setting out the options—naturally, that has been presented as a U-turn. It is nothing of the sort. We want to listen to genuinely held views about the sort of identity card that we should have—if we should have one at all—and about the driving licence and social security options.

I look forward to the outcome of this important national debate and if necessary to taking action on it.

We shall continue to do all that we can to reduce crime and to protect the public. That is one of the first duties of any Government. But the responsibility for preventing crime does not rest solely with the Government, the police, local councils or any single organisation. Respect for the law will be encouraged when everyone joins in—families and parents, schools, the Government, the local community, the business sector, people playing their part in neighbourhood watch schemes and in the special constabulary. If everyone plays his part we can get the crime figures down.

The message of the falling crime figures of the past two years is that it is no use running around wringing our hands and saying that it is all too difficult—where should be start? Nothing will get done that way. But if we tackle burglary and the police mount operations such as Operation Bumblebee, Operation Claw, the Bear Bites Back operation in Warwickshire, Operation Spider and Operation Gemini, involving the community and businesses in genuine partnerships against crime such as the one in Lancashire, we can bring down crime sector by sector. That has to be the right approach.

The community in Ribble Valley are playing an excellent part, and I would ask my hon. Friend to pass on my hope to his constituents that they will keep up the good work and keep supporting their police force, who do an excellent job. I trust that they will continue to shoulder part of the burden, as all good citizens should. What we can do in Lancashire we can do in other parts of the country as well—although my hon. Friend might disagree with me about that.

*Question put and agreed to.*

*Adjourned accordingly at twenty-eight minutes past Seven o'clock.*

# House of Commons

*Wednesday 31 May 1995*

*The House met at half-past Two o'clock*

## PRAYERS

[MADAM SPEAKER *in the Chair*]

### SITTINGS OF THE HOUSE

*Ordered,*

That this House, at its rising this day, do adjourn till Tuesday 6th June.—*[Mr. Wood.]*

## Bosnia

*Motion made, and Question proposed,* That this House do now adjourn.—*[Mr. Wood.]*

2.34 pm

**The Prime Minister (Mr. John Major):** In the three weeks since the House last debated Bosnia, the position has qualitatively changed. Conflict has grown. The shelling of Sarajevo has intensified. UN soldiers have been deliberately targeted and killed by both sides. UN personnel, including officers and men of the Royal Welch Fusiliers, have been taken captive by Bosnian Serbs.

The Government have decided to reinforce our contingent in Bosnia, and the diplomatic pace has quickened. For all those reasons, I thought it right to seek the recall of Parliament to set out the Government's response to this tense and dangerous situation.

Let me recall for the House the evolution of this crisis. The dispute in Bosnia began to crystallise in the spring of 1992, when Bosnia declared its independence. War broke out, and the country split into three parts. I believe that it would have been wrong for us to stand and watch Bosnia burn, and we did not.

In August 1992, I convened the London conference which brought the parties together in search of a political settlement. We set up the Sarajevo airlift, and we were instrumental in establishing the United Nations protection force's Bosnia command. The first British troops arrived in Bosnia in November 1992. Let me remind the House why we sent them. First is the humanitarian case. I believe that we have a duty—a moral responsibility if one likes—to play our part in the relief of suffering. Soldiers were being killed, but we also saw civilian suffering in Bosnia on a massive scale. There was ethnic cleansing—cold-blooded and racial-based murders. There was widespread rape and brutality. As winter approached, there was the clear prospect of widespread starvation.

There had been nothing like it in Europe since the second world war. The aid agencies were doing their best, but they needed protection if the convoys bearing food and medicines were to get through. So we decided to play our part in providing that protection.

Bosnia is close to the borders of the European Union. Even so, precisely the same case for help was seen by countries as far away as Canada, Malaysia and New Zealand, all of which have joined us in the task. Service men and women of 19 nations have stood with our relief agencies and our troops to help alleviate suffering. Many who would have died are alive today because of that effort. We should understand that many alive today would die if that effort were to end.

Secondly, we sent our soldiers there for strategic reasons. The Balkans have often enough been a tinderbox in history, and war memorials throughout the United Kingdom testify to the price paid in British blood for past Balkan turbulence. The Bosnian war by itself might not directly affect our interests, but a wider conflagration across the Balkans—leading to a wider Balkan war—most certainly would affect our strategic interests.

If unchecked, the fighting in Bosnia could have ignited not only a Serb-Croat war in Croatia, but unrest in Kosovo and Macedonia. That could easily have dragged Albania, Bulgaria, Greece and Turkey into confrontation with one another. The Bosnian dispute has always contained within it the seeds of the nightmare of a wider Balkan war.

The consequences of a wider Balkan conflict would be disastrous for Europe as a whole. In my judgment, it is unquestionably in our national interest to prevent that if we are able to do so. The United Nations protection force and British forces may not have extinguished the fighting in Bosnia, but they have contained it and they have prevented it from spreading. That is a remarkable tribute to their efforts. Had they not been there, the circumstances we face today might have been incomparably more serious than those that we are debating this afternoon.

If it is in our national interest to avert a greater calamity in Bosnia and the Balkans, so it is for other members of NATO and the European Union. The strategic case and the humanitarian case were the twin reasons why I thought it right to commit British troops in 1992. Both those cases apply in equal measure today—which is why I expressly do not wish to see the United Nations protection force withdraw until or unless the risks become wholly unacceptable.

I will describe in more detail the developments of the last three weeks. My right hon. Friend the Foreign Secretary warned the House on 9 May that there was a real risk of a relapse into substantial war, in place of the ragged and uncertain peace of previous months. Since then, my right hon. Friend's words, sadly, have been borne out. There has been a chain reaction of attack and counter-attack by Bosnian Government and Bosnian Serb forces. Both parties have violated the Sarajevo exclusion zone by firing heavy weapons on to the confrontation lines and into the city itself.

On 24 May, the UN Secretary-General's special representative and the protection force commander made a further attempt to stop the escalating bombardment. They issued an ultimatum that certain heavy weapons should be returned to the collection points and other heavy weapons be removed from the exclusion zone.

When the Bosnian Serb army ignored that ultimatum, NATO carried out a successful air strike against an ammunition store near Pale. It did so at the United Nations' request.

**Mr. Tam Dalyell** (Linlithgow): Were the Russians consulted about the ultimatum? Were they consulted about the strike against the ammunition dumps? If not, would it not have been wise to do so?

**The Prime Minister:** That was, as it was intended to be, a decision on the ground. No individual national

*[The Prime Minister]*

Government were directly consulted. There is a proper procedure for determining how such strikes are approved, and that procedure was followed. The troops are there as United Nations troops, with a United Nations commander who happens to be a British general, and they proceeded at the request of the United Nations. I believe that they proceeded correctly.

Shortly afterwards—in deliberate escalation—the Bosnian Serbs launched artillery attacks against the populations of Srebrenica, Gorazde and Tuzla. In the bombardment of Tuzla, 70 people were killed and 130 were injured. They were, I understand, for the most part innocent civilians in a marketplace—men, women and children going about their daily business. They were not armed combatants in the conflict.

Following a second NATO air strike against the ammunition storage complex on 26 May, the Bosnian Serb army began to take United Nations military observers and members of the protection force as hostages. Hon. Members will have seen, in the press and on television, that some of these hostages, in an outrageous breach of international law and of their status as United Nations peacekeepers, were chained to potential targets as so-called "human shields".

On 27 May, the Bosnian Serb army attacked and captured a French observation post at Sarajevo. The post was subsequently retaken, but one French soldier was killed, 11 were wounded and 10 were taken captive.

On Sunday 28 May, United Kingdom and Ukrainian soldiers were taken captive at Gorazde. Some of the Ukrainians were taken by Bosnian Government forces.

I have set out in this brief summary only the bare facts of the situation confronting the United Nations and NATO commanders on the ground, but there is no doubt in my mind that these events mark a qualitative change in the conflict, and one to which we and our partners have no choice but to respond very firmly.

**Mr. Tony Benn** (Chesterfield): The House is listening intently, obviously, because of the British soldiers who are being held, but can the Prime Minister tell the House how he reconciles humanitarian aid given by British soldiers in blue berets with bombing attacks by American pilots in blue berets? Is it possible to combine humanitarian aid with a combative role? Is that not the question to which he should address himself?

**The Prime Minister:** I think that the right hon. Gentleman knows precisely what has happened when the NATO attacks—not necessarily American: they are NATO planes—in these circumstances have been used, and they have been used as a deterrent to persuade the Bosnians that that sort of activity is not acceptable to the international community in any way whatever.

It is not very long ago—as the right hon. Gentleman will recall, for he will have hated this as much as anyone else did—that the nature of atrocities that we saw at the beginning of this war spread a darkening stain right the way across the conscience of the whole of Europe and the whole of the world as well. I believe, in these circumstances, that we have not only a right but an obligation to take the action that has been taken, to try to bring this conflict to an end and to end the suffering that so many people have faced in Bosnia.

**Mr. Mike Gapes** (Ilford, South): Does the Prime Minister agree with the French Prime Minister that the preparation of those air strikes was not good, and that it led to putting the peacekeepers at risk in a thoughtless way?

**The Prime Minister:** I said just a moment ago that I thought that it was right for the commanders on the ground to proceed as they did, and I have to say that I do not believe that I am prepared to second-guess the decisions of the commanders on the ground to whom those decisions were delegated, and I do not wish to do so.

Let me now turn to the response that I believe we should make, and first to the matter that I believe is most upon the minds of the House this afternoon: the British and the other United Nations troops who have been taken captive and held hostage.

The situation is that more than 350 United Nations personnel—who, I remind the House, have been serving in an impartial humanitarian and peacekeeping role in Bosnia—are now being illegally held by the Bosnian Serb army. Of these, one is a Royal Air Force officer serving as a United Nations military observer, and 33 are officers and men of the Royal Welch Fusiliers, who were taken captive last Sunday from observation points around the town of Gorazde, where 336 British solders are based.

Six—not five as previously reported—of the soldiers have apparently been injured in a road accident and are in hospital, although none of them, we believe, is in a serious condition. The fusiliers are thought to be in Visegrad and in both good heart and good health.

The taking of United Nations peacekeepers as hostages is a despicable act, which has rightly been condemned around the world. It is without a shred of justification. It will win the Bosnian Serbs no favours and gain them no friends. It will guarantee unremitting hostility to them, and the certainty of pariah status and international isolation.

**Mr. Ieuan Wyn Jones** (Ynys Môn): The Prime Minister will be aware that the whole House and those outside it—particularly in Wales—will be very concerned about the safety and welfare of the 33 young soldiers who have been taken hostage by the Serb aggressors. Will he tell the House today that whatever action he proposes to take will in no way endanger the safety of those young men, and that he will ensure that that action will be taken to secure their early release?

**The Prime Minister:** I will have something to say in a few moments about what we propose to do. I am sure that the hon. Gentleman will understand why it would be neither wise nor prudent for me to say too much about the matter at this time.

Within hours of the capture of the British troops, we took steps to make it clear, directly and unequivocally, to the Bosnian Serb leadership that the safety of our troops in Bosnia is of vital British interest. We have told Mr. Karadzic, the Bosnian Serb leader, that we shall hold him and General Mladic personally responsible for the well-being and the safe return of our troops. These words are not lightly spoken, and, as I shall explain, we are reinforcing our protection force contingent.

No one should doubt our resolve to secure the safe return of our soldiers. Yet, as we embark on the moves towards such a result, I hope that the House will understand if I do not go into detail about the courses that may be available to us.

**Mr. Roy Hughes** (Newport, East): Will the Prime Minister give way?

**The Prime Minister:** In a moment.

With the lives of British soldiers at stake, there will be a need for patience, a time for restraint, perhaps at times a need for silence. But if the silences are long, and if the requirement for restraint and patience becomes frustrating, no one in the House should imagine that those soldiers will be forgotten. The work to secure their release will be unremitting.

**Mr. Hughes:** Does the Prime Minister appreciate that eight members of the Royal Welch Fusiliers are at present unaccounted for? Does he appreciate that there is considerable concern among their relatives back home about their safety?

**The Prime Minister:** I think that the hon. Gentleman is referring to the observation post near Gorazde. I understand entirely the points that he has to make.

Let me turn to the reason why our forces are in Bosnia—and to what they are not there to do. Our troops have not gone to Bosnia to wage war, but even on humanitarian duties we have seen that they need protection. If they are attacked, they must be able to defend themselves robustly.

The protection force commander in Bosnia, General Smith, knows that he has our complete support. The protection force must be able to take whatever action is necessary in justifiable self-defence. When it does so, it will have the unqualified backing of the British Government—and, I believe, of the British nation.

To improve the protection force's capacity to defend itself, the Government on Sunday night decided to enhance the equipment and manpower available to the force.

At present, we have some 3,400 troops in Bosnia, protecting convoys and monitoring local ceasefires. A further 3,000 men and women from the Royal Air Force and Royal Navy are engaged in the airlift from Italy to Sarajevo; in NATO operations to police the air exclusion zone; in the joint enforcement by NATO and the Western European Union of the arms embargo and trade sanctions; and as contingency reinforcements on a carrier task group.

Anyone who has had the privilege of visiting any of those units, as I have, knows that they have carried out their peacekeeping tasks with scrupulous fairness and with a cool resolve—often in the face of provocation. I believe that we can be truly proud of them. But despite their military professionalism, the troops on the ground in Bosnia now need more protection, and the safety of those troops is, as I said, of vital national interest.

So we have decided to dispatch two artillery batteries and an armoured engineer squadron to Bosnia, totalling around 1,000 personnel. The first detachment, from 19 Field Regiment, left for Bosnia yesterday. Those units will increase our contingent's armoured capability. Crucially, they will provide artillery. They will be equipped with 12 105 mm light guns. That will provide the protection forces, for the first time, with the artillery that is now necessary as a deterrent and response to bombardment.

That does not mean that we are taking sides in the conflict. The protection force remains neutral, and it remains impartial. But, to defend itself, it now needs a capability to fill the gap between machine guns and air strikes.

The Government have also announced that 24 Air Mobile Brigade has been placed under orders to prepare to deploy to Bosnia. The order to move will be given unless there is a clear and rapid improvement in the situation. We have proposed to the United Nations that the brigade, as United Nations troops, should come under the command of General Rupert Smith in Sarajevo. We are now discussing the details of the deployment with the United Nations.

Let me say a little more about 24 Air Mobile Brigade. It is a flexible, self-contained force of over 5,000 personnel. It is, as its title suggests, able to deploy very rapidly within theatre. Its equipment includes Army and Royal Air Force helicopters, Milan anti-tank weapons, artillery batteries, an air defence battery and engineer and medical support. We have constantly said that the safety of British troops is crucial; our readiness to deploy the Air Mobile Brigade is ample testimony to that.

Let me emphasise one point that I know is of concern to the House, which should not be misunderstood in the House or beyond it. The protection force is in Bosnia as an humanitarian and peacekeeping force. It is not there to impose peace, and it is not equipped or configured to fight a war. Those points are fundamental, and we do not intend that they should be changed.

**Mr. Simon Hughes** (Southwark and Bermondsey): Does the Prime Minister accept that there will be widespread support, both in the House and outside, for the concept that not just serving the British flag but serving the United Nations is among the most honourable of tasks for our armed forces?

Although some may react by saying that, as soon as there is particular danger, the troops should be withdrawn, it is also true—given that these are among the best armed forces in the world, equipped to deal with particular danger—that many in those forces will regard the job they have started as a job that they would rather continue, if that is possible. Not necessarily success, but the attempt to bring about peace on behalf of the international community, is the reason why the forces are there, and the reason why the Government are right to support them in the way that the Prime Minister has announced.

**The Prime Minister:** I have indicated that I wish our forces to stay there, and I wish the United Nations protection force as a whole to stay there to carry out the job for which it was sent. That job is not yet concluded; I hope that it will be possible for it to remain.

We see a strong case for reducing the vulnerability of United Nations personnel—particularly the United Nations military observers, who have been in the most exposed positions. Some may need to be withdrawn, others concentrated and others given stronger protection. The commanders on the ground are best placed to determine precisely how that should be done, in consultation with the Secretary-General and, through him, with the Security Council. I understand that the Secretary-General will shortly be making his recommendations to the Security Council on the future role of the protection forces.

**Mr. Rhodri Morgan** (Cardiff, West): Will the Prime Minister give way?

**The Prime Minister:** May I make a little progress?

*[The Prime Minister]*

Our decisions have been warmly welcomed by the protection force and by other Governments. The contact group agreed on Monday that the protection force should have a rapid reaction capability. France, which at present has the largest contingent in Bosnia, has sent reinforcements to the Adriatic. Some other troop contributors are also thinking of strengthening their contingents.

Madam Speaker, those decisions are intended to help carry UNPROFOR through a dangerous phase. We hope that they will make it more secure, will help it to fulfil its tasks, and will deter further escalation. If we can damp down the level of violence and make progress towards a lasting cessation, at that point the protection force would no longer need the enhanced protection.

However, success for the protection force rests ultimately with the warring parties. I believe that, at this moment, Bosnia is at a turning point. It must be made clear to the parties that, if they turned to all-out war, the protection force would not be equipped to remain. It would be unable to carry out its tasks, and the risks to the troops of all nationalities would be unacceptable.

Withdrawal is not our objective; but our ability to handle withdrawal, if it is forced upon us, would undoubtedly be helped by the further deployment that I have announced to the House today.

**Mrs. Teresa Gorman** (Billericay): Before we commit more troops to that theatre who may suffer the same fate as the troops who are already there, will my right hon. Friend comment on the report that the Serbs have said that, if we agree to cease bombing, they will release the hostages? Is that report accurate? If it is, what are we doing to make NATO give us that assurance?

**The Prime Minister:** I yield to no one in my wish to have those troops returned safely to their units, but I am not entering into that sort of blackmailing deal.

Madam Speaker, in taking those decisions, we have unequivocally signalled our serious intent. We wish to see the protection force remain in Bosnia and continue its work. We wish to restore equilibrium to a situation that has become dangerously unstable. We continue to believe that only a political settlement will end the conflict. There can be no satisfactory and lasting military solution.

The way ahead may yet be rocky and painful. I know that many people, for good and understandable reasons, may advocate withdrawing the forces and, as I have said to the House, circumstances could arise in which that would become inevitable. But withdrawal is not a policy. No one should believe that leaving Bosnia would end the United Kingdom's interest in the conflict.

**Mr. Morgan:** I wish to put a question to the Prime Minister on behalf of the families of the 30 Welsh soldiers who are being held in Bosnia. Was it primarily the responsibility of the British Government or of the United Nations to have secured in advance some means of escape for those soldiers who were being held in the very difficult pockets of the further extensions of Bosnia in case things got extremely difficult—as they have done—and there was hostage taking? Whose responsibility was that?

**The Prime Minister:** I think that we have a joint interest in securing their release. Of course, their

deployment is a matter that must be determined on the ground, as the hon. Member for Cardiff, West (Mr. Morgan) and the soldiers themselves would well know.

Let me turn to the possible consequences of withdrawing the protection force. If the United Nations left, what would be the likely outcome?

The first likely outcome is that the Muslim areas, including the eastern enclaves, would be likely to come under immediate threat. The bloodshed and loss of life could be massive. Before we sent troops three years ago, Bosnia was on the brink of genocide—of atrocities far worse than we have yet seen. If we depart, I remind the House that those dangers return. Could the west stand idly by and let such actions take place in south-eastern Europe? I doubt it; I truly doubt it. Would we ignore the threat of an all-out Balkan war? Again, I do not believe that we would or should ignore such a threat.

Leaving Bosnia—if the protection force is forced to do so—is neither an easy nor a pain-free option. The threats would return if the United Nations protection force withdrew, and we and our allies would have to find other ways of responding to them—ways which could conceivably impose a greater financial and military burden on us than we are now carrying. Those who contemplate withdrawal must think very carefully about the humanitarian consequences and the strategic implications for European security.

At present, UNPROFOR is holding the ring. It must try to continue to do so, while we seek a political solution. Despite every effort by Governments and individuals—notably Lord Owen and Mr. Stoltenberg—the search for a negotiated settlement has been extremely frustrating. For months, progress has been blocked by the intransigence of the Bosnian Serbs.

Over the past week, we have been in close touch with our partners to reinvigorate diplomatic efforts and maximise the pressure on Pale. I have spoken to the Presidents of Russia, the United States and France, the German Chancellor and the Canadian Prime Minister. My right hon. Friend the Foreign Secretary has attended meetings of the contact group, NATO and the European Union, and this morning had further discussions with the Russian Foreign Minister.

As a result of those meetings, there is a renewed unity of purpose among contact group Governments. The Russian Government condemned the behaviour of the Bosnian Serbs in the strongest possible language. We wish to see an equally clear stance from President Milosevic.

The contact group's emissary is in Belgrade today. If the contact group can secure the recognition of Bosnia-Herzegovina by the former republic of Yugoslavia, fears or ambitions of a greater Serbia should be laid to rest, and the message to the Bosnian Serbs would be absolutely unmistakable.

I have tried to set out the situation as I see it. It is stark and it is serious, but we cannot avoid it. So I hope the word will go out this afternoon from all parts of the House that British peacekeepers, United Nations peacekeepers, must be released unharmed and unconditionally.

Let us show our forces, whether they are on land, at sea or in the air in the former Yugoslavia and the Adriatic, that they have the total support of the House. They have saved many lives. They have brought peace and hope and a semblance of normality to central Bosnia. They have prevented the spread of war. They are defending British interests and international security. Their courage and professionalism have earned the widest admiration. They deserve our wholehearted backing, and I commend it to the House.

3.7 pm

**Mr. Tony Blair** (Sedgefield): We have offered our support to the Prime Minister in his action, as he knows. I believe that the more united the House can be on the issue, the better.

The whole House will want to send a message of the deepest support to those soldiers now taken hostage, particularly the 33 members of the Royal Welch Fusiliers and the RAF officer. Our thoughts and prayers are with them. Their safety is our uppermost priority and their taking as hostages was a barbarous act of terrorism. It was in violation of every canon of international law and we join the Prime Minister in holding the leaders of the Bosnian Serbs personally responsible for their safe return.

The Bosnian Serbs lay claim to some understanding of national sentiment. They should be in no doubt about the national sentiments of the House and the British people, should any harm come to any one of those hostages. We would expect and demand the pursuit of those responsible without let or quarter.

It is worth reflecting on the conduct of British soldiers in this field of conflict. Some 13 have died and they have often borne the brunt of risk and danger. I believe that they have behaved throughout with conspicuous commitment and bravery and we have every reason to be proud of them.

We support the sending of additional troops as protection. As the Prime Minister has said, it will increase the military capability and options open to General Smith; in particular, 24 Air Mobile Brigade can provide further cover if necessary.

I believe that—perhaps the Secretary of State for Defence can say a little more about this in his speech— these troops need to have a clear chain of command and clear rules of engagement. The House would expect to have a clear assessment of that from the Secretary of State for Defence. Of course, in protecting British troops the reinforcements also increase the protection available to all United Nations troops, but we need to be absolutely clear about the terms on which our troops are operating and they must not be given objectives beyond their capability to achieve.

I believe that talk of withdrawal in Bosnia in response to the taking of hostages is deeply unhelpful at this time. It is hardly a message of firm resolve in the face of what is effectively an act of coercive blackmail.

The Bosnian Serbs must understand that they cannot fulfil their aim of an ethnically pure Serbian state by these means. Until they accept the route of diplomacy, they will remain outcasts on the international stage. We should not engage in any truck with them by which the release of hostages is in return for a pledge never to use our air power. That would be a mistake.

In the short term, as the Prime Minister said, our task is to secure the release of the hostages without rewarding the hostage taker.

Inevitably, this debate allows us to take stock of the medium and longer-term strategy in Bosnia. I think that

the beginning of understanding in this matter—indeed, of humility—is to recognise that all options are fraught with difficulty and that there is no difficulty that is not vast in its character and complexity.

Undoubtedly, there have been errors of judgment and there has been indecision at almost every turn by the international community. The early recognition of Croatia without thinking through its evident impact on Bosnia is one example. We were too slow to recognise the need to deter the Serbian army and we were too hesitant when we did recognise it. The contact group has been plagued by divisions and by conflicting interests. The UN involvement has often developed in a piecemeal way, without adequate thought or support.

There is no doubt—there is no point in denying it— that this has been a profoundly unhappy experience for the international community. Yet, the errors and the uncertainty have arisen from the nature of the conflict itself. The choice is, has been and remains: do we stay out and let the conflict be resolved by force or do we become involved in order to provide at least a chance for a diplomatic solution to be found? However long this conflict goes on, that choice remains the same.

I can well understand that public reaction, especially now, favours the first of those choices. Many of our constituents look at this as a faraway war, indecipherable in its rights and wrongs and now putting at risk British lives. But consider the origins of this crisis and the origins of our involvement. There is no doubt that the basic cause of the conflict was the aggressive and violent attempt to bring about a greater Serbia from the ruins of the former Yugoslavia. To those who believe that Bosnia was always a nest of ethnic hatreds, incapable of peaceful coexistence between its different minorities I recommend "Bosnia: A Short History" by Mr. Noel Malcolm. Even allowing for the strongly held views of its author, it is a powerful rebuttal of that myth.

Our involvement began with those vivid pictures of ethnic cleansing, carried out with indescribable brutality. Bosnia is a country whose region borders the European Union; a country in the Balkans where conflict has often spread out to engulf neighbouring states and, indeed, the whole of Europe on occasions; a country whose boundaries were being changed by brute force by an aggressor that went unchecked.

Let us think back to September 1992 and the questions asked in the House at that time. We were warned of millions dying in the winter and of a refugee crisis that could sweep across western Europe. Of course, there has always been a danger that our international response would be governed by television news at any one point in time. In fact, it is interesting to note that in the debate on 9 May there was much criticism of the fact that the United Nations commanders had been overruled on the use of air strikes against the Bosnian Serbs. Days later, such strikes were authorised, hostages taken and, of course, questions began to be put the other way around.

I do not believe, however, that the international community realistically could ever have walked away from Bosnia. Having become involved, there is no easy option of walking away. Even withdrawal, without some agreed solution, would be painfully difficult. Our forces may be under attack and the civilians pleading with us to

[*Mr. Tony Blair*]

stay. That is not a reason for staying if there are not other reasons, but it is something to weigh in the balance and we should do so.

**Mr. Iain Duncan Smith** (Chingford): We accept that the priority is to protect British troops and that the deployment of extra troops to do that task must have our full support. The right hon. Gentleman quoted Noel Malcolm. Does he agree that one of the points that Noel Malcolm would have made was that the unbalanced arms embargo, which did not allow the Bosnian Muslims to defend themselves, has in many ways created the problem and that we have had to step into the gap to do the job? Does he further agree that we should now lift that arms embargo to give the Bosnian Muslims the opportunity to defend themselves?

**Mr. Blair:** No, I do not agree with the hon. Gentleman's suggestion, although I understand why he put that point to me. I well recall our previous debates on that very topic and the concern—which I believe was justified then and is justified now—that lifting the arms embargo would increase the conflagration rather than limit it. However, I accept that such judgments are difficult.

**Sir Peter Tapsell** (East Lindsey): I fully understand— as everyone in the House and the country understands— the force of the right hon. Gentleman's remarks about the humanitarian aspects of this desperate problem. However, bearing in mind the fact that there are terrible civil wars taking place in Angola, Cambodia, Kurdistan, Tibet and Chechnya, among others, is British foreign policy to be based on humanitarian considerations, resulting in our having to send armies to all the countries where civil wars break out? If not, what is it about Bosnia that makes it so different from all the others?

**Mr. Blair:** I do not believe that that is a compelling case for withdrawal from Bosnia and I shall tell the hon. Gentleman why. It is always possible to say that we should have intervened in other conflicts and there can be debates about that. However, the Bosnian conflict is in Europe and the consequences could spread to neighbouring European states. We have to make a judgment about where our national interest lies and take humanitarian concerns into account. I believe that that judgment is overwhelmingly in favour of involvement.

**Mr. Nicholas Budgen** (Wolverhampton, South-West): Three weeks ago, my right hon. Friend the Foreign Secretary said that there was risk of a war that would range the United States and Russia on different sides. If that was true and if there was such a foreseeable risk, is not it unbelievable that there should be any possibility of withdrawing our troops? Was not that argument simply thrown in to justify an intervention that at first hand was done on humanitarian grounds alone?

**Mr. Blair:** Those judgments are best made by those on the ground, but the hon. Gentleman should put that intervention to the Defence Secretary when he begins to reply to the debate. I have to say to him and his hon. Friends who are advocating, in effect, that we withdraw— that we walk away from this—that I do not believe that that would have been in the remotest way acceptable those two or three years ago when we first became involved.

I do not believe that the question is whether we have a responsibility in this area; I believe we do and I also believe that we have a responsibility to explain that to the people whom we represent. The question is not whether we have a responsibility but how we discharge it and what are its limitations.

**Dr. Robert Spink** (Castle Point): Will the right hon. Gentleman give way?

**Mr. Blair:** If the hon. Gentleman will forgive me, I will make some progress. I may give way later.

From the beginning, we have ruled out a role as combatants, taking sides to fight the war. I believe that that is right. Indeed, it is an inexorable consequence of the nature of the situation. For example, simply in military terms, if we compare it with Kuwait, the war there was relatively easy to fight on what was effectively a sand table in the desert. Here, the terrain is unremittingly hostile to outside involvement. The roads and supply lines run through valleys surrounded by wooded hills. It is natural guerilla territory. The fighting force needed would be vast.

It is worth bearing it in mind that the United States has no ground troops in Bosnia. The brunt would therefore fall on France and Britain, and there is just no consent to such a commitment. The entire UN mandate would have to be changed from one of limited engagement for humanitarian and diplomatic purposes to active participation on the side of one of the combatants. I do not believe that that is desirable or feasible.

Our responsibility, therefore, is, and should remain, to enforce the current UN mandate in order to increase the possibility of a negotiated settlement without becoming involved in open-ended combat. That is our strategic, diplomatic and military aim. So long as the United Nations presence in Bosnia is conducive to that end, it should remain.

Let us for a moment assess the role of the UN and what it has achieved. Has it made a difference, and can it continue to do so? That is the question that we need to ask to determine whether we remain.

I do not believe that there can be any serious dispute over whether the UN presence has helped: it has. The policy of containment has, by and large, worked: Macedonia is free of fighting; the awful possibility of general conflict in the Balkans has been avoided; humanitarian aid has helped hundreds of thousands to survive; some semblance of normality has returned to central Bosnia. The Croat-Muslim conflict has been halted, for which, I may say, British troops bear much of the credit. It is worth pointing out that they have been instrumental in Bosnia in reconnecting gas, water and electricity and in rebuilding schools like those at Vitez. Anyone who, like those Conservative Members, doubts whether the United Nations presence has made a difference should ask those on the ground—soldiers or civilians.

Most important, slowly but surely, as a result of this, President Milosevic and Belgrade have been detached from the Bosnian Serbs. This is surely of central importance and it gives the best prospect of pressure on the Bosnian Serbs. That could not have been foreseen or achieved without that United Nations presence; and, of course, the contact group plan for Bosnia has at least gained the acceptance in principle of Bosnia, Serbia and Croatia.

No one doubts, as, indeed, the Prime Minister said earlier, that withdrawal must remain an option if we are advised by our military commanders that their utility is spent or that it is too dangerous for the safety of the men. A definite prospect of some diplomatic movement is essential to prevent there being diminishing returns over time of the UN presence. Without such a prospect, the Bosnian Government have an incentive to try to recapture lost territory and the Bosnian Serbs to pursue their aim of an independent Serbian state. The gains under a UN presence have, I believe, been substantial.

Let us contemplate the impact of a withdrawal now. If we were to announce from the House that we were to going to withdraw, what would be the impact? It would reward the hostage takers. That is a great message, is it not, to send from the international community? It would be terrible to do such a thing. The United Nations would be utterly humiliated for this and future conflicts, the Bosnian Serbs would begin a major offensive and, despite whatever reports there are, the best advice that I can make out is that they might well win in such an offensive. Would Croatia remain stable, or Kosovo or Macedonia? Would Turkey and other Muslim states remain aloof? These are serious considerations and we must weigh them in the balance when we come to our decision.

**Sir Russell Johnston** (Inverness, Nairn and Lochaber): The right hon. Gentleman mentioned Kosovo. He will know that it is widely reported that there are considerable diplomatic efforts to make Milosevic recognise Bosnia, as a result of which sanctions would be raised. That would still leave the Kosovo problem without our having any leverage. Is not that a real difficulty?

**Mr. Blair:** I agree that it is a real difficulty but it should not prevent us from increasing the pressure on President Milosevic to recognise Bosnia because of the impact that would have on the conduct of the Bosnian Serbs.

If we say that the case for staying remains, I believe we must examine how we take firm and clear steps radically to improve the United Nations' position and thus that of our forces. First, the UN mandate should be enforced with clarity and consistency. Mixed messages on the use of force are not helpful and, where they are used, the consequences of their use in terms of retaliation should be carefully provided for. If they are not, the impact of those forces becomes significantly diminished.

Secondly, we must surely back up the UN mandate with the men and weapons necessary to achieve it. For example, the safe area resolution of the UN was passed in June 1993. It was thought at the time that a minimum of some 15,000 personnel was necessary to enforce it. Around 7,000 were promised and, a year later, there were barely 6,000. If we are to enforce that mandate and hold to it, we must make sure that the resources are there, available to do the job properly.

Thirdly, I think that there is a very strong case for the safe areas to be demilitarised. This has surely been a central weakness until now. It has meant that the Bosnian Government have been able to continue fighting from out of the exclusion zone and has loosened the impression of the UN's even-handedness.

Fourthly, we should consider, as I am sure the Foreign Secretary is, how we tighten sanctions still further. In particular, do we have the necessary monitors along the Serbian border to ensure that weapons and fuel cannot get through?

Fifthly, the Government should examine carefully the suggestion of my hon. Friend the shadow Foreign Secretary for ways in which we can counter the virulent nationalism of the Bosnian Serb media and others, which has played such a part in stoking up hatred among the various groups. It is a sensible suggestion worthy of examination.

Above all, the UN's presence can act only as a platform for a diplomatic peace effort. It is now almost a year since the contact group plan was promulgated. The unity of the contact group is the key to its effectiveness. There has to be a major effort to resolve differences within it, both for Russia and for the United States in the increase of pressure on Belgrade. Any increase in military capacity must be accompanied by new investment in diplomacy. We should see whether out of this fresh crisis a clearer, firmer strategy can be produced with the political will to achieve it.

The settlement proposed by the international community in Bosnia has already had its configurations partly determined by battle. We should reflect on what would happen if we allowed the boundaries of Bosnia or any part of former Yugoslavia to be determined solely by force. What message would that send? We must look at the disputes over borders and ethnic groupings just in that region of the world alone; between Turkey and Greece, Greece and Macedonia, Albania and Serbia, Hungary and Romania over Transylvania, and Slovakia and Hungary. If we allowed such force to replace the rules of international law, the reputation of the United Nations would slide into the same abyss into which the League of Nations eventually fell.

Naturally today, the House unites in its support for our troops and its demand that the hostages, so wickedly seized, should be returned. That is our vital national interest and we shall protect it. Britain has always been a country willing to lift its eyes to the far horizon and judge its actions by their immediate impact not only on ourselves but on world events and history. The decisions that we take are of momentous import for the world and its order and stability. Let us ensure that those decisions are the right ones, for we shall live with their consequences.

3.31 pm

**Mr. Paddy Ashdown** (Yeovil): There are many questions about what has happened over the past three years in Bosnia and about Britain's part in it that we could address in this debate, but with British and other United Nations troops being held hostage and with our forces in Bosnia in an increasingly precarious position, such questions are best left for another day. What is vital is not what has happened, or a review of history, or what mistakes have been made, but what happens now. Our first duty, as the Prime Minister has rightly said, is quite clear. Our first duty at the moment is to those who are in Serb hands. They must be our primary consideration and nothing that we say in this debate should damage their chances of return.

There is no point, of course, in pretending that there is an easy solution. There is not. A military answer to the hostage problem is now—probably—increasingly difficult. In the last analysis, decisions have to be left to the commanders on the ground. They are the only ones who know what is possible and what is advisable. They will have their contingency plans and we must have the

[*Mr. Paddy Ashdown*]

patience to let them take effect. Our job is to back the actions which they take and which they feel it is right to take. As the Prime Minister also rightly said, there may well be times when silence is the best kind of response in the face of what happens over the next few weeks and months.

It seems probable that the most likely route to freeing those who are now held is the diplomatic one. If that is the case, the roles of Serbian President Milosevic and the Governments of Russia and Ukraine are absolutely vital. The strong line taken by the Russian envoy Aleksandr Zotov is, in this context, a very welcome sign. A key ingredient to the success of this diplomatic operation will be for the Bosnian Serbs, who have committed this barbarous act of provocation, to hear a single, firm and united response from the international community. In Britain, that united message should come from all parties.

The Government are entitled to expect our support in that situation, and they will get it—although I wish that they had been rather more definite about the role and intention of the new deployment than they appear to have been so far. There is a lack of clarity that gives the impression, rightly or wrongly, of a decision hastily made. That could add to the military muddle on the ground and create misunderstandings in the minds of both the Bosnians and the Bosnian Serbs that might impede that deployment, and perhaps even get in the way of our best efforts to release hostages.

Nevertheless, on Sunday the Prime Minister responded to a request from the commanders on the ground, and he was right to do so. The reinforcements that have been committed to Bosnia will be a signal to the Bosnian Serbs of the seriousness of our intent. Those reinforcements will strengthen the capacity of British and United Nations troops to protect themselves—and, we are told, they provide the necessary cover for a withdrawal should one become unavoidable. For reasons that I shall explain in a moment, I believe that withdrawal should be the last option, because it is the worst option.

I hope that the other major troop-contributing nations will now match Britain's actions. I hope especially that the United States will make the commitment that it has so far failed to make on the ground. No single act would better show the solidarity of the international community or do more to convince the Bosnian Serbs of the seriousness of their position than the commitment of United States ground troops to the operation in Bosnia at this time.

The next questions that we must consider are: how are the troops to be deployed, and—this is crucial—under whose command? The technical position is clear: Britain is entitled to take such actions as we think necessary to ensure the protection of our troops, so it would be perfectly in order for us to station troops in Bosnia under sole British command if we wished to do so. But in my judgment to do so would be to misjudge both what has happened and what needs to happen next.

The events of the past few days have irreversibly changed the position of the UN in Bosnia. Any attempt to fudge the consequences of that change will lead only to further humiliations, further risks for troops on the ground, further muddle over the mandate, and the continuing descent of the UN operation in Bosnia into chaos, farce and eventual retreat.

There are now two routes leading to withdrawal. There is the quick route of a decision to leave today, and there is the long, slow, painful route whereby we would keep on muddling through. In short, we are now being forced by events to take the decisions that we should have taken three or four years ago. There are those who will argue about the benefits of a withdrawal—no doubt we shall hear them later. I am not one of those.

I accept the fact that there may come a time when our commanders on the ground tell us that there is nothing further that we can do without unacceptable risk. Then we shall be forced to go. But we should be absolutely clear about what the consequences would be.

**Mr. Denis MacShane** (Rotherham): Will the right hon. Gentleman give way?

**Mr. Ashdown:** Will the hon. Gentleman let me make a little progress?

Withdrawal will be difficult along the best part of 100 miles of dirt track over the Dinaric alps, and it will almost certainly be extremely costly, both in materials and, almost certainly, in lives. However, it is the consequences of withdrawal even more than its difficulties that make it such a dangerous option.

A United Nations withdrawal without assuring the means by which the Bosnians could defend themselves would leave the United Nations-recognised state of Bosnia to be obliterated by the Serbs, aided by the Croats—probably in short order. It would mean abandoning about 1 million Bosnian Muslims to their fate, with a degree of suffering, visible on our television screens, that would be unacceptable and intolerable to a civilised people.

Withdrawal would almost certainly lead to a wider Balkan war, with incalculable consequences beyond that. It would send a signal to the Muslim world which could be very damaging for world peace in the longer term; and it would be to collude in the death of the United Nations as an organisation capable of contributing to world peace—just as certainly as the failure to confront aggression in Abyssinia marked the end of the League of Nations, with consequences that we know all too well.

What is at risk in this crisis is not just the preservation of the Bosnian state; it is the preservation of the ultimate authority of the UN. Right hon. and hon. Members might like to reflect that there would be consequences closer to home for us in Europe as well, for Europe would have participated in the destruction of the best model it has of a multi-ethnic, multi-religious state. And in an age when fascism and destructive nationalism are once again on the march, we would have sent out a signal that, once again, we do not have the will to stop them.

**Mr. MacShane:** Twice the right hon. Gentleman has referred to commanders on the ground taking decisions about air strikes and deciding whether British troops should be withdrawn. I had rather hoped—based on the first two speeches today—that those decisions would be taken by the elected leaders of this country and by this House.

**Mr. Ashdown:** The hon. Gentleman may not be aware of how military operations are conducted. Politicians set the parameters; military commanders operate within them and take the battlefield decisions. The Prime Minister clearly and rightly set out the conditions in which air strikes could be used. Within those conditions, the timing of the air strikes is then set by the commanders on the ground. In the same way, as the leader of the hon. Gentleman's party has just said, it is the commanders on the ground who will make recommendations as to whether the mandate that we set for them can be carried out without unacceptable risk, and if not, as to whether it is then—but not before—time to think about withdrawal. I should have thought that was clear to anyone with an iota of knowledge of these matters.

**Mr. Edward Leigh** (Gainsborough and Horncastle): Is the right hon. Gentleman's policy, then, that he is prepared to use British troops not just for humanitarian purposes but in a combat role to impose peace on those who will not be pacified and to punish wrongdoing when there has been wrongdoing on both sides? Is he not being rather free with British lives?

**Mr. Ashdown:** The hon. Gentleman may not realise this, but the second part of the UN resolution under which our troops operate in Bosnia already allows punitive action in the case of aggression. He is clearly unaware that the circumstances he describes are in effect at the moment.

I am aware—perhaps painfully aware—of the price that will have to be paid if the UN stays on in Bosnia. That price would have been far lower if appropriate action had been taken three years ago. I understand very well that there are those who say that we should cut our losses: the cost of staying is far too great. To them I would say that the cost of going is in the long term much greater.

When we make this decision, that is the calculation that we shall have to arrive at. It is clear, however, that we shall not be able to return to the old mandate—the old terms of engagement. They were never tenable in any case, not least because they pointed in two opposite directions at the same time—humanitarian aid and punitive action. One of the major flaws in the whole Bosnian operation is the fact that military action on the ground has seemed consistently to have neither co-ordination nor even connection with diplomatic action being taken in Geneva. All that now has to change.

All that has now changed—whether we like it or not. The Bosnian Serbs are now calling the hostages UN prisoners of war. They have made it clear that they will now treat the UN as an enemy. Even if they had not done so, we could surely never again risk placing UN peacekeepers or observers at their mercy, as we have seen the way in which they have exploited the present mandate to take hostages to prevent international action.

A new mandate, a new set of priorities and clear terms of engagement for the military operation in Bosnia will inevitably now be required. That means being prepared to protect the areas which we have defined as safe areas. It means giving our troops on the ground a free hand to defend themselves when they are subject to threats or aggression from Bosnian Serbs, or anybody else. It means consolidating our position into more defensible locations.

There are difficulties involved in that, and I do not underestimate them. But whatever they are, that seems to be the only rational means now open to us. We must reshape the Bosnian operation in a way which gives the UN commanders a clear and achievable aim which is consistent with the UN's diplomatic effort.

**Mr. John Townend** (Bridlington): The right hon. Gentleman talks about the financial cost and the cost in

lives. Does he feel that this country has been asked to carry too great a share of the burden? Is not it incredible that the three wealthiest countries in the UN—the United States, Germany and Japan—are not contributing anything, while we are now contributing the most in men and in treasure?

**Mr. Ashdown:** I take the view that this country has once again had to operate to make something work, and I am rather proud of that. The hon. Gentleman fails to recognise that our membership of the Security Council lays upon us certain duties which would not necessarily be incumbent upon us were we not members. We gain an advantage from our membership, but we also have a responsibility.

I am aware that what I have been saying—

**Mr. Roger Gale** (Thanet, North): Will the right hon. Gentleman give way?

**Mr. Ashdown:** If the hon. Gentleman will forgive me, I should like to make some progress.

What I am saying about a new and clearer mandate carries with it some hard choices. I cannot judge at this moment what the likely options will be, as they will have to be established by the commanders on the ground when they are deciding what they believe to be possible. But whatever the sacrifices involved in changing the posture and the mandate of our troops, they are far less than those involved in withdrawal, or in leaving things as they are, which—in the end—inevitably amounts to the same thing by a longer route.

In the meantime, the process of declaring the so-called Republika Serbska an international pariah state should be accelerated. A key element of that would be the early recognition of Bosnia by President Milosevic, and the stationing of UN observers on the Drina and Sava rivers to monitor embargo breaches into Serbian Bosnia. It is my view that if those two matters were satisfactorily concluded, the international sanctions on Serbia proper could be relaxed, or in due course—perhaps consistent with the situation in Kosovo—lifted.

There are those who will say that all of that is far too difficult, or that we should just muddle through for a little longer. But muddling through for the past three years has got us here. Muddling through will mean months—perhaps years—of being controlled by events, rather than controlling them. Muddling through means more humiliations, more retreats and more soldiers in the firing line in pursuit of an aim that has never been identified and a mandate that has become impossible to fulfil.

Whatever the difficulties, the only rational response to the events of the past week is to face up to the consequences of those events. We must reshape the Bosnian operation in a way which gives the commanders a clear and achievable aim which is consistent with the diplomatic efforts in Geneva. That is the only way in which the UN will have any hope of pulling success out of this disastrous muddle.

**Mr. Gale:** Will the right hon. Gentleman give way now?

**Mr. Ashdown:** If the hon. Gentleman will forgive me, I am reaching the end of my remarks.

This speech amounts to support for the Government's position and for what appears to be the growing NATO consensus. That is the right thing to do when British

*[Mr. Ashdown]*

troops are committed to the field. If that position does not work—and I have my suspicions about that—we may in short order be once again faced with the decision that we ducked three years ago, of whether or not we are prepared to take sides against aggression. None of this will make any sense to our commanders on the ground or to our people until we are prepared to face that decision. If the steps now planned succeed in avoiding that choice, well and good. If they do not, we must be clear that it will always be preferable to take sides against aggression than to run away in the face of it.

**Several hon. Members** *rose*—

**Madam Speaker:** Order. Before I call Sir Edward Heath, I must tell the House that because of the great demand from right hon. and hon. Members to contribute to this debate, speeches made between 7 pm and 9 pm must be limited to 10 minutes.

3.50 pm

**Sir Edward Heath** (Old Bexley and Sidcup): I am sure that the whole House agrees that it was right for the Prime Minister to ask you, Madam Speaker, to recall the House this afternoon, so that we could debate what he rightly described as a serious situation. He explained clearly the thoughts in his mind and emphasised that we started this as a humanitarian act. We have achieved a great deal, working with other countries, and I am certain that work should continue as long as physically possible. The Prime Minister emphasised the protection that we also provided and stated that additional British forces are going to Bosnia to strengthen that protection. That is also justifiable, provided it can be properly undertaken and achieves the results that we require.

When 300 soldiers from different countries were taken hostage, I had to ask myself what was the organisation that allowed that to happen. [HON. MEMBERS: "Hear, hear."] It is astonishing to anyone who has served in the forces, particularly during a war, that those troops could have been exposed in that way, taken and kept. That matter needs urgent attention.

In such a debate, one point always arises. It was dealt with by the Prime Minister when he said that we cannot impose a solution by force—that we cannot do it by going to war. That is critical to the whole of the Government's attitudes and policies. It is critical also in the minds of the people of this country and of the worried parents of the hostages. In that, the Prime Minister is absolutely right.

The right hon. Member for Yeovil (Mr. Ashdown) refused to put it that way. He said that we missed opportunity after opportunity, that we ought to have been stronger and that we should have tackled the situation. That means going to war—there is no other interpretation of that which the right hon. Gentleman has been saying with great force. I cannot accept that; nor will the people of this country accept the position that he described.

**Mr. Ashdown:** The right hon. Gentleman has great experience of military matters and every other matter, so he will understand that the appropriate thing is to take the right action at the right time. He might care to reflect on the fact that every single action that I commended to the Prime Minister—having first visited Sarajevo in August 1992—was said by him to be impossible. Months later,

when it was too late for them to have any effect, the Prime Minister took those actions—putting in troops, undertaking and supporting humanitarian operations, and establishing air and weapons exclusion zones. All those actions were said to be impossible, but all were subsequently taken—but too little, too late.

**Sir Edward Heath:** Even if I cannot say it so forcefully, that does not alter the fact that the right hon. Member for Yeovil refuses to acknowledge that what he is advocating now is that we should be prepared to go to war, and that is something about which he must be honest. The Prime Minister has emphasised this, and quite rightly.

As for the internal situation, the Prime Minister emphasised quite rightly that it is now absolutely impossible to decide between the merits and the faults of one group as against another. I know that there are right hon. and hon. Gentlemen who support particular groups in the former Yugoslavia. I respect their decisions, and they know the area—often very intimately—that they are supporting. But if one looks at the whole picture, as we have to today, and as my right hon. Friend the Prime Minister has done, one will see that it is now impossible to judge and say, "These are the people who ought to be supported for a particular reason." The right hon. Gentleman does not share that view, but that is certainly my view.

Nor can I accept some of the exaggerations. This will not be the end of the United Nations. The United Nations has had to face other great problems as well. It had to face them in Vietnam, the middle east, Africa—

**Mr. Dennis Skinner** (Bolsover): Somalia.

**Sir Edward Heath:** Somalia, yes. Because it did not achieve its aims entirely—sometimes not at all in the case of Vietnam—it was not the end of the United Nations. I suggest that we look at this reasonably and not with exaggeration.

Nor do I believe that, if we act sensibly in the present situation, there is any great danger that the conflict will spread over a lot of countries adjacent to or near Yugoslavia. Turkey has its hands full at the moment; it is not going to join in the conflict, and nor will the countries surrounding Yugoslavia. I think that one has to look sensibly and make a balanced judgment about what will happen in that particular part of the world.

Next, we come to the question of a peaceful solution and a negotiated settlement. I do not share the view which has been expressed that we have not been earnest about this matter. Lord Carrington and Lord Owen have worked extraordinarily hard and very earnestly. What we have to face realistically is that this situation is based on decades of conflict and it cannot be solved and resolved overnight. That does not alter the fact that we have to keep up the efforts to the greatest possible extent. It may be that, as we saw earlier with a smaller country helping in the middle east, someone skilled from a smaller country than the powers directly involved would have a better chance of influencing these people in getting a settlement. We do not know, but if it is being reconsidered, it is worth trying. I suggest that that approach might be looked at by my right hon. Friend the Prime Minister and his colleagues as well.

Then we come to the question of Russia and the help that it could give. It is a practical question. Russia has always objected to the bombing, and it is the bombing that has brought about the present situation. We know that many of our commanders were also opposed to the bombing, because they believed that it was dangerous for the civilian population, that it was very difficult to control militarily, and now, as we have seen, it has caused intense antagonism among the Bosnian Serbs.

The Prime Minister committed himself strongly to the fact that the hostages cannot be freed by an arrangement over bombing. Very well; that is now on the record. But it does not alter the fact that somebody else might deal with the bombing and then get the hostages out, for everybody concerned, not just ourselves. If another country intervenes and is able to persuade the Bosnian Serbs that bombing will not be resumed in that form, there is a chance that we can get a solution to this particular problem, as well as starting on a political settlement for the whole affair.

We come finally to the Prime Minister's statement that there can be no question of going to war. That is the crux of the matter. The Leader of the Opposition said, "Of course we must stiffen up here; we must be better there; we must be much more courageous there." Yes, but we will always come to the question, "But are you prepared to go to war?" And the answer must be no.

3.59 pm

**Mr. Tony Benn** (Chesterfield): I welcome the decision to recall the House and I can understand the Government's reasons for doing it. Not only are the hostages held, but they are held following air strikes that the Government supported. I do not say that they authorised them, but they supported them. The Government also have to consider carefully what foreign policy should be followed in such situations and, as the Prime Minister said, this affects the future of Europe and how its security can be assured.

However, nothing that has been said so far has clarified in my mind the objectives behind the decision to send more troops. Is it to release the hostages? If so, how is that to be achieved? Is it to maintain and develop humanitarian aid? If so, how is that to be achieved? Is it to defeat Serbia? The right hon. Member for Old Bexley and Sidcup (Sir E. Heath) said that if at the back of our mind is the defeat of Serbia, which is clearly what the leader of the Liberal Democrats wants, that can only mean war. Is that one of the objectives? Is one of the objectives to impose a settlement? Is it to cover a withdrawal?

It is a very great pity that this debate should take place without some historical background being set against which we can judge what has happened. The only person who came near to providing such a background was the right hon. Member for Old Bexley and Sidcup, who talked about decades—indeed, centuries—of conflict. The Turks controlled the area. The Austro-Hungarian empire was there. The Germans established a fascist Croatia during the war. Later, the German Government recognised Croatia. The British Government went along with that decision, it is said because of a concession over the social chapter. [HON. MEMBERS: "Rubbish."] Whatever the truth is, there was some negotiation that took a reluctant British Government into recognition of Croatia. Those factors have to be taken into account if we are to assess the motivation and strength of feeling of the warring parties in the old Yugoslavia.

I do not accept for one moment that the only options open are to fight—the Liberal Democrat view is that ultimately we shall have to fight and that we should have done better to fight three years ago—or to withdraw, which is, I understand, the view of some on the Conservative Benches who ask what British interest there is in remaining. My view is straightforward: it is that we should now build policy around the only things that can be done in a civil war—and it is time we got it straight—which are to provide humanitarian aid, mediation, arbitration and negotiation and an arms embargo to ensure that more arms do not get into the area. That is all that we can do.

The first thing that one can do is to provide humanitarian aid. I looked up the history of the Red Cross—because the Red Cross never needs air strikes to back up its work. As I learned this morning, it was set up after the slaughter on the battlefield of Solferino in 1861 and, from 1863 to today, no one has ever doubted that the Red Cross is independent and neutral and provides help for all the victims of war. That is all that can be done in a civil war—unless we follow the fight or withdraw options, both of which I reject.

**Mr. Andrew Hargreaves** (Birmingham, Hall Green): Will the right hon. Gentleman give way?

**Mr. Benn:** No. I am speaking briefly because I am told that 37 right hon. and hon. Members want to speak and my point can be briefly put.

The second thing that can be done is to provide mediation. In the case of a civil war, we need someone who is prepared to talk to both sides, to listen and to try to bring them together. Whether Lord Owen was the right person—

**Ms Clare Short** (Birmingham, Ladywood): Will my right hon. Friend give way?

**Mr. Benn:** That is what I am saying: the only thing that the international community can do is to mediate.

**Ms Short:** I was asking my right hon. Friend to give way.

**Mr. Benn:** I am sorry.

**Ms Short:** My right hon. Friend keeps talking about civil war. Is not the truth of the matter that there has been aggression and a breach of international law? The attempt to build a Greater Serbia breaches international law. It is the duty of the United Nations to uphold international law, otherwise we have chaos. What is happening is not just a civil war.

**Mr. Benn:** I know the argument that my hon. Friend advances. The view is widely shared among Opposition Members that this is not a civil war, but an act of aggression by Serbia against the Bosnian Government. But, if the Serbian Government recognise Bosnia, that will not end the war in Bosnia; it will still be a civil war, with the Bosnian Serbs fighting. The suggestion—which that great peacemonger Michael Foot seems to have overlooked—that the present position is a direct parallel with the position of Czechoslovakia in 1938 strikes me as wholly false. The right hon. Member for Old Bexley and Sidcup—the former Prime Minister—nods, because he remembers that and remembers the stand that he took against appeasement at the time.

**Mr. Hargreaves:** Will the right hon. Gentleman give way?

**Mr. Benn:** I will, but reluctantly.

**Mr. Hargreaves:** I am grateful to the right hon. Gentleman, who is seeing fair play.

The right hon. Gentleman mentioned the Red Cross. On a number of occasions, the Red Cross has expressed its concern about its own members being taken hostage in just such circumstances as these.

**Mr. Benn:** I am not saying that people who exercise a humanitarian function do not get killed; they do. The Red Cross, however, has never corrupted its own purpose or destroyed its credibility by inviting someone to launch air strikes when its workers are killed.

I am making an extremely serious point. As others have pointed out, this is not the only civil war in the world. Some we have disregarded altogether, but in the case of the former Yugoslavia we have become very much involved—correctly in the first instance, I believe, through the provision of humanitarian aid. I am saying that the air strikes have caused the problem, and may have destroyed the humanitarian function—unless we now clarify what our purpose is.

My third point concerns the arms embargo. I read in a newspaper the other day that the United States supplies 72 per cent. of all the arms that are sold around the world, and provides arms in 45 of the 50 regional conflicts taking place in the world. The President, however, sits in the White House and—because he does not want to send in American troops—authorises and encourages air strikes.

Perhaps the Prime Minister cannot say it publicly, but I should be very surprised if he were not warning Washington on the telephone, "Do not do it again or we shall be in deeper trouble." The air strikes were the occasion for the taking of hostages—whom the Serbs now call prisoners of war, because they say that the United Nations has declared war on them—and the air strikes are what now prevent the resumption of the humanitarian role.

I have always thought the arms trade the most criminal trade in the world. Unlike terrorism and drugs, it is sponsored by Governments. Hon. Members may have read the other day that about a quarter of the arms that we sell abroad are covered by the Export Credits Guarantee Department, and the recipients never pay for them. The British taxpayer pays for the supply of those arms.

I have already put this point to the Prime Minister; let me put it again, as vividly as I can. We cannot have British or French soldiers in blue berets acting as humanitarians, and pilots in blue helmets bombing: that is not a sustainable position. That issue must be clarified.

I am also not happy about NATO's taking over the role of the United Nations. We are about to celebrate the 50th anniversary of the establishment of the United Nations, which—as the House must know—was set up to secure the peaceful settlement of differences. I was much moved at the time, as I still am when I reflect on the UN's charter. NATO cannot take over the agency responsibility for the UN; if it does, I envisage many other dangers. NATO may, for instance, aspire to play a larger part in what it calls out-of-area functions, as part of the new world order. That is not at all what the United Nations is about.

What can we do in the House? We have absolutely no power in the matter. In sending troops, the Prime Minister used the royal prerogative of war making. We have no vote on that, for he is not consulting the House today. This is a prerogative power that successive Prime Ministers have used to commit our forces to what may be conflicts abroad. We can debate the matter, like the media, and at the end a sort of Jeremy Paxman will bring the debate to a conclusion; or we can express a view in the Lobbies.

I do not know whether other hon. Members will join me, but tonight I intend to vote against what the Government have done, first, because I think that the Government's policy up to now has endangered the hostages and, secondly, because the uncertainties of our current objectives could put the hostages in greater danger. I do not believe that those of us with no governmental responsibility would be representing the people of the country, including the troops and their families, if we were to give the Government a blank cheque to do what they like with our soldiers in a situation of exceptional danger. Therefore, if the opportunity presents itself, I intend to divide the House for the reasons that I have given.

4.9 pm

**Mr. David Howell** (Guildford): I am very glad that the Leader of the Opposition recognised in his speech the true origins of the horrific saga whose consequences we are discussing today. As he said, those consequences lie in the vicious dream of greater Serbian expansionism, and with those Serbians and their sinister intellectual backers who dreamed up the idea of smashing the Yugoslav federation and of turning areas of relative peace—contrary to the general mythology, families and villages had lived in peace for many years—into areas of ethnic hatred and horror. We should never forget that when we try to analyse how on earth we should wind down the spiral of hatred which has been escalated so viciously by those who are bent on ethnic cleansing.

On this occasion, the media, as is their wont because it is more entertaining, have sought to portray the debate as a conflict between those who wish to see an immediate disengagement and withdrawal of the troops—I think that that would be extremely difficult to achieve—and those who believe that we should become involved on a new and larger scale and wage intensive war against the enemy, whoever it may be. Presumably, the enemy is the Bosnian Serbs in this case. As usual, some of the media analysis is too simplistic; the situation is far too complex to lend itself to that sort of simple labelling.

I believe that the Government are totally correct in acting forcefully to mobilise and send more troops into Bosnia. They have focused the nation's attention—and I hope that of the whole House, whether or not the right hon. Member for Chesterfield (Mr. Benn) divides the House—on our determination to see the hostages returned unharmed.

However, it is not merely a question of returning all of the United Nations hostages, including our own soldiers, unharmed—although that is an absolute priority. There is also the question of ensuring that the troops deployed throughout Bosnia—some of whom are scattered in very remote regions from which it would be extremely hard to disengage and escape—are protected from further hostage taking.

As the saga continues—and it will, possibly for many years—there can be no doubt that more hostages will be taken. No one should be surprised by the recent hostage taking, although it has occurred on a larger scale, as hostages were taken during previous conflicts. There were hideous examples of hostage taking during the Gulf war, as people who watched their televisions and read books will know, and we were bound to reach that point in this conflict. As my right hon. Friend the Member for Old Bexley and Sidcup (Sir E. Heath) said, it was predictable. It raises question marks about the efficiency of an organisation that allowed hostages to be taken and, at the very least, it requires a fundamental rethink of the situation.

I hope that my right hon. Friend the Prime Minister's appeal, backed by the Leader of the Opposition, that we must show unity in the face of the immediate crisis will be recognised and respected in the House. We must get our hostages out unharmed, and we must prevent a further haemorrhaging of the situation through further hostage taking. In the short term, we must demonstrate that we mean business and that we will not merely retire from the conflict or stand paralysed.

I turn to the medium and longer-term situation, and the reasonable proposition that we should understand how we got into the present difficulties, in order to prevent the situation from worsening further.

I have no doubt that those who propose rethinking the United Nations mandate are right. I am glad to hear that Dr. Boutros-Ghali is rethinking the mandate for the protection force. I understand that the right hon. Member for Yeovil (Mr. Ashdown) believes in rethinking the mandate. We shall come in a moment to whether it should be a tougher mandate or a more prudent and limited one.

I could not quite make out whether the Leader of the Opposition wants the present mandate reinforced, as he said at one stage, or whether he is seeking a different mandate for the troops. Apparently, it is all too easy for some of them to be rounded up as hostages.

One thing, however, is clear. It is misleading to describe what the protection forces are doing as a peacekeeping operation, as there is no peace to keep. We recognise—and everyone urged from the start when the British troops were sent in—that there was an important job to do: to protect aid workers, medical supplies and food supplies, and to ensure that men, women and children did not starve and stayed alive. Who could stand against that? We thought that it was the right thing to do—the humanitarian task and the humanitarian role.

What we did not consider at the time—it was not suggested as a likely event, although some of us should have foreseen it—was that the humanitarian role would move from protecting the columns and the aid workers to protecting the troops who were protecting the aid workers, and then to protecting the civilian population in various garrisons and groups, and that ultimately it would become an attempt to maintain neutral ground where there is no neutral ground and to impose peace when it remains absolutely clear that the combatants are not prepared to accept peace.

The Bosnian presidency troops certainly would not accept peace if it meant bisecting their country when the international community had promised to keep Bosnia sacred. Croatia, which is out of the news at the moment, certainly would not accept peace if it meant keeping a quarter of Croatia out of the hands of the Croatian central Government. Those varieties of peace would never be accepted and could not be maintained.

It is completely unfair to ask our troops, or UNPROFOR troops generally, to keep such a peace or attempt to impose it, particularly when the diplomats have notably failed even to get it accepted around the negotiating table.

**Mr. Ashdown:** Surely the right hon. Gentleman was not quite right to say that none of the sides would accept peace. The Bosnian Government have committed themselves to what the international community believes would be a just peace—the five-nation contact group plan. The Serbs have not.

Surely considering whether we are prepared to take sides against aggression does not mean going to war, as the right hon. Gentleman suggests. There is broad battlefield parity between Bosnian and Serb forces, but surely, when we assess our attitudes, the fact that the Bosnian Government have accepted what the international community regards as a fair peace, and the Bosnian Serbs have not, needs to colour our attitude.

**Mr. Howell:** I stand corrected. It is perfectly true that the Bosnian presidency troops—we keep calling them the Bosnian Muslims, but, as the right hon. Gentleman knows, they are not entirely Muslims, or even dedicated Muslims and Islamics in the sense that we see them in parts of the Maghreb—said that they were prepared to accept a settlement which would involve some partition of their country. I find that difficult, and I rather suspect that the small details of that peace proposal would reveal that the Bosnian presidency thought it would not involve partition and that the Bosnian Serbs had every intention it would, so I have little faith that any such peace would stick for a moment.

Most, if not all, of us recognise that, in facing the most hideous choices between the bad and very bad, my right hon. Friends in government have taken a bold and courageous step—the only one open to them in the short term—but in the longer term we have to rethink the situation in which so-called peacekeeping troops are scattered around and vulnerable to precisely the immense dangers into which they have been plunged and which we simply cannot tolerate and allow to continue.

As we have no overall power over what our allies and the United Nations collectively decide, although we have some input, we in the House must suggest what mandate the United Nations should now proceed towards, what objectives we should set ourselves and how to achieve them, and whether military solutions have anything more to add.

**Mr. Michael Connarty** (Falkirk, East): Before moving on to future strategies, would it not be more accurate to explain the mandate fully and to accept that one of the parts of the mandate which has led to this situation is the protection of safe havens, and that the troops were not adequate for the task?

**Mr. Howell:** The hon. Gentleman is right. The safe havens were not mentioned in the original mandate, but the UN came up with the idea later. In some senses, the safe havens have become garrisons, but they are ineffective garrisons. They may be havens, but they are not safe. We saw that with shells whistling into Tuzla the other day, killing 70 people who were drinking coffee in a cafe. That does not amount to a safe haven.

[Mr. Howell]

It would be too sweeping to say that full withdrawal from the safe haven areas and from the safe haven role would not add to the bloodshed, because it would, but where we are now adds to the bloodshed. That emphasises the agony of the dilemma—there is blood and mayhem if we do not act and blood and mayhem if we do.

**Sir Teddy Taylor** (Southend, East): Can my right hon. Friend explain what is so special about Bosnia that we have to commit massive amounts of aid in a rather unclear role, when there are so many other parts of the world where there is ethnic cleansing, massive killing and enormous social distress and starvation? What is so special about this situation?

**Mr. Howell:** The way in which the question was posed suggests that we have power, and have had power all along, to choose what we do there. The difficulty is that we decided three years ago that there was a humanitarian need. The television cameras showed all the terror, and the cry went out, "Send the troops to protect the aid workers." From that, one step has led to another.

If my hon. Friend asks why we took all those steps, we could spend a long time blaming each other and analysing why the policy makers made mistakes. We are where we are. It is not a matter of choice. No one would conceivably choose to be where we are now if we had a free will in the matter—and, of course, we do not have a free will.

I want to try to move away from the endless analysis of the past which, although it is not totally a waste of time, will not help the hostages or the present situation. I want to suggest some guidelines that we should think of following while we try to shape the next stage of this horror.

Do we have the will? I would be in favour of a huge military operation, if for one moment the will existed to mount such a thing, which could isolate and crush the Bosnian Serbs. I believe that that would remove this terror and horror, and would rapidly remove the danger of a spread of the conflagration.

However, it is totally unrealistic to talk in that way. We do not have the will power to do that, and I doubt whether we even have the military capability. We are talking about a vast area of very difficult terrain and a very determined enemy, who believe that it is their land and that they have been there for 1,000 years. The idea that we could take them on militarily is completely unrealistic. However, that is the way that we are being dragged now, because they say that the UN and the British are their enemies. We must resist the logical temptation to say that, if they think that we are the enemy, we should treat them as an enemy as well, and mobilise more and more forces to do something against them. That would be fatal, and would be disastrous for the hostages now being held as prisoners of war, so they say, by these people.

So the military course is not open to us. The diplomatic course should be open, because, as a nation concerned with the stability of Europe, we have a role to play in ensuring that the conflagration does not spread. We must continue with our diplomatic efforts.

**Mr. Michael Lord** (Suffolk, Central): I would not for one moment want to recommend all-out war, but does not history show us that, with aggressors like these, if we do not stop them sooner, we have to stop them later?

**Mr. Howell:** That is easy to say; my hon. Friend knows that such phrases trip off the lips. Historical analogies are not good, because history does not necessarily repeat itself. As Mr. Balfour said, historians repeat each other, which is a different thing. We cannot necessarily learn a precise lesson from one era and then apply it to another.

It would be dangerous to assume that, if outside powers declared war on a particular group, conquered them and crushed them, that would solve the problem. It may be that the Bosnian Serbs will be stopped only by force, but if so, we must determine which force. The obvious answer is the people they are fighting.

If there was a military balance on the battlefield, and the Bosnian Muslims had the same heavy weapons as the Bosnian Serbs, the Serbs would think twice before attacking every morning. We would then begin to fulfil the adage in my hon. Friend's question, that the Bosnian Serbs will be stopped only by force—but it would be the proper force.

To date, that has not been possible, because the international community has denied heavy weapons to the Bosnian Muslim troops. They have a few weapons, but they are lightly armed. The precise way that the war in that area has developed shows that the Bosnian Serbs have succeeded in the areas where they have heavy weapons. That has happened every time, which encourages them to attack again. They know that, with heavy weapons, they will succeed.

I know that that view puts me out of line with most European Governments and in line with the American Congress, which appears to be going through various extraordinary moods. However, I have always believed that, if we want even-handedness in the area and to achieve a military stalemate, we should seriously consider non-intervention in arms supplies, so that the two main combatants have equal fire power and respect each other. I do not believe that that would necessarily make life much more difficult for the remaining humanitarian protection forces.

There is a question whether those forces should be expanded. The answer is yes in the short term, for the immediate purpose of getting the hostages out, but no in the long term, because we should return to the original mandate, which was humanitarian protection as far as possible. That is happening in many areas that are away from significant conflict—areas of Bosnia about which we never hear—where our troops are doing magnificent work. They should continue to do so.

As my right hon. Friend the Foreign Secretary said, when we come to regroup and rethink the deployment of various troops in Bosnia, it may be possible to concentrate more on the humanitarian role and prevent them from being dragged into this mythical peacekeeping exercise, which leads nowhere and exposes our troops to unacceptable dangers.

We return to the basic point that everyone who has spoken so far in the debate has recognised—that we cannot stay with the present position, where troops are likely to be taken hostage by people they were talking to over breakfast. By lunchtime, the Bosnian Serbs may say,

"Come with us: you are hostages." We must ensure that there is a rapid regrouping and reorganisation and, to some extent—although not totally—a withdrawal.

It has been suggested that there has always been conflict in that area, and that the people have always been fighting each other. That is not true—they have been marrying each other and living with each other in villages and communities throughout the Balkan area. They can do that again.

It would be a great pity if the House divided tonight, and I am sorry that the right hon. Member for Chesterfield wants that. It will send the wrong message, I believe that the situation can be calmed by the judicious use of diplomacy and humanitarian work, but not by clumsy interventions in the name of a peace that does not exist. First, let us work on the diplomacy and put pressure on Milosevic and the Serbian nationalists who began it all, and then gradually try to calm the situation.

4.28 pm

**Mr. John Home Robertson** (East Lothian): This debate brings back memories of the debates on the deployments to the Falkland Islands in 1982 and to the Gulf in 1990. As a member of the first generation of Scots in the whole of recorded history which has not been required to go to war with somebody or other, I always feel a certain anxiety about voting to send other people to regions of conflict.

I have discussed that dilemma with a number of service men in recent years. The consensus among them seems to be that they are glad that we take the issues seriously in the House. However, just as they would not flinch from doing their duty, so they do not want us to flinch from taking the right decisions. I approach the debate in that spirit.

I bring a little experience of Bosnia and Herzegovina to the House this evening, from my two visits there with the Defence Select Committee in February 1993 and March this year, and from the four weeks I spent during the last summer recess driving a truck in an aid convoy run by Edinburgh Direct Aid. I hope to go back in the coming summer recess, but the outlook is rather ominous. Denis Rutovitz, the chairman of Edinburgh Direct Aid, was shot and wounded on the way to Sarajevo with another convoy last month.

We have heard a lot about the failures and difficulties of UNPROFOR, and especially about the shortcomings of the so-called safe areas, which are plainly not safe. The main part of the trouble is that they have never been demilitarised. They are clearly not safe for the civilian populations of those towns, which are subject to regular shelling, sniping, and deprivation of supplies. As we now know to our cost, they are not safe for UN troops either. I will come back to that.

I want to highlight the spectacular successes of UNPROFOR, which are not spoken of enough in the press or anywhere else. First, never let us forget that 3 million people who are, in effect, under siege in central Bosnia—including half a million people who are literally under siege in Sarajevo—have been kept supplied, at least with basic materials, for the past three years. That would not have been possible without UNPROFOR.

I can tell the House that it is scary enough to be driving around with supplies on those rough, isolated routes through a civil war zone now; it would be far more hazardous without the United Nations patrols that are currently on those roads. I have with me the card that I carried last year that identified me as being under the auspices of the United Nations High Commissioner for Refugees and asked that everyone should grant me free passage. That card would not be worth much in the absence from those roads of UN warriors and patrols from the UN contingents. It is vital that they should continue in central Bosnia.

The second major success of UNPROFOR is that one lethal part of the three-way civil war has been stopped. The vicious conflict between the Croatian HVO and the Government BiH forces, which claimed hundreds of lives in towns such as Mostar, Gornji Vakuf and other communities, was ended by a United Nations-sponsored truce on 23 February 1994. There is now a peace to be kept in central Bosnia, and that task must continue.

If we were to withdraw the United Nations force now, that fragile peace would be put in jeopardy. It is more than likely that the confederation would disintegrate, and that the Croat-Muslim civil war would break out again. We would be abandoning those 3 million people to an unimaginable fate. After my personal contacts with the decent and heroic people who are running the hospitals, orphanages and caring services of central Bosnia, I would be horrified if we were to abandon them to the mercy of the ethnic cleansers, murderers and rapists who stand ready to prey on this conflict.

That brings me to the third side of the grim Balkan triangle: the Bosnian Serb army. It is undeniably the worst offender, although I stress that it is not the only one. It is the 30 per cent. of the people of Bosnia that has used military superiority to seize 70 per cent. of the territory of Bosnia and Herzegovina and followed that by savage ethnic cleansing and merciless pressure on Sarajevo and other besieged communities. It has never accepted or respected United Nations resolutions or UNPROFOR, and it is now holding United Nations soldiers, including the 33 Royal Welch Fusiliers, as hostages. It calls them prisoners of war. Peacemakers are being treated as prisoners of war; the Bosnian Serb army is despicable.

Through other channels, such as the Select Committee, I will want to hear explanations of why United Nations military observers and our troops in Gorazde were left in vulnerable positions when the situation was escalating. However, that should probably be addressed in private rather than in the context of this debate. This is just the latest in a long string of outrages perpetrated by these people. They are entirely responsible for the escalation of the conflict that led to the present situation, and the whole world knows it.

The Bosnian Serbs are treating the United Nations with contempt. They are cynically exploiting weaknesses and inconsistency in the United Nations' position. I am afraid that it has to be said that the UN deployment in relation to the Bosnian Serb army has been characterised by muddled thinking and undermanning. Whatever happens, the mandate must be clarified, and I believe that the force should be strengthened to ensure maximum effectiveness and minimum risk in future. There has to be a fundamental reappraisal of the deployment.

Surely the time has come to reconsider some of the humiliating compromises that have been made with the Bosnian Serb army. I offer just one example. UNPROFOR is co-operating with the BSA to enforce the siege of Sarajevo. The United Nations has been

[Mr. John Home Robertson]

manoeuvred into a position in which a Bosnian Serb army liaison officer has absolute control over who and what can go in and out of Sarajevo. He makes the decisions, and the United Nations applies them. Diplomats have been kept off aeroplanes and, recently, 40 pallets of material urgently required by Médecins sans Frontières were effectively impounded by the United Nations on Serb instructions at Sarajevo airport for three whole months.

Furthermore, the United Nations is channelling the aid convoys into Sarajevo through Serb checkpoints, where the BSA routinely steals up to 50 per cent. of the loads. Worse, the United Nations cannot even return fire when the BSA uses machine guns and mortars against clearly identified aid convoys with official UNHCR number plates, as happened to my friends in Edinburgh Direct Aid when they went to Sarajevo five weeks ago.

The protection of humanitarian aid is the prime objective of UNPROFOR. That responsibility should not have been abdicated, and should be reaffirmed now. I should like to ask whether the United Nations should go on respecting the status of Bosnian Serb liaison officers while United Nations peacekeepers are being held hostage, but I shall leave that one sticking to the wall.

There is much to say, but I shall confine myself to the most important points. First, the international community has a responsibility to the suffering people of Bosnia and Herzegovina. Secondly, the Bosnian Serb leadership is a serious threat, not only to the people of the Balkans but to the security of Europe. We cannot allow a savage, racist, expansionist force to go on doing its worst on the very doorstep of the European Community and of NATO. It is worth mentioning that Hungary—east of Bosnia—is probably going to be joining the European Community shortly, and that, as NATO members, we are committed to the security of neighbouring countries such as Italy and Greece.

It would be folly to turn a blind eye to the unbridled savagery that is taking place in the adjacent territories of former Yugoslavia. Apart from anything else, it would be intolerable and unthinkable for the Security Council of the United Nations to be driven into submission by Mr. Radovan Karadzic and his Administration.

It is clear from today's speeches that some hon. Members regard Bosnia-Herzegovina as what might be described as a faraway place of which we know little, to borrow a phrase from another era of appeasement. We should be learning some lessons from history, perhaps especially in this anniversary year.

Bosnia-Herzegovina is a great deal closer than the Falkland Islands, and closer even than Kuwait. It is only a very short flight away, or three days' drive in a truck. I suggest that protecting the people of Bosnia is a vital humanitarian interest, that the collective security and stability of Europe is a vital national interest for all of us in Europe, that respect for the United Nations is a vital international interest, and that the safety of the 33 Royal Welch Fusiliers and the RAF officer is an immediate and direct national priority.

The United Kingdom and France in particular can take special pride in our part in the operation so far. We have not been helped by German diplomacy and, frankly, the

United States and the Russians have not exactly covered themselves in glory so far. I hope that they are listening; I hope that they are learning.

**Mr. Andrew Robathan** (Blaby) *rose—*

**Mr. Home Robertson:** I am just concluding, as I know that many hon. Members want to take part in this debate.

The United Nations operation has reached an absolutely critical stage. We can capitulate to naked aggression and oppression, mainly perpetrated by the Bosnian Serbs, or we can continue to stand up for civilisation and international order. I support the Government's decision to reinforce the United Nations presence in Bosnia. I urge the Government to seek similar reinforcement from other contributing countries and I also urge them to press for a stronger and clearer mandate for the UN force.

As a member of the Defence Select Committee, I shall be looking to the Government to ensure that our forces are deployed with the maximum effect and the minimum risk, the first priority being to get the hostages home. Let us stop talking about withdrawal, which means capitulation to sheer tyranny. We must see this thing through.

4.40 pm

**Mr. Tom King** (Bridgwater): The House will have listened with great respect to the hon. Member for East Lothian (Mr. Home Robertson), who spoke of his personal experiences in Bosnia. I am sure that other hon. Members will join me in hoping that when he returns—if he does—in the summer recess, he will be able to do so under the extra security that the Government's measures will provide.

I cannot help reflecting on the fact that this is the second time in five years that the House has expressed outrage about the use of human shields. We expressed outrage during the Gulf war when Saddam Hussein took such action. I remember the importance that we attached to speaking with the clearest possible voice, so that there was no doubt whatever about where the House, the Government and this country stood in defence of our armed forces and the outrage against any taking of hostages.

The lesson that we learned from the Gulf war is that many audiences watch our debates on television, and not only in this country. Saddam Hussein was an avid listener to the House's proceedings, hoping to detect signs of weakness, disunity and encouragement for his cause. I have no doubt that reports will quickly pass to Pale on whether the United Kingdom stands staunchly behind the Government's actions.

I support the Government's action. For very good causes, we have a duty to our forces which are, to use an old phrase, in harm's way. We are clearly concerned to ensure that our hostages, the taking of whom was outrageous, are released immediately and restored to their units.

Despite the few dissenting elements and discordant voices, which echo those expressed in our debates five years ago, when the same war and anti-war parties emerged in the House, I recognise the same spirit among hon. Members that produced the largest majority that I can remember in support of our forces in their time of need. I have no doubt that the same House of Commons will strongly support—if it is needed—our armed forces should they face danger overseas. I welcome the speeches in support of the Government's position made by—of course—my right hon. Friend the Prime Minister, the Leader of the Opposition and the right hon. Member for Yeovil (Mr. Ashdown) on behalf of the Liberal Democrats.

I say to those who might encourage alternative action that, even if it were possible, I would be appalled by the idea of an immediate withdrawal. It would send a message that blackmail works and that people only have to take hostages to be successful. What an effect that would have on any future United Nations effort. Any discordant group would know that all that it had to do was grab a few people who were deployed for humanitarian, peacekeeping purposes and the will of the free world would dissolve rapidly like the mist. As we know, that would encourage the taking of yet more hostages.

I have been enormously impressed by what has been achieved. I say no more because I bow to the experience of the hon. Member for East Lothian. The House and this country should be very proud of what we have done and the part that we have played. Of course we could have stood aside, of course we could have said, as some did, that the conflict was nothing to do with us, that it was a long way away and that although we could see people dying on television, other people were dying in places that television could not reach. We did what we could and I have no doubt that hundreds of thousands of people— arguably, an even greater number—are alive because of the efforts that have been made.

I respect what has been achieved and I am desperately keen to ensure that, if possible, such work continues. If we send additional forces, which I support, we must be clear about the basis on which we do so. We owe it to those forces to ensure that their rules of engagement and the mandate—whatever phrase is used—are clear. The exercise must not become a one-way delivery system of extra equipment to the warring factions. Many envious eyes will be cast on the 105 mm artillery that we are sending. We had better have some very clear rules of engagement to ensure that any valuable or powerful equipment sent out is properly defended.

The number of troops is not the whole matter. It is interesting to note that we are increasing the number of British troops to the number that the French have, effectively, already deployed. There have been 37 French casualties, and a significant number of the 333 hostages are French. The number of troops sent is no guarantee of security unless people are empowered with the right rules of engagement and the right authority to act to protect their position.

The biggest mistake is to imagine that the previous crisis teaches us all the lessons that we need to know about the current crisis, but the clarity of authority was a major factor in the achievement of the rapid and successful completion of the Gulf war. Although that war was certainly under the authority of the United Nations, there was a very clear command structure. We did not engage in endless public ministerial meetings about exactly when, for example, the air campaign would start. We had the authority to proceed and we managed to achieve an element of surprise. We did not have ministerial meetings in public in Brussels, New York,

Washington or elsewhere to determine whether the left hook would be employed for the land attack to outflank the Iraqi defence.

Of course in Bosnia we face a different situation and comparisons cannot be made, but there is no question that such public meetings have put our commanders at a great disadvantage and have made the task on which we have embarked so much more difficult. I therefore hope that, while we will receive considerable advice and persuasion from many countries that are not so involved, the greater responsibility for command and authority will lie with those that are involved, whose troops are present and that are playing their part under the overall authority of the United Nations.

I hope that there is very close co-ordination. I have seen the report that the recapture of the post on the bridge may have been due to a policy change authorised by President Chirac, who ordered that French troops were to cede no more ground and allow no more humiliation. I can understand that reaction in the light of the experiences of the French forces. It is very important that if that is a change of policy—I hope that my right hon. and learned Friend the Secretary of State for Defence will make the position clear in his speech—an absolutely co-ordinated view among the UN forces undertaking this important and valuable role is established.

Much has been said already in support of the Prime Minister's decisions, and there is no need to repeat many of the points that have been made, but one lesson that we must learn from the present crisis is the importance of keeping Russia involved. That is crucial, both in the short and long term—in the short term with regard to the immediate position over the hostages and any opportunity that there may be for Russia to play her part in ensuring their release.

With regard to the longer term, my right hon. Friend the Foreign Secretary has often illustrated the importance of our role in Bosnia by reminding us how many cemeteries in this country are filled with those who died in a war that arose out of the Balkans. Of course that conflict was partly due to the problems of the Balkans themselves but, in the very nature of a world war, it owed more to the fact that other nations then sought to become involved.

Throughout the cold war it was NATO's great dread that Yugoslavia would collapse when Tito died so that, at a time of maximum tension, that cockpit of the struggle for influence would suddenly present problems. We must be thankful that the crisis that NATO expected did not occur until after the end of the cold war. It is crucial that the improvement in relations that is now possible is maintained, and that we keep the closest possible contacts between ourselves and Russia, so as to ensure that, if things do not work out as we hope, there is no risk of the conflagration ever spreading on the scale that we have seen in the past.

4.51 pm

**Mr. Nick Ainger** (Pembroke): I represent the constituency in which the Royal Welch Fusiliers' base is now located, at the former RAF base at Brawdy. The families of seven of the 33 hostages live in my constituency. The rest, of course, are scattered throughout Wales. I am sure that other Welsh Members will join me in welcoming the fact that Parliament has been recalled

*[Mr. Nick Ainger]*

today. It shows the seriousness with which the House takes the hostage issue, and I am sure that that alone will give the families some comfort. Obviously they are extremely worried about the present situation. I am grateful for all the sympathetic comments that have been made by Members from both sides of the House about the families. The whole House shares their concern about their 33 loved ones held hostage in Bosnia.

I understand that the Secretary of State for Defence will wind up, and I should like to draw his attention to a specific question asked by my hon. Friend the Member for Newport, East (Mr. Hughes) about the location of eight of the 33 hostages. There appears to be some confusion, so will the right hon. and learned Gentleman make inquiries before he winds up? If the situation has not been clarified and the eight hostages have not been located, the families' concern will increase.

Unlike my hon. Friend the Member for East Lothian (Mr. Home Robertson), I am no expert on either the immediate circumstances or the long-term background in Yugoslavia—although, having spent two wonderful holidays there, I have a great love for the country. None the less, to me it seems that the description "muddling through" could be applied throughout.

I totally support the Government's position, although many of the families of the hostages are expressing concern and, understandably, may even say that we should withdraw. I appreciate their worries and I understand why they may say that, but withdrawal would be wholly wrong for several reasons.

First, as has been said, withdrawal would give the Bosnian Serbs a signal that such despicable action wins rewards. The safety not only of the other 300-odd Royal Welch Fusiliers but of the other 3,500 British troops and the 7,000 French troops would be put at risk if we decided that such action by the rebel Serbs would be rewarded. If we gave any hint that we were prepared to back down from our current or our proposed position, it would exacerbate the hostages' position.

Secondly, in the wider strategic view, the Balkans are extremely unstable at the moment. I remember being told a story in which a Hungarian was asked, "How many countries surround Hungary?" The answer was, "One— Greater Hungary." Throughout the Balkans, given the wrong circumstances, the ethnic, religious and territorial conflicts could explode, and more countries would be sucked into a conflict that all the resources of the British and French armies could not control or contain.

The United Nations humanitarian aid programme has been successful but unfortunately, because the media like only the bad and the sensational stories, the work that has been going on day in, day out since November 1992 has gone unreported in the main. Sadly, only the tragedies are reported from Bosnia, not the boring but vital everyday successes of delivering aid, reducing conflict and brokering local ceasefires and deals.

That may be why public opinion, as reflected in certain newspaper polls, is that we should pull out. The success of the British and French armies has not been fully reported and only the tragedies, such as that in Tuzla the other day, suddenly appear on our television screens. Then people say, "What a failure that is. The United Nations should be doing more or pulling out." That is understandable if the public's only source of information is our television screens and the other media.

I understand that the position adopted by the Secretary of State and the Prime Minister on the bombing cannot be overstated. However, previous bombings have been ineffective. The targets chosen were not of any great import, and an objective view would be that the previous bombing regime did not achieve the aim intended. Undoubtedly the most recent incident was totally counterproductive.

In the long run we may have to review that policy. I hope that if a different mandate is given to the extra troops going to Bosnia, we can establish a more effective method than the relatively indiscriminate use of air power. But, no, it is unfair to say "indiscriminate". The use has not been indiscriminate, but none the less air power can certainly be construed by the Bosnian Serbs as indiscriminate.

Judging from my research and the information that has recently come out of Bosnia and the former Yugoslavia it seems that the Bosnian Serbs are now becoming increasingly desperate. They have had a number of military set-backs in western Slavonia and in Bosnia. The hostage taking, although undoubtedly related to the bombing, may represent a last desperate throw by the Bosnian Serbs. They certainly want the UN, Britain and France out of Bosnia as quickly as possible, and they hope and pray that British public opinion will persuade the Government and this House to withdraw. That would be wrong for the hostages, and strategically wrong in the longer term for Europe and for the millions of people who depend on the humanitarian aid effort.

I am sure that the Government, with the Russians, are actively trying to persuade President Milosevic to use his best influence to ensure that the 33 British hostages and all the other UN hostages are released. That is the best way forward: diplomatic pressure and a show not just of strength but of resolve by the House that we are not willing to accept this sort of action by the Bosnian Serbs.

My priority is to secure the release of the 33 Royal Welch Fusiliers and the RAF officer. I hope that the action on which the Government have embarked will lead to their release as soon as possible, allowing them to come home safely to their families.

5.1 pm

**Sir John Stanley** (Tonbridge and Malling): Opening the debate, the Prime Minister said that the events of the past few days represented a qualitative change in the situation in Bosnia. That judgment is entirely right. I would go as far as to say that, now that the Bosnian Serbs feel at liberty to engage in mass hostage taking against UN personnel, they have made an undeclared declaration of war against UN personnel in Bosnia. That will necessitate substantial changes in the way UN troops are deployed there and in the resources brought to bear to protect them.

Hostages have been taken on a number of occasions before—civilians and service personnel. Based on my experience of one or two of those incidents I would argue that the families of those taken hostage can be assured that the necessary qualities will be brought to bear on their plight—the qualities of a cool head, a calculating mind and a steely determination to see the matter through, however long it takes. I have every confidence that those with the formidable task of dealing with the problem, the Government and their professional advisers in the armed services and the diplomatic corps, will bring every ounce of their professionalism to bear to secure the release of the hostages.

I am also certain that, whatever options or combination of options my right hon. Friends choose to apply, they will have the full support of the House in doing whatever is necessary to secure a successful outcome for the hostages.

As for the UN and its deployment in Bosnia, as we all well know, UN deployments around the world—including hitherto in Bosnia—have always rested on the central assumption that there will be no direct or immediate risk to the safety of the personnel in question. I refer to UN deployments in peacekeeping and humanitarian roles. That is why UN personnel are usually deployed highly visibly and statically, and no attempt is made to conceal their progress along road or air transport routes.

The new situation will necessitate a fundamental reconsideration of this posture. UN commanders in the field will have to try as far as possible to remove the hostage-taking option from the Bosnian Serbs. This House, like other Parliaments elsewhere, would find it unacceptable if such hostage taking were continuously repeated. In effect, around the clock, seven days a week, the UN will have to have at its disposal, at every location where its personnel are deployed, enough fire power to ensure that hostage taking cannot be repeated.

The new situation also calls for a significant concentration of UN personnel. It will inescapably result in a significant reduction in the number of places where those personnel can be deployed, because of the clear need to reduce their exposure and vulnerability. There will necessarily therefore have to be some reduction in the usefulness of the humanitarian work that they can carry out. My right hon. Friends will have the considerable task of judging whether the residual humanitarian role that the UN can perform is viable.

Moreover, it will be essential to provide an altogether different order of protection for the remaining UN peacekeepers. I welcome the steps that the Prime Minister announced today to ensure that the British contingent receives infinitely more protection. My right hon. Friends will have the formidable task of judging whether the extent and longevity of the new commitment of personnel will be tolerable in the context of British armed services and financial resources. For as long as hostage taking and the risk of it remain, these major changes in our approach to UN deployment will be called for—they follow inescapably from the position in which we find ourselves.

I approach the subject of air strikes from a position different from that of the right hon. Member for Chesterfield (Mr. Benn). I greatly welcome what the Prime Minister said in response to an intervention—that we shall have no truck whatever with the Serbian attempt to exchange hostages for an undertaking that air strikes will never be used. It would be quite wrong to succumb to that form of blackmail, and I was delighted to hear my right hon. Friend rule it out immediately.

As the House is well aware, the utility or otherwise of air strikes has probably been the most hotly debated issue throughout the conflict and the UN's involvement in it. Some people—particularly on the other side of the Atlantic—have given the impression that if only the air strikers were let off the leash, the whole conflict in Bosnia could be rapidly brought to an end. We have taken a different position, and we have constantly advocated caution and care in the use of air strikes.

The pattern of the use of air power in the 50 years since the second world war has demonstrated two things: first, control of the air is indispensable to the protection of ground troops and to the holding and taking of ground; secondly, control of the air alone and the use of air power does not enable one to control the ground unless one is also prepared to make a commitment of ground forces. That commitment has not so far been forthcoming from the international community.

In the context of Bosnia, the limitations of air power are particularly pronounced. Factors such as the terrain, the relative smallness of the targets and the ability to move those targets put considerable constraints on the use of air power. When that is coupled with the vulnerability of UN personnel, the Government's judgment is seen to be entirely right. Air strikes are a blunt weapon which have the undoubted capacity to turn into a boomerang. Following the events of the past 10 days, I hope that our friends on the other side of the Atlantic will make a more realistic assessment of the utility of air strikes.

The House has effectively discussed three options today. In my opinion, only one hon. Member so far has advocated a significant military escalation—the leader of the Liberal Democrats. I am sorry that the right hon. Gentleman is not in his place now, because I particularly wanted to refer to his speech. The record will show that the right hon. Gentleman called on UN forces to increase their military fire power and activity to defend the safe havens. The defence of the safe havens effectively means that they are physically and, if necessary, militarily protected. It means securing ground and weapons beyond the safe havens to make them fire-free.

If that is to be done effectively, the UN will have to go to war to defend the safe havens. My right hon. Friend the Member for Old Bexley and Sidcup (Sir E. Heath) was entirely right to state to the leader of the Liberal Democrats that if it is his policy to safeguard militarily the integrity of the safe havens—apparently it is—he should make it clear what the military implications are of that policy. It would mean taking UN forces into a fighting role.

**Sir Patrick Cormack** (Staffordshire, South): Surely it should mean something if the UN designates an area a safe haven. Should not the combatants respect that? If they do not, what is the point of the designation?

**Sir John Stanley:** I am seeking clarity of the position taken by the leader of the Liberal Democrats. If my hon. Friend is asking me, I would say that we have two choices. We can diplomatically declare a safe haven, while recognising that its integrity may be destroyed militarily—that is the option which the UN, the commanders on the ground and the Governments concerned have adopted—or we can go further and say that we are going to defend militarily the integrity of that safe haven. That appears to be the policy of the leader of the Liberal Democrats.

If that is the right hon. Gentleman's policy, he must spell out the military implications and accept the consequences. We would not merely have to prevent Serb soldiers from getting inside the safe havens, but we would have to do everything necessary to prevent incoming fire of any sort from coming into the safe haven. That would

[*Sir John Stanley*]

entail a considerable military commitment. There may be some Members who believe that we should make that commitment, but one cannot say that we must protect the safe havens while pretending that that does not have far-reaching military consequences.

**Mr. Menzies Campbell** (Fife, North-East): I am sure that the right hon. Gentleman—like all of us—is familiar with UN Security Council resolution 836 of 4 June 1994, which provides for precisely the kind of action to which he has referred. The resolution gives the UN the ability

"to take the necessary measures, including the use of force, in reply to bombardments against the safe areas by any of the parties or to armed incursion into them or in the event of any deliberate obstruction in or around those areas to the freedom of movement of UNPROFOR or of protected humanitarian convoys."

Paragraph 10 of the resolution authorises

"all necessary measures, through the use of air power, in and around the safe areas in the Republic of Bosnia and Herzegovina, to support UNPROFOR in the performance of its mandate".

**Sir John Stanley:** I am well aware of the UN mandate to which the hon. and learned Gentleman has referred. The mandate may say one thing, but the willingness of the leading members of the UN—in particular the United States—to provide the wherewithal to deliver that mandate is not forthcoming. I am afraid that, as the hon. and learned Gentleman will be aware, that is not the only UN mandate which has not been delivered on the ground.

The second option which we have been discussing today is the withdrawal option and—like some hon. Members who have spoken—I strongly oppose withdrawal at present. I believe that withdrawal would result in a significant increase in numbers losing their lives in Bosnia. It would be a dismal course of events if the parliamentary democracies and those who defend human rights were to withdraw after the appalling naked territorial aggression, ethnic cleansing and mass rape and hostage taking—the things which we have been trying to rid Europe of since the events of 50 years ago. I am glad that we are not doing so, at least for the moment.

We are left with the option of remaining. That is a damage-limitation exercise, and I fully appreciate its difficulties and dangers. But it is the only one of the three choices before us that we can follow at the moment. It has some significant advantages. I am certain that it is the option which will result in the least loss of life, and that is a weighty consideration for all hon. Members.

If we left Bosnia now, it could turn into an uncontrolled inferno, and no one could say how high and wide that fire might go. It is a tinderbox, and it has the capacity to spread. We should also remain in Bosnia because we can continue to protect the humanitarian operation which, coupled with the diplomatic efforts we are making, may provide a route to achieving an agreed settlement. We may not get an agreed settlement, but none of the other options provides the means of achieving, by agreement, a settlement of the conflagration. I welcome the statement that my right hon. Friend the Prime Minister has made today, and I wish the Government all the very best as they discharge their heavy responsibilities.

5.19 pm

**Mr. David Winnick** (Walsall, North): I say straight away that I believe that the air strikes were justified. Like others, I have argued that military action was necessary to stop designated areas being shelled by Serbian commanders. I took the opportunity on a number of occasions in recent weeks to question the Secretary of State for Defence and the Foreign Secretary about action to safeguard designated areas. Having urged air strikes where appropriate, I am hardly in a position now to say that they were wrong. They were right in all the circumstances.

I well recall the outrage felt by the House and the country when towns and cities in Bosnia were continuously shelled by Serbian military forces. That brutal and deliberate killing of civilians could not be allowed to go on. The British people saw on their television screens the killing of men, women and children—some while queuing for bread in Sarajevo. In those circumstances, it was right and proper for the UN to designate safe areas. My right hon. Friend the Leader of the Opposition and the Prime Minister referred to the slaughter that occurred last week, when 71 people were murdered in Tuzla. No distinction was made between military personnel and civilians. No distinction was made, as was previously, between men, women and children.

How could it be wrong to designate safe areas? The right hon. Member for Old Bexley and Sidcup (Sir E. Heath) says that he does not favour air strikes, but I do not recall any criticism at the time by hon. Members over the designation of safe areas. That innovation was unanimously agreed. If it was right to declare safe areas to stop the killing of civilians, what should be done when Serbian military commanders decide to act in defiance of UN Security Council resolutions? What is the use of designating safe areas unless military force is taken to defend them under the appropriate Security Council resolutions? If the Serbs are simply allowed to shell and murder, what credibility do Security Council resolutions and the United Nations have? If safe areas are designated, military action must be taken in the face of clear defiance by forces determined to ignore the resolutions of the international community.

**Mr. Robathan:** I take entirely the hon. Gentleman's point about defending safe areas, but perhaps he will work through the logic of his argument. Would he be happy to go to the funerals of 100 of his constituents killed defending a safe area in a civil war? Would he be prepared to write to their mothers and wives to explain why those soldiers died?

**Mr. Winnick:** I do not see the purpose of the hon. Gentleman's question. I have the deepest sympathy for the relatives of all soldiers killed in Bosnia, particularly British service men and women. I hope that the hon. Gentleman genuinely shares that concern and is not merely making a debating point.

**Mr. Robathan:** Will the hon. Gentleman give way again?

**Mr. Winnick:** No, because many other hon. Members wish to speak.

If the international community took the same line as the hon. Gentleman, there would be no purpose at all to any Security Council resolution, or to the United Nations. Any terrorist could threaten a particular action. When the Iranian embassy in London was besieged, the soldiers responsible for that courageous rescue operation could have been killed. According to the hon. Gentleman—who served in the forces—the British Government should have said, "We cannot send in anyone, be they troops or otherwise."

I do not know why my right hon. Friend the Member for Chesterfield (Mr. Benn) compared the Red Cross, which he said never engaged in any form of military action, with the United Nations. I have the highest regard for the Red Cross, which has for more than a century performed great humanitarian work. Newsreels that I have seen showed Red Cross representatives visiting Nazi concentration camps. A show was put on for them, but the Red Cross had no authority. The moment its representatives went away murders continued, of course. If one argues that the UN, regardless of any outrages, should serve as nothing more than the Red Cross, there is no need for the UN. We could have an enlarged Red Cross instead.

Apart from outrages in designated safe areas, there is also the ethnic cleansing to which hon. Members referred, atrocities and rapes. As in all military conflicts, the Bosnian side no doubt committed crimes, which I do not minimise, defend or otherwise act as an apologist for. However, can anyone doubt that the worst atrocities and ethnic cleansing were committed by the Serbian military, in ways that shock us all—perhaps even more as we celebrate the 50th anniversary of the end of the last world war? Was not that about ethnic cleansing—an attempt by the Nazis to do away with people whom they thought inferior? Bosnia is on a much smaller scale fortunately, but that is no consolation for the victims.

I cannot understand those who say, "We are concerned but we do not want action taken." They are wrong, and I hope that the House will, by an overwhelming majority, demonstrate its support for the action of the international community, including this country.

Some people argue that we should withdraw completely from Bosnia, but they are very much in the minority. Other matters aside, the humanitarian work undertaken in Bosnia will be an everlasting tribute to the international community, United Nations and this country. So much has been done to provide food and water, without which people would have starved. Such basic humanitarian work is what the international community and the United Nations are also about.

Some Conservative Members—they may not be present today—have never been keen on the United Nations but I do not share that view. In the Falklands conflict and in the Gulf war, I argued that aggression had to be combated. I am a firm supporter of the United Nations and of international law. I am the first to criticise the British Government when they act in defiance of the UN, as they did over Suez. In 1956, I demonstrated against their actions, and I am proud to have done so. I believe that the United Nations is necessary and I want to see it supported all the way.

The line that was put forward, in an intervention in the Prime Minister's speech, by the hon. Member for Billericay (Mrs. Gorman) was absolutely shameful. If ever there was an illustration of wishing to give in to terrorism, that was it. What could be more shameful than to say to the Serbians, "You have taken our hostages. That is wrong, but we will make a deal with you and do whatever you want."? Surely, hon. Members, like the hon. Lady, time and again in other circumstances would have condemned terrorism, and what has happened over the taking of hostages, the taking of British soldiers, is indeed an act of outright terrorism and should be recognised as

such. There can be no dirty deals or appeasement. I am pleased that hon. Members on both Front Benches fully agree on that.

I am not one of those—if there are any, and I doubt whether there are—who want to see us drifting into a wider war. Far from it. All of us, passionately, I am sure, want to see peace restored in the former Yugoslavia, and certainly in Bosnia. We want to see a political solution, as that is necessary. The Muslims are obviously not going to get all that they want. No one has ever suggested that they are likely to do so. There has to be give and take, and at the end of it all, when the conflict comes to an end, once again, as in all previous times, people from all kinds of ethnic backgrounds—Muslims, Serbs, Jews and the rest—can live together in peace in Bosnia. Every attempt that can be made to isolate the Bosnian Serbs by getting Belgrade to recognise Bosnia is, of course, to be welcomed. I hope that that will achieve its purpose.

As always in these debates, one takes a particular position, and most of us believe—I believe that it will be demonstrated in the vote tonight—that there is overwhelming support against terrorism and against the kinds of outrages and atrocities that have been committed by the Serbs in Bosnia. There will be a recognition by the overwhelming majority of us that international law should be upheld. I believe that, at 10 o'clock tonight, we will not only have a large majority but that we will be right, politically and morally.

5.31 pm

**Sir Nicholas Bonsor** (Upminster): It seems to me that the House is debating two matters today, the first and most immediate of which is the release of the hostages. The second is the much broader issue of whether our troops should be in Bosnia at all.

With regard to the first of those two matters, quite clearly the whole House agrees that we must take every step, whether it is diplomatic or military, to secure the release of our hostages and to ensure that no more such hostages can be taken. I appreciate absolutely the reluctance of my right hon. Friend the Prime Minister to spell out to the House in detail what may be done in that regard and I am sure that the House will back whatever steps the Government find necessary to secure that release. My right hon. and learned Friend the Secretary of State for Defence has told the Bosnian Serb leadership in no uncertain terms that their actions have put them beyond the pale in terms of international acceptance. That must be right.

So, in the short term, I am sure that we must concentrate on taking all steps necessary to secure the release of our troops, of the 34 British and the 350 or so overall who are being illegally held by the Bosnian Serbs in this conflict. I hope also that we will take the steps that some of my right hon. and hon. Friends have specified to ensure that no further hostages are taken. I believe that that will mean securing our positions in a narrower area, that we will have to withdraw, perhaps, from some of the positions where our people are isolated and that we will have to consolidate the position of all United Nations personnel so that they cannot be taken.

I believe also that the rules of engagement must be broadened. It is not acceptable to require the troops to surrender if no shots are fired at them, which I believe to be the case at the moment. The rule that is preventing

*[Sir Nicholas Bonsor]*

them from firing first if necessary to secure their own safety must be reviewed. I believe that the French Government have called for that; indeed, I believe that they have issued specific instructions to their troops to that effect. I hope that the British Government will follow suit and that my right hon. and learned Friend the Secretary of State for Defence, in summing up the debate, will be able to tell us that the rules of engagement are adequate to prevent further hostages being taken.

I now turn briefly to the broader matters, which have already been extensively covered. I welcomed in particular the speech by the hon. Member for East Lothian (Mr. Home Robertson), who has not only been out to Bosnia twice with the Select Committee but driven a lorryload of humanitarian aid through that country. His knowledge and experience there are invaluable to the Committee and to the whole House. He specified—I was extremely glad to hear it—the way in which UNPROFOR has played such a splendid role in Bosnia-Herzegovina. There has been some unfortunate speculation in the more ignorant parts of the press to the effect that our soldiers out there are wasting their time and that their lives are put at risk for no good purpose. Nothing could be further from the truth.

First, were our troops not in Bosnia-Herzegovina, the atrocities that occurred at the beginning of this appalling conflict would undoubtedly be continuing to this day. Because of the presence of United Nations observers, because of the humanitarian aid, because of the presence of the troops on the ground, those atrocities are being largely, although sadly not entirely, curtailed.

Secondly, if the British troops in particular were not there, and if were no military cover in the British sector, I have no doubt whatever that the Muslims and the Croats, who are enjoying a tenuous peace between the two of them, would start fighting within a week. What we saw as a Committee when we went out there was the officers of the British Army, from platoon commanders, sometimes non-commissioned officers as well, right up to the brigadier, having to bash their heads together on a weekly basis, with the Muslim and Croat leaders, to prevent the outbreak of further conflict and the breakdown of the peace between the Muslim and Croat communities. It is bad enough having a war between the Serbian side and the alliance, but, if there were a three-way conflict, I do not believe that it would be possible for very long to maintain the UN presence there or to stop a renewal of the kind of atrocities that we have seen in the past.

Thirdly, the work being done by the Overseas Development Administration, as well as by the humanitarian agencies, is extraordinarily successful. When the Committee was in Zenica, we saw the work that was being done there. Without the presence of the British engineers—I think that there were 12—none of the water supplies would have been running; no water, except for that from the deepest wells, would have been safe for the population to drink, and the electricity supply would have been cut off and remained so. In fact, because of the advice that we are able to give and the aid that we are putting in, that city, and many others, too, are enjoying a comparatively civilised existence with all the necessary basic supplies for the continuation of life.

It would be folly, in my view, for the House to vote in such a way or, indeed, to venture a view that reflected other than support for the Government's line in staying in Bosnia-Herzegovina as long as that is possible without putting British lives at intolerable risk. At the moment, I see no reason to assume that that stage has been reached. I am delighted that we are reinforcing our Army there to ensure that we can defend our own troops, that we can maintain a position in that country and that we will not be forced out by the terrorism in which, currently, the Bosnian Serbs are indulging.

I now deal briefly with some of the other objectives that have been set out by the Government for our existence in Bosnia-Herzegovina. First, on containment, I profoundly disagreed with my right hon. Friend the Member for Old Bexley and Sidcup (Sir E. Heath), who, sadly, is not in his place. I do not think that he is right in his rather optimistic assessment on the likelihood of the war escalating if we cannot contain it within Bosnia. I believe that it would escalate, that we would have the domino effect, which has occurred in similar conflicts. Albania, Kosovo, Macedonia, Greece and Turkey would, over a period, be drawn inexorably into this conflict and go to a state of war. My right hon. Friend said that Greece and Turkey have enough on their hands. Well, of course, they have, but the trouble is that Greece and Turkey find it very difficult to co-exist at all. The tension between them last November almost brought them to war. Were there to be other such sources of conflict between them, that would make it more, rather than less, likely that such a conflict would occur. The consequences for NATO would be catastrophic. I am sure that one of the dangers that we are likely to face in the next decade or so will be some aggressive act from some country in the middle east. If eastern Europe were not part of NATO—if it were not going to be part of our defensive mechanism—the whole of Europe would be put at risk by that fact.

I hope that we shall be able to stay in Bosnia-Herzegovina as long as is necessary to ensure that the lid is kept on this appalling conflict.

5.39 pm

**Mr. John D. Taylor** (Strangford): In Northern Ireland, people have taken and continue to take a considerable interest in the affairs of Bosnia. There are many reasons for that. First, we live on an island, part of which was able to break away in 1921 and exercise its right of self-determination—something that we understand. Secondly, we live in a society that has grievously suffered from ethnic, cultural and religious divisions and, therefore, we recognise perhaps more clearly than others the kind of problems that exist in the Balkans. Thirdly, when our own Army went to Bosnia in 1992, the first two regiments to go were the Cheshires, and the Royal Irish Regiment from Northern Ireland.

During my 30 years as a Member of Parliament I have attended more funerals of service men than any other Member present in the House today. Those funerals were always very sad occasions, but people could understand why the events leading to them had taken place. As a Member of Parliament representing a Northern Ireland constituency, I must say that, when the Royal Irish Regiment was in Bosnia, I dreaded more than ever the prospect of soldiers being brought back dead to Belfast and to the constituency of Strangford. That was because I knew that, even after 30 years of attending funerals, I would find it extremely hard to explain why lives had been lost in Bosnia. If that begins to happen in other parts of the United Kingdom, those hon. Members who are so keen to see the situation develop in one way or another may be given pause for thought. The leader of the Liberal Democrats, for example, said that we should take sides. In the United Kingdom, that means more deaths. [HON. MEMBERS: "He didn't say that."] Oh, he did; read *Hansard*. I noted it down.

First, I want to say how much I sympathise with hon. Members on both sides of the House who represent Welsh constituencies. We are very conscious of the problems facing families in Wales, and all of us urge the Bosnian Serbs to behave properly and in the context of international law and to release the hostages at once. There should be no hostages from Wales or any other part of the world in Bosnia.

I condemn without hesitation the bombing of the Serbs. I know that it was American inspired and I think that it was politically, militarily and diplomatically a disaster: militarily, it did not succeed; politically, it strengthened the ill will that exists in Serbia itself; and, diplomatically, it upset the Russians. Above all, we should understand that—it is perhaps also because I come from Ireland that I know this—one cannot bomb nationalism out of a people, whether they are Serbs, or in Ireland, or Chechens. We condemned the Russians for bombing the people in Chechnya, yet now the Americans urge the bombing of the people in Serbia. It is incredible. There is no consistency in the American approach towards the bombing.

The basic problem is that we were bounced into the recognition of Bosnia. Yesterday, when the Leader of the Opposition—who made an excellent speech today—was in Germany, Chancellor Kohl said that this was one occasion on which Europe should act together. Of course, he is right, but we must recall what happened. Three or four years ago, the European Union Foreign Ministers decided to take no action. Within two weeks, Germany pre-empted everyone and unilaterally decided to recognise Bosnia, thereby bouncing not only the rest of Europe but, a day later, the Americans, into recognising that state. That is the fundamental problem from which the present difficulties have developed, because Bosnia is a failed entity, which had and still has little cohesion as a nation state. We cannot hold Bosnia together by force. That is one of the problems that we must accept. The history of the recent atrocities perpetrated among the various ethnic groups in Bosnia makes a settlement within that state almost impossible.

Two options have been suggested today. One is that we should walk away. There is no way in which we can walk away from the situation in Bosnia today. If we did so, the conflict would develop into a world war. Equally, the option suggested by the Liberal Democrats would lead to a world war, because if we take sides—I am not too sure which side the Liberal Democrats wanted us to take— Turkey would take sides and Greece would take sides. Perhaps even Germany and Russia would take sides. The conflict would develop. So we cannot take sides either.

The third option is the diplomatic way forward. We have to keep our existing troops there—I hope that no more troops will be going in, as we are slowly being sucked further into the conflict—and move as quickly as possible with diplomacy. But what kind of diplomacy should we adopt? That is the question on which I disagree with the Prime Minister. If the recognition of Croatia, Bosnia and the other states of the former Yugoslavia was wrong—if we were bounced into it—why is that now the basis on which we foresee a settlement being made? Recognition was wrong then and it is still wrong today.

The Government should take the initiative to bring the various parties together under the auspices of the contact group. Let us face reality: Bosnia is a failed entity; new international boundaries must be agreed within the former states of Yugoslavia; and those boundaries must be related to the ethnic groups that live in those areas. Only when people support the new boundaries will we finally get a settlement. If the Government think that the way forward is to maintain the present boundaries of Bosnia and to get Serbia to recognise Bosnia, and that that in itself would lead to a settlement, they are badly mistaken. Recognition by Serbia of the present boundaries of Bosnia is not in itself a settlement. A settlement can be achieved only when the people living there identify with its terms. For that reason—because I disagree with the Government's diplomatic approach—if there is a Division tonight, I cannot support the Government.

5.48 pm

**Sir Patrick Cormack** (Staffordshire, South): I could not disagree more with the concluding words of the right hon. Member for Strangford (Mr. Taylor). I commend to him the history of Bosnia by Noel Malcolm— recommended by others this afternoon—because it clearly demonstrates that what he was saying about Bosnia is simply just not so. If the right hon. Gentleman looks back—he will not have to look back far—to the time before this awful war broke out, he will see that Bosnia was, indeed, an entity. That has been said this afternoon and was said three weeks ago when we debated Bosnia. Bosnia was a shining example to people throughout the world of communities living together. The right hon. Gentleman can shake his head, but the fact is that there were more disparate religious buildings—synagogues, Orthodox churches, Roman Catholic churches and mosques—in Bosnia, and particularly in Sarajevo, than in any other comparable area of Europe. People lived together and intermarried. Bosnia was an entity, and to deny that is to fly in the face of the facts. I do not want to digress too far in that direction because I want to refer to what has been said by the Prime Minister and others this afternoon.

A number of hon. Members have referred in passing to the debate on the Falklands. Anyone who was here on that Saturday morning, when the House was absolutely crammed, could not help but note a contrast with the attendance today. That is a pity. The difference may be symptomatic of the life that has gone out of the Chamber over the past few years—much to my regret. I shall merely say that I consider the issue that we are debating now involves far greater potential damage to the world than the Falklands conflict. I entirely supported what the Government did then, but this issue—which, if improperly handled, could lead to a major European war—is of infinitely greater significance, and involves an infinitely greater danger.

I strongly support the Government's clear, firm and decisive response to one of the most despicable acts of international terrorism that we have seen in recent years— for the taking of the hostages is precisely that. My right hon. Friend the Prime Minister made an admirable speech.

*[Sir Patrick Cormack]*

as did the Leader of the Opposition. It was good to see the House united through its two principal Members. I shall be very sorry if there is a Division tonight, and I hope that, if there is, an insignificant number will go into the No Lobby. A Division of any strength would send out all the wrong signals; at a time when members of the armed forces are in grave danger, they deserve the united backing of the House of Commons.

The policy pursued by the international community in Bosnia over the past three years has been bedevilled by lack of the clarity, firmness and decisiveness that we have seen in the past few days. That has been caused by an unwillingness to acknowledge the consequences of recognising Bosnia as an independent state, and by a compulsion to behave as a neutral between victim and aggressor—between those who would protect their nationhood and those who would destroy it.

We must recognise that Bosnia is a state. Whatever the right hon. Member for Strangford and others may think, it has a seat at the United Nations; its Foreign Minister, who was so tragically killed the other day—a brilliant man whom some of us had the honour of knowing—was here just three short weeks ago, representing his country at the VE day celebrations. I have been privileged to take part in a number of discussions between my right hon. Friend the Foreign Secretary and Haris Silajdzic when he was Bosnia's Foreign Minister—he is now its Prime Minister—and there was never any doubt that my right hon. Friend received him not only with the utmost courtesy, as one would expect, but as a fellow Foreign Minister.

Bosnia is a state, and we must recognise that what has gone on over the past three years is an attempt to destroy that state. Under the charter of the United Nations, any state that is threatened with destruction has the right to defend itself or to be defended.

I do not want to digress at length on the reasons for or against the arms embargo, save to say that an acute moral dilemma is involved in not giving a state the means to defend itself while also not coming to its defence. Certain facts stand out in the unhappy history of the past three years. One is that the prime responsibility for the war rests with the Serbs: initially, those in Belgrade, who were bent on creating a greater Serbia—that is why some of us get cross when this is described as an ordinary civil war—and then, increasingly, those Serbs in Bosnia whose aim has been to smash and shatter a tolerant, civilised society.

I say "those Serbs in Bosnia" deliberately. One of the myths that has bedevilled this whole saga—I referred to it in a speech three weeks ago—is the myth that all Serbs in Bosnia support Radovan Karadzic. They emphatically do not. Only this morning I received a copy of the declaration of the Serb Council, which gives unequivocal support to the concept of a multi-ethnic Bosnia, repudiates the use of force by Karadzic and his henchmen and castigates, in the most damning language, the atrocities perpetrated in Bosnia. I have no means of knowing, any more than any other hon. Member, precisely what support each group of Serbs has; but the statement that the Council has the support of 200,000 Serbs currently in Bosnia has never been convincingly challenged. Indeed, it is unlikely that Mr. Karadzic and his henchmen represent more than a maximum of 50 per cent. of the Serbs in Bosnia.

In pursuing their aims, the Karadzic Serbs, as I shall call them—those who follow him and General Mladic—have perpetrated some of the most appalling atrocities suffered in Europe during this century: atrocities that compare in horror with some of the worst atrocities of the last war. I do not for a moment pretend that no atrocities have been committed by the Bosnian Government forces—in a war, terrible things happen on each side—but what is not in doubt is that the vast majority of the horror and mayhem has been caused by Karadzic's Serbs, those same people who now seek to hold the international community to ransom.

If we are to talk of taking sides, let me ask who has taken sides. It is Karadzic and his men who have proclaimed the United Nations force to be an enemy. I shall not describe—as have many hon. Members on both sides of the House—UNPROFOR's splendid achievements in appallingly difficult circumstances; but the branding of those who have brought help and succour to the young, the old and the sick as "the enemy" shows the mentality of Karadzic and his men.

I will not forget, and I am sure that no other hon. Member who saw them will forget, those pictures of French and other soldiers chained to targets and the parading of the so-called prisoners of war before the television cameras. In the light of those latest atrocities, it is essential for the response of the international community to be cool, calm and utterly determined. Karadzic must be in no doubt that, unless he unconditionally releases the hostages and ceases to slaughter innocent civilians—as he did in Tuzla last week—he cannot hope for a place at any conference table. That message must be spelt out clearly by the contact group, at Head of Government level.

President Milosevic—who, properly, has been mentioned several times this afternoon—should be in no doubt that, unless he reinforces that message by recognising Bosnia-Herzegovina, there can be no relaxation of sanctions against Serbia. The honouring of those preconditions will provide an opportunity for a proper peace conference, and an opportunity for Serbia to begin to rebuild itself—for no one should doubt that, although the sufferings of those living in Serbia pale into insignificance beside the sufferings of those living in Bosnia, the people of Serbia have suffered greatly over the past three years.

Unless and until Karadzic complies, the United Nations must strengthen and regroup its forces and it must redefine its mandate—although it is perhaps appropriate to remember that it is Karadzic who has prevented it from fulfilling its existing mandate. In a very well-informed speech, the hon. Member for East Lothian (Mr. Home Robertson) referred to the way in which individual Serb soldiers were able to prevent the distribution of vital medical supplies from the airport in Sarajevo. Serb soldiers have prevented the airport from functioning on many occasions, they have turned back convoys and dealt out all sorts of humiliations to the United Nations. It is crucial that British, French and other soldiers who are serving with such distinction in the face of great difficulty should never again be denied the chance or the means of taking proper anticipatory or retaliatory action if they or any civilian targets are at risk.

For their part, the Bosnian Government must be asked to place all their heavy weaponry under United Nations control. They have shown their willingness to do so in the past, however they can comply only if they are secure in the knowledge that civilian targets will be safe from attack and that we will never again see the sorts of scenes that disfigured our television screens on the weekend when 70 young people, including a child of three, were blown to smithereens during the shelling of Tuzla. They wanted nothing more than to enjoy a quiet coffee and a stroll on a spring evening.

Unity and cohesion on the part of the international community, and particularly among the nations of the contact group, are crucial. I believe that the Prime Minister and the Government have taken a commendable lead this week. The Prime Minister told us this afternoon that he has had individual contact with the President of Russia, the President of the United States, the President of France and the Chancellor of Germany. That is absolutely splendid and as it should be. However, I hope that he will also consider a request that I have made previously and that I do not apologise for making again today. I hope that the Prime Minister will consider calling for a meeting of the contact group at Head of Government level in order to demonstrate our unity and resolve to the whole international community. It would be entirely appropriate to invite President Milosevic to such a meeting at the right time.

If we can unite in support of the new clarity, firmness and resolve that have been demonstrated in the past few days, I think that the horrors of the past three years and the suffering of the people of Bosnia and of Serbia and Croatia may come to an end. If the will weakens, if the resolve crumples and if the unity dissolves, that will be a prelude to even greater horrors—not the least of which would be the humiliation and demonstration of the incompetence of the international community. We cannot afford to let that happen. I congratulate the Prime Minister and the Government on what they have done and I urge them to keep up their excellent work.

6.3 pm

**Mr. Tam Dalyell** (Linlithgow): I am afraid that many of the speeches that we have heard in the past three and a half hours have been laced with wishful thinking. Therefore, it is with a heavy heart that I shall vote against the Government—and indeed against my own Front Bench—at the end of the debate. I should like to put a number of questions to the Government.

**Mr. D. N. Campbell-Savours** (Workington): On the Adjournment.

**Mr. Dalyell:** Yes.

The Prime Minister gave way most courteously during his opening remarks, but I fear that he did not listen carefully to the question that was put to him. That question was: did the Russians agree, or were they consulted, about the ultimatum, let alone the actual use of air strikes? As the former Secretary of State for Defence, the right hon. Member for Bridgwater (Mr. King) said, unless we maintain the closest relations with the Russians, we have no hope of influencing the Serbs.

The Secretary of State may like to answer that question now or in winding up. Were the Russians consulted? I think that the House should be told whether they were consulted and whether they agreed to the air strikes.

**The Secretary of State for Defence (Mr. Malcolm Rifkind):** I think that the hon. Member heard my right

hon. Friend the Prime Minister answer that question quite unambiguously. According to the rules under which the United Nations command operates, the Russian, French, British and American Governments are not consulted. The United Nations commanders in the field make a recommendation as they see fit in favour of an air strike. If Mr. Akashi, the Secretary-General's representative, agrees with it, the request is put to the Commander-in-Chief South—who is a NATO commander—who then initiates the use of air power. That is the way that the procedure has always worked, and that is the way it worked on this occasion.

**Mr. Dalyell:** The Secretary of State is doubtless correct about the procedure; I would not argue with him about the legal small print. However, it is mad beyond measure not at least to seek the agreement of the Russians on a matter about which we know they have the strongest views, even though those views may be unpalatable. Whatever the legal aspects may be, the political judgment exercised on that occasion was absolutely deplorable. Therefore, I am very unhappy with both the Secretary of State's courteous answer and the Prime Minister's response this afternoon.

I turn to a subject that I know is very unpleasant. The Prime Minister has talked both in the House and outside about Serbia becoming a pariah because it has taken hostages. My right hon. Friend the Leader of the Opposition described its behaviour as "barbarous", and an act of terrorism. That is correct, yet perhaps there is another side to the story.

We should not be personal in the debate, but I belong to a generation—I am rather older than most hon. Members—who did national service. During my national service, I served in a tank crew with the Royal Scots Greys, as they then were, or the Dragoon Guards as they are now known, and whose tie I proudly wear. The blunt fact is that my contemporaries and I faced the possibility of being "brewed up" in a tank; that was the situation at the time of the Yalu river crisis.

The thought that one may be destroyed in the most dramatic circumstances really concentrates one's mind. I am not claiming any kind of bravery; I am simply making the point that, if one is faced with the threat of missile attack, one does desperate things in the name of self-preservation.

If the right hon. Member for Old Bexley and Sidcup (Sir E. Heath) had been in the Chamber, I would have reminded him that he and I and my right hon. Friend the Member for Chesterfield (Mr. Benn) have visited Baghdad in different circumstances, and we have witnessed the results of modern missile warfare. It is absolutely traumatic. People who are faced with that kind of attack—like it or not, that was the threat—will act in what we might regard as a very uncivilised way. They will take hostages.

Bluntly, I have to tell the Prime Minister and my right hon. Friend the Leader of the Opposition that all their lecturing and haranguing of the Serbs will not make much difference to the Serbs actually on the spot, who are threatened with missile attack. Is it the loss of face? Why do we not simply say that there will be no more such attacks, which were entirely American-initiated?

I share the resentment expressed by some right hon. and hon. Members, mostly Conservative Members sitting below the Gangway, that Americans such as Madeleine

[*Mr. Dalyell*]

Albright applied so much pressure for missile attacks from the air when we have troops on the ground and the Americans do not. I repeat the question asked by my right hon. Friend the Member for Chesterfield, which has not been answered. Can we continue the threat of aerial attack and at the same time have troops carrying out what is supposed to be a humanitarian mission? We cannot have both. It has to be one or the other. It is make-believe and unreal to think that it can conceivably be both.

In his reply to the debate, the Secretary of State for Defence will have to provide some very good reasons for the threat of aerial attack which, as has been said by hon. Members on both sides of the House, including my right hon. Friend the Member for Strangford (Mr. Taylor), has created considerable doubt. Will we do it again, and if not, had we not better say so?

I am conscious that there is an ethnic problem. Political friends of many years have asked me, "How can you do anything that seems to endorse ethnic cleansing?" But is it ethnic cleansing? Are we quite sure about that, because the history of those particular Muslims is not ethnic? I return for a moment to Baghdad, where the Sunnis and Shi-ites, when asking about Bosnia, say, "These particular Muslims are not quite our kind of Muslims." They are the grandchildren and great-grandchildren of Serbs who tried to ingratiate themselves with the Ottoman Turks by embracing the religion of the Ottoman Turks, often in order to gain position in the Turkish empire and get some kudos from Constantinople, or Istanbul.

I am against massacres, but we should not think that it is straightforward ethnic cleansing. They are interreacting tribal affairs and ancient rivalries. We have to ask ourselves whether the British Army can sort them out. I have the gravest doubts about that.

We are all under a curfew, so I shall be brief. The hon. Member for Staffordshire, South (Sir P. Cormack) led an all-party group to Greece and Macedonia. I hasten to say that we paid for ourselves, so it was not a freebie. In Greek Macedonia—I cannot speak for Yugoslav Macedonia—the general feeling was that there should be no military intervention, so there are differing views in that part of the world. I do not say that there is not a problem of extension to Macedonia and Kosovo, but a large section of the population involved takes a different view.

Those of us who have been in danger and been all right because it did not happen know that the troops are entitled to some cover. What cover is being given to those who are being sent in? As I understand it, there should be heavy artillery cover if not tank cover, but it is not tank country.

The Secretary of State for Defence owes it to the House to be specific about what cover is being provided. If it is essential to have massive cover if it were a matter of withdrawing, why cannot some agreement be reached with people who ostensibly want us to go? I do not see it as an overriding problem.

What is an overriding problem, however, is that it is part of history that Tito's deterrent to Stalin was not atomic bombs, let alone hydrogen bombs; it was the most powerfully trained guerrilla army ever. The hon. Member for Dorset, West (Sir J. Spicer) will remember that our colleague Julian Amery, who knew a good deal of this, would go into detail about the strength, determination and training of Yugoslavian soldiers. We are coping with their sons if not themselves, trained in the tradition of guerrilla warfare.

It is a formidable deterrent. I understand that it was such a deterrent that Marshals Zhukov and Timoshenko told Stalin that on no account should the Red Army take on those people, although in the eyes of Moscow they were guilty of a deviant variety of communism.

I conclude that, unless we are prepared to impose a solution—and it will involve more than the 37 German Panzer divisions that the Yugoslavs tied down during the war—we are in no position for posturing. Whether or not we lose face, we have to talk seriously. If our priority is to rescue the hostages—and that should be one of our top priorities—for heaven's sake let us get around a table, embarrassing as it may be, and talk, talk, talk. We should start by making it clear that never again will there be such a strike as took place so catastrophically and has been the genesis of the debate.

6.17 pm

**Sir Peter Tapsell** (East Lindsey): It is a demonstration of the extent to which this debate has transcended normal party political divisions that I find myself in so much agreement with much of the speeches of the right hon. Member for Strangford (Mr. Taylor), the right hon. Member for Chesterfield (Mr. Benn) and the hon. Member for Linlithgow (Mr. Dalyell).

I was one of those who from the beginning argued against sending troops into Bosnia. Nothing that has happened in recent days has in any way surprised me, because it is exactly what would obviously happen once we had sent in troops. The trouble with politics, as with life generally, is that, however far-sighted one may have been in past years about possible future dangers, one has always to live with the circumstances as they are and not as they might have been had wiser counsels been followed. That is the position we are in now.

The right hon. Member for Strangford was the only one so far in the debate to make so powerfully one of the most important points of all. What will the attitude of the British people who sent us here be when, as may only too possibly happen in future weeks and months, considerable numbers of British troops are sent home in body bags for burial?

The right hon. Member for Strangford told us about his tragic first-hand memories of his Northern Ireland constituency and the service funerals that he had attended. I agree with his judgment that the British people were prepared to accept that we had to fight for the Falkland islands. I know that my constituents are prepared to fight for the union of Northern Ireland and the rest of Britain and, as a Unionist, I am passionately committed to that. However, I have represented my constituents for over 30 years and I have lived in my constituency for all that time, and I doubt whether they will be prepared to see their sons die to protect the people of Bosnia.

My hon. Friend the Member for Staffordshire, South (Sir P. Cormack) was right to paint the appalling picture of what life is like in Bosnia. As individuals, we would all like to be able to stop those appalling atrocities. However, when a boy in their street is killed trying to stop these savages, who have been killing each other in this way for centuries, I believe that British public opinion will quickly turn against the operation.

**Mr. David Wilshire** (Spelthorne): Will it come as any surprise to my hon. Friend to learn that not a single one of my constituents has written to me, telephoned me, come to my surgery or tracked me down in the street to say that they support sending troops to Bosnia, either at the beginning or now—or, I suspect, like my hon. Friend, in the future? Does that surprise my hon. Friend, or does it reinforce his argument?

**Sir Peter Tapsell:** It does not surprise me at all. I have not yet met a constituent of mine in Lincolnshire who is in favour of sending more troops to Bosnia. In my view, the overwhelming majority want the whole lot of them brought out now. That is what they tell me.

**Sir Patrick Cormack:** How does my hon. Friend think his constituents or anybody else's constituents would feel if, as my right hon. Friend the Prime Minister mentioned in his admirable speech, we were landed with a major European war? How would they feel if NATO partners such as Greece and Turkey were fighting each other and we faced the destabilisation of our entire continent and really were drawn into a war? Surely they would think that we had failed to give a lead.

**Sir Peter Tapsell:** Our right hon. Friend the Member for Old Bexley and Sidcup (Sir E. Heath) has more experience in these matters than anybody else in the House. He said that talk of a great increase in the number of wars in the vicinity was greatly exaggerated. Nobody can be certain about the future.

The Leader of the Opposition made an admirable speech, and he mentioned a country that I have known for many years—Turkey. My view—I share the view of my former leader, the right hon. Member for Old Bexley and Sidcup—is that it is most improbable that, at this stage in its history, Turkey would allow itself to be drawn into a Balkan war. It would know for certain that all hope of joining the European Union for the foreseeable future would disappear at once. Knowing some Turkish Ministers as I have, I simply do not believe that they would contemplate that.

We are talking about imponderables, and of course it is a matter of judgment. If my hon. Friend the Member for Staffordshire, South was right and our withdrawal from Bosnia led to the 1914 scenario starting over again, we would be blamed. But we are sent here to exercise our judgment.

As the hon. Member for Linlithgow mentioned, in his speech and in his question to the Prime Minister, if we want to avoid the 1914 scenario, our top priority should be to work closely with Russia. It seems astonishing that we treat the Russians so casually in all this. If there is one overseas subject on which the Russians feel passionately, it is the protection of Serbia.

The reply that my right hon. and learned Friend the Secretary of State for Defence gave a moment ago to the hon. Member for Linlithgow was admirably legalistic, but do Mr. Yeltsin and Mr. Zhirinovsky and people like that read the small print, or do they hear that Americans, against the advice of most of us, have been bombing their Serbian friends without them being told in advance? I do not think that there will be much support for that in Russia.

The hon. Member for Linlithgow and the right hon. Member for Strangford were right to draw attention to the fact that it is the older Members of the House, who have served in the armed forces, who are most concerned about all this. There is a tendency for people who have never been in the armed services to have a slightly glamorous version of what military life is like.

If one has been in the armed services, one knows that there is nothing glamorous about much of it, and that getting hurt or the prospect of getting hurt concentrates the mind considerably. It is people such as my right hon. Friend the Member for Old Bexley and Sidcup and the right hon. Member for Chesterfield, who served in the war, who properly have these great anxieties.

My right hon. Friend the Member for Guildford (Mr. Howell) said that there was no point in looking back over how we reached this point. With great respect to him— and I agree with much of what he said—there is some point in looking back. It is only by doing so that we can learn how we have got to where we are now, and perhaps learn some lessons about where we want to go in the future, and where we do not want to finish.

I wish to give my right hon. and learned Friend the Secretary of State for Defence and my other hon. Friends on the Front Bench three recollections. On 29 June 1992, I said:

"we can hope to restore order in that part of the world"—

that is, Bosnia—

"only with a massive military intervention, which would inevitably lead to large-scale casualties."—[*Official Report*, 29 June 1992; Vol. 210, c. 591.]

In reply, my right hon. Friend the Prime Minister said that the main purpose of the very limited military intervention planned would be to escort Red Cross convoys to Sarajevo.

On 14 January 1993, in a question to my right hon. and learned Friend the Secretary of State for Defence, I told him that, when I first visited the Vietnam war zone, there were 600 American advisers in civilian clothes, but that, on my last visit to that area, there were 500,000 American troops. My right hon. and learned Friend told me that he could reassure me that only the Cheshire Regiment was in Bosnia, and that

"today's announcement will mean that about 89 additional personnel will go into Bosnia. Those are the only people who will enter the former Yugoslavia."—[*Official Report*, 14 January 1993; Vol. 216, c. 1061.]

On 10 March 1994, when it was announced that we were sending a second battalion to Bosnia, I told my right hon. and learned Friend the Secretary of State for Defence that I viewed

"with a sickening sense of the inevitable the slowly unfolding fact that, as we all predicted, we are moving on from protecting the convoys to maintaining the peace. In those circumstances, why are we sending only one battalion, when five divisions will eventually prove insufficient?"

My right hon. and learned Friend said:

"about 30 members of the United Nations are now making some contribution of troops in former Yugoslavia."—[*Official Report*, 10 March 1994; Vol. 239, c. 405.]

He said that, consequently, we had to increase our contribution substantially.

As has been pointed out, Britain and France have made by far the most significant contribution of ground troops in the most dangerous areas, and we are now moving towards a total commitment of British troops approaching

[*Sir Peter Tapsell*]

12,000 in number. So much for the Secretary of State's reassurance about only 89 extra men, as recently as January 1993.

That is a picture of the classic, deadly escalation that was certain to happen from the moment that we sent our first troops—as I said at the time, backed by several hon. Members with military service. Nor will it stop there. Just as we are now sending in another 6,000 troops to protect the 6,000 already there, we will soon be told that we must send another 6,000 to protect that 6,000—ad Vietnam.

The first Candian United Nations commander in Bosnia, General Macdonald—

**Mr. Home Robertson:** General Mackenzie—get something right.

**Sir Peter Tapsell:** I am only half Scot.

That first UN commander, on giving up his command, said that it would take 250,000 troops to maintain anything approaching peace in the area, and that, as soon as those troops were withdrawn, the situation would quickly become as bad as it was before. That is the reality. In my experience, most people outside this House clearly understand that, so let us bring some hard-headed realism into the practical conduct of our Balkan policy.

No important British national self-interest is involved. That is the basic point. The interest is that of common humanity, which is an immensely important point, as I accepted when I intervened in the speech of the Leader of the Opposition. However, as I said then, if humanity is to be the determining factor in British foreign policy, why are not we sending troops to Angola, Rwanda, Cambodia, Kurdistan, Tibet and Chechnya, to mention just a few? What is so very different about Bosnia?

**Sir Patrick Cormack:** It is in Europe.

**Sir Peter Tapsell:** Yes, Bosnia is at the heart of Europe, but I suspect that many people throughout the world will say that what is so very different about Bosnia is that its people are white—[*Interruption.*] That is what they will say. There is another reason, apart from being in Europe, that makes Bosnia so different—it is that, admirable and brave a woman though she is, it is less than satisfactory to have our foreign policy directed by Miss Kate Adie—[*Interruption.*] It is a relevant point.

When the television cameras suddenly moved to Rwanda, people stopped writing to me about Bosnia and wrote about Rwanda instead. Public opinion is important, but we must be careful not to allow vital British foreign policy to be dominated by where the television cameras happen to be.

Some of my hon. Friends seem to think that my remarks are somewhat frivolous and inappropriate on such a serious occasion,, but I draw the attention of the House to the fact that the television pictures of one lorry bomb exploding in the marine barracks in Beirut brought about an immediate and complete change in American policy towards the Lebanon. It took television pictures of just one airman being lynched by an Arab mob to change American policy in Somalia. Are we so sure that our Ministers will be made of sterner stuff when our television cameras are concentrating on dead British soldiers?

It is no wonder that the American President—far more interested in New Hampshire than in old Sarajevo—advocates a Balkan policy of bombing Serbia back into the stone age from a very safe height. He will not put any American boys on the ground, and who can blame him for that? Only yesterday, the American Secretary of State said that there was no issue of sufficient strategic importance in Bosnia to justify the commitment of American ground forces. He was right—and what is true for America is true for both Britain and France.

The war cannot be won; peace cannot be imposed; it is a tragedy deeply embedded in history that should be allowed to continue to unfold. Of course the Serbs have committed and are committing appalling atrocities, but so have the Muslims and the Croats in the past. Indeed, it is well known that the Croats and the Muslims, organised by the Nazis, murdered 500,000 Serbs during the war years, and Serbian memories of that are still vivid.

In fact, the west has consistently underestimated the Serbs. They are one of the fiercest, bravest and most patriotic races on earth, and always have been. Their leaders enjoy the virtually unanimous support of their people, as the recent elections have shown. Greater Serbia is a dream that will never die, however many Serbs may die in its pursuit. Anyone who has read any Balkan history—not just Mr. Noel Malcolm's rather slim volume—will tell us that.

California and Sakhalin are on terrestrial fault lines. In Bosnia, we are dealing with one of the great political fault lines on our planet—ethnic, cultural, religious and historic; the medieval frontier between west and east. If the outside world had not interfered, as we declined to interfere in the civil wars in Nigeria and Angola, I believe that the war in Bosnia would long have been over. We face a disaster in Bosnia that was not only predictable, not only predicted, but certain.

At the apogee of the British empire, we sent General Gordon to Khartoum to restore order. Then we sent an army, under Lord Wolseley, to rescue him. That failed. Then we sent another Army, under Lord Kitchener, to avenge him. It dug up the remains of the dead Mahdi and hung his skeleton in chains. Today, the Sudan is as proud, as savage and as Islamic a country as any in the world. Let us withdraw General Smith and his troops, now.

6.37 pm

**Miss Kate Hoey** (Vauxhall): I am sure that the hon. Member for East Lindsey (Sir P. Tapsell) does not speak for the House when he refers to the role of television journalists and photographers in the war zone in Bosnia. Indeed, I am sure that the House would want to pay tribute to the many journalists who have risked their lives to show people in this country what is happening in Bosnia.

I welcome the debate and the speeches by the Prime Minister, my right hon. Friend the Leader of the Opposition and the right hon. Member for Yeovil (Mr. Ashdown). Hon. Members today, representing our constituencies and speaking as the voice of the nation, must send a clear message throughout the world that we will not allow a bunch of bully-boy thugs to defy the United Nations, to defeat democracy and to use unarmed hostages.

I pay tribute to the hon. Member for Staffordshire, South (Sir P. Cormack) for his speech. Since the beginning of the war three years ago, there has been a lack of firmness, clarity and resolution. I recall our debate in November 1992, when I and a number of other hon. Members who are present today spoke. So many of the events prophesied in that debate have come true. If more resolution had been shown and some of the aggression faced up to, we would not be in this position today.

We have to be very clear about the terms we use when we talk about this serious issue. Bosnia-Herzegovina is a sovereign state recognised by the international community. It is not a Muslim state. It is a state where 30 per cent. of the citizens marry people from different religious groups. That is good evidence of the tolerance that has sustained Bosnia's character and identity.

For centuries, the populations have lived and been educated together. The synagogues, mosques and Orthodox and Roman Catholic churches, as the hon. Member for Staffordshire, South (Sir P. Cormack) mentioned, have existed side by side. Anyone who attended the winter Olympics in Sarajevo in 1984 saw that tolerance.

When I and my hon. Friends the Members for Western Isles (Mr. Macdonald) and for Croydon, North-West (Mr. Wicks) visited the besieged Sarajevo in November 1993, we saw for ourselves the dedication of the Bosnian Government and their people to the idea of a pluralist, multi-ethnic state. We saw a Government who were made up of members of Bosnia's various ethnic groups. We must not continue to talk about a Muslim Government and a Muslim state.

The three years of war have not lessened their commitment to a historic Bosnia existing within its pre-war frontiers, pluralist in culture and with equal rights for all its citizens. The continued existence of thousands of Serbs in Sarajevo, Zenica, Tuzla and elsewhere proves that that remains a viable goal and gives the lie to all those who assert that the war has made it impossible for the communities to live together.

The fact that, under the huge pressure of aggression, terror, ethnic cleansing and genocide, those communities have continued to do so proves not only that it remains possible but that it is the only possibility that most Bosnians can envisage. The Bosnia that they are defending could not be Bosnia if it was not a mix of the Catholic, Orthodox and Muslim traditions.

We must also be clear that this is not a civil war. We should not use the term "warring factions". How can a legitimate, internationally recognised Government be a warring faction? It beggars belief that anyone can attempt to classify in the same category Haris Silajdzic, the Prime Minister of Bosnia, and Karadzic, the leader of a minority of Serbs. Karadzic is a thug, liar and terrorist and the United Nations must not even consider appeasing him. If it does, as has been said, not only will he come back for more but UN soldiers anywhere in the world will be open to being taken hostage.

Karadzic does not speak for all the Serbs in Bosnia. He speaks for only a small number of rebel Serbs. Karadzic is the leader of a criminal minority of the Bosnian Serbs. He does not want peace because he is too deeply involved in crime. He can continue to lead only while there is war. He has no future outside his present world of terror and the hostage taking has stripped any last vestiges of respectability that he had.

The situation in Bosnia-Herzegovina today is a monument to the international community, which has allowed aggression to pay and prevented the victim from defending itself from that aggression.

I pay tribute, as have other hon. Members, to the role that UNPROFOR and our British troops have played. With their hands tied behind their back, they have still managed to save thousands of lives. The international community should condemn and punish the Serbian aggressors who have carried out torture, murder and ethnic cleansing.

I am sad that my hon. Friend the Member for Linlithgow (Mr. Dalyell) talked as if there were some shades of difference in ethnic cleansing. Ethnic cleansing is ethnic cleansing and we should not get into the details of whether one sort is better than others. In spite of all that, the international community has chosen to treat what is happening in Bosnia as a civil war in which the warring parties are equally guilty.

The legitimate Government of Bosnia, recognised as a sovereign state by the international community, have been deprived by the arms embargo of the access to the weapons that they need to defend their people and territory. The UN Security Council resolutions have failed to be implemented and therefore the Serbs do not believe that the world powers have the will to confront them. What message does that send out to other potential aggressors who want to flout international law in pursuit of nationalist ambitions?

Attacks on safe havens by Serb forces should be repelled—as has happened—by NATO military action. We have to make it clear to Serbia that until it recognises unconditionally the independence of Bosnia and Croatia, there will be no lifting of the sanctions against it and that, indeed, sanctions will be tightened.

The Prime Minister and other hon. Members have talked about us not taking sides. How can we be even-handed in the face of aggression? I do not apologise for taking sides. I know what side I am on: I am on the side of the legitimate Bosnian Government. How can we allow the international order to be seen off by a gang of terrorists? What is the point of safe havens if they are not safe?

We have talked a lot about the UN mandate and how it can be changed. As it stands, it allows General Rupert Smith to use whatever force is necessary to deliver humanitarian aid, to enforce the no-fly zone and to deter attacks on safe areas. That sounds like a pretty good mandate to me. The problem is that he has not been able to carry it out.

What kind of message does it give to the world and to those who want to support legitimate Governments when, as my hon. Friend the hon. Member for East Lothian (Mr. Home Robertson) mentioned in his excellent speech, we allow rebel Serbs to close down the airport of Sarajevo—a capital city just two hours flight from here—so that UN officials and aid cannot get there? The city is still besieged as it has been from the start. There has merely been a little bit less shelling and fewer people have been killed.

It is appalling that the only way in which the legitimate Government, recognised by the international community, can get out of their capital city is to go through the tunnel under the airport and up by Mount Igman. That is disgraceful.

[*Miss Kate Hoey*]

The prevention of a full-scale Balkan war is very much a strategic interest for Britain. That is why our troops must stay and why we must give them the power to act. If not, then we have to say quite clearly that we will lift the arms embargo. If the international community is not prepared to act to uphold international law, we must give the people of Bosnia the right to defend themselves.

I am very sorry that my right hon. Friend the Member for Chesterfield (Mr. Benn) is forcing a vote tonight. It was extremely useful that both Front Benches supported each other.

**Mr. Campbell-Savours:** So that people outside the House do not misunderstand what we are doing, would my hon. Friend make it clear that there will be no Division tonight on any resolution or motion? It is simply that some hon. Members intend to divide the House against the debate being terminated at 10 o'clock.

**Miss Hoey:** I thank my hon. Friend for his intervention but I do not think that that is the reason that my right hon. Friend the Member for Chesterfield gave. I am sorry that my right hon. Friend is doing that. If he thinks that that will help in any way to get the release of hostages in Pale, he is wrong.

When we visited Pale, my hon. Friends the Members for Croydon, North-West and for Western Isles met Karadzic. He lied to us absolutely and straight up and down. He simply lied about the shelling; he lied about everything. He will be sitting in Pale tonight and will be delighted to see the House divide. It does not matter about the technicalities. It will send a wrong message from the House. I do not think that the British public want us to send that message.

I support the speeches of the Prime Minister and of my right hon. Friend the Leader of the Opposition. I hope that we will strengthen our resolve to ensure that international law is kept and that we will give what support we can to the people of Bosnia in their endeavours to have a multi-cultural, pluralist and safe society to live in.

6.48 pm

**Sir Geoffrey Johnson Smith** (Wealden): I listened with interest to the speech of the hon. Member for Vauxhall (Miss Hoey) because it was a strong defence of what she described as the integrity of Bosnia. In the end, however, she was asking us to take sides. If we were to do so, we should have to ask the Government to do so on the ground in the former Yugoslavia, which would mean interfering with the warring factions and ceasing to fulfil our mandate. That was the point made by many Conservative and Opposition Members and by the Prime Minister and the Leader of the Opposition.

There is no commitment by the Government to get involved in the enforcement of peace. There is no such commitment among the majority of hon. Members and certainly not among the people outside who do not think that this country should interfere in what they see as an ethnic dispute or civil war, whatever one chooses to call it. They know that, for month after month, some of the wisest people whom we have been able to summon to try to arbitrate or get some agreement have failed in that pursuit. Why have they failed? It is not through a lack of diligence, common purpose or good will towards the warring factions but because the people there do not seem to want agreement.

It is not only a question of the Serbs not wanting agreement, bad though their reputation is. We can point to members of other communities in the former Yugoslavia who have committed the most despicable acts and acted with an obtuseness that has been one of the most appalling demonstrations by a so-called civilised nation that we have experienced since the end of the previous war. On the basis of what we have heard from the two Front Benches, on no account should we be lured into taking sides because the consequence of doing so would be entering the war.

I had not intended to say this, but an article was brought to my attention. It is written by someone living in Belgrade, I assume, and was published in a magazine there called *The Age of Man*, although its title is given in French as *L'Age D'Homme*. It is entitled *Misconceptions about Bosnia-Herzegovina*. I do not know whether it is true but it states:

"The major preoccupation of the Contact group was the territorial partition of Bosnia-Herzegovina . . . The plan of the Contact group was refused by Serbs and that is an irrefutable fact",

or so it is claimed. The article goes on the make a point that was also made—strongly—by the right hon. Member for Strangford (Mr. Taylor), who should know about ethnic disputes. Essentially, the article states:

"It is impossible to create unity without the unanimous will of the people."

I think that we all recognise that. It goes on to say that, if one third of the Bosnian population in the Bosnia-Herzegovina conflict—the Serbs—are not interested in living with the other two thirds, how can we make them? We cannot tell them that they have to; we can suggest that they do so and object to the tactics that they use but if we try to tell a Serb, with his passions and memories, that he has to live with the Croats and Muslims—and the Croats and Muslims do not want to live with him—we shall have a dangerous and explosive cocktail.

**Mr. Calum Macdonald** (Western Isles): Does the hon. Gentleman appreciate that 150,000 Serbs live alongside Muslims in Bosnian Government-controlled territory and that the majority of Serbs in Karadzic-controlled territory have fled, usually to Serbia? Karadzic represents only a minority of the Serb population, most of whom do not want violence and aggression.

**Sir Geoffrey Johnson Smith:** The hon. Gentleman may be right, but it seems to many hon. Members that among the Croats, Muslims and Serbs—I am talking about Bosnian Serbs—there seems to be a lack of the unity and good will that we have every right to expect after three years of bloody war, which we have tried to stop and during which we have given humanitarian relief and risked the lives of our soldiers and those from other countries, some of which are a damn sight poorer than the country that they are helping. It seems that they are refusing to bury their differences, which have been shored up by a history of discontent and exacerbated by the breakdown of the former Yugoslavian state.

It cannot be disputed that in the federation of Yugoslavia two states were based on ethnic grounds—Croatia and Serbia. Bosnia-Herzegovina is based on not one but three ethnic grounds, and Lord knows we have had enough trouble with the others. It may be that diplomacy is the way out of the problem—it is certainly the only way that I can see because I cannot envisage our sending troops to enforce a peace. Nor can I envisage the Americans doing so, and certainly not the Germans or French. It seems, therefore, that we have to go back to the drawing board to find out how to stop Bosnia-Herzegovina becoming the most important and intractable problem of all. It may have something to do with the fact that the passion of the Serbs needs to be resolved in the way suggested by the right hon. Member for Strangford—by a recognition that ethnicity is a vital component in the wretched business of trying to achieve a diplomatic solution.

I refer now to a reaction that some colleagues and some Opposition Members displayed recently. When there is a new drama in international affairs, there is a tendency to make a panic or a sensational response. At the spring meeting of the North Atlantic Assembly in Budapest, the media and some other bodies acted true to form. The options were a panic withdrawal or the sending of more troops and if, ultimately, things do not work out, we should smash the Serbs and tell them what to do.

That, however, was not the reaction of the hon. Member for South Shields (Dr. Clark) or of the hon. and learned Member for Fife, North-East (Mr. Campbell), who has left his place, when I got together with them as the leader of the United Kingdom NAA delegation to see whether we could get some expression of opinion from the many delegates from various Parliaments of western, central and eastern Europe, from the Russian Parliament and from the United States Congress about the taking of hostages. With their help, we were able to propose an initiative that became the resolution supported not only by the NAA's standing committee but the plenary session.

The draft resolution states:

"The Assembly,

Condemns without reservation the unprincipled and barbaric use of unarmed military observers of the United Nations as human shields by Bosnian Serb Forces . . .

Demands the immediate and unconditional release of the unarmed military observers of the United Nations . . .

Calls for an immediate cessation of aggression, in particular towards the civilian population in Bosnia;

Expresses its support for the continuing effort of forces operating under relevant United Nations resolutions to maintain peace and bring humanitarian assistance in certain regions in former Yugoslavia . . .

Strongly endorses the efforts of the Contact Group to achieve a negotiated settlement . . .

Requests that the United Nations Security Council considers amending the mandate of UNPROFOR so that it is able to respond to any aggression to which it is subjected."

The resolution was carried almost unanimously. Two did not support it—a German Green and a German Communist. We wondered how the Russians would respond, but they supported it, too. They did not seem especially concerned about whether they had been consulted on whether there should have been an order for an air strike. However, I would not want to assume too much from the Russians.

Nevertheless, it would be terrible to send the message that people consider it a waste of time for us to try to seek a diplomatic solution or believe that it is wrong for our troops to be out there with those of other nations trying to provide humanitarian assistance. It would be to send a terrible message if that view were expressed in tonight's

vote and interpreted as meaning that we were backtracking on the concept shared by many of us, enshrined in the assembly's resolution and accepted by many countries from central and eastern Europe, many of which had received refugees and sent their men and women to help.

**Mr. Dalyell:** Can the hon. Gentleman and his colleagues envisage circumstances in years to come when it would ever be acceptable for us to withdraw on the basis of the criteria that he has outlined?

**Sir Geoffrey Johnson Smith:** Yes, I think that one has to face up to that reality. That is why I am not one of those who believes that we should go on and on and in the end, as an act of despair, decide to bomb them into subjection. I have heard that phrase used in the United States. It is a ludicrous concept and it would be as counterproductive as some of the actions of the Serbs.

As I see Government policy, it is an each-way bet. The Government have to respond in the way in which they do and I think that that is right. As hon. Members have said, we cannot give way to blackmail; that would be wrong. Withdrawal has its own risks and costs quite apart from its financial costs. It cannot be achieved overnight. If we wanted to withdraw, not only would the humanitarian aid stop, as we know, but we would have the delicate task of trying to withdraw our armed forces which would—perhaps—be resisted by the very people who we have tried to help. People would block the path of troops supplying the humanitarian aid and beg them not to leave. I would like to see the television cameras cover that scene, as British troops withdraw and people stop them to ask for help in administering medical supplies. That picture would tell a story that would shame all of us.

Withdrawal is not an easy moral option; it is very difficult. Nevertheless, patience can run out. As I see it, the Government are sending troops to help make it more possible for the aid to go through, to protect those deployed for peacekeeping and to ensure that they are not isolated. That is an honourable objective. It sends a signal to people who wish us to withdraw that we shall not be bullied out. That seems to be the first objective.

As time goes by—we know that NATO has already made plans for withdrawal—and if further provocative action is taken by whichever side is stupid enough, we would expect the forces to be organised and to be reinforced by other NATO allies to enable their swift and competent exit. Although NATO has thoroughly planned that scenario, the decision has yet to be made. I hope, therefore, that we can be patient and do not rush or be panicked into any immediate withdrawal, or think that the alternative, as I said, is to go to war.

I know that there are still many hon. Members who want to speak, so I shall not go into any further detail about the speeches made from the two Front Benches. Speeches of hon. Members of all parties—I single out that of my right hon. Friend the Prime Minister—have displayed a quality of statesmanship which we ought to respect. The action is both prudent and honourable.

**Mr. Deputy Speaker:** I must remind the House that Madam Speaker has placed a 10-minute limit on speeches between 7 pm and 9 pm.

7.2 pm

**Mr. Andrew Faulds** (Warley, East): Lucky me! Having listened to some of the rubbish that I have had to listen to this afternoon, it is now two minutes past 7. In my 30 years in the House, I have seen some strange liaisons—both in the Chamber and, not surprisingly, outside the Chamber—but tonight's is a collector's piece. We have my much regarded hon. Friend the Member for Linlithgow (Mr. Dalyell) appearing to try to sustain two unacceptable arguments: one, that ethnic cleansing, if it is the descendants of converts, is a little more acceptable, and, secondly, that after four years of discussions with the Serbs, we should sit down with them again because they will suddenly be reasonable. My hon. Friend usually has contact with reality, but tonight I think that he has lost it. The liaison with that and the speech of the hon. Member for East Lindsay (Sir P. Tapsell), who unfortunately has left—[HON. MEMBERS: "He is there."] Ah, there he is. I welcome him to the Chamber—is one of the oddest that I have seen.

The hon. Member for East Lindsay claims to know something about Turkey, but he probably knows rather less about Turkey than I. He may know the bankers, and all those people, but I know a lot more about Turkey than that. He seems to forget when he mentions Turkey that there is a Turkish battalion in UNPROFOR. Are the Turks going to be agreeable to the withdrawal of their battalion when the Serbs are committing Muslim murders? He, too, has lost contact—just a bit—with reality. I have to say that much worse than that was the tone of the hon. Gentleman's comments this afternoon. I am old enough to recall exactly that tone of appeasement by the Tories before the last war. I never thought that I would live—I will probably not live to hear it again—to hear that sort of comment again in the House of Commons.

The Serbs have been the guilty party since the break up of Yugoslavia. I do not think that even the apologists would try to pretend that the situation is anything other than that. The Serbs were the protagonists and the practitioners of ethnic cleansing and the displacement of hundreds of thousands of members of the other communities in the old Yugoslavia. Why? It is because of their lunatic commitment to the Greater Serbia fantasy of the Serbian Orthodox Church. They have been the most criminal—nobody is going to argue with that—in their conduct of organised rape of thousands and thousands of women and the practice of torture and murder of thousands and thousands and thousands of prisoners. And their conduct does not change. It really is beyond the pale of civilised behaviour. Their bombardment of Tuzla, pointless in any military terms, left 200 people either dead or injured. They have taken hostage soldiers of various nationalities in the UN force, which is absolutely unacceptable, and they have even chained them, some of them, as potential targets to try to stop any sort of western action. The Serbs have masqueraded as UN troops and are using UN weapons and equipment.

Those actions, of course, are quite contrary to and an absolute contravention of international agreements. All that is the conduct of Christian soldiers under their two internationally notorious criminal leaders, the fanatic Karadzic and the thug Mladic, who must eventually—I hope that the international community ensures this—be held to account, as must Milosevic, that chief proponent of Greater Serbia, with whom we are now trying to do a political deal. Greater Serbia is a political fantasy as

historically incorrect and offensive as Zionism's Eretz Israel. I have to say that I have no great hope of Mr. Milosevic's conversion.

Having denied the Bosnian Muslims the arms to defend themselves, the international community cannot now allow such people as these criminals Serbs to force a UN withdrawal. That would give ethnic aggression and cleansing its head in various other areas of the world and the effectiveness of the UN would be very much destroyed.

In speeches that I made in this House two and three years ago, I argued that the only realistic way to stop Serb aggression was, first, to withdraw UN forces to prevent their becoming hostages—perhaps I should have been listened to. NATO could then deal with the Serbs, as they are going to have to be dealt with unless we are going to abandon totally any principle in political life in this country and in Europe. We must take out the Serbs' artillery, their air fields. We must disrupt their communications and destroy their arms factories. While the Bosnian Muslims are denied arms, the Serbs are having them manufactured throughout the old Yugoslavia for their use.

Of course, there would have been and there will be heavy, heavy casualties among the Serbs and among the civilians of all faiths if the necessary action is taken. But there have been, over these years, in any case, hundreds of thousands of civilian casualties and there will be many hundreds of thousands more if the international community withdraws and allows the belligerents of all sides to fight it out to the bloody end. That, I believe, is the likely outcome of European procrastination—the Minister of State for the Armed Forces had better listen—and timidity.

I fear that the present performance of sending in numbers of reinforcements is not—do not let us be conned—not in reality to face down the Serbs, to take them on and best them and force a negotiated settlement upon them. I am convinced, regardless of the rhetoric and the pretence, that these reinforcements are a preparation for evacuation. I believe that is what will undoubtedly evolve eventually from all the convocations that have been summoned and are likely to be summoned.

If my suspicions are correct—and I think they are—and the wimps and the wobblies on the other side have their way and withdrawal is undertaken, the war will of course spread, as the Prime Minister, the Leader of the Opposition and the leader of the Liberal Democrats stated. It will spread into Kosovo and Macedonia, and between Greece and Turkey, and a fully fledged Balkans war will ensue, with horrendous slaughter.

As I have warned on a number of occasions, the effect of such developments on our relations with the Muslim world will be immensely damaging—right across the world, in all the Muslim communities throughout the world in both economic and political terms. The world balance of power is changing away from the west and it is time we started to appreciate this fact. There is a gathering together of the immensely increasing political and economic power and resources of Muslim nations and communities throughout Asia, south-east Asia, Africa, the middle east and, of course, in the old Turkic areas of the Soviet Union.

That new world movement will have as its dynamic and its purpose a rejection of all the works and all the interests of the western world. I wish, I wish British politicians had a little more intelligence.

7.10 pm

**Mr. Peter Viggers** (Gosport): I enjoyed the speech by the hon. Member for Warley, East (Mr. Faulds), but I fear that he may not enjoy mine much. The original role in Bosnia was one of distributing humanitarian aid and medical support and of promoting peace. The idea was that the presence of blue berets and blue helmets in that country would promote confidence, and that that in itself would help to promote peace.

Then tasks were added to those that our troops already had through the United Nations. They were given the safe havens to look after, although when they were given the denominated safe havens they were not given the troops to provide the necessary support. Although that role was rather unrealistic, for some time it seemed as if it might have some success. The Muslim-Croat federation emerged, and there was peace between the Muslims and the Croats. In Sarajevo, thanks to the extraordinary courage and leadership of General Sir Michael Rose, the trams were running again, and for a time it seemed as if things were indeed returning to normal. The ceasefire was scheduled to end on 1 May this year, but it looked as though things were moving the right way.

What has become apparent now is the extent to which all that success required consent—consent that is not now present on the Serb side in Bosnia. Things have started going seriously wrong. The Muslims have taken the opportunity to rearm, and it is clear that they are re-equipped and rearmed with all that they need apart from tanks, heavy armour and aircraft.

The Croats in the federation have taken the opportunity to take western Slavonia. Despite the United Nations presence, in the United Kingdom sector alone in the past few months—in Vitez, in Gornji Vakuf and in Novi Travnik—the Defence Committee has seen the extent to which war and ethnic cleansing could go raging through the towns while all that the UN soldiers could do was to stay in their barracks and hope that the problem would resolve itself without their being involved. The troops were in no way equipped to prevent the wars from raging through the towns in which they were based. So it has become increasingly apparent that the position in Bosnia is unrealistic.

As for humanitarian aid, I am always rather suspicious when I am given two good reasons for something. And we are given two good reasons why our troops and the other United Nations troops are in Bosnia at the moment. The first "good reason" is that by being there we are preventing a third world war. Our assistance in the distribution of humanitarian aid is apparently the second valid reason for our being there.

However, it is arguable that humanitarian aid may be extending the conflict, because the United Nations is underwriting the basic needs of the population. I attribute that thought to Patrick Bishop of *The Daily Telegraph*, who spoke to the Conservative defence committee recently; I am following his thought through. He cited Clausewitz, who points out that sometimes for war to end it is necessary for the population to come to a culminating point where such is the exhaustion and war-weariness of all the people that they turn away from war, realising that it is getting them nowhere.

Those who have studied history and politics will realise that that was the case with the hundred years war and the thirty years war. But if one underwrites the basic needs of the population, the population will not come to that point and there will not be that pressure on the war leaders to end the war. So, however unattractive the thought may be, there are two sides to the distribution of humanitarian aid,

What role is there now for the United Nations forces and the United Kingdom contribution? First, of course, we must resolve the hostage situation without benefit to those who set it up. We must be certain that blackmail does not pay; that must be our first priority. Secondly, we need to consolidate our position and ensure that our troops are less exposed in Bosnia.

Thirdly, we need to take account of the fact that there is a total contrast between the manner in which forces can operate with consent and without consent. So far our forces have operated with consent. My right hon. Friend the Member for Old Bexley and Sidcup (Sir E. Heath) said that he found it surprising that hostages could have been taken, because during his time in the armed forces he would not have thought it likely or possible that that could happen. My right hon. Friend is not in the Chamber now, but I must tell him that the situation in Bosnia has been completely different.

When we are operating with consent, the United Nations forces simply go along the street with their guns, walking past people of the three different sides, who also have guns. They are waved through a checkpoint at which Muslims point guns at them, they then go through a Croat checkpoint where a Croat tank is pointed at them, and as they move on they may even pass through a Serbian checkpoint too. All those people have guns. In Tomislavgrad I found that the United Nations forces were sharing barracks with the Croats. Our soldiers are rubbing shoulders with such people all the time. It is the easiest thing in the world for any of the factions or their subordinate gangs to hold up United Nations troops and take them away, simply by pointing guns at them. So it is not surprising that hostages were taken.

There is a total contrast between the manner of operation in areas in which we have consent and areas in which we do not. Without consent we cannot operate in the manner for which the mandate has been set up in Bosnia. It is inconceivable that we can long continue in the position that has existed for some weeks in which our troops are within gun range of the Serb positions while we are bombing the Serbs or calling in air strikes against them.

How can we expect the Serbs not to retaliate if we have ordered air strikes that have killed some of their people or damaged some of their property? Can we seriously expect to walk past them and be waved through the next checkpoint, when they have guns? Of course not. The two methods of operation are inconsistent. Anyone who dreams in that fashion is, as the hon. Member for Linlithgow (Mr. Dalyell) said, misleading himself.

We must resolve that problem, which has now come to a head. If we do not have consent we must work out where we go from here. Both the Prime Minister and the Leader of the Opposition talked about strengthening the forces engaged in humanitarian relief, and about strengthening

*[Mr. Peter Viggers]*

the peacekeepers. But how can we think in those terms when we shall not be permitted to carry those intentions out? I submit that the previous mandate has expired, because it depended on consent.

Is it realistic to think that we can continue to protect the safe havens if we are now under attack there? It is not. Neither is it realistic to imagine that 15,000 troops could defend Sarajevo. We should need many more than that, bearing in mind the fact that it would take only two men felling a tree to block the road leading to the main British positions at Gornji Vakuv and Vitez. As others have already said, we are facing troops with wide experience in an area of the country noted for its guerilla activities. We shall need many more people than the numbers so far contemplated if we are to stand a chance of succeeding in carrying out our mandate there.

The risk in which our troops are positioned is extraordinary. When the Defence Select Committee was in Bosnia two months ago, we were told the following story. The Serbs told a Canadian unit that they proposed to shell it the following day. So the colonel in charge of the Canadian unit quite sensibly thinned out his positions, and sent some of his troops out of the barracks; they were stopped in the street outside by Muslims, who got their people to stand in front of the Canadians' armoured cars—known as grizzlies. The Muslims told the Canadians, "If you keep going, we'll shell you where you are now." The Canadians went back into the barracks, whereupon they were shelled by the Serbs. That is the problem faced in Bosnia, not only with the Serbs but in places such as Gornji Vakuf and Vitez, where the battle is between Muslims and Croats.

We had 3,500 of our troops exposed to this sort of risk last week; next month 9,500 of them will be thus exposed. And for what? My right hon. Friend the Prime Minister referred to a turning point in Bosnia, and thought that it might have come at this time. I do not agree; but he also referred to a time that might come when humanitarian aid and peace promotion became impossible. I submit that that time has come. I believe that no longer should our troops remain in Bosnia on the basis on which they were originally sent there, which depended on consent.

I am not squeamish about troops being engaged in support of the UN in Bosnia—but we cannot carry on with the previous mandate, which depended on consent. We should be considering strategic aims in Bosnia. Then, if we can make a contribution to those revised strategic aims, by all means let us keep our troops there. But on the current mandate—

**Mr. Deputy Speaker:** Order.

7.21 pm

**Mr. Calum Macdonald** (Western Isles): I visited Tuzla during the Easter recess and talked to many of its citizens—Serbs, Croats and Muslims. For all I know, some of the people to whom I talked then have become victims of the shelling of the past few days. I also met the Bosnian Foreign Minister during his last visit to this country. While we are conscious of our own anguish at the fate of our British soldiers, we should also remember that fate against the background of the suffering that the ordinary people of Bosnia have undergone for the past two or three years.

The right hon. Member for Bridgwater (Mr. King)—not in his place now—made a most important speech today. One of his key points concerned the importance of adjusting the current rules of engagement under which all the UN forces operate. That chimed with what Brigadier Michael Harbottle told Members of both Houses when he spoke to us in one of the Committee Rooms in November last year about the nature of UN peacekeeping. He served with the UN forces in Cyprus in the 1960s and went on to write the UN peacekeeping manual.

In his talk, the brigadier described one of his tasks in Cyprus, which was to defend a village which happened to be a Turkish village being threatened by some Greek soldiers. Brigadier Harbottle explained that the advantage he had, as compared with Bosnia, was that he possessed crystal clear rules of engagement. So when the Greek soldiers began moving towards the village and the UN soldiers interposed between the Greeks and the Turks, the brigadier was able to tell the Greek soldiers, "If you move within 200 yd of the UN soldiers, you will be infringing our ability to carry out our mandate and we will shoot." The Greek soldiers withdrew.

That contrasts markedly with what has been happening in recent days in Bosnia. Armed men have been able to walk right up to UN positions and disarm UN soldiers. If the UN rules of engagement in Cyprus in the 1960s were able to prevent such a thing from happening, we have to ask why such rules of engagement have not been applied in the past couple of years in Bosnia.

The hon. Member for Gosport (Mr. Viggers) talked about the importance of consent. I think that he is much mistaken about the auspices under which UN forces in Bosnia are supposed to be operating. The objectives of the UN are clear, as are the objectives for the reinforcements who are being sent out. They are provided by UN resolutions 770, which concerns ensuring the delivery of aid, 816, which is about enforcing the no-fly zone, and 824 and 836, which are about the protection of so-called safe areas and deterring attacks on them. These mandates do not rely on consent, however. They are enforcement resolutions, and they do not depend on the consent of the Bosnian Serbs or of any other party. They demand compliance, and the resolutions authorise their enforcement "by all necessary means".

It is important, too, to remember that these resolutions were passed under chapter 7 of the UN charter, which authorises the use of force without the consent of local parties. Peacekeeping which requires consent is authorised under chapter 6. I agree with those who have said that what is happening is not peacekeeping because there is no peace to keep—that is obvious. I agree, too, that it is not peacemaking; that would require a much larger deployment of forces. It is a humanitarian mission, as set out in the relevant resolutions, but a humanitarian mission under chapter 7, which demands enforcement. That point has escaped many of those who have spoken today.

The problem has been that the UN forces sent out to enforce the mandate have been too lightly armed and have been wrongly deployed to carry out their task. Whenever a mandate has been thwarted by Bosnian Serbs, UNPROFOR has been unable to respond effectively because it has been undergunned and overexposed. Both those problems have crippled the effectiveness of UNPROFOR and have made the jobs of its commanders almost impossible. That is why the reinforcement is so necessary and is to be supported and welcomed.

Over the next few days and weeks, we need a patient build-up and a regrouping and redeployment of UN forces. If there was one thing I was sorry to hear the Prime Minister say, it was that the Air Mobile Brigade had still not been given its orders to be dispatched. Regardless of what happens in the next couple of days, it is crucial that that brigade go if we are to prevent a repetition of events.

Once the regrouping has taken place, we must give full backing and full tactical freedom to General Smith to carry out the job that we have asked him to do: to enforce the mandates. The only restriction on his freedom to call on air support, artillery and indeed all the forces at his disposal should be our humanitarian wish to avoid civilian casualties. But General Smith must have the full support and confidence of the international community when carrying out that task.

Regrouping is certainly the key, but we must also be very careful about certain other aspects. There must be no concessions, for instance, to the hostage takers. It seems obvious that giving concessions will only encourage them to hold on to hostages and to seize more of them. There must be no abandonment of the safe areas. UNPROFOR must maintain a presence—regrouping notwithstanding— even in the most vulnerable safe areas. There must be no more talk by the Government of withdrawal. I cannot think of anything more designed to undermine the sense of purpose and the morale of our troops than Ministers constantly speculating on the possibility of defeat, reversal and withdrawal. By all means let us make contingency plans, but for God's sake let us not talk about them.

There is no need to go beyond the tasks outlined in the UN resolutions. It is not a question of retaking Serb territory or of imposing a ceasefire on a vast territory. The mandate is specific, and lays out clear tasks. We now need a proper enforcement of those tasks. There must be no more fudging or muddling through in the execution of the mandate.

I pay full credit to General Smith for the deliberate and clear way in which he has forced the issue over the past few days. He has refused to play the politicians' game at the expense of the mandate that he was asked to enforce. To insinuate or to suggest—as some have done—that somehow General Smith's hand was forced by the Americans when he called in the air strikes is both insulting and absurd to those who know General Smith and who had the privilege of meeting him early last year. I have no doubt whatsoever that he did what he did for a purpose and to calculated effect.

We should support the deployment of reinforcements. In fact, we should support the deployment of whatever General Smith advises is necessary to enforce the existing mandate. That must be the bottom line. My only complaint would be—

**Mr. Deputy Speaker:** Order.

7.31 pm

**Mr. Cyril D. Townsend** (Bexleyheath): It is excellent that this special debate during the Whit recess has brought forward speeches of such passion and conviction, and it has formed some rather odd alliances across the Floor of the House. I have taken part in three debates on Bosnia; each time the mood has been that we must not put more troops in the area, but each time we have found at the next debate that we have raised the level of our commitment.

As a former Regular soldier and the chairman of the parliamentary UN group, I approach the subject of Bosnia with mixed feelings. My right hon. Friend the Prime Minister, whom I am delighted to see in the Chamber, made an excellent speech. I admire the leadership that my right hon. Friend has shown during the past four days, which I cannot help contrasting with what has come out of the White House in the same period.

I pay tribute to the professionalism and dedication of senior and junior British soldiers in Bosnia in recent months and in the past three years. Although I have not been surprised by that professionalism, or by their logistical abilities and communications skills, the Bosnian crisis has brought those skills to light for many people.

I am concerned at the ever-increasing involvement of the United Kingdom in former Yugoslavia, and at the ever-increasing commitment of the UN. The immediate cause of this debate is the taking of the hostages, a despicable act which goes against all forms of international morality and behaviour. Diplomacy is the immediate way forward, and patience is the key word. I am reminded of the old adage—"Talk softly but carry a big stick".

The hostage takers must be told in person of the resolve of this House and the Government to get every single hostage released. They must have no doubt that we are prepared to be ruthless, and that we will take the most serious steps to achieve that objective if patient negotiation fails. It would be crazy to think of withdrawing our troops in the light of the hostage taking.

Having said that, I want to express my sense of alarm at how events have moved on swiftly and seriously in the past three years. The media love giving labels, and I am a minimalist. I was against sending the Cheshire Regiment, but I pay tribute to it for its performance in the area. I have been alarmed at the declaration of safe zones, because UNPROFOR has had neither the ability nor the backing to guarantee their safety.

The UN has been desperately exposed. I have been told of an occasion a few months ago when Canadian troops were seriously threatened in a safe area and asked the United Kingdom Government if we would be prepared to use our air power to protect their troops on the ground. After a certain amount of argy-bargy, we stated that we would do so. The consequences of using our aircraft in a deployment to defend such a position would be quite extraordinary, and far beyond anything contemplated so far by the Government—let alone the House of Commons.

The concept of the air strikes is highly questionable. As an ex-military man, I am amazed at the idea of using the most advanced fighter bombers in the world to destroy a tank that may be 40 or 50 years old. Such a strike involves putting that plane at risk of an attack from a comparatively unsophisticated surface-to-air missile. I do not believe that these attacks have done much damage to the Serbs, but they have done some damage to NATO and to the UN.

We are talking about the important concept of peacekeeping, and not peacemaking as we had in Korea. There is a subtle difference between them, and we are foolish if we do not understand it. Peacekeeping involves white vehicles and blue helmets which can be seen from a distance. It demands talking to both sides, and walking openly down streets. Conventional warfare involves deceit, deception, camouflage and surprise movements, and it is an entirely different military concept. As events

[*Mr. Cyril D. Townsend*]

have moved on in the past three years, those two concepts have become blurred. I believe that that is highly dangerous.

In two first-class speeches, my right hon. Friend the Prime Minister and the Leader of the Opposition over-egged the case for UNPROFOR, and I am sure that they would admit that. Yes, it is had its successes, and we are proud of those. But the risks have been enormous, and we have been lucky not to have had more British casualties. The French have had a far higher number.

We are proud of the humanitarian record, but we all know that a considerable amount of the food that we have brought to mountain villages has been supplying the forces taking part in the conflict. That is the brutal reality. We may not like it, but we must accept that it is true. We are dealing not with proper standing armies but with voluntary armies. A lad serving in such an army will go back and have supper with his mum, and he will be eating UN rations. The same is true with regard to medical supplies, where the situation has been horrendous. Some of the supplies have gone to the combatants and have helped to shield them from the reality of the civil war which has been raging for so long in that country. That war will continue to rage.

At the moment, the Serbs have probably reached a peak. We are told that their rivals have been getting a considerable number of weapons and recruits, and they are likely to regain some of the ground that they have lost. There is no way in which UNPROFOR can stop the two sides fighting if the Muslims are determined to regain the territory they have lost to the Serbs. So what are my conclusions? When the present hostage-taking episode has passed, as it will, Britain and France—which work well and closely together in the context of Bosnia—should say to their colleagues on the Security Council, "We do not believe that we should shoulder this burden for ever. The United Nations is in danger of becoming part of the problem in that unhappy, troubled country because expectations are too high." The UN can postpone problems but cannot necessarily prevent them. It is hopelessly overextended in the world, particularly in Bosnia. The UN has a role in Bosnia, but does UNPROFOR have a role there over the next five, 10 or 15 years? I have to say no.

It is easy for us all to imagine that the UN in 1995 can take on the burdens of the world and solve Angola and Nagorno Karabakh. In reality, it cannot. If people are determined to fight, rape, pillage, and go in for ethnic cleansing and policies of degradation and despair, the UN cannot stop them. It needs to sort out its new priorities on a global scale. I fear that means scaling down its troops in Bosnia.

7.40 pm

**Mr. Alan Keen** (Feltham and Heston): I pay tribute to the members of the armed forces in the former Yugoslavia, particularly those who have been taken hostage, and sympathise-with their relatives and friends.

It is an understatement to say that we face a difficult situation in the former Yugoslavia. We all, including the Bosnian Serbs, know that the solution will not be military. Eventually, all sides in that troubled area must get together and compromise. We must continue to contribute

to a negotiated and permanent settlement, but until there is movement in that direction we must offer the services of our armed forces in whatever role is necessary on the understanding that there will be a negotiated, not military, settlement.

We must continue to protect and help feed people in the most vulnerable eastern enclaves and elsewhere, and we must use our influence around the world's conference tables to maintain the support of NATO and UN colleagues. It is almost impossible to balance the provision of humanitarian aid and protecting civilians and our own forces—which may at times mean the deterrent of aggression and striking back. It is not easy to reconcile those contradictory roles, but we must persist. We cannot give any undertaking to the Bosnian Serbs in Pale that there will be no further air strikes in return for the release of hostages. As other hon. Members explained that aspect well, I shall not elaborate.

It is time to talk, but talks should be from a position of unbending strength, not weakness. I support the movement of additional ground troops to protect the UN peacekeeping contingent and agencies taking further food, clothing and medical supplies to the enclaves. It is pleasing that there was a consensus at the NATO conference that the method of operation should be changed, with the strengthening of troops on the ground. Those forces have an unenviable role, and the operation is expensive financially and in human terms.

The world is at a crossroads. We have moved on from the stability—if that is the word—of the cold war and can either withdraw behind our own borders and pretend that we have no responsibility to anyone else or work at becoming a proper world community. If we fail to take responsibility in the former Yugoslavia, we will be unable to assist anywhere else in the world and we will send a signal to powers with selfish motives that they can get away with it if they try. We must work and work until we make the UN an effective organisation. That is the only way forward.

That will cost more in the short term, but we must look ahead. I have little interest in rugby, but it has been inspirational to watch nations of the world playing together and South Africa competing again, with teams from Romania and Argentina. When we see such progress, there is hope for the future.

I want no barriers or borders to world travel. Many people in this country question risking the lives of British soldiers and incurring heavy costs to help people who appear to be inflicting damage on each other. Many say that they should be left to fight it out. It is understandable that some factions in the former Yugoslavia earn criticism and disregard, but the children of Bosnia are the children of us all. They are the children of the world and we cannot neglect them, whatever we may think of the adults. I want those children to grow up in a world free of conflict, to live a full life of education and leisure. I want them to look forward to bringing up families of their own in peace and security.

I want my children and grandchildren to be able to visit the former Yugoslavia as holidaymakers among those friendly people, as my parents and I have done. I look forward to the time when the world can be policed without the need for armies, but to achieve that we must make sacrifices now. We must act with restraint but use force when necessary.

We do not need to look back as far as the last war to learn the lessons. We need to look back only at the early stages of the present conflict in the former Yugoslavia, when a more determined and united effort would almost certainly have saved a great number of lives.

7.46 pm

**Sir Jim Spicer** (Dorset, West): The British hostages taken in Bosnia serve in the 1st Royal Welch Fusiliers. I served in the Army in the 53rd Welsh Division alongside men of the 1st Battalion, Royal Welch Fusiliers in 1944-45. It is a chastening thought for me that the men taken hostage are probably the grandsons of men who served alongside me. If they are like their grandfathers, they will face up to the situation—as will their families.

In an article published at the weekend, my right hon. Friend the Prime Minister said:

"Those who felt right from the start that we could solve everything through air strikes have never thought through some of the possible implications. Hostage taking was always one of them."

He was absolutely right. All the lessons of modern war make it clear that air power alone cannot force a determined enemy to the negotiating table. Of course it is comfortable to have aircraft circling above and it makes one feel much better—but, in the end, one must have men on the ground to win battles. I hope that right hon. and hon. Members who, over the past two years, have been harrying members of the Government Front Bench and calling for air strikes now realise the stupidity of that policy. I am delighted to see the Liberal Democrat defence spokesman nodding his head.

**Mr. Menzies Campbell:** The hon. Gentleman has never heard me argue that all the problems could be solved by using air strikes.

**Sir Jim Spicer:** I realise that, but perhaps the hon. and learned Gentleman will have a word with his leader. I am delighted to see that the leader of the Liberal Democrats has rejoined us.

**Mr. Ashdown** *rose*—

**Sir Jim Spicer:** I am afraid that I cannot allow the right hon. Gentleman to intervene because I have only 10 minutes in which to speak.

At the time of Suez, many others and I questioned our country's actions, believing that the politicians had not really thought through our precise objectives, how we could achieve them and where it all might end. Bosnia is a totally different story and the Prime Minister rightly set out the dangers of bloody massacres and of a major conflagration if the UN and, in particular, members of the NATO alliance were to cut and run.

I must take issue with hon. Members who have spoken about Turkey. My right hon. Friend the Member for Old Bexley and Sidcup (Sir E. Heath) said that it is absolute nonsense to talk about Turkey becoming involved. Turkey is involved, not just with a Turkish battalion on the ground but through Turkish public opinion. Senior members of the Turkish Government will not stand by and let their "communities", as they see them, be overrun in Bosnia. So, if anybody has any illusions on that count, may I dispel them here and now? I say with some sincerity that I formed the British-Turkish parliamentary group in 1974 and I know Turkey almost as well as anyone in the House.

The men of the Devon and Dorsets arrived in Bosnia only last month. They are my county regiment and they will serve us well there, but they and all the other service men in Bosnia will be questioning their role at this moment and wondering just where it will all end. I think that they will take heart from the decisions made by our Government last weekend. We all know that our armed forces are the best in the world. Of course they are. They are professional and they have a great sense of purpose, but they need to be reinforced in that sense of purpose so that they can be sure that the job that they are doing is worth while. In Bosnia, there was such a sense of purpose when the role of our armed forces was peacekeeping and humanitarian. They knew exactly where they were. Now we are in more dangerous territory. The line between peacekeeping and peacemaking becomes very blurred. My concern is that we may stumble across that line and become engaged in a savage and brutal war, which would need massive ground reinforcements.

My right hon. Friend the Prime Minister, in his speech today, made it quite clear that, in that case, there might be no alternative but for us to leave. Even taking account of that, from where would such massive reinforcements have come? The reality is that no major nation, other than Britain and France, has either the intention or the will to commit more ground forces. Indeed, many of the national contingents already in Bosnia may well be withdrawn or reduced over the next few months. The question for Ministers tonight is this: are there plans to get the other allies in NATO and the UN to change their minds and to reinforce instead of moving out? We have to decide our priorities in the full knowledge that, from others, we may have only words, not deeds. That said, our Government are absolutely right to reinforce our ground forces and to take every possible contingency action to give them increased protection and fire power in what I hope will be safer base areas, where we do not have people on outposts able to be picked up at the drop of a hat.

The options now are plain: the United Nations must commit more troops, take on the Serbs—or, for that matter, anyone else who cuts across us—or withdraw. Britain and France cannot and should not shoulder the main burden of providing additional ground forces in the future. Neither option, to stay or to go, is palatable. We are absolutely right to prepare and to dispose our forces so that they are ready to do either. I personally hope that, in the circumstances that now exist, we will be able to remain. But if we cannot remain, getting out, as the hon. and learned Member for Fife, North-East (Mr. Campbell) said on the radio yesterday, will be just as difficult as staying. Therefore, let us stay, stick it out and play our part and give a lead to others.

7.53 pm

**Mr. Ieuan Wyn Jones** (Ynys Môn): The hon. Member for Dorset, West (Sir J. Spicer) spoke warmly of the Royal Welch Fusiliers. The thoughts of the people of Wales tonight are with the 33 young men from the Royal Welch Fusiliers who are currently held hostage by the Bosnian Serbs. Our thoughts are with them and their families and we all pray for their safe release and return. We utterly condemn the outrageous actions of the Bosnian Serbs in taking young soldiers as hostages. They are part of the United Nations peacekeeping force, dedicated to ensuring the safety of civilians and the safe passage of humanitarian supplies. To have their lives endangered is totally unacceptable.

[*Mr. Ieuan Wyn Jones*]

United Nations forces, with representatives from 18 nations, have already carried out their duties with great skill and professionalism. Without doubt, their presence, as we have heard today, has saved the lives of thousands of men, women and children. We have all been horrified by the atrocities that have been perpetrated in the former Yugoslavia, in the main by Serbs and Bosnian Serbs. The practice of ethnic cleansing has shocked us beyond belief. In these very difficult circumstances, the troops of the United Nations have carried out their duties, on behalf of all of us who share the view that the west, and Europe in particular in this case, has a responsibility to the innocent people who are caught in the middle of a bloody conflict.

It must be said, however, that, from time to time, United Nations missions in Bosnia have lacked clarity, and a lack of a strategic objective has hampered their operation. We already have three resolutions governing the rules of engagement and the deployment of troops to safe areas. Because some of those safe areas are remote and isolated, troops stationed in them have always been vulnerable to Serb aggression. What happened to the Royal Welch Fusiliers in Gorazde is a case in point.

**The Minister of State for the Armed Forces (Mr. Nicholas Soames):** As the hon. Gentleman takes a close interest in the Royal Welch Fusiliers, who find themselves in these difficulties, does he recall that, as the 23rd of foot, the Royal Welch Fusiliers took part in the siege of Lucknow, the siege of the Pekin legations and at Kohima? They will give a very good account of themselves.

**Mr. Jones:** I am grateful to the Minister for that intervention.

We have to remember that the remaining troops currently in the safe area of Gorazde could be trapped and that they would not be able to leave, except through Serb-held territory. Given those circumstances, however emotional the appeal might be for withdrawal, in these circumstances it is simply neither practical nor logistically possible. We need an assurance from the Government that the deployment of further troops to Bosnia will give better protection to the existing forces, and their withdrawal, if necessary, from the safe areas where the risk to their safety is considered to be unacceptable. We also want assurances that the Government see the deployment of those further troops as a way to increase pressure on the Serbs to release the hostages held by them and that nothing will be done to harm their welfare in the meantime.

We must also accept that much stronger action at an earlier date would have prevented the Serbs from believing that the international community would hold back from action at crucial times. That lack of clear leadership has allowed the Serbs to think that, although strong words have been used to condemn their actions, they have not always been followed by resolute action. We have to criticise, quite forcefully, the decision to launch air strikes when troops were vulnerable. That is an issue on which we should be absolutely clear. I think that there has been a division of opinion between the European nations and the United States on that issue. If the United States felt that the only way in which it could be seen to be taking strong action was to organise air strikes, it has

put European troops in difficulty. In my view, the Government should take up that issue with the United States.

A number of matters are important for us to consider in the light of the announcement by the Government today. I shall make half a dozen short points. First, we recognise that the deployment of further troops is necessary to give support to existing United Nations forces, provided, of course, that we see the release of the hostages as a top priority. We want to see them released safe and well. Secondly, the troops, if necessary, should be removed from the safe areas that are too remote or vulnerable to be given proper support. Thirdly, there should be no withdrawal of peacekeeping forces at present. Not only would that be a massive and, perhaps, fatal blow to the authority of the United Nations but it would be a humiliation and an acceptance that Serb aggression had triumphed. Terrorism perpetrated against 33 young soldiers cannot be rewarded in that way. However, the situation must be closely monitored, and the withdrawal of troops would need to be contemplated at some future date if the situation deteriorated to such an extent that the safety of United Nations troops was unacceptably compromised.

Fourthly, the diplomatic efforts to find a solution should be stepped up. The Bosnian Serbs must be made to understand that they face international isolation as a result of their recent actions. The diplomatic effort should be channelled into securing the recognition of the state of Bosnia, by the international community, the Bosnian Serbs and the Serb nation. That would be the clearest possible signal to the Bosnian Serbs that the international community is serious on this occasion.

Fifthly, the action taken to bolster the security of the troops already deployed would also act as a demonstration of the will of the international community to send a clear message to the warring factions. Although the United Nations should not contemplate all-out war, it should send the clearest possible signal that holding troops as hostages is an act of terrorism and cannot be allowed to pass. A proactive stance in the current situation would send such a signal.

Finally, the United Nations must be clear in its objectives, which must be to secure the recognition of Bosnia by diplomacy, as well as strengthening and supporting the peacekeeping forces and reducing their vulnerability in the face of Serbian aggression. To achieve that end, the Security Council's resolutions may need to be revised to allow greater flexibility of action when necessary.

The people of Wales share the anguish and concern for the welfare and safety of the 33 young men taken by the Bosnian Serbs. I am sure that the whole House will join me in calling for their immediate release and asking that their families be spared further anguish. We recognise the role that they have played, as part of the forces in Bosnia, in securing the delivery of humanitarian aid to the civilian population. They must remain in our thoughts as further action is contemplated, and their release must remain our top priority. They would also wish us, I am sure, to persevere with our efforts to seek a lasting peace in that troubled country.

We ask that those new efforts be channelled through the United Nations—an organisation whose 50th anniversary we celebrate this year. The UN's authority must be maintained, otherwise we are all weakened in our efforts to deter unwarranted military aggression in any part of the world.

8.1 pm

**Mr. Nicholas Budgen** (Wolverhampton, South-West): It is a pleasure and a privilege to take part in this debate. The hon. Member for Ynys Môn (Mr. Jones) did well to end his speech by reminding us of the plight of the families of the 33 soldiers who have been taken hostage. One of the questions that those of my generation ask ourselves before embarking on a political career is in what circumstances we would ask the young men of this country to risk their lives on our behalf. For those of us who were brought up in the shadow of the war, and whose characters were much formed by the consequences of the war, that is a big and important question.

Many Conservative Members fear that we may be slowly becoming embroiled in something not unlike a British Vietnam. We begin to become very concerned as we see the changing role of the British troops in Bosnia.

I do not want to repeat all the arguments put so very well by my hon. Friends the Members for Gosport (Mr. Viggers) and for East Lindsey (Sir P. Tapsell). Three arguments have been advanced as our involvement has become ever greater. The first has been the humanitarian argument. I agree with my hon. Friend the Member for Gosport that it seems that action under that head has failed, and it is certainly highly likely that much of the food and aid has not—[Hon. Members: "Not true."] At any rate, it was hoped that humanitarian aid would end the fighting and the tension and it has not. [Hon. Members: "No."] All right. If it has succeeded, it is rather strange that all these unfortunate persons have been kidnapped and that the House is sitting today.

The second argument for involvement has been the peacekeeping argument, and I should have thought that that, too, had failed. If it had succeeded, there would have been no need for the House to convene for this special debate.

A third argument is now being used—an argument, I may say, that was not being advanced at the beginning—which is that there is a British national interest in attempting to stop a war spreading across the map of Europe, particularly if that war would range the United States and Russia on different sides. That is a proper argument. That argument—the risk of danger to the British national interest—is an argument that we, as Tories, have always advanced to justify any risk to British soldiers. But the British national interest does not exist merely because a politician declares that it exists: it exists because it is felt by the British people and because it is conceived by British mothers and British families to be a purpose for which they are prepared to see their sons die.

That was certainly felt about the Falklands—perhaps to a greater extent by the British people than by the British political class. The strength of feeling, which I recollect, on the Saturday when we debated the Falklands war surprised many people. It certainly surprised many of the people detached from ordinary emotions, who see these things in terms of legalistic peacekeeping, with references to the United Nations, the European Union and the concept of international law. That was not what was being expressed on that important Saturday. Instead, there was the feeling that British people and British territory had

been conquered; that the wrong must be righted as quickly as possible; and that to that end it was justifiable to suffer casualties and the loss of lives. There is at present no such feeling about our involvement in Bosnia.

There is nothing more dangerous than a half-hearted war. It gives the wrong signal to each and every person, section of the community and ally involved. We are in danger of getting sucked into a half-hearted war—a war which will be damaging and dangerous to our service men; which will undermine our honour; which will certainly give us a false impression of our resolve. We should engage in war only if we are satisfied that the British people see that their interest is involved. On that point, I entirely agree with my right hon. Friend the Member for Old Bexley and Sidcup (Sir E. Heath): this is not an occasion on which we should engage in war. We should send some more troops, but we should send them to facilitate the return of those troops already there. We should not get involved in what could become a British Vietnam.

8.8 pm

**Mrs. Ann Clwyd** (Cynon Valley): I join the hon. Member for Ynys Môn (Mr. Jones) and my hon. Friend the Member for Pembroke (Mr. Ainger)—the only two Welsh Members who have spoken during this debate—in voicing concern about the 33 members of the Royal Welch Fusiliers who are now hostages. One of them is a constituent of mine. His family do not want his name to be known. He was married only four days before he was sent to Bosnia in February and his new wife and his family are naturally very concerned about his fate. I hope that the safety of the hostages will be paramount in any discussions that the Government have with those who have any influence in this matter.

We must make it clear to those holding the men that they have absolutely nothing to gain by trying to use them as blackmail material in this awful war. In my view, talk of withdrawal in response to hostage taking is reprehensible and should not on any account be supported. We should now be asking ourselves how we should discharge our responsibilities to enforce the current UN mandate and to bring about a negotiated settlement.

I disagree with the right hon. Member for Guildford (Mr. Howell), who said that we need not analyse the past. I think that we need to analyse the past, however briefly. Past mistakes by the contact group and other external actors on the stage include wholly inadequate political and diplomatic responses to ethnic cleansing and other actions—perpetrated principally by the Serbs, but also by the Croats—wholly inadequate pressure on the Serbians to limit support for Bosnian Serbs, tardy imposition of sanctions and inadequate attempts to achieve unity among the contact group, in particular, the lack of political leadership by France and Britain with regard to resolving US-Russian differences. The hon. Member for East Lindsey (Sir P. Tapsell) described it as treating the Russians casually.

Despite all that, for three years the British troops and other have helped hundreds of thousands of ordinary Bosnians to survive the war. They have aided the starving, provided shelter for the homeless, brought medical aid to the injured and stamped out some of the most awful brutality. We have tried to help, whatever the Bosnian Government say. Pulling out would mean the end of that

[Mrs. Ann Clwyd]

aid and the probable collapse of the enclaves, causing a huge flight of people and leaving thousands defenceless against the ethnic cleansers. Is that what we want?

Three broad options exist, which have been spelt out this afternoon. They are massively to expand military forces to enforce a peace, especially on the Bosnian Serbs; withdrawal of UN military forces and humanitarian relief in the belief that the war will be brought to a conclusion; and continuing peacekeeping operations at broadly current levels, but with changes in rules of engagement coupled with selective withdrawals from exposed areas—all accompanied by systematic increases in diplomatic pressure.

There is clearly not the political will in the House to enforce a peace by military means. Large-scale force might have suppressed the conflict at an earlier stage— and I was in favour of that—but it would probably now incite guerrilla responses, ultimately backed by Serbia. Withdrawal would represent the second UN defeat in recent years—after Somalia—but would be politically much more significant than that. In the likely ensuing upsurge in conflict, any Bosnian Government successes would bring in Serbian support for Bosnian Serbs, leading to an escalation; any Bosnian Serb successes would bring in unofficial—and perhaps official—support from middle east states, leading to an escalation.

Pressure for withdrawal is understandable, but the almost inevitable result would be a substantial widening of the war, heavy civilian casualties and a dangerous regional instability. However unsatisfactory, the UN presence needs to be maintained, concentrating on humanitarian relief, while diplomatic pressures are systematically intensified. In that process, offensive military action and humanitarian relief are fundamentally incompatible.

Given past mistakes and political inadequacies, there are no easy answers; but the current Bosnian Serb belligerence arises partly through desperation, and Serbian support is already succumbing to external pressure. Greatly strengthening such pressure, while attempting wherever possible to suppress and contain the fighting, must surely be the best option.

8.14 pm

**Mr. Andrew Robathan** (Blaby): Some years ago, I dabbled in strategy at the Army staff college. I remember an old adage, which many may have heard before: "Do not march on Moscow, and do not go to war in the Balkans."

I understand—some of it was before my time—that this is the third occasion on which Parliament has been recalled to discuss international military emergencies in the past 13 years. I well remember the recall of Parliament to debate the Falklands. I was in Belize at the time as a serving soldier, but I was keen to go to the Falklands because I saw the national interest: I saw how important it was to go, and I wanted to be there. I also remember the Gulf war. I was a civilian then, but I volunteered to go to the Gulf because that too was an international emergency, and I could see the national and international interest—and, indeed, I went.

I think that everyone realises that Parliament has been recalled today in very different circumstances. It is difficult to see a clear national interest for us, or a clear aim. Sadly, however, because of the last two experiences, the feeling is abroad that whatever we do we shall win— for, notwithstanding the tragic deaths in the Falklands and many fewer deaths in the Gulf, we won relatively easily. This is a great deal less easy.

Let me deal briefly with the diplomatic disasters and failures. I refer to the failure of European Community efforts in Bosnia, and the disaster of the early recognition of Croatia and Bosnia, to which others have referred— driven largely, it must be said, by the Germans when Bosnia was not a real country. It was recognised, and now we learn from yesterday's newspapers that Chancellor Kohl considers it essential for UN troops to remain in Bosnia. We also see the failure of the United States to send any troops, only to give the most extraordinary signals in calling for air strikes—possibly using its aircraft in the process. From the White House there is a stunning silence, and certainly no offer of troops.

The UN structure in Bosnia, certainly the civilian structure, has been at best mixed. It has sent out mixed messages, and has at times been hopeless. If anyone has not read Lewis Mackenzie's book "Peacekeeper", I recommend it for the chapters in which the author describes how impossible it was to secure a clear instruction from the United Nations. The account may not be accurate, but it is an interesting reflection.

Then, last week, there was the disaster of air strikes. Some of us had warned against them for some time. When I went to Pale two years ago, I found two UN soldiers— one British, one Swedish—in a little villa, a skiing lodge on the slopes of Pale, in the sunshine. It was obvious to me then that they were hostages, and I suspect that their successors have now been taken hostage. In the past three years we have heard a good deal about the surgical use of air power, but it is not very surgical. I should like to know what the "bombers" who have called for the surgical use of air power think now; we have heard from one or two. We were told that it would send a signal to the Serbs. The Serbs have heard that signal, and have sent a signal to the United Nations.

There are those here who blame the Serbs alone. The Serbs have acted very aggressively, and have been the most culpable in the war all along; furthermore, they are acting as terrorists now and are becoming our enemies. They are not, however, the only culpable parties in Bosnia.

I should prefer to deal with the military situation. I supported the Government when they first sent troops to Bosnia to deliver aid, but I now question whether I was right to support that decision. I support the Government now, as we send reinforcements, but I urge caution, as I believe everyone has. Like the United States in Vietnam, NATO troops are being sucked into a conflict in which we are outsiders. The Bosnians—be they Serb, Muslim or Croatian in origin, and indeed Serbia and Croatia as countries—are fighting for their survival, like the North Vietnamese and the Vietcong. Some will be happy to die: they feel that they are fighting in a national crusade, for some glorious cause. Our troops, however, do not feel that they are fighting in some national crusade, and I suspect that the French do not either. We are outsiders; we do not understand the passions and the politics of the Balkans. That fact was illustrated by the hon. Member for Vauxhall (Miss Hoey), who said that the conflict was not a civil war but who then referred to Karadzic as a Bosnian Serb. How can it not be a civil war if Bosnian Serbs are fighting Bosnian Muslims and Croatians?

There is no obvious British national interest, so why are our troops in the area? They are there to deliver aid but, sadly, that is no longer possible. My right hon. Friend the Prime Minister said that we will not wage war, so what are we there for? Our first purpose must be to free and to protect our soldiers who are being held hostage, but then what? If we are not waging war and we are unable to deliver aid, what is the mission for our commanders? What is our aim? What orders will we give our soldiers on the ground?

There has been talk about command and control and about giving the United Nations control over the reinforcements that we have sent. I do not think that the United Nations—particularly the civilian structure—has proved to be the best command structure in Bosnia. We may make a disastrous situation worse if we send our reinforcements into the same structure.

The structure of our forces and of all the United Nations forces is in penny packets. Small United Nations military observer teams are scattered around Bosnia. Their purpose is to deliver aid; they are not organised to fight a war. As we have seen in the last week, they are not even organised to defend themselves. They cannot fight at the moment, even if they want to.

The United Nations observers are in the way. The right hon. Member for Yeovil (Mr. Ashdown) called for more observers to be sent to the river Drina where they could be taken hostage. That is a bizarre suggestion. Even with reinforcements, the United Nations and the United Kingdom will not be able to wage war.

There has been much talk about the honour of the United Nations and of international law. In my experience, few soldiers fight for international law. They fight for Queen and country, family, mates, pay, leave and even for excitement; but I doubt that many would fight for international law.

Our troops have got stuck in and they have done incredibly well in the past three years; we all acknowledge that. However, I would suggest that they do not want to die for the cause of international law and a member of the armed forces said exactly that to me last year. For what noble cause could our troops die in Bosnia? It appears that the noble cause may be keeping two bands of cut-throats apart.

The House has enough armchair tacticians, of whom I fear I am one. I do not want to know what tactics will be employed in Bosnia; it is not my business to know the details. The right hon. Member for Yeovil asked for details about what our troops would do. I think that it is quite wrong even to ask. I do not think that the House should ask for such details because it weakens our national hand in Bosnia. If we are to be successful, we must keep the combatants, the press and, I fear, some hon. Members guessing.

General Smith is a first-class leader. I had the honour to attend his O group in the Gulf. He did an excellent job in the Gulf commanding our division and keeping a very low profile. He is extremely capable and he is an excellent person for the United Nations to have in position. He has an impossible task, but I know that the whole House wishes him well.

Many historical analogies have been bandied about today—Czechoslovakia, Munich, the Falklands and the Gulf. My analogies are Vietnam and, perhaps more aptly, Lebanon. The Government are absolutely correct to send reinforcements to Bosnia. I think that the whole House trusts General Smith and almost all hon. Members have put their trust in the decision of my right hon. Friend the Prime Minister and my right hon. and learned Friend the Secretary of State for Defence to send reinforcements. I know that they are receiving excellent advice from the chiefs of staff. They have a difficult task and I do not wish to make it more difficult.

We must defend our soldiers, but what will we do when the hostages are released? That is an impossible question and I have no answers. I do not envy my right hon. Friends having to take those decisions. I remember one more thing from having dabbled in tactics 10 years ago: one should reinforce success and on no account reinforce failure.

8.24 pm

**Mrs. Alice Mahon** (Halifax): The House is united tonight—as I hope it will be in the future—in support of the peacekeepers and deliverers of humanitarian aid in Bosnia who are in a desperate plight. The safety and the rescue of those peacekeepers must be paramount. We should never underestimate how difficult their job has been. The peacekeepers in Bosnia have been continually humiliated, and it must be extremely difficult for a 21-year-old to be taunted time and again as he attempts to carry out his duty. I believe that the peacekeepers have operated quite well in a very dignified manner under a very difficult and narrow mandate. There is universal condemnation of those who would chain peacekeepers like animals and hold them against their will.

Last weekend I attended the spring session of the North Atlantic Assembly in Budapest and during my stay I visited a refugee camp where many Bosnians have lived for some time. I talked to young people, both Serbs and Muslims, who had lived side by side in Bosnia. They condemned their leaders out of hand and referred to them as war criminals and crazy people. I had a very good conversation with a young Serb who spoke English quite well. He urged the west to speak with people other than the self-appointed leaders and to by-pass all those who were responsible for the present carnage in Bosnia.

I admit that that is a difficult task, but it is not impossible. The hon. Member for Staffordshire, South (Sir P. Cormack) referred to the Serb Council and he reminded us how many people belong to that organisation. It may be a good idea to concentrate our efforts on opening a dialogue with the council.

In Budapest we debated an emergency motion about the crisis in Bosnia. My hon. Friend the Member for South Shields (Dr. Clark) seconded the motion and spoke very well on the subject. Speakers from France, the Czech republic, the Netherlands, Poland, Turkey, Canada, Russia and the United States participated in the debate. Speaker after speaker condemned the hostage taking and demanded the release of the prisoners. The speakers also made the point that the problems in Bosnia cannot be resolved by external military force. We must resume negotiations and, if possible, continue to deliver humanitarian aid.

*[Mrs. Alice Mahon]*

I have listened to many defence debates over the years. It is quite difficult to speak in defence debates when one is female, but I have picked up as much information as I can and I believe that we have three options in Bosnia. We could opt for massive air attacks. I think that the recent bombing was a disastrous mistake which led to the hostage taking. Ironically, that option is favoured by the United States, which does not have a single soldier on the ground and which said recently that it would never allow a United States soldier to set foot on Bosnian soil.

However, in answer to a question at the NAA, the Assistant Secretary Holbrooke said that the United States would contribute half the troops in order to facilitate a withdrawal from Bosnia if it proved necessary. We cannot evacuate our troops on the ground in Bosnia by aircraft carrier, no matter how sophisticated or large it may be. We must ask who we would bomb. I think that air strikes have been exposed as a flawed tactic.

I agree with my right hon. Friend the Member for Chesterfield (Mr. Benn) who said that there are blue berets in the air dropping bombs while blue berets on the ground are trying to keep the peace and deliver aid. Those two objectives are incompatible. I believe that air strikes would lead to an increase in hostage taking. It is an impossible strategy and I hope that the Government have enough sense to ignore any advice in its favour.

The second option would be to concentrate all our efforts on trying to isolate the problem and contain it within Bosnia so that it does not spill over into other countries. That containment strategy is being argued tonight, and I have heard it before. It could include withdrawal of peacekeeping if it becomes impossible to deliver aid, although I am not sure how we could manage containment from outside.

The third option, and the one that I favour, is to try to maintain the status quo, difficult as that might be. We have to face the truth, uncomfortable as it might be, that the belligerents in the conflict are not yet ready for peace and there still appears to be bloodlust. The rest of us feel helpless and frustrated, especially our troops on the ground.

Experience teaches us that there are limits to external intervention in civil wars. I also believe that we have become involved in a civil war and that making paper threats has helped us lose credibility.

As many of our military commanders have told us, we should ignore those groups that encourage us to take sides. That is always dangerous. One Opposition Member referred to knowing which side to support; I am on the side of peace in the Balkans and that must be paramount. To be sucked into taking sides would be disastrous and would lead us into another Vietnam. That is why the United States does not want to commit any troops on the ground. The Americans have had their fingers burnt and realise that such a move would be disastrous.

I should make a couple of points about the Russians. If we are serious about peace in the Balkans, we cannot exclude them as we did in the bombing. They did not know of the plans to bomb, yet they constantly warned us about the consequences of such action. This weekend, the Russian delegate told us that it was fairly well-established that the recent breakdown of peace in Bosnia was brought about by Bosnian Government forces taking the first pot shot at a French soldier and that was followed by retaliation.

Obviously, I accept that the greatest brutality has been on the side of the Serbs. They have had the most weapons and have been the most organised militarily, but there have been atrocities on both sides. In civil war, barbarism is the name of the game. It is the most appalling war and it is happening in Bosnia.

When my right hon. Friend the Member for Copeland (Dr. Cunningham) was shadow Foreign Secretary, he told us that senior members of the Bosnian Government had made it clear to him that they thought they could win the war. At that time, they were not interested in talking about peace.

The United Nations and NATO should not look for one guilty party and we must not allow the media to persuade us into reckless action. Russia can play an important part in exerting pressure on the Serbs and the Russians must be consulted. We have been absolutely crazy to exclude them.

I end on a point that has already been made. At present, the House has an overriding duty to rescue our troops as we sent them there. I do not want the Prime Minister or the Secretary of State for Defence to tell me how they plan to do that. As my right hon. Friend the Leader of the Opposition said, we have to be totally united and have a single purpose. We want their safety.

On the wider question of extending our mandate and taking sides in a civil war, we need firmer assurances than we have had so far. I am sure that the Opposition will agree with that because we would never ask the young men and women who volunteer to serve our country in a defensive capacity to be cannon fodder in a Balkan conflict which will be resolved only when the present antagonists want to resolve it. Our role has to be to facilitate peace and to continue trying to provide humanitarian aid.

8.33 pm

**Mr. Jacques Arnold** (Gravesham): Our right hon. Friends were right to take the difficult and awesome decision to send reinforcements into Bosnia following recent events. They will provide British forces under the United Nations with support and protection in carrying out their role and will empower them to be flexible. We have to choose between maintaining the policy of containment and humanitarian support and withdrawal.

The House should reflect carefully before taking that decision, bearing in mind that we remain a great power and that our actions will have consequences. We are a permanent member of the Security Council of the United Nations, a leading nation in the European Union and NATO and a worldwide player in United Nations peacekeeping. Therefore, what we do is of considerable significance.

Would we really withdraw our troops from Bosnia? Are we really prepared to face the scenes of panic and mass slaughter which would be shown on our televisions night after night, with Kate Adie drawing attention to all the blood and gore? There would be massive public revulsion and people would ask Parliament, "What do you plan to do about it?". There would be a complete swing in British public opinion were people to see the slaughter that would follow a withdrawal.

Matters are not that simple. We and the French may withdraw, but our troops make up not even a quarter of UNPROFOR. Would the Muslim United Nations troops abandon their co-religionists? We have to consider the two Pakistani battalions at Vares and Banovici, the Bangladeshi battalion at Bihac, the Malaysian battalion at Konjic and Makarska, the Turkish battalion at Zenica and the Jordanians, who have similar numbers of troops to ours in the former Yugoslavia. It is more likely those Muslim nations' battalions would become partisan combatants rather than withdraw as we would.

What pressures would our withdrawal put on the Russian contingent and their pan-orthodox links with the Serbs? We should reflect carefully before we leave a void into which dark forces would race. Iran is already supplying the Bosnian Muslims, and many other Islamic states would become involved.

Malaysia, Indonesia, Pakistan and the Arab nations, let alone the zealots, not least Libya, would consider themselves under an obligation to their co-religionists. If we were to exacerbate fundamentalism at such a difficult time, we could well reap the results. We should consider the impact on Algeria and other Maghreb countries, and Turkey, which could be dragged backwards from its modern role. All those factors should be taken into account. We should ask ourselves whether we really want Islamic fundamentalism warring in the continent of Europe.

The more likely outcome, however, would be a Serbian short-term victory accompanied by brutality, rape and slaughter, and then what? How long would it be before the Bosnian Serb Republic would merge itself into Greater Serbia? How long would it be before it were joined by the Krajina Serbs from Croatia and what would that do in terms of reigniting the Croatian tinderbox? Would not Belgrade become re-emboldened as the sanctions gripped around her throat were eased, and would not Greater Serbia extrapolate the very lessons that our weakness would reveal?

We have only to examine what is already happening. The two previous autonomous provinces of Yugoslavia and Serbia are already feeling the Serb jackboot. In the Vojvodina, where one quarter of the population is Hungarian, autonomy was scrapped in 1990 and Serbo-Croat was declared the only official language the following year. In Kosovo, where 90 per cent. of the population is Muslim Albanian, autonomy was simultaneously scrapped and repression is increasing.

In the Sandjak on the Serbian-Montenegrin border, which has an 80 per cent. Muslim population, Serb repression is also deepening. Many Muslims from the Sandjak are already fleeing into Bosnia. That is significant. If Bosnia is supposed to be such a dangerous place, what does that say about civil rights and freedoms in the Sandjak?

Perhaps Greater Serbia would acquire an enthusiasm to regain the former Yugoslav Republic of Macedonia. That country, with its volatile mix of Macedonians, Albanians and Serbs, is also coveted by Bulgaria and Greece.

What would Hungary do? Would it tolerate indefinitely the repression by the Serbs of a third of a million Hungarians in Vojvodina? Would Hungary eventually react? That, in turn, could rekindle the interests of Hungary in the substantial minorities that it has in Slovakia where there are 600,000 ethnic Hungarians or Romania where there are 1.6 million ethnic Hungarians in Transylvania.

As we look at the whole issue, the ethnic ripples that could be ignited in Sarajevo go wider and wider. It is trite to say that one of the big conflicts that the continent of

ours has suffered this century also started in Sarajevo in 1914. It would be wrong for the House to echo the exasperation of Neville Chamberlain who complained of

"a quarrel in a far-away country between people of whom we know nothing."

What we need in the House of Commons are cool heads, a wide perspective and wise counsel based on experience, which is what this country has traditionally provided to the world.

8.41 pm

**Mr. Mike Gapes** (Ilford, South): Three weeks ago in the House I was fortunate enough to speak in the debate on Bosnia. I concluded my remarks by saying:

"We must recognise that there is a limit to how long we can simply sit ineffectively hoping for something to turn up."—[*Official Report*, 9 May 1995; Vol. 259, c. 640.]

Regrettably, I did not expect that something to be the events of the past week.

Why are we in this mess? According to a report by Martin Walker in *The Guardian* on 27 May there was a serious bout of arm twisting from the Clinton Administration last week. They were going round world capitals putting pressure on for more and more military action against the Bosnian Serbs. At the same time, there was a report in *The Independent* that Senator Jesse Helms was quite happy with what President Clinton had been doing because it was

"essential in terms of doing something."

That is the problem and it is a problem that occurs in some of the things that we have heard in the debate. There are times when doing something can make situations worse than calmly sitting and waiting for a more opportune moment in the future. The French Prime Minister Alain Juppé is quoted as saying:

"Ultimatums and air strikes must be used after reflection and preparation . . . Last Friday's ultimatum and air strikes were not well prepared and exposed the peacekeepers to thoughtless risks. We must not again carry out this type of operation."

Could the Security Council members and the NATO commanders really not have thought through the consequences of their decision for the peacekeepers? If that is so, it is absolutely appalling.

The situation is perhaps a consequence of different views of the world. Those who have participants on the ground view things differently from those who see the conflict on CNN and think that somehow there can be a quick fix intervention to solve the problem so that they can move on to another problem in the afternoon.

I regret that it is not just CNN. I was in a debate this afternoon on CNN with an American congressman. He argued that British and French forces in Bosnia were an impediment to a solution and that they were standing in the way of the tough action required. He was completely against any deployment of United States ground forces but he was in favour of lifting the arms embargo and of air strikes. That was an eight-term Republican congressman from New Jersey. It worries me that we have a United States congress dominated by such views. Clearly, they are thinking about the world without taking account of the realities.

There has been mention in the debate that the United States might, perhaps, provide half of the 50,000 troops that might be required should there be a withdrawal. I say, "Don't hold your breath." I do not believe that President

[*Mr. Mike Gapes*]

Clinton is capable of getting that through the American Congress. If they are not prepared to put people in at a time like this, I suspect that they would not be prepared to put them in anything like the numbers required for a withdrawal.

I am also conscious of the divisions in the statements that are coming from other quarters. There are clearly differences within the coalition. There are differences between the United States and Europe and there are differences with the Russians. There are potential differences with the Islamic world and we know that if we are to achieve a negotiated settlement, it needs the agreement of the Bosnian Government, the Bosnian Croats, the Bosnian Serbs, and Mr. Abdic's forces as well as the Governments of Croatia and Serbia and, presumably, the other successor states to former Yugoslavia.

I have great worries that we are all being used in different ways by people who are very good at pushing their own propaganda and using their own ploys to try to get us in on their side. Mr. Ejup Ganic, the Vice-President of Bosnia, said that there must be massive intervention by the west to solve the problem.

There is a belief in the Bosnian Government that somehow the cavalry will come over the hill. Therefore, the ceasefire that was negotiated by Jimmy Carter was not to be continued. On the other hand, we have this appalling and outrageous behaviour by the Bosnian Serbs.

How do we get out of this mess? First, we must recognise that there is no easy and quick fix. Secondly, we must face up to the fact that there may not be the possibility of any solution in the foreseeable future. Thirdly, we must recognise that if that is the case, we may have to face some harsh realities. There may come a point at which the humanitarian operation becomes impossible.

If that is the case, the three options that we have currently will be reduced to two. I do not want that. I believe in humanitarian intervention by the United Nations and I believe in internationalism and support for people who are suffering from starvation and oppression. However, I do not believe in being used and manipulated to fight somebody else's war, whether it is being done from across the Atlantic or from our own continent. Therefore, we should not allow the justifiable increase in our forces going in to provide protection for our own peacekeepers to become an incremental escalation towards a longer-term, indefinite involvement.

I am prepared, with some reservations, to support the actions that have been taken in the past few days. However, I want to make it clear that it is not just Conservative Members who have concerns about this matter. I have my concerns about where this is leading. It is important that the House should express the view that is shared by many people out there. They want to know why this is happening and where it will lead.

We did not get a satisfactory clarification from the Prime Minister and I do not expect to get one from the Secretary of State for Defence. Nevertheless, these questions warrant answers. If we return to this subject in a month's time and are asked to approve the sending of another few thousand troops, those questions will have to be put even more strongly than they have been put today.

**8.50 pm**

**Mr. Quentin Davies** (Stamford and Spalding): I listened to the hon. Member for Ilford, South (Mr. Gapes) with much interest. I thought that his approach to the problem and his reaction to the unfortunate events of the last few days showed a characteristic Labour party approach—a great deal of visceral anti-Americanism and a considerable lack of decisiveness about what we should do in difficult circumstances.

I want to make several points in the 10 minutes available to me, so I shall try to be as succinct as possible. My right hon. Friend the Prime Minister spoke today with great resolution and I believe that he will have the overwhelming majority of the country behind him. It is out of the question for this country to yield to threats or to give in to blackmail. We have rarely done so in more than 1,000 years of history. On the rare and shameful occasions that we have, from the Danegeld to Hitler in the 1930s, we have always come to regret it. It is much more expensive to rebuild a country's credibility once it has been damaged than it is to maintain a resolute position in the first place.

But we must not prevaricate. It is no good saying that we will not give in to threats and blackmail, but then saying that in the light of the hostage taking we may have to bring forward a withdrawal from Bosnia or give some assurances about no air strikes. Either of those suggestions immediately offers some reward to the Bosnian Serbs for their bad behaviour. The object of our policy must be the exact reverse—to ensure that the Bosnian Serbs come to regret and to regard as a complete mistake the dastardly action that they have taken against our troops during the past few days.

My second point is that consistent with that overall national objective we must get our hostages out, and by whatever mixture of military means, subterfuge and diplomacy that we can devise. I have every confidence in the Prime Minister and the Defence Secretary, although obviously we must not go into any details today about what they may be considering. However, I want to make a point about diplomacy, a word that has been used on many occasions this evening. Diplomacy is a means to an end; it is a mechanism for enabling parties who desire or have a need for an agreement to reach one. But unless the parties have such a desire or need, diplomacy will be a useless weapon. It cannot be used in a vacuum. Sometimes it is necessary to change the facts of the situation—the balance of forces—to generate that need for an agreement.

Thirdly, some tactical lessons need to be learnt from the taking of the hostages. A number of hon. Members, including myself, were perplexed by the fact that our commanders on the spot, who knew that an air strike was in prospect—indeed, they had called for air strikes—and who knew that the Bosnian Serbs had a history of taking hostages, nevertheless did not deploy the forces available to them in defensible numbers in defensible positions. There may be good reasons for that. Perhaps they were hamstrung by instructions from the special representative of the United Nations Secretary-General.

In the current position, it would not be helpful to have immediate answers to the obvious questions that arise, but in due course we will need to know exactly why such decisions were taken on deployment. I hope that whatever lessons need to be learnt will be learnt rapidly by those who are responsible for our troops.

There is a fourth conclusion to be drawn from the experiences of the past week, which is that Great Britain needs now, and will continue to need, professional, effective, flexible defence forces. We never know from where the threat will come. Who could have predicted the taking of hostages a few weeks or months ago? However, the Government have been able rapidly to mobilise 6,000 men—an armoured brigade—and are prepared to deploy them rapidly in the former Yugoslavia.

Quite simply, we would not have such a flexible range of responsive capabilities, we would not have those extremely well-trained and mobile troops, if we had adopted the defence policies urged on the Government by the two major Opposition parties over the past 15 years.

A number of hon. Members from those parties have made robust statements in the Chamber today and I welcome that unreservedly. However, I hope that they will have the honesty, at least in their private thoughts if not in their public statements, to acknowledge first, that those robust statements are empty and meaningless unless effective defence forces are at the disposal of the Government, and secondly, that the defence policies that their parties have urged on this House would have proved disastrous and would have deprived us of that necessary capability.

Finally, there is a longer-term strategic conclusion to be drawn. The point has already been made that one of the salient features of the present position is that we have engaged our forces in Bosnia, as have the French, whereas we have not been prepared to engage them in humanitarian, peacekeeping or peacemaking operations further afield. We have rightly not deployed our forces in Somalia, Angola, Azerbaijan, Cambodia or all the other places where human beings have been and are being massacred in deplorable circumstances. The reason for that is quite clear—we have a special interest in and a special responsibility for the maintenance of stability on our continent of Europe and on the frontiers of the European Union and the Atlantic Alliance.

We are not the world's policemen. We cannot take upon ourselves responsibility for maintaining order or for supervising the distribution of humanitarian relief across the globe. It is sad, but realistically we cannot do that. However, we can and must take responsibility for stability in our own zone. We and our French allies—and I pay tribute to them—have shouldered that responsibility. We have done so in the Gulf and we are doing so now in Bosnia. We have an interest in doing that. Over the years, the Americans have made it clear that they have a lesser interest because geopolitically they are much further removed from Bosnia. Nevertheless, we must recognise that the interest that we and the French have is fully shared, or ought to be, by our allies in the European Union—the Germans, the Italians, the Spaniards, the Dutch, the Finns and other smaller countries.

There is a very anomalous aspect in the present situation because the fact is that Britain and France have been shouldering a substantial burden in the Gulf, and now in Bosnia, not just in the interests of the stability of our zone and of our own countries but equally in the interests of the other European members of the Atlantic alliance and the other members of the European Union.

The other members of the European Union, one might say, have been free riding. They have been gaining the full benefit that has been secured by the gallantry, courage and sacrifices of our troops and by the financial costs that Britain and France have incurred. That situation is not viable, sensible, or reasonable and it cannot be allowed to continue into the longer term future.

It is necessary that the European Union should take seriously the commitment into which it entered in the Maastricht treaty to develop effective common foreign, security and defence policies. That is necessary in the interests of world peace because our influence on events will be much greater if policy is co-ordinated and focused—indeed, we might, arguably, have been able to avoid conflict in Yugoslavia had it been.

And if we need to engage in military action, it is necessary that the costs are spread through the Union as a whole, just as the benefits are. I hope that my right hon. Friends the Secretary of State for Defence and the Foreign Secretary will take advantage of the lessons that can be learned from Bosnia to press forward the implementation of the foreign, security and defence aspects of the Maastricht treaty.

8.59 pm

**Mr. Robert N. Wareing** (Liverpool, West Derby): There is one issue on which the House is united: the taking of hostages was a wrongful and sinful act by General Mladic and Mr. Karadzic. To say the least, it was very bad public relations on the part of the Bosnian Serbs.

We have to ask what led to that action. The answer was given by the Father of the House, the right hon. Member for Old Bexley and Sidcup (Sir E. Heath), when he pointed out that it would not have happened without the air strikes. Without those air strikes, we would not have sat here all afternoon and evening debating the problems in Bosnia-Herzegovina.

Although I support sending troops to safeguard our people out there and to restore the hostages to freedom, I think that 6,000 is rather a lot and I do not believe that the action which is being taken now, as with many actions that have involved the use of force in the past, is anything other than short-termism in military terms. There is a complete lack of political strategy.

Some hon. Members have argued about whether this is a civil war. My hon. Friend the Member for Vauxhall (Miss Hoey) argued that it was not a civil war on the ground that there is a Government universally recognised throughout the world in Sarajevo. In 1642, we had a Government who were universally recognised throughout the world; that did not stop us having a civil war. In the United States in 1861, they had a Government who were recognised by everyone; that did not stop them having a civil war.

Civil wars arise when one part of a country refuses to recognise the legitimacy of the Government who are installed at the time. That is precisely what has happened in Bosnia-Herzegovina. For all sorts of reasons, some of them historical, the Serbs do not recognise the Government in Sarajevo.

We should ask ourselves—surely the question should have been asked before—what we would do if we were in the position of Serbs living in Bosnia, or Krajina for that matter, when air strikes are launched. Their immediate reaction is that they are not the only ones fighting the civil war. After all, only a few weeks ago, 2,000 Serbs were driven out of their homes in western Slavonia and many Serbs were massacred by Croatian forces. Nobody contemplates sanctions against Croatia, let alone the use of air strikes.

*[Mr. Robert N. Wareing]*

My right hon. Friend the Leader of the Opposition made a very important point, which I hope will be answered, when he suggested that the safe havens should be demilitarised because many of the attacks which have been made, as general after general has said, were launched from inside the safe havens by Muslim forces. Even if the retaliation of the Serbs has sometimes been inordinate, Tuzla and Sarajevo have certainly been used as bases by Muslim forces to break ceasefire after ceasefire. Do we talk about air strikes against the Muslims? Of course we do not.

I am not suggesting that air strikes are justified in any event, but I am pointing out that if we talk about being even-handed, as the Prime Minister still does, we must remember that what is sauce for the goose is sauce for the gander. To act in any other way while putting an extra 6,000 of our troops into Bosnia-Herzegovina is to ensure the inevitability of their being sucked into a civil war on one side against the other. I do not believe that I could support that approach. It is a purely military strategy and there is a complete lack of political strategy.

Any political strategy must take two further factors into account. First, what will be the impact on Serbia itself? Some people are keen to attack President Milosevic, but they should consider the fact that, if we get embroiled in a civil war, it may not be Milosevic with whom we are dealing but Arkan or Seselj or some more extreme fascist elements.

Secondly, the impact on Russia has been mentioned by several hon. Members. Although it is the Government's policy to try to expand the frontiers of NATO—wrongly, in my view—we are ignoring the Russians in the essential matter of future political action in Bosnia-Herzegovina. Russia, one of the contact group's members, is being wholly ignored when it comes to political or military action.

I shall find it very difficult to support the Government; indeed, until I see a political strategy that brings even-handedness back to our approach, I shall not be able to do so.

9.6 pm

**Lady Olga Maitland** (Sutton and Cheam): One thing of which I am absolutely certain is that the country will applaud our Prime Minister for his decisiveness, clarity of mind and sense of purpose in making the important decision to send reinforcements to Bosnia. The country was waiting for decisive action and leadership, and they got it. We needed to be given a sober warning that he feared that, if we did not take decisive action and uphold the authority of the United Nations, a major war in Europe could follow. These are worrying moments, and it is right for us to be deeply concerned.

It is also appropriate and right that the Prime Minister should make it a priority to get the hostages released. However, we have to go a little further: it is important not only to take firm, decisive action to show that the authority of the United Nations cannot be sneered at or swept aside, but to consider what we can do to bring the Bosnian Serbs to sanity. We have to be firm with them, for I have always felt that Karadzic was a bully, a tyrant and a coward. Only cowards attack innocent citizens as he does.

It is significant that there is now evidence from a variety of sources that Karadzic is losing support among his own people. My hon. Friend the Member for Staffordshire, South (Sir P. Cormack) mentioned a document that shows that only 50 per cent. of his people support Karadzic's endeavours. I, too, have had reports that he is losing backing and that people in his country are seeking peace. It is important to take such divisions into account and to emphasise the importance of diplomacy. Diplomacy must be very carefully balanced. On one hand, we have to be firm militarily; we must not allow the Serbs to get away with their tyranny. On the other hand, if we bunker them too hard into a tight corner, I believe, knowing the Serbian personality as I do, that we will have taken a step backwards.

The key to peace lies in Belgrade. At least Milosevic has condemned the taking of those hostages and has accepted the contact group's peace plan. The next stage is to consider how to get him to recognise Bosnia. Recognising Bosnia is a possibility for Milosevic, because it is in his interests. Isolating Karadzic would help Milosevic, bearing in mind that Karadzic has eyes on the presidency in the former Yugoslavia. Therefore we must help Milosevic to facilitate a diplomatic outcome. A face-saving formula may be required, but one thing is for sure: unless we put as much effort into our diplomatic initiatives as we put into our military initiatives, we shall not obtain the peace in Europe that we desperately require.

9.10 pm

**Dr. David Clark** (South Shields): This has been an excellent debate and it has certainly justified the decision of the Government and Madam Speaker to recall Parliament. In all, 35 right hon. and hon. Members will have spoken in the debate, which has been of a very high standard and, naturally, of very high passion. Two sides—indeed, three sides if that is possible—of the argument have been presented. Some hon. Members felt that enough had not been done. My hon. Friends the Members for Vauxhall (Miss Hoey) and for Western Isles (Mr. MacDonald) made that point forcefully. The hon. Member for Staffordshire, South (Sir P. Cormack) shared the same point of view. They have long made their points of view very clear and we all know and appreciate the depth of their feelings on this issue.

Equally, members of all parties have said that we should not be involved, we should not take sides and a war-like posture should not be adopted. The Father of the House, the right hon. Member for Old Bexley and Sidcup (Sir E. Heath), and the hon. Member for East Lindsey (Sir P. Tapsell) spelled out very clearly why they felt that. My hon. Friend the Member for Linlithgow (Mr. Dalyell) and my right hon. Friend the Member for Chesterfield (Mr. Benn) expressed very clearly their reasons why they felt that it was not in Britain's interests to become involved.

We heard, too, a wealth of experience. My hon. Friend the Member for East Lothian (Mr. Home Robertson) talked about taking a convoy across the area. The hon. Member for Wealden (Sir G. Johnson Smith) told us of his experience in the North Atlantic Assembly and with European parliamentarians. Other hon. Members merely put their own views. I thought that the speech of my hon. Friend the Member for Halifax (Mrs. Mahon) was especially balanced, incisive and based on common sense, which we could do with by the bucketful in Bosnia. My hon. Friend the Member for Ilford, South (Mr. Gapes) gave an analytical response. My hon. Friends the Members for Feltham and Heston (Mr. Keen), for Liverpool, West Derby (Mr. Wareing) and for Walsall, North (Mr. Winnick) and, indeed, all hon. Members who have spoken put forward points of view that will be helpful to the Government and to the Secretary of State for Defence in trying to achieve a policy that is acceptable to the House. It is very important—if it is at all possible—that we maintain a consensus across the Chamber.

The Prime Minister set out the reasons why he felt that it was necessary to send British reinforcements. He took time to explain them and to try to take the House with him. My right hon. Friend the Leader of the Opposition made a comprehensive and perceptive speech. Above all, it was a balanced speech which actually managed to avoid the polarisation to which this issue, I am afraid, all too easily lends itself. His analysis, in a sense, served to emphasise that there is no easy solution to this problem. We all know that that is why we must redouble our efforts to try to bring some peace to Bosnia.

That is why we state without hesitation that we are not looking for the withdrawal of British troops. In fact, the barbaric action of the Bosnian Serbs in seizing hostages has once again reunited the House. Almost every Member has spelt that point out and shared that view. It is because of that barbaric action that the United Nations effort in Bosnia has been brought to crisis point yet again.

That crisis must be used for two primary purposes, one immediate and the other longer term. The first objective, one on which I believe there is complete consensus, is a matter of the greatest urgency—the release of the hostages. Of course we shall not probe the Secretary of State for Defence or the Foreign Secretary on that point; we know that they will be using all their best endeavours to ensure that release.

The Opposition believe that the perpetrators of the outrage must be brought to book and charged with war crimes. We have said that repeatedly, and there is no better time than now to press the demand. The behaviour of the Bosnian Serbs has been unforgivable; they have really crossed the rubicon this time. We all hope and pray that the captives will soon be released unharmed—a point made forcefully by the Members from Wales who have spoken on behalf of their constituents. But of course any response must be calculated and balanced. It must not be based purely on anger or revenge, because those motives will not serve us well.

We support and appreciate the Government's speedy reaction in announcing the reinforcements of further British troops. That action was correct, and we recognise that after such haste any decision will need further working out. Some of the answers may not be readily apparent, and we would not expect the Government to provide us with precise details today. However, 72 hours after the initial decision it is important for the Secretary of State to attempt to end some of the confusion and to clarify the situation.

In particular, if we are to put the lives of our young men and women at risk we have the right to expect the Secretary of State to announce the changed nature of the mission. There seems to have been confusion over the past mandate, and as we look towards a changed mandate it is important that the troops whom we are sending to Bosnia are aware of what the new mission is.

That is something that the military always ask me. If they are critical at all—and they rarely are in Bosnia—I think that sometimes, in their heart of hearts, they are a little unsure of what their precise mission is. We shall be rather unhappy if the Secretary of State cannot be a little more forthcoming about what he expects of the troops whom we are sending out there. As he knows, the nature of the troops and the armaments that we are sending add a potential for a great escalation of the situation in Bosnia.

We, and the whole House, want to be certain that the Government have a clearly worked-out strategy. If there has been an undertone running through the debate among certain Members, it has been the fear that we shall be sucked into a quagmire in Bosnia. That could easily happen, but it does not need to happen. That, however, will depend on the Government adopting a strategic approach. We should certainly like to know how they see this aspect of the problem.

I have gone on at some length about this point because I think it is important. It is perhaps worth reflecting on the history of why our troops were first sent to Bosnia and why we have had almost to treble their numbers now. They were, of course, originally sent out to escort the humanitarian convoys—to get the food and medicine through. As time went on, we found that more was needed. The second aspect of their mission then became clear, with the establishment of the safe havens. By definition, safe havens have to be safe. We now know that they are not really safe, because not enough nations were prepared to supply enough troops to make them so.

I was in Gorazde immediately before it was declared a safe area, although in effect it already was one. It was manned, ostensibly, by a Nordic battalion, consisting of a Nordic commander, a Kenyan, a Dutch deputy and seven other ranks—10 soldiers in all to look after an area of 250 sq km.

It is worth reminding ourselves when we talk about Europe and NATO that not only western Europe is involved. We should not forget the Bangladeshis, the Kenyans or the New Zealanders serving in Bosnia. Of course our own troops must be our first priority and interest in the context of military action and changing the mandate, but we must not forget that the United Nations has gone to a great deal of expense and spent a great deal of time in ensuring that some of these troops are adequately kitted out. Some time ago, there were reports of Bangladeshi troops in the Bihac enclave with one rifle between four men. That puts the difficult task of changing the mandate in context.

Several of my right hon. and hon. Friends have tried today to draw out the Secretary of State on the point to which I shall come next. Several countries that belonged to the former Warsaw pact have been active, too: Russia, Ukraine, Poland, the Czech Republic and Slovenia. A number of their troops have been taken hostage as well, which shows how much conditions have changed.

I wish to press the Secretary of State on the safe havens. There have been well-founded reports to the effect that the whole idea is to be abandoned. There are also well-founded reports that the Secretary-General of the United Nations believes that the three eastern safe havens, Zepa, Srebrenica and Gorazde, cannot be sustained and may have to be abandoned. That changes the nature of the game, but we understand why the Secretary-General thinks it necessary.

*[Dr. David Clark]*

When the safe havens were created in 1993, the Secretary-General asked the Security Council for 34,000 additional troops. In the end, he had to be satisfied with 7,500, and not even all of them were delivered. So he has had an impossible task. As the Secretary of State for Defence knows, the Royal Welch Fusiliers in Gorazde were not having an easy time of it even before the kidnappings. They have been short of water and supplies and their lives have been pretty intolerable. We want to know what efforts the Government are making at the United Nations—we are, after all, a permanent member of the Security Council—to deal with that problem. Before I leave the subject of safe havens, I wish to press a point that Labour Members have made for two years. When will the safe havens be demilitarised? It is unacceptable for safe havens to be used for military bases, as it upsets the military balance. Action must be taken if the safe havens are to be meaningful.

The change of policy and responsibility in Bosnia has been gradual. The problems of containment have been put at the top of the Ministry of Defence briefing notes, but they were not made explicit previously. I do not quibble with the present policy, because we must try to stop the flames spreading to the rest of the Balkans. But the pre-emptive stationing of troops in Macedonia—for which we have argued for a long time—means that an extra responsibility is placed on the troops.

We must ensure that the troops have a clear mandate and a clear mission, and that they have the facilities that they need to carry out their duties with the minimum of risk to their lives. We may well be adding to the mandate, and it is important that the Secretary of State for Defence brings the House more into his confidence on this issue without supplying any details that might put at risk our troops or make their tasks more difficult.

The other point which concerns us is the issue of command and control. Clearly, the UN has learnt a great deal, and obviously its experience in Bosnia has been unique. We are all learning as we go on. Things have been better since NATO took on a large part of the command structure, but there are basic problems.

My right hon. Friend the Member for Chesterfield made it clear that it is difficult to have an effective system of unified command and control where the soldiers on the ground who wear the blue helmets are neutral, while at the same time and under an associated command the forces in the air—which are also under the remit of those wearing the blue helmet—are carrying out offensive actions. That problem must be addressed, as it has exacerbated the situation and is certainly responsible for the current hostage situation.

**Sir Patrick Cormack:** Will the hon. Gentleman give way?

**Dr. David Clark:** I apologise, but I am short of time. I want to give the Secretary of State time to answer my questions.

That point must be clarified in relation to the deployment of the extra troops we are sending. As I understand it, the first two tranches of new troops will be working in BRITFOR under Brigadier Pringle in the south-west section. That is fairly clear. But will they be used for any other purpose other than supplementing British troops? Will they be used as a rapid reaction force to go to other parts of Bosnia to relieve and help out other troops under UN command?

Has the Secretary of State clarified the status under which the 24 Air Mobile Brigade group will be operating? The brigade is the largest contingent of our troops. We have seen reports that they will not go under the UN flag or wear the blue helmets, but will be attached to the British contingent. Does that mean that General Smith will have dual command? Will he be a double-hatted general? From where will 24 Air Mobile take its orders? Will it be from the UN in New York, or from the Ministry of Defence in Whitehall? I hope that I am not being too specific, but it is important that the House is aware of the problems.

**Dr. Spink:** The hon. Gentleman asks for too much detail.

**Dr. Clark:** Perhaps, but I am sure that the Secretary of State for Defence can deal with my questions.

Hon. Members on both sides of the House referred to the Russian position. Earlier this week, the hon. Member for Wealden and I visited Budapest to talk to politicians from the east and from the west. We know of the deep concern felt by the Russians, and we are aware of the intricacies and detail of command and control. We appreciate the complications of NATO-delivered air cover in conjunction with the UN, which becomes doubly difficult when other nations are not part of the NATO command structure.

We know the intricacies, details and routine of the command structure, but when it comes to a country that is a member of the contact group and is a major player—Russia—it makes no sense to cause offence by not at least keeping that country informed when air strikes are to take place. Leaders of the Duma whom I met in Budapest felt aggrieved and were reluctant to help—and we may need Russia's help when it comes to relieving the hostages and perhaps in other respects. Britain must be more sophisticated in developing that part of her policy.

The Labour party has made it clear that talk of withdrawal is not on the table. We would not be prepared to give in to blackmailers and terrorism. That is not an option. However, we came to play a role in Bosnia—in delivering humanitarian aid and dousing the flames—at the request of the UN. Our troops have done that well and honourably. However, as the Secretary of State for Defence knows, the scenario has changed. As Britain has a permanent seat in the Security Council, we wonder whether the Government will return and address the original problem and policy. It was envisaged that when troops were sent to Bosnia, they would not remain there permanently. There is a roulement of British troops every six months. The Government have said that they are not prepared to allow British troops to enter Gorazde once the Royal Welch Fusiliers leave. The Dutch troops have the same problem in Srebrenica; they took over from the Canadians and nobody will relieve them.

If policy is to be effective, we must be able to reassure the public that Bosnia is not—to use a phrase bandied around today—another Vietnam or Afghanistan.

I appreciate the difference, to the extent that we are working for the UN. But if we are talking about a long haul of about 10 years—

**Lady Olga Maitland:** Not 10 years.

**Dr. Clark:** Yes. If one talks to military people, that is the length of time that they mention. In that event, we shall need circulation and replacement of national troops. I hope that the Government will take that point on board.

The whole House has paid tribute, rightly, to our troops and to those of other nations, who have acted with great bravery and generosity. We politicians created the war situation and, ironically, have left it to our military to try to maintain the peace. At the end of the day, however, this tragedy will finally be settled around the negotiating table. What we must do, with sending the extra reinforcements, is to try to force, to try to put pressure, to try to bring in as many people as possible to join us, to get the negotiators around the table so that we can finally get a peaceful settlement in Bosnia.

9.34 pm

**The Secretary of State for Defence (Mr. Malcolm Rifkind):** We are now approaching the end of what must have been one of the longest debates that the House has experienced for many years. As has been said, some 35 right hon. and hon. Members have contributed to the debate, making speeches of exceptional quality and seriousness, and showing a great commitment.

The fact that the vast majority of hon. Members— indeed, all the parties represented in the House—have welcomed the decision to send extra reinforcements to Bosnia is a matter that I especially welcome, because, as our forces go to the former Yugoslavia, it is of great significance that they know that they go with the near-unanimous endorsement of the House of Commons.

I welcome the fact also that all parties and most hon. Members support the policy that the Government have been pursuing, but am conscious of the fact that a number of hon. Members, with equal seriousness and equal thought, have come to different conclusions. It is right and proper that we should acknowledge that the subject of our involvement in former Yugoslavia is one that is not easy for any hon. Member. It involves ethical issues, practical questions, moral judgments, as well as coming to a view as to the wider strategic interest both of this country and of the western world as a whole.

There has been an understandable concern that the sending of more British troops to Bosnia could have the result of bogging us further down in the Balkan morass; that it could be a step towards our becoming a combatant in that war, and seeking to achieve a military solution. Comparisons with Vietnam have been made, and also with the Falklands and the Gulf war.

Becoming a combatant is not and will not be our policy. Indeed, far from the events of the past week making it more likely, they should have shown all but the most stubborn the limitations of air power when combined with United Nations ground forces who do not have either the mandate or the equipment with which to wage war.

That has come as no surprise to the British Government, to General Rupert Smith or to the other UNPROFOR commanders, who have always stressed the caution that must be applied with regard to the use of air strikes. I hope that the siren voices from Congress and from some in the House will now be stilled.

**Mr. Benn:** I am grateful to the Secretary of State for giving way. Will he comment on the broadcast by President Clinton that the United States is now contemplating—contemplating—sending in ground troops, and on the statement by Dr. Boutros Boutros-Ghali, the Secretary-General, that, if increased forces are sent in, they should be under national command, because these statements on the "Nine O'clock News" really do transform the situation? I know that the Government will know about them, but I wonder whether the Secretary of State will incorporate that in his speech.

**Mr. Rifkind:** The right hon. Gentleman—and, I am sure, the House as a whole—will wish to study carefully what President Clinton has said today. I understand that he has indicated that there could be circumstances in which he would consider favourably the temporary deployment of US ground forces to help with a redeployment of forces within Bosnia. Naturally, we would wish to study carefully the precise implications of that, and I do not propose to comment on that matter further at this stage.

A recognition that the United Nations is not going to wage war does not leave withdrawal as the only alternative. There is much that has been done and which we can still do to reduce the suffering in Bosnia, to prevent the spread of the war throughout the Balkans and to further the prospects of a political settlement.

My hon. Friend the Member for East Lindsey (Sir P. Tapsell) asked why we were in Bosnia, and why different arguments applied to Bosnia than to Angola, Cambodia or other parts of the world. I have to make two responses to him. First, to some extent, he is incorrect. At this very moment, British forces are in Angola helping in a humanitarian way. They have been in Rwanda and Cambodia and in a number of other countries around the world. I accept that we cannot seek to do all that we might in theory wish to do, but perhaps my hon. Friend and other hon. Members who have spoken in a similar way should reflect on the remark that Edmund Burke once made:

"no one makes a greater mistake than he who does nothing because he, himself, can only do a little."

I ask those who call for the withdrawal of our forces the following questions. Is Britain the sort of country that can stand and watch but do nothing while tens of thousands are being slaughtered in a not so far away country of which we now know quite a lot?

Should Britain be unwilling to play a part, despite its unrivalled experience in peacekeeping, in trying to contain, and in due course end, a European conflict that could destabilise a significant part of our continent for years to come?

Is it being suggested that British troops could withdraw from Bosnia even if French, Dutch, Canadian and other forces stay? Would that be either honourable or in our national interest? Of course peacekeeping in Bosnia is a thankless, dangerous and depressing experience, but that does not make it any less necessary. We have been more cautious than most—less prone to rhetoric as a substitute for policy, and more realistic as to what can be achieved. That is why we have maintained broad support, both in the House and in the country as a whole.

*[Mr. Rifkind]*

We share many of the reservations and concerns that have been expressed during this debate—I do not doubt that for a moment—and we do not dismiss those concerns. But ultimately this country will want to do its duty and to play its part in international efforts to end the bloodshed and restore stability.

Against that background, may I briefly report to the House where we stand with regard to the deployment of certain of the United Kingdom forces about which the hon. Member for South Shields (Dr. Clark) specifically asked me.

Yesterday, the first element of 19 Field Regiment, with its 105 mm light guns, left RAF Lyneham for Split in Croatia by C130 Hercules aircraft. It will continue to deploy by air to Split over the next week. A chartered ro-ro ferry will leave Emden in Germany on 6 June with 31 Armoured Engineer Squadron and elements of 21 Engineer Regiment.

Then, on 8 June, the ship will collect from Marchwood military port combat service support elements and logistics elements of the Household Cavalry Regiment. It should arrive in Split on 17 June. Signals personnel and the two additional Lynx helicopters of 9 Regiment Army Air Corps will leave by air over the next few days.

Why are we sending those initial units—the artillery and the armoured engineers? The reinforcement package includes those elements. They provide essential capabilities to enhance the protection of UNPROFOR and increase the range of options open to UN commanders to respond robustly against the possibility of UN troops having to defend themselves when trying to carry out UNPROFOR's mission in a more hostile environment.

Those assests could be used to counter attacks by parties to the conflict; to ensure that vital aid or resupply routes can be kept open; and to safeguard essential engineer projects such as route maintenance, bridge building or mine-clearing operations. The artillery, for example, will provide an essential defence against artillery and mortar attacks while our forces are carrying out their UN tasks.

The inclusion of artillery and armoured engineer capabilities constitutes an important balancing of the force: as we have already seen, UNPROFOR checkpoints and observation points have in the past been subject to hostile action. Should the need arise, these robust assets will enable commanders to counter such attacks with an all-arms capability.

**Mr. Dalyell:** May we just be clear about this? Are the armoured units and artillery under British control or United Nations control? And are the incoming American forces under Washington control or UN control?

**Mr. Rifkind:** It is premature, to say the least, for the hon. Gentleman to refer to incoming American forces, so I will not try to respond to that point. I am happy to respond on the question of United Kingdom forces, however.

The artillery and armoured regiments that are going in at this moment will be blue helmet and under General Rupert Smith as part of the UNPROFOR force. The hon. Member for South Shields and the Leader of the Opposition asked about 24 Air Mobile Brigade. In fact,

my right hon. Friend the Prime Minister answered that question when he said that that would come under General Rupert Smith and the UNPROFOR force.

Let me expand on that if I may. We have said that the 5,000-strong force comprising 24 Air Mobile, when it arrives in Bosnia, will be there primarily to protect United Kingdom forces. Consistent with that, however, we are willing to see it available for the protection of UNPROFOR as a whole, because anything that protects that force is relevant to our national interest. The force will be commanded by General Rupert Smith; its members will wear blue berets and blue helmets. That meets our requirements.

To consider the alternative would have many disadvantages. While it would theoretically be possible for the force to come under national control rather than that of General Rupert Smith, it would mean our having two groups of British soldiers in Bosnia at the same time—a national element and an UNPROFOR element. That would create considerable inconvenience, confusion and possible danger. We are all conscious of the difficulties that have arisen as a result of the dual key system between air and ground; the last thing we want, if it can be avoided, is a comparable problem on the ground. We are confident that the matter can be dealt with satisfactorily.

**Dr. David Clark:** May I clarify that? Would 24 Air Mobile Brigade be in exactly the same position—in terms of command and control—as all other British troops in the area, or does the Secretary of State's statement that the brigade is there primarily to protect British troops mean that there is an extra command structure involving the British general?

**Mr. Rifkind:** It does not mean that there is any extra command structure. It means what it says—that, in offering these forces to the United Nations, we have indicated that we are offering them on the basis that their primary role will be to enhance the protection of the British forces that are part of UNPROFOR. So far as that objective is not compromised, however, they are also available to be used for other tasks, particularly other protection tasks. That is not a unique position, and it is one that I am confident to recommend.

**Sir Peter Tapsell:** When General Rupert Smith's tour of duty ends, if his successor is not British, will a foreign United Nations commander then command his new troops?

**Mr. Rifkind:** Naturally, whoever is the commander of the UN forces in Bosnia-Herzegovina will have the same duties and responsibilities as General Rupert Smith has now. Of course, General Smith is himself answerable to the French general, General Janvier, who has overall command over the former Yugoslavia. There is no particular point of principle here.

Let me give the House some information that has not been mentioned so far. An important development is now taking place in the force in Bosnia-Herzegovina as a result of an initiative by General Rupert Smith. Following the serious developments over the weekend and at the instigation of General Smith, elements of UNPROFOR— the existing force—will be reorganised to provide a theatre reserve force.

That force will be a mobile reaction force capable of responding to a range of requirements, from protecting UNPROFOR units to a reserve capability that could be deployed at very short notice within theatre, and is robustly equipped to counter potential attacks on UNPROFOR personnel if that became necessary in a more hostile environment.

The theatre reserve force has been placed under the command of Brigadier Pringle, commander of the British contingent and UN commander of Bosnia's sector south-west. It is likely to comprise some of the United Kingdom assets in the reinforcement package—for example, the artillery batteries and the armoured engineer squadron—together with some elements already in theatre, and forces made available by other troop-contributing nations such as the Canadians or the New Zealanders, either from within theatre or as new reinforcements.

The main elements of the reserve force would include an armoured infantry battalion group incorporating three companies of Warrior vehicles from the 1st Battalion the Devonshire and Dorset Regiment, Scimitars of the British Cavalry Battalion already in theatre, and some Lynx helicopters which we had previously offered to the United Nations in support of the now-expired cessation of hostilities agreement.

I was pleased to hear that today the Netherlands has indicated its willingness to contribute to the British forces as part of the new theatre reserve force, while the Dutch Government have mentioned a reinforced company of marines and additional military means. That is something that we welcome very warmly.

The creation of a theatre reserve force is a very important initiative. Last night on television, General Lewis Mackenzie, the former Canadian commander in Bosnia, said:

"every United Nations commander in the 38 missions from 1956 on has wanted a reserve and has never got one. If this gives General Smith a reserve for his entire contingent in Bosnia, I'm sure he'll be delighted."

It is an important initiative, and we are very pleased that the United Kingdom will be intimately involved in the matter.

**Mr. Home Robertson:** I am sure that the whole House welcomes the enhancement of UNPROFOR's ability to protect itself. Will the additional firepower also be available to protect the delivery of humanitarian aid? For example, when aid convoys come under fire from the Serbs or someone else, will UNPROFOR be able to open fire on whoever is responsible for the attack?

**Mr. Rifkind:** Its precise role will be for the UNPROFOR commander to determine, but I have no doubt from what has been said already that he would see part of its role as giving added protection, for example, to a convoy that may be threatened or subject to an assault from hostile forces. General Smith has the flexibility to use the force as a reserve force within Bosnia-Herzegovina to be deployed at his discretion, consistent with the overall terms of the mandate under which he operates.    -

There has been considerable comment about the achievements of UNPROFOR within Bosnia-Herzegovina over the past three years. The right hon. Member for Yeovil (Mr. Ashdown) and my right hon. Friend the Member for Guildford (Mr. Howell) both said that it was

inappropriate to refer to the United Nations force as "peacekeepers" because there is "no peace to keep"—I think that is the phrase that they used. I understand why they have made those observations, but I think that that is an unfair and inaccurate description.

It is true that, in parts of Sarajevo, Bihac and Gorazde, the fighting and conflict is such that it is very difficult to say that the peace is being kept. However, they are only small parts of Bosnia-Herzegovina. In a very large part of Bosnia—particularly central Bosnia, which is where the United Kingdom forces are most concentrated —the peace is being kept, and it has been increasingly well kept for the past 18 months.

The right hon. Member for Yeovil has been to Bosnia-Herzegovina, and if he recollects his visits during that period, I am sure that he will be the first to acknowledge that, a year and a half ago, the Croat and Muslim forces were at each other's throats. It was impossible to travel around central Bosnia without going through dozens of checkpoints. In towns such as Gorni Vakuf, there was severe bloodshed.

If the right hon. Gentleman travels to Bosnia today, he will find that UNPROFOR forces are not under threat. They may travel around without their armoured vehicles and, to a very large extent, they have helped to restore some semblance of normality to a large part of the country.

**Mr. Ashdown:** What the right hon. and learned Gentleman says is entirely true. However, I did not make the comments that he has attributed to me. I did not mention in my speech that there was no peace in certain areas. I said that the present mandate and terms of engagement under which our forces have been operating is manifestly bust. It needs to be reconsidered, and, at the very least, some priority should be established as to the operation of the twin mandates for humanitarian aid and for more aggressive action.

Does the right hon. and learned Gentleman accept that case? The Prime Minister has used the word "consolidation" in the past two or three days. I do not disagree that some consolidation may be necessary. Will the right hon. and learned Gentleman tell the House whether that consolidation will mean any change of policy in respect of the safe havens of Gorazde, Zepa and Srebrenica?

**Mr. Rifkind:** Of course our immediate task is to release the hostages, and much has been said about that subject, particularly by my right hon. Friend the Prime Minister. Consistent with that objective, we have three priorities.

First, we must ensure the enhanced protection of British forces and of the whole UNPROFOR force. I have explained the various ways in which that is being taken forward substantially. Secondly, in the statement issued by the British Government on Sunday night, we said that we believed that it was appropriate to propose to our friends and allies some concentration of United Nations forces within Bosnia.

There is no doubt that, with the present scale of United Nations facilities, it is extremely difficult for them to carry out the many tasks that are currently expected of them. No criticism can be made of the United Kingdom; we are one of the largest contributors in Bosnia, but the overall size of the force is difficult to reconcile with the many demands it faces.

*[Mr. Rifkind]*

For example, it is well worth remembering the inevitable isolation of the United Nations military observers, given the work they have been asked to do. There are a total of 678 UNMOs currently deployed throughout the country. They act as the eyes and ears of the United Nations on the ground. They are specifically responsible for reporting on the state of day-to-day relationship between the parties to the conflict.

We have always been aware, as has UNPROFOR, that military observers in Bosnian Serb, Bosnian Croat or Bosnian Government territory inevitably have been at some risk. They have been subject to harassment, obstruction and humiliation. What has become qualitatively different in the past week is that some of them have now been taken hostage and used as human shields. That degree of risk is unacceptable. We cannot expect individual military observers to be in Bosnia if that is the fate that awaits them; therefore, there may be a need at least to bring them into central Bosnia so that their personal security can be enhanced.

**Mr. Ashdown:** I am afraid that the Secretary of State has not answered my question. Does consolidation mean a change of policy in the three safe havens that are isolated from Bosnia-Herzegovina?

**Mr. Rifkind:** I am dealing first with the United Nations military observers. Another isolated part of the structure is the three safe havens: Gorazde, Zepa and Srebrenica. That will be for the United Nations to decide. We certainly believe that it is appropriate to examine those three safe havens to see whether the policy is tenable and to assess the implications of a possible change of policy. We have reached no judgment or conclusion on that, but it is important that the matter should be addressed. I understand that today the United Nations Secretary-General indicated that it was appropriate to address those matters.

We have all been critical of the United Nations trying to do more than it is capable of doing with the mandate and the forces provided to it. If that is our judgment, if countries are unable to provide additional forces to the extent that would be required, we have a duty to address the issues honestly and frankly and prepare to work out what the implications would be.

With regard to the individuals who have been taken hostage, it is very important to realise the extent to which the Bosnian Serbs acted in a way which is, in effect, akin to terrorism. They cannot say, as they have claimed, that the hostages are prisoners of war, as if that somehow makes it acceptable. Apart from anything else, prisoners of war are entitled to the benefit of the Geneva convention, which would prevent them from being used in exactly the way in which they are being used now, so Mr. Karadzic and General Mladic are in a totally indefensible position.

My hon. Friend the Member for Upminster (Sir N. Bonsor) mentioned the rules of engagements, and asked whether we are satisfied about their robustness. As he is aware, from the very beginning of our forces' presence in Bosnia-Herzegovina, we have told them that the right to self-defence is an absolute entitlement, and they must respond in the way that is judged appropriate to ensure their physical safety.

The rules of engagement, the terms of which we do not comment on publicly, are very robust. Although we shall always look to see whether some change is needed to reflect any change in the mandate or the circumstances, we do not believe that there is any problem with regard to their robustness to entitle them to do what is necessary to defend themselves.

My right hon. Friend the Member for Bridgwater (Mr. King) made an excellent and most informative speech. His comparison between the way in which the individuals who have been taken hostage are being used in Bosnia and the circumstances in Iraq some years ago, when Saddam Hussein applied a similar policy, should remind everyone of the folly of such a policy, and its inevitable failure.

My hon. Friend the Member for Wolverhampton, South-West (Mr. Budgen) sought to use the analogy of Vietnam and to imply that somehow this conflict would move in the same direction. The issue that differentiates this conflict from Vietnam is a fundamental one. The issue in Vietnam was not the number of American troops or the fact that that increased over the years, but the basic fact that the United States was a combatant. It went in to defeat the Vietcong, and took that decision at an early stage. We have not taken such a decision, nor have we any intention of doing so.

The House has an important contribution to make to the well-being of our forces in Bosnia. They need to know that they have the unqualified endorsement of the House. It is important for their morale and for their commitment. It is important that they know that they have the support not only of the United Kingdom but of its Parliament, and I commend that to the House.

*It being Ten o'clock, the motion for the Adjournment of the House lapsed, without Question put.*

## ADJOURNMENT

*Motion made and Question put,* That this House do now adjourn.—*[Mr. Kirkhope.]*

**Hon. Members:** Aye.

**Hon. Members:** No.

**Madam Speaker:** After Ten o'clock is a time of unopposed business, and there can be no vote on the motion for the Adjournment. The Ayes therefore have it.

*Question accordingly agreed to.*

*Adjourned at one minute past Ten o'clock.*

# Written Answers to Questions

*Monday 15 May 1995* ·

## TRANSPORT

### Newbury Bypass

**Mr. Rendel:** To ask the Secretary of State for Transport when he received the report of the Highways Agency reviewing the options for the Newbury bypass.    [23867]

**Mr. Watts:** The Highways Agency has yet to report the final outcome of its review of the Newbury bypass to my right hon. Friend.

### Bull Bars

**Mr. Flynn:** To ask the Secretary of State for Transport if he will make it his policy to introduce new measures to reduce fatal and serious accidents caused by bull bars, including lower speed limits.    [23794]

**Mr. Norris:** We are taking steps to quantify the effects of bull bars in terms of actual accidents on the road. We have no plans to reduce the speed limit of vehicles fitted with bull bars.

### Public Bodies

**Mr. Flynn:** To ask the Secretary of State for Transport which non-departmental public bodies within the responsibility of his Department are subject to scrutiny by *(a)* ombudsmen, *(b)* the National Audit Office, *(c)* the Audit Commission and *(d)* other monitoring officers; which are covered by citizens charters; in which performance indicators apply; and in which members are liable to surcharge.    [23952]

**Mr. Norris:** For *(a)*, *(b)*, *(c)* and points covering citizens charters and performance indicators, I refer the hon. Member to the reply I gave the hon. Member for Cannock and Burntwood (Dr. Wright) on 25 April 1995, *Official Report*, column 505.

For tribunal and advisory bodies within my responsibility not covered by that reply, the answers are, for *(a)* none and for *(b)* and *(c)* none; all are encouraged to follow citizens charter principles: none are subject to performance indicators.

For *(d)*, the answer is that none has a monitoring officer such as that designated by a local authority, but advisory bodies and the traffic commissioners are subject indirectly to scrutiny by the Comptroller and Auditor General as their expenditure arises in my Department. My Department has a monitoring role for bodies that are subject to quinquennial reviews.

No body has members who are liable to surcharge.

### Travelcard

**Mr. Cox:** To ask the Secretary of State for Transport if he will make it the policy of his Department fully to support and develop London Transport's travelcard; and if he will make a statement.    [24148]

**Mr. Norris:** Yes. The Government already recognise the importance and value of the London travelcard and have taken steps to ensure its continued availability.

### Interdepartmental Group

**Ms Walley:** To ask the Secretary of State for Transport if he will list the membership of the interdepartmental group of officers chaired by the Minister for Transport in London.    [21585]

**Mr. Norris:** The membership of the group has not yet been finalised. A further statement will be made shortly.

### Goods Service Operators

**Mr. Heppell:** To ask the Secretary of State for Transport how much money has been paid to goods service operators since 5 November 1993 under provisions of section 137 of the Railways Act 1993.    [21658]

**Mr. Watts:** None as yet. Eleven applications are under consideration.

### Motorways

**Mr. William O'Brien:** To ask the Secretary of State for Transport if he will list the issues other than environmental issues that his Department takes into consideration when considering the routes of new motorways.    [21672]

**Mr. Watts:** The objectives of the road building programme are to assist economic growth, conserve and improve the environment, enhance road safety and make better use of the existing road network. We are no longer making larger-scale additions to the network. The current programme is carefully targeted to focus on improvements to existing road corridors and building bypasses for towns and villages.

**Mr. Gordon Prentice:** To ask the Secretary of State for Transport, which four lane stretches of motorway in the United Kingdom do not have lighting.    [23857]

**Mr. Watts:** This is an operational matter for the Highways Agency. I have asked its chief executive to write to the hon. Member.

*Letter from Lawrie Haynes to Mr. Gordon Prentice, dated 15 May 1995:*

The Minister for Railways and Roads, Mr. John Watts, has asked me to write to you in reply to your recent Parliamentary Question about lighting on four lane motorways.

Road lighting has been installed on all four lane motorways except for a short length on the southbound M6 motorway between junctions 3 and 4 in Warwickshire.

### National Vocational Qualifications

**Mr. Barron:** To ask the Secretary of State for Transport how many, and what proportion of, vacancies advertised by his Department, and by each of his Department's agencies, in the last three years have listed the attainment of NVQs as an acceptable entry requirement; and, of those, how many have required (i) level 1 NVQs, (ii) level 2 NVQs, (iii) level 3 NVQs and (iv) other level NVQs.    [22982]

**Mr. Norris:** The Department of Transport and its agencies accept NVQ qualifications at the following recruitment levels:

Administrative Assistant: Level 1 in Business Administration.

Administrative Officer: Level 2 in Business Administration.

Personal Secretary: Level 2 in Business Administration.

Executive Officer: Level 3 in Business Management and Levels 4 and 5 in Management.

A wide range of academic and vocational qualifications are accepted as meeting initial entry requirements. NVQs are not normally specifically listed in recruitment advertising but reference is made to acceptable alternative qualifications. In five campaigns in the past three years for eight personal secretary posts, NVQs were specifically mentioned as a suitable qualification.

### Road Works (London)

**Mr. Keen:** To ask the Secretary of State for Transport what assessment he has made of the adequacy of current arrangements for co-ordinating road works and other road openings in London; and what plans he has to review the situation. [23951]

**Mr. Norris:** Under the New Roads and Street Works Act 1991 co-ordination on publicly maintained local roads is the responsibility of the local highway authority, while for trunk roads the responsibility rests with the Highways Agency. A code of practice issued under the Act gives practical guidance on the co-ordination of street works and works for road purposes and related matters; we are currently reviewing this and the other codes of practice and regulations governing street works in the light of responses received following a public consultation.

### Road Pricing

**Mr. Gordon Prentice:** To ask the Secretary of State for Transport (1) what is his policy on road pricing; [23859]

(2) when he intends to introduce motorway tolls. [23858]

**Mr. Watts:** As far as policy on road pricing in urban areas is concerned, the Government are considering the report that the Transport Select Committee issued on the subject in April and will respond in due course.

Policy on tolling the motorway network remains as set out by the then Secretary of State for Transport on 2 December 1993, *Official Report*, column *646–49*. Its introduction is subject to the availability of suitable technology, which we are assessing, and Parliament's approval of the necessary legislation.

### LORD CHANCELLOR'S DEPARTMENT

### Appeal Listings

**41. Mr. Mudie:** To ask the Parliamentary Secretary, Lord Chancellor's Department what notice is normally given by his Department to prisoners of the listing of their appeal. [22509]

**Mr. John M. Taylor:** In the Crown court, a minimum of 10 days' notice is usually given to prisoners; in the Criminal Appeal Office, the notice given is normally 10 days but can, on occasions, be less.

### Immigration Appeals

**46. Dr. Spink:** To ask the Parliamentary Secretary, Lord Chancellor's Department what is the total number of appeals awaiting processing by the immigration appeals office. [22514]

**Mr. John M. Taylor:** As at 31 March 1995, there were approximately 13,500 appeals waiting to be heard. In about 25 per cent. of these cases, the immigration appellate authorities were awaiting an indication from the parties that they were ready to proceed before being able to list them.

### Judicial System (Modernisation)

**47. Mr. Mackinlay:** To ask the Parliamentary Secretary, Lord Chancellor's Department what plans he has to review court practices and procedures with a view of the modernisation of the judicial system. [22515]

**Mr. John M. Taylor:** There is a continuing programme to review court practices and procedures. The Royal Commission on criminal justice reported in July 1993 and many of its recommendations are being taken forward. In addition, Lord Justice Woolf is undertaking a comprehensive review of the civil justice system.

### Legal Aid

**48. Mr. Steen:** To ask the Parliamentary Secretary, Lord Chancellor's Department if he will make a statement as to the operation of the legal aid system in civil cases. [22516]

**Mr. John M. Taylor:** The civil legal aid scheme is administered by the Legal Aid Board. The Lord Chancellor will shortly issue a Green Paper making proposals for reforms to the legal aid scheme.

**49. Mr. Mike O'Brien:** To ask the Parliamentary Secretary, Lord Chancellor's Department how many people would have been likely to qualify for legal aid if they had a case in the courts in *(a)* 1979, *(b)* 1985, *(c)* 1993 and *(d)* 1995. [22517]

**Mr. John M. Taylor:** It is not possible to say. Legal aid is available subject to the applicant's financial circumstances and the merits of the case. There is no upper limit for financial eligibility for criminal legal aid.

**Mr. Gapes:** To ask the Parliamentary Secretary, Lord Chancellor's Department if he will make a statement on the workings of the legal aid system. [22510]

**Mr. John M. Taylor:** The Lord Chancellor will shortly issue a Green Paper making proposals for reforms to the legal aid scheme.

### Public Bodies

**Mr. Flynn:** To ask the Parliamentary Secretary, Lord Chancellor's Department which non-departmental public bodies within the responsibility of his Department are subject to scrutiny by *(a)* ombudsmen, *(b)* the National Audit Office, *(c)* the Audit Commission and *(d)* other monitoring officers; which are covered by citizens charters; in which performance indicators apply; and in which members are liable to surcharge. [23953]

**Mr. John M. Taylor:** The Lord Chancellor's Department is responsible for two executive non-departmental public bodies: the Legal Aid Board and the Authorised Conveyancing Practitioners Board. However, the latter has been inactive since March 1992 when the Lord Chancellor announced his decision to postpone implementation of the authorised practitioners scheme.

The Legal Aid Board is not subject to scrutiny by the Audit Commission or other monitoring officers and members are not liable to surcharge. It is subject to scrutiny by the Parliamentary Commissioner and the National Audit Office. It is covered by provisions under the citizens charter and performance indicators apply.

The immigration appeal tribunal and adjudicators, the lands tribunal, the pensions appeal tribunal, the value added tax tribunal and the transport tribunal are subject to the scrutiny of the ombudsman and the National Audit Office, to the extent that the courts are. Tribunals have performance indicators.

The Advisory Committee on Legal Education and Conduct is subject to scrutiny by the National Audit Office. For other advisory committees, and the tribunals, the expenditure which is incurred forms part of the Department's total expenditure. The Department's accounts are subject to scrutiny by the National Audit Office.


# PRIME MINISTER

## Government Announcements

**Mr. Mandelson:** To ask the Prime Minister what is the Cabinet Committee on policy co-ordination and presentation in supervising Government announcements, irrespective of department; and how a distinction is made between the objective presentation and timing of these announcements and their use for party political benefits.        [24325]

**The Prime Minister:** I published the terms of reference of the ministerial committee on the co-ordination and presentation of Government policy on 21 March 1995 *Official Report*, column *112*. The committee's terms of reference make it clear that the committee's role is to consider the co-ordination and presentation of Government, as distinct from party, policy. It is therefore subject to the published conventions relating to Government publicity.

## No. 10 Downing Street

**Mr. Redmond:** To ask the Prime Minister what steps he takes to ensure that the address No. 10 Downing street is not used in connection with private business activities.        [22899]

**The Prime Minister:** I know of no reason to believe that the No. 10 Downing street address has been improperly used.

## Churchill Papers

**Mr. Redmond:** To ask the Prime Minister if he will list the state papers donated to Churchill college, Cambridge, in each case giving the date the item was donated.        [24074]

**The Prime Minister:** The Churchill archive comprises many thousand documents. It would be disproportionately costly to list the state papers in the archive individually.

The papers relating to Sir Winston Churchill's ministerial and prime ministerial appointments, claimed by the Crown as state papers, were transferred to Churchill college on the same day as the agreement to purchase the non-state papers was concluded. The effective date of transfer was 26 April 1995.

## Ministerial Meetings

**Mr. Cox:** To ask the Prime Minister when he last met the current President of the European Commission.        [24149]

**The Prime Minister:** I last saw Mr. Santer in Paris on 8 May, and will see him for substantive talks about when he comes to London on 17 May.

## Official Gifts

**Mr. Tony Banks:** To ask the Prime Minister who is responsible for maintaining the official inventory of gifts given to the office of the Prime Minister and kept at No. 10; and what additions have been made to the list since 1979.        [23782]

**The Prime Minister:** The inventory is maintained by staff within No. 10 in accordance with the rules in "Questions of Procedure for Ministers" and is subject to the normal audit procedures. The details of gifts received are not made public.

**Mr. Tony Banks:** To ask the Prime Minister what official gifts have been received by officials travelling with him abroad during the last 12 months.        [23786]

**The Prime Minister:** Gifts received by officials are dealt with in accordance with the official rules. The details are not made public.

**Mr. Tony Banks:** To ask the Prime Minister how much has been donated to charity arising from the sale of official gifts given to Prime Ministers since 1979.        [23788]

**The Prime Minister:** I have made it a practice to donate to charity all the proceeds from sales of gifts which I have retained under the guidelines set out in "Questions of Procedure for Ministers".

**Mr. Tony Banks:** To ask the Prime Minister what has been the total value of gifts to Prime Ministers since 1979 sold from the official inventory.        [23787]

**The Prime Minister:** Sales from the inventory have been carried out in accordance with "Questions of Procedure for Ministers". It is not the practice to publish details.

**Mr. Tony Banks:** To ask the Prime Minister what record is kept official gifts given to business representatives travelling with him on official visits abroad.        [23789]

**The Prime Minister:** No gifts are given by the British Government. Gifts by foreign Governments are a matter for them.

## Lockerbie

**Mr. Dalyell:** To ask the Prime Minister if he will acquire for the video library of No. 10 Downing street the video of Alan Francovitch's film. "The Maltese Double Cross".        [23721]

**The Prime Minister:** I have no plans to do so.

**Mr. Dalyell:** To ask the Prime Minister for what reason Her Majesty's Government declined to allow Chief Superintendent Gilchrist of Dumfries and Galloway police to interview Mr. O'Neill and Mr. Tuzcu, baggage handlers at the Rhein-Main airport in Frankfurt, when they were brought to the United Kingdom in connection with the destruction of Pan Am 103 over Lockerbie.    [24009]

**The Prime Minister:** Her Majesty's Government did not and would not interfere in decisions regarding the conduct of the Lockerbie investigation.

### Gibraltar

**Mr. Mackinlay:** To ask the Prime Minister on what occasions Gibraltar's status within the European Union has been raised formally in the Heads of Government Council of Ministers since he became Prime Minister.
    [24470]

**The Prime Minister:** I do not recall any such occasion.

**Mr. Mackinlay:** To ask the Prime Minister on what occasions Gibraltar's status *(a)* within the European Union and *(b)* with Spain has been raised by him since he became Prime Minister at his meetings with the Prime Minister of Spain.    [24471]

**The Prime Minister:** I last discussed Gibraltar in detail with the Prime Minister of Spain in May 1991. I have met him since on a number of occasions, but have not discussed the points mentioned by the hon. Member.

### Royal British Legion

**Mr. McMaster:** To ask the Prime Minister when he last met representatives of the Royal British Legion to discuss the establishment of a ministry of veterans affairs; and if he will make a statement.    [24073]

**The Prime Minister:** I have not personally met representatives of the Royal British Legion to discuss a ministry of veterans affairs but my noble Friends Lord Mackay of Ardbrecknish and Lord Henley did so on my behalf on 23 November 1994. My view remains that such a Ministry would add an extra layer of bureaucracy without necessarily resulting in a better service for ex-service men and women. The Government's continuing commitment is to improve standards for every citizen.

### Misuse of Drugs Act 1971

**Mr. McMaster:** To ask the Prime Minister if he will make a statement on the application of the provisions of the Misuse of Drugs Act 1971 to Scotland, by comparison to how they apply in England; and if he will make a statement.    [24079]

**The Prime Minister:** The provisions of the Misuse of Drugs Act 1971 apply equally to all parts of the United Kingdom.

### Departmental Seminars

**Mr. Mandelson:** To ask the Prime Minister whether departmental seminars have been organised under the auspices of the Cabinet Office with the aim of taking the presentational initiative away from the Government's critics.    [24324]

**The Prime Minister:** No.

### No. 10 Policy Unit

**Mr. Mandelson:** To ask the Prime Minister whether the No. 10 policy unit and its head, Norman Blackwell, have any party political responsibilities; and what rules exist on the subject.    [24451]

**The Prime Minister:** The members of the policy unit are either career civil servants or employed as special advisers, and are subject to the general rules applicable to those groups. They have no party political responsibilities at national level. The rules on political activities for special advisers are set out in the model appointment letter for special advisers, a copy of which has been placed in the Library of the House. I refer the hon. Member to the reply of my right hon. Friend the Chancellor of the Duchy of Lancaster to the hon. Member for Darlington (Mr. Milburn) on 24 April 1995, *Official Report*, column *373*.

**Mr. Mandelson:** To ask the Prime Minister what functional relationship exists between the Cabinet committee on policy co-ordination and presentation and the No. 10 policy unit; and how this is discharged.    [24323]

**The Prime Minister:** The Prime Minister's policy unit contributes to the work of the Cabinet committee on policy co-ordination and presentation as appropriate. The head of the policy unit attends meetings of this and other Cabinet committees as required.

### World War Two

**Mr. Mackinlay:** To ask the Prime Minister pursuant to his statement on 25 April, *Official Report*, column 667, if he will list the 18 hon. Members who saw active service in world war two; and if he will also list those who served in the Merchant Navy during the war.    [23010]

**The Prime Minister** *[holding answer 5 May]:* The figure to which I referred on 25 April derived from information provided by the House of Commons authorities. I understand that they now believe that a least 20 hon. Members saw active service in world war two, including those who served in the Merchant Navy. It is a matter for hon. Members whether they wish to make their war record known.

## EDUCATION

### Grant-maintained Schools

**Mr. Blunkett:** To ask the Secretary of State for Education if she will list the applications she has received to establish *(a)* groups and *(b)* clusters of grant-maintained schools.    [23723]

**Mr. Robin Squire:** Although we have not yet received any formal applications to establish clusters of grant-maintained schools under the group or joint scheme arrangement, there has been a steady interest in the initiative since it was launched last year.

### Public Bodies

**Mr. Flynn:** To ask the Secretary of State for Education which non-departmental public bodies within the responsibility of her Department are subject to scrutiny by *(a)* ombudsmen, *(b)* the National Audit Office, *(c)* the Audit Commission and *(d)* other monitoring officers; which are covered by citizens charters; in which performance indicators apply; and in which members are liable to surcharge.    [23963]

**Mr. Boswell:** The information requested is shown, for the Department's executive non-departmental public bodies, in the table.

| Name of body | Parliamentary Commissioner | National Audit Office | Audit Commission | Other monitoring officers[1] | Citizen's charter | Performance indicators | Members' liability to surcharge |
|---|---|---|---|---|---|---|---|
| Centre for Information on Language Teaching and Research (CILT) | no | yes | no | yes | yes | yes | no |
| Education Assets Board (EAB) | yes | yes | no | yes | yes | yes | no |
| Funding Agency for Schools (FAS) | no | yes | no | yes | yes | yes | no |
| Further Education Funding Council (FEFC) | no | yes | no | yes | yes | yes | no |
| Higher Education Funding Council for England (HEFCE) | no | yes | no | yes | yes | yes | no |
| National Council for Educational Technology (NCET) | no | yes | no | yes | yes | yes | no |
| National Youth Agency (NYA) | no | yes | no | yes | yes | yes | no |
| School Curriculum Assessment Authority (SCAA) | no | yes | no | yes | yes | yes | no |
| Teacher Training Agency (TTA) | no | yes | no | yes | yes | yes | no |

[1] Monitoring by the sponsor Department.

## Publicity

**Mr. Blunkett:** To ask the Secretary of State for Education if she will list the expenditure on publicity by her Department for each year since 1979 broken down into spending on *(a)* television, *(b)* radio, *(c)* newspaper and *(d)* other. [24389]

**Mr. Forth:** The expenditure figures for advertising and other promotional material by this Department for the financial years 1979–80 to 1994–95 are given in the table. Final decisions on media in the current financial year have not been taken.

| Year | TV £000 | Radio £000 | Newspaper £000 | Other £000 |
|---|---|---|---|---|
| 1979–80 | — | — | 91.6 | 12.2 |
| 1980–81 | — | — | 8.9 | 58.3 |
| 1981–82 | — | — | 86.9 | 49.9 |
| 1982–83 | — | — | 6.0 | 33.7 |
| 1983–84 | — | — | 9.6 | 74.9 |
| 1984–85 | — | — | 18.5 | 150.6 |
| 1985–86 | — | — | 14.8 | 184.1 |
| 1986–87 | — | — | 532.0 | 533.0 |
| 1987–88 | — | — | 280.0 | 1,459.0 |
| 1988–89 | — | 40.0 | 475.0 | 1,156.0 |
| 1989–90 | — | 11.8 | 238.0 | 1,150.0 |
| 1990–91 | 1,100 | 97.0 | 1,470.0 | 1,916.0 |
| 1991–92 | 800.0 | — | 2,237.9 | 5,842.7 |
| 1992–93 | — | — | 1,086.4 | 5,800.1 |
| 1993–94 | — | 29.2 | 1,413.0 | 8,551.3 |
| 1994–95 | — | — | 159.3 | [1]7,929.0 |

[1] Estimated.

## Public Opinion Surveys

**Mr. Blunkett:** To ask the Secretary of State for Education if she will list each public opinion survey commissioned by *(a)* her Department and *(b)* her agencies for each year since 1992, showing for each the subject, the cost and the organisation from which it was commissioned. [23689]

**Mr. Forth:** The Department has carried out the following public opinion surveys since 1992:

Subject: National Curriculum leaflet for parents
Date: March and December 1992
Company: British Market Research Bureau

Subject: School Performance Tables
Date: December 1992 and January 1994
Company: Taylor Nelson

Subject: Grant-Maintained Schools
Date: July 1992, May 1993, October,1993, February 1994 and February 1995
Company: Audience Selection

Subject: National Curriculum testing of 7, 11 and 14 year olds
Date: April 1993
Company: British Market Research Bureau

Subject: National Curriculum testing of 7, 11 and 14 year olds
Date: May 1993
Company: Bulmershe Research

Subject: Publicity campaign for parents on National Curriculum testing of 7, 11 and 14 year olds
Date: January 1994, July 1994
Company: British Market Research Bureau

Subject: DFE Exhibitions—DFE Touring Roadshow
Date: October 1992, July 1993, July 1994
Company: 1992, 1993 Martin Hamblin; 1994 Alpha Research

Subject: Further and Higher Education Charters
Date: September 1993, November 1993
Company: Martin Hamblin

Subject: Educational Provision for Under 5's
Date: April 1994
Company: Bulmershe Research

Subject: Updated Parent's Charter
Date: June 1994, August 1994
Company: Research Society for Great Britain

Subject: School Performance Tables
Date: November 1994, February 1995
Company: Audience Selection

Subject: Publicity campaign for parents on National Curriculum testing of 7, 11 and 14 year olds.
Date: February 1995, April 1995
Company: British Market Research Bureau

Subject: Parent's Information Needs
Date: March 1995
Company: Research Surveys of Great Britain

Information about the Department's agencies and other related bodies is not held centally. One item of research of which the Department is aware was commissioned by the School Curriculum Assessment Authority and is as follows:

Subject: Public perception of the National Curriculum and the relative priorities of National Curriculum subjects

Date: June 1994

Company: Gallup

To give the cost of the research surveys carried out by the DFE and its agencies would compromise confidential tendering procedures.

## Pupil Expenditure

**Mr. Worthington:** To ask the Secretary of State for Education what has been the expenditure per *(a)* primary school and *(b)* secondary school pupil in real and constant price terms in every year since 1979; and what are the corresponding figures excluding staffing costs. [23395]

**Mr. Robin Squire:** The table shows net institutional expenditure per pupil including and excluding staffing costs, in cash terms and in 1994–95 prices, on LEA-maintained nursery and primary and secondary schools in England from 1979–80 to 1993–94, the latest year for which provisional outturn figures are available. The primary figures include expenditure on nursery provision which cannot be differentiated.

| Year | Net institutional expenditure per pupil Cash terms £ | Net institutional expenditure per pupil 1995 prices £ | Net institutional expenditure per pupil excluding staffing costs Cash terms £ | Net institutional expenditure per pupil excluding staffing costs 1995 prices £ |
|---|---|---|---|---|
| *Nursery primary* | | | | |
| 1979–80 | 429 | 1,074 | 108 | 272 |
| 1980–81 | 546 | 1,157 | 133 | 281 |
| 1981–82 | 621 | 1,198 | 151 | 291 |
| 1982–83 | 682 | 1,229 | 168 | 303 |
| 1983–84 | 732 | 1,260 | 184 | 317 |
| 1984–85 | 767 | 1,257 | 190 | 312 |
| 1985–86 | 817 | 1,270 | 201 | 312 |
| 1986–87 | 905 | 1,366 | 218 | 329 |
| 1987–88 | 1,006 | 1,441 | 239 | 342 |
| 1988–89 | 1,101 | 1,479 | 254 | 340 |
| 1989–90 | 1,210 | 1,519 | 294 | 369 |
| 1990–91 | 1,339 | 1,555 | 347 | 403 |
| 1991–92 | 1,469 | 1,606 | 364 | 398 |
| 1992–93 | 1,583 | 1,664 | 364 | 383 |
| 1993–94 | 1,637 | 1,670 | 385 | 393 |
| *Secondary* | | | | |
| 1979–80 | 607 | 1,520 | 162 | 405 |
| 1980–81 | 765 | 1,618 | 191 | 405 |
| 1981–82 | 865 | 1,668 | 213 | 411 |
| 1982–83 | 942 | 1,696 | 235 | 424 |
| 1983–84 | 1,014 | 1,745 | 255 | 439 |
| 1984–85 | 1,086 | 1,780 | 273 | 447 |
| 1985–86 | 1,177 | 1,829 | 291 | 452 |
| 1986–87 | 1,340 | 2,021 | 334 | 503 |
| 1987–88 | 1,517 | 2,172 | 376 | 538 |
| 1988–89 | 1,692 | 2,272 | 410 | 550 |
| 1989–90 | 1,858 | 2,332 | 472 | 593 |
| 1990–91 | 2,019 | 2,346 | 541 | 629 |
| 1991–92 | 2,145 | 2,345 | 520 | 569 |
| 1992–93 | 2,256 | 2,372 | 503 | 528 |
| 1993–94 | 2,252 | 2,297 | 517 | 527 |

**Mr. Blunkett:** To ask the Secretary of State for Education (1) what was the average unit cost per pupil for 1994–94 in *(a)* each local education authority and *(b)* nationally for (i) provision in nursery schools and nursery classes, (ii) provision in reception classes in primary schools and (iii) all under-fives provision; [23639]

(2) what was the average unit cost per pupil for 1993–94 of educating four-year-olds in *(a)* each local education authority and *(b)* nationally, (i) in nursery schools and nursery classes, (ii) in reception classes in primary schools and (ii) overall. [23638]

**Mr. Robin Squire:** The average unit cost per full-time equivalent pupil in 1993–94 for those categories of under-fives provision for which estimates are available nationally are given below:

*1993–94 estimates (provisional)*

| | £ |
|---|---|
| Nursery schools | 3,250 |
| Nursery classes in primary schools | 2,660 |
| Primary classes including under 5s | 1,590 |
| Average | 2,040 |

Figures for each local authority are not separately available; nor are figures for four-year-olds only.

## Stratford School

**Mr. Timms:** To ask the Secretary of State for Education what payment the newly appointed governors at Stratford grant-maintained school will receive for their work; and what brief they will be working to.          [23855]

**Mr. Forth:** My right hon. Friend announced on 5 May four new appointments to the governing body of Stratford school. Governors of publicly maintained schools do not receive payments for their services, although they may be refunded travel and subsistence expenses.

My right hon. Friend expects the newly constituted governing body as a whole to begin work immediately on a range of strategies to improve the standard of education on offer.

## Autistic Children

**Mr. Alex Carlile:** to ask the Secretary of State for Education which authorities provide specialist facilities for the education of austic children; and if she will make a statement.          [23680]

**Mr. Forth:** This information is not available centrally. However, information provided by the National Autistic Society suggests that a third of LEAs in England and Wales maintain specialist units for autistic children. In addition, LEAs may place autistic pupils at independent schools, including those run by the NAS. The majority of autistic children receive provision in accordance with statements of specialist educational need in other special or mainstream schools.

## Further Education Colleges

**Mr. MacShane:** To ask the Secretary of State for Education what plans she has to revise the enrolment targets for further education colleges.          [23538]

**Mr. Boswell:** My right hon. Friend does not set college targets for enrolment in the further education sector. The Government's planning assumptions continue to imply a significant increase in student numbers between 1993–94 and 1997–98.

**Mr. MacShane:** To ask the Secretary of State for Education what is the Government's assessment of the effect of increased enrolments on teaching loads at further education colleges in terms of teaching standards and levels of stress among lecturers.          [23541]

**Mr. Boswell:** The Government have not conducted a formal assessment of the effect of increased enrolment in the further education sector. The issue of teaching standards in the sector is the responsibility of the Further Education Funding Council.

**Mr. MacShane:** To ask the Secretary of State for Education what steps she is taking to monitor teaching standards at further education colleges.          [23539]

**Mr. Boswell:** The responsibility for ensuring quality in FE sector colleges in England rests with the Further Education Funding Council (England). I have asked Sir William Stubbs, its chief executive, to write to the hon. Member.

## Pupil-teacher Ratios

**Sir Ralph Howell:** To ask the Secretary of State for Education, pursuant to her answer of 25 April, *Official Report,* column *487,* what assessment she has made of the reasons why the average size of single-teacher classes is increasing, while the pupil-teacher ratio is decreasing; and if she will make a statement.          [23408]

**Mr. Robin Squire:** Pupil-teacher ratios are calculated by dividing full-time equivalent pupil numbers by the total number of full-time equivalent qualified teaching staff. Many teachers are not engaged full-time in classroom teaching; these include head teachers and others with management and planning responsibilities, as well as teachers allocated "non-contact" time during the school day for work to support their own teaching. Average class sizes therefore reflect decisions taken at school level about how to allocate available staff time.

PTRs in January 1994 were slightly below those in 1979, while average class sizes were slightly higher. This is because the proportion of teachers' time allocated to activities other than teaching has increased over the period.

**Mr. Worthington:** To ask the Secretary of State for Education what was the pupil-teacher ratio in *(a)* primary schools and *(b)* secondary schools in each year since 1979.          [23624]

**Mr. Robin Squire:** The information requested is shown in the table.

*Pupil: Teacher Ratios in maintained schools in England 1979–1994 position in January each year*

|  | Primary | Secondary |
|---|---|---|
| 1979 | 23.1 | 16.8 |
| 1980 | 22.7 | 16.7 |
| 1981 | 22.6 | 16.7 |
| 1982 | 22.5 | 16.7 |
| 1983 | 22.3 | 16.6 |
| 1984 | 22.1 | 16.4 |
| 1985 | 22.2 | 16.3 |
| 1986 | 22.1 | 16.1 |
| 1987 | 21.9 | 15.8 |
| 1988 | 22.0 | 15.5 |
| 1989 | 22.0 | 15.4 |
| 1990 | 22.0 | 15.4 |
| 1991 | 22.2 | 15.7 |
| 1992 | 22.2 | 15.9 |
| 1993 | 22.4 | 16.2 |
| 1994 | 22.7 | 16.4 |

## Schools, Ealing

**Mr. Harry Greenway:** To ask the Secretary of State for Education, pursuant to her answer of 4 May, *Official Report,* column *288,* what is the total amount spent per pupil in *(a)* primary and *(b)* secondary locally managed schools in Ealing other than that allocated to schools.          [23618]

**Mr. Robin Squire:** The figures are £517.33 for primary and £923.45 for secondary schools. These are derived from the Budget statement for 1995–96 published by the local education authority under section 42 of the Education Reform Act, and relate to all planned expenditure on mandatory and discretionary "excepted items".

## Further Education

**Mr. MacShane:** To ask the Secretary of State for Education what is the Government's assessment of the trend in the percentage of pupils staying on to continue education and training.          [23540]

**Mr. Boswell:** The trend in the proportion of 16-year-old pupils who stay on in full-time or part-time education, including those who attend college while undergoing training, is as follows:

*Percentage of 16-year-olds*

| Academic year | Full time education | Part time education | Total |
|---|---|---|---|
| 1983–84 | 47.8 | 16.5 | 64.3 |
| 1984–85 | 46.7 | 17.8 | 64.6 |
| 1985–86 | 47.3 | 17.7 | 65.0 |
| 1986–87 | 46.8 | 17.9 | 64.7 |
| 1987–88 | 48.5 | 17.2 | 65.7 |
| 1988–89 | 51.5 | 18.4 | 69.9 |
| 1989–90 | 55.0 | 15.9 | 70.8 |
| 1990–91 | 59.3 | 13.3 | 72.6 |
| 1991–92 | 66.6 | 9.7 | 76.3 |
| 1992–93 | 69.9 | 7.9 | 77.8 |
| 1993–94 | 72.5 | 7.5 | 80.0 |

### School Leavers

**Mr. Worthington:** To ask the Secretary of State for Education what proportion of school leavers has attained no academic qualifications in each year since 1979.    [23389]

**Mr. Robin Squire:** The proportion of school leavers, excluding special schools, in England who attained no academic qualifications in each year since 1979 is as follows:

| | Per cent. |
|---|---|
| 1978–79 | 12.8 |
| 1979–80 | 12.2 |
| 1980–81 | 11.4 |
| 1981–82 | 10.6 |
| 1982–83 | 9.6 |
| 1983–84 | 9.5 |
| 1984–85 | 9.4 |
| 1985–86 | 9.6 |
| 1986–87 | 9.4 |
| 1987–88 | 9.5 |
| 1988–89 | 7.9 |
| 1989–90 | 7.6 |
| 1990–91 | 7.0 |

Data on school leavers was collected on a reduced sample in 1991–92 and not collected at all after 1992. However, data from the school performance tables for 1992, 1993 and 1994 show that the percentage of 15-year-old pupils attaining no academic qualification was 8.4 per cent. in 1991-92, 7 per cent. in 1992–93 and 7.7 per cent. in 1993–94.

### Higher Education

**Mr. Blunkett:** To ask the Secretary of State for Education if she will estimate the number of hours which staff in her Department spend on issues relating to (*a*) higher and (*b*) further education in (i) whole-time equivalents and (ii) cost terms.    [23636]

**Mr. Boswell:** The number of hours spent on higher education issues is estimated to be just over 4,000 and on further education issues just under 4,000 per working week. The estimated salary costs are £2.47 million on higher education and £2.33 million on further education in the financial year 1995–96.

### Review Groups (National Curriculum)

**Mr. Timms:** To ask the Secretary of State for Education what assessment she has made of the merits of establishing long-term review groups in each of the national curriculum core subjects of mathematics, English and science; and what plans she has to introduce such groups.    [23156]

**Mr. Forth:** The School Curriculum and Assessment Authority is responsible for advising the Secretary of State on the national curriculum. To that end, it will be monitoring the new curriculum, which will be introduced from September 1995. Precisely how it does so is a matter for the authority itself, and I have asked the chief executive to write to the hon. Member.

## HOME DEPARTMENT

### Dr. Ishan Barbouti

**Mr. Dalyell:** To ask the Secretary of State for the Home Department what is the status in the United Kingdom of the late Dr. Ishan Barbouti.    [22664]

**Mr. Nicholas Baker:** Records relating to individual overseas nationals are held in confidence by the immigration and nationality department and it is not our normal practice to divulge them to third parties.

### Rape in Marriage

**Mr. Cohen:** To ask the Secretary of State for the Home Department what proposals he has for reviewing the law in respect of rape in marriage.    [22507]

**Mr. Maclean:** Under the law as it stands at present, a man may be convicted of raping his wife. The Government have no plans to review the law on this subject.

### Public Bodies

**Mr. Flynn:** To ask the Secretary of State for the Home Department which non-departmental public bodies within the responsibility of his Department are subject to scrutiny by (*a*) ombudsmen, (*b*) the National Audit Office, (*c*) the Audit Commission and (*d*) other monitoring officers; which are covered by citizens charters; in which performance indicators apply; and in which members are liable to surcharge.    [23961]

**Mr. Howard:** In respect of the executive non-departmental bodies sponsored by the Home Office I would refer the hon. Member to the reply given to a question from the hon. Member for Cannock and Burntwood (Dr. Wright) on 1 May, at column *100*. NDPB members are not subject to surcharge but the Alcohol Education and Research Council and the Community Development Foundation are charities and as such the trustees have potential financial liabilities under the Charities Acts 1992 and 1993. The information requested in relation to the 154 non-executive NDPBs sponsored by the Home Office, including 130 boards of visitors, is not held centrally and could be obtained only at disproportionate cost.

## Lockerbie

**Mr. Dalyell:** To ask the Secretary of State for the Home Department if he will acquire for the video library of the Home Office the video of Alan Francovitch's film, "The Maltese Double Cross."                    [23720]

**Mr. Howard:** No.

## Political Refugees, Visitors and Students

**Mr. Dicks:** To ask the Secretary of State for the Home Department (1) how many applicants, including dependants from Bosnia, have been granted entry into the United Kingdom since 1992 as *(a)* political refugees, *(b)* visitors and *(c)* students; and how many have subsequently returned to that country;                    [23419]

(2) how many applicants, including dependants from Somalia, have been granted entry into the United Kingdom since 1992 as *(a)* political refugees, *(b)* visitors and *(c)* students; and how many have subsequently returned to that country.                    [23418]

**Mr. Nicholas Baker** *[holding answer 10 May 1995]:* Information on nationals of the former Yugoslavia and Somalia given leave to enter as visitors, students and "refugees, exceptional leave cases and their dependants" in 1992–93 are given in table 3.1 of "Control of Immigration: Statistics, United Kingdom, 1992", Cm. 2368, and the corresponding publication for 1993, Cm. 2637, copies of which are in the Library. Data for 1994 are given in the table. The data exclude persons granted temporary admission before the resolution of their case. The data available for the new countries of the former Yugoslavia are incomplete because many passengers still have Yugoslav passports. It is not known how many nationals of the former Yugoslavia and Somalia subsequently returned to their home country.

*Persons given leave to enter the United Kingdom in 1994[1]*

*Number of admissions*

| Nationality | Visitors | Students | Refugees, exceptional leave cases and their dependants[2] |
|---|---|---|---|
| Former Yugoslavia | 38,800 | 5,370 | 1,270 |
| Somalia | 1,780 | 20 | 980 |

[1] Data are provisional.

[2] Persons who applied for asylum at a port and were subsequently granted refugee status or exceptional leave to enter the United Kingdom—and their dependants.

## Prisons

**Mr. Hoyle:** To ask the Secretary of State for the Home Department if he will list the figures for the number of prison governors by grade and ethnic origin.                    [23085]

**Mr. Michael Forsyth** *[holding answer 9 May 1995]:* Responsibility for this matter has been delegated to the Director General of the Prison Service, who has been asked to arrange for a reply to be given.

*Letter from Derek Lewis to Mr. Doug Hoyle, dated 15 May 1995:*

The Home Secretary of State has asked me to reply to your recent Question about the number of prison governors by grade and by ethnic origin.

On 1 May 1995 there were 1,020 staff employed in governor grades; 46 at Governor 1 level, 75 at Governor 2 level, 126 at Governor 3 level, 309 at Governor 4 level and 464 at Governor 5 level. Our database of staff ethnic backgrounds, covering 97 per cent of non-industrial staff in the Prison Service, indicates that four members of staff in the governor grades registered that they were members of ethnic minorities. To protect those individuals' privacy, and as the numbers are so small I have not broken down the figures by grade or by ethnic origin.

**Mr. Hoyle:** To ask the Secretary of State for the Home Department what is the policy on the recruitment of ethnic minority prison officers; and what action he is taking to further this policy.                    [23091]

**Mr. Michael Forsyth** *[holding answer 9 May 1995]:* Responsibility for this matter has been delegated to the Director General of the Prison Service, who has been asked to arrange for a reply to be given.

*Letter from A. J. Pearson to Mr. Doug Hoyle, dated 15 May 1995:*

The Home Secretary has asked me, in the absence of the Director General from the office, to reply to your recent Question about the recruitment of prison officers from the ethnic minorities.

The Prison Service is an equal opportunities employer and equality of opportunity is one of the values set out in the Statement of Purpose, Vision, Goals and Values.

Individual prison establishments assumed responsibility for recruiting prison officers in April 1993, (before this there was a centralised system with continuous recruitment). All appointments to the Prison Service are (and must be) made on the basis of merit and fair and open competition. When recruitment was devolved, comprehensive guidance on recruitment procedures was issued to each establishment.

The guidance included specific guidance on recruitment of members of the ethnic minorities. It pointed out that positive discrimination in favour of women or members of the ethnic minorities is unlawful, but the Sex Discrimination Act and Race Relations Act do permit positive action to encourage under represented groups to apply for jobs. Governors, therefore, are expected to take positive action to redress the current under representation of people from the ethnic minorities in the prison officer grades. The guidance suggested various means—such as presentations to local religious and community groups, encouraging ethnic minority groups to attend prison events, development of links with local Race Equality Councils and the Race Relations Employment Advisory Service—by which governors could raise awareness of the work of the Prison Service and encourage members of the ethnic minorities to apply for jobs.

All recruitment is continuously monitored and further advice is issued to Governors in response to any problems or difficulties highlighted by that monitoring process.

## Visitor Passports

**Mr. Nigel Evans:** To ask the Secretary of State for the Home Department how many 12-month visitor passports were issued in 1992, 1993, 1994 and this year to date.                    [23676]

**Mr. Nicholas Baker:** A total of 212,552 British visitor's passports have been issued up to 22 March this year—the latest date for which confirmed figures are available. For the numbers issued in 1992, 1993 and 1994 I would refer the hon. Member to the reply given to the hon. Member for Ravensbourne (Sir J. Hunt) on 2 February, at column *807*.

## 159 Grove Green, Leytonstone

**Mr. Cohen:** To ask the Secretary of State for the Home Department who was present at the meeting on 1 December 1994 at which the operational decision was taken to take physical possession of 159 Grove Green road, Leytonstone; and whom they represented. [23545]

**Mr. Maclean:** I understand that the county court made an order for the possession of this property on 11 July 1994 and that the Metropolitan police were requested to be present on 1 December 1994 when the bailiffs executed the order, to prevent a breach of the peace.

This was an operational matter for the Commissioner of the Metropolitan Police.

## Police Operational Duties and Training

**Mr. Butler:** To ask the Secretary of State for the Home Department for how many hours per day, on average, a police constable *(a)* performs operational duties, *(b)* receives training and *(c)* works on other matters in the latest year for which statistics are available, by police forces. [23599]

**Mr. Maclean:** The only information available relates to the average number of days spent in training by police constables, including probationers, during 1992–93.

| Forces | Training days | Average number of days per PC |
|---|---|---|
| Avon and Somerset | 37,194 | 16 |
| Bedfordshire | 16,717 | 18 |
| Cambridgeshire | 14,056 | 15 |
| Cheshire | 20,773 | 14 |
| City of London | 6,688 | 12 |
| Cleveland | 14,149 | 13 |
| Cumbria | 17,674 | 20 |
| Derbyshire | 30,721 | 22 |
| Devon and Cornwall | 44,487 | 20 |
| Dorset | 15,987 | 16 |
| Durham | 10,614 | 10 |
| Dyfed Powys | 10,241 | 14 |
| Essex | 45,804 | 20 |
| Gloucestershire | 11,930 | 13 |
| Greater Manchester | 65,586 | 13 |
| Gwent | n/a | n/a |
| Hampshire | n/a | n/a |
| Hertfordshire | 18,222 | 14 |
| Humberside | n/a | n/a |
| Kent | 50,259 | 21 |
| Lancashire | 35,215 | 15 |
| Leicestershire | 25,175 | 18 |
| Lincolnshire | 14,391 | 16 |
| Merseyside | 53,859 | 15 |
| Metropolitan | 230,627 | 11 |
| Norfolk | 15,987 | 14 |
| North Wales | 10,829 | 11 |
| North Yorkshire | 20,257 | 19 |
| Northamptonshire | 22,062 | 25 |
| Northumbria | 48,274 | 17 |
| Nottinghamshire | 34,977 | 20 |
| South Wales | 33,019 | 14 |
| South Yorkshire | 36,666 | 16 |
| Staffordshire | 23,603 | 14 |
| Suffolk | 11,940 | 13 |
| Surrey | n/a | n/a |
| Sussex | n/a | n/a |
| Thames Valley | 47,442 | 16 |
| Warwickshire | 8,599 | 11 |

| Forces | Training days | Average number of days per PC |
|---|---|---|
| West Mercia | 26,279 | 17 |
| West Midlands | 105,198 | 20 |
| West Yorkshire | 40,936 | 10 |
| Wiltshire | 19,139 | 22 |

## Campsfield House

**Mr. Rooker:** To ask the Secretary of State for the Home department what is the average weekly cost of detaining a person at Campsfield house. [23358]

**Mr. Nicholas Baker:** The average weekly cost is currently estimated at £413, excluding immigration service and escorting costs.

## Historical Documents

**Mr. Gordon Prentice:** To ask the Secretary of State for the Home Department what special training is given to persons who have responsibility for assessing the historical significance of documents held by his Department. [23285]

**Mr. Howard:** The staff involved receive desk training, carried out under the guidance of the Keeper of Public Records, and are provided with written guidance prepared within the Department and by the Public Records Office. Staff also attend conferences and seminars arranged by the Public Records Office, and are encouraged to attend Civil Service College and Public Records Office courses.

## National Vocational Qualifications

**Mr. Barron:** To ask the Secretary of State for the Home Department how many, and what proportion of, vacancies advertised by his Department, and by each of his Department's agencies in the last three years have listed the attainment of NVQ's as an acceptable entry requirement; and, of those, how many have required (i) level 1 NVQs, (ii) level 2 NVQs, (iii) level 3 NVQs and (iv) other level NVQs. [22974]

**Mr. Howard:** Information is not readily available about vacancies advertised by Prison Service establishments. In the remainder of the Home Office no vacancy advertised in the last three years has specifically listed the attainment of NVQs as an acceptable entry requirement. In both areas, however, NVQs are accepted as a recognised equivalent to the entry qualifications of certain grades.

# LORD PRESIDENT OF THE COUNCIL

## Registered Medical Practitioners

**Mr. Spearing:** To ask the Lord President of the Council how many appeals from decisions of the General Medical Council *(a)* heard, *(b)* which were successful against removal from the list of registered medical practitioners consequent to proceedings in its professional conduct committee, and how many other appeals were *(c)* heard and *(d)* successful since the coming into force of the Medical Act 1983.

**Mr. Newton:** Since 26 October 1983, when the Medical Act 1983 came into force, the Judicial Committee of the Privy Council has heard 33 appeals, of which three were successful, from decisions of the professional conduct committee of the General Medical Council directing the erasure or suspension of a doctor's name from the register. Over the same period, the committee has heard seven appeals against decisions of the health committee of the General Medical Council of which none was successful.

## TRADE AND INDUSTRY

### Military Exports

**Mr. Cousins:** To ask the President of the Board of Trade whether, between December 1984 and August 1990, exporters were required to obtain end user certificates for the export of goods, licensed under the military list, to (a) Thailand, (b) Singapore, (c) Pakistan, (d) Portugal, (e) Cyprus and (f) Hong Kong.        [19402]

**Mr. Ian Taylor:** Where goods were to be exported to a Government Department of the countries listed no end-user certificate was required by the DTI export licensing unit, although a copy of the contract or purchase order was requested. For military list exports to companies and other private consignees, exporters were required to submit sufficient information to enable the ELU to assess the export licence application. The guidance note on filling out an export licence application form said that exporters should supply an end-user certificate, or an end-use statement or an international import certificate, but this was not insisted upon in all cases.

### Richard Budge

**Mr. Betts:** To ask the President of the Board of Trade (1) what account was taken of the role of Richard Budge as a director of AF Budge (Mining) when awarding the franchise to mine coal in the three English coal regions;        [22706]

(2) if the Government were aware of the concerns raised by Coopers and Lybrand, officers in the insolvency unit of his Department and the official receiver about the actions of Richard Budge as a director of AF Budge (a) when the shortlist of companies to be considered for the coal franchise was agreed and (b) when RJB (Mining) was awarded franchises;        [22707]

(3) what consideration Ministers gave to monitoring the concerns being expressed by Coopers and Lybrand, officers in the insolvency unit of his Department and the Official Receiver over the actions of Richard Budge as a director of AF Budge when making statements to the House about the shortlist of firms to be considered for coal franchises and the awarding of franchises to RJB (Mining);        [22708]

(4) what stage had investigations into the actions of Richard Budge reached (a) when RJB (Mining) was shortlisted as a franchisee and (b) when it was given the coal franchises.        [22709]

(5) what consideration was given to the questions still surrounding Richard Budge as a director of AF Budge when deciding not to choose a second, back-up, franchisee for the coal franchises awarded to RJB (Mining).        [22712]

**Mr. Page** *[holding answer 9 May 1995]:* The Department and its advisers undertook a careful assessment of each of the bids for the regional coal companies and care and maintenance collieries when tenders were submitted in September 1994. Bids were assessed on their merits, including the prospects for the long-term viability of the industry and value for money for the taxpayer.

The preferred bidders for the regional coal companies and care and maintenance collieries were announced on 12 October. As envisaged when bids were invited, a single preferred bidder was identified for each regional coal company, with whom detailed negotiations were to take place. It was made clear to the preferred bidders that their identification as preferred bidders did not commit the Government to a sale if the detailed negotiations did not reach a satisfactory conclusion. The position of each of the preferred bidders was kept under close review throughout the course of the negotiations.

Decisions in relation to disqualification were taken on 21 November 1994. The decision not to take proceedings against Mr. Richard Budge and some other former directors of AF Budge Ltd. and related companies was made after careful consideration of the circumstances of the failure and in the light of legal advice.

In the light of consideration of the conduct of Mr. Richard Budge in the context of the failure of the AF Budge companies, as well as the decision on proceedings, the Department reviewed RJB (Mining) plc's status as preferred bidder for the English coal companies, having regard to Mr. Budge's position as chief executive of RJB (Mining) plc. The Department concluded that RJB (Mining) plc should properly continue as preferred bidder.

The contract for the sale of the English Regional Coal Company was signed on 9 December and the sale was completed on 30 December 1994.

**Mr. Betts:** To ask the President of the Board of Trade what investigations are pending or being considered into loans made to Richard Budge as a director RJB (Mining).        [22710]

**Mr. Jonathan Evans** *[holding answer 9 May 1995]:* It is not our practice to comment on the affairs of individual companies.

**Mr. Betts:** To ask the President of the Board of Trade what involvement and knowledge he and his Department had about the agreement reached between Sheffield development corporation and Budge which divided responsibility for providing the infrastructure for an airport at Tinsley, Sheffield, and the authority for opencasting the site.        [22714]

**Mr. Page** *[holding answer 9 May 1995]:* The agreement between Sheffield Development Corporation and AF Budge (Mining) Ltd. is a matter for the Department of the Environment and I refer the hon. Gentleman to the answer given by my hon. Friend the Minister for Local Government on 9 May 1995, *Official Report*, column *421*.

The agreement was disclosed to the official receiver in relation to the subsequent failure of AF Budge Ltd. and related companies.

**Mr. Betts:** To ask the President of the Board of Trade what was the role of Ministers in deciding not to disqualify Richard Budge as a director following his actions as a director of AF Budge.    [22715]

**Mr. Jonathan Evans** *[holding answer 9 May 1995]:* Decisions in relation to the disqualification of directors of failed companies are taken on behalf of the Secretary of State by the Insolvency Service which has operational responsibility. Those decisions are based on statutory provisions, on criteria agreed by Ministers, informed by developing case law, and legal advice where necessary; and the likelihood of a court making a disqualification order. Ministers were advised of the Insolvency Service's decisions on disqualification proceedings relating to the failed AF Budge companies and endorsed them.

**Mr. Byers:** To ask the President of the Board of Trade on what date his Department received the Coopers and Lybrand report into the collapse of AF Budge; and if he will place a copy of the report in the Library.    [22582]

**Mr. Jonathan Evans** *[holding answer 4 May 1995]:* The insolvency service received the report on AF Budge Ltd. on 28 September 1993. Such reports are confidential between the Secretary of State and insolvency practitioners.

**Mr. Byers:** To ask the President of the Board of Trade who took the decision, and on what date, to bring disqualification proceedings against former directors of AF Budge; what criteria were used in selecting the directors; and if he will identify those former directors against whom disqualification proceedings have not been taken.    [22584]

**Mr. Jonathan Evans** *[holding answer 4 May 1995]:* Decisions in relation to the disqualification of directors of failed companies are taken on behalf of the Secretary of State by the Insolvency Service which has the operational responsibility. Those decisions are based on statutory provision, criteria agreed by Ministers, informed by developing case law, and legal advice where necessary; and the likelihood of a court making a disqualification order. Ministers were advised of the Insolvency Service's decisions on disqualification proceedings relating to the failed AF Budge Group and endorsed them. In this case decisions were made on 21 November 1994.

Given the number of companies comprised in the AF Budge Group and the large number of directors, it is not practical to list all former directors from the incorporation of the earliest company in 1967. The following were returned as directors in the three years prior to the first appointments of administrative receivers to AF Budge companies in December 1992, and against whom proceedings have not been taken in relation to the relevant companies:

| Name | Ceased to act (if applicable) |
| --- | --- |
| J. R. Bower | 28 February 1992 |
| R. J. Budge | 22 February 1992 |
| G. W. Jarrett | 20 February 1992 |
| G. Muir | 7 January 1993 |
| D. T. Threadkell | 7 January 1993 |
| S. S. Clarke | 15 December 1992 |
| A. A. Mackintosh | 13 January 1993 |
| M. A. Connolly | — |

| Name | Ceased to act (if applicable) |
| --- | --- |
| R. V. Sallis | 18 December 1992 |
| J. E. Greenhalgh | 11 December 1992 |
| D. T. Trewick | — |
| M. Wainwright | 18 January 1993 |
| C. A. Walton | 22 February 1992 |
| K. Jarrett | 22 February 1992 |
| M. Chick | |
| D. Cowlinshaw | 1 October 1990 |
| G. B. Cowlinshaw | 1 October 1990 |
| P. M. Annington | — |
| R. S. Allan | — |
| E. Bruce | — |
| C. H. Coward | — |
| M. R. Hampton | — |
| M. Shield | — |
| S. G. Mort | 8 January 1993 |
| J. A. Buck | 18 December 1992 |
| N. J. Teal | 16 December 1992 |
| M. F. Vasey | 31 March 1993 |

**Mr. Byers:** To ask the President of the Board of Trade on what dates in 1994 his Department's insolvency service interviewed Mr. Richard Budge; and on what date the Service reported on the conduct of the former directors of AF Budge.    [22585]

**Mr. Jonathan Evans** *[holding answer 4 May 1995]:* The official receiver reported initially on the affairs of AF Budge Ltd. and related companies on 25 July 1994. Following further investigations into those affairs Mr. R. J. Budge and two other directors of the AF Budge Group were interviewed by him on 11, 14 and 15 November respectively and he reported the outcome of those interviews on 15 November 1994. The official receiver's report to the court under the Company Directors Disqualification Act 1986 was made on 7 December 1994.

**Mr. Byers:** To ask the President of the Board of Trade if he will make available to the National Audit Office investigators into the privatisation of the coal industry the Coopers and Lybrand report into the collapse of AF Budge and the report from the insolvency service into the conduct of Mr. Richard Budge as a director of AF Budge.    [22583]

**Mr. Jonathan Evans** *[holding answer 4 May 1995]:* The insolvency service will co-operate fully with the National Audit Office.

**Mr. Byers:** To ask the President of the Board of Trade which Ministers in his Department in the last five years have been a member of a group considering the energy industry policy which had Mr. Richard Budge as one of its members.    [23018]

**Mr. Page** *[holding answer 9 May 1995]:* As far as I am aware, no Minister in this Department, or in the former Department of Energy, in the last five years has been a member of a group considering energy industry policy which had Mr. Richard Budge as one of its members.

**Mr. Byers:** To ask the President of the Board of Trade on what dates in 1992, 1993 and until 12 October 1994, Ministers in his Department met Mr. Richard Budge to discuss the privatisation of the coal industry.    [23016]

**Mr. Page** *[holding answer 9 May 1995]:* I have been asked to reply.

My right. hon. Friend the Minister for Industry and Energy discussed coal privatisation with a number of industry figures in this period. At meetings with

Mr. Richard Budge on 17 June 1992, 29 June 1992, 1 March 1993, 26 March 1993, 15 April 1993, 15 June 1993 and 7 July 1994 a range of issues were discussed. Mr. Budge met the Minister for Industry and Energy both in his capacity as chairman of the trade association Coalpro, and as chief executive of RJB (Mining).

**Mr. Byers:** To ask the President of the Board of Trade if any Ministers in his Department since April 1992 have been on trips overseas in which Mr. Richard Budge was in the party. [23017]

**Mr. Page** *[holding answer 9 May 1995]:* No DTI Minister has been on an overseas visit with Mr. Richard Budge during this period.

**Mr. Byers:** To ask the President of the Board of Trade on how many occasions between 1989 and 1992 advance payments for ordinary soil extraction were made to AF Budge; and what was their total value. [22818]

**Mr. Page** *[holding answer 9 May 1995]:* This is a matter for the British Coal Corporation.

### Cottonware Ltd.

**Mr. Byers:** To ask the President of the Board of Trade what action he proposes to take against the directors of Cottonware Ltd. for not filing their company accounts within the legal deadline. [23970]

**Mr. Jonathan Evans:** There is no company registered with that name on the public record held at Companies House.

### Oil and Gas Pipelines

**Dr. Godman:** To ask the President of the Board of Trade (1) what proposals he has to modify the Petroleum Act 1987 in relation to the dismantling and removal of redundant offshore oil and gas structures and submarine pipeline networks; and if he will make a statement; [24032]

(2) if he will list *(a)* the redundant offshore oil and gas installations which have been dismantled and removed from their sites and *(b)* the redundant submarine pipeline networks which have been dismantled and removed from their sites in accordance with the relevant provisions contained in the Petroleum Act 1987; and if he will make a statement; [23033]

(3) how many programmes of *(a)* abandonment of redundant offshore oil and gas structures, *(b)* abandonment of submarine pipeline networks, *(c)* dismantlement and removal of redundant offshore oil and gas structures and *(d)* dismantlement and removal of submarine pipeline networks he has approved in each of the past seven years; and if he will make a statement; [24034]

(4) if he will list *(a)* the number and location of redundant offshore oil and gas installations which operators have been allowed to abandon and *(b)* the redundant submarine pipeline networks which operators have been allowed to abandon in accordance with the relevant provisions of the Petroleum Act 1987; if he will detail what measures have been taken, in relation to such programmes of abandonment, to protect the safety and commercial interests of other parties engaged in maritime industries; and if he will make a statement; [23036]

(5) what advice is given to commercial fishermen who fish nearby fishing grounds and other users of the local marine environment in relation to the dismantlement and removal of redundant offshore oil and gas structures and redundant submarine pipeline networks; [23037]

(6) if he will list the regulations governing the maintenance and inspection of abandoned offshore oil and gas structures and redundant submarine pipeline networks; and if he will make a statement; [23038]

(7) when Shell UK Exploration, Shell Expro, was given approval under part I of the Petroleum Act 1987 for its abandonment proposal for the Brent Spar, which at present is located in the Brent field; and if he will make a statement; [23377]

(8) what discussions have taken place with Shell UK Exploration and Production, Shell Expro, concerning the removal and disposal of the decommissioned Brent Spar under part I of the Petroleum Act 1987 which at present is located in the Brent field; and if he will make a statement; [23378]

(9) if it is his policy in relation to the Petroleum Act 1987 to allow offshore oil and gas operators to dispose of redundant oil and gas structures and pipeline networks by way of deep-water sinkings; and if he will make a statement; [23379]

(10) how many redundant, or decommissioned, offshore oil and gas structures and pipeline networks have been disposed of under the Petroleum Act 1987 by way of *(a)* onshore scrapping, *(b)* deep-water sinking or *(c)* left in situ in each of the past seven years; and if he will make a statement; [23380]

(11) if he name those persons and companies against whom he has initiated court proceedings in each of the past seven years in relation to offences they were alleged to have committed under sections 2, 5, 9 or 10 of the Petroleum Act 1987, of those so proceeded against how many were found guilty; what were the penalties imposed upon them by the law courts; and if he will make a statement. [24210]

**Mr. Eggar:** My right hon. Friend the President of the Board of Trade and his predecessor the Secretary of State for Energy have approved the following abandonment programmes for offshore installations and pipelines:

| Year | Facilities |
|---|---|
| 1988 | Piper Alpha |
| 1991 | Crawford[1] |
| 1992 | Argyll, Duncan and Innes Blair[1] |
| 1993 | Angus |
| | Forbes |
| | Part of Staffa—Ninian pipe-line |
| 1994 | Fulmar single anchor leg mooring (SALM) buoy Brent Spar oil storage and tanker loading facility |

[1] Includes pipe-lines.

In each case, except Piper Alpha, two Blair pipelines, a redundant part of the Staffa—Ninian pipeline, and the Argyll Base Manifold, the abandonment programme provided for the complete removal of the facilities. The Crawford, Argyll, Duncan and Innes, and Angus floating production facilities have been re-used elsewhere. The Forbes topsides have been sold for re-use and the jacket has been sold for possible re-use or scrapping onshore. The Fulmar SALM buoy has been removed from the field and the disposal options are under consideration.

In accordance with section 4 of the Petroleum Act 1987 the President of the Board of Trade approved the Brent Spar abandonment programme on 20 December 1994.

That programme provides for disposal of the Spar in the deep waters of the north-east Atlantic. That decision was taken following a comparative assessment of the options including an analysis of the best practicable environmental option. My Department had extensive discussions with Shell UK Exploration and Production during the consideration of the abandonment programme and consulted others in Government with an interest in protection of the marine environment and fisheries. Apart from environmental considerations and possible interference with navigation and fisheries, the comparative assessment also examined risk, technical feasibility and cost. Our decision fully meets our international obligations and has been communicated to other countries under the procedural requirements of the Oslo convention.

No regulations have been made in respect of the abandonment provisions of the Petroleum Act 1987. Inspection and maintenance requirements are decided on a case-by-case basis in the light of the circumstances of each abandonment proposal and after consultation with other Government Departments.

In each case, the President of the Board of Trade has required consultations to be carried out with interested parties, including representatives of fishermen's organisations, and that the results of the consultations be reported in the abandonment programme.

Abandonment programmes are considered on a case-by-case basis and their approval must be consistent with our international obligations including the International Maritime Organisations's guidelines and standards for the removal of offshore installations and the London and Oslo conventions.

While decommissioning operations are being undertaken, mariners are advised by notice to avoid the area. An installation which is only partly removed will not be allowed to endanger navigation. The Government are currently considering whether further measures need to be taken to ensure that mariners, including fishermen, are aware of any remains of installations.

Guidance notes for the abandonment of offshore installations and pipelines were issued for consultation on 4 May 1995. A copy of the guidance notes is available in the Library of the House.

I have no proposals at present to modify the Petroleum Act.

I have not initiated any court proceedings in respect of offences under sections 2, 5, 9 or 10 of the Petroleum Act.

**Dr. Godman:** To ask the President of the Board of Trade on how many occasions in each of the past seven years he has used his powers, contained in section 4 of the Petroleum Act 1987, to reject an abandonment programme submitted by offshore oil and gas operators; in how many such cases the programmes were replaced by an abandonment programme prepared by himself; and if he will make a statement. [24204]

**Mr. Eggar:** No abandonment programmes have been rejected under section 4 of the Petroleum Act 1987.

**Dr. Godman:** To ask the President of the Board of Trade when he plans to issue the authorisation anent the laying of the gas pipeline to Premier Transco Ltd. between Scotland and Northern Ireland; when he expects the work to *(a)* commence and *(b)* be completed; and if he will make a statement. [24181]

**Mr. Eggar:** The authorisation under the Pipe-lines Act 1962 for the onshore section of the pipeline was issued on 27 February this year. It is expected that the authorisation for the offshore section required under the Petroleum and Submarine Pipe-lines Act 1975 will be issued shortly. Work has already commenced on the onshore section and work on the whole pipeline is expected to be completed by October 1996.

### Fireworks

**Mr. Burden:** To ask the President of the Board of Trade what are the responsibilities of *(a)* the fire service and *(b)* the trading standards officer for enforcing the law relating to the purchase of fireworks by children under the apparent age of 16 years in Metropolitan areas; and what changes have been made since March. [22819]

**Mr. Jonathan Evans** *[holding answer 9 May 1995]:* Prior to the revocation of the Fireworks (Safety) Regulations 1986, trading standards authorities had responsibility for enforcing those regulations relating to the supply of fireworks to children apparently under the age of 16. The fire service had no such responsibility. Since the coming into force of the Fireworks (Safety) (Revocation) Regulations 1995, section 31 of the Explosives Act 1875, as amended, prohibits the sale of fireworks to those apparently under 16 years of age and the police remain the appropriate enforcement authority.

**Mr. Nigel Griffiths:** To ask the President of the Board of Trade what body will be responsible for enforcing section 31 of the Explosives Act 1875, on the sale of firearms to children under 16 years after the coming into force of the Fireworks (Safety) Revocation Regulations 1995. [23009]

**Mr. Jonathan Evans** *[holding answer 5 May 1995]:* Following the coming into force of the Fireworks (Safety) (Revocation) Regulations 1995, the police remain the appropriate authority to enforce section 31 of the Explosives Act 1875, as amended, which prohibits the sale of fireworks to children apparently under 16 years of age.

### MGM Cinemas

**Mr. Nigel Griffiths:** To ask the President of the Board of Trade (1) what reassurances he has sought from the Office of Fair Trading to ensure that the position of the independent cinema owners is protected in the sale of MGM cinemas by Credit Lyonnais; [24430]

(2) what steps he has taken to ensure that competition in high street cinemas is not reduced as a result of a takeover of MGM cinemas by the Rank Organisation; [24432]

(3) what guarantees he has sought from *(a)* Credit Lyonnais and *(b)* the various bidders for the MGM cinema chain being sold by Credit Lyonnais that they will endeavour where possible to keep open the maximum number of high street and multiple cinemas; [24431]

(4) what steps he has taken to ensure that competition in multiplex cinemas is not reduced as a result of a takeover of MGM cinemas by Time Warner. [24433]

**Mr. Jonathan Evans:** If the sale of MGM cinemas results in a qualifying merger under the Fair Trading Act 1973 it will be for the Director General of Fair Trading to advise my right hon. Friend the President of the Board of Trade whether to refer the merger to the Monopolies and Mergers Commission. In giving his advice, the DGFT will take account of all relevant factors including the impact on competition in the cinema industry and the views of third parties. If appropriate, the DGFT will also advise about possible undertakings which might be given to remedy any adverse effects resulting from the merger.

### Trade Statistics

**Mr. MacShane:** To ask the President of the Board of Trade what is the latest trade balance of *(a)* the United Kingdom, *(b)* Germany, *(c)* France and *(d)* Korea with (i) Poland, (ii) Hungary, (lii) the Czech Republic and (iv) Russia.          [23708]

**Mr. Needham:** Information on the topic is regularly published in the "IMF Direction of Trade Statistics", a copy of which is available in the Library of the House.

### Insolvency Service

**Mr. Byers:** To ask the President of the Board of Trade if he will publish the replies received from the Official Receiver as part of the consultation process for the privatisation of the insolvency service; and if he will consult the official receiver on the detailed specifications for the contracting out of the insolvency service.  [24154]

**Mr. Jonathan Evans:** A digest of official receivers' responses to the consultation process was published and laid in the Libraries of the House and the Vote Office on 3 May 1995. The views of the official receivers have been sought on the draft technical specification and their comments are being considered.

**Mr. Sheerman:** To ask the President of the Board of Trade what estimate he has made of the potential change in public expenditure arising from the proposed privatisation of the insolvency service.          [24375]

**Mr. Jonathan Evans:** It is too early to form any assessment of the effect on public expenditure of the possible contracting out of official receivers' functions. This information will not be available until final bids have been received from the private sector and compared to the benchmark costs of the service. The evaluation of tenders is due to be completed by early December 1995.

**Mr. Sheerman:** To ask the President of the Board of Trade what assessment his Department has made of the potential effect of the privatisation of the insolvency service on fraudulent bankruptcy.          [24377]

**Mr. Jonathan Evans:** Stoy Hayward reported that the contracting out of official receivers' case administration functions upon the making of an insolvency order would enable them to concentrate on their investigatory role.

**Mr. Sheerman:** To ask the President of the Board of Trade what representations he has received about the proposed privatisation of the insolvency service.   [24376]

**Mr. Jonathan Evans:** Both my right hon. Friend the President of the Board of Trade and I have received substantial correspondence concerned with contracting out certain of the official receiver's functions; originating from official receivers staff, members of the public, and members of professional bodies. The official receivers, as statutory office holders, have been formally consulted on proposals for contracting out.

### Convention on Nuclear Safety

**Mr. Llew Smith:** To ask the President of the Board of Trade when he expects the United Kingdom to deposit the United Kingdom's instrument on ratification for the convention on nuclear safety which was signed on 20 September 1994 with the Director General of the International Atomic Energy Agency.          [24292]

**Mr. Page:** Deposit of the United Kingdom's instrument of ratification for the convention on nuclear safety is expected to take place before the end of 1995.

### Overseas Projects Board

**Mr. Wray:** To ask the President of the Board of Trade if he will instruct *(a)* the overseas project board and *(b)* the regional industrial development board to issue an annual report before Parliament.          [24190]

**Mr. Needham:** I shall ensure that any annual report published by the overseas projects board is made available in the Library of the House.

There are seven regional industrial boards covering the 10 English regions. They are non-statutory boards but by tradition each board contributes an annual commentary for inclusion in the annual reports of the Industrial Development Act 1982, copies of which are in the Library of the House.

## NORTHERN IRELAND

### Fish Hatcheries

**Mr. Beggs:** To ask the Secretary of State for Northern Ireland when permission was granted for the operation of a hatchery at Killylough lough, Maghera, County Londonderry; what is the consent discharge number or reference number for this project; and what public notification or consultation took place prior to authorisation for the Killylough lough hatchery, Maghera, County Londonberry, being given.          [23306]

**Mr. Ancram:** There is no fish hatchery of this name and neither has permission been granted for the operation of one at this location. A small unauthorised hatchery was detected and closed in January 1989. In anticipation of an authorised fish hatchery development a consent, No. 89/90, to the discharge of effluent was issued by the Department of the Environment under the terms of the Water Act (Northern Ireland) 1972. The application was not pursued and, as no authorisation was issued for the operation of a hatchery, public notification and consultation procedures were not instigated.

**Mr. Beggs:** To ask the Secretary of State for Northern Ireland if employees of the Fisheries Conservancy Board are required to register an interest when a close relative operates a hatchery or fish farm within or outside the jurisdiction of the Fisheries Conservancy Board for Northern Ireland.          [23305]

**Mr. Ancram:** No.

### Stevens Report

**Mr. Mullin:** To ask the Secretary of State for Northern Ireland, pursuant to his answer of 2 May, *Official Report*, column *160*, if Mr. John Stevens succeeded in identifying those responsible for the killings which were the subject of the shoot to kill inquiry.          [23122]

**Sir John Wheeler:** Mr. Stevens conducted no such inquiry. He conducted an inquiry into allegations of collusion and submitted a report on that inquiry. He conducted further inquiries into the purported activities of Brian Nelson and certain members of the Army. As stated in my reply of 2 May, *Official Report*, column *160*, a direction of no prosecutions was issued on 17 February 1995.

**Mr. Mullin:** To ask the Secretary of State for Northern Ireland, pursuant to his answer of 2 May, *Official Report*, column *160*, on what grounds the direction of no prosecution was issued on 19 February following the report by Mr. John Stevens; and if he will make a statement.          [23121]

**Sir John Wheeler:** In respect of the supplementary reports which were forwarded to the Director of Public Prosecutions (Northern Ireland) on 25 April 1994, 18 October 1994 and 24 January 1995, the director concluded that there was insufficient evidence to warrant prosecution of any persons. A direction of no prosecution was issued on 17 February 1995.

**Mr. Mullin:** To ask the Secretary of State for Northern Ireland, pursuant to his answer of 2 May, *Official Report*, column *160*, if he will place in the Library a survey of the supplementary reports by Mr. John Stevens to his shoot to kill inquiry on 25 April and 18 October 1994 and on 24 January 1995.          [23123]

**Sir John Wheeler:** No. Police reports remain confidential.

### Reservoirs

**Ms Rachel Squire:** To ask the Secretary of State for Northern Ireland if he will make a statement on public access to ownership of water reservoirs in Northern Ireland, with particular reference to the Annalong reservoir.          [23153]

**Mr. Moss:** Ownership of reservoirs used for public water supply purposes is vested in the Department of the Environment for Northern Ireland. Access is granted for specific recreational purposes such as angling, or for general recreation dependent upon consideration of safety, water quality and the nature of the environment. There is no Annalong reservoir. The nearest reservoir is at the Silent valley and the public enjoy full access there. There are no plans to alter these arrangements.

### Local Management of Schools

**Mr. Worthington:** To ask the Secretary of State for Northern Ireland what research he has conducted into the effectiveness and fairness of the local management of schools formula for the delegation of school budgets; and what proposals he has to change it.          [23390]

**Mr. Ancram:** The effects of the local management of schools formula have been closely monitored by the five education and library boards and by the Department of Education. The Department has also commissioned the University of Ulster to undertake a survey of the impact of LMS on school. I have no proposal for changes at this time.

### Industrial Development Board

**Mr. McGrady:** To ask the Secretary of State for Northern Ireland what cash settlement was paid to the former chief executive of the Industrial Development Board to terminate his contract; and if he will make a statement.          [23078]

**Mr. Ancram:** The former chief executive of the Industrial Development Board expressed a wish to return to his private sector business and the Department agreed that he could be released from his contract from 31 March 1995. As his departure was by mutual agreement, no cash settlement was paid.

**Mr. Mallon:** To ask the Secretary of State for Northern Ireland what was the total number of Industrial Development Board sponsored potential investor visits in each of the past five years; and for each year if he will give details of the number of visits to *(a)* Armagh city, *(b)* Newry town, *(c)* Armagh district council area, *(d)* Newry and Mourne district council area, *(e)* Craigavon district, *(f)* Belfast, *(g)* Derry city and *(h)* Antrim borough.          [23722]

**Mr. Ancram:** The number of potential investor visits for the years in question together with the breakdown by district council area are as follows. Information relating to Armagh city and Newry town is not readily available and could be provided only at disproportionate cost.

*Total inward visits to Northern Ireland*

|         | Total |
|---------|-------|
| 1990–91 | 231   |
| 1991–92 | 240   |
| 1992–93 | 216   |
| 1993–94 | 229   |
| 1994–95 | 254   |

*Total visits by potential investors in the following district councils areas*

|                  | 1990–91 | 1991–92 | 1992–93 | 1993–94 | 1994–95 |
|------------------|---------|---------|---------|---------|---------|
| Armagh           | 3       | 2       | 3       | —       | 2       |
| Newry and Mourne | 4       | 4       | 10      | 9       | 19      |
| Craigavon        | 14      | 12      | 15      | 6       | 24      |
| Belfast          | 188     | 213     | 141     | 125     | 138     |
| Derry            | 23      | 28      | 23      | 30      | 31      |
| Antrim           | 61      | 81      | 38      | 55      | 40      |

### Historical Documents

**Mr. Gordon Prentice:** To ask the Secretary of State for Northern Ireland what special training is given to persons who have responsibility for assessing the historical significance of documents held by his Department. [23281]

**Sir John Wheeler:** Assessments of the historical significance of departmental records held in Northern Ireland is the responsibility of the Public Records Office of Northern Ireland. I have asked its chief executive, Dr. Malcomson, to arrange for a reply to be given about the training of his staff.

Assessment of the historical significance of departmental records held in London is done in consultation with the Public Record Office of Northern Ireland. The staff responsible for this work attend courses, conferences and seminars arranged by the Public Record Office, Kew.

*Letter from A. P. W. Malcomson to Mr. Gordon Prentice, dated 5 May 1995:*

I have been asked to reply to your recent Parliamentary Question Number 797 enquiring about the training given to persons who have responsibility for assessing the historical significance of documents held by the Department of the Secretary of State for Northern Ireland.

Documents of historical significance originating in the Northern Ireland Departments are transferred to the Public Record Office of Northern Ireland (PRONI) when they have ceased to have recurrent administrative value—usually at twenty years. By this stage, the assessment of their historical significance will have been carried out by curatorial staff of PRONI, who are all graduates (often in history) and are given a two-year training period before being allowed to make independent, but still supervised, decisions.

I hope you find this information helpful.

### Police Complaints

**Mr. Worthington:** To ask the Secretary of State for Northern Ireland what proposals he has to give powers to the Independent Commission for Police Complaints for Northern Ireland to allow it to supervise inquiries of its own volition. [23600]

**Sir John Wheeler:** There are at present no plans to allow the commission to instigate the supervision of the investigation of a matter which is not the subject of a complaint. However, my right hon. and learned Friend announced on 29 March, *Official Report*, columns 659-61, that the commission will have the power to draw a non-complaint matter to his attention: he will then have the responsibility to refer appropriate cases to the commission for supervision. Draft legislation to give effect to this new power, the Police (Amendment) (Northern Ireland) Order, was published for consultation on 25 April 1995.

### Telephones

**Mr. Donohoe:** To ask the Secretary of State for Northern Ireland how many mobile telephones being utilised by his Department have been cloned during the last 12 months. [23435]

**Sir John Wheeler** [holding answer 9 May 1995]: Three.

**Mr. Donohoe:** To ask the Secretary of State for Northern Ireland what use his Department makes of hand-held and car-based mobile telephones; what were the costs for each financial year of these services since mobile telephones were first introduced to his Department; and how many mobile telephones are currently in use. [23441]

**Sir John Wheeler** [holding answer 9 May 1995]: Within the Northern Ireland Departments and the Northern Ireland Office, hand-held and car-based mobile telephones are used by senior management, private office staff, security personnel, press officers, car pool/official drivers and other staff whose duties require them to be frequently absent from their base and who are required to maintain contact.

The cost of these phones and the number currently in use are as follows:

| Department | Number of mobile phones | 1987–88 £ | 1988–89 £ | 1989–90 £ | 1990–91 £ | 1991–92 £ | 1992–93 £ | 1993–94 £ | 1994–95 £ |
|------------|-------------------------|-----------|-----------|-----------|-----------|-----------|-----------|-----------|-----------|
| Education | 4 | 154 | 335 | 468 | 361 | 450 | 1,214 | 2,346 | 2,807 |
| Agriculture | 69 | nil | [1]10,000 | [1]10,000 | [1]11,000 | [1]11,500 | 13,600 | 16,000 | 22,400 |
| Finance and Personnel | 38 | nil | nil | nil | 1,670 | 8,095 | 9,490 | 17,303 | 16,972 |
| Environment | 235 | [2]Approximately £50,000 pa operating cost excluding call charges | | | | | | | |
| Economic Development | 59 | nil | 500 | 2,781 | 4,077 | 5,935 | 12,611 | 17,552 | 19,909 |
| Health and Social Services | 34 | This information is not recorded centrally and could be obtained only at disproportionate cost. | | | | | | | |
| Northern Ireland Office | 19 | [3] | — | — | — | — | 15,893 | 13,761 | 11,434 |

[1] Estimated expenditure.
[2] Annual breakdown and call charges not available.
[3] Records do not show when mobile phones were first introduced—last three years given only.

**Mr. Donohoe:** To ask the Secretary of State for Northern Ireland what costs his Department has incurred during the last 12 months as a result of cloning of mobile telephones being utilised by his Department, with particular reference to the making of unauthorised calls.        [23481]

**Sir John Wheeler** *[holding answer 9 May 1995]:* None. Unauthorised calls on cloned phones are not paid for by the Department.

### School Leavers

**Mr. Worthington:** To ask the Secretary of State for Northern Ireland what proportion of school leavers has attained no academic qualifications in every year since 1979.        [23393]

**Mr. Ancram:** The proportion of school leavers attaining no academic qualifications from 1979–80 is as follows:

|         | Per cent. |
|---------|-----------|
| 1979–80 | 27.0      |
| 1980–81 | No survey |
| 1981–82 | 24.3      |
| 1982–83 | No survey |
| 1983–84 | 21.1      |
| 1984–85 | No survey |
| 1985–86 | 19.5      |
| 1986–87 | 17.7      |
| 1987–88 | 16.4      |
| 1988–89 | 12.7      |
| 1989–90 | 10.0      |
| 1990–91 | 8.6       |
| 1991–92 | 7.4       |
| 1992–93 | 4.9       |

### Consultants

**Mr. John D. Taylor:** To ask the Secretary of State for Northern Ireland what contracts have been awarded to Capita Management Consultants Ltd. for consultancy work in the Northern Ireland civil service since January 1990; and if he will list the cost of each consultancy to date.        [23661]

**Sir John Wheeler:** Northern Ireland Departments maintain records of consultancy expenditure on a financial year basis. The provision of information from 1 January 1990 to 31 March 1990 can be obtained only at disproportionate cost. During the period 1 April 1990 to 31 March 1995, payments totalling £546,738, excluding VAT, were made by Northern Ireland Departments in respect of consultancy work undertaken by Capita Management Consultants Ltd. Details of the value of individual contracts cannot, however, be released as this would breach commercial confidentiality.

### Public Bodies

**Mr. Flynn:** To ask the Secretary of State for Northern Ireland which non-departmental public bodies within the responsibility of his Department are subject to scrutiny by *(a)* ombudsmen, *(b)* the National Audit Office, *(c)* the Audit Commission and *(d)* other monitoring officers; which are covered by citizens charters; in which performance indicators apply; and in which members are liable to surcharge.        [23959]

**Sir John Wheeler:** In Northern Ireland, the Commissioner for Complaints investigates complaints of alleged injustice in consequence of maladministration by local and public bodies. The current list of non-departmental public bodies within the jurisdiction of the Commissioner for Complaints is as follows:

Agricultural Research Institute of Northern Ireland
Arts Council of Northern Ireland
Council for Catholic Maintained Schools
Education and Library Boards
Enterprise Ulster
Fire Authority for Northern Ireland
Fisheries Conservancy Board for Northern Ireland
Industrial Training Boards
Labour Relations Agency
Laganside Corporation
Livestock and Meat Marketing Commission for Northern Ireland
Local Enterprise Development Unit
Mental Health Commission for Northern Ireland
National Board for Nursing, Midwifery and Health Visiting for Northern Ireland
Northern Ireland Housing Executive
Northern Ireland Local Government Officers Superannuation Committee
Northern Ireland Council for the Curriculum, Examinations and Assessment
Northern Ireland Sports Council
Northern Ireland Tourist Board
Office of the Northern Ireland Commissioner for the Rights of Trade Union Members
Trustees of the Ulster Folk and Transport Museum
Trustees of the Ulster Museum
Youth Council for Northern Ireland

There are no non-departmental public bodies in Northern Ireland which are subject to scrutiny by the Audit Commission.

The following non-departmental public bodies sponsored by the Northern Ireland Office are subject to scrutiny by the National Audit Office:

Police Authority for Northern Ireland
Probation Board for Northern Ireland
Independent Commissioner for Police Complaints
Training Schools Management Board Rathgael and Whiteabbey

The responsibility of the National Audit Office does not extend to the six Northern Ireland Departments, which have their own similarly appointed body—the Northern Ireland Audit Office. The following non-departmental public bodies are subject to scrutiny by the NIAO:

Belfast Education and Library Board
Northern Education and Libary Board
South Eastern Education and Library Board
Southern Education and Library Board
Western Education and Library Board
Enterprise Ulster
Equal Opportunities Commission for Northern Ireland
Executive of the Industrial Development Board for Northern Ireland
Fair Employment Commission for Northern Ireland
Fire Authority for Northern Ireland
General Consumer Council for Northern Ireland
Health and Safety Agency for Northern Ireland
Mental Health Commission for Northern Ireland
National Board for Nursing, Midwifery and Health Visiting for Northern Ireland
Northern Ireland Council for the Curriculum Examinations and Assessments
Northern Ireland Housing Executive

Northern Ireland Tourist Board
Sports Council for Northern Ireland
Staff Commission for Education and Library Boards
Ulster Folk and Transport Museum
Ulster Museum
Youth Council for Northern Ireland

The following non-departmental public bodies are subject to scrutiny by the Fair Employment Commission for Northern Ireland:

Public authorities for the purposes of sections 27 and 42 of the Fair Employment Act of 1989

Any agency established under article 4(1) of the Health and Personal Services (Special Agencies) (Northern Ireland) Order 1990 before the coming into operation of this order

Agricultural Research Institute of Northern Ireland

Arts Council for Northern Ireland

Belfast Harbour Commissioners

British Broadcasting Corporation

Chief Constable of the Royal Ulster Constabulary

Chief Electoral Officer for Northern Ireland

Citybus Ltd.

Coleraine Harbour Commissioners

Comptroller and Auditor General for Northern Ireland

Council for Catholic Maintained Schools

Any district council

Any education and library board established under article 3 of the Education and Libraries (Northern Ireland) Order 1986

Enterprise Ulster

Equal Opportunities Commission for Northern Ireland

Fair Employment Commission for Northern Ireland

Fire Authority for Northern Ireland

Fisheries Conservancy Board for Northern Ireland

Flexibus Ltd.

Foyle Fisheries Commission

General Consumer Council for Northern Ireland

Any health and social services board established under article 16(1) of the Health and Personal Social Services (Northern Ireland) Order 1972

Any health and social services trust established under article 10(1) of the Health and Personal Services (Northern Ireland) Order 1991 before the coming into operation of this order.

Independent Commission for Police Complaints for Northern Ireland

Any industrial training board established under article 14(1) of the Industrial Training (Northern Ireland) Order 1984

Labour Relations Agency

Laganside Corporation

Livestock and Meat Commission

Local Enterprise Development Unit

Local Government Staff Commission for Northern Ireland

Londonderry Port and Harbour Commissioners

Mental Health Commission for Northern Ireland

Milk Marketing Board for Northern Ireland

National Board for Nursing, Midwifery and Health Visiting for Northern Ireland

Northern Ireland Central Services Agency for the Health and Social Services

Northern Ireland Commissioner for Complaints

Northern Ireland Community Relations Council

Northern Ireland Council for the Curriculum, Examinations and Assessment

Northern Ireland Council for Postgraduate Medical and Dental Education

Northern Ireland Economic Development Office

Northern Ireland Fishery Harbour Authority

Northern Ireland Housing Executive

Northern Ireland Local Government Officers Superannuation Committee

Northern Ireland Parliamentary Commissioner for Administration

Northern Ireland Railways Company Ltd.

Northern Ireland Tourist Board

Northern Ireland Transport Holding Company

Pigs Marketing Board (Northern Ireland)

Police Authority for Northern Ireland

Post Office

Probation Board for Northern Ireland

Rathgael and Whiteabbey Schools Management Board

Sports Council for Northern Ireland

Sports Commission for Education and Library Boards

The board of governors of Stranmillis college of education, Belfast

Trustees of the Ulster Folk and Transport Museum

Trustees of the Ulster Museum

Ulster Sheltered Employment Ltd.

Ulsterbus Ltd.

Warrenpoint Harbour Authority

Youth Council for Northern Ireland

The Fire Authority for Northern Ireland is subject to scrutiny by the Home Office fire service inspectorate.

All non-departmental public bodies are subject to internal departmental scrutiny. All executive non-departmental public bodies listed in the publication "Public Bodies 1994" are subject to performance indicators. Information on advisory non-departmental public bodies is not available and could be obtained only at disproportionate cost.

The following non-departmental public bodies in Northern Ireland have published charters:

Northern Ireland Housing Executive tenants charter
Northern Ireland railway passengers charter
Ulsterbus/Citybus passengers charter

The following non-departmental public bodies have published charter standard statements.

Eastern health and social services board
Northern health and social services board
Southern health and social services board
Western health and social services board

Each document sets out the rights and standards of service people can expect.

As part of the charter, Northern Ireland Railways operates a compensation scheme whereby passengers receive discount vouchers or refunds if services are delayed.

In respect of members being liable to surcharge, the education and library boards attract the provisions of sections 31 to 33 of the Local Government Act Northern Ireland 1972 which relate to fraudulent activity.

## AGRICULTURE, FISHERIES AND FOOD

### Agricultural Wages Board

**Mr. MacShane:** To ask the Minister of Agriculture, Fisheries and Food what is the wage-setting role of the Agricultural Wages Board. [23710]

**Mr. Jack:** Under the provisions of the Agricultural Wages Act 1948, as amended, the Agricultural Wages Board has the power to make orders:

(a) fixing minimum rates of wages;

(b) directing holidays to be allowed;

(c) fixing any other terms and conditions of employment;

for workers employed in agriculture.

### Rural White Paper

**Mr. Colvin:** To ask the Minister of Agriculture, Fisheries and Food what is his estimate of the net annual financial saving, or cost, of his Department's submission for the proposed White Paper on the rural economy.

[24334]

**Mr. Jack:** Proposals for the rural White Paper remain subject to continuing collective consideration and discussion. The costs of measures contained in the White Paper will be taken into account in the public expenditure survey.

### Public Bodies

**Mr. Wray:** To ask the Minister of Agriculture, Fisheries and Food if he will introduce legislation to make it a statutory requirement for *(a)* the Advisory Committee on Pesticides, *(b)* the Advisory Committee on Novel Foods and Processes, *(c)* the Food Advisory Committee and *(d)* the Spongiform Encephalopathy Advisory Committee to lay an annual report before Parliament.

[24178]

**Mr. Jack:** The answer to (a), (b), (c) is no. These non-departmental public bodies already produce annual reports, copies of which are placed in the Library of the House.

The answer to (d) is no. This NDPB produces periodic rather than annual reports and these are placed in the Library of the House.

### Intervention Stores

**Mr. Davidson:** To ask the Minister of Agriculture, Fisheries and Food when *(a)* butter and *(b)* cheese was last distributed on a (i) national and (ii) local basis from intervention stores.

[24289]

**Mr. Jack:** Butter released from intervention stores was last distributed during the period September 1992 to March 1993, as part of the 1992 surplus food scheme arrangements. The scheme applied throughout the UK and distribution was undertaken by 1,367 designated organisations. Cheese has never been distributed in the UK from EC intervention stocks.

**Mr. Davidson:** To ask the Minister of Agriculture, Fisheries and Food when and where there have been any distribution of Intervention Board *(a)* butter, *(b)* cheese and *(c)* wine in the UK in the last 12 months.

[24288]

**Mr. Jack:** There has been no distribution by the Intervention Board of butter, cheese or wine in the last 12 months.

### CHURCH COMMISSIONERS

### Investments

**29. Mr. Flynn:** To ask the right hon. Member for Selby, as representing the Church Commissioners what new proposals he has to improve the return of the investments of the Church Commissioners.

[22496]

**Mr. Alison:** DTZ Debenham Thorpe advised on our property investment strategy in March 1994 and is in the course of updating this advice. The commissioners have embarked upon a strategic programme of property sales

to rebalance their investment portfolio in the light of that advice.

Our consulting actuaries have advised on our asset allocation strategy. This advice was recently considered at length by the assets committee and has influenced the committee's aim to combine the maximisation of investment return with an acceptable level of risk and diversification in those investments.

### Staff (Dismissals)

**31. Mr. David Evans:** To ask the right hon. Member for Selby, as representing the Church Commissioners when a member of the commissioners' staff was last dismissed.

[22498]

**Mr. Alison:** The most recent dismissal of a member of the commissioners' staff took place last April, and before that in August 1992.

### Pensions

**32. Mr. Jenkin:** To ask the right hon. Member for Selby as representing the Church Commissioners what discussions the commissioners have had concerning the recent second report of the Social Security Committee on the Church Commissioners and Church of England pensions; and if he will make a statement.

[22499]

**34. Mr. Harry Greenway:** To ask the right hon. Member for Selby, as representing the Church Commissioners if he will make a statement on the recommendations contained in the second report of the Social Security Committee of Session 1994–95, HC 354, on the operation of Church of England pensions.

[22501]

**35. Mr. Corbyn:** To ask the right hon. Member for Selby, as representing the Church Commissioners what action has been taken to carry out the recommendations of the second report of the Social Security Committee, HC 354, in respect of the past use of Church Commissioners' pension fund money.

[22502]

**Mr. Alison:** I refer the hon. Members to the answer I gave earlier to day to the hon. Members for Derbyshire, North-East (Mr. Barnes), and Cirencester and Tewkesbury (Mr. Clifton-Brown).

**33. Mr. Frank Field:** To ask the right hon. Member for Selby, as representing the Church Commissioners how many wives have been divorced from their clergy husbands for each of the last 30 years; and if he will make a statement on the impact of these numbers on pension provision.

[22500]

**Mr. Alison:** Neither the Church Commissioners nor the pensions board holds this information. It is possible that Broken Rites, which, as the hon. Member knows, is an independent association of divorced and separated wives of clergy, may be able to provide certain information.

A survivorship pension is payable to a legal widow— the wife to whom the clergyman was married at the time of his death. No such pension is payable in respect of the ex-wife of a divorced clergyman unless he remarries. In that event, and if he is survived by the second wife, she would receive a pension.

The pensions board makes discretionary grants to a former wife, after the death of her ex-husband, if her total income from all sources is below a certain figure.

## ENVIRONMENT

### G7 Meeting, Hamilton

**Mr. Llew Smith:** To ask the Secretary of State for the Environment what proposals were put forward by the United Kingdom and what decisions taken at the meeting of G7 Environment Ministers in Hamilton from 29 April to 1 May; and if he will place in the Library a copy of the communiqué from the meeting. [22927]

**Mr. Gummer:** The meeting of G7 Environment Ministers was concerned to prepare the response of the most prosperous world economies to the major environmental challenges we face.

We stressed the need to maximise our efforts to implement the biodiversity and climate change conventions. On climate change, we emphasised the importance not only of meeting our targets for the year 2000 but of taking forward the mandate negotiated at the Berlin conference of the parties to consider the position beyond 2000. The UK was able to take the lead in these discussions, and our firm proposition of the need to cut developed country greenhouse gas emissions by the between 5 and 10 per cent. from 1990 levels by the year 2010 is becoming an increasingly important signal as to the direction of the climate change debate.

We discussed the role of international environment institutions, on which we broadly endorsed the conclusions reached at the informal meeting of Environment Ministers, which I hosted at Brocket hall in February. We looked forward to the governing council of the United Nations environment programme in Nairobi next month as an opportunity to confirm the mandate of UNEP as the world's environment voice.

These and other results of the meeting were reported in the form of chairman's highlights, a copy of which I have placed in the Library. I will be reporting the outcome of the meeting to the Prime Minister, as will my G7 colleagues to their Heads of Government. The results will thus feed into the discussions by Heads of Government at the Halifax summit in July.

### Telephones

**Mr. Donohoe:** To ask the Secretary of State for the Environment (1) what cost his Department has incurred during the last 12 months as a result of cloning of mobile telephones being utilised by his Department, with particular reference to the making of unauthorised calls; [23484]

(2) what use his Department makes of hand-held and car-based mobile telephones, what were the costs for each financial year of these services since mobile telephones were first introduced to his Department; and how many mobile telephones are currently in use;

(3) how many mobile telephones being utilised by his Department have been cloned during the last 12 months; [23432]

(4) what steps his Department has taken to prevent the cloning of telephones being utilised by his Department; and if his Department has discussed this matter with any official agencies; [23461]

(5) what representations his Department has made to the Department of Trade and Industry concerning the need for the legislation to prevent the cloning of mobile telephones. [23473]

**Sir Paul Beresford** *[holding answer 9 May 1995]:* Mobile telephones are used by Ministers and officials who, by virtue of their work, need to speak to colleagues when not in the office. The Department does not keep central financial records for mobile telephones but there are currently 230 mobile telephones in use in my Department, of which 16 are car based, at an estimated cost of £74,000 for the rental per annum.

The information that we have suggests that 11 mobile telephones have been cloned in the last 12 months. Service providers have identified incidents of cloning and the Department has not been charged for the calls.

It is difficult to prevent the cloning of analogue mobile telephones but the Department will be discussing this issue with the mobile phone industry and will consider the further use of digital mobile telephones which are not easily cloned.

No Government Departments or official agencies have made representations to the Department of Trade and Industry concerning the need for legislation to prevent the cloning of mobile phones.

### Opencast Mining

**Mr. MacShane:** To ask the Secretary of State for the Environment wht consultations with local communities have taken place in regard to opencast mining in south Yorkshire. [23532]

**Sir Paul Beresford:** There has been no consultation with local communities by my Department regarding opencast mining in south Yorkshire, but local planning authorities and site operators would have been consulted as part of the planning application process.

**Mr. MacShane:** To ask the Secretary of State for the Environment how many compulsory land purchase orders have been exercised by opencast mining operators under the Coal Industry Act 1994; and in what locations. [23536]

**Sir Paul Beresford:** No compulsory land purchase orders have been confirmed under the 1994 legislation.

**Mr. MacShane:** To ask the Secretary of State for the Environment what has been the response of south Yorkshire local authorities to his Department's MPG3 guidance note on opencast mining. [23534]

**Sir Paul Beresford:** My Department has not received any correspondence from south Yorkshire local authorities on the MPG3 guidance note, which was published in July 1994.

**Mr. MacShane:** To ask the Secretary of State for the Environment when he will introduce an environmental test for opencast mining planning applications. [23535]

**Sir Paul Beresford:** Procedures for environmental assessment of new development already exist in compliance with a European directive which came into force in July 1988. Mineral extraction qualifies under the legislation as a schedule 2 project, with respect to which the requirement for environmental assessment depends on a prior assessment of whether the project in question is likely to give rise to significant environmental effects.

**Mr. MacShane:** To ask the Secretary of State for the Environment if he will list the sites where permission for opencast mining has been given in the Rotherham metropolitan borough council area. [23544]

**Sir Paul Beresford:** The following opencast coal sites have been given permission in the Rotherham MBC area:

> Roundwood Phase 1, Rotherham (site now in restoration stage)
>
> Roundwood Phase 2, Rotherham
>
> Cortonwood, Wentworth (site now restored)
>
> Pithouse West, Rother Valley Park (restoration under way)

**Mr. MacShane:** To ask the Secretary of State for the Environment what estimate has been made of increased heavy lorry traffic in Rotherham as a result of proposed opencast mining. [23533]

**Sir Paul Beresford:** No estimate of increased heavy lorry traffic in Rotherham has been made by my Department. However, this matter is one that should have been considered by the local planning authority in its determination of applications for opencast mining permissions.

## Complaints

**Mr. Tony Lloyd:** To ask the Secretary of State for the Environment how many complaints his Department received alleging anti-competitive behaviour by local authorities in England under the terms of the Local Government Act 1988 for the financial years 1990–91, 1991–92, 1992–93 and 1993–94; and how many local authorities were subsequently issued with a section 19A notice or 19B direction as a result. [23340]

**Mr. Curry** *[holding answer 11 May 1995]:* The table gives, for the years in question, the number of complaints received by the Department of the Environment alleging anti-competitive behaviour by local authorities under the Local Government Act 1988. It also indicates the number of authorities on which notices were served under section 13 and to which directions were given under section 14, and the total numbers of notices and directions.

| Year | Total number of complaints | Number of authorities receiving notices | Total number of notices | Number of authorities given directions | Total number of directions |
|---|---|---|---|---|---|
| 1990–91 | 59 | 6 | 6 | 3 | 3 |
| 1991–92 | 41 | 6 | 7 | 2 | 2 |
| 1992–93 | 70 | 8 | 9 | 5 | 6 |
| 1993–94 | 110 | 12 | 13 | 6 | 6 |

**Mr. Tony Lloyd:** To ask the Secretary of State for the Environment how many complaints his Department received alleging anti-competitive behaviour by local authorities in England under the terms of the Local Government, Planning and Land Act 1980 for the financial years 1990–91, 1991–92, 1992–93 and 1993–94; and how many local authorities were subsequently issued with a section 19A notice or 19B direction as a result. [23339]

**Mr. Curry** *[holding answer 11 May 1995]:* The table gives, for the years in question, the number of complaints received by the Department of the Environment alleging anti-competitive behaviour by local authorities under the Local Government, Planning and Land Act 1980. It also indicates the number of authorities on which notices were served under section 19A and to which directions were given under section 19B, and the total numbers of notices and directions.

| Year | Number of complaints | Number of authorities receiving notices | Total number of notices | Number of authorities given directions | Total number of directions |
|---|---|---|---|---|---|
| 1990–91 | 21 | — | 0 | — | 0 |
| 1991–92 | 15 | 3 | 3 | 0 | 0 |
| 1992–93 | 36 | 2 | 3 | 3 | 3 |
| 1993–94 | 40 | 5 | 6 | 6 | 8 |

## City Pride Initiative

**Mr. Alfred Morris:** To ask the Secretary of State for the Environment what plans he has to extend the city pride initiative; and if he will make a statement. [23422]

**Mr. Curry** *[holding answer 11 May 1995]:* Three cities, Birmingham, London and Manchester, are currently taking part in the city pride initiative, and have all made excellent progress in drawing up a prospectus setting out their vision for the future. As my right hon. Friend the Secretary of State said in the House on 4 November 1993, *Official Report*, column 516, these are the pilot areas on which city pride is currently concentrated. We will wish to assess progress with the city pride initiative in these areas before any extension.

## Air Pollution

**Mr. Matthew Taylor:** To ask the Secretary of State for the Environment what action his Department has taken to improve public information on air pollution following the survey on air quality and smog awareness commissioned by his Department last July. [23670]

**Mr. Atkins:** I shall shortly publish a consultation paper, proposing changes to our public information system. I will also announce a major upgrade to the free telephone service which provides the public with continuous access to information about pollution levels and health advice.

## Public Bodies

**Mr. Flynn:** To ask the Secretary of State for the Environment which non-departmental public bodies within the responsibility of his Department are subject to scrutiny by *(a)* ombudsmen, *(b)* the National Audit Office, *(c)* the Audit Commission and *(d)* other monitoring officers; which are covered by citizens charters; in which performance indicators apply; and in which members are liable to surcharge. [23968]

**Sir Paul Beresford:** Details of non-departmental public bodies sponsored by my department are listed in the Cabinet Office publication, "Public Bodies 1994". A copy is available in the House of Commons Library. In respect of executive NDPBs, I refer the hon. Member to my answer to the hon. Member for Cannock and Burntwood (Dr. Wright) on Tuesday 25 April, *Official Report*, column *474–75*.

In respect of the advisory and tribunal NDPBs, the Local Government Commission is subject to scrutiny by the Parliamentary Commissioner. It is also intended to introduce an Order under the Parliamentary Commissioner Act 1994 to extend the commissioner's jurisdiction to the Department's tribunals.

The Local Government Commission and departmental expenditure in respect of advisory bodies and tribunals are subject to inspection by the National Audit Office.

The Local Government Commission, the valuation tribunals and the rent assessment panels are expected to abide by the provisions of the citizens charter. Key performance measures and targets are set for the Local Government Commission, while the tribunals have key objectives or benchmarks.

No members of any NDPBs are liable to surcharge.

### Air Pollution (Bexley)

**Mr. Evennett:** To ask the Secretary of State for the Environment what plans he has to visit the London borough of Bexley to discuss the problems of air pollution in the area. [23729]

**Mr. Atkins:** I have no plans at present to visit Bexley to discuss matters related to air pollution in the area.

**Mr. Evennett:** To ask the Secretary of State for the Environment what proposals he has for improving air quality and reducing air pollution in the London borough of Bexley. [23730]

**Mr. Atkins:** I intend shortly to table amendments to the Environment Bill to implement the proposals on air quality management announced in January.

**Mr. Evennett:** To ask the Secretary of State for the Environment what recent representations he has received about air pollution in the London borough of Bexley. [23731]

**Mr. Atkins:** My officials are in regular contact with local government officers in Bexley in connection with the operation of air quality monitoring facilities in the borough.

### Annual Reports

**Mr. Wray:** To ask the Secretary of State for the Environment if he will introduce legislation to make it a statutory requirement for *(a)* the Advisory Committee on Releases to the Environment, *(b)* the Radioactive Waste Management Committee and *(c)* the Royal Commission on environmental pollution to lay an annual report before Parliament. [24174]

**Sir Paul Beresford:** I see no need to introduce such legislation. The Advisory Committee on Releases to the Environment and the Radioactive Waste Management Advisory Committee already produce annual reports which are placed in the House of Commons Library and the Royal Commission on environmental pollution presents all its reports to Parliament.

**Mr. Wray:** To ask the Secretary of State for the Environment if he will instruct the Inland Waterways Amenity Advisory Council to lay an annual report before Parliament. [24185]

**Mr. Atkins:** The Transport Act 1968 established the Inland Waterways Amenity Advisory Council to advise the British Waterways Board and the Secretary of State on the amenity and recreation aspects of the board's network. Apart from the part-time chairman's salary, which is paid by DOE, IWAAC's expenses are met by the British Waterways Board and recorded in the board's annual report and accounts, copies of which are placed in the Library of the House. Additionally IWAAC carries out regular reviews of its activities, reports of which are made freely available to interested parties.

### Single Regeneration Budget

**Mr. Blunkett:** To ask the Secretary of State for the Environment what is the planned spending on *(a)* task forces, *(b)* compacts, *(c)* teacher placements, *(d)* education business partnerships, *(e)* TEC challenge, *(f)* section 11, *(g)* ethnic minorities grant, *(h)* safer cities and (i) GEST 19 under the single regeneration budget for 1995–96 and 1996–97. [24388]

**Mr. Curry:** Provisional allocations for these programmes are as follows:

| | £ million | |
|---|---|---|
| | *1995–96* | *1996–97* |
| *(a)* Task Forces | 13.0 | 9.6 |
| *(b)* Compacts | 4.3 | 1.1 |
| *(c)* Teacher Placement scheme | 2.0 | 2.0 |
| *(d)* Education Business Partnerships | <0.1 | 0 |
| *(e)* TEC Challenge | 0 | 0 |
| *(f)* Section 11 (part) | 37.3 | 27.4 |
| *(g)* Ethnic Minorities Grant | 2.3 | 0 |
| *(h)* Safer Cities | 5.4 | 6.1 |
| *(i)* GEST 19 | 0.4 | 0 |

These allocations reflect on-going commitments on programmes that now form part of the single regeneration budget. They do not take into account approvals for new schemes under the SRB challenge fund.

### Rural White Paper

**Mr. Colvin:** To ask the Secretary of State for the Environment what is his estimate of the net annual financial saving, or cost, of his Department's submission for the proposed White Paper on the rural economy. [24335]

**Mr. Atkins:** Proposals for the rural White Paper remain subject to continuing collective consideration and discussion. The cost of measures contained in the White Paper will be taken into account in the public expenditure survey.

### Cable Communications Installers

**Mr. Redmond:** To ask the Secretary of State for Environment if he will make it his policy to require cable communication installers to restore all pavements and roads to their former standard and to replace trees which die within five years of the installation work.          [22730]

**Mr. Ian Taylor:** I have been asked to reply.

Cable operators' streetworks are already subject to the New Roads and Street Works Act 1991, and its associated regulations. The Act requires that reinstatement following street works must be carried out to a specified standard, and any defects remedied at the operator's expense. Failure to reinstate is an offence under the Act, as is failure to comply with the prescribed reinstatement standards.

Cable operators are committed to ensuring that the potential for any tree damage is minimised by following best practice when trenching in the vicinity of trees. The cable industry supports the guidelines, published last month by the national joint utilities group, which promote the use of trenchless technology or else hand digging around trees.

# DEFENCE

## Base Purchasers

**Mr. Gordon Prentice:** To ask the Secretary of State for Defence, pursuant to his answer of 3 May, *Official Report,* columns *234–38,* if any of the purchasers listed have as directors or employ as consultants, present or former hon. Members.          [23523]

**Mr. Soames:** The information requested is not held by my Department.

## Northern Ireland Expenditure

**Mr. Worthington:** To ask the Secretary of State for Defence what is the estimated gross cost of British defence policy in Northern Ireland for 1994–95; and what percentage this constitutes of the total defence budget.          [23398]

**Mr. Soames:** The current estimate of costs incurred by the General Officer Commanding, Northern Ireland in 1994–95 on personnel, stores, services, lands and works is some £510,000,000. This amounts to about 2 per cent. of the total estimated expenditure on the defence budget.

**Mr. Worthington:** To ask the Secretary of State for Defence what is the estimated additional cost of the Army's work in Northern Ireland compared with its standard deployment elsewhere; and what percentage this additional cost forms of the total defence budget.          [23399]

**Mr. Soames:** The cost of deploying the Army varies according to its location around the world and the task it is undertaking; there is, therefore, no standard deployment to form the basis of such a comparison.

## Public Bodies

**Mr. Flynn:** To ask the Secretary of State for Defence which non-departmental public bodies within the responsibility of his Department are subject to scrutiny by (a) ombudsmen, (b) the National Audit Office, (c) the Audit Commission and (d) other monitoring officers; which are covered by citizens charters; in which performance indicators apply; and in which members are liable to surcharge.          [23964]

**Mr. Soames:** Although none of my Department's executive non-departmental public bodies is subject to scrutiny by the ombudsmen or the Audit Commission, they are subject to citizens charter and performance indicators. All MOD NDPBs are liable to scrutiny by the National Audit Office and my Department also maintains a monitoring role under which NDPBs are subject to a comprehensive review every five years. None of the MOD's NDPB board members is liable to surcharge.

## Trident

**Mr. Flynn:** To ask the Secretary of State for Defence, pursuant to the statement on the defence estimates, page 38, (a) if HMS Vanguard is deployed with significantly fewer than 96 warheads, (b) under what circumstances Trident submarines may deploy with significantly fewer than 96 warheads and (c) if his Department will seek to publicly announce any future decision to deploy significantly fewer than 96 warheads per submarine.          [23994]

**Mr. Soames:** We will deploy on Trident submarines only the minimum nuclear capability, within our declared ceiling of 96 warheads, which we judge necessary to provide an effective deterrent. It is not our practice to release details of the number of warheads actually carried.

**Mr. Flynn:** To ask the Secretary of State for Defence, pursuant to his oral answer to the hon. Member for Castle Point (Dr. Spink), on 2 May, *Official Report*, column *164,* (a) when his Department first revealed that the Trident warhead has a lower yield than that of Polaris (b) to what extent the yield of the Trident warhead is smaller than the Polaris warhead and (c) if the yield of the Chevaline warhead is smaller than that of the Polaris warhead.          [23993]

**Mr. Soames:** The first explicit comparison of the yield of Trident and Polaris or Chevaline warheads was made in the answer to which the hon. Member refers. The yield of the Chevaline warhead is much the same as that of the Polaris warhead. It is not our practice to comment in more detail on the yield of nuclear warheads.

## Tornado Aircraft

**Dr. David Clark:** To ask the Secretary of State for Defence how many Tornado aircraft based at RAF Coningsby were grounded last year for checks after sand was found in the fuel bowsers; what was the cause of this damage; who was responsible for this damage; which company has the contract to maintain the Tornado aircraft at RAF Coningsby; and if he will make a statement.          [23946]

**Mr. Soames:** Twenty-eight Tornado aircraft were grounded as a precaution when a routine check discovered that fuel in a bowser had been contaminated with grit. The contamination was due to residue remaining after a grit blasting technique had been used to remove the lining from part of a bulk fuel installation. The investigation into the responsibility for this contamination is still under way. The majority of the maintenance of Tornado aircraft at RAF Coningsby is carried out by service personnel; very occasionally, some tasks are undertaken by contractors.

## Training

**Mr. Ian Bruce:** To ask the Secretary of State for Defence what is the distance from (i) RAC Bovington,

(ii) RAF Netheravon and (iii) RAF Swanton Morley to the nearest facilities suitable for armoured reconnaissance vehicles for *(a)* live firing, *(b)* off-road rough training, *(c)* off-road paved track training, *(d)* major overhaul of vehicles, *(e)* training with heavy armour, *(f)* training with infantry, *(g)* training on vehicle maintenance, *(h)* training for drivers, (i) port facilities designed to support loading armoured vehicles, *(j)* training with signals and *(k)* training with helicopters.    [24468]

**Mr. Soames:** For RAF Bovington, Netheravon and RAF Swanton Morley, the information requested is as follows:

- (a) Each armoured unit is obliged to fire at Castlemartin in Wales. Distances are 250 miles from Bovington, 200 miles from Netheravon and 340 miles from Swanton Morley. Movement will usually be by rail.
- (b) Training will be at Salisbury Plain for units from Bovington, 60 miles and Netheravon, three miles; training will be at Stanford for units from Swanton Morley, 20 miles.
- (c) There is a good but heavily used facility at Bovington. There is no access to a facility at Netheravon, Swanton Morley has exclusive use of the on-site airfield perimeter track.
- (d) Repairs will be carried out on site. Major overhaul for CVR(T) vehicles from all three sites, which would take place about every eight years, would be at Donnington in Staffordshire.
- (e and f) There is no mandatory requirement for such training.
- (g) this is provided before joining units, and then continuation training is conducted within the regiment, wherever based.
- (h) Basic training is provided before joining the unit. Continuation training is carried out on local roads and nearby training areas.
- (i) Armoured recce vehicles do not require specialised loading facilities. Nearest port facilities are Marchwood for Bovington, 50 miles, and Netheravon, 40 miles, and Felixtowe for Swanton Morley, 80 miles. Vehicles can also be transported through the channel tunnel.
- (j) This is provided before joining units, and then continuation training is conducted within the regiment, wherever based.
- (k) There is no mandatory requirement, but training can be carried out on most training areas—see answer to (b). In addition, Swanton Morley is close to Wattisham where two Army Air Corps Regiments are based.

### Stanley Barracks, Bovington

**Mr. Ian Bruce:** To ask the Secretary of State for Defence if a study has concluded that there is space at Bovington to locate the Third Armoured reconnaissance regiment; and what is the current area occupied by *(a)* Stanley barracks and *(b)* the area owned by his Department that abuts the barracks.    [24467]

**Mr. Soames:** Studies show that the Stanley barracks site at Bovington does not have the capacity to accommodate all the regiment, and that it would therefore be necessary to split the regiment between two sites, Stanley barracks and the gunnery school, Lulworth, which would have to accommodate garaging, workshops, and stores as well as living accommodation for one squadron.

The current area taken up by Stanley barracks, mess accommodation, married quarters and other buildings is 329 acres. Adjacent training land, which is very heavily utilised, occupies 2,150 acres.

### RAF Swanton Morley

**Mr. Ian Bruce:** To ask the Secretary of State for Defence what savings have been estimated in running costs by closing *(a)* RAF Swanton Morley and *(b)* RAF Northavon; and what was the estimate of the capital value of these sites.    [24469]

**Mr. Soames:** The annual running cost savings resulting from the closure of RAF Swanton Morley are £6,729,000. There are no plans to close Netheravon camp—there is no RAF Northavon—but savings from ceasing Army Air Corps flying activity at the site are expected to be £1,404,000.

As it may be possible to sell Swanton Morley, it is not appropriate to disclose the estimate of likely capital value. Such estimates have, however, been taken into account in the cost appraisal for the options for the future location of the third reconnaissance regiment.

### Sound of Jura Mines

**Dr. Godman:** To ask the Secretary of State for Defence for what reasons the mines have not been recovered from the medium mine field in the sound of Jura; what arrangements have been made to pay compensation to fishing vessel owners and crews in the event of gear being fouled and damaged by such mines; and if he will make a statement.    [24180]

**Mr. Soames:** The practice mines which were laid in the sound of Jura, all of which are inert, could not be recovered as planned because the special clearance vessel which was to have carried out the task had to be diverted to look for the wreckage of a crashed Tornado. This had to be recovered as soon as possible to assist a board of inquiry. The mine clearance operation has, however, now been undertaken.

In the event of gear being fouled and damaged by practice mines, any claims should be submitted to my Department in the usual way through the local Scottish Fisheries Protection Agency fisheries officer.

### Nuclear Committees

**Mr. Wray:** To ask the Secretary of State for Defence if he will introduce legislation for make it a statutory requirement that *(a)* the nuclear powered warships committee and *(b)* the nuclear weapons safety committee lay an annual report before Parliament.    [24186]

**Mr. Soames:** I have no plans to do so.

### Dartmoor Steering Group

**Mr. Wray:** To ask the Secretary of State for Defence what consideration led to the decision not to release externally the annual report of the Dartmoor steering group and working party.    [24188]

**Mr. Soames:** None, as no such decision has been taken. A copy of the 13th annual report of the Dartmoor steering group, December 1994, has been placed in the Library of the House.

### Detention Facilities

**Mr. Wray:** To ask the Secretary of State for Defence what considerations led to the decision not to release externally the annual report of the independent board of visitors for the military corrective training centre and royal naval detention quarters.    [24187]

**Mr. Soames:** The reports rendered by the independent board of visitors for the military corrective training centre and the royal naval detention quarters comprise accounts of their visits to the service detention facilities and are employed as an internal management tool to preserve an impartial overview of the running of the facility. There has previously been no indication of any interest in these reports outside my Department, but consideration will now be given to a formal, wider distribution of them.

### Rural White Paper

**Mr. Colvin:** To ask the Secretary of State for Defence what is his estimate of the net annual financial saving, or cost, of his Department's submission for the proposed White Paper on the rural economy.    [24327]

**Mr. Soames:** Proposals for the rural White Paper remain subject to continuing collective consideration and discussion. The cost of measures contained in the White Paper will be taken into account in the public expenditure survey.

### Job Losses

**Mr. Fatchett:** To ask the Secretary of State for Defence, pursuant to his answer of 9 May, *Official Report*, column *403*, if he will give a breakdown of the 11,167 posts proposed for reduction.    [23992]

**Mr. Soames:** As my right hon. Friend the Minister of State for Defence Procurement made clear in his answer of 9 May, *Official Report*, column *403*, details of the categories of those posts proposed for reduction, by ranks and grades, are not held centrally. A breakdown of the total number proposed for reduction, by main management areas, and showing the likely outcome for the postholders involved, is as follows:

| Main management areas | Outcome for staff in posts proposed for reduction | | | | | | | | | |
|---|---|---|---|---|---|---|---|---|---|---|
| | A | B | C | D | E | F | G | H | I | J |
| Royal Navy | 1,017 | 236 | 41 | 0 | 476 | 11 | 19 | 241 | 1 | 0 |
| Army | 1,891 | 529 | 14 | 11 | 157 | 14 | 875 | 285 | 1 | 5 |
| Royal Air Force | 942 | 120 | 83 | 19 | 691 | 12 | 9 | 12 | 1 | 15 |
| 2nd Permanent Under Secretary of State | 948 | 860 | 50 | 0 | 36 | 2 | 0 | 0 | 0 | 0 |
| Vice Chief of the Defence Staff | 307 | 7 | 2 | 0 | 121 | 0 | 2 | 175 | 0 | 0 |
| Chief of Defence Procurement | 7,920 | 869 | 8,500 | 0 | 14 | 0 | 28 | 509 | 0 | 0 |
| Defence Evaluation and Research Agency | 1,529 | 792 | 0 | 0 | 0 | 587 | 43 | 107 | 0 | 0 |
| Meteorological Office | 146 | 120 | 0 | 0 | 15 | 4 | 0 | 0 | 18 | 0 |
| Total | 14,700 | 3,533 | 6,670 | 30 | 1,512 | 630 | 976 | 1,329 | 21 | 20 |

*Notes:*
A. Number of posts in activity before testing.
B. Number of posts in activity after testing.
C. Transfer to new employer under TUPE.
D. Transfer to new employer not under TUPE.
E. Redeployed within the Department.
F. Voluntary early retirement/redundancy.
G. Compulsory redundancy.
H. Outcome not yet decided.
I. Other (Aga/Medical retirement, End of fixed term and casual service).
J. Outcome not known.

### Defence Export Services Organisation

**Mr. Fatchett:** To ask the Secretary of State for Defence, pursuant to his answer of 20 April, *Official Report*, column *226*, on the Defence Exports Services Organisation, how many applications to engage in work for the private sector have been made in the last 10 years; how many were refused; and if he will make a statement.    [23996]

**Mr. Freeman:** The records available show that in the last 10 years one such application was received and approved from an individual seconded to DESO.

**Mr. Fatchett:** To ask the Secretary of State for Defence, pursuant to his answer of 20 April, *Official Report*, column *227*, if the current offset adviser and international finance adviser of the Defence Export Services Organisation have made applications to engage in work for outside companies.    [23998]

**Mr. Freeman:** The international finance adviser, who is employed on a part-time short-term contract has been granted permission to work for a company in the civil sector when not employed by the MOD. The offset adviser, who is seconded full-time to DESO, has made no application of this kind.

**Mr. Fatchett:** To ask the Secretary of State for Defence, pursuant to his answer of 20 April, *Official Report*, column *226*, on the Defence Exports Services Organisation, if he will list the applications made in the last five years to work for or offer consultancy services to companies int he private sector.    [23997]

**Mr. Freeman:** The records available show that, within the last five years, the only secondee granted permission to work in the private sector was the former head of Defence Export Services who accepted a non-executive directorship in a civil sector company in 1994.

### Private Detective Agencies

**Mr. Fatchett:** To ask the Secretary of State for Defence if he will list the activities for which Brays Detective Agency has been retained in each of the last three years for which information is available; and if he will give the cost for each year.    [23995]

**Mr. Soames:** I refer the hon. Member to the answer given by right hon. and learned Friend the Attorney-General to the hon. Member for Southampton,

Itchen (Mr. Denham) on 23 March 1995, *Official Report*, column *309*.

### Royal Military Academy, Sandhurst

**Mr. Fatchett:** To ask the Secretary of State for Defence if he will list the subjects currently studied by those on the Sandhurst standard military course; and if he will provide an estimate of the time spent on each subject as a proportion of the whole. [23999]

**Mr. Soames:** The commissioning course at the Royal Military Academy, Sandhurst is made up of three 14-week terms with one week of adventurous training in each of the two recesses. The subjects studied and the percentage time spent on each of them, based on the number of periods allocated, are as follows:

| Subject | Percentage |
|---|---|
| Practical exercises | 22.5 |
| Leadership | 4.1 |
| Organisation and concepts | 1.2 |
| Tactics | 8.3 |
| Training a platoon | 1.0 |
| Skill at arms/craft/range management | 8.4 |
| Map reading | 2.4 |
| Signals | 3.4 |
| First aid | 1.1 |
| Nuclear biological chemical | 1.3 |
| Physical training | 5.6 |
| Administration | 2.3 |
| Drill | 6.3 |
| Communication studies | 2.4 |
| Contemporary affairs | 1.4 |
| War studies | 1.4 |
| Adventurous training instr | 0.2 |
| Adventurous training | 4.4 |
| Battlefield technology | 0.6 |
| Military law | 0.1 |
| Combined arms training | 0.5 |
| Information systems | 0.4 |
| Course administration | 7.5 |
| Female (separate) training | 0.6 |
| At college disposal (lectures/discussions etc). | 4.5 |
| Sport | 8.1 |

### Land Mines

**Mr. Alton:** To ask the Secretary of State for Defence, pursuant to his answer of 2 May, *Official Report*, column *202*, how many projector area defence land mines were produced for his Department by Royal Ordnance factories in 1986; when the research was undertaken that revealed that a command detonated point defence weapon such as a projector area defence weapon fell within the standard NATO definition of a land mine; and if he will list the numbers of *(a)* anti-tank, *(b)* anti-personnel, *(c)* area denial and *(d)* any other type of land mine stockpiled by any organisation or body responsible to his Department. [23120]

**Mr. Freeman:** The research which revealed that the projector area defence weapon falls within the NATO standard definition of a land mine was undertaken as part of the preparation for my reply to the question asked by the hon. Member, answered on 2 May 1995, *Official Report*, column *202*.

It is our established policy for security reasons not to reveal quantities of munitions held.

## OVERSEAS DEVELOPMENT ADMINISTRATION

### Aid Programmes

**Miss Lestor:** To ask the Secretary of State for Foreign and Commonwealth Affairs what percentage of the bilateral aid programme budget was allocated to the aid and trade programme for 1994–95. [23182]

**Mr. Baldry:** The original 1994–95 allocation for ATP was set at £100 million, or 9.6 per cent. of the bilateral aid programme. However, as my right hon. Friend the Foreign Secretary announced on 13 December 1994, the cost of four ATP projects—two soft loans and two mixed credits—in 1994–95 and 1995–96 will be met from outside the 1980 Overseas Development and Cooperation Act. As a result, the ATP allocation for 1994–95 was revised to £67,984 million, or 6.1 per cent. of the bilateral aid programme.

**Miss Lestor:** To ask the Secretary of State for Foreign and Commonwealth Affairs if he will list those countries eligible for support under the aid and trade programme. [23181]

**Mr. Baldry:** The list of low income countries eligible for ATP based on GNP per capita of $700, at 1989 prices, is:

> 1. Low income countries where export credit cover is available
>
> Bangladesh, China, Egypt, Ghana, Indonesia, India, Lesotho, Nepal, Pakistan, Philippines, Sri Lanka, Vietnam, Zimbabwe
>
> 2. Other low income countries
>
> Afghanistan, Angola, Benin, Bhutan, Bolivia, Burkina Faso, Burundi, Cambodia, Central African Republic, Chad, Comoros, Djibouti, Eq. Guinea, Ethiopia, Gambia, Guinea, Guinea Bissau, Guyana, Haiti, Kenya, Kiribati, Laos, Liberia, Madagascar, Malawi, Maldives, Mali, Mauritania, Mozambique, Nicaragua, Niger, Nigeria, Rwanda, Sao Tome, Senegal, Sierra Leone, Solomon Islands, Somalia, Sudan, Tanzania, Togo, Tuvalu, Uganda, Yemen, Zaire and Zambia.

### Aid Donors (Kenya)

**Mr. Worthington:** To ask the Secretary of State for Foreign and Commonwealth Affairs when the next meeting will take place of Kenya's major aid donors, including Her Majesty's Government; and if he will make a statement. [23609]

**Mr. Baldry:** The World bank has invited the Government of Kenya, Her Majesty's Government and other donors to a meeting to discuss Kenya in Paris on 24 July. We welcome this and will attend.

### Goldenberg Affair

**Mr. Worthington:** To ask the Secretary of State for Foreign and Commonwealth Affairs what representations he has made to the Government of Kenya about the Goldenberg affair; and to what extent the treatment of that issue by the Kenyan Government has strengthened its eligibility for aid under the good governance criteria. [23610]

**Mr. Baldry:** We have expressed our concerns about the Goldenberg affair to the highest levels of the Kenyan Government. We welcome their recent public commitment to expedite police investigations. Action by the Government of Kenya on corruption is an important factor in determining the level of British aid to Kenya.

## Aid (Kenya)

**Sir Thomas Arnold:** To ask the Secretary of State for Foreign and Commonwealth Affairs if he will make a statement about British bilateral and multilateral aid to Kenya.    [23356]

**Mr. Baldry:** British bilateral aid to Kenya amounted to £31.3 million in 1993–94, We also make substantial contributions to several multilateral organisations which provide aid to Kenya.

## TREASURY

### Rules and Regulations

**Mr. Steen:** To ask the Chancellor of the Exchequer what requirements there are for officials in his Department to introduce a compliance cost assessment for all rules and regulations coming before him and his Ministers; and how many compliance cost assessments have been issued in his Department in the first three months of this year.    [19356]

**Sir George Young** *[holding answer 18 April 1995]:* The Chancellor's departments issued 10 compliance cost assessments in the first three months of 1995. Officials will introduce a compliance cost assessment in all the circumstances set out by my right hon. Friend the President of the Board of Trade in his answer of 19 April at column *190.*

**Mr. Steen:** To ask the Chancellor of the Exchequer how many rules and regulations he repealed in the first three months of 1995; and how many new rules and regulations were introduced in that period by way of statutory instruments, motions or orders.    [19372]

**Sir George Young** *[holding answer 18 April 1995]:* Thirteen rules and regulations were repealed in the first three months of 1995. In the same period, 31 rules and regulations were introduced, not including commencement orders, Orders in Council and instruments not subject to parliamentary procedure. However, most of the new regulations were deregulatory in nature: for example, two orders widened the range of activities exempt from the Financial Services Act 1986. Only one introduced new requirements with any costs for business, and even these costs are small.

Of the 31 regulations:

—10 replaced existing regulations;

—15 amended existing regulations;

—6 were new regulations.

### Mortgage Interest Tax Relief

**Mr. Malcolm Bruce:** To ask the Chancellor of the Exchequer what is his estimate of the cost of mortgage interest tax relief for the financial year 1995–96.    [22275]

**Sir George Young** *[holding answer 2 May 1995]:* In 1995–96, the estimated total cost of mortgage interest relief is about £2.8 billion.

This figure is based on the assumption, by convention, of no change from the current estimated average building society interest rate of 8.1 per cent. The rate of relief is 15 per cent.

## Married Couple's Allowance

**Mr. Malcolm Bruce:** To ask the Chancellor of the Exchequer what is his estimate of the cost of the married couple's allowance tax relief for the financial year 1995–96.    [22274]

**Sir George Young** *[holding answer 2 May 1995]:* The estimated full-year cost in 1995–96 is £3.1 billion. This includes the cost of allowances related to the married couple's allowance—the additional personal allowance and the widow's bereavement allowance.

## European Monetary Institute

**Sir Teddy Taylor:** To ask the Chancellor of the Exchequer if he will make a statement on the work being undertaken by the EMI; and what part the United Kingdom plays in determining its policy.    [22549]

**Mr. Nelson** *[holding answer 4 May 1995]:* The objectives and the tasks of the European monetary institute are set out in articles 109f and 109j, paragraph 1, of the treaty establishing the European Community and the protocol on the statute of the European monetary institute annexed to the treaty. The EMI annual report 1994, published in April 1995, which reports on the activities of the EMI up to 31 December 1994, is available from the House of Commons Library.

The Governor of the Bank of England is a member of the EMI council. Like the central banks of all the other member states, the Bank of England is participating in the EMI's work.

## Uniforms

**Mr. Dicks:** To ask the Chancellor of the Exchequer how many employees who have to wear a uniform at their place of work as part of their contract of employment are currently paying tax because their uniform is counted as a benefit in kind.    [23315]

**Sir George Young** *[holding answer 9 May 1995]:* None, if the clothing is agreed to be a uniform that must be worn as part of the duties of the employment.

**Mr. Dicks:** To ask the Chancellor of the Exchequer what plans the Inland Revenue has to tax, as receiving a benefit in kind, those employees who have to wear uniforms at their place of work as part of their contract of employment; and if he will make a statement.

**Sir George Young** *[holding answer 9 May 1995]:* None. Although a tax charge can arise where employees are provided with clothing, the Inland Revenue accepts that no tax is due if the clothing is a uniform and the wearing of that uniform is a necessary part of the duties of the employment.

## Telephones

**Mr. Donohoe:** To ask the Chancellor of the Exchequer what representations his Department has made to the Department of Trade and Industry concerning the need for legislation to prevent the cloning of mobile telephones.    [23466]

**Mr. Nelson** *[holding answer 9 May 1995]:* The Treasury has made no representations to the Department of Trade and Industry.

**Mr. Donohoe:** To ask the Chancellor of the Exchequer (1) what costs his Department incurred during the last 12 months as a result of cloning of mobile telephones being utilised by his Department, with particular reference to the making of unauthorised calls; [23490]

(2) how many mobile telephones being utilised by his Department have been cloned during the last 12 months. [23426]

**Mr. Nelson** *[holding answer 9 May 1995]:* Two of the Treasury's mobile telephones have been cloned during the past 12 months. No costs were incurred in consequence, all unauthorised calls having been removed from the bill by the mobile telephone's airtime supplier.

**Mr. Donohoe:** To ask the Chancellor of the Exchequer what use his Department makes of hand-held and car-based mobile telephones; what were the costs for each financial year of these services since mobile telephones were first introduced to his Department; and how many mobile telephones are currently in use. [23450]

**Mr. Nelson** *[holding answer 9 May 1995]:* Mobile telephones are used by Treasury Ministers, senior officials and other staff whose duties regularly take them out of their offices but who still need to be contactable. Information relating to rental and call costs is available only for 1993–94 and 1994–95 and amounted to £13,100 and £14,400 respectively, excluding VAT. There are 32 mobile telephones currently in use in the Treasury.

**Mr. Donohoe:** To ask the Chancellor of the Exchequer what steps his Department has taken to prevent the cloning of telephones being utilised by his Department; and if his Department has discussed this matter with any official agencies. [23457]

**Mr. Nelson** *[holding answer 9 May 1995]:* The Treasury is moving away from the use of analogue to the use of digital mobile telephones due to the greater protection against eavesdropping offered by the latter. Digital mobile telephones are thought to be immune to cloning; the matter has not been discussed with any official agency.

### Scott Inquiry

**Mr. Byers:** To ask the Chancellor of the Exchequer on what dates the Chief Secretary to the Treasury submitted written evidence to the Scott inquiry; and what areas were covered in his evidence. [24156]

**Mr. Aitken:** I wrote to the hon. Member on 9 May.

### Smoking

**Mr. Peter Griffiths:** To ask the Chancellor of the Exchequer what facilities are provided and arrangements made for the well-being and comfort of staff who *(a)* smoke and *(b)* do not wish to be affected by smoking at (i) the work station and (ii) rest, recreation and refreshment facilities at the Treasury, Parliament street, London. [24176]

**Mr. Nelson:** The policy on smoking in the Parliament street building has recently been revised to provide a better balance between smokers and non-smokers. Smoking is prohibited in all common areas, including the staff restaurant and recreation rooms. Smoking at work stations is allowed only with the consent of all the occupants of the room. Designated smoking rooms have been set aside for the use of smokers including an area within the coffee lounge in the staff restaurant. The smoking rooms include smoke extraction and air filtering designed to protect non-smokers working in close proximity.

### International Derivative Trading

**Mr. MacShane:** To ask the Chancellor of the Exchequer what assessment he has made of the adequacy of the supervision exercised by the Bank of England and its agencies over international trading in derivatives. [21140]

**Mr. Nelson:** The Bank of England has made clear, on a number of occasions, the risks involved in derivatives and in trading activities more generally. Banks are expected to hold sufficient capital against these risks and to maintain appropriate systems and controls. The supervision of banks is conducted by the Bank of England, where appropriate in collaboration with other regulators in the UK or overseas.

### Tobacco Duty

**Mr. Barron:** To ask the Chancellor of the Exchequer what is the amount of sterling equivalent and/or percentage rate levied on *(a)* hand-rolling tobacco, *(b)* cigars, *(c)* other smoking or chewing tobacco in (i) excise duty and (ii) VAT or other sales tax in each country in (1) the European Union and (2) the Group of 7. [22966]

**Mr. Heathcoat-Amory:** The information for European Union member states is given in the table. The information requested is not readily available for the G7 countries in the form required.

| | Hand-rolling tobacco | | (b) Cigars | | (c) Other smoking tobacco | |
| | (i) Excise Duty | (ii) VAT | (i) Excise Duty | (ii) VAT | (i) Excise Duty | (ii) VAT |
|---|---|---|---|---|---|---|
| Austria | 47 per cent. of RRP | 20.00 per cent. | 13 per cent. of RRP | 20.00 per cent. | 34 per cent. of RRP | 20.00 per cent. |
| Belgium | 37.55 per cent. of RRP | 20.50 per cent. | 10 per cent. of RRP | 20.50 per cent. | 37.55 per cent. of RRP | 20.50 per cent. |
| Denmark | £31.78 per kg | 25.00 per cent. | £22.88 per 1000 + 10 per cent. of RRP | 25.00 per cent. | £40.44 per kg | 25.00 per cent. |
| Finland | 48 per cent. of RRP | 22.00 per cent. | 20 per cent. of RRP | 22.00 per cent. | 48 per cent. of RRP | 22.00 per cent. |
| France | 56.38 per cent. of RRP | 19.50 per cent. | 29.26 per cent. of RRP | 19.50 per cent. | 47.14 per cent. of RRP | 19.50 per cent. |
| Germany | £13.80 + 18.12 per cent. | 15.00 per cent. | 5 per cent. of RRP | 15.00 per cent. | £2.51 per kg + 22 per cent. of RRP15.00 per cent. | |
| Greece | 57.50 per cent. of RRP | 18.00 per cent. | 26 per cent. of RRP | 18.00 per cent. | 57.5 per cent. of RRP | 18.00 per cent. |
| Ireland | £70.82 | 21.00 per cent. | £83.93 per kg | 21.00 per cent. | £58.22 per kg | 21.00 per cent. |

| | Hand-rolling tobacco (i) Excise Duty | (ii) VAT | (b) Cigars (i) Excise Duty | (ii) VAT | (c) Other smoking tobacco (i) Excise Duty | (ii) VAT |
|---|---|---|---|---|---|---|
| Italy | 54.28 per cent. of RRP | 19.00 per cent. | 23 per cent. of RRP | 19.00 per cent. | 54 per cent. of RRP | 19.00 per cent. |
| Luxembourg | 31.50 per cent. of RRP | 12.00 per cent. | 10 per cent. of RRP | 12.00 per cent. | £14.54 per kg + 31.5 per cent. of RRP 12.00 per cent. | |
| Netherlands | £14.34 + 16.53 per cent. of RRP | 17.50 per cent. | 5 per cent. of RRP | 17.50 per cent. | 16.1 per cent. of RRP | 17.50 per cent. |
| Portugal | 30 per cent. of RRP | 16.00 per cent. | 26.21 per cent. of RRP | 16.00 per cent. | 30 per cent. of RRP | 16.00 per cent. |
| Spain | 30 per cent. of RRP | 17.00 per cent. | 10 per cent. of RRP | 17.00 per cent. | 20 per cent. of RRP | 17.00 per cent. |
| Sweden | £32.56 | 25.00 per cent. | £29.68 per 1000 | 25.00 per cent. | £6.36 per kg | 25.00 per cent. |
| UK | £85.94 per cent. | 17.50 per cent. | £85.61 per kg | 17.50 per cent. | £37.64 per kg | 17.50 per cent. |

RRP—Recommended Retail Price.

**Mr. Barron:** To ask the Chancellor of the Exchequer what is the current proportion of the purchase price paid in taxation for an average *(a)* packet of 20 cigarettes, *(b)* 250g of hand-rolling tobacco, *(c)* packet of five cigars and *(d)* 250g of pipe tobacco; and what it has been in each year since 1965. [22964]

**Mr. Heathcoat-Amory:** Information based on actual purchase prices for average cigarettes or other tobacco products is not readily available. Information in the form requested is given in the table based on manufacturers' recommended retail prices during the period 1965–95 for the current leading brands of tobacco products. I regret that the figures for hand-rolling tobacco, cigars and pipe tobacco between 1965 and 1976 could be provided only at disproportionate cost.

*Total tax (Excise and VAT) as a percentage of retail price*

| | Cigarettes | HRT | Cigars | Pipe |
|---|---|---|---|---|
| 1965 | 77 | — | — | — |
| 1966 | 77 | — | — | — |
| 1967 | 69 | — | — | — |
| 1968 | 70 | — | — | — |
| 1969 | 71 | — | — | — |
| 1970 | 71 | — | — | — |
| 1971 | 67 | — | — | — |
| 1972 | 66 | — | — | — |
| 1973 | 64 | — | — | — |
| 1974 | 70 | — | — | — |
| 1975 | 69 | — | — | — |
| 1976 | 70 | — | — | — |
| 1977 | 77 | 27 | 18 | 21 |
| 1978 | 70 | 72 | 44 | 68 |
| 1979 | 70 | 70 | 43 | 66 |
| 1980 | 71 | 69 | 44 | 65 |
| 1981 | 74 | 69 | 46 | 65 |
| 1982 | 75 | 72 | 51 | 68 |
| 1983 | 74 | 71 | 51 | 67 |
| 1984 | 75 | 70 | 50 | 65 |
| 1985 | 75 | 71 | 52 | 63 |
| 1986 | 75 | 71 | 50 | 61 |
| 1987 | 74 | 72 | 49 | 59 |
| 1988 | 75 | 71 | 49 | 58 |
| 1989 | 74 | 71 | 45 | 57 |
| 1990 | 74 | 69 | 44 | 55 |
| 1991 | 76 | 69 | 44 | 53 |
| 1992 | 76 | 71 | 47 | 55 |
| 1993 | 76 | 71 | 48 | 54 |
| 1994 | 76 | 69 | 47 | 53 |
| 1995 | 77 | 73 | 51 | 57 |

Using price at 1 January.

### Tax (Retail Prices)

**Mr. Barron:** To ask the Chancellor of the Exchequer what is the current total tax as a proportion of retail price on *(a)* cigarettes, *(b)* beer, *(c)* whisky, *(d)* wine, *(e)* leaded petrol and *(f)* DERV; and what it has been in each year since 1965. [22968]

**Mr. Heathcoat-Amory:** The information requested is given in the table. I regret that the figures for wine, leaded petrol and DERV between 1965 and 1978 could be provided only at a disproportionate cost.

*Total tax (Excise and VAT) as a percentage of retail price*

| | Cigarettes per 20 | Beer (per pint) | Spirits (per 70cl bottle) | Wine (per 75cl bottle) | Leaded petrol (per litre) | DERV (per litre) |
|---|---|---|---|---|---|---|
| 1965 | 77 | 42.1 | 72.4 | — | — | — |
| 1966 | 77 | 44.3 | 72.7 | — | — | — |
| 1967 | 69 | 44.3 | 77.2 | — | — | — |
| 1968 | 70 | 47.0 | 80.1 | — | — | — |
| 1969 | 71 | 43.5 | 82.9 | — | — | — |
| 1970 | 71 | 40.2 | 83.2 | — | — | — |
| 1971 | 67 | 39.2 | 81.2 | — | — | — |
| 1972 | 66 | 36.2 | 81.5 | — | — | — |
| 1973 | 64 | 31.2 | 78.4 | — | — | — |
| 1974 | 70 | 32.6 | 81.9 | — | — | — |
| 1975 | 69 | 35.5 | 81.1 | — | — | — |
| 1976 | 70 | 33.6 | 80.0 | — | — | — |
| 1977 | 77 | 32.4 | 80.0 | — | — | — |
| 1978 | 70 | 30.5 | 78.5 | — | — | — |
| 1979 | 70 | 33.9 | 81.9 | 49.3 | 50.76 | 54.85 |
| 1980 | 71 | 33.7 | 79.3 | 49.1 | 43.74 | 46.14 |
| 1981 | 74 | 37.7 | 77.9 | 50.6 | 47.47 | 45.62 |
| 1982 | 75 | 38.1 | 74.8 | 51.7 | 52.51 | 47.18 |
| 1983 | 74 | 37.8 | 74.2 | 52.8 | 55.39 | 48.5 |
| 1984 | 75 | 36.4 | 73.4 | 46.4 | 53.44 | 50.62 |
| 1985 | 75 | 36.2 | 73.3 | 49.1 | 54.35 | 48.72 |
| 1986 | 75 | 35.1 | 71.9 | 48.3 | 56.14 | 49.88 |
| 1987 | 74 | 34.1 | 70.7 | 47.1 | 63.49 | 59.87 |
| 1988 | 75 | 33.8 | 68.7 | 47.9 | 65.72 | 61.33 |
| 1989 | 74 | 32.5 | 66.2 | 47.0 | 68.08 | 63.64 |
| 1990 | 74 | 31.9 | 65.9 | 46.6 | 62.99 | 57.14 |
| 1991 | 76 | 33.0 | 64.8 | 47.7 | 62.86 | 65.96 |
| 1992 | 76 | 32.6 | 65.5 | 48.1 | 69.98 | 65.53 |
| 1993 | 76 | 32.5 | 64.3 | 49.1 | 69.10 | 63.46 |
| 1994 | 76 | 31.1 | 64.8 | 49.7 | 74.61 | 68.45 |
| 1995 | 77 | 31.0 | 66.5 | 51.1 | 75.65 | 72.63 |

### Taxation (Leaded Petrol)

**Mr. Barron:** To ask the Chancellor of the Exchequer what is his policy on the taxation of leaded petrol. [22969]

**Mr. Heathcoat-Amory:** Over recent years Government policy has been to charge duty on road fuels at rates which will not only raise sufficient revenue but take account of the need to conserve finite stocks of fossil fuels and protect the general environment. In 1993 we announced that we would raise road fuel duties on average by at least 5 per cent. in real terms in future Budgets. This commitment forms an important part of the Government's strategy to reduce UK greenhouse gas emissions to 1990 levels in the year 2000.

A duty differential in favour of unleaded petrol was introduced in 1987 to discourage the use of leaded petrol. Unleaded petrol became liable to a rebated rate of excise duty while leaded petrol remains liable to the full rate of light oil excise duty. The rebate now stands at 4.82 per litre.

**Mr. Barron:** To ask the Chancellor of the Exchequer if he will list for each 5p between 5p and £1 his estimate of the effect on the retail prices index of an increase in excise duty on an average *(a)* packet of 20 cigarettes, *(b)* 250g of hand-rolling tobacco, *(c)* packet of five cigars and *(d)* 250g of pipe tobacco, if such increases were to be fully reflected in price.                                    [22957]

**Mr. Heathcoat-Amory:** The information is as follows:

| Pence | Cigarettes 20 king size Per cent. | Cigars 5 small cigars Per cent. | Hand rolling 250 grammes Per cent. | Pipe tobacco 250 grammes Per cent. |
|---|---|---|---|---|
| 5 | 0.091 | 0.003 | 0.000 | 0.000 |
| 10 | 0.182 | 0.007 | 0.000 | 0.000 |
| 15 | 0.273 | 0.010 | 0.000 | 0.001 |
| 20 | 0.364 | 0.014 | 0.001 | 0.001 |
| 25 | 0.455 | 0.017 | 0.001 | 0.001 |
| 30 | 0.546 | 0.021 | 0.001 | 0.001 |
| 35 | 0.637 | 0.024 | 0.001 | 0.001 |
| 40 | 0.728 | 0.028 | 0.001 | 0.002 |
| 45 | 0.819 | 0.031 | 0.001 | 0.002 |
| 50 | 0.910 | 0.035 | 0.002 | 0.002 |
| 55 | 1.000 | 0.038 | 0.002 | 0.002 |
| 60 | 1.091 | 0.041 | 0.002 | 0.002 |
| 65 | 1.182 | 0.045 | 0.002 | 0.003 |
| 70 | 1.273 | 0.048 | 0.002 | 0.003 |
| 75 | 1.364 | 0.052 | 0.002 | 0.003 |
| 80 | 1.455 | 0.055 | 0.002 | 0.003 |
| 85 | 1.546 | 0.059 | 0.003 | 0.003 |
| 90 | 1.637 | 0.062 | 0.003 | 0.004 |
| 95 | 1.728 | 0.066 | 0.003 | 0.004 |
| 100 | 1.819 | 0.069 | 0.003 | 0.004 |

### Monetary Policy

**Mr. Austin Mitchell:** To ask the Chancellor of the Exchequer, what assessment he has made of the effect of the statements made by the Governor of the Bank of England in respect of tightening monetary policy on the willingness of British manufacturers in the import-competing and export industries to invest in increased capacity.                                    [23675]

**Mr. Nelson:** The Government can best encourage investment in all sectors by consistently following stable macroeconomic policies, including ensuring that inflation remains permanently low. Over the last year manufacturing investment rose by more than 8 per cent, and investment by machinery and equipment industries was up almost 18 per cent.

### Temazepam

**Mr. McMaster:** To ask the Chancellor of the Exchequer what powers HM Customs and Excise have to monitor and control the import and export of the drug temazepam; what is his latest estimate, expressed in kilogrammes, of the quantities imported and exported in the most recent five years for which figures are available; and if he will make a statement.                                    [24161]

**Mr. Heathcoat-Amory:** Temazepam is not subject to importation or exportation controls under the Misuse of Drugs Act of 1971; therefore, HM Customs and Excise currently has no powers to monitor or control its import or export.

The integrated tariff of the United Kingdom does not separately identify temazepam under a specific heading and commercial importations therefore cannot be identified. Exportation procedures also do not allow the quantity of consignments to be determined.

### Ministerial Meetings

**Mr. Mathew Banks:** To ask the Chancellor of the Exchequer if he will make a statement about the recent spring meetings of the International Monetary Fund and World bank.

**Mr. Kenneth Clarke:** I attended the spring meetings of the International Monetary Fund and World bank on 26 and 27 April.

In the interim committee of the IMF, I spoke mainly about the quality of surveillance by the IMF, its finances and the need for further action on developing country debt.

Consideration of the IMF's surveillance of its members' economies was timely given recent events in Mexico. I welcome the IMF's intention to learn lessons from this experience. I made four proposals: first, for a greater frankness by the IMF in its assessment of members' economies; secondly, a better flow of information from countries both to the IMF and financial markets; thirdly, greater selectivity by the IMF in which economies to subject to close and continual monitoring; and, fourthly, the establishment of an independent evaluation unit at the IMF. The first three of these points were reflected in the committee's communiqué.

On IMF finances, I said that the IMF should have sufficient resources to use its existing facilities at agreed access limits. Resources should not be provided in advance for exceptional circumstances such as Mexico, but where necessary the IMF's first recourse should be activation of the established credit line of the general arrangements to borrow. I did not rule out an increase in IMF quotas if and when justified.

I welcomed the agreement of the Paris Club to offer "Naples Terms" to the poorest countries on bilateral official debt along the lines set out by my right hon. Friend the Prime Minister in 1990. I noted that implementation was now the key issue. I also followed up the initiative I launched last autumn on debt owed to multilateral institutions. The committee agreed to a further study of the IMF's enhanced structural adjustment facility. I will press for greater certainty and increased concessionality of lending for the poorest most indebted countries financed by sale and investment of the proceeds of a small amount of the IMF's gold stocks.

I also took part in the interim committee's discussion of the world economy and looked forward to the review of international institutions at the forthcoming G7 summit in Halifax, Nova Scotia.

In the development committee of the IMF and World bank, in addition to elaborating on my proposals on debt owed to the World bank, I noted the potential that exists for increasing the proportion of infrastructure in developing countries financed by the private sector, drawing on the UK's experience of privatisation and the private finance initiative.

As is customary, there was a meeting of G7 Finance Ministers and central bank governors prior to the spring meetings. Copies of the G7's communiqué and of the interim and development committee's, as well as my speeches to the committees, have been placed in the Library of the House.

## NATIONAL HERITAGE

### National Lottery

**12. Mr. Pike:** To ask the Secretary of State for National Heritage what recent discussions he has had with Oflot regarding the distribution of national lottery proceeds.
[22476]

**Mr. Dorrell:** None. The Office of the National Lottery has no responsibility for the distribution of national lottery proceeds.

**17. Mr. Flynn:** To ask the Secretary of State for National Heritage what is his most recent estimate of the extent of fraud in the national lottery procedures. [22482]

**Mr. Dorrell:** Fraud relating to the handling and sale of national lottery tickets is a matter for Camelot and the relevant authorities. I understand that a few instances of apparent fraud have come to light and that these are being dealt with.

**21. Mr. O'Hara:** To ask the Secretary of State for National Heritage if he will make a statement on the use of national lottery funds to purchase the Churchill papers.
[22487]

**Mr. Dorrell:** Under the National Lottery etc. Act 1993, the national heritage memorial fund is responsible for distributing 20 per cent. of the net proceeds from the national lottery for expenditure on or connected with the national heritage. Individual funding decisions are taken entirely independently of Government.

**Mr. Gapes:** To ask the Secretary of State for National heritage what plans he has to review the expenditure plans of the national lottery.
[22481]

**Mr. Dorrell:** I refer the hon. Member to the reply I gave earlier today to the hon. Member for Pendle (Mr. Prentice).

### Film Industry

**15. Mr. MacShane:** To ask the Secretary of State for National Heritage what steps he is taking to encourage the United Kingdom film industry.
[22479]

**Mr. Dorrell:** The National Heritage Select Committee published its report on the British film industry on 4 April. I shall set out the Government's approach to the industry in my response to the Committee's findings.

### European Football Championships

**16. Mr. Frank Cook:** To ask the Secretary of State for National heritage what meetings he has had with local authorities with a view to exploiting the cultural potential of Euro '96, the European football Championships.
[22480]

**Mr. Sproat:** My officials have had several meetings with local authority representatives to discuss a supporting programme of cultural events.

**22. Mrs. Eagle:** To ask the Secretary of State for National Heritage what assistance he is providing to local authorities with their preparations for the Euro '96 football championships.
[22488]

**Mr. Sproat:** My officials have met local authority representatives several times, and arranged a meeting of local authorities and interested parties to encourage the development of supporting cultural events of match venues.

### National Collection of Fine Art

**18. Mr. Carrington:** To ask the Secretary of State for National Heritage what proposals he has to expand the national collection of fine art heritage objects.
[22483]

**Mr. Sproat:** It is for the trustees of individual museums to decide on acquisitions. The Government have a number of measures which help to develop the national collections. These include the funding of the national heritage memorial fund, the Waverley system of export controls and important tax concessions. The national collections may also benefit from the net proceeds of the national lottery.

### Tourism

**19. Mr. William O'Brien:** To ask the Secretary of State for National Heritage what measures his Department is taking to help tourism; and if he will make a statement.
[22484]

**Mr. Dorrell:** On 1 March, my Department published "Tourism: Competing with the Best" which set out an action programme for Government and the tourist boards aimed at revitalising the accommodation sector and improving marketing effectiveness. We are making good progress and I intend to make announcements at key stages on all of the initiatives we are pursuing.

**25. Mr. Ian Bruce:** To ask the Secretary of State for National Heritage what assessment his Department has made of the effect of the United Kingdom's VAT rate on tourism.
[22491]

**Mr. Dorrell:** I am not aware of any conclusive evidence that the UK's VAT rate places the tourism industry at a competitive disadvantage. The report on VAT published by the British Tourist Authority on 1 May does not take account of all the different costs to tourism business in other EU member states.

**26. Mr. Waterson:** To ask the Secretary of State for National Heritage what measures he is proposing to encourage domestic and inbound tourism; and if he will make a statement.
[22492]

**Mr. Dorrell:** I refer my hon. Friend to the reply I gave earlier today to the hon. Member for Normanton (Mr. O'Brien).

## Sporting Provision

**20. Mr. Cox:** To ask the Secretary of State for National Heritage what plans he has to encourage local authorities' sporting provision. [22486]

**Mr. Sproat:** It is for local authorities to determine their level of expenditure on sporting provision, in the light of their own priorities. The Department recognises the important role that local authorities play in this area and the Sports Council will continue to work closely with them, as appropriate, in pursuing its objectives.

## Millennium Commission

**23. Mr. Cohen:** To ask the Secretary of State for National Heritage what assessment he has made of the most suitable national proposal arising from the consultation on the distribution of the Millennium Commission. [22489]

**Mr. Dorrell:** I understand that the closing date for the first round of applications to the Millennium Commission was Monday 1 May. Around 550 applications have been received, details of which will be published later this month. Successful applicants will be announced in July this year.

**Mr. Fisher:** To ask the Secretary of State for National Heritage if he will list the applications received to date by the Millennium Commission; and if he will place the list in the Library on a monthly basis. [22944]

**Mr. Sproat:** This is a matter for the Millennium Commission. I understand that information on proposals and applications received by the Millennium Commission will be made available by the end of May, and a copy will be placed in the Library of the House. The Millennium Commission will run a series of time-limited application rounds, and similar information will be made available at the end of each round.

## Churchill Papers

**24. Mr. Winnick:** To ask the Secretary of State for National Heritage if he will state the latest position over the Churchill papers. [22490]

**Mr. Dorrell:** The non-state papers have been purchased through lottery proceeds awarded by the national heritage memorial fund and are now held at Churchill college, Cambridge. The state papers have been transferred to Churchill college by the Government to ensure the archive remains intact. The entire archive is therefore secure for the future.

## Team Games

**Mr Harry Greenway:** To ask the Secretary of State for National Heritage what discussion he has had with the Department for Education and with the Treasury with regard to improving the provision of team games in schools; and if he will make a statement. [22850]

**Mr. Sproat:** My Department is working closely with the Department for Education on a major policy paper on sport, including sport in schools, which will be published in early summer. Other Government Departments with an interest, including Her Majesty's Treasury, are in touch with progress.

## Public Libraries

**Mr. Campbell-Savours:** To ask the Secretary of State for National Heritage how many public library authorities there are in England; how many of these have subscribed to the ProdCom statistics; and what assessment he has made of why the other authorities have not subscribed. [22533]

**Mr. Sproat:** There are 108 public library authorities in England. Information about which statistical publications each authority subscribes to is not held centrally by my Department.

**Mr. Campbell-Savours:** To ask the Secretary of State for National Heritage if he will make a statement on his policy for ensuring the availability of statistics through public and other libraries. [22534]

**Mr. Sproat:** The responsibility for providing public library services, and for choosing their stock including sources of statistical information, rests with local library authorities.

# ATTORNEY-GENERAL

## Historical Documents

**Mr. Gordon Prentice:** To ask the Attorney–General what special training is given to persons who have responsibility for assessing the historical significance of documents held by his Department. [23242]

**The Attorney-General:** Training is provided under the guidance of the Keeper of Public Records. It includes desk training, regular meetings between departmental reviewers and officials at the Public Record Office and attendance at conferences and seminars and on courses arranged by the Public Record Office.

# SOCIAL SECURITY

## Benefit Payment Card

**Mr. Dewar:** To ask the Secretary of State for Social Security what savings he expects will arise from the introduction of benefit payment cards; and if he will set out the basis on which this calculation is made, together with the multiplier used. [23007]

**Mr. Arbuthnot:** Annual savings will comprise both administrative savings and programme savings.

The administrative savings comprise costs associated with certain aspects of the order book and girocheque payment systems which would no longer be incurred, or would be significantly reduced, once card payment replaces them. These include administrative procedures associated with the loss of theft of instruments of payment and the actual production of order books and girocheques. The feasibility study estimated savings to be £60 million per annum.

The programme savings are those resulting from a reduction in fraudulent encashments of instruments of payment. Our estimate of the level of this type of fraud is not by use of a multiplier but rather from sampling of encashed order book foils and girocheque reconciliation. Once fully implemented the new payment system is expected to eliminate fraudulent encashment estimated in the feasibility study at £140 million per annum.

## National Insurance Computer Contract

**Mr. Allen:** To ask the Secretary of State for Social Security what steps he has taken to ensure that the bidding process for the national insurance computer contract was fair, allowing no one bidder an undue advantage. [23634]

**Mr. Arbuthnot:** The contract for the national insurance computer replacement system was awarded following a procurement through a competitive tendering exercise, undertaken in accordance with EC regulations governing the award of public service contracts (Public Service Contracts Legislation 1993). Due to the novel nature of the arrangement through the private finance initiative, DSS independent audit carried out surveys at various checkpoints to ensure that suppliers were content with the process and its fairness. None of the three suppliers made any criticism of the Department's efforts to create an unbiased and fair procurement process.

**Mr. Allen:** To ask the Secretary of State for Social Security which of the companies that bid for the national insurance computer contract had previously been involved in drawing up the business case for outsourcing the contract. [23633]

**Mr. Arbuthnot:** The business case for outsourcing was produced soley by civil servants of the Contributions Agency and the Information and Technology Services Agency with legal and financial guidance from external advisers who had no links with any of the companies involved in the bidding process.

## Mortgage Interest

**Mr. Gerrard:** To ask the Secretary of State for Social Security what plans he has, after October, to protect mortgagors who become eligible for income support, but who because of their health status have been refused insurance to cover their mortgage repayments, during those months when, under the new arrangements, such mortgagors will be ineligible for mortgage interest payments from the Benefits Agency. [23360]

**Mr. Roger Evans:** The social security advisory committee has consulted widely on the proposals for changes to assistance with mortgage interest payments, and I expect to receive its report shortly. The effects of those who are refused insurance cover because of their health status will depend on the details of the scheme, which will not be concluded until I have studied the report.

## Free School Meals

**Mr. Bradley:** To ask the Secretary of State for Social Security what is the estimated cost of extending access to free school meals to children whose parents are in receipt of family credit. [23622]

**Mr. Roger Evans:** I refer the hon. Member to the reply I gave him on 16 March, *Official Report*, column *698*. The figure relate to 1993 and are the most up to date available.

## Retirement Pensions

**Mr. David Marshall:** To ask the Secretary of State for Social Security if he will list the total number of people in receipt of *(a)* state retirement pension as single persons, *(b)* state retirement pension as married couples and *(c)* adult dependant's pension. [23690]

**Mr. Arbuthnot:** The information is not available in the form requested. The table gives the number of persons receiving each category of state retirement pension. Details of marital status are available only where shown.

| Category of state retirement pension | Number of recipients |
| --- | --- |
| Category A Men[1] | 3,576,660 |
| Category A Women[1] | 2,565,280 |
| Category BL Wives (married) | 1,397,960 |
| Category ABL Wives (married) | 720,120 |
| Category B Widows (single) | 1,862,290 |
| Category B Widowers (Single) | 840 |
| Graduated retirement benefit only Men[1] | 3,450 |
| Graduated retirement benefit only Women[1] | 126,960 |
| Additional pension only category A Men[1] | 1,330 |
| Additional pension only category A Women[1] | 11,690 |
| Additional pension only category B Widows (single) | 2,570 |
| Adult dependent's pension[1] | 91,800 |

*Note:* [1] Marital status not known.
*Source:*
Retirement Pension biannual enquiry—September 1994.

## Social Fund Commissioner

**Mr. Luff:** To ask the Secretary of State for Social Security whether he has appointed a new social fund commissioner to succeed Mrs. Rosalind Mackworth who retires on 31 May. [24567]

**Mr. Roger Evans:** I am pleased to announce that Mr. John Scampion has agreed to serve as social fund commissioner for a period of three years from 1 June. Mr. Scampion is currently town clerk and chief executive officer of Solihull metropolitan borough council.

## Weekly Incomes

**Mr. Byers:** To ask the Secretary of State for Social Security, pursuant to his answer of 4 April, *Official Report*, column *1074*, on weekly incomes, if he will update the table to show the position in 1995–96. [23796]

**Mr. Burt:** Pursuant to the reply by my hon. Friend, the Under-Secretary of State for Social Security of 4 April, *Official Report*, columns *1074-76*, the table reflects changes to tax, national insurance and social security benefits from last April. Rent and council tax are for 1994–95, the latest year for which information is available.

*Weekly income for various family types at different hours of work*

| Hours of work | Gross earnings | Tax and national insurance contributions | Take home pay | Unemploy-ment benefit | Income support | Family credit | Child benefit | Rent | Housing benefit | Council tax | Council tax benefit | Total net income | Net income after rent and council tax |
| --- | --- | --- | --- | --- | --- | --- | --- | --- | --- | --- | --- | --- | --- |
| Single person—aged 25 or over | | | | | | | | | | | | | |
| 8 | 28.00 | 0.00 | 28.00 | 38.71 | 0.00 | 0.00 | 0.00 | 30.91 | 21.02 | 6.60 | 3.56 | 91.29 | 53.78 |
| 16 | 56.000 | 0.00 | 56.00 | 30.97 | 0.00 | 0.00 | 0.00 | 30.91 | 7.85 | 6.60 | 0.00 | 94.82 | 57.31 |
| 24 | 84.00 | 7.00 | 77.00 | 0.00 | 0.00 | 0.00 | 0.00 | 30.91 | 14.34 | 6.60 | 1.50 | 92.84 | 55.33 |

*Weekly income for various family types at different hours of work*

| Hours of work | Gross earnings | Tax and national insurance contributions | Take home pay | Unemploy- ment benefit | Income support | Family credit | Child benefit | Rent | Housing benefit | Council tax | Council tax benefit | Total net income | Net income after rent and council tax |
|---|---|---|---|---|---|---|---|---|---|---|---|---|---|
| *Married couple—non earning partner* | | | | | | | | | | | | | |
| 8 | 28.00 | 0.00 | 28.00 | 62.58 | 0.00 | 0.00 | 0.00 | 30.91 | 25.98 | 8.60 | 7.08 | 123.64 | 84.13 |
| 16 | 56.00 | 0.00 | 56.00 | 50.07 | 0.00 | 0.00 | 0.00 | 30.91 | 15.91 | 8.60 | 3.99 | 125.97 | 86.46 |
| 24 | 84.00 | 3.76 | 80.24 | 0.00 | 0.00 | 0.00 | 0.00 | 30.91 | 30.91 | 8.60 | 8.60 | 119.75 | 80.24 |
| *Married couple—non earning partner with two children aged 4 and 6 years* | | | | | | | | | | | | | |
| 8 | 28.00 | 0.00 | 28.00 | 62.58 | 10.72 | 0.00 | 18.85 | 36.42 | 36.42 | 11.00 | 11.00 | 167.57 | 120.15 |
| 16 | 56.00 | 0.00 | 56.00 | 0.00 | 0.00 | 67.90 | 18.85 | 36.42 | 24.90 | 11.00 | 7.48 | 175.21 | 127.79 |
| 24 | 84.00 | 3.76 | 80.24 | 0.00 | 0.00 | 62.83 | 18.85 | 36.42 | 12.52 | 11.00 | 3.65 | 178.09 | 130.67 |

*Notes:*

1. Earnings for 8 hours assumed to represent one days employment. Earnings for 16 hours assumed to represent two days employment.
2. All the examples shown assume take-up of full entitlement to the income-related and contributory benefits that would be most advantageous.
3. All the family types shown are assumed to live in local authority accommodation and be liable for average council tax and local authority rent.
4. Earnings are assumed to be £3.50 per hour.

## Public Bodies

**Mr. Flynn:** To ask the Secretary of State for Social Security which non-departmental public bodies within the responsibility of his Department are subject to scrutiny by *(a)* ombudsmen, *(b)* the National Audit Office, *(c)* the Audit Commission and *(d)* other monitoring officers; which are covered by citizens charters; in which performance indicators apply; and in which members are liable to surcharge. [23957]

**Mr. Hague:** The information requested, in respect of those bodies listed in "Public Bodies 1994", is as follows:

(a) The administrative function of the Independent Tribunal Service and Central Adjudication Services is subject to such scrutiny.

Arrangements to bring the Occupational Pensions Board within the jurisdiction of the Parliamentary Commissioner for Administration are well advanced.

(b) All bodies are subject to scrutiny by the National Audit Office.

(c) None.

(d) All bodies are subject to the financial and resource controls set by the Accounting Officer for the Department.

The Occupational Pensions Board is committed to the principles of the citizen's charter, and has published its own charter standard statement and code of practice.

The Independent Tribunal Service and Central Adjudication Services have set performance indicators.

No member of any body is liable to surcharge.

## Residential Care and Nursing Homes

**Mr. Pickthall:** To ask the Secretary of State for Social Security what plans he has to give a higher level of support to elderly people in residential homes who need nursing care as well as residential care. [24362]

**Mr. Roger Evans:** Higher levels of income support are available to people with preserved rights who are resident in residential care and nursing homes. These amounts are linked to the category of care a home is registered to provide and are higher for nursing homes in order to reflect the increased costs of personal care provided.

These higher levels of income support increased last April. This uprating targeted extra help on high dependency cases in both residential care homes and nursing homes. The income support limits will be reviewed later this year as part of the annual uprating exercise.

## Telephones

**Mr. Donohoe:** To ask the Secretary of State for Social Security what use his Department makes of hand-held and car-based mobile telephones; what were the costs for each financial year of these services since mobile telephones were first introduced to his Department; and how many mobile telephones are currently in use. [23439]

**Mr. Hague** *[holding answer 9 May 1995]:* Mobile telephones are widely used across the Department. They help to reduce delays for peripatetic staff, and assist with safety where staff may be placed in potentially difficult situations.

All procurement of mobile telephones must be through the departmental information technology authority procurement services, and procurement guidance and processes have been developed to help managers make informed decisions as to the correct equipment to procure.

Available figures are in the tables.

*Running costs on mobile telephones and pagers*

£

| Year | Benefits agency | Information technology services agency | Contributions agency | Child support agency | War pensions agency | Resettlement agency |
|---|---|---|---|---|---|---|
| 1992–93 | 339,891.87 | [2]283,000.00 | — | — | — | — |
| 1993–94 | 625,738.94 | [3]278,000.00 | 194,183.18 | — | 2,350.00 | — |
| 1994–95 | [1]1,098,227.88 | [4]218,000.00 | 210,050.00 | — | 2,375.00 | — |

*Notes:*

[1] Provisional.
[2] Includes Child Support Agency, Contributions Agency and DSS HQ.
[3] Includes Child Support Agency and DSS HQ.
[4] Includes DSS HQ.

*Number of mobile phones*

|  | Benefits agency | Information technology services agency | Contributions agency | Child support agency | War pensions agency | Resettlement agency | DSS HQ |
|---|---|---|---|---|---|---|---|
| 1994–95 | ¹ n/a | 413 | ¹ n/a | ¹ n/a | 95 | 3 | 94 |

*Notes:*
¹ Budgets for mobile phones and pagers are delegated to individual agency district managers. Details could be obtained only at disproportionate cost.
n/a = not available.

## Vaccine Damage

**Mr. Barry Field:** To ask the Secretary of State for Social Security how many applications have been made under the Vaccine Damage Payments Act 1979; and how many of the cases have *(a)* have been successful or *(b)* still under review since 31 May 1991. [21419]

**Mr. Hague:** The administration of the vaccine damage payment scheme is a matter for Mr. Ian Magee, the chief executive of the Benefits Agency. He will write to the hon. Member.

*Letter from Ian Magee to Mr. Barry Field, dated 15 May 1995:*

The Secretary of State for Social Security has asked me to reply to your recent Parliamentary Question about claims made under the Vaccine Damage Payment Scheme since 31 May 1991.

Since that date a total of 216 claims have been received, 13 of which have been successful. There are a further 21 cases under consideration and awaiting a decision on entitlement.

In addition, since 31 May 1991 there have been 19 awards made relating to applications made prior to that date.

32 cases are awaiting a review by the independent Vaccine Damage Tribunal and there are 10 requests for a review which are currently being processed for submission to the Tribunal.

I hope you find this reply helpful.

## EMPLOYMENT

### Refractory Ceramic Fibre

**Mr. Steen:** To ask the Secretary of State for Employment what representations he is making to DGXI, Brussels with regard to its proposals to label a refractory ceramic fibre with a skull and crossbones; if he will ensure that the European commission working party meeting at Ispra on 20 and 21 April considers whether the dangerous substance directive represents a suitable forum for the classification of fibres; and if a fiche d'impact has been completed on the cost to business in each EEC country so affected. [20014]

**Mr. Oppenheim:** At the meeting on 20 to 21 April, the refractory ceramic fibre industry was given an ample opportunity to present its case. There was sympathy for the UK suggestion that RCFs be uncoupled from other fibres under consideration, to enable their hazard classification, and its implications, to be considered at more length.

The UK will be continuing to explore with the European Commission ways of ensuring that no unintended consequences arise for the RCF industry, and will ask the Commission to complete a fiche d'impact in the event that it presses ahead with a classification proposal.

## Brewing Industry

**Mr. Martyn Jones:** To ask the Secretary of State for Employment how many people were employed in the brewing industry in *(a)* 1980, *(b)* 1985, *(c)* 1990 and *(d)* 1994. [23272]

**Mr. Oppenheim:** Information on employment in the brewing industry is available from the periodic censuses of employment and is as follows:

*Number of employees in employment in the brewing industry¹ in Great Britain, September of each year*

| Year | Number of employees |
|---|---|
| 1981 | 62,100 |
| 1984 | 49,600 |
| 1987 | 43,200 |
| 1989 | 40,800 |
| 1991 | 44,500 |

¹ Group 427 of the standard industrial classification 1980.

## Asbestos

**Mr. McCartney:** To ask the Secretary of State for Employment if he will ask the Health and Safety Executive to conduct an inquiry into school teachers or caretakers exposed to asbestos. [23362]

**Mr. Oppenheim:** No. Recently completed research indicates that school teachers and caretakers are not in occupations with a raised risk of contracting asbestos-related diseases. However, caretakers in all industry sectors, including schools, would be well advised to take the precautions recommended by the Health and Safety Executive when carrying out routine building maintenance and repair work that may involve asbestos materials.

**Mr. McCartney:** To ask the Secretary of State for Employment how many asbestos removal licences have been removed from companies operating in this industry in each year since 1983. [23364]

**Mr. Oppenheim:** The number of asbestos removal licences removed from companies operating in the industry in each year since 1983 are shown in the following table:

| Year | Licences revoked |
|---|---|
| 1983 | 0 |
| 1984 | 0 |
| 1985 | 1 |
| 1986 | 2 |
| 1987 | 2 |
| 1988 | 1 |
| 1989 | 4 |
| 1990 | 0 |
| 1991 | 0 |

| Year | | Licences revoked |
|------|--|------------------|
| 1992 | | 0 |
| 1993 | | 0 |
| 1994 | | 3 |

**Mr. McCartney:** To ask the Secretary of State for Employment how many asbestos removal companies were inspected by the Health and Safety Executive in each year since 1983. [23370]

**Mr. Oppenheim:** Information is not available on the number of asbestos removal companies inspected by Health and Safety Executive inspectors since 1983. The following table shows the total number of visits for each year since 1985 to companies or contractors licensed at that time under the Asbestos (Licensing) Regulations 1983. Information is not available for visits made in 1983 or 1984 as the Asbestos (Licensing) Regulations 1983 did not come into force until August 1984.

| | Number of visits |
|------|------------------|
| 1985 | 2,709 |
| 1986 | 1,654 |
| 1987 | 941 |
| 1988 | 533 |
| 1989 | 677 |
| 1990 | 401 |
| 1991 | 385 |
| 1992 | 373 |
| 1993 | 399 |
| 1994 | 805 |

**Mr. McCartney:** To ask the Secretary of State for Employment how many licensed asbestos removal companies are currently operating in the United Kingdom. [23381]

**Mr. Oppenheim:** There are currently 768 asbestos removal companies licensed to operate in Great Britain. The Health and Safety Executive does not record comparable information for Northern Ireland.

**Mr. McCartney:** To ask the Secretary of State for Employment how many asbestos removal companies have been prosecuted in each year since 1983; what was the average fine; what was the lowest and highest fine; and what offences were committed. [23365]

**Mr. Oppenheim:** Statistics relating to the prosecution of licensed asbestos removal contractors are laid out in the following table. The figures relate only to offences by licensed asbestos removal contractors under the Asbestos (Licensing) Regulations 1983 and the Control of Asbestos at Work Regulations 1987 and the Asbestos Regulations 1969 which CAWR replaced. No information is readily available on the specific offences. There were no prosecutions in 1983; the Asbestos (Licensing) Regulations 1983 did not come into force until 1 August 1984.

| Year | Number | Highest fine (£) | Lowest fine (£) | Average fine (£) |
|------|--------|------------------|-----------------|------------------|
| 1984 | 3 | 1,500 | 200 | 733 |
| 1985 | 31 | 4,500 | 150 | 843 |
| 1986 | 13 | 3,750 | 100 | 800 |
| 1987 | 8 | 2,000 | 100 | 810 |
| 1988 | 6 | 1,500 | 100 | 583 |

| Year | Number | Highest fine (£) | Lowest fine (£) | Average fine (£) |
|------|--------|------------------|-----------------|------------------|
| 1989 | 8 | 9,000 | 250 | 3,237 |
| 1990 | 3 | 2,000 | 650 | 1,117 |
| 1991 | 6 | 3,000 | 250 | 1,348 |
| 1992 | 1 | 150 | 150 | 150 |
| 1993 | 4 | 3,000 | 530 | 1,570 |
| 1994 | 2 | 8,000 | 150 | 4,075 |

**Mr. McCartney:** To ask the Secretary of State for Employment how many (a) improvement and (b) prohibition notices have been served on asbestos removal companies each year since 1983. [23369]

**Mr. Oppenheim:** The following table gives the available information on the number of improvement and prohibition notices issued to licensed asbestos removal companies under the Asbestos (Licensing) Regulations 1983 and the Control of Asbestos at Work Regulations 1987 and the Asbestos Regulations 1969, which CAWR replaced.

| Year | Number of improvement notices | Number of prohibition notices |
|------|-------------------------------|-------------------------------|
| 1983 | Not available | Not available |
| 1984 | Not available | Not available |
| 1985 | 9 | 71 |
| 1986 | 5 | 40 |
| 1987 | 1 | 15 |
| 1988 | 1 | 11 |
| 1989 | 3 | 14 |
| 1990 | 2 | 12 |
| 1991 | Nil | 6 |
| 1992 | 1 | 13 |
| 1993 | Not yet available | Not yet available |
| 1994 | Not yet available | Not yet available |

*Note:*
· Figures for 1983 and 1984 are not available because these years precede the collection of data on prohibition and improvement notices.

### Manslaughter

**Mr. McCartney:** To ask the Secretary of State for Employment how many cases the Health and Safety Executive has referred to the Crown Prosecution Service for potential manslaughter charges in each of the last five years; and how many were accepted. [23366]

**Mr. Oppenheim:** Since April 1992, 26 cases which the Health and Safety Executive has investigated have been referred to the Crown Prosecution Service for consideration of possible manslaughter charges, as follows:

| Year | Number of cases referred to CPS | Prosecutions for manslaughter started by CPS | Cases still under consideration by CPS |
|------|--------------------------------|----------------------------------------------|----------------------------------------|
| 1992–92 | 12 | 2 | — |
| 1993–94 | 5 | 1 | — |
| 1994–95 | 9 | 2 | 3 |

Information for previous years is available only at disproportionate cost.

### Health and Safety Executive Inspections

**Mr. McCartney:** To ask the Secretary of State for Employment how many registered workplaces the Health and Safety Executive has been responsible for, for each of the past five years; and what proportion each year has received an inspection-type visit from a Health and Safety Executive inspector in *(a)* the past year and *(b)* the past five years.                                               [23368]

**Mr. Oppenheim:** It is estimated that some 650,000 premises are registered with the Health and Safety Executive. The HSE's systems are designed to record all those premises in which it has an active interest. It does not readily provide historical data, which could be obtained only at disproportionate cost.

The average numbers of planned inspections completed by each of the HSE's operational divisions, for each of the financial years 1989–90 to 1993–94, are set out in the following table. The table also indicates the numbers of planned inspections that divisions expected to achieve in 1994–95.

*Number of planned inspections completed or planned by HSE operational divisions*

|  | 1989–90 Outturn | 1990–91 Outturn | 1991–92 Outturn | 1992–93 Outturn | 1993–94 Outturn | 1994–95 Planned |
|---|---|---|---|---|---|---|
| Field Operations Division planned inspections | 164,122 | 165,198 | 168,865 | 157,426 | 152,014 | 157,000 |
| Mines Inspectorate planned inspections | 6,290 | 3,064 | 2,462 | 2,190 | 1,707 | 1,290 |
| Offshore Safety Division planned inspections (1) | — | — | 359 | 405 | 467 | 370 |
| Railway Inspectorate planned inspections (2) | — | — | 2,306 | 1,452 | 1,482 | 2,080 |
| Technology and Health Sciences Division planned inspections | 348 | 243 | 285 | 459 | 563 | 480 |

*Notes:*

1. HSE assumed responsibility for offshore safety on 1 April 1991.
2. The Railway Inspectorate transferred from the Department of Transport on 3 December 1990.

### Safety Regulations

**Mr. McCartney:** To ask the Secretary of State for Employment (1) how many improvement and prohibition notices have been served under the Safety Representatives and Safety Committee Regulations 1977 for each year since 1978;                                          [23372]

(2) how many prosecutions there have been under the Safety Representatives and Safety Committee Regulations 1977 for each year since 1978.                                       [23371]

**Mr. Oppenheim:** According to available information, the Health and Safety Executive's field inspectorates issued one improvement notice under these regulations, in 1984. They did not issue a prohibition notice or initiate a prosecution during the period. Details of enforcement action by other inspectorates and by local authorities are not readily available on a regulation-by-regulation basis, and this information could be obtained only at disproportionate cost.

### Workplace Accidental Deaths

**Mr. McCartney:** To ask the Secretary of State for Employment for how many workplace accidental deaths in each of the past five years there were Health and Safety Executive or environmental health officer prosecutions.                                                [23367]

**Mr. Oppenheim:** Except for the Health and Safety Executive offshore safety division, the information requested is either not available or available only at disproportionate cost:

| Year | *(OSD) Prosecutions arising from workplace fatalities* |
|---|---|
| 1989–90 | 0 |
| 1990–91 | 3 |
| 1991–92 | 2 |
| 1992–93 | 2 |
| 1993–94 | 3 |
| Total | 10 |

### Family and Working Lines Survey

**Mr. Morgan:** To ask the Secretary of State for Employment what is the value and duration of the contract awarded to Research Services Ltd. Harrow, Middlesex to undertake the family and working lives survey.   [23643]

**Mr. Oppenheim** *[holding answer 10 May 1995]:* The cost of the working lives survey is £1,231,928, including VAT.

The contract for the project started on 14 October 1993 and is scheduled for completion at the end of September 1996.

**Mr. Morgan:** To ask the Secretary of State for Employment what arrangements there are to sub-contract any of the interview work being carried out by Research Services Ltd. as part of the family and working lives survey to other organisations and colleges; and what are the minimal levels of qualifications required of the sub-contractors to undertake direct market research.               [23645]

**Mr. Oppenheim** *[holding answer 10 May 1995]:* Research Services Ltd. has not sub-contracted any of the interviewing for the family and working lives survey.

**Mr. Morgan:** To ask the Secretary of State for Employment by what method Research Services Ltd. was awarded by the contract to undertake the family and working lives survey; and how the contract was advertised.                                               [23647]

**Mr. Oppenheim** *[holding answer 10 May 1995]:* The contract for the family and working lives survey was awarded by competitive tender. Tenders were invited from four leading social research organisations.

The research was advertised in the Department's "Annual Report on Research" in 1992.

**Mr. Morgan:** To ask the Secretary of State for Employment what is the sample size of the family and working lives survey being carried out by Research Services Ltd.; and how many people are being interviewed in *(a)* England, *(b)* Wales, *(c)* Scotland and *(d)* Northern Ireland.                                  [23644]

**Mr. Oppenheim** *[holding answer 10 May 1995]:* The survey aimed to interview 12,000 respondents and their partners where appropriate. Fieldwork is sill in progress. To date 9,248 have been interviewed in England, 533 in Wales and 976 in Scotland.

The survey does not cover Northern Ireland.

**Mr. Morgan:** To ask the Secretary of State for Employment if he will make a statement on the sampling techniques, including the form of sampling and the sampling frame, being used by Research Services Ltd. in conducting the family and working lives survey. [26346]

**Mr. Oppenheim** *[holding answer 10 May 1955]:* The sampling technique used for the survey was stratified random sampling of census enumeration districts selected with probability proportional to size. All EDs in mainland Britain were included. Islands, such as Jersey and the Scottish islands, were not included and neither was Northern Ireland. Addresses were drawn from the postcode address file with equal probability in the selected EDs. At each address, one adult was selected at random from all those eligible. If this person had a partner living in the same household, a shorter interview was conducted with the partner.

### International Labour Conference

**Mr. MacShane:** To ask the Secretary of State for Employment if he will list the delegation representing the United Kingdom at the forthcoming international labour conference. [23711]

**Miss Widdecombe:** The UK will, as in previous years be sending a tripartite delegation. Members of the delegation are as follows:

INTERNATIONAL LABOUR CONFERENCE

(82nd Session, Geneva, 6 to 23 June 1995)

MEMBERS OF UK DELEGATION

MINISTER ATTENDING THE CONFERENCE

*Miss Ann WIDDECOMBE,* MP

Minister of State for Employment

She will be accompanied by her Private Secretary, *Mr. Simon WOOD,* and Mr. Clive TUCKER, Head of International Division, Employment Department.

GOVERNMENT DELEGATES

*Mr. Mark WESTON,* Head of International Relations Branch, Employment Department.

*Ms Shan MORGAN,* Grade 7, Employment Department

*Advisers and Substitute Delegates*

*Mr. Edward G. M. CHAPLIN* OBE, Deputy Permanent Representative, United Kingdom Mission to the United Nations Office and other International Organisations in Geneva

*Mr. Keith ANDREWS,* Senior Executive Officer, Employment Department

*Advisers*

*Mr. Nigel WILLIAMS* CMG, Permanent Representative, United Kingdom Mission to the United Nations Office and other International Organisations in Geneva

*Mr. Geoff GREEN,* HM Principal Inspector of Mines, Health and Safety Executive

*Mr. Alistair KENNARD,* Grade 7, Employment Department

*Mr. Philip SCOTT,* Field Operations Division, Health and Safety Executive

*Mr. Tim SIMMONS,* First Secretary, United Kingdom Mission to the United Nations Office and other International Organisations in Geneva

*Miss Sarah BOARDMAN,* Third Secretary, United Kingdom Mission to the United Nations Office and other International Organisations in Geneva

*Mr. Herbert LYSK,* Head of Industrial Relations Division, Department of Economic Development (Northern Ireland)

*Mr. Johnathan CLAGUE,* Higher Executive Officer, Department of Industry, Isle of Man

*Mr. Stephen IP,* Commissioner for Labour, Labour Department Hong Kong

*Ms Angella BLAGGROVE,* Executive Officer, Employment Department

EMPLOYERS' DELEGATE

*Miss Anne MACKIE* OBE, CBI Consultant on International Employment Affairs; Member, Governing Body of the International Labour Office

*Adviser and Substitute Delegate*

*Miss Deborah A. FRANCE,* Head, International Social Affairs, Confederation of British Industry

*Advisers*

*Mr. Alan WILD,* Employee Relations Director, Guinness Brewing Worldwide

*Mr. Rod STACE,* Mining Engineer, Operations Department, British Coal Corporation

*Mr. David EVANS,* Confederation of British Industry

*Ms Petunia OGUNLEYE,* Employee Relations Adviser, Shell UK Exploration and Production

*Mr. Sai-chu HO,* Employers' Representative, Labour Advisory Board, Hong Kong

WORKERS' DELEGATE

*Mr. Bill BRETT,* Vice-President, Governing Body of the International Labour Office, General Secretary of the Institution of Professionals, Managers and Specialists

*Adviser and Substitute Delegate*

*Mr. Simon STEYNE,* International Officer, International Department, Trades Union Congress

*Advisers*

*Mr. Chris GIFFORD,* Mine Health and Safety Consultant, National Association of Colliery Overmen, Deputies and Shotfirers/NUM

*Mr. William MORGAN,* Member of the Executive Council of Amalgamated Engineering and Electrical Union; Member of the TUC General Council

*Mr. Gus BOATENG,* Unit Representative and Unit Equal Opportunities Representative, Communication Workers' Union; Member of the TUC General Council

*Ms Ina LOVE,* Member of the National Executive Committee of UNISON; Member of the TUC General Council

*Mr. Ken THOMAS,* Former General Secretary to the Civil and Public Services Association; Former Member of the TUC General Council

*Mr. Ming CHU,* Employees' Representative, Labour Advisory Board, Hong Kong

### Jobcentres

**Mr. Chidgey:** To ask the Secretary of State for Employment what instructions his Department gives to jobcentres on the circumstances in which they can advertise job vacancies that exist at employment agencies. [23682]

**Miss Widdecombe:** Responsibility for the subject of the question has been delegated to the Employment Service under its chief executive. I have asked him to arrange for a reply to be given.

*Letter from M. E. G. Fogden to Mr. David Chidgey, dated 15 May 1995:*

The Secretary of State has asked me to reply to your question about what instructions people in Jobcentres follow when handling vacancies on behalf of employment agencies.

You may be aware of the long standing agreement we have with the Federation of Recruitment and Employment Services (FRES). This enables my Jobcentres to accept individual vacancies for display from an employment agency or business recruiting people to be sub-contracted to companies.

Following a review last year of our vacancy handling policy with agencies, we reached a new agreement with FRES on co-operation between Jobcentres and private employment agencies. Under the new arrangements, agencies may use Jobcentres to advertise vacancies which they have been contracted to fill.

We are keen to introduce jobseekers to all the options available to help them in their search for work and we believe that the new arrangements give unemployed people access to wider range of opportunities.

Further information is included in our publication, Helping People into Jobs, The Guide to Job Broking, copies of which are available in the Library.

I hope this is helpful.

### Fourth World Conference on Women

**Mr. MacShane:** To ask the Secretary of State for Employment what public consultations are planned with *(a)* women's bodies and *(b)* other interested representative bodies prior to deciding United Kingdom policy in regard to the UN's fourth world conference on women in Beijing. [23699]

**Miss Widdecombe:** Throughout the preparatory process for the fourth UN world conference on women, the Government have been in continuous dialogue with women's non-governmental organisations and other interested groups. We consulted widely on the UK national report for the world conference which was released last September, and have invited comments on the draft global platform for action. Members of the delegation to the recent preparatory meeting of the commission on the status of women are meeting NGOs this week to discuss the outcome of that meeting.

**Mr. MacShane:** To ask the Secretary of State for Employment which non-governmental organisations have been in contact with the Government in respect of the UN's fourth world conference on women in Beijing this year. [23696]

**Miss Widdecombe:** A wide range of non-governmental organisations have contacted the Government regarding the fourth UN world conference on women.

### European Structural Funds

**Mr. Byers:** To ask the Secretary of State for Employment what is the estimate of the amount that will have been spent on 1994–95 under objective 3 of the European structural funds; what amount has been applied for in 1995–96; and on what date the application was made. [24155]

**Miss Widdecombe:** The European Commission works on a calendar year cycle for its financial commitments. In 1994, 478 mecu, about £368 million, has been committed to European social fund objective 3 projects in Great Britain. The actual expenditure will not be known until later this year, when our final claims for 1994 are submitted.

In 1995, 497 mecu is available. This is drawn down from the Commission in a series of tranches. The first 50 per cent., 248.5 mecu, was requested on 21 April 1995.

## FOREIGN AND COMMONWEALTH AFFAIRS

### Nuclear Non-proliferation Treaty

**Mr. Menzies Campbell:** To ask the Secretary of State for Foreign and Commonwealth Affairs if he will make a statement on Her Majesty's Government's response to the report of the European Parliament's Committee on Foreign Affairs, Security and Defence Policy on the conference on the extension of the nuclear non-proliferation treaty, adopted by the European Parliament on 5 April. [22350]

**Mr. David Davis** *[holding answer 4 May 1995]:* My right hon. Friend the Secretary of State for Foreign and Commonwealth Affairs will make a statement about the nuclear non-proliferation treaty after the review and extension conference has taken place.

### Mr. Nick Leeson

**Mr. MacShane:** To ask the Secretary of State for Foreign and Commonwealth Affairs what visits have been made to Mr. Nick Leeson in Frankfurt by United Kingdom consular staff. [23709]

**Mr. David Davis:** Our vice-consul saw Mr. Leeson immediately after he was stopped at Frankfurt airport on 2 March. The vice-consul visited him in Hoechst prison, Frankfurt, on 10 March. He will be visited again within the next three weeks. Mr. Leeson is free to contact our consulate at any time.

### Fourth World Conference on Women

**Mr. MacShane:** To ask the Secretary of State for Foreign and Commonwealth Affairs what assurances have been obtained from the Chinese Government in respect of participation by non-governmental organisations in the UN's fourth world conference on women in Beijing this year. [23695]

**Mr. Douglas Hogg:** In accordance with standard UN practice, non-governmental organisations will be admitted as observers at the fourth world conference on women in Peking. Under the terms of the host country agreement, China has agreed to issue visas to all non-governmental organisations properly accredited by the United Nations.

**Mr. MacShane:** To ask the Secretary of State for Foreign and Commonwealth Affairs what guarantees the United Kingdom has obtained from China to the effect that all British-based journalists seeking to cover the UN fourth world conference on Women in Beijing will be granted accreditation. [23698]

**Mr. Douglas Hogg:** Press accreditation for the fourth world conference on women will be arranged by the United Nations. The Chinese have confirmed that they will issue visas to all those so accredited.

**Mr. Macshane:** To ask the Secretary of State for Foreign and Commonwealth Affairs if he will list the composition of the United Kingdom delegation to the UN fourth world conference on women in Beijing. [23700]

**Mr. Douglas Hogg:** I refer the hon. Member to the reply given to the hon. Member for Aylesbury (Mr. Lidington) by my hon. Friend the Minister of State, Department of Employment on 16 March, *Official Report,* column *648.*

### Argentine Postage Stamps

**Mr. Wallace:** To ask the Secretary of State for Foreign and Commonwealth Affairs what consideration Her Majesty's Government have given to making representations to the Universal Postal Union in respect of postage stamps issued by the Argentine postal authorities bearing the words "Islas Malvinas"; and if he will make a statement.    [23714]

**Mr. David Davis:** We have not made representations to the Universal Postal Union about the stamps in question. However, we have protested to the Argentine Government about the issue, reiterating our sovereignty over the Falklands Islands, and informing the Argentines that they have no right to issue such stamps.

### British Diplomatic Staff

**Mr. Tony Banks:** To ask the Secretary of State for Foreign and Commonwealth Affairs if he will list those countries where the British ambassador, high commissioner or charge is female; and in how many countries there is British diplomatic presence.    [23785]

**Mr. Goodlad:** The countries where the head of post is female are:

Irish Republic
Lebanon
Costa Rica
Ivory Coast
Uzbekistan
Zaire

Diplomatic or consular relations are maintained with 183 countries, although in some cases the accredited diplomatic staff reside in a third country.

### Cannes European Council

**Mr. Richard Shepherd:** To ask the Secretary of State for Foreign and Commonwealth Affairs when Her Majesty's Government expect to publish their specific proposals for reform of the European Community for intergovernmental conference; and if they will be in the form of a White Paper.    [23719]

**Mr. David Davis:** We do not expect the Cannes European Council to consider proposals for the IGC, which will not meet until next year. My right hon. Friends the Prime Minister and the Foreign Secretary have set out the Government's approach to the IGC on a number of occasions, including in the Opposition day debated on Europe on 1 March, *Official Report,* columns 1060—74 and 1138–45.

### Indonesia

**Mrs. Clwyd:** To ask the Secretary of State for Foreign and Commonwealth Affairs on what dates he approved the use by the Indonesian Government of British-supplied defence equipment against *(a)* the GAM: Aceh, *(b)* the OPM: West Papua/Irian Jaya; and *(c)* FRETLIN: East Timor.    [23865]

**Mr. Goodlad:** We would not approve the export of defence equipment likely to be used for internal repression in Indonesia or East Timor.

**Mrs. Ann Clwyd:** To ask the Secretary of State for Foreign and Commonwealth Affairs on what dates he protested to the Government of Indonesia about the use of British-supplied defence equipment against *(a)* the GAM: Aceh, *(b)* the OPM: West Papua/Irian Jaya and *(c)* FRETLIN: East Timor.    [23866]

**Mr. Goodlad:** We have no evidence that British-supplied defence equipment has been so used.

### Public Bodies

**Mr. Flynn:** To ask the Secretary of State for Foreign and Commonwealth Affairs which non-departmental public bodies within the responsibility of his Department are subject to scrutiny by *(a)* ombudsmen, *(b)* the National Audit Office, *(c)* the Audit Commission and *(d)* other monitoring officers; which are covered by citizens charters; in which performance indicators apply; and in which members are liable to surcharge.    [23967]

**Mr. Goodlad:** For executive non-departmental public bodies I refer the hon. Member to my answer of 25 April to the hon. Member for Cannock and Burntwood (Dr. Wright), *Official Report,* column *428,* on such bodies sponsored by the FCO (Diplomatic Wing and Overseas Development Administration). Only members of the boards of the British Council and the Britain-Russia Centre are liable to surcharge. For advisory non-departmental public bodies the information requested is shown in the following table.

| | Investigation by Parliamentary Commissioner (a) | Scrutiny by NAO (b) | Subject to: Scrutiny by Audit Commission (c) | Other Monitoring Officers (d)[1] | Citizen's Charter | Performance Indicators | Members Liable to Surcharge |
|---|---|---|---|---|---|---|---|
| Diplomatic Service Appeals Board | No | No | No | No | No | No | No |
| Government Hospitality Fund Advisory Committee for the Purchase of Wine | No | No | No | No | No | No | No |
| Wilton Park Academic Council | Yes | Yes | No | No | Yes | Yes | No |
| Wilton Park International Advisory Council | Yes | Yes | No | No | Yes | Yes | No |
| Advisory Committee on Overseas Economic and Social Research | No | No | No | No | No | No | No |

| | Investigation by Parliamentary Commissioner (a) | Scrutiny by NAO (b) | Scrutiny by Audit Commission (c) | Subject to: Other Monitoring Officers (d)[1] | Citizen's Charter | Performance Indicators | Members Liable to Surcharge |
|---|---|---|---|---|---|---|---|
| Indian Family Pension Funds Body of Commissioners | No | No | No | No | No | No | No |
| Overseas Service Pensions Scheme Advisory Board | No | No | No | No | No | No | No |
| Know-How Fund Advisory Board | No | No | No | No | No | No | No |

[1] All non-departmental public bodies are subject to regular review by the sponsoring FCO department.

## Mercenaries

**Mr. Llew Smith:** To ask the Secretary of State for Foreign and Commonwealth Affairs when Her Majesty's Government intend to sign and ratify the United Nations international convention against the recruitment, use, financing and training of mercenaries. [24293]

**Mr. Douglas Hogg:** I refer the hon. Gentleman to the answer given by my right hon. Friend the Minister of State, Foreign and Commonwealth Office, to the hon. Member for Cynon Valley (Mrs. Clwyd) on 27 March, *Official Report,* column *443.*

## Gibraltar

**Mr. Mackinlay:** To ask the Secretary of State for Foreign and Commonwealth Affairs on what occasions Gibraltar's status *(a)* within the European Union and *(b)* with Spain has been raised by him at his meetings with the Foreign Minister of Spain over the past two years. [24473]

**Mr. David Davis:** My right hon. Friend the Secretary of State for Foreign and Commonwealth Affairs meets the Spanish Foreign Minister regularly. Detailed discussions on Gibraltar are held under the auspices of the Brussels process. The last such meeting was on 20 December 1994 in London.

**Mr. Mackinlay:** To ask the Secretary of State for Foreign and Commonwealth Affairs on how many occasions British citizens using the border between Gibraltar and Spain have been subject to delays initiated by the Spanish authorities during the past 14 days; and if he will make a statement. [24474]

**Mr. David Davis:** British citizens have been subject to some delays on each of the past 14 days. As we have repeatedly made clear, we consider the delays caused by the Spanish controls at the Spain-Gibraltar frontier excessive and unjustified. We have protested vigorously to the Spanish authorities.

**Mr. Mackinlay:** To ask the Secretary of State for Foreign and Commonwealth Affairs on what occasions Gibraltar's status within the European Union has been raised formally in any of the Council of Ministers other than the Heads of Governments Council, over the past two years; and if he will make a statement. [24472]

**Mr. David Davis:** Gibraltar is within the European Union as part of the United Kingdom by virtue of article 227(4) of the EC treaty, although Gibraltar remains outside certain areas of Community policy. These issues have not been formally raised in EU Council of Ministers' meetings over the past two years.

## Gun Running (Rwanda)

**Mr. Worthington:** To ask the Secretary of State for Foreign and Commonwealth Affairs what recent representations he has made to Zaire about gun running in Rwanda and other central African countries. [23615]

**Mr. Baldry:** We have no evidence on which to base formal representations to the Government of Zaire about the illegal supply of arms to Rwanda or other central African countries.

## SCOTLAND

## A1 Dual Carriageway

**Mr. Home Robertson:** To ask the Secretary of State for Scotland if he will make a statement on proposals by the Miller Amey consortium to depart from certain aspects of the confirmed plan for the A1 dual carriageway between Tranent and Haddington, and if he will require the contractor to design and construct this section of road in accordance with the confirmed plan. [21813]

**Lord James Douglas-Hamilton:** The contract awarded to Miller/Amey joint venture was on a "design and build" basis. This form of contract encourages the contractor to optimise the design, thus bringing benefits in which both the taxpayer and the industry can share. The amended proposals are subject to completion of their statutory procedures, including consultation, in the normal way. It is too early to say at this stage what the final outcome will be.

The Scottish Office has found that alternative proposals by contractors can often deliver improved value for money. This, of course, means that the funds voted by Parliament for trunk roads in Scotland will be able to purchase more new construction than would otherwise be possible using traditional tendering methods.

## Gemini Housing Association

**Mr. Michael J. Martin:** To ask the Secretary of State for Scotland (1) what records are kept at the Glasgow office of Scottish Homes of the numbers of hours staff spend with Gemini Housing Association Ltd; and if he will make them available for public inspection; [23111]

(2) which officer in Scottish Homes is empowered to give leave of absence to those employees of Scottish Homes who wish to participate in the activities of Gemini Ltd; [23112]

(3) on what terms the Gemini Housing Association is allowed to use office equipment and stationery belonging to Scottish Homes at its Glasgow offices; and what charge is made;    [23113]

(4) what method is used to fill vacancies which occur on the steering committee of Gemini Housing; and if he will place in the Library a copy of the constitution of the Gemini Housing Association;    [23114]

(5) if he will list the members of Gemini Housing Association and those who have resigned since it was formed;    [23115]

(6) what is the monthly rent and rates that Gemini Housing Association pays to Scottish Homes for use of their Glasgow offices;    [23116]

(7) if the officers of Scottish Homes who attended the Gemini meeting at Campsie street on 28 April were paid from Scottish Homes' budget;    [23117]

(8) to what extent resources given by the chief executive of Scottish Homes to Gemini Ltd exceed the normal start up grants given to newly formed housing associations; and when approval was given by the Scottish Homes Board.    [23118]

**Lord James Douglas-Hamilton:** The information requested is a matter for Scottish Homes. I have asked its chairman, Sir James Mellon, to write to the hon. Member.

### Historical Documents

**Mr. Gordon Prentice:** To ask the Secretary of State for Scotland what special training is given to persons who have responsibility for assessing the historical significance of documents held by his Department.    [23279]

**Lord James Douglas-Hamilton:** Scottish Office documents of historical significance are transmitted to the Keeper of the Records of Scotland, whose staff are responsible for selection on historical grounds. These members of staff—curatorial officers of the Scottish Record Office—are qualified archivists, trained by the SRO itself and, increasingly nowadays in possession also of a diploma in archive administration. In addition, they are supervised in the early stages of their work on these records by senior colleagues to ensure that they

follow consistently general guidelines laid down over the 25 years or so that the present system has been in operation.

### Population Statistics

**Mr. Darling:** To ask the Secretary of State for Scotland what is his estimate of the number of people likely to be living in Scotland aged (i) 65, (ii) 75 and (iii) over 85 years in *(a)* 1996, *(b)* 2000 and *(c)* 2005.    [23157]

**Lord James Douglas Hamilton** *[holding answer 9 May 1995]:* Projected population figures are given in the table.

| Age | 1996 | Year 2000 | 2005 |
|---|---|---|---|
| 65 | 50,600 | 49,000 | 49,800 |
| 75 | 38,600 | 36,100 | 37,300 |
| 85 and over | 82,600 | 92,100 | 96,400 |

### Residential Care

**Mr. Darling:** To ask the Secretary of State for Scotland what is his estimate of the number of private sector long-term residential places for elderly people in Scotland in 1995 and in 2000; and if he will make a statement.    [23159]

**Lord James Douglas-Hamilton** *[holding answer 9 May 1995]:* The number of private sector residential care home places which will be required for elderly people in the year 2000 cannot be estimated as it will depend on a number of factors. These include not only the numbers of elderly people at that time and their state of health but the extent to which this form of care is available in other sectors. Cost and quality of residential care will influence the distribution between sectors. At present, the cost of care in homes run by local authorities is substantially more than in homes in the private and voluntary sectors. However, there is no indication that the quality of local authority care is higher. The numbers of residential care home places for elderly people in each sector in Scotland and England at 31 March 1994 are set out in the table below.

| | Scotland | | England | |
|---|---|---|---|---|
| | *Number of places* | *Places per 1,000 population aged 75+* | *Number of places* | *Places per 1,000 population aged 75+* |
| Local authority | 8,356 | 26.0 | 67,401 | 19.9 |
| Private | 4,693 | 14.6 | 163,202 | 48.3 |
| Voluntary | 4,139 | 12.9 | 39,359 | 11.6 |
| Total | 17,188 | 53.5 | 269,962 | 79.9 |

### Long-stay NHS Patients

**Mr. Darling:** To ask the Secretary of State for Scotland what are the numbers of beds available in each region for long-stay NHS patients in 1995; what is his estimate of the number in 2000; and if he will make a statement.    [23160]

**Lord James Douglas-Hamilton** *[holding answer 11 May 1995]:* The latest available information is as follows:

*Average available beds by Health Board area of treatment; quarter ending 31 December 1994* [12]

| | Geriatric long-stay beds | Young chronic sick beds | Psychiatric speciality total beds | Mental handicap total beds |
|---|---|---|---|---|
| Scotland [3] | 7,393 | 290 | 10,964 | 3,398 |
| Argyll and Clyde | 614 | 38 | 1,094 | 226 |
| Ayrshire and Arran | 460 | — | 651 | 132 |
| Borders | 141 | 3 | 239 | 5 |

*Average available beds by Health Board area of treatment; quarter ending 31 December 1994 [1][2]*

| | Geriatric long-stay beds | Young chronic sick beds | Psychiatric speciality total beds | Mental handicap total beds |
|---|---|---|---|---|
| Dumfries and Galloway | 256 | — | 367 | 86 |
| Fife | 432 | 12 | 685 | 302 |
| Forth Valley | 506 | — | 612 | 523 |
| Grampian | 742 | 24 | 1,041 | 296 |
| Greater Glasgow | 1,392 | 131 | 2,117 | 660 |
| Highland | 308 | 7 | 399 | 106 |
| Lanarkshire | 699 | 19 | 990 | 440 |
| Lothian[4] | 1,080 | 33 | 1, 658 | 435 |
| Orkney | 49 | — | — | — |
| Shetland | 81 | — | — | — |
| Tayside | 587 | 22 | 1,059 | 186 |
| Western Isles | 44 | — | 51 | — |

*Notes:*
[1] Provisional.
[2] Includes Joint User and Contractual hospitals.
[3] Health Board totals may not tally with Scotland totals due to the effects of rounding.
[4] Average available staffed beds. Includes all beds whether classified as long-stay or otherwise.
*Source:*
Information and Statistics Division.

There are no centrally imposed targets for long-stay bed provision in the NHS for the year 2000. The pace of change in the number of long-stay NHS beds is directed by patient needs and by the rate at which alternative provision becomes available in the community. The organisation of long-stay care and care services in the community are determined by continuous joint assessment of local needs involving health boards and local authorities. The aim is to secure the most effective package of services, both in hospital and the community, that meet the specific needs of patients and carers.

### University Entrance

**Mr. Worthington:** To ask the Secretary of State for Scotland what proportion of the appropriate age group has attained university entrance standards in each year since 1979. [23386]

**Lord James Douglas-Hamilton:** The previous general entry requirement of the Scottish Universities Council on entrance was of three or more SCE higher grades at A-C lapsed in 1993. Minimum entry requirements for all ages of applicants are now at the discretion of individual institutions.

The percentage of Scottish school leavers gaining three or more higher grades at A-C is given in the table. Information is not available on the same basis for years earlier than 1981–82.

*Scottish school leavers by highest SCE qualification*

| Academic year | Number of leavers | Percentage with three or more higher grades (A-C) |
|---|---|---|
| 1981–82 | 88,607 | 21 |
| 1982–83 | 90,988 | 21 |
| 1983–84 | 89,737 | 21 |
| 1984–85 | 85,819 | 21 |
| 1985–86 | 83,076 | 21 |
| 1986–87 | 80,356 | 21 |

*Scottish school leavers by highest SCE qualification*

| Academic year | Number of leavers | Percentage with three or more higher grades (A-C) |
|---|---|---|
| 1987–88 | 76,059 | 23 |
| 1988–89 | 72,695 | 24 |
| 1989–90 | 67,900 | 26 |
| 1990–91 | 62,072 | 27 |
| 1991–92 | 60,596 | 28 |
| 1992–93 | 57,796 | 29 |
| 1993–94 | 58,194 | 30 |

### Irvine Housing Association

**Mr. Donohoe:** To ask the Secretary of State for Scotland if he will make a statement indicating the latest position in respect of the bid by Irvine Housing Association to take over some of the housing stock of Irvine development corporation in advance of the general disposal of the corporation housing stock. [23493]

**Mr. Kynoch** *[holding answer 9 May 1995]:* I understand that Irvine Housing Association has yet to finalise its funding from the private sector. I have asked the development corporation to advise the hon. Member with the transaction has been concluded.

### Pupil-teacher Ratios

**Mr. Worthington:** To ask the Secretary of State for Scotland what has been the pupil-teacher ratio in *(a)* primary schools and *(b)* secondary schools in Scotland in each year since 1979. [23603]

**Lord James Douglas-Hamilton:** The information requested, for education authority primary and secondary schools, is given in the table.

The figures for the years 1985 and 1986 are estimates due to industrial action by teachers during those years. The figures for 1994 are provisional.

*Pupil-teacher ratios at September*

| Year | EA Primary | EA Secondary |
|---|---|---|
| 1979 | 20.3 | 14.4 |
| 1980 | 20.3 | 14.4 |
| 1981 | 20.3 | 14.4 |
| 1982 | 20.4 | 14.3 |
| 1983 | 20.3 | 14.0 |
| 1984 | 20.4 | 13.7 |
| 1985 | 20.4 | 13.5 |
| 1986 | 20.4 | 13.2 |
| 1987 | 20.4 | 13.0 |
| 1988 | 20.3 | 12.7 |
| 1989 | 19.7 | 12.4 |
| 1990 | 19.5 | 12.2 |
| 1991 | 19.5 | 12.4 |
| 1992 | 19.3 | 12.6 |
| 1993 | 19.5 | 12.8 |
| 1994 | 19.3 | 12.9 |

### School Leavers

**Mr. Worthington:** To ask the Secretary of State for Scotland what proportion of school leavers has attained no academic qualifications in each year since 1979. [23387]

**Lord James Douglas Hamilton:** The proportion of school leavers who have attained no academic qualifications has dropped from 28 per cent. in 1981–82 to 9 per cent. in 1993–94. The table below covers the period from 1981–94. Information prior to 1981–82 is not available on a comparable basis. The percentages listed do not include school leavers with English GCSEs or A-levels, nor do they include pupils who have attained SCOTVEC modules while at school.

*Scottish school leavers with no SCE qualifications*

| Academic year | Number of leavers | Percentage with no SCE qualifications or none found |
|---|---|---|
| 1981–82 | 88,607 | 28 |
| 1982–83 | 90,988 | 26 |
| 1983–84 | 89,737 | 26 |
| 1984–85 | 85,819 | 25 |
| 1985–86 | 83,076 | 24 |
| 1986–87 | 80,356 | 19 |
| 1987–88 | 76,059 | 15 |
| 1988–89 | 72,695 | 12 |
| 1989–90 | 67,900 | 11 |
| 1990–91 | 62,072 | 10 |
| 1991–92 | 60,596 | 10 |
| 1992–93 | 57,796 | 10 |
| 1993–94 | 58,194 | 9 |

### Epilepsy

**Mr. Battle:** To ask the Secretary of State for Scotland how many deaths were attributed to epilepsy in Scotland in each year since 1990 in each health board area for which information is available.          [22842]

**Lord James Douglas-Hamilton** [*holding answer 11 May 1995*]: The information is given in the table.

*Epilepsy[1] recorded as underlying cause of death*

| Health board area | 1990 | 1991 | 1992 | 1993 | [2]1994 |
|---|---|---|---|---|---|
| Argyll and Clyde | 8 | 8 | 7 | 8 | 11 |
| Ayrshire and Arran | 3 | 7 | 3 | 11 | 10 |
| Borders | 1 | 1 | 2 | 0 | 1 |
| Dumfries and Galloway | 4 | 0 | 0 | 1 | 1 |
| Fife | 3 | 6 | 5 | 2 | 6 |
| Forth Valley | 7 | 5 | 3 | 4 | 5 |
| Grampian | 13 | 12 | 9 | 12 | 13 |
| Greater Glasgow | 26 | 27 | 20 | 13 | 18 |
| Highland | 4 | 0 | 0 | 0 | 1 |
| Lanarkshire | 15 | 10 | 9 | 6 | 7 |
| Lothian | 15 | 16 | 14 | 11 | 7 |
| Orkney | 0 | 0 | 0 | 0 | 2 |
| Shetland | 1 | 0 | 0 | 0 | 0 |
| Tayside | 12 | 7 | 15 | 9 | 7 |
| Western Isles | 2 | 2 | 1 | 0 | 0 |
| Scotland | 114 | 101 | 88 | 77 | 89 |

[1] International Classification of Diseases (9th Revision) Codes 345.0–345.9.
[2] 1994 figures are provisional.

*Epilepsy[1] mentioned on death certificate but not as underlying cause of death*

| Health board area | 1990 | 1991 | 1992 | 1993 | [2]1994 |
|---|---|---|---|---|---|
| Argyll and Clyde | 19 | 21 | 15 | 19 | 22 |
| Ayrshire and Arran | 13 | 11 | 11 | 18 | 18 |
| Borders | 4 | 5 | 1 | 0 | 5 |
| Dumfries and Galloway | 8 | 4 | 2 | 5 | 3 |
| Fife | 11 | 10 | 10 | 7 | 8 |
| Forth Valley | 11 | 10 | 8 | 7 | 6 |
| Grampian | 10 | 16 | 9 | 13 | 17 |
| Greater Glasgow | 29 | 30 | 31 | 43 | 40 |
| Highland | 6 | 8 | 8 | 4 | 7 |
| Lanarkshire | 14 | 12 | 26 | 25 | 27 |

*Epilepsy[1] mentioned on death certificate but not as underlying cause of death*

| Health board area | 1990 | 1991 | 1992 | 1993 | [2]1994 |
|---|---|---|---|---|---|
| Lothian | 28 | 23 | 29 | 20 | 37 |
| Orkney | 1 | 1 | 2 | 0 | 0 |
| Shetland | 3 | 2 | 1 | 1 | 0 |
| Tayside | 17 | 18 | 19 | 16 | 10 |
| Western Isles | 0 | 0 | 1 | 0 | 4 |
| Scotland | 174 | 171 | 173 | 178 | 204 |

[1] International Classification of Diseases (9th Revision) Codes 345.0–345.9
[2] 1994 figures are provisional.

### Cultybraggan Civil Defence Facility

**Mrs. Ewing:** To ask the Secretary of State for Scotland if he will publish a list of (a) Ministers (b) civil servants who are entitled to use the civil defence facility underneath Cultybraggan training camp, near Comrie, in the event of it having to be used as an emergency centre of Government in time of war; and if he will make a statement.          [23188]

**Lord James Douglas-Hamilton** [*holding answer 11 May 1995*]: Arrangements for designating individuals to be deployed to regional Government headquarters have been discontinued and lists of such individuals are no longer maintained.

It is anticipated that formal arrangements for the deployment of designated staff to regional Government headquarters would be reintroduced only in the event of a return to a threat situation such as that which existed during the cold war.

### Fatal Accident Inquiries

**Dr. Godman:** To ask the Secretary of State for Scotland how many fatal accident inquiries are to be held in the current year in relation to the deaths of hospital patients in (a) Strathclyde and (b) Scotland as a whole; and if he will make a statement.          [23374]

**Lord James Douglas-Hamilton** [*holding answer 11 May 1995*]: It is for the Lord Advocate to determine in the light of the circumstances in individual cases whether a fatal accident inquiry is appropriate. It is not possible to estimate how many fatal accident inquiries will be held in any particular year.

**Dr. Godman:** To ask the Secretary of State for Scotland how many fatal accident inquiries are to be held in the current year in relation to the deaths of hospital patients in (a) Strathclyde and (b) Scotland as a whole in each of the past 10 years; how many of these cases led to disciplinary action being taken against medical practitioners and other parties; and if he will make a statement.          [23375]

**Lord James Douglas-Hamilton** [*holding answer 11 May 1995*]: The Crown Office does not hold records centrally of the number of hospital patients whose deaths were subsequently the subject of a fatal accident inquiry. The costs of obtaining this information manually from the records of the 49 procurator fiscal offices in Scotland would be prohibitive. Decisions about disciplinary action following fatal accident inquiries would be for the relevant NHS employer.

## Prosecution of Parents

**Mrs. Fyfe:** To ask the Secretary of State for Scotland what was *(a)* the number of parents prosecuted under section 43 of the Education (Scotland) Act 1980, *(b)* the number of respondents who pleaded guilty, *(c)* the number of respondents found (i) guilty and (ii) not guilty after trial and *(d)* the average penalty, and the scope of penalty from minimum to maximum, imposed on those pleading guilty or found guilty in each full year for which statistic are available.                                    [23190]

**Lord James Douglas-Hamilton:** The information requested is not separately identifiable in the Scottish Office Home and Health Department's classification of crimes and offences.

## Public Bodies

**Mr. Flynn:** To ask the Secretary of State for Scotland which non-departmental public bodies within the responsibility of his Department are subject to scrutiny by *(a)* ombudsmen, *(b)* the National Audit Office, *(c)* the Audit Commission and *(d)* other monitoring officers; which are covered by citizens charters; in which performance indicators apply; and in which members are liable to surcharge.                               [23958]

**Mr. Lang:** As regards executive NDPBs, I refer the hon. Member to the answer that I gave to the hon. Member for Cannock and Burntwood (Dr. Wright) on 1 May, *Official Report*, column *10-11*. No advisory NDPBs are subject to the scrutiny of the Parliamentary Commissioner per se, although the administrative actions of administrative staff of the Scottish Office acting on behalf of the body would fall within his remit, as would those of the Horse Race Betting Levy Appeal Tribunal for Scotland and the Rent Assessment Panel for Scotland. The actions of members of the children's panel advisory commitees, which are administered by the local authorities, are subject to the scrutiny of the Local Authority Commissioner, as are the administrative actions of the administrative staff of children's panels, who are local authority employees. The expenditure of advisory NDPBs, the Horse Race Betting Levy Appeal Tribunal for Scotland and the Rent Assessment Panel for Scotland forms part of the total expenditure of the Scottish Office, whose accounts are audited by the Comptroller and Auditor General. The financial affairs of children's panels, which form part of official authority expenditure, are scrutinised by the Accounts Commission for Scotland. There are no other statutory monitoring officers which scrutinise the work of NDPBs, although all such bodies sponsored by my Department are answerable through me to Parliament. In accordance with the recommendations of a joint report by the Treasury and the Office of the Minister for the Civil Service in 1988, all NDPBs sponsored by my Department are subject to a comprehensive review at least every five years.

The only NDPBs sponsored by my department whose members are subject to surcharge are the seven river purification boards.

## Teacher Training

**Mr. Wallace:** To ask the Secretary of State for Scotland how many people since the 1993 deadline have been refused entry to postgraduate teacher training on the grounds of non-conversion to degree equivalents of non-degree qualifications; and if he will make a statement.                                    [23728]

**Mr. Lang:** All-graduate entry to the teaching profession in Scotland has long been an objective of both Government and teachers. In 1987 the Government announced that only those with degree qualifications would be eligible for entry to postgraduate teacher training after academic session 1989–90. Candidates who had begun a non-degree or degree equivalent course before 31 January 1987 were, however, eligible for entry in the seven years up to and including academic session 1993–94 in recognition of the fact that, prior to 1987, degree equivalent qualifications had been treated on the same basis as degrees.

My Department is aware of 18 cases in which the 1993 deadline for holders of non-degree qualifications was missed. Clearly, it must be disappointing for the individuals involved to have missed this deadline despite the very substantial transitional period which had been allowed. It may be possible for holders of non-degree qualifications to upgrade them to a degree by means of the credit accumulation and transfer scheme operated by higher education institutions.

## Charter Mark

**Mr. McMaster:** To ask the Secretary of State for Scotland which public bodies, arm's-length organisations, executive agencies and quangos under the operational control of the Scottish Office are now in receipt of the charter mark; and which ones are not.        [24062]

**Mr. Lang:** The following seven organisations within the area of responsibility of The Scottish Office (and no others) listed in the Cabinet Office publication "Public Bodies 1994", a copy of which is available in the House of Commons Library have received charter marks:

> *1992*
>
> HM Prison, Dungavel, now part of the Scottish Prison Service executive agency
>
> *1993*
>
> Aberdeen Royal Hospitals NHS Trust
>
> *1994*
>
> Highlands and Islands Enterprise Network
>
> Edinburgh NHS Trust department of chiropody and podiatry
>
> South Ayrshire Hospitals NHS Trust
>
> Law Hospital NHS Trust: William Smellie maternity unit
>
> State hospital, Carstairs

# HEALTH

## Severance Payments

**Mr. Redmond:** To ask the Secretary of State for Health how many applications were received by the NHS management executive for authority to pay severance payments in excess of those laid down by the standard NHS regulations in each year since 1990; how many were approved; and what was the total sum involved each year in each health authority.                         [20681]

**Mr. Malone:** The information requested is shown in the table.

*Applications received by the NHS Executive for authority to pay severance payments in excess of those laid down by standard NHS Regulations*

| Authority | Received | Approved | Amount |
|---|---|---|---|
| *1993–94* | | | |
| Salisbury HA | 1 | 1 | 8,000 |
| *1994–95* | | | |
| Mid-Downs HA | 1 | 1 | 7,000 |
| Anglia and Oxford | 1 | 1 | 20,322 |
| South Thames RHA | 3 | [1]2 | 38,391 |
| North Thames RHA | 1 | 1 | 116,000 |
| Merton, Sutton and Wandsworth IIA | 1 | 1 | 14,000 |
| Camden and Islington | 1 | [2]— | — |
| NHS Supplies Authority | 2 | 1 | 72,881 |

[1] One still under consideration.
[2] Under consideration.

## GP Fundholding

**Mr. Devlin:** To ask the Secretary of State for Health what percentage of the population is covered by general practitioners who are fundholders in *(a)* the north-east region of England and *(b)* each family health service authority in the north-east region of England. [21307]

**Mr. Malone:** The percentage of the population covered by a general practitioner fundholder in family health services authorities in the north-east region of England is shown in the table.

| FHSA | Coverage per cent. |
|---|---|
| Cleveland | 30 |
| Durham | 43 |
| Northumberland | 45 |
| Gateshead | 42 |
| Newcastle | 27 |
| North Tyneside | 16 |
| South Tyneside | 34 |
| Sunderland | 10 |
| North East England | 32 |

## "The Health of the Nation"

**Mr. Alex Carlile:** To ask the Secretary of State for Health what plans she has to introduce social, economic and environmental targets into "The Health of the Nation" programme; and if she will make a statement. [22671]

**Mr. Sackville:** None. "The Health of the Nation" is a Government-wide strategy to improve the health of the population. Many Departments have a role to play within their own policy areas. The immediate priority is to ensure that good progress is made towards achieving the targets already identified, although we keep the range of targets under review.

## Central Register of Suspended Doctors

**Mr. Redmond:** To ask the Secretary of State for Health if she will introduce a central register of doctors suspended by hospitals and require all hospitals to refer to that register before employing a doctor. [22738]

**Mr. Malone:** No.

## Folic Acid

**Mr. Cohen:** To ask the Secretary of State for Health what consideration she has given to making folic acid 0.4mg available on prescription for pregnant women; and if she will make a statement. [23542]

**Mr. Sackville:** Folic acid 0.4mg is already available on prescription for women who are pregnant or planning a pregnancy.

## Cancelled Operations

**Mrs. Beckett:** To ask the Secretary of State for Health how many operations were cancelled in total, in each region and in each district in the fourth quarter of 1994–95. [23621]

**Mr. Malone:** This information is not available centrally.

## Chelsea and Westminster Hospital

**Mrs. Beckett:** To ask the Secretary of State for Health how many wards at Chelsea and Westminster hospital are *(a)* for the use of private patients, *(b)* in use for NHS patients and *(c)* not in use; and how many beds there are in the wards in each category. [23619]

**Mr. Sackville:** This information is not available centrally. The right hon. Member may wish to contact Sir Keith Bright, chairman of Chelsea and Westminster Healthcare NHS trust, for further information.

## Children in Care

**Mr. Robert Ainsworth:** To ask the Secretary of State for Health what research she has funded into how best to improve the standard of care, quality of life and outcome for children in care; and if she will make a statement. [23412]

**Mr. Bowis:** The Department of Health funds an extensive programme of research on child care. The work funded between April 1991 and March 1994 is summarised in "The Centrally Commissioned Research Programme", copies of which are available in the Library. Two research reports which focus specifically on the development of improved methods to assess and monitor outcomes of children in care are the linked HMSO publications—"Looking After Children: Assessing Outcomes in Child Care" and "Looking After Children: Research into Practice". These are also available in the Library.

**Mr. Robert Ainsworth:** To ask the Secretary of State for Health (1) what funding will be available to local authorities to develop detailed records of assessed needs of children in care; [23411]

(2) what funds she has allocated for the monitoring and assessment system being piloted by 39 local authorities as a follow up to, "Looking After Children: Research into Practice"; and if she will list the authorities involved. [23413]

**Mr. Bowis:** About £400,000 has been made available in the financial year 1995–96 to support the "Looking After Children: Good Parenting Good Outcomes" project. The 39 authorities listed will receive free forms, training materials, training courses, access to consultants and a helpline. The Department is currently considering whether the same development package of support can be made available to other authorities, if and when they commit themselves to using this system.

Bedfordshire
Bexley
Bradford
Bromley
Buckinghamshire
Camden
Cumbria
Derbyshire
Dudley
Durham
Gateshead
Gloucestershire
Hackney
Hammersmith and Fulham
Hampshire
Hereford and Worcestershire
Hertfordshire
Islington
Kensington and Chelsea
Kingston
Kirklees
Lambeth
Leicestershire
Lewisham
Merton
Norfolk
Northants
North Yorkshire
Richmond
Salford
Somerset
St. Helens
Stockport
Suffolk
Sunderland
Sutton
Tower Hamlets
Wigan
Wolverhampton

## Parliamentary Questions

**Mrs. Angela Knight:** To ask the Secretary of State for Health what has been the cost of answering questions from the right hon. Member for Derby, South (Mrs. Beckett) since November 1994. [24214]

**Mr. Sackville:** Between November 1994 and 11 May 1995, the right hon. Member for Derby, South (Mrs. Beckett) has tabled 501 parliamentary questions. The cost of producing the replies cannot be separately identified. However, I refer my hon. Friend to the reply my right hon. Friend the then Financial Secretary to the Treasury gave to my hon. Friend the Member for Hertfordshire, West (Mr. Jones) on 30 November 1993, at column *391,* which stated that the average cost of preparing an answer to a written parliamentary question was £97.

## Acute Services, Southport and Ormskirk

**Mr. Pickthall:** To ask the Secretary of State for Health (1) when she plans to meet the chairmen of the South Lancashire health authority and the Ormskirk hospital trust to discuss the health service review in Southport, Formby and West Lancashire; [23973]

(2) what assessment she has made as to whether the health service review in Southport, Formby and West Lancashire, conducted by Sir Duncan Nichol, has been objective; [23972]

(3) when she plans to meet the chairman of the North West regional health authority to discuss the health service review in Southport and Formby and West Lancashire; [23971]

(4) what steps she will take to ensure that the Ormskirk hospital is not closed down by the health service review in Southport, Formby and West Lancashire; [24444]

(5) what considerations led the health service review in Southport, Formby and West Lancashire to come to its decision; and what weight was given to the evidence *(a)* in support and *(b)* against the decision making; [24442]

(6) for what reasons the health service review in Southport, Formby and West Lancashire's conclusions are based on current service and not on the proposed service. [24443]

**Mr. Malone:** The Sefton and South Lancashire health authorities commissioned a review of health services in the Southport and Ormskirk areas. When the health authorities concerned have considered the report and Sir Duncan Nichol's observations on it, their proposals will be the subject of public consultation. As these proposals may be referred eventually to my right hon. Friend the Secretary of State for decision, it would not be appropriate for Ministers to comment at this stage.

## Public Bodies

**Mr. Flynn:** To ask the Secretary of State for Health which non-departmental public bodies within the responsibility of her Department are subject to scrutiny by *(a)* ombudsmen, *(b)* the National Audit Office, *(c)* the Audit Commission and *(d)* other monitoring officers; which are covered by citizens charters; in which performance indicators apply; and in which members are liable to surcharge. [23962]

**Mr. Sackville:** The following non-departmental public bodies sponsored by the Department of Health are:

*Subject to scrutiny by the Ombudsmen:*

Human Fertilisation and Embryology Authority.

Central Council for Education and Training in Social Work.

Standing Committee on Postgraduate Medical and Dental Education.

Public Health Laboratory Service Board.

*Subject to scrutiny by the National Audit Office:*

Public Health Laboratory Service Board.

National Biological Standards Board.

National Radiological Protection Board.

Human Fertilisation and Embryology Authority.

Central Council for Education and Training in Social Work.

United Kingdom Central Council for Nursing, Midwifery and Health Visiting.

English National Board for Nursing, Midwifery and Health Visiting.

Standing Committee on Postgraduate Medical and Dental Education.

*Subject to scrutiny by the Audit Commission:*

Human Fertilisation and Embryology Authority.

English National Board for Nursing, Midwifery and Health Visiting.

*Subject to scrutiny by other monitoring officers*

The Department of Health's internal auditors have access to all the non-departmental public bodies sponsored by the Department of Health (as listed in Public Bodies, 1994).

The following non-departmental public bodies sponsored by the Department of Health are covered by citizens charters:

Human Fertilisation and Embryology Authority.
Standing Committee on Postgraduate Medical and Dental Education.

Performance indicators apply in the following non-departmental public bodies sponsored by the Department of Health:

Public Health Laboratory Service Board.
National Biological Standards Board.
National Radiological Protection Board.
Human Fertilisation and Embryology Authority.
Central Council for Education and Training in Social Work.
English National Board for Nursing, Midwifery and Health Visiting.

None of the members of non-departmental public bodies sponsored by the Department of Health are subject to surcharge.

### Child Care

**Mr. Win Griffiths:** To ask the Secretary of State for Health (1) if she will place in the Library a copy of her report to the European Commission on child care services and facilities; [23725]

(2) if her report for the European Commission on child care services and facilities will have separately identifiable sections on Wales, Scotland, Northern Ireland and the regions of England. [23727]

**Mr. Bowis:** At the end of March 1995, the European Commission asked member states to complete a questionnaire on the European Council's recommendation on child care, 92/241/EEC. This requests a response from the United Kingdom as a whole rather than from its constituent parts. This is currently being considered within relevant departments.

### Cross Infection (Prevention)

**Mr. Pike:** To ask the Secretary of State for Health what assessment she has made of the adequacy of the guidelines to hospitals to ensure prevention of cross infection; what steps exist to ensure other hospitals are made aware of problems that may arise; and if she will make a statement. [23949]

**Mr. Sackville:** The Department of Health recognised the need for revised advice on the control of infection in hospitals and issued guidance prepared by a joint Department of Health and Public Health Laboratory Service working group, under cover of HSG(95)10, copies of which are available in the Library. The guidance includes advice on communications with other relevant hospitals.

### London Ambulance Service

**Mr. Spearing:** To ask the Secretary of State for Health if she will state, subsequent to the demise of the South Thames regional health authority, which body or person other than the national health service executive or herself is responsible for the policy of the London ambulance service. [23870]

**Mr. Sackville:** This will depend on the outcome on any application for trust status for the London ambulance service.

### Burnley General Hospital Ophthalmology Department

**Mr. Pike:** To ask the Secretary of State for Health if she will call for a report on the recent incident in Burnley General hospital ophthalmology department in which three people lost an eye; and if she will make a statement. [23948]

**Mr. Sackville:** We are satisfied that Burnley Health Care National Health Service trust took all the necessary measures to deal with this regrettable incident promptly and effectively. An investigation by the Medical Devices Agency is currently taking place.

### Research Work Force Capacity

**Mrs. Beckett:** To ask the Secretary of State for Health what progress her Department is making with its initiative on research work force capacity; when it plans to publish reports of the work it has commissioned; and if she will place copies of relevant reports in the Library when they are completed. [24140]

**Mr. Malone:** The Department of Health, through the research and development division, has commissioned a number of small-scale projects to provide a systematic description to current problems in ensuring that there is an appropriate research work force to take forward R and D initiatives in the field of health and social care. The information collected is now being used to inform the preparation of a co-ordinated strategy on research work force capacity.

The reports of these complementary projects were produced as working documents for discussion at a workshop with the researchers involved. Following the workshop, further work drawing on the reports and the subsequent discussion was undertaken on one particular study. This report by SCPR—social and community policy research—is now being prepared for publication and will be available shortly. A copy will be placed in the Library.

### Edgware and Barnet Hospitals

**Mr. John Marshall:** To ask the Secretary of State for Health when the joint transport working party dealing with transport links between Edgware and Barnet hospitals first met. [24475]

**Mr. Sackville:** A meeting of officials from the Departments of Health and Transport is being arranged.

### GPs (Out-of-hours Work)

**Mrs. Beckett:** To ask the Secretary of State for Health from what source the proposed offer to GPs for out-of-hours work will be funded. [24141]

**Mr. Malone:** Our proposals will be funded from moneys voted by Parliament.

### Research

**Mrs. Beckett:** To ask the Secretary of State for Health if she will list the research programmes funded by her Department which were in progress on 1 January, with (a) the title of the programme, (b) the location of the research team, (c) the name of the director, (d) the start and end dates of the contract for the programme, (e) the actual or planned amount of funding each year and (f) whether the question of renewal of the contract is being or has been considered and, if so, the outcome of any decision made or whether negotiations are still under way.                                                        [24143]

**Mr. Malone:** The Department of Health has arrangements with 13 universities for long-term research programmes: these are listed in annexe C of the report "Centrally Commissioned Research Programme", copies of which are available in the Library.

Peer review by site visit to all units was completed last year. The outcome of all the visits was favourable and directors have been informed that departmental funding will continue for a further five years after the expiry of their current contracts.

In addition to its long-term funding, the Department currently has in the region of 230 contracts for individual research projects.

## Annual Reports

**Mr. Wray:** To ask the Secretary of State for Health if she will instruct *(a)* the Joint Committee on Vaccination and Immunisation, *(b)* the Committee on Medical Aspects of Radiation in the Environment and *(c)* the Clinical Standards Advisory Group to lay an annual report before Parliament.                                          [24177]

**Mr. Sackville:** There are no plans to introduce legislation to make any of these statutory bodies lay an annual report before Parliament.

The recommendations of the Joint Committee on Vaccination and Immunisation are subject to ministerial acceptance and are published biennially in the memorandum, "Immunisation against infectious disease". The memorandum is published by HMSO and provided to all doctors throughout the United Kingdom; copies are placed in the Library. Advice produced by the Committee on Medical Aspects of Radiation in the Environment is always made available to the public and is available in the Library. The results of studies undertaken by the Clinical Standards Advisory Group are published by HMSO and are available in the Library.

## Hospital Building Costs

**Mr. Pickthall:** To ask the Secretary of State for Health what are the estimated costs of building a new maternity unit at *(a)* Ormskirk hospital and *(b)* Southport hospital.                                                [24445]

**Mr. Sackville:** The cost will depend on proposals for the future pattern of services, as determined by the health service review in South Lancashire and Sefton, which will be the subject of full public consultation.

## NHS Failures

**Mrs. Beckett:** To ask the Secretary of State for Health what representations she has received from Sir Donald Acheson calling for a royal commission to investigate failures in the NHS; and if she will make a statement.                                              [24220]

**Mr. Malone:** None.

## Waiting Times

**Mrs. Beckett:** To ask the Secretary of State for Health what plans she has to set a maximum time that a patient should wait on a trolley.                               [24142]

**Mr. Sackville:** The patients charter for England sets a new national standard for patients waiting to be admitted to a hospital bed from an accident and emergency department. From 1 April 1995, once a doctor has decided that a patient should be admitted, the patient can expect to be given a bed as soon as possible and certainly within three to four hours. The standard will be improved to two hours from April 1996.

## Hospital Closures

**Mrs. Beckett:** To ask the Secretary of State for Health what is the average time it has taken in the last year for her to make a decision on the closure of a hospital after the final plans and proposals have been submitted by the regional health authority.                              [19801]

**Mr. Sackville** *[holding answer 21 April 1995]:* Decisions on closure of a hospital have been referred to my right hon. Friend the Secretary of State on three occasions in the last year. Plans in Sunderland for the closure of Havelock hospital, the royal infirmary and the Ryhope general hospital and for the transfer of their services to the Sunderland district general hospital and the Sunderland eye infirmary were received from the Northern regional health authority on 15 December 1994 and the decision was announced on 22 February 1995. Plans to close the Brook hospital, change the use of the Greenwich district hospital and develop new services at the Queen Elizabeth military hospital were submitted by South Thames regional health authority on 16 March 1995 and announced on 4 April. Plans to bring together the general and specialist services managed by the Royal Hospitals National Health Service trust on the Royal London Whitechapel site and to close over time the London chest hospital and most of the St. Bartholomew's hospital site were submitted to my right hon. Friend the Secretary of State on 23 March and the decision was announced on 4 April.

# WALES

## Telephones

**Mr. Donohoe:** To ask the Secretary of State for Wales (1) what representations his Department has made to the Department of Trade and Industry concerning the need for legislation to prevent the cloning of mobile telephones;                     [23474]

(2) what costs his Department has incurred during the last 12 months as a result of cloning of mobile telephones being utilised by his Department, with particular reference to the making of unauthorised calls.           [23483]

**Mr. Redwood** *[holding answer 9 May 1995]:* None.

**Mr. Donohoe:** To ask the Secretary of Sate for Wales what steps his Department has taken to prevent the cloning of telephones being utilised by his Department; and if his Department has discussed this matter with any official agencies.                                        [23460]

**Mr. Redwood** *[holding answer 9 May 1995]:* We are considering the possibility of making greater use of digital phones which are not susceptible to cloning and are discussing this issue with official agencies.

**Mr. Donohoe:** To ask the Secretary of State for Wales how many mobile telephones being utilised by his Department have been cloned during the last 12 months. [23433]

**Mr. Redwood** *[holding answer 9 May 1995]:* One.

**Mr. Donohoe:** To ask the Secretary of State for Wales what use his Department makes of hand-held car-based mobile telephones; what were the costs for each financial year of these services since mobile telephones were first introduced to his Department; and how many mobile telephones are currently in use. [23443]

**Mr. Redwood** *[holding answer 9 May 1995]:* Mobile phones are issued to Ministers and key personnel for urgent business communications. For safety reasons mobile phones are also available to travelling officers.

Total costs for the last three financial years are:
1992–93: £22,289.98
1993–94: £50,353.32
1994–95: £48,664.90

One hundred and forty-eight mobile phones are currently in use.

### Surplus Accommodation

**Mr. Win Griffiths:** To ask the Secretary of State for Wales if he will list the Welsh Office accommodation which is surplus to its needs, identifying for rented properties the remaining length of the lease and the annual rental for each. [23724]

**Mr. Redwood:** Welsh Office accommodation is part of the common user estate, which is the responsibility of Property Holdings. There may be spare space available within individual buildings but the Welsh Office has no accommodation surplus to its needs. It is my policy to concentrate all of the central Welsh Office staff in Cathays Park. As this happens, other accommodation will be disposed of.

### Child Care

**Mr. Win Griffiths:** To ask the Secretary of State for Wales if he will publish the information relevant to Wales prepared for the European Commission on child care services and facilities in the United Kingdom. [23726]

**Mr. Gwilym Jones:** I refer the hon. Member to the reply given to him today by my hon. Friend the Under-Secretary of State at the Department of Health.

### Public Bodies

**Mr. Flynn:** To ask the Secretary of State for Wales which non-departmental public bodies within the responsibility of his Department are subject to scrutiny by *(a)* ombudsmen, *(b)* the National Audit Office, *(c)* the Audit Commission and *(d)* other monitoring officers; which are covered by citizens charters; in which performance indicators apply; and in which members are liable to surcharge. [23954]

**Mr. Redwood:** I refer the hon. Member to the reply I gave the hon. Member for Cannock and Burntwood (Dr. Wright) on 25 April, *Official Report,* column *514.* None of the members of these bodies is liable to surcharge.

**Mr. Morgan:** To ask the Secretary of State for Wales if he will list all other non-departmental public bodies set up with effect from the same time as the Countryside Council for Wales; and if he will list which of them have had financial management and policy reviews *(a)* commenced and *(b)* completed. [24386]

**Mr. Redwood:** No other executive non-departmental public bodies were established at the same time as the Countryside Council for Wales.

**Mr. Morgan:** To ask the Secretary of State for Wales on how many occasions action plans relating to non-departmental public bodies sponsored by his Department have been published during the course of a bank holiday weekend; and if he will list those NDPBs involved and the dates concerned during the past four years. [24382]

**Mr. Redwood:** The action plan for the Countryside Council for Wales was published on Saturday 6 May 1995. Action plans are published at the earliest possible opportunity. No other publication date within the past four years has coincided with a public bank holiday.

### Countryside Council for Wales

**Mr. Morgan:** To ask the Secretary of State for Wales what was the grade of the civil servant who carried out financial management and policy review of the Countryside Council for Wales and the department or section to which he is attached, when not carrying out FMPRs. [24383]

**Mr. Redwood:** Grade 7. The officer was employed on various duties before undertaking the review. Other senior managers were consulted on the review and a wide range of views was canvassed.

**Mr. Morgan:** To ask the Secretary of State for Wales if he will place in the Library a copy of the financial management policy review of the Countryside Council for Wales carried out by his Department. [24385]

**Mr. Redwood:** The financial management policy review of the Countryside Council for Wales was overtaken by the review of the council's functions which I announced in response to the question by my right hon. Friend the Member for Conwy (Sir Wyn Roberts) on 3 November, *Official Report,* column *1329.* The action plan resulting from that review has been placed in the Library of the House.

**Mr. Morgan:** To ask the Secretary of State for Wales when the financial management policy review of the Countryside Council for Wales was commended; how long the review took to complete; and what was the total cost to public funds of the review. [24384]

**Mr. Redwood:** The financial management policy review of the Countryside Council for Wales was overtaken by the review of the council's functions which I announced in response to the question by my right hon. Friend the Member for Conwy (Sir Wyn Roberts) on 3 November 1994, *Official Report,* column *1329.* The review started on 5 April 1994 and consultations on the action plan are continuing. The cost of staff allocated full-time to the work was about £23,000. They would have been performing other duties within the Welsh Office if they had not been doing this task.

**Mr. Morgan:** To ask the Secretary of State for Wales what consultations he has had with local authorities prior to the publishing of his Department's action plans on the Countryside Council for Wales. [24381]

**Mr. Redwood:** The action plan was drawn up in consultation with the Countryside Council for Wales. I am currently consulting local authority associations in Wales seeking their views on the proposals in the plan which could affect their members.

## South and East Wales Ambulance Trust

**Mr. Morgan:** To ask the Secretary of State for Wales what consultations he has had with the chairman of the South and East Wales ambulance trust concerning the dismissal of the board director responsible for personnel; and if he will make a statement.                    [24281]

**Mr. Redwood:** None. This is a matter for the trust.

## NHS Trust Annual Accounts

**Mr. Morgan:** To ask the Secretary of State for Wales, what guidelines he has issued to NHS trusts with regard to the availability to the public of the last published set of annual accounts at convenient places; and what proposals he has to issue further guidelines.             [24387]

**Mr. Redwood:** NHS trusts are required to prepare an annual report under schedule 2(7) of the National Health Service and Community Care Act 1990. Either the full or an abridged version of the annual accounts must be included within the body of the report. The report must be made available to the public free of charge, be published prior to the annual general meeting, the advertisements for which must state how copies can be obtained and be placed in the Library of the House.

## Employment Statistics

**Mr. Llew Smith:** To ask the Secretary of State for Wales what are the latest available figures for the numbers of people in Blaenau Gwent constituency who are in *(a)* part-time and *(b)* full-time employment.          [24291]

**Mr. Redwood:** According to the 1991 census of employment, there were 4,800 part-time and 14,800 full-time employees in Blaenau Gwent constituency in September 1991.

## Trust Appointments

**Mr. Morgan:** To ask the Secretary of State for Wales when he expects to announce the non-executive members of the boards of the NHS trusts in Wales which became operational on 1 April; what assessment he has made of the impact on the operations of those trusts which have been without boards since 1 April; and if he will make a statement.                              [24283]

**Mr. Redwood:** I hope to make an announcement shortly.

I have received no reports of operational difficulties in trusts established on 1 April 1995.

**Mr. Morgan:** To ask the Secretary of State for Wales how many NHS trusts had the appointment of their non-executive board members announced *(a)* before 1 April, *(b)* before 15 April, *(c)* before 30 April and *(d)* later in each year in which trusts have became operational in Wales.                          [24279]

**Mr. Redwood:** Prior to 1 April 1995, appointments of non-executive board members were announced for 23 of the 24 established NHS trusts before their operational date on 1 April. Board non-executive members were appointed to the remaining trust later in the year.

## Car Leasing

**Mr. Morgan:** To ask the Secretary of State for Wales what guidelines he has issued to NHS trusts concerning the purchase or leasing of cars for executive board members; what proposals he has for the issuing of further guidelines; and what representations he has received concerning the controls on car leasing contracts for board members.                                  [24282]

**Mr. Redwood:** I have not issued guidance to NHS trusts concerning the purchase or leasing of cars for executive board members. However, as set out in the code of conduct and accountability, proper stewardship of public moneys requires all NHS boards to achieve value for money. No representations have been received recently.

**Mr. Morgan:** To ask the Secretary of State for Wales how many executive board members of NHS trusts in Wales have been *(a)* disciplined formally and *(b)* dismissed for breaches of the code of conduct in relation to executive car leasing arrangements.    [24280]

**Mr. Redwood:** The information is not available centrally. This is a matter for individual NHS trusts.

## Pay Rates

**Mr. Llew Smith:** To ask the Secretary of State for Wales if he will make a statement about rates of pay in *(a)* the Blaenau Gwent constituency, *(b)* the rest of Wales and *(c)* the United Kingdom.             [24313]

**Mr. Redwood:** Rates of pay vary widely, depending on the type of work, the level of skill involved and what the employer can afford. Outside the south-east in the UK, there is little evidence to suggest that, for the same job, they vary greatly from area to area.

# Written Answers to Questions

*Tuesday 16 May 1995*

## TREASURY

### Manufacturing Industry

**Mr. Austin Mitchell:** To ask the Chancellor of the Exchequer (1) what assessment he has made of by how much imports of manufactures would have to fall in each industry to take up the spare capacity of each of the principal import-saving and export industries, all other things remaining the same; [23792]

(2) what estimate he has made of by how much exports of manufactures would have to increase in each industry to take up the spare capacity of each of the principal import-saving and export industries, all other things remaining the same. [23791]

**Mr. Nelson:** The Confederation of British Industry's April Quarterly Industrial Trends survey reported the strongest rise in export optimism since July 1973. This does not suggest that manufacturing companies are running short of spare capacity.

### Tobacco

**Mr. Barron:** To ask the Chancellor of the Exchequer if he will list in each year since 1965 the cost, in current and in real terms, of an average *(a)* packet of 20 cigarettes, *(b)* 250g of hand-rolling tobacco, *(c)* packet of five cigars and *(d)* 250g of pipe tobacco. [22960]

**Mr. Heathcoat-Amory:** Information on average prices for tobacco products is not readily available. The table gives information based on manufacturers' recommended retail prices during the period 1965–1995 for the current leading brands of tobacco products. I regret that the figures for hand-rolling tobacco, cigars and pipe tobacco between 1965 and 1976 could be provided only at disproportionate cost.

|  | Cigarettes £ per 20 | | HRT £ per 250g | | Cigars £ per 5 small | | Pipe £ per 250g | |
|---|---|---|---|---|---|---|---|---|
|  | Actual | Real | Actual | Real | Actual | Real | Actual | Real |
| 1965 | 0.27 | 2.72 | | | | | | |
| 1966 | 0.27 | 2.61 | | | | | | |
| 1967 | 0.23 | 2.14 | | | | | | |
| 1968 | 0.24 | 2.18 | | | | | | |
| 1969 | 0.26 | 2.23 | | | | | | |
| 1970 | 0.26 | 2.12 | | | | | | |
| 1971 | 0.26 | 1.96 | | | | | | |
| 1972 | 0.27 | 1.88 | | | | | | |
| 1973 | 0.27 | 1.74 | | | | | | |
| 1974 | 0.32 | 1.84 | | | | | | |
| 1975 | 0.42 | 2.02 | | | | | | |
| 1976 | 0.45 | 1.75 | | | | | | |
| 1977 | 0.49 | 1.64 | [1]7.70 | 25.72 | 0.52 | 1.74 | [1]6.95 | 23.22 |
| 1978 | 0.55 | 1.67 | [1]8.90 | 27.05 | 0.54 | 1.64 | [1]7.50 | 22.80 |
| 1979 | 0.66 | 1.83 | [1]9.20 | 25.57 | 0.55 | 1.53 | [1]7.80 | 21.68 |
| 1980 | 0.73 | 1.71 | 9.10 | 21.37 | 0.63 | 1.48 | 7.70 | 18.08 |
| 1981 | 0.95 | 1.97 | 10.10 | 20.98 | 0.72 | 1.50 | 8.30 | 17.24 |
| 1982 | 1.02 | 1.89 | 13.20 | 24.48 | 0.89 | 1.65 | 10.50 | 19.47 |
| 1983 | 1.09 | 1.93 | 14.60 | 25.80 | 0.97 | 1.71 | 11.60 | 20.50 |
| 1984 | 1.23 | 2.07 | 15.60 | 26.23 | 1.03 | 1.73 | 12.10 | 20.34 |
| 1985 | 1.33 | 2.13 | 17.50 | 28.01 | 1.14 | 1.82 | 12.50 | 20.01 |
| 1986 | 1.48 | 2.25 | 18.90 | 28.67 | 1.18 | 1.79 | 13.10 | 19.87 |
| 1987 | 1.52 | 2.22 | 21.10 | 30.81 | 1.22 | 1.78 | 13.60 | 19.86 |
| 1988 | 1.56 | 2.20 | 21.40 | 30.25 | 1.24 | 1.75 | 13.90 | 19.65 |
| 1989 | 1.63 | 2.14 | 22.30 | 29.33 | 1.29 | 1.70 | 14.30 | 18.81 |
| 1990 | 1.67 | 2.04 | 23.00 | 28.10 | 1.35 | 1.65 | 15.00 | 18.33 |
| 1991 | 1.80 | 2.02 | 25.10 | 28.15 | 1.46 | 1.64 | 15.70 | 17.61 |
| 1992 | 2.08 | 2.24 | 29.00 | 31.22 | 1.64 | 1.77 | 18.00 | 19.38 |
| 1993 | 2.27 | 2.40 | 31.70 | 33.56 | 1.76 | 1.86 | 19.10 | 20.22 |
| 1994 | 2.52 | 2.60 | 35.30 | 36.47 | 1.91 | 1.97 | 21.10 | 21.80 |
| 1995 | 2.70 | 2.70 | 36.80 | 36.80 | 2.02 | 2.02 | 22.60 | 22.60 |

[1] 10 ounces.

*Note:*

Actual prices at 1 January. Real prices at January 1995 prices, calculated using the RPI (All Items).

**Mr. Barron:** To ask the Chancellor of the Exchequer how many representations he has received in the last year concerning tobacco taxation; how many have been in favour of *(a)* an increase and *(b)* a decrease in the level of taxation; and if he will list the representations received. [22961]

**Mr. Heathcoat-Amory:** We have received a number of representations. The majority of these asked that tobacco taxation should be kept at a minimum. I regret that more precise information could be provided only at disproportionate cost.

## Alcohol Smuggling

**Mr. Martyn Jones:** To ask the Chancellor of the Exchequer (1) what is the estimated loss in tax due to illegal imports of *(a)* beer and *(b)* wine for (i) 1980, (ii) 1985, (iii) 1990, (iv) 1994 and (v) 1995.  [23260]

(2) what is the estimated amount of illegal imports of *(a)* beer and *(b)* wine for (i) 1980, (ii) 1985, (iii) 1990, (iv) 1994 and (v) 1995.  [23259]

**Mr. Heathcoat-Amory:** Before the completion of the single market on 1 January 1993 only seizures of spirits were separately recorded as seizures of other alcoholic drinks were insignificant. It is by definition impossible to calculate the true extent of smuggling and there is no current estimate. The actual amount of goods seized and the corresponding revenue evaded during the last two financial years are shown in the table.

| Financial year ending | Beer | | Wine | |
|---|---|---|---|---|
| | Revenue (£000s) | Quantity (hlitres) | Revenue (£000s) | Quantity (hlitres) |
| 31 March 1994 | 500 | 7,000 | 155 | 840 |
| 31 March 1995 | 1,000 | 11,000 | 330 | 1,900 |

## Cross-border Shopping

**Sir Thomas Arnold:** To ask the Chancellor of the Exchequer what is his latest estimate of the loss of revenue from cross-border shopping.  [23357]

**Mr. Heathcoat-Amory:** Estimates for the amount of legal cross border shopping for alcohol and tobacco in the year to December 1994 are now available.

The consequential loss of tax revenue may be expressed in one of two ways. On the traditional measurement, which formed the basis of the Customs and Excise advice to the Treasury and Civil Service Committee in 1994 and excludes both additional consumption effects and pre-single-market purchases, the revenue loss would be £210 million compared with the previous estimate of £200 million. However, given the additional passage of time, I am minded in future estimates to stop deducting the value of the pre-single-market element. On that adjusted basis the total revenue loss is £360 million.

## Privatised Companies

**Ms Armstrong:** To ask the Chancellor of the Exchequer what were the administrative costs of the share offers relating to *(a)* International, *(b)* Associated British Ports, *(c)* British Aerospace, *(d)* the British Airports Authority, *(e)* British Airways, *(f)* British Petroleum, *(g)* the British Steel Company, *(h)* British Telecom, *(i)* Britoil, *(j)* Cable and Wireless, *(k)* Enterprise Oil, *(l)* the National Freight Corporation and *(m)* Rolls-Royce on the basis of the answer of 23 March, *Official Report*, column 287.  [23027]

**Sir George Young** *[holding answer 9 May 1995]:* The table shows the administrative costs for the sales requested. These costs have been shown disaggregated into the same categories as the answer of 23 March, *Official Report*, column 287 to the degree that this information is held centrally. Administrative costs for these sales of just under £1 billion need to be set in the context of their gross proceeds of over £32 billion.

*Administrative costs[1] of privatisation*

£ million

| | Year | Selling and other commissions | Marketing[2] | Receiving bank costs | UK advisers Fees | UK underwriting | Other costs[3] | Total |
|---|---|---|---|---|---|---|---|---|
| Amersham International | 1982 | — | 0.1 | — | — | 0.4 | — | 2.9 |
| Associated British Ports | 1983 | — | 0.3 | — | — | 0.4 | — | 2.6 |
| | 1984 | — | 0.1 | — | — | [4]0.9 | — | 1.4 |
| British Aerospace | 1981 | — | 0.6 | — | — | [4]2.3 | — | 5.6 |
| | 1985 | — | 1.9 | — | — | 7.0 | — | 17.8 |
| BAA | 1987 | 4.2 | 10 | 16.0 | 2.4 | 13.6 | — | 46.2 |
| British Airways | 1987 | 2.9 | 6.2 | 8.3 | 4.3 | 7.8 | 5.2 | 34.7 |
| BP | 1979 | — | — | — | — | 3.8 | — | 7 |
| | 1983 | — | — | — | — | 8.3 | — | 22.8 |
| | 1987 | 2.1 | 48.3 | 4.7 | 5.4 | 38.2 | 55.3 | [5]154.0 |
| British Steel | 1988 | 1.7 | 11.6 | 4.3 | 5.6 | 21.3 | 13.9 | 58.4 |
| BT | 1984 | 13 | 14 | 20 | 6 | 74 | 58 | 185 |
| | 1991 | 30.2 | 38.8 | 39.1 | 7.4 | — | 66.9 | 182.4 |
| | 1993 | 48.5 | 29.2 | 14.9 | 5.6 | — | 32.9 | 131.2 |
| Britoil | 1982 | — | 0.3 | — | — | 9.8 | — | 12.6 |
| | 1985 | — | 4.1 | 3.7 | — | 6.9 | 5.6 | 23.3 |
| Cable and Wireless | 1981 | — | 0.3 | — | — | [4]3.4 | — | 8.9 |
| | 1983 | 0.2 | 0.9 | — | — | 4.3 | — | 12.5 |
| | 1985 | — | 2.8 | — | — | 8.7 | — | 21.4 |
| Enterprise Oil | 1984 | — | 0.2 | — | — | [4]7.0 | — | 10.7 |
| National Freight Consortium | 1982 | — | — | — | — | — | — | 0.3 |
| Rolls-Royce | 1987 | 4.2 | 4.0 | 11.0 | 2.2 | 12.5 | — | 33.9 |

[1] Only costs borne by the Exchequer are shown. Costs shown include VAT and stamp duty, but exclude the cost of incentives and interest earned on application monies.

[2] Including the operation of the Share Information Office (where applicable).

[3] Includes overseas expenses.

[4] Incudes some advisory fees.

[5] Excludes the cost of the Bank of England purchase scheme (27m).

## Income Tax

**Mr. Frank Field:** To ask the Chancellor of the Exchequer (1) if he will publish estimates for the revenue cost in 1996–97 and for a full year of reducing the 20 per cent. tax rate to *(a)* 5 per cent., *(b)* 7 per cent., *(c)* 9 per cent., *(d)* 10 per cent., *(e)* 12 per cent., *(f)* 15 per cent., *(g)* 16 per cent. and *(h)* 18 per cent. on taxable income of (i) £1,000, (ii) £2,000 (iii) £3,000 and (iv) £3,200 retaining any balance of £3,200 at the 20 per cent. rate.

[23354]

(2) if he will provide estimates for the revenue cost in 1995–96 and for a full year of reducing the 20 per cent. tax rate to *(a)* 5 per cent., *(b)* 7 per cent., *(c)* 9 per cent., *(d)* 10 per cent., *(e)* 12 per cent., *(f)* 15 per cent., *(g)* 16 per cent. and *(h)* 18 per cent., on taxable income of (i) £1,000, (ii) £2,000 (iii) £3,000 and (iv) £3,200 retaining any balance of £3,200 at the 20 per cent. rate.

[23974]

**Sir George Young** *[holding answer 9 May 1995]:* The table gives available estimates showing the variation in revenue costs over the specified ranges of tax rates and bands of taxable incomes. No change in the rate of advance corporation tax or the rate of tax on dividends has been assumed.

*Full year revenue cost, at 1995–96 levels*[1]

| Band of taxable income (£) | (£ billion) lower rate | | |
| | 5 per cent. | 10 per cent. | 18 per cent. |
|---|---|---|---|
| 1,000 | 3.8 | 2.5 | 0.5 |
| 2,000 | 7.3 | 4.9 | 1.0 |
| 3,000 | 10.5 | 7.0 | 1.4 |
| 3,200 | 11.1 | 7.5 | 1.5 |

[1] The figures include consequential effects on the yield of capital gains tax.

## Tax Burden

**Mr. Betts:** To ask the Chancellor of the Exchequer if he will set out in the form of table 4A9 of the Financial Statement and Budget Report 1995–96, revised tables, what the average ratio is if non-North sea taxes and national insurance contributions to non-North sea gross domestic product for *(a)* 1965–66 to 1969–70, *(b)* 1970–71 to 1973–74, *(c)* 1974–75 to 1978–79 and *(d)* 1979–80 to 1996–97. [21759]

**Sir George Young** *[holding answer 28 April 1995]:* The figures requested are *(a)* $34\frac{1}{4}$ per cent., *(b)* $34\frac{3}{4}$ per cent., *(c)* 36 per cent. and *(d)* 37 per cent. But the tax burden should not be looked at alone. Since 1979 the public finances have been in much better shape and people are much better off than in the period 1974–75 to 1978–79.

The average public sector borrowing requirement has been 2.5 per cent. of gross domestic product well below the 6.8 per cent. average during the 1974–77 to 1978–79 Government. Sound public finances are the key to lasting improvements in living standards.

## VAT on Fuel

**Mr. Frank Field:** To ask the Chancellor of the Exchequer if he will estimate the amount which will be raised from VAT on domestic fuel in 1995–96, 1996–97 and 1997–98 at its present rate of 8 per cent. [24366]

**Mr. Heathcoat-Amory:** The total revenue raised from the introduction of VAT on domestic fuel is estimated to be as follows:

| Year | £ million |
|---|---|
| 1995–96 | 1,230 |
| 1996–97 | 1,320 |
| 1997–98 | 1,325 |

## Publicity

**Mr. Malcolm Bruce:** To ask the Chancellor of the Exchequer what was the total expenditure on *(a)* all forms of publicity and *(b)* all publications and pamphlets produced for his Department and for all the agencies and public bodies for which his Department and is responsible for each year since 1979, including the budgeted figure for 1995–96, (i) including and (ii) excluding privatization-related expenditures and expressed in 1994 prices; and if he will supply information for the period from 1 April 1993 to 1 March 1995 showing (1) the nature and (2) the purpose of each publicity campaign and of each publication involving the expenditure of more than £50,000.

**Mr. Nelson** *[holding answer 17 March 1995]:* The Treasury has no central budget for publications. Expenditure on publications and pamphlets since 1988–89 was as follows:

| Year | Expenditure | £ At 1994 prices |
|---|---|---|
| 1988–89 | 202,700 | 272,197 |
| 1989–90 | 207,285 | 260,136 |
| 1990–91 | 218,531 | 253,854 |
| 1991–92 | 139,865 | 161,892 |
| 1992–93 | 171,311 | 180,090 |
| 1993–94 | 202,719 | 206,773 |
| 1994–95 | 238,139 | 238,139 |

No individual publication between 1993 to 1995 cost more than £50,000.

Comparable data relating to the agencies and public bodies responsible to the Chancellor of the Exchequer could be obtained only at disproportionate cost.

The Treasury does not have a specific advertising budget. Since 1993, £8.1 million has been spent on advertising the sale of the Government's remaining share in the electricity generating companies in England and Wales.

Information about publicity costs since 1979 including publications and pamphlets, for the Treasury and the Chancellor's agencies and public bodies, could only be obtained at disproportionate cost.

## Unleaded Fuel

**Mr. Wray:** To ask the Chancellor of the Exchequer if he will undertake a review of the excise differential favouring unleaded and super-unleaded fuels. [24182]

**Mr. Heathcoat-Amory** *[holding answer 15 May 1995]:* My right hon. and learned Friend will be reviewing the tax treatment of all road fuels in the run-up to the budget in the normal way.

## FOREIGN AND COMMONWEALTH AFFAIRS

### Malaysia

**Miss Lestor:** To ask the Secretary of State for Foreign and Commonwealth Affairs between which dates in March and April 1989 the Secretary of State for Defence visited Malaysia; which Malaysian Government Ministers he met; and if aid funding for Malaysia was discussed during that visit.     [22675]

**Mr. Goodlad:** My right hon. and noble Friend Lord Younger, while Secretary of State for Defence, paid a visit to Malaysia on 31 March 1989 as part of a tour of the region. He met the Malaysian Ministers of Defence and Finance. The purpose of his visit was to discuss defence matters, but it is normal for a Cabinet Minister on such visits to discuss any important outstanding issues. In a general discussion on bilateral issues with the Finance Minister, he asked about progress on two planned civil infrastructure projects for which aid and trade provision support had been offered—the Pergau dam and another project not in the event won by a British firm.

### Nuclear Weapons

**Mr. Llew Smith:** To ask the Secretary of State for Foreign and Commonwealth Affairs what assessment he has made of the report on dual capable nuclear technology, prepared by John Large, sent to him by Greenpeace on 4 May; and what response he has made to the questions raised about United Kingdom nuclear export policy in the report.     [24399]

**Mr. David Davis:** I have seen the report sent to the Foreign Secretary by Greenpeace. It points to dangers of which we are aware, but it underestimates the complexities of developing nuclear weapons. I am satisfied that our nuclear export policy meets our obligations under the nuclear non-proliferation treaty not to assist, encourage or induce non-weapon states to manufacture or otherwise acquire nuclear weapons.

### Brazil

**Mr. Corbyn:** To ask the Secretary of State for Foreign and Commonwealth Affairs what representations he has made to the Brazilian President on his recent visit to the United Kingdom, regarding human rights abuses and in particular the case of Wagnor dos Santos.     [24487]

**Mr. David Davis:** The Brazilian Government are well aware of the concern felt in Britain about human rights abuses. We are in regular touch with them.

**Mr. Corbyn:** To ask the Secretary of State for Foreign and Commonwealth Affairs if he will seek assurances that the safety of Wagnor dos Santos will be safeguarded by the Brazilian authorities and that the shooting of him will be investigated with a view to bringing those responsible to justice.     [24488]

**Mr. David Davis:** We understand that the case of Wagnor dos Santos is under investigation by the Brazilian authorities. Our embassy is monitoring developments.

### Immigration

**Dr. Kim Howells:** To ask the Secretary of State for Foreign and Commonwealth Affairs how many entry clearance applications were (1) made, (2) granted and (3) refused in (a) New York, (b) Moscow, (c) St. Petersburg, (d) Accra, (e) Lagos, (f) Abuja, (g) New Delhi, (h) Bombay. (j) Calcutta, (k) Madras, (l) Dhaka, (m) Islamabad, (n) Karachi and (o) Colombo in the financial years (i) 1992–93, (ii) 1993–94 and (iii) 1994–95 to the latest convenient date.     [22648]

**Mr. Baldry** *[holding answer 9 May 1995]:* During 1992, 1993 and 1994 calendar years the number of UK entry clearance applications 1) made, 2) granted and 3) refused in the posts listed was as follows:

| | 1992 | | | 1993 | | | 1994 | | |
|---|---|---|---|---|---|---|---|---|---|
| | *Applied* | *Issued* | *Refused* | *Applied* | *Issued* | *Refused* | *Applied* | *Issued* | *Refused* |
| a) New York | 15,425 | 15,033 | 157 | 17,498 | 17,312 | 130 | 18,726 | 18,559 | 110 |
| b) Moscow | 50,303 | 49,732 | 1,502 | 61,367 | 59,743 | 1,624 | 86,661 | 84,761 | 1,900 |
| c) St. Petersburg | — | — | — | 1,429 | 1,313 | 116 | 16,622 | 15,820 | 607 |
| d) Accra | 16,699 | 11,507 | 5,048 | 15,753 | 11,051 | 4,094 | 16,130 | 11,684 | 3,825 |
| e) Lagos | 47,181 | 31,552 | 11,145 | 44,526 | 29,447 | 9,894 | 49,176 | 32,411 | 10,529 |
| f) Abuja | — | — | — | — | — | — | 6,113 | 4,955 | 655 |
| g) New Delhi | 39,291 | 32,261 | 3,464 | 37,148 | 31,652 | 3,708 | 43,258 | 35,857 | 7,373 |
| h) Bombay | 38,913 | 34,905 | 4,301 | 37,988 | 34,125 | 3,785 | 43,425 | 39,924 | 3,342 |
| j) Calcutta | 7,156 | 6,538 | 232 | 6,826 | 6,491 | 253 | 7,308 | 7,139 | 153 |
| k) Madras | 10,363 | 10,079 | 291 | 10,348 | 10,043 | 247 | 12,807 | 12,624 | 204 |
| l) Dhaka | 18,414 | 14,043 | 3,901 | 19,359 | 14,990 | 4,447 | 20,861 | 14,615 | 5,892 |
| m) Islamabad | 45,625 | 31,611 | 10,791 | 41,485 | 30,715 | 9,526 | 42,445 | 29,850 | 10,018 |
| n) Karachi | 23,397 | 19,169 | 2,610 | 24,368 | 20,712 | 2,181 | 28,266 | 22,921 | 2,516 |
| p) Colombo | 9,026 | 7,139 | 1,172 | 9,200 | 7,937 | 874 | 9,969 | 7,610 | 821 |

It should be noted that St. Petersburg started entry clearance work in November 1993 and Abuja in February 1994.

### Nigeria

**Mr. Wray:** To ask the Secretary of State for Foreign and Commonwealth Affairs if he will make a statement on the latest political developments in Nigeria.     [24183]

**Mr. Baldry** *[holding answer 15 May 1995]:* The national constitutional conference is expected to present its report to the Nigerian Government in June. We urge the authorities to respond quickly to the conference recommendations and announce their plans for the next stage of the political process, including a credible timetable for an early transition to civilian democratic rule.

## Sierra Leone

**Mr. Llew Smith:** To ask the Secretary of State for Foreign and Commonwealth Affairs what steps have been taken to prevent the recruitment of mercenaries, including former members of the British armed forces, by the Government of Sierra Leone.   [24296]

**Mr. Baldry** [*holding answer 15 May 1995*]: The recruitment of mercenaries of whatever nationality is a matter for the Government of Sierra Leone.

## Rwanda and Burundi

**Mr. Ottaway:** To ask the Secretary of State for Foreign and Commonwealth Affairs what action he is taking to strengthen the United Kingdom's diplomatic representation in Rwanda and Burundi.   [24916]

**Mr. Baldry:** We have informed the Government of Rwanda of our intention to replace the British Government's liaison office in Kigali with an embassy as soon as protocol and staffing formalities permit. We have also established a temporary office in Bujumbura staffed by a diplomatic service officer.

# TRANSPORT

## Gospel Oak to Barking Line

**Mr. Corbyn:** To ask the Secretary of State for Transport when resignalling of part of the Gospel Oak–Barking line to replace obsolete semaphore and colour light signalling will be undertaken.   [24490]

**Mr. Norris:** I understand form Railtrack there are no current plans to replace the signalling equipment on the Barking–Gospel Oak line.

**Mr. Corbyn:** To ask the Secretary of State for Transport what assessment has been made of the condition of railway viaducts and over-bridges on the north London line, between Gospel Oak and Camden Road stations; if they are able to carry heavy freight trains with special reference to the Mendip rail aggregate trains; what restrictions are currently being imposed on the section of railway between Gospel Oak and Camden Road; and what remedial works are required on the viaducts and over-bridges in the Kentish Town area to permit all freight trains to traverse the line.   [24489]

**Mr. Norris:** Railtrack inform me that work is now under way on the arch at Kentish Town. This is due to be completed in mid-June and there can then be a resumption of freight traffic. Railtrack is at the moment carrying out a complete structural survey of the north London line.

**Mr. Corbyn:** To ask the Secretary of State for Transport if passenger services over the Gospel Oak–Barking line are delayed more than 30 seconds when freight trains are diverted over the line; and if passenger trains are cancelled to avoid Railtrack Anglia incurring financial penalties from the freight train operators.   [24491]

**Mr. Norris:** Railtrack is required to treat both freight and passenger operators fairly. I understand from Railtrack that no passenger trains have been cancelled to avoid Railtrack incurring financial penalties. All train operators are entitled to penalty payments from Railtrack if their services are delayed.

**Mr. Corbyn:** To ask the Secretary of State for Transport how much are the penalties imposed on Railtrack when passenger trains are cancelled on the Gospel Oak–Barking line.   [24492]

**Mr. Norris:** Penalties for the cancellation of trains are payable under the existing track access agreement and are a commercial matter between Railtrack, the train operating unit and the British Railways Board. I understand that a new performance regime is currently being negotiated between the British Railways Board, the Office of Passenger Rail Franchising and Railtrack, and will be subject to the approval of the Rail Regulator.

## Severn Tunnel

**Mr. Flynn:** To ask the Secretary of State for Transport what plans his Department has for the temporary or permanent closure of the Severn tunnel.   [24485]

**Mr. Watts:** There are no plans for the temporary or permanent closure of the Severn tunnel.

## Road Accidents

**Mr. Burden:** To ask the Secretary of State for Transport how many casualties have been killed, seriously injured and slightly injured on (*a*) A-class non-trunks roads, (*b*) trunk roads and (*c*) motorways for each year since 1990 in (i) England and (ii) in the United Kingdom as a whole.   [24452]

**Mr. Norris:** The information requested is shown in the following table. Figures are given for England and Great Britain as equivalent data for Northern Ireland are not available.

*Road accident casualties by severity and road type in England and Great Britain: 1990–93*

| | Non-trunk A-roads | | | Trunk roads | | | Motorways | | |
|---|---|---|---|---|---|---|---|---|---|
| | Killed | Seriously injured | Slightly injured | Killed | Seriously injured | Slightly injured | Killed | Seriously injured | Slightly injured |
| *England* | | | | | | | | | |
| 1990 | 1,781 | 19,078 | 92,325 | 804 | 5,781 | 23,818 | 211 | 1,500 | 8,255 |
| 1991 | 1,604 | 16,441 | 85,628 | 649 | 4,650 | 21,363 | 208 | 1,272 | 7,775 |
| 1992 | 1,435 | 15,844 | 87,383 | 594 | 4,225 | 21,562 | 219 | 1,214 | 8,408 |
| 1993 | 1,374 | 14,724 | 89,209 | 526 | 3,853 | 20,712 | 181 | 1,233 | 8,912 |
| *Great Britain* | | | | | | | | | |
| 1990 | 2,088 | 22,079 | 103,950 | 1,023 | 7,423 | 28,800 | 229 | 1,643 | 8,969 |
| 1991 | 1,855 | 19,160 | 96,429 | 848 | 6,165 | 26,086 | 234 | 1,394 | 8,377 |
| 1992 | 1,671 | 18,407 | 97,790 | 792 | 5,575 | 25,852 | 238 | 1,338 | 9,046 |
| 1993 | 1,589 | 16,871 | 99,160 | 689 | 5,035 | 24,933 | 201 | 1,338 | 9,507 |

## Pedestrian Deaths and Injuries

**Mr. Burden:** To ask the Secretary of State for Transport (1) what were the national quarterly figures for *(a)* pedestrian deaths, (b) pedestrian serious injuries, and *(c)* pedestrian slight injuries for people aged 60 years and over for the period 1990 to 1993; [24453]

(2) what were the national quarterly figures for *(a)* pedestrian deaths, *(b)* pedestrian serious injuries, and *(c)* pedestrian slight injuries for people aged 60 years and over for his Department's baseline years of 1981 and 1985. [24455]

**Mr. Norris:** The information requested is shown in the following table.

*Pedestrian casualties aged 60 and over*

| | | | | | Number of casualties |
|---|---|---|---|---|---|
| | | Fatal | Serious | Slight | Total |
| 1981 | | 947 | 3,912 | 6,334 | 11,193 |
| 1985 | | 869 | 3,866 | 6,060 | 10,795 |
| 1981–1985 Average | | 895.6 | 3,908.8 | 6,340.0 | 11,144.4 |
| 1990 | Quarter 1 | 254 | 968 | 1,806 | 3,028 |
| | Quarter 2 | 167 | 642 | 1,369 | 2,178 |
| | Quarter 3 | 141 | 692 | 1,387 | 2,220 |
| | Quarter 4 | 277 | 1,115 | 1,879 | 3,271 |
| | Total | 839 | 3,417 | 6,441 | 10,697 |
| 1991 | Quarter 1 | 178 | 812 | 1,488 | 2,478 |
| | Quarter 2 | 128 | 619 | 1,308 | 2,055 |
| | Quarter 3 | 172 | 661 | 1,362 | 2,195 |
| | Quarter 4 | 276 | 990 | 1,704 | 2,970 |
| | Total | 754 | 3,082 | 5,862 | 9,698 |
| 1992 | Quarter 1 | 172 | 767 | 1,320 | 2,259 |
| | Quarter 2 | 120 | 545 | 1,170 | 1,835 |
| | Quarter 3 | 156 | 559 | 1,203 | 1,918 |
| | Quarter 4 | 230 | 924 | 1,655 | 2,809 |
| | Total | 678 | 2,795 | 5,348 | 8,821 |
| 1993 | Quarter 1 | 171 | 646 | 1,298 | 2,115 |
| | Quarter 2 | 102 | 515 | 1,168 | 1,785 |
| | Quarter 3 | 119 | 572 | 1,166 | 1,857 |
| | Quarter 4 | 240 | 858 | 1,560 | 2,658 |
| | Total | 632 | 2,591 | 5,192 | 8,415 |

**Mr. Burden:** To ask the Secretary of State for Transport what were the quarterly figures for *(a)* pedestrian deaths, *(b)* pedestrian serious injuries and *(c)* pedestrian slight injuries for people aged 60 years and over in Birmingham for the period 1990 to 1993. [24456]

**Mr. Norris:** The information requested is shown in the following table.

| Year | Quarter | Fatal | Severity Serious | Slight | Total |
|---|---|---|---|---|---|
| 1990 | Q1 | 1 | 23 | 42 | 66 |
| | Q2 | 9 | 17 | 22 | 48 |
| | Q3 | 2 | 7 | 26 | 35 |
| | Q4 | 7 | 25 | 40 | 72 |
| 1991 | Q1 | 5 | 23 | 34 | 62 |
| | Q2 | 2 | 14 | 32 | 48 |
| | Q3 | 3 | 17 | 37 | 57 |
| | Q4 | 6 | 27 | 28 | 61 |
| 1992 | Q1 | 6 | 18 | 36 | 60 |
| | Q2 | 5 | 12 | 46 | 63 |
| | Q3 | 3 | 16 | 30 | 49 |
| | Q4 | 6 | 24 | 47 | 77 |
| 1993 | Q1 | 3 | 19 | 22 | 44 |
| | Q2 | 1 | 9 | 31 | 41 |
| | Q3 | 4 | 19 | 21 | 44 |
| | Q4 | 6 | 26 | 42 | 74 |
| Annual totals | | | | | |
| 1990 | | 19 | 72 | 130 | 221 |
| 1991 | | 16 | 81 | 131 | 228 |
| 1992 | | 20 | 70 | 159 | 249 |
| 1993 | | 14 | 73 | 116 | 203 |

## Kiwi Arrow and Pelander Collision

**Mr. Barry Field:** To ask the Secretary of State for Transport what reports he has received of the collision off the Isle of Wight between the Kiwi Arrow and the Pelander; what were the weather conditions at the time of the collision; what assessment he has made of the bearing the Donaldson report has on the circumstances of this collision; what reports he has had from the port authorities where these two ships docked; if he intends to hold an inquiry; what representations he will be making to the International Maritime Organisation about this accident; what representations he is making to the ship registers of the two vessels; what reports he has received from his inspectors about these two vessels; what reports he has received from Her Majesty's Coastguard about this incident; and if he will make a statement. [23780]

**Mr. Norris:** At the time of the collision between Kiwi Arrow and Pelander the sea was calm and visibility was approximately five nautical miles. The Solent coastguard responded immediately to the distress call, but both ships were able to proceed to Southampton under their own power. Two surveyors from the Marine Safety Agency carried out a port state control inspection of both ships to examine the damage.

As the incident occurred outside the United Kingdom's territorial waters and involved non-UK registered ships, the responsibility for accident investigation rests with the flag states of the Kiwi Arrow and Pelander. However, an inspector from the Marine Accident Investigation Branch visited the ships when in Southampton to obtain background information concerning the incident which has been sent to both administrations.

The flag states have been asked to advise of the outcome of an investigation into the causes of this accident. Under the provisions of the international conventions, any representations made to the International Maritime Organisation on the circumstances of this collision will be a matter for the flag states. The flag states have been asked to inform the MSA of the measures they intend to take to ensure that the ships comply with international requirements before departure. Neither ship will be permitted to leave Southampton until the MSA is satisfied that they are fit to proceed to sea.

Until the full facts of this incident are known and its causes established, it would be premature to make an assessment of any bearing the Donaldson report might have on the circumstances of the incident.

**Mr. Barry Field:** To ask the Secretary of State for Transport what contact his Department has had with the French marine authorities about the collision between the Kiwi Arrow and the Pelander off the Isle of Wight; and what joint action channel marine countries and authorities can take to prevent incidents of this type. [23781]

**Mr. Norris:** The collision was in the UK search and rescue region and the immediate response was coordinated accordingly by Solent coastguard. No assistance was sought from the French authorities because UK lifeboats and other vessels were in the vicinity and were available to render adequate assistance.

No contact with the French has been made since because neither Kiwi Arrow nor Pelander is registered under the French flag and the accident occurred in international waters.

The UK Government and marine authorities will continue to work closely with all our European partners, including our counterparts in the channel, in order to seek to eliminate incidents of this nature and to minimise the pollution of the seas and endangerment of life at sea. My Department, through the Coastguard Agency and the Marine Safety Agency, maintains regular contact with the French authorities about safety, search and rescue and counter-pollution matters in the English channel.

### Heavy Goods Vehicles

**Mr. Redmond:** To ask the Secretary of State for Transport how many foreign HGVs were *(a)* stopped for safety checks, *(b)* found defective and *(c)* not permitted to continue in each of the last three years. [24039]

**Mr. Norris:** The number of foreign HGVs inspected at the roadside and prohibited from use because of defects likely to cause danger of injury is as follows:

| Year | Foreign HGVs inspected at roadside | Immediate prohibitions issued (defect likely to cause danger of injury) |
|---|---|---|
| 1994–95 | 5,575 | 310 |
| 1993–94 | 6,060 | 230 |
| 1992–93 | 6,175 | 413 |

Delayed prohibitions are not issued to foreign vehicles.

### Passenger Boats

**Mr. Hawksley:** To ask the Secretary of State for Transport what assessment he has made of the consequences of the implementation of regulations introduced by the Marine Safety Agency on passenger-carrying boats on narrow, shallow canals; what account was taken of the existing safety record; and if he will make a statement. [24145]

**Mr. Norris:** This is an operational matter for the Marine Safety Agency. I have asked the chief executive to write to my hon. Friend.

*Letter from R. M. Bradley to Mr. Warren Hawksley, dated 16 May 1995:*

The Secretary of State for Transport has asked me to reply to your Question about the regulations for passenger carrying vessels on narrow, shallow canals.

New regulations for passenger vessels operating on inland waterways were introduced in 1992 following an extensive consultation exercise. As a result of the consultation the inland waterways were split into four categories, the required survivability standard and scale of safety equipment varies according to the risk associated with the category of water.

Passenger vessels of the type you have asked are in the least onerous category, narrow waterways with a depth of water of up to 1.5 metres. The requirements applied to these vessels were not significantly changed.

The MSA is currently assessing all merchant shipping regulations as part of the Government initiative on deregulation. This will include the safety requirements for small passenger vessels.

### Herald of Free Enterprise

**Mr. Flynn:** To ask the Secretary of State for Transport (1) which are the two long-term recommendations of the Herald of Free Enterprise inquiry that have not been implemented; and why there were considered unnecessary; [22908]

(2) which are the two long-term recommendations of the Herald of Free Enterprise inquiry that have been implemented in alternative ways, and what these are. [22911]

**Mr. Norris** *[holding answer 9 April 1995]:* The two long-term recommendations of the court of inquiry which were not implemented because they were considered unnecessary were the recommendation that roll-on roll-off passenger ferries should have dedicated pumps capable of stripping at a rate of at least 600 tonnes an hour and that there should be drain valves which must be controlled remotely and operable from the bridge.

Both recommendations were considered, but after consultation were felt to be unnecessary because, in practice, existing drainage arrangements could already cope with amounts of water approaching these levels. Moreover, pumps of the size recommended could not cope with the significantly larger volume of water involved in catastrophic flooding as occurred on the Herald of Free Enterprise and, indeed, on the Estonia. There may also be difficulties in guaranteeing power supplies in situations of catastrophic flooding. Automatic drain valves are now fitted as a matter of course, so there is no need for their remote control.

The two long-term recommendations implemented in alternative ways were the recommendations that the freeboard from the margin line to the vehicle deck should be increased to a minimum of perhaps 1 m, and that attention should be given to achieving substantially higher downflooding angles. These recommendations were addressed through an extensive research programme and the subsequent adoption of the SOLAS 90 survivability standard for existing ships.

### Land Compensation Act

**Mr. Chidgey:** To ask the Secretary of State for Transport what procedures the Highways Agency follows to inform affected individuals of their right to make retrospective claims under part I of the Land Compensation Act 1973, as amended, in respect of any depreciation of more than £50 in the value of certain interests in land caused by the use of new or altered highways and resulting from specified physical factors. [23797]

**Mr. Watts:** This is an operational matter for the Highways Agency. I have asked the chief executive to write to the hon. member.

*Letter from Lawrie Haynes to Mr. David Chidgey, dated 16 May 1995:*

As you know, the Minister for Railways and Roads, Mr John Watts, has asked me to reply to your Parliamentary Question asking the Secretary of State for Transport what procedures the Highways Agency follows to inform affected individuals of their right to make retrospective claims under Part I of the Land Compensation Act 1973 in respect of depreciation in value of interests in land caused by the use of new or altered highways.

The Highways Agency places public notices in the local press at the date of opening of a new or altered road and again shortly before the first date when owners are entitled by the legislation to make Part I claims, which is one year after the road opens. General press releases are also issued.

The Highways Agency also draws attention to the entitlement of owners to make Part I claims in its booklet "Your Home and Trunk Road Proposals" which is made available at public consultations and exhibitions about scheme proposals. This booklet draws attention to further guidance which is available in other booklets and from Highways Agency offices of the particular circumstances which may affect an individual owner's entitlement to claim and action which they should take, if, for example, they wish to sell their property before the date when claims can be accepted.

Special consideration for ex-gratia payment is given to any claims which are made outside the statutory claim period (more than seven years after the road is opened) if it can be shown that initial advertising was inadequate, or there were convincing reasons why an owner could not have submitted a claim which was valid under the statutory provisions.

**Mr. Chidgey:** To ask the Secretary of State for Transport if the Highways Agency sends individual letters to affected individuals informing them of their right to make retrospective claims under part I of the Land Compensation Act 1973, as amended, in respect of any depreciation of more than £50 in the value of certain interests in land caused by the use of new or altered highways and resulting from specified physical factors. [23798]

**Mr. Watts:** This is an operational matter for the Highways Agency. I have asked the chief executive to write to the hon. Member.

*Letter from Lawrie Haynes to Mr. David Chidgey, dated 16 May 1995:*

As you know, the Minister for Railways and Roads, Mr John Watts, has asked me to reply to your Parliamentary Question asking the Secretary of State for Transport if the Highways Agency sends individual letters to affected individuals informing them of their right to make retrospective claims under Part I of the Land Compensation Act 1973 in respect of depreciation in value of interests in land caused by the use of new or altered highways.

The Highways Agency does not send letters to individuals in these circumstances as it is not practicable to attempt to identify every individual who may be entitled to claim. I have explained the existing arrangements publicising the entitlement of owners to claim in my answer to your Parliamentary Question reference 1684/94/95.

We understand that local agents may also contact individual owners, advise them of their entitlements and submit claims on their behalf. The Highways Agency reimburses the cost of any agents fees incurred in submitting a valid claim.

### Ferry Safety

**Mr. Flynn:** To ask the Secretary of State for Transport what assumptions were made in the SOLAS 90 standards for evacuation of roll-on/roll-off ferries of the percentage of passengers who are *(a)* disabled, *(b)* infants, *(c)* drunk, *(d)* wheelchair bound and *(e)* asleep when the emergency occurs. [24483]

**Mr. Norris:** This is an operational matter for the Marine Safety Agency. I have asked the chief executive to write to the hon. Member.

*Letter from R. M. Bradley to Mr. Paul Flynn, dated 16 May 1995:*

The Secretary of State has asked me to reply to your recent Parliamentary Question about the evacuation of various categories of passengers from roll-on-roll-off ferries.

There is no specific reference in the Solas 90 standard as to what percentage of passengers may fall into any of the categories listed in your question. However, minimum training requirements for personnel nominated to assist passengers in emergency situations have been established and are promulgated by way of a Merchant Shipping Notice.

### Road Use

**Mr. Burden:** To ask the Secretary of State for Transport what has the total mileage been of *(a)* all A class non-trunk road, *(b)* all trunk roads and *(c)* all motorways, in each year since 1990 for (i) England and (ii) the United Kingdom as a whole. [24454]

**Mr. Norris:** The table sets out the road length figures by road type for 1990 to 1994.

*miles*

| | A Class Non-trunk | | Trunk | | Motorway | |
|---|---|---|---|---|---|---|
| | England | UK | England | UK | England | UK |
| 1990 | 15,445 | 23,125 | 5,085 | 7,965 | 1,673 | 1,977 |
| 1991 | 15,728 | 23,393 | 4,888 | 7,768 | 1,692 | 1,995 |
| 1992 | 15,748 | 23,424 | 4,890 | 7,754 | 1,699 | 2,016 |
| 1993 | 15,815 | 23,478 | 4,836 | 7,694 | 1,700 | 2,021 |
| 1994 | 15,891 | 23,551 | 4,792 | 7,641 | 1,705 | 2,044 |

*Note:*

Roads in Northern Ireland are not classified in the same way as the rest of Great Britain. Therefore the figures provided for the United Kingdom include the lengths of class 1(A) single carriageway roads and class 1(A) dual carriage roads in Northern Ireland as A class non-trunk roads and trunk roads respectively.

### Driving Standards Agency

**Ms Walley:** To ask the Secretary of State for Transport if he will make a statement on the salary details for the newly appointed chief executive of the Driving Standards Agency and details of any bonus or performance pay schemes. [24424]

**Mr. Norris:** The chief executive of the Driving Standards Agency was appointed on 1 April 1995 at a salary of £58,000 per annum. He is also eligible for an annual performance bonus of up to 15 per cent. of salary.

### Rural Economy

**Mr. Colvin:** To ask the Secretary of State for Transport what is his estimate of the net annual financial saving, or cost, of his Department's submission for the proposed White Paper on the rural economy. [24326]

**Mr. Norris:** Proposals for the White Paper on the rural economy remain subject to continuing collective consideration and discussion. The cost of measures contained in the White Paper will be taken into account in the public expenditure survey.

## Highways Agency

**Ms Walley:** To ask the Secretary of State for Transport if the chief executive of the Highways Agency has received either a performance related bonus or any pay increase since his appointment. [24428]

**Mr. Norris:** The chief executive of the Highways Agency received a 2.5 per cent. pay increase on 1 April 1995. He has received no other pay increase since his appointment. He is, however, eligible for a performance bonus of up to 20 per cent. of salary for the year ending 31 March 1995. This has not yet been assessed.

## OVERSEAS DEVELOPMENT ADMINISTRATION

### Aid and Trade Provision

**Ms Lestor:** To ask the Secretary of State for Foreign and Commonwealth Affairs if he will list aid and trade programme supported projects, since 1993, by country, purpose, all companies involved, and value. [23183]

**Mr. Baldry:** A list of all the companies involved in ATP projects on which ATP agreements have been concluded since 1993 has been placed in the Library of the House.

### Rwanda

**Mr. Worthington:** To ask the Secretary of State for Foreign and Commonwealth Affairs what is his policy in respect of the plan of the European Commission to suspend rehabilitation assistance to Rwanda. [23613]

**Mr. Baldry:** Some aspects of the EC's longer-term aid plans have been temporarily suspended pending the outcome of the Kibeho inquiry. But at our insistence there will be no immediate effect on humanitarian aid, all planned health and education assistance, support for human rights monitoring and the rule of law. The suspension will therefore have little immediate effect. There will be a review at the Development Council on 1 June which my noble Friend the Minister for Overseas Development will attend.

### China

**Mr. MacShane:** To ask the Secretary of State for Foreign and Commonwealth Affairs what protests the United Kingdom has been made to China in respect of *(a)* compulsory abortion policies, *(b)* compulsory sterilisation policies, *(c)* proposed eugenics legislation and *(d)* treatment of women under Chinese legislation since 1990. [23697]

**Mr. Baldry:** We frequently raise with the Chinese authorities our concerns over human rights abuses in China. My right hon. Friend the Secretary of State for Foreign and Commonwealth Affairs raised the issue during his talks with the Chinese Foreign Minister and Vice Premier in New York on 18 April. My right hon. Friend the Minister of State my right hon. Friend the Member for Eddisbury (Mr. Goodlad), also discussed this issue with the Chinese Vice Foreign Minister when he visited China in July last year.

## DUCHY OF LANCASTER

### Science Budget

**Mrs. Angela Knight:** To ask the Chancellor of the Duchy of Lancaster when he expects the Director General of the Research Councils to publish his review of the science budget portfolio; and if he will make a statement. [24367]

**Mr. David Hunt:** I have today placed copies of the Director General's review in the Libraries of both Houses. In addition, I have placed in the libraries copies of the research councils' own analyses of the strengths and weakness of the UK science and engineering base and a summary of the centres that the director general visited and the organisations that he met.

This is an excellent assessment of the state of science and engineering research in Britain today. It shows that we have major strengths in many areas and that we are continuing to build on those strengths for the benefit of Britain and British industry. Although there are no serious problems in the science and engineering base, the review exposes some weaknesses and describes the corrective action taken in the expenditure allocations I announced on 2 February 1995.

### Fluoridation

**Mr. Chidgey:** To ask the Chancellor of the Duchy of Lancaster what research has been carried out by the Medical Research Council into the impact of fluoride on *(a)* the bone structure of children and adults, *(b)* the immune system and *(c)* the incidence of hip fractures. [23737]

**Mr. Horam:** The Medical Research Council is not currently funding any research in these areas.

However, in 1990, scientists at the MRC environmental epidemiology unit in Southampton published findings showing that water fluoridation up to levels of around 1 mg/litre was unlikely to reduce hip fracture incidence. Also, in December 1993, the MRC set up an ad hoc working group to review the evidence regarding the possible effects of fluoridation of public water supply on the incidence of osteoporosis and to suggest guidelines for the formulation of scientific strategy in this field. The working group highlighted the need to establish accurate estimates of total fluoride intake in any future studies.

The MRC is willing to consider high quality research proposals in these areas, in competition with those in other fields.

## PRIME MINISTER

### Engagements

**Mr. Harry Greenway:** To ask the Prime Minister if he will list his official engagements for Tuesday 2 May 1995. [23165]

**Sir Peter Tapsell:** To ask the Prime Minister if he will list his official engagements for Tuesday 16 May. [23164]

**The Prime Minister:** This morning I had meetings with ministerial colleagues and others. In addition to my duties in this House, I shall be having further meetings later today.

### Lockerbie

**Mr. Dalyell:** To ask the Prime Minister if he will raise at the United Nations the letter of 20 February from the Bundesminsterium der Justig to Mrs. Lisa Mosey of Glossop, relating to the Lockerbie bombing, a copy of which has been sent to him. [24499]

**The Prime Minister:** No.

### Review Bodies

**Mr. Shersby:** To ask the Prime Minister if he will list the current membership of the School Teachers Review Body and the Review Body on Doctors and Dentists Remuneration. [24874]

**The Prime Minster:** The current membership, with effect from 1 April 1995, is as follows:

*Review Body on Doctors and Dentists Remuneration*
Mr. Brandon Gough (Chairman)
Ms Christina Boyden
Miss Sally Field
Dr. Elizabeth Nelson
Mr. David Penton
Mr. Michael Innes
Mr. John Bennigsen
Mrs. Beryl Brewer
*School Teachers Review Body*
Mr. John Gardiner (Chairman)
Mrs. Brigita Amey
Mrs. Gill Rostron
Mrs. Anna Vinton
Mr. Michael Harding
Mrs. Julia Cuthbertson
Mr. Phillip Halsey CB LVO
Mrs. Elizabeth Drummond
Sir Alan Cox CBE

### Lady Cobham

**Mr. Redmond:** To ask the Prime Minister how many quangos Lady Cobham has been appointed to; and if he will list them; and what salary is paid to her in respect of each appointment. [24144]

**The Prime Minister:** According to the information available to the public appointments unit, Lady Cobham currently holds four ministerial appointments to public bodies as follows:

| Body | Post | Salary |
|---|---|---|
| London Docklands development corporation | Member | £6,830 |
| Museum and Galleries Commission | Member | Unpaid |
| Victoria and Albert museum | Trustee | Unpaid |
| Historic Palaces advisory group | Member | Unpaid |

### Hong Kong

**Mr. McMaster:** To ask the Prime Minister what is his latest assessment of the potential to maintain and develop trade links with Hong Kong in future years; what action is being taken by Her Majesty's Government to encourage inward investment from and outward investment to Hong Kong; and if he will make a statement.    [24130]

**The Prime Minister:** Hong Kong is our 12th largest market and I expect trading links to continue at this level well into the future. The Department of Trade and Industry maintains a strong promotional programme to encourage British business to take full advantage of the opportunities Hong Kong offers. British investment in Hong Kong, which is very substantial, continues to grow. The Department of Trade and Industry's Invest in Britain Bureau has recently established an office In Hong Kong to encourage greater flows of investment from the Asia Pacific, including Hong Kong.

### Former Prime Ministers

**Mr. McMaster:** To ask the Prime Minister what *(a)* allowances and *(b)* facilities are currently available to former Prime Ministers who serve in (i) either or (ii) neither House of Parliament.    [24014]

**The Prime Minister:** In addition to the normal allowances for which they are eligible as members of either House of Parliament, former Prime Ministers receive a financial allowance to help meet the continuing additional office costs which they are liable to incur because of their special positions in public life. This allowance is payable in respect of actual office and secretarial expenses incurred in connection with public duties arising from their previous tenure of the office of Prime Minister, up to an amount equal to that of the parliamentary office costs allowance. The allowance is not payable to a former Prime Minister occupying the position of Leader of the Opposition and therefore in receipt of Short money.

Other facilities available to all former Prime Ministers are: physical protection, as necessary; the use of an official car; access to the official papers of their Administration. Briefing and help from local posts may also be provided in connection with overseas visits.

### Public Bodies

**Mr. Flynn:** To ask the Prime Minister which non-departmental bodies within the responsibility of his Department are subject to scrutiny by *(a)* the ombudsmen, *(b)* the National Audit Office, *(c)* the Audit Commission and *(d)* other monitoring officers; which are covered by the citizens charters; in which performance indicators apply; and in which members are liable to surcharge.    [23966]

**The Prime Minister** *[holding answer 15 May 1995]:* None.

## LORD CHANCELLOR'S DEPARTMENT

### Legal Aid

**Mr. Boateng:** To ask the Parliamentary Secretary, Lord Chancellor's Department if he will publish the rules on capital, income and contributions governing eligibility for *(a)* criminal legal aid, *(b)* civil legal aid and *(c)* green form cases for each of the previous six financial years.    [24514]

**Mr. John M. Taylor:** The rules governing qualification for civil legal aid, criminal legal aid and green form advice and assistance are set out in full in the legal aid handbook, produced every year by the Legal Aid Board.

**Mr. Boateng:** To ask the Parliamentary Secretary, Lord Chancellor's Department what percentage of the population was eligible for green form assistance in *(a)* 1973, *(b)* 1974, *(c)* 1984 and *(d)* each of the previous six financial years.    [24515]

**Mr. John M. Taylor:** The Department does not generally produce estimates of financial eligibility for green form advice and assistance and figures are not available for 1973, 1974 and 1984. However, in 1993 the Department estimated that around 21 per cent. of households were eligible. The green form disposable income eligibility limit was increased by nearly 15 per cent. to £70 in April 1994 and by a further 1.8 per cent. in April this year. Eligibility is correspondingly now at a higher level, probably somewhere between 25 per cent. and 30 per cent.

**Mr. Boateng:** To ask the Parliamentary Secretary, Lord Chancellor's Department what percentage of gross domestic product was expended on *(a)* civil legal aid and *(b)* criminal legal aid in each of the last six years; and what were the equivalent figures in Canada, Australia, New Zealand, America, France, Germany and Spain.    [24516]

**Mr. John M. Taylor:** The percentage of gross domestic product expended on legal aid in England and Wales in each of the last six years was as follows:

|  | Percentage criminal legal aid | Percentage civil legal aid |
|---|---|---|
| 1988–89 | 0.051 | 0.054 |
| 1989–90 | 0.055 | 0.059 |
| 1990–91 | 0.060 | 0.068 |
| 1991–92 | 0.069 | 0.088 |
| 1992–93 | 0.070 | 0.114 |
| 1993–94 | 0.068 | 0.130 |

It is not possible to provide comparative figures for the other countries in question since the information is not readily available.

**Mr. Boateng:** To ask the Parliamentary Secretary, Lord Chancellor's Department what percentage of the population was eligible for criminal legal aid in *(a)* 1965, *(b)* 1970, *(c)* 1980 and *(d)* each of the previous six financial years.    [24519]

**Mr. John M. Taylor:** There is no upper financial limit for criminal legal aid, so the question of eligible population does not arise. In determining applications, the courts consider whether it is in the interests of justice for legal aid to be granted and whether the defendant needs help with the costs.

**Mr. Boateng:** To ask the Parliamentary Secretary, Lord Chancellor's Department what percentage of the population was eligible for civil legal aid in *(a)* 1965, *(b)* 1969, *(c)* 1979 and *(d)* each of the previous six financial years.    [24520]

**Mr. John M. Taylor:** The Department has no estimates of eligibility for 1965 and 1969. The

Department's estimates of the proportion of households eligible for civil legal aid in the other years requested are as follows:

1979–80: 77 per cent.

1989–90: 58 per cent.

1990–91: 57 per cent.

1991–92: 51 per cent. (53 per cent. for personal injury cases)

1992–93: 53 per cent. (57 per cent. for personal injury cases)

1993–94: 48 per cent. (51 per cent. for personal injury cases)

1994–95: 48 per cent. (51 per cent. for personal injury cases)

Estimates are based on data published in the Family Expenditure Survey.

**Mr. Boateng:** To ask the Parliamentary Secretary, Lord Chancellor's Department what has been the change in total expenditure on legal aid in each of the previous six financial years; and how these changes differ from the changes in the rate of inflation. [24521]

**Mr. John M. Taylor:** Increases in respect of total net expenditure on legal aid in comparison with increases in the rate of inflation, in each of the last six years, were as follows:

| | Percentage change in expenditure | Percentage change in inflation (gdp) |
| --- | --- | --- |
| 1988–89 | 9.4 | 6.7 |
| 1989–90 | 19.1 | 7.0 |
| 1990–91 | 20.7 | 8.1 |
| 1991–92 | 32.8 | 6.3 |
| 1992–93 | 20.7 | 3.8 |
| 1993–94 | 10.7 | 3.3 |

**Mr. Boateng:** To ask the Parliamentary Secretary, Lord Chancellor's Department what was the level of criminal legal aid expenditure *(a)* by region and *(b)* by type of case for each of the last six financial years. [24522]

**Mr. John M. Taylor:** The table shows gross Crown court legal aid expenditure on a regional and case type basis for each of the last six financial years for which records are available.

£ million

| Circuit | Case type | 1988–89 | 1989–90 | 1990–91 | 1991–92 | 1992–93 | 1993–94 |
| --- | --- | --- | --- | --- | --- | --- | --- |
| South Easter | Trials | 57.698 | 63.183 | 75.129 | 88.749 | 106.848 | 111.546 |
| | Appeals | 0.686 | 0.739 | 1.381 | 1.141 | 1.181 | 1.367 |
| | Sentencing | 0.481 | 0.580 | 0.604 | 0.780 | 0.776 | 0.615 |
| Midland and Oxon | Trials | 14.843 | 17.723 | 20.643 | 22.520 | 27.695 | 31.719 |
| | Appeals | 0.367 | 0.631 | 0.477 | 0.495 | 0.528 | 0.704 |
| | Sentencing | 0.285 | 0.285 | 0.359 | 0.460 | 0.392 | 0.277 |
| Northern | Trials | 13.700 | 16.412 | 18.286 | 23.225 | 28.359 | 28.664 |
| | Appeals | 0.360 | 0.436 | 0.474 | 0.640 | 0.666 | 0.713 |
| | Sentencing | 0.172 | 0.192 | 0.257 | 0.343 | 0.310 | 0.242 |
| North Eastern | Trials | 12.472 | 12.955 | 14.469 | 18.151 | 19.890 | 22.697 |
| | Appeals | 0.292 | 0.319 | 0.334 | 0.420 | 0.458 | 0.532 |
| | Sentencing | 0.189 | 0.222 | 0.238 | 0.288 | 0.294 | 0.247 |
| Wales and Chester | Trials | 6.071 | · 6.743 | 7.444 | 9.866 | 10.916 | 14.097 |
| | Appeals | 0.127 | 0.121 | 0.144 | 0.208 | 0.194 | 0.201 |
| | Sentencing | 0.073 | 0.073 | 0.094 | 0.125 | 0.127 | 0.097 |
| Western | Trials | 9.444 | 12.072 | 13.960 | 16.124 | 18.459 | 18.710 |
| | Appeals | 0.262 | 0.264 | 0.363 | 0.422 | 0.453 | 0.438 |
| | Sentencing | 0.134 | 0.140 | 0.190 | 0.224 | 0.212 | 0.163 |

Details of gross criminal legal aid expenditure in the magistrates courts, by region, are given in table general 6 of the Legal Aid Board's annual reports for the years 1990–91 to 1993–94, and in appendix 4D of the annual report of the Law Society for 1988–89 and appendix 4D of the Legal Aid Board's annual report for 1989–90, copies of which are available in the Library. A breakdown of expenditure in each year by type of case is not available.

**Mr. Boateng:** To ask the Parliamentary Secretary,Lord Chancellor's Department what was the level of civil legal aid expenditure *(a)* by region *(b)* by type of case for each of the last six financial years. [24523]

**Mr. John M. Taylor:** Details of gross expenditure on civil legal aid, by region, and giving a limited breakdown of type of case, are given in table general 6 of the Legal Aid Board's annual reports for the years 1990–91 to 1993–94, and in appendix 4D of the annual report of the Law Society for 1988–89 and appendix 4D of the Legal Aid Board's annual report for 1989–90, copies of which are available in the Library.

## Woolf Review

**Mr. Boateng:** To ask the Parliamentary Secretary, Lord Chancellor's Department when he expects to implement those reforms to the civil justice system recommended by Lord Woolf and accepted by the Government; and if *(a)* primary legislation, *(b)* statutory instruments and *(c)* practice directions will be require to implement those recommendations. [24517]

**Mr. John M. Taylor:** Lord Woolf expects to present his interim report to the Lord Chancellor in June and to complete his inquiry by this time next year. When Lord Woolf's proposals are received the Lord Chancellor will consider how best to take matters forward.

**Mr. Boateng:** To ask the Parliamentary Secretary, Lord Chancellor's Department when he expects *(a)* to receive and *(b)* to publish the interim report of Lord Woolf's civil justice review. [24578]

**Mr. John M. Taylor:** Lord Woolf expects to publish his interim report in June.

## WALES

### Suicide

**Mr. Wigley:** To ask the Secretary of State for Wales if he will list the suicide rates for persons employed in agriculture in each county of Wales. [23407]

**Mr. Gwilym Jones:** The latest available information is for deaths registered as suicide in 1993 and is given in the following table:

*Suicide of farmers and farm workers in Wales, 1993*

| | Number | Rate per 1,000 farmers and farm workers[1] |
|---|---|---|
| Clwyd | 1 | 0.14 |
| Dyfed | 5 | 0.28 |
| Gwent | 1 | 0.26 |
| Gwynedd | — | — |
| Mid Glamorgan | — | — |
| Powys | 4 | 0.39 |
| South Glamorgan | — | — |
| West Glamorgan | — | — |
| Wales | 11 | 0.22 |

*Source:*
Office of Population Censuses and Surveys and June Agricultural Census.
*Note:*
[1] At June 1993, as estimated by the Agricultural Census which excludes very small holdings with very little or no agricultural activity.

### Housing Stock

**Mr. Matthew Taylor:** To ask the Secretary of State for Wales if he will publish data relating to the Welsh housing stock that is comparable to the energy supplement to the 1991 "English House Condition Survey". [23671]

**Mr. Gwilym Jones:** Data for the housing stock in Wales comparable to the energy supplement to the 1991 "English House Condition Survey" are not available. The 1993 "Welsh House Condition Survey" did not cover energy consumption or related matters.

### Countryside Council for Wales

**Mr. Morgan:** To ask the Secretary of State for Wales to what extent the action plan he has agreed with the board and chairman of the Countryside Council for Wales differs from the conclusions of his departmental financial management policy review; and if he will make a statement on the principal components. [24478]

**Mr. Redwood:** The financial management policy review of the Countryside Council for Wales was overtaken by the review of the council's functions which I announced in response to the question by my right hon. Friend the Member for Conwy (Sir W. Roberts) on 3 November 1994. The action plan reflects the conclusions of the review of these functions.

### Employment

**Mr. Barry Jones:** To ask the Secretary of State for Wales how many people are currently in full-time employment in Wales; and how many were employed full-time in 1987. [24193]

**Mr. Redwood:** According to the Employment Department, the number of full-time employees in employment in Wales was 677,000 in December 1994 and 704,000 in September 1987.

**Mr. Barry Jones:** To ask the Secretary of State for Wales, if he will list the numbers of long-term unemployed people in each of the constituencies of Wales. [24195]

**Mr. Redwood:** The data requested are available from the NOMIS database, which can be accessed by the staff of the Library of the House.

**Mr. Barry Jones:** To ask the Secretary of State for Wales how many people in the Deeside constituency are self-employed; and how many were self-employed in 1987. [24192]

**Mr. Redwood:** According to the 1991 census of population, the number of self-employed residents aged 16 and over in the Alyn and Deeside constituency was 3,629. Data for 1987 are not available.

### Business Expenditure

**Mr. Barry Jones:** To ask the Secretary of State for Wales what initiatives he has taken to encourage business expenditure on research and development in Wales; and if he will make a statement. [24338]

**Mr. Redwood:** My Department actively encourages business expenditure on research and development through the promotion of a number of Government initiatives to encourage innovation, including the SMART and SPUR schemes.

### Play Areas

**Mr. McMaster:** To ask the Secretary of State for Wales what guidelines he has issued to local authorities to encourage the provision of safety surfacing on play areas; what special financial provision he has made available to local authorities to encourage and enable them to meet this need; and if he will make a statement. [24087]

**Mr. Gwilym Jones:** In January 1992 a joint publication, "Playground Safety Guidelines", was issued by the Department of Education and Science, the National Children's Play and Recreation unit, and the Welsh Office to Welsh local authorities, interested voluntary organisations, the Sports Council for Wales, the Welsh Trades Union Congress, trade unions in the education field and church education authorities.

Local authorities fund the provision of safety surfacing on play areas from resources made available through the annual revenue and capital settlements. It is for individual authorities to determine the priority they give to this provision when apportioning resources between services. Central Government support is provided by way of grant to help meet the costs of Play Wales, an advisory body made up of representatives from county and district councils and the voluntary sector.

### Smoking

**Mr. Peter Griffiths:** To ask the Secretary of State for Wales what facilities are provided and arrangements made for the well-being and comfort of staff who *(a)* smoke and *(b)* do not wish to be affected by smoking, at (i) the work station and (ii) rest, recreation and refreshment facilities at Gwydyr house, Whitehall, London. [24198]

**Mr. Redwood:** The general rule is that staff in Gwydyr house are not allowed to smoke at their work station, unless they are the sole occupier of a room, through smoking is allowed in the locker room for security staff and messengers, which is also used as the work station for the drivers of official cars.

Smoking is not allowed in the room designated as the refreshment-rest room for the building.

### Hospital Visits, Clwyd

**Mr. Barry Jones:** To ask the Secretary of State for Wales if he will visit (a) Dobbs Hill hospital, (b) Deeside hospital and (c) Meadowsleigh hospital.

**Mr. Redwood:** I have no current plans to visit these hospitals.

### Public Bodies

**Mr. Jon Owen Jones:** To ask the Secretary of State for Wales if he will publish his guidelines concerning the declaration of interests of quango board members when dealing with agenda items which may involve pecuniary interests; and what are the Welsh Office guidelines concerning public access to such information. [24339]

**Mr. Redwood:** Guidance on the treatment of the financial interests of board members is included in the "Code of Best Practice for Board Members of Public Bodies" published by H M Treasury in June 1994. All Welsh executive non-departmental public bodies are establishing registers of members' interests which will be published or made available for inspection.

### Giant Hogweed

**Mr. McMaster:** To ask the Secretary of State for Wales what measures he plans to require the owners of land to which the public may have access to eradicate heracleum manteggazzianum; if he will give local authorities a duty to control heracleum manteggazzianum; and if he will make a statement about the dangers associated with this plant. [24100]

**Mr. Gwilym Jones:** Controls on the spread of the plant already exist. It is an offence under the Wildlife and Countryside Act 1981 to introduce the plant into the wild. There is, however, no evidence to show that it is widespread or that it causes a particular problem in Wales. The control of the plant is a matter for relevant local authorities if there is a perceived threat to public health. Direct contact with the plant can cause severe irritation to the skin as well as swelling and painful blistering.

### Planning Policy Guidance

**Mr. Gareth Wardell:** To ask the Secretary of State for Wales if he will make a statement on the future of policy planning guidance in Wales; and if he will make a statement. [24497]

**Mr. Gwilym Jones:** I refer the hon.Member to the reply I gave him on 24 April 1995 at column *371*.

### Sheep

**Mr. Martyn Jones:** To ask the Secretary of State for Wales what was the estimated sheep population in Wales in 1980, 1985, 1990, and 1994; and what percentage of the United Kingdom flock they formed. [24558]

**Mr. Gwilym Jones:** The information requested is given in the following table:

*Sheep population in Wales*

| | Total sheep and lambs (000s)[1] | Total as a percentage of the UK flock |
|---|---|---|
| 1980 | 8,013.8 | 25.5 |
| 1985 | 9,129.7 | 25.6 |
| 1990 | 10,935.3 | 25.0 |
| 1994 | 11,092.6 | 25.6 |

*Source:*
June Agricultural Census and Minor Holdings Census.
*Note:*
[1] At 1 June.

### Operations Cancelled

**Mr. Morgan:** To ask the Secretary of State for Wales if he will set up a system for the collection of data on (a) cancellations and (b) double cancellations of hospital operations; and if he will make a statement. [24718]

**Mr. Redwood:** As part of monitoring the patient's charter, information on cancelled operations is reported regularly to the Welsh Office. Between 1 April and 31 December 1994, 18 patients were admitted to a Welsh hospital more than one month after the second cancellation of a non-urgent operation.

From January 1995 the information collected on cancellations was altered to reflect the tightening of the related charter standard to focus on the number of patients who experience a delay of more than a month after the cancellation of just one non-urgent operation. During the three months to 31 March 1995, Welsh hospitals reported that 27 patients had experienced such a delay during the same quarter hospitals in Wales treated 189,059 as in-patients and day cases.

**Mr. Morgan:** To ask the Secretary of State for Wales what rights under the patient's charter patients whose operations have been cancelled twice, due to shortage of intensive care beds, after they have been prepared for surgery have.

**Mr. Redwood:** The latest edition of the Patient's Charter for Wales, which was published in October 1994, makes it clear that patients should receive priority treatment within a month if they have had to face the cancellation of a non-urgent operation. Hospital performance against the new standard is monitored quarterly by my Department.

### Intensive Care Beds

**Mr. Morgan:** To ask the Secretary of State for Wales what consultations he has had with the chairman of the University Hospital of Wales, Cardiff Royal Infirmary trust concerning patients with liver cancer who have had their operation cancelled twice due to a lack of intensive care beds after being prepared for surgery. [24719]

**Mr. Redwood:** I have not discussed these specific cases with the chairman of the NHS trust involved. However, on 4 April my Department asked all health authorities and hospitals in Wales to review urgently the need for intensive care beds and to ensure adequate provision is available.

## Policy Reviews

**Mr. Sweeney:** To ask the Secretary of State for Wales what arrangements he has made for publishing the conclusion of the 1991–92 financial management and policy reviews of the Welsh development agency, the Development Board for Rural Wales and the Land Authority for Wales.    [24869]

**Mr Redwood:** I have today arranged for copies of the conclusions of all three reviews, and of the action taken in response, to be placed in the Library of the House.

Government thinking and policy on these three bodies has evolved since these reviews, as I have explained to the House.

## Morbidity Rates

**Mr. Ainger:** To ask the Secretary of State for Wales what was the average morbidity in terms of annual admissions to hospital per 100,000 population in each district health authority in *(a)* 1980, *(b)* 1984, *(c)* 1985 and *(d)* each year since 1990–91.

**Mr. Gwilym Jones** *[holding answer 14 March 1995]:* Latest estimates of the number of in-patient cases and day cases per 100,000 population are given in the following table.

*Number of in-patient cases and day cases per 100,000 population*[1]

| Health authority of residence | Discharges and deaths | | | | Completed consultant episodes[2] | | |
| --- | --- | --- | --- | --- | --- | --- | --- |
| | 1980 | 1984–85 | 1985–86 | 1990–91[3] | 1991–92 | 1992–93 | 1993–94 |
| Clwyd | 10,945 | 13,800 | 14,027 | 12,590 | 19,106 | 20,283 | 21,908 |
| East Dyfed | 10,746 | 13,892 | 14,430 | 15,929 | 21,244 | 27,123 | 27,623 |
| Gwent | 9,897 | 14,022 | 15,053 | 17,514 | 18,149 | 20,286 | 21,000 |
| Gwynedd | 11,893 | 15,280 | 17,046 | 17,760 | 21,124 | 17,274 | 21,036 |
| Mid Glamorgan | 11,727 | 16,553 | 18,131 | 21,504 | 25,064 | 25,530 | 26,821 |
| Pembrokeshire | 11,337 | 13,164 | 14,358 | 15,684 | 21,361 | 25,381 | 24,738 |
| Powys | 6,303 | 8,085 | 8,765 | 10,122 | 12,977 | 14,222 | 15,435 |
| South Glamorgan | 10,762 | 16,342 | 17,433 | 18,063 | 20,768 | 21,737 | 22,193 |
| West Glamorgan | 10,329 | 14,305 | 15,045 | 14,212 | 18,326 | 18,434 | 21,527 |

[1] Excluding patients treated outside Wales.
[2] Where there is more than one completed consultant episode during a patient's spell in hospital, only the first of these episodes is counted.
[3] Data for 1990–91 are incomplete in some areas.

## EDUCATION

### Stratford Grant-maintained School

**Mr. Spearing:** To ask the Secretary of State for Education (1) pursuant to her answer to the hon. Member for Aylesbury (Mr. Lidington) of 5 May, *Official Report*, column *338*, on Stratford grant-maintained school, what is the latest date she expects to receive the strategy adopted by the new governing body and the period over which it will be subject to appraisal;    [23872]

(2) if she will name all the governors of Stratford grant-maintained school; when and at what meeting Mrs. Marinda Bailey was elected chairman of the school's governing body; when she was appointed to the governors; and what qualifications, experience or local knowledge she possesses relevant to this post.    [23874]

**Mr. Forth:** My right hon. Friend announced on 5 May four new appointments to the governing body of Stratford school. She expects the newly constituted governing body to begin work immediately on a range of strategies to improve the standards of education on offer. Ofsted will be undertaking another monitoring visit to the school in the autumn term and my right hon. Friend expects there to be significant signs of improvement by then.

I understand that Mrs. Merinda Bailey was elected chairman of governors at the governing body meeting on the 4 May 1995. She was previously vice-chairman and is a parent of a pupil at the school. The names of all the governors can be obtained from the school.

**Mr. Spearing:** To ask the Secretary of State for Education what is the maximum planned intake in September at Stratford grant-maintained school and the number of forms this represents; how many *(a)* pupils and *(b)* forms had entered each September since the school attained grant-maintained status; how many other pupils joined during each academic year as a grant-maintained school; and how many are entered to join in September 1995.    [23873]

**Mr. Robin Squire:** Stratford school's approved admissions number at the time of the decision on grant-maintained status was 180, indicating six forms of entry. The Department does not collect information in the precise form requested. Returns from the school indicate the following first-year intakes, organised in each case in five forms:

> September 1991: 124 pupils
> September 1992: 116 pupils
> September 1993: 129 pupils
> September 1994: 111 pupils

An estimated figure for the 1995 intake can be provided by the school.

**Mr. Spearing:** To ask the Secretary of State for Education, pursuant to her answer to the hon. Member for Aylesbury (Mr. Lidington) of 5 May, *Official Report*, column *338*, on Stratford grant-maintained school, what consultancy help the school has received; for what purpose; at what cost and from whom; and what further grants it has received from the Funding Agency for Schools and for what purposes.    [23875]

**Mr. Forth:** Decisions on the appointment of consultants in a grant-maintained school are the responsibility of the school's governing body. The cost of consultancies is met from within a school's normal recurrent funding, plus any additional grants which may have been agreed.

The funding of Stratford school is a matter for the Funding Agency for Schools. I have asked the chairman of the funding agency to write to the hon. Member with the information requested.

### Mathematics and English Teachers

**Mr. Blunkett:** To ask the Secretary of State for Education how many qualified *(a)* mathematics and *(b)* English teachers there were in secondary schools in each year since 1979; and what proportion of the total of teachers of each subject they represent.        [23982]

**Mr. Robin Squire:** The information requested is available only for 1984, 1988 and 1992 from the secondary school staffing surveys. In those years the number of full-time teachers who were teaching mathematics and English in maintained secondary schools in England and who had post A-level qualifications in the subject were as follows:

| Year | Number of Maths teachers ('000) | Number with Maths qualification ('000) | Percentage with qualification |
|---|---|---|---|
| 1984 | 40.5 | 30.0 | 74 |
| 1988 | 35.5 | 26.1 | 73 |
| 1992 | 31.0 | 23.5 | 76 |

| Year | Number of English teachers (000) | Number with English qualification (000) | Percentage with qualification |
|---|---|---|---|
| 1984 | 42.8 | 30.8 | 72 |
| 1988 | 36.3 | 26.1 | 72 |
| 1992 | 30.8 | 22.4 | 73 |

The total number of full-time teachers with post A-level qualifications in mathematics and English, including those not teaching the subjects, are as follows.

|  |  | *Thousands* |
|---|---|---|
| Year | Mathematics | English |
| 1984 | 47.9 | 54.6 |
| 1988 | 42.0 | 45.7 |
| 1992 | 38.1 | 40.1 |

### School Transport, Brent

**Mr. Pawsey:** To ask the Secretary of State for Education what consideration she gave to issuing a section 68 or 99 direction to Brent borough council in relation to its school transport policy for denominational schools; and if she will make a statement.        [24597]

**Mr. Forth:** My right hon. Friend is currently considering whether in her view Brent local education authority is acting unreasonably or unlawfully when dealing with applications for free transport to denominational schools.

### Public Bodies

**Mr. Blunkett:** To ask the Secretary of State for Education how many people work for *(a)* the Higher Education Funding Council, *(b)* the Funding Agency for Schools, *(c)* the Further Education Funding Council and *(d)* the Teacher Training Agency; and how much was spent on (i) administration and (ii) salaries in respect of each, in the last financial year.        [23983]

**Mr. Boswell:** The information requested is given in the following table:

| | Staff (fte) March 1995 | Administration costs[1] £000 | Salary costs[2] £000 |
|---|---|---|---|
| HEFCE | 193.5 | 6,635 | 5,113 |
| FAS[3] | 261.8 | 6,712 | 4,215 |
| FEFC | 390 | 13,200 | 10,600 |
| TTA[4] | 48.2 | 1,106 | 536 |

[1] Excludes salary costs.
[2] Includes employers national insurance and superannuation costs.
[3] The FAS was established with effect from 1 April 1994. Staff numbers have built up over the year.
[4] The TTA was established on 21 September 1994. Staff numbers have increased gradually over the 6 month period.

### Vocational Training and Education

**Mr. Corbyn:** To ask the Secretary of State for Education if she will make a statement on the priority she attaches to the involvement of industry in vocational training and education.        [24493]

**Mr. Boswell:** The Govnerment attach high priority to the involvement of industry in vocational training and education. In the case of general national vocational qualifications, for which my Department is responsible, industry is involved in the preparation, development and, through work placements, the delivery of the qualifications.

### Student Funding

**Mr. Heald:** To ask the Secretary of State for Education if she will announce the postgraduate bursary and studentship rates payable by this Department for the academic year 1995–96.        [24873]

**Mr. Boswell:** The main maintenance rates under the Department's own postgraduate awards scheme for certain professional and vocational courses in the academic year 1995–96 will be as follows. 1994–95 rates are shown in brackets:

| | 1995–96 £ |
|---|---|
| *Bursaries* | |
| London | 3,375 (3,295) |
| Elsewhere | 2,665 (2,600) |
| Parental home | 2,015 (1,965) |
| *Studentship* | |
| London | 5,695 (5,555) |
| Elsewhere | 4,525 (4,415) |
| Parental home | 3,335 (3,255) |

These represent increases of 2.5 per cent. on the current year's rates. The relevant supplementary allowances will be increased broadly in line.

### Capital Spending, Northamptonshire

**Mr. William Powell:** To ask the Secretary of State for Education if she will list the capital spending approvals allowed for Northamptonshire schools in each year since 1987–88.        [23940]

**Mr. Robin Squire:** Credit approvals for building work at county and voluntary controlled schools in Northamptonshire are as follows:

| Year | Amount £000 |
|------|------------:|
| 1987–88 | 1,460 |
| 1988–89 | 2,823 |
| 1989–90 | 3,676 |
| 1990–91 | 5,218 |
| 1991–92 | 7,887 |
| 1992–93 | 4,107 |
| 1993–94 | 4,558 |
| 1994–95 | 3,404 |
| 1995–96 | 3,454 |

### Grant-maintained Schools

**Mr. Blunkett:** To ask the Secretary of State for Education if she will list the applications she has received to open new grant-maintained schools. [23664]

**Mr. Robin Squire:** Applications to establish new grant-maintained schools have been received from three independent schools:

Oak Hill school, Avon, to establish an all age interdenominational Christian school;

St. Anselm's college, Wirral, to establish an 11–18 Roman Catholic grammar school for boys; and

Upton Hall convent school, Wirral, to establish an 11–18 Roman Catholic grammar school for girls.

A fourth application, for the establishment of a new grant-maintained Jewish high school in Leeds, has been withdrawn. A number of prospective promoters of new grant-maintained schools are currently in consultation with the Funding Agency for Schools.

**Mr. Blunkett:** To ask the Secretary of State for Education what are the arrangements within her Department for monitoring complaints about grant-maintained schools; and how many complaints have been received to date over *(a)* admissions, *(b)* exclusions and *(c)* the conduct of the schools. [23665]

**Mr. Robin Squire:** The Department receives a variety of complaints about schools of all kinds—independent, local authority maintained and grant maintained—which are followed up as appropriate. Details are not aggregated, nor recorded by school type.

**Mr. Blunkett:** To ask the Secretary of State for Education if she will list for each application from a grant-maintained school for a change of character to *(a)* add whole or partial selection of pupils and *(b)* to add or extend a sixth form (i) the number of objections submitted to the Secretary of State, (ii) the number of objections submitted by the governing bodies of other schools and (iii) if an objection was submitted by the local education authority. [23125]

**Mr. Robin Squire** *[holding answer 9 May 1995]:* The information requested has been placed in the Library. The table includes only statutory objections. Some cases were supported by a large a number of signatories.

### Teacher and Pupil Numbers

**Mr. Blunkett:** To ask the Secretary of State for Education what were the numbers in each local education authority area and nationally of *(a)* provisional full-time equivalent teachers for (i) nursery, (ii) primary and (iii) secondary schools as at January 1995 and (v) the provisional pupil numbers in (i) nursery, (ii) primary and (iii) secondary schools as at January 1994. [23666]

**Mr. Robin Squire:** Information on pupils and the full-time equivalent of qualified teachers in maintained schools in each local education authority area in England in January 1994, the latest date for which information is available, is shown in the table. Information for January 1995 will not be available until the autumn.

*Pupils and Full-Time Equivalent of Qualified Teachers in Maintained schools in each local education authority area in England. January 1994*

| Local Education Authority area | Pupils | | | | | FTE Qualified Teachers | | |
|---|---|---|---|---|---|---|---|---|
| | Nursery Part-time | Full-time | Primary Part-time | Full-time | Secondary Full-time | Nursery FTE | Primary FTE | Secondary FTE |
| Corporation of London | 0 | 0 | 20 | 194 | 0 | 0.0 | 13.6 | 0.0 |
| Camden | 33 | 40 | 495 | 10,433 | 10,657 | 3.0 | 521.6 | 696.7 |
| Greenwich | 342 | 332 | 2,298 | 18,782 | 13,980 | 23.0 | 948.9 | 854.5 |
| Hackney | 108 | 62 | 1,398 | 15,485 | 7,445 | 8.0 | 812.7 | 509.5 |
| Hammersmith | 303 | 275 | 600 | 8,591 | 5,885 | 26.3 | 471.2 | 387.7 |
| Islington | 177 | 153 | 579 | 15,078 | 7,215 | 13.2 | 757.6 | 469.7 |
| Kensington and Chelsea | 83 | 169 | 231 | 6,210 | 3,162 | 15.0 | 357.5 | 253.8 |
| Lambeth | 262 | 190 | 1,439 | 17,493 | 6,306 | 20.0 | 953.8 | 425.3 |
| Lewisham | 136 | 97 | 2,122 | 18,692 | 10,888 | 9.0 | 917.9 | 671.1 |
| Southwark | 346 | 199 | 1,894 | 20,626 | 9,384 | 21.6 | 963.4 | 551.2 |
| Tower Hamlets | 280 | 432 | 1,054 | 20,678 | 11,888 | 38.1 | 1,179.5 | 837.2 |
| Wandsworth | 102 | 114 | 1,324 | 16,113 | 8,941 | 9.5 | 845.8 | 606.8 |
| Westminster | 136 | 53 | 581 | 8,645 | 7,464 | 12.0 | 508.4 | 482.0 |
| Barking | 0 | 0 | 1,815 | 14,287 | 9,756 | 0.0 | 687.1 | 570.3 |
| Barnet | 532 | 21 | 2,109 | 21,893 | 18,790 | 15.0 | 1,091.3 | 1,251.8 |
| Bexley | 0 | 0 | 1,425 | 18,083 | 14,525 | 0.0 | 801.1 | 882.4 |
| Brent | 42 | 181 | 1,713 | 20,691 | 12,688 | 15.0 | 978.5 | 799.7 |
| Bromley | 0 | 0 | 169 | 22,261 | 17,150 | 0.0 | 916.8 | 1,059.2 |
| Croydon | 462 | 0 | 1,125 | 25,891 | 14,909 | 13.5 | 1,212.0 | 881.3 |
| Ealing | 498 | 16 | 3,118 | 22,477 | 13,480 | 16.3 | 1,130.8 | 829.2 |
| Enfield | 0 | 0 | 1,713 | 22,110 | 17,848 | 0.0 | 1,018.9 | 1,076.1 |
| Haringey | 71 | 168 | 1,991 | 17,786 | 9,222 | 14.5 | 922.9 | 662.4 |

*Pupils and Full-Time Equivalent of Qualified Teachers in Maintained schools in each local education authority area in England.*
*January 1994*

| Local Education Authority area | Pupils | | | | | FTE Qualified Teachers | | |
|---|---|---|---|---|---|---|---|---|
| | Nursery Part-time | Full-time | Primary Part-time | Full-time | Secondary Full-time | Nursery FTE | Primary FTE | Secondary FTE |
| Harrow | 0 | 0 | 1,016 | 18,332 | 8,320 | 0.0 | 916.9 | 531.6 |
| Havering | 0 | 0 | 1,471 | 18,637 | 14,892 | 0.0 | 837.5 | 901.2 |
| Hillingdon | 120 | 0 | 3,125 | 17,418 | 14,115 | 3.2 | 858.9 | 860.2 |
| Hounslow | 0 | 0 | 2,395 | 17,200 | 14,526 | 0.0 | 872.8 | 894.8 |
| Kingston upon Thames | 157 | 63 | 1,463 | 9,308 | 7,787 | 8.8 | 427.3 | 487.3 |
| Merton | 0 | 0 | 2,866 | 12,788 | 7,313 | 0.0 | 702.7 | 453.7 |
| Newham | 851 | 84 | 3,527 | 22,059 | 14,067 | 27.0 | 981.0 | 823.8 |
| Redbridge | 0 | 0 | 1,264 | 18,443 | 15,362 | 0.0 | 832.3 | 927.4 |
| Richmond upon Thames | 62 | 8 | 1,790 | 9,405 | 7,622 | 2.0 | 500.1 | 451.2 |
| Sutton | 241 | 0 | 1,609 | 11,861 | 11,359 | 6.0 | 518.2 | 671.6 |
| Waltham Forest | 279 | 41 | 2,216 | 17,948 | 11,506 | 9.1 | 870.7 | 722.0 |
| Birmingham | 1,460 | 865 | 6,318 | 101,382 | 64,728 | 71.1 | 4,495.3 | 3,961.2 |
| Coventry | 176 | 30 | 1,946 | 27,879 | 19,013 | 8.4 | 1,272.2 | 1,201.2 |
| Dudley | 60 | 10 | 2,764 | 26,818 | 18,124 | 1.0 | 1,252.7 | 1,083.5 |
| Sandwell | 106 | 111 | 4,308 | 27,983 | 18,418 | 9.0 | 1,339.5 | 1,158.5 |
| Solihull | 0 | 0 | 1,837 | 18,283 | 13,505 | 0.0 | 823.2 | 823.3 |
| Walsall | 719 | 88 | 3,517 | 25,009 | 19,506 | 16.8 | 1,194.9 | 1,233.9 |
| Wolverhampton | 826 | 0 | 2,978 | 22,630 | 16,001 | 20.1 | 1,130.4 | 1,041.1 |
| Knowsley | 0 | 0 | 2,748 | 16,252 | 9,096 | 0.0 | 749.3 | 537.2 |
| Liverpool | 362 | 218 | 5,416 | 46,200 | 30,556 | 22.0 | 2,093.1 | 1,920.8 |
| St. Helens | 70 | 5 | 1,596 | 16,039 | 11,759 | 2.0 | 764.1 | 771.1 |
| Sefton | 313 | 3 | 2,189 | 25,210 | 19,030 | 8.0 | 1,136.0 | 1,159.9 |
| Wirral | 314 | 12 | 1,960 | 29,672 | 21,159 | 8.5 | 1,359.2 | 1,299.3 |
| Bolton | 497 | 27 | 2,278 | 25,360 | 17,031 | 15.0 | 1,201.9 | 1,059.6 |
| Bury | 105 | 56 | 1,224 | 16,024 | 10,332 | 5.4 | 712.1 | 603.6 |
| Manchester | 160 | 417 | 2,842 | 44,081 | 21,693 | 27.6 | 2,040.1 | 1,383.1 |
| Oldham | 0 | 0 | 1,519 | 23,255 | 16,331 | 0.0 | 1,049.9 | 1,050.1 |
| Rochdale | 865 | 50 | 1,107 | 20,551 | 12,942 | 22.5 | 869.9 | 767.6 |
| Salford | 517 | 457 | 852 | 22,413 | 11,639 | 32.0 | 964.9 | 700.2 |
| Stockport | 845 | 81 | 1,050 | 24,545 | 16,019 | 20.0 | 1,061.1 | 977.8 |
| Tameside | 344 | 0 | 2,198 | 21,098 | 13,372 | 10.0 | 891.2 | 767.9 |
| Trafford | 0 | 0 | 2,257 | 18,308 | 11,947 | 0.0 | 795.8 | 735.8 |
| Wigan | 189 | 4 | 2,012 | 27,951 | 19,523 | 6.0 | 1,267.2 | 1,237.2 |
| Barnsley | 181 | 0 | 2,787 | 18,715 | 12,730 | 4.0 | 831.3 | 743.6 |
| Doncaster | 0 | 0 | 3,435 | 26,024 | 21,868 | 0.0 | 1,178.8 | 1,343.8 |
| Rotherham | 401 | 1 | 2,726 | 22,228 | 18,187 | 10.0 | 1,105.6 | 1,148.9 |
| Sheffield | 722 | 129 | 5,058 | 39,505 | 26,981 | 24.6 | 1,873.4 | 1,637.4 |
| Bradford | 320 | 196 | 5,840 | 35,389 | 46,297 | 22.5 | 1,802.5 | 2,680.2 |
| Calderdale | 0 | 0 | 1,566 | 18,315 | 13,390 | 0.0 | 806.8 | 822.1 |
| Kirkless | 569 | 0 | 3,849 | 33,870 | 24,875 | 17.0 | 1,618.3 | 1,572.7 |
| Leeds | 92 | 0 | 8,526 | 60,902 | 43,627 | 4.6 | 2,782.0 | 2,728.1 |
| Wakefield | 478 | 0 | 4,361 | 26,347 | 20,084 | 13.0 | 1,235.5 | 1,232.1 |
| Gateshead | 57 | 7 | 1,770 | 16,596 | 11,751 | 2.0 | 810.8 | 748.7 |
| Newcastle upon Tyne | 30 | 594 | 1,547 | 20,894 | 16,902 | 25.4 | 946.2 | 1,023.6 |
| North Tyneside | 186 | 38 | 2,318 | 14,297 | 14,342 | 6.3 | 667.7 | 844.9 |
| South Tyneside | 408 | 18 | 1,792 | 14,231 | 9,570 | 11.0 | 652.9 | 563.3 |
| Sunderland | 995 | 41 | 2,318 | 27,739 | 19,436 | 29.0 | 1,310.2 | 1,209.1 |
| Isles of Scilly | 0 | 0 | 14 | 155 | 122 | 0.0 | 11.5 | 13.8 |
| Avon | 1,116 | 784 | 3,278 | 77,422 | 54,418 | 68.1 | 3,423.4 | 3,352.3 |
| Bedfordshire | 1,160 | 338 | 4,275 | 39,236 | 44,711 | 47.2 | 1,880.1 | 2,592.5 |
| Berkshire | 2,031 | 134 | 4,259 | 58,196 | 47,005 | 63.2 | 2,630.7 | 2,935.8 |
| Buckinghamshire | 569 | 0 | 4,348 | 58,017 | 37,166 | 12.5 | 2,617.1 | 2,216.8 |
| Cambridgeshire | 715 | 18 | 1,570 | 57,557 | 40,904 | 19.3 | 2,505.7 | 2,398.2 |
| Cheshire | 814 | 25 | 4,686 | 85,258 | 63,583 | 19.0 | 3,665.4 | 3,788.0 |
| Cleveland | 134 | 0 | 9,124 | 55,978 | 36,437 | 4.0 | 2,540.4 | 2,144.3 |
| Cornwall | 96 | 21 | 3,270 | 37,261 | 28,977 | 3.3 | 1,669.5 | 1,678.0 |
| Cumbria | 802 | 1 | 2,252 | 40,588 | 31,215 | 18.0 | 1,853.2 | 1,947.5 |
| Derbyshire | 1,423 | 146 | 9,237 | 76,181 | 57,548 | 43.8 | 3,461.3 | 3,670.5 |
| Devon | 259 | 44 | 2,450 | 78,183 | 58,826 | 6.4 | 3,461.3 | 3,593.7 |
| Dorset | 0 | 0 | 4,570 | 41,233 | 41,286 | 0.0 | 1,859.7 | 2,399.5 |
| Durham | 2,530 | 47 | 4,577 | 51,757 | 37,708 | 63.1 | 2,356.3 | 2,271.6 |
| East Sussex | 300 | 0 | 3,960 | 48,021 | 34,349 | 7.6 | 2,244.8 | 2,129.2 |
| Essex | 296 | 0 | 2,334 | 121,663 | 95,893 | 8.0 | 5,389.3 | 5,594.0 |
| Gloucestershire | 0 | 0 | 15 | 43,582 | 33,389 | 0.0 | 1,940.6 | 1,890.8 |
| Hampshire | 298 | 2 | 5,430 | 131,883 | 79,199 | 8.8 | 5,998.2 | 4,827.8 |
| Hereford and Worcester | 0 | 0 | 1,188 | 48,063 | 47,472 | 0.0 | 2,189.1 | 2,748.4 |

*Pupils and Full-Time Equivalent of Qualified Teachers in Maintained schools in each local education authority area in England.*
*January 1994*

| Local Education Authority area | Nursery Part-time | Nursery Full-time | Pupils Primary Part-time | Primary Full-time | Secondary Full-time | FTE Qualified Teachers Nursery FTE | Primary FTE | Secondary FTE |
|---|---|---|---|---|---|---|---|---|
| Hertfordshire | 1,710 | 53 | 7,709 | 77,116 | 68,347 | 43.2 | 3,654.6 | 4,352.8 |
| Humberside | 967 | 186 | 7,334 | 78,075 | 56,111 | 30.5 | 3,366.5 | 3,212.1 |
| Isle of Wight | 0 | 0 | 175 | 7,039 | 10,498 | 0.0 | 320.1 | 597.5 |
| Kent | 85 | 0 | 5,261 | 123,973 | 102,229 | 2.1 | 5,296.6 | 6,127.3 |
| Lancashire | 3,448 | 87 | 4,294 | 126,282 | 84,257 | 90.9 | 5,592.1 | 5,221.7 |
| Leicestershire | 50 | 0 | 4,253 | 76,195 | 59,963 | 1.1 | 3,488.2 | 3,657.2 |
| Lincolnshire | 187 | 57 | 1,149 | 48,695 | 37,841 | 7.3 | 2,113.2 | 2,391.4 |
| Norfolk | 390 | 7 | 2,211 | 60,354 | 41,078 | 11.0 | 2,804.4 | 2,624.0 |
| North Yorkshire | 402 | 1 | 3,632 | 55,608 | 44,013 | 9.0 | 2,502.5 | 2,757.9 |
| Northamptonshire | 612 | 0 | 2,309 | 48,956 | 44,910 | 16.6 | 2,213.7 | 2,712.6 |
| Northumberland | 90 | 38 | 2,898 | 18,794 | 29,329 | 3.0 | 834.7 | 1,622.4 |
| Nottinghamshire | 598 | 11 | 12,866 | 80,018 | 63,768 | 18.2 | 3,774.4 | 4,027.5 |
| Oxfordshire | 1,137 | 52 | 2,071 | 39,242 | 35,127 | 40.3 | 1,870.9 | 2,090.8 |
| Shropshire | 173 | 0 | 2,057 | 33,934 | 25,223 | 4.0 | 1,515.9 | 1,571.5 |
| Somerset | 0 | 0 | 554 | 35,899 | 28,038 | 0.0 | 1,604.1 | 1,692.6 |
| Staffordshire | 1,392 | 736 | 3,332 | 90,182 | 69,487 | 50.2 | 3,661.2 | 3,971.3 |
| Suffolk | 97 | 0 | 3,031 | 41,324 | 48,024 | 2.1 | 1,981.3 | 2,955.5 |
| Surrey | 334 | 84 | 2,913 | 70,412 | 45,405 | 18.1 | 3,292.3 | 2,698.8 |
| Warwickshire | 758 | 0 | 1,335 | 45,111 | 25,087 | 18.0 | 2,067.5 | 1,562.7 |
| West Sussex | 465 | 18 | 646 | 52,512 | 39,952 | 14.0 | 2,401.3 | 2,420.6 |
| Wiltshire | 0 | 0 | 709 | 47,496 | 34,487 | 0.0 | 2,089.0 | 2,064.5 |
| England | 43,428 | 9,046 | 296,406 | 3,945,344 | 2,933,598 | 1,575.2 | 180,557.7 | 178,780.1 |

## Playing Fields

**Mr. Blunkett:** To ask the Secretary of State for Education how many school playing fields there were in each year since 1979. [23667]

**Mr. Robin Squire:** I refer the hon. Member to the reply that I gave him on 23 January, *Official Report*, columns *37-8.*

## Admission Appeals

**Mr. Blunkett:** To ask the Secretary of State for Education how many admission appeals were made by parents failing to obtain a place for their child in the school of their choice in the latest available year in each local education area and nationally. [23668]

**Mr. Robin Squire:** The information requested is shown in the table.

*Appeals lodged by parents against non-admission of their children to maintained (including Grant maintained) primary and secondary schools in each local education authority area in England.*

*Academic year 1992–93*

| Local Education Authority area | Total appeals lodged |
|---|---|
| Corporation of London | 1 |
| Camden | 378 |
| Greenwich | 393 |
| Hackney | 371 |
| Hammersmith and Fulham | 231 |
| Islington | 392 |
| Kensington and Chelsea | 58 |
| Lambeth | 380 |
| Lewisham | 784 |
| Southwark | 352 |
| Tower Hamlets | 596 |
| Wandsworth | 154 |
| Westminster | 227 |
| Barking and Dagenham | 174 |

*Appeals lodged by parents against non-admission of their children to maintained (including Grant maintained) primary and secondary schools in each local education authority area in England.*

*Academic year 1992–93*

| Local Education Authority area | Total appeals lodged |
|---|---|
| Barnet | 918 |
| Bexley | 434 |
| Brent | 145 |
| Bromley | 879 |
| Croydon | 831 |
| Ealing | 288 |
| Enfield | 710 |
| Haringey | 340 |
| Harrow | 372 |
| Havering | 388 |
| Hillingdon | 314 |
| Hounslow | 318 |
| Kingston upon Thames | 125 |
| Merton | 233 |
| Newham | 39 |
| Redbridge | 503 |
| Richmond upon Thames | 227 |
| Sutton | 572 |
| Waltham Forest | 511 |
| Birmingham | 1,957 |
| Coventry | 437 |
| Dudley | 193 |
| Sandwell | 161 |
| Solihull | 258 |
| Walsall | 39 |
| Wolverhampton | 75 |
| Knowsley | 34 |
| Liverpool | 897 |
| St. Helens | 134 |
| Sefton | 123 |
| Wirral | 438 |
| Bolton | 233 |
| Bury | 619 |
| Manchester | 1,263 |
| Oldham | 378 |

*Appeals lodged by parents against non-admission of their children to maintained (including Grant maintained) primary and secondary schools in each local education authority area in England.*

*Academic year 1992–93*

| Local Education Authority area | Total appeals lodged |
| --- | --- |
| Rochdale | 262 |
| Salford | 134 |
| Stockport | 92 |
| Tameside | 173 |
| Trafford | 237 |
| Wigan | 158 |
| Barnsley | 0 |
| Doncaster | 55 |
| Rotherham | 140 |
| Sheffield | 595 |
| Bradford | 1,457 |
| Calderdale | 138 |
| Kirklees | 221 |
| Leeds | 2,360 |
| Wakefield | 93 |
| Gateshead | 29 |
| Newcastle upon Tyne | 136 |
| North Tyneside | 16 |
| South Tyneside | 45 |
| Sunderland | 73 |
| Isles of Scilly | 0 |
| Avon | 1,115 |
| Bedfordshire | 92 |
| Berkshire | 625 |
| Buckinghamshire[1] | 580 |
| Cambridge | 315 |
| Cheshire | 147 |
| Cleveland | 80 |
| Cornwall | 51 |
| Cumbria | 99 |
| Derbyshire | 485 |
| Devon | 541 |
| Dorset | 340 |
| Durham | 392 |
| East Sussex | 298 |
| Essex | 440 |
| Gloucestershire | 279 |
| Hampshire | 148 |
| Hereford and Worcester | 273 |
| Hertfordshire | 1,071 |
| Humberside | 457 |
| Isle of Wight | 37 |
| Kent[1] | 975 |
| Lancashire | 2,400 |
| Leicestershire | 373 |
| Lincolnshire | 240 |
| Norfolk | 183 |
| North Yorkshire | 533 |
| Northamptonshire | 103 |
| Northumberland | 51 |
| Nottinghamshire | 322 |
| Oxfordshire | 374 |
| Shropshire | 360 |
| Somerset | 379 |
| Staffordshire | 190 |
| Suffolk | 150 |
| Surrey | 640 |
| Warwickshire | 160 |
| West Sussex | 187 |
| Wiltshire | 151 |
| England | 41,927 |

[1] LEAs which did not submit a complete return.

## Physical Education

**Mr. Blunkett:** To ask the Secretary of State for Education if she will list for each year since 1979 *(a)* the number and *(b)* the percentage of qualified physical education teachers in (i) primary and (ii) secondary schools.    [23669]

**Mr. Robin Squire:** The information requested for secondary schools is available only for 1984, 1988 and 1992 from the secondary school staffing surveys. In those years the number of full-time teachers who were teaching physical education in maintained secondary schools in England and who had a post-A-level qualification in physical education was as follows:

| Year | Number of PE teachers ('000) | Number with a PE qualification ('000) | Percentage with qualification |
| --- | --- | --- | --- |
| 1984 | 37.9 | 21.6 | 57 |
| 1988 | 30.3 | 18.4 | 61 |
| 1992 | 24.4 | 16.5 | 68 |

The total number of full-time teachers with a physical education qualification, including those not reaching PE, in each year was:

| Year | All teachers with a PE qualification (thousands) |
| --- | --- |
| 1984 | 36.4 |
| 1988 | 31.6 |
| 1992 | 30.3 |

No figures are available centrally for the number of physical education teachers in primary schools.

## Higher Education

**Mr. Worthington:** To ask the Secretary of State for Education what proportion of the appropriate age group has attained university entrance standards in each year since 1979.    [23388]

**Mr. Boswell:** There is no formal minimum qualification for entrance to higher education; however, the normal requirement for young entrants is that the candidate possesses two or more A-levels, or the equivalent.

Figures for the proportions of students obtaining two or more A-levels are shown in the Department for Education and Office for Standards in Education departmental report which is held in the Library. The figures are in annex B, table D (page 80): GCE A/AS level examinations, England 1979–80 to 1993–94.

## DEFENCE

## Land Mines

**Mr. Wigley:** To ask the Secretary of State for Defence how many representations he has received this year concerning the United Kingdom policy on land mines; and what proposals he has to change Government policy on this issue.    [23941]

**Mr. Freeman:** My Department has received a number of representations this year about land mines. We have no plans to change our policy on this issue.

## Low Flying

**Mr. Blunkett:** To ask the Secretary of State for Defence what trials or low-level flying exercises were undertaken by the RAF over the Sheffield city conurbation on Monday 1 May; for what purpose; and if he will make a statement. [23640]

**Mr. Soames:** Military aircrews are instructed to avoid flying low over major towns and conurbations. We have no record of any specific authority having been given for a waiver of this regulation in respect of Sheffield on Monday 1 May. If the hon. Member is concerned about a particular incident he should provide details, including the times, the names and addresses of any witnesses and, if possible, the number of aircraft involved, to my noble Friend the Parliamentary Under-Secretary of State for Defence who will arrange for the matter to be investigated.

## Mr. Perry Miller

**Dr. David Clark:** To ask the Secretary of State for Defence, pursuant to his Answer of 9 May, *Official Report*, column *401*, how many days' notice his former special adviser, Mr. Perry Miller, was required to give under his terms and conditions of employment following the decision to end his employment; and how many days Mr. Miller actually served following his notification that he wished to end his appointment. [24609]

**Mr. Rifkind:** Under his terms and conditions of employment, Mr. Perry Miller was required to give 35 days notice; he served 57 days following formal notification that he wished to end his employment.

## E-mail

**Dr. David Clark:** To ask the Secretary of State for Defence to what extend his Department uses e-mail to transmit messages and information amongst his staff. [24611]

**Mr. Freeman:** E-mail is being used on various computer systems within the Department, the largest of which is the corporate headquarters office technology system CHOTS currently links 6,700 users at 14 sites by e-mail, including the Secretary of State for Defence's office, and 3,000 Ministry of Defence users in the main building alone. A significant proportion of MOD Departmental business is now conducted on the system.

## CHOTS Computer

**Dr. David Clark:** To ask the Secretary of State for Defence what was the total cost of his Department's corporate head office technology systems computer; what was its original estimated cost at today's prices; when the computer system first began operation; when it will be fully installed; who manufactures the CHOTS system; how many people it serves; to what extent it is out of date; what communications he has had with his departmental staff concerning CHOTS and what were the results of these consultations; what assessment he has made of the adequacy of the CHOTS; and if he will make a statement. [24616]

**Mr. Freeman:** The latest assessment of total cost at current prices, which includes installation and support of the system, MOD manpower costs and enabling works, amounts to £392 million over an agreed 10-year period.

This compares with approved funding agreed in 1991 which uprated to current prices is £394 million.

Operation of CHOTS began in October 1992 and by the end of April 1995 there were 6,700 users. Implementation was originally planned to complete in 1996 but the present plan contains four sites that will be implemented after 1996 because of internal restructuring within the MOD and the armed forces.

Hardware and software from a variety of sources is procured and installed by the prime contractor, ICL. CHOTS has been upgraded four times since the original technical design in 1989 but was not able to support MS Windows applications. A recent review involving a wide range of existing and potential CHOTS users established a clear need to operate a range of modern commercial software on the CHOTS workstation. As a result it was agreed that a further development be undertaken to meet this requirement.

**Dr. David Clark:** To ask the Secretary of State for Defence which computer system is used by his Department's Procurement Executive; if the Procurement Executive is fitted with the corporate headquarters office technology system; how many people at the Procurement Executive use CHOTS; and if he will make a statement. [24617]

**Mr. Freeman:** At present the Procurement Executive utilises a number of computer systems appropriate to its needs. This includes CHOTS for those staff employed in areas in which CHOTS has been introduced. A total of approximately 1560 PE staff currently have access to CHOTS.

## Bosnia

**Dr. David Clark:** To ask the Secretary of State for Defence, pursuant to his answer of 9 May, *Official Report*, column *401*, how many British troops will be located in Bosnia after the withdrawal of British troops from Gorazde in September 1995; and how many British troops are currently stationed in Bosnia. [24608]

**Mr. Soames:** We intend to maintain a major contribution to UNPROFOR for as long as the force can continue to carry out its mandate at an acceptable level of risk, though it is too early to say how many British troops will be in Bosnia after September 1995. There are currently some 3,4000 British troops in the former Yugoslavia.

## Departmental Paperwork

**Dr. David Clark:** To ask the Secretary of State for Defence through what mechanisms his Department monitors the quantity of its internal paperwork. [24610]

**Mr. Freeman:** My Department has no formal mechanism to monitor the quantity of its internal paperwork, nor would it be easy to develop such a mechanism. None the less, the Department is keen to ensure that staff are encouraged to generate no more paperwork than is absolutely necessary to achieve departmental objectives.

As part of the Department's campaign to improve working practices, described in the essay on the "New Working Culture" on page 94 of SDE 1995, new guidelines are to be issued to staff on preparing and circulating written work. In due course, one measure of the effectiveness of this campaign should be a reduction in the amount of paper consumed.

### Tri-service Chaplaincy School

**Mr. Brazier:** To ask the Secretary of State for Defence if he will make a statement on the proposed location of the tri-service chaplaincy school. [24912]

**Mr. Soames:** As part of "Front Line First" we announced our intention to establish a single tri-service chaplaincy school. Further work on this issue has led us to conclude that, subject to consultation, the school should be located at Amport house from 1 April 1996. A consultative document covering this proposal is being issued today. As part of the further work we are examining the future of Eltham palace and Queen Elizabeth barracks Guildford and, if no alternative defence uses are found for either site, we will seek to dispose of our interest in them.

### Postal and Courier Service

**Mr. Brazier:** To ask the Secretary of State for Defence if he has begun the review of the Defence Postal and Courier Services agency. [24913]

**Mr. Soames:** A review of the agency status of Defence Postal and Courier Services is under way. As a Defence agency, the performance of the Defence Postal and Courier Services will be subjected to the prior options review set out in the 1993 "Next Steps Review", CM 2430.

Comments and contributions from those with an interest in Defence Postal and Courier Services and its work will be welcomed and should be sent by 27 June to:

DPCS Review Team,
Log Sp Pol 2,
HQ, QMG,
Andover,
Hants,
SP11 8HT.

### Hydrographic Office

**Mr. Robathan:** To ask the Secretary of State for Defence when the Hydrographic Office Defence agency's triennial review was completed; and what were its conclusions. [24914]

**Mr. Soames:** The Hydrographic Office's triennial review has now been completed and has confirmed that the Hydrographic Office should continue as a Defence agency. In addition, an evaluation study was carried out regarding the agency's performance over the first three years, which has concluded that;

(a) Both commercial and Government customers found that the Hydrographic Office's products were second to none, and its response time had considerably improved, whilst continuing to provide good value for money;

(b) Target setting procedures had been refined and developed which has resulted in robust and realistic targets, most of which have been met;

(c) Agency management had made full use of delegated powers and is actively working to extend them, particularly in the personnel field where it has instigated a pay and grading review.

An executive summary of the evaluation study is being placed in the Library of the House.

## NATIONAL HERITAGE

### National Lottery

**Dr. Godman:** To ask the Secretary of State for National Heritage what recent representations he has received concerning the distribution of national lottery funds to Scottish voluntary organisations for the funding of sports and sports facilities for disabled people; and if he will make a statement. [23343]

**Mr. Dorrell:** I have received no such representations.

### Commonwealth Games

**Mr. Beggs:** To ask the Secretary of State for National Heritage how many technical officials in England received grant aid towards travel expenses in respect of the Victoria, Canada, Commonwealth games in 1994. [23703]

**Mr. Sproat:** Twenty technical officials received grant aid towards travel expenses.

### Welsh Fourth Channel

**Mr. Garel-Jones:** To ask the Secretary of State for National Heritage whether he has now received the report of the inquiry into applications for funding under the business sponsorship incentive scheme in connection with payments made by the Welsh Fourth Channel Authority; and if he will make a statement. [24917]

**Mr. Dorrell:** I announced on 27 February *Official Report*, column *680*, that my Department had commissioned a report from a senior Treasury official, Mr. John Beastall, to review the circumstances of the applications for matching funding under the business sponsorship incentive scheme made by Pengwyn Pinc and certain other Welsh arts bodies. I have now received and considered Mr. Beastall's report. Copies have been placed in the Library.

The report takes account of reports received by the Department of National Heritage from the Association for Business Sponsorship of the Arts, which runs the BSIS on the Department's behalf, and from the Welsh Fourth Channel Authority—S4C. It draws on an examination of the relevant records and a series of interviews with staff of S4C and the companies and organisations involved in the applications conducted, at S4C's request, by Grant Thornton, S4C's auditors. Mr. Beastall has interviewed certain S4C and ABSA staff himself.

The report's main conclusions are:

In 1993 and 1994 S4C made sponsorship payments via intermediary companies to Welsh arts organisations totalling £53,500 in respect of which BSIS matching funding was claimed. These claims were an abuse of the BSIS because of S4C's position as publicly-funded body.

All the intermediary companies were genuinely trading and wholly independent of S4C. Confirmation has been obtained that the relevant arts organisations received the S4C money in full. There is no evidence that any of the intermediary companies, their directors or S4C staff received any financial gain from the transactions. A thorough investigation has revealed no other instances of abuse of the BSIS through sponsorship funds originating from S4C.

The recipient arts bodies, to the extent that they were aware of the ultimate source of the sponsorship funds, must share responsibility for the improper claims because they completed the BSIS application forms without disclosing the true source of the sponsorship funds and because their applications were not consistent with the BSIS objective of encouraging extra sponsorship from businesses. The intermediary companies must similarly share some responsibility.

In two cases, where S4C staff were the prime movers in the setting up of artificial arrangements designed to secure additional public funding for recipient bodies which would not otherwise have been obtainable and which was clearly contrary to the rules and objectives of the BSIS, the main responsibility lies with S4C. S4C staff should in any event have consulted ABSA in all the cases about whether the proposed arrangements were acceptable.

In the Pengwyn Pinc case, ABSA should have checked with S4C whether the claims made by the company about likely future contracts from S4C were valid.

In order to ensure that there is no loss to public funds, S4C have agreed to pay to ABSA from their non-public sector funds a sum equivalent to the BSIS grants which were wrongly made, to the extent that these are not recoverable by ABSA. S4C should consider whether they can appropriately recover the relevant sum from the arts organisations concerned.

Disciplinary action has been taken against one member of S4C's staff. S4C is considering whether there is a case for disciplinary action against any other staff involved.

ABSA should have notified S4C in writing that S4C's sponsorship payments were no longer eligible for BSIS matching after S4C's change in status to a statutory corporation from 1 January 1993.

The new BSIS rule requiring full disclosure if a sponsor is acting as an indirect source of sponsorship from a third party should be amended so that applicants must state that they are not deriving their sponsorship funds from a third party.

In future ABSA should make rigorous checks in any case where there is doubt whether the sponsoring company is making the payment from its own funds. ABSA should also make it clear that in future any arts body or sponsoring company knowingly involved in arrangements designed to secure BSIS funds contrary to the rules or objectives of the BSIS will be disqualified from benefitting from the BSIS either permanently or for a substantial period.

The arrangement between ABSA and the trade association Teledwyr Annibynnol Cymru Cyf—TAC—whereby TAC receives applications from arts organisations and proposes to member companies that they should sponsor particular arts events, should have been referred to ABSA headquarters before it was agreed. It is accepted by ABSA that this arrangement with TAC should now cease. Any future arrangement for BSIS matching of sponsorship by TAC members should require that sponsorship payments made by a company derive solely from that company's own funds and should take appropriate account of previous sponsorships.

In future ABSA should obtain an account or auditor's certificate that the BSIS grant has been spent as intended in all major cases and should establish a procedure for checking a sample of smaller cases. ABSA already have such arrangements in hand.

All future sponsorship payments made by S4C will be clearly identified as such. All sponsorship proposals will be approved by the authority on the recommendation of the chief executive.

S4C has agreed that when it makes sponsorship payments in future:

(a) the payments should be made direct to the final recipient, not via any third party;

(b) the recipient should be explicitly told in writing that the sponsorship payment is not eligible for BSIS matching;

(c) S4C should inform ABSA in confidence of any arts sponsorship payments it makes.

S4C should require a subsequent account or auditor's certificate that sponsorship funding has been spent appropriately. This procedure is now in effect.

S4C's relationship with TAC should be clearly at arm's length. This does not preclude the continuation of the arrangement whereby S4C, on TAC's behalf, deducts a percentage of programme fees due to TAC members and transmits it to TAC for the purpose of funding such activities as training and sponsorship. S4C has agreed that any future contributions by S4C towards TAC's administrative costs should be covered by a contract specifying the services to S4C for which the payment is made.

It has been S4C's policy that fees paid to TAC members should not be higher than the market rate. There needs to be a continuing effective check that this remains the case.

The role of S4C staff who are members of the ABSA Wales Committee should be defined and agreed between S4C and ABSA.

S4C has introduced arrangements to prevent possible conflicts of interest arising in cases where members of the Authority or S4C staff are involved in the work of other companies or organisations.

The chief executive as accounting officer is responsible for ensuring that appropriate standards of financial propriety are maintained within S4C and has already taken action to this end. However to assist him in this a senior member of management below chief executive level should have the clear responsibility of promoting appropriate standards of financial propriety throughout the organisation and of acting as the acknowledged source of advice when any issues of propriety arise.

DNH should check whether there is any risk of the improper use of public funds in any other cases where the department provides funds on a matching basis.

I am grateful to Mr. Beastall for carrying out this thorough review and for making practical recommendations to ensure the proper use of public money. In a number of instances, the bodies concerned have already taken the necessary steps to implement these conclusions. My officials will monitor carefully the action taken by the bodies concerned in response to the report's recommendations.

### Public Library Review

**Mr. Alan Howarth:** To ask the Secretary of State for National Heritage if he will publish the ASLIB consultancy study commissioned as part of the public library review.        [24915]

**Mr. Dorrell:** The ASLIB consultancy was commissioned by my predecessor to produce a report as part of a major review of the public library service in England and Wales. I am today authorising the publication of the report and seeking public reactions to its contents, and depositing copies in the Libraries of the House.

This is a time of major change for the public library service. The review aims to provide fundamental examination of its future, and ASLIB has produced a very full report as part of that process. In doing so, it has examined the public library service currently provided by local authorities in England and Wales and the context within which they operate; and it has consulted widely.

Public libraries are important to all sectors of the community. Each year more than 24 million adults in England and Wales use them. The ASLIB report draws attention to those services which the public values particularly highly, and demonstrates that libraries play a crucial role in the economy of the United Kingdom.

The report addresses a number of recommendations to the Government. We shall of course consider them carefully; but I can make it clear now that:

I have no intention of introducing charges for the present free core of the public library service;

I will be taking forward the proposals that Government should produce guidance notes for local authorities to define more clearly the range of core services which libraries should provide. In doing so, however, I am conscious of the desirability of leaving decisions about how best to provide such services for local authorities to decide in the light of local circumstances.

I am not inclined to establish a new independent library inspectorate; and

I do not intend to change the present legislation governing public library services.

Most of the recommendations in the report are addressed to local authorities, and I am seeking their views. However, I can make it clear now that I support in principle an approach under which local authorities:

state explicitly what kind of library service they want to buy, however that service is delivered; and

explore innovative ways of providing that service, including new technology and diverse sources of finance.

The separate study that I have commissioned of the scope for contracting out public library services will make a valuable contribution to this debate.

Following consultation with local authorities and other interests, I expect to make a further statement on the outcome of the review later this year.

## Telephones

**Mr. Donohoe:** To ask the Secretary of State for National Heritage how many mobile telephones being used by his Department have been cloned during the last 12 months. [23431]

**Mr. Dorrell** *[holding answer 9 May 1995]:* My Department has never been a victim of mobile telephone cloning.

**Mr. Donohoe:** To ask the Secretary of State for National Heritage what use his Department makes of hand-held and car-based mobile telephones; what were the costs for each financial year of these services since mobile telephones were first introduced to his Department; and how many mobile telephones are currently in use.

[23445]

**Mr. Dorrell** *[holding answer 9 May 1995]:* I refer the hon. Member to the answer given by my hon. Friend the Parliamentary Under-Secretary of State to the hon. Member for Leicester East (Mr. Vaz) on 20 May 1994, *Official Report* columns *601-2.* In 1994–95 the costs were £12,600 running costs and £6,800 capital.

## Public Bodies

**Mr. Flynn:** To ask the Secretary of State for National Heritage which non-departmental public bodies within the responsibility of his Department are subject to scrutiny by *(a)* the ombudsmen, *(b)* the National Audit Office, *(c)* the Audit Commission and *(d)* other monitoring officers; which are covered by citizens charters; in which performance indicators apply; and in which members are liable to surcharge. [23960]

**Mr. Dorrell** *[holding answer 15 May 1995]:* My Department's executive and advisory non-departmental public bodies are listed in "Public Bodies 1994". On 4 April 1995, the Advisory Council on Libraries took over from the Library and Information Services Council (England) the statutory responsibilities established under the Public Libraries and Museums Act 1964. The

functions and responsibilities of each body are specified in its founding legislation or charter. The information requested is as follows:

(a) Bodies subject to the jurisdiction of the Parliamentary Commissioner for Administration are listed in schedule 2 of the Parliamentary Commissioner Act 1967 as amended. This includes:

Arts Council of England

British Film Institute

British Library Board

Crafts Council

English Tourist Board

Historic Buildings and Monuments Commission (English Heritage)

Museums and Galleries Commission

Trustees of the National Heritage Memorial Fund

Register of Public Lending Right

Sports Council

(b) All of my Department's executive NDPBs are subject to scrutiny by the Comptroller and Auditor General with the exception of the National Film development fund. The funding of most of the Department's advisory NDPBs forms part of DNH's expenditure and DNH's accounts are audited by the Comptroller and Auditor General. The accounts of the Theatres Trust are audited by a commercial firm.

(c) None.

(d) My Department monitors the performance of its NDPBs as part of the corporate planning process, through which targets and performance indicators are set. The principles of the citizens charter apply to all the Department's NDPBs. There are no surcharging arrangements with regard to members of the Department's NDPBs.

## TRADE AND INDUSTRY

### Electricity Generation Inquiries

**Mr. Ainger:** To ask the President of the Board of Trade if he will list the applications by power generating companies under section 36 of the Electricity Act 1989 that have been referred to a public inquiry *(a)* directly by his Department or *(b)* as a result of a decision by a local authority; and if he will list the length of time between the referral and the completion of the public inquiry in each case. [24297]

**Mr. Page:** The information requested is as follows:

*Public inquiries under section 36 of the Electricity Act 1989*

| Station | Announcement made | Inspector's report |
| --- | --- | --- |
| *(a)* | | |
| Didcot B | 6 September 1991 | 8 June 1992 |
| | | |
| *(b)* | | |
| Hinkley Point C | 21 March 1988 | 4 June 1990 |
| Ryedale | 13 September 1991 | 18 June 1992 |
| Staythorpe C | 29 October 1991 | 19 March 1992 |
| Belvedere | 30 June 1992 | 3 November 1993 |

*Note:*

Pursuant to the Electricity Generating Stations and Overhead Lines (Inquiries Procedure) Rules 1990, SI 1990 No. 528 a period of not less than six weeks from the announcement of an inquiry being made to it opening must be given in order to allow for the serving of statements of case.

## Energy Use Forecasts

**Mr. Robert Ainsworth:** To ask the President of the Board of Trade what assessment he has made of the extent to which 8 per cent. reduction in electricity prices, announced as part of the nuclear review, affects the forecasts for energy use and $CO_2$ emissions contained in Energy Paper 65.    [24217]

**Mr. Eggar:** Energy Paper 65 assumed that the nuclear component of the fossil fuel levy would cease in 1998. It is expected that the early removal of the levy will have a negligible impact on the long-run energy and $CO_2$ projections contained in Energy Paper 65. There will, however, be a small short-run impact on energy and $CO_2$ levels. In view of this, my right hon. Friend the Secretary of State for the Environment announced on 11 May 1995, *Official Report*, columns *564–65*, that he would make available an additional £25 million a year to the Energy Saving Trust to promote energy efficiency measures, from 1996 until the gas and electricity markets are fully liberalised.

## Nuclear Industry

**Mr. Clapham:** To ask the President of the Board of Trade (1) what assessment his Department has made of the effectiveness of the investment of the fossil fuel levy in Sizewell B by Nuclear Electric;    [24570]

(2) what was the application of premium income received by Nuclear Electric under the fossil fuel obligation contract with regional electricity companies, reimbursed through the fossil fuel levy, for each year from 1990–91 to 1994–95; and what estimates have been made for the use of this income up to the end of 1996.    [24572]

**Mr. Eggar:** Payments to Nuclear Electric from the fossil fuel levy are not hypothecated to any particular purpose. It follows that the information requested is unavailable.

The economics of the Sizewell B project were examined exhaustively during the planning inquiry, which gave planning consent for its construction, and again in 1990 by the Government when they confirmed the decision to continue construction.

**Mr. Milburn:** To ask the President of the Board of Trade, pursuant to his answer of 7 December 1994, *Official Report*, columns *257–59*, if he will list those projects in the civil nuclear power industry which have received European regional development funding over the last 10 years indicating, in each case, *(a)* the level of funding and *(b)* when it was received.    [24673]

**Mr. Eggar:** There were no such projects.

**Mr. Llew Smith:** To ask the President of the Board of Trade what is the basis for the assumption made in the footnote to the table at paragraph 5.22 and in paragraph 5.23 of the nuclear review White Paper, Cm 2860, that the lifetime cost for electricity from a Sizewell C pressurised water reactor would fall in the range of 3.5p to 5.75p per kilowatt hour.    [24400]

**Mr. Eggar:** The judgment that lifetime generation costs of Sizewell C would fall within a range of 3.5p to 5.75p per kilowatt hour, expressed in 1990 price,s was based on an assessment of evidence to the nuclear review. The range takes account of uncertainties in such key variables as capital cost, station load factor and the required rate of return for a private sector nuclear generation project. These uncertainties are discussed in chapter 4 of the White Paper. The range quoted in paragraph 5.23 covers the bulk of the range of cost estimates given in evidence to the review as reported in chapter 4.

**Mr. Llew Smith:** To ask the President of the Board of Trade, pursuant to paragraphs 7.30 and 7.31 of the nuclear review White Paper, Cm *2860*, if he will make a statement on the ways in which those existing nuclear plant sites which jointly contain Magnox reactors and advanced gas cooled or pressurised water reactors which currently share common safety, waste management, railhead or other facilities will have these roles and assets divided between the Magnox public company and the private GB Co. operating on the same sites after privatisation.    [24661]

**Mr. Eggar:** Arrangements will be put in place to ensure the continued safe and efficient operation of all the nuclear stations currently operated by Scottish Nuclear and Nuclear Electric when the AGR and PWR stations are privatised and the Magnox stations placed in a new public sector company. Safety will be the paramount consideration and the arrangements will be subject to the requirements of the nuclear installations inspectorate.

**Mr. Llew Smith:** To ask the President of the Board of Trade what evaluation was made in the nuclear review on non-proliferation concerns addressed at paragraphs 10.43 and 10.44 of the nuclear review White Paper, of doubts raised by submissions, including that by the hon. Member for Blaenau Gwent (Mr. Smith), on whether sufficient resources had been allocated to ensure the proper implementation of the nuclear safeguards measures to which reference is made on page 74 of Cm *2860*.    [24420]

**Mr. Eggar:** All submissions to the nuclear review were given careful and detailed consideration. We are satisfied that appropriate resources have been allocated to ensure the proper implementation of nuclear safeguards measures in the UK.

**Mr. Llew Smith:** To ask the President of the Board of Trade if he will list those local authorities and environmental organisations consulted by KPMG Peat Marwick in its evaluation of nuclear liabilities as mentioned at paragraph 8.12 of the nuclear review White Paper, Cm 2860; what criteria were adopted in choosing these bodies for consultation.    [24421]

**Mr. Eggar:** The liabilities management study was carried out as part of the nuclear review. All the documents submitted as part of the nuclear review process were made available to KPMG, and were taken into account by KPMG, in so far as they were relevant to its terms of reference. It was for KPMG to decide what level of further consultation was necessary, and with whom, to enable it to complete its study. I understand that, in the event, KPMG followed up the submissions from Friends of the Earth and Greenpeace by holding direct meeting with them, but that there were no direct meetings with local authorities.

**Mr. Alan W. Williams:** To ask the President of the Board of Trade what was the total cost at 1995 prices of construction of *(a)* the Sizewell pressurised water reactor and *(b)* each of the advanced gas-cooled reactors in Britain.    [23947]

**Mr. Eggar** *[holding answer 15 May 1995]:* I refer the hon. Member to the note on tangible fixed assets on page 67 of the report and accounts of nuclear electric 1993–94. Copies of which are available in the Library of the House.

**Mr. Llew Smith:** To ask the President of the Board of

Trade what is his estimate of the financial value of the liabilities to be transferred to the privatised nuclear holding company and its subsidiaries.          [24290]

**Mr. Eggar** *[holding answer 15 May 1995]:* The Government's aim is to privatise as much of the nuclear liabilities of Scottish Nuclear and Nuclear Electric as possible. The liabilities associated with their AGR and PWR stations will be transferred to the private sector when these stations are privatised under the holding company structure. The Magnox stations and associated liabilities will be retained in the public sector, initially in a stand alone company. The value of the liabilities in each case will be published in the accounts of the various companies in due course.

**Mr. Llew Smith:** To ask the President of the Board of Trade if article 14 of the 1978 tripartite safeguards agreement between the United Kingdom, Euratom and the International Atomic Energy Agency, Cmnd 6730, permitting the withdrawal of civil nuclear materials for national security reasons, will apply to the safeguards arrangements set out at paragraph 10.44 at page 74 of the nuclear review White Paper, Cm 2860.          [24312]

**Mr. Eggar** *[holding answer 15 May 1995]:* Yes.

### Car Seat Covers

**Mr. Nigel Griffiths:** To ask the President of the Board of Trade if he will takes steps to include loose car seat covers and car seats in the definition of furniture in the Furniture and Furnishings (Fire) (Safety) Regulations 1988 as is amended or introduce legislation to set safety standards for car seats and loose car seat covers.  [24434]

**Mr. Jonathan Evans:** I have no present plans to do so. So far, there is no evidence to suggest that the flammability of current loose car seat covers or car seats represents a significant risk to life and would warrant inclusion within the scope of, for example, the Furniture and Furnishings (Fire) (Safety) Regulations 1988, as amended.

### Director General of Fair Trading

**Mr. Nigel Griffiths:** To ask the President of the Board of Trade when the appointment of Sir Bryan Carsberg's successor as Director General of Fair Trading will be announced.          [24439]

**Mr. Jonathan Evans:** Good progress has been made towards making an appointment and I expect an announcement to be made within the next few weeks.

### Monopolies and Mergers Commission

**Mr. Nigel Griffiths:** To ask the President of the Board of Trade (1) what decisions the Office of Fair Trading has taken concerning the provision of misleading information to the Monopolies and Mergers Commission investigation into the supply of ice cream;          [24438]

(2) if any criminal proceedings are either under consideration or pending under section 93B of the Fair Trading Act 1973 as a result of misleading information being provided to the Monopolies and Mergers Commission over the past three years;          [24436]

(3) how many reports from the Monopolies and Mergers Commission in the past three years are considered unsafe and have been or are being reconsidered by the Office of Fair Trading as a result of

powers given to the Director General of Fair Trading by the Deregulation and Contracting Out Act 1994.  [24437]

**Mr. Jonathan Evans:** No reports received from the MMC in the past three years have been considered unsafe. However, the Office of Fair Trading is currently pursuing inquiries concerning allegations that certain evidence presented to the Monopolies and Mergers Commission during its investigation into the supply in the UK of ice cream for immediate consumption was misleading. No decisions have yet been taken concerning any further action which might arise under section 93B of the Fair Trading Act. I am not aware of any other inquiries in connection with section 93B of the Act.

### Energy Research and Development

**Mr. Hardy:** To ask the President of the Board of Trade what has been the expenditure from public funds on research and development relating to the production of energy in each of the last five years; and what expenditure he expects to be devoted to these matters during each of the next three years.          [24201]

**Mr. Eggar:** Details of expenditure in the last five years by DTI and the former Department of Energy on research and development relating to the production of energy are contained in Departmental annual reports and expenditure plans, Cm Nos. 1505, 1905, 2204, 2504. The latest departmental report "Trade and Industry 1995: The Government's Expenditure Plans 1995–96 to 1997–98," Cm 2804, also gives information about the Government's plans for such expenditure in future years.

Information about expenditure on research and development by public corporations is contained in their annual reports and accounts.

These publications are available in the Library of the House.

### VSEL

**Mr. Hutton:** To ask the President of the Board of Trade when he expects to announce his decision on the Monopolies and Mergers Commission report into the future ownership of VSEL.          [24509]

**Mr. Jonathan Evans:** My right hon. Friend the President of the Board of Trade will publish the MMC reports on the proposed acquisition of VSEL, together with any decision which it falls to him to take, as soon as is reasonably practicable.

### Nigeria

**Mr. Wray:** To ask the President of the Board of Trade if he will instruct his officials in the overseas trade division to suspend their trade promotion visits to Nigeria.          [24184]

**Mr. Needham** *[holding answer 15 May 1995]:* The Government recognise the difficulties of conducting business with Nigeria in the present political and economic climate. Nigeria nevertheless remain the United Kingdom's second largest export market in Africa. UK exports in 1994, although significantly down on the previous year, still amounted to £457.9 million. It would not be appropriate to withdraw the support the Department of Trade and Industry gives to UK companies continuing to do business in Nigeria.

## Companies House

**Mr. Morgan:** To ask the President of the Board of Trade if the contract to advise on the contracting out of functions in Companies House was *(a)* competitively tendered for and *(b)* publicly advertised; and if he will make a statement.        [23977]

**Mr. Jonathan Evans** *[holding answer 15 May 1995]:* I can confirm that the appointment of consultants to advise on the contracting out of Companies House, London, and the satellite offices was as a result of a competitive tender following an advertisement in the *Official Journal* of the European Communities.

**Mr. Morgan:** To ask the President of the Board of Trade what is the current estimate of the dates on which he anticipates letting out the contractorisation contracts within Companies House at *(a)* Edinburgh, *(b)* London and *(c)* Cardiff.        [23981]

**Mr. Jonathan Evans** *[holding answer 15 May 1995]:* The London contract is likely to be awarded by the end of January 1996 and the Edinburgh and Cardiff contracts by the end of the current financial year.

**Mr. Morgan:** To ask the President of the Board of Trade if the value of the contract awarded to PA Consulting group to advise on the contracting out of functions at Companies House exceeds £250,000 per annum; on what date PA started the contract; and how long it is estimated to last.        [23976]

**Mr. Jonathan Evans** *[holding answer 15 May 1995]:* While the precise value of the contract with PA Consulting group to provide advice on contracting out Companies House, London, is commercially confidential, I can confirm it is less than £250,000. PA started work in February this year. The target is to have a contractor in place in Companies House, London, by end January 1996.

**Mr. Morgan:** To ask the President of the Board of Trade what guidelines he has given to PA Consulting group debarring the letting of contracts for the contractorisation of Companies House, Edinburgh, London and Cardiff to the same contractor.        [23978]

**Mr. Jonathan Evans** *[holding answer 15 May 1995]:* No such guidelines have been issued.

## PA Consulting

**Mr. Morgan:** To ask the President of the Board of Trade what consultation he had with the special compliance office of the Inland Revenue concerning its allegations of tax irregularities at PA Consulting prior to the appointment of that company to oversee the contracting out of Companies House functions at Edinburgh, London and Cardiff.        [23868]

**Mr. Jonathan Evans** *[holding answer 15 May 1995]:* There were no such consultations. Tax affairs of individual companies are confidential.

## EMPLOYMENT

### Health and Safety

**Mr. McCartney:** To ask the Secretary of State for Employment how many applications to industrial tribunals there have been under the Safety Representatives and Safety Committee Regulations 1977 for each year since 1978.        [23373]

**Mr. Oppenheim:** The number of applications to the industrial tribunals under these regulations was as follows:

| Year | Number of applications |
| --- | --- |
| 1994–95 | 14 |
| 1993–94 | 11 |
| 1992–93 | 2 |
| 1991–92 | 16 |
| 1990–91 | 11 |
| 1989–90 | 7 |
| 1988–89 | 10 |
| 1987–88 | 4 |
| 1986–87 | 5 |

Prior to these dates, applications under the above regulations were not separately identified, but were aggregated with appeals dealt with under the Health and Safety Improvement and Prohibition Notice Appeals Regulations. However, detailed records of applications under these regulations are no longer available for the period prior to January 1984.

### Jobseeker's Allowance

**Mr. McCartney:** To ask the Secretary of State for Employment (1) if he will list the information technology that will be required to implement the jobseeker's allowance; what are its costs; and if it will be installed and ready to use by April 1996;        [23933]

(2) what contingency plans have been developed in case the information technology that will be required to implement the jobseeker's allowance is not installed and ready to use by April 1996; if such plans could process annually *(a)* fewer than 100,000, *(b)* between 100,000 and 250,000, *(c)* between 250,000 and 500,000, *(d)* between 500,000 and 1 million, *(e)* between 1 million and 2 million and *(f)* more than 2 million; and what are its costs.

[23934]

**Miss Widdecombe:** The new computer systems will support the implementation of the jobseeker's allowance. The labour market system will replace current computer systems in Employment Service jobcentres used to support vacancy filling and advisory work, at an implementation cost of around £70 million.

The JSA payments system is being developed to pay JSA, by girocheque or automated credit transfer, at an implementation cost of around £40 million to March 1997.

In addition, the stand-alone computer system currently used in ES sector adjudication offices, adjudication officer automation, will continue to be used to support adjudication and appeals casework.

We are keeping progress on the development and installation of information technology systems and equipment under close review. If we conclude that the arrangements being made cannot be put in place or only at an unacceptable level of risk in April 1996, alternatives will be considered.

**Mr. McCartney:** To ask the Secretary of State for Employment if he will undertake that no job seeker will lose any money due to him or her if the information technology that will be required to implement the jobseeker's allowance is not installed and ready to use by April 1996.                                            [23945]

**Miss Widdecombe:** Yes. The aims of the Jobseekers Bill are to help people into jobs, improve our services to people while they are unemployed and achieve better value for the taxpayer. The Government's priority is to introduce the jobseeker's allowance through the network of 1,200 jobcentres for unemployed people throughout the country. This is a large and complex undertaking. It involves development of two substantial new computer systems and very large-scale training programmes. We have kept the project under close review. Substantial progress has been made but we have now concluded that, in order to deliver an excellent service to unemployed people from day one, JSA should be introduced in October 1996.

The transitional arrangements for JSA will be such that the duration of an unemployed claimant's entitlement to unemployment benefit will, from April 1996, be the same as it would have been had JSA been introduced on that date.

Plans for the introduction of the back-to-work Bonus are unaffected. The bonus will be introduced as planned in October 1996.

### Asbestos

**Mr. McCartney:** To ask the Secretary of State for Employment what inquiry the Health and Safety Executive has conducted into the asbestos removal industry; what its conclusions were; and what plans there are for a further inquiry.                            [23718]

**Mr. Oppenheim:** The Asbestos (Licensing) Regulations 1983, which require contractors to obtain a licence from the Health and Safety Executive to carry out work removing asbestos, have been subject to two reviews. The reviews found that the regulations have been effective in improving the standards of performance of asbestos removal contractors, and that the regulations are working well in practice. No further review is currently considered necessary. HSE's field inspection programmes for 1994–95 and 1995–96 include increased visit targets for asbestos contractors' sites.

### Benefit Fraud

**Mr. David Atkinson:** To ask the Secretary of State for Employment what has been the change since 1992 in personnel involved in investigating fraud and abuse of the unemployment benefit system; and if he will make a statement on the results that have been achieved including a comparison between the cost and the amount saved.
[24450]

**Miss Widdecombe:** Responsibility of the subject of the question has been delegated to the Employment Service agency under its chief executive. I have asked him to arrange for a reply to be given.

*Letter from M. E. G. Fogden to Mr. David Atkinson, dated 16 May 1995:*

The Secretary of State has asked me to reply to your question about the numbers of, and results achieved by, Employment Service (ES) personnel involved in the investigation of fraud and abuse of the unemployment benefit system.

The table below contains the information you requested:

|  | 1992–93 | 1993–94 | 1994–95 |
|---|---|---|---|
| Total number of staff (investigators) | 1,343 (780) | 1,343 (780) | 1,343 (780) |
| Gross savings[1] | £71.15 million | £80.12 million | £92.1 million |
| Cost of fraud operation | £26.44 million | £26.84 million | £27.5 million |
| Net savings | £44.71 million | £53.28 million | £64.6 million |
| Investment return[2] | £2.69 | £2.99 | £3.35 |
| Number of sign-offs[3] | 61,129 | 67,426 | 78,231 |

[1] This figure is calculated by multiplying the weekly amount of benefit saved by 22. The 22 week figure was identified by the Department of Social Security research and represents the average number of weeks claimants would have remained on the register if they had not been investigated by fraud staff.
[2] £s of benefit saved for every £ of cost.
[3] Number of clients withdrawing their claims to benefit after investigation by ES inspectors.

The number of claims withdrawn following investigation by ES inspectors has risen impressively over the past three years, indicating effective targeting of fraudulent activity and increasingly efficient use of resources.

The year on year increase in savings has been achieved without any significant increase in resource.

I hope this is helpful

### Job Vacancy Advertisements

**Mr. Chidgey:** To ask the Secretary of state for Employment what instructions his Department gives to jobcentres on the circumstances in which they can include minimum or maximum age restrictions on advertised job vacancies.                                     [23732]

**Miss Widdecombe:** Jobcentres are instructed to challenge age restrictions placed on job vacancies and to persuade employers to consider all job seekers on their merits. The only exception to this is where age limits are essential to the performance of the job, for example the need for the applicant to hold a driving licence or to qualify for insurance cover.

Where employers insist on imposing age limits, they are reluctantly accepted and included on the displayed vacancy details. However, jobcentre staff are then encouraged to approach and employer on behalf of an otherwise suitable jobseeker who falls outside the stated age limit.

This approach is outlined in the booklet "Too old . . . Who Says?, which gives job search advice to older workers. The Booklet was recently published as part of the campaign to combat age discrimination in the workplace. Copies are available to the public at jobcentres."

### Wages Councils

**Mr. Byers:** To ask the Secretary of State for Employment pursuant to his answer of 5 May, *Official Report*, column 322, if he will identify the industrial sectors in which wages councils mainly operated. [24175]

**Mr. Oppenheim** *[holding answer 15 May 1995]:* Wages Councils mainly operated within the hotel and catering, retailing and clothing manufacture sectors.

### Labour Statistics

**Mr. McCartney:** To ask the Secretary of State for Employment what information has been gathered through surveys and on the basis of notified redundancies on how many jobs have been lost and created, together with their pay rates, in the regions of the United Kingdom in the last quarter. [21797]

**Mr. Oppenheim** [holding answer 1 May 1995]: The labour force survey is the Department's main source of information on the number of redundancies. The latest regional figures from the LFS on redundancies and the net change of numbers in employment are given in the following table. There is no information available on the pay rates of jobs lost and created. Figures for Northern Ireland are only available for the spring quarter of each year.

*Not seasonally adjusted (Thousands)*

| Region | Redundancies[1] Autumn 1994 | Employment change summer 1994–autumn 1994 | Employment change autumn 1994–winter 1994–95 |
|---|---|---|---|
| Great Britain | 190 | 18 | −135 |
| North | 13 | 0 | −23 |
| Yorkshire and Humberside | 16 | 24 | −13 |
| East Midlands | 20 | 16 | 16 |
| East Anglia | [2]— | −3 | 0 |
| South East | 52 | 33 | −57 |
| South West | 14 | 0 | −25 |
| West Midlands | 17 | −20 | 4 |
| North West | 23 | −6 | −18 |
| Wales | [2]— | −9 | −15 |
| Scotland | 17 | −16 | −5 |

[1] Number of redundancies that took place in the three months prior to interview.
[2] Less than 10,000 in cell; estimate not shown.

# HEALTH

## Casualty Units

12. **Mr. Corbyn:** To ask the Secretary of State for Health what plans she has to meet health authorities to discuss casualty units. [22862]

**Mr. Sackville:** We have no such plans.

## Social Deprivation

13. **Mr. Olner:** To ask the Secretary of State for Health if she will make a statement on the link between social deprivation and ill health. [22863]

**Mr. Sackville:** Variations in health status between different socio-economic groups have been documented in Britain since the 1860s and are found across the developed world.

## Dermatology Services, London

14. **Mr. Fraser:** To ask the Secretary of State for Health what is her strategy for dermatology services in London. [22864]

**Mr. Sackville:** It is a matter for local purchasers to determine the most appropriate arrangements for providing dermatology services.

## Smoking

15. **Mr. Steen:** To ask the Secretary of State for Health what steps she is taking to restrict smoking. [22865]

**Mr. Sackville:** On 7 February 1994 the Government published "Smoke Free for Health", an action plan to achieve "The Health of the Nation" targets on smoking, copies of which are available in the Library. The action plan sets out the full range of measures being taken to reduce smoking.

## Sandwell Health Services Authority

16. **Mr. Spellar:** To ask the Secretary of State for Health if she will make a statement regarding the conduct of Sandwell family health services authority and Sandwell health plan. [22866]

**Mr. Malone:** The setting up of Sandwell health plan by Sandwell family health services authority has been the subject of an investigation by the Audit Commission. Its report under section 15(3) of the local Government Finance Act 1982 and the subsequent action proposed by Sandwell family health services authority were discussed at a public meeting of that authority on 30 March 1995.

## NHS Pay

17. **Mr. Mudie:** To ask the Secretary of State for Health how many nurses she estimates will receive at least a 3 per cent. pay award. [22867]

**Mr. Malone:** Across the United Kingdom, 321 national health service trusts and directly managed units have made formal offers or made clear to staff their intentions for local pay increases. Of these, some 75 per cent. have been for proposed increases of around 3 per cent. We have been told by the majority of the remaining 164 trusts that they will have made offers by the end of this month.

24. **Mr. George Howarth:** To ask the Secretary of State for Health what considerations led to the pay offer made to (a) doctors and (b) nurses; and if she will make a statement. [22874]

**Mr. Malone:** Pay for doctors and nurses is based on the recommendations made by the independent pay review bodies which were accepted in full by the Government.

25. **Mr. Canavan:** To ask the Secretary of State for Health how many representations she has received this year about the pay of nurses and other NHS employees; and if she will make a statement. [22875]

**Mr. Malone:** A number of representations have been received this year. Correspondence and some petitions have been received and verbal representations have been made.

## Patient Care

18. **Mr. Brazier:** To ask the Secretary of State for Health what proportion of NHS staff currently provides direct care to patients; and what was the position 10 years ago. [22868]

**Mr. Malone:** The proportion of direct care staff in hospital and community health services has increased from 61.3 per cent. in 1983 to 65.7 per cent. in 1993.

## Conflicts of Interest

19. **Mrs. Dunwoody:** To ask the Secretary of State for Health what action she has taken to prevent potential conflicts of interest between those who hold senior posts in NHS trusts and in private sector health service consultancies. [22869]

**Mr. Malone:** The codes of conduct and accountability, which were issued to all national health service board members in April last year, introduced stringent measures to prevent conflicts of interest arising at board level. All NHS boards now maintain a register of members' relevant private interests and these are available for inspection by the public.

### District Health Authority Funding

20. **Mr. Robert Ainsworth:** To ask the Secretary of State for Health what plans she has to ensure that district health authorities have equality of funding. [22870]

**Mr. Sackville:** We remain committed to the principle of weighted capitation as being the fairest way of achieving equality of funding for health authorities.

### Emergency Hospital Admissions

21. **Mr. Congdon:** To ask the Secretary of State for Health if she will make a statement on the recent change in emergency and urgent hospital admissions. [22871]

**Mr. Sackville:** The number of non-elective admissions has remained constant as a proportion of the total number of admissions for several years.

### Consultant Oncologists

22. **Mrs. Mahon:** To ask the Secretary of State for Health what action her Department is taking in respect of the number of consultant oncologists in the NHS. [22872]

**Mr. Malone:** Establishment of consultant posts is the responsibility of individual employers, who have regard to the needs of the local population and available resources. The specialist work force advisory group advises the Department on the number of higher specialist trainees needed in each specialty to provide an appropriate supply of suitably qualified candidates for consultant posts.

The number of medical staff, including consultants, in oncology is shown in the table.

*Hospital medical staff in medical oncology and clinical oncology (radiotherapy) by grade*

*England—30 September 1993*

| | Whole time equivalent | | |
| | Medical | Clinical | |
| Grade | oncology | oncology | Total |
|---|---|---|---|
| Consultant | 40 | 200 | 240 |
| Senior Registrar | 20 | 50 | 70 |
| Registrar | 10 | 70 | 80 |
| Senior House Officer | 30 | 100 | 130 |
| House Officer | 10 | 10 | 20 |
| Other grades | 10 | 20 | 30 |
| Totals | 120 | 450 | 570 |

*Note:*

Figures are rounded to the nearest 10.

### Heart Surgery, Waiting Lists

23. **Mr. Sutcliffe:** To ask the Secretary of State for Health how many patients are dying each year on the waiting list for heart surgery. [22873]

**Mr. Malone:** I refer the hon. Member to the reply the then Minister for Health, my right hon. Friend the Member for Peterborough (Dr. Mawhinney), gave the

hon. Member for Bristol, South (Ms Primarolo) on 19 May 1994, *Official Report*, column 557.

### Community Care

26. **Mr. Jon Owen Jones:** To ask the Secretary of State for Health when she last met organisations representing carers to discuss the effect of the community care changes. [22876]

**Mr. Bowis:** I meet frequently with organisations representing carers to discuss a range of matters including community care.

29. **Mr. Clifton-Brown:** To ask the Secretary of State for Health what assessment she has made of the future time scale for implementing the supervised discharge provisions of the Mental Health (Patients in the Community) Bill. [22879]

**Mr. Bowis:** The Bill which received its first reading on 11 May, would come into force on 1 April 1996. This is intended to allow sufficient time, following Royal Assent, for the necessary regulations to be made and laid and guidance issued to those who will be responsible for implementing the new provisions.

### Infertility Treatment

27. **Mr. Barron:** To ask the Secretary of State for Health what services are provided under the NHS for the treatment of infertility; and if she will make a statement. [22877]

**Mr. Sackville:** Information on the services available under the national health service for the treatment of infertility is contained in "The Effective Health Care Bulletin" on "The Management of Subfertility", August 1992, published for the NHS management executive by a consortium of Leeds and York universities and the research unit of the Royal College of Physicians. A copy is available in the Library.

Local health authorities are responsible for the provision of local health services, including the provision of infertility services. Decisions about the resources to be made available for these services must be left to individual health authorities as they are in the best position to determine priorities in the light of local needs and circumstances.

**Mrs. Roche:** To ask the Secretary of State for Health (1) what advice New River health authority has sought from her Department in respect of the most efficacious provision of infertility treatment and diagnosis; [23807]

(2) what contracts her Department has had with New River health authority in respect of infertility treatment and investigation in the United Kingdom. [23808]

**Mr. Sackville:** The provision of infertility diagnosis and treatment locally is a matter for New River health authority. Guidance on infertility services has been issued by the Department and as far as I am aware New River health authority has not sought any additional advice from the Department. The hon. Member may wish to contact Mr. David Kleeman, chairman of the authority, for details of local arrangements for fertility services.

**Mrs. Roche:** To ask the Secretary of State for Health (1) what comparative studies her Department has conducted of one type of infertility treatment against another in the United Kingdom; [23806]

(2) what comparative studies of one infertility treatment against another in the United Kingdom have been assessed by her Department. [23805]

**Mr. Sackville:** I refer the hon. Member to the reply I gave my hon. Friend the Member for Gillingham (Mr. Couchman) on 18 April, *Official Report,* column *114.*

### Health Care, London

30. **Mr. Dowd:** To ask the Secretary of State for Health what plans she has for the future of London's health care following the recommendations of the second "King's Fund Monitor", [22880]

**Mr. Malone:** The Government's plans for London's health care are as set out in "Making London Better", published in February 1993, copies of which are available in the Library, and in a number of statements since that date. These include action to develop higher quality, more accessible primary and community health care for Londoners; action to provide a more balanced hospital service to meet the needs of London's resident, working and visiting population; and action to enhance and foster London's role as a centre of high-quality education and research.

On 10 May, a seven-point pledge was given to the House that there would be no closure until alternative and better services are up and running; that there will be modern emergency services, including an improved London ambulance service; that local health authorities will continue to be held to account for providing comprehensive and effective services in each area, including a proper supply of beds to meet demand; waiting times will improve further; patients charter standards must be met; efforts will continue to recruit and retain the very best doctors and nurses; staff and the public will be involved in the changes so they can see and contribute to objectives; and support will be given to innovation and development in teaching and research.

### Primary Care, Ealing

**Mr. Harry Greenway:** To ask the Secretary of State for Health how much is to spent on primary health care in the borough of Ealing; what were the figures three and five years ago; and if she will make a statement. [22010]

**Mr. Malone:** The main elements of primary health care are the demand-led family health services. Expenditure on these services within the borough of Ealing is not separately identifiable from information available centrally. A summary of the total FHS expenditure by the Ealing, Hammersmith and Hounslow family health services authority, whose area of responsibility includes the borough of Ealing, is set out in the following table. Expenditure on the final element of primary health care, the community health services funded by health authorities, is not separately identifiable in data available centrally.

*Gross expenditure on family health services within the Ealing, Hammersmith and Hounslow family health services authority*
*£ million*

|  | 1990–91 | 1992–93 | 1994–95 (provisional) |
|---|---|---|---|
| Total gross expenditure | 78.3 | 96.6 | 108 |

*Notes:*

1. Gross expenditure includes prescription and dental charge income collected from patients.

2. Figures include payments made by the Dental Practice Board to dentists in contract with the Ealing, Hammersmith and Hounslow FHSA. Figures exclude GP fundholders' management costs and budgets for purchasing secondary care services, and the FHSA's administrative costs.

3. Figures for 1990–91 and 1992–93 are based on receipts and payments returns submitted by the FHSA with its annual accounts. The provisional figures for 1994–95 are based on in-year monitoring data.

### Access Committee for England

**Mr. Tom Clarke:** To ask the Secretary of State for Health what plans she has for the future funding of the Access Committee for England. [23590]

**Mr. Bowis:** Funding in the current financial year is £105,000. Decisions on further funding will be taken at the appropriate time and will be based on current core grant tapering policy.

### Doncaster Healthcare NHS Trust

**Mr. Redmond:** To ask the Secretary of State for Health what plans she has to disband Doncaster Healthcare NHS trust. [23864]

**Mr. Malone:** None.

### Burnley Health Care NHS Trust

**Mr. Gordon Prentice:** To ask the Secretary of State for Health if Burnley Health Care NHS trust acted in accordance with the NHS code of openness in respect of the timescale of release of details of the incident at Burnley general hospital in which ophthalmic patients each lost an eye. [23862]

**Mr. Malone:** The code of practice on openness in the national health service, which takes effect on 1 June, will increase public access to information held by the NHS. Burnley Health Care NHS trust, in recognising the sensitivity of the incident, issued a press release as soon as treatment of all the affected patients had been completed and the full facts were known. Its action was entirely in keeping with the spirit of the code of practice.

### London Initiative Zone

**Mr. Timms:** To ask the Secretary of State for Health what capital schemes in the London borough of Newham have been allocated funding through the LIZ initiative; and what sums have been allocated to each of these and on what dates. [23924]

**Mr. Malone:** The London initiative zone capital schemes and sums allocated are as shown in the table.

*LIZ Primary Care Capital Funded Projects in Newham*

| Project name | Capital allocation £000 | | |
|---|---|---|---|
|  | 1993–94 | 1994–95 | 1995–96 |
| *Newham* |  |  |  |
| Essex Lodge (Primary Care Centre) | 25 | 65 | 0 |
| Shrewsbury Road | 285 | 483 | 0 |
| Improvement Grants to GP premises (various) | 279 | 259 | 0 |
| Star Lane (Primary Care Centre) | 470 | 500 | 80 |
| Stratford Corridor (Primary Care Centre) | 310 | 0 | 300 |
| Cyprus Dock (Resource Centre) | 192 | 133 | 675 |
| Freemasons Road | — | — | 40 |
| 326 Stratford High Street | — | — | 80 |

*LIZ Primary Care Capital Funded Projects in Newham*

| Project name | Capital allocation £000 | | |
| --- | --- | --- | --- |
| | 1993–94 | 1994–95 | 1995–96 |
| 140 Claremont Road | — | — | 40 |
| 50 Upper Road | — | — | 150 |
| 497 Barking Road | — | — | 130 |
| 751 Barking Road | — | — | 50 |
| 85 Stopford Road | — | — | 10 |
| 125/127 Prince Regents Lane | — | — | 250 |
| 39/50c Romford Road | — | — | 250 |
| 17 Turley Close | — | — | 300 |
| 533 Barking Road | — | 8 | 0 |
| 1 Kennard Street | — | 89 | 0 |
| Newham GP Forum | — | 71 | 0 |
| Security improvements to GP surgeries | — | 1 | 0 |
| Total Expenditure | 1,561 | 1,649 | 2,355 |

### NHS Estates

**Mr. Alex Carlile:** To ask the Secretary of State for Health what plans she has for the privatisation of NHS Estates; and if she will make a statement. [23681]

**Mr. Sackville:** I refer the hon. and learned Member to the reply I gave my hon. Friend the Member for Sutton and Cheam (Lady Olga Maitland) on 1 December 1994, *Official Report,* column *825.*

### NHS Domestic Cleaning Standards

**Mr. Redmond:** To ask the Secretary of State for Health what plans she has to advise NHS trusts to control domestic cleaning standards by introducing the Asda and Tesco control systems. [23935]

**Mr. Sackville:** National health service trust management determine locally the domestic cleaning standards for each of their units and then monitor to ensure those standards are met. We have recently introduced a patients charter standard which emphasises the need for a clean and safe environment in hospitals.

### Star Lane Medical Centre

**Mr. Timms:** To ask the Secretary of State for Health in which year funding was allocated from North Thames regional health authority for the proposed Star Lane medical centre, London E16; and where that funding currently resides. [23943]

**Mr. Malone:** Funds have been set aside for the proposed Star Lane medical centre in 1993–94 and 1994–95. Funds of £500,000 for 1994–95 have been carried over to the 1995–96 financial year and work will begin on the centre in July 1995.

### GP Suicides

**Mr. Alex Carlile:** To ask the Secretary of State for Health how many suicides by general practitioners took place in each of the last five years for which figures are available in each family health services authority area; and if she will make a statement. [23678]

**Mr. Malone:** The information is not available centrally.

### Gorton Medical Centre

**Mr. Kaufman:** To ask the Secretary of State for Health what action she intends to take to remedy the situation created by the decision of the High Court that the Manchester family health services authority applied more than £250,000 unlawfully; and if she will as a consequence increase the funding allocation to make possible the building work necessary to Gorton medical centre. [23694]

**Mr. Malone:** I am considering the implications of the judgement as a matter of urgency. Separately, I understand that Manchester family health services authority will shortly contact the doctors at the Gorton medical centre to advise what financial assistance can be provided to them to improve their premises.

### Child Labour

**Mr. Jim Cunningham:** To ask the Secretary of State for Health what powers she proposes for local authorities to cope with the problem of child labour. [24031]

**Mr. Bowis:** Local authorities have sufficient powers under existing legislation to deal with any instances of illegal employment of children that may occur.

**Mr. Jim Cunningham:** To ask the Secretary of State for Health what initiatives arising from the UN Year of the Child and the UN Year of the Family have been instituted to deal with the issue of child labour. [24032]

**Mr. Bowis:** I am aware of no initiatives in the United Kingdom on child labour arising from either of these years.

**Mr. Jim Cunningham:** To ask the Secretary of State for Health what resources are available to reduce the use of child labour; and what resources were made available in each of the last five years. [24034]

**Mr. Bowis:** It is for local authorities to devote resources to this activity as they think necessary.

**Mr. Jim Cunningham:** To ask the Secretary of State for Health what assessment has been made by her Department of the numbers of children currently illegally working; what assessment her Department has made of the extent of child labour for each of the last five years; and what comparable information she has about other European countries. [24030]

**Mr. Bowis:** I am not aware of any significant evidence that the illegal employment of children is a widespread problem. We have no information about the situation in other European countries.

**Mr. Jim Cunningham:** To ask the Secretary of State for Health what discussion on child labour took place at the recent UN conference on poverty in Copenhagen; and what contribution the Government made in this regard. [24033]

**Miss Widdecombe:** I have been asked to reply.

The world summit for the social development identified family poverty as a main cause of child labour. The Government demonstrated their commitment to international action in this area by endorsing recommendations to ensure the protection of working children and to promote the elimination of child labour.

### Rural White Paper

**Mr. Colvin:** To ask the Secretary of State for Health what is her estimate of the net annual financial saving, or cost, of her Department's submission for the proposed White Paper on the rural economy.    [24329]

**Mr. Sackville:** Proposals for the rural White Paper remain subject to continuing collective consideration and discussion. The cost of measures contained in the White Paper will be taken into account in the public expenditure survey.

### Census Questions

**Ms Gordon:** To ask the Secretary of State for Health what steps she is taking to ensure that the Office of Population Censuses and Surveys includes questions in the next census to record the number of hours which women and men spend doing unpaid household, caring and voluntary work and to record household income.

[24394]

**Mr. Sackville:** The census offices in Great Britain—Office of Population Censuses and Surveys and the General Register Office for Scotland—have started to consult users about information needs for the next census which is being planned for 2001. Some support has already been expressed both for a question on income, and for a question on unpaid work such as housework, voluntary work, and caring for others.

Users have requested more new and revised questions than can be accommodated on the form without placing an undue burden on the public and a preliminary assessment is being made on whether the census is the most appropriate means of collecting the required information. Questions for which there is likely to be a good case will be tested for acceptability to the public, and for the ability of the public to respond with data of a quality adequate to meet users' needs, in a programme which will run over the next three years.

Formal business cases for including particular questions will be considered in early 1998. The Government's proposals will be published later that year, and the final selection of questions will be approved by Parliament.

### Exeter and North Devon Health Authority

**Mr. Harvey:** To ask the Secretary of State for Health what were the full legal costs incurred by the Exeter and North Devon health authority and its predecessor authorities *(a)* in its dispute with Mrs. Carol Rudd and *(b)* in the cases of (i) Mrs. Mikibbin, (ii) Mrs. Gerlach and (iii) Mrs. Filer Cooper; what reports she has called for into these cases; to what extent the payment of costs complied with her Department's guidelines; and if she will make a statement.    [24706]

**Mr. Malone:** This is a matter for the Exeter and North Devon health authority. The hon. Member may wish to contact Mrs. R.A. Day, chairman of the health authority, for details.

### Hospital Matrons

**Mr. Harry Greenway:** To ask the Secretary of State for Health how many trust and non-trust hospitals use the title matron; and if she will make a statement.    [23166]

**Mr. Sackville:** This information is not available centrally. The exact titles and responsibilities of senior nurses are for local decision. The title "Matron" may be used if appropriate.

### Fluoridation

**Mr. Chidgey:** To ask the Secretary of State for Health which European Union countries currently have artificial fluoridated public water supplies; and which European Union countries have abandoned artificial fluoridated public water supplies in the last 20 years.    [23733]

**Mr. Malone:** This information is shown in the table.

*Water fluoridation in Europe*

|  | Current status | If discontinued in last 20 years |
|---|---|---|
| Austria | Natural only | — |
| Belgium | Natural only | — |
| Denmark | Natural only | — |
| Finland | Natural only | Kuopio fluoridated 1959 to 1992 |
| France | Natural only | — |
| Germany | Natural only | Schemes in GDR ceased on reunification |
| Greece | Actively pursuing | — |
| Ireland | Mandatory, approx 70 per cent. coverage | — |
| Italy | Actively pursuing | — |
| Netherlands | Natural only | Artificial fluoridation 1953 to 1973 |
| Spain | Approx. 2 million people receive artificial fluoridated supplies, actively pursuing extending coverage | — |
| Sweden | Natural only | — |
| United Kingdom | Approximately 10 per cent. coverage, actively pursuing extending coverage to approx. 25 per cent. | — |
| Luxembourg | No data | No data |
| Portugal | No data | No data |

*Source:*
British Fluoridation Society—12 May 1995.

**Mr. Chidgey:** To ask the Secretary of State for Health whether water companies that add fluoride to the public water supplies are indemnified by her Department for legal claims of negative health effects.    [23734]

**Mr. Malone:** The Department of Health, subject to Treasury approval, offers water undertakers wide indemnities against civil liabilities, including costs and expenses in connection with any proceedings, in connection with the fluoridation of the water supply, provided that the actions of the water undertaker are within the terms of the agreement with the health authority.

**Mr. Chidgey:** To ask the Secretary of State for Health what assessment she has made of the extent of medical research on the long-term benefits of artificial fluoridated water supplies for *(a)* children and *(b)* adults, based on detailed studies of the dental records of communities with added artificial fluoridated public water supplies and communities without added artificial fluoridated public water supplies but with similar economic and social backgrounds.    [23736]

**Mr. Malone:** Our assessment is that it has been shown conclusively that water fluoridated at one part per million can result in a 50 per cent. reduction in tooth decay in children and also helps adults to keep their teeth longer.

A number of studies have been carried out into the long term benefits of artificially fluoridated water supplies for both children and adults in comparable fluoridated and non-fluoridated areas of similar social and economic backgrounds. Summaries of such studies and their findings are set out in the recent book "One in a Million: Water Fluoridation and Dental Public Health", published jointly by the Public Health Alliance and the British Fluoridation Society, pages 8 to 18, copies of which are available in the Library.

**Mr. Chidgey:** To ask the Secretary of State for Health what instructions her Department gives to the manufacturers of dental products containing fluoride concerning *(a)* the need for adults and children to be informed of the potential harm of such products if consumed in excess and *(b)* the suitability of such products for young children. [23738]

**Mr. Malone:** The Department of Health is responsible for regulating those dental products containing fluoride and regarded as medicinal. Medicinal products are granted licences on the basis of quality, safety and efficacy. The dangers of excess consumption and the products' suitability for young children are addressed in the licence.

Dental products containing fluoride include toothpaste, gels, mouthwashes, tablets and drops. Some of these products are medicines and come under the responsibilities of the Department of Health, while others are cosmetics and are regulated by the Department of Trade and Industry.

**Mr. Chidgey:** To ask the Secretary of State for Health which health authority areas in England and Wales currently have fluoridated public water supplies; and on what dates the fluoridation of public water supplies commenced in each such area. [23739]

**Mr. Malone:** This information is set out in the book "One in a Million: Water Fluoridation and Dental Public Health", published jointly by the Public Health Alliance and the British Fluoridation Society, pages 33 to 52, copies of which are available in the Library.

## Hip Fractures

**Mr. Chidgey:** To ask the Secretary of State for Health what is the incidence per capita of hip fractures for people aged 60 years or above for each health authority in England and Wales. [23735]

**Mr. Sackville:** In 1993–94, the number of finished consultant episodes of hospital care for fracture of femur suffered by those aged 60 and above, per capita in England, was 0.0052, about one in 200. A breakdown at health authority level is not available.

## NHS Organ Donor Register

**Mr. Churchill:** To ask the Secretary of State for Health how much has been spent so far this year in the campaign to promote the national organ donor register; what has been the response; how many and what proportion of responses are currently awaiting processing; what steps she proposes to take to expedite processing; and what plans she has to carry forward this campaign. [24717]

**Mr. Sackville:** Some £1.53 million was spent in 1994–95 on publicity material and activities to promote the national health service organ donor register which was launched in October 1994. Over 1,300,000[1] applications to join the register have been received so far, of which

nearly 270,000 were received and processed in April. On 12 May, some 86,000 postal applications, 6.5 per cent. of the total applications received, were waiting to be processed. Temporary staff were recruited from April mainly to help process the surge of applications following the March publicity campaign. The register will continue to be promoted in 1995–96.

[1]Includes about 400,000 transferred from the lifeline Wales register.

## Selenium

**Mr. Hain:** To ask the Secretary of State for Health (1) what assessment her Department has made of the effects of selenium deficiency; what those effects are; and what action she recommends to avoid selenium deficiency; [24166]

(2) if she will make a statement setting out her policy for combating dietary deficiency in selenium. [24169]

**Mr. Sackville:** The Department of Health considered selenium deficiency as part of the Committee on Medical Aspects of Food Policy's review of dietary reference values for food energy and nutrients for the United Kingdom. A copy of this report is available in the Library. There is no deficiency disease known to result solely from selenium deficiency, although a specific cardiomyopathy may occur with low selenium intakes which responds to selenium. There is no evidence that selenium deficiency is a problem in the UK. No action is recommended specifically to avoid selenium deficiency.

**Mr. Hain:** To ask the Secretary of State for Health what representations her Department has received regarding research suggesting that selenium deficiency may speed or trigger the growth and spread of the AIDS virus; what action she proposes to take; and if she will make a statement. [24168]

**Mr. Sackville:** The Department of Health has received no such representations. The Department is aware of a number of recent publications in the scientific literature on this topic and continues to monitor the situation. There is currently no clear evidence that selenium supplements produce an improvement in haematological or immunological parameters of disease progression in HIV-AIDS patients.

## Temazepam

**Mr. McMaster:** To ask the Secretary of State for Health, pursuant to her answer of 21 April, *Official Report*, column *309* (1) what is her latest estimate of the total amount of prescription units of the drug temazepam produced and imported into the United Kingdom in the 1994 calendar year; what is the latest estimate of the total amount of prescription units of the drug temazepam required to meet known legitimate use; and if she will make a statement; [22070]

(2) what is her latest estimate of the amount of temazepam required for prescription under the national health service, in kilograms and prescription units, in the 1994 calendar year; and if she will make a statement. [22044]

**Mr. Bowis** [*holding answer 1 May 1995*]: Information on the amount of temazepam manufactured and imported in 1994 is not yet available. Information on total quantities dispensed in family health services authorities in England in 1994 is shown in the table.

*Temazepam dispensed in the family health services authorities in England 1994 (provisional figures)*

|  | | Thousands |
|---|---|---|
|  | Prescription items | Kilograms |
| Tablets | 3,392 | 1,595.6 |
| Capsules | 2,837 | 1,577.3 |
| Oral preparations | 116 | 58.3 |
| Total | 6,345 | 3,231.2 |

*Note:*

The data are from the prescription cost analysis system and include all prescriptions dispensed by community pharmacists, dispensing doctors, and prescriptions submitted by prescribing doctors for items personally administered.

**Mr. McMaster:** To ask the Secretary of State for Health, pursuant to her answer of 21 April, *Official Report,* column *309,* what is her latest estimate of the trend of temazepam production and amount of imports and the amount required for prescriptions by the national health care service over the last five years; if she will give these figures in kilograms, prescription units and the percentage change from year to year and from 1990 to 1994; and if she will make a statement. [22069]

**Mr. Bowis** *[holding answer 1 May 1995]:* Information on the total quantity of temazepam manufactured, held in stock, imported and exported in the United Kingdom during the last five years is shown in table A. Information on total quantities dispensed in family health services authorities in England is given in table B.

*Table A: Summary of annual returns for temazepam from Schedule 4 authority holders in the UK for the period 1989 to 1993 (kilograms)*

| | | | | | Percentage change from previous year | |
|---|---|---|---|---|---|---|
| Year | Quantity manufactured | Manufacturers stocks at 31 December | Total imports | Total exports | Quantity manufactured | Imports |
| 1989 | 2,238.00 | 2,284.311 | 3,672.010 | 752.955 | — | — |
| 1990 | 2,912.70 | 2,226.262 | 2,787.380 | 170.598 | 30.15 | −24.09 |
| 1991 | 2,918.00 | 3,005.970 | 3,442.124 | 712.890 | 0.18 | 23.49 |
| 1992 | 3,271.90 | 3,978.215 | 4,486.190 | 1,018.726 | 12.13 | 30.33 |
| 1993 | 970.20 | 923.039 | 4,505.314 | 1,815.770 | −70.35 | 0.43 |

*Table B: Temazepam dispensed in the family health services authorities in England for the period 1989 to 1994*

| | | | Percentage change from previous year | |
|---|---|---|---|---|
| Year | Prescriptions[1] (000s) | Kilograms of temazepam | Prescription items | Kilograms of temazepam |
| 1989 | [2]5,946 | 3,347 | — | — |
| 1990 | [2]5,985 | 3,297 | 0.7 | −1.5 |
| 1991 | [3]6,427 | 3,449 | — | — |
| 1992 | [3]6,914 | 3,625 | 7.6 | 5.1 |
| 1993 | [3]6,651 | 3,434 | −3.8 | −5.2 |
| 1994 (provisional) | [3]6,345 | 3,231 | −4.6 | −5.9 |

*Source:*
The data are from prescription cost analysis system.

*Notes:*

[1] The data up to 1990 are not consistent with data from 1991 onwards, so it is not possible to give a meaningful figure for percentage changes between 1990 and 1994. Figures for 1989 and 1990 are based on fees and on a sample of one in 200 prescriptions dispensed by community pharmacists and appliance contractors only. Figures for 1991 to 1994 are based on items and cover all prescriptions dispensed by community pharmacists, appliance contractors, dispensing doctors and prescriptions submitted by prescribing doctors for items personally administered.

[2] Fees.

[3] Items.

## NHS Hospitals

**Mrs. Beckett:** To ask the Secretary of State for Health how many NHS hospitals there were in England *(a)* by region and *(b)* in total in each year since 1979. [17068]

**Mr. Malone** *[pursuant to the reply, 30 March 1995, c. 716]:* The number of national health service hospitals as defined by section 128 of the NHS Act 1977 is not available centrally. The information on the number of NHS hospitals in 1994 in the previous reply was estimated from energy consumption returns submitted to NHS Estates by NHS trusts and directly managed units. This number should be treated with caution. Comparable information for previous years is not available centrally. Returns based on a count of hospitals providing residential facilities is available from 1979 until 1991 as follows.

*Table A: Number of hospitals with available overnight beds by regional health authority in England, 1979 to 1990–91*

| RHA | 1979 | 1980 | 1981 | 1982 | 1983 | 1984 | 1985 | 1986 | 1987–88 | 1988–89 | 1989–90 | 1990–91 |
|---|---|---|---|---|---|---|---|---|---|---|---|---|
| Northern | 135 | 131 | 129 | 129 | 128 | 127 | 124 | 124 | 112 | 109 | 105 | 105 |
| Yorkshire | 164 | 159 | 157 | 155 | 155 | 149 | 147 | 144 | 133 | 124 | 120 | 128 |
| Trent | 199 | 194 | 188 | 185 | 185 | 187 | 170 | 170 | 173 | 166 | 150 | 143 |
| East Anglian | 93 | 94 | 90 | 88 | 90 | 85 | 80 | 79 | 78 | 78 | 76 | 75 |
| North West Thames | 118 | 112 | 109 | 102 | 101 | 99 | 99 | 100 | 95 | 102 | 88 | 88 |
| North East Thames | 121 | 114 | 114 | 122 | 121 | 114 | 114 | 114 | 117 | 120 | 117 | 122 |

*Table A: Number of hospitals with available overnight beds by regional health authority in England, 1979 to 1990–91*

| RHA | 1979 | 1980 | 1981 | 1982 | 1983 | 1984 | 1985 | 1986 | 1987–88 | 1988–89 | 1989–90 | 1990–91 |
|---|---|---|---|---|---|---|---|---|---|---|---|---|
| South East Thames | 145 | 141 | 135 | 137 | 138 | 137 | 130 | 129 | 123 | 118 | 122 | 117 |
| South West Thames | 124 | 119 | 112 | 113 | 115 | 112 | 106 | 99 | 115 | 115 | 107 | 108 |
| Wessex | 147 | 146 | 146 | 148 | 154 | 163 | 178 | 187 | 138 | 137 | 134 | 130 |
| Oxford | 92 | 88 | 88 | 88 | 88 | 88 | 84 | 89 | 83 | 83 | 79 | 77 |
| South Western | 223 | 221 | 226 | 224 | 223 | 221 | 221 | 227 | 202 | 203 | 192 | 200 |
| West Midlands | 202 | 201 | 200 | 201 | 203 | 196 | 204 | 203 | 187 | 182 | 174 | 165 |
| Mersey | 87 | 83 | 79 | 79 | 74 | 68 | 65 | 66 | 64 | 62 | 59 | 55 |
| North Western | 130 | 129 | 128 | 126 | 128 | 125 | 123 | 124 | 114 | 105 | 104 | 100 |
| Special Health Authorities | 27 | 26 | 26 | 20 | 20 | 20 | 17 | 17 | 18 | 18 | 17 | 16 |

*Notes:*

1. 1987–88 numbers for South West Thames were estimated as complete numbers were not available.
2. Numbers may include a small number of community units for patients with learning disabilities.
3. From 1987–88 collection of data changed from years ended 31 December to years ended 31 March.
4. Numbers are based on a count of hospitals which provided residential facilities.
5. The table has been estimated from available data which was not used to compile the total figures given in table B. Where possible, account has been taken of changes in the way data was collected over the period, and of boundary charges.

*Table B: Total number of hospitals in England*

| Year | 1979 | 1980 | 1981 | 1982 | 1983 | 1984 | 1985 | 1986 | 1987–88 | 1988–89 | 1989–90 | 1990–91 |
|---|---|---|---|---|---|---|---|---|---|---|---|---|
| Total hospitals | 2,023 | 1,984 | 1,926 | 1,917 | 1,923 | 1,891 | 1,862 | 1,870 | 1,737 | 1,722 | 1,646 | 1,624 |

These figures are taken from the annual published health and personal social services statistics and were not collected after 1990–91. The analysis from which these figures were compiled is no longer available.

### Folic Acid

**Mr. Cohen:** To ask the Secretary of State for Health when the fortification of cereal grain flour with folic acid will take place. [23543]

**Mrs. Browning:** I have been asked to reply.

Currently manufacturers may voluntarily fortify flour with folic acid.

The issue of fortification of foods is currently being considered by the committee on medical aspects of food policy.

## ENVIRONMENT

### Construction Industry

**Mr. Robert Ainsworth:** To ask the Secretary of State for the Environment what plans he has to give small firms in the construction industry protection against unfair terms of contract imposed by larger companies. [23410]

**Mr. Robert B. Jones:** My Department will shortly be issuing a second consultation document taking forward recommendations made in Sir Michael Latham's report "Construction the Team" which will deal with contractual issues in the construction industry.

**Mr. Robert Ainsworth:** To ask the Secretary of State for the Environment what plans he has to introduce a long-term strategy for the construction industry and on maintaining relations between the Government and the industry. [23415]

**Mr. Robert B. Jones:** My Department has a coherent strategy to assist the construction industry and its suppliers by promoting a programme of research, innovation and development; assisting the industry in markets abroad; encouraging the development of technical and professional training; and reviewing the contractual arrangements which operate within the industry. To facilitate this, the Government have joined with the industry on a new forum, the Construction Industry Board, which has been set up to promote dialogue between the various parts of the industry and its clients.

**Mr. Robert Ainsworth:** To ask the Secretary of State for the Environment what plans he has to introduce a Bill on construction contracts. [23409]

**Mr. Robert B. Jones:** The Government will consider legislation in the light of the responses to the consultation exercise now being undertaken.

### Closed Circuit Television

**Sir David Steel:** To ask the Secretary of State for the Environment if he will list the level of funds allocated to local authorities for closed circuit television systems in England and Wales. [23642]

**Mr. Curry:** Support for CCTV schemes may be given through programmes such as the urban programme, the urban crime fund, city challenge, safer cities and under the single regeneration budget. The Home Office CCTV challenge competition also injected £5 million into local schemes.

### House Condition Survey

**Mr. Matthew Taylor:** To ask the Secretary of State for the Environment when he proposes to publish the energy supplement to the already published results of the 1991 English house condition survey. [23672]

**Mr. Robert B. Jones:** Later this year. However, some key findings from the 1991 survey have been included in a guided "Energy Efficiency in Council Housing: Condition of the Stock" which is being sent to all local housing authorities by 19 May. I am arranging for copies of this guide to be placed in the Library.

## Access Committee for England

**Mr. Tom Clarke:** To ask the Secretary of State for the Environment what plans he has for the future funding of the Access Committee for England.    [23588]

**Mr. Robert B. Jones:** I refer the hon. Member to the reply given today by my hon. Friend the Under-Secretary of State for Health, the hon. Member for Battersea (Mr. Bowis).

## Local Government Reorganisation

**Mr. Frank Cook.** To ask the Secretary of State for the Environment which former county boroughs in existence immediately prior to the 1974 local government reorganisation will have their area divided between two or more unitary authorities as a result of proposals from the Local Government Commission.    [23683]

**Mr. Curry:** The area which, between 1968 and 1974, comprised the county borough of Teesside will, from 1 April 1996, constitute parts of the unitary authorities of Middlesbrough, Redcar and Cleveland and Stockton-on-Tees.

**Mr. Frank Cook:** To ask the Secretary of State for the Environment, pursuant to his answer of 30 March to the hon. Member for Burnley (Mr. Pike) *Official Report,* columns *731-33,* what local government structure existed in the Stockton and Langbaurgh areas immediately prior to the local government reorganisation of 1974.    [23685]

**Mr. Curry:** The present district of Stockton-on-Tees is made up of parts of the county borough of Teesside—the Billingham East, Billingham West, Grangefield, Hartburn, Mile House, North End, Norton, Stockton South, Thornaby East and Thornaby West wards—the administrative county of Durham, part of the rural district of Stockton and the administrative county of Yorkshire, North Riding, part of the rural district of Stokesley.

The present district of Langbaurgh-on-Tees is made up of parts of the county borough of Teesside—the Coatham, Eston Grange, Kirkleatham, Ormesby, Redcar and South Bank wards—and the administrative county of Yorkshire, North Riding—the urban districts of Guisborough, Loftus, Saltburn and Marske-by-the-Sea and Skelton and Brotton.

**Mr. Frank Cook:** To ask the Secretary of State for the Environment on what date and from whom he received a copy of the opinion of the Audit Commission on the Local Government Commission's review of the Cleveland and Durham area and if that opinion included the relevant appendices.    [23687]

**Mr. Curry:** A copy of the opinion provided by the Audit Commission to the Local Government Commission in respect of the report containing the latter's draft recommendations for Cleveland and Durham was sent to my Department by the Local Government Commission in November 1993. It included three appendices.

**Mr. Frank Cook:** To ask the Secretary of State for the Environment, pursuant to his answer of 30 March to the hon. Member for Burnley (Mr. Pike), *Official Report,* columns *731–33,* when Middlesbrough ceased to be a county borough council; and what local government structure existed in that area between that date and the subsequent local government reorganisation of 1974.    [23684]

**Mr. Curry:** The area of the county borough of Middlesbrough became part of the county borough of Teesside on 1 April 1968, and remained so until 1 April 1974.

**Mr. Frank Cook:** To ask the Secretary of State for the Environment what steps were taken to ensure that hon. Members were made fully aware, prior to the debate on the Cleveland Structural Change Order, of the view of the Audit Commission on the Local Government Commission's estimates of transitional costs which would result from the proposals for local government change in the Cleveland area.    [23686]

**Mr. Curry:** The Local Government Commission has made available for public inspection all written opinions and other representations it received in response to its draft recommendations for Cleveland and Durham. It also summarised them in its final report for the area. There was no Audit Commission opinion submitted in relation to the estimates of transitional costs set out in that final report.

**Mr. Frank Cook:** To ask the Secretary of State for the Environment if, when he tabled the Cleveland Structural Change Order before the House, he was aware of the view of the Audit Commission on the Local Government Commission's estimates of transitional costs which would be incurred as a result of the order and the views of both the Local Government Commission itself and its financial advisers Ernst and Young on the relative costs of a unitary structure of the kind proposed in the order and the present two-tier local government structure.    [23688]

**Mr. Curry:** When we took our decisions on local government structure in Cleveland, we had before us the estimates of costs and savings contained in the Local Government Commission's report on its draft recommendations for Cleveland and Durham, and the written opinion of the Audit Commission on those estimates. We also had the revised estimates contained in the Local Government Commission's final report for Cleveland and Durham, and the financial appraisal— based on the financial model developed by the Local Government Commission with Ernst and Young—on which those revised estimates were based.

## Giant Hogweed

**Mr. McMaster:** To ask the Secretary of State for the Environment what measures he plans to require the owners of land to which the public may have access to eradicate heracleum mantegazzianum; if he will give local authorities a duty to control heracleum mantegazzianum; and if he will make a statement about the dangers associated with this plant.    [24081]

**Sir Paul Beresford:** It is an offence under the Wildlife and Countryside Act for any person to plant, or otherwise cause to grow in the wild, the giant hogweed.

The control of giant hogweed is a matter for individual local authorities to consider if they believe there is a localised threat to public health.

I understand that contact with giant hogweed can cause a dermatological reaction which, if exposed to strong sunlight, may result in blistering and swelling, however individuals handling the plant only on an occasional basis may experience no reaction at all, or only transient irritation.

## Ozone Levels

**Ms Quin:** To ask the Secretary of State for the Environment if he will make a statement about ozone levels affecting Tyneside on 4 May. [24021]

**Mr. Atkins:** The reported "poor" ozone levels recorded at Newcastle on 4 May between 2 and 3 am were not real levels but due to a technical fault in the analyser, which is currently being corrected by our contractor.

**Ms Quin:** To ask the Secretary of State for the Environment what plans he has to ensure that British cities do not exceed World Health Organisation guidelines for low-level ozone concentrations. [24022]

**Mr. Atkins:** Ozone is a transboundary pollutant, and reductions of ozone concentrations to WHO guideline levels in Europe will not be possible by any one country acting in isolation. The Government believes that harmonised action at an international level is necessary to ensure cost-effective reductions in ozone levels. The Government are pressing for such action in the appropriate international fora.

## Contaminated Land, Liverpool

**Mr. Loyden:** To ask the Secretary of State for the Environment what action he intends to take to deal with the problem of contaminated land on the site of the former synthetic resins plant in the Liverpool, Garston constituency. [24274]

**Sir Paul Beresford:** An investigation of the contamination on the site has recently been funded by English Partnerships. Liverpool city council have subsequently initiated further survey work to examine leeching of contamination into adjoining residential properties at Bradford road. On the basis of these surveys, the city council will consider what remedial work is necessary and how such work should be funded.

## Business Rates

**Mr. Robert Banks:** To ask the Secretary of State for the Environment if he will set out the amounts allowed in reduction of business rates by local authorities in England for the last financial year. [24163]

**Mr. Robert B. Jones:** Figures for 1994–95 are not yet available. In 1993–94, English local authorities granted £1.9 million in hardship relief from non-domestic rates. In addition, £35 million was granted in discretionary relief to charities and other non-profit-making bodies.

## Sheffield Airport

**Mr. Betts:** To ask the Secretary of State for the Environment what information he has about the plans for the development of Sheffield airport by Glenlivet. [24408]

**Sir Paul Beresford:** My Department has received detailed information from the Sheffield development corporation about the plans for the development of Sheffield airport by Glenlivet. This is currently under consideration.

**Mr. Betts:** To ask the Secretary of State for the Environment what advice and evaluation were available to him between 1989 and the present of the possibility that companies in the Budge group or successor companies to the contract could gain the benefit and profit of opencasting at Tinsley, Sheffield, without fulfilling

commitments to provide infrastructure for an airport on the site. [24410]

**Sir Paul Beresford:** My predecessors were aware that there was no contractual linkage between the opencasting operation and the provision of infrastructure for and construction of the airport.

**Mr. Betts:** To ask the Secretary of State for the Environment when he became aware that the guarantee given by A. F. Budge Mining for the construction of Sheffield airport would not be honoured. [24412]

**Sir Paul Beresford:** The guarantee, or surety, for the construction of Sheffield Airport, was held by A. F. Budge Ltd., rather than A. F. Budge (Mining). My Department became aware that A. F. Budge Ltd. would not be in a position to support the airport development when the administrative receivers were appointed to it in December 1992.

**Mr. Betts:** To ask the Secretary of State for the Environment what conditions requiring work towards the construction of an airport at Tinsley, Sheffield, were contained in the original planning application for opencasting awarded to British Coal Opencast; and what conditions in relation to such work were contained in the agreement between British Coal Opencast and A F Budge (Mining) Ltd. [24414]

**Sir Paul Beresford:** The planning permission awarded to British Coal for Opencasting at Tinsley contained the following conditions relating to the construction of an airport.

    i. the construction of a road linking the site to the existing road network

    ii. the site to be reclaimed

    iii. specific parts of the site to be compacted and made suitable for use as an airport

    iv. drainage outfall to be provided for the site.

My Department was not party to the terms of agreement between British Coal and A F Budge (Mining) for the opencast mining of the site.

**Mr. Betts:** To ask the Secretary of State for the Environment whether he will have to give approval before any proposals to develop an airport at Tinsley, Sheffield, are agreed to. [24416]

**Sir Paul Beresford:** Yes.

**Mr. Betts:** To ask the Secretary of State for the Environment (1) what information he has obtained of past or present connections or involvement between Glenlivet and any of its directors and RJB Mining or A F Budge Ltd, or any of their subsidiaries or any of the directors; [24418]

(2) what information he has received on the involvement by RJB Mining or any of its directors in the scheme to develop an airport at Tinsley, Sheffield, proposed by Glenlivet. [24419]

**Sir Paul Beresford:** The only information I have about connections between the directors and the companies mentioned is that a former director of three subsidiary companies of A F Budge Ltd. is currently advising Glenlivet on the aviation elements of its airport proposals.

**Mr. Betts:** To ask the Secretary of State for the Environment how much public money to date has been spent on the infrastructure for the Sheffield airport site at Tinsley; and how much more is committed in the future. [24409]

**Sir Paul Beresford:** Sheffield development corporation has spent £95,000 on the design of infrastructure for the Tinsley site for airport and other development.

In addition, British Coal has spent £1.9 million providing access to the site and has committed £25,000 to provide site drainage. British Coal will also be providing a drainage outfall for the site which is expected to cost in the region of £500,000.

There are plans for a further £5 million of expenditure on roads and drainage funded by Industrial Development Act grants, European funding and the Sheffield development corporation.

All of the infrastructure provided at Tinsley park will benefit commercial development in addition to a proposed airport.

**Mr. Betts:** To ask the Secretary of State for the Environment when he became aware that the guarantee to construct Sheffield airport and the right to opencast the site of Tinsley were invested in separate companies and were not mutually enforceable; when he was officially notified of the separation; and when he gave approval to such a separation.    [24413]

**Sir Paul Beresford:** My Department was notified in December 1991 of the proposed company restructuring which would separate the mining and airport construction interests within the A F Budge group. No approval was required from my Department.

**Mr. Betts:** To ask the Secretary of State for the Environment what financial checks he intends to make of the financial viability of the scheme to develop an airport at Tinsley, Sheffield, proposed by Glenlivet.    [24415]

**Sir Paul Beresford:** Checks on the financial viability of the Glenlivet scheme for the development of Sheffield airport will be carried out by the Sheffield development corporation.

**Mr. Betts:** To ask the Secretary of State for the Environment what information he has about the funding arrangement for the development of an airport at Tinsley, Sheffield, by Glenlivet.    [24417]

**Sir Paul Beresford:** We will wish to be assured that adequate funding will be available to secure the project.

### Opencasting, Tinsley

**Mr. Betts:** To ask the Secretary of State for the Environment when he became aware of the transfer of the opencast contract at Tinsley, Sheffield to RJB Mining; when he was officially informed of it; and when he approved it.    [24411]

**Sir Paul Beresford:** My Department became aware of the proposed transfer of the opencast contract at Tinsley to RJB Mining in December 1991 when informed by Sheffield development corporation. As set out in my answer to the hon. Member on 9 May, *Official Report*, column *421*, no approval was required.

### Security Facilities Executive

**Mr. Mans:** To ask the Secretary of State for the Environment what targets he has set for the Security Facilities Agency for 1995–96.    [24707]

**Sir Paul Beresford:** For 1995–96, the agency has been set the following targets. They require the agency to make further improvements in its performance particularly in the quality of the service it delivers, with the exceptions of the targets for surplus and sales turnover, where a marginal reduction on the previous year acknowledges the reducing need for expenditure on security.

| Category | Measure | Target |
|---|---|---|
| Financial | Cost recovery in accruals terms | 100 per cent. cost recovery including 6 per cent. cost of capital |
| | Outturn on the vote | A surplus of £1 million |
| | Outturn on net running costs | Break even |
| Sales | Sales turnover | Turnover of £40 million |
| Efficiency | Unit costs | 2 per cent. reduction in real terms |
| Quality of service[1] | Customer surveys | 90 per cent. satisfaction rating |
| | Management | Achieve and maintain ISO9000 standard on quality management systems |
| Environmental | Management | Achieve BS7750 standard on environmental management systems |
| | Vehicle fuel efficiency | Annual average of 25 mpg for GCS and IDS fleets |

[1] The quality of service target in addition to requiring an overall 90 per cent. satisfaction rating in customer surveys, comprises also a number of separate targets applying to different ways to each part of the agency's business, viz:

*Notes:*

1. Government car service—90 per cent. customer satisfaction targets for driver appearance, punctuality, driving standards, vehicle presentation; at least 70 per cent. of pool service calls to be met by in-house drivers; all customers to be visited at least once a year to review delivery and needs.

2. Inter-dispatch service—To implement service enhancements resulting from the service's market test, and implement new performance measuring systems; both by June 1995.

3. Special Services Group-security furniture—To keep within 90 per cent. of approved project timetables and estimates; deliver 98 per cent. of SFS standard items within 15 days.

4. Custody service—To achieve a monthly target of 99.5 per cent productive hours as percentage of total hours; a nil target for entry violations; have at least yearly liaison visits to customers; improve image with new uniforms and conduct code.

### Wind Farms

**Mr. Hutton:** To ask the Secretary of State for the Environment how many wind farms are currently operating in each county in England.    [24510]

**Sir Paul Beresford:** The information requested is as follows:

| County | Number of wind farms |
|---|---|
| Cornwall | 6 |
| Cumbria | 3 |
| Lancashire | 2 |
| Norfolk | 1 |
| Northumberland | 1 |
| South Yorkshire | 1 |
| North Yorkshire | 1 |
| West Yorkshire | 1 |

**Mr. Hutton:** To ask the Secretary of State for the Environment (1) how many planning decisions for wind farms were overturned after an appeal by his Department in each of the last 10 years; [24511]

(2) how many planning applications for wind farms were *(a)* granted or *(b)* rejected in each county in England in each of the last 10 years. [24512]

**Sir Paul Beresford:** This information is not kept centrally and would be obtainable only at a disproportionate cost.

### Middlesbrough Football Club

**Mr. Devlin:** To ask the Secretary of State for the Environment what assistance was given to Middlesbrough football club by the Teesside development corporation in respect of its new stadium. [24675]

**Sir Paul Beresford:** The Teesside development corporation has provided no direct assistance to the football club in regard to its new stadium. The corporation is actively promoting access improvements, site preparation and reclamation of the overall Middlehaven site, part of which is occupied by the football club, in order to encourage the economic regeneration of the former dock area.

### North Sea Conference

**Mr. Tyler:** To ask the Secretary of State for the Environment what proposals he will be making concerning protection of the marine environment at the North sea ministerial conference on 8 and 9 June.

[24524]

**Dr. Spink:** To ask the Secretary of State for the Environment what will be his policy objectives for the fourth North sea conference on 8 and 9 June. [24808]

**Mr. Gummer:** I have placed in the Library a statement of the policy objectives of the United Kingdom for the fourth international conference on the protection of the North sea. The topics which we expect to be discussed, and the main points that the United Kingdom would wish to achieve, are:

(a) *protection of species and habitats:* action on the protection of wildlife outside territorial waters, which, with the protection inside territorial waters already offered by the EC birds and habitats directives, will constitute a comprehensive strategy for this purpose;

(b) *fisheries:* getting the European Commission to propose measures to control over-fishing, especially in industrial fisheries, and to carry out more research into the effects of industrial fisheries and how to regulate them;

(c) *prevention of pollution by hazardous substances:* a practical approach built on the concept of sustainable development and the precautionary principle, which aims for goals that are capable of being achieved; and agreement on the urgent need for internationally coordinated research to improve our knowledge of the possible effects of some chemicals on reproductive systems;

(d) *further eduction of nutrient inputs to the North sea:* bearing in mind that the United Kingdom does not contribute to problems in, eg, the German bight and the Kateggat, strategies that are aimed at solving the problems actually faced by different countries; these should address, where appropriate, the problems of agricultural run-off, particularly where this results from unsustainable agriculture supported by feed from industrial fishing;

(e) *the prevention of pollution from shipping:* the need to complete the international framework—for example, ratifying conventions already agreed and completing a

hazardous and noxious substance convention—and effective enforcement by flag, coastal and port sates;

(f) *the prevention of pollution from offshore installations:* commitment to agreeing, if possible by 1996, a harmonised mandatory control scheme for chemicals used and discharged offshore; there is not need for further action on the abandonment of oil rigs, since we have a recent international convention which provides for case-by-case decisions;

(g) *radioactive substances;* the need for commitment by the North sea states who are not members of the board of governors of the International Atomic Energy Agency to the safety fundamentals for radioactive waste recently adopted by the board, and support for the IAEA process aimed at a global convention on radioactive waste management;

(h) *future co-operation:* acceptance of Norway's generous offer to host a fifth North sea conference in 2000–2002, and to link this much more closely with the work of the convention for the protection of marine environment of the north-east Atlantic, the OSPAR convention.

### Crime

**Mrs. Roche:** To ask the Secretary of State for the Environment what percentage of the single regeneration budget since 1994 has gone into projects aimed at tackling crime. [22836]

**Sir Paul Bersford** *[holding answer 10 May 1995]:* The single regeneration budget encompasses 20 programmes from four Departments and tackling crime is a key objective of many of the funded projects. For example, city challenge partnerships, estate action schemes and task forces all tackle crime, or the causes of crime, as part of their regeneration strategies. Because the SRB takes an integrated approach to regeneration, it is not possible to sensibly apportion costs to individual scheme objectives, such as crime prevention, but the estimated total expenditure on SRB programmes in 1994–95 was £1.45 billions. It is expected that substantial funding will be directed to projects aimed at tackling crime through the SRB challenge fund.

The safer cities programme, which is directly aimed at reducing crime and the fear of crime, spent £2 million in 1994–95.

## HOME DEPARTMENT

### Police Authorities

**Mr. Morley:** To ask the Secretary of State for the Home Department if an independent member of a police authority has to resign immediately if elected to a new shadow unitary authority; and whether that person may continue to serve on the police authority until the vesting date. [24732]

**Mr. Maclean:** The interpretation of the law is a matter for the courts. Nevertheless, in our view a new shadow authority becomes a council for a district only when it assumes full powers on re-organisation date. If this view is shared by the courts, then an independent member of a police authority who is elected to a new shadow authority may continue to serve on the police authority until the date on which full powers are assumed by the new authority.

## Asylum Seekers

**Mrs. Roche:** To ask the Secretary of State for the Home Department if he will publish a breakdown of the number of applications for asylum since 1 January by location of application. [23799]

**Mr. Nicholas Baker:** During the period 1 January 1995 to 30 April 1995, 12,720 applications were made for asylum in the United Kingdom. Of these, 3,910 were port applications and 8,810 were applications made after entry into the United Kingdom.

**Mrs. Roche:** To ask the Secretary of State for the Home Department how many applications for asylum have been determined in each month since 1 January 1994; for each month, in how many cases the applicant was granted asylum; in how many cases the applicant was granted exceptional leave to remain; in how many cases the applicant was refused under paragraph 340 of the immigration rules; and in how many cases the application was refused under paragraph 345 of the immigration rules. [23800]

**Mr. Nicholas Baker:** Information on decisions made on asylum applications, by month, since January 1994 is given in the table.

*Decisions[1] on applications[1] received for asylum in the United Kingdom, excluding dependants, 1 January 1994 to 30 April 1995*

*Number of principal applicants*

|  | Total decisions[2] | Recognised as a refugee and granted asylum | Not recognised as a refugee but granted exceptional leave | Total refused | Refused asylum and exceptional leave after full consideration | Refused on safe third country grounds[3] | Refused under para. 340 of Immigration Rules[4] |
|---|---|---|---|---|---|---|---|
| **1994** | | | | | | | |
| January | 1,245 | 45 | 245 | 955 | 740 | 100 | 120 |
| February | 1,430 | 80 | 245 | 1,110 | 925 | 60 | 130 |
| March | 1,685 | 55 | 240 | 1,390 | 1,195 | 85 | 110 |
| April | 1,300 | 35 | 230 | 1,040 | 785 | 125 | 130 |
| May | 1,915 | 110 | 370 | 1,435 | 1,100 | 85 | 250 |
| June | 1,780 | 60 | 350 | 1,365 | 1,125 | 35 | 205 |
| July | 1,835 | 85 | 245 | 1,505 | 1,185 | 35 | 285 |
| August | 1,985 | 75 | 265 | 1,645 | 1,115 | 50 | 485 |
| September | 1,950 | 55 | 355 | 1,540 | 1,045 | 55 | 440 |
| October | 2,170 | 90 | 415 | 1,660 | 1,220 | 75 | 365 |
| November | 2,185 | 70 | 425 | 1,690 | 1,315 | 85 | 290 |
| December | 1,500 | 65 | 275 | 1,160 | 905 | 85 | 175 |
| Total | 20,990 | 825 | 3,660 | 16,500 | 12,655 | 865 | 2,985 |
| **1995** | | | | | | | |
| January | 2,450 | 130 | 435 | 1,885 | 1,435 | 145 | 305 |
| February | 2,385 | 155 | 570 | 1,665 | 1,275 | 100 | 290 |
| March | 2,515 | 135 | 525 | 1,855 | 1,525 | 120 | 210 |
| April | 1,965 | 65 | 470 | 1,430 | 1,195 | 75 | 160 |
| Total | 9,315 | 480 | 2,000 | 6,830 | 5,425 | 440 | 965 |

*Notes:*

[1] Figures rounded to the nearest 5.

[2] Information is of initial determination decisions, excluding the outcome of appeals or other subsequent decisions.

[3] Refusals on the grounds that the applicant had arrived from a safe third country.

[4] Refusals under para 340 (para 180F prior to 1 October 1994 and para 101 prior to 26 July 1993) of the Immigration Rules for failure to provide evidence to support the asylum claim within a reasonable period.

*Source:*

S3 Division.

**Mrs. Roche:** To ask the Secretary of State for the Home Department if he will publish a breakdown of the number of asylum seekers currently detained under Immigration Act powers by *(a)* nationality, *(b)* gender, *(c)* length of detention, *(d)* place of detention and *(e)* immigration status at the time of application. [23801]

**Mr. Nicholas Baker:** As at 10 May 1995, a total of 646 persons who had at some stage sought asylum were detained. This figure includes people awaiting the setting of directions for removal following refusal of the application, as well as those whose applications were under consideration or subject to appeal. Of this figures, 152 had been in detention less than one month, 166 between one and two months, 225 between two and six months, and 103 had been in detention longer than six months.

Information on the gender, immigration status, nationality and location of those detained, as at 10 May 1995, is provided in tables 1 to 3.

*Table 1: Number of people detained on 10 May 1995 who had sought asylum, by immigration status and gender*

| Immigration Status | Male | Female | Total |
|---|---|---|---|
| Port case | 294 | 29 | 323 |
| Illegal entrant case | 253 | 16 | 269 |
| Deportation case | 49 | 5 | 54 |
| Total | 596 | 50 | 646 |

*Table 2: Number of people detained on 10 May 1995 who had sought asylum, by nationality*

| Country | Number |
|---|---|
| Albania | 8 |
| Algeria | 65 |
| Angola | 6 |
| Bangladesh | 19 |
| Cameroon | 1 |
| China | 76 |
| Colombia | 8 |
| Cyprus | 7 |
| Czech Republic | 1 |
| Dominica | 1 |
| Ecuador | 3 |
| Egypt | 2 |
| Eritrea | 1 |
| Ethiopia | 1 |
| Gambia | 5 |
| Georgia | 5 |
| Ghana | 65 |
| India | 84 |
| Iran | 8 |
| Ivory Coast | 4 |
| Jamaica | 5 |
| Kenya | 3 |
| Lebanon | 3 |
| Liberia | 3 |
| Libya | 4 |
| Mauritius | 2 |
| Morocco | 9 |
| Nigeria | 108 |
| Pakistan | 29 |
| Phillippines | 1 |
| Poland | 3 |
| Romania | 7 |
| Russia | 5 |
| Sierra Leone | 5 |
| Sri Lanka | 20 |
| South Africa | 1 |
| Sudan | 5 |
| Tanzania | 1 |
| Trinidad and Tobago | 2 |
| Tunisia | 1 |
| Turkey | 30 |
| Uganda | 3 |
| Former Yugoslavia | 11 |
| Zaire | 10 |
| Zambia | 1 |
| Nationality not known | 4 |
| **Total** | **646** |

*Table 3: Number of persons detained who have claimed asylum as at 10 May 1995, by place of detention*

| Place of detention | Number detained |
|---|---|
| *Prisons* | |
| HMP Haslar | 93 |
| HMP Rochester | 36 |
| HMP Winson Green | 32 |
| HMP Greenock | 14 |
| HMP Manchester | 12 |
| HMP Wormwood Scrubs | 7 |
| HMP Exeter | 5 |
| HMP Wandsworth | 5 |
| HMP Horfield, Bristol | 4 |
| HMP Belmarsh | 3 |
| HMP Brinsford | 3 |
| HMP Brixton | 3 |
| Other HMP Prisons | 23 |

*Table 3: Number of persons detained who have claimed asylum as at 10 May 1995, by place of detention*

| Place of detention | Number detained |
|---|---|
| *Other places of detention* | |
| Campsfield House | 145 |
| Harmondsworth | 80 |
| Police Cells | 42 |
| Gatwick Detention Centre | 38 |
| Dover Harbour Board | 18 |
| Queens Building | 14 |
| Newhaven | 12 |
| Stansted | 8 |
| Manchester Airport Detention Suite | 4 |
| Other[1] | 45 |
| **Total** | **646** |

[1] Includes Immigration Service detention centres, police cells and HM Prisons.

**Mrs. Roche:** To ask the Secretary of State for the Home Department how many asylum seekers have been removed to the Netherlands on safe third country grounds since 26 July 1993, and how many of those removed have been returned to the United Kingdom by the Dutch authorities. [23802]

**Mr. Nicholas Baker:** Seventy-one persons who had been refused asylum in the United Kingdom on safe third country grounds have been removed to the Netherlands since 26 July 1993. Of these, 11 have been returned to the United Kingdom.

**Mrs. Roche:** To ask the Secretary of State for the Home Department if he will publish a breakdown by nationality of the number of asylum seekers removed from the United Kingdom on safe third country grounds since 1 January. [23803]

**Mr. Nicholas Baker:** A list of nationalities removed from the United Kingdom on safe third country grounds is given in the table.

*Table 1: Number of persons who had sought asylum who have been removed from the United Kingdom on safe third country grounds, by nationality, between 1 January—to 10 May 1995*

| | Number |
|---|---|
| Algeria | 18 |
| Romania | 11 |
| China | 9 |
| Poland | 8 |
| Nigeria | 6 |
| Ghana | 5 |
| Afghanistan | 4 |
| Iran | 4 |
| Sri Lanka | 4 |
| Zaire | 4 |
| Lebanon | 3 |
| Pakistan | 3 |
| Somalia | 3 |
| Turkey | 3 |
| Bangladesh | 2 |
| Cameroon | 2 |
| Iraq | 2 |
| Ivory Coast | 2 |
| South Africa | 2 |
| Yugoslavia | 2 |
| Albania | 1 |
| Colombia | 1 |

*Table 1: Number of persons who had sought asylum who have been removed from the United Kingdom on safe third country grounds, by nationality, between 1 January—to 10 May 1995*

|  | Number |
|---|---|
| Ecuador | 1 |
| Eritrea | 1 |
| Ethiopia | 1 |
| Israel | 1 |
| Kenya | 1 |
| Liberia | 1 |
| Morocco | 1 |
| Russia | 1 |
| Rwanda | 1 |
| Uganda | 1 |
| Total | 109 |

**Mrs. Roche:** To ask the Secretary of State for the Home Department how many asylum seekers have been removed to other countries in the last two years; to which countries they have been returned; and how many of those so removed have been returned to the United Kingdom by the authorities of those countries.    [23804]

**Mr. Nicholas Baker:** A total of 824 persons who had been refused asylum were removed on safe third country grounds in 1993 and 1994. Information on the number of persons returned to specific countries and the number returned to the United Kingdom from these countries is not available for 1993 and 1994.

### Wheel Clamping

**Mr. Corbett:** To ask the Secretary of State for the Home Department what consultations he has had with West Midlands police during his review of the practice of wheel clamping on private land.    [24513]

**Mr. Maclean:** The police service, via the Association of Chief Police Officers, has provided an assessment of the current extent of the problems associated with wheel clamping on private land and the practicality of the various proposals to overcome those problems. I understand that the West Midlands police have contributed to providing that ACPO view.

### Passports

**Mr. Frank Field:** To ask the Secretary of State for the Home Department if he will establish a computer system on which all lost or stolen passports can be recorded.

[24615]

**Mr. Nicholas Baker:** The United Kingdom computerised passport issuing system has been in operation since 1988 and has the facility to record machine-readable passports that have been reported lost or stolen.

### Probation Areas, Wales

**Mr. Hendry:** To ask the Secretary of State for the Home Department what changes he plans to make to the boundaries of the probation areas of Mid-Glamorgan and Gwent following the creation of the new unitary authority of Caerphilly.    [24871]

**Mr. Nicholas Baker:** I propose to make a combined probation areas order under the Probation Services Act 1993 altering the boundary between the probation areas of Gwent and Mid-Glamorgan, subject to consultation with the justices concerned and other interested parties. The order would involve combining the petty sessions divisions within the unitary authority Caerphilly with those in the existing probation area of Gwent, and withdrawing the corresponding divisions from the Mid-Glamorgan probation area, with effect from 1 April 1996. Subject to the views of consultees, I believe that this outcome would promote the effective and efficient provision of probation services in South Wales and their co-ordination with other criminal justice services.

### Review Group on Appropriate Adults

**Mr. Hendry:** To ask the Secretary of State for the Home Department if he will publish the findings of the review group on appropriate adults; and if he will make a statement.    [24872]

**Mr. Maclean:** The review group reported its findings on 1 May and I have placed a copy of its report in the Library. Copies will also be sent to interested organisations for its comments. The Government will consider the recommendations made by the review group in the light of any further comments received on its findings.

### Criminal Injuries Compensation

**Mr. Khabra:** To ask the Secretary of State for the Home Department what were the total legal costs of defending the Government's tariff scheme for criminal injuries compensation in the courts up to and including the House of Lords.    [23617]

**Mr. Maclean:** The full costs are unlikely to be known for some time. The accounts settled to date have amounted to some £42,000.

**Mrs. Roche:** To ask the Secretary of State for the Home Department how many *(a)* police officers, *(b)* firefighters, *(c)* nurses and *(d)* shopworkers in each parliamentary constituency were awarded compensation for criminal injuries under the tariff scheme; and in each category how many were (i) women and (ii) received less money under the tariff scheme than they would have done under the old scheme.    [23527]

**Mr. Maclean** *[holding answer 10 May 1995]:* This information is not recorded centrally and could not be obtained without disproportionate cost.

### Football Restriction Orders

**Mr. Pendry:** To ask the Secretary of State for the Home Department how many restriction orders made under section 15 of the Football Spectators Act 1989 were enforced with regard to the Arsenal versus Real Zaragoza football match in Paris on 10 May.    [24395]

**Mr. Maclean:** None.

### MI5

**Mr. Mike O'Brien:** To ask the Secretary of State for the Home Department (1) what consideration he is giving to whether MI5 should take a lead role in work against drug trafficking or organised crime;    [21735]

(2) what consideration he is giving to legislation to change the functions of MI5; and if he will make a statement.    [21736]

**Mr. Howard:** The functions of the Security Service are set out in section 1 of the Security Service Act 1989. The Government has no plans to amend that legislation. If, however, resources were available to the Security Service and if, within their statutory functions, a useful role were identified for them in support of the police and other law enforcement agencies in their work to counter serious crime, I would be ready to consider such proposals.

### Race and Community Relations

**Mr. Bernie Grant:** To ask the Secretary of State for the Home Department how many trainers from Bramshill have undergone training in race and community relations by the HOSSU. [24344]

**Mr. Maclean** [holding answer 15 May 1995]: At present two trainers at the Police Staff College are graduates of courses provided by the Home Office specialist support unit.

**Mr. Bernie Grant:** To ask the Secretary of State for the Home Department (1) what reports he has received from the Association of Chief Police Officers regarding the effectiveness of the training in race and community relations carried out by the HOSSU; [24347]

(2) what representations he has received from the Association of Chief Police Officers regarding the training in race and community relations provided by the HOSSU. [24345]

**Mr. Maclean** [holding answer 15 May 1995]: None. However, the work of the Home Office Specialist Support Unit is overseen by a Management Board on which ACPO is represented.

**Mr. Bernie Grant:** To ask the Secretary of State for the Home Department if the ID codes for negroid types, including mulatto, octoroon, and quadroon have been removed from the pocket books issued to (a) Metropolitan police officers and (b) other forces; and if he will make a statement. [24342]

**Mr. Maclean** [holding answer 15 May 1995]: The provision of pocket books for police officers is a matter for chief officers. I understand that the pocket book issued to officers in the Metropolitan police service was updated in 1993 without these classifications. Some of the old books may remain in circulation but steps are being taken to replace them. I am not aware that the same classifications have been used in other forces.

### Race and Community Relations

**Mr. Bernie Grant:** To ask the Secretary of State for the Home Department who has been awarded the contract for the training of the police officers in race and community relations for 1995–96. [24351]

**Mr. Maclean** [holding answer 15 May 1995]: Equalities Associates' contract to provide the Home Office specialist support unit for police community and race relations training was renewed, for a period of three years, in July last year.

**Mr. Bernie Grant:** To ask the Secretary of State for the Home Department how many (a) senior officers, (b) trainers and (c) others in the Metropolitan police have been sent on the courses in race and community relations provided by the Home Office specialist support unit in each of the last six years; and how many still remain (i) in training at Hendon and (ii) in divisions in the Metropolitan police area. [24346]

**Mr. Maclean** [holding answer 15 May 1995]: I understand from the Commissioner of Police of the Metropolis that 13 senior officers have attended the HOSSU Training for managers course since its introduction in 1992. Seventy-three trainers have attended the six week race and community relations course since 1989. Of the 73 officers who have undergone the training, 15 are currently trainers at the Metropolitan police training school in Hendon. At least 37 trainers continue to have a training responsibility at a division or unit. No other officers have attended this six week course.

**Mr. Bernie Grant:** To ask the Secretary of State for the Home Department (1) what assessment he has made of the standard of training provided by Equalities Associates Ltd; [24349]

(2) if he will make a statement on the results of the latest HMI report on the work of the Home Office specialist support unit for the training of police officers in race relations; and if he will place a copy of the report in the Library. [24350]

**Mr. Maclean** [holding answers 15 May 1995]: The work of the specialist support unit was inspected in 1991 by Her Majesty's inspectorate of constabulary, supported by HMI (Schools) and an independent assessor.

It was found that the provider of the unit, Equalities Associates, was meeting its contractual objectives, and recommendations aimed at further enhancing the effectiveness of the unit's contribution to police service training in community and race relations have been implemented.

I have placed in the Library those parts of the assessment conducted by Her Majesty's inspectorate of constabulary.

**Mr. Bernie Grant:** To ask the Secretary of State for the Home Department what assessment he has made as to whether the police trainers who have undergone training in race and community relations are competent to train their fellow officers in these issues; and if he will make a statement. [24353]

**Mr. Maclean** [holding answer 15 May 1995]: All police trainers are assessed on their competence to deliver training programmes, including those concerning community and race relations.

**Mr. Bernie Grant:** To ask the Secretary of State for the Home Department (1) what is the amount by which the Home Office specialist support unit for the training of police officers in race and community relations, has been reduced for the year 1995–96; and what are the reasons for this budget reduction; [24348]

(2) if (a) the Commissioner of Police for the Metropolis and (b) other chief constables for England, Wales and Scotland were consulted before the decision to reduce the budget of the HOSSU was taken; and what was (i) his and (ii) their response. [24446]

**Mr. Maclean** *[holding answers 15 May 1995]:* The funding of the unit this financial year is £39,000 less than in 1994–95. This reduction reflects public expenditure pressures and the terms of the new contract negotiated with the unit in July 1994.

Issues of funding are discussed by the unit's management board, on which the Metropolitan police and the Association of Chief Police Officers are represented.

**Mr. Bernie Grant:** To ask the Secretary of State for the Home Department what assessment he has made whether all senior police officers have been sufficiently trained in race and community relations.    [24352]

**Mr. Maclean** *[holding answer 15 May 1995]:* All police officers, by the time they have attained a senior rank, will have received training in community and race relations matters. In addition to formal courses the Home Office provides an annual one-week seminar on this subject for senior officers; and steps are being taken with the Home Office specialist support unit to provide further support to senior officers in those forces serving major ethnic minority communities.

**Mr. Bernie Grant:** To ask the Secretary of State for the Home Department how many police trainers who have undergone training in race and community relations are still working as trainers in the police force.    [24343]

**Mr. Maclean** *[holding answer 15 May 1995]:* It is for chief officers to allocate individual officers to appropriate duties. This information is not held centrally.

### Motor Vehicle Theft

**Mr. Robert Ainsworth:** To ask the Secretary of State for the Home Department, pursuant to his answer of 1 May, *Official Report,* column *96,* what was the recorded number of notifiable offences of theft of motor vehicles in 1994.    [24266]

**Mr. Maclean** *[holding answer 15 May 1995]:* The number of notifiable offences of theft or unauthorised taking of a motor vehicle, including aggravated vehicle taking, recorded by the police in England and Wales in 1994 was 534,700.

### Long-handled Batons

**Mr. Bernie Grant:** To ask the Secretary of State for the Home Department how many people have been *(a)* injured and *(b)* killed by the new long-handled batons since their introduction; and what is their ethnicity according to police codes.    [24341]

**Mr. Maclean** *[holding answer 15 May 1995]:* This information is not centrally available and could be obtained only at disproportionate cost.

## NORTHERN IRELAND

### Autism

**Mr. Worthington:** To ask the Secretary of State for Northern Ireland what provision is currently made within Northern Ireland for children with autism.    [23601]

**Mr. Ancram:** It is the responsibility of the five education and library boards in Northern Ireland to make special educational provision for children with special educational needs, and this includes autistic children. Placements may be made in special schools, in special units attached to mainstream schools or in mainstream schools themselves. One board has established an advisory and support service for autistic children and their families.

The Department of Health and Social Services will be providing grant-aid of £25,000 in 1995–96 to autism via the TEACCH programme, a multi-disciplinary project involving professionals from the fields of education and health and social services, now available at all schools for children with severe learning difficulties.

### Schools Expenditure

**Mr. Worthington:** To ask the Secretary of State for Northern Ireland what has been the expenditure per *(a)* primary school and *(b)* primary school pupil in real and constant price terms in each year since 1979.    [23382]

**Mr. Ancram:** The information requested in respect of primary and secondary school pupils is set out in the table for years 1979–80 to 1992–93, which is the latest year for which details are available:

| Year | Primary | | Secondary[1] | |
| --- | --- | --- | --- | --- |
| | Expenditure per pupil £ | Expenditure per pupil at 1992–93 prices £ | Expenditure per pupil £ | Expenditure per pupil at 1992–93 prices £ |
| 1979–80 | 388 | 924 | 597 | 1,442 |
| 1980–81 | 493 | 993 | 749 | 1,508 |
| 1981–82 | 561 | 1,030 | 855 | 1,570 |
| 1982–83 | 599 | 1,027 | 922 | 1,580 |
| 1983–84 | 630 | 1,032 | 977 | 1,600 |
| 1984–85 | 665 | 1,037 | 1,064 | 1,659 |
| 1985–86 | 715 | 1,057 | 1,144 | 1,691 |
| 1986–87 | 807 | 1,158 | 1,305 | 1,873 |
| 1987–88 | 882 | 1,202 | 1,427 | 1,944 |
| 1988–89 | 973 | 1,243 | 1,571 | 2,006 |
| 1989–90 | 1,079 | 1,288 | 1,725 | 2,059 |

| Year | Primary | | Secondary[1] | |
|---|---|---|---|---|
| | Expenditure per pupil | Expenditure per pupil at 1992–93 prices | Expenditure per pupil | Expenditure per pupil at 1992–93 prices |
| | £ | £ | £ | £ |
| 1990–91 | 1,186 | 1,311 | 1,859 | 2,054 |
| 1991–92 | 1,285 | 1,336 | 2,053 | 2,135 |
| 1992–93 | 1,408 | 1,408 | 2,195 | 2,195 |

*Notes:*
[1] Includes preparatory pupils at grammar schools.
1. In the 1992–93 financial year there were 189,995 full-time equivalent pupils at primary schools, 3,659 at preparatory departments in grammar schools and 144,773 at secondary schools.

**Mr. Worthington:** To ask the Secretary of State for Northern Ireland what has been the expenditure per *(a)* primary school and *(b)* secondary school pupil in real and constant price terms in each year since 1979 excluding staff costs.                    [23384]

**Mr. Ancram:** The information requested is set out in the table for years 1979–80 to 1992–93 which is the latest year for which details are available:

| Year | Primary | | Secondary[1] | |
|---|---|---|---|---|
| | Expenditure per pupil | Expenditure per pupil at 1992–93 prices | Expenditure per pupil | Expenditure per pupil at 1992–93 prices |
| | £ | £ | £ | £ |
| 1979–80 | 65 | 155 | 107 | 255 |
| 1980–81 | 76 | 153 | 128 | 258 |
| 1981–82 | 88 | 162 | 145 | 266 |
| 1982–83 | 92 | 158 | 156 | 267 |
| 1983–84 | 93 | 152 | 159 | 260 |
| 1984–85 | 98 | 153 | 193 | 301 |
| 1985–86 | 104 | 154 | 193 | 285 |
| 1986–87 | 139 | 199 | 244 | 350 |
| 1987–88 | 122 | 166 | 237 | 323 |
| 1988–89 | 130 | 166 | 257 | 328 |
| 1989–90 | 161 | 192 | 296 | 353 |
| 1990–91 | 168 | 186 | 317 | 350 |
| 1991–92 | 188 | 195 | 326 | 339 |
| 1992–93 | 217 | 217 | 341 | 341 |

*Notes:*
[1] Includes preparatory pupils at grammar schools.
1. In the 1992–93 financial year there were 189,995 full-time equivalent pupils at primary schools, 3,659 at preparatory departments in grammar schools and 144,773 at secondary schools.

**Mr. Worthington:** To ask the Secretary of State for Northern Ireland what has been the capital expenditure in real and constant price terms on *(a)* primary schools and *(b)* secondary schools in each year since 1979.    [23383]

**Mr. Ancram:** Capital expenditure by education and library boards for each of the financial years from 1979–80 to 1992–93 is analysed by school sector in the statements and summary of the educational and library boards; accounts, Command 8143, 8508, 8816, 9225,

9487, 9820, 255, 388, 690, 1105, 1531, 1977, 2249 and 2603, copies of which are available in the Library. The figures for 1993–94 will be published in July 1995.

Capital grants paid by the Department of Education in respect of approved capital expenditure incurred by voluntary schools and grant-maintained integrated schools since 1984–85 are set out. Information in the form requested for the years 1979–80 to 1983–84 is not readily available and could be obtained only at disproportionate cost.

| Year | Voluntary and grant-maintained integrated primary schools (including Nursery) | | Voluntary and grant-maintained integrated secondary schools | |
|---|---|---|---|---|
| | Grants £ million | 1992–93 Prices £ million | Grants £ million | 1992–93 Prices £ million |
| 1984–85 | 1.983 | 3.092 | 4.072 | 6.350 |
| 1985–86 | 2.457 | 3.632 | 3.809 | 5.631 |
| 1986–87 | 3.064 | 4.397 | 4.860 | 6.975 |
| 1987–88 | 2.294 | 3.126 | 8.268 | 11.266 |
| 1988–89 | 3.497 | 4.466 | 11.148 | 14.237 |
| 1989–90 | 4.389 | 5.239 | 14.229 | 16.985 |

| Year | Voluntary and grant-maintained integrated primary schools (including Nursery) | | Voluntary and grant-maintained integrated secondary schools | |
|---|---|---|---|---|
| | Grants £ million | 1992–93 Prices £ million | Grants £ million | 1992–93 Prices £ million |
| 1990–91 | 6.390 | 7.062 | 19.717 | 21.790 |
| 1991–92 | 6.060 | 6.301 | 25.615 | 26.635 |
| 1992–93 | 6.850 | 6.850 | 23.232 | 23.232 |

### Higher Education

**Mr. Worthington:** To ask the Secretary of State for Northern Ireland what proposals he has to increase the inflow of students from outside Northern Ireland into higher education in Northern Ireland. [23392]

**Mr. Ancram:** None. Universities in Northern Ireland are autonomous and independent bodies and, as such, it is for them to set entry requirements and select students.

**Mr. Worthington:** To ask the Secretary of State for Northern Ireland what percentage of the appropriate age group has progressed to higher education in each year since 1979. [23391]

**Mr. Ancram:** The percentage of young people entering higher education is given by the age participation index—the number of full-time undergraduate new entrants aged under 21 expressed as a percentage of the 18-year-old population. The API is available only from 1985–86 onwards and the information is as follows:

*Age participation index[1]*

| | | | | | | | | Percentage |
|---|---|---|---|---|---|---|---|---|
| 1985–86 | 1986–87 | 1987–88 | 1988–89 | 1989–90 | 1990–91 | 1991–92 | 1992–93 | 1993–94[2] |
| 19.2 | 20.1 | 21.0 | 22.9 | 25.6 | 27.7 | 29.2 | 33.4 | 36.4 |

*Notes:*
[1] Does not include agricultural college or nursing college students or students attending institutions outside the United Kingdom.
[2] 1993–94 figure is provisional.

**Mr. Worthington:** To ask the Secretary of State for Northern Ireland what proportion of the appropriate age group has attained university entrance standards in each year since 1979. [23385]

**Mr. Ancram:** Entrance requirements to university vary enormously. As a general guide 2 A-levels or equivalent is often used as the standard entrance requirement. Figures on this basis are available only for 1991–92 and 1992–93, when 38.1 per cent. and 39.9 per cent. respectively of young people aged 21 or under had achieved this standard.

### Pupil-Teacher Ratios

**Mr. Worthington:** To ask the Secretary of State for Northern Ireland what has been the pupil-teacher ratio in (a) primary schools and (b) secondary schools in Northern Ireland in each year since 1979. [23602]

**Mr. Ancram:** The information is as follows:

| | 1979–80 | 1980–81 | 1981–82 | 1982–83 | 1983–84 | 1984–85 | 1985–86 | 1986–87 |
|---|---|---|---|---|---|---|---|---|
| Primary | 23.8 | 23.6 | 23.5 | 23.3 | 23.4 | 23.3 | 23.4 | 23.4 |
| Secondary | 15.3 | 15.4 | 15.4 | 15.4 | 15.3 | 15.2 | 15.0 | 14.9 |

| | 1987–88 | 1988–89 | 1989–90 | 1990–91 | 1991–92 | 1992–93 | 1993–94 |
|---|---|---|---|---|---|---|---|
| Primary | 23.5 | 23.2 | 23.2 | 22.8 | 22.6 | 22.2 | 21.6 |
| Secondary | 14.8 | 14.8 | 14.7 | 14.7 | 15.1 | 15.2 | 15.1 |

### Drugs White Paper

**Mr. Clifford Forsythe:** To ask the Secretary of State for Northern Ireland when he intends to publish a White Paper for Northern Ireland similar to the recent "Tackling Drugs Together" publication concerning England. [24674]

**Mr. Moss:** The Northern Ireland Committee on Drug Misuse, which advises the Department of Health and Social Services on issues relating to drug and solvent misuse, issued for consultation in March 1995 a draft policy statement on drug misuse. Following the consultation period, which ends on 31 May, the committee will submit a final draft to the Government for consideration as the basis of a policy framework for tackling drug misuse in Northern Ireland. The draft policy statement is designed to be consistent with the "Tackling Drugs Together" White Paper.

## AGRICULTURE, FISHERIES AND FOOD

### Trade Balance (Beer)

**Mr. Martyn Jones:** To ask the Minister of Agriculture, Fisheries and Food what was the United Kingdom's trade balance for beer for the years *(a)* 1980, *(b)* 1985, *(c)* 1990 *(d)* 1994. [23270]

**Mr. Jack:** Official statistics for the United Kingdom's trade balance in beer made from malt, including ale, stout and porter, are shown in the table:

| | Imports | Exports | Value (£000s) trade gap |
|---|---|---|---|
| 1980 | 35,440 | 19,000 | –16,440 |
| 1985 | 84,471 | 42,490 | –41,981 |
| 1990 | 169,493 | 80,854 | –88,639 |
| 1994 | 254,592 | 173,449 | –81,143 |

*Notes:*
1. Because of differences in the valuation principles for imports and exports, the crude trade gap between them overstates the contribution of beer to the deficit on visible trade in the balance of payments statistics.
2. The above figures exclude trade by private persons.
3. Data are provisional.

### Live Animal Exports

**Dr. Lynne Jones:** To ask the Minister of Agriculture, Fisheries and Food what checks have been made on the length of time calves are waiting in transporters at Baginton airport prior to being flown to Europe and on the implications for the maximum journey time limit without food and water. [23361]

**Mrs. Browning:** Arrangements have been made to check consignments of calves awaiting flights from Coventry airport to ensure that their welfare needs are being met. In circumstances where there is the possibility that the 15-hour rule could be breached because of delayed flights, officials have powers to intervene to prevent the journey continuing, and to order the calves to be returned to their premises of origin so as to arrive within 15 hours of the time their journey started.

### Meat Hygiene Service

**Sir Donald Thompson:** To ask the Minister of Agriculture, Fisheries and Food whether he will hold an annual meeting with representatives of the meat and livestock industries to review the performance of the Meat Hygiene Service. [24791]

**Mr. Waldegrave:** Yes. I intend to meet the members of the Meat Hygiene Service's industry forum to discuss the agency's performance as recorded in its annual report. The first annual report is likely to be available in mid-1996.

### Intervention Stores

**Mr. Davidson:** To ask the Minister of Agriculture, Fisheries and Food how much *(a)* beef, *(b)* butter, *(c)* wine and *(d)* cheese is presently held in intervention stores in (i) the United Kingdom and (ii) the EC; how many days' supply this represents and what were the equivalent figures for the previous 12 months. [24287]

**Mr. Jack:** Tables showing levels of all produce held in intervention within the EU are placed in the House Library at regular intervals, most recently on 15 May. The information currently held in the House Library goes back to January 1985.

### Food Surpluses

**Mrs. Ann Winterton:** To ask the Minister of Agriculture, Fisheries and Food if he will publish a breakdown by type of foodstuff of the volumes and tonnage of surplus foodstuffs made available for *(a)* free distribution within member countries of the European Union and *(b)* overseas aid purposes in the most recent year for which figures are available and in each of the previous three years. [242298]

**Mr. Jack:** Details of the quantities of surplus food made available under Council regulation (EEC) 1035/72, on the common organisation of the market in fruit and vegetables, and Council regulation (EEC) 3730/87, on the supply of food from intervention stocks for distribution to the needy, for the most recent four years for which figures are available are given in the table.

There is also provision under Commission regulation (EEC) 1501/83 for the disposal of fishery products which have been withdrawn from the market, including by distribution to the public. This option has not been used in the UK, where the usual method of disposal is for use as animal feed. Information is not available on methods of disposal in other member states.

*Produce made available under Council Regulation (EEC) 1035/72*

(tonnes)

| | 1989–90 | 1990–91 | 1991–92 | 1992–93 |
|---|---|---|---|---|
| Cauliflowers (1 May–30 April) | 1,095 | 368 | 852 | 1,799 |
| Apricots (1 June–31 May) | 88 | 8 | 5 | 24 |
| Nectarines (1 June–31 May) | 716 | 298 | 124 | 364 |
| Peaches (1 June–31 May) | 4,438 | 822 | 438 | 1,155 |
| Lemons (1 June–31 May) | 4,716 | 285 | 291 | 618 |
| Tomatoes (11 June–10 June) | 50 | 217 | 205 | 382 |
| Pears (1 July–30 June) | 51 | 319 | 66 | 768 |
| Apples (1 August–31 July) | 6,090 | 3,656 | 293 | 4,486 |
| Clementines/Mandarins (16 November–15 November) | 105 | 384 | 59 | 274 |
| Oranges (1 December–30 November) | 9,766 | 2,605 | 7,467 | 31,248 |

*Produce made available under Council Regulation (EEC) No 3730/87*

(tonnes)

| | [1]1991–92 | 1992–93 | 1993–94 | 1994–95 |
|---|---|---|---|---|
| Common Wheat | 12,330 | 11,530 | 14,970 | 14,950 |
| Durum Wheat | 42,200 | 42,300 | 49,850 | 55,350 |
| Rice | 9,500 | 10,500 | 4,700 | 4,700 |
| Olive Oil | 2,700 | 4,700 | 7,000 | 9,000 |
| Milk Powder | 4,525 | 4,425 | 7,325 | 8,800 |

*Produce made available under Council Regulation (EEC) No 3730/87*

| | [1]1991–92 | 1992–93 | 1993–94 | 1994–95 |
|---|---|---|---|---|
| | | | | *(tonnes)* |
| Butter | 15,125 | 13,140 | 9,455 | 10,520 |
| Beef/Veal | 30,318 | 34,915 | 33,415 | 34,950 |
| Cheese | 0 | 500 | 2,000 | 2,300 |

[1] 1 October to 30 September.

In most cases, surplus foodstuffs are not suitable for use as food aid. Nevertheless, in 1992, 62,000 tonnes of wheat was released from intervention for famine relief in Somalia.

In addition, since 1992 the EU food aid programme has provided 2.4 million tonnes of food for Africa, while the total value of humanitarian aid from the EU to Rwanda and the former Yugoslavia has now reached £251 million and £524 million respectively. In addition to contributing to these food aid packages, Britain has provided direct bilateral aid, including 450,000 tonnes of food to Africa since 1992 and £88 million worth of aid to the former Yugoslavia.

### Selenium

**Mr. Hain:** To ask the Minister of Agriculture, Fisheries and Food (1) what recent studies have been undertaken by his Department on the consumption levels of selenium; what were the findings of those studies; to what extent the survey indicates that selenium consumption levels are meeting the recommended daily amount; if he intends to publish the results of the surveys; and if he will make a statement;     [24164]

(2) what is the current recommended daily amount of selenium which should be consumed for *(a)* adult men and *(b)* adult women; what steps have been taken to calculate the current actual average daily consumption of selenium by such adult men and women; and how he accounts for differences between the figures for recommended and actual consumption;     [24165]

(3) what is meant by the terms reference nutrient intake and lower reference nutrient intake; what are the amounts of those references in relation to selenium; and how those amounts compare with the actual amounts of selenium currently consumed by the adult population.     [24167]

**Mrs. Browning:** The selenium content of foods was measured as part of the Ministry's total diet study in 1985 and 1991, and as a separate research project in 1994. The estimations of average intake based on these results are either 30–40µg/day or 50–60µg/day, depending on the method of analysis used. The most sensitive method leads to the higher estimate, but further research is planned to resolve this analytical uncertainty. The reports of these analytical studies have been published in the scientific press, or have been announced in the MAFF/DH Food Safety Information Bulletin and are available on request to the MAFF library.

There is no recommended daily intake for selenium. The Department of Health's committee on medical aspects of food policy reported on dietary reference values[1] in 1991, and gave a reference nutrient intake of 75µg/day for men and 60/µgday for women, and a lower reference nutrient intake of 40µg/day for both men and women. The RNI is the amount of a nutrient that is estimated to be enough, or more than enough, for about 97 per cent. of a population to fulfil the functional criterion against which the RNI was set, which in this case is to maintain maximum glutathione peroxidase activity. The LRNI is the amount of a nutrient which is estimated to be sufficient for those in the population who have low needs. Populations with average selenium intakes above 20µg/day are not at risk of clinical adverse effects.

[1] Report on the Panel on Dietary Reference Values of the Committee on Medical Aspects of Food Policy, Department of Health, HMSO, 1991.

### Surplus Wine

**Mr. Davidson:** To ask the Minister of Agriculture, Fisheries and Food what plans he has to distribute the EC wine lake.     [24498]

**Mr. Jack:** Responsibility for management of the EU wine regime rests with the European Commission. Surplus wine is distilled into alcohol. The United Kingdom Government support the Commission in its efforts to dispose of wine alcohol stocks at the best price available; sales are mainly to third countries for use in the fuel sector. The UK also supports the European Commission's aim to reform the EU wine regime so as to bring production into line with demand.

### Ochratoxin A

**Mr. Flynn:** To ask the Minister of Agriculture, Fisheries and Food when he expects his Department's research into the possible toxic effects of ochratoxin A in coffee and other foods to be completed and published.     [23793]

**Mrs. Browning** *[holding answer 15 May 1995]:* I refer the hon. member to my answer of 28 February 1995, *Official Report*, col. *481*, for information on the MAFF-funded research and surveillance concerning the contamination of coffee by Ochratoxin A. In addition the results of surveys of other foodstuffs have been published in the "Food Safety Information Bulletin", September 1994 and January 1995 and in Food Surveillance Paper number 36, "Mycotoxins: Third Report." Copies are available in the Library. We are planning further work to increase our knowledge of UK dietary exposure to Ochratoxin A. This work is scheduled to be completed in 1998 and the results of any surveillance will be published in the usual manner in the bulletin.

### Telephones

**Mr. Donohoe:** To ask the Minister of Agriculture, Fisheries and Food what representations his Department has made to the Department of Trade and Industry concerning the need for legislation to prevent the cloning of mobile telephones.     [23469]

**Mr. Jack** *[holding answer 9 May 1995]:* The Department has made no representations to the Department of Trade and Industry concerning the need for legislation to prevent the cloning of mobile telephones.

**Mr. Donohoe:** To ask the Minister of Agriculture, Fisheries and Food what use his Department makes of hand-held and car-based mobile telephones; what were the costs for each financial year of these services since mobile telephones were first introduced to his Department; and how many mobile telephones are currently in use.     [23456]

**Mr. Jack** *[holding answer 9 May 1995]:* The Ministry and its associated executive agencies have a large number of field officers providing service to food, farming and fishing interests. They are often working in isolated areas away from fixed telephones. In order that the service they provide can be fast and efficient, these officers need to be able to make contact whatever their situation. Senior officers travel more frequently nowadays and they, too, make use of mobile telephones in order to keep in touch and respond quickly.

Local management evaluate the business need and financial justification in order to decide who should be issued with mobile telephones. Financial, technical and procurement advice is available centrally.

The Ministry's estimated costs for service rental, excluding VAT, are broken down into each financial year as follows:

| Financial year | Service Rental (£) |
|---|---|
| 1 April 1990 to 31 March 1991 | 8,640 |
| 1 April 1991 to 31 March 1992 | 45,630 |
| 1 April 1992 to 31 March 1993 | 96,120 |
| 1 April 1993 to 31 March 1994 | 222,480 |
| 1 April 1994 to 31 March 1995 | 379,620 |

The costs for call charges are available centrally for financial year 1994–95 only:

| Financial Year | Call Charges (£) |
|---|---|
| 1 April 1994–31 March 1995 | 206,066 |

The Ministry and its associated executive agencies currently have approximately 1,400 mobile phones.

**Mr. Donohoe:** To ask the Minister of Agriculture, Fisheries and Food, what steps his department has taken to prevent the cloning of telephones being used by his Department; and if his Department has discussed this matter with any official agencies. [23452]

**Mr. Jack** *[holding answer 9 May 1995]:* We are aware of the risks of analogue mobile phones being cloned. For this reason, the Department has issued an advice note to all telecommunications managers which gives advice on the more secure nature of digital mobile phones over analogue. To minimise the potential cost of cloning, one of MAFF's largest agencies has instituted a blanket bar on the majority of their mobile phones on international and premium rate services which will prevent unauthorised calls to expensive numbers.

### Public Bodies

**Dr. Wright:** To ask the Minister of Agriculture, Fisheries and Food if he will list the executive non-departmental public bodies sponsored by his Department which are subject to *(a)* investigation by the Parliamentary Commissioner, *(b)* scrutiny by the Audit Commission, *(c)* scrutiny by the National Audit Office, *(d)* statutory provision for open government, *(e)* performance indicators and *(f)* provisions under the citizens charter. [20651]

**Mr. Jack** *[holding answer 25 April 1995]:* The Milk Development Council is currently being set up. The information required on other executive NDPBs is as follows:

Subject to:
*(a)Investigation by the Parliamentary Commissioner*
—Agricultural Wages Council

*(b) Scrutiny by the Audit Commission*
—None

*(c) Scrutiny by the National Audit Office*
—Wine Standards Board of the Vintners' Company
—Agricultural Wages Committees
—Agricultural Wages Board
—Regional Flood Defence Committees
—Food From Britain
—Sea Fish Industry Authority
—Royal Botanic Gardens, Kew
—Horticulture Research International
    and access rights to the following bodies are under review
—Home-Grown Cereals Authority—review of existing arrangements
—Meat and Livestock Commission—review of existing arrangements
—Horticultural Development Council
—Apple and Pear Research Council

*(d) Statutory Provisions for Open Government*
—There are no statutory provisions for Open Government
*(e) Performance Indicators*
—Wine Standards Board of the Vintners' Company
—Home-Grown Cereals Authority
—Food From Britain
—Sea Fish Industry Authority
—Meat and Livestock Commission
—Royal Botanic Gardens, Kew
—Horticulture Research International
Discussions are in progress with
—Horticultural Development Council
—Apple and Pear Research Council

*(f) Provisions under the Citizens' Charter*
The following NDPBS have produced or are producing service statements
—Home-Grown Cereals Authority
—Meat and Livestock Commission
—Sea Fish Industry Authority
—Horticulture Research International
—Royal Botanic Gardens, Kew
—Wine Standards Boards of the Vintners' Company

## SOCIAL SECURITY

### Retirement Pension

**Mr. Dewar:** To ask the Secretary of State for Social Security what state earnings-related pension would be received in the years 2010 and 2040 by *(a)* a man and *(b)* a woman both with a full national insurance contribution record and earning throughout (i) national average earnings, (ii) one and a half times average earnings, (iii) and half average earnings, using the assumptions used by the Government actuary in Cm. 2714, "Report on the Financial Provisions of the Pension Bill on the National Insurance Fund," before the changes to SERPs introduced in 1988, under the present scheme and on the assumption that the changes in the Pensions Bill, as introduced in the House of Lords, are implemented in full. [22449]

**Mr. Arbuthnot:** The information is in the table.

| 1995–96 prices £s per week | Pre-1988 changes | Present | Proposed |
|---|---|---|---|
| *Male: retiring in 2010–11* | | | |
| Average earnings | 87.90 | 75.30 | 71.60 |
| 1.5 average earnings | 128.40 | 102.90 | 99.30 |
| 0.5 average earnings | 36.90 | 31.60 | 27.90 |

| 1995–96 prices £s per week | Pre-1988 changes | Present | Proposed |
|---|---|---|---|
| *Female: retiring in 2010–11* | | | |
| Average earnings | 87.90 | 75.30 | 71.60 |
| 1.5 average earnings | 128.40 | 102.90 | 99.30 |
| 0.5 average earnings | 36.90 | 31.60 | 27.90 |
| *Male: retiring in 2040–41* | | | |
| Average earnings | 144.60 | 102.70 | 97.50 |
| 1.5 average earnings | 173.60 | 112.10 | 107.00 |
| 0.5 average earnings | 65.30 | 52.20 | 47.00 |
| *Female: retiring in 2040–41* | | | |
| Average earnings | 143.70 | 101.20 | 97.50 |
| 1.5 average earnings | 160.10 | 107.10 | 107.00 |
| 0.5 average earnings | 65.30 | 52.20 | 47.00 |

*Notes:*

1. Pensioners are assumed to retire in the tax years 2010–11 and 2040–41. Under the proposed scheme State pension age for women in 2010–11 will be between 60 years and 1 month and 60 years and 6 months, and in 2040–41 it will be 65. In all other schemes it will be 60.

2. Future real earnings growth is assumed to be 1.5 per cent. per annum.

3. The pre-1988 amounts are based on the best 20 years of revalued earnings.

4. The earnings figures used are national, all adult full-time average earnings.

## Benefits Agency Framework Document

**Mr. Waterson:** To ask the Secretary of State for Social Security, pursuant to his answer of 29 March, *Official Report,* column *687,* when the revised Benefits Agency framework document is to be published. [24837]

**Mr. Roger Evans:** The revised Benefits Agency framework document has been published today, and a copy has been placed in the Library.

## Mortgage Interest

**Mr. David Nicholson:** To ask the Secretary of State for Social Security (1) how many claimants of income support for mortgage interest currently receive assistance with loans taken out to facilitate improvements to a property which are reasonable in the circumstances, as set out in paragraph 8, schedule 3 to the Income Support (General) Regulations 1987; [24677]

(2) how many claimants of income support for mortgage interest currently receive assistance under the deserted partner rule as set out in paragraph 7, schedule 3 to the Income Support (General) Regulations 1987; [24676]

(3) how many claimants of income support for mortgage interest currently receive assistance *(a)* to pay the interest on arrears which have accrued during the first 16 weeks of a claim when only 50 per cent. of the eligible interest is payable, *(b)* to pay the interest on arrears where a mortgage has a deferred interest payment arrangement for at least a two-year period, *(c)* where other arrears of mortgage payments have accrued and a standard amount of £2.35 per week is deducted from the claimant's entitlement to income support and *(d)* the total expenditure in each of these areas. [24678]

**Mr. Roger Evans:** A total of 135,000 income support claimants have an amount deducted from their benefit and paid to their lender to help with the clearing of mortgage interest arrears. This does not involve any additional expenditure on income support. The other information could be obtained only at disproportionate cost.

*Source:*

Income Support Statistics Quarterly Enquiry, May 1994.

*Note:*

The figure has been rounded to the nearest thousand.

## Fraud

**Mr. Frank Field:** To ask the Secretary of State for Social Security (1) how many officials in his Department have been *(a)* suspended, *(b)* disciplined, *(c)* dismissed and *(d)* prosecuted for each of the last 30 years for irregularities in connection with benefit fraud from which they or their associates have gained; [24612]

(2) how many officials working on the departmental central index have been *(a)* suspended, *(b)* disciplined, *(c)* dismissed and *(d)* prosecuted for each of the last 30 years for irregularities in connection with benefit fraud from which they or their associates have gained. [24613]

**Mr. Arbuthnot:** This information is not available in the form requested and can be obtained only at disproportionate cost. Benefit fraud by staff is treated very seriously, resulting in dismissal and prosecution when proven. A total of 34 staff have been prosecuted for matters relating to benefit fraud since 1 April 1994; it is not possible to say how many of these had access to the departmental central index. I refer the hon. Member to the reply that I gave him on 8 March, *Official Report,* columns *693–94.*

**Mr. Frank Field:** To ask the Secretary of State for Social Security if he will list those local authorities who use *(a)* auditors and *(b)* specialist trained fraud investigators to investigate housing benefit fraud; and if he will detail each authority and the total number of staff who have been employed for each of the last 10 years. [24614]

**Mr. Roger Evans:** The information requested is not available.

## Family Credit

**Mr. Bradley:** To ask the Secretary of State for Social Security what proportion of *(a)* new family credit claims and *(b)* renewal family credit claims are being processed within one week, four weeks, six weeks, eight weeks and longer than eight weeks. [23623]

**Mr. Roger Evans:** The administration of family credit is a matter for Mr. Ian Magee, the chief executive of the Benefits Agency. He will write to the hon. Member.

*Letter from Ian Magee to Mr. Keith Bradley, dated 15 May 1995:*

The Secretary of State for Social Security has asked me to reply to your recent Parliamentary Question about the clearance times of new and renewal claims to Family Credit.

The table below details the information you have requested. Such figures are produced on a monthly basis and I have therefore provided information for the month ending 30 April 1995 which is the latest full month available. For the purposes of this question, one week has been calculated as 5 working days.

| | 1 week (1–5 days) | 4 weeks (6–20 days) | 6 weeks (21–30 days) | 8 weeks (31–40 days) | Over 8 weeks (41+ days) |
|---|---|---|---|---|---|
| New claims | 46.65 | 40.34 | 8.08 | 3.01 | 1.92 |
| Renewal claims | 45.92 | 44.6 | 646 | 1.88 | 1.14 |

The Family Credit Unit is currently operating a pilot section, introduced during April 1995, which is processing new claims from customers who have not previously claimed Family Credit. The pilot section accepts new (first-time) claims from one of the ten operational areas that process claims within the Family Credit Unit. These claims can be from customers who have recently started work but have not used the Fast Track service available through the Employment Service, had a change of hours and earnings, or have simply not previously claimed Family Credit.

A claim form is submitted and any additional information required is, wherever possible, taken over the telephone which allows the claims to be processed more quickly. A verification exercise is then conducted on a sample of the claims where telephone evidence has been accepted. Figures for the month ending 30 April showed that 97.5% of customers using this system had their claim decided in 5 working days.

I hope you find this reply helpful.

# SCOTLAND

## Chernobyl

**Mr. Llew Smith:** To ask the Secretary of State for Scotland what is the total compensation paid to farmers for loss of earnings and clean-up of radioactive contamination of Scottish farms arising from the fallout from the Chernobyl nuclear accident in 1986.    [22025]

**Sir Hector Monro:** The sheep compensation scheme was introduced in July 1986 to compensate farmers whose enterprises had been disrupted as a result of statutory movement and slaughter restrictions following the Chernobyl accident. The total paid out under the scheme in Scotland up to the end of March 1995 was £2,491,842.

## Drumkinnon Bay

**Mr. McFall:** To ask the Secretary of State for Scotland what direct representations the Minister with responsibility for industry and local government received in writing or in person from Drumkinnon Development Company Ltd. or any associated companies regarding the latter's negotiations with Dumbarton district council and its subsequent sale of land to Dumbartonshire Enterprise.    [23057]

**Mr. Kynoch:** Neither I nor my predecessor received any representation from Drumkinnon Development Company Ltd. or any associated company on the matter to which the question refers, although the Scottish Office Environment Department was approached by agents of the Drumkinnon Development Company Ltd. in support of a request from Dumbarton district council that the decision on the planning appeal should be deferred for an additional month to allow the discussions between the district council and the Drumkinnon Development Company Ltd. to be completed.

**Mr. McFall:** To ask the Secretary of State for Scotland on what date the Minister with responsibility for industry and local government was informed of Dumbartonshire Enterprise's interest in the acquisition of Drumkinnon bay from the Drumkinnon Development Company.    [23059]

**Mr. Kynoch:** I first learned of Dumbartonshire Enterprise's interest in the acquisition on 8 March 1995.

**Mr. McFall:** To ask the Secretary of State for Scotland (1) on what date the Drumkinnon Development Company approached Dumbartonshire Enterprise to negotiate the purchase by the latter of Drumkinnon bay, Balloch;    [23060]

(2) what information the Drumkinnon Development Company provided to Dumbartonshire Enterprise regarding the original price paid by the former for the land eventually acquired by the latter at Drumkinnon bay;    [23054]

(3) what is the name of the company employed by Dumbartonshire Enterprise which assessed the value of the Drumkinnon bay site at £2.743 million; and what was the date of this assessment;    [23061]

(4) when the Scottish Enterprise Board agreed in principle to allow Dumbartonshire Enterprise to acquire Drumkinnon bay from the developers.    [23063]

**Mr. Kynoch:** This is an operational matter for Scottish Enterprise. I have asked its chairman to write to the hon. Member.

**Mr. McFall:** To ask the Secretary of State for Scotland on what date he became aware of Dumbartonshire Enterprise's interest in acquiring Drumkinnon bay from the developers.    [23062]

**Mr. Kynoch:** My right hon. Friend became aware of Dumbartonshire Enterprise's interest in the acquisition on 8 March 1995.

**Mr. McFall:** To ask the Secretary of State for Sctoland what ministerial discussions took place either with Scottish Enterprise or Dumbartonshire Enterprise regarding the acquisition of Drumkinnon bay by the latter; and on what date ministerial consent was given.    [23056]

**Mr. Kynoch:** No such discussions took place. Ministerial consent was not required in this case and no request for such consent was made.

**Mr. McFall:** To ask the Secretary of State for Scotland what was the involvement of Dumbartonshire Enterprise or Scottish Enterprise in written or oral communication with the Minister with responsibility for industry and local government on the subject of the development at Drumkinnon bay.    [23058]

**Mr. Kynoch:** There has been no written or oral communication between me or my predecessor and Dumbartonshire Enterprise or Scottish Enterprise on the subject of the development at Drumkinnon bay.

## Scottish Enterprise

**Mr. McFall:** To ask the Secretary of State for Scotland what (a) formal or (b) informal reporting mechanisms operate to ensure that Scottish Enterprise is made aware of developments being undertaken by local enterprise councils which involve projects greater than £250,000; and how and to whom these are communicated by Highlands and Islands Enterprise or Scottish Enterprise to the Industry Department.    [23064]

**Mr. Kynoch:** A local enterprise company is required by its operating contract to refer to Scottish Enterprise or Highlands and Islands Enterprise proposals which wouldinvolve expenditure in excess of specified delegated limits. The amounts of these limits vary according to the nature and purpose of the proposed expenditure, but expenditure exceeding £250,000 in any of the categories would require to be referred to Scottish Enterprise or Highlands and Islands Enterprise as appropriate.

Similarly, Scottish Enterprise and Highlands and Islands Enterprise are required to refer to the Secretary of State proposals which would involve expenditure in excess of certain limits, although these limits are generally higher than those which apply to local enterprise companies. Again, the amounts of the limits vary according to the nature and purpose of the proposed expenditure, but are for the most part set at amounts above £250,000. Cases involving property acquisition have to be referred to my right hon. Friend if the expenditure involved exceeds £5 million.

**Mr. McFall:** To ask the Secretary of State for Scotland what is the project capital threshold expended by either Dumbartonshire Enterprise or Scottish Enterprise above which the Minister with responsibility for industry and local government is consulted.

**Mr. Kynoch:** The delegated authorities which apply to the Scottish Enterprise network vary according to the nature and purpose of the proposed expenditure. Cases involving property acquisition have to be referred to my right hon. Friend if the expenditure involved exceeds £5 million.

### Forestry Commission

**Mr. Tipping:** To ask the Secretary of State for Scotland what was the total revenue derived from Forestry Commission woodland disposals for each year since 1981 in (a) England, (b) Wales and (c) Scotland. [23402]

**Sir Hector Monro:** The information is as follows:

|  |  |  | £000s |
| --- | --- | --- | --- |
| Year ended 31 March | England | Wales | Scotland |
| 1982[1] | 8.9 | 2.2 | 13.6 |
| 1983[1] | 8.9 | 2.2 | 13.6 |
| 1984[1] | 8.9 | 2.2 | 13.6 |
| 1985 | 9.2 | 2.4 | 3.7 |
| 1986 | 4.3 | 2.2 | 3.1 |
| 1987 | 4.1 | 1.6 | 2.6 |
| 1988 | 4.4 | 0.9 | 1.5 |
| 1989 | 1.9 | 1.5 | 1.6 |
| 1990 | 2.8 | 1.8 | 2.4 |
| 1991 | 2.8 | 2.0 | 2.3 |
| 1992 | 2.2 | 2.2 | 4.8 |
| 1993 | 1.6 | 1.2 | 2.3 |
| 1994 | 2.0 | 1.7 | 9.7 |
| 1995[2] | 2.2 | 2.3 | 3.6 |

[1] Annual records are not available for this period.
[2] Provisional.

**Mr. Tipping:** To ask the Secretary of State for Scotland what will be the estimated targets in terms of (a) hectarage and (b) revenue for the disposal of Forestry Commission woodlands after 2000 in (i) England, (ii) Wales and (iii) Scotland. [23404]

**Sir Hector Monro:** No decisions have been taken on the Forestry Commission's disposals programme beyond the year 2000.

**Mr. Tipping:** To ask the Secretary of State for Scotland if he will list by county in respect of England and Wales and region in respect of Scotland the name

and hectarage of Forestry Commission woodlands that are currently for sale. [23401]

**Sir Hector Monro:** The following Forestry Commission woodlands are currently for sale on the open market:

| County/Region | Name of Property | Area (hectares) |
| --- | --- | --- |
| *England* | | |
| Cambridgeshire | Langley High Wood | 49 |
| Cornwall | Hay Wood | 54 |
| | Port Elliot, Pathada, Perdredda | 95 |
| | Treworgey Wood | 17 |
| Cumbria | Black Knors | 25 |
| Derbyshire | Moorhall Wood | 8 |
| Devon | Bedpark | 8 |
| | Hawkmoor | 22 |
| Durham | Campville | 30 |
| | Stanley Wood Cottages | 31 |
| Essex | Audley End Estate | 57 |
| Humberside | Greenwickdale Wood | 37 |
| Isle of Wight | Grammars Common | 17 |
| | Timber Copse | 8 |
| Leicestershire | Bolt Wood | 27 |
| Lincolnshire | Hurn Wood | 9 |
| Shropshire | Coed Detton | 14 |
| Somerset | Higher Bitcombe | 30 |
| South Yorkshire | Greensprings Wood | 12 |
| | Old Park Wood | 41 |
| | Owston and Duck Holt Woods | 66 |
| *Scotland* | | |
| Borders | Edgarhope | 143 |
| | Spottiswoode | 191 |
| Dumfries and Galloway | Glaik | 62 |
| Grampian | Aquharney | 128 |
| | Auchinroath | 62 |
| | Glenbuchat | 539 |
| | Greenness | 115 |
| | Longhill (part) | 120 |
| | New Pitsligo | 42 |
| Highland | Abriachan | 865 |
| | Achandounie Woods | 39 |
| | Achrugan | 59 |
| | Ardelve | 26 |
| | Duisky | 89 |
| | Garvan, North | 112 |
| | Garvan, South | 183 |
| | Loch Ashie | 437 |
| | Lundavra | 148 |
| | New Kelso | 43 |
| Strathclyde | Daljarrock | 51 |
| | Docherneil | 83 |
| | Glenmard | 56 |
| Tayside | Camusericht | 295 |
| | Dalguise (part) | 7 |
| | Upper Glenprosen | 230 |
| *Wales* | | |
| Clwyd | Coed Melyn Y Moch | 12 |
| | Fron Plantation | 5 |
| | Gwernto | 15 |
| | Nurse Gwern Y Coed | 5 |
| | Tan Y Fron Woodland | 3 |
| | Trevor Hall Wood | 22 |
| Dyfed | Allt Cil y Llyn Fawr | 3 |
| | Cilflower Wood | 5 |
| | Cynheidre Uchaf | 24 |
| | Glan Teifi Wood | 2 |
| | Llwyn Y Gwair | 13 |
| | Pant Eynon and Allt y Forlan | 29 |
| | Pencwmfawr | 9 |
| | Penhill Wood | 4 |

| County/Region | Name of Property | Area (hectares) |
|---|---|---|
| | Rhos Rhiwlas Isaf | 5 |
| | Ty'r Shyme | 6 |
| Gwent | Coed Chambers | 6 |
| Gwynedd | Aberdunant (part) | 16 |
| | Coed Ty Uchaf | 14 |
| | Rhiwbach and Tyddyn Bach | 106 |
| Mid Glamorgan | Bryncarnau | 23 |
| Powys | Gilfach | 9 |
| West Glamorgan | Bryn Wicket | 33 |
| | Graig Ynysgollen | 10 |
| | Nant Y Stalwyn | 44 |

## NHS Appointments

**Mr. McMaster:** To ask the Secretary of State for Scotland if he will list the *(a)* name, *(b)* place of residence, *(c)* date of appointment and *(d)* honorarium of the chairman, vice-chairman and members of (i) Argyll and Clyde health board, (ii) the Royal Alexandra hospital trust and (iii) Renfrewshire Healthcare NHS trust. [24105]

**Lord James Douglas-Hamilton:** The information requested is as follows:

*Argyll and Clyde Health Board*

| | Residence | Date of appointment | Remuneration £ |
|---|---|---|---|
| **Chairman** | | | |
| Mr. Malcolm Jones | Helensburgh | 1 January 1995 | 17,700 |
| | | | |
| **Non-Executive Members** | | | |
| Mrs. Elizabeth Lander (Vice-Chairman) | Kilmacolm | 1 April 1995 | 5,000 |
| Mrs. Sheenah Nelson | Balloch | 1 April 1993 | 5,000 |
| Mr. Ian Macdonald | Paisley | 7 March 1994 | 5,000 |
| Mr. Robert Anderson | Rothesay | 1 April 1995 | 5,000 |
| Miss Moira Leitch | Islay | 1 April 1995 | 5,000 |
| Mr. John Mullin | Paisley | 1 April 1995 | 5,000 |

*Royal Alexandra Hospital NHS Trust*

| | Residence | Date of appointment | Remuneration £ |
|---|---|---|---|
| **Chairman** | | | |
| Mr. Tom Gibson | Paisley | 1 January 1993 | 17,145 |
| | | | |
| **Non-Executive Directors** | | | |
| Mrs. Audrey Burns | Houston | 1 January 1993 | 5,000 |
| Mrs. Marion Ford | Paisley | 1 January 1993 | 5,000 |
| Mr. Alec MacDonald Gaunt | Paisley | 1 January 1993 | 5,000 |
| Mr. George Murray | Paisley | 1 January 1993 | 5,000 |

*Royal Alexandra Hospital NHS Trust*

| | Residence | Date of appointment | Remuneration £ |
|---|---|---|---|
| Mr. Allan Durward | Bridge of Weir | 1 January 1993 | 5,000 |

*Renfrewshire Healthcare NHS Trust*

| | Residence | Date of appointment | Remuneration £ |
|---|---|---|---|
| **Chairman** | | | |
| Dr. John Moffat | Greenock | 6 December 1993 | 19,285 |
| | | | |
| **Non-Executive Directors** | | | |
| Mr. David McNiven (Vice-Chairman) | Brookfield | 6 December 1993 | 5,000 |
| Mr. Basil Baird | Eaglesham | 6 December 1993 | 5,000 |
| Mrs. Jean Goldie | Elderslie | 6 December 1993 | 5,000 |
| Mrs. Margaret Foggie | Greenock | 6 December 1993 | 5,000 |
| Mr. John Hornibrook | Kilmacolm | 6 December 1993 | 5,000 |

## Cable Installers

**Dr. Godman:** To ask the Secretary of State for Scotland if he will make it his policy to require cable communication installers to restore all pavements and roads to their former standard and to replace trees which die within five years of the installation work; and if he will make a statement. [23298]

**Lord James Douglas-Hamilton:** The New Roads and Street Works Act 1991 and associated regulations and codes of practice already require undertakers, such as cable operators, executing road works to comply with prescribed material specifications and standards of workmanship when reinstating a road or footway and to guarantee the performance of the reinstatement for a minimum period of two years. If an undertaker fails to comply with his duties under the Act regarding reinstatements then he commits an offence. Provision is made for road works authorities to inspect reinstatements and to require corrective work where a reinstatement is defective. Ultimately, the road works authority may carry out the work themselves and recover costs from the undertaker.

Particular attention is drawn by the codes of practice to the need to excavate carefully where trees, shrubs and other planted areas are involved. The National Joint Utilities Group has also recently published, in collaboration with the Cable Communications Association and arboriculturists, "Guidelines for the Planning, Installation and Maintenance of Utility Services in Proximity to Trees". A copy of the paper is available in the Library. The Government do not consider that it is necessary to legislate for the replacement of trees in the way suggested.

## Police Deaths (Convictions)

**Dr. Godman:** To ask the Secretary of State for Scotland if he will name those persons convicted of murdering police officers since 1960 *(a)* who are still serving prison sentences and *(b)* who have been released under licence; and if he will make a statement. [23299]

**Lord James Douglas-Hamilton:** My noble and learned friend the Minister of State will write to the hon. Member.

## NHS Trusts

**Dr. Godman:** To ask the Secretary of State for Scotland if he will include in the new code of openness in the national health service a requirement for NHS trusts to hold their meetings in public and for health authorities to cease the practice of routinely closing their meetings to the public for items on their agendas which are not confidential.    [23300]

**Lord James Douglas-Hamilton:** My noble Friend the Minster of State will be publishing the code of practice on openness in the NHS in Scotland later this month. It will require health boards and NHS trusts to be as open as possible about their activities and plans.

**Mr. Foulkes:** To ask the Secretary of State for Scotland what is the capital allocation for each NHS trust in Scotland for 1995–96, 1996–97 and any subsequent year for which allocations have been made.    [24055]

**Lord James Douglas Hamilton** *[holding answer 15 May 1995]:* The capital provision included in the current external financing limit for 1995–96 is as in the table.

Further provisions will be made throughout 1995–96 as business cases are approved for projects above trust's delegated limits.

Capital provision on a trust-by-trust basis for 1996–97 and subsequent years has yet to be determined.

| Name of NHS trust | 1995–96 Capital provision 000s |
| --- | --- |
| Aberdeen Royal Hospitals | 3,669 |
| Angus | 896 |
| Argyll and Bute | 1,749 |
| Ayrshire and Arran Community Healthcare | 2,044 |
| Borders General Hospital | 816 |
| Borders Community Health Services | 511 |
| Caithness and Sutherland | 589 |
| Central Scotland Healthcare | 3,185 |
| Dumfries and Galloway Acute and Maternity Hospitals | 2,835 |
| Dumfries and Galloway Community Health | 1,918 |
| Dundee Healthcare | 1,280 |
| Dundee Teaching Hospitals | 4,362 |
| East and Midlothian | 1,306 |
| Edinburgh Sick Childrens | 1,206 |
| Edinburgh Healthcare | 2,672 |
| Falkirk and District Royal Infirmary | 949 |
| Fife Healthcare | 2,198 |
| Grampian Healthcare | 5,023 |
| Greater Glasgow Community and Mental Health Services | 8,792 |
| Glasgow Dental Hospital and School | 656 |
| Glasgow Royal Infirmary University | 4,273 |
| Hairmyres and Stonehouse Hospitals | 2,310 |
| Highland Communities | 2,024 |
| Inverclyde Royal | 1,121 |
| Kirkcaldy Acute Hospitals | 1,327 |
| Law Hospital | 2,662 |
| Lanarkshire Healthcare | 4,373 |
| Lomond Healthcare | 1,251 |
| Monklands and Bellshill | 3,494 |
| Moray Health Services | 4,073 |
| North Ayrshire and Arran | 6,206 |
| Perth and Kinross Healthcare | 2,004 |
| Queen Margaret | 1,301 |
| Raigmore Hospital | 3,644 |

| Name of NHS trust | 1995–96 Capital provision 000s |
| --- | --- |
| Renfrewshire Healthcare | 1,358 |
| Royal Alexander Hospital | 1,277 |
| Scottish Ambulance Service | 8,311 |
| South Ayrshire Hospitals | 3,614 |
| Southern General | 4,447 |
| Stirling Royal Infirmary | 2,100 |
| Stobhill | 1,646 |
| The Royal Infuirmary of Edinburgh | 8,371 |
| Victoria Infirmary | 1,443 |
| West Lothian | 1,941 |
| West Glasgow Hospitals University | 5,471 |
| Western General Hospitals, Edinburgh | 3,551 |
| Yorkhill | 2,571 |
| | 132,820 |

## Medical Negligence

**Dr. Godman:** To ask the Secretary of State for Scotland how many cases of alleged medical negligence by *(a)* NHS consultants and *(b)* general practitioners were awaiting settlement or court hearing at 30 March in each of the last six years.    [23301]

**Lord James Douglas-Hamilton:** Details of the number of cases of alleged medical negligence by NHS consultants awaiting either settlement or court hearing is available from 30 March 1991 only. The information available is set out in the table:

| Year | Number of claims awaiting settlement at 30 March |
| --- | --- |
| 1991 | 194 |
| 1992 | 214 |
| 1993 | 222 |
| 1994 | 178 |
| 1995 | 93 |

Information on general medical practitioners is not collected centrally. They are independent contractors and as such insure themselves.

**Dr. Godman:** To ask the Secretary of State for Scotland what is the average time taken for an alleged medical negligence case to be settled; and if he will make a statement on how this average time has changed over the past six years.    [22302]

**Lord James Douglas-Hamilton:** The length of time taken to settle claims on medical negligence will vary depending on the nature of the case. If agreement is reached before the case goes to court, it can be settled within six to nine months of the claim being lodged. Where the claim is determined by the courts, the average time taken to reach a conclusion is around five years. Both averages have remained relatively static since 1990, when information on settlements was first collected centrally.

## Child Protection

**Mrs. Fyfe:** To ask the Secretary of State for Scotland what plans he has to introduce safeguards to protect parents with care and their children from violent or abusive absent parents who wish to claim parental rights and responsibilities.    [24603]

**Lord James Douglas-Hamilton:** As I indicated on 1 May 1995 on the Floor of the House, *Official Report*, column 84, during the Report stage of the Children (Scotland) Bill, the Government will consider whether through rules of court a parent's address might be kept confidential during the lead-up to a court hearing an application for parental rights and responsibilities by the other parent. That apart, we consider the law contains adequate safeguards for a parent and children against the other parent who is violent or abusive.

**Mrs. Fyfe:** To ask the Secretary of State for Scotland if he will make it his policy to reform section 12(7) of the Children and Young Persons (Scotland) Act 1937 to ensure that striking a child so as to cause or risk causing, injury will not be lawful whether or not the action was undertaken in terms of a parental right to chastise.    [24605]

**Lord James Douglas-Hamilton:** My right hon. Friend has no plans to reform section 12(7) of the Children and Young Persons (Scotland) Act 1937 in the way suggested. As was made clear in the Report Stage debate on the Children (Scotland) Bill on 1 May, *Official Report* columns 49-75, the law as it stands—both statutory and common law—already offers sufficient protection to children from assault.

**Mrs. Fyfe:** To ask the Secretary of State for Scotland what plans he has to ensure that registration of an agreement between a mother and a father on parental rights and responsibilities will have safeguards against duress or coercion.    [24604]

**Lord James Douglas-Hamilton:** The arrangements set out in clauses 4 and 11 of the Children (Scotland) Bill

provide adequate protection for the mother and child. This was made clear on 23 February when, in Committee, amendments Nos. 238 and 239 were considered. Consequently, my right hon. Friend has no plans to change the arrangements which the Bill will bring into play.

### NHS Pay

**Mr. Foulkes:** To ask the Secretary of State for Scotland if he will list for each NHS trust in Scotland what decision has been taken on the claim by nurses for an increase in wages for the current year; and if he will make a statement.    [24054]

**Lord James Douglas-Hamilton** *[holding answer 15 May 1995]:* To date, 43 out of the 47 NHS trusts in Scotland have either made offers to nursing staff at local level or have indicated their intention to do so in the near future.

**Mr. Wallace:** To ask the Secretary of State for Scotland what was the total wage and salary costs in each year since 1988 in *(a)* actual terms and *(b)* at current prices, of health service employees, including management and clerical grades, in respect of each health board area and NHS trust in Scotland; and what percentage each sum represented of the total wage and salary costs of the respective health board or NHS trust.    [20606]

**Lord James Douglas-Hamilton** *[holding answer 2 May 1995]:* The information is set out in the table. Figures for 1994–95 are not yet available.

The figures for administrative and clerical staff costs include amounts for those senior nurses and clinicians who have transferred to the general/senior managers' pay scales, particularly in latter years.

*(£ thousands)*

| Health Boards | Administration and clerical | Actual total salaries | Percentage | Administration and clerical | Current prices total salaries | Percentage |
|---|---|---|---|---|---|---|
| *1988–89* | | | | | | |
| Argyll and Clyde | 9,430 | 98,003 | 9.62 | 12,411 | 128,989 | 9.62 |
| Ayr and Arran | 6,666 | 73,464 | 9.07 | 8,775 | 96,691 | 9.07 |
| Borders | 1,911 | 23,088 | 8.28 | 2,515 | 30,388 | 8.28 |
| Dumfries and Galloway | 2,897 | 37,610 | 7.70 | 3,813 | 49,502 | 7.70 |
| Fife | 5,746 | 69,553 | 8.26 | 7,564 | 91,544 | 8.26 |
| Forth Valley | 5,133 | 66,813 | 7.68 | 6,755 | 87,937 | 7.68 |
| Grampian | 11,263 | 125,244 | 8.99 | 14,824 | 164,843 | 8.99 |
| Greater Glasgow | 27,357 | 343,939 | 7.95 | 36,006 | 452,682 | 7.95 |
| Highland | 4,345 | 52,637 | 8.25 | 5,719 | 69,280 | 8.25 |
| Lanarkshire | 8,205 | 111,788 | 7.34 | 10,799 | 147,131 | 7.34 |
| Lothian | 18,674 | 217,879 | 8.57 | 24,578 | 286,765 | 8.57 |
| Orkney | 266 | 3,905 | 6.82 | 350 | 5,140 | 6.82 |
| Shetland | 362 | 4,791 | 7.56 | 477 | 6,306 | 7.56 |
| Tayside | 11,032 | 129,398 | 8.53 | 14,519 | 170,309 | 8.53 |
| Western Isles | 557 | 6,994 | 7.96 | 733 | 9,205 | 7.96 |
| Scotland total | 113,844 | 1,365,106 | 8.34 | 149,838 | 1,796,712 | 8.34 |
| *1989–90* | | | | | | |
| Argyll and Clyde | 10,588 | 104,651 | 10.12 | 13,027 | 128,746 | 10.12 |
| Ayr and Arran | 7,655 | 79,776 | 9.60 | 9,418 | 98,144 | 9.60 |
| Borders | 2,217 | 25,289 | 8.77 | 2,727 | 31,111 | 8.77 |
| Dumfries and Galloway | 3,275 | 39,904 | 8.21 | 4,029 | 49,091 | 8.21 |
| Fife | 6,674 | 74,324 | 8.98 | 8,211 | 91,437 | 8.98 |
| Forth Valley | 5,905 | 71,428 | 8.27 | 7,264 | 87,874 | 8.27 |
| Grampian | 12,837 | 134,462 | 9.55 | 15,793 | 165,420 | 9.55 |
| Greater Glasgow | 31,142 | 359,709 | 8.66 | 38,312 | 442,529 | 8.66 |
| Highland | 5,005 | 56,668 | 8.83 | 6,157 | 69,715 | 8.83 |
| Lanarkshire | 9,325 | 119,097 | 7.83 | 11,472 | 146,518 | 7.83 |
| Lothian | 21,668 | 228,805 | 9.47 | 26,657 | 281,484 | 9.47 |

*(£ thousands)*

| Health Boards | Administration and clerical | Actual total salaries | Percentage | Administration and clerical | Current prices total salaries | Percentage |
|---|---|---|---|---|---|---|
| Orkney | 298 | 4,237 | 7.03 | 367 | 5,212 | 7.03 |
| Shetland | 471 | 5,184 | 9.08 | 579 | 6,378 | 9.08 |
| Tayside | 12,311 | 137,560 | 8.95 | 15,145 | 169,232 | 8.95 |
| Western Isles | 684 | 7,351 | 9.30 | 841 | 9,043 | 9.30 |
| Scotland total | 130,055 | 1,448,445 | 8.98 | 159,999 | 1,781,934 | 8.98 |
| *1990–91* | | | | | | |
| Argyll and Clyde | 12,064 | 112,112 | 10.76 | 13,741 | 127,693 | 10.76 |
| Ayr and Arran | 8,848 | 87,469 | 10.12 | 10,078 | 99,626 | 10.12 |
| Borders | 2,575 | 27,095 | 9.51 | 2,933 | 30,861 | 9.51 |
| Dumfries and Galloway | 3,919 | 43,840 | 8.94 | 4,464 | 49,933 | 8.94 |
| Fife | 8,047 | 81,784 | 9.84 | 9,166 | 93,150 | 9.84 |
| Forth Valley | 7,016 | 77,780 | 9.02 | 7,992 | 88,590 | 9.02 |
| Grampian | 14,963 | 144,566 | 10.35 | 17,043 | 164,658 | 10.35 |
| Greater Glasgow | 36,734 | 378,673 | 9.70 | 41,839 | 431,300 | 9.70 |
| Highland | 6,086 | 62,266 | 9.77 | 6,932 | 70,920 | 9.77 |
| Lanarkshire | 11,246 | 128,742 | 8.74 | 12,809 | 146,634 | 8.74 |
| Lothian | 24,765 | 241,386 | 10.26 | 28,207 | 274,934 | 10.26 |
| Orkney | 402 | 4,775 | 8.42 | 458 | 5,438 | 8.42 |
| Shetland | 653 | 5,775 | 11.30 | 743 | 6,577 | 11.30 |
| Tayside | 14,422 | 149,398 | 9.65 | 16,425 | 170,161 | 9.65 |
| Western Isles | 806 | 8,221 | 9.79 | 917 | 9,363 | 9.79 |
| Scotland total | 152,546 | 1,553,882 | 9.82 | 173,747 | 1,769,838 | 9.82 |
| *1991–92* | | | | | | |
| Argyll and Clyde | 14,178 | 125,534 | 11.29 | 15,194 | 134,527 | 11.29 |
| Ayr and Arran | 10,117 | 96,968 | 10.43 | 10,843 | 103,915 | 10.43 |
| Borders | 2,105 | 27,939 | 7.54 | 2,256 | 29,940 | 7.54 |
| Dumfries and Galloway | 4,277 | 46,844 | 9.13 | 4,583 | 50,200 | 9.13 |
| Fife | 9,508 | 91,140 | 10.43 | 10,189 | 97,670 | 10.43 |
| Forth Valley | 8,381 | 86,562 | 9.68 | 8,981 | 92,763 | 9.68 |
| Grampian | 17,061 | 160,303 | 10.64 | 18,283 | 171,787 | 10.64 |
| Greater Glasgow | 41,749 | 407,459 | 10.25 | 44,740 | 436,649 | 10.25 |
| Highland | 7,263 | 70,321 | 10.33 | 7,783 | 75,359 | 10.33 |
| Lanarkshire | 13,350 | 139,726 | 9.55 | 14,306 | 149,736 | 9.55 |
| Lothian | 28,451 | 264,872 | 10.74 | 30,489 | 283,847 | 10.74 |
| Orkney | 480 | 5,519 | 8.70 | 514 | 5,914 | 8.70 |
| Shetland | 770 | 6,560 | 11.73 | 825 | 7,030 | 11.73 |
| Tayside | 17,108 | 165,259 | 10.35 | 18,334 | 177,098 | 10.35 |
| Western Isles | 919 | 9,370 | 9.81 | 985 | 10,041 | 9.81 |
| Scotland total | 175,717 | 1,704,376 | 10.31 | 188,305 | 1,826,476 | 10.31 |

| Health Boards | Administration and clerical (£000's) | Actual total salaries (£000's) | Percentage | Administration and clerical (£000's) | Current Prices Total Salaries (£000's) | Percentage |
|---|---|---|---|---|---|---|
| *1992–93* | | | | | | |
| Argyll and Clyde | 15,744 | 134,343 | 11.72 | 16,224 | 138,454 | 11.72 |
| Ayr and Arran | 9,603 | 80,727 | 11.90 | 9,897 | 83,198 | 11.90 |
| Borders | 2,518 | 31,628 | 7.96 | 2,596 | 32,596 | 7.96 |
| Dumfries and Galloway | 5,292 | 52,800 | 10.02 | 5,454 | 54,416 | 10.02 |
| Fife | 10,462 | 97,794 | 10.70 | 10,783 | 100,786 | 10.70 |
| Forth Valley | 9,724 | 94,683 | 10.27 | 10,021 | 97,580 | 10.27 |
| Grampian | 14,364 | 110,568 | 12.99 | 14,803 | 113,951 | 12.99 |
| Greater Glasgow | 47,473 | 436,265 | 10.88 | 48,925 | 449,614 | 10.88 |
| Highland | 8,264 | 75,378 | 10.96 | 8,517 | 77,684 | 10.96 |
| Lanarkshire | 14,240 | 146,730 | 9.70 | 14,676 | 151,220 | 9.70 |
| Lothian | 32,352 | 286,483 | 11.29 | 33,342 | 295,249 | 11.29 |
| Orkney | 553 | 6,126 | 9.03 | 570 | 6,313 | 9.03 |
| Shetland | 868 | 6,643 | 13.07 | 895 | 6,846 | 13.07 |
| Tayside | 19,415 | 174,964 | 11.10 | 20,009 | 180,318 | 11.10 |
| Western Isles | 1,107 | 10,512 | 10.53 | 1,141 | 10,833 | 10.53 |
| Sub total | 191,979 | 1,745,644 | 11.00 | 197,853 | 1,799,058 | 11.00 |

| Health Boards | Administration and clerical (£000's) | Actual total salaries (£000's) | Percentage | Administration and clerical (£000's) | Current Prices Total Salaries (£000's) | Percentage |
|---|---|---|---|---|---|---|
| *NHS Trusts* | | | | | | |
| Aberdeen Royal Hospitals | 6,050 | 61,300 | 9.87 | 6,235 | 63,176 | 9.87 |
| South Ayrshire Hospitals | 2,681 | 25,619 | 10.46 | 2,763 | 26,403 | 10.46 |
| Sub total | 8,731 | 86,919 | 10.04 | 8,998 | 89,579 | 10.04 |
| Scotland total | 200,710 | 1,832,563 | 10.95 | 206,852 | 1,888,636 | 10.95 |

| Health Boards | Administration and clerical (£000s) | Actual total salaries (£000s) | Percentage | Administration and clerical (£000s) | Current prices total salaries (£000s) | Percentage |
|---|---|---|---|---|---|---|
| *1993–94* | | | | | | |
| Argyll and Clyde | 14,377 | 110,631 | 13.00 | 14,377 | 110,631 | 13.00 |
| Ayr and Arran | 1,627 | 4,185 | 38.88 | 1,627 | 4,185 | 38.88 |
| Borders | 2,801 | 33,605 | 8.34 | 2,801 | 33,605 | 8.34 |
| Dumfries and Galloway | 5,608 | 51,679 | 10.85 | 5,608 | 51,679 | 10.85 |
| Fife | 11,494 | 96,969 | 11.85 | 11,494 | 96,969 | 11.85 |
| Forth Valley | 7,414 | 59,633 | 12.43 | 7,414 | 59,633 | 12.43 |
| Grampian | 4,725 | 12,449 | 37.96 | 4,726 | 12,449 | 37.96 |
| Greater Glasgow | 37,480 | 316,086 | 11.86 | 37,480 | 316,086 | 11.86 |
| Highland | 5,535 | 39,066 | 14.17 | 5,535 | 316,086 | 14.17 |
| Lanarkshire | 28,033 | 163,861 | 17.11 | 28,033 | 163,861 | 17.11 |
| Lothian | 31,685 | 239,760 | 13.22 | 31,685 | 239,760 | 13.22 |
| Orkney | 671 | 6,619 | 10.14 | 671 | 6,619 | 10.14 |
| Shetland | 1,012 | 6,896 | 10.14 | 1,012 | 6,619 | 14.67 |
| Tayside | 14,716 | 114,533 | 12.85 | 14,716 | 114,533 | 12.85 |
| Western Isles | 1,392 | 11,808 | 11.79 | 1,392 | 11,808 | 11.79 |
| Sub Total | 168,571 | 1,267,781 | 13.30 | 168,571 | 1,267,781 | 13.30 |
| *NHS Trusts* | | | | | | |
| Aberdeen Royal Hospitals | 7,328 | 69,913 | 10.48 | 7,328 | 69,913 | 10.48 |
| South Ayrshire Hospitals | 3,176 | 25,985 | 12.22 | 3,176 | 25,985 | 12.22 |
| Ayrshire and Arran Community Healthcare | 3,831 | 34,782 | 11.01 | 3,831 | 34,782 | 11.01 |
| Caithness and Sutherland | 1,088 | 8,553 | 12.72 | 1,088 | 8,553 | 12.72 |
| Dundee Teaching Hospitals | 7,012 | 65,375 | 10.73 | 7,012 | 65,375 | 10.73 |
| Grampian Healthcare | 10,322 | 81,497 | 12.67 | 10,322 | 81,497 | 12.67 |
| Monklands and Bellshill Hospitals | 3,271 | 31,526 | 10.38 | 3,271 | 31,526 | 10.38 |
| Moray Health Services | 1,697 | 14,773 | 11.49 | 1,697 | 14,773 | 11.49 |
| North Ayrshire and Arran | 5,119 | 44,293 | 11.56 | 5,119 | 44,293 | 11.56 |
| Raigmore Hospital | 2,735 | 25,819 | 10.59 | 2,735 | 25,819 | 10.59 |
| Royal Scottish National Hospital | 654 | 13,203 | 4.95 | 654 | 13,203 | 4.95 |
| Royal Alexandra Hospital | 2,404 | 25,700 | 9.35 | 2,404 | 25,700 | 9.35 |
| Southern General, Glasgow | 4,740 | 46,108 | 10.28 | 4,740 | 46,108 | 10.28 |
| Stirling Royal Infirmary | 2,195 | 23,939 | 9.17 | 2,195 | 23,939 | 9.17 |
| Victoria Infirmary | 4,071 | 36,244 | 11.23 | 4,071 | 36,244 | 11.23 |
| West Lothian | 4,560 | 40,801 | 11.18 | 4,560 | 40,801 | 11.18 |
| Yorkhill | 3,477 | 35,376 | 9.83 | 3,477 | 35,376 | 9.83 |
| Sub total | 67,680 | 623,887 | 10.85 | 67,680 | 623,887 | 10.85 |
| Scotland total | 236,251 | 1,891,668 | 12.49 | 236,251 | 1,891,668 | 12.49 |

## Fishing Industry

**Dr. Goodman:** To ask the Secretary of State for Scotland when he expects European Union PESCA funds to be distributed to fishing communities; how much money he anticipates being paid for *(a)* the fishing industry and *(b)* the retraining of fishermen; if he will make it his policy to invite representatives of the fishing communities to take part in the decision and the distribution of such monies, and if he will make a statement. [24178]

**Sir Hector Monro** *[holding answer 15 May 1995]:* The United Kingdom PESCA programme is still subject to final agreement with the European Commission. It is not yet possible to say when funds will be available. The sum of some 16.5 mecu—£13.8 million at present exchange rates—has been proposed for projects in Scotland over the next five years of which £7.4 million will be available for European regional development fund spending, £2.6 million for European social fund spending, and £3.8 million under the financial instrument of fisheries guidance. The precise allocation will depend on the projects approved for EC support. Decisions on which projects should be supported will be based on discussion in local action groups which may involve representatives of the fishing industry.

## Telephones

**Mr. Donohoe:** To ask the Secretary of State for Scotland how many mobile telephones being used by his Department have been cloned during the last 12 months. [23434]

**Mr. Lang** *[holding answer 9 May 1995]:* I am aware of five instances of cloning of mobile telephones being used by the Scottish Office and its agencies during the last 12 months.

**Mr. Donohoe:** To ask the Secretary of State for Scotland what representations his Department has made to the Department of Trade and Industry concerning the need for legislation to prevent the cloning of mobile telephones. [23475]

**Mr. Lang** *[holding answer 9 May 1995]:* No representations have been made by the Scottish Office to the Department of Trade and Industry concerning the need for legislation to prevent the cloning of mobile telephones.

**Mr. Donohoe:** To ask the Secretary of State for Scotland what use his Department makes of hand-held and car-based mobile telephones; what were the costs for each financial year of these services since mobile telephones were first introduced to this Department; and how many mobile telephones are currently in use. [23442]

**Mr. Lang** *[holding answer 9 May 1995]:* Use of hand-held and car-based mobile telephones is made by travelling officers to facilitate communications while on official business. Mobile telephones were first introduced into The Scottish Office in the financial year 1986–87 but records of costs are only retained for the past three financial years. These indicate total cost of:

1992–93: £110,000

1993–94: £128,000

1994–95: £148,000

Our records show 380 mobile telephones as being currently in use throughout the Scottish Office and its agencies.

**Mr. Donohoe:** To ask the Secretary of State for Scotland what costs his Department has incurred during the last 12 months as a result of cloning of mobile telephones being used by his Department, with particular reference to the making of unauthorised calls. [23482]

**Mr. Lang** *[holding answer 9 May 1995]:* No costs have been incurred during the last 12 months as a result of cloning of mobile telephones.

**Mr. Donohoe:** To ask the Secretary of State for Scotland what steps his Department has taken to prevent the cloning of telephones being used by his Department; and if his Department has discussed this matter with any official agencies. [23462]

**Mr. Lang** *[holding answer 9 May 1995]:* All departmental users are encouraged to ensure the physical security of their mobile telephones but nothing can be done of a technical nature to prevent cloning. There have been no discussions with any official agencies on this subject.

## Civil Defence Facilities

**Mrs. Ewing:** To ask the Secretary of State for Scotland how many civil defence facilities in Scotland it is envisaged would be used as emergency centres of government in time of war; and if he will make a statement. [23171]

**Lord James Douglas-Hamilton** *[holding answer 11 May 1995]:* There is one purpose-built civil defence facility, at Cultybraggan, which would be available to be used as an emergency centre of government during a war.

**Mrs. Ewing:** To ask the Secretary of State for Scotland what future plans he has for the civil defence facility underneath Cultybraggan training camp, near Comrie; and if he will make a statement. [23189]

**Lord James Douglas-Hamilton** *[holding answer 11 May 1995]:* While much of the former civil defence infrastructure has been sold or dismantled, the Cultybraggan facility will be retained, since it houses the central node of the emergency communications network. The ECN links together all local authorities, the emergency services, a number of central Government locations, and other sites such as nuclear industry off-site emergency centres. This network is available to local authorities when responding to civil emergencies in peace time and proved to be most useful during the severe weather emergencies of 1993 and 1994.

**Mrs. Ewing:** To ask the Secretary of State for Scotland what was the final cost of *(a)* constructing the civil defence facility located underneath Cultybraggan training camp, near Comrie and *(b)* the unfinished civil defence facility at the grounds of Peel hospital near Galashiels; and if he will make a statement. [23187]

**Lord James Douglas-Hamilton** *[holding answer 11 May 1995]:* The final cost of the facility at Cultybraggan training camp was £3.6 million. The Scottish Office purchased the site at the former Peel hospital at a cost of £100,000. Because of the change in the perceived threat of a major conflict; no start was made on construction work, and the site is currently being offered for sale.

## Hospital Beds

**Mr. Foulkes:** To ask the Secretary of State for Scotland if he will give the total number of hospital beds in *(a)* medical and *(b)* surgical specialisms in each health board area as at 1st April 1993, 1994 and 1995; and what are the projected figures for 1996 and 1997.        [24053]

**Lord James Douglas-Hamilton** *[holding answer 15 May 1995]:* The information requested is shown in the table.

Hospital bed numbers are not projected on a national basis and the availability of beds in any specialty is primarily a matter for health boards and the appropriate health care providers to agree.

*National Health Service hospitals in Scotland: average available staffed surgical and medical beds*

| | Quarters ending 31 March 1993 | | 31 March 1994 | | 31 December 1994 [1] | |
| --- | --- | --- | --- | --- | --- | --- |
| | Surgical (1) | Medical (2) | Surgical | Medical | Surgical | Medical |
| *Scotland* | 8,568 | 6,260 | 8,051 | 6,117 | 7,856 | 5,942 |
| Argyll and Clyde | 573 | 451 | 541 | 447 | 538 | 439 |
| Ayrshire and Arran | 596 | 371 | 565 | 382 | 557 | 367 |
| Borders | 143 | 95 | 137 | 95 | 131 | 92 |
| Dumfries and Galloway | 210 | 107 | 187 | 136 | 186 | 146 |
| Fife | 391 | 236 | 378 | 240 | 362 | 240 |
| Forth Valley | 354 | 193 | 346 | 196 | 354 | 192 |
| Grampian | 853 | 593 | 838 | 576 | 811 | 576 |
| Greater Glasgow | 2,064 | 1,661 | 1,905 | 1,573 | 1,864 | 1,470 |
| Highland | 384 | 276 | 364 | 258 | 356 | 255 |
| Lanarkshire | 888 | 544 | 845 | 536 | 809 | 520 |
| Lothian | 1,222 | 1,071 | 1,152 | 1,012 | 1,100 | 999 |
| Orkney | 39 | — | 39 | — | 39 | — |
| Shetland | 23 | 24 | 26 | 20 | 26 | 20 |
| Tayside | 777 | 589 | 676 | 601 | 675 | 582 |
| Western Isles | 50 | 50 | 52 | 46 | 51 | 44 |

[1] Provisional.

*Notes:*
1. Surgical: general surgery, orthopaedic surgery, ENT surgery, ophthalmology, urology, neurosurgery, cardiothoracic surgery, plastic surgery, orthodontics and paediatric dentistry, oral surgery and medicine, restorative dentistry, spinal paralysis, paediatric surgery, gynaecology.
2. Medical: general medicine, cardiology, metabolic diseases, neurology, gastroenterology, poisons, dermatology, nephrology, rheumatology, rehabilitation medicine, respiratory medicine, radiotherapy (consultative) paediatric medicine, anaesthetics, haematology.
3. General practice beds are excluded.

## Departmental Accounting Officer

**Mr. Meacher:** To ask the Secretary of State for Scotland how many times in the last 10 years, and on which dates, his departmental accounting officer has issued a minute in that role; and what was the issue in each case.        [22564]

**Mr. Lang** *[holding answer 9 May 1995]:* Where a Minister overrules an accounting officer's advice on an issue of propriety or regularity or one of value for money, the accounting officer should request a written instruction from the Minister to take the action in question.

I refer the hon. Member to the answer I gave to the hon. Member for Merthyr Tydfil and Rhymney (Mr. Rowlands) on 2 March 1994, *Official Report*, column *783*, when I advised that no such occasion had been identified. No direction has been issued since that date.

Any such instruction would be reported to the Comptroller and Auditor General who, after making whatever investigations he considers appropriate, would report his findings to the Committee of Public Accounts.

## NHS Administration

**Mr. Wallace:** To ask the Secretary of State for Scotland how many health service employees, including management and clerical grades, in respect of each health board area and NHS trust in Scotland, were engaged in administration on 31 March in each year since 1988; and what percentage they represented of the total number of persons employed by each health board and NHS Trust in each of these years.        [20605]

**Lord James Douglas-Hamilton** *[holding answer 2 May 1995]:* Information is not available centrally on which staff are engaged in administration as a whole or part of their work. The table shows, therefore, the number of staff employed on senior manager, and administrative and clerical payscales. Increases in numbers can be accounted for in part due to the assimilation of some professional staff into senior manager grades. Data are shown for 30 September, the only date for which a complete census of all NHS staff is available. Information at trust level is not available centrally.

*NHSiS administrative and clerical staff [1][2][3][4][7] by health board as at 30 September*

Whole time equivalent

| | 1988 | 1989 | 1990 | 1991 | 1992[6] | 1993[6] | 1994[6] |
| --- | --- | --- | --- | --- | --- | --- | --- |
| Argyll and Clyde | 1,132 | 1,191 | 1,225 | 1,231 | 1,370 | 1,400 | 1,472 |
| Ayrshire and Arran | 754 | 778 | 810 | 847 | 913 | 957 | 1,019 |
| Borders | 224 | 219 | 231 | 237 | 257 | 272 | 335 |
| Dumfries and Galloway | 339 | 348 | 367 | 412 | 442 | 463 | 496 |
| Fife | 654 | 676 | 722 | 769 | 800 | 920 | 1,022 |
| Forth Valley | 564 | 594 | 632 | 666 | 716 | 758 | 775 |

*NHSiS administrative and clerical staff[1 2 3 4 7] by health board as at 30 September*

Whole time equivalent

| | 1988 | 1989 | 1990 | 1991 | 1992[6] | 1993[6] | 1994[6] |
|---|---|---|---|---|---|---|---|
| Grampian | 1,313 | 1,371 | 1,413 | 1,489 | 1,581 | 1,636 | 1,755 |
| Greater Glasgow | 3,343 | 3,368 | 3,421 | 3,511 | 3,679 | 3,800 | 3,875 |
| Highland | 489 | 504 | 548 | 594 | 627 | 652 | 713 |
| Lanarkshire | 1,009 | 1,019 | 1,091 | 1,097 | 1,159 | 1,240 | 1,322 |
| Lothian | 2,151 | 2,274 | 2,340 | 2,355 | 2,417 | 2,635 | 2,757 |
| Orkney | 21 | 23 | 29 | 30 | 31 | 33 | 37 |
| Shetland | 39 | 43 | 44 | 50 | 55 | 59 | 64 |
| Tayside[5] | 1,230 | 1,229 | 1,347 | 1,399 | 1,509 | 1,478 | 1,564 |
| Western Isles | 50 | 54 | 56 | 65 | 79 | 88 | 91 |
| Total | 13,311 | 13,690 | 14,275 | 14,751 | 15,636 | 16,390 | 17,296 |

*Notes:*
[1] These data need to be interpreted carefully because of the possible inclusion of supra-area functions in the data of some boards, eg., computer consortia staff may appear on one health board payroll but supply a service across several health boards.
[2] Comprises staff on senior management grades and A and C grades one to 10.
[3] The increase in numbers can be partially accounted for by the assimilation of some professional staff to senior manager grades.
[4] Excludes nurses in training.
[5] Data for Tayside in 1989 is at 31 March for staff other than medical and dental staff.
[6] The data include trust staff within the health board area.
[7] The data exclude staff in the Common Services Agency and state hospital, Carstairs.
*Source:*
National Manpower Statistics from Payroll.
Medical and Dental Census.
Information and Statistics Division.

*NHSIS Administration and Clerical Staff[1 2 3 7] as a percentage of all staff[4]: by health board as at 30 September*

Percentage

| County | 1988 | 1989 | 1990 | 1991 | 1992[6] | 1993[6] | 1994[6] |
|---|---|---|---|---|---|---|---|
| Argyll and Clyde | 14.1 | 14.9 | 15.6 | 15.5 | 17.1 | 17.3 | 18.1 |
| Ayrshire and Arran | 12.8 | 12.9 | 13.5 | 13.7 | 14.8 | 15.5 | 16.1 |
| Borders | 12.0 | 11.5 | 12.4 | 12.9 | 13.7 | 14.2 | 16.5 |
| Dumfries and Galloway | 11.3 | 11.7 | 12.2 | 13.4 | 14.2 | 14.7 | 15.5 |
| Fife | 11.5 | 12.3 | 13.0 | 13.6 | 14.1 | 16.0 | 18.3 |
| Forth Valley | 10.3 | 11.0 | 11.4 | 12.1 | 12.6 | 13.5 | 13.9 |
| Grampian | 13.2 | 13.7 | 14.3 | 14.8 | 15.3 | 16.0 | 17.1 |
| Greater Glasgow | 12.6 | 13.4 | 14.5 | 15.2 | 15.9 | 16.5 | 17.0 |
| Highland | 12.3 | 12.7 | 13.6 | 14.4 | 15.0 | 15.8 | 16.6 |
| Lanarkshire | 11.2 | 11.4 | 12.4 | 13.0 | 14.1 | 15.0 | 16.1 |
| Lothian | 13.2 | 14.2 | 15.4 | 15.7 | 16.2 | 17.3 | 17.4 |
| Orkney | 7.3 | 7.8 | 8.9 | 9.0 | 8.9 | 9.0 | 10.1 |
| Shetland | 10.8 | 11.6 | 11.6 | 12.4 | 17.0 | 17.5 | 17.6 |
| Tayside | 11.8 | 11.9 | 13.0 | 13.9 | 15.0 | 15.0 | 15.5 |
| Western Isles | 9.9 | 10.7 | 10.7 | 12.1 | 13.8 | 13.7 | 14.0 |
| Total | 12.4 | 13.0 | 13.9 | 14.4 | 15.2 | 15.9 | 16.7 |

*Notes:*
[1] These data need to be interpreted carefully because of the possible inclusion of supra-area functions in the data of some boards eg computer consortia staff may appear on one health board payroll but supply a service across several health boards.
[2] Comprises staff on senior management grades and A to C grades one to 10.
[3] The increase in numbers can be partially accounted for by the assimilation of some professional staff to senior manager grades.
[4] Excludes nurses in training.
[5] Data for Tayside in 1989 is at 31 March for staff other than medical and dental staff.
[6] The data include trust staff within the health board area.
[7] The data excludes staff in the Common Services Agency and state hospitals, Carstairs.
*Source:*
National Manpower Statistics from Payroll.
Medical and Dental Census.
Information and Statistics Division.

### Cervical Smears

**Dr. Godman:** To ask the Secretary of State for Scotland how many women underwent surgical treatment and medical care as a result of the maladministration of the cervical smear programme at the Inverclyde royal hospital, Greenock; what types of surgical operations and treatment were involved; and if he will make a statement. [21613]

**Lord James Douglas-Hamilton** *[holding answer 2 May 1995]:* Following the re-reading of 1,954 cervical smear slides at Inverclyde royal hospital, 400 women received a result which indicated assessment by colposcopy. Approximately 2,000 additional cervical smear tests were carried out. Some 346 women were assessed for colposcopy in Inverclyde royal hospital. Some 147 had cervical biopsies with associated appropriate treatment of the cervix either in Inverclyde or elsewhere.

The forms of treatment include colposcopy without biopsy, colposcopically directed selective biopsy, cold coagulation and conization of the cervix.

**Dr. Godman:** To ask the Secretary of State for Scotland how many women have instituted legal proceedings against the Argyll and Clyde health board and the Inverclyde royal hospital, Greenock, as a result of the maladministration of the cervical smear programme at the aforesaid hospital; of such cases, how many have *(a)* been settled out of court, *(b)* resulted in court cases and *(c)* are still waiting a court hearing; what financial compensation has been paid; and if he will make a statement. [21614]

**Lord James Douglas-Hamilton** *[holding answer 2 May 1995]:* Argyll and Clyde health board has received 105 legal claims as a result of the re-reading of cervical smear slides at Inverclyde royal hospital. Two claims have proceeded to a settlement. A further 10 settlements are in the process of negotiation. Once all the claims have been settled, I will be in a position to give an indication of the total amount of settlements made. No claims have resulted in a court case or are at present awaiting a court hearing.

# Written Answers to Questions

*Wednesday 17 May 1995*

## DEFENCE

### Nuclear-powered Submarines

**Mr. Hicks:** To ask the Secretary of State for Defence if he will make a statement on the availability of docking facilities for nuclear-powered submarines. [25183]

**Mr. Freeman:** We are currently assessing the availability of the facilities for docking RN nuclear-powered submarines, taking into account nuclear safety requirements and latest estimates of the time the submarines will need to spend in dry dock. The assessment is concerned only with existing facilities and does not involve consideration of future refitting facilities needed for Vanguard class submarines.

Two factors have led to the need for this work. First, an on-going survey of existing docking facilities at both Rosyth and Devonport, taking into account increasingly stringent nuclear safety practices, has identified a requirement for improvements to be made to some facilities. Secondly, in addition to delays arising from this work, the time which some nuclear-powered submarines need to spend in dock during refit has increased, typically by about three months.

We are therefore considering ways of limiting the resulting disruption to the docking programme for nuclear-powered submarines, including the possibility of deferring the ending of nuclear work at Rosyth which was previously planned for 1997. The assessment will include discussions with both the nuclear regulatory authorities and the dockyard companies. No decisions have yet been taken.

### Defence Agency

**Sir John Hannam:** To ask the Secretary of State for Defence if he will be renewing investment decisions on *(a)* the replacement or enhancement of all three services' individual computer systems and *(b)* the establishment of a new Army personnel centre in Glasgow following the Bett study report. [23701]

**Mr. Soames:** Harmonisation of all defence administrative computer systems is a departmental aim arising from the "Front Line First" studies. In the case of personnel administration and pay systems, Mr. Bett has recommended that the harmonisation process should be undertaken by a defence agency, which should be set up within three years. He envisaged that it might then take about five years to develop a fully integrated personnel administration and pay system to operate across the services. We shall be examining this recommendation carefully in consultation with the services. In the meantime, our plans for the creation of the Army personnel centre in Glasgow are not inconsistent with the ultimate creation of a defence agency and we are proceeding with them.

Investment decisions on replacement or enhancement of the services' existing systems will take fully into account the need for harmonisation.

### Dartmouth Royal Regatta

**Mr. Steen:** To ask the Secretary of State for Defence if he will list the guardships which have attended the port of Dartmouth royal regatta in each of the last 15 years, and which ship will be on guard at the August 1995 regatta. [24737]

**Mr. Soames:** The following ships have attended the port of Dartmouth royal regatta during the last 15 years:

1980: Diomede and Alfriston
1981: Alfriston
1982: Alfriston
1983: Achilles
1984: Euryalus
1985: Diomede
1986: Hermione
1987: Plymouth
1988: Avenger
1989: Cardiff
1990: Active
1991: Battleaxe
1992: Sirius
1993: Battleaxe
1994: Battleaxe

Regrettably, there will not be a ship available to attend the 1995 Dartmouth royal regatta due to other operational commitments, and the number required for additional official duties during August, principally as a result of the VJ day commemorations.

### Service Bases

**Mr. Fatchett:** To ask the Secretary of State for Defence if he will list all Navy, Royal Air Force and Army bases which have been sold in the last two financial years and the buyers. [24549]

**Mr. Soames:** I refer the hon. Member to my answer of 3 May, *Official Report*, columns *234-37*, to the hon. Member for Pendle (Mr. Prentice).

### Tornados

**Mr. Gordon Prentice:** To ask the Secretary of State for Defence (1) how many RAF Tornado sorties have flown to the United Kingdom on exercise from their base at RAF Bruggen in the latest 12-month period for which figures are available. [23860]

(2) how many Tornados have participated in training sorties flown from their base in RAF Bruggen to the United Kingdom in the latest 12-month period for which figures are available. [23861]

**Mr. Soames:** RAF Bruggen Tornados flew 2,718 sorties to the United Kingdom between 1 May 1994 and 30 April 1995. Records are not maintained in such a way as to identify the purpose of each flight.

### Old Sarum Airfield

**Mr. Key:** To ask the Secretary of State for Defence how many bids he received for the freehold of Old Sarum airfield; and when he will announce his decision. [24546]

**Mr. Soames:** In all, four tenders were received. One of them has been accepted and the successful party was notified in writing on 10 May.

## LORD CHANCELLOR'S DEPARTMENT

### Early Retirement Packages

**Mr. Milburn:** To ask the Parliamentary Secretary, Lord Chancellor's Department if he will list the individual value of each *(a)* compulsory early retirement and *(b)* flexible early retirement package received by civil servants leaving his Department on the ground of limited efficiency in each of the last five years.

[22082]

**Mr. John M. Taylor** *[holding answer 2 May 1995]:* Compensation payments for early retirement on the ground of limited efficiency are age, salary and service related. Details of limited efficiency early retirements for each of the last five financial years are as follows:

£

| | Annual compensation payment to age 60 (rate pa) | Superannuation lump sum | Lump sum compensation payment | Compensation in lieu of notice (if any) |
|---|---|---|---|---|
| *1990–91* | | | | |
| Compulsory | — | — | — | — |
| Flexible | 20,738.68 | 56,618.79 | — | — |
| *1991–92* | | | | |
| Compulsory | 4,071.45 | 11,383.07 | 6,935.42 | — |
| Flexible | 10,428.50 | 29,935.88 | — | — |
| *1992–93* | | | | |
| Compulsory | 8,809.23 | 26,238.43 | 1,447.29 | — |
| Flexible | — | — | — | — |
| *1993–94* | | | | |
| Compulsory | — | — | — | — |
| Flexible | 35,879.38 | 102,324.52 | — | — |
| *1994–95* | | | | |
| Compulsory | — | — | — | — |
| Flexible | 30,703.19 | 84,945.71 | — | — |

### Legal Aid

**Mr. Butler:** To ask the Parliamentary Secretary, Lord Chancellor's Department when he expects to publish hisGreen Paper proposing reforms to the legal aid system in England and Wales. [25187]

**Mr. John M. Taylor:** The Lord Chancellor has today published a Green Paper, "Legal Aid—Targeting Need, The Future of Publicly Funded Help in Solving Legal Problems and Disputes in England and Wales". I have arranged for copies to be placed in the Library of the House.

## FOREIGN AND COMMONWEALTH AFFAIRS

### Ponsonby Rule

**Mr. Llew Smith:** To ask the Secretary of State for Foreign and Commonwealth Affairs how many objections have been registered by right hon. and hon. Members under the Ponsonby rule procedures, for instruments of ratification laid before Parliament in a Command Paper in the miscellaneous series in each year since 1979; and if he will indicate the resolution of the objection in each case. [24398]

**Mr. Baldry:** I know of none.

### Subsidiarity

**Mr. McMaster:** To ask the Secretary of State for Foreign and Commonwealth Affairs when he next plans to visit Spain and Germany to assess the value of devolved government and subsidiarity; and if he will make a statement. [24060]

**Mr. David Davis:** My right hon. Friend the Foreign Secretary hopes to discuss subsidiarity—the relationship between member states and the European Union—when he has talks with the German Foreign Minister on 26 May, and when he visits Spain under the Spanish presidency of the European Union. Devolution is an entirely separate issue, as all EU Heads of State or Government recognised at the 1992 Birmingham European Council:

"it is for each Member State to decide how its powers should be exercised domestically".

Germany and Spain may, however, be interested in the arrangements in Scotland, for example, which has far greater educational and judicial autonomy than any German land or Spanish autonomous community.

### Czech Republic

**Mr. Dafis:** To ask the Secretary of State for Foreign and Commonwealth Affairs what assessment Her Majesty's Government have made of the contribution of the growth of independent environmental non-governmental organisations in the Czech Republic to democracy there. [24716]

**Mr. Douglas Hogg:** Independent environment non-governmental organisations in the Czech Republic have helped raise public consciousness both before and after the end of the communist regime in 1989, notably in north Bohemia and Prague, the areas worst affected by environmental damage. Together with other independent groups, they have made a positive contribution to the growth of democracy.

## Spain

**Mr. Steen:** To ask the Secretary of State for Foreign and Commonwealth Affairs how much subsidy has been given to Spain in each of the last three years from the European Community for infrastructure; and what is the forecast of funding to Spain for each of the next three years.    [24685]

**Mr. David Davis:** It is not possible to give a global figure for Spanish receipts from the European Community for infrastructure, but I will write to the hon. Member with a breakdown of the figures he requests.

## TRADE AND INDUSTRY

### British Gas (Streetworks)

**Mr. Thurnham:** To ask the President of the Board of Trade what assurances he has received from the chairman of British Gas regarding the impact of the company's streetworks on small business.    [25131]

**Mr. Eggar:** I have received a letter from Richard V. Giordano, KBE, chairman of British Gas plc, the text of which says:

"Thank you for your letter of 28 April regarding possible disruption caused by British Gas in undertaking streetworks. British Gas takes a great deal of care to ensure that disruption caused by streetworks is kept to a minimum and has a liability under the 1986 Gas Act to compensate for physical damage caused directly by those works. Following our recent discussions and the Standing Committee debate, we have been giving further careful consideration to the question of economic loss caused to small businesses in exceptional circumstances of prolonged streetworks disruption.

In order to minimise the risk of such disruption, TransCo is revising its existing Code of Practice in respect of communication and co-operation with owners of commercial premises. In particular, TransCo will identify the nature of the work, explain why it is necessary, the anticipated start date and the likely duration. TransCo will subsequently discuss, with individual business owners, issues including vehicular access, customer access, special notices and any special requirements.

In those exceptional cases where small businesses suffer severe and clearly established loss of business over a prolonged period as a direct result of streetworks carried out by British Gas or its agents, British Gas will give sympathetic consideration to claims in respect of financial loss, on an ex-gratia basis. However, such payments would clearly be inappropriate in respect of escape-related or other emergency works.

For indicative purposes British Gas would regard a business with a turnover of less than £500,000 per annum (in constant 1995 price terms) as a "small business" and streetworks over a period exceeding four weeks as a "prolonged period".

Payment of ex-gratia compensation would be subject to the Director General of Gas Supply providing British Gas with reasonable assurance that such payments will be taken into account in any review of applicable price controls.

I am also concerned that gas should not be unduly disadvantaged vis-a-vis competing fuels and would ask you to take this into account when considering the position of other relevant networks.

I believe that this undertaking, together with TransCo's revised Code of Practice, demonstrates our continued commitment to high levels of performance in relation to streetworks and a responsive approach to the concerns of the small business community"

This undertaking from British Gas, to which the Government expect it to adhere, in the spirit as well as the letter, will address the concerns raised by my hon. Friend in a practical and appropriate way.

### Berkshire

**Mr. Berry:** To ask the President of the Board of Trade if he will make a statement on the implications for the business community of the proposed division of Berkshire into six unitary authorities.    [24537]

**Mr. Eggar:** The potential benefits of unitary authorities include cost-effective service delivery, reduced bureaucracy and clear accountability. These benefits will accrue to the business community, among others.

### Nuclear Electric

**Mr. Clapham:** To ask the President of the Board of Trade what provisions Nuclear Electric has made for decommissioning of Magnex power stations in each year since 1990; and what estimate his Department has made of the provisons that will be outstanding if Magnox stations are transferred to a separate public sector company in 1996.    [24574]

**Mr. Eggar:** I refer the hon. Member to the annual reports and accounts of Nuclear Electric, available in the Library of the House. The estimated provisions outstanding, if Magnox stations are transferred to a separate public sector company in 1996, will be published in the accounts of that company.

**Mr. Clapham:** To ask the President of the Board of Trade (1) what is the current value of investments made by Nuclear Electric to cover decommissioning costs; and what value his Department estimates such investments will have at the end of 1996;    [24571]

(2) what cash balance Nuclear Electric has accumulated in the national loans fund at the end of each financial year form 1990–91 to 1994–95; and what balance his Department expects by the end of 1996.    [24573]

**Mr. Eggar:** I refer the hon. Member to the annual reports and accounts of Nuclear Electric, available in the Library of the House. Information for future years will be published in the accounts of the various companies for those years.

### Rural White Paper

**Mr. Colvin:** To ask the President of the Board of Trade what is his estimate of the net annual financial saving, or cost, of his Department's submission for the proposed White Paper on the rural economy.    [24331]

**Mr. Page:** Proposals for the Rural White Paper remain subject to continuing collective consideration and discussion. The cost of measures contained in the White Paper will be taken into account in the public expenditure survey.

### British Coal Land

**Mr. Hardy:** To ask the President of the Board of Trade if he will advise British Coal to refrain from seeking to dispose of land for development and to seek the removal of land from the green belt where the planning authority and the local community wish that classification to be maintained.    [24199]

**Mr. Page:** The disposal of British Coal property is a matter for the corporation, which is currently considering the detailed options for the transfer of its land holdings, including those with development potential, out of its ownership.

The designation of any land for green belt purposes is not a matter for British Coal.

### National Lottery

**Mr. McMaster:** To ask the President of the Board of Trade what discussions he has had with the chairman of the Post Office about its policy of paying for the television advertising of national lottery instant scratch cards; what steps he has taken to ensure that Camelot contributes towards the cost of this advertising; and if he will make a statement. [24117]

**Mr. Page:** Commercial arrangements between the Post Office and its clients are a matter for the board.

### Companies House

**Mr. Morgan:** To ask the President of the Board of Trade (1) if he will list the total *(a)* set-up and *(b)* recurrent annual costs of the Companies House Cardiff contracting out team; how many civil servants are allocated to it and on what grade they are established; when it was set-up; and for how long he estimates the work of this team will continue; [23980]

(2) if he will list the total *(a)* set-up and *(b)* recurrent annual costs of the Companies House London contracting directorate; how many civil servants are allocated to it and on what grade they are established; when it was set-up; and for how long he estimates the work of this directorate will continue. [23979]

**Mr. Jonathan Evans** *[holding answers 15 May 1995]:* Companies House contracting directorate was set up following my right hon. Friend the President of the Board of Trade's announcement on 20 December 1994, *Official Report*, column *1046*, to implement the contracting out of the London Edinburgh and English satellite offices. At present the directorate comprises of:

1 part time grade 5, 2 grade 7, 1 higher executive officer (D), 1 executive officer, 1 personal secretary and 1 administrative assistant.

It is also planned to recruit another HEO.

The Cardiff-based contracting team presently comprises: one G7, one EO and one AA. The team was set up at the beginning of April. It is envisaged that both teams will remain in place until the completion of the contracting out programme.

The target is to have contractors in place by the end of March 1996. The estimated staff costs for the contracting directorate are £45,000 in financial year 1994–95 and £273,000 in financial year 1995–96. The staff costs for the Cardiff team fall in 1995–96 and are likely to be in the region of £70,000. There will be further costs of contract monitoring and management but it is not possible to specify these at this stage.

### Deregulation

**Mr. Mike O'Brien:** To ask the President of the Board of Trade (1) who commissioned the report "Deregulation Now" published by his Department on 21 March; [24000]

(2) how the membership of the Anglo-German working party on deregulation was determined; who appointed its members; and what are the political affiliations of each of the British members; [24001]

(3) how often the Anglo-German working party on deregulation met; and what resources were available to it to undertake research; [24002]

(4) what parts of the report of the Anglo-German working party on deregulation have not been accepted as his policy; [24003]

(5) what was the cost of setting up, running and publishing the report of the Anglo-German working party on deregulation; how much of these costs were met from public funds; to what extent the Health and Safety Commission was consulted over the health and safety section of the report; and if he will place a copy of its response in the Library; [24004]

(6) which British organisations *(a)* submitted evidence to the Anglo-German working party on deregulation, *(b)* were consulted on it and *(c)* provided staff on research facilities for it; [24005]

(7) what is the constitutional position of a policy document when its contents are not all Government policy, with particular reference to the report of the Anglo-German working party on deregulation from a Government Department submitted to the European Union; [24006]

(8) what relative weight his Department gives to the differing conclusions on health and safety regulation of the Anglo-German working party on deregulation and his own authorised review of UK health and safety regulations; [24008]

(9) how much public money was paid in disbursements or remuneration to members of the Anglo-German working party on deregulation; and if he will place in the Library an itemised list detailing to whom such money were paid. [24010]

**Mr. Jonathan Evans:** The report of the independent group of Anglo-German business men was commissioned by my right hon. Friend the Prime Minister and Chancellor Kohl at the Anglo-German summit in April 1994. Members of the group were appointed by their respective Governments, with United Kingdom members being drawn from the deregulation task force. Apart from the right hon. Francis Maude, I am not aware of the political affiliations of any other UK member of the group.

The group met twice and had access to a small team of UK and German officials who provided secretariat support. Assistance and research facilities were drawn from members' own organisations. Group members conducted independent consultations, collected evidence from sectoral representative bodies and their own organisations.

The report has the status of independent advice from senior business men to Government, and is not a policy document from either the UK or German Governments. I am currently consulting other Whitehall Departments, and the Health and Safety Commission, on their specific recommendations. The UK's share of publication, distribution and related costs totalled £25,240. Members of the group received no remuneration from public funds.

Travel and subsistence expenses totalling £2,930 were met for the five UK members of the group who are listed in the groups's report "Deregulation Now", which is available in the Library of the House.

### Nigeria (Military Equipment)

**Mr. Worthington:** To ask the President of the Board of Trade, pursuant to his answer of 10 May, *Official Report*, columns *517–18*, if he will list the goods that fall under each category in the military list of the Export of Goods (Control) Order. [24663]

**Mr. Ian Taylor:** Export of Goods (Control) Orders contain the details of each of the categories of goods which are controlled. The orders are placed in the Library of the House on the date that they are published. Recent orders' dates of publication are as follows:

EGCO 1989—14 February 1990; EGCO 1991—31 December 1990; EGCO 1992—31 December 1992; EGCO 1994—25 May 1994.

## HOUSE OF COMMONS

### *Official Report*

**Mr. Patrick Thompson:** To ask the right hon. Member for Berwick-upon-Tweed, as representing the House of Commons Commission, what conclusions the House of Commons Commission has reached about the future pricing of the *Official Report* following the adjournment debate on 3 April.

**Mr. Beith:** I am pleased to advise the hon. Member that agreement has been reached with HMSO for a reduction in the price of the *Weekly Hansard* from its present level of £22 to £12. This will enable purchasers to obtain *Hansard* at a price equivalent to £2.40 per sitting day, while for public libraries, which can take advantage of the Government discount scheme provided for in class XVIII, vote 5 of the supply estimates, the price will be equivalent to £1.20 per sitting day. Following advice from the Administration Committee, this price reduction has been endorsed by the House of Commons Commission and will take effect when the House returns after the late spring adjournment. It has been made possible by the computerisation of production in the Department of the *Official Report*, and will be achieved at no additional cost to the House.

Discussions are continuing on a new, long-term agreement with HMSO for the printing and publication of the different categories of House documents. The results of these discussions are expected to be submitted to the Commission later this year. In the meantime, there will be no change in the price of the daily *Hansard*.

## TREASURY

### Central Statistical Office

**Mr. Matthew Banks:** To ask the Chancellor of the Exchequer what key targets have been set for the Central Statistical Office for 1995–96. [25038]

**Mr. Nelson:** The Central Statistical Office's key targets for 1995–96 are set out in "CSO Programme Strategies 1995–98", a copy of which has been placed in the Library of the House. As before, these targets cover the timeliness of published statistics, the size of revisions, the coherence of key economic statistics, the response rates for statistical inquiries, action to minimise the load on respondents, response times to public requests for information and the CSO's running costs, efficiency improvements and receipts. A number of the targets have been tightened for 1995–96 in recognition of the continuing improvements in the CSO's performance.

### European Monetary Institute

**Sir Teddy Taylor:** To ask the Chancellor of the Exchequer how much the Bank of England has now invested in the EMI in Frankfurt. [22448]

**Mr. Nelson** *[holding answer 4 May 1995]:* I refer to the reply I gave to the right hon. Member for Llanelli (Mr. Davies) on 6 February, *Official Report*, column *63*. The position is unchanged since that reply was given.

### Tax Bands

**Mr. Frank Field:** To ask the Chancellor of the Exchequer if he will publish estimates for the revenue cost in 1995–96, 1996–97 and for a full year of extending the 20 per cent. tax band by *(a)* £1,000, *(b)* £2,500, *(c)* £5,000, *(d)* £7,500, *(e)* £10,000, *(f)* £12,500, *(g)* £15,000, *(h)* £17,500 and *(i)* £20,000. [23352]

**Sir George Young** *[holding answer 9 May 1995]:* Available estimates are as follows:

| *Increasing the lower rate band by:* £ | *Full year revenue cost at 1995–96 levels*[1] £ billion |
|---|---|
| 1,000 | 1.0 |
| 2,500 | 2.3 |
| 5,000 | 4.2 |
| 7,500 | 5.6 |
| 10,000 | 6.8 |
| 12,500 | 7.6 |
| 15,000 | 8.3 |
| 17,500 | 8.7 |
| 20,000 | 9.1 |

[1] The figures include consequential effects on the yield of capital gains tax.

### Income Tax

**Mr. Frank Field:** To ask the Chancellor of the Exchequer (1) if he will *(a)* list the rates of income tax below 25 per cent., and the brands of income in (i) local currency terms and (ii) sterling equivalents, to which they apply, for each OECD country and *(b)* provide estimates for the number of different tax bands applying in the income tax system of each OECD country; [24368]

(2) if he will update the answer to the hon. Member for Taunton (Mr. Nicholson) of 28 October 1993, *Official Report*, column *749*, and list the rates of income tax over 25 per cent., and the bands of income, in *(a)* local currency terms and *(b)* sterling equivalents, to which they apply, for each OECD country. [24369]

**Sir George Young** *[holding answer 16 May 1995]:* The information requested in the two questions, giving all rates of tax and income bands for each OECD country, has been placed in the Library of the House.

# EMPLOYMENT

## Take-home Pay

**Mr. Devlin:** To ask the Secretary of State for Employment what is the change in real take-home pay for single wage earners in the bottom 10 per cent. of earnings in the north-east region of England between *(a)* 1974 and 1979 and *(b)* 1979 and 1995.                [21316]

**Mr. Oppenheim:** The real take-home pay for an unmarried man at the bottom 10 per cent. of the full-time male wage distribution in the Northern region increased by 1.2 per cent. or £1.50—in 1993–94 prices—between 1973–74 and 1978–79, and by 17.7 per cent. or £20.50 between 1978–79 and 1993–94.

## Spain

**Mr. Steen:** To ask the Secretary of State for Employment how much subsidy has been given to Spain in each of the last three years from the European Community for employment; and what is the forecast of funding to Spain for each of the next three years. [24682]

**Miss Widdecombe:** The information is not available in the form requested. Amounts committed to Spain from the European social fund to part finance a variety of measures in the field of vocational training and employment in recent years are as follows:

| Period | Source | Amount (Mecu) |
| --- | --- | --- |
| 1989–1993 | Objectives 1, 2, 3, 4, 5b | 4,151.00 |
| 1991–1993 | Community Initiatives | 152.19 |
| 1994–1996 | Objective 2 | 259.90 |
| 1994–1999 | Objective 1, 3, 4 | 7,890.00 |

A commitment of 664 mecu has also been made to Spain for objective 5b across all the structural funds, but information on the proportion that will be committed to ESF activities is not held. Information on community initiatives over the period from 1994 is not yet available.

# OVERSEAS DEVELOPMENT ADMINISTRATION

## Africa

**Mr. Watson:** To ask the Secretary of State for Foreign and Commonwealth Affairs what assistance the Government intend to provide to Africa through *(a)* bilateral channels and *(b)* multilateral channels over the next three years.                [23795]

**Mr. Baldry** *[holding answer 15 May 1995]:* Over the next three years, we plan to provide over £900 million of development assistance to Africa, including the middle east, through our bilateral programme. In addition to this, certain low-income, credit-worthy countries in Africa are eligible for assistance under the aid and trade provision.

We will continue to provide emergency assistance in Africa, as needs arise.

It is not possible to provide planning figures for our contribution to Africa through multilateral institutions. We estimate our share will be around £2 billion based on past experience.

# EDUCATION

## Local Government Reorganisation

**Mr. Berry:** To ask the Secretary of State for Education how many chief education officers are currently employed in Berkshire; and how many she expects will be employed when the proposed reorganisation of local government has been completed.                [24532]

**Mr. Robin Squire:** Under section 88 of the Education Act 1994, each local education authority has to have a chief education officer. Berkshire has one. Following reorganisation, each new LEA in the Berkshire area will have one.

**Mr. Berry:** To ask the Secretary of State for Education if she will make a statement on the expected provision, quality and accountability of education services in the Reading urban area when that area is governed by three education authorities under the proposed reorganisation of local government in Berkshire.                [24534]

**Mr. Robin Squire:** The Government's aim in reorganising local government is to improve cost-effectiveness and the quality and co-ordination of local services. The role of local education authorities will not change specifically as a result of the reorganisation of local government. It will be for the new LEAs to play their part in ensuring that the education service is run at least as effectively as now.

**Mr. Beggs:** To ask the Secretary of State for Education for how many schools and pupils each of the proposed unitary authorities in England will have responsibility.                [24583]

**Mr. Robin Squire:** The information requested is not yet available.

## University Lecturers

**Mr. Sheerman:** To ask the Secretary of State for Education what was the difference in levels of pay for lecturers in the old and new universities in 1988–89; and what is the difference currently.                [24379]

**Mr. Boswell:** Lecturers in the old universities were paid on average £37.10 per week more in April 1989 and £48.80 per week more in April 1994 than those in former local authority further and higher education. It is not possible to give a separate figure for new universities from the "New Earnings Survey".

## Rural White Paper

**Mr. Colvin:** To ask the Secretary of State for Education what is her estimate of the net annual saving, or cost, of her Department's submission for the proposed White Paper on the rural economy.                [24330]

**Mr. Forth:** Proposals for the White Paper remain subject to continuing collective consideration and discussion. The cost of measures contained in the White Paper will be taken into account in the public expenditure survey.

### Professors

**Mr. Sheerman:** To ask the Secretary of State for Education how many professors there were in the *(a)* old and *(b)* new universities for 1988–89; and how many there are currently.     [24380]

**Mr. Boswell:** In the academic year 1988–89 there were 3,442 full-time staff at professorial grade in English former University Funding Council-funded universities. The comparable figure for 1992–93 was 4,391.

In the former PCFC-funded English polytechnics granted university status, there were 3,614 wholly institution financed full-time academic staff at principal lecturer grade, and some 925 full-time academic staff graded above principal lecturer in the academic year 1992–93. Data for 1988–89 were not collected centrally.

### University Promoted Posts

**Mr. Sheerman:** To ask the Secretary of State for Education how many promoted posts there were in the *(a)* old and *(b)* new universities for 1988–89; and how many there are currently.     [24378]

**Mr. Boswell:** Data on promoted posts are not available centrally.

### Student Dependency Grant

**Mrs. Helen Jackson:** To ask the Secretary of State for Education (1) how many students in receipt of dependency grant last year were *(a)* women and *(b)* men;     [24591]

(2) how many students in receipt of dependency grant last year were married;     [24592]

(3) how many students last year received dependency grant; and at what cost to the Exchequer.     [24590]

**Mr. Boswell:** Provisional figures for the academic year 1993–94 show that 27,000 mandatory award holders resident in England and Wales received dependants' allowances. The gross value of these allowances was £55 million. Since these allowances are means-tested, the cost to the Exchequer will have been less that this amount.

Information on the marital status or gender of students in receipt of dependants' allowances is not collected centrally.

**Mrs. Helen Jackson:** To ask the Secretary of State for Education if she will bring forward regulations to ensure that women students with dependent children do not lose their entitlement to dependency grant when they marry.     [24589]

**Mr. Boswell:** Under the Education (Mandatory Awards) Regulations, the additional allowance to the student's grant which can be made for children who are wholly or mainly financially dependent on him or her will continue after marriage if the children remain his or her dependants.

## DUCHY OF LANCASTER

### Complaints

**Ms Hodge:** To ask the Chancellor of the Duchy of Lancaster what policy and procedure exists for dealing with complaints against central Government Departments by members of the public; when each Department last updated its policy; what time limit and target for dealing with complaints by members of the public exists for each central Government Department; and what follow-up procedure exists where complainants against each central Government Department are not satisfied with the Department's response to a complaint.     [23715]

**Mr. Horam:** Each central Government Department is responsible for its own policy and procedure for handling complaints. The information requested is not held centrally.

Any member of the public who is dissatisfied with how a Department has dealt with his complaint may ask a Member of Parliament to submit his complaint to the Parliamentary Commissioner for Administration for investigation and review.

### Departmental Performance

**Ms Hodge:** To ask the Chancellor of the Duchy of Lancaster what performance indicators there are for measuring the performance of central Government Departments in answering letters from members of the public; what is each Government Department's target for answering letters; how performance is monitored by each Government Department; and what is the performance against the target set by each Government Department.     [23717]

**Mr. Horam:** Government Departments are responsible for ensuring that their handling of letters from members of the public is effective, and for setting their own targets. Departments and agencies are encouraged to publish such targets in their charter statements as appropriate.

**Ms Hodge:** To ask the Chancellor of the Duchy of Lancaster what performance indicators there are for measuring the performance of central Government Departments in answering telephone calls from members of the public; what is each Government Department's target for answering calls; how performance is monitored by each Government Department; and what has been the performance against the target set by each Government Department.     [23716]

**Mr. Horam:** It is for individual Departments to decide whether performance standards for answering telephone calls from members of the public should be set, and at what level. Standards may cover all or part of the Department. The monitoring of calls to see whether standards are met, and any resulting management action, is the responsibility of individual Departments. Information on the performance of Government Departments in answering telephone calls is not held centrally and could not be collected without incurring disproportionate cost.

### "People and their Governments in the Information Age"

**Mr. Allen:** To ask the Chancellor of the Duchy of Lancaster if he will make a statement on CCTA's participation in the electronic on-line meetings "People and their Governments", organised by the US Administration. [24598]

**Mr. Horam:** "People and Their Governments in the Information Age" was a two-week electronic on-line conference, held on 1 to 14 May, organised by the US Administration using the world-wide web and the Internet. The purpose of the conference was to garner public opinion on the use of information technology by federal, state and local governments.

I am delighted to report that CCTA, the Government centre for information systems, was the only non-American organisation specifically invited to participate. It did so by establishing an Internet mailbox to facilitate United Kingdom contributions, to be consolidated into a single response.

In the UK we have had collaborative open groups established on the Internet for the past six months, allowing users to contribute to discussions on a wide range of topics relating to the Government's use of information superhighways. We are exploring ways in which the participation in these debates can be widened.

## PRIME MINISTER

### Special Advisers

**Mr. McMaster:** To ask the Prime Minister if he will list the name, former occupation and supervising Minister of each special adviser currently employed from any Government funding source; and if he will list the salary range of such advisers as of 5 May; and if he will make a statement. [24211]

**The Prime Minister:** There are 36 special advisers currently employed by Government Departments; details of their names, former occupations, and Ministers are as follows. For information on the salary range of special advisers I refer the hon. Member to the reply I gave to him on 28 February 1995, *Official Report*, columns *484–85*.

The following is the information:

| Name | Former occupation | Minister |
| --- | --- | --- |
| K. Adams | Personal Assistant to the Right Hon. John Gummer | Secretary of State for the Environment |
| P. Barnes | Management Consultant, Boston Consulting Group | Secretary of State for Social Security |
| J. Bercow | Director, Rowland Sallingbury Casey | Chief Secretary |
| N. Blackwell | Partner, McKinsey and Co. Consultants | Prime Minister |
| C. Blunt | Public Affairs Consultant, PI Political | Secretary of State for Defence |
| Miss A. Broom | Freelance Political Consultant | Secretary of State for Employment |
| T. Burke* | Director, Green Alliance | Secretary of State for Environment |
| J. Caine | Desk Officer, Conservative Research Department | Secretary of State for Northern Ireland |
| T. Collins | Communications Director, Conservative Central Office | Prime Minister |
| Dr. E. Cottrell | Assistant Director, Conservative Research Department | Secretary of State for Education |
| Dr. W. Eltis* | Director General, National and Economic Development Office | President of the Board of Trade |
| Miss C. Fairbairn | Strategy Consultant, McKinsey and Co. Consultants | Prime Minister |
| M. Fraser | Assistant Director, Conservative Research Department | Secretary of State for Foreign and Commonwealth Affairs |
| A. Hockley | Economic Adviser, Air Transport Users Council, and Freelance Adviser | Secretary of State for Health |
| Miss S. Hole | Secretary to Lord Rothschild | Chief Whip |
| M. Izatt | Research Assistant to Mr. Raymond Robertson MP | Secretary of State for Scotland |
| A. Kemp* | Owner of ODP Nexus Ltd. | President of the Board of Trade |
| G. Maclay | Economic Researcher, Pieda plc | Secretary of State for Scotland |
| M. Maclay | Associate Editor, "The European" | Secretary of State for Foreign and Commonwealth Affairs |
| R. Marsh | Writer and Researcher on Environment and Local Government, Conservative Central Office | Secretary of State for Health |
| Ms S. McEwean | Account Executive Namara Cowan Ltd. | Lord Privy Seal |
| M. McManus | Desk Officer for Wales, Conservative Central Office | Chancellor of the Duchy of Lancaster |
| P. Moman | Self Employed Consultant and Writer | Lord President |
| L. O'Connor* | Self Employed Architect | Secretary of State for the Environment |
| Mrs. K. Ramsay | Desk Officer, Conservative Central Office Research Department | Prime Minister |
| P. Rock | Assistant Director Conservative Central Office | Home Secretary |
| D. Ruffley | Solicitor, Clifford Chance | Chancellor of the Exchequer |
| D. Rutley | Business Development Director, Pepsi Cola | Minister of Agriculture, Fisheries and Food |
| M. Simmonds | Researcher, BBC Political Research Unit | Secretary of State for Transport |
| D. Soskin | Chief Executive of Asquith Courts Schools Ltd. | Prime Minister |
| Lady Strathnaver | Adviser to Right Hon. Michael Heseltine MP | President of the Board of Trade |
| N. True | Director, Public Policy Unit | Prime Minister |
| Miss A. Warburton | Private Secretary | Prime Minister |
| Miss R. Whetstone | Head of Political Section, Conservative Central Office | Home Secretary |
| H. Williams | Governing Body of Rugby School, also Freelance Journalist and Writer | Secretary of State for Wales |
| S. Williams | Company Secretary, Williams Lea Group | Prime Minister |

*Note:*

Special advisers fall into two categories, political and those with specialised expertise relevant to their appropriate Secretary of State. The latter are indicated by an asterisk.

## TRANSPORT

### Eastleigh Rail Maintenance Ltd.

**Mr. Chidgey:** To ask the Secretary of State for Transport (1) what is the cost of *(a)* terminating and *(b)* terminating in perpetuity the contractual commitments relating to intellectual property rights of contractors to Eastleigh Rail Maintenance Ltd. for rolling stock maintenance in order to complete the privatisation contract of Eastleigh Rail Maintenance Ltd.; [24045]

(2) what action the British Rail Board has taken in respect of the contractual commitments relating to intellectual property rights of contractors to Eastleigh Rail Maintenance Ltd. in order to complete the privatisation contract of Eastleigh Rail Maintenance Ltd.;    [24044]

(3) what plans the British Rail Board has to enter into contractual commitments relating to intellectual property rights as a consequence of the privatisation process of Eastleigh Rail Maintenance Ltd.;    [24043]

(4) what is the cost to the British Rail Board entering into contractual commitments relating to intellectual property rights as a consequence of the privatisation process of Eastleigh Rail Maintenance Ltd.    [24042]

**Mr. Watts:** The British Railways Board is taking steps to ensure that the BR Maintenance Ltd. depots, including Eastleigh, are transferred to the private sector with adequate access to intellectual property rights. The terms of sale and purchase contracts, both in relation to such rights and generally, are a matter of commercial confidence between the BR Board and purchasers.

### London-Tilbury-Southend Line

**Mr. Mackinlay:** To ask the Secretary of State for Transport on how many occasions over the past 12 months services have been interrupted on the London-Tilbury-Southend line due to broken rail track; and if he will make a statement.    [24496]

**Mr. Watts:** Railtrack informs me that services on the London-Tilbury-Southend line have been affected by broken rails on seven occasions during the past 12 months.

### A303

**Mr. Key:** To ask the Secretary of State for Transport, pursuant to his answer of 27 March, *Official Report*, column 510, when he will announce the date for the start of the round-table conference on improvements to the A303 at Stonehenge; and who will be its chairman.    [24687]

**Mr. Watts:** I will announce the arrangements for a conference including the name of the chairman later in the year.

### M65 (Protestors)

**Ms Walley:** To ask the Secretary of State for Transport which contractor was awarded the contract to clear the protestors involved with the M65 extension; what was the cost of the work undertaken; and whether the contract was subject to competitive tendering.    [24403]

**Mr. Watts:** This is an operational matter for the Highways Agency. I have asked the chief executive to write to the hon. Member.

*Letter from Lawrie Haynes to Ms Joan Walley, dated 17 May 1995:*

Mr. John Watts has asked me to write in reply to your Parliamentary Question asking the Secretary of State for Transport, which contractor was awarded the contract to clear the protestors involved with the M65 extension; what was the cost of the work undertaken; and whether the contract was subject to competitive tendering.

I assume your question refers to the eviction of protestors from Stanworth Woods on the line of the M65 which took place between 1 and 5 May. This action was entirely the responsibility of the Under-Sheriff of Lancashire. He was accompanied by teams of bailiffs and specialist climbers. The Under-Sheriff directly recruited these teams and there was no involvement by the Highways Agency.

The Under-Sheriff will in due course submit a bill to the Treasury Solicitor for the costs he has incurred. The Treasury Solicitor will arrange payment on behalf of the Agency.

The main contractor for the scheme is the Alfred McAlpine-AMEC joint venture. They employ Group 4 Total Security as a security sub-contractor. In accordance with the Agency's current requirements Group 4 were appointed after quotations were obtained from three security firms. During the eviction process Group 4 guards were present, but took no part in the actual evictions. Their job was merely to keep the site secure after the protestors had been evicted. The cost to the Agency of security and other contractor expenses for the week (but excluding the Under-Sheriff's costs) is estimated at some £100,000.

### Driving Standards Agency

**Ms Walley:** To ask the Secretary of State for Transport if he will publish the full cost of his Department, the Driving Standards Agency and the Treasury of the recent market test of the Driving Standards Agency booking service and list the costs according to consultancies, implementation costs, the establishment of residual functions, accommodation and staffing costs including the costs of redundancies and recruitment;    [24426]

(2) what is his estimate of the short and long-term savings which will be made as a result of the market test of the Driving Standards Agency booking service;    [24427]

(3) if he will place in the Library a copy of the successful bid for the Driving Standards Agency booking service.    [24425]

**Mr. Norris:** These are operational matters for the Driving Standards Agency. I have asked the chief executive to write to the hon. Member.

*Letter from B. L. Herdan to Ms Joan Walley, dated 17 May 1995:*

The Secretary of State for Transport has asked me to reply to the following questions concerning the recent Market Test of the Agency's regional booking service.

The costs of the market test exercise up to the announcement of the result were: consultancies £76,647 and staff time and effort £148,000. The implementation exercise has commenced but it is too early to assess the actual costs of redundancies, recruitment and the reorganisation of the residual functions.

The In-House Bid proposals will provide a saving of £1.3 million over the three years of the contract. The anticipated savings over 10 years of implementing the In-House Bid are £5.2 million.

No. The submission made by the successful bidder contains information which is commercial in confidence.

**Mr. McAllion:** To ask the Secretary of State for Transport how many staff are employed in the Scottish booking office of the Driving Standards Agency; how many of them will transfer to Newcastle if the office is relocated there; and what will be the cost to the Exchequer of these transfer and of any voluntary redundancy or early retirement packages taken up because of the relocation decision.    [24277]

**Mr. Norris:** This is an operational matter for the Driving Standards Agency. I have asked the chief executive to write to the hon. Member.

*Letter from B. L. Herdan to Mr. John McAllion, dated 17 May 1995.*

The Secretary of State has asked me to reply to your question about the staff in the Scottish Booking Office.

At present 17 staff are employed in the Booking Office in Edinburgh. None of these staff are expected to transfer with the work to the Newcastle office. Local transfers to other Government Department sin the Edinburgh area have already been agreed for 4 staff and similar transfers are being sought for those remaining.

Two members of staff have sought voluntary early retirement at a total cost of £18,000 compensation. Full estimates of these costs for any remaining staff cannot be given until discussions with other Departments on transfers are complete.

**Mr. McAllion:** To ask the Secretary of State for Transport (1) how many driving tests were booked through the Scottish booking office of the Driving Standards Agency in each of the past three years; [24275]

(2) what is the annual cost of running the (a) the Scottish booking office and (b) the Newcastle office of the Driving Standards Agency; and how many driving tests are booked through each office annually; [24278]

(3) whom he consulted on his proposal to relocate the Scottish booking office of the Driving Standards Agency to Newcastle; how many responses he received as a result; and how many of them supported the relocation. [24276]

**Mr. Norris:** These are operational matters for the Driving Standards Agency. I have asked the chief executive to write to the hon. Member.

*Letter from B. L. Herdan to Mr. John McAllion, dated 17 May 1995:*

The Secretary of State has asked me to reply to your questions concerning the relocation of the driving tests booking responsibility in Scotland from Edinburgh to Newcastle.

The number of applications dealt with by the Agency's Booking Office in Scotland in each of the past three years was, 1992/93 156,594, 1993/94 153,625 and 1994/95 157,004.

The cost of running the office in Haymarket House, Edinburgh during 1995/96 is £119,008 or £268.58 per m2. This takes account of a rent free first quarter agreed when the Agency moved into the accommodation last year. For 1996/97 this would rise to £134,090 or £302.62 per m2. The cost for Westgate House, Newcastle is £212,182 or £226.93 per m2. These do not include staffing costs.

The number of driving tests booked through each office varies from year to year. During the period 1 April 1994–31 March 1995 the office in Edinburgh dealt with 157,004 applications, whilst Newcastle dealt with 234,190 applications.

There is no requirement under the Market Testing guidance to undertake a consultation exercise on proposals in bids. Since the result of the Market Test was announced some 33 items of correspondence have been received opposing the decision; no correspondence has been received supporting the decision.

### Channel Tunnel Rail Link

**Mr. Mills:** To ask the Secretary of State for Transport when he will publish his response to the judgment of the Colonel Owen case on compensation for those affected by public works with special reference to motorways; and if he will make a statement. [24364]

**Mr. Watts:** I refer my hon. Friend to the answer that I gave my right hon. Friend the Member for Tonbridge and Malling (Sir J. Stanley) on 23 March, *Official Report*, column *317*.

### M42

**Mr. Mills:** To ask the Secretary of State for Transport when he will announce the date for the conclusion of the public inquiry on the proposed widening of the M42; and if he will make a statement; [24363]

**Mr. Watts:** This is an operational matter for the Highways Agency. I have asked the chief executive to reply.

*Letter from Lawrie Haynes to Mr. Iain Mills, dated 17 May 1995.*

As you know, the Minister for Railways and Roads, Mr. John Watts, has asked me to reply to your Parliamentary Question asking the Secretary of State for Transport, when he will announce the date for the conclusion of the public inquiry on the proposed widening of the M42; and if he will make a statement.

The Highways Agency have yet to put forward their recommendations to the Secretary of State on the options for widening following last year's public exhibitions. We are still considering carefully all the issues raised.

The question of a public inquiry would not arise until the Secretary of State had announced his preferred option and the Agency had published draft Orders for the widening to which statutory objections have been received.

### Roads Programme Director

**Ms Walley:** To ask the Secretary of State for Transport what assessment he has made of whether all rules relating to outside business appointments have been met following the appointment of the former roads programme director to the company Ove-Arup and Partners; if advice has been sought from the Cabinet Office; and if he will make a statement. [24429]

**Mr. Norris:** The rules relating to outside business appointments were fully complied with prior to the appointment of the former roads programme director to the company Ove-Arup and Partners. The appointment was referred to the Cabinet Office and the relevant trade associations were also content.

### Ferries

**Mr. Flynn:** To ask the Secretary of State for Transport if he will arrange a trial of the dryshod evacuation of (a) 500, (b) 1,000 and (c) 2,000 passengers from roll on/roll off ferries. [24484]

**Mr. Norris** *[holding reply 16 May 1995]:* This is an operational matter for the Coastguard Agency. I have asked the chief executive to write to the hon. Member.

*Letter from C. J. Harris to Mr. Paul Flynn, dated 17 May 1995:*

The Secretary of State for Transport has asked me to reply to your recent Parliamentary Question as the question deals with an operational matter, for which I have responsibility as Chief Executive.

HM Coastguard carries out regular ferry exercises. These exercises normally involve the evacuation of large numbers of passengers and crew and their succour ashore.

Nine such exercises have taken place in the last two years. Further exercises are planned this year, but none of them involve more than 500 "passengers".

I am considering whether the plans for exercises in future years could include one involving larger numbers of passengers.

### Motorways

**Mr. Flynn:** To ask the Secretary of State for Transport what assessment he has made on the affect on accident levels of (a) motorway lane closures and (b) motorway lighting. [24486]

**Mr. John Watts** *[holding reply for 16 May]:* This is an operational matter for the Highways Agency. I have asked the chief executive to write to the hon. Member.

*Letter from L. Haynes to Mr. Paul Flynn, dated 17 May 1995:*

As you know, the Minister for Railways and Roads, Mr. John Watts, has asked me to reply to your Parliamentary Question asking the Secretary of State for Transport, what assessment he has made on the affect on accident levels of (a) motorway lane closures and (b) motorway lighting.

Recent studies have shown that the accident rate at motorway lane closures due to road works is higher than the rate on unrestricted carriageways, although the increased rate is less than on any other category of road. Studies have also shown that lighting can reduce the after dark accident rate on trunk roads and motorways by an average of 30%.

The Highways Agency seeks to minimise accidents on motorways by applying, amongst other techniques, mandatory 50mph speed limits at roadworks enforced by speed detection cameras, and by providing lighting where appropriate and environmentally acceptable. These measures have met with success, but research and innovation are continuing with a view to improve safety further.

# ENVIRONMENT

## Open Spaces

17. **Mr. Harry Greenway:** To ask the Secretary of State for the Environment what steps he is taking to ensure the provision of more open spaces in built-up areas; and if he will make a statement.    [23207]

**Sir Paul Beresford:** We fully recognise the importance of open space for amenity and recreation and our planning policy guidance encourages its provision.

## Council House Sales

20. **Sir David Knox:** To ask the Secretary of State for the Environment how many council houses have been sold to sitting tenants in England since May 1979.    [23210]

**Mr. Curry:** Over 1.42 million tenants bought their homes from English local authorities and new towns between April 1979 and December 1994.

## Homelessness, Leicester

21. **Mr. Janner:** To ask the Secretary of State for the Environment if he will make a statement on the number of homeless people in the city of Leicester.    [23211]

**Mr. Curry:** A total of 1,305 households were accepted as statutorily homeless by Leicester city council during 1994.

## Construction Industry

22. **Mr. William O'Brien:** To ask the Secretary of State for the Environment if he will make a statement about the prospects for the construction industry.    [23212]

**Mr. Robert B. Jones:** Construction output increased by 3 per cent. last year. British firms are doing well abroad and industry forecasts point to continuing modest growth this year and in the future.

## Defence Jobs, Dorset

23. **Mr. Ian Bruce:** To ask the Secretary of State for the Environment what plans his Department has to increase resources to local government in Dorset to help it to cope with the economic effects of defence job losses.    [23213]

**Mr. Curry:** Standard spending assessments use the most up-to-date information available to take account of changes in economic conditions.

In addition, South Dorset is getting £2.7 million over five years from the single regeneration budget in connection with the closure of the Portland naval base. It is also eligible for KONVER funding.

## Eco-labelling

24. **Mr. Bennett:** To ask the Secretary of State for the Environment if he will make a statement about eco-labelling.    [23214]

**Sir Paul Beresford:** I am pleased to report that since my right hon. Friend the Secretary of State for the Environment intervened at the October Environment Council over the continuing delays with this European Community scheme, considerable progress has been made. In all, there are eight product groups for which criteria have been established; including soil improvers, tissue paper, kitchen rolls, household detergents, paints, varnishes and lightbulbs, which significantly improves the prospects for a range of eco-labelled goods being available in the shops later this year. Further speedy progress is anticipated.

## Office for London

25. **Mr. Corbyn:** To ask the Secretary of State for the Environment what steps he proposes to make the Government Office for London open to public scrutiny.    [23215]

**Mr. Gummer:** The Government Office for London is responsible to Ministers, who are answerable to Parliament, in the same way as other parts of the civil service.

## Urban Regeneration, Hackney

26. **Ms Abbott:** To ask the Secretary of State for the Environment what plans he has to visit Hackney to discuss urban regeneration with the new council leadership.    [23216]

**Mr. Curry:** I visited Hackney 6 March 1995.

## New Houses

27. **Mr. Nicholas Winterton:** To ask the Secretary of State for the Environment if he will make a statement on new housing starts in the latest quarter for which figures are available.    [23217]

**Mr. Robert B. Jones:** There were 30,200 private enterprise housing starts in England in the first quarter of this year.

## City Pride

28. **Ms Janet Anderson:** To ask the Secretary of State for the Environment what plans he has to extend the City Pride initiative.    [23218]

33. **Mr. Pike:** To ask the Secretary of State for the Environment what plans he has to extend the City Pride initiative.    [23223]

**Mr. Gummer:** Birmingham, London and Manchester have made tremendous progress in pursuing City Pride. We will look at what they have achieved before extending the initiative.

### SSSIs, East Anglia

30. **Mr. Garrett:** To ask the Secretary of State for the Environment how many sites of special scientific interest in Norfolk and in Suffolk have been damaged in each of the past five years.          [23220]

**Sir Paul Beresford:** The information requested for years 1989–90 to 1991–92 is as follows:

| Year | Norfolk | Suffolk |
|------|---------|---------|
| 1989–90 | 2 | 7 |
| 1990–91 | 2 | 4 |
| 1991–92 | 7 | 3 |

These figures do not reflect the on-going and cumulative damage.

Change were made in 1992 to the method of recording of damage to reflect continuing and cumulative effects. The information for years 1992–93 and 1993–94 reflect this as follows:

| Year | Norfolk | Suffolk |
|------|---------|---------|
| 1992–93 | 21 | 3 |
| 1993–94 | 21 | 4 |

### Urban Regeneration

31. **Mr. Nigel Evans:** To ask the Secretary of State for the Environment if he will make a statement about the total Government spending on regenerating inner cities.          [23221]

**Mr. Curry:** Economic, social and physical regeneration is supported through main programme expenditure by several Government Departments. This is supplemented by targeted programmes which have been brought together into the single regeneration budget. The SRB will fund more than £1.3 billion of regeneration work in 1995–96 in inner city and other areas.

The SRB challenge fund reflects the Government's commitment to encourage local councils, the private sector and community groups to work together in partnership to develop comprehensive strategies which address all of an areas's fundamental problems and opportunities.

### Housing Costs (Young People)

32. **Mr. Soley:** To ask the Secretary of State for the Environment what research information he has on the number of young people living with their parents who are unable to find affordable alternative accommodation.          [23222]

**Mr. Robert B. Jones:** My Department commissioned research in this area in 1990. A copy of the research report, "Shared accommodation in England 1990", is in the House of Commons Library.

### Thames Gateway

34. **Mrs. Gorman:** To ask the Secretary of State for the Environment if he will make a statement on the relationship between the Thames Gateway scheme and local government reorganisation in Essex.          [23224]

**Mr. Curry:** An integrated approach to regeneration will be required to secure the objectives for the Thames Gateway. We wish to consider whether unitary authorities offer advantages, for this purpose, over the two-tier system. This is one of the reasons why we are referring some authorities in the Thames Gateway area, including Thurrock in Essex, to the Local Government Commission for fresh reviews.

### Nuclear Power

35. **Mr. Alan W. Williams:** To ask the Secretary of State for the Environment if he will list his Department's responsibilities in the operation of the nuclear power industry.          [23225]

**Mr. Atkins:** Under the Radioactive Substances Act 1993, my Department—together with the Ministry of Agriculture, Fisheries and Food—is responsible for authorising the disposal of radioactive waste from nuclear licensed sites.

### Council Housing

36. **Mr. Skinner:** To ask the Secretary of State for the Environment how many local authority houses have been built in England and Wales in the last 12 months for which figures are available.          [23226]

**Mr. Robert B. Jones:** Local authorities in England and Wales completed about 1,000 dwellings in the 12 months from April 1994 to March 1995.

39. **Mr. Nigel Griffiths:** To ask the Secretary of State for the Environment what funding is available in this financial year for the improvement of council housing estates.          [23229]

**Mr. Curry:** Under the housing investment programme and other programmes, over £1.2 billion has been allocated to local authorities for 1995–96; a number of the programmes lever in additional resources from the private sector.

Local authorities also fund capital expenditure on housing from usable capital receipts and revenue contributions to capital.

It is up to each local authority to decide how to use its allocation on the basis of local needs.

### Council Tax

37. **Mr. John Marshall:** To ask the Secretary of State for the Environment what recent representations he has received about the principle of council tax capping.          [23227]

**Mr. Gummer:** I have received a number of representations about the principle of council tax capping.

### Beaches

38. **Mr. Waterson:** To ask the Secretary of State for the Environment what progress has been made in achieving cleaner beaches; and if he will make a statement.          [23228]

**Mr. Atkins:** Considerable progress has been made. Compliance with the relevant coliform bacteria standards of the EC directive has risen from 56 per cent. in 1987 to 82 per cent. in 1994. I expect further improvements as the remaining schemes in the clean-up programme are completed.

### Air Quality

40. **Dr. Spink:** To ask the Secretary of State for the Environment what steps he is taking to improve air quality.    [23230]

**Mr. Atkins:** I intend shortly to bring forward amendments to the Environment Bill implementing the proposals set out earlier this year in "Air Quality: Meeting the Challenge".

### Water Pollution

**Sir Teddy Taylor:** To ask the Secretary of State for the Environment what estimate he has made of the capital expenditure of the water industry in providing equipment designed to remove nitrates and pesticides; and if he will make a statement.    [23208]

**Mr. Atkins:** Information published by the Director General of Water Services estimates that £128 million has been spent on removing nitrates up to 1993–94. Similar information was not collected for the removal of pesticides. I estimate that around £430 million has been spent on this up to 1993–94.

### Birds Directive

**Mr. David Shaw:** To ask the Secretary of State for the Environment how many sites the UK has designated under the EC birds directive.    [23219]

**Mr. Atkins:** A total of 105 special protection areas have been designated in the United Kingdom. Further designations are expected shortly.

### Green Belt

**Sir Irvine Patnick:** To ask the Secretary of State for the Environment if he will make a statement on green belt expansion, with special reference to Sheffield.    [24361]

**Sir Paul Beresford:** National planning policy for green belts is set out in "Planning Policy Guidance Note 2". This states that existing green belt boundaries should be altered only in exceptional circumstances. The Sheffield unitary development fund, which is currently being considered at a local public inquiry, proposes a net addition to the green belt of 53 hectares—0.6 per cent. of the total area. It is for the inspector conducting the UDP inquiry to consider the appropriateness of the proposed changes to the green belt and make his recommendations to the city council, who will then be responsible for deciding whether to accept them and reflect them in the final version of the UDP.

### Water Rates

**Mr. Jim Cunningham:** To ask the Secretary of State for the Environment what protection consumers have if a water authority refuses to change business water rates to domestic water rates, in cases where a business property has been changed to a home.    [24037]

**Mr. Atkins:** It is for each water company to decide the basis of charging for water in its area. If the occupant considers that the latest rateable value is no longer appropriate, the occupant has the option of switching to a measured basis of charge. Alternatively, the water company may agree to charge on the basis of a domestic rateable value if such a value is available.

**Mr. Jim Cunningham:** To ask the Secretary of State for the Environment to what extent water authorities are required to take account of changes since the last valuation of a property in calculating water rates; and what proposal he has to improve the situation.    [24035]

**Mr. Atkins:** Where water charges are based on rateable values, the latest available valuations are used by the water companies. Where the occupant considers the subsequent changes to the property render the latest valuation inappropriate, the occupant has the option of switching to a measured basis of charge.

### Units of Measurement Directive

**Dr. Twinn:** To ask the Secretary of State for the Environment what advice his Department has given to local planning authorities and applicants for planning permission on the impact since 1 January of the units of measurement directive.    [24202]

**Sir Paul Beresford:** The interpretation of the directive is ultimately for the courts. However, our advice in response to inquiries is that any risk of successful legal challenge is avoided if a metric conversion is substituted for any imperial measurements in a planning application. The imperial measurements may also be retained as a supplementary indication.

### Construction Contracts

**Mr. Cox:** To ask the Secretary of State for the Environment when he expects to make a statement on his Department's policy on a construction contracts Bill.    [24019]

**Mr. Robert B. Jones:** My Department is currently consulting on proposals for possible legislative provisions arising out of the recommendations in Sir Michael Latham's report, "Construction the Team". The results of the consultation process will be announced in due course.

**Mr. Heald:** To ask the Secretary of State for the Environment what progress he has made in implementing the recommendations in Sir Michael Latham's report, "Construction the Team", on legislation for construction contracts.    [24809]

**Mr. Gummer:** I have today published a consultation document entitled, "Fair Construction Contracts" containing proposals for taking forward the recommendations in "Constructing the Team". These proposals are designed to help reduce the number of disputes in the industry and improve its performance.

Our paper contains proposals for rapid resolution of disputes, limitation of the right of set-off of debts, encouragement of prompt payment and protection against insolvency. It will be widely distributed and we expect both factual comment and informed views from all sectors of the construction industry.

Copies of the document have been placed in the Library of the House.

## Home Loss Payments

**Mr. Jim Cunningham:** To ask the Secretary of State for the Environment what consideration he has given to raising the ceiling for compensation levels for those tenants who are required to leave their property; what representations he has received concerning concerns about the present compensation ceiling; what formula was used to set it; what power local authorities have to set compensation limits to suit local conditions; and if he will consider allowing more discretion for local authorities to decide their own compensation ceiling.    [24029]

**Sir Paul Beresford:** The current level of home loss payment for permanently displaced tenants is £1,500. This level was set during the passage of the Planning and Compensation Act 1991. There are no immediate plans to change it.

The new provisions apply to anyone displaced on or after 16 November 1990. Since they came into force, we have received occasional representations, but there has been no widespread pressure to have this level increased.

Prior to the 1991 Act, the amount of home loss payment was calculated as 10 times the rateable value of the dwelling concerned, subject to a minimum payment of £1,200 and a maximum of £1,500. The minimum period of residence prior to displacement in order to qualify for a payment was five years. The 1991 Act fixed the amount payable to tenants at £1,500 and reduced the minimum period of residence to one year.

The amount of the home loss payment for displaced tenants is fixed at £1,500 and there is no provision for local authorities to vary it.

**Mr. Jim Cunningham:** To ask the Secretary of State for the Environment what guidance he has issued to local authorities as to the levels of compensation a council should provide to tenants who are obliged to move because of redevelopment; and what specific guidelines he provides in respect of compensation for long-term tenants.    [24028]

**Sir Paul Beresford:** Circular 15/91 on land compensation and compulsory purchase, issued jointly by my Department and the Welsh Office, describes the new provisions for home losses payments included in the Planning and Compensation Act 1991. At paragraph 23, it sets out the level of compensation payable to displaced tenants. These provisions apply to tenants who have been in residence for at least one year before displacement. All such tenants receive a home loss payment of £1,500. In addition, my Department issues a series of booklets called "Land Compensation—Your Rights Explained". Booklet number 1 in the series, "Your Home and Compulsory Purchase", provides further information about home loss payments. It is available free of charge to the public as well as to local authorities.

## Housing

**Sir Irvine Patnick:** To ask the Secretary of State for the Environment how many houses have been built in co-operation with the Housing Corporation in each of the last three years: and if he will make a statement.    [24358]

**Mr. Curry:** The table shows the number of houses built through the Housing Corporation's approved development programme and local authority funding of housing associations supported by housing association grant LA HAG in 1992–93 to 1994–95. The table also shows the number of other lettings provided through the ADP and local authority funding of housing associations, through rehabilitation, shared ownership and sale schemes.

|  | 1992–93 | 1993–94 | 1994–95[1] |
|---|---|---|---|
| *New build* |  |  |  |
| ADP | 36,240 | 35,604 | 37,925 |
| LA HAG | 4,480 | 5,894 | 8,487 |
| Total | 40,720 | 41,498 | 46,412 |
| *Other lettings provided* |  |  |  |
| ADP | 25,897 | 20,896 | 21,039 |
| LA HAG | 1,858 | 2,465 | 4,073 |
| Total | 27,755 | 23,361 | 25,112 |
| Total lettings provided | 68,475 | 64,859 | 71,524 |

[1] Figures for 1994–95 are estimates.

## Water Meters

**Mr. Jim Cunningham:** To ask the Secretary of State for the Environment how many water meters have been installed to date in each region and nationally.    [24038]

**Mr. Atkins:** In 1994–95 the number of metered properties in each region of England and Wales covered by Ofwat's customer service committees was:

|  | | Thousands |
|---|---|---|
|  | Domestic | Non-domestic |
| Eastern | 195 | 147 |
| Northumbria | 15 | 45 |
| North West | 89 | 169 |
| Central | 206 | 210 |
| Southern | 149 | 102 |
| South West | 39 | 83 |
| Thames | 207 | 257 |
| Wales | 37 | 77 |
| Wessex | 62 | 68 |
| Yorkshire | 93 | 124 |
| Total | 1,092 | 1,282 |

**Mr. Jim Cunningham:** To ask the Secretary of State for the Environment in what circumstances a water authority can oblige customers to accept water meters.    [24036]

**Mr. Atkins:** It is for water companies to decide on the most appropriate method of charging for water in their area. Since 1990, most companies have had a policy of metering new or substantially converted domestic properties on a compulsory basis. Most companies also have a policy of metering commercial premises on a compulsory basis. Where companies are extending metering to existing domestic properties they may give customers the option of continuing to pay an unmeasured charge.

## Home Energy Efficiency

**Sir Irvine Patnick:** To ask the Secretary of State for the Environment how many households have been insulated under programmes initiated by the energy efficiency office in each of the last two years in (*a*) Sheffield and (*b*) the Sheffield, Hallam constituency; and how many are expected to be insulated in the next year.    [24360]

**Mr. Robert B. Jones:** The home energy efficiency scheme pays grants towards the cost of basic insulation measures in the homes of people who are over 60, receive disability living allowance or an income-related benefit. The information requested, based on financial years, is as follows:

| | 1993–94 | 1994–95 | 1995–96 (estimated) |
|---|---|---|---|
| Sheffield | 3,709 | 6,139 | 7,500 |
| Sheffield, Hallam | 640 | 1,059 | 1,300 |

### Carbon Dioxide Emissions

**Mr. Robert Ainsworth:** To ask the Secretary of State for the Environment what assessment he has made of the effect of an 8 per cent. cut in electricity prices on $CO_2$ emissions. [24218]

**Mr. Atkins:** I refer the hon. Member to the reply given yesterday by my hon. Friend the Minister for Energy and Industry.

**Mr. Robert Ainsworth:** To ask the Secretary of State for the Environment what new measures to cut $CO_2$ emissions as a result of the nuclear review. [24216]

**Mr. Atkins:** I refer the hon. Member to the answer which my right hon. Friend the Under-Secretary for the Environment, gave to my hon. Friend the Member for Croydon, North-East (Mr. Congdon) on 11 May 1995, *Official Report*, column 564–65.

### Spain

**Mr. Steen:** To ask the Secretary of State for the Environment how much subsidy has been given to Spain in each of the last three years from the European Community, for the environment; and what is the forecast of funding to Spain for each of the next three years. [24683]

**Sir Paul Beresford:** The main sources of Community funding for the environment are the structural and cohesion funds, various research programmes and the LIFE grant fund. The information the department has available is as follows. More detailed information will be available from the European Commission.

a) The Structural Funds: allocations for environmental protection and improvement projects—

Objective 1—1730m ecu for 1994–99 (£1437m)

Objective 2—39.5m ecu for 1994–96 (£32.8m)

Objective 5(b)—Spain has been allocated 664m ecu in total at 1994 prices (£551.5m) for 1994–99. Some of this may be allocated to environmental projects, but we do not have details.

*b) The Cohesion Fund*

| | Total (ecu) | Millions<br>Environment (ecu)[1] |
|---|---|---|
| 1993 | 858.45 (£713.0) | 252.08 (£209.37 |
| 1994 | 962.5 (£799.4) | 385 (£319.8) |
| 1995 | 1100 (£913.6) | 440 (£365,4) |
| 1996 | 1,237.5 (£1,027.8) | 495 (£411.1) |
| 1997 | 1,375 (£1,142.0) | 550 (£456.8) |
| 1998 | 1,402.5 (£1,164.9) | 561 (£465.9) |

[1] There are no guidelines for the breakdown of the Fund between environment and transport projects. Estimates for 1994 onwards are based on the Commission's division of 40 per cent. transport and 60 per cent. environment.

*(c) LIFE (Financial Instrument for the Environment)—grants awarded to Spanish projects*

| | |
|---|---|
| 1991–93 | 26 million ecu (£21.6 million) |
| 1994 | 16 million ecu (£13.3 million) |
| 1995–97 | expected range 12–15 million ecu each year (£10–12.5 million) |

*Note:*
Conversion rate used: £1 = 1.204 ecu.

### Air Pollution, London

**Ms Glenda Jackson:** To ask the Secretary of State for the Environment what additional measures he has taken to monitor air pollution in London; and if he will make a statement. [23304]

**Mr. Atkins:** The Government propose to bring forward by a year completion of their current programme of enhanced urban network sites. Suitable locations for a further nine stations will be installed by the end of 1996, two of which will be in London. Additionally, the Government will seek to integrate three further centrally-funded sites and around 35 local authority sites by the end of 1997. My officials are in contact with the Association of London Government and the South East Institute of public health, which co-ordinate the London air quality monitoring network.

### Local Government, Berkshire

**Mr. Berry:** To ask the Secretary of State for the Environment whether he has consulted the Chancellor of the Exchequer about the administrative costs of his proposals for local government reorganisation in Berkshire. [24529]

**Mr. Curry:** Government decisions are collective.

**Mr. Berry:** To ask the Secretary of State for the Environment what estimate he has made of the additional administrative staff required by the six proposed unitary authorities in Berkshire. [24530]

**Mr. Curry:** Staffing structures will be a matter for the newly elected councils.

**Mr. Berry:** To ask the Secretary of State for the Environment if he will make a statement on his proposals for the allocation of standard spending assessments to the proposed new unitary authorities in Berkshire. [24531]

**Mr. Curry:** The standard spending assessments for the new unitary authorities in Berkshire will be calculated on the basis of the services which these authorities provide, using the formulae which are applied to all relevant authorities.

Details of the formulae for 1995–96 are set out in the publication "Standard Spending Assessment handbook, 1995–96" which is available from the Library. Following the review work which we undertake each year with the local authority associations, we will publish our proposals for 1996–97 in the usual way in December.

### Local Government, Reading

**Mr. Berry:** To ask the Secretary of State for the Environment whether he is considering alterations to the boundary of Reading in connection with his proposal that Reading borough council should become a unitary authority. [24528]

**Mr. Curry:** I have accepted the Local Government Commission's final recommendation that Reading should be a unitary authority on existing borough boundaries.

## Urban Development Corporations

**Mr. Nigel Evans:** To ask the Secretary of State for the Environment if he has considered the future of the Birmingham Heartlands and Trafford Park development corporations; and if he will make a statement. [24918]

**Mr. Curry:** Following representations made by each urban development corporation, I have decided to extend their lifetimes for an additional year to 31 March 1998.

In this extra year, they aim between them to secure some 11,000 additional jobs, build 250 homes and attract about £100 million of private sector investment. They will not be given any additional grant in aid, but will be financed from receipts and by European funding.

For Birmingham Heartlands, the extra year will allow the corporation to oversee the complete redevelopment of the "Star Site" near the M6, as well as the adjacent "String of Pearls" sites.

In Trafford Park, the corporation has already assembled and prepared many sites and attracted over 700 companies into the area; it will now be able to increase yet further the level of inward investment and jobs through marketing all the remaining development opportunities.

The UDC programme will end as planned in March 1998 when all corporations will have been wound up.

## Energy Efficiency

**Mr. Peter Ainsworth:** To ask the Secretary of State for the Environment what progress has been made by Government Departments towards the target of improving energy efficiency by 15 per cent. in the five years ending in March 1996. [25184]

**Mr. Robert B. Jones:** The progress of the Departments during 1993–94 is shown in the tables and footnotes. Overall, a 6 per cent. improvement has been achieved which, in the light of increasing demands for energy, represents good progress. I am pleased to note that the performance of my Department shows a 9 per cent. improvement against the standard indicator, with far greater improvements on reducing $CO_2$ emissions.

Energy management in individual Government Departments is a matter for Ministers responsible for those Departments. The Energy Efficiency Office of my Department provides information on good practice and monitors progress towards the target.

*Table 1: Government Estate: Energy Efficiency Performance*

| Civil Departments, Including Agencies | Energy Expenditure 1993–94 £ million | Own investment in Energy Efficiency 1993–94 £ million | Percentage Reduction Relative to 1990–91 | | | | | | Total $CO_2$ Adjusted for weather correction | | |
|---|---|---|---|---|---|---|---|---|---|---|---|
| | | | Energy Cost ("£/sq m") Adjusted for estate changes and weather correction | | | Carbon Dioxide ("$CO_2$/sqm") Adjusted for estate changes and weather correction | | | | | |
| | | | 1991–92 | 1992–93 | 1993–94 | 1991–92 | 1992–93 | 1993–94 | 1991–92 | 1992–93 | 1993–94 |
| MAFF | 2.5 | 0.631 | 0 | 3 | −5 | 3 | 8 | 2 | 4 | 4 | 5 |
| MAFF—Laboratories | 1.5 | — | −12 | −19 | −24 | −5 | −9 | −14 | −12 | −22 | −28 |
| MAFF—Depots | 0.1 | — | 0 | 20 | 12 | 3 | 24 | 19 | 3 | 23 | 34 |
| Cabinet Office | 0.5 | 0.074 | −14 | 0 | 5 | −6 | 5 | 16 | −19 | −9 | 4 |
| Customs and Excise | 3.8 | 0.819 | 2 | 14 | 10 | 1 | 17 | 16 | −53 | −34 | −41 |
| Education | 0.5 | 0.028 | −20 | −82 | −95 | −15 | −58 | −67 | −33 | −7 | −14 |
| Employment | 11.0 | 0.607 | −1 | −4 | −2 | 0 | 0 | 4 | −3 | −4 | 1 |
| Environment | 1.6 | 0.165 | 3 | 5 | 9 | 5 | 9 | 22 | 3 | 13 | 22 |
| Environment—QEII CC | 0.5 | — | −17 | −16 | −14 | −14 | −11 | −8 | −14 | −11 | −8 |
| FCO | 0.6 | 0.045 | −3 | 7 | −9 | 0 | 12 | 0 | −2 | 6 | 38 |
| Health | 1.3 | — | −13 | 0 | −98 | −9 | 4 | −70 | −48 | 0 | −76 |
| Home Office | 2.5 | — | −8 | −8 | −8 | −6 | −3 | −2 | −6 | −3 | −2 |
| Home Office— Prisons | 26.1 | 1.500 | 2 | −4 | −3 | 4 | 3 | 7 | −4 | −6 | −6 |
| Inland Revenue | 13.5 | 1.146 | 1 | 3 | 7 | 3 | 8 | 13 | 0 | 6 | 15 |
| Lord Chancellors' Department | 6.4 | — | 3 | 6 | 11 | 4 | 11 | 17 | −10 | −4 | −1 |
| ODA | 0.7 | 0.017 | n/a | −4 | 0 | n/a | 0 | 5 | n/a | −1 | 4 |
| National Heritage | 0.0 | — | — | — | — | 0 | 0 | 0 | 0 | 0 | 0 |
| National Savings | 1.2 | 0.027 | 3 | 9 | 12 | 6 | 12 | 16 | 6 | 13 | 17 |
| Northern Ireland Office | 9.3 | 0.802 | 7 | 6 | 8 | 8 | 9 | 10 | 4 | 3 | 6 |
| Scottish Office | 1.6 | 0.231 | n/a | −4 | −7 | n/a | −1 | −1 | n/a | 1 | 3 |
| Scottish Courts | 1.1 | 0.080 | n/a | 4 | 9 | n/a | 7 | 13 | n/a | −5 | −1 |
| Scottish Prisons | 3.2 | 0.238 | 0 | 1 | 5 | 2 | 4 | 10 | 0 | 1 | 6 |
| Social Security | 16.1 | 0.657 | −6 | 0 | −2 | −3 | 6 | 7 | −3 | −9 | −8 |
| Trade and Industry | 5.4 | — | 5 | 5 | 0 | 10 | 12 | 9 | 11 | 20 | 19 |
| Transport | 3.5 | 0.359 | 7 | 8 | 12 | 10 | 13 | 19 | 10 | 13 | 22 |
| Treasury | 0.3 | 0.003 | 8 | 4 | −9 | 12 | 10 | 1 | 14 | 33 | 32 |
| Welsh Office | 0.5 | 0.104 | 1 | 2 | 2 | 2 | 7 | 9 | 3 | 18 | 26 |
| Total | 115.4 | 7.533 | 0.6 | 0.4 | 0.3 | 3 | 6 | 8 | −2 | −1 | 1 |

*Notes:*

1. Progress against each performance indicator (PI) is expressed as a percentage relative to the base year (1990–91) value of the PI in question. The standard indicator is weather—corrected consumption, adjusted for estate changes, and converted to costs at fixed prices (Energy Cost). For the civil estate, estate changes are allowed for by dividing by floor area. For the defence estate, a different procedure is used (see notes to table 2 below). The target is to achieve a 15 per cent. improvement against this indicator by March 1996. Positive figures represent progress, negative figures represent regress.

2. The Energy Cost ($£/m^2$) figure is obtained by weather correcting the energy consumption per unit floor area, and converting to costs using "standard" fuel prices (6p/kWh for electricity and 1.25p/kWh for all fossil fuels). This conversion to money was done to reflect the relative costs of electricity and fossil fuels,

and also their relative environmental impact. Fixed prices eliminate the effects of tariff changes, which distort the comparison of annual bills. Normalising by floor area helps overcome problems of changing estate size.

3. The average performance figure for the civil estate cannot be obtained simply by adding together the individual Departmental progress figures and dividing by the number of Departments. This does not allow for the large variations in total consumption. The correct figure can be obtained by calculating the value of the PI for the civil estate as a whole (eg total $CO_2$ divided by total area), then calculating the reduction relative to the base year value.

4. Some Departments have revised earlier years' figures, which explains some differences from previously published results. Equally, some of this year's figures may be subject to revision.

5. Investment figures relate only to clearly identifiable energy efficiency measures undertaken by Departments. Energy efficiency is also an integral part of all major construction projects, including building refurbishment and plant replacement carried out by Departments. However, separating out the energy efficiency component is not always meaningful; for example, a well designed energy efficient new building may actually cost the same or less than a conventional one.

6. Electricity generated on site, eg Combined Heat and Power, is not included under "electricity": but the input fuel to the generator is, of course, included. This therefore accords appropriate credit for CHP. Heating from the Whitehall District Heating Scheme is included.

7. All departments have greatly increased their use of Information Technology, but have not been allowed to offset the increased use of electricity as a result.

8. Expenditure on energy and investment figures are included for information only and do not form part of the Government estate target.

9. MAFF: Main Estate—Energy consumption has risen, as a result of a large increase in the use of Information Technology and business led demands of Agencies.

10. MAFF: Laboratories—Energy consumption has increased as a result of business led demand, and recent legislation which has required a number of old buildings to be replaced with air-conditioned buildings. Own investment in energy efficiency is included with MAFF Main Estate.

11. Customs and Excise: Progress figures partly reflect a widening of the basis for measurement as the Department overcomes problems with the collation of data. Operational changes have allowed greater use of buildings where Customs and Excise control the energy use instead of paying an energy-inclusive charge; this process is continuing and may affect future figures.

12. Education: Consumption is dominated by its headquarters building. This changed from a largely naturally ventilated building in the base year to a completely air-conditioned one, with a much smaller floor area, in 1991–92. This is the explanation for the large increase against the PI since 1992–93.

13. Environment: QEII Conference Centre is reported separately because of its business led demands.

14. Health: Consumption is dominated by its headquarters building. Since the base year this has changed from a largely naturally ventilated building to a fully air-conditioned one, explaining the large increase against the PI.

15. Home Office Prisons: Improved accommodation standards for prisoners are leading to increases in energy consumption.

16. ODA: Base year is 1991–92.

17. National Heritage: Newly formed in 1992 and moved to its own accommodation in 1993. Full year figures are not therefore available.

18. Scottish Office: Base year is 1991–92.

19. Scottish Courts: Base year is 1991–92.

20. Scottish Prisons: Improved accommodation standards for prisoners are leading to increases in energy consumption.

21. Social Security: DSS workload is increasing, affecting occupancy and offices are occupied for longer hours, increasing the use of energy. Electricity consumption has increased as a result of greater demands on the use of Information Technology, expansion in the use of air-conditioning and the upgrading of lighting levels. For example, electricity consumption has increased by 8 per cent. in the Benefits Agency, by 2 per cent. in ITSA, and by 125 per cent. in the CSA: CSA shows an exceptional increase because of the phased occupancy of buildings between 1992 and 1993 prior to full operation in 1993–94.

*Table 2: Government Estate: Energy Efficiency Performance*

| Ministry of Defence | Percentage Reduction for 1993–94 Relative to 1990–91 | | | |
| | Column 1 Energy Consumption | Column 2 Energy Cost | Column 3 Carbon Dioxide | Column 4 Total $CO_2$ Adjusted for Weather Correction |
| | Adjusted for Estate Changes and Weather Correction | | | |
| Civil | 11 | 7 | 12 | 0 |
| Navy | 11 | 14 | 17 | 5 |
| Army | 8 | 8 | 12 | 12 |
| RAF | 10 | 6 | 11 | 19 |
| Procurement Executive | 27 | 18 | 25 | 25 |
| Defence Research Agency | n/a | n/a | n/a | n/a |
| Total | 10 | 9 | 13 | 13 |

*Notes:*

1. The MOD estate is different in nature from the rest of the Government estate, and has been undergoing more radical changes. It is therefore treated in a slightly different way. In common with other Departments, the MOD has greatly increased its reliance on Information Technology, but in many areas, no allowance has been made for the resulting increases in electricity usage. Full data for years between 1990–91 and 1993–94 are not available, so the table shows a comparison between these two years. Positive figures denote progress, negative ones regress.

2. Floor area data cannot be calculated for the majority of the MOD estate. However, to allow comparisons with data from other Departments adjusted for changes in floor area, a proxy has been used. The figures in columns 1 to 3 have been adjusted by estimating changes in consumption resulting from buildings being added to, or leaving, the estate and making an appropriate adjustment to the gross data for years following the change.

3. Column 1 shows changes, after estate adjustments (see above) and weather correction, in energy consumption. This has been the primary measure used by MOD in its efforts to increase energy efficiency.

4. Column 2 shows changes, after estate adjustments and weather correction, in energy cost at "standard" fuel prices calculated in the same way as the civil estate.

5. Column 3 shows changes, after estate adjustments and weather correction, in carbon dioxide emissions.

6. Column 4 shows changes in total carbon dioxide emissions, after weather correction.

*Table 3: Government estate: energy efficiency performance*

| Entire government estate | Per cent. reduction for 1993–94 relative to 1990–91 | | |
| | Energy cost Adjusted for estate changes and weather correction | Carbon dioxide Adjusted for estate changes and weather correction | Total $CO_2$ Adjusted for weather correction |
| Civil departments, including agencies | 0.3 | 8 | 1 |
| Ministry of defence | 9 | 13 | 13 |
| Total | 6 | 11 | 9 |

*Notes:*

1. This shows combined results for the whole of the Government estate based on the data in tables 1 and 2. It is not a simple average of the two, but reflects the proportion of total consumption represented by each part of the estate (see third note to table 1). The Ministry of Defence is the major user of energy on the Government estate, using some 70 per cent. of the energy consumed.

## SCOTLAND

### Forestry

**Mr. Tipping:** To ask the Secretary of State for Scotland how many hectares of Forestry Commission woodlands will be disposed of between now and 2000 in *(a)* England, *(b)* Wales and *(c)* Scotland; and what is the anticipated income from these sales. [23403]

**Sir Hector Monro:** As announced in the Government's expenditure plans 1995–96 to 1997–98, the Forestry Commission plans to sell 15,000 hectares of forest land in Britain in each of the next three years, and to receive some £60 million from the sale of forests and surplus properties. The proportion that will be sold in each of the three countries will depend on the state of the market, but the Commission estimates that around 70 per cent. will be sold in Scotland and 15 per cent. each in England and Wales. As yet, no firm plans have been made for sales in subsequent years.

## Unemployment

**Dr. Godman:** To ask the Secretary of State for Scotland what is his estimate of the number of *(a)* men and *(b)* women aged 40 years and over who are out of work.     [23376]

**Mr. Kynoch** *[holding answer 15 May 1995]:* In Scotland, in January 1995, there were 55,166 males and 15,717 females aged 40 or over who were unemployed.

## Sheltered Housing

**Mr. McMaster:** To ask the Secretary of State for Scotland if he will commission a study to assess the need for sheltered housing to allow people who have grown elderly in peripheral housing schemes and rural areas to remain within their own communities; and if he will make a statement.     [24101]

**Lord James Douglas-Hamilton:** The assessment of demand for sheltered housing is a matter for local housing authorities, working in partnership, as appropriate, with Scottish Homes, housing associations and other housing agencies. This assessment should take into account whether elderly people wish to remain within their communities, and what type of provision is appropriate in local circumstances.

## Judiciary

**Mr. McMaster:** To ask the Secretary of State for Scotland what are the requirements and qualifications for appointment to the judiciary in Scotland; and if he will make a statement.     [24097]

**Lord James Douglas-Hamilton:** The minimum qualifications for appointment to the judiciary in Scotland are set down in a number of statutes, most particularly the Act of Union 1707, the Sheriff Courts (Scotland) Act 1971, the Law Reform (Miscellaneous Provisions) (Scotland) Act 1990, and the Courts and Legal Services Act 1990.

## Free School Meals

**Mr. McMaster:** To ask the Secretary of State for Scotland what was the percentage of pupils entitled to free school meals in each year since 1975 until the latest year for which figures are available in each Scottish region; and if he will make a statement.     [24063]

**Lord James Douglas-Hamilton:** Information on entitlement to free school meals has been collected in the annual January census of school meals since 1989. The available information is given in the table:

*Percentage of pupils on the registers of education authority schools entitled to free meals, at January*

| Education authority | 1989 | 1990 | 1991 | 1992 | ¹1993 | 1994 |
|---|---|---|---|---|---|---|
| Borders | 4.1 | 4.1 | 5.0 | 5.6 | 5.6 | 5.6 |
| Central | 15.7 | 15.6 | 15.7 | 18.4 | 17.7 | 18.6 |
| Dumfries and Galloway | 9.6 | 9.9 | 9.3 | 9.7 | 10.5 | 10.5 |
| Fife | 14.2 | 14.0 | 14.1 | 15.7 | 16.5 | 17.2 |
| Grampian | 6.3 | 5.8 | 6.3 | 6.7 | 7.4 | 7.5 |
| Highland | 12.3 | 10.7 | 10.8 | 11.5 | 12.2 | 14.1 |
| Lothian | 14.7 | 17.7 | 18.5 | 19.0 | 20.8 | 20.7 |
| Strathclyde | 22.1 | 22.0 | 22.3 | 23.7 | 25.4 | 25.6 |
| Tayside | 14.1 | 13.7 | 13.5 | 13.3 | 13.2 | 13.8 |
| Orkney | 8.1 | 6.1 | 6.6 | 7.5 | 7.0 | 7.8 |
| Shetland | 4.1 | 3.8 | 4.3 | 5.6 | 6.2 | 6.2 |
| Western Isles | 17.5 | 14.3 | 14.1 | 13.7 | 14.0 | 12.3 |
| Scotland | 16.8 | 16.9 | 17.2 | 18.2 | 19.3 | 19.7 |

## Industrial Development Advisory Board

**Mr. Wray:** To ask the Secretary of State for Scotland if he will instruct the Scottish Industrial Development advisory board to lay annual reports before Parliament.     [24191]

**Mr. Kynoch** *[holding answer 15 May 1995]:* Sections 11 and 15 of the Industrial Development Act 1982 require an annual report to be laid before Parliament on the exercise of powers under the Act during the year: this is presented jointly by the Secretaries of State for Trade and Industry, for Scotland and for Wales. The report contains commentaries by the Industrial Development advisory boards, including one from the chairman of the Scottish Industrial development advisory board.

## Close Circuit Television

**Mr. McMaster:** To ask the Secretary of State for Scotland if he will now support and contribute towards the introduction of closed circuit television in Paisley: and if he will make a statement.     [24070]

**Lord James Douglas-Hamilton:** The Government remain firmly of the view that funding for the installation of CCTV in Scotland should continue to be provided by joint ventures involving local businesses, local authorities and other groups who derive a direct benefit from the resource. I am glad to hear that a tender has been accepted to provide a CCTV system in Paisley, with substantial public-sector funding.

## Emergency Planning

**Mrs. Ray Michie:** To ask the Secretary of State for Scotland what measures he has taken to ensure that emergency planning teams will be adequately financed and staffed in future years; and if he will make a statement.     [24264]

**Lord James Douglas-Hamilton:** Civil defence grant will continue to be paid to local authorities, police forces and fire brigades, in support of planning which is aimed at developing an effective response to a wide range of emergencies, irrespective of their cause.

The grant is seen as a contribution towards emergency planning and its current total level is expected to be maintained.

**Mrs. Ray Michie:** To ask the Secretary of State for Scotland what consultations he has had with the emergency planning teams to discuss the effects of local government reorganisation. [24265]

**Lord James Douglas-Hamilton:** The Scottish Office wrote to chief executives, offering to discuss emergency planning arrangements in a revised local government structure, in April 1994. This offer was not accepted at the time due to the position of the Convention of Scottish Local Authorities with regard to the then Local Government etc. (Scotland) Bill.

Since the convention's position was relaxed, officials have discussed the matter with regional emergency planning officers in December and will again do so in early June. They have also met representatives of chief executives in February and numerous discussions have taken place at local level during emergency co-ordinating group meetings and various seminars.

**Mrs. Ray Michie:** To ask the Secretary of State for Scotland what measures he has taken to ensure that emergency planning is maintained after the completion of local government reorganisation. [24263]

**Lord James Douglas-Hamilton:** Each of the new authorities will be responsible for civil defence and civil emergency planning arrangements. It is up to each to decide how its responsibilities will be delivered, and there are various powers under local government legislation, including section 58 of the Local Government etc. (Scotland) Act 1994, which provide scope for joint arrangements or other options to be considered. Grant to local authorities, police forces and fire brigades will continue.

**Dr. Godman:** To ask the Secretary of State for Scotland if he will list the names of those persons selected to be the chief executives of the new unitary councils giving their academic and technical qualifications where appropriate and their current employment and employers; and if he will make a statement. [23035]

**Mr. Kynoch** *[holding answer 16 May 1995]:* The appointment of chief executives—strictly speaking heads of paid service—is entirely a matter for the new councils. Information on appointments made to date is given in the table.

*New unitary authorities—appointments of head of paid service*

| New council | Head of paid service | Current position |
|---|---|---|
| Aberdeen, City of | Not yet appointed | — |
| Aberdeenshire | Alan Campbell | Chief Executive, Grampian Regional Council |
| Angus | Sandy Watson | Chief Executive, Tayside Regional Council |
| Argyll and Bute | James McLellan | Director of Administration, Argyll and Bute District Council |
| Borders, The | Alistair Croall | Depute Chief Executive, Borders Regional Council |
| Clackmannan | Robert Allan | Chief Executive, Clackmannan District Council |
| Dumbarton and Clydebank | Not yet appointed | — |
| Dumfries and Galloway | Ian Smith | Chief Executive, Dumfries and Galloway Regional Council |
| Dundee, City of | Alex Stephen | Chief Executive, City of Dundee District Council |
| East Ayrshire | Not yet appointed | — |
| East Dumbartonshire | Cornelius Mallon | Chief Executive, Strathkelvin District Council |
| East Lothian | John Lindsay | Depute Chief Executive and Director of Finance, East Lothian District Council |
| East Renfrewshire | Peter Daniels | Chief Executive, Clydesdale District Council |
| Edinburgh, City of | Tom Aitchison | Chief Executive, Lothian Regional Council |
| Falkirk | Walter Weir | Chief Executive, Falkirk District Council |
| Fife | Dr. John Markland | Chief Executive, Fife Regional Council |
| Glasgow, City of | John Anderson | Depute Chief Executive, Strathclyde Regional Council |
| Highland | Arthur McCourt | Assistant Chief Executive, Tayside Regional Council |
| Inverclyde | Graeme Bettison | Senior Depute Director of Administration, Grampian Regional Council |
| Midlothian | Trevor Muir | Chief Executive, Midlothian District Council |
| Moray | Anthony Connell | Deputy Chief Executive and Director of Administration, Grampian Regional Council |
| North Ayrshire | Bernard Devine | Chief Executive, Cunninghame District Council |
| North Lanarkshire | Andrew Cowe | Managing Director, Renfrew District Council |
| Perthshire and Kinross | Harry Robertson | Chief Executive, Perth and Kinross District Council |
| Renfrewshire | Not yet appointed | — |
| South Ayrshire | George Thorley | Assistant Chief Executive, Strathclyde Regional Council |
| South Lanarkshire | Alastair J. H. MacNish | Depute Director of Social Work, Strathclyde Regional Council |
| Stirling | Keith Yates | Assistant Chief Executive, Central Regional Council |
| West Lothian | Alex Linkston | Chief Executive and Director of Finance, West Lothian District Council |

*Source:* Local Government Staff Commission.

## Suicides

**Mr. Martyn Jones:** To ask the Secretary of State for Scotland what is the most recent available percentage suicide rate for employed 18 to 65-year-olds in Scotland. [24554]

**Lord James Douglas-Hamilton:** The information requested is not available. When a death is registered the registrar obtains information on the last known occupation of the deceased but not on whether he or she was employed at the time of death.

## Planning Inquiries

**Mr. Menzies Campbell:** To ask the Secretary of State for Scotland on how many occasions in the last 10 years for which information is available part-time reporters from outside Scotland have been appointed to conduct planning inquiries. [24542]

**Mr. Kynoch:** None. In April of this year, however, as a temporary measure, five recently retired planning inspectors from the Department of Environment were added to the list of part-time reporters on whom the Secretary of State could call to determine planning appeals submitted under the Town and Country Planning (Scotland) Act 1972. The small number of appeals which have been allocated to the planning inspectors have all been for determination under the written submissions procedure. No public local inquiry appeals have been allocated to these additional reporters.

**Mr. Menzies Campbell:** To ask the Secretary of State for Scotland what is the remuneration of, and what are the rates of expenses paid to, part-time reporters when they conduct planning inquiries. [24544]

**Mr. Kynoch:** The information requested is set out in table:

|  | £ |
| --- | --- |
| Daily Fee | 130.00 |
| Hourly Rate | 17.96 |
| 24 Hour Subsistence | 62.40 |
| Day Subsistence |  |
| Over 5 hours | 4.25 |
| Over 10 hours | 9.30 |

**Mr. Menzies Campbell:** To ask the Secretary of State for Scotland what consideration he gives to proficiency in Scots law when appointing part-time reporters in planning inquiries. [24539]

**Mr. Kynoch:** When making new appointments to the list of part-time reporters, careful consideration is given to the suitability of the candidate. A working knowledge of Scottish planning law, and in particular, development control procedures, is one of the main pre-requisites for appointment. Newly appointed reporters receive induction training and supporting documents, and advice is available on points of law.

**Mr. Menzies Campbell:** To ask the Secretary of State for Scotland if he will list the number of planning inquiries conducted by part-time reporters in the last 10 years for which information is available. [24540]

**Mr. Kynoch:** This information is not recorded.

**Mr. Menzies Campbell:** To ask the Secretary of State for Scotland if he will list the names and qualifications of all part-time reporters who have conducted planning inquiries in the last 10 years for which information is available. [24541]

**Mr. Kynoch:** This information is not recorded.

**Mr. Menzies Campbell:** To ask the Secretary of State for Scotland if he will publish a list of part-time reporters from which appointments are made to conduct planning inquiries. [24543]

**Mr. Kynoch:** The information requested is as follows:

A.G. Bell CB BL
D. Connelly
Miss. E. B. Haran MA BD MRTPI
J. H. Fullerton ARIAS DipTP
G. Pease DipArch DipTP RIBA MRTPI ARIAS
J. M. Webster FRICS MBIM
D. R. Penman ARIAS FRTPI
J. F. Rankin MA LLB
G. Kirkbride Eur Ing FICE FBIM Ceng FIHE ASIArb
M. O'Carroll DipPhil MRTPI
D. C. Price BArch MCD RIBA MRTPI ARIAS

## WALES

### Foxes

**Mr. McMaster:** To ask the Secretary of State for Wales how many fox destruction clubs or societies are registered in Wales; what is the level of assistance they currently receive; what guidelines he issues on how these clubs and societies destroy foxes; what guidelines he issues on the numbers of foxes to be destroyed; how the fox population is assessed; and if he will make a statement. [24127]

**Mr. Gwilym Jones:** There is no requirement for fox destruction clubs or societies to be registered with the Welsh Office and no financial assistance is provided to such organisations. Responsibility for the control of foxes rests with individual owners and occupiers to whom advice is provided through ADAS on request.

### Female Employment

**Mr. Barry Jones:** To ask the Secretary of State for Wales what is his estimate of the number of women employed in Alyn and Deeside, Clwyd, and Wales *(a)* full-time and *(b)* part-time; and what measures he proposes to get the long-term unemployed back to work. [24194]

**Mr. Redwood:** The latest available information on the number of female employees in Alyn and Deeside is from the 1991 census of employment. This, together with the comparable data for Clwyd and Wales, is given in the following table:

*Female employees in employment—September 1991*

|  | Thousands | |
| --- | --- | --- |
|  | Full-time | Part-time |
| Alyn and Deeside district | 6.5 | 4.5 |
| Clwyd | 34.5 | 31.3 |
| Wales | 250.2 | 220.1 |

The Government's policies are aimed at creating the right economic conditions for success—low inflation, sound public finances, markets that work properly, and a minimal regulatory and tax burden on business. That recipe is promoting sustained economic growth.

The training and enterprise councils and the Employment Service provide a wide range of measures to help the long-term unemployed back into work. They include the training for work programme, restart, the job interview guarantee scheme, Workstart and community action.

### Employment (Young People)

**Mr. Barry Jones:** To ask the Secretary of State for Wales what special measures he will adopt to give employment to young people. [24196]

**Mr. Redwood:** Our policies aim to create the right economic conditions for success; low inflation, sound public finances; markets that work properly; and a minimal regulatory and tax burden on business. That recipe is promoting sustained economic growth and higher living standards, from which all age groups will benefit.

Good education and training and sound careers advice are fundamental to a young person's employment prospects. My plan to raise achievement, strengthen standards and widen choice and opportunity is set out in "People and Prosperity: an Agenda for Action", which was published on 20 March 1995.

### Minority Languages

**Mr. Roy Hughes:** To ask the Secretary of State for Wales, pursuant to his answer of 7 March to the hon. Member for Meirionnydd Nant Conwy (Mr. Llwyd), *Official Report*, column *152*, when Government Departments with an interest in the Council of Europe charter for regional or minority languages will have completed their consideration of its implications; and if he will make a statement. [24754]

**Mr. Gwilym Jones:** The decision whether to sign the charter raises a number of different issues, each of which we must consider fully.

### NORTHERN IRELAND

### Housing Executive

**Mr. McGrady:** To ask the Secretary of State for Northern Ireland what consultations have taken place about the amalgamation of the two Housing Executive offices in Newry and the reduced opening hours for the Kilkeel office; and if he will make a statement. [24041]

**Mr. Moss:** This is a matter for the Northern Ireland Housing Executive, but the chief executive has advised me that consultations have taken place with staff and their representatives, the Northern Ireland Public Service Alliance, on the proposed amalgamation of Newry 1 and Newry 2 district offices. In addition, Housing executive officials will consult with Newry and Mourne district council on 7 June 1995.

The Housing Executive's regional director has discussed with local councillors the reduced opening

hours for the Kilkeel office. A new sub-office will be opening in nearby Annalong in the late summer to coincide with the reduced working hours in the Kilkeel office.

### NATIONAL HERITAGE

### Churchill Papers

**Mr. Kaufman:** To ask the Secretary of State for National Heritage what plans he had made to take action to preserve the Churchill papers intact for the nation before the National Heritage Memorial Fund decided to make national lottery funds available for this purpose. [23693]

**Mr. Dorrell:** The Government had commenced proceedings in the High Court with the object of preserving the papers intact for the nation.

**Mr. Gordon Prentice:** To ask the Secretary of State for National Heritage who assessed the historical significance of each of the items in the Churchill papers. [23178]

**Mr. Dorrell:** Following its normal procedures, the NHMF took advice on the content of the archive from the British Library and the Royal Commission on Historical Manuscripts as statutory heritage agencies. Individual historians and other relevant institutions were also consulted.

### Cinemas

**Mr. MacShane:** To ask the Secretary of State for National Heritage which listed buildings in England are used as cinemas. [23537]

**Mr. Dorrell:** The use of listed cinemas can change, and listed buildings built for another purpose may subsequently have been converted into cinemas. My Department does not monitor such changes. However, English Heritage has provided the following details of listed buildings which it believes are currently used as cinemas:

*Pre-1916 Cinemas*
Electric, King's Quay Street, Harwich
Scala, Market Place, Ilkeston
Picture House, Bridge Street, Stafford
Picture Playhouse, Market Place, Beverley
Dome, Worthing
Gem, ex-Palace of Light, Great Yarmouth
Windsor, Broadstairs
King Edward, Blackpool
Torbay Picture Palace, Paignton
Carlton, Westgate
Duke of York's, Brighton
Electric, Portobello Road, Kensington, London[1]
Ritzy, Brixton, London
Cameo/Poly, Upper Regent Street, Westminster, London
*1919–28*
Apollo, Dock Street, Blackburn
MGM Magdalene Street, Oxford
Plaza, Lower Regent Street, Westminster, London
New Gallery, Regent Street, Westminster, London
*1928–40*
Gaumont, (now Odeon), Salisbury
Cannon, Lime Street, Liverpool
Gaumont/Astor, Barnstaple

Embassy (now Cannon), Esher

Odeon, Faversham

Dreamland, Merged

Odeon, Northgate Street, Chester

Odeon, Blackpool

Odeon, East Parade, Harrogate

Odeon, Blossom Street, York

Odeon, Great North Road, Barnet, London

Odeon, (now Coronet), Parson's Hill, Woolwich, London

Odeon, (now Coronet), Well Hall Road, Greenwich, London

Odeon, Fortis Green Road, Muswell Hill, Haringey, London

Granada (now Cannon), Sheepcote Lane, Harrow, London

Granada/Options, Richmond Road, Kingston upon Thames, London

Richmond (now Odeon), Hill Street, Richmond, London

Granada/Cannon, Hoe Street, Walthamstow, London

¹Listed Grade II; all others listed Grade II

### Cockpit Theatre

**Mr. Corbyn:** To ask the Secretary of State for National Heritage what his Department's plans are for the Cockpit theatre, London NW8; what representations he has received regarding the future of the theatre; and if he will make a statement.        [24494]

**Mr. Dorrell** *[holding answer 16 May 1995]:* The Cockpit theatre is owned by the City of Westminster college, and has been made available for the use of the Soho Theatre Company. I have received one representation about the future of the Soho Theatre Company at the Cockpit theatre. That, however, is entirely a matter for negotiation between the company and the college.

### Windsor Castle

**Mrs. Clwyd:** To ask the Secretary of State for National Heritage if he will make a statement on the responsibilities of his Department's fire, health and safety branch following the Windsor castle fire.        [24671]

**Mr. Sproat** *[holding answer 16 May 1995]:* My Department's branch which deals with fire, health and safety is responsible for precautions in the Department's own offices. It does not bear responsibility for premises occupied by other bodies which the Department sponsors or for which it provides funds. For the occupied royal palaces which are funded by the grant in aid these responsibilities lie with the royal household's own fire and safety branch which was strengthened in accordance with the recommendations of the Bailey report.

**Mrs. Clwyd:** To ask the Secretary of State for National Heritage what is the total cost of repair of the fire damage at Windsor castle; if he will list the *(a)* sources and *(b)* amounts of the contributions to the cost of the repairs; and when he expects the work to be completed.        [24672]

**Mr. Sproat** *[holding answer 16 May 1995]:* It is currently estimated that the total cost of the repair of the fire damage at Windsor Castle will be about £35 million, including fees and VAT. Some £24.5 million of the cost will be met from the opening of Buckingham palace and charging for entry to the Windsor castle precincts, with the balance of £10.5 million from the grant in aid allocation for the maintenance of the occupied royal palaces. The work is progressing well and is expected to be completed to schedule by mid-1998.

### Royal Palaces

**Mrs. Clwyd:** To ask the Secretary of State for National Heritage if a full inventory now exists of what is owned by the state in all royal palaces.        [24670]

**Mr. Sproat** *[holding answer 16 May 1995]:* The royal collection is responsible for works of art and other items held by the Crown on behalf of the nation. The royal household is completing an inventory of these items which is scheduled for completion by the end of 1997. For other items such as office furniture, computers, vehicles and so on inventories are currently maintained.

### London Film Commission

**Mr. Soley:** To ask the Secretary of State for National Heritage whether he intends to support the London Film Commission initiative.        [23691]

**Mr. Dorrell:** My Department has consistently supported the efforts by the British Film Commission and the London Film Commission initiative to establish a film commission for London.

### Play Areas (Safety)

**Mr. McMaster:** To ask the Secretary of State for National Heritage what guidelines he has issued to local authorities to encourage the provision of safety surfacing on play areas; what special financial provision he has made available to local authorities to encourage and enable them to meet this need; and if he will make a statement.        [24089]

**Mr. Sproat:** In January 1992, the joint publication "Playground Safety Guidelines" was issued by the Department of Education and Science, the Welsh Office and the National Children's Play and Recreation Unit. This publication provides guidance to playground providers and managers on play safety issues, including safety surfacing, and was sent to all local authorities in England. The publication was updated and reprinted in 1993.

No specific provision is made within the standard spending assessment for the funding of play areas, although provision for services for children is included within the education and social services assessment, and for recreation within the general services assessment.

### Rugby League

**Mr. Pendry:** To ask the Secretary of State for National Heritage if he has *(a)* requested or *(b)* examined a copy of the proposed contract between News International and the Rugby Football League with regard to the sport's television coverage.        [24137]

**Mr. Dorrell:** No. Contracts for the television coverage of sport or any other subject are entirely a matter between rights holders and broadcasters.

### Sport

**Mr. Pendry:** To ask the Secretary of State for National Heritage when he intends to publish his Department's White Paper on sport.        [24139]

**Mr. Sproat:** We intend to publish the sport policy statement early in the summer.

## SOCIAL SECURITY

### Severe Disability Premium

**Mr. Gareth Wardell:** To ask the Secretary of State for Social Security on what date he petitioned the House of Lords for leave to appeal against the decision of the Court of Appeal in the Bate case, regarding eligibility for payment of the severe disability premium.    [24018]

**Mr. Roger Evans:** The petition was lodged on 9 January 1995.

### Expatriate Pensioners

**Mr. David Nicholson:** To ask the Secretary of State for Social Security, pursuant to his answer of 4 May, *Official Report*, columns *307-8*, what is the total number of United Kingdom expatriates receiving uprated United Kingdom pensions in *(a)* Spain and *(b)* Portugal; which Government pay the cost of these upratings; and what considerations underlie the different treatment of pensioners in those two countries and in the four Commonwealth countries referred to in his answer.    [24286]

**Mr. Arbuthnot:** In January 1995, UK pensions were in payment to 28,097 beneficiaries in Spain and 3,208 in Portugal. The entire cost of these pensions is met by the UK Government. Uprated pensions became payable in Spain in April 1975, and in Portugal in October 1979, by virtue of reciprocal social security agreements with those countries. Since 1 January 1986, uprated UK pensions have been payable in Spain and Portugal under the EC regulations on social security for migrant workers. The UK has no similar agreements with the four Commonwealth countries referred to in my previous reply.

### Occupational Injuries Report

**Mr. Ottaway:** To ask the Secretary of State for Social Security if he has received reports on the Industrial Injuries Advisory Council's investigations into hand arm vibration syndrome, disorders of the knee and occupational rhinitis; and if he will make a statement.

[24843]

**Mr. Hague:** My right hon. Friend the Secretary of State for Social Security has today laid copies of the council's reports before Parliament—Cm 2842, 2843, and 2844. We shall give them careful consideration and respond to the council's recommendations once the medical, administrative and financial issues raised by the reports have been examined.

### Child Support Agency

**Mr. Duncan:** To ask the Secretary of State for Social Security when he expects the Government to publish their response to the Third Report of the Select Committee on the Parliamentary Commissioner for Administration published on 20 March about the Child Support Agency.

[24945]

**Mr. Burt:** The Government's response is set out in "The Child Support Agency—Reply by the Government to the Third Report of the Select Committee on the Parliamentary Commissioner Session 1994–95", Cm2865, published today.

### Benefits Agency Nursery, Brixton

**Mr. McNamara:** To ask the Secretary of State for Social Security what plans he has to visit St. Paul's Angels Benefits Agency nursery, Brixton, before its proposed closure.    [24708]

**Mr. Roger Evans:** My right hon. Friend the Secretary of State has no such plans.

### Mortgage Interest

**Ms Armstrong:** To ask the Secretary of State for Social Security how many people received assistance with mortgage interest payments in each year since 1990; and what is the current average level of assistance, by standard economic region.    [23028]

**Mr. Roger Evans** *[holding answer 9 May 1995]:* The information is set out in the table. This shows the numbers of cases and average amount of mortgage interest considered in the assessment of each year since 1990, broken down by region and whether half or full mortgage interest was in payment at the time of the inquiry.

*Source:*

Income Support Statistics Annual Enquiries, May 1990–1993
Income Support Statistics Quarterly Enquiry, May 1994.

*Notes:*

1. Numbers of cases have been rounded to the nearest thousand. Average amounts are correct to the nearest penny.
2. The regions shown are those which have been used, historically, for social security purposes and are identified by an area code which is given to each claim.

*Income support recipients with mortgage interest considered in their assessment*

| | All cases | | Cases with half mortgage interest | | Cases with full mortgage interest | |
| --- | --- | --- | --- | --- | --- | --- |
| | Number of cases | Average MI considered per week £ | Number of cases | Average MI considered per week £ | Number of cases | Average MI considered per week £ |
| *1990:* | | | | | | |
| Great Britain | 310,000 | 34.33 | 40,000 | 33.70 | 270,000 | 34.43 |
| North Eastern | 45,000 | 23.25 | 7,000 | 19.32 | 38,000 | 24.03 |
| London North | 51,000 | 48.12 | 7,000 | 48.17 | 45,000 | 48.11 |
| South Western | 25,000 | 39.05 | 3,000 | 28.64 | 28,000 | 40.34 |
| Wales | 26,000 | 23.58 | 2,000 | 26.90 | 24,000 | 23.31 |
| Midlands | 52,000 | 25.47 | 6,000 | 24.72 | 46,000 | 25.57 |
| North Western | 50,000 | 25.33 | 8,000 | 26.58 | 42,000 | 25.11 |
| Scotland | 14,000 | 32.64 | 2,000 | 41.72 | 12,000 | 31.19 |
| London South | 47,000 | 52.98 | 6,000 | 57.39 | 41,000 | 52.38 |

*Income support recipients with mortgage interest considered in their assessment*

| | All cases | | Cases with half mortgage interest | | Cases with full mortgage interest | |
| | Number of cases | Average MI considered per week £ | Number of cases | Average MI considered per week £ | Number of cases | Average MI considered per week £ |
|---|---|---|---|---|---|---|
| *1991:* | | | | | | |
| Great Britain | 411,000 | 44.41 | 74,000 | 35.61 | 337,000 | 46.34 |
| North Eastern | 52,000 | 29.91 | 9,000 | 20.53 | 43,000 | 31.86 |
| London North | 80,000 | 59.43 | 17,000 | 43.44 | 63,000 | 63.80 |
| South Western | 40,000 | 51.30 | 7,000 | 39.07 | 33,000 | 64.08 |
| Wales | 27,000 | 34.80 | 4,000 | 26.62 | 24,000 | 36.02 |
| Midlands | 69,000 | 35.30 | 12,000 | 31.95 | 57,000 | 36.02 |
| North Western | 58,000 | 28.38 | 7,000 | 22.64 | 51,000 | 29.20 |
| Scotland | 18,000 | 35.33 | 4,000 | 24.69 | 14,000 | 37.99 |
| London South | 67,000 | 63.51 | 14,000 | 49.22 | 53,000 | 67.21 |
| *1992:* | | | | | | |
| Great Britain | 499,000 | 44.02 | 64,000 | 30.59 | 435,000 | 46.01 |
| North Eastern | 60,000 | 29.93 | 7,000 | 21.35 | 52,000 | 31.13 |
| London North | 100,000 | 60.72 | 15,000 | 39.93 | 86,000 | 64.29 |
| South Western | 52,000 | 48.30 | 6,000 | 31.25 | 46,000 | 60.50 |
| Wales | 34,000 | 33.67 | 3,000 | 21.47 | 31,000 | 34.78 |
| Midlands | 80,000 | 33.31 | 10,000 | 22.43 | 70,000 | 34.91 |
| North Western | 68,000 | 27.34 | 8,000 | 24.10 | 60,000 | 27.78 |
| Scotland | 19,000 | 32.59 | 3,000 | 21.49 | 16,000 | 34.50 |
| London South | 87,000 | 61.34 | 13,000 | 39.63 | 74,000 | 64.99 |
| *1993:* | | | | | | |
| Great Britain | 555,000 | 42.18 | 55,000 | 22.76 | 500,000 | 44.31 |
| North Eastern | 69,000 | 26.34 | 8,000 | 15.71 | 60,000 | 22.76 |
| London North | 112,000 | 57.82 | 11,000 | 29.29 | 101,000 | 60.92 |
| South Western | 53,000 | 45.64 | 5,000 | 26.25 | 48,000 | 47.70 |
| Wales | 34,000 | 29.63 | 3,000 | 17.39 | 31,000 | 30.70 |
| Midlands | 89,000 | 32.93 | 8,000 | 18.89 | 81,000 | 34.39 |
| North Western | 73,000 | 27.27 | 7,000 | 16.92 | 66,000 | 28.30 |
| Scotland | 22,000 | 27.99 | 3,000 | 16.46 | 19,000 | 29.81 |
| London South | 103,000 | 59.70 | 10,000 | 29.90 | 93,000 | 62.94 |
| *1994:* | | | | | | |
| Great Britain | 529,000 | 38.18 | 42,000 | 20.87 | 487,000 | 39.69 |
| North Eastern | 68,000 | 25.30 | 7,000 | 16.18 | 61,000 | 26.35 |
| London North | 105,000 | 51.65 | 8,000 | 28.33 | 97,000 | 53.66 |
| South Western | 48,000 | 40.69 | 3,000 | 21.33 | 45,000 | 42.01 |
| Wales | 33,000 | 27.45 | 2,000 | 15.55 | 32,000 | 28.17 |
| Midlands | 83,000 | 29.87 | 6,000 | 17.56 | 77,000 | 30.90 |
| North Western | 70,000 | 26.05 | 6,000 | 16.20 | 65,000 | 26.91 |
| Scotland | 24,000 | 26.26 | 3,000 | 16.00 | 21,000 | 27.78 |
| London South | 97,000 | 54.09 | 7,000 | 27.31 | 89,000 | 56.21 |

### Benefit Statistics

**Ms Harman:** To ask the Secretary of State for Social Security (1) if he will list, for the last available year, the total amount of expenditure on *(a)* income support, *(b)* housing benefit, *(c)* council tax benefit and *(d)* family credit given to (i) families containing one or more adults in work and (ii) people in work with no dependants, expressing the data by benefit office area; [23318]

(2) if he will list, for the last available year, the total amount of expenditure on *(a)* income support, *(b)* housing benefit, *(c)* council tax benefit and *(d)* family credit given to (i) families containing one or more adults in work and (ii) people in work with no dependants, expressing the data by region; [23319]

(3) if he will list the number of *(a)* families containing one or more adults in work and *(b)* people in work with no dependants receiving (i) income support, (ii) housing benefit, (iii) council tax benefit and (iv) family credit, expressing the data by (i) region and (ii) benefit office area for the latest year possible for which figures are available. [23648]

**Mr. Hague** *[holding answer 10 May 1995]:* Information cannot be provided in the precise form requested. No information is available for benefit office areas and information for family credit is available only for social security administrative regions. The available information is shown in the tables:

*Income–related benefit recipients and expenditure by standard statistical region*

| | North | | | York and Humberside | | | East Midlands | | | East Anglia | | | South East (ex London) | | |
|---|---|---|---|---|---|---|---|---|---|---|---|---|---|---|---|
| | IS | HB | CTB | IS | HB | CTB | IS | HB | CTB | IS | HB | CTB | IS | HB | CTB |
| Families in work in receipt (000s) | 11 | 21 | 25 | 11 | 18 | 27 | 10 | 15 | 22 | 5 | 9 | 12 | 23 | 36 | 41 |
| Estimated expenditure (£ million) | 38 | 29 | 8 | 41 | 20 | 7 | 35 | 21 | 6 | 15 | 15 | 3 | 99 | 74 | 12 |
| Number of recipients in work without dependants (000s) | 6 | 11 | 16 | 7 | 10 | 15 | 5 | 9 | 15 | 2 | 7 | 7 | 11 | 25 | 25 |
| Estimated expenditure (£ million) | 12 | 13 | 5 | 12 | 13 | 4 | 8 | 13 | 4 | 4 | 8 | 2 | 29 | 41 | 7 |

| | London (Inner and Outer) | | | South West | | | West Midlands | | |
|---|---|---|---|---|---|---|---|---|---|
| | IS | HB | CTB | IS | HB | CTB | IS | HB | CTB |
| Families in work in receipt (000s) | 10 | 33 | 26 | 13 | 19 | 23 | 12 | 19 | 21 |
| Estimated expenditure (£ million) | 37 | 75 | 9 | 55 | 32 | 7 | 48 | 26 | 6 |
| Number of recipients in work without dependants (000s) | 5 | 21 | 12 | 8 | 12 | 16 | 7 | 13 | 19 |
| Estimated expenditure (£ million) | 8 | 43 | 4 | 21 | 20 | 5 | 14 | 16 | 5 |

| | North West | | | Wales | | | Scotland | | |
|---|---|---|---|---|---|---|---|---|---|
| | IS | HB | CTB | IS | HB | CTB | IS | HB | CTB |
| Families in work in receipt (000s) | 16 | 30 | 45 | 8 | 14 | 12 | 8 | 25 | 25 |
| Estimated expenditure (£ million) | 56 | 41 | 13 | 32 | 21 | 2 | 24 | 29 | 6 |
| Number of recipients in work without dependants (000s) | 8 | 19 | 28 | 4 | 6 | 7 | 6 | 17 | 15 |
| Estimated expenditure (£ million) | 14 | 23 | 7 | 11 | 7 | 1 | 10 | 19 | 4 |

*Family credit recipients and expenditure by social security administrative region*

| | North Eastern FC | London North FC | South Western FC | Wales FC | Midlands FC | North Western FC | Scotland FC | London South FC |
|---|---|---|---|---|---|---|---|---|
| Families in work in receipt (000s) | 89 | 57 | 37 | 31 | 89 | 79 | 57 | 50 |
| Estimated expenditure (£ million) | 204 | 127 | 82 | 70 | 196 | 187 | 128 | 106 |

*Source:*
Housing Benefit Management Information Systems. 1 per cent. sample May 1993.
Income Support Statistics Annual Enquiry May 1993.
Family Credit Statistics Quarterly Enquiry May 1993.
*Notes:*
1. Recipients have been rounded to the nearest thousand, expenditure to the nearest £ million.
2. "People" has been interpreted to mean singles or couples with no dependants, and "families" as singles or couples with dependants.
3. Estimated annual expenditure is the total number of recipients multiplied by the average weekly award multiplied by 52 weeks.

# HEALTH

## Cancer Treatment

**Mrs. Bridget Prentice:** To ask the Secretary of State for Health in which NHS hospitals high dose marrow ablative chemotherapy with autologous bone marrow rescue is available.     [23147]

**Mr. Sackville:** This information is not available centrally.

It is for clinicians to decide upon the most appropriate form of treatment for each individual patient.

**Mrs. Bridget Prentice:** To ask the Secretary of State for Health (1) how many specialists in NHS hospitals have dealt with the condition known as PNET; how many of these are paediatric specialists; and what has been the success rate in each case;     [23149]

(2) how many specialists in NHS hospitals have dealt with the condition known as glioblastoma multiforme;

how many of these are paediatric specialists; and what has been the success rate in each case; [22148]

(3) how many paediatric centres in the United Kingdom currently use high-dose chemotherapy with bone marrow rescue in the treatment of children with malignant brain tumours; [23146]

(4) how many specialists in NHS hospitals have dealt with the condition known as Li Fraumeni syndrome; how many of these are paediatric specialists; and what has been the success rate in each case. [23150]

**Mr. Sackville:** This information is not available centrally.

However, this is an area where doctors are taking a strong lead in auditing the process and outcome of their care. The United Kingdom children cancer study group, which recently met Department of Health officials, registers cases of childhood cancers treated by its members and acts as an organisation for promoting professional standards in the field of paediatric oncology. Childhood tumours are fortunately uncommon, and some types are rare. The UKCCSG is therefore planning a service to help doctors find the best place to treat rare childhood tumours.

The recent report of the chief medical officer's expert advisory group on cancer recommends increasing specialisation and sub-specialisation in cancer to enhance outcomes.

### Hospitals

**Mrs. Beckett:** To ask the Secretary of State for Health (1) if she will list each hospital closure referred to the Secretary of State in the last 16 years; [23597]

2) how many hospitals closures were referred to the Secretary of State for approval due to community health council objection in each year since 1979; and what was the decision of the Secretary of State in each case. [23596]

**Mr. Malone:** I refer the right hon. Member to the reply I gave her on 18 April, column *120* for a list of proposed closures and changes of use considered by Ministers following community health council objection for the period from January 1992 to December 1994. Information before this could be provided only at disproportionate cost. Ministers approved all the proposals except the proposed closure of Ponteland and Lemington hospitals, Newcastle.

**Mrs. Beckett:** To ask the Secretary of State for Health if she will provide official figures for the number of hospitals opened and closed since 1 April 1991. [23593]

**Mr. Malone:** This information is not available centrally.

**Mrs. Beckett:** To ask the Secretary of State for Health on what date her approval ceased to be required for opening or closing a hospital. [23595]

**Mr. Malone:** Ministerial approval has never been required for the opening of a hospital. Ministers continue to make final decisions on closures when they are contested by the local community health council.

**Mrs. Beckett:** To ask the Secretary of State for Health (1) on what date the decision not to collect information centrally on hospital closures and openings was made; and if she will make a statement; [23591]

(2) if she will consider reintroducing centrally held information on hospital closures and openings including size, type and location of the hospital in question. [23592]

**Mr. Malone:** The collection of information centrally on hospital closures ceased during 1991. Information on hospital openings has never been collected centrally. We have no plans to change these arrangements.

**Mrs. Beckett:** To ask the Secretary of State for Health how many hospitals there were in England by region and in total on 1 April. [23598]

**Mr. Malone:** Information on the number of hospitals in England is not available for 1 April 1995. For previous years I refer the right hon. Member to the reply I gave her on 16 May, columns *173–76*.

**Mrs. Beckett:** To ask the Secretary of State for Health what information is provided to her Department by regional health authorities on the number of hospitals opened and closed. [23594]

**Mr. Malone:** Regional health authorities refer to Ministers only those proposals for hospital closures which are contested by the local community health council following RHA consideration.

**Mrs. Beckett:** To ask the Secretary of State for Health, pursuant to her answer of 30 March, *Official Report,* column *716,* how many hospitals provide *(a)* acute services, *(b)* maternity services, *(c)* geriatric services, *(d)* mental health services, *(e)* learning difficulty services and *(f)* specialist services, by region and by total. [22832]

**Mr. Malone** *[holding answer 9 May 1995]:* The information requested is not available centrally.

### Burnley Health Care NHS Trust

**Mr. Gordon Prentice:** To ask the Secretary of State for Health what steps were taken by the Medical Devices Agency or the former relevant authority before it to certify the safety of the probe implicated in the loss of eyes by patients at Burnley general hospital. [23856]

**Mr. Sackville:** Responsibility for the design of individual medical devices resides with the manufacturer of the device. As soon as the problem was identified, Burnley Health Care NHS trust notified the manufacturers and the Medical Devices Agency, which are issuing a hazard notice to all NHS hospitals.

### Criminal Records

**Dr. Lynne Jones:** To ask the Secretary of State for Health if she will make it her policy that a criminal record should play no part in the assessment of medical needs NHS patients. [23854]

**Mr. Bowis:** It would do so only if information about criminal activity was essential in order to decide on the type or location, of care to be provided for a particular condition.

### Human Rights

**Sir Richard Body:** To ask the Secretary of State for Health if it is her policy to accept the provisional recommendations made by the Council of Europe on human rights in its document 1235/1994. [23712]

**Mr. Bowis:** A Government response will be made once final recommendations are formally adopted and published by the Council of Europe.

## Dental Services

**Ms Walley:** To ask the Secretary of State for Health how she plans to develop the role of the community dental service.    [24405]

**Mr. Malone:** The Department of Health circular (89)2 provides guidance for health authorities and sets out the role of the community dental service. This circular is available in the Library. We intend to open discussions with the joint negotiating forum, comprising health departments, the Central Committee for Community Dental Services, and health authorities to consider the present role of the community dental service and to provide revised guidance. The guidance will encourage health authorities to assess the need for the community dental service to act as a "safety net", and to make arrangements for services in the light of these assessments.

## Waiting Times

**Sir Irvine Patnick :** To ask the Secretary for State for Health if she will give the latest waiting list times for (*a*) in-patient and (*b*) out-patient treatment for (i) Trent region and (ii) Sheffield health authority for each of the last five years; and if she will make a statement.    [24401]

**Mr. Malone:** Information on in-patient waiting lists and times by district health authority and region in England is given in "Hospital Waiting List Statistics: England", published twice yearly, copies of which are available in the Library. Information on the waiting times of patients for out-patient assessment has been published for two quarters. In the quarter to 31 December 1994, in Trent region 85 per cent. of patients were seen within 13 weeks and 97 per cent. within 26 weeks of referral by their general practitioner. Information on performance at individual trusts will be placed in the Library once the Audit Commission has completed checks on the trusts' information systems.

## Suicides

**Mr. Martyn Jones:** To ask the Secretary of State for Health what is the most recent available percentage suicide rate for employed 18 to 65 years old in England.    [24553]

**Mr. Bowis:** Information on the number of unemployed people who have committed suicide is not available. At death registration, informants are asked for the last occupation rather than the employment status of the deceased.

## Local Government Reorganisation

**Mr. Berry:** To ask the Secretary of State for Health (1) what assessment she has made of the implications for her community care policy of the absence of private old people's homes in Slough, given the proposal that Slough borough council should become a unitary authority;    [24533]

(2) if she will make a statement on the potential effect on children on the children protection register when Berkshire is divided into six unitary authorities;    [24535]

(3) if she will make a statement on the likely effects on social services provision of the proposed division of Berkshire into six unitary authorities.    [24536]

**Mr. Bowis:** All new unitary authorities will be responsible for deciding how their statutory responsibilities for personal social services can best be discharged. On 12 May, the Department issued an advice document to local authorities entitled "Social Services: Maintaining Standards in A Changing World" under cover of local authority social services letter (95)5. Copies of the advice document are available in the Library. It draws attention to the special features of social services which the new authorities will need to consider if they are to deliver those services effectively to people who need them.

## Prescriptions

**Mr. Battle:** To ask the Secretary of State for Health how many NHS prescriptions for the treatment of epilepsy were dispensed in each of the last five years for which figures are available; and how many of those prescriptions were for products that were licensed (*a*) within the last five years, (*b*) more than 10 years ago and (*c*) more than 20 years ago.    [22840]

**Mr. Malone** [*holding answer 11 May 1995*]: The available information will be placed in the Library.

# AGRICULTURE, FISHERIES AND FOOD

## Fisheries

**Mr. Austin Mitchell:** To ask the Minister of Agriculture, Fisheries and Food (1) if his common fisheries policy review group will be enabled to visit Canada, Iceland or Norway to report on the advantages and disadvantages of national control of national fishing waters;    [23991]

(2) how many members of the review group on the common fisheries policy have been or are in receipt of research grants from his Department or from EEC sources; and if he will list the grants and projects involved;    [23987]

(3) if he will instruct his common fisheries policy review group to make its first priority to report on the financial viability of the English fishing industry;    [23989]

(4) if he will indicate the geographical base of each member of his review group on the common fisheries policy.    [23988]

**Mr. Jack:** I do not intend to dictate to the group what it should or should not discuss, provided that any discussion is about ways of improving the CFP. I am sure there are lessons to be learnt from management regimes operated outside the EU, although I do not anticipate that any foreign visits will be necessary.

Group members' places of residence are:

Mr. Goodland: Shetland isles

Professor McIntyre: Aberdeen

Mr. Thomas: Hull

Dr. Gubbay: Ross-on-Wye

Dr. Cunningham: Portsmouth

Dr Cooke: Brixham

Members of the group involved in research activities may well be associated with organisations which receive grants from this Department or from EC sources.

However, we have no records of members of the group personally receiving research grants from the Department or from EC sources.

**Mr. Brazier:** To ask the Minister of Agriculture, Fisheries and Food how many fishermen *(a)* not belonging to and *(b)* belonging to producer organisations have been prosecuted for illegal catches of fish since 1 January 1990.    [24538]

**Mr. Jack:** Information about illegal catches by sector and non-sector fishermen in the form requested is not readily available. However, I refer my hon. Friend to the answers given to the hon. Member for Pembroke (Mr. Ainger) on 28 and 31 March, *Official Report,* columns *626* and *848* respectively.

### Trading Standards Services Berkshire

**Mr. Berry:** To ask the Minister of Agriculture Fisheries and Food what assessment he has made of the applicability of the views attributed to his Department on pages 42 and 43 of "Renewing of Local Government in the English shires" to the future of the trading standards service after the proposed division of Berkshire into six unitary authorities.    [24548]

**Mrs. Browing:** I hold to our views expressed in the Local Government Commission report, but I accept that the issues of enforcement of food law by trading standards officers were not the only issues that the commission had to consider in making its recommendations on local government re-organisation in Berkshire. Now that it has been agreed what form the reorganisation will take, I am considering what advice on this topic it may be necessary for us to give to the successor authorities.

### Bananas

**Mr. Steen:** To ask the Minister of Agriculture, Fisheries and Food if he will make a statement about the Government's position with regard to the European Community's proposal on bananas.    [24679]

**Mr. Jack:** The Commission has proposed a number of changes to the EU bananas regime. These take account of the accession of the three new member states, make proper provision for response to natural disasters in the production areas, provide for quota transferability amongst African, Caribbean and Pacific suppliers, simplify the arrangements for allocating import licences and remove fig bananas from the scope of the regime.

The Government welcome the proposed improvements in the provisions relating to ACP suppliers. On licence allocation, it will press for simplification of the rules but without undermining existing incentives for wide participation in the development of trade in ACP fruit.

### Lamb Exports

**Mr. Steen:** To ask the Minister of Agriculture, Fisheries and Food what estimate he has as to how many kilos of English lamb exported to France is sold annually in France labelled as French lamb.    [24684]

**Mr. Jack:** I have no reason to believe that any English or other UK lamb exported to France in the form of meat is ever sold labelled as French lamb.

Meat from live sheep exported from the UK to France may be sold labelled as "freshly killed" or "home killed" lamb, but not as French lamb.

### Fish Farms, Salisbury

**Mr. Key:** To ask the Minister of Agriculture, Fisheries and Food how many fish farm sites are located within the boundaries of Salisbury district council.    [24545]

**Mr. Jack:** There are currently 11 fish farm sites registered within the Salisbury postal district area.

### Spain

**Mr. Steen:** To ask the Minister of Agriculture, Fisheries and Food how much subsidy has been given to Spain in each of the last three years from the European Community for agriculture; and what is the forecast of funding to Spain for the next three years.    [24680]

**Mr. Jack:** Receipts by Spain of funds from both the guarantee section, which funds the common agricultural policy, and the guidance section, which funds structural measures in the agricultural sector, of the European agricultural guidance and guarantee fund for the last three years are shown in the table below. The EAGGF guarantee section expenditure contains a small element in respect of fisheries market support.

*Payments to Spain for agriculture from the EC Budget*

|      | CAP (EAGGF guarantee section) | | (of which fisheries market support) | | EAGGF guidance section (agriculture) | |
| --- | --- | --- | --- | --- | --- | --- |
|      | mecu | £ million | mecu | £ million | mecu | £ million |
| 1992 | 3,579 | 2,533 | (12) | (8) | 557 | 394 |
| 1993 | 4,326 | 3,401 | (10) | (8) | 387 | 304 |
| 1994 | 4,255 | 3,287 | (10) | (8) | n/a | n/a |

*Conversion rates:* 1992 £1 = 1.4131 ecu; 1993 £1 = 1.2718 ecu; 1994 £1 = 1.2945 ecu
*Sources:*
CAP - 1992 and 1993 : EAGGF guarantee section annual financial reports; 1994: Commission working document; EAGGF guidance section - annual reports of the European Court of Auditors

With regard to future expenditure, the CAP budget is drawn up only a year in advance, and is set in relation to forecast expenditure throughout the Community, and not on the basis of allocations to individual member states. With regard to agricultural structures, Spain has been allocated 3,640 mecu or £3,023 million from the EAGGF guidance section, under objective 1 and objective 5a for the period 1994–1999. The allocation to Spain under objective 5b—rural development—for the same period is 664 mecu or £551 millions derived from the EAGGF guidance section, European regional development fund and the European social fund combined. A breakdown of the amount to be funded from the EAGGF guidance section alone is not available.

## HOME DEPARTMENT

### Criminal Injuries Compensation

**Mr. Straw:** To ask the Secretary of State for the Home Department (1) how many claims for dependency due to fatal injuries were made for criminal injuries compensation under the common law scheme between April 1993 and April 1994; and how many resulted in an award;                                                    [23772]

(2) what was the highest award made by the Criminal Injuries Compensation Board for psychiatric injury in cases determined under the common law scheme before April 1994;                                                    [23769]

(3) how many criminal injuries compensation cases decided under the common law scheme between April 1993 and April 1994 involved injuries to the dominant hand or arm;                                                    [23773]

(4) what was the highest criminal injuries compensation award made to a child under the common law scheme between April 1993 and April 1994;                    [23765]

(5) how many criminal injuries compensation awards involving fatal injuries were dealt with under the common law scheme between April 1993 and April 1994; and what was the highest award;                                     [23767]

(6) what was the highest criminal injuries compensation award for scarring injuries made under the common law scheme between April 1993 and April 1994;        [23774]

(7) how many fatal criminal injuries compensation cases decided under the tariff scheme would have resulted in a dependency award under the common law scheme;                                                    [23755]

(8) how many criminal injuries compensation cases were determined under the common law scheme in relation to children under 18 years between April 1993 and April 1994;                                                    [23764]

(9) what was the average criminal injuries compensation award made to a victim of child sexual abuse under the common law scheme between April 1993 and April 1994.                                                    [23766]

**Mr. Maclean:** This information is not recorded centrally.

**Mr. Straw:** To ask the Secretary of State for the Home Department how many criminal injuries compensation cases were accepted under the common law scheme between April 1993 and April 1994 which had been lodged out of time; and how many cases were rejected under the common law scheme between April 1993 and April 1994 *(a)* for being out of time and *(b)* under eligibility rules.                                                    [23776]

**Mr. Maclean:** In the year to 31 March 1994, the board received 3,704 out of time applications. In addition, 164 cases were carried forward from 1992–93. At 31 March 1994 the position was:

|                          | Numbers |
|--------------------------|--------:|
| Under consideration      | 356     |
| Accepted                 | 2,715   |
| Refused                  | 766     |
| Abandoned by applicant   | 31      |

Reasons for refusal are not recorded centrally.

**Mr. Straw:** To ask the Secretary of State for the Home Department how many claims for criminal injuries compensation were lodged for consideration under the common law scheme between April 1993 and April 1994; how many were rejected under eligibility rules; and how many resulted in an interim award under the common law scheme.                                                    [23771]

**Mr. Maclean:** In the year ending 31 March 1994, the board received 73,473 applications. Some 23,933 cases were rejected, and interim awards were made in 6,492 cases. The latter two figures include cases received before 1993–94.

**Mr. Straw:** To ask the Secretary of State for the Home Department how many criminal injuries compensation cases were pursued by way of appeal to a member level panel under the common law scheme between April 1993 and April 1994; and how many were successfully appealed.                                                    [23775]

**Mr. Maclean:** The available information is that the board received 15,192 appeals and made 4,094 monetary awards following appeal.

**Mr. Straw:** To ask the Secretary of State for the Home Department if he will list, for each tariff band, the *(a)* longest, *(b)* shortest and *(c)* average periods for an application for criminal injuries compensation to be determined under the tariff scheme;                    [23740]

(2) what was the average length of time to determine an application for criminal injuries compensation under the tariff scheme during the first year of its operation.                                                    [23758]

**Mr. Maclean:** All offers of award made under the tariff scheme will be honoured without prejudice to reassessment under the reinstated—1990—scheme. Applicants have three months in which to accept or reject an offer. The information requested will not therefore be available until at least three months after the last offers were made.

**Mr. Straw:** To ask the Secretary of State for the Home Department (1) how many awards for criminal injuries compensation have been made under the tariff scheme involving *(a)* combination awards for multiple injuries and *(b)* injuries not specified within the tariff of injuries;                                                    [23741]

(2) what have been the highest and lowest awards for criminal injuries compensation under the tariff scheme for an injury not specified within the tariff of injuries; and what were the injuries involved in each case.        [23742]

**Mr. Maclean:** Six hundred and forty-one awards have been offered and accepted in cases involving more than one injury. No awards were made in respect of injuries not specified in the tariff.

**Mr. Jack Straw:** To ask the Secretary of State for the Home Department (1) how many criminal injuries compensation cases involving sexual violence have been determined under the tariff scheme;                    [23743]

(2) how many reviews were lodged under the tariff scheme for criminal injuries compensation against initial determination;                                                    [23756]

(3) what was the average award for criminal injuries compensation under the common law scheme between April 1993 and April 1994;                                     [23777]

(4) how many criminal injuries compensation claimants have received interim payments under the tariff scheme;                                                    [23753]

(5) how many fatal criminal injuries compensation cases have been decided under the tariff scheme; [23754]

(6) what was the highest award made under the common law criminal injuries compensation scheme between April 1993 and April 1994; [23768]

(7) how many awards for criminal injuries compensation were decided under the common law scheme between April 1993 and April 1994. [23778]

**Mr. Maclean:** The answer is 690, 2,918, £4,064, 66, 54, £1,148, 760 and 40,635 respectively.

**Mr. Straw:** To ask the Secretary of State for the Home Department what was *(a)* the average award, *(b)* the highest award and *(c)* the lowest award made in criminal injuries compensation cases involving sexual violence determined under the tariff scheme. [23744]

**Mr. Maclean:** The answer is £4,613, £17,500 and £1,00 respectively.

**Mr. Straw:** To ask the Secretary of State for the Home Department what was *(a)* the average award, *(b)* the highest award and *(c)* the lowest award made under the tariff scheme for criminal injuries compensation involving psychiatric injury. [23745]

**Mr. Maclean:** This answer is £2,791, £20,000 and £1,000 respectively.

**Mr. Straw:** To ask the Secretary of State for the Home Department how many criminal injuries compensation cases determined under the tariff scheme involved *(a)* paralysis of all four limbs, *(b)* paralysis of the lower limbs, *(c)* hemiplegia, *(d)* serious brain damage and *(e)* brain damage with serious impairment. [23746]

**Mr. Maclean:** One award was made in respect of paralysis of all four limbs. No determinations were made in respect of the other categories.

**Mr. Straw:** To ask the Secretary of State for the Home Department how many criminal injuries compensation cases provisionally decided under the tariff scheme are expected to result in a higher award when reconsidered under the common law scheme. [23747]

**Mr. Maclean:** Based on assessments made when the tariff scheme was introduced, 40 per cent. of awards provisionally made might be expected to have been the same as, or less than, awards which would have been made under the scheme based on common law damages and as such to result in higher awards when reconsidered. It should be noted, however, that the provisional awards made are likely to have been typical since, because of the priority which was given to clearing the outstanding cases lodged before 1 April 1994 and the way in which the work was organised, the cases which were settled under the tariff scheme included a high proportion of nil awards.

**Mr. Straw:** To ask the Secretary of State for the Home Department how many criminal injuries compensation cases outstanding under the common law scheme were decided between April 1993 and April 1994. [23748]

**Mr. Maclean:** In the year ending 31 March 1994, the board resolved 65,293 cases.

**Mr. Straw:** To ask the Secretary of State for the Home Department how many criminal injuries compensation claims on behalf of children under the age of 18 years were *(a)* lodged and *(b)* determined under the tariff scheme between April 1994 and April 1995. [23759]

**Mr. Maclean:** Some 12,086 applications were received. Compensation was paid in 1,006 cases.

**Mr. Straw:** To ask the Secretary of State for the Home Department how many child victims of sexual abuse lodged applications for criminal injuries compensation between April 1994 and April 1995; and how many have been determined. [23761]

**Mr. Maclean:** Information about the number of such applications is not recorded. Compensation was paid in 225 cases involving child victims of sexual abuse.

**Mr. Straw:** To ask the Secretary of State for the Home Department (1) what were the administrative costs of the Criminal Injuries Compensation Authority between April 1994 and April 1995; [23763]

(2) what is the estimated administrative cost of dealing with the consequences of the House of Lords decision on the criminal injuries compensation scheme; and how much additional criminal injuries compensation he estimates will have to be paid as a result of the decision in respect of cases lodged between April 1994 and April 1995; [23749]

(3) what was the cost of setting up the Criminal Injuries Compensation Authority. [23762]

**Mr. Maclean:** I would refer the hon. Member to the answers given to the hon. Member for Hornsey and Wood Green (Mrs. Roche) on 25 November 1994, *Official Report*, column *446*, and 26 April, *Official Report*, column *561*.

The additional cost of compensation arising in respect of cases lodged in the year ending 31 March 1995 is likely to be in the order of £85 million.

**Mr. Straw:** To ask the Secretary of State for the Home Department what assessment he has made of the time it will take to reassess those criminal injuries compensation cases previously decided under the tariff scheme, in the light of the House of Lords ruling. [23770]

**Mr. Maclean:** I would refer the hon. Member to the answer given to the hon. Member for Hornsey and Wood Green (Mrs. Roche) on 1 May, *Official Report*, column *92*.

**Mr. Straw:** To ask the Secretary of State for the Home Department what was the average length of time for determining criminal injuries compensation cases under the common law scheme between April 1993 and April 1994; and what was the average award. [23985]

**Mr. Maclean:** The board does not record information about the average length of time for determining cases, although paragraphs 3.11 and 3.12 of its 30th annual report do give some information on the subject. The average award was £4,064.

**Mr. Straw:** To ask the Secretary of State for the Home Department how many criminal injuries compensation claims lodged between April 1994 and April 1995 and not determined under the tariff scheme involve *(a)* fatal injuries, *(b)* injuries sustained in sexual attack, *(c)* paraplegia, *(d)* quadriplegia, *(e)* hemiplegia, *(f)* serious brain damage and *(g)* brain damage resulting in serious impairment. [23750]

**Mr. Maclean:** Some 1,192 cases involving fatal injuries were awaiting initial determination. Information on the other categories is not available.

**Mr. Straw:** To ask the Secretary of State for the Home Department how many criminal injuries compensation claims between April 1994 and April 1995 were *(a)* lodged under the tariff scheme, *(b)* decided under the tariff scheme, *(c)* accepted for eligibility under the tariff scheme, *(d)* rejected for eligibility under the tariff scheme, *(e)* rejected for eligibility under the tariff scheme which would have been eligible under the common law scheme. [23751]

**Mr. Maclean:** The available information is that in the year ending 31 March 1995, 66,387 cases were registered under the tariff scheme. Some 4,891 monetary awards were offered, and 11,076 cases were rejected or received "nil" awards. There is no information as to how many of the cases rejected under the tariff scheme would have been eligible under the common law scheme.

**Mr. Straw:** To ask the Secretary of State for the Home Department how many criminal injuries compensation cases have been decided under the tariff scheme, by tariff band. [23752]

**Mr. Maclean:** The breakdown of awards offered in the year ending 31 March 1995 was as follows:

| Band | Number |
|------|--------|
| 1 | 1,160 |
| 2 | 268 |
| 3 | 1,324 |
| 4 | 76 |
| 5 | 432 |
| 6 | 153 |
| 7 | 736 |
| 8 | 170 |
| 9 | 93 |
| 10 | 72 |
| 11 | 70 |
| 12 | 244 |
| 13 | 50 |
| 14 | 2 |
| 15 | 5 |
| 16 | 24 |
| 17 | 12 |
| 18 | 5 |
| 19 | 2 |
| 25 | 1 |

**Mr. Straw:** To ask the Secretary of State for the Home Department how many criminal injuries compensation cases were *(a)* pursued by way of review to the review panel under the tariff scheme and *(b)* successfully appealed to the review panel under the tariff scheme. [23757]

**Mr. Maclean:** One hundred and twenty appeals were made to the appeals panel. The tariff scheme was withdrawn before the panel considered any cases.

**Mr. Straw:** To ask the Secretary of State for the Home Department when he plans to publish the 30th report of the Criminal Injuries Compensation Board. [23984]

**Mr. Maclean:** It was published on 11 May 1995.

**Mr. Straw:** To ask the Secretary of State for the Home Department what were the highest and lowest criminal injuries compensation awards made to children under the tariff scheme between April 1994 and April 1995. [23760]

**Mr Maclean:** The highest and lowest awards made to persons aged under 18 were £30,000 and £1,000.

### African National Congress (Bombing)

**Mr. Hain:** To ask the Secretary of State for the Home Department, pursuant to his answer of 23 February, *Official Report*, columns *330–31,* what progress has been made in police investigations of the 1982 bombing of the London offices of the African National Congress. [24457]

**Mr. Howard:** I understand that the police have now completed their review of the evidence and are considering whether there is a basis for further action in the light of Mr. Williamson's reported remarks.

### Consultants

**Mr. Roy Hughes:** To ask the Secretary of State for the Home Department what work was carried out on behalf of his Department by EDMC Management Consultants in connection with proposals to privatise the escorting of vehicles carrying abnormal loads on motorways and other roads; and at what cost. [24753]

**Mr. Maclean:** EDMC Management Consultants analysed and defined the skills and competencies which are required for the escorting of abnormal loads on motorways and linked dual carriageways. Its work included advice and recommendations regarding assessment of these competencies and on how possible to draw up a formal qualification in escorting for issue by an awarding body. It is not the Department's policy to waste the value of individual contracts, on the grounds of commercial confidentially.

### Data Protection Registrar

**Mr. Peter Atkinson:** To ask the Secretary of State for the Home Department what plans he has to review the office of the Data Protection Registrar. [25186]

**Mr. Nicholas Baker:** The next five yearly review of the office of the Data Protection Registrar will take place in 1995–96. The first stage of the review will consist of a "prior options" study. In accordance with normal practice, this will consider whether the registrar's functions still need to be performed at all—and, if they do, whether they could be privatised, contracted out, or transferred to some other body. The study will shortly begin, and I would welcome comments from interested parties. Comments should be sent by 16 June 1995 to Mr. M. Jones, Room 978, Home Office, Queen Anne's gate, London SW1H 9AT.

### Passport Agency

**Mr. Atkinson:** To ask the Secretary of State for the Home Department what performance targets he has set for the UK Passport Agency in 1995–96. [25185]

**Mr. Nicholas Baker:** During 1995–96 I shall expect the Passport Agency to continue to improve its standard of service to the public while seeking further efficiency savings in its operations.

I have set the agency the following targets:

(i) to process properly completed straightforward applications within a maximum of 15 working days between April and August 1995, 10 working days between September and February 1996 and 15 working days in March 1996.

(ii) to process such applications within an overall average of seven working days for the year as a whole, and

(iii) to reduce unit costs by a further 5 per cent. in real terms in comparison with the outturn for 1994–95.

The chief executive will remain directly accountable to me for the performance of the Passport Agency. An advisory board, including two private sector members with experience of delivering services to the public, will continue to provide me with an independent assessment of the agency's performance.

## Prisons Expenditure

**Mrs. Roche:** To ask the Secretary of State for the Home Department what proportion of the criminal justice budget has been spent on the prison service, including accommodating prisoners in police cells; and what proportion has been spent on crime prevention in each of the last 16 years. [21607]

**Mr. Howard** [*holding answer 1 May 1995*]: The full information sought is not available. The information readily available is as follows:

£ million

| | 1986–87 | 1990–91 | 1991–92 | 1992–93 | 1993–94 | 1994–95 |
|---|---|---|---|---|---|---|
| Total estimated expenditure on the criminal justice system in England and Wales[1] | 4,596 | 7,629 | 8,770 | 9,204 | 9,524 | 10,100 |
| Expenditure on prisons (including accommodating prisoners in police cells) | 697 | 1,452 | 1,586 | 1,610 | 1,507 | 1,596[2] |

[1] Figures include Home Office expenditure on prisons; Home Office and local authority expenditure on the police and probation services; Lord Chancellor's Department expenditure on criminal business related administration, court services and legal aid; and expenditure on the Crown Prosecution Service.
[2] Supply estimate figure.

One of the principal objectives of the criminal justice system is the prevention of crime. All constituent parts of the system contribute to this objective. Indeed, the Government's White Paper "Police Reform" published in June 1993, Cm 2281, listed fighting and preventing crime as a main aim of the police, who account for over half of all criminal justice expenditure. It is not possible to isolate the resources associated with the crime prevention part of the work of criminal justice agencies. Information about specific Home Office initiatives in crime prevention is set out in paragraphs 4.41 to 4.48 of the Home Office annual report 1995, Cm 2808.

## Probation Service

**Mr. Bermingham:** To ask the Secretary of State for the Home Department if he will publish the terms of the informal agreement between the European Community Commission and Her Majesty's Government on the use of the restricted procedure in procurement process for the probation service house II framework agreement. [24391]

**Mr. Nicholas Baker:** The conditions for use of the restricted procedure in the procurement process are set out in the Public Supply Contract Regulations, S.I.1991. No. 2679, a copy of which is in the Library. These conditions were complied with in the establishment of the house II— Home Office Unix systems environment—framework arrangement used to set up the agreement for probation services.

**Mr. Bermingham:** To ask the Secretary of State for the Home Department if the Treasury has been alerted to the facsimile correspondence from his Department's Mr. Lindsay Watson to Mr. Guy Lougher of Wragge and Co. on 9 February 1995; and if the questions raised about the award of the house II framework contract are factually and legally accurate. [24393]

**Mr. Nicholas Baker:** Mr. Lindsay Watson's letter of 9 February 1995 was prepared in consultation with the Treasury, who is content that the procedure under which the house II framework arrangement was awarded was in compliance with the Public Supply Contracts Regulations, S.I. 1991, No. 2679.

**Mr. Bermingham:** To ask the Secretary of State for the Home Department if the award by a probation committee or board of any contract to Bull Information Systems Ltd. under or in pursuance of the house II framework agreement will need to comply with the relevant European Procurement rules in all respects; and if it will need to be separately advertised or publicised by the said probation committee or board under those rules. [24392]

**Mr. Nicholas Baker:** Since the house II—Home Office Unix systems environment—framework arrangement was awarded in accordance with the Public Supply Contracts Regulations, there is no need to have a further competition each time a probation committee or board awards any contract to Bull Information Systems Ltd. under or in pursuance of the house II framework agreement.

**Mr. Bermingham:** To ask the Secretary of State for the Home Department if the relevant European public procurement regulations and laws in relation to the house II—Bull framework agreement—have been implemented. [24390]

**Mr. Nicholas Baker:** The house II—Home Office Unix Systems Environment—framework arrangement was awarded following a competition which complied with the Public Supply Contracts Regulations, SI 1991, No. 2679. The regulations are the mechanism by which the EC supplies directive is implemented.

## Race Relations

**Mr. Hoyle:** To ask the Secretary of State for the Home Department (1) what race relations policies the Prison Service has; and to what extent they are mandatory; [23087]

(2) what means are in place to check establishments for compliance with race relations policy; and what training is given to those who check compliance; [23088]

(3) what special arrangements the Prison Service provides for prisoners who are foreign nationals; [23089]

(4) how many prison governors have a race relations element in their contracts; and what formal race relations management training is given to prison governors; [23135]

(5) how many prisons have facilities for serving kosher or halal food; [23081]

(6) how many prison race relations management teams have a membership which includes a representative from an outside racial equality organisation; [23082]

(7) how many formal complaints on racial grounds have been received by his Department *(a)* from staff and *(b)* from prisoners in each of the last five years. [23083]

**Mr. Michael Forsyth** *[holding answer 9 May 1995]:* Responsibility for these matters has been delegated to the Director General of the Prison Service, who has been asked to arrange for a reply to be given.

*Letter from Derek Lewis to Mr. Doug Hoyle, dated 17 May 1995:*

The Home Secretary has asked me to reply to your recent Questions about race relations in the Prison Service.

The Prison Service's race relations policy is set out in its policy statement on the subject, a copy of which is attached. This states that all prisoners should be treated impartially and without discrimination on grounds of colour, race and religion. Under the policy, which is mandatory, racially insulting, abusive or derogatory language towards prisoners is not tolerated.

To check establishments are complying with race relations policy, the prison governors' standard business plan includes targets on race issues, for which governors are accountable to their area manager. Governors are also required to complete an annual race relations checklist. These checklist returns form the basis of an annual report on race relations to the Prisons Board. Additionally, annual reports of Boards of Visitors and reports of inspections by HM Chief Inspector of Prisons frequently cover race issues. No specific training for the purpose of checking compliance is given. However, some of those involved, for example, area managers and some Board of Visitors members, will have received general race relations training.

Prison governors' contracts include a race relations element and race relations issues are addressed as part of the modular training course for middle managers, including governor grades. This is delivered by the Prison Service Colleges in conjunction with Leeds Metropolitan University. Governors recruited under the Accelerated Promotion Scheme receive race relations training both as part of initial officer training and on subsequent development courses.

In 1993–94, the latest year for which figures are available, the number of prisons which could provide kosher and halal food were 119 and 117 respectively.

At present, 39 prison race relations management teams have a membership which includes a representative from an outside racial equality organisation.

Information on how many formal complaints on racial grounds have been received by the Prison Service from staff and from prisoners in each of the last five years is not available. However, analysis of the annual checklist returns shows that the number of recorded racial incidents, which includes complaints, is as follows:

| | *Staff* | *Prisoners* |
|---|---|---|
| 1990–91 | 0 | 22 |
| 1991–92 | 11 | 95 |
| 1992–93 | 20 | 121 |
| 1993–94 | 16 | 206 |
| 1994–95 | [1]— | [1]— |

[1] Information not yet available.

With regard to foreign nationals, the Prison Service has produced a Foreign Prisoners' Resource Pack, which provides information and guidance for prison staff working with foreign nationals, and the prisoners themselves. The pack is available in 12 languages and topics include awareness of foreign prisoners' needs and concerns, the criminal justice system, immigration, customs and excise, embassies, interpreting and translating. There is also a Prisoners' Information Pack which is available in 14 languages. In addition the Prison Service has given support for the Nuffield Interpreters Project to encourage accredited interpreters; and has introduced the language line telephone interpreting service into all prisons.

*Prison Service race relations policy statement*

1. The Prison Service is committed absolutely to a policy of racial equality and to the elimination of discrimination in all aspects of the work of the Prison Service. It is opposed also to any display of racial prejudice, either by word or conduct by any member of the Service in his or her dealings with any other person.

2. All prisoners should be treated with humanity and respect. All prisoners should be treated impartially and without discrimination on grounds of colour, race and religion. Insulting, abusive and derogatory language towards prisoners will not be tolerated.

3. Race relations concerns every member of the Prison Service. It is the responsibility of every member of staff to ensure that the Department's policy is carried out in relation to other members of staff as well as prisoners.

4. Members of minority religious groups have the same right to practise their faith as those of the majority faith. Wherever feasible in prison circumstances arrangements are made to give them the same practical opportunity to do so.

5. All inmates should have equal access to the facilities provided in the establishment including jobs. The distribution of inmates throughout the establishment and its facilities should as far as practicable and sensible be broadly responsive to the ethnic mix of the establishment.

6. No particular racial group should be allowed to dominate any activity in the establishment to the unfair exclusion of others.

## Young Offenders

**Mr. Mike O'Brien:** To ask the Secretary of State for the Home Department what were the numbers of offences attributed to juvenile offenders *(a)* in 1979 and *(b)* in 1994; what were the numbers of juveniles given custodial sentences (i) in 1979 and (ii) in 1994; and what were the reasons for trends in those statistics. [23936]

**Mr. Maclean:** It is not possible to present an accurate picture of the nature and extent of crime committed by youths aged 10 to 17, as much crime is unreported and not all reported crime is cleared up. We cannot therefore measure the number of crimes actually committed by young people. The best indicator we have is the number of young people known to have been involved in offending, that is, those cautioned by the police for, or convicted by the courts of, a crime.

Information given in the tables show *(a)* the number of known offenders by age and type of offence and *(b)* persons sentenced to immediate custody by age and type of offence for the years 1979 and 1993.

Reasons for the trends in known offending may include the demographic fall in the general population of persons aged 10 to 17 from 6.4 million in 1979 to 4.9 million in 1993. The trends may also partly reflect the increased use of informal methods for dealing with young offenders.

1994 data will not be available until autumn 1995.

*Table A—Number of persons found guilty at all courts or cautioned by age and type of offence 1979 and 1993*

England and Wales *Thousands*

| | Persons aged 10–17 | | All ages | |
|---|---|---|---|---|
| Type of offence | 1979 | 1993 | 1979 | 1993 |
| *Indictable offences* | | | | |
| Violence against the person[1] | 13.6 | 16.0 | 53.1 | 63.0 |
| Sexual offences | 2.7 | 1.5 | 10.2 | 7.6 |
| Burglary[2] | 36.8 | 19.1 | 66.1 | 53.1 |
| Robbery | 1.1 | 2.1 | 3.3 | 5.8 |
| Theft and handling stolen goods[1] | 128.7 | 73.1 | 295.5 | 238.8 |

*Table A—Number of persons found guilty at all courts or cautioned by age and type of offence 1979 and 1993*

England and Wales                                    Thousands

| | Persons aged 10–17 | | All ages | |
|---|---|---|---|---|
| Type of offence | 1979 | 1993 | 1979 | 1993 |
| Fraud and forgery | 2.8 | 1.9 | 22.1 | 25.5 |
| Criminal damage[1] | 5.3 | 4.3 | 11.2 | 13.5 |
| Drug offences | 0.5 | 7.5 | 11.9 | 57.0 |
| Other (excluding motoring)[2] | 1.9 | 3.8 | 13.4 | 40.4 |
| Motoring offences[1][3] | 3.0 | 0.3 | 21.8 | 10.8 |
| Total indicatable | 196.5 | 129.5 | 508.7 | 515.5 |
| Summary (excluding motoring) | 58.2 | 38.5 | 440.3 | 551.1 |
| All offences (excluding motoring) | 254.6 | 168.0 | 949.0 | 1,066.6 |

[1] A number of indicatable offences were reclassified as summary offences following the Criminal Justice Act 1988.

[2] Offenders found guilty, or cautioned for, "going equipped for stealing etc." were counted against burglary offences until 1986, and against "other" from 1987. Historical data provided in this table have been amended to take account of this change.

[3] Offenders found guilty only; motoring offence may attract written warnings.

*Table B—Number of persons sentenced to immediate custody at all courts by age and type of offence 1979 and 1993*

England and Wales                                    Thousands

| | Persons aged 10–17 | | All ages | |
|---|---|---|---|---|
| Type of offence | 1979 | 1993 | 1979 | 1993 |
| *Indictable offences* | | | | |
| Violence against the person[1] | 1.0 | 0.4 | 6.9 | 7.4 |
| Sexual offences | 0.1 | 0.0 | 1.5 | 2.0 |
| Burglary[2] | 4.3 | 1.4 | 15.4 | 11.8 |
| Robbery | 0.5 | 0.3 | 2.3 | 3.4 |
| Theft and handling stolen goods[1] | 4.9 | 0.9 | 22.9 | 10.1 |
| Fraud and forgery | 0.1 | 0.0 | 2.8 | 2.4 |
| Criminal damage[1] | 0.3 | 0.1 | 1.4 | 0.8 |
| Drug offences | 0.0 | 0.0 | 1.0 | 3.6 |
| Other (excluding motoring)[2] | 0.2 | 0.2 | 1.8 | 4.0 |
| Motoring offences[1][3] | 0.2 | 0.1 | 2.0 | 1.1 |
| Total indicatable | 11.6 | 3.4 | 57.9 | 46.6 |
| Summary (excluding motoring) | 0.4 | 0.4 | 3.9 | 3.6 |
| All offences (excluding motoring) | 12.0 | 3.7 | 61.9 | 50.2 |

[1] A number of indicatable offences were reclassified as summary offences following the Criminal Justice Act 1988.

[2] Offenders found guilty, or cautioned for, "going equipped for stealing etc." were counted against burglary offences until 1986, and against "other" from 1987. Historical data provided in this table have been amended to take account of this change.

[3] Offenders found guilty only; motoring offence may attract written warnings.

## Animal Procedures Committee

**Mr. Strang:** To ask the Secretary of State for the Home Department if he will list the current members of the Animal Procedures Committee; and which members of the Animal Procedures Committee are employed by animal welfare organisations.                    [24014]

**Mr. Nicholas Baker:** The current membership of the Animal Procedures Committee is given. Members' association with animal welfare organisations is shown where appropriate.

Professor Margaret Brazier (Chairman)
Professor Ronald S. Anderson
Professor Margaret Boden
Professor Barry Bridges
Dr. Fiona Broughton Pipkin
Dr. David Christopher
Dr. Yvonne Cripps
Mr. Roger Ewbank—Director of the Universities Federation for Animal Welfare
Dr. John Flack
Dr. Paul Flecknell
Professor Susan Iversen
Mrs. Judy MacArthur Clark
Miss Cindy Milburn—Special Projects Director, World Society for the Protection of Animals
Dr. Iain Purchase
Dr. Jacqueline Southee
Professor Michael Spyer
Dr. Anthony J. Suckling—Director of Scientific Affairs RSPCA
Mr. Les Ward—Director, Advocates for Animals

## Suicides

**Mr. Wigley:** To ask the Secretary of State for the Home Department what is *(a)* the average suicide rate and *(b)* the suicide rates for those employed in agriculture in each county in England and Wales.                    [23406]

**Mr. Bowis:** I have been asked to reply.

The death rates per 100,000 persons aged 16 to 74 for 1991–93 for (i) agricultural workers and (ii) the whole population, from suicide and self-inflicted injury—international classification of diseases code E950–E959—and for injury undetermined whether accidentally or purposely inflicted—international classification of diseases code E980–E989, excluding E988.8—are shown in the table.

| | Suicide | Undetermined |
|---|---|---|
| (i) agricultural workers | 19.9 | 5.2 |
| (ii) all persons | 9.3 | 3.5 |

Information on rates by county could be provided only at disproportionate cost.

# Written Answers to Questions

*Thursday 18 May 1995*

## TRADE AND INDUSTRY

### Defence Role

**Mr. Merchant:** To ask the President of the Board of Trade what are the roles of his Department of Trade and Industry and the Ministry of Defence in regard to the United Kingdom's defence industry.    [25667]

**Mr. Eggar:** The two Departments are in regular contact about the United Kingdom's defence industry.

The Ministry of Defence, as the biggest single customer of UK industry, aims to achieve maximum value for money in procurement, primarily through competition but also, where appropriate, through international collaboration or non-competitive acquisition. It has an interest in ensuring that its supplier base, which includes both specialist defence companies and general companies in most sectors of industry, is efficient, competitive and capable of meeting its needs in both the short and the long term. It works closely with companies to ensure that its requirements are properly understood and to improve the efficiency of the procurement process.

It supports the efforts of UK companies to export defence goods and services.

It funds research and development of technologies needed to meet defence needs. Through the Defence Research Agency it encourages the exploitation of technologies developed for military purposes in civil applications and the exploitation for defence purposes of civil technologies.

The Department of Trade and Industry's objective is to help UK industry compete successfully at home and in world markets. It works closely with the defence industry and related companies, trade associations, universities and other agencies to help improve the industry's international competitiveness. It pursues trade liberalisation world-wide and helps UK industry to take full advantage of market opportunities.

DTI works closely with the Ministry of Defence on issues affecting the competitiveness of the defence industries:

It advises on the industrial implications of MoD procurement policy to ensure that consequences for the competitiveness of the UK defence industrial base are taken into account. On substantial individual defence procurement projects, DTI is consulted well before decisions are taken, to ensure that the industrial implications are considered fully.

Together with MoD it works to promote joint military and civil research activities and adaptation of military technology to civil applications.

It works with MoD to develop a common information base on the defence industries.

### Offshore Licensing

**Mr. Merchant:** To ask the President of the Board of Trade if he will announce the award of licences for the 16th round of offshore licensing; and if he will make a statement.    [25668]

**Mr. Page:** After very careful consideration of applications for exploration licences in the west of Shetlands, we have been able to offer licences for each of the blocks applied for.

Our "fast tracking" of these applications means that over 1,700 sqk of 3D seismic surveys will now be shot this summer with even more to come in 1996. Companies have also committed themselves to drilling 12 wells in the next two years and a further 13 in three years time. This level of commitment demonstrates the keen interest in a very exciting area of the United Kingdom continental shelf.

The blocks attracted a high level of applications with one block receiving eight applications. The competition for some blocks has been intense and some very innovative ideas were presented with a number of very good applications for the same block. A total of 24 applications were received from 17 groups involving 32 companies.

When examining applications we were conscious of the need to protect the environment. Although most of the blocks are some distance from the coast, it is important to ensure that the risks of any oil spills reaching the coasts of the Shetlands and Orkneys are understood and steps taken to minimise the risks and prepare contingency plans. The companies which have been awarded licences have all shown a strong commitment to protecting the environment.

These awards—and the interest in the other blocks offered in the 16th round—shows the continuing high level of commitment by the international oil and gas companies to the UKCS. The opening up of new areas in the west of Shetlands basin as a result of this round will help maintain the UK's position as an oil and gas producer well into the next century.

I plan to announce the remainder of the 16th round awards—for blocks around the coast of Britain and to the north of Scotland—in the summer.

### Copyright Tribunal

**Sir Thomas Arnold:** To ask the President of the Board of Trade what changes he proposes to make to the procedures of the Copyright tribunal; and if he will make a statement.    [24778]

**Mr. Ian Taylor:** Last year, my Department consulted users of the Copyright tribunal on how far they were satisfied with its performance and on how its procedures might be improved. The overwhelming majority of respondents considered that tribunal procedures were fair, flexible, unintimidating and thorough. However, there were some concerns about the cost and speed of procedures and suggestions for improvement in these and other respects were made. The Department is considering these suggestions in consultation with the chairman of the tribunal and it is likely that a statutory instrument providing for some amendments in procedures will be put forward in due course.

## Technopole Information Networks

**Mr. John Battle:** To ask the President of the Board of Trade how much funding he expects to receive from the European Union SPRINT programme for research into technopole information networks.    [24150]

**Mr. Ian Taylor:** The SPRINT programme ended on 31 December 1994. The European Commission was responsible for the selection of SPRINT projects based on merit, and for issuing grants to the successful candidates. My right hon. Friend the President of the Board of Trade did not receive any funding from the programme.

The third activity of the EC fourth framework programme for research and development has superseded SPRINT. It brings together under one programme all the Community's efforts on dissemination and exploitation of research results and technological developments. There are provisions in the third activity for support of science parks and networks in support of innovation, though no specific provisions for research into technopole information networks. Projects involving information networks may be eligible for support under other programmes in the fourth framework.

## Richard Budge

**Mr. Byers:** To ask the President of the Board of Trade, pursuant to his answer of 15 May, *Official Report*, column 25, at what venues the meetings with Mr. Richard Budge took, place and which Government Departments were represented at each of the meetings.    [24941]

**Mr. Page:** Of the seven meetings with Mr. Richard Budge detailed in my previous answer of 15 May, six were conducted in the office of my right hon. Friend the Minister for Industry and Energy. The meeting on 15 April 1993 took place over lunch in central London. No other Government Departments were represented at any of the meetings.

**Mr. Byers:** To ask the President of the Board of Trade, pursuant to his reply of 15 May, *Official Report*, column 25, which other two directors of A. F. Budge were interviewed.    [24939]

**Mr. Jonathan Evans:** David Thomas Trewick and Martin Connolly were interviewed, together with David Threadkell, a former director.

**Mr. Stephen Byers:** To ask the President of the Board of Trade, pursuant to his reply of 15 May, *Official Report*, column 24, what was the cost of the Coopers and Lybrand report on the collapse of A. F. Budge.    [24944]

**Mr. Jonathan Evans:** Administrative receivers have a statutory duty to report under the Company Directors Disqualification Act 1986 and the Department makes no payment in respect of such reports. The administrative receivers and Coopers and Lybrand have carried out further enquiries at the request of the Official Receiver and has submitted invoices to date totalling £51,101.18 plus VAT £8,942.70.

**Mr. Byers:** To ask the President of the Board of Trade which directors of A. F. Budge were recommended by the Official Receiver for action to be taken against them under the Company Directors Disqualification Act 1986.    [24940]

**Mr. Jonathan Evans:** The content of the Official Receiver's report is confidential between the Secretary of State and the Official Receiver.

## Water Treatment Equipment, Iraq

**Mrs. Clwyd:** To ask the President of the Board of Trade if the DTI has received request for export credit licences for sewerage pumps or other water treatment equipment to Iraq; and if these requests have been granted.    [24879]

**Mr. Ian Taylor:** Export Licences for such equipment have been applied for and, in certain cases, issued. Any export of humanitarian goods to Iraq also requires an authorisation from the United Nations Sanctions Committee.

## Construction Contracts

**Mr. Cox:** To ask the President of the Board of Trade when he expects to make a statement on his Department's policy on a construction contracts Bill.    [24020]

**Mr. Eggar:** Matters concerning the construction industry are for my right hon. Friend the Secretary of State for the Environment.

## British Coal Land

**Mr. Ron Davies:** To ask the President of the Board of Trade if he will place in the Library a list of all the properties in Wales that British Coal proposes to offer for sale.    [24774]

**Mr Page:** This is a matter for British Coal. I understand that the corporation is still finalising the list of properties to be offered for sale. Details will be made public as the properties become available.

## Policy Statements

**Mr. Mike O'Brien:** To ask the President of the Board of Trade on how many occasions in each of the last five years his Department published policy statements from non-governmental working parties or organisations; and if he will list the name of the document, the organisation which produced it and the cost to the public purse of publishing it.    [24007]

**Mr. Ian Taylor:** This information is not held centrally and could be obtained only at disproportionate cost.

## Plutonium

**Mr. Llew Smith:** To ask the President of the Board of Trade if he will obtain from his United States counterpart a copy of the US Department of Energy's plutonium working group report on environmental, safety and health vulnerabilities associated with plutonium storage, released in November 1994; and if he will arrange for a copy to be placed in the Library.    [24295]

**Mr. Page:** The report referred to was, I understand, published by the US Department of Energy and is publicly available. It can also be accessed on the Internet.

## OVERSEAS DEVELOPMENT ADMINISTRATION

### Malaysia

**Miss Lestor:** To ask the Secretary of State for Foreign and Commonwealth Affairs how many applications to the aid and trade provision for support for power projects in Malaysia have been rejected during the last 10 years; and if he will list the grounds for rejection, the date of rejection and the names of the United Kingdom companies involved. [22676]

**Mr. Baldry:** On the basis of information available, between 1984 and 1993, applications relating to 11 power projects were rejected because they did not meet the developmental, commercial and industrial criteria for the ATP scheme; or for budgetary reasons; or because they were not accepted by recipient Governments. Ten British companies were involved as lead contractors for these projects. Information on the names of companies is commercial in confidence.

One project was rejected in each of the following years: 1988, 1991 and 1993. Three were rejected in 1990. Information is not readily available concerning the dates of rejection for the other five.

### SCIAF

**Mr. McMaster:** To ask the Secretary of State for Foreign and Commonwealth Affairs when he or his Ministers last met representatives of Scottish Catholic International Aid Fund to discuss overseas development; and if he will make a statement. [24162]

**Mr. Baldry:** There have been no meetings specifically with the Scottish Catholic International Aid Fund—SCIAF—in recent years. My noble Friend, the Minister for Overseas Development, meets non-governmental organisation on a regular basis to discuss emergency and development issues, and has addressed gatherings of NGOs which have included representatives from SCIAF.

### Afghan Refugees

**Mr. Cox:** To ask the Secretary of State for Foreign and Commonwealth Affairs what discussions he has had with the Government of Pakistan regarding the Afghan refugees now living in refugee camps in Pakistan; and if he will make a statement. [24147]

**Mr. Baldry:** We regularly discuss with the Government of Pakistan a wide range of issues including Afghan refugees. This issue was raised last month in talks between officials of the Foreign and Commonwealth Office and the Pakistan high commission, who expressed appreciation of our support for Afghan refugees.

### AIDS Programme

**Mr. Dalyell:** To ask the Secretary of State for Foreign and Commonwealth Affairs what is the policy of Her Majesty's Government on the issue of the withdrawal of the AIDS programme from the World Health Organisation. [24506]

**Mr. Baldry:** We support the establishment of the joint United Nations programme on AIDS—UNAIDS—which will replace the World Health Organisation's global programme on AIDS—WHO/GPA—on 1 January 1996. UNAIDS will be co-sponsored by six United Nations agencies, including the World Health Organisation. The other co-sponsors are: United Nations Population Fund, United Nations Educational, Scientific and Cultural Organisation, United Nations Development Programme, the World Bank and the United Nations Childrens Fund.

## DEFENCE

### Air Training, Germany

**Dr. David Clark:** To ask the Secretary of State for Defence what air training activities are allowed for Royal Air Force aircraft based in Germany. [24801]

**Mr. Soames:** The supplementary agreement to the NATO status of forces agreement of 3 August 1959, governs the way in which the RAF conducts air training in Germany. In general no fixed-wing flying activity is allowed below 1,000 ft above ground level. However, aircraft may be cleared to fly at 50 ft for limited periods during specific exercises. Medium level training is carried out in temporary restricted areas. Weapons training is primarily conducted at the air weaponry range at RAF Nordhorn, although limited use is also made of other ranges from time to time. The rules governing helicopter training activities in Germany are similar to those in operation in the UK.

### UN Peacekeeping Support

**Dr. David Clark:** To ask the Secretary of State for Defence (1) how many British helicopters were operating in support of United Nations operations in each of the last 10 years; [24798]

(2) how many British troops were operating in support of United Nations operations in each of the last 10 years; [24799]

(3) how many British Hercules aircraft were operating in support of United Nations operating in each of the last 10 years. [24800]

**Mr. Soames:** The information requested could be provided only at disproportionate cost. The United Kingdom has contributed troops to United Nations peacekeeping operations in each of the last ten years. In recent years there has been a rapid increase in the level of peacekeeping undertaken by the UN and the UK's contribution has increased substantially. Some 4,600 British personnel are serving in operations under UN command, and about 3,500 more in operations in support of UN Security Council resolutions. Where necessary British personnel are supported by helicopters and Hercules aircraft. Important support is also provided to other elements of UN operations.

### Air Force Personnel

**Dr. David Clark:** To ask the Secretary of State for Defence (1) how many Royal Air Force maintenance and support personnel there were in each of the last 10 years; [24796]

(2) what was the total Royal Air Force manpower in each of the last 10 years; and what is the estimated Royal Air Force manpower strength in 1997–98. [24797]

**Mr. Soames:** The total manpower strength of the Royal Air Force and the RAF's maintenance and support element, as at 1 April in each of the years in question is as follows:

| Date | Total RAF strength (trained and untrained) | Total RAF maintenance and support personnel (trained and untrained) |
|------|-----|-----|
| 1986 | 93,237 | 84,861 |
| 1987 | 93,627 | 85,172 |
| 1988 | 93,291 | 84,890 |
| 1989 | 91,443 | 83,385 |
| 1990 | 89,685 | 81,786 |
| 1991 | 88,371 | 80,505 |
| 1992 | 85,962 | 78,183 |
| 1993 | 80,909 | 73,392 |
| 1994 | 75,681 | 68,642 |
| 1995 | 70,754 | 64,056 |

For the purposes of this question "maintenance and support" personnel has been defined as all personnel other than those employed on general duties (air) and airmen aircrew duties. It is not our practice to provide estimates of manpower strength more than a year in advance, and the forecast total strength for 1 April 1996 is around 66,500.

### Market Testing

**Dr. David Clark:** To ask the Secretary of State for Defence what Royal Air Force activities have been market tested over the last five years. [24795]

**Mr. Soames:** Full details of market-testing activities in the Royal Air Force over the last five years are not available centrally. However, in the three year period from April 1992 to March 1995 six Royal Air Force activities have been market tested, and a further 16 subjected to other CFQ processes, which resulted in either contractorisation or efficiency measures being taken. Detail of the six market-tested activities are as follows:

(a) *Those contractorised following market test:*

Inspectorate of Recruitment Exhibition Production Flight, RAF Henlow

Air Weapon Range, RAF Holbeach

Flight checking, 115 Squadron, RAF Benson

Nimrod Major Serving Unit, RAF Kinloss

(b) *Those won by in-house bid team following market test:*

Air Weapon Range, RAF Cowden

Support Services, Gateway House, RAF Brize Norton

### Information to Members

**Dr. David Clark:** To ask the Secretary of State for Defence, pursuant to his answer of 2 May, *Official Report*, column *201*, what considerations led him not to list the hon. and right hon. Members who have been notified of contracts by his special advisor. [24508]

**Mr. Rifkind:** I do not think listing over 300 contracts, of local rather than national significance, in the *Official Report* would usefully add to the answer I gave to the hon. Gentleman on 2 May, *Official Report*, column *201*.

### Sandia National Laboratories

**Mr. Simpson:** To ask the Secretary of State for Defence if he will list all projects his Department is working on jointly with Sandia National Laboratory. [24783]

**Mr. Freeman:** Under the 1958 UK/US mutual defence agreement, the Atomic Weapons Establishment works closely with Sandia National Laboratory on a number of areas of research. These include:

Neutron Sources

Irradiation Effects on Materials and Components

Non-nuclear Components

Independent Assessment of Nuclear Weapon Safety

Nuclear Weapons Engineering

Nuclear Weapons Physics

Nuclear Accident Response Technology

**Mr. Simpson:** To ask the Secretary of State for Defence what specific support is being provided by Sandia National Laboratory in support of the Trident programme. [24782]

**Mr. Freeman:** Sandia National Laboratory provides engineering support services associated with certain US-supplied components of the United Kingdom Trident system. Further details are classified.

### Latham Report

**Mr. Spellar:** To ask the Secretary of State for Defence what policy his Department has put to the working groups on the Latham report as to the desirability of a single exclusive register for public sector work. [24355]

**Mr. Freeman:** My officials are actively involved in the follow up work to the Latham report, which is being co-ordinated by the Department of the Environment, and also the efficiency scrutiny into construction procurement. Together, these will form the Govnerment response to Latham's recommendations, including the desirability of a single register for public sector work.

### Ground Training

**Mr. Devlin:** To ask the Secretary of State for Defence what plans he has for the future of ground training in the Royal Air Force. [25563]

**Mr. Soames:** Following issue of the consultative document on 22 March 1995 recommending the closure of RAF Locking and the transfer of its training task to RAF Cosford, representations have been made by the hon. Member for Weston-super-Mare (Sir J. Wiggin), and local authorities. My Department has consulted thoroughly with the trade unions and relevant local authorities, and full and careful consideration has been given to all of the representations that we have received.

Following this work I am satisfied that no issues have been raised which call into question the viability of the proposals, which satisfactorily meet our future ground training needs and save £6,000,000 per annum. I have therefore decided that RAF Locking should close by 1 April 1998.

We will, of course, continue to consult the trade unions about the detailed implementation of the closure and transfer of work to RAF Cosford.

## High Velocity Missiles

**Mr. Devlin:** To ask the Secretary of State for Defence when he will place an order with Shorts for high velocity missiles; and if he will make a statement.          [25564]

**Mr. Freeman:** An order for the development and initial production of high velocity missiles was placed with Shorts Missile Systems Ltd. in 1986. In the light of progress on the project, I have given approval for an order for 1,000 missiles to be placed with Shorts, subject to satisfactory contractual conditions being agreed.

## Defence Accounts Agency

**Mr. Devlin:** To ask the Secretary of State for Defence what performance targets have been set for the Defence Accounts Agency for 1995–96.          [25565]

**Mr. Freeman:** The chief executive of the Defence Accounts Agency is responsible for providing accounting services for the Ministry of Defence as defined in the agency framework document. During 1995–96, the DAA will be reorganised and its successor organisations will be set new targets. The chief executive of the DAA will however report progress against the DAA targets during the year in a final annual report.

DAA has been set the following challenging key performance targets in 1995–96:

(a) To complete the following workload within the funds allocated for this purpose:

Manage 89,350 non-industrial pay accounts

Manage 41,5000 industrial pay accounts

Complete 130,000 pensions awards/transactions

Approve 500,000 claims for travel or transfer expenses

Pay 17,000 fees claims

Pay 20,000 miscellaneous personal payments claims

Pay 3,205,000 bills

Process 45,000 invoices

Make 396,500 personal payments

Manage 13,000 imprest accounts

Process 35,000 HQ receipts

Process 2,750 banknote orders

Process 2,250 bank fundings

(b) To meet the agency's quality of service standards in service level agreements and performance targets.

(c) To make efficiency savings with a value of at least 2.5 per cent. of the initial cash allocation.

(d) To compete for payroll and pension awarding business offered through the Government's market testing programme.

(e) To implement the DAA quality strategy by 30 June 1995.

(f) To implement the findings of the agency's first three year review.

## PRIME MINISTER

### Engagements

**Sir Peter Tapsell:** To ask the Prime Minister if he will list his official engagements for Thursday 18 May.  [23663]

**The Prime Minister:** This morning I presided at a meeting of the Cabinet and had meetings with ministerial colleagues and others. In addition to my duties in the House, I shall be having further meetings later today.

## China

**Mr. Winnick:** To ask the Prime Minister if the President of the Board of Trade has been asked to raise the issue of human rights on his visit to China    [24804]

**The Prime Minister:** The President of the Board of Trade has been briefed on all aspects of our bilateral relationship, and more generally on conditions in China, including human rights.

## Lockerbie

**Mr. Dalyell:** To ask the Prime Minister if he will discuss with Chancellor Kohl, the letter from the Bundesministerium der Justif to Ms Lisa Mosey, concerning explosive material and baggage handling at Frankfurt, a copy of which has been sent to him by the hon. Member for Linlithgow.          [24794]

**The Prime Minister:** I have nothing further to add to the reply of 14 March 1995, *Official Report,* column *498.*

## TREASURY

### Building Societies

**Mr. French:** To ask the Chancellor of the Exchequer what assessment he has made of the risk and extent of speculative movement of funds in connection with possible takeovers or conversions of building societies, and the duties of boards of societies in such circumstances; and if he will make a statement.  [23266]

**Mr. Nelson:** Monitoring the movement of funds within the building society sector is one of the tasks of the Building Societies Commission.

Boards of societies faced with speculative flows can respond in a number of ways. These include varying the rates of interest on offer and withdrawing certain types of accounts. In reacting to proposals for takeovers or conversions which may give rise to such flows, the Building Societies Act requires boards to take account not only of the financial interests of their current members, but of the longer-term objectives of the society.

### Rural White Paper

**Mr. Colvin:** To ask the Chancellor of the Exchequer what is his estimate of the net annual financial saving, or cost, of his Department's submission for the proposed White Paper on the rural economy.          [24332]

**Mr. Heathcoat-Amory:** Proposals for the rural White Paper remain subject to continuing collective consideration and discussion. The cost of measures contained in the White Paper will be taken into account in the public expenditure survey.

### Inheritance Tax

**Mr. French:** To ask the Chancellor of the Exchequer (1) what was the yield from inheritance tax arising from United Kingdom securities held by non-United Kingdom residents in each of the last three years.          [24713]

(2) how many non-United Kingdom residents incurred an inheritance tax liability arising from their holdings of United Kingdom securities in each of the last three years.          [24714]

**Sir George Young:** For inheritance tax purposes, it is the country of domicile that determines liability and not the country of residence. I regret that information for estates where the deceased was domiciled outside of the United Kingdom is not held centrally. The information requested could therefore be provided only at disproportionate cost.

### Tax Allowance Transfers

**Mr. Lidington:** To ask the Chancellor of the Exchequer what would be the cost of making individual tax allowances transferable between spouses; and if he will make a statement. [24568]

**Sir George Young:** The full year revenue cost at 1995–96 income levels is estimated to be about £3 billion. This estimate does not take into account any behavioural change which could result from such a measure.

### Mortgage Protection Policies

**Mr. Darling:** To ask the Chancellor of the Exchequer when the review into the taxation of proceeds for mortgage protection policies was set up; what are its terms of reference; who is conducting it; when he expects it to report; and if he will make a statement. [23630]

**Sir George Young** *[holding answer 10 May 1995]:* My right hon. and learned Friend the Chancellor made it clear in the statement he issued on 2 May that benefits under mortgage payment protection policies will be exempt from tax. The decision resulted from a review that had been under way for some months.

### Summer Economic Forecast

**Mr. Andrew Smith:** To ask the Chancellor of the Exchequer what is the expected publication date for the Treasury's summer economic forecast. [24495]

**Mr. Aitken** *[holding answer 17 May 1995]:* We expect to publish the summer economic forecast on a similar date to last year. I will let the hon. Gentleman know the exact date as soon as it is decided.

## EDUCATION

### Pre-school Education

**Mr. MacShane:** To ask the Secretary of State for Education what percentage of children under the age of five years receive nursery or pre-school public education in each member state of the European Union. [24219]

**Mr. Forth:** Information is not collected centrally in the form requested. The latest available international comparisons of under-fives participating in public and private education are shown in the table. Separate participation rates for nursery provision only are not available.

*Under fives participation rates[1] in education, 1992*

|  | Percentages |
| --- | --- |
| Austria | 47 |
| Belgium | 98 |
| Denmark | 46 |
| Finland | 26 |
| France | 100 |
| Former West Germany | 49 |
| Greece | 30 |
| Ireland | 29 |
| Italy[2] | 76 |
| Luxembourg | n/a |
| Netherlands | 49 |
| Portugal[3] | 36 |
| Spain | 67 |
| Sweden | 48 |
| United Kingdom | 53 |

*Sources:*
Education Statistics for the United Kingdom, 1994 edition, HMSO, 1995
 Education at a Glance,. OECD, 1995
*Notes:*
[1] Pupils aged 3 and 4 as percentages of the population aged 3 and 4.
[2] 1988
[3] 1991

### Non-teaching Staff

**Mr. Flynn:** To ask the Secretary of State for Education from which schools she has received reports that *(a)* dinner ladies and *(b)* school crossing patrol persons have undertaken teaching duties. [24422]

**Mr. Robin Squire:** My right hon. Friend is not aware of any such cases. Non-teaching staff are widely used to supervise pupils and to support the work of teachers; decisions on their deployment are for headteachers.

### Supply Cover

**Mr. Simpson:** To ask the Secretary of State for Education what is her estimate of the cost of supply cover for classroom teachers, while primary schools carry out the standard assessment tests. [24781]

**Mr. Forth:** The estimated cost of supply cover for teachers administering the national curriculum tests and tasks to seven and 11-year-olds is around £15 million.

### Schools, Ealing

**Mr. Harry Greenway:** To ask the Secretary of State for Education, pursuant to her answer of 15 May, *Official Report,* column *14* on the educational spending in Ealing, if she will give an expenditure breakdown of the figures of *(a)* £517.33 and *(b)* £923.45 for expenditure per primary and secondary pupil in locally-managed schools other than that allocated to schools under the locally managed school budgets; and if she will make a statement. [24878]

**Mr. Robin Squire:** The following table provides the information requested. It is derived from the planned expenditure totals and pupils numbers shown in the 1995–96 budget statement published by the local education authority under section 42 of the Education Reform Act.

| Item | Primary | Secondary |
| --- | --- | --- |
| | £ | £ |
| Management and Administration | | |
| a. Education Department | 24.98 | 24.85 |
| b. Other Council Departments | 31.41 | 31.34 |
| Advisory and Inspection Services | 2.33 | 2.28 |
| Special Needs Support Services including Special Units | | |
| a. Pupils with Statements | 69.65 | 70.21 |
| b. Other Services | 19.18 | 19.14 |
| Staff Costs (Supply Cover) | 8.43 | 8.49 |
| Structural Repairs and Maintenance | 45.62 | 79.74 |
| Home to School Transport | 7.81 | 69.66 |
| School Meals and Milk | | |
| a. Expenditure to be met from income | 40.39 | 21.09 |
| b. Other Expenditure | 98.60 | 77.46 |
| Inspection Expenditure to be met by Income from OFSTED | 0.00 | 13.21 |
| Pupil Support | 11.46 | 11.56 |
| LEA Initiatives | 0.65 | 0.66 |
| School Specific Contingencies | 20.26 | 20.22 |
| Capital Expenditure | 21.80 | 304.41 |
| Education Welfare Service | 8.79 | 32.01 |
| Education Psychology Service | 3.88 | 2.59 |
| Statementing Costs | 7.10 | 7.16 |
| Premature Retirement Costs | 14.34 | 36.20 |
| Specific Grant Related Expenditure | | |
| a. Expenditure on Section 11 Posts | | |
| (i) to be reimbursed by Government Grant | 18.36 | 18.23 |
| (ii) to be met by LEA | 23.62 | 23.38 |
| b. Other expenditure to be reimbursed by Government Grant | 20.89 | 26.52 |
| c. LEA contribution to Grants at b. | 17.80 | 23.06 |

## EMPLOYMENT

### Remploy

**Mr. Hain:** To ask the Secretary of State for Employment (1) what alterations he has made to the recruitment criteria for disabled persons employed by Remploy;                                    [24885]

(2) what discussions he has held with the management board of Remploy about changes to the recruitment criteria for disabled people.                    [24886]

**Miss Widdecombe:** Responsibility for the subject of the questions has been delegated to the Employment Service Agency under its chief executive. I have asked him to arrange for a reply to be given.

*Letter from M. E. G. Fogden to Mr. Peter Hain, dated 18 May 1995:*

The Secretary of State has asked me to reply to your questions about the recruitment criteria for disabled persons employed by Remploy.

There has been no change to the recruitment criteria for disabled persons employed by Remploy. Remploy is part of the Employment Service's Supported Employment Programme. This programme is open to people with severe disabilities who are registered under the Disabled Persons (Employment) Act 1944 and who, because of the severity of their disability and its effect on their productivity, are unlikely to be able to obtain of retain jobs in open employment.

As there have been no changes to the criteria, we have not held discussions with Remploy management on this subject.

I hope this is helpful.

## LORD CHANCELLOR'S DEPARTMENT

### Maxwell Brothers

**Mr. Byers:** To ask the Parliamentary Secretary, Lord Chancellor's Department what contributions have so far been made from the legal aid fund towards the defence costs of *(a)* Kevin Maxwell and *(b)* Ian Maxwell; and what have been the costs incurred by the defence in carrying out public opinion surveys.          [24925]

**Mr. John M. Taylor:** The total amount of criminal legal aid paid to date to lawyers acting for all six defendants in R *v.* Kevin Maxwell and Others is £4,745,391. This amount includes final costs in the magistrates' court of £829,377 as well as payments on account, as of 24 January 1995, in the Crown Court of £3,916,014. All payments include VAT and disbursements, such as expert witness and accountancy fees, and other expenses necessarily incurred. It would not be appropriate while the case is continuing to give a further breakdown of these figures. Nothing has been paid from the legal aid fund to cover the cost of public opinion surveys conducted by the defence.

### Judges

**Mr. William Powell:** To ask the Parliamentary Secretary, Lord Chancellor's Department if he will list all full-time judges aged over 70 years still sitting on the bench.          [23938]

**Mr. John M. Taylor:** The information requested as at 10 May 1995, is as follows:

*Lords of Appeal in Ordinary*
Lord Jauncey of Tullichettle
Lord Keith of Kinkel
*Heads of Division*
The President of the Family Division (Sir Stephen Brown)
*Lord Justices*
Lord Justice Beldam
Lord Justice Glidewell
Lord Justice Neill
*High Court Judges*
Mr. Justice Drake
Mr. Justice Gatehouse
Mr. Justice Knox
*Circuit Judges*
Judge Allardice DL
Judge Atkinson
Judge Paul Baker QC
Judge David Kt QC, DL
Judge Quentin Edwards QC
Judge Halnan
Judge Harris DSC, QC
Judge Head
Judge Holt
Judge Lownie
Judge Richard Lowry QC
Judge Mildon QC
Judge Phelan
Judge Stroyan QC
Judge Sir Lawrence Verney TD, DL
Judge Ian Webster
*District Judges*
District Judge Goodman
District Judge Hughes
District Judge Keyes
District Judge Lam

**Mr. William Powell:** To ask the Parliamentary Secretary, Lord Chancellor's Department if he will list the names of those judges whose period in office has been extended by the Lord Chancellor beyond their statutory retiring age; and when he now expects each to retire. [23939]

**Mr. John M. Taylor:** The Lord Chancellor exercises the powers available to him under section 26(4) to (6) of the Judicial Pensions and Retirement Act 1993 where he considers it desirable in the public interest to continue a judge in office for a period, or further period, not exceeding one year, up to the age of 75.

Judge David Kt QC is the only circuit judge in office whose appointment has been continued beyond his statutory retirement date. The continuance expires on 30 April 1996. No district judges in office have been continued beyond their statutory retirement date. There are no powers to continue more senior judges in office beyond their statutory retirement date.

# FOREIGN AND COMMONWEALTH AFFAIRS

## Professional Staff

**Mr. MacShane:** To ask the Secretary of State for Foreign and Commonwealth Affairs what are the numbers of professional grade officials employed by the United Nations and its agencies who are citizens of *(a)* the United Kingdom, *(b)* the United States of America, *(c)* France, *(d)* Sweden, *(e)* India, *(f)* Canada, *(g)* the Netherlands, *(h)* Japan, *(i)* Ireland and *(j)* Belgium. [23707]

**Mr. Douglas Hogg:** The numbers of professional staff, including senior officials, employed by the United Nations and its agencies who are citizens of the ten countries listed are given in the following table.

*Number of professional staff[1]*

| | UN | ILO | WHO | ITU | WMO | UPU | WIPO | IAEA | UNIDO | FAO | WFP | IFAD | ICAO | UNESCO | IMO |
|---|---|---|---|---|---|---|---|---|---|---|---|---|---|---|---|
| United Kingdom | 502 | 66 | 123 | 16 | 16 | 4 | 15 | 52 | 32 | 134 | 28 | 9 | 21 | 34 | 16 |
| USA | 1,087 | 72 | 258 | 17 | 11 | 1 | 9 | 129 | 46 | 164 | 49 | 13 | 18 | 45 | 4 |
| France | 595 | 100 | 111 | 33 | 11 | 5 | 34 | 31 | 27 | 165 | 22 | 7 | 22 | 103 | 15 |
| Sweden | 197 | 26 | 22 | 7 | 2 | 1 | 2 | 12 | 8 | 21 | 8 | 2 | 2 | 18 | 5 |
| India | 223 | 28 | 36 | 14 | 2 | 3 | 3 | 12 | 25 | 55 | 9 | 3 | 4 | 14 | 3 |
| Canada | 330 | 27 | 48 | 10 | 4 | 3 | 3 | 24 | 6 | 61 | 36 | 3 | 62 | 24 | 1 |
| Netherlands | 303 | 82 | 49 | 3 | 3 | 1 | 1 | 9 | 18 | 124 | 15 | 5 | 5 | 26 | 2 |
| Japan | 246 | 23 | 46 | 6 | 4 | 5 | 3 | 24 | 22 | 37 | 13 | 3 | 3 | 34 | 5 |
| Ireland | 70 | 5 | 11 | 1 | 1 | 0 | 0 | 1 | 5 | 14 | 5 | 0 | 3 | 6 | 2 |
| Belgium | 181 | 46 | 36 | 4 | 5 | 2 | 4 | 5 | 8 | 122 | 11 | 7 | 2 | 16 | 1 |

[1] UN figures reflecting staff in post on 31 December 1993.

## Peaceful Nuclear Explosions

**Mr. Llew Smith:** To ask the Secretary of State for Foreign and Commonwealth Affairs what was the policy position taken by Her Majesty's Government in regard to the support for article V, on peaceful nuclear explosions, of the nuclear non-proliferation treaty at the review and extension conference of the nuclear non-proliferation treaty in New York. [24423]

**Mr. David Davis:** We expressed the view that there are no useful peaceful applications of nuclear explosions.

## Passports (Date-stamping)

**Mr. Marlow:** To ask the Secretary of State for Foreign and Commonwealth Affairs in what circumstances it is permitted within EU laws or other ordnances for Belgium frontier authorities to date stamp the passports of United Kingdom passport holders on entry into Belgium. [24865]

**Mr. David Davis:** Date-stamping of United Kingdom passports by Belgian immigration authorities would not necessarily be contrary to EC law provided that it could not be construed as an immigration control on a British citizen, and provided that it was not done in circumstances which amounted to discrimination on the ground of nationality. Nevertheless it appears that the few cases reported recently of such date-stamping were the result of administrative error and the Belgian authorities assure us they have taken steps to see that it does not happen again.

## Holy Shrine, Charar-e-Sharief

**Mr. Rooney:** To ask the Secretary of State for Foreign and Commonwealth Affairs what discussions he has had with the Indian and Pakistani Governments regarding the destruction of the holy shrine, Charar-e-Sharief. [24897]

**Mr. Baldry:** My right hon. Friend the Secretary of State for Foreign and Commonwealth Affairs has not had discussions with the Indian and Pakistani Governments regarding the destruction of the shrine at Charar-e-Sharief.

## Social Development Fund

**Mr. Wray:** To ask the Secretary of State for Foreign and Commonwealth Affairs what factors led to the United Kingdom not participating in the Council of Europe's social development fund. [24802]

**Mr. David Davis:** The cost of the United Kingdom joining the social development fund would be prohibitive. As a major contributor to the Council of Europe, our initial investment would be around £30 million, with annual running costs of about £225,000. This could be met only by diverting aid resources from bilateral and multilateral aid programmes.

## Pakistan (Drugs)

**Mr. Madden:** To ask the Secretary of State for Foreign and Commonwealth Affairs, what action Her Majesty's Government are taking *(a)* directly, *(b)* through the EU and *(c)* through other organisations, to assist the

Government of Pakistan in combating drug trafficking; what assistance is being given to the supply of equipment to combat drug trafficking with particular reference to helicopters; and if he will make a statement. [22306]

**Mr. Baldry** *[pursuant to his reply 2 May, Official Report, column 151]:* I regret that the last three paragraphs of my answer of 2 May were inadvertently omitted. The full answer is as follows:

We have given considerable narcotics-related assistance to Pakistan both bilaterally and through multilateral channels. Last financial year, bilateral assistance includes the provision of law enforcement training by HM Customs and Excise. Multilaterally we have pledged over £8 million since 1985 to projects administered by the United Nations drug control programme to strengthen law enforcement control of the Pakistan/Iran/Afghanistan border area and to reduce the supply of opium through rural development.

As part of the programme of assistance, we agreed to fund the purchase of two helicopters to enhance the capacity of the ANF to interdict drugs convoys in the area bordering Afghanistan and Iran.

Assistance by EU Governments is co-ordinated through the forum of the Dublin group both locally and in Brussels. Assistance by the European Commission has been mainly directed towards narcotics demand reduction.

HM Customs and Excise works closely with Pakistani law enforcement agencies. We stand ready to provide further assistance and are considering additional requests from the Pakistan Government for training and equipment to enhance their capability to counter drug trafficking.

# DUCHY OF LANCASTER

## "Management Matters"

**Mr. Mike O'Brien:** To ask the Chancellor of the Duchy of Lancaster what was the cost of printing, publishing and distributing "Management Matters"; who paid this and what charges were made to private organisations who were allowed to insert looseleaf advertisements in the magazine. [24587]

**Mr. Horam:** The average gross cost of printing, publishing and distributing each edition in the 1994–95 financial year was approximately £12,800.

The cost of producing "Management Matters" is met from the Cabinet Office—Office of Public Service and Science—budget.

Organisations which wish to place a looseleaf insert in the magazine are charged at a rate of £38 per 1,000 leaflets. Revenue raised is used to offset the magazine's production costs.

**Mr. Mike O'Brien:** To ask the Chancellor of the Duchy of Lancaster on whose and on what authority the Government publication for civil servants, "Management Matters" included looseleaf advertising for insurance and life assurance. [24585]

**Mr. Horam:** Each looseleaf advertisement that is inserted in "Management Matters" is approved by the magazine's editorial board prior to publication. The board, which comprises officials from the Cabinet Office—OPSS—and HM Treasury, examines each proposed advertisement against pre-determined criteria.

**Mr. Mike O'Brien:** To ask the Chancellor of the Duchy of Lancaster what assessment has been made as to whether the insertion of looseleaf advertising for private organisations selling financial and other services in "Management Matters" might be understood by readers as implying an endorsement of particular commercial products, not withstanding disclaimers; and if he will place in the Library the reports which have evaluated such matters. [24586]

**Mr. Horam:** There are precedents for civil service publications carrying advertising. The editorial board gave careful consideration to the decision to insert looseleaf advertisements in "Management Matters". Taking into account the strict criteria it would apply and the disclaimer included in each edition—on which it took legal advice—the board took the view that such advertisements could not reasonably be regarded as bearing official endorsement.

## Civil Service Pension Scheme

**Mr. Frank Field:** To ask the Chancellor of the Duchy of Lancaster what plans he has to market test the management of the civil service pension scheme; and if he will make a statement. [24371]

**Mr. Horam:** The 1992 efficiency scrutiny identified administration of the principal civil service pension scheme as suitable for market testing. New information technology for administration of the scheme, which will start to become operational towards the end of this year, will facilitate the market-testing process. This will also enable service standards to be raised and costs reduced. It will however first be necessary for Parliament to approve an order under the Deregulation and Contracting Out Act which will remove the legal impediment that at present exists to market testing PCSPS administration.

Occupational pension arrangements for civil servants will continue to be provided through the PCSPS. The PCSPS will be managed and controlled by the Office of Public Service and Science.

## AIDS

**Mr. Alex Carlile:** To ask the Chancellor of the Duchy of Lancaster if he will list the research work his Department sponsors on HIV/AIDS which incorporates international co-operation. [24694]

**Mr. Horam:** A list of current research work into AIDS/HIV funded by my Department through the research councils, and involving international co-operation has been placed in the Libraries of both Houses. This list show the titles of the projects, by whom they were carried out and, where information is available, the resources allocated.

**Mr. Alex Carlile:** To ask the Chancellor of the Duchy of Lancaster if he will list the research work sponsored by his Department and the amount spent on each project for AIDS/HIV treatment and prevention for the last five years for which figures are available; and if he will make a statement. [24693]

**Mr. Horam:** The Medical Research Council provided data in answer to a similar question on 11 May 1995, and this was placed in the Libraries of both Houses. Equivalent information for the other research councils funded by my Department which have undertaken research into AIDS/HIV treatment and prevention is as follows:

| Grant Holder | Grant Title | Duration | Cost |
|---|---|---|---|
| *Research supported by the Economic and Social Research Council* | | | |
| Dr. M. Lyons University of London | AIDS and women—the history of sexually transmitted disease and epidemic of HIV/AIDS in East Africa | 1 November 1992 to 1 October 1995 | £129,460 |
| Dr. P. G. Forster Hull University | AIDS, the local community and traditional health practitioners in Malawi | 30 June 1993 to 30 September 1995 | £2,790 |
| Dr. J. Bujra Leeds University | Gender relations as a key aspect of the fight against AIDS/HIV in Tanzania | 1 September 1994 to 1 September 1996 | £150,000 |
| Dr. N. P. McKeganey Glasgow University | An Ethnography of a late teenage population exposed to intravenous drug misuse and HIV | 1 February 1988 to 31 January 1991 | £137,690 |
| Dr. D. V. McQueen Edinburgh | An integrated study of AIDS-related behaviour | 1 August 1988 to 31 December 1990 | £264,850 |
| Dr. H. A. Klee Manchester Polytechnic | The potential for HIV transmission among amphetamine users in the North West: a study of sexual and social lifestyles | 1 July 1989 to 31 December 1991 | £79,550 |
| Dr. G. M. Breakwell Surrey University | Social and behavioral consequences of HIV/AIDS for 16-21 year olds | 1 October 1988 to 31 March 1993 | £308,621 |
| Dr. R. Ingham Southampton University | Social aspects of risk reduction in the light of the threat of HIV infection | 1 January 1989 to 31 December 1991 | £136,182 |
| Dr. M. J. Bloor | A sociological study of the context of AIDS media messages and audience responses | 1 September 1988 to 31 August 1991 | £198,590 |
| Dr. M. A. Plant | HIV/AIDS risks, alcohol and illicit drug use and young adults | 1 July 1992 to 30 September 1992 | £3,260 |
| Dr. G. Semin Sussex University | The transmission and formation of AIDS-related representations in adolescence | 1 December 1987 to 31 January 1991 | £136,980 |
| Dr. J. Holland London University | Young women, sexuality and the limitation of AIDS | 31 October 1988 to 30 September 1990 | £70,926 |
| *Research supported by the Natural Environment Research Council (all at the Institute for Virology and Environmental Microbiology, Oxford)* | | | |
| Dr. P. A. Nuttall | Aids diagnosis | 1 October 1987 to 31 September 1990 | £60,000 |
| Dr. I. M. Jones | Expression, purification and in *vitro* activity of the HIV encoded regulatory protein ART/TRS | 1 January 1988 to 31 December 1990 | £86,000 |
| Dr. I. M. Jones | AIDS vaccine development | 1 April 1988 to 31 March 1991 | £125,000 |
| Dr. I. M. Jones | Expression of simian immunodeficiency virus proteins | 1 September 1989 to 31 March 1993 | £200,000 |
| Dr. I. M. Jones | Structure and function of recombinant HIV antigens | 1 May 1990 to 30 April 1993 | £114,000 |
| Dr. I. M. Jones | Analysis of CD4 binding repertoire of natural GP120 molecules | 1 July 1992 to 30 June 1995 | £194,000 |
| Dr. I. M. Jones | Furin and maturation of lentivirus glycoproteins | 1 January 1993 to 31 December 1996 | £111,000 |
| Dr. P. A. Nuttall | Virology and environmental microbiology | 12 March 1993 to 1 September 1995 | £65,000 |
| Dr. I. M. Jones | Fundamental and comparative studies on the structural proteins of HIV and SIV | 1 October 1993 to 30 September 1995 | £359,000 |
| Dr. P. Roy | Development of virus-like particle (VLP) candidate vaccines for human immuno-deficiency virus (HIV) produced by baculovirus multigene expression vectors | 1 January 1994 to 31 December 1996 | £58,000 |

## AGRICULTURE, FISHERIES AND FOOD

### EU Fishing Industries

**Mr. Austin Mitchell:** To ask the Minister of Agriculture, Fisheries and Food what information he has about the *(a)* Government construction grants, *(b)* fuel subsidies, *(c)* enforcement of minimum/maximum catch sizes, *(d)* enforcement of log book reporting and *(e)* elimination of secret fish holds in each of the other fishing nations of the EEC.    [23986]

**Mr. Jack:** On construction grants and fuel grants, I refer the Hon. Member to the answer that I gave on 6 February 1995, *Official Report,* column 84.

Latest information on the results of inspections on member states' vessels is provided in the summary tables for 1993, produced by the Commission in accordance with Commission regulation (EEC) No. 3561/85: a copy of which is in the Library of the House.

### Fish Imports

**Mr. Sykes:** To ask the Minister of Agriculture, Fisheries and Food what representations he has received from east coast fishermen regarding the importation of cheap fish from Russia, Norway and Iceland.    [24152]

**Mr. Jack:** I regularly consult producers' interests on the question of imports from outside the European Union and this was one of the issues raised with me by fishermen's leaders on my recent visit to Tynemouth earlier this month. Subsequent to that, I have not heard directly on this matter from east coast fishermen.

**Mr. Sykes:** To ask the Minister of Agriculture, Fisheries and Food if he will impose quota restrictions on the importation of cheap fish from Russia, Norway and Iceland.      [24151]

**Mr. Jack:** Mechanisms already exist within European Union legislation to take action against imports from outside the EU where they can be shown to be having a disruptive effect on the market over a period of time. Unqualified restrictions on imports would serve only to prevent UK processors from obtaining the raw material supplies that they need to maintain the range of fish products available to the consumer. I believe that there is scope for better communication within the industry to help match supply and demand. I hope shortly to call a meeting of interested parties to explore the issue further.

### Access to the Countryside

**Mr. Tipping:** To ask the Minister of Agriculture, Fisheries and Food if he will set out for *(a)* the countryside access scheme allowing public access to set-aside land and *(b)* the scheme allowing access for land in environmentally sensitive areas (i) its number and direction of such agreements, (ii) the location and size of these sites, (iii) what steps have been taken to inform the public of these access opportunities, (iv) the payment made to the landowner of each site, (v) the administrative costs of these schemes, (vi) whether public access was available on each site prior to designation under the schemes.      [24618]

**Mr. Jack:** The information requested is as follows:

*(a) Countryside Access Scheme*

(i) There are currently 78 agreements in England. There are similar schemes in Wales and Scotland.

(ii) Details of access agreements have been lodged in the library of the House. The following table gives a summary of the position by county.

| County | Size (in hectares) |
| --- | --- |
| Bedfordshire | 91.3 |
| Cambridgeshire | 93.63 |
| Essex | 126.93 |
| Hertfordshire | 22.05 |
| Norfolk | 111.06 |
| Buckinghamshire | 21.57 |
| Suffolk | 142.52 |
| Cumbria | 4.45 |
| Wiltshire | 41.09 |
| Warwickshire | 16.7 |
| Gloucestershire | 14.33 |
| Yorkshire | 52.04 |
| Humberside | 14.74 |
| Devon | 15 |
| Cornwall | 15 |
| Oxfordshire | 42.55 |
| Surrey | 7.21 |
| Hampshire | 6.89 |
| Kent | 26.27 |
| Northamptonshire | 75.5 |
| Nottinghamshire | 21.78 |
| Shropshire | 1.68 |

(iii) Participants are asked to send a map of the land opened to public access provided by the Ministry, to their local parish council. Further copies of maps are sent to the Countryside Commission, the Rambler's Association and, where appropriate, the local national park authority. Members of the public can request free copies of these maps.

(iv) The first payments to participants will be made early in 1996. Participants will receive an annual rate of £90 per hectare of route opened and £45 per hectare of open field opened to public access for a period of five years. Participants can normally only claim up to a maximum of 15 hectares of public access on any one farm.

(v) In 1994–95 administrative costs were £300,000 in England. This figure includes significant start-up costs as the scheme only opened for applications in September 1994.

(vi) Project officers inspect every potential public access site, any land where there is evidence of existing de facto public access will not normally be accepted into the scheme. Similarly, land which is designated as a public right of way or land to which public access has been secured under another publicly funded scheme is not eligible.

*(b) Environmentally Sensitive Areas Scheme*

(i) 26 management agreements with access tier.

(ii) Details of the access agreements have been lodged with the library of the House. The following table provides a summary by Environmentally Sensitive Area.

| ESA | Number of agreements | Total length (in kilometres) |
| --- | --- | --- |
| Broads | 4 | 4.62 |
| Pennine dales | 2 | 0.91 |
| Somerset levels and moors | 1 | 0.31 |
| South Downs | 1 | 1.38 |
| Suffolk river valleys | 1 | 0.98 |
| Exmoor | 2 | 1.01 |
| Lake District | 10 | 7.55 |
| South West Peak | 1 | 1.25 |
| Dartmoor | 3 | 5.84 |
| Upper Thames tributaries | 1 | 0.48 |

(iii) Maps of completed access routes are sent to the relevant parish councils, the Countryside Commission, the National Park Authority (Where applicable) and the Rambler's Association. These maps may also be sent to other organisations and members of the public, on request.

(iv) Agreement holders receive £170 per kilometre of access route.

(v) Unlike the countryside access scheme, it is not possible to disaggregate the costs of administration of the public access tier from the total costs of administering the ESA scheme.

(vi) Only land which offers new or additional access opportunities is eligible for the scheme. Land which is subject to an existing right of way is not accepted.

### Bovine Spongiform Encephalopathy

**Mr. Clappison:** To ask the Minister of Agriculture, Fisheries and Food if he will make a statement about bovine spongiform encephalopathy.      [25536]

**Mrs Browning:** A further report on BSE in Great Britain is available today. I have arranged for copies to be placed in the Library of the House.

The report provides information about the continuing decline in incidence of the disease, further proposed changes to the controls and the on-going research programme.

The number of cases of BSE being reported at present is 45.3 per cent. fewer than at the same time last year and there is continued downturn in incidence of BSE in five-year-old and younger animals. Both changes are attributed to the ban on feeding ruminant protein to ruminant animals which was introduced in 1988.

I have also arranged for copies of the BSE progress report presented to the Office International des Epizooties this week to be placed in the Library of the House.

### Countryside Stewardship Scheme

**Mr. Clappison :** To ask the Minister of Agriculture, Fisheries and Food what plans he has for the future of the countryside stewardship scheme. [25537]

**Mr. Waldegrave:** The Government are publishing today a public consultation document which seeks views on the development of the Government's strategy for environmental land management schemes in England. The consultation document results from a review of the future role of the countryside stewardship scheme and of ways of better integrating and focusing all environmental land management schemes in England, announced by my right hon. Friend the Secretary of State for the Environment last year on 21 June 1994, *Official Report,* column *106.* The review was carried out by a working group comprising officials from my Department, the Department of the Environment, the Countryside Commission, English Heritage and English Nature. Copies of the consultation document are available in the Library of the House.

The Government believe that environmental land management schemes are one important means of promoting environmental and amenity benefits in the countryside. The conclusion of the pilot phase of countryside stewardship and the decision that it should be transferred to the Ministry of Agriculture, Fisheries and Food in 1996 represent a landmark in the development of such schemes and an opportune moment to review their strategic development.

The main proposals of the working group are that:

the countryside stewardship scheme should continue to be based on the key principles established during the pilot phase;

subject to the availability of resources, the full range of stewardship options should be retained;

countryside stewardship and the environmentally sensitive areas scheme should be developed into the Ministry's two core environmental schemes when I take over responsibility for stewardship from April 1996;

the farm and conservation grant scheme should not continue as a separate scheme in England but capital grants for conservation purposes should be integrated into other schemes, principally countryside stewardship;

further scheme mergers should be considered once the new agri-environment schemes have been operating long enough to be evaluated;

subject to resources being available, the focus of countryside stewardship should be broadened to include two new options targeting traditional stone walls and banks and the remaining unimproved areas of old meadow and pasture on neutral and acid soils throughout lowland England;

the ministry should develop a fuller information service to act as a first stop shop for information and basic advice on the range of environmental schemes for farmers and land managers.

In addition, I have decided in consultation with my right hon. Friend that a national steering group should be set up to advise the Ministry on the objectives, targets and priorities of all its environmental incentive schemes, their effective development and deployment and their monitoring and evaluation, and that liaison arrangements should also be made regionally.

The objective of these proposals is to improve the integration and focus, and hence the effectiveness and efficiency of the Government's range of environmental land management schemes. They are designed to improve the service provided to land managers and to yield greater environmental benefits in the countryside. As such, they would represent a major development of the Government's strategy for such schemes.

My right hon. Friend and I look forward to receiving the responses to this consultation document, which will be fully taken into account in the Government's preparation of the forthcoming rural White Paper.

## NATIONAL HERITAGE

### Museum Entry Charges

**Mr. Malcolm Bruce:** To ask the Secretary of State for National Heritage what is his estimate of the revenue accruing to the Exchequer from charges for entry to museums. [22400]

**Mr. Dorrell:** Of the 17 museums and galleries directly sponsored by my Department, seven charge for admission to their collections and exhibitions. During 1994–95, the income generated by these organisations for admissions is estimated at £11.39 million.

Information about revenue raised from admissions to local authority and independent museums is not held centrally.

## ENVIRONMENT

### Urban Programmes

**Sir Irvine Patnick:** To ask the Secretary of State for the Environment if he will make a statement on the total amount of resources available for local authorities for urban programmes for the last year for which figures are available; and if he will list the allocations to individual authorities. [24359]

**Mr. Curry:** Urban initiatives by local authorities are supported through main programme expenditure by several Government Departments. This is supplemented by targeted programmes which have been brought together into the single regeneration budget. SRB resources are made available to local authorities and other organisations, reflecting the partnership-based approach of many schemes. In total the SRB will fund more than £1.3 billion of regeneration work in 1995–96 in urban and other areas. The Department's 1995 annual report, a copy of which is in the Library, provides detailed information about the programmes supported.

### Sheltered and Supported Housing

**Mr. Jim Cunningham:** To ask the Secretary of State for the Environment what assessment he and his ministerial colleagues have made of the savings to the Exchequer that voluntary organisations provide with sheltered and supported housing. [24026]

**Mr. Robert B. Jones:** Two of the key voluntary providers of sheltered and supported housing are the Abbeyfield societies and almshouses. In 1990 their housing stock represented 1 per cent. and 3 per cent.

respectively of the total sheltered and supported rented housing available for elderly people. Research published last year by the Department[1] found that 28 per cent. of Abbeyfield societies and 100 per cent. of almshouses capital costs were met from non-exchequer sources. Seven per cent. of Abbeyfield and 25 per cent. of almshouses revenue costs were also met from non-exchequer sources.

1 "Living Independently—A study of the Housing Needs of elderly and disabled people", HMSO 1994.

## Compulsory Competitive Tendering

**Mr. McLoughlin:** To ask the Secretary of State for the Environment what are the Government's conclusions following the completion of consultation on their proposals for extending compulsory competitive tendering to information technology, finance and personnel services.                    [25561]

**Mr. Robert B. Jones:** We have been discussing how best to give effect to the Government's decision to extend compulsory competitive tendering to white collar professional and corporate services with local authority representatives and other interested parties since early 1993. That consultation has proved valuable to all parties and I am grateful to all those who play a part.

Last summer we put in place statutory instruments which extended CCT to legal and construction and property services. In the autumn we issued consultation papers setting out the proposed regime for information technology, finance and personnel services. Those attracted between them over 600 responses to my Department, together with 112 to the Scottish Office and 54 to the Welsh Office.

I have considered all the points made carefully with colleagues in all the departments with an interest in the services concerned and am now able to announce the Government's final decisions on CCT for these remaining services.

*IT Services*

Taking first IT services, we have concluded that both the percentage competition requirement of 70 per cent. for this work and the implementation timetable set out in the consultation paper are reasonable and do not intend to alter either, save that English shire authorities remaining unchanged following review by the Local Government Commission will now be expected to follow the timetable I announced on 29 March at column *644*. There is no case for any other substantive change to the proposals put forward in last year's consultation paper. On matters of detail, I am now able to:

confirm that we intend to make an exemption for fire brigade mobilisation and communications systems. The precise wording of this is being discussed with fire service representatives and a specific exemption order will be brought forward in due course. The defined activity does not include fire brigades' radio systems;

confirm the proposed credit for in-house IT support to contractors who have taken on other work on behalf of a defined authority, allowing the authority to count this work towards satisfying its CCT obligations, provided it had been the contractors decision to use the IT in question.

confirm the proposed amendment to guidance on the avoidance of anti-competitive behaviour which will allow an authority to require that contractors use specified software or hardware, including the authority's own systems, where this can be justified on operational grounds.

I have decided to reject arguments for a short term exemption from CCT for project work underway at the time competition bites.

*Finance Services*

We have given very careful consideration to the competition percentage for finance services. The Government wish to put real pressure on authorities to market test theses services and I am confident that all authorities can achieve the competition requirement of 35 per cent. proposed in the consultation paper We do not, therefore, intend to change this figure.

In reaching this conclusion we have had in our minds the Government's commitment that there should be no pressure for compulsory testing of housing benefit or council tax benefit administration. Similarly, the Government have made clear that we are not seeking to compel market testing of those revenues tasks which are to be the subject of an order under the Deregulation and Contracting Out Act 1994 permitting the work to be undertaken by third parties. My hon. Friend the Parliamentary Under-Secretary for Social Security and I consider that authorities can achieve this figure without necessitating the market testing of benefits work or the revenues tasks I have mentioned.

We accept that there are some statutory constraints to contracting out aspects of revenues or benefits work, and many of the services are sensitive. Nevertheless a number of authorities have already shown that, even with these limitations, market testing of this work can improve the quality of the service they are able to offer, and we would encourage them to explore this option on a voluntary basis. Should they choose to do so, this can be counted towards satisfying their obligations under the CCT regime.

Should the percentage chosen in the event be at such a level as to compel any authority to market test benefits administration or other work which we have said should only be exposed voluntarily, we will consider further the arguments for change. Where individual authorities can demonstrate they cannot meet the figure without being compelled to test benefits work the Parliamentary Under-Secretary for Social Security and I will consider sympathetically any request they may put forward for a specific exemption.

In the case of education-related benefits service and student awards administration my hon. Friend the Parliamentary Under-Secretary of State for Education and I have concluded that this work is more closely integrated with the education service that any other part of the authority. The volume of work these services make up is small, and we have concluded there would be little benefit, and possibly some disruption of services, if they were included in the CCT regime. We will, however, wish to consider carefully other methods for improving the efficiency of these services.

Also on finance services, we intend to make two further changes to the proposed regime. The first is to allow a temporary exemption from CCT for project work on the development and implementation of financial information and management systems underway when CCT bites. This will allow internal management changes, some of which may flow from CCT, to be implemented smoothly.

Secondly, I intend to allow English metropolitan districts and London boroughs an additional six months to implement CCT extension, taking their start date to 1

April 1997. This recognises the foreshortened timescale facing these authorities as they prepare for CCT and the need for an adequate lead-in time before new contracts can become operational. The timetable for reorganised shire authorities remains unchanged from that set out in the consultation paper, that which status quo shires will be expected to meet was explained in my announcement of 29 March.

### Personnel Services

Turning lastly to personnel services, we have concluded that the defined activity should be amended to reflect practical concerns raised about the difficulties of bringing certain work into the CCT regime. We intend to specifically exclude:

> (i) all training undertaken by a local authority on behalf of a Training and Enterprise Council (TEC), or, in Scotland, Local Enterprise Council (LEC).
>
> (ii) personnel work undertaken by local authorities as members of consortia (with educational institutions and others) for the pre- and post-qualification training of social workers.
>
> (iii) operational training of fire fighters.

Colleagues in the Department for Education and I also intend to allow in-service teacher training and other education-related training funded through the grant for education support and training—GEST—to be counted towards satisfying the competition requirement in the same way as we have agreed delegated spending under the LMS initiative should count. In Wales Athrawon Bro services will similarly count.

We have also considered carefully authorities concerns that the competition percentage, which we proposed be 35 per cent., was too high and may compel them to introduce organisational changes or to tender unsuitable work. We have concluded that a reduction in the figure is necessary to accommodate these concerns and therefore intend to set the competition requirement at 30 per cent

The study of the options for setting the competition requirement undertaken by KPMG on our behalf illustrated that many authorities already actively test the market for certain aspects of personnel work. Much specialist training, for example, is already provided through contract by external organisations. Since they already have a good record in market testing, CCT should present no new difficulties to authorities, For this reason, I have concluded that no additional time is required to implement personnel CCT. All authorities will therefore be expected to meet the timetable set out in the consultation paper, with the exception of status quo English shire authorities, for which I announced a revised timetable on 29 March.

Finally for personnel services we also intend to increase the de-minimis exemption for personnel work from £300,000 to £400,000 to permit smaller authorities to protect core services.

### Fire Authorities

The regime I have described will, subject to certain exemptions outlined in the consultation papers, apply to all defined authorities which are subject to CCT, with the exception of police authorities, metropolitan fire and civil defence authorities, including London, and combined fire authorities. CCT for IT, finance and personnel in police authorities is the subject of separate consultation still underway.

For single purpose fire authorities my right hon. and noble Friend the Minister of State at the Home Office and I have now decided that, having exempted operational training the competition requirement for the remaining work within the defined activity of personnel services should be reduced to 15 per cent. For IT and finance work the competition requirements remain at 70 per cent. and 35 per cent. respectively, as for other authorities. The implementation timetable for English single purpose fire authorities will remain aligned with that applying to metropolitan districts and London boroughs, save that any new combined authority created following the implementation of local government reorganisation will have two years from the local date for reorganisation to take effect before CCT will bite.

### Conclusion

I will be bringing forward a draft order to add these new services to the CCT regime shortly. Once the House has had the opportunity to debate and approve this order we will bring forward further regulations to put in place the remainder of the regime I have today announced.

The regime I have described today will apply to defined authorities in England, Scotland and Wales. My right hon. Friend the Secretary of State for Wales is considering comments made on the timetable for implementing CCT extension in Wales and will make an announcement in due course. My right hon. Friend the Secretary of State for Scotland announced the timetable which the new Scottish unitary authorities will be expected to follow on 27 January.

This announcement is intended to give all authorities a clear basis on which to plan for the extension of CCT. We will write with copies of the new statutory instruments and detailed guidance on each of the new services as soon as possible.

Following extensive consultation we have now established the statutory framework on which the extension of CCT to all of the white collar services will proceed. This is challenging but, I believe, fair and offers a flexible regime which meets many of the concerns raised with us. I urge all those concerned to strive for the successful implementation of CCT to ensure that local people receive the acknowledged benefits that competition may bring.

### Anti-competitive Behaviour

**Mr. Nigel Evans:** To ask the Secretary of State for the Environment what action he has decided to take against Ribble Valley district council, Sandwell metropolitan borough council and South Lakeland district council following the notices served on them last year for anti-competitive behaviour.    [25562]

**Mr. Robert B. Jones:** On 20 July 1994, my right hon. Friend, the Secretary of State, served a notice under section 13 of the Local Government Act 1988 on South Lakeland district council, setting out his view that the authority had acted anti-competitively during a competition for ground maintenance work. On 30 September he served a similar notice on Sandwell metropolitan borough council, also for ground maintenance work, and on 21 November he served a similar notice on Ribble Valley district council, for refuse collection work.

My right hon. Friend has given careful consideration to the responses to the notices and has today given the authorities directions under section 14 of the Local Government Act 1988.

South Lakeland is required to retender the grounds maintenance work which was the subject of the notice so that new arrangements are in place by 1 April 1996, and to seek the Secretary of State's consent if it wishes to reassign the work to its direct service organisation.

The direction given to Sandwell requires the authority to seek the Secretary of State's consent if it wishes to award the ground maintenance work which was subject of the notice to its direct service organisation when the current arrangements expire in 1997.

Ribble Valley has been directed to retender its refuse collection work so that new arrangements are in place by 1 July 1996, and to seek the Secretary of State's consent if it wishes to reassign the work to its direct services organisation.

### Minister for Bristol

**Mr. Berry:** To ask the Secretary of State for the Environment what expenditure has been incurred by the office of the Minister for Bristol since the present Minister took up post. [24525]

**Sir Paul Beresford** [holding answer 17 May 1995]: Since taking up post, the total expenditure incurred by Lord Astor's office in making visits to Bristol amounts to £1,159.

**Mr. Berry:** To ask the Secretary of State for the Environment on what dates the present Minister for Bristol has visited the city on official business; and whom he met. [24526]

**Sir Paul Beresford** [holding answer 17 May 1995]: The present sponsor Minister for Bristol has visited the city on six occasions. The dates of these visits were:

14 October 1994
11 November 1994
16 January 1995
17 February 1995
15 March 1995
12 May 1995

During these visits the Minister met the following persons:

| Name | Representing |
| --- | --- |
| Ablett Malcolm | Hanson Properties |
| Baker Simon | Western Development Partnership |
| Bale Simon | Communities Organised for a Greater Bristol |
| Barrett Bill | Communities Organised for a Greater Bristol |
| Barnfield Richard | WESTEC |
| Beales Ian | Western Daily Press |
| Bee Will | Bristol Common Purpose |
| Biddle Norman | University of Bristol Council |
| Blake Michael | Knightstone Housing Association |
| Birtchnell Michael | Communities Organised for a Greater Bristol |
| Brown Jeffrey | South Bristol College |
| Bullard Emma | Bristol Common Purpose |
| Bunyan Diane | Bristol City Council |
| Burge Maureen | Communities Organised for a Greater Bristol |
| Burke John | Bristol and West Building Society |
| Channon John | Western Development Partnership |
| Collinge Miles | Bristol Development Corporation |
| Couper Professor Heather | Millennium Commissioner |
| Courtier Peter | Bristol Racial Equality Council |
| Croucher Neil | Bristol Tourism Forum |
| De Groot Lucy | Bristol City Council |

| Name | Representing |
| --- | --- |
| Durie Robert | Western Chamber of Commerce |
| Ewens Alec | Bristol Old Vic |
| Ferguson George | Ferguson Mann Architects |
| Fudge Colin | University of the West of England |
| Hartnell St John | Bristol 1997 |
| Heighton Martin | Bristol City Council |
| Holland Helen | Deputy Leader, Bristol City Council |
| Hood Nicholas CBE | Bristol 2000 |
| Hood Sam | Knightstone Housing Association |
| Irvine Roy | Bristol City Council |
| Jackson Tess | Bristol Arnolfini |
| Johnson David | Councillor, Avon County Council |
| Kay Richard | Communities Organised for a Greater Bristol |
| Kearney Paul | Bristol United Press |
| Kelly Andrew | Bristol Cultural Development Partnership |
| Kenworthy David | Avon and Somerset Constabulary |
| Kershaw Diana | Bristol City Council |
| Kingman Sir John | Bristol University |
| Lawder Simon | "Building a Better Bristol" Campaign |
| McClure Tim | Churches Council for Industry and Social Responsibility |
| McGahey Michael | Westcountry Tourist Board |
| McGowan Hilary | Bristol City Council |
| McGuire Cecilia | Bristol City Council |
| McInally Brian | Gatehouse Enterprise Centre |
| McIver Barry | South Bristol College |
| McKinlay Bob | Bristol Chamber of Commerce and Initiative |
| MacMahon Clara | Bristol Watershed |
| Marshfield Susan | Bristol Chamber of Commerce |
| Mellor David | Alec French Partnership |
| Mordaunt Terence | Bristol Port Company |
| Morris Alfred | Bristol Old Vic |
| Ord David | Bristol Port Company |
| Osbourne Hazel | Communities Organised for a Greater Bristol |
| Pool John | Bristol 2000 |
| Robertson Graham | Leader, Bristol City Council |
| Rogerson Barry | Bishop of Bristol |
| Rylance Nicola | The Bristol Initiative |
| Sandbrook Martin | WESTEC |
| Savage John | Bristol Chamber of Commerce and Initiative |
| Shepherd Tony | Bristol Chamber of Commerce and Initiative |
| Singh Raj | Communities Organised for a Greater Bristol |
| Smetherham David | South Bristol College |
| Smith Steve | CompuAdd Ltd |
| Symonds Brian | CBI |
| Taylor Prue | South Bristol College |
| Thomas Christopher | Bristol Development Corporation |
| Venn Ian | Communities Organised for a Greater Bristol |
| Vincent Martin | CompuAdd Ltd |
| Wall Robert Sir | Conservative Leader of Bristol City Council |
| Warren Claire | Lord Mayor of Bristol |
| Williams Eric | Avon County Council |
| Wordsworth Chris | Hanson Properties |

**Mr. Berry:** To ask the Secretary of State for the Environment what initiatives the present Minister for Bristol has taken for the benefit of the people of the city. [24527]

**Sir Paul Beresford** *[holding answer 17 May 1995]:* The present sponsor Minister for Bristol has, during the first few months of his appointment, been working to encourage partnerships between the public and private sectors which are vital to the future success of Bristol and to capitalise on the substantial public investment secured for the city through, among other things, the Bristol development corporation and single regeneration budget challenge fund.

### Autistic Children

**Mr. Alex Carlile:** To ask the Secretary of State for the Environment what percentage of local authorities provide specialist facilities for autistic children; and if he will make a statement. [23677]

**Mr. Forth:** I have been asked to reply.

I refer the hon. Member to the reply that I gave him on 15 May, *Official Report,* column *13.*

### SOCIAL SECURITY

#### Industrial Injuries Disablement Benefit

**Mr. Tony Banks:** To ask the Secretary of State for Social Security how many claimants were awarded *(a)* weekly industrial disablement benefit and *(b)* reduced earnings allowance in each of the last five years for which figures are available in Newham; how many claims for industrial disablement benefit and reduced earnings allowance were allowed in each of the last six years for which figures are available; and what were the total amounts of (i) lump sum back payments and (ii) gratuities awarded in each year in Newham. [23790]

**Mr. Hague:** The administration of industrial injuries disablement benefit is a matter for Mr. Ian Magee, the chief executive of the Benefits Agency. He will write to the hon. Member with such information as is available.

*Letter from Ian Magee to Mr. Tony Banks, dated 17 May 1995:*

The Secretary of State for Social Security has asked me to reply to your recent Parliamentary Question about awards of Industrial Injuries Disablement Benefit (IIDB) and Reduced Earnings Allowance (REA) in the Benefits Agency's Newham District.

Information about awards of benefit, or claims allowed, is not available for all of the periods requested because collection of the relevant data on an individual office basis did not begin until October 1991. The figures for 1991–92 relating to awards and claims allowed therefore cover a period of only six months. The available information is at Annex A.

The distinction between the figures for IIDB allowed and awarded is that some successful claims do not attract benefit because they are assessed at less than 14%. On the other hand, all claims allowed for REA result in an award of benefit.

Information about lump sum back payments and gratuities is not readily available and could be obtained only at a disproportionate cost.

I hope you find this reply helpful.

*Annex A: Industrial Injuries Disablement Benefit*

| Year | Claims allowed IIDB | Claims awarded IIDB |
| --- | --- | --- |
| 1991–92 | 98 | 59 |
| 1992–93 | 126 | 50 |
| 1993–94 | 142 | 30 |
| 1994–95 | 77 | 31 |

*Note:*
1994–95 figures are provisional and subject to amendment.

*Reduced Earnings Allowance*

| Year | Claims allowed and awarded REA |
| --- | --- |
| 1991–92 | 22 |
| 1992–93 | 20 |
| 1993–94 | 2 |
| 1994–95 | 0 |

*Note:*
1994–95 figures are provisional and subject to amendment.

### St. Paul's Angels Nursery

**Mr. McNamara:** To ask the Secretary of State for Social Security (1) what was the expected working life of St. Paul's Angels benefit agency nursery, Brixton, when it was opened; [24711]

(2) if St. Paul's angels benefit agency nursery, Brixton, is able to offer vacant places to the general public; [24709]

(3) what are the grounds for closing St. Paul's Angels benefit agency nursery, Brixton, after September. [24710]

**Mr. Roger Evans:** This is a matter for Mr. Ian Magee, the chief executive of the Benefits Agency. He will write to the hon. Member.

*Letter from Ian Magee to Mr. Kevin McNamara, dated 17 May 1995:*

The Secretary of State for Social Security has asked me to reply to your recent Parliamentary Questions about the St Paul's Angels Nursery in Brixton.

The nursery was opened on 19 June 1991. No timescale was put on the life of the nursery, but to ensure continuing value for money it has been subject to financial review since it opened.

Since 1991, with the transfer of the bulk of benefit processing work from Brixton to Belfast there has been a significant reduction of locally based Benefits Agency staff to about 70 on the Brixton site. Despite vigorous efforts by management, take up of places has been low and from September 1995, no District staff plan to use the nursery. A review, conducted in March 1995, shows that the nursery does not satisfy the Treasury value for money criteria and there is a financial shortfall.

I should add that local management have attempted to accommodate domestic arrangements by extensive use of flexible working patterns, including allowing staff to work part time.

It is not possible to open the nursery to the public as the Benefits Agency may not trade as a business in competition with the private sector. The Agency is consulting once more with other Government Departments and Agencies in the locality to see if they would be willing to pay the necessary subsidies in respect of their staff's use of the facility. Until this has been done no decision about the future of the nursery can be taken.

I hope you find this reply helpful.

### Incapacity Benefits

**Mr. Wigley:** To ask the Secretary of State for Social Security on what date he received the memorandum from Disability Wales on incapacity benefits, posted to his Department on 4 December 1994; on what date he sent an acknowledgement of receipt of this letter to Disability Wales; and when he expects his Department to answer the letter. [23950]

**Mr. Hague:** A copy of the letter dated 4 December 1994 from Disability Wales was received on 22 March.

A reply was sent on 17 May.

## Fraud

**Mr. Frank Cook:** To ask the Secretary of State for Social Security what was the estimated amount of benefit fraud in each year since 1979.     [23674]

**Mr. Arbuthnot:** The information requested is not available. The benefit savings figures for the fraud detected from 1986–87 are in the table.

| Year | Benefit Savings £ million |
|------|--------------------------:|
| 1986–87 | [1]144 |
| 1987–88 | [1]196 |
| 1988–89 | [1]262 |
| 1989–90 | [1]309 |
| 1990–91 | [2]341 |
| 1991–92 | [2]427 |
| 1992–93 | [2]558 |
| 1993–94 | [2]654 |

[1] Count by district offices.
[2] Count by area fraud sectors after the internal fraud organisation changed.

## Housing Benefit

**Mr. Jim Cunningham:** To ask the Secretary of State for Social Security, (1) what plans he has to exempt sheltered and supported housing from the remit of the proposed changes to housing benefit;     [24023]

(2) what discussions he has had with the National Federation of Housing Associations and other interested bodies with respect to the proposed housing benefit changes, with particular reference to sheltered and supported housing;     [24025]

(3) what savings he is expecting by the expected reductions in housing benefit for sheltered and supported housing;     [24027]

(4) what analysis was made by his Department of the extra costs that sheltered and supported housing would bear under his proposed housing benefit changes.     [24024]

**Mr. Roger Evans:** My right hon. Friend the Secretary of State has recently received the report of the Social Security advisory committee following its public consultation on the proposed changes to housing benefit. We will be considering carefully the position of sheltered and supported housing under the changes as part of our response to the report.

## Amputees

**Mr. McMaster:** To ask the Secretary of State for Social Security if he will list the (i) categories and (ii) range of clothing grants which may be paid to *(a)* single upper limb amputees, *(b)* double upper limb amputees, *(c)* single lower limb amputees, *(d)* double lower limb amputees, *(e)* amputees who have lost one upper and one lower limb. *(f)* triple amputees and *(g)* those who have had all four limbs amputated.     [24122]

**Mr. Hague:** An allowance may be awarded to an arm or leg amputee or other war disablement pensioners whose pensioned disablement and/or prosthesis causes wear and tear of his clothing. Payment of the allowance is not restricted to amputees. The allowance may be paid at one of two rates as follows:

| | £ per annum |
|---|---:|
| Higher rate | 129.00 |
| Lower rate | 82.00 |

If the pensioner wears a single artificial limb—other than a tilting-table limb—the lower allowance is awarded. If he wears a tilting-table limb or has more than one artificial limb, the higher rate is awarded. In any other case where the Secretary of State is satisfied that as a result of the pensioned disablement there is exceptional wear and tear of the pensioner's clothing, the allowance may be awarded at a rate not exceeding the higher rate.

The rate paid to an amputee pensioner is not solely dependent on the site on amputation nor on the number of amputations but on a medical assessment as to the extent the pensioner's accepted disablement and/or prosthesis causes wear and tear of his clothing.

## Fraud

**Mr. McMaster:** To ask the Secretary of State for Social Security what is his estimate of the number of claimants of incapacity for work benefit who are likely to attempt fraud through the false or unnecessary use of wheelchairs; and if he will make a statement.     [24076]

**Mr. Hague:** We have not made such an estimate.

## Low Income Statistics

**Mr. Clappison:** To ask the Secretary of State for Social Security when he will publish a response to the Social Security Select Committee's report, "Low Income Families: Low Income Statistics:", published on 21 March 1995.     [25538]

**Mr. Burt:** A Government response to the Social Security Select Committee's report, "Low Income Families: Low Income Statistics" has been published today. Copies have been placed in the Library.

## Child Support Agency

**Mr. Timms:** To ask the Secretary of State for Social Security what were *(a)* the running costs of the Child Support Agency and *(b)* the costs incurred by his Department in dealing with Child Support Agency matters in (i) 1993–94 and (ii) 1994–95.     [24831]

**Mr. Burt:** The annual accounts for the year ended 31 March 1994 were published on 28 November 1994. These included an expenditure statement prepared on an accruals basis and show that the net cost of operations during 1993–94 was £139 million. Similar accounts will be prepared for 1994–95 and published in the agency annual report.

It is not possible to identify separately the expenditure incurred by the Departmental headquarters in respect of Child Support Agency matters.

**Mr. Clifton-Brown:** To ask the Secretary of State for Social Security what is the average length of time the Child Support Agency takes to make an assessment; and thereafter in what period those assessed have to make a payment.     [20138]

**Mr. Burt** *[Pursuant to his reply Official Report, column 106, 1 May.]:* The information I gave regarding the time taken to complete an assessment was incorrect. The correct information is as follows:

The length of time taken to complete an assessment is variable as it depends on the receipt of information from various sources. Once the agency has all the information it needs, it is currently taking 99 days to complete an assessment. Where no payment is received within 14 days from notification of the maintenance assessment, the agency can consider enforcement action.

**Mr. Timms:** To ask the Secretary of State for Social Security if he will update (a) table G2.04, relating to benefit status of parent or person with care and absent parent, (b) table G2.07 relating to net income from employment of absent parents where maintenance has been assessed and (c) table G2.08 relating to distribution of maintenance assessments of the "Social Security Statistics 1994" by reference to the most recent data from the caseload of the Child Support Agency. [24836]

**Mr. Burt:** The information requested, based on information available at March 1995, is in the tables.

*Benefit Status of Parent with Care and Absent Parent at 11 March 1995*

*Thousands*

| | | | Absent parents | | |
| --- | --- | --- | --- | --- | --- |
| *Parents with care* | *Total* | *[1]On Income Support* | *On Invalidity Benefit, Sickness Benefit or UB* | *Not on benefit* | *Benefit Status not known* |
| Total | 488.0 | 90.1 | 21.9 | 172.3 | 203.7 |
| IS | 391.0 | 77.8 | 18.2 | 138.9 | 156.1 |
| FAMC/DWA | 63.6 | 9.5 | 2.6 | 19.5 | 32.0 |
| No benefit | 33.4 | 2.8 | 1.1 | 13.9 | 15.6 |

*Notes:*

[1] Includes some cases on Invalidity Benefit, Sickness Benefit or UB. In some cases where the MEF was returned the AP's benefit status was not recorded and so the available information on APs may not be fully representative of all cases.

*Net income from employment of Absent Parents at 11 March 1995 where maintenance has been assessed*

| | *Maintenance Assessments* | | |
| --- | --- | --- | --- |
| | *£ per week* | *000's* | *Percentage* |
| All Absent Parents | — | 267.5 | 100.0 |
| APs with no employment income | — | 117.1 | 43.8 |
| APs with employment income | — | 150.4 | 56.2 |
| Average net employment income (£pw) | 195.67 | — | — |
| Net employment income (£pw) | | | |
| Up to 49.99 | — | 3.9 | 1.5 |
| £50.00–£99.99 | — | 8.2 | 3.1 |
| £100.00–£149.99 | — | 33.5 | 12.5 |
| £150.00–£199.99 | — | 43.0 | 16.1 |
| £200.00–£249.99 | — | 31.1 | 11.6 |
| £250.00–£299.99 | — | 16.9 | 6.3 |
| £300.00 or more | — | 13.8 | 5.2 |

*Note:*

Net income from employment is gross pay less income tax and National Insurance contributions. Average net income is the mean for APs with income from employment.

*Distribution of Maintenance Assessments at 11 March 1995*

| | *Maintenance Assessments* | | |
| --- | --- | --- | --- |
| | *£ per week* | *000's* | *percentage* |
| *Full Maintenance Assessments[1]—AP not on Income support* | | | |
| All assessments | — | 175.0 | 100.0 |
| Average Maintenance Assessment (£pw) | 37.22 | — | — |
| £0 | — | 18.3 | 10.5 |
| £0.01–2.30 | — | 24.4 | 13.9 |
| £2.31–£5.00 | — | 1.8 | 1.0 |
| £5.01–£9.99 | — | 4.5 | 2.6 |
| £10.00–£19.99 | — | 11.8 | 6.7 |
| £20.00–£29.99 | — | 15.1 | 8.6 |
| £30.00–£39.99 | — | 18.8 | 10.7 |
| £40.00–£49.99 | — | 18.6 | 10.6 |
| £50.00–£59.99 | — | 17.0 | 9.7 |
| £60.00–£69.99 | — | 17.8 | 10.2 |
| £70.00–£79.99 | — | 13.1 | 7.5 |
| £80.00–£89.99 | — | 7.7 | 4.4 |
| £90.00–£99.99 | — | 3.6 | 2.1 |
| £100–£109.99 | — | 1.3 | 0.7 |
| £100–£119.99 | — | 0.4 | 0.2 |
| £120+ | — | 0.8 | 0.5 |
| *Full Maintenance Assessments[1]—AP on Income Support* | | | |
| All assessments | — | 82.9 | 100.0 |
| Average Maintenance Assessment (£pw) | 0.93 | — | — |
| £0 | — | 48.8 | 58.9 |
| £2.20 | — | 12.1 | 14.6 |
| £2.30 | — | 22 | 26.5 |
| *Interim Maintenance Assessments[2]* | | | |
| All assessments | — | 87.5 | 100.0 |
| Average Maintenance Assessment (£pw) | 96.34 | — | — |
| Under 30.00 | — | 0.0 | 0.0 |
| £30.00–£39.99 | — | 1.1 | 1.3 |
| £40.00–£49.99 | — | 3.0 | 3.4 |
| £50.00–£59.99 | — | 8.7 | 9.9 |
| £60.00–£69.99 | — | 3.0 | 3.4 |
| £70.00–£79.99 | — | 2.5 | 2.9 |
| £80.00–£89.99 | — | 1.9 | 2.2 |
| £90.00–£99.99 | — | 30.3 | 34.6 |
| £100–£109.99 | — | 12.9 | 14.7 |
| £110–£119.99 | — | 13.3 | 15.2 |
| £120+ | — | 10.8 | 12.3 |

[1] Includes Category 'B' Interim Maintenance Assessments.
[2] Excludes Category 'B' Interim Maintenance Assessments.

*Note:*

Category 'B' Interim Maintenance Assessments are made when insufficient information has been provided about the partners of the AP, PWC or about some other member of their households.

## Severe Disability Premium

**Mr. Alfred Morris:** To ask the Secretary of State for Social Security what are the cost implications for income support for severe disability premium of the Court of Appeal's decision in the case of Anne Marie Bate; how many cases are potentially involved; and if he will make a statement. [24880]

**Mr. Roger Evans:** On 9 May the House of Lords Judicial Committee granted the Secretary of State and chief adjudication officer leave to appeal the Court of Appeal judgment in the case of Anne Marie Bate. This means that the exact impact of the judgment on the payment of the severe disability premium within income support will depend on the decision of the House of Lords.

It is difficult to assess the cost implications and numbers of potential cases. The judgment could result in an estimated 45,000 income support claimants being entitled to between one and eight days severe disability premium as a result of the two day period between the judgment and the introduction of amending legislation restoring the original policy intention behind the premium. Additional costs could also arise from appeals currently within the appeal system or later appeals.

Payment of benefit arising as a result of the case has been suspended pending the result of the appeal.

### Income Support

**Mr. Malcolm Bruce:** To ask the Secretary of State for Social Security what is his estimate of the savings to the Exchequer from the lower rate of income support benefit payable to those aged between 18 and 25 years.    [22407]

**Mr. Roger Evans** [*Pursuant to his reply 9 May Official Report column 391*]: The information I gave regarding the current annual cost of raising the income support rate for 18 to 24-year olds was incorrect due to a typographical error. The correct information is as follows.

The current annual cost of raising the income support rate for 18 to 24 year olds to that payable for single people aged 25 and above would be about £420 million.
Notes:
1. The figure is based on the 1990, 1991, 1992 Family Expenditure Surveys, uprated to 1995–96 prices and benefit levels.
2. The figure includes the additional cost of linked increases in housing benefit and council tax benefit.

## SCOTLAND

### Equal Opportunities

**Ms Eagle:** To ask the Secretary of State for Scotland what progress has been made within his Department on equal opportunities matters.    [21481]

**Mr. Lang:** The Scottish Office as an employer, has made considerable progress on equal opportunities issues. Its initiatives have been based on the 1984 report, on "Equality of Opportunity for Women in the Civil Service", and also on the Cabinet Office "Programmes of Action on Race and Disability".

Details of these initiatives can be found in the following Cabinet Office publications:

Civil Service Data Summary 1994

Equal Opportunities for Women in the Civil Service—10 Year Progress Report 1984–94

Annual Reports on the Progress of Women and People of Ethnic Origin

**Ms Eagle:** To ask the Secretary of State for Scotland what progress he hopes to achieve in his Department over the next three months to push forward the declaration signed in October 1994 at the Vienna conference in preparation for the fourth UN conference on women; and if he will agree to incorporate a section on equal opportunities in his Department's annual report.    [21483]

**Mr. Lang:** The Government are committed to the principles set out in the regional platform for action agreed at the preparatory conference in Vienna for the fourth UN world conference on women. We have taken these forward through a wide range of programmes and initiatives and will continue to do so.

In line with the Government's commitment in the White Paper "Taking Forward Continuity and Change", the Scottish Office is committed to reporting on equal opportunities in its annual report.

**Ms Eagle:** To ask the Secretary of State for Scotland if he will publish the gender assessment being prepared by his Department.    [21482]

**Mr. Lang:** The Scottish Office policy, in line with guidance issued in 1992 by the ministerial group on women's issues, is that policy proposals should ensure that unlawful or unjustifiable sex or race discrimination does not occur and that similar principles apply to people with disabilities, older people or ex-offenders. This scrutiny is part of a continuous and routine process, as part of policy advice to Ministers.

**Ms Eagle:** To ask the Secretary of State for Scotland which Minister in his Department has responsibility for equal opportunities issues.    [21480]

**Mr. Lang:** I am responsible, along with my ministerial team, for ensuring that Government policy on equal opportunities is implemented in the Scottish Office.

### Closed Circuit Television

**Sir David Steel:** To ask the Secretary of State for Scotland what principle determines the levels of funding allocated to local authorities for closed circuit television systems in Scotland as compared with England and Wales.    [23641]

**Mr. Lang:** Capital consent allocations to Scottish local authorities are not project specific and it is for local authorities themselves to determine their own priorities for their areas, including the provision of closed circuit television systems, from within the total resource available to them.

A recent competition by the Home Office to fund closed circuit television systems in England and Wales was not emulated in Scotland. In Scotland we remain firmly of the view that funding for the installation of CCTV should continue to be provided by joint ventures involving local businesses, local authorities and other groups who derive a direct benefit from the resource.

These financial arrangements, involving a large public sector commitment, have worked well. I am glad to say that there are already 13 CCTV schemes in Scotland, with more in prospect.

### Public Bodies

**Mr. McMaster:** To ask the Secretary of State for Scotland if he will list the non-departmental public bodies, arms-length organisations, and executive agencies which can be referred to the Parliamentary Commissioner for Administration.    [24212]

**Mr. Lang:** The following non-departmental public bodies sponsored by my Department fall within the jurisdiction of the Parliamentary Commissioner for Administration.

Crofters Commission
New Town Development Corporations
Red Deer Commission
Scottish Arts Council
Scottish Homes

Scottish Legal Aid Board
Scottish Medical Practices Committee
Scottish Natural Heritage
Scottish Sports Council
Scottish Tourist Board

Executive agencies are within the jurisdiction of the Parliamentary Commissioner in the same way as their parent Department. Scottish Office executive agencies are:

Scottish Prison Service
Historic Scotland
Scottish Fisheries Protection Agency
Scottish Agricultural Science Agency
Scottish Office Pensions Agency
Students Awards Agency for Scotland

### Water Boards

**Mr. Salmond:** To ask the Secretary of State for Scotland how much money has been allocated to set up the three new water boards in Scotland; and if he will make a statement. [24805]

**Mr. Kynoch:** A total of £9.7 million has been allocated for grant-in-aid to the new water authorities in 1995–96. The allocations to individual water authorities is shown in the respective grant-in-aid tables at chapter 4 of the Scottish Office departmental report, published as Cm 2814.

### Lucia Martin Johnson

**Mr. Tom Clarke:** To ask the Secretary of State for Scotland if he will intervene in the case of Lucia Martin Johnson of Craigendmuir park, Cardowan, Stepps, to prevent her removal from the United Kingdom. [24863]

**Lord James Douglas-Hamilton:** Under the provisions of the Hague convention on the civil aspects of international child abduction, which were incorporated in to the laws of the United Kingdom by the Child Abduction and Custody Act 1985, such decisions are for the Court of Session and not for my right hon. Friend.

### Smoking

**Mr. Peter Griffiths:** To ask the Secretary of State for Scotland what facilities are provided and arrangements made for the well-being and comfort of staff who (a) smoke and (b) do not wish to be affected by smoking at (i) the workstation and (ii) rest, recreation and refreshment facilities at Dover house, Whitehall, London. [25233]

**Mr. Lang:** My Department introduced restrictions on smoking in 1990 under which smoking is not permitted by staff at any time in work areas, reception areas, corridors, toilets, lifts, conference rooms and staff restaurants, except where there are designated smoking areas. In Dover house there is a designated smoking room in which staff may smoke.

### Fisheries Committee

**Mr. Wray:** To ask the Secretary of State for Scotland what considerations led to the decision not to release externally the annual report of the electricity Fisheries Committee. [24189]

**Sir Hector Monro:** *[holding answer 15 May 1995]:* The annual reports which the Fisheries Committee has made to my right hon. Friend in recent years, were produced on its own initiative. There is no statutory requirement for them. They were made without any expectation on the part of the committee, or hydro-electric companies, that the reports would be given wider distribution. For that reason, these reports have not been released externally. However, the committee will be informed that any future annual reports will be made available on request.

# HEALTH

### Charges and Receipts

**Mrs. Beckett:** To ask the Secretary of State for Health, pursuant to her answer of 2 May, *Official Report*, column *177*, what assumptions informed her estimate of charges and receipts in tables of the departmental report for 1994–95 and 1995–96. [23620]

**Mr. Sackville:** The estimates of charges and receipts for 1994–95 and 1995–96 were published in table 3 of the departmental report, Cmnd 2812.

The estimates of hospital and community health services charges and receipts for 1994–95 were based on the latest national health service trust audited summarisation accounts and on accounts and estimates from health authorities. The 1995–96 hospital and community health services current estimate is based on projections of past trends in receipts and will be revised in the usual way as further information becomes available. The HCHS capital receipts for 1994–95 and 1995–96 assume that some expected land sales which were not completed in 1994–95 will take place in the following year.

The estimate of family health service charges and receipts for 1994–95, reflected the charge levels then in force and forecasts of the volume of prescriptions and dental treatments. The planned increase for 1995–96 reflects the increase in family health services charges announced on 22 February, updated forecasts of the volume of prescriptions and dental treatments, and the knock on effect on charges of the increase in dental fees from 1 April, following the recommendation of the Doctors and Dentists Review Body.

### Dental Services

**Ms Walley:** To ask the Secretary of State for Health what assessment she has made of the number of adults who no longer have access to NHS dentists. [24406]

**Mr. Malone:** All family health services authorities in England report that they can help patients who contact them to find national health service dentists.

**Mr. Wray:** To ask the Secretary of State for Health if her Department will undertake an assessment of the report commissioned by the Austrian Government in 1993 on the role of fluorides in the prevention of caries. [24803]

**Mr. Malone:** Yes, when it is received.

### Operations

**Mrs. Angela Knight:** To ask the Secretary of State for Health what is the average cost of (a) a hip and (b) a cataract operation undertaken by hospitals in Derby. [24215]

**Mr. Sackville:** The information is not available centrally. My hon. Friend may wish to contact Mr. Graham Rudd, chairman of Southern Derbyshire health authority, for details.

### Annual Reports

**Mr. Wray:** To ask the Secretary of State for Health if she will introduce legislation to make it a statutory requirement for *(a)* the Advisory Committee on National Health Service Drugs, *(b)* the Advisory Committee on the Microbiological Safety of Food, *(c)* the Committee on the Carcinogenicity of Chemicals in Food, Consumer Products and the Environment, *(d)* the Committee on the Medical Aspects of Food Policy, *(e)* the Committee for Monitoring Agreements on Tobacco Advertising and Sponsorships, *(f)* the Committee on the Medical Aspects of Radiation in the Environment, *(g)* the Committee on the Mutagenicity of Chemicals in Food, Consumer Products and the Environment and *(h)* the Committee on Toxicity of Chemicals in Food, Consumer Products and the Environment, to lay an annual report before Parliament. [24203]

**Mr. Sackville:** There are no plans to introduce legislation to make it a statutory requirement for any of these bodies to lay their annual reports before Parliament. The following bodies already publish their annual reports through HMSO:

   Advisory Committee on the Microbiological Safety of Food;

   Committee on the Carcinogenicity of Chemicals in Food, Consumer Products and the Environment;

   Committee for Monitoring Agreements on Tobacco Advertising and Sponsorship;

   Committee on the Mutagenicity of Chemicals in Food, Consumer Products and the Environment.

   Committee on Toxicity of Chemicals in Food, Consumer Products and the Environment.

The annual report for the Committee on the Medical Aspects of Food Policy is available from the body itself. Reports from the Committee on the Medical Aspects of Radiation in the Environment are published by HMSO, although not necessarily annually.

The Advisory Committee on National Health Service Drugs does not publish an annual report. Its recommendations are made to my right hon. Friend the Secretary of State who considers them in the formulation of policy.

### Nurse Training

**Mr. Spellar:** To ask the Secretary of State for Health how many individuals have commenced nursing training in each of the last five years. [24354]

**Mr. Sackville:** Data on the number of entrants to initial pre-registration nursing education are collected by the English National Board for Nursing, Midwifery and Health Visiting. Copies of the board's annual report for 1993–1994 are available in the Library.

### Kawasaki Disease

**Dr. Lynne Jones:** To ask the Secretary of State for Health, pursuant to her answer of 28 February, *Official Report*, column 495, what information about Kawasaki disease has now been made available to doctors through *(a)* her Department and *(b)* health authorities. [24080]

**Mr. Sackville:** The chief medical officer plans to include advice on the diagnosis and treatment of Kawasaki disease in his "Update" newsletter which is sent to all doctors in contract with the national health service. Copies are also placed in the Library.

Details of the information which health authorities make available to doctors is not collected centrally.

### Myalgic Encephalomyelitis

**Mr. McMaster:** To ask the Secretary of State for Health if she will support the campaign to make the people of the United Kingdom more aware of myalgic encephalomyelitis; if she will increase official recognition of the disease; and if she will make a statement. [24096]

**Mr. Sackville:** We recognise what is increasingly being referred to as chronic fatigue syndrome as a potentially debilitating and distressing complex and we would support any informed efforts to raise awareness of this condition. Unfortunately, the causes of CFS are not understood, nor is there a generally agreed method of treatment.

The national task force on CFS, PVFS—post viral fatigue syndrome—and ME, which is independent of the Department, has produced a report. With a view to securing progress and promoting the development of a professional consensus, the chief medical officer has invited the conference of medical royal colleges to consider the report. The views of the conference of colleges will be of much assistance to the Department in helping to determine the best way forward.

### Temazepam

**Mr. McMaster:** To ask the Secretary of State for Health when she next plans to meet representatives of the Advisory Committee on the Misuse of Drugs to discuss the rescheduling of temazepam; and if she will make a statement. [24120]

**Mr Bowis:** I refer the hon. Member to the reply my right hon. Friend the Lord President of the Council gave the hon. Member for Ayr (Mr. Gallie) on 10 May at column 756.

### Capital Expenditure

**Mrs. Angela Knight:** To ask the Secretary of State for Health what has been the capital expenditure on *(a)* the Derbyshire royal infirmary, *(b)* Derby City general hospital and *(c)* the Queens medical centre, Nottingham since (i) 1979 and (ii) 1992. [24213]

**Mr. Sackville:** Information on capital expenditure is not available centrally. My hon. Friend may wish to contact David Dawson, Norman Woods and Martin Suthers, chairmen of Derbyshire royal infirmary, Derby City general hospital and Queen's medical centre, respectively for details.

### Peto Institute

**Mr. Jim Cunningham:** To ask the Secretary of State for Health (1) what discussions she has had with the Foreign Secretary in respect of the transfer of moneys promised to the Peto institute in Hungary to the Peto institute in Britain; [24503]

(2) if the Peto institute complies with the criteria under the section 64 scheme, to apply for a grant this year; and what other financial assistance is available to the Foundation for Conductive Education. [24504]

**Mr. Bowis:** I refer the hon. Member to the reply I gave him on 18 April at column *113*. Any application from the Foundation for Conductive Education for funding in 1996–97 under the section 64 scheme would be considered on its merits. The Health and Education Departments keep in close touch with the Foreign and Commonwealth Office about the agreement between the United Kingdom and Hungarian Governments covering the construction of a new international Peto institute in Budapest and I met the Hungarian Minister of Health in Budapest on 19 September 1994 to discuss progress.

### Rubber Gloves

**Mr. Congdon:** To ask the Secretary of State for Health what dangers her Department has identified in the use of certain types of rubber gloves used by health service workers; what assessment her Department has made of allergic reactions caused by the use of rubber surgical gloves used by health service workers; and what advice her Department gives to DHAs as to the purchasing of rubber surgical gloves. [24580]

**Mr. Sackville:** The Department is investigating claims of an apparent increase in the incidence of latex sensitivity in the last two years. The Medical Devices Agency is consulting experts in the field and reviewing survey information from other countries. A safety notice will be issued shortly drawing attention to the fact of latex sensitivity. Health authorities and national health service trusts are advised to buy surgeon's gloves and examination gloves which meet the Department's specification and quality standards, as do all such gloves supplied through the national and divisional contracts of the NHS Supplies Authority. Non-latex gloves are available under those contracts, if required.

### Richard Linford

**Mr. Cohen:** To ask the Secretary of State for Health (1) if she will call for a report into the medical care given to Mr. Richard Linford and Mr. Christopher Edwards, prior to their imprisonment; and is she will make a statement; [24665]

(2) if she will make a statement on the treatment of Mr. Richard Linford at Broomfield hospital, Chelmsford following his arrest for assault in November 1994. [24664]

**Mr. Bowis:** North Essex health authority, Essex social services and the Home Office, representing the Prison Service, are establishing an independent inquiry into the care of Christopher Edwards and Richard Linford as required by HSG(94)27, copies of which are available in the Library.

### Hib Vaccine

**Mr. Mike O'Brien:** To ask the Secretary of State for Health what impact the Hib vaccine has had on cases of Hib meningitis since its introduction. [24563]

**Mr. Sackville:** The introduction of Hib vaccine, in October 1992, has had a dramatic impact on cases of invasive Hib disease, including meningitis. Disease among young children targeted by Hib immunisation has almost completely disappeared. Laboratory reports show that cases of Hib meningitis in the under-fives fell from 347 in 1991 to just 11 last year; a reduction of 97 per cent.

**Mr. Mike O'Brien:** To ask the Secretary of State for Health what is her Department's policy on advice to be given to parents by GPs about the level and type of protection given against meningitis by the Hib vaccine; and what monitoring is undertaken by her Department to ensure this advice is complied with. [24565]

**Mr. Sackville:** Before the introduction of Hib vaccine into the childhood immunisation programme in October 1992, the Department of Health provided all health professionals with a comprehensive pack of information on the vaccine, including guidance on answering parents' questions. The pack includes information from Hib vaccine trials which showed 95 per cent. of children immunised developed effective levels of protection. It also clearly states that the vaccine gives protection against the invasive forms of Hib disease, including meningitis, but that it will not protect against other types of meningitis. Information about the type of protection Hib vaccine gives against meningitis is also contained in parents' information literature published by the Health Education Authority.

The Health Education Authority conducts a continuous tracking study of parental attitudes and knowledge of all immunisations in the childhood programme, including Hib. for the Department.

### Tuberculosis

**Mr. Mike O'Brien:** To ask the Secretary of State for Health what has been the incidence of tuberculosis among persons who had at some stage had the BCG vaccine in each of the last five years; and what conclusions she has reached concerning the effectiveness of the BCG from this information. [24566]

**Mr. Sackville:** Whether or not a patient with tuberculosis had previously received BCG vaccine is not routinely recorded, nor was this information collected during the 1993 national survey of notifications of tuberculosis.

### Hospitals

**Mr. Devlin:** To ask the Secretary of State for Health if she will set out for *(a)* St. Bartholomew's hospital, London and *(b)* North Tees general hospital, Stockton-on-Tees (i) the catchment population, (ii) the annual revenue and capital budgets, (iii) the number of consultant medical staff, (iv) the number of nursing staff, (v) the average waiting time for patients and (vi) the proximity of the nearest general hospital. [24700]

**Mr. Sackville:** The information on St. Bartholomew's hospital is not available centrally, as St. Bartholomew's is a constituent part of a larger unit—the Royal London Hospitals national health service trust. My hon. Friend may wish to contact the chairman of the trust, Sir Derek Boorman for specific details.

For information about North Tees general hospital, my hon. Friend may wish to contact Ms J. Graham Bowman, chairman of the North Tees health NHS trust, for details.

## Asthma

**Mr. Mike O'Brien:** To ask the Secretary of State for Health how many cases of childhood asthma have been reported in Britain in each of the last 15 years; and what percentage this is of the children in Britain. [24561]

**Mr. Sackville:** Information is not available in the form requested. It has been estimated that 4 to 6 per cent. of children have asthma requiring regular medical supervision.

Earlier this year, the Department of Health published "Asthma—An Epidemiological Overview", copies of which are available in the Library. This overview brings together a range of statistics on asthma.

## Recruitment

**Mrs. Beckett:** To ask the Secretary of State for Health what representations she has received from *(a)* hospitals and *(b)* general practice about difficulties in recruiting doctors; and if she will make a statement. [24721]

**Mr. Malone:** We have received some representations from NHS trusts. However, this may be due to factors such as the geographical location or proposed duties of the posts. The number of NHS consultants continues to rise steadily, with average annual increases over the five years to 1993 well in excess of the Government's 2 per cent. target.

The specialist workforce advisory group, SWAG, recognises the need to have better information about recruitment difficulties in relation to hospital doctors. SWAG has recently conducted a survey on this issue in a small sample of trusts. Most of the responses have now been received, and SWAG will use this information to help it make decisions on the relative priority with which it should examine individual specialties.

Some general medical practitioners have expressed concern about recruitment into general practice. However, the number of general practitioner principals continues to increase year on year.

## Alcohol Consumption

**Mr. Alex Carlile:** To ask the Secretary of State for Health what evidence she has received on the relationship between alcohol consumption and heart disease; and if she will make a statement. [24712]

**Mr. Bowis:** This is one of the matters currently being considered by the inter-departmental group on sensible drinking. The group has received about 90 pieces of evidence on the effects of alcohol consumption on health, including the effects on heart disease.

## Emergency Admissions

**Mrs. Beckett:** To ask the Secretary of State for Health what has been the number of *(a)* surgical, *(b)* adult medical, *(c)* paediatric, *(d)* intensive therapy units, *(e)* A and E and *(f)* other, emergency admissions in each of the last 10 years. [24722]

**Mr. Sackville:** Information for the years 1988–89 to 1993–94 is shown in the table. Comparable data for earlier years are not available centrally. Patients in intensive therapy units are admitted under the care of consultants in the specialties that provide the treatment.

Emergency admissions, numbers of finished consultant episodes:

| | 1993–94 | 1992–93 | 1991–92 | 1990–91 | 1989–90 | 1988–89 |
|---|---|---|---|---|---|---|
| Acute surgical | 1,312,775 | 1,287,166 | 1,213,773 | 1,246,919 | 1,258,519 | 1,234,125 |
| Acute medical (not Paediatrics) | 1,370,415 | 1,258,608 | 1,182,521 | 1,167,393 | 1,158,073 | 1,114,957 |
| Paediatrics | 464,118 | 429,110 | 433,369 | 406,353 | 400,576 | 384,851 |
| A and E speciality | 85,510 | 82,225 | 81,656 | 82,901 | 84,046 | 82,132 |
| Other emergency | 600,680 | 583,786 | 545,991 | 548,859 | 521,520 | 486,005 |

*Source:*
Hospital Episode Statistics.

## World Health Organisation

**Mr. Dalyell:** To ask the Secretary of State for Health what is Her Majesty's Government's policy in respect of the motion made by certain African countries in respect of the position of the current director general of the World Health Organisation. [24507]

**Mr. Malone:** The draft resolution proposed by two African countries in respect of the current director general of the World Health Organisation was withdrawn by its sponsors after it failed to attract support among other African countries, and before member states from other WHO regions had commented on it.

## Junior Doctors

**Mr. Alex Carlile:** To ask the Secretary of State for Health what measures are in place to improve the working conditions, living conditions and terms of employment of junior doctors; what percentage of junior doctors is currently receiving implemented improvements; and if she will make a statement. [24695]

**Mr. Malone:** "The New Deal on Junior Doctors' Hours", copies of which are available in the Library, has resulted in significant improvements in the conditions of junior doctors. Over 96 per cent. of the 27,669 junior doctors and dentists in England now comply with the current new deal contracted hours' targets.

We have devoted over £180 million to support the new deal. Our task forces, working closely with hospitals, have made excellent progress in using this money not only to reduce junior doctors' hours but to make real improvements in their living and working conditions. Over 2,000 new posts for doctors, including over 900 extra consultant posts, have been funded centrally or locally to support the new deal. We have also enabled task forces to spend significant sums in-year on improving living and working conditions.

We introduced in 1992 a new, more flexible, pay system which recognises the diversity of junior doctors' working patterns and rewards them according to their level of work intensity. We have also accepted a recommendation this year from the Doctors and Dentists Pay. Review Body to increase the rate of pay for on-call work for house officers and senior house officers. This improves their position relative to other doctors in training.

We are committed to ensuring that the very encouraging progress made so far is sustained and that we continue to move forward in providing a better working and training environment for junior doctors. This will help to improve the quality of patient care delivered by doctors.

### Medical Graduates

**Mr. Alex Carlile:** To ask the Secretary of State for Health how many medical graduates leave the profession within three years of graduation.                    [24696]

**Mr. Malone:** Data are not available in the form requested.

### Pre-Registration House Officer Posts

**Mr. Alex Carlile:** To ask the Secretary of State for Health if she will make a statement on the process for allocation of pre-registration house officer posts.  [24697]

**Mr. Malone:** The Department seeks the advice of the postgraduate deans and the medical profession's joint consultants committee on the number and distribution of pre-registration house officer posts. The aim is that there should be sufficient posts to ensure that all new graduates are able to obtain a PRHO post. There is a small—currently 12.5 per cent.—excess of posts to ensure that they have some choice.

### Ambulance Services

**Mr. Alex Carlile:** To ask the Secretary of State for Health (1) if she will make a statement on the change in emergency demand and urgent demand for ambulance services in 1994–95;                                [24698]

(2) if she will list the ambulance services which failed to meet patients charter standards in any month for the year 1994–95, and the total number of months in which each ambulance service failed to meet patients charter standards; and if she will make a statement.      [24699]

**Mr. Sackville:** This information is not collected on a monthly basis. Information on ambulance service activity in 1994–95 will not be available until later in the year.

### Read Clinical Codes

**Mrs. Beckett:** To ask the Secretary of State for Health if she will list the total sums paid for the Read code by the NHS; and to whom these sums were paid.    [24762]

**Mr. Sackville:** The sum paid by the Secretary of State for the Read clinical codes is commercial-in-confidence information. The agreed amount was paid directly to the inventor and developer of the codes, Dr. James Read, in April 1990.

### Telephone Links (South Thames Regional Office)

**Mrs. Beckett:** To ask the Secretary of State for Health (1) what is the total cost to South Thames regional health authority of purchasing electronic links computer equipment for new 10 digit telephone numbers within the NHS;                                        [24789]

(2) from which budget South Thames regional health authority is purchasing electronic links computer equipment.                                        [24788]

**Mr. Sackville:** The telephone switchboard at Eastbourne terrace, the location of both South and North Thames regional health authorities, will be upgraded at a cost of £8,500 to make it compatible with the existing Department of Health telephone system. This will have significant benefits and will be funded from the office information system implementation budget for the North and South Thames regional office.

### Breast Cancer

**Ms Lynne:** To ask the Secretary of State for Health what consideration she is giving to extending the age that women are automatically screened for breast cancer.    [24824]

**Mr. Sackville:** A study is being planned looking at the benefits and cost-effectiveness of including women aged 65 or over in the breast screening programme. Research is already under-way on the effectiveness of screening women aged 40 to 50.

**Ms Lynne:** To ask the Secretary of State for Health if she will list the research currently being conducted into *(a)* breast screening of women 65 years and over, *(b)* breast screening of women under 50 and *(c)* the interval between breast screening which her Department has (i) commissioned and (ii) evaluated; and if she will detail for each (1) the body undertaking the research, (2) the geographical areas covered, (3) the sample size, (4) the expected completion date and (5) the cost of the exercise.                                        [24825]

**Mr. Sackville:** The United Kingdom Health Departments, along with the Medical Research Council, which receives its grant-in-aid from the office of my right hon. Friend the Chancellor of the Duchy of Lancaster, and the two major cancer research charities—the Cancer Research Campaign and the Imperial Cancer Research Fund—are currently funding four studies into breast cancer screening costing £5 million over five years. Two of these trials relate to:

(i) *The effects of screening women annually from age 40*

This is a multi-centre trial of some 195,000 women aged 40–41 who were identified and randomly allocated to a study group of 65,000 or a control group of 130,000. An interim analysis will take place in 1996, after which a decision on future funding will be taken.

(ii) *The effects of screening more frequently than every three years in women aged 50 and over*

This is a five-centre randomised trial looking at annual screening. The aim is to recruit 100,000 women aged 50 to 64. This trial is due to finish in 1996.

The trials are being co-ordinated by the United Kingdom co-ordinating committee on cancer research. The Department of Health contributed £270,000 to the trials in 1994–95.

The Department also funds the cancer screening evaluation unit at the Royal Marsden hospital, Sutton, by some £400,000 per year. The CSEU has a wide remit for the evaluation of cancer screening, a large part of which relates to breast cancer screening. This includes the co-ordination of the multi-centre UKCCCR age trial.

A study is planned to look at the benefits and cost-effectiveness of including women aged 65 or over in the breast screening programme.

## Imported Monkeys

**Mrs. Beckett:** To ask the Secretary of State for Health what assessment she has made as to potential health hazards posed by the import of monkeys into the United Kingdom.    [24786]

**Mr. Sackville:** All monkeys imported into Great Britain have to be licensed by the Ministry of Agriculture, Fisheries and Food and must spend six months in quarantine. Importers carry out tests for infectious agents that might be transmitted to humans before importation and during the period of quarantine. Instructions on preventing the spread of infection are given to those who handle monkeys as part of their work. Our medical advice is that these steps are adequate to protect human health.

## Medical Insurance

**Mrs. Beckett:** To ask the Secretary of State for Health what responsibility a family health services authority has to ensure that a general practitioner holds current medical insurance.    [24785]

**Mr. Malone:** None. General practitioners, as self-employed contractors, have responsibility for ensuring where appropriate, that they hold medical insurance. Subscriptions to medical defence bodies are fully reimbursed to the profession through the cost-plus contract.

## Disciplinary Tribunals

**Mrs. Beckett:** To ask the Secretary of State for Health in what circumstances a nurse may present evidence to a hospital disciplinary tribunal.    [24787]

**Mr. Sackville:** There are no special provisions or circumstances which affect the attendance of nurses at disciplinary hearings; like other members of staff they may be called on to give evidence.

## HIV-AIDS

**Mr. Kirkwood:** To ask the Secretary of State for Health what initiatives have been undertaken by her Department to warn young people of the need to protect themselves against HIV when travelling abroad.    [24862]

**Mr. Sackville:** The Health Education Authority which has the responsibility for the national HIV public education programme runs a summer campaign every year to alert travellers to the risk of HIV infection when they go abroad. This year and for the past two years the Department of Health has also run its HIV "Travel Safe Campaign" which is aimed at young, independent travellers. National initiatives are amply supported by travel projects funded at local level in the national health service.

## TRANSPORT

## Motorway Traffic, Hampshire

**Mr. Chidgey:** To ask the Secretary of State for Transport what sections of motorways in Hampshire currently have traffic levels which exceed on average 75,000 vehicles per day; and what sections are expected to have such traffic levels by 2000.    [24299]

**Mr. Watts:** This is an operational matter for the Highways Agency. I have asked the chief executive to write to the hon. Member.

*Letter from Lawrie Haynes to Mr. David Chidgey, dated 18 May 1995:*

As you know, the Minister for Railways and Roads, Mr. John Watts, has asked me to reply to your Parliamentary Question asking the Secretary of State for Transport what sections of motorways in Hampshire currently have traffic levels which exceed on average 75,000 vehicles per day and what sections are expected to have such traffic levels by the year 2000

The following sections of motorway currently have traffic levels in excess of 75,000 vehicles per day:-

M3 Junctions 4–6 (Camberley to Basingstoke)
M27 Junctions 5–9 (Stoneham to Park Gate)
M27 Junctions 11–12 (Fareham to Portsmouth)

By the year 2000, the following additional sections are expected to have flows in excess of 75,000 vehicles per day:-

M3 Junctions 9–14 (Winnall to M27 Chilworth)
M27 Junctions 4–11 (Chilworth to Fareham).

## Road Surfacing

**Mr. Gordon Prentice:** To ask the Secretary of State for Transport what is the cost of *(a)* laying and *(b)* maintaining 100 yards of (i) porous and (ii) conventional asphalt.    [23863]

**Mr. Watts:** This is an operational matter for the Highways Agency. I have asked the chief executive to write to the hon. Member.

*Letter from Lawrie Haynes to Mr. Gordon Prentice, dated 18 May 1995:*

The Minister for Railways and Roads, Mr. John Watts MP, has asked me to write to you in reply to your recent Parliamentary Question concerning the cost of (a) laying and (b) maintaining 100 yards of (i) porous asphalt and (ii) conventional asphalt.

My previous answer of 8 March quoted a range of prices for one kilometre length within a typical surfacing contract. Prices for a 100 yards length would be approximately 10% of those quoted figures. For instance a two lane dual carriageway all purpose road would be £10,000 to £20,000 for porous asphalt and £7,000 to £10,000 for conventional asphalt. I should point out that where only short lengths such as 100 yards are to be surfaced the costs would rise substantially for both porous asphalt and conventional asphalt due to the increased impact of fixed site costs. As we have little experience of such working we are unable to be more precise.

Differences in maintenance cost between porous asphalt and conventional asphalt relate chiefly to the need for more frequent resurfacing with porous asphalt, the extra cost of the porous asphalt material and the more frequent salting operations needed for porous asphalt in winter. It is currently not possible to give any representative information on the additional cost of salting given the limited amount of porous asphalt which has been laid and the recent mild winters. However, I am able to give you an indication of the difference in material and laying costs. Broadly speaking, maintaining a porous asphalt surface over the life of a road will be of the order of double the cost of maintaining a conventional asphalt surface. This does not take into account the effect of traffic delays during roadworks which will add to the cost of maintaining porous asphalt because of the need for more frequent resurfacing.

As explained in my letter the costs are influenced by numerous factors such as traffic and climatic conditions. These also have an influence on the life of a road surface. Consequently the performance of the different surfaces will vary significantly from site to site.

**Mr. Chidgey:** To ask the Secretary of State for Transport what are the locations of the sections of Britain's motorways that currently have porous asphalt surfacing; what total length of motorways is covered in porous asphalt surfacing; and what total length of motorway covered in porous asphalt surfacing currently have traffic levels *(a)* below and *(b)* above 75,000 vehicles per day.                                    [24300]

**Mr. Watts:** This is an operational matter for the Highways Agency. I have asked the chief executive to write to the hon. Member.

*Letter from Lawrie Haynes to Mr. David Chidgey, dated 18 May 1995:*

The Minister for Railways and Roads, Mr. John Watts MP, has asked me to write to you in reply to your recent Parliamentary Question concerning the locations of lengths of porous asphalt laid on motorways throughout Britain and of those the total lengths carrying above and below 75,000 vehicles per day.

You will appreciate that the Secretary of State for Transport and the Highways Agency are responsible only for roads in England. Roads in Scotland and Wales are the responsibility of the appropriate Secretaries of State and I am not able to provide information to you for those areas.

Porous asphalt surfacings have been used within two long term trials on the M1 in Yorkshire and on the M6 in Lancashire. In addition, porous surfaces have been used on the M40 (Junction 6 - Postcombe) and on the M25 widening (Junctions 7-8) currently under construction.

To date the total length of motorway covered with porous asphalt is approximately 4.5 miles excluding the trials. These trials comprise approximately 1.1 miles but in each case it is only one or part of one of the two carriageways which has been treated.

None of the lengths with porous asphalt surfacing carry flows less than 75,000 vehicles per day.

**Mr. Chidgey:** To ask the Secretary of State for Transport, pursuant to his answer of 9 May, *Official Report,* columns *351–52,* in what specific circumstances porous asphalt is considered not to be technically suitable as a noise mitigation measure on motorways.          [24461]

**Mr. Watts:** This is an operational matter for the Highways Agency. I have asked the chief executive to write to the hon. Member.

*Letter from Lawrie Haynes to Mr. David Chidgey, dated 18 May 1995:*

The Minister for Railways and Roads, Mr. John Watts MP, has asked me to write to you in reply to your recent Parliamentary Question concerning the specific circumstances porous asphalt is considered not to be technically suitable as a noise mitigation measure on motorways.

The technical limitations on the use of porous asphalt on motorways and other trunk roads are set out in the Design Manual for Roads and Bridges, Volume 7, Section 2, Part 4, HD27/94 as published by HMSO. This states that porous asphalt should not be used in the following situations:

   a) On areas where the pavement strength is sub-standard.

   b) On areas where there is considerable acceleration, braking, turning and parking.

   c) On tight radius curves, and loops of radii less than 75 metres, or when gradients exceed 10 per cent., without advice from the Overseeing Department.

   d) On areas where excessive deposits of detritus or oil and fuel may be experienced; such as parking areas, exits from farms and quarries and other industrial sites.

   e) On areas where the use of tracked vehicles, construction plant, farm equipment or similar industrial vehicles is expected.

   f) On areas where the cross-fall is insufficient to remove water to the road edge such that flooding may occur in the porous asphalt.

   g) At locations where free drainage cannot be accommodated along the low edge of the surfacing; for example abutting other types of construction such as a concrete carriageway.

   h) Generally on lengths of carriageway less than 100m, because of spray carry-over from adjacent surfacing, unless special conditions prevail.

   i) Where cyclists use the carriageway and where kerbs are provided, unless provision is made to ensure drainage design overcomes any possible safety hazards.

   j) On existing new bridges where it is not possible to adequately drain the surface.

   k) In urban environments, where frequent excavations by statutory undertakers may occur.

   l) Where traffic levels exceed 4,000 commercial vehicles per lane per day, at opening, without reference to the Overseeing Department. This is being extended to embrace traffic levels up to 6,000.

Porous asphalt is not recommended for use on jointed concrete or flexible composite road pavements without seeking advice from the Overseeing Department. Additionally, it is not recommended for certain steel deck bridges.

Whilst the above limitations currently apply the Highways Agency has implemented a research programme to see if it is possible to produce more durable porous asphalt and reduce the number of limitations.

### Motorway Noise

**Mr. Chidgey:** To ask the Secretary of State for Transport, pursuant to his answer of 9 May, *Official Report,* column *345,* what is the definition adopted by his Department of noise levels being unreasonably high at adjacent properties to a motorway; and what consideration is given to the expected increase in noise levels due to the future growth in traffic.          [24458]

**Mr. Watts:** This is an operational matter for the Highways Agency. I have asked the chief executive to write to the hon. Member.

*Letter from Lawrie Haynes to Mr. David Chidgey, dated 18 May 1995:*

The Minister for Railways and Roads, Mr. John Watts MP has asked me to write to you in reply to your recent Parliamentary Question concerning the definition adopted of noise levels being unreasonable adjacent to motorways and what allowance is made for traffic growth.

The level of traffic noise which is taken to be unreasonable is that prescribed by the Noise Insulation Regulations, namely a level which is predicted to exceed 68 db(A) at the facade of a residential property, of which an increase of at least 1db(A) is attributable to traffic on the new or improved road. Future growth of traffic, both on the new road and associated roads in the area, is taken into account by basing predicted noise levels on the most adverse combination anticipated within 15 years of the new road or improvement being open to traffic.

**Mr. Chidgey:** To ask the Secretary of State for Transport, pursuant to his answer of 9 May, *Official Report,* column *344,* for what reasons only motorways which had a start of works prior to April and which are still under construction are considered for the provision of acoustic fencing.          [24459]

**Mr. John Watts:** This is an operational matter for the Highways Agency. I have asked the chief executive to write to the hon. Member.

*Letter from Lawrie Haynes to Mr. David Chidgey, dated 18 May 1995:*

As you know, the Minister for Railways and Roads, Mr. John Watts, has asked me to reply to your Parliamentary Question asking the Secretary of State for Transport for what reasons only motorways which had a start of works prior to April and that are still under construction are considered for acoustic fencing.

The provision of acoustic fencing is considered for all new motorway and motorway widening schemes as the noise mitigation part of a package of environmental measures. But how much is provided in any one year depends on when the particular scheme starts and the contractors programme of work on that scheme.

Thus in answering your previous question, we could only give details of fencing for schemes which had started and therefore had a known contractors works programme. Information for schemes which are due to start this year will become available when the contractors submit their programme and I shall write to you again.

**Mr. Chidgey:** To ask the Secretary of State for Transport, pursuant to his answer of 9 May, *Official Report*, column *346*, how he allows for the cost of compensation for loss in property values under part I of the Land Compensation Act 1973 in making a cost benefit analysis of proposals for acoustic fencing and other noise mitigation measures for motorways in the absence of specific figures. [24400]

**Mr. Watts:** This is an operational matter for the Highways Agency. I have asked the chief executive to write to the hon. Member.

*Letter from Lawrie Haynes to Mr. David Chidgey, dated 18 May 1995:*

The Minister for Railways and Roads, Mr. John Watts MP, has asked me to write to you in reply to your Parliamentary Question concerning how costs of compensation for loss in property values under Part I of the Land Compensation Act 1973 are taken into account in cost benefit analysis of proposals for acoustic fencing.

Composite estimates of the likely amount of compensation payable are provided by the District Valuer at various stage of development of a road proposal. Estimates of the element of compensation attributable to loss in property value under Part I of the Land Compensation Act take into account the mitigating effect of any protective measures included in the options or alternatives which the District Valuer is asked to consider.

## Street Furniture

**Mr. Flynn:** To ask the Secretary of State for Transport, what estimate he has made of the likely reduction in the numbers of serious and fatal accidents if steel or concrete light standards and telegraph poles were replaced by aluminium poles and standards. [24904]

**Mr. Norris:** The information requested is not available.

**Mr. Flynn:** To ask the Secretary of State for Transport how many *(a)* serious and *(b)* fatal accidents involved collision with lighting standards and telephone poles in each of the last five years. [24905]

**Mr. Norris:** The information requested is shown in the table:

*Fatal and serious accidents involving collision with lamp posts, telegraph poles or electricity poles: Great Britain 1989–93*

*Number of accidents*

| Object hit | Year | One vehicle only involved Fatal | One vehicle only involved Serious | Pedestrian and one vehicle involved Fatal | Pedestrian and one vehicle involved Serious |
|---|---|---|---|---|---|
| Lamp post | 1989 | 94 | 866 | 4 | 20 |
| | 1990 | 110 | 854 | 6 | 25 |
| | 1991 | 91 | 683 | 6 | 32 |
| | 1992 | 93 | 627 | 5 | 26 |
| | 1993 | 70 | 586 | 4 | 16 |
| Telegraph pole or electricity pole | | | | | |
| | 1989 | 45 | 290 | 0 | 5 |
| | 1990 | 34 | 288 | 3 | 3 |
| | 1991 | 27 | 234 | 3 | 9 |
| | 1992 | 25 | 213 | 1 | 6 |
| | 1993 | 28 | 182 | 0 | 1 |

## North Sea Conference

**Ms Walley:** To ask the Secretary of State for Transport what proposals he will (i) put forward and (ii) support at the North sea ministerial conference in Denmark on 8 June in respect of shipping; and if he will make a statement. [24404]

**Mr. Norris:** A note on UK policy objectives for the fourth North sea conference was placed in the Library of the House on 16 May. My Department has been fully involved in the preparations for the fourth North sea conference, and has already made a number of proposals consistent with our policy on marine safety and pollution following Lord Donaldson's report, "Safer Ships, Cleaner Seas".

The Government will be represented at the North sea conference by my right hon. Friend the Secretary of State for the Environment. He will be proposing and supporting a wide range of measures to enhance ship safety, to reduce accidental and operational discharges from ships, to improve the clean-up of spills and to secure better compensation for the victims of marine pollution damage, especially through the development and ratification of the convention on hazardous and noxious substances.

## Coast Watch Services

**Mr. Ian Bruce:** To ask the Secretary of State for Transport what instructions he has given to the Coastguard Agency in respect of co-operation with the National Coastwatch Institution; and if he will make a statement. [24669]

**Mr. Norris:** The Coastguard Agency welcomes any useful information which the National Coastwatch Institution may provide. It is always ready to encourage any responsible organisation volunteering information which might assist the coastguard in fulfilling the national responsibility for co-ordination of civil maritime search and rescue.

## Ferry Safety

**Mr. Flynn:** To ask the Secretary of State for Transport when he plans to publish the results of the evacuation trials conducted by the HSA on new high-speed catamaran passenger craft; and if he will make a statement. [24920]

**Mr. Norris:** This is an operational matter for the Marine Safety Agency. I have asked the chief executive to write to the hon. Member.

*Letter from R. M. Bradley to Mr. Paul Flynn, dated 18 May 1995:*

The Secretary of State for Transport has asked me to reply to your Question about evacuation trials on new high-speed catamaran passenger craft.

There are no plans to publish the results of the evacuation trials conducted by the Marine Safety Agency (MSA) on high-speed catamaran passenger craft. The MSA is, however, fully satisfied that the craft currently operating from United Kingdom ports can meet the required evacuation time for this type of vessel.

**Mr. Flynn:** To ask the Secretary of State for Transport what consideration he gave to the evacuations from the Achille Lauro and the Lakonia when postulating evacuation times for ferries using United Kingdom ports; and if he will make a statement. [24922]

**Mr. Norris:** This is an operational matter for the Marine Safety Agency. I have asked the chief executive to write to the hon. Member.

*Letter from R. M. Bradley to Mr. Paul Flynn, dated 18 May 1995:*

The Secretary of State for Transport has asked me to reply to your Question about evacuation times for roll-on roll-off ferries with regard to the cases of the "Achille Lauro" and the "Lakonia".

Responsibility for the investigation of casualties to ships lies with the flag state; neither the "Achille Lauro" nor the "Lakonia" were registered with the United Kingdom. The flag state may thus determine what changes are required to the regulations of the International Convention for the Safety of Life at Sea (SOLAS) and, put forward proposals for discussion within the International Maritime Organization. Any changes agreed, including for example evacuation times, would be implemented by the United Kingdom and other Administrations signatory to the SOLAS Convention.

**Mr. Flynn:** To ask the Secretary of State for Transport for what reasons he has not yet accepted the Marine Safety Committee document 65/4, "RoRo Ferry Safety". [24822]

**Mr. Norris:** The Secretary of State has already broadly welcomed the recommendations of the panel of experts, now issued as Maritime Safety Committee document 65/4, in his oral statement to the House on 5 April 1995, *Official Report*, column 1753. The Government will continue to press for the adoption of measures to enhance ferry safety recommended by the panel.

**Mr. Flynn:** To ask the Secretary of State for Transport, when he expects the review of the financial implications of Marine Safety Committee document 65/4, "RoRo Ferry Safety", to be completed and published. [24823]

**Mr. Norris:** The Secretary of State for Transport, in his oral statement to the House on 5 April 1995, *Official Report*, column 1753, emphasised that any new measures proposed as a result of the recommendation made by the International Maritime Organisation's panel of experts would be subject to a full analysis of the potential costs and benefits. The Marine Safety Agency is currently investigating the costs of implementing various possible new requirements for ro-ro ferries. This information should be available in time for the negotiations on ferry safety at the International Maritime Organisation in November.

**Mr. Flynn:** To ask the Secretary or State for Transport how much time is allocated to muster passengers from 10 decks to lifeboat points in the standard 30-minute evacuation of 2,000 people from roll-on-roll-off ferries. [24919]

**Mr. Norris:** This is an operational matter for the Marine Safety Agency. I have asked the chief executive to write to the hon. Member.

*Letter from R. M. Bradley to Mr. Paul Flynn, dated 18 May 1995:*

The Secretary of State for Transport has asked me to reply to your Question about allocation of the 30 minute evacuation time for roll-on roll-off ferries.

No specific period is allocated for the muster of passengers. The muster of passengers will commence when the general alarm signal is given whereas the 30 minute evacuation period begins with the abandon ship signal which may be given sometime later.

**Mr. Flynn:** To ask the Secretary of State for Transport if he has sought or received views from the Royal Institute of Naval Architects on the estimated costs and timescale of introducing the recommendation in Marine Safety Committee document 65/4,"RoRo Ferry Safety". [24821]

**Mr. Norris:** The Government are aware of the views of the Royal Institution of Naval Architects on the issue of ferry stability, in particular its views submitted to the International Maritime Organisation's panel of experts.

The Government will continue to press for the adoption of recommendations on roll-on roll-off ferry safety made by the International Maritime Organisation's panel of experts on ferry safety. We need to take matters forward on the basis of the panel's recommendations, including a full analysis of the costs and benefits of implementing new measures.

### Marchioness

**Mr. Spearing:** To ask the Secretary of State for Transport what facilities were made available for the Marchioness action group to examine or photograph the hull of the Marchioness *(a)* on the shore at Southwark and *(b)* at any other named location; to whom and on whose authority the hull was sold; and on what date it left the Thames. [24744]

**Mr. Norris:** Although the marine accident investigation branch inspected the hull of the Marchioness in the course of its investigation, at no time was either access to the vessel or sale of the vessel under its control.

The sale of the vessel would have been a matter for the owners, Tidal Cruises Ltd, following its release by the police on completion of their investigations. My Departments has no records relating to the sale of the vessel.

### Accident Inquiries

**Mr. Meacher:** To ask the Secretary of State for Transport if he will accept as a regular procedure that any major transport accident which involves either large-scale loss of life or has significant implications for transport policy should normally lead to the setting up of a public inquiry. [15905]

**Mr. Norris** *[holding answer 24 March 1995]:* Ministers must be free to consider the most appropriate form of inquiry, taking into account the circumstances of the accident and its severity. The purpose of any inquiry must be to establish the facts and cause of the accident, to evaluate what lessons can be learnt and to make recommendations to avoid future recurrence. Technical inquiries, such as those by the independent marine accident investigation branch and the air accident investigation branch have the advantage of being carried out by experienced and expert investigators. A public inquiry is one option that Ministers will consider following a major transport accident but we do not believe that it would be appropriate or effective for this to be accepted as a regular procedure.

## NORTHERN IRELAND

### Autism

**Mr. Alex Carlile:** To ask the Secretary of State for Northern Ireland what services are available for autistic people in Northern Ireland; and if he will make a statement. [23679]

**Mr. Ancram:** I refer the hon. Member to the answer I gave the hon. Member for Clydebank and Milngavie (Mr. Worthington) on 16 May, *Official Report* column *194.*

### Youth Service

**Mr. Beggs:** To ask the Secretary of State for Northern Ireland how much money was allocated to the youth service in Northern Ireland in 1993–94 and 1994–95; how much was allocated to (a) uniformed organisations and (b) non-uniformed organisations; and what was the membership of (i) uniformed and (ii) non-uniformed organisations in each year. [23990]

**Mr. Ancram:** The total allocation was £15.822 million in 1993–94 and £16.010 million in 1994–95.

The information on allocations to uniformed and non-uniformed organisations and their respective memberships details is not held centrally and could be obtained only at disproportionate cost.

### Home Improvement Grants

**Mr. McGrady:** To ask the Secretary of State for Northern Ireland how many applications for each type of home improvement grant at each of the Housing Executive offices were refused because of the means-tested element since the introduction of the Housing (NI) Order 1992. [23706]

**Mr. Moss:** This is a matter for the Northern Ireland Housing Executive but the chief executive has advised me that the Housing Executive does not refuse grant applications on the ground of a means test. The means test determines the contribution which an applicant must make towards the cost of remedial work. The amount of the applicant's contribution can range from nil to the full cost of the works and, depending on this assessment, applicants may decide not to proceed.

**Mr. McGrady:** To ask the Secretary of State for Northern Ireland how long it takes to process each of the nine home improvement grant applications at each of the Housing Executive grants offices in Northern Ireland. [23704]

**Mr. Moss:** This is a matter for the Northern Ireland Housing Executive but the chief executive has advised me that the information requested is not readily available. However, the average time to process applications at three key stages is as follows:

| | Average time |
| --- | --- |
| 1. From receipt of preliminary inquiry form to inspection of the dwelling | 15 weeks |
| 2. From inspection to issue of a schedule of work | 9 weeks |
| 3. From receipt of completed formal application to issue of approval | 4 months |

**Mr. McGrady:** To ask the Secretary of State for Northern Ireland how many applications have been made for each type of home improvement grant at each of the Housing Executive grants offices in Northern Ireland since the introduction of the Housing (NI) Order 1992; and of these how many were (a) approved (b) rejected and (c) withdrawn, giving the reasons for refusal. [23705]

**Mr. Moss:** This is a matter for the Northern Ireland Housing Executive but the chief executive has advised me

that the Executive does not maintain records in the format requested. However table 1 indicates the total number of preliminary inquiry forms received by each grant office, the numbers refused and the numbers not taken forward by the applicant. Table 2 shows the numbers approved by grant type.

*Table 1: Numbers of preliminary enquiries received, refused and withdrawn: October 1992–March 1995*

| | Preliminary enquiries received | Preliminary enquiries refused | Withdrawn |
| --- | --- | --- | --- |
| Belfast: Area 1 | 4,378 | 1,353 | 196 |
| Belfast: Area 2 | 3,897 | 1,641 | 367 |
| Belfast: Area 3 | 4,853 | 1,392 | 301 |
| HMO Unit[1] | 196 | Nil | Nil |
| Ballyclare | 3,312 | 1,506 | 205 |
| Ballymena | 2,401 | 584 | 104 |
| Coleraine | 1,567 | 383 | 281 |
| Derry | 5,127 | 1,383 | 456 |
| Omagh | 4,690 | 587 | 590 |
| Fermanagh | 2,802 | 555 | 56 |
| Newry | 5,559 | 74 | 46 |
| Craigavon | 5,940 | 730 | 393 |
| Lisburn | 3,258 | 717 | 332 |
| Newtownards | 4,374 | 1,508 | 416 |
| Totals: | 52,354 | 12,413 | 3,743 |

The main reasons for refusals are:-
1. the property was considered to be fit for human habitation;
2. the property was less than 10 years old;
3. the applicant did not have the appropriate legal interest in the property.
[1] Houses in multiple occupation.

*Table 2. Formal approvals issued: October 1992–March 1995*

| | Ren | NBG | DFG | MWA | RG | HMO |
| --- | --- | --- | --- | --- | --- | --- |
| Belfast: Area 1 | 413 | — | 52 | 156 | 796 | — |
| Belfast: Area 2 | 415 | — | 21 | 217 | 800 | — |
| Belfast: Area 3 | 403 | — | 63 | 365 | 883 | — |
| HMO Unit | — | — | — | — | — | 50 |
| Ballyclare | 277 | 2 | 71 | 225 | 83 | — |
| Ballymena | 185 | 12 | 65 | 97 | 13 | — |
| Coleraine | 157 | 7 | 56 | 89 | 14 | 3 |
| Derry | 366 | 6 | 165 | 278 | 23 | — |
| Omagh | 228 | 20 | 136 | 335 | 351 | — |
| Fermanagh | 128 | 118 | 50 | 248 | 137 | — |
| Newry | 178 | 15 | 169 | 168 | 998 | — |
| Craigavon | 209 | 33 | 119 | 199 | 1,864 | — |
| Lisburn | 225 | 28 | 65 | 128 | 285 | 1 |
| Newtownards | 299 | 2 | 76 | 268 | 450 | 2 |
| Totals: | 3,483 | 243 | 1,108 | 2,773 | 6,697 | 56 |

*Notes:*

*Ren = Renovation Grant.*
NBG = Replacement Grant.
DFG = Disabled Facilities Grant.
MWA = Minor Works Assistance.
RG = Repairs Grant.
HMO = Houses in Multiple Occupation Grant.

### Road Traffic Legislation

**Mr. Worthington:** To ask the Secretary of State for Northern Ireland what progress he is making in introducing new road traffic legislation in Northern Ireland. [24320]

**Mr. Moss:** The Department of the Environment (Northern Ireland) is carrying forward a programme of road traffic legislation aimed at updating the law in this field. Three Orders in Council are being progressed as follows:

> A draft Road Traffic (Northern Ireland) Order which will update road safety and construction and use of vehicles provisions will be laid before Parliament in the near future.
>
> A proposal for a draft Road Traffic Offenders (Northern Ireland) Order setting out the prosecution and punishment of offenders, including the introduction of a penalty points system, is currently being drafted and will be published for consultation purposes by the autumn.
>
> The modification of the law in relation to the regulation of traffic, parking places and speed limits is to be the subject of a Road Traffic Regulation (Northern Ireland) Order. It is planned to publish a proposal for a draft Order in Council for consultation purposes in the autumn.

### Ports Grants

**Mr. Worthington:** To ask the Secretary of State for Northern Ireland what grants are available from the European Union to Northern Ireland ports in the public sector that would not be available in the event of privatisation.     [24316]

**Mr. Moss:** European Union structural funds grants which are currently available to public sector ports in Northern Ireland would continue to be available in the event of privatisation

### Construction Industry

**Mr. McGrady:** To ask the Secretary of State for Northern Ireland what steps he will adopt to ensure an upturn in the construction industry through investment in schools, hospitals, education, housing, roads and factories.     [23702]

**Mr. Moss:** I have asked my officials to consider, as a matter of urgency, how the construction industry could best be assisted over the coming year. The possibility of increasing expenditure on infrastructure will be borne in mind.

### Railways

**Mr. Worthington:** To ask the Secretary of State for Northern Ireland if he will make a statement on the progress in implementing the consultants' recommendations about Northern Ireland Railways.
[24314]

**Mr. Moss:** I refer the hon. Member to the answer I gave my hon. Friend the Member for Colchester, North (Mr. Jenkin) on 11 January 1995, *Official Report*, column *146*. Since then the Northern Ireland Transport Holding Company has commissioned a study to examine further opportunities for market testing and contracting out and to advise on the scope for sale of Northern Ireland Railways' non-core businesses.

### Giant Hogweed

**Mr. McMaster:** To ask the Secretary of State for Northern Ireland what measures he plans to require the owners of land to which the public may have access to eradicate Heracleum Mantegazzianum; and if he will make a statement about the dangers associated with this plant.     [24082]

**Mr. Moss:** No new measures are planned to require the owners of land to which the public may have access to eradicate Heracleum Mantegazzianum or giant hogweed. The Department of Agriculture and Department of Environment continue to promote a programme of voluntary control.

The existing provisions of the Public Health (Ireland) Act 1888 give district councils powers to deal with "nuisances" in premises, including lands, which are in such a state as to be "injurious to health".

The danger associated with giant hogweed is that the plants release sap when the stems are cut or leaf hairs are broken. On contact with the skin in sunlight, the sap can cause severe blistering.

### Conservation Areas

**Mr. McGrady:** To ask the Secretary of State for Northern Ireland what towns and villages are currently being considered for the designation of conservation area status in the constituency of South Down; and when these designations will take place.     [24761]

**Mr. Moss:** The towns of Saintfield and Ardglass are currently being considered for designation as conservation areas. There is also a proposal to extend the conservation area of the village of Rostrevor, originally designated in 1979. It is not possible at this stage to indicate when the designations will take place.

### US Investment Conference

**Dr. Godman:** To ask the Secretary of State for Northern Ireland what plans he has to review his decision to provide partial funding for support of representatives of non-governmental organisations at President Clinton's investment conference, to be held in Washington DC from 24 to 26 May; and if he will make a statement.     [24857]

**Mr. Ancram:** None.

**Dr. Godman:** To ask the Secretary of State for Northern Ireland if he will make a statement on President Clinton's investment conference to be held in Washington DC in May; and how he intends to maximise the returns for all delegates from Ireland, north and south; and what plans he has for de-briefing, follow-up meetings and dissemination of the results of the aforesaid conference within Northern Ireland.     [24861]

**Mr. Ancram:** The White House conference for trade and investment in Washington offers considerable potential for more investment in Northern Ireland and the six border counties of the Republic of Ireland through new inward investment, trade, business partnerships, technology transfer and tourism. This potential will be released through the various breakout or workshop sessions, individual meetings with key business people and networking at various functions.

Following the conference there will be full follow-up on all prospects for trade, inward investment or technology transfer.

**Dr. Godman:** To ask the Secretary of State for Northern Ireland if he will make available the resources and facilities of Her Majesty's Government's Departments and agencies by way of access to briefings, meetings, and exhibitions organised by Her Majesty's Government's Departments and agencies to assist and facilitate the participation of the representatives of voluntary organisations and community groups, at

President Clinton's investment conference in Washington DC; and if he will make a statement. [24858]

**Mr. Ancram:** Officials in Northern Ireland Departments and agencies have already participated in briefings of community group representatives in preparation for their attendance at the White House trade and investment conference in Washington.

During the conference, officials will be available to provide information and advice for the purpose of facilitating the participation of all representatives.

**Dr. Godman:** To ask the Secretary of State for Northern Ireland what proposals he has for the support of the participation of the community and voluntary sector representatives invited to attend President Clinton's investment conference in Washington DC. [24856]

**Mr. Ancram:** Some financial assistance will be available through the Northern Ireland voluntary trust to community and voluntary sector representatives to enable them to participate in the conference.

A break-out or workshop session has been offered by the conference organisers to provide an opportunity for bringing together the interests of those involved in community development activities in Northern Ireland with those of business leaders from both sides of the Atlantic. Support has also been provided by officials involved in briefing community sector participants.

### Rowe Report

**Mr. Wilshire:** To ask the Secretary of State for Northern Ireland whether he has yet received Mr. J. J. Rowe's report on the operation in 1994 of the Northern Ireland (Emergency Provisions) Act 1991. [25532]

**Sir Patrick Mayhew:** I have received Mr. Rowe's report and it is being published today and copies are being placed in the library. I am most grateful to him for his work.

As the ceasefires continue to hold the powers in the Act are being used less and less. But the Government believe that the Act itself remains necessary. This is also the view of Mr. Rowe. I am therefore laying before the House today an order continuing for a further year those provisions in the Act which are currently in force. We all look forward to the time when there will no longer be a need for them.

### Rate Collection Agency

**Mr. David Wilshire:** To ask the Secretary of State for Northern Ireland what performance targets have been set for the Rate Collection Agency in 1995–96. [25533]

**Mr. Moss:** For 1995–96 the following performance targets have been set for the agency:

1. To collect 98.11 per cent. of the gross collectable rate, excluding late assessments, by 31 March 1996.
2. To achieve a reduction of 2 per cent. in the real value of the unit costs of rate collection per rate account issued.
3. To generate refunds to 97 per cent. of ratepayers so entitled within 14 days of credits being identified.
4. To process by 31 March 1996 90 per cent. of applications for the incoming year received before 15 March 1996 from existing housing benefit recipients.
5. To achieve a reduction of 2 per cent. in the real value of the unit costs of processing Housing Benefit applications.
6. To process 95 per cent. of Housing Benefit claims free of error.

## HOME DEPARTMENT

### Drug Abuse

14. **Mr. Martlew:** To ask the Secretary of State for the Home Department what representations he has received on the problems of drug abuse. [23560]

**Mr. Michael Forsyth:** Apart from several general inquiries from members of the public, we have had 52 letters forwarded by Members of Parliament this year.

The most common inquiry was concerned with the legal status of drugs, usually arguing for or against legalising cannabis, followed by issues such as drugs and crime, the scheduling of temazepam, drug logos on clothing and cuts in the numbers of customs officials at ports.

### Metropolitan Police

16. **Mr. Cyril D. Townsend:** To ask the Secretary of State for the Home Department how many officers there are on duty per 1,000 population in the Metropolitan police; and what is the national average. [23562]

**Mr. Maclean:** I understand from Her Majesty's inspectorate of constabulary that there are 3.6 officers per 1,000 population in the Metropolitan police district. This compares with a national average of 2.2 officers per 1,000 population excluding the Met.

### Identity Cards

17. **Mr. Mullin:** To ask the Secretary of State for the Home Department what assessment he has made of the cost effectiveness of introducing identity cards; and if he will make a statement. [23563]

**Mr. Howard:** The cost-effectiveness of any identity card scheme would depend upon the detailed arrangements for the scheme, the value of the card to the individual holder, the wider value to society, and the costs of the scheme. I intend publishing a consultation document on identity cards shortly.

### Asylum Seekers

18. **Mr. Gerrard:** To ask the Secretary of State for the Home Department what steps he is taking to reduce the delays in making decisions on applications for asylum. [23564]

**Mr. Nicholas Baker:** The Asylum and Immigration Appeals Act 1993 has reduced significantly the average time taken to decide applications made since the Act came into force. But delays persist as a result of a large and continuing increase in the number of asylum applications. Earlier this year, my right hon. and learned Friend announced substantial additional resources to speed up the asylum determination and appeal system. We hope to announce shortly proposals for further improvements.

25. **Mr. Corbyn:** To ask the Secretary of State for the Home Department what recent representations he has received on the number of asylum seekers held in custody. [23571]

**Mr. Nicholas Baker:** Since 1 January 1995 we have received 97 letters on this subject from hon. Members writing on behalf of their constituents and 47 from members of the public writing direct. I have also received a letter, dated 2 May, from the Refugee Legal Centre.

**26. Mr. Eric Clarke:** To ask the Secretary of State for the Home Department how many asylum seekers in the last year have been detained for over six months. [23572]

**Mr. Nicholas Baker:** The information is not available in the form requested. On 9 May 1995, a total of 118 persons who had at some time claimed asylum had been in detention for six months or more. Of these, 114 had their application refused.

**Mr. Robert Ainsworth:** To ask the Secretary of State for the Home Department if he will provide a breakdown of the current establishment of the third country unit within the Home Office's immigration and nationality department; and if he will make a statement on the function of this unit. [24826]

**Mr. Nicholas Baker:** The third country unit is part of the asylum division. It consists of one higher executive officer, four executive officers and one administrative assistant. It is responsible for cases where an asylum applicant has arrived from a safe third country to which he may be returned without substantive consideration of his claim in accordance with paragraphs 337 and 345 of the immigration rules.

**Mr. Robert Ainsworth:** To ask the Secretary of State for the Home Department how many asylum seekers have been removed to Norway on safe third country grounds since 26 July 1993; and how many so removed have been returned to the United Kingdom by the Norwegian authorities. [24827]

**Mr. Nicholas Baker:** Four persons who had been refused asylum in the United Kingdom on safe third country grounds have been removed to Norway since 16 July 1993. Of these, one has been returned to the United Kingdom.

### Crime Statistics

**19. Mr. Clifton-Brown:** To ask the Secretary of State for the Home Department what assessment his Department has made of the trend in the recorded crime figures. [23565]

**Mr. Maclean:** Recorded crime in England and Wales fell by 5 per cent. in 1994. Together with the 1 per cent. fall in 1993, this represents the largest percentage fall over a two-year period for 40 years. This fall is a testament to the success of recent police initiatives which actively target crimes such as burglary.

**Mr. Michael:** To ask the Secretary of State for the Home Department how many crimes were recorded by each police force in England and Wales within each category of crime in 1994; how many incidents of theft or unauthorised taking of a motor vehicle and of theft from a motor vehicle were recorded by each force; and how many of the burglaries recorded by each police force in England and Wales in 1994 were *(a)* in a dwelling and *(b)* in another building. [23876]

**Mr. MacLean:** The information requested is contained in the following table:

*Notifiable recorded by the police by police force area and offence group*

England and Wales 1994 — Number of offences

| Police force area | Total | Violence against the person | Sexual offences | Robbery | Burglary | Theft and handling stolen goods | Fraud and Forgery | Criminal damage | Other offences | Theft of vehicle | Theft from vehicle | Burglary in a dwelling | Burglary in another building |
|---|---|---|---|---|---|---|---|---|---|---|---|---|---|
| Avon and Somerset | 167,975 | 6,791 | 1,091 | 1,714 | 37,397 | 93,164 | 4,316 | 22,532 | 970 | 21,938 | 34,890 | 18,993 | 18,404 |
| Bedfordshire | 55,661 | 1,978 | 426 | 582 | 12,881 | 27,271 | 1,904 | 7,214 | 405 | 7,414 | 10,341 | 6,124 | 6,757 |
| Cambridgeshire | 61,732 | 3,030 | 421 | 242 | 14,099 | 33,942 | 1,460 | 8,087 | 451 | 5,792 | 10,335 | 6,206 | 7,893 |
| Cheshire | 74,926 | 3,245 | 543 | 278 | 19,248 | 34,961 | 2,625 | 12,449 | 1,577 | 7,451 | 11,662 | 9,363 | 9,885 |
| Cleveland | 81,732 | 2,359 | 236 | 466 | 18,428 | 42,931 | 1,287 | 15,621 | 404 | 12,007 | 10,902 | 12,380 | 6,048 |
| Cumbria | 42,492 | 2,153 | 250 | 74 | 10,066 | 20,259 | 1,127 | 8,170 | 393 | 2,555 | 7,586 | 4,156 | 5,910 |
| Derbyshire | 85,915 | 3,984 | 493 | 421 | 24,049 | 38,526 | 1,678 | 15,995 | 769 | 8,564 | 14,190 | 10,112 | 13,937 |
| Devon and Cornwall | 109,396 | 4,603 | 892 | 403 | 30,266 | 54,843 | 3,258 | 13,780 | 1,351 | 6,884 | 21,367 | 15,123 | 15,143 |
| Dorset | 55,590 | 1,885 | 443 | 146 | 9,395 | 31,456 | 3,151 | 8,244 | 870 | 3,564 | 10,111 | 5,740 | 3,655 |
| Durham | 65,029 | 2,665 | 510 | 149 | 12,524 | 33,591 | 2,575 | 12,259 | 756 | 7,989 | 8,995 | 7,709 | 4,815 |
| Essex | 106,025 | 4,505 | 549 | 423 | 23,639 | 55,314 | 2,688 | 17,968 | 939 | 8,346 | 17,352 | 8,606 | 15,033 |
| Gloucestershire | 61,198 | 2,140 | 1,006 | 319 | 15,844 | 31,765 | 2,677 | 6,850 | 597 | 4,528 | 13,671 | 7,685 | 8,159 |
| Greater Manchester | 339,074 | 9,281 | 1,228 | 5,361 | 91,077 | 156,296 | 8,549 | 64,874 | 2,408 | 49,661 | 51,908 | 54,915 | 36,162 |
| Hampshire | 141,271 | 5,704 | 1,056 | 585 | 29,600 | 74,988 | 4,026 | 23,779 | 1,533 | 9,571 | 26,936 | 12,829 | 16,771 |
| Hertfordshire | 54,887 | 1,996 | 305 | 264 | 12,100 | 28,788 | 1,307 | 9,781 | 346 | 5,301 | 12,782 | 4,480 | 7,620 |
| Humberside | 135,826 | 5,054 | 695 | 547 | 43,965 | 62,544 | 3,010 | 19,402 | 609 | 15,023 | 19,356 | 20,127 | 23,838 |
| Kent | 155,345 | 7,128 | 1,099 | 635 | 26,871 | 86,022 | 3,830 | 28,001 | 1,759 | 16,677 | 25,006 | 16,944 | 9,927 |
| Lancashire | 127,302 | 3,232 | 502 | 546 | 27,151 | 63,958 | 3,486 | 27,275 | 1,152 | 11,038 | 21,399 | 17,990 | 9,161 |
| Leicestershire | 99,150 | 4,855 | 617 | 1,158 | 26,109 | 48,279 | 3,326 | 14,238 | 568 | 10,785 | 17,006 | 15,574 | 10,535 |
| Lincolnshire | 47,767 | 2,319 | 393 | 119 | 11,221 | 23,110 | 1,158 | 8,733 | 714 | 3,345 | 5,906 | 6,239 | 4,982 |
| London, City of | 5,272 | 125 | 23 | 29 | 675 | 3,640 | 422 | 267 | 91 | 79 | 541 | 37 | 638 |
| Merseyside | 136,825 | 7,678 | 808 | 2,035 | 33,042 | 65,342 | 3,012 | 23,286 | 1,622 | 15,308 | 16,357 | 20,479 | 12,563 |
| Metropolitan Police | 849,976 | 46,292 | 6,929 | 25,518 | 161,174 | 399,545 | 32,591 | 168,363 | 9,564 | 57,859 | 126,276 | 103,988 | 57,186 |
| Norfolk | 56,075 | 2,187 | 370 | 186 | 13,931 | 29,412 | 1,481 | 7,882 | 626 | 3,614 | 10,179 | 5,081 | 8,850 |
| Northamptonshire | 57,607 | 2,498 | 367 | 306 | 14,521 | 27,199 | 1,559 | 10,701 | 456 | 6,536 | 9,194 | 6,942 | 7,579 |
| Northumbria | 204,057 | 6,185 | 746 | 1,213 | 57,207 | 82,215 | 2,946 | 52,553 | 992 | 25,008 | 23,151 | 29,121 | 28,086 |
| North Yorkshire | 62,153 | 2,082 | 263 | 187 | 16,694 | 31,358 | 1,059 | 10,031 | 479 | 5,235 | 10,876 | 7,152 | 9,542 |
| Nottinghamshire | 152,592 | 7,718 | 1,141 | 1,193 | 34,639 | 71,974 | 3,857 | 31,301 | 769 | 16,010 | 19,072 | 21,735 | 12,904 |
| South Yorkshire | 157,089 | 5,027 | 664 | 1,062 | 51,242 | 69,998 | 2,885 | 24,859 | 1,352 | 21,692 | 23,304 | 25,563 | 25,679 |
| Staffordshire | 93,179 | 6,090 | 551 | 416 | 26,736 | 41,772 | 2,244 | 14,925 | 445 | 9,638 | 16,320 | 12,637 | 14,099 |
| Suffolk | 39,393 | 2,140 | 392 | 118 | 7,778 | 19,624 | 1,544 | 7,137 | 660 | 1,938 | 5,517 | 3,200 | 4,578 |
| Surrey | 46,782 | 2,715 | 463 | 165 | 10,158 | 24,046 | 1,724 | 6,899 | 612 | 3,612 | 8,263 | 4,657 | 5,501 |
| Sussex | 107,105 | 3,420 | 747 | 589 | 24,271 | 56,214 | 2,860 | 17,759 | 1,245 | 6,701 | 18,286 | 13,024 | 11,247 |
| Thames Valley | 186,268 | 5,564 | 870 | 1,130 | 38,254 | 103,974 | 6,115 | 28,763 | 1,598 | 19,618 | 38,460 | 21,187 | 17,067 |
| Warwickshire | 42,592 | 1,411 | 288 | 136 | 11,040 | 21,797 | 1,091 | 6,483 | 346 | 5,004 | 8,363 | 4,548 | 6,492 |
| West Mercia | 83,948 | 3,437 | 473 | 284 | 16,738 | 45,438 | 1,545 | 15,332 | 701 | 8,258 | 13,866 | 8,610 | 8,128 |
| West Midlands | 315,755 | 10,407 | 1,354 | 7,028 | 90,637 | 142,522 | 8,134 | 53,738 | 1,935 | 40,347 | 49,714 | 48,241 | 42,396 |
| West Yorkshire | 289,719 | 9,414 | 1,504 | 2,968 | 87,391 | 134,406 | 5,625 | 45,720 | 2,691 | 34,917 | 44,815 | 55,306 | 32,085 |
| Wiltshire | 38,147 | 2,495 | 364 | 137 | 8,152 | 19,193 | 1,142 | 6,144 | 520 | 2,406 | 6,210 | 4,032 | 4,120 |
| Dyfed-Powys | 21,602 | 2,192 | 250 | 41 | 3,491 | 9,667 | 631 | 4,816 | 514 | 1,110 | 2,372 | 1,396 | 2,095 |
| Gwent | 38,431 | 2,533 | 270 | 79 | 6,639 | 19,841 | 1,160 | 7,047 | 862 | 3,538 | 5,895 | 3,296 | 3,343 |
| North Wales | 43,451 | 2,612 | 352 | 100 | 10,215 | 20,611 | 1,103 | 7,917 | 541 | 2,494 | 7,372 | 3,314 | 6,901 |
| South Wales | 157,748 | 6,141 | 550 | 419 | 37,405 | 77,227 | 3,677 | 30,952 | 1,377 | 25,372 | 26,666 | 14,802 | 22,603 |
| England and Wales | 5,251,059 | 219,270 | 32,494 | 59,771 | 1,257,960 | 2,559,023 | 145,845 | 928,127 | 48,569 | 534,727 | 842,770 | 679,643 | 578,317 |

## Closed Circuit Television

20. **Mr. Simon Hughes:** To ask the Secretary of State for the Home Department what are Her Majesty's Government's plans for *(a)* further funding for closed circuit television and *(b)* further funding for supplementary policing in urban areas.    [23566]

**Mr. MacLean:** The recent CCTV challenge competition has injected £5 million into local CCTV schemes, generating up to £13.8 million in other funding. The possibility of further competitions in the future has not been ruled out, but it is too early to give a firm commitment.

General funding is allocated between police authorities on the basis of a formula which measures relative policing needs. That formula allows for extra demands in urban areas.

24. **Mr. David Atkinson:** To ask the Secretary of State for the Home Department what has been the outcome of the bid for Government funding for a closed circuit television scheme for the Boscombe shopping centre in Bournemouth.    [23570]

**Mr. MacLean:** My right hon. and learned Friend was pleased to announce on Monday 27 March that this scheme was one of the 106 successful schemes to share the £5 million funding provided to spread CCTV technology more widely.

## Female Prisoners

21. **Mr. Enright:** To ask the Secretary of State for the Home Department what is the latest figure for the number of women serving a prison sentence.    [23567]

**Mr. Michael Forsyth:** On 9 May 1995, there were 1,470 sentenced female prisoners in Prison Service accommodation in England and Wales.

## Drug Smuggling, Republic of Ireland

22. **Rev. Martin Smyth:** To ask the Secretary of State for the Home Department what assistance has been requested by the Republic of Ireland to combat drug smuggling into the United Kingdom and the Republic.    [23568]

**Mr. Maclean:** There is close co-operation between police and customs in the United Kingdom and their counterparts in the Republic of Ireland and regular exchanges of information on operational matters. Irish customs has requested some training assistance which HM Customs and Excise is providing.

## Police Salaries

23. **Mr. Mudie:** To ask the Secretary of State for the Home Department if he will make a statement on top salaries in the police force.    [23569]

**Mr. Maclean:** On 22 March, I wrote to Professor Sir Laurie Hunter CBE informing him of the Government's response to the Police Negotiating Board's recommendations for chief officers' pay. The Government approved most of the Police Negotiating Board's proposals for restructuring chief officers' pay. The Association of Chief Police Officers has made representations about the timing of the implementation of part of the new pay arrangements, which the Government are currently considering.

## Criminal Injuries Compensation

27. **Mrs. Roche:** To ask the Secretary of State for the Home Department how long victims of violent crime whose cases were assessed under the tariff scheme will have to wait for the reassessment of their awards.    [23573]

**Mr. Maclean:** I refer the hon. Member to the answer given to her on 1 May, *Official Report,* column 92.

**Mr. Alfred Morris:** To ask the Secretary of State for the Home Department what were the total legal costs of defending the Government's tariff scheme for criminal injuries compensation in the courts up to and including the House of Lords: and if he will make a statement.    [23632]

**Mr. Maclean:** I refer the right hon. Member to the answer given to the hon. Member for Ealing, Southall (Mr. Khabra) on 16 May, *Official Report*, column 190.

## Prisoners (Drug-related Offences)

28. **Mr. Tony Banks:** To ask the Secretary of State for the Home Department what is his current estimate of the numbers in prison for drug-related offences.    [23574]

**Mr. Michael Forsyth:** The number of prisoners serving sentences for offences under misuse of drugs legislation in 1994 was around 10 per cent. of the prison population; but no reliable estimate is yet available of the number of prisoners serving sentences for offences committed under the influence of drugs or to pay for drugs.

## "In the Line of Fire"

29. **Mr Cohen:** To ask the Secretary of State for the Home Department what is his response to the Audit Commission report, "In the Line of Fire".    [23575]

**Mr. Nicholas Baker:** I refer the hon. Member to the reply which I gave earlier today in response to an identical question from the hon. Member for Nottingham, East (Mr. Heppell).

## Criminal Justice and Public Order Act 1994

**Mr. Robert Hughes:** To ask the Secretary of State for the Home Department what effect the Criminal Justice and Public Order Act 1994 will have on the fight against crime; and if he will make a statement.    [23548]

**Mr. Howard:** The Act will make a significant contribution to the fight against crime. As the Police Federation has said, it will

> "enhance the stature and ability of the criminal justice system to reduce crime, bring criminals to justice and significantly reduce the fear of crime, thereby improving the quality of life for many members of our society".

## Jersey

**Mr. Foulkes:** To ask the Secretary of State for the Home Department when he next expects to visit Jersey to meet members of the states to discuss the current constitutional position.    [23561]

**Mr. Nicholas Baker:** My right hon. and learned Friend hopes to visit the Channel Islands, as it is customary for Home Secretaries to do, in the not—too—distant future. Meanwhile, my noble Friend Lady Blatch has recently completed a visit to the Channel Islands, including Jersey, where she held discussions with members of the states.

## Police Station Inquiry Desks

**Mr. Harry Greenway:** To ask the Secretary of State for the Home Department what steps he is taking to improve civilian competence in dealing with the public at police station inquiry desks, with particular reference to the ability to communicate; and if he will make a statement. [23662]

**Mr. Maclean:** This is a matter primarily for each chief officer of police. I am not aware of any problems arising from civilian members of the police service dealing with members of the public, but I, or the relevant chief officer of police, as appropriate, would be happy to respond to any specific concerns.

## Brian Douglas

**Mr. Cohen:** To ask the Secretary of State for the Home Department if he will make a statement on the death of Mr. Brian Douglas on 8 May; and what assessment has been made as to the cause of his injuries. [24692]

**Mr. Maclean:** I understand that the matter is being investigated by the Police Complaints Authority. It would not be appropriate for me to comment at this stage.

## Derek Bentley

**Mr. Michael:** To ask the Secretary of State for the Home Department if he will take steps to order a searching review of the case of Derek Bentley to deal with all outstanding issues of public concern and following the review, consider the appropriateness of recommending a posthumous free pardon. [24901]

**Mr. Nicholas Baker:** I am aware of no present grounds for a further review of this case, which was very thoroughly reviewed in 1991 and 1992.

**Mr. Michael:** To ask the Secretary of State for the Home Department if he will place in the Library full details of investigations carried out by the police at the request of the Home Office and other relevant documents relating to the case of Derek Bentley. [24903]

**Mr. Nicholas Baker:** Police reports are confidential documents which do not fall to be disclosed. A memorandum was published on 1 October 1992, however, explaining in detail the decision then reached that there were no grounds for recommending the grant of a posthumous free pardon to Derek Bentley. This dealt among other things with the alleged inconsistencies in evidence. A copy of the memorandum was placed in the Library.

**Mr. Michael:** To ask the Secretary of State for the Home Department what terms of reference were set by his Department for the investigation of the Derek Bentley case by the Metropolitan police requested by his predecessor in 1991; and what reports were subsequently submitted to his Department. [24923]

**Mr. Nicholas Baker:** The Home Office wrote to the Metropolitan police in August 1991 asking for inquiries to be carried out into certain matters which had been presented to the Home Office by Thames Television and others. The police submitted two reports in October and December 1991.

**Mr. Michael:** To ask the Secretary of State for the Home Department (1) if he will arrange the release of full details of investigations by the police ordered by his predecessors into the case of Derek Bentley; [24902]

(2) if he will review his Department's papers relating to the Derek Bentley case with a view to fulfilling precisely the legal requirements for disclosure of papers and investigations undertaken by, or on behalf of, himself or his predecessors. [24900]

**Mr. Nicholas Baker:** Following a request by solicitors for the family of the late Derek Bentley, we are examining our papers with a view to making appropriate disclosures in full compliance with the Hickey judgment as soon as possible. Such disclosure to affected parties and their legal representatives is not constrained by the provisions of the Public Records Acts which govern the opening of records to the public.

## Detainees

**Mr. Robert Ainsworth:** To ask the Secretary of State for the Home Department if he will provide a breakdown of the current establishment of the detention planning and policy unit within the Home Office immigration and nationality department; and if he will make a statement regarding the function of this unit. [24828]

**Mr. Nicholas Baker:** The immigration service detention policy and planning unit employs a total of some 53 staff including those engaged in detention centres at Campsfield house, nine; Gatwick airport, four; and Harmondsworth, 25, where the staff also have national responsibility for co-ordination of the use of detention places.

The detention policy and planning unit is responsible for ensuring the provision of detention accommodation and escorting services including all commercial, financial and contractual matters and for co-ordinating policy, procedures and practice relating to all aspects of immigration detention management.

**Mr. Robert Ainsworth:** To ask the Secretary of State for the Home Department what was the total cost in the financial year 1993–94 to his Department of detaining persons under the Immigration Act powers in (a) immigration detention centres, (b) Prison Service establishments and (c) police cells. [24855]

**Mr. Nicholas Baker:** The total cost to the immigration service in running its detention accommodation in the financial year 1993–94 was £7,466,352. No separate figures for detaining persons under Immigration Act powers are kept by the Prison Service. The cost of detaining persons under the Act in police cells was £430,152.27.

**Mr. Robert Ainsworth:** To ask the Secretary of State for the Home Department what is the current (a) weekly and (b) monthly cost of detaining persons under Immigration Act powers in (a) an immigration detention centre and (b) a Prison Service establishment. [24854]

**Mr. Nicholas Baker:** The overall cost of detaining a person in accommodation for which the immigration service is responsible is currently estimated at £540 per week, including full immigration service staffing costs. This would equate to £2,340 per month. The current cost of detaining someone in a Prison Service establishment is not available. The latest available figures are for the year 1993–94, which show a cost of £411 a week or £1,780 per month, excluding headquarters costs. In many cases, the carrying company which brought the person to the United Kingdom is liable for all or some the expenses incurred. Therefore, the whole cost does not fall to the taxpayer.

## Paul Malone

**Mr. Miller:** To ask the Secretary of State for the Home Department (1) what plans he has to refer the case of Paul Malone to the Court of Appeal; and if he will make a statement; [24894]

(2) what action he proposes to take following the Metropolitan police investigation into the case of Paul Malone. [24892]

**Mr. Nicholas Baker:** This case was referred to the Court of Appeal by my right hon. and learned Friend under section 17(1)(a) of the Criminal Appeal Act 1968 on 8 December 1994. As the case remains sub judice it is not appropriate for me to comment. As my hon. Friend stated in his reply to a question from the hon. Member on 27 April 1995, *Official Report*, column *679*, the report of the investigation by the Metropolitan police has been referred to the Director of Public Prosecutions who will decide whether any criminal charges should be brought. Once a decision has been made, the chief constable of Cheshire and the Police Complaints Authority will consider whether disciplinary action should be taken against any officer.

## Greater Manchester Fire Authority

**Mr. Cunliffe:** To ask the Secretary of State for the Home Department what discussions he has had with the Greater Manchester fire authority concerning the financing of the service. [23555]

**Mr. Nicholas Baker:** My right hon. and learned Friend has had no such discussions during the course of the past year.

## Pornography

**Dr. Spink:** To ask the Secretary of State for the Home Department if the Indecent Displays (Control) Act 1981 applies to pornographic magazines normally displayed on the top shelf of newsagents. [24477]

**Mr. Nicholas Baker:** The Indecent Displays (Control) Act 1981 applies to any matter, including pornographic magazines, displayed in a public place or where it can be seen from a public place, if such matter is indecent.

**Dr. Spink:** To ask the Secretary of State for the Home Department how many prosecutions have been brought under the Indecent Displays (Control) Act 1981 in the last five years; how many of these were successful; and at what sort of premises the material was displayed. [24480]

**Mr. Maclean:** Information of the number of prosecutions and convictions for 1989 and 1993 is given in the table. 1994 data will not be available until the autumn.

Information is not collected centrally regarding the type of premises where the offence took place.

*Number of defendants prosecuted at magistrates courts and found guilty at all courts of offences under the Indecent Displays (Control) Act 1981, 1989–1993*

England and Wales

|  | 1989 | 1990 | 1991 | 1992 | 1993 |
|---|---|---|---|---|---|
| Prosecutions | 30 | 27 | 9 | 10 | 7 |
| Convictions | 17 | 19 | 4 | 8 | 3 |

**Dr. Spink:** To ask the Secretary of State for the Home Department what assessment he has made of the trends in pornographic publishing and distribution industry in respect of the explicit nature of the material, and what action he is taking to resist the slippage of standards and ensure that the Indecent Displays (Control) Act 1981 is effectively enforced. [24479]

**Mr. Nicholas Baker:** The Government share the widespread concern about the spread of pornography and keep the law in this area under review. Measures to ensure that the law keeps pace with advances in technology and is enforced more effectively were included in the Criminal Justice and Public Order Act 1994.

The recently established interdepartmental group on obscenity will monitor trends in the area of obscenity and pornography with the aim of identifying any actual or potential difficulties in enforcement or weaknesses in the law, including the Indecent Displays (Control) Act 1981.

**Dr. Spink:** To ask the Secretary of State for the Home Department (1) whose responsibility it is to enforce the Indecent Displays (Control) Act 1981; and what arrangements are in place to monitor its enforcement; [24482]

(2) to whom the public should complain in respect of concerns about a magazine cover which they believe is indecent and on display. [24476]

**Mr. Nicholas Baker:** The enforcement of the Indecent Displays (Control) Act 1981 itself is a matter for the police, to whom the public should complain if they are concerned that a magazine cover is indecent and on public display.

The interdepartmental group on obscenity keeps under review the operation of the law on obscenity and pornography, including indecent displays.

## Panic Alarms

**Mr. Jim Cunningham:** To ask the Secretary of State for the Home Department what funding is available for panic alarms to be given to tenants in high crime areas. [24206]

**Mr. Maclean:** Since 1988, a number of vulnerable people have benefitted from personal alarms funded under phase 1 of the safer cities programme. Funding under this programme is restricted to areas in which safer cities projects have been established, and decisions on which schemes to support are taken by local steering committees based on their agreed priorities and action plans.

**Mr. Jim Cunningham:** To ask the Secretary of State for the Home Department what studies have been carried out by his Department or by other bodies into the effectiveness of panic alarms in crime prevention; and what assessment he has made of these studies. [24208]

**Mr. Maclean:** As part of a programme of work on violent crime, the Home Office funded a project in Merseyside aimed at preventing domestic violence. Pendant alarms, linked via a cellular network to the police divisional control room, were loaned to "at risk" victims. At the same time, a database of police calls to domestic incidents was established so that officers responding to one of the alarm calls could be briefed quickly about the previous calls received from that address. Police officers were issued with aide-memoires on their powers for dealing with incidents of domestic violence; and victims were given information cards, and offered help from a domestic violence prevention officer in developing longer term safety plans. Detailed accounts taken from the victims indicate the relief both they and their children experienced as a result of this work. The report of this project was published as crime prevention unit paper 49. I have arranged for a copy of this report to be placed in the Library.

I am not aware of any other research in this area.

### Security Companies

**Mr. McMaster:** To ask the Secretary of State for the Home Department what plans he has to introduce a licensing scheme for security companies; and if he will make a statement.                                          [24158]

**Mr. Maclean:** I am currently looking again at policies in this area and await with interest the report of the Home Affairs Select Committee inquiry into the private security industry which is expected shortly.

### Female Prisoners

**Dr. Lynne Jones:** To ask the Secretary of State for the Home Department how many female prisoners currently share *(a)* two and *(b)* three to a cell.          [24272]

**Mr. Michael Forsyth:** Responsibility for this matter has been delegated to the Director General of the Prison Service, who has been asked to arrange for a reply to be given.

*Letter from Derek Lewis to Dr. Lynne Jones, dated 18 May 1995:*

The Home Secretary has asked me to reply to your recent Question about the number of female prisoners currently sharing two and three to a cell.

At the end of April there were 54 female prisoners in England and Wales sharing two to a cell designed for one. There were no female prisoners sharing three to a cell designed for one.

### Braille Ballot Papers

**Mr. McMaster:** To ask the Secretary of State for the Home Department if he will list those European Union countries which provide ballot papers in local, national and European elections in Braille; and if he will make a statement.                                          [24113]

**Mr. Nicholas Baker:** I am not aware that any of the member states provide ballot papers in Braille. As in this country, blind voters throughout the Community may choose someone to help them to vote.

**Mr. McMaster:** To ask the Secretary of State for the Home Department what plans he has to introduce Braille ballot papers in local, national and European elections; and if he will make a statement.          [24112]

**Mr. Nicholas Baker:** There are no plans to do so.

### Polling Station Ramps

**Mr. McMaster:** To ask the Secretary of State for the Home Department what is his latest estimate of the amount expended in the 1995 local elections in England and Wales on the provision of temporary ramps for access to polling stations; what assessment was made of the comparative cost and cost benefit of providing permanent ramps instead; and if he will make a statement.     [24111]

**Mr. Nicholas Baker:** The provision of temporary ramps for use at local government elections is a matter for local authorities. No grants are made from central funds towards the cost of equipment purchased for local government elections, but returning officers may apply for grants towards the cost of temporary ramps to be used at polling places for parliamentary and European elections. Temporary ramps purchased for parliamentary and European elections under these arrangements can be made available for local government elections and for other purposes by arrangement with the returning officer.

### Returning Officers

**Mr. McMaster:** To ask the Secretary of State for the Home Department how much was paid or payable to each returning officer in England and Wales at the 1995 local elections; what out-of-pocket expenses had to be met from these payments; what was the level of payment to each other grade involved in these elections; and if he will make a statement.                                          [24107]

**Mr. Nicholas Baker:** Returning officers' fees and expenses and other costs relating to the conduct of local government elections are met by local authorities. This information is not collected centrally.

### Crack Cocaine

**Mr. Mike O'Brien:** To ask the Secretary of State for the Home Department what is his policy on cautioning of persons found in possession of crack cocaine.     [24012]

**Mr. Maclean:** It is for the police to decide, on the basis of the guidance on the cautioning of offenders in Home Office circular 18/1994, whether a person found in possession of a controlled drug should be dealt with by means of a caution.

### Rural White Paper

**Mr. Colvin:** To ask the Secretary of State for the Home Department what is his estimate of the net annual financial saving, or cost, of his Department's submission for the proposed White Paper on the rural economy.     [24333]

**Mr. Maclean:** Proposals for the rural White Paper remain subject to continuing collective consideration and discussion. The cost of measures contained in the White Paper will be taken into account in the public expenditure survey.

### Safer Cities Scheme

**Mr. Jim Cunningham:** To ask the Secretary of State for the Home Department what plans he has to extend the funding via the safer cities scheme for a secure room for the safety of witnesses at Salford magistrates' court to Coventry magistrates court and other magistrates courts.                                          [24207]

**Mr. Maclean:** I have no such plans. The Coventry safer cities project closed in March 1994 and the bulk of the safer cities programme now forms part of the single regeneration budget at the Department of the Environment. It is for projects' local steering committees to decide on their funding priorities.

### Witness Liaison Officers

**Mr. Jim Cunningham:** To ask the Secretary of State for the Home Department (1) what plans he has to discuss with Victim Support and other interested groups ways to introduce witness liaison officers *(a)* across the country and *(b)* in the Hillfields and Stoke Aldermoor areas of Coventry; [24209]

(2) what discussions he has had with the Secretary of State for the Environment on funding for witness liaison officers *(a)* across the country and *(b)* in the Willenhall, Hillfields and Stoke Aldermoor areas of Coventry.

[24205]

**Mr. Maclean:** The Government have accepted the recommendation made by the Royal Commission on criminal justice that witness support schemes should be established at all Crown court centres. There are already 40 schemes in operation, including one at Coventry Crown court, and additional Home Office funding, made available in 1994–95 and 1995–96, will enable Victim Support to establish schemes at all 78 Crown court centres by the end of 1995.

My Department has regular contact with Victim Support on a whole range of issues, including witness support. Since the Home Office accepts responsibility for funding the Crown court witness service this is not an issue which I have discussed with my right hon. Friend the Secretary of State for the Environment.

### Car Fires

**Mr. Nigel Griffiths:** To ask the Secretary of State for the Home Department how many fires there were in cars; and how many deaths were caused by those fires in each year since 1993. [24435]

**Mr. Nicholas Baker:** The available information is for 1993 and relates to car fires attended by local authority fire brigades. This is published in table 15 of Home Office "Statistical Bulletin" issue 29/94, "Summary Fire Statistics United Kingdom 1993", a copy of which is in the Library.

### Foundation for Business Responsibilities

**Mr. Robert Ainsworth:** To ask the Secretary of State for the Home Department (1) what plans he has to seek further information on how the Foundation for Business Responsibilities applied its funds; [24705]

(2) what investigations the Charity Commissioners have made into the Foundation for Business Responsibilities; what assessment he has made; if he will seek further investigations; and if he will make a statement. [24704]

**Mr. Nicholas Baker:** The Charity Commissioners have recently concluded their second enquiry into the affairs of the Foundation for Business Responsibilities during which they interviewed a number of further witnesses and sought and obtained further documents. The two inquiries have established that some money was paid improperly to Marketforce Communications and that there were some shortcomings in the controls within the charity. The individual responsible for the payments has left the charity and has repaid the money. The administrative and financial systems of the charity will be closely monitored over the next two years. Responsibility for decisions in relation to individual cases are the responsibility of the Charity Commissioners.

**Mr. Robert Ainsworth:** To ask the Secretary of State for the Home Department when the Metropolitan police received a report of the thefts of documents from the offices of the Foundation for Business Responsibilities;

what investigations were undertaken into these thefts; and what the conclusions and results were. [24703]

**Mr. Maclean:** The information is not readily available and I will write to the hon. Member.

### Nicholas Hill

**Mr. Mike O'Brien:** To ask the Secretary of State for the Home Department if he will write to the hon. Member for Warwickshire, North giving the outcome of the application for parole of Nicholas Hill convicted in 1990 at Birmingham for robbery. [24560]

**Mr. Michael Forsyth:** I will write to the hon. Member once Mr. Hill has been notified of the outcome of his current parole review, which should be known in about three months' time.

### Young Offenders

**Mr. Mike O'Brien:** To ask the Secretary of State for the Home Department how many youths under 18 years were held in Prison Service establishments in 1994. [23937]

**Mr. Michael Forsyth:** Responsibility for this matter has been delegated to the Director General of the Prison Service, who has been asked to arrange for a reply to be given.

*Letter from Derek Lewis to Mr. Mike O'Brien, dated 18 May 1995:*

The Home Secretary has asked me to reply to your recent Question about how many youths under 18 years were held in Prison Service establishments in 1994.

The population of male and female youths aged under 18 at 30 June 1994 was 1,526.

### Prisons (Drug Tests)

**Mr. David Porter:** To ask the Secretary of State for the Home Department (1) if he will list the establishments piloting the first phase of mandatory drug tests in prisons together with the percentages in each prison of prisoners tested positive; and what forms of disciplinary penalty have been chosen by each governor in each case where prisoners have tested positive; [20313]

(2) what estimate he has made of the increase in prison population and average length of sentence, arising from disciplinary actions as a result of the first phase of mandatory drug testing in prisons; and if he will make a statement; [20312]

(3) if he will make a statement on the results to date of the first phase of mandatory drug tests in prisons; what is the percentage of randomly selected prisoners and targeted prisoners who have tested positive; what are the most common drugs identified; and what is the average increase in prison sentence for drug-positive results; [20314]

(4) if he will make a statement on *(a)* the cost to date and *(b)* the anticipated costs of the mandatory drug tests in prisons. [20315]

**Mr. Howard** *[holding answer 24 April 1994]:* Eight prison establishments were selected for the initial phase of the mandatory drug testing programme. These were Bristol, Holloway, Lindholme, Pentonville, Wakefield and Wayland prisons, and Her Majesty's young offenders institution/remand centre, Feltham and HMYOI Stoke Heath. Holloway has only recently begun its testing programme and no results are as yet available.

Random tests have been carried out at each of the other seven sites and, of the total samples taken and submitted for testing between February and the end of April 1995—871—36 per cent. have confirmed positive. The results for individual prisons are shown in the table.

In addition to the random tests, each prison undertakes tests targeted on prisoners who are suspected of misusing drugs and, of the total samples collected on these grounds and submitted for testing between February and April 1995, 62 per cent. have tested positive.

The most common drug identified through the random testing programme is cannabis, which was present in 32 per cent. of the random tests undertaken. Of the other drug types, only opiates—heroin—present in 2 per cent. of tests undertaken, and benzodiazepines—tranquillisers—present in 1 per cent. of tests, appear in any significant quantities.

All prisoners testing positive are informed of the options available for assistance in giving up their drug habits. Reducing the level of drug misuse within prison is one of the Prison Service's strategic priorities for 1995–98. To facilitate this, the Prison Service has recently launched a comprehensive drugs strategy containing a wide range of measures aimed at reducing the supply of drugs into prison, reducing the demand for drugs within prison together with measures to assist in rehabilitating drug misusers. Local drug strategies are being developed at each prison and will form part of each establishment's contract with their area manager.

The disciplinary penalties selected by governors have varied between prisons and in individual cases. A total of 290 prisoners have, up to the end of April, been found guilty of disciplinary charges arising from positive drug tests and penalties have generally included the imposition of added days for those serving determinate sentences. Details of individual punishments for those charges resulting from positive test results will be placed in the Library.

As the number of adjudications following positive tests has been relatively small, the impact of any awards of added days on prison population will have been negligible during the initial phase. Any impact on future prison population is being considered but with the limited information available to date, it is not possible as yet to make any reliable estimates of future trends.

The total costs, excluding staffing costs, incurred during 1994–95 in introducing mandatory drug testing in prisons was £95,000. One of the purposes of the initial phase of mandatory drug testing is to help identify the total costs likely to be involved in the drug testing programme. These costs will not be clear until the initial phase is over and the negotiations are completed with contractors who are bidding for a national contract to provide the Prison Service with drug testing facilities.

| Establishment | Number of random tests carried out | Proportion of random tests confirmed for illicit drugs Per cent. |
|---|---|---|
| Bristol | 145 | 33 (±8) |
| Feltham | 143 | 40 (±8) |
| Lindholme | 46 | 48 (±15) |
| Pentonville | 166 | 46 (±8) |

| Establishment | Number of random tests carried out | Proportion of random tests confirmed for illicit drugs Per cent. |
|---|---|---|
| Stoke Heath | 78 | 23 (±9) |
| Wakefield | 115 | 29 (±8) |
| Wayland | 178 | 35 (± 7) |
| Total | 871 | 36 (±3) |

*Note:*
The plus/minus (±) figures shown in the last column represents the confidence which can be placed in the accuracy of the proportions given the relatively small number of tests undertaken to date.

### Crime Prevention

**Mrs. Roche:** To ask the Secretary of State for the Home Department how much money has been spent on crime prevention in each of the last 10 years; and what percentage this is of the criminal justice budget.   [22837]

**Mr. Howard** *[holding answer 10 May 1995]:* I refer the hon. Member to the reply I gave her yesterday in response to question No. 184.

## WALES

### Careers Service

**Mr. Barry Jones:** to ask the Secretary of State for Wales, if he will make a statement on the running of the careers service in Wales.   [24197]

**Mr. Redwood:** My hon. Friend, the Parliamentary Under-Secretary of State (Mr. Richards), announced on 3 April 1995, details of the contracts agreed for the provision of the careers service from 1 April 1995. Arrangements for contract management were set out in the prospectus published on 8 June 1994.

Copies of the prospectus and the announcement are available in the Library of the House.

### Early Retirement

**Mr. Morgan:** To ask the Secretary of State for Wales on what date his Department's second and enhanced early retirement and voluntary redundancy scheme was advertised; and how many applications have been received so far.   [24928]

**Mr. Redwood:** On 20 December 1994. A total of 163 applications were received.

**Mr. Morgan:** To ask the Secretary of State for Wales, on what date the request for volunteers for the Welsh Office redundancy scheme without enhancement was first posted; and how many staff applied in *(a)* the first and *(b)* the second month.   [24927]

**Mr. Redwood:** On 4 November 1994. There were two applicants in November and one in December.

### NHS Annual Accounts

**Mr. Morgan:** To ask the Secretary of State for Wales, pursuant to his answer of 15 May, if he will ensure that copies of trust annual reports are made available to the public via the public library service and via local authority offices.   [24938]

**Mr. Redwood:** Copies of their annual report may be obtained on request from NHS trusts.

## Trust Appointments

**Mr. Morgan:** To ask the Secretary of State for Wales, pursuant to his answer of 15 May, *Official Report,* columns *103–4,* if he will specify which trust had its non-executive board members announced after 1 April; on what date; and if he will specify which of the trusts which became operational on 1 April 1995 still have not had the non-executive board members' names announced. [24935]

**Mr. Redwood:** Morriston NHS trust became operational on 1 April 1994; its board was completed in February 1995. No announcement was made.

The following trusts became operational on 1 April 1995: Cardiff Community Healthcare NHS trust; University Hospital of Wales Healthcare NHS trust; University Dental Hospital NHS trust; West Wales Ambulance NHS trust; and Glan-y-Mor NHS trust— shadow running until 1 April 1996 I have not yet announced the names of the non-executive directors.

## Countryside Council for Wales

**Mr. Morgan:** To ask the Secretary of State for Wales, pursuant to his answer of 15 May, *Official Report,* column *103,* on what date he initiated the consultations with local authorities or their associations on the implications for authorities of the action plan for the Countryside Council for Wales. [24933]

**Mr. Redwood:** I consulted both the Assembly of Welsh Counties and the Council of Welsh Districts on 4 May 1995.

**Mr. Morgan:** To ask the Secretary of State for Wales, pursuant to his answer of 15 May, *Official Report,* column *103,* in which section of his Department the grade 7 officer was in charge of the financial management policy review of the Countryside Council for Wales immediately before being put in charge of the review. [24942]

**Mr. Redwood:** The officer had a wide range of policy experience before undertaking the review. It is not my Department's practice to give detailed information about the postings of individual officers.

**Mr. Morgan:** To ask the Secretary of State for Wales, pursuant to his answer of 15 May, *Official Report,* column *102,* if the Financial Management Policy Review of the Countryside Council for Wales reached the stage of drawing conclusions before it was overtaken by the review referred to in his answer to the right hon. Member for Conwy (Sir W. Roberts) on 3 November 1994, *Official Report,* column *1329;* and if he will give the cost to public funds separately for each of the two reviews. [24932]

**Mr. Redwood:** The financial management policy review of the Countryside Council for Wales was not completed, although some of the initial conclusions reached were carried forward into the review. Work on the review was carried out by the appropriate divisions in my Department as part of their normal duties and it is not possible to attribute separate costs to the work beyond the information provided in the answer to the hon. Member on 15 May.

## Public Bodies

**Mr. Morgan:** To ask the Secretary of State for Wales, pursuant to his answer of 15 May, *Official Report,* column *102,* for how long the Countryside Council for Wales had been in existence before the financial management policy review was begun; and if he will list all other non-departmental public bodies which have had reviews initiated following a shorter period of existence. [24943]

**Mr. Redwood:** The Countryside Council for Wales was established on 5 November 1990 and assumed its full responsibilities on 1 April 1991. The financial management and policy review started on 5 April 1994. No other reviews of executive non-departmental bodies have been undertaken in a shorter timescale.

## Cardiff East Sewage Works

**Mr. Morgan:** To ask the Secretary of State for Wales (1) what consultation he has had with the National Rivers Authority and Welsh Water concerning the proposed Cardiff East sewage works; what further consideration he has given to the size and scope of the scheme and the date for completion of stage one and stage two; and if he will make a statement; [24929]

(2) what representations he has had concerning the proposed Cardiff East sewage works; and what consultations he has had with the Environment Directorate of the European Commission concerning derogations from the completion dates specified in the municipal waste water treatment directive. [24926]

**Mr. Redwood:** I refer the hon. Member to the reply I gave him on Thursday 20 October 1994, at column *313.*

## GP and Hospital Records

**Mr. Morgan:** To ask the Secretary of State for Wales (1) if he will list the principal aspects of the guidelines governing the conduct of appeal hearings under the health service complaints procedures as they applied in 1991–92, with respect to the safe keeping of original NHS general practitioner and hospital records in his Department's vaults during the adjournments of such hearings; what records are kept of retrievals of such records during any such adjournment of a hearing; what are the rules relating to the notification to appellants or their legal representatives on the resumption of the hearing of such retrieval of documents and records; and if he will make a statement; [24780]

(2) what departmental records exists of retrieval and replacement between 19 March and 7 September 1992 of files held in his departmental vaults containing the original general practitioner records and hospital records of Robert Powell (deceased), of 138 Brecon road, Ystradgynlais, pertaining to the adjournment appeal by Mr. William Powell of the same address and father of the deceased child under the NHS complaints procedure in relation to primary health care. [24784]

**Mr. Redwood:** The regulations governing the handling of complaints against GPs make no specific provision about the safe-keeping of such documents in the circumstances described. The security of all documents is of course subject to the Department's overall policy on record keeping. Only the hospital records of Robert Powell were held by the Department between March and September 1992.

The only record of retrieval during that period concerns the retrieval made in response to a request, made by a letter dated 13 August 1992, from Mr. Powell's solicitors for the hospital records to be subject to scientific testing. The other parties to the appeal were made aware of the request.

### Welsh Assembly

**Mr. Morgan:** To ask the Secretary of State for Wales if he will make a statement on his plans to cost proposals of Her Majesty's Opposition for a Welsh Assembly.    [24931]

**Mr. Redwood:** When I get a clear idea of the Opposition's devolution proposals I will comment on costs.

**Mr. Morgan:** To ask the Secretary of State for Wales, what guidelines he has agreed with his Department to maintain a proper distinction between party political activities and administrative duties in calculating the cost of proposals of Her Majesty's Opposition for a Welsh Assembly; and if he will make a statement.    [24930]

**Mr. Redwood:** Once the Labour party has published its agreed proposals, I shall calculate the costs taking account of published data.

### Local Pay

**Mr. Morgan:** To ask the Secretary of State for Wales, pursuant to his answer of 15 May, *Official Report*, column *103*, what guidelines he has given to trusts which became operational on 1 April but which have not yet had their non-executive board membership appointed, on the negotiations of local pay bargaining with nursing and auxiliary staff; and if he will make a statement.    [24934]

**Mr. Redwood:** None. I hope to complete appointments shortly which will enable all trust boards to authorise settlement.

### Trade (Taiwan)

**Sir Wyn Roberts:** To ask the Secretary of State for Wales what he is doing to promote trade between Wales and Taiwan and whether he will make a statement.    [25535]

**Mr. Redwood:** The Welsh Office actively supports trade and business contacts between Wales and Taiwan—including a successful trade mission to Taiwan last September; by support for inward investment, including the recent announcement of a 100 job project by Ringtel, the first major Taiwanese inward investment into Wales. The Welsh Development Agency has an active programme to develop further investment opportunities and maintains an office in Taipei. I am also aware of and appreciate my right hon. Friend's support for the WDA's efforts through his own forthcoming visit to Taiwan.

# Written Answers to Questions

*Monday 22 May 1995*

## EMPLOYMENT

### Volunteer Work

**Mr. Sheerman:** To ask the Secretary of State for Employment what steps he is taking to encourage unemployed people to seek relevant work experience through volunteering. [24448]

**Miss Widdecombe:** We recognise that volunteering can help unemployed people keep in touch with the labour market and contribute to improving their prospects of getting a job. The potential advantages of undertaking voluntary work while unemployed are set out in an Employment Department leaflet entitled "Voluntary Work When You're Unemployed", copies of which are available in the Library. There are special arrangements in the benefit rules for unemployed people undertaking voluntary work. They are allowed 48 hours' notice to be available for work; and voluntary work is taken into account in determining whether someone is actively seeking employment.

### Jobseeker's Allowance

**Mr. Burden:** To ask the Secretary of State for Employment what trials or pilot schemes of anticipated jobseeker's allowance procedures have been undertaken by his Department; where they have been held; how long they lasted; what they covered; and what were the results. [25575]

**Miss Widdecombe:** The jobseeker's allowance implementation project team is setting up trials of the jobseeker's allowance process in 20 locations throughout England, Scotland and Wales. Three trials, in Newton Abbot, Barnstaple and Exeter, started during April. Other locations where trials are likely to start during June are Bathgate, Alnwick, Jarrow, Middlesbrough, Cheetham Hill, Goole, Porthmadog, Madeley, Halesowen, Norwich, Gabalfa and Victoria Park. Discussions are under way with the Employment Service and the Benefits Agency in other locations where trials might take place.

The trial offices will simulate the jobseeker's allowance process as closely as possible under existing legislation. Evaluation of the trials will inform development of operational procedures.

## PRIME MINISTER

### Nolan Committee

**Mr. Harry Greenway:** To ask the Prime Minister what has been the cost to public funds to date of the Nolan committee; what payments or emoluments have been made to each member of the committee; what are the anticipated on-going costs; and if he will make a statement. [25259]

**The Prime Minister:** I refer my hon. Friend to the Nolan committee's first report, which was published last week and states that the committee's total estimated cost to the end of April 1995 was £317,200.

Lord Nolan, my right hon. Friend the Member for Bridgwater (Mr. King), the right hon. Member for Bethnal Green and Stepney (Mr. Shore) and Ms Diana Warwick do not receive emoluments for their Nolan committee work as they already receive a salary from other public funds. Other members of the committee were paid a salary of £1,000 per month from November 1994 to April 1995. They are now receiving an attendance fee of £155 per day. Members travel and subsistence expenses are met from public funds.

The on-going cost of the committee is estimated to be £500,000 a year.

### Deregulation

**Mr. Harry Greenway:** To ask the Prime Minister what further action he proposes to take to advance the Government's deregulation initiative. [25801]

**The Prime Minister:** I have established a new ministerial committee to co-ordinate the Government's programme of deregulation and consider how the burden of deregulation on business, charities and individuals can be kept to a minimum. Copies of the terms of reference and membership are in the Library of the House.

MINISTERIAL COMMITTEE ON DEREGULATION (EDD)

*Composition*

    President of the Board of Trade (Chairman)
    Lord President of the Council
    Chancellor of the Duchy of Lancaster
    Secretary of State for Employment
    Lord Privy Seal
    Chief Secretary to the Treasury
    Minister of State, Foreign and Commonwealth Office
    Parliamentary Under-Secretary of State for Corporate Affairs, Department of Trade and Industry
    Other Ministers will be invited to attend as necessary.

*Terms of Reference*

    "To co-ordinate the Government's programme of deregulation and to consider how the burden of regulation on businesses, charities and individuals can be kept to a minimum."

## CHURCH COMMISSIONERS

### Resignations

**Mr. Frank Field:** To ask the right hon. Member for Selby, as representing the Church Commissioners (1) if he will list the estimates the Commission has been given by the House of Bishops on the estimated number of resignations and claims which will be made to the Ordination of Women (Financial Provisions) Measure 1993 up until the expiry of the Measure;

(2) what estimates the Church Commission has made of the number of priests who will claim compensation under the Ordination of Women (Financial Provisions) Measure 1993 for each year until the expiry of the Measure.

**Mr. Alison:** The House of Bishops has not itself provided estimates, the Church Commissioners' estimates are their own, following consultation with the Church of England pensions board.

As at 30 April 1995, 265 clergy eligible for financial assistance under the Measure had resigned and so far have received £3.5 million in resettlement grants and periodic payments. A further 40 clergy have indicated their intention to resign. It is difficult to predict the final number of resignations. However, actual expenditure in 1994 and illustrative costings based on a possible total of 350 resignations are set out in the following table. These reflect the pattern of expenditure to date.

*Illustration of costs for 350 resignations*

| Year | Gross Costs to be met from CC Income £ | Housing Capital (funded by CC) £ | Net Costs for Church £ | Net Housing Capital (funded by CC) £ |
|---|---|---|---|---|
| 1994 | 2,452,000 | 5,011,000 | 747,000 | 5,011,000 |
| 1995 | 3,439,000 | 4,770,000 | 1,872,000 | 4,770,000 |
| 1996 | 3,216,000 | 1,370,000 | 1,899,000 | 1,370,000 |
| 1997 | 2,434,000 | 355,000 | 1,226,000 | 54,000 |
| 1998 | 1,731,000 | 213,000 | 706,000 | (100,000) |
| 1999 | 1,250,000 | 111,000 | 433,000 | (215,000) |
| 2000 | 890,000 | 85,000 | 272,000 | (254,000) |
| 2001 | 851,000 | 88,000 | 412,000 | (264,000) |
| 2002 | 707,000 | 91,000 | 413,000 | (274,000) |
| 2003 | 625,000 | 95,000 | 437,000 | (285,000) |
| 2004 | 415,000 | — | 321,000 | (396,000) |
| 2005 | 289,000 | — | 244,000 | (411,000) |
| 2006 | 216,000 | — | 197,000 | (428,000) |
| 2007 | 211,000 | — | 204,000 | (445,000) |
| 2008 | 211,000 | — | 209,000 | (463,000) |
| 2009 | 217,000 | — | 216,000 | (361,000) |
| 2010 | 221,000 | — | 221,000 | (375,000) |
| 2011 | 226,000 | — | 226,000 | (390,000) |
| 2012 | 233,000 | — | 233,000 | (406,000) |
| Total | 19,834,000 | 12,189,000 | 10,488,000 | 6,138,000 |

*Notes:*

(a) The number of resignations shown, 350, is a broad estimate, and the final costs may vary substantially.

(b) Actual costs based on 232 resignations are shown in respect of 1994. A similar pattern of costs has been assumed for future years.

(c) The figures make allowance for future increases in house prices and stipends.

(d) It has been assumed that 50 per cent. of resigners will require housing assistance.

(e) The net figures take account of such variables as stipends savings—assuming at least a temporary reduction in the payroll—allowance for retirement housing provision which would otherwise have arisen on retirement, and the possibility of some people redeeming loans or leaving rented accommodation once they have obtained alternative employment.

### Clergy (Resignations)

**Mr. Clifton-Brown:** To ask the right hon. Member for Selby, as representing the Church Commissioners what redundancy and other terms are being awarded to clergy who have left the Church of England to join the Roman Catholic Church.

**Mr. Alison:** Clergy who resign from ecclesiastical service and apply for assistance under the Ordination of Women (Financial Provisions) Measure 1993 are entitled to the various payments stipulated by the Measure, irrespective of whether they join another church. Provision is made for periodical payments and a resettlement grant. Additional discretionary payments may be made in cases of hardship, and access is also granted to the Church's housing assistance for the retired ministry scheme. Clergy in receipt of assistance under the Measure are obliged to disclose the income or other benefits derived from any new employment or office, and their periodical payments may be reduced or terminated to take account of this.

## FOREIGN AND COMMONWEALTH AFFAIRS

### Nuclear Non-proliferation Treaty

**Mr. Llew Smith:** To ask the Secretary of State for Foreign and Commonwealth Affairs if he will place in the Library *(a)* a copy of the paper on the United Kingdom's activities relating to the objectives of the nuclear non-proliferation treaty, to which reference was made by Sir Michael Weston in his presentation to main committee I of the non-proliferation treaty conference on 19 April, *(b)* all other working papers submitted by the United Kingdom delegation to the main and sub-committees, *(c)* details of responses made by other delegations to United Kingdom submissions and *(d)* a copy of the final declaration from the conference; and if he will make a statement on the outcome of the non-proliferation treaty review and extension conference.

**Mr. David Davis:** Copies of the paper have been placed in the Library providing information on the activities and views of the United Kingdom on the principal objectives of the nuclear non-proliferation treaty, and of our statements to main committees I, II, and III. Copies of the verbatim records of the open debates in the main committees will also be placed in the House Library. It is not our practice to disclose working papers. The conference did not adopt a final declaration. The Secretary of State for Foreign and Commonwealth Affairs made a statement to the House on 16 May, *Official Report,* columns 151–61.

### China (Nuclear Tests)

**Mr. Llew Smith:** To ask the Secretary of State for Foreign and Commonwealth Affairs what representations Her Majesty's Government have made to China about the nuclear weapons test conducted in China on 14 May. [24882]

**Mr. David Davis:** We have made no formal representations to the Chinese. We have noted their repeated commitment to abide by a comprehensive test ban treaty and look forward to their active participation in the negotiations on that treaty, which we hope will reach an early conclusion.

**Mr. Llew Smith:** To ask the Secretary of State for Foreign and Commonwealth Affairs what indication the Chinese delegation at the recent nuclear non-proliferation treaty conference in New York gave to the United Kingdom diplomatic delegation of the intention of China to conduct a nuclear weapons test on 14 May. [24881]

**Mr. David Davis:** None.

### Iran (Nuclear Weapons)

**Mr. Llew Smith:** To ask the Secretary of State for Foreign and Commonwealth Affairs what recent information has been provided to Her Majesty's Government by the Government of the United States concerning the technical capability and aspirations of Iran to obtain nuclear weapons. [24883]

**Mr. David Davis:** We remain in close touch with the US Government on this issue. However, it is not our practice to reveal details of confidential exchanges with other Governments. We have grave concerns about the nuclear weapon aspirations of Iran, and we continue to work closely with the United States and our European partners to prevent the proliferation of nuclear weapons.

### Staff

**Ms Hodge:** To ask the Secretary of State for Foreign and Commonwealth Affairs how many posts were lost in *(a)* the Foreign and Commonwealth Office and *(b)* agencies for which the Foreign and Commonwealth Office is responsible, listing the total lost posts agency by agency in (i) 1993–94 and (ii) 1994–95; and how many posts are proposed to be lost in 1995–96. [25080]

**Mr. Goodlad:** Details of reductions in job slots resulting from efficiency measures taken in the Foreign and Commonwealth Office and Overseas Development Administration up to 1993–94 have been published annually in the citizens charter White Paper.

The number of job slots reduced in 1994–95 was: FCO, 1985; ODA, 32; and Natural Resources Institute, 49. The following reductions in 1995–96 have also been identified: FCO, 92; ODA, 50; and NRI, 140.

There have been no reductions in slots at Wilton Park, the FCO agency, nor are there plans for reductions in 1995–96.

**Ms Hodge:** To ask the Secretary of State for Foreign and Commonwealth Affairs what changes there have been in the numbers of staff employed by *(a)* the Foreign and Commonwealth Office and *(b)* agencies for which the Foreign and Commonwealth Office is responsible, listing the changes in the number of staff agency by agency in (i) 1993–94 and (ii) 1994–95; and what changes are projected for 1995–96. [25062]

**Mr. Goodlad:** The members of permanent and casual staff employed by the Foreign and Commonwealth Office diplomatic wing and its executive agency and the Overseas Development Administration in 1993–94, projected outturn for 1994–95, and plans for 1995–96 are published in this Department's annual report, a copy of which is in the Library of the House.

The breakdown for the Overseas Development Administration and its agency, the Natural Resources Institute, is:

| | 1993–94 | 1994–95 | 1995–96 |
|---|---|---|---|
| *ODA* | | | |
| Civil Service full-time equivalents | 1,190 | 1,137 | 1,120 |
| Overtime | 21 | 17 | 17 |
| Casuals | 56 | 63 | 70 |
| | 1,267 | 1,217 | 1,207 |
| *NRI* | | | |
| Civil Service full-time equivalents | 428 | 341 | 341 |
| Overtime | 3 | 3 | 3 |
| Casuals | 25 | 25 | 25 |
| | 456 | 369 | 369 |

### Immigration

**Mr. Madden:** To ask the Secretary of State for Foreign and Commonwealth Affairs when a decision is to be taken on the application made by Arshad Iqbal—ref: IMM/C8387—to the post in Islamabad to join his wife in the United Kingdom; and if he will make a statement. [25049]

**Mr. Baldry:** I have asked the high commission in Islamabad for details and will arrange for the hon. Member to receive a substantive reply from the migration and visa correspondence unit as soon as possible.

### UN Conference on Women

**Mr. Alton:** To ask the Secretary of State for Foreign and Commonwealth Affairs what information he has on the size and membership of the International Planned Parenthood Federation and United Nations Family Planning Association delegations to the UN conference on women to be held in Beijing and of his Department's delegation. [25315]

**Mr. Douglas Hogg:** We have no information on the size or composition of the International Planned Parenthood Federation and the United Nations Family Planning Association delegations to the fourth world conference on women. On the British delegation, I refer the hon. Member to the reply given to the hon. Member for Aylesbury (Mr. Lidington) by my hon. Friend the Minister of State, Department of Employment on 16 March, *Official Report*, column *648*.

**Mr. Alton:** To ask the Secretary of State for Foreign and Commonwealth Affairs what assessment he has made of the human rights implications of choosing Beijing as the venue for the UN conference on women; what consideration was given to China's population programme in the choice of venue; what were the reasons for the choice; what representations Her Majesty's Government made to the conference organisers on the issue; and what provision is being made on the agenda to discuss the programme.

**Mr. Douglas Hogg:** Peking was nominated as the venue for the fourth world conference on women in accordance with the United Nations principle of geographical rotation. Population will be discussed in one of the critical areas of concern in the global platform for action.

### Indonesia

**Mr. Andrew Smith:** To ask the Secretary of State for Foreign and Commonwealth Affairs what plans he has to send a delegation of hon. Members and military experts to East Timor to assess whether British arms including Hawk aircraft are being used against the local civilian population by the Indonesian army. [25168]

**Mr. Goodlad:** None.

We have closely considered the latest allegations that Hawk aircraft have used to attack villages in East Timor and found no evidence from any source to support them.

Our embassy staff visit East Timor regularly, as do other western diplomats. The all-party Anglo-Indonesian parliamentary group visited East Timor from 17 to 19 September 1994.

**Mr. Andrew Smith:** To ask the Secretary of State for Foreign and Commonwealth Affairs what guarantees he has received that Scorpion tanks exported to Indonesia will not be used against either Indonesia or East Timorese civilians. [25169]

**Mr. Goodlad:** I refer the hon. Gentleman to the statement made by my right hon. Friend the President of the Board of Trade on 2 March, *Official Report*, column *716*.

### Romania

**Sir John Gorst:** To ask the Secretary of State for Foreign and Commonwealth Affairs what progress has been made by Her Majesty's Government to promote and sustain the reform process in Romania; and what results have been achieved by the establishment of the Romania information service. [25241]

**Mr. Douglas Hogg:** We continue to support the reform process in Romania through a variety of means including the know-how fund. Romania is now a member of the Council of Europe and has an association agreement with the European Union. We also support financially the Romanian information centre which responds to the needs for advice and support for over 500 British charities and non-governmental organisations working in Romania.

### Charar-e-Sharief Shrine

**Mr. Pike:** To ask the Secretary of State for Foreign and Commonwealth Affairs what discussions he has had with the representatives of the Governments of India and Pakistan following the destruction of the holy shrine Charar-e-Sharief; and if he will make a statement. [25249]

**Mr. Baldry:** My right hon. Friend the Secretary of State for Foreign and Commonwealth Affairs has not had any discussions with the representatives of the Government of India and Pakistan following the destruction of the holy shrine at Charar-e-Sharief.

### Iraq

**Mr. David Young:** To ask the Secretary of State for Foreign and Commonwealth Affairs what recent actions he has taken to ascertain the fate of Kuwaiti military personnel and civilians abducted by the Iraqis; and if he will make a statement. [25389]

**Mr. Douglas Hogg:** We raise this issue at the United Nations at every opportunity and did so most recently when the Security Council reviewed sanctions against Iraq on 12 May. We have made it clear to the Iraqis that the lack of progress to date is unacceptable. We will continue to play a leading role in the tripartite commission and its technical sub-committee set up last December to speed up the review of case files on the detainees.

### Uzbekistan

**Mr. David Atkinson:** To ask the Secretary of State for Foreign and Commonwealth Affairs what recent reports he has received of the harassment of Christians in Uzbekistan; and if he will make a statement. [25592]

**Mr. Douglas Hogg:** We have received reports of a meeting in Tashkent in April 1994 at which all religious organisations in Uzbekistan were warned against missionary activity, in particular the publishing and distribution of religious literature. We are not aware of any specific cases of harassment of Christians in Uzbekistan.

### Instruments of Torture

**Mrs. Clwyd:** To ask the Secretary of State for Foreign and Commonwealth Affairs what advice has been given to his Department to (a) the Secretary of State for Defence and (b) the President of the Board of Trade on the transfer of weapons that can be used for torture overseas. [25674]

**Mr. David Davis:** A wide variety of weapons could conceivably be used for torture. If this Department judged that defence equipment, if transferred, would be likely to be so used, it would advise against the transfer.

## ENVIRONMENT

### Mortgage Arrears and Repossessions

**Mr. Nicholas Winterton:** To ask the Secretary of State for the Environment (1) what are the main conclusions of his Department's report on mortgage arrears and repossessions; if he will identify, specifically, all the conclusions which refer to problems associated with the widespread promotion and uptake of private insurance to cover mortgage interest in the event of redundancy; and if he will make a statement; [24846]

(2) if he will list all the individuals, companies and organisations which were consulted by his officials in preparing their report on mortgage arrears and repossessions; [24845]

(3) what has been the cost of producing his Department's report on mortgage arrears and repossessions; and if he will be arranging a press conference to publish that report; [24847]

(4) when he intends to publish the full results of the report undertaken by his Department on mortgage arrears and repossessions; if he intends to circulate that report with an appropriate press release to the media; if he will make it his policy to make copies of that report immediately available through the Vote Office to all right hon. and hon. Members, and if he intends to make a statement in the House on the conclusions of that report; [24844]

(5) what plans he has to make available to the Secretary of State for Social Security copies of his Department's report on mortgage arrears and repossessions. [24848]

**Mr. Curry:** On 18 May 1995, my Department published the report of a £313,000 study commissioned from the university of Loughborough and the Policy Studies Institute into mortgage arrears, possessions and voluntary surrenders. Copies of the report, entitled "Mortgage arrears and possessions: perspectives from borrowers, lenders and the courts", have been placed in the Library. Copies have been sent to other Government Departments with an interest in the study, the Council of Mortgage Lenders, the Association of British Insurers, the Audit Commission, the Housing Corporation and the local authority associations. Further copies are available from HMSO outlets.

In the course of the study, the researchers carried out surveys and interviews with representative borrowers, lenders and district judges. The methods used and number of respondents of each type are described on pages 115 to 121 of the report. The main conclusions of the study are set out in pages 107 to 113 of the report, and those relating to mortgage protection insurance are on pages 60 to 62.

### Radioactive Waste, Milton

**Mrs. Anne Campbell:** To ask the Secretary of State for the Environment what representations he has received about the dumping of low-level radioactive waste on the Milton landfill site; and how many of them were in favour of the proposal to dump low-level radioactive waste on the Milton landfill site.                    [24816]

**Mr. Atkins:** Low-level radioactive waste from "small users" such as hospitals and research laboratories has been disposed of by "controlled burial" at the Milton landfill site for a number of years. The Department's consultation document, "Review of Radioactive Waste Management Policy: Preliminary Conclusions", published in August 1994, suggested that greater use should be encouraged of controlled burial by radioactive waste producers including the nuclear industry. No proposals were made for specific sites. The conclusions of the radioactive waste review will be published in a White Paper in the summer.

The Department has received 220 letters opposing the disposal of low-level radioactive waste from the nuclear industry at the Milton site, together with two petitions— one with 766 signatures, the other with five. I also understand that the operators of the Milton site have said that they will not accept radioactive waste from the nuclear industry.

### Water Quality

**Mr. Matthew Taylor:** To ask the Secretary of State for the Environment what guidance on appraisal, covering environmental, economic and financial costs to industry, he has given to the National Rivers Authority to assist it when it draws up its recommendations for statutory water quality objectives for the pilot rivers; and what arrangements he has made for the appraisals to be made available to the public.                    [24772]

**Mr. Atkins:** It is for the National Rivers Authority to support its recommendations for statutory water quality objectives with an assessment of the anticipated costs and benefits of achieving them. It is intended that this should form part of the public consultation document on the proposals.

### Energy Efficiency

**Mr. Thomason:** To ask the Secretary of State for the Environment what provisional resources his Department makes available to assist low-income households improve the energy efficiency of their homes.                    [25145]

**Mr. Robert B. Jones:** Our major energy efficiency programme for low-income households is the home energy efficiency scheme. More than 1 million households have benefited since 1991 from this scheme, which pays grants for basic home insulation measures and energy advice to householders who are over 60, receive an income-related benefit or disability living allowance. We have increased provision for the scheme substantially. During 1995–96, some £100 million will be made available for grants, and a similar sum has been set aside for each of the next two years. Over the next three years, I expect almost 2 million households to benefit from grants.

**Mr. Thomason:** To ask the Secretary of State for the Environment what assessment he has made of the results of the funding by Midlands Electricity of neighbourhood energy action projects to benefit low-income consumers in the west midlands; and if he will commend the extension of private and voluntary sector partnership to other utilities.                    [25146]

**Mr. Robert B. Jones:** More than 20 different projects in the west midlands, ranging in scope from the provision of energy advice to non-English-speaking communities to home improvement programmes building on the energy efficiency measures available under our home energy efficiency scheme, have resulted from Midland Electricity's generous contribution to a partnership with the charity Neighbourhood Energy Action. My right hon. Friend the Secretary of State visited one of these projects in the Sparkbrook area of Birmingham on 20 March this year, and was impressed with the energy efficiency improvements for the benefit of low-income households. This initiative is a good example of the kind of partnership between the private and voluntary sectors which many other energy companies have already adopted or are considering.

### Landfill Sites

**Mr. Sheerman:** To ask the Secretary of State for the Environment what assessment his Department has made of the safety of the United Kingdom's landfill sites.                    [24992]

**Mr. Atkins:** All landfill sites are required to be licensed by waste regulation authorities in accordance with part II of the Environmental Protection Act 1990. A waste regulation authority is required to reject an application for a licence unless it is satisfied that the landfill operation will not lead to pollution of the environment, harm to human health or serious detriment to the amenities of the locality. Conditions are attached to licences to ensure that operations do not lead to pollution or harm. Waste regulation authorities should regularly review licences to ensure that the conditions remain appropriate and effective. Authorities have powers to suspend or revoke licences if the licensed activities would cause pollution or harm.

### Local Government Reorganisation

**Mr. Frank Cook:** To ask the Secretary of State for the Environment if he will make a statement on his proposals for the allocation of standard spending assessments to the new unitary authorities created as a result of local government reorganisation in Cleveland.                    [25220]

**Mr. Curry:** The standard spending assessments for the new unitary authorities in Cleveland will be calculated on the basis of the services which these authorities provide, using the formulae which are applied to all relevant authorities.

Details of the formulae for 1995–96 are set out in the publication "Standard Spending Assessment Handbook, 1995–96", which is available from the Library. Following the review work which we undertake each year with the local authority associations, we will publish our proposals for 1996–97 in the usual way in December.

## UN Conference on Environment and Development

**Mr. Sheermen:** To ask the Secretary of State for the Environment what assessment his Department has made of the progress of our European partners towards satisfying the recommendations of the United Nations conference on environment and development.        [24986]

**Mr. Atkins:** The primary responsibility for carrying forward the commitments entered into at the Rio Earth summit lies with individual countries. At the request of my right hon. Friend the Prime Minister, EU colleagues adopted an action plan to implement the Rio commitments. Progress on meeting these commitments, and reviewing them as appropriate, is discussed at international fora such as the UN Commission on Sustainable Development, and the recent Berlin meeting of parties to the convention on climate change. The European Community's fifth environmental action programme, "Towards Sustainability", is linked closely to the principles and themes of Agenda 21. The UK is contributing fully to the present review of the programme by the European Commission.

## Compulsory Competitive Tendering

**Mr. Patrick Thompson:** To ask the Secretary of State for the Environment what steps he is taking to ensure housing management services are exempt from compulsory competitive tendering during local government reorganisation and that those authorities with only boundary changes following the review are exempted in the same way as those with structural changes. [25560]

**Mr. Robert B. Jones:** On 12 December, the Government made regulations—the Local Government Changes for England (Direct Labour and Service Organisations) Regulations 1994—to exempt local authorities undergoing reorganisation from most of the requirements of compulsory competitive tendering. However, the regulations as drafted did not extend to housing management services or to authorities which will undergo functional changes but where the transferor authority has not been abolished. I have now made amendment regulations to rectify these omissions. These are being laid before the House today.

I have also taken the opportunity in these same amendment regulations to extend the exemption to local authority subject to boundary changes but not structural changes as a result of the implementation of the recommendations of the Local Government Commission made in pursuance of a direction given before the date these regulations were made. I think it only fair that such authorities are treated in a similar way as those that have been restructured. They also will face problems arising from the need to take decisions on appropriate new patterns of service delivery.

## Abandoned Mine Workings

**Mrs. Helen Jackson:** To ask the Secretary of State for the Environment what resources, capital and revenue have been allocated to the National Rivers Authority, in the current year and in the next three years' projections specifically for clean up operations of ferruginous discharges from abandoned mine workings.        [24907]

**Mr. Atkins:** The National Rivers Authority receives an annual block allocation of resources to cover the gap between income and expenditure on its functions other than flood defence. Subject to ministerial guidance on priorities the amount used to cover clean-up of ferruginous discharges from abandoned mines is a matter for the NRA. The NRA's corporate plan has made provision for £2 million expenditure for clean-up of ferruginous discharges from abandoned mines in 1995–96 and envisages provision of a similar amount in the three following years.

**Mrs. Helen Jackson:** To ask the Secretary of State for the Environment if he will list the projects, both proposed and in operation, relating to discharges from abandoned mine workings, for which the National Rivers Authority has applied for resources.        [24908]

**Mr. Atkins:** The National Rivers Authority receives an annual block allocation of resources to cover the gap between income and expenditure on its functions other than flood defence. Subject to ministerial guidance on priorities, the use of these resources is a matter for the NRA. Except in the case of Wheal Jane, the NRA has not applied for resources for individual mine-water projects.

## Wading Birds, Cardiff Bay

**Mr. Morgan:** To ask the Secretary of State for the Environment what consultations he has had with the European Union environment directorate concerning compliance with the undertaking given to create alternative bird reserves to mitigate the loss of wading birds' habitat in Cardiff bay.        [25281]

**Sir Paul Beresford:** The European Commission was consulted about a review of the options for suitable sites for mitigating measures. The Commission is being kept informed of progress.

## Majority Shareholdings

**Mr. Byers:** To ask the Secretary of State for the Environment if he will list those companies in which the holder of his office is a majority shareholder which (a) are currently in existence and (b) have been wound up in the past five years.        [25718]

**Sir Paul Beresford:** None.

## National Parks

**Mr. Peter Atkinson:** To ask the Secretary of State how he intends to respond to the concerns of those who live and work in the national parks that their views should be properly represented in the management of these special areas.        [25745]

**Mr. Atkins:** I am well aware of the concerns expressed during the Bill's passage that local people should have greater involvement in the running of the parks and management of parks affairs. We have already made a number of amendments to the Bill to strengthen the part which local people should play in the parks' affairs. These have generally been welcomed, but we have been giving further thought to the membership of the NPAs, so as to ensure that the interests of park residents are properly represented on the new authorities.

Under the proposals, a third category of membership would be added to the current provisions of the Bill, which allow for two thirds of the members of the new authorities to be appointed by the local authorities—county, district and metropolitan district councils—with land in the parks and one third by the Secretary of State. The new category would be allocated to parishes which lie wholly or partly within the parks.

It is proposed that the new authorities would be constituted along the following lines:

i) one half of the members plus 1 to be appointed by local authorities with land in the parks; and

ii) the remainder to be appointed by the Secretary of State, of whom one half of his members minus 1 would be drawn from the relevant parishes.

Parish members would be drawn from parishes wholly or partly in the parks, and would be serving parish councillors or, where there is no parish council, chairmen of parish meetings.

Nominations to the Secretary of State for parish members would be sought from any or all of the following: the National Association of Local Councils, groupings of parishes within the parks or individual parishes. Nominations could also come from other sources, including individuals with an interest in park affairs.

Parish members would be appointed by the Secretary of State, after consulting the Countryside Commission, as is already the case for his direct appointments, and would be subject to the same provisions as set out in the Bill as regards, for example, attendance, disqualification from holding office, members' interests, allowances, as apply to local authority and other members appointed by the Secretary of State. I have placed a copy of the letter which I have sent to local authorities in the Libraries of the Houses.

These proposals apply to the English national parks. Because of commitments which have already been made in respect of the membership of the national park board being established under the Local Government (Wales) Act 1994, and the circular letters already issued for consultations about establishing Welsh NPAs, the Secretary of State for Wales is proposing to leave unchanged the provisions for membership of the NPAs as they apply in Wales.

### Radioactive Waste Management Advisory Committee

**Mr. Hawkins:** To ask the Secretary of State for the Environment if he will make a statement on the chairmanship of the Radioactive Waste Management Advisory Committee. [25767]

**Mr. Gummer:** Together with my right hon. Friends the Secretaries of State for Scotland and for Wales, I have today appointed Sir Gordon Beveridge to succeed Sir John Knill as chairman of the Radioactive Waste Management Advisory Committee, when his appointment ends on 31 May. Sir Gordon's appointment is for a three-year term ending on 31 May 1998.

I have written to Sir John Knill to thank him for the excellent work he has done for the Committee over a period of nearly 10 years, for more than seven of which he has been chairman.

### Sewage Sludge

**Mr. Sumberg:** To ask the Secretary of State for the Environment what progress has been made on the Government's response to the recommendations from the review on the current rules on sewage sludge use in agriculture; and if he will make a statement. [25746]

**Mr. Atkins:** Environment and Agriculture Ministers have considered the two reports from the review which examined the soil fertility aspects and the food safety and relevant animal health aspects. We are reassured by their general conclusions on the level of protection afforded by the current rules on sewage sludge use in agriculture.

Following consultation with appropriate bodies, we have decided to reduce the advisory limit for zinc in the code of practice on sludge use in agriculture. We shall review the limit again when results from recently commissioned, long-term research become available.

We have also decided to reduce the advisory limit for cadmium where sewage sludge is applied to grass managed in rotation or grown for conservation. In addition, research will be undertaken to address the review's recommendation on dropping the pH banding for metal limits.

The water industry has been successful in effectively controlling direct and identifiable metal inputs to sewers, and achieving reductions in metal concentrations in sewage sludge. Trade effluent charges based on the polluter pays principle should lead to continuing improvements in sludge quality. In addition, we expect further reductions in cadmium and mercury concentrations in sewage sludge as we continue implementation of integrated pollution control.

As recommended, we are also considering the need for controls on heavy metals from other waste materials and products, including animal manures, to protect soil fertility. Results from a study investigating metal inputs to agricultural soils from all sources will shortly be available.

The decisions we have taken will enable sewage sludge to continue to beneficially recycled to agriculture land, while ensuring that soil microbial processes and human, animal plant health are not put at risk from potentially toxic elements which may be present in sludge.

### British Gas Sites

**Mr. Robert Ainsworth:** To ask the Secretary of State for the Environment if he will list the sites formerly owned by British Gas where *(a)* discussions regarding grant aid have occurred, *(b)* grant aid has been formally applied for and *(c)* grant aid has been approved in order to redevelop the sites giving, in each case, the amount of aid involved and including grant aid from (i) his Department and (ii) urban development corporations and other publicly funded bodies. [24599]

**Sir Paul Beresford:** Information on the former ownership of sites which have been subject to applications for grant is not readily available. In many cases, the previous landowner is unknown. I will, however, write to the hon. Gentleman with such further information as we can gather.

## NATIONAL HERITAGE

### Public Library Review

**Mr. Maclennan:** To ask the Secretary of State for National Heritage when he expects to publish the findings of the public library review and the study of the possibilities for contracting out in public libraries; what proposals he has to consult with local authorities and the Library Association; and if he will make a statement. [24407]

**Mr. Sproat:** I refer the hon. Gentleman to the statement about the public library review that my right hon. Friend the Secretary of State made on Tuesday 16 May, *Official Report*, columns *150-51*. The separate contracting out study was completed and received by my Department after the Aslib report and we are looking carefully at its findings. We expect to make a further statement in due course.

## DEFENCE

### Gulf War Syndrome

**Mr. McMaster:** To ask the Secretary of State for Defence what is his current policy in respect of the recognition of Gulf war syndrome; and if he will make a statement. [24125]

**Mr. Soames:** No evidence has emerged to support the existence of a medical condition peculiar to those who served in the Gulf which would justify recognition of the term Gulf war syndrome. We will, however, continue to investigate all those with Gulf-related health concerns and all allegations, both scientific and anecdotal, which bear on this issue.

### Former Service Personnel

**Mr. McMaster:** To ask the Secretary of State for Defence when he last met representatives of the Royal British Legion to discuss the establishment of a Ministry for Veterans Affairs as a sub-department of MOD; and if he will make a statement. [24072]

**Mr. Soames:** Following a meeting last November between the Minister of State for Social Security, the Under-Secretary of State for Defence and representatives of the Royal British Legion, it was agreed that many matters relating to the welfare of former service personnel fall within the scope of the Department of Social Security. That Department is now taking the lead on these issues.

### Plutonium

**Mr. Llew Smith:** To ask the Secretary of State for Defence if he will obtain a copy of the United States Department of Energy's plutonium working group report on environmental safety and health vulnerabilities associated with the department's plutonium storage published in November 1994; and if he will evaluate its relevance for the situation at sites and facilities operated by the Atomic Weapons Establishment and British Nuclear Fuels plc on behalf of his Department. [24294]

**Mr. Soames:** My Department's study of the report is currently in progress. The UK's position is, however, different from that of the US in that our holding of fissile materials is broadly in balance with national needs at any given time and is, in the main, embodied in manufactured warheads. The question of managing a substantial reserve stockpile does not, therefore, arise.

### Western European Union

**Mr. Llew Smith:** To ask the Secretary of State for Defence what proposals were put by the United Kingdom to the meeting of Western European Union Defence and Foreign Affairs Ministers in Lisbon on 15 May. [25292]

**Mr. Soames:** The WEU Ministerial Council met to consider a number of issues, including the contribution that we expect the WEU to make to the 1996 intergovernmental conference to review the provisions of the Maastricht treaty, and the internal development of the WEU itself to provide it with new decision-making and planning mechanisms and structures. The WEU Council also met associate partners to review progress on a study of the new security conditions in Europe. The UK has made a significant contribution to the debate on all these topics, both at the ministerial meeting and in the preceding months. In particular, we have made proposals for the development of the WEU as the defence arm of the European Union, which were set out in the "Memorandum on the UK's approach to the treatment of European defence issues at the 1996 Inter-Governmental Conference", a copy of which is in the Library of the House. WEU Ministers welcomed the UK's contribution in this regard, as noted in the Lisbon declaration, a copy of which will be placed in the Library of the House shortly. The UK has also worked with Italy to develop proposals for a WEU task force for humanitarian missions, which Ministers endorsed at Lisbon.

### Russia

**Mr. Gill:** To ask the Secretary of State for Defence what assessment he has made of the recent evaluation of the current military threat posed by Russia made by the Chief of the Defence Staff. [25264]

**Mr. Soames:** Although Russia currently poses no direct military threat to the United Kingdom, it retains immense military forces, both conventional and nuclear; the progress of reform, which we all hope will succeed, will remain an important determinant of our security and defence policies.

### Crown Housing Trust

**Mr. Jamieson:** To ask the Secretary of State for Defence, pursuant to his answer of 24 January, *Official Report*, column *192*, what amount of performance-related bonus was received by the chief executive of the Crown Housing Trust on the anniversary of his appointment. [25178]

**Mr. Soames:** The chief executive (designate) of the Crown Housing Trust received a total of £19,900 in performance bonus for his service, which was terminated on 31 March 1995.

### Empty Dwellings

**Mr. Jamieson:** To ask the Secretary of State for Defence what action his Department has taken to reserve all empty MOD dwellings that have been standing empty for six months or more and negotiate their disposal by lease or sale to local authorities of housing associations. [25175]

**Mr. Soames:** The majority of my Department's empty dwellings are not surplus to requirements but are undergoing or awaiting major maintenance work, already allotted to service families due to move in shortly, or form part of the management margin needed to ensure that accommodation is available for entitled service families. Those properties which are surplus are, wherever possible, offered for sale to service personnel through the services' discount scheme to enable them to purchase a home of their own. Surplus properties not suitable for this scheme are normally offered in the first instance to housing associations or local authorities before being offered for sale on the open market. In addition, we are planning an enhanced programme of leasing to housing associations or local authorities of properties which are temporarily surplus to requirements but which will be needed again in the long term.

**Mr. Hall:** To ask the Secretary of State for Defence how many MOD homes in Cheshire are empty; and how many of these homes have been empty for more than six months. [25177]

**Mr. Soames:** As at 31 March, my Department owned 107 empty houses in Cheshire, of which 26 had been empty for more than six months. Many of the vacant properties were either undergoing or awaiting major maintenance work, already allotted to service families due to move in shortly or formed part of the management margin needed to ensure that accommodation is available for entitled service families. Twenty-eight of the 107 empty properties were in the process of being sold.

### US Air Bases

**Mr. Hall:** To ask the Secretary of State for Defence if he will list the UK American air base sites that have been declared surplus to requirement and sold between April 1991 and April 1995; and the total income generated. [25180]

**Mr. Soames:** The only American air base site that has been declared surplus to requirement and sold between April 1991 and April 1995 is RAF Chessington, Surrey. The income generated from this sale is commercial in-confidence between my Department and the purchaser.

### Surplus RAF Sites

**Mr. Hall:** To ask the Secretary of State for Defence if he will list the RAF sites that have been declared surplus to requirement and sold between April 1991 and April 1995; and the total income generated. [25179]

**Mr. Soames:** The RAF sites which were declared surplus to requirement and sold between April 1991 and April 1995 are:

RAF Chessington, Surrey, formerly UK American air base
RAF Barnwood, Gloucestershire
RAF Collaton Cross, Deveon
RAF Mountbatten, Devon
RAF Bawdsey, Suffolk
RAF Ely, Cambridgeshire
RAF Greatworth, Northamptonshire
RAF Northcoates, Lincolnshire
RAF Orfordness, Suffolk
RAF Jurby Head, Isle of Man
RAF Bishopscourt, Northern Ireland

The total income generated from these sales was £18,988,689.

### Bovington

**Mr. Ian Bruce:** To ask the Secretary of State for Defence how many people are employed at Bovington and Lulworth broken down by types of employee; and whether they live on or off site. [25587]

**Mr. Soames:** There are at present 686 military personnel, about 400 civilian staff and 205 contractors employed at Bovington. Nearly all the military live on site; and nearly all the civilians live off site. This does not include trainees who come to Bovington for courses, who number around 3,500 a year.

**Mr. Ian Bruce:** To ask the Secretary of State for Defence what estimate he has made of the cost of building sufficient facilities for the 3rd Armoured Reconnaissance Regiment at Bovington on land abutting Stanley barracks, by comparison to splitting the regiment between Bovington and Lulworth; and what studies have been carried out to look at these two options. [25505]

**Mr. Soames:** The two options were both examined in the study of the comparative costs of future locations of the 3rd Armoured Reconnaissance Regiment. This work showed that the cost of building facilities at Bovington alone would be about £7 million higher than the costs of splitting the regiment. Moreover, building extra facilities on a green field site at Bovington would disrupt training activity.

**Mr. Ian Bruce:** To ask the Secretary of State for Defence if he will give a breakdown of the living accommodation at Bovington and Lulworth including the number of vacancies; how much of the accommodation is occupied by people on courses; what other accommodation the MOD owns within a 20-mile radius; and what are the vacancies. [25588]

**Mr. Soames:** At Stanley barracks, Bovington there are 550 bed spaces, 336 of which are for trainees. At present, there are 150 vacancies, although these vary from week to week depending on course loading.

At Allenby barracks, Bovington there are 567 bed spaces, all of which are occupied.

At Lulworth, there are 465 bed spaces. There are currently 142 vacancies, but these also vary depending on course loading.

Within a 20-mile radius of Bovington and Lulworth my Department owns three sites; West Moors petroleum training school which has 30 spare bed spaces and Blandford school of signals which has 121 spare bed spaces. The number of spare bed spaces at both sites depends on course loading and will often reduce to nil. In addition to the above two sites there is a hutted and tented training camp at Wyke Regis. This camp does not possess permanent living accommodation.

**Mr. Ian Bruce:** To ask the Secretary of State for Defence what training activities are carried out at Bovington camp in areas designated on the Bovington and Lulworth Ordnance Survey map as *(a)* S1, *(b)* W1 and *(c)* W2; how many days per year these activities are carried out; and what is the area of each of these sites. [25584]

**Mr. Soames:** The activities are as follows:

(a) Recruit driver training, Territorial Army training, and infantry tactics; about 100 days a year; 180 acres.

(b) Engineer training—bridging and digging, driver training, infantry tactics; 280 days a year; 165 acres.

(c) Driving circuit used for low level infantry training and the armoured trials and development unit; about 100 days a year; 140 acres.

**Mr. Ian Bruce:** To ask the Secretary of State for Defence if he will name the consultants who were employed to advise on the location of the 3rd Armoured Reconnaissance Regiment; what were their terms of reference; if these included calculating the cost of locating the whole of the regiment at Bovington; and if he will publish their report. [25586]

**Mr. Soames:** The consultants were Sawyer Architects of Winchester. Their terms of reference which are set out, required them to consider and comment on the option of locating the 3rd Armoured Reconnaissance Regiment in the Bovington area, taking into account a number of factors.

*Terms of Reference*

(1) All the land and buildings associated with Stanley barracks, Bovington and areas available for development at Lulworth camp for satisfying the statement of requirement. The married quarters are not to be considered as part of the study. Any shortfall in existing buildings is to be costed as a new build, and any shortfall of land is to be addressed with a statement on how this shortfall can be overcome.

(2) The study is to comment on the adequacy of existing, and future requirements for land, buildings and facilities for single living, eating, sleeping, recreation, administration offices, training and working accommodation and the storage, servicing, maintenance and operation of vehicles and equipment.

(3) Identify in conjunction with the Defence Land Agent any known or anticipated environmental constraints, planning constraints including any historical listings.

(4) As a desk study examine information available on ground conditions, ground water table which may have a bearing on the options.

(5) Any proposed new builds, modernisations, extensions of maintenance projects in planning/design or construction.

(6) For each option give estimated costs of the annual maintenance for the option as a whole as well as any anticipated major maintenance items, and the year in which you estimated they will occur, over a 60-year period.

(7) Identify with the client representative the security needs for both the active and passive ie fences, lighting, perimeter intruder defence systems, close circuit television and security of buildings.

(8) The report should identify, consider and make a brief statement on the implications of the feasibility, planning, costing, phasing and execution of the works with the current or proposed occupants in occupation during the construction of any works identified within the options.

A number of options were investigated including the cost of locating the whole regiment at Bovington. The consultants' report contains much information that is commercial in-confidence, and will not therefore be published. The conclusions of their report, along with other relevant factors, will, however, be made clear by the Ministry of Defence when a final decision on the future location of the 3rd Armoured Reconnaissance Regiment is made.

### Nuclear-powered Submarines

**Dr. David Clark:** To ask the Secretary of State for Defence, pursuant to his answer of 17 May to the hon. Member for Cornwall, South-East (Mr. Hicks), *Official Report*, column 229, what new nuclear safety practices have been introduced; what improvements need to be made to the Devonport facilities; how much these changes will cost and when they will be completed; how many nuclear-powered submarines will be refitted at Rosyth; when a final decision will be announced; and if he will make a statement.                          [25694]

**Mr. Freeman:** It is Government policy that naval nuclear reactors are operated with at least as high a regard for safety standards as any other nuclear facility in the UK. Civil practice now requires a wide variety of both manmade and naturally occurring environmental hazards to be considered in the safety assessment of nuclear plant including earthquakes, extremes of wind and temperature on the environmental side, and aircraft crash, blast and dropped loads on the manmade side. In line with the developments in civil practice, additional assessment techniques have been used in this process including probabilistic risk and statistical analysis techniques.

We are at present assessing the extent of the improvements required to existing nuclear docking facilities at Devonport. Until the assessment is complete, it would be premature to speculate on cost or time scale. We expect that the assessment will complete during this summer. Decisions will be announced shortly thereafter.

Regarding docking facilities for nuclear-powered submarines, I refer the hon. Member to the answer I gave to hon. Member for Cornwall, South-East on 17 May, *Official Report*, column 229.

### Devonport Dockyard

**Dr. David Clark:** To ask the Secretary of State for Defence what geological surveys have been carried out at the Devonport dockyard; when these surveys were carried out; what were the problems identified by the surveys; and how much money it will cost to rectify these problems.                          [25695]

**Mr. Freeman:** Site investigations, including borehole surveys, and desk studies have been carried out to verify that the nature of the underlying geology is suitable to support the development of nuclear submarine refitting facilities at Devonport dockyard. The site surveys were carried out in 1993, with laboratory testing and desk study work completed predominantly during 1994. The surveys confirmed that the site is underlain by competent rock which will form a suitable foundation for the proposed nuclear installations.

No significant geological problems have been encountered on site to date.

### Accidental Shootings

**Dr. David Clark:** To ask the Secretary of State of Defence how many accidental shootings have occurred in the armed forces in each of the last 10 years; how many of these have resulted in compensation payments to those involved; what was the total amount of these payments; and how many of those accidentally shot in the last 10 years left the armed forces as a result of the shooting.                          [25566]

**Mr. Soames:** In the time available about 20 cases have been identified, in which compensation has been paid to Army personnel following injuries, in some cases minor injuries, resulting from accidental shooting. The total compensation paid in these cases so far is about £250,000; this includes interim payments. Since 1987, service personnel have had the same legal rights as civilians to seek compensation for injuries at work: any dispute over my Department's liability to pay compensation, or on the amount payable, can be taken to the civil courts.

### Old Sarum Airfield

**Mr. Key:** To ask the Secretary of State for Defence who was the successful bidder for the freehold of Old Sarum airfield.                          [25677]

**Mr. Soames:** The successful bidder for the freehold of Old Sarum airfield was Megastream Ltd., trading as the Old Sarum flying club.

# OVERSEAS DEVELOPMENT ADMINISTRATION

## Job Creation

41. **Mr. Butler:** To ask the Secretary of State for Foreign and Commonwealth Affairs what estimate he has made of the number of British jobs in the United Kingdom and abroad, which have been secured as a result of ODA-funded projects in the most recent period for which figures are available. [23925]

**Mr. Baldry:** An indirect benefit of aid and the economic development promotes, but there is no ready means of assessing how many or at what cost.

## South Africa

42. **Mr. Hain:** To ask the Secretary of State for Foreign and Commonwealth Affairs what aid provision he has made for sport in South African townships. [23927]

**Mr. Baldry:** I refer the hon. Member to the reply I gave on 24 April, *Official Report,* column *328.*

## Poverty Reduction

**Mr. Denham:** To ask the Secretary of State for Foreign and Commonwealth Affairs what measures he has taken to ensure that structural adjustment programmes alleviate poverty. [23923]

**Mr. Baldry:** Poverty reduction is at the heart of structural adjustment, which restores the economic growth essential for reducing poverty. Our measures alleviate poverty by promoting a framework which protects the poor and by directing our financial support for these programmes to their specific needs whenever possible.

## Aid (Overseas Jobs)

**Mr. Harry Greenway:** To ask the Secretary of State for Foreign and Commonwealth Affairs how many overseas jobs in how many countries and at what cost are dependent upon United Kingdom overseas aid; and if he will make a statement. [24301]

**Mr. Baldry:** The primary purpose of UK aid is to improve the welfare of those who live in poorer countries than ourselves. An indirect benefit of aid is that jobs can be created in developing countries. But we have no means of assessing how many or at what cost. Any attempt to produce such figures would be complex, and not particularly meaningful.

# LORD CHANCELLOR'S DEPARTMENT

## Law Reform

**Mr. Jim Cunningham:** To ask the Parliamentary Secretary, Lord Chancellor's Department what consideration he is giving to examine the Law Commission's proposals to clarify legislation. [23909]

**Mr. John M. Taylor:** Careful consideration is given to all such proposals. Recommendations for reform in five Law Commission reports were implemented in the last Session of Parliament, and it is anticipated that at least eight further reports will be implemented this Session, together with seven consolidation and statute law repeal Bills produced by the Law Commission.

## Remand Prisoners

**Mr. Bermingham:** To ask the Parliamentary Secretary, Lord Chancellor's Department what is the number of remand prisoners in England and Wales who had waited more than six months for the commencement of their trial; and what was the number of these who *(a)* received custodial sentence, *(b)* received non-custodial sentence and *(c)* were acquitted or not proceeded with, for the latest date for which information is available. [24374]

**Mr. John M. Taylor:** The question concerns a specific operational matter on which the chief executive of the Court Service is best placed to provide an answer and I have accordingly asked the chief executive to reply direct.

*Letter from M. D. Huebner to Mr. Gerald Bermingham, dated 22 May 1995:*

The Parliamentary Secretary, Lord Chancellor's Department, has asked me to reply to your Question about remand prisoners in England and Wales.

In reply to the first part of your Question, I can tell you that in the year ending 31 March 1995, 3042 remand prisoners waited over 6 months from the date of committal to the Crown Court to the commencement of their trial.

Information on the sentences of those defendants is not available and could only be obtained at disproportionate cost. However, you may like to know that in the year ending 31 March 1995, a total of 24812 defendants on remand were committed to the Crown Court for trial. Of these 73.7 per cent received custodial sentences, 18.9 per cent. received non-custodial sentences and 7.4 per cent were acquitted on all counts.

## Legal Aid

**Mr. John Marshall:** To ask the Parliamentary Secretary, Lord Chancellor's Department how much money has been dispersed by the legal aid fund under the Dangerous Dogs Act 1989; and what is the maximum hourly rate paid to experts with particular reference to animal psychiatrists. [24730]

**Mr. John M. Taylor:** No separate records are kept on the specific cost of legal aid for cases relating to the Dangerous Dogs Act. There is no prescribed rate for the use of expert witnesses, but all bills are subject to taxation based on the merits of the case.

## Sukhwinder Kaur

**Mr. Winnick:** To ask the Parliamentary Secretary, Lord Chancellor's Department, further to the letter of the Parliamentary Secretary to the hon. Member for Walsall, North dated 16 May concerning the appeal of Sukhwinder Kaur, for what reason the registration number TH/21452/95 was given to this case by the immigration appellate authority. [25603]

**Mr. John M. Taylor:** In accordance with information provided by the immigration appellate authorities, my letter of 16 May explained that Sukhwinder Kaur's appeal had not been received. Subsequent inquiries show that the appeal had been received on 13 April and allocated a reference number on 25 April. I apologise for this error. The computer system used by the appellate authorities is being upgraded and difficulties have been experienced in recent weeks. It is therefore possible that the inaccurate information given in my letter was the result of a manual, but less reliable, search being made for Mrs. Kaur's appeal.

The progress of the appeal has not been hampered by this error and a hearing date will be offered as soon as Mrs. Kaur's representatives indicate that they are ready.

## Majority Shareholdings

**Mr. Byers:** To ask the Parliamentary Secretary, Lord Chancellor's Department if he will list those companies in which the holder of his office is a majority shareholder which *(a)* are currently in existence and *(b)* have been wound up in the last five years.    [25713]

**Mr. John M. Taylor:** I am not the majority shareholder in any company, nor have I been the majority shareholder in any company wound up in the last five years.

## TRANSPORT

### Manchester Metrolink

**12. Mr. Bryan Davies:** To ask the Secretary of State for Transport when he expects Manchester Metrolink to be extended to Oldham.    [23889]

**Mr. Norris:** The timing of the extension will depend on progress with development of the scheme, the priority attached to it by the Greater Manchester local authorities and the availability of resources.

### Lorry Safety

**13. Mrs. Mahon:** To ask the Secretary of State for Transport when he will next be meeting BRAKE to discuss lorry safety.    [23890]

**Mr. Norris:** I told representatives of the Brake Lorry Safety campaign at my meeting with them on 6 March that I would be prepared to meet them again in approximately six months.

### East London Line

**14. Mr. Simon Hughes:** To ask the Secretary of State for Transport how much of the total planned repair and maintenance work has been carried out to date on the east London line; and what is the latest expected completion date of the works.    [23891]

**Mr. Norris:** Good progress has been made on the foundations for the new Jubilee line station at Canada Water, and on upgrading the existing track, signalling, stations, and pumps and drains.

The final completion date will depend on the outcome of London Underground's application for listed building consent to strengthen and waterproof the Thames tunnel.

### Fare Increases

**15. Mr. Nigel Griffiths:** To ask the Secretary of State for Transport what has been the average fare increase between 1985 and 1995.    [23892]

**Dr. Mawhinney:** The answer depends on the mode of transport being considered. Between March 1985 and March 1995, the average increase above inflation in rail fares, as measured by the retail prices index, was 2.3 per cent. Bus and coach fares increased by an annual average of 1.9 per cent.

### South Yorkshire Supertram

**16. Mr. Betts:** To ask the Secretary of State for Transport if he will reconsider the method of funding the south Yorkshire supertram so that the expenditure is not caught by the capping rules for local authorities.    [23893]

**Mr. Norris:** I have no plans to reconsider the method of funding the south Yorkshire supertram.

### Railway Station Staff

**17. Mrs. Roche:** To ask the Secretary of State for Transport if he will make a statement regarding the destaffing of British Rail stations in London.    [23894]

**Mr. Norris:** Staffing levels are a management matter for the railway industry. Like the Government, it wants passengers to have a good service in a safe and secure environment.

### Disabled People

**18. Mr. Barnes:** To ask the Secretary of State for Transport if he will make a statement on his Department's policy on the needs of disabled people in all modes of transport.    [23895]

**Mr. Norris:** We are committed to the development of accessible public transport systems which can provide effective and sustainable transport services for all passengers, including those with disabilities.

### Ferry Safety

**20. Mr. Miller:** To ask the Secretary of State for Transport which organisations he intends to consult regarding the report of the International Maritime Organisation's panel of experts inquiring into roll-on roll-off ferry safety.    [23898]

**Dr. Mawhinney:** We are already consulting interested parties, and have been since the IMO's panel of experts was set up, through a shadow panel organised by the Marine Safety Agency. The shadow panel includes representatives from the Chamber of Shipping, major UK ferry operators, the Consumers Association and trade unions.

Further consultation will be carried out once we have fully considered the reaction of the IMO's maritime safety committee to the work of the panel of experts.

### Crossrail

**21. Mr. Khabra:** To ask the Secretary of State for Transport what is the projected timetable for the completion of the crossrail project; and if he will make a statement.    [23899]

**Mr. Norris:** The promoters of crossrail continue to prepare their application for powers under the Transport and Works Act 1992 to build crossrail. This is being done in parallel with the study which the promoters are undertaking at my request, with my Department.

**Mr. Timms:** To ask the Secretary of State for Transport what are the implications of studies other than the Montagu committee of public transport in London for the timetable for the deposit of a draft order application in respect of crossrail.    [24820]

**Mr. Norris:** The impact of studies other than the crossrail study, which the promoters are undertaking at my request, with my Department, is marginal. In parallel with this study, the promoters of crossrail continue to prepare their application for powers under the Transport and Works Act 1992 to build crossrail.

### Sleeper and Motorail Services

22. **Mr. Robert G. Hughes:** To ask the Secretary of State for Transport what representations he has received about the withdrawal of sleeper services and motorail services. [23900]

**Mr. Watts:** I have received a number of representations concerning British Rail's plans to withdraw motorail and certain sleeper services.

**Mr. Tyler:** To ask the Secretary of State for Transport what were the passenger loading figures for the Night Scot for stations between Plymouth and Glasgow inclusive, and for the Night West Countryman in the reverse direction, for each quarter in 1991, 1992, 1993, 1994 and to the latest available date. [25243]

**Mr. Watts:** In 1993–94, 32,000 passengers travelled on the sleeper service between Plymouth and Glasgow and Edinburgh. Figures are not available for each direction, intermediate stations, by quarter or for other years.

### Local Rail Services

24. **Mr. Illsley:** To ask the Secretary of State for Transport if he will make a statement on the future funding of local rail services. [23903]

**Mr. Watts:** The Government will continue to provide funding, through the franchising director, to support local rail services. With regard to revenue support for railway passenger services funded by English passenger transport executives, my right hon. Friend intends to replace the current temporary arrangements with an enhancement of the standard spending assessment "bolt on" grant, with effect from 1996–97.

### Road and Rail Building Blight

25. **Mrs. Lait:** To ask the Secretary of State for Transport what progress is being made to reduce blight stemming from road and rail building. [23904]

**Mr. Watts:** The 1994 trunk roads programme review which prioritised schemes has reduced blight by removing some schemes from the programme. A review of safeguarding on all schemes in the trunk roads programme will be continued with the aim of reducing blight. Safeguarding directions for the channel tunnel rail link project were issued in December 1994, which effectively reduced blight by removing uncertainty about which land will be required. Considerable effort will be made to minimise the physical impact from construction and operation of the CTRL.

### Rail Freight

27. **Mr. Hendry:** To ask the Secretary of State for Transport what steps his Department is taking to encourage heavy loads to be transported by rail rather than road. [23906]

**Mr. Watts:** We have already opened up access to the rail network for private sector rail hauliers. In conjunction with the BR board, we are currently progressing plans for the privatisation of the British Rail freight businesses. We also make available capital grants for rail freight facilities and revenue grants to assist in defraying track access charges levied by Railtrack. For example, a recent freight facilities grant award of £2.6 million to a company based in Derbyshire will secure traffic to rail which would have otherwise gone by road, thereby avoiding an estimated 45,000 lorry journeys per year.

### Vehicle Emissions

28. **Mr. Harry Greenway:** To ask the Secretary of State for Transport what steps he is taking to reduce exhaust emissions from cars and other vehicles; and if he will make a statement. [23907]

**Dr. Mawhinney:** A range of measures has been introduced to reduce vehicle pollution substantially both for new vehicles and by controlling emissions in service. Stringent standards for all new vehicle types which substantially reduce levels of carbon dioxide, hydrocarbon, nitrous oxide and particulates from cars, lorries and buses were introduced from 1993. These promoted the widespread use of catalysts on petrol cars which typically reduce emissions of the main pollutants by 75 to 80 per cent. Diesel cars have to meet the same standards and, additionally, have to comply with a stringent particulate limit. Legislation is already in place for a further tightening which will, in particular, more than halve particulate standards for diesels in 1996. The Government are also playing a leading role in the European Union to secure a further reduction in levels for new vehicles from 2000. These measures will be reinforced by tighter in-service standards for diesel and conventional petrol-engined vehicles from 1 September this year and for catalyst-equipped petrol-engined vehicles from 1 January 1996, together with a continuing intensified roadside enforcement programme to remove the worst offenders from the road.

### Traffic Pollution

**Mr. Win Griffiths:** To ask the Secretary of State for Transport if he will make a statement about the impact of transport pollution. [23880]

**Dr. Mawhinney:** Vehicle emissions can contribute to global warming and poor local air quality. The Government are pursuing a range of measures to reduce such pollution.

### Road Building, North-east England

**Ms Quin:** To ask the Secretary of State for Transport what recent representations he has received about the road building programme in the north-east of England. [23897]

**Mr. Watts:** Recent representations include a petition in respect of the A1 Gateshead western bypass proposal. I met a delegation led by Sir Ralph Carr-Ellison on 30 March following which I invited Gateshead metropolitan borough council to work with the Highways Agency in considering a trial of junction closures and the development of a local traffic management scheme.

### London-Tilbury-Southend Rail Services

**Sir Teddy Taylor:** To ask the Secretary of State for Transport if he will make a statement on the timetable for privatising the London-Tilbury-Southend rail service. [23902]

**Mr. Watts:** The franchising director issued invitations to tender for LTS rail on 17 May. Indicative bids must be submitted by 28 July. Formal tenderers will be selected in September. The franchising director intends to let the franchise by the end of the year.

### Cambridge-St. Ives Railway Line

**Mrs. Anne Campbell:** To ask the Secretary of State for Transport if he expects that the Cambridge-St. Ives railway line will become fully operational for passenger transport. [23905]

**Mr. Norris:** The Cambridge to St. Ives railway line is currently the subject of a feasibility study by Cambridgeshire county council into the likely use of the line should it be reopened for passenger traffic. It is too early to say whether a viable scheme is likely to emerge, but I have suggested that the county council continue the study work and prepare cost estimates.

### Tolls

**Mr. Harris:** To ask the Secretary of State for Transport when he will announce plans to deregulate the tolls of the 10 bridges and ferries that are still subject to statutory controls. [25474]

**Mr. Watts:** I have today published a consultation paper, "Regulation of Tolls at Statutory Undertakings". The paper examines options for replacing the current procedures governing toll revisions of crossing such as private ferry undertakings and private and local authority-owned bridges and tunnels.

The three main options outlined are continued regulation, but with improvements in the criteria and procedures; partial deregulation, with tolls rising annually up to a prescribed limit; and full deregulation, with undertakings setting their own charges.

Current procedures are cumbersome and protracted for the 16 private and local authority river crossings that were promoted by statute, and the criteria by which toll revisions have to be judged are unclear and difficult to apply. We are inviting users and operators of the relevant crossings to comment on alternatives to the present system. If some measure of deregulation is the outcome, I envisage consulting further on measures under the Deregulations and Contracting Out Act 1994.

I have placed a copy of the consultation paper in the Library.

### Bull Bars

**Mr. Flynn:** To ask the Secretary of State for Transport what is his estimate of the numbers of vehicles now fitted with front bull bars; what the numbers will be over the next five years if present trends continue; and what affect he expects the increase to have on accident figures in each of the next five years. [25268]

**Mr. Norris:** My reply to the hon. Gentleman on the 30 March, *Official Report*, columns *786-87*, gave the Transport Research Laboratory's estimate of the extra deaths and injuries to vulnerable road users that could result from collisions with vehicles fitted with bull bars. It is estimated that in 1993, on the latest figures available,

3 per cent. of the vehicle fleet were off-road vehicles and 9 per cent. were delivery vans. The TRL's injury projections were based on 20 per cent. of these vehicles having bull bars.

Information on trends is not recorded. We cannot therefore estimate the effects of bull bars on future accident figures.

**Mr. Scott:** To ask the Secretary of State for Transport if he will instigate an investigation into the effect of bull bars in traffic accidents in the Metropolitan police district and publish a report. [25261]

**Mr. Norris:** The Metropolitan police, on their own initiative, are collecting details of traffic accidents involving vehicles fitted with bull bars. We will be analysing the results of this work in due course as part of our wider analysis of the effects of bull bars in accidents.

### Rail Fares

**Ms Glenda Jackson:** To ask the Secretary of State for Transport (1) how much additional grant his Department will provide to London Transport to compensate for loss of revenue as a result of the franchising director's decision to cap British Rail fares; [25088]

(2) what is the effect on London Transport revenue forecasts of the franchising director's decision to cap British Rail fares in *(a)* 1996, *(b)* 1997, *(c)* 1998, *(d)* 1999 and *(e)* 2000. [25087]

**Mr. Norris:** The effect will depend on the future relationship between London Transport and rail fares, and the fares which LT would have charged in the absence of the franchising director's decision. All relevant factors will be taken into account when LT's future funding requirements are considered.

**Mr. Barry Jones:** To ask the Secretary of State for Transport what assessment he has made of his recent statements on rail fares upon the *(a)* Crewe to Holyhead rail line and *(b)* Wrexham to Birkenhead rail line; and if he will make a statement. [24838]

**Mr. Watts:** The regulation of fares is a matter for the franchising director. Except in passenger transport executive areas, the franchising director will regulate all Saver tickets, unrestricted standard returns where there are no Savers, and all standard weekly season tickets. Prices for these tickets will be capped by the increase in the retail prices index for the next three years, and 1 per cent. per annum below the RPI for the following four years. Regulation will apply to British rail as well as franchised services. PTEs will continue to be able to control fares in their areas.

### Rail Franchises

**Ms Glenda Jackson:** To ask the Secretary of State for Transport, pursuant to his answer of 4 May, *Official Report*, column *255*, what plans he has to impose restrictions on *(a)* the Rahahane Djjomhouriye Eslami Iran, *(b)* the Socialist People's Libyan Araya Jamihiriya Department of Road Transport and *(c)* the Iraqi Republic Railways Organisation from bidding to operate rail franchises in Great Britain. [25410]

**Mr. Watts:** The choice of bidders for passenger rail franchises is a matter for the franchising director, but I understand that none of these organisations has expressed any interest in pre-qualification.

**Ms Glenda Jackson:** To ask the Secretary of State for Transport what assessment he has made of the additional subsidy required for private franchise operators if rail fares are to be raised in line with the retail prices index; and if he make a statement. [23896]

**Mr. Watts:** Level of subsidy will be determined by the tendering process for each franchise. The Government have stated their commitment to continuing to pay subsidy needed to support passenger services, including the effect of the new fares policy.

### Rail Privatisation

**Mr. Denham:** To ask the Secretary of State for Transport if he will make a statement on progress towards rail privatisation. [23901]

**Dr. Mawhinney:** Restructuring in preparation for privatisation is mostly complete and invitations to tender have issued for the first three franchises and the three rolling stock leasing companies. Sales of BR's support businesses have commenced and sales of the domestic freight businesses are planned this year. Railtrack will be floated in the life of this Parliament.

### Hayes-London Rail Service

**Mr. Bayley:** To ask the Secretary of State for Transport, pursuant to his answer of 20 December 1994, *Official Report*, column *1091*, if all rail services on the Hayes (Kent) to London line are operated by Networker trains; and what is the average age of the rolling stock used on this line at peak times. [25147]

**Mr. Watts:** Yes. Two years or less.

### Railtrack (Contaminated Land)

**Mr. Matthew Taylor:** To ask the Secretary of State for Transport if he will list every contaminated site owned by Railtrack, together with the total area; and what is his estimate of the cost of cleaning it up. [24770]

**Mr. Watts:** This is a matter for Railtrack. Railtrack will be considering the environmental condition of its property as part of the preparations for privatisation.

**Mr. Matthew Taylor:** To ask the Secretary of State for Transport what survey his Department has carried out of contaminated land owned by Railtrack. [24771]

**Mr. Watts:** My Department has not carried out any surveys, but Railtrack will be considering the environmental condition of its property as part of the preparations for privatisation.

### Shipping Collisions

**Mr. Flynn:** To ask the Secretary of State for Transport what was the number of collisions between vessels in *(a)* the North sea, *(b)* the English channel and *(c)* St. George's channel in each of the last 10 years. [25574]

**Mr. Norris:** The figures in the table relate to collisions involving one or more UK registered vessels where the location of the accident has been established.

The figures are given only for the years shown, as information relating to a particular sea area and type of accident can readily be obtained only from the marine accident investigation branch computerised accident database. The database contains data from 1991 onwards only.

| Year | Collisions |
| --- | ---: |
| *North Sea* | |
| 1991 | 14 |
| 1992 | 18 |
| 1993 | 15 |
| 1994 | 7 |
| 1995 to date | 4 |
| | |
| *English Channel* | |
| 1991 | 9 |
| 1992 | 6 |
| 1993 | 8 |
| 1994 | 10 |
| 1995 to date | 2 |
| | |
| *St George's Channel* | |
| 1991 | 2 |
| 1992 | 2 |
| 1993 | 6 |
| 1994 | 3 |
| 1995 to date | 2 |

## HEALTH

### Sir Duncan Nichol

**Mr. Redmond:** To ask the Secretary of State for Health for what reasons Sir Duncan Nichol was made redundant. [24440]

**Mr. Sackville:** Sir Duncan Nichol had been seconded to the national health service executive by Mersey regional health authority. At the termination of the secondment arrangement, he was unable to return to his contracted post in Mersey RHA because, through restructuring, it was no longer available. Since there was no alternative employment available to Sir Duncan, the health authority declared him redundant.

### Care for the Elderly

**Mr. Pickthall:** To ask the Secretary of State for Health what is the average cost of keeping an elderly infirm person *(a)* in hospital and *(b)* in a residential care home. [24402]

**Mr. Bowis:** The cost per patient week for the geriatric specialty is provisionally estimated at £791.42 in 1993–94, the latest year for which figures are available. This amount does not include expenditure on people over 65 who use acute hospital services or community health services, as such expenditure is not apportioned according to age. In the same year, the average expenditure by local authorities for each supported resident in residential care homes for elderly people was approximately £260 per week. Comparisons of costs between types of care should be treated with caution as dependency levels and other characteristics will vary considerably.

### Immunisation

**Mr. Mike O'Brien:** To ask the Secretary of State for Health what research has been conducted by or on behalf of her Department into damage to the body's immune system caused by immunisation; and what conclusions have been reached. [24562]

**Mr. Sackville:** The Department of Health is not aware of evidence that immunisation causes damage to the immune system.

The main agency through which the Government support biomedical and clinical research is the Medical Research Council which receives its grant in aid from the office of my right hon. Friend the Chancellor of the Duchy of Lancaster.

## Tobacco Advertising

**Mr. Barron:** To ask the Secretary of State for Health what assessment she has made of the extent to which the Benson and Hedges "Gratis" campaign breaches the voluntary agreement on tobacco advertising in respect of *(a)* the encouragement of smoking in general, *(b)* the offering of incentives to smoke more than the average, *(c)* the linkage of smoking with a healthy life style and *(d)* the linkage of smoking with children's gifts; what action she intends to take in respect of the campaign; and if she will make a statement. [24662]

**Mr. Sackville:** The content of advertisements is governed by the cigarette code, which forms part of the voluntary agreement. It is for the Advertising Standards Authority to arbitrate on whether the cigarette code has been breached. I understand that a formal complaint about the "Gratis" campaign has been made to the ASA, and it will be conducting an investigation.

## Residential Homes

**Mr. Hendry:** To ask the Secretary of State for Health which local authorities do not directly manage *(a)* residential homes for the elderly, *(b)* residential homes for the mentally ill, *(c)* residential homes for the physically disabled, *(d)* residential homes for people with learning disabilities and *(e)* residential homes for expectant mothers. [24893]

**Mr. Bowis:** Homes are categorised on the basis of their primary function. Homes classified in one client group may also contain residents from other client groups. The absence of a directly managed home does not therefore mean that the authority provides no places for that client group within its own homes.

The information available at 31 March 1994 shows:

*Local authorities not directly managing residential homes for the elderly are:*

Tameside, Knowsley, City of London, Somerset.

*Local authorities not directly managing residential homes for the mentally ill are:*

Durham, North Tyneside, Barnsley, Bolton, Bury, Manchester, Knowsley, Warwickshire, Dudley, Sandwell, Buckinghamshire, Essex, Oxfordshire, Southwark, Tower Hamlets, City of London, Barking, Barnet, Bexley, Bromley, Harrow, Havering, Kingston Upon Thames, Merton, Newham, Waltham Forest, Hampshire, Isle of Wight, Kent, East Sussex, West Sussex, Cornwall, Devon, Gloucestershire, Isles of Scilly.

*Local authorities not directly managing residential homes for the physically disabled are:*

Newcastle Upon Tyne, North Tyneside, South Tyneside, Sunderland, Humberside, North Yorkshire, Barnsley, Rotherham, Calderdale, Wakefield, Bolton, Bury, Oldham, Rochdale, Stockport, Trafford, Knowsley, Sefton, Shropshire, Warwickshire, Sandwell, Solihull, Wolverhampton, Derbyshire, Lincolnshire, Buckinghamshire, Oxfordshire, Suffolk, Greenwich, Hackney, Kensington, Lambeth,

Lewisham, Wandsworth, Westminster, City of London, Barnet, Bexley, Brent, Bromley, Enfield, Haringey, Harrow, Hillingdon, Kingston Upon Thames, Merton, Newham, Redbridge, Richmond Upon Thames, Sutton, Waltham Forest, Dorset, Isle of Wight, Kent, Wiltshire, Isles of Scilly.

*Local authorities not directly managing residential homes for people with learning disabilities are:*

Manchester, Warwickshire, City of London, Bexley, Redbridge, Isles of Scilly.

Centrally available information does not separately identify residential homes for expectant mothers.

## Nurseries

**Mr. Robert Ainsworth:** To ask the Secretary of State for Health (1) what action she has taken in conjunction with the Department for Education regarding the situation where a deregistered nursery can reopen as an independent school; and if she will make a statement; [25137]

(2) what are her plans to deal with those who escape the provisions of the Children Act 1989 on registration of nurseries, by registering as an independent school. [25609]

**Mr. Bowis:** If a private nursery school provides full-time education for five or more children of compulsory school age, it must register with the Department for Education, which will monitor the quality of the service being provided.

My Department works closely with the Department for Education and other relevant organisations to ensure that facilities offering services to young children are of an acceptable standard. We shall continue to keep these arrangements under review.

## Weighted Capitation

**Mr. Bayley:** To ask the Secretary of State for Health, pursuant to her answer about weighted capitation of 20 December 1994, *Official Report*, column *1152*, if she will specify the 1995–96 *(a)* cash allocation, *(b)* weighted capitation target in cash terms calculated on the basis used for table 8.3 in the Health Committee's first special report of Session 1993–94 on public expenditure, HC617, and *(c)* weighted capitation target in cash terms on the basis of the modified formula described in annexe 1 of the NHS executive's hospital and community health services revenue resource allocation: weighted capitation formula of October 1994; and if she will list *(b)* and *(c)* as percentage of *(a)*. [25002]

**Mr. Sackville:** The table shows:

(i) 1995–96 hospital and community health services revenue allocations to regional health authorities for resident population.

(ii) 1995–96 weighted capitation targets for regional health authorities in cash terms using the modified formula.

(iii) 1995–96 weighted capitation targets as a percentage of revenue allocations.

1995–96 regional health authority weighted capitation targets on the same basis as used for table 8.3 are not available as there are no operational reasons for these to be calculated.

| Regional health authority | 1995–96 HCHS revenue allocation for resident population £000s | 1995–96 weighted capitation target £000s | Target as percentage of allocation Percentage |
|---|---|---|---|
| Northern and Yorkshire | 3,184,616 | 3,150,160 | 98.92 |
| Trent | 2,181,505 | 2,191,435 | 100.46 |
| Anglia and Oxford | 2,183,496 | 2,236,531 | 102.43 |
| North Thames | 3,551,835 | 3,499,064 | 98.51 |
| South Thames | 3,330,776 | 3,383,899 | 101.59 |
| South and west | 2,953,543 | 2,946,094 | 99.75 |
| West Midlands | 2,438,538 | 2,399,624 | 98.40 |
| North west | 3,199,588 | 3,217,091 | 100.55 |
| England | 23,023,897 | 23,023,897 | 100.00 |

## General Practitioner Fundholding

**Mr. Clappison:** To ask the Secretary of State for Health if she will make a statement about the payment of management allowances to general practitioner fundholders. [25321]

**Mr. Malone:** Payments from management allowances are made to fundholding practices to reimburse the additional costs incurred in directly managing national health service resources on behalf of their patients. Section 15 of the National Health Service and Community Care Act 1990 enables fundholders to receive a sum determined in such manner and by reference to such factors as the Secretary of State may direct. However, our legal advice is that payments by fundholders for the sole purpose of management expenses need to be specified within regulations. This has now been provided for under the National Health Service (Fund-holding Practices) Amendment Regulations 1995. The regulations are in line with guidance previously issued by the NHS executive on this matter, copies of which are routinely placed in the Library. Extra-statutory management allowance payments of this kind, made between 1990–91 and 1994–95, estimated at around £165 million, have now been authorised.

## NHS Accounts

**Mr. Milburn:** To ask the Secretary of State if she will list those instances in each of the last three financial years for which accounts have been finalised when a qualified opinion was issued against the final accounts of any NHS body, with the name of the body concerned and the reason for the qualified opinion. [24911]

**Mr. Sackville:** This information will be placed in the Library.

## World Health Organisation

**Dr. Goodson-Wickes:** To ask the Secretary of State for Health what consultations she has had over Government liaison with the World Health Organisation. [23926]

**Mr. Malone:** The Department of Health has lead responsibility for World Health Organisation matters. Departmental officials are in regular and frequent contact with officials at the Foreign and Commonwealth Office and the Overseas Development Administration throughout the year and particularly in the build-up to meetings of the WHO executive board and the World Health Assembly. These contacts cover the whole range of issues relating to the United Kingdom's input to WHO, including budgetary and programme matters.

## London Ambulance Service

**Sir John Gorst:** To ask the Secretary of State for Health how much extra money will be given to the London ambulance service to be used specifically in the catchment area of Edgware general hospital. [25242]

**Mr. Sackville:** Barnet health authority will fund two additional ambulance crews at a cost of £320,000 a year before the Edgware hospital accident and emergency department closes.

## Edgware General Hospital

**Sir John Gorst:** To ask the Secretary of State for Health what plans exist to extend the opening hours of the planned minor accident treatment service unit at Edgware general hospital, once it is in operation, beyond those normally operated. [25240]

**Mr. Sackville:** Such decisions are for the Wellhouse national health service trust and will depend on local circumstances. My hon. Friend may wish to contact the chairman, David Phillips, for details.

## Primary Health Care

**Sir John Gorst:** To ask the Secretary of State for Health, pursuant to her oral statement of 10 May, *Official Report*, column *785*, (1) what discussions she has had with the chairmen of the relevant health authorities in connection with the extra £2 million provision to improve primary health care in West Barnet; how these funds are to be administered; and what plans there are for minister to monitor the utilisation of these funds. [25244]

(2) how much of the extra £2 million to improve primary care in West Barnet will be allocated to fund improvements in the Hendon, North constituency; and how the remainder will be allocated accordingly to neighbouring parliamentary constituencies. [25245]

**Mr. Malone:** It is the responsibility of local health authorities, working in conjunction with others, to assess the needs of their populations and to balance service and spending requirements both in the medium term and on a year to year basis. Following discussion with the chairman and regional director of North Thames regional health authority, criteria have been set by which effective implementation of the changes in north London will be judged and on the importance of maintaining high-quality standards for patients. The chairman of the regional health authority will take this forward with chairmen of the relevant health authorities. Arrangements are in place for regular progress meetings with the regional chairman. The chief executive of the NHS executive will also continue to work closely with the regional director.

## Special Transitional Grants

**Mr. Hinchliffe:** To ask the Secretary of State for Health if she will list those authorities which have not yet submitted audited returns of expenditure of the 1993–94 special transitional grant. [25322]

**Mr. Bowis:** Local authorities are required to submit returns to district auditors who, in turn, submit them to the Department. We could not therefore know whether returns that have not yet been submitted to the Department have or have not been submitted by local authorities to their respective district auditors.

## Majority Shareholdings

**Mr. Byers:** To ask the Secretary of State for Health if she will list those companies in which the holder of her office is a majority shareholder which (a) are currently in existence and (b) have been wound up in the past five years. [25717]

**Mr. Sackville:** None.

## Breastfeeding

**Mr. Morgan:** To ask the Secretary of State for Health (1) what information she has on commencement levels of breastfeeding in each member state of the European Union; and if she will publish the most recent sets of data available; [25607]

(2) if she will publish league tables for the different regional health authorities for percentage breastfeeding commencement levels. [25723]

**Mr. Sackville:** Information is not available in the form requested. The five-yearly surveys of infant feeding undertaken by the Office of Population Censuses and Surveys on behalf of the United Kingdom Health Departments provide information, on a national basis, on breastfeeding levels in the UK. A copy of the 1990 infant feeding survey is available in the Library. Field work for the 1995 study will start later this year. We do not have information on breastfeeding levels in other member states of the European Union.

## EDUCATION

## Conductive Education

**Mr. Jim Cunningham:** To ask the Secretary of State for Education (1) what funding has been provided by her Department to the Foundation for Conductive Education in the past; and what are her future plans for funding in the United Kingdom; [24818]

(2) what representations she has received regarding funding for the Foundation for Conductive Education in the United Kingdom. [24817]

**Mr. Forth:** The Department has not received any bids for funding from the Foundation for Conductive Education in the United Kingdom, and has not financed the foundation in the past.

The Department would consider any such representations, with other Government Departments, on their merits. But the statutory responsibility for special educational provision rests in the first instance with local education authorities, to be decided in the light of local needs and resources.

**Mr. Jim Cunningham:** To ask the Secretary of State for education what funding has been provided from her Department to the Peto Institute in Budapest; and how much funding has been provided over the last three years. [24819]

**Mr. Forth:** The Department for Education provided £600,000 in 1991, as part of an initial Government package totalling £1.75 million. No funding has been provided over the last three years.

## Teacher Numbers

**Mr. Steinberg:** To ask the Secretary of State for Education if she will list the number of licensed teachers in each local authority and funding agency area.

**Mr. Robin Squire:** Centrally held information about the number of licensed teachers in post in England on 31 March 1995 is given in the table. On 1 April 1995 responsibility for issuing new licences became the responsibility of the Teacher Training Agency.

| Local authority or funding agency area | LEA-maintained schools | Self-governing (grant-maintained) schools |
|---|---|---|
| Avon | 3 | 0 |
| Barking and Dagenham | 14 | 0 |
| Barnet | 8 | 3 |
| Bedfordshire | 21 | 3 |
| Berkshire | 17 | 4 |
| Bexley | 14 | 0 |
| Birmingham | 0 | 2 |
| Bolton | 1 | 0 |
| Bradford | 1 | 2 |
| Brent | 27 | 0 |
| Bromley | 9 | 3 |
| Buckinghamshire | 5 | 5 |
| Calderdale | 2 | 2 |
| Cambridgeshire | 11 | 3 |
| Camden | 9 | 2 |
| Cleveland | 3 | 0 |
| Cornwall | 5 | 0 |
| Coventry | 2 | 0 |
| Croydon | 7 | 0 |
| Cumbria | 7 | 0 |
| Derbyshire | 8 | 1 |
| Devon | 6 | 1 |
| Dorset | 3 | 0 |
| Dudley | 0 | 1 |
| Ealing | 10 | 1 |
| East Sussex | 3 | 0 |
| Enfield | 4 | 0 |
| Essex | 33 | 17 |
| Gloucestershire | 2 | 0 |
| Greenwich | 21 | 0 |
| Hackney | 29 | 0 |
| Hammersmith and Fulham | 4 | 3 |
| Hampshire | 32 | 5 |
| Haringey | 2 | 0 |
| Harrow | 6 | 0 |
| Havering | 4 | 0 |
| Hereford and Worcester | 7 | 0 |
| Hertfordshire | 30 | 6 |
| Hillingdon | 9 | 4 |
| Hounslow | 8 | 0 |
| Islington | 36 | 0 |
| Kensington and Chelsea | 0 | 1 |
| Kent | 40 | 13 |
| Kingston upon Thames | 2 | 2 |

| Local authority or funding agency area | LEA-maintained schools | Self-governing (grant-maintained) schools |
|---|---|---|
| Lambeth | 6 | 1 |
| Lancashire | 18 | 1 |
| Leicestershire | 5 | 0 |
| Lewisham | 7 | 0 |
| Lincolnshire | 19 | 1 |
| Liverpool | 0 | 2 |
| Manchester | 1 | 0 |
| Newham | 19 | 0 |
| Norfolk | 3 | 4 |
| Northamptonshire | 23 | 2 |
| Northumberland | 2 | 0 |
| North Yorkshire | 7 | 0 |
| Nottinghamshire | 3 | 1 |
| Oxfordshire | 5 | 0 |
| Redbridge | 15 | 1 |
| Richmond upon Thames | 2 | 0 |
| Rochdale | 3 | 0 |
| Sandwell | 1 | 0 |
| Sefton | 2 | 0 |
| Sheffield | 1 | 0 |
| Shropshire | 5 | 1 |
| Solihull | 2 | 0 |
| Somerset | 6 | 0 |
| Southwark | 6 | 0 |
| Staffordshire | 3 | 0 |
| Stockport | 1 | 0 |
| Suffolk | 9 | 0 |
| Surrey | 21 | 7 |
| Sutton | 4 | 1 |
| Tower Hamlets | 16 | 0 |
| Trafford | 1 | 1 |
| Walsall | 1 | 0 |
| Waltham Forest | 4 | 1 |
| Wandsworth | 9 | 0 |
| Warwickshire | 3 | 1 |
| Westminster | 18 | 0 |
| West Sussex | 8 | 0 |
| Wiltshire | 10 | 1 |

## Jean Monnet Programme

**Sir Richard Body:** To ask the Secretary of State for Education if she will publish a list of Jean Monnet projects in the United Kingdom.

**Mr. Boswell:** The Department has no direct involvement with or responsibility for the Jean Monnet programme, which is wholly administered by the European Commission. However, I understand that the following UK universities have applied successfully to the Commission for funding in 1995:[1]

| University | Project |
|---|---|
| Bath | European integration and international business |
| | European integration and the multinationalisation of European business |
| Queen's Belfast | History of the European integration |
| Birmingham | European co-operation and integration: national European élites and European institution building |
| Derby | Party systems in contemporary Europe and European international law |
| | The language and politics of identity in Europe |
| Dundee | European energy, environmental and economic law |
| | Energy and economic regulatory theory and practice in the context of the European single market in energy |
| Durham | Annual Jean Monnet public lecture |
| East London | Patterns of intellectual integration in Europe |
| Essex | European Union law |
| Glamorgan | European law |
| | European integration and regionalism |
| Glasgow | European politics |
| | Decision making in the European Union |
| Humberside | European studies minor |
| Keele | European unification |
| Kent at Canterbury | Politics of European integration |
| | Regional initiative/seminars |
| La Sainte Union College of HE | European integration: history and institutions |
| Leeds Metropolitan | Economics of the European Union |
| Loughborough | The European Union and negotiation in the new Europe |
| Luton | Western European integration |
| Manchester | Organisation and policy for European RTD |
| Newcastle upon Tyne | Rural development in the European Union |
| Oxford Brookes | The business environment in Europe |
| | A social anthropological approach to integration |
| Paisley | European integration and public policy |
| | Introduction to European institutions/introduction to EU policies |
| | Research into European policies for care of the aged |
| | European law and European legal order |
| Reading | The international dimension of European integration |
| | Assessment of the role of the European Parliament in the development of a European foreign and security policy: case of ex-Yugoslavia |
| Salford | European studies |
| Southampton | Economics |
| | Labour markets and macro-economic institutions and policy |
| South Bank | The history and theory of European integration |
| | Reform of European Community and European Union institutions |
| Strathclyde | To establish 2 or 3 "Jean Monnet Scholarships in European Law" for students of Scottish universities to attend the LLM |
| Surrey | The evolution of an integrated Europe |
| Ulster | Organisation of Jean Monnet lectures |
| University College London | Teaching materials |
| Westminster | European integration studies |
| | European business and the environment |

[1] The information given has been provided by the European Commission.

## GCSE Study Leave

**Mr. French:** To ask the Secretary of State for Education if she will discuss with as many head teachers as possible the practice of releasing GCSE candidates from attendance at school for about three weeks prior to their exams; and if she will make a statement. [24815]

**Mr. Forth:** Following consultation with the head teacher associations and other interested parties, the Department issued guidance on the categorisation of absence to all schools in May 1994. The guidance included advice on study leave. It recommended that it should be normally available for year 11 pupils only, that it should be granted sparingly and that it should not normally exceed a maximum of two weeks.

## Education Authority Reorganisation, Teesside

**Mr. Frank Cook:** To ask the Secretary of State for Education if she will make a statement on the expected provision, quality and accountability of education services in the former Teesside county borough area when services in that area are provided by three education authorities as a result of local government reorganisation. [25217]

**Mr. Robin Squire:** The Government's aim in reorganising local government is to improve cost-effectiveness and the quality and co-ordination of local services. The role of local education authorities will not change specifically as a result of the reorganisation of local government. It will be for the new LEAs to play their part in ensuring that the education service is run at least as effectively as now.

## University Staff-Student Ratios

**Mr. Sheerman:** To ask the Secretary of State for Education if she will list the average student/lecturer ratio in United Kingdom universities (a) currently, (b) in 1979, (c) in old universities and (d) in the new universities. [25019]

**Mr. Boswell:** Information on the student: staff ratios in former English Universities Funding Council and Polytechnics and Colleges Funding Council funded institutions was presented in table G of the Department's annual report, Cm 2810, published in March this year, a copy of which is in the Library. This table provides information for both sectors for the academic years 1990–91 to 1992–93. Information on the same basis for earlier years is not available.

## Nursery Education

**Mr. Robert Ainsworth:** To ask the Secretary of State for Education what action she has taken in conjunction with the Department of Health regarding deregistered nurseries reopening as independent schools. [25003]

**Mr. Forth:** Private nursery establishments providing full-time education for five or more pupils of compulsory school age must by law register with the Department as independent schools. The Department works closely with the Department of Health and other relevant agencies to ensure that such establishments meet the statutory requirements for registration and make appropriate provision for pre-school age pupils. If they fail to do so, those establishments may be removed from the register and may not then lawfully operate as independent schools. We continue to keep these arrangements under review.

## Biotechnology Research

**Mr. Sheerman:** To ask the Secretary of State for Education what steps she is taking to encourage co-operation between United Kingdom industries and universities in biotechnology research. [24993]

**Mr. Boswell:** My right hon. Friend provides grant to the Higher Education Funding Council for England to support research in universities. The council is allocating some £10 million in 1994–95 and £20 million in 1995–96 to reward co-operation between universities and industry on generic research that may lead to a range of applications. This includes biotechnology research.

## School Transport

**Mr. Pawsey:** To ask the Secretary of State for Education what consultation took place between her Department and the Welsh Office before the issue of her Department's letter of 21 June 1994 and Welsh Office circular 19/95 about home-to-school transport. [25135]

**Mr. Forth:** The Department consulted the Welsh Office about the text of our letter of guidance which issued on 21 January 1994. Circular 19/95, which is the responsibility of my right hon. Friend the Secretary of State for Wales, is based closely on the text of that letter. These documents do not provide an authoritative interpretation of the law; that is a matter for the courts.

## Student Employment

**Mr. Sheerman:** To ask the Secretary of State for Education what estimate her Department has made of the number of (a) undergraduates and (b) postgraduates undertaking paid employment during their studies due to financial hardship. [25024]

**Mr. Boswell:** Information on student employment is not collected by the Department. However, the latest student income and expenditure survey, which looked at full-time undergraduate students, found that 22 per cent. of younger students and 23 per cent. of mature students received some income from paid employment during term time.

## Chief Education Officers, Cleveland

**Mr. Frank Cook:** To ask the Secretary of State for Education how many chief education officers are currently employed in Cleveland; and how many she expects will be employed when the reorganisation of local government in that county has taken place. [25216]

**Mr. Robin Squire:** Under section 88 of the Education Act 1944 each local education authority has to have a chief education officer. Cleveland has one. Following reorganisation, each of the four new LEAs in the Cleveland area will have one.

## Teachers (Early Retirement)

**Mr. Byers:** To ask the Secretary of State for Education what is the total number of teachers for each year over the last 10 years taking early retirement; how many of these retirements were on medical or breakdown grounds; and what was the total annual cost of these retirements. [24937]

**Mr. Robin Squire:** The total number of teachers granted early retirement and, of these, the number granted infirmity and premature retirement in each of the years

1984–85 to 1993–94 is given in table 1. The first year cost to the teachers superannuation scheme of these retirements and the total expenditure by LEAs on pension enhancements and Crombie compensation for each year from 1989–90 to 1993–94 is given in table 2. Figures for the first year cost to the TSS of early retirements for the years 1984–85 to 1988–89 and for the total annual cost to the TSS of all early retirements could be produced only at disproportionate cost. Figures for LEA expenditure on pension enhancements and Crombie compensation for the years 1984–85 to 1988–89 are not available.

*Table 1: Numbers of teachers granted early retirement*
*(England and Wales)*

| Year | Total | Infirmity | Premature |
|------|-------|-----------|-----------|
| 1984–85 | 13,166 | 2,449 | 10,717 |
| 1985–86 | 12,976 | 2,698 | 10,278 |
| 1986–87 | 11,794 | 2,707 | 9.087 |
| 1987–88 | 10,103 | 2,544 | 7,559 |
| 1988–89 | 15,769 | 3,423 | 12,346 |
| 1989–90 | 16,516 | 4,182 | 12.334 |
| 1990–91 | 16,626 | 4,934 | 11,692 |
| 1991–92 | 14,943 | 4,656 | 10,287 |
| 1992–93 | 17,081 | 4,867 | 12,214 |
| 1993–94 | 17,798 | 5,565 | 12,233 |

*Table 2: Costs (in £ million) of early retirements*
*(England and Wales)*

| Year | First year cost to TSS Infirmity | Premature | LEA expenditure PRC and Crombie |
|------|------|-----------|------|
| 1989–90 | 23.7 | 71.0 | 53.9 |
| 1990–91 | 29.7 | 71.7 | 58.8 |
| 1991–92 | 30.9 | 68.8 | 79.1 |
| 1992–93 | 36.4 | 90.4 | 91.9 |
| 1993–94 | 44.8 | 95.3 | 96.6 |

### Drug Education Programmes

**Mr. Flynn:** To ask the Secretary of State for Education what assessment she has made of which drug education programmes in the United Kingdom or elsewhere have resulted in a reduction in drug use.    [25174]

**Mr. Forth:** My right hon. Friend took into account available research evidence when planning the Department's initiatives to support drug education in schools. The innovative drug education and prevention projects supported under the Department's grants for education support and training programme in 1995–96 will be evaluated. At my right hon. Friend's request, the Office for Standards in Education will undertake a specific study of provision for drug education in schools during the academic year 1995–96 in the light of existing research findings on effective drug education.

### Higher Education Funding Council

**Mr. Hinchliffe:** To ask the Secretary of State for Education if she will require the Higher Education Funding Council to reply to Mr. Anthony Murray of Wakefield, following his letter to it of 6 March.    [25363]

**Mr. Boswell:** This is a matter for the Higher Education Funding Council for England. I have asked the chief executive to write to the hon. Member.

### Majority Shareholdings

**Mr. Byers:** To ask the Secretary of State for Education if she will list those companies in which the holder of her office is a majority shareholder which (a) are currently in existence and (b) have been wound up in the past five years.    [25720]

**Mr. Boswell:** There are no companies, either currently in existence or which have been wound up in the past five years, in which the Secretary of State is or was a majority shareholder. The Student Loans Company Ltd., established in 1989, is owned jointly—50 per cent. each—by the Secretaries of State for Education and for Scotland.

# TRADE AND INDUSTRY

### Radiocommunications Agency

**Mr. Lester:** To ask the President of the Board of Trade what targets he has set his Department's Radiocommunications Agency for 1995–96.    [25864]

**Mr. Heseltine:** I have set my Department's Radiocommunications Agency the following quality of service targets for 1995–96 covering its licensing work and enforcement activities. These are in addition to the target of an overall efficiency improvement of 5 per cent.

*Licensing*

99 per cent. of new aeronautical and aircraft applications and amendments to be processed within three working days of receipt in the agency;

98 per cent of maritime business radio cases to be processed within one month;

99 per cent. of new on-site paging applications and amendments to be processed and dispatched within three working days;

90 per cent. of new private mobile radio applications and amendments that require no international co-ordination to be processed and dispatched within 15 and 20 working days respectively.

*Enforcement*

100 per cent. of safety of life services complaints to be investigated within 24 hours;

98 per cent of business complaints to be investigated within five working days; and

98 per cent. of domestic interference complaints to be investigated within one month.

In addition, I expect the agency's enquiry point to continue to answer 90 per cent. of all calls within 30 seconds and the chief executive to reply within 10 working days to all letters from Members of Parliament delegated to him for reply.

### Gas Licences

**Mr. Byers:** To ask the President of the Board of Trade on what date his Department was made aware that the Office of Gas Supply intended to show draft licences under the Gas Bill to independent gas suppliers.    [25696]

**Mr. Eggar:** Following a major consultation last year on the introduction of competition into the domestic gas market, the Department and Ofgas followed up the responses received by meeting a number of organisations—both in the industry and consumer groups. In the later stages, DTI and Ofgas discussed draft licence conditions with British Gas and, where appropriate, other parties in the industry. This was necessary to ensure that DTI had a sufficient grasp of the technical issues to publish worthwhile draft licences on 20 and 27 March as the basis for parliamentary consideration and wider consultation.

In addition to the comments made in Committee on the Bill by hon. Members, a variety of parties including the industry, consumer groups and other affected organisations have made detailed comments on the Bill and draft licences to DTI. These will be carefully considered in preparing any Government amendments to the Bill and revising the draft licences.

### Local Government Reorganisation, Cleveland

**Mr. Frank Cook:** To ask the President of the Board of Trade if he will make a statement on the implications for the business community in the Teesside area of the division of Cleveland into four unitary authorities; and what guidance he has issued as to the maintenance of important business support services, such as the Cleveland European advice team.                     [25223]

**Mr. Ian Taylor:** The Local Government Commission for England, in its report on the future local government of Cleveland and Durham, recommended that the four new unitary authorities, plus Darlington, should work together in the setting up of a strategic alliance—Tees Valley Development Company—in relation to economic development and other activities. This will include private sector members and has been warmly welcomed by bodies such as the Northern Development Company and the business community on Teesside.

The future of business support services now lies with the newly created Business Link Teesside and its partners, which began operations on 10 April 1995. Partners include all the local authorities, the TEC, the chamber, NDC, Teesside Small Business Club, university of Teesside, and local development and enterprise agencies.

### VSEL

**Mr Cousins:** To ask the President of the Board of Trade, pursuant to his answer to the hon. Member for Glasgow, Garscadden (Mr. Dewar) of 27 March, *Official Report*, column *408*, when he proposes to announce his decision on the bids for VSEL; and what was the advice of the Monopolies and Mergers Commission on those bids.                                      [25364]

**Mr. Jonathan Evans:** My right hon. Friend the President of the Board of Trade will publish the MMC reports on the proposed acquisitions of VSEL, together with the announcement of any decision which it falls to him to take, as soon as is reasonably practicable. Until then, the advice of the Monopolies and Mergers Commission remains confidential.

### Scott Inquiry

**Mr. Fisher:** To ask the President of the Board of Trade if he has yet received the draft report of Lord Justice Scott.                                        [23913]

**Mr. Heseltine:** No.

Sir Richard Scott has not yet finished his report. As the report is written, draft extracts are being circulated by the inquiry to a range of persons referred to in the report for comment.

**Mr. Gordon Prentice:** To ask the President of the Board of Trade what steps he has taken to ensure that Whitehall Departments co-operate fully with Lord Justice Scott to ensure the earliest possible publication of his inquiry report.                                   [23911]

**Mr. Heseltine:** Officials are under instruction to co-operate fully with Sir Richard Scott's inquiry. As I told my hon. Friend the Member for Hazel Grove (Sir T. Arnold) on 11 July 1994, *Official Report*, column *387*, the timing of the report is a matter for Sir Richard Scott.

### Pergau Dam

**Mr. Nigel Griffiths:** To ask the President of the Board of Trade what is his latest estimate of the United Kingdom contribution to the Pergau dam project.     [23918]

**Mr. Needham:** The cost is presently estimated at £233 million, as compared to £255.31 million previously quoted in my answer of 18 April 1994, *Official Report*, column *360*. Some £10 million of the £22 million reduction will be offset by increased costs against other items in Export Credits Guarantee Department's fixed interest support programme.

### Staff

**Ms Hodge:** To ask the President of the Board of Trade, (1) how many posts were lost in *(a)* the Department of Trade and Industry and *(b)* agencies for which the Department of Trade and Industry is responsible, listing the total lost posts agency by agency in (i) 1993–94 and (ii) 1994–95; and how many posts are proposed to be lost in 1995–96;                                     [25084]

(2) what changes there have been in the numbers of staff employed by *(a)* the Department of Trade and Industry and *(b)* agencies for which the Department of Trade and Industry is responsible, listing the changes in the number of staff agency by agency in (i) 1993–94 and (ii) 1994–95; and what changes are proposed for 1995–96;                                            [25058]

(3) what changes there have been in the number of staff in employment by grade in *(a)* his Department and *(b)* each agency for which his Department is responsible in (i) 1993–94 and (ii) 1994–95; and what are the projected figures for 1995–96;          [25627]

(4) how many staff of *(a)* the Department of Trade and Industry and *(b)* agencies for which the DTI is responsible, were employed on a casual or short-term basis in (i) 1993–94 and (ii) 1994–95; and what are the projected figures for 1995–96.           [25415]

**Mr. Ian Taylor:** The numbers of permanent and casual staff employed by my Department and each of its executive agencies in 1993–94, projected outturn for 1994–95; and plans for 1995–96 are published in my Department's annual report, Cm 2804, a copy of which is in the Library of the House. No projections broken down by grade are available. Separate numbers are not shown in the report for the Insolvency Service and the National Weights and Measures Laboratory executive agencies. These are included in the report in the numbers for the gross control area. The numbers of permanent and casual staff for these agencies are as follows:

| | | | *Man years* |
|---|---|---|---|
| | *1993–94* | *1994–95* | *¹1995–96* |
| *Permanent staff* | | | |
| Insolvency Service | 1,592.5 | 1,548.2 | 1,566 |
| National Weights and Measures Laboratory | 46 | 44.5 | 46 |
| *Casual Staff* | | | |
| Insolvency Service | 227 | 285 | 120 |
| National Weights and Measures Laboratory | 0.5 | 0 | 0.5 |

¹In 1995–96 plans are provisional subject to the final outcome of the MINIS scrutiny.

### Private Payphones

**Mr. Janner:** To ask the President of the Board of Trade (1) if he will consider ensuring the Office of Telecommunications takes action against owners of private payphones who charge unreasonably high multiples of the standard rate of a telephone call and fail to display a statement of pricing at the phones;   [24970]

(2) if he will ask Oftel to ensure that offenders who have operated payphones with illegally high charges either return their illegal earnings of pay or offer them to local charities;   [24969]

(3) if he will investigate the level of monitoring by Oftel of the pricing practices of operators of private payphones in public houses, garages, clubs, supermarkets and shops.   [24971]

**Mr. Ian Taylor:** Provision of private payphones has been liberalised so as to encourage their installation, and with great success—an estimated 500,000 payphones are now in place, giving wider access to public telephony than would otherwise be the case. Tariffs of private payphones have never been regulated, but they are required to be displayed. The question of whether Oftel should investigate "illegally high" charges, or pricing practices generally, therefore does not arise. Enforcement of the requirement to display tariffs is a matter for Oftel, which pursues those cases brought to its attention. Oftel is also discussing with representatives of trading standards officers how compliance with this requirement might be improved.

### Companies House

**Mr. Morgan:** To ask the President of the Board of Trade what checks Companies House carries out of its records before the awarding of government contracts and to the existence of an Inland Revenue interest in the affairs of those companies.   [25669]

**Mr. Jonathan Evans:** Companies House carries out checks, relating to compliance with the Companies Act, when requested to do so by Government Departments.

Any Inland Revenue interest in a company would be confidential to the tax authorities, and such checks by my Department would be precluded on taxpayer privacy grounds.

### Coal Prices

**Mr. Milburn:** To ask the President of the Board of Trade what has been the change in real terms of the price of coal used in electricity generation over the period 1989 to 1994.   [25189]

**Mr. Page:** Between 1989 and 1994 the price of coal used in electricity generation by major power producers fell by 29 per cent. in real terms.

### Gas Prices

**Mr. Milburn:** To ask the President of the Board of Trade what has been the change in real terms of the price of materials and fuel purchased by the gas supply industry between 1986 and 1994.   [25192]

**Mr. Page:** Between 1986 and 1994 the price of gas purchased by the gas supply industry fell by 23 per cent. in real terms.

### Electricity Prices

**Mr. Pike:** To ask the President of the Board of Trade if he will list the maximum and minimum price of electricity on the pool basis on a monthly basis since privatisation.   [25234]

**Mr. Eggar:** The information, expressed in money of the day, is as follows:

| | Pool Selling Price | |
|---|---|---|
| *Date* | *Minimum* £/MWh | *Maximum* £/MWh |
| April 1990 | 12.37 | 37.00 |
| May 1990 | 11.16 | 38.15 |
| June 1990 | 9.41 | 44.56 |
| July 1990 | 0.00 | 32.76 |
| August 1990 | 8.00 | 39.97 |
| September 1990 | 10.91 | 33.44 |
| October 1990 | 8.00 | 65.57 |
| November 1990 | 8.00 | 37.35 |
| December 1990 | 12.40 | 74.51 |
| January 1991 | 12.26 | 51.16 |
| February 1991 | 13.22 | 47.79 |
| March 1991 | 14.30 | 35.08 |
| April 1991 | 15.74 | 60.67 |
| May 1991 | 16.01 | 67.57 |
| June 1991 | 15.47 | 68.63 |
| July 1991 | 13.50 | 34.87 |
| August 1991 | 7.13 | 37.05 |
| September 1991 | 5.00 | 170.20 |
| October 1991 | 14.90 | 145.46 |
| November 1991 | 14.15 | 134.26 |
| December 1991 | 16.35 | 375.79 |
| January 1992 | 16.95 | 115.23 |
| February 1992 | 13.39 | 66.59 |
| March 1992 | 16.57 | 39.11 |
| April 1992 | 16.68 | 35.68 |
| May 1992 | 10.99 | 37.40 |
| June 1992 | 17.35 | 48.06 |
| July 1992 | 17.43 | 43.66 |
| August 1992 | 12.71 | 40.41 |
| September 1992 | 17.46 | 39.22 |
| October 1992 | 17.44 | 117.57 |
| November 1992 | 17.46 | 82.22 |
| December 1992 | 17.40 | 67.68 |
| January 1993 | 17.41 | 67.22 |
| February 1993 | 17.52 | 54.22 |
| March 1993 | 17.49 | 84.13 |
| April 1993 | 17.57 | 86.30 |
| May 1993 | 18.03 | 94.09 |
| June 1993 | 16.50 | 66.36 |
| July 1993 | 16.50 | 125.48 |
| August 1993 | 6.04 | 82.12 |
| September 1993 | 17.96 | 70.83 |
| October 1993 | 17.97 | 74.70 |
| November 1993 | 18.01 | 208.60 |
| December 1993 | 17.95 | 72.37 |
| January 1994 | 10.67 | 63.20 |

| Date | Pool Selling Price Minimum £/MWh | Maximum £/MWh |
|---|---|---|
| February 1994 | 10.61 | 134.52 |
| March 1994 | 10.53 | 37.46 |
| April 1994 | 10.56 | 66.83 |
| May 1994 | 9.75 | 56.51 |
| June 1994 | 9.50 | 61.85 |
| July 1994 | 9.50 | 60.50 |
| August 1994 | 9.50 | 55.19 |
| September 1994 | 9.51 | 46.99 |
| October 1994 | 8.07 | 213.59 |
| November 1994 | 8.07 | 200.67 |
| December 1994 | 8.08 | 414.55 |
| January 1995 | 6.74 | 724.66 |
| February 1995 | 6.15 | 239.25 |
| March 1995 | 6.87 | 65.71 |
| April 1995 | 7.23 | 841.24 |

*Source:*
Offer

**Mr. Alan W. Williams:** To ask the President of the Board of Trade what was the average cost of generation of electricity in 1994 for the United Kingdom's *(a)* coal power stations, *(b)* oil power stations, *(c)* gas power stations, *(d)* Magnox reactors and *(e)* advanced gas-cooled reactors. [25274]

**Mr. Eggar:** These are commercial matters for the companies concerned.

**Mr. Alan W. Williams:** To ask the President of the Board of Trade what plans the electricity regulator has to review the pool price paid for base load electricity generation. [25283]

**Mr. Eggar:** This is a matter for Professor Littlechild.

### Electricity Users

**Mr. Pike:** To ask the President of the Board of Trade if he will make it his policy to collate data on the number of large industrial and commercial electricity users committed to buying electricity at pool prices; and if he will make a statement. [25235]

**Mr. Eggar:** All consumers with premises which take more than 100 kW of electricity are now free to contract with the supplier of their choice. The terms that they negotiate, including whether the price to be paid is related to short-term variations in the pool price, are commercial matters between the parties concerned.

### Recycling

**Mr. Sheerman:** To ask the President of the Board of Trade what steps he is taking to encourage British industries to develop end products for recycled materials. [25023]

**Mr. Page:** Identifying end markets for recycled materials has been an important feature in the Government's "producer responsibility" dialogue with a range of industrial sectors. Industry recognises the crucial need for demand to be developed ahead of collection. The Government, for their part, have taken a number of steps to stimulate demand, providing support for R and D projects investigating new uses for recovered materials, including glass, rubber and plastics, and arranging for UK standards to be examined with a view to removing unnecessary discrimination against the use of recycled materials.

### Trade Statistics

**Mr. Thurnham:** To ask the President of the Board of Trade what has been the trend of Britain's share of world trade over the last 30 years, per *(a)* invisibles, *(b)* visibles and *(c)* invisibles and visibles combined. [24569]

**Mr. Needham:** The available information is given in the table.

*UK value share of world exports in visibles, invisibles and both combined.*

(Per cent.)

| | visibles | invisibles | visibles and invisibles |
|---|---|---|---|
| 1963 | 7.9 | — | — |
| 1964 | 7.2 | — | — |
| 1965 | 7.3 | — | — |
| 1966 | 6.9 | — | — |
| 1967 | 6.7 | — | — |
| 1968 | 6.4 | — | — |
| 1969 | 6.4 | — | — |
| 1970 | 6.2 | — | — |
| 1971 | 6.4 | — | — |
| 1972 | 5.9 | — | — |
| 1973 | 5.1 | — | — |
| 1974 | 4.5 | 9.5 | 5.5 |
| 1975 | 5.0 | 9.1 | 5.8 |
| 1976 | 4.6 | 8.8 | 5.5 |
| 1977 | 5.0 | 8.3 | 5.7 |
| 1978 | 5.2 | 8.2 | 5.9 |
| 1979 | 5.3 | 8.9 | 6.0 |
| 1980 | 5.5 | 8.7 | 6.2 |
| 1981 | 5.2 | 12.9 | 7.3 |
| 1982 | 5.3 | 13.0 | 7.6 |
| 1983 | 5.0 | 12.1 | 7.3 |
| 1984 | 4.9 | 12.0 | 7.1 |
| 1985 | 5.7 | 11.9 | 7.6 |
| 1986 | 5.0 | 11.1 | 7.0 |
| 1987 | 5.3 | 10.8 | 7.1 |
| 1988 | 5.2 | 11.0 | 7.1 |
| 1989 | 5.1 | 10.9 | 7.1 |
| 1990 | 5.5 | 10.6 | 7.3 |
| 1991 | 5.4 | 9.7 | 7.0 |
| 1992 | 5.2 | 8.6 | 6.5 |
| 1993 | 4.9 | 8.0 | 6.0 |

*Source:*
IMF International Financial Statistics.
Balance of Payment Statistics Part 2.

### Sound Recordings

**Mr. Wigley:** To ask the President of the Board of Trade what is the Government's position with regard to EU directive 92/100 on guaranteeing performers 50 per cent. of the receipts of a recording company when the record is broadcast or used in public; and what reasons underlie the difference in approach between the UK and other member states. [25007]

**Mr. Ian Taylor:** Directive 92/100/EEC requires member states to ensure that a single equitable remuneration is paid by users for broadcasting or other communication to the public of sound recordings, and that the remuneration is shared between performers and record producers. It does not specify that performers are to receive a 50 per cent. share of the remuneration. The proposals we have made in the recent consultative draft of regulations to implement the directive aim at flexibility as technical developments increase the ways in which sound recording are communicated to the public, and are intended to ensure that performers receive an equitable share, while leaving the precise amount to be agreed between the parties and determined by the Copyright Tribunal in default of agreement. We are aware that performers are dissatisfied with this approach, and will look carefully at the matter again before submitting the legislation to Parliament. Clearly, however, given the various options open to us under the directive, we will also have to consider the views of users and producers on how the legislation should be framed in the UK.

### Nuclear Power

**Mr. Alan W. Williams:** To ask the President of the Board of Trade what has been the load factor at each of Britain's nuclear power stations in the last year for which figures are available. [25272]

**Mr. Eggar:** These are commercial matters for the companies concerned.

**Mr. Alan W. Williams:** To ask the President of the Board of Trade how many staff were employed at each of Britain's advanced gas-cooled reactor power stations *(a)* in 1989 and *(b)* in 1994. [25273]

**Mr. Eggar:** These are matters for Nuclear Electric and Scottish Nuclear.

**Mr. Alan W. Williams:** To ask the President of the Board of Trade when the licence for the operation of the Sizewell pressurised water reactor and each of Britain's advanced gas-cooled reactors was last issued by the nuclear installations inspectorate; what is the period of the licence; what are the consent conditions; how often inspections are carried out; and what modifications there have been in each licence since first issued. [25287]

**Mr. Eggar:** The table gives the dates on which the current nuclear site licences were granted for the sites listed and the number of times the licences have been varied.

| Site name | Date licence last granted | Number of variations since last licence was granted |
| --- | --- | --- |
| Sizewell | 1 March 1990 | 4 |
| Dungeness | 1 March 1990 | 5 |
| Hinkley Point | 30 July 1993 | 5 |
| Hartlepool | 1 March 1990 | 3 |
| Heysham 1 and 2 | 1 March 1990 | 5 |
| Hunterston | 1 March 1990 | 5 |
| Torness | 1 March 1990 | 3 |

Nuclear site licences are granted to nuclear operators for the sites on which installations are situated and not for the individual facilities such as reactors. For example, the Sizewell B pressurised water reactor is situated on the Sizewell site, for which the last licence was issued on 1 March 1990, as indicated in the table.

Nuclear site licences may be varied for a number of reasons—for example, the commissioning of full power.

A complete list of the variations that have been made to each of the site licences listed is not readily available and could be provided only at a disproportionate cost.

The Health and Safety Executive grants a nuclear site licence for an indefinite period. The licence can be revoked by the HSE and can also be surrendered by the licensee, who is responsible for the safety of activities on the site. HSE's publication, "Nuclear Site Licences under the Nuclear Installations Act 1965 (As Amended), Notes for Applicants", sets out the current conditions attached to a licence. A copy of this is in the Library of the House.

In 1994, on average, HSE's nuclear installations inspectorate inspected each nuclear power station every 2.5 weeks. The operation of each reactor is constrained by HSE using controls, including consents, derived from the conditions attached to the licence.

### Electricity Demand

**Mr. Alan W. Williams:** To ask the President of the Board of Trade what were the United Kingdom's *(a)* base load and *(b)* peak electricity demands during 1994. [27276]

**Mr. Eggar:** The simultaneous maximum demand for electricity in the United Kingdom met during the winter 1993–94 was 54.8 GW and during the winter of 1994–95 was 52.4 GW. The lowest demand met in the UK during the year 1994 was 20.2 GW. Base load varies according to season, with the minimum load on the day of maximum winter demand almost twice the minimum load in mid-summer. There is thus no single measurement for base load.

### Nuclear Decommissioning

**Mr. Alan W. Williams:** To ask the President of the Board of Trade what are the latest projections for the total cost of decommissioning *(a)* Berkeley and *(b)* Trawsfynydd nuclear power stations at 1995 prices, and what are the anticipated dates when these costs will accrue. [25280]

**Mr. Eggar:** These are matters for Nuclear Electric plc.

**Mr. Alan W. Williams:** To ask the President of the Board of Trade what is the total amount of money set aside to date by Nuclear Electric and Scottish Nuclear for decommissioning *(a)* Magnox reactors and *(b)* advanced gas-cooled reactor power stations. [25275]

**Mr. Eggar:** I refer the hon. Member to the annual reports and accounts of Nuclear Electric and Scottish Nuclear, available in the Library of the House.

### Sizewell

**Mr. Alan W. Williams:** To ask the President of the Board of Trade what is the total insurance cover for an accident at the Sizewell pressurised water reactor; and how such risks are insured against. [25290]

**Mr. Eggar:** The insurance of Nuclear Electric's own property and other commercial risks is a matter for the company.

With regard to insurance cover for third party liability claims resulting from a nuclear occurrence, Nuclear Electric is insured in accordance with the requirements of the Nuclear Installations Act 1965, which reflected international agreements. This requires the operator to take out insurance for £140 million.

## Fossil Fuel Levy

**Mr. Alan W. Williams:** To ask the President of the Board of Trade how much has been raised by the non-fossil fuel obligation in each financial year since 1989; and how the total levy proceeds have been distributed. [25286]

**Mr. Eggar:** The fossil fuel levy was introduced on 1 April 1990. The information requested is:

£ million

|  | Amount raised | Payments to: Nuclear Electric | Renewable generators |
|---|---|---|---|
| 1990–91 | 1,175 | 1,135 | 6 |
| 1991–92 | 1,324 | 1,281 | 12 |
| 1992–93 | 1,348 | 1,291 | 29 |
| 1993–94 | 1,233 | 1,139 | 68 |
| 1994–95[1] | 1,204 | 1,081 | 96 |

[1]Estimate.

*Sources:*

Office of Electricity Regulation, amounts raised, and Non-Fossil Purchasing Agency Ltd. payments.

The balance of levy receipts is used to finance payments to British Nuclear Fuels plc in respect of nuclear electricity generated by its plant, and to cover certain other costs such as administration costs.

## Electricity Supplies

**Mr. Alan W. Williams:** To ask the President of the Board of Trade what determines which power stations provide base load electricity supply within the pool pricing arrangements. [25278]

**Mr. Eggar:** The order of priority for calling stations to run is determined by the England and Wales grid code and by the pool rules.

**Mr. Alan W. Williams:** To ask the President of the Board of Trade if purchases from the French interconnector are to provide base load electricity supply; and if prices are discounted on the basis of the guarantee to run continuously. [25285]

**Mr. Eggar:** The interconnector was built for mutual system support and to trade electricity when one country could supply it more cheaply than the other. Because of low avoidable generation costs at its nuclear plants, Electricité de France has been able to bid into the pool to supply electricity at prices lower than the marginal cost of indigenous fossil-based supplies. As a consequence of the level of EdF's bids, the interconnector has normally supplied base load electricity from France to England.

**Mr. Alan W. Williams:** To ask the President of the Board of Trade (1) what percentage of Britain's electricity is provided by companies other than National Power, PowerGen and the nuclear industry; and if he will list the main contributors; [25270]

(2) what percentage of Britain's electricity supply in 1994 were provided by *(a)* National Power, *(b)* PowerGen and *(c)* advanced gas-cooled reactors. [25271]

**Mr. Eggar:** In the United Kingdom in 1994, provisional data show that 62 per cent. of electricity generated was by the former nationalised industries in Britain—National Power, PowerGen, Scottish Power and Hydro-Electric—26 per cent. by Nuclear Electric and Scottish Nuclear, 7 per cent. by new entrants to generation

and 5 per cent. by other generators, including those generating electricity for their own use. Information about individual generators cannot be provided. Advanced gas-cooled reactors generated 19 per cent. of UK electricity in 1994.

The new entrants to electricity generation are: Barking Power Ltd., Corby Power Ltd., Elm Energy and Recycling Ltd., Fellside Heat and Power Ltd., Fibropower Ltd., Fibrogen Ltd., Keadby Generation Ltd., Lakeland Power Ltd., Peterborough Power Ltd., Regional Power Ltd., South East London Combined Heat and Power Ltd. and Teesside Power Ltd.

**Mr. Alan W. Williams:** To ask the President of the Board of Trade what was the average price paid by the distribution companies to the generating companies during 1994 *(a)* for base load electricity supply and *(b)* for electricity supply at peak demand. [25279]

**Mr. Eggar:** Supply companies, rather than distribution companies, purchase electricity from generating companies. The price paid is dependent upon commercially confidential contracts between the parties.

## Nestles-Rowntree Factory, Norwich

**Ms Harman:** To ask the President of the Board of Trade (1) if he plans to meet representatives of the management of Rowntree, trade unions representing employees at Rowntree and other interested parties in relation to the proposed closure of the Nestles-Rowntree factor in Norwich; [24756]

(2) what discussions his Department has had with the Department of Employment and other Government Departments concerning the proposed closure of the Nestles-Rowntree factory in Norwich and the effect of the closure on the local economy; [24758]

(3) if he will make a statement on the proposed closure of the Nestles-Rowntree factory in Norwich; [24759]

(4) how many jobs in total will be lost in Norwich and the surrounding areas as a result of the proposed closure of the Nestles-Rowntree factory in Norwich; [24755]

(5) what representations he has received regarding the proposed closure of the Nestles-Rowntree factory in Norwich. [24757]

**Mr. Jonathan Evans** *[holding answers 17 May 1995]:*Neither my right hon. Friend the President of the Board of Trade nor my right hon. Friend the Secretary of State for Employment has had representations about the proposed closure of the factory. Nor do we have any immediate plans to make a statement on the proposed closure of the factory. The closure decision was taken on purely commercial grounds and is expected to involve the loss of some 900 jobs. We have no plans to meet with the management of Nestle or with the trade unions at the plant. My right hon. Friend the President of the Board of Trade hopes, however, to visit Norwich in the autumn and in the course of his visit expects to hear at first hand more about the impact of the closure and the immediate and longer-term response of the business and other communities in the town. Since the closure announcement was made, the Government office for eastern region, which embraces the Departments of Trade and Industry, of Employment, of the Environment and of Transport, has kept closely in touch with business, local government and the training and enterprise council in Norwich and is providing help and advice to the emerging partnership which is addressing economic development and competitiveness in the area.

## Public Bodies

**Mr. Flynn:** To ask the President of the Board of Trade which non-departmental public bodies within the responsibility of his Department are subject to scrutiny by *(a)* the ombudsmen, *(b)* the National Audit Office, *(c)* the Audit Commission and *(d)* other monitoring officers; which are covered by citizens charters; in which performance indicators apply; and in which members are liable to surcharge. [23956]

**Mr. Heseltine** *[holding answer 15 May 1995]:* The information in relation to DTI's executive NDPBs is as follows:

(a) The Coal Authority

(b) The NAO's access to DTI's NDPBs is detailed in "Public Bodies 1994" which is available in the Library of the House. The newly created Coal Authority is not listed but is audited by the NAO.

(c) None.

(d)  (i) All DTI's NDPBs are appropriately monitored by the relevant divisions of the Department.

(ii) All DTI's NDPBs are encouraged to follow citizens charter principals where they are appropriate.

(iii) DTI's NDPBs are encouraged to introduce performance indicators where they are appropriate. So far, the following bodies have adopted or are soon to adopt indicators:

Coal Authority—precise indicators to be agreed in 1995–96

Simpler Trade Procedures Board

United Kingdom Atomic Energy Authority

National Consumer Council—precise indicators to be agreed in 1995–96

Gas Consumers Council

(iv) Although board members of DTI's NDPBs may in certain circumstances be liable for wrongful or negligent actions, individual members are not subject to surcharge of a statutory nature.

## Trading Standards Service

**Mr. Berry:** To ask the President of the Board of Trade what assessment he has made of the applicability of the views attributed to his Department on pages 42 and 43 of "Renewing Local Government" in the English shires to the future of the trading standards service after the proposed division of Berkshire into six unitary authorities. [24547]

**Mr. Jonathan Evans** *[holding answer 17 May 1995]:* The Government remain committed to the continued provision of an effective and efficient trading standards service following the reorganisation of local government. However, responsibility for particular organisational arrangements, including, allocation of resources to provide the necessary services, such as trading standards services, which will best service the needs of their respective communities, is a matter for individual authorities.

Where they are unable to provide a satisfactory service from their own resources, it is opened to new unitary authorities to enter into voluntary co-operative arrangements with neighbouring authorities. Smaller

authorities in particular may wish to consider entering into such arrangements. In areas where reorganisation leaves in place a previous provider of the service, new authorities may wish to consider the scope for sharing an existing capability.

## Nigeria

**Mr. Byers:** To ask the President of the Board of Trade, pursuant to his reply of 20 January, *Official Report*, column 759, what is the total amount paid to date by the Export Credits Guarantee Department in respect of defaults on credits to Nigeria; and what sum relates to contracts for defence equipment. [24686]

**Mr. Needham:** *[holding answer 17 May 1995]:* From the period 1 April 1980 to 31 March 1994, ECGD paid claims of £1,449 million in respect of capital goods and project business in Nigeria.

It is not practicable to extract the amounts that relate to contracts for defence equipment in Nigeria.

# SOCIAL SECURITY

## Social Fund

**Dr. Godman:** To ask the Secretary of State for Social Security if he will list the annual social fund allocated to each local office of his Department when the fund was introduced in April 1988. [24463]

**Mr. Roger Evans:** The information requested is in the Library.

**Dr. Godman:** To ask the Secretary of State for Social Security what percentage of income support claimants were repaying a social fund loan in *(a)* Scotland and *(b)* Britain as a whole at the end of each financial year between 1988–89 and 1994–95. [24464]

**Mr. Roger Evans:** The available information is set out in the table. Information on the percentage of income support recipients who are repaying a social fund loan is available only at the end of May of each year. Data are unavailable for May 1993.

|  |  | *Per cent.* |
| --- | --- | --- |
| Year | Scotland | Great Britain |
| 31 May 1989 | 14.6 | 8.5 |
| 31 May 1990 | 15.7 | 9.2 |
| 31 May 1991 | 17.2 | 9.9 |
| 31 May 1992 | 18.1 | 11.5 |
| 31 May 1994 | 17.2 | 11.7 |

**Dr. Godman:** To ask the Secretary of State for Social Security if he will list the criteria by which the social fund budget allocations were made to local offices in his Department when the fund was introduced in April 1988. [24465]

**Mr. Roger Evans:** The information requested is in annexe 3 of the Secretary of State's annual report on the social fund 1988–89, Cm 748, a copy of which is in the Library.

## Majority Shareholdings

**Mr. Byers:** To ask the Secretary of State for Social Security if he will list those companies in which the holder of his office is a majority shareholder which *(a)* are currently in existence and *(b)* have been wound up in the past five years. [25708]

**Mr. Hague:** My right hon. Friend the Secretary of State does not, in his official capacity, hold shares in any company.

## Access Committee for England

**Mr. Tom Clarke:** To ask the Secretary of State for Social Security what plans he has for the future funding of the Access Committee for England. [23589]

**Mr. Hague:** I refer the hon. Member to the reply given on 16 May, *Official Report*, column *165*, by the Under-Secretary of State for Health, my hon. Friend the Member for Battersea (Mr. Bowis).

## Child Support Agency

**Mr. Timms:** To ask the Secretary of State for Social Security (1) how many of the parents with care in the case load of the Child Support Agency are caring for *(a)* one, *(b)* two or *(c)* three or more children; [24830]

(2) what is the average maintenance requirement assessed by the Child Support Agency in cases where the parent with care is not in receipt of benefit; [24832]

(3) what proportion of maintenance collected through the Child Support Agency is retained by parents with care; [24834]

(4) what is the average maintenance assessment made by the Child Support Agency in cases where there is *(a)* one child, *(b)* two children and *(c)* three or more children. [24829]

**Mr. Burt:** The administration of the Child Support Agency is a matter for the chief executive, Miss Ann Chant. She will write to the hon. Member.

*Letter from Tony Ward to Mr. Stephen Timms, dated 18 May 1995:*

In the absence of Miss Chant, the Chief Executive, I am replying to your recent Parliamentary Questions to the Secretary of State for Social Security about parents with care (PWC) who have had child maintenance arranged by the Child Support Agency.

Information relating to the number of PWCs caring for up to three or more children and the average maintenance payable in such cases is only available in relation to the total number of children in the PWCs household. There will be instances where some of the children in the PWCs household do not qualify for a child maintenance assessment to be carried out by the Agency.

As at 11 March 1995, 190,700 PWCs cared for one child; 166,500 cared for two children and 97,400 cared for three or more children. The average maintenance assessed for households with one, two, three or more children was £41.62, £45.88 and £42.79 respectively. The average weekly maintenance assessed in cases where the PWCs household was not in receipt of benefit was £61.48. These figures are all estimates taken from a one per cent sample of Agency cases.

From launch to the end of March 1995, a total of £86.81 million was received and allocated by the Agency. Of this, 36% (£30.88 million) has been paid to PWCs.

I hope this is helpful.

**Mr. Timms:** To ask the Secretary of State for Social Security what proportion of absent parents in the case load of the Child Support Agency has second families. [24833]

**Mr. Burt:** The administration of the Child Support Agency is a matter for Miss Ann Chant, the chief executive. She will write to the hon. Member.

*Letter from Tony Ward to Mr. Stephen Timms, dated 18 May 1995:*

In the absence of Miss Chant, the Chief Executive, I am replying to your recent Parliamentary Question to the Secretary of State for Social Security about the number of absent parents with second families.

As at 11 March 1995, it is estimated that the absent parents who had returned a maintenance enquiry form, 6.5 percent had second families.

I hope this is helpful.

**Mr. Timms:** To ask the Secretary of State for Social Security what benefit savings he estimates to have been achieved through the Child Support Agency in *(a)* 1993–94 and *(b)* 1994–95. [24835]

**Mr. Burt:** The administration of the Child Support Agency is a matter for Miss Ann Chant, the chief executive. She will write to the hon. Member.

*Letter from Tony Ward to Mr. Stephen Timms, dated 18 May 1995:*

In the absence of Miss chant, the Chief Executive, I am replying to your recent parliamentary Question to the Secretary of State for Social Security about the benefit savings achieved by the Agency.

During 1993/94 the Agency achieved £418 million in benefit savings. The estimated figure for 1994/95 is £479.05 million.

## Income-related Benefits

**Mr. Jenkin:** To ask the Secretary of State for Social Security (1) what is the total of households in the United Kingdom; and what proportion there are on means-tested benefits; [24607]

(2) how many pensioner households there are in the United Kingdom; and what proportion there are on means-tested benefits. [24606]

**Mr. Burt** *[holding answer 16 May 1995]:* The information requested is not available for households and has therefore been provided for benefit units. A benefit unit is defined as a single person or a couple, with or without children. There may be more than one benefit unit within a household. Information is available only for Great Britain.

The available information is in the table.

*Benefit units (Great Britain)—totals and proportion receiving an income-related benefit*

|  | Total | Pensioners |
|---|---|---|
| Benefit units (millions) | 29.5 | 8.6 |
| Proportion of benefit units receiving an income-related benefit | 29 per cent. | 40 per cent. |

*Notes:*
1. People may be in receipt of more than one income-related benefit. Overlap between benefits has been taken into account.
2. Pensioners have been defined as those eligible for the income support pensioner premiums, that is, where the claimant and/or partner are aged 60 or over.
3. Information is for May 1993, the latest date for which figures are available for all benefits.

*Source:*
Income support annual statistical inquiry, 5 per cent. sample
Family credit statistical system, 5 per cent. sample of awards made
Disability working allowance statistical system, 100 per cent. count
Housing benefit/council tax benefit MIS annual 1 per cent. sample
Family expenditure survey

### Jobseeker's Allowance

**Mr. Sheerman:** To ask the Secretary of State for Social Security what representations he has received from voluntary organisations regarding the potential effects of the Jobseekers Bill on voluntary work.     [24449]

**Miss Widdecombe:** I have been asked to reply.

Ministers in the Employment Department and the Department of Social Security have received a number of representations from voluntary organisations. As my noble Friend Lord Inglewood indicated during discussion on the Jobseekers Bill in Committee, we will consider the view of the representatives of the voluntary sector before jobseeker's allowance regulations are drafted.

**Mr. Sheerman:** To ask the Secretary of State for Social Security what assessment he has made of the effect of the Jobseekers Bill on the numbers of people gaining work experience through long-term voluntary work.     [24447]

**Miss Widdecombe:** I have been asked to reply.

People who undertake voluntary work must still be available for employment and must actively seek employment in order to receive unemployment benefit or income support for the unemployed. Current provision in regulations however, allow unemployed people who undertake voluntary work 48 hours' notice to be available to take up an offer of employment. Current provisions also enable a person's voluntary work to be taken into account when considering whether he has met the actively seeking employment condition for receipt of benefit. As my noble Friend Lord Inglewood indicated during discussion of the Jobseekers Bill, we will be following this approach in jobseeker's allowance.

**Mr. Burden:** To ask the Secretary of State for Social Security what trials or pilot schemes of anticipated jobseeker's allowance procedures have been undertaken by his Department; where they were held; how long they lasted; what they covered; and what were their results.     [25575]

**Mr. Roger Evans:** I refer the hon. Member to the reply given today by my right hon. Friend the Minister of State for Employment.

## NORTHERN IRELAND

### Hospital Study

**Mr. McGrady:** To ask the Secretary of State for Northern Ireland if he will place in the Library a copy of the complementarity study undertaken in respect of hospitals within the Eastern health and social services board's area. [23051]

**Mr. Moss:** I will write to the hon. Gentleman about this matter.

### Hospital Agency Staff

**Mr. Spellar:** To ask the Secretary of State for Northern Ireland what has been the cost of employing agency staff in hospitals covered by the Eastern health and social services board in each of the last four years. [24446]

**Mr. Moss:** The information requested is only available from 1992–93 and is as follows:

| Year | Total cost (£) |
|---|---|
| 1992–93 | 21,325 |
| 1993–94 | ¹45,048 |
| 1994–95 | ²Nil |

*Notes:*

¹ In 1993–94 two units of management increased their use of agency staff.

² By 1994–95 all directly managed units within the Eastern health and social services board were established as health and social services trusts. The board's accounts for 1994–95 remain subject to audit.

### Public Service Offices

**Mr. Trimble:** To ask the Secretary of State for Northern Ireland if he will list all the public service offices, other than local government offices, and the number of persons employed in such offices, in Armagh district council in *(a)* January 1992, *(b)* January 1993, *(c)* January 1994 and *(d)* January 1995. [23528]

**Sir John Wheeler:** The information requested is listed in the table:

| Office | January 1992 | January 1993 | January 1994 | January 1995 |
|---|---|---|---|---|
| *Department of Agriculture* | | | | |
| The Mall West, Armagh | 163 | 157 | 150 | 140 |
| Divisional Veterinary Office, Alexander Road, Armagh | 33 | 37 | 37 | 38 |
| Newry Road, Armagh | 23 | 24 | 29 | 27 |
| Manor House, Loughgall | 87 | 86 | 83 | 79 |
| Cornmarket Street, Tandragee | Nil | 1 | 1 | 1 |
| Kinelowen Street, Keady | 4 | 4 | 4 | 3 |
| Gosford Forest Park, Markethill | 25 | 23 | 22 | 22 |
| *Department of Finance and Personnel* | | | | |
| Ballynahonemore Road, Armagh | Nil | Nil | Nil | 1 |

| Office | January 1992 | January 1993 | January 1994 | January 1995 |
|---|---|---|---|---|
| *Department of Economic Development* | | | | |
| Training and Employment Agency, Armagh | 14 | 14 | 13 | 14 |
| Trading Standards Branch, Armagh | 3 | 5 | 4 | 4 |
| *Department of Environment* | | | | |
| Ardmore Road, Armagh¹ | 31 | 31 | 23 | 19 |
| Ballynahonemore Road, Armagh¹ | 28 | 26 | 26 | 19 |
| Hamiltonsbawn Road, Armagh¹ | 10 | 10 | 11 | 10 |
| Dobbin Street, Armagh¹ | Nil | 1 | 1 | 1 |
| Dobbin Centre, Armagh¹ | 11 | 11 | 11 | 12 |
| Roads Service, Cornmarket Street, Tandragee | 10 | 9 | 9 | 5 |
| Environment Service Markethill Depot | 5 | 5 | 5 | 6 |
| Water Executive, Ardmore Road, Armagh | 47 | 47 | 41 | 42 |
| Roads Service, Ballynahonemore Road, Armagh | 92 | 85 | 79 | 48 |
| *Department of Health and Social Services* | | | | |
| Social Security Office, Armagh² | 70 | 73 | 73 | 70 |

*Notes:*

¹ Figures apply to non-industrial staff in months of April.

² Includes Keady community benefit office which is staffed by members from the Armagh Office.

Department of Agriculture figures for 1992, 1993 and 1994 are estimated.

**Mr. Molyneaux:** To ask the Secretary of State for Northern Ireland if he will list all the public service offices, other than local government offices, and the number of persons employed in such offices, in Down district council in *(a)* January 1992, *(b)* January 1993, *(c)* January 1994 and *(d)* January 1995. [23531]

**Sir John Wheeler:** The information requested is listed in the table:

| Office | January 1992 | January 1993 | January 1994 | January 1995 |
|---|---|---|---|---|
| *Department of Agriculture* | | | | |
| Crown Buildings, Ballynahinch | 2 | 2 | 4 | 3 |
| Main Street, Newcastle | 6 | 6 | 6 | 6 |
| Rathkeltair House, Downpatrick | 3 | 4 | 5 | 5 |
| Castlewellan Forest Park | 53 | 58 | 55 | 52 |
| The Harbour, Ardglass | 1 | 1 | 2 | 1 |
| *Department of Finance and Personnel* | | | | |
| Valuation and Lands Agency, Downpatrick | 11 | Nil | Nil | Nil |
| Rathkeltair House, Downpatrick | Nil | Nil | Nil | 2 |

| Office | January 1992 | January 1993 | January 1994 | January 1995 |
|---|---|---|---|---|
| **Department of Economic Development** | | | | |
| Training and Employment Agency, Ballynahinch | 6 | 6 | 5 | 5 |
| Training and Employment Agency, Downpatrick | 14 | 15 | 15 | 13 |
| Training and Employment Agency, Newcastle | 4 | 6 | 5 | 5 |
| | | | | |
| **Department of Health and Social Services** | | | | |
| Social Security Office, Ballynahinch | 33 | 32 | 34 | 32 |
| Social Security Office, Downpatrick | 53 | 55 | 52 | 46 |
| Social Security Office, Newcastle | 53 | 55 | 52 | 46 |
| | | | | |
| **Department of Environment** | | | | |
| Castlewellan Demesne[1] | 1 | 1 | 1 | 1 |
| Ferry Terminal, Strangford[1] | 2 | 2 | 2 | 2 |
| Flying Horse Industrial Estate, Downpatrick[1] | 10 | 10 | 9 | 12 |
| Cloonag Road, Downpatrick[1] | 21 | 21 | 18 | 21 |
| 129 Newcastle Road, Seaforde[1] | 8 | 9 | 9 | 9 |
| 13 Newcastle Road, Seaforde[1] | 17 | 17 | 17 | 18 |
| Mourne Countryside Centre, Newcastle[1] | 2 | 2 | 2 | 2 |
| Rathkeltair House, Downpatrick[1] | 200 | 207 | 203 | 187 |
| Quay Road, Downpatrick[1] | 3 | 3 | 3 | 3 |
| Water Executive, Cloonagh Road, Downpatrick | 52 | 48 | 47 | 50 |
| Roads Service, Castlenavan, Seaforde | 127 | 124 | 104 | 61 |
| Castlewellan Depot | 11 | 12 | 10 | 10 |
| Environment Service, Quoile, Quay Road, Downpatrict | 4 | 3 | 3 | 3 |
| Environment Service, Mourne Countryside Centre, Newcastle | 1 | 1 | 1 | 2 |

*Note:*

[1] Figures apply to non-industrial staff in months of April.

Department of Agriculture figures for 1992, 1993, 1994, are estimated

**Mr. John D. Taylor:** To ask the Secretary of State for Northern Ireland if he will list the public service offices, other than local government offices, and the number of persons employed in such offices, in *(a)* Ards, *(b)* Castlereagh and *(c)* North Down borough councils in (i) January 1992, (ii) January 1993, (iii) January 1994 and (iv) January 1995.          [23625]

**Sir John Wheeler:** The information requested is listed in the table:

| Office | January 1992 | January 1993 | January 1994 | January 1995 |
|---|---|---|---|---|
| *(a) Ards Borough Council* | | | | |
| **Department of Agriculture** | | | | |
| Divisional Veterinary Office, Robert Street, Newtownards | 34 | 37 | 38 | 43 |
| Portaferry Road, Newtownards | 8 | 8 | 9 | 9 |
| The Harbour, Portavogie | 1 | ? | 2 | 2 |
| | | | | |
| **Department of Economic Development** | | | | |
| Training and Employment Agency, Newtownards | 18 | 17 | 15 | 14 |
| | | | | |
| **Department of Health and Social Services** | | | | |
| Social Security Office, Newtownards | 67 | 65 | 65 | 62 |
| | | | | |
| **Department of Environment** | | | | |
| Church Street, Greyabbey[1] | 1 | 1 | 1 | 1 |
| Jubilee Road, Newtownards[1] | 26 | 27 | 25 | 28 |
| Scrabo Country Park, Newtownards | 5 | 5 | 5 | 7 |
| Roads Service, Jubilee Road, Newtownards | 44 | 42 | 42 | 9 |
| Environment Service, Church Street, Greyabbey | 11 | 11 | 9 | 9 |
| | | | | |
| *Northern Ireland Office* | | | | |
| Prison Service College | 47.5 | 75.5 | 51.5 | 77.5 |
| Ulster Bank Building, Newtownards | 8 | 8 | 8 | 8 |
| | | | | |
| *(b) Castlereagh Borough Council* | | | | |
| **Department of Agriculture** | | | | |
| Houston Road, Crossnacreevy | 35 | 36 | 35 | 35 |
| Knockbreda Crown Buildings, Belfast | 16 | 17 | 28 | 27 |
| Belvoir Forest Park | 13 | 11 | 11 | 10 |
| | | | | |
| **Department of Economic Development** | | | | |
| Training Centre, Dundonald | 107 | 100 | 99 | 83 |
| | | | | |
| **Department of Health and Social Services** | | | | |
| Social Security Office, Knockbreda | 86 | 87 | 83 | 74 |
| | | | | |
| **Department of Environment** | | | | |
| Road Service, Newtownbreda | 24 | 21 | 18 | Nil |
| Prince Regent Road, Belfast | 14 | Nil | Nil | Nil |
| | | | | |
| *Northern Ireland Office* | | | | |
| HM Young Offenders Centre | 250.5 | 240.5 | 248.5 | 248 |
| NI Forensic Science Laboratory | 141.5 | Nil | Nil | Nil |
| | | | | |
| *(c) North Down Borough Council* | | | | |
| **Department of Finance and Personnel** | | | | |
| Crown Buildings, Bangor | 29 | 29 | 27 | 29 |

| Office | January 1992 | January 1993 | January 1994 | January 1995 |
|---|---|---|---|---|
| **Department of Education** | | | | |
| Rathgael House, Bangor | 674 | 684 | 572 | 480 |
| **Department of Economic Development** | | | | |
| Training and Employment Agency, Bangor | 17 | 18 | 16 | 16 |
| **Department of Health and Social Services** | | | | |
| Social Security Office, Bangor | 80 | 83 | 76 | 71 |
| **Department of Environment** | | | | |
| Crawfordsburn Country Park[1] | 2 | 3 | 3 | 2 |
| Crown Buildings, Bangor[1] | 17 | 17 | 19 | 15 |
| Green Road Industrial Estate, Conlig[1] | 33 | 32 | 33 | 30 |
| N Down Section Office, Balloo Road, Bangor[1] | 10 | 11 | 11 | 11 |
| Rathgael House, Bangor[1] | 10 | 10 | 11 | 10 |
| Roads Service, Balloo Industrial Estate, Bangor | 42 | 40 | 36 | 57 |
| Water Executive, Conlig | 63 | 56 | 65 | 59 |
| Environment Service, Crowfordsburn Country Park | 10 | 10 | 10 | 5 |

*Note:*

[1] Figures apply to non-industrial staff in months of April.

Department of Agriculture figures for 1992, 1993 and 1994 are estimated.

**Mr. Trimble:** To ask the Secretary of State for Northern Ireland if he will list all the public service offices, other than local government offices, and the number of persons employed in such offices in Newry and Mourne district council in *(a)* January 1992, *(b)* January 1993, *(c)* January 1994 and *(d)* January 1995.

[23529]

**Sir John Wheeler:** The information requested is listed in the table.

| Office | January 1992 | January 1993 | January 1994 | January 1995 |
|---|---|---|---|---|
| **Department of Agriculture** | | | | |
| Divisional Veterinary Office, Crown Buildings, Newry | 47 | 53 | 55 | 54 |
| Holts Building, Newry | 11 | 12 | 15 | 17 |
| Bridge House, Kilkeel | 3 | 3 | 3 | 3 |
| The Harbour, Kilkeel | 2 | 2 | 2 | 2 |
| Forest Service, Rostrevor | 16 | 14 | 15 | 14 |
| The Harbour, Warrenpoint | 3 | 3 | 1 | Nil |
| The Square, Crossmaglen | 1 | 1 | 1 | 1 |
| Armagh Street, Newtownhamilton | 2 | 2 | 2 | 2 |

| Office | January 1992 | January 1993 | January 1994 | January 1995 |
|---|---|---|---|---|
| **Department of Economic Development** | | | | |
| Training and Employment Agency, Kilkeel | 1 | 2 | 2 | 2 |
| Training and Employment Agency, Newry | 28 | 29 | 24 | 24 |
| Training Centre, Newry | 48 | 53 | 48 | 41 |
| Trading Standards Branch, Newry | 2 | 2 | 2 | 2 |
| **Department of Environment** | | | | |
| Cecil Street, Newry[1] | 19 | 16 | 15 | 15 |
| Rathfriland Road, Newry[1] | 10 | 10 | 10 | 11 |
| Carnbane Industrial Estate, Newry[1] | 32 | 33 | 27 | 26 |
| Bank Parade, Newry[1] | 11 | 11 | 10 | 9 |
| Roads Service, Newry Road, Rathfriland | 21 | 14 | 15 | 16 |
| Road Service, Greencastle Street, Kilkeel | 9 | 8 | 8 | 6 |
| Road Service, Cragganduff, Crossmaglen | 5 | 5 | 4 | 4 |
| Roads Service, Cecil Street, Newry | 52 | 51 | 50 | 40 |
| Water Executive, Carnabane Industrial Estate, Newry | 65 | 67 | 69 | 62 |
| **Department of Health and Social Services** | | | | |
| Social Security Office, Kilkeel | 35 | 36 | 34 | 32 |
| Social Security Office, Newry[2] | 139 | 149 | 141 | 138 |
| Child Support Agency, Newry | Nil | Nil | 6 | 6 |

*Notes:*

[1] Figures apply to non-industrial staff in months of April.

[2] Includes Crossmaglen community benefit office which is staffed by members from the Newry office.

Department of Agriculture figures for 1992, 1993 and 1994 are estimated.

**Mr. Molyneaux:** To ask the Secretary of State for Northern Ireland if he will list all the public service offices, other than local government offices, and the number of persons employed in such offices, in Lisburn borough council in *(a)* January 1992, *(b)* January 1993, *(c)* January 1994 and *(d)* January 1995.

[23530]

**Sir John Wheeler:** The information requested is listed in the table:

| Office | January 1992 | January 1993 | January 1994 | January 1995 |
|---|---|---|---|---|
| **Department of Agriculture** | | | | |
| Ravarnet House, Lisburn | 187 | 177 | 168 | 145 |
| Large Park, Hillsborough | 15 | 15 | 14 | 14 |
| Batchelor's Walk Lisburn | 9 | 10 | 10 | 9 |
| **Department of Finance and Personnel** | | | | |
| The Sidings, Lisburn | 23 | 34 | 31 | 38 |

| Office | January 1992 | January 1993 | January 1994 | January 1995 |
|---|---|---|---|---|
| *Department of Economic Development* | | | | |
| Industrial Science Centre, Lisburn | 100 | 110 | 117 | 122 |
| Training and Employment Agency, Lisburn | 20 | 28 | 19 | 19 |
| Training Centre, Lisburn | 43 | 41 | 37 | 30 |
| *Department of Health and Social Services* | | | | |
| Social Security Office, Lisburn | 95 | 96 | 92 | 81 |
| *Department of Environment* | | | | |
| Ballinderry Industrial Estate, Lisburn[1] | 11 | 11 | 11 | 12 |
| Benson House, Lisburn[1] | 16 | 17 | 15 | 13 |
| Bow House, Lisburn[1] | 13 | 13 | 13 | 12 |
| Derryvolgie House, Lisburn[1] | 23 | 23 | 22 | 22 |
| Roads Service, Sprucefield, Lisburn | 86 | 76 | 73 | 64 |
| Environment Service, Station Road, Moira | 35 | 35 | 34 | 31 |
| Water Executive, Belfast Road, Lisburn | 62 | 62 | 56 | 51 |
| *Northern Ireland Office* | | | | |
| HMP Maze | 1,336 | 1,077 | 1,059 | 1,122.5 |
| HMP Maghaberry | 670 | 664 | 655 | 647 |
| Hillsborough Castle | 5.5 | 5.5 | 5.5 | 6.5 |

*Note:*
[1] Figures apply to non-industrial staff in months of April.
Department of Agriculture figures for 1992, 1993 and 1994 are estimated.

## Road Safety

**Mr. Worthington:** To ask the Secretary of State for Northern Ireland what proposals he has for improving road safety in Northern Ireland. [24318]

**Mr. Moss:** The Government will publish Northern Ireland's first road safety plan later this year, which is intended to increase the effectiveness of their road casualty reduction measures by providing a more strategic approach to the planning, co-ordination and delivery of road safety activities. Strong emphasis will continue to be placed on road safety education and publicity and on enforcement of traffic law. Increased resources have been provided and further increases planned, for accident remedial measures and traffic calming schemes at locations where accidents are known to occur.

Northern Ireland's road traffic legislation is being strengthened and brought more closely in line with the rest of the United Kingdom; legislative proposals include the introduction of a penalty points scheme for traffic offences.

**Mr. Worthington:** To ask the Secretary of State for Northern Ireland what comparison he has made between road safety standards in Northern Ireland and those in the rest of the United Kingdom. [24321]

**Mr. Moss:** Road safety standards, when measured in terms of accident, death and casualty rates, are published annually in "Northern Ireland Transport Statistics". This publication is available from the House of Commons Library. These statistics permit comparisons between Northern Ireland and the rest of the United Kingdom and are summarised in the tables.

Table 2.6: Road traffic accidents

| Year | Per 100,000 population | | | | Per 10,000 vehicles | | | |
|---|---|---|---|---|---|---|---|---|
| | N. Ireland | England | Scotland | Wales | N. Ireland | England | Scotland | Wales |
| 1984 | 386 | 474 | 388 | 375 | 118 | 122 | 138 | 105 |
| 1985 | 371 | 455 | 402 | 364 | 123 | 116 | 141 | 99 |
| 1986 | 394 | 459 | 387 | 373 | 130 | 114 | 133 | 99 |
| 1987 | 403 | 442 | 365 | 371 | 130 | 108 | 117 | 96 |
| 1988 | 440 | 455 | 375 | 391 | 139 | 106 | 114 | 97 |
| 1989 | 455 | 478 | 404 | 411 | 139 | 107 | 118 | 99 |
| 1990 | 450 | 472 | 395 | 411 | 132 | 105 | 111 | 97 |
| 1991 | 385 | 427 | 372 | 375 | 111 | 96 | 103 | 90 |
| 1992 | 411 | 423 | 353 | 363 | 115 | 94 | 95 | 85 |
| 1993 | 399 | 417 | 326 | 346 | 111 | 92 | 86 | 80 |

Table 2.7: Road traffic deaths

| Year | Per 100,000 population | | | | Per 10,000 vehicles | | | |
|---|---|---|---|---|---|---|---|---|
| | N. Ireland | England | Scotland | Wales | N. Ireland | England | Scotland | Wales |
| 1984 | 12.2 | 10.1 | 11.6 | 8.9 | 3.7 | 2.6 | 4.1 | 2.5 |
| 1985 | 11.4 | 9.2 | 11.7 | 8.7 | 3.8 | 2.3 | 4.1 | 2.4 |
| 1986 | 15.1 | 9.6 | 11.7 | 8.3 | 5.0 | 2.4 | 4.0 | 2.2 |
| 1987 | 13.6 | 9.2 | 10.9 | 7.8 | 4.4 | 2.2 | 3.5 | 2.0 |
| 1988 | 11.3 | 9.0 | 10.7 | 7.9 | 3.6 | 2.1 | 3.2 | 2.0 |
| 1989 | 11.4 | 9.6 | 10.9 | 8.1 | 3.5 | 2.2 | 3.2 | 1.9 |
| 1990 | 11.6 | 9.2 | 10.7 | 8.5 | 3.4 | 2.0 | 3.0 | 2.0 |
| 1991 | 11.6 | 8.0 | 9.5 | 7.9 | 3.3 | 1.8 | 2.6 | 1.9 |
| 1992 | 9.3 | 7.3 | 9.0 | 7.6 | 2.6 | 1.6 | 2.4 | 1.8 |
| 1993 | 8.8 | 6.7 | 7.8 | 6.4 | 2.4 | 1.5 | 2.1 | 1.5 |

*Table 2.8: Road traffic casualties*

| Year | Per 100,000 population | | | | Per 10,000 vehicles | | | |
| | N. Ireland | England | Scotland | Wales | N. Ireland | England | Scotland | Wales |
|---|---|---|---|---|---|---|---|---|
| 1984 | 564 | 604 | 508 | 504 | 173 | 156 | 181 | 141 |
| 1985 | 554 | 586 | 531 | 492 | 184 | 149 | 187 | 134 |
| 1986 | 603 | 593 | 510 | 512 | 200 | 147 | 175 | 136 |
| 1987 | 631 | 574 | 484 | 504 | 203 | 140 | 156 | 131 |
| 1988 | 695 | 592 | 499 | 531 | 219 | 138 | 152 | 132 |
| 1989 | 733 | 623 | 540 | 563 | 224 | 140 | 158 | 136 |
| 1990 | 740 | 611 | 534 | 571 | 217 | 135 | 150 | 134 |
| 1991 | 644 | 562 | 496 | 521 | 185 | 126 | 137 | 125 |
| 1992 | 696 | 562 | 473 | 508 | 195 | 125 | 127 | 120 |
| 1993 | 680 | 555 | 438 | 493 | 189 | 123 | 116 | 115 |

*Source:* DOE (NI). RUC, DOE (L), Scottish Office, Welsh Office.

## Play Areas (Safety Surfacing)

**Mr. McMaster:** To ask the Secretary of State for Northern Ireland what guidelines he has issued to local authorities to encourage the provision of safety surfacing on play areas; what special financial provision he has made available to local authorities to encourage and enable them to meet this need; and if he will make a statement. [24088]

**Mr. Ancram:** A handbook, "Playground Safety Guidelines", prepared by the national Children's Play and Recreation Unit, was issued in 1992 to the Association of Local Authorities of Northern Ireland for distribution to local district councils. These guidelines include a section on safety surfacing of play areas.

No special financial provision has been made available to local authorities for improvement works in this area.

## Foxes

**Mr. McMaster:** To ask the Secretary of State for Northern Ireland how many fox destruction clubs or societies are registered in Northern Ireland; what is the level of assistance they currently receive; what guidelines he issues on how these clubs and societies destroy foxes; what guidelines he issues on the numbers of foxes to be destroyed; how the fox population is assessed; and if he will make a statement. [24128]

**Mr. Moss:** There are no fox destruction clubs or societies registered in Northern Ireland, nor is there any mechanism for registering them.

No scientific monitoring of the fox population in Northern Ireland is carried out.

## Belfast Harbour Commissioners

**Mr. Worthington:** To ask the Secretary of State for Northern Ireland what development land is possessed by the port of Belfast. [24319]

**Mr. Moss:** The Belfast Harbour Commissioners currently own 226 acres of commercial development land, the majority of which is on the County Down side of the harbour estate.

## Occupational Therapists

**Mr. McGrady:** To ask the Secretary of State for Northern Ireland how many occupational therapists are employed in each health and social services trust; and what were the figures five years ago. [24015]

**Mr. Moss:** The information requested is set out in the table.

*Occupational therapists in HSS trusts*

| Trust | 30 September 1994 [1] | | 30 September 1990 [2] | |
| | WTE [3] | SIP [4] | WTE [3] | SIP [4] |
|---|---|---|---|---|
| Belfast City Hospital | 16.5 | 17 | 16.3 | 17 |
| Greenpark Healthcare | 20.8 | 22 | 25.0 | 26 |
| South and East Belfast | 29.9 | 33 | 29.4 | 31 |
| Ulster, North Down and Ards | 19.6 | 22 | 16.1 | 20 |
| Royal Group | 17.0 | 17 | 16.0 | 16 |
| Mater Infirmorum | 2.0 | 2 | 3.0 | 3 |
| North and West Belfast | 21.1 | 23 | 12.8 | 14 |
| Down and Lisburn | 22.3 | 26 | 16.0 | 20 |
| North Down and Ards | 11.8 | 15 | 6.2 | 9 |
| Causeway | 12.1 | 13 | 6.0 | 6 |
| Newry and Mourne | 13.0 | 13 | 11.0 | 11 |
| Craigavon and Banbridge | 19.9 | 23 | 3.5 | 4 |
| Craigavon Area Hospital | — | — | 13.5 | 14 |

*Notes:*

[1] Latest available figures.

[2] Information as requested is not available as trusts were not set up in 1990. However, figures for occupational therapists within the units have been provided for that year.

[3] WTE = Whole-time equivalent.

[4] SIP = Staff in post.

**Mr. McGrady:** To ask the Secretary of State for Northern Ireland how many vacant positions exist in respect of occupational therapists in each health and social services trust in Northern Ireland. [24016]

**Mr. Moss:** The information requested is set out in the table.

*Occupational therapists in HSS trusts*

| Trust | Vacancies[1] WTE[2] |
|---|---|
| Belfast City Hospital | 1.0 |
| Greenpark Healthcare | 2.0 |
| South and East Belfast | 4.0 |
| Ulster, North Downs and Ards | 4.0 |
| Royal Group | 2.0 |
| Mater Infirmorum | 2.0 |
| North and West Belfast | 0.5 |
| Down and Lisburn | 3.5 |
| North Down and Ards | 2.5 |
| Causeway | 2.0 |
| Newry and Mourne | 0.5 |
| Craigavon and Banbridge | 2.0 |
| Craigavon Area Hospital | — |

*Notes:*
[1] Latest available figures.
[2] WTE = Whole-time equivalent.

### Ports (European Grant Aid)

**Mr. Worthington:** To ask the Secretary of State for Northern Ireland what grant ports in Northern Ireland have received or are receiving from the European Union; and whether these would have to be repaid in the event of privatisation. [24317]

**Mr. Moss:** Details of grant paid prior to 1986 are incomplete.

Details of grant paid to Northern Ireland ports from 1986 to date are as follows:

| Ports | £ |
|---|---|
| Belfast Port | 70,388,570 |
| Londonderry Port | 18,071,419 |
| Warrenpoint Harbour | 6,841,407 |
| Larne Harbour | 7,164,729 |
| Coleraine Harbour | 403,467 |
| Total | 102,869,592 |

In the event of the privatisation of a trust port, the question of repayment of grant aid would be a matter for discussion between the Commission and the Government.

### Northern Ireland Railways

**Mr. Worthington:** To ask the Secretary of State for Northern Ireland if he will make a statement about the involvement of private sector finance in Northern Ireland Railways. [24315]

**Mr. Moss:** The Northern Ireland Transport Holding Company, which is the parent company of Northern Ireland Railways, has commissioned a study which will consider the scope for attracting private finance into Northern Ireland Railways's capital programme.

### Housing Associations

**Mr. John D. Taylor:** To ask the Secretary of State for Northern Ireland for what purposes he requires *(a)* names of children, *(b)* names of spouse and *(c)* details of member's hobbies from all members and senior staff of the housing associations in Northern Ireland; and if he will make a statement about the relevance of these personal details to the performance of all the housing association members and staff involved. [24501]

**Mr. Moss:** The information was sought in order to obtain up-to-date and accurate pen pictures of members and senior staff of housing associations. Such information is already sought routinely by the Department from associations on an ad hoc basis. There is no link whatever between the personal details and performance. The provision of the information is entirely voluntary and will be treated as confidential.

### Craigakulliar Quarry

**Mr. William Ross:** To ask the Secretary of State for Northern Ireland whether he will now visit Craigakulliar quarry. [24584]

**Mr. Moss:** I have no plans to do so at present.

**Mr. William Ross:** To ask the Secretary of State for Northern Ireland when the commissioner who heard the inquiry into the planning application to use the Craigakulliar quarry as a dump completed his report; when the other commissioners finished their consideration of that report; when they decided to overturn the recommendations of the commissioner who held the inquiry; and when their decision was *(a)* first communicated to the officers and town clerk of Coleraine borough council and *(b)* published. [24588]

**Mr. Moss:** This is a matter for the Planning Appeals Commission. I have asked the chief commissioner to write to the hon. Gentleman.

### National Insurance Numbers

**Mr. Clifford Forsythe:** To ask the Secretary of State for Northern Ireland (1) how many national insurance numbers existing on 31 March were being held as a record following the death of the owner; [24595]

(2) how many national insurance numbers existing on 31 March 1995 *(a)* referred to owners living abroad and *(b)* were cancelled between 1 April 1994 and 31 March 1995; [24596]

(3) how many national insurance numbers existed in Northern Ireland on 31 March 1995. [24594]

**Mr. Moss:** Responsibility for the subject in question has been delegated to the Social Security Agency under its chief executive, Mr. Alec Wylie. I have asked him to arrange a reply to be given.

*Letter from Alec Wylie to Mr. Clifford Forsythe, dated 18 May 1995:*

I have been asked to reply to your three recent Parliamentary Questions relating to National Insurance numbers.

I should first explain that all National Insurance records for the United Kingdom are held centrally in Newcastle-upon-Tyne and Northern Ireland National Insurance numbers are not held separately from the rest of the United Kingdom. The information you require is not readily available and to disaggregate the National Insurance numbers for Northern Ireland would incur disproportionate costs.

I can, however, tell you that at July 1994, for the United Kingdom as a whole, there was 8.8 million National Insurance numbers being held as a record following the death of the owner. This can be for a number of reasons including to support payment of a Widow's Pension. At July 1994, again for the United Kingdom as a whole, there were 6.1 million National Insurance numbers which referred to owners living abroad.

Finally, from 1 April 1994 to 31 March 1995, there were 10,421 National Insurance Numbers cancelled in the United Kingdom.

I am sorry that I cannot provide the information in the format you require but I hope that the information I have given you will be helpful.

### Roman Catholic Council for Maintained Schools

**Mr. Beggs:** To ask the Secretary of State for Northern Ireland, pursuant to his answer of 9 May, *Official Report*, column *433*, if he will make a statement on the role of the Roman Catholic Council for Maintained Schools.

[24667]

**Mr. Ancram:** The functions of the Roman Catholic Council for Maintained Schools are set out in part IX of the Education Reform (Northern Ireland) Order 1989, a copy of which is available in the Library.

### National Lottery Grants

**Mr. Worthington:** To ask the Secretary of State for Northern Ireland on what occasions he as used his powers under the National Lottery etc. Act 1993 to direct the administrators of lottery grants to withhold grants to groups; and what proposals he has to use these powers in future.

[24601]

**Mr. Ancram:** The Secretary of State for Northern Ireland has not to date used his powers under the National Lottery etc. Act 1993 to prohibit the distribution of money to any group and has at present no proposals to do so.

### Suicides

**Mr. Martyn Jones:** To ask the Secretary of State for Northern Ireland what is the most recent available percentage suicide rate for employed 18 to 65-year-olds in Northern Ireland.

[24555]

**Sir John Wheeler:** Information on the number of employed people who have committed suicide is not available. At death registration, informants are asked for the last occupation rather than the employment status of the deceased.

### Education and Library Boards

**Mr. Beggs:** To ask the Secretary of State for Northern Ireland for how many pupils in each education and library board area in Northern Ireland the area board has a responsibility to provide services.

[24666]

**Mr. Ancram:** Details of the services provided for pupils by the education and library boards are contained in their annual reports, copies of which are available in the Library.

### Pupil Numbers

**Mr. Beggs:** To ask the Secretary of State for Northern Ireland what is the total number of children enrolled in *(a)* maintained, *(b)* voluntary, *(c)* integrated and *(d)* independent schools in each area board in Northern Ireland.

[24668]

**Mr. Ancram:** The information requested is as follows:

| | *Belfast* | *Western* | *North-Eastern* | *South-Eastern* | *Southern* | *Total* |
|---|---|---|---|---|---|---|
| Maintained | 28,149 | 37,149 | 20,348 | 17,105 | 38,789 | 141,540 |
| Voluntary | 15,652 | 8,528 | 9,234 | 7,580 | 8,674 | 49,668 |
| *Integrated:* | | | | | | |
| Grant-maintained | 1,050 | 918 | 512 | 1,028 | 665 | 4,173 |
| Controlled | 167 | — | 51 | 155 | 266 | 639 |
| Independent | 100 | 65 | 109 | 552 | 117 | 943 |

### Public Health Notices

**Mr. McGrady:** To ask the Secretary of State for Northern Ireland how many public health notices have been issued by each district council in respect of properties between 1 April 1993 to 31 March 1995; and what were the reasons for such notices.

[24745]

**Mr. Moss:** The service of public health notices is a statutory duty of district councils. The information requested is not held centrally and could be obtained only at disproportionate cost.

**Mr. McGrady:** To ask the Secretary of State for Northern Ireland how many home improvement grant applications were approved as a result of public health notices issued by each district council in Northern Ireland since 1 April 1993 to 31 March 1995; what were the budgetary amounts allocated; and if each application fulfilled the criteria for unfitness as laid down in the Housing (NI) Order 1992.

[24750]

**Mr. Moss:** This is a matter for the Northern Ireland Housing Executive. However, the chief executive has provided in the table, for each district council area, the numbers of repairs grants approved on foot of the service of public health notices and the amount of grant paid for the period April 1993 to March 1995. Applications for grant aid resulting from the service of public health notices do not have to fulfil the criteria for unfitness as laid down in the Housing (NI) Order 1992.

*Numbers of repairs grants approved and amount of grant paid, by district council area, between April 1993 and March 1995*

| District council | Repairs grants approved | Amount of grant paid £ |
|---|---|---|
| Belfast | 2,479 | 769,492 |
| Newtownabbey | 23 | 13,071 |
| Carrickfergus | 48 | 14,651 |
| Larne | 12 | 2,120 |
| Ballymena | 6 | 3,466 |
| Moyle | — | — |
| Antrim | 7 | 10,083 |
| Coleraine | 10 | 9,956 |
| Ballymoney | 4 | 3,453 |
| Derry | 10 | 7,277 |
| Magherafelt | 6 | 714 |

*Numbers of repairs grants approved and amount of grant paid, by district council area, between April 1993 and March 1995*

| District council | Repairs grants approved | Amount of grant paid £ |
|---|---|---|
| Strabane | 7 | 5,468 |
| Limavady | — | — |
| Omagh | 82 | 110,809 |
| Dungannon | 254 | 330,486 |
| Cookstown | 15 | 31,519 |
| Fermanagh | 137 | 116,308 |
| Newry and Mourne | 625 | 946,749 |
| Banbridge | 373 | 467,318 |
| Craigavon | 913 | 1,154,827 |
| Armagh | 951 | 1,290,249 |
| Lisburn | 246 | 284,237 |
| Down | 39 | 50,852 |
| North Down | 157 | 140,218 |
| Castlereagh | 90 | 75,810 |
| Ards | 203 | 137,955 |
| Totals: | 6,697 | 5,977,088 |

### Downpatrick Regeneration Project

**Mr. McGrady:** To ask the Secretary of State for Northern Ireland when he will fill the vacant project officer position in the Downpatrick regeneration project. [24746]

**Mr. Moss:** The Department is actively seeking to fill the vacant post and it is hoped that an appointment will be made shortly.

### Conservation Area Grants

**Mr. McGrady:** To ask the Secretary of State for Northern Ireland what consultations have taken place about increasing the level of conservation area grants. [24747]

**Mr. Moss:** Consultations about increasing the level of conservation area grants have taken place with the Historic Buildings Council. In the light of these, it was decided that grants should remain unaltered.

### Housing Executive

**Mr. McGrady:** To ask the Secretary of State for Northern Ireland what plans he has to sell off the Housing Executive's stock to the private sector, and if he will make a statement. [24748]

**Mr. Moss:** There are no plans to sell off the Housing Executive's stock to the private sector. The executive, however, does have powers to sell houses to the private sector to complement its own developments or to tenants under its house sales scheme.

### Planning Applications

**Mr. McGrady:** To ask the Secretary of State for Northern Ireland what consultations took place about the recent price increase in respect of certain planning applications. [24751]

**Mr. Moss:** It is Government policy to achieve full recovery of the costs of processing applications and current planning fees do not meet these costs. The recent increase was designed to close this gap and external consultations were not considered appropriate.

### Disclosure in Criminal Cases

**Mr. Trimble:** To ask the Secretary of State for Northern Ireland if he will publish the consultation paper on disclosure in criminal cases in Northern Ireland; and if the consultation period will conclude after 31 July. [25176]

**Sir John Wheeler:** My right hon. and learned Friend the Secretary of State published such a paper on 19 May, seeking comments by 31 July.

### Miss Markievicz Gorman

**Mr. William Ross:** To ask the Secretary of State for Northern Ireland whether the shot which wounded Markievicz Gorman was fired before the stolen car in which she was a passenger had passed the Army patrol. [22917]

**Sir John Wheeler** *[holding answer 9 May 1995]:* It has not been established at what stage Miss Gorman received her wound.

Miss Gorman herself did not appear to have realised at what stage she received her injury and in fact became aware that she was injured only after the shooting had stopped and she was removed from the car by Army personnel.

## ATTORNEY-GENERAL

### Inquests

32. **Ms Hoey:** To ask the Attorney-General what criteria he uses when deciding to exercise his discretion under section 13 of the Coroners Act 1988 to grant a fresh inquest. [23914]

**The Solicitor-General:** The Attorney-General considers whether an application to the High Court would have a reasonable prospect of establishing that it is necessary or desirable in the interests of justice for a fresh inquest to be held.

### Private Lee Clegg

33. **Sir Michael Neubert:** To ask the Attorney-General, pursuant to his oral answer of 6 February, *Official Report*, column 13, what further representations he has received on the case of Private Clegg. [23915]

**The Attorney-General:** The Law Officers have received 42 individual representations since 6 February and two petitions, one bearing 18 names and the other 45.

### Stefan Kiszko Case

34. **Mr. Mullin:** To ask the Attorney-General what plans he has to appeal against the decision of Rochdale's stipendiary magistrate to drop charges of perverting the course of justice in the Stefan Kiszko case against former Superintendent Richard Holland and Mr. Ronald Outteridge; and if he will make a statement. [23916]

**The Solicitor-General:** The Crown Prosecution Service is carefully considering and taking counsel's advice on the possibility of an appeal.

## War Crimes Act 1991

**35. Mr. John Marshall:** To ask the Attorney-General what recent representations he has received about the workings of the War Crimes Act 1991.          [23917]

**The Attorney-General:** With regard to second world war crimes, following initial advice from Treasury counsel, further inquiries are in hand in relation to certain potential defendants. Decisions as to possible prosecutions will be taken as soon as all the relevant evidence has been fully considered and analysed.

## Treasury Counsel

**Mr. Byers:** To ask the Attorney-General how many barristers on the panel of Treasury counsel received more than £200,000 in fees from public funds for the latest year for which information is available.          [25055]

**The Attorney-General:** There are two Treasury counsel retained for Government civil work. A supplementary panel of counsel is also maintained and used in suitable cases. Both Treasury counsel received more than £200,000 in fees from public funds in the financial year 1994–95.

There were 14 Treasury counsel based at the central criminal court to represent the Crown in serious criminal cases until Easter 1995, when three resigned having accepted appointments as Her Majesty's counsel. On the information currently available, seven of those received in excess of £200,000 from the Crown Prosecution Service over the same period. However, criminal Treasury counsel are not exclusively retained by the Crown Prosecution Service and may work for other Government Departments and undertake legal aid defence work. Information on fees from those sources can be determined only at disproportionate cost.

The information referred to is based on payments made inclusive of value added tax.

**Mr. Byers:** To ask the Attorney-General how many barristers are presently on the panel of the Treasury counsel.          [25056]

**The Attorney-General:** There are two Treasury counsel retained for government civil work. A supplementary panel of counsel is also maintained and used in suitable cases.

There are at present 11 Treasury counsel based at the central criminal court to represent the Crown in serious criminal cases.

## Majority Shareholdings

**Mr. Byers:** To ask the Attorney-General if he will list those companies in which the holder of his office is a majority shareholder which *(a)* are currently in existence and *(b)* have been wound up in the past five years.          [25714]

**The Attorney-General:** There are no companies in which the Attorney-General is a majority shareholder and no such companies have been wound up in the past five years.

## Electro-shock Batons

**Mrs. Clwyd:** To ask the Attorney-General if he will make a statement about the outcome of the investigation by the Crown Prosecution Service relating to British Aerospace and the export of electro-shock batons.          [25567]

**The Attorney-General:** The Crown Prosecution Service does not itself conduct investigations. The relevant police investigation is not yet concluded.

## DUCHY OF LANCASTER

## Majority Shareholdings

**Mr. Byers:** To ask the Chancellor of the Duchy of Lancaster if he will list those companies in which the holder of his office is a majority shareholder which *(a)* are currently in existence and *(b)* have been wound up in the past five years.          [25710]

**Mr. David Hunt:** None.

## Parliamentary Council

**Mr. McMaster:** To ask the Chancellor of the Duchy of Lancaster what is the role of the Office of Parliamentary Counsel in relation to *(a)* public Bills, *(b)* private Bills and *(c)* private Members' Bills; how this has changed over the past 20 years, with specific instances; and if he will make a statement.          [24132]

**Mr. David Hunt:** Parliamentary counsel are responsible for drafting Government Bills, except common form ones and those relating exclusively to Scotland. Parliamentary counsel advise on all aspects of parliamentary procedure in connection with these Bills. On the instructions of sponsoring Departments, they are responsible for drafting Government amendments and a procedural and other motions.

The Office is not involved in the production of private Bills. It may, however, provide drafting assistance on private Members' Bills on the instructions of Departments acting with the authority of Ministers.

There has been no change in the role of the Office of Parliamentary Counsel over the past 20 years.

## Science Budget

**Mr. Battle:** To ask the Chancellor of the Duchy of Lancaster if he will place in the Library the Director General of the Research Councils' review of the science budget published at the press briefing on Tuesday 16 May, together with accompanying press releases and press pack; and if he will make a statement.          [25688]

**Mr. David Hunt:** I refer the hon. Member to the answer that I gave to the hon. Member for Erewash (Mrs. Knight) on 16 May, *Official Report*, column *123*.

I have today deposited in the Libraries of the House the press pack issued at the press briefing on 16 May. The text of the director general's review is also available on the Internet through http://www.open.gov.uk/ost/osthome.htm.

## Civil Servants

**Mr. McAllion:** To ask the Chancellor of the Duchy of Lancaster if he will list the grade on entry to the civil service of all current permanent secretaries, including those officials nominally graded at permanent secretary level.                                    [25067]

**Mr. Horam:** The following list gives details of all current permanent secretaries, including those nominally graded, within the home civil service and their grade on entry to the civil service:

| Name | Entry grade |
| --- | --- |
| Adye Sir J. A. | Executive Officer |
| Battishill Sir A. M. W. | Assistant Principal |
| Bichard M. G, | Grade 3 |
| Brown Sir A. P. | Principal |
| Budd A. P. | Grade 1A |
| Burns Sir T. | Grade 1A |
| Butler Sir F. E. R. | Assistant Principal |
| Calman K. C. | Grade 1A |
| Chilcot Sir J. A. | Assistant Principal |
| Culpin R. P. | Assistant Principal |
| Davies D. E. N. | Grade 1A |
| Gregson Sir P. L. | Assistant Principal |
| Hart G. A. | Assistant Principal |
| Hillhouse Sir R. R. | Assistant Principal |
| Hosker Sir G. A. | Legal Assistant |
| Jenkins J. C. | Assistant Parliamentary Counsel |
| Langlands A. | Grade 2 |
| Lankester Sir T. P. | Principal |
| Legg Sir T. S. | Legal Assistant |
| McIntosh Dr. M. K. | Grade 1 |
| Mills Mrs B. J. L. | Grade 2 |
| Mottram R. C. | Assistant Principal |
| Mountfield R. | Assistant Principal |
| Packer R. J. | Inspector of Taxes |
| Partridge Sir M. J. A. | Assistant Principal |
| Phillips G. H. | Assistant Principal |
| Rimington J. D. | Assistant Principal |
| Scholar M. C. | Assistant Principal |
| Stewart J. M. | Assistant Principal |
| Strachan Mrs. V. P. M. | Assistant Principal |
| Turnbull A. | Assistant Principal |
| Vereker J. M. M. | Assistant Principal |
| Wicks Sir N. L | Assistant Principal |
| Wilson R. T. J. | Assistant Principal |

In July, Professor Tim Holt will take up the post of director at the Central Statistical Office. This appointment was made following an open competition. He will join the civil service directly as a grade 1A.

### "Forward Look" 1995

**Mrs. Gillan:** To ask the Chancellor of the Duchy of Lancaster when he expects to publish the "1995 Forward Look of Government Funded Science, Engineering and Technology" and the report of the technology foresight steering group.                                    [25769]

**Mr. David Hunt:** I am today publishing the report of the technology foresight steering group and the "1995 Forward Look of Government Funded Science, Engineering and Technology". Copies of both reports are being placed in the Library and summaries are available from the Vote Office.

The report on technology foresight is from an independent steering group chaired by the Government's chief scientific adviser, Sir William Stewart. I am grateful to Sir William and his colleagues for their report. This builds on those of the 15 technology foresight sector panels, all of which have already been published by my Department. They have been widely welcomed. The steering group report provides an overarching assessment of the broad areas of science, engineering and technology that will help the UK capture national and global markets over the next 10 to 20 years. The report also makes recommendations concerning basic research, skills, finance and regulation.

The Government will respond vigorously to the steering group and panel reports. Their recommendations will inform policy and priorities in Government, the research councils and universities. My Department, in partnership with the DTI, will also be undertaking a major campaign to spread awareness of foresight findings throughout industry.

The key to success will be to get industry and the science and engineering base working in partnership to address the opportunities which foresight has identified. To stimulate this, I am announcing today a foresight challenge. This will be financed through an extra £40 million of public money which I will make available over the next three years, for collaborative initiatives which address foresight priorities. The challenge will be based on existing mechanisms for industry/science base collaboration, in particular the successful LINK scheme. It will attract matching funds from industry—making £80 million of new resources. I intend to consult the scientific and business communities about the detailed arrangements for the challenge.

Further details of the Government's plans for the next stage of the foresight exercise are set out in the 1995 "Forward Look". This report provides an up-to-date statement on the ways in which public funds for science, engineering and technology are being spent throughout Government and the challenges and opportunities that lie ahead. Particular emphasis is given to the ways in which Government Departments and the research councils are refocusing their programmes in support of wealth creation and quality of life in line with the policy objectives of the 1993 White Paper "Realising our Potential".

Taking account of technology foresight, the Government will continue to work towards a much closer coupling between publicly funded research and development and the wealth-creating private sector, to help deliver the goals of enhanced national prosperity and quality of life.

## AGRICULTURE, FISHERIES AND FOOD

### Food Labelling

**Mr. McMaster:** To ask the Minister of Agriculture, Fisheries and Food what further measures he plans to introduce to ensure that food labelling is truthful and accurate about its impact on animal welfare and the environment; and if he will make a statement.    [24065]

**Mrs. Browning:** The Food Safety Act 1990 already requires that food labelling shall neither falsely describe the food nor mislead as to the nature or substance or quality of the food concerned. Statements on food labels concerned with animal welfare must therefore comply with those requirements. I have no plans to introduce any more specific requirements; advice I received from the Independent Food Advisory Committee indicated that it would not be appropriate so to do and there are no proposals at European Community level to introduce any such requirement.

## Foxes

**Mr. McMaster:** To ask the Minister of Agriculture, Fisheries and Food how many fox destruction clubs or societies are registered in England; what is the level of assistance they currently receive; what guidelines he issues on how these clubs and societies destroy foxes; what guidelines he issues on the numbers of foxes to be destroyed; how the fox population is assessed; and if he will make a statement. [24129]

**Mrs. Browning:** Fox destruction clubs or societies are neither required to be registered with nor are they financially assisted by the Ministry and information is not collected on the number of such organisations.

Responsibility for the control of foxes rests with those who most benefit from such control, that is, individual landowners and occupiers. The actual method of control is also at the discretion of individual landowners and occupiers, provided that the method does not contravene current legislation, such as the Wildlife and Countryside Act 1981 and the Control of Pesticides Regulations 1986.

## Plant Labelling

**Mr. McMaster:** To ask the Minister of Agriculture, Fisheries and Food what measures are in place to ensure that containerised and container-grown decorative house plants destined for sale in supermarkets which also sell food are clearly labelled with any potential dangers associated with their natural features or pesticide treatments by growers or suppliers; what further measure he plans to introduce; and if he will make a statement. [24160]

**Mrs. Browning:** The risks associated with the sale of potentially hazardous plants by supermarkets and other outlets is a matter which has been considered in a horticultural industry initiative. A voluntary code of practice on handling, retailing and labelling of poisonous plants has been drawn up for adoption. This is a good example of self-regulation. The risk of contamination of food by pesticides used on ornamental plants sold in the same store is extremely small. We have no plans to require growers or suppliers to label plants with the treatments applied.

## Fish Imports

**Mr. Sykes:** To ask the Minister of Agriculture, Fisheries and Food what assessment he has made of the economic impact of cheap fish imported from non-EEC countries on the livelihoods of east coast fishermen. [24153]

**Mr. Jack:** No specific assessment has been made in relation to the situation on the east coast of England, but last year's broad-based analysis by the European Commission indicated that underlying structural problems rather than non-EU imports were responsible for the generally depressed state of the fish market within the European Union. The EU market depends increasingly on imports for its supplies and fish processors in particular depend heavily on imported raw material because their needs cannot be met from EU resources.

## Live Animal Exports

**Sir Terence Higgins:** To ask the Minister of Agriculture, Fisheries and Food, pursuant to his answer of 18 April, *Official Report*, columns *103-104*, regarding the conformity of the vessel Northern Star to the provisions of the Welfare of Animals during Transport Order 1994, by what authority his Department takes the view that point 18 of schedule 3 to the order, which implements EC directive 91/628, does not apply to roll-on roll-off ferries. [24441]

**Mrs. Browning:** My previous answer to which my right hon. Friend refers gave the view which the Department takes when assessing roll-on roll-off ferries for compliance with the law.

**Mr. Olner:** To ask the Minister of Agriculture, Fisheries and Food, pursuant to his answer of 11 May, *Official Report*, column *581*, when he expects his Department's consideration of the Royal Society for the Prevention of Cruelty to Animals' latest legal advice on the export of live animals to be completed. [24779]

**Mr. Waldegrave:** I have now received advice from lawyers on the opinion from Mr. Gerald Barling QC entitled "Welfare of Calves: Lawfulness of Export Restrictions".

My legal advice in the light of that opinion remains: namely, that a ban on calf exports—whether a blanket ban or a selective ban on exports to certain countries or to rearing units using veal crates—would be at serious risk of successful challenge under European law.

There are also policy considerations. By far the best outcome, which I believe is achievable, would be EU measures to prohibit the use of the veal crate across Europe. That, I am sure all would agree, would be the best way of achieving a real increase in the sum of animal welfare. A unilateral restriction on exports from the UK— if it could be made to stick—would be only a gesture in terms of animal welfare: continental rearers would carry on using veal crates, and would obtain calves from alternative, more distant, sources from which they would probably be transported in conditions less humane than those we impose on our own exports. There would be no net gain across Europe in animal welfare terms.

In addition, to attempt to introduce a unilateral ban would be counter-productive in relation not only to the chances of getting a Euro-wide ban, but to the very delicate negotiations on welfare in transit in general. We would have antagonised other member states, some of them at present our allies, and might indeed give them a pretext for declining to take matters further, pending resolution of the legal issues. These are strong reasons for not introducing a ban, even if I thought—as I do not— that I had discretion to do so in legal terms. The fact is that I am still being advised that I do not have that discretion.

Mr. Barling's opinion does, however, raise an interesting new point in highlighting the fact that the provisions of Community directive 91/629 on the welfare of calves fail to reflect those of appendix C to the recommendation on cattle which the Council of Europe adopted under the European convention for the protection of animals kept for farming purposes. As I have said, this does not alter the legal position in respect of a unilateral ban on calf exports. However, I am, as the House will know, already pressing the Council of Ministers to revise directive 91/629 so as to prohibit the use of the veal crate throughout the Community. In support of this aim, I intend drawing Mr. Barling's argumentation over the Council of Europe texts to the Commission's attention. I hope it will see this as a powerful reason for it to make proposals to the Council for the Community's own rules to be brought into line with the rules to which the Community has subscribed in the Council of Europe.

I believe that the RSPCA—and other animal welfare organisations—can play an important role in our efforts to achieve changes in the Community rules. I am today conveying to it my views in the light of Mr. Barling's opinion, and inviting it to meet me to discuss how matters can now be taken forward.

### Head of EC Tobacco Sector

**Mr. Marlow:** To ask the Minister of Agriculture, Fisheries and Food what was the result of the Belgian police investigation into the circumstances surrounding the suicide of the former head of the tobacco sector of the EC.     [24867]

**Mr. Jack:** The Belgian police investigated the immediate circumstances surrounding the death of the former head of the tobacco sector of the EC, with the assistance of the Commission, and concluded that he took his own life. They did not carry out a further investigation into the alleged case of fraud. The Commission, from its own internal investigation, passed dossiers of information to the Italian and Greek authorities, and the state prosecutors in Rome and Athens are now pursuing their own inquiries with the full assistance of the Commission's anti-fraud squad.

### Public Bodies

**Mr. Flynn:** To ask the Minister of Agriculture, Fisheries and Food which non-departmental public bodies within the responsibility of his Department are subject to scrutiny by *(a)* the ombudsmen, *(b)* the National Audit Office, *(c)* the Audit Commission and *(d)* other monitoring officers, which are covered by citizens charters, in which performance indicators apply, and in which members are liable to surcharge.     [23965]

**Mr. Jack** *[holding answer 15 May 1995]:* I refer the hon. Member to the reply given to the hon. Member for Cannock and Burntwood (Mr. Wright) on 16 May 1995, *Official Report,* columns *203–204,* as regards the role of the ombudsmen and the NAO in relation to the Ministry's executive NDPBs and the applicability of the citizens charter and performance indicators. The ombudsmen and NAO may also scrutinise funding and secretariat support for other NDPBs. The Audit Commission has no role in relation to MAFF's NDPBs, but NDPBs are subject to internal and external audit. The normal legal rules on liability to surcharge apply to board members of NDPBs, whose liability is not limited.

## WALES

### Nurses' Pay

**Mr. Barry Jones:** To ask the Secretary of State for Wales if he will make a statement concerning nurses' pay in Wales.     [24336]

**Mr. Richards:** The independent pay review body has recommended a 1 per cent. increase in national salaries to be supplemented by local negotiations on pay which are expected to lead to improvements in total of between 1.5 and 3 per cent. These recommendations have been accepted in full by the Government.

Some 13 trusts and units in Wales have made offers known—all at the 3 per cent. mark. The remainder are expected to make offers soon.

Negotiations are still continuing between the management and staff sides of the Nursing and Midwifery Staffs Council to translate the pay review body recommendations into an agreement for promulgation to the service.

### Community Care Charters

**Mr. Gareth Wardell:** To ask the Secretary of State for Wales on what date he intends to issue his consultation paper on community care charters for Wales.     [24017]

**Mr. Richards:** We intend to issue our draft framework for community care charters in Wales for consultation within the next few weeks. The new health and local authorities will be asked to have their charters in place by April 1997.

### Unitary Authorities (School Pupils)

**Mr. Beggs:** To ask the Secretary of State for Wales for how many school pupils each of the proposed unitary authorities in Wales will be responsible.     [24582]

**Mr. Richards:** The following table shows at January 1994 the number of pupils attending LEA-maintained schools in each unitary authority area. These pupils may not be residents of the unitary authority in which their school is located.

*Number of pupils on roll at January 1994[1]*

| Unitary Authority | Part-time | Full-time | Total |
|---|---|---|---|
| Anglesey | 219 | 10,703 | 10,922 |
| Caernarfonshire and Merionethshire | 221 | 17,078 | 17,299 |
| Aberconwy and Colwyn | 774 | 11,051 | 11,825 |
| Denbighshire | 1,063 | 14,201 | 15,264 |
| Flintshire | 1,745 | 22,979 | 24,724 |
| Wrexham | 1,694 | 18,160 | 19,854 |
| Powys | 32 | 18,844 | 18,876 |
| Cardiganshire | 163 | 10,445 | 10,608 |
| Pembrokeshire | 549 | 18,451 | 19,000 |
| Carmarthenshire | 524 | 27,011 | 27,535 |
| Swansea | 3,350 | 34,261 | 37,611 |
| Neath and Port Talbot | 2,256 | 21,418 | 23,674 |
| Bridgend | 537 | 21,917 | 22,454 |
| Vale of Glamorgan | 890 | 17,087 | 17,977 |
| Rhondda, Cynon, Taff | 214 | 43,027 | 43,241 |
| Merthyr Tydfil | 701 | 10,931 | 11,632 |
| Caerphilly | 1,174 | 29,224 | 30,398 |
| Blaenau Gwent | 808 | 10,967 | 11,775 |
| Torfaen | 935 | 15,402 | 16,337 |
| Monmouthshire | 408 | 11,554 | 11,962 |
| Newport | 1,588 | 22,870 | 24,458 |
| Cardiff | 2,759 | 47,616 | 50,375 |
| Wales | 22,604 | 455,197 | 477,801 |

[1] Includes pupils on roll at all LEA-maintained nursery, primary, secondary and special schools.

## Suicides

**Mr. Martyn Jones:** To ask the Secretary of State for Wales what is the most recent available percentage suicide rate for employed 18 to 65-year-olds in Wales.    [24556]

**Mr. Richards:** Information on the number of employed people who have been recorded as having committed suicide is not available. At death registration, it is the last occupation rather than employment status of the deceased that is recorded.

## Live Sheep Exports

**Mr. Martyn Jones:** To ask the Secretary of State for Wales how many sheep were exported live from Wales in 1980, 1985, 1990 and 1994.    [24557]

**Mr. Gwilym Jones:** The number of sheep exported live from Wales in recent years are as follows:

    1980:  86,500
    1985:  18,500
    1990: 128,500
    1994: 242,000

## Abattoirs

**Mr. Martyn Jones:** To ask the Secretary of State for Wales what was the number of abattoirs in Wales in 1980, 1985, 1990 and 1994.    [24559]

**Mr Gwilym Jones:** Since the beginning of 1993, agriculture departments have been responsible for licensing fresh meat premises including abattoirs; prior to that local authorities had this responsibility. Figures for the numbers of abattoirs before 1993 are derived from records of state veterinary service visits made at the end of each year as set out in the chief veterinary officer's reports for those years. The number of abattoirs operating in Wales was 62 in 1980, 72 in 1985, and 60 in 1990. At the end of 1994, the number of abattoirs licensed by the Welsh office was 40—not 39 as previously advised to the hon. Members for North Cornwall (Mr. Tyler) and for Glanford and Scunthorpe (Mr. Morley).

## Education Funding

**Mr. Barry Jones:** To ask the Secretary of State for Wales what action he has taken to ensure increased funding for school budgets in 1996–97; and if he will make a statement.    [24850]

**Mr. Richards:** When making its public expenditure decisions for 1996–97, the Government will give careful consideration to the spending needs of unitary authorities, taking account of the views of the Welsh Consultative Council on Local Government Finance.

## Smoking

**Mr. Barry Jones:** To ask the Secretary of State for Wales what advances his anti-smoking campaigns have achieved; and if he will make a statement on specific results achieved.    [25160]

**Mr. Richards:** In Wales there has been an encouraging decrease in the level of smoking prevalence in recent years. Studies carried out by the Health Promotion Authority for Wales show that the percentage of men aged 18 to 64 smoking daily has fallen from 35 per cent. in 1985 to 27 per cent. in 1993. The equivalent change for women of the same age group was from 30 to 25 per cent.

## Countryside Council for Wales

**Mr. Wigley:** To ask the Secretary of State for Wales what consultations he held with (a) the Campaign for the Protection of Rural Wales and (b) local government in Wales, concerning his proposals for the future of the Countryside Council for Wales; and if he will make a statement.    [25005]

**Mr. Redwood:** Copies of the Countryside Council for Wales action plan were sent to the local authority associations and to the Campaign for Rural Wales.

## GP Fundholders

**Sir Wyn Roberts:** To ask the Secretary of State for Wales if he will make a statement about the payment of GP fundholder management allowances.

**Mr. Redwood:** Management allowances are paid to GP fundholders to reimburse the additional costs incurred in directly managing NHS resources on behalf of their patients. Section 15 of the NHS and Community Care Act 1990 enables fundholders to receive a sum determined in such manner and by reference to such factors as the Secretary of State may direct. However, legal advice is that payments by fundolders for the sole purpose of management expenses need to be specified within regulations. This has now been provided for under the NHS (Fundholding Practices) Amendment Regulations 1995, which came into force on 1 April 1995. Extra-statutory management allowance payments of this kind, made between 1990–91 and 1994–95—which are estimated at around £9 million—have now been authorised.

## Nuclear Waste

**Mrs. Clwyd:** To ask the Secretary of State for Wales if he will make it his policy that nuclear industrial waste will not be disposed of within (a) the boundaries of the Cynon Valley and (b) the boundaries of Mid Glamorgan.    [25025]

**Mr. Gwilym Jones:** There are no sites in the Cynon Valley or in Mid Glamorgan which are authorised by Her Majesty's inspectorate of pollution for the disposal of radioactive waste from nuclear licensed sites. The Government's overall policy in this area will be set out this summer when the conclusions to their review of radioactive waste management are published.

## Welsh Office Accommodation

**Mr. Win Griffiths:** To ask the Secretary of State for Wales, pursuant to his answer of 15 May, *Official Report*, column *101*, if he will list all the accommodation rented by the Welsh Office in Cardiff and elsewhere, indicating the percentage of use in each case and the remaining length of the lease and annual rental.    [25167]

**Mr. Redwood:** For reasons of commercial confidentiality, it is Government policy not to disclose information about rent levels for individual properties. The total amount of rent paid in 1994–95 was £4,131,761. Other information requested is given in the following table.

*Welsh Office accommodation on the Common User Estate (CUE)*

| Property | Welsh[1] Office occupation (per cent.) | Tenure | Lease expiry |
|---|---|---|---|
| Cathays Park, Crown Building (CP1) | 100.00 | Freehold | — |
| Cathays Park, New Crown Building (CP2) | 69.95 | Freehold | — |
| Government Buildings, Llanishen | 10.80 | Freehold | — |
| Caradog House, Cardiff | 5.53 | Leasehold | 28 September 2000 |
| Golate House, Cardiff | 100.00 | Leasehold | 29 September 1999 |
| Bessemer Road, Cardiff | 100.00 | Leasehold | 31 January 1999 |
| John Williams Building, Cardiff | 74.28 | Leasehold | 23 June 2000 |
| Southgate House, Cardiff | 4.85 | Leasehold | 22 September 2019 |
| Brunel House, Cardiff | 56.00 | Leasehold | 24 March 1999 |
| Ty Nant, Swansea | 2.58 | Freehold | — |
| Pontfaen Road, Lampeter | 20.97 | Freehold | — |
| Picton Terrace, Carmarthen | 53.03 | Freehold | — |
| Jobs Well Lane, Carmarthen | 100.00 | Freehold | — |
| 8 Barn Street, Haverfordwest | 43.13 | Freehold | — |
| 4 and 5 Hamilton Terrace, Milford Haven | 100.00 | Leasehold | 10 September 1998 |
| Spa Road East, Llandrindod Wells | 88.87 | Freehold | — |
| Park Street, Newtown | 16.00 | Freehold | — |
| Canal Road, Brecon | 35.81 | Freehold | — |
| Royal Welsh Pavillion Showground, Builth Wells | 100.00 | Leasehold | 31 December 2082 |
| Y Buarth, Aberystwyth | 100.00 | Leasehold | 24 December 2054 |
| Bryn Adda, Bangor | 2.20 | Freehold | — |
| Dinerth Road, Colwyn Bay | 33.99 | Freehold | — |
| New Crown Building, Ruthin | 46.35 | Freehold | — |
| Penrallt, Caernarfon | 52.00 | Freehold | — |
| Newry Street, Holyhead | 18.25 | Leasehold | 24 December 2009 |
| Arran Road, Dolgellau | 1.81 | Freehold | — |
| Chartist Tower, Newport | 1.06 | Leasehold | 23 June 1998 |
| 23 Gold Tops, Newport | 100.00 | Leasehold | 23 June 1997 |
| 14 King Street, Carmarthen | 50.96 | Freehold | — |
| Gwydyr House, Whitehall | 100.00 | Freehold | — |

[1] Represents the amount of accommodation within each of the respective CUE properties occupied by the Welsh Office. Where there is a balance of space it is not the responsibility of the Welsh Office. There is no space currently within Welsh Office occupations which is surplus to its needs.

## Cardiff Bay

**Mr. Morgan:** To ask the Secretary of State for Wales what representations he has received from the World Wide Fund for Nature concerning breaches of faith in relation to the Government's creation of alternative bird reserves to mitigate the loss of wading birds' habitat in Cardiff bay. [25282]

**Mr. Redwood:** The director of the World Wide Fund for Nature (UK) wrote to me on 22 February 1994 seeking a meeting to discuss the progress made on the Cardiff bay barrage scheme and associated bird compensation measures. A meeting involving officials from my Department, Cardiff Bay development corporation and the WWF about the Government's commitment to the undertakings given to Parliament was held on 27 June 1994.

**Mr. Morgan:** To ask the Secretary of State for Wales what further progress he has to report on the proposal to spend £5.8 million on the Gwent levels to create bird reserves to mitigate the loss of wading birds from Cardiff bay. [25269]

**Mr. Redwood:** Cardiff Bay development corporation has completed a site options study. This has been considered by a working group comprising representatives from the Countryside Council for Wales, the Royal Society for the Protection of Birds and the Land Authority for Wales. More detailed investigations are being undertaken to determine which sites present the best options. These should be completed by September.

## Drug Strategy

**Mr. Flynn:** To ask the Secretary of State for Wales what progress has been made in the drug strategy for Wales. [25171]

**Mr. Richards:** I hope to publish the Welsh drug and alcohol strategy for consultation in the next few weeks.

## Majority Shareholdings

**Mr. Byers:** To ask the Secretary of State for Wales if he will list those companies in which the holder of his office is a majority shareholder which *(a)* are currently in existence and *(b)* have been wound up in the past years. [25704]

**Mr. Redwood:** There are no such companies in either category.

## Deprivation Payments Scheme

**Mr. Morgan:** To ask the Secretary of State for Wales if he will make a statement on the amended basis for calculating the deprivation index for awarding supplementary payments to GPs in Wales; how many *(a)* GP practices and *(b)* individual GPs in each family health services authorty area qualified for supplementary payment under the deprivation payment scheme in 1994–95; and what estimate he has made of the figures for the present year. [25606]

**Mr. Redwood:** The Review Body on Doctors and Dentists Remuneration has recommended that payments under the deprivation payments scheme should be based on the 1991 census Jarman scores. The Government have accepted its recommendation, which will take effect in 1995–96 and is likely to lead to a further £1.2 million being paid to doctors in Wales, an increase of 66 per cent. This excludes the increase due to the upgrading of the payment levels per patient in each of the deprivation bands following the review body's award for 1995–96.

The number of GP practices and individual GPs with patients in deprived wards at 1 April 1994 is given in the following table:

| FHSA | GP practices | GPs |
|---|---|---|
| Clwyd | 19 | 45 |
| Dyfed | 1 | 1 |
| Gwent | 64 | 134 |
| Gwynedd | 28 | 70 |
| Mid Glamorgan | 95 | 224 |
| Powys | 6 | 22 |
| South Glamorgan | 49 | 131 |
| West Glamorgan | 43 | 111 |
| Wales | 305 | 738 |

As a result of the revision of the scheme, it is not yet possible to make a reliable estimate in respect of the present year.

### Building Process Work

**Ms Hodge:** To ask the Secretary of State for Wales for each piece of work subject to a building process under the auspices of *(a)* his Department and *(b)* agencies for which his Department is responsible (i) who the successful bidders were where work was contracted out and (ii) which contracts were won by in-house bidders in (1) 1993–94, (2) 1994–95 and (3) 1995-96. [25546]

**Mr. Redwood:** This information is not held centrally.

## TREASURY

### Medals and Decorations

**Mr. Flynn:** To ask the Chancellor of the Exchequer what was the cost of producing the conspicuous gallantry cross medal awarded to Corporal Wayne Mills; and what will be the unit cost of future medals. [25170]

**Mr. Nelson:** The Royal Mint supplied the medal under contract to the Ministry of Defence. The terms on which the Royal Mint supplyies medals to its customers are not disclosed for commercial reasons.

**Mr. Flynn:** To ask the Chancellor of the Exchequer what plans he has to bring the intrinsic financial value of medals in line with the valour honoured by their award. [25173]

**Mr. Nelson:** None.

**Mr. Flynn:** To ask the Chancellor of the Exchequer, pursuant to his answer of 24 April, *Official Report*, columns *266–67*, what are the reasons for the costs of those medals whose cost exceeds £3,000. [25181]

**Mr. Nelson:** The cost of insignia is dictated by the complexity of the design, the materials used and the labour costs.

**Mr. Flynn:** To ask the Chancellor of the Exchequer what plans he has to continue recycling the insignia of the Order of the Garter; what is the cost of recycling; and what plans he has to recycle other insignia. [25172]

**Mr. Nelson:** Current practice will continue. The insignia of the Order of the Garter is always returned on the death of a holder, renovated and reissued when another knight is appointed. Renovation costs depend upon its condition on return, but represent a significant saving over replacement by new insignia. All other insignia that are returned—for example, on promotion within the same order—are already also renovated and reissued.

### Majority Shareholdings

**Mr. Byers:** To ask the Chancellor of the Exchequer if he will list those companies in which the holder of his office is a majority shareholder which *(a)* are currently in existence and *(b)* have been wound up in the past five years. [25705]

**Mr. Nelson:** There are no companies in either category.

### Value Added Tax

**Mr. Dobson:** To ask the Chancellor of the Exchequer if he will estimate the yield from 2.5 percentage points on value added tax in each year since 1991–92, showing separately the estimated yields in respect of the United Kingdom and England. [25409]

**Mr. Heathcoat-Amory:** The estimated revenue yield from an increase of 2.5 percentage points on the standard rate of VAT—£ million—is as follows:

| | UK | England |
|---|---|---|
| 1991–92 | 5,200 | 4,400 |
| 1992–93 | 5,800 | 4,900 |
| 1993–94 | 6,200 | 5,200 |
| 1994–95 | 5,900 | 5,000 |
| 1995–96 | 6,300 | 5,300 |
| 1996–97 | 6,900 | 5,900 |

**Mr. Milburn:** To ask the Chancellor of the Exchequer what is the estimate for VAT receipts in 1995–96; and what it would be if the 1978–79 VAT regime still applied. [25194]

**Mr. Heathcoat-Amory:** The estimate for VAT receipts in 1995–96 was published in the revised 1995–96 "Financial Statement and Budget Report". Any attempt to estimate under the 1978–79 VAT regime would require the revisiting not only of the legislation as it then stood, but the reinterpretation of many changes in practice since that time. I do not think this would be a meaningful exercise.

### Biodiesel Fuels (Excise Duty)

**Mr. Soley:** To ask the Chancellor of the Exchequer what plans he has to implement section 11 of the Finance Act 1993 dealing with excise duty on biodiesel fuels. [23713]

**Mr. Heathcoat-Amory:** Section 11 of the Finance Act 1993 provides for excise duty to be charged on fuel substitutes, including biofuels. The necessary commencement order is currently being drafted. The intention is that the order will be made and laid before

Parliament in accordance with negative procedures, and be subject to the scrutiny of the Statutory Instruments Committee. It is expected to take effect later this year.

### Tax Fraud

**Mr. Frank Cook:** To ask the Chancellor of the Exchequer what was the estimated amount of tax fraud in each year since 1979. [23673]

**Sir George Young:** No official estimates have been made, but the annual yield from the Inland Revenue's counter-evasion and anti-avoidance work rose from £137.9 million in 1979–80 to £1,609.6 million in 1993–94.

A significant part of this arises from improved targeting of cases and more effective working methods.

### Charitable Donations

**Mr. Robert Ainsworth:** To ask the Chancellor of the Exchequer what investigations the Inland Revenue have made into the charitable donations made by *(a)* the Porter Foundation, *(b)* G G M Newton Charitable Trust, *(c)* Robert McAlpine Ltd., *(d)* the liquidators of London and Paris Property Group plc., *(e)* Wimpey Group Services Ltd., *(f)* Regalian Properties plc and *(g)* Hammerson Group Management Ltd. to the Foundation for Business Responsibilities; what conclusions these have drawn; and what further investigations are planned. [24701]

**Sir George Young:** The tax affairs of all charities, companies and trusts, like those of all taxpayers, are protected by strict rules of confidentiality. The Inland Revenue is unable to provide any information which might breach these rules.

### Privatisation

**Mr. Hardy:** To ask the Chancellor of the Exchequer what is the total of the sums paid or which are due to be paid to financial institutions or companies in respect of their services or advice in regard to those privatisations which have been completed or partially completed since 1979 or which are in preparation or under consideration at this time; and what payments have been or are expected to be paid to the seven businesses or institutions which have received the largest share of these payments. [24200]

**Sir George Young:** For the sale costs of privatisations that have been completed, I refer the hon. Member to the reply I gave at 27 April 1995, *Official Report,* column *646.* Details of disaggregated costs can be found in my replies of 23 March 1995, *Official Report,* column *287,* and 16 May 1995, *Official Report,* column *108.* Sale costs for those privatisations that have yet to be completed will be announced in the normal manner following the completion of each sale. Details of the firms which have been the seven largest recipients of privatisation sale fees are not held centrally and could be obtained only at disproportionate cost.

**Mr. Milburn:** To ask the Chancellor of the Exchequer what will be the cumulative total for privatisation receipts from 1979–80 to 1995–96 in 1995–96 prices. [25196]

**Sir George Young:** Privatisation proceeds from 1979–80 to 1995–96 are expected to total £82.4 billion in 1995–96 prices.

### Forged Currency

**Mr. French:** To ask the Chancellor of the Exchequer what estimate he has made of the fact value of forged currency in currency in circulation in the form of *(a)* notes and *(b)* coinage. [24715]

**Mr Nelson:** The Bank of England is not in a position to provide a meaningful estimate of the number of counterfeit notes in circulation. A record is maintained of the number which are received from circulation but the Bank, in common with most note-issuing authorities, does not publish details of the counterfeits it receives. However, despite an increase in counterfeiting over the last few years, counterfeit notes detected still represent only a fraction of 1 per cent. of the total notes in circulation.

The Royal Mint is not in a position to provide an estimate of the number of counterfeit coins in circulation.

### Improper Financial Advice (Compensation)

**Sir David Steel:** To ask the Chancellor of the Exchequer (1) if he will make a statement on the implications for compensation of investors who have been improperly advised by a firm of its takeover by another; [24752]

(2) what plans he has for compensation to be paid to investors who have been wrongly advised by financial advisers before the coming into force of the Financial Services Act 1986. [24731]

**Mr. Nelson:** Investors who were given advice which breaches the rules of a regulator under the Financial Services Act 1986 once the relevant provisions of the Act came into force and who suffer loss as a result may be entitled to compensation. This compensation comes either from the firm concerned, or from the investors compensation scheme if the firm defaults. In either case, compensation payments are not affected by any takeover.

Compensation for wrong advice given before the Financial Services Act came into force is a private matter between the investor and the firm concerned. The Government do not intend to provide for compensation to be paid in respect of loss suffered as a result of bad advice given before the relevant provision of the Act came into force.

### Long-term Investment

**Mr. Sheerman:** To ask the Chancellor of the Exchequer what recent discussions he has had with the Governor of the Bank of England regarding long-term investment in British industry. [25021]

**Mr. Nelson:** My right hon. and learned Friend and I meet regularly with the Governor to discuss the prospects for inflation and the current state of the economy, including long-term investment in British industry. Recent figures for investment show some very encouraging signs. For example, in the fourth quarter of 1994, manufacturing investment in plant and machinery was over 10 per cent. up on a year earlier.

### Retail Prices Index

**Mr. Milburn:** To ask the Chancellor of the Exchequer if he will provide forecasts of the percentage change on the previous financial year for the retail prices index excluding and including mortgage interest payments for 1994–95 and 1995–96. [25198]

**Mr. Nelson:** The November "Financial Statement and Budget Report" forecast that underlying inflation would be $2\frac{1}{4}$ per cent. in the second quarter of 1995 and $2\frac{1}{2}$ per cent. both in the fourth quarter of 1995 and in the second quarter of 1996. These forecasts will be updated in the summer economic forecast.

### Oil and Gas Revenues

**Mr. Milburn:** To ask the Chancellor of the Exchequer what will be the cumulative total for Government revenues from oil and gas production from 1979–80 to 1995–96 expressed in 1995–96 prices. [25195]

**Sir George Young:** Total revenues to the Exchequer from North sea oil and gas production from 1979–80 to 1995–96, at 1995–96 prices, are expected to be £128 billion.

### Currency Values

**Mr. Austin Mitchell:** To ask the Chancellor of the Exchequer if he will list the tests which he applies in considering whether a currency is overvalued. [25476]

**Mr. Nelson:** The values of currencies are determined in foreign exchange markets. The Government do not have a target for sterling's exchange rate.

### Procurement Strategy

**Mr. Matthew Banks:** To ask the Chancellor of the Exchequer if he will publish a statement on the Government's procurement strategy. [25927]

**Mr. Kenneth Clarke:** I am today presenting to Parliament a White Paper entitled "Setting New Standards: A Strategy for Government Procurement", Cm 2840. Copies of the White Paper are being placed in the Libraries of both Houses.

With the development of the Government's policies for private finance, market testing, contracting out and internal markets, Departments are doing more of their business than ever before through procurement as against in-house provision. The annual spend is now about £40 billion a year and, in addition, purchasing authorities in the national health service internal market spend more than £20 billion. These policies have brought immense benefits to the country. Their full potential has still to be realised. The more procurement there is, the more important it becomes that Government Departments should make a first-class job of it. The Government owe nothing less to citizens, taxpayers and suppliers. Ten years have passed since the Government's first major statement on procurement strategy, in 1984. That statement, which came to be known as the Government's purchasing initiative, was an excellent beginning but much has happened since then. The Government now need a new strategy to carry it forward for the next 10 years and beyond. "Setting New Standards" provides this strategy. Key points from the strategy include:

> A clear objective throughout Government, and at all levels of management, to achieve world-class standards in procurement.
> A broader interpretation of procurement to cover all non-pay, non-transfer expenditure.
> A continuing emphasis on fair competition, as being the cornerstone of good procurement, coupled with constructive co-operation between customers and suppliers.

> Emphasis on integrated procurement processes focused on whole-life costs and benefits, non-short-term lowest price, and on intelligent management of risks.
> A step change in professionalism and skill development among officials with procurement responsibilities.
> A clear pinning of responsibility on contract managers and project sponsors, supported by multi-disciplinary teams.
> An agenda for benchmarking of processes and performance to world standards.
> A new statement of good practice designed to promote fair competition, constructive co-operation between customers and suppliers, and world-class suppliers.

The objectives of Government procurement are to achieve best value for taxpayers' money and to increase the competitiveness of their suppliers. The strategy set out in "Setting New Standards" is therefore an essential part of the Government's commitment to improved competitiveness, described in "Competitiveness: Forging Ahead", Cm 2867, which my right hon. Friend the President of the Board of Trade is publishing today.

### Civil Service Appointments

**Mr. Ainger:** To ask the Chancellor of the Exchequer how many civil service appointments were made to administrative assistant and administrative officer posts in his Department and the agencies for which he is accountable in each quarter from September 1993 until April 1995. [21777]

**Mr. Nelson** *[holding answer 1 May 1995]:* The information for the Treasury and the Chancellor of the Exchequer's four agencies is as follows:

*HM Treasury*

| | Administrative assistant | | Administrative officer | |
| | Permanent | Casual | Permanent | Casual |
|---|---|---|---|---|
| Q4 1993 | 3 | 6 | 0 | 4 |
| Q1 1994 | 1 | 6 | 0 | 3 |
| Q2 1994 | 1 | 0 | 0 | 2 |
| Q3 1994 | 6 | 1 | ¹1 | 3 |
| Q4 1994 | 0 | 7 | 0 | 2 |
| Q1 1995 | 0 | 6 | 0 | 0 |
| Total (52) | 11 | 26 | 1 | 14 |

*Notes:*
Dates refer to date of taking up post.
¹ Transferred from MOD.

*Central Statistical Office*

| | Administrative assistant | | Administrative officer | |
| | Permanent | Casual | Permanent | Casual |
|---|---|---|---|---|
| Q4 1993 | 0 | 8 | 3 | ¹11 |
| Q1 1994 | 0 | 26 | 3 | ¹18 |
| Q2 1994 | 0 | 11 | ˙2 | ¹25 |
| Q3 1994 | ˙1 | 13 | 1 | ¹25 |
| Q4 1994 | 0 | 5 | ˙1 | ¹19 |
| Q1 1995 | 0 | 4 | ˙1 | ¹23 |
| Total (200) | 1 | 67 | 1 | 121 |

*Notes:*
Dates refer to date of taking up post.
Includes ¹ 6 fixed-term appointments (1993).
  ˙ 4 transfers (1994).
  ¹ 18 fixed-term appointments (1994).
  ˙ 1 transfer (1995).
  ¹ 17 fixed-term appointments (1995).

### Royal Mint

| | Administrative assistant Permanent | Casual | Administrative officer Permanent | Casual |
|---|---|---|---|---|
| Q4 1993 | [1]4 | 1 | 0 | 3 |
| Q1 1994 | 0 | [1]5 | 0 | 1 |
| Q2 1994 | 0 | 1 | 0 | 4 |
| Q3 1994[2] | 0 | 0 | 3 | 1 |
| Q4 1994[2] | 0 | 1 | 0 | [1]1 |
| Q1 1995[2] | 0 | 6 | 2 | [1]5 |
| Total (38) | 4 | 14 | 5 | 15 |

*Notes:*

Dates refer to date of taking up post.

[1]Includes 1 transfer, 2 part-time AA (1993)
         1 part-time AA/1 part-time AO (1994)
         1 part-time AO (1995)

[2]From 1 August 1994 recruitment is to Royal Mint equivalent grades.

### Paymaster

| | Administrative assistant Permanent | Casual | Administrative officer Permanent | Casual |
|---|---|---|---|---|
| Q4 1993 | 0 | 2.5 | 0 | 0.5 |
| Q1 1994 | 0 | 3[1] | 0 | 3[1] |
| Q2 1994 | 0 | 1[1] | 0 | 1 |
| Q3 1994 | 0 | 24 | 0 | 0 |
| Q4 1994 | 0 | 21[1] | 0 | 2 |
| Q1 1995[2] | 0 | 20.5[1] | 0 | 0 |
| Total (78.5) | 0 | 72 | 0 | 6.5 |

*Notes:*

Dates refer to date of taking up post.

[1]Includes 13 fee paid AA/3 fee paid AO/1 short notice AA contract (1994)
        3 fee-paid AA (1995).

### Valuation Office

| | Administrative assistant Permanent | Casual | Administrative officer Permanent | Casual |
|---|---|---|---|---|
| Q4 1993 | 34 | 172 | 1 | 6 |
| Q1 1994 | 11 | [1]157 | 0 | [1]11 |
| Q2 1994 | 18 | [1]508 | 0 | [3]2 |
| Q3 1994 | 6 | [1]170 | 0 | [1]13 |
| Q4 1994 | 7 | [1]146 | 0 | [1]18 |
| Q1 1995 | 7 | [1]204 | 2 | [1]10 |
| Total (1,533) | 83 | 1,357 | 3 | 90 |

*Notes:*

Dates refer to date of taking up post.

[1]Includes  465  fixed-term  appointment  AA/31  fixed-term appointment AO (1994).
         47   fixed-term  appointment  AA/4  fixed-term appointment AO (1995).

## Income Tax

**Mr. Frank Field:** To ask the Chancellor of the Exchequer if he will publish estimates of the revenue cost of (i) allowances set against income tax and (ii) reliefs set against income tax for *(a)* the top 1 per cent. of taxpayers, *(b)* the top 5 per cent., *(c)* the top 10 per cent., *(d)* the top 25 per cent., *(e)* the top 50 per cent., *(f)* the top 70 per cent. and *(g)* all taxpayers. [23348]

**Sir George Young** *[holding answer 9 May 1995]:* Estimated full-year revenue costs at 1995–96 income levels are in the table. Separate costings have been produced for allowances and reliefs. The combined cost of both allowances and reliefs would be greater than the sum of the individual figures. Since 1979, income tax rates have been lowered and real incomes have increased by 40 per cent.

| | Cost of Allowances and Reliefs Allowances £ billion | Reliefs £ billion |
|---|---|---|
| Group of taxpayers | | |
| Top 1 per cent. | 0.4 | 0.7 |
| Top 5 per cent. | 2.1 | 1.9 |
| Top 10 per cent | 4.1 | 2.9 |
| Top 25 per cent. | 8.3 | 4.6 |
| Top 50 per cent. | 15.0 | 6.5 |
| Top 70 per cent. | 20.3 | 7.3 |
| All taxpayers | 27.8 | 7.7 |

**Mr. Frank Field:** To ask the Chancellor of the Exchequer if he will publish a table showing the increase in income tax in 1995–96 compared with the 1992–93 indexed regime broken down into the top 1 per cent., top 5 per cent., top 10 per cent., top 50 per cent. and bottom 50 per cent., showing the total increase and the average loss. [23351]

**Sir George Young** *[holding answer 9 May 1995]:* Provisional estimates are given in the table. These figures reflect a larger working population and the fact that more people are better off—real incomes have grown by 40 per cent. since 1979—both largely due to economic growth.

*Total increase and average increase in 1995–96 compared with 1992–93 indexed regime.*

| Group of taxpayers | Total increase in income tax £ million | Average increase in income tax £ |
|---|---|---|
| Top 1 per cent. | 190 | 740 |
| Top 5 per cent. | 910 | 710 |
| Top 10 per cent. | 1,540 | 600 |
| Top 50 per cent. | 3,390 | 260 |
| Bottom 50 per cent. | 1,120 | 90 |

**Mr. Frank Field:** To ask the Chancellor of the Exchequer if he will update his answer to the hon. Member for Hartlepool (Mr. Mandelson), of 1 July 1993, *Official Report,* columns *598-600,* providing estimates for 1995–96 and 1996–97 of the revenue yield of introducing upper limits for tax allowances and reliefs, and the number of individuals affected. [23522]

**Sir George Young** *[holding answer 9 May 1995]:* Since the married couple's allowance and mortgage interest relief are now given at a rate of 15 per cent., the terms of the original question are no longer meaningful.

**Mr. Frank Field:** To ask the Chancellor of the Exchequer if he will estimate, on the same basis as in his answer to the hon. Member for Hartlepool (Mr. Mandelson) of 30 November 1993, *Official Report,* columns *385-86, (a)* the total income, earned and unearned, *(b)* the total national insurance contributions and *(c)* the total income tax paid by (i) the top 1 per cent., (ii) the top 5 per cent., (iii) the top 10 per cent., (iv) the bottom 50 per cent. and (v) all taxpayers in 1983–84, 1985–86, 1987–88, 1988–89 and 1995–96. [24370]

**Sir George Young** [*holding answer 16 May 1995*]: Final estimates for 1992–93 and provisional estimates for 1993–94 to 1995–96 based on a projection of the 1992–93 survey of personal incomes are given in the table. The estimates of total income relate to income subject to tax and exclude non-taxable income such as certain social security benefits. These figures reflect a larger working population and the fact that more people are better off—real incomes have grown by 40 per cent. since 1979—both largely due to economic growth.

Analyses for the earlier years are not available, but extensive analyses of the distribution of income and income tax are published as follows:

| Year | Publication |
|------|-------------|
| 1983–84 | The Survey of Personal Incomes 1983–84 |
| 1984–85 | The Survey of Personal Incomes 1984–85 |
| 1985–86 | Inland Revenue Statistics 1988 |
| 1986–87 | Inland Revenue Statistics 1989 |
| 1987–88 | Inland Revenue Statistics 1990 |
| 1988–89 | Inland Revenue Statistics 1991 |

| Quantile group of taxpayers<br>Per cent. | Total income<br>£ million | Income tax liability<br>£ million | Employees' and self-employed national insurance contributions liability<br>£ million |
|---|---|---|---|
| *1992–93* | | | |
| Top 1 | 29,300 | 9,500 | 300 |
| Top 5 | 72,000 | 19,800 | 1,600 |
| Top 10 | 108,100 | 26,500 | 3,100 |
| Bottom 50 | 96,900 | 8,000 | 4,000 |
| All taxpayers | 373,700 | 60,700 | 16,300 |
| *1993–94* | | | |
| Top 1 | 30,000 | 9,800 | 300 |
| Top 5 | 74,300 | 20,500 | 1,700 |
| Top 10 | 111,700 | 27,600 | 3,400 |
| Bottom 50 | 97,300 | 8,200 | 3,900 |
| All taxpayers | 382,800 | 63,200 | 17,200 |
| *1994–95* | | | |
| Top 1 | 31,800 | 10,700 | 400 |
| Top 5 | 78,300 | 22,600 | 1,900 |
| Top 10 | 117,500 | 30,400 | 3,900 |
| Bottom 50 | 99,400 | 9,000 | 4,400 |
| All taxpayers | 398,500 | 69,000 | 19,900 |
| *1995–96* | | | |
| Top 1 | 33,700 | 11,400 | 400 |
| Top 5 | 82,700 | 24,100 | 2,000 |
| Top 10 | 124,400 | 32,700 | 4,100 |
| Bottom 50 | 104,300 | 9,800 | 4,500 |
| All taxpayers | 420,900 | 74,600 | 20,800 |

### Gross Domestic Product

**Mr. Frank Field:** To ask the Chancellor of the Exchequer what estimate he has of the total gross domestic product for 2000–01. [25676]

**Mr. Aitken:** For projections of growth in total gross domestic product up to 1999–2000, I refer the hon. Member to the "Financial Statement and Budget Report 1995–96", table 3A.2, a copy of which can be found in the House Library.

### PA Consulting Group

**Mr. Morgan:** To ask the Chancellor of the Exchequer what guidelines he has issued to other Government Departments in relation to the use of PA Consulting Group, pending the outcome of the tax compliance inquiries by the special compliance office of the Inland Revenue; and if he will make a statement. [23869]

**Sir George Young** [*holding answer 15 May 1995*]: The tax affairs of this company are, like those of all taxpayers, protected by strict rules of confidentiality.

## SCOTLAND

### Agricultural Colleges

**Mr. McMaster:** To ask the Secretary of State for Scotland if he will make a statement on the development, funding and future of the Scottish agricultural colleges. [24085]

**Sir Hector Monro:** The three former Scottish agricultural colleges at Aberdeen, Edinburgh and Auchincruive were merged into a single Scottish Agricultural College in 1990. The administrative and financial relationship between the college and the Scottish Office Agriculture and Fisheries Department is set out in a memorandum of understanding, which recognises that the board of the college is solely responsible for the conduct of its business. It also places a requirement on the college, in line with the Government's policy, to find an increasing proportion of its funding from sources other than SOAFD, and I have no plans to change the present policy. In 1995–96 the grant in aid from SOAFD to the college will be £19.7 million.

## Drug Dealers

**Mr. McMaster:** To ask the Secretary of State for Scotland what powers are available to local authorities, housing associations, housing co-operatives and the private rented sector to evict people convicted of drug dealing and drug-related offences; what plans has he to introduce further measures; and if he will make a statement. [24093]

**Lord James Douglas-Hamilton:** I refer the hon. Member to the answer I gave to him on 8 March 1995, *Official Report*, column 227.

I have no plans to introduce further measures specifically in relation to people convicted of drug dealing and drug-related offences, but I am issuing a consultation paper to local authorities and other bodies seeking their views on the introduction of probationary tenancies to help to deal with anti-social behaviour more generally.

**Mr. McMaster:** To ask the Secretary of State for Scotland (1) what measures he plans to introduce to support the chief constable and officers of Strathclyde police in their efforts to bring drug dealers, money lenders and professional intimidators to justice; and if he will make a statement; [24133]

(2) what further measures he plans to deal with drug dealing and illegal money lending; what plans he has to introduce any pilot measures in the Paisley area; and if he will make a statement. [24058]

**Lord James Douglas-Hamilton:** Decisions about tackling drug dealing and illegal money lending and about bringing professional intimidators to justice are operational matters for the police. My right hon. Friend will continue to seek to ensure that the police have adequate resources and equipment to tackle the full range of policing requirements for which they have responsibility.

## Braille Ballot Papers

**Mr. McMaster:** To ask the Secretary of State for Scotland what plans he has to introduce Braille ballot papers for local elections in Scotland. [24109]

**Lord James Douglas-Hamilton:** There are no plans to do so.

## Buses

**Mr. McMaster:** To ask the Secretary of State for Scotland what plans he has to introduce measures to ensure that deregulated bus companies are required to provide local services until at least 10 pm; and if he will make a statement. [24057]

**Lord James Douglas-Hamilton:** My right hon. Friend has no plans to introduce measures to regulate service provision. It is for bus operators to decide, on the basis of commercial viability, which services will be provided. Local authorities may, however, subsidise routes which

they consider are socially necessary, including off-peak and late-night services.

**Mr. McMaster:** To ask the Secretary of State for Scotland what assessment he has made of the impact of deregulated bus services in Scotland, particularly in relation to evening and late-night services; and if he will make a statement. [24056]

**Lord James Douglas-Hamilton:** An independent study of the effect of privatisation and deregulation on the former Scottish Bus Group companies was commissioned by the Scottish Office from the transport operations research group at Newcastle university. The TORG report was published in 1993 and concluded that deregulation of the bus industry in Scotland has stimulated competition, increased efficiency and made more cost-effective the provision of socially necessary services, including off-peak and late-night services.

## Local Government Reorganisation

**Mr. McMaster:** To ask the Secretary of State for Scotland what is his latest assessment of the impact that the provisions of the Local Government (Scotland) Act 1994 will have on the occupation of office buildings in each Scottish region post-1996; what assessment he has made of the effect on property prices in each region; and if he will make a statement. [24061]

**Mr. Kynoch:** My right hon. Friend will be issuing shortly for comment a draft property transfer order which will set down broad guidelines for the transfer of property to the new councils. Only when the councils work through that process will it be possible for them to assess the extent of surplus property and possible ramifications for the property market.

**Mr. McMaster:** To ask the Secretary of State for Scotland what estimate he has made of compulsory redundancies during the transition from the current local government structure in Scotland to the new unitary authorities; and if he will make a statement. [24094]

**Mr. Kynoch:** The Government have not made forecasts about the number of compulsory redundancies arising from the move to single-tier councils. Decisions on management of the local authority work force and new staffing structures will be the responsibility of the new councils, but the Government hope that most, if not all, changes can be managed by means of early retirements, voluntary severance and the retraining of existing employees.

**Mr. McMaster:** To ask the Secretary of State for Scotland how many *(a)* local authority, *(b)* Scottish Homes, *(c)* housing association, *(d)* housing co-operative, *(e)* private sector rented and *(f)* owner-occupied homes, are contained within the boundaries of (i) Renfrew district and (ii) Eastwood district; and how many will be contained within the boundaries of the new unitary authorities of (1) Renfrewshire and (2) East Renfrewshire, based upon current figures. [24095]

**Lord James Douglas-Hamilton:** The available information is set out in the table:

|  | Local Authority[1] | Scottish Homes[2] | Housing Associations[3] | Housing Co-operative[3] | Private Rented[4] | Owner Occupied[4] |
|---|---|---|---|---|---|---|
| (i) Renfrew | 27,524 | 4,391 | 2,262 | 0 | 2,088 | 42,221 |
| (ii) Eastwood | 1,602 | 10 | 95 | 0 | 654 | 20,475 |

| | Local Authority[1] | Scottish Homes[2] | Housing Associations[3] | Housing Co-operative[3] | Private Rented[4] | Owner Occupied[4] |
|---|---|---|---|---|---|---|
| (1) Renfrewshire | 24,410 | 3,339 | 2,020 | 0 | 1,967 | 36,920 |
| (2) East Renfrewshire | 4,716 | 1,062 | 337 | 0 | 775 | 25,776 |

*Notes:*
[1] Source: The Scottish Office. Estimates at 30 September 1995.
[2] Source: Scottish Homes. Figures at 1 May 1995. Estimates for Renfrewshire and East Renfrewshire calculated using breakdown in 1991 census of population.
[3] Source: Scottish Homes. Figures at 31 March 1995. Estimates for Renfrewshire and East Renfrewshire calculated using breakdown in 1991 census of population.
[4] Estimates based on 1991 census of population.

**Mr. McMaster:** To ask the Secretary of State for Scotland what is his latest estimate of the number of job losses created by the provisions of the Local Government (Scotland) Act 1994; and if he will make a statement.

[24098]

**Mr. Kynoch:** The Government have estimated that the move to single-tier local authorities will result in a reduction in posts in a range between 220 and 1,800. The eventual number of jobs in the unitary councils will, however, depend on decisions taken by them in the light of the services to be provided.

### Railway Stations (Disabled Access)

**Mr. McMaster:** To ask the Secretary of State for Scotland when he next plans to meet representatives of ScotRail, Railtrack and Strathclyde regional council to discuss the provision of disabled access to (a) Johnstone High station, (b) Gilmour Street station in Paisley and (c) Milliken Park station in Johnstone; and if he will make a statement. [24121]

**Lord James Douglas-Hamilton:** My right hon. Friend has no plans to meet representatives of the organisations listed to discuss the specific issue of disabled access to stations in Paisley and Johnstone. I understand however that plans have been advanced to provide disabled access to Gilmour Street station and further improvements at Milliken Park. Johnstone High station already has disabled access facilities.

### Myalgic Encephalomyelitis

**Mr. McMaster:** To ask the Secretary of State for Scotland what guidance he has issued to health boards in Scotland relating to the diagnosis, recognition and treatment of myalgic encephalomyelitis; and if he will make a statement. [24075]

**Lord James Douglas-Hamilton:** As a matter of principle, the Government do not issue clinical guidance, since that is the responsibility of the medical profession.

**Mr. McMaster:** To ask the Secretary of State for Scotland if he will support the campaign to make the people of Scotland more aware of myalgic encephalomyelitis, if he will increase official recognition of the disease; and if he will make a statement. [24099]

**Lord James Douglas-Hamilton:** We recognise myalgic encephalomyelitis as a potentially debilitating and distressing complex, and would support informed efforts to raise awareness of the condition, which is increasingly being referred to as chronic fatigue syndrome.

We have awarded the ME Association a three-year core grant under the National Health Service (Scotland) Act

1978. One of the association's main aims is to increase public awareness of the condition.

### Paisley Pattern Design

**Mr. McMaster:** To ask the Secretary of State for Scotland when he next plans to meet the chairman of Scottish Enterprise to discuss the potential of the Paisley pattern design in the economic regeneration of Renfrewshire; and if he will make a statement. [24135]

**Mr. Kynoch:** My right hon. Friend meets the chairman of Scottish Enterprise regularly to discuss a range of issues.

Local economic initiatives generally fall to be pursued by the local enterprise companies. While my right hon. Friend is aware of the planned initiative by Renfrewshire Enterprise and Renfrew district council to promote for economic development purposes the link between the Paisley pattern design and the town of Paisley, he has no plans at present to discuss these with the chairman of Scottish Enterprise.

### Construction Industry

**Mr. Spellar:** To ask the Secretary of State for Scotland what policy his Department has put to the working groups on the Latham report as to the desirability of a single exclusive register for public sector work. [24357]

**Lord James Douglas-Hamilton:** The Scottish Office Environment Department has expressed no policy view to the working groups as to the desirability of an exclusive register. It is participating in the Capita Management Consultancy Ltd. study and will consider the results before reaching conclusions.

### Flood Prevention

**Mr. McMaster:** To ask the Secretary of State for Scotland when he will introduce a flood prevention Bill for Scotland. [24067]

**Sir Hector Monro:** There are no plans to introduce such a Bill. The powers available to local authorities under the Flood Prevention (Scotland) Act 1961 are already sufficient to enable authorities to act in the public interest.

### Johnstone

**Mr. McMaster:** To ask the Secretary of State for Scotland if he will visit Johnstone to assess the success of the multi-agency investment in Houston square in the town's main shopping centre; if he will also visit derelict buildings in high street, Johnstone, to assess how this multi-agency approach to investment could be extended; and if he will make a statement. [24071]

**Mr. Kynoch:** My right hon. Friend has no immediate plans to visit Johnstone. He is aware, however, of the Houston square project in Johnstone which is due to be completed shortly and has been financed by Renfrewshire Enterprise, Renfrew district council and the European Commission. The need for further investment in Johnstone is, in the first instance, a matter for the local agencies concerned.

### Law Reform

**Mr. McMaster:** To ask the Secretary of State for Scotland when he will introduce a bill which brings forward further measures to outlaw and punish *(a)* illegal intimidation and harassing of potential witnesses, *(b)* illegal possession of shotguns, *(c)* illicit drugs dealing and *(d)* illegal money lending.    [24131]

**Lord James Douglas-Hamilton:** My right hon. Friend has no plans to introduce such a Bill.

A combination of Scots common law offences and a wide range of statutory measures ensures that all these activities are already illegal. The maximum penalties available for these common law and statutory offences enable the courts to punish severely those who are convicted of serious offences.

### Illegal Money Lending

**Mr. McMaster:** To ask the Secretary of State for Scotland, what are the maximum penalties for those convicted of illegal money lending; what plans he has to stiffen the maximum sentences; and if he will make a statement.    [24091]

**Lord James Douglas-Hamilton:** The penalties would depend upon the specific charges brought and proved and whether the case was prosecuted summarily or on indictment. These are matters for my right hon. and learned Friend the Lord Advocate.

### Solicitor-General for Scotland

**Mr. McMaster:** To ask the Secretary of State for Scotland what parliamentary facilities are available to a Solicitor-General for Scotland who is not a member of either House of Parliament; if a holder of this position in such circumstances benefits from the use of a ministerial car; what is his annual salary; how it relates to ministerial salaries, how it is voted by each House; and if he will make a statement.    [24115]

**Lord James Douglas-Hamilton:** The privileges accorded to the Solicitor-General for Scotland, when not a member of the House of Commons, are as follows:

*(a)* Access to the Members' Lobby

*(b)* Admission to a seat under the Gallery

*(c)* Access to:

    (i) The Strangers Dining Room

    (ii) The Churchill Room

    (iii) The Strangers' Bar;

A holder of this position has the use of a ministerial car shared with the Lord Advocate.

The salary of the Solicitor-General for Scotland with effect from 1 January 1995 is £47,697. It is a ministerial salary which is voted as part of the total expenditure of the Crown Office, Procurator Fiscal Service and Lord Advocate's Department.

**Mr. McMaster:** To ask the Secretary of State for Scotland if he will give the *(a)* name and *(b)* period of

office of Solicitors-General for Scotland since 1965 who have been members of neither House of Parliament; and if he will make a statement.    [24114]

**Lord James Douglas-Hamilton:** The information is as follows:

| Name | Period for which Solicitor-General not a member of either House |
|---|---|
| Henry Stephen Wilson | 1965–67 |
| Ewan George Francis Stewart | 1967–70 |
| David William Robert Brand | 1970–72 |
| William Ian Stewart | 1972–74 |
| John Herbert McCluskey | 1974–76 |
| Peter Lovat Fraser | 1987–89 |
| Alan Ferguson Rodger | 1989–92 |
| Thomas Cordner Dawson | 1992–95 |
| Donald Sage Mackay | 1995– |

### Ombudsman

**Mr. McMaster:** To ask the Secretary of State for Scotland how hon. Members and individual members of the public should refer cases involving Scottish Homes and housing associations for consideration by the appropriate ombudsman.    [24078]

**Lord James Douglas-Hamilton:** Details of how hon. Members and individual members of the public refer cases to the parliamentary ombudsman, the local government ombudsman and the housing association ombudsman are set out in information leaflets which give guidance on the procedure to be followed when lodging complaints, including those against Scottish Homes and housing associations. Copies of these leaflets are available in the House of Commons Library.

### Windyhill Farm, Elderslie

**Mr. McMaster:** To ask the Secretary of State for Scotland what is the current position on the proposal by Scottish Aggregates to turn Windyhill farm, Elderslie into a quarry; and if he will make a statement.    [24086]

**Mr. Kynoch:** The Reporter is presently considering comments received from parties in regard to part 1 of her report containing the summary of evidence and her findings of fact. The revised part 1 will shortly be re-circulated to parties. Thereafter, the Reporter will complete her report with recommendations and submit it to my right hon. Friend. A decision on this application is expected in late summer.

### Polling Station Ramps

**Mr. McMaster:** To ask the Secretary of State for Scotland what is his latest estimate of the amount expended in the 1995 local elections in Scotland on the provision of temporary ramps for access to polling stations; what assessment was made of the comparative cost and cost benefit of providing permanent ramps instead; and if he will make a statement.    [24110]

**Lord James Douglas-Hamilton:** Grants are not made towards the cost of temporary ramps for use at local government elections. However, grants are available towards the cost of temporary ramps to be used at parliamentary and European parliamentary elections. A total of £11,914 has been paid in the last three financial years. Temporary ramps purchased for parliamentary and European parliamentary elections can be made available for local government elections and for other purposes by arrangement with the returning officer. Grants are not available towards the cost of building permanent ramps.

### Foxes

**Mr. McMaster:** To ask the Secretary of State for Scotland how many fox destruction clubs or societies are registered in Scotland; what is the level of assistance they currently receive; what guidelines he issues on how these societies destroy foxes; what guidelines he has issued on the number of foxes to be destroyed; how the fox population is assessed; and if he will make a statement.
[24126]

**Sir Hector Monro:** Grants are paid to 29 societies or clubs throughout Scotland to meet 50 per cent. of the approved cost of carrying out systematic fox control within a clearly defined area of adequate size. Grants amounting to £68,000 were paid in 1994–95. Records are not kept of clubs not in receipt of grant.

Foxes may be killed legally by shooting, snaring or cage trapping followed by humane dispatch. The Scottish Office Agriculture and Fisheries Department does not advise on the number of foxes to be destroyed. The fox is not an endangered species and there is no reason to engage in regular surveys.

### Scottish Council for Spastics Centre

**Mr. McMaster:** To ask the Secretary of State for Scotland if he will visit the residential centre operated by the Scottish Council for Spastics at Wallace court in Elderslie to assess the value of such initiatives. [24134]

**Lord James Douglas-Hamilton:** My right hon. Friend has no plans to visit the centre. However, the Government fully recognise the contribution made by the council in meeting the care needs of people with cerebral palsy and other disabled people with similar needs.

### Argyll and Clyde Health Board

**Mr. McMaster:** To ask the Secretary of State for Scotland how many complaints were received by Argyll and Clyde health board in each year since 1980 until the latest year for which figures are available; and if he will make a statement. [24159]

**Lord James Douglas-Hamilton:** This information is not available for the full period requested. Information about complaints has been collected centrally since January 1993. The number of complaints received by Argyll and Clyde health board for the period 1 January 1993 to 31 March 1994 and the nine months to 31 December 1994 is as follows:

1 January 1993—31 March 1994: 263
1 April 1994—31 December 1994: 75

**Mr. McMaster:** To ask the Secretary of State for Scotland which facilities, units and buildings within the area of Argyll and Clyde health board have not been transferred to NHS trusts; which of these are seeking, or are likely to seek, trust status within the next year; and if he will make a statement. [24124]

**Lord James Douglas-Hamilton:** There are no remaining facilities which the Argyll and Clyde health board either requires or intends to transfer to NHS trusts in its area.

### Play Areas (Safety Surfacing)

**Mr. McMaster:** To ask the Secretary of State for Scotland what guidelines he has issued to local authorities to encourage the provision of safety surfacing on play areas; what special financial provision he has made available to local authorities to encourage and enable them to meet this need; and if he will make a statement. [24090]

**Mr. Kynoch:** My right hon. Friend has not issued any guidelines on the provision of safety surfacing for play areas. However, local authorities should be aware of the new British standard on impact-absorbing playground surfaces which came into effect on 31 August 1989. On the question of special financial provision, there are no plans to target resources in this way. Local authorities have complete freedom to determine their own priorities from within the total resources available to them. It is therefore for individual local authorities to consider whether safety surfacing of play areas is a priority and, if so, to direct the necessary resources towards it.

### Dykebar Hospital, Paisley

**Mr. McMaster:** To ask the Secretary of State for Scotland when he last discusses the future of Dykebar hospital, Paisley with representatives of *(a)* Argyll and Clyde health board and *(b)* Renfrewshire Healthcare trust; and if he will make a statement. [24106]

**Lord James Douglas-Hamilton:** My noble and learned Friend the Minister of State meets the chairmen of health boards and NHS trusts in Scotland from time to time when he discusses a range of matters.

The future of Dykebar hospital will be considered in the context of Argyll and Clyde health board's community care plan which is still in preparation. Once finished, the plan will be subject to extensive public consultation.

### Security Companies

**Mr. McMaster:** To ask the Secretary of State for Scotland what plans he has to introduce a licensing scheme for security companies; and if he will make a statement. [24157]

**Lord James Douglas-Hamilton:** My right hon. Friend has no immediate plans to do so, but he will be considering the position on the publication of the report of the Home Affairs Select Committee inquiry into the private security industry in England and Wales. This report is expected shortly.

### NHS Acute Beds

**Mr. Galbraith:** To ask the Secretary of State for Scotland when he last discussed with any member or official of the Greater Glasgow health board the acute bed strategy; what changes he suggested; and if he will make a statement. [24040]

**Lord James Douglas-Hamilton:** My right Friend has been kept informed by the health board as its strategy has developed. Public consultation on the acute elements of the board's strategy ended on 30 April; consultation on the maternity services elements is still under way. I expect the health board to submit its proposals formally for my right hon. Friend's consideration once it has considered the response to the consultation exercise.

### Mortgage Repossessions

**Mr. McMaster:** To ask the Secretary of State for Scotland how many court actions relating to mortgage repossessions in Paisley were heard in Paisley sheriff court in each year since 1980; and if he will make a statement. [24068]

**Lord James Douglas-Hamilton:** Comprehensive information is not available in the form requested, but 206 such actions were initiated at Paisley sheriff court in 1994 and decrees in absence were granted in 188 actions at the court during the same 12-month period.

### Operation Dragon

**Mr. McMaster:** To ask the Secretary of State for Scotland if he will make a statement on Operation Dragon in Strathclyde. [24084]

**Lord James Douglas Hamiliton:** My right hon. Friend fully supports the chief constable of Strathclyde police in mounting of Operation Dragon which is well organised and well resourced. The objective of the operation is to curb the recent outbreak of violent crime and to enable the police to identify and arrest those responsible. A number of arrests have been made and the police have recovered a number of shotguns and ammunition, handguns and replica handguns. The operation is continuing.

### Temazepam

**Mr. McMaster:** To ask the Secretary of State for Scotland what are the maximum penalities for those convicted of the illegal dealing in the drug temazepam; what plans he has to stiffen such sentences; and if he will make a statement. [24092]

**Lord James Douglas-Hamilton:** Offences under Sections 4(3) and 5(3) of the Misuse of Drugs Act 1971 in relation to the supply of, or intent to supply, class C drugs, including temazepam, carry a maximum penalty of five years' imprisonment and/or a fine of up to £2,500 when tried on indictment.

The maximum fine for these offences was increased from £500 to £2,500 as recently as February of this year, when the relevant section of the Criminal Justice and Public Order Act 1994 came into effect. There are no present plans to increase further the maximum penalties available to the courts for such offences.

### Returning Officers

**Mr. McMaster:** To ask the Secretary of State for Scotland if he will publish a table showing the amount paid or payable to each returning officer in Scotland at the 1995 local elections; what out-of-pocket expenses had to be met from these payments; what was the level of payment to each other grade involved in these elections; and if he will make a statement. [24108]

**Lord James Douglas-Hamilton:** This information is not collected centrally. Returning officers' fees and expenses and other costs relating to the conduct of local government elections are met by the local authority. A total of £5 million was, however, made available

exceptionally by the Scottish Office to regional councils to cover the cost of the elections to the shadow councils in April.

### Scottish Homes

**Mr. McMaster:** To ask the Secretary of State for Scotland what is the current and specific remit of the national housing agency, Scottish Homes. [24116]

**Lord James Douglas-Hamilton:** The Housing (Scotland) Act 1988 established Scottish Homes and gave it a wide range of functions and powers to promote housing in Scotland. Scottish Homes' current aim, which reflects the Government's objective for housing in Scotland and is endorsed by my right hon. Friend, is to ensure the quality of housing and variety of housing options available in Scotland are substantially improved. It has six specific main objectives to achieve this aim. These were set out in Scottish Homes' recently published strategic plan for the period up to 1997–98.

### Electricity Prices

**Mr. Salmond:** To ask the President of the Board of Trade, pursuant to his oral statement of 9 May, *Official Report,* column 565, if he will break down into its constituent parts the components of his forecast of an 8 per cent. fall in electricity prices in Scotland with particular reference to savings accruing from the ending of the nuclear premium. [24146]

**Mr. Kynoch:** The premium element in the price which Scottish Nuclear receives for its output from Scottish Power and Hydro-Electric under the nuclear energy agreement began to reduce in 1994–95. It was due to end entirely in 1998–99. The Government have now decided that the remaining element of the premium will not continue until 1998; instead it will be ended at the point of privatising Scottish Nuclear's two advanced gas-cooled reactor stations. It is proposed that changes will be made in the supply price control to ensure that the savings to ScottishPower and Hydro-Electric will be passed through to Scottish franchise customers. The Office of Electricity Regulation has calculated that the removal of the premium between 1994–95 and 1996–97 will result in franchise electricity prices in Scotland reducing by around 8 per cent. in real terms over that period.

**Mr. Home Robertson:** To ask the Secretary of State for Scotland what will be the net effect on electricity bills per household in Scotland of the premature abolition of the nuclear premium under the Government's plans to privatise the nuclear industry. [24502]

**Mr. Kynoch:** The premium element in the price which Scottish Nuclear receives for its output from ScottishPower and Hydro-Electric under the nuclear energy agreement began to reduce in 1994–95. It was due to end entirely in 1998–99. The Government have now decided that the remaining element of the premium will not continue until 1998 but will be ended at the point of privatising Scottish Nuclear's two AGR stations. At that time, changes will be made in the supply price control to ensure that the resultant savings to ScottishPower and Hydro-Electric are passed through to Scottish franchise customers. The Office of Electricity Regulation has calculated that the removal of the premium between 1994–95 and 1996–97 will result in franchise electricity prices in Scotland reducing by around 8 per cent. in real terms over that period, of which around 3 to 4 per cent. will be delivered in 1996–97.

# HOME DEPARTMENT

## Derek Bentley

**Mr. Michael:** To ask the Secretary of State for the Home Department (1) if he will review the release dates set by his predecessors for papers in the Derek Bentley case to conform fully with subsequent legal rulings on the obligations of the Home Office to disclose information;

[24910]

(2) if he will place in the Library a copy of the report submitted to his Department by the investigating officer on behalf of the Commissioner of Police of the Metropolis regarding inconsistencies in the evidence, including evidence not available to the court or the public, relating to the case of Derek Bentley. [24936]

**Mr. Nicholas Baker:** I refer the hon. Member to the reply given to his question of 18 May, at columns *363–64.*

## Probation Services, Mid Glamorgan

**Dr. Howells:** To ask the Secretary of State for the Home Department which of the newly formed unitary authorities will have responsibility for the provision of probation services currently provided by officers of Mid Glamorgan county council in *(a)* the Rhymney Valley, *(b)* Merthyr, *(c)* Aberdare and *(d)* Porth *(e)* Bridgend.

[25050]

**Mr. Nicholas Baker:** Local authorities contribute to the costs of, but do not have responsibility for, the provision of probation services. Such services are provided by probation committees. The Mid Glamorgan probation committee is responsible for the provision of services in its area. On 16 May, our intention to make changes to the Mid Glamorgan probation area was announced, and I refer the hon. Member to the answer

given to the hon. Member for High Peak (Mr. Hendry) of that date, at columns *189–90.*

## Probation Service, South Glamorgan

**Mr. Morgan:** To ask the Secretary of State for the Home Department what is the total grant given by his Department to South Glamorgan probation service this year and each of the last three years in *(a)* cash terms and *(b)* real terms. [25602]

**Mr. Nicholas Baker:** Information is given in the table.

|  | 1992–93 | 1993–94 | 1994–95 | 1995–96 |
|---|---|---|---|---|
| Cash terms | 2,642,191 | 2,785,037 | 3,038,229 | 2,018,655 |
| Real terms | 2,642,191 | 2,702,345 | 2,890,215 | 2,781,206 |

The figures are in terms of specific grant cash limits. In addition to the cash terms figure shown for 1995–96, a further £202,486 is added to support probation service partnerships with the independent sector previously funded by the Home Office.

## Fine Defaulters

**Mr. Michael:** To ask the Secretary of State for the Home Department how many people were imprisoned because of default on fines levied by the courts in the last year for which figures are available, and in each of the previous 20 years. [25318]

**Mr. Michael Forsyth:** Responsibility for this mater has been delegated to the Director General of the Prison Service, who has been asked to arrange for a reply to be given.

*Letter from Derek Lewis to Mr. Alun Michael, dated 22 May 1995:*

The Home Secretary has asked me to reply to your recent Question about how many people were imprisoned because of fine default on fines levied by the courts in the last year for which figures are available, and in each of the previous 20 years.

Provisional information shows that 22,400 persons in 1993 and 22,700 persons in 1994 were received into Prison Service establishments in England and Wales for fine default. Information for earlier years is published in "Prison Statistics, England and Wales" (Table 7.1 of the 1992 edition, Cm 2581), an extract of which is attached.

Table 7.3:  *Receptions into prison in default of payment of a fine: by period and sex, 1974–84*

*Number of persons*

| Period imposed in default | 1974 | 1975 | 1976 | 1977 | 1978 | 1979 | 1980 | 1981 | 1982 | 1983 | 1984 |
|---|---|---|---|---|---|---|---|---|---|---|---|
| *Males* | | | | | | | | | | | |
| Up to and including 1 week | 1,000 | 1,032 | 1,015 | 1,526 | 3,606 | 3,624 | 3,210 | 3,670 | 4,052 | 3,726 | 3,576 |
| Over 1 week up to and including 2 weeks | 1,875 | 1,751 | 1,705 | 1,660 | 2,937 | 3,101 | 2,731 | 3,801 | 4,468 | 4,183 | 4,480 |
| Over 2 weeks up to and including 1 month | 3,487 | 3,669 | 3,646 | 3,371 | 4,494 | 5,208 | 5,011 | 7,425 | 9,283 | 9,086 | 8,154 |
| Over 1 month up to and including 2 months | 3,215 | 3,749 | 4,208 | 4,113 | 2,710 | 2,689 | 2,629 | 3,583 | 3,867 | 3,517 | 3,099 |
| Over 2 months up to and including 3 months | 1,959 | 2,799 | 3,645 | 3,617 | 1,304 | 948 | 927 | 1,063 | 1,070 | 966 | 684 |
| Over 3 months up to and including 6 months | 516 | 717 | 903 | 838 | 467 | 484 | 434 | 474 | 391 | 406 | 258 |
| Over 6 months | 62 | 85 | 73 | 59 | 29 | 38 | 34 | 30 | 37 | 36 | 24 |
| Total | 12,114 | 13,802 | 15,195 | 15,184 | 15,547 | 16,092 | 14,976 | 20,046 | 23,168 | 21,920 | 20,275 |
| *Females* | | | | | | | | | | | |
| Up to and including 1 week | 71 | 41 | 55 | 89 | 249 | 223 | 230 | 214 | 252 | 289 | 439 |
| Over 1 week up to and including 2 weeks | 87 | 112 | 106 | 144 | 213 | 263 | 236 | 287 | 323 | 314 | 376 |
| Over 2 weeks up to and including 1 month | 233 | 262 | 247 | 273 | 280 | 306 | 331 | 425 | 530 | 499 | 485 |
| Over 1 month up to and including 2 months | 64 | 122 | 184 | 188 | 100 | 119 | 123 | 136 | 157 | 165 | 149 |
| Over 2 months up to and including 3 months | 44 | 63 | 109 | 132 | 41 | 31 | 33 | 33 | 39 | 40 | 33 |

Table 7.3:   *Receptions into prison in default of payment of a fine: by period and sex, 1974–84*

Number of persons

| Period imposed in default | 1974 | 1975 | 1976 | 1977 | 1978 | 1979 | 1980 | 1981 | 1982 | 1983 | 1984 |
|---|---|---|---|---|---|---|---|---|---|---|---|
| Over 3 months up to and including 6 months | 8 | 12 | 14 | 27 | 9 | 9 | 7 | 10 | 21 | 12 | 4 |
| Over 6 months | 1 | 3 | 1 | 3 | 3 | 1 | 2 | 2 | 2 | 2 | — |
| Total | 508 | 615 | 716 | 856 | 895 | 952 | 962 | 1,107 | 1,324 | 1,321 | 1,486 |
| Males and females total | 12,622 | 14,417 | 15,911 | 16,040 | 16,442 | 17,044 | 15,938 | 21,153 | 24,492 | 23,241 | 21,761 |

*Source:*
Extract from Prison Statistics England and Wales.

Table 7.1:   *Population, receptions and estimated average time spent in Prison Service establishments: by sex, 1982–92*
England and Wales

Fine defaulters

| | 1982 | 1983 | 1984 | 1985 | 1986 | 1987 | 1988 | 1989 | 1990 | 1991 | 1992 |
|---|---|---|---|---|---|---|---|---|---|---|---|
| *Population at 30 June* | | | | | | | | | | | |
| All fine defaulters | 909 | 900 | 792 | 563 | 511 | 626 | 576 | 484 | 466 | 409 | 382 |
| Males | 871 | 854 | 752 | 540 | 491 | 598 | 549 | 460 | 441 | 397 | 359 |
| Females | 38 | 46 | 40 | 23 | 20 | 28 | 27 | 24 | 25 | 12 | 23 |
| Total sentenced population | 36,000 | 35,438 | 35,496 | 37,344 | 36,450 | 39,303 | 38,548 | 38,013 | 35,220 | 35,114 | 35,564 |
| Fine defaulters as a percentage of total sentenced population | 2.5 | 2.5 | 2.2 | 1.5 | 1.4 | 1.6 | 1.5 | 1.3 | 1.3 | 1.2 | 1.1 |
| Population serving sentences of imprisonment of 6 months or less[1] | 5,588 | 6,006 | 6,205 | 6,285 | 4,787 | 4,856 | 3,563 | 3,744 | 3,238 | 3,650 | 3,621 |
| Fine defaulters as a percentage of population serving sentences of imprisonment of 6 months or less | 16.3 | 15.0 | 12.8 | 9.0 | 10.7 | 12.9 | 16.2 | 12.9 | 14.4 | 11.2 | 10.5 |
| *Receptions* | | | | | | | | | | | |
| All fine defaulters | 24,492 | 23,241 | 21,761 | 20,493 | 19,159 | 18,723 | 16,817 | 16,985 | 16,659 | 18,973 | 19,826 |
| Males | 23,168 | 21,920 | 20,275 | 19,108 | 18,084 | 17,804 | 15,881 | 16,117 | 15,814 | 17,997 | 18,782 |
| Females | 1,324 | 1,321 | 1,486 | 1,385 | 1,075 | 919 | 936 | 868 | 845 | 976 | 1,044 |
| All receptions under sentence | 94,377 | 93,414 | 92,810 | 96,189 | 86,153 | 86,358 | 81,836 | 76,430 | 67,510 | 72,313 | 69,832 |
| Fine defaulters as a percentage of all receptions under sentence | 26.0 | 24.9 | 23.4 | 21.3 | 22.2 | 21.7 | 20.5 | 22.2 | 24.7 | 26.2 | 28.4 |
| All receptions under sentence of imprisonment of 6 months or less[1] | 52,195 | 51,415 | 50,242 | 49,287 | 43,109 | 41,446 | 39,391 | 42,209 | 36,813 | 41,245 | 40,509 |
| Fine defaulters as a percentage of all receptions under sentence of imprisonment of 6 months or less | 46.9 | 45.2 | 43.3 | 41.6 | 44.4 | 45.2 | 42.7 | 40.2 | 45.3 | 46.0 | 48.9 |
| *Average time served (days)[2]* | | | | | | | | | | | |
| Males | 14.1 | 14.1 | 12.9 | 11.3 | 10.9 | 10.9 | 9.9 | 8.1 | 7.0 | 7.5 | [3]7.3 |
| Females | 11.0 | 10.1 | 8.7 | 8.1 | 7.9 | 8.4 | 7.1 | 6.0 | 6.0 | 6.8 | [3]6.8 |

[1] Excludes detention centre trainees; includes youth custody trainees and persons sentenced to detention in a young offender institution.
[2] Excluding those remaining in custody as fine defaulters on completion of a custodial sentence for criminal offence.
[3] January to June.
*Source:*
Extract from Prison Statistics England and Wales.

### Jewish Burial Ground, London

**Mr. Corbyn:** To ask the Secretary of State for the Home Department when he gave approval for the removal of bodies from the Jewish burial ground at Kingsbury road off Balls Pond road, London N1; and what representations he has received about this.          [25404]

**Mr. Nicholas Baker:** The Secretary of State's directions with respect to the removal and reinterment of human remains interred in the Jewish burial ground at Kingsbury road, London N1 were given on 13 October 1994, in accordance with the provisions of the Disused Burial Grounds (Amendment) Act 1981. My right hon. and learned Friend the Secretary of State has since received four letters of representation on the matter. His involvement is limited to ensuring that the removal and reinterment of human remains are carried out with due care and attention to decency. Before any removals can take place, the applicants will be required, under the 1981 Act, to advertise their intentions in the local press, and by notices posted at the burial ground, so that interested parties may have the opportunity to object to the proposals.

### Consultancy Costs

**Ms Hodge:** To ask the Secretary of State for the Home Department what is the level of expenditure on consultancy by (i) the Home Office and (ii) agencies for which the Home Office is responsible for *(a)* 1993–94, *(b)* 1994–95 and *(c)* the projected figure for 1995–96.
          [25522]

**Mr. Howard:** Information on the level of expenditure for consultancy contracts let by the Home Office, and agencies for which the Home Office is responsible, during the period specified is not recorded centrally and could be obtained only at disproportionate cost.

## Majority Shareholdings

**Mr. Byers:** To ask the Secretary of State for the Home Department if he will list those companies in which the holder of his office is a majority shareholder which *(a)* are currently in existence and *(b)* have been wound up in the past five years.    [25715]

**Mr. Howard:** The Secretary of State for the Home Department is not a major shareholder in any company, nor has he held a majority shareholding in any company which has been wound up in the past five years.

## Mr. Richard Linford

**Mr. Cohen:** To ask the Secretary of State for the Home Department what assessment was made by *(a)* Essex police and *(b)* the Prison Service of Mr. Richard Linford's psychiatric condition prior to his imprisonment.    [24691]

**Mr. Michael Forsyth:** Responsibility for this matter has been delegated to the Director General of the Prison Service, who has been asked to arrange for a reply to be given.

*Letter from Derek Lewis to Mr. Harry Cohen, dated 22 May 1995:*

The Home Secretary has asked me to reply to your recent Question asking what assessment was made by Essex police and the Prison Service of Mr. Richard Linford's psychiatric condition before his imprisonment.

Mr. Linford was remanded in custody by Chelmsford Magistrates Court on 28 November 1994. The Prison Service did not, therefore, have any opportunity to assess his psychiatric condition prior to his reception into its custody. The matter of what assessment was made of Mr. Linford's psychiatric condition by the police prior to his reception or by the Prison Service after his reception into prison will be one of the questions to be examined in the course of the independent inquiry the Prison Service is jointly commissioning with North Essex Health Authority and Essex Social Services into the circumstances surrounding the death of Mr. Christopher Edwards.

## Secure Mental Hospitals (Manslaughter Detainees)

**Mrs. Roche:** To ask the Secretary of State for the Home Department, pursuant to his answer of 11 May, *Official Report,* column *554,* what proportion of patients with secure mental hospital orders for manslaughter has been given any kind of leave of absence it the last 10 years.    [25157]

**Mr. Michael Forsyth:** This information is not available.

**Mrs. Roche:** To ask the Secretary of State for the Home Department, pursuant to his answer of 11 May, *Official Report,* column *554,* in which secure mental hospitals each of the patients who pleaded guilty to manslaughter was detained.    [25134]

**Mr. Michael Forsyth:** Information on the plea entered by defendants is not available centrally for those sentenced to detention in a secure mental hospital. The following information is based on those restricted patients with a hospital order who were sentenced for manslaughter.

*List of hospitals to which each of the patients who were convicted of manslaughter and given a hospital order were initially admitted (1985–94)*

| Hospital name | Admissions |
| --- | --- |
| Broadmoor | 67 |
| Rampton | 60 |

*List of hospitals to which each of the patients who were convicted of manslaughter and given a hospital order were initially admitted (1985–94)*

| Hospital name | Admissions |
| --- | --- |
| Ashworth | [1]58 |
| Arnold Lodge | 2 |
| Bexley | 3 |
| Calderstones | 1 |
| Camlet Lodge | 2 |
| Cane Hill | 1 |
| Caswell Clinic | 2 |
| Central Hospital, Warwick | 2 |
| Claybury | 1 |
| Clent Unit | 1 |
| Doncaster Gate | 3 |
| East Glamorgan | 1 |
| Edenfield Centre | 1 |
| Fairmile | 1 |
| Friern | 1 |
| Goodmayes | 1 |
| Hackney | 6 |
| Knapsbury | 2 |
| Kneesworth | 2 |
| Knowle | 2 |
| Langdon | 1 |
| Long Grove | 2 |
| Maidstone | 2 |
| Mapperley | 1 |
| Moorgreen | 1 |
| Newton Lodge | 1 |
| North Wales Hospital | 2 |
| Northern General, Sheffield | 2 |
| Northgate | 1 |
| Norvic Clinic | 2 |
| Pastures | 1 |
| Pen y Fai | 1 |
| Poole Hospital | 5 |
| Prestwich | 5 |
| Rainhill | 1 |
| Reaside | 10 |
| Roundway | 1 |
| Runwell | 3 |
| Scott Clinic | 5 |
| Severalls | 1 |
| St. Bernard's, Ealing | 12 |
| St. James' | 1 |
| St. Augustine's | 1 |
| St. Nicholas, Newcastle | 1 |
| St. Francis, Hayward's Heath | 2 |
| St. Andrew's, Northampton | 1 |
| Stanley Royd | 2 |
| Storthes Hall | 1 |
| Three Bridges | 4 |
| Towers | 2 |
| Trevor Gibbens Unit | 1 |
| Waddilove's | 1 |
| Warlingham | 1 |
| Whittingham | 1 |
| Winterton | 1 |

[1] Moss Side and Park Lane merged to become Ashworth in February 1990.

**Mrs. Roche:** To ask the Secretary of State for the Home Department what consultation is required by his Department before people being detained in secure mental hospitals after conviction for manslaughter with diminished responsibility are released into the community.    [23526]

**Mr. Michael Forsyth** *[holding answer 10 May 1995]:* Where such a person is subject to both a hospital and a restriction order, the powers of the responsible medical officer to grant leave to, or discharge, the patient may be exercised only with the consent of my right hon. and learned Friend the Secretary of State. Discharge may also be directed by a mental health review tribunal. In considering whether it is safe for a restricted patient to be granted leave or discharged, the Home Office takes account of all relevant information including reports by the responsible medical officer and members of the care team.

### Abdelaziz Bouteraa

**Mrs. Roche:** To ask the Secretary of State for the Home Department what assurances his Department has sought regarding the proposed release into the community from Chase Farm hospital of Abdelaziz Bouteraa.

[23520]

**Mr. Michael Forsyth** *[holding answer 10 May 1995]:* I am not aware of any current proposal to discharge Mr. Bouteraa from hospital. Mr. Bouteraa has overstayed his permitted leave to remain in the United Kingdom and has been served with a notice of intention to deport him. He has appealed against this decision to the independent appellate authorities. His immigration status will be reviewed in the light of his medical condition and the outcome of appeal proceedings.

### Disclosure Demands

**Mr. Mullin:** To ask the Secretary of State for the Home Department, pursuant to his oral statement of 16 May, *Official Report*, columns 167-71, if he will list the criminal cases drawn to his attention which had to be abandoned due to unreasonable demands by defence lawyers for disclosure.

[25260]

**Mr. Howard:** Paragraph 15 of the consultation document which I published on 16 May lists examples of cases drawn to my attention which have been abandoned following a court ruling on the disclosure of sensitive material.

### Prison Staff

**Mrs. Roche:** To ask the Secretary of State for the Home Department what proportion of prison staff on the accelerated promotion scheme are women.

[25150]

**Mr. Michael Forsyth:** Responsibility for this matter has been delegated to the Director General of the Prison Service, who has been asked to arrange for a reply to be given.

*Letter from Derek Lewis to Mrs. Barbara Roche, dated 22 May 1995:*

The Home Secretary has asked me to reply to your recent Question about the number of women on the Prison Service Accelerated Promotion Scheme.

There are, at present, 89 members of the Prison Service on the Accelerated Promotion Scheme, 34 of whom are women.

### Remand Prisoners

**Mr. Bermingham:** To ask the Secretary of State for the Home Department how many remand prisoners in England and Wales had been in custody for *(a)* up to three months, *(b)* from three to six months, *(c)* for six to nine months, *(d)* from nine to 12 months and *(e)* more than 12 months, on the latest date for which information is available.

[24373]

**Mr. Michael Forsyth:** Responsibility for this matter has been delegated to the Director General of the Prison Service, who has been asked to arrange for a reply to be given.

*Letter from Derek Lewis to Mr. Gerald Bermingham dated, 22 May 1995:*

The Home Secretary has asked me to reply to your recent Question about how many remand prisoners in England and Wales had been in custody for (a) up to three months, (b) from three to six months, (c) from six to nine months, (d) from nine to 12 months and (e) more than 12 months, on the latest date for which information is available.

The latest available provisional data for England and Wales is for 31 December 1994 and is shown in the attached table.

*Remand prisoners in Prison Service establishments in England and Wales by length of time since first reception[1] on 31 December 1994*

| Time since first remand | 31 December 1994 [2] |
| --- | --- |
| Less than 3 months | 6,660 |
| More than 3 months, up to and including 6 months | 2,660 |
| More than six months, up to and including 9 months | 940 |
| More than 9 months, up to and including 12 months | 840 |
| Over 12 months | 320 |
| | 11,420 |

[1] Awaiting trial or sentence. Time since first reception on remand into a Prison Service establishment. This includes any intervening time spent on bail, but excludes time spent in police cells beforehand.
[2] Rounded estimates which therefore may not add to the totals.

**Mr. Bermingham:** To ask the Secretary of State for the Home Department what is the remand population in England and Wales for the latest available date.   [24372]

**Mr. Michael Forsyth:** Responsibility for this matter has been delegated to the Director General of the Prison Service, who has been asked to arrange for a reply to be given.

*Letter from Derek Lewis to Mr. Gerald Bermingham, dated 22 May 1995:*

The Home Secretary has asked me to reply to your recent Question about the remand population in England and Wales for the latest available date.

The latest available figure is for 28 February 1995, when there was a total of 11,970 prisoners on remand in England and Wales, including 124 being held in police cells.

### Crack Cocaine

**Mr. Mike O'Brien:** To ask the Secretary of State for the Home Department how many people have been cautioned for possession of crack cocaine in each of the last five years.   [24011]

**Mr. Michael Forsyth:** Home Office records show that one person was cautioned for possession of crack cocaine in 1990. Three persons were so cautioned in 1991, and 14 persons in 1992. Information for 1993 is not available separately and that for 1994 is not yet available.

**Mr. Mike O'Brien:** To ask the Secretary of State for the Home Department which police stations have cautioned persons in respect of possession of crack cocaine in 1994. [24013]

**Mr. Michael Forsyth:** Information regarding individual police stations is not collected centrally. The only readily available information regarding cautioning for possession of crack cocaine relates to the years 1990 to 1992 and shows that all but two of the 18 cautions administered during that time were given by the Metropolitan police.

### Women (Sentences)

**Dr. Lynne Jones:** To ask the Secretary of State for the Home Department what was the sentenced female population in England and Wales on the latest date available, broken down by type of offence, length of sentence and previous convictions. [24269]

**Mr. Michael Forsyth:** Responsibility for this matter has been delegated to the Director General of the Prison Service, who has been asked to arrange for a reply to be given.

*Letter from Derek Lewis to Dr. Lynne Jones, dated 22 May 1995:*

The Home Secretary has asked me to reply to your recent Question about the sentenced female population in England and Wales on the latest date available, broken down by type of offence, length of sentence and previous convictions.

The latest date for which figures are available is 28 February 1995. Figures for female population on this date by type of offence and length of sentence are contained in the attached tables.

The latest available published information on the previous convictions of females was given in "Prison Statistics England and Wales 1992" Cm 2581, Table 5.2, an extract of which is attached.

*Female sentenced population, England and Wales, on 28 February 1995, by type of offence:*[1] [2]

| Offence group | |
| --- | --- |
| Violence against the person | 268 |
| Sexual offences | 11 |
| Burglary | 51 |
| Robbery | 93 |
| Theft and handling | 251 |
| Fraud and forgery | 92 |
| Drugs offences | 330 |
| Other offences | 124 |
| Offence not recorded | 163 |
| **Total** | **1,383** |

[1] Excludes fine defaulters.
[2] Provisional figures.

*Female sentenced population, England and Wales, on 28 February 1995, by length of sentence*[1] [2]

| Sentence length | |
| --- | --- |
| Up to and including 3 months | 94 |
| Over 3 months and up to 6 months | 146 |
| Over 6 months and up to 12 months | 198 |
| Over 12 months and up to 18 months | 127 |
| Over 18 months and up to 3 years | 279 |
| Over 3 years and up to 4 years | 125 |
| Over 4 years and up to 5 years | 102 |
| Over 5 years and up to 10 years | 178 |
| Over 10 years and less than life | 26 |
| Life | 106 |
| **Total** | **1,383** |

[1] Excludes fine defaulters.
[2] Provisional figures.

Table 5.2: Population in Prison Service establishments under sentence on 30 June 1992: by offence group and previous convictions[1]
England and Wales

Number of persons

| Offence group | All adult females | Number of preivous convictions[2] | | | | |
| --- | --- | --- | --- | --- | --- | --- |
| | | nil | 1–2 | 3–5 | 6–10 | 11 and over |
| Violence against the person | 158 | 60 | 20 | 20 | 20 | 20 |
| Rape | 2 | — | — | — | — | 0 |
| Other sexual offences | 7 | — | — | — | — | 0 |
| Burglary | 40 | 10 | 10 | 10 | 10 | 10 |
| Robbery | 37 | — | 10 | 10 | 10 | 10 |
| Theft and handling | 172 | 30 | 40 | 30 | 40 | 40 |
| Fraud and forgery | 52 | 20 | 10 | 10 | 10 | 10 |
| Drugs offences | 245 | 130 | 30 | 30 | 30 | 30 |
| Other offences | 143 | 60 | 20 | 20 | 20 | 20 |
| Offence not recorded | 160 | 50 | 30 | 30 | 30 | 30 |
| *Offences with immediate custodial sentence* | 1,016 | 360 | 160 | 160 | 160 | 170 |

*Source:*
Extract from: "Prison Statistics England and Wales 1992", Cm 2581.
[1] Estimated using self-reporting of previous criminal history in the national prison survey 1991 and the distribution of previous convictions in the 1991 prison population. Excludes fine defaulters.
[2] Rounded estimates to the nearest 10, which therefore may not add to the totals.

### Female Prisoners

**Dr. Lynne Jones:** To ask the Secretary of State for the Home Department what additional cell and bed space had been made available during the last six months in each female gaol in England and Wales. [24273]

**Mr. Michael Forsyth:** Responsibility for this matter has been delegated to the Director General of the Prison Service, who has been asked to arrange for a reply to be given.

*Letter from Derek Lewis to Dr. Lynne Jones, dated 22 May 1995:*

The Home Secretary has asked me to reply to your recent Question about the additional cell and bed space made available during the last six months in each female prison in England and Wales.

Establishments that have provided additional cell and bed space during the last six months are given in the table below:

*Certified Normal Accommodation (CNA) available for use in Female Prison Establishments in England and Wales on 30 November 1994 and 28 April 1995*

| Establishment | CNA in use | | Increase |
| | 30 November 1994 | 28 April 1995 | |
|---|---|---|---|
| New Hall | 169 | 207 | +38 |
| Risley | 132 | 154 | +22 |
| Winchester | 0 | 60 | +60 |
| Total | 1,948 | 2,068 | +120 |

*Note:*
Cell and bed space in all other female establishments has remained unaltered in the last six months.

**Dr. Lynne Jones:** To ask the Secretary of State for the Home Department what was the female prisoner population in England and Wales on the last day of April in 1994, 1993, 1992 and 1991 broken down by category of offence. [24268]

**Mr. Michael Forsyth:** Responsibility for this matter has been delegated to the Director General of the Prison Service, who has been asked to arrange for a reply to be given.

*Letter from Derek Lewis to Dr. Lynne Jones, dated 22 May 1995:*

The Home Secretary has asked me to reply to your recent Question about the female prisoner population in England and Wales on the last day of April in 1994, 1993, 1992 and 1991 broken down by category of offence.

The available information relates to the sentenced female prison population on 30 June each year. This information was published on 27 April 1995 in a Home Office Statistical Bulletin entitled "The prison population in 1994" (table 6, Issue 8/95), an extract of which is attached.

*Table 6:　Population in Prison Service establishments under sentence on 30 June by sex and offence group, 1989–94*
*England and Wales*

Number of persons

| Sex and offence group | 1989 | 1990 | 1991 | 1992 | 1993 | 1994[1] |
|---|---|---|---|---|---|---|
| **MALES** | | | | | | |
| *Offences with immediate custodial sentence* | | | | | | |
| Violence against the person | 8,449 | 7,477 | 6,945 | 6,893 | 7,273 | 7,600 |
| Rape | 1,343 | 1,441 | 1,508 | 1,582 | 1,593 | 1,650 |
| Other sexual offences | 1,639 | 1,577 | 1,585 | 1,564 | 1,572 | 1,650 |
| Burglary | 7,038 | 5,885 | 5,082 | 5,349 | 4,690 | 5,100 |
| Robbery | 4,151 | 4,052 | 3,990 | 4,174 | 4,856 | 5,040 |
| Theft and handling | 4,073 | 3,042 | 2,910 | 2,910 | 2,578 | 3,030 |
| Fraud and forgery | 937 | 795 | 791 | 800 | 826 | 890 |
| Drugs offences | 2,896 | 2,829 | 2,584 | 2,899 | 2,900 | 3,140 |
| Motoring offences | 902 | 659 | 861 | 967 | 1,045 | 1,510 |
| Other offences | 3,225 | 2,621 | 2,311 | 2,490 | 2,248 | 2,290 |
| Offence not recorded[2] | 1,621 | 3,148 | 5,002 | 4,402 | 1,794 | 2,060 |
| All offences | 36,274 | 33,526 | 33,569 | 34,030 | 31,375 | 33,970 |
| In default of payment of a fine | 460 | 441 | 397 | 359 | 522 | 510 |
| All males all offences | 36,734 | 33,967 | 33,966 | 34,389 | 31,897 | 34,480 |
| **FEMALES** | | | | | | |
| *Offences with immediate custodial sentence* | | | | | | |
| Violence against the person | 218 | 201 | 189 | 184 | 216 | 270 |
| Rape | 7 | 3 | 1 | 2 | 1 | 1 |
| Other sexual offences | 16 | 8 | 15 | 8 | 14 | 10 |
| Burglary | 68 | 51 | 39 | 51 | 39 | 40 |
| Robbery | 82 | 51 | 46 | 56 | 77 | 90 |
| Theft and handling | 230 | 203 | 175 | 190 | 207 | 230 |
| Fraud and forgery | 63 | 50 | 42 | 53 | 64 | 70 |
| Drugs offences | 317 | 318 | 272 | 259 | 308 | 320 |
| Motoring offences | 2 | 5 | 2 | 3 | 7 | 20 |
| Other offences | 174 | 207 | 174 | 155 | 118 | 120 |
| Offence not recorded[2] | 78 | 131 | 181 | 191 | 74 | 100 |
| All offences | 1,255 | 1,228 | 1,136 | 1,152 | 1,125 | 1,270 |
| In default of payment of a fine | 24 | 25 | 12 | 23 | 24 | 20 |
| All females all offences | 1,279 | 1,253 | 1,148 | 1,175 | 1,149 | 1,290 |
| All males and females | 38,013 | 35,220 | 35,110 | 35,564 | 33,046 | 35,770 |

[1] Provisional rounded estimates. Components may not add to totals because they have been rounded independently.
[2] Includes 30 court martial prisoners for 1989 with "not recorded", from 1990 court martial prisoners are included under the appropriate offence.

**Dr. Lynne Jones:** To ask the Secretary of State for the Home Department how many female prisoners were received on remand during 1993 and 1994; and how many were eventually *(a)* given a custodial sentence, *(b)* given a non-custodial sentence and *(c)* acquitted or not proceeded with. [24271]

**Mr. Michael Forsyth:** Responsibility for this matter has been delegated to the Director General of the Prison

Service, who has been asked to arrange for a reply to be given.

*Letter from Derek Lewis to Dr. Lynne Jones, dated 22 May 1995:*

The Home Secretary has asked me to reply to your recent Question about how many female prisoners were received on remand during 1993 and 1994, and how many were eventually *(a)* given a custodial sentence, *(b)* given a non-custodial sentence and *(c)* acquitted or not proceeded with.

Information on the number of females received on remand into Prison Service establishments in England and Wales in 1993 and 1994 is shown in table 1, attached. Information on the court outcome is only available for 1993 from court remand statistics and is given in table 2.

*Table 1:   Receptions[1] into Prison Service establishments of untried and convicted unsentenced female prisoners in 1993 and 1994*

| Females | 1993[2] | 1994[2] |
|---|---|---|
| Untried prisoners | 2,647 | 2,891 |
| Convicted unsentenced prisoners | 1,505 | 1,728 |
| All remand prisoners | 3,322 | 3,679 |

[1] The figures for "all remand" record once only a person received as an untried prisoner who is subsequently received also as a convicted unsentenced prisoner.
[2] Provisional figures.

*Table 2:   Final court outcome for females remanded in custody at some stage in magistrates' court proceedings[1] in 1993 England and Wales*

| Females | Estimated percentages |
|---|---|
| Final court outcome[2] | |
| Acquitted not proceeded with etc. | 21 |
| Non-custodial sentence: | 53 |
| Community sentence[3] | 26 |
| Fine | 10 |
| Absolute or conditional discharge | 12 |
| Other non-custodial sentence | 5 |
| Custodial sentence | 26 |
| Total | 100 |

[1] Includes persons remanded in custody by magistrates during proceedings or on committal.
[2] Includes estimated outcome at the Crown Court for those committed for trial or sentence.
[3] Includes CSO, probation, supervision orders, attendance centre orders.

**Dr. Lynne Jones:** To ask the Secretary of State for the Home Department what was the female prison population in England and Wales on 28 April broken down by category of prisoner.    [24267]

**Mr. Michael Forsyth:** Responsibility for this matter has been delegated to the Director General of the Prison Service, who has been asked to arrange for a reply to be given.

*Letter from Derek Lewis to Dr. Lynne Jones, dated 22 May 1995:*

The Home Secretary has asked me to reply to your recent Question about the female prison population in England and Wales on 28 April broken down by category of prisoner.

The latest available information is for 28 February 1995 and is given in the attached table.

*Female population in Prison Service establishments and police cells on 28 February 1995 by type of custody*

| Type of custody | Number |
|---|---|
| Remand prisoners | |
| Untried | 346 |
| Convicted Unsentenced | 165 |
| Sentenced prisoners | |
| Young Offenders | 189 |
| Adults | 1,194 |
| Fine defaulters | 10 |
| Non-criminal prisoners | 26 |
| Total in custody | 1,930 |

### Transsexual Prisoners

**Dr. Lynne Jones:** To ask the Secretary of State for the Home Department what guidelines relate to the type of prison establishment to which transsexual offenders are committed; and if he will make it his policy to house pre-operative transsexuals in the gaols of their new gender if they have had two or more years of hormone therapy.    [23853]

**Mr. Michael Forsyth:** Responsibility for this matter has been delegated to the Director General of the Prison Service, who has been asked to arrange for a reply to be given.

*Letter from Derek Lewis to Dr. Lynne Jones, dated 22 May 1995:*

The Home Secretary has asked me to reply to your recent Question about the guidelines which relate to the type of prison establishment to which transsexual offenders are committed.

The particular difficulties experienced by transsexual prisoners have always been accepted by the Prison Service, which recognises it has a duty of care towards those committed by the courts, while at the same time having to take account of a prisoner's legal gender, as currently determined by a prisoner's birth certificate—a document at present understood in law to be immutable.

It is well understood that where transsexual offenders are concerned, a wide and complex range of physical, presentational, and psychiatric needs exist. For this reason the Prison Service adopts, in practice, a pragmatic approach once a full physical and psychiatric assessment has been made and the help of any specialist psychiatrist already involved in that individual's care before imprisonment has been sought. In virtually all such cases, the initial placement of an offender will correspond to his genetic gender and birth certificate: definitive location will be arranged only after careful, and often necessarily lengthy, assessment.

Following assessment, the principal issues which the Prison Service takes into account when considering allocation are the anticipated reaction of other prisoners and the difficulties likely to be encountered by a transsexual who may be allocated to an establishment which he/she considers to be inappropriate. While it is important that such prisoners should be offered, and avail themselves of, as wide a regime of activities as any other prisoners, in our experience many will request (and manage best) under the protection afforded by Prison Rule 43. A proportion will prefer to remain in the Prison Health Care Centre.

In view of the fact that in many instances gender dysphoria is only one facet of a very complex set of personality difficulties, it would be impractical to seek to prescribe anything other than these general guidelines for the management of transsexuals. By their nature, each particular individual will require a solution specific to himself/herself at that particular time in his/her history.

### Temazepam

**Mr. McMaster:** To ask the Secretary of State for the Home Department what measures are in place to ensure that imports of the drug temazepam are intended for legitimate prescribed use within the United Kingdom; what plans he has to introduce further measures; and if he will make a statement. [24118]

**Mr. Michael Forsyth:** Controls on the licit trade in temazepam are contained in schedule 4 to the Misuse of Drugs Regulations 1985. Imports and exports are not controlled, but records must be kept. The supply of the drug, whatever its source, is subject to authorisation, and records are required to be kept for two years. The possession of the drug in non-medicinal form, which is the form in which most importation takes place, also requires authorisation. It is permissable to import temazepam for further processing and re-export.

The Government are continuing to give careful consideration to the recommendation that temazepam be moved from schedule 4 to schedule 3 to the regulations; this would introduce, among other things, a licensing requirement for imports and exports.

### Postal and Proxy Voting

**Mr. McMaster:** To ask the Secretary of State for the Home Department which newspapers, magazines and periodicals will be used in England, Scotland, Wales and Northern Ireland during the period before the next general election to advertise postal and proxy voting; what assessment he has made of the coverage that these have across all parliamentary constituencies in the United Kingdom; and if he will make a statement. [24069]

**Mr. Howard:** In England and Wales, advertising giving details of absent voting procedure will be booked in all national daily and Sunday newspapers and in some ethnic minority language newspapers. A television advertisement will be transmitted in England and Wales, two days in advance of the press advertising to alert the public to the press campaign. Electoral registration officers in England and Wales will be provided with artwork for use in local advertising that they might wish to book.

The Central Office of Information estimates that the national newspaper advertising will be seen by 75 per cent. of the adult population throughout England and Wales.

Advertising in Scotland and Northern Ireland is arranged by the Scottish Office and the Northern Ireland Office.

### Anabolic Steroids

**Mr. Pendry:** To ask the Secretary of State for the Home Department what progress he has made towards banning the supply of anabolic steroids; and when he intends to introduce legislation. [24136]

**Mr. Michael Forsyth:** The Advisory Council on the Misuse of Drugs agreed on 11 May which substances to recommend for control, and we hope to bring forward the necessary draft modification order to the Misuse of Drugs Act 1971 shortly.

### Telephones

**Mr. Donohoe:** To ask the Secretary of State for the Home Department what use his department makes of hand-held and car-based mobile telephones; what were the costs for each financial year of those services since mobile telephones were first introduced to his department; and how many mobile telephones are currently in use. [23449]

**Mr. Howard** *[holding answer 9 May 1995]:* There are about 1,400 mobile telephones in use in my department, including the executive agencies. Fewer than 50 of these are installed in cars. Mobile telephones are used mainly by operational staff in HM Prison Service and HM immigration service who need to maintain immediate contact with their offices or other officials. Current costs were about £580,000 in 1994–95 and about £495,000 in 1993–94. Figures for capital costs and for previous years are not available.

**Mr. Donohoe:** To ask the Secretary of State for the Home Department what steps his department has taken to prevent the cloning of telephones being utilised by his department; and if his department has discussed this matter with any official agencies. [23455]

**Mr. Howard** *[holding answer 9 May 1995]:* The cloning of analogue mobile telephones can be detected, but not prevented. Cloning will cease to be a problem as my Department changes from analogue to digital telephones over the next three years. There have been no discussions, other than with the mobile telephone operators.

**Mr. Donohoe:** To ask the Secretary of State for the Home Department what cost his department has incurred during the last 12 months as a result of cloning of mobile telephones being utilised by his department, with particular reference to the making of unauthorised calls. [23489]

**Mr. Howard** *[holding answer 9 May 1995]:* None. Any such costs have been borne by the mobile telephone operators.

**Mr. Donohoe:** To ask the Secretary of State for the Home Department how many mobile telephones being utilised by his Department have been cloned during the last 12 months. [23427]

**Mr. Howard** *[holding answer 9 May 1995]:* Twelve.

### Prisons (Racial Discrimination)

**Mr. Hoyle:** To ask the Secretary of State for the Home Department (1) how many *(a)* prison staff and *(b)* prisoners have been charged with offences under race legislation in each of the last five years; [23086]

(2) how many representations he has received on racial discrimination against prisoners in prison work in each year since the case of Alexander *v.* Home Office 1987. [23084]

**Mr. Michael Forsyth** *[holding answer 9 May 1995]:* Responsibility for these matters has been delegated to the Director General of the Prison Service, who has been asked to arrange for a reply to be given.

*Letter from Derek Lewis to Mr. Doug Hoyle, dated 22 May 1995:*

The Home Secretary has asked me to reply to your recent Questions about race relations in prisons.

There are no records of any representations having been made to Ministers on racial discrimination against prisoners in prison work since the case Alexander v Home Office 1987. However, there have been approximately 55 official complaints made by prisoners to prison staff of racial discrimination on prison work since 1987.

Information on the number of prison staff and prisoners that have been charged with offences under race legislation in the last five years is not recorded centrally and could be obtained only at disproportionate cost.

## Mr. Christopher Edwards

**Mr. Cohen:** To ask the Secretary of State for the Home Department (1) if he will make a statement into the killing of Mr. Christopher Edwards by Mr. Richard Linford in Chelmsford prison on 28 November 1994; [24688]

(2) what warnings Chelmsford prison received to the effect that Mr. Richard Linford was potentially dangerous; and on what basis he was placed in a cell with another inmate; [24689]

(3) if he will list those prison service procedures which have been reviewed and changed since the killing of Mr. Christopher Edwards in Chelmsford prison; and if he will make a statement. [24690]

**Mr. Michael Forsyth** *[holding answers 18 May 1995]:* Responsibility for these matters has been delegated to the Director General of the Prison Service, who has been asked to arrange for a reply to be given.

*Letter from Derek Lewis to Mr. Harry Cohen, dated 22 May 1995:*

The Home Secretary has asked me to reply to your recent Questions about the death of Mr Christopher Edwards in Chelmsford prison on 28 November 1994.

The internal investigation conducted by the Prison Service into the circumstances surrounding the death concluded that existing procedures at Chelmsford prison had been followed satisfactorily. There was no evidence on which to recommend changes in procedures.

In view of the wider issues raised by the case, the Prison Service is jointly commissioning an independent inquiry with North Essex Health Authority and Essex Social Services. All the matters which you raise will be considered in the light of the findings of this independent inquiry.

I will write to you again when the terms of reference have been agreed, with details of members of the inquiry panel.

## Prison Proposals

**Mr. Roche:** To ask the Secretary of State for the Home Department what estimate his Department has made of the cost of building and running a super-max prison of the kind the Director General of the Prison Service is currently visiting in the United States of America. [22311]

**Mr. Michael Forsyth** *[holding answer 3 May 1995]:* Although some early work has been done on possible construction costs, specific estimates can be prepared only when we know more clearly the requirement for such prisons, how many prisoners they might hold, their location and likely regime. I shall also want to consider the views of Sir John Learmont, who will report shortly on his wide-ranging inquiry into prison security.

# Written Answers to Questions

*Tuesday 23 May 1995*

## DEFENCE

### Meteorological Office

**Mr. French:** To ask the Secretary of State for Defence what plans he has to privatise the Meteorological Office. [24812]

**Mr. Freeman:** There are no such plans.

**Mr. French:** To ask the Secretary of State for Defence when he proposes to meet Professor Julian Hunt, chief executive of the Meteorological Office to discuss the accuracy of weather forecasts. [24814]

**Mr. Freeman:** My noble Friend the Under-Secretary of State for Defence maintains regular contact with the chief executive of the Meteorological Office.

**Mr. French:** To ask the Secretary of State for Defence what assessment he has made of the effect of introducing competition for the Meteorological Office on the quality of weather forecasts. [24813]

**Mr. Freeman:** The Meteorological Office and the private sector have been competing for a number of years for commercial contracts for meteorological services. The competition helps to ensure that the Met Office maintains a very high-quality forecasting service.

### Base Closures

**Mr. Martlew:** To ask the Secretary of State for Defence if he will list the MOD bases where closures have been announced in the last five years; and in which parliamentary constituency they are located. [25188]

**Mr. Soames:** My Department does not hold information in the form requested and it could not be provided without disproportionate cost. I would, however, refer the hon. Member to my answer to the hon. Member for Pendle (Mr. Prentice) of 3 May, *Official Report,* columns *234–38.* which listed bases sold by my Department since 1990.

### Nuclear Emergencies

**Mr. Llew Smith:** To ask the Secretary of State for Defence what is the total number of departmental staff and members of the armed services available for mobilisation in the event of a nuclear accident emergency as described at pages 39-40 of the Statement on the Defence Estimates, 1995, Cm. 2800; and what level of training is given to departmental staff on nuclear emergency response. [25263]

**Mr. Soames:** In addition to a small full-time staff in MOD headquarters, the Nuclear Accident Response Organisation could draw on the skills of many hundreds of personnel across the armed forces and the MOD. Their precise number and specialisation would be dependent on the particular circumstances of an accident but it might include medical experts, health physicists, technical/design specialists, radiation monitoring experts, engineering teams and associated logistic and other support staff. In addition to the training given to ensure day-to-day expertise in these functions, appropriate training is also provided to ensure familiarisation with specific procedures relevant to a nuclear accident; the exercises described in the Statement on the Defence Estimates are an essential element in ensuring an effective response organisation.

### Auxiliary Oiler Replenishment Vessels

**Mr. Fatchett:** To ask the Secretary of State for Defence if he is now in a position to announce the agreed final costs for AORO1 and AORO2; and if he will make a statement. [24868]

**Mr. Freeman:** The total cost to the end of April 1995 to my Department is £154.890 million and £204.701 million, actual prices, for AORO1 and AORO2 respectively. Final costs for both vessels have still to be agreed.

### Princess Alexandra Hospital

**Dr. David Clark:** To ask the Secretary of State for Defence what has been the total amount of money spent by his Department on civilians receiving medical treatment at the Princess Alexandra hospital, RAF Wroughton, in each of the last five years. [25598]

**Mr. Soames:** No separate records are maintained of the costs of treating civilian NHS patients at service hospitals. The element of total running costs at the Princess Alexandra RAF hospital, Wroughton, proportionate to the percentage of patients treated on behalf of the NHS in each of the last five years is as follows:

1990–91: £8,100,000
1991–92: £6,200,000
1992–93: £7,600,000
1993–94: £8,400,000
1994–95: £8,100,000

These figures include fixed costs which would in any case have been incurred in the treatment of service patients. In addition, because of changes in budgetary responsibility and accounting procedures during the period, the costs are not entirely comparable year on year.

### Tornado Aircraft

**Dr. Clark:** To ask the Secretary of State for Defence, pursuant to his answer of 15 May, *Official Report,* column *49,* what was the total cost of the damage done to 28 Tornado aircraft based at RAF Coningsby; who will carry out the repairs to the damaged aircraft; when the investigation into the contamination will be concluded; and if he will make a statement on the conclusions of the investigation when he has received it. [25597]

**Mr. Soames:** Necessary work to allow the aircraft to resume normal operations was conducted by service personnel immediately after the contamination was discovered. Once full and careful consideration has been given to the investigation I will write to the hon. Member.

### Tri-service Hospital, Haslar

**Dr. David Clark:** To ask the Secretary of State for Defence what is the estimated total cost of accommodation at the proposed tri-service hospital at

Haslar. [25599]

**Mr. Soames:** Existing single accommodation will be made available for the staff of the Royal hospital, Haslar. Although some refurbishment may be necessary, the cost of this work is as yet unquantified. Estimates for the requirement of additional married quarters, which will be met in the short term by hiring property or payment of excess rent allowance, are not yet available, although these costs will be partially offset by savings at current locations.

## Personal Protection Weapons

**Rev. Martin Smyth:** To ask the Secretary of State for Defence if he will make a statement on the removal of personal protection weapons from soldiers in the Royal Irish Regiment. [25353]

**Mr. Soames:** There has been no change in our policy on soldiers from the Royal Irish Regiment holding personal protection weapons. The requirement for individual soldiers to retain army-issue weapons is kept under review on a case-by-case basis, and there are no plans to institute a general policy of withdrawing such weapons.

## TREASURY

### Inflation

**Sir Thomas Arnold:** To ask the Chancellor of the Exchequer what plans he has to alter the inflation target. [24876]

**Mr. Kenneth Clarke:** The Government's aim is to keep underlying inflation in the range 1 to 4 per cent. and to bring it down into the lower half of this range by the end of the present Parliament. I have no plans to change the objective for that period.

**Mr. Malcolm Bruce:** To ask the Chancellor of the Exchequer, whether it remains his policy to keep RPIX inflation below 2.5 per cent. at the end of the current Parliament. [24552]

**Mr. Nelson:** The Government's policy is to keep underlying inflation, as measured by the retail prices index excluding mortgage interest payments, in the range 1 to 4 per cent. and to bring it down to the lower half of the range by the end of the present Parliament.

### Capital Gains Tax

**Mr. Frank Field:** To ask the Chancellor of the Exchequer if he will estimate for 1995–96 the number of individuals whose gross income and capital gains exceed *(a)* £70,000, *(b)* £80,000 and *(c)* £100,000, in each case specifying the number paying capital gains tax. [25011]

**Sir George Young:** Available information is in terms of taxable income and capital gains. Provisional estimates are given in the table:

*Number of individual taxpayers, excluding trusts, 1995–96*

| Taxable income[1] and gains[2] over: | Total | Paying capital gains tax[3] |
|---|---|---|
| £70,000 | 220,000 | 19,000 |
| £80,000 | 170,000 | 17,000 |
| £100,000 | 110,000 | 14,000 |

[1] Taxable income is defined as gross income for income tax purposes less those allowances and reliefs which are available at the taxpayer's marginal rate.

[2] Taxable gains are chargeable gains net of reliefs and the annual exempt amount.

[3] Figures exclude gains made by companies which are included under corporation tax.

### Public Expenditure

**Mr. Matthew Banks:** To ask the Chancellor of the Exchequer when the Government intend to publish provisional outturn figures for public expenditure in 1994–95. [25997]

**Mr. Aitken:** The Government propose to replace the annual Cash Limits Outturn White Paper by a comprehensive outturn document covering not just cash limited expenditure but all expenditure within the control total. The aim is to publish the first document in the new early July, a week or so before the normal publication date for the CLOWP. The document will show provisional outturn for 1994–95 for the control total by Department compared with plans, and for individual votes and voted cash limits, non-voted cash limits, external financing limits, and gross and net running costs limits compared with original and final provision.

**Mr. Milburn:** To ask the Chancellor of the Exchequer if he will update the figures contained in tables 1.2, 1.3, 1.4 and 1.5 of the public expenditure statistical supplement to the Financial Statement and Budget Report 1995–96 to show the outturn for 1994–95 and estimated outturn for 1995–96. [25193]

**Mr. Aitken:** My answer today to the hon. Member for Southport (Mr. Banks) described the arrangements for publishing provisional outturn data on public expenditure for 1994–95. For 1995–96, following usual practice, forecast outturn figures will be published in the Financial Statement and Budget Report 1996–97 for the control total by Department, and in more detail in the statistical supplement to that report.

### Private Nursing Homes

**Mr. Hood:** To ask the Chancellor of the Exchequer with what frequency the Inland Revenue performs spot checks on the accounting practices of owners of private nursing homes. [25488]

**Sir George Young** *[holding answer 22 May 1995]:* All businesses are liable to have their accounts inspected by the Inland Revenue and investigations are carried out where there is reason to believe the accounts may not be correct. Specific figures relating to nursing homes are not compiled.

### Banks (Tax Relief)

**Mr. Foulkes:** To ask the Chancellor of the Exchequer how much has been granted in tax relief to United Kingdom banks against possible default on third world debts in each of the last 10 years; and what is the rationale for such tax relief. [25373]

**Sir George Young:** Provisions by banks operating in the United Kingdom for doubtful sovereign debt—mostly of third world countries, but which may include relatively small amounts for other countries—are estimated to have reduced corporation tax receipts in the last nine years by the following amounts:

| | £ million |
|---|---|
| 1986–87 | 70 |
| 1987–88 | 190 |
| 1988–89 | 550 |
| 1989–90 | 490 |
| 1990–91 | 880 |
| 1991–92 | 120 |
| 1992–93 | 120 |
| 1993–94 | 120 |
| 1994–95 (provisional) | 120 |

Estimates for earlier years are zero or small.

Third world debt is a feature of banking and losses on sovereign debt represent real losses arising in the normal course of such business. Losses or potential losses on sovereign debt therefore attract relief in broadly the same way as losses or potential losses on trading debts of other businesses.

### Exporters

**Mr. Austin Mitchell:** To ask the Chancellor of the Exchequer if he has asked the Deputy Governor of the Bank of England to substantiate the claim of December 1993 that exporters were profiteering by raising prices excessively instead of increasing sales. [25478]

**Mr. Kenneth Clarke:** I regularly discuss a wide range of economic issues with both the Governor and Deputy Governor of the Bank of England. Export sales have clearly increased since December 1993, growing by 11 per cent. in 1994, the strongest increase in more than 20 years.

### VAT on Spectacles

**Mr. Donohoe:** To ask the Chancellor of the Exchequer if he will make a statement on the state of discussions between British ophthalmic physicians and his Department relating to the overpayment of tax under European directives; and how much his Department estimates is owed by the Customs and Excise to British opticians in overpaid tax. [25343]

**Mr. Heathcoat-Amory:** Customs and Excise met opticians' representatives on 11 May and discussed the matters arising from the recent High Court decision on the VAT liability of supplies of spectacles. Proposals are awaited from the trade representatives on a number of the issues discussed and these will be considered at a further meeting planned for mid June. It is difficult to estimate the total amount of tax to be refunded to opticians, because the impact of the High Court decision will vary significantly from business to business; Customs estimate that the figure may be of the order of £250 million including statutory interest.

## TRADE AND INDUSTRY

### South Africa

**Mr. Caborn:** To ask the President of the Board of Trade (1) if he will make a statement on the draft negotiating mandate for a new trade regime between the European Union and South Africa; [25610]

(2) if he will undertake a study into the effect of the proposed free trade area between the European Union and South Africa on the economies of the other member states of the Southern African Customs Union and the Southern African Development Community. [25609]

**Mr. Needham:** The draft negotiating directives presented by the European Commission propose that the EU should respond positively if the South African Government were willing to negotiate a bilateral free trade agreement. The Government believe that such an agreement offers the greatest potential for delivering improvements in access to the EU market for South African products and promoting our long-term trade relations.

We therefore support the Commission proposal, on the understanding that any free trade agreement negotiated between the EU and South Africa is compatible with World Trade Organisation rules and takes account of South Africa's regional commitments. I believe that this is in line with the recommendation on the future relationship between the EU and South Africa made in the Trade and Industry Select Committee's report on trade with southern Africa published on 27 July 1994. In the process of negotiation, we will urge the European Commission to take into account the possible effects of such an agreement on the economies of South Africa's neighbours and we will also listen carefully to the views of South Africa's partners in the Southern African Customs Union and the Southern African Development Community.

### Balance of Trade

**Mr. Milburn:** To ask the President of the Board of Trade (1) what has been the balance of trade in oil in 1994 prices for each year since 1978; [25191]

(2) what has been the balance of trade in manufactured goods in 1994 prices for each year since 1978. [25190]

**Mr. Needham:** The information is published for 1994 by the Central Statistical Office in the "Monthly Review of External Trade Statistics", available in the Library of the House. The information is not available in 1994 prices for other years, although data at 1990 prices is available from the CSO's central shared database, also in the Library of the House.

## AGRICULTURE, FISHERIES AND FOOD

### Trading Standards Services, Cleveland

**Mr. Frank Cook:** To ask the Minister of Agriculture, Fisheries and Food what assessment he has made of the applicability of the views attributed to his Department on pages 42 and 43 of "Renewing Local Government in the English Shires" to the future of trading standards services in Cleveland after the division of those services among four unitary authorities as a result of local government reorganisation. [25215]

**Mrs. Browning:** I refer the hon. Member to the reply that I gave to the hon. Member for Kingswood (Mr. Berry) on 17 May, *Official Report*, column *283*. The same considerations apply in Cleveland as in Berkshire.

### Animal Health and Veterinary Group

**Mr. William Ross:** To ask the Minister of Agriculture, Fisheries and Food if he will now publish the Lebrecht report. [24955]

**Mrs. Browning:** This report on an internal management review of the functions and organisation of the Ministry's animal health and veterinary group was not written with publication in mind and is not suitable for publication. My right hon. Friend did, however, issue a consultation document last October setting out the basis for his provisional conclusions following the review and took the many comments received into account in reaching the decisions that he announced in a written answer to my hon. Friend the Member for Gloucester (Mr. French) on 4 May.

### Fisheries

**Mr. Austin Mitchell:** To ask the Minister of Agriculture, Fisheries and Food why Irish vessels currently enjoy fishing rights off Spitzbergen. [25383]

**Mr. Jack:** For 1995 the European Union has a cod quota of 24,220 tonnes at Spitzbergen and Bear island. In accordance with the traditional allocation key, Council Regulation 3362/94 divides this between the member states as follows:

|  | Tonnes |
| --- | --- |
| France | 2,130 |
| Germany | 4,820 |
| Portugal | 2,390 |
| Spain | 11,500 |
| United Kingdom | 3,130 |
| Other member states except France, Germany, Portugal, Spain, United Kingdom, Finland and Sweden | 250 |

**Mr. Austin Mitchell:** To ask the Minister of Agriculture, Fisheries and Food what red fish quotas were offered in Iceland waters in 1994 and 1995 to *(a)* Britain and *(b)* Germany; which British firms were offered catches there by his Ministry; and whether they took up the offer. [25384]

**Mr. Jack:** Germany and the United Kingdom were allocated quotas for respectively 1690 tonnes and 1160 tonnes of red fish in Icelandic waters for both 1994 and 1995. The Fish Producers Organisation of Grimsby was offered the UK quota for 1994 but did not take up the

opportunity. For 1995 the United Kingdom quota has not yet been allocated; it is not available before 1 July each year.

### Regional Service Survey

**Mr. Michael Brown:** To ask the Minister of Agriculture, Fisheries and Food if he will publish the results of the recent survey of satisfaction with the levels of service his Department's regional organisation provides for the farming public. [26098]

**Mr. Waldegrave:** In accordance with the principles of the citizens charter, a survey of customers of the MAFF regional service centre was carried out by a firm of independent consultants in early 1995. The overall results are very positive and show that nearly nine in 10 customers felt their MAFF centre had done a good, very good or excellent job in dealing with their most recent scheme or licence application. We will be considering carefully what can be done to address those areas where our customers feel that there is scope for improvement in our performance.

I have placed copies of the consultants' report in the Library of the House.

### Baby Milk

**Mr. Morgan:** To ask the Minister of Agriculture, Fisheries and Food what consultations she has had with community nurses, health visitors, midwives and other professionally involved groups concerning the effect of banning the advertising of baby milk within national health service premises on levels of breast feeding commencement; and if she will make a statement. [25605]

**Mrs. Browning** *[holding answer 22 May 1995]:* I refer the hon. Member to the answer that I gave to the right hon. Member for Tweeddale, Ettrick and Lauderdale (Sir D. Steel) on 14 March 1995, *Official Report*, columns *550-51.*

**Mr. Morgan:** To ask the Minister of Agriculture, Fisheries and Food, what information he has on which European Union member states permit the advertising of baby milk *(a)* in generally available media and *(b)* health-specific premises on what dates changes in permission for either category of advertising was amended in either direction what subsequent changes occurred in breast feeding commencement levels; and if she will make a statement. [25604]

**Mrs. Browning** *[holding answer 22 May 1995]:* I have no such information; there is no requirement on member states to supply it to one another.

### Spanish Veterinary Inspections

**Mr. Morley:** To ask the Minister of Agriculture, Fisheries and Food, pursuant to his answer of 24 April, *Official Report*, column *379*, how many vets are employed by the Spanish authorities; how many of these have undertaken spot checks of sheep being imported into Spain; how many spot checks were undertaken by the Spanish authorities in the last year for which figures are available; and what assessment he has made as to the extent to which the welfare of British sheep exported to Spain is adequately provided for. [21851]

**Mrs. Browning** *[holding answer 22 May 1995]:* The level of spot checking and the resources devoted to it are matters for the Spanish authorities. We maintain contact with them, and understand from them that they are satisfied on the basis of their checks that the animals' welfare is satisfactorily protected.

### Live Animal Exports

**Mr. Morley:** To ask the Minister of Agriculture, Fisheries and Food how many inspections of live animals for export were made by Ministry vets at *(a)* Shoreham and *(b)* Brightlingsea, since 1 January. [24736]

**Mrs. Browning** *[holding answer 18 May 1995]:* Between 1 January and 12 May there were 60 sailings from Shoreham carrying animals for slaughter or for further fattening and 70 from Brightlingsea. Veterinary inspectors were present at the ports for each sailing, when visual checks were made of the animals on board lorries and export paperwork checked. Veterinary inspection of animals for fitness to travel is carried out at point of departure, not at the port.

**Mr. Morley:** To ask the Minister of Agriculture, Fisheries and Food how many *(a)* calves and *(b)* sheep arriving at (i) Shoreham and (ii) Plymouth, in the period between 1 November 1994 and 30 April 1995 were (1) dead on arrival, (2) judged to be unfit to travel and (3) destroyed because of injury or disease; and if he will make a statement. [24735]

**Mrs. Browning** *[holding answer 16 May 1995]:* The figures for the period specified are as follows:

| | Number of animals | | | | | |
| | Dead on arrival | | Unfit to travel | | Destroyed | |
| Port | calves | sheep | calves | sheep | calves | sheep |
|---|---|---|---|---|---|---|
| Shoreham | none | 1 | 1 | 2 | none | none |
| Plymouth | none | none | none | none | none | none |

### PRIME MINISTER

### North-West Kent

Q7. **Mr. Dunn:** To ask the Prime Minister what plans he has to visit north-west Kent. [23845]

**The Prime Minister:** Although I have no current plans to do so, I hope such a visit will be possible in the near future.

### Scotland

Q8. **Mr. David Marshall:** To ask the Prime Minister when he next intends to visit Scotland. [23846]

**The Prime Minister:** I have at present no plans to do so.

### Engagements

**Mr. Harry Greenway:** To ask the Prime Minister if he will list his official engagements for Tuesday 23 May 1995. [24304]

**Sir Peter Tapsell:** To ask the Prime Minister if he will list his official engagements for Tuesday 23 May. [24304]

**The Prime Minister:** This morning I had meetings with ministerial colleagues and others. In addition to my duties in the House, I shall be having further meetings later today.

### Intelligence and Security Committee

**Mr. Peter Ainsworth:** To ask the Prime Minister whether he has yet received a report from the Intelligence and Security Committee on the discharge of its functions under the Intelligence Services Act 1994. [25998]

**The Prime Minister:** I can confirm that I have recently received an interim report from the Intelligence and Security Committee, setting out the broad pattern of its work to date and outlining some of its future priorities for inquiry. I do not consider that the report contains any matter whose publication would be prejudicial to the continued discharge of the functions of the Secret Intelligence Service, Security Service or Government Communications Headquarters, and I have therefore today placed copies of it, as submitted by the Committee, in the Libraries of both Houses.

### Nolan Committee

**Mr. Austin Mitchell:** To ask the Prime Minister if he will seek to extend the recommendations of the Nolan Committee concerning the conduct of Ministers and officials to include the Governor of the Bank of England and all senior members of his staff. [25379]

**The Prime Minister:** I have no plans to do so.

### Antanas Gecas

**Mr. Foulkes:** To ask the Prime Minister for what period Antanas Gecas was employed by British intelligence. [25622]

**The Prime Minister:** It remains the Government's policy not to provide information on the operations at the security and intelligence agencies.

### Majority Shareholdings

**Mr. Byers:** To ask the Prime Minister if he will list those companies in which the holder of his office is a majority shareholder which *(a)* are currently in existence and *(b)* have been wound up in the past five years. [25722]

**The Prime Minister** *[holding answer 22 May 1995]:* None.

### Bank of England

**Mr. Austin Mitchell:** To ask the Prime Minister if the statement of Government policy set out in paragraph 5 of the Bank of England press release of the text of the Deputy Governor's speech to the City branch of the Institute of Directors on 13 December was authorised by him. [25683]

**The Prime Minister:** I refer the hon. Member to the answer that I gave him on 29 March 1995 *Official Report*, column *640*.

### OVERSEAS DEVELOPMENT ADMINISTRATION

### Recycling

**Mr. Sheerman:** To ask the Secretary of State for Foreign and Commonwealth Affairs what plans he has to introduce recycling programmes as part of the work of the Overseas Development Administration. [24991]

**Mr. Baldry:** We are ready to consider support to recycling programmes whenever invited to do so by partner countries. We are, for example, discussing recycling as part of current environmental management projects in India and Egypt.

### Micro-enterprise Development

**Ms Glenda Jackson:** To ask the Secretary of State for Foreign and Commonwealth Affairs what progress has been made with regard to the Grameen trust's training programme application for support. [25090]

**Mr. Baldry** [*holding answer 22 May 1995*]: We are keen supporters of micro-enterprise development. We have advised the Garmeen trust that the managers of our micro-enterprise projects in recipient countries will seek to identify suitable opportunities for project beneficiaries to use the trust's training facilities.

### Bangladesh

**Mr. Alton:** To ask the Secretary of State for Foreign and Commonwealth Affairs if he will list the amount donated by the Overseas Development Administration department for primary health care in Bangladesh, excluding family planning provision, for the last year in which figures are available. [25309]

**Mr. Baldry** [*holding answer 22 May 1995*]: Our expenditure on primary health care projects in Bangladesh in 1993–94 was £2.55 million.

### Aid and Trade Programme

**Dr. Lynne Jones:** To ask the Secretary of State for Foreign and Commonwealth Affairs what has been the total expenditure on the aid and trade programme in each of the last five years; and which British companies have won contracts under this programme. [24884]

**Mr. Baldry:** The final outturn of expenditure for ATP in 1994–95 is not yet available.

Expenditure for ATP for each of the previous five years was:

| Financial year | ATP actual expenditure £ million |
| --- | --- |
| 1989–90 | 61.671 |
| 1990–91 | 94.424 |
| 1991–92 | 101.183 |
| 1992–93 | 93.019 |
| 1993–94 | 84.687 |

For lists of which British companies have won contracts under the ATP in the last five years I refer the hon. Member to the answer that I gave to the hon. Member for Eccles (Miss Lestor) *Official Report*, 16 May, column *121*, covering 1993–95 and, for the years 1991–1992, to the answer that I gave to the hon. Member for Carrick, Cumnock and Doon Valley (Mr. Foulkes) on 23 November 1994 at column *199*.

### Population Control

**Mr. Alton:** To ask the Secretary of State for Foreign and Commonwealth Affairs (1) what action the Overseas Development Administration takes to ensure that money donated by Her Majesty's Government for family planning purposes is not used as part of a coercive family planning programme or to free resources in recipient countries for such programmes; [25313]

(2) what legal provisions govern the funding of coercive population programmes overseas; and what plans he has to promote legislation banning such funding. [25316]

**Mr. Baldry** [*holding answer 22 May 1995*]: Bilateral programmes are designed and monitored to ensure that they promote reproductive choice on an entirely voluntary and informed basis. We ensure that organisations to which we give funds for reproductive health activities operate similar policies and approaches. We do not believe that it is necessary to introduce legislation to ensure that aid funds for reproductive health programmes are used effectively and in accordance with our policies.

**Mr. Alton:** To ask the Secretary of State for Foreign and Commonwealth Affairs if he will make a statement on the Overseas Development Administration's policy on the provision of financial, personal or community incentives to encourage contraceptive use in developing countries. [25312]

**Mr. Baldry** [*holding answer 22 May 1995*]: We believe that decisions by couples and individuals about the use of particular methods of contraception should be made on an entirely voluntary and informed basis and that the use of incentives which are likely to prejudice this principle should be discouraged.

**Mr. Alton:** To ask the Secretary of State for Foreign and Commonwealth Affairs if he will list the officials from the Overseas Development Administration who sit on any board, committee, or regular meeting of the International Planned Parenthood Federation and the UN Family Planning Association. [25299]

**Mr. Baldry** [*holding answer 22 May 1995*]: The British Government have a seat on the executive board of the United Nations development programme, which is also the governing body of the United Nations fund for population activities. Part of each board meeting is devoted to UNFPA business. The United Kingdom is invited to the annual donors meeting of the International Planned Parenthood Federation. In both cases meetings are attended by officials from the Overseas Development Administration's health and population division.

**Mr. Alton:** To ask the Secretary of State for Foreign and Commonwealth Affairs what visits officials from his Department have made to China to assess the Chinese population control programme or the work of the Chinese Family Planning Association or the UN fund for population activities in China; and what reports exist on such visits. [25303]

**Mr. Baldry** [*holding answer 22 May 1995*]: Officials from the British embassy in Peking have regular meetings with the relevant Chinese authorities to discuss a range of issues, including China's population policies.

**Mr. Alton:** To ask the Secretary of State for Foreign and Commonwealth Affairs to which countries the Overseas Development Administration donates money, directly or via a non-governmental organisation, where overseas aid is tied to acceptance of family planning programmes; and if he will make a statement on his Department's policy on tying overseas aid to acceptance of family planning programmes. [25311]

**Mr. Baldry** *[holding answer 22 May 1995]:* None. We do not support making the provision of overseas aid conditional on the implementation of family planning programmes.

**Mr. Alton:** To ask the Secretary of State for Foreign and Commonwealth Affairs (1) what considerations underlie the policy of donating funds from the Overseas Development Administration budget to the core funds of the International Planned Parenthood Federation and the UN Family Planning Association rather than to specific earmarked projects undertaken by those organisations;     [25298]

(2) if he will list those organisations involved in family planning projects to which the Overseas Development Administration makes donations to their core funds, together with the amount donated for the last year for which figures are available.     [25306]

**Mr. Baldry** *[holding answer 22 May 1995]:* The United Nations Population Fund and the International Planned Parenthood Federation have the capacity to allocate and spend their resources in an effective manner. Together with other Governments we set policy for UNFPA and provide guidance for IPPF on the use of resources. Her Majesty's Government representatives seek to ensure that funds are used in ways which are fully in line with British aid policy and priority objectives. On this basis, we and other Governments provide the large majority of funds without earmarking. The efficiency and effectiveness of both organisations would be impeded if the United Kingdom and other donors earmarked their contributions for specific activities.

In 1994 we gave £7.5 million to the general funds of IPPF and £8.5 million to those of UNFPA.

**Mr. Alton:** To ask the Secretary of State for Foreign and Commonwealth Affairs (1) if he will place in the Library all reports submitted to the Overseas Development Administration since 1989 by the International Planned Parenthood Federation on population policies in China.     [25317]

(2) what written statements by the International Planned Parenthood Federation, the UN Family Planning Association or the Chinese Family Planning Association condemning or disassociating themselves from any instance of coercive population control in China are held on the files of his Department; and if he will list in each case the instance condemned and the date of the document.     [25301]

**Mr. Baldry** *[holding answer 22 May 1995]:* The latest annual report from the International Planned Parenthood Federation covering its worldwide operations, together with a sample of statements, by both the United Nations Population Fund and the IPPF, opposing coercion, have been placed in the Libraries of the House.

**Mr. Alton:** To ask the Secretary of State for Foreign and Commonwealth Affairs what information he has on links between the International Planned Parenthood Federation and the British eugenics movement and the Gaton Institute.     [25300]

**Mr. Baldry** *[holding answer 22 May 1995]:* We understand from the International Planned Parenthood Federation that some individual members at its founding in 1952 may have had links with the eugenics movement. However, eugenics views have never influenced IPPF's policies or programmes. IPPF makes it an unequivocal condition for membership that each autonomous family planning association commits itself to fight all discrimination and coercion based on social or economic status, gender, race, colour, creed or political beliefs.

**Mr. Alton:** To ask the Secretary of State for Foreign and Commonwealth Affairs what definition the Overseas Development Administration uses of what constitutes coercive population control; and in which countries such practices have been identified.     [25307]

**Mr. Baldry** *[holding answer 22 May 1995]:* Population activities would be considered coercive if they sought to infringe the basic right of couples and individuals to decide freely and responsibly the number and spacing of their children. Population programmes funded by the Overseas Development Administration safeguard and promote this right and facilitate the exercise of such a right by individuals. The Overseas Development Administration does not hold authoritative information on instances of coercion in overseas countries.

**Mr. Alton:** To ask the Secretary of State for Foreign and Commonwealth Affairs what information he has on the numbers of volunteers provided by the Chinese Family Planning Association to assist in family planning initiatives in China; what assessment he had made of the level of independence of the Chinese Family Planning Association from the central Chinese Government; what information he has on the role played by the Chinese Family Planning Association in recent Chinese "population high tides"; what information he has on the liaison between the Chinese Family Planning Association and the International Planned Parenthood Federation; and what documentation the Overseas Development Administration has received arising from such liaison.     [25310]

**Mr. Baldry** *[holding answer 22 May 1995]:* The China Family Planning Association is a member of the International Planned Parenthood Federation. We understand that there are some 75 million volunteers in CFPA, including many doctors and nurses, who assist with counselling and providing information on family planning. The CFPA does not provide clinical services.

The CFPA is a non-profit, non-governmental organisation, governed by a board of volunteers drawn from all sections of national society. The CFPA has been appointed by the Chinese Government to monitor the national family planning programme and help to ensure that coercion does not take place in the programme. The IPPF provides information on the activities of CFPA as and when required.

**Mr. Alton:** To ask the Secretary of State for Foreign and Commonwealth Affairs what assessments his Department has made for the unmet need for family planning overseas; and on what assumptions such assessments are made.     [25308]

**Mr. Baldry** *[holding answer 22 May 1995]:* We use estimates of unmet demand for family planning prepared by the United Nations Population Fund and other organisations with expertise in this area. Such estimates are based on demographic and health survey data collected from individual countries. These surveys collect information about couples using family planning and about couples who do not, but who express a desire to limit their family size. Where necessary, we also undertake our own small-scale studies to assess specific reproductive health needs.

## Child Mortality Rates

**Ms Glenda Jackson:** To ask the Secretary of State for Foreign and Commonwealth Affairs what additional bilateral aid will be provided to meet the goals set at the 1990 world summit for children, to reduce *(a)* infant mortality rates and *(b)* under-five mortality rates, by one third by 2000. [25089]

**Mr. Baldry** *[holding answer 22 May 1995]:* We are increasing our support for reproductive health programmes, which will enable children and women to enjoy better health through improved child spacing, safer childbirth, and improved access to other essential health care. We expect to commit, over the years 1994 and 1995, at least £100 million for these purposes and in support of other reproductive health goals.

# HEALTH

## Nursing Services

**Mrs. Beckett:** To ask the Secretary of State for Health if she will make a statement on the change in episodes in *(a)* health visiting, *(b)* community nursing services, *(c)* district nursing, *(d)* community mental handicap nursing and *(e)* occupational therapy between 1988–89 and 1992–93. [21743]

**Mr. Sackville:** The information available is set out in the table.

*New episodes of care*

| | 1988–89 (000's) | 1992–93 (000's) |
|---|---|---|
| Community psychiatric nursing | 229.7 | 303.4 |
| Community mental handicap nursing | 21.2 | 20.5 |
| District nursing | 2,383.2 | 2,152.5 |
| Occupational therapy[1] | 774.1 | 879.4 |

[1] Figures for occupational therapy are provisional.

New episodes of care have increased by 32.1 per cent. in community psychiatric nursing and by 13.6 per cent. in occupational therapy. Numbers of new episodes in community mental handicap nursing have remained virtually constant over the period 1988–89 to 1992–93.

The number of new episodes has reduced by 9.7 per cent. in district nursing. This may reflect the increasingly complex treatment they provide, requiring a longer time to be spent with each patient, and also their role as team leaders. Simpler treatments often administered by district nurses in the past may now increasingly be provided by other members of the care team or through self-medication by patients, enabling district nurses to devote more time to individual patients who require their specialist skills.

Information on episodes of care for health visitors is not held centrally.

## Surgeons (Suspension)

**Mr. Cann:** To ask the Secretary of State for Health (1) how many surgeons suspended on full pay by NHS hospital trusts have later been *(a)* dismissed and *(b)* reinstated; and how many cases await a decision on the surgeon's future; [24729]

(2) how many surgeons have been suspended on full pay because of concern about their professional competence by NHS hospital trusts since their inception; [24728]

(3) what discussions she has had with the General Medical Council on the employment of suspended surgeons in hospitals, other than those in respect of which they were suspended; and what further discussions she plans to have; [24726]

(4) what advice her Department gives to NHS hospital trusts about the employment of surgeons who have been suspended by other NHS hospital trusts. [24727]

**Mr. Malone:** The General Medical Council, an independent statutory body, is responsible for protecting the public by regulating the medical profession. Its professional conduct committee may attach conditions to a doctor's registration, or suspend or remove a doctor from the register, if the doctor is found guilty of serious professional misconduct. The committee may immediately suspend a doctor, notwithstanding that he may appeal. In exceptional circumstances, interim suspension for two months may be imposed pending a hearing by the professional conduct committee. A doctor whose name is suspended or erased cannot practise in the national health service.

The GMC's powers are being widened. We have introduced the Medical (Professional Performance) Bill this Session, based on proposals by the GMC, to allow it to take action in cases of seriously deficient professional performance by doctors. This action may include suspension of registration. My right hon. Friend the Secretary of State will meet the new president of the GMC, when he is elected, to discuss these and other matters.

A doctor suspended by a NHS trust needs the trust's permission to work elsewhere. We would expect the trust to consider carefully the circumstances in which the doctor was suspended before agreeing to any other employment. Working without permission is a breach of contract. All NHS trusts should obtain references from previous employers as part of their duty to ensure that the competence and integrity of a doctor is not in doubt.

A decision to disqualify a general practitioner is made by the NHS tribunal. We have supported the Bill introduced this Session by the hon. Member for Woolwich (Mr. Austin-Walker)—the NHS (Amendment) Bill— which will enable the tribunal to protect patients by suspending a GP before a full hearing takes place.

Guidance on doctors' registration and employment was issued in EL(92)84, copies of which are available in the Library. Figures on the number of suspensions by NHS trusts are not available centrally.

## London Health Services Report

**Mr. Spearing:** To ask the Secretary of State for Health what response she has made to the report on London health services prepared by the Greater London Association of Community Health Councils for London Members of Parliament, dated 10 May, a copy of which has been sent to her. [24739]

**Mr. Malone:** No formal response has been made. However, the report on admissions times which monitors the progress of hospitals towards the new patients charter standard, launched in January 1995 is welcomed. From April 1995, all patients should be given a bed within three to four hours. The community health council figures show that progress has been made and it is encouraging to note the relatively small numbers outside the target last year before management attention was focused on this important issue.

### Northern Birmingham Mental Health Trust

**Mr. Mike O'Brien:** To ask the Secretary of State for Health when a negotiating body was formed by Northern Birmingham Mental Health trust to deal with pay and other trade union related matters. [24777]

**Mr. Malone:** This is a matter for the trust. The hon. Member may wish to contact the chairman, Mrs. Judith Mackay, for details.

### Hepatitis C

**Mr. Wigley:** To ask the Secretary of State for Health how many *(a)* letters and *(b)* other representations she has received in the current year concerning the need to compensate those people who are infected by the hepatitis C virus from contaminated blood; and if she will make a statement. [24946]

**Mr. Sackville:** Representations about payments include four parliamentary questions, a short debate in the House of Lords and three early-day motions. In addition, Ministers have received 196 letters.

### Bull Bars

**Sir Nicholas Scott:** To ask the Secretary of State for Health how many admissions to hospital in *(a)* the London area and *(b)* nationally have to a significant extent been due to accidents involving bull bars on road vehicles in the latest available year. [25262]

**Mr. Sackville:** This information is not available centrally.

### Abortions

**Mrs. Bridget Prentice:** To ask the Secretary of State for Health how many abortions involving admission and discharge the same day were performed on women resident in each district health authority and in each regional health authority in England and Wales in 1993; and how many of these operations were performed in NHS hospitals. [25047]

**Mr. Sackville:** This information will be placed in the Library.

### Medical and Dental Education

**Mr. Kirkwood:** To ask the Secretary of State for Health what plans there are to introduce the model of the Scottish Council for Postgraduate Medical and Dental Education for the delivery of postgraduate medical and dental education in England; and if she will make a statement. [25048]

**Mr. Malone:** None. The national health service executive is considering the future arrangements for postgraduate medical and dental education in England and a document entitled "Options for the Future Management of Postgraduate Medical and Dental Education" was issued for consultation on 27 March 1995, copies of which are available in the Library. Responses to the document are being considered.

**Mrs. Gorman:** To ask the Secretary of State for Health what plans the NHS has to support medical undergraduates' education. [26202]

**Mr. Malone:** I have placed in the Library a copy of the report, "SIFT into the Future", from an advisory group on future arrangements for the service increment for teaching—SIFT—chaired by Dr. Graham Winyard, health care director of the national health service executive.

I welcome the direction of change proposed by the advisory group. The report recommends development in the way we meet the additional NHS costs to hospitals, community trusts and general practitioners associated with teaching medical undergraduates. Payments will be based progressively on the demonstrated costs of clinical placements and of facilities to support teaching, within a sound framework of responsibilities, relationships and accountability. The report has been welcomed by the steering group on undergraduate medical and dental education and research.

I am sending copies of the report to health authorities, family health services authorities, trusts, universities and other interested bodies, seeking views on the detailed recommendations and on plans for implementation.

Comments are also sought on separate proposals for changes in the service increment for teaching dental students, which follow from the recommendations of the dental hospital subgroup of SGUMDER. I have placed in the Library a copy of the consultation paper about the proposals for change.

Subject to consultation and to detailed development work, changes will take effect from 1 April 1996.

### London Initiative Zone, Newham

**Mr. Timms:** To ask the Secretary of State for Health, pursuant to her answer of 16 May, *Official Report,* column *166* how much of the amount allocated has been spent in *(a)* 1993–94, *(b)* 1994–95 and *(c)* 1995–96 on each scheme funded through the LIZ initiative in Newham listed in her answer. [25214]

**Mr. Malone:** The information is shown in the table:

|  | Capital spend £ | |
| --- | --- | --- |
|  | *1993–94* | *1994–95* |
| *Newham* | | |
| Essex Lodge (primary care centre) | 22,373 | 40,439 |
| Shrewsbury Road | 217,000 | 432,000 |
| Improvement grants to GP premises | 283,472 | 97,373 |
| Star Lane (primary care centre) | 470,128 | 130,533 |
| Stratford Corridor (primary care centre) | 304,132 | 188 |
| Cyprus Dock (resource centre) | 192,000 | 138,495 |

*Notes:*

1. Figures for 1995–96 schemes are not yet available.

2. Some 1994–95 projects have been carried over into the 1995–96 financial year. These are 533 Barking road, 1 Kennard street, Newham GP Forum and security improvements to GP surgeries.

### Thalidomide Trust

**Mr. Tom Clarke:** To ask the Secretary of State for Health what measures she has considered in response to the 1994 report of the Thalidomide Trust National Advisory Council, with particular reference to the actuarial projections on the life of the trust. [24972]

**Mr. Sackville:** The Government have not been asked to respond to this report. Representations have, however, been made by Thalidomide disabled people that the moneys held by the Thalidomide Trust are insufficient to meet their needs, and the Government have brought these concerns to the attention of the trust. The Government welcome the further financial help promised by Guinness plc to secure the future of the Thalidomide Trust and underpin the beneficiaries' needs, but have made it clear that adequacy of the settlement with Distillers—now Guinness—is not a matter in which the Government can intervene.

### Dental Services

**Mr. Gordon Prentice:** To ask the Secretary of State for Health what is the number and percentage of the population *(a)* across the United Kingdom, *(b)* in the north-west and *(c)* in Lancashire which have dental treatment outside the NHS for each year since 1979. [25152]

**Mr. Malone:** Information about the number and percentage of the population who have dental treatment outside the national health service is not available centrally.

### New Hospitals, London

**Mr Michael Spicer:** To ask the Secretary of State for Health if she will list the number of new hospitals which have opened in central London in the last 10 years, together with their numbers of beds. [25136]

**Mr. Malone:** This information is not available centrally. My hon. Friend may wish to contact Sir William Staveley and Mr. William Wells, chairmen of North Thames and South Thames regional health authorities respectively, for details.

### Contraception

**Mrs. Bridget Prentice:** To ask the Secretary of State for Health what is the cost of *(a)* the registered morning-after pill and *(b)* the equivalent oral contraceptive; and if she will make a statement. [25046]

**Mr. Sackville:** Schering PC4 is the only product marketed in the United Kingdom for use as a morning-after pill. The cost of a pack of four tablets is £1.40. Oral contraceptives range in price from 37p to £2.77 per cycle, but none is licensed for post-coital use.

### Glaucoma

**Mr. Chidgey:** To ask the Secretary of State for Health (1) what steps her Department is taking to inform *(a)* people of Afro-Caribbean origin, *(b)* diabetics and *(c)* individuals aged over 40 years with a family history of glaucoma of the increased risks that they face of developing glaucoma; [25029]

(2) what steps her Department is taking to inform blood relatives of glaucoma sufferers of the availability of free glaucoma checks after they reach the age of 40 years. [25030]

**Mr. Sackville:** All close relatives aged 40 and over—parents, brothers and sisters, and children—of diagnosed glaucoma sufferers are entitled to free national health service sight tests. All optometrists are required to display in their practices a notice advising of the services available under the general ophthalmic services.

Information about glaucoma, and the groups most at risk from it, is also available from the International Glaucoma Association. It would not be appropriate to disclose information about a person's health to third parties.

**Mr. Chidgey:** To ask the Secretary of State for Health what statistical evidence she has on whether improvements in the early detection of glaucoma have occurred in the last five years. [25031]

**Mr. Sackville:** There is no centrally collected statistical data on prevalence of glaucoma.

**Mr. Chidgey:** To ask the Secretary of State for Health what steps her Department is taking to ensure that uneven standards in testing for glaucoma are minimised. [25032]

**Mr. Sackville:** Screening for diseases of the eye, of which glaucoma is one, is part of the routine sight test procedure carried out by optometrists and ophthalmic medical practitioners. We have no evidence which would lead us to believe that standards of sight testing are uneven.

**Mr. Chidgey:** To ask the Secretary of State for Health what consideration her Department has given to widening the availability of free eye tests to all groups that face a significantly higher than average risk of developing glaucoma. [25036]

**Mr. Malone:** Close relatives—parents, children, brothers and sisters—aged 40 or over of diagnosed glaucoma sufferers are already eligible for free sight tests. We have no plans to alter these categories.

## ATTORNEY-GENERAL

### Serious Fraud Office

**Mr. Byers:** To ask the Attorney-General how much was paid to leading counsel for the Serious Fraud Office in the prosecution against Roger Levitt; and how much was paid to the counsel team prosecuting in the Barlow Clowes case. [25780]

**The Attorney-General:** Leading counsel for the prosecution in the Roger Levitt case acted for the Serious Fraud Office from January 1991 to December 1993 and was paid a total of £137,405 in fees.

Over the period 1988 to 1993, covering preparation, trial, and appeal, a total of nine counsel were instructed at different times as part of the prosecution team in the Barlow Clowes case. Five of those nine either were Queen's Counsel or were appointed queen's counsel during the course of the case. The total paid to the team in fees was £1,109,261.80.

The information referred to above is based on payments made inclusive of value added tax.

## ENVIRONMENT

### Industrial Waste

**Mr. Sheerman:** To ask the Secretary of State for the Environment (1) what new steps he is taking to maximise the recycling of industrial waste materials; [24987]

(2) what plans he has to encourage the minimisation of industrial waste.                                    [24989]

**Mr. Atkins:** The "Waste Strategy for England and Wales", a consultation draft published in January 1995, sets out the steps the Government are taking to minimise the production of and maximise the recycling of industrial waste materials. A copy is in the Library.

**Mr. Sheerman:** To ask the Secretary of State for the Environment what percentage of industrial waste is recycled.                                    [24988]

**Mr. Atkins:** The "Waste Strategy for England and Wales", a consultation draft published in January 1995, includes an estimate that approximately 18 per cent. of industrial waste in the UK is recycled or re-used—table 1.2, page 6. A copy is in the Library.

**Mr. Sheerman:** To ask the Secretary of State for the Environment when he next expects to meet representatives from local authorities to discuss waste minimisation and recycling issues.               [24990]

**Mr. Atkins:** Representatives from local authorities have regular meetings with the Department to discuss a wide range of waste related issues, including proposals set out in the draft "Waste Strategy for England and Wales".

### Local Government Reorganisation

**Mr. Frank Cook:** To ask the Secretary of State for the Environment what estimate he has made of the additional administrative staff who will be required by the four unitary authorities created as a result of local government reorganisation in Cleveland.               [25219]

**Mr. Curry:** Staffing structures are a matter for the newly elected councils.

**Mr. Frank Cook:** To ask the Secretary of State for the Environment what consultations he has had with the Chancellor of the Exchequer about both the transitional and continuing administrative costs of the reorganisation in Cleveland; and what was the outcome of those consultations.                                    [25218]

**Mr. Curry:** Government decisions are collective. The Cleveland (Structural Change) Order 1995, which implements reorganisation in Cleveland, was made on 30 January.

**Mr. Frank Cook:** To ask the Secretary of State for the Environment if he will make a statement on the views he has received from the business community in the Teesside area, prior to and since the decision to divide the Teesside conurbation among three unitary authorities.   [25224]

**Mr. Curry:** Following publication of the Local Government Commission's final recommendations for Cleveland, we received representations from the local business community both in support of and opposing the commission's proposals. We took these into account, together with other representations, when we decided to put the Cleveland (Structural Change) Order 1995 before the House.

### European Regional Development Fund

**Mr. Jim Cunningham:** To ask the Secretary of State for Environment at what stage is Teesside airport's bid to gain the funding from the ERDF; and what guidelines he proposes to issue in respect of future bids by airports for funds from the ERDF.                    [24979]

**Sir Paul Beresford:** The application from Teesside airport for ERDF grant is being considered alongside other bids which have been submitted under the north-east objective 2 structural funds programme for funding. There are no proposals to issue guidelines in respect of future bids by airports for funds from ERDF.

**Mr. Jim Cunningham:** To ask the Secretary of State for the Environment what representations he has made to the European Commission to reconsider the priority that airports have within the European regional development fund.                                    [24976]

**Sir Paul Beresford:** None.

**Mr. Jim Cunningham:** To ask the Secretary of State for the Environment what *(a)* European and *(b)* national alternatives there are for bidders who fail to gain funds for capital projects from the European regional development fund through overbidding.          [24978]

**Sir Paul Beresford:** Competitive bidding for resources available under the structural funds programme plays a major part in ensuring good value for money. Bids for European regional development fund grants have generally exceeded the resources available under current programmes. This has helped to ensure that grant has been made only to those projects which best met the aims and objectives of each programme. Bids which fail to gain ERDF funding may be eligible to receive resources available under other European or national programmes. However, this will depend very much on the activity concerned and whether this is eligible for support under a particular programme.

### Staff

**Ms Hodge:** To ask the Secretary of State for the Environment how many posts were lost in *(a)* the Department of the Environment and *(b)* agencies for which the Department of the Environment is responsible, listing the total lost posts agency by agency in (i) 1993–94 and (ii) 1994–95; and how many posts are proposed to be lost in 1995–96.          [25076]

**Sir Paul Beresford:** The numbers of staff employed by my Department and each of its executive agencies in 1993–94 and 1994–95, and plans for 1995–96, are published in my Department's annual report, a copy of which is in the Library of the House. This shows the reduction of posts between years.

### Pollution

**Mrs. Helen Jackson:** To ask the Secretary of State for the Environment if he will list by volume, and rivers affected, the annual discharges from abandoned mines and tips in the Yorkshire National Rivers Authority area.                                    [24909]

**Mr. Atkins** *[holding answer 22 May 1995]:* The information requested, so far as it is available, has been provided by the National Rivers Authority and is as follows:

*Discharges from abandoned mines and tips in the southern Yorkshire NRA area*

| Location | Type | Receiving river | Volume of Minewater (M³/day) |
|---|---|---|---|
| Clayton West | AM | Dearne Tributary | 1,360 |
| Silkstone | AM | Banks Bottom Dyke | not known |
| Flockton | AM | Flockton Beck Tributary | not known |
| Flockton | TL | Flockton Beck Tributary | not known |
| Dodworth | TL | Silkstone Beck Tributary | not known |
| Wath on Dearne | CL | Groundwater | not known |
| Killamarsh | TL | Park Brook | not known |
| Upstream of Silkstone Sewage Treatment Works | AM | Silkstone Beck | not known |
| Wooley | PM | Dearne | 17,000 |
| Sheffield | CL | Rother | not known |
| Chesterfield | CL | Rother | not known |
| North Doncaster | TL | Swan Sike Drain | not known |
| A1 North of Doncaster | TL | Groundwater | not known |
| Castleford | CL | Carr Beck | not known |
| Thornton | AM | Pitty Beck | not known |
| Todmorden | AM | Mitgelde Brook/Calder | 1,000 |
| Todmorden | AM | Beater Clough/Calder | 500 |
| Holmfirth | AM | Calder | 1,000 |
| Chesterfield | AM | Hipper | 60 |
| Dronfield | AM | Barlow Brook | 1,100 |
| Dronfield | AM | Drone | 1,100 |
| Dronfield | AM | Drone | 45 |
| Dronfield | AM | Drone | 1,100 |
| Dronfield | AM | Drone | 25 |
| Chesterfield | AM | Whitting | 110 |
| Chesterfield | AM | County Dike | 45 |
| Chesterfield | AM | Drone Tributary | 50 |
| Chesterfield | AM | Rother | 100 |
| Chesterfield | AM | Hipper | 50 |
| Chesterfield | AM | Rother | 40 |
| Chesterfield | AM | Redlead Mill Brook | 50 |
| Chesterfield | AM | Whitting | 50 |
| Penistone | AM | Don | 2,900 |
| Stocksbridge | AM | Little Don | 1,000 |

*Discharges from abandoned mines and tips in the southern Yorkshire NRA area*

| Location | Type | Receiving river | Volume of Minewater (M³/day) |
|---|---|---|---|
| Sheffield | AM | Don | 500 |
| Stocksbridge | AM | Don | 200 |
| Sheffield | AM | Don | 200 |
| Sheffield | AM | Loxley | 100 |

*Notes:*

Type of discharge.
AM Abandoned Minewater.
TL Tip Leachate.
CL Contaminated Land.
PM Pumped Minewater.

**Mrs. Helen Jackson:** To ask the Secretary of State for the Environment how many court actions were taken in each of the last three years by Her Majesty's inspectorate of pollution; what were the gross and net legal costs of Her Majesty's inspectorate of pollution in each of the past three years; how many of the court actions taken by Her Majesty's inspectorate of pollution in each of the last three years resulted in prosecution and fines; and what were the total fines imposed by Her Majesty's inspectorate of pollution in respect of pollution incidents in each of the past three years. [25778]

**Mr. Atkins:** The tables give details of the court actions taken by Her Majesty's inspectorate of pollution in each of the financial years 1992–93, 1993–94 and 1994–95. Fines imposed by the courts and details of costs are also included. All this information is available in HMIP's annual reports, the latest one of which, for the year 1994–95, is due for publication on 21 July. When considering what level of enforcement action to take, HMIP considers not only the environmental consequences and operator culpability, but whether it will be sufficient to ensure that remedial action to prevent a recurrence is carried out. Prosecution is not the only solution in every case, as HMIP endeavours to make the level of enforcement action proportionate to the offence. Enforcement may take the form of a letter of admonishment, an enforcement notice, a prohibition notice, prosecution or even revocation of the authorisation.

*HMIP prosecutions 1992–1993 (1 April–31 March)*

| Division | Name | Act | Offence | Date of hearing | Verdict | Fine | Cost |
|---|---|---|---|---|---|---|---|
| West | Bloxham Laboratories | HSW 1974 | Failure to comply with conditions of registration to ensure supervision of the competent use of radioactive material. | 28 April 1992 | G | £750 | £500 |
| East | Harrow Health Authority | HSW 1974 | Failure to use the best practicable means in operating incineration plant. | 5 May 1992 | G | £1,000 | £3,468.75 |
| East | Esselte Letraset | RSA 1960 | Failure to comply with condition of registration to prevent unauthorised access to a radioactive source. | 29 June 1992 | G | £100 | £1,000 |
| East | Foster Yeoman | 1906 alkali | Operating without a certificate of registration. | 2 July 1992 | G | £3,000 | £2,000 |
| East | White Mountain Roadstone | HSW 1974 | Failure to use the best practicable means in operating roadstone coating plant. | 9 July 1992 | G | £500 | £1,000 |

*HMIP prosecutions 1992–1993 (1 April–31 March)*

| Division | Name | Act | Offence | Date of hearing | Verdict | Fine | Cost |
|---|---|---|---|---|---|---|---|
| North | Gath Drums (Shipley) Ltd. | HSW 1974 | Failure to comply with two improvement notices. | 26 August 1992 | G | Conditional discharge | £3,905 |
| West | Xidex (UK) Ltd. | RSA 1960 | Breach of conditions relating to storage of radioactive material. | 7 September 1992 | G | £6,000 | £5,000 |
| West | British Coal | RSA 1960 | Breach of conditions relating to storage of radioactive material. | 12 October 1992 | G | £20,000 | £6,410 |
| North | Pozzolanic Lytag Ltd | HSW 1974 | Failure to use best practicable means to prevent emissions of noxious or offensive substances into the atmosphere. | 21 October 1992 | G | £3,500 | £3,500 |
| West | British Steel | HSW 1974 | Failure to use best practicable means to prevent emission of noxious or offensive substances. | 26 October 1992 | G | £2,000 | £19,000 |
| West | Rhone-Poulenc | HSW 1974 | Failure to use the best practicable means to prevent emission of sulphur dioxide from their sulphuric acid plant. | 16 November 1992 | G | £10,000 | £4,048 |
| West | West Midlands Regional Health Authority | RSA 1960 | Breaching 17 offences under Section 13(1)(c) of the RSA. | 18 December 1992 | G | £51,000 | £8,000 |
| East | Knauf UK | HSW 1974 | Failure to use BPM to prevent unfiltered processed gypsum from escaping into the atmosphere. | 26 January 1993 | G | £1,500 | £3,270 |
| West | Brookridge Timber Ltd | EPA 1990 | First HMIP prosecution under EPA 1990. Breach of Section 6(1) and section 23(1)—using a toxic substance without authorisation. | 16 March 1993 | G | £1,650 | £3,000 |

*Summary detail:*
Total prosecutions: 14.
Total fines: £101,000.
Total costs: £64,101.75.

*HMIP Prosecutions 1993–1994 (1 April–31 March)*

| Region | Name | Act | Offence | Date of hearing | Verdict | Fine | Cost |
|---|---|---|---|---|---|---|---|
| Anglian | Nichols Institute Diagnostics | RSA 1960 | Breach of conditions relating to accumulation of radioactive waste without authorisation. | 6 April 1993 | G | £10,000 | £2,726 |
| Southern and HMNII | UK Atomic Energy Authority | RSA 1960 | Failure to use BPM to limit the activity of radioactive waste released and to make a record of the means employed. | 16 April 1993 | G | £5,000 | N/A |
| Wales | Evans Group Ltd. | Alkali Act 1906 and HSW 74 | Failure to apply for registration for crushing equipment operated on site and failure to apply BPM to prevent emissions into the atmosphere. | 17 May 1993 | G | £6,000 | £5,000 |
| Anglian | Plessey GEC Semiconductors Ltd. | RSA 1960 | Holding a radioactive source without a certificate of registration. | 17 May 1993 | G | £1,000 | £2,261 |
| Anglian | Essex University | RSA 1960 | Exceeding their authorised limit for the incineration of radioactive waste. | 21 May 1993 | G | £800 | £2,651 |
| North West | North West Aggregates Ltd. | HSW 1974 | Failure to use BPM to prevent the release of offensive and noxious fumes. | 7 January 1994 | G | £8,000 | £11,000 |
| Wales | Glan Clwyd District Hospital NHS Trust | RSA 1960 | Unauthorised disposal of radioactive waste. | 9 February 1994 | G | £5,500 | £1,775 |

HMIP Prosecutions 1993–1994 (1 April–31 March)

| Region | Name | Act | Offence | Date of hearing | Verdict | Fine | Cost |
|--------|------|-----|---------|-----------------|---------|------|------|
| Southern | National Power Littlebrook "D" Power Station | EPA 1990 | Two offences involving discharges of oil to the River Thames. | 16 February 1994 | G | £7,500 | £13,248 |
| South West | ICI Nitram Plant, Severnside, Bristol | HSW 1974 | Failure to use BPM to prevent discharge of ammonia to atmosphere. | 18 February 1994 | G | £2,000 | £9,195.18 |

*Summary Detail:*
Total prosecutions: 9
Total fines: £45,800
Total costs: £47,856

HMIP prosecutions 1994–95 (1 April—year to date)

| Region | Name | Act | Offence | Date of hearing | Verdict | Fine | Costs |
|--------|------|-----|---------|-----------------|---------|------|-------|
| Midlands | AGA Gas Ltd., Bardon Filling Plant, Leics | EPA 1990 | Operation of an unauthorised acetylene plant. | 10 May 1994 | G | £10,000 | £5,135 |
| Midlands | Wednesbury Tubes Ltd., Bilston, W Midlands | HSW 1974 | Failure to use BPM to prevent the emission into the atmosphere of noxious or offensive substances. | 11 May 1994 | G | £4,000 | £1,540 |
| Southern | Acal Auriema, Slough | RSA 1960 /IRR 1985 /HSW 1974 | Two charges—failure to hold an authorisation certificate to collect waste radioactive sources for disposal/damage of a waste source. | 20 May 1994 | G | £14,000 | £2,842.61 |
| Southern | Drum Laundry Services Ltd., Aldershot | EPA 1990 | Failure to prevent a release to controlled waters. | 20 June 1994 | G | £5,000 | £5,000 |
| North East | Safety-Kleen UK Ltd., Rotherham | EPA 1990 | Failure to prevent a release to controlled waters. | 5 September 1994 | G | £7,500 | £6,040 |
| Southern | Enichem Elastomers Ltd., Hythe, Hampshire | EPA 1990 | Failure to use BATNEEC to prevent an unauthorised release of styrene. | 9 November 1994 | G | £5,000 | £12,062 |
| North East | British Coal, Wearmouth | RSA 1993 | Breach of RSA93 over the loss of a radioactive source. | 14 November 1994 | G | £5,000 | £7,561 |
| Wales | Coalite Products Ltd., Beddau | EPA 1990 | Exceedance of ammonia release limits for discharges to controlled waters. | 21 November 1994 | G | £22,500 | £10,000 |
| South West | Rhone-Poulenc Chemicals Ltd. | HSW 1974 | Failure to use BPM to prevent an unauthorised release of ammonia. | 28 November 1994 | G | £12,000 | £5,400 |
| South | CET Flexitec Ltd. | RSA 1993 | Failure to comply with registration condition relating to storage of radioactive source. | 30 November 1994 | G | £7,000 | £2,500 |
| South | Southern Refining Services Ltd. | EPA 1990 | Failure to comply with conditions of authorisation. | 5 December 1994 | G | £12,000 | £6,571.85 |
| North West | Vinamul Ltd. | EPA 1990 | Unauthorised escape of substances and failure to ensure control during production. | 31 January 1995 | G | £19,000 | £13,716 |
| North East | ICI Wilton | EPA 1990 | Failure to prevent an unauthorised release of degraded organic peroxide. | 2 February 1995 | G | £10,000 | £10,250 |

*HMIP prosecutions 1994–95 (1 April—year to date)*

| Region | Name | Act | Offence | Date of hearing | Verdict | Fine | Costs |
|--------|------|-----|---------|-----------------|---------|------|-------|
| North East | Hickson Fine Chemicals | EPA 1990 | Failure to prevent a release to controlled waters. | 13 February 1995 | G | £5,000 | £10,694.50 |
| Anglian | IGE Medical Systems | RSA 1993 | Loss of radioactive source. | 24 February 1995 | G | £5,000 | £5,754.75 |

*Summary detail:*
  Total prosections: 15.
  Total fines to date: £143,000.
  Total costs: £105,066.71.

**Mrs. Helen Jackson:** To ask the Secretary of State for the Environment how many court actions were taken in each of the last three years in total and in each authority area by the waste regulation authorities; what was the gross and net costs to each waste regulation authority and in total of legal action taken in each of the past three years; what were the total fines imposed by each waste regulation authority and in total in respect of pollution incidents in each of the past three years; and how many of the court actions taken by waste regulation authorities in each of the past three years resulted in a prosecution and fine. [25779]

**Mr. Atkins:** The information requested is not held centrally. Information on the number and description of prosecutions brought by waste regulation authorities under part II of the Environmental Protection Act 1990 must be included in the annual reports authorities are required to publish under section 67 of the Act. Authorities are required to publish their reports within six months of the end of each financial year and the first such reports will be those for the financial year 1994–95.

### Contracting Out

**Ms Hodge:** To ask the Secretary of State for the Environment (1) what work has been contracted out *(a)* by his Department and *(b)* by agencies for which his Department is responsible in (i) 1993–94, (ii) 1994–95 and (iii) projected for 1995–96; [25524]

(2) for each piece of work subject to a bidding process under the auspices of *(a)* the Department of the Environment and *(b)* agencies for which the Department is responsible where work was contracted out who were the successful bidders; and which contracts were won by in-house bidders in (i) 1993–94, (ii) 1994–95 and (iii) projected for 1995–96. [25526]

**Sir Paul Beresford:** Under the competing for quality programme, results during the 1 October 1993 to 30 September 1994 market testing year are:

| Department of the Environment project | Successful tenderer |
|---|---|
| *Security guarding:* | |
| (daytime hours) | Royal British Legion Attendants Co. Ltd. |
| (silent hours) | Security Facilities Executive |
| Management Audit Services | In-house team |
| | |
| *Construction research:* | |
| Ventilation of underground car parks | TBV Science |
| Scoping study for HVAC system | Centre for Configurational Studies—The Open University |
| Water economy | BSRIA |

| Department of the Environment project | Successful tenderer |
|---|---|
| Identification and development of source datafor fire risk assessments, part 1 | Four Elements Ltd. |
| Identification and development of source data for fire risk assessments, part 2 | Fire SERT Centre (University of Ulster) |
| Alternative aggregates | Mott MacDonald Consultants |
| Fire resistance behaviour of trussed rafters | Trada Technology |
| Performance of emulsion preservatives | Building Research Establishment |
| Sprinkler system cost benefit study | Building Research Establishment |
| Comparative strength of masonry walls | Building Research Establishment |

| Agencies | Successful tenderer |
|---|---|
| *Security Facilities Executive:* | |
| Cleaning of Ponton Road premises | Mayfair Window Cleaning Co Ltd. |
| Inter-Departmental Despatch Service | In-house team |
| | |
| *Planning Inspectorate* | |
| Secretarial and typing | In-house team |
| | |
| *Building Research Establishment:* | |
| Office and printing services | In-house team |
| Audio Visual | In-house team |

| 1994–95 Department of the Environment | Successful tenderer |
|---|---|
| *Construction Research* | |
| Organically coated metal phase 2 | BDA |
| Masonry clad steel frame buildings | Taywoods |
| Timber panels | CERAM |
| Assessment of ground defamation properties | Building Research Establishment |

*Notes:*
No other results are available, and no results can be projected for 1995–96.
Results of market tests are published in the monthly Market Testing Bulletin, copies of which are available in the House of Commons Library.

### Contaminated Land

**Mr. Harry Greenway:** To ask the Secretary of State for the Environment what arrangements he has made in regard to the allocation of capital resources for local authorities to tackle contaminated land in 1995–96. [26101]

**Mr. Atkins:** The Department of the Environment has today written to 49 local authorities and waste disposal authorities informing them of the Secretary of State's intention to issue supplementary credit approvals for 1995–96 totalling nearly £8 million in respect of capital expenditure on 109 new projects to investigate or carry our remedial work to contaminated land.

The Department has already written to 40 authorities about making SCAs totalling £6.7 million available this year in respect of 127 on-going projects from previous years.

Between 1990–91 and 1993–94 SCAs worth nearly £40 million were issued to enable work to be undertaken on over 800 contaminated sites. A figure for SCAs spent for 1994–95 is not yet available as authorities are in the process of submitting final returns for that financial year.

The SCA programme for contaminated land is aimed at tackling problems on sites in local authority ownership or where they have responsibility to take action and cannot recover their costs. The Department operates an assessment and prioritisation procedures to ensure that the available funding goes to projects representing the greatest threat to health or the environment.

### Local Government Commission

**Mr. Haselhurst:** To ask the Secretary of State for the Environment what decisions he has reached on the Local Government Commission's final recommendations on electoral, boundary and other non-structural matters. [26203]

**Mr. Curry:** The Local Government Commission made a number of recommendations on boundary and electoral matters in its final reports on the future of local government in the shire countries of England. My right hon. Friend has now reached decisions on these recommendations.

Among other factors, he has had regard to the possible interaction between these recommendations and the programme of fresh structure reviews of individual districts which he announced on 2 March. Where the commission has recommended further reviews of boundaries or electoral arrangements he has considered the implications for the commission's programme of periodic electoral reviews and other work. In each case he has considered the commission's reports and the representations he has received, and is satisfied that these decisions will best reflect the identities and interests of local communities and will best secure effective and convenient local government.

My right hon. Friend accepts the recommendations made for a boundary change in Gloucestershire between the parishes of West Dean and Coleford in the district of the Forest of Dean, and the consequential changes to parish, district and county electoral arrangements. He also accepts the recommended change in boundary between Colchester borough and Tendering district in the Wivenhoe area of Essex, the recommended re-warding of East Hertfordshire district and the recommended re-warding of Newbury district in Berkshire.

Basildon, Thurrock and Peterborough will be subject to fresh district reviews. My right hon. Friend has already announced that the recommended boundary changes around Basildon which would transfer Wickford to Rochford and Billericay to Brentwood will not be acted upon pending the fresh reviews. It follows that he should defer a decision on the recommended changes in electoral representation in Wickford, Billericay, Basildon and the county, which are based on this boundary change. He considers that a decision on the electoral change recommended for Thurrock—an extra two councillors— should also await the fresh review. Similarly, in Peterborough, a decision on the recommended boundary change which would transfer the southern township area from Huntingdonshire to Peterborough will be made in the light of the outcome of the fresh review of Peterborough. He also expects the commission to look again at the re-warding of Peterborough as part of that review.

In a number of cases the commission suggested it be directed to undertake further reviews. My right hon. Friend will be considering the case for undertaking a review of Cambridge City's boundaries in due course. As he has already announced, he will consider asking the commission to look again at the proposed boundary change around Southend airport. On electoral matters, the commission recommended an early review of electoral arrangements at district and county level in those areas of Essex affected by structural change, the six districts in Berkshire which will gain unitary status and the Suffolk Coastal district. He accepts the case for each of these, and will be discussing with the commission how they may be given priority in its programme of work.

Decisions in principle on all the commission's structural recommendations have now been announced. Decisions on the remaining planning recommendations were announced on 11 April, and an announcement on the parishing recommendations will be made very shortly. Other matters, such as recommendations for police and fire service arrangements, flow directly from the structural decisions, and will be set out in draft orders for structural change which are the subject of consultation. Similarly, ceremonial matters will be covered in general regulations and in structural change orders which are subject to public consultation.

## FOREIGN AND COMMONWEALTH AFFAIRS

### Official Gifts

**Mr. Tony Banks:** To ask the Secretary of State for Foreign and Commonwealth Affairs if he will list those gifts received by Ministers in their official capacities and reported to the Permanent Secretary in each of the last five years. [23783]

**Mr. Goodlad:** The details of gifts received by Ministers are not made public. Their retention or disposal is dealt with in accordance with "Questions of Procedure for Ministers".

### Nuclear Safety

**Mr. Maclennan:** To ask the Secretary of State for Foreign and Commonwealth Affairs what steps he will take to support the international action plan and fund proposed by Norway to address (a) safety at nuclear installations, (b) the sound management of nuclear waste and (c) problems associated with the dumping of nuclear waste and arms-related environmental hazards in the Kola peninsula. [25182]

**Mr. Douglas Hogg:** We share Norway's concerns about nuclear safety and radioactive waste management problems in Russia. The majority of international assistance in this area is currently focused on improving the safety of nuclear reactors. Our main contributions to these efforts are channelled through the European Union's PHARE and TACIS programmes, as well as the G7 multilateral programme of action. As projects in these nuclear safety related programmes begin to bear fruit, increasing emphasis is likely to be placed on the specific problem of radioactive waste management.

### Immigration

**Mr. Madden:** To ask the Secretary of State for Foreign and Commonwealth Affairs what assistance is being offered to Mrs. Abida Noreen and her daughter, Muneeza Khan (Ref: Imm/C8970) by the United Kingdom post in Islamabad to return as residents of the United Kingdom; and if he will make a statement. [25699]

**Mr. Baldry:** I have asked the high commission at Islamabad for details and will arrange for the hon. Member to receive a substantive reply from the migration and visa correspondence unit as soon as possible.

### Intergovernmental Conference

**Mr. Nicholas Winterton:** To ask the Secretary of State for Foreign and Commonwealth Affairs what are the main constitutional issues on the Government's agenda for the 1996 inter-governmental conference. [25776]

**Mr. David Davis:** We shall not make proposals at the 1996 intergovernmental conference which would involve significant constitutional change. We will also, as my right hon. Friend the Prime Minister said on 23 May, block any attempt to extend Community competence into intergovernmental areas such as foreign affairs, defence and home affairs.

### NORTHERN IRELAND

### Police Order

**Mr. Worthington:** To ask the Secretary of State for Northern Ireland whether comments on the draft proposals to change the Police (Northern Ireland) Order will be placed in the Library at the conclusion of the period of consultation on 6 June. [24322]

**Sir John Wheeler:** No substantive comments on the draft order have yet been received. I will, however, keep the suggestion under review, bearing in mind that some comments may be offered on a confidential basis.

### Housing Benefit

**Mr. McGrady:** To ask the Secretary of State for Northern Ireland what plans he has to introduce into Northern Ireland proposals in relation to the capping of housing benefit similar to those made for England and Wales. [24749]

**Sir John Wheeler:** The implications for Northern Ireland of the proposals for amending the housing benefit scheme in Great Britain are currently being considered.

Account will be taken of the different arrangements in Northern Ireland for administering the housing benefit scheme.

### Health Service Contracts

**Mr. Trimble:** To ask the Secretary of State for Northern Ireland if he will make a statement on all contracts placed by (a) each health board and (b) each health trust with Grafton Recruitment. [24505]

**Mr. Moss** [holding answer 17 May 1995]: There are currently 52 nursing agencies licensed by the Department, of which two have been issued in respect of Grafton Recruitment. Information on contracts placed by the health and personal social services with these agencies is not held centrally, but by individual health and social services boards and trusts.

### Majority Shareholdings

**Mr. Byers:** To ask the Secretary of State for Northern Ireland if he will list those companies in which the holder of his office is the majority shareholder which (a) are currently in existence and (b) have been wound up in the past five years. [25711]

**Mr. Ancram** [holding answer 22 May 1995]: None in either category.

### DUCHY OF LANCASTER

### Advisory Committee on Business Appointments

**Mr. Mullin:** To ask the Chancellor of the Duchy of Lancaster how many civil servants applied to the advisory committee on business appointments for approval for a job offer in the private sector in each of the last five years; and in how many cases the application was refused. [25016]

**Mr. Horam:** The information requested, including information on members of the diplomatic service, is set out in the table. Separate applications must be submitted for each appointment or consultancy commission an individual wishes to accept. Under the business appointment rules applications cannot be rejected outright, but approval may be made subject to behavioural conditions or to waiting periods of up to a maximum of two years.

*Number of applications (number of applicants)*

| Financial year | Unconditionally approved | Conditionally approved | Total |
|---|---|---|---|
| 1990–91 | 12 | 9 | 21 (16) |
| 1991–92 | 17 | 14 | 31 (21) |
| 1992–93 | 11 | 25 | 36 (20) |
| 1993–94 | 8 | 15 | 23 (13) |
| 1994–95 | 13 | 17 | 30 (16) |

*Note:*

The figures in brackets refer to the number of individuals who applied; all other figures refer to the number of applications received.

**Mr. Mullin:** To ask the Chancellor of the Duchy of Lancaster if he will list by name and profession the members of the advisory committee on business appointments.        [25017]

**Mr. Horam:** The members of the Prime Minister's advisory committee on business appointments are:

> The right hon. the Lord Carlisle of Bucklow QC—Chairman
> The Lord Bridges GCMG—Deputy Chairman
> Sir John Blelloch KCB
> Sir Denys Henderson
> Sir Charles Huxtable KCB CBE
> Sir Robin Ibbs KBE
> The right hon. Peter Shore MP
> The right hon. the Lord Thomson of Monifieth KT

Lord Carlisle, Lord Thomson and Mr. Peter Shore are senior parliamentarians and former Ministers. Lord Bridges is a retired diplomat; Sir John Blelloch is a retired senior civil servant; Sir Charles Huxtable is a retired senior army officer; Sir Robin Ibbs is chairman of Lloyds Bank plc; and Sir Denys Henderson is chairman of the Rank Organisation.

**Mr. Mullin:** To ask the Chancellor of the Duchy of Lancaster if he will list by Government Department the number of civil servants who have applied to the advisory committee on business appointments for approval to take a job in the private sector in each of the last five years.        [25018]

**Mr. Horam:** The number of civil servants, including members of the diplomatic service, who have applied to the advisory committee for approval to take a job in the private sector in each of the last five financial years is set out in the table:

| | *Number of applicants* | | | | |
| --- | --- | --- | --- | --- | --- |
| | *1990–91* | *1991–92* | *1992–93* | *1993–94* | *1994–95* |
| Cabinet Office | 2 | 0 | 2 | 1 | 1 |
| Ministry of Defence | 4 | 2 | 1 | 2 | 1 |
| Department for Education | 0 | 0 | 0 | 1 | 1 |
| Department of Employment | 0 | 1 | 0 | 0 | 0 |
| Department of Energy | 0 | 0 | 0 | 1 | 0 |
| Department of the Environment, including PSA | 1 | 3 | 1 | 2 | 1 |
| Export Credits Guarantee Department | 0 | 1 | 1 | 0 | 0 |
| Foreign and Commonwealth Office | 5 | 9 | 12 | 3 | 5 |
| Department of Health | 1 | 0 | 0 | 1 | 1 |
| Home Office | 0 | 0 | 0 | 0 | 1 |
| Lord Chancellor's Department | 0 | 0 | 1 | 0 | 0 |
| Northern Ireland Office | 0 | 2 | 0 | 0 | 0 |
| Scottish Office | 0 | 0 | 1 | 0 | 0 |
| Department of Social Security | 0 | 0 | 0 | 0 | 1 |
| Department of Trade and Industry | 1 | 1 | 1 | 1 | 1 |
| Department of Transport | 0 | 1 | 0 | 0 | 2 |
| Her Majesty's Treasury | 2 | 1 | 0 | 1 | 1 |

# EDUCATION

## Dance and Drama

9. **Mr. Fisher:** To ask the Secretary of State for Education if she has met the Secretary of State for National Heritage to discuss the future of dance and drama training.        [23818]

**Mr. Boswell:** My right hon. Friend has done so.

## Higher Education Review

14. **Sir Fergus Montgomery:** To ask the Secretary of State for Education what are the aims of her departmental review of higher education.        [23824]

**Mr. Boswell:** My right hon. Friend is reviewing the aims and purposes of higher education with a view to determining its appropriate shape and size at the end of the century and beyond.

## Mathematics and Engineering

15. **Mr. Dalyell:** To ask the Secretary of State for Education, pursuant to letters to the hon. Member for Linlithgow from the Minister of State, what proposals Her Majesty's Government have for relating mathematics teaching in schools to the requirements of the engineering profession as set out by the Engineering Council.        [23825]

**Mr. Forth:** The mathematics curriculum is relevant to many professions, including engineering. As the hon. Member is aware, the Government are committed to higher standards and higher quality teaching in mathematics for all pupils.

## History Teaching

16. **Mr. Hawkins:** to ask the Secretary of State for Education what plans she has to review the teaching of history in schools.        [23826]

**Mr. Forth:** None.

## School Funding

17. **Mr. Tipping:** To ask the Secretary of State for Education what representations she has received asking her for increased funding for school budgets in 1996–97.        [23827]

**Mr. Robin Squire:** My. right hon. Friend has received a number of representations on school finances, many of which have requested increased funding for school budgets in 1995–96.

23. **Mr. Skinner:** To ask the Secretary of State for Education how many representations she has now received from *(a)* parents, *(b)* teacher and *(c)* governors regarding school funding for 1995–96.        [23834]

**Mr. Robin Squire:** My right hon. Friend has received a number of such representations. It is not possible to break down this total into separate categories.

24. **Mr. Clifton-Brown:** To ask the Secretary of State for Education what estimate she has made of the effect of a national funding formula for primary and secondary schools on financial distribution to local education authorities.        [22835]

**Mr. Robin Squire:** The detailed effects of a national funding formula would depend on how it was constructed. It is clear, however, that redistributing a national funding total using identical formula factors across the country would result in large numbers of schools gaining, and large number of schools losing compared with their existing levels of funding.

### Selective Grammar Schools

18. **Mr. Lidington:** To ask the Secretary of State for Education if she will make a statement about the Government's policy towards selective grammar schools.    [23828]

**Mr. Robin Squire:** The Government believe that schools which select pupils by ability, or which specialise in particular subjects, have an important part to play in giving parents a choice of schooling for their children.

### Nursery Education

19. **Mr. Denham:** To ask the Secretary of State for Education what assessment she has made of the need for nursery education in Hampshire.    [23829]

**Mr. Forth:** It is for local education authorities to determine the need for education provision for children below compulsory school age.

22. **Sir David Madel:** To ask the Secretary of State for Education what are her future plans for the development of nursery education; and if she will make a statement.    [23832]

**Mr. Forth:** My right hon. Friend the Prime Minister has set a target to provide, over time, a pre-school place for all four-year-olds whose parents wish to take it up. My right hon. Friend the Secretary of State and the official task force have been consulting widely with a view to drawing up detailed proposals for the expansion.

**Mr. Cox:** To ask the Secretary of State what has been the amount of money given from her Department to London borough councils to help with the provision of nursery schooling in each of the last two years.    [23823]

**Mr. Forth:** In 1994–95 local education authorities in London received in total in their education standard spending assessment some £189.870 million in respect of the population of children aged 0 to 4 in their area. In 1995–96 the figure was £199.198 million. How much each local authority spends on nursery provision is a matter solely for the local authority concerned.

### Primary School Pupils

20. **Mr. Robert Ainsworth:** To ask the Secretary of State for Education what guidelines her Department issues on the optimum number of pupils per class in primary schools.    [23830]

**Mr. Robin Squire:** None. It is for the governors and head teachers of individual schools to decide how to organise their classes.

### Grant-maintained Schools

21. **Mr. Dunn:** To ask the Secretary of State for Education how many grammar and high schools in Kent have successfully applied for grant-maintained status; and if she will make a statement.    [23831]

**Mr. Robin Squire:** Eighteen grammar schools and 46 other secondary schools in Kent have successfully applied for grant-maintained status. This means that half the state secondary schools in the county are now self-governing— a clear illustration of the extent to which Kent parents have appreciated the benefits of GM status for their children's schools.

### Assisted Places

25. **Mr. Clappison:** To ask the Secretary of State for Education what proportion of pupils on the assisted places scheme receive a free place.    [23836]

**Mr. Robin Squire:** Over 42 per cent. of assisted place holders are receiving a free place in the current academic year 1994–95.

**Mr. Brandreth:** To ask the Secretary of State for Education what plans she has to review the assisted places scheme; and if she will make a statement.    [23833]

**Mr. Robin Squire:** The assisted places scheme is an outstanding success and popular with parents. It is here to stay under this Government. We will continue to keep its detailed operation under regular review.

### Further Education

26. **Mrs. Anne Campbell:** To ask the Secretary of State for Education if she expects to maintain the unit of resource per student in the further education sector over the next two years.    [23837]

**Mr. Boswell:** The Government's expenditure plans mean that the funding available for colleges will increase by 4 per cent. in 1995–96 and by a further 3 per cent. in 1996–97. The plans assume that FE sector colleges will make real terms efficiency gains of 5 per cent. in 1995–96 and 3 per cent. in 1996–97.

### Ethnic and Religious Facilities

27. **Mr. Dykes:** To ask the Secretary of State for Education to what extent her Department wishes to encourage the development of additional ethnic and religious facilities in English primary and secondary schools in the future.    [23838]

**Mr. Forth:** My right hon. Friend considers proposals from promoters of a variety of new voluntary and grant-maintained schools. She takes into account a number of factors, including the extent to which the proposals would enhance the choice, diversity and quality of education in the area; the overall need for additional school places locally and therefore the cost-effective use of public money; and evidence that the new school would be able to deliver the national curriculum.

### Teaching Methods

**Mr. Harry Greenway:** To ask the Secretary of State for Education what guidance her Department is giving for methods of teaching classes of all sizes; and if she will make a statement.    [24302]

**Mr. Robin Squire:** None. The Teacher Training Agency and Ofsted are to take joint action to identify good teaching methods and improve teachers' effectiveness. The agency is conducting a fundamental national review of in-service training.

## Autism

**Sir Michael Neubert:** To ask the Secretary of State for education what plans she has to increase the level of provision for autistic children in north-east London; and if she will make a statement.          [24046]

**Mr. Forth:** The assessment of autistic children and the identification of a suitable school for them is the responsibility of the LEA in whose area they live. Not every LEA will be able to, or need to make its own specialist provision. In some cases collaboration between LEAs might be desirable; if this led one or more LEAs to publish statutory proposals for new schools or units, or to the development of additional provision in non-maintained special schools, the Secretary of State would consider any proposals carefully.

## Medical Students

**Mr. Wray:** To ask the Secretary of State for Education if she or her ministerial colleagues will agree to meet medical student representatives from the British Medical Association to discuss the current level of student loans and other relevant matters.          [23817]

**Mr. Boswell:** The pressure of other commitments means that my right hon. Friend and I are unable to meet representatives of the medical students committee. I am well aware of the arguments advanced by the BMA medical students committee, and have answered the points raised by them in correspondence.

## Special Needs

**Mr. Blunkett:** To ask the Secretary of State for Education if she will list by local education authority those secondary schools which are grant maintained, giving for each the number of pupils with a statement of special educational needs for each year since the school became grant-maintained.          [25678]

**Mr. Robin Squire:** The information requested will take a little time to assemble. I will write to the hon. Member as soon as possible and place a copy in the Library.

Statements of special educational needs are drawn up by the local education authority and name the school which the pupil in question should attend, taking account of parents' preferences and consultation with the schools' governors. A grant-maintained school can neither draw up a statement itself nor refuse admission to a pupil whose statement names that school.

## HOME DEPARTMENT

### Assaults (Police Officers)

**Mr. Chidgey:** To ask the Secretary of State for the Home Department how many physical assaults on police officers were recorded in Hampshire and the Isle of Wight for each year since 1990.          [25034]

**Mr. Maclean:** The information available centrally relates to assaults on police officers recorded for the Hampshire police force area as a whole. Separate information for the Isle of Wight is not available centrally. There were 343 assaults in 1990, 374 in 1991, 388 in 1992 and 355 in 1993. Information for 1994 is not yet available.

## Asbestos Ash

**Mr. Chidgey:** To ask the Secretary of State for the Home Department what instructions his Department has given to police force and fire brigade services to co-ordinate strategies in evacuating communities that are at risk from dispersed asbestos ash following fires on buildings containing asbestos material.          [25035]

**Mr. Nicholas Baker:** Guidance has been issued to fire brigades on dealing with incidents involving asbestos and to the police on any type of incident where evacuation is to be considered.

## Prison Statistics

**Mr. Michael:** To ask the Secretary of State for the Home Department (1) what was the total number of sentenced offenders, including fine defaulters, received into prison in *(a)* 1993 and *(b)* 1994; and how many had committed offences involving (i) violence, (ii) sex and (iii) robbery;          [25319]

(2) what was the total number of sentenced offenders, excluding fine defaulters, received into prison in *(a)* 1993 and *(b)* 1994; and how many had committed offences involving (i) violence, (ii) sex and (iii) robbery.          [25320]

**Mr. Michael Forsyth:** Responsibility for these matters has been delegated to the Director General of the Prison Service, who has been asked to arrange for a reply to be given.

*Letter from Derek Lewis to Mr. Alun Michael, dated 23 May 1995:*

The Home Secretary has asked me to reply to your recent Questions about the total number of sentenced offenders, both including and excluding fine defaulters, received into prison in (a) 1993 and (b) 1994; and how many had committed offences involving (i) violence, (ii) sex and (iii) robbery.

Provisional information for receptions of sentenced prisoners in 1993 and 1994 is contained in the attached table.

*Receptions into Prison Service Establishments, 1993 and 1994, by offence group, including and excluding fine defaulters*

| Principal offence | Receptions: Including fine defaulters | | Receptions: Excluding fine defaulters | |
|---|---|---|---|---|
| | *1993* | *1994* | *1993* | *1994* |
| Violence against the person | 8,823 | 9,979 | 7,317 | 8,667 |
| Sexual offences | 1,926 | 1,905 | 1,899 | 1,895 |
| Robbery | 2,934 | 2,933 | 2,895 | 2,912 |
| Other offences | 59,283 | 69,165 | 38,452 | 47,784 |
| All offences | 72,966 | 83,982 | 50,563 | 61,258 |

## Prison Golf Courses

**Mr. Byers:** To ask the Secretary of State for the Home Department what was the estimated cost of providing a golf course at Swaleside prison on the Isle of Sheppey; what costs had been incurred when the work was stopped; what is the estimated cost of restoring the land to its original condition; what amount was spent to purchase golf clubs and balls; and how many clubs and balls were brought.          [17340]

**Mr. Michael Forsyth** *[holding answer 3 April 1995]:* Responsibility for this matter has been delegated to the Director General of the Prison Service, who has been asked to arrange for a reply to be given.

*Letter from Derek Lewis to Mr. Stephen Byers, dated 23 May 1995:*

The Home Secretary has asked me to reply to your recent Question about the costs incurred in the abandoned project to construct a three hole golf course at Swaleside prison. I am sorry for the delay in replying to your Question.

At the time of the cancellation of the project, the cost that had been incurred as a result of labour costs, plant hire and materials was £14,275. Some of the aggregate materials that had already been delivered to the site were recovered and used for construction purposes elsewhere in the prison estate. There have subsequently been cancellation costs of £8,043.

Some ground work had already been carried out at Swaleside. The work to restore the land will be done by prisoners under the supervision of staff and will need no additional resources.

The cost of 24 golf clubs, 150 golf balls and 200 practice balls was £709. It is hoped to recover some of this cost through negotiation with equipment suppliers.

As a result of what happened at Swaleside, it has been made clear to governors that there should be no further proposals to use public funds in this way.

## Al Fayed Brothers

**Mr. Madden:** To ask the Secretary of State for the Home Department who signed (a) notices refusing applications by Mr. A. and Mr. M. Al Fayed to be granted British citizenship and (b) letters refusing to explain the reasons for such refusal notices submitted by either applicant or their representatives; and on whose behalf such notices or letters were signed. [25700]

**Mr. Nicholas Baker:** It is not our practice to disclose details relating to individual applications for British citizenship.

## Police Vehicle Accidents

**Mr. Flynn:** To ask the Secretary of State for the Home Department what was the percentage of police vehicles involved in (a) serious and (b) fatal accidents in each of the last 15 years. [25426]

**Mr. Maclean:** The available information on the number of police vehicle accidents in England and Wales is for the period 1988–1993 and is given in the table. The figures shown for casualties relate only to death or serious injury in the course of either police pursuits or responses to emergency calls.

*Police vehicle accidents (England and Wales)*

| Year | Total police vehicle accidents | [1]Fatal injuries | [1]Serious injuries |
| --- | --- | --- | --- |
| 1988 | 18,917 | 22 | 282 |
| 1989 | 18,481 | 39 | 333 |
| 1990 | 18,941 | 24 | 317 |
| 1991 | 18,445 | 32 | 271 |
| 1992 | 19,560 | 30 | 300 |
| 1993 | 19,504 | 34 | 300 |

[1]Arising in the course of police pursuits or responses to emergency calls.

## Criminal Injuries Compensation

**Mr. Michael:** To ask the Secretary of State for the Home Department (1) what was the average award for rape plus a serious injury given under the criminal injuries compensation scheme under the tariff scheme operating from April 1994; [24887]

(2) if he will list for each of the last five years the number of claimants for criminal injuries compensation who were incapacitated for more than 28 weeks and the percentage they represented of (a) the total number and (b) the total cost of claimants in each year; [24889]

(3) what was the number of awards and total value of awards made (a) in respect of rape and (b) in respect of rape plus a serious injury in each of the last six financial years. [24888]

**Mr. Maclean** *[holding answer 18 May 1995]:* This information is not recorded centrally.

**Mr. Michael:** To ask the Secretary of State for the Home Department (1) if he will list the criteria he intends to use in reviewing the criminal injuries compensation tariff once it is in place; [24891]

(2) if it is his policy that the tariff published with the Criminal Injuries Compensation Bill should be uprated to allow for inflation; and if it is his policy to ensure that the tariff rates are subsequently uprated each year; [24896]

(3) if it is his policy that the tariff published with the Criminal Injuries Compensation Bill should be implemented as it stands. [24895]

**Mr. Maclean** *[holding answer 18 May 1995]:* It is the intention that the tariff which was published on 11 May should be the one which is used when the enhanced tariff scheme starts.

The injury descriptions in the tariff will be monitored on a continuing basis, and can be adjusted as necessary with the consent of Parliament. It is intended that the tariff levels will be reviewed every three years. No criteria for such reviews have yet been set, but might be expected to include reference to inflation more generally and other pressures on public expenditure.

**Mr. Michael:** To ask the Secretary of State for the Home Department (1) if he will make it his policy that the time limit for applications under the criminal justice compensation tariff should be not less than three years; [24899]

(2) what will be the time limit for applications under the recently announced tariff scheme for criminal injury compensation. [24898]

**Mr. Maclean** *[holding answer 18 May 1995]:* The intention is to set the time limit at two years. Police and other records are often weeded at about three years and this can make it more difficult to obtain documentary evidence to substantiate claims. However, there will continue to be discretion for the scheme administrators to waive the time limit in exceptional cases.

**Mr. Michael:** To ask the Secretary of State for the Home Department if he will define the terms dependency/loss of support payments used in note 4 to his paper on the proposed tariff scheme published with the Criminal Injury Compensation Bill, together with the circumstances in which they are relevant and the means by which this relevance would be assessed in a specific case. [24890]

**Mr. Maclean** *[holding answer 18 May 1995]:* Payments for dependency and loss of support will be made to those relations who are able to show that they were financially dependent on the deceased at or before his or her death, or a probability that the deceased would have provided some sort of financial support in the future had he or she lived. They will be calculated by reference to the deceased's contribution to the household budget and the probable length of the dependency.

### Europol Drugs Unit

**Dr. Howells:** To ask the Secretary of State for the Home Department how many staff *(a)* in his Department and *(b)* in other Government Departments have specific duties relating to the Europol drugs unit. [25051]

**Mr. Maclean** *[holding answer 22 May 1995]:* Within the National Criminal Intelligence Service two members of staff currently work full-time on liaison duties associated with the Europol drugs unit. Other members of NCIS, the Home Office and Customs and Excise undertake duties associated with the work of the unit as part of their wider responsibilities for national and international police and customs co-operation.

**Dr. Howells:** To ask the Secretary of State for the Home Department what was the cost in 1994–95 of the United Kingdom's participation in the Europol drugs unit. [25052]

**Mr. Maclean** *[holding answer 22 May 1995]:* For the financial year 1994–95 the United Kingdom's contribution towards the running and staff costs of the Europol drugs unit in The Hague was £849,000. Some additional costs were incurred in the United Kingdom as a result of staff time spent on representational, liaison and other duties associated with the work of the unit.

**Dr. Howells:** To ask the Secretary of State for the Home Department, how many United Kingdom police officers are currently serving *(a)* full-time and *(b)* part-time with the Europol drugs unit. [25057]

**Mr. Maclean** *[holding answer 22 May 1995]:* *(a)* Three; *(b)* none.

### National Criminal Intelligence Service

**Dr. Howells:** To ask the Secretary of State for the Home Department how many United Kingdom police officers are currently serving *(a)* full-time and *(b)* part-time with the National Criminal Intelligence Service. [25053]

**Mr. Maclean** *[holding answer 22 May 1995]:* As at 1 May there were 248 police officers serving with the National Criminal Intelligence Service, all full-time. Of these, 229 were seconded on central service terms and 19 were on periods of attachment.

**Dr. Howells:** To ask the Secretary of State for the Home Department what was the cost in 1993–94 and 1995 of the National Criminal Intelligence Service. [25054]

**Mr. Maclean** *[holding answer 22 May 1995]:* In 1993–94 the net outturn for the National Criminal Intelligence Service was £20.068 million. The outturn in 1994–95, which has yet to be confirmed, is estimated to be £23.508 million.

### Forensic Science Service Agency

**Mrs. Gillan:** To ask the Secretary of State for the Home Department what targets he has set for the Forensic Science Service agency for 1995–96. [26102]

**Mr. Howard:** During 1995–96 I expect Forensic Science Service to continue to improve its efficiency and effectiveness. The financial targets for the year are recovery of full economic costs; and a cash unit cost target of £484.91 based on an efficiency gain of 1.98 per cent. The service level targets are to meet 90 per cent. of delivery dates agreed with customers; and to maintain accreditation to national measurement accreditation service and BS5750 standards.

### Boards of Visitors

**Mr. McLoughlin:** To ask the Secretary of State for the Home Department if he has reviewed the role of boards of visitors. [26103]

**Mr. Michael Forsyth:** On 1 February 1995 I made an announcement in the House that I would conduct a review of the role of boards of visitors. My right hon. and learned Friend and I place great value on the work of boards and on the participation of lay people from the local community in the prison system. There has been considerable change within the Prison Service, particularly after it became an agency, which has placed new and increased demands on boards of visitors. The objective of the review was to find ways to strengthen the role of boards and help them undertake their duties more effectively.

My review group consisted of Mrs. Lindsay Addyman JP, Mrs Mary Bentall OBE JP, Mr. Colin Edwards, Ms Freda Evans, Mrs Denise Hurst, Mr. Alfred Mossop JP, Mrs Sylvia Peach JP, Mr. Jim Romer, and Mrs Judy Veale OBE JP, all of whom are current or past members of boards of visitors, and Judge Stephen Tumim, Her Majesty's Chief Inspector of Prisons. The governor of HM prison, Maidstone was co-opted. Support was provided by a small team of officials.

Written representations within the terms of reference were invited by 3 March from a wide variety of groups interested in penal affairs including boards of visitors, prison governors and others. I chaired a number of meetings during March and April at which the review group considered these representations and in the light of their own wide practical experience, developed the recommendations.

The main recommendations are that:

the title "board of visitors" should be replaced by "advisory council";

a code of practice should be produced and all boards should follow it; a statement of purpose and a common constitution should be adopted by all boards;

all training for new and experienced members and new chairmen should become mandatory; and a training-needs analysis should be completed;

there should be a new elected body under the title "national advisory council" to represent to the Secretary of State matters of common concern to boards;

there should be a director of boards, appointed by open competition, supported by a secretariat based in the Home Office; additional funds of about £300,000 per annum will be necessary; the director's role will be to provide support to boards and to enhance their performance of the watchdog role on behalf of ministers;

the chairman and vice-chairman of a board should be appointed by the Secretary of State after they have been nominated by a secret ballot of its members;

the role of the board chairman should be strengthened, his duties should include ensuring the best use of resources within a notional budget set by the Secretary of State, and agreeing with the governor (or prison director) in writing the level of administrative support required from the clerk to the board and other secretarial staff; and

a 12-month probation period should be introduced for all new members; a new power should be introduced enabling the Secretary of State to suspend a member from duty as a matter of urgency; and objectives should be introduced for members and chairman together with a system of open appraisal.

One of the remarkable features of the review group was the unanimous agreement on the nature of the problems faced by boards and about their solutions. I am confident that the recommendations will command widespread support. The aim is to have them in place by January 1996.

Copies of the report of the review have been placed in the Library.

### Crime Statistics

**Dr. Lynne Jones:** To ask the Secretary of State for the Home Department if he will list the percentage change in each category of recorded crime and in total recorded crime *(a)* between the last two years for which figures are available and *(b)* between 1979 and the last year for which figures are available (i) in England and Wales and (ii) in each police force area.          [25258]

**Mr. Maclean:** The information requested is contained in the tables:

### Identity Cards

**Mr. Hawkins:** To ask the Secretary of State for the Home Department when he will publish the consultation paper on identity cards.          [26104]

**Mr. Howard:** I will lay before Parliament and publish tomorrow a Green Paper on identity cards.

### Fireworks

**Mr. Burden:** To ask the Secretary of State for the Home Department how many shops and businesses were successfully prosecuted for selling fireworks to children under the apparent age of 16 years by *(a)* the police

and *(b)* trading standards officers, in each year since 1985.          [23572]

**Mr. Maclean** *[holding answer 22 May 1995]:* Statistics relating to prosecutions undertaken by trading standard officers cannot be identified centrally.

The table shows the number of police and non-police prosecutions and convictions under section 31 of the Explosives Act 1875, as amended, from 1985 to 1993: 1994 data will not be available until autumn 1995.

It should, however, be noted that the statistics of court proceedings are based on returns made by the police to the Home Office and although these include offences where there has been no police involvement, such as those prosecutions instigated by Government Departments, local authorities—in this case, probably trading standards officers—and private organisations and individuals, the reporting of these types of offence is known to be incomplete.

*Number of defendants prosecuted and convicted at magistrates' courts for selling fireworks to any child apparently under 16 years of age[1] by type of proceeding 1985–1993*

*England and Wales*

| Year | Prosecutions | | Convictions | |
|---|---|---|---|---|
| | Police | Others | Police | Others |
| 1985 | — | — | — | — |
| 1986[2] | 6 | — | — | — |
| 1987[3] | 1 | — | 1 | — |
| 1988 | 1 | 1 | — | 1 |
| 1989 | — | — | — | — |
| 1990 | — | 1 | — | 1 |
| 1991 | — | — | — | — |
| 1992 | — | — | — | — |
| 1993 | — | — | — | — |

[1] Section 31 of the Explosives Act 1875 as amended by the Explosives (Age of Purchase, etc) Act 1976, s1 and the Consumer Protection Act 1987, sch 4.
[2] A further offender found guilty at the Crown Court.
[3] A further offender found guilty at the Crown Court.

### Telephones

**Mr. Donohoe:** To ask the Secretary of State for the Home Department what representations his Department has made to the Department of Trade and Industry concerning the need for legislation to prevent the cloning of mobile telephones.          [23467]

**Mr. Howard** *[holding answer 9 May 1995]:* None.

*Percentage change in numbers of notifiable offences recorded by police force area and offence group 1993–94*

*England and Wales*                                                      *Percentage change*

| Police force area | Total | Violence against the person | Sexual offences | Robbery | Burglary | Theft and handling stolen goods | Fraud and forgery | Criminal damage | Other offences |
|---|---|---|---|---|---|---|---|---|---|
| Avon and Somerset | −5 | +18 | +22 | −8 | −8 | −6 | −14 | +4 | +30 |
| Bedfordshire | −11 | +2 | +2 | +7 | −17 | −11 | −18 | −1 | +34 |
| Cambridgeshire | −6 | +7 | +7 | −21 | −6 | −10 | −18 | +10 | +6 |
| Cheshire | −7 | +9 | +17 | −19 | −13 | −10 | −3 | +4 | +46 |
| Cleveland | +4 | +6 | +9 | +39 | −2 | +4 | −14 | +14 | +24 |
| Cumbria | −3 | +11 | +2 | (−19) | −6 | −7 | +11 | +7 | +5 |
| Derbyshire | −6 | −3 | +3 | +18 | −6 | −10 | +2 | +1 | +11 |
| Devon and Cornwall | −10 | +12 | −9 | −5 | −7 | −12 | −15 | −13 | +16 |
| Dorset | +7 | +9 | +39 | +8 | 2 | +6 | −16 | +38 | +1 |
| Durham | −3 | +11 | +3 | −9 | −8 | −5 | −11 | +6 | +8 |
| Essex | −7 | +8 | −23 | −2 | −13 | −9 | −11 | +4 | +15 |
| Gloucestershire | 0 | +22 | +220 | +5 | −8 | −4 | +13 | +28 | +30 |

*Percentage change in numbers of notifiable offences recorded by police force area and offence group 1993–94*

*England and Wales*                                                   *Percentage change*

| Police force area | Total | Violence against the person | Sexual offences | Robbery | Burglary | Theft and handling stolen goods | Fraud and forgery | Criminal damage | Other offences |
|---|---|---|---|---|---|---|---|---|---|
| Greater Manchester | −7 | −8 | −10 | −1 | −7 | −11 | −17 | +6 | −11 |
| Hampshire | −4 | +7 | −25 | +4 | −10 | −4 | −24 | +7 | +11 |
| Hertfordshire | −3 | +4 | +11 | −3 | −10 | −3 | −14 | +5 | −16 |
| Humberside | −4 | +2 | −13 | +4 | −8 | −1 | −11 | −2 | +35 |
| Kent | −4 | +15 | +17 | +1 | −13 | −5 | −10 | +3 | +20 |
| Lancashire | −5 | +3 | +7 | +1 | −8 | −9 | +2 | +5 | +17 |
| Leicestershire | −1 | +29 | +31 | +11 | +4 | −6 | −6 | +1 | +10 |
| Lincolnshire | −9 | +2 | +26 | −25 | −14 | −12 | −10 | +2 | +9 |
| London, City of | −6 | −47 | (0) | (−43) | −13 | −2 | −13 | +3 | (+11) |
| Merseyside | −4 | +4 | +5 | −8 | −2 | −4 | −39 | −1 | −1 |
| Metropolitan Police | −7 | +17 | +8 | +4 | −8 | −11 | −5 | −4 | +41 |
| Norfolk | −13 | +7 | +1 | −14 | −23 | −13 | −9 | +2 | +32 |
| Northamptonshire | −4 | −5 | +26 | +2 | −9 | −6 | −14 | +12 | +2 |
| Northumbria | −5 | −3 | +5 | −1 | −9 | −7 | −4 | +4 | +2 |
| North Yorkshire | +7 | +4 | −1 | +52 | +3 | +3 | −13 | +39 | −3 |
| Nottinghamshire | −4 | 0 | −2 | −1 | −13 | −8 | −10 | +22 | +8 |
| South Yorkshire | 0 | +4 | +4 | +13 | −2 | −3 | +24 | +7 | +28 |
| Staffordshire | −5 | +6 | +6 | 0 | −11 | −6 | +1 | +2 | +20 |
| Suffolk | −9 | +1 | +3 | +1 | −15 | −14 | −14 | +13 | +18 |
| Surrey | −11 | +25 | +23 | −23 | −21 | −12 | −21 | +1 | +37 |
| Sussex | −4 | +5 | +8 | +8 | −9 | −3 | −10 | −3 | −2 |
| Thames Valley | −7 | +18 | +11 | +24 | −5 | −8 | −18 | −9 | +20 |
| Warwickshire | −6 | −3 | −13 | +4 | −12 | −5 | −21 | −1 | +21 |
| West Mercia | +1 | +4 | +13 | +9 | −7 | −2 | +1 | +23 | +54 |
| West Midlands | −4 | −5 | −10 | +18 | −9 | −5 | −14 | +6 | +5 |
| West Yorkshire | −4 | +2 | +3 | −6 | −7 | −5 | −8 | +5 | +10 |
| Wiltshire | −8 | −5 | −5 | −7 | −11 | −10 | −16 | +1 | +8 |
| Dyfed Powys | −13 | +8 | −31 | (+32) | −25 | −16 | −20 | −3 | +41 |
| Gwent | −4 | +6 | −14 | (−32) | −6 | −9 | +2 | +3 | +91 |
| North Wales | −10 | −9 | −37 | −15 | −15 | −11 | −3 | +2 | +35 |
| South Wales | −5 | +2 | −8 | −13 | −2 | −1 | −14 | −17 | +30 |
| England and Wales | −5 | +7 | +4 | +3 | −8 | −7 | −10 | +2 | +19 |

*Note:*

Figures in brackets are based on totals of less than 100.


*Percentage change in numbers of notifiable offences recorded by police force area and offence group 1979–94*

*England and Wales*                                                   *Percentage change*

| Police force area | Total | Violence against the person | Sexual offences | Robbery | Burglary | Theft and handling stolen goods | Fraud and forgery | Criminal damage | Other offences |
|---|---|---|---|---|---|---|---|---|---|
| Avon and Somerset | +227 | +239 | +120 | +965 | +313 | +200 | +68 | +286 | +708 |
| Bedfordshire | +87 | +36 | +71 | +299 | +172 | +73 | +7 | +93 | +65 |
| Cambridgeshire | +150 | +201 | +54 | (+426) | +237 | +119 | +57 | +207 | +370 |
| Cheshire | +147 | +128 | +75 | (+435) | +188 | +107 | +167 | +215 | +1,847 |
| Cleveland | +135 | +69 | −12 | (+718) | +133 | +132 | −40 | +243 | +778 |
| Cumbria | +118 | +188 | +82 | (+208) | +165 | +86 | +3 | +192 | +836 |
| Derbyshire | +122 | +108 | +21 | (+378) | +197 | +100 | −34 | +158 | +442 |
| Devon and Cornwall | +152 | +133 | +55 | (+343) | +296 | +113 | +42 | +175 | +1,017 |
| Dorset | +139 | +196 | +93 | (+224) | +135 | +130 | +39 | +267 | +375 |
| Durham | +138 | +109 | +119 | (+217) | +108 | +136 | +85 | +200 | +1,382 |
| Essex | +96 | +111 | +6 | +166 | +130 | +75 | +18 | +157 | +676 |
| Gloucestershire | +269 | +312 | +447 | (+867) | +427 | +220 | +243 | +229 | +1,198 |
| Greater Manchester | +100 | +93 | −13 | +985 | +133 | +63 | +6 | +238 | +330 |
| Hampshire | +111 | +144 | +28 | +179 | +136 | +98 | −5 | +172 | +909 |
| Hertfordshire | +41 | +65 | +14 | (+267) | +163 | +24 | −62 | +64 | +230 |
| Humberside | +182 | +90 | +12 | +431 | +303 | +147 | +147 | +168 | +459 |
| Kent | +181 | +257 | +111 | +443 | +157 | +170 | +43 | +276 | +462 |
| Lancashire | +123 | +62 | −7 | +363 | +118 | +108 | +39 | +221 | +345 |
| Leicestershire | +227 | +243 | +100 | (+1,159) | +358 | +172 | +147 | +297 | +312 |
| Lincolnshire | +172 | +165 | +29 | (+358) | +242 | +134 | +58 | +261 | +1,110 |
| London, City of | −23 | −25 | (+53) | (−33) | −41 | −20 | +4 | −41 | (+82) |
| Merseyside | +26 | +102 | +62 | +134 | +6 | +13 | −10 | +123 | +270 |
| Metropolitan Police | +52 | +189 | +153 | +309 | +38 | +26 | +26 | +136 | +457 |
| Norfolk | +148 | +168 | +83 | (+313) | +224 | +123 | +34 | +184 | +229 |
| Northamptonshire | +151 | +154 | +16 | (+260) | +226 | +112 | +21 | +270 | +365 |

*Percentage change in numbers of notifiable offences recorded by police force area and offence group 1979–94*

England and Wales     *Percentage change*

| Police force area | Total | Violence against the person | Sexual offences | Robbery | Burglary | Theft and handling stolen goods | Fraud and forgery | Criminal damage | Other offences |
|---|---|---|---|---|---|---|---|---|---|
| Northumbria | +105 | +87 | +10 | +519 | +112 | +51 | +22 | +358 | +720 |
| North Yorkshire | +184 | +130 | +11 | (+367) | +250 | +162 | –16 | +281 | +685 |
| Nottinghamshire | +110 | +97 | +20 | +479 | +110 | +77 | +35 | +326 | +134 |
| South Yorkshire | +179 | +70 | –6 | +548 | +307 | 130 | +56 | +234 | +784 |
| Staffordshire | +146 | +103 | +57 | (+486) | +234 | +114 | +35 | +194 | +45 |
| Suffolk | +95 | +130 | +85 | (+219) | +173 | +67 | +13 | +162 | +159 |
| Surrey | +73 | +163 | +29 | (+166) | 1112 | +58 | –20 | +114 | +695 |
| Sussex | +120 | +74 | +18 | (+495) | +162 | +100 | –7 | +238 | +513 |
| Thames Valley | +146 | +144 | +34 | +436 | +176 | +129 | +21 | +254 | +813 |
| Warwickshire | +205 | +146 | +89 | (+216) | +291 | +181 | +87 | +220 | +918 |
| West Mercia | +139 | +104 | +30 | (+373) | +182 | +140 | –8 | +144 | +294 |
| West Midlands | +102 | +75 | 0 | +580 | +127 | +69 | +75 | +180 | +420 |
| West Yorkshire | +125 | +86 | +28 | +517 | +172 | +99 | +51 | +154 | +436 |
| Wiltshire | +86 | +244 | +29 | (+140) | +131 | +66 | +9 | +89 | +326 |
| Dyfed Powys | +84 | +334 | +2 | (+71) | +104 | +61 | –38 | +129 | +286 |
| Gwent | +87 | +143 | +6 | (+126) | +100 | +70 | –8 | +147 | +2,055 |
| North Wales | +84 | +127 | +8 | (+156) | +119 | +61 | –48 | +224 | +641 |
| South Wales | +120 | +153 | +17 | +152 | +109 | +106 | +24 | +207 | +806 |
| England and Wales | +107 | +131 | +49 | +379 | +131 | +81 | +24 | +190 | +454 |

*Note:*
Figures in brackets are based on totals of less than 100.

## Body Armour

**Mrs. Roche:** To ask the Secretary of State for the Home Department which European countries routinely supply their police officers with body armour. [25149]

**Mr. Maclean:** We do not have this information.

**Mrs. Roche:** To ask the Secretary of State for the Home Department (1) how many *(a)* bullet-proof and *(b)* knife-proof vests have been supplied to police officers in each police division in England; [25148]

(2) how many police officers have been supplied with *(a)* knife-proof body armour and *(b)* bullet-proof body armour; and what proportion this constitutes of all police officers. [25141]

**Mr. Maclean:** This information is not kept centrally.

**Mrs. Roche:** To ask the Secretary of State for the Home Department what research his Department is carrying out into body armour for police officers which is both knife and bullet proof. [25155]

**Mr. Maclean:** The police scientific development branch of the Home Office has a continuous programme of evaluating the latest developments in this field. It has in addition, developed test standards and procedures which are provided to manufacturers.

**Mrs. Roche:** To ask the Secretary of State for the Home Department when he expects body armour to be supplied to all police officers in England and Wales. [25142]

**Mr. Maclean:** This is a matter for chief officers of police. I understand, however, that all officers involved in firearms operations are issued with ballistic protection.

## Police Discipline

**Mr. Mullin:** To ask the Secretary of State for the Home Department (1) further to the recent report of the Police Complaints Authority, how many police officers were allowed to retire early on medical grounds while facing disciplinary charges in each of the last five years; and if he will make a statement; [25015]

(2) how many police officers facing disciplinary charges retired early on medical grounds in each of the last five years. [25740]

**Mr. Maclean:** In 1993, 39 officers retired on the grounds of ill health during the course of investigations into their conduct or whilst facing disciplinary action or criminal proceedings.

Information for earlier years is not available in the form requested.

**Mr. Mullin:** To ask the Secretary of State for the Home Department (1) further to the recent report of the Police Complaints Authority, what form of disciplinary action was imposed on 1,228 police officers in 1994; [24983]

(2) further to the recent report papers of the Police Complaints Authority, what was the nature of the 1,228 offences for which disciplinary action was imposed in 1994. [24982]

**Mr. Maclean:** The information available on punishments resulting from disciplinary hearings, including those originating from a complaint, will appear in the Home Office's annual statistical bulletin on police complaints and discipline, which is expected to be published in June.

Information on the types of complaint which resulted in disciplinary action recorded by the Police Complaints Authority in 1994 will appear in the authority's annual report, which is due to be published shortly.

## Police Training

**Mr. Mike O'Brien:** To ask the Secretary of State for the Home Department, pursuant to his answer of 11 May, *Official Report*, column 555, what estimates were made of the training costs needed to enable police in England and Wales to be fully aware of the provisions of the Criminal Justice and Public Order Act 1994; and to what extent these were taken into consideration when assessing police funding. [25232]

**Mr. Maclean:** No additions to funding have been made for local training requirements in relation to this Act which were expected to vary according to individual and operational needs. Police funding generally takes into account increasing costs, but forces have to work within budgets to meet changing demands.

### Name Badges (Prison Service)

**Mr. Cox:** To ask the Secretary of State for the Home Department if he will make a statement on the policy of his Department that all members within the Prison Service should wear name badges. [22206]

**Mr. Michael Forsyth:** I have asked the Prison Service to review the policy.

## WALES

### Nursery Education

**Mr. Barry Jones:** To ask the Secretary of State for Wales what review he is making of nursery school provision in Wales; and if he will make a statement. [24849]

**Mr. Richards:** My right hon. Friend and I are considering a number of options on how to fulfil the Government's commitment to provide pre-school places for all four-year-olds whose parents wish to take them up.

In Wales the office of Her Majesty's chief inspector of schools is undertaking a survey of existing provision in the maintained and voluntary sectors.

### Education Funding

**Mr. Barry Jones:** To ask the Secretary of State for Wales what representations he has received concerning school funding in 1995–96 from *(a)* teachers, *(b)* governors and *(c)* parents; and if he will make a statement. [24853]

**Mr. Richards:** My right hon. Friend and I have received many representations concerning school funding in 1995–96 from many parties. The funding of schools is a local government responsibility. We have made it clear that in our view there is sufficient scope for local authorities in Wales to fund schools appropriately from within the overall settlement they have received. By long-standing arrangement, it is for local authorities in Wales to decide their priorities for spending.

### Doctors (Suspension)

**Mr. Barry Jones:** To ask the Secretary of State for Wales (1) what measures he will take to ensure that general practitioners found guilty of professional misconduct do not continue to practise pending the outcome of their appeal; [24860]

(2) how many general practitioners found guilty of professional misconduct are continuing to practise pending their appeal; and if he will make a statement; [24839]

(3) what representations he has received concerning general practitioners who continue to practise pending their appeal; and if he will make a statement. [24859]

**Mr. Richards:** The General Medical Council is the independent statutory authority responsible for regulating the medical profession. In the last two years the GMC has used its powers to suspend doctors in almost 50 per cent. of cases. Representations have been received on individual cases, but these are matters for the GMC, not the Government.

A Bill currently before Parliament would give the NHS tribunal new powers of suspension.

### School Class Sizes

**Mr. Barry Jones:** To ask the Secretary of State for Wales what guidelines his Department issues on the optimum number of pupils per class in primary schools; and if he will make a statement. [24851]

**Mr. Richards:** Class sizes are a matter for individual school governing bodies.

### Assisted Places Scheme

**Mr. Barry Jones:** To ask the Secretary of State for Wales what was the amount of Government funding given to each of the public schools in Wales via the assisted places schemes in *(a)* 1993–94 *(b)* 1994–95; and if he will make a statement. [24852]

**Mr. Richards:** The information requested is as follows:

*Total payments to APS schools 1993–94 and 1994–95*

| Name of school | Total payments 1993–94 £ | Total payments 1994–95 £ |
| --- | --- | --- |
| Monmouth Boys | 456,071 | 468,332 |
| Penrhos College | 295,428 | 309,809 |
| Howells, Cardiff | 430,751 | 452,598 |
| Rydal School | 252,589 | 289,112 |
| Llandovery College | 256,648 | 279,489 |
| Christ College | 389,754 | 410,476 |
| Howells, Denbigh | 353,064 | 365,186 |
| Monmouth Girls | 186,956 | 196,502 |
| Total expenditure | 2,621,261 | 2,771,504 |

### National Lottery

**Mr. Barry Jones:** To ask the Secretary of State for Wales if he will list the sports bodies in *(a)* Wales and *(b)* Clwyd to which grants from national lottery proceeds have been made; and if he will give the amounts given. [24840]

**Mr. Richards:** The first allocation of grants from Sportlot, the Lottery Sports Fund for Wales, has been distributed throughout Wales as follows:

| Applicant | Amount of grant £ |
| --- | --- |
| Cardiff Central Youth Club | 95,192 |
| Llandaff Rowing Club | 150,623 |
| Y Pant Comprehensive School | 4,500 |
| Builth Wells Rugby Club | 60,398 |
| Llanfapley Cricket Club and Llanfapley Sports and Social Committee | 34,498 |
| Llanwrda Cricket Club | 10,675 |
| Clwb Rygbi Castell Newydd Emlyn | 100,000 |
| Dyffryn Cricket Club/Bryncoch Sports Club | 4,000 |

| Applicant | Amount of grant £ |
|---|---|
| Lampeter AFC | 20,000 |
| Aberporth and District Youth Club | 45,000 |
| Pembroke Dock Bowling Club | 10,000 |
| Dale Yacht Club | 5,000 |
| Solva Rowing and Watersports Club | 5,000 |
| Rhydymwyn Football Club | 26,125 |
| Total | 571,011 |

In Clwyd one grant of £26,125 has been made to Rhydymwyn football club.

### Welsh Patients Treated in Chester

**Mr. Barry Jones:** To ask the Secretary of State for Wales what is the percentage of beds taken annually by people from Clwyd in Chester hospitals; and if he will make a statement. [25163]

**Mr. Richards:** Reliable information is not available centrally.

### Infertility Treatment

**Mr. Barry Jones:** To ask the Secretary of State for Wales what is his policy concerning treatment for infertility. [25162]

**Mr. Richards:** The NHS in Wales provides a wide range of services for the investigation and treatment of infertility. It is for individual health authorities to determine the extent and type of services in the light of local needs and priorities.

The Welsh Office has provided guidance in the protocol, "Investment in Health Gain for Health Living", and has drawn attention to the advice contained in "The Effective Health Care Bulletin on the Management of Subfertility", published for the NHS management executive by a consortium of Leeds and York universities and the research unit of the Royal College of Physicians, and the Royal College of Obstetricians and Gynaecologists publication "Infertility—Guidelines for Practice". Copies of these documents are available in the Library of the House.

### European Structural Funds

**Mr. Wigley:** To ask the Secretary of State for Wales what contributions are planned from his Department during 1995–96 for funding to facilitate the optimising of take-up of EU grants under the objective 5b programme in Wales; and if he will make a statement. [25008]

**Mr. Redwood:** I refer the hon. Member to the reply that I gave him on 11 May, *Official Report,* column *585.*

Support for the objective 5b programme can come from a variety of public sector sources, including my own Department. The amount of assistance actually made available from any source in direct support of objective 5b projects will depend on the nature and quality of projects put forward.

### Care in the Community

**Mr. Barry Jones:** To ask the Secretary of State for Wales if he will make a statement on the working so far of care in the community in Wales. [25164]

**Mr. Richards:** Local authorities in Wales have made generally good progress since April 1993 with community care. The Welsh Office departmental report, Cm2815, records that in the first year of the new arrangements local authorities assessed over 50,000 people for community care services and over 28,000 were provided with care to help them stay in their own homes.

### Contracting Out

**Ms Hodge:** To ask the Secretary of State for Wales what work has been contracted out *(a)* by his Department and *(b)* by agencies for which his Department is responsible in (i) 1993–94 and (ii) 1994–95; and what is projected for 1995–96. [25544]

**Mr. Redwood:** As a result of my Department and its agency's competing for quality programmes the following services have been contracted out: 1993–94 building maintenance management; 1994–95 staff training; 1995–96 to date, architects and surveyors services and careers service in Wales. Contracting out of further work in 1995–96 is dependent on the outcome of current market testing exercises.

### Elderly People

**Mr. Foulkes:** To ask the Secretary of State for Wales what was the total income in 1993–94 to each local authority and in total from placements of old people in *(a)* registered and *(b)* unregistered independent residential care and nursing homes, inside and outside the local authority area and from placements in local authority homes for older people; and if he will break down by income from (i) government grants, inside aggregate external finance and outside aggregate external finance, (ii) sales, (iii) fees and charges, (iv) other income and (v) joint arrangements. [25393]

**Mr. Gwilym Jones:** The information requested is given in the following tables, based on revenue outturn forms from local authorities in Wales. Local authorities received no income in 1993–94 from placements in unregistered independent residential care and nursing homes.

*(a) Income from residential care and nursing placements in registered independent homes for the elderly 1993–94*[1]

£000

| | Total income | (i) Government grants[2] | (ii) Sales | (iii) Fees and charges | (iv) Other income | (v) Joint arrangements |
|---|---|---|---|---|---|---|
| Clwyd | 27 | 0 | 0 | 27 | 0 | 0 |
| Dyfed | 1,248 | 0 | 0 | 1,248 | 0 | 0 |
| Gwent | 1,203 | 0 | 0 | 1,203 | 0 | 0 |
| Gwynedd | 0 | 0 | 0 | 0 | 0 | 0 |
| Mid Glamorgan | 0 | 0 | 0 | 0 | 0 | 0 |

*(a) Income from residential care and nursing placements in registered independent homes for the elderly 1993–94[1]*

£000

| | Total income | (i) Government grants[2] | (ii) Sales | (iii) Fees and charges | (iv) Other income | (v) Joint arrangements |
|---|---|---|---|---|---|---|
| Powys | 121 | 0 | 0 | 121 | 0 | 0 |
| South Glamorgan | 94 | 0 | 0 | 94 | 0 | 0 |
| West Glamorgan | 5 | 0 | 0 | 5 | 0 | 0 |
| Total Wales | 2,698 | 0 | 0 | 2,698 | 0 | 0 |

[1]Provisional. Includes placements in independent sector homes which are not required to register under the Registered Homes Act 1984 because they are managed or provided by an exempt body.
[2]Includes specific government grants inside and outside Aggregate External Finance.

*(b) Income from Local Authority Homes for the elderly 1993–94[1]*

£000

| | Total income | (i) Government grants[2] | (ii) Sales | (iii) Fees and charges | (iv) Other income | (v) Joint arrangements |
|---|---|---|---|---|---|---|
| Clwyd | 2,252 | 0 | 107 | 2,036 | 109 | 0 |
| Dyfed | 4,537 | 0 | 21 | 3,812 | 704 | 0 |
| Gwent | 3,103 | 54 | 19 | 2,548 | 474 | 35 |
| Gwynedd | 2,621 | 0 | 0 | 2,559 | 62 | 0 |
| Mid Glamorgan | 5,146 | 35 | 43 | 5,068 | 0 | 0 |
| Powys | 1,502 | 0 | 10 | 1,475 | 17 | 0 |
| South Glamorgan | 1,876 | 0 | 22 | 1,637 | 209 | 8 |
| West Glamorgan | 2,371 | 17 | 33 | 2,201 | 120 | 0 |
| Total Wales | 23,435 | 106 | 255 | 21,336 | 1,695 | 43 |

[1]Provisional. Includes income from placements of the elderly mentally infirm, the physically disabled and blind and deaf people. Excludes income from sheltered accommodation.
[2]Includes specific government grants inside and outside Aggregate External Finance.

### Schools Inspectors

**Mr. Win Griffiths:** To ask the Secretary of State for Wales if he will publish a list of all schools inspectors indicating those who have undertaken further training to become registered inspectors and are able to tender for school inspections and lead inspection teams.    [25391]

**Mr. Richards** *[holding answer 22 May 1995]:* This is a matter for Her Majesty's chief inspector to deal with and I have arranged for him to write to the hon. Member about it.

### Radioactive Waste

**Mr. Win Griffiths:** To ask the Secretary of State for Wales what plans he has to allow radioactive waste from the nuclear power industry to be accepted by local landfill disposal sites.    [25773]

**Mr. Gwilym Jones:** This is one of the issues being considered in the current review of radioactive waste management policy, as part of which a major consultation exercise was undertaken last autumn. The Government's conclusions on this matter and other aspects of radioactive waste management policy will be published in a White Paper in the summer.

**Mr. Win Griffiths:** To ask the Secretary of State for Wales if he will list the local landfill disposal sites that accept low level radioactive waste for disposal; and if he will make a statement about the sources of such waste.    [25775]

**Mr. Gwilym Jones:** In Wales only one landfill site has been authorised for this purpose—Cilgwyn quarry, near Caernarfon. The very small amounts of waste involved have come from the university sector and have been regulated in accordance with the Radioactive Substances Act 1993.

### Welsh Language

**Mr. Win Griffiths:** To ask the Secretary of State for Wales what plans he has to ensure that the privatised utilities in Wales develop comprehensive bilingual policies.    [25774]

**Mr. Richards:** It was not intended that the provisions of the Welsh Language Act 1993 should apply to the private sector. However, many private companies, including privatised utilities, have produced Welsh language schemes voluntarily and in response to customer demand. The privatised utilities have, I believe, a particularly good record of operating bilingual policies successfully.

## SOCIAL SECURITY

### Income Support

**Mr. David Nicholson:** To ask the Secretary of State for Social Security what representations his Department and its agencies have received since 1 January about delays in paying income support in respect of persons with extreme difficulties in specialised units *(a)* nationally and *(b)* in Somerset; what trends there have been in the time taken to settle these claims; and if he will make a statement.    [24285]

**Mr. Roger Evans:** The administration of income support is a matter for Mr. Ian Magee, the chief executive of the Benefits Agency. He will write to the hon. Member.

*Letter from Ian Magee to Mr. David Nicholson, dated 22 May 1995:*

The Secretary of State for Social Security has asked me to reply to your recent Parliamentary Question asking about delays in making payment of Income Support to customers with extreme difficulties living in specialised units in Somerset and elsewhere in Great Britain.

I understand that the Manager of the Benefits Agency's District Office in Somerset wrote to you on 17 May concerning the Income Support claims of four residents of a specialised unit, two of whom had their cases immediately resolved. Since that date the two outstanding cases have also been resolved and full entitlement to benefit including all arrears due has been sent.

I am very sorry that there have been difficulties in respect of these particular cases. I am assured, however, that this is an isolated matter and we have no evidence or indication that there is a problem of delays in the payment of Income Support either in Somerset or nationally to customers in these circumstances.

I hope you find this reply helpful.

**Mr. Corbyn:** To ask the Secretary of State for Social Security how many people have been refused income support after failing the habitual residence test since its introduction, in the Euston district office of Glasgow; how many have appealed against this decision; how many of those appeals have now been heard by a tribunal; how many claimants won their appeals; how many are still waiting for an appeal date to be given; and how many of those claimants appealing, have applied for an interim payment, and how many of those applicants have been refused. [25403]

**Mr. Roger Evans:** The administration of income support is a matter for Mr. Ian Magee, the chief executive of the Benefits Agency. He will write to the hon. Member.

*Letter from Ian Magee to Mr. Jeremy Corbyn, dated 22 May 1995:*

The Secretary of State for Social Security has asked me to reply to your recent Parliamentary Question about the operation of the habitual residence test (HRT) for Income Support customers of the Benefits Agency (BA) District Office in Euston.

The full range of information is not available. Information about the number of customers who pass or fail the HRT is collected and maintained centrally for BA management information purposes. Information is not routinely collected about appeals specifically against HRT decisions, the result of those appeals, or of requests for interim payments on account of Income Support entitlement.

However, as an aid to their resource planning and management team at Glasgow Benefit Centre has kept an informal record of appeals against Income Support disallowances from customers of Euston District Office who fail the HRT, and of the decisions of the Social Security Appeal Tribunals, for which a notification has been received, in those appeals. The data available is:

Habitual Residence Test disallowances—3966

Habitual Residence Test appeals—364

Appeals heard—97

Appeals allowed—72

Hearing date awaited—116

It should be noted that in a number of cases the local adjudicating authorities revised the disallowance of Income Support as part of a routine review of the decision following receipt of an appeal; a number of appeals have been heard but notification of the Tribunal decision is awaited; and in a number of cases hearing dates have been notified to customers.

I hope you find this reply helpful.

**Mr. Frank Field:** To ask the Secretary of State for Social Security if he will re-institute the collection and publishing of data on the length of time claimants have

been drawing income support by each year of duration above two years, and up to 20 years plus. [25140]

**Mr. Roger Evans:** It is no longer possible to collect reliable information on durations of claims for those people who have been in receipt of income support for relatively long periods. A full explanation is given in the introduction to the 1993 annual statistical enquiry, a copy of which is in the Library.

### National Insurance Contributions

**Mr. Jon Owen Jones:** To ask the Secretary of State for Social Security how far back computerised records of national insurance contributions extend. [25040]

**Mr. Arbuthnot:** The administration of national insurance is the responsibility of Mrs. Faith Boardman, the chief executive of the Contributions Agency. She will write to the hon. Member.

*Letter from Mrs. Faith Boardman to Mr. Jon Owen Jones, dated 19 May 1995:*

As Chief Executive of the Contributions Agency, I have responsibility for answering questions about operational matters relating to the National Insurance scheme, I have been asked to reply to your question about how far back computerised records of National Insurance contributions extend.

A cumulative total is held on each contributor's computer account of all National Insurance contributions from April 1948 to March 1975.

From April 1975, detailed annual records of all National Insurance contributions are held on each contributor's account.

I hope you will find this reply helpful. If I can be of any further assistance, please let me know.

### HIV Infection

**Mr. Frank Field:** To ask the Secretary of State for Social Security what steps his Department is taking to disseminate the guidance to Benefits Agency medical services on HIV infection to doctors and staff. [25247]

**Mr. Roger Evans:** This is a matter for Mr. Ian Magee, the chief executive of the Benefits Agency. He will write to the hon. Member.

*Letter from Ian Magee to Mr. Frank Field, dated 22 May 1995:*

The Secretary of State for Social Security has asked me to reply to your recent Parliamentary Question about the guidance that is issued by the Benefits Agency on HIV infection.

"A Guide to Benefits and HIV" was produced by the Benefits Agency in June 1993. It was written in co-operation with many organisations including the Terrence Higgins Trust. The Guide was distributed widely throughout the Agency, and provides advice for staff, including the Agency's medical advisors, and customers about the benefit and welfare issues which affect people with HIV positive related illnesses. There is also advice on other agencies and outside organisations from whom help may be obtained; a list of related publications is also included.

Additionally, during 1994 guidance was issued to staff, including the Agency's medical advisors, on the following topics:-

    i) the safe disposal of hypodermic needles discarded by the public in Benefits Agency District and Branch Offices.

    ii) precautions to be taken by those administering First Aid, particularly in the avoidance of blood contact.

    iii) the Benefits Agency Policy Statement covering employees and clients who may have AIDS or be HIV positive.

I have enclosed both "A Guide to Benefits and HIV" and the further guidance I have mentioned, copies of which have been placed in the Library.

I hope you find this reply helpful.

## Benefit Take-up

**Mr. Milburn:** To ask the Secretary of State for Social Security how many people received social security benefits *(a)* in total and *(b)* as a percentage of the eligible population in each year since 1979. [25757]

**Mr. Hague:** The information is not available in the form requested.

## Sickness and Maternity Pay

**Mr. Jim Cunningham:** To ask the Secretary of State for Social Security (1) how many people have been denied statutory sick pay because their earnings were too low in the last year for which figures are available; [25001]

(2) how many women in the last year for which figures are available have been denied statutory maternity pay because their earnings were too low. [24994]

**Mr. Hague:** The information is not available. Employers are not required to keep information on exclusions.

## Incomes

**Mr. Byers:** To ask the Secretary of State for Social Security what would be the weekly income of *(a)* a single person aged 25 years or over, *(b)* a married couple with a non-earning partner and *(c)* a married couple with a non-earning partner with two children aged four and six years when the person in work was employed for (i) 16 hours and (ii) 40 hours a week at (1) £2.50 an hour, (2) £3 an hour, (3) £3.50 an hour, (4) £4 an hour and (5) £4.15 an hour, assuming full take-up of benefits and assuming that they lived in local authority accommodation paying average council tax and local authority rent. [25045]

**Mr. Roger Evans:** The information is set out in the tables.

From July, families working 30 or more hours per week will be entitled to an extra £10 family credit A new benefit to provide help to couples and single people without children in low-paid work of 16 or more hours per week is to be piloted from October 1996.

*Single Person—Aged 25 or over*

£

| Hours Worked | Rate per hour | Gross earnings | Tax and N.I. Contributions | Take home pay | Un-employment benefit | Income support | Family Credit | Child Benefit | Rent | Rent Rebate | Council tax | Council tax benefit | Total net income | Net income after rent and Council tax | Net income after rent and Council tax if no UB entitlement |
|---|---|---|---|---|---|---|---|---|---|---|---|---|---|---|---|
| 16 | 2.50 | 40.00 | 0.00 | 40.00 | 30.97 | 0.00 | 0.00 | 0.00 | 30.91 | 18.25 | 6.60 | 2.71 | 91.93 | 54.42 | 40.00 |
| 16 | 3.00 | 48.00 | 0.00 | 48.00 | 30.97 | 0.00 | 0.00 | 0.00 | 30.91 | 13.05 | 6.60 | 1.11 | 93.13 | 55.62 | 48.00 |
| 16 | 3.50 | 56.00 | 0.00 | 56.00 | 30.97 | 0.00 | 0.00 | 0.00 | 30.91 | 7.85 | 6.60 | 0.00 | 94.82 | 57.31 | 52.18 |
| 16 | 4.00 | 64.00 | 1.76 | 62.24 | 30.97 | 0.00 | 0.00 | 0.00 | 30.91 | 3.80 | 6.60 | 0.00 | 97.01 | 59.50 | 53.11 |
| 16 | 4.15 | 66.40 | 2.00 | 64.40 | 30.97 | 0.00 | 0.00 | 0.00 | 30.91 | 2.39 | 6.60 | 0.00 | 97.76 | 60.25 | 53.44 |
| 40 | 2.50 | 100.00 | 11.80 | 88.20 | 0.00 | 0.00 | 0.00 | 0.00 | 30.91 | 7.06 | 6.60 | 0.00 | 95.26 | 57.75 | — |
| 40 | 3.00 | 120.00 | 17.80 | 102.20 | 0.00 | 0.00 | 0.00 | 0.00 | 30.91 | 0.00 | 6.60 | 0.00 | 102.20 | 64.69 | — |
| 40 | 3.50 | 140.00 | 24.34 | 115.66 | 0.00 | 0.00 | 0.00 | 0.00 | 30.91 | 0.00 | 6.60 | 0.00 | 115.66 | 78.15 | — |
| 40 | 4.00 | 160.00 | 31.34 | 128.66 | 0.00 | 0.00 | 0.00 | 0.00 | 30.91 | 0.00 | 6.60 | 0.00 | 128.66 | 91.15 | — |
| 40 | 4.15 | 166.00 | 33.44 | 132.56 | 0.00 | 0.00 | 0.00 | 0.00 | 30.91 | 0.00 | 6.60 | 0.00 | 132.56 | 95.05 | — |

*Notes:*
1. Earnings for 16 hours assumed to represent two days employment.
2. All the examples shown assume take-up of full entitlement to the income-related and contributory benefits that would be most advantageous.
3. All the family types shown are assumed to live in local authority accommodation and be liable for average council tax and local authority rent.
4. Benefit Rates reflect increases from April 1995—apart from rent and council tax which remain at April 1994 rates.

*Married couple—Non earning partner*

£

| Hours worked | Rate per hour | Gross earnings | Tax and N.I. contributions | Take home pay | Un-employment benefit | Income support | Family credit | Child benefit | Rent | Rent Rebate | Council tax | Council tax benefit | Total net income | Net Income after rent and council tax | Net income after rent and council tax if no UB entitlement |
|---|---|---|---|---|---|---|---|---|---|---|---|---|---|---|---|
| 16 | 2.50 | 40.00 | 0.00 | 40.00 | 50.07 | 0.00 | 0.00 | 0.00 | 30.91 | 26.31 | 8.60 | 7.19 | 123.57 | 84.06 | 40.00 |
| 16 | 3.00 | 48.00 | 0.00 | 48.00 | 50.07 | 0.00 | 0.00 | 0.00 | 30.91 | 21.11 | 8.60 | 5.59 | 124.77 | 85.26 | 48.00 |
| 16 | 3.50 | 56.00 | 0.00 | 56.00 | 50.07 | 0.00 | 0.00 | 0.00 | 30.91 | 15.91 | 8.60 | 3.99 | 125.97 | 86.46 | 56.00 |
| 16 | 4.00 | 64.00 | 1.76 | 62.24 | 50.07 | 0.00 | 0.00 | 0.00 | 30.91 | 11.86 | 8.60 | 2.74 | 126.91 | 87.40 | 62.24 |
| 16 | 4.15 | 66.40 | 2.00 | 64.40 | 50.07 | 0.00 | 0.00 | 0.00 | 30.91 | 10.45 | 8.60 | 2.31 | 127.23 | 87.72 | 64.40 |
| 40 | 2.50 | 100.00 | 6.84 | 93.16 | 0.00 | 0.00 | 0.00 | 0.00 | 30.91 | 24.31 | 8.60 | 6.57 | 124.04 | 84.53 | — |
| 40 | 3.00 | 120.00 | 12.84 | 107.16 | 0.00 | 0.00 | 0.00 | 0.00 | 30.91 | 15.21 | 8.60 | 3.77 | 126.14 | 86.63 | — |

*Married couple—Non earning partner*

£

| Hours worked | Rate per hour | Gross earnings | Tax and N.I. contri- butions | Take home pay | Un- employ- ment benefit | Income support | Family credit | Child benefit | Rent | Rent Rebate | Council tax | Council tax benefit | Total net income | Net Income after rent and council tax | Net income after rent and council tax if no UB entitlement |
|---|---|---|---|---|---|---|---|---|---|---|---|---|---|---|---|
| 40 | 3.50 | 140.00 | 19.37 | 120.63 | 0.00 | 0.00 | 0.00 | 0.00 | 30.91 | 6.45 | 8.60 | 1.07 | 128.15 | 88.64 | — |
| 40 | 4.00 | 160.00 | 26.37 | 133.63 | 0.00 | 0.00 | 0.00 | 0.00 | 30.91 | 0.00 | 8.60 | 0.00 | 133.63 | 94.12 | — |
| 40 | 4.15 | 166.00 | 28.47 | 137.53 | 0.00 | 0.00 | 0.00 | 0.00 | 30.91 | 0.00 | 8.60 | 0.00 | 137.53 | 98.02 | — |

*Notes:*

1. Earnings for 16 hours assumed to represent two days employment.
2. All the examples shown assume take-up of full entitlement to Income-related and contributory benefits that would be most advantageous
3. All the family types shown are assumed to live in local authority accommodation and be liable for average countil tax and local authority rent.
4. Benefit Rates reflect increases from April 1995—apart from rent and council tax which remains at April 1994 rates.

*Married couple—non earning partner with two children aged 4 and 6 years*

| Hours worked | Rate per hour | Gross earnings | Tax and N.I. contributions | Take home pay | Unemployment benefit | Income support | Family credit | Child benefit | Rent | Rent rebate | Council tax | Council tax benefit | Total net income | Net income after rent and council tax |
|---|---|---|---|---|---|---|---|---|---|---|---|---|---|---|
| 16 | £2.50 | 40.00 | 0.00 | 40.00 | 0.00 | 0.00 | 67.90 | 18.85 | 36.42 | 35.38 | 11.00 | 10.68 | 172.81 | 125.39 |
| 16 | £3.00 | 48.00 | 0.00 | 48.00 | 0.00 | 0.00 | 67.90 | 18.85 | 36.42 | 30.18 | 11.00 | 9.08 | 174.01 | 126.59 |
| 16 | £3.50 | 56.00 | 0.00 | 56.00 | 0.00 | 0.00 | 67.90 | 18.85 | 36.42 | 24.98 | 11.00 | 7.48 | 175.21 | 127.79 |
| 16 | £4.00 | 64.00 | 1.76 | 62.24 | 0.00 | 0.00 | 67.90 | 18.85 | 36.42 | 20.92 | 11.00 | 6.23 | 176.14 | 128.72 |
| 16 | £4.15 | 66.40 | 2.00 | 64.40 | 0.00 | 0.00 | 67.90 | 18.85 | 36.42 | 19.52 | 11.00 | 5.80 | 176.47 | 129.05 |
| 40 | £2.50 | 100.00 | 6.84 | 93.16 | 0.00 | 0.00 | 53.79 | 18.85 | 36.42 | 10.00 | 11.00 | 2.87 | 178.67 | 131.25 |
| 40 | £3.00 | 120.00 | 12.84 | 107.16 | 0.00 | 0.00 | 43.99 | 18.85 | 36.42 | 7.27 | 11.00 | 2.03 | 179.30 | 131.88 |
| 40 | £3.50 | 140.00 | 19.37 | 120.63 | 0.00 | 0.00 | 34.56 | 18.85 | 36.42 | 4.64 | 11.00 | 1.22 | 179.90 | 132.48 |
| 40 | £4.00 | 160.00 | 26.37 | 133.63 | 0.00 | 0.00 | 25.46 | 18.85 | 36.42 | 2.11 | 11.00 | 0.44 | 180.49 | 133.07 |
| 40 | £4.15 | 166.00 | 28.47 | 137.53 | 0.00 | 0.00 | 22.73 | 18.85 | 36.42 | 1.35 | 11.00 | 0.21 | 180.67 | 133.25 |

*Notes:*

1. Earnings for 16 hours assumed to represent two days employment.
2. All the examples shown assume take-up of full entitlement to the income-related and contributory benefits that would be most advantageous.
3. All the family types shown are assumed to live in local authority accommodation and be liable for average council tax and local authority rent.

4. Benefit Rates reflect increases from April 1995—apart from rent and council tax which remain at April 1994 rates.

### Home Responsibilities Protection

**Mr. Corbyn:** To ask the Secretary of State for Social Security what consideration his Department is giving to the treatment of a male claimant of home responsibilities protection credits, for looking after and taking responsibility for his children while his partner is working, in a way which differs from what would apply if the roles were reversed; what plans he has to equalise the treatment; and if he will make a statement. [25789]

**Mr. Arbuthnot:** Home responsibilities protection protects a person's basic retirement pension by reducing the number of years of contributions otherwise needed for a full pension. The provisions apply equally to both men and women. HRP is available to those with child-caring responsibilities provided that they are entitled to child benefit for a child under age 16. In cases where the caring roles are reversed, it is open to a woman to forgo her CHB entitlement so that her partner can claim it and thus have access to HRP.

### In-work Benefit Scheme

**Mr. Bradley:** To ask the Secretary of State for Social Security what progress has been made regarding the setting up and running of family credit pilot schemes for families without children; and for how long he intends these pilot schemes to run. [25802]

**Mr. Roger Evans:** The pilot of a new in-work benefit for those not able to take advantage of family credit is one of a number of measures which we announced last November to help unemployed people move back into work more easily and increase the opportunities and rewards of work.

The pilot will run for three years to enable the impact of the new benefit to be properly evaluated. A Green Paper to be published shortly will set out our proposals in detail.

## EMPLOYMENT

### Unemployment

**Mrs. Wise:** To ask the Secretary of State for Employment how many people are recorded as having been unemployed for more than six months; and what proportion this is of the total number recorded as unemployed. [22318]

**Mr. Oppenheim:** In April 1995 there were 1,361,160 claimants who had been unemployed for six months or more. This represents 57.3 per cent. of the total number of claimant unemployed. In autumn 1994, according to the labour force survey, there were 1,499,000 people who had been unemployed for six months or more on the internationally standard ILO definition. This represents 59.6 per cent. of the corresponding ILO total. Both figures are on the unadjusted basis.

### Minimum Wage

**Mr. Harry Greenway:** To ask the Secretary of State for Employment what is the minimum wage in other EC countries; which EC countries have a minimum wage of £180 per week equivalent; what assessment he has made of the effect of these minimum wages on jobs and the economy; and if he will make a statement. [23692]

**Mr. Oppenheim:** The table gives the most up-to-date information available on national minimum wages in other European Union countries:

| Minimum wage level | Own currency | UK equivalent converted at market exchange rates £ per hour (estimated) |
| --- | --- | --- |
| Belgium | 42,808 BF monthly | 5.30 |
| France | 35.56 FF hourly | 4.60 |
| Greece | 4,934 Dr daily | 1.70 |
| Luxembourg | 42,677 LF per month | 5.30 |
| Netherlands | 2,163.2 Hfl monthly | 4.90 |
| Portugal | 52,000 Esc monthly | 1.30 |
| Spain | 62,700 Pts monthly | 1.80 |

*Note:*
Table uses latest information available in April 1995. Wage rates converted to UK equivalent using spot exchange rates for May 9 1995.

On the above estimates, on the assumption of a 40-hour working week, France, Belgium, the Netherlands and Luxembourg would have minimum wages of £180 per week or more.

Minimum wages destroy jobs, particularly among young people. This was the conclusion of the OECD jobs study.

### Correspondence

**Mr. Tom Clarke:** To ask the Secretary of State for Employment when he intends to reply to the letter from the hon. Member for Monklands, West of 27 April, regarding the access to work programme. [25159]

**Miss Widdecombe:** The letter was replied to on 16 May 1995, before the hon. Member tabled this question and well within the normal time scale for ministerial reply.

### Health and Safety Executive Publications

**Mrs. Wise:** To ask the Secretary of State for Employment how the price for the Health and Safety Executive's publication, "New and Expectant Mothers at Work—A Guide for Employers", HS(G) 122, was arrived at; what the profit margin is; what profit he expects to make on sales; and what assessment he has made of the deterrent effect of the price on availability of this information to those who need it in order to comply with legal duties. [25211]

**Mr. Oppenheim:** In accordance with Treasury guidelines the Health and Safety Executive aims to recover the costs of production and distribution of its priced publications. There is no profit element built into the price.

**Mrs. Wise:** To ask the Secretary of State for Employment what considerations underlie the refusal by the Health and Safety Executive to allow trade unions to photocopy the Health and Safety Executive publication, "New and Expectant Mothers at Work—A Guide for Employers", HS(G) 122, for use by union health and safety representatives. [25213]

**Mr. Oppenheim:** I understand that there has been no such refusal by the Health and Safety Executive.

**Mrs. Wise:** To ask the Secretary of State for Employment how many copies of the Health and Safety Executive publication, "New and Expectant Mothers at Work—A Guide for Employers, HS[G]122, have so far been sold; how many would need to be sold to give a substantially complete coverage of employers; and what percentage of employers he estimates will have been reached so far. [25212]

**Mr. Oppenheim:** Over 10,000 copies of this guidance have been sold since it was published in December 1994. It is not feasible to estimate the size of the market for the publication.

### Staff

**Ms Hodge:** To ask the Secretary of State for Employment what changes there have been in the numbers of staff employed by *(a)* the Department of Employment and *(b)* agencies for which the Department of Employment is responsible, listing the changes in the number of staff agency by agency in (i) 1993–94 and (ii) 1994–95; and what changes are proposed for 1995–96. [25059]

**Miss Widdecombe:** Information on staff numbers for the Department can be found in annexe A to table (iii) of the Department's annual report, Cm 2805. A copy of this publication is available in the Library.

### Age Discrimination

**Mr. Jim Cunningham:** To ask the Secretary of State for Employment (1) what inter-departmental discussions he has conducted to prohibit age discrimination in the civil service; [24996]

(2) what assessment he has made of the effect of age discrimination legislation in Canada and New Zealand; [24999]

(3) what discussions *(a)* have been held or *(b)* are proposed to be held by his Department with employers' organisations on age bars on young and older people. [24995]

**Miss Widdecombe:** The Government are firmly committed to countering discrimination on age grounds in the workplace. I launched a campaign in 1993 to highlight the unfairness of such discrimination. As part of the campaign the Employment Department published in 1994 a booklet, "Getting On", aimed specifically at employers. It urges them to recruit on merit and drop age bars in job vacancies. A series of regional seminars is currently spreading this message among locally invited employers and their organisations.

Staff in Employment Service jobcentres have been given clear guidance to challenge employers over restrictive upper and lower age limits and to try to persuade them to consider all jobseekers on merit.

Responsibility for promoting equality of opportunity in the civil service, in particular in the areas of gender, race and disability, but including age discrimination, lies with the Office of Public Service and Science. Civil service policy is that all eligible people have equal opportunities for employment and advancement on the basis of their suitability. A 1990 ruling not to set age limits on recruitment was extended in 1994 to cover those adverts which give preferred age ranges of applicants. This enables the civil service to benefit from the skills, experience and commitment which older workers can offer. Discrimination on grounds of age alone is now permitted only in exceptional circumstances—for example where there are statutory requirements, and with the prior consent of OPSS.

In June 1994, the Employment Department published a report entitled "An International Overview of Employment Policies and Practices Towards Older Workers", research series No. 29, containing research into the policies and practices towards older workers in 22 countries, including Canada and New Zealand. The research found no evidence that anti-discrimination legislation has been successful in improving either the economic activity rates of older workers or their employment prospects. A copy of the report is available in the Library.

### Wage Studies

**Mr. Jim Cunningham:** To ask the Secretary of State for Employment what studies he has initiated to ascertain how many workers receive less than £66.50 per week.    [24997]

**Mr. Oppenheim:** The Department has undertaken no such study.

### Statutory Employment Rights

**Mr. Jim Cunningham:** To ask the Secretary of State for Employment to what extent he monitors the impact of statutory employment rights on the economic effectiveness of the work force.    [24953]

**Mr. Oppenheim:** The Department conducts research from time to time to assess the effect of statutory employment rights, including on employment and the economy.

### Graduate Unemployment

**Mr. Sheerman:** To ask the Secretary of State for Employment what percentage of graduates was unemployed one year after leaving higher education *(a)* currently *(b)* in 1979.    [25020]

**Mr. Oppenheim:** The latest available estimates for Great Britain from the spring 1994 labour force survey show that 16.6 per cent. of graduates of working age who were not full-time students when interviewed, but were full-time students one year prior to interview were ILO unemployed. There is no information for 1979.

### Access to Work Programme

**Mr. Tom Clarke:** To ask the Secretary of State for Employment what is his policy regarding items of equipment purchased under the access to work programme where the beneficiary has ceased to be employed but is actively seeking work.    [25323]

**Miss Widdecombe:** Responsibility for the subject of the question has been delegated to the Employment Service under its chief executive. I have asked him to arrange for a reply to be given.

*Letter from A. G. Johnson to Mr. Tom Clarke, dated 23 May 1995:*

The Secretary of State has asked me, in the absence of the Chief Executive, to reply to your question about the policy regarding items of equipment purchased under the Access to Work programme where the beneficiary has ceased to be employed but is actively seeking work.

Special aids and equipment are supplied under the Access to Work programme to help overcome work related needs that arise because of disability. Where a person in receipt of such help is no longer employed but is actively seeking employment and continued use of that equipment would benefit them in finding work, they may retain the equipment for an agreed period at the discretion of the Employment Service. The equipment may then be used in their new job if appropriate.

I hope this is helpful.

### Majority Shareholdings

**Mr. Byers:** To ask the Secretary of State for Employment, if he will list those companies in which the holder of his office is a majority shareholder which *(a)* are currently in existence and *(b)* have been wound up in the past five years.    [25719]

**Miss Widdecombe** *[holding answer 22 May 1995]:* None.

### Job Clubs

**Mr. Gordon Prentice:** To ask the Secretary of State for Employment what is his policy regarding smoking at job clubs.    [25750]

**Miss Widdecombe:** Responsibility for the subject of the question has been delegated to the Employment Service under its chief executive. I have asked him to arrange for a reply to be given.

*Letter from M. E. G. Fogden to Mr. Gordon Prentice, dated 23 May 1995:*

The Secretary of State has asked me to reply to your question about the smoking policy in Jobclubs.

In 1994 a policy on smoking in all Employment Service (ES) programmes, including Jobclub, was introduced. The principle of the policy is that participants shall be entitled to a smoke free environment. In practice this means that unrestricted smoking is not allowed on any ES workshops, seminars or courses, including Jobclub. Wherever possible, designated areas and times should be provided for smokers.

Jobclubs continue to be both popular with the people who join and an effective way of helping them back to work. We are now able to help more members than at any time before and over 266,000 unemployed people joined Jobclub last year.

I hope this is helpful.

## Disqualification Periods

**Mr. Flynn:** To ask the Secretary of State for Employment what are the latest statistics of the periods of disqualification for benefit for those who have voluntarily left employment. [25427]

**Miss Widdecombe:** Responsibility for the subject of the question has been delegated to the Employment Service under its chief executive. I have asked him to arrange for a reply to be given.

*Letter to M. E. G. Fogden to Mr. Paul Flynn dated 23 May 1995:*

The Secretary of State has asked me to reply to your question about statistics held on the periods of disqualification of benefit for clients who have voluntarily left employment.

The regular statistics regarding disqualifications are broken down into subjects, not the length of disqualification and I am therefore unable to provide the information you have requested. I am however able to advise that the number of decisions affecting clients who have left employment voluntarily during the three months to 31 December 1994 was 58,425. Of these, 50.2 percent were Adverse Decisions.

These figures are taken from the unemployment benefit statistics. A copy of this quarterly publication which is an Analysis of Adjudication Officers' Decisions has been placed in the Library.

A one-off survey, which was part of a larger project looking at adjudication issues carried out in late 1994, gave a snap shot picture of average periods of disqualification during October 1994. The findings showed that for those who left their employment voluntarily, 25 percent were disqualified for the maximum period of 6 months.

I hope this is helpful.

## TRANSPORT

### Driving Theory Test

**Mr. Peter Bottomley:** To ask the Secretary of State for Transport how he proposes to implement the driving theory test; and if he will make a statement. [26194]

**Mr. Norris:** The previous Secretary of State set in hand detailed developmental work on a separate theory test, *Official Report,* 9 February 1994, columns *270–71.* I announced earlier today that the test will be in the form of a written test lasting about half an hour and consisting of about 35 multiple choice questions on the main principles of safe driving and the responsible use of vehicles on the road. The theory test will need to be passed before a candidate can take the practical test. We see the new test as making an important contribution to safer driving, especially by new drivers.

Introduction of the new theory test will be the responsibility of the Driving Standards Agency, which plans to contract out the practical implementation work to the private sector. Tenders will shortly be invited from non-governmental bodies for the operation of the theory test through a network of local centres. We shall be seeking a reputable body with experience in conducting assessments and with no financial interest in driving tuition.

We have carefully considered the alternative of a computerised test involving hazard perception and concluded that for the present this option would be too costly and needs further development. We shall be monitoring the effect of the separate theory test with a view to developing it in ways which will further improve road safety, one of which may well be the use of computers.

We shall be making further announcements in due course on the details of the test.

### Rail Privatisation

**Mr. Chidgey:** To ask the Secretary of State for Transport, pursuant to his answer of 10 May, *Official Report,* column *457* (1) if he will make it his policy to ensure that the public expenditure cover he will make available to the British Railways Board in regard to the contractual and other obligations of the board will be sufficient to cover all industrial injury claims brought by retired British Rail employees following privatisation of British Rail; [25028]

(2) whether the amount of public expenditure cover that will be made available by his Department to the British Railways Board in regard to the contractual and other obligations of the board will be financially limited. [25027]

**Mr. Watts:** In setting the annual level of public expenditure provision to support British Rail, the Government have regard to all aspects of the board's financial position, including any contractual obligations and any need to make payments arising from industrial injury claims awards.

### Collision Research

**Mr. Flynn:** To ask the Secretary of State for Transport what new proposals he has to make road vehicle fronts more absorbent to the force of collision. [25428]

**Mr. Norris:** The United Kingdom has taken a leading role on pedestrian protection research for many years. We have in particular encouraged the preparation of a draft EU directive which would require car fronts to be designed with pedestrian accidents in mind and will continue to press the European Commission to bring forward a proposal without further delay.

**Mr. Flynn:** To ask the Secretary of State for Transport if he will investigate the evidence on the safety value of the use of airbags on the front of cars in Japan. [25529]

**Mr. Norris:** No. Very little information is yet available on this system.

**Mr. Flynn:** To ask the Secretary of State for Transport what research he has evaluated into the effects on driver and passenger on vehicles with bull bars when involved in accidents, listing the studies *(a)* conducted in the United Kingdom and *(b)* conducted overseas. [25425]

**Mr. Norris:** None. We are not aware of any relevant research.

### Majority Shareholdings

**Mr. Byers:** To ask the Secretary of State for Transport if he will list those companies in which the holder of his office is a majority shareholder which *(a)* are currently in existence and *(b)* have been wound up in the past five years. [25706]

**Dr. Mawhinney** *[holding answer 22 May 1995]:* On *(a),* majority shareholdings are currently held in the following five companies: Railtrack Group PLC, Union Railways Ltd, European Passenger Services Ltd, National

Bus Company Pension Trustees Ltd and National Bus Nominees Ltd.

On *(b)*, a majority shareholding was held in the Red Sea Lights Company, prior to the company being wound up in 1991.

## Marine Safety Exercises

**Mr. Flynn:** To ask the Secretary of State for Transport what percentage of the passengers and crew involved were able-bodied; and in what time periods the passengers were evacuated and succoured ashore in the evacuation exercises carried out by the coastguard.    [25573]

**Mr. Norris** *[holding answer 22 May 1995]:* This is an operational matter for the Coastguard Agency. I have asked the chief executive to write to the hon. Member.

*Letter from C. J. Harris to Mr. Paul Flynn, dated 23 May 1995:*

The Secretary of State for Transport has asked me to reply to your recent Parliamentary Question as the question deals with an operational matter, for which I have responsibility as Chief Executive.

PQ 1811/94/95 The information requested in this PQ is detailed below:

| Exercise | Number of evacuees | Percentage able bodied[1] | Time: evacuation to reception ashore |
|---|---|---|---|
| Common Aim 3 | 183 | 91 | 2 Hrs |
| Claymore | 243 | 66 | 2 Hrs 44 min |
| Goodwin | 160 | 94 | 2 Hrs 17 min |
| Liverpool Bay | 42 | 86 | 2 Hrs 17 min |
| Eddystone | 277 | 84 | 2 Hrs 54 min |
| Webex | 50 | 0 | 3 Hrs 15 min |
| Seafire | 207 | 69 | 3 Hrs 32 min |
| Beauforts Dyke | 210 | 62 | 4 Hrs 02 min |
| Sovereign | 250 | 94 | 2 Hrs 30 min |

[1] Remainder Injured (simulated).

## Munitions Transport

**Mr. Wilshire:** To ask the Secretary of State for Transport if permission was granted by the Civil Aviation Authority for British Airways to transport munitions from Hong Kong to London on 4 April.    [25571]

**Mr. Norris:** I understand that British Airways was granted permission by the Civil Aviation Authority to carry munitions of war from Hong Kong on 4 April.

**Mr. Wilshire:** To ask the Secretary of State for Transport what controls exist to regulate the transport of weapons and ammunition as cargo on scheduled civil air services.    [25568]

**Mr. Norris:** Article 46 of the Air Navigation Order 1989—Article 51 of the 1995 order—sets out the conditions under which weapons and munitions of war can be carried on civil aircraft. The Air Navigation (Dangerous Goods) Regulations 1994 set out the conditions under which dangerous goods, including ammunition, can be carried on civil aircraft.

## Vehicle Licence Payments

**Mrs. Helen Jackson:** To ask the Secretary of State for Transport if he will bring in a scheme to allow the payment of the vehicle licence by monthly instalments, at no extra cost.    [25540]

**Mr. Norris:** No. This would be costly to administer, and is unnecessary since, under the existing stamp saving scheme, £5 stamps can be purchased at post offices throughout the year for use towards payment of the vehicle licence.

## Contracting Out

**Ms Hodge:** To ask the Secretary of State for Transport (1) for each piece of work subject to a bidding process under the auspices of *(a)* his Department and *(b)* agencies for which his Department is responsible (i) where work was contracted out, who were the successful bidders and (ii) which contracts were won by in-house successful bidders in (1) 1993–94, (2) 1994–95 and (3) 1995–96;    [25664]

(2) what work has been contracted out *(a)* by his Department and *(b)* by agencies for which his Department is responsible in (i) 1993–94 (ii) 1994–95 and (iii) projected for 1995–96.    [25662]

**Mr. Norris:** The information requested is given in the table. It is not possible to forecast which work will be contracted out in 1995–96 but items in the Department's competing for quality programme which are not yet completed are listed.

*Results of competing for quality programme for 1 April 1992—30 September 1993*

| DOT or Agency | Activity | Outcome | Winner where contracted out |
|---|---|---|---|
| DVLA | Despatch | In-house team won | — |
| DVLA | Security | In-house team won | — |
| DVOIT | IT and facilities management for DOT | Privatised | EDS |
| MSA | Register of shipping and seamen | In-house team won | — |
| TRL | Research commissions | In-house team win and contracted out | [1]Various |

[1] Various covers those case where a number of different firms have been awarded contracts or where a range of call-off contracts has taken the place of a single supplier.

*Results of competing for quality programme for 1 October 1993—30 September 1994*

| DOT or Agency | Activity | Outcome | Winner where contracted out |
|---|---|---|---|
| Coastguard | Property management | Contracted out | Various[1] |
| DOT | Computer bureau facilities | Contracted out | Digital |
| DOT | Eastcote services: distribution | Contracted out | EROS Marketing Support |
| DOT | Other distribution | In-house team won[2] | HMSO |
| DOT | Stationery supplies | Contracted out | Dudley Stationery Ltd |
| DOT | Book and periodical procurement | Two items: One contracted out and one in-house team won | Dawson UK Ltd and HMSO |

*Results of competing for quality programme for
1 October 1993—30 September 1994*

| DOT or Agency | Activity | Outcome | Winner where contracted out |
|---|---|---|---|
| DOT | Office machinery | Contracted out | Various[1] |
| DOT | Reprographics | Transferred to HMSO | HMSO |
| DVLA | Reprographics | In-house team won | — |
| DVLA | Telesales | Contracted out | Teledata Ltd |
| DVLA | Forms design | Contracted out | Claydon Heely international |
| VCA | Microfilm, data storage and reprographics | Contracted out | REM Office Systems (Bristol) Ltd |
| VI | IT strategy support | Contracted out | EDS |
| VI | Roller brake testing maintenance | Contracted out | VL Test Systems |
| VI | Weighbridge Maintenance | Contracted out | Metler Toledo |
| VI | Library Services | Contracted out | Various[1] |
| VI | Building and estate management | Contracted out | Various[1] |
| VI | Workshop and stores | Contracted out | VLT Limited |

[1] Various covers those cases where a number of different firms have been awarded contracts or where a range of call-off contracts has taken the place of a single supplier.

[2] In-house team for these items is a team from another Government Department.

*Results of competing for quality programme for
1 October 1994–31 March 1995*

| DOT or Agency | Activity | Outcome | Winner where contracted out |
|---|---|---|---|
| DOT | Managed voice telephony service | In-house team won[1] | CCTA |
| DOT | Records service | Two items: one contracted out, one in-house team won | Brittania Data Management (BDM) |
| DSA | Driver test booking service | In-house team won | — |
| DVLA | Waste collection | Contracted out | ISS Contract Clean (Southern) Ltd. |
| DVLA | Stores and waste management | In-house team won | — |
| DVLA | Messenger services | In-house team won | — |
| DVLA | Internal Audit | Contracted out | Ernst and Young |

[1] In-house team for these items is a team from another Government Department.

*Competing for quality items not yet completed*

| DOT or agency | Activity |
|---|---|
| DOT | Payroll |
| DOT | Library |
| DOT | Enquiry service |
| DOT | New HQ: |

*Competing for quality items not yet completed*

| DOT or agency | Activity |
|---|---|
| DOT | Telecommunications |
| | Post and messengers |
| | Central Services: |
| | IT communications network |
| DOT | Correspondence location unit |
| DOT | IDS and couriers |
| DOT | Telecoms |
| DOT | Printing |
| DOT | DOT publications |
| Coastguard | Training |
| Coastguard | Messengers and post room services |
| DVLA | Personnel group |
| Highways | Topographical/architectural model making |
| Highways | Management of land and property acquired for roads programme |
| Highways | Procurement and maintenance of vehicles for winter maintenance of motorways |
| Highways | Administrative arrangements for public inquiries into road schemes |
| TRL | Privatisation of Agency |

### Stationary Buses (Pollution)

**Mr. John Morris:** To ask the Secretary of State for Transport what consideration he is giving to the practice of stationary tourist buses with their engines running for long periods. [25407]

**Mr. Norris:** The Government deplore the actions of any motorist who leaves an engine running unnecessarily. It is already illegal to do so in certain circumstances.

### London Transport Staff

**Mr. Dowd:** To ask the Secretary of State for Transport how many staff were employed by London Transport on 1 April. [25790]

**Mr. Norris:** London Transport employed 18,602 permanent staff, full-time equivalent, on 31 March, the nearest date for which figures are available from its management accounts.

### Train Repair Services

**Ms Lynne:** To ask the Secretary of State for Transport what facilities are currently available to repair a train on the InterCity west coast service which develops a fault on its southbound journey; and what facilities will be available in six months' time. [24810]

**Mr. Watts:** This is an operational matter which is the responsibility of British Rail.

I understand that scheduled maintenance activities on InterCity west coast are carried out principally at Glasgow Polmadie, Manchester Longsight, Wolverhampton Oxley and London Wembley. BR is in consultation with the rail regulator about the future of Wembley depot.

## SCOTLAND

### Public Bodies

**Mr. McMaster:** To ask the Secretary of State for Scotland what plans he has to introduce, further *(a)* non-governmental departments, *(b)* arms-length bodies, *(c)* trusts and *(d)* executive agencies in Scotland.

**Mr. Lang:** The three new water authorities are expected to be public corporations. In 1996, the Scottish Environment Protection Agency, the Scottish Children's Reporter Administration and the Scottish Water and Sewerage Customers Council, all of which will be non-departmental public bodies, will come into operation. No decisions have yet been taken on the establishment of bodies under section 18, residuary bodies, or section 19, property commission, of the Local Government etc. (Sootland) Act 1994. There are no plans at present to create further NHS trusts. Forest Enterprise, which has a Great Britain-wide remit and for which I am lead Minister, will be established as an executive agency within the Forestry Commission later this year. In addition, the Scottish Office fisheries research services is a potential candidate for agency status.

### Housing (Disabled Access)

**Mr. Chisholm:** To ask the Secretary of State for Scotland if and when he will take steps to make barrier-free standards mandatory for new Scottish housing.    [25132]

**Lord James Douglas-Hamilton:** My right hon. Friend is currently considering a number of options for amendment of the Building Standards (Scotland) Regulations to extend access for disabled people to new dwellings, taking into account responses to a consultation document issued by the Scottish Office on 8 February 1995.

### Child Witnesses

**Dr. Godman:** To ask the Secretary of State for Scotland which recommendations contained in the report "Live Television Links: An Evaluation of its use by Child Witnesses in Scottish Criminal Trials", central research unit, Scottish Office, 1995 he plans to implement; and if he will make a statement.    [24462]

**Lord James Douglas-Hamilton** *[holding answer 22 May 1995]:* Provisions in the current Criminal Justice (Scotland) Bill implement a number of the recommendations in this report which was published last month. The other recommendations in the report are being carefully examined and decisions on the outcome will be announced in due course.

### NHS Consultants

**Dr. Godman:** To ask the Secretary of State for Scotland what recent representations he has received from *(a)* health boards and *(b)* NHS trusts about difficulties in the recruitment and selection of consultants and other hospital-based medical practitioners in *(a)* Strathclyde and *(b)* Scotland; which specialist areas have the greatest problems on such recruitment and selection; and if he will make a statement.    [24866]

**Lord James Douglas-Hamilton** *[holding answer 22 May 1995]:* We are aware of the difficulties of NHS trusts in recruitment of senior house officers, particularly in accident and emergency medicine and in paediatrics, and

of consultants. NHS trusts last year reported 120 consultant vacancies with the largest numbers in anaesthetics and general psychiatry. To increase the number of candidates for consultant posts, the establishment of senior registrars in Scotland this year has been increased from 473 to 500. Increases have been made in anaesthetics, general medicine, medical paediatrics, diagnostic radiology, ear, nose and throat surgery, ophthalmology, orthopaedic surgery and urology.

### Coronary Heart Disease

**Mr. Stewart:** To ask the Secretary of State for Scotland what progress has been made towards the eradication of premature deaths caused by coronary heart disease in Scotland.    [24906]

**Mr. Lang** *[holding answer 22 May 1995]:* Deaths from coronary heart disease among people under 65 have fallen from 94 per 100,000 population in 1986 to 72 per 100,000 in 1993, the latest year for which figures are available. The target set in "Scotland's Health—A Challenge To Us All", the policy statement issued in 1992, is to reduce mortality in this age group by 40 per cent. between 1990 and 2000. This will require a further decrease to 46 deaths per 100,000 population. A wide range of initiatives is in train to facilitate progress towards the target by addressing the risk factors associated with coronary heart disease and encouraging the life-style changes which can help prevent it.

### A77

**Mr. McKelvey:** To ask the Secretary of State for Scotland if there is to be a public inquiry into the upgrading of the A77 from Fenwick to Malletsheugh; and if he will make a statement.    [25246]

**Lord James Douglas-Hamilton** *[holding answer 22 May 1995]:* There are a number of objections to the order published for the scheme and negotiations are continuing to see whether these can be resolved by agreement. A decision on whether a public local inquiry will be required will be taken later this summer.

### Nurses' Pay

**Mr. Foulkes:** To ask the Secretary for State for Scotland, pursuant to his answer to the hon. Member for Carrick, Cumnock and Doon Valley, *Official Report,* 16 May 1995, column *216* if he will list which NHS trusts have offered nurses a wage increase *(a)* in excess of 3 per cent., *(b)* at 3 per cent., with no attached conditions, *(c)* at 3 per cent., with conditions, *(d)* under 3 per cent. but above 1 per cent., *(e)* at 1 per cent. and *(f)* under 1 per cent.    [25248]

**Lord James Douglas-Hamilton** *[holding answer 22 May 1995]:* The information requested is as detailed. This covers formal offers and notice by trusts of intent to offer. All the offers are, of course, subject to local negotiations.

NHS Trust

*(a) offers in excess of 3 per cent.*

Dundee Teaching Hospitals
Edinburgh Healthcare
Scottish Ambulance Service

*(b) offers at 3 per cent. with no attached conditions*

Aberdeen Royal Hospitals
East and Midlothian
Grampian Healthcare
Lanarkshire Healthcare
North Ayrshire and Arran

*(c) offers at 3 per cent. with conditions*

Argyll and Bute
Ayrshire and Arran Community Healthcare
Caithness and Sutherland
Dumfries and Galloway Acute and Maternity
Dundee Healthcare
Falkirk and District Royal Infirmary
Fife Healthcare
Hairmyres and Stonehouse Hospitals
Highland Communities
Inverclyde Royal
Law Hospital
Lomond Healthcare
Monklands and Bellshill
Perth and Kinross
Queen Margaret Hospital
Raigmore Hospital
Royal Infirmary of Edinburgh
South Ayrshire Hospitals
Southern General Hospital
Stirling Royal Infirmary
West Glasgow Hospitals University
West Lothian
Western General Hospitals
Yorkhill

*(d) offers under 3 per cent. but above 1 per cent.*

Borders Community Services
Borders General Hospital
Central Scotland Healthcare
Dumfries and Galloway Community Services
Edinburgh Sick Children's
Greater Glasgow Community and Mental Health Services
Moray Health Services
Renfrewshire Healthcare
Royal Alexandra Hospital
Stobhill

*(e) offers at 1 per cent.*

Victoria Infirmary

*(f) offers under 1 per cent.*

None.

### Drumkinnon Bay

**Mr. McFall:** To ask the Secretary of State for Scotland, pursuant to his answer of 16 May, *Official Report*, columns *207–208*, on what date *(a)* his predecessor as Minister with responsibility for industry and *(b)* officials in his Department were first informed of Dunbartonshire Enterprise's interest in the acquisition of Drumkinnon bay from the Drumkinnon Development Company.    [25265]

**Mr. Kynoch** *[holding answer 22 May 1995]:* I understand that, during his tenure as a Minister, my predecessor was not advised of Dunbartonshire Enterprise's interest in acquiring Drumkinnon bay.

Officials of the Scottish Office Industry Department first became aware of that interest in early December 1994, although the matter was not formally referred to the Department.

### Nursing Homes

**Mr. Hood:** To ask the Secretary of State for Scotland if he will list the criteria for owning a registered nursing home in Lanarkshire; and if he will make a statement.    [25487]

**Lord James Douglas-Hamilton** *[holding answer 22 May 1995]:* The requirements for the registration of nursing homes are set out in the Nursing Homes Registration (Scotland) Act 1938 as amended. Health boards, as registering authorities, make copies of relevant guidance available to those seeking registration. A copy of the Lanarkshire health board guidance notes on "Registration and Inspection of Nursing Homes" has been placed in the Library.

**Mr. Hood:** To ask the Secretary of State for Scotland if he will initiate an independent inquiry into the care for the elderly in the Lanarkshire health board area.    [25485]

**Lord James Douglas-Hamilton** *[holding answer 22 May 1995]:* My right hon. Friend has no plans to initiate an independent inquiry into the care for the elderly in the Lanarkshire health board area.

### Rural Child Care

**Mrs. Fyfe:** To ask the Secretary of State for Scotland if he will undertake to carry out the recommendations of the European Commission network on child care on child care services for rural families.    [25582]

**Lord James Douglas-Hamilton** *[holding answer 22 May 1995]:* My right hon. Friend understands that the European Commission's report on child care services for rural families was launched in Scotland earlier this month. He will study it with interest.

### Socialist Education Association

**Mrs. Fyfe:** To ask the Secretary of State for Scotland if he will include the Socialist Education Association in any relevant lists of bodies to be consulted on educational matters.    [25583]

**Lord James Douglas-Hamilton** *[holding answer 22 May 1995]:* Yes.

### Technical Plastics Ltd.

**Mrs. Clwyd:** To ask the Secretary of State for Scotland when the investigation by Strathclyde police into matters arising from a television documentary programme relating to ICL Technical Plastics Ltd. in Glasgow was concluded; and if any prosecution arises as a result.    [25615]

**Lord James Douglas-Hamilton** *[holding answer 22 May 1995]:* The investigation is not yet concluded.

### Torness Power Station

**Mr. Ingram:** To ask the Secretary of State for Scotland what funds were provided by the European Commission for the building of Torness nuclear power station; and what terms were applied to the provision of the funds. [25493]

**Mr. Kynoch** *[holding answer 22 May 1995]:* No funds were provided by the European Commission for the building of Torness power station.

### Dounreay

**Mr. Llew Smith:** To ask the Secretary of State for Scotland when he received from the Radioactive Waste Management Advisory Committee its report on the radioactive contamination arising from the nuclear waste disposal deep shaft at Dounreay, and what remedial action he intends should be taken to clean up the contamination. [25411]

**Sir Hector Monro:** My right hon. Friend awaits the committee's report on the radioactive particles found at Dounreay and will consider it carefully as soon as he receives it.

### Prescriptions

**Mr. Donohoe:** To ask the Secretary of State for Scotland if he will make a statement about the guidance he has issued to Scottish health boards concerning the issuing of private medical prescriptions to patients where the costs of obtaining the medication on an NHS prescription are greater than those in buying the medication through a private prescription. [25330]

**Lord James Douglas-Hamilton:** No such guidance has been issued to Scottish health boards.

**Mr. Donohoe:** To ask the Secretary of State for Scotland how many prescriptions were issued by general practitioners in each health board in Scotland in each year since 1979–80. [25351]

**Lord James Douglas-Hamilton:** The information for each health board for the financial years 1979–80 to 1993–94 is set out in the tables. The figures include prescriptions written by general medical practitioners and dentists, as well as hospital-generated prescriptions from England and prescriptions written for personnel serving in the armed forces.

*Number of prescriptions issued*

| Health Board | 1979–80 | 1980–81 | 1981–82 | 1982–83 | 1983–84 | 1984–85 | 1985–86 | 1986–87 |
|---|---|---|---|---|---|---|---|---|
| Argyll and Clyde | 3,020,887 | 3,119,305 | 3,080,779 | 3,215,820 | 3,308,346 | 3,387,998 | 3,416,920 | 3,477,819 |
| Ayrshire and Arran | 2,917,102 | 2,950,691 | 2,925,920 | 2,995,259 | 3,034,920 | 3,072,132 | 3,057,375 | 3,108,628 |
| Borders | 696,541 | 713,847 | 718,828 | 727,461 | 741,681 | 750,546 | 762,220 | 771,461 |
| Dumfries and Galloway | 998,184 | 1,016,422 | 1,006,361 | 1,047,110 | 1,066,906 | 1,070,408 | 1,083,736 | 1,116,269 |
| Fife | 2,302,688 | 2,330,990 | 2,325,161 | 2,361,160 | 2,383,291 | 2,418,429 | 2,435,329 | 2,460,693 |
| Forth Valley | 1,885,324 | 1,888,929 | 1,850,223 | 1,929,467 | 1,989,505 | 2]024,173 | 2,044,775 | 2,087,639 |
| Grampian | 3,181,513 | 3,232,774 | 3,194,810 | 3,291,698 | 3,333,170 | 3,356,741 | 3,350,591 | 3,387,637 |
| Greater Glasgow | 7,429,534 | 7,430,775 | 7,292,301 | 7,506,305 | 7,665,852 | 7,776,269 | 7,745,029 | 7,882,635 |
| Highland | 1,220,693 | 1,228,673 | 1,215,931 | 1,234,509 | 1,240,427 | 1,233,964 | 1,227,784 | 1,248,755 |
| Lanarkshire | 4,011,256 | 4,152,073 | 4,094,760 | 4,225,707 | 4,360,576 | 4,468,827 | 4,472,930 | 4,543,104 |
| Lothian | 4,551,022 | 4,665,377 | 4,598,347 | 4,721,963 | 4,801,780 | 4,854,429 | 4,872,711 | 4,962,619 |
| Orkney | 127,037 | 130,326 | 129,043 | 132,617 | 132,909 | 134,321 | 132,101 | 134,106 |
| Shetland | 167,798 | 174,244 | 167,464 | 165,460 | 162,268 | 159,572 | 161,387 | 165,194 |
| Tayside | 2,595,660 | 2,659,792 | 2,621,910 | 2,708,202 | 2,775,500 | 2,829,288 | 2,865,689 | 2,931,406 |
| Western Isles | 187,125 | 211,517 | 203,002 | 207,764 | 216,435 | 221,481 | 221,113 | 222,552 |
| Total | 35,292,364 | 35,905,735 | 35,424,840 | 36,470,502 | 37,213,656 | 37,758,578 | 37,849,690 | 38,500,517 |

*Number of prescriptions issued*

| Health board | 1987–88 | 1988–89 | 1989–90 | 1990–91 | 1991–92 | 1992–93 | 1993–94 |
|---|---|---|---|---|---|---|---|
| Argyll and Clyde | 3,616,334 | 3,732,573 | 3,942,096 | 4,079,891 | 4,300,725 | 4,508,277 | 4,682,393 |
| Ayrshire and Arran | 3,226,280 | 3,316,494 | 3,518,006 | 3,604,259 | 3,788,332 | 3,940,976 | 4,073,508 |
| Borders | 803,902 | 821,439 | 865,944 | 891,690 | 947,609 | 1,007,194 | 1,049,644 |
| Dumfries and Galloway | 1,152,765 | 1,190,874 | 1,262,296 | 1,308,771 | 1,382,936 | 1,443,633 | 1,514,202 |
| Fife | 2,540,786 | 2,632,029 | 2,757,067 | 2,841,090 | 2,967,220 | 3,071,638 | 3,186,806 |
| Forth Valley | 2,156,792 | 2,199,241 | 2,297,756 | 2,394,187 | 2,537,797 | 2,649,311 | 2,761,543 |
| Grampian | 3,556,224 | 3,653,754 | 3,813,054 | 3,898,337 | 4,007,418 | 4,137,204 | 4,288,124 |
| Greater Glasgow | 8,203,693 | 8,344,864 | 8,779,589 | 8,919,678 | 9,374,723 | 9,756,522 | 10,143,448 |
| Highland | 1,304,758 | 1,349,094 | 1,441,004 | 1,503,594 | 1,603,834 | 1,677,624 | 1,771,531 |
| Lanarkshire | 4,735,156 | 4,886,894 | 5,179,521 | 5,270,290 | 5,557,051 | 5,831,177 | 6,105,927 |
| Lothian | 5,160,088 | 5,289,043 | 5,517,844 | 5,656,233 | 5,848,567 | 6,021,362 | 6,249,471 |
| Orkney | 136,015 | 136,385 | 140,905 | 146,725 | 154,508 | 162,625 | 167,126 |
| Shetland | 174,867 | 172,265 | 178,670 | 184,071 | 186,501 | 190,354 | 203,180 |
| Tayside | 3,076,554 | 3,200,984 | 3,344,626 | 3,465,036 | 3,611,409 | 3,686,056 | 3,783,897 |
| Western Isles | 228,612 | 224,569 | 237,024 | 237,018 | 242,910 | 254,958 | 276,615 |
| Total | 40,072,826 | 41,150,502 | 43,275,402 | 44,400,870 | 46,511,540 | 48,338,911 | 50,257,415 |

## Local Government Reorganisation

**Mr. Donohoe:** To ask the Secretary of State for Scotland when he will notify Scottish local authorities of the relevant date under the Local Government etc. (Scotland) Act 1994 when they should statutorily consult the new unitary authorities before taking decisions with revenue implications for the new councils. [25331]

**Mr. Kynoch:** Section 55 of the Local Government etc. (Scotland) Act 1994 requires existing local authorities to gain the agreement of their successors from a date to be specified by my right hon. Friend before committing themselves to major financial transactions. Existing and new authorities are currently being consulted on the proposal that the specified date should be 1 August 1995. A copy of the consultation letter has been placed in the Library.

**Mr. Stewart:** To ask the Secretary of State for Scotland if he will make a statement on the framework which will be adopted for transferring staff on 1 April 1996 from existing regional and district councils to their successor bodies. [26100]

**Mr. Kynoch:** Following discussions with the Local Government Staff Commission (Scotland) and consultations with Scottish local authorities, the Convention of Scottish Local Authorities and staff representative bodies, I have today laid before Parliament the Local Authorities (Staff Transfer) (Scotland) Order 1995 which requires outgoing local authorities and their successor bodies to draw up and agree detailed schemes for the transfer of staff to the new bodies on 1 April 1996.

This is an important step in the reorganisation process. The order is designed to ensure a fair and ordered transfer of staff to the new councils, the water and sewerage authorities and the Scottish children's reporter administration. Successful transition to the new authorities is dependent on the efforts of both councillors and staff.

## Education Consultation

**Mrs. Fyfe:** To ask the Secretary of State for Scotland what criteria he uses to establish which bodies should be consulted on educational matters. [25589]

**Lord James Douglas-Hamilton** *[holding answer 22 May 1995]:* Consultees are selected from lists held by the Scottish Office Education Department of organisations which may have an interest in educational matters. As account is taken of the relevance of each subject to particular bodies, all the organisations listed do not necessarily receive all consultation papers as a matter of course. The aim, however, is always to include the widest appropriate range of interests in any consultation exercise.

## Traffic Calming

**Mr. Donohoe:** To ask the Secretary of State for Scotland what guidelines his Department has issued to the roads departments of Scottish local authorities relating to the provision of traffic calming measures with particular reference to the traffic flows necessary to justify these measures. [25333]

**Lord James Douglas-Hamilton:** The Scottish Office Industry Department issued guidance on traffic calming to local roads authorities in October 1994. This refers to traffic flows and advises local authorities that traffic calming is more suited to roads which have lower traffic levels and is likely to be inappropriate on high-speed roads with high volumes of through traffic. The guidance also indicates that traffic calming should not be discounted on busier routes since such treatment may be used to tackle a particular road safety problem. The final decision on which roads, other than trunk roads, should be treated with traffic calming rests with the local roads authorities themselves.

## Ayr Road

**Mr. Donohoe:** To ask the Secretary of State for Scotland how much policing operations at the Ayr road route arising out of roads construction at the location have cost thus far. [25335]

**Lord James Douglas-Hamilton:** As at 14 May 1995, policing costs associated with the construction of the Ayr road route amounted to £145,526.

## Expelled Pupils

**Mr. Donohoe:** To ask the Secretary of State for Scotland how many pupils were *(a)* suspended and *(b)* expelled in each financial year since 1979–80 in each education authority in Scotland. [25336]

**Lord James Douglas-Hamilton:** The information sought is not at present held centrally. However, following a circular issued by the Scottish Office Education Department last year, education authorities are to collect and provide information on exclusions on a school-by-school basis with effect from the current school session as part of the annual exercise to collect statistics on attendance and absence.

Returns provided in 1993 by education authorities for a working group, comprising representatives from the Scottish Office and the Association of Directors of Education in Scotland, indicated that there were around 25,000 exclusions from school in total during the school year 1992–93.

## Regional Selective Assistance

**Mr. Donohoe:** To ask the Secretary of State for Scotland what was *(a)* the amount of regional selective assistance recovered from Scottish companies and *(b)* the number of companies involved for each financial year since 1979–80; [25348]

(2) if he will list for each financial year since 1979–80 those Scottish companies where regional selective assistance was recovered because of the original terms of the offer not being met. [25349]

**Mr. Kynoch:** Recovery figures are given in the table for all assisted projects in Scotland. Details of grant recoveries from individual companies are commercially confidential and are not divulged.

| Financial year | Amount recovered £000 | Number of companies |
|---|---|---|
| 1989–90 or earlier | 67 | 4 |
| 1990–91 | 1,106 | 10 |
| 1991–92 | 557 | 7 |
| 1992–93 | 491 | 4 |
| 1993–94 | 1,817 | 12 |
| 1994–95 | 866 | 7 |

### Planning Applications

**Mr. Donohoe:** To ask the Secretary of State for Scotland what was *(a)* the total number of public inquiries held by the Scottish Office into planning applications, *(b)* the total costs of these inquiries and *(c)* the number of public inquiries for each Scottish local authority, for each financial year since 1979–80.    [25340]

**Mr. Kynoch:** This information is available only by callendar year. The answer to part *(a)* is set out. Regarding part *(b)*, the Scottish Office is responsible for the reporter's salary, travelling and subsistence expenses and the hire of the accommodation. The remainder of the costs are borne by the participating parties. It is therefore not possible to give details of the total costs of these inquiries. Information regarding part *(c)* is not available.

| Calendar Year | Public Local enquiries held |
| --- | --- |
| 1979 | 163 |
| 1980 | 121 |
| 1981 | 166 |
| 1982 | 155 |
| 1983 | 158 |
| 1984 | 123 |
| 1985 | 116 |
| 1986 | 122 |
| 1987 | 95 |
| 1988 | 99 |
| 1989 | 96 |
| 1990 | 116 |
| 1991 | 87 |
| 1992 | 78 |
| 1993 | 88 |
| 1994 | 47 |

**Mr. Donohoe:** To ask the Secretary of State for Scotland what was the total number of *(a)* planning applications passed to the Scottish Office for consideration and *(b)* planning application refusals overturned by the Scottish Office for each year since 1979–80.    [25341]

**Mr. Kynoch:** This information is only available by calendar year and is as set out.

| Calendar year | Planning appeals | Appeals allowed | ¹Applications notified to the Secretary of State |
| --- | --- | --- | --- |
| 1979 | 446 | 68 | 62 |
| 1980 | 569 | 75 | 65 |
| 1981 | 549 | 117 | 60 |
| 1982 | 500 | 136 | 63 |
| 1983 | 533 | 144 | 54 |
| 1984 | 566 | 149 | 42 |
| 1985 | 606 | 166 | 75 |
| 1986 | 723 | 193 | 87 |
| 1987 | 724 | 223 | 129 |
| 1988 | 764 | 233 | 93 |
| 1989 | 959 | 247 | 63 |
| 1990 | 1,139 | 348 | 85 |
| 1991 | 1,130 | 313 | 67 |
| 1992 | 1,019 | 294 | 45 |
| 1993 | 916 | 267 | 41 |
| 1994 | 871 | 177 | 56 |

¹ These figures relate to the number of applications, in each given year which planning authorities were minded to grant consent to, but which, for various reasons, were required to be notified to the Secretary of State so that he could decide whether or not to call them in for his own determination.

### Scottish Prison Service

**Mr. Stewart:** To ask the Secretary of State for Scotland what targets he has set the Scottish Prison Service for 1995–96, its third year of agency status.    [26099]

**Mr. Lang:** I have set the chief executive of the Scottish Prison Service the following targets:

| Performance measures | Key targets |
| --- | --- |
| The number of prisoners unlawfully at large. | —No A category prisoners should escape.<br>—The number of escapes by B category prisoners should be no higher that 2.3 per 1,000 prisoners. |
| The number of significant incidents. | The number of significant incidents should be no higher than 10. |
| The number of serious assaults on staff and prisoners. | —The number of serious assaults on staff should be no higher than four per 1,000 staff.<br>—The number of serious assaults on other prisoners should be no higher than 10 per 1,000 prisoners. |
| Basic quality of life for prisoners. | By April 1996, 63 per cent. of available prisoner places will have access to forms of night sanitation. |
| The amount of available opportunities for prisoners' self development. | 85 per cent. of convicted prisoners should have the opportunity of at least seven hours per working day of programmed activities. |
| Time out of cell for unconvicted prisoners. | On average, 30 per cent. of unconvicted prisoner hours— seven in 24— should be available for out of cell activities. |
| Average annual cost per prisoner place. | To keep costs within £26,724 per place available for use. |
| The level of absence through staff sickness. | To reduce the average number of days lost per person per year through staff sickness to 17. |

### Councils (Political Restrictions)

**Mr. Donohoe:** To ask the Secretary of State for Scotland what was *(a)* the total number of appeals lodged against the classification of posts in Scottish councils as politically restricted and the total number of successful appeals against political restriction, *(b)* the number of these appeals lodged for each local authority in Scotland, *(c)* the number of successful appeals against political restriction for each Scottish local authority and *(d)* the percentage figure for successful appeals for each Scottish local authority, for each financial year since 1989–90.    [25337]

**Mr. Kynoch:** Appeals relating to the rules on political restrictions are considered by the political restrictions exemptions adjudicator. Information supplied by his office indicates that the total number of applications for exemption from political restrictions since 1989–90 is 168. Of these, 141 have been granted. Of the remaining 27, 20 were unsuccessful, two were withdrawn, four were declared invalid and one case has still to be determined. The percentage of successful applications was 84 per cent. Statistics are not recorded on a local authority basis.

# Written Answers to Questions

*Wednesday 24 May 1995*

## FOREIGN AND COMMONWEALTH AFFAIRS

### Contracting Out

**Ms Hodge:** To ask the Secretary of State for Foreign and Commonwealth Affairs for each piece of work subject to a bidding process under the auspices of *(a)* his Department and *(b)* agencies for which his Department is responsible (i) where work was contracted out and who the successful bidders were and (ii) which contracts were won by 1995–96. [25552]

**Mr. Goodlad:** The information requested in respect of the work subject to a bidding process in (a) the Foreign and Commonwealth Office, (b) its agency, Wilton Park, and (c) the Overseas Development Administration is shown in the table. To date there have been no bids for work in 1995–96.

|  | Contract won by: |
|---|---|
| **FCO** | |
| *1993–94* | |
| Travel services | Thomas Cook |
|  | |
| *1994–95* | |
| Unclassified mails | In-house bid |
| Home security service | Security Facilities Executive |
| Reprographics | In-house bid |
|  | |
| **Wilton Park** | |
| *1994–95* | |
| Cleaning services | Coastline Cleaning Company |
|  | |
| **ODA** | |
| *1993–94* | |
| Facilities management, Victoria street | In-house bid |
| Facilities management, Abercrombie house | In-house bid |
|  | |
| *1994–95* | |
| Information systems services | In-house bid |
| Payroll services | ¹Defence Accounts Agency |

¹ Notification of award made 1994–95, contract to commence in 1995–96.

**Ms Hodge:** To ask the Secretary of State for Foreign and Commonwealth Affairs what work has been contracted out *(a)* by his Department and *(b)* by agencies for which his Department is responsible in (i) 1993–94 and (ii) 1994–95; and what are the projected figures for 1995–96. [25550]

**Mr. Goodlad:** Work contracted out in *(a)* the Foreign and Commonwealth Office, *(b)* its agency, Wilton Park and *(c)* the Overseas Development Administration is shown in the table.

In 1995–96, an exercise to decide on the future ownership of the Natural Resources Institute will also be completed.

| *FCO* | *Wilton Park* | *ODA* |
|---|---|---|
| 1993–94 Travel services | | |
| 1994–95 Home security service | Cleaning services | |

The following services will be investigated in 1995–96 with a view to possible contracting out:

|  | *Service* |
|---|---|
| Travel accounts unit | Payroll services |
| Pensions | Daytime security |
|  | Messenger services for travel implant |

*Note:*
Additional candidates for contracting out are currently under consideration.

### Retirements and Redundancies

**Ms Hodge:** To ask the Secretary of State for Foreign and Commonwealth Affairs what is the annual cost to his Department of staff leaving under redundancy/early retirement schemes to incorporate *(a)* added years lump sum payments, *(b)* redundancy payments, *(c)* pension payments, including enhancements and *(d)* any other special arrangements for (i) 1993–94 (ii) 1994–95, (iii) projected for 1995–96 and (iv) projected for 1996–97. [25664]

**Mr. Goodlad:** The costs to the Department of early retirement and redundancies are borne form the Department's running costs provision.

A detailed breakdown of the various cost could be obtained only at disproportionate cost.

The total costs borne on the Department's running costs in 1993–94 and 1994–95 were £3,777,329 and £6,017,362 respectively. For 1995–96, the amount is estimated at £3,598,324. The figures cover both the diplomatic wing and the Overseas Development Administration. Projections for 1996–97 will be determined during the coming public expenditure survey.

### Armenia

**Mr. David Atkinson:** To ask the Secretary of State for Foreign and Commonwealth Affairs, what recent reports he has received of attacks and violence against Pentecostal and other evangelical Christians, and members of the Baha'i and Hare Krishna communities in Armenia; and if he will make a statement. [25593]

**Mr. Goodlad:** We have received no reports of such incidents.

### Staff

**Ms Hodge:** To ask the Secretary of State for Foreign and Commonwealth Affairs what changes there have been in the number of staff in employment by grade in *(a)* his office and *(b)* each agency for which his office is responsible (i) 1993–94 and (ii) 1994–95; and what are the projected figures for 1995–96. [25624]

**Mr. Goodlad:** The numbers of permanent staff employed by the Foreign and Commonwealth Office diplomatic wing and its executive agency and the Overseas Development Administration in 1993–94, projected out-turn for 1994–95, and plans for 1995–96 are published in my Department's annual report, a copy of which is in the Library of the House. No projections broken down by grade are available.

**Ms Hodge:** To ask the Secretary of State for Foreign and Commonwealth Affairs how many staff of *(a)* the Foreign and Commonwealth Office and *(b)* agencies for which the FCO is responsible, were employed on a casual or short-term basis in (i) 1993–94 and (ii) 1994–95; and what are the projected figures for 1995–96.     [25480]

**Mr. Goodlad:** I refer the hon. Member to reply that I gave on 22 May, *Official Report,* column *381.*

### Consultancy Expenditure

**Ms Hodge:** To ask the Secretary of State for Foreign and Commonwealth Affairs what is the level of expenditure on consultancy by *(a)* his Department and *(b)* agencies for which his Department is responsible for (i) 1993–94 and (ii) 1994–95; and what are the projected figures for 1995–96.     [25551]

**Mr. Goodlad:** The table shows the level of expenditure on consultancy by the Foreign and Commonwealth Office Diplomatic and Aid Wings for 1993–94 and 1994–95 and projected figures for 1995–96 including the aid wing's agency, the Natural Resources Institute. Figures for the aid wing exclude expenditure under the aid programme.

| | £ millions | | |
| --- | --- | --- | --- |
| | 1993–94 | 1994–95 | 1995–96 Projected |
| Diplomatic wing | 14.2 | 12.4 | 16 |
| Aid wing | 0.7 | 0.5 | 0.8 |
| Natural Resources Institute | 0.02 | 0.04 | 0.05 |

### British Prisoners Overseas

**Mr. Ottoway:** To ask the Secretary of State for Foreign and Commonwealth Affairs what is the policy of Her Majesty's Government on appeals for clemency on behalf of British nationals who are sentenced to death overseas.     [26110]

**Mr. Baldry:** An appeal for clemency is a request to foreign authorities to exercise such leniency as they can under their own legal and constitutional system.

We do not automatically appeal for clemency on behalf of British nationals sentenced to death overseas. Appeals for clemency are considered case by case, normally once the domestic legal process has been exhausted.

We take a number of factors into account in deciding whether to appeal for clemency, including considering whether the sentence complies with established international standards on the application of the death penalty. For example:

—Is the sentence disproportionate to the crime?

—Are there grounds to believe there has been a denial or miscarriage of justice?

—Is an appeal for clemency by the prisoner allowed locally?

We also take into consideration whether the accused is a dual national, any humanitarian grounds for concern, and the likely effect of an appeal for clemency.

An appeal for clemency on behalf of a British national is in principle a bilateral matter between ourselves and the state concerned. Where a bilateral appeal has been rejected, we may consider asking our EU partners to join us in supporting an appeal.

### Falklands Islands (Oil)

**Mr. Hendry:** To ask the Secretary of State for Foreign and Commonwealth Affairs what agreement British Gas has reached with Her Majesty's Government on obtaining exclusive rights to explore for oil off the Falkland Islands.     [26584]

**Mr. David Davis:** No special agreements have been entered into between any company and either the British or the Falkland Islands Governments. The Falkland Islands Government are responsible for awarding licences to explore for hydrocarbons off the islands. They intend to seek expressions of interest in licences from all companies wishing to be involved in oil exploration.

## ATTORNEY-GENERAL

### Mr. Jonathan Carrington Miller

**Ms Estelle Morris:** To ask the Attorney-General if he will review the sentence given to Mr. Jonathan Carrington Miller at Hereford Crown court in May.     [24793]

**The Attorney-General:** I am unable to review the sentence in this case as the offences for which the sentence was imposed fall outside the scope of my powers under the Criminal Justice Act 1988.

## WALES

### Public Bodies

**Mr. Jon Owen Jones:** To ask the Secretary of State for Wales (1) what date his Department has set by which all Welsh executive non-departmental public bodies must *(a)* establish and *(b)* publish registers of members' interests;     [25387]

(2) if it is his policy to ensure that all Welsh executive non-departmental public bodies publish registers of members' interests; and what steps he has taken to instigate their publication     [25388]

**Mr. Redwood:** I refer the hon. Member to the reply I gave him on 16 May, *Official Report,* column *131.* I expect all Welsh executive non-departmental public bodies to establish a register within the current year.

### Disabled Parking

**Mr. Roy Hughes:** To ask the Secretary of State for Wales what guidelines he issues to ensure that spaces allocated in public car parks for the disabled are left executively for them; and what measures he is taking to ensure that those guidelines are complied with.     [25761]

**Mr. Gwilym Jones:** Designated bays can be provided on the highway or in off-street car parks under the Road Traffic Regulation Act 1984. These are enforceable by law.

Guidelines for the provision and enforcement of spaces for the disabled are contained in traffic advisory leaflet 5/95 issued by the Department of Transport. Copies of the leaflet are available in the Library of the House.

In privately owned and operated car parks, it is for individual operators to take whatever steps they consider necessary to see that reserved spaces are not misused.

### Further Education Funding Council

**Mr. Sweeney:** To ask the Secretary of State for Wales when he expects to announce the new membership of the Further Education Funding Council for Wales; and if he will make a statement. [26433]

**Mr. Richards:** The following have accepted invitations to be members of the Further Education Funding Council for Wales:

    Mr. Richard Webster, Chairman
    Mr. Stephen Dunster
    Mr. Shaun Dyke
    Mr. Osborn Jones
    Mrs. Caroline Lewis
    Mr. Idris Price
    Mr. Ken Thomas
    Mr. Grant Walshe
    Mr. Trevor Wilmore

Mr. Dunster, Mr. Thomas and Mr. Walshe have been reappointed for two years from 6 May 1995, and the other members appointed for three years from the same date.

Professor John Andrews continues as chief executive and member until 5 May 1997.

## HOUSE OF COMMONS

### Parliamentary Questions

**Mr. McMaster:** To ask the Lord President of the Council what is the procedure for obtaining parliamentary answers in the House of Commons from the Lord Advocate and the Solicitor-General for Scotland; and if he will make a statement. [24077]

**Mr. Newton:** Parliamentary questions relating to matters which fall within the responsibility of the Lord Advocate or Solicitor General for Scotland are addressed to the Secretary of State for Scotland and answered by a Scottish Office Minister.

## LORD PRESIDENT OF THE COUNCIL

### Child Care

**Mr. McNamara:** To ask the Lord President of the Council what are the child care or nursery facilities within his Department; and what is the breakdown in their use (a) by grade and (b) by gender. [15233]

**Mr. Newton:** Privy Council Office staff are able to use the Westminster holiday play scheme, which is organised by the Office of Public Service and Science. So far, no staff have made use of this facility.

## TREASURY

### Treasury Reserve

**Miss Lestor:** To ask the Chancellor of the Exchequer if he will list all the occasions when the Treasury reserve was used in 1994–95; how much was drawn; and which Departments or Ministries were involved. [25734]

**Mr. Aitken:** Provisional outturn figures for public expenditure for 1994–95 will be published as described in the answer I gave to my hon. Friend the Member for Southport (Mr. Banks) on 23 May. The information published will include revised plans and provisional outturn by Department, and the difference between these constitutes the net claim on the reserve. Because these are net figures which include offsets for underspending, it is not possible to break them down into individual claims.

**Miss Lestor:** To ask the Chancellor of the Exchequer if he will list the occasions in the last five years when the Overseas Development Administration has had to draw on Treasury reserves. [25735]

**Mr. Aitken:** The ODA has drawn on the reserve 22 times in the past five years. The claims were agreed in the usual way on the occasions listed:

    1990–91 Main Estimates
    1990–91 Summer Estimates
    1991–92 Winter Supplementary
    1991–92 Main Estimates
    1991–92 winter Supplementary
    1991–92 Spring Supplementary
    1992–93 Winter Supplementary
    1993–94 Spring Supplementary
    1994–95 Main Estimates
    1994–95 Winter Supplementary
    1994–95 Spring Supplementary
    1995–96 Main Estimates

### Staff

**Ms Hodge:** To ask the Chancellor of the Exchequer (1) what changes there have been in the numbers of staff employed by (a) the Treasury and (b) agencies for which the Treasury is responsible, listing the changes in the number of staff agency by agency in (i) 1993–94 and (ii) 1994–95; and what changes are projected for 1995–96; [25063]

(2) how many posts were lost in (a) the Treasury and (b) agencies for which the Treasury is responsible, listing total posts lost agency by agency in (i) 1993–94 and (ii) 1994–95; and how many posts are proposed to be lost in 1995–96;

(3) what changes there have been in the number of staff in employment by grade in (a) the Treasury and (b) each agency for which the Treasury is responsible in (i) 1993–94 and (ii) 1994–95; and what are the projected figures for 1995–96; [25628]

(4) how many staff of (a) the Treasury and (b) agencies for which the Treasury is responsible were employed on a casual or short-term basis in (i) 1993–94 and (ii) 1994–95; and what are the projected figures for 1995–96. [25417]

**Mr. Heathcoat-Amory:** The numbers of permanent and casual staff employed by the Treasury in 1993–94, projected outturn for 1994–95 and plans for 1995–96 are published in the Departmental report of the Chancellor's smaller Departments, a copy of which is in the Library of the House. Projections by grade are not available. The Treasury does not have any executive agencies.

## Bank of England Inflation Report

**Mr. Malcolm Bruce:** To ask the Chancellor of the Exchequer what plans he has to instigate an inquiry into the disclosure of the Bank of England's inflation report conclusions before the release time of 11.30 am on 11 May.

**Mr. Nelson** *[holding answer 23 May 1995]:* The bank's inflation report was published at 11.30 am on Thursday 11 May. I have no reason to believe that any unauthorised person had access to the report or its conclusions prior to that time.

## HEALTH

### City and East London FHSA

**Mr. Timms:** To ask the Secretary of State for Health on what date she received the section 20(3) report referred to in the City and East London family health services authority 1994 management letter.        [23944]

**Mr. Malone:** On 2 February 1995.

**Mr. Timms:** To ask the Secretary of State for Health if she will list the *(a)* chairmen and *(b)* members of the City and East London family health services authority since 1 January 1990; and what were their terms of office.        [25558]

**Mr. Malone:** The City and East London family health services authority was established on 17 September 1990. Those who have served as chairmen since then are:

Ms Jacqui Lait from 17 September 1990 to 31 October 1991;

Mr. Norman Warner from 1 November 1991 to 31 August 1994; and Mr. Peter Holwell from 1 September 1994. Mr. Holwell's term of office is due to expire on 31 March 1996.

The appointment of non-executive members to City and East London FHSA is a matter for North Thames regional health authority, the hon. Member may wish to contact Sir William Staveley, the chairman, for details.

### Skin Cancer

**Mr. Congdon:** To ask the Secretary of State for Health (1) what information campaigns her Department is funding to increase understanding and awareness of the dangers of exposure to the sun;        [24578]

(2) what work her Department has undertaken in the past year to raise awareness of the dangers to the skin of exposure to sunlight;        [24579]

(3) what steps her Department is taking to ensure that children are protected from exposure to the sun during the summer months; and if she will make a statement.        [25477]

**Mr. Sackville:** Skin cancer is a serious public health problem—and one that is largely preventable. In pursuit of "The Health of the Nation" strategy to halt the year on year increase in the incidence of skin cancer, the

Department is collaborating with a number of organisations on a range of initiatives and "health alliances" aimed at tackling skin cancer. These include:

surveys on behaviour and attitudes to sun exposure in order to refine targeting of action;

research projects on the nature of skin cancer to help provide a better understanding of prevention and treatment strategies;

the issue of comprehensive guidance to the NHS on local skin cancer prevention strategies;

public information initiatives, such as ultraviolet radiation levels on Television weather forecasts; a Freephone Helpline, and a factsheet on UVR from the National Radiological Protection Board;

the launch of a "sun know-how" programme of skin cancer prevention initiatives by the Health Education Authority involving more than 1,000 local organisations;

the issue earlier this month of "Sun Awareness and Protection Guidelines for Schools" to encourage the implementation of prudent sun protection policies in schools;

most recently, the launch of a poster from the Cancer Research Campaign and the Department aimed specifically at primary health care teams giving prevention and early diagnosis advice.

In addition, the Health Education Authority is participating in a Sun Awareness Week starting on 5 June, when a number of mainly local events will be mounted.

The Department will continue to work actively with others to reduce the rising incidence of skin cancer over the next decade and beyond.

### Immunisation

**Mr. Mike O'Brien:** To ask the Secretary of State for Health how many cases of adverse reaction among children to immunisation have been reported by the medical profession to her Department in each of the last five years.        [24564]

**Mr. Sackville:** The number of reports of adverse reactions to all vaccines in children reported to the Medicines Control Agency is shown in the table, with the total number of immunisations given to children as part of the childhood vaccine programme:

| Time period | Number of UK reports of adverse reactions (children aged 16 years or less) | Estimated number of immunisations given as part of the UK childhood vaccine programme (children aged 16 years or less) |
| --- | --- | --- |
| June 91–May 92 | 481 | 8,000,000 |
| June 92–May 93 | 1,585 | 11,000,000 |
| June 93–May 94 | 1,125 | 10,000,000 |
| June 94–present | 1,844 | 18,000,000 |

*Notes:*

1. Information about the adverse reactions for the period June 1991 to May 1992 has not been provided because of disproportionate cost. A report of a reaction does not necessarily mean that it was caused by the vaccine.

2. In the time period shown, considerable changes have been made to the childhood immunisation programme. Hib vaccine was introduced in October 1992 and the measles and rubella immunisation campaign was carried out during November 1994.

### Local Government Reorganisation, Cleveland

**Mr. Frank Cook:** To ask the Secretary of State for Health (1) what assessment she has made of the implications for the implementation of effective care in the community services in Cleveland when the Tees health authority makes arrangements with four social services departments following local government reorganisation;    [25221]

(2) if she will make a statement on the implications for child protection services and procedures in the Cleveland area—including the effect on children on the child protection register—resulting from local government reorganisation in Cleveland; and what guidance she has issued in relation to how other agencies, including health, probation and police should maintain effective and consistent working arrangements with four social services departments.    [25222]

**Mr. Bowis:** I refer the hon. Member to the reply that I gave to the hon. Member for Kingswood (Mr. Berry) on 17 May, *Official Report,* columns *281–82.*

### Consultancy Expenditure

**Ms Hodge:** To ask the Secretary of State for Health what is the level of expenditure on consultancy by *(a)* her Department and *(b)* agencies for which her Department is responsible for (i) 1993–94, (ii) 1994–95 and (iii) the projected figures for 1995–96.    [25634]

**Mr. Sackville:** The Department of Health and its agencies have spent the following amounts from running costs on consultancy.

    1993–94 : £15,933,037
    1994–95 : £18,479,405

The projected figure for 1995–96 is in the region of £15,600,000 and is based on 1993–94 prices.

Separate expenditure for the Department and agencies could be provided only at disproportionate cost.

### Patients Charter

**Mr. Milburn:** To ask the Secretary of State for Health if she will provide details of the 10 trusts which came closest to meeting each of the new patients charter targets on out-patient waiting times and the area trusts which were furthest from meeting the targets in the latest quarter for which figures are available, indicating the percentages of patients concerned.    [25572]

**Mr. Malone:** Data on out-patient waiting times at individual trusts will be published in full shortly and placed in the Library.

### Staff Contracts

**Mr. Nicholas Brown:** To ask the Secretary of State for Health what plans she now has to require NHS trusts to remove gagging clauses from the terms of staff contracts.    [26077]

**Mr. Malone:** The contents of employment contracts are a matter to be decided between national health service trusts and their staff and must be expressed in a way which does not conflict with the principles and advice outlined in the NHS Executive's document, "Guidance to staff on relations with the public and the media—EL(93)51". Copies of the guidance are available in the Library.

### Mental Health Funding

**Mr. Nicholas Brown:** To ask the Secretary of State for Health to what extent a social deprivation score is included as a weighting factor in allocation formulae for mental health funding.    [26073]

**Mr. Malone:** There is no index of deprivation in the formula. Instead it uses two needs indices, one for acute services and the other for psychiatric services, both of which take account of a number of health and socio-economic factors.

### Private Finance Initiative

**Mr. Nicholas Brown:** To ask the Secretary of State for Health (1) if she will list by cost all the NHS projects that have been fully or partly funded under the private finance initiative, and all those currently under discussion;    [26106]

(2) how much investment has been made in the NHS under the private finance initiative in each year since the scheme began.    [26105]

**Mr. Sackville:** I refer the hon. Member to the reply that I gave to the right hon. Member for Derby, South (Mrs. Beckett) on 21 April at cols *312–13.*

### Hospital Maintenance

**Mr. Nicholas Brown:** To ask the Secretary of State for Health if she will list by region the hospital maintenance backlog as at 31 March.    [26078]

**Mr. Sackville:** I refer the hon. Member to the reply that I gave him on 8 December 1994 at cols *359-60* for the latest information available.

### Competitive Tendering

**Mr. Nicholas Brown:** To ask the Secretary of State for Health if she will place in the Library a list of the contracts for hospital and health services awarded so far under the competitive tendering process by each district health authority.    [26072]

**Mr. Sackville:** This information is not available centrally.

### Departmental Plans

**Mr. French:** To ask the Secretary of State for Health what are her plans for the work of the Department in 1995–96 and beyond.    [26434]

**Mrs. Virginia Bottomley:** I have agreed a statement of the aims, goals and priorities for my Department for 1995–96 and subsequent years.

The statement covers the whole range of the Department's work relating to health and social services, European Union and other international issues, and internal management.

The statement includes our specific priorities for the National Health Service Executive, which are taken forward in more detail in the NHS Executive's business plan for 1995–96, approved by the NHS Policy Board, and which was published on 5 April 1995.

Copies of the statement will be placed in the Library.

### Statement of Responsibilities and Accountabilities

**Mr. French:** To ask the Secretary of State for Health when she intends to publish the statement of responsibilities and accountabilities foreshadowed in the document published in October 1993 on changes in the NHS, "Managing the new NHS".    [26435]

**Mrs. Virgina Bottomley:** The statement of responsibilities and accountabilities is being published today. It explains how the Government's responsibilities for health and social care in England are discharged by the Department of Health and the national health service, and the lines of accountability within both organisations to the Secretary of State and to Parliament. Copies of the statement will be placed in the Library.

### Community Care Conferences (Wheelchair Access)

**Mr. Hinchliffe:** To ask the Secretary of State for Health if all the venues for local community care charter regional conferences had wheelchair access facilities; and if she will list all the venues. [25397]

**Mr. Bowis:** Arrangements were made at all the venues used for the regional conferences on local community care charters to allow attendance by disabled delegates. Disabled delegates were invited to contact the conference organisers to specify their needs. Conferences have been arranged at the following locations: Grand hotel, Broad street, Bristol; Wigan conference centre, Waterside drive, Swan Meadow road, Wigan; Civic centre, Newcastle-upon-Tyne; Hotel Russell, Russell square, London WC2 and Jarvis Grand hotel, Granby street, Leicester.

### Treatment Costs

**Mrs. Beckett:** To ask the Secretary of State for Health, pursuant to her answers of 9 and 11 May, *Official Report*, columns *409–10* and *574*, (1) if she will make a statement on the relationship between the reductions in treatment costs and length of stay in hospital between 1982–83 and 1992–93; [25904]

(2) if she will make a statement on the average cost of treating an acute patient contained in the departmental report, Cm 2812, between 1982–83 and 1990–91. [25903]

**Mr. Sackville:** Over the 10-year period from 1982–83 there has been a shift towards day case treatments and shorter hospital stays. These changes reflect improving clinical practice and have brought benefits to patients, who recover better at home with their families, and economic advantages to the national health service, which can treat more patients within the same resources, while maintaining high standards of care.

### Casualty Officer Posts

**Mrs. Beckett:** To ask the Secretary of State for Health if she will make a statement on the number of vacancies in medical posts in casualty units around the country. [25900]

**Mr. Malone:** The available information is shown in the table.

*Whole-time equivalent vacant posts not occupied by a locum in England as at 30 September 1993, accident and emergency, by grade*

| | Number |
|---|---|
| Consultant | 10 |
| Staff grade | 4 |
| Senior registrar | 2 |
| Registrar | 4 |
| Senior house officer | 4 |
| Total | 24 |

*Note:*
All figures are rounded to the nearest whole number.

### GP Fundholding

**Mrs. Beckett:** To ask the Secretary of State for Health what percentage of general practitioners are fundholders in each region. [25899]

**Mr. Malone:** From April 1995, it is estimated that 39 per cent. of general practitioners in England are fundholders, serving over 41 per cent. of the population.

Information, by region, on the general practitioner fundholding scheme is shown in the table.

*GP fundholding scheme by region—1994–95*

| Region | Number of funds | Number of fundholding practices | Number of fundholding GPs | Percentage of GPs[1] that are fundholders | Population served by a fundholding GP (percentage) |
|---|---|---|---|---|---|
| Northern and Yorkshire | 265 | 321 | 1,500 | 41 | 40 |
| Trent | 237 | 314 | 1,138 | 45 | 48 |
| Oxford and Anglia | 208 | 233 | 1,145 | 40 | 43 |
| North Thames | 270 | 373 | 1,292 | 34 | 40 |
| South Thames | 290 | 383 | 1,507 | 42 | 44 |
| South and West | 200 | 230 | 1,180 | 31 | 33 |
| West Midlands | 285 | 405 | 1,399 | 50 | 51 |
| North West | 252 | 344 | 1,249 | 37 | 37 |
| England | 2,007 | 2,603 | 10,410 | 39 | 41 |

*Source:*
Estimates from regional health authorities.
*Note:*
[1] Unrestricted principals taken from April 1994 GP Census.

**Mr. Hinchliffe:** To ask the Secretary of State for Health how many general practitioner fundholders have contracted with (a) NHS trusts and (b) district health authorities for (i) health visiting services and (ii) community psychiatric nursing services in each of the last five years. [25759]

**Mr. Malone:** The information requested is not available centrally.

Community health services have been included in the general practitioner fundholding scheme since April 1993. GP fundholders are required to contract for health visiting services with an established national health service provider of community nursing services, or with a provider of community mental health services for community psychiatric nursing services.

**Mrs. Beckett:** To ask the Secretary of State for Health if she will make a statement on geographical variations in the uptake of general practitioner fundholding.    [25890]

**Mr. Malone:** The strength of general practitioner fundholding is its voluntary nature. It is to be expected therefore that the rate at which family doctors take up the opportunities of fundholding will vary, depending on local circumstances and the state of their practice development. The extensions to fundholding announced last October provide a wider range of options for general practitioner teams to improve services for patients in this way.

### Hospitals

**Mrs. Beckett:** To ask the Secretary of State for Health, pursuant to her answer of 30 March, *Official Report*, col *716*, what indication the information obtained from energy consumption returns gives of the change in the number of hospitals between 1 April 1994 and 1 April 1995; and if she will publish the numbers and make a statement.    [25897]

**Mr. Malone:** The change in the number of hospitals in England between 1 April 1994 and 1 April 1995 obtained from energy consumption returns is not yet available. These figures have to be treated with caution because they do not define hospitals in accordance with section 128 of the National Health Service Act 1977 and include estimates for incomplete returns.

### Primary Care, London

**Mrs. Beckett:** To ask the Secretary of State for Health what are the projected revenue savings from the closure of London hospitals in the next three years in real terms; and what is the projected extra money spent in London on primary care in each of the next three years.    [25901]

**Mr. Malone:** The revenue savings expected to be released following the changes announced on 4 April are currently estimated to be around £75 million per year. The timing of the release of the savings will depend on the detailed implementation of proposals. Figures for total projected expenditure on primary care are not available. Most elements of family health services expenditure are primarily demand-led and funded accordingly. However, investment in primary and community health services in the London initiative zone area alone is likely to exceed £200 million over the next three years.

### Broadmoor Hospital

**Mr. Hinchliffe:** To ask the Secretary of State for Health what independent monitoring there has been of the Broadmoor hospital re-build fund; and if she will make a statement.    [25760]

**Mr. Bowis:** This is the responsibility of the Special Hospitals Service Authority. The hon. Member may wish to contact the chairman of the authority for details.

### Organ Donation

**Mrs. Beckett:** To ask the Secretary of State for Health what training programmes have been initiated for doctors in respect of requesting permission from relatives prior to organ donation.    [25881]

**Mr. Sackville:** Much is being done by hospitals in education of their staff about organ donation and approaches to bereaved relatives, including bereavement counselling. As part of this the Government, following consultation with the royal colleges, are piloting a programme of information and training for doctors and nurses working in intensive care units development by the European donor hospital education programme.

**Mrs. Beckett:** To ask the Secretary of State for Health if she will make a statement on the proposed national registration day to promote the national computerised registration system for organ donors.    [25889]

**Mr. Sackville:** We will as usual be supporting the publicity activities organised by the group of charities known as "Transplants in Mind" during its National Transplant Week which is held each year in conjunction with the British Transplant Games in July. This year their activities will focus on the national health service organ donor register.

**Mrs. Beckett:** To ask the Secretary of State for Health what support her Department has provided for the national computerised registration scheme for organ donors; what is its advertising budget; and what has been the expenditure to date on information packs.    [25882]

**Mr. Sackville:** The Department set up the national health service organ donor register in October 1994. In addition to funding the cost of setting up and maintaining the Register, which is held at the United Kingdom Transplant Support Service Authority, we spent £1.53 million in 1994–95 on publicity material and activities to promote the register. It is planned to spend a similar sum in the current year. This has included national, regional and local newspaper advertisements and the production of 10 million information leaflets—"Life Don't Keep it to Yourself"—containing registration forms of which more than 7 million have already been distributed. About £7,500 was spent on producing 20,200 copies of the "NHS Organ Register and General Practitioners" booklet which were sent to every general practice in England. The United Kingdom Transplant Support Service Authority has also produced an information leaflet for the general public and a resources and an information pack for the transplant community.

### Treatment Numbers

**Mrs. Beckett:** To ask the Secretary of State for Health (1) how many bed days of finished episodes there were in each of the last 10 years;    [25883]

(2) how many people were treated as a hospital in-patient or day-care patient without going on to a waiting list in each of the last 10 years.    [25885]

**Mr. Sackville:** The available information for the years 1988–89 to 1993–94 has been published in the annual volumes of Hospital Episode Statistics. Information for the years 1986 and 1987–88 is not available. For 1984 and 1985 information was published in the relevant volumes of Hospital In-Patient Enquiry, but because of changes to information systems in the NHS after 1985, figures are not directly comparable with HES. Copies of the publications are available in the Library.

The latest available information for patients admitted immediately is shown in the table. Comparable figures are not available for earlier years.

| Year | Patients admitted immediately |
|---|---|
| 1988–89 | 3,597,501 |
| 1989–90 | 3,748,774 |
| 1990–91 | 3,786,756 |
| 1991–92 | 3,829,414 |
| 1992–93 | 4,037,827 |
| 1993–94 | 4,291.304 |

*Source:* Hospital Episode Statistics.

### Hospital Transport

**Mrs. Beckett:** To ask the Secretary of State for Health how many free hospital bus services are provided by *(a)* her Department, *(b)* trust hospitals and *(c)* in total; what was the total expenditure on these services; and what proposals she has to reduce them. [25887]

**Mr. Sackville:** This information is not available centrally.

### Tobacco Advertising

**Mrs. Beckett:** To ask the Secretary of State for Health, pursuant to her answer of 9 May, *Official Report,* columns 412–13, if she will define the meaning of the phrase "not have a major impact" in terms of a percentage reduction in the consumption of tobacco if tobacco advertising were banned. [25891]

**Mr. Sackville:** It is not possible to quantify this phrase in terms of a percentage reduction in tobacco consumption.

### Information Dinner

**Mrs. Beckett:** To ask the Secretary of State for Health what was the budget for her Department's information dinner in each of the last five years. [25893]

**Mr. Sackville:** The Department does not have an information dinner. The right hon. Lady may wish to provide clarification.

### "Making London Better"

**Mrs. Beckett:** To ask the Secretary of State for Health what estiamte she has made of public support for her document entitled "Making London Better". [25895]

**Mr. Malone:** "Making London Better" set out the strategic direction for health services in London and the framework within which change would take place. It stated that, where appropriate, there would be statutory consultation before decisions were taken. Proposals for a number of changes have already been the subject of local public consultation by health authorities in the usual way. Detailed information on the public response to those consultations may be obtained from the health authorities concerned.

### Local Pay

**Mrs. Beckett:** To ask the Secretary of State for Health pursuant to her answer of 2 May, *Official Report* column 713, what projected savings in staff costs will result from the estimated cost of £500,000 for the financial year 1994–95 for the National Health Service Executive support programme for the introduction of local pay. [25898]

**Mr. Malone:** The purpose of the introduction of local pay throughout the health service, facilitated by this support programme, is to provide more flexible working, to redeploy finite resources and to target them more closely on improvements in the quality and quantity of healthcare. The support programme is designed to facilitate the spread of good practice developed by trusts which have made significant progress in developing local pay schemes for different staff groups.

### Cancelled Operations

**Mrs. Beckett:** To ask the Secretary of State for Health pursuant to her answer of 16 March, *Official Report,* column *704,* how many operations were cancelled on the day or after the date when the patient was due to be admitted to hospital by regional health authority, district health authority and in total; and how many were not readmitted within one month for the fourth quarter of 1994–95. [25902]

**Mr. Malone:** This information will be placed in the Library when available.

### Termination Payments

**Mr. Byers:** To ask the Secretary of State for Health how many termination payments have been made by national health service trusts to *(a)* chief executives, *(b)* general managers and *(c)* senior managers; and what was the total amount for each trust since 30 September 1994. [25788]

**Mr. Malone:** Since 30 September 1994 national health service trusts have reported to the National Health Service Executive three termination payments made to chief executives and 38 payments made to both general and senior managers(1).

The total amount for each trust is as follows:

| NHS trust | Amount £ |
|---|---|
| Broadgreen Hospital NHS Trust | 86,167 |
| Bromley Hospitals NHS Trust | 25,400 |
| Burnley Health Care NHS Trust | 245,000 |
| Dudley Priority Health NHS Trust | 17,120 |
| East Hertfordshire NHS Trust | 22,500 |
| Enfield Community Care NHS Trust | 35,522 |
| Frimley Park Hospital NHS Trust | 6,328 |
| Kingston Hospital NHS Trust | 37,402 |
| Kings Health Care NHS Trust | 23,627 |
| Mid Anglia Community Health NHS Trust | 5,449 |
| New Possibilities NHS Trust | 65,199 |
| Northgate and Prudhoe NHS Trust | 6,500 |
| North Middlesex Hospital NHS Trust | 11,328 |
| North West London NHS Trust | 6,500 |
| Northern Birmingham Mental Health NHS Trust | 74,526 |
| Nottingham City Hospital NHS Trust | 54,960 |
| Nottinghamshire Ambulance Service NHS Trust | 17,500 |
| Plymouth Hospitals NHS Trust | 21,900 |
| Royal Free Hampstead NHS Trust | 35,295 |
| Royal Liverpool Children's Hospital NHS Trust | 12,122 |
| Royal Liverpool University Hospital NHS Trust | 35,626 |
| Royal National Orthopaedic Hospital NHS Trust | 7,130 |
| Salford Mental Health Services NHS Trust | 15,874 |
| South Devon Health Care NHS Trust | 37,740 |
| South Downs Health NHS Trust | 8,727 |
| South Kent Community Healthcare NHS Trust | 30,636 |
| Southmead Health Services NHS Trust | 30,649 |

| NHS trust | Amount £ |
|---|---|
| Stockport Healthcare NHS Trust | 21,940 |
| West Herts Community Health NHS Trust | 69,505 |
| Winchester and Eastleigh NHS Trust | 19,504 |
| York Health Services NHS Trust | 55,000 |

[1] Payments made to general managers and payments made to senior managers are not separately identified in the information held centrally.

### Kidney Patients

**Mrs. Beckett:** To ask the Secretary of State for Health what assessment she has made of the adequacy of Manchester Royal Infirmary's provision for kidney transplant patients.        [25879]

**Mr. Sackville:** This is a matter for district health authorities, in consultation with the North West regional health authority, to decide. The right hon. Member may wish to contact Sir Donald Wilson, regional chairman, for further information.

**Mrs. Beckett:** To ask the Secretary of State for Health what estimate she has made of how many patients die each year from kidney failure; how many of these did not receive dialysis; and what assessment she has made of how many would have survived if they had received a transplant.        [25880]

**Mr. Sackville:** In 1992, the latest year for which figures are available, 856[1] people died from chronic renal failure. Information on how many of these were not receiving dialysis is not available. It is not therefore known how many were on the active kidney transplant waiting list. No estimate can be made of how many would have survived if they had received a transplant.

[1] Data received from the Office of Population, Censuses and Surveys.

**Mrs. Beckett:** To ask the Secretary of State for Health how many hospitals provide kidney dialysis treatment in each region of the NHS; how many patients there are in the catchment area of each hospital; and how many hospitals provide kidney transplants.        [25888]

**Mr. Sackville:** The information is not available in the form requested. Kidney dialysis and transplant provision for England in 1993 will be placed in the Library. It is not possible to show numbers of patients per catchment area, as the number of renal units are limited and there is much cross-boundary activity. There are 30 hospitals in England that provide kidney transplants for adult patients.

### St. Bartholomew's Hospital

**Mrs. Beckett:** To ask the Secretary of State for Health, how many patients are seen on average each week at the minor injuries unit at St. Bartholomew's hospital.  [25896]

**Mr. Malone:** The average figure for weekdays is 36 people per day and for weekends 13 people per day.

### Waiting Lists

**Mrs. Beckett:** To ask the Secretary of State for Health (1) how many people waited for hospital in-patient or day-care treatment for *(a)* nought to three months and *(b)* nought to six months in each of the last 10 years;        [25884]

(2) what percentage of patients treated in hospital have come from a waiting list in each of the last 10 years.        [25886]

**Mr. Malone:** Such information as is available is given in "Hospital Episode Statistics, England". The latest year for which information has so far been published is 1993–94. Copies are available in the Library.

### Dr. Johnstone

**Mrs. Beckett:** To ask the Secretary of State for Health if she will publish communications between the Department of Health NHS Management Executive and Camden and Islington health authority over the last six years in relation to Dr. Johnstone's legal action.   [25892]

**Mr. Malone:** This information could be provided only at disproportionate cost.

### London Hospital

**Mrs. Beckett:** To ask the Secretary of State for Health how many name changes the London Hospital has had in the last five years; and what those names were.   [25894]

**Mr. Malone:** The name of the Royal London hospital has not changed.

# LORD CHANCELLOR'S DEPARTMENT

### Legal Aid

**Mr. Matthew Taylor:** To ask the Parliamentary Secretary, Lord Chancellor's Department how much has been spent on legal aid in each of the five years.  [24790]

**Mr. John M. Taylor:** Net expenditure on legal aid in each of the last five years was as follows:
    1990–91: £682 million
    1991–92: £906 million
    1992–93: £1,093 million
    1993–94: £1,210 million
    1994–95[1]: £1,294 million
    [1] Estimated outturn

**Mr. Matthew Taylor:** To ask the Parliamentary Secretary, Lord Chancellor's Department what percentage of the overall cost of legal aid has been spent on administration in each of the last five years.        [24769]

**Mr. John M. Taylor:** The total cost of legal aid over the past five years has been:
    1990–91: £682 million
    1991–92: £906 million
    1992–93: £1,093 million
    1993–94: £1,210 million
    1994–95[1]: £1,294 million

The Legal Aid Board is responsible for administering the majority of that expenditure, namely:
    1990–91: £526 million
    1991–92: £720 million
    1992–93: £873 million
    1993–94: £974 million
    1994–95[1]: £1,032 million

The cost of the Legal Aid Board's administration are met by separate provision as follows:
    1990–91: £33.2 million
    1991–92: £41.2 million
    1992–93: £43.7 million
    1993–94: £47.5 million
    1994–95[1]: £49.0 million

This gives the following figures for the board's administration costs as a percentage of the legal aid money that the board deals with:

1990–91: 5.9 per cent.
1991–92: 5.4 per cent.
1992–93: 4.8 per cent.
1993–94: 4.7 per cent.
1994–95[1]: 4.5 per cent.

The remainder of legal aid expenditure relates to criminal legal aid in the higher criminal courts, which is administered by the courts concerned. It is not possible to isolate the costs to the courts of administering this part of the legal aid scheme.

*Note:*
[1]Figures for 1994–95 are estimated.

### Official Print of Statutes

**Mr. Gordon Prentice:** To ask the Parliamentary Secretary, Lord Chancellor's Department when he expects there to be an official print of all statutes.   [25513]

**Mr. John M. Taylor:** An official print of all statutes is published by HMSO immediately upon Royal Assent. An annual volume of Public General Acts and Measures is prepared by the Statutory Publications Office for publication by HMSO. The four parts constituting the 1993 volume were published in March of this year.

## SOCIAL SECURITY

### Contributions Agency

**Mr. Wigley:** To ask the Secretary of State for Social Security how many people are currently employed *(a)* in Wales and *(b)* in Newcastle upon Tyne in the work of the National Insurance Contributions Agency; and what were the corresponding figures for five and 10 years ago.   [25014]

**Mr. Arbuthnot:** The administration of the Contributions Agency is the responsibility of Mrs. Faith Boardman, the chief executive. She will write to the hon. Member.

*Letter from Mrs. Faith Boardman to Mr. Dafydd Wigley, dated 23 May 1995:*

As Chief Executive of the Contributions Agency, I have responsibility for answering on operational matters relating to the Agency. I have been asked to reply to your question about how many people are currently employed in a) Wales and b) Newcastle Upon Tyne in the work of the Contributions Agency; and what were the corresponding figures for five and ten years ago.

The Agency currently employs 205 staff in Wales. This includes staff both in Field Operations and the Agency's Civil Recovery Section in Cardiff.

In being asked to supply a figure for the number of staff employed in Newcastle Upon Tyne I have interpreted this to mean those staff who work on the Agency's Newcastle Estate (ie excluding those staff employed in Field Operations offices in the Newcastle area). The number of staff currently employed by the Agency at its Newcastle estate is 5598.

The Contributions Agency was established as a "Next Steps" agency in April 1991, and prior to that the Contributions Unit had operated within the Department of Social Security from April 1990. Whilst I cannot provide exact details of the number of staff employed by the Contributions Unit in Wales five years ago, I can tell you that the total number of staff employed in our Wales and Severn Estuary Divisions at 1 May 1990 was 307. However, some of the staff from the Severn Estuary Division would have been working in its two offices located in England, and records of the precise split in staff numbers between England and Wales have not been kept.

The number employed by the Contributions Unit at the Newcastle estate on 1 May 1990 was 2029.

I regret that I am unable to supply corresponding figures for ten years ago as they are not kept in that form. The records of the number of staff actually employed on contributions duties cannot be dis-aggregated from the overall staffing of the Department of Social Security.

I hope you will find this answer helpful. If I can be of any further assistance please let me know.

**Mr. Wigley:** To ask the Secretary of State for Social Security how many jobs will be lost from the Porthmadog office of the Contributions Agency as a result of the centralisation of the work of the agency to North East England; and if he will make a statement.   [25006]

**Mr. Arbuthnot:** The administration of the Contributions Agency is the responsibility of Mrs. Faith Boardman, the chief executive. She will write to the hon. Member.

*Letter from Mrs. Faith Boardman to Mr. Dafydd Wigley, dated 23 May 1995:*

As Chief Executive of the Contributions Agency, I have responsibility for answering questions on operational matters relating to the Agency. I have been asked to reply to your question about how many jobs will be lost from the Porthmadog office of the Contributions Agency as a result of centralisation of work to North East England.

Over the last four years the Contributions Agency has centralised some work in Newcastle Upon Tyne while maintaining a local presence. In many areas we have also gradually been reducing the number of local offices by concentrating Field staff in larger, more viable units. Nationally, the combined effect has been to improve the flexibility, efficiency and quality of the service provided. At present I am looking at proposals to establish a Call Centre to handle, on a national basis, all unsolicited telephone calls, but as yet no decision has been made as to where this would be located, and we are conducting a comprehensive national review of the overall organisation and numbers of our Field Offices in order to see how far we should extend the efficiencies already achieved in some areas.

Since the Contributions Agency was formed in April 1991 four staff have been employed at the Porthmadog Office. However, with the need to achieve operational efficiencies it has quite recently been decided to transfer the processing of clerical work dealt with at Porthmadog to our office in Rhyl. This has resulted in a reduction of two clerical staff at Porthmadog.

As has been the case since April 1991, the Benefits Agency in Porthmadog will continue to provide a counter service for customers making enquiries about National Insurance matters. If a customer wishes a private interview with a Contributions Agency officer this can be arranged and can take place in the Porthmadog office. Additionally, there is a Customer Access Telephone in the reception area of Porthmadog office which allows the customer to speak directly to Contributions Agency staff free of charge.

### Retirement Pension

**Mr. Jon Owen Jones:** To ask the Secretary of State for Social Security if his Department automatically sends letters notifying people of their eligibility for a pension when they reach retirement age to people *(a)* who have worked and paid national insurance contributions in the last 25 years and *(b)* who have not worked and not paid national insurance contributions in the last 25 years.   [25039]

**Mr. Arbuthnot:** The administration of retirement pensions is a matter for Mr. Ian Magee, the chief executive of the Benefits Agency. He will write to the hon. Member.

*Letter from Ian Magee to Mr Jon Owen Jones, dated 23 May 1995:*

The Secretary of State for Social Security has asked me to reply to your recent Parliamentary Question about the Department automatically sending letters to people at retirement age concerning their eligibility for Retirement Pension.

Approximately four months before a person reaches State pension age (60 for a woman and 65 for a man), the Benefits Agency automatically sends them, by computer process, a form on which to claim Retirement Pension; this is provided they have established some entitlement to a pension, however small. In the case of a man, two claim forms are sent. This is to enable a wife to also make a claim on her husband's National Insurance record. An accompanying form sets out the amount of pension to which it is known the person is so far entitled. Both Welsh and English versions of the forms are sent to addresses in Wales.

Even if there is no entitlement to any pension at the time the claim forms would be sent, they would still be sent if it was known the person had previously lived abroad or if the person is shown to be either widowed or divorced. In these cases, contributions paid abroad or paid by the former spouse may help establish entitlement to pension.

The automatic issue of forms to claim Retirement Pension is not a legal requirement, but it is in line with the Agency's aim to provide a high level of Customer Service.

I hope you find this reply helpful.

## Bronchitis and Emphysema

**Mr. Mike O'Brien:** To ask the Secretary of State for Social Security how many chronic bronchitis and emphysema claims have been *(a)* instigated and *(b)* successful in each of the last five years (i) in total and (ii) in each benefits area directorate.    [24773]

**Mr. Hague:** The administration of industrial injuries disablement benefit is a matter for Mr. Ian Magee, the chief executive of the Benefits Agency. He will write to the hon. Member.

*Letter from Ian Magee to Mr. Mike O'Brien, dated 23 May 1995:*

The Secretary of State for Social Security has asked me to reply to your recent Parliamentary Question about claims made for chronic bronchitis and emphysema both nationally and in each area directorate in the last five years.

Information about the number of claims and successful claims is not available for all the period requested because chronic bronchitis and emphysema did not become a prescribed disease until 13 September 1993. The available information has been provided at Annex A.

There was a "take on" exercise which lasted twelve months and the data shown in the table, under the heading September 1993–September 1994, covers this exercise. The data under the heading October 1994–March 1995 covers the six month period from the end of the exercise to the end of the 1994–95 statistical year.

I hope you find this reply helpful

### Scotland and Northern Territorial Directorate

| | Claims | | | |
| --- | --- | --- | --- | --- |
| | September 1993 to September 1994 | | October 1994 to March 1995 | |
| | Made | Successful | Made | ¹Successful |
| ADI. Tyne Tees | 7,142 | 587 | 185 | 33 |
| AD2, South Yorkshire and Humberside | 6,521 | 776 | 214 | 33 |
| AD3, North and West Yorkshire | 2,676 | 422 | 121 | 20 |
| AD4, Glasgow and Paisley | 242 | 8 | 5 | 0 |
| AD5, North, Central and West Scotland | 1,895 | 60 | 24 | 1 |
| AD6, East of Scotland | 2,394 | 94 | 29 | 2 |

¹ Includes claims received but not decided in the earlier period.

### Wales and Central Territorial Directorate

| | Claims | | | |
| --- | --- | --- | --- | --- |
| | September 93 to September 94 | | October 94 to March 95 | |
| | Made | Successful | Made | ¹Successful |
| AD1. East Midlands | 5,685 | 613 | 234 | 53 |
| AD2. Midlands South West | 652 | 55 | 8 | 8 |
| AD3. West Mercia | 3,668 | 383 | 100 | 9 |
| AD4. Wales | 9,388 | 1,347 | 416 | 97 |
| AD5. Merseyside | 501 | 49 | 14 | 0 |
| AD6. Greater Manchester | 328 | 31 | 14 | 1 |
| AD7. Lancashire and Cumbria | 2,270 | 151 | 53 | 6 |

¹ Includes claims received but not decided in the earlier period.

### Southern Territorial Directorate

| | Claims | | | |
| --- | --- | --- | --- | --- |
| | September 1993 to September 1994 | | October 1994 to March 1995 | |
| | Made | Successful | Made | ¹Successful |
| AD1. Anglia | 25 | 3 | 0 | 0 |
| AD2. Chilterns | 22 | 4 | 0 | 0 |
| AD3. South London and West Sussex | 0 | 0 | 0 | 0 |
| AD4. West Country | 144 | 3 | 8 | 3 |
| AD5. East London and Essex | 0 | 0 | 42 | 0 |
| AD6. South East | 470 | 32 | 17 | 1 |
| AD7. Wessex | 0 | 0 | 0 | 0 |

¹ Includes claims received but not decided in the earlier period. Claims for AD3, AD5 and AD7 are dealt with by AD6.

*National*

| | Claims | | | |
| --- | --- | --- | --- | --- |
| | September 1993 to September 1994 | | October 1994 to March 1995 | |
| | Made | Successful | Made | Successful |
| | 44,023 | 4,618 | 1,477 | 267 |

Included in the successful claims are 48 in 1993–94 and 3 in 1994–95 where although assessed as having a percentage of disability it was below 14 per cent. and therefore did not attract an award of benefit.

## National Insurance Contributions

**Mr. Foulkes:** To ask the Secretary of State for Social Security what would be the additional revenue gained to the national insurance fund if women aged between 60 and 65 years were subject to national insurance contributions.                    [24947]

**Mr. Arbuthnot:** The effect on the national insurance fund for 1995–96 is estimated to be a gain a of some £70 million.

Note: figures are for Great Britain.

**Mr. Foulkes:** To ask the Secretary of State for Social Security what would be the additional cost to the national insurance fund of exempting men aged over 60 years from paying national insurance contributions                    [24949]

**Mr. Arbuthnot:** The effect on the national insurance fund for 1995–96 is estimated to be a loss of some £350 million.

*Note:* figures are for Great Britain.

## Staff

**Ms Hodge:** To ask the Secretary of State for Social Security (1) what changes there have been in the numbers of staff employed by *(a)* the Department of Social Security and *(b)* agencies for which the Department of Social Security is responsible, listing the changes in the number of staff agency by agency in (i) 1993–94 and (ii) 1994–95; and what changes are projected for 1995–96;                    [25064]

(2) what changes there have been in the number of staff in employment by grade in *(a)* his Department and *(b)* each agency for which his Department is responsible in (i) 1993–94 and (ii) 1994–95; and what are the projected figures for 1995–96;                    [25629]

(3) how many staff of *(a)* the Department of Social Security and *(b)* agencies for which the DSS is responsible were employed on a casual or short-term basis in (i) 1993–94 and (ii) 1994–95; and what are the projected figures for 1995–96.                    [25419]

**Mr. Hague:** The numbers of permanent and casual staff employed by this Department and each of its executive agencies in 1993–94, projected outturn for 1994–95, and plans for 1995–96 are published in the Department's annual report, a copy of which is in the Library.

A breakdown by grade reflecting staff in post at the commencement of each of the financial years is in the tables:

*Departmental Staff in Post—April 1993*

| | HQ SIP | ISB SIP | BA SIP | CA SIP | CSA SIP | ITSA SIP | RA SIP | WPA SIP | DSS Total |
| --- | --- | --- | --- | --- | --- | --- | --- | --- | --- |
| Grade 1–4 | 15.5 | 1.0 | 11.0 | 1.0 | 1.0 | 2.0 | 0.0 | 0.0 | 31.5 |
| Grade 5 | 48.5 | 20.0 | 41.0 | 2.0 | 3.0 | 5.5 | 0.0 | 0.0 | 120.0 |
| Grade 6 | 40.0 | 3.0 | 235.5 | 7.0 | 4.0 | 17.0 | 1.0 | 1.0 | 308.5 |
| Grade 7 | 188.0 | 16.0 | 253.5 | 30.0 | 14.5 | 81.0 | 5.0 | 4.0 | 592.0 |
| SEO | 119.0 | 38.0 | 617.0 | 110.5 | 32.0 | 238.0 | 9.0 | 13.0 | 1,176.5 |
| HEO/HEO(D) | 340.0 | 189.5 | 3,140.0 | 458.0 | 178.5 | 742.5 | 26.5 | 55.5 | 5,130.5 |
| LOI–EO–AT | 279.0 | 170.5 | 16,016.5 | 2,580.0 | 1,260.5 | 1,455.0 | 46.5 | 298.0 | 22,106.0 |
| LOII–AO | 245.5 | 406.0 | 32,100.5 | 3,966.0 | 1,246.0 | 1,073.5 | 62.0 | 534.5 | 39,634.0 |
| AA | 98.0 | 164.0 | 8,272.0 | 1,804.0 | 168.0 | 264.0 | 4.0 | 366.0 | 11,140.0 |
| SPES–PES | 78.5 | 20.5 | 105.5 | 10.0 | 10.5 | 27.0 | 2.0 | 1.0 | 255.0 |
| Typing Grades | 27.5 | 53.5 | 1,278.0 | 110.0 | 8.5 | 18.0 | 3.5 | 76.0 | 1,575.0 |
| SM1 | 0.0 | 0.0 | 2.0 | 0.0 | 0.0 | 0.0 | 0.0 | 0.0 | 2.0 |
| SM2 | 0.0 | 0.0 | 7.0 | 4.0 | 0.0 | 1.0 | 0.0 | 0.0 | 12.0 |
| SM3 | 1.0 | 0.0 | 27.0 | 10.0 | 0.0 | 4.0 | 134.0 | 0.0 | 176.0 |
| SG1 | 9.0 | 0.0 | 374.5 | 57.5 | 0.5 | 54.0 | 0.0 | 0.0 | 495.5 |
| SG2 | 40.0 | 19.0 | 1,520.0 | 205.0 | 10.0 | 84.0 | 0.0 | 5.0 | 1,883.0 |
| Professionals | 0.0 | 0.0 | 36.0 | 0.0 | 0.0 | 2.0 | 0.0 | 0.0 | 38.0 |
| Others | 0.0 | 0.0 | 18.5 | 15.0 | 0.0 | 0.0 | 11.0 | 29.0 | 73.5 |
| Industrial | 0.0 | 0.0 | 0.0 | 0.0 | 0.0 | 0.0 | 54.0 | 21.0 | 75.0 |
| | | | | | | | | | |
| Permanent Posts | 1,529.5 | 1,101.0 | 64,055.5 | 9,370.0 | 2,937.0 | 4,068.5 | 358.5 | 1,404.0 | 84,824.0 |
| Casual | 32.0 | 143.0 | 3,327.5 | 331.0 | 42.0 | 501.0 | 23.0 | 148.5 | 4,548.0 |
| Fixed Term contract | Figures not available for 1993 | | | | | | | | |

1. Independent statutory Bodies (ISB). 2. Benefits Agency (BA).

3. Contributions Agency (CA).

4. Child Support Agency (CSA).

5. Information and Technology Services Agency (ITSA)

6. Resettlement Agency (RA).

7. War Pensions Agency (WPA).

8. Staff in Post (SIP).

*Departmental Staff in Post—April 1994*

| | HQ<br>SIP | ISB<br>SIP | BA<br>SIP | CA<br>SIP | CSA<br>SIP | ITSA<br>SIP | RA<br>SIP | WPA<br>SIP | DSS<br>Total |
|---|---|---|---|---|---|---|---|---|---|
| Grade 1–4 | 15.0 | 1.0 | 12.0 | 1.0 | 1.0 | 2.0 | 0.0 | 0.0 | 32.0 |
| Grade 5 | 54.0 | 36.0 | 43.0 | 3.0 | 3.0 | 6.0 | 1.0 | 1.0 | 147.0 |
| Grade 6 | 35.0 | 3.0 | 214.5 | 8.0 | 6.0 | 16.5 | 0.0 | 1.0 | 284.0 |
| Grade 7 | 183.0 | 13.0 | 272.5 | 40.0 | 18.0 | 108.0 | 4.0 | 8.0 | 646.5 |
| SEO | 128.0 | 40.0 | 587.0 | 155.0 | 62.5 | 361.0 | 7.0 | 15.5 | 1,356.0 |
| HEO/HEO(D) | 343.0 | 180.0 | 3,000.0 | 572.0 | 286.5 | 917.0 | 24.5 | 68.0 | 5,391.0 |
| LOI–EO–AT | 334.0 | 215.5 | 16,003.0 | 2,631.0 | 1,488.0 | 1,449.5 | 40.5 | 330.0 | 22,491.5 |
| LOII–AO | 244.0 | 490.5 | 32,481.5 | 4,167.0 | 2,505.0 | 864.5 | 42.5 | 594.5 | 41,389.5 |
| AA | 97.0 | 220.0 | 8,035.5 | 1,829.5 | 344.0 | 109.5 | 3.0 | 323.0 | 10,961.5 |
| SPES–PES | 82.0 | 25.5 | 94.0 | 14.0 | 10.0 | 32.0 | 2.0 | 0.0 | 259.5 |
| Typing Grades | 26.0 | 62.5 | 1,192.0 | 80.0 | 12.5 | 9.0 | 1.0 | 73.5 | 1,456.5 |
| SM1 | 0.0 | 0.0 | 2.0 | 0.0 | 0.0 | 0.0 | 0.0 | 0.0 | 2.0 |
| SM2 | 0.0 | 0.0 | 10.0 | 9.0 | 0.0 | 1.0 | 0.0 | 0.0 | 20.0 |
| SM3 | 1.0 | 0.0 | 28.0 | 4.0 | 0.0 | 2.0 | 101.0 | 0.0 | 136.0 |
| SG1 | 5.0 | 0.0 | 366.0 | 86.0 | 0.0 | 36.5 | 0.0 | 0.0 | 493.5 |
| SG2 | 27.0 | 35.5 | 1,335.5 | 212.0 | 12.0 | 80.5 | 0.0 | 5.0 | 1,707.5 |
| Professionals | 0.0 | 0.0 | 174.5 | 0.0 | 0.0 | 0.0 | 0.0 | 0.0 | 174.5 |
| Others | 0.0 | 0.0 | 45.5 | 9.0 | 3.0 | 3.0 | 11.0 | 54.5 | 126.0 |
| Industrial | 0.0 | 0.0 | 0.0 | 0.0 | 0.0 | 0.0 | 38.5 | 20.5 | 59.0 |
| Permanent Posts | 1,574.0 | 1,322.5 | 63,896.5 | 9,820.5 | 4,751.5 | 3,988.0 | 276.0 | 1,494.5 | 87,133.5 |
| Casual | 61.0 | 45.0 | 3,922.0 | 209.0 | 494.5 | 611.0 | 47.5 | 145.5 | 5,535.5 |
| Fixed Term Contract | 25.0 | 47.0 | 1,594.0 | 543.0 | 138.0 | 270.0 | 36.0 | 58.0 | 2,711.0 |

*Departmental Staff in Post—April 1995*

| | HQ<br>SIP | ISB<br>SIP | BA<br>SIP | CA<br>SIP | CSA<br>SIP | ITSA<br>SIP | RA<br>SIP | WPA<br>SIP | DSS<br>Total |
|---|---|---|---|---|---|---|---|---|---|
| Grade 1–4 | 15.0 | 1.0 | 12.0 | 1.0 | 1.0 | 1.0 | 0.0 | 0.0 | 31.0 |
| Grade 5 | 50.8 | 1.0 | 42.0 | 3.0 | 3.0 | 7.0 | 0.0 | 1.0 | 107.8 |
| Grade 6 | 42.3 | 4.0 | 277.9 | 11.0 | 4.0 | 17.0 | 1.0 | 1.0 | 358.2 |
| Grade 7 | 192.2 | 13.7 | 300.1 | 40.0 | 22.0 | 104.0 | 4.0 | 6.0 | 682.0 |
| SEO | 130.1 | 37.0 | 628.1 | 172.0 | 65.5 | 301.2 | 6.0 | 14.0 | 1,353.9 |
| HEO/HEO(D) | 360.7 | 181.0 | 3,189.0 | 640.0 | 324.7 | 813.3 | 12.6 | 70.9 | 5,592.2 |
| LOI–EO–AT | 313.6 | 213.8 | 17,391.1 | 2,767.1 | 1,822.4 | 1,296.9 | 30.3 | 387.1 | 24,222.3 |
| LOII–AO | 220.7 | 482.6 | 34,880.9 | 3,701.7 | 3,198.4 | 800.1 | 19.0 | 513.2 | 43,816.6 |
| AA | 85.5 | 175.4 | 7,727.2 | 1,323.4 | 497.6 | 80.3 | 1.0 | 207.2 | 10,099.6 |
| SPES–PES | 80.7 | 25.6 | 85.3 | 14.9 | 9.5 | 28.4 | 1.0 | 1.0 | 246.4 |
| Typing Grades | 18.2 | 76.9 | 632.0 | 70.1 | 14.2 | 7.5 | 0.0 | 65.3 | 884.2 |
| SM1 | 0.0 | 0.0 | 2.0 | 0.0 | 0.0 | 0.0 | 0.0 | 0.0 | 2.0 |
| SM2 | 0.0 | 0.0 | 7.0 | 3.0 | 0.0 | 2.0 | 0.0 | 0.0 | 12.0 |
| SM3 | 0.0 | 0.0 | 27.0 | 4.0 | 0.0 | 1.4 | 43.0 | 0.0 | 75.4 |
| SG1 | 5.0 | 0.0 | 260.7 | 39.2 | 0.0 | 25.0 | 0.0 | 0.0 | 329.9 |
| SG2 | 21.0 | 28.2 | 1,007.0 | 98.6 | 12.0 | 54.8 | 0.0 | 1.8 | 1,223.4 |
| Professionals | 0.0 | 0.0 | 0.0 | 0.0 | 0.0 | 0.0 | 0.0 | 0.0 | 0.0 |
| Others | 0.0 | 40.0 | 215.9 | 0.0 | 0.0 | 0.0 | 0.0 | 0.0 | 255.9 |
| Industrial | 0.0 | 0.0 | 0.0 | 0.0 | 0.0 | 0.0 | 14.9 | 26.0 | 40.9 |
| Permanent Posts | 1,535.8 | 1,280.2 | 66,687.2 | 8,889.0 | 5,974.3 | 3,539.9 | 132.8 | 1,294.5 | 89,333.7 |
| Casual | 40.0 | 64.9 | 3,473.0 | 491.0 | 205.0 | 387.0 | 5.0 | 263.0 | 4,928.9 |
| Fixed Term Contract | 7.0 | 60.0 | 2,441.0 | 121.0 | 79.0 | 414.0 | 21.0 | 23.0 | 3,166.0 |

## Agency Job Losses

**Ms Hodge:** To ask the Secretary of State for Social Security how many posts were lost in *(a)* the Department of Social Security and *(b)* agencies for which the Department of Social Security is responsible, listing the total lost posts agency by agency in (i) 1993–94 and (ii) 1994–95; and how many posts are proposed to be lost in 1995–96.        [25078]

**Mr. Hague:** The information is not available in the form requested.

## Income Distribution

**Mr. Amess:** To ask the Secretary of State for Social Security if he will provide an analysis and examples of the family types and occupational groups who appear in the top 10 per cent. of the income distribution.        [26387]

**Mr. Lilley:** In 1991–92, the latest period for which figures are available, there were 5.7 million people in the top tenth of the income distribution in the UK, of whom 13 per cent. were pensioners, 41 per cent. couples without children, 26 per cent. couples with children and 19 per cent. single, all after housing costs.

Analysis of the patterns of personal disposable income throughout the UK income distribution will be included in the next edition of households below average income statistics, covering the period 1979 to 1992–93, which will be published on Friday 2 June.

## EMPLOYMENT

### Training and Enterprise Council Licences

**Mr. Heald:** To ask the Secretary of State for Employment what progress Hertfordshire training and enterprise council is making in meeting the criteria for the award of a three-year licence. [26341]

**Mr. Paice:** I am pleased to announce that Hertfordshire training and enterprise council has now completed the process of meeting the rigorous standard we set for the award of the new three-year licences.

**Mr. Lidington:** To ask the Secretary of State for Employment what progress Thames Valley Enterprise TEC is making in meeting the criteria for the award of a three-year licence. [26342]

**Mr. Paice:** I am pleased to announce that Thames Valley Enterprise TEC has now completed the process of meeting the rigorous standard we set for the award of he new three-year licences.

**Mr. Biffen:** To ask the Secretary of State for Employment what progress Shropshire training and enterprise council is making in meeting the criteria for the award of a three-year licence. [26583]

**Mr. Paice:** I am please to announce that Shropshire training and enterprise council has now completed the process of meeting the rigorous standard we set for the award of the new three-year licences.

## EDUCATION

### Staff

**Ms Hodge:** To ask the Secretary of State for Education (1) what changes there have been to the number of staff employed by (i) her Department and (ii) each agency for which the DFE is responsible in (a) 1993–94 and (b) 1994–95; and what are the projected figures for 1995–96; [25491]

(2) what changes there have been to the number of staff employment by grade in (i) the Department for Education and (ii) each agency for which the DFE is responsible in (a) 1993–94 and (b) 1994–95; and what are the projected figures for 1995–96; [25422]

(3) how many staff of (a) the Department for Education and (b) agencies for which the Department for Education is responsible, were employed on a casual or short term basis in (i) 1993–94 and (ii) 1994–95; and what are the projected figures for 1995–96; [25506]

(4) how many posts were lost in (a) the Department for Education and (b) agencies for which the Department for Education is responsible, listing the total posts agency by agency in (i) 1993–94 and (ii) 1994–95 and how many posts are proposed to be lost in 1995–96. [25073]

**Mr. Boswell:** The numbers of permanent and casual staff employed by the Department, including the Teachers

Pensions Agency, in 1993–94, projected outturn for 1994–95, and plans for 1995–96 are published in the departmental report, a copy of which is in the Library of the House. No projections broken down by grade are available.

### Consultancy Expenditure

**Ms Hodge:** To ask the Secretary of State for Education what is the level of expenditure on consultancy by (a) her Department and (b) agencies for which her Department is responsible for (i) 1993–94 and (ii) 1994–95; and what are the projected figures for 1995–96.

**Mr. Boswell:** The level of expenditure committed by the Department's central purchasing unit on consultancy for the periods requested is as follows:

| | £ |
|---|---|
| *(a) Department* | |
| 1993–94 | 1,300,000 |
| 1994–95 | 1,400,000 |
| 1995–96 | ¹3,000,000 |
| | |
| *(b) Agencies* | |
| 1993–94 | 190,000 |
| 1994–95 | 285,000 |
| 1995–96 | ¹240,000 |

¹ Projected.

### Retirements and Redundancies

**Ms Hodge:** To ask the Secretary of State for Education how many staff of (a) the Department for Education and (b) agencies for which the Department for Education is responsible (i) took early retirement, (ii) took voluntary redundancy, (iii) took compulsory redundancy and (iv) were retired on medical grounds in (1) 1993–94 and (2) 1994–95; and what are the projected figures for 1995–96. [25505]

**Mr. Boswell:** Information on DFE staff working in the Teachers' Pensions Agency cannot be separately identified from the Department as a whole without disproportionate cost.

During 1993–94, a total of 45 staff took early retirement and 10 retired on medical grounds.

In 1994–95, 20 staff took early retirement and 11 were retired on medical grounds.

There were no redundancies during either of these years. None are planned for 1995–96, though the Department keeps its staffing requirements under constant review.

**Ms Hodge:** To ask the Secretary of State for Education what is the annual cost to the Department of staff leaving under redundancy/early retirement schemes to incorporate (i) added years lump sum payments, (ii) redundancy payments, (iii) pension payments including enhancements and (iv) any other special arrangements for (a) 1993–94, (b) 1994–95, and projected for (c) 1995–96 and (d) 1996–97. [25643]

**Mr. Boswell:** The costs to the Department of early retirement and redundancies are borne from the Department's running costs provision.

A detailed breakdown of the various costs could be obtained only at disproportionate cost.

The total costs borne on the Department's running costs in 1993–94 and 1994–95 were £4.9 million and £2.8 million respectively. For 1995–96, the amount is estimated not to exceed £2.4 million. Projections for 1996–97 will be determined during the coming Public Expenditure Survey.

## Contracting Out

**Ms Hodge:** To ask the Secretary of State for Education, for each piece of work subject to a bidding process under the auspices of *(a)* her Department and *(b)* agencies for which her Department is responsible (i) where work was contracted out, who were the successful bidders and (ii) which contracts were won by in-house bidders in (1) 1993–94, (2) 1994–95, and (3) 1995–96.

**Mr. Boswell:** The information requested, resulting from market tests, is as follows:

| Market Test | Year | Name of Contractor |
|---|---|---|
| *(i) Successful bidders for work contracted out* | | |
| Provision of data preparation services | 1994–95 | Compower Ltd. |
| Provision of banking services to the Teachers Pensions Agency | 1995–96 | Midland Bank |
| Development and management of a computerised register of schools | 1995–96 | The Schools Register |
| *(ii) Work won by in-house bidders* | | |
| Provision of telephone network management | 1993–94 | — |
| Development of small IT systems | 1993–94 | — |
| Provision of central support services (London) | 1993–94 | — |
| Provision of central support services (Darlington) | 1994–95 | — |

All of the tests were under the auspices of the Department, apart from provision of banking services to the Teachers Pensions Agency.

**Ms Hodge:** To ask the Secretary of State for Education what work has been contracted out *(a)* by her Department and *(b)* by agencies for which her Department is responsible in (i) 1993–94, (ii) 1994–95 and (iii) projected for 1995–96.

**Mr. Boswell:** Information on work which has been contracted out during the years in questions is as follows:

| Description of work | Year |
|---|---|
| *(a) Department* | |
| Provision of data preparation services | 1994–95 |
| Development and management of a computerised register of schools | 1995–96 |
| *(b) Agencies* | |
| Provision of internal audit services to the Teacher Training Agency (TTA) | 1994–95 |
| Provision of banking services to the Teachers Pensions Agency | 1995–96 |

There is no projection for future work to be contracted out in 1995–96, and no work was contracted out in 1993–94.

## Schools Budget

**Mr. Streeter:** To ask the Secretary of State for Education if she will show for each local education authority for the year 1995–96 the element of the potential schools budget which is not delegated to schools through the aggregated schools budget, expressed *(a)* as a percentage of the potential schools budget and *(b)* as a sum of money per pupil in schools covered by the LMS scheme. [25037]

**Mr. Robin Squire:** The percentage of the potential schools budget not delegated to schools in 1995–96 through the aggregated schools budget is shown for each local education authority in the following table, which is derived from the percentages shown as delegated in the LMS budget statements for 1995–96 published by local education authorities under section 42 of the Education Reform Act.

The Department is not yet in a position to provide the information requested at *(b)*. I will write to my hon. Friend when these figures are available later in the year.

| Local education authority | PSB Percentage not delegated |
|---|---|
| Avon | 11.9 |
| Barking and Dagenham | 10.9 |
| Barnet | 9.8 |
| Barnsley | 10.9 |
| Bedfordshire | 8.7 |
| Berkshire | 7.1 |
| Bexley | 8.8 |
| Birmingham | 9.7 |
| Bolton | 11.1 |
| Bradford | 11.9 |
| Brent | 7.0 |
| Bromley | 12.2 |
| Buckinghamshire | 11.6 |
| Bury | 8.2 |
| Calderdale | 10.9 |
| Cambridgeshire | 10.7 |
| Camden | 12.6 |
| Cheshire | 9.1 |
| City | 11.0 |
| Cleveland | 10.6 |
| Cornwall | 11.1 |
| Coventry | 8.7 |
| Croydon | 10.0 |
| Cumbria | 8.2 |
| Derbyshire | 10.6 |
| Devon | 8.1 |
| Doncaster | 10.0 |
| Dorset | 10.4 |
| Dudley | 4.2 |
| Durham | 11.5 |
| Ealing | 10.1 |
| East Sussex | 10.8 |
| Enfield | 10.6 |
| Essex | 11.0 |
| Gateshead | 13.4 |
| Gloucestershire | 8.9 |
| Greenwich | 7.3 |
| Hackney | 13.0 |
| Hammersmith and Fulham | 9.0 |
| Hampshire | 11.4 |
| Haringey | 12.8 |
| Harrow | 9.8 |
| Havering | 8.3 |
| Hereford and Worcester | 9.0 |
| Hertfordshire | 5.8 |
| Hillingdon | 10.1 |
| Hounslow | 11.0 |
| Humberside | 11.3 |

| Local education authority | PSB Percentage not delegated |
| --- | --- |
| Isle of Wight | 9.8 |
| Isles of Scilly | n/a |
| Islington | 5.9 |
| Kensington and Chelsea | 10.0 |
| Kent | 12.5 |
| Kingston | 10.8 |
| Kirklees | 12.9 |
| Knowsley | 6.1 |
| Lambeth | 13.6 |
| Lancashire | 12.3 |
| Leeds | 6.6 |
| Leicestershire | 11.6 |
| Lewisham | 12.5 |
| Lincolnshire | 10.5 |
| Liverpool | 7.7 |
| Manchester | 8.0 |
| Merton | 10.8 |
| Newcastle | 11.8 |
| Newham | 14.0 |
| Norfolk | 8.6 |
| North Tyneside | 8.2 |
| North Yorkshire | 10.2 |
| Northamptonshire | 7.1 |
| Northumberland | 9.2 |
| Nottinghamshire | 11.2 |
| Oldham | 9.4 |
| Oxfordshire | 8.4 |
| Redbridge | 9.4 |
| Richmond | 9.6 |
| Rochdale | 7.1 |
| Rotherham | 10.6 |
| Salford | 9.3 |
| Sandwell | 11.9 |
| Sefton | 11.0 |
| Sheffield | 12.2 |
| Shropshire | 11.8 |
| Solihull | 6.0 |
| Somerset | 8.9 |
| South Tyneside | 10.8 |
| Southwark | 12.0 |
| St. Helens | 14.5 |
| Staffordshire | 7.2 |
| Stockport | 9.1 |
| Suffolk | 9.4 |
| Sunderland | 7.7 |
| Surrey | 10.2 |
| Sutton | 9.8 |
| Tameside | 10.7 |
| Tower Hamlets | 9.0 |
| Trafford | 11.4 |
| Wakefield | 12.1 |
| Walsall | 9.7 |
| Waltham Forest | 6.1 |
| Wandsworth | 14.6 |
| Warwickshire | 11.6 |
| West Sussex | 11.1 |
| Westminster | 9.8 |
| Wigan | 7.3 |
| Wiltshire | 10.4 |
| Wirral | 9.7 |
| Wolverhampton | 8.1 |

*Notes:*

1. n/a = budget statement not yet received.
2. Figures rounded to one decimal place where given to two places in LEA's statement.

## National Curriculum (Gardening)

**Mr. Battle:** To ask the Secretary of State for Education what plans she has to introduce gardening into the national curriculum so as to equip school-leavers with the skills needed to grow vegetables.    [15259]

**Mr. Forth:** The national curriculum has just been subject to a major review, and the revised curriculum will be introduced in schools from this September. The Government have announced that we have no plans to make any further major changes for at least five years.

# TRANSPORT

## Vehicle Testing

**Mr. Hinchliffe:** To ask the Secretary of State for Transport if local authority DOT—approved testing facilities will continue to test Hackney carriages and private hire vehicles to MOT standards.    [25354]

**Mr. Norris:** Any local authority MOT testing stations must test to MOT standards. The Government have announced that taxis and private hire vehicles will in future be treated by suitably equipped MOT testing stations, and is currently considering whether taxis would be subject either to more frequent or more rigorous inspections than under the current MOT scheme.

**Mr. Hinchliffe:** To ask the Secretary of State for Transport, if private hire vehicle operators with their own garages will be permitted to undertake MOT testing for private hire vehicles.    [25355]

**Mr. Norris:** This is permissible at present. The criterion that any prospective MOT tester must satisfy is that they have the necessary skills and facilities to MOT test vehicles. The issue of whether or not they might test their own vehicles as well as others is irrelevant to that question.

**Mr. Hinchliffe:** To ask the Secretary of State for Transport if higher standards of MOT testing are required for taxis, public hire vehicles and other public service vehicles.    [25356]

**Mr. Norris:** Some licensed taxis are currently exempt from MOT testing on the basis that they are subject to an annual licensing inspection carried out by the licensing authority which is at least as rigorous as the MOT test. In most cases licensing authorities who test taxis require comfort and cleanliness to be tested as well as the roadworthiness of the vehicle. These additional aspects are also included in the annual MOT tests of public service vehicles. Where the licensing authority does not test taxis or private hire vehicles, vehicles are subject to the MOT test as for private cars.

## London-Tilbury-Southend Line

**Mr. Mackinlay:** To ask the Secretary of State for Transport what policy considerations underlie the decision to allocate the older rolling stock to the London-Tilbury-Southend line under the cascade arrangements; on what occasion this has occurred over the past decade; and if he will make a statement.    [25360]

**Mr. Watts:** These decisions have been an operational matter for British Rail.

## Wheelchair-accessible Taxis

**Mr. Hinchliffe:** To ask the Secretary of State for Transport if flexibility will be granted to local authorities discretion, in circumstances where wheelchair-accessible vehicles are taken off the road for short periods following accidents or awaiting repair, to allow taxis which are not wheelchair accessible to be operated in the interim period, where the original vehicle will return to use. [25359]

**Mr. Norris:** If a taxi is taken off the road for a period, there is nothing to stop an owner transferring the taxi licence to a substitute vehicle, but the substitute will have to meet the local taxi standards, including wheelchair accessibility where appropriate; it may have to be tested if the licensing authority requires, and licensing fees may be payable.

### Rail Fares

**Mr. Dafis:** To ask the Secretary of State for Transport, what Exchequer funding will be made available for each of the next seven years to meet the cost of pegging rail fares; and if he will make a statement. [25613]

**Mr. Watts:** The Government remain firmly committed to the franchising process and to providing the subsidy needed to support passenger railway services, including the effects of the new policy on fares. The level of funding needed for the railways will depend on the bids received by the franchising director for franchises. The Government believe that privatisation will bring efficiency and other improvements to services. All these factors will affect the level of funding required by the railways.

### ENVIRONMENT

### Local Minerals Plans

**Mr. Batiste:** To ask the Secretary of State for the Environment how many local minerals plans are currently in force in England and Wales. [24973]

**Sir Paul Beresford:** Eighteen mineral local plans have been adopted and are currently in force in England. Planning matters in Wales are the responsibility of my right hon. Friend the Secretary of State for Wales.

### Retirements and Redundancies

**Ms Hodge:** To ask the Secretary of State for the Environment what is the annual cost to the Department of staff leaving under redundancy/early retirement schemes to incorporate (i) added years lump sum payments, (ii) redundancy payments, (iii) pension payments including enhancements and (iv) any other special arrangements for *(a)* 1993–94, *(b)* 1994–95 and projected for *(c)* 1995–96 and *(d)* 1996–97.

**Sir Paul Beresford:** The costs to the Department of early retirements and redundancies are borne from its running costs provision. A detailed breakdown of the various costs could be obtained only at disproportionate cost.

The total cost borne on my Department's running costs provisions for 1993–94 and 1994–95 were:

| | 1993–94 £ | 1994–95 £ |
|---|---|---|
| DOE[1] and next steps agencies | 2,601,328 | 2,408,042 |
| Property Services Agency | 73,668,000 | 68,944,000 |

For 1995–96, the amount is estimated at:

| | £ |
|---|---|
| DOE[1] and next steps agencies | 1,752,600 |
| Property Services Agency | 28,500,000 |

1. The figures for 1994–95 and 1995–96 are net of Treasury funding (ie 80 per cent.) of the cost of retirements occurring after 1 October 1994).
[1] excludes Property Holdings, on which information is temporarily unavailable. I will write to the hon. Member in due course.

Projections for 1996–97 will be determined during the current Public Expenditure Survey.

**Ms Hodge:** To ask the Secretary of State for the Environment how many staff of *(a)* the Department of the Environment and *(b)* agencies for which the Department of the Environment is responsible (i) took early retirement, (ii) took voluntary redundancy, (iii) took compulsory redundancy and (iv) were retired on medical grounds in (1) 1993–94 and (2) 1994–95; and what are the projected figures for 1995–96. [25517]

**Sir Paul Beresford:** The following information covers staff in my Department, excluding Ordnance Survey and PSA Services.

| | 1993–94 | | | | 1994–95 | | | |
|---|---|---|---|---|---|---|---|---|
| | (i) | (ii) | (iii) | (iv) | (i) | (ii) | (iii) | (iv) |
| DOE | 120 | 31 | 0 | 38 | 26 | 3 | 2 | 32 |
| SAFE | 7 | 2 | 0 | 1 | 0 | 0 | 0 | 0 |
| Planning Inspectorate | 2 | 0 | 0 | 5 | 7 | 0 | 0 | 4 |
| Building Research Establishment | 10 | 0 | 0 | 3 | 19 | 0 | 0 | 3 |
| The Buying Agency | 0 | 0 | 0 | 1 | 0 | 0 | 0 | 0 |
| QEII Conference Centre | 0 | 1 | 0 | 2 | 0 | 0 | 0 | 0 |

*Notes:*

(i) Early retirement.

(ii) Voluntary redundancy.

(iii) Compulsory redundancy.

(iv) Medical grounds.

Projections for 1995–96 which are not able to be broken down by those categories:

|  | Number |
| --- | --- |
| DOE | 175 |
| SAFE | 0 |
| Planning Inspectorate | 8 |
| Building Research Establishment | n/a |
| The Buying Agency | 0 |
| QEIICC Conference Centre | 0 |

## Planning Regulations

**Mr. Tom Clarke:** To ask the Secretary of State for the Environment if he will review the provisions of the Town and Country Planning (General Development) Order 1988, in respect of permission granted to a householder to construct an outbuilding two metres from a neighbouring dwelling without permission, in circumstances where the neighbouring householder is housebound and the erection of the outbuilding will obstruct his view.    [24974]

**Sir Paul Beresford:** My Department keeps the General Development Order under constant review. If I find that the permitted development rights granted by it are being widely abused, I shall consider taking action. I cannot, however, intervene in individual cases.

## Staff

**Ms Hodge:** To ask the Secretary of State for the Environment, how many staff of (a) the Department of the Environment and (b) agencies for which the Department of the Environment is responsible were employed on a casual or short-term basis in (i) 1993–94 and (ii) 1994–95; and what are the projected figures for 1995–96.    [25515]

**Sir Paul Beresford:** The numbers of casual staff employed by my Department and each of its executive agencies in 1993–94, projected outturn for 1994–95, and plans 1995–96 are published in my Department's Annual Report, a copy of which is in the Library of the House.

**Ms Hodge:** To ask the Secretary of State for the Environment, what changes there have been in the number of staff in employment by grade in (a) his Department and (b) each agency for which his Department is responsible in (i) 1993–94 and (ii) 1994–95; and what are the projected figures for 1995–96.    [25633]

**Sir Paul Beresford:** The numbers of staff employed by my Department and each of its executive agencies in 1993–94, projected outturn for 1994–95, and plans 1995–96 are published in my Department's annual report, a copy of which is in the Library of the House. No information or projections broken down by grade are available.

**Ms Hodge:** To ask the Secretary of State for the Environment, what changes there have been in the number of staff employed by (i) his Department and (ii) each agency for which his Department is responsible in (a) 1993–94 and (b) 1994–95; and what are the projected figures for 1995–96.    [25494]

**Sir Paul Beresford:** The numbers of staff employed by my Department and each of its executive agencies in 1993–94, projected outturn for 1994–95, and plans 1995–96 are published in my Department's annual report, a copy of which is in the Library of the House.

## Right to Buy

**Mrs. Gorman:** To ask the Secretary of State for the Environment how many people in (a) London and (b) the rest of the country have exercised their right to buy their council house since the right was introduced.    [25528]

**Mr. Robert B. Jones:** Between October 1980 and September 1994 some 185,000 council homes in London were purchased by tenants under the right-to-buy legislation. During the same period, about 1,025,000 sales were made to local authority and new town tenants in the rest of England.

## Construction Contracts

**Mr. Cox:** To ask the Secretary of State for the Environment which Government Department he is consulting as to a construction contracts Bill, and if he will make a statement.    [25755]

**Mr. Robert B. Jones:** A number of Government Departments have received copies of my Department's consultation documents, "Latent Defects Liability and 'Build' Insurance" and "Fair Construction Contracts", which follow up proposals for legislation set out in Sir Michael Latham's report, "Constructing the Team".

## City Pride

**Mr. Vaz:** To ask the Secretary of State for the Environment on which dates he received the city pride documents from (a) Manchester, (b) Birmingham and (c) London; and if he will estimate the cost of implementing the proposals submitted so far from each.    [25768]

**Mr. Curry:** My right hon. Friend the Secretary of State for the Environment received the Manchester, Birmingham and London city pride prospectuses on 8 September 1994, 18 April 1995 and 23 January 1995 respectively. The promoters of city pride and the Government have not costed the proposals set out in the prospectuses, most of which are at a provisional stage.

## Houses in Multiple Occupation

**Mr. Cox:** To ask the Secretary of State for the Environment how many responses he has received in reply to the consultation paper on the case for licensing houses in multiple occupation; and when he expects to issue his report.    [25754]

**Mr. Robert B. Jones:** I refer the hon. Member to the reply that I gave to the hon. Members for Cardiff, Central (Mr. Jones) and for Sheffield, Heeley (Mr. Michie) on 20 March 1995, *Official Report*, columns 57-58.

## Housing, Yorkshire and Humberside

**Mr. Hinchliffe:** To ask the Secretary of State for the Environment (1) what sum for new rented housing association homes in 1995–96 would have been available if funding outlined in the 1992 Autumn Statement had been maintained for each local authority in Yorkshire and Humberside;    [25399]

(2) what estimate he has for the number of housing association homes for rent which will be built in 1995–96 in each local authority in Yorkshire and Humberside; [25398]

(3) what is the total central Government funding for new rented housing association homes for 1995–96, excluding tenant incentive schemes, do it yourself shared ownership and major repairs or sales programmes for each local authority in Yorkshire and Humberside. [25358]

**Mr. Robert B. Jones:** Allocations made in Yorkshire and Humberside from the Housing Corporation's 1995–96 approved development programme for the provision of new-build rented housing are as follows, together with the Housing Corporation's estimate of what the allocations may have been for 1995–96 if funding plans in the 1992 Autumn Statement had been maintained.

| Local authority | Allocation (£m) | Related units | 1992 Autumn Statement estimated allocation (£m) | Related units |
|---|---|---|---|---|
| Barnsley | 0.88 | 33 | 2.18 | 82 |
| Beverley | 0.41 | 11 | 1.02 | 27 |
| Boothferry | 0.30 | 12 | 0.74 | 30 |
| Bradford | 5.44 | 212 | 13.55 | 528 |
| Calderdale | 1.21 | 47 | 3.01 | 117 |
| Cleethorpes | 0.37 | 17 | 0.91 | 42 |
| Craven | 0.19 | 7 | 0.47 | 17 |
| Doncaster | 1.59 | 70 | 3.95 | 174 |
| East Yorkshire | 0.43 | 25 | 1.06 | 62 |
| Glanford | 0.31 | 16 | 0.76 | 40 |
| Great Grimsby | 1.11 | 51 | 2.76 | 127 |
| Hambelton | 0.38 | 16 | 0.95 | 40 |
| Harrogate | 0.82 | 31 | 2.03 | 77 |
| Holderness | 0.25 | 15 | 0.63 | 37 |
| Kingston upon Hull | 1.84 | 87 | 4.59 | 217 |
| Kirklees | 3.13 | 116 | 7.79 | 289 |
| Leeds | 4.71 | 231 | 11.73 | 576 |
| Richmondshire | 0.25 | 11 | 0.62 | 27 |
| Rotherham | 0.58 | 30 | 1.44 | 75 |
| Ryedale | 0.44 | 22 | 1.11 | 55 |
| Scarborough | 0.55 | 23 | 1.38 | 57 |
| Scunthorpe | 0.16 | 10 | 0.39 | 25 |
| Selby | 0.37 | 40 | 0.92 | 100 |
| Sheffield | 2.79 | 121 | 6.94 | 302 |
| Wakefield | 1.13 | 52 | 2.81 | 130 |
| York | 0.67 | 42 | 1.67 | 105 |

Further social lettings will also be made available through vacancies in local authority and housing association properties; through the Housing Corporation's new-build programme for shared rent/sale; through the corporation's other home ownership initiatives and rehabilitation; through housing association developments funded by local authority housing association grant; and through the cash incentive scheme.

**Mr. Hinchliffe:** To ask the Secretary of State for the Environment if he will list the number of applicants on council waiting lists for each local authority in Yorkshire and Humberside. [25357]

**Mr. Robert B. Jones:** Local authorities in England report the numbers of households on their housing waiting lists at 1 April each year in their annual housing investment programme returns.

The latest available data for individual local authorities in Yorkshire and Humberside can be found in section B of the "1994 HIP1 All Items Print", a copy of which is in the Library.

### English Partnerships

**Mr. Evenett:** To ask the Secretary of State for the Environment when English Partnerships' management statement and financial memorandum will be available [26195]

**Mr. Curry:** Both documents have today been placed in the Library. The management statement defines the strategic relationship between the Secretary of State and English Partnerships, and the financial memorandum set out the framework for financial control within which English Partnerships must operate.

### Housing Repairs

**Mr. Purchase:** To ask the Secretary of State for the Environment how many cases have been brought in England under housing and public health legislation to oblige local authorities to (a) carry out essential repairs to their own dwellings and (b) to give essential repairs grants to owners of private dwelling in each year since 1990. [25803]

**Mr. Robert B Jones** [*holding answer Tuesday 24 May 1995:*]: The local Government and Housing Act 1989 requires local authorities to give mandatory renovation grants to owners of unfit private dwellings. Mandatory grants given annually since 1990 to the nearest thousand, are:

1990 : 2.6

1991 : 29.7

1992 : 35.5

1993 : 37.4

1994 : 37.8

The Department does not collect data on the number of repairs local authorities are obliged to carry out to their own dwellings under housing and public health legislation.

# OVERSEAS DEVELOPMENT ADMINISTRATION

## Railway Projects

**Mr. Bayley:** To ask the Secretary of State for Foreign and Commonwealth Affairs if he will list the railway infrastructure and rolling stock projects supported in the last five years by (a) Overseas Development Administration bilateral aid, (b) EU aid and (c) other multilateral donors to which the Overseas Development Administration contributes giving the date each project was approved, its value and the European companies which obtained contracts as suppliers or consultants to those projects. [24951]

**Mr. Baldry:** Details of railway infrastructure and rolling stock projects supported by ODA in the last five years have been placed in the Libraries of the House. These involve only British companies. ODA is unable to list the projects supported by the European Union and other multilateral donors.

## Loan to Grant Conversion

**Mr. Foulkes:** To ask the Secretary of State for Foreign and Commonwealth Affairs what is the cost in each of the last five years of converting Overseas Development Administration loans to developing countries into grants; and whether conversion of Overseas Development Administration loans into grants is registered as expenditure in the year in which conversion is made. [25376]

**Mr. Baldry:** The cost in each of the last five years of converting Overseas Development Administration loans to developing countries into grants is shown on the attached table; conversion of Overseas Development Administration loans into grants is not registered in the year in which conversion is made. The repayment amounts are cancelled over the period of the original loan repayment dates.

*Debt cancellation*

|  | | | £ Thousands |
|  | Principal | Interest | Total |
|---|---|---|---|
| 1990–91 | 21,424 | 637 | 22,061 |
| 1991–92 | 20,925 | 489 | 21,414 |
| 1992–93 | 19,717 | 382 | 20,099 |
| 1993–94 | 21,995 | 1,698 | 23,694 |
| 1994–95 | 25,041 | 3,104 | 28,144 |

## Aid and Trade Projects

**Miss Lestor:** To ask the Secretary of State for Foreign and Commonwealth Affairs how many aid and trade provision projects were refused or postponed solely on financial grounds in 1993–94. [25736]

**Mr. Baldry:** No aid and trade provision projects were refused or postponed solely on financial grounds in 1993–94.

## South Africa

**Mr. Caborn:** To ask the Secretary of State for Foreign and Commonwealth Affairs if he will seek an amendment to the draft negotiating mandate on future relations between the European Union and South Africa to enable South African bodies to tender for contracts under the VIII European development fund on the preferential terms available to the African, Caribbean and Pacific group states under the Lomé convention. [25612]

**Mr. Baldry** *[holding answer 23 May 1995]:* There are good prospects that the negotiating mandate on future relations between the European Union and South Africa will enable South African bodies to tender for contracts under the European development fund. The idea of granting to South Africa the ACP's preferential status in EDF tenders, however, raises a number of additional issues which are still under discussion between member states in Brussels.

## Population Control

**Mr. Alton:** To ask the Secretary of State for Foreign and Commonwealth Affairs if he will list those countries in which the Overseas Development Administration has funded family planning initiatives together with the number of projects, their nature and the amount spent in each case for the last year for which figures are available. [25305]

**Mr. Baldry** *[holding answer 22 May 1995]:* The table lists the countries in which ODA supported reproductive health projects in 1994 through the bilateral aid programme, together with the number of such projects, where expenditure exceeded £50,000 per project, and the total amount spent for each country. These projects aim to enable men and women to have better access to family planning; enable women to experience safer motherhood and childbirth; and to improve sexual health. In addition, ODA contributed £19,435,000 in 1994 to the United Nations Population Fund, the International Planned Parenthood Federation and special programmes of the World Health Organisation for population and reproductive health work.

*Reproductive health projects—calendar year 1994*

| Country | Number of projects | Total expenditure (£) |
|---|---|---|
| Bangladesh | 5 | 3,551,847 |
| India | 5 | 1,973,618 |
| Pakistan | 9 | 1,976,910 |
| Malaysia | 1 | 131,026 |
| Sri Lanka | 1 | 102,735 |
| Cambodia | 1 | 135,227 |
| El Salvador | 1 | 80,000 |
| Nicaragua | 1 | 93,548 |
| Mexico | 1 | 752,366 |
| Peru | 2 | 1,399,441 |
| Oceania Regional | 1 | 214,211 |
| Russian Federation | 1 | 143,475 |
| Africa Regional | 1 | 76,828 |
| Burkina Faso | 1 | 81,764 |
| Ethiopia | 2 | 125,414 |
| Ghana | 2 | 197,250 |
| Kenya | 4 | 1,454,581 |
| Nigeria | 1 | 57,390 |
| Tanzania | 4 | 1,287,399 |
| Togo | 1 | 75,000 |
| Uganda | 4 | 520,712 |
| Malawi | 7 | 809,200 |
| Sierra Leone | 1 | 65,304 |
| South Africa | 1 | 120,016 |
| Zaire | 2 | 50,951 |
| Zambia | 2 | 252,101 |
| Zimbabwe | 2 | 737,598 |
| Total | 63 | 16,463,918.00 |

## DEFENCE

### Flight Simulators

**Mr. Gordon Prentice:** To ask the Secretary of State for Defence to what extent flight simulators are used to train RAF jet pilots as an alternative to flying using terrain-following radar. [25156]

**Mr. Soames:** Flight simulators are used for initial and continuation procedural training of crews in the use of terrain following radar; simulators are not, however, sufficiently sophisticated at present to provide a realistic alternative to low level flying training.

### Gulf War Medical Assessment Programme

**Dr. David Clark:** To ask the Secretary of State for Defence how many members of the armed forces have taken part in his Department's Gulf war medical assessment programme to date; how many of these have since left the services; and for what reason. [25165]

**Mr. Soames:** To date, a total of 246 individuals have been medically examined as part of the Department's Gulf war medical assessment programme, 70 of whom were serving members of the armed forces at the time of their appointment. As it is not relevant to the conduct of the programme, information is not at present available on subsequent changes of status. I will write to the hon. Member when it has been collected.

**Dr. David Clark:** To ask the Secretary of State for Defence, when Colonel Johnson left his post in the Gulf war medical assessment programme and for what reason; and what is the name of his replacement. [25166]

**Mr. Soames:** Arrangements were made earlier this year for the temporary attachment of an additional consultant, Colonel J. H. Johnston, to the Gulf war medical assessment programme in order to reduce patient waiting times. He participated in the programme between 22 February 1995 and 23 March 1995, by which time waiting times has been brought within acceptable limits. Colonel Johnston will again participate in the programme during the month of June 1995 to cover for a period of leave and other professional commitments of the resident consultant physician.

### Draft Reserve Forces Legislation

**Dr. David Clark:** To ask the Secretary of State for Defence how many representations to date he has received concerning the draft Reserve Forces Bill. [25781]

**Mr. Soames:** The draft reserve forces legislation was published on 30 March, and the consultation period continues until Thursday 15 June 1995. By Monday 22 May, some 217 written responses had been received. In addition, many of those present at the Department's series of presentations on the Bill have taken the opportunity to make comments orally.

### Bosnia

**Dr. David Clark:** To ask the Secretary of State for Defence, how many breaches of the no-fly zone in Bosnia have been recorded in each of the last three months. [25782]

**Mr. Soames:** NATO published figures show that between 1 February and 30 April there were 1,283 reported violations. The monthly breakdown is as follows:

February : 399

March : 292

April : 592

A further 242 violations have been reported up to 15 May.

**Dr. David Clark:** To ask the Secretary of State for Defence, how many breaches of the ceasefire in Sarajevo have been detected by the British army mortar locating troop in each of the last three months. [25783]

**Mr. Soames:** British mortar and artillery locating personnel in Sarajevo have recorded a total of 683 incidents over the last three months which have involved the firing of one or more mortar or artillery rounds. The figures are broken down as follows:

March : 63

April : 74

May : 546 (figures to 19 May)

**Dr. David Clark:** To ask the Secretary of State for Defence when he announced the decision not to replace Britain's contribution to UNPROFOR based in Gorazde; and if he will state the reasons for this decision. [25784]

**Mr. Soames:** The UN were informed in April of the Government's intention not to replace British troops in Gorazde when the present detachment's tour of duty expires in September. By then, British troops will have been in the isolated enclave for 18 months and the Government believe it is time for another UN contingent to take on the responsibility.

### Corporal Neil Hughes

**Dr. David Clark:** To ask the Secretary of State for Defence when the board of inquiry took place into the death of Corporal Neil Hughes of the Duke of Wellington Regiment; what was the result of the board of inquiry; what conclusions have been reached as to the responsibility for the death of Corporal Hughes; and if compensation has been made to the widow of Corporal Hughes. [25785]

**Mr. Soames:** A board of inquiry was not held, as all the facts relating to this matter were established during the coroner's inquest and subsequent civil police inquiries. The case was referred to the Crown Prosecution Service, which decided to take no further action. The compensation claim from the widow of Corporal Hughes has been accepted and an interim payment agreed.

### Lance Corporal Robert Strong

**Dr. David Clark:** To ask the Secretary of State for Defence what factors underlay the imprisonment of Lance Corporal Robert Strong, formerly of the Parachute Regiment; where he was imprisoned; and what assistance and advice was offered to Lance Corporal Strong following the incident in which he was shot. [25787]

**Mr. Soames:** Lance Corporal Strong has never been imprisoned. He received treatment at the Queen Elizabeth military hospital Woolwich between February and June 1993; and prior to his medical discharge, in line with my Department's policy, he would have been given resettlement advice including information on how to make a claim for benefits.

## Injuries due to Negligence

**Dr. David Clark:** To ask the Secretary of State for Defence what forms of assistance and advice are made available to members of the armed forces who have been injured as a result of the negligent discharge of weapons. [25786]

**Mr. Soames:** All personnel who are injured while serving in Her Majesty's forces are given appropriate treatment by the armed forces medical service, including psychiatric help if necessary. Comprehensive assistance is given to all those disabled however the injury is sustained. Assistance includes intreatment, rehabilitation, and, wherever necessary, retraining and resettlement into civilian life.

Where death or injury is attributable to service, benefits may be paid from both the Department of Social Security's war pensions scheme and from my Department's armed forces pension scheme. The definition of attributability is widely drawn; accidental death or injury in training or on duty is normally accepted as attributable to service.

Following the passing of the Crown Proceedings (Armed Forces) Act 1987 serving and former service personnel have had the same rights as those in civilian life and are able to make a claim in common law against my Department for compensation for personal accident or injury through negligence.

The procedure for anyone contemplating a claim for compensation is set out in a Defence Council instruction published each year which specifically recommends that prospective claimants approach the Royal British Legion initially as the organisation best placed to liaise with my Department's claims department.

# NORTHERN IRELAND

## Abortion Law

**Mr. Robathan:** To ask the Secretary of State for Northern Ireland whether he is yet in a position to respond to the recommendations on abortion law in Northern Ireland made by the Standing Advisory Commission on Human Rights. [24870]

**Mr. Moss:** The Secretary of State wrote to the chairman of the commission on 10 May indicating that he does not propose to suggest any changes in the law at present. A copy of the Secretary of State's letter has been placed in the Library.

## Home Improvement Grants

**Mr. McGrady:** To ask the Secretary of State for Northern Ireland what was the budgetary allocation in respect of home improvement grants to each Housing Executive grants office since 1 April 1993. [24763]

**Sir John Wheeler:** This is a matter for the Northern Ireland Housing Executive, but the chief executive has advised me that the expenditure figures for each financial year were as follows:

| | | £ million |
|---|---|---|
| | Expenditure | |
| Office | 1993–94 | 1994–95 |
| Belfast[1] | 9.6 | 9.3 |
| Newtownards | 2.0 | 1.9 |
| Lisburn | 2.2 | 2.5 |
| Newry | 3.2 | 3.8 |
| Craigavon | 2.6 | 3.3 |
| Ballymena | 1.8 | 1.6 |
| Ballyclare | 1.4 | 1.2 |
| Coleraine | 1.5 | 1.6 |
| Londonderry | 3.2 | 2.6 |
| Omagh | 3.0 | 3.9 |
| Fermanagh | 1.9 | 2.3 |
| Total | 32.4 | 34.0 |

[1] For budgetary purposes three Belfast offices are treated as one unit.

**Mr. McGrady:** To ask the Secretary of State for Northern Ireland what was the budgetary allocation in respect of home improvement grants to each grants office for the 1995–96 financial year. [24764]

**Sir John Wheeler:** This is a matter for the Northern Ireland Housing Executive, but the chief executive has advised me that the allocations for the financial year 1995–96 are as follows:

| | Allocation |
|---|---|
| Office | £ million |
| Belfast[1] | 10.5 |
| Newtownards | 2.6 |
| Lisburn | 3.0 |
| Newry | 4.4 |
| Craigavon | 4.2 |
| Ballymena | 2.6 |
| Ballyclare | 1.4 |
| Coleraine | 1.5 |
| Londonderry | 4.3 |
| Omagh | 3.4 |
| Fermanagh | 4.1 |
| Total | 42.0 |

[1] For budgetary purposes 3 Belfast offices are treated as one unit.

## Environmental Improvement Schemes

**Mr. McGrady:** To ask the Secretary of State for Northern Ireland what environmental improvement schemes have been funded for the 1995–96 financial year; and what have been the financial amounts allocated to each scheme. [24766]

**Sir John Wheeler:** The environmental improvement schemes which have been funded in the 1995–96 financial year are as follows:

*Environmental improvement schemes to be undertaken or completed in financial year 1995–96*

| | 1995–96 |
|---|---|
| Town/Scheme | £000 |
| Dromore Town Centre/Conservation Area | 14 |
| Markethill | 17 |
| Town Hall, Newry | 7 |
| Riehhill | 71 |
| Loughgall | 13.5 |
| Market Square/Town Centre, Downpatrick | 6 |
| Lower Irish Street, Downpatrick | 30 |
| Market Street/Bow Street, Lisburn | 5 |
| Castlewellan | 25 |

*Environmental improvement schemes to be undertaken or completed in financial year 1995–96*

| Town/Scheme | 1995–96 £000 |
|---|---|
| Market Place, Carrickfergus | 6 |
| Town Centre/Taxi Rank, Antrim | 1 |
| Bowling Green, Strabane | 13.5 |
| Mews Lane, Enniskillen | 14 |
| War Memorial, Omagh | 2.5 |
| Churches Avenue, Omagh | 20 |
| Market Square, Dungannon | 6 |
| Foundry Lane, Omagh | 12 |
| High Street/Town Centre, Ballymoney | 5 |
| Dunluce Avenue, Portrush | 85 |
| | |
| *Londonderry* | |
| Walled City conservation area phase 5D | 20 |
| Foyleside A (Foyle Street) | 242.5 |
| Foyleside B (Orchard Street, Newmarket Street, Bridge Street, Water Street) | 284.5 |
| Bank Place | 84.5 |
| Artillery Street | 141 |
| Strand Road Upper | 50 |
| Meadowbank River Scheme | 50 |
| Additional cleansing/graffiti removal etc | 50 |
| Union Hall Place | 22.5 |
| | |
| *Belfast* | |
| Donegall Square | 1,400 |

**Mr. McGrady:** To ask the Secretary of State for Northern Ireland what has been the budgetary allocation in respect of environmental improvement schemes in each financial year since 1 April 1990. [24767]

**Sir John Wheeler:** The information is as follows:

| | £ million |
|---|---|
| 1990–91 | 5.6 |
| 1991–92 | 6.4 |
| 1992–93 | 4.6 |
| 1993–94 | 3.5 |
| 1994–95 | 3.5 |
| 1995–96 | 2.7 |

**Mr. McGrady:** To ask the Secretary of State for Northern Ireland what environmental improvement schemes were funded in each financial year since 1 April 1990, and what were the financial amounts allocated to each scheme. [24768]

**Sir John Wheeler:** The following list sets out the environmental improvement schemes and the financial amounts allocated to each scheme from 1 April 1993 only. Information in respect of earlier years could be provided only at disproportionate cost.

*Environmental Improvement Schemes Funded 1st April 1993—31 March 1995*

| Town/Scheme | 1993/94 £000 | 1994–95 £000 |
|---|---|---|
| Dromore Town Centre/Conservation Area | 72 | 86 |
| Market Square, Armagh | 1 | 8 |
| St Patrick's, Armagh | 153 | 28 |
| Markethill | 2 | 54 |
| Town Hall, Newry | 122 | 18 |
| Canal Bank, Newry | 13 | 3 |
| Lurgan Town Centre | 26 | 42 |

*Environmental Improvement Schemes Funded 1st April 1993—31 March 1995*

| Town/Scheme | 1993/94 £000 | 1994–95 £000 |
|---|---|---|
| Hill Street/John Mitchell Place, Newry | - | 70 |
| Richhill | — | 4 |
| Loughgall | — | 12 |
| Spruce-Up, Craigavon | — | 2 |
| Project Office, Newry | — | 3 |
| West Street/Church Place, Portadown | — | 3 |
| Queens Parade, Bangor | 171 | 27 |
| Down District Council | 2 | — |
| Floodlighting, Lisburn | 1 | 9 |
| Market Street/Town Centre, Downpatrick | 1 | 64 |
| Fair Green, Ballynahinch | 33 | 106 |
| Lower Irish Street, Downpatrick | 73 | – |
| Market Street/Bow Street, Lisburn | — | 94 |
| Spruce-Up, Downpatrick | — | 17 |
| Lighting Scheme, Donaghadee | — | 23 |
| Killyleagh | — | 4 |
| Provision of Town Parks, D/patrick | — | 26 |
| Minor Scheme—Newtownards, Bangor, Holywood | — | 18 |
| Heritage Plaza, Carrickfergus | 77 | 13 |
| Rainey Street, Magherafelt | 7 | — |
| Market Place, Carrickfergus | 154 | 14 |
| Irish Gate, Carrickfergus | 4 | 2 |
| Draperstown | 23 | 120 |
| Whitehead | 5 | 9 |
| Spruce-Up, Ballymena | 9 | 30 |
| Joymount, Carrickfergus | — | 5 |
| Town Centre/Taxi Rank, Antrim | — | 34 |
| Fairhill Square, Ballymena | — | 5 |
| Phase II, Carnlough | — | 12 |
| Bowling Green, Strabane | 5 | 52 |
| Mews Lane, Enniskillen | 96 | 66 |
| Linear Parks, Dungannon | 12 | — |
| Abercorn Square, Strabane | — | 6 |
| War Memorial, Omagh | 1 | — |
| Churches Avenue, Omagh | 29 | 9 |
| Spruce-Up, Omagh | 3 | 17 |
| Town Centre, Cookstown | — | 15 |
| Market Square, Dungannon | — | 5 |
| Hanover Square, Coagh | — | 66 |
| Foundry Lane, Omagh | — | 1 |
| Cushendall | — | 6 |
| Castle Street, Ballycastle | 17 | — |
| O'Connor Memorial,Ballycastle | 1 | — |
| High Street/Town Centre, Ballymoney | 20 | 135 |
| Cricket Link, Ballymoney | 60 | — |
| Dunluce Avenue, Portrush | — | 186 |
| Spruce-Up, Northern | — | 9 |
| Project Office, Ballymoney | — | 10 |
| | | |
| *Belfast* | | |
| St Anne's Square | 30 | 39 |
| Chichester Street, Tree Planting | 17 | 3 |
| Blackstaff Square | 20 | 1 |
| Marquis Street Open Space | 31 | — |
| Royal Avenue | 23 | — |
| Belfast Harbour Local Plan | 220 | 299 |
| Falls Road SSO | 105 | 40 |
| City Centre Floodlighting Scheme | 41 | — |
| Pottinger's Entry | 3 | — |
| St Peter's Cathedral | 211 | 189 |
| Bedford Street | 10 | — |
| Henry Place | 17 | — |
| Craven Street Landscaping | 16 | — |
| Donegall Square | 58 | 8 |
| BBC Cliftonville Playing Fields | 18 | — |
| NIHE David St/Conway Street Junction | 5 | — |
| NIHE Roden Street | 5 | — |
| Arthur Square Bandstand | — | 17 |
| Castle Lane | — | 118 |
| Traffic Calming Studies | 7 | 18 |

*Environmental Improvement Schemes Funded*
*1st April 1993—31 March 1995*

| Town/Scheme | 1993/94 £000 | 1994–95 £000 |
|---|---|---|
| Suffolk Road Apartments | — | 16 |
| QCA Lighting | — | 50 |
| Planning MBW Schemes | — | 225 |
| NIHE Upper Library Street | — | 24 |
| Urban Forestry Schemes | 60 | 79 |
| Maintenance of Landscape Areas | 146 | 228 |
| Belfast CC Maintenance | 123 | 68 |
| Graffitti | 100 | 100 |
| | | |
| *Londonderry* | | |
| Walled City Conservation Area Phase 5D | 23.5 | 107 |
| Market Street | 6.5 | — |
| Carlisle Square | 7 | — |
| Dorman's Wharf | 19 | 14.5 |
| Waterloo Street Upper (Part) | 45.5 | — |
| City Walls, Phase 5C | 102.5 | — |
| Clooney Terrace | 28.5 | — |
| Gartan Square | 11 | — |
| Floodlighting City Gates | 8 | — |
| General Soft Landscaping | 36 | — |
| City Walls, Phase 5D | 107 | — |
| Victoria Market Car Park/ Strand Road | 68.5 | 34 |
| Union Hall Place | 36 | 62.5 |
| Additional Cleansing/Graffiti Removal etc | 86.5 | 85 |
| City Walls Interpretive Plaques | 18.5 | — |
| Direction Signs | 4 | — |
| Londonery Lighting Vision | 51.5 | — |
| Miscellaneous Minor Projects (by Roads Service etc) | 127 | 44.5 |
| William Street | 112 | 147.5 |
| Madam's Bank | 26 | 12.5 |
| Expressway Central Reservation | 12.5 | 14.5 |
| City Walls Interpretive Strategy | 18.5 | 85.5 |
| Foyleside A (Foyle Street) | — | 57.5 |
| Foyleside B (Orchard Street, Newmarket Street, Bridge Street, Water Street | — | 180.5 |
| Painting etc (Street Furniture) | — | 9 |
| Bank Place | — | 10.5 |
| Additional Street Furniture (Litter bins, fingerposts etc) | — | 23 |
| City Walls Lighting | — | 6.5 |
| Artillery Street | — | 4 |

### St. Columban's College, Kilkeel

**Mr. McGrady:** to ask the Secretary of State for Northern Ireland what plans he has to make provisions for a special needs unit at St. Columban's college, Kilkeel, Co Down.     [24775]

**Mr. Ancram:** Responsibility for making proposals to my Department to establish new special units at Catholic maintained schools rests with the education and library boards in conjunction with the Council for Catholic Maintained Schools. No proposal has been made to establish such a unit at St. Columban's college, Kilkeel.

### Compulsory Competitive Tendering

**Mr. Spellar:** To ask the Secretary of State for Northern Ireland what representations he has received from local authorities regarding compulsory competitive tendering in the last two years.     [25238]

**Sir John Wheeler:** In the last two years representations about compulsory competitive tendering have been received from Ards borough council, Ballymoney borough council, Banbridge district council, Belfast city council, Castlereagh borough council, Limavady borough council, Lisburn borough council, Newry and Mourne district council, Newtownabbey borough council and North Down borough council. These representations, which were made following the issue of draft regulations to all district councils on 12 October 1994 setting out the proposed arrangements for the second round of compulsory competitive tendering, sought an abandonment of compulsory competitive tendering or, alternatively, an increase in the "deminimis" level of £100,000 and changes to the phasing arrangements. In addition, during the Prime Minister's meeting with the mayors, chairmen and chief executives of district councils on 23 January, the mayor of Ballymena borough council advocated a moratorium on compulsory competitive tendering.

### Job Losses

**Ms Hodge:** To ask the Secretary of State for Northern Ireland how many posts were lost in *(a)* the Northern Ireland Office and *(b)* agencies for which the Northern Ireland Office is responsible, listing the total lost posts agency by agency in (i) 1993–94 and (ii) 1994–95; and how many posts lost are proposed to be lost in 1995–96.     [25071]

**Sir John Wheeler:** Information on the number of staff in the Northern Ireland Office, as published in the Supply Estimates, is as follows. Figures for 1992–93 are included to allow comparison with 1993–94.

| Year | NIO | Compensation Agency | Northern Ireland Prison Service[1] | Total |
|---|---|---|---|---|
| 1992–93 | 4,640 | 145 | — | 4,785 |
| 1993–94 | 4,730 | 150 | — | 4,880 |
| 1994–95 | 4,810 | 150 | — | 4,960 |
| 1995–96 | 1,080 | 150 | 3,590 | 4,820 |

[1] Launched as an agency in April 1995.

The figures include prison officers and are rounded to the nearest five.

### Bus Companies

**Mr. Worthington:** To ask the Secretary of State for Northern Ireland what proposals he has to give greater commercial freedom to Ulsterbus and Citybus.     [25725]

**Sir John Wheeler:** None.

**Mr. Worthington:** To ask the Secretary of State for Northern Ireland what proposals he has to improve the speed of response of his Department so as to meet the commercial needs of Ulsterbus and Citybus.     [25726]

**Sir John Wheeler:** The regulatory framework which governs the relationship between the Department of the Environment for Northern Ireland and the transport companies is kept under constant review to ensure its continued effectiveness.

**Mr. Worthington:** To ask the Secretary of State for Northern Ireland nif he will make a statement on the age and quality of the fleets of Ulsterbus and Citybus relative to deregulated services in Great Britain.     [25727]

**Sir John Wheeler:** The different methodology used in preparing such statistics in Northern Ireland and Great Britain makes comparison difficult. At March 1994 the average age of the Ulsterbus fleet was just under eight years old and that of the Citybus fleet 8.75.

In Great Britain, at December 1993, 19 per cent. of the fleet was less than four years old, 27 per cent. between four and seven years old, 20 per cent. between eight and 11 years old, leaving 34 per cent. 12 years old or over. Information as to the respective quality is not available.

## Environmentally Sensitive Areas

**Dr. Strang:** To ask the Secretary of State for Northern Ireland how many hectares of land *(a)* are eligible for entry into each environmentally sensitive area in Northern Ireland and *(b)* have been entered in each tier of each environmentally sensitive area in Northern Ireland. [25791]

**Mr. Ancram:** The information is as follows:

| ESA | Eligible area (hectares) | Tier 1 | Under agreement Tier 2 | Tier 3 |
|---|---|---|---|---|
| Antrim Coast, Glens and Rathlin | 34,600 | 9,500 | 780 | — |
| Slieve Gullion | 13,800 | 90 | 10 | — |
| Mourne Mountains and Slieve Croob | 29,000 | 5,710 | 180 | — |
| West Fermanagh and Erne Lakeland | 57,400 | 7,290 | 3,060 | 130 |
| Sperrins | 82,950 | 3,090 | 2,240 | — |

## Crown Buildings (Fire Safety)

**Mr. Spellar:** To ask the Secretary of State for Northern Ireland what plans he has to allow the Northern Ireland Fire Brigade to assume responsibility for the fire safety inspections and issue of fire certificates for Crown buildings in Northern Ireland. [25866]

**Sir John Wheeler:** This matter is currently under consideration.

## RUC Annual Report

**Mr. McLoughlin:** To ask the Secretary of State for Northern Ireland when he will lay before the House the annual report for 1994 of the chief constable of the Royal Ulster Constabulary. [26386]

**Sir Patrick Mayhew:** Copies of the chief constable's annual report 1994 have today been placed in the Library. It is a general report on the carrying out by the RUC of its functions during 1994 which is submitted to the Police Authority for Northern Ireland and transmitted to me for laying before Parliament in accordance with section 15 of the Police Act (Northern Ireland) 1970.

# SCOTLAND

## George Beattie Case

**23. Mr. Hood:** To ask the Secretary of State for Scotland if he will make a statement on the results of his investigations into the new evidence given to the Under-Secretary of State during the Adjournment debate on the George Beattie case on 29 March; and if he will make a statement. [24247]

**Lord James Douglas-Hamilton:** The documents handed to me by the hon. Member on 29 March are being examined and relevant inquiries are in hand. The hon. Member will be kept informed of developments.

## Scottish Economy

**24. Mr. McKelvey:** To ask the Secretary of State for Scotland what plans he has to meet the Scottish TUC to discuss the Scottish economy. [24248]

**Mr. Kynoch:** My right hon. Friend meets the Scottish TUC from time to time and officials maintain regular contacts. My right hon. Friend is therefore kept fully aware of the STUC's views on all matters concerning the Scottish economy.

**33. Mr. Salmond:** To ask the Secretary of State for Scotland when he last met the Scottish Council Development and Industry to discuss trends in the Scottish economy; and if he will make a statement. [24257]

**Mr. Kynoch:** Scottish Office Ministers and officials maintain regular contact with the Scottish Council Development and Industry to discuss economic and other issues. My right hon. Friend last met the Scottish Council Development and Industry when he addressed the annual dinner of the council's London committee on 22 March 1995.

## Scottish Homes

**25. Mr. Michael J. Martin:** To ask the Secretary of State for Scotland when he will next meet Scottish Homes to discuss transfer of property; and if he will make a statement. [24249]

**Lord James Douglas-Hamilton:** My right hon. Friend has no plans to meet Scottish Homes to discuss transfer of property. He issued guidance to Scottish Homes on this matter following which it published procedures for the disposal of its stock.

**Mr. Donohoe:** To ask the Secretary of State for Scotland, pursuant to his answer of 21 March, *Official Report*, column *174*, on Scottish Homes, when the hon. Member for Cunninghame, South can expect a reply from Sir James Mellon. [25352]

**Lord James Douglas-Hamilton:** Sir James Mellon wrote to the hon. Member on 28 March and sent me a copy of his letter. I have arranged for a further copy of the correspondence to be sent to the hon. Member.

## Voluntary Organisations

**26. Sir David Knox:** To ask the Secretary of State for Scotland what was the value of grants from his Department to voluntary organisations in each of the last three years. [24250]

**Lord James Douglas-Hamilton:** Grants paid to voluntary organisations by the Scottish Office in the last three years for which information is available were £20.7 million in 1991–92, £25.7 million in 1992–93 and £21.6 million in 1993–94.

## Engineering Jobs

**27. Mr. Dunnachie:** To ask the Secretary of State for Scotland what plans he has to meet the Scottish TUC to discuss the continuing loss of skilled engineering jobs in Scotland. [24251]

**Mr. Kynoch:** My right hon. Friend meets the Scottish TUC from time to time and officials maintain regular contacts. My right hon. Friend is therefore kept fully aware of the STUC's views on all matters concerning the Scottish economy.

### Waste Disposal

28. **Mr. McAvoy:** To ask the Secretary of State for Scotland what proposals he has to encourage local authorities to find alternatives to landfill as a method of waste disposal. [24252]

**Sir Hector Monro:** The Government favour waste management methods such as recycling and incineration with energy recovery which are higher in the waste management hierarchy than landfill. By requiring local authorities to prepare and update waste disposal plans and waste recycling plans the Government ensures they keep their waste management options under review. Together with the landfill tax which we intend to introduce, this will encourage authorities to respond to our target for recycling household waste.

### Local Government Finance

29. **Mr. Ernie Ross:** To ask the Secretary of State for Scotland when he last met Convention of Scottish Local Authorities to discuss local government finance. [24253]

**Mr. Kynoch:** My right hon. Friend last met representatives of the Convention of Scottish Local Authorities to discuss local government finance on 20 January. He also addressed the convention's annual conference on 10 March.

31. **Mrs. Adams:** To ask the Secretary of State for Scotland when he next plans to meet the Convention of Scottish Local Authorities to discuss local government finance. [24255]

**Mr. Kynoch:** My right hon. Friend and I are due to meet representatives of the Convention of Scottish Local Authorities on 12 June as part of the normal consultation on local government finance matters.

### Tree Planting

30. **Mr. Pawsey:** To ask the Secretary of State for Scotland if he will set out the tree planting programme for England, Scotland and Wales for 1995–96. [24254]

**Sir Hector Monro:** As announced in the Government's expenditure plans, we expect about 38,000 hectares of woodland to be planted in 1995–96, including restocking.

### Strengths of the Union

32. **Mr. Thurnham:** To ask the Secretary of State for Scotland what recent representations he has received about maintaining the strengths of the Union; and if he will make a statement. [24256]

**Mr. Lang:** I have received a number of expressions of support for the maintenance of the Union.

### South East Asia

34. **Mr. Norman Hogg:** To ask the Secretary of State for Scotland when he next expects to visit south-east Asia to promote Scotland for inward investment and jobs; and if he will make a statement. [24258]

**Mr. Kynoch:** My right hon. Friend intends to visit Japan later this year to promote Scotland as a location for inward investment but he has no plans at present to visit South East Asia. The benefits of Scotland as a business location are promoted within South East Asia by Locate in Scotland's representatives in Taiwan and Singapore.

### Forestry Policy

35. **Sir Thomas Arnold:** To ask the Secretary of State for Scotland if he will make a further statement about forestry policy. [24259]

**Sir Hector Monro:** We remain committed to the forestry policy set out in "Forestry Policy for Great Britain" and "Sustainable Forestry: The UK Programme", copies of which are in the Library of the House.

### Combating Crime

36. **Mr. McMaster:** To ask the Secretary of State for Scotland when he next plans to meet representatives of Scottish police forces to discuss combating crime.

**Lord James Douglas-Hamilton:** My right hon. Friend meets representatives of Scottish police forces from time to time, most recently on 10 February.

### Private Finance Initiative

**Mr. Darling:** To ask the Secretary of State for Scotland if he will list those capital projects within the NHS in Scotland that are currently being considered under the private finance initiative; and if he will make a statement. [24242]

**Lord James Douglas-Hamilton:** All capital projects currently being proposed in the NHS in Scotland have been considered, or are being considered, as opportunities under the private finance initiative. A list of these projects has been placed in the Library of the House.

### Sports Facilities

**Mr. Canavan:** To ask the Secretary of State for Scotland if he will make a statement about improvement of sports facilities in Scotland. [24230]

**Sir Hector Monro:** The provision of sports facilities in Scotland has been significantly enhanced in recent years. More, however, remains to be done. The national lottery now provides a marvellous opportunity to develop a wider range of facilities to meet the nation's sporting needs.

### Temazepam

**Mr. McMaster:** To ask the Secretary of State for Scotland when he next plans to meet representatives of the Advisory Committee on the Misuse of Drugs to discuss the rescheduling of Temazepam; and if he will make a statement. [24119]

**Lord James Douglas-Hamilton:** My right hon. Friend has no plans for such a meeting. The reply that my right hon. Friend the Lord President of the Council gave to my hon. Friend the Member for Ayr (Mr. Gallie) on 10 May, *Official Report*, column *756*, described the immediate steps being taken to reduce the misuse of Temazepam and confirmed that careful consideration is being given to the advisory council's recommendation on rescheduling the drug.

### Police (Body Armour)

**Mrs. Roche:** To ask the Secretary of State for Scotland what plans he has to ensure that all police officers are supplied with body armour.  [25143]

**Lord James Douglas-Hamilton:** It is for individual chief constables to take decisions about providing body armour for their officers. The Scottish Office would pay police grant in the usual way at 51 per cent. of the expenditure on any such provision.

### Appeals

**Mr. McMaster:** To ask the Secretary of State for Scotland how many appeals against conviction and applications for pardon or the prerogative of mercy have been lodged with his office in each of the past 10 years; how long, on average, it took to process each one; how many are still outstanding; how much, on average, such cases cost in terms of time, salaries and expenses for all Government and local government authorities, including the Scottish Office, the Crown Office, procurators fiscal offices and police; and if he will make a statement.  [25158]

**Lord James Douglas-Hamilton:** The number of cases in respect of which representations were received by my right hon. Friend are as follows:

    1984: 54
    1985: 43
    1986: 39
    1987: 61
    1988: 46
    1989: 60
    1990: 39
    1991: 54
    1992: 58
    1993: 52
    1994: 30

Representations in respect of 20 cases are at present under consideration. The average time taken to process cases received and cleared in 1994 was 55 working days. Additionally, on 1 January 1995 there were five major cases which had been under consideration for more than 12 months. Comparable figures for earlier years are not available because statistics were not kept in that form. The costs of processing cases are not available in the form requested.

### Job Losses

**Ms Hodge:** To ask the Secretary of State for Scotland how many posts were lost in *(a)* the Scottish Office and *(b)* agencies for which the Scottish Office is responsible, listing the total lost posts agency by agency in (i) 1993–94, and (ii) 1994–95; and how many posts are proposed to be lost in 1995–96.  [25072]

**Mr. Lang:** The numbers of permanent and casual staff employed by the Scottish Office and each of its executive agencies in 1993–94, estimated outturn for 1994–95, and plans for 1995–96 are published in appendix 4 of my departmental report for 1995, a copy of which is in the Library of the House.

### Staff

**Ms Hodge:** To ask the Secretary of State for Scotland (1) what changes there have been to the number of staff in employment by grade in *(a)* the Scottish Office and *(b)* each agency for which the Scottish Office is responsible, in (i) 1993–94 and (ii) 1994–95; and what are the projected figures for 1995–96;

(2) how many staff of *(a)* the Scottish Office and *(b)* agencies for which the Scottish Office is responsible, were employed on a casual or short-term basis in (i) 1993–94 and (ii) 1994–95; and what are the projected figures for 1995–96.  [25504]

**Mr. Lang:** The numbers of permanent and casual staff employed by the Scottish Office and each of its executive agencies in 1993–94, estimated outturn for 1994–95, and plans for 1995–96 are published in appendix 4 of my departmental report for 1995, a copy of which is in the Library of the House. No projections broken down by grade are available.

### Mental Health Guidance

**Dr. Bray:** To ask the Secretary of State for Scotland when he proposes to revise the code of practice for the guidance of medical practitioners and others in accordance with the requirements of the Mental Health Act (Scotland) 1984.  [25877]

**Lord James Douglas-Hamilton:** Under section 119 of the Mental Health (Scotland) Act 1984, my right hon. Friend the Secretary of State for Scotland is required to prepare, and from time to time revise, this code of practice. The original code of practice for this Act was laid before Parliament on 16 November 1989.

It is currently proposed in the Mental Health (Patients in the Community) Bill, which recently received its Third Reading in another place, that the ambit of the code of practice should be widened to include after-care services for patients subject to the proposed community care orders and existing provisions for guardianship. We intend to begin a review of the code of practice after the provisions in this Bill have entered into force; the proposed commencement date for the provisions is 1 April 1996.

### Environmentally Sensitive Areas

**Dr. Strang:** To ask the Secretary of State for Scotland how many hectares of land *(a)* are eligible to be entered into each environmentally sensitive area in Scotland and *(b)* have been entered into each tier of each environmentally sensitive area in Scotland.  [25795]

**Sir Hector Monro:** The number of hectares eligible to be entered into the schemes in each designated area is not known as eligibility depends on the individual circumstances of the agricultural business and the land on the unit. The estimated number of hectares of agricultural land in each designated area and the number of hectares which have been covered by agreements under the schemes are set out in the following table.

| | Number of hectares in each designated area | Hectares covered by tier 1 agreements by 30 April 1995 |
|---|---|---|
| Breadalbane | 140,000 | [1]67,966 |
| Loch Lomond | 36,875 | [1]20,789 |
| Stewartry | 48,535 | [1]19,626 |
| Central Borders (formerly Whitlaw and Eildon) | 28,785 | [1]2,395 |
| Machair of the Uists and Benbecula, Barra and Vatersay | 16,230 | [1]3,911 |
| Central Southern Uplands | 220,289 | 49,625 |
| Western Southern Uplands | 131,004 | 18,721 |
| Cairngorms Straths | 236,138 | 10,493 |
| Argyll Islands | 177,420 | 34,103 |
| Shetland Islands | 64,090 | 633 |
| | 1,099,366 | 228,262 |

[1] Excludes hectares covered by expired agreements under the original Schemes.

All the land entered into tier 1 agreements can be considered for tier 2 of the scheme. The precise requirements of the agreement under tier 2 will depend on the types of land and features of conservation interest on the farm or croft and will be set out in the agreed farm or croft conservation plan.

**Dr. Strang:** To ask the Secretary of State for Scotland how many farms *(a)* are eligible to have land entered into each environmentally sensitive area in Scotland and *(b)* have had land entered into each environmentally sensitive area in Scotland. [25796]

**Sir Hector Monro:** The precise number of farmers and crofters eligible to enter land into the schemes in each designated area is not known, as eligibility depends on the individual circumstances of the agricultural business and the land on the unit. However, all agricultural units will land in a designated area are eligible to apply. The number of agricultural units in each designated area and the number of farmers and crofters who have had land covered by agreements under the schemes are set out in the following table:

| | Number of agricultural units in each designated area | Farmers/crofters who have had land covered by ESA agreements by 30 April 1995 |
|---|---|---|
| Breadalbane | 203 | [1]91 |
| Loch Lomond | 77 | [1]40 |
| Stewartry | 340 | [1]134 |
| Central Borders (formerly Whitlaw and Eildon) | 190 | [1]15 |
| Machair of the Uists and Benbecula, Barra and Vatersay | 789 | [1]400 |
| Central Southern Uplands | 633 | 107 |
| Western Southern Uplands | 455 | 49 |

| | Number of agricultural units in each designated area | Farmers/crofters who have had land covered by ESA agreements by 30 April 1995 |
|---|---|---|
| Cairngorms Straths | 284 | 12 |
| Argyll Islands | 435 | 50 |
| Shetlands Islands | 1,350 | 13 |
| | 4,756 | 911 |

[1] Excludes farmers/crofters whose agreements under the original Schemes have expired.

### Mink Farms

**Mr. Morley:** To ask the Secretary of State for Scotland, pursuant to his answer of 3 May, *Official Report*, column *252*, if he will refuse to license any future mink farms. [25738]

**Sir Hector Monro:** Any future applications will be considered on their merits. There are no mink farms in Scotland.

### Sandeel Fishing

**Mr. Morley:** To ask the Secretary of State for Scotland what assessment he is carrying out of the environmental impact of sandeel fishing in Shetland waters; and if he will make a statement. [25739]

**Sir Hector Monro:** The Scottish Office marine laboratory has an ongoing programme of research on sandeels and associated environmental issues. In 1993 it published a report entitled "Biology of Sandeels in the vicinity of seabird colonies at Shetland".

### Fisheries Research Vessel

**Dr. Godman:** To ask the Secretary of State for Scotland if he will make a statement on the timetable for the invitation and assessment of tenders for the construction of a fisheries research vessel; when he expects to announce the successful bid; and if he will make a statement. [25362]

**Sir Hector Monro:** By the end of this year, I hope to be in a position to announce the award of the contract to build a replacement fisheries research vessel. Invitations to tender will be issued by late summer, allowing nine weeks for their submission. A similar period will be devoted to the assessment of tenders.

### European Parliamentary Constituencies

**Mr. Stewart:** To ask the Secretary of State for Scotland when the Boundary Commission for Scotland intends to begin its review of European parliamentary constituencies in Scotland. [26582]

**Mr. Lang:** The Boundary Commission for Scotland has informed me that its review of the boundaries of the eight European parliamentary constituencies in Scotland will commence on 2 June 1995.

The Commission is unable to forecast at this stage how long the review is likely to take.

## Local Government Employees (Political Restrictions)

**Mr. Donohoe:** To ask the Secretary of State for Scotland what conditions the Scottish Office would require to be fulfilled before removing the political restriction of local government employees. [25395]

**Mr. Kynoch** [*holding answer 23 May 1995*]: Following the report of the Widdicombe committee, it was agreed that there were certain key posts in local government where it was particularly important that the postholder should be seen to be politically impartial. This remains just as valid today, and we therefore have no intention of abolishing the rules on politically restricted posts.

## Rent-to-mortgage Scheme

**Mr. Donohoe:** To ask the Secretary of State for Scotland how much the Scottish Office *(a)* is planning to spend in the current year and *(b)* has spent in previous financial years on promoting the rent-to-mortgage scheme; and how much is being and was spent during these periods on television advertising for the campaign. [25344]

**Lord James Douglas-Hamilton** [*holding answer 23 May 1994*]: Advertising of the pilot rent-to-mortgage scheme took place in spring 1991 and spring 1992. Subsequently the right to buy and statutory rent-to-mortgage schemes have been promoted together. No decision has yet been taken on any further advertising in 1995–96. Expenditure in each financial year is as follows:

|  | *Total* £ | *Television Advertising* £ |
|---|---|---|
| 1995–96 | ¹186,000 | ¹111,600 |
| 1994–95 | 220,000 | 116,600 |
| 1993–94 | 312,420 | 122,100 |
| 1992–93 | nil | nil |
| 1991–92 | 186,290 | 45,600 |
| 1990–91 | 194,710 | 64,750 |

¹Estimate.

## TRADE AND INDUSTRY

### European Regional Development Fund

**Mr. Lester:** To ask the President of the Board of Trade how the private sector can be involved in European Regional Development Fund projects in the United Kingdom. [25863]

**Mr. Eggar:** It is Government policy to encourage private sector participation in projects partly financed by the European regional development fund. This also accords with the aims of the private finance initiative.

We have today introduced new criteria for this purpose. These arrangements will help to provide a significant boost to the regeneration of ERDF areas.

I have tabled a copy of the criteria in the Library of the House. Projects, which may include industrial, transport, environmental, tourism and other economic infrastructure, will need to be of general economic benefit to eligible areas and to meet the other conditions of ERDF grant. Companies wishing to inquire about the possibility of

ERDF grant for such projects should contact the Government Office for their English region, or the Scottish Office, Welsh Office, or Northern Ireland Departments.

To encourage maximum private sector involvement, the private sector will be able to make a reasonable profit on investment. Conditions attached to grants will ensure that any excessive profits that might be derived from ERDF grants continue to be used for the general economic benefit of the area and that risks will be shared appropriately between the public and private sectors. Grant will normally be routed through a public sector participant, which will be accountable for proper project administration for grant purposes. Where this is not appropriate, grant may be paid direct to the private sector.

Regional single programming documents, agreed between the Government and the European Commission, set aggregate targets for private sector contributions, alongside totals of public expenditure and of ERDF grant.

### Research Laboratories

**Mr. Nicholls:** To ask the President of the Board of Trade what targets he has set his Department's research laboratories for 1995–96. [26388]

**Mr. Heseltine:** In the light of the announcement I made on 14 April 1994, *Official Report,* columns *251-53* on the future management of the DTI's laboratories, the targets I have set the Laboratory of the Government Chemist and the National Engineering Laboratory for 1995–96 are set out below. In addition, I expect the chief executives of the laboratories, including the National Physical Laboratory, to continue to reply within 10 working days to all letters from Members of Parliament delegated to them for reply.

*Primary Financial Targets*

LGC Recovery of full costs from income for customer work.

NEL Recovery of full costs through "arms-length" contracts from customers.

*Secondary Targets*

LGC : To achieve an average rate of 93 per cent for completion of reports on analysis of (or research into) samples by the date agreed with customers for the year as a whole.

To achieve more than 87 per cent. of contract research milestones within the time scale agreed with the customer.

To maintain NAMAS accreditation for the categories of work in which the Laboratory operates, registration for Good Laboratory Practice (GLP) and Laboratory-wide registration to BS EN ISO 9001.

NEL: To increase the number of non-DTI customers who provide revenues of more than £100,000 per annum by 25 per cent.

To increase the number of hours charged to customers per staff member by 10 per cent.

To carry out post completion reviews, with customers, on 20 per cent. of all contracts valued in excess of £250,000.

Bids are currently being considered from the private sector for the contractorisation of NPL. For the time it is expected to remain an agency, its primary target is to recover its full costs from income for customer work after taking account of the special circumstances arising from the task of preparing for transfer to private management. NEL and LGC are expected to have been privatised by the end of 1995–96 and hence to cease to be agencies.

## Fire Safety

**Mr. Beith:** To ask the President of the Board of Trade what plans he has to publish the report of the steering committee which reviewed responses to the report of the interdepartmental review team on fire safety legislation and enforcement. [25859]

**Mr. Jonathan Evans:** Ministers are currently considering the Government's response to the recommendations of the interdepartmental review of fire safety legislation and enforcement, and we hope to make an announcement in the coming weeks on the way forward.

**Mr. Cox:** To ask the President of the Board of Trade if he has now received a report from the steering committee reviewing responses to the inter-departmental review on fire safety legislation and enforcement; and if he will make a statement. [25756]

**Mr. Jonathan Evans:** I refer the hon. Member to the reply I gave today to the right hon. Member for Berwick upon Tweed (Mr. Beith).

## Local Government Reorganisation

**Mr. Frank Cook:** To ask the President of the Board of Trade what assessment he has made of the applicability of the views attributed to his Department on pages 42 and 43 of "Renewing Local Government in the English Shires" to the future of trading standards services in Cleveland after the division of those services amongst four unitary authorities as a result of local government reorganisation. [25225]

**Mr. Jonathan Evans:** I refer the hon. Member to the reply that I gave to hon. Member for Kingswood (Mr. Berry) on 22 May 1995, *Official Report*, columns *429–30*. The same considerations apply to Cleveland as to Berkshire.

## Internal Market Advisory Committee

**Sir Cranley Onslow:** To ask the President of the Board of Trade if he will list the specific complaints his Department has raised at the internal market advisory committee since its inception. [25594]

**Mr. Needham:** My Department's single market compliance unit has arranged for 14 cases to be raised at the internal market advisory committee since specific single market complaints were first placed on its agenda last year. These have covered:

restrictions on the provision of auctioneering services in France;

Italian taxation of cars over 2 litres;

Dutch waste water regulations;

requirements for tyre inflators to be tested to German standards;

requirements for stack gas analisyers to be tested to German standards;

Greek regulations on the content of soft drinks;

discriminatory provisions concerning the operation of security firms in Portugal;

Dutch requirements involving the double-testing of electric fencing;

restrictions on the operation of UK qualified accountants in Greece;

Greek restrictions on the operation of a speedboat for business purposes;

restrictions on the establishment of private language schools in Greece;

Portuguese requirements concerning lighting devices on tractors;

German refusal to accredit non-German bodies to issue the GS mark;

German requirements for re-testing of samples for liquid density standards.

## Overseas Posts

**Mr. Austin Mitchell:** To ask the President of the Board of Trade what evidence has resulted from major export drives as to the effectiveness of the establishment of commercial posts overseas in terms of increasing exports. [25495]

**Mr. Needham:** The FCO's commercial Posts play a crucial role in the delivery of the Government's export promotion drive. It would be impossible to mount major campaigns such as "Action Japan" or the "Indo-British Partnership" without the support of commercial officers overseas. The "Indo-British Partnership" has been associated with an increase of 50 per cent. in bilateral trade between the UK and India. A new office was opened in Bangalore to help prepare this initiative. Business demand for charged services has nearly tripled. During the period of "Action Japan" and its predecessor, "Priority Japan", exports to Japan have risen significantly. This trend continues as visible exports are 35 per cent. higher in the first three months of 1995 than for the same period last year. I am confident from my recent visit that the 35 Japanese specialists we have in Tokyo contribute a great deal to this success story.

## Manufacturing Companies

**Mr. Gordon Prentice:** To ask the President of the Board of Trade what estimates he has made of the number of companies engaged in manufacturing that have closed their United Kingdom operation and have transferred production overseas to plants owned by those companies or in which they otherwise have a stake since 1990. [25512]

**Mr. Page:** This information is not available.

## Insider Dealing

**Mr. Gordon Prentice:** To ask the President of the Board of Trade if he will make a statement on the application of section 5(3) of the Public Records Act 1958 to information on inside dealing under section 179 of the Financial Services Act 1986. [25510]

**Mr. Heseltine:** Section 179 of the Financial Services Act 1986 prohibits the disclosure of certain information obtained for the purposes of, or in the discharge of functions under, that Act. Section 179 is therefore a statutory bar on disclosure of the type referred to in section 5(3) of the Public Records Act 1958. Section 5(3), which otherwise places a duty on the Keeper of Public Records to arrange that reasonable facilities are available for public inspection of public records, does not apply to information covered by section 179. Therefore such information will not be made available in the Public Record Office.

## CIS Countries

**Mr. Sheerman:** To ask the President of the Board of Trade what new steps he is taking to maximise the involvement of United Kingdom companies in the economic development of the CIS countries. [25022]

**Mr. Needham:** My right hon. Friend the President of the Board of Trade announced on 22 May 1995, *Official Report,* columns *597-99* a package of additional support measures for exporters including trade fairs, inward and outward missions and business links export services. Additional staff will be deployed on the DTI market desks and in our overseas posts and in September an additional export promoter from the private sector will join those already working in the developing CIS markets. These additional resources will help companies take advantage, including through new sector specific initiatives, of the increasing opportunities in these markets.

### Local Bus Services

**Ms Walley:** To ask the President of the Board of Trade if he will list for each of the last 10 years the number of complaints received by the Office of Fair Trading regarding the operation of local bus services and the actions of bus companies reported to his Department. [25911]

**Mr. Jonathan Evans:** The numbers of complaints about competition aspects of local bus operation received by the Office of Fair Trading since bus services outside London were deregulated are as follows.

| | *Number* |
| --- | --- |
| 1987 | 57 |
| 1988 | 58 |
| 1989 | 53 |
| 1990 | 51 |
| 1991 | 68 |
| 1992 | 90 |
| 1993 | 108 |
| 1994 | 56 |
| Total | 541 |

Complaints which my Department receives regarding unfair competition in the industry are referred to the Director General of Fair Trading, who has the initial responsibility for considering them.

### Monopolies and Mergers Commission

**Mr. Wigley:** To ask the President of the Board of Trade (1) what powers he has to direct the Monopolies and Mergers Commission to reconsider its decision on a case if it appears to him that it may have been given inaccurate information; [25730]

(2) how many prosecutions there have been since 1973 under section 93(b) of the Fair Trading Act 1973. [25731]

**Mr. Jonathan Evans:** I have no powers to direct the Monopolies and Mergers Commission to reconsider its reports. If it were found that the commission had been misled, a further reference to the commission could be considered.

I am not aware of any previous prosecutions under section 93B of the Fair Trading Act 1973.

### Bird's Eye Walls Ltd.

**Mr. Wigley:** To ask the President of the Board of Trade if he will ensure that the report of the Office of Fair Trading on the investigation into the Bird's Eye Walls freezer exclusivity case, will be published. [25729]

**Mr. Jonathan Evans:** The Office of Fair Trading will make a statement when it has completed its investigation into the evidence given to the Monopolies and Mergers Commission by Bird's Eye Walls Ltd.

### Majority Shareholdings

**Mr. Byers:** To ask the President of the Board of Trade if he will list those companies in which the holder of his office is a majority shareholder which *(a)* are currently in existence and *(b)* have been wound up in the past five years. [25707]

**Mr. Heseltine** *[holding answer 22 May 1995].* The President of the Board of Trade is, by virtue of that office, the majority shareholder in British Nuclear Fuels plc and Nuclear Electric plc. There have been no instances in the last five years of companies, in which I or my predecessors have by virtue of our office been majority shareholders, being wound up.

### General System of Preferences

**Mr. Caborn:** To ask the President of the Board of Trade if he will ask the European Commission to bring forward proposals for the provision of the general system of preferences to agricultural produce from South Africa. [25611]

**Mr. Needham** *[holding answer 23 May 1995]:* From 1 January 1995, South Africa was granted GSP benefits for a limited range of agricultural products. The European Commission is committed, under the terms of the current GSP regulation for agricultural products, to bring forward a proposal to re-examine the scope of those benefits to enable the Council to take a decision to enter into force on 1 July 1995. Her Majesty's Government take the view that South Africa should have access to the full range of agricultural concessions available under the scheme.

### RJB (Mining)

**Mr. Byers:** To ask the President of the Board of Trade, pursuant to his answer to the hon. Member for Sheffield, Attercliffe (Mr. Betts) of 15 May, *Official Report*, column 22, on what date the decision was taken to review the status of RJB (Mining) as preferred bidder; and continue as preferred bidder. [25392]

**Mr. Page** *[holding answer 23 May 1995]:* The position of each of the preferred bidders was kept under review throughout the course of negotiations. Following the decision on proceedings against former directors of the AF Budge companies, which was made on 21 November, the Department specifically reviewed RJB (Mining) plc's status as preferred bidder for the English coal companies in the light of the consideration of the conduct of Mr. Richard Budge in the context of the failure of the AF Budge companies and the decision on those proceedings. The Department concluded on 25 November that RJB (Mining) should properly continue as preferred bidder.

## NATIONAL HERITAGE

### Job Losses

**Ms Hodge:** To ask the Secretary of State for National Heritage how many posts were lost in *(a)* the Department of National Heritage and *(b)* agencies for which the

Department of National Heritage is responsible, listing the total lost posts agency by agency in (i) 1993–94 and (ii) 1994–95; and how many posts are proposed to be lost in 1995–96. [25074]

**Mr. Dorrell:** The information in respect of the Department of National Heritage and its two agencies is as follows:

| | 1993–94 | 1994–95 | ¹1995–96 |
|---|---|---|---|
| DNH central Department | nil | nil | nil |
| Historic Royal Palaces Agency | 11.5 | nil | 70 |
| Royal Parks Agency | nil | nil | nil |

¹ Estimate.

## Churchill Papers

**Mr. Gordon Prentice:** To ask the Secretary of State for National Heritage how many separate items there are in the Churchill papers; and what are the professional qualifications of those persons who advised him that none of the papers to be sold was a state paper. [25153]

**Mr. Dorrell:** I have never been advised that none of the Churchill papers is a state paper. There are estimated to be around 1.5 million separate papers in the Churchill archive. The archive comprises both state and non-state papers. The papers which were purchased with lottery funds were the non-state papers.

**Mr. Gordon Prentice:** To ask the Secretary of State for National Heritage, pursuant to his answer of 17 May, *Official Report,* column 270 on the value of the Churchill archive, what advice he received from each of the bodies listed, the individual historians and relevant institutions as to the appropriate monetary value of the papers. [25600]

**Mr. Dorrell:** My answer of 17 May related to a question about the historical significance of the papers. As to the value, the National Heritage Memorial Fund took independent advice from a different source; this was from a well respected dealer in the field of antiquarian books.

**Mr. Gordon Prentice:** To ask the Secretary of State for National Heritage if the Churchill papers are fully catalogued. [25154]

**Mr. Dorrell:** An outline catalogue is available at Churchill college, Cambridge, and at the national register of archives in Chancery lane.

Work on a detailed catalogue began at Churchill college in 1991. It is expected to take a further five years to complete.

## British Broadcasting Corporation

**Mr. Jim Cunningham:** To ask the Secretary of State for National Heritage to what extent the closure of BBC Radio CWR and other local radio stations will affect the BBC's statutory obligations in its charter. [25230]

**Mr. Dorrell:** The BBC's royal charter requires the corporation to provide such broadcasting services and facilities as may be required by any licence granted to, or any agreement made with, the BBC by the Secretary of State. Under the terms of the annex to its current licence and agreement the board of governors recognises that the BBC has a duty to undertake to provide a properly balanced service displaying a wide range of subject matter. Subject to meeting this obligation, it is for the BBC to decide how best to allocate its resources.

**Mr. Jim Cunningham:** To ask the Secretary of State for National Heritage how many licences have been issued to private radio stations to replace those stations that will be reduced or merged by the BBC. [25229]

**Mr. Dorrell:** It is for the Radio Authority to determine the pattern for licensing independent local radio stations.

**Mr. Jim Cunningham:** To ask the Secretary of State for National Heritage what discussions he has had with the BBC management following the decisions to close BBC Radio CWR and other local BBC radio stations, in respect of the transparency of the BBC's decision-making progress. [25226]

**Mr. Dorrell:** None. The transparency of the BBC's decision-making process is a subject which is being reviewed in the context of discussions about its new charter and agreement.

**Mr. Jim Cunningham:** To ask the Secretary of State for National Heritage if he will make it his policy to demand full disclosure of the BBC's future financial plans with particular regard to (a) programme production and (b) local services. [25227]

**Mr. Dorrell:** The White Paper on the future of the BBC proposed that the BBC should publish objectives for each of its services and for programme production, and should undertake public consultation prior to making any material change to the nature of its services.

**Mr. Jim Cunningham:** To ask the Secretary of State for National Heritage how many local radio stations are to be merged with other radio stations; and if he will list the radio stations that will be merged or lose their licence to broadcast. [25228]

**Mr. Dorrell:** These are matters for the BBC and the Radio Authority. It is for the BBC to determine what local radio services it will provide and for the Radio Authority to license and oversee the development of independent local radio.

## Tourism-related Regulations

**Mr. Pendry:** To ask the Secretary of State for National Heritage if he will list all those tourism-related regulations that have been amended or repealed as part of the Government's deregulation initiative. [24138]

**Mr. Dorrell:** A complete list of regulations amended or repealed which affect the tourist industry could only be assembled at disproportionate cost, but progress has been made in several of the key areas identified during my Department's inquiry into regulatory burdens on tourism. Examples include food hygiene regulation, road signposting and the Electricity at Work Regulations. We are continuing to follow up a number of issues made to me in the course of the inquiry.

## National Lottery

**Mr. Harry Greenway:** To ask the Secretary of State for National Heritage if he will list the arts and sports bodies in the London borough of Ealing to which grants have been given from national lottery proceeds; what sum of money was involved in each case; and if he will make a statement. [24811]

**Mr. Dorrell:** There have as yet been no national lottery awards made to arts or sports organisations based in the London borough of Ealing.

**Mr. Barry Jones:** To ask the Secretary of State for National Heritage if he will summarise the criteria used for the allocation of national lottery money in Wales. [24841]

**Mr. Dorrell:** The national lottery distributing bodies operating in Wales have each developed their own eligibility criteria for lottery funding, within the framework provided by the directions made under section 26 of the National Lottery etc. Act 1993, and the individual bodies' governing legislation. Copies of the directions have been placed in the Library of the House.

**Mr. Barry Jones:** To ask the Secretary of State for National Heritage how he expects the national museums of Scotland, Northern Ireland and Wales to benefit from national lottery money; and if he will make a statement. [24842]

**Mr. Dorrell:** The national museums of Scotland, Northern Ireland and Wales are eligible for national lottery funding from the National Heritage Memorial Fund.

**Mrs. Fyfe:** To ask the Secretary of State for National Heritage if he will consider relaxing the restrictions for the national lottery on publishing information about the district in which a winning ticket was sold. [25579]

**Mr. Dorrell** *[holding answer 22 May 1995]:* Protection of winners' anonymity is a section 5 licence condition and therefore a matter for the director general of the national lottery. I have asked him to write to the hon. Member, placing copies of his response in the Library of the House.

**Mrs. Fyfe:** To ask the Secretary of State for National Heritage what measures he plans to enable the owners of unclaimed winning lottery tickets to come forward. [25580]

**Mr. Dorrell** *[holding answer 22 May 1995]:* This is an operational matter for Camelot Group plc. I have therefore asked the director general of the national lottery, who is responsible for regulating the operation of the lottery, to write to the hon. Member, placing copies of his response in the Library of the House.

### Historic Documents

**Mr. Gordon Prentice:** To ask the Secretary of State for National Heritage what special training is given to persons who have responsibility for assessing the historical significance of documents held by his Department. [23282]

**Mr. Dorrell:** Training in assessing the historical significance of departmental records is carried out under the guidance of the keeper of public records. It is provided in a number of different ways, including courses on the appraisal of records and through conferences and seminars arranged by the Public Record Office.

### Rural Economy

**Mr. Colvin:** To ask the Secretary of State for National Heritage what is his estimate of the net annual financial saving, or cost, of his Department's submission for the proposed White Paper on the Rural Economy. [24328]

**Mr. Dorrell:** Proposals for the rural White Paper remain subject to continuing collective consideration and discussion. The cost of measures contained in the White Paper will be taken into account in the Public Expenditure Survey.

### VE Day

**Mr. McMaster:** To ask the Secretary of State for National Heritage what plans he has to congratulate the staff of the royal parks for their part in the VE day commemorations; and if he will make a statement. [24123]

**Mr. Dorrell:** The VE day commemorations in Hyde park were a great success and I am conveying appropriate congratulations and thanks to all those involved in the organisation of the events, including staff of the Royal Parks Agency.

### Evidence to Select Committees

**Mr. Flynn:** To ask the Secretary of State for National Heritage, what training his civil servants receive in preparation to give evidence to select committees with special reference to *(a)* watching a video, *(b)* written information and *(c)* oral information. [25577]

**Mr. Dorrell** *[holding answer 22 May 1995]:* Training is available from the Civil Service College for those civil servants who are likely to appear in person to give evidence. A number of senior civil servants in my Department have already attended such courses.

A copy of the Cabinet Office guidance "Departmental Evidence and Response to Select Committees" is sent to all grade 5s and above in my Department. Copies of the guidance are available in the House Libraries.

### Welsh Fourth Channel

**Mr. Morgan:** To ask the Secretary of State for National Heritage, pursuant to his answer of 16 May, *Official Report,* columns *148–50,* to the right hon. Member for Watford (Mr. Garel-Jones) if he will state the basis for the Beastall report's conclusions that all five intermediary companies used were genuinely trading; what checks were made with Companies House and each company's auditors with respect to annual reports and accounts pertinent to that issue; and if he will make a statement. [25698]

**Mr. Dorrell** *[holding answer 22 May 1995]:* Mr. Beastall's concern was to check that the companies involved had not been created merely as vehicles for sponsorship payments. His conclusion that they were genuinely trading was based on evidence from S4C, the proprietors of the companies and, in some cases, ABSA that they were engaged in film, video or programme production or related activities at the time that the sponsorship payments were made.

**Mr. Morgan:** To ask the Secretary of State for National Heritage, pursuant to his answer of 16 May to the right hon. Member for Watford (Mr. Garel-Jones), *Official Report,* columns *148–50,* what consultations he has had with the chairman of the Welsh Fourth Channel Authority concerning the date on which the disciplinary action was taken against the member of S4C in relation to the Pengwyn Pinc issue; and what form the disciplinary action took. [25267]

**Mr. Dorrell** *[holding answer 22 May 1995]:* I have had no discussions with the chairman of the Welsh Fourth Channel Authority on this topic. The timing and form of any disciplinary action is a matter for S4C.

**Mr. Morgan:** To ask the Secretary of State for National Heritage, pursuant to his answer of 16 May to the right hon. Member for Watford (Mr. Garel-Jones), *Official Report,* columns *148–50,* what proposals he has for submitting a report to the Comptroller and Auditor-General; and if he will make a statement on the accountability of the Welsh Fourth Channel Authority to the Committee of Public Accounts. [25266]

**Mr. Dorrell** *[holding answer 22 May 1995]:* A copy of the report by Mr. John Beastall has been sent to the Comptroller and Auditor General. The chief executive of S4C is designated as the accounting officer for payments made to S4C under the Broadcasting Act 1990. He may be called upon to appear before the Committee of Public Accounts.

### Tourism (EC Funding)

**Mr. Hawksley:** To ask the Secretary of State for National Heritage if private sector applications are eligible for moneys under European structural fund objective 5B, priority 3 measure 3.1 in the tourism sector. [24581]

**Mr. Eggar:** I have been asked to reply.

European regional development fund grants in the tourism sector are covered in all the UK objective 5b single programming documents, although the precise priorities and measures involved vary. I refer the hon. Member to the reply that I gave to my hon. Friend the Member for Broxtowe (Mr. Lester) today, on new rules on private sector involvement in ERDF projects. Tourism projects are treated in the same way as other projects.

### HOME DEPARTMENT

### Prison Governors

**Mr. Hoyle:** To ask the Secretary of State for the Home Department, pursuant to his answer of 15 May, *Official Report,* column *17,* what steps are being taken to recruit more members of the ethnic minorities to governor grades. [25530]

**Mr. Michael Forsyth:** Responsibility for this matter has been delegated to the Director General of the Prison Service, who has been asked to arrange for a reply to be given.

*Letter from Derek Lewis to Mr. Doug Hoyle, dated 24 May 1995:*

The Home Secretary has asked me to reply to your recent Question about the recruitment of members of the ethnic minorities to the prison governor grades.

During a voluntary survey of staff ethnic origins, four members of the governor grades indicated that they were members of the ethnic minorities. There are a further 520 members of the prison officer grades of ethnic minority origin, who have an avenue of promotion into the governor grades. We expect that the currently small number of governor grades from ethnic minority backgrounds will increase over time, as some of these officers progress through the ranks under the normal arrangements for promotion. The Prison Service is continuing to try and increase the level of recruitment to the prison officer grades from ethnic minority groups.

The Prison Service's Acceleration Promotion Scheme is attempting to recruit ethnic minority graduates by a range of means. We have taken part in a mentoring scheme with one of the London universities, which arranges for black and Asian students to shadow a manager from the ethnic minorities, and an undergraduate is shortly to be sponsored by the Prison Service through the Windsor Fellowship Scheme. Last autumn, the Accelerated Promotion Scheme's national recruitment campaign placed advertisements in ethnic minority newspapers—The Voice, The Weekly Journal, Asian Times and Eastern Eye—as well as in the national broadsheets. Advertising is also placed in careers publications aimed specifically at ethnic minority undergraduates, such as Hobsons' Racial Equality Casebook and Kaleidoscope, both of which are circulated widely among universities and community relations organisations. Attempts will be made late this year to target universities with high numbers of black and Asians students, where we hope to offer presentations outlining career options in the Prison Service, under both the Accelerated Promotion Scheme and more generally.

**Mr. Hoyle:** To ask the Secretary of State for the Home Department what number of prison governors, by grade, are women. [25531]

**Mr. Michael Forsyth:** Responsibility for this matter has been delegated to the Director General of the Prison Service, who has been asked to arrange for a reply to be given.

*Letter from Derek Lewis to Mr. Doug Hoyle, dated 24 May 1995:*

The Home Secretary has asked me to reply to your recent Question about the number of female governors in the Prison Service.

As at 1 May 1995 there are 1,020 staff employed in governor grades, of whom 96 (9.4%) are women. Broken down by grade the numbers are as follows:

| Grade | Number of women in grade (%) | Total number of staff in grade |
|---|---|---|
| Governor 1 | 2 (4.4%) | 46 |
| Governor 2 | 5 (6.7%) | 75 |
| Governor 3 | 16 (12.7%) | 126 |
| Governor 4 | 37 (12%) | 309 |
| Governor 5 | 26 (7.8%) | 429 |
| Governor 5 (APS)[1] | 10 (28.6%) | 35 |

[1]Accelerated Promotion Scheme, the Prison Service's fast-track management development scheme.

The number of female governing governors has increased steadily over the last few years.

There are now eight male establishments and four female establishments where the governing governor is a woman. These are:

    Bullingdon
    Bullwood Hall (f)
    East Sutton Park (f)
    Erlestoke
    Holloway (f)
    Kirklevington
    Low Newton
    The Mount
    Norwich
    Pucklechurch (f)
    Swinfen Hall
    Woodhill

The controller at Buckley Hall, a contracted prison, is a woman.

### Lotteries

**Mr. Corbett:** To ask the Secretary of State for the Home Department if he will summarise the outcome of the Schindler case concerning the United Kingdom's ban on EC lotteries before the European Court of Justice, and its practical effects. [25763]

**Mr. Nicholas Baker:** The judgment in the Schindler case was delivered by the European Court of Justice on 24 March 1994.

The court found that the importation of lottery advertisements and tickets into a member state relates to a service within the meaning of the treaty of Rome and that the UK lotteries legislation is an obstacle to the freedom to provide this service. However, the court also found that the aims of the UK legislation were to protect the users of the service as well as consumers generally and social order, and that such aims justified the restrictions on the freedom to provide services.

The practical effect of the judgment has been the continued ability of the UK to ban advertising and promotion of lotteries not permitted by our legislation, including those operating in other member states, under section 2 of the Lotteries and Amusements Act 1976.

## Job Losses

**Ms Hodge:** To ask the Secretary of State for the Home Department how many posts were lost in *(a)* the Home Office and *(b)* agencies for which the Home Office is responsible, listing the total lost posts agency by agency in (i) 1993–94 and (ii) 1994–95; and how many posts are proposed to be lost in 1995–96. [25075]

**Mr. Howard:** Changes in the numbers of posts are not recorded centrally. Consequently the information sought could be provided only at disproportionate cost.

Staff in post information can be found in the annual publication "Civil Service Statistics" and in annex 4 of the Department's annual report, Cm 2508, both of which are available in the Library.

## Action Against Crime Pack

**Mrs. Roche:** To ask the Secretary of State for the Home Department what was the cost of publishing the Action Against Crime pack; and what proportion of this represents the time spent by his officials. [25151]

**Mr. Howard:** For information on the cost of publication, I refer the hon. Member to the answer that I gave to the hon. Member for Bristol, South (Ms Primarolo) on 24 April, *Official Report*, column *385*. The pack was drafted by my officials from existing material in the course of their normal duties and was not costed separately.

## Prisons (Market Testing)

**Mr. Streeter:** To ask the Secretary of State for the Home Department what progress has been made on the selection of prisons for market testing. [26488]

**Mr. Howard:** In August last year, the Prison Service announced a shortlist of establishments which were either poor performers or had been judged to have particular scope for improvement. The Prisons Board intended to select for market testing one or two establishments from this list, but in an attempt to resolve a complaint to the central arbitration committee about this process, selection was deferred.

The central arbitration committee heard the complaint 1 February and published its determination 27 March. I will place a copy in the Library. The Prison Service is today responding to the central arbitration committee

determination by providing some additional information about the basis on which the short list was prepared.

Because of this regrettable delay, the information on which the present short list was prepared is now out of date. A fresh selection process will instead be conducted in due course.

## Prisoner Transfers

**Mr. Corbyn:** To ask the Secretary of State for the Home Department how many prisoners have been transferred from prisons in the mainland UK to prisons in Northern Ireland and Ireland over the past 10 years. [25401]

**Mr. Michael Forsyth** *[holding answer 22 May 1995]:* The number of prisoners transferred from prisons in England and Wales to prisons in Northern Ireland over the past 10 years is given in the table. It is not possible for prisoners to be transferred to prisons in the Republic of Ireland because although the Irish Republic has signed the Council of Europe convention it has not yet ratified it.

*Transfer of prisoners to Northern Ireland*

| Year | Number |
| --- | --- |
| 1984 | 1 |
| 1985 | 4 |
| 1986 | 2 |
| 1987 | 3 |
| 1988 | 5 |
| 1989 | 17 |
| 1990 | 13 |
| 1991 | 25 |
| 1992 | 26 |
| 1993 | 7 |
| 1994 | 19 |

## Foundation for Business Responsibilities

**Mr. Robert Ainsworth:** To ask the Secretary of State for the Home Department what plans the fraud division at the Crown Prosecution Service has to investigate the affairs of the Foundation for Business Responsibilities. [24702]

**The Attorney-General:** I have been asked to reply.

The investigation of alleged criminal offences is a police function. The papers submitted to the CPS by the deputy leader of the opposition of Westminster city council will be referred to the police.

## Derek Bentley

**Mr. Michael:** To ask the Secretary of State for the Home Department if he will place in the Library a copy of the report submitted to his Department by the investigating officer on behalf of the Commissioner of Police of the Metropolis regarding inconsistencies in the evidence, including evidence not available to the court or the public, relating to the case of Derek Bentley. [24936]

**Mr. Nicholas Baker:** I refer the hon. Member to the reply given to his question of 18 May, *Official Report*, column *363*.

# Written Answers to Questions

*Thursday 25 May 1995*

## LORD CHANCELLOR'S DEPARTMENT

### Immigration Adjudicators

**Mr. Robert Ainsworth:** To ask the Parliamentary Secretary, Lord Chancellor's Department how many full-time and part-time immigration adjudicators employed by the Immigration Appellate Authority are currently designated as special adjudicators to hear appeals against a refusal of asylum; and what plans he has to increase that number.                    [26179]

**Mr. John M. Taylor:** Of the 20 full-time and 91 part-time immigration adjudicators appointed by the Lord Chancellor, 20 and 57 respectively are currently designated as special adjudicators to hear appeals against a refusal of asylum. Increases in the numbers of full-time and part-time immigration adjudicators are planned during the course of 1995.

It is expected that all full-time immigration adjudicators appointed will be designated as special adjudicators. Increases in the number of part-time immigration adjudicators designated as special adjudicators will be made as they gain sufficient experience of immigration work, the number depending on the work load of the Immigration Appellate Authority.

### Mrs. Kuldip Kaur

**Mr. Madden:** To ask the Parliamentary Secretary, Lord Chancellor's Department, pursuant to his answer of 4 May, *Official Report,* column *259,* concerning Mrs. Kuldip Kaur, what decision was taken by the regional adjudicator on whether her appeal may proceed out of time; and if he will make a statement.          [25996]

**Mr. John M. Taylor:** I now understand that the Immigration Appellate Authority sent copies of the case papers to the former address of Mrs. Kaur's representatives. These were returned by the Post Office undelivered, and as Mrs. Kaur's representatives had not had an opportunity to submit their written observations, a decision was not taken by the adjudicator on 12 May.

The case papers have now been sent to Mrs. Kaur's representatives at their current address. I apologise for the delay to Mrs. Kaur's case and confirm that it is now due to be placed before the regional adjudicator on 23 June.

### Legal Aid

**Mr. Boateng:** To ask the Parliamentary Secretary, Lord Chancellor's Department if he will list the day and exact time when his Department's press office released copies of the Green Paper on legal aid published on 17 May to *(a)* legal correspondents of the broadsheet newspapers, *(b)* the Bar Council, *(c)* the Law Society, *(d)* the National Association of Citizen's Advice Bureaux, *(e)* the National Consumer Council, *(f)* the Consumers' Association, *(g)* the Law Centres' Federation and *(h)* the Legal Action Group; and if he will make a statement.          [26020]

**Mr. John M. Taylor:** The Lord Chancellor's Department's press office invited representatives of the media, including the legal correspondents of the broadsheet newspapers, to collect one copy each of the Green Paper on legal aid, embargoed for 16.00 on 17 May, from the Department's headquarters building at 11.15 on 17 May. Representatives of the Bar Council, the Law Society, the National Association of Citizen's Advice Bureaux, the National Consumer Council, the Law Centres' Federation, and the Legal Action Group received advance copies on the same basis. A copy of the Green Paper on legal aid was sent to the Consumers' Association by post on 17 May.

## DEFENCE

### Chinook Crash, Mull of Kintyre

**Mr. Sykes:** To ask the Secretary of State for Defence when he expects to publish the results of the inquiry into the Chinook crash on the Mull of Kintyre on 2 June 1994.          [26619]

**Mr. Soames:** The circumstances of this tragic accident have been the subject of a most exhaustive investigation. The proceedings are now almost complete and I hope to release the findings by the middle of June. A summary will be placed in the Library of the House in the usual way.

### Defence Postal and Courier Services

**Mr. Sykes:** To ask the Secretary of State for Defence what plans he has to rationalise the activities of the Defence Postal and Courier Services agency.          [26751]

**Mr. Soames:** As part of "Front Line First", my Department announced its intention to integrate departmental mail services, rationalise vehicle fleets, provide better training of all personnel and set up a strategic management structure across all three services.

These proposals were explained in a consultative document issued on 9 March 1995. No objections to the proposals were received during the consultation period, and I have therefore decided that we shall begin work on rationalising the mail and courier operations of the Department. A number of activities previously carried out at several separate locations in the centre of London will be rationalised, and concentrated at the British forces post office site, in Mill Hill, north-west London. This will involve the main MOD mail sorting operation and the Defence Postal and Courier Service terminal centred on St. Giles court, London WC2, and mail and courier vehicles currently located at Regents Park barracks.

Inglis barracks, Mill Hill is the headquarters of the Defence Postal and Courier Service agency and will absorb the additional personnel management and training commitment implicit in the rationalisation.

We will of course continue to consult staff and trade unions about the detailed implementation of this rationalisation.

## Royal Marines School of Music, Deal

**Mr. Heald:** To ask the Secretary of State for Defence if his Department has concluded its consideration of the future of the Royal Marines school of music, Deal; and if he will make a statement. [26693]

**Mr. Soames:** Our proposal to transfer the Royal Marines school of music from Deal was announced by my right hon. and learned Friend the Secretary of State for Defence on 14 July 1994, *Official Report*, column *1171*. A consultation document was issued on 17 October. We have considered very carefully all the representations made during the consultation period.

I can now announce that we have decided to confirm the preferred option contained in the consultative document. The Royal Marines school of music will therefore transfer from Deal to Portsmouth, by spring 1966, where it will be housed in the Royal Naval detention quarters. They will not be required for their present purpose from the autumn of this year, and can be refurbished at modest cost to adapt them for the Royal Marines school of music.

The move will result in significant savings for the Defence budget. The closure of the stand-alone site at Deal, which is far too large for its present purpose, and the removal of the school to within the perimeter of the larger naval base at Portsmouth will save about £3 million per year in support costs. No significant additional support costs will be incurred at Portsmouth where the naval base has adequate infrastructure to absorb the relatively small school of music. The case for the transfer of the Royal Marines school of music has been thoroughly discussed with all interested parties including the hon. Member for Dover (Mr. Shaw), who has represented his constituents' views with understandable vigour. Indeed, of the many measures arising as a result of the "Defence Costs Study", the decision to close the Royal Marines school of music at Deal is one taken only with the greatest regret and in view of the clear financial case. We fully recognise the warm and close relationship which has grown up between the people of Deal and the Royal Marines in an association which dates back to 1664. I know that successive generations of recruits have been grateful for the friendliness and support they have received.

## Advisers

**Dr. David Clark:** To ask the Secretary of State for Defence if he will publish the names of the individuals who were recruited from outside the civil service and the military to advise him on "Options for Change" and "Front Line First", respectively. [26143]

**Mr. Freeman:** No external advisers were recruited for "Options for Change". For external advisers on "Front Line First", I refer the hon. Member to the answer my right hon. Friend the Member for Richmond and Barnes (Mr. Hanley) gave to the hon. Member for Leyton (Mr. Cohen) on 29 April 1994, *Official Report*, column *399*.

**Dr. David Clark:** To ask the Secretary of State for Defence if his previous paid special adviser, Perry Miller, underwent security clearance. [26146]

**Mr. Rifkind:** Yes.

**Dr. David Clark:** To ask the Secretary of State for Defence (1) what restrictions on future employment were made when Perry Miller was recruited as his special adviser. [26142]

(2) what written agreement on the scope of employment to be undertaken by Perry Miller when he left his Department as special adviser was reached with his private sector employer. [26144]

**Mr. Rifkind:** None, as special advisers are at present explicitly excluded from the business appointments rules.

**Dr. David Clark:** To ask the Secretary of State for Defence if his unpaid adviser, David Hart, underwent security clearance. [26147]

**Mr. Rifkind:** Mr. Hart has been subject to the checks necessary to permit him from time to time to have access to classified information.

## Trident

**Dr. David Clark:** To ask the Secretary of State for Defence (1) what assurances were provided by his Department to Devonport Management Ltd. in relation to the refitting of Trident submarines; and if he will make a statement; [26130]

(2) what is his Department's policy concerning the location of the refitting of Trident submarines; and what change there has been in his Department's policy in the last two years; [26132]

(3) what recent discussions he has had with Babcock International concerning the refitting of Trident submarines. [26131]

**Mr. Freeman:** It was announced by my right hon. and learned Friend the Secretary of State for Defence on 24 June 1993, *Official Report*, column *447*, that, subject to satisfactory contractual negotiations, refitting of Trident submarines will be undertaken at Devonport. Contractual negotiations are continuing, the details of which are commercially confidential, and no assurances have been provided to Devonport Management Ltd. There has been no change to that policy and Babcock International has no involvement of which I am aware with the provision of nuclear facilities at Devonport.

## Anti-ballistic Missile Defence System

**Dr. David Clark:** To ask the Secretary of State for Defence what is his Department's policy on the development of a European anti-ballistic missile defence system. [26128]

**Mr. Freeman:** The UK is currently considering whether a requirement exists for ballistic missile defence and this will be informed by the programme of pre-feasibility studies which I announced in the House on 18 October 1994, at columns 239–400. This assessment will include opportunities for European collaboration.

## Royal Welch Fusiliers, Gorazde

**Dr. David Clark:** To ask the Secretary of State for Defence if the Royal Welch Fusiliers based in Gorazde have *(a)* an adequate supply of fuel and *(b)* adequate stocks of food. [26252]

**Mr. Soames:** Yes, although restrictions on the movement of convoys to and from Gorazde have limited the use of fuel to essential tasks.

**Dr. David Clark:** To ask the Secretary of State for Defence what was the date of the three most recent deliveries of mail to the Royal Welch Fusiliers based in Gorazde. [26251]

**Mr. Soames:** On 21 April, 28 April and 19 May.

**Dr. David Clark:** To ask the Secretary of State for Defence what assessment he has made of the morale of the Royal Welch Fusiliers based in Gorazde; and if he will make a statement. [26124]

**Mr. Soames:** The British contingent in Gorazde is in good spirits and morale is high. Regular contact is maintained with the base and the situation is closely monitored.

**Dr. David Clark:** To ask the Secretary of State for Defence (1) if the Royal Welch Fusiliers based in Gorazde are under water rationing; and if water is available for washing purposes; [26250]

(2) if the Royal Welch Fusiliers based in Gorazde are under water rationing; and if water is available for washing purposes. [26250]

**Mr. Soames:** In order to preserve fuel, the water purification plant at the British base in Gorazde is running at a reduced rate and consequently some rationing of purified water has been introduced. However, supplies are being supplemented with sterilised water and adequate stocks are available. Water is also freely available for washing purposes.

**Dr. David Clark:** To ask the Secretary of State for Defence (1) if he will make a statement on the *(a)* leave roster for the Royal Welch Fusiliers based in Gorazde and *(b)* backlog in the granting of leave to members of the Royal Welch Fusiliers in Gorazde; [26122]

(2) what effect recent fighting in Gorazde has had on the granting of leave to members of the Royal Welch Fusiliers in Gorazde. [26123]

**Mr. Soames:** Restrictions on the movement of UN personnel to and from Gorazde have caused some difficulties for the leave roster of the Royal Welch Fusiliers. There are currently some 42 personnel with a backlog of leave which they are expected to be able to take before the end of their current tour of duty.

### Nimrod Aircraft

**Dr. David Clark:** To ask the Secretary of State for Defence which company is responsible for the maintenance and support of the Nimrod aircraft which crashed off the coast of Scotland on 16 May; when the contract with the company commenced; how many of his Department's aircraft are maintained by this company; who was responsible for the maintenance and support of the Nimrod aircraft before this contract came into force; and if he will list the dates and circumstances of any previous accidents involving Nimrod aircraft in the last five years. [26090]

**Mr. Soames:** Maintenance and servicing of RAF Nimrod aircraft is currently undertaken by RAF personnel at the Nimrod major servicing unit at RAF Kinloss. As a result of the "Competing for Quality" initiative, the work of the NMSU has been market tested and FRA Serco will assume responsibility for Nimrod servicing next month.

**Dr. David Clark:** To ask the Secretary of State for Defence what was the conclusion of the investigation into the recent crash off Scotland of a Nimrod aircraft; if he will place a copy of the report in the Library; and if he will make a statement. [26126]

**Mr. Soames:** A RAF board of inquiry was convened immediately after the accident; it is not, however, expected to report for some time. A copy of the summary of the inquiry's findings will be placed in the Library of the House.

**Dr. David Clark:** To ask the Secretary of State for Defence what was the base of the Nimrod which recently crashed off the Scottish coast; what operational duties it was carrying out at the time of the crash; and how many crew were on board the aircraft. [26089]

**Mr. Soames:** The Nimrod aircraft which ditched in the Moray firth on 16 May 1995 was based at RAF Waddington. It was engaged in a post-servicing air test. A total of seven crew were on board.

**Dr. David Clark:** To ask the Secretary of State for Defence how many Nimrod maritime patrol aircraft his Department possesses; what was the total cost of purchase of the aircraft; and where the aircraft are stationed. [26125]

**Mr. Freeman:** There are 26 operational Nimrod MR2 aircraft, including two in use reserves plus four spares. All are stationed at RAF Kinloss. The original total cost of these aircraft is not readily available and could be provided only at disproportionate cost.

### Nuclear Test Ban Treaty

**Dr. David Clark:** To ask the Secretary of State for Defence what changes to his Department's policy on a comprehensive nuclear test ban treaty have been made in the last four years. [26176]

**Mr. Freeman:** For many years, HMG have been committed to achieving the conclusion of an effective and verifiable comprehensive nuclear test ban treaty. We welcomed in August 1993 the conference on disarmament mandating an ad hoc committee on a nuclear test ban to negotiate such a treaty. We have kept our policy under close review and, for example, on 6 April this year announced in the conference on disarmament that we have now accepted that there should be no exemption in the draft treaty for tests in exceptional circumstances.

### Office Accommodation

**Dr. David Clark:** To ask the Secretary of State for Defence if he maintains a record of the total office area of his Department's main building on Whitehall which remains unused. [26175]

**Mr. Freeman:** My Department does record office accommodation which becomes temporarily vacant in main building. This record is updated on a regular basis.

### Compulsory Drug Tests

**Dr. David Clark:** To ask the Secretary of State for Defence how many members of the Army have taken part in compulsory drug tests; how many of these were positive drug tests and what has happened to these people; if individuals or units are selected for compulsory drug tests; which units have had compulsory drug tests; and how people are selected for compulsory drug tests. [26082]

**Mr. Soames:** At present, 4,420 officers and soldiers have provided specimens of urine as part of the compulsory drug testing programme. To date, 21 soldiers have tested positive; and of these, 15 have been either discharged or recommended for discharge; two are recommended to be given formal warnings, one of whom it is also recommended should be reduced in rank; two have elected for premature voluntary release; a decision on the remaining two is awaited. Units or sub-units have been selected at random, and individuals within them have been chosen by random selection of surname initial. The units and sub-units selected are as follows:

> Ministry of Defence, (Army department Main Building)
> Headquarters Northern Ireland
> Headquarters 1st (UK) Armoured Division
> Headquarters 42nd (Northern Western) Brigade
> Headquarters Herford Garrison
> Headquarters Lisburn Station
> Headquarters Joint Support Group Northern Ireland
> 16 Air Defence Regiment Royal Artillery
> 47th Field Regiment Royal Artillery
> 33 Engineer Regiment Royal Engineers
> 1st (UK) Armoured Division Headquarters and Signal Regiment
> 15th Signal Regiment
> 16th Signal Regiment
> 241 Signal Squadron
> 253 Signal Squadron
> Joint Communications Unit (Northern Ireland)
> 1st Battalion The Grenadier Guards
> 1st Battalion The Scots Guards
> 1st Battalion The Kings Own Scottish Borderers
> 1st Battalion The Queens Lancashire Regiment
> 1st Battalion The Highlanders
> 2nd Battalion The Parachute Regiment
> 9th Regiment Army Air Corp
> 5 Airborne Brigade Combat Services Support Battalion
> 12 Supply Regiment Royal Logistic Corp
> 15 Supply Regiment Royal Logistic Corp
> 21 Logistic Support Regiment Royal Logistic Corp
> 221 Explosive Ordnance Disposal Squadron Royal Logistic Corp
> 321 Explosive Ordnance Disposal Squadron Royal Logistic Corp
> 5 Field Ambulance Royal Army Medical Corp
> Army Pay and Documentation Office (Northern Ireland)
> Royal Military Police Training Centre Chichester
> 2nd Regiment Royal Military Police
> 74 Provost Company Royal Military Police
> 115 Provost Company Royal Military Police
> 36 Detachment Special Investigation Branch Royal Military Police
> 32 Army Education Centre
> 45 Army Education Centre
> Education Services
> 7 Dental Group
> 9 Dental Group
> Garrison Labour Support Unit Herford, Germany
> Army Families and Welfare Services Herford, Germany
> Army Careers and Information Office Herford, Germany
> Station Services Office Herford, Germany

Where parts of the units only are to be tested, individuals are selected by random selection based on surname initials. The selection involves the commanding officer and the drug testing officer completing separately a matrix. One matrix lists initials and the other contains numbers. Once completed, one matrix is then placed on the top of the other, and the surname initials are listed in order of priority according to the random selection. Personnel are then tested until the number of specimens allocated for testing that day are collected. If a whole unit is to be tested, as has been the policy since the beginning of March, the unit is selected by my Department at random from those available, and all personnel in barracks on that day are tested.

### Western European Union

**Dr. David Clark:** To ask the Secretary of State for Defence what is his policy concerning the creation of a WEU military satellite capability; and if he will make a statement. [26127]

**Mr. Soames:** The Western European Union is currently studying the possibilities of co-operation on a military satellite capability. The United Kingdom is contributing fully to that work. No decisions have yet been taken.

### Nuclear Test Veterans

**Dr. David Clark:** To ask the Secretary of State for Defence what is his Department's policy in respect of nuclear test veterans, and if he will make a statement. [26177]

**Mr. Soames:** Over a period of more than 40 years from the atmospheric nuclear tests in the 1950s and early 1960s, up to the end of 1990, there has been no overall excess of death and malignant disease among British nuclear test veterans. Out of over 20,000 veterans studies by the National Radiological Protection Board, more than 3,000 would have died, over 900 of them from cancer, if the veterans had suffered the same death and cancer rates as members of the public in the same age groups. In fact, fewer than 2,800 veterans died, fewer than 800 of them from cancer, these figures being no higher than for the matched control group in the NRPB study. These facts do not sustain a case for compensation.

### Manpower Reductions

**Dr. David Clark:** To ask the Secretary of State for Defence what is to be the percentage fall in the manpower strength of *(a)* the Army, *(b)* the Royal Air Force and *(c)* the Royal Navy between January 1990 and the completion of his Department's plans under the "Options for Change" and "Front Line First" initiatives. [26129]

**Mr. Soames:** The percentage fall in manpower strength of the Army, Royal Air Force and the Royal Navy on completion of MOD's plans under "Options for Change" and the "Front Line First" initiatives will depend on such factors as recruiting and turnover of personnel. Some of the "Front Line First" initiatives are still being considered. Manpower forecasts indicate that by 1995–96, manpower strengths will have fallen by 26 per cent. in the Army, 24 per cent. in the Royal Air Force and 21 per cent. for the Royal Navy since January 1990. These figures include some of the "Options for Change" measures already implemented.

### Gibraltar Garrison

**Mr. Mackinlay:** To ask the Secretary of State for Defence, pursuant to the oral statement of the Minister of State, the hon. Member for Eddisbury (Mr. Goodlad) of 20 December 1994, *Official Report*, column 1535, how many people have benefited from the tailored training courses provided by the Ministry of Defence for those affected by the drawdown of the Gibraltar garrison; and if he will make a statement. [26267]

**Mr. Soames:** To ease the impact of reductions in the garrison, the Ministry of Defence in Gibraltar provides training and retraining opportunities for its locally entered civilian staff. Courses are conducted either internally or by employing external educational authorities for vocational training. They include driver instruction, information technology, management, administration and engineering, all of which are recognised by the Gibraltar Government as valuable skills for future employment. Some 250 personnel have so far benefited from these training initiatives.

### EC Explanatory Memoranda

**Mrs. Gorman:** To ask the Secretary of State for Defence how many explanatory memoranda on EC proposals his Department has prepared since 19 July 1993; and for how many explanatory memoranda on EC proposals compliance cost assessments have been drawn up. [25799]

**Mr. Freeman:** None.

### Building Works

**Ms Hodge:** To ask the Secretary of State for Defence for each piece of work subject to a building process under the auspices of *(a)* the Ministry of Defence and *(b)* agencies for which the Ministry of Defence is responsible, where work was carried out, who were the successful bidders, and which contracts were won by in-house bidders in (1) 1993–94 and (2) 1994–95 and (3) 1995–96. [25498]

**Mr. Freeman:** The MOD assumed responsibility for the management and procurement of its works services from the PSA in April 1990. This was a new sphere of activity for the Department for which it had no in-house capacity. To meet this requirement, MOD set up Defence Works Services to act as its intelligent customer capability.

All of the information requested is not available centrally and could be provided only at disproportionate cost. However, it is possible to provide details of works contracts placed by my Department for construction projects, each costing more than £24,000, excluding VAT.

|  | Contracts | Value (inc. VAT) £ million |
|---|---|---|
| a) 1993–94 | 568 | 720 |
| b) 1994–95 | 479 | 545 |
| c) 1995–96 | 22 | '25 |

*Note:*
¹ April 1995 only.

My Department has no in-house capability for construction contracts and therefore there are no in-house bids.

Details of MOD works requirements are published fortnightly in the "Works Services Opportunities" bulletin—an example of which has been placed in the House of Commons Library—which is widely available on subscription.

### Retirements and Redundancies

**Ms Hodge:** To ask the Secretary of State for Defence how many people in *(a)* the Defence Department and *(b)* agencies for which the Defence Department is responsible (i) took early retirement, (ii) took voluntary redundancy, (iii) took compulsory redundancy and (iv) were retired on medical grounds in (1) 1993–94 and (2) 1994–95; and what is the projected figure for 1995–96. [25475]

**Mr. Freeman:** Details of staff who left my Department early are set out in the table. Records held centrally do not distinguish between staff of individual top level budgets or agencies, or terms of redundancy. Such information could be obtained only at disproportionate cost. Our present plans assume that more than 2,000 staff will leave under early retirement or redundancy terms in 1995–96.

| Year | Early retirement | Redundancy | Ill-health retirement |
|---|---|---|---|
| 1993–94 | 399 | 2,639 | 1,200 |
| 1994–95 | 166 | 3,058 | 1,120 |

**Ms Hodge:** To ask the Secretary of State for Defence what is the annual cost to his Department of staff leaving under redundancy/ early retirement schemes to incorporate *(a)* added years lump sum payments, *(b)* redundancy payments, *(c)* pension payments, including enhancements and *(d)* any other special arrangements for (i) 1993–94, (ii) 1994–95, (iii) projected for 1995–96 and (iv) projected for 1996–97. [25663]

**Mr. Freeman:** The costs to my Department of early retirement and redundancies are borne from the running costs provision. A detailed breakdown of the various costs could be obtained only at disproportionate cost. The total costs borne on my Department's running costs in 1993–94 and 1994–95 were £62 million and £59 million respectively. For 1995–96, the amount is estimated at £51 million. Projections for 1996–97 will be determined during the coming public expenditure survey.

**Ms Hodge:** To ask the Secretary of State for Defence how many posts were lost in *(a)* the Defence Department and *(b)* agencies for which the Defence Department is responsible, listing the total lost posts agency by agency for (i) 1993–94 and (ii) 1994–95; and how many posts are proposed to be lost in 1995–96. [25085]

**Mr. Freeman:** Historical information on posts lost is not kept centrally by my Department and could be provided only at disproportionate cost. The total number of permanent UK-based posts which it is estimated will be lost in 1995–96 is some 6,000.

**Ms Hodge:** To ask the Secretary of State for Defence (1) what changes there have been in the numbers of staff employed by *(a)* the Ministry of Defence and *(b)* agencies for which the Ministry of Defence is responsible, listing the changes in the number of staff agency by agency in (i) 1993–94 and (ii) 1994–95; and what changes are projected for 1995–96; [25066]

(2) how many staff of *(a)* the Defence Department and *(b)* agencies for which the Defence Department is responsible, were employed on a casual or short-term basis in (i) 1993–94 and (ii) 1994–95; and what are the projected figures for 1995–96; [25482]

(3) what changes there have been in the number of staff in employment by grade in *(a)* his Department is responsible in (i) 1993–94 and (ii) 1994–95; and what are the projected figures for 1995–96. [25555]

**Mr. Freeman:** The numbers of permanent and casual staff employed by my Department in 1993–94, projected outturn for 1994–95, and plans for 1995–96 are published annually in the departmental report by the Ministry of Defence, a copy of which is in the Library of the House.

No projections broken down by grade are available.

### Defence Export Services Organisation

**Dr. David Clark:** To ask the Secretary of State for Defence how many people work on the Iranian desk of the Defence Export Services Organisation. [26134]

**Mr. Freeman:** The DESO does not have a desk responsible specifically for Iran. Inquiries are handled by a section of three people, who are also responsible for seven other countries.

## FOREIGN AND COMMONWEALTH AFFAIRS

### Intergovernmental Conference on Political Union

**Mr. Spearing:** To ask the Secretary of State for Foreign and Commonwealth Affairs if, in respect of the intergovernmental conference on political union convened by the European Council at its meeting in Dublin on 25 and 26 June 1990, he will state *(a)* the date and location of each meeting, *(b)* the names of those representing the United Kingdom, *(c)* the relevant duration of each meeting and *(d)* which parts of the draft treaty on political union (i) were, and (ii) were not incorporated into the draft treaty on European Union signed at Maastricht on 9 and 10 December 1991.

**Mr. David Davis** *[holding answer 7 March 1995]:* Ministerial meetings were held on the following dates as part of the 1990–91 intergovernmental conference on political union:

| Date | Representative | Location |
|------|----------------|----------|
| *1990*<br>15 December | (Formal Opening of IGC) Prime Minister and Foreign Secretary | Rome |
| *1991*<br>4–5 February | Foreign Secretary | Brussels |
| 4 March | Foreign Secretary and the right hon. Member for Watford (Mr. Garel-Jones) | Brussels |
| 26 March | (Informal Foreign Ministers meeting) Foreign Secretary | Luxembourg |
| 8 April | (Special European Council) Prime Minister and Foreign Secretary | Luxembourg |
| 15 April | Right hon. Member for Watford (Mr. Garel-Jones) | Luxembourg |
| 27–28 April | (Informal Foreign Ministers meeting) Foreign Secretary | Luxembourg |

| Date | Representative | Location |
|------|----------------|----------|
| 13–14 May | Foreign Secretary and the right hon. Member for Watford (Mr. Garel-Jones) | Brussels |
| 3 June | (Informal Foreign Ministers meeting) Foreign Secretary | Dresden |
| 17–18 June | Foreign Secretary | Luxembourg |
| 23 June | Right hon. Member for Watford (Mr. Garel-Jones) | Luxembourg |
| 28–29 June | (European Council) Prime Minister and Foreign Secretary | Luxembourg |
| 29–30 July | Right hon. Member for Watford (Mr. Garel-Jones) | Brussels |
| 30 September | Foreign Secretary and the right hon. Member for Watford (Mr. Garel-Jones) | Brussels |
| 5–6 October | (Informal Foreign Ministers meeting) Foreign Secretary | The Hague |
| 28 October | Right hon. Member for Watford (Mr. Garel-Jones) | Brussels |
| 4–5 November | Foreign Secretary and the right hon. Member for Watford (Mr. Garel-Jones) | Brussels |
| 12–13 November | Foreign Secretary and the right hon. Member for Watford (Mr. Garel-Jones) | The Hague |
| 2–3 December | Foreign Secretary and the right hon. Member for Watford (Mr. Garel-Jones) | Brussels |
| 9–10 December | (European Council) Prime Minister and Foreign Secretary | Maastricht |

This was an on-going negotiation, none of which was finalised until the Maastricht European Council on 10 December 1991, following which the treaty on European Union was signed at Maastricht on 7 February 1992.

### Nuclear Non-proliferation Treaty

**Mr. Menzies Campbell:** To ask the Secretary of State for Foreign and Commonwealth Affairs if he will make a statement on Her Majesty's Government's policy in respect of the recommendations made in the European Parliament's motion on the extension of the nuclear non-proliferation treaty, adopted on 5 April, relating to *(a)* nuclear weapon states opening all their nuclear facilities to inspection by the International Atomic Energy Agency, *(b)* the creation of an international office to control plutonium and highly enriched uranium, *(c)* nuclear weapon states declaring that they will refrain from the first use of nuclear weapons against non-nuclear states, *(d)* for the conference of disarmament to begin negotiations on a nuclear weapons convention, *(e)* for the nuclear weapons states to agree a timetable and funding for fulfilling their obligations under article VI of the nuclear non-proliferation treaty and (*f*) for the creation of a nuclear weapons register; and if he will list those recommendations which Her Majesty's Government (i) support and (ii) do not support.

**Mr. David Davis** [*holding answer 4 May 1995*]: My right hon. Friend the Secretary of State for Foreign and Commonwealth Affairs made a statement on the nuclear non-proliferation treaty review and extension conference on 16 May. Our civil nuclear facilities are subject to international safeguards. We do not support any of the other recommendations.

### European Union

**Mr. Austin Mitchell:** To ask the Secretary of State for Foreign and Commonwealth Affairs which east European states he expects to be eligible for EEC membership; what timetable he envisages; and what size of fishing fleet each of these states has.        [25381]

**Mr. David Davis:** The Copenhagen European Council in 1993 agreed that the associated countries of central and eastern Europe that so desired would become members of the European Union. Their accessions would take place once they were able to assume the obligations of membership. The present associates are Poland, Hungary, the Czech Republic, Slovakia, Romania and Bulgaria. Similar association agreements are expected to be signed with the Baltic states at the 12 June Foreign Affairs Council, and another is being negotiated with Slovenia.

According to the latest FAO figures, for 1992, the Polish fishing fleet has 521 vessels, 249,079 gross tonnage; the Bulgarian, 38 vessels, 86,600 gross tonnage; the Latvian, 141 vessels, 343,236 gross tonnage; the Lithuanian, 162 vessels, 236,268 gross tonnage; the Estonian, 249 vessels, 180,921 gross tonnage; and, according to 1989 OECD figures, the Romanian fleet has 106 vessels, 237,457 gross tonnage. Figures are not available for Slovenia.

**Mr. Gill:** To ask the Secretary of State for Foreign and Commonwealth Affairs what are the specific contributions to the nation's security which arise from membership of the European Union which are not adequately covered by membership of the North Atlantic Treaty Organisation, the Western European Union, the United Nations and Organisation of Security and Co-operation.        [25770]

**Mr. David Davis:** The security of the United Kingdom is enhanced by the contribution that membership of the European Union makes to our prosperity. It benefits from intergovernmental co-operation under the Maastricht treaty in the fields of justice and home affairs, especially with respect to fighting cross-border crime and drug trafficking. Our participation in the common foreign and security policy enables us to exercise greater influence in foreign affairs, including relations with Russia, Ukraine and central and eastern Europe.

### National Minorities

**Sir Donald Thompson:** To ask the Secretary of State for Foreign and Commonwealth Affairs, pursuant to his answer of 3 March, *Official Report*, column *731*, what further actions are necessary prior to ratification by the United Kingdom of the Council of Europe framework convention for the protection of national minorities; when he expects these actions to be completed; and if he will make a statement.        [25473]

**Mr. David Davis:** The framework convention accords closely with our national legislation and policies on non-discrimination equality of opportunity, hence our decision in principle to ratify it. There are some technical points which we wish to consider further before ratifying.

### Ms Mukhtaj Bibi

**Mr. Madden:** To ask the Secretary of State for Foreign and Commonwealth Affairs when Ms Mukhtaj Bibi, ref: GV100/21701/VT, is going to be interviewed and the United Kingdom post in Islamabad in connection with her application to enter the United Kingdom.        [25990]

**Mr. Baldry:** I have asked the high commission at Islamabad for details and will arrange for the hon. Member to receive a substantive reply from the migration and visa correspondence unit as soon as possible.

### Turkey

**Sir Russell Johnston:** To ask the Secretary of State for Foreign and Commonwealth Affairs if he will make it the policy of Her Majesty's Government to support the proposal of the Parliamentary Assembly of the Council of Europe, in recommendation 1266–1995, that the Committee of Ministers should call on Turkey to withdraw its forces from northern Iraq and set a specific timetable for Turkey to bring its constitution and legislation in line with the principles and standards of the Council of Europe; and if he will make a statement.        [25860]

**Mr. David Davies:** At its meeting on 11 May, the Committee of Ministers took note of the Parliamentary Assembly's recommendation 1266–1995 on

"Turkey's military intervention in norther Iraq and on Turkey's military intervention in northern Iraq and on Turkey's respect of commitments concerning constitutional and legislative reforms",

and instructed its deputies to prepare a reply.

We have noted with satisfaction the announcement by the Turkish Government on 4 May that their forces have withdrawn completely form northern Iraq. We are urging the Turkish Government to take equal account of our concerns over democratisation and human rights.

### Gibraltar

**Mr. Mackinlay:** To ask the Secretary of State for Foreign and Commonwealth Affairs what reply he has received to his representation made on 19 April to Foreign Minister Carlos Westendorp about the delays on the Gibraltar-Spain border.        [26260]

**Mr. David Davis:** None.

**Mr. Mackinlay:** To ask the Secretary of State for Foreign and Commonwealth Affairs (1) pursuant to the oral statement of the Minister of State, the right hon. Member for Eddisbury (Mr. Goodlad) of 20 December, *Official Report*, column 1535, what courses of action Her Majesty's Government have taken as a consequence of the deliberations of the Gibraltar joint economic forum;        [26268]

(2) what assistance and advice has been offered to the Gibraltar Government to expand and diversify their economy; and if he will make a statement.        [26255]

**Mr. David Davis:** We have provided extensive advice and assistance to the Government of Gibraltar. An economic study, identifying market opportunities which could be exploited by Gibraltar, was supplied in 1993, and another dealing with the impact of MOD drawdown and ways to compensate for that in 1994. In 1994, we set up the joint economic forum to consider ways of assisting Gibraltar in the wake of that rundown. We have also negotiated considerable EC structural funds help for Gibraltar. The MOD runs a training programme.

All this took place against the background of the completion of the 1986 to 1990 development grant, following which the Gibraltar Government have not requested further UK bilateral assistance.

**Mr. Mackinlay:** To ask the Secretary of State for Foreign and Commonwealth Affairs if he will give details of the longest wait and extent of delays for pedestrians and cars in either direction on the Gibraltar-Spain border, for each day since 17 May. [26259]

**Mr. David Davis:** I will write to the hon. Member shortly.

**Mr. Mackinlay:** To ask the Secretary of State for Foreign and Commonwealth Affairs, pursuant to the oral statement of the Minister of State, the hon. Member for Boothferry (Mr. Davis), of 17 May, *Official Report,* column 307, if he will amplify on the method by which Her Majesty's Government have stood up for the rights of Gibraltarians in the current border problems; and what is the measure of success to date. [26257]

**Mr. David Davis:** The oral statement of the Minister of State referred to set out the position.

**Mr. Mackinlay:** To ask the Secretary of State for Foreign and Commonwealth Affairs, pursuant to the oral statement of the Minister of State, the right hon. Member for Eddisbury (Mr. Goodlad) of 20 December, *Official Report,* column 1534, if he has anything to add to his comments about spurious claims by the Spaniards in regard to the success rate of the Royal Gibraltar police in seizing illegal substances. [26265]

**Mr. David Davis:** I have nothing further to add to the remarks made by my right hon. Friend the Member for Eddisbury, except to add my own congratulations to the splendid achievements of the members of the Royal Gibraltar police. The continued achievements this year are worthy of the highest praise.

**Mr. Mackinlay:** To ask the Secretary of State for Foreign and Commonwealth Affairs what is the current status of the talks under the Brussels process in respect of Gibraltar; and if he will make a statement. [26254]

**Mr. David Davis:** The last ministerial meeting under the Brussels process took place on 20 December 1994. I refer the hon. Gentleman to the answer the Minster of State, my right hon. and learned Friend the Member for Grantham (Mr. Hogg), gave the hon. Member for Uxbridge (Mr. Shersby) on 10 January 1995, *Official Report,* column 62.

**Mr. Mackinlay:** To ask the Secretary of State for Foreign and Commonwealth Affairs what reply the United Kingdom ambassador to Spain has received following his representations on 21 April to the Spanish Foreign Minister about the delays on the Gibraltar-Spain border. [26261]

**Mr. David Davis:** None. I made clear in my oral statement of 17 May, *Official Report,* columns 300–7, the attitude of the Spanish Government to the delays at the Spain-Gibraltar frontier remains unacceptable.

**Mr. Mackinlay:** To ask the Secretary of State for Foreign and Commonwealth Affairs, pursuant to the oral statement of the Minister of State, the right hon. Member for Eddisbury (Mr. Goodlad), of 20 December, *Official Report,* column 1533, if it is Her Majesty's Government's

policy to abide by the democratically expressed wish of the people of Gibraltar, in respect of their links with the Crown. [26269]

**Mr. David Davis:** Yes. Our commitment remains firm, as set out in the preamble to the 1969 Gibraltar constitution.

**Mr. Mackinlay:** To ask the Secretary of State for Foreign and Commonwealth Affairs, pursuant to his oral answer of 20 December 1994, *Official Report,* column 1535, what response has been received to the request that the Spanish Government substantiate their allegations that Gibraltar is a money laundering centre. [26188]

**Mr. David Davis:** None.

**Mr. Mackinlay:** To ask the Secretary of State for Foreign and Commonwealth Affairs if he will list those European directives which the United Kingdom Government have requested the Gibraltar Government to enact in their legislature. [26263]

**Mr. David Davis:** As in any other part of the EU, the Gibraltar Government must implement all applicable EU legislation.

**Mr. Mackinlay:** To ask the Secretary of State for Foreign and Commonwealth Affairs what representations have been made by the United Kingdom Government to the Spanish Government since 17 May about the delays on the Gibraltar-Spain border; and what replies have been received. [26258]

**Mr. David Davis:** My right hon. Friend the Secretary of State for Foreign and Commonwealth Affairs has made our views clear to the Spanish Foreign Minister.

**Mr. Mackinlay:** To ask the Secretary of State for Foreign and Commonwealth Affairs, pursuant to the oral statement of the Minister of State, the right hon. Member for Eddisbury (Mr. Goodlad), of 20 December, *Official Report,* column 1532, if he will detail the protests previously made by Her Majesty's Government to Spain about border controls and delays. [26266]

**Mr. David Davis:** On 1 December 1994, I summoned the Spanish ambassador to express our strong concern at the intrusive and disruptive checks in question; and made clear that they should cease. We also repeatedly and vigorously protested at the highest levels to the Spanish authorities on other occasions.

**Mr. Mackinlay:** To ask the Secretary of State for Foreign and Commonwealth Affairs if he has in his discussions and communications with the Chief Minister of Gibraltar, intimated circumstances where the United Kingdom Government might suspend the Gibraltar constitution or dismiss the Gibraltar Government. [26253]

**Mr. David Davis:** No.

**Mr. Mackinlay:** To ask the Secretary of State for Foreign and Commonwealth Affairs if he will list the legislation, other than that derived from European directives, which the United Kingdom Government have requested the Gibraltar Government to enact in their legislature; and if he will detail the reason in each case. [26262]

**Mr. David Davis:** We have asked the Government of Gibraltar to enact a number of pieces of legislation relating to good government and fulfilling the UK's international obligations.

**Mr. Mackinlay:** To ask the Secretary of State for Foreign and Commonwealth Affairs, pursuant to his answer of 20 December 1994, *Official Report*, column 1535, what response has been received to the request that the Spanish Government substantiate their allegation that the co-operation of Gibraltar has been refused in respect of combating money laundering. [26189]

**Mr. David Davis:** None. We have asked the Spaniards twice since then at trilateral talks with Gibraltar, and have received no response.

**Mr. Mackinlay:** To ask the Secretary of State for Foreign and Commonwealth Affairs, pursuant to the oral statement of the Minister of State, the hon. Member for Boothferry, (Mr. Davis), of 17 May, *Official Report*, column 307, what response has been received in respect of United Kingdom protests at the delays on the Gibraltar-Spain border from *(a)* the Schengen states, *(b)* the European Commission, *(c)* the Schengen secretariat and *(d)* the Schengen presidency. [26256]

**Mr. David Davis:** We cannot provide details of confidential discussions; but we are confident that our concerns are fully understood by all those to whom we have spoken.

**Mr. Mackinlay:** To ask the Secretary of State for Foreign and Commonwealth Affairs what quantity of illegal substances has been seized by the Royal Gibraltar police in each of the past two years. [26264]

**Mr. David Davis:** In 1993, approximately 1.5 tonnes were seized or found. In 1994, over 2 tonnes were seized or found.

### Western Sahara

**Mr. Corbyn:** To ask the Secretary of State for Foreign and Commonwealth Affairs what protests have been made to the Moroccan Government over the arrests of Polisario supporters on 11 and 12 May during a peaceful demonstration; and if he will make a statement on Her Majesty's Government's policy towards the Western Sahara. [26270]

**Mr. Douglas Hogg:** The UN is investigating the incident and will report to the Security Council. We continue to support the efforts of the UN Secretary-General to bring about an early resolution of the dispute concerning the Western Sahara in accordance with the UN's settlement plan.

### Armenia

**Mr. Madden:** To ask the Secretary of State for Foreign and Commonwealth Affairs on what date he now expects a British embassy to be established in Armenia; and if he will make a statement. [25983]

**Mr. Douglas Hogg:** We expect our ambassador, Mr. David Miller OBE, to arrive at post in Yerevan by the end of July.

### Iran

**Dr. David Clark:** To ask the Secretary of State for Foreign and Commonwealth Affairs what is his Department's policy on the export of arms to Iran; and what changes there have been to it there have been in the last two years. [26135]

**Mr. Douglas Hogg:** There have been no changes to our policy on arms exports to Iran since it was announced by my right hon. Friend the Secretary of State for Foreign and Commonwealth Affairs on 1 March 1993. We continue to apply the following criteria in considering applications for the export of licensable goods to Iran:

(i) With two exceptions we should not approve licences for any goods or technology on the military or atomic energy lists— schedule 1, part 3, groups 1 and 2—of the Export of Goods (Control) Order 1992, as amended. The exceptions are:

(a) goods essential for the safety of civil aircraft and air traffic control systems;

(b) radioactive material in the form of sources for medical equipment and deuterium labelled compounds for medical use.

(ii) We should not approve licences for any equipment, including the exceptions to the complete ban mentioned above, where there was knowledge or reason to suspect that it would go to a military end-user or be used for military purposes.

Existing export licences, approved under the old guidelines, will remain valid. We shall support efforts among supplier countries, in particular the G7 and our European partners, to promote a harmonised approach to effective controls on the export of dual-use goods to countries of particular concern.

### TRANSPORT

#### Smoked Glass Windows (Cars)

**Mr. John Morris:** To ask the Secretary of State for Transport if he will introduce legislation to prohibit motorcars having smoked glass in their side and rear windows. [25408]

**Mr. Norris:** No. Regulation 32 of Road Vehicles (Construction and Use) Regulations 1986 already prohibits, with certain limited exceptions, the fitment of excessively dark or smoked glass in the windows of motorcars first used on or after 1 June 1978.

#### British Rail Employees (Statutory Rights)

**Mr. Chidgey:** To ask the Secretary of State for Transport if former employees of British Rail working for a new railway contractor following the privatisation of British Rail will be entitled to statutory redundancy pay and statutory sick pay based upon their cumulative employment under both employers. [25806]

**Mr. Watts:** Provided a move from one employer to another is part of a transfer of an undertaking where employees are transferred with their existing contracts of service to the new undertaking—that is, a transfer to which the provisions of the Transfer of Undertakings (Protection of Employment) Regulations 1981 apply— then continuity of employment is maintained. This means that employment with both employers counts towards any statutory or contractual entitlements which have a minimum qualifying period or are based on length of service.

#### Road Accident Victims (Compensation)

**Mr. Colvin:** To ask the Secretary of State for Transport if he will review the Road Traffic Acts with a view to providing scope for compensation for the victims of driving offences. [26190]

**Mr. Norris:** There are no plans for such a review.

## Motor Cycle Tests

**Mr. Madden:** To ask the Secretary of State for Transport (1) how many motor cycle testing stations there are in *(a)* Bradford and *(b)* Leeds; what is the current waiting list at each of these stations; how many test inspectors are employed at each station; how many hours and on what days each station holds tests; what contingency arrangements are to be introduced if motor cyclists are unable to be tested before the expiry of a provisional licence; and if he will make a statement;                 [26138]

(2) what action he is taking to facilitate motor cyclists living in *(a)* Bradford and Leeds and *(b)* other parts of West Yorkshire to take any tests they are required to take without undue delay.                 [26137]

**Mr. Norris:** These are operational matters for the Driving Standards Agency. I have asked the chief executive to write to the hon. Member.

*Letter from B. I. Herdan to Mr. Max Madden, dated 25 May 1995:*

The Secretary of State for Transport has asked me to reply to your questions about motorcycle tests in Bradford and Leeds.

The Agency offers motorcycle tests at the centres at Wibsey, Bradford and Horsforth, Leeds. At these centres local demand is such that current waiting times are 2 and 9 weeks respectively. These include test slots provisionally reserved by Approved Training Bodies where payment is required not later than 10 clear working days before the day of the test. Earlier dates may therefore become available at Horsforth if provisionally reserved slots are not taken up, or there are cancellations, and the centre is within reasonable travelling distance of Wibsey where current demand is not so great. There is one motorcycle examiner at each centre who conducts tests three days a week. At Wibsey this is on Monday, Tuesday and Wednesday, and at Horsforth on Tuesday, Wednesday and Thursday. These involve full daily programmes of 8 tests a day.

Where there is a specific need for an earlier test date, for example the expiry of a provisional licence, our Regional Office in Newcastle which currently deals with the books for West Yorkshire always endeavours to make additional programmes available to meet this need. This will obviously depend on the examiner resources available at the time and the method of notice given by the candidate.

## Lorry Registration

**Mr. Flynn:** To ask the Secretary of State for Transport what evidence he has that United Kingdom lorry firms are registering their vehicles elsewhere in the European Union; and what loss of revenue is involved.      [26027]

**Mr. Norris:** I know of no such evidence.

## A13

**Mr. Mackinlay:** To ask the Secretary of State for Transport what is the latest date when the construction of the new A13 road between the Heathway-Thames avenue and Mardyke-Wennington sections must commence before compensation or penalty payments may be invoked by the promoters of the channel tunnel rail link route; and if he will make a statement.      [26026]

**Mr. Watts:** The competition to select the private section promoter is still under way, and the details of the contract between the promoter and the Secretary of State are not yet finalised. However, the environmental statement for the hybrid Bill assumed that these sections of the A13 would be completed before the relevant part of CTRL construction commenced.

## Taxis (Smoking Ban)

**Mr. Bendall:** To ask the Secretary of State for Transport what is the Government's policy on allowing licensed taxi drivers to ban smoking in their cabs; and what plans the Government have to allow them to do so.      [26184]

**Mr. Norris:** Taxi drivers may request passengers not to smoke in their cabs.

The courts, in interpreting the compellability law, have ruled that the fact that an intending passenger was smoking was not a "reasonable excuse" for the driver to refuse to carry him or her.

The Government have already announced in "The Health of the Nation" White Paper that they propose to change the law to allow a taxi driver to designate his or her cab as a "no smoking" one and then to refuse passengers that are smoking. This proposal awaits a suitable legislative opportunity.

## Driving Tests

**Mr. Dalyell:** To ask the Secretary of State for Transport, pursuant to his letter M/PSO/5928/95 of 1 May, when he expects to complete his assessment of hazard perception tests and to reach decisions about heavy elements in driving tests as required by the second EC directive on driver licensing.      [25761]

**Mr. Norris** *[holding answer 24 May 1995]:* I refer the hon. Member to the written answer that I gave my hon. Friend the Member for Eltham (Mr. Bottomley) on 23 May, *Official Report,* columns *567–68.*

## Double Glazing Grails

**Mr. Chidgey:** To ask the Secretary of State for Transport what grants his Department provides for double glazing of residential properties adjacent to motorways where noise levels are unreasonably high.      [25033]

**Mr. Watts** *[holding answer 23 May 1995]:* This is an operational matter for the Highways Agency. I have asked the chief executive to write to the hon. Member.

*Letter from Lawrie Haynes to Mr. David Chidgey, dated 25 May 1995:*

The Minister for Railways and Roads, John Watts, has asked me to reply to your recent question about the provision of double glazing adjacent to motorways where noise levels are unreasonably high.

The Highways Agency does not provide specific grants for double glazing of residential properties.

Owners of properties eligible under the Noise Insulation Regulations 1975 are offered a provision of insulation or grant in lieu in accordance with the relevant specifications set out in Schedule 1 of the Regulations. The regulations specify secondary glazing of existing windows or exceptionally a new replacement double window.

## Bus Services (Complaints)

**Ms Walley:** To ask the Secretary of State for Transport if he will list by traffic area office for each of the last five years the number of complaints received from members of the public regarding the operation of local bus services.      [25912]

**Mr. Norris:** The available information is given in the attached table.

*Number of complaints received by Traffic Area Offices from the general public since 1990*

| Traffic Area | 1990–91 | 1991–92 | 1992–93 | 1993–94 | 1994–95 |
|---|---|---|---|---|---|
| WTA | 84 | 53 | 87 | 101 | 105 |
| SEMTA | 34 | 40 | 62 | 42 | 69 |
| NWTA | 41 | 59 | 52 | 35 | 32 |
| SCOT | 37 | 63 | 55 | 95 | 120 |
| ETA | 98 | 103 | 76 | 71 | 109 |
| NETA | ¹220 | ¹230 | 237 | 321 | 205 |
| WMTA | n/a | n/a | 90 | 133 | 109 |
| SWTA | n/a | n/a | 96 | 60 | 110 |

*Note:*

¹ Estimated figures.

## Road Scheme Acquisitions

**Mr. Spearing:** To ask the Secretary of State for Transport under what Acts and statutory instruments road scheme acquisitions have or will have been made of *(a)* housing north and south of the A40 Western avenue in the London borough of Hammersmith and *(b)* housing on the north side of the A13 Newham way west of its intersection with the A112 Prince Regent land; and in respect of each scheme (i) what are the costs of housing acquisitions and compensations, (ii) what is the total cost of the scheme, (iii) what statutory procedures are outstanding and (iv) what are the firm dates of commencement and completion. [24481]

**Mr. Watts:** This is an operational matter for the Highways Agency. I have asked the chief executive to write to the hon. Member.

*Letter from Lawrie Haynes to Mr. Nigel Spearing, dated 25 May 1995:*

I have been asked to write to you with the information you requested in your question in the house about the trunk road improvement schemes at A40 Western Circus and A13/A112 Prince Regent Land junctions.

The Secretary of State for Transport acquires properties for road construction under the Highways Act 1980, the Acquisition of Land Act 1981 and the Compulsory Purchase Act 1965 and, in planning blight cases, under the Town and Country Planning act 1990. He pays compensation for the properties acquired under the Land Compensation Acts 1961 and 1973.

The Highways Agency, on behalf of the Secretary of State, requires (a) houses north and south of the A40 for the trunk road improvement scheme at Western Circus in the Borough of Hammersmith and (b) houses north of A13 Newham Way to the west of A112 Prince Regent Land for the improvement of the A13/A112 junction.

(1) The total cost of the housing and compensation for these properties is estimated for (a) at £3.1 million and for (b) £3.4 million.

(ii) The total estimated costs of the schemes are (a) £48 million and (b) £40 million; including costs already incurred of £10 million and £3 million respectively.

(iii) The statutory procedures for (a) are complete, and for (b) are awaiting a decision by the Secretaries of State whether the scheme should proceed, following the public inquiry held last year. The outstanding statutory procedures for (b) are: the A13 Trunk Road (A112 Prince Regent Lane Junction Improvement, The Trunk Road and Slip Roads) Order 19;

the A13 Trunk Road (A112 Prince Regent Lane Junction Improvement, Side Roads) Order 19;

the A13 Trunk Road (A112 Prince Regent Lane Junction Improvement) Compulsory Purchase Order (No.) 19; and

the proposal to issue a certificate of exchange land; entitled, The Open Space Land at Canning Town Recreation Ground, former Beckton Lido Site and Prince Regent Lane Playing Field.

(iv) The main construction of the A40 Western Circus scheme is planned to start in the first quarter of 1996; a firmer date for start of works will not be available until tenders for the project have been assessed. The improvement scheme for the A13/A112 junction will proceed to construction after the statutory procedures are completed, provided resources are available.

## TRADE AND INDUSTRY

### Export Licences

**Mr. Bennett:** To ask the President of the Board of Trade (1) under which military list specifications, as specified in group 1 of part III of schedule 1 of Statutory Instrument 1992 No. 3092 goods for export to Argentina were refused five export licences in 1993; [25751]

(2) goods for export to China were refused three export licences in 1993. [25752]

**Mr. Ian Taylor:** The goods in question were classified under ML5, ML9 and ML10 in respect of Argentina and ML5, ML11 and ML15 in respect of China.

**Mr. Byers:** To ask the President of the Board of Trade, pursuant to his answer of 30 March, *Official Report*, column 777 if the exporters of goods with potential defence applications were required in every case to obtain end user certificates for the export of goods licensed under the military list. [25697]

**Mr. Ian Taylor** *[holding answer 22 May 1995]:* Where military list goods were to be exported to an overseas Government Department, no end-user certificate was required by the DTI export licensing unit, though a copy of the contract or purchase order was requested.

For military list exports to companies and private consignees, exporters were required to submit sufficient information to enable the ELU to assess the export licence application. The guidance note on filling out an export licence application said that exporters should supply an end-user certificate, or an end-use statement or an international import certificate, but this was not insisted upon in all cases.

**Mrs. Clwyd:** To ask the President of the Board of Trade if he will list the companies to which export licences were granted for the export of electronic batons in 1991. [25614]

**Mr. Ian Taylor** *[holding answer 22 May 1995]:* No licences were granted for these goods in 1991.

### Iraq (Export Credit Guarantees)

**Mr. Byers:** To ask the President of the Board of Trade, pursuant to his answer of 30 March, *Official Report*, column 777, if BMARC received support from the Export Credits Guarantee Department for contracts with Iraq between 1985 and 1990. [25684]

**Mr. Ian Taylor:** No.

### Instruments of Torture

**Mrs. Clwyd:** To ask the President of the Board of Trade if he will further regulate the sale of equipment which can be used, and has been designated, for use against persons in repressive conditions. [25693]

**Mr. Ian Taylor** *[holding answer 22 May 1995]:* It is not feasible to control the export of the many innocuous goods that can be misused for torture. Exports of weapons, security and para-military police goods are controlled under the terms of the Export of Goods (Control) Order. Licences are granted only after careful consideration of the political and military implications of the proposed sale, with particular attention paid to the human rights record of the proposed recipient country. The Department would not knowingly give any support to promote sales overseas of torture equipment. I see no need for further regulation.

The regulation of firearms sales within Great Britain is a matter for my right hon. and learned Friend the Secretary of State for the Home Department.

### Regional Airports

**Mr. Jim Cunningham:** To ask the President of the Board of Trade what recent economic assessment he has made of the economic benefits of regional airports to regional economies. [24977]

**Mr. Eggar:** The Department of Trade and Industry has not made any such recent economic assessment. The Department is aware of a recent study by the Civil Aviation Authority entitled "The Economic Impact of New Air Services", which examines the impact of new long haul services from Manchester and Birmingham airports. This contains useful references to other similar studies.

### Consultants

**Ms Hodge:** To ask the President of the Board of Trade what is the level of expenditure on consultancy by *(a)* his Department and *(b)* agencies for which his Department is responsible for (i) 1993–94 and (ii) 1994–95; and what are the projected figures for 1995–96. [25542]

**Mr. Ian Taylor:** I refer the hon. Member to the answer I gave to the hon. Member for Gordon (Mr. Bruce) on 10 February 1995, *Official Report,* column *429,* which shows the fees paid by the Department for general consultancies for 1993–94. Corresponding provisional outturn figures for 1994–95, budget figures for 1995–96 and a breakdown of the 1993–94 figure between the Department and its agencies are detailed in the following table.

*£000*

|  | *1993–94* | *1994–95* | *1995–96* |
|---|---|---|---|
| Department | 3,345 | 4,445 | ¹— |
| Executive Agencies | 1,429 | 1,734 | 1,584 |
| Total | 4,774 | 6,179 | 1,584 |

*Note:*
¹ The Department's allocation for 1995–96 will be set shortly in the light of the outcome of MINIS 95.

### Retirements and Redundancies

**Ms Hodge:** To ask the President of the Board of Trade how many staff of *(a)* the Department of Trade and Industry and *(b)* agencies for which the DTI is responsible (i) took early retirement, (ii) took voluntary redundancy, (iii) took compulsory redundancy and (iv) were retired on medical grounds in (i) 1993–94 and (ii) 1994–95; and what are the projected figures for 1995–96. [25416]

**Mr. Ian Taylor:** The figures requested are shown in the following table. The 1995–96 projections represent current estimates which may be modified during the course of the year. In preparing these tables, redundancies have been taken as covering those cases which involve early severance on redundancy.

|  | *Early retirement* | | *Voluntary redundancy* | | *Compulsory redundancy* | | *Medical retirement* | | *Current total projections 1995–96 (all categories)* |
|---|---|---|---|---|---|---|---|---|---|
|  | *1993–94* | *1994–95* | *1993–94* | *1994–95* | *1993–94* | *1994–95* | *1993–94* | *1994–95* |  |
| DTI | 302 | 64 | 5 | 28 | 22 | 16 | 31 | 34 | 300 |
| *Agencies:* | | | | | | | | | |
| CH | 0 | 0 | 0 | 0 | 2 | 0 | 8 | 13 | 0 |
| INSS | 10 | 18 | 0 | 0 | 0 | 7 | 13 | 11 | 13 |
| LGC | 14 | 7 | 0 | 10 | 0 | 1 | 0 | 1 | 5 |
| NEL | 0 | 0 | 69 | 44 | 0 | 0 | 0 | 0 | 10 |
| NPL | 35 | 1 | 0 | 0 | 1 | 0 | 8 | 0 | 55 |
| NWML | 1 | 0 | 0 | 0 | 0 | 0 | 1 | 1 | 0 |
| PATS | 1 | 7 | 0 | 0 | 0 | 1 | 7 | 13 | 18 |
| RA | 10 | 5 | 0 | 0 | 4 | 0 | 5 | 2 | 6 |

**Ms Hodge:** To ask the President of the Board of Trade what is the annual cost to his Department of staff leaving under redundancy/early retirement schemes to incorporate (i) added years lump sum payments, (ii) redundancy payments, (iii) pension payments, including enhancements and, (iv) any other special arrangements for *(a)* 1993–94, *(b)* 1994–95, and projected for *(c)* 1995–96 and *(d)* 1996–97. [25635]

**Mr. Ian Taylor:** Most of the costs to the Department of early retirement and redundancies are borne from the Department's running costs provision. A detailed breakdown of the various costs could be obtained only at disproportionate cost.

The total costs borne by the Department in 1993–94 and 1994–95 were £13,498,000 and £13,515,000 respectively. For 1995–96, the amount is estimated at £3,634,000. Projections for 1996–97 will be determined during the coming public expenditure survey.

### Contracting Out

**Ms Hodge:** To ask the President of the Board of Trade what work has been contracted out *(a)* by his Department and *(b)* by agencies for which his Department is responsible in (i) 1993–94 and (ii) 1994–95; and what is projected for 1995–96. [25541]

**Mr. Ian Taylor:** The following areas of work have been contracted out under the "Competing for Quality" programme. For those areas where work is shown as under way in 1995–96, contracting out will be dependent on the Department or agency receiving bids which offer value for money compared with keeping the activity in-house.

(a) Areas of work contracted out by the Department in:

   *(i) 1993–94*

   Central Training

   Offshore Geology

   Stationery Supply

   Translation

   *(ii) 1994–95*

   IT Services

   Accounts Services Agency

Work is under way to contract out the following in 1995–96:

   Services Management Division Building Management

   National Physical Laboratory

In addition, the following areas of work were contracted out in part under partnership arrangements between the private sector and in-house staff in 1994–95:

   Mail and Messengers

   Reprographics

   Central File Store

   Internal Audit

   Oil and Gas IT Services

(b) Areas of work contracted out by agencies for which the Department is responsible in:

   *(i) 1993–94*

   Patent Office

     Various Support Services

   *(ii) 1994–95*

   Radiocommunications Agency

     Ships Radio Licensing

Work is under way to contract out the following in 1995–96:

   Companies House

     London Office and satellites

     Edinburgh Office

     Cardiff Office; range of activities

   Insolvency Service

     Official Receivers' Administrative Functions

   Patent Office

     Various support services

   Radiocommunications Agency

     Various Support Services

### Regional Challenge

**Mr. Tony Lloyd:** To ask the President of the Board of Trade if he will give details of the cost of the launch of regional challenge and the cost of administering it; and if he will make a statement. [25701]

**Mr. Eggar:** The cost to Government Departments of the launch of regional challenge has been less than £10,000. The challenge will be administered within the normal running cost budgets of the various Departments and Government offices responsible for structural funds administration.

**Mr. Tony Lloyd:** To ask the President of the Board of Trade if moneys from European Union sources will be used to fund regional challenge. [25702]

**Mr. Eggar:** Yes. Regional challenge is a competition for grants from the European regional development and social funds.

### Petrol

**Sir Irvine Patnick:** To ask the President of the Board of Trade what proportion of the total sales of petrol in the United Kingdom are now accounted for by the sale of unleaded and super unleaded fuel. [26013]

**Mr. Page:** In the first quarter of 1995, premium unleaded petrol and super unleaded petrol accounted for 56.3 per cent. and 4.7 per cent. respectively of total sales of petrol in the United Kingdom. Thus, 61 per cent. of total petrol sales were unleaded.

### Fire Safety

**Mr. Pike:** To ask the President of the Board of Trade if the review team's report regarding fire safety legislation and enforcement matters arising from the deregulation proposals has now been considered; and when he expects to be able to make a statement on the outcome. [26245]

**Mr. Jonathan Evans:** I refer the hon. Member to the reply I gave to the right hon. Member for Berwick-upon-Tweed (Mr. Beith) on 24 May 1995, *Official Report*, column *643*.

### Import and Export Controls

**Mr. Gordon Prentice:** To ask the President of the Board of Trade to what extent the emergency powers contained in the Import, Export and Customs Powers (Defence) Act 1939 have been made permanent by subsequent amending legislation. [25511]

**Mr. Heseltine:** The judgment handed down by the Court of Appeal on 22 May confirmed on all counts the continuing validity of the powers to control imports and exports in the Import, Export and Customs Powers (Defence) Act 1939, and in the orders made under that Act. The Import and Export Control Act 1990 made the powers in the Act permanent.

### Nuclear Power

**Mr. Alan W. Williams:** To ask the President of the Board of Trade (1) if the special status of nuclear power stations that guarantees that they run continuously to provide base load electricity will be reviewed as a result of privatisation; [25284]

(2) by what authority nuclear power stations are empowered to provide their maximum output whenever available to base load electricity supply. [27277]

**Mr. Eggar** *[holding answer 22 May 1995]:* For safety reasons, Nuclear Electric's plants are permitted by the National Grid Company to offer a level of flexible operation less than that of other generating plant. In Scotland, arrangements dealing with SNL's access to the Scottish distribution system are covered by the Nuclear Energy Agreement between SNL and Scottish Power and Hydro-Electric.

I understand that Nuclear Electric and the National Grid Company are in discussion about ways in which the flexibility of their plant can be increased without in any way compromising rigorous standards of safety.

**Mr. Alan W. Williams:** To ask the President of the Board of Trade what restrictions will be imposed on the new privatised nuclear company from diversifying into building gas-fired power stations. [25291]

**Mr. Eggar** *[holding answer 22 May 1995]:* Decisions on new generating plant will be a commercial matter for the privatised companies, subject to meeting the appropriate regulatory requirements.

## PRIME MINISTER

### Engagements

**Mr. Harry Greenway:** To ask the Prime Minister if he will list his official engagements for Thursday 25 May. [24806]

**Sir Peter Tapsell:** To ask the Prime Minister if he will list his official engagements for Thursday 25 May. [24807]

**The Prime Minister:** This morning, I presided at a meeting of the Cabinet and had meetings with Ministerial colleagues and others. In addition to my duties in the House, I shall be having further meetings later today.

### Lockerbie

**Mr. Dalyell:** To ask the Prime Minister if he will place in the Library the correspondence between Nelson Mandela and himself on the issue of Lockerbie. [25952]

**The Prime Minister:** No. It is not my normal practice to do so.

### Wild Mammals (Protection) Bill

**Mr. Chidgey:** To ask the Prime Minister, what amount of correspondence he has received requesting that extra parliamentary time be given to the Wild Mammals (Protection) Bill. [26133]

**The Prime Minister:** I have received a substantial number of representations on the Wild Mammals (Protection) Bill.

### Intergovernmental Conference

**Mr. Marlow:** To ask the Prime Minister by what date he expects to decide whether Her Majesty's Government's submission to the reflections group of the inter-governmental conference should be placed before Parliament either as a White or Green Paper. [25390]

**The Prime Minister** *[holding answer 22 May 1995]:* I have made it clear that Parliament will have a full opportunity to discuss the issues relating to the intergovernmental conference before that conference gets under way. Precisely when the conference will start is not yet clear. Meanwhile the Government are examining in detail what the British position should be. The purpose of the study group is explanatory. My hon. Friend the Minister of State for Foreign and Commonwealth Affairs will represent the Foreign Secretary. We do not intend to make a single written submission, although we naturally contributed to the Council submission which has been published as Command Paper 2866. Parliament will be kept informed of the study group's progress.

## AGRICULTURE, FISHERIES AND FOOD

### Large Narcissus Fly

**Mr. Matthew Taylor:** To ask the Minister of Agriculture, Fisheries and Food (1) what research her Department has carried out into methods of controlling the large narcissus fly; [24740]

(2) what research her Department has carried out into the effect of the large narcissus fly on daffodil crops; [24741]

(3) how much money has been spent on research into methods of controlling the large narcissus fly in each year for the last five years; [24742]

(4) what plans her Department has to fund research into alternative methods of controlling the large narcissus fly. [24743]

**Mr. Jack:** The large narcissus fly is widely recognised as representing a serious problem for commercial bulb production. Consequently, our research has focused on methods of control. This has included studies of the efficacy of insecticides; the susceptibility of narcissus varieties to the fly; and the effects of a range of growing practices. The Department's spend on this strategic research, on behalf of the industry, since 1991 was as follows:

1991–92 : £32,000
1992–93 : £34,000
1993–94 : £35,000
1994–95 : £36,000

In April 1995, the Department established a new, four-year project estimated to cost £40,000 in 1995–96, investigating the relationship between the large narcissus fly and the chemicals emitted by narcissus plants. The identification of such chemicals may offer some opportunity for attracting flies to decoy plants and then destroying them, repelling flies from narcissus crops or for breeding varieties resistant to attack by the fly.

### New Zealand Flatworm

**Mrs. Wise:** To ask the Minister of Agriculture, Fisheries and Food (1) if he will list the areas in which the New Zealand flatworm has now been observed; and what guidelines he has issued to growers and gardeners in those areas; [25203]

(2) what steps he is taking to deal with the spread of the New Zealand flatworm and its threat to the United Kingdom worm population; [25205]

(3) what discussions he has held with his New Zealand counterpart as to how the New Zealand flatworm is dealt with in its native habitat with particular reference to its predators. [25204]

**Mrs. Browning:** The Government have sponsored research which shows that the New Zealand flatworm has been found in certain areas of the United Kingdom. These findings have been sporadic and have largely been confined to private gardens, allotments and some garden centres and the flatworm is not considered likely to pose a major threat to the agricultural and horticultural industries in the United Kingdom. A code of practice is planned to supplement information and advice already provided by the Agricultural Departments to industry and the public. This advice emphasises the need to avoid spreading the New Zealand flatworm. Since 1992, it has been an offence in Great Britain under the Wildlife and Countryside Act 1981 to release flatworms, or allow them to escape, into the wild. It is understood from contacts in

New Zealand that in its natural environment a number of factors combine to maintain a balance between the flatworm and the native earthworm population.

## Tuberculin Testing

**Mr. William Ross:** To ask the Minister of Agriculture, Fisheries and Food if he will publish the qualifications he will require to allow lay personnel to carry out tuberculin testing under veterinary direction. [24954]

**Mrs. Browning:** My Department is consulting with the Royal College of Veterinary Surgeons on this matter. If and when an order is made to allow lay personnel to carry out tuberculin testing, the necessary qualifications will be published.

## Live Animal Exports

**Mr. Etherington:** To ask the Minister of Agriculture, Fisheries and Food what representations he has received from Compassion in World Farming on the lawfulness of restrictions on *(a)* the export of calves for rearing in veal crates and *(b)* the export of all live farm animals; and if he will make a statement on them. [24984]

**Mrs. Browning:** Compassion in World Farming wrote to my right hon. Friend on 4 April advising him to consider the lawfulness of restrictions of this type. My right hon. Friend wanted, before replying, to have the advice he had sought from lawyers on the legal opinion, commissioned from Gerald Barling QC by the RSPCA, which argued that a ban on the export of calves would be legal. My right hon. Friend's conclusions in the light of that legal advice were set out in his reply of 22 May to the hon. Member for Nuneaton, (Mr. Olner), column *456*, and conveyed to CIWF in a letter which he sent on the same date. The letter also explained that he saw no reason to change his view that a ban on the export of all live farm animals would be incompatible with European law, as well as with the Government's policy.

**Mr. Morley:** To ask the Minister of Agriculture, Fisheries and Food for how long the MV Northern Cruiser carrying livestock trucks from Dover to Boulogne on Friday 12 May was delayed outside Boulogne; what was the cause of delay, when he was informed of the delay by the boat's operators; whether, as a result of the delay, any of the animals went without being offered food and water for more than 15 hours; if any prosecutions are to be brought; and if he will make a statement. [25581]

**Mrs. Browning:** We have not at present received any information which suggests that an offence occurred under the Welfare of Animals during Transport Order 1994, in relation to the voyage of the Northern Cruiser on 12 May 1995.

## Retirements and Redundancies

**Ms Hodge:** To ask the Minister of Agriculture, Fisheries and Food what is the annual cost to his Department of staff leaving under redundancy/early retirement schemes to incorporate *(a)* added years lump sum payments, *(b)* redundancy payments, *(c)* pension payments, including enhancements and *(d)* any other special arrangements for (i) 1993–94 (ii) 1994–95, (iii) projected for 1995–96 and (iv) projected for 1996–97. [25665]

**Mr. Waldegrave:** The cost to the Department, including its agencies, of early retirements and

redundancies are borne from the Department's running costs provision.

A detailed breakdown of the various costs could be obtained only at disproportionate cost.

The total costs borne on the Department's running costs in 1993–94 and 1994–95 were £7 million and £9 million respectively. For 1995–96, the total amount is estimated at £7 million. Projections for 1996–97 will be determined during the coming public expenditure survey.

## Vessel Engine Capacity

**Mr. Austin Mitchell:** To ask the Minister of Agriculture, Fisheries and Food what assessment he has made of whether the engine capacity registered by *(a)* British, *(b)* Spanish and *(c)* Dutch vessels under the multi-annual guidance targets is accurate; what steps are taken to check this in each country; and if he has asked the Commissioner to verify registered capacities under the programme. [25385]

**Mr. Jack:** It is the European Commission's responsibility to ensure that member states comply with Community obligations, and for member states authorities to ensure proper administration in relation to their own vessels. In the United Kingdom, it is the responsibility of the chief executive of the Marine Safety Agency to ensure that the details entered on a vessel's certificate of registry accurately reflect that vessel's characteristics. The characteristics of the engine of each vessel on the UK register are obtained by a surveyor approved by the Marine Safety Agency before registration of the vessel takes place.

Where specific instances of discrepancies arise or are brought to my attention, they are taken up with the Commission or, in the case of a UK-registered vessel, with the Marine Safety Agency.

## Eastern European Fishing Fleets

**Mr. Austin Mitchell:** To ask the Minister of Agriculture, Fisheries and Food what information he has on the size of the fishing fleets of Bulgaria, Poland, Latvia, Lithuania and Estonia; and what historic fishing rights each of these nations can claim in British or European waters before the Fishing Limits Act 1976. [25382]

**Mr. Jack:** The latest year for which information on the size of nations' fishing fleets is available is 1992, showing the following:

| Country | Number of vessels | Size |
|---|---|---|
| Bulgaria | 38 | [1]86,600 GRT |
| Poland | 521 | 249,079 GRT |
| Latvia | 141 | 343,236 GRT |
| Lithuania | 162 | 236,268 GRT |
| Estonia | 249 | 180,921 GRT |

*Source:* FAO fleet statistics.
[1] GRT = gross registered tonnage.

Before the Fishery Limits Act 1976, British waters extended only to 12 miles. None of the above countries fished within our 12 mile limits, nor have they claimed historic fishing rights within the British fishing limits established in 1976. The EU currently has reciprocal fishing agreements with Poland and the three Baltic states, but these are confined to the Baltic sea. We have no record of Bulgarian vessels having fished in waters around the United Kingdom.

## Coarse Fish Close Season

**Sir Cranley Onslow:** To ask the Minister of Agriculture, Fisheries and Food what research into the likely effects of the ending of the coarse fish close season his Department has considered. [25595]

**Mr. Jack:** We have not commissioned any special research into the likely effects of ending the coarse fish close season. However, in coming to a conclusion on a recent proposal from the National Rivers Authority to dispense with the coarse fish close season on lakes, ponds and reservoirs, we took account of opinions expressed by a wide range of expert bodies. We also noted that in those parts of England and Wales in which the close season had already been dispensed with, there was no evidence that this had an adverse effect on either fisheries or fish.

## Bovine Immunodeficiency

**Mr. Martyn Jones:** To ask the Minister of Agriculture, Fisheries and Food what survey he has made of research into BIV being undertaken in other countries. [25857]

**Mrs. Browning:** In September 1994, senior veterinarians from the Veterinary Investigation Service, and the virology department of the Central Veterinary Laboratory carried out a study tour of North America, where research into bovine immunodeficiency-like virus has been undertaken for a number of years. Discussions were held with the veterinary regulatory authorities in Washington and Ottawa and with veterinarians and research workers at the National Animal Disease Centre, Ames, Iowa; the National Cancer Institute, Frederick, Maryland; the Louisiana State university; the Animal Disease Research Institute, Ottawa; Ontario Veterinary college, Guelph; and the veterinary laboratory services, Ministry of Agriculture and Food, Guelph, Ontario.

The veterinary regulatory authorities in the USA and Canada confirmed that they had no concerns whatsoever over food safety with respect to BIV and were unaware of any concern by the public health authorities with regard to BIV. They also confirmed that there was no scientific evidence that the lentivirus in question caused immunodeficiency in cattle.

**Mr. Martyn Jones:** To ask the Minister of Agriculture, Fisheries and Food what assessment he has made of whether it has been proved that the BIV organism is destroyed by normal dairy pasteurization. [25855]

**Mrs. Browning:** Judging from the similarities with other lentiviruses, we would expect that bovine immunodeficiency-like virus would get into milk but that pasteurisation would kill it. We are carrying out experimental work at the Department's Central Veterinary Laboratory to investigate this hypothesis.

**Mr. Martyn Jones:** To ask the Minister of Agriculture, Fisheries and Food, what research is being conducted into BIV and cross infection to humans. [25852]

**Mrs. Browning:** None. Bovine immunodeficiency-like virus infection of cattle has been known for a long time. There is no evidence that it affects humans, whether through contact with animals, through drinking milk or eating meat or indeed when injected into the body, as happened, accidentally, to two US researchers who suffered no ill effects. Experimental efforts in the USA to grow the virus in human cells have failed. It is characteristic of these types of viruses to be highly species specific.

**Mr. Martyn Jones:** To ask the Minister of Agriculture, Fisheries and Food what number and percentage of United Kingdom herds are infected by BIV. [25856]

**Mrs. Browning:** A limited laboratory investigation was carried out by the Central Veterinary Laboratory in 1990. Several hundred cattle sera, from a considerable number of cattle herds spread throughout Great Britain, were tested as part of a programme to develop a diagnostic test for bovine immunodeficiency-like virus. Approximately 10 per cent. of the samples tested were serologically positive for BIV using the tests being developed at that time. This level of infection is consistent with what has been found in other countries but the investigation was not structured nor were the results validated and for that reason it is not possible to estimate with any precision what is the actual level of incidence of BIV infection in the United Kingdom.

A full-scale survey would currently be inappropriate, particularly in the absence of a specific and sensitive test suitable for widespread application.

## Environmentally Sensitive Areas

**Dr. Strang:** To ask the Minister of Agriculture, Fisheries and Food how many hectares of land *(a)* are eligible for entry into each environmentally sensitive area in England and *(b)* have been entered into each tier of each environmentally sensitive areas in England. [25793]

**Mr. Waldegrave:** The information for environmentally sensitive areas in England is as follows:

| | Eligible area in hectares | Area currently under agreement in hectares |
| --- | --- | --- |
| *Stage I ESAs* *(launched in 1987)* | | |
| Broads | 24,000 | Tier 1–8,596 |
| | | Tier 2–5,906 |
| | | Tier 3–354 |
| | | Tier 4–256 |
| Total | | 15,112 |
| Pennine Dales | 39,100 | Tier 1–24,280 |
| | | Tier 2–1,198 |
| Total | | 25,478 |
| Somerset Levels and Moors | 25,900 | Tier 1–10,630 |
| | | Tier 2–2,244 |
| | | Tier 3–881 |
| Total | | 13,755 |
| South Downs | 51,700 | Tier 1–4,810 |
| | | Tier 2–408 |
| | | Tier 3–5,964 |
| Total | | 11,182 |
| West Penwith | 6,900 | Tier 1–6,125 |

| | Eligible area in hectares | Area currently under agreement in hectares |
|---|---|---|
| *Stage II ESAs (launched in 1988)* | | |
| Breckland | 51,600 | Tier 1–2,595 |
| | | Tier 2–99 |
| | | Tier 3–2,431 |
| | | Tier 4–281 |
| Total | | 5,406 |
| Clun | 18,900 | Tier 1–12,125 |
| | | Tier 2–1,142 |
| | | Tier 3–178 |
| Total | | 13,445 |
| North Peak | 50,500 | Tier 1–22,980 |
| | | Tier 2–11,244 |
| Total | | 34,224 |
| Suffolk River Valleys | 32,600 | Tier 1–6,910 |
| | | Tier 2–1,607 |
| | | Tier 3–324 |
| | | Tier 4–98 |
| Total | | 8,939 |
| Test Valley | 3,300 | Tier 1–934 |
| | | Tier 2–116 |
| Total | | 1,050 |
| *Stage III ESAs (launched in 1993)* | | |
| Avon Valley | 3,800 | Tier 1–572 |
| | | Tier 2–42 |
| Total | | 614 |
| Exmoor | 67,700 | Tier 1–38,529 |
| | | Tier 2–931 |
| Total | | 39,460 |
| Lake District | 219,300 | Tier 1–87,280 |
| | | Tier 2–4,066 |
| Total | | 91,346 |
| North Kent Marshes | 11,600 | Tier 1–3,030 |
| | | Tier 2–599 |
| Total | | 3,629 |
| South Wessex Downs | 38,300 | Tier 1–17,583 |
| | | Tier 2–1,218 |
| Total | | 18,801 |
| South West Peak | 27,000 | Tier 1–11,279 |
| | | Tier 2–3,043 |
| Total | | 14,322 |
| *Stage IV ESAs (launched in 1994)* | | |
| Blackdown Hills | 32,200 | Tier 1–3,162 |
| | | Tier 2–49 |
| Total | | 3,211 |
| Cotswold Hills | 66,100 | Tier 1–20,128 |
| | | Tier 2–939 |
| Total | | 21,067 |

| | Eligible area in hectares | Area currently under agreement in hectares |
|---|---|---|
| Dartmoor | 89,000 | Tier 1–6,729 |
| | | Tier 2–324 |
| Total | | 7,053 |
| Essex Coast | 23,000 | Tier 1–1,925 |
| | | Tier 2–115 |
| | | Tier 3–223 |
| Total | | 2,263 |
| Shropshire Hills | 34,900 | Tier 1–7,035 |
| | | Tier 2–32 |
| Total | | 7,067 |
| Upper Thames Tributaries | 18,000 | Tier 1–2,264 |
| | | Tier 2–312 |
| | | Tier 3–262 |
| Total | | 2,838 |

**Dr. Strang:** To ask the Minister of Agriculture, Fisheries and Food how many farms *(a)* are eligible to have land entered into each environmentally sensitive area in England and *(b)* have had land entered into each environmentally sensitive area in England.

**Mr. Waldegrave:** Records are not kept of the number of farms in each designated environmentally sensitive area in England which are eligible to enter the scheme.

The number of agreements in each ESA in England is as follows:

| | Number |
|---|---|
| *Stage I ESAs (launched in 1987)* | |
| Broads | 740 |
| Pennine Dales | 716 |
| Somerset Levels and Moors | 888 |
| South Downs | 213 |
| West Penwith | 187 |
| *Stage II ESAs (launched in 1988)* | |
| Breckland | 113 |
| Clun | 195 |
| North Peak | 76 |
| Suffolk River Valleys | 396 |
| Test Valley | 32 |
| *Stage III ESAs (launched in 1993)* | |
| Avon Valley | 32 |
| Exmoor | 390 |
| Lake District | 812 |
| North Kent Marshes | 52 |
| South Wessex Downs | 130 |
| South West Peak | 320 |
| *Stage IV ESAs (launched in 1994)* | |
| Blackdown Hills | 126 |
| Cotswold Hills | 276 |
| Dartmoor | 156 |
| Essex Coast | 62 |
| Shropshire Hills | 123 |
| Upper Thames Tributaries | 106 |

## French Pig Sector (Illegal Aid)

**Mr. Morley:** To ask the Minister of Agriculture, Fisheries and Food what progress has been made in relation to his representations to the EU for the recovery of illegal aid to the French pig sector. [25742]

**Mr. Jack:** After sustained pressure from the United Kingdom, the European Commission finally initiated article 93(2) procedure against two schemes in the pigmeat sector in April 1994. The two schemes were a FF30 million scheme for relieving pig producers of the high cost of commercial loans already taken out and a reduced rate loan arrangement through Stabiporc using Government funds, and Government guarantees for loans given by commercial banks and other organisations.

The Commission's decisions announcing that it had found elements of both schemes to be illegal and requiring the repayment of the illegal aid were published on 8 and 10 November and 23 December 1994. The French Government are required to advise the Commission of steps they have taken to recovers the illegal aid.

I understand that the Commission is in dialogue with the French Government. We shall persist with our pressure on the Commission to ensure that the French Government recover the aid which was illegally paid.

## Sheep Slaughter (France)

**Mr. Dowd:** To ask the Minister of Agriculture, Fisheries and Food what reports he has received on the recent slaughter in Paris of sheep exported from Britain; what assessment he has made of compliance with the EU directive on the slaughter of animals; what representations he has made to the French Government in the light of the article; and if he will make a statement. [25800]

**Mrs. Browning:** The allegations in a daily newspaper about the slaughter of sheep in Paris have been discussed with officials of the French Ministry of Agriculture. I am advised that such slaughtering elsewhere than in a slaughterhouse is illegal under French law, although the European directive on the protection of animals at slaughter permits it, subject to certain conditions. I understand that the French Government are discussing this matter with the relevant organisations and therefore, neither my right hon. Friend nor I believe that it is necessary to make representations to them on this matter.

## Farm and Conservation Grant Scheme

**Mr. Morley:** To ask the Minister of Agriculture, Fisheries and Food what expenditure has been saved as a result of the ending of the farm and conservation grant scheme; and if that saving has been redirected to other areas of MAFF expenditure. [25744]

**Mr. Jack:** No decision has yet been made to discontinue the farm and conservation grant scheme. An official working group reviewing the development of environmental land management schemes in England has proposed that the F and CGS should not continue as a separate scheme in England after February 1996, but that capital grants for conservation purposes should then be integrated into the countryside stewardship scheme. The working group's proposals were published for public consultation on 18 May. Current expenditure on conservation grants under the F and CGS in England amounts to £4 million in a full year.

## Majority Shareholdings

**Mr. Byers:** To ask the Minister of Agriculture, Fisheries and Food if he will list those companies in which the holder of his office is a majority shareholder which (a) are currently in existence and (b) have been wound up in the past five years. [25703]

**Mr. Waldegrave** [*holding answer 22 May 1995*]: None.

## Water Level Management Plans

**Sir Cranley Onslow:** To ask the Minister of Agriculture, Fisheries and Food (1) what steps his Department took to consult representatives angling organisations before publishing the procedural guide for operating authorities entitled water level management plans; [23103]

(2) for what reasons no angling organisations are included in the list of useful contacts and addresses in annex II of his Department's guide water level management plans. [23104]

**Mr. Jack** [*holding answer 11 May 1995*]: The main purpose of the procedural guide to which my right hon. Friend refers is to help flood defence authorities to draw up water level management plans in areas of conservation importance so as to balance the needs of flood defence, economic activity, and conservation. Such plans are prepared at local level and the guide emphasises the importance of consultations with all those affected, including recreational and sporting interests, during the preparation of a water level management plan for a particular area.

Although representative angling organisations were not consulted prior to publication of the Ministry's procedural guide, such organisations should be consulted by local flood defence authorities when individual plans are in preparation. Annex II of the guide is not intended as an exhaustive list of all those who should be consulted, but to meet my right hon. Friend's point representative angling organisations and other recreational and sporting interests will be added when the guide is next reprinted.

# EDUCATION

## Area Cost Adjustment

**Mr. Blunkett:** To ask the Secretary of State for Education if she will list for each education authority (a) not in receipt and (b) in receipt of area cost adjustment for the last year that figures are available. [25953]

**Mr. Robin Squire:** The information requesed is set out in the attached lists.

LEAs WHICH RECEIVE AREA COST ADJUSTMENT
CITY OF LONDON
*Inner London Boroughs*
  Camden
  Greenwich
  Hackney
  Hammersmith and Fulham
  Islington
  Kensington and Chelsea
  Lambeth
  Lewisham

Southwark
Tower Hamlets
Wandsworth
Westminster

*Outer London Boroughs*
Barking
Barnet
Bexley
Brent
Bromley
Croydon
Ealing
Enfield
Haringey
Harrow
Havering
Hillingdon
Hounslow
Kingston upon Thames
Merton
Newham
Redbridge
Richmond Upon Thames
Sutton
Waltham Forest

*Shires*
Bedfordshire
Berkshire
Buckinghamshire
East Sussex
Essex
Hampshire
Hertfordshire
Kent
Oxfordshire
Surrey
West Sussex
Isle of Wight
Isles of Scilly

LEAs WHICH DO NOT RECEIVE AREA COST ADJUSTMENT
*Metropolitan Authorities*
Birmingham
Coventry
Dudley
Sandwell
Solihull
Walsall
Wolverhampton
Knowsley
Liverpool
St. Helen's
Sefton
Wirral
Bolton
Bury
Manchester
Oldham
Rochdale
Salford
Stockport

Tameside
Trafford
Wigan
Barnsley
Doncaster
Rotherham
Sheffield
Bradford
Calderdale
Kirklees
Leeds
Wakefield
Gateshead
Newcastle upon Tyne
North Tyneside
South Tyneside
Sunderland

*Shire Counties*
Avon
Cambridgeshire
Cheshire
Cleveland
Cornwall
Cumbria
Derbyshire
Devon
Dorset
Durham
Gloucestershire
Hereford and Worcester
Humberside
Lancashire
Leicestershire
Lincolnshire
Norfolk
North Yorkshire
orthamptonshire
Northumberland
Nottinghamshire
Shropshire
Somerset
Staffordshire
Suffolk
Warwickshire
Wiltshire

### Complaints

**Ms Hodge:** To ask the Secretary of State for Education what policy and procedures exists for dealing with complaints against her Department by members of the public; when the policy was last updated; what time limit and target for dealing with such complaints her Department has; and what follow-up procedure exists where complainants are not satisfied with her Department's response to a complaint.     [26224]

**Mr. Boswell:** Any complaint about the conduct of a member of the Department would be dealt with under the Department's agreed disciplinary procedures. These are set out in its terms and conditions handbook, which was revised in 1994 and made available to all staff. If a complainant remains dissatisfied with the handling of a complaint, it is open to them to take further action through the Parliamentary Commissioner for Administration.

### Information Technology Teachers

**Mr. David Shaw:** To ask the Secretary of State for Education how many qualified information technology teachers there were in secondary schools in each year since 1979; and what proportion of the total number of teachers in this subject they represent. [25772]

**Mr. Robin Squire:** The information requested is available only for 1984, 1988 and 1992 from the secondary school staffing surveys. In those years, the number of full-time teachers who were teaching information technology, including computer studies, in maintained secondary schools in England and who had a post A-level qualification in information technology was as follows:

| Year | Number of IT teachers (000) | Number with an IT qualification (000) | Percentage with qualification |
|------|------|------|------|
| 1984 | 9.4 | 2.3 | 24 |
| 1988 | 12.1 | 3.1 | 26 |
| 1992 | 10.4 | 2.8 | 27 |

The total number of full-time teachers with an information technology qualification, including those not teaching IT, in each year was:

| Year | All teachers with an IT qualification (000) |
|------|------|
| 1984 | 4.1 |
| 1988 | 6.4 |
| 1992 | 7.1 |

It should be noted that the definition of information technology has changed slightly over the years, so the figures quoted may not be strictly comparable.

## SOCIAL SECURITY

### VAT on Fuel (Compensation)

**Mr. Foulkes:** To ask the Secretary of State for Social Security, what is the total cost of the compensation for VAT on fuel given annually to women aged between 60 and 65 years. [24948]

**Mr. Roger Evans:** The information is not available.

### Benefit Fraud

**Mr. Etherington:** To ask the Secretary of State for Social Security if he will list, by town or city and region, all his Department's research trials, conducted since 1990, aimed or associated with trials testing procedures to prevent the fraudulent encashment of instruments of payment, giving *(a)* the cost of each trial, *(b)* the target population, *(c)* the period of trial, *(d)* other joint/collaborative agencies and *(e)* schemes involving incentive payments to participants. [24985]

**Mr. Arbuthnot:** This information is laid out by geographical area since January 1994, the first date for which information is available. No specific target population was sought, since this was not an important factor in any of the trials.

*Devon*

Hole punching of order books by Postmasters prior to their return to BA offices, to render them valueless.

Cost: £ Nil

Period: 05 September 1994–02 December 1994

Other agencies: Post Office Counters Ltd.

Incentive involved: No

*Sunderland*

Identity trial

Cost: £ Nil

Period: 06 March 1995 due to end 03 June 1995

Other agencies: Post Office Counters Ltd.

Incentives involved: No

*London and Clyde Valley*

Secure delivery order books

Cost: £ Nil

Period: 10 October 1994–02 December 1994

Other agencies: Post Office Counters Ltd.

Incentives involved: No

*London*

Alert-Computerised system to prevent fraudulent encashment of lost or stolen order books.

Cost: £2.4 million

Period: 30 November 1992–31 August 1994

Other agencies: Post Office Counters Ltd.

Incentives involved: No

*London*

Secure delivery of order books

Cost: £21,936

Period: 22 March 1993–02 April 1995

Other agencies: Post Office Counters Ltd. and Royal Mail

Incentives involved: No

*Manchester*

UV lamps—Post Office use

Cost: £11,808

Period: 04 July 1994–31 August 1994

Other agencies: Post Office Counters Ltd

Incentives involved: No

*Birmingham*

Post Office Reward Scheme

Cost: £18,594

Period:25 October 1993–29 August 1994

Other Agencies: Post Office Counters Ltd

Incentives involved: Yes

*Midlands Area*

Post Office Reward Scheme

Cost: £95,931

Period: 30 August 1994-ongoing

Other agencies: Post Office counters Ltd.

Incentives involved: Yes

**Benefit Recipients**

**Ms Short:** To ask the Secretary of State for Social Security what percentage of claimants for each benefit were *(a)* male and *(b)* female for the latest available year.    [25138]

**Mr. Hague:** The information is in the table.

*Figures rounded to nearest Thousand*

| Benefit | Total claimants (000s unless indicated) | Total males (000s) | Males as percentage of total claimants | Total females (000s) | Females as percentage of total claimants | Date of enquiry |
|---|---|---|---|---|---|---|
| *Non-means tested benefits* | | | | | | |
| Attendance allowance[1] | 996 | 286 | 29 | 710 | 71 | 31 March 1994 |
| Child benefit | 6,905 | 227 | 3 | 6,678 | 97 | 31 December 1994 |
| Child's special allowance[3] | 69 | n/a | n/a | n/a | n/a | 31 December 1994 |
| Disability living allowance[1] | 1,491 | 769 | 52 | 723 | 48 | 28 February 1995 |
| Guardian's allowance[3] | 2,125 | n/a | n/a | n/a | n/a | 31 December 1995 |
| Invalid care allowance | 127 | 39 | 31 | 88 | 69 | 31 March 1995 |
| Industrial death benefit | n/a | n/a | n/a | n/a | n/a | |
| Industrial injuries disablement[2] | 209 | 180 | 86 | 29 | 14 | 3 April 1993 |
| Invalidity benefit | 1,580 | 1,156 | 73 | 424 | 27 | 3 April 1993 |
| Maternity allowance | 16 | — | — | 16 | 100 | 31 March 1993 |
| Non contributory retirement pension | 28 | 6 | 20 | 22 | 80 | 30 September 1994 |
| One parent benefit | 925 | 80 | 9 | 845 | 91 | 31 December 1994 |
| Other industrial injuries benefits[3] | 312 | n/a | n/a | n/a | n/a | 1994 |
| Reduced earnings allowance/retirement allowance[2] | 155 | 125 | 81 | 30 | 19 | 3 April 1993 |
| Retirement pension | 10,139 | 3,579 | 35 | 6,560 | 65 | 30 September 1994 |
| Sickness benefit | 534 | 312 | 58 | 222 | 42 | 3 April 1993 |
| Severe disablement allowance | 316 | 121 | 38 | 195 | 62 | 3 April 1993 |
| Unemployment benefit | 2,341 | 1,784 | 76 | 556 | 24 | 10 November 1994 |
| Widow's benefit | 324 | — | — | 324 | 100 | 30 September 1994 |
| War pension[4] | 99 | n/a | n/a | n/a | n/a | 31 March 1995 |
| *Means tested benefits* | | | | | | |
| Council tax benefit[5] | 5,641 | n/a | n/a | n/a | n/a | 30 November 1994 |
| Disability working allowance | 5 | 3 | 60 | 2 | 40 | 31 October 1994 |
| Family credit[6] | 578 | 250 | 43 | 327 | 57 | October 1994 |
| Housing benefit | 4,711 | n/a | n/a | n/a | n/a | 30 November 1994 |
| Rent rebate | 3,009 | n/a | n/a | n/a | n/a | 30 November 1994 |
| Rent allowance | 1,702 | n/a | n/a | n/a | n/a | 30 November 1994 |
| Income support | 5,675 | 2,702 | 48 | 2,973 | 52 | May 1994 |

*Notes:*
[1] Beneficiaries.
[2] Assessments current at 3 April 1993.
[3] Extract figures quoted.
[4] All claims includes first and subsequent claims.
[5] Figure includes 53,000 second adult rebate cases.
[6] Figures based on sex of main earner.
[7] Male and female recipients may not total due to rounding.

**Retirements and Redundancies**

**Ms Hodge:** To ask the Secretary of State for Social Security how many staff of *(a)* the Department of Social Security and *(b)* agencies for which the DSS is responsible (i) took early retirement, (ii) took voluntary redundancy, (iii) took compulsory redundancy and (iv) were retired on medical grounds in *(a)* 1993–94 and *(b)* 1994–95; and what are the projected figures for 1995–96.    [25420]

**Mr. Hague:** The information is not readily available in the form requested and could be obtained only at disproportionate cost. The available information is in the table.

| | Retirement on medical grounds | | Compulsory redundancy | | Other early retirement/voluntary redundancy | |
|---|---|---|---|---|---|---|
| | 1993–94 | 1994–95 | 1993–94 | 1994–95 | 1993–94 | 1994–95 |
| Department of Social Security[1] | 472 | 650 | 64 | 41 | 352 | 823 |
| Benefits Agency | 395 | 513 | 0 | 0 | 207 | 294 |
| Child Support Agency | 13 | 21 | 0 | 0 | 6 | 4 |

| | Retirement on medical grounds | | Compulsory redundancy | | Other early retirement/voluntary redundancy | |
|---|---|---|---|---|---|---|
| | 1993–94 | 1994–95 | 1993–94 | 1994–95 | 1993–94 | 1994–95 |
| Contributions Agency | 37 | 49 | 0 | 0 | 67 | 244 |
| Information Technology Services Agency | 15 | 27 | 0 | 0 | 50 | 246 |
| Resettlement Agency | 2 | 0 | 64 | 41 | 15 | 15 |
| War Pensions Agency | — | 14 | 0 | 0 | — | 2 |

*Notes:*

No projections are available for 1995–96.

[1] The number of retirements and redundancies in the executive agencies are included in the departmental figures.

**Ms Hodge:** To ask the Secretary of State for Social Security what is the annual cost to the Department of staff leaving under redundancy/early retirement schemes to incorporate (i) added years lump sum payments, (ii) redundancy payments, (iii) pension payments including enhancements and (iv) any other special arrangements *(a)* 1993–94, *(b)* 1994–95, and projected for *(c)* 1995–96 and *(d) 1996–97.* [25638]

**Mr. Hague:** The costs to the Department of early retirement and redundancies are borne from the Department's running costs provision.

A detailed break-down of the various costs could be obtained only at disproportionate cost.

The total costs borne on the Department's running costs in 1993–94 and 1994–95 were £23.975 million and £17.903 million—provisional—respectively. For 1995–96, the amount is estimated at £22.607 million. Projections for 1996–97 will be determined during the coming public expenditure survey.

### Motability

**Mr. Alex Carlile:** To ask the Secretary of State for Social Security what measures are in place to ensure the best use of public money by Motability and its associate companies and charities and that those bodies are accountable to his Department; and if he will make a statement. [25947]

**Mr. Hague:** Motability is an independent charity which receives grant in aid from the Department for all its administration costs and part of its grant-making provision. A comprehensive financial agreement exists between the Department and Motability which has been drawn up in accordance with Government accounting procedures. This gives Motability the responsibility for ensuring it obtains good value for money in its dealings with suppliers to the scheme.

### Contracting Out

**Ms Hodge:** To ask the Secretary of State for Social Security what work has been contracted out *(a)* by his Department and *(b)* by agencies for which his Department is responsible in (i) 1993–94 and (ii) 1994–95 and (iii) the projected figures for 1995–96. [25657]

**Mr. Roger Evans:** The value of work previously carried out by civil servants and contracted out by the Department and each of its agencies in 1993–94 and 1994–95 is shown in the tables. In 1995–96, we will be examining running costs of some £166 million with a view to contracting out. We will examine a further £27 million with a view to inviting in-house bids, together with bids from the private sector, in market tests. We cannot predict in advance of the market tests the value of work that will be contracted out.

*Financial year April 1993–March 1994*

| | Value £ |
|---|---|
| *Benefits Agency* | |
| Travel Services | 200,000 |
| Accommodation and Office Services | 840,000 |
| Training | 3,609,191 |
| Storage Archives | 490,000 |
| *Headquarters* | |
| Accommodation and Office Services | 722,734 |
| Facilities Management | |
| Accommodation and Office Services | 2,114,000 |
| *Information Technology Services Agency* | |
| Audit | 1,200,000 |
| *Contributions Agency* | |
| Cleaning (Emerson house) | 732,202 |

*Financial year April 1994–March 1995*

| | |
|---|---|
| *Benefits Agency* | |
| Publishing | 4,326,046 |
| Accommodation and Office Services (19 Contracts) | 43,707,618 |
| Storage Printed Material | 2,711,019 |
| *Information and Technology Services Agency* | |
| Security Guarding | 422,000 |
| Area Computer Centre | 6,100,000 |

**Ms Hodge:** To ask the Secretary of State for Social Security for each piece of work subject to a bidding process under the auspices of *(a)* his Department and *(b)* agencies for which his Department is responsible (i) where work was contracted out, who were the successful bidders and (ii) which contracts were won by in-house bidders in (1) 1993–94, (2) 1994–95 and (3) 1995–96. [25651]

**Mr. Roger Evans:** The Department and its agencies procure a wide range of goods and services by competitive tender. I have provided information showing the outcomes of competitive tenders of work carried out by civil servants and a copy has been placed in the Library.

### Consultants

**Ms Hodge:** To ask the Secretary of State for Social Security what is the level of expenditure on consultancy by *(a)* his Department and *(b)* agencies for which his Department is responsible for (i) 1993–94 and (ii) 1994–95; and what are the projected figures for 1995–96. [25644]

**Mr. Hague:** The available information is in the table. Information on projected levels of expenditure for 1995–96 is not available.

| Agency | Financial Year 1993–94 £ | 1994–95 £ |
|---|---|---|
| Benefits Agency | 8,111,715 | 5,730,220 |
| Contributions Agency | 3,170,895 | 1,113,425 |
| Information Technology Services Agency | 17,996,000 | 9,660,000 |
| Child Support Agency | 2,300,000 | 7,426,938 |
| Resettlement Agency | 95,111 | 65,203 |
| War Pensions Agency | ¹— | 456,798 |
| Sub totals | 31,673,721 | 24,452,584 |
| DSS Headquarters | 2,322,877 | 1,653,173 |
| Grand total | ²33,996,598 | 26,105,757 |

¹ War Pensions Agency set up 1 April 1994. Consultancy expenditure for 1993–94 included in Benefits Agency total.

² This figure has been adjusted from those previously quoted due to accounting adjustments.

### Family Credit

**Mr. Chidgey:** To ask the Secretary of State for Social Security what steps his Department are taking to inform family credit claimants of the extra money they are entitled from July for working full time.    [25808]

**Mr. Roger Evans:** We plan to undertake extensive publicity to inform people about the new premium for working 30 hours or more a week on family credit and the associated extra help in housing benefit, council tax benefit and disability working allowance. People already receiving family credit or disability working allowance will receive a new claim pack shortly before their renewal claim is due to be made. The claim pack will advise them of the new premium.

We plan also to provide information to advisors of people likely to be affected to inform them of the new premium.

*Notes*:

1. Because approval for expenditure on the campaign cannot be given until regulations have been laid, we cannot be explicit at this stage on the form the advertising will take.

2. The new claim pack is planned to be available a few days in advance of the change.

**Mr. Chidgey:** To ask the Secretary of State for Social Security what percentage of family credit claims from employees currently take five working days to be dealt with from the time of the claim being received by his Department; and if he will give the figures for each working day up 30 working days.    [25807]

**Mr. Roger Evans:** The administration of family credit is a matter for Mr. Ian Magee, the chief executive of the Benefits Agency. He will write to the hon. Member.

*Letter from Ian Magee to Mr. David Chidgey, dated 25 May 1995:*

The Secretary of State for Social Security has asked me to reply to your recent Parliamentary Question about the clearance times of claims made by employees to Family Credit.

The table below details the information that you have requested. Such figures are produced on a monthly basis and I have therefore provided information for the month ending 30 April 1995 which is the latest full month available. The figures provided relate only to employees and do not include claims made by self-employed people.

| Days | Percentage cleared |
|---|---|
| 5 | 47.2 |
| 6 | 52.3 |
| 7 | 54.8 |
| 8 | 57.7 |
| 9 | 63.9 |
| 10 | 67.1 |
| 11 | 71.5 |
| 12 | 73.6 |
| 13 | 75.6 |
| 14 | 79.4 |
| 15 | 81.1 |
| 16 | 83.7 |
| 17 | 84.8 |
| 18 | 85.8 |
| 19 | 87.8 |
| 20 | 88.6 |
| 21 | 90.0 |
| 22 | 90.5 |
| 23 | 91.0 |
| 24 | 92.0 |
| 25 | 92.5 |
| 26 | 93.1 |
| 27 | 93.4 |
| 28 | 93.7 |
| 29 | 94.3 |
| 30 | 94.5 |

I hope you find this reply helpful.

## HOME DEPARTMENT

### Asylum Seekers

**Mrs. Roche:** To ask the Secretary of State for the Home Department, pursuant to his answer of 16 May, *Official Report*, columns *185-88*, if he will publish a breakdown of the location of asylum seekers as at 10 May listed as 'other' in table 3 of the answer.    [25810]

**Mr. Nicholas Baker:** This information is not readily available as comprehensive statistics are not currently compiled on all the places of detention of persons who have sought asylum. For this reason, only the main places were separately identified.

**Mrs. Roche:** To ask the Secretary of State for the Home Department, pursuant to his answer of 16 May, *Official Report*, columns *185-88*, when he now expects to phase out the detention of asylum seekers in prisons and police cells.    [25811]

**Mr. Nicholas Baker:** The plans to expand and improve the detention accommodation for which the immigration service is responsible will reduce the need to hold immigration detainees in prisons and police cells in the future.

There will, however, always be a need for some immigration detainees to be accommodated in prisons, either because of known violent tendencies or because of a need for closer supervision than can be provided in immigration detention centres. Similarly, there will be a continuing need to use police cells for the initial detention of immigration offenders detected within the United Kingdom.

**Mr. Robert Ainsworth:** To ask the Secretary of State for the Home Department how many asylum-seekers have been removed to Sweden on safe third country grounds since 26 July 1993; and how many of those so removed have been returned to the United Kingdom by the Swedish authorities.    [26174]

**Mr. Nicholas Baker:** The available information identifies 29 persons who had been refused asylum in the United Kingdom on safe third country grounds having been removed to Sweden since 26 July 1993. Of these, four have been returned to the United Kingdom.

**Mr. Robert Ainsworth:** To ask the Secretary of State for the Home Department how many applications for asylum are currently outstanding.    [26180]

**Mr. Nicholas Baker:** As at 31 April 1995, there were 57,610 applications for asylum outstanding in the United Kingdom.

**Mr. Gerrard:** To ask the Secretary of State for the Home Department, pursuant to his answer of 15 February, *Official Report*, column *695*, to the hon. Member for Chesham and Amersham (Mrs. Gillan), if he will identify the evidence which indicates that in the bulk of cases the asylum application is not made immediately after leave to enter or remain has been granted, but shortly before it is due to expire.    [25692]

**Mr. Nicholas Baker:** An analysis of the available information for 1994 suggests that some 60 per cent. of asylum applications made by in-time visitors had not been made within one month of arrival in the United Kingdom, and about 40 per cent. had not been made within three months.

### Immigration Officers

**Mr. Madden:** To ask the Secretary of State for the Home Department what plans he has to increase the establishment of immigration officers at Leeds–Bradford airport; and if he will make a statement.    [26139]

**Mr. Nicholas Baker:** I refer the hon. Member to my answer of 31 March, *Official Report*, column *860*. As part of the routine review of staffing and work load levels, the complement of immigration officers at Leeds–Bradford has recently been increased by one.

### Eurostar

**Mr. Robert Ainsworth:** To ask the Secretary of State for the Home Department how many applications for asylum have been made by individuals arriving at Waterloo railway station on board Eurostar trains since January.    [26181]

**Mr. Nicholas Baker:** Between 1 January 1995 and 24 May 1995, a total of 148 applications for asylum were made by passengers arriving at Waterloo international terminal on Eurostar trains.

### Detention Costs

**Mr. Robert Ainsworth:** To ask the Secretary of State for the Home Department, pursuant to his answer of 18 May, *Official Report*, column *364*, what was the total amount of detention costs reclaimed from carrying companies in *(a)* the most recent financial year for which information is available, *(b)* 1994 and *(c)* 1995 to date.    [26273]

**Mr. Nicholas Baker:** The total amount of detention costs reclaimed from carrying companies in the financial year 1994–95 is £674,538.51. The total for 1994 is £597,125.21, and the total for this year to 23 May is £289,136.07.

### Data Protection

**Mr. Cohen:** To ask the Secretary of State for the Home Department, pursuant to his answer of 8 March, *Official Report*, column *181*, if he will make a statement on the parameters applying to filing systems under the draft data protection directive; and if he will make a statement on the implementation of the data protection directive.    [26448]

**Mr. Nicholas Baker:** In implementing the directive in respect of manual data, member states must have regard to the definition of a "personal data filing system" contained in article 2. Subject to this, the directive allows member states some flexibility in determining precisely the types of manual records to which the directive should apply. Once the final form of the directive is known, we shall be consulting widely on how these and other provisions should be implemented in United Kingdom law.

**Mr. Cohen:** To ask the Secretary of State for the Home Department what assessment he has made of the effectiveness of the new offence of procuring unregistered disclosures, under the Criminal Justice and Public Order Act 1994; and what discussions he has had with the Data Protection Registrar in relation to this offence.    [26449]

**Mr. Nicholas Baker:** On the information available to me, I believe that the new offence, which was brought into force in February this year, has had a positive effect upon the unacceptable activities at which it was aimed. The Data Protection Registrar has kept Home Office officials closely informed of her plans for enforcing the offence.

### Equine Crime Unit

**Mr. Harry Greenway:** To ask the Secretary of State for the Home Department what measures he is taking to enhance the work and performance of the Metropolitan equine intelligence unit; and if he will make a statement.    [25596]

**Mr. Maclean** *[holding answer 22 May 1995]:* I understand from the Commissioner of Police of the Metropolis that he plans to make more resources available to the equine crime unit, including personnel and information technology. The unit is now based in New Scotland Yard.

### Immigration

**Mr. David Shaw:** To ask the Secretary of State for the Home Department what plans he has to introduce application forms for use by foreign nationals wishing to apply for leave to remain in the United Kingdom.    [26623]

**Mr. Nicholas Baker:** Application forms will enable the Immigration Department to provide a more efficient service to applicants at a lower cost to the public purse. Genuine applicants will receive a speedier decision while those not entitled to further leave to stay will be refused more quickly, strengthening the immigration control. From 5 June, application forms for requests for limited leave to remain will be available from the application forms unit of the Immigration Department. Forms for settlement applications are in preparation. The scheme will not include applications under European Community law or applications for asylum. The operation of the scheme will be reviewed later this year following which we envisage making the use of application forms compulsory.

## Departmental Performance

**Ms Hodge:** To ask the Secretary of State for the Home Department what performance indicators and performance targets there are for measuring the performance of his Department in *(a)* answering letters from members of the public and *(b)* answering telephone calls from members of the public; how performance is monitored; and what are the latest figures for performance measured against the target set. [26234]

**Mr. Howard:** Individual units and agencies are required to set clear targets for the time taken to deal with correspondence from the public and to monitor performance against those standards. The targets set range from five to 30 working days. Some parts of the Department use computerised tracking systems to monitor performance, and others take samples periodically. No records are however kept centrally of performance against targets.

There is no similar system of targets for answering telephone calls in most parts of the Department, but standards relating to courtesy and helpfulness have been laid down.

## Complaints

**Ms. Hodge:** To ask the Secretary of State for the Home Department what policy and procedures exist for dealing with complaints against his Department by members of the public; when his Department last updated its policy; what time limit and target for dealing with such complaints his Department has; and what follow-up procedure exists where complainants are not satisfied with his Department's response to a complaint. [26218]

**Mr. Howard:** There are various arrangements for dealing with complaints in different parts of the Department. These involve a range of time limits and targets. For example, the UK Passport Agency aims to deal fully with all problems raised within 15 working days, or to acknowledge them within five working days if they are not straightforward, and the Immigration and Nationality Department aims to respond within eight weeks of receiving a complaint.

The IND complaints system is monitored by an independent Complaints Audit Committee, which ensures that procedures are working effectively. The leaflets on complaints procedures produced by the Passport Agency and by IND make it clear that complainants who are not satisfied with the response they receive can raise the matter with the Home Office Minister responsible for the service, or with the Parliamentary Commissioner for Administration.

## Contracting out

**Ms Hodge:** To ask the Secretary of State for the Home Department for each piece of work subject to a bidding process under the auspices of *(a)* the Home Office and *(b)* agencies for which the Home Office is responsible where work was contracted out, who were the successful bidders; and which contracts were won by in-house bidders in (i) 1993–94; (ii) 1994–95; and (iii) 1995–96. [25523]

**Mr. Howard:** The table set out, for 1993–94 and 1994–95, the results of those "Competing for Quality" exercises in the Home Office, including the Prison Service, which proceeded to competition.

| Activity | Result |
|---|---|
| *(i) 1993–94—Prison Service* | |
| Court Escort and Custody Services—Metropolitan Area | Contract awarded to Securior Services |
| Doncaster Prison | Contract awarded to Premier Prison Services |
| Manchester Prison | In-house win |
| *(ii) 1993–94—rest of Home Office* | |
| Statistical Data Collection | In-house win |
| Internal Audit | In-house win |
| Immigration and Nationality Department Security Guards | In-house win |
| *(iii) 1994–95—Prison Service* | |
| Buckley Hall Prison | Contract awarded to Group 4 |
| Court Escort and Custody Services—East Anglia, the North West and North Wales | Contract awarded to Group 4 |
| Facilities Management at the Prison Service College, Newbold Revel | In-house win for administration, works and ground maintenance. Contract awarded to Taylorplan Services for catering and housekeeping |
| IT Helpdesk | Contract awarded to Serco |
| *(iv) 1994–95—rest of Home Office* | |
| Central Typing Services | In-house win |
| Records Storage and Retrieval | In-house win |
| Administrative Computer Services | Contract awarded to Sema Group plc |
| Central Training Services | In-house win |
| Central Reprographics and Design and Illustration Services | Service Level Agreement awarded to Her Majesty's Stationery Office (HMSO) |
| Central Office Keeping and Messengerial Services | In-house win |
| Immigration and Nationality Department Typing Services | In-house win |
| Immigration and Nationality Department Messengerial and Reprographic Services | In-house win |
| Immigration and Nationality Department File Management | Contract awarded to Britannia Data Management (BDM) |

No contracts or service level agreements have yet been awarded as a result of "Competing for Quality" exercises in 1995–96.

The estimated annual savings figures arising so far from the "Competing for Quality" programme since April 1992 are £19 million for the Prison Service and £11 million for the rest of the Home Office.

A substantial number of competitions also take place outside the "Competing for Quality" programme, mainly to meet requirements for a wide range of specialist services. Information on the results of these competitions is not readily available and could be obtained only at disproportionate cost.

### Dangerous Dogs Act

**Mr. Barry Jones:** To ask the Secretary of State for the Home Department (1) what has been the total cost so far of keeping dogs held under the Dangerous Dogs Act 1991 in kennels; and if he will make a statement;    [25671]

(2) what has been the total cost so far of the Dangerous Dogs Act 1991; and if he will make a statement.    [25670]

**Mr. Nicholas Baker:** Information on the cost to the police, local authorities, the Crown Prosecution Service, and the courts of operating the Dangerous Dogs Act 1991 is not held centrally.

### Staff

**Ms Hodge:** To ask the Secretary of State for the Home Department (1) what changes there have been in the number of staff employed by (i) the Home Office and (ii) each agency for which the Home Office is responsible in *(a)* 1993–94 and *(b)* 1994–95; and what are the projected figures for 1995–96;    [25496]

(2) what changes there have been in the number of staff in employment by grade in *(a)* his Department and *(b)* each agency for which his Department is responsible in (i) 1993–94 and (ii) 1994–95; and what are the projected figures for 1995–96;    [25632]

(3) how many staff of *(a)* the Home Office and *(b)* agencies for which the Home Office is responsible, were employed on a casual or short-term basis in (i) 1993–94 and (ii) 1994–95 and what are the projected figures for 1995–96.    [25514]

**Mr. Howard:** The numbers of permanent and casual staff employed by my Department and each of its executive agencies in 1993–94, projected outturn for 1994–95, and plans for 1995–96 are published in my Department's annual report, a copy of which is in the Library. No projections broken down by grade are available.

### Contracting Out

**Ms. Hodge:** To ask the Secretary of State for the Home Department what work has been contracted out by (i) his Department and (ii) by agencies for which the Department is responsible in *(a)* 1993–94, *(b)* 1994–95 and projected for 1995–96.    [25521]

**Mr. Howard:** Details of work contracted out by my Department and agencies for which my Department is responsible for the specified years, are as follows:

*1993–94*

i. Court Escorts— Greater London (Area 3).

ii. HMP Doncaster

iii. Education services in some prison establishments following the Further and Higher Education Act.

iv. HMP Reading (staff and inmate catering).

*1994–95*

i. Campsfield House Immigration Detention Centre

ii HMP Buckley Hall

iii. Banking Services

iv. Court Escorts—East Anglia (Area 4).

v. Court Escorts—Merseyside, Greater Manchester, North Wales (Area 6).

vi. Legal Services—Fire Service College.

vii.Radio link installation and maintenance—Police Department.

viii.Immigration and Nationality Department—File storage and retrieval services.

ix. Building support services—Forensic Science Service

x. Administrative Computer Services.

xi. IT Helpdesk.

*Projected work— 1995–96*

i. Court Escorts—South West, South Wales (Area 1).

ii. Court Escorts—South, South East (Area 2)

iii. Court Escorts—West Midlands, Mid Wales (Area 5).

iv. HMP Bridgend—Design, Construct, Manage and Finance.

v. HMP Fazakerley—Design, Construct, Manage and Finance

vi. HMP Lowdham Grange—Rebuild on Existing site.

vii. HMP Coldingley—Staff/Inmate catering and prison shop.

viii. HMP Brixton—Staff Catering

ix. HMP Wealstun—Staff catering and prison shop.

x. HMP Highpoint—Prison Shop

xi. Transport for Police Staff College Bramshill.

Information on low-value work that has been contracted out during the period specified is not recorded centrally and could be obtained only at disproportionate cost.

### Talbot Bail Hostel

**Mr. John Morris :** To ask the Secretary of State for the Home Department when the report on the Port Talbot bail hostel will be published.    [25406]

**Mr. Nicholas Baker:** Early in the summer.

### Trespassers

**Mrs. Gorman:** To ask the Secretary of State for the Home Department on how many occasions the police have used their discretionary power to direct trespassers to leave land since 8 November 1994.    [25539]

**Mr. Maclean:** This information is not available centrally and could be obtained only at disproportionate cost.

### Lewis Probation Centre

**Mr. Morgan:** To ask the Secretary of State for the Home Department what representations he has received, and what consultations he has had, concerning the closure of Lewis probation centre, Neville street, Riverside, Cardiff; and what proposals he has to fund alternative specialist provision.    [25601]

**Mr. Nicholas Baker:** My right hon. and learned Friend has received no representations concerning the decision of the South Glamorgan probation committee to relocate its probation centre, with Home Office capital grant support, from Lewis street to Westgate street, Cardiff.

### Fire Safety

**Mr. Beith:** To ask the Secretary of State for the Home Department (1) what plans he has to reform the legislation in respect of Crown buildings which require a fire certificate but are not obliged to apply for one; and if he will make a statement;     [25861]

(2) when he expects to lay before the House the Fire Precautions (Places of Work) Regulations to be made under section 12 of the Fire Precautions Act 1971.     [25862]

**Mr. Nicholas Baker:** Action on both these issues will depend on the outcome of the Government's consideration of the recommendations of the interdepartmental review of fire safety legislation and enforcement on which we hope to make an announcement shortly.

### Mentally Ill Offenders

**Mr. Nicholas Brown:** To ask the Secretary of State for the Home Department how many places were available in secure units for mentally ill offenders (a) in 1990 and (b) in the latest year for which figures are available.     [26081]

**Mr. Bowis:** I have been asked to reply.

In 1990, there were 572 places in medium secure units. By March 1995, this had increased to 792. The completion of our centrally funded building programme, to which we have allocated more than £47 million between 1991 and 1995, will take the total to over 1,150 by the end of 1996. There are also about 450 places in interim secure psychiatric units, many of which are of medium secure standard, and others which are funded by health authorities in independent sector facilities.

In addition, there are about 1,600 places in the three special hospitals at Ashworth, Broadmoor and Rampton. The number of secure places in local hospitals is not recorded centrally but is estimated at about 2,000.

There were no purpose-built NHS medium secure places in 1979, despite the fact that the Glancy committee had recommended them in its 1974 report.

### WALES

### Industrial Development

**Mr. Wigley:** To ask the Secretary of State for Wales, pursuant to his oral answer of 24 April, *Official Report*, columns 504-5, concerning Government grants and locational incentives, if he will ensure that no jobs are lost in the food processing industry in Wales as a direct displacement arising from grant-aided new jobs being created in the same industrial sector in Northern Ireland.     [24950]

**Mr. Redwood:** When applications for assistance are being assessed displacement is always considered and the same criteria apply throughout the United Kingdom. The hon. Gentleman has written to me about a particular case and I will reply to him as soon as possible.

### Water Treatment Directive

**Mr. Ainger:** To ask the Secretary of State for Wales (1) if he will list those areas of the Welsh coastline that have been designated (a) less sensitive and (b) high natural dispersion areas under the urban waste water treatment directive, 91/271/EEC; and if he will make a statment;     [25991]

(2) what criteria has been used to designate those areas of the Welsh coastline as less and high natural dispersion areas under the urban waste water treatment directive, 91/271/EEC; and if he will make a statement;     [25993]

(3) what plans he has to reclassify the Severn and Afan estuaries as coastal waters under the urban waste water treatment directive, 91/271/EEC, and what practical effect reclassification will have on existing or future sewage discharges in these estuaries     [25992]

**Mr. Gwilym Jones:** I refer the hon. Member to the reply given on 18 May 1994 by my hon. Friend the Minister of State for the Environment and Countryside, columns *511-12*.

The criteria for identifying high natural dispersion areas—otherwise known as less sensitive areas—are set out in annex II B of the urban waste water treatment directive. A map showing all the areas identified in England and Wales as high natural dispersion areas was placed in the Library of the House. Maps defining, for the purposes of the directive, the outer limits of estuaries, including the Severn and Afan, are available for inspection at the National Rivers Authority's principal offices. The Government have no plans to redefine these limits.

### Staff

**Ms Hodge:** To ask the Secretary of State for Wales (1) what changes there have been in the numbers of staff employed by (a) the Welsh Office and (b) agencies for which the Welsh Office is responsible, listing the changes in the number of staff agency by agency in (i) 1993–94 and (ii) 1994–95; and what changes are projected for 1995–96.     [25060]

(2) what changes there have been in the number of staff in employment by grade in (a) his office and (b) each agency for which his office is responsible in (i) 1993–94 and (ii) 1994–95; and what are the projected figures for 1995–96     [25625]

(3) how many staff of (a) the Welsh Office and (b) agencies for which the Welsh Office is responsible, were employed on a casual or short-term basis in (i) 1993–94 and (ii) 1994–95; and what are the projected figures for 1995–96.     [25490]

**Mr. Redwood:** The numbers of permanent and casual staff employed by my Department and Cadw in 1993–94, projected outturn for 1994–95 and plans for 1995–96 are published in my Department's annual report, a copy of which is in the Library of the House.

**Ms Hodge:** To ask the Secretary of State for Wales how many posts were lost in (a) the Welsh Office and (b) agencies for which the Welsh Office is responsible, listing the total lost posts agency by agency in (i) 1993–94 and (ii) 1994–95; and how many posts are proposed to be lost in 1995–96.     [25082]

**Mr. Redwood:** This information is not held centrally.

**Ms Hodge:** To ask the Secretary of State for Wales how many staff of (a) the Welsh Office and (b) agencies for which the Welsh Office is responsible (i) took early retirement, (ii) took voluntary redundancy, (iii) took compulsory redundancy and (iv) were retired on medical grounds in (1) 1993–94 and (2) 1994–95; and what are the projected figures for 1995–96. [25479]

**Mr. Redwood:** The information is set out as follows:

| | Welsh Office | | | Cadw | | |
|---|---|---|---|---|---|---|
| | 1993–94 | 1994–95 | 1995–96 | 1993–94 | 1994–95 | 1995–96 |
| Early Retirement | 4 | 39 | 16 | — | 1 | — |
| Redundancy | 9 | 25 | — | — | — | — |
| Ill Health | 19 | 28 | 3 | 3 | 3 | 1 |
| | 32 | 92 | 19 | 3 | 4 | 1 |

These figures include those who chose redundancy as an alternative to employment at other locations. Projected figures are not available.

## TREASURY

### Debt Management

**Mr. Matthew Banks:** To ask the Chancellor of the Exchequer if he will make a statement on Government debt management. [26624]

**Mr. Nelson:** Yes. The current tax rules for gilts and bonds inhibit the development of new types of gilts and bonds and make the introduction of an official gilt strips market impossible. They also offer scope for tax avoidance and hence necessitate lengthy and complex anti-avoidance legislation.

The Inland Revenue has therefore today published a consultative document outlining a much simpler system, under which all returns on gilts and bonds would be taxed as income. This would also provide a consistent framework for the taxation of new types of bonds and gilts.

Reform on these lines is a necessary precondition for the introduction of an official gilt strips market. The Bank of England is today publishing a consultative document on the introduction of a strips market.

The consultative period will end on 30 June and the Government will make an announcement shortly afterwards on how they intend to proceed.

Copies of both consultative documents have been placed in the Libraries of both Houses.

### Environmental Satellite Accounts

**Mr. Dafis:** To ask the Chancellor of the Exchequer if he has set a date for the establishment within the Central Statistical Office of a new unit to develop a pilot system of environmental satellite accounts linked to national accounts. [25293]

**Mr Nelson:** The Central Statistical Office is in the course of establishing the unit which will carry out this development.

### Real Net Capital Stocks

**Mr. Milburn:** To ask the Chancellor of the Exchequer if he will provide estimates of real net capital stocks by industry at 1990 replacement cost for each year since 1979. [25197]

**Mr. Nelson:** Estimates of real net capital stock by industry at 1990 replacement cost are unavailable.

Estimates of gross capital stock by industry at 1990 replacement cost are shown in table 14.8 of "United Kingdom National Accounts", a copy of which is available in the House of Commons Library.

### Sterling-dollar Exchange Rate

**Mr. Austin Mitchell:** To ask the Chancellor of the Exchequer what was the change in the real exchange rate of the dollar to the pound in terms of relative export unit values for manufactures in the second quarter of 1994 compared to the first quarter of 1980; and what estimate he has made of the effect of this change on the balance of trade between *(a)* the United States of America and (1) the world and (2) the United Kingdom and *(b)* the United Kingdom and (1) the United States of America and (2) the world. [25675]

**Mr. Nelson:** The sterling-dollar real exchange rate in terms of export unit values for manufactures can be calculated from data available on the Central Statistical Office database, which can be accessed through the Library of the House.

The balance of trade between countries depends on a variety of factors, including price and non-price competitiveness, domestic demand, and overseas demand, none of which are easy to isolate.

### Retirements and Redundancies

**Ms Hodge:** To ask the Chancellor of the Exchequer what has been the annual cost to the Treasury of staff leaving each Department under redundancy or early retirement schemes, to incorporate *(a)* added years lump sum payments, *(b)* redundancy payments, *(c)* pension payments, including enhancements and *(d)* other special arrangements for (i) 1993–94, (ii) 1994–95, (iii) projected for 1995–96 and (iv) projected for 1996–97. [25471]

**Mr. Nelson:** The costs of early retirement and redundancies are borne from individual Departments' running costs provision in respect of their own staff. But in the case of individuals leaving the civil service in the period 1 October 1994 to 31 March 1997, Departments will bear 20 per cent. of such costs, with the remaining 80 per cent. being covered by the Treasury, through the civil superannuation vote, as announced in the civil service White Paper (Cm 2627).

For 1994–95, the cost to the civil superannuation vote of the 80:20 central funding scheme was £26.9 million. Provision for £150 million has been taken in main estimates for 1995–96. Projections for 1996–97 will be determined during the coming public expenditure survey.

### Contracting Out

**Ms Hodge:** To ask the Chancellor of the Exchequer for each piece of work subject to a bidding process under the auspices of *(a)* the Treasury and *(b)* agencies for which the Treasury is responsible (i) who the successful bidders were when work was contracted out and (ii) which contracts were won by in-house bidders in (1) 1993–94, (2) 1994–95 and (3) 1995–96. [25559]

**Mr. Nelson:** The table shows the work subjected to competition by the Treasury under the "Competing for Quality" initiative, who won the contracts and in which year.

| *Successful Bidders* | | | |
| --- | --- | --- | --- |
| *Contract* | *1993–94* | *1994–95* | *1995–96* |
| Library Services | In house Team Touche Ross | Nil | Nil |
| Internal Audit | Price Waterhouse | Nil | Nil |
| Security Guarding | Nil | SAFE | Nil |

### Mortgage Holders (Compensation)

**Mr. Wray:** To ask the Chancellor of the Exchequer what plans he has to compensate mortgage holders unable to meet their mortgage costs owing to rises in interest rates. [24222]

**Mr. Nelson** *[holding answer 24 May 1995]:* The Government have no such plans. Home ownership is very affordable in the UK: less than one third of the total increase in base rates since September 1994 has been passed through by building societies to average variable mortgage rates. Even allowing for that increase, the overall reduction in mortgage interest rates since October

1990 has resulted in a net saving of £130 per month for the average mortgage holder. Fixed-rate mortgages are available for borrowers who want certainty about the level of their mortgage payments over a given period.

## Taxation

**Mr. Frank Field:** To ask the Chancellor of the Exchequer (1) if he will publish estimates for the revenue cost/yield in 1996–97 and for a full year of levying a new top rate of tax of *(a)* 30 per cent., *(b)* 35 per cent., *(c)* 45 per cent., *(d)* 50 per cent., *(e)* 55 per cent., *(f)* 60 per cent., and imposing it on incomes above (i) £27,825, (ii) £30,000, (iii) £40,000, (iv) £50,000, (v) £60,000, (vi) £70,000, (vii) £80,000, (viii) £90,000, (ix) £100,000 and, (x) £110,000 (xi) £120,000, (xii) £130,000, (xiii) £140,000 and, (xiv) £150,000, and assuming that where the new top rate is lower than 40 per cent., the 40 per cent. band is abolished, and where it is higher, the 40 per cent. band remains in place;                    [23349]

(2) if he will provide estimates for the revenue cost or yield in 1995–96 and for a full year of levying a new top rate of tax of *(a)* 30 per cent., *(b)* 35 per cent., *(c)* 45 per cent., *(d)* 50 per cent., *(e)* 55 per cent. and *(f)* 60 per cent. and imposing it on incomes above (i) £27,825, (ii) £30,000, (iii) £40,000, (iv) £50,000, (v) £60,000, (vi) £70,000, (vii) £80,000, (viii) £90,000, (ix) £100,000, (x) £110,000 (xi) £120,000, (xii) £130,000, (xiii) £140,000 and (xiv) £150,000 assuming that where the new top rate is lower than 40 per cent., the 40 per cent. band is abolished, and where it is higher, the 40 per cent. band remains in place.                    [23975]

**Sir George Young** *[holding answer 9 May 1995]:* To provide all of the details sought could be done only at disproportionate cost. Therefore, the table gives available estimates showing the variation in revenue costs over the specified ranges of tax rates and bands of taxable income. These estimates do not allow for any behavioural changes that might result from the introduction of the new tax rate.

*£ billion*

| Lower limit taxable income £ | Full year revenue cost (-)/yield (+) at 1995–96 levels[1] Higher rate | | |
|---|---|---|---|
| | 30 per cent. | 45 per cent. | 60 per cent. |
| 24,300 | −4.7 | 2.4 | 9.3 |
| 50,000 | −6.2 | 1.0 | 3.9 |
| 70,000 | −6.5 | 0.7 | 2.7 |
| 100,000 | −6.8 | 0.5 | 1.9 |

[1] The figures include consequential effects on the yield of capital gains tax.

**Mr. Frank Field:** To ask the Chancellor of the Exchequer if he will estimate the revenue yield in 1995–96 and in a full year of introducing an alternative minimum tax of *(a)* 20 per cent., *(b)* 25 per cent., *(c)* 30 per cent. and *(d)* 35 per cent. at the levels of income of (i) £50,000, (ii) £60,000, (iii) £70,000, (iv) £80,000, (v) £90,000, (vi) £100,000, (vii) £110,000, (viii) £120,000, (ix) £130,000, (x) £140,000 and (xi) £150,000.                    [24365]

**Sir George Young** *[holding answer 16 May 1995]:* The table gives available estimates showing the variation in revenue yields over the specified ranges of tax rates and thresholds of gross income up to £100,000. Reliable estimates are not available for higher thresholds of gross income.

*£ million*

| Gross income | Full year revenue yield at 1995–96 levels Rate of minimum tax | | | |
|---|---|---|---|---|
| | 20 per cent. | 25 per cent. | 30 per cent. | 35 per cent. |
| Over £50,000 | 15 | 60 | 510 | 2,030 |
| Over £70,000 | 10 | 20 | 100 | 700 |
| Over £100,000 | 5 | 10 | 40 | 250 |

*Note:*
The estimates do not take account of any behavioural effects which might result from the introduction of the new arrangements.

## VAT (Tour Operators)

**Mr. Malcolm Bruce:** To ask the Chancellor of the Exchequer if he will delay the introduction of VAT on tour operators total margin until he has reviewed the equity of the exemption of operators with an in-house travel capacity; and if he will make a statement.   [24760]

**Mr. Heathcoat-Amory** *[holding answer 17 May 1995]:* No. The proposed changes which bring the VAT scheme for tour operators into line with a judgment of the European Court of Justice were announced by Customs and Excise last October, over 14 months before the implementation date of 1 January 1996. While I recognise that some concern has been expressed about possible distortions of competition, there are differing views within the industry and this is one of several complex issues which does not relate solely to the 1 January 1996 changes and which can be addressed only in the longer term and in full consultation with industry representatives. It will therefore be included in a wide-ranging review of the tour operators' margin scheme which Customs proposes to begin next month.

I am satisfied that, in the meantime, the changes must be made, and a Treasury order will be laid before the House.

**Mr. David Atkinson:** To ask the Chancellor of the Exchequer what representations he has received from *(a)* the Association of Independent Tour Operators and *(b)* other small companies in the outbound travel industry to his VAT changes to tour operators margin scheme; and if he will make a statement.                    [25590]

**Mr. Heathcoat-Amory:** The Association of Independent Tour Operators and others have raised several concerns about the proposed changes to the tour operators' margin scheme. The changes, which were announced by Customs and Excise last October and will be implemented on 1 January 1996, bring the scheme into line with a judgment of the European Court of Justice. Many, but not all, wish to see the implementation of the changes delayed.

Some concern has been expressed about possible distortions of competition. This is one of several complex issues connected with the scheme which do not solely relate to the 1 January 1996 changes and which can be addressed only in the longer term and in full consultation with industry representatives. Customs propose to begin just such a wide-ranging review of the scheme next month.

There will also be further contacts between Customs and Excise and the Association of Independent Tour Operators to discuss the position, but I am satisfied that the changes must be made, and a Treasury order will be laid before the House.

### Leeds/Bradford Airport

**Mr. Madden:** To ask the Chancellor of the Exchequer when a flexible anti-smuggling team of Customs and Excise was first established at Leeds/Bradford airport; and how many Customs and Excise staff are based permanently at the airport; how many people arriving at the airport have telephoned requesting to declare goods for excise charges to be levied; and if he will make a statement. [26140]

**Mr. Heathcoat-Amory:** Flexible anti-smuggling teams were introduced by Customs at Leeds/Bradford airport in early 1992. There are no Customs staff based permanently at the airport. Local Customs management estimate that about six telephone calls per month are made to declare goods for which excise charges are to be levied.

There are no Customs-free ports or airports. Over recent years, Customs enforcement strategy has progressively moved away from a static presence at all ports and airports towards more flexible checks operated by fast response teams targeted at both areas and times of highest risks. At major ports and airports these anti-smuggling teams are based on site, the smaller places being covered by mobile anti-smuggling strategy, which encompasses both anti-smuggling and fiscal controls, there are some locations where passengers can telephone Customs if they have anything to declare for fiscal purposes. This facility is not a part of anti-smuggling controls.

**Mr. Madden:** To ask the Chancellor of the Exchequer what representations he has received about the absence of permanent Customs and Excise staff at Leeds/Bradford airport. [26141]

**Mr. Heathcoat-Amory:** Since 1 January 1994, two representations have been received referring specifically to concerns about the absence of permanently based Customs staff at Leeds/Bradford airport, and a further representation expressed concern about airports, including Leeds/Bradford, which have no permanently based staff.

### Developing Countries (Debt)

**Miss Lestor:** To ask the Chancellor of the Exchequer (1) if he will list the total stock of existing and estimated debt outstanding to the United Kingdom by developing countries for each year from 1990 to 2000; [22674]

(2) if he will list by country the total stock of existing and estimated debt outstanding to the United Kingdom by developing countries for each year from 1900 to 2000. [22677]

**Mr. Nelson:** The figures for the Export Credit Guarantees Department are not readily available. To assemble them manually would incur disproportionate costs. Figures for outstanding ECGD debt stock as at 31 March 1995 are below. For the ODA figures, I refer the hon. Member to the reply given to her by the Under-Secretary of State for the Foreign and Commonwealth Office on 10 May 1995, *Official Report*, column *463*.

*Outstanding debt stock as at 31 March 1995—ECGD*

| | £ million |
| --- | --- |
| **Africa** | |
| Algeria | 70.69 |
| Angola | 56.97 |
| Benin | 3.83 |
| Burkina Faso | 1.94 |
| Cameroon | 58.61 |
| C A R | 0.25 |
| Congo | 106.96 |
| Cote d'Ivoire | 30.25 |
| Egypt | 345.48 |
| Ethiopia | 9.80 |
| Gabon | 118.06 |
| Gambia | 2.36 |
| Ghana | 8.34 |
| Guinea Republic | 5.06 |
| Kenya | 57.45 |
| Liberia | 6.64 |
| Madagascar | 18.14 |
| Malawi | 0.72 |
| Mali | 11.36 |
| Mauritania | 7.50 |
| Morocco | 121.73 |
| Mozambique | 87.66 |
| Niger | 10.64 |
| Nigeria | 2,304.30 |
| Senegal | 2.62 |
| Sierra Leone | 3.62 |
| Somalia | 16.22 |
| Sudan | 168.23 |
| Tanzania | 163.31 |
| Togo | 13.22 |
| Uganda | 25.33 |
| Zaire | 80.03 |
| Zambia | 236.45 |
| | 4,153.77 |
| **America** | |
| Argentina | 142.29 |
| Bolivia | 41.47 |
| Brazil | 861.44 |
| Chile | 0.00 |
| Costa Rica | 1.72 |
| Cuba | 28.55 |
| Ecuador | 60.85 |
| Guyana | 117.21 |
| Jamaica | 4.32 |
| Mexico | 193.65 |
| Nicaragua | 0.91 |
| Peru | 130.60 |
| Trinidad and Tobago | 12.24 |
| | 1,595.25 |
| **Asia and Middle East** | |
| Indonesia | 3.55 |
| Philippines | 53.83 |
| Vietnam | 10.40 |
| Jordan | 365.21 |
| | 432.99 |
| | 6,182.01 |

## DUCHY OF LANCASTER

### Departmental Committees

**Mr. Forman:** To ask the Chancellor of the Duchy of Lancaster if he will list all the departmental committees of inquiry which have been established since November 1990, and in each case the date of establishment and the name of the chairman. [23145]

**Mr. David Hunt:** I list in the table those inquiries of which I am aware. I assume that "departmental committee of inquiry" should include any ad hoc inquiry set up by a Minister or Ministers bringing in expert or lay opinion and chaired by someone from outside Government to investigate either a specific event or a more general issue.

I have not included inquiries set up routinely in pursuance of responsibilities under a statutory requirement, for example public inquiries held under planning legislation.

*Departmental Committees of Inquiry*

| Department | Committee | Established | Chairman |
|---|---|---|---|
| MAFF | Advisory Committee on Flood and Coastal Defence Research and Development | December 1990 | Mr. P. Ackers |
| MAFF | Expert Group on Animal Feeding-stuffs | February 1991 | Professor G. E. Lamming |
| MAFF | Committee on Sea Level and Wave Recording | February 1991 | Mr. M. J. Tucker |
| MAFF | Committee on the Ethics of Genetic Modification and Food Use | September 1992 | Reverend Dr. J. C. Polkinghorne FRS |
| MAFF | Review of the Hygiene and Structural Requirements in a Sample of Slaughterhouses which have applied for temporary derogations under the Fresh Meat (Hygiene and Inspection) Regulations 1992 | October 1992 | Dr. A. M. Johnston Mr. B. J. Spurr |
| MAFF | Committee to Review Fertility Aspects of Sewage Sludge Application to Agricultural Land | January 1993 | Professor A. D. Bradshaw |
| MAFF | Ad Hoc Committee to consider the Ethical Implications of Emerging Technologies in the Breeding of Farm Animals | May 1993 | Professor Michael Banner |
| Attorney General | Possible merger of SFO with CPS | July 1994 | Rex Davie |
| MOD | MOD Policy Study | December 1993 | Sir John Blelloch |
| MOD | Independent Review of Armed Forces' Manpower, Career and Remuneration Structures | April 1994 | Michael Bett |
| MOD | Review of Representational Entertainment in the Armed Forces | October 1994 | Sir Peter Cazalet |
| DFE | Review of the Further Education Unit and Further Education Staff College | January 1993 | Ken Young CBE |
| DFE | Review of the National Curriculum and Assessment Framework | April 1993 | Sir Ron Dearing |
| DFE | A short study to investigate the potential of emerging technologies to improve the effectiveness of the learning process for pupils of statutory school age | January 1995 | Peter Seaborne |
| DFE | Review of the 16–19 Qualifications Framework | April 1995 | Sir Ron Dearing |
| DOE | Inquiry into the Rating of Plant and Machinery | June 1991 | Derek Wood QC |
| DOE | Enquiry into the Planning System in North Cornwall District | August 1992 | Miss Audrey M. Lees |
| DOE | Task Force on Government Departments' Empty Houses | December 1992 | John Baker |
| DOE | Inquiry into the Investment arrangements of the National Rivers Authority | March 1993 | Sir Michael Kerry |
| DOE | Review of the Procurement and Contracting in the Construction Industry | July 1993 | Sir Michael Latham |
| DoH | Committee of Enquiry into Complaints about Ashworth Hospital | April 1991 | Sir Louis Blom-Cooper |
| DoH | Fundamental Review of the Existing System of Remuneration of General Dental Practitioners | July 1992 | Sir Kenneth Bloomfield KCB |
| DoH | Panel of persons appointed under the Medicines Act 1968 to hear company representations on the proposed revocations of the product licences for Halcion/Triazolam | January 1993 | Miss Diana Cotton QC |
| DoH | The Allitt Enquiry | May 1993 | Sir Cecil Clothier |
| DoH | Review of NHS Complaints Procedures | June 1993 | Professor Alan Wilson |
| DoH | Advisory Group on Osteoporosis | November 1993 | Professor P. J. Barlow |
| DoH | Task Force to Review Services for Drug Misusers | May 1994 | Reverend Dr. John Polkinghorne FRS |
| DoH | Expert Group to Investigate Cot Death Theories | November 1994 | Lady Sylvia Limerick |
| HO | Royal Commission on Criminal Justice | July 1991 | Viscount Runciman of Droxford |
| HO | Enquiry into Police Rewards and Responsibilities | July 1992 | Sir Patrick Sheehy |
| HO | Enquiry into the Escape of IRA Prisoners from Whitemoor Jail | September 1994 | Sir John Woodcock |
| HO | Enquiry into Prison Security | December 1994 | Sir John Learmont |
| LCD | An Inquiry into Access to Civil Justice | March 1994 | Conducted by Lord Justice Woolf |
| DNH | Review of press Self-Regulation | July 1992 | Conducted by Sir David Calcutt QC |
| DNH | Fire protection measures for the Royal Palaces | January 1993 | Sir Alan Bailey |
| NI | Taxi Industry | November 1991 | Mr. R. Stirling |
| NI | Operational Policy in Belfast Prison from Management of Paramilitary Prisoners | December 1991 | Viscount Colville of Culrose QC |
| NI | Overtime Inquiry | January 1993 | Sir John Blelloch |
| NI | Northern Ireland Energy Efficiency Action Group | March 1993 | Dr. William J. McCourt |
| NI | Stormont Fire and Safety in Crown Buildings | January 1995 | Sir Reginald Doyle |

*Departmental Committees of Inquiry*

| Department | Committee | Established | Chairman |
|---|---|---|---|
| OPSS | Expert Working Group on Human Genome Research | February 1993 | Professor Kay E. Davies |
| OPSS | Review of UK Microbial Culture Collections | January 1994 | Professor Roger Whittenbury CBE |
| OPSS | Committee to Review the Contribution of Scientists and Engineers to the Public Understanding of Science, Engineering and Technology | January 1995 | Sir Arnold Wolfendale FRS |
| PM | Committee on Standards in Public Life | October 1994 | Lord Nolan |
| SO | Committee to review Curriculum and Examination in the Fifth and Sixth years of Secondary Education in Scotland | March 1990 | Prof. John M. Howie CBE |
| SO | The Cairngorms Working Party | March 1991 | Magnus Magnusson KBE |
| SO | The Loch Lomond and Trossachs Working Party | November 1991 | Sir Peter Hutchinson Bt CBE |
| SO | Committee to review Initial Training of Further Education College Lecturers | May 1992 | Prof. Janette Anderson |
| SO | Inquiry into Cervical Cytopathology at Inverclyde Royal Hospital, Greenock | April 1993 | Dr. Euphemia McGoogan |
| DSS | The Pension Law Review Committee | June 1992 | Prof. Roy Goode |
| DTI | Coal Task Force | November 1990 | Dr. Eoin Lees |
| DTI | Renewable Energy Advisory Group | September 1991 | Dr. Martin Holdgate |
| DTI | Radio Spectrum Review Committee Stage 3: 28–470 Mhz | July 1992 | Sir Colin Fielding CB |
| DTI | Inquiry into the Export of Defence Equipment and Dual-Use Goods to Iraq 1984–90 | November 1992 | Sir Richard Scott |
| DTp | Review of London Underground Limited's response to fires and other emergencies | September 1991 | Dr. Brian Appleton |
| DTp | Inquiry into river safety | December 1991 | John W. Hayes |
| DTp | Inquiry into the prevention of pollution from merchant shipping | January 1993 | Lord Donaldson |
| DTp | Assessment of what further work should be undertaken to identify the cause of the sinking of the MV Derbyshire | March 1995 | Lord Donaldson |
| DTp | Review of Coastguard actions during and after the Lyme Bay canoe tragedy | May 1995 | John Reeder QC |
| DTp | Study into aircraft noise mitigation measures at Redhill Aerodrome and Wycombe Air Park | November 1990 | A. J. O'Connor |
| HMT | Inquiry into the Supervision of the Bank of Credit and Commerce International | July 1991 | Rt Hon. Lord Justice Bingham |
| HMT | Report on the role and functions of the Securities and Investments Board | July 1992 | Andrew Large |

## NATIONAL HERITAGE

### Children's Play Funds

**Mrs. Golding:** To ask the Secretary of State for National Heritage in what areas of children's play funds will be available to bid for in the coming year. [25771]

**Mr. Sproat:** Bids will be invited in the near future for funds to carry out work in the areas of information dissemination, playwork education and training, and play safety.

### National Vocational Qualifications

**Ms Hoey:** To ask the Secretary of State for National Heritage if he will list the centres and the sports concerned in the awarding of national vocational qualifications.

[25043]

**Mr. Sproat:** Thirty-three sports were included in a pilot project to establish national vocational qualification centres.

These are:

archery
association football
athletics
badminton
basketball
bowls
canoeing
cricket
cycling
dinghy sailing
exercise and fitness
fencing
gymnastics
hockey
judo
mountaineering
movement and dance
netball
orienteering
rowing
rugby league
rugby union
skiing
squash
sub aqua
surfing
swimming
table tennis
target shooting
tennis
trampolining
volleyball

Currently, there are 12 fully approved centres in the following sports:

- association football
- swimming
- hockey
- gymnastics
- tennis
- basketball
- karate
- yachting

A number of other centres are in line for approval by the end of this year.

**Ms Hoey:** To ask the Secretary of State for National Heritage (1) how many national vocational qualifications have been awarded in martial arts;    [25042]

(2) what assessment he has made of the progress of awarding national vocational qualifications for martial arts.    [25041]

**Mr. Sproat:** National vocational qualifications will not be awarded in the category "martial arts". There are eight different recognised martial arts, each with varying styles and techniques and each has to be treated separately in its preparation for NVQ centre approval. Details of awards in the eight recognised martial arts are not available.

### Contracting Out

**Ms Hodge:** To ask the Secretary of State for National Heritage (1) what work has been contracted out *(a)* by his Department and *(b)* by agencies for which his Department is responsible in (i) 1993–94, (ii) 1994–95 and (iii) projected for 1995–96;    [25661]

(2) for each area of work subject to a bidding process under the auspices of (i) his Department and (ii) agencies for which his Department is responsible where work was contracted out who were the successful bidders; and which contracts were won by in-house bidders in (i) 1993–94, (ii) 1994–95 and (iii) 1995–96.    [25518]

**Mr. Dorrell:** Details of work contracted out for the first time which would previously have been carried out in-house by (i) my Department and (ii) the two agencies for which I am responsible in (i) 1993–94, (ii) 1994–95 and (iii) 1995–96 are given in the table below. Only one of the tenders was subject to an in-house bid, which was successful.

| Let by | Activity | Name of successful bid | Won by in-house bid |
|---|---|---|---|
| *(i) 1993–94* | | | |
| DNH | Consultancy for advice on competitive tendering of works management functions | Watts and Partners | No in-house bid |
| DNH | Reprographics | William Lea FM | No in-house bid |
| DNH | Central Typing and Secretarial | Manpower plc | No in-house bid |
| DNH | Mailroom | Security Despatch Group | No in-house bid |
| DNH | Security | Royal British Legion association | No in-house bid |
| DNH | Minor Maintenance | Richard Devine | No in-house bid |
| DNH | Cleaning | Ramoneur | No in-house bid |
| DNH | Reception | Manpower plc | No in-house bid |
| DNH | Payments and Accounts Services | Accounts Services Agency | No in-house bid |
| The Royal Parks | Property maintenance management | Tarmac Facilities Management | No in-house bid |
| Historic Royal Palaces | Kew Palace—Security Services | Royal British Legion | No in-house bid |
| Historic Royal Palaces | Hampton Court Palace—Gardens Litter Clearance | SITA | No in-house bid |
| Historic Royal Palaces | Hampton Court Palace | Initial Cleaning Services | No in-house bid |
| Historic Royal Palaces | Kensington Palace—Catering | De blanks | No in-house bid |
| Historic Royal Palaces | Kensington Palace—Cleaning | Swanlux | No in-house bid |
| Historic Royal Palaces | Kensington Palace—Cash Collection | Armaguard/Security Express | No in-house bid |
| Historic Royal Palaces | Banqueting House—Cleaning Services | Sloane Cleaning | No in-house bid |
| Historic Royal Palaces | Banqueting House—Security | Royal British Legion | No in-house bid |
| Historic Royal Palaces | Banqueting House—Porterage | Universal | No in-house bid |
| Historic Royal Palaces | Banqueting House—Catering | 10 companies used—selected by tender | No in-house bid |
| Historic Royal Palaces | Banqueting House—Floristry | Nancy Ford | No in-house bid |
| *(ii) 1994–95* | | | |
| DNH | Provision of works management services for certain properties in central London | E C Harris | No in-house bid |

| Let by | Activity | Name of successful bid | Won by in-house bid |
|---|---|---|---|
| DNH | Provision of works management services for central ceremonial activities | Unicorn Consultancy Ltd. | No in-house bid |
| DNH | Provision of works services management at the Royal Naval College, Greenwich | Taylor Woodrow Facilities Management | No in-house bid |
| DNH | Statue maintenance services | Stonewest Ltd. | No in-house bid |
| DNH | Services relating to Trafalger Square Christmas Tree and New Year works | Building and Property Facilities Management Ltd. | No in-house bid |
| DNH | Record Storage, Retrieval and Review | Britannia Data Management | No in-house bid |
| The Royal Parks | Management of Car Parking Facilities | Apcoa Parking Ltd. | No in-house bid |
| The Royal Parks | Audit Services | Price Waterhouse | No in-house bid |
| The Royal Parks | Estate management duties | Daniel Smith | No in-house bid |
| Historic Royal Palaces | IT Consultants | Internet Solutions | No in-house bid |
| Historic Royal Palaces | Ticketing/EPOS Systems | MHG Systems Select Ticketing | No in-house bid |
| Historic Royal Palaces | HM Tower of London—Window Cleaning | Metropolitan | No in-house bid |
| Historic Royal Palaces | HM Tower of London—Computer Maintenance | HMSO | No in-house bid |
| Historic Royal Palaces | HM Tower of London—Commercial Guard Force | RBLA | No in-house bid |
| Historic Royal Palaces | HM Tower of London—Signage—Moat Gardens | HB Sign Company | No in-house bid |
| Historic Royal Palaces | HM Tower of London—Costumed Interpretation | Past Pleasures | No in-house bid |
| Historic Royal Palaces | HM Tower of London—Garden Maintenance | Ground Control | No in-house bid |
| Historic Royal Palaces | Hampton Court Palace—Catering | Town and County | No in-house bid |
| Historic Royal Palaces | Hampton Court Palace—Costumed Interpretation | Past Pleasures | No in-house bid |
| Historic Royal Palaces | Hampton Court Palace—Recorded Tour Service | Acoustiguide | No in-house bid |
| Historic Royal Palaces | Hampton Court Palace—Warding Services | Group 4 | In-house bid unsuccessful |
| Historic Royal Palaces | Kensington Palace—Catering | De blanks/Diby Trout | No in-house bid |
| Historic Royal Palaces | Kensington Palace—Catering | Securicor | No in-house bid |
| Historic Royal Palaces | Kensington Palace—Cash Collection | Armaguard/Security Express | No in-house bid |
| *(iii) 1995–96* | | | |
| DNH | Consultancy for provision of professional support and advisory services relating to other Royal Estate Division works responsibilities | Tenders under consideration | No in-house bid |
| DNH | Services relating to Remembrance Day ceremony works | Tendering exercise planned for later in the year | No in-house bid |
| DNH | Stationery | Not yet awarded | No in-house bid |
| DNH | Payments and Accounts Services | CSL Managed Services | No in-house bid |
| The Royal Parks | Car Park Security duties | Reliance Security | No in-house bid |
| The Royal Parks | Entertainment organiser | Not yet awarded | — |
| Historic Royal Palaces | Computer Maintenance | LCE Computer Systems | No in-house bid |
| Historic Royal Palaces | HM Tower of London—Cash Collection/Counting | Security Express | No in-house bid |
| Historic Royal Palaces | Kensington Palace— Catering | Securicor | No in-house bid |
| Historic Royal Palaces | Kensington Palace—Cleaning | Securicor | No in-house bid |
| Historic Royal Palaces | Kensington Palace—Cash Collection | Armaguard/Security Express | No in-house bid |

## Archaeological Sites

**Mr. Dafis:** To ask the Secretary of State for National Heritage if it remains Her Majesty's Government's policy to legislate, as parliamentary time permits, to implement proposals for new controls for archaeological sites. [24723]

**Mr. Dorrell:** The Ancient Monuments and Archaeological Areas Act 1979 is the primary legislation in operation to safeguard ancient monuments and archaeological remains in England, Wales and Scotland. Proposals to update and improve the 1979 Act will be included in the Heritage Green Paper which I intend to publish later this year.

## Consultants

**Ms Hodge:** To ask the Secretary of State for National Heritage what is the level of expenditure on consultancy by (i) his Department and (ii) agencies for which his Department is responsible for (a) 1993–94, (b) 1994–95 and (c) projected for 1995–96.

**Mr. Dorrell:** My Department's expenditure on consultancy for the years 1993–94, 1994–95 and the forecast expenditure for 1995–96 is as follows:

| | DNH £ | Agencies £ |
|---|---|---|
| 1993–94 | 1,547,125 | 4,456,430 |
| 1994–95 | 1,145,996 | 2,470,325 |
| 1995–96(est) | 761,000 | 2,430,921 |

## Staff

**Ms Hodge:** To ask the Secretary of State for National Heritage (1) how many staff of (a) the Department of National Heritage and (b) agencies for which the Department of National Heritage is responsible, were employed on a casual or short-term basis in (i) 1993–94 and (ii) 1994–95; and what are the projected figures for 1995–96; [25508]

(2) what changes there have been in the number of staff employed by (i) his Department and (ii) each agency for which his Department is responsible in (a) 1993–94 and (b) 1994–95; and what are the projected figures for 1995–96. [25497]

**Mr. Dorrell:** The numbers of permanent and casual staff employed by my Department and its two executive agencies—the Royal Parks agency and the Historic Royal Palaces agency—in 1993–94; projected outturn for 1994–95; and plans for 1995–96 are published in my Department's annual report, a copy of which is in the Library of the House. No projections broken down by grade are available.

### Majority Shareholdings

**Mr. Byers:** To ask the Secretary of State for National Heritage if he will list those companies in which the holder of his office is a majority shareholder which *(a)* are currently in existence and *(b)* have been wound up in the past five years.    [25712]

**Mr. Dorrell** *[holding answer 22 May 1995]:* In my capacity as Secretary of State for National Heritage, I am not a majority shareholder in any companies which are either *(a)* currently in existence or *(b)* have been wound up in the past five years.

### EMPLOYMENT

#### Staff

**Ms Hodge:** To ask the Secretary of State for Employment how many staff of *(a)* the Department of Employment and *(b)* agencies for which the Department is responsible (i) took early retirement, (ii) took voluntary redundancy, (iii) took compulsory redundancy and (iv) were retired on medical grounds in (i) 1993–94 and (ii) 1994–95; and what are the projected figures for 1994–95.    [25414]

**Miss Widdecombe:** The information is not readily available in the form requested. The total number of staff who left on voluntary early retirement schemes in 1993–94 and 1994–95 were 1,909 and 1,884 respectively. The total number of staff who left on ill health retirement in 1993–94 and 1994–95 were 291 and 328 respectively. It is too soon to project the likely outcomes for 1995–96.

**Ms Hodge:** To ask the Secretary of State for Employment what is the annual cost to his Department of staff leaving under redundancy/early retirement schemes to incorporate (i) added years lump sum payments, (ii) redundancy payments, (iii) pension payments, including enhancements and (iv) any other special arrangements for *(a)* 1993–94, *(b)* 1994–95, and projected for *(c)* 1995–96 and *(d)* 1996–97.    [25636]

**Miss Widdecombe:** The cost to the Department of early retirement and redundancies are borne from the department's running costs. A detailed breakdown of the various costs could be obtained only at disproportionate cost.

The total costs borne on the Department's running costs in 1993–94 and 1994–95 were £61.87 million and £25.7 million respectively. It is too soon to project the costs to be borne for 1995–96 or 1996–97.

**Ms Hodge:** To ask the Secretary of State for Employment (1) how many staff of *(a)* the Department of Employment and *(b)* agencies for which the Department is responsible, were employed on a casual or short-term basis in (i) 1993–94 and (ii) 1994–95; and what is the projected figure for 1995–96;    [25413]

(2) what changes there have been in the number of staff in employment by grade in *(a)* his Department and *(b)* each agency for which his Department is responsible in (i) 1993–94 and (ii) 1994–95; and what are the projected figures for 1995–96.    [25626]

**Miss Widdecombe:** The numbers of permanent and casual staff employed by the Department and the Employment Service agency in 1993–94, estimated outturn for 1994–95, and plans for 1995–96 can be found in annexe A table iii of the Department's annual report, Cm 2805, a copy of which is available in the Library. No projections broken down by grade are available.

### Job Vacancies

**Mr. Chidgey:** To ask the Secretary of State for Employment, pursuant to his answer of 16 May, *Official Report*, column *160*, what consideration he has given to instructing jobcentres to refuse the acceptance of job vacancies with age restrictions in all circumstances where the employer cannot prove that age limits are essential to the performance of the job.    [25804]

**Miss Widdecombe:** The Government are not convinced that refusing to accept vacancies with age restrictions would persuade many employers to change their attitudes. Those employers who currently insist on imposing age restrictions may choose to fill their vacancies by other means. We are concerned that any movement away from using jobcentres would have a harmful effect on the job prospects of the unemployed, especially those who are disadvantaged.

### Minicab Drivers

**Mr. Bendall:** To ask the Secretary of State for Employment how many operations against benefit fraud by minicab drivers have been mounted by the Employment Service since January 1991; how many investigations were carried out; how many minicab drivers were found to be claiming social security benefits; what was the value of the benefits saved; and what was the cost of the operation.    [26182]

**Miss Widdecombe:** Responsibility for the subject of the question has been delegated to the Employment Service agency under its chief executive. I have asked him to arrange for a reply to be given.

*Letter from A. G. Johnson to Mr. Vivian Bendall, dated 25 May 1995:*

The Secretary of State has asked me, in the absence of the Chief Executive, to reply to your question about investigations by Employment Service (ES) Inspectors into mini cab drivers since 1991.

Unfortunately, the information you requested is not available.

Over the last 18 months (the period for which details concerning individual investigations is kept) ES Inspectors have carried out over 400,000 investigations covering all areas of the economy. However case files are held under clients' names and not by occupation or industry.

Experience has shown that benefit fraud is more prevalent in certain areas of employment, mini cab driving being one. My inspectors have and will continue to target these areas. Often it has been legitimate licensed taxi drivers and their trade associations who have provided information for my inspectors to act on.

Although I am unable to supply the information you seek on the investigation of mini cab drivers, the table below shows the performance of the ES Inspectors over the last three years.

|  | 1992–93 | 1993–94 | 1994–95 |
|---|---|---|---|
| Total number of staff | 1,343 | 1,343 | 1,343 |
| (investigators) | (780) | (780) | (780) |
| Gross savings[1] | £71.15 million | £80.12 million | £92.1 million |
| Cost of fraud operation | £26.44 million | £26.84 million | £27.5 million |
| Net savings | £44.71 million | £53.28 million | £64.6 million |
| Investment return[2] | £2.69 | £2.99 | £3.35 |
| Number of sign-offs[3] | 61,129 | 67,426 | 78,231 |

[1] This figure is calculated by multiplying the weekly amount of benefit saved by 22. The 22-week figure was identified by the Department of social Security research and represents the average number of weeks claimants would have remained on the register if they had not been investigated by fraud staff.

[2] Pounds of benefit saved for ever £ of cost.

[3] Number of clients withdrawing their claims to benefit after investigation by ES inspectors.

I hope this is helpful.

### Workstart

**Mr. Chidgey:** To ask the Secretary of State for Employment how many unemployed people will be taking part in the new workstart pilot schemes running in *(a)* the west midlands and *(b)* the north-west. [25805]

**Miss Widdecombe:** The new workstart pilots, which pay a subsidy to employers who recruit very long-term unemployed people, began last month in the west midlands conurbation, Greater Manchester and Cheshire.

No targets have been set for the number of people who will participate on the individual workstart pilots. However, 5,000 places are available for the pilots as a whole.

**Mr. Chidgey:** To ask the Secretary of State for Employment what steps his Department is taking *(a)* to evaluate the workstart pilot scheme in the west midlands in which a subsidy for placing an unemployed person is negotiated with an employer on an individual basis and *(b)* to monitor the workstart pilot scheme in the north-west in which the use of a subsidy varies according to the duration of a client's unemployment; and when he expects to publish the results of his evaluations. [25809]

**Miss Widdecombe:** Information on the workstart pilots is being collected in three ways: routine management information; a database which will contain details of participants' characteristics and a survey of employers.

A final report will be available in late 1996.

### Information Technology

**Mr. Madden:** To ask the Secretary of State for Employment what studies have been commissioned by Her Majesty's Government into the impact on employment over the next decade from information technology; and if he will make a statement. [25984]

**Miss Widdecombe:** Several studies have been commissioned into the future impact on employment of information technology:

The Government's technology foresight programme has examined a wide range of technology developments which will underpin improvements in the UK's wealth creating capacity. This has included the IT sector and developments of new IT-based businesses.

Several Government Departments co-funded the "Britain in 2010" study which included an assessment of the impact of new technology on jobs.

The Department of Trade and Industry has commissioned a feasibility study into the impact of telecommunications and computer applications on the international mobility of jobs.

A major study of teleworking, carried out for the Employment Department in 1992, highlighted the ways in which this new form of working can create employment opportunities.

A recent study for the Department of Trade and Industry highlighted the potential of telework for increasing the competitiveness of British industry.

Advances in IT play a key role in helping to increase productivity and enhance the competitiveness of British industry, contributing to employment growth and improving living standards. IT has facilitated the growth of new forms of working such as telework, which give more people the opportunity to participate in the labour force, help businesses to retain skilled workers and increase employment opportunities in remote areas.

### Allerton Outreach Team

**Mr. Madden:** To ask the Secretary of State for Employment what further funding he has authorised to support two staff and running costs of the Allerton outreach team in Bradford; and if he will make a statement. [25987]

**Miss Widdecombe:** The original Employment Service source of funding for the Allerton outreach team has been absorbed into the single regeneration budget and the Employment Department no longer has a direct involvement in funding this project, which is managed by Bradford council.

However, for 1995–96, the Bradford and district training and enterprise council has made available £10,000 towards the cost of an outreach worker. I understand that the balance of the cost is being met by Bradford council. The TEC has also arranged for up to £10,000 of guidance vouchers to be available for Allerton's residents. I do understand that a trainee under the training for work programme continues to provide a second team member. A full range of ED programmes are available to help unemployed people in Bradford including the residents of Allerton.

### Disabled People

**Mr. Alan Howarth:** To ask the Secretary of State for Employment what response he received from the National Advisory Council on Employment of People with Disabilities to his consultation on Government measures to tackle discrimination against disabled people with regard to *(a)* the remit of the new advisory body proposed in the consultation document, *(b)* additional functions which the new advisory body might undertake, over and above those proposed in the consultation document, *(c)* infrastructure and resources for the new advisory body and *(d)* exclusion of small firms from the new statutory requirements proposed in the consultation document; and if he will place in the Library a copy of the response of the National Advisory Council on Employment of People with Disabilities. [26084]

**Miss Widdecombe:** The Government have published a full analysis of the responses to the consultation exercise entitled "A Consultation on Government Measures to Tackle Discrimination Against Disabled People: An Analysis of the Responses", and a copy of this has been placed in the Library. Our general policy is not to publish particular responses to the consultation document.

The National Advisory Council on Employment of People with Disabilities advised my right hon. Friend the Secretary of State. The council's advice was sought on the employment and training implications of the consultation proposals. NACEPD's advice is provided direct to Ministers or to officials, and its views are subsequently made known publicly through periodic reports on its activities. Such a report is not due yet, so I have arranged for a copy of NACEPD's response to the consultation document to be placed in the Library.

### Public Bodies

**Mr. Flynn:** To ask the Secretary of State for Employment which non-departmental public bodies within the responsibility of his Department are subject to scrutiny by *(a)* the ombudsmen, *(b)* the National Audit Office, *(c)* the Audit Commission and *(d)* other monitoring officers; which are covered by citizens charters; in which performance indicators apply; and in which members are liable to surcharge.    [23969]

**Miss Widdecombe** *[holding answer 15 May 1995]:* I refer the hon. Member to the reply given to the hon. Member for Cannock and Burntwood (Dr. Wright) on 25 April 1995, *Official Report*, column *477*. In addition to the executive non-departmental public bodies listed in that reply, the Department sponsors the following NDPBs:

> The National Advisory Council on the Employment of People with Disabilities;
>
> Committees for the Employment of Disabled People, around 60 local committees;
>
> Supported Employment Consultative Group;
>
> Race Relations Advisory Group.

These advisory bodies are convened to advise the Department on the impact of Government employment policies on people with disabilities and ethnic minorities. They have no grant in aid are supported within the Department's running costs. None of them provides a service direct to the public. They are therefore all potentially subject to scrutiny by the National Audit Office but not by the Parliamentary Commissioner or the Audit Commission. None is covered by citizens charters or performance indicators. In none of the NDPBs for which the Department is responsible are the members liable to surcharge and none is subject to scrutiny by monitoring officers other than those referred to above and those carrying out normal audit functions.

### SCOTLAND

### Former Ministers

**Mr. McFall:** To ask the Secretary of State for Scotland what rules and regulations are laid down by his office regarding former Ministers taking up appointments with companies with which they have been involved while Ministers.    [23053]

**Mr. Lang:** No specific rules or regulations are laid down by my office. Existing guidance is contained in paragraph 105 of "Questions of Procedures for Ministers", a copy of which is available in the House of Commons Library.

### Departmental Property

**Mr. McMaster:** To ask the Secretary of State for Scotland what have been the total capital and recurring costs of improvements and replacements in relation to the fabric, decoration, carpeting and facilities of *(a)* Dover house, *(b)* Bute house and *(c)* Alhambra house in each year since 1979.    [24103]

**Mr. Lang:** The information available for each full financial year for which detailed records are held by the Scottish Office is as in the table. Works in previous years were carried out by the Property Services Agency and my Department does not hold information from which these buildings could be identified separately:

| Building | Year | Capital £ | Maintenance £ |
|---|---|---|---|
| Alhambra House | 1990–91 | 90,778.31 | 15,121.03 |
|  | 1991–92 | 76,349.69 | 15,638.30 |
|  | 1992–93 | 6,685.10 | 45,274.75 |
|  | 1993–94 | 13,616.11 | 6,279.37 |
|  | 1994–95 | 4,059.52 | 35,944.66 |
| Dover House | 1990–91 | 100,056.43 | 16,094.90 |
|  | 1991–92 | 107,643.96 | 12,400.31 |
|  | 1992–93 | 184,779.49 | 35,283.21 |
|  | 1993–94 | 64,555.14 | 17,971.33 |
|  | 1994–95 | 80,186.26 | 66,570.16 |
| Bute House | 1990–91 | 21,828.12 | 20,700.76 |
|  | 1991–92 | 19,347.71 | 24,802.82 |
|  | 1992–93 | 8,407.70 | 20,731.24 |
|  | 1993–94 | 14,153.23 | 17,946.15 |
|  | 1994–95 | 7,490.65 | 35,104.58 |

Dover house and Bute house are both grade A listed buildings. Alhambra house was vacated by the Scottish Office in November 1994.

### Giant Hogweed

**Mr. McMaster:** To ask the Secretary of State for Scotland what measures he plans to require the owners of land to which the public may have access to eradicate heracleum mantegazzianum; if he will give local authorities a duty to control heracleum mantegazzianum; and if he will make a statement about the dangers associated with this plant.    [24083]

**Sir Hector Monro:** There are no plans to bring forward legislation to impose new duties in relation to heracleum mantegazzianum on landowners or local authorities. Heracleum mantegazzianum contains large amounts of sap whose toxins can cause painful blistering, and humans coming into contact with the plant may require medical treatment.

### Health Boards

**Mr. Galbraith:** To ask the Secretary of State for Scotland if he has any plans to alter the boundaries of health boards; and if he will make a statement.    [24975]

**Lord James Douglas-Hamilton:** My noble and learned Friend the Minister of State is considering, in consultation with relevant interests, whether adjustments should be made in the small number of cases where the boundaries of the new local authorities intersect those of health boards.

### Retirements and Redundancies

**Ms Hodge:** To ask the Secretary of State for Scotland how many staff of *(a)* the Scottish Office and *(b)* agencies for which the Scottish Office is responsible (i) took early retirement, (ii) took voluntary redundancy, (iii) took compulsory redundancy and (iv) were retired on medical grounds in (1) 1993–94 and (2) 1994–95; and what are the projected figures for 1995–96.          [25503]

**Mr. Lang:** The information requested is set out in the table below. Staff numbers for the Scottish Prison Service are shown separately.

|  | *1993–94* | *1994–95* | *Projected 1995–96* |
| --- | --- | --- | --- |
| *(a) The Scottish Office* |  |  |  |
| (i) Early retirement | 35 | 30 | 25 |
| (ii) Voluntary redundancy | 47 | 144 | 100–200 |
| (iii) Compulsory redundancy | — | — | — |
| (iv) Medical grounds | 26 | 19 | 20 |
|  |  |  |  |
| *(b) Agencies* |  |  |  |
| (i) Early retirement | 3 | 4 | 2 |
| (ii) Voluntary redundancy | 3 | 12 | 6 |
| (iii) Compulsory redundancy | 1 | — | 1 |
| (iv) Medical grounds | 3 | 31 | 6 |
|  |  |  |  |
| *(c) Scottish Prison Agency* |  |  |  |
| (i) Early retirement | 50 | 160 | 150 |
| (ii) Voluntary redundancy | 3 | 3 | ¹— |
| (iii) Compulsory redundancy | — | — | — |
| (iv) Medical grounds | 80 | 60 | 60 |

¹ None expected.

**Ms Hodge:** To ask the Secretary of State for Scotland what is the annual cost to his Department of staff leaving under redundancy/early retirement schemes to incorporate (i) added years lump sum payments, (ii) redundancy payments, (iii) pension payments, including enhancements and (iv) any other special arrangements for *(a)* 1993–94, *(b)* 1994–95, *(c)* projected for 1995–96 and *(d)* projected for 1996–97.          [25470]

**Mr. Lang:** The costs to the Department of early retirement and redundancies are borne from the Department's running costs provision.

A detailed breakdown of the various costs could be obtained only at disproportionate cost.

The total costs borne on the Scottish Office running costs in 1993–94 and 1994–95 were £900,000 and £1.5 million respectively. For 1995–96 the amount is estimated at £1.6 million.

For the Scottish Prison Service the total costs borne in 1993–94 and 1994–95 were £900,000 in each year and for 1995–96 the amount is estimated at £800,000.

Projections for 1996–97 will be determined during the coming public expenditure survey.

### Consultants

**Ms Hodge:** To ask the Secretary of State for Scotland what is the level of expenditure on consultancy by *(a)* his Office and *(b)* agencies for which his Office is responsible for (i) 1993–94, (ii) 1994–95 and (iii) projected for 1995–96.          [25645]

**Mr. Lang:** The information requested is currently not held centrally and is therefore not available. Steps are, however, being taken to establish a central record of such information. I shall write to the hon. Member with the information requested as soon as it becomes available and place a signed copy of the letter in the Library of the House.

### Contracting Out

**Ms Hodge:** To ask the Secretary of State for Scotland for each piece of work subject to a bidding process under the auspices of *(a)* his Department and *(b)* agencies for which his Department is responsible (i) where work was contracted out, who were the successful bidders and (ii) where contracts were won by in-house bidders in (1) 1993–94, (2) 1994–95 and (3) 1995–96.          [25656]

**Mr. Lang:** The information requested is as set out:

*(a) The Scottish Office core*

| Activity | Successful bidder(s) |
| --- | --- |
| *(1) 1993–94* |  |
| Superannuation | Ministry of Defence |
| Animal House Services | Western General Hospital |
| Audit of NHS Boards | KPMG Peat Marwick; Coopers and Lybrand; Price Waterhouse |
| Scottish Fire Service Training School Catering | Gardner Merchant |
| Design, Print and Publication Services | HMSO |
| Education, Social Work and Transport Statistics | In-house teams |
| Recruitment | In-house teams |
| Drawing Office | In-house team |
| Telecommunications Depots | In-house team |
|  |  |
| *(2) 1994–95* |  |
| Additional typing services | Carol Jones Recruitment Ltd. |
| Data Preparation | Saztec and AlphaNumeric |
| Mainframe Applications Support | FI Group plc |
| Audit of second wave NHS trusts | KPMG Peat Marwick; Price Waterhouse; Ernst and Young |
| Audit of third wave NHS trusts | Ernst and Young; Scott Moncrieff; KPMG Peat Marwick; Price Waterhouse |
| Facilities management and messengerial services at Victoria Quay | Serco Services Ltd. |
| Security at Victoria Quay | In-house team |
|  |  |
| *(3) 1995–96* |  |
| Publications distribution and sales | HMSO |

*Agencies*

| Activity | Successful bidder(s) |
| --- | --- |
| *(1) 1993–94* |  |
| Scottish Prison Service—Building and Electrical Maintenance Work atHM Prison, Barlinnie | AMEC |
| Scottish Prison Service—Building and Electrical Maintenance Work at three establishments (Perth, Shottsand Edinburgh) | In-house team |
| Scottish Prison Service, Central Stores | In-house team |

*Agencies*

| Activity | Successful bidder(s) |
| --- | --- |
| *(2) 1994–95* | |
| Scottish Prison Service—Building and Electrical Maintenance Work at six establishments (Longriggend, Aberdeen, Peterhead, Corntonvale,Polmont, Glenochil) | In-house team |
| Security at the Scottish Agricultural Science Agency | Burns Security |
| Scottish Office Pensions Agency—Development, Supply and Maintenance of Pensions Administration Systems | McDonnel Information Systems |
| Prison-based Education, Scottish Prison Service | Motherwell College, Stoke College, James Watt College, Falkirk College, Aberdeen College, Angus College, Coatbridge College, Highland Regional Council |
| Historic Scotland, Patrolmen at Edinburgh Castle | Pinkerton Security Services |
| Historic Scotland—Gardening and Grounds maintenance work at Palace of Holyroodhouse and Holyrood Park | In-house team |
| Typing and clerical support at Registers of Scotland | In-house team |

No external contracts have yet been awarded during 1995–96 in respect of agencies for which my Department is responsible.

**Ms Hodge:** To ask the Secretary of State for Scotland what work has been contracted out *(a)* by his Department and *(b)* by agencies for which his Department is responsible in (i) 1993–94, (ii) 1994–95 and (iii) projected for 1995–96. [25659]

**Mr. Lang:** The information is as set out.

*(a) The Scottish Office*

*(i) 1993–94*

Superannuation
Animal House Services
Audit of NHS Boards
Scottish Fire Service Training School Catering
Design, Print and Publication Services

*(ii) 1994–95*

Additional typing services
Data Preparation
Mainframe Applications Support
Audit of 2nd wave NHS trusts
Audit of 3rd wave NHS trust
Facilities management and messengerial services at Victoria Quay

*(iii) 1995–96*

Publications distribution and sales

*(b) Agencies*

*(i) 1993–94*

Scottish Prison Service—Building and Electrical Maintenance and minor works at HMP Barlinnie.

*(ii) 1994–95*

Scottish Agricultural Science Agency—Security
Scottish Office Pensions Agency—Development, Supply and Maintenance of Pensions Administration Systems
Historic Scotland—Patrolmen at Edinburgh Castle
Scottish Prison Service—Prison-based education

*(iii) 1995–96*

Scottish Prison Service—Maintenance and minor works at Castle Huntly, Dumfries, Penninghame, Noranside, Friarton, Greenock, Inverness, Low Moss and Dungavel establishments.
Registers of Scotland—Pre-application reports.

## Departmental Performance

**Ms Hodge:** To ask the Secretary of State for Scotland what performance indicators and performance targets there are for measuring the performance of his Department in *(a)* answering letters from members of the public and *(b)* answering telephone calls from members of the public; how performance is monitored; and what are the latest figures for performance measured against the target set. [26232]

**Mr. Lang:** Where members of the public write to Ministers and the reply is made on their behalf by departmental officials, there is a target of 20 days for doing so. In 1994, 14,846 such replies were issued—76 per cent. within the target of 20 days.

Where members of the public write direct to departmental officials, the setting of targets for the issue of replies is a matter for individual divisions and units. There is no centrally laid down target and no central collection of performance figures by individual divisions and units.

The target for answering telephone calls to the Scottish Office central inquiry unit is an average of 10 seconds. Weekly performance is monitored electronically. During a recent 10-day period, 14,208 calls were handled. The average response time was 11 seconds.

## Complaints

**Ms Hodge:** To ask the Secretary of State for Scotland what policy and procedure exist for dealing with complaints against his Department by members of the public; when his Department last updated its policy; what time limit and target for dealing with such complaints his Department has; and what follow-up procedure exists where complainants are not satisfied with his Department's response to a complaint. [26216]

**Mr. Lang:** My Department provides a wide range of services to the public. A single department-wide complaints procedure would not be appropriate. Our complaints procedures are tailored to the particular circumstances of the service provided and the needs of the users. A comprehensive review of our complaints procedures was carried out in 1992. Time limits for dealing with complaints were introduced. They vary from service to service. Most of our complaints procedures provide for complainants to refer their complaint to a more senior level if they are dissatisfied. If the matter is not resolved to the complainant's satisfaction he or she can ask a Member of Parliament to refer the matter to the Parliamentary Commissioner for Administration.

## Belvidere Hospital

**Mr. David Marshall:** To ask the Secretary of State for Scotland if he will publish the names of all the bodies which have any responsibility for all or part of the services provided at Belvidere hospital, Parkhead, Glasgow; and to which organisation the hospital belongs. [26186]

**Lord James Douglas-Hamilton:** The Glasgow Royal Infirmary University NHS trust, The Southern General Hospital NHS trust and the West Glasgow Hospitals University NHS trust have responsibility for the services provided at Belvidere hospital.

Greater Glasgow health board is in discussion with the Glasgow Royal Infirmary University NHS trust over the transfer of the assets of the hospital to that trust.

### Glasgow City Council

**Mr. David Marshall:** To ask the Secretary of State for Scotland what is the electorate for each of the new unitary authority wards in the Glasgow city council area as at 6 April. [26187]

**Mr. Kynoch:** The electorate for each of the new unitary authority wards for the city of Glasgow council at the latest available date, 15 February 1995, are given in the table:

| Electoral ward | Total electorate |
| --- | --- |
| 1. Drumry | 5,997 |
| 2. Summerhill | 5,821 |
| 3. Blairdardie | 5,309 |
| 4. Knightswood Park | 6,502 |
| 5. Knightswood South | 5,556 |
| 6. Yoker | 6,048 |
| 7. Anniesland | 6,081 |
| 8. Jordanhill | 5,813 |
| 9. Kelvindale | 6,326 |
| 10. Scotstoun | 5,812 |
| 11. Victoria Park | 5,898 |
| 12. Broomhill | 6,348 |
| 13. Hyndland | 7,272 |
| 14. Hillhead | 6,197 |
| 15. Partick | 7,064 |
| 16. Kelvin | 7,242 |
| 17. Firhill | 5,916 |
| 18. Woodlands | 6,532 |
| 19. Kelvingrove | 5,699 |
| 20. Anderston | 5,232 |
| 21. Merchant City | 6,044 |
| 22. Milton | 5,680 |
| 23. Possil | 5,258 |
| 24. Keppochhill | 5,643 |
| 25. Summerston | 5,797 |
| 26. Maryhill | 5,493 |
| 27. Wyndford | 5,521 |
| 28. Robroyston | 4,989 |
| 29. Gartcraig | 6,211 |
| 30. Carntyne | 5,870 |
| 31. Royston | 6,299 |
| 32. Milnbank | 6,350 |
| 33. Dennistoun | 5,626 |
| 34. Springburn | 6,038 |
| 35. Cowlairs | 6,099 |
| 36. Wallacewell | 6,027 |
| 37. Calton | 4,780 |
| 38. Bridgeton | 5,610 |
| 39. Dalmarnock | 5,112 |
| 40. Queenslie | 5,367 |
| 41. Greenfield | 6,029 |
| 42. Barlanark | 5,851 |
| 43. Tollcross Park | 5,198 |
| 44. Braidfauld | 5,176 |
| 45. Shettleston | 6,132 |
| 46. Mount Vernon | 6,606 |
| 47. Garrowhill | 5,988 |
| 48. Baillieston | 6,494 |
| 49. Garthamlock | 4,694 |
| 50. Wellhouse | 5,579 |
| 51. Easterhouse | 5,466 |

| Electoral ward | Total electorate |
| --- | --- |
| 52 Drumoyne | 5,804 |
| 53. Govan | 5,121 |
| 54. Ibrox | 5,755 |
| 55. Kingston | 5,109 |
| 56. Pollokshields East | 5,784 |
| 57. Maxwell park | 5,506 |
| 58. Penilee | 6,034 |
| 59. Craigton | 6,972 |
| 60. Cardonald | 5,376 |
| 61. Pollok | 5,145 |
| 62. Mosspark | 6,693 |
| 63. Crookston | 5,563 |
| 64. South Pollok | 5,034 |
| 65. Arden | 4,217 |
| 66. Levernholm | 5,582 |
| 67. Carnwadric | 5,964 |
| 68. Newlands | 6,211 |
| 69. Cathcart | 5,957 |
| 70. Pollokshaws | 5,633 |
| 71. Strathbungo | 6,153 |
| 72. Langside | 5,355 |
| 73. Hutchesontown | 4,418 |
| 74. Oatlands | 5,807 |
| 75. Govanhill | 6,415 |
| 76. Battlefield | 6,832 |
| 77. Mount Florida | 5,274 |
| 78. Aitkenhead | 5,642 |
| 79. Carmunock | 5,007 |
| 80. Castlemilk | 5,393 |
| 81. Glenwood | 4,203 |
| 82. Toryglen | 4,689 |
| 83. King's Park | 3,650 |
| | 474,990 |

### NHS Numbers

**Mr. Cohen:** To ask the Secretary of State for Scotland if he will give an undertaking that the new NHS number will be used only with respect to the provision of health-related services; and if he will make a statement. [26399]

**Lord James Douglas-Hamilton:** There are no proposals to reissue the NHS number in Scotland where a community health index number has been in use for many years. We have no plans to use the community health index number for anything other than health-related purposes.

### Local Government Finance

**Mr. Donohoe:** To ask the Secretary of State for Scotland when his Department will issue the new Scottish unitary authorities with their indicative budgets for 1995–96. [25332]

**Mr. Kynoch** *[holding answer 23 May 1995]:* My right hon. Friend intends to lay a report before the House, in accordance with section 24 of the Local Government etc. (Scotland) Act 1994, in the autumn specifying the amounts which he will use as the baseline for considering capping action in 1996–97. However, in recognition of the shadow councils' need to have early knowledge of the amounts for the purpose of beginning to prepare budgets for 1996–97, my right hon. Friend hopes to be able to issue his proposed figures by about the end of June.

The Convention of Scottish Local Authorities is being fully consulted about the preparation of the figures and those existing local authorities which are being disaggregated have agreed to have discussions with relevant shadow councils about the appointment of their 1995–96 budgets to the new council areas.

## NHS Trusts

**Mr. Donohoe:** To ask the Secretary of State for Scotland what was the number of *(a)* applications for trust status which have been turned down by the Scottish Office, *(b)* applicants involved and *(c)* amounts of money spent by the national health service management executive in supporting these unsuccessful applicants for each year since 1991–92.                              [25329]

**Lord James Douglas-Hamilton** *[holding answer 23 May 1995]:* Four applications for trust status have been rejected. These were as follows:

Princess Margaret Rose Orthopaedic Hospital
Lothian College of Nursing and Midwifery
Forth Valley Healthcare
Western Isles Health Unit

The costs incurred by the NHS in supporting these applications amounted to:

1991–92: £50,000
1992–93: £69,730
1993–94: £195,000

The application made by Forth Valley Healthcare was subsequently re-submitted and accepted as a conjoint application with the Royal Scottish National Hospital and Community NHS trust to form Central Scotland Healthcare NHS trust.

**Mr. Donohoe:** To ask the Secretary of State for Scotland if he will list the correspondence addresses and the names of the executive and non-executive directors of the NHS trusts established in April.          [25345]

**Lord James Douglas-Hamilton** *[holding answer 23 May 1995]:* The executive and non-executive directors of the NHS trusts established in April are as follows:

*Argyll and Bute NHS Trust (Aros, Lochgilphead, Argyll PA31)*

| Non-executive directors | Executive directors |
| --- | --- |
| Mrs. Hester Gardiner | Chief Executive: |
| | Mr. Jonathan R. Best |
| Dr. J. Stewart Moffat | Medical Director: |
| | Dr. Angus MacKay |
| Mr. John Wilson | Nursing Director: |
| | Mr. Rob Brown |
| Miss Catherine Pollock | Finance Director: |
| | Mr. Graeme Oram |
| Mr. Ian Smyth | Human Resources Director: |
| | Mr. John McCormick |
| | Business and Operations Director: |
| | Mr. Steven Gallagher |

*Borders Community Health Services NHS Trust (Dingleton Hospital, Melrose, TD6 9HN)*

| Non-Executive Directors | Executive Directors |
| --- | --- |
| Dr. Daniel Jones | Chief Executive: |
| Mrs. Marie Mackie | Mr. John Turner |
| Dr. Andrew Simpson | Medical Director: |
| Mrs. Marni Lamb | Dr. Bruce Low |
| Mr. Angus Davidson | Nursing Director: |
| | Mr. Paul Martin |
| | Finance Director: |
| | Mr. Robert Kemp |
| | Human Resources Director: |
| | Miss Janet Kyle |
| | Mental Health Director: |

*Borders Community Health Services NHS Trust (Dingleton Hospital, Melrose, TD6 9HN)*

| Non-Executive Directors | Executive Directors |
| --- | --- |
| | Mr. Hector Christie |
| | Clinical Services Director: |
| | Mrs. Irene Morris |
| | Estate Director: |
| | Mr. Bill Wilkie |

*Borders General Hospital NHS Trust (Borders General Hospital, Melrose, Roxburghshire TD6 9BS)*

| Non-Executive Directors | Executive Directors |
| --- | --- |
| Mrs. Ann Bryce | Acting Chief Executive: |
| | Mr. Allistair Matheson |
| Professor Kenneth Fowler | Medical Director: |
| | Dr. Peter Buchan |
| Mr. George Finlay | Nursing Director: |
| | Vacant |
| Mrs. Elspeth Bruce | Finance Director: |
| | Mr. Allistair Matheson |
| Mr. Graham Watt | Human Resources Director: |
| | Mr. Simon Crouch |

*Dumfries and Galloway Community Services NHS Trust (Crichton Hall, Crichton Royal Hospital, Glencapple Road, Dumfries DG1 4TF)*

| Non-Executive Directors | Executive Directors |
| --- | --- |
| Dr. Robert Grieve | Chief Executive: |
| | Dr. Tom Shearer |
| Mr. Alexander Scott | Medical Director: |
| | Dr. John Waterhouse |
| Mr. Ronald Percy | Nursing Director: |
| | Mr. Richard Swift |
| Mr. William Alexander | Finance Director: |
| | Mr. Keith Stephenson |
| Mrs. Janette Richardson | Human Resources Director: |
| | Miss Dorothy Elsey |

*Glasgow Dental Hospital and School NHS Trust (378 Sauchiehall Street, Glasgow G2 3JZ)*

| Non-executive directors | Executive directors |
| --- | --- |
| Rev. Malcolm Cuthbertson | Chief Executive: |
| | Dr. Doreen Steele |
| Mrs. Elspeth Farmer | Dental Director: |
| | Vacant |
| Sir David Mason | Nursing Director: |
| | Ms Teresa Kemp |
| Mr. John Bannon | Finance Director: |
| | Mr. Colin Brown |
| Mrs. Joy Travers | Human Resources Director: |
| | Dr. Doreen Steele |
| | Research Director: |
| | Vacant |

*Lanarkshire Healthcare NHS Trust (Strathclyde Hospital, Airbles Road, Motherwell ML1 3BW)*

| Non-executive directors | Executive directors |
| --- | --- |
| Mrs. Peggy Murphy | Chief Executive: |
| | Mr. David Parr |
| Mrs. Winifred Sherry | Medical Director: |
| | Dr. Allan Sinclair |
| Ver Rev. Dr. Hugh Wyllie | Nursing Director: |
| | Mrs. Helen Scott |

*Lanarkshire Healthcare NHS Trust (Strathclyde Hospital, Airbles Road, Motherwell ML1 3BW)*

| Non-executive directors | Executive directors |
|---|---|
| Mrs. Mary Smith | Finance Director: Miss Elaine Ramage |
| Mr. Robert Thomson | Human Resources Director: Mr. Kenny Small |
| | Planning and Contracts Director: Mr. Kenny Small |
| | Director of Estates: Mr. Leslie Lambert |

*Lomond Healthcare NHS Trust (Vale of Leven District General Hospital, Alexandria, Dunbartonshire, G83 OUA)*

| Non-executive directors | Executive directors |
|---|---|
| Mrs. Eileen Gorie | Chief Executive: Mr. Stephen Hayes |
| Rev. Ian Miller | Medical Director: Mr. Eric W. Taylor |
| Mrs. Elizabeth McHard | Nursing Director: Vacant |
| Mr. Archibald Mackenzie | Finance Director: Mr. Ross Arbuckle |
| Mr. David Morrell | Human Resources Director: Mrs. Francine G. Ewen |

*Scottish Ambulance Service NHS Trust (National Headquarters, Tipperlinn Road, Edinburgh EH10 5UU)*

| Non-Executive Directors | Executive Directors |
|---|---|
| Mr. William Campbell | Chief Executive: Mr. Andrew Freemantle |
| Mr Greer Johnston | Medical Director: Mr. Andrew Marsden |
| Mr. Neil Menzies | Finance Director: Mr. Brian J. Roy |
| Dr. David Cormack | Human Resources Director: Mr. John Bateman |
| Miss Ann Foster | Logistics Director: Mr. Clive Wooller |

## Dental Services

**Mr. Donohoe:** To ask the Secretary of State for Scotland how many dental patients were registered at 31 March in each health board area in Scotland. [25350]

**Lord James Douglas-Hamilton** *[holding answer 23 May 1995]:* The number of patients registered with a dentist at 31 March in each health board area in Scotland is shown in the table.

*Dental patients registered at 31 March 1995—by Health Board area in Scotland*

| Health board | Patients registered |
|---|---|
| Scotland | 2,473,758 |
| Argyll and Clyde | 204,708 |
| Ayrshire and Arran | 192,382 |
| Borders | 55,105 |
| Dumfries and Galloway | 65,869 |
| Fife | 170,247 |
| Forth Valley | 132,150 |
| Grampian | 256,628 |
| Greater Glasgow | 458,436 |
| Highland | 82,613 |
| Lanarkshire | 241,947 |
| Lothian | 375,991 |
| Orkney | 4,766 |
| Shetland | 6,822 |
| Tayside | 217,007 |
| Western Isles | 9,087 |

## Non-domestic Rates

**Mr. Donohoe:** To ask the Secretary of State for Scotland how much the Scottish Office estimates will be raised through the imposition of non-domestic rates charges on empty properties during the financial year 1995–96. [25338]

**Mr. Kynoch** *[holding answer 23 May 1995]:* It is estiamted that the additional rates income due to changes in unoccupied property relief will be £23.5 million in 1995–96. This was taken fully into account in determining the level of the unified business rate for 1995–96, so there is no additional burden on business ratepayers in aggregate as a result of this measure.

## Official Visits

**Mr. Donohoe:** To ask the Secretary of State for Scotland how many official visits on ministerial business each Minister in his Department undertook during the last 12 months to each parliamentary constituency in Scotland. [25339]

**Mr. Lang** *[holding answer 23 May 1995]:* To list visits made to each Scottish constituency in the last 12 months would involve disproportionate costs. However, since 20 May 1994, Scottish Office Ministers have made a total of 313 visits to Scottish constituencies.

## Planning Applications

**Mr. Donohoe:** To ask the Secretary of State for Scotland what was *(a)* the number of planning application refusals considered by the Scottish Office and *(b)* the number of planning application refusals which were overturned by the Scottish Office for each year since 1979–80 and for each planning authority. [25342]

**Mr. Kynoch** *[holding answer 23 May 1995]:* This information is available only by calendar year. The answer to part *(a)* of the question is as set out. The answer to part *(b)* regarding the number of planning applications which were overturned by the Scottish Office for each year since 1979 is also set out, but it is not possible to break this down for each planning authority.

| Calendar year | Planning appeals decided | Planning appeals allowed |
|---|---|---|
| 1979 | 319 | 68 |
| 1980 | 320 | 75 |
| 1981 | 415 | 117 |
| 1982 | 409 | 136 |
| 1983 | 445 | 144 |
| 1984 | 396 | 149 |
| 1985 | 508 | 166 |
| 1986 | 542 | 193 |
| 1987 | 589 | 223 |
| 1988 | 636 | 233 |
| 1989 | 702 | 247 |
| 1990 | 960 | 348 |
| 1991 | 923 | 313 |
| 1992 | 886 | 294 |
| 1993 | 765 | 267 |
| 1994 | 643 | 177 |

## Residential Homes

**Mr. Foulkes:** To ask the Secretary of State for Scotland what was the total income in 1993–94 of each local authority and in total from placements of old people in *(a)* registered and *(b)* unregistered independent residential care and nursing homes, inside and outside the local authority area and from placements in local authority homes for older people; and if he will break down by income from (i) government grants, inside aggregate external finance and outside aggregate external finance, (ii) sales, (iii) fees and charges, (iv) other income and (v) joint arrangements. [25394]

**Lord James Douglas-Hamilton** *[holding answer 23 May 1995]:* The available information is shown in the following table:

*Local Authority Income relating to fully staffed residential homes for older people: 1993–94 (Provisional)*

£ *thousands*

| Income source | Borders | Central | Dumfries and Galloway | Fife | Grampian | Highland |
|---|---|---|---|---|---|---|
| (i) Government grants | — | — | — | — | — | — |
| (ii) Sales | — | — | — | 59 | — | 42 |
| (iii) Rents, fees and charges | 1,522 | 1,701 | 1,013 | 1,453 | 3,525 | 1,337 |
| (iv) Other accounts and authorities[1] | — | 257 | 5 | — | — | 6 |
| (v) Other incomes | — | — | — | 6 | 280 | — |
| Total income | 1,522 | 1,958 | 1,018 | 1,518 | 3,805 | 1,385 |

*Notes:*
[1] Includes income for other accounts in the same local authority and from other local authorities.
*Source:*
Local financial returns made by local authorities to Scottish Office.

£ *thousands*

| Income source | Lothian | Strathclyde | Tayside | Orkney | Shetland | W Isles | Scotland |
|---|---|---|---|---|---|---|---|
| (i) Government grants | — | — | — | — | — | 45 | 45 |
| (ii) Sales | 20 | 47 | — | — | 76 | — | 244 |
| (iii) Rents, fees and charges | 4,482 | 10,230 | 2,689 | 242 | 296 | 399 | 28,889 |
| (iv) Other accounts and authorities[1] | 2 | 173 | — | — | — | — | 443 |
| (v) Other income | — | 1 | 10 | 5 | 4 | — | 306 |
| Total income | 4,504 | 10,451 | 2,699 | 247 | 376 | 444 | 29,927 |

*Note:*
[1] Includes income for other accounts in the same local authority and from other local authorities.
*Source:*
Local financial returns made by local authorities to Scottish Office.

### Nursing Homes

**Mr. Hood:** To ask the Secretary of State for Scotland what assessment he has made of the adequacy of the procedures that operate in the Lanarkshire health board area for inspecting nursing homes; and if he will make a statement. [25484]

**Lord James Douglas-Hamilton** *[holding answer 22 May 1995]:* The Nursing Homes Registration (Scotland) Act 1938, as amended, places the responsibility for the registration and inspection of nursing homes on the local health board. The Scottish Office Home and Health Department has issued model guidelines for the registration and inspection of nursing homes for elderly people, for people with dementia, for people with a learning disability and for homes providing acute services. All health boards are expected to follow this national guidance.

**Mr. Hood:** To ask the Secretary of State for Scotland if he will visit Orchard house nursing home to assess the quality of care provided for the elderly residents at that home. [25486]

**Lord James Douglas-Hamilton** *[holding answer 22 May 1995]:* My right hon. Friend understands that an inquiry by Lanarkshire health board into the standards of care at Orchard house nursing home has been under way for some months, and is expected to report to the board in early June.

### Lanarkshire Health Board

**Mr. Hood:** To ask the Secretary of State for Scotland if he will give details as to the length of service, salary and qualifications of the Lanarkshire health board's senior nursing officer. [25483]

**Lord James Douglas-Hamilton** *[holding answer 22 May 1995]:* Such information is not held centrally. The hon. Member may therefore wish to pursue his query with Lanarkshire health board.

### Forestry Commission

**Mr. Tipping:** To ask the Secretary of State for Scotland if he will list by English county and Scottish region Forestry Commission woodland currently offered for sale, under offer or proposed for sale within the next six months; and if he will state for each piece of woodland its size and the steps which have been taken to ensure that public access on foot is permitted after any sale takes place. [24619]

**Sir Hector Monro** *[holding answer 18 May 1995]:* The information is as follows:

| County/Region | Name of property | Area (hectares) | Continued public access |
|---|---|---|---|
| WOODLAND CURRENTLY FOR SALE ON THE OPEN MARKET | | | |
| *England* | | | |
| Cambridgeshire | Langley High Wood | 49 | d |
| Cornwall | Hay Wood | 54 | d |

| County/Region | Name of property | Area (hectares) | Continued public access |
|---|---|---|---|
| | Port Elliot, Pathada, Perdredda | 95 | d |
| | Treworgey Wood | 17 | d |
| Cumbria | Black Knors | 25 | b |
| Derbyshire | Moorhall Wood | 8 | d |
| Devon | Bedpark | 8 | d |
| | Hawkmoor | 22 | b |
| Durham | Campville | 30 | b |
| | Stanley Wood Cottages | 31 | c |
| Essex | Audley End Estate | 57 | d |
| Humberside | Greenwickdale Wood | 37 | d |
| Leicestershire | Bolt Wood | 21 | d |
| Lincolnshire | Hurn Wood | 9 | d |
| Shropshire | Coed Detton | 14 | b |
| Somerset | Higher Bitcombe | 30 | d |
| South Yorkshire | Greensprings Wood | 12 | a |
| | Old Park Wood | 41 | c |
| | Owston and Duck Holt Woods | 66 | d |

*Scotland*

| County/Region | Name of property | Area (hectares) | Continued public access |
|---|---|---|---|
| Borders | Edgarhope | 143 | d |
| | Spottiswoode | 191 | b |
| Dumfries and Galloway | Glaik | 62 | b |
| Grampian | Aquharney | 128 | a |
| | Auchinroath | 62 | b |
| | Glenbuchat | 539 | d |
| | Greenness | 115 | d |
| | Longhill (part) | 120 | b |
| | New Pitsligo | 42 | e |
| Highland | Abriachan | 865 | b |
| | Achrugan | 559 | a |
| | Ardelve | 26 | b |
| | Cuidrach | 58 | b |
| | Duisky | 89 | d |
| | Garvan, North | 112 | d |
| | Garvan, South | 183 | d |
| | Loch Ashie | 437 | d |
| | Lundavra | 148 | a |
| | New Kelso | 43 | d |
| | Tote | 421 | b |
| | Uig | 40 | b |
| Strathclyde | Daljarrock | 51 | b |
| | Docherneil | 83 | b |
| | Glenmard | 56 | b |
| Tayside | Camusericht | 295 | d |
| | Upper Glenprosen | 230 | d |

WOODLANDS CURRENTLY UNDER OFFER
*England*

| County/Region | Name of property | Area (hectares) | Continued public access |
|---|---|---|---|
| Berkshire | Lot Wood (part) | 6 | d |
| Cambridgeshire | West Wood | 30 | d |
| Cornwall | Branchecombe | 2 | d |
| | Coldgear | 4 | d |
| | Cutmere and Bara | 4 | d |
| | Moor/Scullop | 3 | d |
| Cumbria | Foulshaw Big Belt | 13 | b |
| | Warriners Wood | 4 | b |
| Isle of Wight | Timber Copse | 8 | a |
| Kent | Post Wood | 26 | a |
| Lancashire | Long Ellers Wood | 2 | d |
| Lincolnshire | Halstead Wood | 26 | d |
| Somerset | Frys Wood | 25 | e |
| South Yorkshire | Walkers Wood | 6 | b |
| Suffolk | Wrights Wood | 5 | d |

*Scotland*

| County/Region | Name of property | Area (hectares) | Continued public access |
|---|---|---|---|
| Borders | Fruid, land at | 62 | b |
| | Gala Blocks | 153 | a |
| Central | Stronvar | 2 | b |
| Fife | Kirkton Barns | 26 | d |
| Grampian | Lenabo | 332 | a |
| | Moreseat of Hatton | 38 | d |
| | Oldtown Belt | 3 | c |
| | White Cow Wood | 448 | a |
| | Wood of Wrae | 50 | a |
| Highland | Clava and Craggie | 34 | d |
| | Craskie Woods | 49 | b |
| | Eilean Darach and Dundonnel | 110 | b |
| | Faichem Wood | 7 | b |

| County/Region | Name of property | Area (hectares) | Continued public access |
|---|---|---|---|
| | Garbole Forest | 699 | b |
| | Glencannich Wood | 70 | b |
| | Lochlait Wood | 90 | a |
| | Muchrachd Wood | 29 | b |
| | Rebeg | 77 | b |
| Strathclyde | Kirnan Wood | 222 | d |
| Tayside | Claysykes | 17 | b |

a. Access agreement has been concluded.
b. Local authority declined to enter an access agreement.
c. Local authority is considering whether to enter an access agreement.
d. A third party with an interest has declined to enter an access agreement or restrictions in the Commission's title prevented the offer of an access agreement.
e. Sale commenced before the introduction of the arrangements for access agreements.

Advance notification of areas being considered for sale is given in the "Estates Gazette" in respect of all woodlands of more than five hectares, together with any other land having a known conservation, recreation or amenity interest. Copies of the "Estates Gazette" are held in the Library of the House.

## Entrepreneurship

**Mr. Stewart:** To ask the Secretary of State for Scotland if he will make a statement on his policy for the encouragement of entrepreneurship in Scotland; and what assessment he has made of the effectiveness of this policy. [22651]

**Mr. Lang** *[holding answer 9 May 1995]:* Entrepreneurship is essential to the continued competitiveness of the Scottish economy. The Government have in place a range of initiatives aimed at encouraging young people to consider a career in business, supporting such careers with an appropriate training infrastructure and providing assistance and advice on the creation and development of small businesses. Specific initiatives include the recent publication of a new framework for action for the development of improved education/industry links; the business birth rate strategy operated by Scottish Enterprise, which is aimed at increasing the number of business start-ups in Scotland; and the promotion by Scottish Enterprise of 1995 as "The Year of the Entrepreneur"—a concept which acts as a framework for a series of events and presentations aimed specifically at encouraging entrepreneurship. More generally, all local enterprise companies are pursuing policies aimed at promoting business activity and entrepreneurship throughout Scotland. The effectiveness of this policy is evidenced by the continuing success of the Scottish economy, both domestically and in terms of its export performance.

## ATTORNEY-GENERAL

### Roger Levitt

**Mr. John Marshall:** To ask the Attorney-General (1) what discussions he has had about the Roger Levitt case since 21 May; [26281]

(2) when plea bargaining began in the case of Roger Levitt. [26246]

**The Attorney-General:** Since 21 May, I have discussed the case with officials simply for the purpose of preparing answers to parliamentary questions. I refer my hon. Friend to my earlier written answers on the 9 December 1993, and 17 December 1993 at columns *332–33* and *1045–46* respectively, which explained the events that led up to Mr. Levitt's plea.

### Butte Mining

**Mr. Morgan:** To ask the Attorney-General what consultations he has had with the director of the Serious Fraud Office concerning the investigation into the company affairs of Butte Mining.    [26592]

**The Attorney-General:** I frequently meet the director of the Serious Fraud Office for discussions about matters of departmental interest, including casework. It is my policy not to divulge the subject matter of such meetings or operational details of current investigations.

### "Tomorrow's Job" Investigation

**Mr. Madden:** To ask the Attorney-General how many reports have been referred by the Metropolitan police to the Crown Prosecution Service from the "Tomorrow's Job" investigation; how many have been referred to him by the Crown Prosecution Service; and what action he has taken.    [25986]

**The Attorney-General:** The police have forwarded one interim report to the Crown Prosecution Service which specifically arises out of their inquiries concerning "Tomorrow's Job". The Crown Prosecution Service is considering this report and will submit it to me if it concludes that proceedings may be justified against any person for an offence requiring my consent.

### Crown Prosecution Service Report

**Mr. Madden:** To ask Mr. Attorney General on what date the Crown Prosecution Service referred to him a report, concerning a printer, received by the Crown Prosecution Service last August from the Metropolitan police; and what action he is taking in this matter.    [25988]

**The Attorney-General:** Papers relating to the case to which the hon. Member refers were submitted to me by the Crown Prosecution Service on 13 April 1995. I requested and am awaiting a more detailed analysis of the relevant material.

### "Red Watch"

**Mr. Madden:** To ask Mr. Attorney General when the Crown Prosecution Service received from the Metropolitan Police the third issue of "Red Watch"; and what action has been taken by the Crown Prosecution Service.    [25989]

**The Attorney-General:** The publication "Red Watch" is a part of the "Combat 18" magazine issue No. 3. The Metropolitan police supplied the Crown Prosecution Service with a copy of that magazine on 20 January 1995, for information only. A police report and the evidence gathered in the investigation into the publication of "Combat 18" magazine issue No. 3 has been delivered to the Crown Prosecution Service on 6 April 1995 and a prosecution is under consideration.

### Disciplinary Proceedings

**Mr. Straw:** To ask the Attorney-General how many solicitors employed by the Crown Prosecution Service since 1987 have been the subject of disciplinary proceedings by the Law Society *(a)* before their employment with the Crown Prosecution Service commenced and *(b)* during their employment with the Crown Prosecution Service.    [25994]

**The Attorney-General:** The information sought by the hon. Member could be definitively obtained only by a trawl of the personal files relating to all solicitors currently employed, as well as those previously employed. That exercise would involve disproportionate costs.

A review by the Department, with the assistance of the Law Society had identified *(a)* three solicitors who were the subject of disciplinary proceedings before their employment commenced with the Crown Prosecution Service, whom one remains in the employment of the Crown Prosecution Service, with the agreement of the Law Society. The other two ceased to be employed in 1989. The answer to *(b)* is that two solicitors have been the subject of disciplinary proceedings during their employment with the Crown Prosecution Service, but neither has had their practising certificate withdrawn. Both are still employed by the Crown Prosecution Service.

## OVERSEAS DEVELOPMENT ADMINISTRATION

### Global Environment Facility

**Mr. Dafis:** To ask the Secretary of State for Foreign and Commonwealth Affairs who is Her Majesty's Government's representative on the council of the global environment facility; and what arrangements have been made for his or her accountability to Parliament.    [24724]

**Mr. Baldry:** The executive director for the United Kingdom's constituency in the council of the Global Environment Facility is Mr. David Turner, head of environment policy department in the Overseas Development Administration. The Government are accountable to Parliament for expenditures under the global environmental assistance programme through the Minister for Overseas Development.

### Countdown 2000

**Sir David Steel:** To ask the Secretary of State for Foreign and Commonwealth Affairs what plans the Overseas Development Administration has to assist the Leprosy Mission for the Countdown 2000 campaign.    [25876]

**Mr. Baldry:** The Overseas Development Administration is not directly involved in the Countdown 2000 campaign, but has supported the Leprosy Mission's work in developing countries for some years and will continue to do so. Current funding involves programmes in Bangladesh, Indonesia and Chad.

### Family Planning

**Mr. Alton:** To ask the Secretary of State for Foreign and Commonwealth Affairs if he will list the amounts spent by the Overseas Development Administration in the overall sum spent on family planning on *(a)* advertising and information, *(b)* abortion and abortifacients, *(c)* barrier methods of contraception, *(d)* chemical methods of contraception and *(e)* sterilisation. [25310]

**Mr. Baldry** *[holding answer 22 May 1995]:* The table lists the relevant bilateral commitments in 1994:

| | £ million |
|---|---|
| Family planning component | 1994 Commitment |
| Abortion and abortifacients | nil |
| Barrier methods (condoms) | 3.339 |
| Chemical (hormonal) methods | 7.12 |

*Notes·*
1. Support for voluntary surgical contraception, as one of a variety of methods of contraception available, has been an element of commitments for projects in previous years. There were no such commitments in 1994.
2. All the projects in question provide information about family planning and the range of contraceptive methods available. Such information is provided as part of an overall service to clients and is not separately costed.

**Mr. David Alton:** To ask the Secretary of State for Foreign and Commonwealth Affairs what records his Department keeps of instances or reports of coercive family planning overseas. [25304]

**Mr. Baldry** *[holding answer 22 May 1995]:* I refer the hon. Member to the reply I gave him on 23 May at column *514.*

# NORTHERN IRELAND

## Waste Disposal

11. **Mr. William O'Brien:** To ask the Secretary of State for Northern Ireland if he will make a statement on the future provision for waste disposal in Northern Ireland. [24631]

**Sir John Wheeler:** Arrangements for the disposal of waste will be determined by district councils, taking into account the specific needs of their areas, the costs to the community and the requirement for proper environmental safeguards.

## Bodies (Information)

12. **Mr. Barnes:** To ask the Secretary of State for Northern Ireland if he raised with the Sinn Fein delegation in his bilateral talks the question of the fate of those killed by the Provisional IRA who are still unburied; and if he will make a statement. [24632]

**Mr. Acnram:** Yes. During yesterday's meeting in exploratory dialogue with Sinn Fein I raised this important issue and called upon it to use its influence to ensure that the families of the bereaved were given such information as the IRA had about their fate and the whereabouts of their bodies.

## Peace Process

13. **Mr. McFall:** To ask the Secretary of State for Northern Ireland what progress has been made by the Secretary of State in his discussions with the Dublin Government on the peace process. [24633]

**Mr. Ancram:** My right hon. and learned Friend last met the Tanaiste at the intergovernmental conference in Dublin on 28 April; the Prime Minister and the Taoiseach met in the margins of the VE ceremonies in Moscow. On both occasions, the progress of the peace process and the right ways of advancing it were discussed.

17. **Mr. Hunter:** To ask the Secretary of State for Northern Ireland if he will make a further statement on the progress of the exploratory dialogue and substantive talks which he is conducting with political parties in Northern Ireland. [24637]

**Mr. Ancram:** Exploratory dialogue with the loyalists and Sinn Fein continue on the basis set out in the reply I gave the hon. Members for Walsall, North (Mr. Winnick) for Pendle (Mr. Prentice) and for Falkirk, West (Mr. Canavan) earlier today.

As for substantive talks, my right hon. and learned Friend has invited the four main parties to discuss with him bilaterally the issues on which there would need to be agreement if there is to be a comprehensive settlement. So far, a meeting has been held with the Ulster Unionist party, and meetings with the alliance and SDLP are currently being arranged. The DUP has regrettably not responded formally to my right hon. and learned Friend's invitation—at least not at this stage.

19. **Mr. Hain:** To ask the Secretary of State for Northern Ireland if he will make a statement about latest progress in the peace negotiations. [24639]

**Mr. Ancram:** I refer the hon. Member to the answer I gave the hon. Members for Walsall, North, (Mr. Winnick) for Pendle (Mr. Prentice) and for Falkirk, West (Mr. Canavan) earlier today.

## Irish Medium Schools

15. **Mr. Flynn:** To ask the Secretary of State for Northern Ireland what new proposals he has to improve the work of Irish medium schools. [24635]

**Mr. Ancram:** Improvements in the work of Irish medium schools are primarily a matter for their boards of governors. All grant-aided Irish medium schools can avail themselves of the extensive curriculum advisory and support services provided by the education and library boards.

## Northern Ireland-Scotland Co-operation

16. **Mr. John D. Taylor:** To ask the Secretary of State for Northern Ireland when he last met the Secretary of State for Scotland to promote trade, tourism and greater co-operation between Northern Ireland and Scotland. [24636]

**Sir John Wheeler:** My right hon. and learned Friend meets the Secretary of State for Scotland frequently to discuss matters of common interest.

## Private Lee Clegg

18. **Sir Michael Neubert:** To ask the Secretary of State for Northern Ireland what representations he has received

about the case of Private Clegg in the last three months; and what response he has made to them. [24638]

**Sir John Wheeler:** Private Clegg's case has generated very great interest, including a number of petitions and over 4,000 individual letters from the public. Approximately half the correspondents have been sent replies.

### Royal Ulster Constabulary

20. **Mr. Corbyn:** To ask the Secretary of State for Northern Ireland what plans he has to restructure the Royal Ulster Constabulary. [24640]

**Sir John Wheeler:** None at present. The Government published proposals for reform of the tripartite structure in 1994. The Police Authority and the RUC are currently conducting public consultations on policing services. The RUC is engaged in a detailed consultation process, both within the force and externally, which will identify future policing strategy. Any change to the structure of the RUC will be based on careful professional evaluation of policing needs, and take into account the consultation processes.

### Terrorist Disarmament

21. **Mr. Cyril D. Townsend:** To ask the Secretary of State for Northern Ireland what progress is being made over the handing over and destruction of terrorist arms and explosives in Northern Ireland. [24641]

**Sir John Wheeler:** I refer my hon. Friend to the answer I gave earlier today to my hon. Friend the Member for Macclesfield (Mr. Winterton).

### Abortion

22. **Mrs. Ann Winterton:** To ask the Secretary of State for Northern Ireland how many right hon. and hon. Members representing Northern Ireland constituencies have made representatives *(a)* supporting and *(b)* opposing extension to the Province of the Abortion Act 1967. [24642]

**Mr. Ancram:** In the last three years, no Northern Ireland Member has made representations supporting the extension of the Abortion Act 1967 to Northern Ireland. Seven Northern Ireland Members have made representations to Ministers expressing their opposition to the extension of the Act.

### Police (Seat Belts)

23. **Mr. Peter Bottomley:** To ask the Secretary of State for Northern Ireland if police officers will now wear seat belts in cars. [24643]

**Sir John Wheeler:** The Royal Ulster Constabulary will keep its policy on the wearing of seat belts under review, but it must continue to be a matter of judgment as to whether or not a police officer wears a seat belt according to the prevailing circumstances and assessment of the security risk.

### Benefit Applications

24. **Mr. Clifford Forsythe:** To ask the Secretary of State for Northern Ireland what steps are taken to apply the parity of treatment arrangement between Northern

Ireland and Great Britain to ensure equality of treatment between identical social security benefit applicants residing in Northern Ireland and Great Britain. [24644]

**Mr. Ancram:** Although social security benefits are available in Northern Ireland on the same basis as they are in Great Britain, Northern Ireland has its own social security legislation and the independent adjudication authorities are obliged to apply this in deciding on applications for benefit having regard to the particular circumstances of the applicant only. The statutory appeal procedures can be invoked if the applicant is dissatisfied with the decision in their case.

### Inward Investment

25. **Mr. Spring:** To ask the Secretary of State for Northern Ireland what effort are being made to attract inward investment into the Province. [24645]

**Mr. Ancram:** The Industrial Development Board for Northern Ireland acting through the Department of Economic Development has overall responsibility for attracting inward investment to Northern Ireland. It has representative offices in Great Britain, Germany, the United States and Asia. In light of a more positive business climate in Northern Ireland, the IDB plans substantially to increase its overseas representation. Already, an office has been opened in Atlanta, Georgia and a person has been appointed in Singapore to research and to identify foreign investment potential.

26. **Mr. Simon Coombs:** To ask the Secretary of State for Northern Ireland if he will make a statement on the level of inward investment in Northern Ireland since the ceasefires. [24646]

**Mr. Ancram:** Investment inquiries have risen dramatically since the ceasefires to 743 in the six months ended 31 March compared to 189 in the corresponding period last year. First-time visits also rose from 146 in 1993–94 to 163 in 1994–95. However, because of the long lead time on decisions by companies about their internationally mobile investments, it will be some time before the practical benefits of the ceasefires are seen in terms of much needed additional jobs on the ground.

### Industrial Disputes

27. **Mr. John Marshall:** To ask the Secretary of State for Northern Ireland if he will make a statement about the number of days lost in industrial disputes in Northern Ireland. [24647]

**Sir John Wheeler:** In Northern Ireland the number of days lost due to industrial disputes has fallen significantly in recent years. It fell to a record low of nine days per 1,000 employees in 1994 from an average of 76 days over the previous 10-year period.

### Irish Constitution

28. **Dr. Godman:** To ask the Secretary of State for Northern Ireland when he last met the Taoiseach to discuss articles of the Irish constitution. [24648]

**Mr. Ancram:** My right hon. and learned Friend last met the Taoiseach at a memorial ceremony at Islandbridge on 28 April. The purpose of the ceremony was to pay tribute to those Irish people who fought and died in the British forces in the last war.

The Irish constitution and any possible changes to it are a matter for the Irish Government, Parliament and people. "A New Framework for Agreement" sets out the Irish Government's commitment to remove any jurisdictional or territorial claim of legal right over the territory of Northern Ireland contrary to the will of its people.

**Mr. Peter Robinson:** To ask the Secretary of State for Northern Ireland if he will seek to persuade the Government of Ireland to declare that they have no selfish, political economic or strategic interest in Northern Ireland.     [25954]

**Mr. Ancram:** The Irish Government have made it clear that, as part of a wider agreement, they will introduce and support changes in the Irish constitution. The Taoiseach has said that those changes would remove any jurisdictional or territorial claim of legal right over the territory of Northern Ireland contrary to the will of its people.

### Energy Costs

**Mr. Foulkes:** To ask the Secretary of State for Northern Ireland when he next expects to meet the Northern Ireland Chamber of Commerce to discuss energy costs in the Province.     [24649]

**Sir John Wheeler:** There are no plans for such a meeting.

### Police Complaints

**Mr. Butler:** To ask the Secretary of State for Northern Ireland when he will lay before Parliament copies of the annual report of the Independent Commission for Police Complaints for Northern Ireland; and if he will make a statement.

**Mr. Patrick Mayhew:** The commission's report for 1994, which is the seventh annual report to be produced by the commission since its establishment in 1988, was laid before Parliament on 26 April. The report sets out the purpose and values of the commission. It provides details of the commission's work during the year in supervising the investigation of complaints against the police and of its role in disciplinary proceedings.

The report shows clearly the valuable work which is carried out by the commission in ensuring that complaints against the police are dealt with independently and in effective manner.

I am grateful to the chairman and members of the commission for the important work they do to sustain and increase public confidence in the police complaints system.

### Tape-recorded Interviews

**Mr. Mullin:** To ask the Secretary of State for Northern Ireland when he last discussed the tape recording of interviews with suspects with the Chief Constable of the RUC; and what plans he has to bring practice in Northern Ireland into line with that elsewhere in the UK.     [24634]

**Sir John Wheeler:** My right hon. and learned Friend and I have regular meetings with the Chief Constable.

Tape recording of interviews under the Police and Criminal Evidence (Northern Ireland) Order 1989 follows guidelines similar to the English PACE codes. I intend to replace these guidelines in a revised set of codes for Northern Ireland in early 1996.

### Housing Executive

**Mr. McGrady:** To ask the Secretary of State for Northern Ireland if he will list the existing Housing Executive developments which have been transferred for management purposes to housing associations.     [25923]

**Mr. Ancram:** A number of housing executive properties in the streets listed have been transferred to housing associations for management purposes:

*South Region (Portadown)*
Corcain park
Millington park
Moeran park

*North-east Region (Coleraine)*
Glenvarra drive

**Mr. McGrady:** To ask the Secretary of State for Northern Ireland if he will list the Housing Executive new build schemes which will be transferred to housing associations for implementation and management.     [25924]

**Mr. Ancram:** The new build schemes, which it has been agreed will transfer from the Housing Executive to housing associations for implementation and management, are as follows:

Maphoner road, Mullaghbawn, phase 2, Co Armagh
Ballygowan road, phase 2, Banbridge, Co Down
Bowtown road, phase 5, Newtownards, Co Down
Camphill, Newtownbutler, phase 6, Co Fermanagh
Ballyekelly, phase 1, Co Londonderry
Burnside road, Coleraine, Co Londonderry
2–20 Charleville street, Belfast

### Market Testing

**Mr. Spellar:** To ask the Secretary of State for Northern Ireland what considerations underlay the requirements on health authorities to submit quarterly reports on competitive tendering; and what consideration was given to adopting the English model of an annual report.     [25239]

**Mr. Ancram:** The White Paper "Competing for Quality" requires all UK health Departments to monitor and report annually on progress by their agent bodies in market testing. The Department of Health and Social Services has therefore adopted this process. In addition, the Department has asked for the co-operation of boards and trusts in providing interim quarterly updates of the same information as is contained in the annual returns, to assist in responses to inquiries and to meet the reporting requirements of the efficiency unit.

**Mr. Spellar:** To ask the Secretary of State for Northern Ireland what instructions his Department has issued to health boards and health trusts regarding competitive tendering.     [25236]

**Mr. Ancram:** Health and social services boards and trusts have been advised that they must implement Government policy set out in the White Paper "Competing for Quality". In addition, and in keeping with the NHS in Great Britain, there is a management requirement to market test the specific services of domestic, laundry and catering.

### RUC Drug Squad

**Mr. John D. Taylor:** To ask the Secretary of State for Northern Ireland what was the average number of officers of the Royal Ulster Constabulary in the drug squad in each of the past 10 years; and if he will make a statement about the presence of illegal drugs in Northern Ireland.

[24957]

**Sir John Wheeler:** Every operational RUC officer is aware of the drugs issue and is a resource in combating drugs offences within Northern Ireland. At sub-divisional level, there are some 70 officers operating within 30 drugs liaison units whose sole responsibility is to address the problems of drug offences at a local level.

The headquarters drugs squad itself over the past 10 years has had on average 36 officers, arising from 34 in 1985 to a present strength of 44 officers, including the recent upgrading to Detective Superintendent of the post of head of drugs squad.

Northern Ireland, like other parts of the UK and Europe, does have an identifiable problem in the availability of illegal drugs, although it does not yet suffer the widespread abuse of drugs found elsewhere. One indicator of the availability of illegal drugs is the rate of seizures by the RUC; the Chief Constable's report for 1994 gives full details of drug seizures by the RUC and other agencies, which show a clear upward trend.

The Government, together with the RUC and other agencies, both statutory and voluntary, are committed to a robust multi-agency approach to tackle effectively all aspects of the drugs problem in Northern Ireland.

### Sheep Subsidy

**Mr. John D. Taylor:** To ask the Secretary of State for Northern Ireland how many farmers receive the subsidy of £39.80 per head for sheep which are neither kept for breeding lambs nor for having their wool shorn; and if he will make a statement on the practice of keeping non-productive sheep for the purpose of collecting the sheep subsidy. [24958]

**Mr. Ancram:** To be eligible for sheep annual premium, animals need only be females at least 12 months of age or have given birth to a lamb. Northern Ireland statistics on this scheme do not identify the purposes for which eligible animals are kept.

### Retirements and Redundancies

**Ms Hodge:** To ask the Secretary of State for Northern Ireland what is the annual cost of his Department of staff leaving under redundancy/early retirement schemes to incorporate (i) added years lump sum payments, (ii) redundancy payments, (iii) pension payments, including enhancements and (iv) any other special arrangements for (a) 1993–94, (b) 1994–95, (c) projected for 1995–96 and (d) projected for 1996–97. [25469]

**Sir John Wheeler:** For staff leaving the Northern Ireland Office and other Northern Ireland Departments these costs are accounted for as non-departmental running costs, exempt, until 31 March 1994. From 1 April 1994, these costs are accounted for as departmental running costs as in the home civil service.

A detailed breakdown of the various costs could be obtained only at disproportionate cost.

The total costs in respect of officers leaving the Northern Ireland Office and the other Northern Ireland Departments in 1993–94 and 1994–95 were £10,900,000 and £7,082,000 respectively.

The planning of early retirements which will take place in 1995–96 are still at an early stage, and for this reason it is not possible to provide projected costs although there is estimates provision for £3,000,000 expenditure at this time. Projections for 1996–97 will be determined during the coming public expenditure survey.

**Ms Hodge:** To ask the Secretary of State for Northern Ireland, how many staff of (a) the Northern Ireland Office and (b) agencies for which the Northern Ireland Office is responsible (i) took early retirement, (ii) took voluntary redundancy (iii) took compulsory redundancy and (iv) were retired on medical grounds in (1) 1993–94 and (2) 1994–95; and what are the projected figures for 1995–96. [25501]

**Sir John Wheeler:** The information is as follows:

|  | 1993–94 | 1994–95 | 1995–96 |
|---|---|---|---|
| *(i) Took early retirement* |  |  |  |
| NIO (excluding agencies) | 2 | 1 | 0 |
| Agencies | 1 | 0 | 0 |
| *(ii) Took voluntary redundancy* |  |  |  |
| NIO (excluding agencies) | 13 | 12 | 0 |
| Agencies | 0 | 0 | 15 |
| *(iii) Took compulsory redundancy* |  |  |  |
| NIO (excluding agencies) | 0 | 0 | 0 |
| Agencies | 0 | 0 | 0 |
| *(iv) Were retired on medical grounds* |  |  |  |
| NIO (excluding agencies) | 11 | 15 | n/a |
| Agencies | 1 | 2 | n/a |

It is not possible to forecast the number of retirements on medical grounds.

### Belvoir Park Hospital

**Mr. John D. Taylor:** To ask the Secretary of State for Northern Ireland (1) what hospital costs and what increase in revenue costs have been anticipated as a result of the decision by the Eastern area health board to remove the infectious diseases service from Belvoir Park hospital;

[24963]

(2) if the fixed costs of the infectious diseases service at Belvoir Park hospital, following its closure, will be transferred to the other service at Belvoir hospital; what will be the consequences for all area boards and general practitioner fundholders who purchase cancer treatment services at Belvoir hospital; and to what extent these consequences were taken into consideration by the Eastern area health board prior to its decision to close down the infectious diseases service at Belvoir hospital;

[24966]

(3) if he will make available the option appraisals and business case which identified benefits against the costs involved in the transfer of the infectious diseases service from Belvoir Park hospital; [24968]

(4) if the Eastern area health board consulted with the Northern and Southern area health boards prior to the decision by the Eastern board to close the infectious diseases service at Belvoir Park hospital; what representations he has received from the Northern and Southern health boards; and to what extent these area health boards presently use the infectious diseases service at Belvoir Park hospital; [24964]

(5) to which hospital the infectious diseases service at Belvoir Park hospital will be transferred; and what is the target date for completion of this transfer. [24967]

**Mr. Ancram:** The Eastern health and social services board's original proposal concerning the transfer of the infectious diseases service was incorporated in its acute hospital services strategy, published in November 1993 after consultation with wide range of groups and individuals including the other three boards. The Under-Secretary, my hon. Friend the Member for Cambridgeshire, North-East (Mr. Moss), has not had any representations from any of these boards about this proposal. The latest figures available show that in 1993–94 354 patients from the Northern board and 336 from the Southern board used this service at Belvoir Park.

My noble Friend Baroness Denton approved the board's strategy in March 1994. After detailed investigation and further consideration of the proposal for infectious diseases the board has now decided that the service should be split and that it should be provided by the Royal Group of Hospitals trust and the Ulster, North Down and Ards Hospital trust. A steering group is to be established to take this forward and to complete the transfer by June 1996. It is hoped to do so on a revenue neutral basis. Any capital requirements linked to the transfer will be for the two trusts to meet, within available resources, and in the face of competing priorities.

With regard to fixed costs, when a service is transferred from one provider to another, the original provider is expected to reduce so far as possible any fixed costs associated with that service over a reasonable period of time.

Finally, any option appraisal and business case in support of the decision are a matter for the Eastern board and the chairman has been asked to write to the right hon. Gentleman.

**Mr. John D. Taylor:** To ask the Secretary of State for Northern Ireland how many cases of infectious diseases used the service at Belvoir Park hospital in each of the past 10 years; and how many of these cases each year had to be sent to an intensive care facility at another location.

[24965]

**Mr. Ancram:** The table shows the number of cases treated in the infectious diseases speciality in Belvoir Park hospital in the last 10 years. Information on the number of cases transferred to an intensive care facility at another location is not available.

| | Number |
|---|---|
| 1984 | 1,988 |
| 1985 | 2,259 |
| 1986 | 2,018 |
| 1987 | 2,090 |
| 1988–89 | 1,889 |
| 1989–90 | 2,253 |
| 1990–91 | 2,241 |
| 1991–92 | 2,048 |
| 1992–93 | 2,079 |
| 1993–94 | 2,295 |

### Government Cleaning Contracts

**Mr. Spellar:** To ask the Secretary of State for Northern Ireland if Government cleaning remains on the approved list for tenders for contracts in the health sector in Northern Ireland. [25237]

**Mr. Ancram:** The health and personal social services in Northern Ireland do not operate an approved list system.

### Housing, South Down

**Mr. McGrady:** To ask the Secretary of State for Northern Ireland (1) what steps have been taken to replace the remaining Orlit dwellings in the constituency of South Down; [25325]

(2) how many Orlit dwellings have been replaced with new build in the constituency of South Down since 1 April 1987 to 31 March 1995; and how many have still to be replaced. [25326]

**Mr. Ancram:** These are matters for the Northern Ireland Housing Executive, but I have been advised by the chief executive that 163 Orlit dwellings have been replaced in the period 1 April 1987 to 31 March 1995 in the South Down constituency. A further 42 Orlit dwellings remain in Housing Executive ownership. The replacement of these dwellings at the end of their useful economic lives depends on a number of factors including housing need in the areas where the dwellings are sited. The Housing Executive has programmed for eight of these dwellings to be replaced in 1996–97.

### Police Body Armour

**Mrs. Roche:** To ask the Secretary of State for Northern Ireland what plans he has to ensure that all police officers are supplied with body armour. [25144]

**Sir John Wheeler:** The Royal Ulster Constabulary has provided body armour for its members since 1972. It is on issue at every station and is available to all officers.

### Job Displacement Criteria

**Mr. Wigley:** To ask the Secretary of State for Northern Ireland if he will ensure that the same rules are applied with regard to job displacement criteria when industrial development grants are paid to create additional manufacturing capacity in Northern Ireland, as are applied to projects in Wales, Scotland and England; and if he will make a statement. [25004]

**Mr. Ancram:** The rules applied in Northern Ireland regarding job displacement criteria are exactly the same as those applied in all other parts of the United Kingdom.

### International Fund for Ireland

**Mr. Worthington:** To ask the Secretary of State for Northern Ireland what representations he has made to the United States Government about the importance of Congress *(a)* maintaining and *(b)* increasing support to the International Fund for Ireland. [25728]

**Sir John Wheeler:** The Government are very supportive and appreciative of the work of the International Fund for Ireland. Ministers use every opportunity, both at home and abroad, to express the Government's appreciation of the generous international contributions to the fund, in particular the donations made by the United States. We are most grateful to President Clinton for his continuing support and look forward to Congress ratifying an increased US donation of $30 million in 1996 and 1997.

### Environmentally Sensitive Areas

**Dr. Strang:** To ask the Secretary of State for Northern Ireland how many farms *(a)* are eligible to have land entered into each environmentally sensitive area in Northern Ireland and *(b)* have had land entered into each environmentally sensitive area in Northern Ireland.

[25792]

**Mr. Ancram:** The information is as follows:

| ESA | Eligible farms | Under agreement (25 April 1995) |
|---|---|---|
| Antrim Coast, Glens and Rathlin | 1,200 | 229 |
| Slieve Gullion | 808 | 1 |
| Mourne Mountains and Slieve Croob | 1,846 | 321 |
| West Fermanagh and Erne Lakeland | 2,815 | 303 |
| Sperrins | 2,170 | 37 |

### Roads, South Down

**Mr. McGrady:** To ask the Secretary of State for Northern Ireland what plans he has to improve the roads infrastructure within the constituency of South Down.

[25748]

**Mr. Ancram:** In addition to a substantial programme of maintenance work, a number of minor improvement schemes will be carried out on the A2, A7, A22, A25, A50, B1, B2, B7 and B8 routes in the 1995–96 and 1996–97 financial years. Work on the Church street/Scotch street scheme in Downpatrick is programmed to start in the current financial year subject to the completion of the statutory processes.

### Ambulance Response Times

**Mr. Trimble:** To ask the Secretary of State for Northern Ireland how many emergency calls for ambulances there have been in *(a)* Craigavon, *(b)* Newry and Mourne, and *(d)* Down districts from January 1995 to 30 April 1995; what has been the (i) longest, (ii) shortest and (iii) average time before the dispatch of an ambulance; and what has been the (1) longest, (2) shortest and (3) average time between the receipt of the call and the arrival of the patient at hospital.

[24500]

**Sir John Wheeler:** This information is not available in the format requested. The table shows how many emergency calls were received by the Eastern ambulance trust and the Southern health and social services board during the quarter 1 January 1995 to 31 March 1995.

Activation times, defined as the time from receipt of an ermgency call until an ambulance is on its way, and response times, defined as the time from receipt of an emergency call until the arrival of an ambulance with the patient, are also shown. Information on the time from the receipt of an emergency call to the arrival of the patient at hospital is not collected centrally.

| Board/trust | Total number of emergency calls received | Total number of emergency calls activated within 3 minutes | Total number of emergency calls responded to within | |
|---|---|---|---|---|
| | | | 8 mins | 18/21mins |
| Eastern | 6,819 | 5,726 | 3,355 | 6,493 |
| Southern | 1,345 | 1,168 | ¹667 | ¹1,255 |

*Notes:*
Information is not collected centrally below board/trust level. Abortive calls have been excluded.
¹ The response time was not recorded for one emergency call.

### Race Relations

**Mr. Worthington:** To ask the Secretary of State for Northern Ireland if he will make a statement on his proposals for race relations legislation and his proposals for consultation thereon.

[24600]

**Mr. Ancram:** Following a period of public consultation, in response to a question from the hon. Member for Torfaen (Mr. Murphy) on 27 April 1995, *Official Report,* column *705,* my right hon. and learned Friend made clear his intention to introduce race relations legislation to Northern Ireland by means of an Order in Council.

A draft proposal for an Order in Council will be published and comments sought in due course.

## HEALTH

### Staff

**Ms Hodge:** To ask the Secretary of State for Health (1) how many posts were lost in *(a)* the Department of Health and *(b)* agencies for which the Department of Health is responsible, listing the total lost posts agency by agency in (i) 1993–94, (ii) 1994–95; and how many posts are proposed to be lost in 1995–96;

[25077]

(2) what changes there have been in the numbers of staff employed by *(a)* the Department of Health and *(b)* agencies for which the Department of Health is responsible, listing the number of staff agency by agency in (i) 1993–94, (ii) 1994–95; and what changes are projected for 1995–96;

[25065]

(3) what changes there have been in the numbers of staff in employment by grade in *(a)* her Department and *(b)* each agency for which her Department is responsible in (i) 1993–94, (ii) 1994–95; and what are the projected figures for 1995–96;

[25630]

(4) how many staff of *(a)* the Department of Health and *(b)* for which the DOH is responsible were employed on

a casual or short-term basis in (i) 1993–94, (ii) 1994–95; and what are the projected figures for 1995–96.    [25421]

**Mr. Sackville:** The number of permanent and casual staff employed by my Department and each of its executive agencies in 1993–94, projected outturn for 1994–95, and plans for 1995–96 are published in my Department's annual report, a copy of which is in the Library. No projections broken down by grade are available.

**Ms Hodge:** To ask the Secretary of State for Health how many staff of *(a)* the Department of Health and *(b)* agencies for which the Department of Health is responsible (i) took early retirement, (ii) took voluntary redundancy, (iii) took compulsory redundancy and (iv) were retired on medical grounds in (1) 1993–94 and (2) 1994–95; and what were the projected figures for 1995–96.    [25516]

**Mr. Sackville:** The information is shown in the table.

| | 1993–94 | 1994–95 | 1995–96 |
|---|---|---|---|
| *Department of Health* | | | |
| Early retirement | 105 | 33 | 137 |
| Voluntary redundancy | 0 | 104 | 237 |
| Compulsory redundancy | 0 | 54 | 0 |
| Retired on medical grounds | 38 | 37 | 0 |
| | | | |
| *Medicines Control Agency* | | | |
| Early retirement | 5 | 5 | 2 |
| Voluntary redundancy | 0 | 3 | 0 |
| Compulsory redundancy | 0 | 0 | 0 |
| Retired on medical grounds | 1 | 2 | 1 |
| | | | |
| *National Health Service Estates* | | | |
| Early retirement | 6 | 1 | 7 |
| Voluntary redundancy | 0 | 3 | 9 |
| Compulsory redundancy | 0 | 1 | 0 |
| Retired on medical grounds | 0 | 0 | 1 |
| | | | |
| *National Health Service Pension Agency* | | | |
| Early retirement | 15 | 6 | 37 |
| Voluntary redundancy | 0 | 4 | 24 |
| Compulsory redundancy | 0 | 0 | 0 |
| Retired on medical grounds | 0 | 0 | 5 |
| | | | |
| *Medical Devices Agency* | | | |
| Early retirement | 0 | 0 | 16 |
| Voluntary redundancy | 0 | 3 | 7 |
| Compulsory redundancy | 0 | 0 | 0 |
| Retired on medical grounds | 0 | 0 | 0 |

*Notes:*

The Medical Devices Agency did not become an Agency until 27 September 1994 and the figures quoted for it represent the numbers leaving from that date. Figures relating to staff leaving prior to the Agency launch are included in the figures for the Department of Health.

**Ms Hodge:** To ask the Secretary of State for Health what is the annual cost to the Department of staff leaving under redundancy/early retirement schemes to incorporate (i) added years lump sum payments for (ii) redundancy payments, (iii) pension payments including enhancements and (iv) any other special arrangements for *(a)* 1993–94, *(b)* 1994–95 and projected for *(c)* 1995–96 and *(d)* 1996–97.    [25639]

**Mr. Sackville:** The costs to the Department of early retirement and redundancies are borne from the Department's running costs provision.

A detailed breakdown of the various costs could be provided only at disproportionate cost.

The total costs borne on the Department's running costs in 1993–94 and 1994–95 were £4.51 million and £6.51 million respectively. For 1995–96, the amount is estimated at £2.73 million. Projections for 1996–97 will be determined during the coming public expenditure survey.

*Notes:*

1. Figures include ongoing costs of redundancies/early retirements from previous years.

2. Costs shown for 1993–94 and 1994–95 include moneys paid to paymaster to offset costs of redundancies/early retirements in future years.

3. Costs take into account Treasury contribution, from 1 October 1994 to 31 March 1997, of 80 per cent. of costs of reducing staff numbers in that period.

## Hospital providers

**Mr. Mike O'Brien:** To ask the Secretary of State for Health how much as a percentage and in real terms hospital provider prices have changed in each of the last two years for providers serving Warwickshire residents, identifying each hospital provider's individual price change.    [25206]

**Mr. Sackville:** This information is not available centrally.

## Mental Disorder

**Sir Andrew Bowden:** To ask the Secretary of State for Health what contribution she expects her Department to make to the committee of specialists recently appointed by the Committee of Ministers to the Council of Europe to consider revision of Committee of Ministers' recommendation No. R(83)2 on the legal protection of persons suffering from mental disorder placed as involuntary patients following recommendation 1235(1994) of the Parliamentary Assembly of the Council of Europe; and if she will make a statement.    [25327]

**Mr. Bowis:** I understand that the members of this committee have not yet been appointed. We are currently considering how we can most effectively contribute to its work.

## Contracting Out

**Ms Hodge:** To ask the Secretary of State for Health (1) for each piece of work subject to a bidding process under the auspices of *(a)* her Department and *(b)* agencies for which her Department is responsible (i) where work was contracted out, who were the successful bidders and (ii) which contracts were won by in-house bidders in (1) 1993–94, (2) 1994–95 and (3) 1995–96;    [25652]

(2) what work has been contracted out *(a)* by her Department and *(b)* by agencies for which the Department is responsible in (i) 1993–94, (ii) 1994–95 and (iii) projected for 1995–96.    [25527]

**Mr. Sackville:** Available information of all contracts awarded, as part of the Department's "Competing For Quality" market-testing programme, will be placed in the Library.

Detailed information of contract awards can be found in the "Market Testing Bulletin". This is issued monthly, and copies are available in the Library.

## Medicines Commission

**Ms Hodge:** To ask the Secretary of State for Health if she will list the occasion in the last five years upon which the Medicines Commission has reviewed the functions of the Committee on the Safety of Medicines and of the Medicines Control Agency; and if she will publish the findings of the reviews.    [25608]

**Mr. Sackville:** The Committee on the Safety of Medicines, together with all other committees established under section 4 of the Medicines Act 1968, reports with respect to the performance of its functions to the Medicines Commission on an annual basis. These reports are available in the Library.

The functions of the Medicines Control Agency are not within the remit of the Medicines Commission.

## Dental Services

**Mr. Martyn Jones:** To ask the Secretary of State for Health (1) what is the estimated percentage of the population with tooth decay, giving the figures for *(a)* the total United Kingdom population and *(b)* those aged one to 10 years;    [25365]

(2) what is the estimated number of cases amongst those aged one to 10 years of *(a)* tooth decay and *(b)* tooth extraction due to tooth decay.    [23569]

**Mr. Malone:** The table shows the proportion of children in England aged from 0 to 10 years with permanent teeth which are actively decayed, filled or missing due to decay. In young children, it is difficult to establish whether a tooth has been lost naturally or through decay. The Office of Population Censuses and Surveys adult dental survey, 1988, shows that in England, 43 per cent. of dentate adults in the survey had decayed or unsound teeth. For further explanation of decay in primary teeth and levels of adult tooth decay, I refer the hon. Member to the following OPCS publications—"Adult Dental Survey (1988)" and "Children's Dental Health in the United Kingdom (1993)". These publications are held in the Library. Information relating to Scotland, Wales and Northern Ireland are matters for my right hon. Friends the Secretaries of State for Scotland and for Wales and my right hon. and learned Friend the Secretary of State for Northern Ireland.

*General Dental Service: percentage of children aged 0–10 years*
*with permanent teeth which are actively decayed, filled or missing*
*due to decay*

England

| Tooth condition | Age | | | | | |
| | 5 | 6 | 7 | 8 | 9 | 10 |
|---|---|---|---|---|---|---|
| Actively decayed | [1]— | 3 | 8 | 11 | 13 | 14 |
| Filled (otherwise sound) | [2]— | 1 | 4 | 7 | 14 | 16 |
| Missing due to decay | [1]— | [1]— | 1 | 1 | 1 | 3 |

*Source:*
Children's dental health survey OPCS.
[1] indicates a proportion of less than 0.5 per cent.
[2] indicates zero value.

*General Dental Service: average number of permanent teeth for children*
*aged 0–10 years which are actively decayed, filled or missing*
*due to decay*

England

| Tooth condition | Age | | | | | |
| | 5 | 6 | 7 | 8 | 9 | 10 |
|---|---|---|---|---|---|---|
| Actively decayed | [1] | [1] | 0.1 | 0.2 | 0.2 | 0.3 |
| Filled (otherwise sound) | [2]— | [1] | [1] | 0.1 | 0.2 | 0.3 |
| Missing due to decay | [1] | 0.1 | 0.2 | 0.3 | 0.5 | 0.6 |

*Source:*
Children's dental health survey OPCS.
[1] Indicates a proportion of less than 0.5 per cent.
[2] Indicates zero value.

**Mr. Martyn Jones:** To ask the Secretary of State for Health (1) how many cases of tooth decay were treated in the United Kingdom in *(a)* 1994–95 and *(b)* 1990 to 1995;    [23566]

(2) what is the estimated cost of treating tooth decay for *(a)* the NHS and *(b)* patients for (i) 1994–95 and (ii) 1990 to 1995.    [23568]

**Mr. Malone:** Information is not available about the cost of treating tooth decay or the number of cases. The total costs of the general dental service in England and the total number of adult courses of treatments are shown in the table. Since 1990, the majority of treatment for children has been paid for on a capitation basis and courses of treatment are not separately identifiable. Information relating to Scotland, Wales and Northern Ireland are matters for my right hon. Friends the Secretaries of State for Scotland and for Wales and my right hon. and learned Friend the Secretary of State for Northern Ireland.

*General Dental Service: number of adult courses of treatment and cost*[1]

England

| Year | Number of adult courses of treatment | Total NHS gross expenditure (millions) £ | Cost of the GDS borne by the Exchequer (millions) £ | Cost borne by patient (millions) £ |
|---|---|---|---|---|
| 1990–91 | 22,558,739 | 1,039.996 | 660.267 | 379.729 |
| 1991–92 | 24,273,099 | 1,245.970 | 842.000 | 403.970 |
| 1992–93 | 25,141,300 | 1,305.879 | 911.092 | 394.787 |
| 1993–94 | 24,847,648 | 1,221.719 | 854.695 | 367.024 |
| 1994–95 | 24,913,096 | 1,282.294 | 897.266 | 385.028 |

[1] The cost of figures for 1994–95 are provisional.

**Mrs. Beckett:** To ask the Secretary of State for Health how many patients have been deregistered from NHS dental treatment; and how many NHS dentists have given up NHS dental work entirely since July 1992.    [26292]

**Mr. Malone:** Since July 1992, 891,554 patients have been deregistered by their dentists for reasons other than retirement. In the same period, a total number of 426 dentists removed their names completely from the dental list for reasons other than retirement. The number of dentists contracted to provide national health service general dental services has, however, increased in the period by over 2 per cent.—15,745 on 31 March 1995 compared with 15,426 on 30 June 1992—and, over the same period, there have been some 33 million additions to NHS dentists' lists. These additions include patients moving from one dentist to another and patients re-registering with the same dentist after a gap.

## Heart Disease

**Mr. Martyn Jones:** To ask the Secretary of State for Health how many *(a)* cases of heart disease and *(b)* deaths due to heart disease were recorded for (i) 1994–95 and (ii) 1990 to 1995.    [23567]

**Mr. Sackville:** The number of finished consultant episodes for hospital in-patients suffering from heart diseases is published in "Hospital Episode Statistics" which are available from 1988–89 to 1993–94. Copies of the publications are available in the Library.

The table shows the number of deaths due to heart disease—ICD[1] codes 390–429—in England and Wales, 1990–93.

    1990: 173,453

    1991: 174,447

    1992: 169,539

    1993: 178,963

This information is not yet available for 1994 and 1995.

[1] International Classification of Diseases, 9th Revision.

**Mr. Martyn Jones:** To ask the Secretary of State for Health what is the estimated cost to the NHS of treating heart disease for *(a)* 1994–95 and *(b)* 1990 to 1995.    [23570]

**Mr. Sackville:** This information is not available centrally.

## Yellow Card Scheme

**Ms Hodge:** To ask the Secretary of State for Health what is her Department's latest estimate of the percentage of adverse drug reactions which are reported by general practitioners via the yellow card system.    [25520]

**Mr. Sackville:** The percentage of all adverse drug reactions reported by general practitioners is not known, as there is no means of knowing the total number of adverse drug reactions. A recent survey found that 77 per cent. of general practitioners have used the yellow card reporting scheme. Of 17,635 reports received in 1994 through the scheme, approximately 63 per cent. originated from general practitioners. Most of the remainder were reported by hospital doctors and pharmaceutical companies.

## Committee on the Safety of Medicines

**Ms Hodge:** To ask the Secretary of State for Health if she will consider inviting a consumer representative to sit on the Committee on the Safety of Medicine to complement the medical experts.    [26243]

**Mr. Sackville:** The Committee on the Safety of Medicines is an expert scientific advisory body, and as such members need to have relevant and appropriate expertise. Members do not represent organisations, but contribute by their individual expertise and judgment to the advice given by the body to the licensing authority.

## Chelation Therapy

**Mr. David Atkinson:** To ask the Secretary of State for Health what research has been undertaken into chelation therapy; what consideration has been made to make it available within the national health service on a non-discretionary basis; and if she will make a statement. [25591]

**Mr. Sackville:** None.

As with all other forms of treatment, it is for local purchasers to decide in the light of available resources and competing priorities, on the purchase of the most appropriate forms of treatment to meet the assessed health needs of their population.

## GP Fundholding

**Mrs. Beckett:** To ask the Secretary of State for Health (1) what research she has commissioned to evaluate general practitioner fundholding against joint commissioning; [25920]

(2) what evidence she has evaluated to the effect that general practitioner fundholding is more cost effective than joint commissioning. [25921]

**Mr. Malone:** As independent studies have shown, general practitioner fundholding has been a major success since 1991 in improving services for patients. Over 41 per cent. of the population is now registered with a fundholding GP. Joint commissioning is a subsequent development which involves both fundholding and non-fundholding general practitioners working in partnership with health authorities to plan and purchase services. We will be developing our research programme to assess these developments, including the full evaluation of the 51 total purchasing sites, over the coming months.

**Mr. Alex Carlile:** To ask the Secretary of State for Health how many general practitioner fundholding practices per family health service authority are currently in dispute, arbitration or subject to appeal over one or more of their budgets; and if she will make a statement. [25932]

**Mr. Malone:** This information is not available centrally.

**Mr. Nicholas Brown:** To ask the Secretary of State for Health how many first, second, third and fourth wave fundholders have since left the scheme. [26199]

**Mr. Malone:** This information is not available centrally. Indications are that the small number of fundholders who have left the scheme have done so largely because of changes in the practice partnership.

## Hospital Closures

**Mrs. Beckett:** To ask the Secretary of State for Health if she will list all hospitals with overnight beds closed in each year since 1979. [25922]

**Mr. Malone:** Information on closures of hospitals has never been collected centrally in the form requested.

## Special Hospitals

**Mr. Nicholas Brown:** To ask the Secretary of State for Health what plans there are to grant trust status to Ashworth hospital on Merseyside, Broadmoor hospital in Berkshire and Rampton hospital in Nottinghamshire; and if she will make a statement. [26200]

**Mr. Bowis:** I expect to be making a statement shortly about future management arrangements for the special hospitals.

## Mental Health

**Mr. Alex Carlile:** To ask the Secretary of State for Health what guidelines are in place for the management and multi-agency response to the initial onset of an acute psychiatric emergency occurring in the community; and if she will make a statement. [25931]

**Mr. Bowis:** The Mental Health act code of practice provides guidance to practitioners on the steps to be taken if a patient requires emergency psychiatric assessment in the community. Copies of the code are available in the Library.

**Mr. Nicholas Brown:** To ask the Secretary of State for Health if her Department has, within the past year, made strategic recommendations on how best to allocate mental health expenditure in relation to needs for services. [26075]

**Mr. Bowis:** The annual priorities and planning guidance for the national health service sets the broad direction for the planning and delivery of health services for the coming year. The guidance for 1995–96 identifies mental health as a priority for the medium term. It is the responsibility of district health authorities to prepare local health strategies and purchasing plans to address the national priorities whilst also taking full account of local health needs. A copy of the guidance for 1995–96—EL(94)55—is available in the Library.

**Mr. Nicholas Brown:** To ask the Secretary of State for Health if she will list the organisations that were involved in her Department's consultation process prior to the publication of the Mental Health (Patients in the Community) Bill. [26019]

**Mr. Bowis:** The information will be placed in the Library.

## Local Pay

**Mr. Alex Carlile:** To ask the Secretary of State for Health how many local pay offers from NHS trusts to nurses, midwives and professions allied to medicine have been connected to changes in employment and working conditions in the current pay round; and if she will make a statement. [25937]

**Mr. Malone:** This information is not available centrally. Terms of local pay offers are a matter for employers.

## Ethnic Minorities

**Mr. Alex Carlile:** To ask the Secretary of State for Health what measures are in place to address the specific health needs of different ethnic minority groups; and if she will make a statement. [25938]

**Mr. Sackville:** We are totally committed to ensuring that people from ethnic minorities should benefit fully from the national health service. The reforms we have introduced into the NHS require health authorities to assess the health needs of their local population and to deliver the services to meet these needs. To improve information about the use of health services by people from ethnic minorities from 1 April 1995 it is mandatory to record the ethnic group of patients who use in-patient or day-case services. This data will enable purchasers and providers to examine the uptake of services, monitor standards and identify any gaps in service provision.

Since 1989, we have made available £3 million to provide funding for projects to improve access to health services and information for ethnic minorities. The projects are now related specifically to "The Health of the Nation" key areas and to the rights and standards outlined in the patients charter. The patients charter is available in 11 ethnic languages and has been widely distributed.

We have also established the ethnic health unit as part of the NHS Executive. The aim of the unit is to promote good practice in the NHS, support managers in developing links with local communities and to build ethnic health into the mainstream work of the NHS. The unit has funded many local initiatives to improve services to ethnic minorities.

### Child Abuse

**Mr. Nicholas Brown:** To ask the Secretary of State for Health when the social services departmental inspectorate last inspected Newcastle city council social services department; when it next intends to do so; what specific advice has been given to Newcastle social services department in respect of the issues raised in the Hunt report into a multiple child abuse case in Newcastle; and what assessment she has made of the adequacy of remedial action taken to deal with the shortcomings identified by the Hunt report. [26206]

**Mr. Bowis:** The social services inspectorate has undertaken a number of inspections relating to different services provided by Newcastle city council's social services department, the most recent in January this year.

Mr. Hunt's report following his independent inquiry into multiple abuse of children in nursery classes raised issues for several local authority departments and the area child protection committee as well as the Newcastle city council social services department. I am advised that the recommendations requiring immediate action have now been implemented and inspectors from my social services inspectorate are continuing to monitor progress.

### Oculogenital Clinic, Moorfields Eye Hospital

**Mr. Chris Smith:** To ask the Secretary of State for Health if statutory consultation requirements were met in relation to the decision by Moorfields Eye hospital to close its oculogenital clinic. [25962]

**Mr. Sackville:** The decision on whether to consult is a matter for the local health authority. The hon. Member may wish to contact Mr. Roland Everington, chairman of Camden and Islington health authority, for details.

### Air Pollution

**Mr. Alex Carlile:** To ask the Secretary of State for Health what consultations she has had in the last year with other Ministers and Departments concerning combating the levels of air pollution and its effect on health; and if she will make a statement. [25960]

**Mr. Sackville:** Ministers in the Department of Health hold frequent meetings with other Ministers to discuss a variety of matters, which will sometimes include the effects of air pollutants upon health. On this issue we are advised in particular by the Committee on the Medical Aspects of Air Pollution Episodes.

**Mr. Watson:** To ask the Secretary of State for Health if she will specify the air-borne pollution most damaging to health as indicated by Her Department's research into the causes of asthma and links with air pollution. [26602]

**Mr. Sackville:** Levels of air pollution vary considerably from place to place and at different times, and there is no one pollutant which is consistently the most damaging. The effects on individuals are determined by the duration of exposure as well as the level of pollution, and sensitivity to pollutants may also vary between individuals. The Department of the Environment's air quality information line—0800 556677—provides information on the levels of pollutants.

### Sex Change Operations

**Mr. Gordon Prentice:** To ask the Secretary of State for Health what is the cost to public funds of a sex change operation carried out on the NHS. [26017]

**Mr. Sackville:** As there are a wide range of patient conditions and particular treatment needs, it is not possible to state, with certainty, how much a sex change operation costs.

**Mr. Gordon Prentice:** To ask the Secretary of State for Health what is the current waiting list for sex change operations. [26016]

**Mr. Sackville:** For waiting list purposes, sex change operations are included in the plastic surgery speciality. It is not possible to identify sex change operations data separately.

**Mr. Gordon Prentice:** To ask the Secretary of State for Health how many sex change operations (a) from male to female and (b) from female to male, have been carried out under the national health service in each year since 1990. [26018]

**Mr. Sackville:** Data on sex change operations data are not recorded separately from data on other plastic surgery operations.

### GP Lists

**Mr. Nicholas Brown:** To ask the Secretary of State for Health what plans her Department has to ensure that general practitioners tell patients the reason why they have been struck off family doctor lists. [26079]

**Mr. Malone:** I refer the hon. Member to the reply I gave to the hon. Member for Stockport (Mrs. Coffey) on 2 March, column *647*.

**Mr. Nicholas Brown:** To ask the Secretary of State for Health what plans her Department has to overhaul the rules regarding the deregistration of patient from general practitioners' practice lists. [26070]

**Mr. Malone:** None.

**Mr. Milburn:** To ask the Secretary of State for Health, pursuant to her answer of 16 March, *Official Report*, column *707*, when she will publish data for 1993 on patients removed from general practitioner lists. [26083]

**Mr. Malone:** It is planned to include the available information in the health service indicators package due to be published later this year.

### Remedial Training for Doctors

**Mr. Nicholas Brown:** To ask the Secretary of State for Health how much money was spent on remedial training of (a) general practitioners and (b) hospital doctors in each regional health authority in each of the last 10 years. [26208]

**Mr. Malone:** Remedial training is not separately identified within the overall cost of postgraduate and continuing medical education in the national health service.

### Residential Care

**Mr. Bayley:** To ask the Secretary of State for Health how many people in England aged over 64 years live in *(a)* private residential homes, *(b)* private nursing homes, *(c)* local authority part III homes and *(d)* national health service nursing homes; and, of these, how many have the cost of their care paid wholly or partly by (i) their local authority, (ii) their health authority, and (iii) the Department of Social Security; and how many pay for their care wholly from private sources. [25971]

**Mr. Bowis:** At 31 March 1994, there were 142,000 and 53,600 long-stay residents aged over 64 in private residential homes and local authority part III homes respectively. A further 37,000 people were in residential homes provided by the voluntary sector. An estimated 132,000 beds were occupied by people over 64 years in nursing homes registered under section 23 of the Registered Homes Act 1984. Information on national health service nursing homes is not available centrally.

The numbers of long-stay residents aged over 64 in residential or nursing homes whose costs are met wholly or in part by the local authority are shown in the table.

No information is available centrally on the numbers of people whose costs are met wholly or in part by their health authority nor on numbers who pay for their care wholly from private sources. Information on numbers supported wholly or in part by the Department of Social Security is a matter for my right hon. Friend the Secretary of State for Social Security.

*Long-stay residents aged over 64 in residential or nursing homes whose costs are met wholly or in part by their local authority, England at 31 March 1994.*

*Numbers*

| Sector | Residential homes | Nursing homes |
| --- | --- | --- |
| Private | 21,900 | 20,600 |
| Local authority | 51,500 | — |
| Voluntary | 6,800 | 1,100 |

*Source:*
Department of Health return SR1.

### In Vitro Fertilisation

**Mr. Matthew Taylor:** To ask the Secretary of State for Health what plans she has to ensure that in vitro fertilisation treatment is provided on the NHS by the Cornwall health authority. [26161]

**Mr. Sackville:** It is the responsibility of each individual health authority to determine its provision of infertility treatment in the light of local needs and the availability of resources. The hon. Member may wish to contact Dr. Stanley Dennison, chairman of the Cornwall and Isles of Scilly health authority for details.

**Mr. Matthew Taylor:** To ask the Secretary of State for Health what plans she has to ensure that in vitro fertilisation treatment is provided on the NHS by every health authority. [26162]

**Mr. Sackville:** Local health authorities are responsible for the provision of local health services, including the provision of infertility services. Decisions about the resources to be made available for these services must be left to individual health authorities as they are in the best position to determine priorities in the light of local needs and circumstances.

### Departmental Performance

**Ms Hodge:** To ask the Secretary of State for Health what performance indicators and performance targets there are for measuring the performance of her Department in *(a)* answering letters from members of the public and *(b)* answering telephone calls from members of the public; how performance is monitored; and what are the latest figures for performance measured against the target set. [26235]

**Mr. Sackville:** The Department has an explicit aim to answer all letters from members of the public within 28 days. This is included in departmental business plans, and monitored as part of local management responsibilities.

The majority of telephone calls received from members of the public relate to the national health service and are passed initially through the Department's public inquiry office. Questions that cannot be answered by the inquiry office are passed to relevant parts of the Department for reply. As with written communications, performance targets are set internally and achievement against those targets monitored by local management.

### Asthma

**Mr. Alex Carlile:** To ask the Secretary of State for Health what is her estimate of the number of people currently diagnosed as asthmatic. [25955]

**Mr. Sackville:** There are no comprehensive data on the number of people with a diagnosis of asthma. However, it has been estimated that the prevalence of asthma sufficiently severe to require regular medical supervision is from 4 to 6 per cent. in children and about 4 per cent. in adults. More information is given in "Asthma: An Epidemiological Overview", published on 22 March, copies of which are available in the Library.

### Preventive Medicine

**Sir Irvine Patnick:** To ask the Secretary of State for Health if she will make a statement outlining her Department's latest initiatives in preventive medicine. [26014]

**Mr. Sackville:** The Government launched "The Health of the Nation" strategy in July 1992 as a long-term strategy emphasising disease prevention and health promotion. The strategy involves a wide range of partners both within and outside Government. Already, we are seeing results. For 19 of the 24 targets where data are available, movement is in the right direction.

### Psychiatric Beds

**Mr. Nicholas Brown:** To ask the Secretary of State for Health how many *(a)* long-stay and *(b)* acute psychiatric beds there were in each regional health authority and district health authority in (i) 1979, (ii) 1990 and (iii) the last year for which figures are available. [26080]

**Mr. Bowis:** Information is not available in the form requested. The available information for 1979 has been published in "SH3 National and Regional Summaries (DHSS Hospital Statistics) 1979" and for later years in "Bed availability in England", copies of which are available in the Library. Because of changes in the classifications of beds and health authority boundaries over the period, figures are not strictly comparable.

## Complaints

**Ms Hodge:** To ask the Secretary of State for Health what policy and procedures exist for dealing with complaints against her Department by members of the public; when the policy was last updated; what time limit and target for dealing with such complaints her Department has; and what follow-up procedure exists where complainants are not satisfied with her Department's response to a complaint. [26219]

**Mr. Sackville:** The majority of complaints received by the Department from members of the public relate to the national health service.

Complaints relating specifically to the Department are handled as any other correspondence, and are subject to performance targets set and monitored by local departmental management.

Any member of the public who is dissatisfied with how the Department has dealt with his complaint may ask a Member of Parliament to submit the complaint to the Parliamentary Commissioner for Administration for investigation and review.

## Residential Homes

**Mr. Bayley:** To ask the Secretary of State for Health how many people in England aged over 64 years and living in *(a)* private residential homes, *(b)* private nursing homes, *(c)* local authority residential homes and *(d)* national health service nursing homes have spouse living elsewhere. [25972]

**Mr. Bowis:** This information is not available centrally.

## Malaria Prophylaxis

**Mr. Nicholas Brown:** To ask the Secretary of State for Health what plans she has to make all malaria prophylaxis available over the counter in United Kingdom pharmacies. [26076]

**Mr. Malone:** There are no plans to change the status of those malaria prophylactics which are prescription-only medicines.

## University College Hospital

**Mrs. Beckett:** To ask the Secretary of State for Health how many beds of each type will be lost under the proposed reorganisation of University College London hospital. [26315]

**Mr. Malone:** Camden and Islington health authority is consulting on those proposals. Details are set out in the public consultation document issued on 24 April.

## Swindon Health Care

**Mr. Illsley:** To ask the Secretary of State for Health (1) what steps he is taking to ensure sufficient in-patient accommodation will be available for Swindon and district between the closure of the Princess Alexandra hospital in 1996 and the refurbishment of the Princess Margaret hospital; [26305]

(2) what steps she is taking to ensure the health care needs of Swindon and district are met following the closure of the Princess Alexandra hospital 1996. [27307]

**Mr. Sackville:** These are matters for the Wiltshire and Bath health authority. The hon. Member may wish to contact the chairman, Mr. Alastair Service CBE, for details.

## Minor Injury Units

**Mrs. Beckett:** To ask the Secretary of State for Health what evidence she has of the effect of the replacement of accident and emergency centres with trauma centres and minor injuries units on the level of deaths. [26309]

**Mr. Sackville:** We set up a pilot trauma centre at the North Staffordshire Hospitals NHS trust in 1990. This followed a report from the Royal College of Surgeons on the management of patients with major injuries that found that one in every five deaths from major trauma was potentially preventable. The pilot has been evaluated by the medical care research unit at the university of Sheffield and we expect to receive its findings in the summer.

There is, however, a considerable body of scientific evidence showing that patients with major injuries receive more effective care in large, appropriately staffed, accident and emergency centres, backed up by the main hospital specialties. A review of the literature on the relationship between the size of accident and emergency departments and clinical outcomes prepared by my Department is available in the Library.

Studies of minor injury units have shown them to be effective in treating patients with minor conditions. The studies also found that nearly all patients use minor injury units appropriately.

## Fluoridation

**Mr. Gordon Prentice:** To ask the Secretary of State for Health which water companies add fluoride to the water supply; and which have chosen not to do so. [26572]

**Mr. Malone:** United Kingdom companies which are currently operating—or have at some point operated—fluoridation plant include:

  Severn Trent Water
  South Staffordshire Water
  East Worcestershire Waterworks Company (now part of severn Trent)
  North East Water
  North West Water
  Welsh Water
  Yorkshire Water
  Anglian Water
  Colne Valley Water Company

It is for a health authority, following extensive public consultation, to submit a request to the water undertakers to fluoridate the water supply on behalf of the local population. Yorkshire Water decided recently not to agree to fluoridate the regions's water supply. The fluoridation of water supplies accords with Government policy and underpins the objectives of the oral health strategy.

## Blood-lead Levels

**Mr. Watson:** To ask the Secretary of State for Health (1) what continuous monitoring of blood-lead levels in children is carried out by her Department; if she will publish the results for the last three years for which such information is available; and if she will make a statement; [26591]

(2) what evidence she has evaluated to indicate that blood-lead levels in children have reached levels *(a)*

potentially affecting the central nervous system and *(b)* causing other effects damaging to health; and if she will make a statement;    [26606]

(3) if she will publish the latest available figures her Department has evaluated on the contribution of air-borne lead to children's blood-lead levels;    [26604]

(4) if she will list the latest available figures her Department has evaluated on the contribution to children's blood-lead levels caused by *(a)* petrol, *(b)* food and *(c)* lead water pipes.    [26607]

**Mr. Sackville:** Since 1974, it has been the policy of successive Governments to contain and reduce exposure to lead wherever practicable, particularly in those circumstances where people are most exposed.

Monitoring programmes have shown a continuing fall in blood-lead levels in children and adults since the early 1970s as controls on sources of lead exposure have been introduced. Since action has been taken to reduce exposure from a wide range of sources including petrol, drinking water, air, food, industrial emissions, paint, cosmetics, ceramic glazes and toys, the contribution made to blood-lead levels by any one source is difficult to estimate and will vary with location and age of the person.

Continuous monitoring of children's blood-lead levels is not carried out in the United Kingdom. However, lead will be determined in blood samples collected for the 1995 health survey for England from a sample of adults and children aged 11 and over.

### Meals on Wheels

**Mr. Hinchliffe:** To ask the Secretary of State for Health how much was spent on meals on wheels by each authority in each of the last 10 years, expressed in 1995 prices.    [25764]

**Mr. Bowis:** The information, expressed in 1994–95 prices, will be placed in the Library. The figures should be treated with caution as local authorities differ from year to year in their respective treatment of administrative and other overhead costs. Year-on-year variations may also reflect changes in type or method of meal service and changes of contract. New guidelines for future social services accounting have been drawn up by the Chartered Institute of Public Finance and Accounting and the local authorities, which should result in greater consistency.

### North Tees NHS Trust

**Mr. Milburn:** To ask the Secretary of State for Health is she will provide details of the early retirement package given to Mr. Belton, the former chief executive of North Tees NHS trust.    [26185]

**Mr. Malone:** Mr. Belton is still employed as chief executive of North Tees NHS trust.

### Medical Records

**Mr. Ron Davies:** To ask the Secretary of State for Health (1) what guidance she issues as to the grounds on which a health authority may restrict an individual's access to their own medical records;    [25948]

(2) what is her Department's policy on procedure when individuals request their medical records;    [25949]

(3) what guidelines her Department offers to health authorities on how to respond when patients request their medical records.    [25950]

**Mr. Sackville:** Patients have a legal right to see their own health records. For records kept on paper and compiled on or after 1 November 1991, access is provided for by the Access to Health Records Act 1990. For records held on computer, access is provided for by the Data Protection Act 1984. Access may be denied to all or part of the record if disclosure of any information in it might cause serious harm to the physical or mental health of the patient. Access may also be denied if it contains information which would identify a third party, other than a health professional, unless that person has consented to the disclosure. The Access to Health Records Act also permits access to be withheld to protect the health of another person.

Guidance on the Access to Health Records Act 1990 was issued to the National Health Service in England in August 1991. Guidance on the Data Protection Act 1984 was issued to the NHS in England in 1987 and 1989. Guidance was also issued to the NHS in Wales. A revised handbook, "Introduction to Data Protection in the NHS" was issued in July 1994. All guidance contains advice on procedures to enable patients to see their records. Copies of the guidance are available in the Library.

### Breast Cancer Screening

**Ms Lynne:** To ask the Secretary of State for Health (1) how many women *(a)* in England and *(b)* in the United Kingdom aged (i) 50 to 54, (ii) 55 to 59 (iii) 60 to 64, (iv) 65 and, (v) 66 years or over were screened for breast cancer following an invitation from the national health service breast screening programme in each of the last five years;    [26021]

(2) what percentage of women aged 65 years or over *(a)* in England and *(b)* in the United Kingdom were screened for breast cancer through the national health service breast screening programme at their own request or the request of their general practitioner, excluding women who are screened through the diagnostic service, in the latest year for which figures are available;    [26023]

(3) how many women *(a)* in England and *(b)* in the United Kingdom aged: (i) 50 to 54, (ii) 55 to 59, (iii) 60 to 64, (iv) 65 to 69, (v) 70 to 74, (vi) 75 to 79, (vii) 80 to 84 (viii) 85 years or over were screened for breast cancer through the national health service breast screening programme at their own request or the request of their general practitioner, excluding women who are screened through the diagnostic service, in each of the last five years.    [26022]

**Mr. Sackville:** This information is not available centrally in the form requested. The available information is shown in the tables.

*Breast cancer screening—number of women tested or screened as a result of self or GP referral*

| Age | 1992–93 | 1993–94[1] |
| --- | --- | --- |
| 50–54 | 7,393 | 7,068 |
| 55–59 | 6,405 | 6,893 |
| 60–64 | 5,220 | 5,652 |
| 65–69 | 11,136 | 12,828 |
| 70–74 | 3,194 | 4,635 |
| 75 and over | 636 | 892 |

[1] Provisional data only.

*Breast cancer screening—number of women tested or screened as a result of first invitation, or routine recall*

| Age | 1992–93 | 1993–94[1] |
|---|---|---|
| 50–54 | 310,028 | 324,239 |
| 55–59 | 302,167 | 314,387 |
| 60–64 | 279,605 | 291,090 |
| 65–69 | 28,700 | 29,922 |
| 70–74 | 1,053 | 187 |
| 75 and over | 56 | 10 |

[1] Provisional data only.

*Percentage of women aged 65 and over tested or screened as a result of a GP or self referral*

| | 1992–93 | 1993–94[1] |
|---|---|---|
| Percentage | 0.33 | 0.44 |

[1] Provisional data only.

**Ms Lynne:** To ask the Secretary of State for Health what is the average cost per person screened on the national health service breast screening programme. [26025]

**Mr. Sackville:** The estimated average cost per person screened under the national health service breast screening programme in England in 1993–94 was £27.

**Ms Lynne:** To ask the Secretary of State for Health what amount the national health service breast screening programme spends on screening women 65 years or over; and what percentage of the total budget this is. [26024]

**Mr. Sackville:** It is estimated that in 1993–94 in England, about £1.4 million, representing 5 per cent. of the total breast cancer screening budget, was spent on testing women aged 65 years or over for breast cancer.

### Capital Underspending

**Mr. Milburn:** To ask the Secretary of State for Health, pursuant to her answer of 23 January, *Official Report,* columns 13–14, if she will provide 1994–95 information on regional health authority capital underspending. [26088]

**Mr. Sackville:** Details of underspending on regional health authority capital cash limits will not be available until all authorities have completed their annual accounts for 1994–95.

### Staff Cars

**Mrs. Beckett:** To ask the Secretary of State for Health how much was expended on cars for staff by *(a)* trusts and *(b)* in total in each of the last five years. [26288]

**Mr. Sackville:** I refer the right hon. Member to the replies I gave to the hon. Member for Wakefield (Mr. Hinchliffe) on 19 December 1994, column *990;* the hon. Member for Sheffield, Brightside (Mr. Blunkett) on 24 October 1994, column *450;* the reply my right hon. Friend the then Minister for Health gave the hon. Member for Lewisham, East (Mrs. Prentice) on 1 March 1994, columns *678–79;* and the reply I gave the hon. Member for Brightside on 6 December 1993, columns *70–71.*

### GP Vacancies

**Mr. Milburn:** To ask the Secretary of State for Health how many general practitioner posts were *(a)* filled and *(b)* vacant in each health region in each year since 1988. [26087]

**Mr. Malone:** The information is not available centrally.

### Private Patients

**Mrs. Beckett:** To ask the Secretary of State for Health how many bed days of finished episodes have been provided for private patients treated in NHS hospitals in total and by regional health authority in each of the last five years. [26289]

**Mr. Sackville:** The information requested is detailed in "Hospital Episode Statistics Volume 1", copies of which are available in the Library.

### Vacant Medical Posts

**Mr. Milburn:** To ask the Secretary of State for Health if she will list the number of *(a)* consultant, *(b)* senior registrar, *(c)* registrar and *(d)* senior house officer posts that were vacant in each region, by speciality, in each year since 1988. [26085]

**Mr. Malone:** The available information has been placed in the Library in crown copyright table R5 of the Department's census of the medical and dental work force. As these relate to a single date each year, they may not fairly reflect the trend for the number of vacancies in the stated grades over the year as a whole.

### Cardiac Services, Plymouth

**Mrs. Beckett:** To ask the Secretary of State for Health what cardiac services are available to patients in the Plymouth area. [26286]

**Mr. Sackville:** This is a matter for the South and West Devon health commission. The right hon. Member may wish to contact Mrs. Judy Leverton, chairman of the health commission, for details.

## ENVIRONMENT

### Local Government Finance

**Mr. Clifton-Brown:** To ask the Secretary of State for the Environment if he will list those local authorities which are considered to be debt free; and what are the Government guidelines on debt to equity ratio for local authorities.

**Mr. Robert B. Jones:** *[pursuant to his reply, 4 April 1995, c. 1049–50]:* the list of local authorities which were debt free as at 30 September 1994 given in that answer was incomplete and should have included Wansdyke. The complete list should therefore read:

Dorset
Bedford
Bracknell
Breckland
Broadland
Chiltern
Christchurch
Corby
Dacorum
Daventry
East Cambridgeshire
East Devon
East Dorset
Epsom and Ewell
Hambleton
Hertsmere

Leominster
Medina
Mid Bedfordshire
Mid Sussex
Newbury
Rochester upon Medway
Ryedale
St. Edmundsbury
South Bucks
South Northampton
South Shropshire
South Wight
Suffolk Coastal
Surrey Heath
Swale
Tonbridge and Malling
Tunbridge Wells
Wansdyke
West Sussex
Barking and Dagenham
City of London

## West Midlands Housing Corporation

**Dr. Lynne Jones:** To ask the Secretary of State for the Environment if he will list the West Midlands housing corporation cash allocations for 1995–96 and each of the previous five years broken down into *(a)* regional cash limit, *(b)* new rent allocations, *(c)* new sale allocations, *(d)* new do-it-yourself sale allocations and *(e)* rehabilitation-renovation with an indication as to the proportion of these allocations that are within (i) the west midlands metropolitan area and (ii) Birmingham. [24593]

**Mr. Robert B. Jones:** The table shows the housing corporation allocations in 1995–96 and each of the previous five years, by the headings requested, for the corporation's west midlands region; and how much of these were allocated to Birmingham and the west midlands metropolitan area, which has been taken to be Coventry, Dudley, Sandwell, Solihull, Walsall and Wolverhampton. The allocations represent housing corporation resources going into new housing association scheme starts whilst the cash limit represents expenditure on new and existing schemes.

### Housing Corporation Allocations 1990–91—1995–96 to West Midlands an Birmingham

| Year | Rent (new build) £ million | Rent (rehab) £ million | Total rent £ million | Percent. of total rent | Sale (new build) £ million | Sale (rehab) £ million | Total sale £ million | Percent. of total sale | DIYSO £ million | Total £ million | Percent. of total £ million | Regional cash limit £ million |
|---|---|---|---|---|---|---|---|---|---|---|---|---|
| **1990–91** | | | | | | | | | | | | |
| Birmingham | 10.45 | 5.19 | 15.64 | 41.2 | 0.31 | 0.00 | 0.31 | 23.5 | 0.00 | 15.95 | 40.6 | — |
| West Midlands Metropolitan Area (excl. Birmingham) | 10.33 | 2.46 | 12.79 | 33.7 | 0.47 | 0.00 | 0.47 | 35.6 | 0.00 | 13.26 | 33.7 | — |
| Rest of West Midlands Region | 8.93 | 0.64 | 9.57 | 25.2 | 0.54 | 0 | 0.54 | 40.9 | 0.00 | 10.11 | 25.7 | — |
| West Midlands (HC Regions) | 29.71 | 8.29 | 38.00 | 100.0 | 1.32 | 0.00 | 1.32 | 100.0 | 0.00 | 39.32 | 100.0 | 101.77 |
| **1991–92** | | | | | | | | | | | | |
| Birmingham | 30.77 | 6.97 | 37.74 | 33.6 | 2.03 | 1.07 | 3.10 | 33.0 | 0.05 | 40.89 | 33.5 | — |
| West Midlands Metropolitan Area (excl. Birmingham) | 26.09 | 4.83 | 30.92 | 27.5 | 1.49 | 0.34 | 1.83 | 19.5 | 0.16 | 32.91 | 27.0 | — |
| Rest of West Midlands Region | 37.6 | 6.08 | 43.679 | 38.9 | 4.47 | 0 | 4.47 | 47.6 | 0.07 | 48.22 | 39.5 | — |
| West Midlands (HC Region) | 94.46 | 17.88 | 112.34 | 100.0 | 7.99 | 1.41 | 9.40 | 100.0 | 0.28 | 122.02 | 100.0 | 140.37 |
| **1992–93** | | | | | | | | | | | | |
| Birmingham | 29.83 | 6.83 | 36.66 | 27.0 | 1.14 | 0.84 | 1.98 | 20.3 | 1.76 | 40.40 | 26.8 | — |
| West Midlands Metropolitan Area (excl. Birmingham) | 32.28 | 11.13 | 43.41 | 32.0 | 3.86 | 0.75 | 4.61 | 47.3 | 1.23 | 49.25 | 32.7 | — |
| Rest of West Midlands Region | 49.25 | 6.32 | 55.57 | 41.0 | 2.77 | 0 | 3.16 | 32.4 | 2.24 | 60.97 | 40.5 | — |
| West Midlands (HC Region) | 111.36 | 24.28 | 135.64 | 100.0 | 7.77 | 1.98 | 9.75 | 100.0 | 5.23 | 150.62 | 100.0 | 154.82 |
| **1993–94** | | | | | | | | | | | | |
| Birmingham | 32.49 | 12.38 | 44.87 | 35.1 | 3.13 | 0.41 | 3.54 | 31.9 | 4.55 | 52.96 | 34.9 | — |
| West Midlands Metropolitan Area (excl. Birmingham) | 34.24 | 4.11 | 38.35 | 30.0 | 3.28 | 0.15 | 3.43 | 30.9 | 3.62 | 45.40 | 29.9 | — |
| Rest of West Midlands Region | 39.03 | 5.47 | 44.5 | 34.8 | 4.13 | 0 | 4.14 | 37.3 | 4.69 | 53.33 | 35.2 | — |
| West Midlands (HC Region) | 105.76 | 21.96 | 127.72 | 100.0 | 10.54 | 0.57 | 11.11 | 100.0 | 12.86 | 151.69 | 100.0 | 162.03 |
| **1994–95** | | | | | | | | | | | | |
| Birmingham | 23.53 | 12.61 | 36.14 | 35.8 | 1.41 | 0.40 | 1.81 | 25.1 | 3.27 | 41.22 | 34.7 | — |
| West Midlands Metropolitan Area (excl. Birmingham) | 21.30 | 7.89 | 29.19 | 28.9 | 1.40 | 0.85 | 2.25 | 31.2 | 3.47 | 34.91 | 29.4 | — |
| Rest of West Midlands Region | 29.37 | 6.33 | 35.7 | 35.3 | 2.37 | 0 | 3.16 | 43.8 | 3.74 | 42.6 | 35.9 | — |
| West Midlands (HC Region) | 74.20 | 26.83 | 101.03 | 100.0 | 5.18 | 2.04 | 7.22 | 100.0 | 10.48 | 118.73 | 100.0 | 134.21 |
| **1995–96** | | | | | | | | | | | | |
| Birmingham | 6.93 | 4.89 | 11.82 | 36.0 | 1.04 | 0.29 | 1.33 | 39.8 | 3.62 | 16.77 | 36.7 | — |
| West Midlands Metropolitan Area (excl. Birmingham) | 5.67 | 3.26 | 8.93 | 27.2 | 0.86 | 0.27 | 1.13 | 33.8 | 2.83 | 12.89 | 28.2 | — |
| Rest of West Midlands Region | 9.25 | 2.83 | 12.08 | 36.8 | 0.68 | 0 | 0.88 | 26.3 | 3.05 | 16.01 | 35.1 | — |
| West Midlands (HC Region) | 21.85 | 10.98 | 32.83 | 100.0 | 2.58 | 0.76 | 3.34 | 100.0 | 9.50 | 45.67 | 100.0 | 103.15 |

## Union Flag

**Mr. David Young:** To ask the Secretary of State for the Environment what guidelines his Department issued to local authorities in respect of the flying of flags on *(a)* VE day and *(b)* VJ day; and to what extent local authorities are free to determine their own policy.

[25328]

**Sir Paul Beresford:** My Department issued no guidelines to local authorities about flying the Union Flag on VE or VJ Day. Local authorities are completely free to determine their own policy in this respect.

## HM Inspectorate of Pollution

**Mr. Battle:** To ask the Secretary of State for the Environment how many scientists employed by Her Majesty's inspectorate of pollution are specialists in air pollution. [25690]

**Mr. Atkins:** Under HMIP's integrated structure, work on air pollution is undertaken by staff working in multi-disciplinary teams where individuals address all aspects of the inspectorate's responsibilities for pollution regulation and control.

**Mr. Battle:** To ask the Secretary of State for the Environment what is the current starting salary for a professional at Her Majesty's inspectorate of pollution now; and what it was in each of the years since 1990. [25686]

**Mr. Atkins:** The information is as follows:

£

| Grade | Location | 1 January 1990 | 1 August 1990 | Salary minimum 1 April 1991 | 1 August 1991 | 1 August 1992 | 1 August 1993 | 1 April 1994 |
|---|---|---|---|---|---|---|---|---|
| Assistant Pollution Inspector | London | — | 18,194 | 18,194 | 19,377 | 20,961 | 21,275 | 21,275 |
| | National | — | 18,194 | 18,194 | 19,377 | 20,152 | 20,454 | 20,454 |
| Pollution Inspector | London | 18,488 | 20,059 | 21,905 | 24,379 | 25,330 | 25,330 | 25,837 |
| | National | 18,488 | 20,059 | 21,905 | 23,329 | 24,239 | 24,239 | 24,724 |

**Mr. Battle:** To ask the Secretary of State for the Environment how many times Her Majesty's inspectorate of pollution has had to re-advertise to fill vacancies in professional posts since 1990. [25689]

**Mr. Atkins:** Since 1990, seven recruitment campaigns have been held to increase the number of inspectors in line with the progressive growth in HMIP's complement over this period.

**Mr. Battle:** To ask the Secretary of State for the Environment how many of the professional posts at Her Majesty's inspectorate of pollution are currently vacant. [25691]

**Mr Atkins:** Three.

**Mr. Battle:** To ask the Secretary of State for the Environment how many people holding professional posts with Her Majesty's inspectorate of pollution have resigned since 1990. [25687]

**Mr. Atkins:** Nine.

### Environment Bill

**Mr. Colvin:** To ask the Secretary of State for the Environment what plans he has, following the House of Lords' decision on 17 November 1994, in support of the Yorkshire Water Company against the National Rivers Authority under section 107 of the Water Act 1989, to bring forward amendments to the Act of the Environment Bill currently before Parliament. [25906]

**Mr. Atkins:** We have no such plans. Our views on this issue were fully set out by my hon. Friend, Viscount Ullswater, during consideration of the Environment Bill in another place.

### Water Pollution

**Mr. Martyn Jones:** To ask the Secretary of State for the Environment (1) how many of the cases of water pollution due to agriculture, recorded in 1994 occurred as a result of (a) pesticides on crops, (b) silage and (c) fertilizers; [25853]

(2) what was the number of recorded cases of water pollution caused by agricultural practice in 1994. [25854]

**Mr. Atkins:** The National Rivers Authority publishes a detailed annual statistical report on water pollution incidents in England and Wales. The report for 1994 will be published this summer. However, on the basis of the information currently available which is still being validated, the NRA estimates that there were 3,329 pollution incidents arising from agriculture in 1994, of which 26 can be attributed to pesticides, 259 to silage and

17 to solid and liquid fertilizers. In addition, eight can be attributed to sheep dip.

**Mr. Colvin:** To ask the Secretary of State for the Environment how many prosecutions there have been in each of the last five years of water companies for illegally breaching consents to discharge treated sewage. [25905]

**Mr. Atkins:** I understand that there have been 58 such prosecutions of water companies since 1989–90. The annual figures are:

1989–90: 4
1991: 17
1992: 17
1993: 11
1994: 9

**Mrs. Helen Jackson:** To ask the Secretary of State for the Environment how many court actions were taken in each of the last three years in total and in each region by the National Rivers Authority; at what gross and net cost to the authority; how many court actions were taken in each of the last three years in total and against each of the water and sewerage companies by the National Rivers Authority; at what gross and net costs; how many of the court actions taken by the National Rivers Authority in each of the last three years in each region resulted in the polluter being prosecuted; and what were the total fines imposed by the National Rivers Authority on (a) polluters and (b) statutory water undertakers in each of the last three years in each region. [25777]

**Mr. Atkins** *[holding answer 23 May 1995]:* The National Rivers Authority publishes an annual statistical report on water pollution incidents in England and Wales. The report for 1994 will be published later this year but the latest estimates for that year are included in the tables. In some cases the information is not available in exactly the form requested. As regards the cost of court actions, the NRA does not keep records of its costs categorised annually for individual regions or water and sewerage companies. The average cost to the NRA of bringing a prosecution—reflecting a wide range of prosecutions—is £660. Costs imposed by the courts can vary widely and can rarely be compared with the actual cost of taking a prosecution.

*Total court actions (in respect of incidents occurring in the relevant calendar year and heard by the end of the relevant financial year)*

| Region | 1992 | 1993 | 1994 |
|---|---|---|---|
| Anglian | 34 | 45 | 45 |
| Northumbria and Yorkshire | 22 | 26 | 13 |

*Total court actions (in respect of incidents occurring in the relevant calendar year and heard by the end of the relevant financial year)*

| Region | 1992 | 1993 | 1994 |
|---|---|---|---|
| North West | 61 | 61 | 49 |
| Severn-Trent | 72 | 56 | 32 |
| Southern | 5 | 5 | 9 |
| South Western | 37 | 26 | 29 |
| Thames | 32 | 31 | 32 |
| Welsh | 34 | 36 | 28 |
| Totals | 297 | 286 | 237 |

*Court actions against water and sewerage companies*

| Company | 1992 | 1993 | 1994 |
|---|---|---|---|
| Southern Water | 4 | 1 | 1 |
| Severn Trent Water | 1 | 4 | 2 |
| South West Water | 2 | — | — |
| Wessex Water | 2 | 4 | 1 |
| Northumbria Water | 3 | — | — |
| Yorkshire Water | 1 | 11 | 1 |
| Anglian Water | 7 | 1 | 2 |
| Thames Water | 5 | 7 | 4 |
| North West Water | 4 | 6 | 13 |
| Welsh Water | 11 | 2 | 1 |
| Total | 40 | 36 | 25 |

*Fines against water and sewerage undertakers*

£

| Company | 1992 | 1993 | 1994 | Total |
|---|---|---|---|---|
| Southern Water | 4,800 | 5,000 | 4,000 | 13,800 |
| Severn Trent Water | 2,000 | 8,750 | 11,000 | 21,750 |
| South West Water | 6,000 | — | — | 6,000 |
| Wessex Water | 4,500 | 6,700 | — | 11,200 |
| Northumbria Water | 6,750 | — | — | 6,750 |
| Yorkshire Water | 6,000 | 101,000 | 5,000 | 112,000 |
| Anglian Water | 30,750 | 4,000 | 2,500 | 37,250 |
| Thames Water | 20,000 | 23,500 | 15,000 | 58,500 |
| North West Water | 34,000 | 33,000 | 56,500 | 123,500 |
| Welsh Water | 39,600 | 9,000 | 20,000 | 68,600 |
| Totals | 154,900 | 190,950 | 114,000 | 459,350 |

*Enforcement*
*Successful prosecutions (all polluters) (in respect of incidents occurring in the relevant calendar year)*

| Region | 1992 | 1993 | 1994 |
|---|---|---|---|
| Anglian | 34 | 42 | 45 |
| Northumbria and Yorkshire | 22 | 24 | 13 |
| North West | 60 | 60 | 46 |
| Severn Trent | 72 | 56 | 31 |
| Southern | 4 | 5 | 5 |
| South Western | 36 | 25 | 27 |
| Thames | 30 | 29 | 28 |
| Welsh | 32 | 36 | 27 |
| Total | 290 | 277 | 222 |

*Total fines (all polluters)*

£

| Region | 1992–93 | 1993–94 |
|---|---|---|
| Northumbria and Yorkshire | 144,150 | 176,100 |
| North West | 167,700 | 256,600 |
| Welsh | 91,775 | 74,050 |
| Severn Trent | 139,550 | 172,440 |

*Total fines (all polluters)*

£

| Region | 1992–93 | 1993–94 |
|---|---|---|
| Anglian | 164,850 | 168,650 |
| Thames | 202,000 | 111,000 |
| Southern | 80,540 | 32,500 |
| South Western | 100,460 | 97,280 |
| Total | 1,091,025 | 1,088,580 |

## Recycling

**Mr. Matthew Taylor:** To ask the Secretary of State for the Environment (1) what action his Department has taken to encourage the use of remanufactured goods;

[26163]

(2) what plans he has to encourage investment and expansion in the remanufactured products industry.

[26164]

**Mr. Atkins:** The draft "Waste Strategy for England and Wales", published for consultation in January 1995, has opened up a wide debate to identify ways in which all of our waste can be managed in a more sustainable way including the promotion of recycling and manufacture using waste materials. Recycling rates reflect market forces including the costs of recyclate against virgin material, consumer preference and the way in which business buying specifications are set out. Several of the Government's policies set out in the strategy will help secure significant increases in recycling rates, and in particular the producer responsibility initiative which gives an incentive to businesses to increase the amount of recyclate which re-enters the productive loop.

## Air Pollution

**Mr. Matthew Taylor:** To ask the Secretary of State for the Environment what assessment he has made of the effects on *(a)* public health, *(b)* asthma sufferers, *(c)* the elderly and *(d)* pregnant women, when ground level ozone reaches 90PPB. [26171]

**Mr. Atkins:** Within Government, the Department of Health takes the lead in assessing the health effects of air pollutants, including advice from its Committee on the Medical Aspects of Air Pollutants. The effects of exposure to ozone depend on the duration of the exposure as well as on the level of the pollutant. The main effects are on the respiratory system and vary considerably from individual to individual. In 1991, the expert advisory group on the medical aspects of air pollution episodes published a report on ozone. A copy is in the Library of the House.

## Nuclear Waste

**Mr. Allen:** To ask the Secretary of State for the Environment whether any landfill sites within the parliamentary constituency of Nottingham, North will be used for the disposal of nuclear waste. [26244]

**Mr. Atkins:** At the present moment, there are no proposals for the disposal of radioactive waste from nuclear sites to Nottingham, North. My Department has no knowledge of any future plans in this regard.

## Members' Interests

**Mr. Nicholas Brown:** To ask the Secretary of State for the Environment what proposals he has to regulate possible conflicts of interest arising when an elected member of a local authority or appointed member of other public bodies acts in a professional capacity for individual employees of the same authority where the employee faces serious disciplinary action.          [26204]

**Mr. Robert B. Jones:** We have no proposals to add to the existing legislation and guidance about members' interests,

## Uniform Business Rate

**Mr. Bayley:** To ask the Secretary of State for the Environment (1) how many appeals against uniform business rate valuations were received from businesses in *(a)* York and *(b)* north Yorkshire following the 1987 revaluation; how long on average these appeals took to resolve; and on what date the last of these appeals was resolved;          [25965]

(2) how many appeals against uniform business rate valuations were received from businesses in *(a)* York and *(b)* north Yorkshire following the 1992 revaluation; how long on average these appeals are taking to resolve; and how many currently are outstanding.          [25966]

**Mr. Curry:** I take it that the hon. Member is referring to the revaluations which took effect on 1 April 1990 and 1 April 1995. A total of 3,677 proposals to alter the 1990 rating list had been received in York and 21,899 in north Yorkshire by 30 April 1995, of which 903 and 4,616 respectively were outstanding at that date. Proposals to alter this list can still be made in some circumstances up to 31 March 1996. One hundred and forty proposals to alter the 1995 rating list had been received in York and 991 in north Yorkshire by 30 April 1995. None have yet been resolved.

**Mr. Bayley:** To ask the Secretary of State for the Environment what percentage of uniform business rate charged in each local authority in England is allocated, according to the uniform business rate distribution formula, to the business ratepayers own authorities.          [25968]

**Mr. Curry:** National non-domestic rates—business rates—are collected by billing authorities during the year and paid into the NNDR pool. Funds from the pool, the "distributable amount" are re-distributed on a population basis to all classes of authority in line with the formula set out in the local government finance report. This includes distribution to police and fire and civil defence authorities which do not all operate within the boundary of a single billing authority.

Billing authorities may make adjustments during the year of the sums contributed to the pool, in line with their collection rates. No adjustments are made in year to the distributed amount.

It is not therefore possible to calculate the final amount of NDR charged by each billing authority until after the end of the relevant financial year.

As the distributable amount is calculated on a population basis for each year and the amount collected in that year is not known until the following year, the information could be obtained only at disproportionate cost in the form requested.

## Toner Cartridges

**Mr. Matthew Taylor:** To ask the Secretary of State for the Environment what percentage of toner cartridges have been recycled or remanufactured in each year for the last five years.          [26164]

**Mr. Atkins:** My Department does not hold this information, but I understand that the United Kingdom Cartridge Recyclers Association, established in March 1993 to promote the use of remanufactured toner cartridges, may be able to supply industry estimates of the current levels of toner cartridges remanufactured.

## North Sea

**Mr. Matthew Taylor:** To ask the Secretary of State for the Environment (1) what research his Department has carried out into the levels of hydrocarbons in the North sea;          [26167]

(2) if he will list the research work sponsored by his Department into the effects of oil-based drilling muds in the North sea;          [26169]

(3) what estimates he has made of *(a)* the average level of hydrocarbons in the North sea and *(b)* the level of hydrocarbons in the 8 km radius of oil drilling platforms;          [26168]

(4) what assessment his Department has made of contamination around oil drilling platforms in the North sea;          [26166]

(5) what assessment his Department has made of the effects of oil-based drilling muds on the North sea.          [26170]

**Mr. Atkins:** Marine laboratories of the fisheries departments carry out research into this area and relevant data are compiled by the Oslo and Paris Commission from information provided by all North sea states involved in offshore activities. This information was reported in the 1993 "North Sea Quality Status" report and its associated sub-regional reports, copies of which are in the House Library.

In the North sea as a whole, oil concentrations in water are generally low. These reports state that levels of oil may be higher close to production platforms than elsewhere in the North sea. Such concentrations influence the sea floor community in the immediate vicinity and some effects may persist up to several kilometres from the drilling site.

## Going for Green Initiative

**Mr. Dafis:** To ask the Secretary of State for the Environment what have been the results so far of the going for green initiative.          [24725]

**Sir Paul Beresford:** On 6 February 1995, the going for green national committee launched its campaign to catalyse people's interest in the environment, inform their understanding of the consequences of the choices they make as consumers, and endorse actions to improve their environment, whether through managing resources better, reducing pollution or cultivating the local environment. Going for green is currently preparing a business plan which includes a strategy for a national campaign, the sustainable communities pilot project and the further development of the eco-schools programme.

### Tinsley, Sheffield

**Mr. Betts:** To ask the Secretary of State for the Environment (1) if he will make available to the National Audit Office, all agreements relating to the building of an airport at Tinsley, Sheffield.          [25868]

(2) if he will make available to the National Audit Office all agreements relating to opencasting at Tinsley, Sheffield.          [25869]

**Sir Paul Beresford:** No request has been received from the NAO for information relating to the building of an airport or the opencasting at Tinsley, Sheffield.

**Mr. Clive Betts:** To ask the Secretary of State for the Environment (1) if he will place in the Library all agreements relating to the operating at Tinsley, Sheffield;          [25870]

(2) if he will place in the Library all the agreements relating to the building of an airport at Tinsley, Sheffield;          [25871]

(3) if he will place in the Library such information held by Sheffield development corporation in respect of opencasting at Tinsley, Sheffield as would have been publicly available if the opencasting had been the responsibility of a local authority;          [25872]

(4) if he will place in the Library information in respect of Tinsley airport such as would have been publicly available had the development been the responsibility of a local authority.          [25873]

**Sir Paul Beresford:** Documentation relating to the planning decisions for the open casting and the building of an airport at Tinsley is available for inspection at the offices of Sheffield city council and Sheffield development corporation.

Documentation relating to the development, rather than the planning decisions, at Tinsley is commercially confidential and is not publically available.

**Mr. Clive Betts:** To ask the Secretary of State for the Environment if he will undertake an investigation to determine if the land at Tinsley, Sheffield being prepared for building an airport runway has been properly compacted following opencasting.          [25874]

**Sir Paul Beresford:** It is for Sheffield development corporation as landowner and local planning authority to be satisfied that the land at Tinsley has been properly compacted in accordance with the planning conditions.

**Mr. Betts:** To ask the Secretary of State for the Environment which body currently has responsibility for defects resulting from compaction work on the opencast site at Tinsley, Sheffield.          [25875]

**Sir Paul Beresford:** British Coal retains responsibility to deal with defects resulting from the compaction of the site.

### Allerton Outreach Team

**Mr. Madden:** To ask the Secretary of State for the Environment what further funding to support two staff and running costs of the Allerton Outreach team in Bradford has been secured; and if he will make a statement.          [25981]

**Sir Paul Beresford:** I refer the hon. Member to the reply given today by my hon. Friend the Minister of State for Employment.

### Lister Mills

**Mr. Madden:** To ask the Secretary of State for the Environment how much public money, including the cost of official time, he estimates has been spent to date on the re-development of Lister mills in Bradford, with particular reference to the establishment of a northern branch of the Victoria and Albert museum.          [26136]

**Sir Paul Beresford:** My Department contributed £18,500 towards a feasibility study funded jointly with Bradford metropolitan district council and Listers plc in 1989. Information on the cost of the official time spent by public organisations on the wide range of proposals under consideration since 1988 is not recorded.

**Mr. Madden:** To ask the Secretary of State for the Environment what indication he has given formally or informally to Millview Developments, owners of Lister Mills in Bradford, that public financial support from his Department will be available to pay for redevelopment at the mills; and if he will make a statement.          [26367]

**Sir Paul Beresford:** My Department has given no formal or informal indication to Millview Developments that public financial support will be available to pay for development at Lister Mills, Bradford.

### Drinking Water

**Mrs. Helen Jackson:** To ask the Secretary of State for the Environment what are the limits of chlorine and chlorinated substances imposed by the current European Council drinking water regulations.          [26394]

**Mr. Atkins:** The EC drinking water directive—80/778/EEC—does not include a maximum admissible concentration for chlorine. Persistent organochlorine insecticides, polychlorinated biphenyls and polychlorinated terphenyls are included within the pesticides and related products parameter and maximum admissible concentrations of 0.1 and 0.5 microgram per litre apply for individual and total substances respectively. There are no maximum admissible concentrations for other organochlorine compounds although there is a comment that haloform—trihalomethanes—concentrations must be as low as possible.

The Water Supply (Water Quality) Regulations 1989 set standards of 100 microgram per litre for total trihalomethanes and 3, 30 and 10 microgram per litre for the chlorinated solvents tetrachloromethane, trichloroethene and tetrachloroethane respectively in addition to those required by the EC directive.

### Dry Stone Walls

**Mr. Gordon Prentice:** To ask the Secretary of State for the Environment what is the cost of rebuilding a derelict dry stone wall for any length for which figures are available.          [26450]

**Mr. Atkins:** My Department has not carried out specific research into the costs of rebuilding dry stone walls. The costs in particular cases are likely to be subject to considerable variation depending on a number of factors including a wall's design, height and width, the extent of dereliction, the availability of stone and the nature of the terrain.

**Mr. Gordon Prentice:** To ask the Secretary of State for the Environment what steps he is taking, following the Countryside Commission's national survey of the condition of dry stone walls, to ensure that walls which have major signs of advancing or potential deterioration or are in early stages of dereliction are rebuilt or otherwise repaired. [26436]

**Mr. Atkins:** The Government already offer payments for the repair and restoration of stone walls in landscapes eligible for support under the countryside stewardship scheme, the farm and conservation grant scheme and in environmentally sensitive areas. Proposals for the integration and focus of environmental land management schemes in England were published on 18 May by my right hon. Friends the Secretary of State and the Minister of Agriculture, Fisheries and Food. Copies of the consultation document have been placed in the Library of the House.

### Fire Authorities

**Mr. Sheerman:** To ask the Secretary of State for the Environment what plans he has to extend the discretionary powers of fire authorities in county council offices to metropolitan fire authorities under section 137 of the Local Government Act 1972. [26313]

**Mr. Robert B. Jones:** There are no plans to extend the provisions of section 137 of the Local Government Act 1972 to apply to metropolitan fire authorities.

### Leaseholders

**Mr. Denham:** To ask the Secretary of State for the Environment when he will publish his proposals to assist local authority leaseholders to sell their flats. [26525]

**Mr. Robert B. Jones:** We plan to announce a package of measures in the next few weeks.

### Revenue Support Grant

**Mr. Gordon Prentice:** To ask the Secretary of State for the Environment what is the level of revenue support grant per head in *(a)* Pendle, *(b)* Ribble valley, *(c)* the City of Westminster, *(d)* Wandsworth and *(e)* the City of London for 1994–95 and 1995–96. [26565]

**Mr. Curry:** The revenue support grant per head of these authorities is shown in the first row of figures in each of the tables. The tables also show the revenue support grant per head of the other types of authority which serve these areas, since the division of responsibilities for services between types of authorities is different in Lancashire, inner London and the City of London. In particular, in Pendle and Ribble valley, Lancashire county council provides major services which, in London, are provided by the borough and city authorities.

*1994–95 revenue support grant*

| | | | | | £ per head of population |
|---|---|---|---|---|---|
| | Pendle | Ribble Valley | Westminster | Wandsworth | City of London |
| District, etc | 43 | 19 | 760 | 507 | 13,105 |
| County council | 308 | 308 | — | — | — |
| Police authority | — | — | 38 | 38 | — |
| Fire authority | — | — | 22 | 22 | 22 |

*1995–96 revenue support grant*

| | | | | | £ per head of population |
|---|---|---|---|---|---|
| | Pendle | Ribble Valley | Westminster | Wandsworth | City of London |
| District, etc. | 40 | 15 | 804 | 501 | 12,166 |
| County council | 282 | 282 | — | — | — |
| Police authority | 23 | 23 | 61 | 61 | — |
| Fire authority | — | — | 22 | 22 | 22 |

### North Sea Conference

**Mrs. Helen Jackson:** To ask the Secretary of State for the Environment what policy on toxic discharges into the North sea Her Majesty's Government will advance at the fourth North sea Ministers Conference in Esbjerg; and if he will make a statement. [26395]

**Mr. Atkins:** The Secretary of State announced on 16 May, columns *183–84* the United Kingdom's priorities for the North sea conference including that relating to toxic discharges. A note on our objectives was placed in the Library of the House.

### Housing (Elderly and Disabled People)

**Mr. Sheerman:** To ask the Secretary of State for the Environment how many specialist housing schemes and associations providing care and support for vulnerable residents and those at risk there are in the United Kingdom. [26539]

**Mr. Robert B. Jones:** Research published last year by the Department[1] found that there were a total of 14,206 units of very sheltered accommodation for elderly and disabled people provided in England by local authorities, registered housing associations, Abbeyfield societies and almshouses in 1990.

There were a further 52,679 supported units provided for non-elderly vulnerable residents in England through the Housing Corporation in 1994–95. The Housing Corporation supported a total of 317 housing associations providing care and support to their tenants.

[1]Living Independently—A study of the Housing Needs of elderly and disabled people, HMSO 1994.

### Nuclear Waste

**Mr. Ashton:** To ask the Secretary of State for the Environment if he will give undertaking that no nuclear industry waste will be disposed of inside the boundary of the Bassetlaw constituency or the boundary of the Bassetlaw district council in north Nottinghamshire.

**Mr. Atkins:** There are no sites in the Bassetlaw constituency or the boundary of Bassetlaw district council which are authorised by Her Majesty's inspectorate of pollution for the disposal of waste from nuclear licensed sites. The Government's overall policy in this area will be set out this summer when the conclusions to its review of radioactive waste management are published.

## Nitrate Consultation

**Mr. Stephen:** To ask the Secretary of State for the Environment what progress has been made on the Government's response to last year's consultation on proposed nitrate vulnerable zones under the EC nitrate directive; and if he will make a statement.    [26621]

**Mr. Atkins:** My right hon. Friends the Minister of Agriculture, Fisheries and Food, the Secretary of State for Wales and I issued today our response to last year's consultation. As with the original consultation document, the response document is being sent to farmers in parishes and communities containing a proposed nitrate vulnerable zone, and to other interested groups.

A major purpose of the consultation was to confirm the accuracy of the proposed zones, using farmers' local knowledge, before their formal designation. Over 500 sets of written comments were received, in the main from farmers in the proposed zones, and in each case an individual response has been sent out. In addition many points have been addressed directly at a local level by the National Rivers Authority and the Agricultural Development and Advisory Service.

The response document indicates how the Government propose to proceed with designations in the light of comments received. In all, the proposed boundaries for 31 of the 72 zones have been altered and it is proposed that two small groundwater zones should be deferred for further consideration. Maps of the revised zones are available free from MAFF regional services centres and WOAD divisional offices.

As foreshadowed in last year's consultation document, we have set up an independent review panel, chaired by Mr. Terence Etherton QC and assisted by Dr. Richard Downing and Mr. Alastair Allcock. The panel will assess whether the Government's published methodology has been correctly and consistently applied in drawing up the boundaries in those cases where consultees are dissatisfied with the amended boundaries as set out in the response document. In addition, because of the uniqueness of the proposed surface water zone at Nayland, we have asked the independent review panel to consider the case for and against its designation.

I am placing copies of the response document in the Library.

## Environment Agency

**Mr. Jacques Arnold:** To ask the Secretary of State for the Environment what steps are being taken to appoint senior directors of the proposed environment agency.
    [26620]

**Mr. Atkins:** I have informed the environment agency advisory committee that it may commence the recruitment of senior directors of the proposed environment agency. Approval has already been given for the recruitment of the chief executive, as announced in my reply of 21 April to my hon. Friend the Member for Wyre Forest (Mr. Coombs), columns *288–89*.

Parliamentary approval to this new service will be sought in a summer supplementary estimate for the Department of the Environment's environmental protection and water vote, class VII, vote 3. Pending that approval, urgent expenditure estimated at £135,000 will be met by repayable advances from the contingencies fund.

This expenditure is required to meet the cost of recruiting up to six directors. Its urgency reflects the need to have directors in place as soon as possible after Royal Assent, so that they can support the chief executive in planning for the agency to take over its functions from predecessor bodies on 1 April 1996. The successful candidates will not be formally appointed as directors until after the Bill has received Royal Assent.

## Packaging

**Mr. Dicks:** To ask the Secretary of State for the Environment if he will make a statement on his proposals for producer responsibility for packaging.    [26622]

**Mr. Gummer:** When my right hon. Friend the President of the Board of Trade and I launched the producer responsibility challenge on 17 July 1993, we took the view that only industry could provide the leadership and know-how necessary to achieve a successful UK initiative on recycling and recovery of packaging waste. Nearly two years later, that industry-led approach has enabled us to meet many of our key objectives. The producer responsibility group of leading businesses involved in packaging has achieved widespread industry support for its plan to secure the recovery and recycling of 58 per cent. of United Kingdom packaging waste and create close to home recycling facilities for eight out of 10 households by the year 2000. After extensive negotiation, in which the UK played a leading part, the European Community has adopted a packaging and packaging waste directive which we now need to implement.

A major challenge remains. In its first report, the producer responsibility group made it very clear that the initiative could not be successful without legislative underpinning to deter "free riders". Enabling powers to provide that legislative underpinning are included in the Environment Bill, now being considered by Parliament. But we need to specify precisely who in business will be subject to a legal obligation and what action is required to satisfy it. Such an obligation must be simple and clear if it is to be effective and enforceable—in industry's interests as much as Government's. It must also be consistent with wider Government policies, for example on ensuring competition and minimising burdens on business.

The Government are today publishing, "Producer Responsibility for Packaging Waste—a Consultation Paper", which sets out a variety of options on how such a legal obligation might work and includes a compliance cost assessment. Copies are being placed in the Library. These options have been the subject of lengthy and detailed deliberation by different industry groups in the light of the legislative tests set out in the answer given by my hon. Friend the Minster of State to my hon. Friend the Member for Plymouth, Sutton (Mr. Streeter) on 2 February, *Official Report,* columns *763–64*.

Several of the options have been put forward by the VALPAK—working representative advisory group—V—WRAG—the industry body which has succeeded PRG and which will continue to be a focus for discussions. Alternative approaches may emerge in consultation but they will need to demonstrate that they have been widely publicised in industry and tested against the same criteria as the options in this paper. The Government will need to make a decision to adopt a proposal based on one of these approaches and are keen to have the views of all sectors of industry and commerce, and others who will be involved in achieving our aims, including local authorities and consumers.

What is most needed now is further work by the proponents of different approaches to help build a consensus behind the best option. The Government would prefer to proceed on the basis of a board consensus on an approach which best meetws the test we have published. We invite all those involved in the production, distribution and use of packaging to meet this challenge.

## Housing

**Mr. Hinchcliffe:** To ask the Secretary of State for the Environment what is his estimate of the number of housing association homes for rent which could have been constructed at funding levels announced in the 1992 autumn statement.                                [25396]

**Mr. Robert B. Jones** *[holding answer 24 May 1995]:* Such estimates depend on the assumptions made. But if allocations and unit costs had been on the same basis as for the current programme, the Housing Corporation estimates that the 1995–96 approved development programme would have provided some 35,900 new build homes for rent if funding levels in the 1992 autumn statement had been maintained.

# INDEX TO THE

# PARLIAMENTARY DEBATES

## OFFICIAL REPORT

**SIXTH SERIES**

SESSION 1994–95

**VOLUME 260**

*15th May—31st May 1995*

## SCOPE OF THE INDEX, ARRANGEMENT AND ABBREVIATIONS

This index is derived from the House of Commons Library's Parliamentary On-Line Information System (POLIS), and the subject terms used are based on those used in POLIS. There are often changes in column numbering, etc., between the daily part or weekly Hansard (which simply collects together the daily parts without revision) and the bound volume. The index for the bound volume is revised to take account of these changes and cannot therefore, be used in connection with the daily part or weekly Hansard. For these versions use the Fortnightly Index.

### Scope and arrangement of the Index

Oral and Written Parliamentary Questions are indexed under subject headings and the names of Members asking and Ministers replying to them. Questions are not listed under the names of Departments replying. Departmental listings can be arrived at indirectly by looking under the names of the Minister(s) of that Department. There are, however, the headings 'Northern Ireland', 'Scotland', and 'Wales' under which one can find not only most Questions answered by the Northern Ireland Office, Scottish Office, Welsh Office but also Questions about these areas of the United Kingdom which are answered by other Departments. Ministerial statements are indexed under subject headings, under 'Ministerial statements' and the names of Ministers making them and Members speaking on them. General debates are indexed under broad subject headings and under the names of all Members and Ministers taking part. Debates on legislation (Bills, Orders, Regulations etc.) are indexed under the name of the Bill, Statutory Instruments etc, under subject headings and under the names of those taking part.

Rulings and Statements by Speaker and deputies are brought together under the heading 'Speaker's rulings and statements'.

Other contributions by Speaker and deputies appear under the heading Speaker.

Opposition Day Debates and Estimates Day Debates and Standing Order No. 10 applications are listed under those respective headings and under subject headings too.

The date of each item except Parliamentary Questions is inserted immediately before the reference.

Members' names are given in the form by which they prefer to be known and are printed in bold italics. Under their names, entries are arranged under one of the two headings *Debates, etc.* (to include interventions on statements, points of order and so on) or *Questions.*

### Abbreviations

*Bills* 1R = first reading, 2R = second reading, Money res = money resolution, Comm = Committee stage, Rep = Report stage, 3R = third reading, amendt/amendts = amendment/amendments, * = matter taken formally, without debate.

Column numbers followed by the letter W refer to Written Questions. These appear at the end of each daily part or volume with their own sequence of column numbers printed in italics.

**Ballot papers**
Braille 367w, 473w
Scotland 473w

**Bananas**
EC action 283–4w

**Banbridge**
Tourism 929–30

**Bangladesh**
Grameen Bank 511w
Health aid 511w

**Bank of England**
510w
Disclosure of information 591w
Investment in financial assets 58w

**Banks**
Tax allowances 505w

*Banks, Mr Matthew*
*Debates etc.*
Gas Bill, Rep (15.05.95) 31–2
*Questions*
Central Statistical Office, Performance
standards 237–8w
Government securities 711w
International Monetary Fund 62–3w
Procurement 467–8w
Public expenditure, Departmental
publications 504w

*Banks, Mr Robert*
*Debates etc.*
Gas Bill, Rep and 3R (16.05.95) 198–200
*Questions*
Non-domestic rates 179w

*Banks, Mr Tony*
*Debates etc.*
House purchase (17.05.95) 249, 254–6,
264
Oral question time intervention (15.05.95)
15
*Questions*
Business questions 476, 942
Diplomatic service, Women 81w
Drugs and crime 362w
House renovation grants 331
Industrial disablement benefits, Newham
327–8w
Judiciary, Codes of practice 18–20
Motor vehicles, Greater London 583
National Lottery 8–9
Official gifts 6w, 532w
Stratford School 694
Thatcher, RtHonBaroness 707–8

**Barbouti, Ishan**
British national (overseas) 16w

**Barlow Clowes**
Prosecutions 520w

*Barnes, Mr Harry*
*Debates etc.*
Committee on Standards in Public Life
(18.05.95) 559
Competition (22.05.95) 609
*Questions*
Business questions 478, 946
Church of England, Pension funds 12–3
Public transport, Mobility of disabled
400w
Terrorism, Northern Ireland 747w

**Barnet**
Primary health care 410w

**Barnet Hospital**
98w

*Barron, Mr Kevin*
*Questions*
Excise duties 60w
Fertility, Medical treatments 164w
Hydrocarbon oil duties 60–1w
National vocational qualifications, Dept of
Transport 2–3w
National vocational qualifications, Home
Office 20w
Tobacco, Prices 106w
Tobacco advertising 407w
Tobacco duties 58–61w, 105–6w

**Bassetlaw**
Radioactive waste disposal 788w

*Batiste, Mr Spencer*
*Debates etc.*
Conditional fee agreements orders
(15.05.95) 111, 114–5
*Questions*
Mineral resources, Planning permission
617w
Opencast mining 316
Prison staff, Medals 457

*Battle, Mr John*
*Questions*
Epilepsy, Prescription drugs 282w
Epilepsy, Scotland 89–90w
HM Inspectorate of Pollution 778–80w
Horticulture, Curriculum 615–6w
Science and technology research, EC
grants and loans 299w
Science budget 452w
Supermarkets, Planning permission 327–8

*Bayley, Mr Hugh*
*Debates etc.*
ABB Transportation (24.05.95) 877–81,
884
Railway travel (17.05.95) 356, 372–4,
385–6
*Questions*
NHS finance 408–9w
Overseas aid, Railway transport 623w
Railway network, Kent 405w
Residential care, Elderly 769w, 771w
Uniform business rate 783w
Uniform business rate, York 783w

**BBC**
Local radio 647–8w

**Beaches**
Sea pollution 252–3w

**Bear Island**
Fishing quotas 507w

**Beattie, George**
Convictions 633–4w

**Beckett, Margaret**
House of Commons questions 95w

*Beckett, Rt Hon Margaret*
*Questions*
Accident and emergency departments,
Hospital beds 99–100w
Accident and emergency departments,
Vacancies 596w
Acute beds, Per capita costs 595–6w
Community health services 515w
Computers in National Health Service
343w
Dental services 763w
Dept of Health, Official hospitality 599w
Dept of Health, Research 98–9w
Family doctors, Insurance 345w
Family doctors, Working hours 98w
GP fundholders 141, 596–7w, 765w
Health service staff, Company cars 775w
Health service staff, Pay 599–600w
Health services, Greater London 599w
Heart diseases, Plymouth 776w
Hospital admissions, Emergencies 342w
Hospital closures 100w, 136, 279w, 765w
Hospital closures, Greater London 597w
Hospital doctors, Recruitment 341–2w
Hospital patients 598–9w
Hospital waiting lists 601–2w
Hospitals 173–6w, 279–80w, 597w
Johnstone, Chris, Compensation 602w
Kidney patients 601w
Manchester Royal Infirmary, Kidney
patients 601w
NHS, Royal commissions 99w
NHS charges 336w
Nurses, Tribunals 345w
Organ donors 597–8w
Patients' transport 599w
Primates, Health hazards 345w
Private patients 776w
Royal London Hospital 602w
St Bartholomew's Hospital, Out-patients
601w

*Beckett, Rt Hon Margaret—continued*
South Thames Regional Health Authority,
Telephone systems 343–4w
Surgery, Hospital waiting lists 94w, 600w
Tobacco advertising 599w
Trauma centres 772w
University College Hospital 771w
Westminster and Chelsea Hospital,
Hospital wards 94w

**Beer**
199w

*Beggs, Mr Roy*
*Questions*
Commonwealth Games 148w
Council for Catholic Maintained Schools
447w
Fish farming, Northern Ireland 31w
Local education authorities, Local
government reform 240w
Northern Ireland education and library
boards 448w
School population, Northern Ireland 448w
School population, Wales 458w
Youth services, Northern Ireland 353w

*Beith, Rt Hon A J*
*Questions*
Business questions 940–1
Fire regulations 707w
Fire Safety Enforcement Agencies Review
643w
Official report 237w
Prison employment 457–8

**Belfast Harbour Commissioners**
Land ownership and tenure 444w

**Belgium**
Passports 311w

*Bell, Mr Stuart*
*Debates etc.*
Coal Industry (Restructuring Grants) Order
(25.05.95) 950–4

**Belling**
Pension funds (24.05.95) 847–8

*Bellingham, Mr Henry*
*Questions*
Northern Ireland government 923

**Belvidere Hospital Glasgow**
734–5w, 901–2

**Belvoir Park Hospital**
Infectious diseases 754–5w

*Bendall, Mr Vivian*
*Questions*
Taxis, Smoking 674w
Taxis, Social security abuse 726–7w

**Benefits Agency**
see Social Security Benefits Agency

*Benn, Rt Hon Tony*
*Debates etc.*
Bosnia-Herzegovina, Armed forces
deployment (31.05.95) 1001, 1019–22,
1096
Committee on Standards in Public Life
(18.05.95) 485, 532–4, 569
Members' conduct, Points of order
(17.05.95) 336
Wilson of Rievaulx, RtHonLord, Death
(24.05.95) 911–3

*Bennett, Mr Andrew F*
*Questions*
Arms trade, Argentina 676w
Ecolabelling 250w

**Bentley, Derek**
363–4w, 483w, 654w

*Beresford, Sir Paul, Parliamentary
Under-Secretary of State, Dept of the
Environment*
*Questions*
Airports, EC grants and loans 522w
Allerton Outreach Team 785w
Annual reports, Dept of the Environment
45w

**Government assistance to industry**
Northern Ireland 924

**Government buildings**
Ministry of Defence 660w
Scottish Office 730w
Welsh Office 460–2w

**Government Chemist**
Performance standards 642w

**Government contracts**
Capita 35w
Northern Ireland Office 35w

**Government departments**
Energy conservation 260–2w
Inquiries 716–20w
Performance standards 242w

**Government grants to local authorities**
Closed circuit television 176w
Community care 411w

**Government grants to voluntary organisations**
Scotland 634w

**Government information services**
Internet 243w

**Government Office for London**
250w

**Government securities**
711w

**Government shareholding**
Attorney General 451w
Chancellor of the Duchy of Lancaster 452w
Dept for Education 418w
Dept of Employment 566w
Dept of Health 411w
Dept of National Heritage 725w
Dept of Social Security 431w
Dept of the Environment 388w
Dept of Trade and Industry 646w
Dept of Transport 568–9w
Home Office 487w
Lord Chancellor's Dept 399w
Ministry of Agriculture Fisheries and Food 690w
Northern Ireland Office 534w
Prime Minister 510w
Treasury 464w
Welsh Office 462w

**GP fundholders**
140–2, 409w, 596–7w, 765w
Community health services 595–7w
North East region 93w
Wales 460w

**Graduates**
Unemployment 565–6w

**Grafton Recruitment**
534w

***Graham, Mr Thomas***
*Debates etc.*
Nuclear power (17.05.95) 410

**Grameen Bank**
Bangladesh 511w

**Grammar schools**
537w

**Grampian**
Skillseekers' scheme 893

***Grant, Mr Bernie***
*Questions*
Metropolitan Police, Race relations 191w
Police equipment, Death 194w
Police training, Inspections 192w
Police training, Race relations 191–3w

**Grant maintained schools**
8w, 137–8w, 701
East Sussex 693–4
Kent 537–8w
Lancashire 698
North West region 697–8, 702
Special education 539w

**Greater Glasgow Health Board**
Acute beds 480–1w

***Greater Glasgow Health Board—continued***
Long stay patients 898

**Greater London**
Accident and emergency departments 134–5
Air pollution monitoring 258w
Bus services 580–2
Community health services 516–7w
Dermatology 161w
Film industry 272w
Health services 165w, 599w
Hospital closures 144–5, 597w
Hospitals 133
Motor vehicles 583–4
Nursery schools 537w
Primary health care 133, 597w
Railway stations 400w
Road works 3w
Theatres 271w
Travel cards 2w

**Greater Manchester Fire Authority**
365w

**Greenbelt**
Sheffield 253w

***Greenway, Mr Harry***
*Debates etc.*
Oral questions, Points of order (17.05.95) 333
*Questions*
Agricultural land, Scotland 893–4
Bus services, Greater London 580–1
Business questions 476, 946
Church of England, Pension funds 40w
Committee on Standards in Public Life 377–8w
Cost per pupil, Ealing 14w, 308–9w
Deregulation Ministerial Committee 378w
Elstree Studios 5
Exhaust emission controls 402w
Family practitioner services, Ealing 165–6w
Health service staff 169w
Horses, Crime prevention 702w
Land pollution, Local government finance 530–1w
Minimum wage 467–8
Minimum wage, EC countries 563w
National Lottery, Ealing 648w
Official engagements 123–4w, 509w, 681w
Overseas aid, Employment opportunities 397w
Physical education 65w
Police civilians, Police stations 363w
Recreation spaces, Urban areas 249w, 332
Teacher training 538w
Teaching methods, Northern Ireland 925–6

***Greenway, Mr John***
*Debates etc.*
Evidence, Ministerial statements (16.05.95) 170–1

***Griffiths, Mr Nigel***
*Debates etc.*
Gas Bill, Rep (15.05.95) 39–44, 50–2, 77–9, 91–4, 97–8
Gas Bill, Rep and 3R (16.05.95) 180–1, 183–5, 190–1, 211–3
*Questions*
Bus fares 399w
Committee on Standards in Public Life 145
Council housing, Housing improvement 252w
Fire resistant materials, Motor vehicle parts 155w
Fires, Cars 369w
Fireworks, Children 28w
Metro Goldwyn Mayer, Rank Organisation 28–9w
Monopolies and Mergers Commission, Evidence 155–6w
Office of Fair Trading, Public appointments 155w
Pergau dam 420w

***Griffiths, Mr Peter***
*Questions*
Smoking, Scottish Office 335w

***Griffiths, Mr Peter—continued***
Smoking, Treasury 58w
Smoking, Welsh Office 130–1w

***Griffiths, Mr Win***
*Questions*
Child care 97w
Child care, Wales 101w
Exhaust emission controls 402w
NHS, Statistics 143
Radioactive waste disposal, Tipping of waste 555w
Radioactive waste disposal, Wales 555–6w
Schools, Inspections 555w
Taxpayers 148
Welsh language, Public utilities 556w
Welsh Office, Empty property 101w
Welsh Office, Government buildings 460–2w

***Grocott, Mr Bruce***
*Debates etc.*
Railway travel (17.05.95) 354

***Grylls, Sir Michael***
*Debates etc.*
Railway travel (17.05.95) 363

**Gulf War syndrome**
391w, 625w

***Gummer, Rt Hon John, Secretary of State for the Environment***
*Questions*
Building industry, Contracts 254w
City pride 250–1w, 323–5
Council tax capping 252w
Environment protection 41w
Government Office for London 250w
International Conference on the Protection of the North Sea 183–4w, 318–9, 331
Packaging industry, Recycling 790–1w
Radioactive Waste Management Advisory Committee, Public appointments 389w
Supermarkets, Planning permission 327–8
Water charges 328–9
Water meters 329–30
Wind power 327

***Gunnell, Mr John***
*Debates etc.*
Committee on Standards in Public Life (18.05.95) 551–2
Criminal Injuries Compensation Bill, 2R (23.05.95) 795–7
*Questions*
GP fundholders 140–1
Rolling stock 582

**Habitual residence test**
Glasgow 557w
Income support 557w

**Hackney**
Urban planning 250w

**Haemophilia**
Hepatitis (24.05.95) 834–6

***Hague, Mr William, Minister of State, Dept of Social Security***
*Questions*
Access Committee for England, Government grants 431w
Cellular phones, Dept of Social Security 70–2w
Civil service manpower, Dept of Social Security 608–10w
Civil service redundancies, Dept of Social Security 609w
Consultants, Dept of Social Security 698–9w
Early retirement, Dept of Social Security 695–8w
Government shareholding, Dept of Social Security 431w
Handicapped, Social security benefits 329–30w
Incapacity benefit, Social security abuse 330w
Incapacity benefit, Wales 328w
Industrial disablement benefits, Newham 327–8w

**Northern Ireland Industrial Development Board**
see Industrial Development Board for Northern Ireland

**Northern Ireland Office**
Archives 33–4w
Cellular phones 34–5w
Civil service redundancies 632w
Early retirement 753–4w
Government contracts 35w
Government shareholding 534w
Non-departmental public bodies 35–8w

**Northern Ireland Railways**
355w
Private investment 445w

**Northern Ireland Rate Collection Agency**
Performance standards 357w

**Norway**
Political refugees 359–60w

**Norwich**
Redundancy 428–9w

**Nottinghamshire**
Radioactive waste disposal 782w

**Nuclear accidents**
Chernobyl 207w
Emergency planning 501–2w

**Nuclear Electric**
Finance 234w

**Nuclear Non Proliferation Treaty**
80w, 311w, 380w, 666–7w
Ministerial statements (16.05.95) 151–61

**Nuclear power**
680–1w
Departmental responsibilities 252w
EC grants and loans 153w
Opposition days (17.05.95) 394–444
Privatisation 154–5w, (17.05.95) 394–444

**Nuclear power stations**
425w
Decommissioning 426w
Fossil fuel levy 153w

**Nuclear review**
153–5w
Air pollution control 257w

**Nuclear safety**
532–3w
Plutonium 300w, 391w
Treaties 30w

**Nuclear submarines**
Dockyards 229w, 395–6w, 658w

**Nuclear test ban**
660w

**Nuclear weapons**
111–2w
Iran 380–1w
Military alliances 304w

**Nuclear weapons tests**
China 380w
Exservicemen 662w

**Nursery schools**
408w, 415w, 537w, 692
Brixton 274w
Greater London 537w
Hampshire 537w

**Nurses**
742w
Pay 162w, 216w, 574–5w
Scotland 216w, 574–5w, 891
Training 337w
Tribunals 345w
Wales 457–8w

**Nursing homes**
Lanarkshire 576w, 741w
Tax collection 504w

**O'Brien, Mr Mike**
*Debates etc.*
Competition (22.05.95) 610
Criminal Injuries Compensation Bill, 2R (23.05.95) 736–7, 768, 780–4, 804

**O'Brien, Mr Mike**—*continued*
Educational finance, Warwickshire (18.05.95) 571–5, 578
Evidence, Ministerial statements (16.05.95) 170
*Questions*
Anglo-German Deregulation Group 235–7w
Asthma, Children 341w
Business questions 945–6
Cocaine, Police cautions 368w
Crack, Police cautions 490–1w
Criminal Justice and Public Order Act 1994, Police training 550–1w
Dept of Trade and Industry, Non-governmental organisations 300w
Hill, Nicholas, Parole 370w
Hospitals, Warwickshire 760w
Industrial diseases benefits, Social security claims 606–7w
Legal aid 4w
"Management Matters" 313–4w
Meningitis, Vaccination 339–40w
MI5, Drug crimes 190–1w
Northern Birmingham Mental Health NHS Trust 517w
Prisoners, Northern Ireland 930
Tuberculosis 340w
Vaccination 406–7w
Vaccination, Children 592w
Young offenders, Custodial treatment 294–5w
Young offenders, Prison population 370w

**O'Brien, Mr William**
*Questions*
Building industry 249w
Educational finance 697
House renovation grants 332
Legal aid 16
Motorways, Road construction 2w
Tourism 12, 64w
Waste disposal, Northern Ireland 747w

**Occupational therapists**
Northern Ireland health and social services trusts 444–5w

**OECD countries**
Income tax 238–9w

**Office of Fair Trading**
Birds Eye 645–6w
Bus services 645w
Public appointments 155w

**Office of Gas Supply**
Disclosure of information 418–9w

**Office of Parliamentary Counsel**
see Parliamentary Counsel

**Offices**
Northern Ireland Housing Executive 269–70w
Public service 435–41w

**Official engagements**
123–4w, 305w, 509w, 681w

**Official gifts**
6w, 532w

**Official hospitality**
Dept of Health 599w

**Official publications**
Statute law 603w

**Official receiver**
Contracts for services (25.05.95) 982

**Official report**
237w

**Official visits**
Scottish Office 740w

**Offshore drilling**
Oil pollution 784w

**Offshore structures**
Decommissioning 25–7w

**O'Hara, Mr Edward**
*Debates etc.*
Shipbuilding (17.05.95) 282–4

**O'Hara, Mr Edward**—*continued*
Wilson of Rievaulx, RtHonLord, Death (24.05.95) 917–8
*Questions*
Assisted places scheme 699–700
Broadgreen Hospital, Accident and emergency departments 142
Churchill, Winston LS, Archives 63w
Manchester Airport, Passengers 589
Mortgages, Repossession orders 320–1

**Oil pollution**
Offshore drilling 784w

**Oil revenues**
467w

**Old Sarum**
Airports 230–1w, 396w

**Olner, Mr Bill**
*Debates etc.*
Oral question time intervention (22.05.95) 590
*Questions*
Export of live animals, Animal welfare 456–7w
Health, Poverty 161w

**Ombudsman**
Housing associations 478w
Scottish Homes 478w

**Oncology**
Hospital consultants 163w

**O'Neill, Mr Martin**
*Debates etc.*
Gas Bill, Rep (15.05.95) 26–8, 36, 53–8, 61–7, 79–84, 91–2, 98–104
Gas Bill, Rep and 3R (16.05.95) 197–8, 204–7
Nuclear power (17.05.95) 419, 431–4

**Onslow, Rt Hon Sir Cranley**
*Questions*
Fishing, Flood control 690w
Freshwater fishing 685w
Internal Market Advisory Committee 643–4w

**Opencast mining**
(16.05.95) 223–46, 316–7
Asthma 316
Compulsory purchase 42w
Environmental impact assessment 42w
Rotherham 42–3w
Sheffield 22–3w, 179–81w, 785w
South Yorkshire 42w

**Opening hours**
Public houses 454

**Operation Dragon**
Strathclyde Police 481w

**Ophthalmic services**
Burnley General Hospital 98w, 280w

**Oppenheim, Mr Phillip,** *Parliamentary Under-Secretary of State, Dept of Employment*
*Questions*
Asbestos, Industrial health and safety 72–4w, 159w
Brewing industry, Manpower 72w
Ceramic industries, Hazardous materials 71w
Employment protection 565w
Family and working lives survey 76–7w
Hard core unemployed 563w
Industrial accidents, Prosecutions 74–5w
Industrial health and safety, Inspections 74–6w
Low pay 565w
Low pay, North East region 239w
Minimum wage, EC countries 563w
"New and Expectant Mothers at Work" 564w
Redundancy 160–1w
Safety Representatives and Safety Committee Regulations 1977, Industrial tribunals 157–8w

**Sub judice**
Speaker's rulings and statements (24.05.95) 890

**Subsidiarity**
231–2w

**Succession**
(23.05.95) 811

**Suffolk**
Arts 6

**Suicide**
281w
Agricultural workers 129w, 296w
Family doctors 167w
Northern Ireland 448w
Scotland 267w
Wales 459w

**Sumberg, Mr David**
*Questions*
Residential care, Capital rules 138
Sewage, Agricultural land 389–90w

**Sunday trading**
Scotland 899–900

**Supermarkets**
328
Kirkstall Valley 327–8
Planning permission 327–8

**Supply teachers**
Educational assessment 308w

**Surgery**
Eye disorders 336–7w
Geriatric patients 171w
Heart diseases 163–4w
Hospital waiting lists 94w, 132–3w, 600w
Wales 132–3w

**Sutcliffe, Mr Gerry**
*Questions*
Heart diseases, Surgery 163–4w

**Swaleside Prison**
Golf 540–1w

**Sweden**
Political refugees 700–1w

**Sweeney, Mr Walter**
*Debates etc.*
Criminal Injuries Compensation Bill, 2R (23.05.95) 749, 755, 782, 783–6
*Questions*
Further Education Funding Council for Wales, Public appointments 589w
Welsh Development Agency 133–4w

**Swindon**
Hospitals 771–2w

**Sykes, Mr John**
*Debates etc.*
Nuclear power (17.05.95) 404
*Questions*
Defence Postal and Courier Services 656w
Environment Agency 320
Fire engines, Scarborough 462–3
Fish, Imports 316–7w
Fisheries 455w
Foreign investment in UK, Northern Ireland 928
Helicopters, Air accidents 656w

**Taiwan**
Trade promotion 376w

**Takeovers**
Building societies 306w
Vickers Shipbuilding and Engineering 156w, 419w

**Tape recorded evidence**
Northern Ireland 751w

**Tapsell, Sir Peter**
*Debates etc.*
Bosnia-Herzegovina, Armed forces deployment (31.05.95) 1009, 1050–4, 1098
*Questions*
Official engagements 123–4w, 305w, 509w, 681w

**Tax allowances**
Banks 505w
Costs 469–70w
Married people 307w
Tax yields 470w

**Tax burden**
109w, 145–6

**Tax collection**
Nursing homes 504w

**Tax evasion**
465w

**Tax rates and bands**
238w, 706–7, 713–4w

**Tax yields**
Tax allowances 470w
VAT 464w

**Taxation**
937–8
Charitable donations 465w
Uniforms 56w

**Taxis**
Mobility of disabled 616–7w
Motor vehicle testing 616w
Smoking 674w
Social security abuse 726–7w

**Taxpayers**
148

**Taylor, Mrs Ann**
*Debates etc.*
Committee on Standards in Public Life (18.05.95) 482–3, 494–505, 570
Jobseeker's allowance, Points of order (16.05.95) 174
Members' conduct, Points of order (17.05.95) 335
*Questions*
Business statements 471–2, 939–40

**Taylor, Mr Ian,** *Parliamentary Under-Secretary of State, Dept of Trade and Industry*
*Questions*
Arms trade, Argentina 676w
Arms trade, Export controls 21w
Arms trade, Iraq 676w
Arms trade, Nigeria 237w
Audio recordings, Copyright 424–5w
Business, Teesside 419w
Cable systems, Road works 46–7w
Civil service redundancies, Dept of Trade and Industry 420–1w
Consultants, Dept of Trade and Industry 677–8w
Contracts for services, Dept of Trade and Industry 678–9w
Copyright Tribunal 298w
Dept of Trade and Industry, Non-governmental organisations 300w
Early retirement, Dept of Trade and Industry 677–8w
Electric shock equipment, Export licensing 676w
Export credit guarantees, Iraq 676w
Export licensing, Iraq 300w
Public telephones 421w
Science and technology research, EC grants and loans 299w
Torture, Export controls 676–7w

**Taylor, Rt Hon John David**
*Debates etc.*
Bosnia-Herzegovina, Armed forces deployment (31.05.95) 1042–4
*Questions*
Belvoir Park Hospital, Infectious diseases 754–5w
Capita, Government contracts 35w
Housing associations, Northern Ireland 445–6w
MacBride principles, Northern Ireland 925
Public service, Offices 437–9w
Royal Ulster Constabulary, Manpower 752–3w
Sheep premiums, Northern Ireland 753w
Trade promotion, Northern Ireland 748w

**Taylor, Mr John M,** *Parliamentary Secretary, Lord Chancellor's Dept*
*Debates etc.*
Conditional fee agreements orders (15.05.95) 109–11, 115–7, 123–4
*Questions*
Civil Court Procedures Review 128w
Civil service retirement, Lord Chancellor's Dept 231–2w
Court rules and procedures 4w
Court Service Agency 18
Criminal appeals, Prisoners 3w
Dangerous Dogs Act 1989, Legal aid 398w
Government shareholding, Lord Chancellor's Dept 399w
Immigration appeals 4w
Immigration appeals, India 655w
Immigration applications, India 398–9w
Judges 310w
Judges, Retirement 311–2w
Judiciary, Codes of practice 18–20
Law Commission 397w
Legal aid 4w, 14–7, 125–8w
Legal aid, Civil proceedings 4w
Legal aid scheme 4w, 231w, 655–6w
Legal aid scheme, Administrative costs 602–3w
Legal aid scheme, Expenditure 602w
Lockerbie, Bombings 17–8
Maxwell, Kevin, Legal costs 310w
Non-departmental public bodies, Lord Chancellor's Dept 4–5w
Political refugees, Immigration appeals 655w
Prisoners on remand 398w
Public Record Office 18
Statute law, Official publications 603w

**Taylor, Mr Matthew**
*Debates etc.*
Nuclear power (17.05.95) 399, 417–23
*Questions*
Air pollution, Information services 43–4w
Air pollution monitoring 782w
Housing standards 176w
Housing stock, Wales 129w
In vitro fertilisation 769–70w
In vitro fertilisation, Cornwall and Isles of Scilly Health Authority 769w
Insects, Pest control 682w
Legal aid scheme, Administrative costs 602–3w
Legal aid scheme, Expenditure 602w
Oil pollution, Offshore drilling 784w
Railtrack, Land pollution 405w
Recycling 782w
Recycling, Toner cartridges 784w
River pollution 385w
Water charges 329

**Taylor, Sir Teddy**
*Debates etc.*
Bosnia-Herzegovina, Armed forces deployment (31.05.95) 1025
*Questions*
European Monetary Institute 56w, 238w
London Tilbury and Southend line, Privatisation 402–3w
School transport, Southend 701
Water treatment, Nitrates 253w

**Teacher training**
538w
Scotland 91–2w

**Teachers**
Early retirement 416–7w
Information technology 693w
Kent 694
Manpower 138–42w
Physical education 144w

**Teaching methods**
Northern Ireland 925–6

**Teesside**
Business 419w
Local education authorities 415w

**Teesside Airport**
521–2w